LEGAL
THESAURUS

Second Edition

William C. Burton

MACMILLAN PUBLISHING COMPANY
New York

Maxwell Macmillan Canada
Toronto

Macmillan Publishing Company
A Division of Macmillan, Inc.
866 Third Avenue
New York, NY 10022

Maxwell Macmillan Canada, Inc.
1200 Eglinton Avenue East, Suite 200
Don Mills, Ontario M3C 3N1

Macmillan Publishing Company is part of the Maxwell Communication Group
of Companies

Library of Congress Catalog Card Number: 91-37968

Printed in the United States of America

printing number
1   2   3   4   5   6   7   8   9   10

Library of Congress Cataloging-in-Publication Data
Burton, William C.
    Legal thesaurus/William C. Burton.—2nd ed.
        p.   cm.
    Includes index.
    ISBN 0-02-897077-2 (alk. paper)
        1. Law—United States—Terms and phrases.   2. Law—Terms and
    phrases.   I. Title.
    KF156.B856   1992
    340′.14—dc20   91-37968
    ISBN 0-02-897079-9 (pbk)   CIP

The paper used in this publication meets the minimum requirements of American
National Standard for Information Sciences—Permanence of Paper for Printed Library
Materials. ANSI Z39.48-1984.   ∞™

EDITORIAL STAFF

Steven C. DeCosta
Editor

Michal Hoschander Malen
Associate Editor

John Drukker
Assistant Editor

EDITORIAL BOARD

Legal Editorial Consultant
Joan Gudesblatt

Editorial Consultants
Barbara Wiberg Alverson
Arline S. Rogat

Editorial Assistant
Yvonne Antokas Montesantos

Compilation Editors
Dorit King
Ethel Jane Osterman (First Edition)
Camille Capobianco Taranto

Assistants
Karen Dritto
Ronald M. Malen
Michele M. Mandelbaum

WILLIAM C. BURTON received his J.D. from Hofstra University, and has served as a New York State assistant attorney general and as assistant to the New York State special prosecutor. The author of many articles in professional publications, he is currently vice president and director of government affairs for the Continental Insurance Companies.

CONTENTS

FOREWORD

In the legal community absolute understanding is the measure of perfection. Perfection in the realm of the courts is the just resolution of issues of fact and questions of law. The primary tool for resolving conflicts among civilized people is through communication by written and oral language. The root of all language is the individual word.

In the English language, each word may have several meanings. Often, it is the use of a specific word or term upon which a case or controversy may hinge. Only by using precise language can the waters remain clear and unmuddied allowing justice to take its course unfettered by those who would mislead or misrepresent.

It is through the use of such a tool as the *Legal Thesaurus* that one may find the precise term to fit the nuances of a particular situation. It may be too much to expect such a tool to eradicate the confusion between "scienter" and "malice." The difference between "no law" and "no unreasonable law" may also be beyond its scope. But it should clearly demonstrate that "all deliberate speed" is not synonymous with "as slowly as feasible."

WILLIAM O. DOUGLAS
Justice, U.S. Supreme Court
1939–1975

October 22, 1979

INTRODUCTION

For over a century, writers have had the benefit of using Roget's *Thesaurus* for literary composition. During that time other general thesauri have been prepared, but members of the legal profession never had a thesaurus to assist them in their professional work.

For the members of the judiciary, clear and precise language is not only important, it is indispensible. Every word that is written is subject to close scrutiny and interpretation. These words and their usage become precedents and shape the future development of the law.

To members of the bar, persuasive language is extremely important. Written arguments are regularly submitted to the Courts to sway the outcome of pending litigation. Plain-language laws also require lawyers to simplify complex legalistic language and use clear and understandable wording.

To students of the law, precise and accurate expression is similarly critical whenever the nature and functions of jurisprudence are evaluated and these assessments are reduced to writings.

This reference book was compiled to assist judges, lawyers, and students of the law in their desire to convey their thoughts, arguments, and contentions, effectively and persuasively.

The concept of a legal thesaurus was born out of necessity. It has its beginning in 1974 when the author was preparing a memorandum of law and found himself continuously repeating the same legal words. He looked for a legal thesaurus and learned that no such volume had ever been published. He resolved to have such a book compiled. Five years later, under his direction, a staff of lawyers, librarians and trained professionals have fulfilled the need that was foreseen. This second edition, which augments the first work, was compiled over a two-year period.

This book provides the broadest array of words that fit the thoughts to be conveyed. All expressions and colloquialisms that are unrelated to the law have been omitted.

Since a wide range of words is provided, some of which are not exact synonyms, the user should consult a legal dictionary to determined precise meanings, nuances, and variations in usage. Only when the true meaning of each word offered is understood can the user select the most appropriate term. The words provided are not always synonyms but are related in their meaning and use provide a full panoply of possible words to be used by a writer.

At the outset, three criteria were used by the editors to select the main entries which are included in this book: First, those words that are strictly legal; second, those words that are not strictly legal but which are commonly used by members of the legal profession; and third, those words that are not legal and not widely used by lawyers, but are sufficiently sophisticated to warrant their use by attorneys. Through this new edition a fourth category was added which includes words which are regularly used by lawyers. In addition the new edition further supplements the book by adding words that have become more popularly used by attorneys.

In selection of the main headings, words that have multiple parts of speech were evaluated. In each case the noun, adjective, verb or adverb form was selected which was most commonly used by attorneys.

Whenever a main heading has more than one usage it is divided into separate subheadings. For the convenience of the user, these subheadings are arranged alphabetically.

The book also provides an alphabetical listing of associated legal concepts under each main entry. In this way, writers will be able to find complete legal concepts when only a single, central word comes to mind.

Foreign phrases, which are used in the practice of law, are also included under each main heading. Most reference books list foreign phrases alphabetically under the first letter of the foreign word. This book, however, lists foreign phrases under their pivotal English concept.

To assist the user in locating synonyms, in addition to the alphabetically arranged listings in the main entries, there is also a full index.

The author would welcome and appreciate suggestions of additional entries and changes for the expansion and improvement of the next edition.

ACKNOWLEDGMENTS

I gratefully acknowledge, with profound gratitude, the assistance, cooperation, and inspiration given me by my loving parents Martin and Ellen Burton. I am forever indebted to them for providing me with the educational background to undertake this effort.

I am fortunate and thankful to have had the professional guidance, skill, and expertise of Phil Friedman, President and Publisher of Macmillan Reference. It is a pleasure working with him on the revision and gaining his keen insights and in-depth knowledge. I am also appreciative to Editor Melissa Solomon for capably overseeing the second edition and contributing zeal, true interest, and unwavering dedication.

HOW TO USE THIS BOOK

Here are samples of the comprehensive, easy-to-use listings:

MAIN ENTRY

Definition
(when there is more than
one meaning)

Parts of Speech

Synonyms

Associated Legal Concepts

Foreign Phrases and
Translations
(keyed to concepts)

Multiple Meanings

Alternate Parts of Speech

---

questionable, refutable, suspect, unsustainable

DUE *(Owed)*, **adjective**   chargeable, claimable, collectable, condign, *debitus*, delinquent, deserved, earned, in arrears, merited, outstanding, owing, to be paid, uncompensated, unpaid, unrewarded, unsettled
ASSOCIATED CONCEPTS: amount due, balance due, debt due, due bills, due date, due on demand, indebtedness due, justly due and owing, legally due, money due, payment due, rent due, taxes due
FOREIGN PHRASES: *Nihil peti potest ante id tempus, quo per rerum naturam persolvi possit.* Nothing can be demanded before the time when, in the nature of things, it can be paid.

DUE *(Regular)*, **adjective**   according to law, allowable, appropriate, authorized, befitting, correct, expedient, fit, lawful, legal, legislated, legitimate, licit, nomothetic, permitted, proper, rightful, sanctioned, statutory
ASSOCIATED CONCEPTS: due acknowledgment, due administration of justice, due and proper care, due and reasonable care, due care, due compensation, due consideration, due course, due course of business, due course of law, due diligence, due execution, due exercise of discretion, due process of law, due proof, due proof of death, due proof of loss, due regard, holder in due course

DUE, **noun**   accounts collectable, accounts outstanding, arrears, balance to pay, charge, claim, compensation owed, *deberi*, debit, debt, deficit, droit, entitlement, favor owed, fee, indebtedness, lawful claim, liability, obligation accrued, outstanding debt, overdue payment, pledge, right, something owed, that which is owing,

---

misguide, mis
wit, play a t
something ov
advantage of,
ize

DUPLICAT
ditto, doubl
geminatior
enactmen
duction, t
ASSOCIAT
nal

DUPLICI
deceitfulne
duality, dup
falsehearted
sincerity, pe

DURABLE
amaranthi
continual,
eternal, e
holding u
perishable
deciduous,
haustible,
intransmuta
movable, l
long-enduri
longevous,
out, of long
manent, perp
remaining, re

INDEX

Synonym

(Main Entries under
which the synonym
is listed.)

Note Readable Type

(Sample Excerpts, Exact Size)

MAIN ENTRIES

A

A FORTIORI, *adverb*   above all, accordingly, all the more, by a stronger reason, by inference, certainly, chiefly, consequently, *ergo,* especially, even more, for a certainty, for a still stronger reason, in chief, in the main, mainly, over and above, paramountly, particularly, primarily, thus, with the greater force

A PRIORI, *adverb*   accordingly, as a consequence, as a result of, as is, because of this, by reason of, consequently, deducibly, deductively, derivatively, doubtlessly, *ergo, ex concesso,* for that reason, for this reason, for which reason, from a general law to a particular instance, from cause to effect, from that cause, from this cause, in consequence, inferentially, necessarily, on account of this, on that account, on that ground, proceeding from antecedent to consequent, thusly, to that end

A SAVOIR, *adverb*   below, details now to be provided, the following, hence, hereunder, hereupon, namely, next, now to be accounted for, now to be announced, now to be described, now to be enunciated, now to be itemized, now to be listed, now to be mentioned, now to be narrated, now to be presented, now to be read, now to be recited, now to be recounted, now to be reported, now to be set forth, now to be stated, now to follow, subsequently set down, the succeeding, that is, that is to say, to wit, *videlicet*

ABALIENATE, *verb*   assign, bequeath, convey, demise, grant, hand down, hand over, pass on, transfer, transfer by deed, transfer by will

AB INITIO, *adverb*   *ab origine, ab ovo,* as a start, at first, at the beginning, at the start, chiefly, first, first and foremost, first of all, firstly, for a beginning, from its birth, from the beginning, in its infancy, in the beginning, in the first place, initially, mainly, originally, primarily, principally
ASSOCIATED CONCEPTS: void ab initio

ABANDON *(Physically leave),* *verb*   abscond, absent oneself, back out, be gone, be off, cast off, decamp, defect, depart from, desert, *destituere,* disappear, emigrate, evacuate, forsake, *hominem deserere,* leave behind, leave in the lurch, make one's exit, move off, quit, remove from, retreat, run away, secede from, set off, slip away from, take leave, take one's departure, take one's leave, turn one's back on

ASSOCIATED CONCEPTS: abandoned husband, abandoned land, abandoned property, abandoned wife, desertion

ABANDON *(Relinquish),* *verb*   abjure, abstain, apostasize, cast aside, cast away, cast off, cease, cede, concede, demit, desert, desist, discard, discontinue, dispense with, dispose of, dispossess oneself of, disuse, divest oneself of, drop, forbear, forego, forsake, forswear, give away, give over, give up, give up claim to, go back on, jettison, lay aside, part with, put aside, quit, render up, renounce, repudiate, resign, sacrifice, set aside, surrender, tergiversate, throw away, throw off, turn away, yield
ASSOCIATED CONCEPTS: abandon a claim, abandon a crime, renunciate a claim, surrender property

ABANDON *(Withdraw),* *verb*   *ab re desistere,* abdicate, back down, back off, back out, forsake, *omittere,* pull out, quit, *rem relinquere,* renege, retire, retract, retreat, stand aside, tender one's resignation, vacate office

ABANDONMENT *(Desertion),* *noun*   abrogation, apostasy, cession, decampment, defection, demission, departure, dereliction, disaffection, disavowal, evacuation, flight, hasty departure, relinquishment, repudiation, retirement, vacating, withdrawal
ASSOCIATED CONCEPTS: abandonment of a child, abandonment of a husband, abandonment of a property, abandonment of a wife, abandonment of land, dissolution of marriage, Enoch Arden laws
FOREIGN PHRASES: *Occupantis fiunt derelicta.* Things abandoned become the property of the first who is the occupant.

ABANDONMENT *(Discontinuance),* *noun*   abdication, abrogation, cessation, *derelictio,* desistance, discontinuation, disjunction, disruption, relinquishment, surrender, suspension, withdrawal
ASSOCIATED CONCEPTS: abandonment of a crime, abandonment of a pleading, abandonment of an easement, abandonment of assets in bankruptcy, abandonment of proscriptive rights

1

ABANDONMENT (Repudiation), **noun** abnegation, cancellation, declination, denial, disapprobation, disapproval, disavowal, dismissal, disownment, rejection, renouncement, renunciation, reprobation, rescission

ABATE (Extinguish), **verb** abolish, abrogate, annul, *cadere*, cancel, defeat, destroy, discontinue, dissolve, eliminate, exterminate, invalidate, nullify, obliterate, put an end to, quash, quell, repeal, rescind, revoke, terminate, void
ASSOCIATED CONCEPTS: abate a bequest, abate a cause of action, abate a debt, abate a devise, abate a legacy, abate an action

ABATE (Lessen), **verb** alleviate, curtail, decline, decrease, *decrescere*, diminish, *imminui*, lighten, limit, mitigate, modify, palliate, reduce, relieve, *remittere*, suppress, temper
ASSOCIATED CONCEPTS: abate a nuisance, abate a tax

ABATEMENT (Extinguishment), **noun** abolition, abrogation, annulment, cancellation, deadening, defeat, destruction, discontinuance, dissolution, elimination, extermination, invalidation, nonuse, nullification, obliteration, *remissio*, repeal, rescindment, revocation, termination, voidance
ASSOCIATED CONCEPTS: abatement by death, abatement of a bequest, abatement of a cause of action, abatement of a freehold, abatement of a legacy, abatement of an action, abatement of debts, abatement of taxes, plea in abatement
FOREIGN PHRASES: *Cassetur billa.* That the bill be quashed. *Cassetur breve.* That the writ be quashed.

ABATEMENT (Reduction), **noun** alleviation, curtailment, declination, decline, decrease, decrement, *deminutio,* diminishing, diminution, lessening, lightening, limitation, mitigation, modification, palliation, reduction, relief, *remissio,* suppression, tempering
ASSOCIATED CONCEPTS: abatable nuisance, abatement of a tax

ABDICATION, noun abandonment, *abdicatio,* abjuration, demission, departure, deposition, dethronement, *eiuratio,* leaving, quitting, relinquishment, renunciation, resignation, surrender, surrender of control, uncrowning, vacating, vacation, withdrawal
FOREIGN PHRASES: *Cessa regnare, si non vis judicare.* Cease to reign, if you don't wish to adjudicate.

ABDUCT, verb carry away, convey away, decamp, denude, deprive, ensnare, impress, kidnap, pirate, purloin, ravish, shanghai, spirit away, subjugate, take away, take by force, take surreptitiously
ASSOCIATED CONCEPTS: kidnapping
FOREIGN PHRASES: *A piratis aut latronibus capti liberi permanent.* Persons taken by pirates or robbers remain free.

ABDUCTION, noun child-stealing, impressment, kidnapping, overmastering, *raptus,* ravishment, shanghaiing, spiriting away, subjugation, taking away

ABEREMURDER, noun assassination, carnage, dealing death, decimation, destruction of life, elimination, extermination, extinction, homicide, killing, killing with malice aforethought, liquidation, massacre, slaughter, slaying, taking of life, unlawful homicide

ABET, verb *adiuvare,* advance, advocate, afford aid, aid, arouse, assist, back, contribute, cooperate with, embolden, encourage, endorse, facilitate, foment, foster, furnish aid, goad, help, incite, instigate, nourish, nurture, prompt, second, serve, spur, stimulate, succor, supply aid, support, urge
ASSOCIATED CONCEPTS: accessory, accomplice, aid and abet, co-conspirator, facilitation

ABETTOR, noun accessory, accomplice, accomplice in crime, actuator, adjutant, advocate, aide, aider, assistant, associate, auxiliary, backer, coadjutor, collaborator, confederate, conspirator, cooperator, encourager, exponent, favorer, fomentor, helper, henchman, impeller, inducer, inspirer, instigator, mainstay, maintainer, motivator, *particeps criminis,* patron, promoter, prompter, protagonist, second, support, supporter, sustainer, upholder
ASSOCIATED CONCEPTS: aiding and abetting, conspiracy, renunciation

ABEYANCE, noun arrest, cessation, check, deadlock, delay, desistance, discontinuance, discontinuation, dormancy, halt, immobility, *in dubio esse,* inaction, inactivity, inertion, inertness, *intermitti,* interim, interlude, intermission, interregnum, interruption, interval, lapse, quiescency, recess, recumbency, *rem integram relinquere,* repose, reprieve, respite, rest, stalemate, stay, stillness, stoppage, suspension
ASSOCIATED CONCEPTS: contingency, escrow, fee held in abeyance, held in abeyance, in expectation

ABIDE, verb accept, acknowledge, acquiesce, adhere, agree, assent, carry into execution, comply, concur, conform, cooperate, endure, execute, follow, heed, obey, observe, perform, permit, respect, sanction, *stare,* submit, subscribe to, suffer, tolerate, yield
ASSOCIATED CONCEPTS: abiding conviction

ABILITY, noun ableness, adaptability, adeptness, adequacy, aptitude, aptness, capability, capacity, competence, competency, enablement, *facultas,* faculty, fitness, fittedness, *ingenium,* mastership, mastery, potentiality, *potestas,* proficiency, prowess, skill, versatility, *vires*
ASSOCIATED CONCEPTS: ability to contract, ability to earn, ability to pay, ability to perform, ability to provide, ability to purchase, ability to support, capacity, financial ability, readiness, testamentary ability

ABJURATION, verb abandonment, defection, denial, disaffirmation, disallowance, disavowal, disclaimer, disclamation, disownment, forswearing, recall, recantation, rejection, renouncement, renunciation, repudiation, retraction, revocation, revokement
ASSOCIATED CONCEPTS: abjuration of allegiance, law of sanctuary, oath of abjuration

ABODE, noun address, domicile, *domus,* dwelling, dwelling place, fixed residence, *gite,* habitancy, habitat, habitation, home, homestead, house, inhabitancy, inhabitation, living place, place of dwelling, residence, residency
FOREIGN PHRASES: *Constitutum esse eam domum unicuique nostrum debere existimari, ubi quisque sedes et tabulas haberet, suarumque rerum constitutionem fecisset.* It is established that the home of each of us is considered to be the place of his abode and books, and where he may have made an establishment of his business.

ABOLISH, *verb*   abate, *abolere,* abrogate, annihilate, annul, cancel, declare null and void, *delere,* delete, deprive of force, destroy, disannul, discontinue, disestablish, dispense with, dispose, dissolve, eliminate, eradicate, *exstinguere,* exterminate, extinguish, extirpate, invalidate, negate, nullify, obliterate, overturn, override, overrule, prohibit, quash, raze, render null and void, repeal, repudiate, rescind, retract, revoke, set aside, squelch, *subvertere,* supersede, supplant, suppress, terminate, *tollere,* undo, vacate, vitiate, void, wwithdraw
ASSOCIATED CONCEPTS: repeal by amendment

ABOLITION, *noun*   abolishment, abrogation, annihilation, annulment, cancellation, defeasance, deposal, destruction, desuetude, discontinuance, *dissolutio,* dissolution, disusage, disuse, elimination, eradication, extermination, extinction, extinguishment, extirpation, invalidation, nonuse, nullification, obliteration, recantation, recision, repeal, repudiation, rescindment, rescission, retraction, revocation, revokement, vacation, voidance
ASSOCIATED CONCEPTS: abolition of a remedy, abolition of an action, abolition of office, abolition of slavery, express abolition, implied abolition
FOREIGN PHRASES: *Cujus est instituere, ejus est abrogare.* Whoever may institute, his right it is to abrogate.

ABORTION *(Feticide), noun*   aborticide, *abortio,* expulsion of a fetus, termination of a pregnancy

ABORTION *(Fiasco), noun*   blunder, clumsiness, dereliction, disablement, disaster, failure, folly, frustration, inability, incapacity, incompetence, incompetency, ineffectuality, inefficacy, ineptitude, inexpertness, insufficiency, nonfulfilment, quackery, unskillfulness, vain attempt, vain effort, want of success

ABRIDGE *(Divest), verb*   attach, deprive of, dispossess of, disseise, divest of, expropriate, limit, restrict, seize, strip, take away, usurp, wrest from

ABRIDGE *(Shorten), verb*   abbreviate, bate, boil down, capsulize, *circumcidere,* compress, condense, contract, *contrahere,* curtail, cut down, decrease, diminish, epitomize, foreshorten, give the sum and substance, lessen, *praecidere,* reduce, shrink, sketch, subtract, summarize, synopsize, take away, telescope, trim, whittle

ABRIDGMENT *(Condensation), noun*   abbreviation, abbreviature, abstract, *aperçu,* brief, capsule, compendium, compression, consolidation, conspectus, contraction, curtailment, digest, epitome, epitomization, extract, *précis,* reduction, sketch, summary, synopsis
ASSOCIATED CONCEPTS: abridgment of time

ABRIDGMENT *(Disentitlement), noun*   abatement, curtailment, deprivation, deprivement, dispossession, divestiture, limitation, loss, privation, restriction
ASSOCIATED CONCEPTS: abridgment of rights

ABROGATE *(Annul), verb*   abjure, abnegate, abolish, *abrogare,* cancel, contradict, contravene, declare null and void, disannul, disapprove, dissolve, eliminate, impair, invalidate, make void, negate, nullify, obstruct, prohibit, quash, rebuff, refuse, reject, renounce, repudiate, retract, reverse, undo, void

FOREIGN PHRASES: *Cujus est instituere, ejus est abrogare.* Whose right it is to institute anything may abrogate it. *Non impedit clausula derogatoria, quo minus ab eadem potestate res dissolvantur a qua constituuntur.* A derogatory clause does not prevent things from being dissolved by the same power by which they were originally created.

ABROGATE *(Rescind), verb*   abolish, annul, bar, cancel, countermand, declare null and void, deprive of power, destroy, disannul, eliminate, exclude, invalidate, not accept, nullify, omit, override, overrule, prohibit, recall, recant, repeal, repudiate, *rescindere,* retract, reverse, revoke, set aside, supersede, terminate, vacate, void, waive
ASSOCIATED CONCEPTS: abrogating an appeal, express abrogation
FOREIGN PHRASES: *Clausula quae abrogationem excludit ab initio non valet.* A clause which precludes repeal is void from the beginning. *Perpetua lex est nullam legem humanam ac positivam perpetuam esse, et clausula quae abrogationem excludit ab initio non valet.* It is a perpetual law that no human and positive law can be perpetual, and a clause which precludes the power of abrogation or repeal is void from the beginning.

ABSCOND, *verb*   absent oneself, avoid, bolt, decamp, *delitescere,* depart, desert, disappear, dodge, elude, emigrate, escape, , eschew, evade, expatriate oneself, flee, hide, *latere,* leave, levant, make off, *occultari,* remove, run, run away, steal away, take flight, withdraw, withdraw clandestinely
ASSOCIATED CONCEPTS: abscond on bail, absconding debtor, attachment, fugitive, *quasi in rem jurisdiction*

ABSENCE *(Nonattendance), noun*   abandonment, *absentia,* abstention, avoidance, defection, desertion, nonappearance, nonpresence, removal, truancy, withdrawal
ASSOCIATED CONCEPTS: absence from the state, absent creditors, absent debtor, absent defendant, absent from a jurisdiction, leave of action
FOREIGN PHRASES: *Absentem accipere debemus eum qui non est eo loci in quo petitur.* We must consider absent he who is not in that place in which he is sought.

ABSENCE *(Omission), noun*   deficiency, deprivation, disappearance, hiatus, inadequacy, lack, need, negation, nonbeing, nonexistence, shortage, unavailability, void, want
ASSOCIATED CONCEPTS: absence of fraud, absence of funds, absence of heirs, absence of issue, absence of negligence, absence of notice, absence of wrongdoing

ABSOLUTE *(Complete), adjective*   *absolutus,* blanket, comprehensive, downright, entire, exhaustive, final, finished, full, sheer, total, unbounded, unconditional, unconstrained, unlimited, unqualified, unreserved, unrestrained, unrestricted, unstinted, utter, whole, without qualification
ASSOCIATED CONCEPTS: absolute acceptance, absolute admission, absolute assignment, absolute bequest, absolute control, absolute deed, absolute devise, absolute fee, absolute gift, absolute immunity, absolute insuror, absolute owner, absolute power of alienation, absolute power of disposition, absolute sale, absolute transfer, fee simple absolute

ABSOLUTE *(Conclusive)*, **adjective** accurate, actual, axiomatic, beyond doubt, categorical, certain, clear, clearly defined, decided, decisive, definite, definitive, determinate, exact, explicit, express, final, fixed, inalienable, indisputable, indubitable, obvious, positive, precise, real, settled, straightforward, true, unconditioned, undoubted, unequivocal, unerring, unimpeachable, unmistakable, unmitigated, unmixed, unquestionable, veritable, well-defined
ASSOCIATED CONCEPTS: absolute certainty, absolute conviction, absolute discretion, absolute duty, absolute liability, absolute moral certainty, absolute pardon, absolute privilege, absolute right, absolute title

ABSOLUTE *(Ideal)*, **adjective** best, beyond compare, champion, consummate, crowning, defectless, excelling, exemplary, faultless, flawless, highest, immaculate, impeccable, incomparable, matchless, model, *ne plus ultra*, paramount, peerless, perfect, preeminent, pure, spotless, stainless, superior, superlative, supreme, taintless, unblemished, unequaled, unexcelled, unrivaled, unsurpassed, untainted, untarnished

ABSOLUTION, *noun* acquittal, amnesty, clearance, deliverance, discharge, dismissal, dismissal of an accusation, exculpation, exoneration, forgiveness, forgiveness of sins, grace, liberation, pardon, purgation, release, release from punishment, remission, reprieve, vindication

ABSOLVE, *verb* *absolvere*, acquit, adjudge innocent, clear, discharge, exculpate, excuse, exonerate, find not guilty, forgive, free, let off, *liberare*, liberate, pardon, prove innocent, prove not guilty, *purgare*, purge, release from imputation, remit, reprieve, set free, vindicate
ASSOCIATED CONCEPTS: absolve of blame

ABSTENTION, *noun* abstainment, abstemiousness, abstinence, abstinence from action, avoidance, elusion, eschewal, evasion, forbearance, holding off, inaction, nonparticipation, refrainment
ASSOCIATED CONCEPTS: abstention awaiting the state court's decision, abstention based on deferral, abstention based on state issues, doctrine of abstention

ABSTRACT, *noun* abbreviation, abbreviature, abridgment, analect, brief, capsule, compendium, compilation, compression, condensation, consolidation, conspectus, contraction, digest, *epitoma*, epitome, extract, pandect, precis, reduction, summary, synopsis
ASSOCIATED CONCEPTS: abstract idea, abstract of a record, abstract of judgment, abstract of title, abstract proposition of law, abstracts of evidence, marketable title acts, title search

ABSTRACT *(Separate)*, *verb* detach, disengage, disjoin, dissociate, disunite, isolate, remove, take out of context

ABSTRACT *(Summarize)*, *verb* abbreviate, abridge, capsulize, compact, compress, condense, contract, epitomize, reduce, shorten, synopsize, telescope

ABUSE *(Corrupt practice)*, *noun* baseness, breach of trust, deviation from rectitude, dishonesty, distortion, erroneous use, excessive use, exploitation, fraudulency, ill usage, ill use, improper usage, improper use, jobbery, malfeasance, malversation, misap-plication, misappropriation, misdirection, misemployment, mishandling, mismanagement, misrepresentation, misstatement, misusage, misuse, perversion, *usus perversus,* violation, want of principle, wrong use
ASSOCIATED CONCEPTS: abuse of a mandate, abuse of a proceeding, abuse of authority, abuse of discretion, abuse of executive authority, abuse of legal process, abuse of power, neglect
FOREIGN PHRASES: *Ab abusu ad usum non valet consequentia.* A conclusion as to the use of a thing from its abuse is invalid. *Confirmat usum qui tollit abusum.* He confirms a use who removes an abuse. *Omnium rerum quarum usus est, potest esse abusus, virtute sola excepta.* There may be an abuse of everything of which there is a use, virtue alone excepted.

ABUSE *(Physical misuse)*, *noun* atrocity, bad treatment, damage, debasement, defilement, dishonor, dishonoring, hurt, ill treatment, ill usage, ill use, impairment, indecent assault, injury, maltreatment, mishandling, mistreatment, misusage, molestation, outrage, persecution, victimization, violation
ASSOCIATED CONCEPTS: abuse of a child, wife-beating

ABUSE *(Misuse)*, *verb* *abuti,* ill-use, injure, make excessive use of, make improper use of, maltreat, manhandle, misapply, misappropriate, misemploy, mishandle, mistreat, pervert, use improperly, use wrongly
ASSOCIATED CONCEPTS: abuse of a minor

ABUSE *(Victimize)*, *verb* injure, maltreat, manhandle, mistreat, molest, oppress

ABUSE *(Violate)*, *verb* debauch, defile, degrade, dishonor, harm, ill-use, persecute, pollute, profane, wrong

ABUSIVE, *adjective* detracting, insulting, maledictory, menacing, quarreling, reviling, threatening, ungracious
ASSOCIATED CONCEPTS: abusive language, abusive letter, abusive manner

ABUT, *verb* *aboutir,* adjoin, attach, be adjacent to, be contiguous, border on, bound, butt, conjoin, connect, end at, extend to, join, lean against, meet, reach, *rei adiacere, rem attingere,* touch, verge on
ASSOCIATED CONCEPTS: abutting land, abutting on the improvement, abutting owner, abutting property owner

ACCEDE *(Concede)*, *verb* abide by, accept, accord, acknowledge, acquiesce, admit, agree to, approve, assent, back down, capitulate, comply, concur, conform, consent, deign, give assent, give in, grant, obey, permit, submit, subscribe to, succumb, surrender, vouchsafe, yield, yield assent

ACCEDE *(Succeed)*, *verb* assume, attain, become heir to, come after, come next, displace, follow in order, inherit, reach, replace, supersede, supplant, take the place of

ACCELERATED JUDGMENT, *noun* accelerated decision, expedited determination, expedited judgment, facilitated decision, speeded adjudication

ACCELERATION, *noun* dispatch, expedition, expeditious performance, hastening, hurrying, increase of speed, quickening, shortening of time, speedup, spurt, stepping up a pace

ASSOCIATED CONCEPTS: acceleration clause, acceleration doctrine, acceleration of a testamentary gift, acceleration of payments, acceleration of remainders

ACCEPT *(Admit as sufficient),* **verb**   accede to, acquiesce, admit as satisfactory, agree to, allow, comply, confirm

ACCEPT *(Assent),* **verb**   accede to, acquiesce, affirm, agree to, allow, authorize, comply, confirm, endorse, ratify, sanction, tolerate
ASSOCIATED CONCEPTS: accept a contract, ratification

ACCEPT *(Embrace),* **verb**   adopt, consider as true, embrace, internalize

ACCEPT *(Recognize),* **verb**   accord recognition to, acknowledge, allow, honor
ASSOCIATED CONCEPTS: accept a bill, accept a check, accept a draft

ACCEPT *(Take),* **verb**   *accipere,* acquire, obtain, receive, receive with approval, secure, take control of, take hold of, take possession of
ASSOCIATED CONCEPTS: accept a bribe, accept gainful employment

ACCEPTANCE, **noun**   accedence, *acceptio,* accession, accordance, acknowledgment, acquiescence, adoption, agreement, allowance, approbation, approval, assent, assurance, compliance, *comprobatio,* concordance, consent, endorsement, ratification, receipt, receptiveness, resignation, sanction, tolerance, toleration
ASSOCIATED CONCEPTS: acceptance by a grantee to a deed, acceptance by conduct, acceptance in a sale, acceptance of a bill of exchange, acceptance of a bribe, acceptance of a check, acceptance of a contract, acceptance of a draft, acceptance of a gift by a donee, acceptance of an insurance application, acceptance of an offer, acceptance of an order, acceptance of benefits, acceptance of employment, acceptance of goods, acceptance of risk, blank acceptance, conditional acceptance, constructive acceptance, conversion by acceptance, implied acceptance
FOREIGN PHRASES: *Cum in corpore dissentitur, apparet nullam esse acceptionem.* When there is a disagreement in the substance of a thing, it appears that there is no acceptance.

ACCESS *(Opening),* **noun**   accessibility, approachability, availability, chance, means, occasion, open position, opportunity, possibility, unfilled place, vacancy

ACCESS *(Right of way),* **noun**   *accessus,* adit, *aditus,* admission, admittance, approach, course, direct approach, entrance, entrance way, entry, ingress, inlet, means of access, means of approach, opening, passage, passageway, path, right of entry, road, route, way, way in, way of approach, way through

ACCESSION *(Annexation),* **noun**   *accessio,* addition, adherence, adhesion, adjoining, affixation, annexing, appendage, attachment, binding, cementation, cohesion, combination, combining, conjoining, consolidation, coupling, fastening, fusion, inclusion, incorporation, joining, merger, putting together, securing, subjoining, subjunction, supplementation, unification, union, uniting
ASSOCIATED CONCEPTS: accession of fixtures, accession of property

ACCESSION *(Enlargement),* **noun**   accretion, accrual, accumulation, acquisition, addition, advance, aggrandizement, amplification, appreciation, attainment, augmentation, broadening, burgeoning, development, elaboration, enhancement, expansion, extension, gain, growth, increase, multiplication, progress, progression, supplementation, swelling
ASSOCIATED CONCEPTS: accession of property, accretion, acquisition of title by accession, doctrine of accession, permanent accession, riparian accession

ACCESSORY, **noun**   abettor, accomplice, accomplice in crime, advisor, aider, assistant, coconspirator, codirector, collaborator, confederate, *confrère, conscius,* consociate, cooperator, copartner, coworker, *culpae socius,* encourager, fellow conspirator, helper, helpmate, partaker, *particeps criminis,* participant, participator, partner, partner in crime, planner, *socius criminis*
ASSOCIATED CONCEPTS: accessory after the fact, accessory before the fact, accessory contract, accessory during the fact, accessory obligation, accessory to a crime, accessory to an offense, aiding and abetting, principal
FOREIGN PHRASES: *Accessorium non ducit, sed sequitur suum principale.* That which is the accessory or incident does not lead, but follows its principals. *Accessorius sequitur naturam sui principales.* An accessory follows the nature of his principal, thus, an accessory can not be found guilty of a greater crime than his principal. *Cujus juris est principale, ejusdem juris erit accessorium.* He who has jurisdiction of the principal thing also has jurisdiction of the accessory. *Nullus dicitur accessorius post feloniam, sed ille qui novit principalem feloniam fecisse, et illum receptavit et comfortavit.* No one is called an "accessory" after the fact but the one who knew the principal had committed a felony, and who received and comforted him. *Omne principale trahit ad se accessorium.* Every principal thing draws the accessory to itself. *Res accessoria sequitur rem principalem.* An accessory follows the principal. *Ubi non est principalis, non potest esse accessorius.* Where there can be no principal, there cannot be an accessory. *Quae accessionum locum obtinent, extinguuntur cum principales res peremp tae fuerint.* When the principal thing is destroyed, those things which are accessory to it are also destroyed.

ACCIDENT *(Chance occurrence),* **noun**   adventitiousness, befalling, blind chance, *casus,* circumstance, fortuitous event, fortuity, happening, hazard, incident, inevitable occurrence, sudden happening, unanticipated event, undesigned occurrence, unexpected misfortune, unexpected occurrence, unforeseen occurrence
ASSOCIATED CONCEPTS: accidental cause, accidental loss, accidental means
FOREIGN PHRASES: *Casus fortuitus non est sperandus, et nemo tenetur devinare.* A fortuitous event is not to be foreseen, and no one is bound to expect it. *Casus fortuitus non est supponendus.* A fortuitous happening is not to be presumed.

ACCIDENT *(Misfortune),* **noun**   adversity, affliction, calamity, casualty, *contretemps,* disaster, injurious occurrence, misadventure, miscarriage, mischance, mishap, unfortunate event
ASSOCIATED CONCEPTS: accident arising out of the course of employment, accidental bodily injury, acci-

dental fires, collision, disability caused by an accident, expectable loss, external, foreseeable loss, violent and accidental means

ACCOMMODATE, *verb* accept, *accommodare,* adapt, adjust, administer to, agree, aid, arrange, assist, attune, be capable of holding, benefit, bring into consistency, bring to terms, comfort, compose, contain, convenience, defer, do a favor for, do a service for, favor, fit, furnish, gratify, harmonize, have, have capacity for, help, hold, meet the wants of, minister to, oblige, provide, render a service, serve, settle, settle amicably, suit, supply the wants of, support, yield

ACCOMMODATION *(Adjustment),* *noun* accordance, adaptation, agreement, arrangement, *compositio,* composition of differences, compromise, friendly agreement, harmonization, mutual understanding, obliging, provision, readjustment, *reconciliatio,* rectification, settlement

ACCOMMODATION *(Backing),* *noun* assistance, assurance, championing, cooperation, endorsement, guarantee, seconding, security, sponsorship, succor, support, surety
ASSOCIATED CONCEPTS: accommodated endorser, accommodated party, accommodated payee, accommodation acceptance, accommodation bill, accommodation guarantor, accommodation endorsement, accommodation maker, accommodation note, accommodation paper, accommodation signer, *cautio fidejussoria*

ACCOMPANY, *verb* associate with, coexist, commingle, consort, convoy, join, keep, keep company with

ACCOMPLICE, *noun* abettor, accessory, accessory after the fact, accessory before the fact, advisor, aid, aider, aider and abettor, assistant, associate, associate in crime, associate in guilt, coactor, coconspirator, codefendant, codirector, collaborator, comate, confederate, *confrère, conscius,* consociate, contriver, cooperator, coworker, *culpae socius,* encourager, fellow conspirator, helper, helpmate, partaker, *particeps criminis,* participant, participator, partner, partner in crime, partner in wrongdoing, planner, principal, *socius criminis,* supporter
ASSOCIATED CONCEPTS: accomplice witness, aiding and abetting, complicity, inchoate crimes, mens rea, vicarious liability, Wharton's rule
FOREIGN PHRASES: *Agentes et consentientes pari poena plectentur.* Acting and consenting parties are liable to the same punishment.

ACCOMPLISH, *verb* achieve, attain, bring about, complete, consummate, discharge, dispatch, effect, enact, execute, finish, fulfill, realize, succeed

ACCORD, *noun* accommodation, accordance, adjustment, agreement, arrangement, compromise, concession, concord, concordance, mutual understanding, settlement, understanding
ASSOCIATED CONCEPTS: accord and satisfaction, disputed claims, executed accord, executory accord, novation, payment of a debt, release, satisfaction, substituted agreement, unliquidated claim
FOREIGN PHRASES: *Concordare leges legibus est optimus interpretandi modus.* To reconcile laws with other laws is the best method of interpreting them.

ACCORDANCE *(Compact),* *noun* accommodation, accord, adjustment, agreement, arrangement, conciliation, concord, concordance, concurrence, consonance, contract, *entente cordiale,* pact, reconcilement, reconciliation, settlement, unison, unity

ACCORDANCE *(Understanding),* *noun* accommodation, adjustment, agreement, amity, assent, assonance, common view, communion, compatibility, compliance, concinnity, concurrence, conformance, conformity, consensus, consentience, consonance, consonancy, harmonization, harmony, meeting of minds, rapport, reconcilement, reconciliation, unanimity, understanding

ACCOST, *verb* address, *adoriri,* affront, ambush, approach, assail, assault, assault belligerently, attack, beset, *compellare,* confront, draw near, fall upon, rise in hostility before, set upon, strike at, thrust at, waylay

ACCOUNT *(Evaluation),* *noun* appraisal, assessment, *compte rendu,* enumeration, financial statement, ledger, list of receipts and payments, *ratio,* register, statement, statement of debits and credits, statement of pecuniary transactions, tally, valuation
ASSOCIATED CONCEPTS: account rendered, account stated, accounts payable, accounts receivable, bank account, joint account, liquidated account, open account, totten trust account

ACCOUNT *(Report),* *noun* brief, description, history, memoir, *memoria, narratio,* narration, presentation, recapitulation, recital, record, review, saga, summary, summation

ACCOUNTABLE *(Explainable),* *adjective* construable, deducible, definable, describable, determinable, explicable, inferential, interpretable, renderable, translatable

ACCOUNTABLE *(Responsible),* *adjective* answerable, beholden, bound, chargeable, devolving on, liable, obligated, obliged, owing, under obligation
ASSOCIATED CONCEPTS: held accountable for one's actions

ACCOUNTANT, *noun* bookkeeper, calculator, certified public accountant, chartered accountant, clerk, reckoner, recorder, registrar, statistician

ACCOUNTING, *noun* auditing, bookkeeping, complete report, computation, full report, fully detailed analysis, reckoning
ASSOCIATED CONCEPTS: account stated, accounting officer, accounts receivable

ACCREDIT, *verb* accept, affirm, approve, authenticate, authorize, certify, confirm, endorse, ratify, sanction, validate, vouch for
ASSOCIATED CONCEPTS: accredited law school, accredited representative

ACCRETION, *noun* addition, advance, annexation, augmentation, enlargement, extension, gain, growth, increment

ACCROACH, *verb* appropriate, arrogate, assume, break bounds, encroach, impose upon, infringe, interlope, intrude, invade, obtrude, overstep, presume on, take over, transgress, trespass, usurp

ACCRUE *(Arise), verb*   acquire, be derived, become due, become enforceable, become present, come, develop, emanate, ensue, eventuate, fall due, flow, follow, inure, issue, mature, occur, originate, proceed, progress, result from, rise from, spring, yield
ASSOCIATED CONCEPTS: accrual accounting method, accrual of a cause of action, accrued benefit, accrued claims against a municipal corporation, accrued debt, accrued rights, statute of limitations, tolls
FOREIGN PHRASES: *Confirmare nemo potest prius quam jus ei acciderit.* No one can confirm a right before the right accrues to him.

ACCRUE *(Increase), verb*   accumulate, acquire, add on, advance, aggrandize, amass, amplify, annex, appreciate, augment, become added, become greater, become larger, branch out, broaden, build, build up, collect, enlarge, escalate, expand, extend, further, gain, gather, greaten, grow, heighten, improve, intensify, mount, multiply, raise, redouble, supplement, swell, widen
ASSOCIATED CONCEPTS: accrual accounting method, accrual of compensation, accrual of taxes, accrued basis, accrued costs, accrued dividend, accrued earnings, accrued income, accrued interest, accrued overtime, accrued taxes

ACCRUED, *adjective*   accumulated, added to, annexed, grew, increased, mounted, multiplied
ASSOCIATED CONCEPTS: accrued debts, accrued depreciation, accrued dividends, accrued income, accrued interest, accrued installments, accrued rent, accrued rights, accrued taxes

ACCUMULATE *(Amass), verb*   *accumulare,* agglomerate, aggregate, assemble, bring together, *coacervare,* collect, collect into a mass, collect together, colligate, combine, compile, concentrate, cumulate, garner, gather, gather into a mass, gather together, gather up, hoard, mass, pile up, stockpile, store up, unite
ASSOCIATED CONCEPTS: accumulate dividends, accumulate funds, accumulate income, accumulated damages, accumulated deductions, accumulated earnings, accumulated profits, accumulated reserve, accumulated sick leave, accumulated surplus, accumulation in a trust, accumulative judgment, accumulative sentence, consecutive sentence

ACCUMULATE *(Enlarge), verb*   accrue, add to, aggrandize, amplify, augment, broaden, build up, enlarge in size, *exaggerare,* expand, extend, gain, greaten, grow, grow larger, increase, make greater, multiply, redouble, reinforce, spread, swell
FOREIGN PHRASES: *Alienatio rei praefertur juri accrescendi.* The law prefers the alienation of property rather than accumulation.

ACCURATE, *adjective*   actual, authentic, bona fide, careful, clear-cut, conscientious, correct, defect-free, dependable, direct, errorless, exact, executed with care, explicit, factual, faithful, faultless, free of error, genuine, inerrant, literal, meticulous, minute, particular, perfect, precise, proper, punctilious, realistic, reliable, right, rigorous, scrupulous, thorough, true, trustworthy, truthful, unambiguous, unchallenged, uncolored, undenied, undeviating, undisguised, undisputed, undistorted, unerring, unimpeachable, unmistaken, unperjured, unquestionable, unrefuted, unvarnished, valid, veracious, verbatim, verifiable, well-defined

ACCUSATION, *noun*   accusal, *accusatio,* allegation, ascription, assertion, attribution, bill of indictment, charge, citation, *crimen, criminatio,* crimination, delation, filing of charges, formal charge, imputation, imputation of blame, incrimination, inculpation, indictment, information, preferring of charges, true bill, true charge
ASSOCIATED CONCEPTS: accusatory instrument, complaint, grand jury report, indictment, information, presentment, warrant
FOREIGN PHRASES: *Accusare nemo se debet, nisi coram deo.* No one is bound to accuse himself, except before God.

ACCUSE, *verb*   *accusare, arguere,* attack, blame, bring a charge, bring accusation, bring in a true bill, charge with, *citare,* cite, complain against, criminate, denounce, expose, fix blame, impeach, implicate, incriminate, inculpate, indict, lodge a complaint, prefer charges, prosecute, report against
ASSOCIATED CONCEPTS: accusatory instruments

ACCUSED *(Attacked), verb*   attacked, defamed, imputed, maligned, reproached, reproved

ACCUSED *(Charged), verb*   arraigned, brought charges, charged, complained of, filed charges, have charges against, held responsible, impeached, indicted

ACCUSER, *noun*   accusatrix, accusant, challenger, complainant, delator, denouncer, impeacher, incriminator, indictor, informer, libelant, litigant, party to a suit, petitioner, prosecutor

ACCUSTOMED *(Customary), adjective*   *adsuetus,* common, commonplace, confirmed, consuetudinal, consuetudinary, conventional, established, fixed, habitual, normal, ordinary, prevailing, regular, routine, *solitus,* traditional, usual
ASSOCIATED CONCEPTS: accustomed practice, accustomed use

ACCUSTOMED *(Familiarized), adjective*   acclimated, acclimatized, acquainted, adapted, addicted, adjusted, conditioned, familiar, familiar through use, given to, habituated, in the habit of, ingrained with

ACKNOWLEDGE *(Declare), verb*   admit, affirm, ascribe, assert, asseverate, attest to, avow, bear witness, certify, depone, depose, disclose, endorse, express, implicate oneself, state, swear

ACKNOWLEDGE *(Respond), verb*   accede, agree, answer, be responsive, concur, ratify, rejoin, remark, reply, signify assent

ACKNOWLEDGE *(Verify), verb*   admit, admit a right, admit the charge, concede, confess, confirm, defer to, recognize, recognize authority of, testify, yield
ASSOCIATED CONCEPTS: acknowledge a document, acknowledge the signatures on a will

ACKNOWLEDGMENT *(Acceptance), noun*   accession, acquiescence, admittance, agreement, answer, assent, compliance, concession, concurrence, endorsement, ratification, recognition, replication, reply, response, verification
ASSOCIATED CONCEPTS: acknowledgment to an offer

ACKNOWLEDGMENT *(Avowal),* **noun** admission, affirmation, assertion, asseveration, authentication, avowance, certification, *confessio,* confession, confirmation, declaration, formal declaration, statement, validation
ASSOCIATED CONCEPTS: acknowledgment in a deposition, acknowledgment of a conveyance, acknowledgment of a debt, acknowledgment of a deed, acknowledgment of a mortgage, acknowledgment of a will, acknowledgment of an illegitimate child, acknowledgment of indebtedness, acknowledgment of liability, certificate of acknowledgment, public acknowledgment

ACQUAINTED, *adjective* advised, apprised, attuned to, awakened, aware of, briefed, *cognitus,* cognizant of, conscious of, conversant with, enlightened, informed, instructed, introduced to, knowledgeable, notified, *notus, peritus,* posted, primed, told

ACQUIESCENCE, *noun* accedence, acceptance, accession, accordance, acknowledgment, *adsensus,* agreement, allowance, assent, compliance, concession, concordance, concurrence, consent, grant, implied consent, nonresistance, observance, passive agreement, passive consent, permission, permittance, resignedness, sanction, subjection, submission, submissiveness, submittal, sufferance, tacit assent, willingness
ASSOCIATED CONCEPTS: acquiescence in judgment, acquiescence to a breach of contract, acquiescence to a breach of covenant, acquiescence to boundaries, acquiescence to the terms of a contract, ratification by acquiescence
FOREIGN PHRASES: *Agentes et consentientes pari poena plectentur.* Acting and consenting parties are liable to the same punishment. *Longa patientia trahitur ad consensum.* Long sufferance is interpreted as consent.

ACQUIRE *(Receive),* **verb** accept, achieve, *adipisci,* adopt, be given, come into possession of, derive, gain, glean, obtain, reap, take in, win

ACQUIRE *(Secure),* **verb** *adquirere,* annex, appropriate, assume, assume ownership, attain, exact, extort, extract, force from, gain, get, make one's own, obtain by any means, procure, purchase, realize, steal, take, take possession, wrest from
ASSOCIATED CONCEPTS: acquire a business, acquire by fraud, acquire by gift, acquire by inheritance, acquire by will, acquire for resale, acquire ownership
FOREIGN PHRASES: *Incorporalia bello non adquiruntur.* Things incorporeal are not acquired in war.

ACQUISITION, *noun* acceptance, acceptation, acquirement, appropriation, assumption, attainment, find, gain, gleaning, intaking, obtainment of property, possession, procuration, procurement, realization, receival, receiving, reception, recipience, stealing, taking
ASSOCIATED CONCEPTS: acquisition by purchase, acquisition of assets, acquisition of property, acquisition value
FOREIGN PHRASES: *Qui acquirit sibi acquirit haeredibus.* He who acquires for himself acquires for his heirs.

ACQUIT, *verb* absolve, *absolvere,* clear, compurgate, declare innocent, discharge, discharge from accusation, exculpate, excuse, exempt, exonerate, find not guilty, give a favorable verdict, grant remission, let off, *liberare,* liberate, make free, pardon, pronounce not guilty, prove innocent, *purgare,* release, remit, reprieve, set at liberty, set free, vindicate
ASSOCIATED CONCEPTS: acquittal in fact, acquittal in law

ACQUITTAL, *noun* *absolutio,* absolution, acquitment, acquittance, amnesty, clearance, compurgation, discharge, dismissal, exculpation, exoneration, favorable verdict, letting off, *liberatio,* liberation, pardon, purgation, quittance, release, remission, reprieve, restoration, verdict of not guilty, vindication
ASSOCIATED CONCEPTS: acquittal by a jury
FOREIGN PHRASES: *Paribus sententiis reus absolvitur.* When the opinions are equal, where the court is equally divided, the defendant is acquitted.

ACQUITTED, *adjective* cleared, exculpated, exonerated, freed of wrongdoing, let go, let off, not guilty, proved innocent, vindicated

ACT *(Enactment),* **noun** *acte,* administration, bill, code, deed, dictate, edict, law, legislation, legislative decree, *lex,* mandate, ordinance, precept, prescript, *règlement,* regulation, resolution, rule, ruling, statute, written law
ASSOCIATED CONCEPTS: Congressional act, legislative act
FOREIGN PHRASES: *Actus legis nemini est damnosus.* The act of the law shall prejudice no one.

ACT *(Undertaking),* **noun** accomplishment, achievement, action, commission, course, dealing, deed, doing, effectuation, enterprise, execution, feat, implementation, maneuver, manipulation, measure, method, move, operation, performance, perpetration, step, stratagem, task, transaction
ASSOCIATED CONCEPTS: act in official capacity, act of bankruptcy, act of commission, act of cruelty, act of embezzlement, act of flight, act of God, act of infringement, act of insolvency, act of larceny, act of law, act of misfeasance, act of necessity, act of omission, act of ownership, act of providence, act of reckless disregard, act of violence, act of war, *actus reas,* judicial act, mala prohibita act, overt act
FOREIGN PHRASES: *Actus me invito factus non est meus actus.* An act done by me, against my will, is not my act. *Actus non facit reum, nisi mens sit rea.* An act does not render a person guilty, unless the mind is guilty. *Idem est facere, et non prohibere cum possis.* It is the same thing to commit an act as not to prohibit it, when it is in your power. *Facta sunt potentiora verbis.* Acts or deeds are more powerful than words.

ACTING, *adjective* adjutant, deputative, deputy, functioning, holding legal rights conferred by another, impermanent, replacing, representative, representing, short-term, speaking by delegated authority, standing in the place of, substituting for, temporary, transient
ASSOCIATED CONCEPTS: acting illegally, acting in a boisterous manner, acting in concert with others, acting in good faith, acting judge, acting mayor, acting officer, acting within the course of employment, acting within the scope of employment

ACTION *(Performance),* **noun** accomplishment, achievement, administration, carrying out, concrete results, consummation, course of conduct, discharge, doing, effectuation, enforcement, execution, *factum,* implementation, line of action

FOREIGN PHRASES: *Non quod dictum est, sed quod factum est inspicitur.* Not what is said, but what is done, is to be regarded. *Factum cuique suum, non adversario, nocere debet.* A man's own acts should prejudice himself, not his adversary. *Factum infectum fieri nequit.* A thing which has been done cannot be undone. *Les lois ne se chargent de punir que les actions exterieures.* Laws do not assume to punish other than overt acts.

ACTION *(Proceeding), noun*   *actio,* action at law, case, cause, cause in court, court proceeding, formal prosecution, hearing, hearing on the merits, judicial contest, judicial proceeding, lawsuit, legal action, legal contest, legal proceeding, *lis,* litigation, litigation of the charges, prosecution, suit, suit at law, suit in law, trial, trial of a case, trial of the issues

ASSOCIATED CONCEPTS: abatement, action arising under the laws of the United States, action at law, action brought, action by one party against another, action ex delicto, action ex parte, action for a declaratory judgment, action for bodily injury, action for breach of a contract, action for damages, action for deceit, action for disparagement, action for dissolution, action for divorce, action for fraud, action for injury to property, action for liquidated damages, action for misrepresentation, action for money damages, action for rescission and restitution, action for recovery of chattel, action in assumpsit, action in conversion, action in detinue, action in ejectment, action in equity, action in interpleader, action in personam, action in quantum meruit, action in rem, action in replevin, action in tort, action in trespass, action in trover, action of foreclosure, action of garnishment, action on a contract, action on a debt, action on account rendered, action on contract, action quasi in rem, action to quiet title, action to remove a cloud, affirmative action, cause of action, chose in action, civil action, class action, commence an action, consolidation, continuance of action on submitted facts, criminal action, cross action, derivative action, independent actions, joinder of actions, joint action, legal action, local actions, main action, multiplicity of actions, pending action, right of action, severance of actions, stockholders' action, third-party action

FOREIGN PHRASES: *Ex nudo pacto non oritus nascitur actio.* No action arises on a contract without a consideration. *Cum actio fuerit mere criminalis, institui poterit ab initio criminaliter vel civiliter.* When an action is merely criminal, it can be instituted either criminally or civilly at the outset. *In rem actio est per quam rem nostram quae ab alio possidetur petimus, et semper adversus eum est qui rem possidet.* An action in rem is one by means of which we seek our property which is owned by another, and is always against him who possesses the property. *Actio quaelibet it sua via.* Every action proceeds in its own course. *Secta est pugna civilis; sicut actores armantur actionibus, et, quasi, gladiis accinguntur, ita rei muniuntur exceptionibus, et defenduntur, quasi, clypeis.* A suit is a civil battle; for as the plaintiffs are armed with actions, and as it were, girded with swords, so the defendants are fortified with pleas, and defended, as it were, by shields. *Remoto impedimento, emergit actio.* The impediment being removed, the action emerges. *Omnis quereia et omnis actio injuriarum limita est infra certa tempora.* Every complaint and every action for injuries is limited within

certain times. *Omnes actiones in mundo infra certa tempora habent limitationem.* All actions in the world are limited within certain periods of time. *In haeredes non solent transire actiones quae poenales ex maleficio sunt.* Penal actions arising from anything of a criminal nature do not pass to heirs. *Actio personalis moritur cum persona.* A personal action dies with the person. *Ex tupi causa non oritur actio.* No cause of action arises out of an immoral or illegal consideration.

ACTIONABLE, *adjective*   accountable, amenable, answerable, bound, causidical, chargeable, controvertible, disputable, justiciable, liable to prosecution, litigable, litigant, litigious, pertaining to litigation, remediable by an action at law, *res cuius actio est,* responsible, suable, under legal obligation, under obligation, unexempt from

ASSOCIATED CONCEPTS: actionable cause of action, actionable charges, actionable claim, actionable words, actionable wrongdoing

ACTIVE, *adjective*   assiduous, at work, busily employed, busily engaged, busy, effective, effectual, efficacious, efficient, energetic, enterprising, functioning, *impiger,* in a state of action, in actual process, in operation, in practice, industrious, *industrius, navus,* operant, operating, performing, sedulous, trenchant, vigorous, working

ASSOCIATED CONCEPTS: active concealment, active negligence, active participant, active tort feasor, active trust, active wrongdoing, passive negligence, passive tort feasor

ACTIVITY, *noun*   assignment, campaign, cause, crusade, drive, endeavor, enterprise, function, interest, movement, operation, pursuit, undertaking, venture, work

ACT OF GOD, *noun*   accident, chance occurrence, fortuitousness, fortuity, random luck

ACTOR, *noun*   *actor,* aggrieved party, complainant, intervener, litigant, malcontent, man with a grievance, operator, participant, party, performer, person, petitioner, plaintiff, *qui facit*

ASSOCIATED CONCEPTS: an actor as a witness in a prosecution, an actor in a legal proceeding

ACTUAL, *adjective*   absolute, accurate, as represented, ascertained, authentic, authenticated, *bona fide,* categorical, categorically true, certain, concrete, correct, *de facto,* decided, defined, definite, demonstrable, demonstrated, determinate, essential, exact, existent, existing, factual, faithful, genuine, honest, in fact, *ipse,* literal, nonabstract, not fictitious, not imaginary, not merely supposed, objective, official, palpable, positive, precise, present, real, realistic, right, rightful, specific, substantial, substantive, tangible, true, true to the facts, true to the letter, truthful, unerring, unerroneous, unfallacious, unfalse, unimagined, unimpeachable, unmistaken, unrefuted, unsupposed, valid, veracious, veritable, *verus,* well-founded, well-grounded

ASSOCIATED CONCEPTS: actual authority, actual bailment, actual book value, actual case or controversy, actual cash receipts, actual cash value, actual damages, actual delivery, actual earnings, actual eviction, actual expense, actual force, actual fraud, actual income, actual intent, actual intent to defraud, actual knowledge, actual loss, actual malice, actual market value, actual notice, actual occupancy, actual possession, actual residence, actual use, actual value, actual waste, actually engaged in business, actually occupied, actually owing, actually owning, actually receive, fair, fair reasonable cash price, reasonable cash price

ACTUARY, noun calculator of insurance risks, compiler of tables of mortality, insurance adviser, statistician
ASSOCIATED CONCEPTS: actuarial bureaus, actuarial solvency, actuarial tables

ACUTE, adjective acer, acuminate, acutus, alert, apt, astute, aware, clear-sighted, critical, crucial, cutting, discerning, fine, foreseeing, intense, intuitive, keen, keenly sensitive, knowledgeable, penetrating, perceptive, perspicacious, perspicax, piercing, pointed, prompt, provident, prudent, quick-witted, sagax, sapient, sharp, sharp-edged, sharp-witted, subtilis, trenchant, vivid

AD DAMNUM CLAUSE, noun claim for damages, demanded damages, fixed amount of damages, monetary clause, provision for damages

AD HOC, adjective extemporaneous, for the sake of, for this case alone, improvised, in consideration of, on account of, special
ASSOCIATED CONCEPTS: ad hoc appointment, ad hoc committee

AD INFINITUM, adverb boundlessly, endlessly, eternally, illimitably, immeasurably, incalculably, incomprehensibly, indefinitely, indeterminately, innumerably, interminably, limitlessly, measurelessly, to infinity, without end

AD INTERIM, adverb at the same time, during, during the interval, en attendant, for a time, for the time being, in the course of, in the interim, in the intervening time, in the meantime, in the meanwhile, meantime, meanwhile, pending, throughout, till, until, when, while
ASSOCIATED CONCEPTS: ad interim copyright, ad interim restraining order

AD VALOREM, adjective according to value, appraised, appraisement, assessable, assessment, charge, chargeable, charged, dutiable, duty, evaluated, excisable, imposition, leviable, levy, ratable, taxation, valorization, value added tax, valued at
ASSOCIATED CONCEPTS: ad valorem tax

ADAPT, verb acclimatize, accommodate oneself, adjust, alter, aptare, arrange, change, comply with, conform, convert, correlate, fashion, fit, make conformable, make suitable, modify, modulate, readjust, reconcile, regularize, render accordant, revise, standardize, temper, transform, work a change

ADDENDUM, noun additament, addition, adjunct, affix, annex, annexation, annexe, appanage, appendage, appendix, attachment, codicil, complement, concomitant, inclusion, insertion, postscript, rider, subscript, supplement, supplementation
ASSOCIATED CONCEPTS: addendum to a contract, pocket part

ADDICT, noun adherent, ardent admirer, believer, creature of habit, devotee, disciple, enthusiast, fan, fanatic, fancier, follower, frequenter, partisan, practitioner, pursuer, votary, zealot

ADDICTED, adjective accustomed, attached, fanatic, given over, habituated, imbued with, in the habit, indulgent, obsessed with, prone to, rei deditus, surrendered to, under the influence of, wedded to
ASSOCIATED CONCEPTS: addicted to alcohol, addicted to drugs, addicted to pills

ADDITION, noun accessio, accession, accessory, addend, addendum, additament, additive, adiectio, adjunct, adjunction, annex, annexation, attachment, augmentation, complement, enlargement, extension, increase, increment, joining, pendant, subjunction, supplement
ASSOCIATED CONCEPTS: addition to a structure

ADDITIONAL, adjective accessory, added, additive, additus, adiectus, another, appended, auxiliary, collateral, extra, further, included, joined, more, other, superadded, supervenient, supplemental, supplementary, ulterior
ASSOCIATED CONCEPTS: additional assured, additional burden, additional charges, additional compensation, additional consideration, additional coverage, additional duties, additional insured, additional relief, additional servitude

ADDITIVE, noun accrual, addendum, addition, adjunct, appurtenance, attachment, augmentation, enhancement, extension, increment, supplement

ADDITUR, noun assessment of damages, increase of damages, increase of jury award

ADDRESS, noun abode, box number, domicile, dwelling, dwelling place, habitation, headquarters, home, inhabitancy, inscriptio, legal residence, locus, lodging, lodging place, lodgment, place of business, residence, seat, street number
ASSOCIATED CONCEPTS: business address, last known address, local address, office address, post office address, residence

ADDRESS (Direct attention to), verb apply oneself to, approach, be occupied with, bring to attention, bring to notice, call attention to, call to notice, concern oneself with, devote oneself to, direct to, occupy oneself with

ADDRESS (Petition), verb appeal, call upon, enter a plea, enter a suit for, plead, prepare a complaint, prepare a formal request, prepare a petition, seek redress
ASSOCIATED CONCEPTS: address the court

ADDRESS (Talk to), verb deliver a talk, discourse, discuss, give a speech, harangue, hominem adloqui, lecture, orate, preach, se rei dedere, sermonize, speak to

ADDUCE, verb adducere, advance, allege, allude, assert, assign, aver, bring to the fore, claim, declare, disclose, divulge, evidence, evince, furnish, give, indicate, introduce, manifest, mention, offer, place in the foreground, plead, present, produce, producere, proferre, proffer, propound, reveal, show, state
ASSOCIATED CONCEPTS: adduce evidence, adduce testimony

ADEEM, *verb*   abnegate, abolish, abrogate, annul, avoid, cancel, declare null and void, deny, deprive of, disinherit, disseise, divest, make void, negate, nullify, obliterate, offset, remove, render null and void, render void, repeal, repudiate, rescind, retract, revoke, take away, take back, take from, vacate, void, withdraw
ASSOCIATED CONCEPTS: adeem a bequest, adeem a devise, adeem a gift, adeem a legacy

ADEMPTION, *noun*   abnegation, abolishment, abolition, abrogation, annulment, cancellation, cancellation of a legacy, contravention, disclamation, discontinuance, disownment, dissolution, extinction, invalidation, negation, nullification, recall, renouncement, renunciation, repeal, repudiation, rescindment, rescission, retraction, revocation, revokement, vacation, vacatur, voidance, withdrawal, withdrawment
ASSOCIATED CONCEPTS: ademption of a bequest, ademption of a devise, ademption of a gift, ademption of a legacy, operation of law, satisfaction

ADEQUATE, *adjective*   able, acceptable, *accommodatus,* ample, *aptus,* availing, capable, commensurate, competent, effectual, enough, equal to the need, fair, fit, fully sufficient, *idoneus,* proportionate, reasonable, reasonably sufficient, satisfactory, satisfying, serving, sufficient, sufficient for the purpose, sufficing, suitable, valid
ASSOCIATED CONCEPTS: adequate administrative review, adequate care, adequate cause, adequate consideration, adequate notice, adequate remedy at law, adequate support, fair and adequate consideration

ADEQUATE NOTICE, *noun*   ample notice, commensurate notice, fair notice, good notice, satisfactory notice, sufficient notice, suitable notice, valid notice
ASSOCIATED CONCEPTS: adequate care, adequate compensation, adequate remedy at law, adequate security

ADHERE *(Fasten), verb*   agglutinate, anchor, attach, band together, cement, clamp, clasp, cling to, coalesce, cohere, compound, fuse, glue, hold fast, hold firmly, *inhaerere,* join, latch, secure, stick to, stick together, tighten, unite

ADHERE *(Maintain loyalty), verb*   abide by, act in support, advocate, argue for, back, be devoted, be faithful, be loyal, be partisan, be steadfast, be true, champion, comply, conform, *deditum esse,* defend, devote oneself, espouse, follow, give support, keep faith, obey, pay allegiance, preserve, show devotion, stand by, *studere,* support, uphold

ADHERE *(Persist), verb*   abide, be constant, be devoted, be obstinate, be steadfast, be steady, be unyielding, carry on, cling tenaciously, continue, endure, go to any lengths, go to the limit, have tenacity, hold on, hold tight, *in re stare,* keep going, keep on, maintain, *manere,* persevere, persist in, pursue, show determination, stand firm, stick to, sustain, work unceasingly
ASSOCIATED CONCEPTS: adhere to the Constitution, adhere to the terms of a contract

ADHERENCE *(Adhesion), noun*   attachment, bond, cementation, coherence, cohesion, cohesiveness, concretion, conglutination, connectedness, firmness, fixedness, holding together, sticking together, tenaciousness, tenacity, tie

ADHERENCE *(Devotion), noun*   allegiance, attachment, *bona fide,* bond, compliance, constancy, dedication, devotedness, faithfulness, fealty, fidelity, homage, loyalty, obedience, observance, steadfastness, tenaciousness, tenacity, tie, troth
ASSOCIATED CONCEPTS: adherence to a contract, adherence to the principles of the Constitution

ADHESION *(Affixing), noun*   adherence, adhesiveness, agglomeration, agglutination, aggregation, attachment, cementation, clinging, close contact, coadunation, coagulation, coherence, cohesion, cohesiveness, concretion, condensation, congelation, conglomeration, conglutination, conjunction, connection, consolidation, fusion, glutinosity, gumminess, gummosity, inseparability, inseparableness, iron grip, junction, prehension, solidification, stickiness, union, unity, viscidity, viscosity
ASSOCIATED CONCEPTS: contract of adhesion, unequal bargaining power

ADHESION *(Loyalty), noun*   adherence, adherence to duty, allegiance, alliance, ardor, association, attachment, attention, *bona fide,* bond, close identification, commitment, conscientiousness, consecration, constancy, dependability, devotedness, devotion, devoutness, dutifulness, earnestness, faithfulness, fealty, fidelity, firmness, homage, incorruptibility, integrity, obedience, reliability, resolution, scrupulousness, sense of duty, sense of responsibility, service, servitude, single-mindedness, stanchness, steadfastness, strong connection, submission, submissiveness, subservience, support, tenaciousness, tenacity, tie, troth, trueness, trustiness, trustworthiness, union, unswerving fidelity, vote of confidence, willingness, zeal

ADJACENT, *adjective*   abutting, adjoining, alongside, beside, bordering, conterminous, contiguous, *contiguus,* continuous, convergent, *finitimus,* juxtaposed, meeting, neighboring, next to, proximal, touching, verging on, vicinal, *vicinus*
ASSOCIATED CONCEPTS: adjacent county, adjacent land, adjacent owners, adjacent property

ADJECTIVE LAW, *noun*   legal course to adhere to, legal methods, procedural law

ADJOIN, *verb*   abut on, *adiacere,* appose, *attingere,* be adjacent to, be contiguous to, be joined to, border on, cohere, conjoin, connect, converge, juxtapose, juxtaposit, lie beside, lie near to, meet, neighbor, place side by side, reach to, stand by, *tangere,* touch

ADJOINER, *noun*   addition to, appendage, attachment, conjoiner, connection, convergence, subjoiner

ADJOURN, *verb*   *ampliare,* continue, defer, delay, hold in abeyance, hold over, intermit, keep pending, postpone, prorogue, put off, recess, reserve, stop, suspend, terminate
ASSOCIATED CONCEPTS: adjourn a case, adjourn a proceeding, adjourn for a session of the court, adjourn for the term of the court, adjourn on consent, adjourned term

ADJOURNMENT, *noun*   adjournal, break, continuation, deferment, *dilatio,* discontinuation, extension, hold-over, intermission, interruption, moratorium, postponement, prolongation, prorogation, protraction,

recess, reservation, respite, stay, suspension, termination
ASSOCIATED CONCEPTS: adjournment for a session, adjournment for the term, adjournment in contemplation of dismissal, adjournment of a trial, adjournment of a hearing, adjournment of the court, *sine die*

ADJUDGE, *verb*   *addicere, adiudicare,* adjudicate, arbitrate, award, conclude, decide, decree, deem, deliver judgment, determine, dispense, dispense judgment, exercise judgment, find, give an opinion, hold, judge, judicate, judicially determine, make a decision, order, pass judgment, pronounce formally, rule, sentence, settle, sit in judgment
ASSOCIATED CONCEPTS: adjudge bankrupt, adjudge guilt, adjudge incompetent, adjudge innocence, adjudge insolvent, adjudge liability
FOREIGN PHRASES: *Res judicata pro veritate accipitur.* A thing which is adjudicated is accepted or received for the truth.

ADJUDICATE, *verb*   adjudge, arbitrate, award, award judgment, conclude, decide, decree, deem, deliver judgment, determine, determine finally, exercise judicial authority, find, give judgment, hear, hear the case, hold court, judge, make a decision, mediate, order, pass judgment, pass sentence, pronounce, referee, render judgment, rule, rule upon, settle, sit in judgment, try, try the cause
ASSOCIATED CONCEPTS: adjudicate a juvenile delinquent, adjudicate a youthful offender, adjudicate an incompetent, adjudicate bankruptcy, adjudicate guilt, adjudicate innocence, adjudicate insolvency, adjudicate jurisdictional questions, adjudicate liability
FOREIGN PHRASES: *Cessa regnare, si non vis judicare.* Cease to reign, if you don't wish to adjudicate. *In propria causa nemo judex.* No one can be a judge in his own cause.

ADJUDICATION, *noun*   act of judgment, adjudgment, arbitrage, arbitrament, arbitration, authoritative decision, award, conclusion, decision, declaration, decree, deliberate determination, determination, determination of issues, disposition, edict, final determination, final judgment, finding, irrevocable decision, judgment, judgment on facts, judicial decision, opinion, order, order of the court, proclamation, pronouncement, reasoned judgment, *res judicata,* resolution, result, ruling, sentence, settled decision, verdict
ASSOCIATED CONCEPTS: adjudication of a court of competent jurisdiction, adjudication of bankruptcy, adjudication of guilt, adjudication of incompetency, adjudication of innocence, adjudication of insolvency, adjudication of liability, adjudication on the merits, adjudication under law, adjudicative facts, judicial assessment
FOREIGN PHRASES: *Novum judicium non dat novum jus, sed declarat antiquum; quia judicium est juris dictum et per judicium jus est noviter revelatum quod diu fuit velatum.* A new adjudication does not promulgate a new law, but declares the old; because adjudication is the utterance of the law, and by adjudication the law is newly revealed which was for a long time hidden. *Res judicata pro veritate accipitur.* A thing which is adjudicated is accepted or received for the truth.

ADJUNCT, *adjective*   accessory, addendum, additament, addition, appanage, appendage, augmentation, auxiliary, branch, complement, component, corollary, extension, subordinate part, supplement

FOREIGN PHRASES: *Sublato principali, tollitur adjunctum.* By the removal of the principal thing, the adjunct is taken also.

ADJURATION, *noun*   affirmation, attestation, averment, avouchment, avowal, avowance, declaration, legal pledge, oath, pledge, solemn avowal, swearing, sworn statement, testimony, vouching, vow

ADJUST *(Regulate),* *verb*   *accommodare,* accommodate, adapt, *aptare,* attemper, balance, calibrate, coordinate, establish equilibrium, even, methodize, moderate, normalize, reset, restore equilibrium, stabilize, standardize, strike a balance, systematize, temper, tune
ASSOCIATED CONCEPTS: adjust differences, adjusted, adjusted cost basis, adjusted gross income

ADJUST *(Resolve),* *verb*   accord, amend, arrange, bring to agreement, change, clarify, complete, conclude, conform, correct, curb, emendate, fix, mitigate, rectify, redress, remedy, set, settle, solve, treat
ASSOCIATED CONCEPTS: adjust a claim

ADJUSTER, *noun*   arbitrater, interagent, interceder, intercessor, interlocutor, intermediary, intermediate, intermediator, intermedium, intervener, mediator, negotiant, negotiator, reconciler

ADJUSTMENT, *noun*   abatement of differences, *accommodatio,* accommodation, accord, accordance, adaptation, agreement, arrangement, attunement, bargain, binding agreement, coaptation, compact, composition, compromise, concurrence, conformance, conformation, conformity, congruence, congruity, consistency, contract, coordination, correction, covenant, disposition, harmony, mutual concession, mutual understanding, negotiation, pact, reconcilement, reconciliation, rectification, regulating, settlement, stipulation, terms, understanding, uniformity
ASSOCIATED CONCEPTS: adjusted basis, adjusted reserves, adjustment of contracts, adjustment of loss, adjustments in wills

ADMINISTER *(Conduct),* *verb*   administrate, carry out, control, direct, dispose of, effect, effectuate, enforce, engineer, govern, guide, handle, have executive charge of, manage, mastermind, minister, officiate, operate, overlook, oversee, pilot, prescribe, preside over, *procurare,* put in force, regulate, *rem administrare, rempublicam gubernare,* settle, steer, superintend, supervise
ASSOCIATED CONCEPTS: administer a bankrupt's assets, administer an estate, administer the law

ADMINISTER *(Tender),* *verb*   accord, afford, bestow on, confer, deal out, disburse, dispense, disperse, distribute, dole out, extend, give, impart, issue, measure out, mete out, offer, *procurare,* provide with, render
ASSOCIATED CONCEPTS: administer drugs, administer oaths

ADMINISTRATION, *noun*   *administratio,* care, conduct, control, direction, dispensation, disposal, disposition, distribution, execution, executive charge, guardianship, guidance, handling, keeping, management, ministration, oversight, performance of executive duties, practical management, *procuratio,* regulation, settlement of an estate, superintendence, supervision

ASSOCIATED CONCEPTS: administration of a bankrupt's estate, administration of an estate, administration of expenses, administration of the laws, fair administration of justice, trust administration

FOREIGN PHRASES: *Nihil infra regnum subditos magis conservat in tranquilitate et concordia quam debita legum administratio.* Nothing better preserves in tranquillity and concord those subjected to the same government than the due administration of the laws.

ADMINISTRATIVE, *adjective* directorial, guiding, managerial, managing, ministerial, regulative, superintending, supervising, supervisory

ASSOCIATED CONCEPTS: administrative act, administrative action, administrative agency, administrative board, administrative body, administrative capacity, administrative discretion, administrative function, administrative hearings, administrative judges, administrative law, administrative procedures, administrative proceeding, administrative process, administrative regulations, administrative remedy, administrative rulings

ADMINISTRATOR, *noun* administrative head, chief executive, curator, custodian, director, executive, guardian, head of affairs, intendant, leader, legal representative, manager, officer of the court, overseer, personal representative, supervisor, supervisor of an estate, trustee

ASSOCIATED CONCEPTS: *administrator cum testamento annexo, administrator de bonis non, administrator de bonis non cum testamento annexo,* administrator executor, administrator general, *administrator pendente lite,* administrator's bond, administratrix, administratrix general, ancillary administrator, *executrix administrator ad prosequendum,* legal representative, supervisor of an estate

ADMISSIBILITY, *noun* acceptability, adequateness, allowableness, applicability, appositeness, appropriateness, aptness, eligibility, fitness, justifiability, legality, legitimacy, permissibility, presentability, propriety, reasonability, sanctionability, sanctionableness, sufficiency, suitability, tolerability, unexceptionability, unobjectionability, warrantability, warrantableness

ASSOCIATED CONCEPTS: affirmative evidence, confessions, decedent's statements, extrajudicial statements, hearsay, objections, secondary evidence

ADMISSIBLE, *adjective* à propos, acceptable, *aequus,* allowable, allowed, applicable, appropriate, approvable, authorized, eligible, justifiable, legal, legitimate, licensed, passable, permissible, permitted, presentable, proper, qualified, sanctionable, sanctioned, suitable, tolerable, unexceptionable, unforbidden, unobjectionable, unprohibited, warrantable, warranted

ASSOCIATED CONCEPTS: admissions of party-opponent, confessions, declarations against interest, limited admissibility, McNabb-Mallory rule, Miranda rule, nolo contendere, offer of proof, probative value, requests for admissions, secondary evidence

ADMISSIBLE EVIDENCE, *noun* acceptable evidence, creditable evidence, legal evidence, permissible evidence

ADMISSION *(Disclosure), noun* acknowledgment, assertion, attestation, avowal, communication, *concessio,* concession, confession, declaration, divulgence, enlightenment, exposure, expression, profession, revealment, revelation, statement, testimonial averment, testimony, unmasking, unveiling, voluntary acknowledgment

ASSOCIATED CONCEPTS: acknowledged adversary's claim, admission against interest, admission against pecuniary interest, admission as an exemption to the hearsay rule, admission by conduct, admission by flight, admission implied from silence, admission in a pleading, admission in an answer from a failure to deny, admission of a debt, admission of a fact, admission of a party, admission of guilt, admission of liability, admission to a crime, admission to bail, admissions by a representative, declaration against interest, direct admissions, expression admissions, extrajudicial admissions, implied admission, incidental admissions, inconsistent statement, judicial admissions, oral admissions, plenary admissions, written admissions

FOREIGN PHRASES: *Qui non negat fatetur.* He who does not deny admits.

ADMISSION *(Entry), noun* access, admittance, avenue, course, entrance, entryway, ingress, inlet, opening, passage, passageway, path, road, roadway, route, way

ASSOCIATED CONCEPTS: admission to bail, admission to practice law, admission to the bar

ADMIT *(Concede), verb* accede, accept, acknowledge, acquiesce, affirm, agree, assent, *concedere,* concur, confess, confirm, declare, disclose, divulge, enlighten, expose, *fateri,* grant, recognize, relate, reveal, unmask, unveil

ASSOCIATED CONCEPTS: admit fault, admit in a reply, admit in an answer, admit liability, admit to probate

ADMIT *(Give access), verb* adeundi copiam, admittere, allow entrance, create an opening, give right of entry to, inaugurate, induct, initiate, install, institute, invest, open a passage, open a path, open a road, open a route, open an entryway, open an inlet, *recipere,* throw open, vest, yield passage to

ASSOCIATED CONCEPTS: admit to bail, admit to practice

ADMITTANCE *(Acceptance), noun* admission, confirmation, designation, entrance, entree, entry, inclusion, induction, initiation, permission

ADMITTANCE *(Means of approach), noun* access, admission, approach, avenue, course, entrance, entry, entryway, ingress, inlet, liberty of approach, opening, passage, passageway, path, portal, road, route, way

ADMITTEDLY, *adverb* acceptedly, allowedly, assuredly, authentically, authoritatively, avowedly, certainly, concededly, confessedly, doubtlessly, genuinely, incontestably, incontrovertibly, indisputably, indubitably, irrefragably, irrefutably, surely, truly, undeniably, undoubtedly, unquestionably, validly, veritably

ADMONISH *(Advise), verb* admonere, advocate, alert, call attention to, charge, correct, counsel, enjoin, exhort, give advice, give counsel, give notice, inform, instruct, notify, offer counsel, prescribe, propound, recommend, submit, suggest, urge

ADMONISH *(Warn), verb* address a warning to, administer a rebuke, advise against, caution, censure, *commonere,* counsel against, dehort, deprecate, exhort, expostulate, forebode, forewarn, give warning, *monere,* objurgate, premonish, prewarn, rebuke, remonstrate, reprehend, reprimand, reprove, warn against

ADMONITION, noun admonishment, advance notice, advice, alarm, animadversion, caution, *caveat,* censure, commonition, contraindication, contrariety, contrary advice, counsel, dehortation, deprecation, dissuasion, exhortation, expostulation, foreboding, forewarning, hindrance, increpation, indication, instruction, intimidation, judicial reprimand, monition, notice, notification, object lesson, objection, protest, rebuke, reminder, remonstrance, reprimand, reproach, reprobation, reproof, signal, stricture, warning

ADOLESCENCE, noun *adulescentia,* immaturity, juniority, juvenility, minority, nonage, puberty, pubescence, puerility, youth

ADOLESCENT, noun junior, juvenile, minor, teenager, young person, youngling, youngster, youth

ADOPT, verb accept, *ad sententiam,* admit, *adoptare,* affiliate, annex, appropriate, arrogate, assimilate, assume, attach oneself to, avail oneself of, borrow, choose, co-opt, conform to, *constituere,* denizenize, elect, embrace, endenizen, espouse, exercise one's option, follow, foster, imitate, make one's own, naturalize, raise, seize, select, select as one's own, take, take on, take possession of, take up, try, usurp, utilize, vote to accept **ASSOCIATED CONCEPTS:** adopt a child, adopt a law, adopt a philosophy, legitimation, support

ADOPTION (*Acceptance*), **noun** acknowledgment, admission, approbation, approval, assimilation, assumption, attachment to, choice, co-optation, election, embracement, espousal, favorable reception, ratification, reception, recognition, sanction, selection **ASSOCIATED CONCEPTS:** adoption by estoppel, adoption of a contract, adoption of a proposal, adoption of domicile, arrogation

ADOPTION (*Affiliation*), **noun** *adoptio,* custody, fosterage, guardianship, parentage, protection, protectorship, wardship **ASSOCIATED CONCEPTS:** adoption decree, adoption petition, custody, foster care, foster parent, inheritance by adoption, intestate succession, legitimation, legitimation of child, parental rights, paternity proceedings, support, wards of the juvenile court

ADOPTIVE, adjective *adoptivus,* appointive, choosing, discretional, elective, preferential, selective **ASSOCIATED CONCEPTS:** adoptive father, adoptive mother, adoptive parent, foster care, inheritance by adoptive parents, inheritance from adoptive parents, intestate succession, parental rights, wards of the juvenile court

ADULT, noun *adultus,* elder, fully developed person, fully grown person, grown-up person, mature person, one who has attained legal majority, person of age, person of voting age, *pubes,* senior **ASSOCIATED CONCEPTS:** adult male, adult person, adult woman, age of majority

ADULTERATE, verb abase, *adulterare,* change for the worse, contaminate, *corrumpere,* corrupt, debase, debilitate, defile, degrade, denature, depreciate, deteriorate, devalue, devitalize, impair, infect, lessen, lower

the standard, make impure, make lower in quality, mar, pervert, pollute, render spurious, spoil, taint, tamper with, *vitiare,* vitiate, weaken

ADULTERY, noun *adulterium,* criminal unchastity, cuckoldry, extramarital promiscuity, extramarital relations, illicit intercourse, illicit love, illicit sexual intercourse, infidelity, marital infidelity, sexual unfaithfulness of a married person, unfaithfulness, unlawful carnal connection, unlawful carnal knowledge, unlawful carnality, violation of the marriage vows **ASSOCIATED CONCEPTS:** adultery by collusion, adultery by connivance, condonation of adultery, criminal conversation, dissolution of marriage, recrimination of an action of adultery

ADVANCE (*Allowance*), **noun** accommodation, anticipated loan, cash payment, compensation, credit, defrayment, disbursement, emolument, expenditure, fee, giving beforehand, installment, investment, pay, payment beforehand, remuneration, subscription **ASSOCIATED CONCEPTS:** advance as against profits, advancement from an estate grant, future advances

ADVANCE (*Increase*), **noun** amplification, augmentation, elaboration, enhancement, enlargement, enrichment, expansion, extension, improvement, increase, increment, intensification, prolongation, protraction

ADVANCE (*Progression*), **noun** elevation, expedition, facilitation, forward motion, forward movement, forwarding, headway, progress, progression, *progressus,* promotion, upsurge **ASSOCIATED CONCEPTS:** advance payment, advance sheets, anticipatory repudiation, contract breached in advance

ADVANCEMENT (*Improvement*), **noun** aggrandizement, amplification, betterment, development, elaboration, elevation, emendation, enlargement, expansion, furtherance, gain, *gradus amplior,* growth, increase, progress, progression, promotion, rise

ADVANCEMENT (*Loan*), **noun** accommodation, advance, allowance, anticipation, concession, consideration, investment, realization in advance **ASSOCIATED CONCEPTS:** intestate succession, statute of distribution

ADVANTAGE, noun accommodation, aid, approval, ascendancy, asset, assistance, authority, avail, behoof, benefit, choice, convenience, dominance, easement, edge, eminence, expedience, favor, favorable opportunity, favoring circumstance, gain, good, head start, help, hold, improvement, influence, lead, leverage, mastery, odds, patronage, plus, position, power, precedence, predominance, preeminence, preference, prestige, primacy, privilege, profit, protection, resources, sake, sanction, success, superior situation, superiority, support, supremacy, sway, upper hand, utility, welfare, worth

ADVERSARY, adjective *adversarius,* adverse party, antagonist, competitor, contender, contestant, contester, corival, disputant, dissentient, enemy, foe, litigant, opponent, opposer, opposing party, oppositionist, oppugnant, resister, rival **ASSOCIATED CONCEPTS:** adversary parties, adversary proceeding

ADVERSE *(Hostile)*, **adjective** antagonistic, antagonistical, deprecatory, disagreeable, discordant, disinclined, disobedient, dissuasive, fractious, inauspicious, indisposed, *infensus,* inimical, intolerant, opposed, recalcitrant, renitent, repugnant, resistive, restive, uncooperative, unfriendly, unpropitious, unreconciled, untoward, unwilling

ASSOCIATED CONCEPTS: adverse claim, adverse effect, adverse enjoyment of property, adverse interest, adverse possession, adverse use, adverse user, adverse witness

FOREIGN PHRASES: *Longa possessio parit jus possidendi, et tollit actionem vero domino.* Long possession creates the right of possession, and ripens into a right of action against the real owner.

ADVERSE *(Negative)*, **adjective** afflictive, calamitous, catastrophic, corrosive, deleterious, destructive, detrimental, dire, disadvantageous, disastrous, disserviceable, dreadful, harmful, hurtful, injurious, insalubrious, malefic, maleficent, prejudicial, ruinous, scatheful, unadvisable, unfavorable, unfortunate

ASSOCIATED CONCEPTS: adverse determination of the court, adverse effect, adverse holding of the court, adverse interest

ADVERSE *(Opposite)*, **adjective** *adversus,* antipodal, antipodean, antithetical, antonymous, at variance, conflicting, conflictive, contradictory, contradistinct, contrapositive, contrariant, contrarious, *contrarius,* contrary, contrastable, converse, counter, counteractive, diametrically opposite, inverse, irreconcilable, obverse, reverse

ASSOCIATED CONCEPTS: adverse action, adverse party

ADVERSE POSSESSION, *noun* acquisition, appropriation, assumption, attainment, obtainment, ownership, procurement, proprietorship, recovery, seizure

ASSOCIATED CONCEPTS: adverse claim, adverse holding, adverse interest, adverse party, adverse user, adverse verdict, adverse witness

ADVERSITY, *noun* adverse circumstances, adverse fortune, affliction, bale, *calamitas,* calamity, catastrophe, *contretemps,* difficulty, disaster, distress, hardship, injuriousness, injury, misadventure, mischance, *miseria,* misfortune, mishap, oppression, perdition, *res adversae,* ruination, ruinousness, setback, suffering, tragedy, visitation

ADVICE, *noun* advisement, advocacy, communication of knowledge, *consilium,* counsel, direction, guidance, information, instruction, legal counsel, notice, notification, opinion, prompting, proposal, proposition, recommendation, rede, suggestion, view, warning

ASSOCIATED CONCEPTS: advice of counsel, privilege

FOREIGN PHRASES: *Incivile est, nisi tota lege perspecta, una aliqua particula ejus proposita, judicare, vel respondere.* Unless the entire law has been examined, it is improper to pass judgment upon a single portion of it. *Nemo ex consilio obligatur.* No one is obligated as a consequence of giving advice. *Simplex commendatio non obligat.* A mere recommendation is not binding.

ADVISE, *verb* advocate, alert, apprise, *auctorem esse,* caution, coach, communicate, confer with, *consiliari, consilium dare,* consult with, convey, counsel, direct, enlighten, express, familiarize, forewarn, give advice, give an opinion, give counsel, give information, give notice, give one to understand, give suggestions, give warning, guide, *homini suadere,* impart, inform, intimate, make known, mention, notify, offer an opinion, offer counsel, opine, prescribe, propose, recommend, remind, represent, reprove, submit, suggest, warn

ASSOCIATED CONCEPTS: advisory opinion, declaratory judgment

FOREIGN PHRASES: *Consilia multorum quaeruntur in magnis.* The advice of many are required in affairs of magnitude.

ADVISORY, *adjective* cautionary, communicatory, consulting, counselling, directing, enlightening, expressive of opinion, guiding, inducive, instructing, recommendatory, suggesting

ASSOCIATED CONCEPTS: advisory board, advisory opinion, advisory referendum

ADVOCACY, *noun* active espousal, advancement, advice, aid, approbation, approval, assistance, auspices, backing, championship, constructive criticism, countenance, defense, encouragement, endorsement, forceful persuasion, furtherance, guidance, help, intercession, interest, patronage, plea, praise, promotion, recommendation, sanction, seconding, sponsorship, subscription, suggestion, support, vindication, vouching, warranting

ADVOCATE *(Counselor)*, **noun** adviser, apologist, attorney, attorney-at-law, barrister, barrister-at-law, champion, counsel learned in the law, counselor-at-law, defender, friend at court, friend in court, interagent, interceder, intercessor, interlocutor, intermediary, intermediate, intermediate agent, intermediator, intermedium, internuncio, intervener, interventionist, interventor, jurisconsult, jurist, justifier, lawyer, learned counsel, legal adviser, legal practitioner, legal representative, legate, legist, maintainer, man of law, mediator, medium, member of the legal profession, mover, negotiant, negotiator, one called to the bar, paraclete, patron, *patronus,* pleader, proctor, prompter, protector, representative, seconder, solicitor, spokesman, spokeswoman, *suasor,* upholder, votary

ADVOCATE *(Espouser)*, **noun** abettor, adherent, apologist, *auctor,* backer, champion, countenancer, defender, encourager, exponent, expounder, favorer, maintainer, partisan, patron, promoter, propagandist, propagator, proponent, seconder, sectary, spokesman, spokeswoman, support, supporter, sympathizer, upholder, votary

ASSOCIATED CONCEPTS: advocate the abolishment of the death sentence, advocate the commission of a crime, advocate the overthrow of government

ADVOCATE, *verb* advise, allege in support, approve, argue for, assert, back, champion, commend, consent, contend for, counsel, defend, endorse, espouse, exhort, favor, give advice, plead for, plead in favor of, plead one's case, plead one's cause, prescribe, promote, prompt, propose, propound, recommend, sanction, second, speak in favor of, *suadere,* subscribe to, suggest, support, uphold, urge

ASSOCIATED CONCEPTS: advocate the commission of a crime, advocate the overthrow of government

AESTHETIC, *adjective* artistic, cultured, discriminative, ornamental, refined, tasteful

AFFAIRS, *noun* activities, concerns, interests, matters, proceedings, pursuits, topics, transactions

AFFECT, *verb* act on, *adficere,* bear upon, cause to alter, cause to vary, change, *commovere,* conduce, exert influence, have an effect upon, have influence, impress, induce, influence, introduce a change, make a change, play a direct part, prevail upon, produce a change, produce an effect, superinduce, *tangere,* transfigure, work a change, work upon
ASSOCIATED CONCEPTS: affect an action, affected with public interest, affecting a substantial right

AFFECTION, *noun* admiration, adoration, amorousness, ardor, attachment, closeness, devotion, enchantment, endearment, excitation of feeling, fancy, feeling, fervency, fervor, firm attachment, fondness, fullness of heart, inclination, infatuation, kindness, love, mutual attraction, partiality, passion, penchant, *pietas,* popular regard, predisposition, proneness, regard, sentiment, sentimental attachment, sentimentality, state of excitement, tender feeling, tender passion, tenderness, understanding, warmth, zealous attachment
ASSOCIATED CONCEPTS: alienation of affection

AFFIANT, *noun* attestant, attester, deponent, signer, subscriber, swearer, testifier, voucher

AFFIDAVIT, *noun* affirmation under oath, assertory oath, attested statement, averment, avouchment, avowal, avowance, confirmation under oath, declaration under oath, evidence on oath, instrument in proof, solemn affirmation, statement, statement under oath, sworn evidence, sworn statement, testification under oath, *testimonium per tabulas datum,* voluntary attestment under oath, written declaration upon oath, written statement under oath
ASSOCIATED CONCEPTS: affidavit of defense, affidavit of demand, affidavit of judicial power, affidavit of merit, affidavit of service, affidavit to advise the court of a right or on an issue, affidavit to hold to bail, affirmation, verified deposition, verified pleading

AFFILIATE, *noun* arm, assistant, associate, auxiliary, branch, branch organization, chapter, colleague, component, division, offshoot, subdivision, subsidiary, wing

AFFILIATE, *verb* ally, associate, attach, belong to, bring into close connection, bring into close relation, cement a union, confederate, connect, consociate, embrace, federalize, federate, form a connection, join, join forces, join together, make common cause, pertain to, relate to, unite

AFFILIATED, *adjective* allied, associated, closely allied, closely related, confederated, connected, coupled, federated, incorporated, intimately allied, intimately related, joined with, leagued, linked, related, united
ASSOCIATED CONCEPTS: affiliated association, affiliated company, affiliated corporation, affiliated firm, affiliated organization

AFFILIATION *(Amalgamation),* *noun* aggregation, alliance, association, centralization, coalition, combination, confederacy, confederation, consortium, corporation, embodiment, federation, fusion, integration, league, merger, unification, union, unity, voluntary association

AFFILIATION *(Bloodline),* *noun* agnation, ancestry, apparentation, blood relation, blood relationship, common derivation, consanguinity, descent, family, family connection, family tie, filiality, filiation, heredity, kindred, kinfolk, kinship, kinsmen, line of descent, lineage, next of kin, origin, parentage, relation, relationship, ties of blood, ties of race
ASSOCIATED CONCEPTS: affiliation proceedings, paternity proceedings

AFFILIATION *(Connectedness),* *noun* alignment, appositeness, apposition, association, band of union, bond, coaction, coadjuvancy, coalition, colleagueship, combination, concert, conjunction, connection, consociation, copartnership, coworking, friendly association, implication, inclusion, intimate connection, involvement, joint enterprise, link, linkage, membership, participation, partnership, relation, relationship

AFFINITY *(Family ties),* *noun* affiliation, ancestry, blood relative, brethren, clan, *cognatio,* cognation, common ancestry, *coniunctio,* connection, *consanguinitas,* consanguinity, family, family connection, filiation, heritage, kindred, kinship, lineage, linkage, *necessitudo,* offspring, parentage, *propinquitas,* relation, relation by blood, relationship, tribe
ASSOCIATED CONCEPTS: challenge to a prospective juror based on affinity
FOREIGN PHRASES: *Affinis mei affinis non est mihi affinis.* One who is related by marriage to a person who is related to me by marriage has no affinity to me.

AFFINITY *(Regard),* *noun* affection, attachment, attraction, closeness, concern, devotion, fondness, friendliness, friendship, good will, inclination, liking, love, natural liking, partiality, predilection, proclivity, propensity, sympathy, tenderness

AFFIRM *(Claim),* *verb* assert, asseverate, aver, declare to be fact, enunciate, establish, express, make a positive statement, make an assertion, proclaim, profess, pronounce, state, state positively, state with conviction

AFFIRM *(Declare solemnly),* *verb* asseverate, attest, aver, avouch, avow, declare solemnly, depone, depose, give oral evidence, give sworn evidence, give verbal evidence, make a solemn declaration, make an asseveration, make an attestation, make an averment, pronounce, take one's oath, testify, vouch
ASSOCIATED CONCEPTS: affirm a contract
FOREIGN PHRASES: *Affirmanti, non neganti incumbit probatio.* The proof is borne by the person who affirms, rather than the person who denies. *Affirmantis est probare.* He who is affirming must prove. *Ei incumbit probatio, qui dicit, non qui negat; cum per rerum naturam factum negantis probatio nulla sit.* The burden of proof lies upon him who asserts it, not upon him who denies; since, by the nature of things, he who denies a fact cannot produce any proof of it.

AFFIRM *(Uphold),* *verb* *adfirmare,* approve, authenticate, certify, confirm, *confirmare,* endorse, establish, make firm, ratify, substantiate, support, sustain, validate, verify, vouch for, warrant
ASSOCIATED CONCEPTS: affirm a judicial decision, affirm on appeal, affirmed in part, affirmed in whole

AFFIRMANCE *(Authentication),* *noun* acknowledgment, assertion, assurance, attestation, certification, confirmation, countersignature, declaration, endorsement, establishment, predication, pronouncement, ratification, substantiation, validation, verification

ASSOCIATED CONCEPTS: affirmance of a contract, confirmation of a judgment, ratification of a voidable contract

FOREIGN PHRASES: *Posito uno oppositorum, negatur alterum.* By the establishment of one of two opposite propositions, the other one is denied.

AFFIRMANCE *(Judicial sanction),* **noun** acceptance, acquiescence, assent, concord, concordance, countersignature, endorsement, legal approval, legal authorization, legal ratification, subscription

ASSOCIATED CONCEPTS: affirmed without opinion, en banc affirmance, unanimous affirmance

AFFIRMANCE *(Legal affirmation),* **noun** absolute assertion, adjuration, assertory oath, asseveration, attestation, averment, avouchment, avowal, evidence on oath, legal evidence, legal pledge, oral evidence, positive declaration, positive statement, pronouncement, proposition, solemn averment, solemn avowal, statement on oath, sworn evidence, testimony, verbal evidence, written evidence

ASSOCIATED CONCEPTS: affirmation of a statement

AFFIRMANT, *noun* affirmer, apprizer, attestant, attestator, attester, confirmist, deponent, one who testifies under oath, testifier, voucher

ASSOCIATED CONCEPTS: affidavit, affirmation, deponent, oath, perjury

AFFIRMATION, *noun* absolute assertion, acknowledgment, acquiescence, *adfirmatio,* adjurement, affirmance, approval, assertion, assertory oath, asseveration, attest, attestation, authentication, averment, avouchment, avowal, certification, confirmation, declaration, deposition, endorsement, establishment, factual statement, formal declaration, legal evidence, legal pledge, oath, oath-giving, oath-taking, positive statement, predication, profession, pronouncement, ratification, solemn affirmation, solemn averment, solemn avowal, solemn declaration, statement, statement on oath, substantiation, swearing, sworn evidence, sworn statement, testification, testimonial, testimonium, testimony, validation, verification

ASSOCIATED CONCEPTS: affirmation of fact, affirmation to a will, attorney's affirmation

FOREIGN PHRASES: *Affirmatio unius exclusio est alterius.* The affirmance of one thing is the exclusion of the other.

AFFIRMATIVE, *adjective* absolute, affirmatory, categorical, certain, confirmative, confirmatory, convinced, decided, persuaded, positive, sure, undoubting, unqualified

ASSOCIATED CONCEPTS: affirmative action, affirmative action for past discrimination, affirmative action in hiring, affirmative allegation, affirmative authorization, affirmative charge, affirmative covenant, affirmative defense, affirmative easement, affirmative negligence, affirmative plea, affirmative proof, affirmative relief, affirmative showing, affirmative statute, affirmative warranty, affirmative wrongdoing

AFFIX, *verb* add, *adfigere,* adhere, adjoin, *adligare, adnectere,* agglutinate, annex, append, attach, bind, co-

here, combine, conjoin, connect, couple, enclose, fasten, fix, incorporate, insert, join, link, put together, secure, subjoin, supplement, unite

ASSOCIATED CONCEPTS: affix a seal to an instrument, affix a signature, affix exhibits to a pleading, affix process to the door

AFFRAY, *noun* agitation, altercation, battle, brabble, brawl, brush, clash, combat, commotion, conflict, contestation, disturbance, embroilment, encounter, fight, fisticuffs, fracas, fray, free fight, hand-to-hand fight, *melee,* passage at arms, *pugna, rixa,* row, scrimmage, scuffle, set-to, skirmish, sortie, squabble, struggle, tumult, tumultuous assault, *tumultus,* turmoil, tussle, violence

AFFRONT, *verb* afflict, aggrieve, antagonize, be offensive, be rude, cause dislike, cause offense, chafe, disconcert, disdain, disoblige, disquiet, distress, disturb, embitter, encounter, gall, give offense to, grieve, hurt the feelings, ill-treat, insult, irritate, make angry, offend, pique, rankle, scorn, slight, snub, sting, vex, wound the feelings, wrong

AFORESAID, *adjective* above-mentioned, afore-cited, aforedescribed, aforegiven, aforegoing, aforementioned, aforenamed, aforestated, already mentioned, already said, antecedent, anterior, before-mentioned, beforesaid, foregoing, forenamed, former, introductory, mentioned, mentioned previously, named, precedent, preceding, precursive, precursory, preexistent, preluding, prelusory, prevenient, previous, previously specified, prior, recited, said, said in a preceding part, specified

AFORETHOUGHT, *adjective* beforehand, calculated, contrived, contrived in advance, deliberate, designed, intended, planned, planned beforehand, prearranged, preconceived, preconsidered, predeliberated, predetermined, premeditated, prepared, prepense, preresolved, previously in mind, purposed, purposive, reflective, studied, well-considered, with forethought

ASSOCIATED CONCEPTS: malice aforethought

AGE, *noun* *aetas,* date, duration of existence, eon, epoch, era, interval of years, longevity, maturity, period, seniority, stage of life, term of life, time of life, vintage, years

ASSOCIATED CONCEPTS: age of consent, age of majority, legal age, statutory age

AGENCY *(Commission),* **noun** administration, authority, bureau, charge, command, committee, control, delegation, department, office

ASSOCIATED CONCEPTS: administrative agency, governmental agency

AGENCY *(Legal relationship),* **noun** activity, appointment, assignment, authority, care, charge, command, commission, conduct, conduct of affairs, control, delegation, deputation, derivative authority, direction, dominion, duty, employ, employment, function, governance, handling, instrumentality, intermediation, intervention, jurisdiction, management, mandate, mission, procuracy, procuration, proxy, quest, representation, responsibility, role, service, services, superintendence, supervision, task, trust

ASSOCIATED CONCEPTS: actual agency, agency by estoppel, agency coupled with an interest, agency of ne-

cessity, deed of agency, exclusive agency, express agency, general agency, implied agency, scope of the agency, undisclosed agency, vicarious liability
FOREIGN PHRASES: *Actus me invito factus non est meus actus.* An act done against my will is not my act. *Qui facit per alium facit per se.* He who acts through another acts himself. *Qui mandat ipse fecissi videtur.* He who orders or commands is deemed to have done the thing himself. *Quod per me non possum, nec per alium.* What I cannot do myself, I cannot do through the agency of another. *Vicarius non habet vicarium.* A vicar has no deputy.

AGENDA, *noun*   blueprint, business, business affairs, business on hand, calendar, docket, items of business, legal program, main business, matters to be attended to, order, order of the day, plan, planning, procedure, program of business, program of operation, proposal, proposed action, proposition, schedule, schedule of affairs, scheme

AGENT, *noun*   alternate, appointee, assistant, delegate, emissary, envoy, functionary, go-between, intermediary, intermediate, intermedium, mediary, medium, middleman, negotiant, negotiator, procurator, proxy, representative, solicitor, substitute
ASSOCIATED CONCEPTS: agent to accept process, authorization of an agent, bailee, common agent, employee, escrow agent, general agent, implied agent, independent contractor, insurance broker, joint venture, managing agent, master-servant relationship, owner-operator relationship, partnership, principal-agent relationship, real estate agent, real estate broker, special agent, subagents, undisclosed agency, warranty of authority
FOREIGN PHRASES: *Idem agens et patiens esse non potest.* A person cannot be at the same time the person acting and the person acted upon. *Delegatus non potest delegare.* A representative cannot delegate his authority. *Qui facit per alium facit per se.* He who acts by or through another acts for himself.

AGGLOMERATION, *noun*   accumulation, agglomerate, agglutination, aggregate, aggregation, amassment, assemblage, cluster, coagulation, collection, congeries, conglomerate, conglomeration, consolidation, cumulation, glomeration, mass, pile, solidification

AGGRAVATE *(Annoy),* *verb*   acerbate, aggrieve, annoy, bother, cause pain, chafe, dismay, disturb, enrage, envenom, exasperate, excite, give pain, hurt, incense, inflame, infuriate, injure, irk, irritate, madden, miff, nettle, offend, pain, pique, provoke, rankle, ruffle, sour, sting, trouble, vex
ASSOCIATED CONCEPTS: aggravating circumstances

AGGRAVATE *(Exacerbate),* *verb*   add to, add weight to, amplify, augment, complicate, deepen, deteriorate, further, heighten, impair, increase, intensify, magnify, make more offensive, make more serious, make more severe, make worse, render less excusable, render less tolerable, render worse, worsen
ASSOCIATED CONCEPTS: aggravated assault, aggravating circumstances

AGGRAVATION *(Annoyance),* *noun*   complication, difficulty, distress, frustration, grievance, harassment, inconvenience, irritant, irritation, nuisance, ordeal, pressure, provocation, strain, stress

AGGRAVATION *(Exacerbation),* *noun*   agitation, amplification, augmentation, deepening, enlargement, excitation, fomentation, heightening, increase, inflammation, intensification, magnification, stimulation, worsening
ASSOCIATED CONCEPTS: aggravated assault, aggravation of a crime, aggravation of damages, aggravation of injury, aggravation of the disability
FOREIGN PHRASES: *Omne crimen ebrietas et incendit et detegit.* Drunkenness both inflames or aggravates, and uncovers every crime.

AGGREGATE, *noun*   agglomerate, aggregation, amount, assemblage, assembly, body, collection, conglomeration, entire number, entire quantity, entirety, gross, gross amount, indissoluble entity, indivisible entity, mass, sum, sum total, total, totality, whole
ASSOCIATED CONCEPTS: aggregate corporation, aggregate income, combine

AGGREGATE, *verb*   accumulate, acquire, add together, agglomerate, aggroup, amass, amount to, assemble, bring together, build up, clump, cluster, collect, collect into a mass, colligate, compile, conglomerate, cumulate, gather, gather together, group, integrate, join, mass, total, unite
ASSOCIATED CONCEPTS: aggregate claims

AGGRESSOR, *noun*   antagonist, assailant, assailer, assaulter, attacker, belligerent, besieger, combatant, contender, criminal, fighter, foe, initiative seizer, invader, militant, prime mover, provocator, ravager, ruffian, stormer, violator

AGGRIEVED *(Harmed),* *adjective*   abused, afflicted, anguished, bilked, damnified, deprived of legal rights, distressed, grieved, having suffered invasion of legal rights, hurt, ill-treated, incommoded, injured, misused, pained, preyed upon, provoked, swindled, tyrannized, vexed, wounded
ASSOCIATED CONCEPTS: aggrieved heirs, aggrieved party, aggrieved person

AGGRIEVED *(Victimized),* *adjective*   adversely affected, cheated, damaged, defrauded, fleeced, harrassed, harried, ill-used, imposed upon, injured, justly complaining, misserved, offended, oppressed, persecuted, taken advantage of, wronged

AGITATE *(Activate),* *verb*   actuate, arouse, coax, electrify, energize, excite, exhort, ferment, foment, goad, impel, incite, induce, inflame, influence, inspire, inspirit, instigate, irritate, kindle, persuade, prompt, provoke, roil, rouse, spur, stimulate, stir up, urge on

AGITATE *(Perturb),* *verb*   alarm, concern, discomfort, disconcert, dismay, displease, disquiet, disturb, fluster, fret, jar, perplex, perturbate, shake up, throw into confusion, trouble, unsettle, upset, worry

AGITATE *(Shake up),* *verb*   convulse, disarrange, dishevel, disorder, impart motion to, mix, mix up, put in motion, ruffle, stir, throw out of order, tousle, tumble

AGREE *(Comply),* *verb*   accede, accept, accommodate, accord, acknowledge, acquiesce, adapt, adjust differences, adopt, allow, approve, assent, avow, be accordant, be at one with, be in harmony with, be in unison, be willing, coincide, come to an understanding, come to terms, comply with, *componere,* concede, *concinere,* con-

cord, concur, confirm, *congruere,* consent, cooperate, correspond, fit, give assent, give consent, homologate, ratify, reconcile, settle, subscribe to, suit, understand, unite, yield assent
ASSOCIATED CONCEPTS: agreed case, agreed order, agreed statement of facts

AGREE *(Contract), verb* adjust differences, arrive at a settlement, bargain, bring into concord, come to an agreement, come to an understanding, come to terms, compromise, consent, *consentire, constituere,* cooperate, covenant, engage, give assurance, make a bargain, make an agreement, make terms, mutually assent, *pacisci,* pact, pledge, promise, settle, settle by covenant, stipulate, undertake

AGREED *(Harmonized), adjective* accordant, adapted, appeased, arbitrated, arranged, balanced, coherent, compromised, conceded, conciliated, concordant, conforming, correlative, correspondent, counterbalanced, equable, equal, equalized, equivalent, matching, mediated, negotiated, parallel, propitiated, reconciled, settled, suited
ASSOCIATED CONCEPTS: agreed case, agreed price, agreed statement of facts, agreed submission of a case, agreed upon price, agreed value
FOREIGN PHRASES: *Ad quod curia concordavit.* To which the court agreed.

AGREED *(Promised), adjective* affirmed, approved, arranged, assured, attested, avowed, committed, confirmed, contracted, covenanted, declared, endorsed, guaranteed, insured, pledged, stipulated, sworn, warranted
ASSOCIATED CONCEPTS: agreed price, agreed value

AGREEMENT *(Concurrence), noun* accord, amity, arrangement, assent, common assent, common consent, common view, community of interests, concord, concordance, conformance, congruence, congruency, congruity, consent, consentaneity, consentaneousness, consentience, consonance, cooperation, good understanding, harmony, meeting of the minds, mutual assent, mutual promise, mutual understanding, oneness, reciprocity of obligation, settlement, unanimity, understanding, uniformity, unison, unity
FOREIGN PHRASES: *Aggregatio mentium.* Meeting of the minds. *Bona fides exigit ut guod convenit fiat.* Good faith demands that what is agreed upon shall be done. *Consensus ad idem.* An agreement of parties for the same thing; a meeting of minds without which no contract exists. *Conventio privatorum non potest publico juri derogare.* An agreement of private parties cannot derogate from public right. *Conventio vincit legem.* The agreement of parties controls the law. *Modus et conventio vincunt legem.* Custom, convention, and agreement of the parties overrule the law. *Ratihabitio mandato aequiparatur.* Ratification is equivalent to an express command. *Quando verba et mens congruunt, non est interpretationi locus.* When the words and the mind agree, there is no room for interpretation. *Privatorum conventio juri publico non derogat.* The agreement of private persons cannot derogate from public law. *Modus et conventio vincunt legem.* Custom and agreement control the law. *Non differunt quae concordant re, tametsi non in verbis iisdem.* Those matters do not differ which agree in substance, though not in the same words.

AGREEMENT *(Contract), noun* alliance, arrangement, bargain, binding promise, bond, commitment, compact, concordat, *concordia,* contractual statement, convention, covenant, deal, engagement, legal document, mutual pledge, obliga, obligation, pact, pledge, settlement, stipulation, transaction, understanding, undertaking
ASSOCIATED CONCEPTS: abrogate an agreement, agency agreement, agreement implied in fact, agreement of sale, agreement to answer for the debt of another, agreement to purchase, agreement under seal, agreements in contemplation of marriage, antenuptial agreement, area-wide agreement, articles of agreement, articles of impeachment, articles of incorporation, articles of partnership, articles of war, express agreement, illusory agreement, implied agreement, implied agreement in law, sale agreement, settlement agreement, support agreement
FOREIGN PHRASES: *Contractus ex turpi causa, vel contra bonds mores nullus est.* A contract founded on an evil consideration, or against good morals, is void. *Contractus legem ex conbentione accipiunt.* Contracts take their law from the agreement of the parties. *Ex pacto illicito non oritur actio.* An action will not lie on an agreement to do something unlawful. *Ex maleficio non oritur contractus.* No contract is born of wrongdoing. *Nudum pactum est ubi nulla subest causa praeter conventionem; sed ubi subest causa, fit obligatio, et parit actionem.* A naked contract is where there is no consideration except the agreement; but, where there is a consideration, an obligation is created and gives rise to a right of action. *In stipulationibus cum quaeritur quid actum sit verba contra stipulatorem interpretanda sunt.* In the construction of agreements words are interpreted against the person offering them. *Ea quae dari impossibilia sunt, vel quae in rerum natura non sunt, pro non adjectis habentur.* Those things which cannot be given, or which are not in existence, are regarded as not included in the contract. *Conventio facit legem.* The agreement creates the law; i.e., the parties to a binding contract must keep their promises. *Ex nudo pacto non oritur actio.* No action arises on a contract without a consideration. *Ea quae, commendandi causa, in venditionibus dicuntur, si palam appareant, venditorem non obligant.* Those things which are said as praise of the things sold, if they are openly apparent do not bind the seller. *In contrahenda venditione, ambiguum pactum contravenditorem interpretandum est.* In a contract of sale, an ambiguous agreement is to be interpreted against the seller. *In conventionibus, contrahentium voluntas potius quam verba spectari placuit.* In contracts, it is the rule to regard the intention of the parties rather than the actual words. *Omne jus aut consensus fecit, aut necessitas constituit aut firmavit consuetudo.* All right is either made by consent, constituted by necessity, or confirmed by custom. *Pacta conventa quae neque contra leges neque dolo malo inita sunt omni modo observanda sunt.* Agreements which are not contrary to the laws nor entered into with a fraudulent design must be observed in all respects. *Pacta dant legem contractui.* Stipulations constitute the law for the contract. *Pacta quae contra leges constitutionesque, vel contra bonos mores fiunt, nullam vim habere, indubitati juris est.* It is unquestionably the law that contracts which are made contrary to the laws or against good morals, have no force in law. *Pacta quae turpem causam continent non sunt observanda.* Contracts which are based on unlawful

consideration will not be enforced. *Quae dubitationis tollendae causa contractibus inseruntur, jus commune non laedunt.* Those clauses which are inserted in agreements to avoid doubts and ambiguity do not offend the common law. *Nuda pactio obligationem non parit.* A naked agreement does not effect an otherwise binding obligation. *Privatis pactionibus non dubium est non laedi jus caeterorum.* There is no doubt that private contracts cannot prejudice the rights of others.

AID *(Help),* **noun**   abetment, accommodation, advance, advocacy, aidance, assistance, auspices, backing, benefit, coadjuvancy, cooperation, countenance, endorsement, espousal, facilitation, furtherance, guidance, help, helpfulness, maintenance, ministration, ministry, patronage, promotion, reinforcement, relief, rescue, service, sponsorship, subscription, subsidy, subsistence, succor, support, sustainment, sustenance, tutelage, willing help
ASSOCIATED CONCEPTS: aid and abet, aid and comfort

AID *(Subsistence),* **noun**   benefaction, benefit, charity, compensation, endowment, humanitarianism, maintenance, ministration, ministry, patronage, relief, subsidy, support, sustainment, sustenance

AID, **verb**   abet, advance, assist, augment, avail, be auxiliary to, be of service, benefit, collaborate, cooperate with, facilitate, further, give aid, give support, help, minister to, nurture, oblige, promote, provision, reinforce, relieve, render help, rescue, second, serve, service, strengthen, subserve, succor, supplement, support, sustain, uphold
ASSOCIATED CONCEPTS: aid and abet, aid and comfort

AIR POLLUTION, **noun**   contamination, defilement, impure air, unhealthy air

AKIN *(Germane),* **adjective**   affiliated, alike, allied, analogous, appertaining, applicable, apropos, associated, closely related, collateral, connected, correlative, correspondent, corresponding, interchangeable, like, linked, parallel, pertinent, related, relating, relevant, resembling, similar

AKIN *(Related by blood),* **adjective**   affiliated, connate, consanguine, consanguinean, consanguineous, *consanguineus,* fraternal, kindred, of the same stock

ALCOHOL, **noun**   alcoholic beverage, inebriant, intoxicant, intoxicating liquor, liquor, potation, spirits

ALEATORY *(Perilous),* **adjective**   adventurous, beset with perils, dangerous, endangered, exposed, exposed to risk, fraught with danger, full of risk, hazardous, imperiled, minatory, ominous, parlous, precarious, riskful, risky, treacherous, unsafe, venturesome, venturous

ALEATORY *(Uncertain),* **adjective**   alterable, ambiguous, capricious, changeable, changeful, depending, dubious, equivocal, in question, incalculable, indefinite, mutable, not fixed, open, permutable, protean, undecided, unsettled, unstable, unsure, variable
ASSOCIATED CONCEPTS: aleatory contract

ALERT *(Agile),* **adjective**   alive, animated, expeditious, nimble, quick, spirited, sprightly, spry

ALERT *(Vigilant),* **adjective**   active, alive, attentive, guarded, observant, on guard, prepared, wary, watchful

ALERT, **verb**   advise, alarm, arouse, caution, give notice, notify, put on one's guard, sound the alarm, warn

ALIAS, **adverb**   acknowledged elsewhere as, a.k.a., *alias dictus,* also, also acknowledged as, also acknowledging the name of, also answering to, also called, also known as, also known by, also known under the name of, also recognized as, at other times known as, elsewhere known as, known elsewhere as, known elsewhere by, known otherwise under the name, known otherwise as, known previously as, known variously as, *nomen alienum,* otherwise called, otherwise known as, otherwise known by, otherwise named, previously called, variously called, variously known as
ASSOCIATED CONCEPTS: alias execution, alias process, alias subpoena, alias summons, alias writ, assumed name

ALIBI, **noun**   corroborative excuse, declaration, defense, defensive evidence, defensive plea, exculpatory excuse, excuse, explanation, justifiable excuse, justification, justificatory excuse, plausible excuse, plea in being elsewhere, proof of absence, verifiable excuse, verificative excuse
ASSOCIATED CONCEPTS: affirmative defense, notice of intention to introduce alibi defense, traverse of indictment

ALIEN *(Foreign),* **adjective**   coming from another land, external, extrinsic, foreign-born, from abroad, immigrant, imported, not domestic, not indigenous, not native, not naturalized, of foreign origin, outside, unnaturalized

ALIEN *(Unrelated),* **adjective**   detached, different, digressive, disconnected, disjoined, disrelated, dissociated, from nowhere, inappropriate, independent, insular, irrelated, no relation, not comparable, of external origin, outside, unaffiliated, unallied, unassociated, unconnected, ungermane, unrelated, without context, without relation

ALIEN, **noun**   *advena, alienigena,* emigrant, *étranger,* expatriate, foreigner, immigrant, interloper, intruder, noncitizen, one excluded from some privilege, outlander, outsider, *peregrinus,* person coming from a foreign country, person from foreign parts, refugee, stranger

ALIENATE *(Estrange),* **verb**   *abalienare,* aggravate, antagonize, *avertere,* be hateful, be unfriendly, bear malice, break off, cause dislike, cause loathing, come between, destroy goodwill, detach, disaffect, disunite, divide, embitter, enrage, envenom, fall out, harden the heart, incense, make averse, make indifferent, make inimical, make unfriendly, part, pit against, provoke hatred, repel, separate, set against, set at odds, set at variance, sow dissension, take umbrage, turn away, turn off, wean, withdraw the affections of
ASSOCIATED CONCEPTS: alienation of affections, alienation of power

ALIENATE *(Transfer title),* **verb**   *abalienare,* abalienate, assign, barter, consign, convey, deed, deliver

over, demise, devolve, enfeoff, part with, pass, pass over, remise, sign away, sign over, substitute, surrender, transfer ownership, turn over
ASSOCIATED CONCEPTS: alienation of property
FOREIGN PHRASES: *Regulariter non valet pactum de re mea non alienanda.* It is a rule that an agreement not to alienate my property is not binding.

ALIENATION *(Estrangement), noun* abhorrence, abomination, acrimony, *alienatio,* animosity, antagonism, antipathy, aversion, bitterness, breach, break, deflection, disaffection, disfavor, disruption, division, enmity, execration, hostility, implacability, loathing, malevolence, malice, odium, rancor, rift, rupture, schism, separation, split, umbrage, unfriendliness, variance, withdrawal
ASSOCIATED CONCEPTS: alienation of affections, alienation of power
FOREIGN PHRASES: *Alienatio rei praefertur juri accrescendi.* Alienation is favored by the law rather than accumulation.

ALIENATION *(Transfer of title), noun* abalienatio, abalienation, assignation, assignment, cession, conferment, conferral, consignation, consignment, conveyance, conveyancing, deeding, deliverance, delivery, demise, enfeoffment, limitation, nonretention, selling, surrender, transference, transmission
ASSOCIATED CONCEPTS: alienation clause, alienation of property

ALIGHT, *verb* climb down, depart, descend, *descendere,* disembark, dismount, egress, evacuate, exit, get down, get off, ground oneself, land, leave, part, set down, step down

ALIMONY, *noun* allotment, allowance, care, dispensation, emolument, grant, income, maintenance, maintenance allowance, pecuniary aid, pecuniary assistance, personal allowance, provision, recompense, remuneration, separate maintenance, separation money, settlement, stipend, subsidization, subsidy, subvention, support, sustenance, sustentation, upkeep
ASSOCIATED CONCEPTS: alimony award, alimony judgment, alimony penpendente lite, division of property, divorce, necessaries, permanent alimony, separation, support, temporary alimony

ALLAY, *verb* abate, alleviate, appease, assuage, blunt, calm, cause to be still, cause to subside, check, compose, constrain, control, curb, curtail, deaden, decrease, diminish, dull, hush, *lenire,* lessen, lighten, lull, minimize, *mitigare,* mitigate, moderate, mollify, pacify, palliate, qualify, quell, quench, quiet, reduce, reduce in severity, relieve, repress, restrain, *sedare,* silence, slake, smooth, soften, soothe, still, subdue, suppress, temper, tone down, tranquilize

ALLEGATION, *noun* *adfirmatio,* assertion, averment, bill of complaint, charge, claim, complaint, crimination, declaration, denunciation, formal averment, imputation, inculpation, *ipse dixit,* plea, positive assertion, positive declaration, positive statement, pronouncement, statement
ASSOCIATED CONCEPTS: allegation of fact, allegation of law, allegation of wrongdoing

ALLEGE, *verb* adduce, advance, affirm, announce, annunciate, assert, asseverate, attest, aver, avouch, charge, cite, claim, contend, declare, enunciate, express, maintain, make an assertion, plead, present, profess, pronounce, propound, recite, relate, say, set forth, state, state as true, urge as a reason
ASSOCIATED CONCEPTS: allege a crime

ALLEGED, *adjective* acknowledged, adduced, advanced, advocated, affirmed, affirmed, announced, argued, asserted, asserted formally, asseverated, assured, averred, avouched, avowed, certified, cited, claimed, contended, declared, divulged, enunciated, imparted, imputed, insisted, introduced, maintained, positively declared, presented, proclaimed, produced, professed, promulgated, pronounced, propounded, put forward, reported, set forth, stated, stressed, testified to, uttered with conviction, vouched

ALLEGIANCE, *noun* adherence, adherence to duty, attachment, bounden duty, call of duty, case of conscience, commitment, constancy, deference, devotedness, devotion, duteousness, dutifulness, faith, faithfulness, fealty, fidelity, *fides,* homage, imperative duty, inescapable duty, loyalty, matter of duty, moral obligation, obedience, obligation, obsequiousness, observance, observance of obligation, onus, pledge, promise, responsibility, sense of duty, steadfastness, subjection, submission, subordination, support, trueness
FOREIGN PHRASES: *Nemo patriam in qua natus est exuere, nec ligeantiae debitum ejurare possit.* No man can renounce his native country nor adjure his obligation of allegiance. *Ligeantia est quasi legis essentia; est vinculum fidei.* Allegiance is the essence of law; it is the bond of faith.

ALLEVIATE, *verb* abate, *adlevare,* allay, assuage, attenuate, blunt, calm, check, compose, console, dampen, diminish, disburden, divert, dulcify, dull, ease, ease the burden, extenuate, free, lessen, lighten, lull, mitigate, moderate, modulate, nullify, pacify, palliate, quell, quiet, reduce, relieve, remedy, remit, slacken, slow down, smooth, soften, solace, soothe, still, subdue, succor, tame, temper, tranquilize, unburden, unload, weaken

ALLIED, *adjective* affiliated, affinitive, akin, associated, bonded, confederate, connected, federate, kindred, leagued, related

ALLOCATE, *verb* administer, allot, appoint, apportion, appropriate, arrange, assign, assort, cast, class, classify, collocate, consign, deal, deal out, designate, destine, detail, dispense, disperse, dispose, distribute, divide, divide and bestow in shares, dole out, earmark, fix, give out, grant, group, hand out, intend, line up, locate, marshal, mete, parcel out, place, portion off, portion out, prescribe, prorate, ration, render, set apart, set aside, set out, share, situate, specify
ASSOCIATED CONCEPTS: allocate funds, special allocatur

ALLONGE, *noun* addendum, additament, addition, adjunct, affix, appendage, appendix, attachment, complement, postscript, rider, supplement

ALLOT, *verb* *addicere,* administer, *adsignare,* allocate, appoint, apportion, assign, deal, delimit, demarcate, designate, dispense, disperse, dispose, *distribuere,* distribute, divide, dole, earmark, indicate, measure, mete, mete out, parcel out, partition, portion out, prorate, ration, share, specify

ALLOTMENT, noun *adsignatio,* allocation, annuity, appointment, apportionment, appropriation, arrangement, assignment, assignment by share, designation, dispensation, disposal, disposition, distribution, distribution by lot, dole, ordering, partition, portion, proportion, ration
ASSOCIATED CONCEPTS: allotment certificate, allotment note, allotment system

ALLOW *(Authorize),* **verb** accredit, acknowledge, approve, certify, charter, commission, empower, enable, endorse, enfranchise, entitle, give, give authority, give leave, give permission, grant, grant permission, invest, legalize, legitimatize, license, permit, privilege, qualify, sanction, support, sustain, vouchsafe, warrant
ASSOCIATED CONCEPTS: allow to bail, allowable debt, allowable loss, allowed by law, allowed claim
FOREIGN PHRASES: *Est quiddam perfectius in rebus licitis.* There is something more perfect in things permitted.

ALLOW *(Endure),* **verb** abide, accede, accept, accord, acquiesce, afford, agree, approve, assent, be answerable, be indulgent of, bear, brook, carry on under, concede, consent, countenance, forbear, permit, submit to, suffer, suffer to occur, sustain, take patiently, tolerate, undergo, withstand, yield
FOREIGN PHRASES: *Tout es que la loi ne defend pas est permis.* Everything which the law does not forbid is permitted.

ALLOWABLE, adjective acceptable, accepted, admissible, approvable, approved, authorized, excusable, granted, justifiable, lawful, legal, legalized, legitimate, licit, not impossible, not improper, not objectionable, pardonable, passable, permissible, proper, right, sanctionable, sanctioned, sufferable, suffered, suitable, tolerable, tolerated, unforbidden, unobjectionable, unprohibited, venial, warrantable
ASSOCIATED CONCEPTS: allowable claims

ALLOWED, adjective acceptable, accepted, acknowledged, admissible, admitted, allowable, approvable, approved, authorized, certified, chartered, commissioned, conceded, consented, eligible, empowered, endorsed, enfranchised, granted, justified, lawful, legal, legalized, legitimate, licensed, licit, passed, permissible, permissioned, permitted, ratified, recognized, rightful, sanctioned, sanctioned by the law, suitable, supported by authority, tolerable, tolerated, unforbidden, unprohibited, valid, validated, vouchsafed, warranted, within the law
ASSOCIATED CONCEPTS: allowed claim, allowed into evidence
FOREIGN PHRASES: *Est quiddam perfectius in rebus licitis.* There is something more perfect in things permitted.

ALLUDE, verb advert, *attingere,* bring to mind, cite, connote, convey, *designare,* evince, hint, imply, import, indicate, infer, insinuate, leave an inference, make indirect reference, mention, point to, refer to, relate, *significare,* signify, suggest, touch upon

ALLUSIVE, adjective allusory, ambiguous, clandestine, connotative, covert, eclipsed, evasive, imperspicuous, implicational, implicative, indicative, indirect, inferential, inferred, notional, obscure, screened, suggestive, tacit, vague, veiled
ASSOCIATED CONCEPTS: evasive contempt

ALLUVION, noun *batture,* deposit, deposition, residuary, sediment, settlement, settlings
ASSOCIATED CONCEPTS: accretion, alluvial accretion, alluvial land, riparian lands, riparian rights

ALMOST, adverb approximately, close to, nearly, on the brink of, on the verge of, scarcely, within sight of

ALONE *(Solitary),* **adverb** apart, detached, in solitude, independently, insular, isolated, privately, removed, separate, solo

ALONE *(Unsupported),* **adverb** unabetted, unaccompanied, unaided, unassisted, unattended, unseconded

ALONG, adverb coupled with, forward, in company with, in conjunction with, lengthwise, side by side, together, with

ALSO, adverb additionally, as well, besides, extra, furthermore, in addition, including, likewise, moreover, over and above, plus, similarly, then again, together with, too

ALTER, verb adapt, adjust, amend, change, *commutare,* commute, convert, deviate, *immutare,* innovate, invert, make innovations, metamorphose, moderate, modify, modulate, *mutare,* qualify, rearrange, recast, reconstruct, reorganize, temper, transform, transmogrify, transmute, turn, variegate, vary
ASSOCIATED CONCEPTS: alter a document, alter a will, forgery, fraud

ALTER EGO, noun alternate, counterpart, double, living image, match, other, other half, other person, other self, perfect substitute, second self, shadow, stand-in, twin
ASSOCIATED CONCEPTS: agent, alter ego doctrine, corporate alter ego, piercing the corporate veil, separate corporate entity

ALTERCATION, noun affray, *altercatio,* angry dispute, argument, bickering, broil, commotion, conflict, contestation, controversy, disaccord, disputation, dispute, disturbance, feud, fight, fracas, heated debate, *iurgium,* jangle, jangling, melee, noisy quarrel, quarrel, *rixa,* row, scuffle, snarl, squabble, strife, wrangle, wrangling
FOREIGN PHRASES: *Veritas nimium altercando amittitur.* Truth is lost by too much altercation.

ALTERNATE *(Fluctuate),* **verb** be periodic, be unsettled, oscillate, pendulate, show indecision, vacillate, vary, waver

ALTERNATE *(Take turns),* **verb** act interchangeably, *alternare, alterner,* change by alternation, follow one another interchangeably, follow one another reciprocally, interchange, interchange regularly, interchange successively, perform by turns, perform reciprocally, perform responsively, permute, substitute, switch
ASSOCIATED CONCEPTS: alternate causes of action, pleading in the alternate

ALTERNATIVE *(Option),* **noun** alternate choice, choice, conclusion, decision, determination, discernment, discretion, discrimination, distinction, election, embracement, espousal, free selection, judgment, pick,

recourse, remaining course, selection, voluntary decision
ASSOCIATED CONCEPTS: alternative conditions

ALTERNATIVE *(Substitute), noun*   change, other choice, replacement, succedaneum, superseder, supplanter
ASSOCIATED CONCEPTS: alternative conditions, alternative contract, alternative covenant, alternative judgment, alternative legacy, alternative obligation, alternative plea, alternative pleading, alternative relief, alternative remedies, alternative writs

ALWAYS *(Forever), adverb*   all the time, all the while, at all times, for all history

ALWAYS *(Without exception), adverb*   by and large each and every time, invariably, universally

AMALGAMATE, *verb*   admix, bind, blend, centralize, coadunate, coalesce, combine, commingle, commix, conflate, consolidate, fuse, inosculate, join, meld, merge, mix, solidify, syndicate, unify, unite
ASSOCIATED CONCEPTS: amalgamated labor organizations

AMANUENSIS, *noun*   clerk, recorder, recording secretary, scribe, scrivener, secretary, writer

AMATEUR, *adjective*   inept, unaccomplished, unadroit, undextrous, unfit, ungifted, unskilled, untalented

AMATEUR, *noun*   apprentice, aspirant, beginner, disciple, entrant, fledging, freshman, inexperienced person, initiate, layman, neophyte, novice

AMBIGUITY, *noun*   abstruseness, *ambiguitas,* bafflement, bewilderment, confounded meaning, confused meaning, confusion, disconcertion, doubtful meaning, doubtfulness, dubiety, dubiousness, duplexity in meaning, equivocalness, equivocation, incertitude, indefinite meaning, indefiniteness, indeterminacy, obscure meaning, obscurity, puzzlement, reconditeness, uncertainty of meaning, unintelligibility, vagueness
ASSOCIATED CONCEPTS: ambiguity upon the factum, latent ambiguity, patent ambiguity
FOREIGN PHRASES: *Cum in testamento ambigue aut etiam perperam scriptum est benigne interpretari et secundum id quod credibile est cogitatum credendum est.* Where an ambiguous, or even an erroneous, expression occurs in a will, it should be interpreted liberally, and in accordance with the intention of the testator. *Ambiguitas verborum latens verificatione suppletur; nam quod ex facto oritur ambiguum verificatione facti tollitur.* A latent verbal ambiguity may be removed by evidence; for whatever ambiguity arises from an extrinsic fact may be explained by extrinsic evidence. *Ambiguum placitum interpretari debet contra proferentem.* An ambiguous plea ought to be interpreted against the party entering it. *Quae cubitationis tollendae causa contractibus inseruntur, jus commune non laedunt.* Those clauses which are inserted in agreements to avoid doubts and ambiguity do not offend the common law. *Quoties in verbis nulla est ambiguitas, ibi nulla expositio contra verba fienda est.* Whenever there is no ambiguity in the words, then no exposition contrary to the words should be made. *Quum in testamento ambigue aut etiam perperam scriptum est, benigne*

interpretari et secundum id quod credib le et cogitatum, credendum est. When an ambiguous or even an erroneous expression occurs in a will, it should be construed liberally and in accordance with what is thought the probable meaning of the testator. *Ubi jus incertum, ibi jus nullum.* Where the law is uncertain, there is no law. *Verbis standum ubi nulla ambiguitas.* Where there is no ambiguity, one must abide by the words.

AMBIGUOUS, *adjective*   abstruse, *ambiguus,* ambivalent, confused, difficult to comprehend, doubtful, dubious, equivocal, having a double meaning, indefinite, indistinct, inexact, lacking clearness, not clear, not plain, obscure, open to various interpretations, uncertain, unintelligible, vague
ASSOCIATED CONCEPTS: ambiguous language
FOREIGN PHRASES: *Ambigua responsio contra proferentem est accipienda.* An ambiguous answer is to be taken against him who offers it. *In ambigua voce legis ea potius accipienda est significatio quae vitio caret, praesertim cum etiam voluntas legis ex hoc colligi possit.* In an ambiguous expression of law, that interpretation is to be preferred which is consonant with equity, especially where it is in conformity with the purpose of the law. *In ambiguis orationibus maxime sententia spectanda est ejus qui eas protulisset.* In ambiguous expressions, the intent of the person using them is particularly to be regarded. *In ambiguo sermone non utrumque dicimus sed id duntaxat quod volumus.* In ambiguous discourse, language is not used in a double sense, but in the sense in which it is meant.

AMBIT, *noun*   border, boundary, boundary line, bounds, circumference, contour, delineation lines, domain, dominion, furthest extent, furthest point, jurisdiction, limit, lines, orbit, outline, outer limit, pale, perimeter, periphery, province, realm, sphere
ASSOCIATED CONCEPTS: ambit of a statute, within the ambit of the law

AMBIVALENCE, *noun*   dubiety, dubitancy, equivocalness, hesitation, incertitude, indecision, indecisiveness, indeterminacy, indetermination, irresoluteness, irresolution, mental reservation, prevarication, uncertainty, undecidedness, undetermination, vacillation

AMBULATORY, *adjective*   able to be altered, alterative, amendable, amendatory, changeable, emendable, emendatory, modifiable, movable, mutable, not fixed, permutable, renunciatory, repudiative, repudiatory, reversible, reversional, revisional, revisory, revocable, revocatory, subject to change, variable
ASSOCIATED CONCEPTS: ambulatory deed, ambulatory patient, ambulatory will
FOREIGN PHRASES: *Ambulatoria est voluntas defuncti usque ad vitae supremum exitum.* The will of a deceased person is ambulatory until the latest moment of life.

AMBUSH, *verb*   assail, assault, attack, attack from a concealed position, bait a trap, catch by perfidy, ensnare, entrap, lay a trap for, lie in wait for, set a trap for, snare, trap, waylay

AMELIORATE, *verb*   advance, allay, better, change for the better, correct, *corrigere,* cultivate, develop, ease, elevate, enhance, forward, fructify, help, improve, make better, make progress, meliorate, mend,

mitigate, palliate, promote, raise, rectify, reform, upgrade
ASSOCIATED CONCEPTS: ameliorating facts and circumstances, ameliorating waste

AMENABILITY, *noun* accessibleness, accommodativeness, acquiescence, adaptability, agreeableness, compliance, compliancy, conformability, docility, ductility, flexibility, flexibleness, inclination, influenceability, malleability, manageability, mansuetude, obligingness, persuasibility, placability, plasticity, pliability, pliancy, readiness, receptiveness, responsiveness, servility, submission, submissiveness, tractability, versatility, willingness, yieldingness

AMENABLE, *adjective* accessible, acquiescent, agreeable, amiable, available, compliant, *dicto oboediens,* flexible, impressionable, influenceable, movable, obedient, open to suggestions, persuadable, persuasible, pervious, pliable, pliant, reasonable, responsible, suasible, tractable, yielding
ASSOCIATED CONCEPTS: amenable to process

AMEND, *verb* add to, adjust, alter, ameliorate, better, change, correct, *corrigere,* edit, emend, *emendare,* emendate, enhance, enrich, improve, mend, modify, perfect, polish, rectify, refashion, refine, reform, remedy, remove faults, renew, revamp, revise, rework, rewrite, upgrade
ASSOCIATED CONCEPTS: amend a certificate of incorporation, amend a law, amend a pleading, amend a statute, amend a will

AMENDMENT (Correction), *noun* adjustment, amelioration, betterment, change, *correctio,* elaboration, *emendatio,* emendation, enhancement, improvement, melioration, modification, perfection, refinement, reformation, remedy, revampment, revisal, revision, supplement
ASSOCIATED CONCEPTS: amendment in a statute, amendment to a will

AMENDMENT (Legislation), *noun* act, bill, clause, legislation, legislative act, legislative bill, measure, modification of the law, rider, supplement
ASSOCIATED CONCEPTS: amendment to a charter, amendment to the Constitution, Bill of Rights

AMENITY, *noun* accommodation, agreeable manner, agreeable way, agreeableness, allure, *amoenitas,* appeal, attractive feature, attractive quality, attractiveness, civility, delightfulness, desirable feature, grace, invitingness, lure, mildness, niceness, pleasantness, pleasingness, refinement

AMERCEMENT, *noun* damages, fine, forfeit, forfeiture, pecuniary penalty, penalty

AMICABLE, *adjective* affable, amiable, cordial, friendly, genial, harmonious, sociable, unhostile

AMICUS CURIAE, *noun* advocate, champion, exponent, friend in court, intercessor, intervening party, intervenor, party, reresentative, speaker
ASSOCIATED CONCEPTS: amicus brief, amicus motion to intervene

AMMUNITION, *noun* *apparatus belli,* armament, armature, arms, ballistics, cartridges, charge, defense, deterrent, explosive, firearms, gunnery, gunpowder, materials of combat, means of attack, muniment, munition, panoply, propellants, provisions, weapons

AMNESTY, *noun* absolution, acquittance, act of grace, act of mercy, conciliation, condonation, discharge, disculpation, exculpation, exoneration, forgiveness, general pardon, grace, *ignoscere,* pardon, quittance, release, reprieve, universal forgiveness of past offenses, *venia*
ASSOCIATED CONCEPTS: express amnesty, implied amnesty, presidential pardon

AMONG, *adverb* amid, amidst, between, in the middle of, parenthetically

AMORTIZATION, *noun* clearance, defrayal, defrayment, disbursement, discharge, extinction of a debt, extinguishment of claim, liquidation of a debt, payment, remittance, satisfaction
ASSOCIATED CONCEPTS: amortization contract, amortization of a mortgage, amortize a loan

AMOUNT (Quantity), *noun* aggregate, bulk, count, extent, magnitude, mass, measure, measurement, net quantity, number, numeration, strength, substance, sum, *summa,* total, whole
ASSOCIATED CONCEPTS: amount of evidence, amount of loss
FOREIGN PHRASES: *Major numerus in se continet minorem.* The greater number contains in itself the lesser.

AMOUNT (Result), *noun* conclusion, consequence, effect, end result, full effect, import, net quantity, outcome, outgrowth, product, purport, resultant, sum, sum total, upshot

AMOUNT (Sum), *noun* account, count, rate, reckoning, statement, summation, tally, value, worth
ASSOCIATED CONCEPTS: amount allowed, amount due, amount in controversy, amount in dispute, amount of loss, amount recovered, jurisdictional amount

AMPLE, *adjective* abounding, abundant, adequate, bountiful, broad enough, capacious, commodious, comprehensive, copious, expansive, extensive, generous, large enough, liberal, many, plenteous, satisfactory, sufficient

AMPLIFY, *verb* add to, augment, delineate, develop, elaborate, enlarge, expand, extend, increase, specify, specify in greater detail

ANACOLUTHON, *noun* broken thread, disconnectedness, discontinuity, lost connection, non sequitur, unwarranted conclusion

ANALOGOUS, *adjective* akin, alike, allied, analogical, associated, coequal, cognate, comparable, correlative, correspondent, corresponding, equipollent, equivalent, homologous, kindred, like, matching, parallel, related, resembling, same, similar, *similis*

ANALOGY, *noun* affinity, agreement, close relation, close resemblance, common feature, comparability, comparison, congruity, correlation, correspondence, equivalence, homology, like quality, likeness, logical relation, parallel relation, parallelism, parity, partial similarity, point in common, point of resemblance, points of comparison, relation, relativeness, relativity, resemblance, semblance, similar appearance, similar form, similar relation, similarity, similitude, *similitudo,* symmetry

FOREIGN PHRASES: *De similibus ad similia eadem ratione procedendum est.* Proceeding in similiar matters we are to proceed by the same rule.

ANALYSIS, *noun*   ascertainment, assay, audit, canvassing, close inquiry, consideration, critical examination, critique, delineation, dissection, examination, exhaustive inquiry, *explicatio,* exploration, inquiry, investigation, perusal, probe, research, review, scrutinization, scrutiny, searching inquiry, sifting, strict inquiry, study, survey, treatment

ASSOCIATED CONCEPTS: chemical analysis, lab analysis

ANALYZE, *verb*   anatomize, audit, canvass, conduct an inquiry, consider, delineate, delve into, dissect, examine, examine critically, explore, hold an inquiry, inquire into, institute an inquiry, investigate, make an analysis, make an inquiry, probe, question, reason, research, review, scan, scrutinize, set up an inquiry, sift, study, subject to examination, survey

ANARCHY, *noun*   absence of authority, breakdown of administration, chaos, confusion, discord, disobedience, disorder, disorderliness, disorganization, disregard, disunion, indiscipline, insubordination, insurgence, insurrection, interregnum, irresponsibility, lawlessness, *licentia,* misgovernment, misrule, mob law, mob rule, nihilism, political disorder, rebellion, revolution, riot, sedition, terrorism, tumult, turmoil, unruliness, uprising

ASSOCIATED CONCEPTS: criminal anarchy

ANCESTOR, *noun*   ascendant, *auctor generis, auctor gentis,* forebear, forefather, foregoer, forerunner, genitor, grandsire, parent, patriarch, precursor, predecessor, primogenitor, procreator, progenitor

ASSOCIATED CONCEPTS: ancestral estate, ancestral property, descendant, immediate ancestor, inheritance, lineal ancestor, maternal ancestor, paternal ancestor

ANCESTRY, *noun*   affiliation, ascendants, blood, blood relationship, blood tie, bloodline, cognation, connection, consanguinity, derivation, descent, family, family connection, family tree, filiation, forebears, forefathers, former generations, genealogy, genesis, *genus,* heredity, history, kinship, line, lineage, origin, origination, *origo,* parentage, parents, patriarchs, pedigree, predecessors, procreators, stirps, strain

ASSOCIATED CONCEPTS: ancestral estate, ancestral property

ANCILLARY *(Auxiliary),* **adjective**   abetting, accessory, added, additioional, adjunct, adjuvant, advantageous, aidful, aiding, assistant, attendant, beneficial, coadjuvant, collateral, completing, conducive, contributory, cooperative, extra, helpful, in addition, ministrant, more, other, serving as an adjunct, serving as an aid, spare, supernumerary, supplemental, supplementary, supporting

ASSOCIATED CONCEPTS: ancillary acts, ancillary agreements, ancillary attachment, ancillary covenants, ancillary jurisdiction, ancillary proceeding, ancillary relief, ancillary remedies

ANCILLARY *(Subsidiary),* **adjective**   complementing, dependent, derivational, derivative, ensuing, following, lesser, resultant, resulting, secondary, sequential, subaltern, subordinate

ANEW, *adverb*   afresh, again, another time, newly, once more, over again

ANIMAL, *noun*   *animans,* beast, beast of burden, beast of the field, brute, brute creation, created being, creature, pet, wild being

ASSOCIATED CONCEPTS: animals of a base nature, domestic animals, wild animal

FOREIGN PHRASES: *Animalia fera, si facta sint mansueta et ex consuetudine eunt et redeunt, volant et revolant, ut cervi, cygni, etc., eo usque nostra sunt, et ita intelliguntur quamdium habuerunt animum revertendi.* Wild animals, if they are tamed, and are accustomed to leave and return, fly away and fly back, as stags, swans, etc., are considered to belong to us so long as they have the intention of returning to us.

ANIMUS, *noun*   bent, character, decision, deliberateness, design, determination, disposition, fixed purpose, inclination, intendment, intent, intention, intentionality, mind, motive, nature, penchant, predetermination, predilection, predisposition, propensity, purpose, resolution, resolve, set purpose, settled purpose, temper, tendency, volition, will

ASSOCIATED CONCEPTS: *animus derelinquendi, animus et factum, animus furandi, animus revertendi, animus testandi,* anti-union animus

ANNEX *(Add),* **verb**   affix, append, attach, bind, bring together, combine, conjoin, connect, consolidate, fasten, fix, hold together, incorporate, interlink, intertwist, join, merge, put together, subjoin, supplement, unite

ASSOCIATED CONCEPTS: annex an exhibit, annex court papers, annex to a pleading, annexed writing, fixtures

ANNEX *(Arrogate),* **verb**   accroach, appropriate, assume, assume ownership, confiscate, convert, disseise, distrain, expropriate, impound, seize, take over, take possession, take summarily, usurp

ASSOCIATED CONCEPTS: annex a territory

ANNOY, *verb*   acerbate, affront, aggravate, badger, bedevil, bother, chafe, cross, discommode, discompose, displease, disquiet, distress, disturb, enrage, exasperate, fester, fret, gall, get on the nerves of, grate, grieve, harass, harm, harry, heckle, hector, importune, incommode, inconvenience, infest, irk, irritate, nag, needle, offend, pain, pester, pique, plague, provoke, rankle, roil, ruffle, thwart, torment, trouble, upset, vex

ANNUITY, *noun*   allotment, allowance, *annua pecunia,* annual allowance, earnings, income, pension, remuneration, retirement income, return, specified income payable for life, stipend, subsidy, subvention, yearly payment

ASSOCIATED CONCEPTS: annuity by a trust, annuity by will, annuity contract, annuity policy, antenuptial annuity, life insurance annuity, verifiable annuity

FOREIGN PHRASES: *Annua nec debitum judex non separat ipsum.* A judge does not divide annuities nor debt.

ANNUL, *verb*   abnegate, *abolere,* abolish, *abrogare,* abrogate, annihilate, avoid, call back, cancel, cancel

out, contradict, contravene, countermand, counterorder, deny, destroy, discontinue, disestablish, efface, end, expunge, exterminate, extinguish, invalidate, make illegal, make void, negate, nullify, obliterate, overrule, put an end to, recall, reduce to nothing, reduce to nought, relinquish, render null and void, render void, renege, repeal, repudiate, rescind, retract, reverse, revoke, set aside, *solvere,* strike out, supersede, terminate, unmake, vitiate, void, withdraw
ASSOCIATED CONCEPTS: annul a marriage, annul a statute, nol-pros

ANNULMENT, *noun* abolishment, abolition, abrogation, cancellation, contravention, decree of nullity, deletion, discontinuance, disestablishment, dissolution, effacement, invalidation, negation, nullification, obliteration, rasure, rescindment, retraction, reversal, revocation, revokement, undoing, vitiation, voidance
ASSOCIATED CONCEPTS: alimony, annulment of a marriage, dissolution of marriage, divorce, separation, voidable marriage

ANNUM, *noun* age, *annus,* continuum of days, cycle, fifty-two weeks, full round of the seasons, period, time, twelve months, year

ANNUNCIATE, *verb* advise, affirm, announce, apprise, assert, aver, communicate, convey, declare, dispatch news, disseminate, enunciate, explain, express, get across, get through, give notice, impart, inform, keep posted, make known, make known publicly, make proclamation, notify, pass on, pass on information, post, proclaim, profess, promulgate, pronounce, propound, publicize, publish, report, specify, state, tell, transmit

ANOMALOUS, *adjective* aberrant, abnormal, anomalistic, atypical, awry, breaking with tradition, deranged, deviating from the common rule, deviative, disarranged, disjunct, dislocated, disordered, disorganized, divergent, eccentric, erratic, in disorder, in the wrong place, inconsistent, irregular, misplaced, nonstandard, nonuniform, not conforming to the usual, out of keeping, out of order, out of the ordinary, peculiar, solecistic, uncommon, unconventional, uncustomary, unnatural, unrepresentative, untypical, unusual

ANONYMOUS, *adjective* authorless, bearing no name, having no acknowledged name, incognito, innominate, nameless, of unknown authorship, secret, *sine nomine,* unacknowledged, unclaimed, undesignated, unidentified, unknown, unnamed, unsigned, unspecified, without a name, without the name of the author
ASSOCIATED CONCEPTS: anonymous donor

ANSWER *(Judicial response),* **noun** confutation, contradictory evidence, countercharge, counterclaim, counterevidence, counterreply, counterstatement, defense, denial, legal argument, negation, negative evidence, official reply, opposite evidence, plea, plea in rebuttal, rebuttal, rebutting evidence, recrimination, refutation, rejoinder, replication, reply to a charge, surrebuttal, surrebutter, surrejoinder
ASSOCIATED CONCEPTS: amended answer, appearance by an answer, frivolous answer, general appearance, notice of appearance, responsive answer, sham answer, supplemental answer
FOREIGN PHRASES: *Ambigua responsio contra proferentem est accipienda.* An ambiguous answer is to be taken against him who offers it.

ANSWER *(Reply),* **noun** acknowledgment, denial, negation, reaction, rebuttal, refutal, rejoinder, repartee, replication, respondence, response, retort, return, riposte
ASSOCIATED CONCEPTS: argumentative answer, irrelevant answer, nonresponsive answer, responsive answer

ANSWER *(Solution),* **noun** cause, elucidation, explanation, finding, outcome, reason, resolution, result, revelation, verdict

ANSWER *(Be responsible),* **verb** be accountable, be answerable, be bound, be chargeable, be compelled, be liable, be obligated, be obliged, be subject, be surety, be under legal obligation, undertake responsibility

ANSWER *(Reply),* **verb** acknowledge, act in response to, be responsive, confute, contend, contest, contradict, contravene, controvert, counter, counterclaim, debate, defeat, defend, deny, disclaim, disprove, dispute, forswear, impugn, make a rejoinder, oppose, oppugn, plead, rebut, refute, rejoin, repudiate, *rescribere,* respond, *respondere,* retaliate, retort, return, riposte, say in reply, *se defendere,* traverse
ASSOCIATED CONCEPTS: answer in the alternative, argumentative answer

ANSWER *(Respond legally),* **verb** contest, controvert, counterblast, countercharge, counterclaim, defend, plead, rebut, recriminate, rejoin, reply, surrejoin
ASSOCIATED CONCEPTS: appearance by an answer, argumentative answer, supplemental answer

ANTAGONIZE, *verb* act in opposition to, aggress, alienate, cause dislike, cause offense, cause umbrage, compete with, conflict with, contend against, counteract, cross, destroy good will, disaffect, displease, embitter, envenom, estrange, excite hate, go against, incur the hostility of, irritate, make an antagonist of, make unfriendly, offend, oppose, provoke, render inimical, repel, rival, run counter to, set against, set at odds, show ill will, spite, take issue with, take one's stand against, turn against, work against

ANTECEDE, *verb* antedate, forerun, go before, have precedence, precede, predate, prevene
ASSOCIATED CONCEPTS: ancestor, antecedent creditor, antecedent debt, antecedent encumbrance, antecedent fraud, antecedent promise

ANTECEDENT, *adjective* *antecedens,* anterior, earlier, fore, foregoing, forerunning, former, going before in time, introductory, precedent, preceding, precursive, precursory, preexistent, prefatory, preliminary, prelusive, prelusory, prevenient, previous, prior
ASSOCIATED CONCEPTS: antecedent creditors, antecedent debt

ANTEDATE, *verb* affix an earlier date, anachronize, assign to an earlier date, date back, date before the true date, date before the true time, date earlier than the fact, foredate, predate, set an earlier date, transfer to an earlier date

ANTENUPTIAL AGREEMENT, *noun* agreement before marriage, concord before marriage, contract before marriage, legal arrangement before marriage, pact before marriage, understanding before marriage

ANTICIPATE *(Expect)*, **verb**   *antevertere,* assume, be ready for, calculate on, consider in advance, contemplate, count on, forearm, get the start on, guard against, have in prospect, hold in view, intuit, make preparations, plan on, preconceive, predispose, prepare for, suppose, surmise, wait for
ASSOCIATED CONCEPTS: anticipated profits, anticipating defenses, anticipation notes, anticipatory breach, anticipatory repudiation, anticipatory warrant, duty to anticipate in negligence

ANTICIPATE *(Prognosticate)*, **verb**   announce in advance, augur, auspicate, betoken, conjecture, divine, forebode, forecast, foreknow, foreshow, forespeak, harbinger, have a presentiment, herald, look forward to, omen, portend, *praevertere,* preannounce, precognize, predetermine, predict, premonish, presage, prophesy, vaticinate

ANTIPATHETIC *(Distasteful)*, **adjective**   abhorrent, bitter, disagreeable, disgusting, displeasing, hateful, loathsome, odious, offensive, repellent, repugnant, repulsive, undesirable, uninviting, unsatisfactory, virulent

ANTIPATHETIC *(Oppositional)*, **adjective**   adverse, alien, alienated, antagonistic, antipodean, antithetic, antithetical, at cross-purposes, averse, conflicting, constitutionally opposed, contradictory, contradistinct, contrapositive, contrary, contrasted, converse, counter, diametrically opposite, having a natural contrariety, inimical, negatory, opposed, opposing, opposite, oppositive, oppugnant, resistant, reverse, unfriendly, unpropitious

ANTIPODE, **noun**   absolute difference, adverseness, *adversus,* antimony, antipathy, *antipodes,* antipole, antithesis, collision, conflict, contradiction, contradistinction, contraindication, contraposition, contrariety, contrariness, contrary, contrast, converse, counteraction, countermeaning, counterpart, counterpole, direct opposite, disagreement, inconsistency, inverse, inversion, negation, obverse, opposite, opposite extreme, opposite pole, opposite side, oppositeness, opposition, other extreme, polarity, repugnance, reverse, vis-à-vis

ANTIQUE, **adjective**   ancient, antedeluvian, archaic, bygone, old, old fashioned, older, superannuated, time worn, venerable

ANTITHESIS, **noun**   absolute difference, adverseness, antipode, balanced contrast, conflict, *contentio,* contradiction, contradistinction, contraposition, contrariety, *contrarium,* contrary, contrast, converse, counterpart, counterpole, direct opposite, disagreement, divergence, incompatibility, inverse, irreconcilability, mutual exclusiveness, opposite, opposite pole, opposition, other extreme, polarity, reverse, strong contrast

ANTITRUST ACT, **noun**   against fair trade, against free commerce, against free mercantilism, against free trade, against open business, against open markets, contrary to good business

APART, **adjective**   alien, alone, asunder, detached, disconnected, disengaged, disjoined, disjoint, disjointed, disjunct, disrelated, dissociated, *distare,* disunited, *diversus,* foreign, having independent qualities, having unique features, having unique qualities, independent, irrelative, isolated, no relation, removed, *separare,* sep-

arate, separated, solo, *solus,* unaffiliated, unallied, unassociated, unattached, unconnected, unjoined
ASSOCIATED CONCEPTS: living apart

APARTMENT, **noun**   home, premises, residence, place of residence
ASSOCIATED CONCEPTS: condominium, cooperative apartment

APOLOGIST, **noun**   advocate, arguer in defense, champion, defender, *defensor,* disputant, excuser, exponent, expositer, expounder, favorer, justifier, pleader, proponent, protector, supporter, upholder

APPARENT *(Perceptible)*, **adjective**   able to be seen, clear, conspicuous, definite, detectable, discernible, distinct, easily seen, evident, explicit, exposed, express, *fictus,* identifiable, in sight, in view, indubitable, known, manifest, *manifestus,* noticeable, notorious, obvious, open, open to view, overt, palpable, patent, perceivable, plain, real, recognizable, self-evident, showing, *species,* tangible, uncovered, undisguised, *videor,* viewable, visible
ASSOCIATED CONCEPTS: apparent ability, apparent agency, apparent authority, apparent cause, apparent danger, apparent defect, apparent easement, apparent from the record, apparent necessity, apparent ownership, apparent partnership, apparent risk, apparent scope of authority, apparent use

APPARENT *(Presumptive)*, **adjective**   appearing, assumptive, conjectural, contemplated, evidential, expected, hopeful, intended, likely, logical, manifest, ostensible, plausible, premised, presumable, probable, proposed, propositional, prospective, seeming, suggestive, supposable, supposed, suppositional, suppositionary, suppositive, taken for granted, to be supposed
ASSOCIATED CONCEPTS: apparent heir, apparent validity
FOREIGN PHRASES: *Quod constat clare non debet verificari.* What is clearly apparent is not required to be proved. *Quod constat curiae opere testium non indiget.* That which appears to the court needs not the help of witnesses.

APPEAL, **noun**   appellate review, *appellatio,* application for retrial, application for review by a higher tribunal, bid, complaint to a superior court, *obtestatio,* petition, *provocatio,* reconsideration, recourse to some higher power, reexamination, rehearing, reopening, request for another decision, request for retrial, request for review, resort to superior authority, retrial, review
ASSOCIATED CONCEPTS: appellate courts, appellate jurisdiction, *certiorari*
FOREIGN PHRASES: *De fide et officio judicis non recipitur quaestio, sed de scientia, sive sit error juris, sive facti.* The good faith and honesty of a judge are not to be questioned, but his knowledge, whether it be in error of law or fact, may be.

APPEAL, **verb**   *appelare,* apply for a reexamination of a case, apply for a retrial, apply for a review of a case to a higher tribunal, bid, bring new evidence, claim, consider again with a view to a change or action, contest, contest a case by asking for review, *homini placere, obsecrare,* reconsider, reexamine, refer to, rehear, reopen, request another decision, request reexamination, request reopening of a case, retry, review, seek reexamination, seek reference of a case from one court to another, seek review of a case, sue

ASSOCIATED CONCEPTS: appeal as a matter of right, appeal bond, appeal in forma pauperis, appealable interest, appealable judgment, appealable order, appealed from an order of the court, discretionary appeal, perfect on appeal

APPEAR *(Attend court proceedings)*, *verb* *adesse*, answer, be in attendance, be manifest, be present, be present to answer, come formally before a tribunal, come into court, *comparere*, enter an appearance, *in iudicium venire*, make an appearance, present an answer, present oneself, put in an appearance, submit oneself to
FOREIGN PHRASES: *Idem est non esse, et non apparere.* Not to exist is the same thing as not to appear.

APPEAR *(Materialize)*, *verb* *apparere*, arise, be in sight, be manifest, become visible, come into sight, come into view, come to light, *conspici*, emerge, *exsistere*, manifest itself, occur, present to the view

APPEAR *(Seem to be)*, *verb* be patent, convey the impression, create the impression, give the effect, give the impression, have a certain semblance, have every indication, look, look as if, present the appearance, resemble, seem like, strike one as being, take on the aspect, take on the manner, *videri*, wear the aspect

APPEARANCE *(Coming into court)*, *noun* answer, entrance in a case, presence in court, response to an action, submission to a court's jurisdiction
ASSOCIATED CONCEPTS: compulsory appearance, general appearance, limited appearance, special appearance, specific appearance, voluntary appearance

APPEARANCE *(Emergence)*, *noun* *adventus*, arrival into view, coming, evincement, introduction, manifestation, occurrence, rise

APPEARANCE *(Look)*, *noun* air, aspect, *aspectus*, complexion, demeanor, embodiment, external aspect, face, form, guise, likeness, manner, mien, outward look, outward show, personal presence, physiognomy, posture, pretense, *rem simulare*, show, sight, *species*
ASSOCIATED CONCEPTS: appearance of authority, appearance of validity

APPELLANT, *noun* aggrieved party, appealer, *appellator*, contender, delator, litigant, objector, party, party to a suit, petitioner, suitor
ASSOCIATED CONCEPTS: appellee, respondant

APPELLATE COURT, *noun* court of appellate jurisdiction, court of review, higher court, senior court
ASSOCIATED CONCEPTS: appellate division, appellate jurisdiction, appellate term

APPEND, *verb* add, *addere*, *adiungere*, affix, annex, attach, augment, conjoin, connect, extend, fasten, include, insert, join, subjoin, supplement

APPENDIX *(Accession)*, *noun* accessory, additament, *adiungere*, annexation, appendage, attachment, complement, extension, inclusion, insertion, pendant

APPENDIX *(Supplement)*, *noun* *accessio*, *addendum*, *addere*, addition, adjunct, appendage, attachment, codicil, continuation, excursus, rider
ASSOCIATED CONCEPTS: pocket part

APPERTAIN, *verb* affect, allude to, apply to, associate, be akin, be applicable, be characteristic of, be concerned with, be congruent, be connected with, be dependent upon, be incident to, be intrinsic, be part of, be pertinent, bear on, belong as a part, belong as an attribute, concern, deal with, depend upon, have reference, have relation, inhere, interest, involve, link, pertain, refer, regard, relate, touch

APPLIANCE, *noun* accessory, adjunct, apparatus, appurtenance, attachment, commodity, contrivance, convenience, device, equipment, facility, implement, instrument, *instrumentum*, labor-saving device, machine, means, mechanism, piece of apparatus, precision tool, tool, utensil, utility
ASSOCIATED CONCEPTS: fixtures

APPLICABLE, *adjective* *à propos*, acceptable, adaptable, adapted to, appertaining, appliable, appropriate, apt, befit, befitting, belonging, fit, fitting, germane, pertinent, proper, relevant, right, sortable, suitable, to the point, usable, useful, utilizable
ASSOCIATED CONCEPTS: applicable law, applicable local law

APPLICANT *(Candidate)*, *noun* aspirant, bidder, entrant, inquirer, candidate under consideration

APPLICANT *(Petitioner)*, *noun* claimant, moveant, party, petitioner, solicitant

APPLICATION, *noun* advancement, bid, motion, *petitio*, petition, presentation, proposal, proposition, request, requisition, requisition to the court, submission
ASSOCIATED CONCEPTS: application duly made, application for a change of venue, application for a discharge, application for a review, application for adjournment, application of payments, application to the court, insurance application, motion
FOREIGN PHRASES: *Contemporanea expositio est optima et fortissima in lege.* A contemporaneous construction is the best and strongest in the law.

APPLY *(Pertain)*, *verb* affect, be applicable, be concerned with, be connected with, be pertinent, be proper to, be relevant, bear upon, belong to, concern, deal with, have a connection to, have bearing on, have reference, have relation, involve, *pertinere ad*, refer, regard, relate, touch

APPLY *(Put in practice)*, *verb* adapt, adjust, *admovere*, adopt, carry out, convert to use, employ, execute, exercise, exert, put in action, put in operation, put to use, use, utilize

APPLY *(Request)*, *verb* *ad hominem confugere*, ask, *hominem adire*, make formal request, petition, pray, seek, solicit
ASSOCIATED CONCEPTS: motion

APPOINT, *verb* approve, assign, authorize, charge, charter, choose, commission, confirm, *constituere*, *creare*, create, delegate, depute, designate, *destinare*, *dicere*, direct, employ, empower, engage, enlist, entrust, establish, *facere*, give a mandate, license, name, pick, pick out, proclaim, require, sanction, select
ASSOCIATED CONCEPTS: appoint to fill a vacancy, appoint under a will, appointing officer, appointing power, appointive office, public officers

APPOINTMENT *(Act of designating)*, **noun** allocation, allotment, assignment, authorization, certification, charter, choice, decree, delegation, deputation, designation to office, dispensation, distribution, installation, naming, nomination, order, ordination, placing in office, requirement, selection
ASSOCIATED CONCEPTS: agency, delegation, limited power of appointment

APPOINTMENT *(Meeting)*, **noun** agreement as to time and place of meeting, date, engagement, interview, rendezvous, tryst, visit

APPOINTMENT *(Position)*, **noun** capacity, chargeship, employment, function, incumbency, job, living, occupation, office, post, profession, sphere of occupation, station, undertaking, vocation, work
ASSOCIATED CONCEPTS: agency, authority

APPORTION, *verb* administer, *adsignare*, allocate, allot, assign, assort, award, carve up, classify, deal out, delimit, demarcate, dispense, *dispertire*, disseminate, *distribuere*, distribute, distribute proportionately, divide, divide according to rule, divide into shares, divide proportionately, divide up, dole out, measure out, mete, mete out, parcel out, partition, place in order, portion out, portion out equitably, prorate, set in order, share, split, subdivide

APPORTIONMENT, *noun* administration, allocation, allotment, allowance, assignment, assignment in proportion, consignment, disposition, distribution, division, division in proportion, doling out, issuance, just division, measuring out, meting out, partition, partitionment, proportionment
ASSOCIATED CONCEPTS: apportionment of blame, apportionment of damages, apportionment of liability, apportionment of taxes, comparative negligence, doctrine of apportionment, *pro tanto*

APPOSITE, *adjective* accordant, *ad rem*, adapted, affiliated, affinitive, allied, applicable, applying to, appropriate, appurtenant, apropos, apt, associated, associative, bearing upon, befitting, belonging to, cognate, comparable, compatible, congeneric, congenerous, congenial, connatural, connected, consistent, consonant, correlated, correlative, correspondent, corresponding, fit, fitting, germane, in accordance with, in conjunction with, *in loco*, in relation with, pertinent, reconcilable, relating to, relative, relevant, seasonable, suitable, suited, timely, to the point, to the purpose, well-adapted, with reference to

APPRAISAL, *noun* appraisement, assessment, calculation, computation, determination, estimate, estimated value, estimation, evaluation, examination, fixing a price, measurement, quantification, reckoning, setting a price, setting the value, survey, valuation
ASSOCIATED CONCEPTS: appraisal at actual value, appraisal at estimated value, appraisal at market value, appraisal value

APPRECIABLE, *adjective* appraisable, ascertainable, assessable, calculable, capable of being perceived, cognizable, computable, concrete, considerable, conspicuous, countable, detectable, determinable, discernible, discoverable, distinguishable, estimable, evident, fathomable, gaugeable, knowable, manifest, material, measurable, mensurable, mensural, meterable, notable, noticeable, observable, palpable, patent, perceivable, perceptible, perspicuous, ponderable, prominent, recognizable, seeable, sizable, substantial, substantive, surveyable, tangible, visible, weighable
ASSOCIATED CONCEPTS: appreciable damages, appreciable losses

APPRECIATE *(Comprehend)*, *verb* acknowledge, apprehend, be aware of, be cognizant of, be conscious of, conceive, discern, know, notice, perceive, realize, recognize, take into consideration, take notice, understand
ASSOCIATED CONCEPTS: appreciate a risk, appreciate the danger

APPRECIATE *(Increase)*, *verb* advance, become greater, become more numerous, become of greater value, enhance the degree of, gain in worth, grow in value, improve, increase the market price of, make of greater value, rise, rise in value
ASSOCIATED CONCEPTS: appreciate in value

APPRECIATE *(Value)*, *verb* adequately perceive, *aestimare*, esteem, perceive the worth of, realize the worth of, recognize the worth of

APPRECIATION *(Increased value)*, *noun* accrual, accruement, accumulation, added monetary worth, addition, advance in worth, gain, gain in worth, growth, growth in value, increase, increased price, increment, realization, rise, rise in value

APPRECIATION *(Perception)*, *noun* apperception, appraisal, appraisment, assessment, awareness, clear perception, cognition, cognizance, comprehension, consciousness, correct valuation, discernment, estimation, full appraisal, just estimation, measurement, recognition, valuation

APPREHEND *(Arrest)*, *verb* capture, catch, commit, *comprehendere*, confine, constrain, detain, detain by legal process, fetter, hold, legally restrain, place under arrest, put in restraint, put under arrest, restrain, seize, send to prison, take, take by authority, take captive, take into custody, take prisoner

APPREHEND *(Perceive)*, *verb* appreciate, be acquainted with, be apprized of, be aware of, be cognizant of, be conscious of, be under the impression, become aware of, cognize, come to know, comprehend, *comprehendere*, conceive of, detect, discern, discover by observation, fathom, have an understanding of, have cognizance of, have knowledge of, have an impression, ken, know entirely, know of, know well, learn, master, realize, recognize, regard as, see, sense, surmise, understand, view

APPREHENSION *(Act of arresting)*, *noun* arrest, caption, capture, catch, confinement, detention, holding in custody, imprisonment, incarceration, internment, restraint, retention, seizure, taking, taking hold

APPREHENSION *(Fear)*, *noun* agitation, alarm, anticipation of adversity, anxiety, apprehensiveness, care, concern, consternation, distrust, foreboding, misdoubt, misgiving, mistrust, overanxiety, perturbation, phobia, presentiment, qualm, sense of danger, suspicion, threat, trepidation, uneasiness, worry

APPREHENSION *(Perception)*, *noun* cognition, cognizance, comprehension, conception, discernment, grasp, idea, image, impression, intellection, judgment, knowledge, mastery, mental capacity, notion, observation, opinion, recognition, reflection, sense, thought, understanding, view

APPRENTICE, *noun* beginner, learner, novice, novitiate, probationer, worker

APPRISE, *verb* acquaint, advise, alert, announce, brief, communicate, convey knowledge, counsel, describe, disclose, divulge, enlighten, familiarize, give information, give notice, impart knowledge, inform, instruct, let know, make aware, make cognizant, make known, notify, orient, point out, publish, report, reveal, tell, warn
ASSOCIATED CONCEPTS: apprise of the facts

APPROACH, *verb* *accedere,* accost, advance, *adventare, appropinquare,* be in proximity, be in sight of, be in the neighborhood of, be in the vicinity of, be near, come forward, come near, confront, converge upon, draw near, edge close to, get near, go near, move near, move toward, pursue, stalk, step up to, verge on

APPROACHES, *noun* accesses, avenues, channels, entrances, entranceways, entryways, gates, highways, ingresses, inlets, intakes, means of access, passages, routes, ways

APPROPRIATE, *adjective* *accommodatus,* accordant, accurate, adapted to, admissible, applicable, apposite, apropos, apt, *aptus,* befitting, concordant, condign, conformable, *congruens,* congruous, consistent, consonant, correct, correspondent, exact, expedient, fine, fit, fitting, germane, good, harmonious, likely, meet, opportune, pertinent, practicable, precise, proper, relevant, right, rightful, seemly, suitable, suited, timely, well-suited
ASSOCIATED CONCEPTS: appropriate bargaining unit, appropriate cause of action, appropriate remedy

APPROPRIATE, *verb* acquire, adopt, annex, arrogate, assume, assume ownership, borrow, capture, claim, possess, take, take over

APPROPRIATION (*Allotment*), ***noun*** allocation, allowance, apportionment, budget, budgeting, concession, designation of use, dispensation, distribution, setting apart
ASSOCIATED CONCEPTS: appropriation bill, appropriation for public use, appropriation of money, budgetary appropriation

APPROPRIATION (*Donation*), ***noun*** benefaction, bestowal, contribution, disbursement, endowment, funding, gift, grant, guerdon, meed, sponsorship

APPROPRIATION (*Taking*), ***noun*** accroachment, acquisition, adoption, annexation, apprehension, assumption, capture, confiscation, conversion, dispossession, disseisin, divestment, expropriation, impoundment, impropriation, seizure, snatching, taking possession
ASSOCIATED CONCEPTS: appropriation from revenues, appropriation of land, appropriation of payment

APPROVAL, *noun* acceptance, accord, acknowledgment, acquiescence, adoption, affirmance, affirmation, agreement, allowance, *approbatio,* approbation, assent, assurance, authentication, authorization, com-

probatio, concordance, concurrence, confirmation, consent, countenance, encouragement, endorsement, expression of satisfaction, favor, license, nod of approbation, permit, ratification, recognition, sanction, support, toleration, validation, verification
ASSOCIATED CONCEPTS: acceptance by a bank, approved endorsed note, sale on approval
FOREIGN PHRASES: *Qui non improbat, approbat.* He who does not disapprove, approves. *Quod approbo non reprobo.* That which I approve I do not later reject.

APPROVE, *verb* accede to, accept, acquiesce in, adopt, advocate, affirm, agree to, allow, *approbare,* approbate, assent to, authenticate, authorize, be in favor of, be satisfied with, certify, *comprobare,* concur in, confirm, consent to, countenance, endorse, favor, make valid, *probare,* ratify, sanction, second, support, sustain, uphold, validate

APPROXIMATE, *adjective* alike, almost, approaching, close, comparable, estimated, imprecise, in the vicinity of, inexact, like, much the same, nearly accurate, nearly correct, nearly equal, nearly perfect, nearly resembling, nigh, not perfectly accurate, *propinquus,* proximal, proximate, similar, surmised, uncertain, unprecise
ASSOCIATED CONCEPTS: approximate value

APPROXIMATE, *verb* *accedere ad,* advance near to, approach, approach closely, approach in amount, be in the vicinity of, be near, border on, closely resemble, come close in estimation, come close to, come near, come near in position, compare with, draw near, nearly equal, nearly rival, resemble

APPURTENANCE, *noun* accession, accessory, accompaniment, addendum, additament, addition, adjunct, annex, annexation, *annexe,* appanage, appendage, appendant, appendix, attachment, auxiliary, concomitant, dependency, extension, incidental, pendant, something added, subsidiary, supplement
ASSOCIATED CONCEPTS: accession, appurtenance to realty, appurtenant right, conveyance of property, covenants, deeds of conveyance, easement appurtenant, easements, fixture

APPURTENANT, *adjective* accessory, adjunct, ancillary, annexed, appended, appertaining, attached, auxiliary, belonging, connected, dependent on, incident, necessarily connected, subsidiary, used with another thing
ASSOCIATED CONCEPTS: appurtenant passage of air, appurtenant passage of light, appurtenant to land, appurtenant watercourse, *causa rei,* dominant land, servient land

APTITUDE, *noun* ability, applicability, bent, endowment, faculty, fitness, flair, gift, inclination, innate ability, intelligence, learning, propensity, propriety, suitability, talent, tendency

ARBITER, *noun* adjudicator, advisor, *arbiter,* arbitrator, determiner, *disceptator,* final authority, interagent, interceder, intercessor, intermediary, intermediate, intermediator, intervener, mediator, moderator, negotiant, negotiator, prescriber, recommender, reconciler, referee
ASSOCIATED CONCEPTS: arbitrament, final arbiter

ARBITRARY, *adjective*   according to desires, capricious, contrary to reason, determined by no principle, done at pleasure, fanciful, illogical, independent of law, independent of rule, *infinitus,* injudicious, irrational, *libidinosus,* nonrational, perverse, unaccountable, unjustified, unreasonable, unreasoned, without adequate determining principle, without consideration, without reason, without substantial cause
ASSOCIATED CONCEPTS: arbitrary act, arbitrary action, arbitrary and capricious, arbitrary classification, arbitrary determination, arbitrary standards, arbitrary verdict

ARBITRARY AND CAPRICIOUS, *adjective*   absolute, authoritative, baseless, dictatorial, dogmatic, fanciful, groundless, impetuous, motiveless, purposeless, restrictive, unduly, whimsical, willful

ARBITRATE *(Adjudge),* **verb**   adjudicate, arrange, arrive at a conclusion, ascertain after reasoning, assess, conciliate, decide, decide between opposing parties, decree, decree authoritatively, determine, determine a controversy, determine a point at issue, *dijudicare,* end by a decision, fix conclusively, give judgment, judge, judicate, lead to a decision, make a decision, mete out, order, pass judgment, pronounce formally, pronounce judgment, resolve, rule, settle, settle by authoritative decision, sit in judgment
ASSOCIATED CONCEPTS: mediate

ARBITRATE *(Conciliate),* **verb**   accord, adjust differences, arrange, bring into agreement, bring into harmony, bring to terms, bring together, *disceptare,* harmonize, intercede, intervene, make compatible, make peace between, moderate, negotiate, prevail with, propitiate, put in accord, reconcile, referee, regulate, render compatible, render concordant, render no longer opposed, restore harmony, settle, settle differences

ARBITRATION, *noun*   adjudgment, adjustment, apportionment, appraisal, arbitrage, *arbitrium,* assessment, conciliation, decision, decree, determining of a controversy, finding, intercession, interjacence, intermediation, interposition, intervention, judgment, *rapprochement,* resolution, settlement
ASSOCIATED CONCEPTS: advisory arbitration, arbitrability, arbitration agreement, arbitration and award, arbitration award, arbitration clause, arbitration provision, arbitrators, binding arbitration, compulsory arbitration, grievance arbitration, interest arbitration, proceeding to confirm arbitration award, voluntary arbitration

ARBITRATOR, *noun*   adjudicator, arbiter, determiner, *disceptator,* interagent, interceder, intercessor, intermediary, intermediate, intervenor, interventionist, judicator, moderator, negotiant, negotiator, reconciler, referee, referendary, ruler
ASSOCIATED CONCEPTS: arbitration and award, arbitrator's authority, arbitrator's award, board of arbitrators, scope of arbitrator's authority

ARCHITECT, *noun*   *architectus,* artificer, author, begetter, builder, composer, constructor, contriver, creator, designer, deviser, draftsman, enterpriser, founder, framer, generator, introducer, inventor, maker, organizer, originator, planner, prime mover, projector, schemer

ARDOR, *noun*   ardency, *ardor,* drive, eagerness, effusiveness, *élan,* emotion, energy, enthusiasm, excitation of feelings, excitement, exhilaration, fanaticism, fervency, fervidness, *fervor,* feverishness, fire, force, forcefulness, furor, impassionedness, intense desire, liveliness, magniloquence, passion, passionateness, perfervor, spirit, state of excitability, *studium,* verve, vigor, vigorousness, vitality, vivacity, warmth of feeling, zeal

AREA *(Province),* **noun**   *area,* arena, bounds, confines, demesne, domain, expanse, field, jurisdiction, limits, location, orbit, place, premises, purview, range, realm, region, scope, sphere, territory, vicinage, vicinity, zone
ASSOCIATED CONCEPTS: area variance, specific areas of the law

AREA *(Surface),* **noun**   amount of surface, dimensions, expanse, expansion, extent of surface, measured size, measurements, plane surface, proportions, real size, *superficies,* true dimensions

ARGUABLE, *adjective*   at issue, contestable, controversial, controvertible, debatable, disputable, in dispute, in question, up for discussion
ASSOCIATED CONCEPTS: arguable claim, arguable contention

ARGUE, *verb*   advance, affirm, allege, *argumentari,* assert, challenge, claim, confute, *conligere,* contend, contend in argument, contest, controvert, *de re disserere,* debate, disagree, dispute, elucidate, emphasize, enunciate, establish, explain, expostulate, express, maintain, make an assertion, oppose, present reasons against, present reasons for, proclaim, pronounce, propose, propound, put forth, reason upon, remonstrate, set forth, show, state with conviction, stress, submit, urge
ASSOCIATED CONCEPTS: *a posteriori, a priori, ab inconvenienti, ad hominem, arguendo*

ARGUENDO, *adverb*   for mere discussion only, for the sake of argument, hypothetically

ARGUMENT *(Contention),* **noun**   altercation, antagonism, belligerency, bickering, breach, clashing, conflict, contentiousness, controversy, cross-purposes, debate, difference of opinion, disaccord, disagreement, discord, *disputatio,* disputation, dispute, dissension, dissent, dissidence, disunion, disunity, division, divisiveness, feud, hard feelings, hostility, ill feeling, ill will, lack of concord, misunderstanding, opposition, oral contention, polemics, quarrel, quarreling, strife, variance, verbal conflict, war of words, wrangle, wrangling
ASSOCIATED CONCEPTS: *a posteriori, a priori, apex juris*
FOREIGN PHRASES: *In rebus manifestis, errat qui auctoritates legum allegat; quia perspicua vera non sunt probanda.* In clear cases, he errs who cites legal authorities because obvious truths are manifest and do not have to be proved. *Argumentum ab inconvenienti est validum in lege; quia lex non permittit aliquod inconveniens.* An argument drawn from what is inconvenient is good in law, because the law will not permit any inconvenience.

ARGUMENT *(Pleading),* **noun**   argument at the bar, counterstatement, course of reasoning, defense, demonstration, discourse designed to convince, disputation, expression of opinion for or against, plea, pleading,

rationale, rebuttal, refutation, statement of defense, statement offered in proof, statement tending to prove a point, submission
ASSOCIATED CONCEPTS: argument submitted to the court, closing argument, equittable argument, legal argument, opening argument, oral argument, preargument statement
FOREIGN PHRASES: *In rebus manifestis, errat qui auctoritates legum allegat; quia perspicua vera non sunt probanda.* In clear cases, he errs who cites legal authorities because obvious truths are manifest and do not have to be proved.

ARGUMENTATIVE, *adjective* belligerent, characterized by argument, combative, contentious, dialectical, discordant, disputatious, dissentient, eristic, eristical, factious, given to controversy, litigious, logomachic, logomachical, petulant, pilpulistic, polemic, polemical, pugnacious, quarrelsome
ASSOCIATED CONCEPTS: argumentative denial

ARISE *(Appear), verb* become manifest, become noticeable, become visible, come forth, come in sight, come in view, come to light, come to notice, emerge, make an appearance, manifest itself, present itself, reveal itself, show itself
ASSOCIATED CONCEPTS: arise under an obligation, arise under the laws of the United States, arising out of a contract, arising out of and in the course of employment, arising out of employment, arising under federal law, arising under the Constitution, arising upon contract, cause of action arising, counterclaim arising out of the plaintiff's claim

ARISE *(Occur), verb* become operative, come about, come to pass, eventuate, get under way, happen, proceed, take place, transpire

ARISE *(Originate), verb* accrue, be born, be derived, become, begin, come from, come into action, come into being, come into existence, come to be, emanate, ensue, eventuate, evolve, flow, follow, grow out of, have origin, initiate, issue forth, proceed from, spring forth, spring up, start, start out, take birth, take origin

ARMED, *adjective* *armatus,* bristling with arms, equipped with arms, fortified, furnished with weapons, in arms, issued weapons, panoplied, provided with arms, supplied with arms, under arms, well-armed
ASSOCIATED CONCEPTS: armed burglary, armed felony, armed forces, armed guards
FOREIGN PHRASES: *Arma in armatos sumere jura sinunt.* The laws permit the taking up of arms against armed persons. *Ligna et lapides sub "armorum" appellatione non continentur.* Sticks and stones are not included within the definition of "arms."

ARRAIGN, *verb* *accusare,* accuse, accuse of wrong, blame, brand, brand with reproach, bring accusation, bring before a court, bring to trial, bring up for investigation, bring up on charges, call before a court, call to account, charge, *citare,* cite, complain against, criminate, denounce, denunciate, formally accuse, formally charge, formally criminate, formally incriminate, implicate, incriminate, inculpate, *postulare,* prefer charges, prosecute

ARRAIGNMENT, *noun* accusation, accusation in court, allegation of criminal wrongdoing, crimination

through law enforcement, delation by criminal charges, formal accusal, imputation from criminal proceeding, incrimination, inculpation by prosecution, judicial charge, prosecution
ASSOCIATED CONCEPTS: arrest, bail, felony hearing, indictment

ARRANGE *(Methodize), verb* adapt, adjust, allocate, apportion, bring into order, bring to terms, collocate, come to an agreement, come to terms, *componere, constituere,* coordinate, determine, devise, *digerere,* direct, fix, fix the order, group, manage, marshal, order, *ordinare,* organize, place in order, program, put in readiness, reduce to order, regulate, resolve, schematize, set in order, settle, size, space, straighten out, systematize

ARRANGE *(Plan), verb* blueprint, calculate, contrive, design, devise, engineer, formulate, frame, make arrangements, make preparations, mark out a course, prepare, program, project, schedule, shape a course, sketch out

ARRANGEMENT *(Ordering), noun* adaption, arraying, collocation, *compositio,* composition, conformation, *conlocatio,* formation, method, regularity, schematism, symmetry, systematization, uniformity

ARRANGEMENT *(Plan), noun* conception, concoction, contrivance, course of action, ground plan, layout, master plan, method, outline, program of action, schema, scheme, system
ASSOCIATED CONCEPTS: arrangement for the benefit of creditors

ARRANGEMENT *(Understanding), noun* abatement of differences, accommodation, accord, accordance, adjustment, adjustment by agreement, agreement, compact, compromise, concord, contract, entente, harmonization, mutual agreement, mutual assent, mutual promise, mutual undertaking, pact, proviso, reconciliation, restoration of harmony, settlement, terms
ASSOCIATED CONCEPTS: arrangement through a marital settlement

ARRANT *(Definite), adjective* clear, complete, confirmed, conspicuous, consummate, identifiable, obvious, palpable, plain, recognizable, salient, striking, through, uncontestable, unmistakable, utter

ARRANT *(Onerous), adjective* accursed, atrocious, base, characterless, deplorable, discreditable, disgraceful, disreputable, evil, execrable, flagrant, flagrantly bad, foul, fulsome, glaringly bad, grievous, guilty, heinous, immeritorious, infamous, monstrous, outrageous, patently bad, preeminently bad, scandalous, shameful, shameless, shocking, sinful, sinister, unmistakably bad, unscrupulous, vile, wicked, wrong, wrongful

ARRAY *(Jury), noun* body of jurors, good men and true, jurors, jurymen, panel, trier, trier of the facts
ASSOCIATED CONCEPTS: challenge to the array

ARRAY *(Order), noun* arrangement, classification, collocation, composition, course, design, disposition, disposure, due order, fixed order, good order, gradation, layout, logical order, marshaling, method, methodicalness, methodology, ordering, organization, pattern, placing, progression, regularity, rule, schematic arrangement, sequence, state of order, strict order, subordination, system, systematization, unbroken order, uniformity

ARREARS, noun arrearage, back payments, balance due, debit, debt, debt unpaid though due, default, deferred payment, deficit, delinquency, indebtedness, indebtment, liability, obligation, outstanding debt, overdue bill, overdue payment, payments past due, *pecuniae residuae,* state of indebtedness, unpaid bill, unpaid debt
ASSOCIATED CONCEPTS: arrears in taxes, arrears of alimony, arrears of assessment, arrears of dues, arrears of interest, arrears of premiums, arrears of rent, arrears of taxes, judgment on arrears

ARREST, noun apprehension, capture, confinement, custodial detention, imprisonment, incarceration, internment, prehension, restraint, restriction, retention, seizure
ASSOCIATED CONCEPTS: extradition, rendition

ARREST *(Apprehend),* **verb** arrêt, capture, cast into prison, catch, commit, commit to an institution, commit to prison, *comprehendere,* confine, constrain, *deprehendere,* deprive of liberty, detain, detain by criminal process, entrammel, give in custody, hold, immure, imprison, incarcerate, *in custodiam dare,* intern, jail, lay under restraint, legally restrain, make captive, make prisoner, place in confinement, put in durance, put in duress, put under restraint, restrain, secure, seize, seize by legal warrant, send to jail, shackle, take by authority, take captive, take charge of, take into custody, take into preventive custody, take into protective custody, take prisoner, throw into prison
ASSOCIATED CONCEPTS: arrest warrant, false arrest, false imprisonment, illegal arrest, prior arrest, probable cause, resisting arrest, search incident to an arrest, warrant of arrest

ARREST *(Stop),* **verb** avert, block, bring to a standstill, bring to a stop, check, countercheck, curb, curtail, delay, detain, deter, end, enjoin, foil, foreclose, forestall, frustrate, hinder, hold, hold back, impede, inhibit, interfere, interrupt, keep back, obstruct, prevent, quell, repel, restrain, stall, stay, stifle, subdue, suppress, suspend, thwart, withhold
ASSOCIATED CONCEPTS: arrest of inquest, arrest of judgment

ARRESTED *(Apprehended),* **adjective** captured, caught, collared, committed, confined, constrained, detained, held, held in custody, immurred, imprisoned, incarcerated, interned, jailed, kept in custody, legally restrained, made captive, made prisoner, remanded, remanded into custody, restrained, seized, sent to prison, taken by force by the authorities, taken into custody, taken prisoner, under arrest
ASSOCIATED CONCEPTS: arrest warrant, body execution, civil arrest, detention and custody, false arrest, false imprisonment, habeas corpus, imprisonment, malicious prosecution, probable cause to arrest, resisting arrest, restraint of liberty, search incident to an arrest, unlawful arrest

ARRESTED *(Checked),* **adjective** adjourned, blocked, bridled, circumscribed, contained, controlled, curbed, deferred, delayed, deterred, discouraged, encumbered, governed, hampered, held back, hindered, impeded, inhibited, interrupted, limited, obstructed, postponed, prescribed, prevented, repressed, restrained, restricted, retarded, slowed down, stayed, stopped, suppressed, suspended, withheld

ARROGATION, noun accession, adoption, application, appropriation, ascription, assignation, assignment, assumption, attachment, attribution, impropriation, placement, requisition, seizure, taking, usurpation

ARSENAL, noun accumulation, agglomeration, ammassment, conglomeration, depository, garnering, repository, reservoir, storage, treasury

ARSON, noun criminal setting of fires, deliberate burning of property, destruction of property by fire, fire-raising, firing, incendiarism, malicious burning of property, pyromania, set conflagration, willful burning of property

ARTFUL, adjective able, acute, adept, adroit, apt, artistic, astute, *astutus,* aware, calculating, *callidus,* canny, capable, characterized by art, clever, contriving, crafty, cunning, deft, devious, dexterous, done with skill, experienced, facile, gifted, imaginative, ingenious, intriguing, knavish, Machiavellian, masterly, plotting, proficient, quick, rascally, ready, resourceful, scheming, serpentine, sharp, sharp-witted, shrewd, skillful, sly, stealthy, subtle, talented, versatile, *versutus,* vulpine, well-planned, wily

ARTICLE *(Commodity),* **noun** effect, item, lifeless object, material, material object, matter, object, particular object, *res,* subject, substance, thing

ARTICLE *(Distinct section of a writing),* **noun** chapter, clause, contractual clause, division, item, portion, provision, proviso, *res,* section, subject, term of reference
ASSOCIATED CONCEPTS: article in a statute, paragraph of a statute, subdivision of a statute

ARTICLE *(Precept),* **noun** canon, *caput, condicio,* dictated term, dogma, mandate, maxim, principle, requirement, rubric, set of terms, tenet
ASSOCIATED CONCEPTS: articles of incorporation

ARTIFICE, noun artful contrivance, artfulness, artificiality, beguilement, charlatanry, cheating, chicanery, circumvention, cleverness, concealment, connivance, contrivance, cover, cozenage, craftiness, crafty device, cunning, cunningness, deceit, deception, delusion, design, device, disguise, distortion, dodgery, duplicity, *espieglerie,* evasion, expediency, fabrication, false claim, false pretensions, falsification, feint, finesse, forgery, fraudulence, guile, hoax, illusion, impersonation, imposture, ingenuity, insidiousness, insubstantiality, intrigue, jobbery, knavery, Machiavellism, machination, maneuvering, mendacity, misrepresentation, perfidy, pettifoggery, ploy, pretense, pretension, pretext, rascality, ruse, scheme, sham, sharp practice, slyness, snare, stratagem, subterfuge, tactics, trap, trick, trickery, wile, wiliness, wrinkle

ARTIFICIAL, adjective adulterine, *artificiosus,* assumed, casuistic, concocted, counterfeited, deceptive, ersatz, faked, false, feigned, fictitious, forged, illusory, imaginary, imagined, imitation, imitative, man-made, not natural, pretended, simulated, simulative, spurious, superficial, unauthentic, ungenuine, unnatural, unreal

ASSOCIATED CONCEPTS: artificial boundaries, artificial ingredients, artificial monuments, artificial person, artificial pond, artificial presumption, artificial watercourse

ARTISAN, noun *artifex,* artificer, craftsman, craftworker, *faber,* handicraftsman, journeyman, laborer, machiner, master craftsman, master workman, mechanic, mechanician, one engaged in a manual enterprise, one skilled in an industrial art, one trained in a mechanic trade, operator, *opifex,* skilled laborer, skilled worker, technician, tradesman, worker, workingman, workingwoman, workman, workwoman

ASSOCIATED CONCEPTS: artisan lien

AS A MATTER OF RIGHT, adverb be entitled to, by right, correctly, duly, fitting, properly, rightfully, with authority

AS A RULE, adverb as a matter of course, by and large, chiefly, commonly, customarily, for the most part, generally, generally speaking, in general, in most cases, in the main, in the usual course of things, mainly, most frequently, most often, mostly, normally, on the whole, ordinarily, principally, regularly, substantially, to all intents and purposes, usually

AS AGREED UPON, adverb according to contract, according to the agreement, according to the bargain, according to the contract, as agreed to, as arranged by the agreement, as contracted for, as negotiated for, as pledged, as promised, as settled upon, consistent with the agreement, corresponding to the contract, in accordance with the contract, in correspondence with the contract, in obedience to the agreement

AS IS, adjective as it is, as it stands, as offered, as presented, as represented, as seen, as shown, as things are, in its present condition, in its present form, in its present state, in the same way, just the same, without warranty

ASSOCIATED CONCEPTS: as is contract, caveat emptor, without covenants or warranties

AS PROVIDED BY LAW, adverb as contained in the statutes, as set forth by law, as specified in the law

AS SO DEFINED, adverb as contained, as delineated, as explained, as set forth, as specified

AS SOON AS FEASIBLE, adverb as soon as possible, as soon as reasonably possible, at the first possible moment, at the first opportunity, expeditiously, forthwith, promptly, without delay

ASCENDANT, noun ancestor, antecedent, forebear, forefather, forerunner, genitor, *praestare,* precursor, predecessor, procreator, progenitor, sire, *summus, superior*

ASCERTAIN, verb acquire information, acquire intelligence about, adjudge, arrive at a conclusion, assure oneself, become acquainted with, certify, clear from obscurity, clear of doubt, clear of obscurity, *cognoscere,* come to a conclusion, come to know, *comperire,* conclude, confirm, decide, decipher, deduce, derive, descry, determine, discover, disentangle, draw a conclusion, establish, establish with certainty, *explorare,*

fathom, ferret out, figure out, find, find out, find out exactly, find the answer, find the solution, learn about, make certain, make oneself acquainted with, make sure, prove, ravel, reassure oneself, remove doubt, render certain, render definite, resolve, satisfy oneself, solve, unearth, unravel, unriddle, unscramble, untangle, verify

ASSOCIATED CONCEPTS: ascertain loss, ascertained by law

ASCERTAINABLE, adjective answerable, certifiable, cognizable, confirmable, conprehensible, decipherable, definable, demonstrable, determinable, discernible, discoverable, distinguishable, evincible, explainable, fixable, knowable, learnable, perceptible, recognizable, understandable, verifiable

ASSOCIATED CONCEPTS: ascertainable consequences, ascertainable damages, ascertainable debt, ascertainable loss

ASCRIBE, verb accord, accredit, *adsignare,* affiliate, allege to belong, apply, appropriate, *ascribere,* assign, attach, *attribuere,* attribute, charge with, connect with, credit with, derive from, filiate, give, impute, point to, predicate, refer to, trace to

ASSOCIATED CONCEPTS: ascribe a motive

ASPECT, noun appearance, *aspectus,* condition, element, facet, factor, feature, *forma,* look, mien, part, peculiar feature, perspective, phase, position, posture, regard, relative position, salient characteristic, situation, slant, *spectare,* state, view, viewpoint, visage, vista

ASPERSION, noun abuse, affront, *calumnia,* calumniation, calumny, censure, condemnation, contumely, defamation, denigration, denunciation, derision, derogatory criticism, detraction, dishonor, disparagement, envenomed tongue, execration, imputation, insult, invective, libel, malediction, objurgation, obloquy, *opprobrium,* railing, rebuke, reproach, reproof, reviling, scurrility, slander, slight, slur, stricture, traducement, vilification, vituperation

ASPORTATION, noun criminal ablation, criminal remotion, criminal removement, criminal transmission, delocalization, felonious abreption, felonious removal, felonious transference, felonious translocation, furtive removal, illegal amotion, illegal carriage, illegal subduction, illegal transmittance, illegal transplantation, illegal transshipment, wrongful displacement, wrongful removal, wrongful transfer

ASSOCIATED CONCEPTS: burglary, conversion and trover, larceny, robbery

ASSAIL, verb accost, *adgredi, adoriri,* advance against, advance upon, aggress, assault, assault belligerently, attack, beset, encounter, fall upon, invade, mug, oppugn, *oppugnare,* rush upon, savage, set upon, set upon with violence, storm, thrust at, waylay

ASSOCIATED CONCEPTS: assailant

ASSAILANT, noun accoster, aggressor, antagonist, assailer, assaulter, attacker, bludgeon man, criminal, felon, invader, obstructionist, *qui oppugnat,* ravager, terrorist, thug, violator

ASSASSINATION, noun annihilation, *caedes,* destruction, dispatching, execution, homicide, killing, liq-

uidation, murder, murder by stealth, slaying, treacherous killing, unlawful homicide
ASSOCIATED CONCEPTS: *aestimatio capitis,* conspiracy, murder, political assassination

ASSAULT, *noun*   act of hostility, aggression, aggressive action, assailment, attack, besiegement, encounter, *impetus,* incursion, *incursus,* injury, intrusion, irruption, offense, onset, onset with force, onslaught, *oppugnatio,* siege, strike, sudden attack, violation of another's rights
ASSOCIATED CONCEPTS: aggravated assault, assault and battery, assault with a deadly weapon, assault with intent to commit a felony, assault with intent to commit murder, assault with intent to maim, assault with intent to rape, assault with intent to rob, battery, felonious assault, simple assault

ASSAULT, *verb*   accost, accost bellicosely, *adgredi, addriri,* affront hostilely, aggress, *appetere,* assail, assault belligerently, attack, attack physically, attempt violence to, besiege, deal a blow, harm, oppugn, set upon, set upon with force, set upon with violence, strike, thrust at

ASSEMBLAGE, *noun*   accumulation, acervation, agglomeration, aggregation, amassment, array, *assemblage,* assembly, association, audience, bale, band, batch, bevy, body, bolt, bulk, bunch, bundle, caucus, claque, clump, cluster, collection, colligation, combination, committee, company, compilation, concentration, conclave, concourse, confluence, conflux, congeries, conglomerate, conglomeration, congregation, congress, convention, convocation, corps, coven, cumulation, drove, ensemble, flock, flood, gang, gathering, group, heap, horde, ingathering, legion, lot, lump, mass, mass meeting, medley, meeting, miscellany, mob, multitude, outfit, pack, packet, party, pile, queue, rally, *réunion,* series, set, sheaf, squad, stack, string, swarm, symposium, thicket, throng, tribe, troop, troupe, union
ASSOCIATED CONCEPTS: disorderly assemblage, unlawful assemblage

ASSEMBLY, *noun*   aggregation, assemblage, body, caucus, collection, company, conclave, concourse, conference, congregation, *consilium, contio,* convention, *conventus,* convocation, crowd, gathering, group, mass, meeting, multitude

ASSENT, *noun*   acceptance, accord, accordance, acknowledgment, acquiescence, *adsensio, adsensus,* affirmance, affirmation, agreement, approbation, approval, authorization, compliance, concord, concordance, concurrence, confirmation, consent, consentaneity, consonance, endorsement, permission, ratification, recognition, sanction, submission, willing consent, willingness
ASSOCIATED CONCEPTS: legal assent
FOREIGN PHRASES: *Nemo videtur fraudare eos qui sciunt et consentiunt.* No one is considered as deceiving those who know and consent to his acts. *Non refert an quis assensum suum praefert verbis, aut rebus ipsis et factis.* It is immaterial whether a man gives assent by his words or by his acts and deeds.

ASSENT, *verb*   accede, accept, accord, acknowledge, acquiesce, *adnuere, adsentari,* agree, allow, approve, authorize, comply, concede, concur, confirm, conform to, consent, embrace an offer, endorse, express concur-

rence, favor, give consent, homologate, permit, ratify, recognize, sanction, subscribe to
ASSOCIATED CONCEPTS: assent by acts, assent by gestures, assent by silence, express assent, implied assent, judicial assent, mutual assent
FOREIGN PHRASES: *Qui non prohibet id quod prohibere potest assentire videtur.* He who does not forbid what he is able to prevent, is deemed to assent. *Qui tacet consentire videtur, ubi tractatur de ejus commodo.* He who is silent is deemed to consent.

ASSERT, *verb*   *adfirmare,* advance, affirm, allege in support, announce, annunciate, argue for, assever, asseverate, attest, aver, avouch, avow, certify, claim, *confirmare,* contend, declare, depose, *dicere,* emphasize, enunciate, espouse, express, insist upon, maintain, plead one's case, plead one's cause, profess, pronounce, propound, recite, relate, set forth, state, state as true, stress, urge, urge reasons for

ASSERTION, *noun*   *adfirmatio,* affirmation, allegation, announcement, asseveration, attestation, averment, avouchment, avowal, declaration, *defensio,* disclosure, enunciation, expression, insistence, insistence on a claim, insistence on a right, *ipse dixit,* positive declaration, positive statement, predication, profession, pronouncement, representation, statement, *vindicatio*
ASSOCIATED CONCEPTS: admission, confession, criminal accusation, false accusation

ASSERTIVE, *adjective*   authoritative, confident, dogmatic, influential, potent, powerful, self-assured, strong

ASSESS *(Appraise), verb*   *aestimare,* apprize, ascertain, calculate, calibrate, consider, compute, count, determine, estimate, evaluate, fix the value, gauge, judge, measure, mensurate, mete, rate, reckon, set, valuate, value, weigh
ASSOCIATED CONCEPTS: assess a penalty, assess damages, assessed valuation

ASSESS *(Tax), verb*   affix an impost, charge with one's share, demand a payment, demand toll, exact a charge, exact a toll, excise, fix a valuation, impose a charge, impose a levy, lay an impost, levy
ASSOCIATED CONCEPTS: assess taxes

ASSESSMENT *(Estimation), noun*   *aestimatio,* appraisal, appraisement, calculation, determination, estimate, measure, mensuration, rating, reckoning, survey, valuation
ASSOCIATED CONCEPTS: assessment of damages

ASSESSMENT *(Levy), noun*   amount assessed as payable, capitation, *census,* cess, charge, charge levied, exaction, exactment, imposition, impost, rate, tallage, tax, toll
ASSOCIATED CONCEPTS: assessed valuation, assessment and collection of taxes, assessment district, assessment for benefits, assessment for special improvements, assessment insurance, assessment lien, assessment of property, assessment roll, assessor, equalized assessment, improvements, municipal improvements, public improvements, special assessment, tax assessment, valuation of property

ASSESSOR, *noun*   *censor,* charger, collector, exciseman, official receiver, one who exacts, one who im-

poses a charge, one who levies, tax collector, tax gatherer, tax man, tax receiver, tax taker, taxer
ASSOCIATED CONCEPTS: tax assessor

ASSETS, *noun* available means, belongings, *bona,* capital, chattels, effects, estate, funds, goods, holdings, inventories, money, pecuniary resources, personal effects, personal resources, possessions, principal, property, reserves, resources, riches, valuables, wealth, wherewithal
ASSOCIATED CONCEPTS: assets of a trust corpus, assets of an estate, capital assets, concealment of assets, contingent assets, corporation's assets, depletion of assets, disposal of assets, equitable assets, fixed assets, foreign assets, fraudulent transfer of assets, liquid assets, partnership assets, personal assets, real assets, sale of assets, testamentary assets

ASSEVERATION, *verb* acknowledgment, adjuration, affirmance, affirmation, assertion, attestation, averment, avouchment, avowal, certification, confirmation, declaration, emphatic assertion, legal pledge, oath, positive declaration, positive statement, profession, pronouncement, solemn averment, solemn avowal, solemn declaration, sworn statement, vow

ASSIGN *(Allot), verb* allocate, apportion, appropriate, *attribuere,* deal out, dispense, distribute, divide in portions, dole out, give out, mete out, partition, portion out, *rem homini adsignare,* share
ASSOCIATED CONCEPTS: assign a cause of action, assign a chose in action, assign a lease, assign over, assign without recourse, assignable interest, assigned counsel, assigned risk, sublease

ASSIGN *(Designate), verb* appoint, ascribe, attribute, authorize, charge, commission, commit powers to another, delegate, depute, detail, empower, entrust, invest, name, prescribe, put in commission, set, specify
FOREIGN PHRASES: *Assignatus utitur jure auctoris.* An assignee is clothed with the right of his principal.

ASSIGN *(Transfer ownership), verb* abalienate, alienate, commit to another's trust, consign, convey, deliver, devolve upon, dispose of, endorse over, entrust, grant, make over to another, negotiate, refer, release, relegate, sign over, surrender to another, transfer to another, transmit

ASSIGNABLE, *adjective* consignable, conveyable, deliverable, devisable, disposable, exchangeable, grantable, negotiable, transferable, transmissible, transmittable
ASSOCIATED CONCEPTS: assignable contract, assignable interest

ASSIGNATION, *noun* application, arrogation, ascription, assignment, attribution, blame, charge, imputation, placement

ASSIGNEE, *noun* accipient, allottee, donee, grantee, receiver, recipient, transferee
ASSOCIATED CONCEPTS: lessee
FOREIGN PHRASES: *Assignatus utitur jure auctoris.* An assignee has the rights of his principal.

ASSIGNMENT *(Allotment), noun* allocation, allowance, apportionment, appropriation, assignation, dispensation, distribution, division, partition, portion
ASSOCIATED CONCEPTS: assignment of choses in action

ASSIGNMENT *(Designation), noun* appointment, authorization, commission, delegation, deputation, mandate, nomination, placing in office, prescription, selection, signification, specification, stipulation
ASSOCIATED CONCEPTS: assignment of error

ASSIGNMENT *(Task), noun* business, charge, chore, commission, duty, function, mission, part, pursuit, responsibility, role, stint, work

ASSIGNMENT *(Transfer of ownership), noun* abalienation, alienation, assignation, cession, conferment, conferral, consignation, consignment, conveyance, conveyancing, delivery, demise, devolvement, disposition, distribution, grant, impropriation, mutual transfer, nonretention, relegation, transfer, transference, transmission, transmittal
ASSOCIATED CONCEPTS: assignment by operation of law, assignment for the benefit of creditors, assignment for value, assignment of a cause of action, assignment of a chose in action, assignment of an account, assignment of claim, assignment of dower, assignment of lease, assignment of rents and profits, assignment of wages, consignment, general assignment, lease, license, partial assignment, promise to make assignment, voluntary assignment
FOREIGN PHRASES: *Assignatus utitur jure auctoris.* An assignee is clothed with the right of his principal.

ASSIST, *verb* abet, accommodate, act as assistant to, administer to, afford aid, aid, *auxiliari,* back, be of help, be of use, come to the aid of, cooperate with, do a service, endorse, foster, furnish aid, further, give a hand, give aid, give support, help, help along, intercede for, minister to, nurture, oblige, *opitulari,* participate, promote, reinforce, relieve, second, serve, stand by, subserve, subsidize, *subvenire,* succor, supply aid, support, take part with
ASSOCIATED CONCEPTS: accessory, aiding and abetting, complicity

ASSISTANCE, *noun* accommodation, *adiumentum,* adjuvancy, advocacy, aid, *auxilium,* benefit, benevolence, championship, cooperation, furtherance, help, helpfulness, intercession, participation, reinforcement, subsidy, succor, support
ASSOCIATED CONCEPTS: able assistance of counsel, writ of assistance

ASSISTANT, *noun* abettor, accessory, accomplice, *adiutor, adiutrix,* adjutant, adjuvant, advocate, agent, aide, *aide-de-camp,* aider, apprentice, associate, backer, champion, clerk, coadjutor, coaid, collaborator, colleague, confederate, *confrère,* cooperator, copartner, coworker, deputy, employee, helper, helpmate, partner, right-hand man, second, seconder, subaltern, subordinate, supporter, underling, underworker
ASSOCIATED CONCEPTS: accessory, accomplice, coconspirator

ASSOCIATE, *noun* adjunct, aid, aide-de-camp, assistant, auxiliary, coadjutant, coadjutor, coadjuvant, cohelper, cohort, collaborator, colleague, comate, companion, compeer, confederate, confidante, confrere, cooperator, copartner, coworker, fellow worker, friend, partner, *socius, sodalis*
ASSOCIATED CONCEPTS: associates in a law office, confederacy, partner, union

ASSOCIATED, *adjective*   affiliated, agnate, akin, allied, closely allied, closely related, coactive, coadunate, combined, concerted, confederated, conjoint, conjunct, connate, connected, cooperant, cooperative, coupled, coworking, federate, federated, incorporated, inosculated, interallied, joined, leagued, linked, related, synergetic, united
ASSOCIATED CONCEPTS: associated companies

ASSOCIATION *(Alliance), noun*   affiliation, amalgamation, coalition, combination, combine, company, confederacy, confederation, *conlegium,* corporation, coterie, federation, guild, league, syndicate, union
ASSOCIATED CONCEPTS: articles of association, bar associations, beneficial associations, convenant of associations, joint stock associations, mutual benefit associations, professional associations, unincorporated associations, voluntary associations

ASSOCIATION *(Connection), noun*   bond, coadjuvancy, coalition, colleagueship, combination, conjunction, *conlegium,* connectedness, consociation, copartnership, coworking, involvement, joint enterprise, link, linkage, organization, participation, partnership, relatedness, relation, relationship, *societas,* working in concert

ASSUAGE, *verb*   abate, allay, alleviate, appease, attemper, blunt, chasten, check, comfort, compose, curb, diminish, ease, lessen, *levare, mitigare,* mitigate, moderate, mollify, obtund, pacify, palliate, quell, quench, reduce, relieve, remedy, salve, sate, satiate, satisfy, *sedare,* slake, smother, soften, solace, soothe, still, temper, tranquilize

ASSUME *(Seize), verb*   accroach, adeem, adopt, *adsumere,* annex, appropriate, arrogate, commandeer, confiscate, dispossess, distrain, expropriate, help oneself to, make free with, *occupare,* possess oneself of, *rem sibi adrogare,* take as one's own, usurp

ASSUME *(Simulate), verb*   act as, counterfeit, dissemble, dissimulate, don, feign, impersonate, make believe, outwardly seem, pass for, personate, play the part, pose as, pretend to be, profess, put on deceitfully, represent as, take the part of, take the semblance of

ASSUME *(Suppose), verb*   be inclined to think, be of the opinion, conclude, conjecture, consider, deduce, deem true, divine, draw the inference, find probable, gather, have an idea that, hold the opinion, infer, predicate, premise, presume, presuppose, suspect, take for granted, take without proof, theorize, think credible, think likely, think probable

ASSUME *(Undertake), verb*   accept, accept an obligation, attempt, attend to, be willing to bear, become responsible for, begin, broach, commit oneself, contract, contract for, embark upon, engage, enter upon, incur a duty, manage, proceed to, pursue, set about, shoulder, *suscipere,* take care of, take charge, take on oneself, take up, venture upon
ASSOCIATED CONCEPTS: assume a debt, assume a lease, assume a mortgage, assume responsibility, assumed name, assumed risk

ASSUMED *(Feigned), adjective*   adopted, apocryphal, bogus, contrived, counterfeit, deceptive, delusive, disguised, fabricated, factitious, fake, false, fictitious, fraudulent, invented, manufactured, misleading, misrepresented, pretended, pretexted, spurious, synthetic, unauthentic, ungenuine, unreal
ASSOCIATED CONCEPTS: allegation of fact, allegation of law, alleged fact, material allegation, pleading, responsive allegation, specific allegation

ASSUMED *(Inferred), adjective*   accepted, conjectured, connoted, considered true, given, granted, hypothesized, implicit, indicated, insinuated, intimated, posited, postulated, presumed, presupposed, stated, supposed, suppositional, taken for granted, understood

ASSUMPTION *(Adoption), noun*   acceptance, acquisition, receiving, reception, recipience, selection, taking on, undertaking
ASSOCIATED CONCEPTS: *assumpsit on quantum meruit,* assumption agreement, assumption of debt, assumption of facts, assumption of indebtedness, assumption of jurisdiction, assumption of liability, assumption of mortgage, assumption of obligation, assumption of risk

ASSUMPTION *(Seizure), noun*   annexation, appropriation, arrogation, dispossession, encroachment, exaction, expropriation, impropriation, infringement, usurpation

ASSUMPTION *(Supposition), noun*   basis, belief, conjecture, foundation, ground, hypothesis, hypothesization, impression, notion, opinion, personal judgment, postulate, premise, presumption, presupposition, *sumptio,* supposal, surmise, theory, thinking, view

ASSURANCE, *noun*   adjuration, affirmation, assuredness, attestation, averment, avow, avowal, avowance, commitment, confidence, confidentness, *confirmatio,* covenant, declaration, earnest declaration, engagement, *fiducia,* guaranty, oath, obligation, pact, paction, pledge, promise, reassurance, security, solemn assertion, solemn promise, surety, voucher, vow, warranty
ASSOCIATED CONCEPTS: assurance of title, covenant of future assurances

ASSURE *(Give confidence to), verb*   buoy up, cause to feel certain, cheer, comfort, confirm in conviction, console, convince, deliver from uncertainty, dismiss all doubt, embolden, encourage, enhearten, free from doubt, free from uncertainty, give hope, hearten, inspire, inspire hope, lead to believe, make certain, make confident, offer assurances to, persuade, put at ease, raise expectations, reassure, render certain, restore one's faith, satisfy, set at ease, solace

ASSURE *(Insure), verb*   affirm, agree to indemnify for loss, answer for, asseverate, attest, aver, avouch, avow, certify, confirm, endorse, espouse, give security, guarantee, make a promise, make certain, make sure, pledge, profess, promise, render certain, render safe, secure against loss, solemnly promise, subscribe to, swear, underwrite, verify, vouch for, vow, warrant

ASTRAY, *adjective*   aberrant, adrift, afield, amiss, awry, circuitous, deviating, errant, erratic, indirect, lost, misguided, misled, off-center, out of one's bearings, out of one's reckoning, random, round-about, straying, undirected, unguided

ASTRINGENT, *adjective*   acid, acrid, acrimonious, *adstrictorius,* austere, bitter, caustic, dour, exigent, harsh, mordant, rough, severe, stern, strict, stringent, tart

ASYLUM *(Hiding place)*, **noun**   covert, exile, haven, inviolable refuge, place of immunity, place of refuge, refuge, retreat, safehold, sanctuary, *sanctum sanctorum,* secure retreat, shelter, temporary refuge

ASYLUM *(Hospital)*, **noun**   lazaretto, mental hospital, mental institution, nursing home, psychiatric hospital, psychiatric ward, sanitorium, shelter for the afflicted, state hospital, state institution

ASYLUM *(Protection)*, **noun**   freedom from danger, refuge, safeguard, safety, sanctuary, security, shelter
ASSOCIATED CONCEPTS: granted asylum

AT FAULT, *adverb*   culpable, erring, in error, guilty, liable, responsible for, wrong

AT ISSUE, *adverb*   being analyzed, in question, in contemplation, in dispute, on the agenda, under advisement, under consideration, under examination

AT RISK, *adverb*   at peril, capable of loss, involved, potentially liable

ATMOSPHERE, *noun*   air, airspace, ambience, aura, background, circumambience, climate, climatic condition, element, environing influence, environment, medium, milieu, mood, setting, space, surroundings, weather
ASSOCIATED CONCEPTS: clouding the atmosphere, polluting the atmosphere

ATROCITY, *noun*   abomination, abuse, act of ferocity, atrocious crime, *atrocitas,* barbarity, deed of savagery, ferity, ferocity, fiendishness, flagitious villainy, flagitiousness, flagrancy, gross offense, heinousness, holocaust, infamy, inhumanity, iniquity, maltreatment, malevolence, mercilessness, monstrosity, nefariousness, *nefas, res atrox,* ruthlessness, savagery, truculence, victimization, villainy, wantonly wicked conduct, wickedness
FOREIGN PHRASES: Patria potestas in pietate debet, non in atrocitate, consistere. Paternal power should consist of affection not of atrocity.

ATTACH *(Join)*, *verb*   add, add as an accessory, *adfigere,* adhere, adjoin, *adligare,* affix, agglutinate, annex, append, assemble, bind, cohere, combine, conjoin, connect, consolidate, couple, embody, embrace, fasten, fasten together, incorporate, insert, link, make one, merge, put together, secure, subjoin, supplement, unite
ASSOCIATED CONCEPTS: attach exhibits

ATTACH *(Seize)*, *verb*   adeem, annex, appropriate, arrogate, confiscate, disseise, distrain, distress, exact, expropriate, garnish, impound, impress, levy, overcome, preempt, press, replevy, retake, secure, seize summarily, sequester, sequestrate, take, take over, take possession of, take summarily, usurp
ASSOCIATED CONCEPTS: attach property, provisional remedy

ATTACHED *(Annexed)*, *adjective*   added, affixed, agglutinated, appendant, appended, *aptus,* bound, conjoined, connected, fastened, fixed, joined, paired, subjoined, united

ATTACHED *(Seized)*, *adjective*   adeemed, annexed, appropriated, arrogated, confiscated, disseised, distrained, expropriated, foreclosed, forfeited, garnisheed, impounded, levied, replevied, sequestered, usurped
ASSOCIATED CONCEPTS: provisional remedy

ATTACHMENT *(Act of affixing)*, **noun**   adjunction, affixation, annexation, annexion, attaching, binding, bond, cohesion, confixation, conjunction, connection, fastening, fixing, insertion, joinder, joining, junction, ligation, nexus, subjunction, that which attaches, tie
ASSOCIATED CONCEPTS: attachment of a security interest, garnishment, in rem jurisdiction, provisional remedy, quasi in rem jurisdiction

ATTACHMENT *(Seizure)*, **noun**   annexation, apprehending, confiscation, deprivation, deprivement, disownment, dispossession, distrainer, distraint, distress, divestment, *embargo,* execution, expropriation, foreclosure, garnishment, impoundage, impoundment, impressment, seizing, sequestration
ASSOCIATED CONCEPTS: ancillary attachment, attachment execution, attachment of persons, attachment of property, attachment proceedings, attachment to obtain jurisdiction, attachment upon mesne process, body attachment, execution, extraordinary remedy, lien or incumbrance, proceeding in rem, property subject to attachment, provisional remedy, sequestration, writ of attachment, wrongful attachment

ATTACHMENT *(Thing affixed)*, **noun**   accessory, addendum, additum, adjunct, affixture, annex, appendage, appendix, appurtenance, fixture, postfix, supplement, supplementary device

ATTACK, *verb*   abuse, *adgredi, adoriri,* advance upon, aggress, assail, assault, assume the offensive, bear down upon, beat, begin hostilities against, beleaguer, beset, besiege, bombard, charge, combat, commit hostilities, descend on, engage in hostilities, fall upon, fight offensively, fly at, force, hit, impugn, invade, *invehi in,* lay hands on, lay into, make an onset against, open fire upon, oppugn, *oppugnare,* pitch into, pounce upon, raid, revile, run at, rush upon, set upon with force, shoot at, spring upon, start a fight, start a war, storm, strike, strike the first blow, tackle, take offensive action, take the initiative, take the offensive, tear into, throw oneself upon, waylay
ASSOCIATED CONCEPTS: assault, attack on credibility, collateral attack, direct attack, impeach, provocation of attack

ATTAIN, *verb*   accomplish, achieve, acquire, *adsequi,* arrive at, be successful, bring about, bring off successfully, bring to pass, carry through, come by, come to, complete, *consequi,* consummate, earn, effect, effectuate, finish, gain, gain one's end, get, get by effort, get done, get possession of, obtain, perfect, procure, put through, reach, reach one's goal, realize, reap, score a success, secure, succeed, succeed in reaching

ATTAINT, **noun**   abasement, bad name, bad reputation, bad repute, brand, debasement, defilement, degradation, derogation, deviation from rectitude, disapprobation, discredit, disesteem, disgrace, dishonor, disreputability, disrepute, disrespect, humiliation, ignominy, ill fame, ill favor, ill repute, improbity, imputation, infamy, ingloriousness, loss of reputation, mark, obloquy,

odium, opprobrium, reproach, shame, smear, smirch, stain, stigma, taint, tarnish, tarnished honor
ASSOCIATED CONCEPTS: attainder, *autrefois attaint,* bill of attainder, civil death

ATTEMPT, *verb* aim at, assay, be at work, be in action, bid for, carry on, *conari,* do one's best, do the needful, drive at, employ oneself, endeavor, essay, exert oneself, go after, go all out for, intend, labor for, make a bid, make a try, make an effort at, make the effort, ply one's task, pursue, put forth an effort, quest, seek to, set out to, strive, take on, *temptare,* test, try, try hard, try one's best, undertake, use one's best endeavors, venture
ASSOCIATED CONCEPTS: attempt to commit a crime, attempt to defraud, attempt to prove, conspiracy, failure of intended act, preparatory acts, renunciation
FOREIGN PHRASES: *Affectus punitur licet non sequatur effectus.* The intention is punished although the intended result does not follow. *Non officit conatus nisi sequatur effectus.* An attempt does not harm unless a consequence follows. *In maleficiis voluntas spectatur, non exitus.* In criminal offenses, the intention and not the result must be regarded. *Officit conatus si effectus sequatur.* The attempt becomes of consequence, if the effect follows.

ATTEND *(Accompany), verb* be associated with, be connected with, go along with

ATTEND *(Be present at), verb* frequent, go to, visit

ATTEND *(Heed), verb* be attentive to, give heed to, listen, mark, mind, note, notice, take notice of

ATTEND *(Take care of), verb* be attendant on, care for, guard, minister to, see to, serve, wait upon, watch over

ATTENDANCE, *noun* accompaniment, ministration, presence

ATTENUATE, *verb* *attenuare,* bate, constrict, constringe, contract, curtail, debilitate, decrease, deflate, devitalize, diminish, diminish in effect, *extenuare,* extenuate, lessen, lighten, make thin, narrow, reduce, reduce in intensity, reduce in strength, render threadlike, taper, weaken, weaken in force
ASSOCIATED CONCEPTS: attenuation between a cause and the result, proximate cause, remote cause

ATTEST, *verb* adjure, affirm, assert, authenticate, aver, bear out, bear witness to, certify, confirm, corroborate, declare, declare the truth of, depone, depose, endorse, evince, ratify, *rem testari,* speak on oath, subscribe, substantiate, support, swear, take one's oath, *testem facere, testificari,* testify to, validate, verify, vouch for, witness
ASSOCIATED CONCEPTS: affidavit, interrogatory

ATTESTATION, *noun* act of bearing witness, adjuration, affirmation, allegation, assertion, asseveration, attest, attesting declaration, authentication, averment, avouchment, avowal, certification, declaration, endorsement, oath, solemn averment, solemn avowal, solemn declaration, statement, substantiation, swearing, sworn evidence, *testificatio,* testification, *testimonium,* testimony, validification, verification, witnessing
ASSOCIATED CONCEPTS: acknowledgment, attestation clause, attestation of chattel mortgage, attestation of deed, attestation of note, attestation of will, attesting witnesses

ATTORN, *verb* allot, assign, cede, confer, confer ownership, consign, convey, deliver, demise, devise, devolve upon, dispose of, give, grant, impart, let, part with, pass down, relinquish, transfer, turn over

ATTORNEY, *noun* advocate, attorney-at-law, barrister, counsel, counselor, counselor-at-law, jurisconsult, jurisprudent, jurist, lawyer, learned counsel, legal adviser, legal practitioner, legist, member of the bar, officer of the court, pleader, practitioner, procurator, publicist, solicitor
ASSOCIATED CONCEPTS: attorney of record, staff attorney
FOREIGN PHRASES: *Consilia multorum quaeruntur in magnis.* The advice of many is required in affairs of magnitude.

ATTORNEY IN FACT, *noun* alternate, legal appointee, legal representative, proxy, surrogate

ATTORNMENT, *noun* agreement, arrangement, commitment, compact, condition, deal, liability, prerequisite, provision, proviso, requisite, stipulation, understanding

ATTRACTIVE, *adjective* adorable, agreeable, alluring, appealing, attracting, attrahent, beauteous, beautiful, beckoning, becoming, beguiling, bewitching, captivating, catching, catchy, charming, comely, delightful, desirable, drawing, elegant, enchanting, engaging, enthralling, enticing, entrancing, exquisite, fair, fascinating, fetching, glamorous, interesting, intriguing, inviting, likeable, luring, magnetic, pleasant, pleasing, prepossessing, pretty, ravishing, seductive, sightly, sweet, tasteful, tempting, titillating, to one's liking
ASSOCIATED CONCEPTS: attractive nuisance doctrine

ATTRIBUTE, *verb* accredit with, *adsignare,* ascribe, assign, charge with, connect with, consider as belonging to, impute, point to, predicate, set down to, *tribuere*
ASSOCIATED CONCEPTS: attribute a cause to an individual

ATTRIBUTION, *noun* accounting, acknowledgment, affirmation, allusion, ascription, assignation, assignment, association, connection, implication, imputation, incrimination, indication, insinuation, mention, quotation, reference, relation

ATTRITION, *noun* decrease, disintegration, dwindling, erosion, fading, falling off, lessening, waning, wearing away

ATTUNE, *verb* acclimatize, accommodate, accord, adapt, adjust, attemper, be harmonious, blend, bring into accord, bring into agreement, fit for a purpose, harmonize, make accordant, make adjustments, make agree, readapt, readjust, rectify, regulate, render accordant, resolve a discord, restore harmony, set right

ATYPICAL, *adjective* aberrant, abnormal, anomalous, dissimilar, diverse, exceptional, never the same, non-uniform, unalike, unrepresentative, variable

AUCTION, *noun* *auctio, auctione vendere,* public sale, public sale of property, sale by bid, sale by outcry, sale to the highest bidder, *sub hasta vendere,* vendue
ASSOCIATED CONCEPTS: auction license, auction sale, auctioneer, highest bidder, public sale

AUDACITY, noun *audacia,* audaciousness, bold front, boldness, bravado, brave face, bravura, confidence in one's powers, daring, defiance of danger, derring-do, hardihood, intrepidity, nerve, overboldness, overdaring, *protervitas,* rashness, recklessness, scorn of the consequences, temerity, undauntedness, want of caution

AUDIT, verb bring into question, certify, check, check on, conduct an inquiry, examine, examine financial accounts, examine the accounts officially, go through the books, hold an inquiry, inspect, inspect accounts officially, investigate, monitor, probe, pursue an inquiry, *rationes dispungere,* reexamine, research, review, scrutinize, search, study, subject to examination
ASSOCIATED CONCEPTS: allowance of claim, audit of account, audited claims, auditor, auditor's report, disallowance of claim, fraudulent audit

AUGMENTATION, noun *accessio,* accessory, accrual, accruement, accumulation, adding, advance, advancement, aggrandizement, *amplificatio,* amplification, appreciation, appurtenance, broadening, build-up, cumulative effect, cumulativeness, development, enhancement, enlargement, enlarging, expansion, extension, gain, growth, improvement, increase, increasing, increment, intensification, magnification, progress, proliferation, redoubling, reinforcement, rise, something added, spread, supplement, widening
ASSOCIATED CONCEPTS: augmentation of assets, augmentation of estate

AUSPICES, noun abetment, aegis, assistance, *auspicium,* authority, backing, benign favor, care, charge, countenance, custody, encouragement, favor, favoring influence, fosterage, guardianship, guidance, management, oversight, patronage, protection, protectorship, recommendation, safeguard, sponsorship, superintendence, supervision, support, tutelage, wardenship, wardship
ASSOCIATED CONCEPTS: under governmental auspices

AUSPICIOUS, adjective betokening success, encouraging, favorable, favored by fortune, favoring, felicitous, *felix,* fortunate, good, hopeful, inspiriting, lucky, of good omen, of promise, opportune, portending happiness, presaging good fortune, promising, propitious, *prosper,* providential, roseate, successful

AUSTERITY, noun abstemiousness, *austeritas,* bare subsistence, chariness, closed purse, economicalness, economy, frugality, frugalness, good management, husbandry, lack of luxury, meagerness, scantiness, scrimping, self-denial, self-restraint, severe discipline, *severitas,* severity, stinginess, stint, strictness, stringency, subsistence level, temperance, thrift, thriftiness, unwastefulness
ASSOCIATED CONCEPTS: austerity budget

AUTHENTIC, adjective accordant with the facts, according to the facts, accredited, accurate, actual, as represented, attested, authoritative, bona fide, *certus,* credible, demonstrated, dependable, documented, entitled to acceptance and belief, factual, faithful, founded on fact, from competent sources, from the original data, genuine, genuine in origin, honest, inartificial, legitimate, literal, not apocryphal, not false, not fictitious, not spurious, not tampered with, of the origin reputed, original, positive, pure, real, reliable, solid, sound, true, trusted, trustworthy, unadulterated, uncounterfeited, undisguised, undistorted, unexaggerated, unfabricated, unfaked, unfeigned, unfictitious, unplagiarized, unquestionable, unsimulated, unspecious, unspurious, unsynthetic, valid, verifiable, veritable, *verus,* well-based, well-founded, well-grounded, worthy of belief
ASSOCIATED CONCEPTS: authentic act, authenticate, forgery, notaries

AUTHOR (Originator), noun architect, *auctor,* begetter, causer, composer, contriver, creator, deviser, discoverer, effecter, fabricator, founder, generator, inaugurator, initiator, innovater, institutor, introducer, inventor, maker, manufacturer, occasioner, organizer, parent, prime mover, producer, sire
ASSOCIATED CONCEPTS: copyright
FOREIGN PHRASES: *Culpa tenet suos auctores.* Fault binds its own authors.

AUTHOR (Writer), noun compiler, composer of a literary work, drafter, essayist, literary person, man of letters, person who writes, *scriptor,* verse maker
ASSOCIATED CONCEPTS: copyright, plagiarism

AUTHORITIES, noun administration, commanders, directors, executives, government, heads, *magistratus,* management, officeholders, officials, persons in office, persons of commanding influence, *potestates,* powers that be, rulers, those holding power, those in command, those in control, those of influence, those who rule
ASSOCIATED CONCEPTS: competent authorities, governmental authorities, lawful authorities, local authorities, municipal authorities, port authorities, turnpike and toll authorities

AUTHORITY (Documentation), noun authoritative example, authoritative rule for future similar cases, court rule, decision, judgment, judicial decision establishing a rule, judicial precedent, legislative precedent, order, precedent, precept, prior instance, *ratio decidendi,* ruling, sanction, statute
ASSOCIATED CONCEPTS: established authority

AUTHORITY (Power), noun *auctoritas,* authoritativeness, control, dominance, domination, force, governance, importance, influence, position of influence, position of power, powers that be, seniority, source, supremacy, sway
ASSOCIATED CONCEPTS: abuse of authority, acting under authority, actual authority, agency, apparent authority, authority by estoppel, authority coupled with an interest, authority of law, authority of the court, colorable authority, constituted authority, de facto authority, delegation of authority, express authority, general authority, implied authority, incidental authority, indicia of authority, lawful authority, legislative authority, limited authority, local authority, municipal authority, naked authority, parental authority, power of attorney, proxy, public authority, real authority, scope of authority, special authority, under cover of authority, unlimited authority, want of authority, written authority
FOREIGN PHRASES: *Argumentum ab auctoritate est fortissimum in lege.* An argument drawn from authority is the strongest in the law. *Majus dignum trahit ad se minus dignum.* The greater authority appropriates to itself the lesser authority. *Nihil tam proprium imperio quam legibus vivere.* Nothing is so becoming to authority as to live in conformity with the laws. *Non debet*

cui plus licet, quod minus est non licere. He who is given a greater authority ought not to be forbidden that which is less. *Ubi non est condendi auctoritas, ibi non est parendi necessitas.* Where there is no authority for establishing a rule, there is no need for obeying it. *Firmior et potentior est operatio legis quam dispositio hominis.* The operation of the law is more firm and more powerful than the will of man. *Fortior et potentior est dispositio legis quam hominis.* The disposition of the law has greater force and stronger effect than that of man. *Judici officium suum excedenti non paretur.* No obedience is to be given to a judge exceeding his office or jurisdiction. *Legitime imperanti parere necesse est.* One who commands lawfully must be obeyed. *In maxima potentia minima licentia.* In the greatest liberty there is the least freedom. *Semper praesumitur pro legitimatione puerorum.* The presumption always is in favor of the legitimacy of children.

AUTHORITY *(Right), noun*   jurisdiction, legal power, legitimacy, prerogative, right to adjudicate, right to command, right to determine, right to settle issues, rightful power
FOREIGN PHRASES: *Omnis ratihabitio retrotrahitur et mandato priori aequiparatur.* Every ratification relates back and is taken to be the equal of prior authority. *Nullius hominis auctoritas apud nos valere debet, ut meliora non sequeremur si quis attulerit.* No man's influence ought to prevail upon us, that we should not follow better opinions should anyone present them. *Nemo potest facere per obliquum quod non potest facere per directum.* No man can do indirectly that which he cannot do directly. *In rebus manifestis, errat qui auctoritates legum allegat; quia perspicua vera non sunt probanda.* In clear cases, he errs who cites legal authorities because obvious truths are manifest and do not have to be proved.

AUTHORIZE, *verb*   accord, accredit, acquiesce in, admit, advocate, affirm, agree to, allow, appoint, approve, assent to, assign, *auctor esse,* be favorable to, be in favor of, certify, charge, charter, commission, concede, confer a privilege, confer a right, confirm, confirm officially, consent to, consign, countenance, credit, declare lawful, delegate to, depute, empower, enable, endorse, endow, endow with power, enfranchise, entitle, entrust, establish, formalize, formally sanction, give a right, give authority, give leave, give permission, give power, go along with, grant, grant claims, grant permission, have no objection, homologate, interpose no obstacles, invest with power, legalize, legislate, legitimate, legitimatize, legitimize, license, maintain, make legal, make valid, permit, *potestatem facere,* prescribe, privilege, pronounce legal, put in force, put up with, recognize, recommend, release, restore permission, sanctify, sanction, sanction a claim, sign, subscribe to, suffer to occur, support by authority, sustain, sustain by authority, tolerate, underwrite, validate, vest with a title, vouch for, vouchsafe, warrant
ASSOCIATED CONCEPTS: agency, delegation
FOREIGN PHRASES: *Semper qui non prohibet pro se intervenire, mandare creditur.* He who does not prohibit the intervention of another in his behalf is deemed to have authorized it.

AUTONOMOUS *(Independent), adjective*   detached, existing as an independent entity, free, free to choose, self-contained, self-reliant, self-sufficient, self-

supporting, uncoerced, uncompelled, unconstrained, uncontrolled, unrestricted

AUTONOMOUS *(Self governing), adjective*   at liberty, autarchic, autonomic, enfranchised, free, politically independent, self-determined, self-directing, self-ruling, sovereign

AVAIL *(Be of use), verb*   aid, assist, assist in accomplishing a purpose, be good to, be of service, be of value, be profitable, be useful, benefit, bestead, bring to bear, confer a benefit on, do service, have efficacy, help, perform a function, *prodesse,* promote, serve, service, subserve, succor, suit one's purpose, *valere*

AVAIL *(Bring about), verb*   accomplish, bear fruit, bring forth, cause, conduce, effect, effectuate, engender, evolve, generate, give origin to, give rise to, have force, meet the demand, occasion, produce, profit, provide, *re uti,* realize, render, succeed, suffice

AVAILABLE, *adjective*   accessible, approachable, at hand, at one's disposal, attainable, convenient, fit, handy, obtainable, on call, on the market, open, reachable, ready, receptive, securable, suitable, to be had, unfilled, untaken, usable, vacant, willing, within reach
ASSOCIATED CONCEPTS: available remedies

AVENUE *(Means of attainment), noun*   approach, course, course of action, customary way, definite procedure, formula, manner, manner of working, means of access, method, method of attack, mode, mode of operation, procedure, process, scheme, standard procedure, system, tack, technique, way, ways and means

AVENUE *(Route), noun*   approach, boulevard, channel, corridor, course, egress, entrance, entry, ingress, passage, passageway, path, principal thoroughfare, road, roadway, street, way

AVERAGE *(Midmost), adjective*   center, centermost, intermediate, mean, mean proportioned, medial, median, mediate, medium, mid, middle, middle class, middle grade, middlemost, middling
ASSOCIATED CONCEPTS: average annual earnings or wages, average capital, average charges, average daily attendance, average daily balance, average daily wage, average price, average speed, average value, average weekly wage, general average, gross average, income averaging, particular average, petty average, simple average

AVERAGE *(Standard), adjective*   common, commonplace, conventional, fair, mediocre, moderate, normal, normative, ordinary, passable, prosaic, stock, typical, unexceptional, unnoteworthy, usual
ASSOCIATED CONCEPTS: average man, average person, average quality

AVERMENT, *noun*   adjuration, adjurement, affirmance, affirmation, announcement, assertion, assertment, assertory oath, asseveration, attest, attestation, avouchment, avowal, confirmation, declaration, formulation, instrument in proof, positive declaration, positive statement, profession, pronouncement, solemn affirmation, statement of facts, statement on oath, swearing, testification, vouching, written statement
ASSOCIATED CONCEPTS: averment of facts, descriptive averment, general averment, material averment, negative averment, particular averments, pleading, unnecessary averments

AVERSE, adjective adverse, *alienus,* antagonistic, antipathetic, *aversus,* disinclined, disliking, hostile, indisposed, inimical, loath, opposed, reluctant, repelled, repugnant, revolted, undesirous, unfavorable, unwilling

AVERT, verb *amovere,* arrest, *avertere,* avoid, change the course of, check, counteract, deflect, deter, divert, fend off, forestall, head off, intercept, make possible the avoidance of, parry, prevent, *prohibere,* shove aside, shunt, stave off, thwart, turn, turn aside, turn away, turn to the side, ward off
ASSOCIATED CONCEPTS: averting danger

AVOID (Cancel), verb annul, defeat, destroy the efficacy of, invalidate, make inoperative, make of no effect, make void, make wholly without effect, refute, vacate, void

AVOID (Evade), verb abstain from, avert, balk at, decline, depart from, dodge, elude, escape, eschew, flee from, forbear, forsake, have nothing to do with, hold back, keep at a distance from, keep away from, keep clear of, make off, part company, refrain from, retreat, shun, shy away from, *vitare*

AVOIDANCE (Cancellation), noun abrogation, annulling, annulment, cancelling, cessation, discontinuation, dismissal, invalidation, making useless, nullifying, quashing, removal, rendering void, rescission, setting aside, vacating, vacation, voidance
ASSOCIATED CONCEPTS: avoidable preference, avoidance of contract, avoidance of will
FOREIGN PHRASES: *Falsa demonstratione legatum non perimi.* A legacy is not nullified by an erroneous description.

AVOIDANCE (Evasion), noun bypass, detour, deviation, dodge, elusion, eschewment, evasion, evasive action, parrying, refraining, retreat, shunning, sidestep
ASSOCIATED CONCEPTS: avoidable consequences, avoidance by the courts of question of constitutionality, avoidance of consequences, avoidance of risk, confession and avoidance, last clear chance, pleading in avoidance

AVOUCH (Avow), verb acknowledge, affirm, affirm with confidence, allege, allege as a fact, assert, assert peremptorily, assert positively, assert under oath, asseverate, attest, aver, bear witness, certify, confirm, confirm by oath, contend, declare, declare openly, declare with positiveness, depose, maintain, make an assertion, make open affirmation, make solemn affirmation, proclaim, profess, pronounce, propound, put in an affidavit, reaffirm, reassert, solemnly affirm, state, state as true, state with conviction, swear, swear an oath, swear the truth, testify, vouch, vow

AVOUCH (Guarantee), verb assume responsibility for, assure, authenticate, back, be answerable for, be surety for, certify, endorse, ensure, give assurance, insure, pledge, pledge one's word, sponsor, underwrite, verify, vouch for, warrant

AVOUCHMENT, noun acknowledgment, adjuration, affirmance, affirmation, assertion, asseveration, assurance, attest, attestation, averment, avowal, avowance, declaration, formulation, oath, open statement of affirmation, positive assertion, positive statement, proclamation, pronouncement, public declaration, solemn averment, solemn avowal, solemn declaration, statement of facts, swearing, testification, vouch, vow
ASSOCIATED CONCEPTS: affidavit

AVOW, verb acknowledge, admit, admit frankly, affirm, allege as a fact, articulate, assert, assert on oath, assert peremptorily, assert under oath, asseverate, attest, authenticate, aver, avouch, be bound, bear witness, certify, commit oneself, confess, confirm, *confiteri,* contend, declare, declare openly, declare positively, declare the truth of, depose, enunciate, express, *fateri,* formulate, maintain, make a statement, make an assertion, postulate, predicate, proclaim, profess, *profiteri,* pronounce, propound, protest, set down, speak, state, state as true, state with conviction, swear, take one's oath, testify, vouch, vow, witness
ASSOCIATED CONCEPTS: affidavit, testimony

AVOWAL, noun acknowledgment, adjurement, affirmance, affirmation, assertion, asseveration, attestation, authentication, averment, *aveu,* avouchment, avowance, *confessio,* confession, confirmation, contention, corroboration, declaration, endorsement, legal pledge, open declaration, positive statement, profession, pronouncement, protestation, statement, statement on oath, testimony, validation, verification

AVULSION, noun divulsion, evulsion, forcible extraction, plucking out, ripping out, tearing away, tearing off, violent separation, wresting
ASSOCIATED CONCEPTS: accretion, erosion, riparian rights

AWARD, noun act of judgment, action, adjudgment, adjudication, authoritative decision, decision, decree, determination, edict, finding, grant, judication, judicial decision, judicial sentence, opinion, order, order of the court, pronouncement, pronouncement by a court, recorded expression of a formal judgment, resolution, result, ruling, ruling of the court, verdict, warrant
ASSOCIATED CONCEPTS: arbitration and award, award of damages, compensatory award, confirmation of an award, monetary award, punitive award

AWARD, verb act on, *addicere, adiudicare,* adjudge, adjudge to be due, adjudicate, bestow by judicial decree, bring in a verdict, conclude, decide, decree, decree by deliberate judgment, decree to be merited, deliver judgment, determine, establish, find, fix, ordain, order, pass judgment, pass sentence, pass upon, pronounce, pronounce judgment, pronounce on, rule, settle

AXIOMATIC, adjective a priori, absolute, aphoristic, apodictic, apparent, ascertained, assured, beyond all question, beyond dispute, categorical, certain, decided, decisive, definite, determinate, doubtless, incontestable, incontrovertible, indubious, indubitable, irrefutable, manifest, positive, questionless, self-evident, sententious, solid, sure, unambiguous, unchallengeable, uncontested, undeniable, undisputed, undoubted, unequivocal, unimpeachable, unmistakable, unquestionable, unquestioned, well-founded

B

BACK *(In arrears), adjective*   behind, behind time, belated, deferred, delayed, detained, earlier, elapsed, expired, fore, forgotten, former, in abeyance, late, long-delayed, overdue, past, prior, tardy, unpunctual, unready

ASSOCIATED CONCEPTS: back pay, back taxes, back time doctrine, back wages

BACK *(In reverse), adjective*   backward, hindermost, hindmost, hindward, posterior, rearmost, rearward, retrogressive, retrospective, reversed, turned around

ASSOCIATED CONCEPTS: back lands

BACKER, *noun*   abettor, adherent, adjunct, adjutant, adjuvant, advocate, aider, ally, assister, auxiliary, benefactor, champion, coadjutant, coadjutor, coadjuvant, defender, endorser, ensurer, exponent, fautor, guarantor, helper, investor, lender, mainstay, maintainer, mortgagee, partisan, patron, promoter, protagonist, protector, reliever, second, seconder, sectary, sponsor, subsidizer, supporter, sustainer, sympathizer, upholder, warrantor

BAD *(Inferior), adjective*   adultered, base, decaying, defective, degenerative, degraded, deleterious, deplorable, deteriorated, detrimental, dreadful, faulty, foul, fulsome, imperfect, impure, injurious, malignant, *malus,* noxious, objectionable, ruined, undesirable, unfit, unsound, unsuitable

ASSOCIATED CONCEPTS: bad bargain, bad check, bad title

BAD *(Offensive), adjective*   abhorrent, abominable, accusable, amoral, arrant, atrocious, baleful, baneful, base, contemptible, corrupt, cruel, debauched, degenerate, degraded, demoralized, deplorable, depraved, derogatory, despicable, destructive, detrimental, diabolic, dire, disastrous, disgraced, disgusting, dishonorable, disreputable, evil, execrable, flagitious, flagrant, fulsome, heinous, ignoble, immoral, *improbus,* improper, indecent, infamous, iniquitous, injurious, insidious, loathsome, maleficent, malevolent, malific, *malus,* miscreant, monstrous, nasty, nefarious, *nequam,* nocuous, objectionable, obnoxious, odious, offensive, onerous, oppressive, opprobrious, peccant, perfidious, pernicious, reprehensible, reprobate, repugnant, repulsive, retro-gressive, revolting, ruined, ruinous, scandalous, sinful, sinister, treacherous, troublous, turpitudinous, undesirable, unfit, unsuitable, unvirtuous, venal, vicious, vile, villainous, virtueless, wicked

ASSOCIATED CONCEPTS: bad behavior, bad character, bad faith, bad influence, bad motive, bad reputation, bad repute

FOREIGN PHRASES: *In facto quod se habet ad bonum et malum, magis de bono quam de malo lex intendit.* In an act or deed which may be considered as both good and bad, the law directs its attention more to the good than the bad.

BAD CHARACTER, *noun*   bad name, bad reputation, bad repute, baseness, discredit, discreditableness, disesteem, disfavor, disgrace, dishonor, dishonorableness, disreputability, disrepute, ignobility, ignominy, ill favor, ill repute, infamy, lowness, reproachability, undesirability, unrespectability

ASSOCIATED CONCEPTS: character evidence, credibility, impeachment of credibility, imputation of character, reputation, slander

BAD CHECK, *noun*   deceptive check, defective check, forged check, fraudulent check, inutile check, invalid check, nugatory check, returned check, rubber check, suppositious check, unmarketable check, unserviceable check, unsound check, useless check, valueless check, void check, worthless check

ASSOCIATED CONCEPTS: criminal charge of worthless check-writing

BAD DEBT, *noun*   dishonored bill, inconvertible bill, irredeemable bill, irretrievable debt, loss, outstanding debt, protested bill, uncollectible debt, write-off

ASSOCIATED CONCEPTS: bad debt loss, bad debt tax deduction

BAD FAITH, *noun*   abjection, abjectness, absconddence, apostasy, artifice, base conduct, betrayal, betrayment, breach of faith, broken faith, broken promise, collaboration, collusion, complicity, connivance, cozenage, debasement, deceit, deceitfulness, deception, defalcation, defection, delusion, delusiveness, dereliction, dereliction of duty, deviation from rectitude, deviousness, disaffection, disavowal, dishonesty, dishonor,

disingenuousness, disloyalty, disobedience, disrepute, double-dealing, duplicity, fallaciousness, false pretenses, false pretension, false swearing, falseheartedness, falseness, forswearing, fraud, fraudulency, furtiveness, guile, hypocrisy, ignominy, improbity, indiscretion, infidelity, infraction, insidiousness, insincerity, inveracity, lack of conscience, lack of fidelity, lack of principle, lack of probity, *mala fides,* malversation, mendaciousness, mendacity, meretriciousness, misfeasance, misrepresentation, obliquity, peculation, perfidiousness, perfidy, pettifoggery, pretense, pretext, punic faith, recantation, recreancy, reprobacy, sedition, seditiousness, spuriousness, subterfuge, subversion, subversive activity, suppression of truth, surreptitiousness, suspiciousness, traitorousness, treacherousness, treachery, truthlessness, turpitude, unauthenticity, unconscientiousness, underhand dealing, unfairness, unfaith, unfaithfulness, unfaithworthiness, ungenuineness, unloyalty, unscrupulousness, unsteadfastness, untrueness, untrustiness, untrustworthiness, untruthfulness, unveraciousness, unveracity, unverity, venality, violation of allegiance, violation of duty
ASSOCIATED CONCEPTS: fraud

BAD REPUTE, *noun* abasement, abjection, abjectness, abomination, allegation, amoralism, amorality, animadversion, antagonism, aspersion, attaint, bad character, bad influence, bad name, betrayal, calumniation, calumny, castigation, censoriousness, censure, charge, condemnation, confutation, contemptibility, contumely, corruption, criminality, crimination, criticism, debasement, decrial, defilement, degeneracy, degradation, delinquency, demoralization, denigration, denunciation, depravity, deprecation, derision, derogation, despicability, despicableness, detraction, deviation from rectitude, deviation from virtue, deviousness, disapprobation, discommendation, discountenance, discredit, disesteem, disfavor, disgrace, disgracefulness, dishonor, dishonorableness, disparagement, displacency, disreputability, disreputableness, disrepute, disrespectability, disrespectfulness, excoriation, exposure, flagitiousness, flagrancy, fraud, fraudulence, ignobility, ignominiousness, ignominy, ill repute, immorality, impaired reputation, improbation, improbity, impropriety, impugnation, increpation, inculpation, indecorum, infamousness, infamy, infidelity, insolence, irreverence, lack of integrity, laxity, loss of honor, loss of reputation, low regard, low standard, maculation, malevolence, malignity, malversation, misbehavior, moral degeneracy, moral turpitude, notoriety, objurgation, obliquity, obloquy, obnoxiousness, obtrectation, odiousness, odium, opprobrium, peccability, peculation, perfidiousness, perfidy, perversity, prodition, profligacy, public reproach, rapacity, rebuke, reflection, reprehension, reprimand, reproach, reprobation, reproof, revilement, scurrility, sedition, shame, shamefulness, slight, stigma, stricture, suspiciousness, taint, traducement, transgression, turpitude, unacceptableness, unrespectability, unscrupulousness, venality, vice, vilification, vilipendency, want of principle
ASSOCIATED CONCEPTS: character evidence, credibility of witness, moral turpitude, reputation

BADGER, *verb* abuse, afflict, aggravate, aggrieve, annoy, annoy excessively, assail, bait, beset, bother, bully, chafe, discomfort, discommode, discompose, disconcert, disquiet, distress, disturb, disturb keenly, exasperate, excruciate, fret, goad, grate, harass, harrow,

harry, heckle, hector, hound, importune, incommode, irk, irritate, mortify, nettle, oppress, perplex, persecute, perturb, pester, pique, plague, provoke, rile, roil, ruffle, taunt, tease, torment, torture, trouble, try one's patience, vex, worry

BAIL, *noun* assurance, bond, caution money, collateral, earnest, gage, guaranty, indemnity, *pignus,* pledge, security, surety, undertaking
ASSOCIATED CONCEPTS: admission to bail, bail bond, bail piece, bonds, cash bail, common bail, excessive bail, execute on bail, forfeiture of bail, *ne exeat,* recognizance, reduction of bail, release on bail, revocation of bail, special bail, straw bail

BAILIWICK, *noun* area, arena, authority, circle, department, district, domain, dominion, enclave, field, haunt, jurisdiction, orbit, precinct, province, purlieu, realm, region, specialty, sphere, sway, territory, ward

BAILMENT, *noun* giving up, held in pledge, in escrow, transferred, under control

BAIT *(Harass),* *verb* afflict, affront, aggravate, aggrieve, agitate, agonize, anger, annoy, arouse, attack, badger, be malevolent, be offensive, beset, besiege, bother, browbeat, cause resentment, chafe, compel, deride, detract, discommode, displease, distract, distress, disturb, dragoon, embitter, enflame, enrage, envenom, exasperate, excite, excite indignation, exhort, give offense to, give umbrage to, goad, grate, harry, haze, heckle, hector, hound, impel, importune, incense, incite, incommode, inconvenience, inflame, inflict, infuriate, instigate, insult, intimidate, irk, irritate, macerate, make wrathful, malign, maltreat, menace, offend, oppress, outrage, peeve, perplex, persecute, perturb, pique, plague, prey upon, provoke, pursue, put out of countenance, put pressure on, raid, rankle, rile, rouse, solicit insistently, spur, taunt, tease, terrorize, threaten, torment, trouble, try one's patience, tyrannize, urge, vex, victimize, worry

BAIT *(Lure),* *verb* actuate, allure, appeal to, attract, bamboozle, befool, beguile, bias, chouse, compel, cozen, deceive, decoy, delude, dispose, draw, dupe, enlist, enmesh, ensnare, entangle, entice, entrap, entreat, entreaty, evoke, excite, exert pressure, exhort, forelay, gammon, goad, hold out allurement, impel, importune, incite, induce, influence, inveigle, lead astray, lead into temptation, lobby, persuade, predispose, press, prevail upon, provoke, seduce, snare, solicit, stimulate, suborn, swindle, take advantage of, tantalize, tease, tempt, titillate, trap, trepan, trick, urge
ASSOCIATED CONCEPTS: bait advertising, entrapment

BALANCE *(Amount in excess),* *noun* carry-over, excess, extra, leftover, margin, oddments, overflow, overmeasure, overplus, overrun, oversupply, plus, *reliquus,* remainder, remaining portion, remains, remnant, residual, residual portion, residue, residuum, spare, superfluity, superfluousness, superplus, surfeit, surplus, surplusage
ASSOCIATED CONCEPTS: balance due

BALANCE *(Equality),* *noun* analagousness, commensurability, comparability, comparableness, comparativeness, correspondence, equalization, equation, equilibration, equilibrium, equipoise, equipollence, equiponderance, equivalence, homeostasis, level, *libro,*

neutralization of forces, parity, stabilization, stable equilibrium, state of equilibrium, symmetrical scales, symmetry
ASSOCIATED CONCEPTS: balance account, balance of convenience, balance of hardship, balance sheet, balancing equities

BALK, *verb*   avert, baffle, bar, be obstructive, block, check, counter, counteract, countercheck, curb, defeat, delay, detain, *eludere,* estop, foil, forefend, forestall, *frustrari,* frustrate, give trouble, halt, hamper, hinder, hold in check, hold back, impede, impedite, interlope, interrupt, keep in check, nullify, obstruct, obturate, obviate, occlude, prevent, put in check, restrain, stall, stand in the way, stay, stop, stop short, stultify, stymie, suspend, thwart, traverse

BAN, *verb*   abrogate, banish, bar, block, censor, check, declare illegal, deny, disallow, disqualify, embargo, enjoin, estop, exclude, forbid, foreclose, forefend, interdict, obstruct, outlaw, prevent, prohibit, proscribe, refuse, refuse permission, repress, restrain, say no to, shut off, shut out, stay, stop, suppress, taboo, veto, withhold permission
ASSOCIATED CONCEPTS: ban on Sunday sales

BAND, *noun*   alliance, army, array, association, bevy, body, cabal, coalition, collection, combination, confederation, congregation, corps, coterie, covey, crew, detail, force, gang, *grex,* group, horde, league, legion, movement, outfit, pack, panel, phalanx, squad, team, tribe, troop, troupe, *turba,* unit

BANISHMENT, *noun*   deportation, discharge, dismissal, displacement, ejection, eviction, excommunication, exile, exilement, expatriation, expulsion, extradition, *interdictio aquae et ignis,* involuntary exile, ostracism, ostracization, ousting, outlawry, *relegatio,* removal

BANK, *noun*   bursary, cash box, coffer, depository, monetary reservoir, money box, pecuniary resource, promptuary, public treasury, repository, reserve, safe, safe-deposit vault, storehouse, strongroom, till, vault
ASSOCIATED CONCEPTS: bank account, bank bill, bank certificate, bank check, bank collections, bank deposit, bank draft, bank examiner, bank money order, bank note, bank of deposit, bank of issue, bank robber, bank stock, bank transaction, bank withdrawal, bankbook, banker's acceptance, banker's lien, banking hours, banking powers, banking privileges, commercial bank, savings bank

BANKRUPT, *adjective*   bereft, broke, broken, *decoctor,* defaulting, destitute, failed, impecunious, impoverished, in receivership, in the hands of receivers, incapable of discharging liabilities, indigent, insolvent, left in penury, moneyless, out of funds, out of money, pauperized, penniless, poverty-stricken, ruined, unable to make both ends meet, unable to pay matured debts, unable to satisfy creditors, unmoneyed
ASSOCIATED CONCEPTS: bankruptcy, bankruptcy court, discharge in bankruptcy, estate of the bankrupt

BANKRUPTCY, *noun*   defaulting, destituteness, destitution, failure, financial disaster, financial failure, financial ruin, impecuniosity, inability to pay, indigence, insolvency, involuntary liquidation, loss, loss of fortune, pauperism, penury, privation, ruin, ruination

ASSOCIATED CONCEPTS: adverse claims, arrangement for the benefit of creditors, bankruptcy act, bankruptcy assets, bankruptcy court, bankruptcy estate, bankruptcy proceedings, composition in bankruptcy, composition proceedings, discharge in bankruptcy, foreclosure, fraudulent conveyance, fraudulent transfers, involuntary bankruptcy, preferences, priorities, provable debts, receivers in bankruptcy, referees in bankruptcy, reorganization proceedings, sale of assets, schedules, trustee in bankruptcy, valuation, void preference, voidable transfer

BAR *(Body of lawyers),* *noun*   advocates, attorneys, attorneys-at-law, barristers, counsel, counselors, counselors-at-law, jurists, lawyers, the legal fraternity, legal profession, legists, solicitors
ASSOCIATED CONCEPTS: bar association, member of the bar

BAR *(Court),* *noun*   assize, bench, court of justice, court of law, *curia, forum,* judicature, judiciary, seat of justice, sessions, tribunal
ASSOCIATED CONCEPTS: bar of justice

BAR *(Obstruction),* *noun*   balk, ban, barricade, barrier, block, blockage, circumscription, constraint, curb, difficulty, embargo, enjoining, estoppel, exclusion, forbiddance, foreclosure, forestalling, hindrance, hurdle, impediment, impedition, infarction, injunction, interdict, interference, limit, limitation, nonadmission, noninclusion, obstacle, preclusion, prevention, prohibition, proscription, refusal, rejection, restraint, stoppage, stopper, stumbling block, suppression
ASSOCIATED CONCEPTS: bar by former judgment, estoppel

BAR *(Exclude),* *verb*   ban, blacklist, circumscribe, debar, deny, disallow, except, exile, forbid, interdict, keep out, leave out, limit, lock out, occlude, omit, ostracize, outlaw, preclude, prevent, prohibit, refuse, reject, relegate, restrict, shut out, spurn, suspend

BAR *(Hinder),* *verb*   avert, barricade, block, blockade, bolt, bridle, choke, choke off, curb, embar, enjoin, erect a barrier, estop, fasten, fence, forbid, foreclose, frustrate, hamper, impede, inhibit, interfere with, obstruct, obviate, occlude, preclude, prevent, prohibit, proscribe, put an embargo on, put one's veto upon, repress, restrain, retard, seal, secure, shut off, stand in the way, stay, stop, thwart, trammel

BAR SINISTER, *noun*   bastardism, bastardization, bastardy, baton, birth out of wedlock, champain, illegitimacy, illegitimateness, illegitimation, illicit procreation, misbegetting, unlawful begetting

BARE, *verb*   admit, air, announce, appear, be disclosed, be public, bring into view, bring out in evidence, bring to light, confess, declare, denude, disclose, display, divulgate, divulge, evince, evulgate, exhibit, expose, expose to view, lay bare, lay open, make apparent, make evident, make known, make manifest, make public, manifest, open, open up, publicize, represent, reveal, set forth evidence, show, surface, tell the truth, uncloak, unclothe, unconceal, uncover, uncurtain, undisguise, undrape, unfold, unfurl, unmask, unscreen, unseal, unsheathe, unshield, unshroud, unveil, unwrap, vent, ventilate

BARGAIN, noun accord, accordance, agreement, arrangement, collective agreement, compact, compromise, concord, concordance, concordat, contract, convention, covenant, entente, mutual agreement, mutual pledge, mutual understanding, mutual undertaking, pact, *pactio,* settlement, stipulation, treaty, understanding

ASSOCIATED CONCEPTS: arm's-length bargain, bargain and sale deed, bargain and sale in a conveyance, bargain collectively, bargain in good faith, bargain in restraint of trade, bargaining agent, bargaining unit, benefit of the bargain rule, collective bargaining, collective bargaining agreement

BARRAGE, noun artillery fire, assault, attack, blare, blast, blitz, bombardment, bombings, boom, broadside, burst, cannonade, clamor, concentration, covering fire, cross fire, explosions, fire, gunfire, protective fire, roar, salvo, shelling, shower, siege, spray, storm, storming, thunder, verbal assault, volley

BARRED, adjective banned, debarred, disallowed, excepted, excluded, precluded, prohibited, proscribed, shut out

BARREN, adjective arid, bare, childless, desolate, disused, empty, fallow, fruitless, functionless, idle, impotent, inactive, inane, infecund, infertile, insufficient, issueless, nonfertile, nonproducing, nonproductive, profitless, scarce, shallow, sparse, stagnating, sterile, teemless, unable to yield, unfertile, unfruitful, ungerminating, unprocreant, unproductive, unprofitable, unprolific, unrewarded, unrewarding, unsalable, unyielding, vacant, vacuous, valueless, void, void of contents, waste, wasteful, without issue, worthless

ASSOCIATED CONCEPTS: barren land

BARRIER, noun bar, barricade, bound, boundary, bulwark, check, confines, enclosure, encumbrance, fence, fortification, hindrance, hurdle, impediment, interference, limit, obstacle, obstruction, partition, prevention, preventive, prohibition, protective device, rampart, restraining device, restraint, restriction, safeguard, stay, stop, stumbling block, termination, wall

BARRISTER, noun advocate, attorney, attorney-at-law, counsel, counselor, counselor-at-law, jurisconsult, jurisprudent, jurist, lawyer, learned counsel, legal adviser, legal practitioner, legist, member of the bar, procurator, publicist, solicitor

BARTER, verb bargain, buy and sell, deal, dicker, exchange, give and take, give in exchange, haggle, interchange, make exchanges, market, *merces mutare,* merchandise, peddle, *rem pro re pacisci, rem re mutare,* strike a bargain, swap, switch, trade, trade by exchange, trade off, traffic by exchange, vend

BASE *(Bad),* **adjective** contemptible, cowardly, despicable, despised, disreputable, heinous, immoral, odious, virtueless, wicked

BASE *(Inferior),* **adjective** abject, cheap, common, dilapidated, dirty, lowly, mean, menial, poor

BASE *(Foundation),* **noun** basis, cause, pivotal argument, starting point, support

BASE *(Place),* **noun** abode, center, central headquarters, headquarters, place, station

BASED ON, adverb bear upon, built on, contingent upon, dependent on, founded on, grounded on, relying on, rested on

BASELESS, adjective bottomless, empty, erroneous, false, foundationless, gratuitous, groundless, having no foundation, idle, ill-founded, illogical, nonactual, not well-founded, rootless, unbased, uncaused, uncorroborated, unfounded, ungrounded, unjustifiable, unprincipled, unreasonable, unsound, unsubstantial, unsubstantiated, unsupportable, unsupported, unsustainable, unsustained, untenable, unwarranted, vain, without base, without basis, without cause, without reality, without reason

BASIC FACTS, noun essentials, the case, the facts in the matter, the facts of the case, the whole story

BASIS, noun assumption, authority, background, base, cause, essence, foundation, fulcrum, fundamentals, *fundus,* ground, groundwork, hypothesis, justification, motive, origin, premise, principle, proposition, purpose, *raison d'être,* rationale, reason, root, source, support, underlying principle, warrant

ASSOCIATED CONCEPTS: basis of cost, basis of keeping accounts, basis of the bargain, cash basis, contingency basis, cost-plus basis

BASTARD, noun adulterine, bantling, child born before marriage, child born out of wedlock, illegitimate child, *nothus, nullius filius,* spurious issue

ASSOCIATED CONCEPTS: acknowledgment, bastardy proceeding, illegitimate, inheritance, legitimacy support, putative father

FOREIGN PHRASES: *Bastardus non potest habere haeredem nisi de corpore suo legitime procreatum.* A bastard cannot have an heir unless he is one lawfully begotten of his own body. *Bastardus nullius est filius, aut filius populi.* A bastard is the son of no one, or the son of the people. *Non est justum aliquem antenatum post mortem facere bastardum qui toto tempore vitae suae pro legitimo habebatur.* It is not just to make anyone a bastard after his death, who during his lifetime was regarded as legitimate. *Qui nascitur sine legitimo matrimonio, matrem sequitur.* He who is born out of lawful matrimony succeeds to the condition of his mother. *Partus ex legitimo thoro non certius noscit matrem quam genitorem suum.* The offspring of a legitimate marriage knows not his mother more certainly than his father. *Qui ex damnato coitu nascuntur inter liberos non computentur.* They who are born of an illicit union should not be reckoned among the children.

BATTERY, noun assault, attack, beating, harmful physical contact, injurious force, offensive action, onslaught, thrashing, unlawful hitting, unlawful striking, unlawful touching

ASSOCIATED CONCEPTS: assault and battery, simple battery

BEAR *(Adduce),* **verb** acknowledge, acknowledge openly, adjure, admit, affirm, afford proof of, allege, allude to, argue, ascertain, assent, assert, assert absolutely, asseverate, assure, attest, authenticate, aver, avouch, avow, bring forward, bring to light, bring up, call to mind, certify, circumstantiate, cite, claim, contend, corroborate, declare, declare to be fact, demonstrate, denote, depone, depose, display, divulge, document, elucidate, emphasize, endorse, establish, evidence, evince, exemplify, exhibit, expose, express, for-

mulate, furnish evidence, give evidence, give information, give one's word, give witness, guarantee, have evidence, illustrate, imply, indicate, inform, introduce, invoke, involve, maintain, make a statement, make an assertion, make evident, make reference to, make solemn, manifest, name, plead, pledge, point out, point to, present, proclaim, produce, produce the evidence, profess, promulgate, propound, prove, publish, ratify, refer to, represent, show, signify, stand firm, state as fact, state on oath, stipulate, submit, subscribe, substantiate, sustain, swear, take one's oath, testify, validate, verify, vindicate, vouch for, vow, warrant, witness to
ASSOCIATED CONCEPTS: bear false witness, bear witness

BEAR *(Support), verb*   abet, aid, ally, assist, back, back up, bolster, brace, bulwark, buoy up, buttress, carry, champion, contribute to, cradle, cushion, *ferre,* finance, fortify, fortress, foster, furnish assistance, furnish support, furnish sustenance, garrison, *gestare,* give base, give foundation, give ground, give support, hold a brief for, hold up, justify, lend support, maintain, nourish, oblige, plead for, *portare,* promote, prop, provide for, rally to, reinforce, safeguard, sanction, second, shoulder, steady, strengthen, succor, supply aid, supply support, sustain, truss, upbear, uphold, vindicate
ASSOCIATED CONCEPTS: bear the expense, bear weight

BEAR *(Tolerate), verb*   abide, accede to, accept, acquiesce, adhere to, allow, approve, be lenient, be patient, be subjected to, brave, carry on, concede, condone, continue, endure, experience, forbear, go through, keep on, keep one's countenance, labor under, live through, meet with, obey, observe, *pati,* permit, persevere, persist in, plod, put up with, recognize, resign oneself, sanction, show forbearance, spare, stand, stand the strain, submit to, suffer, suffice, support, sustain, *sustinere,* take patiently, *tolerare,* treat with indulgence, undergo, weather

BEAR *(Yield), verb*   accrue, afford, aggrandize, allot, assign, augment, bestow, breed, bring about, bring forth, bring in a supply, cause, confer, contribute, convey, create, deliver, develop, dispense, earn, effectuate, emit, endow, engender, enlarge, equip, evolve, fructify, fund, furnish, gain, generate, give, give increase, grant, impart, make payment, make provision, manifest, minister to, multiply, offer, *parere,* pay back, procreate, produce, profit, proliferate, propagate, provide, provision, purvey, reinforce, remit, render, replenish, reproduce, restore, return, supply, surrender, transfer
ASSOCIATED CONCEPTS: bear interest

BEAR FALSE WITNESS, *verb*   abrogate, affirm the contrary, apostatize, be deceitful, be devoid of truth, be dishonest, be erroneous, be faithless, be fallacious, be false, be forsworn, be fraudulent, be insincere, be mendacious, be perfidious, be perjured, be spurious, be untruthful, belie, betray, break faith, contradict, deny, deviate from the truth, distort, falsely testify, falsify, forswear, go back on one's word, impugn, lie, miscite, misreport, perjure oneself, pervert, prevaricate, revoke, speak falsely, swear falsely, take back, tell a lie, utter a falsehood
ASSOCIATED CONCEPTS: false swearing, perjury

BEAR THE EXPENSE, *verb*   bear the cost, compensate, defray, defray expenses, defray the cost, discharge, expend, give money, incur costs, incur expenses, indemnify, make compensation, make expenditure, make payment, make restitution, meet the bill, outlay, pay an indemnity, pay compensation, pay damages, pay for, pay in full, pay on demand, pay the bill, pay the costs, pay wages, recompense, refund, reimburse, remit, remunerate, render, repay, restitute, stand the cost

BEARER, *noun*   acceptor, carrier, casher, check holder, draft holder, grantee, holder, possessor, receiver, recipient, taker, transferee
ASSOCIATED CONCEPTS: bearer check, bearer instrument, bearer note, bearer paper, negotiable instruments

BEAT *(Defeat), verb*   be superior, be supreme, be victorious over, bring to terms, checkmate, claim a victory, conquer, crush, dash, discomfit, excel, get the best of, get the better of, have the advantage, hold the advantage, lay waste, obtain a victory, outclass, outdo, outflank, outmaneuver, outplay, outpoint, outrange, outrival, overbear, overbid, overcome, overmaster, overmatch, overpower, override, overtake, overthrow, overtrump, overwhelm, predominate, preponderate, prevail over, put to rout, quell, ravage, reduce, repulse, rout, seize the advantage, subdue, subjugate, succeed in winning, *superare,* suppress, surmount, surpass, take precedence, thwart, trample upon, transcend, triumph over, undo, upset, vanquish, *vincere,* win the battle

BEAT *(Pulsate), verb*   alternate, come and go, convulse, ebb and flow, falter, flicker, flitter, fluctuate, flutter, move up and down, oscillate, palpitate, pass and repass, pendulate, pound, pulse, quake, quaver, quiver, reciprocate, seesaw, shake, shiver, shuffle, strike, sway, swing, teeter, throb, thump, toss, tremble, undulate, vacillate, vibrate, wave, waver, writhe

BEAT *(Strike), verb*   abuse, afflict, attack, baste, bastinado, batter, bruise, buffet, *caedere,* club, concuss, contund, contuse, cudgel, cuff, *ferire,* fight, flagellate, flail, flog, fustigate, give a blow, give a thrashing, hit, inflict, kick, knock down, lambaste, land a blow, lash, lunge at, maul, pelt, *percutere,* pound, *pulsare,* pummel, punch, punish, rap, slam, slap, slug, smack, smite, swing, thrash, thresh, trounce, truncheon, *verberare,* whip
ASSOCIATED CONCEPTS: assault, assault and battery, battery

BEFORE MENTIONED, *adjective*   above, above-cited, above-mentioned, above-named, above-stated, aforehand, aforenamed, aforesaid, aforestated, antecedent, anterior, earlier, foregoing, forementioned, forenamed, former, latter, named, precedent, preceding, precursive, precursory, preexistent, prefatory, preliminary, prepositive, prevenient, previous, prior, prodromal, said

BEHALF, *noun*   account, advantage, advocacy, aid, aidance, assistance, auspices, avail, behoof, benefaction, benefit, benevolence, betterment, boon, contribution, countenance, defense, endowment, expedience, favor, furtherance, gift, good, help, improvement, increment, interest, ministration, opportunity, preferment, profit, promotion, propriety, protection, sponsorship, stead, support, sustenance, utility, welfare
ASSOCIATED CONCEPTS: agency, representative capacity

BEHAVIOR, *noun*　　actions, air, bearing, beliefs, carriage, character, comportment, conduct, consuetude, course, course of conduct, course of life, decorum, demeanor, deportment, habits, habituation, habitude, inveteracy, line of conduct, manner, manner of life, manners, matter of course, mien, mode of action, *mores,* personal bearing, presence, propriety, ritual, ritualism, routine, way of acting, way of life
ASSOCIATED CONCEPTS: bad behavior, contemptuous behavior, good behavior, indecent behavior
FOREIGN PHRASES: *Ad vitam aut culpam.* For life, or until guilty of misbehavior. *De bono gestu.* For or during good behavior.

BELAUD, *verb*　　compliment, eulogize, exalt, extol, glorify, laud, make much of, pay tribute, praise, sing the praises of

BELIEF *(Something believed),* *noun*　　canon, conclusion, conviction, credo, creed, doctrinal statement, doctrine, dogma, expectation, maxim, persuasion, precept, principle, rule, tenet
ASSOCIATED CONCEPTS: beyond reasonable doubt, presumption

BELIEF *(State of mind),* *noun*　　absoluteness, assurance, assuredness, certainty, certitude, conclusion, confidence, conviction, credence, credulity, definiteness, expectation, intuition, judgment, *opinio,* opinion, *persuasio,* positiveness, sanguineness, understanding, unequivocalness
ASSOCIATED CONCEPTS: good faith belief, suspicion
FOREIGN PHRASES: *Cuilibet in arte sua perito est credendum.* Credence should be given to one skilled in his particular art. *Cuique in sua arte credendum est.* Everyone is to be believed in reference to his own art or profession. *Testibus deponentibus in pari numero, dignioribus est credendum.* When the number of testifying witnesses is equal on both sides, the more worthy are to be believed.

BELIEVABLE, *adjective*　　conceivable, convincing, credential, credible, creditable, dependable, incontestable, incontrovertible, indisputable, indubitable, irrefragable, irrefutable, likely, persuasive, plausible, presumable, probable, reliable, sure, tenable, trustworthy, trusty, undeniable, unimpeachable, unquestionable, verisimilar, well-founded, well-grounded
ASSOCIATED CONCEPTS: evidence of trustworthiness

BELLIGERENCY, *noun*　　affray, aggression, aggressiveness, altercation, animosity, antagonism, assault, attack, battling, bellicosity, belligerance, clashing, combat, combativeness, conflict, contentiousness, contestation, controversy, disagreement, discord, disputation, dissension, disturbance, embroilment, encounter, enmity, feud, fighting, fracas, hostility, impugnation, impugnment, inimicality, malevolence, martiality, melee, militancy, opposition, oppugnancy, oppugnation, pugnaciousness, pugnacity, resort to arms, revengefulness, riot, rivalry, scuffle, siege, sparring, state of siege, state of war, strife, time of war, tumult, tussle, unpeacefulness, violence, warfare, warlikeness, wartime, wrangle
ASSOCIATED CONCEPTS: adverse possession, belligerency de facto, international law, national defense

BENCH, *noun*　　bar, bar of justice, board, cabinet, chamber, circuit, council, court, court of justice, court of law, forum, forum of justice, judge, judgment seat, judicatory, judicature, judicial assembly, judicial forum, judicial tribunal, judiciary, *judicium,* justice, justice seat, law court, legal administration, magistracy, magistrate, magistrature, open court, panel of judges, privy council, seat of judgment, seat of justice, tribunal
ASSOCIATED CONCEPTS: at the bench, bench docket, bench notes, bench warrant

BENEFACTOR, *noun*　　abettor, advocate, aid, aider, ally, altruist, assister, backer, beneficent friend, benefiter, champion, contributor, defender, donor, favorer, free giver, friend, giver, Good Samaritan, help, helper, humanitarian, kind person, maintainer, ministrant, patron, philanthropist, promoter, protector, redeemer, rescuer, seconder, succorer, supporter, sustainer, upholder, well-doer

BENEFICIAL, *adjective*　　advantageous, aidful, aiding, anodyne, availing, beneficent, benign, benignant, conducive, constructive, contributive, contributory, convenient, cooperative, edifying, efficacious, favorable, fertile, for one's good, for one's interest, functional, gainful, good for one's advantage, helpful, helping, improving, invaluable, obliging, of general utility, of service, of value, paying, practicable, practical, productive, proficuous, profitable, prolific, promoting, propitious, prosperous, remunerative, salubrious, *salutaris,* salutary, salutiferous, serendipitous, to one's advantage, usable, useful, *utilis,* utilitarian, valuable, worthwhile
ASSOCIATED CONCEPTS: beneficial association, beneficial enjoyment, beneficial estate, beneficial gift, beneficial interest, beneficial owner, beneficial power, beneficial purposes, beneficial use

BENEFICIARY, *noun*　　*bènèficiare,* donee, grantee, heir, heiress, inheritor, legatee, one who receives, payee, receiver, recipient, usufructuary
ASSOCIATED CONCEPTS: beneficiary of a trust, beneficiary under a will, *cestui que trust*

BENEFIT *(Betterment),* *noun*　　accommodation, advantage, assistance, avail, behoof, benefaction, comfort, convenience, enjoyment, expediency, gain, good, gratification, improvement, interest, pleasure, profit, promotion, relief, return, satisfaction, solace, success, succor, usufruct, utility, utilization, welfare, well-being, worth
ASSOCIATED CONCEPTS: beneficial use, benefit of clergy, benefit of counsel, benefit of creditors, benefit of estate, benefit of the bargain, benefit of third person
FOREIGN PHRASES: *In favorabilibus magis attenditur quod prodest quam quod nocet.* In things favored, what is beneficial is more regarded than what is harmful. *Privatum incommodum publico bono pensatur.* Private inconvenience is compensated for by public benefit.

BENEFIT *(Conferment),* *noun*　　aid, award, benefaction, beneficience, benevolence, bequest, bestowal, bonus, boon, charity, compensation, contribution, courtesy, devise, dispensation, donation, endowment, favor, gift, good turn, gratuity, kindness, largess, legacy, liberality, oblation, offering, offertory, philanthropy, present, presentation, remittance, reward, subsidy, subvention
ASSOCIATED CONCEPTS: benefit certificate
FOREIGN PHRASES: *Invito beneficium non datur.* A benefit is not conferred upon a person against his will.

Privilegium est beneficium personale, et extinguitur cum persona. A privilege is a personal benefit, and is extinguished with the death of the person. *Omnes licentiam habere his quae pro se indulta sunt, renunciare.* All are free to renounce those privileges which have been allowed for their benefit.

BENEVOLENCE *(Act of kindness),* **noun** assistance, benefaction, beneficence, *benevolentia,* boon, charitable effort, charity, favor, good deed, good treatment, good turn, helpfulness, kind office, kind treatment, philanthropy, relief, service, succor, support

BENEVOLENCE *(Disposition to do good),* **noun** affection, agreeableness, altruism, amiability, amicableness, beneficence, benignancy, bountifulness, brotherliness, charitableness, charity, clemency, compassion, consideration, cordiality, courtesy, forbearance, friendliness, friendship, generosity, good disposition, good intention, good nature, good will, goodness, goodness and mercy, graciousness, helpfulness, humaneness, humanism, humanity, indulgence, kindheartedness, kindliness, kindndness, liberality, mercy, munificence, obligingness, philanthropy, placability, Samaritanism, softheartedness, solicitousness, solicitude, tenderness, thoughtfulness, tolerance, understanding, unselfishness, warmheartedness

BENEVOLENT, *adjective* accommodating, affable, agreeable, altruistic, amiable, amicable, bearing good will, beneficent, *benevolus,* benign, big-hearted, bounteous, bountiful, charitable, complacent, condolent, considerate, cooperative, cordial, decent, disposed to good, doing good, eleemosynary, empathetic, freehanded, friendly, full of good will, generous, genial, good-humored, good-natured, gracious, helpful, hospitable, humane, humanitarian, indulgent, kind, kindhearted, kindly, kindly disposed, liberal, magnanimous, merciful, munificent, neighborly, obliging, openhanded, philanthropic, softhearted, solicitous, supportive, sweet-tempered, sympathizing, tender, thoughtful, tolerant, understanding, ungrudging, unselfish, unsparing, unstinting, warm, warmhearted, well-intentioned, well-meaning, well-meant
ASSOCIATED CONCEPTS: benevolent and charitable organization, benevolent and charitable purposes, benevolent association, benevolent corporation, benevolent institution, benevolent use, charitable corporation

BEQUEATH, *verb* administer to, afford, allow, assign dower, bestow upon, cede, change hands, contribute, deliver to, demise, devise, devolve upon, dispense, dispose of, distribute, donate, endow with, enfeoff, furnish, give, give away at death, give by will, grant, hand down, hand on, hand over to, interchange, invest, leave, leave a legacy, leave by will, leave to, make a bequest, make a present of, make legacies, pass on to, pass over to, provide, put in possession, remit, render, transfer ownership, vest in, will to
ASSOCIATED CONCEPTS: bequest
FOREIGN PHRASES: *Da tua dum tua sunt, post mortem tunc tua non sunt.* Give that which is yours while it is yours, after death it is not yours.

BEQUEST, *noun* bequeathal, birthright, demise, devisal, devise, endowment, entail, gift, heirdom, heirloom, hereditament, heritable, heritage, inheritance, legacy, *legatum,* patrimony, testamentary disposition, testamentary gift

ASSOCIATED CONCEPTS: bequest by implication, bequest for life, bequest in trust, devise, gift, inheritance
FOREIGN PHRASES: *Nemo plus commodi haeredi suo relinquit quam ipse habuit.* No one leaves a greater advantage for his heir than he himself had.

BESPEAK, *verb* argue, attest, call, connote, convey, denote, express, imply, import, indicate, mean, purport, signify, speak of, suggest, tell of, testify

BEST, *adjective* above the average, beyond compare, brought to perfection, chief, choice, crowning, distinguished, exceptional, exemplary, extraordinary, faultless, favorite, first-class, first-rate, flawless, foremost, greater, highest, impeccable, incomparable, inimitable, matchless, maximum, most desirable, most excellent, optimal, *optimus,* outstanding, paramount, peerless, perfect, preeminent, quintessential, record-breaking, *sans pareil,* second to none, select, superfine, superior, superlative, supernormal, supreme, surpassing, top-level, top-notch, topmost, transcendent, unapproached, unequaled, unparalleled, unrivaled, uppermost, without comparison
ASSOCIATED CONCEPTS: best ability, best and highest use, best bid, best efforts, best energies, best evidence, best interests, best interests of a child, best interests of the public, best judgment, best quality, best skill and discretion or judgment, best testimony

BESTIALITY, *noun* animalism, barbarity, barbarousness, beastliness, bloodthirstiness, brutality, brutishness, cruelty, ferociousness, ferocity, fiendishness, fierceness, grossness, inhumanity, monstrousness, savagery, unnaturalness, viciousness

BESTOW, *verb* accord, accredit, address, administer, afford, allot, allow, appoint, apportion, *attribuere,* authorize, award, be favorable to, be prodigal, bequeath, cater, cede, charter, commission, communicate, *conferre,* concede, confer, confer a privilege, confer distinction, consent, contribute, convey, deal, deign, deliver, dignify, dispense, dispose of, distribute, dole, donate, empower, endow, enfranchise, enrich, entitle, equip, extend, facilitate, facultate, favor with, finance, foster, fund, furnish, give, give a present, give approval, give assent, give away, give back, give clearance, give consent, give dispensation, give freely, give leave, give one's hand to, give out, give out in shares, give permission, give power, give up, grant, grant a boon, grant a request, grant permission, gratify, hand out, hand over, heap upon, help to, honor with, impart, *impertire,* indulge, install, invest, issue, *largiri,* lavish, lend, let, license, maintain, make a benefaction, make a loan, make a present of, make provision for, mete, minister to, oblige, ordain, part with, pay tribute, permit, philanthropize, present, proffer, promise, provide, provision, ratify, recognize, recommend, reflect honor upon, release, relinquish, remit, render, replenish, restore, sanction, serve, show favor, shower upon, spare, spend, sponsor, submit, supply, tender, transmit, vest, vouchsafe, yield
ASSOCIATED CONCEPTS: bestow a present upon, gifts

BET, *verb* adventure, ante, ante up, cast lots, chance, chance the odds, draw, draw lots, encounter the risk, flip a coin, gamble, game, hazard, incur the risk, lay a wager, lay even money, lay money down, lay odds, leave to chance, parlay, play, play a long shot, play for, punt, put money down, raffle, rely on fortune, risk, run

the risk, speculate, sport, stake, stand the hazard, take a chance, take the chances of, toss up, trust to chance, try one's fortune, try one's luck, venture, wager
ASSOCIATED CONCEPTS: betting on horse races, betting on numbers, bettor, gambling, lottery

BETRAY *(Disclose),* **verb**   acknowledge, admit, air, *aperire,* avow, bare, bear witness against, bring into the open, bring to light, come clean, confess, declare, *detegere,* divulge, double-cross, expose, give away, give utterance to, impart, inform, inform against, inform on, lay bare, let slip, make a clean breast, make known, make public, own up, *prodere,* report, reveal, sell out, show, tattle, tell, tell on, turn informer, uncover, unearth, unfold, unmask, violate a confidence
ASSOCIATED CONCEPTS: confidences, privileges, professional secrets, trade secrets, trusts, wrongful disclosure

BETRAY *(Lead astray),* **verb**   abandon, abase, bamboozle, be dishonest, be false to, befool, beguile, bluff, break faith with, break one's promise, cheat, circumvent, corrupt, cozen, debauch, deceive, deceive by treachery, decoy, defile, defraud, deliver up, delude, dupe, enmesh, ensnare, entice, entrap, fleece, forswear, fraud, gammon, give over to the foe, give up treacherously, hoax, hoodwink, inveigle, let down, lure, misinform, mislead, outwit, overreach, play false, prostitute, put on, put something over on, ruin, seduce, sell out, swindle, take in, trick, undo, victimize, violate

BETTOR, **noun**   better, gambler, gamester, gentleman of fortune, hazarder, piker, player, player for stakes,   plunger,   punter,   risk-taker,   sharper, speculatist, speculator, venturer, wagerer

BEWARE, **verb**   be careful, be cautious, be chary, be circumspect, be forewarned, be guarded, be on one's guard, be on the alert, be on the lookout, be on the watch, be prepared, be prewarned, be prudent, be warned, be wary, have a care, keep out of harm's way, look about one, look out, mind, receive notice, stop look and listen, take care, take heed, take precautions, take warning, think twice, watch out

BIAS, **noun**   bigotry, disinclination, disposition, favoritism, foregone conclusion, *inclinatio,* inclination, intolerance, jaundice, partiality, partisanism, partisanship, penchant, preapprehension, preconceived idea, preconception, predetermination, predilection, predisposition, preference, prejudgment, prejudication, prejudice, prenotion, proclivity, proneness, *propensio animi,* propensity, susceptibility, tendency, trend, undetachment, undispassionateness
ASSOCIATED CONCEPTS: actual bias, bias of mind

BICAMERAL, **adjective**   bifurcated, bipartite, bisected, divided, dual chambered, multipartite, separated

BICKER, **verb**   agitate, altercate, argue, argue to no purpose, bandy words, battle, be at loggerheads, be at variance, be discordant, brabble, brangle, brawl, cavil, clash, conflict, contend, contest, controvert, differ, disaccord, disagree, dispute, dissent, disunite, embroil, entangle, equivocate, fall foul of, fall out, fence, fight, have an altercation, have it out, have words, jar, join issue, nag, parry, pick a quarrel, pull different ways, quarrel, scrap, spar, spat, split hairs, squabble, take sides, tiff, tilt, wrangle

ASSOCIATED CONCEPTS: bicker over the terms of an agreement, bicker over trivial provisions in a contract

BID, **noun**   advance, approach, estimate, *licitatio,* offer, offered price, overture, presentation, price, proffer, proposal, proposition, quotation, quoted price, submission, tender
ASSOCIATED CONCEPTS: auction sale, bid bond, bid in, bid off, bidder, biddings, by-bidding, competitive bidding, proposal, upset bid, with reserve, without reserve

BIFURCATE, **verb**   bisect, branch, branch off, branch out, cleave, cut in two, dichotomize, dimidiate, divaricate, diverge, divide into two, fork, form a fork, furcate, halve, part, partition, ramify, separate, split, sunder
ASSOCIATED CONCEPTS: bifurcated trial

BIGOT, **noun**   die-hard, doctrinaire, dogmatic theorist, dogmatist, dogmatizer, energumen, extremist, fanatic, illiberal, infatuate, intolerant, *ipse dixit,* know-all, know-it-all, monomaniac, opinionated person, opinionist, persecutor, ranter, red neck, rigorist, stickler, stubborn person, zealot

BILATERAL, **adjective**   bi-facial, dual, two-sided
ASSOCIATED CONCEPTS: bilateral contract, bilateral option, bilateral record

BILIOUS, **adjective**   bileful, choleric, dyspeptic, jaundiced, spiteful, spleenful

BILK, **verb**   appropriate fraudulently, bait, bamboozle, befool, beguile, betray, bluff, cheat, chisel, circumvent, cozen, cully, deceive, defraud, delude, dupe, elude, embezzle, ensnare, entangle, evade, exploit, foist upon, fool, fraud, hoax, hoodwink, humbug, inveigle, levant, misapply, misappropriate, misinform, mulct, peculate, purloin, put something across, put something over, shuffle, swindle, take advantage of, take in, trick, use for one's own needs, utilize for profit, victimize

BILL *(Formal   declaration),* **noun**   allegation of facts, claim, contractual obligation, customs documents, formal petition, indictment, itemized specification, legislative declaration, petition, promissory obligation, specification of details, statement of facts, written certificate, written complaint
ASSOCIATED CONCEPTS: bill for discovery, bill for fraud, bill for new trial, bill in equity, bill in nature of interpleader, bill of attainder, bill of entry, bill of exceptions, bill of health, bill of indictment, bill of instructions, bill of interpleader, bill of particulars, bill of review, Bill of Rights, bill to quiet title, no true bill, true bill

BILL *(Invoice),* **noun**   account, accounts payable, amount due, audit, balance due, charges, check, cost, deferred payment, demand for payment, expenditures, expenses, figure, itemized account, list, manifest, postponed payment, reckoning, record, report, request for payment, score, statement, statement of indebtedness, *syngrapha,* tally
ASSOCIATED CONCEPTS: bank bill, bill book, bill for account, bill of costs, bill of credit, bill of exchange, bill of lading, bill of sale, bill payable, bill receivable, bond, creditor's bill

BILL *(Proposed act),* **noun**   draft, legislation, measure, projected law, proposal, proposed enactment, pro-

posed law, proposed regulation, proposed rule, proposed statute, protocol, resolution, *rogatio*
ASSOCIATED CONCEPTS: act of legislature, law, omnibus bill, private bill, revenue bill

BIND (*Obligate*), *verb* *adstringere,* burden, charge, compel, confirm, conscript, constrain, drive, encumber, exact, force, impose, indent, indenture, *obligare,* oblige, pledge, promise, require, sanction, set a task, warrant
ASSOCIATED CONCEPTS: bind a deal, binding authority, binding instruction, binding receipt, binding transaction
FOREIGN PHRASES: *Nuda ratio et nuda pactio non ligant aliquem debitorem.* Naked intention and naked promise do not bind any debtor. *Quodque dissolvitur eodem modo quo ligatur.* A thing is unbound in the same manner that it is made binding.

BIND (*Restrain*), *verb* block, check, compel, confine, constrain, encumber, fetter, fix, hamper, hinder, immobilize, impede, inhibit, limit, repress, secure, shut in
ASSOCIATED CONCEPTS: bind over

BINDER, *noun* assurance, caution money, collateral, collateral security, deposit, earnest, escrow, expense outlay, gage, guaranty, handsel, indemnity, installment, investment, payment, pledge, receipt, receipt for payment, recognizance, security, stake, token, token payment
ASSOCIATED CONCEPTS: binder receipt, insurance binder, real estate binder

BINDING, *adjective* coercive, compelling, compulsory, confining, constraining, *de rigueur,* final, hampering, hindering, imperative, incumbent, inhibiting, limiting, mandatory, necessary, obligatory, obliging, required, requisite, restrictive
ASSOCIATED CONCEPTS: binding agreement, binding instruction, binding offer, binding over, binding receipt, binding sale

BIPARTITE, *adjective* apart, being in two corresponding parts, bicameral, bifurcated, bifurcous, bisected, detached, dichotomous, disconnected, disengaged, disjoined, disjointed, disjunct, disunited, divaricate, divided, furcate, furcular, halved, in two, partitioned, separate, separated, severed, subdivided

BIRTH (*Beginning*), *noun* animation, arrival, commencement, creation, debut, embarkation, establishment, *exordium,* genesis, inauguration, inception, incipience, incipiency, incunabula, infancy, introduction, nascency, onset, origin, origination, *ortus,* vitalization
ASSOCIATED CONCEPTS: *ante natus*

BIRTH (*Emergence of young*), *noun* arrival, childbirth, delivery, nativity, parturition, vivification
ASSOCIATED CONCEPTS: birth certificate, birth control, issue, pretermission
FOREIGN PHRASES: *Non nasci, et natum mori, paria sunt.* Not to be born, and to be born dead, are the same.

BIRTH (*Lineage*), *noun* ancestry, bloodline, derivation, descent, extraction, heredity, heritage, inheritance, line, line of descent, parentage, provenance, succession
ASSOCIATED CONCEPTS: birth certificate, legitimacy

FOREIGN PHRASES: *Qui in utero est pro jam nato habetur, quoties de ejus commodo quaeritur.* He who is in the womb is regarded as already born, whenever a question arises for his benefit.

BIRTHRIGHT, *noun* absolute right, ancestry, droit, due, entitlement, heritage, heritance, indefeasible right, inheritance, inherited rights, interest, legal right, one's due, *patrimonium,* patrimony, prerogative, primogeniture, privilege, right, rights and privileges, vested interest, vested right

BITTER (*Acrid tasting*), *adjective* absinthal, absinthian, acerbate, acerbic, *acerbus,* acid, acidulous, *acidus,* acrid, *asper,* biting, caustic, cutting, disagreeable, distasteful, pungent, sharp, sour, soured, sourish, tart, unappetizing, unpalatable, unpleasant, unsavory, unsweet, vinegarish

BITTER (*Penetrating*), *adjective* acrimonious, afflictive, astringent, austere, bilious, biting, brutal, burning, choleric, constringent, corrosive, cutting, double-edged, dyspeptic, harsh, incisive, keen, mordant, nasty, piercing, poignant, pricking, scathing, scorching, severe, smarting, sore, stabbing, stern, stinging, trenchant, venomous, virulent, withering

BITTER (*Reproachful*), *adjective* acrimonious, antipathetic, biting, caustic, cross, despiteful, embittered, envenomed, hostile, hurtful, indignant, piqued, provoked, rancorous, resentful, sarcastic, sardonic, scornful, sorrowful, sour-tempered, spiteful, splenetic, unamiable, unhappy, venomous, vexed, vitriolic

BLACKMAIL, *noun* exaction, extortion, hush money, illegal compulsion, oppressive exaction, protection, ransom, shakedown, taking by undue exercise of power

BLAME (*Culpability*), *noun* accusal, accusation, blameworthiness, castigation, censurability, censurableness, censure, chargeability, condemnation, crimination, criticism, *culpa,* culpableness, damnation, decrial, delation, delinquency, denouncement, denunciation, dereliction, deviation from rectitude, disapproval, disparagement, dispraise, excoriation, expostulation, exprobation, fault, guilt, guiltiness, incrimination, inculpation, malfeasance, misconduct, neglect, objurgation, obloquy, opprobrium, peccability, rebuke, remonstrance, *reprehensio,* reprehension, reproach, reprobation, reproof, *vituperatio,* wrong
ASSOCIATED CONCEPTS: culpable negligence, *mens rea*
FOREIGN PHRASES: *Culpa caret qui scit sed prohibere non potest.* One is clear of blame who knows, but cannot prevent.

BLAME (*Responsibility*), *noun* accountability, ascription, assignation, assignment, attribution, charge, implication, imputation, liability
ASSOCIATED CONCEPTS: allocation of blame, blameworthy, culpability, placing the blame

BLAME, *verb* abhor, accuse, administer a rebuke, admonish, anathematize, animadvert, arraign, ascribe to, assign to, attribute to, berate, call to account, carp, cast a slur on, castigate, cavil, censure, charge, chastise, chide, cite, complain against, condemn, criminate, criticize, *culpare,* denounce, deplore, deprecate, depreciate, detract, disapprove, discommend, discountenance, disparage, dispraise, execrate, expostulate, fault, find fault, hold no brief for, hold responsible, hold up to reprobation, impeach, implicate, impugn, impute to, incriminate, inculpate, indict, lodge a complaint, objurgate, rebuke, recriminate, remonstrate, reprehend, *reprehendere*, reprimand, reproach, reprobate, reprove, revile, show disapproval, upbraid, vilipend, *vituperare*

BLAMEFUL, *adjective* abject, accusable, at fault, blamable, blameworthy, censorious, censurable, censured, chargeable, compunctious, condemnable, condemned, contemptible, contemptuous, corrupt, criminal, criminous, criticized, culpable, damnatory, decried, delinquent, deplorable, deplored, despicable, disapproved, discommendable, discreditable, discredited, dishonorable, disowned, dispraised, disreputable, disreputed, errant, exceptionable, execrable, faulty, flagitous, found guilty, found wanting, guilty, heinous, held in contempt, ignominious, illaudable, immeritorious, impeachable, imputable, in the wrong, indefensible, indictable, inexcusable, iniquitous, insalubrious, liable, liable to prosecution, nefarious, neglectful, negligent, objectionable, objurgatory, open to criticism, opprobrious, out of favor, peccable, peccant, reprehensible, reprimanded, reproachable, reproachful, reprobate, reprobative, reprovable, responsible, unacceptable, uncommendable, unjustifiable, unpardonable, unpraiseworthy, unworthy, venal, vile, without defense, without excuse, wrongful

BLAMELESS, *adjective* above reproach, above suspicion, absolved, acquitted, clean, clear, condonable, entirely defensible, exculpable, exculpated, exonerated, faultless, free from guilt, free from wrong, guilt-free, guiltless, immaculate, impeccable, incensurable, incorrupt, inculpable, innocent, innocuous, inoffensive, irreprehensible, irreproachable, irreprovable, moral, not guilty, not liable, not tainted, offenseless, perfect, pure, reprieved, rightful, sinless, stainless, taintless, unblamable, unblameworthy, unblemished, uncensurable, uncondemned, uncorrupt, uncorrupted, unculpable, undefiled, unfallen, unguilty, unimpeachable, uniniquitous, unobjectionable, unoffending, unreproachable, unreproached, unreproved, unsoiled, unspotted, unsullied, untainted, upright, vindicated, virtuous, without blame, without fault, without reproach

BLAMEWORTHY, *adjective* abject, accusable, answerable, arrant, at fault, beneath contempt, blamable, blameful, censurable, chargeable, condemnable, condemnatory, condemned, contemned, contemptible, contemptuous, contumelious, convicted, corrupt, criminal, criminous, criticized, culpable, damnatory, delinquent, deplorable, depraved, despicable, devious, discreditable, discredited, disdainful, dishonorable, disreputable, disrespectable, errant, erring, execrable, flagitious, flagrant, *flagrante delicto*, found guilty, guilty, ignominious, illaudable, impeachable, in fault, in the wrong, indefensible, indictable, infernal, inglorious, iniquitous, injurious, insalubrious, irremediable, justiciable, liable, liable to prosecution, nefarious, negligent, not honorable, not respectable, not to be recommended, objectionable, obnoxious, odious, of no repute, open to criticism, opprobrious, peccable, peccant, questionable, reprehensible, reprimanded, reproachable, reprobate, reprobative, reprovable, responsible, ribald, scandalous, sentenced, sinister, tainted, transgressing, uncommendable, unjustifiable, unpraiseworthy, unrespected,

unrighteous, unvirtuous, unworthy, venal, without defense, woeful, wrong, wrongful

BLANK (*Emptiness*), *noun* absence, barrenness, cipher, hiatus, hollowness, inexistence, insubstantiality, nil, *non-esse,* nonexistence, nonsubsistence, nonentity, nothing, nothingness, nullity, *tabula rasa,* unsubstantiality, vacancy, vacuousness, vacuum, *vacuus,* void, zero

ASSOCIATED CONCEPTS: blank acceptance, blank bond, blank check, blank endorsement, blank instrument, blank verdict, endorsement in blank, signed in blank

BLANK (*Form*), *noun* data sheet, document, dossier, instrument, legal document, paper, questionnaire

BLASPHEMY, *noun* apostasy, blasting, cursing, derogation of religion, desecration, disrespect, epithet, execration, expletive, heresy, iconoclasm, impiety, impious utterance, impiousness, imprecation of evil, irreverence, irreverent behavior, lack of piety, lack of reverence, malediction, profanation, profane oath, profaneness, revilement of religion, sacrilege, sacrilegiousness, sanctimoniousness, solemn mockery, swearing, unholiness, unorthodoxy, unsacredness

ASSOCIATED CONCEPTS: freedom of religion, libel and slander

FOREIGN PHRASES: *Nec veniam, l'aeso numine, casus habet.* Where the divinity is insulted the case cannot be pardoned.

BLATANT (*Conspicuous*), *adjective* apparent, celebrated, clear, discernible, exposed, famous, manifest, noticeable, notorious, observable, obvious, outstanding, overt, patent, perceivable, plain, prominent, public, sensational, well-known

BLATANT (*Obtrusive*), *adjective* bellowing, boisterous, braying, clamorous, coarse, common, crass, crude, crying, flaring, flaunting, gaudy, glaring, gross, harsh, ill-behaved, ill-bred, ill-mannered, improper, indecorous, indelicate, loud, noisy, obstreperous, offensive, offensively assertive, offensively obtrusive, raffish, ribald, rough, rowdy, rude, screaming, scurrilous, tawdry, ululant, uncivil, uncouth, uncultured, undignified, ungenteel, ungentlemanly, ungracious, unladylike, unpolished, unpresentable, unrefined, unseemly, vociferous, vulgar, vulgarian

BLEAK (*Exposed and barren*), *adjective* bare, barren, blank, cold, deserted, desolate, exposed, unpopulated, unsheltered, waste

BLEAK (*Not favorable*), *adjective* dark, depressing, disheartening, dismal, distressing, forbidding, gloomy, grave, grim, inauspicious, joyless, ominous, somber, sombrous, unfavorable

BLEAK (*Severely simple*), *adjective* austere, cheerless, cold, comfortless, depressing, dismal, dour, drear, dreary, dull, gloomy, grim, joyless, somber, sombrous, uninviting

BLEMISHED, *adjective* besmirched, blistered, bruised, chipped, damaged, defaced, defective, deformed, dented, deteriorated, discolored, discredited, disfigured, disgraced, dishonored, faded, faulty, flawed, imperfect, impure, injured, malformed, marred, misshapen, pitted, pock-marked, soiled, spotted, stained, sullied, tainted, tarnished

BLIND *(Concealed), adjective* buried, camouflaged, covered, covert, dim, disguised, hidden, imperceptible, inconspicuous, indiscernible, latent, masked, obscure, out of view, private, screened, secreted, shadowy, sheltered, shrouded, unapparent, undetected, unexposed, unknown, unobserved, unperceived, unrevealed, unseen, unsuspected

BLIND *(Impassable), adjective* barred, barricaded, blanked, blockaded, blocked, closed, dead-end, leading nowhere, obstructed, sealed, shut, shut-off, stopped-up, without exit

BLIND *(Not discerning), adjective* benighted, careless, deluded, headlong, heedless, inadvertent, inattentive, incognizant, inconsiderate, indifferent, indiscriminate, indiscriminating, insensible, insensitive, led astray, mindless, misled by deception, nescient, obtuse, *oculis captus,* rash, thoughtless, unacquainted, unapprised, uncomprehending, unconscious, unconversant, undiscerning, unenlightened, uninformed, unknowing, unlucid, unmindful, unobservant, unobserving, unperceiving, unreflecting, unseeing, unversed, without insight
ASSOCIATED CONCEPTS: blind allegiance, blind amendments

BLIND *(Sightless), adjective* caecus, deprived of sight, dim-sighted, eyeless, feeble-eyed, groping, in darkness, unseeing, visionless, weak-eyed

BLIND *(Deprive of sight), verb* blight one's optical powers, destroy one's perception, extinguish visual discernment, make eyeless, make sightless, make unable to see, obstruct one's vision, render eyeless, render sightless, render visionless, ruin one's eyesight, strike sightless, strike visionless

BLIND *(Obscure), verb* adumbrate, becloud, becurtain, bedim, befog, bemask, benight, blanket, blear, blur, blur the outline, camouflage, cloak, cloud, conceal, conceal from sight, cover, cover up, curtain, dim, eclipse, ensconce, enshroud, envelop, hide, hide away, hide the identity of, hide underground, keep clandestine, keep out of sight, make inconspicuous, make indiscernible, make unapparent, make unperceptible, muddle, obfuscate, occult, overcloud, put in concealment, put out of sight, render dim, render invisible, render uncertain, screen, screen from observation, screen from sight, seclude, secrete, shade, shadow, shield, shroud, veil, veil the brightness

BLOCK, *verb* arrest, avert, ban, bar, barricade, blockade, bridle, check, choke, clog, close, cohibit, constrict, cramp, curb, dam, debar, delay, encumber, estop, exclude, fend off, forbid, foreclose, frustrate, halt, hamper, hinder, hobble, impede, intercept, interdict, interfere with, jam, leave out, limit, obstruct, occlude, oppose, parry, plug up, preclude, prevent, prohibit, proscribe, repulse, restrain, restrict, retard, shut off, shut up, snag, stall, stand in the way, stay, stem, stop, stop up, thwart, trammel, wall up

BLOCKADE *(Barrier), noun* bar, barricade, block, blockage, bottleneck, cordon, curb, impediment, *obsessio, obsidio,* obstacle, obstruction, stop, stumbling block

BLOCKADE *(Enclosure), noun* circumjacence, circumscription, circumvallation, compass, containment, encincture, encirclement, enclosing, encompassment, envelopment, framing, girdling, sealing off, surrounding
ASSOCIATED CONCEPTS: capture and prize, commercial blockade

BLOCKADE *(Limitation), noun* compression, confinement, contraction, debarring, exclusion, obturation, occlusion, preclusion, restriction, shutdown, stoppage, strangulation

BLOOD, *noun* affinity, agnation, ancestry, breed, brethren, brood, children, clan, cognation, common ancestry, consanguinity, derivation, descent, ethnic group, extraction, family connection, family relationship, family tie, family tree, filiation, genealogical tree, genealogy, gentility, *genus,* heredity, heritage, issue, kind, kindred, kinsfolk, kinship, kinsman, kinsmen, kinswoman, line, lineage, nationality, next of kin, offspring, one's people, parentage, pedigree, propinquity, relations, *sanguis,* stock, strain, ties of family, tribe
ASSOCIATED CONCEPTS: blood heirs, blood issue, blood relatives, full blood, half blood, mixed blood
FOREIGN PHRASES: *Consanguineus est quasi eodem sanguine natus.* A person related by consanguinity is, as it were, one born from the same blood. *Pueri sunt de sanguine parentum, sed pater et mater non sunt de sanguine puerorum.* Children are of the blood of their parents, but the father and mother are not of the blood of their children.

BLOODLINE, *noun* affiliation, ancestry, birth, blood, caste, derivation, descent, dynasty, extraction, family, family tree, genealogy, heredity, history, line, line of ancestors, lineage, origin, parentage, pedigree, progeniture, root, stem, stock, strain, succession
ASSOCIATED CONCEPTS: pedigree

BLUE SKY LAW, *noun* canons regarding securities, precepts on securities, securities law, securities oversight, securities rules, securities statutes

BLUEPRINT, *noun* design, detailed plan, diagram, draft, ground plan, map, master plan, mechanical drawing, outline, plan, scheme, sketch

BLUSTER *(Commotion), noun* boisterousness, brawl, disturbance, embroilment, eruption, flare-up, fracas, frenzy, hubbub, maelstrom, melee, outbreak, outburst, pandemonium, racket, rampage, riot, row, rumpus, scramble, storm, tempest, temptestuousness, tumult, tumultuousness, turbulence, turmoil, upheaval, uproar

BLUSTER *(Speech), noun* boast, bragging, *declamatio,* ebullition, ranting, raving, swaggering, talking big

BOARD, *noun* bureau, cabinet, commission, *con-legium,* consistory, consultative body, council, court, *curia,* department, directorate, directorship, governing body, judicatory, management, presidium, tribunal
ASSOCIATED CONCEPTS: advisory boards, board of aldermen, board of arbitrators, board of directors, board of education, board of elections, board of equalization, board of examiners, board of finance, board of health, board of medical examiners, board of public works, board of review, board of special inquiry, board of supervisors, board of trade, board of trustees, de facto

boards, draft board, local board, maritime board, qualification board, revenue board, welfare board, zoning board

BODILY, *adjective*   carnal, corporal, corporeal, corporeous, *corporeus,* de facto, embodied, existent, existing, human, incarnate, living, manifest, material, materiate, natural, organic, palpable, perceptible, physical, solid, somatic, somatical, tactile, tangible, visible
ASSOCIATED CONCEPTS: bodily condition, bodily contact, bodily function, bodily harm, bodily heirs, bodily infirmity, bodily injury, bodily issue, bodily pain or suffering

BODY *(Collection), noun*   aggregation, assemblage, batch, colligation, community, company, compilation, congeries, conglomeration, entity, gathering, host, mass, multitude, plenum, polity, sodality, troupe, wholeness
ASSOCIATED CONCEPTS: body corporate, body politic, governmental body, reviewing body

BODY *(Main part), noun*   core, *corpus,* essential part, exposition, figure, form, greater part, hub, main part, major part, principal part, shape, structure, substance
ASSOCIATED CONCEPTS: body of an instrument

BODY *(Person), noun*   anatomy, cadaver, carcass, carrion, corporality, corporalness, corporeality, corpse, *corpus,* embodiment, entity, human being, material existence, personage, physical being, physique
ASSOCIATED CONCEPTS: bogus ceremony, bogus certificate, bogus check

BOGUS, *adjective*   affected, artificial, counterfeit, false, phony, sham, spurious, unauthentic, ungenuine, unreal, untrue
ASSOCIATED CONCEPTS: bogus ceremony, bogus certificate, bogus check

BOILER PLATE, *adjective*   accepted, after the same pattern, common, commonplace, consonant, conventional, customary, dictated, formulary, habitual, homogeneous, patterned, prescribed, regulation, standardized, stereotyped, stock, typical, undeviating, uniform, universal, unvaried, wonted
ASSOCIATED CONCEPTS: boiler plate clause, boiler plate language

BOLSTER, *verb*   aid, back, buoy up, lift, prop, shore up, shoulder, succor, support, sustain, underpin, uphold

BOMB, *noun*   ammunition, armament, blockbuster, bombshell, charge, detonator, dynamite, explosive, explosive device, fireball, grenade, gunpowder, hand grenade, high explosive, infernal machine, instrument of warfare, mine, missile, Molotov cocktail, munitions, petard, shell, T.N.T., torpedo, weapon

BOMBAST, *noun*   affectation, boastfulness, boasting, braggery, chatter, declamation, diatribe, embellishment, empty talk, enlargement, euphemism, exaggeration, expansion, flatulence, floridness, fustian, garnishing, grandiloquence, grandiosity, harangue, high coloring, high-sounding words, hyperbole, idle speeches, inanity, inflation, loftiness, magnification, magniloquence, oration, ornamentation, orotundity, ostentation, overstatement, polysyllabic profundity,

pomposity, pompous prolixity, prate, preciosity, preciousness, pretentiousness, rant, raving, rhetoric, rhetoricalness, rodomontade, sesquipedalian words, sesquipedalism, sesquipedality, superlative, swelling utterance, swollen diction, tirade, tumidity, tumidness, turgescence, turgidity, vainglory, verbiage

BOMBSHELL, *noun*   astonishment, bewilderment, blow, consternation, eye opener, inexpectation, jolt, nonexpectation, shock, startler, stupefaction, sudden attack, sudden burst, surprisal, surprise, surprise package, thunderbolt, thunderclap, unawaited event, unexpected event, the unforeseen

BONA FIDE, *adjective*   aboveboard, accurate, actual, as represented, candid, faithful, forthright, genuine, honest, honorable, in good faith, ingenuous, intended, just, legitimate, meant, open, plain-speaking, principled, real, reliable, rightful, scrupulous, straightforward, trustworthy, unaffected, uncounterfeited, undisguised, undissembling, undistorted, unexaggerated, unfaked, unfeigned, unperfidious, unperjured, unpretended, unpretentious, unreserved, unsimulated, unspecious, unspurious, veracious, veridical
ASSOCIATED CONCEPTS: bona fide assignment, bona fide belief, bona fide business purpose, bona fide claimant, bona fide controversy, bona fide creditors, bona fide domicile, bona fide holder, bona fide holder for value, bona fide holder in due course, bona fide labor dispute, bona fide members, bona fide operation, bona fide purchaser in good faith, bona fide sale, bona fide seller

BOND, *noun*   assurance, certificate of debt, certificate of indebtedness, *chirographum,* debenture, evidence of a debt, government paper, guarantee, guaranty, indenture, obligation, promise, promissory note, real security, security, surety, *syngrapha,* voucher, warrant, warranty
ASSOCIATED CONCEPTS: back bond, bearer bond, bond discount, bond for costs, bond for deed, bond for title, bond holder, bond issue, bond of matrimony, bond premium, bonded indebtedness, bondsman, cash bond, construction bond, coupon bond, defense bond, delivery bond, fidelity bond, governmental bond, indemnity bond, interest-free bond, municipal bond, *ne exeat,* serial bond, state bond, supersedeas bond, tax-exempt bond
FOREIGN PHRASES: *Eodem ligamine quo ligatum est dissolvitur.* A bond is released by the same formalities by which it was made binding.

BOND *(Hold together), verb*   attach, blend, cement, coagulate, coalesce, cohere, combine, conglutemate, connect, consolidate, couple, fix, fuse, glue, interlock, join, merge, secure, stick, unite

BOND *(Secure a debt), verb*   agree, assure, certify, confirm, contract, covenant, endorse, ensure, give security, guarantee, hypothecate, indenture, insure, pledge, post, promise, secure, stake, underwrite, warrant

BONDAGE, *noun*   abject slavery, arrest, bond of slavery, bonds, captivity, chains, coarctation, compulsory service, confinement, constraint, constraint by force, custodianship, custody, detention, durance, enslavement, entombment, fetters, forced confinement, forced labor, forcible restraint of liberty, guardianship, guarding, helotry, immuration, immurement, impoundment, imprisonment, incarceration, internment,

involuntary servitude, loss of freedom, manacles, penal restraint, penal servitude, prison, refusal of bail, reins, remand, restraint, restriction, restriction on movement, servitude, slavery, slavishness, subduing, subjection, subjugation, subordination, subservience, surveillance, thralldom, yoke
ASSOCIATED CONCEPTS: involuntary servitude, kidnapping

BONUS, *noun* additive, benefit, *boni,* boon, bounty, dividend, donation, extra, gift, gratuity, honorarium, incentive, perquisites, *pourboire,* premium, *prime,* reward, something over and above, surplus, surplusage, tip
ASSOCIATED CONCEPTS: bonus stock

BOOK, *verb* accuse, arrest, chronicle, docket, engage, enter, enumerate, file, index, inscribe, insert, list, log, make an entry, mark down, note, order, post, prefer charges, record, register, report, schedule, seize legally, tabulate, take into custody, write down

BOOM *(Increase), noun* acceleration, accretion, accrual, accruement, accumulation, additament, addition, additory, advance, advancement, amplification, amplitude, annexation, appreciation, appurtenance, attachment, augment, augmentation, boost, broadening, burgeoning, complement, deepening, development, distension, doubling, duplication, enhancement, enlargement, escalation, expansion, extension, gain, growth, heightening, hike, improvement, increasement, increasing, increment, intensification, interest, magnification, production, progress, progression, proliferation, prolongation, protraction, raise, reinforcement, reproduction, rise, spread, spreading, sprouting, strengthening, supplement, swell, swelling, upgrowth, upsurge

BOOM *(Prosperity), noun* abundance, accomplishment, accumulation, achievement, acquisition, advance, advancement, affluence, aggrandizement, amelioration, amplitude, attainment, augmentation, auspiciousness, avails, benefaction, booming economy, bountifulness, burgeoning, capital gains, copiousness, cornucopia, development, earnings, economic prosperity, escalation, excess, exorbitance, exorbitancy, expansion, expediency, favorable trade balance, flourishing condition, gain, good fortune, great quantity, growth, impetus, improvement, increment, inflation, lucre, mutual profit, opulence, opulency, outgrowth, outpouring, plentifulness, plentitude, prevalence, production, productivity, profit, profit making, profluence, profluency, profuseness, profusion, progress, progression, progressiveness, proliferation, prosperous issue, prosperous outcome, prosperousness, recovery, remuneration, revenue, richness, rising prices, spiral inflation, superabundance, superfluity, surplus, thriving conditions, thriving economy, upgrading, upgrowth, upsurge, upward curve, upward trend, weal, wealth, welfare, well-being

BOOTLEGGER, *noun* black marketeer, contrabandist, gunrunner, illicit dealer, moonshiner, runner, smuggler
ASSOCIATED CONCEPTS: prohibition, sale of intoxicating liquor

BORDER, *noun* ambit, borderland, boundary, bounds, brim, brink, circumference, circumjacence, confine, contiguity, edge, edging, end, enframement, ex-tremity, flange, frame, fringe, frontier, hem, ledge, limit, line of demarcation, marge, margin, outline, outpost, outside, outskirts, pale, perimeter, periphery, purlieus, rim, selvedge, side, skirt, terminal, termination, verge
ASSOCIATED CONCEPTS: border search

BORDER *(Approach), verb* abut upon, adjoin, align convergently, approximate, be in the vicinity of, be near, close on, come close, come to a point, concentrate, converge, draw near, encroach, gravitate toward, join, juxtapose, juxtaposit, lie near, meet, move toward, near, neighbor, place in juxtaposition, place near, place parallel, proximate, put along side, skim, skirt, unite, verge, verge upon

BORDER *(Bound), verb* abut upon, *adiacere,* adjoin, appose, attach, *attingere,* be adjacent to, be circumjacent to, be conterminous, be contiguous, be in conjunction with, be in contact with, be juxtaposed, butt, cincture, circumpose, circumvalate, circumvent, close in, confine, conjoin, connect, contain, corral, cut off, define, delimit, delimitate, delineate, demarcate, edge, embrace, encase, enchase, encircle, enclose, enclose within bounds, encompass, ensphere, envelop, environ, extend to, flank, frame, gird, hem in, impinge, join, juxtapose, juxtaposit, lean against, lie contiguous to, lie next to, limit, mark off, meet end to end, meet with, outline, place limitations, proscribe, restrain, restrict, shut in, specify limits, stake out, surround

BORN *(Alive), adjective* animated, begotten, breathing, enlivened, live, living, quick, vital, vitalized

BORN *(Innate), adjective* congenital, connate, connatural, fundamental, genetic, hereditary, immanent, in the blood, inborn, inbred, incarnate, indigenous, ingrained, inherited, instinctive, instinctual, intrinsic, inwrought, native, natural, organic

BORROW, *verb* accept the loan of, apply for a loan, ask for credit, get on credit, get temporary use of, *mutuari,* obtain a mortgage, obtain the use of, take an advance, take on credit, take on loan
ASSOCIATED CONCEPTS: borrowed capital, borrowed employees, borrowed servant, borrowing statute
FOREIGN PHRASES: *In satisfactionibus non permittitur amplius fieri quam semel factum est.* In settlements more must not be received than was received once for all.

BOUND, *adjective* accountable, answerable, beholden, called by duty, chargeable, committed, compelled, constrained, destined, engaged, forced, having no alternative, impelled, liable, necessitated, obligated, obliged, pledged, pressed by duty, required, responsible, restrained, tied, under a vow, under compulsion, under necessity, under obligation
FOREIGN PHRASES: *Naturale est quidlibet dissolvi eo modo quo ligatur.* It is natural for a thing to be unbound in the same way in which it was made binding. *Nemo tenetur ad impossibile.* No one is bound to do an impossibility. *Quo ligatur, eo dissolvitur.* By the same means by which a thing is bound, it is released.

BOUNDARY, *noun* border, borderline, bound, circumscription, compass, configuration, confine, confinement, contour, delimitation, delineation, division line, edge, enclosure, extremity, *finis,* limit, limitation, limits, line of circumvallation, line of demarcation, lineaments, lines, outline, perimeter, periphery, radius, rim, *terminus,* verge

ASSOCIATED CONCEPTS: adjoining landowners, boundary line, boundary of a water course, boundary suit, metes and bounds, surveys and surveyors, trespass to try title, zoning

BOUNTY, *noun* award, benefaction, benevolence, bonanza, bonus, boon, *cadeau,* conferment, emolument, favor, gift, grant, gratification, gratuity, guerdon, handsel, honorarium, largess, *largitas, liberalitas,* perquisite, *pourboire,* premium, prize, reward, reward for service, tip, token, tribute

ASSOCIATED CONCEPTS: bounty lands

BOWDLERIZE, *verb* censor, curtail, cut, cut out, delete, edit out, emasculate, eviscerate, excise, expunge, expurgate, extirpate, remove

ASSOCIATED CONCEPTS: censorship, freedom of speech

BOYCOTT, *noun* abstention from buying, abstention from using, avoidance, ban, banning, black-listing, blackballing, debarring, embargo, exclusion, ostracism, proscription, refusal to do business, rejection, shunning, strike, withholding of patronage

ASSOCIATED CONCEPTS: primary boycott, secondary boycott

BRAND, *noun* badge, colophon, copyright label, disgrace, earmark, emblem, hallmark, identification mark, identification tag, impress, imprint, insignia, label, mark, *nota,* owner's mark, owner's sign, *piste,* seal, sigil, sign, signet, smirch, stain, stamp, sticker, stigma, stigmatism, tag, taint, ticket, token, trade name, trademark, watermark

ASSOCIATED CONCEPTS: brand name

BRAND *(Mark), verb* autograph, blaze, distinguish by mark, earmark, emblaze, emboss, endorse, engrave, identify, impress, imprint, inscribe, label, *notam homini inurere, notare,* print, put a mark on, put an indication on, seal, sign, stamp, tag

BRAND *(Stigmatize), verb* asperse, attaint, besmear, besmirch, bespatter, blacken, blot, bring into discredit, cast a slur upon, cast aspersions at, corrupt, debase, decry, defame, defile, deride, derogate, dirty, discredit, disgrace, dishonor, disparage, excite disapprobation, hold up to shame, impugn, involve in shame, malign, pillory, put to shame, reflect upon, slur, smear, smirch, smudge, soil, stain, sully, taint, tar, tarnish, throw dishonor upon, vilify, vilipend

ASSOCIATED CONCEPTS: libel, reputation, slander

BRANDISH, *verb* dangle before the eyes, display, draw one's sword, exhibit, flap, flaunt, flourish, gesture, rattle the saber, shake, show, swing, threaten, *vibrare,* wag, waggle, wave, wield

ASSOCIATED CONCEPTS: harassment, menacing

BRAWL, *noun* altercation, brangle, breach of the peace, broil, commotion, deafening row, din, dispute, disturbance, embranglement, embroilment, feud, fight, fisticuffs, fracas, fray, hubbub, imbroglio, jangle, *jurgium, mêlée,* noisiness, outbreak, pandemonium, quarrel, racket, rampage, riot, *rixa,* row, rowdiness, ruction, scramble, scrimmage, scuffle, squabble, tumult, turmoil, uproar, wrangle

ASSOCIATED CONCEPTS: disorderly conduct

BRAWL, *verb* altercate, be noisy, bicker, brangle, break the peace, broil, clamor, create a disturbance, create a riot, dispute angrily, fight, have a row, have words with, jangle, make a commotion, make a racket, make an uproar, quarrel noisily, rampage, riot, *rixari,* row, run riot, scrap, scrimmage, scuffle, set to, spat, squabble, tiff, wrangle

ASSOCIATED CONCEPTS: disorderly conduct

BRAZEN, *adjective* arrogant, assuming, audacious, aweless, barefaced, blatant, bluff, bold, boldfaced, brash, conscienceless, daring, defiant, disrespectful, familiar, flagrant, flaunting, flippant, forward, immodest, immoral, impertinent, *impudens,* impudent, indecent, indecorous, insolent, malapert, obtrusive, of loose morals, outspoken, pert, petulant, presumptuous, *risqué,* rude, saucy, shameless, unabashed, unashamed, unblushing, unembarrassed, unmannerly, unmodest, unreserved, unseemly

BREACH, *noun* break, contravention, default, delinquency, dereliction, *discutere,* disobedience, disregard, dissension, dissentience, encroachment, enmity, failure, illegal evasion, illicitness, impropriety, infidelity, infraction, infringement, inobservance, neglection, nonadherence, noncompletion, nonconformity, nonfulfilment, nonobservance, nonperformance, omission, perfidy, *perfringere,* rejection, repudiation, retraction, shortcoming, tergiversation, transgression, trespass, unconformity, undueness, unduteousness, undutifulness, unfaithfulness, unobservance, violation, violation of law

ASSOCIATED CONCEPTS: anticipatory breach, breach of bond, breach of contract, breach of covenant, breach of duty, breach of faith, breach of lease, breach of marriage promise, breach of promise, breach of the close, breach of the covenant of warranty, breach of the peace, breach of trust, breach of warranty, constructive breach, continuing breach, material breach, partial breach, total breach

BREAK *(Fracture), verb* burst, cave in, comminute, cut, destroy, fissure, fragment, hew, interpenetrate, *interrumpere,* penetrate, pierce, pulverize, puncture, rend, rupture, scatter, shatter, shiver, smash, splinter, stave in

ASSOCIATED CONCEPTS: breakage, breaking a close, breaking and entering, burglary, forcible entry and detainer

BREAK *(Separate), verb* cleave, crack, detach, disband, disconnect, disengage, disentangle, disintegrate, disjoin, dislocate, dismantle, dispart, disperse, dissociate, disunite, divaricate, force apart, force open, get free, get loose, incise, lop, open, part, rive, sever, split, split off, subdivide, sunder, take apart, take to pieces, unbind, unchain, unclinch, uncouple, unfetter, unknot, unloose, untie

ASSOCIATED CONCEPTS: break in occupancy, break in the chain of events

BREAK *(Violate), verb* abscind, be derelict, be guilty of infraction, breach, defy, disobey, disregard, infringe, invade, neglect, trample upon, transgress, trespass

BREVET, *noun* authorization, charge, charter, declaration, decree, edict, fiat, grant, law, license, mandate, manifesto, ordinance, ordination, *placet,* precept, prescription, rule, sanction, warrant, writ

BRIBE, noun corrupt money, corrupt offering, graft, hush money, illegal donation, illegal incentive, illegal incitation, illegal inducement, illegal lure, illegal offer, illegal offering, illegal present, illegal reward, offering, *pretium,* protection money, sop, unlawful bait, unlawful compensation, unlawful gift, unlawful gratuity

ASSOCIATED CONCEPTS: acceptance of a bribe, bribe-giving for public office, bribe-receiving, bribery, bribing a witness, corruption, obstructing justice, offer to bribe, official misconduct, rewarding official misconduct, solicitation of a bribe, unlawful gratuities

BRIBERY, noun allurement, baiting, blandishment, breach of faith, bribing, cajolement, cajolery, collusion, complicity, connivance, corrupt inducement, corrupt payment, corruptibility, corruption, crime, criminality, enticement, illegal incitation, illegal inducement, improbity, inducement, inveiglement, jobbery, lawbreaking, luring, misdealing, opportunism, perfidy, pettifoggery, plying, pressure, prodition, seducement, snaring, tantalization, temptation, tempting, unlawful encouragement, venality

ASSOCIATED CONCEPTS: commercial bribery, obstruction of justice, official misconduct, public bribery

BRIEF, adjective abbreviated, abridged, aphoristic, bare, brisk, close, cometary, compact, compendious, compressed, concise, condensed, contracted, cursory, curtailed, cut short, elliptical, ephemeral, epigrammatic, epitomized, exact, fading, fleeting, hasty, hurried, laconic, limited, meteoric, momentary, not protracted, passing, pauciloquent, pithy, precise, quick, reduced, sententious, short, short-term, slight, small, sparing of words, speedy, succinct, sudden, summarized, summary, swift, temporary, to the point, transient, transitory, trenchant, unprolonged, volatile

ASSOCIATED CONCEPTS: brief description, brief statement, brief summary

BRIEF, noun abridgment, account, argument, capsule, compendium, condensation, conspectus, depiction, description, digest, extract, legal abstract, legal document, legal epitome, legal memorandum, memorandum, memorandum of law, outline, outline on the law, profile, representation, resume, sketch, statement of the case, summary, summary on the law, synopsis, thumbnail sketch, vignette

ASSOCIATED CONCEPTS: *amicus curiae,* appellate brief, brief of evidence, points and authorities, reply brief, responsive brief

BROAD, adjective ample, amplitudinous, *amplus,* blanket, collective, comprehensive, covering all cases, deep, diffuse, encyclopedic, expansive, extended, extending, extensive, far-flung, far-reaching, far-spread, full, general, generalized, generic, immense, inclusive, indefinite, indeterminate, indiscriminate, large, large-scale, latitudinous, *latus,* liberal, liberalistic, nonspecific, outspread, outstretched, pervasive, representative, spacious, spreading, standard, sweeping, synoptic, typical, ubiquitous, unbiased, unconfined, unspecified, vague, wide, widespread

ASSOCIATED CONCEPTS: broad appeal, broad definition, broad interpretation, broad meaning, broad sense, broad spectrum

BROKEN *(Fractured),* **adjective** crumbled, damaged, defective, destroyed, disintegrated, dismembered, divided, fractional, fragmentary, injured, lacerated, mangled, mutilated, pulverized, riven, ruptured, sectional, separated, severed, shattered, shivered, slivered, splintered

BROKEN *(Interrupted),* **adjective** checked, deranged, desultory, disarranged, disconnected, discontinuous, disjunct, disordered, divided, erratic, fitful, halting, hindered, incomplete, inconstant, intermittent, irregular, obstructed, spasmodic, sporadic, stopped, suspended, unequal, uneven, unsteady, unsuccessive, variable

BROKEN *(Unfulfilled),* **adjective** contravened, delinquent, derelict, disloyal, disobedient, disregarded, disregardful, dutiless, encroached upon, infringed, infringing, inobservant, insubordinate, lawless, nonadhering, nonobservant, repudiated, transgressed, uncompliant, undutiful, unfaithful, unlawful, unloyal, unobservant, untrue, violated, violative

BROKER, noun agent, bargaining agent, commission agent, commission merchant, customers' man, dealer, deputy, factor, go-between, intermediary, intermedium, internuncio, *interpres,* link, matchmaker, mediator, medium, middleman, monger, negotiant, negotiator, realtor, regrater, representative, trader

ASSOCIATED CONCEPTS: brokerage, broker's commission, exchange broker, insurance broker, merchandise broker, notebroker, pawnbroker, real estate broker, stockbroker

BROKERAGE, noun agio, charge, charges, commission, compensation, discount, emolument, factorage, fee, recompense, remuneration

ASSOCIATED CONCEPTS: agents, brokerage business, brokerage commission, brokerage contract, brokers, commissions

BROOD, verb agonize, be dejected, cogitate, consider, contemplate, deliberate over, despair, despond, dwell upon, fret, grieve, *incubare,* meditate on, mope, morbidly meditate, mull over, muse, ponder, reflect, ruminate, study, sulk, think anxiously, think over, weigh

BROWBEAT, verb abash, badger, beat down, bully, chide, cow, daunt, deflate, discourage, dishonor, domineer, dress down, drive, exert pressure on, frighten, give one a talking to, goad, harass, humble, humiliate, intimidate, make nervous, make one feel small, nag, overawe, overbear, override, petrify, prevail upon, push into, put in fear, put pressure on, raise apprehensions, reprove, scare, set down, shame into, subdue, trounce

BRUTAL, adjective atrocious, barbarous, bearish, beastly, bestial, bloody, brute-like, brutish, churlish, coarse, cruel, despotic, domineering, excessive, extreme, fell, ferocious, *ferus,* fierce, flint-hearted, grim, gross, gruff, hardhearted, harsh, *immanis,* inexorable, inhuman, *inhumanus,* mean, merciless, oppressive, over-harsh, overbearing, persecuting, pitiless, primitive, remorseless, rough, rugged, ruthless, sadistic, savage, severe, stonyhearted, truculent, tyrannical, tyrannous, uncivilized, unfeeling, ungentle, unmerciful, unrelenting, untamed, vicious, violent

BRUTALITY, noun act of inhumanity, barbarity, bestiality, brutalness, brutilization, brutishness, cruelness, cruelty, grossness, hardness, hardness of heart, harshness, heart of stone, heartlessness, *immanitas,* inhumanity, lack of feeling, mercilessness, moral insensibility, pitilessness, ruffianism, ruthlessness, savageness, savagery, truculence, truculency, unfeelingness, violence

ASSOCIATED CONCEPTS: cruel and inhuman treatment, cruel and unusual punishment

BRUTALIZE, *verb* barbarize, be pitiless, be vicious to, be wicked to, brutify, bully, corrupt, decivilize, deform one's character, dehumanize, demoralize, hurt, injure, lead astray, make insensitive, make wicked, maltreat, mislead, molest, oppress, persecute, pervert, render evil, run down, seduce, teach wickedness, tyrranize

ASSOCIATED CONCEPTS: assault, cruel and inhuman punishment

BUDGET, *noun* accountancy, accounts, allocation, allotment, allowance, appropriation, balance sheet, balance statement, distribution, estimated expenditures, planned disbursement, profit and loss account, provision, ration, statement, statement of account

ASSOCIATED CONCEPTS: appropriations, budget bill, budget notes, itemized budget, municipal budget, public debt limitations

BUFFER ZONE, *noun* added protection, bulkhead, bulwark, insulation, medium, rampart, screen, territory for defense

BUILD *(Augment),* *verb* add to, aggrandize, amplify, develop, elevate, enhance, enlarge, expand, extend, grow, heighten, increase, lift, magnify, make higher, make larger, parlay, pyramid, raise, rise, swell

BUILD *(Construct),* *verb* achieve, assemble, carpenter, cast, compile, compose, construct, contrive, create, devise, elevate, engineer, erect, establish, evolve, fabricate, fashion, figure, form, found, frame, lay the foundation, make, manufacture, model, originate, produce, put up, raise, set up, shape, superstruct, upbuild

BUILDING *(Business of assembling),* *noun* *aedificatio,* amalgamation, architecture, arrangement, assembling, causation, collocation, compilation, composition, compounding, conformation, conjunction, constitution, construction, contriving, craftsmanship, creating, design, development, devising, effectuation, efformation, engineering, establishment, fabrication, fashioning, formation, formulation, foundation, framing, grouping, handiwork, implementation, incorporation, industry, installation, institution, interrelation, making, manufacture, organization, origination, plan, prefabrication, preparation, production, shaping, structuring, synthesis

ASSOCIATED CONCEPTS: building for a particular use
FOREIGN PHRASES: *Aedificare in tuo proprio solo non licet quod alteri noceat.* It is not lawful to build upon one's own land what may injure another.

BUILDING *(Structure),* *noun* abiding place, abode, address, *aedificium,* boardinghouse, construction, domicile, *domus, dulce domum,* dwelling, dwelling place, edifice, elevation, erection, establishment, fabric, frame, framework, habitat, habitation, headquarters, home, homestead, house, institute, living quarters, lodging, lodging house, lodging place, lodgings, lodg-

ment, piece of architecture, place, place of habitation, premises, quarters, residence, shelter, site, station, superstructure

ASSOCIATED CONCEPTS: building and construction contracts, building code, building contract, building inspector, building laws, building lien, building lines, building loan, building loan mortgage, building material, building or other improvement, building permit, building purposes, building restriction, building site, building superintendent, building trades

BULK, *noun* abundance, accumulation, a commanding portion, amount, *amplitudo,* batch, block, chief part, clump, cluster, corpus, greatest part, heap, lot, magnitude, *magnitudo,* main part, major part, majority, mass, *moles,* overwhelming part, predominant part, principal part, quantity, quantum, size, stack, substance, substantial number, substantial part, substantial quantity, volume

ASSOCIATED CONCEPTS: bulk assignments, bulk cargo, bulk price, bulk property, bulk sale, bulk sales, bulk sales act, bulk sales laws, bulk shipment, bulk storage, bulk transaction, stored in bulk

BULK TRANSFER, *noun* large asset transfer, main asset transfer, major business asset transfer

BULWARK, *noun* abutment, asylum, barricade, barrier, bastion, battlement, buffer, bulkhead, buttress, citadel, defense, embankment, fort, fortification, fortress, guard, haven, insulation, insulator, palladium, parapet, preservation, *propugnaculum,* protection, rampart, refuge, safeguard, sanctuary, security, shelter, shield, stockade, stronghold, support

BUMPTIOUS, *adjective* audacious, contumelious, forward, obtrusive, procacious

BUNKO, *noun* bamboozlement, cheating, chicanery, con game, confidence trick, defraudation, doubledealing, dupery, ensnarement, flimflam, gyp, hoax, legal chicanery, pettifogging, racket, ruse, skulduggery, *supercherie,* swindle, trick, victimization, wile

ASSOCIATED CONCEPTS: bunko men, bunko steering, confidence game, fraud, gambling, larceny, wagering

BURDEN, *noun* accountability, adversity, affliction, anxiety, assignment, bother, botheration, bounden duty, brunt, call of duty, care, charge, chore, cumbrance, *devoir,* difficulty, drawback, duty, encumbrance, engagement, errand, handicap, hardship, hindrance, impediment, imposition, job, liability, line of duty, load, mandate, necessity, obligation, onus, oppression, ordeal, pains, requirement, requisite, responsibility, strain, task, tribulation, trouble, undertaking, vexation, weight, work

ASSOCIATED CONCEPTS: burden of covenant, burden of easement, burden of going forward with evidence, burden of loss, burden of persuasion, burden of proof, burden upon commerce, shifting of burden

FOREIGN PHRASES: *Non debet alteri per alterum iniqua conditio inferri.* A burdensome condition ought not to be imposed upon one man by the act of another. *Cum par delictum est duorum, semper oneratur petitor et melior habetur possessoris causa.* When there is equal fault on both sides, the burden is always placed on the plaintiff, and the cause of the possessor is preferred. *Actus curiae neminem gravabit.* An act of the court shall prejudice no one. *Probandi necessitas incumbit* *illi qui agit.* The necessity of proving lies with the person who sues. *Qui sentit onus sentire debet et commodum.* He who assumes the burden ought to derive the benefit.

BUREAU, *noun*   administration, administrative unit, agency, authority, board, branch, commission, committee, department, division, ministry, office, specialized administrative unit, specialized unit

BUREAUCRACY, *noun*   administration, agency, authorities, delegated authority, departmentalization, governance, government, government by bureaus, government office, governmental procedure, governmental system for decision-making, inflexible routine, management, ministration, official procedure, officialdom, officiation, organization, powers that be, process of governing, red tape, regulation, reins of government, rigid routine, rule, service, sovereignty, state management, strict procedure, system

BURGLAR, *noun*   bandit, bank robber, criminal, despoiler, filcher, gangster, holdup man, *homo trium literarum,* housebreaker, larcener, marauder, pilferer, pillager, plunderer, prowler, raider, rifler, robber, safebreaker, safecracker, second-story thief, sneak thief, spoiler, stealer, stickup man, thief
ASSOCIATED CONCEPTS: burglar's tools, criminal trespass

BURGLARY, *noun*   breaking and entering, crime, *effractura,* felony, filching, forcible entry, *furtum,* housebreaking, illegality, larceny, lawlessness, looting, marauding, pilfering, pillaging, plunderage, plundering, prowling, purloinment, raiding, robbery, robbing, spoiling, stealing, theft, thievery, unlawful act, unlawful breaking and entering, unlawfulness
ASSOCIATED CONCEPTS: burglar's tools, burglary insurance, common law burglary, receiving stolen goods, robbery, statutory burglary

BURN, *verb*   blaze, blister, brand, burn to a cinder, burst into flame, catch fire, cauterize, char, conflagrate, consume, cremate, deflagrate, enkindle, fire, flame up, flare, gut, ignite, incandesce, incendiarize, incinerate, inflame, kindle, light up, melt, overheat, parch, relume, scald, scorch, scorify, sear, seethe, singe, sizzle, smelt, smolder, strike a light, vesicate
ASSOCIATED CONCEPTS: arson, revocation of wills

BUSINESS *(Affair),* *noun*   activity, concern, duty, interest, matter, mission, proceeding, proposition, responsibility, task, undertaking
FOREIGN PHRASES: *Aliena negotia exacto officio geruntur.* The business of another is to be carried out with particular care. *Constitutum esse eam domum unicuique nostrum debere existimari, ubi quisque sedes et tabulas haberet, suarumque rerum constitutionem fecisset.* It is established that the home of each of us is considered to be the place of his abode and books, and where he may have made an establishment of his business. *In suo quisque negotio hebetior est quam in alieno.* Everyone is more dull in his own business than in that of another.

BUSINESS *(Commerce),* *noun*   barter, buying and selling, commercial intercourse, dealings, exchange, industry, intercourse, merchandising, merchantry, production, trade, trading, traffic, transaction, ventures

ASSOCIATED CONCEPTS: business address, business agent, business corporation, business crimes, business district, business done in state, business enterprise, business expenses, business hours, business interruption insurance, business invitees, business license, business losses, business name, business paper, business purposes, business records, business restrictions, business secrets, business situs, business trust, business venture, business visitor, doing business, good will of business, in the course of business, interference with business, ordinary course of business, transacting business
FOREIGN PHRASES: *Ea quae raro accidunt non temere in agendis negotiis computantur.* Those things which rarely happen are not to be taken into account in the transaction of business without sufficient reason.

BUSINESS *(Commercial enterprise),* *noun*   cartel, combine, company, concern, corporation, establishment, firm, industry, manufacture, organization, private enterprise, shop, store, syndicate, venture

BUSINESS *(Occupation),* *noun*   activity, avocation, calling, career, craft, duty, employment, endeavor, following, function, handicraft, job, line, livelihood, living, means of support, mission, office, practice, profession, pursuit, specialty, trade, undertaking, vocation, walk of life, work

BUY, *verb*   acquire by purchase, acquire ownership of, bargain for, complete a purchase, contract, get in exchange, make a purchase, make one's own, *mercari,* obtain, order, pay a price for, pay cash for, pay for, procure, procure title to, purchase, redeem, secure, secure for a consideration, trade
ASSOCIATED CONCEPTS: buy and sell agreement, buy in the ordinary course of business, buy long, buy out, buy short, buyer beware, buyer's needs, buyer's option, buyer's risk, buying a note or a bill, buying and receiving stolen goods, buying broker
FOREIGN PHRASES: *Caveat emptor, qui ignorare non debuit quod jus alienum emit.* Let a purchaser beware since he ought not to be ignorant that he is purchasing whatever rights another has. *Emptor emit quam minimo potest, venditor vendit quam maximo potest.* The buyer purchases for the least he can; the seller sells for the most he can. *In pretio emptionis et venditionis, naturaliter licet contrahentibus se circumvenire.* In respect to the price, in buying and selling, it is naturally permitted to the contracting parties to overreach one another.

BYLAW, *noun*   canon, charter, code, municipal regulation, ordinance, prescript, prescription, *reglement,* regulation, rubric, rule, standard
ASSOCIATED CONCEPTS: amendment of bylaws, authorization for bylaws, enactment of bylaws, interpretation of bylaws, repeal of bylaws

BYSTANDER, *noun*   apprizer, attestant, attester, audience, beholder, corroborator, earwitness, enlightener, eyewitness, indicator, informant, informer, insider, listener, looker, looker-on, monitor, observer, one who bears witness, onlooker, passer-by, reporter, seer, spectator, swearer, teller, testifier, tipster, tout, undercover man, viewer, viewership, watcher, witness, witness, witness to a crime, witness as to character
ASSOCIATED CONCEPTS: accessory, disinterested party, Good Samaritan, innocent bystander, third persons

C

CABAL, *noun*   band, camarilla, clique, coalition, collusion, combination, complicity, complot, confederacy, connivance, conspiracy, council, design, *factio,* faction, gang, intrigue, junta, league, machination, plot, ring, scheme, secret group, secret plot, *societas clandestina,* union

CACHE *(Hiding place), noun*   *abri,* ambuscade, backroom, confinement, hideaway, inmost recesses, place of concealment, protectory, refuge, safe place, safe retreat, secret place, shelter, undercover

CACHE *(Storage place), noun*   depository, place of deposit, place of safety, promptuary, repertory, repository, reservoir, safe, safe place, secret storehouse, stockroom, storage, store of provisions, storehouse, storehouse for safekeeping, storeroom, warehouse

CADAVER, *noun*   carcass, corpse, corpus delecti, dead body, victim

CADUCITY, *noun*   decadence, decay, decline, decrepitude, degeneracy, deterioration, dotage, feebleness, infirmity of old age, senility, weakness

CAJOLE, *verb*   allure, bait, coax, entice, importune, lure, ply, pressure, push, tease, tempt, urge

CAITIFF, *adjective*   abject, afraid, base, baseborn, brutish, churlish, craven, currish, dastardly, despicable, faint-hearted, fear-stricken, ignoble, ignominious, low, lowborn, mean-spirited, of low extraction, of low origin, of mean extraction, of mean origin, poltroonish, pusillanimous, raffish, recreant, rude, scared, spiritless, uncivilized, uncourageous, unpolished, vile, vulgar, weak-minded

CALAMITY, *noun*   act of God, adverse fortune, adversity, affliction, bad fortune, blight, *calamitas,* cataclysm, catastrophe, *clades,* destruction, disaster, evil fortune, evil lot, evil luck, grievous harm, hardship, ill fortune, loss, major misfortune, mischance, misery, misfortune, stroke, tragedy
ASSOCIATED CONCEPTS: calamity bonds

CALCULATE, *verb*   account, appraise, ascertain mathematically, assess, average out, cast accounts, cipher, *computare,* compute, consider, count, design, determine, devise, enumerate, estimate, evaluate, figure, figure out, form an estimate, furnish an estimate, gauge, make a computation, make an estimate, measure, mete, number, place a value on, plan, predict, quantify, rank, rate, reckon, score, set a value on, size, suit, take an account of, take into account, take stock, take the dimensions, tally, think out, totalize, valorize, valuate, value, work out

CALENDAR *(List of cases), noun*   agenda, cases ready for argument, court's log, docket, enumeration of causes arranged for trial, list of cases set down for hearing, list of causes arranged for trial, list of causes instituted in court, list of causes ready for trial, motion docket, order of cases, record, register, register of cases, schedule, systematic arrangement of cases, table of cases, timetable, trial list
ASSOCIATED CONCEPTS: calendar practice, court calendar, *fasti*

CALENDAR *(Record of yearly periods), noun*   agenda, almanac, annals, chronicle, chronology, daybook, diary, docket, established division of time, history, journal, list of appointments, list of events, log, logbook, memoranda, menology, order of business, plans, program, record, record of yearly periods, register, schedule, schedule of events, sequence of events, system of reckoning time, table, tabular register of the year, timetable
ASSOCIATED CONCEPTS: calendar day, calendar month, calendar week, calendar year, Gregorian calendar

CALIBER *(Measurement), noun*   amount, amplitude, area, breadth, broad guage, broadness, compass, cross dimension, cross measurement, degree, diameter, diameter of a cylindrical body, dimensions, expanse, extent, full size, girth, grade, guage, magnitude, mass, measure, measured size, measurement across, proportion, scale, size, thickness, width

CALIBER *(Mental capacity), noun*   ability, ableness, acumen, acuteness, adequacy, aptitude, arguteness, attainment, capability, capableness, capacity, competence, comprehension, depth, discernment, discrimination, efficacy, efficiency, endowment, faculty, genius, gift, good judgment, instinct, intellect, intellectual power, intelligence, judgment, knowledge, mentality, perspicacity, proficiency, qualification, reach of mind, sagacity, sapience, specialty, talent, understanding, wisdom

CALIBER *(Quality),* **noun**   attribute, capability, character, distinctiveness, eminence, excellence, grade, importance, merit, potency, rate, standing, state, station, status, value, virtue, worth

CALL *(Appeal),* **noun**   address, adjuration, application, beseechment, bid, cry, earnest request, entreaty, impetration, imploration, importunity, insistent demand, instance, invocation, invocatory plea, invocatory prayer, motion, obsecration, obtestation, petition, plea, prayer, request, requirement, requisition, solemn entreaty, solicitation, suit, supplication, *vox*
ASSOCIATED CONCEPTS: adjournment of a term of the court subject to call, calendar call, call contract, call prior to maturity, calls for more margin, dismissal for failure to answer a call

CALL *(Option),* **noun**   alternative, choice, decision, demand made on a stock holder, discretion, discretionary order, freedom of choice, liberty of action, opportunity, requirement, requisition, right of put and call, stock agreement
ASSOCIATED CONCEPTS: "call" option on stock or assessments, calls and assessments, "puts" and "calls" as options in a contract

CALL *(Title),* **noun**   agnomen, alias, antonomasia, appellation, appellative, application, baptism, byword, caption, cognomen, cognomination, compellation, convertible terms, description, designation, epithet, eponym, expression, given name, head, indication, matronymic, name, namesake, naming, nomenclature, patronymic, praenomen, prenomen, proper name, sign, signature, sobriquet, style, surname, synonym, term, trope

CALL *(Appeal to),* **verb**   address a petition, address a request, address oneself to, adjure, appeal, apply to, ask, ask for, be a suppliant, beg a favor, beg leave, beseech, bespeak, call for aid, call for help, call upon, *clamare,* cry, cry to, entreat, impetrate, implore, importune, invite, invoke, make a petition, make a request, make a requisition, make appeal, make application, make bold to ask, make earnest entreaty, petition, plead for, plead with, prefer a petition, prefer a request, prefer an appeal, press, put to, put up a request, request, solicit, sue, supplicate, turn to, urge

CALL *(Demand),* **verb**   ask for with authority, assert a right to, claim, claim as a right, clamor for, command, cry for, demand, *deposcere,* exact, *flagitare,* insist on, lay claim to, make a demand, make an authoritative request, make claims upon, make requisition, necessitate, oblige, order, prescribe, present an ultimatum, present one's claim, press, put in a claim for, render necessary, require, require of others, requisition, send an order for

CALL *(Summon),* **verb**   *advocare,* ask to come, assemble, assemble by summons, beckon, bid come, command to appear, convene, *convocare,* convocate, convoke, desire the presence of, gather, group, invite, invoke, issue an invitation, mobilize, muster, muster up, page, rally, request the presence of, reunite, send for, serve with a writ, subpoena, summon forth, unite
ASSOCIATED CONCEPTS: call as a witness, call for trial, called in question, called to testify, calling the docket

CALL *(Title),* **verb**   characterize, christen, classify, define, denominate, designate, determine, *dicere,* differentiate, discriminate, distinguish, entitle, give a name, identify, identify by name, individualize, label, name, *nominare,* personalize, provide with nomenclature, specify, supply with an epithet, tag, term, *vocare*

CALLING, **noun**   activity, business, career, chosen work, concern, craft, employment, endeavor, enterprise, field, function, industry, job, learned profession, lifework, line, line of achievement, line of business, line of work, livelihood, living, means of earning a living, metier, mission, *munus,* occupation, office, operation, position, post, practice, profession, pursuit, specialization, specialty, sphere of activity, task, trade, undertaking, vocation, walk of life, work
ASSOCIATED CONCEPTS: trade or calling, unlawful calling

CALLOUS, **adjective**   adamant, adamantine, brutal, *callosus,* cold, cold of heart, coldblooded, coldhearted, *durus,* hard, hard of heart, hardened, hardhearted, heartless, impassive, impenetrable, impenitent, imperturbable, impervious, implacable, inclement, indifferent, indisposed to mercy, indurate, indurated, inexcitable, inexorable, inflexible, infrangible, insensate, insensible, insensitive, insentient, intolerant, obdurate, persecuting, pitiless, relentless, remorseless, rigorous, seared, severe, shock-proof, steeled against, stubborn, tearless, thick-skinned, toughened, unbending, unblushing, uncaring, uncomforting, uncompassionate, uncondoling, unconsoling, unfeeling, unforgiving, unimpressed, unimpressible, unimpressionable, unmelting, unmerciful, unmoved, unpardoning, unpitying, unrelenting, unruffled, unstirred, unsusceptible, unsympathetic, unsympathizing, unyielding

CALUMNIOUS, **adjective**   abusive, blackening, calumniatory, castigatory, caustic, censorious, comminatory, compromising, condemnatory, contemptuous, contumelious, criminatory, *criminosus,* damaging, damnatory, decrying, defamatory, denigratory, denunciatory, deprecatory, depreciative, depreciatory, derisive, derogatory, detractory, disapproving, discreditable, disparaging, disrespectful, evil-speaking, ignoble, ignominious, imprecative, imprecatory, imputative, injurious, insinuating, insolent, insulting, libelous, maledictory, malevolent, obloquial, obloquious, offensive, opprobrious, pejorative, scandalous, scurrile, scurrilous, slanderous, slighting, smearing, stigmatizing, unflattering, vilifying, vituperative
ASSOCIATED CONCEPTS: contempt of court, defamation

CAMOUFLAGE, **verb**   adumbrate, alter the appearance of, assume a mask, be concealed, becloud, becurtain, bedim, befog, bemask, blanket, blind, bury, change the face of, cloak, close the curtain, cloud, color, conceal, couch, cover, cover up, curtain, deceive, deform, disguise, dissemble, distort, draw the veil, dress up, embellish, embroider, ensconce, enshroud, envelop, fake, gild, give a color to, give a false appearance, give a false coloring, hide, hide away, hide one's identity, keep from sight, keep from view, keep in the dark, keep in the shade, keep out of view, keep secret, make unrecognizable, mask, masquerade, miscolor, obfuscate, obscure, occultate, pervert, put in concealment, reshape, screen, screen from observation, screen from sight, se-

clude, secrete, shade, shroud, suppress, throw a veil over, twist, twist the meaning of, veil
ASSOCIATED CONCEPTS: fraudulent misrepresentation

CAMPAIGN, *noun* action, activism, activity, cause, course of action, course of conduct, course of proceeding, crusade, design, drive, effort, emprise, endeavor, enterprise, exercise, exertion, expedition, hard task, implementation, large undertaking, line of action, line of conduct, line of proceeding, maneuvering, maneuvers, measures, method, mobilization, motion, movement, operation, organization, plan, plan of offensive, plot, procedure, program, project, proposal, proposition, quest, scheme, self-imposed task, steps, *stipendium,* stratagem, strategy, struggle, tactics, task, undertaking, voluntary work, warfare
ASSOCIATED CONCEPTS: campaign committee, campaign contributions, campaign expenditures, campaign expenses, campaign funds, election campaign, political campaign

CANARD, *noun* deceit, deception, fabrication, false report, false rumor, false statement, falsehood, falsification, fiction, fraud, groundless story, hoax, lie, report intended to delude, roorback, rumor, ruse, trick, unfounded story, untruth, untruthful report

CANCEL, *verb* abolish, abort, abrogate, annihilate, annul, avoid, countermand, counterorder, counterpoise, declare invalid, declare null and void, *delere,* deny, deprive of force, discard, disclaim, discontinue, disestablish, dismiss, dissolve, drop, end, eradicate, excise, expunge, exterminate, extinguish, *inducere,* invalidate, make void, negate, not proceed with, nullify, obliterate, override, overrule, put an end to, quash, quell, quench, recall, recant, remove, render invalid, render useless, render void, renege, repeal, repudiate, rescind, restrain, retract, reverse, revoke, set aside, suspend, terminate, *tollere,* vacate, void, withdraw
ASSOCIATED CONCEPTS: cancel a contract, cancel a debt, cancel an instrument, cancel an order, obsolete, rescission, termination, void

CANCELLATION, *noun* abandoning, abandonment, abolishing, abolishment, abolition, abrogation, abscission, annulling, annulment, cassation, circumduction, countermand, counterorder, deletion, discontinuance, dismissal, dissolution, dissolving, disuse, elimination, eradication, erasure, excision, expunction, extinction, invalidating, invalidation, liquidation, moratorium, negation, nonuse, nullification, nullifying, overruling, rasure, recall, recalling, recantation, relinquishment, renunciation, repeal, repudiation, rescinding, rescindment, rescission, retracting, retraction, reversal, reversing, revocation, revokement, revoking, supersession, surrender, suspension, termination, unmaking, vacation, vacatur, voidance, voiding, waiver, withdrawal, withdrawing
ASSOCIATED CONCEPTS: abatement, cancellation of a contract, cancellation of a lease, cancellation of a mortgage, cancellation of a will, cancellation of an insurance policy, cancellation of bills, cancellation of certificate of registration, cancellation of instruments, cancellation of judgment, cancellation of notes, judicial cancellation

CANDID, *adjective* aboveboard, *apertus sincerus,* apparent, blunt, *candidus,* categorically true, creditworthy, direct, explicit, express, forthright, frank, frankhearted, honest, ingenuous, *liber,* not lying, objec-

tive, open, outright, outspoken, overt, realistic, reliable, scrupulous, *simplex,* sincere, straightforward, substantially true, true, true to scale, true to the facts, trustworthy, truthful, unconstrained, undisguised, undissembling, undistorted, uninhibited, unperfidious, unperjured, unreserved, unshaded, untreacherous, veracious, veridical, veritable, *verus*

CANDIDATE, *noun* applicant, aspirant, aspirer, *candidatus,* challenger, competitor, contender, contestant, designee, desirer, entrant, hopeful, job seeker, nominee, office hunter, office seeker, petitioner, political aspirant, political contestant, runner, seeker, struggler
ASSOCIATED CONCEPTS: candidate for election, candidate for political office, candidate for public office, judicial candidate, legislative candidate, political candidate

CANDOR *(Impartiality),* ***noun*** detachment, disinterestedness, disinterestness, dispassionateness, equitableness, equity, even-handedness, evenness, fair treatment, fairness, justness, liberality, neutrality, nonpartisanship, objectivity, probity, unbias, unprejudicedness

CANDOR *(Straightforwardness),* ***noun*** bluntness, candidness, directness, forthrightness, frankness, genuineness, guilelessness, honesty, ingenuousness, openness, outspokenness, reliability, sincerity, unaffectedness, unpretentiousness, uprightness

CANNABIS, *noun* arouser, bhang, cannabis sativa, drug, grass, hash, hashish, hemp, marijuana, narcotic, opiate, pot, weed
ASSOCIATED CONCEPTS: drug laws

CANON, *noun* act, behest, citation, code, command, commandment, criterion, decree, demand, dictate, dictation, dictum, direction, edict, established principle, fiat, fundamental principle, general rule, imperative, imposition, instruction, interdiction, law, legislation, *lex,* mandate, manifesto, *norma,* order, ordinance, precept, prescript, prescription, proclamation, pronunciamento, public announcement, *regula,* regulation, requirement, requisition, rescript, rule, rule of conduct, ruling, standard, statute, test, ultimatum, warrant, word, writ
ASSOCIATED CONCEPTS: canon law, canons of construction, canons of ethics, canons of judicial ethics, canons of justice, professional canon, rule of construction

CANVASS, *verb* *ambire,* analyze, ask, ask earnestly, audit, bring in question, carry on an inquiry, conduct an inquiry, count, delve into, dig into, discuss, dissect, examine, examine searchingly, explore, follow up an inquiry, hold an inquiry, inquire, inquire into, inspect, institute an inquiry, investigate, look about for, look into, make a survey, petition, poll, preexamine, probe, pursue an inquiry, question, report, request, research, review, scan, scrutinize, search, set up an inquiry, study, subject to examination, survey, take up an inquiry, throw open to inquiry
ASSOCIATED CONCEPTS: canvass a jury, canvass the members of a class

CAP, *noun* ceiling, greatest amount, lid, limit, maximum amount

CAP, *verb* complete, conclude, end, finish, finish off, get done, get through with, perfect, terminate

CAPABLE, *adjective*   able, accomplished, adept, adequate, adroit, *aptus,* competent, deft, effective, effectual, equal to, expert, facile, fit, fitted, gifted, *idoneus,* masterly, potent, proficient, qualified, skillful, suited, worthy
ASSOCIATED CONCEPTS: capable of assisting with one's defense, capable of contracting, capable of inheriting, capable of taking and holding property, capable to inherit, capable to marry, competence capable of distinguishing right from wrong

CAPACIOUS, *adjective*   able to contain a great deal, ample, big, broad, capable of holding much, colossal, commodious, comprehensive, deep, expanded, expansive, extended, extensive, generous, gigantic, great, huge, immense, large, massive, roomy, spacious, substantial, vast, vasty, voluminous, wide

CAPACITY *(Aptitude),* *noun*   ability, ableness, aptness, capability, capableness, competence, competency, effectuality, faculty, giftedness, potentiality, power, proficiency, qualification, range, reach, scope, skill, talent
ASSOCIATED CONCEPTS: full capacity, lack of capacity, legal capacity, lessened capacity, mental capacity, private capacity, proprietary capacity, quasi-judicial capacity, representative capacity, testamentary capacity, want of capacity
FOREIGN PHRASES: *Sola ac per se senectus donationem testamentum aut transactionem non vitiat.* Old age does not alone and of itself vitiate a will, gift, or transaction. *Furiosus stipulare non potest nec aliquid negotium agere, qui non intelligit quid agit.* An insane person who knows not what he is doing, cannot contract nor transact any business. *Furiosus nullum negotium contrahere potest.* An insane person can make no contract. *Furiosi nulla voluntas est.* A madman has no will. *Homo potest esse habilis et inhabilis diversis temporibus.* A man is capable and incapable at different times.

CAPACITY *(Authority),* *noun*   accordance, allowance, authorization, certification, charter, consent, control, dispensation, droit, enablement, jurisdiction, justification, leave, legal capacity, liberty, license, permission, permit, power, prerogative, privilege, qualification, right, sanction, sovereignty, stature, supremacy, warrant
ASSOCIATED CONCEPTS: capacity to sue

CAPACITY *(Job),* *noun*   assignment, function, occupation, position, role, situation, task

CAPACITY *(Maximum),* *noun*   ampleness, amplitude, breadth, compass, comprehensiveness, containing power, extent, full complement, full extent, full volume, fullness, greatest amount, greatest extent, greatest size, holding ability, largeness, limit, limit of endurance, limitation, measure, physical limit, plenitude, reach, room, scope, spaciousness, stretch, tankage, upper limit, volume

CAPACITY *(Sphere),* *noun*   ambit, area, arena, boundaries, bounds, division, domain, extent, field, jurisdiction, limits, orbit, pale, province, reach, realm, region, scope, specialty, stretch, territory

CAPITAL, *noun*   assets, available means, balances, bank annuities, belongings, *caput,* cash supplies, credits, economic resources, finances, financial provision, financial resources, funds, funds for investment, funds in hand, holdings, income, investment portfolio, investments, line of credit, liquid assets, money, pecuniary resources, property, ready cash, receipts, reserves, resources, revenue, savings, *sors,* working assets
ASSOCIATED CONCEPTS: authorized capital, capital account, capital assets, capital budget, capital case, capital construction, capital contribution, capital crime, capital expenditure, capital gains, capital gains tax, capital improvement, capital in a corporation, capital investment, capital loss, capital of a state, capital offense, capital outlay, capital paid-in, capital project, capital punishment, capital reserve, capital stock, capital surplus, circulating capital, distribution of capital, equity capital, fixed capital, floating capital, impairment of capital, reduction of capital, return of capital, stated capital, working capital
FOREIGN PHRASES: *Excusat aut extenuat delictum in capitalibus quod non operatur idem in civilibus.* That excuses or extenuates a wrong in capital cases which would not have the same effect in civil suits.

CAPITAL PUNISHMENT, *noun*   dealing death, death, death sentence, execution, extreme penalty, judicial murder, killing
ASSOCIATED CONCEPTS: cruel and unusual punishment

CAPITALIZE *(Provide capital),* *verb*   advance, afford aid, afford support, aid, aid with a subsidy, back, back up, bring aid, contribute, extend credit, favor, finance, fund, furnish aid, furnish foundations, furnish support, give aid, give support, help, invest, lend, lend one's aid, lend support, loan, *pecuniam mutuam dare,* pension, promote, provide capital for, provide for, provide funds for, provide money for, set up, set up in business, sponsor, subsidize, supply aid, supply support, supply with a subsidy, support, venture capital
ASSOCIATED CONCEPTS: capitalization of income, capitalization of net income, capitalization of stabalized income, capitalize earning

CAPITALIZE *(Seize the chance),* *verb*   avail oneself of, benefit, convert to use, create an opening, employ, exploit, find one's advantage in, make an opening, make the most of, make use of, manipulate, profit, put in operation, put to advantage, put to service, reap the benefit of, render useful, take advantage of, take the opportunity, turn to good account, turn to one's advantage, utilize, utilize for profit

CAPITULATION, *noun*   abandonment, acquiescence, assent, compliance, consent, docility, giving way, nonresistance, obedience, passiveness, passivity, recedence, recession, relinquishment, resignation, resignedness, self-abnegation, submission, submissiveness, submittal, surrender, unresistingness, yielding
ASSOCIATED CONCEPTS: confession, *nolo contendere,* plea of guilty

CAPRICIOUS, *adjective*   apt to change suddenly, changeable, changeful, changing, erratic, everchanging, fanciful, fantasied, fantastical, fickle, flighty, fluctuating, frivolous, giddy, *inconstans,* inconstant, irresolute, irresponsible, *levis,* mercurial, reversible, uncertain, uncontrolled, undisciplined, unmethodical, unreliable, unrestrained, unstable, unsystematic, vacillating, vagarious, variable, wavering, whimsical, without rational basis

ASSOCIATED CONCEPTS: arbitrary and capricious, arbitrary, capricious and unlawful, review of administrative determination

CAPSULE, noun abbreviation, *abrégé,* abridgment, abstract, analysis, brief, capitulation, compend, compendium, compression, condensation, conspectus, contents, digest, epitome, essence, minute, note, outline, pandect, precis, recapitulation, reduction, resumé, review, skeleton, sketch, substance, sum and substance, summary, syllabus, synopsis

CAPTION, noun annotation, banner, banner head, banner line, characterization, clause, description, designation, display line, head, heading, headline, headnote, imprint, indication of contents, inscription, legend, mark of identification, notes, preface, rubric, section head, specification, statement, subhead, subheading, subtitle, superscription, title, topic
ASSOCIATED CONCEPTS: caption of a petition, caption of a pleading, caption of indictment

CAPTIVE, noun bondman, bondsman, *captivus,* captured person, *captus,* convict, felon, helot, hostage, imprisoned person, incarcerated person, inmate, internee, one held in captivity, one held in confinement, one held in subjegation, pawn, person under arrest, prisoner, slave, subject, thrall, victim

CAPTIVITY, noun bondage, *captivitas,* commitment, committal, confinement, constraint, custody, detention, durance, duress, enslavement, entombment, immuration, immurement, impoundment, imprisonment, incarceration, internment, jail, prison, quarantine, quarantine station, restraint, slavery, subjection, subjugation, term of imprisonment
ASSOCIATED CONCEPTS: domestic animals in captivity

CAPTURE, verb apprehend, arrest, *capere,* carry away, catch, *comprehendere,* confine, hold captive, hold in captivity, immure, impress, imprison, incarcerate, jail, lock up, make an arrest, make prisoner, net, repress, restrain, restrict, seize, subdue, take by assault, take by force, take captive, take into custody, take possession of, take prisoner
ASSOCIATED CONCEPTS: capture of a criminal defendant, capture of wild animals, captured property

CARDINAL (Basic), adjective apical, basal, capital, central, chief, controlling, elemental, elementary, essential, first, foremost, fundamental, indispensable, key, main, material, necessary, overruling, pivotal, *praecipuus,* preponderant, primal, primary, prime, *primus,* principal, rudimentary, strategic, substantial, substantive, summital, underlying, undermost, uppermost, utmost, vital
ASSOCIATED CONCEPTS: cardinal rule

CARDINAL (Outstanding), adjective absolute, all-powerful, best, central, chief, commanding, controlling, crowning, dominant, eventful, excellent, finest, foremost, greatest, greatest possible, highest, incomparable, inimitable, insurmountable, key, leading, major, maximal, momentous, most important, notable, paramount, *praecipuus,* predominant, preeminent, preponderant, prevailing, prime, *primus,* second to none, supereminent, superlative, supreme, top, unequaled, unexcelled, unparalleled, unsurpassed, uppermost, utmost

CARE (Be cautious), verb be cautious, be concerned, bear in mind, beware, consider, *curare,* give heed to, guard, have regard, heed, look out for, mind, pay attention to, protect, take precautions, watch out for, watch over
ASSOCIATED CONCEPTS: care and caution, care and skill, careful, careless, degree of care, due care, extraordinary care, great care, lack of care, ordinary care, slight care, want of care

CARE (Regard), verb administer to, attend, attend to, be concerned, be concerned for, become involved, bother, *curare,* foster, mind, minister to, nurture, pay attention to, protect, serve, supervise, support, sustain, tend, watch over
ASSOCIATED CONCEPTS: care and custody, care and maintenance, custody or control

CAREER, noun activity, avocation, business, calling, chosen work, craft, *curriculum, cursus,* employment, field, job, lifework, line, livelihood, metier, occupation, office, position, post, profession, pursuit, situation, skilled occupation, specialty, trade, vocation, work

CAREFUL, adjective *accuratus,* alert, attentive, *attentus,* cautious, circumspect, concerned, *diligens,* discreet, foresighted, guarded, heedful, judicious, meticulous, mindful, on one's guard, on the alert, overcautious, painstaking, precautious, provident, prudent, regardful, scrupulous, thoughtful, unadventurous, unenterprising, vigilant, watchful, wide-awake
ASSOCIATED CONCEPTS: careful and prudent manner, caution, diligence, due care, protection, prudence, reasonable care

CARELESS, adjective casual, cursory, disregardful, forgetful, hasty, heedless, hurried, impetuous, improvident, imprudent, impulsive, inadvertent, inattentive, incautious, inconsiderate, indifferent, indiscreet, injudicious, insouciant, irresponsible, lackadaisical, lax, loose, neglectful, *neglegens,* negligent, nonchalant, oblivious, overhasty, perfunctory, pococurante, precipitant, precipitate, rash, reckless, regardless, remiss, slack, slipshod, sloppy, superficial, temerarious, thoughtless, unapprehensive, uncalculating, uncircumspect, unconcerned, unguarded, unmindful, unobservant, unthinking, unwary, wasteful
ASSOCIATED CONCEPTS: careless and imprudent manner, careless and negligent manner, grossly careless, negligence, recklessly careless, standard of care, wantonly careless

CARETAKER (One caring for property), noun archivist, attendant, *concierge,* convoy, curator, custodian, governor, guard, guardian, keeper, lookout, overseer, porter, sentry, sexton, steward, superintendent, supervisor, warden, watchman

CARETAKER (One fulfilling the function of office), noun administrator, collector, commissioner, controller, director, district officer, government servant, grand vizier, high official, key person, magistrate, manager, minister, officeholder, officer, officer in charge, officer of state, overseer, person in charge, public servant, state servant, superintendent

CARGO, noun baggage, boatload, bulk, capacity, carload, cartload, charge, commodities, consignment, contents, conveyance, freight, freightage, furnishings, goods, haul, impedimenta, lading, lading of a ship, load, luggage, merchandise, *onus,* pack, packages, payload, produce, provisions, shipload, shipment, shipping, stock, tonnage, trainload, transfer, truckload, vanload, ware, wares

ASSOCIATED CONCEPTS: carriers, delivery contract, hot cargo, risk of loss of cargo

CARICATURE, *noun*   apery, cartoon, characterization, depiction, exaggerated likeness, exaggeration, farce, graphic treatment, grotesque portrayal, grotesque rendition, hyperbole, imitation, lampoon, mimicking, mimicry, mockery, overcoloring, overdrawing, overestimation, parody, personation, portrayal, satire, travesty

CAROUSE, *verb*   be a drunkard, be convivial, be drunk, be immoderate, be intemperate, carry to excess, celebrate, *comissari,* commit a debauch, debauch, dissipate, drink, drink to excess, enervate oneself, exceed, feast, frolic, go on a spree, imbibe, indulge in dissipation, indulge oneself, lack self-control, live dissolutely, lose control, overindulge, *potare,* quaff, revel, spree, tipple, wallow

ASSOCIATED CONCEPTS: breach of peace, disorderly conduct, disturbing the peace

CARRIAGE, *noun*   affreightment, airfreight, carrying, cartage, conveyance, drayage, portage, porterage, shipment, shipping, transfer, transference, translocation, transportation, transshipment, truckage, *vehiculum*

ASSOCIATED CONCEPTS: affreightment, carriage of goods, Carriage of Goods by Sea Act

CARRIER, *noun*   conveyor, dispatcher, express shipper, ferrier, shipper, steamship company, transferor, transport company

ASSOCIATED CONCEPTS: air carriers, baggage, carrier by air, carrier engaged in interstate commerce, carrier for hire, carrier of goods, carrier of passengers, carrier's lien, common carriers, forwarding carriers, initial carriers, motor vehicle carrier, operating carriers, private carriers, public carriers, railroad carriers

CARRY *(Succeed), verb*   accomplish, achieve, attain, be victorious, bring to pass, cause to happen, complete, culminate, effect, effectuate, gain, prevail, score, succeed, triumph, win

ASSOCIATED CONCEPTS: carry a vote

CARRY *(Transport), verb*   bear, bring, cart, convey, convoy, haul, move, take, tote, transport

ASSOCIATED CONCEPTS: carry a concealed weapon, carry a weapon, carry back, carry on a business, carry on trade, carrying charges, carrying on a trade or business, carrying on any trade or business, carrying on business, larceny, take and carry away

CARRY AWAY, *verb*   abduce, abduct, capture, carry off, commandeer, convey away, drag away, expropriate, kidnap, make off with, overcome, overpower, purloin, ravish, remove, remove bodily, run off with, seize, shanghai, spirit away, steal, take away, take by assault, take by stealth, take captive, take forcibly, take prisoner, thieve, waylay

ASSOCIATED CONCEPTS: abduction, asportation, kidnapping, theft

FOREIGN PHRASES: *Cepit et asportavit.* He took and carried away.

CARTEL, *noun*   accord, accordance, affiliation, agreement, alliance, amalgamation, association, bloc, body corporate, coadjuvancy, coalition, colleagueship, combination, combine, common consent, community of interest, compact, concert, concord, concordance, concordat, concurrence, confederation, conjunction, consenus, consociation, consonancy, consort, consortium, contract, cooperation, covenant, federation, fusion, group, joint concern, league, merger, mutual understanding, organization, pact, sodality, syndicate, trust, union, unity

ASSOCIATED CONCEPTS: business cartel, international cartel

CASE *(Example), noun*   demonstration, exemplification, illustration, instance, model, occurrence, paradigm, representative, representative selection, sample, specimen, type

CASE *(Lawsuit), noun*   action, cause, claim, contention, controversy, court action, dissension, judicial contest, legal argument, legal dispute, legal issue, legal proceedings, litigation, matter, matter for judgment, proceedings, suit, suit at law

ASSOCIATED CONCEPTS: case arising under laws of the United States, case arising under the Constitution, case at common law, case in equity, case law, case of fraud, case on appeal, case or controversy, criminal case, dismissal of a case, divorce case, equity case, homicide case, injunction case, judicial case, jury case, justiciable case, law case, law of the case, leading case, meritorious case, pending case, prima facie case, sufficient case for jury, trespass on the case

FOREIGN PHRASES: *Secta est pugna civilis; sicut actores armantur actionibus, et, quasi, a ccinguntur gladiis, ita rei muniuntur exceptionibus, et defenduntur, quasi c lypeis.* A suit is a civil battle; for as the plaintiffs are armed with actions, and, as it were, girded with swords, so the defendants are fortified with pleas, and are defended, as it were, with shields. *In consimili casu, consimile debet esse remedium.* In similar cases, the remedy should be similar. *Ubi non est directa lex, standum est arbitrio judicis, vel procedendum ad similia.* Where there is no direct law, the decision of the judge is to be taken, or references to be made to similar cases. *Certa debet esse intentio, et narratio, et certum fundamentum, et certa res quae deducitur in judicium.* The intention, declaration, foundation, and matter brought to the court to be tried ought to be certain.

CASE *(Set of circumstances), noun*   affairs, arrangement, background, circumstance, condition, conjuncture, context, course of events, existing state, factors, grounds, juncture, milieu, occurrence, place, plight, point, position, posture, predicament, set of facts, setting, situation, standing, state, state of affairs, status, terms

CASH, *noun*   available means, bill, capital, coin, coin of the realm, coinage, currency, dollar currency, finances, funds, hard money, legal tender, medium of exchange, monetary unit, money, moneys, *pecunia praesens,* pecuniary resources, principal, ready money, reserve, resources, riches, specie, treasure, working assets

ASSOCIATED CONCEPTS: cash and securities, cash assets, cash bail, cash bond, cash dividend, cash down, cash method, cash on delivery, cash on hand, cash surrender value, cash value

CAST *(Register), verb*   assert, ballot, commit oneself, deposit formally, effect, establish, exercise one's choice, exercise one's options, give a vote, go to the polls, hold up one's hand, make a choice, make a decision, make a selection, make an entry, make one's choice, make one's selection, mark down, place on record, poll, put down, put on record, record, register one's vote, select, tabulate, vote
ASSOCIATED CONCEPTS: votes cast

CAST *(Throw), verb*   bestrew, catapult, *conicere,* disseminate, distribute, eject, emit, fling, force, hurl, *iactare,* impart, impel, launch, let off, *mittere,* project, propel, put into motion, radiate, send forth, send off, shed, spread, toss

CASTIGATE, *verb*   admonish, be severe, berate, call to account, *castigare,* caution, censure bitterly, chasten, chastise, chide, criticize severely, deal retributive justice, discipline, excoriate, execrate, expostulate, objurgate, rebuke, remonstrate, reprehend, reprimand, reproach, reprove, scold, take to task, upbraid, vituperate
ASSOCIATED CONCEPTS: judicial censure

CASUAL, *adjective*   aimless, apathetic, blase, causeless, cursory, designless, desultory, fortuitous, haphazard, inattentive, incidental, indeterminate, indifferent, indiscriminate, informal, insouciant, irregular, nonchalant, occasional, orderless, perfunctory, pococurante, purposeless, superficial, thoughtless, unarranged, uncertain, unconcerned, uncritical, undetermined, undirected, unexacting, unfixed, unmethodical, unmeticulous, unmindful, unordered, unorganized, unparticular, unprecise, unpunctilious, unstudied, unsystematic, unweighed
ASSOCIATED CONCEPTS: casual act, casual employment, casual transaction

CASUALTY, *noun*   accident, adversity, affliction, backset, bad fortune, blight, calamity, catastrophe, contretemps, *débâcle,* disaster, emergency, hardship, ill fortune, ill hap, incident, infliction, injury, misadventure, mischance, misfortune, mishap, serious accident, setback, tragedy, unforeseen accident, unfortunate accident, unfortunate occurence
ASSOCIATED CONCEPTS: casualty insurance, casualty loss

CASUISTRY, *noun*   behaviorism, deontology, empiricism, ethical philosophy, ethology, idealism, moral science, perfectionism, sophistry, utilitarianism

CATACHRESIS, *noun*   distortion, exaggeration, false coloring, false construction, false reading, garbling, incorrect usage, misapplication, misapprehension, miscitation, misconception, misconstruction, misexplanation, misexplication, misexposition, misinterpretation, misjudgment, misquotation, misreading, misrendering, misrepresentation, mistake, mistranslation, misunderstanding, misusage, solecism, strained sense, wrong interpretation, wrong usage

CATACLYSM, *noun*   alluvion, avalanche, convulsion, crash, debacle, deluge, disaster, disturbance, earthquake, eruption, extensive flood, flood, holocaust, inundation, overflow, overflowing, overrunning, quake, storm, temblor, tidal wave, tremor, upheaval, violent upheaval
ASSOCIATED CONCEPTS: act of God, state of emergency

CATALYST, *noun*   abettor, activator, active element, active partisan, active reformer, actuator, *agacerie, agent provocateur,* agitator, animator, catalytic agent, cause, encouragement, encourager, excitant, exciter, ferment, force, goad, impeller, impetus, impulse, incentive, incitation, incitement, inducement, inspiration, inspirer, instigator, maneuverer, modifying cause, motivating force, motivation, mover, moving spirit, planner, popular ringleader, power, prompter, *provocateur,* provocation, provocative, spur, stimulant, stimulator, strategist, suggester

CATASTROPHE, *noun*   accident, adversity, affliction, *calamitas,* calamity, cataclysm, collapse, contretemps, *débâcle,* decimation, desolation, destruction, devastation, disaster, downfall, emergency, eradication, extinction, great misfortune, hardship, havoc, holocaust, infliction, misadventure, mischance, misfortune, mishap, notable disaster, obliteration, ravage, ruin, ruination, scourge, serious calamity, tragedy
ASSOCIATED CONCEPTS: act of God, natural catastrophe, state of emergency

CATCHALL, *noun*   container, depository, holder, receiver, receptacle, repository
ASSOCIATED CONCEPTS: catchall clause to a contract

CATCHWORD, *noun*   adage, byword, catch phrase, clew, cliché, clue, colloquialism, common saying, cue word, key, maxim, mot, password, pithy saying, saying, shibboleth, slogan, stock saying, tag, vogue word, watchword
ASSOCIATED CONCEPTS: trademarks

CATEGORICAL, *adjective*   absolute, apodictic, assured, authoritative, beyond a shadow of doubt, beyond all question, clear-cut, complete, conclusive, confident, convinced, convincing, decided, decisive, definite, definitive, *definitus,* distinct, dogmatic, doubtless, emphatic, evidential, final, forceful, incontestable, incontrovertible, indisputable, indubitable, inevitable, irrefragable, irrefutable, past dispute, positive, settled, *simplex,* strong, total, ultimate, unambiguous, unassailable, unchangeable, unconditional, unconditioned, uncontested, undeniable, undisputed, unequivocal, unhesitating, unmitigated, unqualified, unquestionable, unquestioning, vehement, without a shade of doubt, without appeal, without reserve

CATHARSIS, *noun*   abreaction, acting out, deliverance, detersion, discharge of emotions, emotional release, outlet, purgation, purge, release, riddance, ventilation

CAUCUS, *noun*   assemblage, *assemblée,* assembly, *attroupement,* body of partisans, committee, conclave, concourse, conference, consultation, convention, convergence, convocation, council, council meeting, discussion, foregathering, gathering, ingathering, mass meeting, meet, meeting, meeting of political leaders, policy-fixing meeting, political confluence, *pourparler,* rally, session, subcommittee, summit, top-level meeting
ASSOCIATED CONCEPTS: congressional caucus, legislative caucus

CAUSAL, *adjective*   causative, compelling, conductive, constitutive, creative, determinant, determinative, effective, effectual, formative, generating, generative, inception, inducing, influential, institutive, instrumental, originating, originative, productive
ASSOCIATED CONCEPTS: causal connection, causal negligence, causal relationship

CAUSATIVE, *adjective*   beginning, causal, caused, constitutive, constructive, creative, determinant, directive, dominant, formative, generative, impelling, inceptive, induced, inducing, inductive, influential, inspired, institutive, original, originative, pivotal, predominant, primary, procreative, productive, responsible, stimulating

CAUSE *(Lawsuit), noun*   action, action in court, case, legal action, legal proceedings, litigation, proceedings, subject of dispute, suit, suit at law, trial
ASSOCIATED CONCEPTS: accrual of a cause of action, adversary cause, cause of action, cause pending, meritorious cause, trial of a cause

CAUSE *(Reason), noun*   agent, aim, allurement, base, basis, *causa,* causation, consideration, derivation, design, determinative, end, enticement, factor, foundation, generator, genesis, goal, ground, impulse, incitement, inducement, influence, instigation, intent, intention, mainspring, motivation, motive, object, objective, origin, prompting, purpose, rationale, root, source, spur, stimulant, stimulation, stimulus, temptation, underlying principle
ASSOCIATED CONCEPTS: accidental cause, adequate cause, cause and consequence, cause and effect, cause for removal, cause of death, cause of loss, cause of the injury, cause shown, challenge for cause, compelling cause, concurrent cause, contributing cause, controlling cause, dependent cause, direct cause, discharged for cause, dominant cause, due cause, effective cause, efficient cause, external cause, for cause, good cause, immediate cause, independent cause, initial cause, intervening cause, just cause, justifiable cause, legal cause, meritorious cause, natural cause, nature of the cause, originating cause, primary cause, probable cause, proper cause, proximate cause, reasonable cause, related concepts, remote cause, removal for cause, resulting cause, show cause, sole cause, sufficient cause, superseding intervening cause, supervening cause, unforeseen cause, without cause, without just cause

CAUSE, *verb*   be responsible, be the author of, breed, bring, bring about, bring down, bring into existence, bring on, bring to pass, *causa,* compel, conduce to, contribute to, contrive, create, cultivate, develop, direct, effect, effectuate, elicit, engender, engineer, evoke, foment, generate, give occasion for, give origin to, give rise to, inaugurate, incite, induce, influence, initiate, inspire, institute, launch, lay the foundations, lead to, make, motivate, occasion, originate, precipitate, produce, prompt, provoke, sow the seeds of, start, stimulate, superinduce
ASSOCIATED CONCEPTS: *causa causans, causa remota, causa sine qua non*
FOREIGN PHRASES: *Causa et origo est materia negotii.* The cause and its origin are the essence of a transaction. *Causa proxima non remota spectatur.* The direct and not the remote cause is regarded. *Causa vaga et incerta non est causa rationabilis.* A vague and uncer-

tain cause is not a reasonable cause. *Cessante causa, cessat effectus.* The cause ceasing, the effect ceases. *Effectus sequitur causam.* The effect follows the cause. *Eventus est qui ex causa sequitur; et dicitur eventus quia ex causis evenit.* An event is that which follows from the cause, and is called an "event" because it eventuates from causes. *Malum non habet efficientem, sed deficientem, causam.* Evil has not an efficient, but a deficient, cause. *Scire proprie est rem ratione et per causam cognoscere.* To know properly is to know a thing by its cause and its reason. *Ubi lex aliquem cogit ostendere causam, necesse est quod causa sit justa et legitima.* Where the law compels a man to show cause, it is necessary that the cause be just and legal. *Causae dotis, vitae, libertatis, fisci, sunt inter favorabilia in lege.* Causes of dower, life, liberty, revenue are among the things favored in law.

CAUSE OF ACTION, *noun*   action, action at law, basis for relief, cause, claim, claim for relief, demand, enforceable claim, ground, issue, just claim, lawful cause, legal assertion, reason for legal pursuit, reason for relief, reasonable claim, redressible wrong, right, right of action, right of recovery, right to relief
ASSOCIATED CONCEPTS: accrual of a cause of action, capacity to institute a cause of action, collateral estoppel, derivative cause of action, facts giving rise to a cause of action, facts sufficient to constitute a cause of action, inconsistent claims, joint interest in a cause of action, limitation of actions, meritorious cause of action, relief splitting a cause of action, res judicata, venue

CAUSEWAY, *noun*   acceleration lane, access road, *agger,* approach road, arterial, arterial highway, artery, avenue, by-passage, causey, concourse, crossroad, drive, driveway, express, express highway, expressway, freeway, highroad, highway, lane, motor road, motorway, parkway, paved road, paved way, post road, raised path, raised road, road, roadway, service road, side road, speed track, speedway, state highway, street, superhighway, thoroughfare, through road, thruway, trunk road, turnpike

CAUSTIC, *adjective*   abrasive, abrupt, *acerbus,* acrid, acrimonious, acute, astringent, austere, biting, brash, burning, corroding, corrosive, cruel, curt, cutting, derisive, derisory, envenomed, erosive, excoriating, excruciating, harsh, hurtful, insulting, invidious, irritating, lashing, malevolent, malicious, malignant, mocking, mordacious, *mordax,* mordent, piercing, pungent, pyrotic, rancorous, rude, scalding, severe, sharp, short, stinging, tart, tormenting, tortuous, trenchant, ungentle, unkind, venomous, virulent

CAUTION *(Vigilance), noun*   attention, attentiveness, care, carefulness, *cautio,* circumspection, concern, conscientiousness, consideration, *cura,* diligence, exactitude, exactness, forethought, guardedness, heed, heedfulness, meticulousness, mindfulness, prudence, *prudentia,* regard, thoroughness, wariness, watchfulness
ASSOCIATED CONCEPTS: due caution, ordinary caution

CAUTION *(Warning), noun*   admonition, alarm, alert, augury, caveat, exhortation, foreboding, foretelling, forewarning, monition, notice, omen, portent, precursor, prefiguration, presage, prognosis, prognostic
ASSOCIATED CONCEPTS: cautionary instructions

CAUTION, *verb*　admonish, advise against, apprise, be vigilant, communicate to, counsel, dissuade, exhort, exhort to take heed, forearm, foreshow, forewarn, give advice, give fair warning, give intimation of impending evil, give notice, give warning, give warning of possible harm, inform, make aware, *monere,* notify of danger, persuade against, precaution, predict, prenotify, prepare for the worst, prescribe, presignify, prewarn, put on guard, remonstrate, serve notice, sound the alarm, spell danger, take precautions, urge, warn
ASSOCIATED CONCEPTS: due caution, ordinary caution, unusual caution
FOREIGN PHRASES: *Abundans cautela non nocet.* Extreme caution does no harm.

CAVEAT, *noun*　admonishment, admonition, advance notice, advisement, alert, announcement, augury, bodement, caution, communication, direction, foretoken, forewarning, implication, indication, instruction, lesson, monition, notice, notification, order, portendance, portendment, portention, prefiguration, premonition, prewarning, telling, warning, warning sign
ASSOCIATED CONCEPTS: caveat emptor, caveat venditor

CAVEAT EMPTOR, *noun*　at one's own risk, purchase without a guaranty, purchase without a warranty, purchased at one's risk, unassured purchase, uncovenanted purchase, unendorsed purchase, unguaranteed purchase, unwarranted purchase

CAVIL, *verb*　attack, belittle, *calumniari,* carp, *carpere,* censure frivolously, complain frivolously, condemn, criticize frivolously, decry, denigrate, denounce, deprecate, deride, disapprove, discredit, disparage frivolously, faultfind, find fault with, haggle, object frivolously, protest frivolously, raise frivolous objection to, raise objections frivolously, raise specious objection to, reprehend, ridicule irresponsibly, upbraid, *vellicare*

CEASE, *verb*　abate, abrogate, abstain from, adjourn, annul, arrest, be all over, be at an end, be silent, become void, bring to an end, cancel, cause to halt, check, close, come to a close, come to a standstill, come to an end, conclude, consummate, culminate, *desinere,* desist, *desistere,* discontinue, draw to a close, drop, end, expire, extinguish, finish, forbear, get through, give over, halt, hold off, intermit, interrupt, lapse, leave off, make an end of, pause, put a stop to, put an end to, quell, quit, refrain, relinquish, remain, run its course, stanch, stay, stem, stop, stop work, surcease, suspend, terminate, vacate, withdraw
ASSOCIATED CONCEPTS: cease and desist order, cease doing business, cease from occupying, cease to act, cease to do business
FOREIGN PHRASES: *Cessante causa, cessat effectus.* When the cause ceases, the effect ceases. *Cessante ratione legis, cessat et ipsa lex.* The reason of the law ceasing, the law itself also ceases.

CEDE, *verb*　abalienate, abandon, abdicate, abjure, accede, alienate, assign, bequeath, concede, *concedere,* confer, consign, convey, deed, deliver, devolve, dismiss, donate, give, give away, give up, give up claim to, grant, part with, quitclaim, release, relinquish, remise, render, renounce, renounce claim to, resign, sign away, submit, succumb, surrender, tender, transfer, transmit, turn over, vouchsafe, yield

ASSOCIATED CONCEPTS: cede jurisdiction, cede territory

CEILING, *noun*　acme, altitude, apex, apogee, climax, culmination, extreme, extremity, farthest point, height, highest degree, highest point, limit, maximum, optimum, peak, pinnacle, record, roof, summit, *tectum,* top, ultimate, utmost, utmost extent, utmost height, uttermost, vertex, zenith
ASSOCIATED CONCEPTS: maximum income ceiling, maximum rent ceiling

CELL, *noun*　cage, *cella,* chamber, compartment, confined room, confinement, cubicle, *cubiculum,* enclosed cage, incarceration, jail, jailhouse, penitentiary, pound, prison, prison house, small cavity, small room, solitary abode

CEMENT, *verb*　accouple, adhere, affix, agglomerate, agglutinate, amalgamate, annex, attach, bind, braze, coagulate, coalesce, cohere, combine, concrete, congeal, *conglutinare,* conglutinate, conjoin, connect, consolidate, couple, crystallize, fasten, fix, fix together, fuse, glue, harden, hold together, incorporate, join, make firm, merge, mortar, put together, secure, set, solder, solidify, stick, unite, weld

CENSOR, *verb*　ban, bar, blot out, bowdlerize, cancel, *censor,* control, control the flow of news, cut, delete, disallow, disapprove, discountenance, dispense with, disqualify, eject, eliminate, enforce censorship, eradicate, erase, exclude, expunge, expurgate, forbid, impose a ban, inhibit, interfere, judge, keep within bounds, leave out, limit, not include, omit, oversee, pass under review, police, preclude, prevent, prevent publication, prohibit, proscribe, quash, refuse, refuse permission, reject, restrain, restrict, review, rub out, scratch out, sift, submerge, supervise communications, suppress, withhold permission
ASSOCIATED CONCEPTS: censorship, Federal Communications Act

CENSORSHIP, *noun*　abolition, abridgment, bar, blackout, block, blockage, blue-penciling, bowdlerization, cancellation, control, curb, deprivation, elimination, expurgation, forbidding, governmental control, hindrance, impediment, imposition of veil of secrecy, inhibition, limitation, news blackout, obliteration, prohibition, repression, restraint, restriction, rigid control, seal of secrecy, stifling, suppression
ASSOCIATED CONCEPTS: censorship of books, censorship of films, censorship of First Amendment rights, censorship of mail, censorship of the theatre

CENSURE, *verb*　administer a rebuke, admonish, animadvert upon, assail, attack, berate, blame, bring into discredit, cast a reproach, cast a slur upon, cast blame upon, cast reflection upon, castigate, chastise, chide, condemn, declaim against, decry, denigrate, denounce, denunciate, deprecate, depreciate, descant, disapprove, disparage, dispraise, exclaim against, excoriate, execrate, expostulate, expurgate, find fault with, *fronder,* fulminate against, hold up to execration, hold up to reprobation, impugn, inveigh against, not speak well of, objurgate, raise a hue and cry against, rebuff, rebuke, recriminate, remonstrate, reprehend, *reprehendere,* reprimand, reproach, reprobate, reprove, speak ill of, upbraid, view with disfavor, vilipend, *vituperare*

ASSOCIATED CONCEPTS: censure for improper conduct, censure for prejudicial conduct, letter of admonition, reprimand

CENSUS, *noun* account, calculation, *census,* ciphering, computation, count, counting, demography, enumeration, evaluation, figure-work, figures, figuring, list, listing, measurement, numbering, numeration, official count, official enumeration of inhabitants, official enumeration of the population, official reckoning, official registration, poll, reckoning, recount, registering, registration, score, statement, statistical inquiry, statistics, supputation, tables, tabulation, tally, valuation, vital statistics
ASSOCIATED CONCEPTS: federal census, representation based upon the last census

CENTER *(Central position),* *noun* axis, center of gravity, central point, convergence, converging point, core, epicenter, equidistance, eye, focal point, focus, focus of attention, fulcrum, half distance, halfway, *media pars, medius,* middle, middle distance, middle point, middle position, midmost point, midpoint, midst, point of convergence
ASSOCIATED CONCEPTS: center lane, center line, center of gravity, grouping of contacts doctrine

CENTER *(Essence),* *noun* base, basis, bedrock, cardinal point, central nature, chief part, constitutive principle, core, essential part, gist, gravamen, heart, hypostasis, important part, inmost nature, inmost substance, inner reality, main part, main point, nature, nucleus, pith, primary element, prime constituent, prime ingredient, principal part, quid, quiddity, quintessence, *sine qua non,* soul, substance, sum and substance, vital element, vital part

CENTRAL *(Essential),* *adjective* basal, basic, capital, cardinal, chief, crucial, dominant, elemental, first, foremost, foundational, fundamental, highly important, indispensable, intrinsic, intrinsical, key, main, major, necessary, paramount, pivotal, primal, primary, principal, requisite, ruling, significant, supreme, underlying, vital

CENTRAL *(Situated near center),* *adjective* center, centermost, centric, centrical, equidistant, focal, halfway, inmost, inner, medial, median, mesial, middle, middlemost, midmost
ASSOCIATED CONCEPTS: central board of appeals, central filing, centralization center of gravity doctrine

CENTRALIZATION, *noun* absorption, aggregation, alliance, amalgamation, amassing, assembling, association, bringing together, centering, centralism, coalescence, coalescing, coalition, combination, compacting, compilation, compression, concentralization, concentration, condensation, conglomeration, congregation, consolidation, convergence, converging, coordinate, focalization, fusion, gathering together, grouping, incorporation, massing, merging, narrowing, nucleation, organization, synthesis, systematization, unification, union, unity
ASSOCIATED CONCEPTS: centralization of administration, centralization of government, decentralization

CEREMONY, *noun* *caerimonia,* celebration, commemoration, conventionality, festive occasion, festivity, formal occasion, formality, memorialization, observance, official reception, prescribed procedure, reception, rite, ritual, *ritus,* solemn observance, solemnity, solemnization, state occasion
ASSOCIATED CONCEPTS: ceremonial marriage, marriage ceremonies, testimentary ceremonies

CERTAIN *(Fixed),* *adjective* absolute, assured, attested, certified, changeless, conclusive, confident, confirmed, decided, decisive, definite, determinate, determined, firm, guaranteed, incontestable, incontrovertible, indisputable, indubitable, inescapable, inevitable, infallible, irrefragable, irrefutable, official, positive, reliable, settled, stable, static, sure, unambiguous, unanswerable, unappealable, unavoidable, unchanging, undeniable, undisputed, unerring, unfailing, unmistakable, unpreventable, unquestionable, unquestioned
ASSOCIATED CONCEPTS: absolutely certain, capable of being rendered certain, certain powers and privileges, sum certain

CERTAIN *(Particular),* *adjective* *certus,* distinct, especial, exact, exclusive, individual, marked, peculiar, precise, singular, special, specific, specified, unique

CERTAIN *(Positive),* *adjective* absolute, actual, ascertained, assertive, assured, attested, authoritative, avoidless, axiomatic, beyond a shadow of doubt, beyond all dispute, beyond all question, capable of proof, certified, *certus,* changeless, clear, clear-cut, clearly known, cognizant, conclusive, concrete, confident, consistent, convinced, correct, credulous, decided, decisive, definite, demonstrable, demonstrated, dependable, distinct, doubtless, ensured, established, evident, evidential, existing, factual, final, fully convinced, guaranteed, inalterable, inappealable, incommutable, incontestable, incontrovertible, inconvertible, indefeasible, indestructible, indisputable, indubitable, inerrant, inescapable, inevitable, inexorable, inextinguishable, infallible, inflexible, invariable, inviolate, invulnerable, irreducible, irrefragable, irrefutable, irresistible, irresoluble, irreversible, irrevocable, knowing, past dispute, persuaded, questionless, real, reliable, right, satisfied, secure, self-evident, settled, stated, sure, tangible, true to the facts, unaltered, unambiguous, unassailable, unavoidable, unchangeable, unconfuted, undeniable, undeviating, undisputed, undoubted, undoubtful, undoubting, unequivocal, unerring, unfailing, unhesitating, unimpeachable, unmistakable, unqualified, unquestionable, unquestioned, unrefuted, unshakable, unsusceptible of change, unvarying, unwavering, valid, veracious, verifiable, void of suspicion
ASSOCIATED CONCEPTS: capable of being rendered certain

CERTAIN *(Specific),* *adjective* appropriate, ascertained, assigned, bounded, categorical, characteristic, choice, circumscribed, clear-cut, clearly defined, clearly stated, concrete, definite, designated, determinate, distinct, distinguished, esoteric, especial, exact, exclusive, explicit, express, expressed, fixed, individual, limited, marked, noteworthy, particular, peculiar, precise, prescribed, *quidam,* respective, restricted, select, settled, singular, special, specified, stated, well-defined

CERTAINTY, *noun* absence of doubt, absolute confidence, absoluteness, assurance, assuredness, authoritativeness, certification, certitude, *certus,* complete conviction, conclusiveness, confidentness, conviction, corroboration, definiteness, firmness, firmness of belief, inability to doubt, incontestability, incontrovertibility, indisputability, indubitability, indubitableness, inerrability, inerrancy, inexorability, infallibility, irrefragability, irrefutability, knowledge, objective certitude, positiveness, quality of being certain, questionlessness, reassurance, reliability, secureness, security, solidity, soundness, stability, substantiality, sure presumption, sureness, surety, unconfutability, undeniability, unequivocalness, unimpeachability, unmistakability, unqualification, unquestionability, unquestionableness, verification, warranty

ASSOCIATED CONCEPTS: absolute certainty, certainty to a common intent, moral certainty, proof to a reasonable certainty, reasonable certainty

FOREIGN PHRASES: *Certum est quod certum reddi potest.* That is certain which is capable of being rendered certain. *Terminus annorum certus debet esse et determinatus.* A term of years ought to be certain and determinate.

CERTIFICATE, *noun* affidavit, attestation, authentication, authorization, certification, charter, covenant, credentials, declaration, endorsement, guarantee, instrument, license, matter of record, muniment, official writing, paper, testament, voucher, warrant, writ, written contract, written evidence

ASSOCIATED CONCEPTS: allotment certificate, certificate of authority, certificate of deposit, certificate of incorporation, certificate of indebtedness, certificate of occupancy, certificate of probable cause, certificate of public convenience and necessity, certificate of reasonable doubt, certificate of stock, certificate under seal, death certificate, demand certificate, land certificate, marriage certificate

CERTIFICATION (*Attested copy*), *noun* affirmation, assurance, attestation, attesting declaration, authenticated confirmation, authentification, authoritative attestation, avouchment, confirmation, corroboration, declaration, documentary evidence, documentation, endorsement, evidence, instrument of proof, legal pledge, proof, ratification, reassurance, reassurement, solemn declaration, statement, substantiation, support, swearing, sworn evidence, testification, testimony, validation, verification, written evidence

ASSOCIATED CONCEPTS: audited and paid, certification of loss reserves, certification of stock, certified, certified according to law, certified check, false certification, fraudulent certification

CERTIFICATION (*Certainness*), *noun* absolute certainty, absolute confidence, ascertained fact, ascertainment, assurance, assuredness, authoritativeness, certain knowledge, certainty, certitude, complete conviction, conclusive proof, conclusiveness, confidence, conviction, dependability, freedom from error, incontestability, incontrovertibility, indisputability, indubitability, indubitable fact, inerrancy, inevitableness, infallibility, irrefragability, irrefutability, knowledge, matter of fact, objective certainty, positive fact, positiveness, proof, reliability, reliableness, rigorous proof, sureness, trustworthiness, unambiguity, unimpeachability, unquestionability, unquestionableness, utter reliability

CERTIFICATION (*Certification of proficiency*), *noun* affirmance, authority, authorization, citation, confirmation, copy, credential, credentials, declaration, docu-

mentation, entitlement, indorsement, letter of recognition, license, recognition

ASSOCIATED CONCEPTS: certification to practice law

CERTIFY (*Approve*), *verb* accede to, accept, accord, accord one's approval, accredit, acknowledge, admit, agree, agree to, allow, assent, assent to, authorize, charter, coincide, concur, concur in, confirm, confirm officially, consent, countenance, empower, endorse, entitle, establish, give assent, give clearance, give consent, give permission, indorse, legalize, license, make valid, permit, pronounce legal, ratify, sanction, uphold, validate, yield assent

CERTIFY (*Attest*), *verb* acknowledge, advance, advocate, affirm, affirm explicitly, affirm in an official capacity, allege, assert, assert formally, assert oneself, assert positively, assert under oath, asseverate, assure, attest, authenticate, aver, avouch, avow, be sworn, bear out, bear witness, bear witness to, bring forward, claim, confess, confirm, confirm as correct, *confirmare*, convenant, corroborate, countersign, declare the truth of, declare to be true, deliver as one's act and deed, depone, depose, document, endorse, ensure, evidence, evince, execute, fortify, give a guarantee, give one's word, guarantee, guaranty, insist, insure, issue a statement, make absolute, make certain, make one's oath, make sure, proclaim, pronounce, ratify, reaffirm, reassure, reinsure, set one's hand and seal to, solemnly affirm, state emphatically, state with conviction, stress, sustain, swear, swear an affidavit, take one's oath, testify, utter with conviction, validate, verify, vouch, vouch for, vouch for as genuine, warrant

ASSOCIATED CONCEPTS: certification of pleadings

CERTIORARI, *noun* appeal to a higher court, application for retrial, course of law, legal procedure, legal process

CERTITUDE, *noun* absolute certainty, absoluteness, ascertained fact, assurance, assuredness, attestation, certainness, certainty, certainty of meaning, conclusiveness, confidence, confidentness, conviction, dead certainty, definiteness, freedom from error, incontestability, incontrovertibility, indisputability, indubitability, indubitable fact, indubitableness, inerrability, inerrancy, inevitableness, inexorability, infallibilism, infallibility, infallibleness, irrefragability, irrefutability, irrevocability, moral certainty, objective certainty, positiveness, sure assumption, sure presumption, sureness, surety, unambiguity, undeniability, unequivocalness, unimpeachability, unquestionableness

ASSOCIATED CONCEPTS: proof beyond a reasonable doubt

CESSATION (*Interlude*), *noun* abeyance, adjournment, armistice, arrest, break, ceasing, cloture, delay, desistance, discontinuance, discontinuation, dormancy, *embolium*, halt, hiatus, inaction, inactivity, interim, intermediate time, *intermissio*, intermission, interregnum, interruption, interval, intervening episode, intervening period, intervening space, intervening time, lapse, latency, lull, moratorium, pause, pendency, postponement, procrastination, quiescence, remission, respite, rest, standstill, stay, stop, suspension, temporary inaction, truce, wait

CESSATION *(Termination), noun* abandonment, climax, close, closing, closure, completion, conclusion, consummation, curtain, *dénouement,* determination, dissolution, end, ending, expiration, finale, *finis,* finish, fulfillment, *intermissio,* issue, outcome, realization, retirement, stoppage, surcease, terminus
ASSOCIATED CONCEPTS: cessation of business, cessation of hostilities, cessation of occupation, cessation of possession, cessation of work

CESSION, *noun* abalienation, allowance, assignment, award, bestowal, concession, conveyance, delivery, disposal, disposition, donation, gift, giving up, giving up claim to, grant, handing over, nonretention, parting with, presentation, release, relinquishing claim to, relinquishment, resignation, submittal, surrender, transfer, waiver, yielding

CHAIN *(Nexus), noun* act of coming together, act of coupling, act of joining, act of uniting, affiliation, affinity, alliance, association, attachment, attraction, bond, bond of union, bridge, conjunction, connectedness, connecting link, connecting medium, connection, correlation, interconnection, intermedium, interrelation, junction, kinship, liaison, ligament, ligature, link, linkage, privity, relatedness, relation, relationship, relativity, tie, union

CHAIN *(Series), noun* array, *catena,* catenation, classification, concatenation, connected series, consecution, constant flow, continuity, cordon, gradation, line, links, order, procession, progression, range, round, row, run, scale, sequence, *series,* set, succession, suit, suite, train, unbroken line, *vinculum*
ASSOCIATED CONCEPTS: chain of causation, chain of circumstances, chain of custody, chain of title

CHAIRMAN, *noun* chair, conductor, director, head, headman, key man, leader, master of ceremonies, moderator, monitor, overseer, person in authority, presider, presiding officer, principal, *qui conventui praeest,* speaker, supervisor, symposiarch
ASSOCIATED CONCEPTS: chairman of a committee, chairman of the board of directors

CHALLENGE, *verb* *ad pugnam provocare,* affront, appeal, argue, bid defiance to, call out, call to answer, combat an opinion, confront, confute, contradict, controvert, cry out against, debate, defy, denounce, differ, disagree, disapprove, dispute, dissent, enter a protest, hurl defiance at, invite competition, invite to contest, menace, negate, negative, object to, oppose, protest, quarrel, query, question, raise a question, raise objections, raise one's voice against, reject, remonstrate, repudiate, resist, say no, show reluctance, stand up against, take exception to, threaten, wrangle
ASSOCIATED CONCEPTS: challenge for cause, challenge jurisdiction, challenge of ownership, challenge to a finding of a lower court, challenge to a Grand Jury's composition, challenge to sufficiency of pleading, challenge to the array, challenge to the panel, challenge to the venire, preemptory challenge

CHAMBER *(Body), noun* aggregation, *assemblée,* assembly, bench, bench of judges, board, body of judges, cabinet, caucus, collocation, committee, confederacy, confederation, conflux, congress, constituency, convocation, council, court, federation, forum, gathering, group, ingathering, institute, judicial branch, judicial department, judicatory, law-making body, lawmakers, league, legislative body, legislature, mass, meeting, members of the bar, organization, panel, panel of judges, parliament, plenum, representatives, session, society, tribunal, union
ASSOCIATED CONCEPTS: chamber of commerce

CHAMBER *(Compartment), noun* alcove, antechamber, anteroom, apartment, box, camera, cell, *chambre,* closet, court, cubicle, *cubiculum,* den, division, enclosure, hall, hold, hollow, hollow place, lodging, meeting hall, office, parlor, *pars interior,* partitioned space, reception room, retreat, room, *salle,* section, separate part, sitting room, stall, stateroom, *thalamus*
ASSOCIATED CONCEPTS: chambers of the court, judicial chambers, legislative chambers

CHANCE *(Fortuity), noun* advantage, befalling, *casus,* circumstance, event, favorable time, fortuitousness, good fortune, happening, occasion, opening, suitable circumstance, time
ASSOCIATED CONCEPTS: arise by chance, last clear chance

CHANCE *(Possibility), noun* aptitude, attainability, bare possibility, conceivability, conceivableness, contingency, favorable prospect, hope, imaginability, indeterminacy, indeterminateness, liability, likelihood, possibleness, potential, potentiality, probability, prospect, *spes,* uncertainty, unexpectedness, unpredictability
ASSOCIATED CONCEPTS: chance verdict, games of chance
FOREIGN PHRASES: *Casus fortuitus non est supponendus.* A chance happening is not to be presumed. *Casus fortuitus non est sperandus, et nemo tenetur devinare.* A chance happening is not to be expected, and no one is bound to foresee it.

CHANGE, *verb* adapt, adjust, alter, be converted, be inconstant, be irresolute, convert, *convertere in,* deviate, displace, diverge, evolve, exchange, fluctuate, give in exchange, go through phases, *immutare,* innovate, interchange, make a transition, make different, make over, metamorphose, modify, modulate, permute, put in the place of, recast, recondition, reconstruct, reform, regenerate, remake, reorganize, replace, resolve into, restyle, revise, revive, revolutionize, show phases, subrogate, substitute, switch, switch around, transfigure, transform, transmogrify, transmute, transubstantiate, turn from, turn into, variegate, vary
ASSOCIATED CONCEPTS: additions and alterations, change in circumstances, change in conditions, change in occupancy, change in ownership, change in title, change of address, change of beneficiary, change of domicile, change of duties, change of name, change of ownership, change of parties, change of position, change of possession, change of venue, immaterial change, major change, minor change, permanent change, proposed change

CHAPTER *(Branch), noun* affiliate, associate, branch member, branch office, bureau, component, department, division, local, local office, lodge, member, office, organ, section, subdivision, subsidiary

CHAPTER *(Division), noun* article, *caput,* clause, column, component, fragment, head, heading, paragraph, part, partition, passage, phrase, portion, section, sector, segment, separate part, subdivision, subgroup **ASSOCIATED CONCEPTS:** chapter 10 reorganization, paragraphs, sections

CHARACTER *(An individual),* **noun** being, body, figure, human, human being, man, mortal, party, person, personage, personality, self-determined being, somebody, someone

CHARACTER *(Personal quality),* **noun** *animus,* aspects, attribute, bent, characteristic mood, constitution, description, disposition, dominant quality, essence, essential part, essential quality of one's nature, essentialness, ethos, features, fiber, frame of mind, grain, inclination, individualism, individuality, *ingenium,* inherited characteristics, inner nature, intellect, intrinsicality, intrinsicalness, kind, leaning, makeup, manner, marked traits, mental and spiritual makeup, mettle, mold, moral qualities, *mores, natura,* natural turn of mind, nature, peculiarity, personal traits, personality, predilection, prime ingredients, proclivity, proneness, propension, propensity, *proprietas,* psychological habits, qualities, quiddity, quintessence, slant, striking qualities, style, substantiality, susceptibility, temper, temperament, tendency, tone, trait

CHARACTER *(Reputation),* **noun** celebrity, credit, deference, distinction, eminence, esteem, estimation, *existimatio, fama,* fame, grandeur, high reward, honor, *locus standi,* name, nobility, notability, notice, notoriety, notoriousness, *opinio,* place, popular favor, popularity, position, position in society, preeminence, prestige, prominence, public esteem, publicly recognized standing, recognition, regard, renown, reputableness, repute, respect, respectability, standing, station, status **ASSOCIATED CONCEPTS:** character evidence, character witness

CHARACTERISTIC, *noun* aspect, attribute, cast, constitution, differentia, differential, distinction, distinctive feature, distinguishing trait, essence, essential part, feature, humor, idiocrasy, idiosyncrasy, immanence, inclination, individuality, inherence, inhersion, leaning, liability, makeup, mannerism, marked feature, marked quality, nature, particularity, peculiar idiom, peculiarity, penchant, personal equation, point of difference, predilection, proclivity, proneness, propensity, property, *proprietas,* quality, quintessence, speciality, specialty, specific quality, tendency, trait, type, uniqueness **ASSOCIATED CONCEPTS:** characteristic of and peculiar to business of an employer, characteristic of work performed by an employee

CHARACTERIZE, *verb* classify, construe, delineate, depict, descend to particulars, describe, *designare,* detail, diagram, differentiate, distinguish, draw, elucidate, exemplify, express precisely, formalize, give an account of, give precise meaning to, give the details of, identify, illustrate, individualize, individuate, interpret, make apparent, make clear, make vivid, mark, mark off, *notare,* outline, personify, picture, portray, profile, reflect, render precise, represent, set apart, set forth the character of, specify, specify the peculiarities of

CHARGE *(Accusation),* **noun** *accusatio,* allegation, arraignment, attack, blame, castigation, censure, citation, complaint, condemnation, count, countercharge, *crimen,* crimination, delation, denouncement, denunciation, disapprobation, formal complaint, impeachment, imputation, incrimination, inculpation, indictment, information, insinuation, objurgation, plaint, presentment, recrimination, reproach, reproof, summons **ASSOCIATED CONCEPTS:** charge of a crime, charges of misconduct, criminal charge, indictment, offense charged, specifically charged

CHARGE *(Command),* **noun** call, commandment, commission, dictate, direction, imperative, imposition, injunction, instruction, mandate, *mandatum,* order, precept, proclamation, request, requirement, requisition, subpoena, summons, ultimatum, writ **ASSOCIATED CONCEPTS:** charge with responsibility

CHARGE *(Cost),* **noun** assessment, debit, disbursement, due, dues, exaction, exactment, expenditure, expense, fee, obligation, outlay, payment, pecuniary burden, *pretium,* price, quotation, rate, rent, tax, toll, valuation, value, worth **ASSOCIATED CONCEPTS:** charge against an estate, charge-off, chargeback, charging lien, deferred charges, minimum charge

CHARGE *(Custody),* **noun** administration, auspices, care, chaperonage, concern, control, *curare, custodia,* entrusted cause, entrusted object, guardianship, guidance, jurisdiction, keeping, object of responsibility, patronage, protection, safekeeping, superintendence, supervision, trust, trusteeship, *tutela,* tutelage, ward, wardship, watch

CHARGE *(Lien),* **noun** accountability, bond, burden, claim on property, commitment, debenture, duty, encumbrance, guarantee, guaranty, hold on property, hypothecation, indebtedness, liability, obligation, pecuniary burden, *pignus judiciale,* pledge, real security, right to dispose of property, security, security on property, tie, *vadium mortuum, vadium vivum* **ASSOCIATED CONCEPTS:** charging lien, incumbrance

CHARGE *(Responsibility),* **noun** accountability, accountableness, allegiance, appointment, assignment, burden, commitment, engagement, function, imperative duty, inescapable duty, mission, obligation, one's duty, responsibleness, sense of duty, task, undertaking **ASSOCIATED CONCEPTS:** public charge

CHARGE *(Statement to the jury),* **noun** address to the jury, adjuration, admonition, advice, declamation, definitions on the law, details on the law, direction, discourse, disquisition, exhortation, guidance, instructions, lecture, legal instructions **ASSOCIATED CONCEPTS:** charge to the jury

CHARGE *(Accuse),* **verb** *accusare, arguere,* arraign, attack, blame, bring accusation, censure, challenge, cite, complain against, condemn, criminate, denounce, denunciate, expostulate, file a claim, hold responsible, impute, incriminate, inculpate, indict, issue a writ, lay responsibility upon, lodge a complaint, put the blame on, recriminate, reprehend, stigmatize **ASSOCIATED CONCEPTS:** charged with crime

CHARGE *(Assess), verb* appraise, assess a tax upon, assess pro rata, assign, assign one's share to, bill, compute, demand payment, dun, estimate, exact, fix a charge, fix the price at, give a final notice, impose, incur a debt, invoice, lay a duty upon, levy, make claims upon, present an ultimatum, present one's claim, pricing, prorate, rate, send a final demand, tax, value

CHARGE *(Empower), verb* appoint, assign, authorize, authorize formally, commission, confer power on, delegate, delegate authority to, deputize, emper, enable, endow, endow the power, engage, entrust, give authority to, give power to, grant, invest the power, invest with authoritative power, make able, mission, nominate, permit, put in care of, warrant

CHARGE *(Instruct on the law), verb* admonish, advise, caution, counsel, detail the law, direct, exhort, give advice, give suggestions to, guide, inform, instruct, offer counsel, point out, prepare, prescribe the law, press advice on, propose legal instructions, recommend points of law, suggest, suggest conclusions of law, urge
ASSOCIATED CONCEPTS: charging a jury

CHARITABLE *(Benevolent), adjective* almsgiving, altruistic, beneficent, *beneficus, benignus,* bounteous, eleemosynary, freehanded, generous, giving, gracious, greathearted, liberal, magnanimous, munificent, openhanded, philanthropic, princely, unselfish, unsparing, unstinting

CHARITABLE *(Lenient), adjective* accommodating, acquiescent, beneficent, benevolent, benign, benignant, clement, compliant, condoning, considerate, empathetic, exorable, forbearing, forgiving, free from vindictiveness, gracious, helpful, humane, humanitarian, kind, kindhearted, liberal, *liberalis,* merciful, obliging, patient, permitting, sensitive, soft, softhearted, sympathetic, sympathizing, temperate, tolerant, understanding, warm, yielding

CHARITY, *noun* active giving, aid, almsgiving, altruism, assistance, backing, benefaction, *beneficentia,* benevolence, benevolentness, bestowal, bounteousness, bountifulness, clemency, considerateness, consideration, contribution, donation, dotation, endowment, generosity, generous giving, gift, good will, grace, grant, help, hospitality, humaneness, humanitarianism, humanity, kindness, *liberalitas,* liberalness, magnanimity, munificence, patronage, philanthropic gift, philanthropy, relief, support, unselfishness, willing help
ASSOCIATED CONCEPTS: charitable and benevolent institution, charitable association, charitable bequest, charitable contributions, charitable corporation, charitable enterprise, charitable gift, charitable institution, charitable organization, charitable purposes, charitable trusts, charitable use

CHARTER *(Declaration of rights), noun* announcement, constitution, decree, official announcement, proclamation, promulgation, pronouncement, public announcement, public statement, publication, writing
ASSOCIATED CONCEPTS: amendment of a charter, amendment to a charter, articles of incorporation, charter of a foreign corporation, charter of a municipal corporation, charter of an association, corporate charter, county charter, municipal charter, partnership charter, reform a charter, repeal of a charter, special charter, state charter

CHARTER *(License), noun* authority, certificate, certificate of permission, dispensation, express permission, grant, imprimatur, instrument, muniment, official document, patent, permit, written permission
ASSOCIATED CONCEPTS: chartered bank, chartered by law, expiration of a charter, renewal of a charter

CHARTER *(Sanction), noun* acceptance, acknowledgment, acquiescence, admission, allowance, approval, assent, authority, authorization, concurrence, confirmation, consent, countenance, delegation, empowerment, endorsement, enfranchisement, entitlement, franchise, grant, leave, liberty, license, permission, permit, pragmatic sanction, privilege, ratification, recognition, sufferance, support, tolerance, toleration, vested right
ASSOCIATED CONCEPTS: chartered by the law

CHASE, *verb* endeavor to overtake, follow, go after, go in pursuit of, go in quest of, hunt, pursue, run after, run in pursuit, search, seek, track, trail, try to overtake

CHATTEL, *noun* asset, belonging, commodity, effect, equipment, fortune, holding, movable article of property, movables, personal effect, personalty, possession, property, resource, trapping, valuable
ASSOCIATED CONCEPTS: action to recover a chattel, chattel interest, chattel mortgage, chattel trust, chattels real, conveyance of a chattel, household chattels, lien upon a chattel, personal chattels, personal property
FOREIGN PHRASES: *Catalla juste possessa amitti non possunt.* Chattels justly possessed cannot be lost. *Catalla reputantur inter minima in lege.* Chattels are considered in law of lesser importance.

CHEAT, *verb* act dishonestly, be cunning, be dishonest, befool, beguile, betray, break faith, commit breach of trust, cozen, deceive, defalcate, defraud, deprive of dishonestly, dissemble, dupe, embezzle, *fraudare,* ignore ethics, inveigle, lack honesty, obtain money by false pretenses, peculate, pettifog, play false, practice chicanery, practice fraud, prevaricate, purloin, represent falsely, sharp, swindle
ASSOCIATED CONCEPTS: cheating by false weights and measures, false pretenses, larceny

CHECK *(Bar), noun* abeyance, arrest, barricade, barrier, block, blockage, cessation, checkmate, control, curb, damper, deadlock, deadstop, delay, detainment, detention, disruption, drawback, embargo, estoppel, foil, frustration, full stop, halt, hindrance, impediment, *impedimentum,* impedition, injunction, interference, interruption, limitation, *mora,* obstacle, obstruction, opposition, preclusion, prohibition, proscription, rebuff, regulation, rejection, restraint, restriction, retardation, retardment, standstill, stop, stoppage, stopper, suspension, trammel

CHECK *(Instrument), noun* bank paper, banknote, bill, bill of exchange, certificate, commercial instrument, commercial paper, debenture, draft, fiduciary currency, money order, negotiable paper, note, order on a bank, paper money, security, sight draft, treasury note
ASSOCIATED CONCEPTS: acceptance of a check, altered check, bad check, bank check, bearer check, bill of exchange, cashier's check, certified check, check payable on demand, conditional check, conversion of a check,

delivery of a check, deposit of a check, dishonored check, drawee, drawer, endorsed check, endorsement, forged check, holder in due course of a check, insufficient funds, order check, pay check, payee, payment of a check, postdated check, presentment of a check, registered check, time check, unauthorized endorsement, worthless check

CHECK *(Inspect),* **verb**   audit, balance accounts, canvass, case, check up, examine, experiment, explore, go over, inquire into, inventory, investigate, keep watch, look for flaws, look into, look over, make a reconnaissance, make a trial run, monitor, observe, overhaul, overlook, oversee, peruse, probe, query, question, quiz, reconnoiter, reexamine, regard carefully, regulate, review, run checks on, run tests on, sample, scan, scrutinize, search into, see about, study, subject to scrutiny, superintend, supervise, survey, take stock, test, try, verify, watch

CHECK *(Restrain),* **verb**   abate, adjust, arrest, attemper, bate, block, bring to a standstill, call a halt, cause a stoppage, constrain, control, countercheck, curb, cut off, delay, detain, deter, diminish, discourage, dissuade, draw rein, encumber, estop, freeze, frustrate, halt, head off, hinder, hold in check, impair, impede, impedite, inhibit, intercept, interrupt, intervene, keep back, keep under control, lay under restraint, limit, obstruct, overpower, put a restraint upon, put a stop to, put an end to, put under restraint, restrain, restrict, retard, run counter, set back, slow, slow down, stalemate, stand in the way, stem, stop, stultify, suppress, thwart, undermine

CHIEF, *noun*   boss, captain, *caput,* chairman, chairperson, chief controller, chieftain, commandant, commander, directing head, director, *dux,* employer, foreman, foreperson, general, head, headman, headperson, highest ranking person, leader, manager, organizer, overlooker, overseer, person in authority, person in charge, president, primate, *princeps,* principal, principal person, senior, superior, supervising director
ASSOCIATED CONCEPTS: chief agent, chief counsel, chief deputy, chief examiner, chief executive, chief executive officer, chief fiscal officer, chief judge, chief justice, chief of fire department, chief of police, chief officer of a corporation or business, chief place of business

CHILD, *noun*   adolescent, boy, daughter, *filia, filius,* foster child, girl, grandchild, *infans,* infant, ingenue, issue, juvenile, lineal descendant, minor, newborn, offspring, progeny, *pueri,* scion, young, young boy, young descendant, young girl, youngling, youngster, youth
ASSOCIATED CONCEPTS: abandoned child, abortive child, adopted child, afterborn child, child born out of wedlock, child by future marriage, child custody, child labor, child support, childbirth, childcare, childhood, *en ventre sa mere,* foster child, illegitimate child, legitimate child, minor child, natural child, neglected child, orphan, posthumous child, pretermitted child, stepchild

CHILDREN, *noun*   babies, brood, descendants, heirs, infants, innocents, issue, lineage, minors, offspring, progeny, *pueri,* rising generation, seed, young people, younger generation, youngsters, youth
ASSOCIATED CONCEPTS: descendants, disinheriting, illegitimate children, legal heirs, legitimate children, limitation, purchase, surviving children

CHILLING EFFECT, *adjective*   benumbing, damaging, deterring, discouraging, effect, intimidating, paralyzing, threatening

CHOATE LIEN, *noun*   according to law, allowed, binding, brought to fruition, compulsory, consummated, enforceable, finished, lawful, legal, legalized, legitimate, legitimized, matured, obligatory, official, perfected, ratified, refined, validated

CHOICE *(Alternatives offered),* **noun**   *delectus,* discretion, discrimination, election, opportunities, option, pick, remaining courses, remaining options, selection, substitutes
ASSOCIATED CONCEPTS: alternative causes of action, counsel of one's own choosing, election of remedies, splitting a cause of action

CHOICE *(Decision),* **noun**   act of judgment, analysis, appraisal, assessment, conclusion, considered decision, *delectus,* designation, determination, disposition, election, finding, judgment, order, outcome, predilection, preferability, preference, pronouncement, resolution, resolve, selection, settlement
ASSOCIATED CONCEPTS: domicile of choice, freedom of choice

CHOOSE, *verb*   act on one's own authority, adopt, appoint, be disposed to, be resolute, be so minded, coopt, commit oneself to a course, cull, decide, *deligere,* desire, determine, determine upon, discriminate, discriminate between, do of one's own accord, draw, elect, eliminate the alternatives, embrace, excerpt, exercise one's choice, exercise one's discretion, exercise one's option, exercise one's preference, exercise the will, have volition, make a decision, make one's choice, make one's selection, mark out for, opt for, pick, pick out, prefer, put to the vote, resolve, select, set apart, settle, side, support, take a decisive step, take one's choice, take up an option, use one's discretion, use one's option, will
ASSOCIATED CONCEPTS: election of remedies, freedom of choice, voluntary choice

CHRONIC, *adjective*   ceaseless, confirmed, constant, continual, continuing, continuous, cyclical, deep-rooted, deep-seated, drawn out, endless, enduring, entrenched, established, ever-present, everlasting, extended, forever, frequent, habitual, immedicable, incessant, inextinguished, invariable, lasting, lingering, long-continuing, long-lived, long-standing, longstanding, maintained, never-ceasing, never-stopping, not averruncated, not restorable, of long duration, often, ongoing, perdurable, perennial, permanent, perpetual, persevering, persistent, persisting, prolonged, protracted, recurrent, recurring, regular, repeating, repetitious, repetitive, resisting, returning, returning at intervals, serious, set, settled, steadfast, stubborn, sustained, tenacious, unalleviated, unceasing, uncorrectable, undestroyed, undying, unending, unerasable, unfading, unhealable, unintermitting, uninterrupted, unmitigated, unmitigating, unrelievable, unremedied, unremittent, unremitting, unshifting, unslackening, unstopped, unstopping, unsubsiding, unsuppressed, unvarying, unyielding, virulent, wearing

CHURN, *verb*   convulse, shake up, stir up, whip, work up

CIRCUIT, noun ambit, area, *arrondissement,* bounds, *circuitus, circulus,* confines, district, domain, dominion, exclusive area, extent, field, hemisphere, jurisdiction, land, *locus, orbis,* orbit, pale, part, place, precinct, province, quarter, range, realm, region, section, site, situs, sphere, territory, zone

ASSOCIATED CONCEPTS: circuit court, circuit court of appeals, circuit judge, circuit officers, judicial circuits, riding circuit

CIRCUITOUS, adjective ambagious, anfractuous, anguilliform, anguine, circumfluent, circumambulating, circumfluous, circumlocutory, complicated, contorted, convoluted, convolutional, crooked, curved, deviating, deviatory, devious, digressive, discursive, eel-shaped, eellike, excursive, flexuous, helical, helicoid, helicoidal, indirect, intorted, labyrinthine, mazy, meandering, meandrous, oblique, out of the way, rambling, roundabout, roving, serpentiform, serpentile, serpentine, serpentoid, sigmoid, sinuate, sinuous, skirting, snakelike, snaky, spiriferous, tortile, tortuous, turning, twining, twisting, undulate, undulated, undulating, undulative, undulatory, wandering, whorled, winding, zigzag

ASSOCIATED CONCEPTS: circuitous proceedings, circuitous route, circuity of action

CIRCULATE, verb acquire currency, announce, bandy, be public, be published, become public, bring before the public, bring out, broadcast, bruit abroad, change hands, change places, circuit, circularize, *circumagere,* come out, communicate, convey, diffuse, *dispergere,* disperse, disseminate, distribute, *divulgare,* divulgate, divulge, flow, get abroad, give currency to, give forth, give out, give to the world, go forth, have currency, issue, lay before the public, make known, make public, make the round of, noise abroad, pass, pass current, pass from one to another, pass round, print, proclaim, promulgate, propagate, publish, put about, put forward, put into circulation, radiate, reissue, repeat, reveal, rumor, rumor about, send forth, speak of, spread, spread a report, spread abroad, talk of, transmit, trumpet, ventilate, voice

CIRCULATION, noun allocation, allotment, branching out, *circumagere,* diffusion, dispensation, dispensing, *dispergere,* dispersal, dispersion, dissemination, distribution, divergence, *divulgare,* emanation, flow, flowing, flux, issuance, motion, movement, passage, passing, scattering, spread, spreading, transit, transition, transmigration, transmission

CIRCUMSCRIBE *(Define),* **verb** border, *circumscribere, definire,* delimit, delineate, demarcate, demark, determine, distinguish, establish, outline

CIRCUMSCRIBE *(Surround by boundary),* **verb** begird, belt, border, bound, circuit, circumvallate, cloister, close around, close in, compass, confine, contain, contour, delineate, determine boundaries, edge, embrace, encircle, enclose, encompass, engird, ensphere, envelop, fence in, fix bounds, fix limits, form a circle round, frame, gird, girdle, hedge in, hem in, include, keep in, mark off, mark out, outline, shut in, surround

CIRCUMSPECT, adjective alert, assiduous, astute, attending, attentive, careful, cautious, *cautus,* chary, circumspective, cognizant, conscientious, conscious, considerate, contemplative, deliberate, delibera-

tive, diligent, discerning, discreet, discretionary, discriminating, discriminative, exacting, guarded, heedful, intent, introspective, judicious, meditative, meticulous, mindful, observant, observing, on guard, painstaking, particular, percipient, perspicacious, precautionary, precautious, precise, premeditative, prepared, *providus, prudens,* prudent, reflecting, reflective, regardful, scrutinizing, sensitive, thinking, thorough, thoroughgoing, thoughtful, vigilant, wary, watchful, well-considered

CIRCUMSTANCES, noun accompanying events, attendant conditions, bases, changes, conditions, controlling factors, course of events, details, events, factors, facts, features, full particulars, governing factors, grounds, happenings, incidentals, instances, items, minutiae, occasions, occurrences, particulars, qualifying factors, situations, special points, state of affairs, surrounding facts, surroundings, terms imposed, vicissitudes

ASSOCIATED CONCEPTS: aggravating circumstance, change of circumstances, changed circumstance, circumstances beyond control, exceptional circumstances, extraordinary circumstances, like circumstances, mitigating circumstances, special circumstances, unusual circumstances

CIRCUMSTANTIAL, adjective accessory, *accuratus,* additional, adscititious, apparent, by inference, collateral, conditional, conjectural, construable, contingent, deduced, extraneous, founded on circumstances, implicational, implicative, implicatory, incidental, inconclusive, indecisive, indicative, indicatory, indirect, inessential, inferential, insinuatory, insubstantial, likely, nonessential, ostensible, presumable, presumptive, probable, second rank, secondary, subsidiary, suggestive, unnecessary, verisimilar

ASSOCIATED CONCEPTS: circumstantial errors, circumstantial evidence, circumstantial inference, corroborating evidence, inference

CIRCUMVENT, verb avoid doing, be cunning, be sly, beguile, bypass, *circonvenir, circumscribere, circumvenire,* cloak, conceal, confuse, contravene, contrive, counteract, counterwork, cover, deceive, defeat, defraud, delude, devise, disrupt, elude, escape, evade, foil, hoax, mislead, outmaneuver, outreach, outwit, pettifog, practice chicanery, prevaricate, proceed by stratagem, scheme, swindle, thwart, *tourner la loi,* traverse, trick

ASSOCIATED CONCEPTS: circumvent the law

CITATION *(Attribution),* **noun** ascription, assignment, credit, derivation, designation, mention, organization, parentage, quotation, reference, source

ASSOCIATED CONCEPTS: citation of authorities, citation of tables

CITATION *(Charge),* **noun** command to appear, decree, dictate, interpellation, legal process, mandate, mittimus, monition, notice, notice to appear, notification, official notice, ordination, precept, prescript, prescription, rescript, subpoena, ukase, warrant, writ, writ of summons

ASSOCIATED CONCEPTS: citation for a crime, citation for a violation, citation for contempt

CITE *(Accuse),* **verb** allege, blame, bring a charge, bring an action, call to account, censure, challenge, charge, complain, denounce, discredit, impeach, implicate, impute, incriminate, inform against, lodge a complaint, make a complaint

CITE *(State), verb*   advance, attest, authenticate, bring forward, certify, circumstantiate, document, enunciate, establish, evidence, evince, exemplify, exhibit, express, give as example, illustrate, indicate, introduce as an example, maintain, make evident, make reference to, manifest, mention, name, point to, predicate, present as proof, prove, quote, recite, refer to, refer to legal authorities, set forth, show, show evidence, show proof, specify, substantiate, use in support of propositions of law
ASSOCIATED CONCEPTS: cite a case as precedence

CITIZEN, *noun*   *civis,* denizen, dweller, habitant, *indigen,* indigene, indweller, inhabitant, inhabiter, inmate, native, occupant, occupier, residencer, resident, resider
ASSOCIATED CONCEPTS: adopted citizens, citizen of a state, citizen of the United States of America, citizens of different states, diversity of citizenship, domicile of a citizen, foreign citizen, native-born citizen, natural-born citizen, naturalized citizen, nonresident citizen, privilege and immunities of citizens, renunciation of citizenship
FOREIGN PHRASES: *Semel civis semper civis.* Once a citizen always a citizen.

CITY, *noun*   megalopolis, metropolis, metropolitan area, municipality, polis, urban district, urban place, urbanization, *urbs*
ASSOCIATED CONCEPTS: city attorney, city council, city court, city districts, city employee, city hall, city limits, city marshal, city officer, city purpose, municipal corporations

CIVIC, *adjective*   *civicus,* civil, *civilis,* common, communal, community, government, governmental, juridical, lawful, legal, metropolitan, municipal, neighborhood, official, political, public, regulatory, town, urban
ASSOCIATED CONCEPTS: civic affairs, civic enterprise, civic organizations

CIVIL *(Polite), adjective*   accommodating, affable, amiable, chivalric, chivalrous, civilized, cordial, courteous, courtly, cultivated, deferential, dignified, diplomatic, easy-mannered, fine-mannered, genial, genteel, gentlemanlike, gentlemanly, gracious, mannerly, mild, obliging, polished, refined, respectful, urbane, well-behaved, well-bred, well-brought up, well-mannered, well-spoken

CIVIL *(Public), adjective*   civic, civilian, communal, governmental, laic, laical, metropolitan, mundane, municipal, noncriminal, nonecclesiastical, nonmilitary, oppidan, political, secular, social, societal, temporal, unspiritual, urban, worldly
ASSOCIATED CONCEPTS: civil action, civil aeronautics board, civil arrest, civil authorities, civil case, civil cause, civil ceremony, civil contempt, civil contract, civil courts, civil damages, civil death, civil defense, civil disabilities, civil jurisdiction, civil law, civil liability, civil liberties, civil matters, civil officer, civil proceedings, civil rights, civil service, civil service commission, civil suit, civil unrest, civil war

FOREIGN PHRASES: *Cum actio fuerit mere criminalis, institui poterit ab initio criminaliter vel civiliter.* When an action is merely criminal, it can be instituted from the beginning either criminally or civilly.

CIVILIZATION, *noun*   accomplishments, acquired knowledge, advancement, advancement of knowledge, civilized life, civilized society, cultivation, culture, enlightenment, evolution, *humanitas,* illumination, level of education, national culture, progress, progression, refinement, social adjustment, social elevation, society, sophistication, state of refinement

CLAIM *(Assertion), noun*   affirmation, allegation, asseveration, averment, avouchment, avowal, declaration, position, predication, presentation, proposition, statement
ASSOCIATED CONCEPTS: claimed use, disputed claims, doubtful claims, false claim, fictitious claims, fraudulent claims
FOREIGN PHRASES: *Debitorum pactionibus creditorum petitio nec tolli nec minui potest.* The rights of creditors to sue cannot be prejudiced or diminished by agreements between their debtors.

CLAIM *(Legal demand), noun*   accusation, adjuration, bill of complaint, cause of action, challenge, command, complaint, counterclaim, declaration, exaction, obsecration, plea, postulate, *postulatio,* presentment, requirement, suit, ultimatum
ASSOCIATED CONCEPTS: allowed claim, claim against bankrupt estate, claim against estate, claim and demand, claim arising on contract, claim for alternative relief, claim for support, claim of a creditor, claim of interest, claim or defense notice of claim, claimed on appeal, claimed use, claims ex delicto, colorable claim, common law claim, compensation claim, conflicting claims, contingent claims, counter claim, court of claims, cross claim, disputed claims, doubtful claims, equitable claims, fictitious claims, fixed claims, fraudulent claims, frivolous claims, illegal claims, indeterminate claims, individual claim, insurance claim, just claim, lawful claim, money claim, moral claims, particular nature of claims, prior claim, proof of claim, provable claim, secured claim, settlement of claim, stale claim, subordination of claim, subsequent claims, undisputed claim, unliquidated claims, unmatured claims
FOREIGN PHRASES: *Rogationes, quaestiones, et positiones debent esse simplices.* Demands, questions, and claims ought to be simple.

CLAIM *(Right), noun*   beneficial interest, contingent interest, due, equitable interest, expectancy, heritage, interest, legacy, ownership, privilege, share, stake, title, vested interest
ASSOCIATED CONCEPTS: claim of ownership, claim of right, claim of title

CLAIM *(Demand), verb*   ask for, assert as one's own, assert as one's right, declare one's right, dun, exact as due, have a right, insist upon, make demands on, petition, press, pretend, reclaim, request, require, requisition, seek as due, sue, think one deserves, vindicate a right, vindicate a title
ASSOCIATED CONCEPTS: claim against an estate, claim and demand, claim arising from a contract, claim for relief, claim of right, claim of title, compensation claim, contingent claim, counterclaim, court of claims, fraud

claim, insurance claim, money claim, ownership claim, valid claim

CLAIM *(Maintain), verb*   advocate, affirm, allege, assert, asseverate, attest, aver, avouch, avow, certify, charge, contend, declare, hold, insist, make a statement, make an assertion, predicate, profess, propound, put forward, say, stand firm, state, utter with conviction, vow, warrant
ASSOCIATED CONCEPTS: claimed use

CLAIMANT, *noun*   accusant, accuser, appellant, applicant, asserter, claimer, complainant, libelant, litigant, one who asserts a demand, one who claims a right, party to a suit, person who makes a claim, person with a grievance, petitioner, plaintiff, pleader, postulant, solicitant, solicitor, suitor
ASSOCIATED CONCEPTS: lien claimant, subsequent claimant, suit by claimant
FOREIGN PHRASES: *Semper necessitas probandi incumbit ei qui agit.* The burden of proof always lies upon the claimant.

CLANDESTINE, *adjective*   arcane, behind the scenes, camouflaged, *clandestinus,* cloaked, collusive, concealed, confidential, conspiring, covert, cunning, disguised, ensconced, evasive, furtive, *furtivus,* hidden, in the background, irrevealable, masked, obscure, screened, secluded, secret, secretive, shrouded, sneaking, stealthy, stifled, subterranean, suppressed, surreptitious, undercover, underground, underhand, underhanded, undisclosed, unknown, unrevealed, unseen, veiled, with secret design
ASSOCIATED CONCEPTS: clandestine adultery, clandestine importation, clandestine marriage, clandestine meeting

CLARIFICATION, *noun*   amplification, apostil, clarification, commentary, deciphering, definition, delineation, demonstration, description, elimination of ambiguousness, elimination of complexity, elimination of complication, elucidation, enlightenment, epexegesis, erasure of ambiguity, exemplification, explanation, explication, exposition, illumination, illustration, increase of clarity, increase of clearness, increase of intelligibility, interpretation, making apparent, making distinct, making evident, making lucid, making perspicuous, making precise, making specific, making trenchant, presentation, refinement, rendering explicit, rendering incisive, rendering unequivocal, rendering unmistakable, scholium, simplification, specification

CLARIFY, *verb*   articulate, bare, bring to light, clear up, comment upon, construe, decipher, define, delineate, *deliquare,* demonstrate, disentangle, elucidate, enlighten, exemplify, explain, explicate, expose, exposit, expound, free from ambiguity, free from confusion, illuminate, illustrate, interpret, lay open, make clear, make comprehensible, make explicit, make intelligible, make lucid, make understood, refine, render intelligible, shed light on, show, simplify, spell out, subtilize, unfold, unmask, unravel, unscramble, unveil
ASSOCIATED CONCEPTS: clarify and amplify a complaint, clarify the pleadings

CLASS, *noun*   assortment, bracket, branch, brand, breed, caste, category, classification, *classis,* denomination, designation, division, echelon, genera, genre,

genus, gradation, grade, group, grouping, hierarchy, ilk, kind, layer of society, order, *ordo,* place, position, rank, rating, sect, set, social rank, social status, sort, standing, station, status, stratum, subdivision, subgroup, suborder, subspecies, type, variety
ASSOCIATED CONCEPTS: class action, class gifts, class interest, class legislation, class suit, definite class, gift to a class
FOREIGN PHRASES: *Clausula generalis de residuo non ea complectitur quae non ejusdem sint generis cum iis quae speciatim dicta fuerant.* A general clause of remainder does not include those things which are not of the same kind as those which have been specially mentioned.

CLASSIFICATION, *noun*   allocation, allotment, analysis, apportionment, arrangement, assignment, assortment, cataloguing, categorization, category, class, codification, denomination, designation, disposition, distribution, division, gradation, group, grouping, identification, methodization, nomenclature, order, ordering, orderly arrangement, ordination, organization, placement, ranking, reducing to order, regulation by a system, specification, subgroup, syntaxis, systematization, taxis, type
ASSOCIATED CONCEPTS: arbitrary classification, illegal classification, unreasonable classification

CLASSIFY, *verb*   allocate, allot, analyze, apportion, arrange, assort, brand, break down, catalogue, categorize, class, classify as, codify, collocate, coordinate, correlate, dispose, distinguish, distribute, divide, file, form into classes, grade, group, identify, *in genera describere,* index, introduce a system, label, list, marshal, methodize, name, organize, partition, pigeonhole, place in a category, place in order, put in array, put in order, range, rank, rate, reduce to order, segregate, separate, seriate, set in order, size, sort, specify, subsume, systematize, tag, type
ASSOCIATED CONCEPTS: arbitrary classification, illegal classification, unreasonable classification

CLAUSE, *noun*   article, *caput,* condition, *conditiosine qua non,* contract, covenant, exception, exemption, limitation, *membrum,* paragraph, *pars,* passage, phrase, proposition, provision, proviso, qualification, section, sentence, specification, stipulation, term
ASSOCIATED CONCEPTS: commerce clause, commercial clause, enacting clause, escalation clause, forfeiture clause, grandfather clause, incontestable clause, loss payable clause, most favored nation clause, penalty clause, residuary clause, saving clause, specific clause, spendthrift clause, standard mortagagee clause, sunsetting clause
FOREIGN PHRASES: *Clausula generalis de residuo non ea complectitur quae non ejusdem sint generis cum iis quae speciatim dicta fuerant.* A general clause concerning the remainder does not include those matters which are not of the same kind with those which have been specially expressed. *Clausula generalis non refertur ad expressa.* A general clause does not refer to things expressly mentioned. *Clausula quae abrogationem excludit ab initio non valet.* A clause which forbids its abrogation is invalid from the beginning. *Clausula vel dispositio inutilis per praesumptionem remotam, vel causam ex post facto non fulcitur.* A useless clause or provision is not supported by a remote presumption, or by a cause that arises afterwards. *Clausulae incon-*

suetae semper inducunt suspicionem. Unusual clauses always arouse suspicion.

CLEAN, *adjective* above suspicion, acquitted, angelic, blameless, bloodless, cleanhanded, cleanminded, clear, decent, entirely defensible, fair, faultless, free from guilt, free from impurities, free from sin, good, guileless, guiltless, high-minded, high-principled, honest, honorable, immaculate, impeccable, in the clear, incorrupt, incorruptible, innocent, inviolable, inviolate, irreprehensible, irreproachable, irreprovable, law-abiding, lawful, moral, *mundus,* not guilty, not responsible, pure, pure-hearted, pure in heart, *purus,* right-minded, righteous, scrupulous, snowy, spotless, stainless, straight, strictly honest, taintless, unblamable, unblemished, unbribed, uncorrupted, unculpable, unerring, unexceptionable, unguilty, unimpeachable, uninvolved, unmuddied, unobjectionable, unoffending, unsoiled, unspotted, unstained, unsullied, untarnished, unviolated, upright, veracious, virtuous, white, wholesome, without a stain, without reproach
ASSOCIATED CONCEPTS: clean bill of lading, clean credit, clean docket receipt, clean hands doctrine, clean money

CLEAR *(Apparent),* *adjective* blunt, clarified, clear-cut, demonstrative, direct, distinct, downright, emphatic, *évident,* evident, exact, explicit, express, expressive, frank, glaring, graphic, identifiable, in bold relief, in evidence, in strong relief, intelligible, limpid, manifest, observable, outspoken, overt, patent, pellucid, perceivable, perceptible, perspicuous, plain, prominent, pronounced, pure, salient, self-evident, showing, shown, straightforward, striking, transparent, unadorned, unambiguous, unblurred, unclouded, uncovered, understood, undisguised, unequivocal, unevasive, unmistakable, visible, vivid, well-defined, well-marked, well-seen
ASSOCIATED CONCEPTS: clear and convincing danger, clear and present danger, clear-cut question of law, clear meaning, clear preponderance, clear proof, clearly ascertainable, last clear chance

CLEAR *(Certain),* *adjective* absolute, actual, ascertained, authoritative, beyond a shadow of a doubt, beyond all dispute, categorical, cogent, conclusive, definite, definitive, doubtless, free from doubt, incontestable, incontrovertible, indefeasible, indisputable, indubitable, irrefragable, irrefutable, positive, questionless, settled without appeal, sure, unassailable, unchallengeable, unconfutable, uncontested, uncontroversial, undeniable, undisputed, undoubted, unequivocal, unerring, unhesitating, unimpeachable, unmistakable, unqualified, unquestionable, unquestioned, unrefutable
ASSOCIATED CONCEPTS: clear legal right, clear right, clearly erroneous

CLEAR *(Free from criminal charges),* *adjective* absolved, acquitted, at liberty, cleared, condoned, delivered, disburdened, discharged, disculpated, dismissed, exculpated, excused, exempted, exonerated, forgiven, freed, guiltless, immune, justified, manumitted, nonliable, not guilty, pardoned, purged, released, remitted, reprieved, spared, unburdened, uncensurable, unchastised, uncondemned, unpunished, vindicated

CLEAR *(Unencumbered),* *adjective* disburdened, disencumbered, exempt, free, free from burden, free from encumbrance, free from hindrance, free from impediment, free from limitation, free from obstruction, not answerable, not responsible, unaccountable, unbound, unbridled, unburdened, unconstrained, uncurbed, unfettered, unhampered, unhindered, unobstructed, unrestrained, untrammeled
ASSOCIATED CONCEPTS: clear title

CLEAR, *verb* absolve, acquit, amnesty, deliver, disburden, discharge, disembroil, disencumber, disentangle, dismiss, exculpate, excuse, exempt, exonerate, *explicare,* extricate, find not guilty, forgive, free, give a reprieve, give absolution, grant a reprieve, grant amnesty, grant remission, let go, let off, liberate, pardon, pronounce not guilty, prove innocent, purge, quash the conviction, release, render free, reprieve, rescue, set at large, set at liberty, set free, shrive, vindicate
ASSOCIATED CONCEPTS: clear and convincing evidence, clear and convincing standard of proof, clear and present danger, clear title, last clear chance doctrine

CLEMENCY, *noun* absolution, amnesty, benefaction, beneficence, benevolence, benignity, charity, *clementia,* clementness, commutation, compassion, consideration, decency, disposition to mercy, disposition to pardon, excuse, exemption, extenuation, forbearance, forgiveness, forgivingness, generosity, generousness, gentleness, good will, grace, humaneness, humanity, indemnity, indulgence, kindness, lenience, leniency, lenity, liberality, magnanimity, magnanimousness, *mansuetuda,* mercifulness, mercy, obligingness, pardon, pardoning, purgation, release, reprieve, respite, temperance, tolerance, toleration, willingness to forgive
ASSOCIATED CONCEPTS: clemency by the Governor, clemency by the President of the United States, Executive clemency

CLERICAL, *adjective* accessory, *ad administrationem pertimens,* administrating, administrative, assistant, assisting, attendant, attending, auxiliary, *ex officio,* helping, instrumental, intermediary
ASSOCIATED CONCEPTS: clerical acts, clerical duties, clerical errors, clerical mistakes, clerical omissions

CLERK, *noun* archivist, chronicler, copyist, court employee, court official, court scribe, judicial administrator, judicial assistant, judicial recorder, judicial secretary, office holder, office worker, official, prothonotary, recorder, record keeper, registrar, *scriba,* scribe, scrivener, secretary
ASSOCIATED CONCEPTS: clerk of the county, clerk of the court, county clerk, papers filed with the clerk, town clerk
FOREIGN PHRASES: *Errores scribentis nocere non debent.* An error made by a clerk ought not to prejudice.

CLERK, *verb* aid a judge, assist a judge, help a judge, work for a judge

CLIENT, *noun* business contact, buyer of labor, *cliens, consultor,* consumer, customer, employer of legal advice, hirer, offerer, patron, patron of professional servies, patronizer, person employing advice, person represented, person represented by counsel, purchaser, retainer of counsel
ASSOCIATED CONCEPTS: attorney-client privilege, attorney-client relationship

CLIMATE, *noun* atmosphere, aura, *caelum,* circumambiency, clime, condition, environment, environmental conditions, feeling, forces of nature, influences, mood, prevailing attitudes, prevailing conditions, prevailing standards, surrounding influence, surroundings

CLINICAL, *adjective* analytical, detached, dispassionate, impersonal, imperturbable, unemotional, unimpressionable

CLOAK, *verb* beguile, belie, blind, bluff, bury, camouflage, cloud, conceal, conceal the truth, construe falsely, couch, cover, cover up, curtain, deceive, decoy, disguise, dissemble, *dissimulare,* dissimulate, distort, divert, dress up, dupe, eclipse, embellish, embroider, ensconce, enshroud, envelop, exaggerate, fake, falsify, feign, forswear, garble, give a false coloring, gloss over, go undercover, hide, hide away, keep a secret, keep hidden, keep in ignorance, keep secret, keep undercover, mask, miscolor, misinform, mislead, misrepresent, muffle, obscure, obstruct the view of, occult, pretend, put out of sight, render invisible, screen, seclude, secrete, shade, shadow, sham, shelter, shroud, sneak, stifle, suppress, swear falsely, *tegere,* veil
ASSOCIATED CONCEPTS: cloaked with authority

CLOG, *verb* arrest, astrict, bar, barricade, be obstructive, block, block up, bridle, burden, checkmate, choke, close, close off, constrict, cumber, dam, deadlock, detain, exclude, forbid, foreclose, forestall, frustrate, hamper, handicap, hinder, hold back, hold in check, hold up, impede, *impedire,* impedite, intercept, interfere, keep out, obstruct, occlude, place limitations, plug, plug up, preclude, prevent, prevent passage, prohibit, put a stop to, repress, restrain, restrict, retard, shut off, stall, stand in the way of, stay, stifle, stop, stop short, stop up, stultify, stymie, suppress

CLOSE *(Intimate), adjective* allied, bosom, brotherly, confidential, dear, devoted, faithful, familiar, fast, fraternal, friendly, inseparable, strongly attached
ASSOCIATED CONCEPTS: close corporation, closely held

CLOSE *(Near), adjective* adjacent, adjoining, approaching, approximate, at hand, bordering, close at hand, close by, coming, contiguous, forthcoming, handy, imminent, impending, in close proximity, in the area, in the neighborhood, in the vicinity, near at hand, nearby, neighboring, nigh, *propinquus,* proximal, proximate, tangent, touching, vicinal
ASSOCIATED CONCEPTS: close confinement, close proximity

CLOSE *(Rigorous), adjective* assiduous, attentive, careful, conscientious, diligent, earnest, exact, hard, harsh, intense, keen, meticulous, *parcus,* precise, punctilious, relentless, rigid, scrupulous, severe, sharp, stiff, strict, stringent, *tenax,* uncompromising, unremitting, unsparing

CLOSE *(Conclusion), noun* adjournment, cessation, closing, closure, completion, *conclusio,* consummation, discontinuance, discontinuation, end, ending, expiration, finale, *finis,* finish, last part, last stage, omega, peroration, shutdown, stoppage, termination, *terminus,* windup
ASSOCIATED CONCEPTS: the close of a trial, the closing on a real estate transaction

CLOSE *(Enclosed area), noun* compound, confine, court, courtyard, enclosure, grounds, pen, precinct, square, yard
ASSOCIATED CONCEPTS: breaking the close

CLOSE *(Agree), verb* accept an offer, arrive at an agreement, bargain, come to an arrangement, come to an understanding, come to terms, consent, endorse, enter into a contractual obligation, establish by agreement, execute, finalize, finalize an agreement, fix by agreement, give assurance, go to contract, guarantee, make a bargain, make an agreement, negotiate, *pacisci,* seek accord, settle, strike a bargain, subscribe, undertake, underwrite
ASSOCIATED CONCEPTS: close a business transaction, close a real estate transaction

CLOSE *(Terminate), verb* apply the closure, break off, bring to an end, call a halt, cause a stoppage, cease, *claudere,* come to a stop, come to an end, complete, conclude, consummate, discontinue, dispatch, dispose of, eliminate, end, expire, finish, finish up, fulfill, halt, have run its course, interrupt, make an end of, make inactive, *operire,* prosecute to a conclusion, put a stop to, run out, shut down, stop, surcease, suspend, suspend operation, wind up
ASSOCIATED CONCEPTS: close a bank account, close a case, close a grand jury investigation, close an investigation

CLOTHE, *verb* accouter, *amicire,* appoint, arm, array, attire oneself, bedeck, bedrape, cloak, conceal, costume, cover, cover up, disguise, drape, dress, embroider, empower, enable, encase, endow, enfold, enrobe, envelop, enwrap, equip, fit out, frock, furnish, garb, gear, *induere sibi vestem,* invest, invest with power, outfit, provide, put in uniform, robe, suit, supply, uniform, *vestire,* wrap
ASSOCIATED CONCEPTS: clothe with authority to act, clothe with indicia of ownership

CLOTURE, *noun* abandonment, abeyance, adjournal, adjournment, arrest, break, cease, cessation, check, closing, closure, desistance, discontinuance, discontinuation, halt, interruption, lapse, letup, lull, noncontinuance, prorogation, recess, standstill, stay, stop, stoppage, suspension, withdrawal

CLOUD *(Incumbrance), noun* burden, charge, claim, claim on property, commitment, debt, hold on property, hypothecation, indebtedness, indebtment, liability, mortgage, obligation, obstruction, outstanding debt, *pignus judiciale, pignus legale,* pledge, prescription, real security, restraint, security, security on property, state of indebtedness, *vadium mortuum*
ASSOCIATED CONCEPTS: a cloud on personalty, a cloud on real property

CLOUD *(Suspicion), noun* apprehension, apprehensiveness, consternation, contestability, controvertibility, deniability, disbelief, disputability, distrust, distrustfulness, doubt, fear, hesitation, incredulity, incredulousness, intimation, lack of certainty, lack of confidence, lack of faith, misdoubt, misgiving, mistrust, mistrustfulness, *onus probandi,* perplexity, puzzlement, questionability, refusal to believe, refutability, reluctance to believe, skepticism, trepidation, unbelief, uncredulousness, want of certainty, want of confidence, want of faith

CLOUT, noun authoritative power, authority, consequence, controlling power, directing power, dominancy, dominion, eminence, force, hegemony, importance, influence, influentiality, leverage, mastership, notability, potency, power, power of impelling, predominancy, prestige, prominence, puissance, significance, weight

CLUE, noun data, evidence, finding, guide, hint, idea, index, indication, indicator, information, inkling, insinuation, intimation, key, lead, mark, reason to believe, scent, sign, signal, token

COACTION, noun alliance, association, coalition, cohesion, collaboration, colleagueship, collective action, collusion, combined effort, common effort, complicity, concert of action, concourse, concurrence, confederacy, cooperancy, cooperation, cooperativeness, coworking, federation, fellowship, fraternity, fusion, joint effort, joint participation, league, mutual assistance, mutuality, partnership, solidarity, teamwork, union, union of action, united action, working together

COACTOR, noun abettor, accessory, accessory after the fact, accessory before the fact, accomplice, accomplice in crime, acolyte, adjunct, adjutant, adjuvant, advocate, aid, aide-de-camp, aider, aider and abettor, ally, assistant, associate, attendant, auxiliary, coadjutant, coadjutor, cohelper, collaborationist, collaborator, colleague, colluder, confederate, consociate, consort, conspirator, conspirer, contriver, cooperator, copartner, coworker, deviser, fellow conspirator, helper, henchman, joint-operator, partner, partner in crime, planner, plotter, promoter, promotor, schemer, strategist, supporter

COADJUTANT, noun abettor, accessory, accomplice, adjutant, adjuvant, aid, aide, aider, ally, apprentice, assistant, associate, attendant, auxiliary, coadjutor, collaborator, colleague, confederate, consociate, cooperator, coworker, deputy, fellow worker, follower, help, helper, henchman, lieutenant, mate, partner, subordinate, supporter, teammate, underling

COADUNATE, adjective adherent, adhering, adhesive, agglomerate, aggregate, aggregated, allied, amalgamative, assembled, associated, centralized, clinging, coagulated, coagulative, coalesced, coalescent, cohering, cohesive, combined, compact, concerted, confluent, conglomerate, conglomeratic, congregated, conjoined, conjoint, conjugate, conjunct, connected, consolidated, cooperative, fused, incorporated, integrated, interlinked, interlocked, interrelated, joined, leagued, linked, related, unified, united

COALESCENCE, noun abutting, accordance, adherence, adhesion, admixture, affiliation, agglomeration, agglutination, alliance, amalgamation, annexation, annexing, assemblage, association, attachment, binding, bond, centralization, closeness, coadunation, coagulation, coalition, coherence, cohesion, cohesiveness, combination, commixture, compound, concrescence, concurrence, confederacy, confederation, confluence, conglomeration, conglutination, conjugation, conjunction, connection, consociation, consolidation, contact, convergence, converging, coupling, federation, fusing, fusion, immixture, incorporation, interconnection, interfusion, joining, junction, league, linkage, merger, merging, mixture, solidification, symbiosis, synthesis, unification, union

COALITION, noun affiliation, alliance, amalgamation, association, binding, bond, cartel, combination, combine, coming together, community, concurrence, confluence, conglomerate, congress, conjoining, *conjunctio*, conjunction, conjuncture, connection, consociation, consolidation, consortium, *conspiratio*, convergence, cooperation, federation, fellowship, fusing, fusion, fusion of interests, group, integration, interlocking, joint concern, joint endeavor, junction, league, meeting, merger, merging, mixture, mutual concern, partnership, society, sodality, syndicate, unification, union, union of factions, unity

COAX, verb allure, appeal, attract, bait, blandish, bribe, cajole, captivate, convince, encourage, engage, enlist, ensnare, entice, evoke, exert pressure, exhort, *hominem permulcere, homini blandiri*, impel, incite, induce, influence, insist, inspire, intrigue, inveigle, keep in countenance, lead, lure, manipulate, motivate, offer an inducement, persuade, press, prevail, prevail upon, procure, prod, prompt, provoke, rally, recommend, rouse, spellbind, stimulate, suborn, suggest, sway, tempt, urge

COCONSPIRATOR, noun abettor, accessory, accessory after the fact, accessory before the fact, accomplice, adjunct in crime, adjutant in crime, adjuvant in crime, aide in crime, aide in wrongdoing, aider in wrongdoing, ally in crime, ally in wrongdoing, assistant, associate in crime, associate in guilt, auxiliary in crime, coactor in crime, coadjutor, coaider in crime, collaborator, colleague in crime, colluder, companion in crime, comrade in crime, comrade in wrongdoing, confederate, consociate in crime, cooperator in crime, copartner in crime, coworker in crime, fellow conspirator, fellow machinator, fellow plotter, fellow schemer, fellow strategist, fellow traiter, partner, partner in crime, partner in wrongdoing, supporter

CODE, noun arrangement of statutes, body of laws, bylaw, canon, capitulary, charter, civil code, codification, codified law, collection, collection of laws, collection of statutes, compilation, compilation of law, compilation of laws, constitution, *corpus juris,* digest, enactment, enactment of rules, established law, established order, firm principle, formulary, formulation, guide, guideline, laws, legal code, legislation, *lex,* maxim, model, norm, ordinance, precedent, precept, precepts, prescript, prescription, principles, regulation by law, regulation by statute, regulations, rubric, rules, ruling, settled law, standard, statute, statute book, statute law, subsidiary law, system of law, system of rules, written constitution, written law

ASSOCIATED CONCEPTS: building code, civil code, code of criminal procedure, code of ethics, code of fair competition, Code of Hammurabi, code of judicial conduct, code of law, code of procedure, code of professional responsibility, code pleading, criminal code, ethics code, Napoleonic code, penal code, probate code

FOREIGN PHRASES: *Ad ea quae frequentius accidunt jura adaptantur.* Laws are adapted to those cases which most commonly occur.

CODICIL, noun accessory, accompaniment, addendum, additament, addition, addition to a will, additive, additum, adjunct, affixation, affixture, annex, annexa-

tion, appanage, appendage, appendix, attachment, augmentation, complement, epilogue, insertion, postscript, sequel, sequela, subscript, suffix, supplement, supplement to a will, testament, will addendum, will supplement
ASSOCIATED CONCEPTS: will

CODIFICATION, *noun*   act, arrangement of laws, arrangement of rules, arrangement of statutes, authoritative law, bill, bylaws, canon, capitulary, categorization of laws, collection of statutes, commandment, compendium, compilation, decree, doctrine, enactment, formalization of laws, formulation of laws, lawmaking, legislation, ordinance, precept, prescription, regulation, rule, rules and regulations, rulings, sanctions, scheduling, scheme, set of rules, standardization of laws, statute, statute book, statute law, system, system of laws, system of regulations, systematic arrangement of laws, systematization of laws, tabulation, written law
ASSOCIATED CONCEPTS: codification act, codification of statutes

CODIFY, *verb*   accumulate, arrange, assemble, assort, break down, bring into order, catalog, categorize, classify, collect, compile, coordinate, *digerere,* divide, formalize, formulate, group, index, introduce order, list, methodize, organize, rank, reduce to a code, reduce to a digest, reduce to order, regularize, sort, subdivide, systematize, systemize, tabulate
ASSOCIATED CONCEPTS: codifying act

COEQUAL, *adjective*   *aequalis,* agreeing, analogous, as great as another, coextensive, coincident, commensurate, comparable, congruent, coordinate, correlative, correspondent, corresponding, equal, equibalanced, equipollent, equiponderant, equivalent, even, homologous, identical in value, interchangeable, level, like in degree, like in quantity, matching, neither more nor less, of equal dignity, of equal power, of like rank, of the same rank, on a footing with, on a level with, on a par, on a par with, on the same footing, parallel, reciprocal, symmetrical, synonymous, tantamount, uniform, up to the mark

COERCE, *verb*   apply pressure, bear down, bludgeon, bring pressure to bear, *coercere,* command, compel, conscript, constrain, demand, dictate, dominate, draft, dragoon, drive, elicit by threat, enjoin, enthrall, exact, exhort, extort, foist, force, impel, impose, impose restrictions, impress, induce, insist, interdict, intimidate, issue threats, necessitate, oblige, oppress, order, press, pressure, prod, push, put pressure on, put under restraint, require, rule, subjugate, suppress, terrorize, threaten, use force upon, wrest from
ASSOCIATED CONCEPTS: duress, harassment
FOREIGN PHRASES: *Ejus nulla culpa est cui parere necesse sit.* No guilt attaches to him who is compelled to obey.

COERCION, *noun*   blackmail, bondage, brute force, *coercitio,* command, compulsion, constraint, constraint by force, control, dictation, duress, exaction, exigency, extortion, force, forcing, illegal compulsion, impelling, inducement, insistence, intimidation, moral compulsion, necessity, negative compulsion, oppression, oppressive exaction, pressure, prevailing, prohibition, repression, restraint, strong arm tactics, threat, undue influence, unlawful compulsion

ASSOCIATED CONCEPTS: coercive conduct, duress, extortion, coercion of employees
FOREIGN PHRASES: *Extortio est crimen quando quis colore, officii extorquet quod non est debitum, vel supra debitum, vel ante tempus quod est debitum.* Extortion is a crime when, by color of office, any person extorts that which is not due, or more than is due, or before the time when it is due. *Nihil consensui tam contrarium est quam vis atque metus.* Nothing is so opposed to consent as force and fear. *Vis legibus est inimica.* Force is inimical to the laws.

COEXTENSIVE, *adjective*   agreeing, aligned, analagous, balanced, coequal, coextending, collateral, comparable, concentric, concurrent, congruent, coordinate, correlative, correspondent, corresponding, equable, equal, equal in scope, equal in space, equal in time, equalized, equidistant, equilateral, equipollent, equiponderant, equipondious, equivalent, even, even-sided, homologous, in equilibrium, lined up, matched, parallel, proportioned, symmetrical, synonymous
ASSOCIATED CONCEPTS: coextensive with rights under the United States Constitution

COFFER, *noun*   *arca,* bank, *cista,* container, depository, holder, locker, money chest, receptacle, safe, safe deposit box, storage, strongbox, till, treasury, vault

COGENT, *adjective*   appealing conclusively, appealing forcibly, authoritative, commanding, compelling, conclusive, convincing, definite, definitive, demonstrable, demonstrating, determinative, effective, effectual, efficacious, evidential, forceful, forcible, incontestable, incontrovertible, indubitable, inducive, influential, irrefragable, irrefutable, irresistible, logical, meritorious, of consequence, past dispute, persuasive, potent, powerful, proving, puissant, reliable, solid, sound, strong, suasive, substantial, telling, to the point, trenchant, trustworthy, unanswerable, unconfuted, undeniable, undoubtable, undoubted, unequivocal, unquestionable, valid, veridical, weighty, well-founded, well-grounded

COGITATIVE, *adjective*   contemplative, deliberate, deliberative, ideative, introspective, meditative, museful, pensive, philosophical, pondering, reflective, ruminant, ruminative, speculative, thinking, thoughtful

COGNATE, *adjective*   affiliated, affined, agnate, akin, alike, analogical, analogous, appertaining, appurtenant, associated, bearing upon, belonging, close, closely allied, closely related, coordinate, commensurate, common, comparable, comparative, compared, complementary, concurrent, congeneric, congenerous, congenial, connected, consanguine, consanguineous, correlated, correlative, correspondent, corresponding, entwined, equal, equivalent, germane, homogeneous, homologous, in common with, in the same category, interchangeable, interdependent, interrelated, intimately allied, intimately related, like, linked, mutual, near, of that kind, of that sort, parallel, proportionable, reciprocal, related, relating to, relative, same, serial, sharing, similar, something like, synonymous

COGNITION, *noun*   acquaintance, apperception, appreciation, apprehension, awareness, *cognitio,* cognitive process, cognizance, comprehension, conception, consciousness, discernment, enlightenment, familiarity, grasp, illumination, insight, intellection, ken, knowledge, mastery, perception, percipience, realization, recognition, sensibility, understanding, wisdom

COGNIZABLE, *adjective* accountable, apprehensible, ascertainable, ascertained, capable of being examined, capable of being tried in the court, clear, comprehensible, decipherable, definite, discernible, discoverable, distinct, distinguishable, explicable, explicit, familiar, fathomable, intelligible, jurisdictionally sound, knowable, known, lucid, luminous, meaningful, pellucid, penetrable, perceived, perceptible, perspicuous, readable, realizable, realized, recognizable, scrutable, straightforward, unblurred, understandable, understood, unequivocal, unevasive, uninvolved, unmistakable, well-written
ASSOCIATED CONCEPTS: cognizable by the courts

COGNIZANT, *adjective* accomplished, acquainted, alert, apperceptive, apprehensive, apprised, astute, aware, clear-sighted, cognitive, comprehending, conscious, *conscius,* conversant, discerning, discriminating, educated, endowed with consciousness, endowed with reason, enlightened, erudite, expert, familiar, informed, keen, knowing, knowledgeable, learned, lettered, mindful, perceptive, percipient, perspicacious, possessed of knowledge, posted, practiced, proficient, regardful, sagacious, sage, sensible to, sharp, understanding, versed, well-advised, well-educated, well-grounded, well-informed, well-read, well-versed, wise

COGNOMEN, *noun* appelation, appellative, byname, byword, denomination, designation, name, nickname, sobriquet, style

COGNOVIT, *noun* acknowledged judgment, adjudication, admitted judgment, conceded judgment, confessed judgment, confirmed judgment, decision, declaration, decree, determination, disclosed judgment, finding, legal decision

COHABIT, *verb* abide together, be intimate, conjugate, *consuescere,* copulate, couple, dwell together, live in sexual intimacy, live together, live with, lodge together, reside together, room together, share an address, share bed and board, stay together
ASSOCIATED CONCEPTS: cohabit as husband and wife

COHABITATION (*Living together*), ***noun*** abiding together, act of dwelling together, alliance, living together in sexual intimacy, lodging together, lodging together as husband and wife, occupying the same domicile, residing together, rooming together
ASSOCIATED CONCEPTS: cohabiting in a state of adultery, fornication, illicit cohabitation, lewd and lascivious cohabitation
FOREIGN PHRASES: *Nuptias non concubitus sed consensus facit.* Not cohabitation but consent makes the valid marriage.

COHABITATION (*Married state*), ***noun*** act of living together as husband and wife, act of pairing, bond of matrimony, conjugal bliss, conjugality, connubiality, coverture, domestication, legal relation of spouses to each other, legal union of a man and a woman, marriage, married status, matrimony, nuptial bond, nuptial tie, state of matrimony, union, *vinculo matrimonii,* wedded state, wedded status, wedlock

ASSOCIATED CONCEPTS: bigamous cohabitation, cohabiting in a state of adultery, matrimonial cohabitation, polygamous cohabitation
FOREIGN PHRASES: *Nuptias non concubitus sed consensus facit.* Not cohabitation but consent makes the marriage.

COHERE (*Adhere*), ***verb*** affix, agglomerate, agglutinate, attach, be dense, be tacked together, become solid, cement, clasp, cleave, cling, clot, coagulate, coalesce, *cohaerere,* combine, come together, compress, congeal, conjoin, consolidate, fasten, grasp, grow together, hang on, harden, hold fast, hold on, hold together, hold up, mass, quadrate with, solidify, stay, stick, stick close, stick on to, stick together, unify, unite

COHERE (*Be logically consistent*), ***verb*** accord, agree, be a sound argument, be accordant, be clear, be coherent, be congruous, be intelligible, be logical, be lucid, be rationally connected, be reasonable, be understandable, *cohaerere,* comport with, conform, correspond, hang together, harmonize, hold together, make sense

COHERENCE, *noun* adherence, adhesion, adhesiveness, agreement, apprehensibility, attachment, blending, cleavage, coherency, cohesion, cohesiveness, comprehensibility, concert, congruence, congruity, conjunction, connectedness, connection, consistency, consolidation, consonance, *contextus,* continuity, *convenientia,* correspondence, correspondency, firm hold, fusion, harmony, holding together, intelligibility, interrelation, rationality, sticking together, understandability, union, unity

COHERENT (*Clear*), ***adjective*** adapted to the understanding, apparent, apprehensible, articulate, audible, clear-cut, cogent, cognizable, *cohaerens,* comprehensible, concise, *congruens,* decipherable, defined, definite, direct, discernible, distinct, easily understood, easy to grasp, easy to understand, evident, exact, exoteric, exoterical, explained, explanatory, explicable, explicatory, explicit, express, expressive, fathomable, forthright, graphic, illuminated, in evidence, intelligible, interpreted, knowable, legible, logical, logically appealing, logically consistent, lucid, luminous, making sense, manifest, meaningful, obvious, palpable, pellucid, penetrable, perceivable, perceptible, perspicuous, plain, precise, realizable, recognizable, scrutable, self-evident, simple, straightforward, unambiguous, unblurred, unconfused, understandable, understood, undisguised, unequivocal, unmistakable, visible, vivid, well-defined, well-marked

COHERENT (*Joined*), ***adjective*** accreted, accretive, adherent, adhering, adhesive, agglutinate, agglutinative, allied, amalgamative, cleaving, cleaving together, clinging, close, coadunate, coagulate, coagulated, coalescent, *cohaerens,* cohering, cohesive, combined, composite, compressed, congealed, conglomerate, conglomeratic, *congruens,* conjoined, conjunct, connected, consolidated, *contextus,* coupled, fused, holding together, incorporated, indivisible, inseparable, interlinked, interlocked, interrelated, sticking, sticking together, united, viscous

COHESIVE (*Compact*), ***adjective*** close, compressed, concentrated, concise, concrete, conjacent, conjunct, consolidated, dense, firm, hard, impenetrable, impermeable, indivisible, inseparable, pressed together, solid, strong, substantial, terse, thick, tight, to the point, well-knit

COHESIVE *(Sticking)*, **adjective**   adherent, adhering, adhesive, agglutinate, agglutinative, attached, cementitious, cleaving, clinging, coherent, cohering, conglutinative, connected, consistent, glutinous, holding together, resisting, sticking, tenacious, tied, united

COHORT, **noun**   abettor, accessory, accomplice, aider and abettor, ally, assistant, associate, attendant, auxiliary, coadjutor, cohelper, *cohors*, collaborator, colleague, comate, companion, comrade, confederate, consociate, cooperator, coworker, faithful companion, fellow, fellow conspirator, follower, friend, helper, *particeps criminis,* partner, *socius criminis,* stalwart, supporter

COINCIDE *(Concur)*, **verb**   accede, accept, accord, acquiesce, agree, approve, arrive at an agreement, arrive at an understanding, arrive at terms, assent, be accordant, be at one with, be of the same mind, be one with, come to an agreement, come to an understanding, come to terms, conform to, consent, correspond, endorse, give assent, go along with, harmonize, meet, merge, nod assent to, subscribe to, synchronize, unite, yield assent

COINCIDE *(Correspond)*, **verb**   accompany, be concomitant, be congruent, be contemporaneous, be identical, be simultaneous, coexist, *concurrere,* conform to, *congruere, convenire,* exist together, fall exactly together, fill identical times, fit exactly, go with, happen together, match

COINCIDENTAL, **adjective**   accidental, accompanying, at the same time, by circumstance, casual, chance, circumstantial, coexistent, coexisting, coincident, coinciding, coinstantaneous, concomitant, concurrent, conjunctional, contemporaneous, corresponding, fortuitous, *fortuitus,* occurring simultaneously, occurring together, simultaneous, surprising, unexpected, unplanned

COLD-BLOODED, **adjective**   aloof, barbarous, brutal, brutish, calculated, calculating, callous, cold, cold-hearted, cruel, cruel hearted, deliberate, demoniac, devilish, diabolic, dispassionate, feelingless, fiendish, frigid, hard, hardhearted, hardened, heartless, imperturbable, impervious, indifferent, indurate, indurated, inhumane, insensitive, malevolent, malicious, malign, obdurate, passionless, pitiless, pococurante, relentless, remorseless, ruthless, savage, soulless, truculent, uncaring, unconcerned, unemotional, unfeeling, unimpressible, uninterested, unkind, unmerciful, unmindful, unmoved, unperturbed, unrelenting, unresponsive, unsolicitous, unsusceptible, unsympathetic, untouched, untroubled, without heart, without warmth
ASSOCIATED CONCEPTS: cold-blooded murder

COLLATERAL *(Accompanying)*, **adjective**   accessory, additional, affiliated, ancillary, appertaining, associated, attendant, auxiliary, belonging, closely related, concomitant, concurrent, conjoined, connected, correlated, correspondent, corresponding, coupled with, entwined, interrelated, parallel, related, simultaneous, supplemental, supplementary
ASSOCIATED CONCEPTS: collateral action, collateral agreement, collateral attack, collateral contract, collat-

eral estoppel, collateral note, collateral powers, collateral proceeding, collateral promise, collateral source rule, collateral undertaking, collateral warranties

COLLATERAL *(Immaterial)*, **adjective**   being of no importance, extraneous, impertinent, inapplicable, inappropriate, incidental, inconsequential, indifferent, insignificant, insubstantial, irrelevant, meaningless, minor, negligible, nonessential, nugatory, of little moment, peripheral, secondary, trifling, trivial, unconnected, unessential, unimportant
ASSOCIATED CONCEPTS: collateral evidence, collateral facts, collateral fraud, collateral impeachment, collateral inquiry, collateral issue, collateral matter, collateral question, collateral testimony
FOREIGN PHRASES: *Frustra probatur quod probatum non relevat.* It is useless to prove that which when proved is irrelevant.

COLLATION, **noun**   analogical procedure, analogy, appositeness, ascertainment, balance, check, checking, comparability, comparative estimate, comparison, confirmation, *conlatio,* contrast, correlation, cross-check, determination, differentiation, examination, juxtaposition, relation
ASSOCIATED CONCEPTS: collation of seals, collation of the property in an estate

COLLEAGUE, **noun**   abettor, accessory, accompanier, accomplice, adjunct, adjutant, adjuvant, advocate, aider and abettor, ally, assistant, associate, attendant, auxiliary, backer, brother, champion, coadjutant, coadjutor, coadjutress, coadjutrix, coadjuvant, coaid, codirector, cohelper, collaborator, comate, companion, compeer, comrade, confederate, *confrère, conlega,* consociate, consort, cooperator, coworker, fellow, fellow companion, fellow conspirator, fellow worker, helper, mate, *particeps criminis,* participator, partner, seconder, *socius criminis,* stalwart, stand-by, votary

COLLECT *(Gather)*, **verb**   accumulate, acquire, add to, aggregate, amalgamate, amass, assemble, bring to a common center, bring to a point of union, bring together, compile, concentrate, *conferre, congerere,* conglomerate, consolidate, convene, *convocare,* draw together, embrace, gain, garner, gather together, group, incorporate, join, mass, muster, pile, put together, reunite, roll into one, unify, unite
ASSOCIATED CONCEPTS: collect rent, collect special assessments

COLLECT *(Recover money)*, **verb**   accept, acquire, appropriate, arrogate, assume, be given, be paid, collect payment, demand and obtain payment, exact payment, execute, gain, get back, get money, get possession of, levy, obtain payment, profit, raise, raise contributions, raise funds, reacquire, realize, receive money, receive payment, reclaim, recompense, recoup, recover, redeem, regain, retrieve, secure, secure payment, sequester, settle accounts with, take back again, take possession
ASSOCIATED CONCEPTS: collect a debt, collect on delivery, collect taxes, collecting bank

COLLECTION *(Accumulation)*, **noun**   accession, accretion, acervation, *acervus,* acquisition, addition, agglomeration, aggregate, aggregation, amassment, amount accrued, compilation, concentration, *congestus,* conglomerate, conglomeration, convergence, cumula-

tion, group, growth by addition, heap, hoard, mass, obtainment, pile, stockpile, store
ASSOCIATED CONCEPTS: collection of trust funds

COLLECTION *(Assembly)*, **noun** aggregation, assemblage, association, audience, colligation, collocation, company, conflux, congregation, conventicle, convention, *conventus,* crowd, forgathering, gathering, group, ingathering, meet, meeting, multitude, muster, rally, reassembly, reunion, throng
ASSOCIATED CONCEPTS: freedom of assembly

COLLECTION *(Payment)*, **noun** acquittance, adjustment, amends, bearing the cost, cash payment, clearance, *compensatio,* compensation, contribution, defrayal, defrayment, disbursement, discharge, enforcement of judgment, expenditure, fulfilment, full satisfaction, guerdon, indemnification, indemnity, installment, making amends, money paid, paying for, payment, price, propitiation, *quid pro quo,* quittance, receipted payment, recompense, rectification, redress, reimbursement, remission, remittance, remuneration, reparation, repayment, requital, restitution, restoration
ASSOCIATED CONCEPTS: collecting bank, collection agencies, collection agent, collection and payment, collection attorney, collection districts, collection of money, collection of taxes, collection officer, for collection only endorsements

COLLECTIVE, *adjective* accumulated, accumulative, aggregate, aggregated, amalgamated, amassed, assembled, associated, broad, brought together, combined, compiled, composite, compound, comprehensive, concentrated, concerted, concurrent, confederate, congregate, congregational, congregative, considered together, consolidated, corporate, cumulative, each and every, encyclopedic, entire, every, federative, gathered, general, grouped, integrated, integrative, joined, leagued, massed, mutual, of the same mind, total, unified, united, universal, unspecified, whole, widespread
ASSOCIATED CONCEPTS: collective bargaining, collective bargaining agreement

COLLECTIVE BARGAINING, *noun* abatement of differences, adjustment, arbitrage, arbitrament, arbitration, bargaining, compromise, conciliation, conference, intercession, intermediation, interposition, intervention, mediation, mediatorship, negotiation, package bargaining, pattern bargaining, umpirage
ASSOCIATED CONCEPTS: collective bargaining unit

COLLIDE *(Clash)*, *verb* altercate, antagonize, argue, be antagonistic, be at cross-purposes, be at variance, be contrary, be discordant, be in antagonism, be incompatible, be inimical, be mutually opposed, conflict with, confront, contend, contradict, contrast with, contravene, controvert, counter, counteract, countervail, counterwork, differ, differ in opinion, differ violently, disaccord, disagree, dispute, dissent, embroil, encounter, entangle, feud, go contrary to, go in opposition to, hold opposite views, interfere with, join issue, object, oppose, oppugn, quarrel, resist, run afoul of, run against, run at cross-purposes, run counter to, run foul of, show hostility, smash up, take issue, traverse, vary, withstand, work against, wrangle

COLLIDE *(Crash against)*, *verb* bump, bump into, butt against, come in contact, come into collision, come together, *confligere,* converge, crash into, crash to-

gether, drive against, drive into, encounter with a shock, enter into collision, hit, hurtle against, impinge, knock against, knock into, make contact, make impact, meet, run into each other, run together, slam into, smash into, strike, strike against, strike at, strike forcibly against each other

COLLISION *(Accident)*, *noun* concussion, contact, convergence, crash, encounter, impact, impingement, jar, jolt, meeting, percussion, pileup, shock, striking together, sudden contact, violent contact
ASSOCIATED CONCEPTS: avoidable collision, collision auto insurance, collisions by carriers

COLLISION *(Dispute)*, *noun* affray, altercation, antagonism, battle, clash, combat, *concursio, concursus,* conflict, contention, contradiction, contrariety, counteraction, disagreement, discord, disputation, embroilment, encounter, fight, fracas, fray, friction, hostility, interference, *mêlée,* opposition, resistence, skirmish

COLLUSION, *noun* abetment, act of working together, agreement, agreement for fraud, alliance, association, cabal, chicanery, coadjuvancy, coagency, collaboration, combination for fraud, combined operation, complicity, complot, concert, concord, concurrence, confederacy, conjunction, *conlusio,* connivance, conspiracy, contrivance, contriving, cooperation, cooperation for fraud, counterplot, covin, deceit, deceitful agreement, deceitful compact, deceitfulness, deception, double-dealing, duplicity, foul play, fraud, fraudulence, guile, hoax, illegal pact, intrigue, intriguery, joint effort, joint planning, junction, knavery, league, liaison, participation, participation in fraud, perfidy, plotting, *praevaricatio,* schemery, scheming, secret association, secret fraudulent understanding, secret understanding, secret understanding for fraud, synergism, synergy, treachery, trickery, underhand dealing, underplot, union
ASSOCIATED CONCEPTS: collusion in divorcing a spouse, collusion in obtaining the grounds of a divorce, collusion in procurement of a judgment, collusion to create diversity of citizenship, collusive action, collusive effort, collusive suit, connivance, conspiracy

COLLUSIVE, *adjective* artful, beguiling, calculating, clandestine, confidential, connivant, conniving, conspirational, conspirative, conspiratorial, conspiring, covinous, cunning, deceitful, deceptive, defrauding, designing, fraudulent, furtive, guileful, illicitly covert, indirect, insidious, intriguing, obreptitious, perfidious, plotting, schemeful, scheming, subreptitious, surreptitious, treacherous, undercover, underhanded, wily
ASSOCIATED CONCEPTS: collusion as a divorce defense, collusive claim, collusive suit, conspiracy, fraud and collusion

COLOR *(Complexion)*, *noun* apparent character, aspects, attribute, bearing, character, characteristics, component, constitution, denomination, description, designation, distinction, endowment, faculty, features, fettle, figure, flavor, form, hue, image, inclination, kind, likeness, lineament, make, manner, mark, nature, particularity, peculiarities, posture, principle, quality, shape, *species,* style, temperament, tendency, tone, trim, type, variety
ASSOCIATED CONCEPTS: the color of a case

COLOR *(Deceptive appearance)*, **noun**   act of dissembling, affectation, allegation, alleged motive, apparent right, appearance, cloak, concealment, cunning, deceit, deception, deceptive covering, device, disingenuousness, display, dissemblance, dissimulation, distortion, equivocalness, equivocation, evasion, exaggeration, external appearance, false appearance, falseness, falsification, feint, gloss, guile, guise, impression, misrepresentation, misstatement, outward appearance, *praetextus*, pretense, pretext, representation, show, *simulacrum*, simulation, subterfuge, *suggestio falsi*, *suppressio veri*
ASSOCIATED CONCEPTS: color a cause of action, color of authority, color of claim, color of interest, color of jurisdiction, color of law, color of office, color of right, color of state law, color of title, color of title in adverse possession, under color of, under color of law

COLORABLE *(Plausible)*, **adjective**   *ad captandum*, alleged, apparent, apparently right, *ben trovato*, conceivable, conjecturable, convincing, credible, feasible, *in posse*, logical, ostensible, persuasive, presumable, presumptive, rational, reasonable, seeming, seemingly fair, seemingly sound, seemingly valid, sensible, supposable, surmisable, tenable, thinkable, *verisimilis*, warrantable
ASSOCIATED CONCEPTS: colorable authority, colorable cause, colorable claim, colorable invocation of jurisdiction, colorable title

COLORABLE *(Specious)*, **adjective**   appearing, artful, crafty, deceitful, deceiving, deceptive, delusive, delusory, factitious, false, feigned, fraudulent, sham, trumped up, untrue

COMAKER, **noun**   certifier, coapplicant, coborrower, co-obligor, coratifier, cosignatory, cosigner, endorser, party to an instrument

COMBINATION, **noun**   affiliation, aggregate, aggregation, amalgamation, arrangement, assemblage, bringing together, coadjutorship, coalescence, coalition, collection, composition, compound, *coniunctio*, congregation, conjugation, conjunction, consolidation, fusion, incorporation, joining, junction, merger, pool, *societas*, unification, union
ASSOCIATED CONCEPTS: combination in restraint of trade, combination patent, combination to restrict competition and commerce, combination trademark, combined offense, combined property, illegal combination, patentable combination

COMBINE *(Act in concert)*, **verb**   act as one, act jointly, affiliate with, ally, associate, band together, coact, collaborate, collude, concert, confederate, conspire, cooperate, coordinate, enlist with, enter into partnership with, federate, form a union, harmonize, join forces, join with, league with, make common cause with, marry, pair with, participate with, pool, rally, syncretize, syndicate, take part, team up with, unite, work in unison, work together
ASSOCIATED CONCEPTS: Anti-Monopoly Act, antitrust

COMBINE *(Join together)*, **verb**   admix, affix, agglutinate, amalgamate, annex, append, attach, bind, blend, coalesce, cohere, colligate, commingle, commix, compound, concatenate, conglomerate, conglutinate, *coniungere*, conjoin, connect, *consociare*, consolidate, couple, entwine, fasten, form a union, fuse, glue, group,

immix, inosculate, interblend, interfuse, interlink, intermix, intertwine, intertwist, interweave, intwine, link, make a mixture, meld, merge, mingle, *miscere*, mix, paste, piece together, secure, splice, stick together, tack together, tie, unify, unite
ASSOCIATED CONCEPTS: combined offense, combined property

COMITY, **noun**   accommodation, accord, affability, agreeableness, amenity, amiability, amity, benevolence, camaraderie, civility, compliance, concord, considerateness, consideration, cordiality, courtesy, courtly politeness, deference, disposition to please, fellow feeling, friendliness, general reciprocity, gentility, good-fellowship, good will, graciousness, harmony, mansuetude, mutual consideration, mutual respect, neighborliness, obligingness, politeness, *prévenance*, reciprocity, respect, respectfulness
ASSOCIATED CONCEPTS: comity between courts, comity in conflict of laws, comity of nations, comity of states

COMMAND, **verb**   adjure, authorize, bid, call for, call upon, charge, compel, constrain, decree, demand, direct, direct imperatively, enact, exact, exercise authority, force, give directions, give orders, govern, have control, *hominem iubere facere, homini imperare, homini praecipere ut faciat, imminere*, impose, instruct, issue a command, issue a decree, issue an order, lead, mandate, ordain, order, order with authority, prescribe, proclaim, promulgate an order, require, rule, state authoritatively, take charge, take the lead
FOREIGN PHRASES: *In maleficio, ratihabitio mandato comparatur.* In tort, a ratification is regarded as a command. *Qui mandat ipse fecisse videtur.* He who gives an order is held to be the doer. *Ratihabitio mandato aequiparatur.* Ratification is equivalent to an express command. *Remissius imperanti melius paretur.* He who commands more gently is better obeyed.

COMMENCE, **verb**   arise, auspicate, begin, bring, broach, come into existence, come into the world, embark on, engage in, enter upon, inaugurate, incept, *incipere*, initiate, install, institute, introduce, launch, lay the foundations, make one's debut, open, originate, pioneer, put in execution, rise, set forth, set in operation, start, take the initiative, undertake, venture on
ASSOCIATED CONCEPTS: commence a prosecution, commence a suit, commence by filing, commence by summons, commencement of a proceeding, commencement of a suit, commencement of a trial, commencement of action, duly commenced

COMMENSURABLE, **adjective**   analagous, analogical, coequal, coextensive, coherent, commensurate, comparable, concordant, concurrent, conformable, congruous, consistent, consonant, coordinate, correspondent, equal, equivalent, even, identical in size, level, matching, of an equal size, of equal length or volume, parallel, proportional, proportionate, relative, similar

COMMENSURATE, **adjective**   acceptable, accordant, adequate, agreeing, analagous, appropriate, coequal, coextensive, commeasurable, commensurable, comparable, concordant, congruent, congruous, consistent, corresponding, equal in extent, equal in measure, equal to, equivalent, fitted, having a common measure, in accord, in agreement, in exact agreement, matching, of equal duration, of equal extent, of equal rank, on a par, on a proper scale, on a suitable scale, on even terms, paralleling, proportional, proportionate, relative, similar, sufficient, sufficing, suitable, synchronal

COMMENT, *noun* animadversion, annotation, assertion, averment, *censeo,* clarification, commentary, dictum, elucidation, enucleation, example, exegesis, exemplification, explanation, explanatory note, explication, exposition, expounding, expression, finding, footnote, gloss, illumination, illustration, interpretation, marginal annotation, mention, notation, note, note of explanation, observation, postulate, reflection, remark, report, scholium, statement, utterance, word of explanation
ASSOCIATED CONCEPTS: comment on defendant's failure to testify, comment on evidence, comment on witness' credibility, comment upon the testimony, comments on the weight of evidence

COMMENT, *verb* allege, animadvert, annotate, assert, bring out, *censere,* clarify, clear, criticize, declare, define, descant, dilate upon, discourse upon, discuss, elucidate, enlighten, enucleate, exemplify, expand on, explain, explicate, exposit on, expound, express, give a sense to, gloss, illuminate, illustrate, interject, interpose, interpret, make clear, make notes, make observations, make remarks, mention, note, notice, observe, opine, pass on, point out, posit, postulate, put a meaning on, rationalize, remark, remark upon, render intelligible, reprove, review, say, *sententiam dicere,* shed light upon, spell out, state, touch upon, treat, utter
ASSOCIATED CONCEPTS: comment on defendant's failure to testify, comment on evidence, comment on witness' credibility, comment upon the testimony, comments on the weight of evidence, prosecutor's comments on evidence

COMMERCE, *noun* interstate commerce, bargaining, barter, bartering, business, business affairs, business deals, business intercourse, business transactions, buying and selling, chaffering, commercial intercourse, *commercium,* dealing, exchange, fiscal exchange, industry, industry and trade, interchange, interchange of commodities, interchange of goods, intercourse, marketing, mercantile business, mercantile relations, mercantilism, *mercatura,* merchandising, merchantry, monetary exchange, multilateral trade, *negotia,* negotiation, private enterprise, production and distribution, reciprocal trade, system of exchanges, trade, trading, traffic, traffic of commodities, transportation of commodities, transportation of goods
ASSOCIATED CONCEPTS: affect commerce, affect interstate commerce, arising under a law regulating commerce, commerce among the several states, commerce clause, commerce power, commerce with foreign nations, commercial code, commercial paper, industry affecting commerce, international commerce, intrastate commerce, law regulating commerce, navigation and commerce, regulate commerce, restraint of commerce
FOREIGN PHRASES: *Commercium jure gentium communeesse debet, et non in monopolium et privatum paucorum quaestum convertendum.* Commerce, by the law of nations, ought to be common, and not converted into monopoly and the private gain of a few persons. *Jus accrescendi inter mercatores, pro beneficio commercii, locum non habet.* The right of survivorship does not exist between merchants for the benefit of commerce.

COMMERCIAL, *adjective* business, businesslike, *commercium,* economic, engaged in commerce, finan-

cial, fiscal, in the market, industrial, jobbing, manufactured for sale, mercantile, merchandising, monetary, pecuniary, pertaining to business, pertaining to merchants, pertaining to trade, prepared for sale, skilled in commerce, supplying, trade, trading
ASSOCIATED CONCEPTS: commercial agency, commercial bank, commercial bribery, commercial business, commercial consumption, commercial endorsement, commercial frustration, commercial insolvency, commercial law, commercial letter of credit, commercial loan, commercial mark, commercial partnership, commercial purpose, commercial use, commercial zone

COMMINGLE, *verb* admix, alloy, amalgamate, assemble, associate, band, bind together, blend, bring in contact with, coalesce, *commiscere,* combine, commix, compound, conglomerate, conjoin, connect, consolidate, consort with, couple, cross with, embody, entwine, fasten, fuse, harmonize, hybridize, immix, incorporate, interbreed, interlace, interlard, intermingle, intermix, involve together, join, league, link, lump together, merge, mix, mix together, pair with, piece, put together, run together, scramble, stir, unite
ASSOCIATED CONCEPTS: commingling of assets, commingling of funds by an agent, commingling of property

COMMISSION *(Act),* *noun* accomplishment, achievement, actualization, actuation, attainment, carrying out, completion, consummation, discharge, dispatch, doing, effecting, effectuation, enactment, enforcement, execution, exercise, exercising, fruition, fulfilment, implementation, inflicting, infliction, making, *mandatum,* operation, perpetration, realization, transaction
ASSOCIATED CONCEPTS: commission of crime

COMMISSION *(Agency),* *noun* advisory group, appointed group, board, board of inquiry, body of commissioners, body of delegates, body of deputies, bureau, cabinet, consultants, convocation, council, delegation, deliberative group, embassy, executive committee, investigating committee, planning board, representatives, standing committee, trustees
ASSOCIATED CONCEPTS: advisory body, Federal Trade Commission, Municipal Commission, Public Service Commission

COMMISSION *(Fee),* *noun* allotment, allowance, bonus, compensation, consideration, defrayment, disbursement, dividend, earnings, emolument, extra compensation, increment, interest, pay, pay-off, payment, percentage, percentage compensation, portion, proceeds, profit, recompense, reimbursement, remuneration, repayment, return, reward, salary, share of profits, stipend, subsidy, wage
ASSOCIATED CONCEPTS: broker's commission, commission merchant, compensation, fees, finder's commission, profits

COMMIT *(Entrust),* *verb* allot, assign, authorize, charge, charge with, commission, confer a trust, confide, consign, convey, delegate, employ, empower, engage, grant authority to, invest, invest with power, make responsible for, put an obligation upon, put in the hands of, relegate to, trust, turn over to, vest in
ASSOCIATED CONCEPTS: commit to a writing

COMMIT *(Institutionalize),* *verb* arrest, confine, consign, constrain, deliver into custody, enthrall, hold

in constraint, hold in restraint, immure, impound, imprison, incarcerate, intern, jail, lock up, place in confinement, put in custody, recommit to custody, remand to custody, remit to custody, restrain, send to an asylum, send to jail, send to prison
ASSOCIATED CONCEPTS: commit to a hospital, commit to a mental institution, commit to prison, committing magistrate

COMMIT *(Perpetrate), verb*   accomplish, achieve, act, act on, administer, apply oneself to, be a participator in, be a party to, be an accomplice, be engaged in, be engrossed in, bring about, bring to pass, carry into execution, carry on, carry out, carry through, complete, consummate, discharge, discharge the duties of, effect, employ oneself, execute, finish, fulfill, go through with, inflict, occupy oneself with, operate, participate in, perform, realize, transact
ASSOCIATED CONCEPTS: commit an offense against the United States

COMMITMENT *(Confinement), noun*   committal, confining, constraint, detention, durance, handing over into custody, holding in constraint, holding in restraint, immuring, impoundment, imprisonment, incarcerating, incarceration, interning, internment, jailing, legal confinement, legal constraint, locking up, mittimus, placing in confinement, putting in custody, remanding to custody, remitting to custody, restraint, restriction, sending to jail, sentencing
ASSOCIATED CONCEPTS: commitment to an institution, commitment to jail

COMMITMENT *(Responsibility), noun*   accountability, accountableness, agreement, allegiance, assignment, assurance, burden, call of duty, charge, conscience, contract, covenant, devoir, duty, engagement, faithfulness, incumbency, mission, obligation, onus, pledge, promise, sense of duty, solemn declaration, trust, undertaking, vow, warrant

COMMITTEE, *noun*   advisory group, agency, alliance, appointed group, association, board, body, body of consultants, bureau, cabinet, commission, confederacy, confederation, congregation, *consilium,* council, delegation, federation, fellowship, group of delegates, league, organization, organized group, representatives, staff, syndicate, trustees
ASSOCIATED CONCEPTS: campaign committee, committee of the whole, political committee, standing committee

COMMODITIES, *noun*   articles, articles of commerce, articles of merchandise, articles of trade, assets, chattels, goods, holdings, items, merchandise, *merx,* movables, objects, possessions, produce, produced materials, products, properties, raw materials, *res,* specialties, staples, stock, stock in trade, vendibles, wares
ASSOCIATED CONCEPTS: agricultural commodity, commodity rate, horticultural commodity, public utility commodity, stocks and bonds

COMMON *(Customary), adjective*   accepted, ascertained, commonplace, conventional, current, currently perceived, established, everyday, familiar, frequent, generally known, natural, normal, often met with, ordinary, popular, prevailing, prevalent, publicly known, received, recognized, repeatedly recognized, traditional,

typical, universally known, usual, usually understood, well-known, widely known, widespread
ASSOCIATED CONCEPTS: common assault, common-law, common-law burglary, common-law contempt, common-law copyright, common-law crime, common-law forgery, common-law jurisdiction, common-law larceny, common-law lien, common-law marriage, common-law misdemeanor, common-law murder, common-law nuisance, common-law remedy, common-law trademark, common-law trust, common-law wife, common liability, common peril, common question of law or fact, common seal, common source of title, common stock, common thief, common use

COMMON *(Shared), adjective*   belonging equally to, belonging to all, belonging to many, collective, communal, *communis,* commutual, conjoint, cooperative, for the use of all, in partnership, joint, mutual, owned jointly, participating, participatory, pertaining to the whole community, pooled, popular, public, *publicus,* reciprocal, shared among several, shared by two or more, universal, used by all
ASSOCIATED CONCEPTS: common adventure, common belief, common boundary line, common carrier, common council, common directors, common disaster, common driveway, common enemy doctrine, common enterprise, common good, common interest, common jurisdiction, common knowledge, common labor, common lands, common necessity, common plan, common plea courts, common property, common recovery, common rights, common scheme, common stock, common wall, common walls

COMMON KNOWLEDGE, *noun*   accepted fact, acknowledgment, announcement, annunciation, avowance, declaration, disclosure, dissemination, experience, *exposé,* familiarity, general information, history, learning, manifestation, notoriety, *patefactio,* public disclosure, public knowledge, public notice, publicness, state of being public

COMMON SENSE, *noun*   acumen, astuteness, balanced judgment, calmness, clear thinking, composure, experience, experienced view, good judgment, good sense, intelligence, intuition, judgment, level-headedness, logic, mental poise, native reason, natural sagacity, ordinary judgment, ordinary sense, plain sense, plausibility, practical discernment, practical knowledge, practicality, presence of mind, prudence, rational faculty, rationality, reason, reasonableness, resourcefulness, sagacity, sapience, *savoir faire,* sensibleness, sober-mindedness, sobriety, solidity, sound perception, sound sense, sound understanding, unbiased impulse, understanding, unemotional consideration, wisdom, worldly wisdom
ASSOCIATED CONCEPTS: commonsense reading of a statute, commonsense ruling

COMMOTION, *noun*   affray, *agitatio,* agitation, altercation, brawl, clamor, clash, conflict, confusion, convulsion, disorder, disorderliness, disorganization, disquiet, disquietude, disturbance, ebullition, embroilment, encounter, entanglement, eruption, excitement, ferment, fermentation, fight, fomentation, fracas, fray, furor, imbroglio, inquietude, insurgence, insurrection, maelstrom, mayhem, *mêlée,* moil, *motus,* noisy strife, overthrow, pandemonium, perturbation, public disturbance, quarrel, racket, rampage, rebellion, restlessness, rising insubordination, row, ruction, scuffle, skirmish, stir, struggle, tempest, tumult, *tumultus, turba,* turbulence, turmoil, tussle, unruliness, upheaval, uprising, uproar, violence, welter, whirl

COMMUNICATE, *verb*   acquaint, advertise, advise, announce, apprise, articulate, assert, bandy words, breathe, bring word, broadcast, commerce with, commune, *communicare,* confabulate, converse, convey, correspond, deal with, declare, demonstrate, disclose, discourse with, divulge, engage in a conversation, enlighten, enunciate, express, familiarize, find words to express, give an account, give expression, give notice, give notification, give one to understand, give the facts, give tongue, give utterance, give voice, have intercourse, impart, inform, instill, instruct, interchange thoughts, intercommunicate, lay before, let know, let out, make known, mention, narrate, notify, parley, present facts, proclaim, pronounce, publicize, put forth, put in words, relate, reveal, say, send word, serve notice, set forth, signify, sound, speak one's mind, speak, specify, talk, teach, tell, traffic with, transmit, utter, verbalize, vocalize, voice, write

COMMUNICATION *(Discourse), noun*   collocution, colloquy, *communicatio, communiqué,* conference, conversation, correspondence, dialogue, dissertation, exchange, interchange, intercommunication, intercourse, interlocution
ASSOCIATED CONCEPTS: attorney and client communication, conditionally privileged communication, confidential communication, husband and wife communication, physician and patient communication, privileged communication, telegraph communication, telephonic communication, verbal communication, written communication

COMMUNICATION *(Statement), noun*   announcement, annunciation, declaration, disclosure, dissemination, divulgement, information, message, news, notification, proclamation, report, revelation, utterance, writing

COMMUNITY, *noun*   body, body politic, borough, citizenry, city, civilization, *civitas,* commonalty, commonwealth, commune, group, inhabitants, kinship, locality, municipality, neighborhood, partnership, people, polity, populace, population, *respublica,* society, town
ASSOCIATED CONCEPTS: community estate, community interest, community of right or interest, community property

COMMUTE, *verb*   abate, abbreviate, abridge, allay, alleviate, alter, ameliorate, bate, change, change penalties, curtail, cut, decrease a punishment, dilute, diminish, ease, exchange, exchange penalties, lessen, lighten, limit, make less extreme, make less harsh, make less intense, make less rigorous, make less rough, make less severe, make lighter, make milder, meliorate, minimize, mitigate, modify sentence, palliate, reduce, reduce a punishment, reduce in asperity, relax severity, relieve, render less difficult, shorten, shrink, slacken, slash, soften, substitute, temper, tone down, trim, truncate
ASSOCIATED CONCEPTS: commute a sentence

COMPACT *(Dense), adjective*   arranged within a small space, bunched, close, close-knit, close-set, close together, closely united, clustered, cohesive, compacted,

compressed, concentrated, condensed, consolidated, constricted, constringed, contracted, crammed, crowded, densified, economical of space, firm, firmly united, forced into smaller space, hard, massed, massive, packed, populous, pressed into smaller compass, pressed together, rammed, serried, solid, solidified, space saving, squeezed together, stuffed, thick, tight, tightly knit

COMPACT *(Pithy), adjective*   abbreviated, abbreviatory, abridged, abstracted, aphoristic, aphoristical, apothegmatic, apothegmatical, brief, compendious, concise, condensed, contracted, crisp, curt, digested, direct, epigrammatic, epitomized, expressed concisely, gnomic, gnomical, laconic, meaty, outlined, pointed, recapitulated, sententious, short, shortened, shrunk, straightforward, succinct, summarized, summary, summed up, synoptic, telescoped, terse, tidy, to the point, trim

COMPACT, *noun*   agreement, agreement between parties, arrangement, bargain, cartel, commitment, compromise, concord, concordat, contract, contractual obligation, contractual statement, convention, *conventus,* covenant, deal, entente, *entente cordiale,* indenture, mutual pledge, mutual promise, obligation, pact, *pactio, pactum,* pledge, promise, stipulation, treaty, understanding
ASSOCIATED CONCEPTS: interstate compact
FOREIGN PHRASES: *Pacta privata juri publico derogare non possunt.* Private compacts cannot derogate from public right. *Re, verbis, scripto, consensu, traditione, junctura vestes sumere pactasolent.* Agreements usually take their clothing from the thing itself, from words, from writing, from consent, from delivery.

COMPANY *(Assemblage), noun*   aggregation, assembled body, *assemblée,* assembly, *attroupement,* caucas, coalition, conclave, conference, confluence, conflux, congregation, congress, convention, convergence, convocation, crowd, gathering, group, ingathering, league, meeting, mustering, *societas*

COMPANY *(Enterprise), noun*   association, body corporate, business, business establishment, *coetus,* combination, commercial enterprise, concern, confederacy, consociation, copartnership, corporate body, corporation, establishment, federation, firm, *grex,* guild, institute, joint concern, organization, partnership
ASSOCIATED CONCEPTS: affiliated company, company union, construction company, corporation, holding company

COMPARABLE *(Capable of comparison), adjective*   akin, alike, analogous, analogical, approximate, associated, close, cognate, commensurable, *comparabilis,* congeneric, correlative, homogeneous, homologous, kindred, like, much the same, parallel, related, resembling, similar

COMPARABLE *(Equivalent), adjective*   coequal, commensurate, equable, equal in value, equipollent, even, identical, interchangeable, matched, matching, on par, tantamount, undeviating, uniform, unvarying, without distinction

COMPARATIVE, *adjective*   analogous to, comparable, *comparativus,* connected with, contrastive, correlative, corresponding to, estimated by comparison, in

connection with, in proportion to, in relation to, in relation with, in respect to, in the same category, judged by comparison, matching, metaphorical, pertaining to, pertinent to, referable to, referential, referring, relating to, relational, relative, rivaling, similar to, similitudinous, vying with, with reference to, with regard to, with relation to
ASSOCIATED CONCEPTS: comparative injury, comparative negligence, comparative rectitude

COMPARE, *verb* *aequiperare,* analogize, balance against, bring into comparison, bring into meaningful relation with, bring into relation, *comparare, componere, conferre,* contrast, correlate, differentiate, discriminate between, distinguish between, draw a parallel, equate, estimate relatively, exercise critical judgment, identify with, juxtapose, liken, match, measure, note the similarities and differences, parallel, parallelize, place in juxtaposition, put alongside, relate, represent as resembling, set side by side, show correspondence, show to be analagous, show to be similar, weigh
ASSOCIATED CONCEPTS: comparative negligence, comparing equities

COMPARISON, *noun* alikeness, analogical procedure, analogy, association, balance, *comparatio,* comparative estimate, *conlatio,* contrast, correlation, equation, measurement, nearness, parallel, *rapprochement,* relative estimate, relative estimation, resemblance
ASSOCIATED CONCEPTS: comparison of negligence of opposing parties

COMPATIBILITY, *noun* acclimation, accommodation, accord, accordance, adjustment, affiliation, agreement, amity, attunement, balance, coexistence, comity, common view, companionship, compliance, concord, concordance, concurrence, conformity, congeniality, congruity, congruousness, *consensus omnium,* consent, consentaneity, consistency, consonance, cooperation, coordination, *entente,* equanimity, harmony, mutual understanding, rapport, reconciliation, unanimity, union, unity
ASSOCIATED CONCEPTS: incompatibility

COMPEL, *verb* bear down against, bear hard upon, blackmail, bring pressure to bear upon, burden, cause, coerce, *cogere,* command, *compellere,* constrain, control, decree, demand, dictate, distrain, drive, elicit, employ force, enforce, exact, force, impel, impose, impose a duty, inflict, insist, leave no option, limit, necessitate, obligate, oblige, obtrude on, order, press, pressure, put under obligation, require, restrict, *subigere,* subject, take no denial, threaten, urge, urge forward
ASSOCIATED CONCEPTS: compel accused to give evidence against himself, compel by legal process, compel to testify under a grant of immunity

COMPELLING, *adjective* absolute, assertive, authoritative, binding, categorical, coercive, commanding, compulsive, compulsory, constraining, decisive, dominant, driving, emphatic, enforcing, forcible, *gravis,* great, impelling, imperative, incisive, inducive, influential, involuntary, irresistible, necessary, obligatory, obsessing, obsessional, obsessive, of necessity, omnipotent, overpowering, overriding, overruling, overwhelming, peremptory, potent, predominant, preeminent, preponderant, pressing, propulsive, puissant, strong, thrustful, trenchant, unavoidable, *validus, vehemens,* vigorous, weighty

ASSOCIATED CONCEPTS: compelling interest, compelling necessity, compelling need

COMPENDIUM, *noun* abbreviation, abridgment, abstract, breviary, brief, capsule, compend, concise treatment, condensation, conspectus, contraction, digest, *epitoma,* epitome, essence, extract, outline, pandect, precis, recapitulation, review, summary, survey, syllabus, synopsis

COMPENSATE *(Counterbalance), verb* act against with equal force, allow for, atone, balance, be equivalent, *compensare,* correspond, counteract, counterpoise, countervail, counterweigh, equalize, equate, equilibrate, even, furnish an equivalent, level off, make equal, make level, make steady, make up for, neutralize, offset, oppose, produce equilibrium, restore to equilibrium, set off, square, stabilize, strike a balance

COMPENSATE *(Remunerate), verb* allow for, defray, discharge a debt, give equal value, give satisfaction for damage, give satisfaction for injury, honor, indemnify, make payment, make restitution, pay damages, pay for, pay in full, pay the equivalent, pay the value, pay wages, recompense, redress, refund, reimburse, remit, *remunerari,* remunerate for injury, repay, repay for a loss, return, reward, reward for a loss, reward for an injury, salary, satisfy, settle accounts with
ASSOCIATED CONCEPTS: compensation for expenses, compensation for goods sold and delivered, compensation for hospital bills, compensation for injuries, compensation for out-of-pocket expenses, compensation for pain and suffering, compensation for the negligent acts of another, compensation for wrongdoing, costs, fair and reasonable compensation, fees, penalties, reimbursement, wages, workmen's compensation

COMPENSATION, *noun* amends, atonement, commutation, *compensatio,* consideration, damages, defrayal, defrayment, earnings, emolument, equivalent given for injury, equivalent given for loss sustained, fee, financial remuneration, guerdon, indemnification, indemnity, meed, monetary remuneration, pay, payment, payment of damages, quittance, reclamation, recompensation in value, recompense, recoupment, recovery, rectification, reimbursement, remuneration, remuneration for injury, reparation, repayment, requital, restoration, retainer, retaining fee, retrieval, return, reward, reward for injury, reward for loss, reward for service, salary, satisfaction, satisfaction for damage, satisfaction for injury, settlement, solatium, wages
ASSOCIATED CONCEPTS: adequate compensation, adjusted compensation, agreement for compensation, compensatory damages, fair and reasonable compensation, full compensation, just and adequate compensation, payments of compensation, reasonable compensation
FOREIGN PHRASES: *Corporalis injuria non recipit aestimationem de futuro.* A personal injury cannot be compensated for by later acts.

COMPENSATORY, *adjective* atoning, balancing, compensating, compensative, equivalent, expiating, expiatory, in compensation, indemnificatory, paying, propitiating, recompensive, redemptive, refunding, reimbursing, remitting, remunerative, reparative, repaying, restitutive, restitutory, retributive, rewardful, rewarding, satisfying, unindebted

ASSOCIATED CONCEPTS: compensatory damages, compensatory penalties

COMPETE, *verb*   battle, be a candidate, be in the running, *certare,* challenge, clash, combat, contend, contest, *cum homine contendere,* duel, employ stratagem, encounter, engage in a contest, enter, enter competition, joust, match strength with, match wits with, oppose, participate in, rival, spar, strive, struggle, take part, tilt, vie with, wrestle

COMPETENCE *(Ability),* **noun**   adequacy, adroitness, aptitude, capability, capacity, conversance, dexterity, effectiveness, effectuality, efficacy, eligibility, enablement, endowment, equipment, experience, facility, faculty, fitness, flair, forte, gift, grasp, intelligence, legal competence, legal fitness, mastery, potency, proficiency, qualifications, responsibility, skill, skillfulness, sufficiency, suitability, talent, training
ASSOCIATED CONCEPTS: competency of a witness, competent and intelligent waiver of counsel, competent authority, competent jurisdiction, legally competent
FOREIGN PHRASES: *Homo potest esse habilis et inhabilis diversis temporibus.* A man may be capable and incapable at different times. *Nemo praesens nisi intelligat.* One is not present unless he understands. *Nullus idoneus testis in re sua intelligitur.* No person is deemed to be a competent witness in his own behalf. *Pupillus pati posse non intelligitur.* An infant is not considered able to do an act to his own prejudice. *Sola ac per se senectus donationem testamentum aut transactionem non vitiat.* Old age alone and of itself will not vitiate a will or gift.

COMPETENCE *(Sanity),* **noun**   capability, clearmindedness, coherence, healthy mindedness, lucidity, mental balance, mental capacity, mental equilibrium, mental health, normalcy, normality, normalness, rationality, reason, reasonability, sanemindedness, saneness, sense, senses, sound mind, soundmindedness, soundness, soundness of mind
ASSOCIATED CONCEPTS: age of maturity, competency of a witness, competent and intelligent waiver of counsel, age of maturity, infancy, legally competent, mental competence, *non compos mentis*
FOREIGN PHRASES: *Furiosi nulla voluntas est.* A madman has no will.

COMPETENT, *adjective*   able, accomplished, adept, adequate, adroit, artful, capable, *competere,* conversant, credible, deft, dexterous, effective, effectual, efficacious, efficient, enterprising, excellent, experienced, expert, fit, good, ingenious, learned, masterful, masterly, mentally capable, practiced, prepared, proficient, properly qualified, qualified, ready, resourceful, responsible, satisfactory, skilled, skillful, sufficient, suitable, trained, versed, well-fitted
ASSOCIATED CONCEPTS: *capax negotii,* competent and intelligent waiver of counsel, competent authority, competent court, competent evidence, competent jurisdiction, competent witness, legally competent, mentally competent

COMPETITION, *noun*   attempt to equal, bout, challenge, combat, conflict, *contentio,* contest, corrivalry, encounter, engagement, open contest, opposition, outrivalry, pitting of strength, pitting of wits, race, rivalry, scramble, strife, striving for superiority, struggle for superiority, trial of superiority, vying for ascendance
ASSOCIATED CONCEPTS: competitive bidding, competitive class, competitive examination, fair competition, free and open competition, unfair competition, unreasonable interference with competition

COMPETITIVE *(Antagonistic),* **adjective**   adverse, at issue, at variance, challenging, clashing, colliding, combatant, combative, combatting, competing, competitory, conflicting, contending, contentious, contrary, counteractive, decided by competition vying, discordant, disputatious, dissident, emulative, in competition, opposing, oppugnant, rival, rivaling, striving, vying
ASSOCIATED CONCEPTS: competitive bidding, competitive class, competitive examination, unfair competition

COMPETITIVE *(Open),* **adjective**   accessible to all, common, comprehensive, equal, free, free to all, general, nonexclusive, not partial, not privileged, open to the public, popular, public, unbounded, unclosed, unconfined, universal, unrestrained, unrestricted
ASSOCIATED CONCEPTS: fair competition, free and open competition, unreasonable interference with competition

COMPILATION, *noun*   accretion, accumulation, agglomeration, aggregation, anthology, arrangement, assemblage, classification, codification, collection, colligation, collocation, combination, conglomeration, consolidation, gathering, incorporation, miscellany, selection
ASSOCIATED CONCEPTS: Official Compilation of Codes Rules, and Regulations

COMPILE, *verb*   accumulate, agglomerate, aggregate, amass, anthologize, arrange, arrange materials for publication, assemble, bring together, bunch, bunch together, cluster, collect, combine, *componere,* compose, conglomerate, cull, cumulate, draw together, draw up, extract from other works, garner, gather, gather together, glean, group, group together, lump together, make up, mass, prepare, recapitulate, select, select and arrange, unite, write

COMPLACENT, *adjective*   at ease, carefree, complaisant, compliable, compliant, composed, content, contented, fulfilled, gratified, peaceful of mind, placid, pleased, *qui sibi placet,* reposeful, resigned, satisfied, self-content, self-satisfied, serene, smug, *suffisant,* tranquil, unvexed

COMPLAIN *(Charge),* **verb**   *accusare,* accuse, arraign, blame, bring a suit, bring an action, bring charges, bring proceedings against, bring up on charges, censure, challenge, charge with, cite, criminate, declaim against, delate, denounce, denunciate, file a charge, file a claim, file a suit, implicate, impute, incriminate, inculpate, inform against, institute a lawsuit, lay an information, lay blame upon, lay responsibility on, lay the blame on, lodge a complaint, make an accusation, prefer charges, prosecute, reprehend, reproach, reprobate, start an action, state a grievance, sue, take action
ASSOCIATED CONCEPTS: complain of a criminal act, complain of a tortious act

COMPLAIN *(Criticize)*, *verb*   accuse, admonish, animadvert, asperse, assail, be critical, be dissatisfied, berate, blame, carp, cast aspersions, castigate, cavil, censure, chastise, chide, condemn, *conqueri de rem,* contravene, decry, defy, denounce, deprecate, differ, disagree, disapprove, disparage, faultfind, find fault, find fault with, malign, object, object to, oppose, protest, rebuke, remonstrate, repine, reprehend, reprimand, reproach, reprove, speak ill of, take exception, take exception to, upbraid

COMPLAINANT, *noun*   accusant, accuser, aggrieved party, challenger, charger, claimant, complaining party, delator, denouncer, impeacher, incriminator, indicter, indictor, libelant, litigant, one instigating an action, opposing party, party, party to a suit, petitioner, petitioner for legal redress, plaintiff, preferror of charges, prosecution, prosecutor, public prosecutor, relator, suitor
ASSOCIATED CONCEPTS: complainant's costs, complaining witness

COMPLAINT, *noun*   accusal, accusation, allegation, bill of indictment, case, case for the prosecution, charge, citation, count, crimination, criticism, denouncement, denunciation, expostulation, first pleading, formal allegation, gravamen of a charge, grievance, incrimination, indictment, information, information against, litigation, main charge, objection, particular charge, petition, plaint, plaintiff's initiatory pleading, pleading in a civil action, preferment of charges, prosecution, protest, protestation, *querimonia,* remonstrance, statement of the plaintiff's cause, substance of a charge
ASSOCIATED CONCEPTS: bill of complaint, petition, cross-complaint, verified complaint

COMPLEMENT, *noun*   companion, *complementum,* completion, congener, coordinate, correlate, correspondent, corresponding part, counterpart, pendant, reciprocal, remainder, rest, supplement

COMPLETE *(All-embracing)*, *adjective*   absolute, all, all-comprehending, all-comprehensive, all-covering, all-inclusive, all-pervading, all-sufficing, blanket, broad-based, capacious, comprehensive, consummate, developed, encyclopedic, entire, exhaustive, expansive, extensive, full, global, inclusive, of great scope, over-all, plenary, sweeping, thorough, thoroughgoing, total, unconditional, undiminished, undivided, unimpaired, unqualified, unreduced, unreserved, unrestricted, unsevered, utter, very thorough, wide-embracing, with no exception, without omissions
ASSOCIATED CONCEPTS: complete abandonment, complete and adequate remedy at law, complete contract, complete coverage, complete delivery, complete jurisdiction, complete liquidation, complete ownership, complete record, complete relief, complete remedy, complete title, completed instrument

COMPLETE *(Ended)*, *adjective*   accomplished, achieved, at an end, brought to a conclusion, carried through, closed, completed, completive, concluded, conclusive, consummated, culminated, decided, definitive, disposed of, done, effected, effectuated, executed, final, finished, over, performed, realized, set at rest, settled, terminated, terminational, terminative, through

COMPLETE, *verb*   accomplish, achieve, apply a closure, bring to a close, bring to an end, bring to conclusion, bring to maturity, bring to perfection, carry out, carry through, carry to completion, clinch, close, conclude, consummate, determine, discharge, dispatch, dispose of, draw to a close, end, finalize, finish, follow through, fulfill, perfect, polish, realize, seal, succeed, terminate, wind up
FOREIGN PHRASES: ***Extincto subjecto, tollitur adjunctum.*** When the substance is extinguished, the incident ceases.

COMPLEX, *adjective*   abstruse, bewildering, chaotic, circuitous, complicated, confused, convoluted, difficult, elaborated, enigmatic, entangled, flexuous, impenetrable, implicated, inextricable, inscrutable, interlaced, interwoven, intricate, involuted, involutional, involved, irreducible, jumbled, kaleidoscopic, knotted, labyrinthine, mingled, muddled, *multiplex,* obscure, perplexing, recondite, sinuous, snarled, tangled, tortuous, unarranged, unclassified, undecipherable, unfathomable, unorganized, varied
ASSOCIATED CONCEPTS: complex issues to be tried

COMPLEX *(Development)*, *noun*   aggregate, aggregation, association, collectivity, compages, composite, compound, conglomerate, conglomeration, group, network, organization, structure, system, totality, unity
ASSOCIATED CONCEPTS: building complex, industrial complex, residential housing complex

COMPLEX *(Entanglement)*, *noun*   clutter, complexus, complication, confusion, convolution, derangement, difficulty, disarrangement, disarray, disorder, disorganization, enmeshment, imbroglio, intricacy, involution, involvement, jumble, labyrinth, maze, muddle, *multiplex,* snag, snarl, tangle, twist

COMPLEXION, *noun*   apparent character, apparent state, appearance, aspect, carriage, character, *color,* contour, demeanor, display, disposition, external appearance, facet, fashion, favor, feature, figure, form, guise, image, impression, look, manifestation, manner, mien, nature, outline, outward appearance, port, posture, presence, quality, regard, respect, semblance, shape, slant, spirit, style, temper, tenor, tone, view, visage
ASSOCIATED CONCEPTS: complexion of the case

COMPLIANCE, *noun*   accedence, acceptance, accommodation, accord, accordance, acquiescence, adaptability, adherence, agreeability, agreement, assent, bowing, compliancy, concession, concord, concurrence, conformability, conformance, conformity, consent, consonance, consonancy, cooperation, dutifulness, harmony, keeping, nonresistance, obedience, *obsequium,* observance, pliancy, submission, tractability, tractableness, willingness to comply, yielding, yieldingness
ASSOCIATED CONCEPTS: compliance with the law, in compliance with statute, strict compliance, substantial compliance
FOREIGN PHRASES: ***Impotentia excusat legem.*** The impossibility of performing a legal duty is an excuse from the performance. ***Obedientia est legis essentia.*** Obedience is the essence of the law.

COMPLICATION, *noun*   aggravation, bafflement, barrier, complexity, complexness, *complexus,* complicated state, confusion, development, difficulty, dilemma, entanglement, hindrance, imbroglio, impediment, *implicatio,* incomprehensibility, inextricability, inscrutability, intricacy, intrigue, involution, involved state, involvement, labyrinth, obscurity, obstacle, obstruction, perplexity, predicament, puzzle, quandary, sinuosity, stumbling block, unforeseen circumstance

COMPLY, *verb* abide by, accede to, accept, accommodate, acknowledge, acquiesce in, adhere to, agree with, assent to, attend to orders, be faithful to, be willing, carry into effect, carry into execution, carry out, cease resistance, complete, *concedere,* concur, conform to, consent to, cooperate with, defer to, fall in with, fit, fulfill, give consent to, go along with, harmonize with, *morem gerere,* not resist, obey, observe, *parere,* perform, relent, resign oneself to, respect, satisfy, stoop, submit to, succumb, yield to
ASSOCIATED CONCEPTS: compliance with statutes

COMPONENT, *noun* aspect, basic substance, complement, component part, constituent, constituent part, content, division, element, elementary unit, factor, feature, fragment, fundamental part, ingredient, installment, integral part, item, material part, one of the contents, part, particular part, physical element, piece, portion, principle part, section, sector, segment, subdivision, unit, unit of composition
ASSOCIATED CONCEPTS: component parts

COMPORT *(Agree with),* *verb* accord with, attune, be accordant, be applicable, be apposite, be appropriate, be apt, be consistent, be consonant, be in accordance with, be in keeping, be in tune with, be suitable, become, befit, belong, chime in with, click, cohere, coincide, concur, conform, correspond, fall in with, fit, fit in, fit together, harmonize, jibe, match, mesh with, quadrate, reconcile, render accordant, square with, suit, tally

COMPORT *(Behave),* *verb* acquit, act, appear, conduct, demean, deport, discipline, manage, perform, present oneself, quit, represent, seem, show manner, show mien
ASSOCIATED CONCEPTS: demeanor of a witness

COMPOSE, *verb* accomplish, achieve, actualize, arrange, author, be responsible, be the agent, be the cause of, be the reason, bring about, bring into being, bring into effect, bring into existence, build, call into being, call into existence, carry into execution, cause, cause to be, cause to exist, chalk out, compile, *componere,* conceive, construct, contrive, develop, devise, draft, draw out, draw up, effect, *efficere,* efform, engineer, envisage, execute, express, fashion, form, formulate, frame, generate, give rise to, imagine, improvise, invent, orchestrate, organize, originate, pattern, produce, shape, use one's imagination, visualize, work out, work up, write

COMPOSITE, *adjective* accompanied, admixed, agglomerate, aggregate, aggregated, all-embracing, alloyed, amalgamated, amassed, assembled, assorted, blended, clustered, collected, collective, combined, commixed, complex, *compositus,* compound, compounded, conglomerate, conjoint, conjunct, conjunctive, connected, coupled, diversified, fused, gathered, gathered into a whole, glomerate, heterogeneous, incorporated, integrated, intermixed, joined, medley, miscellaneous, mixed, mosaic, motley, multifarious, multiple, *multi-*

plex, scrambled, sundry, united, unseparated, varied, variegated, wedded
ASSOCIATED CONCEPTS: composite class, composite facts, composite instrument, composite knowledge, composite statements

COMPOSITION *(Agreement in bankruptcy),* *noun* agreement, arrangement, clearance, compact, compromise agreement, contract, discharge, liquidation, mutual agreement, mutual concession, payment in lieu, reciprocal concession, release, settlement, settlement by mutual agreement, settlement on account
ASSOCIATED CONCEPTS: composition agreement, composition in bankruptcy, contract of composition, reorganization

COMPOSITION *(Makeup),* *noun* arrangement, array, combination, compilation, *compositio,* compounding, comprisal, concoction, conformation, constitution, construction, contents, creation, design, efformation, embodiment, establishment, fabrication, formation, formulation, inclusion, manufacture, nature, organization, preparation, production, structure, synthesis, union

COMPOSURE, *noun* *aequus animus,* aplomb, balance, calm, calmness, command of one's faculties, command of temper, complacence, constraint, content, contentment, control, equability, equanimity, equilibrium, evenness, forbearance, fortitude, harmony, imperturbability, imperturbation, indisturbance, inexcitability, moderation, patience, peace, peace of mind, peacefulness, placidity, placidness, poise, presence of mind, quiescence, quietude, repose, reserve, rest, restraint, sedateness, self-assurance, self-command, self-possession, self-restraint, serenity, stability, tolerance, tranquil mind, *tranquillitas,* tranquillity

COMPOUND, *adjective* aggregate, aggregated, amalgamated, assimilated, associated, blended, combined, commixed, complex, complicated, composite, *compositus,* conglomerate, congregated, conjoint, conjugate, conjunct, connected, convoluted, elaborate, embodied, entangled, fused, hybridized, incorporated, infused, inseparable, integrated, interlaced, intermingled, interwoven, intricate, involved, manifold, merged, mingled, mixed, mosaic, motley, multifarious, multiform, multiple, *multiplex,* solid, tangled, tied, united, varied, variegated, woven
ASSOCIATED CONCEPTS: compound a crime, compound interest, compound larceny, compounding a felony
FOREIGN PHRASES: **Aestimatid praeteriti delicti ex postremo facto nunquam crescit.** The weight of an offense committed in the past is never increased by a subsequent fact.

COMPOUND, *verb* accrue, add to, advance, aggrandize, aggravate, amount, *ampliare, amplificare,* annex, append, *augere,* be augmented, be numerous, become greater, become larger, branch out, build up, burgeon, contribute to, develop, *dilatare,* dilate, distend, elaborate, enhance, enlarge, enrich, exacerbate, exaggerate, exalt, expand, extend, fill in, fill out, fortify, further, gain ground, gain strength, get ahead, give strength to, glorify, greaten, grow larger, heighten, increase, increase the numbers, inflate, intensify, lend force to, lengthen, magnify, make greater, make larger, multiply, open out, parlay, pile up, prolong, protract,

raise, refine, reinforce, restrengthen, spread out, strengthen, subjoin, superadd, supplement, widen
ASSOCIATED CONCEPTS: compounding a crime, compounding a debt, compounding a felony, compounding penalty
FOREIGN PHRASES: *Aestimatio praeteriti delicti ex postremo facto nunquam crescit.* The weight of a past crime is never increased by a subsequent fact.

COMPREHEND *(Include), verb*   be composed of, be comprised of, be made up of, circumscribe, compass, comprise, consist of, constitute, contain, cover, embody, embrace, encircle, encompass, envelop, incorporate, involve, possess, span, take in
ASSOCIATED CONCEPTS: comprehensive zoning

COMPREHEND *(Understand), verb*   absorb, appreciate, apprehend, assimilate, be acquainted, be apprized, be aware, be cognizant, be conscious, be conversant with, be in possession of the facts, be informed, cognize, come to understand, *comprehendere,* conceive, descry, detect, discern, fathom, gain insight, grasp, grow aware, ken, know, master, perceive, realize, recognize, see, take in, understand fully
ASSOCIATED CONCEPTS: comprehend the nature and consequences of an act, intent, scienter

COMPREHENSIBLE, *adjective*   apprehensible, articulate, ascertainable, clear, clear-cut, cognizable, cognoscible, comprehendable, conceivable, decipherable, defined, disclosed, easily understood, easy to understand, evident, exoteric, explicable, explicit, express, fathomable, graphic, graphical, intelligible, knowable, legible, lucid, luculent, manifest, obvious, overt, palpable, patent, pellucid, penetrable, perceivable, perceptible, perspicuous, *perspicuus,* plain, realizable, recognizable, revealed, self-evident, self-explanatory, simple, unambiguous, unclouded, unconcealed, unconfused, understandable, unhidden, unmistakable, unobscure, unveiled

COMPREHENSION, *noun*   ability to know, alertness, appreciation, apprehension, attentiveness, awareness, awareness of, capability, capacity to understand, cognition, cognizance, command of thought, *comprehensio,* conception, consciousness, discernment, enlightenment, erudition, expertise, familiarity, grasp, imagination, information, insight, intellect, intellectual power, intellectualism, intellectuality, *intellegentia,* intuition, keenness, knowledge, learning, mastery of thought, mental capacity, mental grasp, mentality, mind, mindfulness, observation, penetration, perception, perspicaciousness, power to grasp ideas, power to understand, rationality, reach of mind, realization, reason, recognition, sagacity, sageness, sense, understanding, wisdom

COMPREHENSIVE, *adjective*   all-covering, all-embracing, all-inclusive, all-pervading, broad, capacious, compendious, complete, completive, comprising, consummate, containing, copious, discursive, encircling, encyclopedic, exhaustive, expansive, extended, extensive, far-reaching, full, fully realized, having no limit, inclusive, intensive, *late patens,* overall, panoramic, sweeping, synoptic, thorough, thoroughgoing, total, unconditional, unexclusive, universal, unmitigated, unqualified, unreserved, unrestricted, wide, wide-reaching, widespread
ASSOCIATED CONCEPTS: comprehensive coverage, comprehensive findings, comprehensive plan, comprehen-

sive police power, comprehensive statute, comprehensive zoning

COMPRISE, *verb*   aggregate, amount to, be composed of, be formed of, be made of, consist of, constitute, contain, embody, embrace, encapsulate, encompass, hold, include, incorporate, involve, subsume, total
ASSOCIATED CONCEPTS: comprising a cause of action

COMPROMISE, *noun*   abatement of differences, adaptation, adjustment, agreement, bargain, commutation, composition, concession, deal, happy medium, middle ground, mutual concession, negotiation, peacemaking, settlement, terms
ASSOCIATED CONCEPTS: accord and satisfaction, compromise a claim, compromise agreement, compromise and settlement, compromise of a claim, compromise verdict, discharge or release, novation, offer of compromise
FOREIGN PHRASES: *Compromissum ad similitudinem judiciorum redigitur.* A compromise is brought into affinity with judgments.

COMPROMISE *(Endanger), verb*   bring into danger, expose to danger, hazard, imperil, jeopardize, make liable to danger, make vulnerable, place in a dubious position, put at hazard, put in jeopardy, put under suspicion, risk, stake, venture

COMPROMISE *(Settle by mutual agreement), verb* accommodate, adjust, agree, arrange by mutual concession, bargain, come to an agreement, come to an understanding, come to terms, *compromittere,* concede, conciliate, find a middle ground, harmonize, maintain a middle position, make a compromise, make a deal, make an adjustment, make concessions, mediate, meet halfway, negotiate, reconcile, settle, settle differences, strike a balance
ASSOCIATED CONCEPTS: accord and satisfaction, compromise a claim, compromise agreement, compromise verdict, discharge, discontinuance, negotiation, novation, offer of compromise, quotient verdict, settlement, substitute contract

COMPTROLLER, *noun*   accountant, auditor, banker, bookkeeper, bookkeeping expert, bursar, business manager, cashier, chartered accountant, chief accounting officer, depositary, examiner of business accounts, financial officer, inspector of accounts, inventory expert, manager, purser, reckoner, registrar, supervisor of accounts, treasurer, trustee
ASSOCIATED CONCEPTS: city comptroller, state comptroller

COMPULSION *(Coercion), noun*   application of force, constraint, constraint to obedience, constriction, demand, dictation, domination, duress, duty, employment of force, enforcement, force, forcible inducement, forcible urging, forcing, high pressure methods, imposition, impressment, limitation, *necessitas,* necessity, objective necessity, obligation, oppression, physical force, pressure, requirement, restraint, restriction, spur of necessity, stress, subjection to force, urgency, urging by force, urging by moral constraint, urging by physical constraint, *vis*
ASSOCIATED CONCEPTS: compulsion of law, compulsory act, compulsory contributions, compulsory demand, compulsory liquidation, compulsory nonsuit, compulsory payment, compulsory process, compulsory sale

COMPULSION *(Obsession), noun*   ardor, besetting idea, craze, drive, earnestness, enchantment, engrossment, enthusiasm, fanaticism, fancy, fascination, fervency, fetish, fixation, fixed conviction, fixed idea, infatuation, intentness, irresistible impulse, mania, need, one-track mind, possession, predilection, preoccupation, prepossession, quirk, zeal

COMPULSORY, *adjective*   against one's will, authoritative, binding, coactive, coercive, commanded, compelling, constraining, decretive, demanded, enforced, exigent, forced, forcible, imperative, incumbent upon, indefeasible, indispensable, inescapable, irresistible, irrevocable, mandatory, necessary, obligatory, peremptory, prerequisite, prescriptive, pressing, required, requisite, restraining, restrictive, stringent, unable to be evaded, unavoidable, unpreventable, urgent, vital, without choice
ASSOCIATED CONCEPTS: compulsory arbitration, compulsory counterclaim, compulsory education, compulsory insurance, compulsory joinder of parties, compulsory performance of duties, compulsory testimony

COMPURGATION, *noun*   absolution, acquittal, acquittance, alibi, benefit of doubt, clearance, defeat of the prosecution, defense, dismissal, exculpation, excuse, exoneration, favorable verdict to the defendant, innocence, just cause, justification, legal defense, liberation, nonprosecution, pardon, reprieve, verdict of not guilty, vindication, withdrawal of the charge

COMPUTATION, *noun*   account, accountancy, accounting, adding, amount computed, appraisal, appreciation, assessment, audit, bookkeeping, calculation, count, counting, deduction, enumeration, estimate, estimation, evaluation, figure work, figuring, measurement, numeration, reckoning, score, statistic, sum, summation, tally, total, valuation

CONATUS, *noun*   attempt, choice, conation, conative will, desire, determination, direction, disposition, drift, endeavor, fancy, inclination, intention, leaning, mind, natural impulse, natural tendency, nisus, option, penchant, predilection, predisposition, preference, proclivity, proneness, propensity, temperament, tendency, trend, trial, unprompted will, volition, voluntariness, voluntary activity, want, will, wish

CONCEAL, *verb*   camouflage, cloak, confine, cover, cover up, curtain, disguise, eclipse, enshroud, entomb, envelop, harbor, hide, keep clandestine, keep from, keep out of sight, keep secret, keep to oneself, keep underground, make inconspicuous, make indiscernible, make unapparent, make unperceptible, mask, not reveal, obscure, *occulere,* protect, render invisible, screen, seclude, secrete, shade, shadow, shield, shroud, store, suppress, throw a veil over, veil, withdraw from observation, withold, withold information
ASSOCIATED CONCEPTS: conceal assets, conceal information, conceal material facts
FOREIGN PHRASES: *Fraus est celare fraudem.* It is fraud to conceal a fraud.

CONCEALMENT, *noun*   camouflage, confinement, cover, deceitfulness, disappearance, disguise, disguisement, duplicity, evasion, furtiveness, hiding, incognito, inconspicuousness, invisibility, nonappearance, obfuscation, obscurity, obsuration, privacy, seclusion, secrecy, secretion, secretiveness, silence, stealthiness, subterfuge, suppression, suppression of the truth
ASSOCIATED CONCEPTS: concealment of assets, concealment of information, concealment of material fact, concealment voiding an insurance policy., concealment with intent to defraud creditors, evasive contempt
FOREIGN PHRASES: *Aliud est celare, aliud tacere.* To conceal is one thing; to be silent is another. *Suppressio veri, suggestio falsi.* The suppression of truth is equivalent to the suggestion of what is false.

CONCEDE, *verb*   abide by, accede, accept, acknowledge, acquiesce, affirm, agree, agree in principle, allow, arrive at an agreement, assent, be persuaded, come to terms, comply with, *concedere,* consent, endorse, endure, give in, grant, impart, permit, *permittere,* profess, recognize, respect, sanction, settle, submit, submit to, succumb, tolerate, withdraw one's objections, yield
ASSOCIATED CONCEPTS: conceded facts
FOREIGN PHRASES: *Qui concedit aliquid, concedere videtur et id sine quo concessio est irrita, sine quo res ipsa esse non potuit.* He who concedes anything is considered as conceding that without which his concession would be idle, without which the thing itself is worthless.

CONCEIVE *(Comprehend), verb*   absorb, accept, appreciate, apprehend, assimilate, conceptualize, conjure up, digest, discern, envisage, envision, fathom, figure out, form a conception, grasp, have an idea, ideate, image, imagine, know, perceive, picture, realize, see, understand, visualize

CONCEIVE *(Invent), verb*   begin, bring into being, bring into existence, coin, compose, *concipere,* concoct, contrive, create, design, develop, devise, draft, dream up, excogitate, fabricate, formulate, frame, generate, give birth to, hatch, inchoate, initiate, innovate, make up, originate, plan, prepare, start
ASSOCIATED CONCEPTS: conceive a criminal plan

CONCENTRATE *(Consolidate), verb*   accumulate, agglomerate, aggregate, amass, assemble, bring into a small compass, bring toward a central point, center, centralize, cluster, coalesce, collect, combine, compact, compress, concenter, condense, congest, conglomerate, congregate, conjoin, *conligere,* constrict, *contrahere,* converge, crowd together, densify, focalize, focus, gather, make firm, make solid, mass, strengthen, unite

CONCENTRATE *(Pay attention), verb*   *animum attendere,* apply the mind, attend, attend minutely, be engrossed in, consider closely, contemplate, direct the mind upon, examine closely, fix one's attention, focus, focus attention on, give attention to, give heed, hearken, listen, meditate, muse, occupy the mind with, occupy the thoughts with, peruse carefully, ponder, put one's mind to, regard carefully, ruminate, scrutinize, study deeply, think intensely

CONCEPT, *noun*   abstract idea, abstraction, appraisal, appreciation, apprehension, assessment, assumption, belief, conception, conclusion, conjecture, consideration, deduction, doctrine, estimate, evaluation, fancy, feeling, formative notion, guess, idea, image, impression, intellectualization, judgment, knowledge, mental image, mental impression, mental representation, notion, observation, opinion, percept, perception, persuasion, picture, point of view, postulate, presumption, reflection, representation, supposition,

surmise, tenet, theory, thought, understanding, view, visualization
ASSOCIATED CONCEPTS: legal concept

CONCERN *(Business establishment),* **noun**   business, company, corporation, establishment, firm, house, institution, organization
ASSOCIATED CONCEPTS: partnership, proprietorship

CONCERN *(Interest),* **noun**   anxiety, attention, care, concernment, consequence, consideration, disquietude, importance, regard, solicitude, *sollicitudo,* uneasiness, worry

CONCERN *(Care),* **verb**   administer to, attend, attend to, be mindful, be vigilant, be watchful, check, consider, *curare,* devote oneself to, direct the attention to, examine intently, foster, give attention, give one's attention, keep, look after, mind, minister to, pay attention to, regard, respect, safeguard, take care of, take into consideration, take note of, tend, watch

CONCERN *(Involve),* **verb**   absorb, affect, appertain to, apply, *attinere,* be a factor, be applicable to, be interdependent with, be involved, be one of, be pertinent to, be related to, be relevant, deal with, embody, embrace, enclasp, entail, have a bearing on, have a connection, have a reference, have a relation, have interrelationship with, immerse, influence, interest, pertain to, *pertinere,* refer to, regard, relate to, respect, stand in relation, *versari in re*
ASSOCIATED CONCEPTS: concerned in interest, concerning a matter of law, general state concern, local concern

CONCERT, **noun**   accord, accordance, agreement, alliance, coaction, coadjument, coadjuvancy, coagency, coalition, coefficiency, collaboration, combination, combined action, combined effort, compatibility, complicity, concord, concordance, concurrence, concurrency, confederation, conjunction, consentaneity, consonance, cooperation, fusion of interests, harmony, joint action, joint operation, merger, mutual assistance, pool, rapport, synergy, teamwork, unanimity, unison, unity
ASSOCIATED CONCEPTS: acting in concert

CONCERTED, **adjective**   abetting, accordant, agreed, agreeing, aiding and abetting, aligned, amalgamated, assenting, blended, bonded, coacting, coactive, coadjutant, coadjuvant, coalescent, coeval, coexistent, coexisting, cohesive, coincident, coinciding, collaborating, colluding, combined, combining, commixed, composite, concordant, concurrent, concurring, conformable, conforming, congruent, congruous, conjoined, conjoint, conjunct, connective, conniving, consensual, consentaneous, consentient, consenting, consistent with, consolidated, consonant, contributing, converging, cooperating, cooperative, corresponding, coworking, fused, harmonious, harmonized, in accord, in accordance with, in agreement, in alliance, in unison, interactive, joined, joint, merging, mutually agreed, parallel, simultaneous, sympathetic, synergic, united, uniting

CONCESSION *(Authorization),* **noun**   allowance, authority, authorization, bestowal, clearance, *concessio,* conferment, conferral, endowment, giving, grant, impartment, leave, license, permission, permit, presentation, privilege, sanction, vouchsafement, warrant

CONCESSION *(Compromise),* **noun**   acceptance, accord, acknowledgment, acquiescence, admission, ad-

mitting, agreement, allowance, assent, capitulation, concurrence, giving in, grant, granting, recognition, recognizance, reconciliation, relinquishment, settlement, submission, surrender, yielding

CONCILIATION, **noun**   abatement of differences, accommodation, accord, accordance, adaptability, adjustment, agreement, appeasement, arrangement, bipartisanship, compact, compliance, compromise, concert, concession, *conciliatio,* concord, concurrence, conformability, conformity, consonance, cooperation, entente, harmony, league, mediation, mutual accord, mutual agreement, mutual concession, mutual understanding, negotiation, pacification, peacemaking, placation, propitiation, reconcilement, reconciliation, reunion, satisfaction, settlement, settlement of differences, solidarity, submission, truce, unanimity, understanding, uniformity, union, unity
ASSOCIATED CONCEPTS: conciliation in a marriage

CONCISE, **adjective**   abbreviated, abridged, abstracted, brief, capsule, capsulized, compact, compacted, compendious, compressed, condensed, contracted, curtailed, curtate, epigrammatic, epitomized, laconic, pithy, short, shortened, succinct, summarized, summary, synoptic, to the point, trenchant

CONCLUDE *(Complete),* **verb**   abort, adjourn, break off, bring to a close, bring to an end, bring to rest, carry to completion, cease, climax, close, *conficere,* consummate, culminate, discharge, discontinue, dispose of, end, execute, exhaust, finalize, *finire,* finish, fulfill, halt, make an end of, make complete, maturate, prosecute to a conclusion, render complete, seal, set at rest, settle, shut down, stop, surcease, terminate
ASSOCIATED CONCEPTS: conclude a hearing, conclude a trial

CONCLUDE *(Decide),* **verb**   choose, come to a determination, *concludere, conligere,* decide upon, declare, decree, decree by judicial authority, deduce, deem, deliver judgment, determine, end by a decision, find, form a judgment, form a resolution, form an opinion, give a ruling, give an opinion, give judgment, hold, infer, judge, make a decision, make a resolution, make terms, make up one's mind, pass judgment, pronounce a judgment, resolve, rule, seal, settle, settle in one's mind, settle upon, take a decisive step
ASSOCIATED CONCEPTS: conclusion of guilt, findings

CONCLUSION *(Determination),* **noun**   adjudication, arbitrament, ascertainment, assessment, authoritative opinion, *conclusio,* consideration, decision, declaration, decree, deduction, derived principle, discernment, estimation, evaluation, final judgment, finding, inference, judgment, observation, opinion, persuasion, pronouncement, realization, reasoned judgment, report, resolution, resolve, result, result ascertained, result of judicial inquest, ruling, settling, solution, surmise, valuation, verdict, view
ASSOCIATED CONCEPTS: conclusion as to intent, conclusion as to motive, conclusion of a trial, conclusion of guilt, conclusion of innocence, conclusion of law, conclusion of mixed law and fact

CONCLUSION *(Outcome),* **noun**   cessation, close, closure, completeness, completion, *conclusio,* consequence, consequent, consummation, culmination, denouement, effect, effectuation, end, end product, end result, ending, eventuality, final result, finale, finalty, *finis,* finish, fulfillment, last stage, outcome, outgrowth, product, repercussion, result, resultance, resultant action, termination, upshot

FOREIGN PHRASES: *Ab abusu ad usum non valet consequentia.* A conclusion as to the use of a thing from its abuse is invalid. *Inclusio unius est exclusio alterius.* The inclusion of one is the exclusion of another. *In propria causa nemo judex.* No one can be judge in his own cause. *Negatio conclusionis est error in lege.* The denial of a conclusion is in error in law.

CONCLUSIVE *(Determinative),* **adjective** absolute, apparent, ascertained, assured, categorical, certain, conspicuous, definite, demonstrated, evident, final, guaranteed, immutable, incommutable, incontestable, incontrovertible, indefeasible, indisputable, indubitable, infallible, irrefragable, irrefutable, irrepealable, irrevocable, mandatory, obligatory, positive, tested, tried, ultimate, unambiguous, unchallengeable, unchangeable, uncontested, undeniable, undoubted, unequivocal, unimpeachable, unmistakable, unquestionable

ASSOCIATED CONCEPTS: conclusive admission, conclusive beyond a reasonable doubt, conclusive evidence, conclusive judgment, conclusive presumption, conclusive presumption of validity, conclusive proof

CONCLUSIVE *(Settled),* **adjective** ascertained, beyond dispute, *certus,* clear, closing, complete, completed, completing, completive, conclusory, confirming, culminating, decided, decisive, definitive, determining, evidential, extreme, final, finished, finishing, terminal, terminative, ultimate

ASSOCIATED CONCEPTS: conclusive adjudification, conclusive as to the facts

CONCOMITANT, *adjective* accompanying, aligned, allied, associated, attendant, attending, coincident, complemental, concurrent, conjoint, conjunctional, conjunctive, contemporaneous, contemporary, correlative, correspondent, corresponding, coupled, joint, parallel, simultaneous, synergic

FOREIGN PHRASES: *Principia data sequuntur concomitantia.* Given principles are followed by their concomitants.

CONCORDANCE, *noun* accord, accordance, agreement, amity, assent, coaction, coincidence, common assent, communion, compact, concert, concord, concurrence, concurrence in opinions, conformance, conformity, congeniality, congruence, congruency, conjunction, consensus, consent, consentaneity, consentaneousness, consistency, consonance, cooperation, correspondence, fraternity, friendship, harmony, like-mindedness, neighborliness, oneness, peace, rapport, sympathy, understanding, unity

CONCORDANT, *adjective* accommodative, accordant, agreeable, agreeing, aligned, allied, assenting, assentive, at one, banded together, blending, bonded, cemented, coexistent, coexisting, coinciding, combinative, compatible, complementary, compliant, *concors,* concurrent, concurring, conformable, conforming, congruent, congruous, conjoined, conjunctional, consensual, consentaneous, consenting, consistent, consonant, coordinate, correlated, correlative, correspondent, corresponding, fusing, harmonious, in accord, in agreement, in concert, in conjunction, in harmony, in rap-

port, in unison, joint, merged, merging, mutual, of the same mind, reconcilable, sympathetic, unanimous, uniform, united, uniting

CONCRESCENCE, *noun* adherance, amalgamating, blending, coalescence, combining, consolidation, fusion, making one, mingling, mixing, symphysis, uniting

CONCRETE, *adjective* bodily, certain, cognizable, definite, demonstrable, determinate, distinct, embodied, existent, existing, explicit, firm, material, palpable, particular, perceptible, physical, real, solid, solidified, *solidus,* specific, substantial, substantive, tangible

ASSOCIATED CONCEPTS: concrete cause of action, concrete idea, concrete interest

CONCUR *(Agree),* **verb** accede to, accept, accord, accredit, acknowledge, acquiesce, act in concert, affirm, allow, approbate, approve, assent to, band together, come to an agreement, come to an understanding, come to terms, come together, comply, condone, conform with, consent, cooperate, countenance, defer to, echo, endorse, favor, give credit, go along with, harmonize, hold with, homologate, jibe, join forces, join in, join together, join with, league together, meet, operate jointly, ratify, sanction, say yes, second, side with, signify assent, subscribe to, suit, support, sustain, sympathize with, unite efforts, unite with, uphold, work jointly, yield

ASSOCIATED CONCEPTS: concurring opinion

CONCUR *(Coexist),* **verb** accompany, be concomittant, be contemporaneous, be contemporary, be parallel, coincide, exist together, happen at the same time, happen simultaneously, happen together, keep pace with, occur at the same time, occur concurrently

ASSOCIATED CONCEPTS: concurrent acts, concurrent causes, concurrent conditions, concurrent contracts, concurrent covenants, concurrent jurisdiction, concurrent negligence, concurrent power, concurrent sentences, consecutive sentences

CONCURRENT *(At the same time),* **adjective** accompanying, associated, at the same instant, attendant, attending, coacting, coactive, coetaneous, coeval, coexistent, coexisting, coincident, coinstantaneous, collateral, concerted, concomitant, conjunctive, contemporaneous, contemporary, convergent, converging, coupled, occurring at the same time, parallel, synchronal, synchronistic, synchronistical, synchronous

ASSOCIATED CONCEPTS: concurrent actions, concurrent findings, concurrent legislation, concurrent remedies, concurrent sentences, concurrent stipulations

CONCURRENT *(United),* **adjective** abetting, accordant, acquiescent, acting in conjunction, agreeing, aiding, allied, amalgamated, assenting, associating, assonant, banded together, binding, blended, bonded, cemented, centralized, coacting, coactive, coalitional, cohesive, collaborative, combinative, combined, common, communal, commutual, compatible, complementary, concerted, concordant, concurring, confederated, conforming, conjoined, connected, consentaneous, consolidated, consonant, contributing, cooperative, coupled, coworking, *en rapport,* fused, harmonizing, in accord, in agreement, in unison, interallied, joined, joint, leagued, linked, meeting, merged, of one accord, paired, participating, shared, synergic, undivided, unified, united, wedded, well-matched

CONDEMN *(Ban), verb*   abhor, abnegate, abrogate, banish, bar, blackball, block, boycott, call a halt, cancel, cast aside, cast out, censor, check, counter, debar, deny, deprive, disallow, disapprove, discommode, discountenance, disfavor, disown, disqualify, embargo, enjoin, exclude, excommunicate, expel, forbid, forestall, frustrate, halt, hamper, impede, interdict, interrupt, keep in bounds, keep out, keep within bounds, lay an embargo on, limit, make impossible, object, obstruct, oppose, ostracize, outlaw, preclude, prevent, prohibit, proscribe, put a stop to, put an embargo on, put an end to, put one's veto to, put under an injunction, put under an interdiction, put under prohibition, quash, quell, refuse, reject, repress, reprobate, restrain, restrict, restrict access, retard, seclude, shut out, stop, suppress, thwart, *vetare,* withhold

CONDEMN *(Blame), verb*   accuse, anathematize, animadvert, asperse, assail with censure, attack, berate, bring into discredit, call to account, cast blame upon, castigate, charge, chide, *condemnare,* criticize, *culpare,* declaim against, decry, denigrate, denounce, deprecate, derogate, disapprove, discountenance, disdain, disparage, dispraise, execrate, find guilty, fulminate against, impeach, implicate, impugn, incriminate, indict, inveigh against, pass censure on, publicly accuse, rebuke, reprehend, reproach, reprove, repudiate, revile, take to task, upbraid, vilify, *vituperare,* vituperate

CONDEMN *(Punish), verb*   adjudge, administer correction, bring to account, carry out a sentence, convict, *damnare,* deal retributive justice, discipline, doom, exact a penalty, exact retribution, execute a sentence, execute justice, impose a penalty, impose penalty, inflict penalty, inflict punishment, pass sentence on, penalize, prescribe punishment, pronounce judgment, pronounce sentence, *punire,* reprimand, reprove, sentence, subject to penalty, take disciplinary action

CONDEMN *(Seize), verb*   accroach, acquire, appropriate, arrogate, assume, assume ownership, attach, compulsorily acquire, confiscate, declare to be forfeited, deprive of corporal possession, deprive of ownership, disentitle, dispossess, disseise, distrain, divest of property, expropriate, foreclose, impound, impropriate, municipalize, nationalize, *publicare,* sequestrate, take for public use, take over, take possession, usurp
ASSOCIATED CONCEPTS: eminent domain

CONDEMNATION *(Blame), noun*   accusation, animadversion, ascription, attack, castigation, censure, charge, chastening, chastisement, chiding, complaint, *condemnatio,* criticism, denigration, denunciation, deprecation, derogation, disapprobation, disapproval, discountenance, discredit, disdain, disfavor, disparagement, dispraise, execration, expostulation, impeachment, implication, imputation, incrimination, inculpation, invective, objection, objurgation, opposition, rebuke, recrimination, reprehension, reprimand, reproach, reprobation, reproof, repudiation, stricture, vilification, vituperation

CONDEMNATION *(Punishment), noun*   conviction, disciplinary action, exaction of penalty, execration, finding of guilty, guilty verdict, infliction, judgment, justice, penalization, penalty, punishing experience, punishment, punition, retribution, retributive justice, sentence

CONDEMNATION *(Seizure), noun*   abrogation, acquisition by right of eminent domain, appropriation, arrogation, assumption, commandeering, compulsory acquisition, confiscation, deprivation, dispossession, distraint, distress, divestment, expropriation, forced sale, forcible seizure, foreclosure, impounding, impropriation, municipalization, nationalization, prehension, takeover, taking of property for public use, taking possession
ASSOCIATED CONCEPTS: condemnation of land for public use, condemnation proceedings, reverse condemnation, title by condemnation

CONDENSE, *verb*   abbreviate, abridge, abstract, capsulize, compress, consolidate, contract, curtail, cut short, detruncate, digest, epitomize, foreshorten, make brief, make concise, make denser, make terse, outline, precis, reduce, render more compact, shorten, shrink, summarize, sum up, synopsize, truncate

CONDESCEND *(Deign), verb*   accommodate oneself, accord, be courteous, be gracious, descend, *descendere,* disregard prestige, grant, humble oneself, lower oneself, sacrifice pride, *se submittere,* stoop, tolerate, unbend, vouchsafe, waive privilege, yield

CONDESCEND *(Patronize), verb*   assume a patronizing air, be contemptuous, be overbearing, belittle, care nothing for, consider beneath notice, contemn, disdain, disparage, disrespect, hold in contempt, hold in disrespect, look down on, look with scorn upon, spurn, talk down to

CONDIGN, *adjective*   appropriate, befitting, *debitus,* deserved, due, earned, fit, fitting, just, justified, merited, *meritus,* right, suitable, warranted, well-deserved, well-earned, worthy

CONDITION *(Contingent provision), noun*   article, clause, *condicio,* contractual terms, desideratum, essential provision, exception, final terms, limitation, obligation, pact, postulate, postulation, prerequirement, prerequisite, prescription, presumption, presupposition, promise, provision, proviso, qualification, regulation, requirement, requisite, reservation, restriction, rule, ruling, specification, stated term, stipulation, supposal, supposition, term, ultimatum, uncertain event
ASSOCIATED CONCEPTS: cause, condition implied in law, condition of employment, condition precedent, condition running with the land, condition subsequent, conditions and exceptions, conditions and restrictions, express condition, implied condition, sale on condition, terms and conditions, warranties
FOREIGN PHRASES: *Ea quae dari impossibilia sunt, vel quae in rerum natura non sunt, pro non adjectis habentur.* Those things which can not be given, or which are not in the nature of things, are regarded as not included in the agreement. *Conditiones quaelibet odiosae; maxime autem contra matrimonium et commercium.* Any conditions are odious, but especially those which are in restraint of marriage and commerce. *Proviso est providere praesentia et futura, non praeterita.* A proviso is to provide for the present and the future, notthe past. *Conditio illicita habetur pro non adjecta.* An unlawful condition is deemed not to be annexed. *Conditio praecedens adimpleri debet prius quam sequatur effectus.* A condition precedent must be fulfilled before the effectcan follow. *Conditio dicitur, cum quid in casum incertum qui potest tendere ad esse*

aut non esse, confertur. It is called a "condition", when something is given on an uncertain event, which may or may not come into existence. *Conditio beneficialis, quae statum construit, benigne secundum verborum intentionem est interpretanda; odiosa autem. quaestatum destruit, stricte secundum berborum proprietatem accipienda.* A beneficial condition, which creates an estate, ought to be interpreted favorably, according to the intention of the words; but a condition which destroys an estate is odious, and ought to be construed strictly according to the letter.

CONDITION *(State), noun* appearance, aspect, character, circumstance, complexion, *condicio,* crasis, grade, habitude, look, plight, position, posture, predicament, quality, rank, shape, situation, state of being, station, *status,* temperament, tenor
ASSOCIATED CONCEPTS: dangerous condition, emergency condition, financial condition, good operating condition, physical condition

CONDITIONAL, *adjective* alterable, changeable, conditioned, containing stipulations, contingent on, dependent on, depending on, depending on a future event, determined by, equivocal, granted on certain terms, hypothetical, imposing a condition, indefinite, indeterminable, indeterminate, liable to, limitative, limited, modified by conditions, negotiable, not absolute, not certain, not sure, pending, possible, provisional, provisionary, provisory, qualified, regulated by, restricted, specified, stipulative, subject to, subject to chance, subject to change, subject to terms, suspenseful, tentative, unassured, uncertain, undecided, under the control of, undetermined, unpositive, unpredictable, unsettled, unsure
ASSOCIATED CONCEPTS: conditional acceptance, conditional agreement, conditional bequest, conditional bill of sale, conditional bond, conditional charge, conditional consent, conditional contract, conditional conveyance, conditional delivery, conditional devise, conditional endorsement, conditional estate, conditional execution, conditional fee, conditional gift, conditional guaranties, conditional judgment, conditional lease, conditional legacy, conditional liability, conditional limitation, conditional obligations, conditional pardon, conditional payment, conditional promise, conditional release, conditional revocation of a will, conditional rights, conditional sale, conditional sales act, conditional sales contract, conditional subscription, conditional will

CONDONATION, *noun* absolution, accommodation, acquittal, allowance, amnesty, cancellation, charity, clearance, clemency, compassion, conciliation, concord, discharge, dismissal, disposition to pardon, disregard, excusal, exemption, exoneration, expiation, extenuation, extrication, forgiveness, full pardon, grace, impunity, indemnity, indulgence, lenience, magnanimity, mercy, nonliability, overlooking, pardon, reconcilement, reprieve, sympathy, vindication, willingness to forgive
ASSOCIATED CONCEPTS: condonation as grounds for a dissolution of a marriage

CONDONE, *verb* absolve, accept, allow, assoil, be lenient, be merciful, be reconciled, be tolerant, bear with, blot out, clear, countenance, dismiss, disregard, excuse, exempt, exonerate, forbear, forget, forgive, free,

give a reprieve, give absolution, give amnesty, grant amnesty, grant immunity, let pass, make allowance, overlook, overlook an offense, palliate, pardon, pass over, permit, recommend to pardon, refrain from punishing, release, relent, remit, reprieve, set free, show mercy, spare, tolerate, vindicate, waive punishment, yield

CONDUCE, *verb* abet, advance, aid, assist, augment, bring about, bring on, cause, *conducere,* contribute toward, cooperate, effect, encourage, expedite, favor, foment, foster, incline to, increase the chances, influence, lead to, make probable, predispose to, promote, put ahead, put forward, tend to, work toward

CONDUCT, *noun* actions, acts, address, air, aspect, attitude, bearing, behavior, behavior pattern, breeding, carriage, code, compliance, comportment, conformance, correctness, course of behavior, dealings, decorum, deeds, demeanor, deportment, established practice, ethics, etiquette, fashion, guise, habits, management, manner, manners, method, mien, mode of action, mode of behavior, morals, operation, performance, personal bearing, port, posture, practice, presence, procedure, propriety, public manners, role, seemliness, social behavior, social graces, style, way, way of acting, ways, wise
ASSOCIATED CONCEPTS: coercive conduct, course of conduct, disorderly conduct, good conduct, immoral conduct, improper conduct, inequitable conduct, justifiable conduct, reasonable conduct, standard of conduct, unprofessional conduct
FOREIGN PHRASES: For his good behavior.

CONDUCT, *verb* administer, *administrare,* administrate, assume responsibility, carry on, carry out, command, control, deal with, direct, direct affairs, discharge, dispatch, do, enact, execute, *gerere,* guide, handle, have control, lead, look after, manage, officiate at, operate, oversee, *perducere,* pilot, preside over, proceed with, regulate, run, superintend, supervise, take care of, take charge of, transact, usher
ASSOCIATED CONCEPTS: conduct a business, conduct a sale, conducted for profit, conducting business
FOREIGN PHRASES: *Melius est recurrere quam malo currere.* It is better to recede than to proceed in error.

CONDUIT *(Channel), noun* agency, artery, avenue, contrivance, course, device, instrument, machinery, manner, means, medium, method, mode, path, process, route, way
ASSOCIATED CONCEPTS: intermediary and accomplice to a crime

CONDUIT *(Intermediary), noun* advocate, agent, delegate, deputy, emissary, envoy, functionary, go-between, intermedium, mediary, mediator, medium, middleman, negotiator, proxy, representative, substitute, surrogate

CONFEDERACY *(Compact), noun* affiliation, alignment, alliance, association, body, cartel, coalition, combination, combine, concurrence, confederation, confraternity, consolidation, coterie, federation, fellowship, *foedus,* fusion, guild, league, *pactum,* set, *societas,* society, solidarity, syndicate, trust, unification, union

CONFEDERACY *(Conspiracy), noun* cabal, collusion, complicity, complot, *coniuratio,* connivance, criminal agreement, illegal agreement, illegal compact, intrigue, plot, schemery, treasonable alliance

CONFEDERATE, *noun*   abettor, accessory, accomplice, adjunct, adjutant, adjuvant, aid, aider, ally, assistant, associate, auxiliary, coactor, coadjutant, coadjutor, collaborator, colleague, colluder, comate, companion, comrade, confidant, confrere, consociate, conspirator, conspirer, cooperator, coworker, fellow, friend, helper, helpmate, intrigant, participator, partner, support, supporter

CONFER *(Consult), verb*   advise, compare opinions, confide in, consult with, *consultare,* counsel, deliberate, discuss, exchange observations, exhort, give advice, hold a conference, hold a consultation, interchange views, negotiate, palaver, parley, refer, seek advice, take counsel, talk over
ASSOCIATED CONCEPTS: confer with a client, confer with an associate

CONFER *(Give), verb*   accord, adjudge, administer, award, bestow, cede, *conferre,* convey, deliver, dispense, endow, give, grant, hand down, impart, invest, issue, pass down, present, relinquish, tender, transfer, transmit, yield
ASSOCIATED CONCEPTS: confer authority, confer jurisdiction, conferred powers

CONFERENCE, *noun*   assembly, colloquy, conclave, confabulation, consultation, consultation meeting, convention, conversations, convocation, deliberation, dialogue, discussion, exchange, forum, gathering, interchange of opinions, interlocution, meeting, negotiation, negotiations, palaver, parlance, parley, premeditation, seminar, symposium, talks

CONFESS, *verb*   acknowledge, acknowledge one's guilt, admit, admit guilt, bare, come forth, compurgate, concede, *confiteri,* declare, disburden one's conscience, disclose, divulge, expose, *fateri,* give evidence, inculpate, lay open, make a confession, make solemn affirmation, own up, purge oneself, reveal, tell all, turn state's evidence, utter, yield
ASSOCIATED CONCEPTS: confess guilt, confess judgment, confess participation
FOREIGN PHRASES: *Qui tacet non utique fatetur, sed tamen verum est eum non negare.* He who is silent does not confess, but it is nevertheless true that he does not deny.

CONFESSION, *noun*   acknowledgment, acknowledgment of guilt, acquiescence, admission, admission of fault, admission of guilt, assertion, avowal of guilt, confirmation, declaration, disclosure, disclosure of fault, divulgement, divulgence, exclamation, exomologesis, incriminating statement, inculpatory statement, pronouncement, purgation, revealment, self-accusation, self-condemnation, statement, utterance
ASSOCIATED CONCEPTS: confessed judgment, confession and avoidance, confession of error, extrajudicial confessions, implied confession, involuntary confession, judgment by confession, judicial confession, voluntary confession, written confession
FOREIGN PHRASES: *Confessus in judicio pro judicato habetur, et quodammodo sua sententia damnatur.* A person confessing his guilt in court is deemed to have been found guilty, and is, in a manner, condemned by his own sentence. *Cum confitente sponte mitius est*

agendum. One making a voluntary confession is to be dealt with more leniently.

CONFIDE *(Divulge), verb*   disclose, disclose something secret, discuss private affairs, divulgate, entrust with private information, let know, make known, reveal something private, share secrets, tell a secret, tell with assurance of secrecy, trust to keep secret

CONFIDE *(Trust), verb*   believe in, commit, consign, deliver to the care of, entrust, feel sure of, give in trust, have confidence in, have faith in, hold responsible for, place reliance on, put faith in, put in care of, rely on, rely upon
ASSOCIATED CONCEPTS: attorney-client privilege, confidential creditor, confidential informant, confidential relation, fiduciary relationship, husband-wife privilege, physician-patient privilege, priest-penitant privilege, privileged against self-incrimination, privileged communications

CONFIDENCE *(Faith), noun*   affiance, aplomb, assurance, boldness, certainty, certitude, cocksureness, confidentness, conviction, courage, credence, credulity, fearlessness, *fides, fiducia,* firm belief, heart, intrepidity, morale, nerve, optimism, poise, positiveness, reliance, sanguineness, security, sureness, surety, trust
FOREIGN PHRASES: *Multa fidem promissa levant.* Many promises lessen confidence. *Fides servanda est.* Good faith must be observed.

CONFIDENCE *(Relation of trust), noun*   assurance of secrecy, classified communication, concealment, confidential communication, confidential matter, intimacy, personal matter, privacy, private, private affair, privileged communication, secrecy, secret, secret communication
ASSOCIATED CONCEPTS: attorney-client confidence, confidential communications, husband-wife confidence, physician-patient confidence, priest-penitent confidence

CONFIDENTIAL, *adjective*   arcane, *arcanus,* auricular, classified, concealed, *fidus,* hidden, imparted in secret, irrevealable, not for publication, not to be communicated, not to be disclosed, not to be quoted, not to be spoken of, off the record, private, restricted, secret, spoken in confidence, told in confidence, top-secret, undercover, unmentionable, unrevealed
ASSOCIATED CONCEPTS: confidential communication, confidential information, confidential proceeding, confidential relationship, fiduciary relationship, privilege

CONFIGURATION *(Confines), noun*   borders, boundary, bounds, circumscription, contour, delineation, dimensions, edges, extent, framework, frontiers, limitations, limits, line of demarcation, outline, perimeter

CONFIGURATION *(Form), noun*   anatomy, appearance, arrangement, body, cast, character, composition, conformation, constitution, construction, contour, design, external form, features, figuration, figure, format, formation, frame, framework, *galbe,* layout, lines, look, makeup, outline, outward form, pattern, physique, profile, rough outline, scheme of arrangement, shape, silhouette, skeleton, structural composition, structural design, structure

CONFINE, *verb*   arrest, barricade, bind, bound, cage, capture, circumscribe, *coercere, cohibere,* commit, commit to prison, constrain, contain, control, detain, enchain, enclose, enthrall, fence in, harness, hold, hold as a hostage, hold back, hold captive, hold in captivity, hold in check, hold in thrall, hold prisoner, immure, impound, imprison, incarcerate, *includere,* institutionalize, intern, jail, keep in custody, keep under control, keep within bounds, limit, lock up, pen in, place in durance, place under protective custody, put into isolation, put under arrest, put under restraint, quarantine, recommit, remand, repress, restrain, restrict, restrict access, seclude, send to jail, shut in, subdue, subjugate, suppress, take into custody, take prisoner, trammel
ASSOCIATED CONCEPTS: actual confinement, confine to an asylum, confinement to a jail, false imprisonment, kidnapping, solitary confinement

CONFINES, *noun*   borders, boundaries, boundary lines, bounds, compound, confinements, curbs, curtilages, division lines, edges, enclosures, ends, environs, extents, extremities, fringes, limitations, limits, lines of demarcation, metes, outer edges, outlines, perimeter, precincts, restraints, skirts
ASSOCIATED CONCEPTS: within the confines of the law

CONFIRM, *verb*   accede, accord, accredit, acknowledge, acquiesce, add strength to, adhere, agree to, agree with, ally, approve, assent, attest, authenticate, authorize, avow, charter, commend, *comprobare,* concede, concur, consent, corroborate, countersign, document, endorse, establish, fortify, give one's word for, give security, guarantee, homologate, join in a compact, legalize, license, make firm, make valid, pass, permit, prove, ratify, recognize, *sancire,* sanction, seal, second, support, sustain, uphold, validate, verify, vote for, vouch for
FOREIGN PHRASES: *Confirmare nemo potest prius quam jus ei acciderit.* No one can confirm a right before it accrues to him. *Confirmare est id firmum facere quod prius infirmum fuit.* To confirm is to make firm that which had been infirm. *Confirmat usum qui tollit abusum.* He confirms a use who removes an abuse.

CONFIRMATION, *noun*   acceptance, accord, accordance, acknowledgment, acquiescence, admission, affidavit, affirmance, affirmation, approval, assent, assertion, assurance, attestation, authentication, authorization, averment, avouchment, certification, corroboration, corroborative statement, declaration, deposition, documentation, endorsement, legal pledge, oath, proof, ratification, sanction, seal, solemn averment, solemn avowal, solemn declaration, stamp of approval, subscription, substantiation, support, swearing, validation, verification, *visé,* warrant
ASSOCIATED CONCEPTS: confirmation of judgment, confirmation of sale
FOREIGN PHRASES: *Non valet confirmatio, nisi ille, qui confirmat, sit in possessione rei vel juris unde fieri debet confirmatio; et eodem modo, misi ille cui confirmatio fit sit in possessione.* Confirmation is not valid unless he who confirms is either in possession of the thing itself or of the right of which confirmation is to be made, and, in like manner, unless he to whom confirmation is made is in possession. *Confirmatio est nulla ubi donum praecedens est invalidum.* Confirmation is a nullity where the preceding gift is invalid. *Confirmatio omnes supplet defectus, licet id quod actum est ab* *initio non valuit.* Confirmation supplies all defects, though that which had been done was not valid at the beginning.

CONFISCATE, *verb*   adeem, annex, appropriate, appropriate to public use, assume, attach, cause to be forfeited, compulsorily acquire, condemn, condemn to public use, deprive, deprive of, disentitle, disinherit, dispossess, disseise, distrain, divest, expropriate, foreclose, forfeit, impound, impress, levy, *publicare,* seize, seize and appropriate, seize as forfeited to the public treasury, seize by authority, sequester, sequestrate, take away from, take over, take possession of, take summarily, wrench away from, wrest away from, wring away from
ASSOCIATED CONCEPTS: condemn, eminent domain, exercise the right of

CONFISCATORY, *adjective*   acquisitive, appropriating, attaching, capturing, commandeering, conquering, deprivative, depriving, disseizing, distraining, divesting, exacting, expropriatory, extortionary, foreclosing, forfeiting, garnishing, impounding, rapacious, requisitory, seizing, sequestrating, taking, usurpatory
ASSOCIATED CONCEPTS: confiscatory orders, confiscatory rates

CONFLAGRATION, *noun*   blaze, bonfire, deflagration, destructive fire, devastation, devouring element, fire, general fire, *ignis,* incendiarism, *incendium,* sheet of flame, wall of flame, wholesale destruction, wild-fire

CONFLICT, *noun*   adverseness, affray, altercation, animosity, antagonism, antipathy, argument, argumentation, battle, belligerency, breach, challenge, clash, clash of arms, collision, combat, competition, conflict of opinion, contention, contentiousness, contest, contradiction, contraposition, contrariety, contrariness, contrast, contravention, controversy, corrivalry, counteraction, debate, defiance, difference, disaccord, disagreement, disapprobation, discord, discordance, discrepancy, disharmony, dislike, dispute, disputed point, *dissensio,* dissension, dissent, dissidence, dissonance, disunion, disunity, divergence, divergent opinions, division, embroilment, encounter, engagement, enmity, faction, failure to agree, fight, fighting, firm opposition, friction, hatred, hostilities, hostility, incompatibility, incongruence, incongruity, inconsistency, infringement, inharmoniousness, inimicality, interference, irreconcilability, mismatch, misunderstanding, opposing causes, opposition, oppugnancy, polarity, quarrel, quarreling, question at issue, rencounter, renitency, resistance, rivalry, subject of dispute, tension, turmoil, unharmoniousness, variance, want of harmony, wrangle
ASSOCIATED CONCEPTS: center of gravity theory, conflict of interest, conflict of laws, conflicting clauses, conflicting evidence, conflicting findings, conflicting jurisdiction, conflicting provisions, irreconcilable conflict

CONFLICT, *verb*   ablude, argue, be at cross purposes, be at variance, be contrary, be different, be discordant, be inconsistent, be inharmonious, be opposed, be opposed to, be unwilling, change, clash, collide, combat, come into collision, contend, contest, contradict, contrast, controvert, counteract, cross, debate, defy, depart from, deviate, differ, differ in opinion, disaccord, disagree, disapprove, *discrepare,* dislike, dispute, dissent, *dissentire,* divaricate, diverge from, go contrary to,

go in opposition to, have differences, hinder, hold opposite views, interfere with, not abide, not accept, not conform, not have any part of, object, oppose, play at cross purposes, protest, quarrel, refute, *repugnare,* resist, revolt, rival, run against, run at cross purposes, run counter to, run in opposition to, schismatize, set oneself against, strike back, strive against, struggle, take exception, vary, wrangle
ASSOCIATED CONCEPTS: conflicting claim, conflicting clauses, conflicting evidence, conflicting findings, conflicting interests, conflicting jurisdiction, conflicting provisions

CONFORM, verb abide by, accede, accept, acclimatize, accommodate, accord, adapt, adhere to, adjust, agree, align, approve, arrive at terms, assimilate, attend to instructions, attune, be at one with, be in harmony, be in keeping, be regulated by, become like, become similar, bend, come round, comply, concede, concur, conventionalize, coordinate, correlate, correspond, equalize, fall in, fall into line, fit, fit in, follow, follow precedent, follow routine, go along with, join the majority, keep to, liken, make uniform, match, measure up to, obey, obey orders, obey regulations, obey rules, observe, observe discipline, *obtemperare,* reconcile, render accordant, side with, stand together, standardize, submit, suit, support, synchronize, systematize, tailor, yield, yield assent
ASSOCIATED CONCEPTS: conformed copies, conformed to the law

CONFORMITY *(Agreement),* **noun** accommodation, accord, accordance, acquiescence, adjustment, affinity, agreement, alliance, assent, coincidence, collaboration, combined operation, compatibility, concert, concinnity, concord, concurrence, concurrent opinion, conformance, conformation, congeniality, congruence, congruency, congruity, conjunction, consensus, consent, consonance, *convenientia,* convention, cooperation, correspondence, harmony, joint effort, joint planning, league, likeness, oneness, similarity, uniformity, union
ASSOCIATED CONCEPTS: conformity in pleadings

CONFORMITY *(Obedience),* **noun** adherence, assimilation, association, close observance, compliance, conformance, conformation, consent, consistency, conventionality, dutifulness, faithfulness, fidelity, full observance, obeisance, observance, submission, submissiveness, subordination, willingness, yielding

CONFOUND, verb abash, astonish, astound, baffle, be uncertain, becloud, bewilder, bring into disorder, complicate, *confundere,* confuse, dumbfound, embrangle, embroil, entangle, involve, make havoc, mingle confusedly, mislead, muddle, mystify, nonplus, obfuscate, obscure, *obstupefacere, per miscere,* perplex, put into disorder, puzzle, scramble, throw into confusion

CONFRONT *(Encounter),* **verb** accost, brave, breast, come across, come face to face with, come in contact, face, meet, stand facing, stand opposite

CONFRONT *(Oppose),* **verb** act in opposition to, argue against, assail, be against, be at cross-purposes, be opposite, challenge, come in conflict with, contend against, contend with, contradict, contrapose, contrast with, contravene, controvert, count against, counteract, counterattack, counterwork, cross, defy, deny, disagree with, disapprove, dispute, engage in conflict with, go against, mark against, match against, meet in conflict, object, offer resistance, oppugn, protest, put in opposition, rebuff, recalcitrate, repel, resist, rise against, rival, run counter, run counter to, *se opponere,* set oneself against, skirmish, stand firm, stem, strike back, struggle, take exception to, turn against, wrangle, wrestle with
ASSOCIATED CONCEPTS: right of cross-examination, right to confront witnesses

CONFRONTATION *(Act of setting face to face),* **noun** act of facing, approach, audience, colloquy, coming together, conference, consultation, dialogue, discussion, encounter, engagement, interview, meeting, parley, rencounter
ASSOCIATED CONCEPTS: right of confrontation, right of cross-examination, right to confront witnesses

CONFRONTATION *(Altercation),* **noun** affray, argument, battle, bout, brawl, brush, clash, collision, combat, conflict, confrontment, contention, contestation, disagreement, discord, dispute, engagement, fight, fracas, fray, hostile contest, hostile encounter, *mêlée,* opposition, opposure, quarrel, rencounter, row, scuffle, skirmish, squabble, struggle, velitation, wrangle

CONFUSE *(Bewilder),* **verb** abash, addle, astonish, baffle, befog, befuddle, bemuddle, confound, *confundere,* daze, discompose, disconcert, distract, embarrass, flurry, fluster, fog, jumble, mislead, mix up, muddle, mystify, nonplus, obfuscate, *permiscere,* perplex, *perturbare,* puzzle, rattle, render uncertain, stump, stupefy, throw into confusion, unhinge, unsettle

CONFUSE *(Create disorder),* **verb** clutter, derange, disarrange, disarray, disorder, disorganize, displace, disturb, embroil, entangle, intermingle, jumble, mess, mess up, mingle, mix up, muddle, snarl, throw into confusion, throw into disorder, unsettle
ASSOCIATED CONCEPTS: mistake, mistake of fact, mistake of law

CONFUSION *(Ambiguity),* **noun** bafflement, befuddlement, bewilderment, complication, confoundment, confusedness, consternation, difficulty, dilemma, discomfiture, disconcertion, distraction, doubt, doubtfulness, dubiety, dubiousness, dubitation, embarrassment, enigma, fluster, fuddle, haziness, incertitude, indecisiveness, indefiniteness, indeterminableness, indeterminateness, indistinctness, inexactness, labyrinth, lack of clearness, miscalculation, misconception, mystification, nonplus, perplexity, perturbation, predicament, puzzle, puzzlement, quandary, uncertainty, unclearness, vagueness
ASSOCIATED CONCEPTS: confusion of corporate names, confusion of trademark

CONFUSION *(Turmoil),* **noun** anarchy, chaos, clamor, clutter, commotion, complexity, *confusio,* congestion, demoralization, difficulty, disarrangement, disarray, discord, disorder, disorderliness, disorganization, disquiet, disquietude, distraction, disturbance, entanglement, farrago, ferment, frenzy, havoc, imbroglio, inseparable intermixture, muddle, pandemonium, *perturbatio,* rampage, shapelessness, tumult, turbulence, unrest, unsettlement, upheaval, uproar

CONFUTATION, noun abjurement, challenge, condemnation, contradiction, contrariety, contrary assertion, contravention, countercharge, counterevidence, counterstatement, disavowal, disproof, effective rejoinder, evidence against, evidence on the other side, negation, plea in rebuttal, rebuttal, rebutter, redargution, refutation, rejoinder, renunciation, reply, repudiation, retort, surrejoinder

CONGEALMENT, noun act of hardening, coagulation, cohesion, compactness, concreteness, concretion, condensation, congelation, consistence, consolidation, crystallization, gelatinization, gelling, hardness, impenetrability, impermeability, incompressibility, indivisibility, jellification, petrification, precipitation, solidification, solidity, solidness, thickening, thickness

CONGLOMERATE, adjective accumulated, agglomerate, aggregate, amalgamated, amassed, assembled, blended, brought together, collected, collectivized, combined, complex, composite, compound, compounded, congregate, congregated, cumulated, gathered into a round mass, glomerate, indiscriminate, inseparable, mass, mingled, miscellaneous, mixed, united, varied

CONGLOMERATION, noun accumulation, agglomeration, aggregate, aggregation, amassment, array, assembly, assortment, collection, compilation, consolidation, cumulation, forgathering, glomeration, group, ingathering, lot, mass, miscellany, multitude, quantity

CONGREGATE, verb accumulate, aggregate, aggroup, amass, assemble, bring together, bring together in a crowd, bunch, cluster, collect, collect into a focus, come in contact, come together, compile, concentrate, conglomerate, *congregari,* convene, converge, convocate, crowd together, gather, get together, group, herd together, ingather, join, mass, meet, meet in a body, rally, receive, throng, unite
ASSOCIATED CONCEPTS: breach of the peace, congregate in a public place

CONGREGATION, noun aggregate, aggregation, amassment, assemblage, assembly, assembly of persons, association, audience, batch, *coetus,* collection, conclave, conference, congregated body, convention, *conventus,* convergence, convocation, crowd, forgathering, gathering, getting together, horde, ingathering, mass, mass meeting, meeting, multitude, reunion, session

CONGRESS, noun advisory body, assemblage, assembly, consultive body, council, governmental body, legislative body, legislature, political body

CONGRUOUS, adjective accordant, acquiescent, adapted, agreeable, agreed, akin, analogical, analogous, applicable, apposite, appropriate, assenting, coexistent, coexisting, coincident, coinciding, combining, commendable, commensurate, compatible, concordant, concurrent, conformable, conforming, congruent, consensual, consentaneous, consentient, consistent with, consonant, consubstantial, correlative, correspondent, corresponding, equal, equivalent, fit, fitting, germane, harmonious, harmonized, identified with, in accord, in accordance with, in harmony with, in point, in rapport, in unison with, like, matching, near, parallel, proportional, proportionate, reconcilable, relevant, representative, representing, resembling, similar, similative, suiting, synchronized, synchronous, synonymous

CONJECTURE, noun assumption, belief, guess, guesswork, hypothesis, imputation, inference, opinion, postulate, postulation, presumption, presupposition, presurmise, speculation, supposal, supposition, surmise, suspicion, theory, thesis, unverified supposition
FOREIGN PHRASES: *In claris non est locus conjecturis.* In matters which are obvious there is no room for conjecture.

CONJOIN, verb accumulate, add, add to, ally, amass, annex, assemble, attach, be joined, blend, bring together, cement, clap together, clasp together, coalesce, cohere, collect, combine, compound, connect, consolidate, entwine, fuse, gather, hold together, incorporate, interlace, interlock, intertwist, interweave, join together, make one, mass, merge, mix, reunite, unify, unite
ASSOCIATED CONCEPTS: conjoint legacy, conjoint robbery, conjoint wills

CONJOINT, adjective affiliated, affixed, agreed, allied, amalgamated, assimilated, associated, attached, banded together, blended, bound together, cemented, coalescent, coalitional, cohesive, collective, combined, common, commutual, compact, compatible, composite, concerted, concomitant, concurrent, confederate, confederated, congruent, conjunct, conjunctive, connected, consolidated, corporate, coupled, coworking, *en rapport,* fastened together, federated, federative, fused, in alliance, in common, in conjunction, in league, incorporated, indivisible, inseparable, integrated, interclasped, interdependent, interfused, intermixed, joined, joined together, joint, leagued, linked, locked, merged, mixed, paired, partnered, pieced together, pooled, reciprocally attached, spliced, tied together, together, unified, united, wedded, welded
ASSOCIATED CONCEPTS: conjoint legacy, conjoint robbery, conjoint wills

CONJUGAL, adjective betrothed, bridal, cojugate, *coniugalis,* connubial, coupled, espoused, marital, married, matched, mated, matrimonial, nuptial, paired, partnered, united, wedded
ASSOCIATED CONCEPTS: conjugal rights

CONJUNCTION, noun adjacency, agreement, alliance, association, compliance, concatenation, concert, concomitance, concord, concurrence, concurrent opinion, conformity, conjoining, connection, cooperation, harmony, joint effort, junction, network, union, united action

CONJURE, verb call to mind, conceive, conceptualize, contemplate, create, devise, dream up, envisage, *excogitare,* excogitate, fabricate, fancy, *fingere,* form an image, formulate, frame, give play to the imagination, have a vision, imagine, improvise, invent, *machinari,* make up, nurture, originate, perceive, produce, realize, represent to oneself, think of, think up, visualize
ASSOCIATED CONCEPTS: conjure up a cause of action

CONNECT *(Join together),* **verb** *adligare,* amalgamate, annex, append, assemble, attach, band, band together, bind, blend, bridge, bring in contact with, cement, coalesce, cohere, combine, conjoin, *connectere,* consolidate, couple, entwine, fasten together, fuse, gather, graft, harness together, hook, hyphenate, interlink, interlock, intertwine, interweave, *iungere,* join, knit, lace, league, link together, lock, marry, match, meet, merge, pair, partner, put together, solder, subjoin, tie, touch, unite, verge on, wed

CONNECT *(Relate), verb* affiliate, ally, appertain to, associate, bracket, bridge, cohere, consociate, correlate, draw a parallel, group, integrate, interconnect, interrelate, link together, make relevant, match, pertain to, relate, show a relationship, show affinity, show as cognate, show as kindred, show relation, show resemblance, show similarity, span
ASSOCIATED CONCEPTS: connect the suspect to the crime

CONNECTION *(Abutment), noun* abuttal, border, contact, contiguousness, junction, juxtaposition, nearness, tangency, union

CONNECTION *(Fastening), noun* attachment, binder, bond, bridge, catch, catenation, cohesion, combination, concatenation, conjunction, consolidation, copula, couple, fastener, hitch, holdfast, interconnection, joiner, joint, junction, juncture, knot, liaison, ligature, link, linkage, nexus, splice, tie, unifier, union

CONNECTION *(Relation), noun* affiliation, alliance, analogy, applicability, application, association, bearing, coalition, coherence, coherency, common denominator, common reference, consanguinity, consociation, correlation, identification, interrelation, kinship, league, liaison, link, linkage, match, parallel, pertinence, propinquity, rapport, reference, relatedness, relationship, relevance, tie
ASSOCIATED CONCEPTS: connection between a suspect and a crime

CONNIVANCE *, noun* act of maneuvering, act of scheming, alliance, association, chicanery, coagency, coincidence, collaboration, collusion, combined operation, complicity, complot, concert, concord, concurrence, concurrent opinion, confederacy, conjunction, conspiracy, contrivance, cooperation, corrupt agreement, corrupt collusion, corrupt consent, corrupt consenting, corrupt cooperation, implied assent, *indulgentia,* intrigue, joint effort, joint planning, junction, league, liaison, machination, manipulation, participation, plot, scheme, secret approval, underhand participation, underhanded complicity, underplot, voluntary oversight, working together
ASSOCIATED CONCEPTS: connivance as a defense to a divorce

CONNIVE *, verb* act in concert, be a party to, be in collusion with, collude, combine, complot, concert, conspire, cooperate, cooperate with secretly, countermine, counterplot, engineer, *in re connivere,* intrigue, join forces, join with, machinate, make an agreement with, maneuver, participate, participate surreptitiously, plot, *rem dissimulare,* scheme

CONNOTATION *, noun* allusion, application, bearing, broad meaning, coloring, comprehension, construction, context, denotation, derivation, drift, essence, essential meaning, expression, force, general meaning, gist, hint, idea, impact, implication, import, inference, information, innuendo, insinuation, intent, intention, interpretation, literal interpretation, literal meaning, literal sense, literality, meaning, natural meaning, object, obvious interpretation, obvious meaning, obvious sense, original meaning, plain meaning, point of, primary meaning, purport, range of meaning, real interpretation, real meaning, real sense, reference, scope, secondary implied meaning, sense, significance, signification, simple meaning, source, spirit, substance, substantial meaning, suggestion, symbolization, tenor, true meaning, unstrained meaning, worth

CONNOTE *, verb* allude to, carry a suggestion, communicate, convey, denote, designate, evidence, express, give indirect information, hint, imply, indicate, infer, insinuate, intimate, involve, make indirect suggestion, mean, point to, refer to, represent, signify, speak of, stand for, suggest, symbolize, tell of, touch on

CONSANGUINEOUS *, adjective* affiliated, agnate, akin, allied, ancestral, blood related, closely allied, closely related, cognate, collateral, congenerous, connatural, consanguine, distantly related, family related, fraternal, hereditary, intimately related, kindred, maternal, matrilinear, nearly allied, nearly related, of the blood, of the same family, of the same kind, paternal, patriarchal, patrilinear, related, relative
ASSOCIATED CONCEPTS: lineal consanguinity

CONSCIENCE *, noun* categorical imperative, code of duty, code of honor, compunction, *conscientia,* conscientiousness, ethical judgment, ethical philosophy, ethical self, ethics, high ideals, high standards, honesty, honor, ideals, inner voice, integrity, inward monitor, mind, moral consciousness, moral faculty, moral obligation, moral principles, moral sense, principle, probity, professional ethics, rectitude, scruples, sense of duty, sense of moral right, sense of right and wrong, standards, superego, uprightness
ASSOCIATED CONCEPTS: conscientious objector
FOREIGN PHRASES: *Fides est obligatio conscientiae alicujus ad intentionem alterius.* A trust is an obligation of conscience of one to the will of another. *Judex habere debet duos sales, - sales, salem sapientiae, ne sit insipidus; et salem conscientiae, ne sit diabolus.* A judge ought to have two salts, - the salt of wisdom, lest he be insipid; and the salt of conscience, lest he be devilish. *La conscience est la plus changeante des regles.* Conscience is the most changeable of rules.

CONSCIENTIOUS *, adjective* assiduous, attentive, careful, diligent, duteous, dutiful, exacting, faithful, fastidious, heedful, honest, honorable, incorruptible, just, meritorious, meticulous, minute, moral, observant, painstaking, particular, precise, principled, punctilious, regardful, reliable, *religiosus,* reputable, righteous, *sanctus,* scrupulous, strict, thorough, trustworthy, trusty, uncorrupt, upright, virtuous

CONSCIOUS *(Awake), adjective* able to recognize, active, acute, alert, alive, animate, astir, breathing, endowed with life, enlivened, existent, existing, extant, imbued with life, in existence, inspirited, live, living, mortal, vivified

CONSCIOUS *(Aware), adjective* acquainted with, apperceptive, appreciative, apprehending, apprised, attentive, cognizant, comprehending, *conscius,* discerning, heedful, informed, knowing, mindful, observant, perceptive, percipient, rational, regardful, sensible, sentient, undeceived, understanding, vigilant, watchful
ASSOCIATED CONCEPTS: conscious act, conscious disregard for others, conscious indifference, conscious reaction

CONSECUTIVE, *adjective*　　chronological, coming after, connected, consequent, *continens,* continual, continuing, continuous, cumulative, ensuing, following in a series, in a line, in a row, in order, in regular order, in sequence, in turn, in unbroken sequence, in uninterrupted succession, nonstop, one after another, one after the other, perennial, recurrent, repeated, repetitive, running, sequent, sequential, serial, serialized, seriate, seriatim, steady, subsequent, succeeding, successive, unbroken, uninterrupted, uninterrupted in course, unremitting

ASSOCIATED CONCEPTS: consecutive sentences

CONSENSUAL, *adjective*　　accordant, acquiesced in, acquiescent, agreeable, agreed upon, approving, assented, at one with, attuned to, carried, coherent, coincident with, collaborating, compatible, compliant, conceded, concomitant, concordant, concurred in, concurrent, confirming, conforming to, congruent, conjunct, consentaneous, consentient, consistent with, cooperative, endorsed, granted, harmonious, harmonized, in agreement, in alliance, joint, like-minded, mutually agreeable, mutually understood, of one accord, of one mind, of the same mind, parallel, popularly believed, reconciled, sympathetic, synergic, unanimous, unchallenged, uncontested, uncontradicted, uncontroversial, uncontroverted, understood, undisputed, united, unopposed, unquestioned, voted

CONSENSUS, *noun*　　acclamation, accord, acknowledgment, affirmance, affirmation, agreement, assonance, attonement, bipartisanship, common consent, compact, compatibility, concent, concentus, concert, concinnity, concord, concordance, concurrence, conformance, conformation, conformity, congruence, consentaneity, consentaneousness, consentience, consistency, consonance, cooperation, correspondence, general agreement, harmony, mutual agreement, mutual sympathy, mutual understanding, reconcilement, solid vote, synchronization, unanimity, uniformity, union, unison

ASSOCIATED CONCEPTS: consensus of opinion, per curiam opinion

CONSENT, *noun*　　accedence, acceptance, accord, acknowledgment, acquiescence, admission, adoption, affirmance, affirmation, agreement, allowance, approbation, approval, assent, assurance, authentication, authority, authorization, certification, commendation, compliance, concession, concord, concordance, concurrence, confirmation, *consensus,* corroboration, countenance, empowering, endorsement, entitlement, grace, grant, guarantee, harmony, indulgence, leave, legalization, license, permission, permit, ratification, sanction, stipulation, subscription, sufferance, support, tolerance, toleration, unison, unity, validation, verification, vouchsafement, warrant, warranty, willingness

ASSOCIATED CONCEPTS: consent decree, consent in writing, consent judgment, consent of adoptive parents, consent of owner, consent of parties, consent to a taking, consent to an act, consent to search, express consent, implied consent, legal consent, limited consent, mutual consent, parental consent, qualified consent, removal of an action by consent, voluntary consent, without consent

FOREIGN PHRASES: *Consensus non concubitus facit nuptias vel matrimonium et consentire non possunt ante annos nubiles.* Consent, not cohabitation, consti-

tutes nuptials or marriage, and persons cannot consent before marriageable years. *Consensus voluntas multorum ad quos res pertinet, simul juncta.* Consent is the united will of several interested in one subject matter. *Consentientes et agentes pari poena plectentur.* Persons who consent and those who perform are subject to the same penalties. *Longa patientia trahitur ad consensum.* Long sufferance is construed as consent. *Itelius estomnia mala pati quam malo consentire.* It is better to suffer every ill than to consent to evil. *Nihil consensui tam controrium est quam vis atque metus.* Nothing is as much opposed to consent as force and fear. *Non consentit qui errat.* He who makes a mistake does not consent. *Non refert an quis assensum suum praefert verbis aut rebus ipsis et factis.* It matters not whether a man gives his consent by his words or by his acts and deeds. *Non videntur qui errant consentire.* Those who err are not deemed to consent. *Non videtur consensum retinuisse si quis ex praescripto minantis aliquid immutavit.* He does not appear to have retained consent who has changed anything through menaces. *Nuptias non cuncubitus sed consensus facit.* Not cohabitation but consent makes the marriage. *Omne jus aut consensus fecit, aut necessitas constituit aut firmavit consuetudo.* Consent created, necessity established, or custom has confirmed every law. *Omnis consensus tollit errorem.* Every consent removes error. *Qui tacet, consentire videtur.* He who is silent, is deemed to consent. *Actus me invito factus non est meus actus.* An act done against my will is not my act. *Agentes et consentientes pari poena plectentur.* Acting and consenting parties are liable to the same punishment. *Consensus est voluntas plurium ad quos res pertinet, simul juncta.* Consent is the conjoint will of several persons to whom the thing belongs. *Consensus facit legem.* Consent makes the law. *Consensus tollit errorem.* Consent removes or obviates mistake. *Quod meum est sine me auferri non potest.* What is mine cannot be taken away without my consent. *Volenti non fit injuria.* He who consents cannot receive an injury.

CONSENT, *verb*　　accede, accept, accord, acquiesce, *adsentire,* affirm, agree, allow, approve, assent, authorize, be in favor of, be willing, come to terms, comply, concur, *consentire,* endorse, give approval, give consent, give permission, grant, gratify, have no objection, indicate willingness, license, permit, ratify, sanction, suffer, support, tolerate, warrant, yield

ASSOCIATED CONCEPTS: consent to an adjournment, consent to jurisdiction

CONSENTING, *adjective*　　accommodating, accordant, acquiescent, acquiescing, agreeable, agreeing, allowing, approving, assentient, assenting, assentive, compliable, compliant, concordant, consentaneous, consentient, favorably inclined, in accord, in agreement, in harmony with, inclined to assent, likeminded, marked by consent, of one accord, permitting, voluntary, willing, yielding

ASSOCIATED CONCEPTS: abetting, consenting to be adjudged a bankrupt, permitting, ratifying

CONSEQUENCE *(Conclusion),* *noun*　　aftereffect, aftergrowth, aftermath, climax, completion, conclusion, *consecutio,* consummation, culmination, decision, deduction, denouement, derivation, derivative, determination, development, effect, emanation, ensual, eventuality, execution, final result, finale, finding, finish, fruition, illation, induction, logical result, offshoot, outcome, outgrowth, product, reaction, resolution, response, result, resultant action, settlement, upshot, verdict

ASSOCIATED CONCEPTS: consequential benefits, consequential contempt, consequential contracts, consequential damages, consequential injuries, consequential loss
FOREIGN PHRASES: *Consuetudo non trahitur in conseqentiam.* Custom is not drawn into consequence. *Non officit conatus nisi sequatur effectus.* An attempt does not harm unless a consequence follows. *Officit conatus si effectus sequatur.* The attempt becomes of consequence, if the effect follows.

CONSEQUENCE *(Significance),* **noun**   accent, *auctoritas,* base, basis, core, distinction, effect, essence, essential quality, force, germ, heart, import, importance, influence, magnitude, marrow, materialness, meaning, merit, nature, notable feature, nucleus, point, primary element, principle, prominence, purport, quintessence, relevance, self-consequence, self-importance, seriousness, signification, soul, substance, usefulness, vital part

CONSEQUENTIAL *(Deducible),* **adjective**   derivative, following, inferential, resultant, sequential
ASSOCIATED CONCEPTS: consequential contempt, consequential damages

CONSEQUENTIAL *(Substantial),* **adjective**   authoritative, considerable, eminent, great, important, influential, momentous, powerful, self-important, significant, weighty

CONSEQUENTLY, *adverb*   accordingly, as a consequence, as a matter of course, as a result, as matters stand, as the case may be, because, by reason of, by the same sign, by the same token, *ergo,* finally, for reasons given, for that cause, for that reason, for this reason, for which reason, from that cause, hence, *igitur,* in accordance therefore, in conclusion, in that case, in that event, in which case, it follows that, *itaque,* logically then, naturally, necessarily, of course, of necessity, on account of this, on that account, on this account, such being the case, that being so, that being the case, therefore, thus, thusly, to that end, under the circumstances, wherefore

CONSERVATION, *noun*   economy, fostering, guarding, harboring, keeping, maintaining, maintenance, nourishing, nursing, preservation, preserving, protecting, protection, providing sanctuary, safeguarding, safekeeping, saving, sheltering, shielding, sparing, storage, support, sustaining, sustentation, upholding, upkeep
ASSOCIATED CONCEPTS: conservation of assets, conservation of property

CONSERVE, *verb*   avoid using, *conservare,* expend gradually, expend slowly, guard, keep, keep from loss, keep in existence, keep safe, keep unimpaired, maintain, omit using, preserve, prolong, protect, refrain from using, refuse to waste, safeguard, save, save from loss, secure, *servare,* shield, spare, store up, sustain, treasure, use carefully, use frugally, use sparingly, use thriftily

CONSIDER, *verb*   advert to, analyze, appraise, assess, be attentive, cerebrate, cogitate, confer, *considerare,* consult, contemplate, debate, deliberate, de-

vote attention to, digest, evaluate, examine, *expendere,* gauge, heed, inspect, investigate, mark, meditate on, mull over, muse, notice, observe, pay attention to, ponder, pore over, probe, reckon, reflect upon, regard, *respicere,* ruminate, scrutinize, study, take into account, think about, turn over in one's mind, weigh
ASSOCIATED CONCEPTS: adjudge, consider on its merits

CONSIDERABLE, *adjective*   abundant, ample, cardinal, commanding, compelling, consequential, dominant, estimable, a good deal of, *gravis,* great, important, impressive, influential, large, *magnus,* marked, material, momentous, not to be overlooked, notable, noteworthy, of importance, of note, overruling, plentiful, potent, powerful, predominant, puissant, reasonable, remarkable, respectable, significant, sizable, special, substantial, tolerable, valuable, worthy of consideration
ASSOCIATED CONCEPTS: considerable damage, considerable provocation, considerable time

CONSIDERATION *(Contemplation),* **noun**   advertency, advisement, attention, attentiveness, cogitation, *consideratio,* examination, forethought, heed, judgment, meditation, pondering, premeditation, reckoning, reflection, review, rumination, serious thought, speculation, study
ASSOCIATED CONCEPTS: due consideration

CONSIDERATION *(Recompense),* **noun**   accommodation, benefits, bounty, compensation, defrayment, disbursement, emolument, fees, financial assistance, gratuity, guerdon, incentive, indemnification, indemnity, inducement, largess, payment, pecuniary aid, prize, reckoning, refund, reimbursement, remittance, remuneration, reparation, repayment, requital, restitution, return, reward, satisfaction, settlement, solatium, something of value, stipend, subsidy, sum
ASSOCIATED CONCEPTS: adequate consideration, collateral consideration, complete failure of consideration, consideration for a contract, due consideration, failure of consideration, fair and valuable consideration, fictitious consideration, founded on a consideration, fraud in consideration, full and adequate consideration, good and sufficient consideration, illegal consideration, illusory consideration, immoral consideration, lack of consideration, legal consideration, meritorious consideration, moral consideration, mutual consideration, new consideration, nominal consideration, partial failure of consideration, past consideration, pecuniary consideration, present consideration, sufficiency of consideration, valid consideration, want of consideration
FOREIGN PHRASES: *Ex turpi causa non oritur actio.* No cause of action arises out of an immoral or illegal consideration. *In omnibus contractibus, sive nominatis sive innominatis, permutatio continetur.* In all contracts, whether nominate or innominate, there is implied an exchange. *L'obligation sans cause, ou sur une fausse cause, ou sur cause illicite, ne peut avoir aucun effet.* An obligation without consideration, or with a false one, or with an unlawful one, cannot have any effect. *Nuda pactio obligationem non parit.* A naked promise does not create a binding obligation. *Nudum pactum est ubi nulla subest causa praeter conventionem; sed ubi subest causa, fit obligatio, et parit actionem.* A naked contract is where there is no consideration for the undertaking or agreement; but where there is a consideration, an obligation is created, and an

action arises. *Pacta quae turpem causam continent non sunt observanda.* Agreements founded upon an immoral consideration are not to be enforced.

CONSIDERATION *(Sympathetic regard),* **noun** accommodation, attentiveness, beneficence, benevolence, benignity, care, chivalry, civility, clemency, compassion, complaisance, concern, considerateness, cordiality, courteousness, courtesy, courtliness, deference, delicacy, diplomacy, esteem, estimation, friendliness, gallantry, generosity, geniality, gentleness, good manners, graciousness, helpfulness, humanity, kindheartedness, kindliness, kindness, mercy, neighborliness, obligingness, politeness, regard, respect, solicitousness, solicitude, tact, tenderness, thought, thoughtful regard, thoughtfulness, understanding, unselfishness, willingness to please

CONSIGN, *verb* abalienate, assign to, authorize, charge, commit, commit to another's trust, *committere,* convey, deliver, deliver formally, deliver over, deposit with, entrust, give in trust, hand over, have conveyed, send, ship, transfer, transfer for sale, transmit, transplant, transport, turn over
ASSOCIATED CONCEPTS: bailment, conditional sale, consignment contract of goods

CONSIGNMENT, *noun* allocation, allotment, appropriation, assignation, assignment, cession, concession, consignation, conveyance, conveyancing, delivering to, dispatchment, distribution, expressage, goods shipped, interchange, merchandise sent, sending, shipment, shipping, transfer, transference, transferring, transmission
ASSOCIATED CONCEPTS: consignment for sale, consignment shipper

CONSIST, *verb* add up to, amount to, be composed of, be comprised of, be contained in, be formed of, be made of, be made up of, comprise, *consistere,* constitute, contain, cover, embody, encompass, enfold, entail, envelop, form, has as a component, have as its foundation, hold, in essence is, in nature is, in substance is, include, incorporate, involve, is composed of, is essentially, make up, occupy, synthesize

CONSISTENT, *adjective* accordant, agreeing, alike, coherent, cohering, compatible, compliable, concordant, conformable, congruent with, congruous, consonant, *constans, conveniens,* correspondent, equable, equal, harmonious, logical, not contradictory, regular, self-consistent, unchanging, undeviating, uniform
ASSOCIATED CONCEPTS: consistent cases, consistent causes of action, consistent construction of sales contracts, consistent decisions, consistent defenses, consistent interpretation of the Constitution, consistent precedence, consistent with the public interest

CONSOCIATE, *noun* abettor, accessory, accomplice, adherent, adjunct, adjutant, aide, ally, assistant, associate, attendant, auxiliary, coadjutor, cohelper, cohort, collaborator, colleague, comate, companion, comrade, confederate, confidant, confrere, consort, cooperator, copartner, coworker, fellow companion, fellow conspirator, fellow worker, follower, helper, helpmate, intimate, mate, participator, partner, retainer, side-partner
ASSOCIATED CONCEPTS: accomplice

CONSOLIDATE *(Strengthen),* **verb** add to, amass, bind, blend, bring together, build up, coalesce, cohere, combine, compact, compound, compress, concatenate, concentrate, condense, congeal, conjoin, conjoint, connect, contract, crystallize, densify, fortify, fuse, harden, intensify, make firm, make solid, mass, mix, put together, render solid, settle firmly, solidify, squeeze together, unify

CONSOLIDATE *(Unite),* **verb** accumulate, affiliate, ally, amalgamate, amass, band, become one, bring together, centralize, coact, coadjuvate, coalesce, combine, compound, compress, concentrate, concert, confederate, congeal, conglomerate, conjoin, connect, cooperate, couple, cowork, draw together, federate, fuse, gather together, incorporate, interblend, interfuse, intertwine, join, join forces, join forces with, league, link, lump together, make one, meet, melt into one, merge, mix, mobilize, piece together, put together, roll into one, shade into, solidify, stay together, stick together, synthesize, unionize, work together
ASSOCIATED CONCEPTS: consolidate actions

CONSOLIDATION, *noun* affiliation, aggregation, amalgamation, assemblage, association, centralization, coadunation, combination, compact, confederation, conjunction, conjuncture, consortium, federation, fusion, incorporation, integration, junction, league, merger, mixture, pool, solidification, strengthening, unification, union
ASSOCIATED CONCEPTS: consolidated laws, consolidated school district, consolidation of actions, consolidation of stock

CONSONANT, *adjective* accordant, adapted, agreeing, alike, answerable, appropriate, apt, arranged, at one, attuned, balanced, becoming, coherent, coincident, commensurate, compatible, concerted, concordant, concurrent, conformable, conforming, congenial, *congruens,* congruent, congruous, consentaneous, *consentaneus,* consentient, consequent, consistent, *conveniens,* cooperating, correspondent, corresponding, equable, equal, fit, fitting, harmonious, in accord, in agreement, in concord, in harmony, in rapport, in unison, logically consistent, parallel, reconcilable, related, self consistent, similar, suitable, synchronal, synchronized, unchangeable, unchanged, unchanging, undeviating, undiscordant, unified, uniform, unisonant, unisonous

CONSORT, *noun* accompanier, associate, colleague, comate, *comes,* companion, compeer, comrade, *confrère,* conjugal partner, copartner, escort, fellow, fellow companion, helpmate, husband, marital partner, *maritus,* marriage partner, mate, partner, *socius,* spouse, wife
ASSOCIATED CONCEPTS: alienation of affections, criminal conversation, loss of consortium

CONSORTIUM *(Business cartel),* **noun** association, business agreement, business combine, business entente, cartel, coalition, combination, combination of financial institutions, confederacy, consolidation, league, merger, monopoly, partnership, pool, syndicate, trust, union

CONSORTIUM *(Marriage companionship),* **noun** accommodation, affiliation, affinity, alliance, assistance, association, attachment, closeness, comfort, com-

pact, companionship, compliance, comradeship, concordance, congruity, congruousness, consocation, consortship, correspondence, familiarity, friendship, help, intercommunion, intimacy, league, marriage accord, marriage compatibility, marriage concord, partnership, reciprocal feeling, understanding
ASSOCIATED CONCEPTS: loss of consortium

CONSPICUOUS, *adjective* apparent, *clarus,* clear, clear-cut, *conspicuus,* definite, discernible, discoverable, distinct, distinguishable, distinguished, evident, exposed, exposed to view, flagrant, in bold relief, in evidence, in plain sight, in the foreground, in view, manifest, *manifestus,* marked, notable, noticeable, notorious, observable, obvious, open, overt, patent, perceivable, perceptible, plain, pointed, preeminent, prominent, pronounced, public, recognizable, remarkable, renowned, self-evident, spectacular, standing out, striking, tending to attract attention, unblurred, unclouded, uncovered, undisguised, unhidden, unmistakable, visible, well-defined, well-marked, well-seen
ASSOCIATED CONCEPTS: conspicuous places

CONSPIRACY, *noun* abetment, agreement to accomplish an unlawful end, agreement to commit a crime, coalescence, coalition, collusion, combination, combined operation, compact, compliance, complicity, composition, concert, confederacy, *coniuratio,* connivance, contrivance, corrupt agreement, countermine, counterplot, duplicitous agreement, intrigue, intriguery, joint effort, joint planning, maneuvering, plan, plot, proposal, scheme, treasonable alliance, underplot, unlawful combination, unlawful contrivance, unlawful plan, unlawful scheme
ASSOCIATED CONCEPTS: conspiracy in restraint of interstate trade, conspiracy in restraint of trade, conspiracy to commit felony, conspiracy to defraud, conspiracy within the Sherman Anti-trust Act, continuing conspiracy, entered into a conspiracy, furtherance of the conspiracy, overt act

CONSPIRATOR, *noun* abettor, colluder, complotter, confederate, *coniuratus,* conniver, deceiver, intrigant, intriguer, machinator, plotter, schemer, spy, strategist

CONSPIRE, *verb* abet, act in combination, act in concert, act in harmony, agree, aid, associate, be banded together, be stealthy, cabal, calculate, coact, cohere, collude, combine, combine for some evil design, combine operations, concert, concoct a plot, concur, confederate, confederate for an unlawful purpose, *coniurare,* conjoin, connive, *conspirare,* contribute toward, contrive, cooperate, countermine, counterplot, cowork, design, devise, devise treachery, form a coalition, form plots, frame, hatch a plot, hold together, intrigue, join, join forces, league together, league with, machinate, make an agreement with, make secret arrangements, maneuver, participate in an unlawful scheme, plan, plan a crime, plan an unlawful act, plan secretly, plan to commit a crime, plot, plot an action in advance, plot craftily, plot together, scheme, take part in, take part with, unify, unite
ASSOCIATED CONCEPTS: conspire to commit a crime, conspire to defraud the United States Government

CONSPIRER, *noun* abettor, accessory, accessory after the fact, accessory before the fact, accomplice, accomplice in crime, adjutant, agent provocateur, aid, aider, aider and abettor, assistant, associate, coactor, coadjutant, coadjutor, cohelper, collaborationist, collaborator, colleague, colluder, confederate, consociate, conspirator, contriver, cooperator, counterpart, fellow conspirator, helper, helpmate, intrigant, intriguer, partner, partner in crime, planner, plotter, promoter, saboteur, schemer, strategist, subversive, traitor
ASSOCIATED CONCEPTS: accomplice

CONSTANT, *adjective* abiding, aeonian, certain, changeless, chronic, consistent, *constans,* continual, continually recurring, continuing, continuous, dependable, durable, endless, enduring, entrenched, eternal, faithful, firm, *firmus,* fixed, habitual, immortal, immutable, imperishable, inalterable, incessant, inconvertible, indeciduous, indelible, indestructible, indissoluble, inextinguishable, inflexible, invariable, invariant, inveterate, lasting, loyal, perdurable, perennial, permanent, perpetual, regular, reliable, sempiternal, *stabilis,* stable, steadfast, steady, sure, sustained, unchanging, undeviating, undying, unequivocal, uninterrupted, unrelenting, unshaken, unswerving, unvarying, unwavering

CONSTANT, *noun* certainty, conformity, consistency, constancy, *constans,* convention, firmness, *firmus,* fixation, form, immutability, inextricability, invariability, invariable, invariant, inveteracy, maxim, pattern, permanence, prescribed form, procedure, prototype, regularity, reliability, rule, sameness, *stabilis,* stability, standard, standard practice, standard procedure, staunchness, steadfastness, steadiness, symmetry, unchangeableness, uniformity

CONSTERNATION, *noun* affright, agitation, alarm, anxiety, anxious concern, anxiousness, apprehension, apprehensiveness, aversion, boding, despair, dismay, disquiet, disquietude, disturbance, dread, fear, fearfulness, fright, horror, inquietude, *pavor,* perturbation, sudden fear, trepidation

CONSTITUENCY, *noun* affiliates, associates, body of members, chapter, collective members, community, constituents, delegation, district, division, electorate, electors, enrollment, faction, group, interest group, lobby, members, membership, partisanship, party, polity, voters, voting district, voting list

CONSTITUENT *(Member)*, *noun* associate, constituency, resident, voter

CONSTITUENT *(Part)*, *noun* balloter, component, component part, division, element, *elementum,* factor, feature, fraction, fragment, included, ingredient, installment, integral part, integrant, integrant part, one of, *pars,* part, part and parcel, particle, piece, section, sector, segment, subdivision
ASSOCIATED CONCEPTS: constituent elements, constituent members, constituent parts

CONSTITUTE *(Compose)*, *verb* be a feature, be inherent, be part of, belong, belong intrinsically, classify as, *componere,* comprise, consist of, contain, create, *efficere,* embody, embrace, encompass, form, include, incorporate, inhere in, involve, make up, produce, put together

CONSTITUTE *(Establish)*, *verb* bring about, bring about by legislation, charter, codify, commission, *constituere,* create, create by law, declare lawful, decree, *designare,* determine, develop, devise, effect, effect by legislation, effectuate, empower, enact, endorse, engender, formulate, formulate by law, give legal form to, inaugurate, install, institute, invest, legalize, legislate, legitimate, legitimatize, legitimize, license, make legal, ordain, organize, originate, pass, prescribe, prescribe by law, put in force, sanction, set up, *statuere,* validate **ASSOCIATED CONCEPTS:** constitute a cause of action, constitute a crime, constitute a fraud, constitute an obstruction

FOREIGN PHRASES: *Eodem modo quo quid constituitur, dissolvitur.* A thing is discharged in the same way in which it was created.

CONSTITUTION, *noun*   act, body of law, body of rules of government, canon, charter, civil law, *civitatis,* code of laws, codification, codified law, collection of laws, compact to govern, compilation of law, dictate, edict, enactment, fundamental law, law, legal code, maxim, organic law, pandect, paramount law, precept, prescription, principles of government, regulation, rubric, statute, supreme law, written law **ASSOCIATED CONCEPTS:** action arising under Constitution or laws, Amendment to the Constitution, Constitutional Amendment, Constitutional Convention, Constitutional court, Constitutional officer, Constitutional question, Constitutional right

CONSTRAIN *(Compel), verb*   actuate, apply pressure, assert oneself, bring about by force, bring pressure to bear upon, burden, cause to, charge, coerce, *cogere,* command, command influence, compel, *compellere,* decree, demand, dominate, drive, enforce, enforce obedience, exact, exert influence, force, goad, have influence, impel, impose, impose a duty, induce, insist, insist on, issue a command, leave no option, make necessary, move, move to action, necessitate, obligate, oblige, order, press, pressure, prevail upon, prod, propel, push, put pressure on, put under obligation, require, secure by force, squeeze, subject, take no denial, tell, urge, urge forward, work upon

CONSTRAIN *(Imprison), verb*   arrest, bind, bridle, chain, circumscribe, commit, commit to an institution, commit to prison, confine, confine forcibly, detain, enclose, enthrall, entomb, harness, hold, hold as hostage, hold back by force, hold captive, hold in restraint, immure, impound, incarcerate, institutionalize, intern, isolate, jail, keep as captive, keep in custody, keep in detention, keep prisoner, limit, manacle, put in a cell, put under arrest, put under restraint, restrain, restrict, send to prison, shackle, take captive, take into custody, trammel

CONSTRAIN *(Restrain), verb*   ban, bar, block, bridle, censor, chain, check, control, curb, debar, deny, disallow, forbid, hamper, harness, hinder, hold back, hold back by force, hold down, hold in, hold in check, impede, impose restrictions, inhibit, keep back, keep in check, lay under restraint, limit, obstruct, oppress, preclude, prevent, prohibit, proscribe, put a stop to, put under restraint, refuse, refuse to grant, repress, restrain, restrict, restrict access, subdue, subjugate, suppress, withhold

CONSTRAINT *(Imprisonment), noun*   act of keeping in, apprehension, arrest, bondage, bonds, bounds, captivity, care, charge, commitment, confinement, con-

tainment, control, custodianship, custody, detainment, detention, encincture, enclosure, enthrallment, fetter, immuration, immurement, impoundment, incarceration, internment, keeping, legal restraint, preventive custody, preventive detention, prison, prohibition, protective custody, quarantine, remand, restriction

CONSTRAINT *(Restriction), noun*   act of forestalling, act of hampering, act of quelling, act of stifling, act of strangling, act of thwarting, astriction, bar, circumscription, coercion, compulsion, constriction, curb, deprivation, detainment, determent, disallowance, disapprobation, duress, encumbrance, enthrallment, fetter, forbiddance, force, hindrance, impediment, inhibition, interdict, interdiction, limitation, muzzle, obstruction, obstructionism, preclusion, pressure, prevention, prohibition, proscription, rein, repression, restraint, restrictive practice, strangulation, stultification, suppression, temperance, trammel
ASSOCIATED CONCEPTS: estoppel

CONSTRICT *(Compress), verb*   abbreviate, abridge, astringe, bind, capsulize, cause to contract, clench, coarct, compact, concentrate, condense, consolidate, constringe, contract, cram, cramp, crowd, crush, draw together, make brief, make dense, make smaller, narrow, pack tightly, pinch, press, press together, ram, reduce, reduce volume, restrict in area, shorten, shrink, squeeze, telescope, tighten

CONSTRICT *(Inhibit), verb*   arrest, astrict, barricade, be an impediment, be an obstacle, block, check, choke, close, constrain, control, curb, dam, delay, detain, deter, estop, fetter, foil, frustrate, halt, hamper, handicap, hinder, hold back, impede, interfere, keep, keep back, limit, obstruct, occlude, rein in, repress, restrain, restrict, retard, set back, set limitations, set limits, slow, stall, staunch, stay, stem, stifle, stop, strangulate, stymie, suppress, thwart, tie up, withhold

CONSTRUCTION, *noun*   clarification, comment, commentary, configuration, conformation, constitution, construability, construal, deduction, definability, definition, delineation, description, diagnosis, exegesis, exemplification, explanation, explicability, explication, exposition, expounding, form, formulation, frame, framework, illumination, inference, interpretability, *interpretatio,* interpretation, meaning, rationale, sense, significance, structure, substance, translation, understanding, version
ASSOCIATED CONCEPTS: construction of a contract, construction of a statute, construction of a writing, construction of will, contemporaneous construction, liberal construction, rule of construction, statutory construction, strict construction

FOREIGN PHRASES: *Contemporanea expositio est optima et fortissima in lege.* Contemporaneous exposition is the best and most powerful in the law. *Quum in testamento ambigue aut etiam perperam scriptum est, benigne interpretari et secundum id quod credible et cogitatum, credendum est.* When an ambiguous or even an erroneous expression occurs in a will, it should be construed liberally and in accordance with what is thought the probable meaning of the testator. *Copulatio verborum indicat acceptationem in eodem sensu.* The coupling of words indicates that they are to be taken in the same sense. *Cum duo inter se pugnantia reperiuntur in testamento, ultimum ratum est.* When two repugnant matters are found in a will, the last will be confirmed. *Curiosa et captiosa interpretatio in lege reprobatur.* A curious and captious interpretation is disapproved. *Verbis standum ubi nulla ambiguitas.* Where there is no ambiguity, one must abide by the words. *Designatio unius est exclusio alterius, et expressum facit cessare tacitum.* The designation of one is the exclusion of the other, and that which is expressed prevails over that which is implied. *In ambigua voce legis ea potius accipienda est significatio quae vitio caret, praesertim cum etiam voluntas legis ex hoc colligi possit.* In an ambiguous expression of law, that interpretation is to be preferred which is consonant with equity, especially where it is in conformity with the purpose of the law. *Non aliter a significatione verborum recedi oportet quam cum manifestum est, aliud sensisse testatorem.* The ordinary meaning of the words ought not to be departed from unless it is evident that the testator intended otherwise. *Non est novum ut priores leges ad posteriores trahantur.* It is not novel that prior statutes should give place to later ones. *Non in legendo sed in intelligendo legis consistunt.* The laws consist not in being read, but in being understood. *Omnis definitio in lege periculosa.* All definition in law is dangerous. *Omnis interpretatio si fieri potest ita fienda est in instrumentis, ut omnes contrarietates amoveantur.* Every interpretation of instruments is to be made, if they will admit of it, so that all contradictions may be removed. *In ambiguo sermone non utrumque dicimus sed id duntaxat quod volumus.* In ambiguous discourse, we do not use language in a double sense, but in the sense in which we mean it. *Benedicta est expositio quando res redimitur a destructione.* Blessed is the exposition when a thing is saved from destruction. *Benignior sententia in verbis generalibus seu dubiis, est praeferenda.* The more favorable construction is to be placed on general or doubtful expressions. *Benignius leges interpretandae sunt quo voluntas earum conservetur.* Laws are to be liberally construed, in order that their intent may be preserved. *Lex non exacte definit, sed arbitrio boni viri permittit.* The law does not define exactly, but trusts to the judgement of a good man. *Lex posterior derogat priori.* A later statute takes away the effect of a prior one. *Magis de bono quam de malo lex intendit.* The law favors a good rather than a bad interpretation. *Maledicta est expositio quae corrumpit textum.* It is a cursed construction which corrupts the text. *Mandata licita strictam recipiunt interpretationem, sed illicita latam et extensam.* Lawful commands receive a strict interpretation, but unlawful commands a broad and extended one. *Neque leges neque senatus consulta ita scribi possunt ut omnis casus qui quandoque in sediriunt comprehendatur; sed sufficit ea quae plaerumque accidunt contineri.* Neither laws nor acts of a legislature can be so written as to include all actual or possible cases; it is sufficient if they provide for those things which frequently or ordinarily may happen. *In stipulationibus cum quaeritur quid actum sit verba contra stipulatorem interpretanda sunt.* In the construction of agreements words are interpreted against the person offering them. *Omne majus minus in se complectitur.* Every greater thing embraces within itself the less. *Partem aliquam recte intelligere nemo potest, antequam totum, iterum atque iterum, perlegerit.* No one can rightly understand any part until he has read the whole over again. *Quamvis lex generaliter loquitur, restringenda tamen est, ut,*

cessante ratione, ipsa cessat. Although a law speaks generally, yet it is to be restrained, so that when its reason fails, it should cease also. *Quotiens idem sermo duas sententias exprimit, ea potissimum accipiatur, quae rei gerendae aptior est.* Whenever the same words express two meanings, that is to be adopted which is the better fitted for carrying out the proposed end. *In ambiguis orationibus maxime sententia spectanda est ejus qui eas protulisset.* In ambiguous expressions, the intent of the person using them is particularly to be regarded. *Statutum generaliter est intelligendum quando verba statuti sunt specialia, ratio autem generalis.* When the words of a statute are special, but the reason general, the statute is to be understood generally. *Tortura legum pessima.* The torture or wresting of laws is the worst. *Verba accipienda sunt secundum subjectam materiam.* Words are to be understood with reference to the subject-matter. *Verba chartarum fortius accipiuntur contra proferentem.* The words of a grant are to be taken most strongly against the person offering them. *Verba generalia generaliter sunt intelligenda.* General words are to be understood generally. *Verbis standum ubi nulla ambiguitas.* Where there is no ambiguity, the words are adhered to. *Semper sexus masculinus etiam femininum sexum continet.* The masculine sex of gender always includes the feminine also. *Semper specialia generalibus insunt.* Special expressions are always included in general ones. *Si nulla sit conjectura quae ducat alio, verba intelligenda sunt ex proprietate, non grammatica sed populari ex usu.* If there be no inference which leads to a different conclusion, words are to be understood according to their proper meaning, not according to a grammatical usage but to a popular and ordinary one. *Statuta pro publico commodo late interpretantur.* Statutes enacted for the public good ought to be liberally construed. *Quando charta continet generalem clausulam, posteaque descendit ad verba specialia quae clausulae generali sunt consentanea, interpretanda est charta secundum verba specialia.* When a deed contains a general clause, and afterwards descends to special words which are consistent with the general clause, the deed is to be interpreted according to the special words. *Quando lex est specialis, ratio autem generalis, generaliter lex est intelligenda.* When the law is special, but its reason is general, the law is to be understood generally. *Quando licet id quod majus videtur et licere id quod minus.* When the greater is allowed, the less is to be deemed to be allowed also. *Quod in minori valet valebit in majori; et quod in majori non valet nec valebit in minori.* That which is valid in the greater shall be valid in the less; and that which is not valid in the greater shall not be valid in the less. *Quum in testamento ambigue aut etiam perperam scriptum est, benigne interpretari et secundum id quod credibile et cogitatum, credendum est.* Where an ambiguous or even an erroneous expression occurs in a will, it should be construed liberally and in accordance with what is thought the probable meaning of the testator. *Semper in dubiis benigniora praeferenda sunt.* In doubtful cases, the more liberal constructions are always to be preferred. *Transgressione multiplicata, crescat poenae inflictio.* Upon the multiplication of the transgression, let the infliction of punishment increase. *Ex tota materia emergat resolutio.* The construction should arise out of the whole subject-matter. *Expressio unius est exclusio alterius.* The expression of one thing is the exclusion of another. *Generale dictum generaliter est interpretandum.* A general expression is to be construed generally. *Generale nihil certum implicat.* A general expression implies nothing certain. *In dubio haec legis constructio quam verba ostendunt.* In a doubtful case, that construction which the words indicate should be adopted. *In expositione instrumentorum, mala grammatica, quod fieri potest, vitanda est.* In the drafting of instruments, bad grammar is to be avoided as much as possible. *In his enim quae sunt favorabilia animae, quamvis sunt damnosa rebus, fiat aliquando extentio statuti.* In matters that are favorable to the spirit, though injurious to property, an extension of the statute should sometimes be made. *In rebus quae sunt favorabilia animae, quamvis sunt damnosa rebus, fiat aliquando extensio statuti.* In matters that are favorable to the spirit, though injurious to things, an extension of a statute should sometimes be made. *In stipulationibus cum quaeritur quid actum sit verba contra stipulatorem interpretanda sunt.* In the construction of agreements terms are interpreted against the person using them. *In verbis non verba, sed res et ratio, quaerenda est.* In the construction of words, not the mere words, but the thing and the meaning, are to be inquired into. *Injustum est, nisi tota lege inspecta, de una aliqua ejus particula proposita judicare vel respondere.* It is unjust to give judgement or advice concerning any particular clause of a law without having examined the whole law. *Interpretatio fienda est ut res magis valeat quam pereat.* Construction should be such that the transaction may be effective rather than fall. *Interpretare et concordare leges legibus, est optimus interpretandi modus.* To interpret and harmonize laws with laws is the best mode of interpretation. *Interpretatio talis in ambiguis semper fienda est ut evitetur inconveniens et absurdum.* In ambiguous things, such a construction should be always made that the inconvenient and absurd may be avoided. *Legis constructio non facit injuriam.* The construction of law does no wrong. *Generalis clausula non porrigitur ad ea quaeantea specialiter sunt comprehensa.* A general clause is not extended to include those things that have been previously provided for specially. *Leges posteriores priores contrarias abrogant.* Subsequent laws repeal prior laws that are repugnant to them. *Id quod est magis remotum, non trahit ad se quod est magis junctum, sed e contrario in omni casu.* That which is more remote does not draw to itself that which is nearer, but the contrary in every case. *In ambigua voce legis ea potius accipienda est significatio quae vitio caret, praesertim cum etiam voluntas legis ex hoc colligi possit.* In an ambiguous expression of law, that signification is to be preferred which is consonant with equity, especially when the spirit of the law can be collected from that. *In obscuris, inspici solere quod verisimiltus est, aut quod plerumque fieri solet.* In obscure cases, we usually regard what is most probable or what is done. *In obscuris, quod minimum est sequimur.* In obscure or doubtful cases, we follow that which is the least. *In poenalibus causis benignius interpretandum est.* In penal causes or cases, the more liberal interpretation should be adopted. *In re dubia, benigniorem interpretationem sequi, non minus justius est quam tutius.* In a doubtful matter, to follow the more liberal interpretation is no more just than it is the more safe. *Generale tantum valet in generalibus, quantum singulare in singulis.* That which is general prevails in general matters, as that which is particular prevails in particular matters. *In ambiguo sermone non utrumque*

dicimus sed id duntaxat quod volumus. In ambiguous language, we do not use it in a double sense, but in the sense in which we mean it. *Generalia specialibus non derogant.* General words do not derogate from special. *Generalia sunt praeponenda singularibus.* General things are to be put before particular things. *Generalia verba sunt generaliter intelligenda.* General words are to be understood generally in a general sense. *Generalibus specialia derogant.* Special words derogate from the meaning of general ones. *Verba posteriora propter certitudinem addita, ad priora quae certitudine indigent, sunt referenda.* Subsequent words, added for the purpose of certainty, are to be referred to the preceding words which are need of certainty. *Verbis standum ubi nulla ambiguitas.* One must abide by the words where there is no ambiguity. *Generalia praecedunt, specialia sequuntur.* Things general precede, things special follow. *In ambiguis orationibus maxime sententia spectanda est ejus qui eas protulisset.* When there are ambiguous expressions, the intentions of the person who uses them is chiefly to be regarded. *A verbis legis non est recendendum.* From the words of a statute, there must be no departure. *Aliud est distinctio, aliud separatio.* Distinction is one thing; separation is another.

CONSTRUCTIVE *(Creative),* **adjective** advantageous, applicable, causative, contributive, convenient, cooperative, desirable, developmental, effective, effectual, efficient, fabricative, favorable, formative, generative, helpful, important, improving, instrumental, invaluable, operative, originative, practical, productive, profitable, resultant, serviceable, significant, stimulating, suitable, usable, useful, valuable, worthy, yielding

CONSTRUCTIVE *(Inferential),* **adjective** apparent, assumable, conceivable, connoted, constructional, implicative, implicatory, implicit, implied, implied in law, in effect, in essence, in practice, indicated, indirect, indirectly meant, inferable, inferred, inferred in law, insinuated, involved, parallel, potential, pragmatic, presumable, presumed, probable, seeming, suggested, supposable, tacit, tacitly assumed, tantamount to, understood, virtual

ASSOCIATED CONCEPTS: constructive contempt, constructive contract, constructive control, constructive conversion, constructive delivery, constructive desertion, constructive escape, constructive eviction, constructive force, constructive fraud, constructive gift, constructive intent, constructive knowledge, constructive malice, constructive mortgage, constructive notice, constructive possession, constructive receipt, constructive total loss, constructive trespass, constructive trust, constructively present

CONSTRUE *(Comprehend),* **verb** *accipere,* analyze, apprehend, ascertain the meaning of, assimilate, be aware of, be given to understand, cognize, conceive of, conclude, conclude from evidence, consignify, decipher, decode, deduce, deduce by interpretation, deduce the meaning of, deduct, derive by reasoning, determine, determine exactly, discern, disentangle, divine, draw an inference, draw as an implication, explain, fathom, figure out, find out the meaning of, form an opinion, gather, glean, grasp mentally, grow aware, infer, interpret, judge, ken, make deductions, master, opine, perceive, ratiocinate, realize, reason, represent, see through, seize, show the meaning of, solve, take one's meaning, understand, understand by, understand the meaning of

CONSTRUE *(Translate), verb*   analyze, assign a meaning to, characterize, characterize precisely, clarify, clear up, connote, convey, decipher, decode, define, delineate, demonstrate, denote, depict, describe, disclose, elucidate, enlighten, enunciate, explain, explicate, exposit, expound, express, give explanation to, give sense to, illuminate, illustrate, indicate, inform, interpret, *interpretari,* literalize, make intelligible, of, outline, paraphrase, put a meaning on, put an interpretation, put in other words, render, render intelligible, rephrase, restate, retranslate, reveal, reword, signify, transfuse the sense, unfold, unravel
ASSOCIATED CONCEPTS: construe the law

CONSULT *(Ask advice of), verb*   advise with, ask, ask advice, ask an opinion, ask for recommendations, ask for suggestions, call in, confer, *consultare,* deliberate, discuss, exchange observations, interchange views, parley, question, seek counsel, seek guidance, seek the opinion of, take counsel, talk over, turn to, ventilate
ASSOCIATED CONCEPTS: consult with counsel

CONSULT *(Seek information from), verb*   check a reference, check a source, examine a source, inquire of, look up information in, refer to, refer to for information, search for an answer, seek facts from

CONSUME, *verb*   *absumere,* annihilate, burn up, *consumere,* demolish, destroy, devour, disappear, drain, dwindle, eat, empty, eradicate, evaporate, exhaust, expend, spend, squander, swallow, use up, utilize, waste, wear away, wear out

CONSUMER, *noun*   buyer, buyer of labor, client, clientele, coemptor, customer, emptor, leaser, lessee, obtainer, patron, procurer, purchaser, purchaser of goods, shopper, transferee, vendee
ASSOCIATED CONCEPTS: consumer action, consumer credit, consumer fraud, consumers sales tax, ultimate consumer

CONSUMMATE, *verb*   accomplish, achieve, actualize, attain, attain the goal, bring to a close, bring to effect, carry into effect, carry out, carry through, carry to completion, complete, conclude, *conficere, consummare,* do thoroughly, effect, effectuate, end, execute, finalize, finish, follow through, fulfill, implement, leave nothing to be desired, perfect, *perficere,* prosecute to a conclusion, reach the goal, realize, render complete, terminate, to bring to completion
ASSOCIATED CONCEPTS: consummate dower, consummation of a marriage, consummation of an agreement, constructive service
FOREIGN PHRASES: *Omne testamentum morte consummatum est.* Every will is consummated by death.

CONSUMPTION, *noun*   *confectio, consumptio,* decay, decomposition, decrement, depletion, desolation, destruction, devastation, diminishment, diminution, dissipation, exhaustion, expenditure, loss, ravage, ruin, ruination, squandering, usage, use, using up, utilization, wastage, waste, wastefulness, wear, withering
ASSOCIATED CONCEPTS: business consumption, consumption in interstate commerce, consumption of goods, consumption of intoxicating liquors, for use and consumption

CONTACT *(Association), noun*   accord, acquaintanceship, affiliation, alliance, bond, camaraderie, close union, cooperation, coalition, combination, commerce, communication, community, companionship, conjunction, connection, consanguinity, consociation, consortium, cooperation, dealings, exchange, federation, fellowship, interchange, intercommunication, intercommunion, intercourse, interrelation, intimacy, kinship, liaison, link, linkage, mutual intercourse, participation, rapport, relation, relationship, tie, transmission, union
ASSOCIATED CONCEPTS: contacts theory in conflicts of law, grouping of contacts

CONTACT *(Touching), noun*   abutment, abuttal, adhesion, adjacency, coherence, *contactus,* connection, connective, contiguity, contiguousness, contingence, convergence, impact, joining, junction, junction of bodies, juncture, juxtaposition, meeting, nexus, taction, tangency, union

CONTACT *(Communicate), verb*   call, consociate, *contactus,* correspond, establish connection, get through to, get to, have an exchange, have dealings with, inform, interchange, intercommunicate, make connection, meet with, notify, reach, relate, serve notice, signal

CONTACT *(Touch), verb*   abut, adjoin, annex, attach, be contiguous, border, border on, bridge, butt against, cohere, collide with, come together, conjoin, connect, converge, embrace, encounter, establish connection, graze, hit, impinge, inosculate, interconnect, join, lie adjacent to, link, meet, osculate, overlap, reach, rub, strike, unite, verge upon

CONTAGIOUS, *adjective*   catching, communicable, contaminating, conveyable, epidemic, impartible, infectious, infective, pathogenic, pestiferous, spreading, transferable, transmissible, transmissive

CONTAIN *(Comprise), verb*   be composed of, be compounded of, be constituted of, be formed of, *capere, comprehendere,* consist of, embody, embrace, enfold, envelop, hold, include, incorporate, number, reckon among, subsist of
ASSOCIATED CONCEPTS: containing facts sufficient to constitute a cause of action

CONTAIN *(Enclose), verb*   beleaguer, belt, bind, blockade, border, close in, confine, *continere,* embox, embrace, encapsulate, encase, encincture, encircle, enclasp, encompass, engird, ensphere, envelop, enwrap, fence in, frame, immure, incase, inclose, infold, keep in, quarantine, seal up, shut in, surround

CONTAIN *(Restrain), verb*   arrest, barricade, bind, block, bridle, cage, chain, check, commit to prison, confine, constrain, control, curb, detain, enchain, encumber, enjoin from, fetter, forfend, hinder, hold back, hold in check, hold in custody, impede, impound, imprison, incarcerate, inhibit, jail, keep in captivity, keep in check, keep prisoner, keep under arrest, keep under control, lock up, manacle, obstruct, pinion, place in durance, prohibit, quash, quell, repress, restrict, shackle, stave off, stop, subdue, suppress, thwart, trammel, ward off

CONTAMINATE, noun abomination, adulteration, befoulment, contagion, defilement, infection, poisoning, pollution, taint, vitiation

CONTAMINATE, verb adulterate, befoul, corrupt, debase, defile, degenerate, degrade, denaturalize, desecrate, disease, impair, infect, mar, poison, pollute, profane, sully, tamper with, taint, tarnish, vitiate

CONTEMN, verb abhor, abominate, accuse, asperse, be contemptuous of, belittle, besmirch, calumniate, cast aspersions, censure, criticize, debase, debauch, decry, defile, denigrate, denounce, depreciate, deride, derogate, desecrate, despise, detest, disapprove, discredit, disdain, disesteem, dishonor, disparage, disprize, disrate, disregard, disrespect, execrate, expose, exprobate, feel contempt for, flout, hold in contempt, hold in despite, inveigh against, loathe, malign, misprize, not respect, objurgate, oppress, overlook, rebuff, reject, reproach, repudiate, repulse, resent, revile, ridicule, scandalize, scoff at, scorn, slight, slur, smear, spurn, taint, vilify, vilipend, vituperate

CONTEMPLATION, noun absorption, aim, attention, brooding, calculation, cerebration, cogitation, concentration, consideration, *contemplatio,* deliberateness, deliberation, design, determination, engrossment, envisagement, envisionment, examination, excogitation, expectance, expectation, forethought, goal, inspection, intellectualization, intent, intention, introspection, musing, observance, pensiveness, plan, pondering, preoccupation, prospect, purpose, ratiocination, reasoning, reflection, resolve, reverie, review, rumination, scrutiny, seriousness, speculation, study, surveillance, thought, thoughtfulness, weighing
ASSOCIATED CONCEPTS: contemplation of assignment, contemplation of bankruptcy, contemplation of insolvency, contemplation of marriage, contemplation of parties, in contemplation of death

CONTEMPORANEOUS, adjective coeval, coexistent, coexisting, coincident, coinciding, coinstantaneous, concomitant, concurrent, concurring, contemporary, correspondent, corresponding, *quod eodem tempore est,* simultaneous, synchronal, synchronistic, synchronous
ASSOCIATED CONCEPTS: contemporaneous agreement, contemporaneous declaration, contemporaneous exposition, contemporaneous forgeries, contemporaneous memorandum, contemporaneous transaction

CONTEMPORARY, adjective co-existent, latest, modern, new, present day, up to date, up to the minute

CONTEMPT *(Disdain),* **noun** abhorrence, abomination, animosity, arrogance, aspersion, aversion, condemnation, contemptuousness, *contemptus,* contumely, debasement, defilement, denigration, denunciation, deprecation, depreciation, derision, derogation, detestation, detraction, disapprobation, disapproval, disdainfulness, disesteem, disfavor, disgust, dislike, disparagement, dispraise, disregard, disrepute, disvaluation, *fastidium,* imprecation, incivility, indignant aversion, infamy, insolence, malediction, misprision, objurgation, obloquy, odium, opposure, opprobrium, rebuff, reproach, reprobation, reproof, reproval, repugnance, revilement, revulsion, ridicule, scorn, scurrility
FOREIGN PHRASES: *Qui contemnit praeceptum contemnit praecipientem.* He who contemns a precept contemns the party who gives it.

CONTEMPT *(Disobedience to the court),* **noun** audacity, contemptuous resistance, contumaciousness, contumacy, contumely, defiance of orders, deprecation, dereliction, disaffection, disobedience, disposition to resist, disregard of orders, disrespect, disrespectfulness, dissension, encroachment, fractiousness, impertinence, improbity, impudence, indiscipline, indocility, infringement, inobservance, insolence, insubmission, insubordination, intractableness, irreverence, nonadherence, noncompliance, noncooperation, nonobservance, obstinacy, obstructionism, perverseness, recalcitrance, recusancy, refractoriness, refusal to obey orders, reproach, repudiation, repulsion, resistance, resistance to authority, restiveness, rudeness, undutifulness, unobservance, unruliness, unsubmissiveness, unwillingness, violation of orders, willful disregard
ASSOCIATED CONCEPTS: aggravated contempt, civil contempt, common-law contempt, constructive contempt, contempt of court, continuing contempt, criminal contempt, evasive contempt, judicial contempt, obstruction of justice, summary contempt

CONTEMPTIBLE, adjective abhorrent, *abiectus,* abject, abominable, atrocious, base, blameworthy, censurable, condemnable, condemnatory, contemned, *contemnendus, contemptus,* contumelious, corrupt, culpable, damnable, deplorable, depraved, despicable, despised, detestable, discreditable, disgraceful, disgusting, dishonorable, disreputable, egregious, evil, execrable, foul, fulsome, hateful, heinous, horrendous, horrible, ignominious, infamous, inglorious, insidious, insufferable, loathsome, nefarious, noxious, objurgatory, odious, offensive, opprobrious, perfidious, repellent, reprehensible, reproachful, reprobative, repugnant, repulsive, shameful, shameless, unworthy, vile, villainous, wicked, worthless
ASSOCIATED CONCEPTS: contemptible criminal act

CONTEMPTUOUS, adjective abasing, abject, abominable, abusive, accusatory, arbitrary, arrogant, base, brazen, bumptious, calumniating, calumniatory, calumnious, challenging, compromising, contemptible, contumelious, damaging, decrying, defamatory, defiant, defying, denigratory, denunciatory, depreciating, depreciative, derisive, derisory, derogative, derogatory, detestable, detracting, disapproving, discourteous, disdainful, dishonorable, dishonoring, dislikable, disparaging, disregardful, disrespectful, execrable, expressing disdain, flouting, forward, harsh, hateful, ignominious, impertinent, impudent, indignant, infamous, injuring, injurious, insinuating, insolent, insulting, irreverent, libelous, maledicent, malevolent, malicious, malignant, maligning, manifesting contempt, nefarious, objectionable, obnoxious, obtrusive, offensive, opprobrious, repellent, reproachful, reproaching, repugnant, repulsive, reviling, rude, scandalous, scornful, slighting, spiteful, uncivil, vile, vituperative

CONTEND *(Dispute),* **verb** altercate, argue, battle, be discordant, bicker, brawl, carry on an argument, challenge, clash, combat, compete, conflict, *contendere,* contest, contradict, *decernere,* differ, disaccord, disagree, discept, discord, dissent, encounter, engage, fight, gainsay, have an altercation, have words with, impugn, litigate, make an issue, oppose, *pugnare,* quarrel, reluct, rival, skirmish, spar, spat, squabble, strike at, strive, struggle, take on, vie with, war, wrangle

CONTEND (*Maintain*), *verb*   *adfirmare*, advance, affirm, argue, assert, asseverate, assure, attest, aver, avow, claim, claim to know, *confirmare, contendere,* declare, emphasize, express, hold, hold the opinion, insist, make a statement, make an assertion, predicate, profess, say, set forth, state, state emphatically, stress, utter with conviction, vouch, warrant

CONTENDER, *noun*   adversary, adverse party, antagonist, appellant, applicant, arguer, aspirant, campaigner, candidate, challenger, charger, claimant, combatant, competitor, complainant, contestant, contester, controversialist, corrival, debater, denouncer, disputant, entrant, examinee, feuder, fighter, foe, libelant, litigant, litigator, nominee, office-seeker, opponent, opposer, opposition, oppositionist, party, party to a suit, petitioner, polemist, the prosecution, pugilist, respondent, rival, striver, suitor

CONTENT (*Meaning*), *noun*   accepted meaning, aim, basis, bearing, cardinal point, chief constituent, chief part, denotation, design, drift, emphasis, essence, essential matter, essential meaning, essential part, exegesis, explanation, explication, exposition, force, general meaning, gist, gravamen, impact, implication, import, intent, intention, interpretation, literal interpretation, literal meaning, literal sense, literality, main point, matter, matter of cognition, meaningfulness, motif, nature, object, obvious interpretation, obvious meaning, obvious sense, plain meaning, point, *prima facie,* primary element, primary meaning, purport, purpose, quiddity, quintessence, salient point, scope, sense, *sensus, sententia,* significance, significant part, signification, *significatio,* spirit, subject, subject matter, substance, substantial meaning, sum, sum and substance, tenor, text, theme
ASSOCIATED CONCEPTS: content contained in an instrument, content of a contract, content of a note

CONTENT (*Structure*), *noun*   anatomy, arrangement of parts, body, combination, complement, composite, composition, configuration, conformation, constitution, construction, contexture, core, design, form, format, formation, framework, interrelation, makeup, nature, organization, pattern, plan, setup, style of arrangement

CONTENTION (*Argument*), *noun*   allegation, area of disagreement, argumentation, cause, conflict, contest, controversy, debate, discord, *disputatio,* disputation, dispute, disputed point, ground, issue, legal dispute, legal issue, plea, point, polemic, proposition, reason, root of dissension

CONTENTION (*Opposition*), *noun*   antagonism, challenge, clashing, combat, competition, competitiveness, conflict, contentiousness, contest, contestation, contrariety, contravention, controversy, counteraction, cross purposes, debate, difference, disaccord, disagreement, discord, disharmony, disputation, dispute, dissension, dissent, dissidence, dissonance, divergence, enmity, faction, factiousness, feud, fight, friction, hostility, inimicality, irreconcilability, protest, protestation, quarrel, quarreling, quarrelsomeness, recrimination, resistance, rivalry, schism, strife, struggle, unappeasability, velitation, wrangling

CONTENTIOUS, *adjective*   aggressive, argumentative, bellicose, belligerent, cantankerous, captious, caviling, combative, competitive, contrary, contumacious, cross, discordant, disputatious, dissentious, factious, inimical, irascible, litigious, militant, noncooperating, nonpacific, obstinate, perverse, polemical, pugnacious, *pugnax,* quarrelsome, recalcitrant, schismatic, stubborn, uncooperative, unfriendly, unpacific, unpeaceful, wrangling

CONTENTS, *noun*   components, constituents, details, drift, essence, gist, items, meaning, parts, pith, scope, sense, subject, subject matter, subject of thought, substance, text, themes, thesis, topics
ASSOCIATED CONCEPTS: contents of a chose in action, contents of a note

CONTEST (*Competition*), *noun*   bout, *certamen, certatio,* challenge, clash, corrivalry, emulation, encounter, engagement, game, match, opposition, pitting of strengths, race, rivalry, rivalship, sport, sporting event, struggle, test of endurance, tournament, tourney, trial
ASSOCIATED CONCEPTS: election contest

CONTEST (*Dispute*), *noun*   action, altercation, antagonism, argument, battle, bickering, brawl, challenge, clash, combat, contention, controversion, controversy, debate, difference of opinion, disaccord, disagreement, disceptation, discord, disharmony, disputation, dispute, dissension, dissent, dissonance, embroilment, encounter, failure to agree, feud, fight, fracas, fray, impugnation, impugnment, inharmony, litigation, monomachy, noncomformity, obstinacy, opposition, oppugnancy, polemics, quarrel, recalcitrance, recusancy, resistance, revolt, skirmish, squabble, strained relations, strife, variance, verbal contention, verbal engagement, war, war of words, wrangle
ASSOCIATED CONCEPTS: notice of contest, will contest

CONTEST, *verb*   altercate, argue, battle, call to answer, challenge, combat, conflict, contend, *contendere,* contradict, contravene, controvert, counter, debate, defy, disaffirm, disagree, dispute, fight, gainsay, grapple with, impugn, object, oppose, oppugn, quarrel over, question, refuse to accept, refuse to admit, resist, struggle, take exception to, traverse, vie with
ASSOCIATED CONCEPTS: contest a will, contest an election, contest an insurance policy, contested case

CONTESTABLE, *adjective*   at issue, close, competing, confutable, controversial, controvertible, debatable, deniable, disputable, questionable, refutable

CONTESTANT, *noun*   adversary, adverse party, *aemulus,* antagonist, appellant, battler, belligerent, candidate, challenger, claimant, combatant, complainant, contender, contester, corrival, disputant, foe, libelant, litigant, opponent, opposer, opposing party, opposition, oppositionist, participant, party to a suit, *petitor,* rival, suitor
ASSOCIATED CONCEPTS: contestant to a will

CONTEXT, *noun*   *argumentum,* background, circumstance, coloring, connection, connotation, extended meaning, force, gist, implication, import, main meaning, meaning, mode of expression, purport, range of meaning, scope, sense, subject matter, sum and substance, surroundings, tenor, text, topic
FOREIGN PHRASES: *Nemo enim aliquam partem recte intelligere possit antequam totum iterum atque iterum*

perlegerit. No one can rightly understand one part before he has again and again read the whole.

CONTIGUOUS, *adjective*   abutting, adjacent, adjoining, against, at close quarters, beside, bordering, bounding, close, *confinis,* conjoining, conjunct, connected, conterminous, *continens,* convergent, coupled, edging, end to end, fringing, in close proximity, in common boundaries with, in contact, joined, meeting, near, neighboring, next to, on the confines of, on the edge of, proximal, proximate, side by side, touching, verging
ASSOCIATED CONCEPTS: contiguous lands, contiguous municipalities, contiguous property, contiguous territory

CONTINENCE, *noun*   abstainment, abstention, abstinence, asceticism, chastity, conservatism, *continentia,* eschewal, forbearance, moderateness, moderation, prudence, renunciation, restraint, self-command, self-control, self-denial, self-discipline, self-restraint, sobriety, stoicism, temperance, *temperantia,* temperateness
ASSOCIATED CONCEPTS: continuance of a law suit

CONTINGENCY, *noun*   accident, befalling, *casus,* chance, circumstance, circumstantial event, coincidence, conditional event, contingence, contingent, contingent event, dependent event, doubtful event, fortune, hap, happening, inadvertence, incident, luck, occurrence, possibility, uncertain event, uncertainty, unforeseen occurrence, unintentional happening
ASSOCIATED CONCEPTS: contingency contract, double contingency, unavoidable contingency, unforeseen contingency, unusual or extraordinary contingencies
FOREIGN PHRASES: *Casus fortuitus non est sperandus, et nemo tenetur devinare.* A fortuitous event is not to be expected, and no one is bound to foresee it.

CONTINGENT, *adjective*   attributed to, coincidental, conditioned, consequential, dependent, dependent on, dependent on circumstances, depending, due to, in a state of uncertainty, incident to, possible, provisional, resulting from, subject to, subject to terms, subsidiary
ASSOCIATED CONCEPTS: contingent basis, contingent claim, contingent contract, contingent debt, contingent demand, contingent estate, contingent event, contingent expectancy, contingent fee, contingent fund, contingent gift, contingent interest, contingent legacy, contingent liability, contingent life estate, contingent obligation, contingent remainder, contingent right, contingent use, contingent will

CONTINUAL (*Connected*), *adjective*   constant, constantly recurring, continued, continuing, *continuus,* nonstop, of regular recurrence, perennial, persistent, proceeding without cessation, proceeding without interruption, regular, steadfast, steady, sustained, unbroken, unceasing, unchanging, unintermitted, uninterrupted, unremitting, unstopped

CONTINUAL (*Perpetual*), *adjective*   *adsiduus,* boundless, ceaseless, continuous, endless, eternal, everlasting, incessant, infinite, interminable, never-ending, permanent, *perpetuus,* sempiternal, unceasing, unending, unstopped, unvarying

CONTINUANCE, *noun*   abiding, adjournment of a cause, adjournment of a proceeding, admission of postponement, *adsiduitas, continuatio,* continuation, endurance, extension, lasting, lengthening, perpetuation,

perpetuitas, perseverance, persistence, postponement, prolongation, protraction, stay, sustained action
ASSOCIATED CONCEPTS: continuance in office, continuance of a nonconforming use, continuance of a partnership, continuance of a proceeding, continuance of criminal case, presumption of continuance

CONTINUATION (*Prolongation*), *noun*   addition, adherence, *adsidritas,* augmentation, continuance, *continuatio,* extension, lengthening, maintenance, perpetuation, *perpetuitas,* perseverance, persistence, preservation, protraction, stretching, sustaining, sustenance
ASSOCIATED CONCEPTS: continuation of a business, continuation of a condition, continuation of a fact, continuation of a lien, continuation of an easement, continuation of service

CONTINUATION (*Resumption*), *noun*   carrying on, continuance, fresh start, new beginning, new start, proceeding, reestablishment, recommencement, recurrence, reinstatement, reinstitution, renewal, reopening, restoration, return, reversion, supplementation
ASSOCIATED CONCEPTS: continuation of a proceeding, continuation of a suit

CONTINUE (*Adjourn*), *verb*   arrest temporarily, defer, delay, discontinue, hold over, interrupt, keep pending, lay aside, lay over, postpone, prorogue, put over, put over to a future date, recess, respite, restrain, set for a later time, shelve, stall, stay, suspend, table, tide over
ASSOCIATED CONCEPTS: continue an action, grant of a continuance

CONTINUE (*Persevere*), *verb*   abide, be durable, be permanent, bide, exist, forge ahead, go on, keep, last, linger, maintain, move ahead, *pergere, perseverare,* persevere, persist, *persistere,* press onward, prevail, progress, promote, pursue, stay on, subsist, sustain
ASSOCIATED CONCEPTS: continuing application, continuing contracts, continuing nuisance, continuing offer, continuing trespass, continuing wrong

CONTINUE (*Prolong*), *verb*   arrange in succession, drag out, draw out, *durare,* extend, extend in duration, lengthen, maintain, maintain continuity, perpetuate, preserve, protract, retain, *stare,* sustain, uphold
ASSOCIATED CONCEPTS: continue in force and effect, continue in office, continue to carry on business, continued and uninterrupted use, continued concealment, continued good health, continued possession, continuing accumulation, continuing affirmative act, continuing and subsisting trust, continuing body, continuing conspiracy, continuing contempt, continuing crime, continuing duty, continuing guaranty, continuing jurisdiction, continuing loan, continuing obligation, continuing offense, continuing offer, continuing proceeding, continuing representation, continuing right, continuing tort, continuing trust

CONTINUE (*Resume*), *verb*   begin again, begin over, carry on, carry over, go back to, make a new beginning, proceed, reestablish, rebegin, recommence, reinstate, reinstitute, renew, *renovare,* reopen, restore, return to, take up again

CONTINUITY, *noun*   coherence, connectedness, connection, consecution, consecutiveness, consistency, constancy, continualness, continuance, *continuatio,* continuation, continuousness, continuum, incessancy, permanence, *perpetuitas,* perpetuity, progression, protraction, sequence, succession, successiveness, unintermittedness, uninterrupted connection, uninterruptedness, uninterruption

CONTINUOUS, adjective   ceaseless, consecutive, constant, continual, continuing, endless, extended, following, incessant, never ending, perennial, perpetual, progressive, prolonged, repeated, running, sequential, steady, sustained, unbroken, unceasing, unending, unfaltering, unintermittent, unintermitting, uninterrupted, unremitting, unstopped, without cessation, without interruption
ASSOCIATED CONCEPTS: continuous absence, continuous account, continuous activity, continuous adverse possession, continuous and unbroken, continuous and uninterrupted use, continuous course of business, continuous crime, continuous disability, continuous easement, continuous guaranty, continuous injury, continuous nuisance, continuous possession, continuous residence, continuous servitude, continuous tort, continuous use, continuous wrong, continuously carry on, continuously confined, continuously disabled, continuously employed

CONTORT, verb   bend, bend out of shape, deform, *depravare, detorquere,* dislocate, *distorquere,* distort, knot, misshape, pervert, turn, twine, twist, twist and turn, wind, wrench, wrest, wrinkle, writhe

CONTOUR *(Outline),* **noun**   ambit, bounds, circle, circuit, circumference, circumscription, configuration, delineation, diagram, figuration, figure, form, frame, framework, laterality, *lineamenta,* lines, main features, outside, perimeter, periphery, picture, plan, profile, relief, rough sketch, silhouette, skeleton, sketch, structure, *tournure*

CONTOUR *(Shape),* **noun**   configuration, conformation, feature, *figura,* figuration, figure, form, *forma,* formation, frame, lines, profile, relief, sculpture, silhouette, structure, substance, substantial form, turn

CONTRA, adverb   adverse to, against, con, contrarily, contrariwise, contrawise, conversely, counter, in conflict with, in contrast to, in opposition to, inversely, loathe to, on the contrary, on the other hand, opposed to, opposite, oppositely, otherwise, *per contra,* quite the contrary, to the contrary, vice versa, *versus*

CONTRA, noun   antipode, antithesis, antonym, contrary, converse, counter, extreme, inverse, obverse, offset, opposite, reverse, the other side

CONTRA, preposition   adverse to, against, at cross purposes, athwart, contrariwise, counter, in conflict with, in opposition to, opposed to, opposite to, over against, versus, vis-à-vis

CONTRABAND, noun   banned goods, bootlegged commerce, bootlegged goods, bootlegged trade, bootlegged traffic, captured goods, confiscated goods, confiscated property, embargoed goods, goods exported illegally, goods imported illegally, goods subject to confiscation, goods subject to seizure, illegal property, illegal traffic, illegally exported goods, illegally imported goods, illicit gains, *merces vetitae,* poached trade, poached traffic, prohibited articles, prohibited import,

restricted goods, seized articles, seized goods, smuggled commerce, smuggled goods, smuggled trade, smuggled traffic, stolen article, stolen goods, swag
ASSOCIATED CONCEPTS: contraband articles, contraband goods

CONTRACT, noun   accord, accordance, agreement, arrangement, articles of agreement, assurance, avouchment, avowal, bargain, binding agreement, bond, charter, collective agreement, commitment, compact, compromise, concordat, *condicio, conductio,* confirmation, *conventio,* covenant, deal, embodied terms, engagement, *entente,* guarantee, instrument evidencing an agreement, ironclad agreement, legal document, mutual agreement, mutual pledge, mutual promise, mutual undertaking, negotiated agreement, obligation, pact, paction, *pactum,* pledge, pledged word, private understanding, promise, ratified agreement, set terms, settlement, stated terms, stipulation, terms for agreement, understanding, undertaking, warranty, written terms
ASSOCIATED CONCEPTS: acceptance of a contract, accessory contract, action on contract, adhesion contract, aleatory contract, alteration of a contract, alternative contract, anticipatory breach of contract, assent to a contract, assignment of a contract, bilateral contract, breach of a contract, breach of contract, cancellation of a contract, claim arising on contract, collateral contract, collective agreement, commercial contract, concurrent contracts, conditional acceptance of a contract, conditional agreement, conditional contract, consideration in a contract, constructive contract, contingency contract, continuing contract, contract action, contract carrier, contract for an option, contract implied in fact, contract obligation, contract of agency, contract of carriage, contract of employment, contract of guaranty, contract of hire or hiring, contract of indemnity, contract of insurance, contract of record, contract of sale, contract of subscription for stock, contract of suretyship, contract price, contract rights, contract to lease, contract to purchase, contract to sell, contracting out work, de facto contract, divisible contract, endowment contract, enforceable contract, exclusive contract, executed contract, executory contract, express contract, fictitious contract, fiduciary contract, formal contract, fraudulent contract, future contract, general contract, government contract, gratuitous contract, guaranty contract, illegal contract, illusory contract, immoral contract, impairing the obligation of contract, implied contract, indivisible contract, inequitable contract, installment contract, joint contract, liberty of contract, lump sum contract, marriage contract, material alteration of contract, material breach of contract, obligation of contract, optional contracts, oral contract, parol agreement, parties to a contract, passive breach of contract, performance of a contract, preexisting contracts, private contract, privity of contract, public contract, quasi contract, reformation of a contract, release from a contract, renunciation of a contract, repudiation of a contract, requirements contract, rescission of a contract, restitution on a contract, revival of a contract, right to contract, sealed contract, separable contract, service contract, severable contract, specialty contract, subcontract, surety contract, third-party beneficiary contract, unconditional contract, unconscionable contract, unenforceable contract, unilateral contract, unlawful contract, valid contract, verbal contract, void contract, written contract

FOREIGN PHRASES: *Vox emissa volat; litera scripta manet.* Words spoken vanish; the written letter remains. *Qui cum alio contrahit, vel est, vel debet esse non ignarus conditionis ejus.* He who contracts with another is not, or ought not to be ignorant of his condition. *Praescriptio et executio non pertinent advalorem contractus, set ad tempus et modum actionis instituendae.* Prescription and execution do not affect the validity of the contract, but the time and manner of instituting an action. *Ex turpi contractu actio non oritur.* From an immoral contract an action does not arise. *Dolo malo pactumse non servaturum.* An agreement induced by fraud is not valid. *Pacto aliquod licitum est, quid sine pacto non admittitur.* By agreement, things are allowed which are not otherwise permitted. *Nulla pactione effici potest ne dolus praestetur.* By no agreement can it be effected that a fraud shall be maintained. *In contractibus, benigna, in testamentis, benignior; inrestitutionibus, benignissima interpretatio facienda est.* In contracts, the interpretations should be liberal, in wills, more liberal; in restitutions, most liberal. *Scientia utrinque par pares contrahentesfacit.* Equal knowledge on both sides makes the contracting parties equal. *Pacta conventa quae neque contra leges, neque dolo malo inita sunt, omni modo observanda sunt.* Agreements which are not contrary to the laws, nor fraudulently entered into, are in all respects to be observed. *Pactis privatorum juri publico non derogatur.* Private contracts do not derogate from public law. *In stipulationibus cum quaeritur quid actum sit verba contrasti pulatorem interpretanda sunt.* In agreements, when the question is what was agreed upon, the terms are to be interpreted against the party offering them. *Privatis pactionibus non dubium est non laedi jus caeterorum.* There is no doubt that the rights of others cannot be prejudiced by private agreements. *In omnibus contractibus, sive nominatis sive innominatis, permutatio continetur.* In all contracts, whether nominate or innominate, an exchange, i.e., a consideration, is implied. *Pacta quae contra leges constitutionesque vel contra bonos mores fiunt, nullam vim habere, indubitati juris est.* It is unquestionably the law that contracts which are made contrary to the laws or against good morals, have no force in law. *Nemo tenetur ad impossibile.* No one is bound to an impossibility. *Pacta dant legem contractui.* Stipulations constitute the law for the contract. *Pacta que turpem causam continent non sunt observanda.* Contracts which are based on an unlawful consideration will not been forced. *Conventio vincit legem.* The agreement of parties controls the law. *Contractus ex turpi causa, vel contra bonos mores, nullus est.* A contract founded on a base consideration, or one against good morals, is null. *Nudum pactum est ubi nulla subest causa praeter conventionem; sed ubi subest causa, fit obligatio, et parit actionem.* A naked contract is where there is no consideration for the agreement; but, where there is a consideration, an obligation is created and gives rise to a right of action. *Modus et conventio vincunt legem.* Custom, convention and an agreement of the parties overrule the law. *Conventio facit legem.* An agreement creates the law, i.e. the parties to a binding contract will be held to their promises. *Ex nudo pacto non oritur actio.* No action arises on a contract without a consideration. *Contractus legem ex conventione accipiunt.* Contracts receive legal sanction from the agreement of the parties. *Naturale est quidlibet dissolvi eo modo quo ligatur.* It is natural for a thing to be unbound in the same way in which it was made binding. *Nihil tam conveniens est naturali aequitati quam unumquodque dissolvi eo ligamine quo ligatum est.* Nothing is so agreeable to natural equity as that a thing should be dissolved by the same means by which it was bound. *In conventionibus, contrahentium voluntas potius quam verba spectari placuit.* In contracts, it is the rule to regard the intention of the parties rather than the actual words. *Ex maleficio non oritur contractus.* No contract is born of wrongdoing. *Ex pacto illicito non oritur actio.* From an unlawful agreement, no action will lie. *In contrahenda venditione, ambiguum pactum contra venditorem interpretandum est.* In the negotiation of a sale, an ambiguous agreement is to be interpreted against the seller. *In contractibus, rei veritas potius quam scriptura perspici debet.* In contracts, the truth of the matter ought to be regarded as more important than the writing. *In contractibus, tacite insunt quae sunt moris et consuetudinis.* In contracts, matters of custom and usage are tacitly implied. *Incerta quantitas vitiat actum.* An uncertain quantity vitiates the act. *Legem enim contractus dat.* The contract makes the law. *Nuda pactio obligationem non parit.* A naked promise does not create a binding obligation. *Eisdem modis dissolvitur obligatio quae nascitur ex contractu, vel quasi, quibus contrahitur.* An obligation which arises in contract, or quasi contract, is dissolved in the same ways in which it is contracted.

CONTRACT, *verb* accept an offer, agree, *contrahere,* covenant, engage, enter into, *locare,* make a bargain, make terms, obligate oneself, pledge, promise, undertake, undertake by contract
ASSOCIATED CONCEPTS: contract to perform services

CONTRACTOR, *noun* architect, artificer, builder, constructor, designer, deviser, engineer, maker, planner

CONTRACTUAL, *adjective* accordant, agreed, agreed to, arranged, binding, collectively agreed, committed, consensual, consentient, in accord, in accordance with, in conformity, negotiated, obligated, obligatory, pledged, promised, settled, signed, signed and sealed, stipulated, understood
ASSOCIATED CONCEPTS: contractual agreement, contractual assumption of risk, contractual consideration, contractual liability, contractual obligation, contractual relationship, contractual right, contractual status

CONTRADICT, *verb* *ab re discrepare,* abrogate, affirm the contrary, annul, answer back, argue, assert the contrary, assert the opposite, challenge, clash, come in conflict with, conflict, confute, *contradicere,* contrast, contravene, controvert, counter, counteract, countervail, counterwork, deny, differ, disagree, disclaim, disprove, dispute, dissent, give denial to, go against, go contrary to, go counter to, go in opposition to, impugn, *inter se repugnare,* negate, negative, oppose, oppugn, prove the contrary, quarrel, rebut, refuse to accept, refute, repudiate, reverse, run counter to, take issue with, traverse
ASSOCIATED CONCEPTS: contradiction by a witness on the stand

CONTRADICTION, *noun* adverseness, antipathy, antithesis, assertion of the contrary, assertion of the opposite, conflict, conflicting evidence, confutation, contradistinction, contraindication, contraposition, con

traries, contrariety, contrariness, contrary assertion, contrast, contravention, controversion, controversy, counteraccusation, counteraction, counterargument, countercharge, counterevidence, counteroath, counterstatement, defiance, denunciation, difference of opinion, direct opposite, disaccord, disagreement, discord, *discrepantia,* disproof, dispute, dissension, dissent, divergence, divergent opinion, incongruity, inconsistency, negation, negative evidence, opposite extreme, oppositeness, opposites, opposition, other extreme, rebuttal, rebutting evidence, refutal, refutation, rejoinder, *repugnantia,* variance
ASSOCIATED CONCEPTS: contradiction in terms, contradiction of a witness, contradiction of a writing, impeachment of a witness

CONTRADICTORY, *adjective* abjuratory, absonant, adversative, adverse, antagonistic, antithetical, asserting the contrary, asserting the opposite, at odds, at variance, clashing, conflicting, confutative, confuting, contradicting, contradistinct, contraindicating, contrapositive, contrarious, *contrarius,* contrary, contrary to reason, contrasted, contravening, converse, counter, counteractant, countervailing, counterworking, denying, diametrically opposite, disagreeing, disclaiming, discordant, discrepant, dissentient, dissenting, *diversus,* in the opposite scale, inconsistent, inverse, irreconcilable, negating, negatory, obverse, opponent, opposed, opposing, opposite, oppositional, oppositive, rebutting, refutative, refutatory, refuting, *repugnans,* repugnant, reverse, *tout au contraire,* unreconciled
ASSOCIATED CONCEPTS: contradiction of a writing, contradictory evidence, contradictory findings, contradictory instructions, contradictory statement
FOREIGN PHRASES: *Allegans contraria non est audiendus.* One making contradictory allegations is not to be heard. *Cum duo inter se pugnantia reperiuntur in testamento, ultimum ratum est.* When two things repugnant to each other are found in a will, the last shall be confirmed.

CONTRADISTINCTION, *noun* antagonism, antithesis, clashing, contradiction, contradictoriness, contrariety, contrast, counterpoint, departure from, difference, disparity, dissimilarity, distinction, distinctness, divergence, oppositeness, opposition

CONTRAPOSITION, *noun* antagonism, antithesis, confrontation, confrontment, contradiction, contradistinction, contrariety, contrast, converse, counterpart, disagreement, disparity, dissimilarity, incompatibility, obverse, odds, opposite, opposite side, opposition, otherness, placement against, placement opposite, reverse, unlikeness

CONTRARY, *adjective* abnegative, adversative, adverse, *adversus,* answering, antagonistic to, antipathetic, antithetic, antithetical, at cross purposes, at issue, at variance, averse, captious, clashing, confutative, confuting, contradicting, contradictory, contradistinct, contraindicating, contrapositive, *contrarius,* contrasted, contrasting, contraway, converse, counter, counteracting, countervailing, denying, diametrically opposite, different, disaffirming, disagreeing, disavowing, discordant, in opposition to, inverse, negative, negatory, obverse, opposed, opposing, opposite, opposite in character, opposite in nature, opposi-

tional, oppugnant, rebutting, refutative, refutatory, refuting, *tout le contraire,* vis-à-vis
ASSOCIATED CONCEPTS: contrary intent, contrary to evidence, contrary to good morals, contrary to law, contrary to public interest, contrary to statute

CONTRARY, *noun* antilogy, antipode, antithesis, conflict, contradiction, contradistinction, contrast, converse, incompatibility, inconsistency, opposite, opposition, other extreme, reverse, vice versa
ASSOCIATED CONCEPTS: contrary to the law

CONTRAST, *verb* appose, bring into comparison, *comparare,* compare by observing differences, compare to, compare with, confront, differ, differentiate, *discrepare,* discriminate, distinguish, distinguish between, draw a comparison, exhibit the differences between, institute a comparison, make a comparison, oppose, place against, place in juxtaposition, set in opposition, set off against, set off by opposition, stand out in opposition

CONTRAVENE, *verb* balk, be contrary to, be in conflict with, clash, conflict with, contest, contradict, counteract, cross, defeat, defy, deny, disagree, dispute, disregard, foil, frustrate, gainsay, go against, impugn, infringe, negate, nullify, oppose, rebut, refute, run counter to, thwart, transgress, traverse, violate
ASSOCIATED CONCEPTS: contravene a statute, contravene the law

CONTRAVENTION, *noun* antagonism, argument, breaking an obligation, clash, conflict, confrontation, contention, contest, contradiction, controversion, counteraction, countervail, debate, denial, disagreement, discord, dissent, dissidence, disunion, disunity, divisiveness, friction, gainsaying, infringement, lack of concord, negation, opposing, opposition, oppugnancy, quarrel, rebuttal, resistance, transgression, traversal, variance, violation, vying with, wrangle
ASSOCIATED CONCEPTS: contravention of a contract, contravention of a statute, contravention of an agreement

CONTRIBUTE (Assist), *verb* abet, accommodate, *adiuvare,* advance, advise, afford aid, aid, assist, assist substantially, be a party to, be helpful, be of service, bear a part, bring aid, conduce, cooperate, encourage, enter into, furnish aid, give aid, help, intercede for, join in, lend assistance, minister, partake, partake of, participate, *prodesse,* render help, serve, stand by, subscribe to, succor, support, take an active part in, tend
ASSOCIATED CONCEPTS: contributing cause, contributing to delinquency of a minor, contributing to support a dependent

CONTRIBUTE (Indemnify), *verb* compensate, give back, indemnity, make compensation, make reparation, make restitution, pay back, pay damages, recompense, reimburse, remit, remunerate, restore, return, satisfy, tender

CONTRIBUTE (Supply), *verb* accord, add, administer, afford, allot, assign, award, bequeath, bequest, bestow, cede, commit, confer, consign, convey, deed, deliver, demise, devote, dispense, dispose of, dole out, donate, endow, enrich, equip, furnish, give, give away, grant, hand over, impart, invest, mete out, pass down, pay, present, proffer, relinquish, remit, render, share, subsidize, supply, tender, transmit, will

ASSOCIATED CONCEPTS: contributed capital, contributing fault, contributing negligence, contributing proximate cause

CONTRIBUTION (*Donation*), **noun**   alms, assistance, award, benefaction, benefit, bequest, bestowal, bestowment of a share, bonus, boon, bounty, charity, conferment, *conferre, contribuere,* dispensation, endowment, generosity, gift, grant, grant of a share, gratuity, honorarium, lagniappe, largesse, offering, present, presentation, provision, remembrance, subsidy, subvention, succor, sustenance, tribute

CONTRIBUTION (*Indemnification*), **noun**   compensation, guerdon, indemnity, need, offsetting, paying back, payment, quittance, reckoning, recompense, redress, reimbursement, remuneration, reparation, repayment, requital, requitement, restitution, restoration, return, satisfaction, substitution
ASSOCIATED CONCEPTS: contribution among joint tort feasors, subrogation

CONTRIBUTION (*Participation*), **noun**   abetment, aid, alliance, assistance, association, coaction, coalition, collaboration, collusion, combination, complicity, comradeship, concert, confederation, consent, cooperation, coordination, encouragement, federation, fellowship, harmony, help, interest, league, partnership, pool, shareholding, sharing, teamwork, union
ASSOCIATED CONCEPTS: accumulated contributions, contributing to the injury, contribution to capital, contributory fault, contributory infringer, contributory negligence, indemnity

CONTRIBUTOR (*Giver*), **noun**   almoner, almsgiver, altruist, assignor, benefactor, bestower, donator, donor, granter, grantor, investor, patron, philanthropist, presenter, subscriber, supplier, supporter, testator, vouchsafer

CONTRIBUTOR (*Contributor*), **noun**   abettor, accessory, accomplice, aide, ally, assistant, associate, auxiliary, coadjutor, cohelper, collaborator, colleague, compeer, comrade, confederate, confrere, consort, cooperator, copartner, coworker, fellow, helper, helpmate, mate, participant, participator, partner, party, peer, shareholder, sharer, teammate, teamworker, workfellow

CONTRIBUTORY, *adjective*   accessory, additional, aiding, assisting, auxiliary, beneficial, conducive, contributing, determining, helpful, helping, influential, instrumental, lending assistance, salutary, secondary, tributary, useful
ASSOCIATED CONCEPTS: contributory cause, contributory negligence

CONTRITE, *adjective*   apologetic, broken in spirit, chastened, compunctious, conscience-smitten, conscience-stricken, desirous of forgiveness, full of regrets, full of remorse, guilty, humble, humbled, *paenitet,* penitent, penitential, regretful, regretting, remorseful, repentant, rueful, self-accusing, self-condemnatory, self-convicted, self-denunciatory, self-reproachful, sorrowful, sorry, soul-searching

CONTRIVANCE, *noun*   artifice, collusion, complicity, connivance, craft, deception, design, designing power, device, dodge, engineering, *excogitatio,* intrigue,

inventio, invention, inventiveness, machination, maneuver, manipulation, means to an end, mechanism, method, plan, plot, scheme, stratagem, strategics, subterfuge, tactics, wile, wily device

CONTRIVE, *verb*   arrange, cause, collude, compose, conceive, concoct, connive, consider, conspire, counterplot, design, develop a course, devise, draft, effect, *excogitare,* fabricate, fashion, forecast, form, frame, imagine, improvise, induce, intrigue, *invenire,* invent, lay plans, *machinari,* machinate, make up, maneuver, mine, organize, pattern, plan, plot, predesign, preestablish, prepare, procure, project, provoke, scheme, shape out a course, sketch, systematize
ASSOCIATED CONCEPTS: contrive a cause of action

CONTROL (*Restriction*), **noun**   blockade, brake, check, constraint, curb, deterrence, deterrent, disallowance, exclusion, inhibition, limitation, moderation, prevention, prohibition, qualification, rationing, repression, restraint, restrictive practice, subdual, suppression
ASSOCIATED CONCEPTS: institution of controls, price control

CONTROL (*Supervision*), **noun**   administration, auspices, authority, care, charge, command, custody, direction, discipline, dominance, domination, dominion, government, guardianship, guidance, jurisdiction, keeping, management, managership, mastery, ministry, *moderatio,* oversight, patronage, power, proctorship, protectorship, *regimen,* regulation, stewardship, superintendence, *temperantia,* ward, wardenship, wardship
ASSOCIATED CONCEPTS: absolute control, circumstances beyond control, complete control, constructive control, exclusive control, immediate control, indirect control, joint control, loss of control, mutuality of control, parental control, reasonable control

CONTROL (*Regulate*), *verb*   administer, administrate, check, *coercere,* command, conduct, direct, dominate, engineer, govern, guide, handle, have charge of, have in one's charge, have the direction of, have under control, instruct, lead, look after, maintain, manage, manipulate, *moderari,* operate, order, overlook, oversee, pilot, preside over, regiment, rule, superintend, supervise, take care of
ASSOCIATED CONCEPTS: Bureau of Control and Accounts, control board, controlled corporation, controlled substance, controlling clause, controlling influence, controlling interest, controlling issues, controlling question of law or fact

CONTROL (*Restrain*), *verb*   arrest, confine, constrain, *continere,* guard, hamper, hinder, hold back, hold in check, impede, inhibit, keep in check, keep under control, limit, obstruct, prohibit, put under restraint, restrict, retard, subdue, suppress, *temperare,* trammel
ASSOCIATED CONCEPTS: controlled substance

CONTROLLED (*Automatic*), *adjective*   contrived, devised, machine like, mechanical, mechanistic

CONTROLLED (*Restrained*), *adjective*   aloof, calm, conditioned, constrained, cool, detached, disciplined, disengaged, distant, guarded, impassive, imperturbable, in check, inhibited, moderate, obedient, passionless, reflex, restrained, self-controlled, steady, stoical, temperate unconcerned, undemonstrative, unemotional, unexcitable, unruffled

CONTROVERSIAL, *adjective*   arguable, at issue, at odds, at variance, confutable, contestable, *controversus,* controvertible, debatable, dialectic, disputable, doubtful, dubious, dubitable, eristic, exhibiting pros and cons, factious, in dispute, in question, not axiomatic, open to discussion, open to doubt, open to question, polemical, problematical, questionable, refutable, speculative, suspect, uncertain, uncertified, undecided, under inquiry, unsure, unverifiable

CONTROVERSY *(Argument),* **noun**   altercatio, altercation, antagonism, argumentation, brawl, break, broil, clashing, conflict, conflict of opinion, contention, contest, contestation, *controversia,* debate, difference of opinion, disaccord, disagreement, *disceptatio,* disceptation, discongruity, discord, discordance, disharmony, disputation, dispute, disputed point, disputed question, dissension, dissidence, dissonance, disunion, disunity, divergence, divergent opinions, embroilment, failure to agree, feud, friction, impugnation, inaccordance, incongruence, inconsistency, inharmoniousness, inharmony, jangle, lack of concord, opposition, polemics, quarrel, question at issue, rupture, set-to, split, squabble, strife, subject of dispute, unconformity, variance, wrangle
ASSOCIATED CONCEPTS: arbitrable controversy, matters in controversy, submission of a controversy

CONTROVERSY *(Lawsuit),* **noun**   action, case, case at law, cause, contest, judicial contest, legal action, legal argument, legal proceeding, legal process, litigation, matter for judgment, process in law, suit in law
ASSOCIATED CONCEPTS: actual present controversy, amount in controversy, case or controversy, controversies in bankruptcy, controversy arising under Constitution, controversy arising under laws of the United States, controversy at law or in equity, controversy between citizens of a state and a foreign country, controversy between citizens of different states, controversy over claim, justiciable controversy, real controversy, settlement of controversy in bankruptcy, subject of controversy, sum in controversy

CONTROVERT, *verb*   abjure, abnegate, abrogate, answer, answer conclusively, argue, argue the case, argue the point, attack, confute, contend against in discussion, contest, contradict, contradict absolutely, contravene, counter, debate, defeat, deny, disaffirm, disagree with, disallow, disavow, disclaim, discuss, dismiss, disprove, dispute, give denial to, make a rejoinder, negate, oppose, overwhelm, rebuff, rebut, *refellere, refutare,* refute, repudiate
ASSOCIATED CONCEPTS: controverted question of fact, controverting plea

CONTUMACIOUS, *adjective*   anarchistic, contankerous, contemptuous, *contumax,* defiant, defying lawful authority, disobedient, *entêté,* factious, fractious, headstrong, indocile, indomitable, insolent, insolently disobedient, insubordinate, intractable, mutinous, not compliant, obstinate, *pertinax,* perverse, rebellious, recalcitrant, recusant, refractory, refusing to obey, renitent, repulsive, resistant, resisting authority, resisting control, restive, stubbornly disobedient, stubbornly rebellious, uncomplying, ungovernable, unman-

ageable, unreasonable, unsubmissive, willfully disrespectful
ASSOCIATED CONCEPTS: contumacious conduct, contumacious witness

CONTUMELY, *noun*   abuse, affront, arrogance, aspersion, berating, castigation, contempt, contemptuous treatment, contemptuousness, *contumelia,* derision, despite, despiteful treatment, discourtesy, disdain, disdainfulness, dishonor, disrespect, effrontery, haughtiness, humiliating rudeness, humiliation, indignity, insolence, insult, invective, objurgation, obloquy, opprobrium, presumptuousness, reproach, revilement, rudeness, scornful insolence, scornful treatment, scornfulness, scurrility, vilification, vituperation

CONVENE, *verb*   accumulate, aggroup, amass, assemble, bring together, call, call together, call up, collect, congregate, consolidate, converge, *convocare,* convoke, draw together, gather, gather together, group, hold a meeting, hold a session, meet, mobilize, muster, rally, reunite, round up, summon, unite
ASSOCIATED CONCEPTS: convene a session of a court, convene a term of the court

CONVENIENT, *adjective*   acceptable, accessible, *accommodatus,* advantageous, agreeable, applicable, appropriate, available, befitting, beneficial, carefree, commodious, conducive, desirable, easily accessible, easily done, easy, effortless, eligible, expedient, fitted, fitting, *habilis,* helpful, *idoneus,* opportune, presenting few difficulties, requiring no effort, serviceable, suitable, suited, useful
ASSOCIATED CONCEPTS: balance of convenience, certificate of public convenience and necessity, convenience and necessity, convenience of parties, enforcement in convenience, greatest convenience, public convenience, reasonably convenient, rule of convenience
FOREIGN PHRASES: *Non solum quid licet, sed quid est conveniens, est considerandum; quia nihil quod est inconveniens est licitum.* Not only that which is lawful, but that which is convenient is to be considered, because nothing which is inconvenient is lawful.

CONVENTIONAL, *adjective*   acceptable, accepted, accustomed, approved, classical, common, conformable, conforming, conforming to accepted standards, customary, established, established by general consent, everyday, familiar, fitting, fixed, general, habitual, in established usage, long-established, natural, normal, of long standing, ordinary, orthodox, permanent, prevalent, regular, routine, standard, time-honored, tradition-bound, traditional, *translaticius,* typical, usual, widely used, wonted
ASSOCIATED CONCEPTS: conventional interest, conventional life estate, conventional mortgage, conventional obligation, conventional sequestration, conventional subrogation, conventional trust

CONVERGE, *verb*   approach, approach one another, assemble, blend, bring into focus, bring near, bring together, center upon, centralize, close in upon, coalesce, *coire,* come closer, come to a focus, come to a point, come together, concenter, concentralize, concentrate, congregate, consolidate, convene, convocate, draw gradually together, draw in, focalize, focus, gather, *in unum vergere,* incline toward each other, interfuse, join together, meet, merge, taper, unite

CONVERSATION, noun articulation, *causerie,* chat, collocution, colloquial discourse, colloquy, communication, confabulation, *conloquium,* consultation, conversing, deliberation, dialogue, discourse, discussion, dissertation, exchange, exchange of views, familiar discourse, imparting of thoughts, inquiry, interchange, interchange of information, interchange of opinions, interchange of speech, interchange of thoughts, intercommunication, interlocution, interview, oral communication, parley, questioning, speaking, talk, telling, verbal intercourse
ASSOCIATED CONCEPTS: confidential conversations, criminal conversation, wiretapping conversations

CONVERSE, verb address, advise, allocute, answer, articulate, attest to, carry on a conversation, comment on, commune with, communicate with, confabulate, confer with, *conferre,* consult with, debate, descant, discourse, discuss, dissertate, exchange ideas, exchange views, have dialogue, have verbal intercourse, hold conference, impart thoughts, inform, interchange ideas, interchange information, interchange opinions, interchange thoughts, interview, make a rebuttal, make a speech, make a statement, parley, perorate, recite, recount, relate, relate ideas, relay ideas, say, speak with, state, talk, utter

CONVERSION (Change), noun alteration, interchange, metamorphosis, passage, reconstruction, shift, switch, transformation, transition, transmutation
ASSOCIATED CONCEPTS: conversion of a security

CONVERSION (Misappropriation), noun appropriation, defraudation, deprivation, embezzlement, fraud, larceny, malfeasance, misapplication, misappropriation of funds, misemployment, misuse, peculation, theft, thievery, unauthorized assumption of property, unlawful appropriation, unlawful use of another's property, wrongful assumption, wrongful exercise of dominion
ASSOCIATED CONCEPTS: action for conversion, attachment, constructive conversion, conversion by assertion of ownership, conversion of goods, conversion of property, conversion of stock, detinue, fraudulent conversion, innocent conversion, involuntary conversion, larceny by conversion, technical conversion, trover, wrongful conversion

CONVERT (Change use), verb alter, amend, become, change, change into, change over, commute, *convertere,* denature, develop, diversify, emend, evolve, exchange, interchange, make into, make over, metabolize, metamorphose, modify, mutate, permute, rearrange, recast, reconstitute, reconstruct, refashion, reform, regenerate, remake, remodel, remold, render different, renovate, reorganize, replace, reshape, restyle, revamp, revise, shift, substitute, switch, transfer, transfigure, transform, transmogrify, transmute, transpose, transshape, transubstantiate, turn, vary
ASSOCIATED CONCEPTS: basic converter, convert bonds, innocent converter

CONVERT (Misappropriate), verb apply dishonestly, appropriate wrongfully, assume unlawful rights of ownership, embezzle, expropriate, misapply, misdirect, misemploy, mismanage, misuse, peculate, put to a wrong use, steal, take illegally
ASSOCIATED CONCEPTS: convert to one's own use, fraudulently convert

CONVERT (Persuade), verb align, brainwash, bring around, convince, enlist, induce, influence, lead to believe, prevail, propagandize, proselytize, reform, sway, talk into, win an argument, win over

CONVERTIBLE, adjective capable of being exchanged, changeable, commutable, commutative, complementary, compromisable, correlative, counterchangeable, exchangeable, interchangeable, mutable, permutable, reciprocative, reversible, substitutive, transformable, transmutable, transposable
ASSOCIATED CONCEPTS: convertible bond rule, convertible bonds, convertible coupon bonds, convertible securities

CONVEY (Communicate), verb acquaint, advise, affirm, announce, annunciate, apprise, articulate, assert, aver, avow, bare, become known, broadcast, comment, confide, contact, declare, describe, detail, direct the attention to, disclose, disseminate, divulgate, divulge, educate, elucidate, enlighten, evince, explain, expose, express, get across, get in touch, give an account, give notice, impart, indicate, inform, instruct, keep posted, make acquainted, make aware, make known, make public, manifest, mention, narrate, notify, pass on, point out, post, proclaim, promulgate, pronounce, publish, recite, recount, relate, remark, render an account, report, represent, reveal, share, signify, speak, specify, state, suggest, teach, tell, transmit, uncover, vent

CONVEY (Transfer), verb abalienate, alienate, assign, award, bequeath, carry, cede, consign, contribute, deed, deliver, deliver over, demise, devolve, dispense, donate, endow, enfeoff, give, grant, hand down, hand out, impart, lease, pass, pass down, pass title, present, relinquish, shift, transfer title, transmit, transport, transpose
ASSOCIATED CONCEPTS: lawfully convey, quitclaim and convey

CONVEYANCE, noun alienation, alienation of property, assignation, assignment, bestowal, bestowment, conferment, consignation, delivery, demise, devise, devolution, disposal, sale, shift, testamentary disposition, tranmission, transfer, transfer of property, transfer of title, transference, transmission, transmittal
ASSOCIATED CONCEPTS: absolute conveyance, conveyance by deed, encumbrance, fraudulent conveyance, involuntary conveyance, presumptive conveyance
FOREIGN PHRASES: *Transit terra cum onere.* Land passes subject to any encumbrances affecting it. *Nihil tam conveniens est naturali aequitati quam voluntatem domini rem suam in alium transferre ratam habere.* Nothing is more conformable to natural equity than to confirm the intention of an owner who desires to transfer his property.

CONVICT, noun accused, accused person, bad example, captive, condemned person, condemned prisoner, criminal, crook, culprit, defaulter, defendant, delinquent, desperado, desperate criminal, escapee, evildoer, felon, first offender, fugitive, guilty man, guilty person, inmate, internee, jail inmate, lawbreaker, malefactor, malevolent, malfeasant, malfeasor, miscreant, misdemeanant, misfeasor, offender, outlaw, parolee, prisoner, prisoner at the bar, prisoner behind bars, prisoner of state, public enemy, recidivist, recreant, reprobate, rogue, scoundrel, sinner, thief, transgressor, villain, wrongdoer

ASSOCIATED CONCEPTS: certificate of relief from disabilities

CONVICT, *verb*　　attaint, bring to justice, call to account, cast blame upon, censure, condemn, condemn after judicial investigation, declare guilty of an offense, denounce, denunciate, doom, find against, find guilty, find liable, give a guilty verdict, hold liable, hold responsible, impose a penalty on, inflict a penalty on, inflict punishment, pass censure on, pass sentence on, penalize, prescribe punishment, pronounce judgment, pronounce sentence, punish, put the blame on, sentence, utter judicial sentence against

ASSOCIATED CONCEPTS: convict of a crime, convict of wrongdoing, sentence

CONVICTION *(Finding of guilt),* **noun**　　adjudgment, adjudication, aspersion, avengement, blame, censure, charge, condemnation, criminality, culpability, *damnatio,* damnation, decision, decree, decrial, denouncement, denunciation, determination, exaction of penalty, execution of sentence, final condemnation, finding, hostile verdict, imposition, judgment, passing judgment, penalization, penalty, prescribed punishment, proof of guilt, punishment, punition, reprehension, reprisal, reprobation, reproof, retribution, retributive justice, ruling, sentence, sentencing, unfavorable verdict, verdict

ASSOCIATED CONCEPTS: certificate of conviction, criminal conviction, felony conviction, final conviction, guilty verdict, nolo cotendere plea, record of conviction, sentencing

CONVICTION *(Persuasion),* **noun**　　ascertained principle, assumption, assurance, assured belief, attitude, avowal, certainty, certitude, concept, conception, conclusion, consideration, credence, creed, declaration of faith, doctrine, dogma, faith, firm belief, fixed opinion, impression, inclination, judgment, leaning, mind, *opinio,* opinion, outlook, personal judgment, point of view, position, positiveness, postulation, posture, predilection, predisposition, presupposition, principle, proclivity, profession, propensity, rooted belief, *sententia,* sentiment, settled belief, settled judgment, standpoint, staunch belief, supposition, sureness, tenet, theory, thinking, understanding, unshakable opinion, view, viewpoint, way of thinking, well-founded opinion

CONVINCE, *verb*　　allure, argue into, assure, bring to reason, carry conviction, clinch an argument, compel, compel belief, convert, dispose, enlist, exert influence, extort belief, gain the confidence of, impel, impress, incline, indoctrinate, induce, influence, inspire, inveigle, lead to believe, make confident, make realize, outweigh, overcome by argument, overweigh, persuade, persuade by argument, *persuadere,* predispose, prevail upon, produce conviction, prompt, propagandize, prove, prove one's point, satisfy, satisfy by evidence, satisfy by proof, suborn, sway, win over

CONVINCING, *adjective*　　absolute, *ad persuadendum accommodatus,* assured, assuring, attestable, authentic, believable, believed, believing, bona fide, categorical, certain, cogent, coherent, commanding, compelling, conclusive, confirmable, confirmatory, confirming, convictive, corroborating, corroborative, credal, credible, creditable, decisive, deducible, demonstrable, docu-

mentary, documented, establishable, established, evident, evincible, forceful, genuine, influential, irrefragable, irrefutable, likely, logical, maintaining, moving, persuasive, plausible, positive, possible, potent, powerful, practiced, prevailing, profound, provable, proving, rational, real, reasonable, reliable, secure, self-evident, stated, strong, suasive, substantial, supportable, sustainable, swaying, tenable, to be believed, tried, true, trusted, trusting, trustworthy, unconfutable, undeniable, undisputed, unrefutable, valid, verifying, well-founded, well-grounded, worthy of credence

ASSOCIATED CONCEPTS: clear and convincing proof, convincing proof

COOPERATE, *verb*　　act in concert, act jointly, act together, *adiuvare,* ally, amalgamate, associate, be a party to, cabal, coact, cofunction, collaborate, collude, combine, combine forces, concert, concord, concur, confederate, conjoin, connive, conspire, contribute, cowork, federate, fraternize, go along with, go into partnership, join forces, join in, join with, league, lend one's support to, lend oneself to, make an agreement with, make common cause with, partake in, participate, pool, pull together, rally round, share in, side with, stand together, take part in, take part with, unite ones efforts, unite with, work as a team, work side by side with, work together

COOPERATIVE, *noun*　　alliance, association, collective, communal business establishment, communal society, commune, concurrent effort, federation, guild, joint action, joint operation, joint possession, partnership, teamwork, union

COORDINATE, *verb*　　adjust, arrange, assimilate, balance, combine, equalize, harmonize, homologize, integrate, methodize, organize, proportion, regularize, regulate, schematize, set in order, synchronize, systematize

COPARTNER *(Business associate),* **noun**　　adjuvant, associate, auxiliary, coadjutant, cohelper, collaborator, colleague, comate, companion, compeer, *confrère,* consociate, consort, cooperator, coworker, fellow, fellow worker, helper, mate, partner, peer, *personnel,* sharer

COPARTNER *(Coconspirator),* **noun**　　abettor, accessory, accessory after the fact, accessory before the fact, accompanier, accomplice, accomplice in crime, adjunct, adjutant, adjuvant, aid, aide-de-camp, aider and abettor, assistant, associate, attendant, *camarade,* coadjutant, coadjutor, coadjutress, coaid, cohelper, cohort, collaborator, colluder, comate, companion, comrade, confederate, *confrère,* consociate, conspirer, cooperator, copartner in crime, helper, helpmate, *intrigant,* intriguer, machinator, *particeps criminis,* partner in crime, *socius criminis,* supporter

ASSOCIATED CONCEPTS: joint adventure, joint enterprise, tenant in copartnership

COPIOUS, *adjective*　　abounding, abundant, ample, bountiful, considerable, *copiosus,* countless, extravagant, exuberant, filled, flowing, full, generous, gigantic, great, in profusion, inexhaustible, innumerable, large, lavish, liberal, luxuriant, massive, more than enough, numerous, of great extent, opulent, overflowing, plenteous, plentiful, populous, producing abundantly, productive, profitable, profuse, profusive, prolific, replete, rich, streaming, superabundant, supernumerary, teeming, unlimited, unmeasured, unrestricted, unsparing, unstinting, voluminous, well-provided, well-stocked, wide, yielding abundantly

COPY, *noun*   cast, counterfeit, counterpart, duplicate, duplication, ectype, facsimile, fake, forgery, image, imitation, impress, impression, imprint, likeness, offprint, personation, print, reissue, repetition, replica, representation, reprint, reproduction, simulation, tracing, transcript, transfer
ASSOCIATED CONCEPTS: certified copy, conformed copy, correct copy, true copy

COPY, *verb*   adopt, ape, approximate, assume, borrow, caricature, cartoon, cheat, conform, depict, ditto, do like, double, draw, duplicate, echo, emulate, falsify, follow, follow suit, follow the example of, forge, give an encore, *imitari,* imitate, impersonate, infringe copyright, iterate, make a duplicate of, make a transcript of, make a replica, mirror, mock, model, parrot, pattern after, personate, pirate, plagiarize, portray, pretend, print, rebuild, recapitulate, reconstruct, recreate, reduplicate, reecho, reestablish, refashion, rehash, reiterate, remake, repeat, replicate, represent, reprint, reproduce, republish, restate, retell, retrace, revive, rewrite, simulate, take after, trace, transcribe
ASSOCIATED CONCEPTS: counterfeit, impersonate, infringe

COPYRIGHT, *noun*   authority, authorization, certificate of invention, certification, concession, enfranchisement, entitlement for a term of years, exclusive privilege of publication, exclusive privilege of publication and sale, exclusive right of production, grant, license, permit, privilege to publish, privilege to reproduce, right of literary property, sanction
ASSOCIATED CONCEPTS: copyright license, patent

CORNERSTONE, *noun*   backbone, base, body, cardinal point, core, corpus, critical point, crucial point, crux, essence, essential matter, exigency, foundation, frame of reference, fundamental, gravamen, groundwork, heart, highlight, key, keynote, keystone, landmark, main body, main element, main point, main thing, mainstay, major event, major part, material point, matter of concern, matter of importance, milestone, nucleus, pedestal, pivot, principal part, principle, purport, purpose, quintessence, rudiment, salient point, *sine qua non,* standard, substance, substantiality, support, *terra firma,* threshold

COROLLARY, *noun*   addition, adjunct, appurtenance, complement, correlation, correspondence, deduction, derivation, derived principle, logical sequence, offshoot, outcome, outgrowth, propinquity, sequent, supplement, syllogism

CORPORAL, *adjective*   bodily, corporeal, fleshy, incarnate, material, not spiritual, palpable, physical, somatic, substantial, tangible
ASSOCIATED CONCEPTS: corporal imbecility, corporal oath, corporal punishment

CORPORATE *(Associate), adjective*   affiliate, allied, banded, federative, incorporate, leagued, partnered
ASSOCIATED CONCEPTS: corporate act, corporate assets, corporate authorities, corporate body, corporate bonds, corporate commission, corporate conduct, corporate div-

idends, corporate existence, corporate franchise, corporate name, corporate officer, corporate powers and privileges, corporate property, corporate purpose, corporate rights, corporate seal, corporate securities, corporate stock

CORPORATE *(Joint), adjective*   associated, coincident, compact, concurrent, conjoint, conjunct, correal

CORPORATION, *noun*   affiliate, affiliation, agglomerate, alliance, artificial entity, artificial person, associate, association, body, body corporate, business, business association, business establishment, coalition, combination, combine, commercial enterprise, company, concern, confederacy, conglomerate, *conlegium,* consociation, consolidation, corporate body, enterprise, establishment, federation, firm, foundation, holding company, industry, institute, institution, joint concern, legal body, legal entity, operating company, organization, sodality, stock company, syndicate, union
ASSOCIATED CONCEPTS: alter ego, business trust, cartel, closed corporation, closely held corporation, consolidation, corporate charter, corporate officers dissolution, corporate structure, de facto corporation, de jure corporation, derivative action, directors, dissolution, domestic corporation, fictitious corporations, foreign corporation, joint stock associations, limited partnerships, membership corporation, merger, municipal corporation, officers, parent corporation, public corporation, partnership, proxies, self-dealing, shareholders, sole proprietorship, stockholders, subsidiaries, voting trusts
FOREIGN PHRASES: *Jus quo universitates utuntur est idem quod habent privati.* The law which governs corporations is the same as that which governs individuals. *Corporatio non dicitur aliquid facere nisi id sit collegialiter deliberari, etiamsi major pars id faciat.* A corporation is not said to do anything unless it be deliberated upon collectively, although the majority should do it.

CORPOREAL, *adjective*   actual, appreciable, bodily, *bona fide,* certain, concrete, corporal, definite, demonstrable, embodied, existent, firm, fleshly, having substance, in existence, incarnate, material, palpable, physical, real, solid, substantial, substantive, tangible, temporal, unspiritual
ASSOCIATED CONCEPTS: corporeal hereditaments
FOREIGN PHRASES: *Haereditas, alia corporalis, alia incorporalis; corporalis est, quae tangi potest et videri; incorporalis quae tangi non potest nec videri.* An inheritance is either corporeal or incorporeal. corporeal is that which can be touched and seen; incorporeal, that which can neither be touched nor seen.

CORPSE, *noun*   body, *cadaver,* carcass, carrion, casualty, corpus, dead body, dead person, deceased, departed, individual, lifeless body, mortal remains, murder victim, organic remains, remains, victim
ASSOCIATED CONCEPTS: *corpus delicti*

CORPUS, *noun*   aggregate, aggregation, amassment, assemblage, body, bulk, chief part, collection, collectivity, colligation, compages, compilation, complexus, comprehensiveness, concentration, concretion, confluence, conglomerate, core, cornerstone, corporality, corporeity, cumulation, distillation, embodiment, ensemble, essence, fullness, grand total, gross amount, grouping, import, importance, inclusiveness, integrality, integration, keynote, legal body, legal en-

tity, main body, main part, major part, mass, materiality, materialization, matter, pith, plenum, principal, principle, quantity, quintessence, res, signification, solid substance, solidarity, structure, substance, substantiality, sum, sum and substance, sum total, summation, total, totality, weight, whole, wholeness
ASSOCIATED CONCEPTS: *corpus delicti, corpus juris,* corpus of a trust

CORRECTION *(Change),* **noun**   adjustment, alteration, amelioration, amending, amendment, betterment, *correctio,* curative, cure, *emendatio,* emendation, improved version, improvement, melioration, mending, modification, qualification, readjustment, reconstruction, rectification, redaction, reform, reformation, rehabilitation, remedy, removal of errors, renovation, repair, repairing, replacement, rescript, restoration, retraction, revampment, revisal, revised edition, revision, rewrite, righting
ASSOCIATED CONCEPTS: corrective action, corrective procedures

CORRECTION *(Punishment),* **noun**   amercement, *animadversio,* animadversion, *castigatio,* castigation, censure, chastening, chastisement, condemnation, corrective measure, disciplinary action, discipline, infliction, invective, lesson, payment, penal retribution, penal servitude, penalization, penalty, punition, reprobation, reproval, retribution, retributive justice, scourging, stricture
ASSOCIATED CONCEPTS: board of corrections, correctional facility, house of correction

CORRELATE, **noun**   affiliate, agnate, ally, analogue, associate, cognate, companion, comparison, complement, complemental term, congener, coordinate, correspondent, counterpart, double, duplicate, equal, equivalent, fellow, like, match, mate, parallel, pendant, reciprocal, reciprocator, relation, similitude, supplement, twin

CORRELATIVE, *adjective*   accordant, adapted, affiliate, affiliated, affined, affinitive, agnate, agreeing, akin, allied, amalgamated, analogous, anent, applicable, apposite, appropriate, associated, associative, belonging, cognate, coinciding, collateral, commensurable, commensurate, commutual, comparable, comparative, compatible, complemental, complementary, concerning, concordant, concurrent, conformable, congeneric, congenerous, congruent, congruous, conjoint, conjunct, conjunctive, connate, connatural, connected, connective, consentaneous, consociate, consonant, conspecific, contingent, coordinate, correspondent, corresponding, dependent, equivalent, exchangeable, fellow, fitting, germane, homological, interacting, interdependent, interlinked, interrelated, joined, linked, matched, mutual, mutually related, paired, parallel, pertaining, proportionate, reciprocal, reconcilable, related, relating to, relative, relevant, resembling, similar, suitable, suited
ASSOCIATED CONCEPTS: correlative rights doctrine

CORRESPOND *(Be equivalent),* **verb**   adapt to, agree, answer the purpose, appertain, approach, approximate, be accordant, be akin, complement, be complemental, be congruent, be related, bear resemblance, belong, border on, bring into relation with, cohere, coincide, compare, comply with, comport with, concur, conform, *congruere,* conjoin, coordinate, copy, correlate,

deal with, dovetail, draw a parallel, equal, harmonize, have a comparison, have a connection, have a relation, homologate, homologize, join, liken, match, parallel, pertain, reciprocalize, reconcile, relate, resemble, run parallel to, support an analogy, tie in with, to be similiar, touch, unite
ASSOCIATED CONCEPTS: corresponding tax

CORRESPOND *(Communicate),* **verb**   acknowledge, contact, disseminate, epistolize, exchange letters, notify, publicize, relate, reply, respond, send a message, transmit, write

CORRESPONDENCE *(Communication by letters),* **noun**   communication, dispatches, *epistulae,* exchange of letters, letter writing, letters, *litterae,* mail, missives, writings

CORRESPONDENCE *(Similarity),* **noun**   accord, agreement, analogy, comparability, conformity, congruence, *congruentia,* congruity, correlation, equivalence, harmony, likeness, parity, resemblance, sameness, semblance, similitude, symmetry, uniformity

CORRIGIBLE, *adjective*   able to improve, adaptable, alleviative, alterative, ameliorable, amenable, amendable, beneficial, controllable, correctable, curable, developmental, emendable, extricable, fixable, functional, governable, improvable, manageable, mendable, perfectible, progressive, reclaimable, recoverable, rectifiable, redeemable, reformable, reformational, reformatory, remediable, renewable, repairable, reparable, replaceable, rescuable, resilient, restorable, resurgent, retrievable, revisable, revisional, salvageable, subject to revisal, submissive to correction, tameable, teachable, tractable

CORROBORATE, *verb*   acknowledge, adduce evidence, advocate, affirm, assent, assure, attest, authenticate, aver, avouch, bear out, bear witness, bolster up, buttress, call to witness, certify, circumstantiate, *comprobare,* confirm, countersign, defend, document, endorse, fortify, guarantee, justify, maintain, manifest, prove, ratify, reassure, reinforce, sanction, strengthen, subscribe, substantiate, support, sustain, testify to, undersign, uphold, uphold in evidence, validate, verify, vouch for, warrant
ASSOCIATED CONCEPTS: corroborating evidence, corroborating witness

CORROBORATION, *noun*   acknowledgment, affirmation, assurance, attestation, authentication, averment, avouchment, bearing out, certification, circumstantiation, conclusive evidence, conclusive proof, confirmation, demonstrability, demonstration, documentation, endorsement, establishment, establishment of proof, evidence, exemplification, fortification, legal evidence, presentation of evidence, proof, ratification, strengthening, substantiation, support, supportability, supporting evidence, sustaining, testification, testimony, upholding, validation, validification, verifiability, verification, vindication, voucher, witness
ASSOCIATED CONCEPTS: corroborating circumstances, corroborating evidence, corroborative proof, corroborative testimony

CORRUPT, *verb*   adulterate, befoul, bribe, cause to be dishonest, contaminate, corrode, *corrumpere,* debase, debauch, decay, defraud, degenerate, *depravare,* de-

prave, devalue, distort, lead astray, misdirect, mislead, pervert, pollute, prostitute, seduce, spoil, suborn, subvert, taint, undermine, *vitiare,* vitiate, vulgarize, warp
ASSOCIATED CONCEPTS: corrupt a minor

CORRUPTION, *noun*   abuse of public trust, act of bribing, act of profiteering, baseness, breach of faith, breach of trust, bribery, complicity, conduct involving graft, corrupt inducement, *corruptela,* corruptibility, *corruptio,* crime, criminality, debasement, deception, *depravatio,* deviation from rectitude, deviousness, disgrace, dishonesty, dishonor, disloyalty, disrepute, feloniousness, fraudulence, fraudulency, graft, illegality, improbity, indirection, injustice, jobbery, knavery, lack of conscience, lack of principle, lack of probity, malignancy, obliquity, perfidiousness, perfidy, perversion of integrity, scoundrelism, turpitude, unscrupulousness, venality, villainousness, villainy, want of principle, wickedness
ASSOCIATED CONCEPTS: corruption in public office
FOREIGN PHRASES: *Corruptio optimi est pessima.* The corruption of the best is worst. *Maledicta est expositio quae corrumpit textum.* It is a cursed interpretation which corrupts the text.

COSIGN, *verb*   accredit, answer for, approve, assure, authorize, back, be surety for, certify, confirm, countersign, endorse, give assurance, give one's signature, guarantee, indorse, insure, promise, ratify, secure, support, undersign, underwrite, validate, vouch for
ASSOCIATED CONCEPTS: accommodation indorser, accommodation party

COST *(Expenses), noun*   business expense, charge, disbursement, expenditure, legal expense, money expended, obligation incurred, outgo, outlay, overhead, payment, running expense
ASSOCIATED CONCEPTS: awarding costs, bill of costs, costs and disbursements

COST *(Penalty), noun*   amercement, bereavement, damage, damages, fine, forfeiture, harm, impairment, injury, loss, penal retribution, penalization, penance, privation, punishment, sacrifice, unfortunate consequence
ASSOCIATED CONCEPTS: court costs, treble costs

COST *(Price), noun*   appraisal, asking price, assessment, carrying charge, charge, consideration, expensiveness, face value, high worth, *impensa,* mark up, marked price, purchase price, quotation, quoted price, reckoning, sum asked for, valuation, value
ASSOCIATED CONCEPTS: accrued costs, actual cost, all costs, cost basis, cost of administration, cost of doing business, cost of materials, cost of repair, cost of replacement, cost-plus contract, costs and expenses, costs of suit, disbursements, fixed costs, full costs, legal costs, legitimate cost, marginal cost, operating costs, sheriff's costs, total cost, wholesale cost

COTENANT, *noun*   another addressee, another denizen, another dweller, another inhabitant, another inhabiter, another leaseholder, another lessee, another lodger, another occupant, another occupier, another paying guest, another possessor, another renter, another resident, another residentiary, coaddressee, codenizen, codweller, cohouseholder, coinhabitant, coinhabiter, coleaseholder, colessee, cooccupant, cooccupier, copossessor, corenter, coresident, coresidentiary

COUNCIL *(Assembly), noun*   advisory board, board, committee, conclave, conference, forum, judicature, palaver, parley, parliament, synod, tribunal

COUNCIL *(Consultant), noun*   advocate, counselor, deliberation

COUNSEL, *noun*   adviser, advocate, attorney, attorney-at-law, barrister, barrister-at-law, *consilium,* counselor, counselor-at-law, jurisconsult, jurist, lawyer, legal adviser, legal practitioner, legist, member of the bar, member of the legal profession, officer of court, pleader, solicitor
ASSOCIATED CONCEPTS: advice of counsel, aid of counsel, assigned counsel, assistance of counsel, attorney's fees, benefit of counsel, counsel in a cause, counsel of record, denial of counsel, effective counsel, Escobedo Rule, of counsel, opposing counsel, sixth amendment, waiver of counsel
FOREIGN PHRASES: *Consilia multorum quaeruntur in magnis.* The advice of many is required in great affairs. *Praepropera consilia raro sunt prospera.* Rash counsels are rarely prosperous.

COUNSEL, *verb*   advise, advocate, caution, coach, commend, confer, consult, direct, discuss, dissuade, encourage, exchange observations, expostulate, forewarn, give a recommendation, give advice, give suggestions to, guide, instruct, offer an opinion to, opine, persuade, prescribe, prompt, propose, reason with, recommend, seek advice, seek to persuade, submit, suggest, suggest a proposed claim, suggest a proposed contention, urge, warn

COUNSELOR, *noun*   advisor, advocate, attorney, attorney-at-law, barrister, barrister-at-law, counsel, counselor-at-law, individual admitted to the bar, instructor, intercessor, jurisconsult, jurist, lawyer, legal adviser, legal defender, legal practitioner, legal representative, legist, member of the bar, member of the legal profession, officer of court, one called to the bar, solicitor
ASSOCIATED CONCEPTS: counselor at law, of counsel

COUNT, *noun*   accusation, allegation, assertion, averment, case for the prosecution, charge, citation, claim, *comes,* condemnation, countercharge, crimination, declaration, delation, denunciation, distinct statement, imputation, inculpation, indictment, item, item in the indictment, main charge, particular charge, statement of a cause of action
ASSOCIATED CONCEPTS: count in an accusatory instrument, omnibus count

COUNTENANCE, *verb*   abet, accede to, accredit, acquiesce in, adjust oneself to, advocate, affirm, agree to, aid, allow, *approbare,* approbate, approve, approve of, assent to, assist, back, be in favor of, charter, commend, concur in, confirm, consent to, corroborate, empower, endorse, favor, forward, further, give one's blessing, go along with, help, hold with, homologate, license, make allowances for, make valid, *permittere,* ratify, recognize, recommend, sanction, stand by, subscribe to, support, sustain, view with favor

COUNTER, *verb*   act against, act in opposition to, agitate against, antagonize, avert, be at cross purposes, be contrary, be inimical, be obstructive, bid against, challenge, clash, collide, come in conflict with, compete with, conflict with, confute, contend, contradict, contravene, counteract, countercheck, countermand, countervail, cross, deflect, defy, disapprove, fend, fight against, fight off, foil, frustrate by contrary action, go against, go contrary to, go in opposition to, hinder, hold at bay, hold off, hold out against, impede, inhibit, interfere, make a stand against, militate against, negate, not support, object, obstruct, oppose, pit against, play against, prevent, prohibit, protest, protest against, put in check, raise objections, rebuff, repel, resist, run in opposition to, set against, side against, stand against, strike back, suppress, take a stand against, take evasive action, take issue with, thwart, ward off, work against, work at cross purposes

COUNTERACT, *verb*   act in opposition to, agitate against, annul, antagonize, be at cross purposes, be contrary, bid against, cancel out, clash, collide, come in conflict with, conflict with, confute, contend, contradict, counter, counterbalance, countermand, countermine, counterpoise, countervail, counterwork, cross, deactivate, defeat, defy, destroy the effect of, disconcert, disrupt, equalize, equiponderate, fight against, find a remedy, foil, frustrate, frustrate by contrary action, go against, go in opposition to, hinder, inhibit, interfere with, make a stand against, match against, militate against, negate, neutralize, nullify, offset, oppose, oppugn, pit against, play against, play at cross purposes, prevent, protest, protest against, rebuff, repress, resist, *resistere,* reverse, rival, run against, run counter, run counter to, run in opposition to, set against, set at naught, side against, squelch, stand against, take issue with, take one's stand against, traverse, undo, withstand, work against

COUNTERARGUMENT, *noun*   answer, *audi alteram partem,* challenge, confutation, contradiction, contraremonstrance, contravention, controversion, counteraccusation, countercharge, counterclaim, counterprotest, counterreply, counterstatement, defense, denial, disproof, gainsaying, invalidation, negation, opposition, plea, plea in rebuttal, proof, rebuttal, rebutter, *reductio ad absurdum,* refutation, rejoinder, replication, reply, response, retort, subversion, surrebuttal, surrebutter, surrejoinder, traversal, upset

COUNTERATTACK, *noun*   counteraction, counterassault, counterblast, counterblow, countermeasure, countermovement, counteroffensive, counterplot, counterpush, counterstrike, counterstroke, counterthrust, cross fire, reprisal, retaliation, retort, retortion, revenge, riposte

COUNTERCHARGE, *verb*   abnegate, answer, answer back, be respondent, be responsive, confute, contradict, counter, defend, negate, oppose by contrary proof, provide the answer, rebut, rebut the charge, recriminate, refute, refute by argument, rejoin, reply, respond, respond conclusively, retort, riposte, say in reply
ASSOCIATED CONCEPTS: counterclaim, cross-claim

COUNTERCLAIM, *noun*   action to defeat plaintiff's demand, assertion against the plaintiff, cause against an opposing party, cause of action in favor of defendants, claim advanced by defendant, claim for relief by defendant, claim presented by defendant, contraremonstrance, counteraction, counterapplication, countercharge, counterdeclaration, counterdemand,

countermotion, counterpetition, counterpostulation, counterproposal, counterreclamation, counterrequest, countersuit, cross-action, cross-bill, opposing suit, rejoinder, set-off
ASSOCIATED CONCEPTS: compulsory counterclaim, cross-complaint, cross-demand, cross-petition, equitable counterclaim, permissive counterclaim, set-off, sham counterclaim

COUNTERFEIT, *noun*   act of copying, bogus, copy, criminal imitation, deception, ersatz, fabrication, fake, false copy, false duplication, false representation, false reproduction, falsehood, falseness, falsification, falsity, *falsus,* forged copy, forgery, fradulent copy, fraudulent imitation, imitation, plagiarism, plagiary, pretense, simulation, unauthorized copy
ASSOCIATED CONCEPTS: counterfeit bill, counterfeited written instrument

COUNTERMAND, *noun*   abolishment, abolition, abrogation, annulment, ban, cancellation, counterorder, defeasance, disallowance, invalidation, nullification, prohibition, recall, recantation, repeal, repudiation, rescindment, rescission, retraction, reversal, revocation, revocation of orders, revokement, suppression, vacation, veto, voidance, withdrawal
ASSOCIATED CONCEPTS: countermand an order

COUNTEROFFER, *noun*   *casus foederis,* contractual terms, counterbid, counterclause, counterconditions, counterexception, counterlimitation, countermeasure, counterplan, counterpresentation, counterproposal, counterproposition, counterprovision, counterqualification, counterrecommendation, counterrequest, counterreservation, counterstipulation, countersuggestion, hard bargaining, negotiation, new offer, part of the bargain, responsive offer, set of terms, terms proposed

COUNTERPART *(Complement), **noun***   alter ego, analogue, brother, coequal, congener, coordinate, correlate, correlation, correlative, correspondent, *doppelganger,* homologue, mate, obverse, pendant, reciprocal, reverse

COUNTERPART *(Parallel), **noun***   carbon, carbon copy, copy, corresponding part, double, duplicate, duplication, *effigies,* effigy, equal, equivalent, image, likeness, match, replica, reproduction, *res simillima,* twin

COUNTERSIGN, *verb*   certify, confirm, corroborate, endorse, execute, ratify, sanction, second, support

COUNTERVAIL, *verb*   abrogate, act against with equal force, agitate against, alter, avail against, balance, be contrary, cancel, cancel out, check, conflict with, confute, contradict, contravene, counter, counteract, counterpoise, cross, damage, destroy, equiponderate, go counter to, hinder, inhibit, interfere, match, militate against, negate, neutralize, offset, oppose, outbalance, prevent, rebut, refute, resist, run counter to, set off, suppress, thwart, traverse, undermine, weaken, weigh against, work against

COUPON, *noun*   allocation, card, certificate, check, cheque, credit, credit check, detachable part of a certificate, detachable portion, dividend, interest certificate, interim dividend, negotiable instrument, note, premium bond, premium certificate, redeemable part, re-

demption slip, separable part of a certificate, separate ticket, share-out, slip, stub, ticket, token, voucher, written instrument
ASSOCIATED CONCEPTS: coupon bond, coupon book, coupon interest, coupon note

COURSE, noun act, act of pursuing, action, activity, advance, approach, arrangment, attack, campaign, completion, conduct, customary manner of procedure, delivery, design, direction, effectuation, effort, employment, endeavor, evolution, execution, exercitation, furtherance, handling, implementation, interaction, *iter*, line of action, line of conduct, management, manner, measures, method, mode, mode of management, mode of procedure, *modus operandi*, motion, movement, operation, order, particular manner of proceeding, performance, perpetration, plan, policy, positive action, practice, praxis, prescribed system, procedure, process, program, pursuance, pursuit, road, route, scheme, succession of acts, system
ASSOCIATED CONCEPTS: arising out of and in course of employment, course of business, course of conduct, course of dealings, course of employment, courses and distances, direct course, general course, water course
FOREIGN PHRASES: *In dubio, pars mitior est sequenda.* In doubt, the safer course is to be followed.

COURT, noun bar, bar of justice, *basilica*, bench, forum for adjusting disputes, forum of justice, *iudicium*, judgment seat, judicial assembly, judicial forum, judicial tribunal, justice, justice seat, lawcourt, magistrates, place where justice is administered, tribunal
ASSOCIATED CONCEPTS: adjournment of the court, appearance in court, application addressed to the court, civil court, clerk of court, competent court, contempt of court, county court, court-appointed receiver, court below, court calendar, court costs, court in banc, court martial, court of appeals, court of bankruptcy, court of chancery, court of claims, court of common pleas, court of competent jurisdiction, court of first instance, court of general jurisdiction, court of inquest, court of justice, court of last resort, court of limited jurisdiction, court of probate, court of record, court's own motion, court's own witness, criminal court, district court, family court, federal court, fraud upon the court, inferior courts, inherent right of court, jurisdiction of a court, leave of court, legislative courts, local court, municipal courts, opinion of the court, order of the court, power of the court, probate court, proceedings in court, state court, Supreme Court, tax court, term of court, United States courts
FOREIGN PHRASES: *Actus curiae neminem gravabit.* An act of the court shall prejudice no man. *Cursus curiae est lex curiae.* The practice of the court is the law of the court. *Ea quae in curia nostra rite acta sunt debitae executioni demandari debent.* Those things which are properly transacted in our court ought to be committed to a due execution. *Nihil habet forum ex scena.* The court has nothing to do with what is not before it. *Nulla curia quae recordum non habet potest imponere finem neque aliquem mandare carceri; quia ista spectant tantummodo ad curias de recordo.* No court which has not a record can impose a fine or commit any person to prison; because those powers belong only to courts of record.

COURTESY, noun affability, amenity, amiability, chivalry, civility, *comitas*, comity, complaisance, consideration, cordiality, courteous conduct, courteousness, courtliness, deference, elegance of manners, etiquette, excellence of behavior, friendliness, gallantry, geniality, gentility, good behavior, good breeding, good manners, graciousness, manners, *officium*, polished manners, polite act, politeness, refinement, respect, reverence, suavity, tact, thoughtfulness, *urbanitas*, urbanity

COURTROOM, noun court, lawcourt, part, room in which a court of law is held, room in which a lawcourt is held, room used for the application of the laws, room used for the public administration of justice, room where justice is administered

COVENANT, noun agreement, arrangement, avowal, binding agreement, collective agreement, commitment, compact, concordat, contract, contractual obligation, contractual statement, *conventio*, convention, engagement, guarantee, mutual understanding, oath, *pacisci*, pact, *pactio, pactum*, pledge, promise, stipulation, understanding, undertaking, warranty, written agreement, written pledge
ASSOCIATED CONCEPTS: breach of covenant, collateral covenants, concurrent covenants, covenant against incumbrances, covenant appurtenant to the land, covenant for quiet enjoyment, covenant not to institute suit, covenant in praesenti, covenant not to convey, covenant of future assurrence, covenant of general warranty, covenant of title, covenant of warranty, covenant running with the land, covenant to pay, dependent covenant, doctrine of implied covenants, joint covenant, negative covenants, restrictive covenant

COVER (Pretext), noun alleged reason, camouflage, claim, disguise, excuse, guise, mask, *obtegere, operire*, pretense, profession, screen, sham, subterfuge, *velare*

COVER (Protection), noun blanket, coating, covering, coverture, guard, integument, safeguard, sheath, shelter, shield, veneer

COVER (Substitute), noun alternate, alternative, equivalent item, exchange, replacement, similar item, stand-in, substitution

COVER (Conceal), verb becloud, befog, bury, camouflage, cloak, curtain, disguise, enshroud, hide, keep out of sight, mask, obscure, put out of sight, screen, seclude, secrete, shroud, veil, *velare*
ASSOCIATED CONCEPTS: cover one's assets

COVER (Guard), verb care for, defend, ensure, harbor, insure, keep in safety, keep safe from harm, keep under close watch, make safe, protect, safeguard, secure, sheathe, shelter, shield, take care of, watch over, wrap

COVER (Provide for), verb compensate for, counterbalance, insure, make compensation, make provision for, offset, pay, recompense, replace, substitute, suffice to defray
ASSOCIATED CONCEPTS: buyer's right to cover

COVERAGE (Insurance), noun act of promise-making, amount for which anything is insured, assurance, backing, bond, covenant, guarantee, guaranty, indemnity, obligation, pledge, promise, promise to pay, protection, reassurance, reinsurance, safeguard, secu-

rity against loss, support, surety, undertaking, under-writing, warrant, warranty
ASSOCIATED CONCEPTS: blanket coverage, casualty coverage, comprehensive coverage, extended coverage, fire coverage, theft coverage

COVERAGE *(Scope), noun*   accommodation, act of compassing, act of comprehending, act of containing, act of embracing, act of encircling, act of encompassing, act of engrossing, act of spanning, act of subsuming, act of surrounding, ambit, bounds, capacity, circulation, circumscription, composition, comprehension, comprehensiveness, comprisal, domain, dominion, embodiment, embrace, enclosure, encompassment, envelopment, expanse, extent of view, fact of comprehending, field, formation, grasp, inclusion, inclusiveness, inclusivity, incorporation, latitude, measure, participation, province, purview, range, range of view, reach, realm, region, room, space, sphere, spread, sweep, that which is comprehended, view, volume, wide currency, zone

COVERT, *adjective*   clandestine, cloaked, concealed, covered, cryptic, cryptical, dark, delitescent, disguised, furtive, hidden, insidious, invisible, latent, muffled, mysterious, mystic, mystical, nonapparent, occult, out of sight, private, screened, secluded, secret, sheltered, shrouded, sly, sneaky, stealthy, surreptitious, tacit, undercover, underground, underhand, undisclosed, unknown, unobtrusive, unseen, unsuspected, veiled

COVERTURE, *noun*   condition of a married woman, conjugality, legal status of a married woman, living as man and wife, marriage lines, married state, married tie, matrimony, matronage, matronhood, matronship, nuptial bond, state of a married woman, state of matrimony, union, wedded state, wifedom

CREATE, *verb*   be responsible, be the agent, be the author, be the cause of, be the reason, beget, bring about, bring into being, bring on, bring out, bring to effect, bring to pass, build, carve, cause, cause to exist, chisel, compose, conceive, concoct, constitute, construct, contribute, contrive, *creare,* develop, devise, effect, engender, engineer, erect, establish, fabricate, fashion, *fingere,* forge, form, formulate, found, frame, generate, give birth to, give origin to, give rise to, ideate, improvise, inaugurate, induce, initiate, institute, invent, kindle, launch, lay the foundations, make, make up, occasion, organize, originate, pattern, procreate, produce, put together, set going, set up, shape, spawn, start, think up
ASSOCIATED CONCEPTS: create a debt, create a liability, create a lien, created by fraud, created by law

CREATION, *noun*   arrangement, artistic effort, authorship, beginning, birth, bringing forth, building, causation, composition, concoction, constituting, construction, contriving, defiance of precedent, designing, development, devising, endeavor, engenderment, establishment, expression, fabrication, fashioning, formation, forming, formulation, formulation of a mental image, formulation of a principle, formulation of an idea, foundation, framing, fruition, imagination, *initium,* invention, manufacture, molding, new departure, original work, origination, patterning, preparation, procreation, producing, production, productiveness, productivity, realization, shaping

CREDENCE, *noun*   acceptance, act of believing, assurance, belief, certainty, complete trust, confidence, conviction, credit, dependence on, faith, firm belief, fixed belief, full assurance, full belief, implicit belief, instinctive belief, persuasion, reliance, subjective belief, sureness, surety, suspension of disbelief, trust, unshaken belief, view
FOREIGN PHRASES: *Culbet in arte sua perito est credendum.* Credence should be given to one skilled in his peculiar profession.

CREDENTIALS, *noun*   authorization, certificates, certification, documents, identification, papers, passport, proof of authority, recommendations, records, references, testimonials, vouchers

CREDIBILITY, *noun*   appearance of truth, *auctoritas,* believability, believableness, credibleness, faithfulness, *fides,* integrity, plausibility, probity, rectitude, reliability, tenability, tenableness, trustworthiness, truthfulness, uprightness, veracity, verisimilitude
ASSOCIATED CONCEPTS: credibility of a witness, impeachment of credibility

CREDIBLE, *adjective*   assured, believable, commanding belief, commanding confidence, convincing, *credibilis,* creditworthy, dependable, deserving belief, deserving of confidence, faithful, faithworthy, frank, honest, incorruptible, indisputable, indubitable, ingenuous, irrefutable, not improbable, of repute, reliable, reputable, scrupulous, sound, straightforward, to be depended on, to be relied upon, true, trusted, trustworthy, truth telling, truthful, uncorrupt, uncorruptible, undeniable, unequivocal, unfailing, unfalse, upright, veracious, verisimilar, void of suspicion, well-grounded, worthy of belief, worthy of confidence, worthy of credence
ASSOCIATED CONCEPTS: attack on credibility, credible evidence, credible person, credible witness

CREDIT *(Recognition), noun*   commendation, consideration, distinction, esteem, fame, favorable opinion, good name, high regard, honor, merit, power, prestige, rank, regard, reputableness, reputation, repute, respect, standing, status, worth
FOREIGN PHRASES: *Judiciis posterioribus fides est adhibenda.* Faith or credit is to be given to the more recent decisions.

CREDIT *(Delayed payment), noun*   advance, chance to borrow money on time, confidence, future payment, installment buying, loan, opportunity to obtain goods on time, permission to defer payment, purchase on time, purchase on trust, reliance
ASSOCIATED CONCEPTS: confirmed credit, consumer credit, contingent creditors, credit agreement, credit association, credit bureau, credit rating, credit union, creditor and debtor, creditor-beneficiary, creditor of bankrupt, creditor of estate, creditor's bill, creditor's committee, creditor's reference, creditor's suits, establishment of credit, extension of credit, general creditors, judgment creditors, junior creditors, letter of credit, line of credit, paper credit, personal credit, preferred creditors, renewal of credit, secured creditors, unconditional credit

CREDITOR, *noun*   backer, debtee, investor, lender, mortgagee, pledgee, seller, sponsor

FOREIGN PHRASES: *Debitorum pactionibus creditorum petitio nec tolli nec minui potest.* The rights of creditors to sue cannot be prejudiced or diminished by agreements between their debtors.

CREDULITY, noun   belief, blind faith, *credulitas,* credulousness, deceivability, disposition to believe, easiness of belief, foolishness, gullibility, gullibleness, impressibility, innocence, lack of doubt, lack of dubiety, lack of dubiousness, lack of skepticism, lack of sophistication, lack of suspicion, naiveness, naivete, overtrustfulness, persuasibility, pliability, pliancy, readiness to believe, simpleness, simplicity, suggestibility, susceptibility, susceptivity, tractability, trust, trustfulness, uncritical acceptance, unquestioning belief, unsophistication, unsuspectingness, unsuspiciousness

CREDULOUS, adjective   believing, *credulus,* deceivable, disposed to believe, easily convinced, easily deceived, easily duped, easily taken in, green, gullible, misjudging, naive, overly trustful, persuasible, prone to believe, simple, trusting, undoubting, unquestioning, unsophisticated, unsuspecting, unsuspicious

CRIME, noun   act prohibited by law, breach of law, contravention, corruption, criminal activity, criminal offense, delict, *delictum,* delinquency, dereliction, deviation from rectitude, encroachment, *facinus,* felony, flagitiousness, fringement, graft, gross offense against law, guilty act, illegality, indictable offense, infringement, jobbery, *maleficium,* malfeasance, malversation, misconduct, misdealing, misdeed, misdemeanor, misdoing, misfeasance, misprision, noncompliance with law, nonobservance of law, nonfeasance, obliquity, offence, offense, offense against the law, offense against the state, official misconduct, omission prohibited by law, public wrong, serious infraction of the law, violation of law, wrong

ASSOCIATED CONCEPTS: accessory to crime, acquittal of crime, antecedent crime, attempted crime, capital crime, commission of a crime, common-law crimes, compounding a crime, concealment of a crime, convicted of a crime, crime against law of nations, crime against nature, crime involving moral turpitude, crime mala in se, crime mala prohibita, crime of violence, *crimen falsi,* element of the crime, guilt, implement a crime, imprisonment, indictable crime, infamous crime, necessarily included crime, pary to crime, proceeds of crime, prosecution for a crime, punishment for a crime, quasi crime, victim

FOREIGN PHRASES: *Crescente malitia crescere debet et poena.* Punishment ought to be increased as malice increases. *Aestimatio praeteriti delicti ex postremo facto nunquam crescit.* The weight of a past crime is never increased by a subsequent fact. *Receditur a placitis juris, potius quam injuriae et delicta maneant impunita.* Settled rules of law will be departed from rather than that crimes should remain unpublished. *Peccata contra naturam sunt gravissima.* Crimes against nature are the most heinous. *Nemo punitur pro alieno delicto.* No one is to be punished for the crime of another. *Ubi culpa est, ibi poena subesse debet.* Where a crime is committed, there punishment should be inflicted. *Impunities semper ad deteriora invitat.* Impunity always invites to greater offenses. *Melior est justitia vere praeveniens quam severe puniens.* Truly preventive justice is better than severe punishment. *Multiplicata transgressione crescat poenae inflictio.*

The inflicton of punishment should be increased in proportion to the repetition of the offense. *Poena non potest, culpa perennis erit.* Punishment cannot be everlasting, but crime will be. *In atrocioribus delictis punitur affectus licet non sequatur effectus.* In the more atrocious crimes the intent is punished, although an effect does not follow. *Crimen laesae majestatis omnia alia crimina excedit quoad poenam.* The punishment for treason exceeds that for all other crimes. *Crimen omnia ex se nata vitiat.* Crime vitiates all which springs from it. *Crimina morte extinguuntur.* Crimes are extinguished by death. *Culpae poena par esto.* Let the punishment fit to the crime. *Venia facilitas incentivum est delinquendi.* Facility of pardon is an incentive to crime. *Voluntas et propositum distinguunt maleficia.* The will and purpose distinguish offenses. *Multiplioata transgressione crescat poenae inflictio.* The inflicton of punishment should be increased in proportion to the repetition of the offense. *In criminalibus, voluntas reputabitur pro facto.* In criminal cases, the intent will be taken for the deed. *In maleficiis voluntas spectatur, non exitus.* In offenses, the intention is regarded, not the result. *In omnibus poenalibus judiciis, et aetatl et imprudentiae succurritur.* In all penal judgments, allowance is made for youth and lack of prudence. *In criminalibus, sufficit generalis malitia intentionis, cum facto paris gradus.* In crimes, a general malicious intent suffices where there is an act of equal degree. *Interest reipublicae quod homines conserventur.* It is in the interest of the state that men be preserved.

CRIMINAL, noun   bandit, blackguard, buccaneer, burglar, convict, defrauder, evildoer, extortionist, felon, filcher, fugitive, gangster, grafter, guilty person, gunman, hardened offender, juvenile delinquent, kidnapper, killer, knave, lawbreaker, malefactor, malfeasant, manslayer, marauder, misdemeanant, murderer, offender, outlaw, pilferer, pillager, pirate, plunderer, public enemy, recidivist, recreant, reprobate, *reus,* robber, *sceleratus,* smuggler, sneak thief, swindler, terrorist, thief, transgressor, underworld character, villain, worker of iniquity, wrongdoer

ASSOCIATED CONCEPTS: convicted criminal, criminal action, criminal attempt, criminal capacity, criminal case or cause, criminal charge, criminal code, criminal conduct, criminal conspiracy, criminal contempt, criminal conviction, criminal courts, criminal information, criminal intent, criminal judgments, criminal jurisdiction, criminal motive, criminal negligence, criminal offense, criminal procedure, criminal process, criminal prosecution, criminal responsibility, criminal sanctions, criminal solicitation, criminal statute, criminal syndicalism, criminal transaction, criminal trial, habitual criminal, known criminals

FOREIGN PHRASES: *Frustra legis auxilium invocat qui in legem committit.* He vainly seeks the aid of the law who transgresses the law.

CRIMINALITY, noun   blameworthy conduct, corruptness, criminal attitude, criminal conduct, crookedness, culpability, culpable conduct, felonious conduct, feloniousness, fraudulence, guilt, heinous conduct, illegality, illicitness, infamous conduct, infamous misbehavior, lawlessness, malversation, misdoing, official misconduct, outlawry, transgression, unlawfulness, wrongdoing

ASSOCIATED CONCEPTS: criminal culpability, criminal intent

CRITERION, *noun* barometer, basis, code, custom, design, discipline, example, exemplar, form, formula, foundation, frame of reference, gauge, ground rules, guide, ideal, law, measure, model, norm, *obrussa*, pattern, point of comparison, precedent, prescribed form, principle, regulation, rule, rules and regulations, shape, standard, standard of comparison, standard of criticism, standard of judgment, test, test case, type, yardstick

CRITICAL *(Crucial),* **adjective** acute, *anceps,* chief, climacteric, climactic, commanding, considerable, deciding, decisive, determining, *dubius,* essential, eventful, exigent, far-reaching, fateful, foremost, grave, imperative, important, imposing, key, major, material, momentous, never to be forgotten, notable, of decisive importance, of great consequence, of importance, of vital importance, outstanding, overruling, overshadowing, paramount, pivotal, pressing, primary, principal, prominent, serious, significant, solemn, strategic, substantial, turning, urgent, vital, weighty
ASSOCIATED CONCEPTS: critical stage of a trial

CRITICAL *(Faultfinding),* **adjective** accusing, blaming, captious, carping, castigating, caustic, caviling, censorious, censuring, chiding, choleric, comminatory, condemnatory, condemning, criminative, criminatory, criticizing severely, cynical, damnatory, defamatory, denunciatory, derogatory, disapproving, *elegans,* exacting, hard upon, hardhitting, hypercritical, inclined to judge with severity, nagging, objecting, objurgatory, overcritical, rebuking, recriminative, reprehensive, reproachful, reprobative, reproving, scarifying, scathing, scolding, severe, taunting, ultracritical, uncomplimentary, upbraiding

CRITICISM, *noun* abuse, accusation, admonition, adverse comment, analysis, animadversion, aspersion, blame, carping, caviling, censure, charge, chiding, commentary, complaining, complaint, condemnation, contravention, critical examination, critical remarks, critique, denunciation, deprecation, depreciation, derogation, detraction, disapproval, discommendation, disdain, disparagement, dispraise, disvaluation, exception, expostulation, fault-finding, grievance, grumbling, imputation, indictment, insinuation, *iudicium,* lecture, objection, obloquy, odium, opposition, opprobrium, protestation, reflection, rejection, remonstrance, reprehension, reprimand, reproach, reproof, review, revilement, scolding, upbraiding
ASSOCIATED CONCEPTS: fair and honest criticism, freedom of speech, privileged criticism

CRITICIZE *(Evaluate),* **verb** adjudge, appraise, assess, consider, examine, gauge, *iudicare,* judge, measure, rank, rate, reckon, review, scrutinize, sum up, take stock of, value, weigh

CRITICIZE *(Find fault with),* **verb** animadvert, berate, blame, castigate, censure, chide, complain, condemn, *culpare,* decry, deprecate, depreciate, disapprove, disparage, dispraise, express dissatisfaction, find cause to blame, impugn, object to, objurgate, rebuke, reprehend, *reprehendere,* reprimand, reproach, reprobate, reprove, upbraid

CROSS *(Disagree with),* **verb** act in opposition to, argue, be opposed to, collide, conflict with, confront, confute, contend, contest, contradict, contravene, controvert, debate, defy, dispute, gainsay, *homini obsistere,* make a stand against, neutralize, oppose, protest, refuse to conform, refute, repudiate, resist, run counter to, speak against, take exception, traverse
ASSOCIATED CONCEPTS: cross action, cross-appeal, cross-claim, cross-complaint, cross-demand, cross-examination, cross-interrogatories, cross libels, cross-motions, cross-petition, cross-remainders, cross section, cross-suit, crosswalk

CROSS *(Intersect),* **verb** bisect, braid, crisscross, crosscut, cut across, divide, go across, halve, intercross, interrupt, intersect, lie across, move across, section, segment, separate, split, traverse

CROSS-EXAMINATION, *noun* asking questions, challenge, checking, cross interrogation, cross questioning, enquiry, evidence-seeking, examination, exploration, formulating questions, grilling, inquest, inquiry, inquisition, interpellation, interrogation, investigation, leading inquiry, minute examination, probe, prosecution, query, quest, questioning, reexamination, scrutiny, search, search into facts, searching inquiry, trial
ASSOCIATED CONCEPTS: right to cross-examine, scope of cross-examination

CROSS-EXAMINE, *verb* ask questions, catechize, challenge, check, cross interrogate, cross question, examine, ferret out, grill, inquire of, interpellate, interrogate, petition, probe, query, question, quiz, reexamine, subject to examination
ASSOCIATED CONCEPTS: cross-examination limited to the scope of the direct examination, direct examination, impeachment, right to cross-examine

CROSS-QUESTIONING, *noun* close inquiry, cross-examination, cross-interrogation, exploration, inquiry, inspection, interrogation, investigation, probe, query, questioning, reexamination, review, scrutiny

CROSS SECTION, *noun* average, characterization, composite representation, embodiment, epitome, example, exemplar, *exempli gratia,* exemplification, *exemplum,* fair sample, *locus classicus,* norm, part exemplifying a mass, part exemplifying a number, profile, random sample, representation, representative sampling, representative section, representative selection, sample

CROSSROAD *(Intersection),* **noun** confluence, conjuncture, cross-way, crossing, crossways, four corners, interchange, intercrossing, intersecting road, intersection, joining road, junction, vertex

CROSSROAD *(Turning point),* **noun** calm before a storm, climacteric, climax, conjuncture, crisis, critical moment, critical period, critical point, crossways, crowning point, crucial moment, culmination, decisive moment, dividing point, eleventh hour, floodgate, hinge, hour of decision, juncture, landmark, line of demarcation, meeting of events, milestone, pivot, point of no return, relapse, turn, turn of the tide, watershed, well-chosen moment, well-timed initiative

CRUCIAL, adjective acute, climacteric, conclusive, consequential, critical, deciding, decisive, definitive, determining, essential, exigent, final, grave, imperative, important, influential, instant, material, momentous, of moment, of note, of supreme importance, pivotal, pressing, severe, significant, supreme, urgent, valuable, vital

CRUEL, adjective acrimonious, agonizing, atrocious, barbarous, blood-thirsty, brutal, cold, cold-blooded, cold-hearted, *crudelis,* demoniacal, devilish, diabolical, distressing, evil-minded, ferocious, fiendish, fierce, hard, hardhearted, harsh, heartless, hellish, ill-intentioned, ill-natured, ill-willed, implacable, indifferent to suffering, inhuman, inhumane, insensitive, malevolent, malicious, malign, malignant, merciless, oppressive, painful, pitiless, punishing, relentless, remorseless, ruthless, sadistic, satanic, savage, severe, spiteful, tortuous, treacherous, tyrannical, unbenevolent, uncompassionate, unfeeling, unkind, unmerciful, unnatural, unpitying, unrelenting, unsympathetic, unsympathizing, vicious
ASSOCIATED CONCEPTS: cruel and abusive treatment, cruel and barbarous treatment, cruel and inhuman punishment, cruel and inhuman treatment, cruel and unusual punishment, cruel disposition, cruel treatment

CRUELTY, noun atrocity, austerity, barbarity, barbarousness, bloodthirstiness, brutality, brutalness, brutishness, *crudelitas,* cruel act, cruel conduct, deliberate malice, deviltry, enmity, ferity, ferociousness, ferocity, fierceness, harshness, heartlessness, ill-nature, ill-usage, ill-will, infliction of pain, inhumanity, intolerance, malice, malice aforethought, malice prepense, maliciousness, malignance, malignancy, malignity, mercilessness, oppression, outrage, persecution, rancor, relentlessness, remorselessness, ruthlessness, savageness, savagery, severity, spite, sternness, torture, tyranny, uncompassionateness, unkindness, unremorsefulness, viciousness, victimization, violence
ASSOCIATED CONCEPTS: cruelty of treatment, cruelty to animals, cruelty to children, extreme cruelty, habitual cruelty, mental cruelty, unneccessary cruelty

CRYSTALLIZE, verb accumulate, amalgamate, arrange itself, assume a pattern, assume definite characteristics, be solid, become a reality, become definite, become delineated, become firm, become settled, become solid, become visible, bring together, cement, coagulate, cohere, combine, come together, compact, compress, condense, conglomerate, consolidate, develop, eventuate, fall into line, fashion, form, form a core, formulate, set, shape up, solidify, take form, take on character, take order, take shape, thicken, unfold, unify

CUDGEL, noun arm, *baculum,* bar, bastinado, bat, battering ram, billy, blackjack, bludgeon, cane, club, cosh, deadly device, deadly weapon, deterrent, ferule, *fustis,* instrument for use in combat, instrument of war, lethal instrument, lethal weapon, mallet, means of offense, night stick, pole, shillelagh, staff, stick, truncheon, war hammer, weapon
ASSOCIATED CONCEPTS: deadly weapons

CULL, verb accumulate, amass, *carpere,* choose, collect, *decerpere,* gather, glean, *legere,* make a selection, pick, pick out, pluck, round up, select, separate, sift, single out, sort out, winnow

CULMINATE, verb accomplish, cap, climax, close, complete, conclude, consummate, crown, effect, end, execute, finish, reach a peak, reach the highest point, reach the zenith, terminate, top

CULMINATION, noun acme, apex, apogee, cap, climax, crest, crown, crowning touch, head, height, highest point, peak, pinnacle, summit, top, topmost point, utmost height, zenith

CULPABILITY, noun blame, blameworthiness, censurableness, chargeableness, criminality, delinquency, dereliction, failure in duty, fault, guilt, guiltiness, improbity, misbehavior, misconduct, misdoing, peccability, peccancy, remissness, reprehensibility, reproachableness, transgression, wrongdoing
ASSOCIATED CONCEPTS: culpable recklessness, culpably negligent

CULPABLE, adjective accusable, at fault, blamable, blameworthy, censurable, chargeable, condemnable, convictable, criminal, criminous, *culpandus,* delinquent, deserving blame, deserving censure, discreditable, dishonest, disorderly, dissolute, encroaching, felonious, guilty, having violated the law, improper, in error, in the wrong, indictable, indiscreet, lawbreaking, lawless, meriting censure, meriting condemnation, misdemeanant, peccant, punishable, responsible, transgressing, unrighteous, worthy of blame, wrong

CULTIVATE, verb advance, *colere,* develop, elevate, enrich, farm, forward, foster, further, garden, improve, make better, nourish, nurture, polish, prepare for crops, promote, rarefy, refine, till, train, work

CUMULATION, noun accession, accretion, accruement, accumulation, acervation, acquisition, addition, agglomerate, agglomeration, aggregate, aggregation, amassment, ammount accrued, assemblage, assembly, *attroupement,* augmentation, bringing together, build up, bulk, collection, compilation, concentration, conglomerate, conglomeration, congregation, glomeration, growth by addition, mass, pile, reserve, stock, stockpile, storage, store, supply

CUMULATIVE (Increasing), adjective accruing, accumulative, added together, additional, additive, additory, advancing, becoming greater, becoming larger, broadening, continually increasing, enlarging, ever-widening, expanding, flourishing, growing, growing by successive additions, incremental, lengthening, multiplying, on the increase, piling up, strengthening, successively gaining in force, successively waxing in force, swelling, thriving, widening
ASSOCIATED CONCEPTS: cumulative criminal acts, cumulative sentences, cumulative voting

CUMULATIVE (Intensifying), adjective accelerating, aggravative, amplifying, augmentative, becoming more intense, boosting, concentrating, deepening, enhancing, escalating, exaggerating, extending, heightening, intensive, magnifying, maximizing, multiplying, quickening, sharpening, strengthening

CURATIVE, adjective analeptic, corrective, emendatory, healing, relieving, remedial, reparative, restorative, therapeutic

CURB, verb arrest, brake, check, control, delay, detain, govern, harness, hinder, hold back, hold in check, hold up, impede, inhibit, keep within limits, limit, mitigate, moderate, muzzle, obstruct, prohibit, repress, restrain, retard, snub, stay, suppress, temper, throttle down, trammel, yoke

CURE, noun antidote, antipoison, antitoxin, assuager, balm, catholicon, corrective, counteractant, elixir, emollient, healing agent, medical treatment, medicament, medicine, method of treatment, palliative, panacea, recovery, recuperation, redress, relief, remedy, restoration to health, restorative, salve, *sanatio,* successful remedial treatment, therapeutic, tonic

CURE, verb ameliorate, apply a remedy, correct, doctor, effect a cure, heal, improve, make well, make whole, *mederi,* medicate, meliorate, mend, minister to, nurse, palliate, recall to life, reclaim, recover, rectify, recuperate, redeem, redress, regenerate, rehabilitate, rejuvenate, relieve, relieve of something detrimental, remedy, renew, repair, restore, resuscitate, revive, revivify, right, salve, *sanare,* soothe, treat
ASSOCIATED CONCEPTS: cured by verdict, curing defect, curing error, curing title, opportunity to cure

CURRENCY, noun bank notes, bills, cash, circulating medium, coin, government notes, hard cash, legal tender, medium of exchange, *moneta,* money, money in actual use, notes, paper money, ready money, specie
ASSOCIATED CONCEPTS: lawful currency

CURRENT, adjective being done, belonging to the time, concurrent, contemporaneous, contemporary, customary, existent, existing, *hic,* immediate, in fashion, in style, in the fad, in vogue, instant, latest, latter day, new, occurring, of the moment, of the present, of this date, of todays date, popular, present, present day, prevailing, prevalent, recent, revised, stylish, topical, up to date, up to the minute, *usitatus,* widespread
ASSOCIATED CONCEPTS: current account, current assets, current basis, current business expenses, current debts, current events, current expenditures, current market value, current obligations, current operating expenses, current rate of exchange, currently distributable

CURSORY, adjective apathetic, brief, careless, casual, desultory, hasty, heedless, hurried, immethodical, inattentive, incautious, indifferent, lax, offhand, passing, perfunctory, quick, rapid, regardless, shallow, short, slapdash, slipshod, speedy, summary, superficial, surface, thoughtless, undiscerning, unmindful, unthorough
ASSOCIATED CONCEPTS: cursory examination

CURTAIL, verb abate, abbreviate, abridge, clip, *coartare,* cut, cut down, cut short, decrease, diminish, halt, lessen, lop, make smaller, *minuere,* pare, pare down, reduce, retrench, shorten, subtract, trim

CURTAILMENT, noun abatement, abbreviation, abbreviature, abridgment, compression, condensation, constriction, contraction, cut-back, cutting down, cutting off, declension, decline, decrease, decrescence, depression, deprivation, diminishment, diminution, divestment, elimination, lessening, minimization, modification, privation, reduction, retrenchment, shortening, shrinkage, subduction, subtraction, trimming

CURTILAGE, noun court, courtyard, enclosure, fenced, garden, land, yard

CUSTODIAN (Protector), noun champion, curator, defender, guardian, keeper, manager, overlooker, overseer
ASSOCIATED CONCEPTS: custodian of assets, gratuitous custodian
FOREIGN PHRASES: *Nemo alienae rei, sine satisdatione, defensor idoneus intelligitur.* No one is considered a competent defender of another's property, without security.

CUSTODIAN (Warden), noun caretaker, jailer

CUSTODY (Incarceration), noun arrest, arrestment, bondage, bounds, captivity, circumscription, commitment, confinement, constraint, detention, durance, enthrallment, fetter, holding, immuration, immurement, impoundment, imprisonment, limitation, restraint, restriction, safekeeping, thralldom
ASSOCIATED CONCEPTS: arrest, bail, constructive custody, hold in custody, parole, probation
FOREIGN PHRASES: *Fortior est custodia legis quam hominis.* The custody of the law is stronger than that of man. *In custodia legis.* In the custody of the law.

CUSTODY (Supervision), noun act of protecting, administration, aegis, auspices, *carcer,* care, charge, control, *custodia,* custodianship, direction, guardianship, guidance, jurisdiction, keeping, management, preservation, preservation from harm, preservation from injury, protection, regulation, safeguard, safekeeping, stewardship, superintendence, trusteeship, wardship, watch
ASSOCIATED CONCEPTS: custody and control, custody decree, custody of children, custody of property, custody order, custody proceeding, guardianship

CUSTOM, noun ceremony, characteristic way, common usage, consuetude, convention, conventionalism, conventionality, course of business, dictates of society, established way of doing things, etiquette, familiar way, fashion, fashionableness, formality, habit, habit of a majority, habitual activity, habitual practice, habituation, habitude, institution, manner, matter of course, observance, ordinary manner, practice, prescribed form, prevailing taste, prevalence, rite, ritual, routine, routine procedure, social usage, style, tradition, traditionalism, traditionality, unwritten law, usage, usual manner, vogue, wont, wontedness
ASSOCIATED CONCEPTS: custom of merchants, custom or practice, custom or usage, general custom, local customs, usual course and custom, waiver by custom
FOREIGN PHRASES: *Servanda est consuetudo loci ubi causa agitur.* The custom of the place where the action is brought should be observed. *In contractibus, tacite insunt quae sunt moris et consuetudinis.* In contracts, matters of custom and usage are tacitly implied. *Consuetudo tollit communem legem.* Custom supersedes the common law. *Consuetudo non trahitur in consequentiam.* Custom is not drawn into consequence. *Consuetudo manerii et loci observanda est.* Custom of a manor and a locality is to be observed. *Consuetudo est optimus interpres legum.* Custom is the best interpreter of the laws. *Consuetudo est altera lex.* Custom is another law. *Consuetudo contra rationem introducta potius usurpatio quam consuetudo appellari debet.* A

custom introduced contrary to reason ought rather to be called a usurpation than a custom. ***Ratio est formalis causa consuetudinis.*** Reason is the source and cause of custom. ***Quae praeter consuetudinem et morem majorum fiunt neque placent neque recta videntur.*** Things which are done contrary to the custom and manner of our ancestors neither please nor appear right. ***Optimus interpres rerum usus.*** Usage is the best interpreter of things. ***Optima est legis interpres consuetudo.*** Custom is the best interpreter of the law. ***Omne jus aut consensus fecit, aut necessitas constituit aut firmavit consuetudo.*** Every right is either derived from consent, established by necessity, or is confirmed by custom. ***Minime mutanda sunt quae certam habuerunt interpretationem.*** Those matters which have had a certain interpretation are to be altered as little as possible. ***Obtemperandum est consuetudini rationabili tanquam legi.*** A reasonable custom is to be obeyed like law. ***Malus usus abolendus est.*** A bad custom is to be abolished. ***Consuetudo volentes ducit, lex nolentes trahit.*** Custom leads the willing, the law compels the unwilling. ***Consuetudo vincit communem legem.*** Custom overrules the common law. ***In consuetudinibus, non diuturnitas temporis sed soliditas rationis est consideranda.*** In customs, not lapse of time, but the soundness of reason should be considered. ***Consuetudo semel reprobata non potest amplius induci.*** Custom once disallowed cannot again be invoked. ***Consuetudo praescripta et legitima vincit legem.*** A prescriptive and lawful custom prevails over the law. ***Consuetudo neque injuria oriti neque tolli potest.*** Custom can neither arise from nor be abolished by a wrongful act. ***Consuetudo loci observanda est.*** The custom of a locality is to be observed. ***Consuetudo, licet sit magnae auctoritatis, nunquam tamen, praejudicat manifestae veritati.*** A custom, though it be of great authority, should never be prejudicial to manifest truth. ***Consuetudo ex certa causa rationabili usitata privat communem legem.*** A custom, based on a certain and reasonable cause, supersedes the common law. ***Consuetudo et communis assuetudo vincit legem non scriptam, si sit specialis; et interpretatur legem scriptam, si lex sit generalis.*** Custom and common usage override the unwritten law, if it be special; and interprets the written law, if the law be general.

CUSTOMARY, *adjective* accepted, according to usage, accustomed, acknowledged, average, characteristic, common, commonly observed, commonly practiced, commonplace, confirmed, consuetudinary, conventional, established, established by custom, everyday, expected, familiar, fashionable, fixed, frequent, general, habitual, in established usage, long-established, normal, of long standing, oft-repeated, ordinary, popular, predominant, prevailing, prevalent, *quotidianus*, recognized, regular, routine, set, standard, traditional, *tritus*, typical, *usitatus*, usual, well-known, wonted

ASSOCIATED CONCEPTS: customary business, customary interpretation, customary practice

CUSTOMER, *noun* acceptor, bargainer, bidder, business contact, buyer, buyer of labor, client, consumer, *emptor*, investor, leaser, lessee, one of the clientele, one of the purchasing public, patron, prospect, purchaser, purchaser of goods from another, redeemer, share buyer, shopper, taker, user, vendee

ASSOCIATED CONCEPTS: buyer in the ordinary course of business, cash customer, customer in ordinary course of business, duty to customers, interference with customers, loss of customers, occasional customer, solicitation of customers

CY PRES, *adverb* as near as may be, as near as practicable, as near as possible

CYCLE, *noun* age, alternation, circle, circuit, *circulus*, consecution, course, eon, epoch, era, flow, period, progression, recurrence, recurring period, regular return, regularity of recurrence, repetitiveness, revolution, rotation, round, sequence, succession

CYNICAL, *adjective* acrimonious, apt to distrust, arrogant, caustic, cavalier, censorious, condemnatory, contemptuous, contumelious, critical, decrying, defamatory, defeatist, denunciatory, derisive, derogative, derogatory, despising, disapproving, disdainful, disillusioned, disparaging, disposed to doubt, distrustful, distrusting the motives of others, doubtful, doubting, dubious, fault finding, haughty, holding a low opinion of mankind, inconvincible, indisposed to believe, misanthropic, mistrustful, mocking, *mordax*, pessimistic, questioning, ridiculing, sarcastic, sarcastical, sardonic, scoffing, scornful, skeptical, sneering, supercilious, suspecting, suspicious, unbelieving, untrustful

D

DAILY, *adjective*　　accustomed, common, diurnal, established, habitual, ordinary, quotidian, *quotidie,* regular, routine, usual

ASSOCIATED CONCEPTS: daily attendance, daily balance, daily occupation, daily output, daily publication, daily rate of pay, daily wages

DAMAGE, *noun*　　adversity, affliction, aggravation, casualty, declination, decline, decrement, depravation, depreciation, destruction, deterioration, detriment, dilaceration, diminution, disrepair, exacerbation, grievance, hardship, harm, hurt, impairment, infliction, injury, loss, ruin, ruination, spoiling, vexation, vitiation, weakening, wreck, wrong

ASSOCIATED CONCEPTS: actual loss, ad damnum clause, aggravation of damages, business damage, conjectural damages, consequential damages, contingent damages, damages actually sustained, damages by fire, damages by the elements, damages in contemplation of party, damages to land, damages to person, damages to property, damages to realty, *damnum absque injuria,* excessive damages, exemplary damages, future damages, general damages, incidental damages, *injuria absque damno,* limitation of liability, liquidated damages, measure of damages, minimizing damages, nominal damages, personal injury, property damage, punitive damages, remote damages, special damages, treble damages, unliquidated damages, unusual or extraordinary damage

FOREIGN PHRASES: *Nemo damnum facit, nisi qui id fecit quod facere jus non habet.* No one is considered as doing damage, except he who does that which he has no right to do. *Nul sans damage avera error ou attaint.* No one shall have error or attaint unless he has suffered damage. *Ubicunque est injuria, ibi damnum sequitur.* Wherever there is a wrong, there damage follows. *Quod quis ex culpa sua damnum sentit non intelligitur damnum sentire.* He who incurs a damage by his own fault is not held to suffer damage. *Damnum sine injuria esse potest.* There can be damage or injury inflicted without any act of injustice. *Actus legis nemini est damnosus.* An act of the law shall prejudice no one.

DAMAGE, *verb*　　abase, abuse, blemish, blight, break, break down, bruise, cause detriment, cause injury, cause mischief, cheapen, contaminate, corrupt, cripple, crush, debase, deface, defile, deform, degrade, demolish, destroy, devalue, devastate, diminish, disable, disfigure, disparage, disrupt, disserve, do disservice to, do violence to, harm, hurt, impair, incapacitate, injure, lacerate, lay waste, maim, make unsound, malign, maltreat, mangle, mar, mutilate, pervert, pollute, prejudice, ravage, ruin, sabotage, scathe, spoil, stain, taint, tamper with, trample on, traumatize, vandalize, violate, vitiate, weaken, wound, wreck, wrong

ASSOCIATED CONCEPTS: damage from negligence, damage to goods, destruction, estimated damage, latent damage, loss, mitigation of damages, opportunity to repair, patent damage, permanent damage, recovery for damage, water damage

DAMAGES, *noun*　　amends, compensation, costs, expenses, expiation, fine, indemnification, indemnity, injury, just compensation, legal costs, legal liability, loss, penalty, recompense, recovery, reimbursement, remuneration for injury suffered, reparation, repayment for injury sustained, repayment for loss, restitution, restoration

ASSOCIATED CONCEPTS: actual loss, addamnum clause, additur, aggravation of damages, amercement, apportionment of damages, assessment of damages, civil damages, claim for damages, compensatory damages, conjectural damages, consequential damages, contingent damages, continuing damages, damages accrued, damages actually sustained, damages to person, damages to property, damages to realty, *damnum absque injuria,* direct damages, division of damages, duty to minimize damages, estimated damages, excessive damages, exemplary damages, future damages, general damages, incidental damages, intervening damages, irreparable damages, irreparable injury, lawful damages, limitation of liability, liquidated damages, measure of damages, minimizing damages, mitigation of damages, nominal damages, ordinary damages, pecuniary damages, pecuniary loss, permanent damages, presumptive damages, property damage, prospective damages, proximate damages, punitive damages, reasonable certainty of damages, remote damages, special damages, speculative damages, substantial damages, treble damages, unliquidated damages

FOREIGN PHRASES: *Ubi damna dantur, victus victori in expensis condemnari debet.* Where damages are given, the losing party ought to be condemned to pay costs to the victor.

133

DAMPER *(Depressant)*, **noun**   backset, bleakness, cheerlessness, chill, cloud, crushed spirits, depressing influence, discouragement, disheartener, downheartedness, feeling of dejection, feeling of depression, gloom, glumness, heaviness, heaviness of spirit, joylessness, lack of spirit, lack of warmth, letdown, low spirits, pessimism, sadness, setback, shadow, unhappiness

DAMPER *(Stopper)*, **noun**   bar, barricade, barrier, block, blockage, bridle, check, clog, control, cork, curb, delay, determent, deterrent, difficulty, disadvantage, discouragement, encumbrance, hamper, hindrance, hitch, impediment, impedition, inhibition, interference, interruption, limitation, muffler, obstacle, obstruction, occlusion, oppilation, plug, preclusion, prevention, rein, restraint, restriction, retardation, snag, stoppage, stopper, stopple

DANGER, noun   assailability, crisis, defenselessness, *discrimen*, exposure to harm, hazard, helplessness, imperilment, jeopardy, lack of protection, lack of safety, liability to injury, menace, nonimmunity, penetrability, *periculum*, peril, perilousness, precariousness, pregnability, risk, susceptibility, threat, unguardedness, vincibility, vincibleness, vulnerability
ASSOCIATED CONCEPTS: apparent danger, appreciation of danger, assumption of risk, avoidance of danger, clear and present danger, danger invites rescue doctrine, danger signal, danger zone, foreseeable dangers, hidden danger, imminent danger, impending danger, inherent danger, intrinsic danger, knowledge of danger, known danger, latent danger, obvious danger, obvious risks, patent danger, unavoidable danger, unnecessary exposure to danger, zone of apprehendable danger
FOREIGN PHRASES: *Periculosum existimo quod bonorum virorum non comprobatur exemplo.* I think that dangerous which is not approved by the example of good men.

DANGEROUS, adjective   alarming, assailable, attended with risk, baleful, baneful, beset with danger, breakneck, causing danger, deadly, destructive, disastrous, explosive, exposed to risk, fearsome, fraught with danger, fraught with peril, full of risk, harmful, hazardous, hurtful, injurious, involving risk, likely to harm, maleficent, malignant, menacing, minatory, ominous, perilous, pestiferous, risky, serious, threatening, treacherous, unprotected, unreliable, unsafe, unsheltered, unstable, unsteady, unstrengthened, untrustworthy, venomous, vicious, viperine, viperous, virulent
ASSOCIATED CONCEPTS: attractive nuisance, danger to the community, dangerous animal, dangerous business, dangerous condition, dangerous contraband, dangerous defect, dangerous drug, dangerous employment, dangerous instrument, dangerous instrumentality, dangerous machinery, dangerous occupation, dangerous or defective condition, dangerous place, dangerous premises, dangerous propensities, dangerous structures, dangerous to health, dangerous to life, dangerous trap, dangerous weapon, deadly weapon

DATA, noun   back-up, documents, evidence, facts, grounds, information, logic, papers, proof, specifics

DATE, noun   assigned time, day, day of the week, *dies*, marked time, moment, particular point of time, period, period of time, point of time, specified period of time, *tempus*, time, time during which anything occurs

ASSOCIATED CONCEPTS: antedating, certainty of date, date certain, date of acceptance, date of acknowledgment, date of application, date of appointment, date of availability, date of award, date of birth, date of commencement of action, date of death, date of default, date of enactment, date of execution, date of final judgment, date of injury, date of issue, date of loss, date of maturity, date of notice, date of publication, date of sale, date of taking, date on which a cause of action accrues, delivery date, due date, effective date, expiration date, filing date, future date, publication date, return date, termination date
FOREIGN PHRASES: *In omnibus obligationibus in quibus dies non ponitur, praesenti die debetur.* In all obligations in which no time is designated for their payment, the obligation is due immediately.

DATE, verb   affix a date to, appoint the time of, ascertain the time of, assign a time to, calendar, chronologize, fix the date, fix the time, furnish with a date, mark the time of, note the time of, reckon from some point in time, record, register, *rem tempore tribuere, rem tempori adsignare*, set the date, time
ASSOCIATED CONCEPTS: post date

DAY IN COURT, noun   action, case, complete lawsuit, full chance, hearing, legal action, legal contest, legal trial, litigation, occasion, opportunity, proceeding, trial

DE FACTO, adjective   absolutely, actual, actually, as a matter of fact, authentic, *bona fide*, certain, demonstrable, determinate, existent, existing, existing in fact, factual, genuine, in existence, in fact, in point of fact, in reality, positively, present, real, substantive, tangible, true, truly, unquestionable, valid, veritable, well-founded, well-grounded, with validity
ASSOCIATED CONCEPTS: de facto administrator, de facto admissions, de facto apprenticeship, de facto appropriation, de facto authority, de facto board, de facto board of directors, de facto contract of sale, de facto court, de facto contract, de facto corporation, de facto director, de facto dissolution, de facto districts, de facto domicile, de facto government, de facto guardian, de facto judge, de facto officer, de facto trust, de facto trustee

DE JURE, adjective   according to law, authorized, authorized by law, by law, by order, by right of law, by statute, in accordance with law, in accordance with the ordinance, in accordance with the statute, in the eyes of the law, lawful, lawfully, legal, legally, legitimate, legitimately, licit, licitly, nomothetical, of right, sanctioned by law, within the law
ASSOCIATED CONCEPTS: de jure board, de jure corporation, de jure director, de jure dissolution, de jure election, de jure judge, de jure marriage, de jure office, de jure officer, de jure sovereignty, de jure title

DE MINIMUS, adjective   inconsequential, insignificant, meager, modest, moderate, negligible, of minor importance, of no account, paltry, petty, obscure, scanty, slight, trifling, trivial, unworthy of serious consideration

DE NOVO, adverb   afresh, again, anew, another time, encore, freshly, from the beginning, new, newly, once more, over, over again, revived, second time
ASSOCIATED CONCEPTS: de novo proceeding, hearing de novo, trial de novo

DEAD, *adjective*   at rest, bereft of life, breathless, buried, cadaverous, deceased, defunct, demised, departed, departed this life, deprived of life, destitute of life, devoid of life, dormant, ended, exanimate, expired, extinct, extinguished, inactive, inert, lifeless, long gone, no longer living, not possessing life, passed away, still, terminated, without a sign of life, without life, without the appearance of life
ASSOCIATED CONCEPTS: dead-born, next of kin, presumed dead, surviving spouse, wrongful death
FOREIGN PHRASES: *Cadaver nullius in bonis.* A dead body is no one's property.

DEAD, *noun*   corpse, the deceased, decedent, the defunct, the departed, *exanimis, exanimus,* fatal casualty, fatality, the late, the late lamented, *mortuus*
ASSOCIATED CONCEPTS: autopsy, dead-born, dead man's statute, decedent's estates, next of kin, presumed dead, surviving spouse, wrongful death
FOREIGN PHRASES: *Extra legem positus est civiliter mortuus.* He who is placed outside the law is civilly dead.

DEADLOCK, *noun*   block, blockage, check, checkmate, dead end, dead heat, dilemma, draw, drawn battle, drawn game, frustration, impasse, insoluble difference, no decision, obstruction, paralysis, predicament, quandary, stalemate, stand off, standstill, state of inaction, state of indecision, state of inertia, state of neutralization, stoppage, stumbling block, tie
ASSOCIATED CONCEPTS: deadlock breaking instructions, deadlocked corporation, jury deadlocked, tie vote

DEADLY, *adjective*   aiming to destroy, aiming to kill, annihilating, attended with death, baleful, calamitous, capital, cataclysmic, consuming, dangerous, dangerous to life, death-bringing, death-dealing, deathful, deathly, destroying, destructive, disastrous, envenomed, *exitialis,* fatal, feral, grave, homicidal, incurable, internecine, killing, lethal, lethiferous, malignant, mephitic, miasmic, mortal, *mortifer,* mortiferous, murderous, noxious, *perniciosus,* pernicious, pestiferous, poisoned, poisonous, ruinous, sanguinary, seriously dangerous, slaughterous, steeped in poison, stifling, suffocating, tending to cause death, toxic, toxicant, unhealthy, unsafe, venomous
ASSOCIATED CONCEPTS: armed with a deadly weapon, assault with a deadly weapon, deadly attack, deadly force, deadly weapon, possession of a deadly weapon

DEAL, *noun*   agreement, arrangement, bargain, business transaction, commerce, commercial transaction, compromise, contract, exchange, merchantry, negotiation, operation, pact, pledge, purchase, trade, transaction, understanding
ASSOCIATED CONCEPTS: agreement to sell or exchange, dealer, dealings, lump sum deal, trade deals

DEAL, *verb*   bargain, barter, buy and sell, carry on negotiations, commercialize, do business, do business with, drive a trade, exchange, export and import, handle, have business relations, have commerce, have dealings with, have to do with, make arrangements, market, merchandise, negotiate, open a trade, open an account with, sell, trade, trade with, traffic, traffic in, turn over
ASSOCIATED CONCEPTS: agreement to sell or exchange, cessation of dealing, dealer, dealing and trading, dealing at arm's length, dealing in, dealing in goods, dealing in property, dealing in securities, dealings, trade deals, transacting business

DEALER, *noun*   agent, broker, businessman, businessperson, chandler, changer, *colporteur,* commission agent, commission man, conduit, consigner, exporter, factor, hawker, huckster, jobber, local representative, man of business, *mercator,* merchandiser, merchant, middleman, monger, *negotiator,* one engaged in buying and selling, operator, packman, packwoman, peddler, retailer, salesman, salesperson, saleswoman, seller, shipper, shopkeeper, shopman, shopperson, shopwoman, storekeeper, street vendor, trader, tradesman, tradesperson, tradeswoman, trafficker, vendor, wholesale trader, wholesaler
ASSOCIATED CONCEPTS: agent, authorized dealer, broker-dealer, dealer at retail, dealer in goods, dealer in real estate, dealer in securities, dealer's talk, established dealer, merchant, retail vendor or dealer, wares and merchandise, wholesale dealer

DEALINGS, *noun*   actions, activities, acts, affairs, arrangements, barter, business, business intercourse, business transaction, buying and selling, commerce, commercial enterprise, commercial intercourse, contracts, deals, deeds, doings, exchange, executions, intercourse, interests, manner of conduct, matters, method of business, practice, proceedings, relations, trade, traffic, transactions, understandings, undertakings
ASSOCIATED CONCEPTS: commercial dealings, continuous dealings, direct dealings, mutual dealings, unfair dealings
FOREIGN PHRASES: *Scire debes cum quo contrahis.* You ought to know with whom you are dealing.

DEARTH, *noun*   absence, *caritas,* deficiency, destitution, exiguity, exiguousness, impoverishment, inadequacy, inadequateness, incompleteness, indigence, *inopia,* insufficiency, lack, leanness, littleness, meagerness, need, paucity, *penuria,* penury, pinch, poorness, poverty, privation, rareness, scantiness, scantness, scarceness, scarcity, short supply, shortage, smallness of number, sparsity, want, wantage

DEATH, *noun*   cessation of life, decease, demise, departure from life, dying, ebb of life, end of life, expiration, extinction, extinguishment, failure of vital functions, fatality, loss of life, mortality, passing away, termination of life
ASSOCIATED CONCEPTS: accidental death, capital punishment, *causa mortis,* cause of death, civil death, Dead Man's Statute, death action, death benefits, death by accidental means, death by natural causes, death by violence, death certificate, death gamble, death penalty, death resulting from accident, death resulting from injury, death sentence, death tax, death trap, death warrant, death without issue, deathbed will, homicide, in contemplation of death, injuries resulting in death, instantaneous death, last illness, life expectancy, likely to produce death, mortality tables, natural death, penalty of death, presumption of death, presumptive death, proof of death, registration of death, right to die, simultaneous death, sudden death, time of death, transfer in contemplation of death, unreasonable risk of death, wrongful death
FOREIGN PHRASES: *Crimina morte extinguuntur.* Crimes are extinguished by death. *Actio personalis moritur cum persona.* A personal action dies with the person.

DEBACLE, *noun* adversity, blow, breakdown, calamity, cataclysm, catastrophe, collapse, contretemps, crash, defeat, demolishment, demolition, destruction, devastation, disaster, disruption, dissolution, downfall, emergency, failure, fall, fiasco, havoc, misadventure, mischance, misfortune, mishap, overthrow, overturn, ravage, reverse, rout, ruin, ruination, setback, smash, tragedy, upset, wreck

DEBAR, *verb* abrogate, arrest, astrict, ban, bar, barricade, block, cancel, check, confine, constrain, countermand, curb, detain, deter, disallow, discourage, dispose of, dissuade, eliminate, embargo, enjoin, estop, exclude, *excludere,* excommunicate, forbid, forestall, gainsay, halt, hamper, hinder, hold back, impede, inhibit, interdict, interfere, limit, obstruct, occlude, outlaw, paralyze, preclude, prevent, *prohibere,* prohibit, proscribe, refuse, remove, restrain, restrict, retard, revoke, shut out, stall, stifle, stop, stymie, suppress, suspend, trammel, veto, ward off, withdraw, withhold

DEBASE, *verb* abase, adulterate, bastardize, befoul, cheapen, coarsen, contaminate, *corrumpere,* corrupt, debauch, defile, degrade, dehumanize, demoralize, deprave, depreciate, depress, desecrate, deteriorate, discredit, disgrace, dishonor, downgrade, foul, humble, humiliate, impair, impair in worth, injure, lower, lower in value, pervert, pollute, profane, reduce in quality, soil, stain, taint, tarnish, *vitiare,* vitiate, vulgarize, weaken

DEBATABLE, *adjective* admitting of doubt, ambiguous, arguable, at issue, baffling, capable of being debated, changeable, confutable, conjecturable, conjectural, contentious, contestable, controversial, controvertible, cryptic, deniable, disposed to question, disputable, disputatious, doubtable, doubtful, dubious, dubitable, dubitative, enigmatic, eristic, hard to believe, hypothetical, in dispute, in issue, in question, inconceivable, incredible, indecisive, indefinite, indeterminate, nebulous, obscure, open to debate, open to discussion, open to dispute, open to doubt, open to question, open to suspicion, paradoxical, perplexing, possible, precarious, problematic, problematical, puzzling, questionable, refutable, speculative, subject to argument, subject to contention, subject to contravention, subject to controversy, suppositious, suspect, suspicious, theoretical, unaffirmed, unascertained, unbelievable, uncertain, unconfirmed, undecided, undemonstrable, undemonstrated, under discussion, under examination, undetermined, unfixed, unpredictable, unproven, unreliable, unresolved, unsettled, unsure, unsustainable, unsustained, unverifiable, up for discussion, up in the air, vague
ASSOCIATED CONCEPTS: debatable issue, debatable question

DEBATE, *verb* agitate, altercate, argue, argue pros and cons, attempt to disprove, bandy, battle verbally, canvass, confer with, confute, consider, consult with, contend, contest, controvert, deliberate, disagree, discept, discuss, dispute, engage in oral controversy, examine a question, examine by argument, moot, negotiate, ponder, present reasons for and against, present varied opinions, ratiocinate, reason, refute, weigh, wrangle
ASSOCIATED CONCEPTS: debates of Constitutional Convention, freedom of debate, legislative debate

DEBAUCH, *verb* abuse, be intemperate, *corrumpere,* corrupt, debase, degenerate, degrade, *depravare,* deprave, despoil, dissipate, lead astray, molest, pervert, ruin, stuprate, sully, violate, *vitiare,* vitiate

DEBAUCHERY, *noun* bacchanalia, debauchment, dissipation, dissoluteness, excess, excessiveness, grossness, immoderation, impudicity, incontinence, intemperance, lasciviousness, lechery, lewdness, libertinage, libertinism, licentiousness, lust, obscenity, orgy, profligacy, salacity, seduction, *stuprum,* unrestraint

DEBAUCHMENT, *noun* defilement, defloration, deflowering, perversion, seduction, violation, vitiation

DEBENTURE, *noun* bond, negotiable instrument, paper money, pledge, title deed

DEBILITATE, *verb* cripple, denature, deprive of strength, devitalize, emasculate, enervate, enfeeble, eviscerate, exhaust, impair, incapacitate, injure, lessen, make feeble, make languid, reduce, render weak, sap the strength of, undermine, weaken

DEBIT, *noun* amount due, amount payable, arrears, bills, commitment, debt, deferred payment, *expensum,* indebtedness, liability, obligation, pecuniary due, sum owing, that which is owed
ASSOCIATED CONCEPTS: debit agent, debit and credit system, debit life insurance
FOREIGN PHRASES: *Perjuri sunt qui servatis verbis juramenti decipiunt aures eorum qui accipiunt.* They are perjured, who, by preserving the words of an oath, deceive the ears of those who receive it. *Non decipitur qui scit se decipi.* A person is not deceived who knows she is being deceived. *Fraus et dolus nemini patrocinari debent.* Fraud and deceit should not excuse anyone.

DEBT, *noun* account owing, account outstanding, *aes alienum,* amount due, amount owing, arrearage, arrears, balance owed, balance to pay, bill, debit, deferred payment, deficit, encumbrance, indebtedness, liability, money due, money owed, nonpayment, obligation, sum owed
ASSOCIATED CONCEPTS: action for debt, admission of debt, antecedent debt, bad debt, bad debt loss, bona fide debt, bonded debt, book debt, business debt, common debt, contingent debt, continuing debt, contract debts, corporate debt, creating a debt, creation of a debt, debt against estate, debt arising on contract, debt by contract, debt by loan, debt discharged, debt due, debt founded on contract, debt incurred, debt instruments, debt not yet due, debt of another, debt of bankrupt, debt of municipality, debt of record, debt owed, debt provable in bankruptcy, debt which is to become due, debtor and creditor, debts of deceased, dischargeable debt, equitable debt, evidence of debt, evidence of indebtedness, existing debt, fiduciary debt, fixed debt, floating debt, fraudulent debt, funded debt, holder of debt, imprisonment for debt, inability to pay debts as they mature, just debt, lawful debt, liquidated debt, moral debt, mutual debts, nonpayment of debt, partnership debt, pecuniary debt, preexisting debt, promise to pay, provable debt, public debt, public debt limitations, recovery of debt, secured debt, simple debt, situs of indebtedness, unliquidated debt, unsecured debt, worthless debt
FOREIGN PHRASES: *Debita sequuntur personam debitoris.* Debts follow the person of the debtor. *Debitor non praesumitur donare.* A debtor is not presumed to

make debts. *Reprobata pecunia liberat solventem.* Money refused releases the debtor. *Nemo potest sibi debere.* No one can be indebted to himself. *Incendium aere alieno non exuit debitorem.* A fire does not discharge a debtor from his debt. *Id solum nostrum quod debitis deductis nostrum est.* That only is ours which remains to us after deduction of our debts. *Chirographum non extans praesumitur solutum.* An evidence of debt not existing is presumed to have been paid. *Chirographum apud debitorem repertum praesumitur solutum.* An evidence of debt found in the debtor's hands is presumed to be paid. *Annua nec debitum judex non separat ipsum.* A judge does not divide annuities nor debt. *In satisfactionibus non permittitur amplius fieri quam semel factum est.* In settlements more must not be received than was received once for all. *Minus solvit, qui tardius solvit; nam et tempore minus solvitur.* He does not pay who pays too late; for, from the lapse of time, he is judged not to pay. *In omnibus obligationibus in quibus dies non ponitur, praesenti die debetur.* In all obligations in which no time is fixed for their fulfillment, the obligation is due immediately.

DEBTOR, *noun*   account debtor, borrower, drawee, loanee, mortgagor, obligor, pledgor

DEBUNK, *verb*   cast doubt upon, decry, deflate, derogate, detract, disabuse, disdain, disenchant, disillusion, disparage, expose, puncture, set right, undeceive

DECADENT, *adjective*   breaking down, cankered, corrosive, corrupt, crumbling, debauched, decaying, declining, decomposing, decrepit, degenerate, degenerating, depraved, deteriorated, deteriorating, dilapidated, disintegrating, effete, failing, falling, falling into ruin, feeble, immoral, in decadence, in decline, moldering, moribund, on the wane, regressive, retrograde, retrogressive, rotting, shabby, sinking, spoiled, spoiling, unprogressive, wasting, wasting away, weakened, withering, worn out

DECAY, *verb*   addle, atrophy, be reduced in worth, become enfeebled, become lower in quality, become putrescent, blight, break down, break up, canker, consume, corrode, corrupt, crumble, decline, decompose, decompound, degenerate, depreciate, deteriorate, dilapidate, disintegrate, fade, fail, fall apart, fall to pieces, grow worse, languish, molder, putrefy, render putrid, retrograde, retrogress, rot, ruin, shrivel, sink, spoil, waste away, wear away, wither, worsen

DECEASE, *verb*   cease existing, cease living, cease to be, cease to exist, cease to live, come to an end, demise, depart, depart from life, die, end one's life, expire, lose life, meet death, pass away, pass on, perish, succumb
ASSOCIATED CONCEPTS: decedent's estate

DECEASED, *adjective*   bereft of life, dead, defunct, demised, departed, deprived of life, destitute of life, devoid of life, exanimate, former, late, lifeless, no longer living, passed away, passed on, perished
ASSOCIATED CONCEPTS: dead man's statute, deceased child, deceased debtor, deceased persons, estate of deceased person, transaction or communication with deceased person, transaction with person since deceased
FOREIGN PHRASES: *Cadaver nullius in bonis.* A dead body is no one's property.

DECEDENT, *noun*   dead man, dead person, deceased, deceased person, demised, departed, he who has passed away, intestate individual, she who has expired, testator
ASSOCIATED CONCEPTS: decedent's estate, obligation of the decedent, transaction with decedent

DECEIT, *noun*   beguilement, camouflage, cheating, collusion, cozenage, craftiness, cunning, deceitfulness, deception, deceptiveness, delusiveness, dissembling, dissimulation, *dolus,* double-dealing, duplicity, equivocation, fabrication, *fallacia,* fallaciousness, falseheartedness, falsehood, falseness, falsification, falsity, forgery, fraud, fraudulence, *fraus,* furtiveness, indirection, insidiousness, insincerity, jugglery, lying, mendacity, misrepresentation, perfidy, perjury, pretense, prevarication, sham, sneakiness, subreption, surreptitiousness, treachery, trickery, underhanded practice, underhandedness, untruth, untruthfulness
ASSOCIATED CONCEPTS: action for fraud or deceit, discovery of the fraud or deceit, fraud or deceit, misrepresentation

DECEIVE, *verb*   befool, beguile, belie, blind, cheat, chicane, circumvent, cog, cozen, decoy, defraud, delude, dissemble, dissimulate, dupe, ensnare, entrap, fainaigue, fake, falsify, fool, forswear, gull, hoax, hoodwink, humbug, intrigue, inveigle, lie, misdirect, misguide, misinform, mislead, misrepresent, mulct, practice chicanery, practice deception, prevaricate, snare, sneak, swindle, take advantage, trap, trick, victimize

DECENTRALIZATION, *noun*   apportionment, branching out, breakdown, delegation, diffusion, disbandment, disintegration, disjoining, disjunction, dispersal, dispersion, dissipation, dissolution, distribution, division, fragmentation, partition, scattering, scission, section, separation, severance, subdivision

DECEPTION, *noun*   artifice, beguilement, blind, bluff, camouflage, charlatanry, cheat, chicane, chicanery, circumvention, con, counterfeit, cozenage, craft, craftiness, cunning, deceit, decoy, defraudation, defraudment, delusion, device, disguise, dishonesty, dissimulation, dodge, double-dealing, dupery, duplicity, equivocation, fabrication, fake, false appearance, false front, falsehood, falseness, falsification, feint, forgery, fraud, fraudulence, fraudulency, guile, hoax, humbuggery, illusion, imposition, imposture, indirection, indirectness, insincerity, intrigue, knavery, legerdemain, lie, machination, masquerade, mendacity, mirage, misrepresentation, obliquity, pretext, prevarication, rascality, roguery, ruse, sham, simulacrum, snare, stratagem, subterfuge, swindle, trap, trepan, trick, trickery, trickiness, trumpery, untruth, untruthfulness, unveracity, wile
ASSOCIATED CONCEPTS: confusion, deception doctrine
FOREIGN PHRASES: *Non decipitur qui scit se decipi.* He is not deceived who knows that he is being deceived. *Decipi quam fallere est tutius.* It is safer to be deceived than to deceive.

DECEPTIVE, *adjective*   artificial, beguiling, bogus, calculated to give a false impression, camouflaged, cheating, collusive, counterfeit, covinous, crafty, cunning, deceitful, deceiving, delusive, delusory, designing, disguised, dishonest, disingenuous, double dealing, fallacious, false, feigned, fraudulent, illusive, illusory, impostrous, indirect, insidious, insincere,

knavish, lying, mendacious, misleading, mock, oblique, obliquitous, pretended, prevaricating, scheming, seeming, sham, slippery, sly, sneaky, sophistic, sophistical, specious, spurious, subdolous, tricky, underhanded, untrue, wily
ASSOCIATED CONCEPTS: deceptive acts, deceptive advertising, deceptive practice, deceptively misdescriptive, deceptively similar

DECIDE, verb adjudge, adjudicate, adjust, agree, arbitrate, arrive at a judgment, ascertain, award, choose, choose a course of action, choose an alternative, choose an option, come to a conclusion, come to an agreement, come to terms, commit oneself, conclude, *constituere, decernere,* decree, determine, diagnose, *diiudicare,* dispose of, elect, end, establish, finalize, find, fix, form a resolution, form an opinion, hold, judge, make a choice, make a decision, make a selection, make up one's mind, opt, ordain, pass, pass judgment, pass sentence, pick, pronounce, reach a decision, reach a verdict, referee, resolve, rule, select, sentence, settle, sit in judgment, terminate, umpire, vote
ASSOCIATED CONCEPTS: decide a case, decide a motion, decided adversely, decided as a matter of law, decided on the merits, decided upon legal principles, jurisdiction to decide

DECISION *(Election),* **noun** choosing, judgment, pick, selection, will
ASSOCIATED CONCEPTS: appellate decision, decision upon the merits, lower court decision

DECISION *(Judgment),* **noun** choice, decree, determination, placitum, resolution, verdict

DECISIVE, adjective absolute, assured, authoritative, beyond all dispute, beyond all question, categorical, certain, characterized by decision, clear, clearly defined, commanding, compelling, conclusive, conclusory, consequential, critical, crucial, culminating, definite, definitive, determinant, determinative, determining, effectual, ernest, final, forceful, impelling, imperative, important, incontestable, indubious, inflexible, influential, intent upon, irreversible, irrevocable, momentous, of great consequence, peremptory, pivotal, positive, powerful, purposeful, questionless, resolute, resolved, significant, summary, thrustful, undoubted, unequivocal, unhesitating, unqualified, unquestionable, unquestioned, without doubt, without question
ASSOCIATED CONCEPTS: decisive proof

DECLAIM, verb address, deliver oratorically, descant, dilate, discourse, dissertate, expand, expatiate, expound, give a formal speech, harangue, hold forth, lecture, make a speech, orate, perorate, preach, prelect, proclaim, rant, recite, rhetorize, sermonize, speak, speak publicly, speak rhetorically, talk

DECLAMATION, noun address, allocution, art of speaking, *declamatio,* discourse, elocution, grandiloquence, harangue, lecture, oration, oratorical display, oratory, orotundity, *pronuntiatio,* public speaking, reading, recital, recitation, rhetoric, screed, sermon, speech, speechification, talk, tirade

DECLARANT, noun affiant, affirmant, complainant, one who affirms, one who asserts, one who proclaims, person who makes allegations, proclaimor, witness

DECLARATION, noun admission, affirmation, announcement, annunciation, assertion, attestation, bulletin, communication of knowledge, *communiqué, declaratio,* decree, decreement, *dictum,* edict, *edictum,* explicit utterance, exposition, expression, fiat, formal assertion, formal notice, *ipse dixit,* notice, notification, official bulletin, positive statement, *praedicatio,* presentation, proclamation, profession, promulgation, pronouncement, public announcement, publication, public notice, recitation, resolution, revelation, solemn averment, solemn avowal, statement, statement of facts, transmission of knowledge, ukase
ASSOCIATED CONCEPTS: declaration against interest, declaration against pecuniary interest, declaration against penal interest, declaration of candidacy, declaration of deceased person, declaration of dividends, declaration of estimated tax, declaration of homestead, declaration of independence, declaration of intent, declaration of intention, declaration of law, declaration of parties, declaration of public necessity, declaration of rights, declaration of trust, declaration of value, declaration of war, dying declarations, extrajudicial declaration, judicial declaration, narrative declaration, res gestae, self-serving declaration, spontaneous declaration

DECLARATORY, adjective annunciative, annunciatory, assertative, assertive, communicative, declarative, decretal, decretive, decretory, demonstrative, elucidating, enunciative, enunciatory, explanatory, expository, express, expressive, notificatory, proclamatory, promulgatory, serving to declare
ASSOCIATED CONCEPTS: declaratory act, declaratory action, declaratory decree, declaratory judgment, declaratory order, declaratory statute

DECLARATORY JUDGMENT, noun affirmation, announcement, declaration, enunciation, judgment of the court, non-executionary judgment

DECLARE, verb advance, affirm, announce, assert, asseverate, assure, aver, avow, bruit, claim, come out, communicate, contend, *declarare,* disclose, divulge, enounce, enunciate, herald, inform, maintain, make a declaration, make a statement, make known, *praedicare,* predicate, proclaim, profess, *profiteri,* pronounce, put forward, reveal, say, set forth, state, tell, utter
ASSOCIATED CONCEPTS: declare a nullity, declare insolvent, declare null and void

DECLINATION, noun abnegation, denial, disavowal, disclaimer, negation, nonacceptance, noncompliance, nonconsent, refusal, refusal of consent, rejection, renunciation, repudiation, unwillingness

DECLINE, noun abatement, act of crumbling, act of dwindling, act of falling away, act of lessening, act of losing ground, act of shrinking, act of slipping back, act of wasting away, act of weakening, act of worsening, atrophy, backward step, cheapening, collapse, consumption, contraction, corrosion, corruption, decadency, decay, decrease, decrement, decrepitude, decurrence, deflation, degeneracy, degenerateness, degeneration, *deminutio,* depreciation, descension, descent, deterioration, devaluation, dilapidation, diminishing, dissolution, downfall, downgrade, downhill, downtrend, downturn, downward inclination, downward incline, downward trend, drop, ebb, enfeeblement, erosion, fail-

ing, fall, falling away, falling-off, gradual crumbling, gradual impairment, lessening, loss, loss of value, lowering, marcescence, pejoration, period of decrease, plunge, recession, regress, regression, relapse, retreat, retroaction, retrocession, retrogradation, retrogression, reversion, ruin, setback, shrinkage, sinkage, sinking, slump, subsidence, wane
ASSOCIATED CONCEPTS: spoilage, waste

DECLINE *(Fall), verb*   come down, decay, degenerate, deteriorate, drop, drop in strength, ebb, fall, lapse, stoop, trend downward, wane, wither
ASSOCIATED CONCEPTS: decline in price

DECLINE *(Reject), verb*   abnegate, abstain, eschew, excuse oneself, hold back, rebuff, *recusare,* refuse, refuse to accept, renounce, *renueve,* repel, repudiate, resist, spurn, turn away, turn down, veto
ASSOCIATED CONCEPTS: decline an appointment, decline to accept an offer

DECONTAMINATE, *verb*   absterge, antisepticize, clean, cleanse, depurate, deterge, disinfect, fumigate, hygienize, lustrate, make aseptic, make disease-free, make germ-free, make healthful, make hygienic, make innoxious, make pure, make salubrious, make wholesome, purge, purify, rarefy, refine, remove pollutants, remove unhealthy agents, render harmless, render sanitary, render sterile, sanitize, scour, scrub, sterilize, unadulterate, uncorrupt, unpollute, untaint

DECORUM, *noun*   act demanded by social custom, amenability, amenableness, amenities, appropriate behavior, appropriateness, best behavior, best of taste, *bienséance,* civility, civilized behavior, code of what is fitting, conduct, conformity, consideration, *convenance,* convention, conventionality, conventions, conventions of society, correctness, courtesy, cultivated taste, custom, decencies, decency, decorousness, *decorum,* delicacy, demeanor, dictates of society, dignity, discrimination, etiquette, fastidiousness, fittingness, form, formalities, formality, gentility, gentlemanliness, good form, good manners, good taste, goodness, grace, mannerliness, manners, modesty, mores, natural courtesy, nice appreciation, nicety, orderliness, point of etiquette, poise, polish, polished manners, politeness, prescribed code of conduct, proper thing to do, properness, propriety, protocol, punctilio, punctiliousness, refined manners, refined taste, refinement, requirement of polite society, respect, respectability, respectful deportment, right note, right thing to do, rules of conduct, sedateness, seemliness, social code, social conduct, social graces, social procedures, social usage, standard, suitability, suitableness, tact, tastefulness, that which is proper

DECOY, *noun*   allure, allurement, ambush, attraction, bait, blind, camouflage, deception, disguise, diversion, enticement, imitation, inducement, *inlex,* inveiglement, misleader, simulation, trap, trick
ASSOCIATED CONCEPTS: entrapment

DECREASE, *noun*   abatement, abbreviation, abridgment, alleviation, attenuation, constriction, contraction, curtailment, cut, cutback, deceleration, declension, declination, decline, decline and fall, decrement, decrescence, deduction, deflation, *deminutio,* depreciation, depression, deterioration, devaluation, diminishment, diminution, dissipation, downtrend,

downturn, downward trend, drop, dwindling, ebb, fall, falling-off, getting less, *imminutio,* lessening, loss, loss of value, lowering, making less, mitigation, narrowing, reduction, reflux, restriction, retrenchment, shortening, shrinkage, shrinking, sinking, slowing down, slump, subduction, subsidence, subtraction, wane, waning, weakening
ASSOCIATED CONCEPTS: decrease in payment, decrease in price, decrease in value, decreased capacity, decreased cost, decreased earning capacity, decreased or diminished mental capacity

DECREASE, *verb*   abate, abbreviate, abridge, allay, attenuate, bate, be consumed, become smaller, blunt, cause to diminish, coarctate, compact, compress, concentrate, condense, constrict, constringe, contract, curtail, cut, cut back, cut down, cut off, cut short, dampen, decelerate, decline, deduct, deflate, *deminuere,* depreciate, depress, detract from, die down, diminish, drain, drop, dwindle, ebb, emaciate, *extenuare,* fall, fall behind, fall below, fall off, go downhill, grow less, *imminuere,* lessen, level off, lower, make brief, make less, make smaller, mark down, melt away, minimize, mitigate, narrow, pare, prune, quell, rake off, recede, reduce, render less, retrench, roll back, run down, scale down, shave, shorten, shrink, sink, slacken, slash, slump, strike off, subduct, subside, subtract, suffer loss, take away, take off, taper, trim, wane
ASSOCIATED CONCEPTS: decrease in payment, decrease in price, decrease in value, decreased capacity, decreased cost, decreased earning capacity, decreased or diminished mental capacity

DECREE, *noun*   adjudgment, adjudication, authoritative decision, award, command, commandment, decision, declaration, *decretum,* dictate, direction, edict, *edictum,* fiat, final judgment, finding, imperative, interdiction, judgment, judicial decision, mandate, opinion, order, order of the court, *placitum,* proclamation, pronouncement, *pronunciamiento,* resolution, ruling, ruling of the court, *senatus consultum,* sentence, standing order, ukase, verdict
ASSOCIATED CONCEPTS: alimony decree, annulment decree, bankruptcy decree, consent decree, declaratory decree, decree for payment of money, decree for possession of property, *decree nisi,* decree of a court of competent jurisdiction, decree of court of record, decree of dismissal, decree of distribution, decree of nullity, decree of support, *decree pro confesso,* default decree, deficiency decree, divorce decree, entry of decree, final decree, foreclosure decree, foreign decree, interlocutory decree, joint decree, judicial decree, summary decree, supplemental decree

DECREE, *verb*   adjudge, adjudicate, award, charge, command, deliver judgment, dictate, direct, establish, exact, find, give judgment, give orders, impose, instruct, issue a fiat, issue a proclamation, issue a ukase, issue an edict, judge, order, pass judgment, prescribe, proclaim, promulgate, pronounce, require, rule, sanction
ASSOCIATED CONCEPTS: alimony decree, annulment decree, bankruptcy decree, consent decree, decree by confession, *decree nisi,* decree of dismissal, *decree pro confesso,* default decree, deficiency decree, divorce decree, entry of decree, final decree, foreclosure decree, foreign decree, interlocutory decree, summary decree, supplemental decree

DECREMENT, noun abatement, abridgment, contraction, curtailment, cut, damage, declension, decrease, decrescence, deduction, deficit, depletion, diminishment, diminution, dissipation, drain, erosion, exhaustion, expenditure, leak, leakage, lessening, loss, shortcoming, shortening, shrinkage, spoilage, subtraction, wastage, waste, wear and tear

DECRETAL, adjective binding, commanded, commanding, decreed, decretive, decretory, demanded, directive, instructive, jussive, law-giving, mandatory, nomothetic, ordered, preceptive, prescriptive
ASSOCIATED CONCEPTS: decretal paragraph

DECRY, verb admonish, be unable to respect, belittle, berate, bring discredit on, bring into disrepute, censure, censure as faulty, clamor against, condemn, condemn as worthless, contemn, criticize, cry down, cry out against, declaim against, degrade, denigrate, denounce, deny respect, deprecate, depreciate, depreciate publicly, deride, derogate, despise, detract, detract from, disapprove, disapprove of, discredit, disdain, disesteem, dismiss, disparage, dispraise, disprize, disrespect, fail to appreciate, fault, feel utter contempt for, find fault, find nothing to praise, have no regard for, have no respect for, have no use for, hold cheap, hold in contempt, inveigh against, make little of, malign, not respect, not speak well of, *obtrectare*, protest against, raise a hue and cry against, raise one's voice against, reject, remonstrate against, reprehend, revile, ridicule, scorn, set at nought, set no value on, speak disparagingly of, speak ill of, speak slightingly of, spurn, vilify, vilipend, *vituperare*

DEDICATE, verb address to, award, bestow, confer, confer honor on, *consecrare*, consecrate, convey, *dedicare*, devote, do honor, donate, endow, enshrine, give, give a prize, give earnestly, give honor, hallow, honor, immortalize, inscribe, offer to give, pay honor, philanthropize, present, reflect honor on, render honor to, set apart, set apart for special use, set aside, vest

DEDICATION, noun bestowal, celebration, consecration, devotion, endowment, enshrinement, giving, gratuity, honoring, immortalization, inscription, offering, ordination, philanthropy, presentation, presentment, setting apart, setting aside for a particular purpose, solemn appropriation
ASSOCIATED CONCEPTS: act of dedication, actual dedication, appropriation for a public use, appropriation of a charitable use, common-law dedication, constructive dedication, dedication by estoppel, dedication of property for public use, dedication to a charitable use, dedication to a public use, express dedication, implied dedication, irrevocable dedication, manner of dedication, private dedication, public dedication, public easement, revocation of offer of dedication, statutory dedication, unaccepted dedication

DEDUCE, verb apply reason, arrive at a conclusion, ascertain, assume, calculate, come to a conclusion, conclude, conjecture, consider probable, construe, deduct, deem, derive, determine, divine, draw a conclusion, educe, extract, gather, guess, infer, judge, ratiocinate, rationalize, reason, suppose, surmise, think, think likely, trace, understand

DEDUCT *(Conclude by reasoning)*, **verb** apply reason, arrive at a conclusion, ascertain, assume, calculate, come to a conclusion, conclude, conjecture, consider probable, construe, deduce, deem, derive, determine, divine, draw a conclusion, educe, extract, gather, guess, infer, judge, rationalize, ratiocinate, reason, suppose, surmise, think, think likely, trace, understand

DEDUCT *(Reduce)*, **verb** abate, attentuate, bate, cheapen, cut, cut down, decrease, deflate, deplete, depreciate, devaluate, dilute, diminish, discount, downgrade, dwindle, lessen, lower, make less, make smaller, mark down, remove, render few, shrink, slash, strike off, strip, subduct, subtract, take away, take off, trim, truncate, withdraw
ASSOCIATED CONCEPTS: tax credit, tax deduction

DEDUCTIBLE *(Capable of being deducted from taxes)*, **adjective** able to be subducted, able to be subtracted for tax purposes, allowable, capable of being deducted, capable of being rebated, discountable, likely to decrease taxes, recoupable, removable
ASSOCIATED CONCEPTS: deductible business expense, deductible debt, deductible expense, deductible loss, deductible policy

DEDUCTIBLE *(Provable)*, **adjective** able to be confirmed, able to be shown, ascertainable, based on evidence, based on proof, capable of being figured out, capable of being proved, conclusible, corroborative, deducible, demonstrable, derivable, documentable, expectable, following, illative, inferable, inferential, likely, presumed, presumptive, probable, ratiocinative, substantiable, supportable, sustainable, testable, traceable, valid, verifiable

DEDUCTION *(Conclusion)*, **noun** assumption, calculation, divination, hypothesis, illation, implication, logical process, logical sequence, opinion, postulate, postulation, ratiocination, rationalization, reasoned judgment, supposal, supposition, surmise, theory, thesis

DEDUCTION *(Diminution)*, **noun** abatement, abridgment, attenuation, cut, decline, decrease, decrement, decrescence, *deductio, deminutio*, discount, dwindling, elimination, lessening, lowering, making less, minimization, reduction, removal, shortening, shrinkage, subduction, subtraction, withdrawal
ASSOCIATED CONCEPTS: allowable deduction, business deductions, deduction directed by law, deduction from purchase price, deduction of cost, deduction of expense, deductions from account, deductions from salary, income tax deductions, marital deduction, special deduction

DEDUCTIVE, adjective analytic, analytical, deducible, evidential, following, inferable, inferential, logical, rational, reasoned, resultant

DEED, noun assignment, authentication, certificate, charter, conveyance, covenant, document, document which passes a present interest, instrument, instrument which transfers title to realty, muniments, record, release, signed and delivered instrument, transfer, transference
ASSOCIATED CONCEPTS: ancient deed, bargain and sale deed, commissioner of deeds, contract for deed, deed by way of mortgage, deed duly registered, deed for a nominal sum, deed in fee simple, deed in the nature of a mortgage, deed of assignment, deed of conveyance, deed

of covenant, deed of gift, deed of land, deed of trust, deed with covenant of warranty, estoppel by deed, executed deed, general warranty deed, gift deed, good and effectual deed, good and sufficient deed, joint deeds, mineral deed, quitclaim deed, recorded deed, registers of deeds, rescission of deed, reservation in a deed, sheriff's deed, simultaneous deeds, special warranty deed, tax deed, trust deed, void or voidable deeds, warranty deed
FOREIGN PHRASES: *Interpretatio chartarum benigne facienda est, ut res magis valeat quam pereat.* The construction of deeds should be liberal in order that the transaction may be effective rather than fail. *Traditio loqui facit chartam.* Delivery gives voice to the words of a deed. *Mala grammatica non vitiat chartam; sed in expositione instrumentorum ma la grammatica quo ad fieri possit evitanda est.* Bad grammar does not vitiate a deed; but, in the drafting of instruments, bad grammar should, as far as possible, be avoided. *Grammatica falsa non vitiat chartam.* False grammar does not vitiate a deed. *Charta de non ente non valet.* A deed of a thing not in being is invalid. *Facta tenent multa quae fieri prohibentur.* Deeds contain many things which are prohibited to be done. *Allegatio contra factum non est admittenda.* An allegation contrary to the deed is not admissible.

DEEM, *verb*   account, adjudge, adopt an opinion, assume, be inclined to think, be of the opinion, be under the impression, believe, believe on consideration, call, conceive, conclude, consider, decide, determine, embrace an opinion, esteem, feel, form a judgment, form an opinion, have an opinion, have the impression, hazard an opinion, hold, hold an opinion, hold in belief, imagine, judge, look upon, opine, perceive, presume, pronounce judgment, regard, suppose, surmise, suspect, take for, take it to be, think, view as
ASSOCIATED CONCEPTS: deemed advisable, deemed to be in the best interests of the child

DEFACE, *verb*   begrime, blacken, blemish, blot, blot out, blotch, blur, cover up, crack, cross out, damage, deform, *deformare,* delete, deprive of form, despoil, destroy, destroy form, disfigure, distort, efface, erase, expange, flaw, *foedare,* foul, hurt, impair, impair the legibility of, impair the looks of, injure, make illegible, make ugly, make unsightly, mangle, mar, mar the appearance of, mark, misshape, mutilate, obliterate, render illegible, rub off, rub out, scar, scratch, scratch out, smear, smudge, soil, spoil, spoil the look of, spot, stain, strike out, sully, tarnish, unshape, warp, wipe away
ASSOCIATED CONCEPTS: cancellation by defacing, defacing public property

DEFACEMENT, *noun*   blemish, blot, blotch, blotting out, crack, damage, defect, deformation, deformity, destruction, discoloration, disfiguration, disfigurement, distortion, effacement, erasure, fault, flaw, impairment, injury, injury to outward appearance, marring, mutilation, obliteration, scar, scratch, smear, smudge, soiling, splotch, spot, stain, tarnish, unsightliness, vandalism, wear and tear, wrecking activities
ASSOCIATED CONCEPTS: defacement of ballots, defacement of documents, defacement of labels, defacement of monuments, defacement of public property

DEFALCATE, *verb*   appropriate to one's own use, cheat, defraud, divert funds, embezzle, falsify accounts,

misapply funds, misappropriate money, misemploy funds, misuse entrusted monies, obtain money under false pretenses, peculate, purloin, rob, steal, swindle, take by fraud, thieve

DEFAMATION, *noun*   abuse, aspersion, calumniation, calumny, denigration, derogation, detraction, discommendation, disparagement, disrepute, false accusation, false publication, false report, imputation, infamy, insinuation, insult, invective, libel, obloquy, scandal, slander, slur, smear, smirch, traducement, untruth
ASSOCIATED CONCEPTS: defamation against title, defamation of business or profession, defamation of character, defamation per quod, defamation per se, defamatory publication, defamatory upon its face, defamatory words, injury to character or reputation, injury to profession or business
FOREIGN PHRASES: *Inveniens libellum famosum et non corrumpens punitur.* A person who finds a libel and does not destroy it is punished.

DEFAME, *verb*   accuse, accuse falsely, anathematize, asperse, assail, belittle, berate, besmear, besmirch, bespatter, blacken, blemish, brand, bring disrepute upon, call names, *calumniari,* calumniate, cast aspersions on, censure, charge, condemn, criticize, damage one's reputation, decry, degrade, denigrate, denounce, depreciate, destroy one's reputation, discredit, disgrace, dishonor, disparage, dispraise, falsify, fulminate, gibbet, give a bad name, impeach, indict, injure the good name of, injure the good reputation of, inveigh against, lessen one's reputation, libel, lower, malign, objurgate, *obtrectare,* ostracize, pillory, put in a bad light, reprehend, revile, run down, scandalize, shame, slander, slur, smear, smirch, spatter, speak evil, speak ill, speak ill of, speak of slightingly, stain the character of, stigmatize, sully, taint, tarnish, traduce, vilify, vilipend, vituperate
ASSOCIATED CONCEPTS: defamation, defamation per quod, defamation per se, defamatory per se, defamatory upon its face, defamatory words, disparagement, injury to character or reputation, injury to profession or business, libel, slander

DEFAULT, *noun*   abrogation, *ad vadimonium non venire,* arrear, avoidance, bankruptcy, breach, breach of orders, delinquence, delinquency, dereliction, dereliction of duty, dishonoring, disregard, evasion of duty, failure of credit, failure of duty, failure to answer, failure to appear, failure to meet one's obligations, failure to pay, financial disaster, insolvency, insufficient funds, neglect, nonfulfillment, nonobservance, nonperformance, omission, pretermission, refusal to pay, repudiation, *vadimonium deserere,* violation of duty
ASSOCIATED CONCEPTS: date of default, declaration of default, default decree, default in payment, default of issue, default or misconduct in office, excusable default, failure to pay money due, failure to perform duty, judgment by default, material default, motion for default, motion to open default, motion to vacate default judgment, willful default

DEFAULT, *verb*   *ad vadimonium non venire,* avoid, be deficient, be delinquent, be derelict, be faithless, be in arrears, be in debt, be neglectful, be negligent, be remiss, be unfaithful, become unable to meet obligations, breach the agreement, break one's trust, break the contract, desert, dishonor, disregard one's duty, dis-

regard one's obligations, dodge, elude, evade, fail, fail in duty, fail to act, fail to answer, fail to appear, fail to meet financial engagements, fail to pay, fail to perform, forsake, ignore one's obligations, lapse, lose by failure to appear, neglect one's duty, not pay, omit what is due, renege, repudiate, shirk, shirk one's duty, shun, stop payment, *vandimonium deserere,* withhold payment
ASSOCIATED CONCEPTS: date of default, default decree, default in office, default in payment, default of issue, default or misconduct in office, excusable default, judgment by default, motion for default, motion to open default, motion to vacate default judgment, opening of default, willful default

DEFEASANCE, noun abolishment, abolition, abrogation, annulment, breakup, canceling, cancellation, cassation, cessation, close, conclusion, deprivation, disallowance, discharge, discontinuance, disendowment, disestablishment, dissolution, end, end of the matter, ending, expiration, finish, invalidation, limit, negation, nullification, ousting, recall, removal, repeal, replacement, rescindment, rescission, retractation, retraction, reversal, reversion, revocation, revokement, stoppage, supersession, suppression, undoing, vacation, voidance, windup, withdrawal
ASSOCIATED CONCEPTS: condition, defeasance clause, defeasance of contract, defeasance of title, defeasible estate

DEFEASIBLE, adjective confutable, dismissible, disprovable, dissoluble, *functus officio,* nullifiable, refutable, removable, revocable, subject to being abrogated, subject to being annulled, subject to being cancelled, subject to being divested, subject to being invalidated, subject to being repealed, subject to being retracted, subject to being revoked, subject to being taken away, subject to being withdrawn, terminable, voidable
ASSOCIATED CONCEPTS: defeasible deed, defeasible estate, defeasible fee, defeasible interest, defeasible remainder, defeasible title, determinable fee

DEFEAT, noun beating, breakdown, collapse, confutation, default, destruction, disappointment, downfall, failure, invalidation, loss, nonfulfillment, overthrow, refutation, *repulsa,* ruin, ruination, setback, thwarting, undoing, vanquishment
ASSOCIATED CONCEPTS: defeat a cause of action, defeat the purpose, defeat the rights, defeated candidate, defeated party

DEFEAT, verb beat, block, checkmate, confound, conquer, contravene, crush, demolish, drub, foil, frustrate, gain control over, halt, master, outwit, overcome, overmaster, overpower, overthrow, overwhelm, prevail over, put down, quell, refute, rout, smash, squelch, subdue, subjugate, *superare,* suppress, surmount, thwart, triumph over, trounce, upset, vanquish, *vincere,* victimize
ASSOCIATED CONCEPTS: defeat a cause of action, defeat a will, defeat or impair jurisdiction, defeat the purpose, defeat the rights

DEFECT, noun blemish, blot, damage, deficiency, deformity, demerit, deviation, drawback, failing, fault, faultiness, flaw, foible, frailty, impairment, imperfection, impotency, inadequacy, incompleteness, incompletion, infirmity, insufficiency, lack, *mendum,* mistake, mutilation, shortcoming, weakness

ASSOCIATED CONCEPTS: actionable defect, concealed defect, cure of defects, dangerous defect, defect appearing upon face of record, defect in description, defect in form, defect in material or workmanship, defect in title, defect of parties, defect of substance, hidden defects, immaterial defects, inherent defect, jurisdictional defect, knowledge of defect, latent defect, legal defect, material defect, mental defect, obvious defect, open and obvious defect, patent defect, products liability, structural defects

DEFECT, verb abandon allegiance, abdicate, abscond, apostasize, back out, be disloyal, betray, break away, break fealty, break with, cast off, change sides, default, demit, depart, desert, disavow, disobey, disown, forsake, leave, leave unlawfully, mutiny, prove treacherous, quit, rebel, reject, renege, renounce, repudiate, resign, revolt, run away, secede, tergiversate, transfer, violate one's oath, withdraw one's support

DEFECTIVE, adjective amiss, awry, below par, below standards, beneath standards, blemished, broken, bruised, crippled, damaged, deficient, deformed, distorted, falling short, faultful, faulty, flawed, impaired, imperfect, *imperfectus,* inadequate, incomplete, incondite, incorrect, infirm, injured, inoperative, insufficient, lacking, lame, marred, mutilated, out of order, unfinished, unsound, wanting, warped, weak
ASSOCIATED CONCEPTS: defective and unsafe condition, defective condition, defective construction, defective in form, defective in substance, defective instrumentality, defective machinery, defective materials, defective or dangerous condition, defective product, defective service of process, defective title, defective workmanship or material, defective writ, mentally defective, products liability

DEFEND, verb advocate, allege in support, argue for, champion, espouse, guard, justify, maintain, plead for, plead one's cause, promote a cause, propound, protect, safeguard, shield, stand up for, support, sustain, uphold, urge reasons for
ASSOCIATED CONCEPTS: effectiveness of counsel, opportunity to defend

DEFENDANT, noun the accused, accused litigant, accused party, charged party, party against whom a complaint is lodged, party against whom charges are pending, party who is sued, respondent
ASSOCIATED CONCEPTS: codefendant, defendant's rights, indispensable party defendant, necessary party defendant, nominal defendant, party defendant, principal defendant, proper party defendant, third party defendants
FOREIGN PHRASES: *Favorabiliores rei potius quam actores habentur.* The condition of the defendant is to be favored rather than that of the plaintiff. *Reus excipiendo fit actor.* The defendant by his pleading may make himself a plaintiff. *Melior est conditio possidentis, et rei quam actoris.* The condition of the possessor and that of the defendant is better than that of the plaintiff. *Habemus optimum testem, confitentem reum.* We have the best witness, a confessing defendant. *Melior est conditio defendentis.* The position of the defendant is the better one.

DEFENSE, noun confutation, counterargument, espousal, justification, parry, preservation, protection, rebuttal, resistance against attack, support, warding off

ASSOCIATED CONCEPTS: affirmative defense, alibi defense, anticipating a defense, assist in his own defense, coercion as a defense, complete defense, defense of a third person, defense of action, defense of estoppel, defense of insanity, defense on the merits, defensive pleading, equitable defense, frivolous defense, ground of defense, incomplete defense, inconsistent defenses, legal defenses, meritorious defense, motion to strike defense, negative defense, new defense, partial defense, personal defense, self-defense, sham defense, special defense

FOREIGN PHRASES: *Peccatum peccato addit qui culpae quam facit patrocinium defensionis adjungit.* He adds one offense to another who connects a wrong which he has committed with his defense. *Vani timoris justa excusatio non est.* A frivolous fear is not a lawful excuse. *Nemo prohibetur pluribus defensionibus uti.* No one is prohibited from making use of several defenses. *Impotentia excusat legem.* Performing a legal duty excuses from the performance. *Quodcunque aliquis ob tutelam corporis sui fecerit, jure id fecisse videtur.* Whatever any one does in defense of his person, that he is deemed to have done legally. *Vim vi repellere licit. modo fiat moderamine inculpatae tutelae, non ad sumendam vindictam, sed ad propulsandam injuriam.* It is lawful to repel force by force, provided it be done with the moderation of blameless defense, not for the purpose of taking revenge, but to repel injury.

DEFENSIBLE, adjective armed, believable, condonable, credible, defendable, exculpatory, excusable, impregnable, invincible, invulnerable, justifiable, justified, maintainable, pardonable, plausible, prepared, sound, supportable, tenable, unassailable, unattackable, vindicable, vindicatory, warrantable

DEFER *(Put off), verb* adjourn, arrest, be dilatory, bide, delay, detain, *differre,* discontinue, extend, file, forbear, forestall, gain time, hesitate, hinder, hold back, hold in abeyance, hold off, hold up, impede, interfere, interrupt, intervene, keep pending, lay aside, linger, *obsequi,* obstruct, pause, pigeonhole, postpone, pretermit, procrastinate, prolong, prorogue, put aside, recess, respite, retard, set aside, shelve, stall, stave off, stay, suspend, table, wait, withhold
ASSOCIATED CONCEPTS: deferred charges, deferred compensation, deferred dividend, deferred income, deferred legacy, deferred payments, deferred premiums, deferred sentence, deferred wage

DEFER *(Yield in judgment), verb* abide by, abstain, accede, accept, accord, accord superiority to, acknowledge, acquiesce, agree, assent, capitulate, cede, comply, conform to, consent, do honor to, esteem, fall in with, give assent, give consent, give in, give way, go along with, hearken, hold in esteem, honor, *obsequi,* pay respect to, regard, respect, show courtesy, show respect, submit, submit for determination, submit in judgment to, subscribe to, venerate, yield, yield in opinion to
ASSOCIATED CONCEPTS: defer to an administrative agency's decision

DEFERENCE, noun acquiescence, assent, complaisance, compliance, consideration, courtesy, esteem, honor, nonresistance, obedience, politeness, regard, respect, respectfulness, submission, submissiveness, submittal, willingness

DEFERMENT, noun adjournment, cunctation, dalliance, deferral, delay, dilatoriness, extension, extension of time, interruption, moratorium, postponement, procrastination, prolongation, prorogation, putting off, respite, stoppage, suspension, tabling, tarrying, wait
ASSOCIATED CONCEPTS: deferment of action, draft deferment

DEFIANCE, noun affront, challenge, contumacy, dare, daring, disobedience, disregard, disregard of orders, gage, impudence, impudency, insolence, insubmission, insubordination, insurgence, insurgency, insurrection, invitation to combat, mutiny, noncompliance, noncooperation, opposition, oppugnation, *provocatio,* rebellion, rebelliousness, recalcitrance, recalcitrancy, recalcitration, recusancy, resistance, revolt, revolution, sedition, strike, stubbornness, unruliness, uprising
ASSOCIATED CONCEPTS: in defiance of the law

DEFICIENCY, noun absence, dearth, defect, deficit, deprivation, destitution, failing, failure to comply, falling short, fault, faultiness, flaw, foible, impairment, imperfection, inadequacy, inadequateness, incompleteness, incompletion, infirmity, insufficiency, lack, loss, meagerness, need, noncompletion, nonfulfillment, nonperformance, omission, paucity, penury, poverty, privation, scarcity, short supply, shortage, shortcoming, sparsity, ullage, want, weakness
ASSOCIATED CONCEPTS: deficiency assessment, deficiency bill, deficiency decree, deficiency judgment, deficiency tax, income tax deficiency, liability for deficiency, mental deficiency, notice of deficiency, recovery of deficiency, tax deficiency

DEFICIENT, adjective attenuated, barren, below par, blemished, defective, depleted, devoid, disappointing, discontenting, empty, falling short, faulty, few, flawed, hollow, impaired, imperfect, impoverished, in arrears, inadequate, incompetent, incomplete, inferior, *inops,* insubstantial, insufficient, jejune, lacking, less than necessary, *mancus,* marred, meager, missing, not enough, not satisfying, not up to normal, not up to par, paltry, partial, poor, scant, scanty, scarce, short, shy, sketchy, skimpy, slight, small, sparing, sparse, starved, substandard, thin, too little, unample, uncompleted, undeveloped, unequal to, unfinished, unfulfilled, unfurnished, unnourishing, unsatisfactory, unsound, unsufficing, unsupplied, unprovided, void of, wanting, weak
ASSOCIATED CONCEPTS: deficiency judgment, mentally deficient, totally deficient

DEFICIT, noun absence, arrears, balance to pay, dearth, default, deficiency, financial shortage, inadequacy, incompleteness, insufficiency, lack, loss, meagerness, omission, overdraft, paucity, scantiness, scarcity, shortage, shortcoming, shortness

DEFILEMENT, noun abomination, adulteration, besmirching, blackening, contamination, corruption, corruption of purity, debasement, debauchment, deflowering, degradation, demoralization, denigration, depravation, desecration, despoilment, devastation, dirtiness, disgrace, dishonor, filthiness, foulness, impairment, indignity, insult, *macula,* outrage, ravagement, ruination, shamefulness, smearing, sullying, turpitude, uncleanliness, uncleanness, violation

DEFINE, *verb*   characterize, characterize precisely, *circumscribere,* clarify, construe, *definire,* delineate, denominate, depict the essential qualities of, describe, describe the properties of, designate, determine the essential qualities of, determine with precision, differentiate, elucidate, enumerate, establish, exemplify, explain, explain the nature of, expound, fix, fix the meaning, fix with precision, formalize, formulate, give the meaning, identify, illustrate, individualize, individuate, interpret, label, limit, make clear, mark the limits, name, prescribe, render, render precise, specify, spell out, state the meaning of, state the meaning precisely, tell the meaning, term, throw light upon, translate
ASSOCIATED CONCEPTS: defined by law, defined by statute

DEFINITE, *adjective*   absolute, accurate, actual, allowed, ascertained, assured, attested, authoritative, axiomatic, beyond all dispute, beyond all question, bound, bounded with precision, categorical, certain, certified, *certus,* clear, clear-cut, conclusive, confident, *constitutus,* convinced, correct, decided, decisive, *definitus,* demonstrable, determinate, determined, distinct, doubtless, ensured, established, evident, evidential, exact, existing, express, firm, fixed, fully convinced, granted, guaranteed, having fixed limits, immutable, inappealable, incommutable, incontestable, indefeasible, indisputable, indubious, indubitable, inescapable, inevasible, inevitable, inexorable, inflexible, insured, intransmutable, invariable, inviolate, irrefragable, irrefutable, irresistible, irreversible, irrevocable, persuaded, positive, precisely bounded, quantified, questionless, real, reliable, resolute, satisfied, secure, settled, stated, strictly defined, tested, true, unchanging, unconfuted, uncontested, undeniable, undisputed, undoubting, unequivocal, unerring, unfailing, unfaltering, unhesitating, unimpeachable, univocal, unmistakable, unqualified, unquestioned, unrefuted, unshaken, unsuspecting, unsuspicious, unwavering, veritable, well-defined, well-marked
ASSOCIATED CONCEPTS: definite and certain, definite class, definite description, definite failure of issue, definite interest, definite location, definite period, definite quantity, definite sentence, definite term

DEFINITION, *noun*   clarification, decipherment, decoding, delimitation, delineation, demarcation, description, elucidation, equivalent meaning, exact meaning, exact statement, explanation, explication, expressed meaning, formulation, identification, illumination, interpretation, making intelligible, meaning, representation, simplification, statement of meaning, synonym, translation
FOREIGN PHRASES: *Omnis definitio in jure civili periculosa est, parum est enim ut non subverti possit.* Every definition in the law is dangerous, because there is little that cannot be subverted.

DEFINITIVE, *adjective*   absolute, accurate, ascertained, authentic, authenticated, authoritative, beyond a doubt, beyond all dispute, closing, complete, completed, conclusive, conclusory, confirmative, consummate, crowning, decided, decisive, definite, determinate, determinative, determining, exact, exhaustive, final, fixed, incontestable, incontrovertible, indisputable, indubitable, irrefutable, last, most complete, most precise, perfect, supreme, terminational, terminative, thorough, ultimate, unassailable, uncontested, undeni-

able, undisputed, undoubted, unimpeachable, unquestionable, without doubt, without question
ASSOCIATED CONCEPTS: definitive decree, definitive judgment, definitive order

DEFLAGRATE, *verb*   blaze, burn, burn fiercely, burn up, burst into flame, conflagrate, consume, cremate, fire, flame, flame up, flare, flare up, flash, ignite, incandesce, incinerate, inflame, reduce to ashes, scorch, sear, singe, torrefy

DEFRAUD, *verb*   befool, beguile, bilk, cheat, cheat out of money, *circumscribere,* commit breach of trust, cozen, *defraudare,* deceive, delude, deprive dishonestly, dupe, embezzle, fleece, fool, hoax, inveigle, levant, mislead, mulct, obtain money on false pretenses, peculate, practice chicanery, practice fraud upon, swindle, take advantage of, take by fraud, take in, trick
ASSOCIATED CONCEPTS: conspiracy to defraud, intent to defraud, use of mails to defraud

DEFRAY, *verb*   adjust, bear the cost, bear the expense, compensate, contribute, disburse, discharge, expend, foot the bill, give compensation for, honor a bill, indemnify, liquidate, make payment, make repayment, make restitution, meet the bill, pay, pay an indemnity, pay compensation, pay for, pay one's way, pay reparations, pay the costs, redeem, refund, reimburse, remit, remunerate, repay, requite, satisfy a claim, *solvere,* spend, stand the cost, *suppeditare*
ASSOCIATED CONCEPTS: defraying cost, defraying expenses

DEFT, *adjective*   able, accomplished, adept, adroit, agile, apt, canny, capable, clever, competent, cunning, dexterous, efficient, expert, facile, flexible, gifted, good at, handy, ingenious, light, masterful, masterly, nimble, nimble-fingered, practiced, proficient, qualified, quick, resourceful, sharp, skilled, skillful, slick, smooth, talented

DEFUNCT, *adjective*   abrogated, all gone, all over with, annulled, cancelled, dead, deceased, demised, departed, devoid of life, exanimate, expired, extinct, finished, gone, gone out of existence, inactive, inefficacious, inoperative, lifeless, *mortuus,* no longer living, no more, not endowed with life, not existing, not in action, not in force, obsolete, old-fashioned, out of fashion, passed away, past, perished, terminated, unknown, unobserved, unused, vanished, void, without life
ASSOCIATED CONCEPTS: defunct business, defunct corporation

DEFY, *verb*   affront, assume a fighting attitude, battle, beard, brave, breast, buck, challenge, conflict with, confront, dare, disobey, disregard, flout, front, mutiny, oppose, outface, *provocare,* rebel, resist, resist openly, stand up against, withstand
ASSOCIATED CONCEPTS: defy a court order

DEGENERATE, *noun*   corrupt person, debased person, debauchee, decadent person, degraded person, depraved person, derelict, disreputable person, immoral person, pervert, rapscallion, recreant, scamp, scapegrace, transgressor, wastrel, worthless person

DEGENERATE, *verb*   atrophy, be destroyed, be reduced in worth, be worse, become depraved, become deteriorated, become enfeebled, become impaired, become lower in quality, become notably worse, become perverted, become tainted, become worse, break up, canker, come down, consume, corrupt, crumble, debase, debase in quality, debauch, decay, decline, decompose, *degenerare,* degrade, deprave, derange, deteriorate, dilapidate, disband, disintegrate, disorder, dissolve, ebb, erode, fall apart, fall away, fall into decay, fall off, fall to pieces, get worse, go bad, go to pieces, grow weak, grow worse, languish, lapse, lessen in worth, lose morale, make inferior in value, make lower in character, make worse, moulder, poison, pollute, putrefy, render chaotic, retrogress, rot, run down, shrivel, sicken, sink, sink to a lower condition, taint, vitiate, wane, waste, wear, wear away, wither, worsen

DEGRADATION, *noun* abasement, abjection, baseness, debasement, decadence, decadency, declension, declination, decline, *dedecus,* degeneratess, degeneration, demotion, deprival of honor, deterioration, discredit, disgrace, dishonor, dismissal from office, disrepute, fall from repute, humiliation, *ignominia,* ignominy, ingloriousness, obloquy, odium, opprobrium, reduction in rank, retrogradation, retrogression, shame

DEGREE *(Academic title), noun* academic honor, award, certificate, collegiate distinction, credentials, credit, dignification, diploma, distinction, graduation certificate, qualification, title, title of honor

DEGREE *(Kinship), noun* affiliation, blood relation, blood relationship, cognation, connation, connection, consanguinity, extraction, family connection, family relationship, family tie, filiation, line of descent, proximity of blood, relatedness, relationship between persons, ties of blood
ASSOCIATED CONCEPTS: degree of descent, degree of kindred

DEGREE *(Magnitude), noun* amount, amplitude, caliber, consequence, dimension, enormity, expanse, extent, greatness, import, importance, intensity, largeness, measure, measurement, might, moment, proportions, range, reach, scope, seriousness, significance, strength, tenor, value, vastness, volume, weight
ASSOCIATED CONCEPTS: degree of care, degree of certainty, degree of crime, degree of disability, degree of offense, degree of proof, degrees of criminality, highest degree of care, lesser included offenses
FOREIGN PHRASES: *Quae sunt minoris culpae sunt majoris infamiae.* Those things which are less culpable may be more infamous.

DEGREE *(Station), noun* classification, echelon, gradation, grade, *gradus,* level of development, manner, mark, *ordo,* plane, point, position, rank, ranking, relative position, rung, situation, stage, stage of advancement, standing, status, step, tier

DEIGN, *verb* allow, allow with condescension, be so good as to, condescend, descend, favor, grant, patronize, stoop, vouchsafe

DELAY, *noun* *cunctatio,* cunctation, dalliance, deceleration, deferment, demurral, detainment, detention, dilatoriness, impediment, intermission, interruption, lag, lateness, *cessatio, mora,* moratorium, pause, postponement, procrastination, prolongation, prorogation, putting off, retardation, setback, slowness, stall, stay, suspension, tardiness, tarriance, wait

ASSOCIATED CONCEPTS: dilatory motions
FOREIGN PHRASES: *De morte hominis nulla est cunctatio longa.* When the death of a human being may be concerned, no delay is considered long. *Justitia non est neganda non differenda.* Justice is neither to be denied nor delayed. *Dilationes in lege sunt odiosae.* Delays are odious to the law.

DELAY, *verb* adjourn, arrest, arrest temporarily, be dilatory, block, bring to a standstill, curb, defer, detain, *detinere,* hamper, hinder, hold, hold back, hold in abeyance, hold over, hold up, impede, impede the progress of, interfere, intermit, keep back, keep from proceeding, keep one waiting, keep pending, lay over, linger, loiter, make inactive, obstruct, postpone, prevent, prolong, protract, put off, remit, retard, set back, shelve, slacken, slow, slow down, slow up, stall, stall for time, stand in the way, stay, stop, stymie, table, *tardare,* tarry, temporize
ASSOCIATED CONCEPTS: accidental delays, damages for delay, delay beyond the seller's control, delay occasioned by the defendant, delayed compensation, dilatory delay, excusable delay, excuse for delay, hinder and delay, inexcusable delay, justifiable delay, laches, unavoidable delay, unreasonable delay, without delay

DELEGATE, *verb* accord, accredit, allocate, allot, appoint, appoint as agent, appoint as representative, assign, assign a duty, assign power of attorney to, assign to a position, authorize, authorize formally, authorize to represent, award, bestow, call upon, charge, charge with an errand, charter, choose, commission, commit, commit powers to another, commit to the hands of, *committere,* confer power on, confide, confide for care, confide for use, consign, convey, *credere, delegare,* deliver, deliver in trust, deliver over, deposit with, depute, designate, designate to a post, despatch, detail, devolve on, dispatch, employ, empower, empower to act for another, enable, engage, entitle, entrust, entrust to the care of another, give, give a mandate, give a responsibility to, give authority to, give employment, give in charge, give in trust, give power, give power of attorney, give to, hand over, hire, hold responsible, impose a duty, impower, instate, intitle, intrust, invest, invest with authoritative power, license, make someone a trustee of, make someone guardian of, *mandare,* name, name to fill an appointment, nominate, oblige, offer a job to, offer a post, order, parcel out to, place in an office, place in charge of, place trust in, put in commission, put in one's hands, put in safekeeping, qualify, refer, relegate, sanction, select, send, send as deputy, send on a commission, send on a mission, send on an errand, send out, substitute, swear in, transfer, transmit, trust with, turn over to, vest in, warrant
ASSOCIATED CONCEPTS: delegated legislative function, delegated power, delegated state function, delegation of authority

DELEGATION *(Assignment), noun* agency, agentship, appointment, authorization, charge, commission, commissioning, consigning, consignment, delegating, deputation, deputization, designation, devolution, entrusting, entrustment, giving over, investing with authority, investiture, license, mandate, ordination, procuration, proxyship, referrence, referring, warrant
ASSOCIATED CONCEPTS: delegation of authority, delegation of duty, delegation of governmental power, dele-

gation of judicial power, delegation of legislative functions, delegation of legislative power, delegation of power

FOREIGN PHRASES: *Vicarius non habet vicarium.* A deputy cannot have a deputy. *Quod per me non possum, nec per alium.* What I cannot do myself, I cannot do through another. *Delegatas potestas non potest delegari.* A delegated power cannot be further delegated. *Delegatus non potest delegare.* A representative cannot delegate his authority.

DELEGATION *(Envoy), noun* body of delegates, body of representatives, commission, committee, delegates, deputies, embassy, legation, mission, people delegated, procuracy, representatives

DELETE, *verb* blot out, cancel, censor, cross off, cross out, cut, cut out, dele, discard, do away with, drop, edit out, efface, elide, eliminate, eradicate, erase, excise, expel, expunge, extirpate, get rid of, leave out, modify by excisions, obliterate, omit, remove, rub out, rule out, scratch out, strike off, strike out, take out, weed, wipe out

DELETERIOUS, *adjective* adverse, bad, baleful, baneful, consuming, corroding, corrosive, damaging, deadly, disadvantageous, disserviceable, envenomed, fatal, foul, harmful, injurious to health, insalubrious, lethal, malefic, maleficent, malignant, miasmal, morbiferous, morbific, nocuous, noisome, noxious, *noxius,* pernicious, pestilential, poisonous, ruinous, septic, toxic, unadvantageous, unfavorable, unhealthful, unhealthy, unsatisfactory, venomous, virulent, wasting
ASSOCIATED CONCEPTS: deleterious drug, deleterious substance

DELIBERATE, *adjective* advised, aimed, attentive, calculated, careful, carefully considered, carefully weighed, cautious, characterized by reflection, cogitative, *cogitatus,* conscious, *consideratus,* considered, contemplated, contemplative, controlled, deliberative, designed, determined, dispassionate, done on purpose, excogitative, fixed, full of thought, given due consideration, gradual, intended, intentional, judged, leisurely, maturely considered, measured, meditated, meditative, outlined beforehand, planned, planned in advance, plotted, pondered, prearranged, preconsidered, predeliberated, predesigned, predetermined, premeditated, prepense, *prudens,* prudent, purposed, purposeful, reasoned, reflective, resolved, slow, slow-moving, slow-paced, sober, speculative, studied, thought-out, thoughtful, unhasty, unhurried, volitient, volitional, volitive, voluntary, wary, weighed, well-considered, willed, willful, with forethought
ASSOCIATED CONCEPTS: deliberate act, deliberate and premeditated killing, deliberate and premeditated malice, deliberate and premeditated murder, deliberate and willful misconduct, deliberate assumption of risk, deliberate killing, deliberate or intentional wrongdoing, deliberate speed, deliberately and with premeditation, deliberative body

DELIBERATE, *verb* advise together, advise with, analyze, brood, cerebrate, cogitate, confer formally, consider, consider attentively, consider carefully, consider pro and con, *considerare,* consult, *consultare,* contemplate, debate, *deliberare,* discourse about, discuss, examine, examine carefully, excogitate, go into, hold a consultation, hold conclave, investigate, judge, medi-

tate, mull over, negotiate, parley, ponder, ponder over, ponder reasons for and against, ratiocinate, reason, reason out, reason the point, reflect, reflect over, reflect upon, regard upon, review, ruminate, sit in conclave, sit in council, study, take counsel with oneself, take into consideration, take under consideration, think carefully, think over, weigh, weigh in the mind

DELIBERATION, *noun* advisement, analysis, brooding, calculation, careful consideration, carefulness, caution, cautiousness, cerebration, circumspection, close attention, close study, cogitation, conscious purpose, consideration, *consultatio,* contemplation, contemplativeness, counsel, debate, *deliberatio,* determination prepense, discussion, distinct intention, examination, excogitation, forethought, heed, heedfulness, inquiry, inspection, intellection, judgment, level-headedness, logical discussion, mature consideration, mature reflection, meditation, pondering, premeditation, prudence, ratiocination, reflection, rumination, sobriety, study, taking counsel, thinking out, thought, thoughtfulness, unhurriedness, wariness, watchfulness, weighing

DELICT, *noun* corruption, crime, *delictum,* dereliction of duty, duty unfulfilled, felony, injurious act, injury, malefaction, malfeasance, malversation, misdemeanor, misfeasance, misprision, neglect of duty, negligent act of injury, negligent offense, negligent wrongdoing, nonfeasance, obligation repudiated, offense, official misconduct, tort, violation, violation of a duty, wrong
ASSOCIATED CONCEPTS: quasi delict

DELIMIT, *verb* allot, bound, circumscribe, confine, define, demarcate, determine, draw the line, edge, encircle, enclose, encompass, fixix, lay out a boundary, mark limits, mark off, mark out, measure, surround

DELINEATE, *verb* adumbrare, block out, blueprint, circumscribe, construct a figure, contour, convey an impression of, define, depict, *depingere,* describe, *describere,* detail, determine, diagram, draft, draw, draw a picture, engrave, etch, figure, frame, give the details of, illuminate, illustrate, itemize, limn, make a likeness, make apparent, make clear, make vivid, map, mold, outline, paint, paint a picture, particularize, picture, picturize, plot, portray, portray in words, profile, recite, recount, relate, report, represent, represent by diagram, represent by outlines, represent pictorially, set forth, shape, silhouette, sketch, sketch in outline, sketch out, specify, specify the particulars of, survey, tell vividly, trace, trace out, trace the outline of, traverse the outline of

DELINEATION, *noun* abstract, account, act of setting forth, the act of tracing, *adumbratio,* blueprint, chart, circumscription, configuration, contour, *débauche,* depiction, depiction of essential features, *descriptio,* description, design, diagram, enumeration of the essential qualities, facsimile, form, framework, graph, line drawn round, map, outline, pattern, plan, plot, portrayal, profile, recital, recitation, relation, rendition, report, representation, representation by words, rough draft, shape, silhouette, skeleton plan, sketch, specification, statements that describe, structure, tracing, verbal portraiture, word picture

DELINQUENCY *(Failure of duty),* **noun** breach, breach of a promise, carelessness, default, dereliction of duty, error, failure, failure of obligation, failure to act, incompletion, indifference to act, inobservance, lapse in conduct, malpractice, misprision, neglect, neglect of obligation, negligence, noncompletion, noncompletion of a task, nonfulfillment, nonobservance, nonperformance, omission, omission of duty, omission of obligation, oversight, repudiation of one's duty, slight, slip, unfulfillment of an assignment, unfulfillment of duty

DELINQUENCY *(Misconduct),* **noun** atrocity, badness, baseness, breach of the law, corruption, crime, criminality, culpability, decadence, degeneracy, *delictum,* depravity, dereliction, devilishness, dissoluteness, evil, evil behavior, fault, *flagrante delicto,* foulness, heinousness, immorality, improbity, impropriety, indiscretion, infraction, infraction of the law, infringement, iniquity, lawbreaking, lawlessness, malefaction, malfeasance, *malum,* malversation, misbehavior, misdeed, misdoing, misstep, nefariousness, obliquity, offense, outrage, peccability, peccancy, prodigality, profligacy, reprobacy, tort, transgression, trespass, turpitude, unvirtuousness, viciousness, vileness, villainousness, villainy, violation, wantonness, waywardness, wickedness, wrong, wrongdoing
ASSOCIATED CONCEPTS: contributing to delinquency, delinquency proceeding, juvenile delinquency

DELINQUENCY *(Shortage),* **noun** arrearage, arrears, dearth, debt, default, deficiency, deficit, depletion, inability to pay, inadequacy, indebtment, insufficiency, lack, late payment, liability, nonfulfillment, nonpayment, obligation, outstanding debt, paucity, scantiness, scarcity, short measure, short supply, shortage, shortness, sparseness, sparsity, unpaid amount
ASSOCIATED CONCEPTS: delinquency assessment, delinquency charges

DELINQUENT *(Guilty of a misdeed),* **adjective** accusable, at fault, bad, blamable, blameful, blameworthy, censurable, condemnable, conscienceless, corrupt, criminal, culpable, derelict, dishonest, disreputable, erring, evil, evil-doing, evil-minded, flagrant, guilty, *homo maleficus,* immoral, improper, in error, in fault, in the wrong, incorrigible, iniquitous, irredeemable, lawbreaking, maleficent, malevolent, malfeasant, misbehaving, monstrous, nefarious, negligent, offending, peccant, profligate, punishable, remiss, reprehensible, reproachable, reprobate, scandalous, sinful, to blame, transgressing, unjust, unlawful, unprincipled, unscrupulous, unseemly, unvirtuous, unworthy, vicious, villainous, virtueless, wicked, worthless
ASSOCIATED CONCEPTS: delinquent child, delinquent minors

DELINQUENT *(Overdue),* **adjective** back, behind, behindhand, chargeable, defaultant, defaulting, deficient, due, failing in duty, in arrears, lacking, missing, neglectful of obligation, not discharged, not met, not paid on time, outstanding, owed, owing, past due, payable, receivable, remiss, short, to be paid, undefrayed, unliquidated, unpaid, unsatisfied, unsettled, wanting
ASSOCIATED CONCEPTS: delinquent assessments, delinquent debtor, delinquent lands, delinquent payment, delinquent premiums, delinquent property, delinquent taxes, delinquent taxpayer

DELINQUENT, noun criminal, culprit, dangerous person, evildoer, guilty man, *homo maleficus,* insolvent debtor, law-breaker, malefactor, malfeasor, mischief-maker, miscreant, misdemeanant, misdoer, misfeasor, neglector of duty, nonpayer, offender, recidivist, recreant, reprobate, rogue, ruffian, scofflaw, swindler, transgressor, trouble maker, undesirable, worker of iniquity, wrong-doer
ASSOCIATED CONCEPTS: delinquent child, delinquent neglected and dependent children, delinquent premiums, delinquent taxes, juvenile delinquent

DELIVER, verb carry, cart, commit, communicate, convey, *dedere,* delegate, entrust, forward, give into another's keeping, give out, hand, hand down, haul, impart, make over, pass on, place in the possession of, *prodere,* put into the hands of, relay, remit, send, ship, surrender, *tradere,* traject, transfer by deed, transfer property, transfer right, transfuse, translate, translocate, transmit, transplant, transport, turn over
ASSOCIATED CONCEPTS: agreement to deliver, constructively delivered, deliver himself up, deliver in trust, deliver possession, deliver up, delivered for shipment, executed and delivered, sold and delivered, writing signed and delivered

DELIVERY, noun *actio,* conveyance, conveyancing, deliverance, *dictio, elocutio,* impartment, mutual transfer, remittance, rendering, sending, shipment, surrender, transfer, transference, transferral, transmission, transmittal, transmittance, transposal, transposition
ASSOCIATED CONCEPTS: absolute delivery, acceptance, acknowledgment of delivery, actual delivery, complete delivery, conditional delivery, constructive delivery, contingent delivery, delivery and acceptance, delivery bond, delivery f.o.b., delivery in escrow, delivery of a deed, delivery of an instrument, delivery of deed, delivery of freight, delivery of goods, delivery of instrument, delivery of mail, delivery of possession, delivery terms, delivery to a third person, failure of delivery, failure to make delivery, immediate delivery, improper delivery, misdelivery, nondelivery, partial delivery, personal delivery, prompt delivery, proper delivery, sale and delivery, sale for future delivery, substituted delivery, symbolic delivery, tender of delivery, unconditional delivery, valid delivery
FOREIGN PHRASES: *In traditionibus scriptorum, non quod dictum est, sed quod gestum est, inspicitur.* In the delivery of writings, not what is said, but what is done, is regarded. *Periculum rei venditae, nondum traditae, est emptoris.* The risk of a thing sold, but not yet delivered, is the purchaser's. *Traditio nihil amplius transferre debet vel potest, ad eum qui accipit, quam est apud eum qui tradit.* Delivery ought to, and can, transfer nothing more to him who receives than is in possession of him who makes the delivery. *Traditio loqui facit chartam.* Delivery makes the deed speak.

DELUDE, verb be cunning, befool, beguile, bluff, cause error, cheat, cozen, create a false impression, cully, dazzle, deceive, decoy, defraud, *deludere,* dissemble, dupe, falsify, fool, give a false idea, give a false impression, gull, hoax, hoodwink, illude, inveigle, lead astray, lead into error, make a fool of, misdirect, misguide, misinform, mislead, misrepresent, misstate, mystify, persuade to believe error, play a trick on, practice chicanery, practice fraud upon, practice upon one's credulity, swindle, take advantage of, take in, trick

DELUSIVE, *adjective* artful, beguiling, bogus, chimerical, crafty, cunning, deceitful, deceiving, deceptive, deluding, delusory, dreamy, elusive, fallacious, *fallax,* false, *falsus,* fancied, fanciful, fantastic, fantastical, feigned, fraudulent, guileful, hallucinative, hallucinatory, illusionary, illusive, illusory, imaginary, imagined, insubstantial, make-believe, misleading, mock, notional, phantasmal, pretended, sham, sleightful, specious, spurious, tricky, unactual, unfounded, unreal, unsubstantial, untrue, *vanus,* visionary, wily

DELVE, *verb* ask for, burrow, carry on intensive research, conduct an inquiry, dig down into, dig into, examine, explore, fathom, ferret out, *fodere,* follow the trail, go deep into, go in pursuit of, go in search of, go through, hold an inquiry, hunt for, hunt through, inquire for, inquire into, institute an inquiry, investigate, look around for, look behind the scenes, look for, look into, look through, make inquiry, peer, penetrate, poke, probe, probe to the bottom, prosecute an inquiry, pry, pursue, quest, research, rummage, search, search for, search laboriously, search through, seek, seek a clue, set up an inquiry, track, trail, unearth

DEMAGOGUE, *noun* agitator, charismatic leader, declaimer, exciter, factionary, factioneer, factious leader, fanatic, firebrand, fomenter, haranguer, incentor, inciter, inflamer, instigator, leader, mob swayer, *plebicola, plebis dux,* politician, popular agitator, provocator, provoker, rabble-rouser, radical, ranter, rebel, revolutionary, ringleader, rouser, trouble-maker, unprincipled politician, unscrupulous agitator, unscrupulous haranguer, urger

DEMAND, *noun* asking for what is due, assertion of legal right, authoritative request, behest, bidding, call, claim, command, emphatic inquiry, exigency, imperative request, imposition, legal claim, notice of claim, order, peremptory claim, request to perform, requirement, requisite, statement of claim, ultimatum
ASSOCIATED CONCEPTS: actual demand, cross demand, demand and refusal, demand certificates, demand deposits, demand for payment, demand for relief, demand instruments, demand note, excessive demands, legal demand, notice and demand, on demand, presentment and demand, unreasonable demand
FOREIGN PHRASES: *Rogationes, quaestiones, et positiones debent esse simplices.* Demands, questions, and claims ought to be simple.

DEMAND, *verb* arrogate, ask, ask for with authority, assert a right to, assert one's rights, call for, claim, claim as one's due, command, direct, enjoin, exact, give notice, impose, insist, make application, order, present one's claim, press, request, require, urge
ASSOCIATED CONCEPTS: actual demand, cross demand, demand and refusal, demand certificates, demand deposits, demand for payment, demand for relief, demand instruments, demand note, excessive demands, legal demand, notice and demand, on demand, presentment and demand, unreasonable demand
FOREIGN PHRASES: *Nihil peti potest ante id tempus quo per rerum naturam persolvi possit.* Nothing can be demanded before the time when, in the nature of things, it can be paid. *Judex non reddit plus quam quod petens ipse requirit.* A judge should not render judgments for a larger sum than the plaintiff demands.

DEMARCATE, *verb* allocate, allot, apportion, assign, border, bound, circumscribe, compass, confine, contradistinguish, define, delimit, delimitate, demark, determine, determine boundaries, differentiate, discriminate, distinguish, disunite, divide, enclose, encompass, establish boundaries, fence off, fix limits, lay down limits, limit, mark, mark limits, mark out, outline, partition, rope off, segregate, separate, set apart, set bounds to, set off, stake out, zone

DEMEAN *(Deport oneself),* *verb* acquit, act, appear, bear, behave, carry, comport, conduct, convey the impression, create the impression, function, have the mien, leave the impression, look, manage, present oneself, present the appearance, quit, represent oneself, resemble, seem, seem to be, show, take on the manner

DEMEAN *(Make lower),* *verb* abase, belittle, bring down, bring into disrepute, bring low, cheapen, conquer, crush, debase, deflate, degrade, depreciate, derogate, descend, detract from, diminish, discredit, disgrace, dishonor, disparage, humble, humiliate, lower, make ashamed, make lowly, mortify, put down, reduce, shame, stain, take down, tarnish, vanquish

DEMEANOR, *noun* appearance, aspect, attitude, bearing, behavior, carriage, comportment, conduct, countenance, deportment, expression, guise, look, manner, mien, physical appearance, poise, posture, presence, way
ASSOCIATED CONCEPTS: demeanor of witnesses

DEMESNE, *noun* acquest, chattels real, domain, dominion, empire, estate, freehold, hereditament, holding, land, landed estate, landed property, manor, one's own land, property, real estate, real property, realm, realty
ASSOCIATED CONCEPTS: demesne lands

DEMISE *(Conveyance),* *noun* abalienation, alienation, bequeathal, cession, conferment, conferral, conveyancing, deeding, deliverance, delivery, testamentary disposition, transfer, transference, transmission, transmittal

DEMISE *(Death),* *noun* annihilation, cessation of life, decease, departure, end of life, expiration, extinction, extinguishment, loss of life, mortality, necrosis, passing away

DEMISE, *verb* award, bequeath, bestow by will, confer by will, convey, deliver over, devise, devolve upon, endow, give by will, grant by will, hand down, leave, leave a legacy, leave by will, make a bequest, make a legacy, make testamentary disposition, pass by will, pass down, transfer by will, transfer ownership, transmit, will
ASSOCIATED CONCEPTS: demise and grant, demise for a term of years, demise for life, demised premises

DEMIT, *verb* abdicate, give up, go into retirement, hand in one's resignation, lay down one's office, leave, make way for, quit, relinquish, renounce, resign, retire, retire from office, stand aside, stand down, tender one's resignation, vacate office, vacate one's seat, withdraw

DEMONSTRABLE, *adjective* absolute, apparent, assured, beyond a question, beyond all doubt, clear, clear-cut, conclusive, decided, definite, dependable, determinate, doubtless, established, evident, incontestable, indisputable, indubitable, not to be disputed, positive, stable, trustworthy, unambiguous, unequivocal, unimpeachable, unmistakable, unqualified, unquestionable, valid, veracious, without doubt, workable

DEMONSTRATE *(Establish), verb* authenticate, circumstantiate, clarify, confirm, corroborate, display, elucidate, evince, exemplify, exhibit, illuminate, illustrate, indicate, instruct, lay out, make clear, make evident, make plain, manifest, perform, point out, prove, set forth, show, show by example, substantiate, support, sustain, teach by example, uphold, validate, verify

DEMONSTRATE *(Protest), verb* challenge, clamor, complain publicly, contravene, controvert, counter, counteract, cry out against, declare opposition, demur, denounce, dissent, expostulate, express disagreement, express disapproval, express dissatisfaction, impugn, inveigh, march, negate, object, oppose, parade, picket, rail, reject, reluct, remonstrate, resist, show disagreement, show disapproval, show opinion publicly, show opposition, spurn, state opposition, storm, traverse

DEMONSTRATIVE *(Expressive of emotion), adjective* communicative, effusive, emotional, emotive, excitable, expressive, fanatical, fervent, feverish, fierce, fiery, free in expression, furious, histrionic, maudlin, overflowing, overwrought, passionate, prone to display of feeling, prone to emotional display, talkative, temperamental, unrestrained, vehement, violent, without reserve

DEMONSTRATIVE *(Illustrative), adjective* affording proof, allegorical, analytical, annotative, characteristic, clarifying, confirmative, confirmatory, confirming, connotative, corroborating, declarative, delineatory, depictive, descriptive, elucidative, enlightening, exegetic, exegetical, explanatory, explicative, explicatory, explicit, expository, expressive, graphic, illuminating, illuminative, informative, informing, interpretative, interpretive, representative, revealing, showing, substantiative, suggesting, suggestive, supportive, telling, typical, verificative, verifying
ASSOCIATED CONCEPTS: demonstrative bequest, demonstrative evidence, demonstrative gift, demonstrative legacy, demonstrative words

DEMOTE, *verb* abase, belittle, bring down, bring low, cashier, cause to descend, cause to sink, debase, decrease in importance, dedecorate, deflate, degrade, demean, depose, depreciate, deprive, dethrone, diminish, discrown, dismiss from favor, dispossess, disrate, divest, downgrade, drop, humble, impose a penalty, lessen importance of, lower, lower in rank, make less important, otherwordly, penalize, reduce, reduce to inferior rank, reduce to the ranks, relieve, remove from office, strip, take down, unseat
ASSOCIATED CONCEPTS: demotion in rank, demotion in salary, demotion of employee

DEMUR, *verb* beg to differ, challenge, contradict, contravene, controvert, deny, differ, disagree, disapprove, disavow, dissent, enter a demurrer, *exceptionem facere,* not confirm, object, oppose, protest, raise objections, reject, repudiate, scruple, take exception, traverse, withhold assent

DEMURRAGE, *noun* compensation for delay, payment for delay, penalty for delay, remittance for delay

DEMURRER, *noun* be at variance, challenge, challenge to the sufficiency of the pleading, confutation, denial of the allegations, denial of the pleading, denial of the statements, exception, exception to a pleading, general denial, negation of allegations, objection, objection to a pleading, opposition to allegations, refusal to answer, refutation, repudiation of the allegations, take exception to the allegations, take issue with, traversal
ASSOCIATED CONCEPTS: argumentative demurrer, demurrer to a pleading, demurrer to evidence, demurrer to interrogatories, frivolous demurrer, general demurrer, special demurrer

DENATURE, *verb* adulterate, alter, attemper, bemingle, blend, change, cheapen, convert, corrupt, deform, denaturalize, devalue, dilute, disguise, distort, doctor, impair, infuse, intermix, introduce changes, invalidate, make lower in quality, make impure, mask, mix, pervert, pollute, sophisticate, tamper with, transfigure, transform, transmute, vitiate, water down, weaken
ASSOCIATED CONCEPTS: denatured food

DENIAL, *noun* abjuration, abnegation, abridgment, challenge, confutation, contradiction, contrary assertion, contravention, deprivement, disaffirmation, disallowance, disavowal, disclaimer, disclamation, disentitlement, dissent, divestment, gainsaying, *negatio,* negation, negative answer, nonacceptance, nonconsent, objection, privation, prohibition, protest, protestation, rebuttal, recantation, refutation, rejection, relinquishment, renouncement, renunciation, *repudiatio,* repudiation, retraction, revocation, spurning, swearing off
ASSOCIATED CONCEPTS: argumentative denial, denial of admittance, denial of civil rights, denial of claim, denial of counsel, denial of due process, denial of equal protection, denial of knowledge or information, denial of liability, denial of motion, denial of relief, general denial, specific denial
FOREIGN PHRASES: *Per rerum naturam, factum negantis nulla probatio est.* It is the nature of things that a person who denies a fact is not bound to give proof. *Justitia non est neganda, non differenda.* Justice is neither to be denied nor delayed. *Qui non negat fatetur.* He who does not deny, admits. *Posito uno oppositorum negatur alterum.* One of two opposite positions being established, the other is denied. *Semper praesumitur pro negante.* A presumption is always in favor of the person who denies.

DENIGRATE, *verb* abase, accuse, asperse, attack, attaint, belittle, besmear, besmirch, bespatter, blacken, blacken one's good name, blemish, brand, call names, calumniate, cast aspersions, charge, compromise, condemn, criticize, decry, defame, degrade, delate, denounce, depreciate, deride, dishonor, expose, gibbet, give a bad name, humiliate, implicate, incriminate, inculpate, insult, libel, lower, malign, pillory, put in in a bad light, put to shame, reflect poorly upon, reproach, reprove, revile, run down, shame, slander, smear, smirch, sneer at, soil, speak ill of, stain, stigmatize, sully, tarnish, taunt, traduce, vilify, vilipend, vituperate

DENIZEN, *noun* burgher, citizen, dweller, habitant, *incola,* indweller, inhabitant, inmate, occupant, occupier, oppidan, resident, residentiary, sojourner, tenant, townsman

DENOMINATE, *verb*   call, call by name, christen, classify, coin, *denominare*, denote, designate, distinguish by name, dub, entitle, give a name to, give title to, label, name, phrase, signify, specify, style, term, title

DENOMINATION, *noun*   appellation, association, band, branch, brotherhood, caption, categorization, category, characterization, class, classification, clique, community, coterie, description, designation, differentiation, distinction, division, faction, genre, group, grouping, heading, identification, kind, label, movement, name, nomenclature, order, organization, party, persuasion, religious order, sect, section, species, subdivision, term, terminology, title, trademark, type, variety

ASSOCIATED CONCEPTS: denomination of money, denominational institution, denominational school, religious denomination

DENOTE, *verb*   be a name for, be a sign of, be an indication of, bespeak, betoken, convey a meaning, denominate, denotate, depict, depicture, *designare*, designate, express, imply, *indicare*, indicate, label, mark, mean, note, point out, portray, refer to, represent, show, signal, *significare*, signify, stand for, suggest, symbolize, tell the meaning of, token

ASSOCIATED CONCEPTS: denoting ownership, denoting possession

DENOUEMENT, *noun*   apodosis, climax, close, closing, closure, completion, conclusion, consummation, *dénouement*, determination, development, disclosure, disentanglement, dissolution, end, ending, epilogue, eventuation, *fait accompli,* final happening, final statement, final touch, *finale,* finalization, finis, finish, finishing stroke, fruition, issue, last act, outcome, outgrowth, *quietus,* realization, resolution, result, settlement, solution, summation, termination, *terminus,* unfolding, unraveling, unraveling of plot, unveiling, upshot, windup

DENOUNCE *(Condemn),* *verb*   anathematize, animadvert, asperse, assail, assail with censure, assault, attack, be censorious, belittle, berate, besmear, besmirch, blackball, blacken, blacklist, brand, bring into discredit, bring to account, call to account, calumniate, cast a slur upon, cast aspersions, cast reflection upon, cast reproach upon, castigate, cavil, censure, challenge, chastise, chide, cite, comminate, condemn openly, contemn, criminate, criticize, criticize severely, cry down, cry out against, declaim against, decry, defame, deflate, degrade, denigrate, denunciate, deprecate, depreciate, derogate, destroy, detract, disapprove, discommend, discountenance, discredit, dishonor, disparage, dispraise, disvalue, dress down, excite disapprobation, exclaim against, excoriate, execrate, find fault with, frown upon, fulminate against, gibbet, impugn, inculpate, inveigh, lash, malign, ostracize, pass censure on, pillory, protest against, publicly accuse, put in a bad light, rebuke, recriminate, reflect upon, remonstrate, reprehend, reprimand, reproach, reprobate, revile, scold, slur, smear, speak ill of, stigmatize, take exception to, take to task, traduce, upbraid, vilify, vilipend, vituperate

DENOUNCE *(Inform against),* *verb*   accuse, arraign, bear witness against, blame, bring accusation, bring charges, charge, complain against, divulge, hold accountable, hold responsible, impeach, implicate, impute, incriminate, inculpate, incur blame, indict, inform, inform on, involve, lay blame upon, lay charges against, lodge a complaint, make charges against, make formal accusation against, name, point at, publicly accuse, report against, turn informer

DENSITY, *noun*   closeness, compactness, concentration, concretion, intransparency, opacity, opaqueness, palpability, solidity, thickness

DENUDE, *verb*   bare, bring to light, defoliate, denudate, disclose, disfurnish, disrobe, divest, doff, exhibit, expose, flay, lay bare, lay open, lay waste, make naked, make public, manifest, open, pare, peel, present to view, publicize, reveal, shed, show, shuck, skin, slough, strip, tear off, uncase, uncloak, unclothe, uncover, uncurtain, undo, undrape, undress, unfold, unfrock, unrobe, unscreen, unsheathe, unshroud, unveil, unwrap, vent

DENUNCIATION, *noun*   accusal, *accusatio,* accusation, anathema, aspersion, backbiting, blame, calumny, carping, castigation, censure, charge, chiding, commination, complaint, condemnation, contumely, *coup de bec,* criticism, damnation, decrial, defamation, *delatio,* delation, denigration, denouncement, deprecation, depreciation, derogation, detraction, diatribe, disapprobation, disapproval, discommendation, discountenance, disparagement, dispraise, excoriation, execration, *exposé,* faultfinding, fulmination, incrimination, inculpation, indictment, informing against, invective, malediction, objurgation, obloquy, opprobrium, Philippic, plaint, rebuke, recrimination, reprehension, reprimand, reproach, reprobation, reproof, revilement, severe censure, slur, smear, stigmatization, stricture, tirade, tongue-lashing, traducement, upbraiding, utter disapproval, vehement condemnation, vilification, vituperation

DENY *(Contradict),* *verb*   contravene, controvert, declare to be false, declare to be untrue, disaffirm, disagree, disallow, disavow, disclaim, disown, dispute, dissent, forswear, gainsay, *infitias ire, negare,* negate, refuse to acknowledge, refuse to admit, refuse to allow, reject as erroneous, repudiate, traverse

FOREIGN PHRASES: *Ei incumbit probatio, qui dicit, non qui negat; cum per rerum naturam factum negantis probatio nulla sit.* The burden of proof lies upon him who asserts it, not upon him who denies; since, by the nature of things, he who denies a fact cannot produce any proof of it.

DENY *(Refuse to grant),* *verb*   abnegate, forbid, keep from, *negare,* prohibit, refuse to allow, refuse to bestow, refuse to give, refuse to permit, refuse to supply, reject, renege, renounce, withhold

ASSOCIATED CONCEPTS: deny a claim, deny a motion, deny a right, deny due process, deny liability

DEPART, *verb*   abscond, absent oneself, be gone, decamp, desert, deviate, differ, digress, disappear, disassociate, *discedere,* disengage, disjoin, dissociate, diverge, divorce, emigrate, evacuate, exit, expatriate oneself, fade, flee, forsake, issue forth, leave, make an exit, march off, part, recede, resign, retire, set out, start out, swerve, vacate, vanish, vary from, withdraw

ASSOCIATED CONCEPTS: depart from scope of employment, depart from terms of a trust, depart from the state, departure in pleading, material departure

DEPARTMENT, *noun*   agency, area, assignment, branch, bureau, categorization, category, chapter, class, classification, designation, district, division, domain, field, field of activity, jurisdiction, ministry, *munus, pars,* part, precinct, province, *provincia,* realm, section, sector, specialty, sphere, station, subdivision, subsection, zone
ASSOCIATED CONCEPTS: department of government, department of state, department rules and regulations, executive department, judicial department, legislative department, municipal department

DEPENDABLE, *adjective*   assured, certain, conscientious, constant, devoted, faithful, guaranteed, incorrupt, loyal, proved, proven, reliable, reputable, responsible, solid, stable, staunch, steadfast, steady, sure, tested, tried, true, trustable, trusted, trustworthy, trusty, unchanging, unfailing, upright, veracious
ASSOCIATED CONCEPTS: dependable evidence

DEPENDENT, *adjective*   ancillary, conditional, conditioned, contingent, controlled by, derivative, derived from, due to, evolved from, granted on certain terms, helpless, imposing a condition, incident to, limited, minor, modified by conditions, needing outside support, *obnoxius,* pendent, provisory, qualified, regulated by, reliant, restricted, resulting from, servile, subject, subject to, subordinate, subservient, sustained by, unable to exist without, weak

DEPENDENT, *noun*   charge, child, helpless person, individual under guardianship, juvenile charge, minor, minor under guardianship, minor under protectorship, pensioner, person under guardianship, vassal, ward
ASSOCIATED CONCEPTS: actual dependent, dependent and neglected child, dependent person, dependent wife, lawful dependent, legal dependent, minor dependent, partial dependency, total dependency

DEPICT, *verb*   characterize, communicate, connote, convey, delineate, *depingere,* describe, *describere,* detail, diagram, draw, *effingere,* embody, enunciate, evince, evoke, exemplify, exhibit, explain, explicate, express, give an account, give expression to, illuminate, illustrate, indicate, limn, manifest, outline, particularize, personify, picture, portray, recite, recount, relate, render an account, report, represent, reveal, set forth, show, signify, sketch, specify, symbolize, tell, tell vividly, typify

DEPLETE, *verb*   beggar, bleed, consume, decrease, dissipate, drain, drain of resources, dry up, eliminate, empty, empty out, evacuate, exhaust, expend, finish, impoverish, lessen, lose, pauperize, purge, reduce, render insufficient, run down, spend, unload, use up, void, waste, weaken, wear out

DEPLORABLE, *adjective*   afflicted, appalling, atrabilious, atrocious, bad, black, calamitous, catastrophic, demoralizing, depressing, depressive, despicable, dire, disagreeable, disastrous, disheartening, dismal, displeasing, distasteful, distressing, doleful, dolorous, dreadful, dreary, *flebilis,* frightful, ghastly, grievous, horrible, horrid, horrific, horrifying, insufferable, intolerable, lamentable, *miserabilis,* miserable, outrageous, pathetic, piteous, pitiable, pitiful, poor, regrettable, sad, shocking, sorrowful, sorry, terrible, tragic, tragical, unbearable, undesirable, unfortunate, unhappy, unpleasant, unpleasing, unsatisfactory, untoward, vile, wretched

DEPLORE, *verb*   be sorry for, bemoan, bewail, brood over, complain, cry over, *deflere, deplorare,* express deep grief for, fret over, grieve for, groan, lament, moan, mourn, regard with sorrow, regret, regret profoundly, repine, rue, shed tears over, show concern for, sigh for, sorrow over, view with regret, weep over

DEPLOY, *verb*   assign to battle stations, assign to positions, branch out, broaden, diffuse, *dilatare,* distribute, diverge, expand, *explicare,* extend, fan out, outspread, place, radiate, scatter, splay, spread, spread out in battle formation, stretch out, thin out, unfold, unfurl, widen

DEPONENT, *noun*   affiant, apprizer, attestant, attestator, attester, attestor, communicant, communicator, compurgator, enlightener, indicator, informant, informer, one who attests, one who bears witness, one who gives evidence, one who makes an affidavit, one who testifies under oath, party making an affidavit, reporter, swearer, teller, testifier, voucher, witness, witness who gives testimony
ASSOCIATED CONCEPTS: witness

DEPORT *(Banish), verb*   bar, cast out, dislodge, dismiss, displace, drive away, drive out, eject, evict, exclude, exile, expatriate, expel, extradite, force out, oust, outlaw, remove, send away, thrust out, transfer, transport, turn out

DEPORT *(Conduct oneself), verb*   acquit, act, bear oneself, behave, carry oneself, comport oneself

DEPORTATION, *noun*   banishment, casting out, dislocation, dismissal, displacement, driving out, ejection, ejectment, elimination, eviction, exclusion, exile, exilement, expatriation, expulsion, extradition, extrusion, forced departure, forced leave taking, ouster, purge, removal, riddance, sending away, thrusting out

DEPORTMENT, *noun*   actions, address, air, appearance, aspect, attitude, bearing, behavior, breeding, carriage, comportment, conduct, decorum, demeanor, dignity, guise, *habitus,* look, manner, mien, personal bearing, poise, port, posture, practice, presence, propriety, way, ways

DEPOSE *(Remove), verb*   cast away, cast out, demote, deprive of rank, dethrone, discard, discharge, discharge from office, disemploy, disentitle, disestablish, dislodge, dismiss, displace, dispossess, divest, drive out, drop, eject, evict, exile, expel, fire, impeach, *loco movere,* oust, oust from office, put out, put out of possession, recall, reduce, turn away, turn out, unseat, usurp

DEPOSE *(Testify), verb*   adduce, affirm, affirm under oath, asseverate, attest, aver, avouch, avow, bear witness to, certify, declare under oath, depone, give a solemn declaration, give an account of, give evidence, give proof, give proof by a witness, give sworn testimony, make an affidavit, make deposition, plead, profess, promise, relate, say under oath, swear, swear under oath, *testari, testificari,* verify, vouch, vouch for, witness
ASSOCIATED CONCEPTS: depose a witness

DEPOSIT, *noun*   accumulation, collateral, collateral security, *depositum,* down payment, earnest pledge, forfeit, gage, guarantee, installment, money in bank, part payment, pawn, payment, pledge, retainer, security, stake, surety

ASSOCIATED CONCEPTS: binder, certificate of deposit, earnest money, escrow, interpleader, savings deposit, security deposit, time deposit

DEPOSIT *(Place), verb*   *deponere,* dump, install, lay, locate, lodge, place in a receptacle, plant, put, quarter, reposit, rest, set, settle, situate, stash, store, stow

DEPOSIT *(Submit to a bank), verb*   bank, commit, enter into an account, entrust, invest, keep an account, lay by, present money for safekeeping, put at interest, save
ASSOCIATED CONCEPTS: interpleader, stake

DEPOSITION, *noun*   compurgation, declaration under oath, disclosure, documentation, oral evidence, oral statement under oath, proof by a witness, solemn declaration, statement on oath, statement under oath, sworn evidence, testification, testimonial, *testimonium,* testimony, transcript of testimony, vouching, written declaration under oath

DEPOSITORY, *noun*   *apotheca,* archives, bunker, cache, catchall, coffer, collection, container, depot, hold, holder, magazine, place for safe keeping, place of deposit, receptacle, *receptaculum,* repertory, repository, reservoir, safe, safe-deposit box, storage, store, storehouse, vault, warehouse
ASSOCIATED CONCEPTS: depository box, legal depository, reservoir

DEPRAVED, *adjective*   abominable, bad, base, base-minded, contemptible, corrupt, debased, debauched, degenerate, degraded, deteriorated, disreputable, dissipated, dissolute, evil, execrable, flagitious, foul, gross, heinous, horrendous, immeritorious, immoral, indecent, iniquitous, lecherous, lewd, licentious, low, low-minded, obscene, perverted, profligate, rank, ruined, salacious, shameful, shameless, sinful, unprincipled, unscrupulous, vile, vitiated, vulgar, warped, wicked
ASSOCIATED CONCEPTS: depraved act, depraved indifference, depraved mind

DEPRECATE, *verb*   *abominari,* asperse, belittle, berate, cast aspersions, charge, decry, demean, denigrate, denounce, deplore, derogate, detract, disapprove, disclaim, discommend, discredit, disdain, disfavor, dislike, disparage, dispraise, disvalue, excoriate, exprobate, fault, find fault, impugn, inculpate, object, objurgate, oppose, protest, reject, repudiate, traduce, view with disfavor, vilipend

DEPRECIATE, *verb*   atrophy, attenuate, become deteriorated, become of less worth, belittle, censure, cheapen, contemn, corrode, cut, debase, debilitate, decay, decline, decrease, decry, deduct, defame, deflate, degenerate, degrade, denigrate, denounce, depress, deride, derogate from, deteriorate, detract from, *detrectare,* devaluate, devalue, dilute, diminish the price of, diminish the value of, discount, discredit, disesteem, disgrace, disparage, dispraise, drop, dwindle, ebb, enervate, enfeeble, erode, fall, fault, find fault with, get worse, grow less, grow worse, impoverish, lessen, lessen the price of, lose value, lower, lower in price, lower in reputation, lower in value, lower the value of, make little of, malign, minimize, misprize, *obtrectare,* readjust downward, reduce the purchasing value of, reduce the strength of, retrograde, run down,

shrink, sink, slight, slur, soil, spoil, stain, sully, taint, take away, tarnish, traduce, underestimate, underpraise, underprize, underrate, underreckon, undervalue, weaken, wear, worsen
ASSOCIATED CONCEPTS: depreciate a loss, obsolescence

DEPREDATION, *noun*   foray, havoc, marauding, raid, rapine, ravaging, sack, spoliation

DEPRESS, *verb*   abase, bring down, bring low, cause to sink, cheapen, dampen, darken, decline, decrease, deflate, deject, depreciate, deteriorate, devaluate, devalue, diminish, discourage, dispirit, drop, ebb, flatten, indent, lessen, lower, make despondent, make sad, plunge, press down, reduce, sadden, shrink, sink, slump, squash, weaken

DEPRESSION, *noun*   debasement, decline, deflation, dejection, depreciation, despondence, despondency, disheartenment, dispiritedness, dolefulness, economic decline, gloom, lowering, lowness, *maeror,* sinking, slump, *tristitia*
ASSOCIATED CONCEPTS: economic depression

DEPRIVE, *verb*   arrogate, attach, bereave, capture, commandeer, confiscate, convert, denude, despoil, disendow, disentitle, disherit, disinherit, disown, dispossess, disseize, distrain, divest, expropriate, extort, fleece, foreclose, impound, impoverish, leave destitute, mulct, pauperize, purloin, rob, seize, sequester, sequestrate, steal, strip, take away, tear away, usurp, wrench, wrest
ASSOCIATED CONCEPTS: deprivation of liberty, deprivation of property, deprivation of right, deprive of employment, deprive of life, deprived of liberty, deprived of substantial right
FOREIGN PHRASES: *Privatio praesupponit habitum.* A deprivation presupposes something possessed.

DEPUTATION *(Delegation), noun*   agents, body of delegates, body of representatives, commissaries, commission, committee, consulate, delegates, delegation, emissaries, envoys, factors, *legati, legatio,* legation, mission, plenipotentiaries, proxies, representation, representatives

DEPUTATION *(Selection of delegates), noun*   appointing, appointment, assignment, authorization, authorizing, commission, conferment, delegation, deputization, designation, devolution, empowering, entrustment, installation, investiture, investment, nomination, procuration

DEPUTY, *noun*   agent, alternate, ambassador, appointee, assignee, broker, commissary, commissioner, delegate, emissary, envoy, factor, intermediary, *legatus,* lieutenant, minister, plenipotentiary, proctor, procurator, proxy, representative, second, secondary, substitute, surrogate, vicar, *vicarius,* vicegerent
ASSOCIATED CONCEPTS: de facto deputy, deputy commissioner, deputy marshal, deputy officer, deputy sheriff, general deputy, special deputy
FOREIGN PHRASES: *Vicarius non habet vicarium.* A deputy cannot have a deputy.

DERANGED, *adjective*   bereft of reason, confused, *demens,* demented, disarranged, disconcerted, disjointed, dislocated, disordered, disorganized, displaced, dissonant, distraught, frenetic, frenzied, in disorder, incompetent, inconsistent, insane, *insanus,* insensate, mad, maddened, maniacal, of unsound mind, rabid, reasonless, unbalanced, unsettled

DERELICT *(Abandoned),* **adjective**   adrift, avoided, cast aside, cast off, castaway, deserted, desolate, discarded, disowned, dispensed with, excluded, forgotten, forlorn, forsaken, friendless, given up, helpless, homeless, ignored, isolated, jettisoned, left, lonely, lonesome, neglected, on the fringe of society, outcast, rejected, relinquished, repudiated, scorned, scrapped, set adrift, shunned, solitary, thrown overboard, uncared for, unclaimed, unfortunate, unfriended, unowned, unpossessed, unwanted, wretched, written off
ASSOCIATED CONCEPTS: derelict property

DERELICT *(Negligent),* **adjective**   careless, delinquent, disregardful, dutiless, failing in duty, faithless, faulty, heedless, improvident, inattentive, inconsiderate, indifferent, lax, neglectful, neglecting, regardless, remiss, slack, thoughtless, uncircumspect, unconcerned, unfaithful, unheedful, unheeding, uninterested, unmindful, unobservant, unwatchful

DERELICT, *noun*   displaced person, drifter, exile, fugitive, ne'er-do-well, outcast, pariah, scamp, tramper, vagrant, wanderer, wastrel

DERELICTION, *noun*   abandonment, breach, carelessness, culpa, default, defection, delinquency, desertion, disregard, dutilessness, evasion, failure in duty, faithlessness, heedlessness, indifference, laxity, laxness, misprision, neglect, neglectfulness, negligence, noncooperation, nonfeasance, nonobservance, nonperformance, omission, relinquishment, remissness, truancy, unconcern, unfaithfulness
ASSOCIATED CONCEPTS: dereliction of duty, moral dereliction

DERIVATION, *noun*   ancestor, ancestry, antecedent, author, authority, base, basis, begetter, beginning, birth, birthplace, causality, causation, cause, commencement, creator, descent, determinant, extraction, family, first cause, first occasion, foundation, fount, fountainhead, generator, genesis, ground, head, inception, issue, line, lineage, mainspring, origin, origination, parent, parentage, prime motive, primogenitor, producer, progenitor, provenance, provenience, reference, root, *source,* source material, spring, springhead, starting point, stem, stock, tracing back, ultimate cause

DERIVATIVE, *adjective*   ascribable, attributable, caused, coming from, consequent, consequential, derivate, derivational, derived, deriving, descendant, descended, ensuing, evolved, following, hereditary, imitative, resultant, resulting, secondary, sequent, subordinate, subsequent, subsidiary, vicarious
ASSOCIATED CONCEPTS: derivative action, derivative authority, derivative deed, derivative jurisdiction, derivative liabilities, derivative powers, derivative rights, derivative stockholder's suit, derivative title

DERIVE *(Deduce),* **verb**   conclude, construe, *deducere,* draw a conclusion, draw an inference, extract, infer, make a deduction, obtain by reasoning, reason, theorize, trace

DERIVE *(Receive),* **verb**   acquire, come into possession, draw from, extract, get, glean, obtain, procure, secure, take, *trahere*

DEROGATE, *verb*   abase, asperse, be derogatory, belittle, besmirch, bespatter, blacken, blot, brand, bring down, bring into discredit, bring low, bring shame upon, calumniate, cast a slur upon, cast aspersions, debase, decry, defame, demean, demote, denigrate, depreciate, depress, deprive, *derogare,* detract, *detrahere,* diminish, discredit, disgrace, dishonor, disparage, dispraise, disprize, disrate, humble, incur disgrace, lessen, lessen the reputation of, lower, make ashamed, make little of, make lowly, make smaller, malign, misprize, not do justice to, pull down, put down, reduce, revile, ridicule, run down, scoff, shame, smirch, sneer at, speak evil of, speak ill of, speak slightingly of, stain, subtract from, sully, taint, take something from, tarnish, traduce, underestimate, underrate, underreckon, undervalue, vilify, vilipend, weaken
ASSOCIATED CONCEPTS: derogation of common law, derogation of deed, derogation of right

DEROGATORY, *adjective*   belittling, calumniatory, calumnious, censorious, condemnatory, contumelious, defamatory, denunciatory, deprecatory, depreciative, depreciatory, detracting, detractory, disapprobatory, disapproving, discrediting, disdainful, dishonoring, disparaging, faultfinding, injurious, lessening, libelous, objurgatory, pejorative, slanderous, slighting, uncomplimentary, unfavorable, unflattering
ASSOCIATED CONCEPTS: derogatory statements
FOREIGN PHRASES: *Quae legi communi derogant stricte interpretantur.* Those things which derogate from the common law are strictly interpreted. *Quae legi communi derogant non sunt trahenda in exemplum.* Those things which derogate from the common law are not to be drawn into precedent.

DESCEND, *verb*   bequeath, bestow, come down by transmission, come down lineally, deed, demise, *descendere,* endow, entrust, give, give by will, grant, hand down, hand on, leave a legacy, make a bequest, make a legacy, pass by devise, pass by inheritance, pass by operation of law, pass by succession, pass down from generation to generation, pass on, settle upon, transmit, will, will and bequeath

DESCENDANT, *noun*   child, family, future generation, heir, issue, kin, lineage, offshoot, offspring, posterity, progeny, scion, succeeding generation, successor
ASSOCIATED CONCEPTS: descendants of the line, direct descendant, lawful descendants, lineal descendant or heir, lineal descendants

DESCENT *(Declination),* **noun**   change from higher to lower, comedown, coming down, downrush, droop, drop, falling, going down, inclination downward, lapse, settlement, sinking, subsidence

DESCENT *(Lineage),* **noun**   ancestry, birth, birthright, blood, bloodline, breed, clan, derivation, dynasty, extraction, family tree, filiation, genealogy, heredity, heritage, kin, line, line of ancestors, origin, parentage, paternity, pedigree, race, stock, strain
ASSOCIATED CONCEPTS: ancestors, collateral descent, descendants, line of descent, right and interest by descent, title by descent

DESCRIBE, *verb*   annotate, be specific, characterize, clarify, define, delineate, depict, *depingere, describere,* detail, elucidate, explain, *explicare,* expound, give an account, identify, illuminate, illustrate,

itemize, make clear, make plain, make vivid, outline, paint, particularize, picture, portray, portray in words, represent by words, specify, spell out
ASSOCIATED CONCEPTS: falsely describe

DESCRIPTION, noun account, characterization, definition, delineation, depiction, *descriptio,* details, *enarratio,* explanation, *expositio,* formulation, narrative, outline, particulars, portrayal, profile, sketch, specification
ASSOCIATED CONCEPTS: correct description, description in a will, description of goods, description of land, description of persons, description of property, specific description
FOREIGN PHRASES: *Veritas demonstrationis tollit errorem nominis.* In all penal judgments, allowance is made for youth and lack of prudence. *Falsa demonstratione legatum non perimi.* A legacy is not nullified by an incorrect description. *Praesentia corporis tollit errorem nominis; et veritas nominis tollit errorem demonstrationis.* The presence of the body cures an error in the name; and the accuracy of the name cures an error of description. *Non accipi debent verba in demonstrationem falsam, quae competunt in limitationem veram.* Words ought not to be taken to import a false description which may be taken to describe a true limitation.

DESCRIPTIVE, adjective characterizing, circumstantial, classificatory, clear, definitional, definitive, delineative, designating, detailed, eloquent, explanatory, explicatory, expositive, expository, graphic, identifying, illuminating, illuminative, illustrative, interpretive, lifelike, narrative, particularized, photographic, pictorial, realistic, representational, representative, revealing, specific, true to life, vivid, well-drawn
ASSOCIATED CONCEPTS: descriptive calls, descriptive term, descriptive trade name, descriptive trademark, descriptive word

DESEGREGATE, verb admix, agglomerate, amalgamate, assimilate, associate, band, be mixed, blend, coalesce, combine racially, combine with, commingle, commix, compound, confederate, conglomerate, conjoin, connect, consolidate, eliminate racial segregation, fuse, incorporate, institute commingling of races, integrate, interblend, interfuse, interlace, interlard, intermingle, intermix, join together, make no racial distinctions, mass, meld, merge, merge in, mingle, mix, promote racial harmony, promote racial mixing, to bring together, unify, unite

DESERTION, noun abandonment, abandonment of allegiance, abjuration, absence without leave, act of forsaking, apostasy, AWOL, defection, departure, *derelictio,* disaffection, disloyalty, flight, forsaking, forswearing, leaving, mutiny, quitting, recreancy, renouncement, renunciation, repudiation, resignation, secession, unlawful departure, willful abandonment
ASSOCIATED CONCEPTS: constructive desertion, willful desertion

DESIDERATUM, noun aim, ambition, aspiration, desideration, desire, essential object of desire, exigency, goal, necessary, necessity, need, objective, requirement, requisite, requisition, want

DESIGN *(Construction plan),* **noun** blueprint, chart, conception, delineation, depiction, *descriptio,* diagram, draft, drawing, *forma,* graph, layout, *lineamenta,* map, model, outline, picture, plan, preliminary drawing, projection, proof, rendering, representation, rough cast, rough copy, rough representation, skeleton, sketch, treatment

DESIGN *(Intent),* **noun** aim, ambition, animus, approach, aspiration, bent, *consilium, consulto,* contemplation, course of action, desire, destination, determination, direction, end, end in view, expectation, fixed purpose, forethought, goal, hope, inclination, intention, intentionality, meaning, mission, motive, object, objective, plan, plan of attack, predetermination, projected goal, proposed action, proposed sequence of action, purport, purpose, purpose in view, pursuit, resolve, scheme, set purpose, settled purpose, stratagem, strategy, target, ultimate end, view, way of doing things, will
ASSOCIATED CONCEPTS: common design, formed design, premeditated design

DESIGNATE, verb appoint, assign, authorize, be specific, characterize, choose, commission, declare, define, denominate, denote, *designare,* detail, determine, discriminate, earmark, enter into detail, entitle, express, fix, formulate, indicate, itemize, mark, mark out, mention, name, *nominare,* nominate, *notare,* note, particularize, pinpoint, point out, select, set, set apart, set aside, show, signify, specify, stipulate
ASSOCIATED CONCEPTS: designate as a beneficiary, designate as an agent, designate as an executor

DESIGNATION *(Naming),* **noun** appellation, appointment, approval, assigning, assignment, authorization, calling, categorization, choosing, commissioning, delegating, delegation, denomination, denotation, deputation, description, *designatio,* fixing, identification, indication, installation, label, ordainment, ordination, particularization, placing in office, pointing out, selection, signification, specification, stipulation
ASSOCIATED CONCEPTS: designated agent, designated document, designation of beneficiary

DESIGNATION *(Symbol),* **noun** badge, cipher, distinguishing mark, earmark, emblem, hallmark, identification mark, indicator, indicium, initial, insignia, label, mark, name, representation, sign, standard, title, token, totem, trademark, type

DESIRABLE *(Pleasing),* **adjective** enjoyable, gratifying, pleasant, pleasurable, pleasureful, welcome

DESIRABLE *(Qualified),* **adjective** acceptable, eligible, entitled, qualified, recommendable, suitable, worthy

DESIRE, noun ambition, appetency, appetite, *appetitio,* ardent impulse, ardor, aspiration, attraction, avidity, bent, concupiscence, covetousness, craving, *cupiditas,* cupidity, *desiderium,* eagerness, fancy, fondness, hankering, hunger, impulse, inclination, liking, longing, lust, motive, predilection, proclivity, propensity, rapaciousness, thirst, urge, want, will, wish, yearning, yen
ASSOCIATED CONCEPTS: precatory words

DESIRE, verb apply for, ask, ask for, aspire, be after, be bent upon, be eager, beg a favor, call for, clamor for, covet, crave, cry out for, *cupere, desiderare,*

desiderate, entreat, *expetere,* express a wish to obtain, have a impulse, have a proclivity, have a yearning, have an appetite, have designs on, have one's heart set on, hope for, incline, like to, long for, make a request for, make application for, press, pursue, put in a claim for, request, solicit, supplicate, urge, want, wish for
ASSOCIATED CONCEPTS: precatory words

DESIST, *verb*   abstain, arrest, be quiescent, call off, cease, check, *desinere, desistere,* discontinue, end, finish, forbear, freeze, halt, intermit, interrupt, leave off, make inactive, put a stop to, refrain, repose, rest, stand, stay, stop, surcease, suspend, terminate
ASSOCIATED CONCEPTS: cease and desist order

DESPOIL, *verb*   assail, attack, bereave, consume, denude, deplume, depredate, deprive, desolate, devastate, devour, dispossess, divest, forage, foray, impoverish, invade, lay waste, leave destitute, loot, make off with, maraud, overrun, pilfer, pillage, plunder, purloin, raid, ransack, ravage, raven, rifle, rob, ruin, ruinate, sack, seize, spoliate, steal, strip, take, take by force, thieve, wreck

DESPONDENT, *adjective*   aggrieved, beaten, defeated, defeatist, dejected, depressed, desolate, despairing, disconsolate, dismal, dispirited, dolorous, downcast, dreary, gloomy, hopeless, in despair, inconsolable, joyless, listless, lugubrious, melancholic, melancholy, moody, mournful, pessimistic, rueful, sad, sluggish, somber, sorrowful, sullen, unhappy, unhopeful

DESTINATION, *noun*   aim, aspiration, bourn, conclusion, consummation, debarkation point, destiny, end, end result, ending, finish, goal, intent, intention, journey's end, last stop, object, objective, planned place of arrival, point of cessation, point of disembarkation, port, purpose, resting place, result, stop, stopping-place, target, terminal, terminal point, termination, terminus
ASSOCIATED CONCEPTS: destination contracts, final destination, place of destination, point of destination

DESTITUTE, *adjective*   bankrupt, beggarly, bereft, depleted, deprived, distressed, impecunious, impoverished, indigent, *inops,* insolvent, lacking funds, moneyless, necessitous, needful, needy, out of money, penniless, poor, poverty-stricken, reduced in means, short of money, squalid, unmoneyed, wanting, without resources
ASSOCIATED CONCEPTS: destitute children, destitute of means of support, destitute of property, destitute persons

DESTROY *(Efface), verb*   abort, annihilate, blast, blight, blot out, break to pieces, bring to ruin, burn, consume, corrode, deal destruction, decimate, deface, demolish, desolate, destruct, *destruere,* devastate, devour, *diruere,* disintegrate, dissolve, do away with, eliminate, eradicate, erase, expunge, exterminate, extinguish, extirpate, gut, incinerate, kill, lay waste, level, liquidate, murder, mutilate, obliterate, overthrow, overturn, *perdere,* pulverize, put to death, quell, ravage, raze, reduce to nothing, rend, root out, rub out, ruin, ruinate, scratch out, slay, subvert, uproot, waste, wipe out, wreck
ASSOCIATED CONCEPTS: destroy a will, fraudulently destroyed, lost or destroyed

DESTROY *(Void), verb*   abolish, annul, break up, bring to naught, completely end, dismantle, extinguish, invalidate, make null, nullify, put an end to, render ineffective, terminate, unmake
ASSOCIATED CONCEPTS: destruction of contingent remainders

DESTRUCTIBLE, *adjective*   accessible, assailable, breakable, delicate, depletable, destroyable, dissolvable, eradicable, exhaustible, extinguishable, ruinable, scissile, unsafe, vulnerable

DESTRUCTION, *noun*   abolition, annihilation, breaking down, collapse, consumption, decimation, decomposition, demolishment, demolition, devastation, dissolution, eradication, extinction, extirpation, nullification, obliteration, perdition, ruin, ruination, tearing down, undoing, unmaking
ASSOCIATED CONCEPTS: destruction of business, destruction of records, total destruction, willful destruction
FOREIGN PHRASES: *Res periit domino.* A thing which has been destroyed is lost to its owner.

DESTRUCTIVE, *adjective*   annihilating, baleful, damaging, destroying, detrimental, feral, harmful, injurious, internecine, malign, miasmal, miasmatic, miasmic, pernicious

DESUETUDE, *noun*   abandonment, abeyance, abrogation, absence, abstention, archaism, arrest, cancellation, cessation, desistance, *desuetudo,* discarding, discontinuance, disusage, disuse, dormancy, failure to use, halt, idleness, impotence, inaction, inactivity, inanimation, inertia, inusitation, inutility, neglect, nonavailability, nonobservance, nonretention, nonuse, obsolescence, obsoleteness, omission, relinquishment, stagnation, standstill, state of being unused, stop, stoppage, stoppage of use, surrender, suspension, termination

DESULTORY, *adjective*   broken, deviating, diffuse, digressive, disarranged, disconnected, discontinuous, discursive, disjoined, disjunct, dispersed, erratic, inconsistent, *inconstans,* inconstant, interrupted, lacking continuity, nonrecurrent, nonuniform, rambling, random, spasmodic, uncohesive, unconnected, unmethodical, unrepeated, unsuccessive, unsystematic, varying

DETACH, *verb*   break off, cleave, disconnect, disengage, disentangle, *disiungere,* disjoin, dispart, dissever, dissociate, disunite, divide, divorce, part, remove, *seiungere, separare,* separate, sever, split, uncouple, unfasten, unlink, unplug, unstick
ASSOCIATED CONCEPTS: detached dwelling houses, detached pages in a will

DETAIL, *noun*   aspect, circumstance, circumstantiality, component, component part, division, element, feature, fractional part, fragment, individual part, ingredient, instance, integral part, integrant, item, minor part, minute part, part, particular, particularity, piece, point, portion, section, *singula,* special point, specification, subdivision, technicality, trivia

DETAIL *(Assign), verb*   allocate, appoint, authorize, bid, call, charge, command, commission, compel, consign, decree, delegate, demand, depute, designate, devolve, dictate, distribute, empower, enjoin, entrust, impose, obligate, oblige, order, prescribe, relegate

DETAIL *(Particularize),* **verb**   amplify, analyze, be precise, catalogue, chronicle, circumstantiate, clarify, delineate, depict, describe, draw, elucidate, enumerate, explain, give an account, give details, go into the particulars, illuminate, illustrate, individualize, itemize, make clear, make vivid, narrate, particularize, picture, portray, recite, recount, relate, report, set forth, show, specify, tell, tell details, tell fully, tell particulars

DETAILED, *adjective*   accounted, accurate, all-inclusive, annotated, complete, comprehensive, delineated, described, descriptive, elaborated, enumerated, exact, exhaustive, explicit, full of details, graphic, inclusive, itemized, meticulous, minute, particular, particularized, plenary, precise, punctilious, replete, representational, specific, thorough, total, vivid, whole
ASSOCIATED CONCEPTS: detailed account, detailed audit, detailed report, detailed statement

DETAIN *(Hold in custody),* **verb**   apprehend, arrest, capture, commit, confine, contain, control, enthrall, guard, hold, hold captive, hold in check, hold in preventive custody, hold in thrall, hold under duress, immure, impound, imprison, incarcerate, intern, isolate, jail, keep in custody, keep in detention, keep under arrest, keep under control, keep within bounds, lock up, mure, pen, place in durance, put under arrest, put under restraint, quarantine, remand, retain, secure, shut in, surround, take captive, take into custody, take prisoner, trammel
ASSOCIATED CONCEPTS: detained in custody, detained in jail

DETAIN *(Restrain),* **verb**   arrest, bind, bound, chain, check, circumscribe, confine, constrain, contain, control, curb, delay, encumber, fetter, filibuster, forestall, gyve, halt, hamper, hinder, hold back, hold up, impede, inhibit, keep, keep back, keep under control, keep within bounds, lay under restraint, limit, manacle, obstruct, prevent, rein in, restrict, *retinere,* shackle, stall, stay, stop, suppress, *tenere,* trammel
ASSOCIATED CONCEPTS: unlawfully detained

DETAINER, *noun*   detainment, illegal custody, illegal detention, illegal restraint, illegal withholding, unlawful detention, unlawful restriction, unlawful retention, wrongful impoundment, wrongful keeping

DETECT, *verb*   be conscious of, become aware of, behold, bring to light, decipher, deduce, descry, determine, diagnose, diagnosticate, discern, discover, disinter, distinguish, divine, educe, espy, expose, extract, feel, ferret out, find, find out, gain knowledge, identify, learn, locate, make out, notice, observe, *patefacere,* perceive, realize, recognize, *rem invenire, reperire,* reveal, see, sense, sight, spot, trace, track, uncover, unearth, unmask, unravel, unveil, view

DETECTION, *noun*   apprehension, ascertainment, disclosure, discovery, exposure, finding, learning, perception, sighting, spotting, unearthing, unfolding

DETECTIVE, *noun*   agent, criminologist, espier, examinant, examiner, indagator, inquirer, inquiry agent, inquisitor, inspector, investigator, prober
ASSOCIATED CONCEPTS: police detectives, private detective

DETENTION, *noun*   arrest, captivity, circumscription, committal, commitment, confinement, constraint, control, *custodia,* custodianship, custody, detainment, durance vile, fetter, guardianship, immuration, immurement, impoundment, imprisonment, incarceration, internment, keeping, keeping back, keeping in, keeping in custody, legal restraint, limitation, preventive custody, prison, protective custody, quarantine, restraint, restriction, restriction on movement, *retentio*
ASSOCIATED CONCEPTS: detention facility, detention of property, illegal detention, lawful detention, preventive detention
FOREIGN PHRASES: *Furtum non est ubi initium habet detentionis per dominium rei.* It is not theft where the commencement of the detention arises through the consent of the owner.

DETER, **verb**   *absterrere,* avert, avoid, ban, bar, barricade, block, blunt, caution, check, chill, circumscribe, constrict, cow, cramp, cumber, dampen, deflect, deny access, *deterrere,* detour, discommode, discountenance, discourage, disenchant, disencourage, dishearten, disincline, dismay, dissuade, divert, divert from, fend, fend off, fetter, foil, forbid, foreclose, forestall, forfend, frustrate, hamper, hamstring, hinder, hold back, hold up, impede, incommode, indispose, inhibit, interclude, interfere with, intimidate, keep back, keep from, keep off, limit, nip in the bud, obstruct, obturate, obviate, overawe, persuade against, put a stop to, put off, quell, quench, remonstrate, render averse, repel, repress, reprove, restrain, restrict, rule out, set one back, shake one's faith, stave off, stop, stultify, thwart, turn aside, undermine one's belief, ward off, warn
ASSOCIATED CONCEPTS: deter from crime

DETERIORATE, *verb*   adulterate, aggravate, atrophy, become worse, collapse, corrode, *corrumpere,* corrupt, debase, debauch, debilitate, decay, decline, decompose, decrease, defile, degenerate, degrade, demoralize, denature, *depravare,* depreciate, devalue, dilapidate, downgrade, ebb, lapse, lower, pervert, pollute, prostitute, regress, retrograde, retrogress, spoil, taint, vitiate, wane, waste, weaken, worsen
ASSOCIATED CONCEPTS: deteriorating building, deteriorating goods

DETERIORATION, *noun*   abasement, abrasion, atrophy, caducity, consumption, corrosion, corruption, debasement, decadence, decay, declension, declination, decomposition, decrepitude, degradation, demission, depreciation, destruction, *deterior condicio,* dilapidation, disintegration, disrepair, emaciation, erosion, gradual decline, gradual impairment, impairment, irrepair, putrefaction, putridity, reduction, retrogradation, retrogression, ruin, ruination, senescence, spoliation, unrepair
ASSOCIATED CONCEPTS: property deterioration

DETERMINABLE *(Ascertainable),* **adjective**   accountable, admitting of decision, amenable to measurement, appraisable, appreciable, assessable, capable of decision, certifiable, cognizable, computable, construable, countable, decipherable, deducible, definable, detectible, discernible, discoverable, distinguishable, estimable, explainable, explicable, fathomable, fixable, gaugeable, interpretable, judicable, knowable, measurable, mensurable, noticeable, observable, perceivable, perceptible, resolvable, solvable, subject to measurement, surveyable, that may be determined, translatable, verifiable, workable

ASSOCIATED CONCEPTS: determinable period of usefulness

FOREIGN PHRASES: *Terminus annorum certus debet esse et determinatus.* A term of years ought to be certain and determinate.

DETERMINABLE (*Liable to be terminated*), *adjective* approaching an end, approaching the finish, coming to an end, drawing to a close, having the possibility of termination, liable to be completed, liable to be discontinued, liable to be dropped, liable to be ended, liable to come to an end, liable to expire, nearing completion, subject to be concluded, subject to cancellation, subject to discontinuance, subject to termination, terminable, with the end in sight

ASSOCIATED CONCEPTS: determinable fee, determinable interest, determinable remainder in fee

DETERMINANT, *noun* agent, authority, background, base, basis, consideration, constitutive element, contributing force, contributor, decisive factor, determining circumstance, determining element, determining influence, driving force, element, factor, fomentor, generator, genesis, impetus, inducement, instigation, justification, leaven, means, medium, motivation, motive, object, origin, prime mover, producer, root, source, ultimate cause, ultimate motive

DETERMINATION, *noun* adjudgment, adjudication, appraisal, appraisement, appreciation, apprisement, apprizement, *arbitrium*, ascertainment, assessment, authoritative estimate, authoritative opinion, award, conclusion, consideration, considered opinion, *consilium*, conviction, court decision, decision, declaration, decree, diagnosis, evaluation, final assessment, finding, *institutum, iudicium,* judgment, judgment on facts, opinion, order, pronouncement, reasoned judgment, reckoning, recommendation, resolution, resolve, result, result ascertained, ruling, sentence, settlement, solution, verdict

ASSOCIATED CONCEPTS: actual determination, determination of a suit, determination of claims, determination of fact, determination of guilt, final determination, judicial determination, official determination, review a determination, self-determination

FOREIGN PHRASES: *Judicia in deliberationibus crebro maturescunt, in accelerato processu nunquam.* Judgments frequently mature by deliberations, never by hurried process. *De audiendo et terminando.* To hear and determine. *In propria causa nemo judex.* No one can be judge in his own case.

DETERMINATIVE, *adjective* authoritative, conclusive, convincing, deciding, decisive, decretal, definitive, directing, *ex parte,* final, important, judgmatic, judicious, limiting, limitive, persuasive, shaping, significant, telling, weighty

DETERMINE, *verb* adjudge, adjudicate, arrive at a conclusion, ascertain, award, bring in a verdict, bring to an end, bring to justice, choose, come to a conclusion, come to a decision, come to a determination, conclude, confirm, *constituere, decernere,* decide, decide upon, declare, decree, decree by judicial authority, deduce, delimit, deliver judgment, direct, draw a conclusion, end by a decision, estimate, exercise the judgment, find, fix upon, form a judgment, form a resolution, give a ruling, give an opinion, give judgment, hold, infer, interpret, judge, limit, make a decision, make a resolution, make

one's choice, make terms, make up one's mind, opine, pass an opinion, pass judgment, pass sentence, prescribe punishment, pronounce, pronounce a judgment, pronounce guilty, reckon, referee, regulate, remain firm, resolve, rule, seal, seal the doom of, settle, settle in one's mind, settle upon, sit in judgment, *statuere,* stipulate, take a decisive step, utter judicial sentence against, weigh, will

ASSOCIATED CONCEPTS: determine the nature of the loss, finally determined, legally determine the rights of the parties to an action

DETERRENCE, *noun* abridgment, active discouragement, admonition, barrier, block, blockade, caveat, check, compulsion, constraint, constriction, contraindication, *contretemps,* control, curb, detainment, deterrent, discouragement, disincentive, dissuasion, extinguishment, forestalling, frustration, halt, hindrance, hurdle, impediment, impedition, inhibition, interference, intimidation, legal restraint, limitation, means of restraint, monition, obstacle, obstruction, opposition, preclusion, prevention, prohibition, prophylaxis, proscription, quashing, repression, resistance, restraint, restriction, stop, striction, stumbling block, suppression, thwarter

ASSOCIATED CONCEPTS: deterrence of crime

FOREIGN PHRASES: *Nemo prudens punit ut praeterita revocentur, sed ut futura praeveniantur.* No wise man punishes in order that past things may be revoked, but that future wrongs may be prevented. *Poena ad paucos, metus ad omnes perveniat.* If punishment be inflicted on a few, a fear comes to all.

DETERRENT, *noun* admonishment, admonition, barrier, barring, block, caution, caveat, constraint, constriction, contraindication, counteraction, counterpressure, curb, damper, deactivation, determent, deterrence, discouragement, disincentive, dissuasion, forestalling, hampering, hinderer, hindrance, hurdle, impedance, impeder, inhibition, inhibitor, insuperable obstacle, interference, interposition, intimidation, legal restraint, limitation, means of restraint, monition, obstacle, obstructer, obstruction, obstructive, obtrusion, occlusion, opposition, preclusion, prevention, proscription, repression, restraint, restriction, retardation, suppression, thwarter, warning

DETOUR, *noun* alternate route, by-pass, by-passage, circuitous route, deflection, departure, deviation, deviation from a direct course, digression, diversion, excursion, indirect path, loop, roundabout course, temporary route, wrong course

ASSOCIATED CONCEPTS: detour from course of employment, frolic and detour

DETOUR, *verb* *aberrare,* alter one's course, avoid, by-pass, change direction, change the bearing, circuit, circumambulate, deflect, depart from, depart from one's course, deviate, deviate from a direct course, *digredi,* digress, diverge, divert, divert from its course, drift, encircle, excurse, go around, go out of one's way, go out of the path, go out of the way, go round about, make a circuit, meander, perform a circuit, ramble, sidestep, skirt, stray, swerve, take a circuitous route, take a roundabout course, take a temporary route, take an alternate highway, take an alternate route, take an indirect way, turn aside, vary, veer

ASSOCIATED CONCEPTS: detour from course of employment, frolick and detour

DETRIMENT, noun adulteration, adversity, affliction, aggravation, atrophy, bane, bedevilment, blemish, blow, collapse, contamination, corrosion, corruption, cost, crippling, damage, *damnum,* decadence, decay, deformation, degeneration, demolishment, deprivation, destruction, deterioration, detraction, *detrimentum,* dilapidation, disability, disablement, disadvantage, disintegration, disorder, disturbance, erosion, evil, forfeit, forfeiture, handicap, hardship, harm, hurt, impairment, impotence, inadequacy, inadvisability, *incommodum,* inconvenience, ineffectualness, inefficiency, inexpedience, inexpediency, injuriousness, injury, insufficiency, laming, liability, loss, misfortune, mutilation, obstacle, poisoning, pollution, prejudice, privation, ruin, ruination, undesirability, undoing, unprofitability, weakness
ASSOCIATED CONCEPTS: legal detriment

DETRIMENTAL, adjective adverse, afflicting, bad, corrupting, crippling, damaging, deleterious, destructive, disadvantageous, disastrous, discommodious, distressing, disturbing, dreadful, extirpative, fulsome, grievous, harmful, hindering, hurtful, ill-advised, ill-contrived, impolitic, inappropriate, inimical, *iniquus,* injurious, inopportune, insalubrious, insidious, internecine, malefic, malignant, noisome, noxious, oppressive, *perniciosus,* pernicious, pestilential, prejudicial, toxic, treacherous, undermining, unfit, unhealthy, unhelpful, unprofitable, unpropitious, unsatisfactory, unsuitable, untoward, unwholesome, unwise
ASSOCIATED CONCEPTS: actively detrimental, detrimental to the best interests of the child, detrimental to the public interest

DEVASTATE, verb demolish, depopulate, depredate, desolate, despoil, destroy, gut, lever, overwhelm, pillage, plunder, raid, ransack, ravage, raze, ruin, sack, wreck

DEVELOP, verb accrue, *adolescere,* advance, advance in successive gradation, *alere,* amplify, arise from, *augeri,* augment, become, become apparent, begin from, bring forth, bring into being, bring to a complete condition, bring to a more advanced state, bring to light by degrees, broaden, build up, cause to expand, cause to grow, change into, come gradually into existence, come to be, come to maturity, *crescere,* cultivate, derive from, descend from, detail, *educare,* elaborate, emanate, emerge, enlarge, enlarge upon, enter into detail, evolve, *excolere,* expand, expand upon, extend, fill in, fill out, further, germinate, give being to, give forth, give rise to, go into detail, grow, grow better, grow from, improve, increase the strength of, infuse, intensify, invigorate, magnify, make headway, make progress, mature, meliorate, mend, perfect, proceed, produce, progress, promote, raise, reach manhood, refine, reinforce, revive, ripen, shape up, show improvement, stimulate, strengthen, stretch, swell, take form, take shape, unfold, widen, work out in detail

DEVELOPER, noun builder, building entrepeneur, creator, designer, enterpriser, establisher, land developer, organizer, originator, planner, promoter
ASSOCIATED CONCEPTS: commercial developer, residential developer

DEVELOPMENT *(Building),* **noun** commercial building, construction, creation of housing project, development of industrial sites, erection, house-building program, housing, industrial area, industrial building, institution of commercial sites, residential building, urbanization

DEVELOPMENT *(Outgrowth),* **noun** accomplishment, achievement, aftergrowth, aftermath, attainment, by-product, conclusion, consequence, consequent, derivation, effect, emanation, ending, ensual, event, eventuality, eventuation, occurrence, offshoot, outcome, product, realization, result, resultant, sequel, side issue, upshot

DEVELOPMENT *(Progression),* **noun** accretion, accumulation, advance, advancement, amelioration, ampliation, amplification, anabasis, *auctus,* betterment, change, cultivation, effectuation, elaboration, enhancement, enrichment, evolution, evolvement, expansion, *explicatio,* extension, furtherance, gain, germination, gradual evolution, growth, improvement, increase in size, lengthening, melioration, modernization, progress, progress to maturity, progressive growth, *progressus,* promotion, refinement, reform, reformation, regeneration, remodeling, renovation, reorganization, revision, stimulation, strengthening, supplementation, transfiguration, transformation, unfolding, unravelment, upgrowth, uptrend
ASSOCIATED CONCEPTS: development costs

DEVIANT, adjective aberrant, abnormal, adverse to, against the rules, atypical, clashing, contrary, counter to, departing from, desultory, deviating, discordant, discrepant, dissident, dissonant, divergent, eccentric, errant, heretical, in violation of, irregular, nonconformist, nonuniform, oblique, out of order, out of step, recalcitrant, stray, unconventional, unfashionable, unorthodox, variant
ASSOCIATED CONCEPTS: deviant behavior

DEVIATE, verb *aberrare,* alter course, angle off, be at variance, be different, be distinguished from, be oblique, bear no resemblance, bear off, branch out, break bounds, break the pattern, change direction, clash, clash with, conflict with, contrast, *declinare,* deflect, *degredi,* depart from, depart from one's course, differ, digress, disagree, divaricate, diverge, divert from its course, drift, err, fall into error, fly off at a tangent, get off the subject, glance off, go adrift, go amiss, go astray, go awry, go off on a tangent, go out of one's way, go round about, go wrong, infringe a law, infringe custom, make a detour, meander, not conform, perform a circuit, show variety, slip, stand apart, step aside, stray, swerve, take a different course, turn, turn aside, turn out of one's way, vary, veer, wander from the subject

DEVIATION, noun aberrance, aberrancy, aberration, abnormality, alteration, anomalousness, anomaly, antipathy, antithesis, branching off, breach of practice, change of direction, change of position, contrast, *declinatio,* defiance of custom, departure, departure from usage, detour, difference, *digressio,* disaccord, disaccordance, disagreement, discongruity, discontinuity, discord, discrepancy, disharmony, disparity, dissidence, dissimilarity, dissonance, distinctness, divagation, divergence, diverseness, diversion, incongruity, inconsistency, inconsonance, inharmoniousness, irregularity, nonconformism, nonconformity, nonimitation, nonobservance, nonuniformity, straying, swerve, swerving, unconformity, unlikeness, unorthodoxy, variability, variance, variation

ASSOCIATED CONCEPTS: deviation doctrine, deviation from scope of employment, deviation from the norm

DEVICE *(Contrivance),* **noun**   artifice, circumvention, craft, design, gimmick, *machina,* machination, maneuver, means to an end, method, plan, program of action, project, resort, ruse, scheme, setup, stratagem, subtle maneuver, system, trick, wile, working plan, working proposition

DEVICE *(Distinguishing mark),* **noun**   badge of office, design, designation, earmark, emblem, ensign, hallmark, identification mark, indicant, *inscriptio,* insignia, label, mark that designates, sign, symbol, token, trademark

DEVICE *(Mechanism),* **noun**   apparatus, appliance, equipment, facility, fixture, gadget, gear, implement, instrument, invention, mechanical aid, tool, utensil
ASSOCIATED CONCEPTS: safety device

DEVIOUS, *adjective*   aberrant, ambagious, artful, circuitous, crafty, crooked, cunning, deceitful, designing, deviating, deviative, *devius,* errant, excursive, foxy, indirect, insidious, labyrinthine, roundabout, scheming, serpentine, sinuous, sly, sneaking, tortuous, tricky, uncandid, unstraightforward, wily

DEVISE *(Give),* **verb**   allot, assign, bequeath, bestow, confer, convey, endow, give, give and bequeath, give away, give by will, grant, leave, leave by will, make a bequest, make testamentary dispositions, transfer, transmit, transmit by will, will and bequeath, will to
ASSOCIATED CONCEPTS: absolute devise, alienation, bequest, conveyance, demonstrative devise, executory devise, general devise, legacy, testamentary disposition
FOREIGN PHRASES: *Nemo plus commodi haeredi suo relinquit quam ipse habuit.* No one leaves a greater benefit to his heir than he had himself. *Da tua dum tua sunt, post mortem tunc tua non sunt.* Give that which is yours while it is yours; after death it is not yours. *Quando aliquis aliquid concedit, concedere videtur et id sine quo res unon potest.* When anyone grants anything, he is deemed to grant also that without which the thing granted cannot be used.

DEVISE *(Invent),* **verb**   arrange, calculate, compose, conceive, construct, contrive, create, design, draw up, engineer, erect, evolve, *excogitare,* fabricate, fashion, find a way, form, formulate, frame, have an idea, imagine, improvise, *invenire,* lay down a plan, lay out, make a plan, make arrangements, make up, maneuver, manufacture, map out, piece together, plan, plan out, prearrange, predetermine, prepare, proceed by stratagem, put together, schematize, scheme, set up, shape, sketch out, take steps, work out

DEVISEE, *noun*   acceptor, beneficiary, donee, grantee, heir, inheritor, legatee, recipient, successor, transferee

DEVOID, *adjective*   bare, barren, bereft of, blank, bleak, deficient, denuded of, deprived of, deserted, desolate, destitute of, empty, empty of, found wanting, ill-furnished, ill-provided, ill-stored, impotent, in default of, in the absence of, in want of, incomplete, insufficient, lacking, missing, out of, poor, *re vacuus,* scant of, short, short of, sparing, stinted, tenantless, unacquired, unexisting, uninhabited, unmanned, unoccupied, unofficered, unpeopled, unpossessed of, unprovided, unreplenished, unstaffed, unsupplied, untenanted, vacant, vacuous, void of, wanting, without, without content, without resources

DEVOLUTION, *noun*   assignment, bequeathal, bequest, change of hands, change-over, conveyance, delegation, delegation of duties, deliverance, delivery, demise, devise, interchange, nonretention, reversion, substitution, succession, succession of property rights, transfer, transfer of property, transference, transmission
ASSOCIATED CONCEPTS: devolution of liability, devolution of property

DEVOLVE, *verb*   be handed down to, be handed over, be transferred, bequeath, cause to pass to another, cede, change from one to another, change ownership, confer ownership, convey, *deferre,* delegate upon another, deliver, deliver over to a successor, descend by inheritance, descend upon, fall by inheritance, fall by succession, give, grant, interchange, invest with, leave to, make over, *mandare,* pass to, *permittere,* put in possession, sign away, substitute, trade, transfer, transfer ownership, transfer to, transmit, turn over
ASSOCIATED CONCEPTS: devolution of a lease

DEVOTE, *verb*   allot, apply, apportion, appropriate, assign, attend, be absorbed in, be attentive, be engrossed in, concentrate, concern, *consecrare,* consecrate, contemplate, *dedere,* dedicate, *devovere,* direct attention, focus, give attention, heed, meditate upon, occupy oneself with, pay attention, pay heed, set apart, set aside, think about, turn attention
ASSOCIATED CONCEPTS: devote attention, devote to a public use

DIABOLIC, *adjective*   accursed, amoral, amoralistic, bad-hearted, brutal, brutalized, callous, conscienceless, cruel, cursed, deadly, dehumanized, demonic, devil-like, devilish, evil, evil-doing, evil-minded, execrable, fiendish, fiendlike, full of sin, god-forsaken, guilty, heinous, hellish, hopeless, horrible, immoral, impious, infernal, inhuman, iniquitous, irredeemable, irreligious, maleficent, malevolent, malignant, Mephistophelian, merciless, monstrous, murderous, nefarious, outrageous, pitiless, possessed, profane, ruinous, ruthless, sadistic, Satanic, sin-laden, sinful, sinister, sinning, transgressing, unnatural, unprincipled, unredeemed, unrighteous, unscrupulous, unvirtuous, vicious, virtueless, wicked

DIAGNOSE, *verb*   analyze, appraise, classify, compare critically, discern, distinguish, estimate, examine critically, have insight, identify, judge, make a judgment, recognize, see the difference, sort out, specify, weigh

DIAGNOSIS, *noun*   analysis, appreciation of differences, assay, breakdown, careful appreciation, categorization, category, classification, classificatory description, conclusion, critical appraisal, critical scrutiny, critique, designation, differentiation, discernment, discretion, discriminating judgment, discrimination, estimation, interpretation, judgment, perception of difference, scientific determination, specification, symptomatology
ASSOCIATED CONCEPTS: faulty diagnosis, malpractice

DIALECTIC, *noun*   applied logic, apprehension, argumentation, brainwork, cerebration, chain of reasoning, cogitation, concluding, consideration, contemplation, deducing, deduction, deliberation, deriving, discursive reasoning, drawing conclusions, force of argument, induction, inferring, judgment, logic, logic of discursive argument, logical argumentation, logical discussion, logical process, logical sequence, mode of reasoning, ratiocination, rationalism, rationalization, rationalizing, reasoning, reflection, rumination, thinking

DIATRIBE, *noun*   abuse, abusive harangue, abusive language, accusation, act of berating, admonition, adverse comment, animadversion, backbiting, bitter harangue, bitter words, blame, carping, castigation, censure, chiding, complaining, condemnation, countercharge, *coup de bec,* criticism, cutting words, denunciation, deprecation, depreciation, discommendation, disparagement, dispraise, dressing down, faultfinding, gainsaying, harangue, hostile attack, hostile criticism, hostile eloquence, hypercriticism, inculpation, indictment, insult, invective, long vehement speech, objurgation, obloquy, oration, prolonged outburst of denunciation, railing, rebuke, remonstrance, reprehension, reprimand, reproach, reproof, revilement, reviling, sarcasm, scolding, scurrility, sermon, stinging words, strain of invective, stream of abuse, tirade, tonguelashing, upbraiding, verbal onslaught, vilification, vituperation

DICHOTOMIZE, *verb*   apportion, bifurcate, bisect, branch, cleave in two, cut in halves, cut in two, detach, disconnect, disjoin, dissect, dissever, disunite, divaricate, diverge, divide, fragment, furcate, halve, keep apart, part, partition, rend, rive, section, sectionalize, segment, separate, separate in two, sever, split, subdivide, transect

DICHOTOMY, *noun*   bifurcation, bipartition, bisection, dissection, divarication, division, halving, separation, severance, split, subdivision

DICKER, *verb*   adjust differences, arbitrate terms, argue price, arrange terms, arrive at a price, bargain, barter, bicker, bid for, come to terms, confer on price, contend, deal, drive a bargain, give terms, haggle, have dealings, make terms, negotiate, put through a deal, state one's terms, strike a bargain, trade, transact, wrangle
ASSOCIATED CONCEPTS: dicker over terms of a contract

DICTATE, *noun*   act, authoritative suggestion, behest, charge, command, commandment, commission, decree, demand, direction, edict, enactment, fiat, imperative, imperious direction, injunction, instruction, judgment, law, mandate, order, ordinance, ordination, precept, prescript, prescription, proclamation, regulation, requirement, rescript, rubric, rule, ruling, ultimatum

DICTATE, *verb*   bid, charge, command, compel, decree, demand, direct, enjoin, exercise authority, give orders, impose an order, instruct, issue a command, issue an order, oblige, ordain, order, prescribe, require, require authoritatively, rule

DICTATOR, *noun*   absolute leader, absolute ruler, autarch, autocrat, autocratic master, despot, despotic commander, despotic master, dictatorial mogul, disci-

plinarian, imperious commandant, inquisitor, martinet, oppressive taskmaster, oppressor, repressive governor, strict disciplinarian, totalitarian, tyrannical leader, tyrant

DICTATORIAL, *adjective*   absolutistic, arbitrary, arrogant, authoritarian, authoritative, autocratic, censorious, commanding, compelling, controlling, despotic, *dictatorius,* dogmatic, domineering, enslaving, exacting, fanatic, fascist, highhanded, imperative, *imperiosus,* imperious, inexorable, inquisitorial, intimidating, ironhanded, lordly, masterful, monocratic, officious, oppressive, overbearing, peremptory, pompous, power-crazed, power-hungry, power-mad, relentless, repressive, severe, suppressive, supreme, totalitarian, tyrannical, tyrannous, uncompromising, undemocratic, unlimited, unrelenting, unrestricted, with an iron hand

DICTUM, *noun*   announcement, assertion, authoritative assertion, declaration, extrajudicial opinion, finding, gratuitous remark, illustrative statement, incidental opinion, judicial assertion, judicial comment, judicial remark, observation, opinion, pronouncement, recommendation, remark, statement, statement by way of illustration
ASSOCIATED CONCEPTS: judicial dictum, obiter dictum

DIDACTIC, *adjective*   academic, adapted to teach, curricular, edifying, educating, educational, educative, enlightening, enriching, erudite, expository, fitted to teach, informational, informative, instructional, instructive, intended for instruction, intended for teaching, learned, pedagogic, propaedeutic, scholarly, scholastic, teaching, tutorial

DIE, *verb*   be no more, breathe one's last, cease living, cease to exist, decease, demise, depart, end one's life, expire, lose one's life, meet one's death, *mori, mortem obire,* part with life, pass away, pass on, perish, relinquish life, rest in peace, succumb to death, suffer death, *vita decedere*
ASSOCIATED CONCEPTS: die at any time without issue surviving, die by his own hand or act, die in performance of duty, die intestate, die leaving issue, die seised and possessed, die simultaneously, die without children or issue, die without heirs, die without issue, die without lawful issue, testamentary dispositions

DIFFER *(Disagree), verb*   be discordant, be incongruent, be inharmonious, bicker, cavil, clash, conflict with, contend, contradict, dispute, divide on, hold different views, object, oppose, protest, raise objections, reject, repudiate, take exception, take issue, think differently, withhold assent

DIFFER *(Vary), verb*   argue, be at cross purposes, be at variance, be contrary, be dissimilar, be distinct, be distinguished from, be inharmonious, be opposite, be unique, be unlike, bear no resemblance, contrast, depart from, deviate from, digress, disaccord, disaccord with, disagree, discept, *discrepare,* dissent, *dissentire, dissidere,* divaricate from, diverge from, diversify, have a dissimilar opinion, lack resemblance, not agree, not compare with, not conform, not equate, show contrast, show variety, take exception, take issue, think differently, vary, withhold assent
FOREIGN PHRASES: *Non differunt quae concordant re, tametsi non in verbis iisdem.* Those matters do not differ which agree in substance, though not in the same words.

DIFFERENCE, noun adverseness, antipathy, antithesis, antitheticalness, asymmetry, atypicality, breach, change, clash of temperament, clashing, conflict of opinion, contradiction, contradistinction, contraposition, contrariety, contrariness, contrast, controversy, counterpoint, departure, departure from, deviation, differentiation, disaccord, disagreement, discongruity, disconnection, discontinuity, discord, discordance, discrepancy, *discrepantia,* discrimination, disequilibrium, disharmony, disjunction, disparity, disproportion, dissemblance, dissension, dissimilarity, dissimilitude, dissonance, distinction, distinctness, distortion, divergence, diverseness, *diversitas,* diversity, failure to agree, heterogeneity, imbalance, imparity, inaccordance, incommensurability, incongruence, incongruity, incongruousness, inconsistency, inconsonance, individuality, inequality, inharmoniousness, inharmony, irreconcilability, irrelation, lack of connection, lack of resemblance, misunderstanding, multifariousness, mutual exclusiveness, nonconformity, nonimitation, nonuniformity, nuance, oppositeness, opposition, schism, separateness, state of being different, unconformity, unequalness, uniqueness, unlikeness, unrelatedness, variance, variation, variegation, *varietas,* variety
ASSOCIATED CONCEPTS: difference in degree, difference in kind, difference in the nature and elements of a crime, difference in value, difference of opinion, settling of differences

DIFFERENT, adjective alien, *alius,* altered, antagonistic, antithetic, atypical, changed, clashing, contradictory, contradistinct, contradistinctive, contrary, contrasting, contrastive, deviating, diametric, discordant, *discrepans,* discrepant, disparate, dissimilar, dissonant, distinct, distinctive, divergent, diverse, diversiform, *diversus,* foreign, heterogeneous, idiosyncratic, in disagreement, incommensurable, incomparable, incompatible, incongruous, individual, inharmonious, mismatched, mismated, nonidentical, not the same, novel, opposed, other than, out of the ordinary, peculiar, separate, set apart, singular, unidentical, unique, unlike, unmatched, unrelated, unusual, unwonted, variant, varied, varietal, various, varying
ASSOCIATED CONCEPTS: different causes of action, different offenses

DIFFERENTIAL, noun attribute, characteristic, constituting a difference, contrasting quality, delicate distinction, difference of degree, differentiating trait, distinction, distinctive feature, distinguishing feature, feature, gradation, grade, graduation, nuance, particularity, peculiarity, property, proportion, quality, rate, ratio, relative quantity, scale, shade of difference, singularity, subtle difference, trait, variant
ASSOCIATED CONCEPTS: wage differential

DIFFERENTIATE, verb characterize, classify, contrast, demarcate, discern between, discriminate, distinguish, diversify, draw the line, exercise discrimination, make a distinction, make distinctive, mark off by differences, mark out, particularize, perceive clearly, recognize as separate, segregate, separate as different, set apart as different, set off, show a difference, single out, sort out, subtilize, tell apart, tell from

DIFFICULT, adjective arduous, attended by obstacles, awkward, beset with difficulty, beyond one's reach, bothersome, burdensome, complex, complicated, convoluted, *difficile, difficilis,* encompassed with difficulties, enigmatic, entangled by difficulties, fatiguing, grueling, hard, hard to deal with, hard to manage, hard to understand, impassable, *impeditus,* impenetrable, incomprehensible, insoluble, insurmountable, intractable, involved, labored, laborious, labyrinthine, obscure, obstinate, offering a problem, operose, out of reach, painstaking, perplexing, perverse, problematic, puzzling, recondite, refractory, strenuous, stubborn, surrounded by difficulties, too hard, troublesome, unachievable, unapproachable, unavailable, uncertain, unclear
ASSOCIATED CONCEPTS: difficult and extraordinary action, difficult and extraordinary case or proceeding

DIFFIDENT, adjective abashed, awestricken, awestruck, bashful, blushful, blushing, cautious, demure, deprecating, deprecative, *diffidens,* embarrassed, fainthearted, faltering, hesitating, humble, humbled, lacking self-confidence, modest, overanxious, overapprehensive, overshy, qualmish, quiet, reserved, retiring, self-conscious, self-effacing, shaky, shameful, sheepish, shrinking, shy, timid, timorous, treading warily, tremulous, unambitious, unassuming, unboastful, unheard, unimposing, unobstrusive, unostentatious, unpretentious, unpushing, unsure of oneself, *verecundus,* wary, without vanity

DIFFUSE, verb bespread, besprinkle, bestrew, break up, broadcast, cast forth, circulate, circumfuse, commingle, deal out, decentralize, *diffundere, diffundi,* disband, disintegrate, disperse, dispread, disseminate, dissipate, distribute, effuse, go in different directions, go in many directions, intermix, intersperse, mix, overspread, *permeare,* permeate, pervade, promulgate, propagate, put into circulation, radiate, scatter, send abroad, send forth, sow, spatter, spread, spread about, spread abroad, spread around, spread far and wide, spread widely, strew, unloose

DIGAMY, noun deuterogamy, finding another mate, finding another spouse, marriage to a second partner, remarriage, second legal marriage, second marriage, wedding a second time

DIGEST, noun abbreviation, abridgment, abstract, analysis, anthology, arrangement, brief, capsule, code, collection, compendium, compilation, condensation, consolidation, conspectus, contraction, epitome, essence, extract, outline, pandect, recapitulation, review, summary, synopsis
ASSOCIATED CONCEPTS: digest of cases, digest of laws

DIGEST (Comprehend), verb absorb, analyze, appreciate, assimilate, cognize, consider, contemplate, fathom, grasp, incorporate, ken, know, muse, register, think about, understand, weigh

DIGEST (Summarize), verb abbreviate, abridge, abstract, capsulize, catalogue, classify, codify, condense, cut down, edit, excerpt, make a summary of, make brief, make concise, outline, recapitulate, reduce, select, shorten, sum up, survey

DIGRESS, verb *aberrare,* alter course, be diffuse, branch out, change direction, depart, detour, deviate, *digredi,* divagate, divaricate, diverge, divert, drift, expatiate, fly off at a tangent, go astray, meander, ramble, rove, shift, sidestep, sidetrack, skirt, stray, swerve, turn, veer, wander

DIGRESSION, *noun* aberrancy, aberration, alteration, break, change, circuity, convolution, departure, detour, deviation, *digressio,* divagation, divarication, divergence, diversion, drift, excursus, misdirection, periphrasis, roundabout way, shift in topic, sideslip, sidestep, swerve, variance, variation
ASSOCIATED CONCEPTS: dictum

DILAPIDATED, *adjective* altered for the worse, condemned, damaged, decomposed, decrepit, fallen into ruin, far-gone, frayed, friable, impaired, imperfect, marred, mouldering, *obsoletus,* on the wane, ramshackle, ruined, shabby, stale, tabid, timeworn, used, weatherbeaten, wilted, withering, worn, worn out
ASSOCIATED CONCEPTS: depreciation, obsolescence

DILATORY, *adjective* after time, behind time, belated, deferring, delayed, delaying, deliberately slow, eleventh hour, inclined to delay, indolent, intended to bring about delay, intended to defer decision, intended to gain time, lackadaisical, last minute, late, overdue, pausing, procrastinating, procrastinative, procrastinatory, remiss, tardy, unpunctual
ASSOCIATED CONCEPTS: dilatory defense, dilatory exceptions, dilatory motion, dilatory plea, dilatory practice

DILEMMA, *noun* awkward predicament, awkward situation, baffle, bafflement, confoundment, confusion, decision, difficult choice, difficulty, imbroglio, impasse, indecision, limited choice, perplexity, predicament, puzzle, puzzlement, puzzling alternative, quandary, uncertainty, unfair choice, vexed question

DILIGENCE *(Care),* *noun* absorption of mind, active application, active attention, active study, active thought, *adsiduitas,* advertence, advertency, alertness, application, attention, attention to detail, carefulness, caution, check-up, circumspection, close application, close attention, close study, close thought, concern, consideration, contemplation, deep application, deep attention, deep study, deep thought, deliberate application, deliberate attention, deliberate study, deliberate thought, diligent application, diligent attention, diligent study, diligent thought, *diligentia,* earnestness, exactitude, exactness, exclusive application, exclusive attention, exclusive study, exclusive thought, fastidiousness, foresight, guard, heed, heedfulness, *industria,* inquisitive attention, inspection, intense application, intense study, intense thought, intentness, meticulousness, mindfulness, minute application, minute attention, minute study, minute thought, minuteness, observation, orderliness, painstaking, particularity, pedantry, preparedness, profound application, profound attention, profound study, profound thought, prudence, rapt attention, readiness, regard, review, scrutiny, seriousness, single-mindedness, studiousness, study, thoroughgoingness, thoroughness, undivided attention, utmost care, vigilance, wakefulness, wariness, watchfulness, whole attention, whole mind
ASSOCIATED CONCEPTS: due diligence, lack of diligence, ordinary diligence, reasonable diligence, utmost diligence

DILIGENCE *(Perseverance),* *noun* application, ardor, assiduity, assiduousness, constancy, continuance, determination, devotedness, devotion, doggedness, earnestness, endurance, firmness of purpose, fixity of purpose, habitual devotion, indefatigability, industriousness, insistence, intentness, intrepidity, meticulosity, patience, persistence, persistency, persistent exertion, pertinacity, purposefulness, relentlessness, resolution, restlessness, sedulity, sedulousness, singleness of purpose, staying power, steadfastness, steadiness, steady application, strength of will, stubbornness, tenaciousness, tenacity, tirelessness, undauntedness, undivided attention, vigilence, vigor, zeal, zealousness
ASSOCIATED CONCEPTS: diligence in prosecution

DILIGENT, *adjective* assiduous, attentive, busily intent, businesslike, busy, conscientious, constant, dependable, *diligens,* dogged, enduring, exact, faithful, fastidious, hardworking, heedful, indefatigable, industrious, *industrius,* never idle, never tiring, operose, painstaking, perseverant, persevering, persistent, pertinacious, punctilious, relentless, reliable, resolute, responsible, scholarly, sedulous, steadfast, studious, tenacious, thorough, thoroughgoing, tireless, trustworthy, undaunted, unfaltering, unrelenting, unremitting, untiring, unwavering, unwearying, watchful
ASSOCIATED CONCEPTS: diligent creditor, diligent efforts, diligent inquiry, diligent prosecution, diligent search, diligent use, due diligence

DILUTE, *verb* abbreviate, add water, attenuate, bate, belittle, cheapen, combine with water, depreciate, detract from, *diluere,* extenuate, lessen the strength of, make less concentrated, make more fluid, make more liquid, make thin, make weak, minimize, mitigate, reduce the strength of, render weak, subtract, take away, thin, thin out, thin with liquid, water, weaken

DIMENSION, *noun* area, boundaries, configuration, conformation, measure, outline, proportions, shape, size, square measure, surface, territorial shape

DIMINISH, *verb* abate, abbreviate, abrade, abridge, alleviate, assuage, bate, become smaller, belittle, bound, cause to be smaller, cause to taper, cheapen, compress, consume, contract, curb, curtail, cut back, cut down, damp down, dampen, decelerate, decimate, decrease, deduct, deflate, delete, *deminuere,* depopulate, depreciate, depress, deprive, derogate, detract, detract from, dilute, divest, do subtraction, dock, drain, drop off, dull, dwindle, eat away, ebb, economize, empty, erode, excise, expurgate, extenuate, fade away, fall away, grow less, lessen, lighten, limit, lower, make less, make smaller, make thin, minify, minimize, *minuere,* mitigate, pare, prune, quell, quiet, recede, reduce, relieve, remit, render few, render smaller, restrain, retard, retrench, roll back, rub away, run down, run low, scale down, shave off, shorten, shrink, slow down, step down, stifle, subdue, subside, subtract, take away, take from, take off, taper, thin, thin out, tone down, tune down, unload, use up, wane, waste, waste away, weaken, wear away, wear down, wear out, weed out, whittle, withdraw, wither
ASSOCIATED CONCEPTS: diminished responsibility, diminished use, diminishing returns

DIMINUTION, *noun* abatement, abbreviation, contraction, decrease, deduction, deflation, diminishment, lessening, let up, lowering, mitigation, reduction, remission, shrinkage

DINT, *noun* ableness, authority, control, effectiveness, effectuality, efficacy, force, forcefulness, greatness, influence, might, mightiness, potence, potency, power, powerfulness, prepotency, pressure, puissance, strength, superiority, sway, vigor, weight

DIPLOMATIC, adjective adept, artful, cautious in dealing, cunning, deft, dexterous, discreet, graceful, polite, politic, prudent, scheming, skillful in handling others, smoothly, strategic, tactful
ASSOCIATED CONCEPTS: diplomatic immunity, diplomatic recognition, diplomatic relations, diplomatic status

DIPSOMANIA, noun acute alcoholism, addictedness, addiction, alcoholic addiction, alcoholism, bibacity, cacoethes, chronic alcoholism, compulsion, crapulence, craving for drink, drunkenness, ebriosity, excessive drinking, excessiveness, inebriation, inebriety, insobriety, intemperance, intoxication, obsession, potation

DIRE, adjective annihilative, appalling, awful, baleful, calamitous, cataclysmic, catastrophic, catastrophical, deadly, demolishing, destroying, destructive, devastating, direful, disastrous, dismal, dreaded, dreadful, eradicative, exterminative, extirpative, extirpatory, extreme, fatal, fearful, fell, frightening, grave, grievous, grim, horrible, horrid, horrifying, ill-boding, ill-omened, inauspicious, lethal, ominous, portentous, ruinous, serious, sinister, terrible, tragic, tragical, unfortunate, unlucky, unpropitious, woeful, worst

DIRECT (Forthright), adjective aboveboard, blunt, candid, clear, explicit, face to face, forthright, frank, genuine, guileless, honest, ingenuous, open, outspoken, plain, point-blank, pointed, *rectus,* sincere, straightforward, summary, transparent, truthful, unaffected, unambiguous, unassuming, unconstrained, undeceitful, undeceiving, undeceptive, undesigning, undisguising, unfeigning, unpretending, unpretentious, unreserved, unrestrained, veracious, veridical

DIRECT (Straight), adjective aimed, guided, immediate, linear, rectilineal, steered, straightaway, true, unbent, unbroken, undeflected, undeviating, undistorted, unswerving, unturned, unwarped, without a bend, without circumlocution, without divergence
ASSOCIATED CONCEPTS: direct and proximate cause, direct attack, direct benefit, direct cause, direct contempt, direct control, direct damages, direct descendants, direct evidence, direct interest, direct knowledge, direct loss, direct result, direct route, direct tax, direct testimony, direct trust

DIRECT (Uninterrupted), adjective connected, consecutive, continual, continuous, progressive, steady, straight, successive, unbroken, unending, unfaltering, unstopped

DIRECT (Order), verb adjure, bid, call upon, charge, command, decree, demand, dictate, enjoin, give a directive, give an order, give directions, give instructions, give orders, govern, instruct, issue a command, issue a decree, issue an order, ordain, prescribe, rule, set a task, signal, tell
ASSOCIATED CONCEPTS: directed verdict

DIRECT (Show), verb conduct, designate, guide, *homini viam monstrare,* indicate, instruct, lead, navigate, point, point out, steer

DIRECT (Supervise), verb administer, *administrare,* administrate, assign, be master, boss, coach, command, conduct, control, *dirigere,* dominate, educate, engineer, exercise authority, exercise supervision, govern, guide, head, lead, look after, manage, mastermind, oversee, preside, preside over, *regere,* regulate, rule, stage, steer, superintend, take command

DIRECTION (Course), noun aim, approach, bearing, bent, blueprint, course of action, *cursus,* design, draft, drift, heading, inclination, line, map, master plan, method, outline, plan, policy, procedure, program, range, *regio,* route, scheme, strategy, tactics, tendency, trend, *via,* way

DIRECTION (Guidance), noun administration, admonition, advice, advocacy, auspices, care, charge, coaching, conduct, *consilium,* counsel, design, directorship, education, enlightenment, exhortation, governorship, *gubernatio,* headship, information, injunction, instruction, jurisdiction, leadership, management, managership, ministration, officiation, oversight, pilotage, preparation, protection, recommendation, regulation, steerage, superintendence, supervision, surveillance, teaching, training, tuition, tutelage, tutoring
ASSOCIATED CONCEPTS: directions of donor, under the direction of

DIRECTION (Order), noun adjudication, canon, charge, citation, command, commandment, decree, demand, dictate, directive, *edico,* edict, enactment, fiat, imperative, *imperium,* injunction, instructions, *iubeo,* judgment, mandate, ordinance, precept, prescript, prescription, proscription, regulation, rescript, rubric, rule, subpoena, summons, warrant, writ
ASSOCIATED CONCEPTS: direction of verdict, express direction, specific direction of court

DIRECTIVE, noun behest, bidding, charge, command, commandment, declaration, decree, decretal, demand, dictate, direction, edict, enjoinment, fiat, hest, imperative, instruction, mandate, notification, order, ordinance, precept, prescript, prescription, proclamation, requirement, rescript, ukase, writ

DIRECTOR, noun administrator, boss, chief, curator, executive, executor, foreman, governor, guide, inspector, intendant, leader, manager, overseer, presiding officer, principal, proctor, procurator, superintendent, supervisor
ASSOCIATED CONCEPTS: board of directors, de facto director, de jure director, director's liability, dummy director, interlocking directorates

DIRECTORY, noun catalogue, guidebook, handbook, index, manual, reference book, reference work

DISABILITY (Legal disqualification), noun disablement, impairment, invalidation, invalidity, legal incapacity, unfitness, unqualification, unqualifiedness, unsuitability, unsuitableness, unsuitedness, want of legal capacity, want of legal qualification
FOREIGN PHRASES: Contra non valentem agere nulla currit praescriptio. No prescription runs against a person who is unable to act.

DISABILITY (Physical inability), noun affliction, ailment, debilitation, debility, deterioration, disablement, disorder, disqualification, feebleness, frailty, handicap, helplessness, illness, impairment, impotence, impotency, inability, inability to work, inadequacy, incapability, incapacitation, incapacity, incompetence, incompetency, indisposition, ineffectiveness, ineffectuality, ineffectualness, inefficacy, inefficiency, infirmity, insufficiency, malady, powerlessness, sickness, unfitness, unsoundness, weakness

ASSOCIATED CONCEPTS: complete disability, continuous disability, disability benefits, disability compensation, disability insurance, general disability, medical disability, mental disability, partial disability, physical disability, proof of disability, temporary disability, total disability

DISABLE, *verb*   annul, bar, becripple, break, cancel, cripple, crush, damage, deactivate, debar, *debilitare,* debilitate, deflate, deprive of power, deprive of strength, devalue, devitalize, disarm, disassemble, disenable, disenfranchise, disfranchise, dismantle, disqualify, emasculate, endamage, *enervare,* enervate, enfeeble, exhaust, harm, hinder, hurt, impair, inactivate, incapacitate, indispose, injure, invalidate, lame, maim, make inactive, make incapable, make unfit, make useless, mangle, mutilate, neutralize, nullify, paralyze, preclude, prostrate, put out of action, render helpless, render impotent, render incompetent, render powerless, render unfit, ruin, sabotage, scathe, sicken, spoil, stultify, take to pieces, undermine, unnerve, vitiate, weaken, wound, wreck

ASSOCIATED CONCEPTS: disabled from holding office, disabled vehicle, disabled veterans, disabled worker, partially disabled, wholly disabled, workmen's compensation

DISABLED *(Deprived of legal right),* **adjective**   disenabled, disqualified, helpless, impotent, incapacitated, ineffectual, inoperative, invalid, invalidated, legally incapable, unable, unendowed, unfit, unqualified, untenable

DISABLED *(Made incapable),* **adjective**   bedridden, crippled, debilitated, decrepit, defenseless, deprived of strength, devitalized, disarmed, disenabled, enfeebled, handicapped, helpless, *hors de combat,* impaired, impotent, incapacitated, incompetent, indisposed, ineffective, inefficacious, inept, invalid, maimed, paralytic, paralyzed, pregnable, shattered, unendowed, unfit, unfitted, unfortified, unqualified, useless, vincible

ASSOCIATED CONCEPTS: veterans' rights

DISABLING, *adjective*   crippling, damaging, debilitating, enfeebling, harming, hurting, impairing, incapacitating, injuring, maiming, paralyzing, weakening

DISABUSE, *verb*   acquaint, admonish, advise, air, announce, apprise, awaken, brief, clear the mind, communicate, convey, correct, debunk, direct the attention to, disclose, disillusion, divulge, edify, educate, enlarge the mind, enlighten, *eripere,* expose, fill with information, free from a mistaken belief, free from error, give to understand, illumine, impart, indicate, inform, instruct, lay open, let know, make known, manifest, notify, open the mind, point out, prove, put right, put straight, recount, rectify, relate, remedy, remove falsehood, report, reveal, rid of deception, set right, set straight, specify, state, straighten out, teach, tell the truth, unbeguile, unblindfold, uncover, undeceive, unfold, unfool, unmask, unveil, vent

DISACCORD, *noun*   affray, animosity, antagonism, argument, argumentation, brawl, broil, caviling, clashing, cleavage, conflict, conflict of opinion, confrontation, contention, contradiction, contrariety, contrariness, controversy, cross-purposes, debate, difference, disaffection, disagreement, discongruity, discord, discordance, discordancy, discrepancy, disharmony, disparity, disputation, dispute, disruption, dissension, dissent, dissidence, dissonance, disunion, disunity, divergence, diversity of opinion, division, embranglement, embroilment, enmity, faction, failure to agree, falling out, feud, fracas, friction, heterodoxy, imbroglio, incompatibility, incongruence, incongruity, inconsistency, inconsonance, inharmoniousness, inharmony, maladjustment, misalliance, nonagreement, nonconformity, noncooperation, odds, opposition, polemics, protest, quarrel, rift, row, schism, skirmish, split, squabble, strained relations, strife, tension, unconformity, variance

DISACCORD, *verb*   ablude, altercate, argue, be at variance, bicker, brabble, brangle, break with, challenge, clash, conflict, contend, contradict, contravene, controvert, debate, deny, deviate, differ, differ in opinion, disaffirm, disagree, disapprove, disavow, discept, disclaim, discredit, disharmonize, dispute, dissent, disunite, divaricate, diverge, divide, fall out, gainsay, have differences, have words with, hold opposite views, impugn, join issue, lack harmony, negate, object, oppose, protest, quarrel, rebut, redargue, refuse assent, refuse to accept, refuse to acknowledge, refuse to admit, refuse to consent, refute, reject, remonstrate, repudiate, repugn, resist, run counter to, split, squabble, take exception, traverse, vary, withhold approval, withhold assent, wrangle

DISADVANTAGE, *noun*   adverse circumstance, adversity, block, blockade, blockage, burden, check, curb, damage, defect, deficiency, detainment, determent, deterrence, deterrent, detriment, difficulty, disability, disablement, discommodity, discouragement, drawback, embarrassment, encumbrance, failing, fault, frailty, hamper, handicap, harm, hindrance, holdback, impediment, imperfection, imperfectness, imposition, inadequacy, inaptitude, *incommodum,* inconvenience, inexpedience, inferiority, infirmity, inhibition, *iniquitas,* injury, insalubriousness, insufficiency, interference, lack, liability, limitation, loss, nuisance, objection, obstacle, obstruction, penalty, prejudice, prevention, problem, repression, resistance, restraint, restriction, retardation, retardment, setback, shortcoming, stifling, stumbling block, suppression, taint, unfavorable circumstance, unfavorableness, weak point, weakness

FOREIGN PHRASES: *Cujus est commodum ejus debet esse incommodum.* He who receives a benefit should also bear the disadvantage.

DISADVANTAGE, *verb*   astrict, baffle, balk, bridle, burden, cause problems, check, circumscribe, constrain, cramp, cumber, curb, damage, deprive of advantage, disaccommodate, discommode, encumber, foil, frustrate, hamper, handicap, harm, hinder, hold back, hold in check, impair, impede, impedite, incommode, *incommodum,* inconvenience, inhibit, injure, interfere with, limit, muzzle, obstruct, overburden, overload, prejudice, put out, rein, repress, restrict, retard, saddle, shackle, stall, stymie, suppress, thwart, trammel, weaken, weigh down

DISADVANTAGED, adjective burdened, deprived, handicapped, impeded, prejudiced, retarded, weakened

DISADVANTAGEOUS, adjective adverse, baleful, baneful, biased, corrosive, counteractant, damaging, deleterious, destructive, detrimental, disapproved, disserviceable, gainless, harmful, hindering, hurtful, impolitic, inadvisable, *incommodus,* injurious, inopportune, insalubrious, malefic, maleficent, malignant, negative, pernicious, prejudicial, profitless, thwarting, unadvisable, unavailing, unfavorable, unfruitful, unhealthy, unhelpful, unprofitable, unpropitious, unwise

DISAFFECT, verb alienate, antagonize, cause a rift, cause dislike, cause hostility, come between, destroy the affection of, disenchant, disfavor, disillusion, disoblige, dissatisfy, disunite, divide, envenom, estrange, incense, irritate, make discontented, make disloyal, make hostile, make inimical, make less friendly, make unfaithful, mislike, provoke hatred against, render averse, rile, separate, set against, set at odds, sow dissension, turn away, wean away, withdraw the affections of

DISAFFIRM, verb abjure, abnegate, abolish, challenge, conflict with, contravene, controvert, defy, demur, deny, differ, disaffiliate, disagree, disallow, disavow, disclaim, disown, dispute, disregard, dissent, forswear, gainsay, impugn, negate, object, oppose, oppugn, overrule, overturn, protest, raise objections, rebut, recant, refuse, refute, reject, renounce, repudiate, resist, retract, reverse, run counter to, traverse
ASSOCIATED CONCEPTS: disaffirmance of contract

DISAGREE, verb argue, battle, be at variance, be contrary, be discordant, be disunited, be in opposition, be of different opinions, be opposed, bicker, break with, cavil, challenge, clash, collide, conflict, confute, contest, contradict, contravene, controvert, create strife, debate, defy, demonstrate, demur, deny, depart, deviate, differ, differ in opinion, disapprove, discord, *discrepare,* dispute, dissent, *dissentire, dissidere,* dissociate oneself, divaricate, diverge, divide, fight, gainsay, have dissension, hold opposite views, lack harmony, not accept, object, oppose, oppugn, protest, quarrel, raise objections, refuse assent, refuse to agree, refute, remonstrate, repudiate, repugn, revolt, split, take a stand against, take exception, take issue, think differently, traverse, vary, wrangle

DISAGREEMENT, noun altercation, argument, argumentation, challenge, conflict, conflict of interest, conflict of opinion, contention, contradiction, contraposition, contrariety, contrariness, contravention, controversy, debate, demurral, difference, difference of opinion, disaccord, discord, discordance, discordancy, discrepancy, *discrepantia,* disharmony, disputation, *dissensio,* dissension, dissent, dissidence, *dissidium,* dissimilitude, dissonance, disunion, disunity, divergent opinions, diversity of opinion, exception, faction, failure to agree, feud, gainsaying, incompatibility, inconsonance, inharmoniousness, negation, nonconsent, objection, odds, opposition, oppugnancy, polemics, quarrel, rebuttal, recusancy, strife, unconformity, variance
FOREIGN PHRASES: *Cum in corpore dissentitur, apparet nullam esse acceptionem.* Where there is a disagreement on the substance, it appears that there is no acceptance.

DISALLOW, verb abjure, abnegate, abrogate, contradict, contravene, controvert, deny, disaffirm, disagree, disapprove, disavow, disclaim, discredit, disown, dispute, dissent, impugn, negate, not accept, not comply, not confirm, object, oppose, protest, rebuff, rebut, refuse, refuse to acknowledge, refuse to allow, refuse to corroborate, refuse to grant, refute, reject, renunciate, repudiate, repulse, resist, spurn, *vetare,* withhold approval
ASSOCIATED CONCEPTS: disallow a claim, notice of disallowance

DISAPPEAR, verb *abire,* abscond, be effaced, be erased, be lost to view, become extinct, become imperceptible, decamp, dematerialize, dissipate, dissolve, escape, evanesce, *evanescere,* evaporate, exit, extinguish, fade, fade away, flee, leave, leave no trace, melt away, pass out of sight, recede from view, retreat, take flight, take wing, undergo eclipse, vacate, vanish, vaporize
ASSOCIATED CONCEPTS: unexplained disappearance

DISAPPOINT, verb break one's promise to, cause discontent, dash one's expectation, *deicere,* discourage, disenchant, disgruntle, dishearten, disillusion, disillusionize, displease, dissatisfy, fail, *frustrari,* hinder, let down, make dissatisfied, ruin one's prospects, *spe depellere*

DISAPPOINTED, adjective crestfallen, dashed, defeated, dejected, despondent, discontented, discouraged, disenchanted, disgruntled, disillusioned, displeased, dissatisfied, distressed, foiled, forlorn, frustrated, let down, put out, successless, thwarted, unsatisfied, unsuccessful

DISAPPROBATION, noun abhorrence, admonishment, adverse comment, animadversion, aspersion, ban, bar, caviling, censure, chiding, commination, complaint, condemnation, contumely, criticism, damnation, decrial, denouncement, denunciation, deprecation, depreciation, derogation, detraction, diatribe, disagreement, disapproval, discommendation, discontent, discountenance, disdain, disesteem, disfavor, dislike, disparagement, displeasure, dispraise, disrespect, dissatisfaction, dissent, dissidence, exclusion, excoriation, execration, expostulation, gainsaying, imputation, indictment, lamentation, negation, nonapproval, objection, objurgation, opposition, opprobrium, protest, protestation, rating, rebuke, rejection, remonstrance, remonstration, reprehension, reprimand, reproach, reproof, reproval, repudiation, repugnance, repugnancy, revilement, revulsion, scurrility, shunning, vilipendency, vitriol

DISAPPROVAL, noun abhorrence, adverse comment, animadversion, censure, complaining, complaint, condemnation, contradiction, contravention, criticism, demurrer, demurring, denial, denouncement, denunciation, deprecation, detraction, difference, difference of opinion, disagreement, disallowance, disapprobation, discommendation, discordance, discountenance, disdain, disesteem, disfavor, dislike, disparagement, displeasure, dissatisfaction, dissent, dissentience, dissidence, exception, faultfinding, *improbatio,* low opinion, negation, nonacceptance, nonapproval, nonconsent, objection, opposition, protestation, refusal, rejection, remonstrance, remonstration, reprehension, reproach, repudiation, resistance, shunning, traversal, unacceptance, veto

FOREIGN PHRASES: *Qui non improbat, approbat.* He who does not disapprove, approves.

DISAPPROVE *(Condemn), verb* admonish, animadvert, belittle, berate, brand, call to account, cast aspersions on, cast blame upon, castigate, cavil, censure, chastise, chide, criticize, debase, declaim against, decry, denounce, denunciate, deprecate, discommend, discountenance, discredit, disfavor, dislike, disparage, dispraise, dress down, exclaim against, excoriate, find fault with, fulminate against, hold up to execration, hold up to reprobation, impeach, impugn, malign, muckrake, not take kindly to, object to, objurgate, pass censure upon, pass unfavorable judgment upon, rebuff, rebuke, regard as wrong, regard with blame, remonstrate, reprehend, reprimand, reproach, reprobate, reprove, repudiate, revile, run down, scold, set oneself against, sully, take a dim view of, take exception to, take to task, think ill of, think reprehensible, think wrong, upbraid, view with disfavor, vilipend

DISAPPROVE *(Reject), verb* abnegate, be against, be contrary, be opposed to, boycott, come in conflict with, *condemnare,* confute, contradict, contravene, controvert, debunk, decline to sanction, demur, deny, deprecate, disaccord with, disagree with, disallow, disavow, disclaim, dispute, gainsay, go against, negate, negative, not abide, not accept, not admit, not approve, not consider, not countenance, not have any part of, not support, object, oppose, pass up, protest, rebuff, refuse, refuse assent to, refuse consent, refuse to confirm, refuse to ratify, refuse to receive, refuse to sanction, reject as inadmissable, renounce, repel, repudiate, resist, scorn, set aside, shun, side against, speak against, spurn, stand against, take exception, take exception to, turn away, turn down, turn from, veto, vote against, vote down, withhold approval from, withhold one's assent, withhold permission

DISARM *(Divest of arms), verb* *arma homini adimere,* attenuate, cripple, deactivate, debilitate, decimate, deescalate, demilitarize, demobilize, deprive of arms, deprive of means of defense, deprive of power, deprive of strength, deprive of weapons, devitalize, dilute, disable, disenable, disinvigorate, enervate, enfeeble, *hominem armis exuere,* incapacitate, invalidate, make inactive, make useless, muzzle, neutralize, paralyze, put out of combat, reduce forces, reduce in strength, reduce the armament, render harmless, render innocuous, render powerless, render weak, strip, unarm, undermine, weaken

DISARM *(Set at ease), verb* allay fears, allay mistrust, appease, assuage, assure, beguile, bring around, bring over, conciliate, content, divest of suspicion, gain over, gain the confidence of, make friendly, mollify, pacify, placate, propitiate, quell suspicion, reconcile, remove suspicion, restore harmony, satisfy, smooth over, subdue, touch, tranquilize, win over

DISASSOCIATION, *noun* breach, break, breakdown, detachment, dichotomy, discerption, disconnection, discontinuation, disengagement, disjointure, disjunction, dismemberment, disruption, disseverence, dissociation, dissolution, disunion, divarication, divergence, division, divorce, divorcement, interruption, partition, rift, rupture, schism, segmentation, separation, severence, split, sunderance

DISASTER, *noun* adversity, affliction, bale, bane, blight, blunder, breakdown, *brutum fulmen, calamitas,* calamity, casualty, cataclysm, catastrophe, *clades,* collapse, *contretemps,* crushing reverse, *déabacle,* devastation, downfall, emergency, extremity, failure, fell stroke, fiasco, great misfortune, great mishap, hard blow, harm, holocaust, misadventure, miscarriage, misery, misfortune, misventure, nasty blow, ravage, ruin, ruination, ruinousness, scourge, setback, sudden misfortune, terrible accident, tragedy, travail, trouble, undoing, unfortunate event, upheaval, upset, woe
ASSOCIATED CONCEPTS: common disaster

DISASTROUS, *adjective* all-destroying, annihilative, appalling, bad, baneful, blighting, *calamitosus,* calamitous, cataclysmic, cataclysmal, catastrophic, crushing, damaging, deadly, deleterious, demolishing, desolating, destroying, destructive, detrimental, devastating, dire, disheartening, distressing, dreadful, eradicative, exterminative, exterminatory, extirpative, fell, fraught with harm, frightful, *funestus,* grievous, grim, harmful, harrowing, heartbreaking, horrendous, horrible, horrid, hurtful, ill-omened, injurious, malefic, malign, oppressive, perilous, *perniciosus,* pernicious, ravaging, ruining, ruinous, sinistrous, tragic, tragical, unfavorable

DISAVOW, *verb* abnegate, back down, back out, call back, declare not to be true, decline, deny, deny absolutely, deny connection with, deny emphatically, deny entirely, deny peremptorily, deny responsibility for, deny wholly, *diffiteri,* disaffirm, disbelieve, discard, disclaim, discredit, disdain, disown, dispense with, dissent, dissociate oneself, forswear, *infitiari, infitias ire,* invalidate, negate, negative, not accept, not admit, not approve, not confirm, not maintain, not pass, nullify, pass up, protest, recall, recant, refuse, refuse credence, refuse to accept, refuse to acknowledge, refuse to admit, refuse to corroborate, reject, relinquish, renounce, repel, repudiate, repulse, rescind, retract, revoke, scorn, send back, set aside, set at naught, shun, spurn, take back, traverse, turn away from, turn back, turn from, veto, withdraw

DISBAND, *verb* break apart, break the association of, break up, cut off, deactivate, demobilize, detach, *dimittere,* discharge, disconnect, disembody, disengage, disjoin, disjoint, dislocate, dismember, dismiss, dismiss from service, disorganize, dispel, disperse, dissever, dissociate, dissolve by dismissal, disunite, divorce, *exauctorare,* go apart, go different ways, go separate ways, let go, let out, part, part company, release, scatter, separate, sever, sunder, unbind, uncouple, withdraw from association

DISBAR, *verb* disbench, dismiss from the bar, dismiss from the legal profession, disqualify as an attorney, divest of legal office, drum out of the legal profession, exclude from the profession of law, expel from the bar, expel from the legal profession, invalidate an attorney's license, remove from legal office, remove from the practice of law, remove from the roll of attorneys, render an attorney's license null and void, rescind an attorney's license to practice, revoke one's license to practice law, strike off the roll of lawyers, suspend from the practice of law, suspend from the profession of law, void the license of an attorney
ASSOCIATED CONCEPTS: disbarment proceedings

DISBELIEVE, *verb*   be doubtful, be incredulous, be skeptical, be unconvinced, challenge, consider implausible, consider not to be true, consider unproven, consider untrue, discredit, dispute, distrust, doubt, give no credence to, give no credit to, harbor doubts, harbor suspicions, have doubts, have qualms, have reservations, hold not to be true, lack faith, mistrust, *non credere,* not accept, not believe, not find tenable, question, refuse credence, refuse to admit, refuse to believe, refuse to credit, reject, reject as untrue, remain unconverted, set no store by, suspect, take no stock in, withhold assent

DISBURSE *(Distribute),* **verb**   administer, allocate, allot, apportion, assign, circulate, deal out, diffuse, discharge, dispense, disseminate, divide, dole out, give, give away, give out, hand out, make available, make distribution of, mete, parcel out, pass out, prorate, ration, scatter, share, spread

DISBURSE *(Pay out),* **verb**   bear the cost of, bear the expense of, compensate, defray, defray the cost, *dissolvere,* endure the cost of, expend, *exsolvere,* give money, give out in payment, incur costs, incur expenses, lay out, make expenditure, make payment, meet charges, meet the bill, meet the expense of, outlay, pay, pay off, recompense, reimburse, remunerate, render payment, repay, requite, reward, *solvere,* spend, stand the cost of, support the expense of, tender payment, undergo the cost of, undergo the expense of

DISBURSEMENT *(Act of disbursing),* **noun**   allotting, allotment, apportioning, apportionment, assigning by lot, compensating, dealing out, dispersal, disposal, disseminating, dissemination, dividing, handing out, laying out, outgo, outlay, parceling out

DISBURSEMENT *(Funds paid out),* **noun**   allowance, compensation, costs, defrayal, defrayment, emolument, expenditure, expense, fees, money going out, moneys expended, moneys paid out, outgo, outlay, pay, payment, recompense, redress, reimbursement, remittance, remuneration, repayment, restitution, spendings
ASSOCIATED CONCEPTS: disbursements necessarily paid or incurred, legal disbursements, necessary disbursements

DISCARD, *noun*   castaway,   castoff,   debris, *déclassé,* derelict, detritus, *évacué,* foundling, leaving, oddment, *proscrit,* reject, remainder, remnant, waste

DISCERN *(Detect with the senses),* **verb**   appreciate, apprehend, apprehend clearly, ascertain, awake to, become acquainted with, become apprized, become aware of, become informed, behold, cast eyes on, catch sight of, cognize, command a view of, comprehend, descry, detect, discover, espy, examine, experience, fathom, have in sight, inspect, know, lay eyes on, look at, look on, look upon, make out, mentally appreciate, note, notice, observe, perceive, realize, recognize, regard, scrutinize, see, see at a glance, set eyes on, sight, spot, spy, view, visualize, witness

DISCERN *(Discriminate),* **verb**   detect differences, differentiate, distinguish, exercise discretion, have insight, judge, keep in perspective, make distinctions, note the distinctions, recognize as distinct, see as distinct, see the difference

DISCERNIBLE, *adjective*   apparent, beholdable, cognizable, detectable, evident, in sight, knowable, manifest, observable, perceivable, perceptible, recognizable, seeable, self-evident, viewable, visible, visual

DISCHARGE *(Annulment),* **noun**   abolishment, abolition, abrogation, canceling, cancellation, cessation, defeasance, discontinuance, dissolution, invalidation, negation, nullification, recall, repeal, repudiation, rescission, retractation, reversal, revocation, voidance

DISCHARGE *(Dismissal),* **noun**   *dimissio,* displacement, ejection, elimination, eviction, expulsion, firing, ouster, ousting, removal, removal from employment, replacement, unseating
ASSOCIATED CONCEPTS: cause for discharge, conditional discharge, discharge from army, discharge from employment, discharge of employee, discriminatory discharge, improper discharge

DISCHARGE *(Liberation),* **noun**   absolution, acquittal, clearance, deliverance, disenthrallment, emancipation, exculpation, exemption, exoneration, extrication, legal release from confinement, loosing, release, release from custody, reprieve, salvation, setting free

DISCHARGE *(Payment),* **noun**   acquitment, acquittal, acquittance, amortization, amortizement, annulment of debt, clearance, compensation, defrayal, defrayment, full satisfaction, liquidation, paying off, recompense, redemption, refund, reimbursement, remittance, reparation, repayment, restitution, retirement of a debt, return, satisfaction, settlement, settlement on account

DISCHARGE *(Performance),* **noun**   accomplishment, achievement, attainment, carrying through, commission, completion, conclusion, consummation, culmination, dispatch, effectuation, enforcement, execution, fruition, fulfillment, implementation, observance, perpetration, production, realization, termination
ASSOCIATED CONCEPTS: discharge of duty, faithful discharge of official duties

DISCHARGE *(Release from obligation),* **noun**   abolition, abrogation, absolution, acquittal, cancellation, defeasance, deliverance, delivery, dismissal, dispensation, emancipation, exception, exculpation, excuse, exemption, exoneration, extrication, invalidation, loosing, nullification, pardon, repeal, reprieve, rescission, revocation, voidance

DISCHARGE *(Shot),* **noun**   blast, blasting, bombardment, burst, *coniectio, coniectus,* crash, detonation, emanation, *emissio,* emmission, explosion, firing, firing a charge, flare, flash, fulguration, fulmination, fusillade, igniting, salvo, spray, volley

DISCHARGE *(Dismiss),* **verb**   cashier, cast, cast loose, depose, deprive of office, *dimittere,* disbar, discard, disemploy, displace, drop, eject, exclude, expel, fire, get rid of, give notice, impeach, let go, let loose, *missum facere,* put on the retired list, release, relieve, remove, remove from office, replace, retire, shut out, strike off the roll, suspend, throw out, turn loose, turn out, unseat
ASSOCIATED CONCEPTS: discharged for cause, lawfully discharged, reinstatement

DISCHARGE *(Liberate)*, **verb**   absolve, acquit, bail out, clear, deliver, emancipate, exculpate, excuse, exonerate, extricate, forgive, free, let go, let loose, let out, let out of prison, loose, pardon, parole, purge, release, relieve, render free, set at liberty, set free, turn loose
ASSOCIATED CONCEPTS: discharge from imprisonment, discharge from prison

DISCHARGE *(Pay a debt)*, **verb**   adjust, amortize, clear, hand over, honor, liquidate, make reparation, make restitution, meet, pay in full, pay off, pay up, recompense, redeem, refund, repay, satisfy, satisfy in full, settle, settle accounts, square accounts, strike a balance, take up
ASSOCIATED CONCEPTS: discharge from obligation

DISCHARGE *(Perform)*, **verb**   accomplish, achieve, act on, adjust, administer, attain, bring about, bring to pass, carry into effect, carry into execution, carry out, carry through, complete, comply, concern oneself with, conclude, consummate, culminate, devote oneself to, dispatch, dispose of, do, effect, effectuate, enforce, execute, fulfill, go about, go through with, implement, *munus obire,* proceed with, produce, realize, render, resolve, succeed, transact
ASSOCIATED CONCEPTS: properly discharge one's responsibilities

DISCHARGE *(Release from obligation)*, **verb**   abolish, abrogate, absolve, annul, cancel, declare null and void, discontinue, dismiss, dissolve, excuse, exempt, exonerate, forgive, invalidate, make void, nullify, quash, recall, relieve, relieve of responsibility, remove, render void, repeal, rescind, retract, reverse, revoke, set aside
ASSOCIATED CONCEPTS: discharge of a debt
FOREIGN PHRASES: *Eodem modo quo oritur, eodem modo dissolvitur.* It is discharged in the same manner in which it was created.

DISCHARGE *(Shoot)*, **verb**   blast, burst, deliver a charge, detonate, emit, expel, explode, fire, fire at, fulminate, ignite, launch, *mittere,* open fire, send forth
ASSOCIATED CONCEPTS: discharge of a weapon

DISCIPLE, **noun**   accepter, adherent, admirer, advocate, ally, apostle, apprentice, *auditor,* backer, believer, condisciple, devotee, *discipulus, élève,* favorer, follower, hanger-on, imitator, learner, loyalist, promoter, protegé, pupil, receiver, recruit, scholar, student, supporter, sympathizer, true believer, truster, votary

DISCIPLINARY *(Educational)*, **adjective**   academic, cultural, didactic, didactical, doctrinal, educative, informational, informative, instructional, instructive, paedeutic, pedagogic, pedagogical, preceptive, preceptoral, scholarly, scholastic, training, tuitionary, tutorial

DISCIPLINARY *(Punitory)*, **adjective**   amercing, castigatory, chastening, corrective, inflictive, penal, penological, punishing, punitive, reformational, reformative, reformatory, regulatory, retaliatory, retributive, talionic
ASSOCIATED CONCEPTS: disciplinary action, disciplinary hearing, disciplinary power, disciplinary proceeding

DISCIPLINE *(Field of study)*, **noun**   area of education, area of learning, branch of instruction, branch of knowledge, course, curriculum, doctrine, education, field of interest, field of learning, learning, lore, teaching

DISCIPLINE *(Obedience)*, **noun**   acquiescence, compliance, constancy, constraint, control, curb, deference, devotion, *disciplina,* dutifulness, faithfulness, fidelity, limitation, loyalty, malleability, nonresistance, obsequiousness, observance, pliancy, repression, restraint, self-command, self-conquest, self-denial, self-direction, self-mastery, self-regulation, self-restraint, servility, stoicism, strength of character, strength of will, submission, submissiveness, subordination to rules, will power
ASSOCIATED CONCEPTS: disciplinary proceeding

DISCIPLINE *(Punishment)*, **noun**   amercement, castigation, chastening, chastisement, correction, deprivation, infliction, judgment, just deserts, penal retribution, penalty, penance, penology, reprimand, reproof, retribution, retributive justice, scourge, suffering, trial

DISCIPLINE *(Training)*, **noun**   coaching, conditioning, conduct, cultivation, development, diligent exercise, diligent practice, drill, drilling, exercise, grooming, guidance, inculcation, indoctrination, initiation, instruction, practice, preparation, qualification, readying, regulation, rehearsal, schooling, system of drill, systematic training

DISCIPLINE *(Control)*, **verb**   administer, bridle, bring to a state of obedience, bring under subjection, check, command, curb, direct, dominate, *exercere,* exercise direction over, govern, govern strictly, harness, hold in leash, hold in line, limit, make toe the line, manage, muzzle, oversee, pull in, regulate, rein in, restrain, restrict, stand over, subjugate, superintend, supervise

DISCIPLINE *(Punish)*, **verb**   administer correction, bring to retribution, call to account, carry out a sentence, castigate, chasten, chastise, correct, deal retributive justice, exact a penalty, exact retribution, execute a sentence, execute judgment, execute justice, get even with, give one his deserts, impose a penalty, inflict penalty, inflict penance upon, make an example of, penalize, reprove, scourge, sentence, subject to punishment, take to task, visit punishment
ASSOCIATED CONCEPTS: deterrence, disciplinary proceeding, isolation, rehabilitation, retribution

DISCIPLINE *(Train)*, **verb**   accustom, break in, bring up, coach, condition, cultivate, direct, educate, enlighten, form, foster, give directions, give instructions, give lessons in, groom, guide, habituate, impress upon the mind, inculcate, indoctrinate, infuse, instill, *instituere,* instruct, nurture, prepare, put through paces, qualify, raise, ready, rear, school, show, train by instruction

DISCLAIM, **verb**   abandon, abnegate, abrogate, annul, cancel, declare null and void, deny, deny any knowledge of, desert, disaffirm, disannul, disavow, disbelieve, discard, discharge, discountenance, disown, dispense with, divest oneself of, forego, forsake, forswear, give up, not accept, not admit, recant, reject, renounce, *repudiare,* repudiate, rescind, retract, set aside, spurn, take back, take exception to, turn away, unsay

DISCLAIMER, noun abandonment, abjuration, abjurement, annulment, denial, disaffirmation, disallowance, disavowal, disclamation, disownment, dissociation, negation, nullification, recantation, refusal, rejection, relinquishment, renouncement, renunciation, repudiation, revocation
ASSOCIATED CONCEPTS: disclaimer of interest, disclaimer of knowledge, disclaimer of liability, disclaimer of title, disclaimer of warranties, innocent bystanders, liability to third parties, third parties

DISCLOSE, verb acknowledge, acquaint, admit, advise, air, allude to, announce, *aperire,* apprise, bare, blazon, bring into the open, bring into view, bring out, bring to light, circulate, communicate, confess, declare, describe, *detegere,* dismask, disseminate, divulge, enlighten, evidence, evince, exhibit, expose, give utterance to, impart, *indicare,* indicate, inform, lay bare, make known, make public, mention, notify, present, proclaim, promulgate, publish, report, reveal, speak out, speak the truth, tell, uncover, unearth, unfold, unmask, unscreen, unseal, unshroud, unveil, utter, vent, voice
ASSOCIATED CONCEPTS: disclose assets, disclose the location of a debtor's residence, disclose wrongdoing, disclosed principal, disclosure of public information

DISCLOSURE (*Act of disclosing*), **noun** admission, advisement, announcement, appraisal, assertion, communication, concession, confession, declaration, disclosing, dissemination, divulgation, divulgement, divulgence, enlightenment, enumeration, exposition, exposure, informing, making aware, making public, mention, notification, *patefactio,* presentation to view, proclamation, production, profession, publication, recital, recitation, relation, representation, revealing, revealment, showing, telling, uncovering, uncovery, unfolding, unfoldment, unmasking, unveiling, uttering
ASSOCIATED CONCEPTS: disclosure device, disclosure of assets, disclosure of interest, duty of disclosure, false disclosure, nondisclosure, right to disclosure, voluntary disclosure
FOREIGN PHRASES: *Suppressio veri, suggestio falsi.* The supression of truth is equivalent to the suggestion of what is false.

DISCLOSURE (*Something disclosed*), **noun** acknowledgement, admission, affirmation, announcement, answer, assertion, averment, avowal, communication, concession, confession, confirmation, declaration, deposition, discovery, divulgence, enunciation, explanation, exposé, exposition, expression, *indicium,* information, inside information, knowledge, manifestation, message, news, notice, notification, presentation, proclamation, profession, publication, recital, remark, report, revealment, revelation, statement, testimony, utterance, word

DISCOMMEND, verb asperse, attack, belittle, bring into discredit, censure, clamor against, condemn, contemn, criticize, decry, denigrate, denounce, deprecate, depreciate, deride, derogate, detract, disapprove, discredit, disfavor, disparage, dispraise, disvalue, fault, find fault, malign, reflect discredit upon, revile, ridicule, scoff at, slight, slur, sneer at, speak ill of, speak slight-

ingly of, spurn, traduce, underrate, undervalue, view with disfavor, vilify, vilipend

DISCOMMODE, verb afflict, affront, aggravate, agitate, annoy, arouse, astound, badger, beset, bother, chafe, contravene, counteract, disaccommodate, disadvantage, disconcert, dishearten, disoblige, displease, disquiet, distress, disturb, exasperate, grieve, harry, hinder, impede, impose upon, incommode, inconvenience, irk, irritate, make uneasy, oppress, perplex, perturb, pique, plague, provoke, put to inconvenience, trouble, undermine, unnerve, upset, vex, worry

DISCOMPOSE, verb addle, afflict, aggravate, agitate, annoy, appall, astound, badger, bedazzle, bedevil, befuddle, bewilder, bring into disorder, browbeat, carp at, chafe, confound, confuse, convulse, cross, daze, dazzle, dement, demoralize, derange, disarrange, discomfit, discomfort, discommode, disconcert, dishevel, dislocate, dismay, disorder, disorganize, displace, disquiet, distemper, disturb, disturb the composure of, embitter, enrage, envenom, exasperate, excite, ferment, fluster, fog, fret, goad, gripe, harass, harry, heckle, hurt the feelings, incense, inflame, infuriate, irk, irritate, jar, jolt, jumble, make uneasy, mix up, mortify, muddle, nettle, nonplus, perplex, perturb, pester, pique, plague, provoke, put out, rattle, rile, roil, ruffle, shake, shake up, shatter, stir, taunt, tease, throw into confusion, torment, tousle, trouble, try the patience, unbalance, unhinge, unsettle, upset, vex, worry

DISCONCERT, verb abash, agitate, alarm, annoy, appall, astound, bedazzle, bedevil, cause discontent, chagrin, confound, confuse, discomfit, discomfort, discompose, discountenance, dismay, disquiet, disrupt, disturb, fluster, give cause for alarm, *percellere,* perplex, perturb, *perturbare,* puzzle, ruffle, startle, throw into confusion, upset

DISCONNECTED, adjective abstracted, adrift, apart, asunder, broken, broken off, cut apart, cut in two, detached, disassociated, discontinuous, discrete, disembodied, disjoined, disjointed, disjunct, disjunctive, disparate, disunited, divergent, divorced, incoherent, inconsistent, interrupted, irrational, irrelative, isolated, jumbled, loose, noncohesive, partitioned, put asunder, scattered, separate, separated, set apart, set asunder, severed, sundered, switched off, unaffiliated, unallied, unannexed, unassociated, unattached, uncohesive, unconnected, uncoupled, unintelligible, unjoined, unlinked, unrelated

DISCONSOLATE, adjective afflicted, anguished, atrabilious, bereaved, brokenhearted, burdened, careworn, cast down, cheerless, comfortless, crestfallen, crushed, dejected, depressed, desolate, despairing, despondent, discouraged, disheartened, dismal, dispirited, distressed, doleful, dolorous, downcast, downhearted, elegiac, encumbered, forlorn, funereal, gloomy, glum, grief-stricken, grieved, grieving, heartbroken, heartsick, heavy-laden, hopeless, hurt, in despair, in heavy spirits, inconsolable, infelicitous, joyless, lachrymose, lamenting, languishing, lost, low spirited, *maestus,* melancholic, melancholy, miserable, moody, morose, mournful, mourning, overcome, pained, pathetic, pessimistic, plaintive, sad, saturnine, sober, somber, sorrowful, spiritless, stricken, tearful, *triste,* troubled, unconsolable, unhappy, unnerved, wan, weeping, woebegone, woeful, wretched

DISCONTINUANCE (*Act of discontinuing*), **noun** abeyance, abolishment, abolition, adjournment, breaking off, cancellation, cancelling, cessation, defeasance, desistance, discontinuation, dismissal, disruption, disuse, interruption, interval, invalidation, nonuse, nullification, pause, postponement, recess, remission, stop, stoppage, suspension, termination, withdrawal

DISCONTINUANCE (*Interruption of a legal action*), **noun** ampliation, cessation, desistance, discontinuation, dismissal, moratorium, termination, withdrawal

DISCONTINUE (*Abandon*), **verb** abolish, abort, abrogate, abstain, annul, apostasize, arrest, break, break off, bring to a close, bring to an end, call off, cancel, cause a discontinuance, cease, cease using, check, close, complete, conclude, consummate, demit, desist, desist from, destroy, discard, disconnect, disjoin, dismiss, dissever, dissolve, disunite, drop, end, expire, finish, forfeit, forsake, give up, halt, have done with, invalidate, leave, leave off, let lapse, play out, put an end to, quit, relinquish, renounce, repeal, resign, retire, revoke, separate, sever, shut down, stop, sunder, surrender, suspend, terminate, vacate, void, waive, withdraw
ASSOCIATED CONCEPTS: discontinuance of an action, dismissal, judgment of discontinuance, lack of prosecution, nonsuit, voluntary discontinuance

DISCONTINUE (*Break continuity*), **verb** adjourn, arrest, balk, break, break off, bring to a standstill, check, cut, cut short, dam up, defer, delay, disconnect, disengage, disjoin, disrupt, dissever, dissolve, disturb, disunite, divide, foil, frustrate, hesitate, hinder, hold in abeyance, intercept, interfere with, interject, intermit, interpose, interrupt, intervene, intrude, leave off, obstruct, part, postpone, punctuate, recess, remit, retard, separate, sever, sunder, suspend, thwart, wait, waive

DISCORD, **noun** animosity, antagonism, argumentation, bickering, clashing, conflict, contention, controversy, difference, disaccord, disaccordance, disagreement, discongruity, discordance, *discordia,* discrepancy, disharmony, disparity, dispute, *dissensio,* dissension, dissent, dissentience, dissidence, *dissidium,* dissimilarity, dissonance, disunion, disunity, divergent opinions, diversity, division, divisiveness, enmity, faction, failure to agree, friction, hostility, ill feeling, ill will, incompatibility, incongruence, incongruity, lack of concord, nonagreement, opposition, quarreling, schism, split, strained relations, strife, unharmoniousness, variance, wrangling

DISCORDANT, **adjective** adverse, antagonistic, antipathetical, antithetical, antonymous, at cross purposes, at variance, cacophonous, clashing, colliding, conflicting, conflictory, contradictory, contradistinct, contrarious, contrary, counter, differing, disaccordant, disagreeing, *discors, discrepans,* discrepant, dissentient, dissenting, dissident, dissimilar, dissonant, *dissonus,* divergent, diverse, hostile, in disagreement, inaccordant, incompatible, incongruent, incongruous, inconsistent, inconsonant, inharmonious, inimical, inverse, irreconcilable, opposed, opposing, opposite, oppositional, oppugnant, out of accord, strident, unagreeing, variant

DISCOUNT, **noun** abatement, allowance, amount deducted, bargain, *decessio,* decrease, decrement, deductio, deduction, diminution, lower price, markdown, reduction, special price, subtraction
ASSOCIATED CONCEPTS: discount a loan, discount bills, discount notes, trade discount

DISCOUNT (*Disbelieve*), **verb** be indifferent to, belittle, brush aside, *decessio, deductio,* depreciate, discountenance, discredit, disdain, disesteem, disparage, disregard, distrust, doubt, gloss over, harbor suspicions, ignore, make light of, misprize, mistrust, pass over, pay no attention, pay no heed, pay no mind, question, slight, spurn, suspect

DISCOUNT (*Minimize*), **verb** abate, abbreviate, abridge, allay, attenuate, condense, curtail, deflate, detract, diminish, lessen, minimalize, pare, reduce, render less, scale down, shorten, underestimate, understate, undervalue

DISCOUNT (*Reduce*), **verb** abate, allow a margin, cut, decrease, deduct from, depreciate, detract, lower, lower the sale price, make allowance for, mark down, rebate, reduce the mark-up, sell below par, slash prices, strike off, subduct, subtract, take from, take off, underprice, undersell, undervalue

DISCOURAGE, **verb** advise against, affright, *animum frangere,* argue against, avert, cast down, cause discontent, cause dislike, cause doubt, caution, contraindicate, convince to the contrary, dampen, daunt, deflect, dehort, deject, demoralize, deprecate, depress, deprive of courage, destroy confidence, deter, *deterrere,* disaffect, discountenance, disenchant, disgruntle, dishearten, disillusion, disincline, disinterest, dismay, dispirit, dissuade, divert, expostulate, forestall, frighten away, give one pause, hinder, impose difficulties, indispose, inspire fear, intimidate, keep back, keep from, lessen the self-confidence of, lower the courage of, obstruct by opposition, oppose, persuade against, put a damper on, quench, remonstrate, render averse, repel, reprove, restrain, sadden, scare, set against, thwart, turn aside, turn from, unnerve, upset, warn, weaken the resolution of

DISCOURSE, **noun** address, allocution, argument, argumentation, commentary, conference, *conlocutio, conloquium,* conversation, declamation, dialogue, discussion, disquisition, dissertation, elucidation, exchange of views, excursus, exhortation, exposition, expression of views, formal discussion, interchange of views, interlocution, language, lecture, oral communication, oration, prelection, recital, recitation, rhetorical presentation, *sermo,* speech, talk, verbal communication, verbal exposition, verbal intercourse

DISCOURSE, **verb** address, comment, commune with, communicate orally, confabulate, confer, *conloqui,* converse, debate, deliver a speech, deliver a talk, deliver an address, dilate, discuss, dissertate, exchange observations, expatiate, explain, expound, give a speech, give a talk, give an address, hold a conference, lecture, make a speech, orate, *orationem facere, orationem habere,* parley, perorate, prelect, recite, sermonize, speak, talk, talk over, talk together

DISCOVER, **verb** ascertain, awake to, become informed, behold, bring to light, chance upon, *cognoscere,* collect knowledge, come to know, come upon, *comperire,* deduce, descry, detect, determine, diagnose, discern, divine, elicit, encounter, expose, ferret out, find out, get a glimpse of, identify, *invenire*, investigate, learn, learn for a certainty, learn of, locate, manifest, observe, perceive, pinpoint, realize, see, turn up, uncover, understand, unearth, unravel

ASSOCIATED CONCEPTS: discover facts and information known by an adverse party, discovered negligence, doctrine of discovered peril, proceeding to discover assets

DISCOVERY, *noun*   acquisition of knowledge, ascertainment, checking, declaration, descrial, detection, discernment, disclosure, disclosure proceedings, distinguishing, divulgence, espial, examination for the purpose of ascertaining facts, exploration, exposition, exposure, finding out, first sight, identification, inquiry, inspection, investigation, investigation to uncover facts, observation, perception, perusal, pretrial examination proceedings, quest, reconnoitering, revealment, revelation, scrutiny, sighting, surveying, uncovering, unearthing

ASSOCIATED CONCEPTS: discovery of deceit, discovery of facts, discovery of fraud, discovery of loss, discovery of mistake, discovery proceeding, discovery which can be patented, doctrine of discovered peril

DISCREDIT, *noun*   animadversion, aspersion, attaint, baseness, castigation, censure, condemnation, contumely, criticism, debasement, *dedecus*, degradation, denunciation, derogation, disapprobation, disapproval, disbelief, disesteem, disfavor, disgrace, dishonor, disparagement, dispraise, disreputability, disrepute, distrust, *ignominia*, ignominy, impaired reputation, imputation, incredulity, *infamia*, infamy, ingloriousness, lack of confidence, lack of esteem, loss of belief, loss of credence, loss of credit, loss of repute, mistrust, odium, opprobrium, *probrum*, reflection, remonstrance, reprehension, reproach, reprobation, repudiation, revilement, scandal, shame, slur, stain, stigma, stricture, taint, tarnish, turpitude

ASSOCIATED CONCEPTS: discredit a witness

DISCREDIT, *verb*   *abrogare,* asperse, besmirch, brand, bring disgrace upon, bring into disfavor, bring reproach upon, cast aspersions on, cast shame upon, debase, decry, degrade, denigrate, deprecate, depreciate, deprive of credit, *derogare,* derogate from, discount, disgrace, dishonor, disparage, downgrade, hold up to shame, impair the reputation of, impute shame to, injure the credit of, involve in shame, make distasteful, malign, reflect dishonor upon, reprehend, scandalize, stain, stigmatize, taint, tarnish

ASSOCIATED CONCEPTS: discredit a witness, discredited witness

DISCREET, *adjective*   astute, calculating, careful, cautious, *cautus,* chary, circumspect, *consideratus,* deliberate, diplomatic, discerning, discretional, discretionary, discriminate, discriminating, discriminative, distinguishing, forethoughtful, guarded, intelligent, judicious, mindful, perceptive, polite, politic, precautious, prepared, *prudens,* prudent, refined, reflecting, regardful, reserved, reticent, sensible, sensitive, subtle, thoughtful, vigilant, watchful, well-advised, wise

DISCREPANCY, *noun*   aberration, anomaly, asymmetry, clash, conflict, contradiction, contrast, departure, deviation, difference, differential, differentiation, disaccord, disagreement, discongruity, discord, discordance, disharmony, disparity, disputed point, dis-

similarity, dissimilitude, dissonance, divergence, failure to correspond, ground of argument, inaccordance, incompatibility, incongruence, incongruency, incongruity, inconsistency, inequality, irreconcilability, lack of accord, lack of agreement, lack of concert, lack of conformity, lack of congruence, lack of congruity, lack of consonance, lack of resemblance, matter of disputation, nonagreement, nonconformity, nonuniformity, split, subject of controversy, subject of dispute, unconformity, unlikeness, variance, variation

DISCRETE, *adjective*   apart, asunder, cut off, detached, different, disassociated, disconnected, *discontinu,* discontinuous, discretive, disengaged, disjoined, disjoint, disjunct, dissociated, distinct, distinguished, disunited, divided, individual, isolated, noncontinuous, parted, removed, separate, separated, sundered, unannexed, unassimilated, unassociated, unattached, unconnected, unfastened, unjoined

DISCRETION *(Power of choice), noun*   analysis, appraisal, assessment, choice, consideration, contemplation, decision, designation, determination, discrimination, distinction, election, evaluation, examination, free decision, free will, freedom of choice, liberty of choosing, liberty of judgment, license, option, optionality, permission, pick, power of choosing, review, right of choice, sanction, selection, self-determination, suffrage, *suo arbitrio,* volition, will

ASSOCIATED CONCEPTS: absolute discretion, abuse of discretion, administrative discretion, arbitrariness, capriciousness, certiorari, judicial discretion, legal discretion, mandemus, prohibition, unreasonableness

FOREIGN PHRASES: *Optima est lex quae minimum relinquit arbitrio judicis; optimas judex qui minimum sibi.* That is the best system of law which leaves the least to the discretion of the judge; that judge is the best who leaves the least to his own discretion. *Optimam esse legem, quae minimum relinquit arbitrio judicis; id quod certitudo ejus praestat.* That law is the best which leaves the least discretion to the judge; this is an advantage which results from its certainty. *Optimus judex, qui minimum sibi.* He is the best judge who leaves the least to his own discretion. *Quam longum debet esse rationabile tempus non definitur in lege, sed pendet ex discretione justiciariorum.* How long a reasonable time ought to be is not defined by law, but is left to the discretion of the judges. *Quam rationabilis debet esse finis, non definitur, sed omnibus circum stantiis inspectis pendet ex justiciariorum discretione.* What a reasonable fine ought to be is not defined, but is left to the discretion of the judges, all the circumstances being considered.

DISCRETION *(Quality of being discreet), noun*   ability to get along with others, acuteness, aesthetic judgment, appreciation, appreciativeness, art of negotiating, artful management, artfulness, artistic judgment, attention, care, carefulness, caution, cautiousness, chariness, circumspection, circumspectness, cleverness, competence, concern, considerateness, consideration, craft, deftness, deliberation, delicacy, diplomacy, discernment, discreetness, discriminating taste, discrimination, discriminatory powers, distinction, expertness, facility, finesse, good sense, guardedness, heed, heedfulness, insight, intuition, *iudicium,* judiciousness, mature responsibility, maturity, mindfulness, nicety, particularness, perception, perspicacity, polish, precaution, presence of mind, providence, prudence, *prudentia,* qualification, quick judgment, refined discrimination, refinement, regardfulness, resourcefulness, safeguard, sagacity, *sagesse, savoir faire,* sensitiveness, sensitivity, sharpness, shrewd diagnosis, shrewdness, skill, sound judgment, sound reasoning, statesmanship, strategy, subtlety, sympathetic perception, tact, tactfulness, taste, technique, thoughtfulness, wariness, watchfulness, wisdom

ASSOCIATED CONCEPTS: absolute discretion, abuse of discretion, administrative discretion, discretion to set aside a judgment, improper exercise of discretion, judicial discretion, prosecutorial discretion, sound discretion

FOREIGN PHRASES: *Discretio est scire per legem quid sit justum.* Discretion consists in knowing through the law what is just.

DISCRETIONARY, *adjective* conative, discretional, discriminative, elective, left to discretion, left to individual judgment, optional, selective, volitional, volitive

ASSOCIATED CONCEPTS: discretionary authority, discretionary damages, discretionary power of the court, discretionary trusts

DISCRIMINATE (*Distinguish*), *verb* characterize, classify, compare, contrast, designate, determine the essentials, differentiate, *diiudicare, discernere, distinguere,* divide, draw the line, individualize, *internoscere,* label, make a choice, make a distinction, make a selection, mark, mark the difference between, note differences, point out, recognize as separate, see the difference, separate, set apart, set off, sift, sort out, tell apart

DISCRIMINATE (*Treat differently*), *verb* avoid, be partial, be predisposed, bear a grudge against, bear malice, disapprove of, disfavor, favor, have an affection for, have ill feelings toward, incline toward, lean toward, look down upon, make a distinction, object to, prefer, reject, show an aversion, show bias, show preference, show prejudice, shun, tend toward

ASSOCIATED CONCEPTS: age discrimination, discriminate against an employee, discriminate in price, discriminatory tax, equal protection, invidious discrimination, race discrimination, religious discrimination, sex discrimination, unlawful discrimination

DISCRIMINATING (*Distinguishing*), *adjective* contradistinct, contrasting, diacritical, differentiating, differentiative, differing, discriminate, distinctive, inconsistent, individualizing, selective, separative

ASSOCIATED CONCEPTS: discrimination because of race, discrimination in hiring, discriminatory practices, equal protection, illegal discrimination, invidious discrimination, racial discrimination, reverse discrimination

DISCRIMINATING (*Judicious*), *adjective* appraising, astute, clear-sighted, critical, discerning, dispassionate, fastidious, impartial, judgmatic, keen, knowing, meticulous, perceptive, perspicacious, rational, reasonable, sagacious, sapient, selective, sober, sound, thoughtful, unbiased, well-advised, wise

DISCRIMINATION (*Bigotry*), *noun* bias, blind zeal, class prejudice, favoritism, illiberality, intolerance, opinionativeness, preference, prejudice, race ha-

tred, race prejudice, racialism, racism, unfairness, want of forbearance

ASSOCIATED CONCEPTS: blacklist, civil rights act, compelling state interest, discrimination based on sex, discrimination in hiring and tenure, due process clause, equal protection, illegal discrimination, invidious discrimination, overwhelming state interest, prejudicial discrimination, race discrimination, rational basis, reasonable classification, unjust discrimination

DISCRIMINATION (*Differentiation*), *noun* analysis, appraisal, appreciation, assessment, comprehension, consideration, contemplation, contrasting, demarcation, *discrimen,* disequalization, *distinctio,* distinction, distinguishment, division, estimation, examination, evaluation, individualization, segregation, separation, setting apart, weighing

ASSOCIATED CONCEPTS: compelling state interest, equal protection

DISCRIMINATION (*Good judgment*), *noun* acumen, acuteness, circumspection, discernment, discreetness, discretion, good sense, insight, *intellegentia,* intelligence, intuition, *iudicium,* judiciousness, knowledge, perception, perspicacity, perspicuity, prudence, *prudentia,* rationality, reason, sagacity, shrewdness, sound reasoning, thoughtfulness, understanding

DISCURSIVE (*Analytical*), *adjective* a fortiori, a posteriori, a priori, analytic, argumentative, deductive, dialectic, disquisitional, epagogic, inductive, inferential, interpretative, logical, ratiocinative, ratiocinatory, rational, rationalistic, reasoning

DISCURSIVE (*Digressive*), *adjective* aimless, circuitous, desultory, deviating, deviative, devious, disconnected, drifting, errant, indirect, meandering, rambling, random, ranging, roaming, roundabout, roving, shifting, straying, undirected, unsystematic, *vagus, varius,* wandering

DISCUSS, *verb* *agitare,* air, analyze, argue for and against, argue the case, argue the point, bandy words, carry on a conversation, comment, comment upon, confabulate, confer, confer with, consider, consult, contend in words, contest, converse, debate, deliberate upon, dialogize, *disceptare,* discourse, discourse about, *disputare, disserere,* dissertate, engage in a conversation, engage in conversation, engage in oral controversy, exchange observations, exchange opinions, explain, have a conference on, hold conclave, hold conference, hold conversations, hold intercourse, indulge in argument, interchange views, join in a conversation, negotiate, parley, partake in a symposium, present varied opinions, reason about, reason with, recite, review, speak of, speak on, take into account, take up in conference, talk about, talk it over, talk of, talk out, talk over, talk together

ASSOCIATED CONCEPTS: confidential information, privileged information

DISDAIN, *noun* abhorrence, abjuration, abnegation, act of despising, act of discrediting, act of loathing, act of scorning, act of shunning, act of spurning, act of taunting, airs, arrogance, contempt, *contemptio,* contemptuousness, contumeliousness, declination, denial, derision, detestation, detraction, disapprobation, disapproval, disavowal, disclamation, discountenancing, disesteem, disfavor, dislike, disownment, disregard, disrespect, *fastidium,* haughtiness, haughty contempt, haughty indifference, *hauteur,* icy aloofness, indignant aversion, insolence, nonacceptance, nonrecognition, opprobrium, proud contempt, rebuff, rejection, renunciation, reprobation, repudiation, repulse, repulsion, revilement, scoff, scorn, scornfulness, scorning, sneer, spurning, superciliousness, supreme contempt, unutterable contempt, utter contempt

DISDAIN, verb   abhor, *aspernari,* avoid, be contemptuous of, belittle, brush aside, care nothing for, consider beneath notice, consider beneath oneself, consider unworthy of regard, contemn, decline, decry, deem unbecoming, deem unsuitable, deride, *despicere,* despise, detest, disavow, discard, disclaim, disesteem, disown, disparage, disregard, esteem of no account, esteem of small account, *fastidire,* feel contempt for, feel utter contempt for, flout, gibe, have no use for, hold cheap, hold in contempt, ignore, jeer, laugh at, loathe, look down on, look with scorn on, misprize, mock, not accept, not consider, not respect, pass by, pass over, rebuff, recoil from with pride, regard with proud contempt, reject, renounce, repudiate, repulse, ridicule, scoff, scorn, shun, slight, sneer at, snub, *spernere,* spurn, think nothing of, think unworthy of notice, treat with contempt, turn one's back upon, turn to scorn, view with a scornful eye

DISDAINFUL, adjective   aloof, arrogant, audacious, bumptious, cavalier, cold, condescending, contemptuous, contumelious, cynical, deprecating, derisive, despising, disapproving, discourteous, disrespectful, distant, *fastidiosus,* filled with pride, flouting, full of contempt, haughty, high, icy, imperious, indifferent, indignant, insolent, insulting, intolerant, jeering, lordly, mocking, overbearing, overweening, proud, ridiculing, rude, sardonic, scornful, sneering, snobbish, snobby, snooty, supercilious, superior, unapproachable, uncivil, unmannerly, unsociable

DISEASE, noun   affliction, ailment, attack, bodily deviation from health, bout of sickness, breakdown, chronic disability, collapse, condition, contagion, defect, deterioration, disability, discomfort, disorder, distemper, epidemic, handicap, ill health, illness, indisposition, infection, infirmity, insalubrity, invalidism, loss of health, malady, *morbus,* physical derangement, plague, scourge, sickness, taint, unhealthiness, unsoundness, unwholesome condition, virus, weakness

DISENCUMBER, verb   alleviate, cast off, clear, clear away, deliver from a hindrance, disburden, disembroil, disengage, disentail, disentangle, disjoin, ease, ease the burden, emancipate, exonerate, extract, extricate, free, free from encumbrance, liberate, lighten the labor, loose, loosen, release, relieve, remove, remove a hindrance, remove a restraint, remove an impediment, rescue, save from, set at large, set free, unbar, unbind, unburden, unchain, unclog, unfasten, unfetter, unhamper, unharness, unload, unlock, unloose, unshackle, untie, untrammel, unyoke

DISENGAGE, verb   *avocare,* become detached, break the connection with, cut loose, cut off, decontrol, deliver, detach, disconnect, disembroil, disencumber, disentangle, disenthrall, disjoin, dislodge, dispart, displant, dissever, dissociate, disunite, divorce, draw off, emancipate, *expedire,* extricate, free, free from engagement, free from pledge, free from vow, let out, *liberare,*

liberate, liberate from connection, lift controls, loose, make free, manumit, part, release, release from attachment, relieve of obligation, separate, set at liberty, set free, sever, *solvere,* sunder, unattach, unbar, unbind, unbolt, unbuckle, unchain, unclasp, undo, unfasten, unfetter, unfix, unglue, unhamper, unhitch, unhook, unknot, unlace, unlatch, unlock, unloose, unpin, unravel, unscrew, unshackle, unsnap, unstick, unstrap, untie, withdraw

DISENTANGLE, verb   arrange, clear, detach, disburden, disconnect, disembroil, disencumber, disengage, disinvolve, disjoin, ease, *expedire, explicare, exsolvere,* extricate, free, liberate, loosen, methodize, organize, release, relieve, relieve of complication, separate, set free, straighten out, unfasten, unfetter, unhamper, unknot, unloose, unravel, untie, untwist

DISENTHRALL, verb   bail out, deliver, deliver from bondage, discharge, disengage, emancipate, enfranchise, extricate, free, free from bondage, free from thralldom, give liberty to, let go, let loose, let out, let out of prison, liberate, liberate from oppression, loosen, make free, manumit, redeem, release, release from bondage, release from restraint, render free, rescue, rescue from imprisonment, rescue from oppression, rescue from slavery, set at large, set at liberty, set free, turn loose, unbar, unbind, unchain, unfetter, unlock, unmanacle, unshackle, untie
ASSOCIATED CONCEPTS: Emancipation Proclamation

DISFAVOR, verb   avoid, be loath, deny respect, despise, disaffect, disapprove, discountenance, discredit, disdain, dishonor, dislike, disregard, disrespect, frown on, have no regard for, have no respect for, have no use for, hold cheap, *invidia,* look askance at, look down on, misprize, not care for, not like, not respect, object to, *offensa,* rebuff, regard unfavorably, reject, repel, repulse, turn away, turn from, view with disfavor

DISFRANCHISE, verb   deprive, forfeit, illegalize, limit, make illegitimate, outlaw, prohibit, restrict

DISGRACE, noun   abasement, abjectness, abomination, attaint, bad character, bad name, bad report, bad reputation, bad repute, badge of infamy, baseness, blemish, blot, brand, cause of reproach, cause of shame, comedown, condition of infamy, contempt, debasement, defame, defilement, deflation, degradation, derogation, detestation, deviation from rectitude, disapprobation, disapproval, discredit, disesteem, disfavor, dishonor, disparagement, disreputability, disrepute, disrespect, embarrassment, exclusion from favor, humbled pride, humbling, humiliation, *ignominia,* ignominy, ill-favor, ill-repute, imputation, indignity, *infamia,* infamy, ingloriousness, loss of honor, loss of reputation, mortification, notoriety, obloquy, odium, opprobrium, reproach, scandal, sense of shame, setdown, shame, shamefacedness, shameful notoriety, slur, smear, smirch, stain, stigma, taint, tarnish, tarnished honor, *turpitudo*
ASSOCIATED CONCEPTS: character evidence, reputation

DISGRACE, verb   abase, abash, affect dishonorably, attaint, be a reproach to, be unable to respect, besmear, blacken, blot, brand, bring down, bring into discredit, bring reproach upon, bring shame upon, cast a slur upon, cast dishonor upon, cast reproach upon, corrupt, debase, debunk, *dedecorare, dedecori esse,* defile, deflate, defrock, degrade, *dehonestare,* demean, demoralize, deny respect, depress, deride, derogate, diminish, disbar, discredit, dishonor, dismiss from favor, disrespect, downgrade, embarrass, fling dishonor upon, have no respect for, hold up to shame, humiliate, impute shame to, involve in shame, lower, make unclean, mock, mortify, pillory, pollute, reflect discredit upon, reflect dishonor upon, reflect shame upon, ridicule, scandalize, shame, slur, smirch, soil, stain, stigmatize, sully, taint, tarnish, throw dishonor upon, treat with disfavor

DISGRACEFUL, adjective abominable, atrocious, base, beneath one's dignity, blameworthy, censurable, compromising, contemptible, damaging, deflated, degrading, demeaning, demoralizing, deplorable, derogatory, deserving reproach, despicable, detestable, discreditable, dishonest, dishonorable, disreputable, *flagitiosus,* flagitious, flagrant, foul, heinous, horrible, humiliating, humiliative, ignoble, ignominious, improper, indecent, infamous, inglorious, *inhonestus,* iniquitous, odious, opprobrious, outrageous, peccant, *probrosus,* recreant, reprobate, scandalous, shameful, shocking, sinful, tarnished, *turpis,* unseemly, unworthy, vile, worthy of contempt

DISGUISE, noun artifice, camouflage, caricature, cloak, concealment, counterfeit, cover, covering, deception, deceptive covering, dissimulation, facade, faking, false appearance, false colors, false copy, false front, guise, hiding, imitation, mask, masquerade, pose, posture, pretense, pretension, pretext, representation, screen, semblance, sham, shield, *simulacrum, simulatio,* simulation, smoke screen, veneer, *vestis mutata*

DISGUISE, verb alter the appearance of, becloud, belie, bemask, camouflage, change the appearance of, change the face of, change the guise of, cloak, conceal, counterfeit, cover, curtain, deceive, dissemble, dissimulate, distort, dress to conceal, dress up, fake, falsify, feign, give a false coloring, give color to, hide, hide one's identity, make unrecognizable, mask, masquerade, misrepresent, muffle, obscure, *occultare,* pass off for, put a false appearance upon, *rem dissimulare,* screen, shield, shroud, simulate, veil

DISHONEST, adjective beguiling, bogus, cheating, conniving, conscienceless, contrary to fact, corrupt, corruptible, counterfeit, cunning, deceitful, deceiving, deceptive, delusive, delusory, designing, destitute of good faith, destitute of integrity, devoid of truth, discreditable, dishonorable, disingenuous, disposed to cheat, disreputable, double-dealing, faithless, fake, faked, fallacious, false, false-hearted, falsified, feigned, fraudulent, *fraudulentus,* guileful, hypocritical, immoral, *improbus,* iniquitous, insidious, insincere, lying, *malus,* meretricious, misleading, nefarious, not honest, not true, perfidious, perjured, scheming, shameless, shifty, spurious, surreptitious, treacherous, truthless, unauthentic, undependable, underhanded, unethical, unfaithful, ungenuine, unprincipled, unreal, unreliable, unscrupulous, untrue, untrustworthy, untruthful, unveracious, unvirtuous, void of truth, wanting in probity, without probity, without truth
ASSOCIATED CONCEPTS: dishonest act, dishonest practice, fraudulent or dishonest acts

DISHONESTY, noun bad faith, cheating, chicane, chicanery, corruption, corruptness, cozenage, deceit, de-

ceitfulness, deception, deviation from probity, dishonor, disingenuousness, disposition to deceive, disposition to defraud, disposition to lie, duplicity, faithlessness, false swearing, falseheartedness, falsehood, falseness, falsification, falsity, fraudulence, fraudulency, *fraus,* furtiveness, *improbitas,* improbity, infidelity, insincerity, inveracity, knavery, knavishness, lack of conscience, lack of honesty, lack of integrity, lack of principle, lack of probity, lying, mendaciousness, mendacity, perfidiousness, perfidy, perjury, prevarication, surreptitiousness, thievishness, treacherousness, trickiness, truthlessness, undependability, underhand dealing, underhandedness, unreliability, unscrupulousness, unstraightforwardness, untrustworthiness, untruth, untruthfulness, violation of trust, want of integrity, wiliness
ASSOCIATED CONCEPTS: criminal acts, dishonest acts, fraudulent acts

DISHONOR (Nonpayment), noun breach of faith, breach of promise, declination, default, delinquency, disregard, failure, improbity, inability to pay, inattention, inobservance, insolvency, nonacceptance, nonadherence, noncompletion, noncompliance, nonfeasance, nonfulfillment, nonobservance, nonpayment at maturity, omission, refusal to accept, refusal to pay, rejection, repudiation of payment
ASSOCIATED CONCEPTS: dishonor of checks, dishonor of negotiated instruments, notice of dishonor

DISHONOR (Shame), noun abasement, abjection, abjectness, aspersion, attaint, bad character, bad favor, bad name, bad reputation, bad repute, badge of infamy, baseness, blemish, blot, brand, calumny, contempt, contumely, debasement, decrial, defamation, defilement, degradation, depravity, derogation, detraction, deviation from rectitude, disapprobation, discredit, disesteem, disfavor, disgrace, disparagement, disreputability, disrepute, disrespect, humiliation, ignobility, *ignominia,* ignominy, ill-fame, ill-favor, ill-repute, improbity, imputation, indignity, *infamia,* infamy, ingloriousness, lack of conscience, lack of honor, lack of principle, lack of probity, loss of reputation, low estimation, mockery, no repute, no standing, notoriety, obloquy, opprobrium, outrage, public disgrace, reproach, ridicule, scandal, scorn, shamefulness, slur, smear, stain, stigma, taint, tarnish, tarnished honor, traducement, turpitude, *turpitudo,* vileness, vilification, wickedness

DISHONOR (Deprive of honor), verb abase, asperse, attaint, besmear, besmirch, blot, brand, bring into discredit, bring shame upon, cast a slur on, cast aspersions, cast reproach upon, contemn, debase, debauch, *dedecorare,* defame, defile, deflower, degrade, *dehonestare,* denigrate, denounce, deride, desecrate, despise, discredit, disgrace, disparage, expose, malign, pillory, reflect discredit upon, reproach, slur, smear, smirch, speak ill of, stain, stigmatize, *stuprare,* taint, tarnish, vilify

DISHONOR (Refuse to pay), verb decline to pay, decline to redeem, disallow payment, disregard, evade, not observe, not pay, refuse payment, refuse to honor, repudiate, stop payment, withhold payment
ASSOCIATED CONCEPTS: dishonor a check, notice of dishonor

DISINCENTIVE, noun averseness, check, constraint, curb, damper, determent, deterrence, deterrent, discouragement, disinclination, dissuasion, hindrance, indisposition, lack of allurement, lack of charm, lack of desire, lack of enticement, lack of impetus, lack of incentive, lack of inducement, lack of motivation, lack of stimulus, lack of temptation, reluctance, restraint, unprovocativeness, unwillingness

DISINCLINED, *adjective* adverse, against, antagonistic, antipathetic, antipathetical, averse, *aversus*, balking, contrary, counter, demurring, dissenting, faltering, grudging, hesitant, hesitating, indisposed, laggard, loath, noncooperating, opposed, qualmish, recalcitrant, refusing, reluctant, renitent, restive, shirking, shrinking, squeamish, unaccommodating, unconsenting, uncooperative, unenthusiastic, uninclined, unpersuaded, unreconciled, unwilling, unzealous

DISINGENUOUS, *adjective* artful, artificial, conscienceless, counterfeit, crafty, cunning, deceitful, deceiving, deceptive, delusive, delusory, designing, devious, dishonest, dodging, evasive, false, false hearted, feigned, fraudulent, hypocritical, insidious, insincere, lacking frankness, lying, mendacious, misdealing, misleading, *parum candidus,* perfidious, prevaricating, scheming, shifty, sly, spurious, surreptitious, tricky, truthless, uncandid, underhanded, unethical, ungenuine, unprincipled, unscrupulous, unstraightforward, untrustworthy, untruthful, wanting in candor, wily, without truth

DISINHERIT, *verb* abandon, abrogate, annul, cast out, cut off, cut off from inheritance, cut out of one's will, deprive, deprive of hereditary succession, disaffirm, discard, disclaim, disendow, disentitle, disherit, disown, dispossess of hereditary right, divest, exclude from inheritance, *exheredare,* forfeit, forsake, nullify, oust, quash, recall, recant, renounce, replace, repudiate, rescind, retract, revoke, supersede, take away from, turn out, withdraw, withhold
ASSOCIATED CONCEPTS: disinherit a husband, disinherit a wife, disinherit an adopted child, disinherit pretermitted children

DISINTEGRATE, *verb* break up, crumble, decay, decompose, diffuse, disband, disperse, dissolve, disunite, fall to pieces, fragment, shatter, split up

DISINTER, *verb* bare, bring from obscurity into view, bring out, deracinate, detect, dig out, dig up, dig up out of the earth, discover, disentomb, disinhume, display, draw forth, draw out, educe, *effodere,* elicit, *eruere,* evince, evoke, evulse, excavate, exhibit, exhume, expose to view, extract, extricate, ferret out, find, find out, lay open, make known, manifest, present to view, pull out, pull up, remove, resurrect, reveal, root out, root up, show, take out of the place of interment, turn up, unbury, uncover, unearth, unroot, unsepulcher, untomb, unveil, withdraw

DISINTEREST *(Lack of interest),* **noun** aloofness, apathy, boredom, callousness, carelessness, coolness, detachment, disdain, disinterestedness, disregard, heedlessness, inappetence, inappetancy, inattention, inattentiveness, inconsideration, incuriosity, incuriousness, indifference, insensitivity, insouciance, lack of attention, lack of concern, langour, languidness, laxity, listlessness, mindlessness, neglect, neglectfulness, negligence, nonchalance, noninvolvement, obliviousness, perfunctoriness, phlegm, pococurantism, spiritlessness,

supineness, tepidity, thoughtlessness, unconcern, unmindfulness, unsolicitousness, want of attention, want of interest

DISINTEREST *(Lack of prejudice),* **noun** broadmindedness, candor, catholicity, detachment, dispassion, dispassionateness, equitableness, equity, evenhandedness, fair play, fair treatment, fairness, freedom from bias, freedom from prejudice, freedom from self-interest, impartiality, impartialness, impersonality, indiscrimination, justice, justness, liberality, neutrality, noninvolvement, nonpartisanship, objectivity, openmindedness, tolerance, toleration, unbiasedness, unprejudice, unselfishness, unslantedness
ASSOCIATED CONCEPTS: disinterested judge, disinterested party, disinterested persons, disinterested witness, without pecuniary interest

DISJOINT, *verb* break apart, break up, carve, cleave, cut up, detach, disarticulate, disassemble, disassociate, disband, disconnect, disengage, disjoin, dislocate, dismantle, dismember, dispart, displace, dissect, dissever, dissociate, disunite, divaricate, divide, divorce, luxate, part, quarter, rend, rive, section, segment, separate, sever, split, subdivide, sunder, take apart, tear apart, uncouple, unfasten, unhinge, unjoint, unloosen

DISJOINTED, *adjective* aimless, confused, deranged, desultory, disarranged, disassociated, discerpted, discordant, disjunctive, disordered, disorderly, disorganized, erratic, in disarray, in disorder, incoherent, *incompositus,* incongruent, incongruous, indiscriminate, interrupted, jumbled, lacking order, nonuniform, orderless, out of order, spasmodic, unclassified, uncohesive, unsorted, unsuccessive, unsystematic

DISJUNCTIVE *(Alternative),* **adjective** alternate, discretional, discretionary, elective, equivalent, having the privilege to choose, interchangeable, noncompulsory, nonobligatory, not compulsory, open to choice, optional, selective, subject to preference, substitute, substitutional, substitutive
ASSOCIATED CONCEPTS: disjunctive allegations, disjunctive covenants, disjunctive relief, disjunctive words of a statute

DISJUNCTIVE *(Tending to disjoin),* **adjective** broken, desultory, detached, disarticulated, disconnected, discrete, disjoined, disjoint, disjointed, dismembered, distinct, disunited, divided, divorced, eratic, fitful, inconsistent, individual, insular, intermittent, intermitting, interrupted, irregular, isolated, loose, noncontinuous, not cohesive, not integrated, parted, partitioned, periodic, punctuated, separate, severed, spasmodic, successive, suspended, unannexed, unassociated, unconnected, unjoined, unsuccessive

DISLOCATE, *verb* agitate, cast out, complicate, confound, confuse, derail, derange, disarrange, disconnect, disjoin, disjoint, dislodge, disorder, disorganize, disorient, displace, disturb, disunite, eject, evacuate, evict, expel, luxate, mislay, misplace, move, oust, remove, scatter, throw into confusion, throw out of joint, throw out of order, unseat, unsettle, upset

DISLODGE, *verb* banish, carry off, cart away, cashier, cast out, *deicere,* delocalize, demote, *depellere,* deport, depose, deracinate, dethrone, detrude, disbar, discharge, disemploy, disenthrone, disestablish, dislocate, dismiss, displace, displant, dispossess, disturb, divest of office, eject, eliminate, evacuate, evict, exclude, exile, expatriate, expel, *expellere,* expropriate, extract, force out, lay off, oust, overthrow, push out, put out, relegate, remove, retire, rid, send away, supersede, supplant, take away, throw away, throw out, thrust out, turn out, unload, unseat, uproot, usurp

DISLOYALTY, *noun* apostasy, barratry, betrayal, betrayal of trust, breach, breach of faith, breach of promise, breach of trust, broken promise, contumacy, defection, dereliction of allegiance, desertion, disobedience, faithlessness, falseness, falsity, fickleness, improbity, inconstancy, *infidelitas,* infidelity, insincerity, insubordination, insurgency, insurrection, lack of fidelity, lack of loyalty, malfeasance, mutineering, mutinousness, mutiny, perfidiousness, perfidy, rebellion, recreancy, revolt, sabotage, sedition, seditiousness, subversion, subversive activity, traitoriousness, treachery, treason, treasonable activities, unfaithfulness, unsteadfastness, venality, violation of allegiance, violation of trust, want of loyalty

DISMISS (*Discharge*), *verb* cashier, cast out, demobilize, depose, deprive of force, disemploy, dispatch, dispense with, displace, dispossess, eject, expel, fire, lay off, oust, purge, release, remove, remove from office, send away, send off, set free, suspend, turn away, turn out, unseat, vacate
ASSOCIATED CONCEPTS: dismiss a cause of action, dismissal because of laches, dismissed for cause, dismissed with prejudice, dismissed without prejudice, motion to dismiss, motion to dismiss for failure to state a claim, motion to dismiss for lack of jurisdiction, nonsuit

DISMISS (*Put out of consideration*), *verb* brush aside, decline, deny, disallow, disavow, discountenance, disregard, ignore, lay aside, not hear of, pass over, pay no regard to, put out of mind, refuse, reject, rule out, set aside, take no notice, think no more of

DISMISSAL (*Discharge*), *noun* cashiering, deposition, *dimissio,* discharge from employment, disemployment, dislodgment, displacement, ejection, elimination, exclusion, expulsion, firing, layoff, ouster, release from employment, removal from a job, removal from a position, removal from office, severance

DISMISSAL (*Termination of a proceeding*), *noun* annulment, cancellation, conclusion of a proceeding, conclusion of an action, discontinuance, disposal, ending of a proceeding, ending of an action, invalidation, nonsuit, quashing, rejection, removal of a cause out of court, termination of an action
ASSOCIATED CONCEPTS: dismissal for cause, dismissal for failure to prosecute, dismissal for want of jurisdiction, dismissal for want of substantial federal question, dismissal of a cause for want of prosecution, dismissal of a charge, dismissal of an action with prejudice, dismissal of an employee, dismissal of an appeal, dismissal of proceedings, dismissal on the merits, dismissal without prejudice

DISOBEDIENT, *adjective* apostatizing, arbitrary, averse, contrary, contumacious, culpable, defiant, delinquent, derelict, disloyal, disorderly, disregarding, disrespectful, fractious, froward, headstrong, hostile, ill-behaved, incorrigible, indisposed, insubordinate, in-

surgent, insurrectional, intractable, irascible, irresponsible, lawbreaking, lawless, licentious, loath, misbehaving, mutinous, neglectful, negligent, *non obsequi,* noncompliant, obdurate, objecting, obstinate, obstreperous, opposed, opposing, perfidious, perverse, rebellious, recalcitrant, recusant, refractory, reluctant, remiss, renitent, resistant, resistive, restive, riotous, stubborn, traitorous, transgressive, treasonous, trespassing, truant, uncompliant, uncomplying, unconsenting, uncooperative, undependable, undisciplined, undutiful, unfaithful, ungovernable, unmanageable, unmindful, unreliable, unruly, unsubmissive, unwilling, unyielding, violating, violative, wayward, wild, willful
ASSOCIATED CONCEPTS: disobedience to lawful mandate of court, lawful disobedience, willful disobedience

DISOBEY, *verb* act illegally, arise, be derelict, be disloyal, be insubordinate, be mutinous, be negligent, be perfidious, be recalcitrant, be recusant, be treasonous, be undisciplined, be unruly, betray, break a law, break a rule, break the law, commit a crime, contravene, cross, defy, deviate, disregard, fail to comply, go counter to, ignore, infringe, insurrect, misbehave, mutiny, negate, neglect, not comply, not cooperate, not heed, not listen, not mind, not obey, oppose, pay no attention to, rebel, recalcitrate, refuse, refuse to obey, reject, repudiate, resist, revolt, revolutionize, rise, shirk, transgress, traverse, trespass, violate
ASSOCIATED CONCEPTS: disobedience, disobedience to a lawful mandate of the court, failure to comply, willful disobedience

DISOBLIGE, *verb* act contrary, affront, antagonize, balk, be unaccommodating, be unwilling, cause displeasure, debase, decline, degrade, demur, denigrate, denounce, deprecate, disaccommodate, discommode, disdain, dishonor, disparage, disregard, fail to accommodate, fail to comply with, give offense to, ignore, incommode, incur disapproval, insult, malign, maltreat, neglect to obey, not accept, not comply with, not obey, offend, *offendere,* put out, rebuff, refuse, refuse to oblige, reject, repel, repudiate, scorn, shrink, slight, spite, spurn, traduce, treat with indignity, turn down, vilipend, withhold consent

DISORDER (*Abnormal condition*), *noun* affliction, ailment, complaint, condition, disability, disease, distemper, handicap, illness, indisposition, infirmity, malady, malfunction, sickness

DISORDER (*Lack of order*), *noun* anarchism, anarchy, breach of peace, chaos, commotion, confusion, derangement, disarrangement, disarray, discomposure, disharmony, dishevelment, disorderly conduct, disorganization, disturbance, fracas, irregularity, lack of regular order, lawlessness, muddle, pandemonium, racket, riot, slipshodness, tumult, tumultuousness, turbulence, turmoil, unrest, uproar
ASSOCIATED CONCEPTS: breach of the peace, disorderly conduct

DISORDERED, *adjective* aberrant, abnormal, agitated, amiss, anarchical, anomalous, askew, atypical, awry, bedraggled, bemuddled, capricious, changeable, changeful, chaotic, confused, deviating, disarranged, discomposed, discontinuous, disheveled, disjunct, dislocated, disorganized, divergent, diverse, entangled, heterogeneous, illogical, immethodical, impetuous, in chaos, in disarray, in hysterics, incoherent, inconsistent, incontrollable, inverted, involved, jumbled, lawless, messy, nonuniform, not belonging, orderless, out of order, out of place, patternless, random, raveled, shapeless, tangled, tumultuary, tumultuous, turbulent, twisted, unarranged, unassembled, unclassified, uncoordinated, undisciplined, uneven, unkempt, unmanageable, unmethodical, unorganized, unpatterned, unruly, unsystematic, untidy, without method

DISORDERLY, *adjective*   aberrant, aggressive, agitated, anarchic, anarchical, anarchistic, barbaric, barbarous, bellicose, blustering, blustery, boisterous, brutal, careless, churlish, confused, contumacious, defiant, deranged, destructive, disagreeable, disarranged, discomposed, discontinuous, discourteous, disgraceful, disheveled, disjointed, disobedient, disorganized, dissolute, disturbed, explosive, fitful, fluctuating, froward, heinous, ill-mannered, immethodical, immoderate, impolite, improper, incendiary, incorrigible, indecorous, inflammatory, insolent, insurrectionary, intemperate, irregular, lawbreaking, lawless, licentious, loud, mannerless, misbehaved, misbehaving, mutinous, nihilistic, nonobservant, obstreperous, orderless, out of order, outrageous, quarrelsome, rackety, raging, rampant, random, rebellious, recalcitrant, refractory, resisting, restive, revolutionary, riotous, rough, rowdy, rude, ruffianly, savage, scampish, scandalous, slovenly, stormy, strong, tangled, tempestuous, tumultous, tumultuary, turbulent, unauthorized, unbridled, uncivil, uncivilized, uncommendable, uncontrolled, uncourtly, uncurbed, undisciplined, uneven, ungenteel, ungentle, ungentlemanlike, ungentlemanly, ungoverned, unladylike, unmanageable, unmannered, unmannerly, unmethodical, unmitigated, unquelled, unregulated, unrepressed, unruly, unseemly, unsettled, unsteady, unsubmissive, unsystematic, untidy, untrained, uprisen, uproarious, violent, warlike, wayward, wild
ASSOCIATED CONCEPTS: breach of the peace, disorderly conduct, disorderly houses, disorderly persons, disturbance of the public peace

DISORGANIZE, *verb*   abolish the organization of, agitate, bedevil, befog, befuddle, bewilder, bother, clutter, come to pieces, complicate, confound, *confundere,* confuse, daze, deactivate, decompose, deform, demobilize, deprive of organization, derange, destroy the form of, deteriorate, disarrange, disband, discompose, disconcert, dishevel, disintegrate, disjoin, dismantle, disorder, disorientate, dispel, disperse, disrupt, dissipate, dissolve, distract, disturb, embrangle, entangle, interrupt, invert, liquidate, make havoc, misarrange, *miscere,* misplace, muddle, obfuscate, obscure, perplex, perturb, *perturbare,* play havoc with, put out of order, ravel, render uncertain, revert, scatter, scramble, separate, tangle, tear up, throw into confusion, throw into disorder, throw out of order, tumble, twist, unbalance, undo, unmake, unsettle, upset

DISORIENT, *verb*   abash, baffle, befuddle, bewilder, confound, dement, derange, disarrange, discompose, disconcert, dislocate, dislodge, disorder, disorganize, distract, disturb, fluster, impair, invert, make havoc, misdirect, mislay, mislead, misplace, muddle, mystify, nonplus, obfuscate, obscure, overturn, perturb, render uncertain, ruffle, scramble, throw into confusion, throw into disorder, throw out of order, trouble, unbalance, unsettle, upset

DISOWN *(Deny the validity),* **verb**   abjure, abnegate, affirm the contrary, annul, call in question, challenge, confute, contest, contradict, contravene, controvert, countermand, demur, deny, deny absolutely, deny peremptorily, deny the possibility, deny wholly, disaffirm, disagree, disallow, disannul, disavow, disbelieve, disclaim, disprove, disregard, dissent, forswear, hold no brief for, impugn, *infitiari,* invalidate, negate, negative, not accept, not admit, not confirm, not maintain, nullify, object, oppose, overrule, protest, rebut, recant, refuse credence, refuse to accept, refuse to admit, refuse to corroborate, refute, reject, render null and void, *repudiare,* repudiate, rescind, retract, reverse, revoke, set aside, set at nought, stand up to, take issue with, traverse, undo, vacate, void

DISOWN *(Refuse to acknowledge),* **verb**   abandon, abjure, alienate, cast away, cast off, cede, cut off, cut out of one's will, deprive of hereditary succession, deprive of the right to inherit, disaffiliate, disallow, disclaim, disclaim the responsibility for, disdain, disendow, disinherit, dispense with, dispossess, dispossess of hereditary right, dissociate oneself, divest, divorce, forsake, get rid of, give up, have nothing to do with, *infitiari,* jettison, let go, not maintain, oust, part with, rebuff, refuse to recognize, relinquish, renounce, *repudiare,* repudiate, repulse, scorn, spurn
ASSOCIATED CONCEPTS: disown a child

DISPARAGE, *verb*   affront, asperse, be insolent, be rude, belittle, bemock, besmear, bespatter, blacken, blot, bring reproach upon, calumniate, cavil, censure, cheapen, condemn, contemn, criticize, debase, decry, defame, deflate, degrade, denigrate, depreciate, deride, derogate, detract, *detrectare,* discount, discredit, disesteem, disfavor, disgrace, dishonor, disregard, disrespect, downgrade, *elevare, extenuare,* find fault with, frown upon, gibe, humiliate, imitate insultingly, insult, jeer, lampoon, laugh at, look down on, lower the estimation of, make fun of, make light of, make sport of, malign, minimize, misprize, mock, play down, reflect poorly upon, ridicule, run down, scoff, scorn, shame, slander, slight, slur, smear, sneer, speak ill of, stain, stigmatize, sully, taint, tarnish, taunt, think little of, traduce, underrate, undervalue, vilify, vilipend
ASSOCIATED CONCEPTS: disparage a name, disparage a product

DISPARAGEMENT, *noun*   accusation, act of berating, act of running down, admonishment, adverse criticism, aspersion, bad review, belittlement, belittling, blame, brand, castigation, complaint, condemnation, confutation, contempt, criticism, damnation, decrial, denigration, *dénigrement,* denouncement, denunciation, deprecation, depreciation, derogation, destructive criticism, detraction, disapprobation, disapproval, discontent, discourtesy, disesteem, disfavor, dishonor, disillusionment, dislike, displeasure, disrepute, disrespect, disrespectfulness, exception, faultfinding, hostile criticism, hypercriticism, impeachment, impugnation, imputation, indignation, insinuation, invective, irreverence, low estimation, low opinion, low valuation, mockery, muckraking, nonapproval, objection, objuration, obloquy, *obtrectatio,* outcry, overcriticalness, poor opinion, protest, rebuke, rejection, reprehension, reprimand, reproach, reprobation, reproof, revilement, ridicule, rude reproach, rudeness, scant respect, scolding, scorn, slighting language, stigma, tirade, uncomplimentary remark, vilification, vilipendency, vituperation, want of respect

ASSOCIATED CONCEPTS: disparagement of goods, disparagement of property, disparagement of title

DISPARATE, adjective aberrant, atypical, clashing, conflicting, contradictory, contrasting, departing from, deviating, different, differentiated, differing, digressive, disagreeing, discordant, discrepant, disproportionate, dissimilar, distinct, distinguished, divaricating, divergent, essentially different, ill-matched, incommensurable, incongruent, incongruous, inconsistent, inconsonant, independent, irreconcilable, irregular, nonuniform, not comparable, not the same, out of proportion, separate, unconformable, unequal, uneven, unlike, unmatched, varied

ASSOCIATED CONCEPTS: disparate award, disparate relief

DISPARITY, noun argument, asymmetry, conflict of opinion, contradiction, contradistinction, contraposition, contrast, controversy, deviation, difference, disaccord, disagreement, discord, discordance, discrepancy, disequilibrium, disharmony, *dissimilitudo,* dissimilitude, dissonance, disunity, divergence, diversity, failure to agree, imbalance, incommensurability, incompatibility, incongruence, incongruity, inequality, inharmoniousness, irreconcilability, irrelation, lack of relation, lack of symmetry, nonagreement, nonconformity, nonuniformity, unconformity, unlikeness, variance, variation

DISPASSIONATE, adjective aloof, ascetic, *blasé,* calm, *calme,* cold, cold-blooded, cold-hearted, collected, composed, controlled, cool-headed, detached, disengaged, disinterested, even-handed, even-tempered, fair, heartless, immovable, impartial, impassive, impersonal, imperturbable, indifferent, inexcitable, inscrutable, neutral, nonchalant, objective, open-minded, passionless, peaceful, phlegmatic, *placatus, placidus, sang-froid,* self-controlled, selfless, steady, stoical, stolid, subdued, temperate, tolerant, tranquil, *tranquillus,* unaffected, unbiased, uncorrupted, undemonstrative, undisturbed, unemotional, unexcited, unfeeling, ungrudging, unimpassioned, unimpressible, unimpressionable, uninfluenced, uninvolved, unirritable, unjealous, unmindful, unnervous, unoffended, unpassionate, unperturbed, unprejudiced, unprepossessed, unresponsive, unruffled, unsentimental, unshaken, unstirred, unsusceptible, unswayed, untouchable, without nerves, without warmth

DISPATCH (Act of putting to death), noun act of killing, act of slaying, assassination, bloodshed, death by violence, deathblow, destruction, disposal, doing away with, execution, extermination, homicide, killing, liquidation, massacre, murder

DISPATCH (Message), noun aviso, bulletin, circular, communication, *communiqué,* correspondence, enlightenment, epistle, *epistula,* information, instruction, letter, *litterae,* mail, missive, monition, news, note, notice, notification, official correspondence, postal communication, report, statement, stream of correspondence, telegram

DISPATCH (Promptness), noun alacrity, briskness, bustle, celerity, dash, *dépêche, diligence,* excitation, expediousness, *expédition,* expeditious perfor-

mance, fast rate, fastness, *festinatio,* feverish haste, flurry, haste, hastiness, hurry, immediateness, impetuosity, inability to wait, instantaneity, liveliness, lively pace, movement, nimbleness, precipitance, precipitancy, precipitation, precipitousness, *promptitude, properatio,* punctuality, punctualness, quick discharge, quick riddance, quickness, rapidity, readiness, rush, scramble, scurry, speed, speediness, speedy completion, speedy disposition, speedy transaction, spurt, suddenness, summariness, swift execution, swift rate, timeliness, urgency

ASSOCIATED CONCEPTS: with all possible dispatch

DISPATCH (Dispose of), verb *absolvere,* accomplish, achieve, attain, bring about, bring off, bring to a conclusion, bring to an end, bring to pass, carry out, carry through, carry to completion, close, complete, conclude, *conficere,* consummate, deal with definitely, do the deed, effect, effectuate, execute, finish, fulfill, implement, make an end of, make final disposition of, *perficere,* perform, realize, see through, set at rest, succeed, work out

DISPATCH (Put to death), verb assassinate, bring down, commit murder, *coup de grâce,* cut down, deal a death blow, deprive of life, destroy, dispose of, do away with, end, end life, execute, exterminate, give the death blow, hasten one's end, *interficere, interimere,* kill, liquidate, make away with, massacre, murder, put an end to, put down, put out of the way, put to death, remove from life, slaughter, slay, take life, take one's life away

DISPATCH (Send off), verb address, detail, direct, expedite, fling, forward, get under way, hasten, hasten on, have conveyed, hurry, hurry along, hurry on, impart motion, impel, *mittere,* mobilize, move on, post, propel, push, push through, put in motion, remit, rush, rush off, send, send away, send forth, send through the mail, set going, ship, speed, speed along, speed on its way, transfer, transmit

ASSOCIATED CONCEPTS: with all due dispatch

DISPEL, verb banish, bestow, bestrew, break up, broadcast, cast adrift, cast off, cast out, deal out, diffuse, discharge, *discutere,* disintegrate, dismiss, *dispellere,* disperse, disperse completely, disseminate, *dissipare,* dissipate, dissolve, do away with, drive away, drive away by scattering, drive off in various directions, eject, expel, fling off, get rid of, loose, push away, put into circulation, radiate, release, remove, rout, scatter, send, send flying, send home, set abroach, set aside, set asunder, shake off, spread, strew, string out, throw away, throw off, turn adrift, utterly disperse

ASSOCIATED CONCEPTS: dispel an inference

DISPENSATION (Act of dispensing), noun accommodation, administration, allocation, allotment, appointment, apportionment, assignment, bestowal, bestowment, conferment, conferral, dispersal, dispersion, disposal, disposition, dissemination, distribution, division, fair sharing, impartation, impartment, issuance, partition, presentation, presentment, provision, repartition, share, subvention, transfer

DISPENSATION (Exception), noun absolution, acquiescence, allowance, amnesty, approval, authorization, *carte blanche,* certificate of exemption, clearance, *congé,* consent, deliberate omission, escape-clause, exception, exception in favor of, exclusion, exculpation,

excuse, exemption, exemption from law, exoneration, forgiveness, freedom, grace, grant, immunity, indulgence, leave, liberty, license, noninclusion, nonliability, nonresponsibility, omission, pardon, permission, permit, privilege, relaxation of law, release from obligation, sanction, special privilege, sufferance, tolerance, toleration, warrant
ASSOCIATED CONCEPTS: concession, franchise, special dispensation

DISPENSE, *verb*   administer, allocate, allot, appoint, apportion, appropriate, assign, bestow, bestow upon, confer, deal, deal to, detail, *dimittere,* dispense, disperse, dispose of, disseminate, *distribuere,* distribute, divide in portions, do away with, do without, dole out, donate, give out, grant, hand out, issue, mete, parcel out, portion out, proportionate, provide, ration, *re carere,* render, scatter, serve, share, tender
ASSOCIATED CONCEPTS: dispense with

DISPERSE *(Disseminate), verb*   administer, allocate, apportion, assign, bestow in shares, bestrew, cast forth, cast off, circulate, consign, convey, deal, deal out, dispense, dispose, distribute, divide, dole, dole out, give away, give out among a number, issue, mete out, parcel out, partition, pass out, pay dividends, pay out, portion out, propagate, scatter abroad, spread, spread abroad, spread out, strew
ASSOCIATED CONCEPTS: disperse public information

DISPERSE *(Scatter), verb*   asunder, decentralize, depart, diffuse, disband, disintegrate, disjoin, dispart, dispel, *dispellere, dispergere, dissipare,* dissipate, dissolve, disunite, divide, go different ways, go in different directions, go separate ways, part, partition, rend, rive, scatter abroad, separate, split up, spread widely

DISPLACE *(Remove), verb*   banish, carry away, cart away, cast out, change the place of, clear away, convey, delocalize, deport, detach, discard, discharge, dislocate, dislodge, dismiss, dispatch, disperse, dispossess, disturb, eject, evict, exclude, exile, expatriate, expel, export, expropriate, *loco suo movere,* move, not retain, oust, purge, put out, send, send away, shift from its place, take away, throw out, transfer, turn out, unhouse, unjoint, unseat
ASSOCIATED CONCEPTS: displaced person, displaced worker

DISPLACE *(Replace), verb*   act for, act the part of, answer for, change for, count for, double for, exchange, fill another's position, fill in for, interchange, make a shift with, make way for, offer in exchange, pass for, put in the place of, replace with, stand in for, substitute, succeed, supersede, supplant, switch, take another's place, take in exchange, take over another's duties, take the place of, transfer, transpose, understudy for

DISPLAY, *verb*   brandish, bring to light, demonstrate, disclose, divulge, evidence, evince, exhibit, express, flaunt, flourish, illustrate, indicate, parade, present, reveal, show, wave

DISPOSABLE, *adjective*   adaptable, advantageous, available, consumable, dispensable, employable, expendable, exploitable, fit for use, free for use, helpful, movable, of service, of use, on call, open to, pervious, procurable, reachable, ready for use, realizable, salable,

securable, serviceable, spendable, suitable, to be had, usable, useful, utilitarian, utilizable, within reach
ASSOCIATED CONCEPTS: disposable assets

DISPOSE *(Apportion), verb*   deal out, distribute, dole out, fix, mete out, parcel out, place

DISPOSE *(Incline), verb*   affect, arrange, bend, bias, decide, determine, incline, induce, influence, put, sway, tend, verge
ASSOCIATED CONCEPTS: disposing mind and memory

DISPOSITION *(Determination), noun*   adjustment, conclusion, decision, disposal, final settlement of a matter, finding, order, pronouncement, putting in order, resolution, settlement, solution
ASSOCIATED CONCEPTS: disposition of a case

DISPOSITION *(Final arrangement), noun*   adjustment, administration, arrangement, array, *conlocatio,* control, direction, dispensation, disposal, *dispositio,* distribution, grouping, management, marshaling, method, order, ordering, *ordinatio,* organization, placement, regulation, settlement
ASSOCIATED CONCEPTS: conditional disposition, final disposition, fraudulent disposition, power of disposition, testimentary disposition
FOREIGN PHRASES: *Cujus est dare, ejus est disponere.* Whoever has the right of giving a thing, has the right of any disposition of it.

DISPOSITION *(Inclination), noun*   aptitude, bent, bias, cast, character, characteristic, characteristic mood, constitution, frame of mind, grain, humor, idiosyncrasy, inclination, individualism, *indoles, ingenium,* leaning, liking, makeup, mental constitution, mold, mood, native character, *natura,* natural fitness, natural tendency, nature, penchant, personality, predilection, predisposition, preference, proclivity, proneness, propensity, spirit, temper, temperament, tendency, turn of mind
FOREIGN PHRASES: *Impunitas continuum affectum tribuit delinquendi.* Impunity confirms the disposition of a delinquent.

DISPOSITION *(Transfer of property), noun*   alienation, arrangement for disposal, assignment, conveyance, conveyancing, deliverance, delivery, dispensation, disposal, distribution, giving, manner of disposal, release, relinquishment, relinquishment by gift, sale, surrender, transfer, transference, vouchsafement, yielding
ASSOCIATED CONCEPTS: dispose of and convey, disposition by will, final disposition, fraudulent disposition, power of disposition, sale or other disposition, testamentary disposition
FOREIGN PHRASES: *Cujus est dare, ejus est disponere.* He who has a right to give, has the right to dispose of the gift.

DISPOSSESS, *verb*   cause to forfeit, declare forfeit, depose, deprive, deprive of occupancy, *deturbare,* disendow, disentitle, dislodge, displace, disseise, disseize, divest, eject from possession, evict, expel, expropriate, foreclose, oust, *possessione depellere,* relieve of, remove, turn out
ASSOCIATED CONCEPTS: dispossess a tenant, eviction, foreclosure, summary proceedings

DISPROPORTIONATE, *adjective*   assymetrical, at odds, at variance, conflicting, contrary to reason, disaccordant, discordant, discrepant, disparate, divergent, excessive, ill-adapted, ill-matched, ill-proportioned, illsorted, ill-suited, illogical, *impar,* improperly proportioned, *inaequalis,* inapplicable, inapposite, inappropriate, incommensurable, incommensurate, incompatible, inconformable, incongruent, incongruous, inconsequent, inconsistent, inconsonant, infelicitous, inharmonious, inordinate, irrational, irreconcilable, lacking proportion, mismatched, not following, not in keeping, out of joint, out of keeping, out of place, out of proportion, overcharged, overmuch, poorly adapted, superfluous, too much, unapt, unbalanced, unbefitting, uncalled for, unconformable, undeserved, undeserving, undue, unequal, uneven, unfitting, unjustifiable, unreasonable, unseemly, unsuitable, unsymmetrical, untoward, unwarrantable, unwarranted, wanting in proportion

ASSOCIATED CONCEPTS: disproportionate penalty, disproportionate to the value, punishment disproportionate to the crime

DISPROVE, *verb*   belie, confute, contravene, controvert, counteract, countervail, deny, discredit, dispel, find unfounded, invalidate, negate, nullify, oppugn, prove false, prove the contrary, prove to be wrong, prove to the contrary, rebut, *redarguere, refellere,* refute, show the fallacy of, show to be false, traverse

DISPUTABLE, *adjective*   admitting of doubt, ambiguous, apocryphal, appealing to reason, arguable, arguing, argumentative, at issue, confutable, conjectural, contestable, controversial, controvertible, cryptic, debatable, deniable, disputatious, doubtable, doubtful, doubting, dubious, dubitable, dubitative, enigmatic, equivocal, eristic, fallible, hard to believe, hypothetical, improbable, in dispute, in doubt, in issue, in question, incredible, indefinite, indeterminate, *infamis,* not axiomatic, not to be believed, of doubtful certainty, open to debate, open to discussion, open to doubt, open to question, open to suspicion, paradoxical, perplexing, polemic, problematic, questionable, refutable, speculative, subject to argument, subject to controversy, suppositional, suspect, suspicious, theoretical, to be decided, unaffirmed, unascertained, unbelievable, uncertain, unconfirmed, undecided, undemonstrable, undemonstrated, under discussion, undetermined, unfixed, unknown, unlikely, unproven, unreliable, unresolved, unsettled, unsure, unsustainable, unsustained, unverifiable, vague

ASSOCIATED CONCEPTS: disputable presumption

DISPUTANT, *noun*   adversary, adverse party, antagonist, argumentative person, assailant, belligerent, caviler, combatant, contender, contestant, controversialist, controvertist, discussant, dissenter, litigant, objector, obstructionist, opponent, opposer, oppositionist, polemicist, resister, rival, wrangler

DISPUTE, *noun*   aggressive argument, *altercatio,* altercation, argument, bickering, challenge, clash of opinions, conflict, conflict of opinion, contention, *controversia,* controversy, debate, *démêlé,* difference, difference of opinion, disaccord, disagreement, *disceptatio,* discord, dissension, dissentience, dissidence, disturbance, disunity, divergence, divergent opinions, embranglement, embroilment, failure to agree, feud, imbroglio, impugnation, legal battle, litigation, nonagreement, opposition, polemic, remonstrance, remonstration, strife, variance, verbal contention, verbal controversy, verbal engagement, wrangle

ASSOCIATED CONCEPTS: amount in dispute, dispute as to the amount, dispute concerning terms or conditions of employment, jurisdictional dispute, labor dispute, matter in dispute, undisputed claim

DISPUTE *(Contest),* *verb*   *altercari,* altercate, argue against, argue vehemently, be at cross purposes, be at variance, bring in question, call in question, challenge, clash, collide, combat, compete, *concertare,* conflict, confute, contend, contend for, contradict, contravene, controvert, deny, deny absolutely, deny emphatically, deny entirely, deny flatly, deny peremptorily, deny the genuineness of, differ, disagree with, dissent from, doubt, gainsay, give denial to, have a feud with, have an altercation, have differences, have words with, impugn, negative, not agree, object to, oppose by argument, quarrel over, query, question the truth of, recriminate, refute, *rixari,* strive against, struggle against, take exception, take issue with, traverse

ASSOCIATED CONCEPTS: disputed claim, disputed demand, disputed issue, disputed question of fact, disputed writing, labor dispute

FOREIGN PHRASES: *Non est certandum de regulis juris.* There is no disputing about rules of the law.

DISPUTE *(Debate),* *verb*   *ambigere,* argue, argue a case, argue a point, argue in opposition, argufy, bandy words, be contrary, bicker, carry on an argument, confute, contend in argument, contradict, controvert, differ, disagree, discept, *disceptare, disputare,* dissent, divide on, have a verbal controversy over, hold an argument, indulge in argument, make a rejoinder, not agree, parry, rebut, refute, wrangle

DISQUALIFICATION *(Factor that disqualifies),* *noun*   defect, disability, disablement, failure, handicap, inability, inadequacy, inaptitude, incapability, incapacitation, incapacity, incompetence, incompetency, ineptitude, inexpertness, insufficiency, invalidation, invalidity, lack of dexterity, lack of proficiency, lack of qualification, shortcoming, unaptness, undeftness, undesirability, unfitness, unfittedness, unpreparedness, unproficiency, unqualifiedness, unskillfulness, unsuitability, want of ability, want of skill

DISQUALIFICATION *(Rejection),* *noun*   banishment, deposal, deprivation, dethronement, disapprobation, disbarment, discharge, disentitlement, disfavor, disfranchisement, dislodgment, dismissal, displacement, dispossession, ejection, elimination, eviction, exclusion, expulsion, forfeiture, inadmissibility, ineligibility, invalidation, loss of right, nonadmission, noninclusion, ouster, preclusion, rejecting, rejection, repudiation, throwing out

ASSOCIATED CONCEPTS: disqualification to hold office, legal disqualification

DISQUALIFY, *verb*   bar, block, check, counteract, debar, deny, deprive of power, disable, disarm, disenable, disentitle, disfranchise, dispossess of right, divest of right, *excipere,* exclude, incapacitate, inhibit, interfere, invalidate, make impossible, make useless, neutralize, preclude, prevent, prohibit, reject, render impotent, render unfit, restrain, restrict, rule out, stop, strip of right, undermine, unfit

ASSOCIATED CONCEPTS: disqualified for interest, disqualified to act, disqualifying interest, disqualifying opinion, permanently disqualified

DISREGARD (*Lack of respect*), *noun* affront, aloofness, bad manners, belittlement, callousness, contempt, contemptousness, contumely, depreciation, discourtesy, disdain, disesteem, disfavor, dishonor, disobedience, disregardfulness, disrespect, heedlessness, impoliteness, impudence, inappreciation, inattentiveness, incivility, inconsiderateness, inconsideration, indifference, insensitivity, insolence, insult, low estimation, outrage, regardlessness, rudeness, scoffing, scorn, slight, snub, thoughtlessness, underestimation, undervaluation, unheedfulness, unmindfulness, want of thought

DISREGARD (*Omission*), *noun* breach of orders, default, delinquency, dereliction of duty, disregardfulness, failure to carry out, infraction, infringement, malefaction, malpractice, misbehavior, misconduct, neglect, neglectfulness, noncompliance, nonobservance, preterition, pretermission, refusal to obey, regardlessness, remissness, transgression, trespass, violation

DISREGARD (*Unconcern*), *noun* carelessness, disinterest, disinterestedness, disregardfulness, exclusion, heedlessness, improvidence, imprudence, inattention, inattentiveness, incaution, inconsideration, indifference, inobservance, insouciance, lack of care, lack of consideration, lack of interest, lack of observation, leaving out, mindlessness, neglect, neglectfulness, negligence, nonobservance, oblivion, obliviousness, overlooking, oversight, regardlessness, unconsciousness, unheedfulness, unmindfulness, unthinkingness, unwariness, unwatchfulness, want of notice, want of thought

DISREGARD, *verb* be incurious, be indifferent, be insensitive, dismiss, fail to notice, fail to observe, feel no concern, give no heed, ignore, leave out, leave out of consideration, neglect, *neglegere,* not bother with, not consider, not hear, not heed, not include, not listen, not think about, not think of, not trouble oneself, *omittere,* overlook, *parvi facere,* pass by, pay no attention, pay no regard to, pretermit, refuse to hear, refuse to know, refuse to regard, snub, spurn, take no account of, take no interest, take no note of, take no notice of, think little of, think nothing of, treat without due respect
ASSOCIATED CONCEPTS: disregard for the law, instruct the jury to disregard testimony, reckless disregard

DISREPAIR, *noun* collapse, corrosion, damage, decadence, decadency, decay, decrepitude, degeneration, deterioration, dilapidation, impaired condition, impairment, lack of maintenance, neglect, ruination

DISREPUTABLE, *adjective* abominable, arrant, bad, base, beastly, being in ill repute, characterless, cheap, coarse, conscienceless, contemptible, corrupt, crass, degraded, demoralizing, deplorable, despicable, despised, detestable, devious, discreditable, discredited, disgraced, disgraceful, dishonest, dishonorable, disliked, disrespectable, dissolute, dreadful, foul, hateful, having a bad reputation, heinous, held in contempt, horrendous, horrid, ignoble, ignominious, immoral, improper, impure, in disgrace, indecent, indecorous, indelicate, inelegant, *infamis,* infamous, inglorious, iniquitous, insincere, knavish, licentious, loathsome, meretri-

cious, misdealing, nefarious, not reputable, not respectable, not thought much of, notorious, objectionable, obnoxious, odious, of bad character, of ill fame, opprobrious, prevaricating, profligate, recreant, rejected, reprehensible, reproached, ribald, shameful, shameless, spurious, suspicious, tasteless, undignified, unethical, unprincipled, unrefined, unrespectable, unsavory, unscrupulous, untrustworthy, untruthful, unworthy

DISREPUTE, *noun* abasement, abjectness, abominableness, bad character, bad reputation, bad repute, baseness, beastliness, brand, contemptibility, debasement, degradation, despicability, despicableness, discreditableness, disesteem, disgracefulness, dishonor, dishonorableness, disparagement, disreputability, disreputableness, disrespect, execrableness, heinousness, ignobility, ignominiousness, ignominy, ill-fame, ill-favor, ill-repute, *infamia,* infamousness, infamy, ingloriousness, loathsomeness, loss of honor, loss of reputation, monstrousness, nefariousness, no reputation, no repute, obloquy, obnoxiousness, odiousness, odium, opprobrium, shady reputation, shame, shamefulness, shoddiness, stain, taint, turpitude, vileness, want of esteem, wickedness, wretchedness

DISRESPECT, *noun* abruptness, affront, arrogance, audacity, bluntness, brashness, brazenness, brusqueness, cavalierness, condescension, contempt, contemptuousness, contumacy, contumely, curtness, defiance, depreciation, derision, derisiveness, detraction, discourteousness, discourtesy, disdain, disesteem, dishonor, disobedience, disparagement, disregard, disrespectfulness, effrontery, flippancy, flout, impertinence, impoliteness, impudence, incivility, indecorum, insolence, *insolentia,* insubordination, insult, inurbanity, irreverence, lack of consideration, lack of courteousness, lack of courtesy, lack of politeness, lack of respect, mockery, offense, pertness, presumption, presumptuousness, rebuff, ridicule, rude behavior, rudeness, sauciness, scoffing, scorn, shortness, slight, sneer, snub, spurn, superciliousness, tactlessness, uncourtliness, ungallantness, ungentlemanliness, ungraciousness, unmannerliness, unmannerly conduct, unpoliteness, vilification, vilipendency, want of esteem
ASSOCIATED CONCEPTS: disrespect to flag

DISRUPT, *verb* agitate, annoy, break apart, cause chaos, cause confusion, cause scission, confuse, create a disturbance, create disorder, derange, disarrange, discompose, discontinue, dishevel, disjoin, disorder, disorganize, disquiet, dissociate, distract, disturb, embroil, fluster, get in the way, hinder, impede, infringe, intercept, interfere, intermit, interrupt, intervene, intrude, meddle, mess up, mix up, obstruct, overturn, perturb, prevent, rend asunder, ruffle, rupture, split up, stir up, stop, sunder, suspend, thwart, unsettle, upset

DISSATISFACTION, *noun* annoyance, chagrin, complaint, dejection, disaffection, disagreement, disappointment, disapprobation, disapproval, discomfort, discontent, discontentedness, discontentment, discouragement, disesteem, disfavor, disgruntlement, disgust, dislike, displeasure, disquiet, dissatisfiedness, dissent, distaste, fault-finding, grievance, grudge, inquietude, irritation, *molestia,* nonapproval, nonfulfillment of one's hopes, *offensa, offensio,* opposition, pique, querulousness, regret, state of not being satisfied, umbrage,

uncomfortableness, uneasiness of mind, unhappiness, unhappiness with one's lot, unsatisfaction, vexation
ASSOCIATED CONCEPTS: express dissatisfaction

DISSEISIN, noun   arrogation, assuming ownership, attachment, capture, commandeering, compulsory acquisition, confiscation, deprivation, deprivation of possession, disendowment, displacement of rightful owner, dispossession, distraint, distress, divestment, exclusion of entitled owner, expropriation, forcible seizure, foreclosure, impropriation, ouster, prehension, privation of seisin, seizure, sequestration, take-over, taking, taking possession, taking without compensation, wrongful dispossession
ASSOCIATED CONCEPTS: adverse possession, disseisin by election

DISSEMINATE, verb   announce, annunciate, apprise, broadcast, bruit, carry a report, circulate, communicate, convey, deal out, diffuse, dispatch news, dispense, *dispergere,* disperse, *disseminare,* distribute, impart, inform, issue, make public, notify, promulgate, propagate, publicize, publish, publish abroad, radiate, relay, report, *spargere,* spread a report, spread far and wide, strew, transmit, utter
ASSOCIATED CONCEPTS: publication of a libel

DISSENSION, noun   angry disagreement, argumentation, bickering, *brouillerie,* caviling, clashing, conflict, conflict of opinion, contention, controversy, difference of opinion, differences, disaccord, disaffection, disagreement, discord, discordance, *discordia,* disharmony, dispute, dissent, dissentience, dissidence, dissonance, disunion, disunity, divergence, divergent opinions, diversity of opinion, division, friction, lack of harmony, nonagreement, nonassent, nonconcurrence, protest, protestation, quarrel, refusal of agreement, remonstrance, resentment, rift, schism, strife, strong dissension, violent disagreement, wrangling

DISSENT (Difference of opinion), noun   apostasy, argument, caviling, challenge, clash, confirmed opposition, conflict, conflict of opinion, contraposition, demur, disaccord, disagreement, discord, discordance, disharmony, disparity, *dissensio,* dissension, dissentience, dissidence, dissonance, divergence, diversity of opinion, expostulation, failure to agree, friction, lack of harmony, nonagreement, noncompliance, objection, oppositeness, opposition, schism, unconformity, variance

DISSENT (Nonconcurrence), noun   contrariety, disagreement, disapproval, disavowal, disclaimer, discontent, dissatisfaction, dissension, dissentient voice, disunity, nonagreement, nonassent, nonconformity, nonconsent, nonobservance, objection, opposition, repudiation, variance
ASSOCIATED CONCEPTS: dissenting opinion, dissenting vote

DISSENT (Differ in opinion), verb   argue, be at variance, be contrary, be of contrary sentiment, bicker, clash, collide, conflict, confute, contradict, differ, differ in sentiment, disagree, disagree in opinion, dispute, *dissentire, dissidere,* not agree, oppose, quarrel, take exception, take issue with
ASSOCIATED CONCEPTS: dissenting fiduciary, dissenting stockholders

DISSENT (Withhold assent), verb   be unwilling, challenge, decline, decline to agree, defy, demur, disallow, disapprove, negate, negative, nonconsent, not accept, not approve, not consider, not defend, not hold with, object, oppose, prohibit, protest, raise objections, raise one's voice against, rebuff, refuse, refuse assent, refuse to admit, reject, repudiate, repulse, resist, spurn
ASSOCIATED CONCEPTS: dissent from the majority opinion

DISSENTING, adjective   arguing, argumentative, at cross-purposes, at issue, at loggerheads, at odds, at variance, caviling, clashing, conflicting, conflictive, conflictory, contentious, contradicting, controverting, debating, declining to agree, demurring, denying, differing, disaccordant, disagreeing, disapproving, discordant, discrepant, disharmonious, disputatious, disputative, disputing, dissentient, dissentious, dissident, dissonant, disunited, divergent, divided on, factious, going contrary to, in conflict, in disagreement, incongruous, inconsistent, inharmonious, irreconcilable, not abiding, not accepting, not agreeing, not conforming, objecting, opposing, polemical, protesting, quarreling, quarrelsome, questioning, recusant, refusing to admit, refusing to agree, refuting, repudiating, repugning, resisting, running counter to, taking exception, taking issue with, unconsenting, varying, withholding approval, withholding assent, wrangling
ASSOCIATED CONCEPTS: dissenting judges, dissenting opinion, dissenting shareholders

DISSERVICE, noun   bad turn, damage, detriment, *detrimentum,* harm, ill turn, *incommodum,* injury, injustice, malfeasance, mischief, misdeed, misdoing, mistreatment, outrage, unkindness, wrong

DISSIDENCE, noun   argument, bickering, clashing, conflict, contradiction, contrariety, controversy, contumaciousness, difference, disaccord, disagreement, discongruity, discord, discordance, discordancy, disharmony, dissension, dissent, dissonance, disunion, disunity, divergence, faction, incongruence, incongruity, inharmoniousness, noncompliance, nonconcurrence, nonconformity, opposition, quarrel, recusancy, schism, strife, unconformity, variance, wrangle

DISSIDENT, adjective   antagonistic, at odds with, at variance with, challenging, clashing, contrary, differing, disagreeing, discontented, discordant, discrepant, disinclined, disobedient, dissatisfied, dissentient, dissenting, dissentious, divergent, divided, factious, inaccordant, inacquiescent, incompatible, inconsistent with, irreconcilable, loath, malcontent, noncompliant, nonconforming, nonconformist, nonobservant, not consenting, objecting, opposing, protestant, protesting, quarreling, rebellious, recalcitrant, recusant, refusing, resistant, unassenting, unconformable, unconsenting, unwilling

DISSIMILAR, adjective   aberrant, asymmetrical, atypical, clashing, contrary, contrasted, contrasting, deviating, different, differing, disagreeing, discordant, discrepant, *dispar,* disparate, *dissimilis,* divergent, divers, diverse, diversified, heterogeneous, incongruent, irregular, irrelative, mismatched, mixed, multiform, nonidentical, nonuniform, not comparable, not similar, odd, of a different kind, of all sorts, of many kinds, unalike, unconformable, unidentical, unlike, unmatched,

unpaired, unrelated, unresembling, unsame, unsimilar, untypical, varied, variegated, variform, various
ASSOCIATED CONCEPTS: dissimilar condition

DISSIPATE *(Expend foolishly),* **verb**   abuse, be extravagant, be immoderate, be intemperate, be prodigal, burn up, consume, consume one's substance, deny oneself nothing, deplete, drain, empty, exhaust, expend, indulge in extravagance, indulge oneself, live idly, misspend, misuse, overdraw, overspend, overstrain, practice extravagance, prodigalize, spend, spend lavishly, spend wastefully, use up, waste
ASSOCIATED CONCEPTS: dissipation of assets, dissipation of property, waste

DISSIPATE *(Spread out),* **verb**   bestrew, break up, cast forth, cease, cease to be, dematerialize, diffuse, disappear, disintegrate, disperse, disseminate, *dissipare,* dissolve, diverge, evanesce, fade, fade away, overspread, radiate, scatter, scatter thinly, scatter to the winds, scatter widely, sow, spread, spread over, sprinkle, strew, vanish

DISSOCIATE, *verb*   break up, cut adrift, cut off, demobilize, detach, disassociate, disband, disconnect, disencumber, disengage, disjoin, dispart, disperse, displace, dissever, disunite, divide, divorce, free, have no concern with, isolate, keep apart, liberate, loosen, part, release, remove, scatter, segregate, separate, set free, sever, sunder, take leave, unbind, unchain, uncouple, undo, unlock, unloose, unyoke, withdraw

DISSOLUTE, *adjective*   abandoned, base-minded, carnal, concupiscent, corrupt, corrupted, debased, debauched, decadent, degenerate, degraded, depraved, dissipated, *dissolutus,* evil-minded, free-living, graceless, immoderate, immoral, impure, incontinent, incorrigible, indecent, indulgent, iniquitous, intemperate, lascivious, libertine, libidinous, licentious, low-minded, lustful, *luxuriosus,* perverted, polluted, prodigal, profligate, prurient, rakish, reprobate, salacious, satyric, sensual, shameless, unashamed, unbridled, unchaste, uncurbed, unprincipaled, unrestrained, unvirtuous, warped, wayward
ASSOCIATED CONCEPTS: dissolute person

DISSOLUTION *(Disintegration),* **noun**   adulteration, atomization, atrophy, breaking up, corrosion, corruption, crumbling, decay, decomposition, demolition, deterioration, dilapidation, disassembly, disbanding, dismantlement, disorganization, dispersal, disruption, dissipation, erosion, rotting, separation, spoilage, spoliation, undoing

DISSOLUTION *(Termination),* **noun**   abolishment, abolition, abrogation, annihilation, annulment, breaking up, cancellation, cancelling, cessation, close, closing, completion, conclusion, death, defeasance, demise, destruction, discontinuance, dismissal, *dissolutio,* disuse, effacement, elimination, end, ending, eradication, erasure, expiration, expunction, extinction, extinguishment, extirpation, finis, finish, invalidation, liquidation, nullification, obliteration, overthrow, prorogation, repeal, rescission, revocation, revokement, ruin, ruination, suppression, voidance
ASSOCIATED CONCEPTS: corporate dissolution, de facto dissolution, de jure dissolution, dissolution of marriage, dissolution of partnership, dissolution proceeding

DISSOLVE *(Disperse),* **verb**   atomize, decompose, diffuse, disintegrate, dispel, dissipate, *dissolvere,* evanesce, intersperse, *liquefacere,* melt away, radiate, scatter, spread

DISSOLVE *(Separate),* **verb**   break apart, break up, decentralize, demobilize, detach, disband, disconnect, disengage, disjoin, dismantle, dispart, dissever, dissociate, disunite, divide, divorce, part, set asunder, sever, split up, sunder, take apart, uncouple, undo

DISSOLVE *(Terminate),* **verb**   abort, abrogate, break up, bring to an end, bring to conclusion, call off, cancel, cease, conclude, desist, destroy, disband, discontinue, dispose of, draw to a close, efface, effect a dissolution, end, erase, expire, finish, halt, neutralize, nullify, obliterate, quash, render inert, revoke, split up, stop, undo, vitiate, wipe out
ASSOCIATED CONCEPTS: dissolving an injunction

DISSUADE, *verb*   abash, advise against, argue against, attempt to divert, attempt to prevent, cause doubt, caution, convince to the contrary, daunt, *dehortari,* deter from one's purpose, *deterrere,* discourage, disenchant, dishearten, disillusion, dispirit, *dissuadere,* divert by appeal, divert from, exhort against, frighten away, raise apprehension, remonstrate, render averse, stave off, talk out of, turn from a purpose, urge not to

DISTILL, *verb*   boil down, clarify, concentrate, condense, decoct, *destillare,* draw forth, draw out, draw out the essence, drop, expel, extract, filtrate, filter, free from extraneous matter, press out, purify by removing the foreign and nonessential, reduce to extreme purity and strength, separate, squeeze out, *stillare,* strain, strain out, take out, trickle, vaporize and condense, wring
ASSOCIATED CONCEPTS: distilled liquor, distilled spirits, distilling apparatus, distilling the essence out of a case

DISTINCT *(Clear),* **adjective**   apparent, *clarus,* clear-cut, clear to the mind, clear to the senses, clearly defined, concrete, conspicuous, crystal clear, definite, *distinctus,* distinguishable, easily perceived, easily understood, eidetic, evident, explicit, exposed to view, express, for all to see, glaring, graphic, in full view, indubitable, intelligible, lucid, manifest, noticeable, obvious, palpable, particular, pellucid, perceivable, perceptible, *perspicuus,* positive, precise, pronounced, recognizable, self-evident, sharp, striking, unambiguous, unclouded, uncovered, undisguised, undistorted, unequiv-

ocal, unhidden, visible, visualized, vivid, well-defined, well-drawn, well-marked
ASSOCIATED CONCEPTS: clear and distinct, distinct action

DISTINCT *(Distinguished from others),* **adjective** characteristic, contrasted, contrasting, decidedly different, departing from, different, differing, disassociated, discrepant, discrete, discriminate, dissimilar, distant, distinctive, *distinctus,* distinguished by nature, distinguished by station, divergent, diverse, divorced, idiosyncratic, incongruent, incongruous, individual, marked, nonuniform, not identical, not the same, observably different, out of the ordinary, particular, peculiar, poles apart, removed, separate, *separatus,* set apart, singular, special, standing apart, uncommon, unconfused, unimitated, unique, unlike, unlike others, unusual
ASSOCIATED CONCEPTS: distinct entity, distinct interests

DISTINCTION *(Difference),* **noun** antithesis, characteristic difference, contrariety, contrast, differentia, differential, differentiation, disaccord, disagreement, discongruity, discrepancy, *discrimen,* discrimination, disharmony, disparity, dissension, dissonance, *distinctio,* distinguishing characteristic, distinguishing quality, diverseness, earmark, individuality, irrelation, nonuniformity, peculiarity, perceivable dissimilarity, point of difference, special marking, unconformity, unique feature, uniqueness, unlikeness, variance, variant, variation
ASSOCIATED CONCEPTS: substantial distinction

DISTINCTION *(Reputation),* **noun** account, *aura popularis,* brilliance, celebrity, credit, *dignitas,* dignity, eminence, exaltation, fame, grandeur, greatness, honor, illustriousness, immortality, importance, loftiness, marked superiority, name, nobility, notability, note, noteworthiness, popular favor, prestige, prominence, public esteem, renown, reputability, repute, respectability, significance, special favor, superiority

DISTINCTIVE, **adjective** characteristic, conspicuous, contrasting, diacritical, different, differentiating, differentiative, differing, discriminating, distinct, distinguishing, exclusive, idiomatic, idiosyncratic, indicating difference, indicative, individualistic, individualizing, marked, noteworthy, noticeable, particular, peculiar, *proprius,* salient, separative, serving to distinguish, singular, special, uncommon, unimitated, unique, unlike
ASSOCIATED CONCEPTS: distinctive characteristic, distinctive name

DISTINGUISH, **verb** ascertain, characterize, classify, contradistinguish, define, demarcate, differentiate, discern, discriminate, *distinguere,* divide, draw a distinction, exercise discretion, exercise discrimination, individualize, *internoscere,* judge, make distinctions, mark out, note differences, particularize, perceive clearly, point out an essential difference, recognize as different, *secernere,* separate, set apart, specify, winnow
ASSOCIATED CONCEPTS: distinguish between right and wrong, distinguishing cases, distinguishing characteristics, distinguishing mark
FOREIGN PHRASES: *Ubi lex non distinguit, nec nos distinguere debemus.* Where the law does not distin-

guish, we ought not to distinguish. *Qui bene distinguit bene docet.* He who distinguishes well, teaches well.

DISTORT, *verb* bend, camouflage, caricature, change out of recognition, change the face of, conceal, contort, corrupt, deform, disguise, disproportion, dissemble, *distorquere,* exaggerate, falsify, give a false idea, give a false impression, give a strained meaning, give a turn, give twist, inflate, make unlike, miscite, miscolor, misconstrue, misdescribe, misdirect, miseducate, misestimate, misexplain, misexpress, misinform, misinstruct, misinterpret, mislead, misquote, misread, misreckon, misreport, misrepresent, misshape, misteach, mistranslate, overdo, overdramatize, overstate, palter with the truth, paralogize, parody, pervert, play upon words, put a false construction on, put a false sense on, put an erroneous construction on, reshape, strain, strain the meaning, strain the sense, strain the truth, stretch, stretch the meaning, transfigure, transform, turn awry, twist, twist the meaning, twist the sense, twist the words, understate, warp, wrench, wrench the meaning, wrench the sense
ASSOCIATED CONCEPTS: distort the truth

DISTORTION, **noun** anamorphosis, camouflage, caricature, contortion, convolution, deception, deformation, deformity, disguise, disparity, disproportion, dissemblance, dissimilarity, dissimilitude, *distortio,* embroidery, enlargement, exaggeration, expansion, false coloring, false construction, false copy, false reading, falsification, gloss, hyperbole, illusion, imbalance, irrelation, magnification, misapplication, misconstruction, misdirection, misexplanation, misinformation, misinstruction, misinterpretation, misquotation, misrendering, misrepresentation, mistranslation, misusage, misuse of words, one-sided conception, one-sided view, over-coloring, overstatement, perversion, *pravitas,* satire, simulacrum, strained sense, stretch, travesty, twist, unlikeness, warped judgment, wrong interpretation

DISTRAIN, *verb* annex, appropriate, assume ownership, attach, bear away, carry away, carry off, compulsorily acquire, confiscate, deprive of, divest, garnish, *hominis bona vendere,* hurry off with, impound, impress, lay hold of, levy, levy a distress, make away with, possess oneself of, preempt, replevy, seize, sequester, sequestrate, take away, take into custody, take over, take possession of

DISTRAINT, **noun** annexation, appropriation, attachment, capture, confiscation, dispossession, distress, divestment, execution, expropriation, forcible seizure, garnishment, impoundage, impoundment, levy, obtainment, securement, seizure and appropriation, seizure to procure satisfaction of a debt, sequestration
ASSOCIATED CONCEPTS: distraint for rent, process of distraint

DISTRESS *(Anguish),* **noun** agitation, agony, anxiety, anxiousness, blight, depression, desolation, despair, despondency, discomfort, difficulty, discomposure, disquiet, disquietude, dissatisfaction, infelicity, inquietude, mental agony, misery, pain, perturbation, sadness, sorrow, suffering, torment, trial, tribulation, trouble, uneasiness, unhappiness, vexation, woe, worry, wretchedness
ASSOCIATED CONCEPTS: distress for rent, distress warrant, mental distress, unreasonable distress, warrant of distress

DISTRESS *(Seizure),* **noun**   acquirement, acquisition, adoption, annexation, appropriation, arrogation, assumption, attachment, capture, confiscation, deprivation, deprivement, dispossession, disseisin, distraint, divestment, expropriation, impoundage, impoundment, impress, impressment, impropriation, levy, removal, seizing, sequestration, snatching, taking, usurpation

DISTRESS, *verb*   afflict, aggravate, aggrieve, agitate, agonize, annoy, bedevil, bother, cause suffering, chagrin, discompose, disgust, disquiet, disturb, exacerbate, grieve, harass, harrow, harry, hurt, irk, irritate, make miserable, make sorrowful, make unhappy, molest, offend, pain, perturb, sadden, subject to strain, torment, trouble, upset, vex, worry

DISTRIBUTE, *verb*   admeasure, administer, allocate, allot, appropriate, arrange, array, assign, assign places to, assort, class, classify, deal, decentralize, dispense, *dispertire,* disseminate, *distribuere,* divide, *dividere,* dole, file, give out, mete, parcel out, portion out, prorate, ration, scatter, set in order, share, sort, sow, space, spread, sprinkle, systematize
ASSOCIATED CONCEPTS: distributed among creditors, distributed because of liquidation, distribution of an estate

DISTRIBUTION *(Apportionment),* **noun**   allocation, allotment, appropriation, assignment, dealing out, dispensation, disposal, dissemination, division, dole, handing out, issuance, parceling out, partition, placement, proporting, rationing, repartition, sharing
ASSOCIATED CONCEPTS: capital distribution, distribution by operation of law, distribution of assets, distribution of capital, distribution of corporate assets, distribution of earnings or profits, distribution of powers and functions, distribution of proceeds, distribution points, just and equal distribution, partial distribution, per capita distribution, per stirpes distribution, pro rata distribution, ratable distribution

DISTRIBUTION *(Arrangement),* **noun**   assemblage, categorization, classification, collocation, disposition, disposure, formation, gradation, graduation, grouping, management, marshaling, ordering, organization, placement, regimentation, serialization, systematization

DISTRICT, *noun*   *ager,* area, circuit, constituency, department, domain, locale, locality, neighborhood, pale, precinct, province, quarter, realm, *regio,* region, section, sphere, *terra,* territorial division, territory, tract, ward, zone
ASSOCIATED CONCEPTS: business district, collection district, election district, federal district, improvement district, judicial district, school district, tax district

DISTRICT ATTORNEY, *noun*   accuser, attorney for the people, attorney representing the state's interest, law enforcement agent, the people, prosecuting attorney, the prosecution, prosecutor, public attorney, public pleader, public prosecutor, the state, state's attorney
ASSOCIATED CONCEPTS: attorney general, county attorney, prosecuting attorney, state's attorney

DISTURB, *verb*   agitate, alarm, annoy, arouse, badger, bedevil, befuddle, bewilder, bother, churn, *commovere,* confound, confuse, *conturbare,* derange, disarrange, discomfit, discompose, disconcert, dishevel, dislocate, dislodge, dismay, disorder, disorganize, disorientate, displace, displant, displease, disquiet, distemper, distract, distress, enrage, exasperate, ferment, fluster, havoc, incommode, interfere, interrupt, intrude, irk, make uneasy, meddle, molest, nettle, nonplus, outrage, overturn, perplex, perturb, *perturbare,* pique, plague, puzzle, rearrange, roil, rouse, ruffle, shake, shake up, startle, stir up, subvert, tamper, trouble, unbalance, unnerve, unseat, unsettle, upset, vex, worry
ASSOCIATED CONCEPTS: disturbing the peace, right to quiet enjoyment

DISTURBANCE, *noun*   affray, agitation, annoyance, anxietude, anxiety, anxiousness, commotion, confusion, disarrangement, discomfiture, discomposure, disconcertion, discontinuity, dishevelment, dislocation, disorder, disorganization, displacement, disquiet, disquietude, embroilment, eruption, faction, ferment, fomentation, fracas, fuss, hindrance, inquietude, interruption, intrusion, maelstrom, misarrangement, misgiving, molestation, *motus,* perturbation, quandary, rebellion, restiveness, restlessness, revolt, revolution, state of disorder, trepidation, tumult, *tumultus, turbatio,* turbulence, turmoil, unrest, unruliness, unsettlement, uprising, uproar
ASSOCIATED CONCEPTS: creating a disturbance, disorderly conduct, disturbance of court, disturbance of possession, disturbance of quiet possession, disturbing the peace, nuisance

DISUSE, *noun*   abandonment, abolishment, abolition, abstinence, archaism, cessation of use, decay, desuetude, discontinuance, discontinuation, disregard, disusage, failure to use, ignorement, inattention, inusitation, neglect, nonemployment, nonuse, obsolescence, staleness, suspension, unemployment

DIVERGENT, *adjective*   aberrant, bifurcate, bifurcated, branching, departing, deviating, deviative, deviatory, different, differing, discrepant, disharmonious, disparate, dissimilar, divaricating, diverging, diverse, diversified, eccentric, factional, factious, forking, furcate, furcated, incompatible, inconsistent, nonuniform, parting, radiating, ramified, separating, straying, taking different courses, unconventional, untraditional, variant, varying
ASSOCIATED CONCEPTS: divergent interests

DIVERSE, *adjective*   *alius,* assorted, contrastive, deviative, different, differing, disagreeing, discrepant, *dispar,* disparate, dissimilar, distinct, distinguishable, divergent, divers, diversified, diversiform, *diversus,* heterogeneous, incomparable, manifold, miscellaneous, mixed, motley, multifarious, multiform, several, sundry, unidentical, unlike, unmatched, variant, varied, variegated, various, varying
ASSOCIATED CONCEPTS: diverse citizenship, diverse interests, diversity jurisdiction

DIVERSIFICATION, *noun*   alteration, assortment, change, contrast, deviation, difference, differentiation, heterogeneity, multifariousness, multiformity, separation, shift, variation
ASSOCIATED CONCEPTS: diversification of investments

DIVERSITY, *noun*   assortment, discongruity, *discrepantia,* dissimilarity, dissimilitude, diverseness, *diversitas,* heterogeneity, inconformity, irregularity,

manifoldness, medley, miscellany, mixture, multifariousness, multiformity, multiplicity, nonuniformity, unconformity, unevenness, unlikeness, variability, variation, variegation, variety, variousness
ASSOCIATED CONCEPTS: diversity jurisdiction, diversity of citizenship

DIVERT, *verb*   *avertere,* cause to bend, cause to curve, cause to deviate, cause to turn from, change the course of, *deducere,* deflect, *derivare,* deter, deviate, distract, draw aside, draw away, misappropriate, misdirect, mislead, parry, pull aside, push aside, put off the track, redirect, shift, shunt, sidetrack, swerve, turn aside, veer
ASSOCIATED CONCEPTS: diversion of assets, diversion of corporate funds, diversion of proceeds, diversion of public funds to a private purpose, diversion of trust funds, illegal diversion, unlawful diversion

DIVEST, *verb*   attach, confiscate, depose, deprive, despoil, discharge, disendow, disentitle, dislodge, displace, dispossess, disrobe, disseize, distrain, drive out, evict, expel, expropriate, forfeit, lay bare, lay open, oust, reduce, relieve, remove, seize, strip, take away, uncover, unseat
ASSOCIATED CONCEPTS: divesting of title, divestiture of rights

DIVIDE *(Distribute), verb*   admeasure, administer, allocate, allot, apportion, appropriate, assign, carve, consign, dispense, disperse, dispose, *distribuere, dividere,* dole, dole out, endow, give out, issue, mete, mete out, parcel out, pass out, pay out, portion out, prorate, ration, serve, share

DIVIDE *(Separate), verb*   bisect, cleave, cut, demarcate, detach, disconnect, disengage, *disiungere,* disjoin, dismember, dispart, dissever, dissociate, disunite, *dividere,* divorce, fractionize, fragment, halve, part, partition, section, sectionalize, segment, segregate, *separare,* separate, sever, split, sunder, tear, unbind, uncouple
ASSOCIATED CONCEPTS: divide and distribute, divided according to law, divided court, divided equally, divided share and share alike

DIVIDEND, *noun*   advantage, allotment, benefit, distribution of earnings, distribution of profits, gain, increment, interest, net profit, profit, return, share
ASSOCIATED CONCEPTS: cumulative dividends, dividend accumulations, dividend additions, dividend earned or declared, dividend in liquidation, dividend in scrip, dividend payable in stock, dividend-paying corporation, dividends paid, guaranteed dividends, life insurance dividend, liquidation dividend, participating dividend, preferential dividend, preferred dividend, regular dividend, stock dividend, taxable dividend, unauthorized dividends, unpaid dividends

DIVISIBLE, *adjective*   apportionable, bisectable, breakable, capable of being divided, cleavable, detachable, disconnectable, dissectible, disseverable, dividable, dividual, fissile, fissionable, partible, scissile, separable, severable, subdivisible, susceptible of apportionment, susceptible of division, tearable
ASSOCIATED CONCEPTS: divisible contract, divisible covenant, divisible divorce, divisible guaranty, divisible offense

DIVISION *(Act of dividing), noun*   allocation, allotment, apportionment, breaking, breakup, cleavage, cut, cutting, departmentalization, detachment, disaccord, disagreement, disassociation, disbandment, disconnection, discord, disengagement, disharmony, disjunction, disjuncture, dismemberment, dispersal, dispersion, dissemination, dissension, disseverance, dissipation, dissociation, dissonance, distribution, disunion, disuniting, disunity, *divisio,* divorce, faction, noncooperation, opposition, parcelling, parting, *partitio,* partition, portioning, rationing, schism, scission, section, segmentation, segregation, sejunction, separation, severance, sharing, split, splitting, spread, sunderance, tearing, uncoupling, untying
ASSOCIATED CONCEPTS: division of costs, division of damages, division of governmental powers, division of property, equitable division, final division and distribution, political subdivision

DIVISION *(Administrative unit), noun*   area, branch, cadre, canton, category, chapter, class, classification, department, district, group, grouping, province, region, ward, zone

DIVISIVE, *adjective*   bisected, causing disagreement, causing disassociation, causing disjunction, causing separation, cleavable, creating dissension, creating disunity, creating hostility, discordant, discrepant, disengaging, disjoined, disjunctive, dissentient, dissident, dissonant, diverging, dividing, divisible, factious, fragmentable, inharmonious, partible, schismatic, separable, severable, split, subdivisive

DIVORCE, *noun*   annulment of marriage, broken marriage, conclusion, decree of nullity, *discidium,* dissolution of marriage, dissolution of the marriage bond, disunion, *divortium,* finality, judgment dissolving a marriage, judicial separation of a husband and wife, legal dissolution of marriage, legal nullification of marriage, legal termination of a marriage, *repudium*
ASSOCIATED CONCEPTS: absolute divorce, alimony, annulment of marriage, comparative rectitude, custody of children, decree for divorce, divisible divorce, divorce action, divorce proceeding, divorce suit, foreign divorce, grounds for divorce, judgment of divorce, legal separation, limited divorce

DIVORCE, *verb*   annul, annul a marriage, detach, disjoin, dissociate, dissolve of the bonds of matrimony, dissolve the marriage of, disunite, legally discard a spouse, nullify a marriage, part, put asunder, put out of matrimony, put out of wedlock, release from matrimonial status, release from matrimony, release from wedlock, sever, split up, sunder, uncouple, unmarry, unyoke
ASSOCIATED CONCEPTS: separation

DIVULGATION, *noun*   disclosure, dissemination, divulgement, divulgence, evulgation, making public, proclamation, promulgation, spreading abroad

DIVULGE, *verb*   acquaint, advertise, air, apprise, bare, blurt out, break news, breathe, bring to light, broadcast, communicate, confide, disclose, divulgate, enlighten, evince, expose, impart, inform, lay bare, lay open, leak, let drop, let slip, make known, make public, manifest, noise abroad, proclaim, promulgate, publicize, publish, relate, report, reveal, spread abroad,

squeal, tattle, tell, unbosom, uncover, unmask, unveil, voice
ASSOCIATED CONCEPTS: divulge or publish

DOCKET, noun   agenda, calendar, catalog, entry book, enumeration, list, list of cases, listing, order of the day, program, record, record of proceedings, register, registry, roll, schedule, slate
ASSOCIATED CONCEPTS: bench docket, court docket, docket book, docket entry, docketing a judgment, docketing cases

DOCTRINE, noun   belief, canon, credendum, credo, creed, dogma, formulated belief, gospel, maxim, orthodoxy, philosophy, precept, principle, professed belief, rule, system, system of belief, teaching, teachings, tenet, universal principle
ASSOCIATED CONCEPTS: added risk doctrine, avoidable consequences doctrine, beneficial consideration doctrine, collateral source doctrine, cy pres doctrine, de facto doctrine, doctrine of abstention, doctrine of assumed risk, doctrine of avoidable consequences, doctrine of last clear chance, doctrine of recrimination, doctrine of relation back, doctrine of res judicata, doctrine of subrogation, doctrine of the law of the case, doctrine of unclean hands, doctrine of unjust enrichment, emergency doctrine, exclusive control doctrine, exhaustion of remedies doctrine, humanitarian doctrine, imminent peril doctrine, last clear chance, main purpose doctrine, res ipsa loquitur doctrine, rescue doctrine

DOCUMENT, noun   book, certificate, confirmation, diploma, evidence, evidentiary record, instrument, *instrumentum, litterae,* official publication, paper, proof, record, recorded material, register, report, *tabula,* verification, writ, written material
ASSOCIATED CONCEPTS: allograph, ancient documents, cancellation of document, document of a public nature, document of title, integrated document, legal documents, public document

DOCUMENT, verb   assemble the facts, authenticate, back, bear out, buttress, circumstantiate, collect evidence, confirm, corroborate, demonstrate, establish, evidence, exhibit, fortify, give references, justify, make certain, make evident, manifest, prove, provide with documents, provide with proof, show, strengthen, substantiate, support, sustain, uphold, validate, verify

DOCUMENTARY, adjective   accredited, accurate, actual, attested, authentic, authoritative, certified, chronicled, correct, described, documental, documented, evidential, factual, founded on fact, genuine, in writing, not fictitious, on record, real, recorded, reported, true, valid, veracious, veritable, written
ASSOCIATED CONCEPTS: defense based upon documentary evidence, documentary evidence, documentary stamp

DOCUMENTATION, noun   annals, authentication, authority, basis, certification, circumstantiation, confirmation, corroboration, data, evidence, evidential record, evidentiary record, exhibit, factual basis, grounds, grounds for belief, medium of proof, proof, record, recorded material, reference, source, substantiation, support, supporting evidence, validation, verification

DOGMA, noun   article of faith, axiom, belief, canon, conviction, credendum, credo, creed, declaration of faith, dictum, doctrinaire opinion, doctrine, *dogma,* doxy, maxim, orthodoxy, persuasion, *placitum,* precept, principle, professed belief, rule, tenet

DOGMATIC, adjective   absolute, arrogant, assertive, assertory, assured, authoritarian, authoritative, canonical, categorical, certain, confident, creedal, decided, definite, definitive, dictatorial, doctrinaire, doctrinal, domineering, emphatic, fanatical, forceful, imperious, insistent, intolerant, magisterial, narrow-minded, opinionated, opinionative, orthodox, overbearing, pedantic, peremptory, positive, positivistic, sure, tenacious, unequivocal, unshakable, unyielding

DOLE, verb   admeasure, allocate, allot, allow, apportion, appropriate, assign, award, bestow, contribute, deal, deliver, dispense, distribute, divide, furnish, give, give away, give out, grant, hand out, hand over, issue, measure out, mete, mete out, parcel out, pay out, portion, present, ration, share, spare, supply

DOMAIN (Land owned), **noun**   alodium, demesne, estate, freehold, hereditament, holding, land, manor, *possessio,* property, real estate, real property, realty, seigniory, tenure
ASSOCIATED CONCEPTS: eminent domain

DOMAIN (Sphere of influence), **noun**   bailiwick, department, dominion, jurisdiction, kingdom, province, realm, region, signory, territory
ASSOCIATED CONCEPTS: private domain, public domain

DOMESTIC (Household), **adjective**   belonging to the house, domiciliary, family, home, homemaking, household, housekeeping, internal, pertaining to one's household, pertaining to the family, pertaining to the home, relating to the family, relating to the home
ASSOCIATED CONCEPTS: domestic animals, domestic duties, domestic employment, domestic fixtures, domestic purposes, domestic relations, domestic servants, domestic service, domestic status, domestic use

DOMESTIC (Indigenous), **adjective**   endemic, home, homemade, local, national, native, native grown, not foreign, not imported
ASSOCIATED CONCEPTS: domestic commerce, domestic corporation, domestic judgment

DOMICILE, noun   abiding place, abode, accommodations, address, billet, *domicilium, domus,* dwelling, habitance, habitancy, habitat, habitation, home, house, inhabitance, inhabitancy, living quarters, lodging, lodgment, place of occupancy, place of residence, quarters, residence, residency, tabernacle
ASSOCIATED CONCEPTS: abandonment of domicile, acquisition of domicile, bona fide domicile, change of domicile, de facto domicile, family domicile, legal domicile, matrimonial domicile, plural domiciles
FOREIGN PHRASES: *Uxor sequitur domicilium viri.* The wife follows the domicile of her husband. *Domus sua cuique est tutissimum refugium.* Everyone's home is his safest refuge.

DOMICILIARY, noun   citizen, denizen, dweller, habitant, indweller, inhabitant, inhabiter, native, occupant, occupier, resident, settler

DOMINANCE, *noun* ascendance, ascendancy, authority, control, dominancy, domination, dominion, eminence, force, governance, hold, importance, influence, mastery, mightiness, power, predominance, predominancy, prepollence, prepollency, preponderance, prepotency, primacy, sovereignty, supremacy, sway, weight

DOMINANT, *adjective* ascendant, authoritative, cardinal, chief, commanding, controlling, eminent, first, foremost, governing, hegemonical, influential, leading, main, master, overshadowing, paramount, predominant, predominating, preeminent, preponderant, prepotent, prevailing, prevalent, primary, prime, principal, regnant, ruling, sovereign, superior, supreme, unsurpassed, weighty
ASSOCIATED CONCEPTS: dominant aspect rule, dominant estate, dominant land, dominant party, dominant right, dominant tenant, serviant land

DOMINATE, *verb* administer, carry authority, command, compel, control, dictate, domineer, govern, have power, hold down, influence, keep subjugated, lead, manage, master, oppress, overrule, predominate, preponderate, preside over, prevail, reign over, repress, rule, rule over, subdue, subject, subjugate, sway, tame, tyrranize

DOMINION *(Absolute ownership),* **noun** claim, control, deed, demesne, domain, freehold, holding, interest, lawful possession, manor, ownership, possession, possessorship, power of disposal, property, proprietorship, right, right of possession, right to property, rightful possession, seignorage, seisin, stake, territory, title
ASSOCIATED CONCEPTS: act of dominion

DOMINION *(Supreme authority),* **noun** ascendancy, authority, command, control, *dicio,* dominance, dominancy, domination, eminent domain, empery, government, grip, hegemony, hold, *imperium,* jurisdiction, lordship, management, mastery, *potestas,* power, primacy, regency, reign, rule, sovereignty, supremacy, sway

DONATION, *noun* alms, benefaction, bequest, bestowment, bounty, charity, contribution, dispensation, *donum,* dotation, endowment, gift, grant, gratuity, handout, impartation, impartment, largess, munificence, offering, philanthropy, present, presentation, provision, subsidy, subvention
ASSOCIATED CONCEPTS: charitable donation, donation deed, donation causa mortis, donation of land, gratuitous donation, special donation

DONATIVE, *adjective* aiding, awarding, beneficent, benevolent, bestowing, bountiful, charitable, conferring, contributing, contributory, conveying, dispensing, eleemosynary, endowing, freehanded, furnishing, generous, given away, giving, granting, gratuitous, imparting, openhanded, philanthropic, presenting, providing, supplying
ASSOCIATED CONCEPTS: donative intent, donative trust

DONEE, *noun* acceptor, beneficiary, devisee, grantee, legatee, recipient

DONOR, *noun* aider, almsgiver, altruist, assignor, backer, benefactor, benefactress, bequeather, bestower, cheerful giver, conferrer, consignor, contributor, deliv-

erer, devisor, distributor of largess, donator, free giver, generous giver, giver, Good Samaritan, grantor, helper, humanitarian, patron, patroness, philanthropist, presenter, rewarder, subscriber, vouchsafer
FOREIGN PHRASES: *Voluntas donatoris in charta doni sui manifeste expressa observetur.* The will of the donor which is clearly expressed in his deed of gift should be observed.

DORMANT, *adjective* abeyant, asleep, at rest, becalmed, deactivated, hibernating, *iacere,* in abeyance, in suspense, inactive, inert, inoperative, latent, passive, quiescent, quiet, resting, sleeping, slumbering, smoldering, static, still, suspended, torpid, unaroused, unawakened, undeveloped, unwakened
ASSOCIATED CONCEPTS: dormant case, dormant corporation, dormant judgment, dormant partner, dormant powers, dormant season

DOSSIER, *noun* archive, brief, case history, data, document, documentation, facts, file, journal, papers, portfolio, record, recorded information, recorded material, resumé

DOUBLE JEOPARDY, *noun* double prosecution, double punishment, re-charged, re-litigated, re-prosecuted, re-tried, tried for the same crime

DOUBT *(Indecision),* **noun** ambiguity, anxiety, apprehension, apprehensiveness, confusion, *dubitatio, dubito,* faltering, feeling of uncertainty, hesitancy, improbability, inability to decide, incertitude, indefiniteness, indeterminateness, indetermination, infirmity of purpose, insecurity, instability, irresolution, lack of certitude, lack of confidence, lack of conviction, lack of faith, matter of dubitation, misgiving, perplexity, precariousness, qualification, qualm, qualmishness, quandary, question, reluctance, reservation, reserve, self-doubt, state of suspense, suspended judgment, suspense, uncertain state, uncertainness, uncertainty, undecidedness, undeterminedness, unsettled opinion, unsettlement, unsteadiness, unsureness, vacillation, vagueness, want of confidence, want of faith, wavering
ASSOCIATED CONCEPTS: beyond a reasonable doubt standard, rational doubt, reasonable doubt
FOREIGN PHRASES: *Nobiliores et benigniores praesumptiones in dubiis sunt praeferendae.* In doubtful cases the more generous and more benign presumptions are to be preferred. *Ambiguitas verborum latens verificatione suppletur; nam quod ex facto oritur ambiguum verificatione facti tollitur.* A latent verbal ambiguity may be removed by evidence; for whatever ambiguity arises from an extrinsic fact may be explained by extrinsic evidence. *Quae dubitationis tollendae causa contractibus inseruntur, jus commune non laedunt.* Those clauses which are inserted in agreements to avoid doubts and ambiguity do not offend the common law.

DOUBT *(Suspicion),* **noun** apprehension, chariness, consternation, critical attitude, disbelief, discredit, dismay, distrust, distrustfulness, doubtfulness, dubiety, dubiousness, dubitation, faithlessness, hesitation, improbability, incredibility, incredulity, incredulousness, lack of confidence, lack of faith, lack of trust, matter of dubitation, misdoubt, misgiving, mistrust, mistrustfulness, qualm, qualmishness, question in one's mind, refusal to believe, reluctance to believe, skepticalness, skepticism, *suspicio,* suspiciousness, unbelief, uncredulousness, want of confidence, want of faith, want of trust, wariness

DOUBT (*Distrust*), *verb*   awake a suspicion, be apprehensive, be doubtful, be dubious, be incredulous, be nervous, be skeptical, be suspicious, be uncertain, challenge, disbelieve, discredit, dispute, entertain doubts, entertain suspicions, feel distrust, find hard to believe, give no credence to, greet with skepticism, half believe, harbor doubts, harbor suspicions, have doubts, have fears, have misgivings, have questions, have suspicions, impugn, lack confidence in, misbelieve, misdoubt, misgive, mistrust, not admit, not believe, object, query, question, raise a question, raise a suspicion, refuse to believe, refuse to trust, regard with suspicion, suspect, withhold reliance
ASSOCIATED CONCEPTS: doubt the credibility of a witness

DOUBT (*Hesitate*), *verb*   be in a quandary, be irresolute, be puzzled, be uncertain, be undecided, be undetermined, debate, delay, deliberate, demur, dubitate, equivocate, falter, feel unsure, fluctuate, have qualms, have reservations, hold off, pause, ponder, push aside, put off a decision, puzzle over, scruple, stop to consider, table, think it over, vacillate, waver, withhold judgment
ASSOCIATED CONCEPTS: beyond a reasonable doubt, beyond a shadow of a doubt, free from all doubt

DOUBTFUL, *adjective*   arguable, at issue, conditional, conjectural, contestable, controvertible, debatable, disbelieving, disposed to question, disputable, distrustful, doubtable, doubting, dubious, dubitable, *dubius,* equivocal, implausible, improbable, in a dilemma, in a quandary, in dispute, in doubt, in question, in suspense, inconceivable, inconvincible, incredible, indecisive, indistinct in character or meaning, irresolute, misbelieving, mistrustful, mistrusting, of uncertain issue, open to doubt, open to question, open to suspicion, problematic, questionable, questioning, speculative, suppositional, unbelievable, unconvincing, unlikely, unresolved, unsettled in opinion, unsolved, unsure, unsustainable, untenable
ASSOCIATED CONCEPTS: doubtful cases, doubtful credit, doubtful debts, doubtful title

DOWER, *noun*   allotment, allowance, appanage, award, bequest, bestowal, bestowment, *dos,* dotation, effects, endowment, estate, inheritance, jointure, legacy, remainder, settlement, widow's estate, widow's portion
ASSOCIATED CONCEPTS: consummated right of dower, curtesy, dower interest, dower right, election of dower, estate in dower, inchoate right of dower, right of dower, widow's dower
FOREIGN PHRASES: *Favorabilia in lege sunt fiscus, dos, vita, libertas.* Favorites of the law are the treasury, dower, life, and liberty.

DOWNPAYMENT, *noun*   collateral, deposit, installment, payment, retainer, stake, surety

DOXOLOGY, *noun*   adulation, compliment, glorification, hero worship, idolatory, laudation, overpraise, paean, praise

DRACONIAN, *adjective*   austere, exacting, extreme, fanatical, formalistic, harsh, inflexible, insensi-

tive, intolerant, precise, punctilious, puritanical, relentless, rigid, rigorous, ruthless, severe, Spartan, stiff, strict, stringent, unbending, uncompassionate, uncompromising
ASSOCIATED CONCEPTS: Draconian laws

DRAFT, *noun*   acceptance bill, bank check, bank note, bank paper, bill, bill of exchange, cashier's check, check, commercial paper, debenture, letter of credit, *"lettre de change",* money order, negotiable instrument, negotiable paper, note, order, order for payment, promissory note, voucher, warrant
ASSOCIATED CONCEPTS: bill of exchange, check, overdraft, sight draft

DRASTIC, *adjective*   acting with force, desperate, dire, exceeding, excessive, extreme, fanatic, fanatical, forceful, harsh, immoderate, improper, inordinate, intemperate, intense, outrageous, powerful, radical, severe, strict, strong, undue, unmitigated, unreasonable, vigorously effective, violent
ASSOCIATED CONCEPTS: drastic remedy, extraordinary remedy

DRAW (*Attendance*), *noun*   frequence, level of attendance

DRAW (*Attraction*), *noun*   attractiveness, enticement, force, gravity, influence, magnetism, pull

DRAW (*Tie*), *noun*   dead heat, deadlock, impasse, stalemate, standoff

DRAW (*Depict*), *verb*   delineate, describe, picture, portray, represent, sketch

DRAW (*Extract*), *verb*   concentrate, condense, derive, pull, receive

DRAWBACK, *noun*   damage, decremental, defect, disadvantage, discount, fault, flaw, harm, hurt, impediment, inconvenience, injury, liability, objection, obstacle, prejudice, protest, protestation, qualification, setoff

DROIT, *noun*   appurtenance, authority, authorization, birthright, certification, claim, due, dueness, easement, eligibility, empowerment, entitlement, faculty, franchise, just claim, legal power, legal right, legal title, license, licitness, power, prerogative, prescriptive right, pretension, privilege, right, sanction, vested right, warrant
ASSOCIATED CONCEPTS: right

DRUG, *noun*   alterant, analgesic, anesthetic, anesthetic agent, anodyne, antibiotic, chemical substance, curative preparation, medical preparation, medicament, *medicamentum,* medication, medicinal component, medicinal ingredient, narcotic preparation, narcotic substance, nepenthe, opiate, painkiller, palliative, physic, prescription, remedy, sedative, soporific, stimulant, stupefacient
ASSOCIATED CONCEPTS: adulterated drugs, dangerous drugs, drug addiction, habit-forming drug, influence of drugs, labeling of drugs, poisonous drugs or chemicals, possession of drugs, preparation of drugs, prescription drugs, regulation of drugs, sale of drugs

DRUG, *verb*   administer, anesthetize, anoint, apply a remedy, benumb, cure, deaden, desensitize, dose, dull,

heal, inject, *medicare,* medicate, narcotize, numb, palliate, physic, poultice, prescribe, put to sleep, stun, stupefy, treat
ASSOCIATED CONCEPTS: drug addicts

DRUNK, *adjective* *ebrius,* inebriated, intemperate, intoxicated, overcome, overcome by liquor, riotous, saturated, sottish, *temulentus,* uncontrolled, under the influence of liquor, unsober
ASSOCIATED CONCEPTS: alcoholism, delirium tremens, driving while intoxicated, drunkometer test, intoxication, voluntary intoxication

DUBIOUS, *adjective* ambiguous, *anceps,* arguable, chancy, conditional, confusing, confutable, contestable, contingent, controversial, controvertible, debatable, dependent, disputable, doubtful, dubitative, *dubius,* equivocal, fallible, hazy, in dispute, in doubt, in question, *incertus,* insecure, moot, perplexing, provisional, questionable, refutable, shadowy, skeptical, speculative, suppositional, unascertained, unassured, unauthentic, unauthenticated, unauthoritative, uncertain, uncertified, unconfident, unconfirmed, undemonstrated, undetermined, unexplained, unlikely, unreliable, unresolved, unsound, unsure, unverifiable, vacillating, vague, wavering

DUBITATIVE, *adjective* contestable, controversial, controvertible, deniable, disputable, doubtable, doubtful, dubious, dubitable, in doubt, open to question, questionable, refutable, suspect, unsustainable

DUE (Owed), ***adjective*** chargeable, claimable, collectable, condign, *debitus,* delinquent, deserved, earned, in arrears, merited, outstanding, owing, to be paid, uncompensated, unpaid, unrewarded, unsettled
ASSOCIATED CONCEPTS: amount due, balance due, debt due, due bills, due date, due on demand, indebtedness due, justly due and owing, legally due, money due, payment due, rent due, taxes due
FOREIGN PHRASES: *Nihil peti potest ante id tempus, quo per rerum naturam persolvi possit.* Nothing can be demanded before the time when, in the nature of things, it can be paid.

DUE (Regular), ***adjective*** according to law, allowable, appropriate, authorized, befitting, correct, expedient, fit, lawful, legal, legislated, legitimate, licit, nomothetic, permitted, proper, rightful, sanctioned, statutory
ASSOCIATED CONCEPTS: due acknowledgment, due administration of justice, due and proper care, due and reasonable care, due care, due compensation, due consideration, due course, due course of business, due course of law, due diligence, due execution, due exercise of discretion, due process of law, due proof, due proof of death, due proof of loss, due regard, holder in due course

DUE, *noun* accounts collectable, accounts outstanding, arrears, balance to pay, charge, claim, compensation owed, *deberi,* debit, debt, deficit, droit, entitlement, favor owed, fee, indebtedness, lawful claim, liability, obligation accrued, outstanding debt, overdue payment, pledge, right, something owed, that which is owing, vested right
ASSOCIATED CONCEPTS: due and payable, due in full, due on demand, having become due, payable upon sight

DULY, *adverb* accurately, as required, correctly, deservedly, fairly, legitimately, rightfully
ASSOCIATED CONCEPTS: duly adjudged, duly allowed, duly appointed, duly assigned, duly awarded, duly certified, duly commenced, duly commissioned, duly completed, duly convened, duly directed, duly enacted, duly entered into, duly established, duly executed, duly filled, duly found, duly given, duly issued, duly made, duly organized, duly presented, duly prosecuted, duly qualified, duly recorded, duly rendered, duly served, duly shown, duly summoned, duly sworn, duly verified

DUN, *noun* bill of accounts, bill of costs, claim, demand, entreaty, exaction, final demand, final notice, forcible demand, *fuscus,* impetration, importunity, insistence, insistent demand, levy, notice, obsecration, obtestation, peremptory demand, reckoning, request, requisition, solicitation, statement, strong request, *suffuscus,* threat, ultimatum, warning notice

DUN, *verb* beseige, beset, clamor for payment, demand, demand payment, demand with threats, exact, *exposcere, flagitare,* give final notice, importune, insist, make claims upon, make demands on, plague, press a claim, request, require

DUPE, *verb* befool, beguile, bilk, cheat, circumvent, counterfeit, cozen, create a false impression, cully, deceive, defraud, delude, ensnare, entrap, fleece, fool, gull, hoax, inveigle, *lactare,* make a fool of, misdirect, misguide, mislead, mulct, outmaneuver, outsmart, outwit, play a trick, play upon, practice chicanery, put something over, set a trap for, sport with, swindle, take advantage of, take by fraud, take in, trap, trick, victimize

DUPLICATE, *noun* carbon, carbon copy, copy, ditto, double, ectype, *exemplar, exemplum,* facsimile, gemination, imitation, likeness, match, photostat, reenactment, repetition, replica, representation, reproduction, twin
ASSOCIATED CONCEPTS: duplicate copy, duplicate original

DUPLICITY, *noun* artifice, casuistry, chicanery, deceitfulness, deception, dissimulation, double-dealing, duality, duplexity, equivocation, evasion, false conduct, falseheartedness, falseness, fraud, guile, hypocrisy, insincerity, perfidy, sham, trickery, two-facedness

DURABLE, *adjective* abiding, aeonian, ageless, amaranthine, ceaseless, changeless, chronic, constant, continual, continuing, endless, enduring, established, eternal, everlasting, firm, *firmus,* fixed, hard, hardy, holding up well, immortal, immovable, immutable, imperishable, impervious to change, incessant, indeciduous, indelible, ineradicable, inerasable, inexhaustible, inexpungeable, interminable, intransmutable, invariable, inveterate, inviolate, irremovable, lasting, lifelong, living, long-continuing, long-enduring, long-lasting, long-lived, long-standing, longevous, maintained, never-ending, not easily worn out, of long duration, of long standing, perdurable, permanent, perpetual, persevering, persistent, persisting, remaining, resistant, robust, rocklike, sempiternal, settled, *solidus,* sound, *stabilis,* stable, staying, steadfast, strong, sturdy, substantial, surviving, sustained, tenacious, timeless, tough, unaltered, unceasing, unchangeable, undying, unending, unfading, unfailing, unintermitting, uninterrupted, unyielding, without end

DURANCE, noun　　arrest, bondage, bonds, captivity, commitment, confinement, custody, detention, forced confinement, forcible detention, immurement, incarceration, internment, legal restraint, *lettre de cachet,* quarantine, restraint, restriction on movement, thrall, thralldom

DURATION, noun　　age, continuance, continuance in time, continuation in time, course, epoch, era, extension in time, extent, interregnum, interval, lasting period, length of time, limit, period, period of time, phase, season, space of time, span, spell, stage, stretch, *temporis spatium,* tenancy, tenure, term, time, while
ASSOCIATED CONCEPTS: duration of any office, duration of contract, duration of emergency, duration of liability, duration of possession, duration of use, duration of war

DURESS, noun　　bondage, captivity, coaction, coercion, compulsion, confinement, constraint, control, dominance, enforcement, exaction, force, high pressure, impressment, necessitation, obligation, press, pressure, repression, requirement, restriction, stress, subjection, subjugation, threat
ASSOCIATED CONCEPTS: actionable duress, business compulsion, defense of duress, duress of goods, duress of property, legal duress, moral duress, payment under duress, undue influence
FOREIGN PHRASES: *Vani timores sunt aestimandi, qui non cadunt in constantem virum.* Those fears are to be regarded as groundless which do not affect an ordinary man. *Nihil consensui tam contrarium est quam vis atque metus.* Nothing is so contrary to consent as force and fear. *Vani timoris justa excusatio non est.* A frivolous fear is not a lawful excuse.

DUTY *(Obligation), noun*　　accountability, allegiance, answerability, assignment, burden, charge, chore, commission, commitment, debt, dictate of conscience, engagement, *fides,* function, indebtedness, liability, moral necessity, moral obligation, *munus,* obedience, office, *officium,* pledge, promise, responsibility, role, task, work
ASSOCIATED CONCEPTS: absolute duty, breach of duty, conditional duty, continuing duty, delegation of duty, duty enjoined by law, duty of support, equitable duty,

imperative duty, in performance of duty, in the line of duty, lawful duty, legal duty, ministerial duty, moral duty, neglect of duty, nondelegatable duty, nondiscretionary duty, official duty, on duty, private duty, public duty, relief from duty, scope of servant's duties, statutory duty, unfit for duty, violation of duty
FOREIGN PHRASES: *Qui jussu judicis aliquod fecerit non videtur dolo malo fecisse, quia parere necesse est.* He who does anything by command of a judge will not be deemed to have acted from an improper motive, because it was necessary to obey. *Judicis officium est opus diei in die suo perficere.* It is the duty of a judge to finish the day's work within that day. *Judicis est judicare secundum allegata et probata.* It is the duty of a judge to decide according to the allegations and proofs.

DUTY *(Tax), noun*　　assessment, burden, capitation, charge, exaction, exactment, excise, imposition, impost, levy, onus, rate, revenue, tallage, tariff, task, tax on demand, taxation, toll, tribute, *vectigal*
ASSOCIATED CONCEPTS: duty on exports, duty on imports

DWELL *(Linger over), verb*　　accent, accentuate, brood over, continue, emphasize, extend, harp upon, impress, *in re commorari,* insist, intensify, point up, prolong, prolongate, reiterate, *rem longius prosequi,* stress

DWELL *(Reside), verb*　　abide, be located, be present, be settled, be situated, be stationed, billet, bunk, denizen, domicile, domiciliate, *domicilium, habere, habitare,* have a habitation, have one's address at, indwell, inhabit, live, lodge, make one's home, occupy, populate, quarter, remain, reside, room, settle, sojourn, stay, stop, take up one's abode, take up residence, tarry, tenant
ASSOCIATED CONCEPTS: citizenship

DWELLING, noun　　abode, camp, domicile, *domicilium, domus,* dormitory, edifice, habitation, homestead, house, living quarters, lodging, lodging place, lodgment, place of residence, quarters, residence, *sedes,* shelter, tabernacle
ASSOCIATED CONCEPTS: dwelling house purposes, inhabited dwelling house, multiple dwelling, principal dwelling place, private dwelling

DYSEPTIC, adjective　　bilious, bitter, choleric, embittered, jaundiced, sour, sour-tempered, spiteful

E

EAGER, *adjective* agressive, alacritous, ambitious, anxious, appetent, ardent, aspiring, assiduous, athirst, avid, *avidus,* bent upon, covetous, craving, desirous, diligent, disposed, earnest, enthusiastic, excited, fanatic, fanatical, fervent, *fervidus,* forward, full of enterprise, full of enthusiasm, full of initiative, impassioned, impatient, inclined, industrious, intense, interested, keen, longing, passionate, perfervid, pushy, ravenous, ready, spirited, tantalized, tempted, unable to resist, vehement, voracious, willing, wishful, yearning, zealous, zestful

EARMARK, *noun* brand, cachet, designation, distinguishing mark, emblem, identification, indication, label, mark, mark of identification, mark of identity, sign, symbol

EARN, *verb* achieve, achieve by continued effort, acquire by service, attain, be deserving, be entitled to, be successful, be worthy, clear, deserve, gain, gain by labor, gain by service, get a profit, get by effort, have a right to, *merere,* merit, merit as compensation, net, obtain a victory, procure by effort, profit, prosper, realize, reap, receive compensation, secure, succeed in reaching, win
ASSOCIATED CONCEPTS: ability to earn, earned commissions, earned income, earned premiums, earned surplus, earned wages, a sum earned and unpaid

EARNEST, *adjective* assiduous, bent upon, concentrating, conscientious, determined, devoted, diligent, eager, *enixus,* enthusiastic, fervent, firm, grave, *gravis,* impassioned, intent, *intentus,* purposeful, resolute, serious, set upon, sincere, sober, solemn, staid, strong-willed, thoughtful, zealous

EARNINGS, *noun* balance, commission, compensation, earned income, emolument, fruit of labor, gains, income, *lucrum,* money earned, pay, payment, personal gain, proceeds, profit, profits, profits from employment, *quaestus,* rate, receipts, recompense, remuneration, returns, revenue, reward, reward of labor, reward of office, salary, takings, wages, winnings
ASSOCIATED CONCEPTS: accrued earnings, annual earnings, corporate earnings, earning capacity, future earnings, gross earnings, individual earnings, loss of earnings, net earnings, profits, rents, surplus earnings, total earnings

EASE, *verb* abate, alleviate, ameliorate, bate, calm, comfort, console, cushion, disburden, disencumber, ease the burden, expedite, extenuate, facilitate, free from anxiety, give repose, give rest, help along, lessen, let up, lighten, loosen, make comfortable, make easy, mitigate, moderate, *otium,* pacify, *quies,* quiet, reduce tension, relax, release from pressure, relieve, render less difficult, slacken, soften, *tranquillitas,* unburden, unload, unstrain

EASEMENT, *noun* advantage in land, convenience, gateway, interest in land, liberty of use, privilege, right of passage, right of use, right of way, serviceway, way over land
ASSOCIATED CONCEPTS: affirmative easement, apparent easement, appurtenance, appurtenant easement, discontinuing easement, dominant and servient estates, easement by grant, easement by necessary implication, easement by prescription, easement in gross, easement of access, easement of convenience, easement of necessity, equitable easement, implied easement, implied reservation of easement, incorporeal hereditament, incumbrance, intermittent easement, irrevocable license, license in nature of easement, natural easement, necessary easement, negative easement, noncontinuous easement, prescription, private easement, profit a prendre, public easement, quasi easement, right of way, right of way in gross, secondary easement, servitude, visible easement
FOREIGN PHRASES: *Iter est jus eundi, ambulandi hominis; non etiam jumentum agendi vel vehiculum.* A way is the right of going or walking by man, and does not include the right of driving a beast of burden or a vehicle.

EAVESDROP, *verb* hearken, intercept, listen, listen stealthily, overhear, tap the lines, wiretap
ASSOCIATED CONCEPTS: eavesdropping device, search warrant, suppression hearing, wiretapping

EBB, *verb* crumble, decay, decline, decrease, degenerate, deteriorate, drop, drop off, dwindle, fade away, fail, fall, fall away, fall off, move back, recede, *recedere,* retire, retreat, shrink, sink, slide, slip, slip back, subside, wane, waste away, withdraw

ECCENTRIC, *adjective* aberrant, anomalous, bizarre, contrary, curious, departing from the usual course, deviant, deviating, deviative, different, differing, divergent, erratic, extraordinary, idiosyncratic, independent, individual, *inusitatus,* irregular, *mirus,* nonconforming, nonconformist, *novus,* odd, out of the common run, out of the ordinary, outlandish, peculiar, quaint, queer, singular, strange, uncommon, unconforming, unconventional, unfashionable, unimitative, unique, unorthodox, unusual, wayward

ECOLOGY, *noun*   antipollution project, bioecology, bionomics, conservation, environmental science, environmental studies, human environment, maintenance, management of natural resources, natural science, nature study, pollution control, preservation, protection, study of ecosystems, study of environs, study of surroundings, support, survival studies, sustainment, sustenance

ECONOMIC, *adjective*   cost effective, cost reducing, economical, labor saving, money saving, time saving, thrifty
ASSOCIATED CONCEPTS: economic activity, economic conditions, economic depression, economic groups, economic factors, economic interest, economic policy, economic segregation, economic status, economic value

ECONOMICAL, *adjective*   *attentus,* avoiding extravagance, careful, chary of expense, cheap, cost-reducing, *diligens,* economizing, efficient, financially prudent, forehanded, free from waste, frugal, *frugi,* inexpensive, labor-saving, money-conscious, money-saving, niggardly, parsimonious, provident, prudent, saving, sparing, thrifty, time-saving, unlavish, unwasteful

ECONOMY *(Economic system),* *noun*   administration, administration of economics, administration of resources, economic science, management, management of resources, regulation of finances, system of distributing wealth, wealth

ECONOMY *(Frugality),* *noun*   avoidance of waste, careful management, carefulness, carefulness in outlay, chariness, cheapness of operation, economicalness, forehandedness, freedom from extravagance, frugalness, good management, husbanding of resources, management, paring, *parsimonia,* prevention of waste, providence, prudence, restriction, saving, scheduling, sound stewardship, sparing, thrift, thriftiness

ECSTATIC, *adjective*   approving, beatific, beside oneself, blissful, carried away, delighted, delirious with joy, dithyrambic, elated, elevated, emotional, enchanted, enraptured, enthusiastic, entranced, excited, exultant, felicitous, full of feeling, glad, happy, heartfelt, joyful, joyous, jubilant, overjoyed, overpowered with emotion, passionate, radiant, rapt, rapturous, rhapsodical, thrilled, tingling, transported

EDGE *(Advantage),* *noun*   advantageous position, benefit, favorable position, head start, jump, lead, odds, superiority, upper hand, vantage

EDGE *(Border),* *noun*   bank, boundary, bounds, brim, brink, confines, corner, demarcation line, dividing line, edging, extremity, *fimbriae,* frame, fringe, frontier, limit, lip, margin, *margo,* molding, *ora,* outer edge, outline, outskirts, periphery, point, rim, side, skirts, tip, verge

EDICT, *noun*   authoritative command, canon, command, *consultum,* declaration, decree, *decretum,* dictate, *edictum,* enactment, fiat, judgment, law, legislation, mandate, order, ordinance, precept, pronouncement, regulation, regulation by law, regulation by statute, rule, ruling, statute

EDIFICATION, *noun*   acquirement, advancement, advantage, attainment, avail, benefit, betterment, direction, education, educational clarification, educational knowledge, enlightenment, gain, guidance, improvement, information, instruction, knowledge, learning, mental cultivation, preparation, profit, progress, schooling, spiritual upbuilding, teaching, training, tuition, tutelage, uplifting

EDIFICE, *noun*   architectural monument, building, building of imposing appearance, construction, high structure, imposing building, piece of architecture, public building, skyscraper, structure, tower

EDIFY, *verb*   brief, coach, direct, discipline, *docere,* educate, enlarge the mind, enlighten, guide, improve, inform, instruct, prime, school, show, strengthen, teach, train, tutor, upbuild, uplift

EDIT, *verb*   alter, amend, annotate, arrange, choose, comment on, correct, cross out, cut, dele, delete, emend, emendate, erase, expunge, improve, *librum edere,* make corrections, make improvements, make ready for publication, modify by excisions, polish, prepare for publication, put right, rearrange, rectify, redact, redraft, refine, remove errors, revamp, revise, rework, rewrite, select, strike out, trim, weed, write notes for

EDUCATE, *verb*   brief, bring up, civilize, coach, cultivate, direct, discipline, drill, edify, *educare,* enlighten, *erudire,* explain, familiarize, give lessons, guide, implant, inculcate, indoctrinate, inform, initiate, *instituere,* instruct, interpret, nurture, preach, prepare, prime, rear, school, show, teach, train, tutor, wipe out illiteracy

EDUCATION, *noun*   accomplishments, acquirements, acquisition of knowledge, body of knowledge, coaching, cultivation, culture, direction, edification, elucidation, enlightenment, erudition, explanation, general information, guidance, imparting of skill, improvement of the mind, inculcation, indoctrination, instruction, intellectuality, knowledge, learning, letters, literacy, pedagogy, preparation, propaedeutics, qualification, scholarship, schooling, science of teaching, store of knowledge, studies, system of knowledge, systematic training, teaching, training, tuition, tutelage, tutoring, upbringing
ASSOCIATED CONCEPTS: board of education, educational corporation, educational facilities, educational institution, educational purposes, educational trust, educational uses

EDUCE, *verb*   bring forth, bring out, bring to light, call forth, deduce, derive, discover, draw, draw forth, draw out, elicit, evoke, evolve, extract, extricate, ferret out, infer, lay open, make obvious, obtain, procure, pull, pull out, secure, summon forth, unearth, unfold, unveil
ASSOCIATED CONCEPTS: educe evidence

EFFECT, *noun*   accomplishment, achievement, aftermath, *consecutio,* consequence, development, effectuation, *effectus,* end product, end result, eventuation, *eventus,* final result, fruit, fruition, impact, issue, outcome, outgrowth, payoff, product, reaction, repercussion, response, result, resultant, resultant action, sequel, termination, upshot

ASSOCIATED CONCEPTS: cause and effect, chilling effect, effective procuring cause, force and effect, natural effect, personal effects

FOREIGN PHRASES: *Effectus sequitur causam.* The effect follows the cause. *Verba accipienda sunt cum effectu, ut sortiantur effectum.* Words are to be received with effect, so that they may be productive of effect. *Cessante causa, cessat effectus.* The cause ceasing, the effect must cease. *Cum quod ago non valet ut ago, valeat quantum valere potest.* When that which I do is of no effect as I do it, it shall be as effective as it can (otherwise) be made. *Nova constitutio futuris formam imponere debet non praeteritis.* A new law ought to affect the future, not what is past. *Non efficit affectus nisi sequatur effectus.* The intention amounts to nothing unless some effect follows. *Verba accipienda ut sortiantur effectum.* Words should be taken so that they may have some effect. *Cuicunque aliquis quid concedit concedere videtur et id, sine quo res ipsa esse non potuit.* Whoever grants anything to another is supposed to grant that also without which the grant itself would be of no effect. *Juris affectus in executione consistit.* The effectiveness of a law lies in its execution. *Quando quod ago non valet ut ago, valeat quantum valere potest.* When that which I do does not have effect as I do it, let it have as much effect as it can. *Cessante ratione legis, cessat et ipsa lex.* Where the reason for a law ceases, the law itself also ceases. *Officit conatus si effectus sequatur.* The attempt becomes of consequence, if the effect follows.

EFFECTIVE *(Efficient),* **adjective** able, adapted, adequate, advantageous, capable, competent, convenient, effectual, efficacious, *efficax,* equal to, expedient, fit, functional, handy, helpful, implemental, instrumental, of service, of use, practicable, practical, pragmatic, productive, proficient, profitable, serviceable, skillful, successful, to the purpose, unerring, up to, useful, utilitarian, valid

EFFECTIVE *(Operative),* **adjective** active, at work, effectual, fit for use, having legal force, in action, in effect, in force, in operation, operational, ready for use, usable, valid, working

ASSOCIATED CONCEPTS: effective assignment, effective at death, effective date, effective dissolution

EFFECTS, *noun* assets, belongings, *bona,* chattel property, chattels, contents, estate, goods, holdings, legal estate, means, movable property, paraphernalia, personal property, personalty, possessions, property, *res,* resources, things, wealth, worldly substance

ASSOCIATED CONCEPTS: household effects, personal effects, personal property, personalty

EFFECTUATE, *verb* accomplish, achieve, attain, bring to maturity, bring to pass, carry into effect, carry into execution, carry through, cause, cause to happen, complete, effect, enact, enforce, execute, fulfill, manage, perform, produce, put in force, realize, succeed, work

EFFICIENCY, *noun* ability, ableness, adeptness, adroitness, capability, capableness, command, competence, competency, deftness, dexterity, dexterousness, effectiveness, efficacy, *efficientia,* excellence, expert-

ness, handiness, helpfulness, mastery, potency, productiveness, proficiency, prowess, quickness, resourcefulness, skill, skillfulness, *vis*

EFFICIENT, *adjective* able, adroit, capable, competent, deft, dexterous, effective, effectual, expedient, expeditious, expert, functional, *habilis,* mighty, potent, powerful, practical, productive, proficient, puissant, skilled, skillful

ASSOCIATED CONCEPTS: efficient cause, efficient intervening cause

EFFORT, *noun* applied energy, arduousness, assiduity, assiduousness, attempt, *conatus, contentio,* endeavor, essay, exertion, expenditure of energy, hard work, industry, laboriousness, *opera,* pains, strain, strenuousness, struggle, toil, travail, trial, vigor, vigorousness

EGREGIOUS, *adjective* absurd, appalling, arrant, bizarre, excessive, extravagant, flagrant, glaring, immoderate, inordinate, intemperate, outrageous, outre, remarkable, uncomfortable

EGRESS, *noun* departure, discharge, doorway, egression, *egressus,* emergence, emersion, emigration, escape, evacuation, exit, *exitus,* exodus, gate, gateway, leavetaking, means of exit, opening, outlet, parting, passage out, place of exit, way out, withdrawal

EJECT *(Evict),* **verb** cast out, *deicere,* dislodge, displace, dispossess, divest, expel, get rid of, oust, put out, put out of possession, remove, remove from premises, rid, summarily dispossess, throw out, thrust out, turn out, turn out of possession

EJECT *(Expel),* **verb** cast forth, cast out, detrude, discard, discharge, disgorge, dismiss, *eicere,* eliminate, eruct, eructate, exclude, *expellere, extrudere,* force out, jettison, oust, push away, push out, remove, throw out, thrust out

ELABORATE, *adjective* baroque, beautified, bedecked, complex, complicated, daedal, decorated, deluxe, detailed, developed minutely, done with thoroughness, *elaboratus,* embellished, executed with exactness, fancy, festooned, flamboyant, flashy, garnished, grandiose, highly wrought, intricate, intricately wrought, involute, involved, labored, marked by excessive effort, ornamented, ornate, ostentatious, painstaking, palatial, perfected, rich, showy, studied, sumptuous, wrought with labor

ELABORATE, *verb* add to, amplify, augment, be more specific, detail, develop, *elaborare,* enlarge upon, enrich, expand, give additional information, go into detail, improve upon, magnify, perfect, refine, state something in detail

ELDERLY, *adjective* advanced in years, *aetate provectus,* aged, along in years, hoary, matured, old, seasoned, senescent

ELECT *(Choose),* **verb** *creare,* decide, *deligere,* determine in favor of, distinguish by special selection, *eligere,* eliminate the alternatives, exercise an option, exercise discretion, make a choice, make a selection, name, opt for, pick, select, settle on, will

ASSOCIATED CONCEPTS: election of remedies, election of rights, election under a will, equitable election, right of election

ELECT *(Select by a vote), verb*   appoint by vote, cast the majority of ballots for, choose for office, designate for office by vote, place in office, select for office, vote into office

ASSOCIATED CONCEPTS: election by ballot, election contest, election day, election district, election laws, election returns, electioneering, elective office, general election, notice of election, popular election, primary election, public election, regular election, special election

ELECTION *(Choice), noun*   appointment, choice between alternatives, cooptation, decision, deliberate choice, designation, determination, *electio,* option, pick, preference, selection, *suffragia,* volition

ASSOCIATED CONCEPTS: election between inconsistent remedies, election of remedies, election of rights, election under a will, equitable election, estoppel by election

FOREIGN PHRASES: *Consecratio est periodus electionis; electio est praeambula consecration is.* Consecration is the termination of election; election is the preamble of consecration. *Electio est interna libera et spontanea separatio unius rei ab alia sine compulsione, consistens in animo et voluntate.* Election is an internal, free, and spontaneous separation of one thing from another, without compulsion, consisting of intention and will. *Electio semel facta, et placitum testatum non patitur regressum.* An election once made, and the intent shown, cannot be recalled. *Electiones fiant rite et libere sine interruptione aliqua.* Elections should be made in due form, and freely, without any interruption.

ELECTION *(Selection by vote), noun*   appointment by vote, balloting, choosing by vote, plebiscite, poll, referendum, representation, selection for office by vote, vote-casting

ASSOCIATED CONCEPTS: ballots, caucus, election contest, election district, election law, election petitions, election returns, general election, primary election, referendum, regular election, special election

ELECTIVE *(Selective), adjective*   alternative, bestowed by ballot, by vote, choosing, cooptive, disjunctive, on approval, open to choice

ASSOCIATED CONCEPTS: elective franchise, elective office

ELECTIVE *(Voluntary), adjective*   appointive, discretionary, gratuitous, not required, optional, spontaneous

ELEGANT, *adjective*   aesthetic, beautiful, chic, deluxe, dignified, distinguished, *elegans,* exquisite, fashionable, gorgeous, graceful, grand, handsome, in good taste, lovely, magnificent, proportioned, refined, sophisticated, splendid, stately, stylish, tasteful, unmeretricious

ELEMENT, *noun*   cantle, component, component part, constituent, content, detail, *elementum,* essential part, factor, feature, fraction, fragment, fundamental part, ingredient, integral part, item, member, part, particle, piece, portion, rudiment, section, segment, substance

ASSOCIATED CONCEPTS: elements of a cause of action, elements of a crime, elements of recovery

ELEMENTARY, *adjective*   abecedarian, apparent, basal, basic, beginning, crude, easy, easy to understand, elemental, foundational, fundamental, inceptive, initiatory, introductory, obvious, plain, precursory, prefatory, primary, primitive, *primus,* proemial, rudimental, rudimentary, simple, simplified, starting, uncomplex, uncomplicated, understandable, unraveled, unsophisticated

ASSOCIATED CONCEPTS: elementary canon of interpretation

ELEVATE, *verb*   advance, aggrandize, *attollere,* beatify, boost, build up, canonize, cause to rise, confer an honor, consecrate, deify, dignify, distinguish, erect, exalt, glorify, heave up, heft, heighten, hoist, hold aloft, hold up, honor, improve, jack up, *levare,* lift, make higher, pick up, pitch, promote, prop, put on a pedestal, raise, raise aloft, raise to a higher position, sanctify, sublimate, upgrade, uplift, upraise

ELEVATION, *noun*   advancement, aggrandizement, altitude, canonization, consecration, coronation, deification, dignification, *elatio,* elevated place, eminence, eminency, erection, exaltation, height, high land, highness, lift, loftiness, promotion, rise, sanctification, stature, steepness, tallness, uplift, upright distance

ELICIT, *verb*   arouse, author, awaken, beget, bring about, bring forth, bring forward, bring out, call forth, cause, draw forth, draw out, *eblandiri,* educe, effect, effectuate, *elicere, evocare,* evoke, extract, generate, initiate, make manifest, stimulate, summon forth

ELIGIBLE, *adjective*   acceptable, appropriate, approved, befitting, capable, desirable, *dignus,* employable, fit, fit for appointment, fit for election, fit for selection, fit to be chosen, fitting, *idoneus,* legally qualified, *opportunus,* proper, qualified, right, satisfactory, suitable, usable

ASSOCIATED CONCEPTS: eligible to hold public office

ELIMINATE *(Eradicate), verb*   abolish, annihilate, blot out, cancel, clear out, consume, cut out, decimate, delete, demolish, deracinate, desolate, destroy, devour, dispatch, dispose of, dissolve, do away with, efface, end, erase, evacuate, expunge, expurgate, exterminate, extirpate, get rid of, kill, lay waste, liquidate, nullify, obliterate, overthrow, purge, put a stop to, put an end to, quash, quell, raze, remove, render useless, slaughter, stamp out, strike out, suppress, sweep away, tear out, terminate, uproot, void, weed out, wipe out

ELIMINATE *(Exclude), verb*   ban, banish, bar, blockade, cashier, cast out, censor, count out, debar, deport, disallow, disbar, discard, disdain, dismiss, disqualify, disregard, do away with, eject, elide, evacuate, evict, except, exclude, excommunicate, exempt, exile, expatriate, expel, keep out, leave out, lock out, omit, ostracize, oust, outlaw, preclude, prevent, prohibit, proscribe, put aside, rebuff, reject, remove, renounce, repulse, rule out, set aside, shed, shut out, spurn, throw out, thrust out, turn out, weed

ELITE, *noun*   aristocracy, best part, best people, choice group, chosen few, cream of society, fashionable society, gentry, high society, most carefully selected group, nobility, optimates, privileged class, select body, select few, superior group, top people, upper circles, upper classes

ELOQUENT, *adjective* articulate, calculated to stir, communicative, compelling, convincing, *disertus,* effective, *eloquens,* expressive, flowing, fluent, forceful, full of feeling, full of meaning, full of substance, graceful, impassioned, impressive, incisive, informative, meaningful, mellifluous, moving, movingly expressive, persuasive, pithy, pointed, powerful, powerfully expressive, pregnant, rich, spellbinding, striking, telling, trenchant, vivid

ELUCIDATE, *verb* annotate, ascertain, bring out more clearly, cast light upon, clarify, clear of obscurity, clear up, comment upon, commentate, construe, decipher, decode, define, demonstrate, describe, detail, determine, disentangle, enlighten, enucleate, exemplify, explain, *explanare,* explicate, *exponere,* exposit, expound, find a clue, give an explanation, give an interpretation, illuminate, illustrate, interpret, *interpretari,* lay open, make apparent, make clear, make intelligible, make less confusing, make lucid, make plain, make sense of, make simple, make understandable, manifest, paraphrase, popularize, put in other words, ravel, rephrase, restate, shed light upon, simplify, solve, spell out, teach, throw light upon, translate, unfold, unravel, unriddle, unscramble, untangle

ELUDE, *verb* abscond, avoid, baffle, be concealed, break away, break loose, dodge, *eludere,* escape, escape by artifice, escape detection, escape notice, evade, *evitare,* flee, get away, hide, keep aloof, keep out of sight, make an escape, mystify, outmaneuver, outwit, parry, remain hidden, remain undiscovered, shun, slip away, slip out, steal away, take evasive action

ELUSIVE, *adjective* abstruse, apt to flee, baffling, difficult, difficult to catch, difficult to comprehend, difficult to understand, eluding clear perception, elusory, enigmatic, equivocal, escaping, evanescent, evasive, fleeting, fugitive, hard to define, hard to express, hard to grasp, hard to maintain, hard to understand, impalpable, intangible, liable to disappear, mysterious, nebulous, obscure, occult, puzzling, runaway, shadowy, shunning, slippery, tending to elude, tending to escape, tending to slip away, uncertain, unclear, vanishing

EMANATE, *verb* arise from, come forth, come from, debouch, derive from, descend from, *effundi,* effuse, eject, *emanare,* emerge, emit, ensue from, exude, fall out, flow forth, *fluere,* follow from, go out of, grow from, grow out of, issue, originate in, pour out of, proceed, project, radiate, result, spring from, stream out

EMANCIPATION, *noun* acquittal, deliverance, deliverance from bondage, discharge, enfranchisement, extrication, freedom, *liberatio,* liberation, liberty, *manumissio,* manumission, pardon, possession of full rights, release, release from custody, reprieve, salvation, setting free, unshackling
ASSOCIATED CONCEPTS: complete emancipation, emancipation of minors, Emancipation Proclamation, express emancipation, implied emancipation, partial emancipation

EMBARGO, *noun* authoritative stoppage of trade, ban, bar, control of trade, debarment, denial, detention of ships, disallowance of trade, exclusion from commerce, forbiddance, freeze, governmental order of prohibition, halt, interference, legal restraint, preclusion, prohibition, restraint, restriction, stop, stoppage
ASSOCIATED CONCEPTS: embargo of commerce, embargo of goods, embargo of products

EMBARK, *verb* auspicate, begin, commence, *conscendere,* engage in an enterprise, enter, enter upon, get under way, go into, inaugurate, initiate, institute, launch, make a beginning, originate, plunge into, *rationem inire,* set out, start, start out, take on, take the first step, take up, undertake, venture

EMBARRASS, *verb* abash, annoy, baffle, bedevil, beset, bewilder, bother, burden, cause confusion, cause discomfort, cause to feel ill at ease, chagrin, confuse, *conturbare,* discomfit, discomfort, discompose, disconcert, disquiet, distress, disturb, encumber, fluster, *impedire,* incommode, make self-conscious, make uncomfortable, mortify, nonplus, perturb, plague, put at a disadvantage, render flustered, render ill at ease, shame, trouble, upset, vex, worry

EMBARRASSMENT, *noun* abashment, awkward situation, awkwardness, bafflement, chagrin, confusion, constraint, discomfiture, discomfort, discomposure, disturbance, fluster, humiliation, *implicatio,* mortification, perturbation, pudency, *scrupulus,* self-consciousness, shame, uneasiness

EMBASSY, *noun* ambassadorial function, ambassadorial office, ambassadorial residence, commission, consulate, delegation, deputation, diplomatic corps, embassage, establishment of an ambassador, legateship, *legatio,* legation, mission, mission of the ambassador, official headquarters of an ambassador, official mission
ASSOCIATED CONCEPTS: consular and diplomatic officers

EMBED, *verb* bury, deposit, engraft, entrench, fix, fix firmly, implant, impress, imprint, infix, ingrain, insert, lodge, plant, press in, root, seat, set, set firmly, settle, stamp

EMBELLISH, *verb* add details, adorn, array, beautify, bedeck, bedizen, bejewel, beribbon, bespangle, better, blazon, chase, dandify, deck, *decorare,* decorate, dizen, dress up, elaborate, emblazon, emboss, embroider, encrust, enhance, enrich, *exornare,* fix up, frill, garnish, gild, glamorize, grace, illuminate, illustrate, improve, make beautiful, make elaborate, make improvements, make resplendent, meliorate, ornament, polish, rubricate, smarten, spangle, spruce up, stretch, tool, touch up, trim, varnish

EMBEZZLE, *verb* appropriate fraudulently, appropriate to one's own use, *avertere,* commit larceny, defalcate, defraud, divert to one's own use, filch, *intercipere, intervertere,* misapply, misappropriate, misappropriate funds, misappropriate intrusted funds, misuse, pilfer, purloin, swindle, take by fraud, take feloniously, thieve
ASSOCIATED CONCEPTS: convert

EMBEZZLEMENT, *noun* appropriation, breach of trust, cheating, defalcation, fraud, fraudulent appropriation, fraudulent appropriation of money, fraudulent

conversion, larceny, malversation, misappropriation, peculation, pilfering, purloining, stealing, swindle, theft, theft of money entrusted to one's care, theft of money entrusted to one's management, thievery, wrongful appropriation
ASSOCIATED CONCEPTS: conversion, corporate embezzlement, embezzlement of public funds, larceny, misappropriation, theft by means of embezzlement

EMBEZZLER, noun   cheater, criminal, crook, culprit, defalcator, defrauder, evildoer, *interceptor,* lawbreaker, malefactor, one who commits larceny, peculator, *pecuniae aversor,* pilferer, purloiner, swindler, thief

EMBODIMENT, noun   actualization, bodily presentation, bodily representation, concrete expression, corporeity, definite form, *effigies,* form, formation, incarnation, manifestation, material figuration, material representation, materialization, personification, realization, representation, *simulacrum,* substantiality, synthesis, tangibility, tangible form, visible form
ASSOCIATED CONCEPTS: embodied in a contract, embodied in the instrument

EMBODY, verb   actualize, constitute, corporealize, exhibit in visible form, express in concrete form, form, give concrete form to, give definite form to, give tangible form to, incarnate, *includere,* incorporate, integrate, interblend, interfuse, intermix, invest with a body, invest with matter, make corporeal, make visible, manifest, materialize, personify, put into bodily form, substantialize, syncretize, synthesize

EMBRACE *(Accept), verb*   adopt, advocate, affiliate, agree to, assume, be in favor of, concur in, consent to, countenance, endorse, espouse, favor, make one's own, ratify, sanction, seize, subscribe to, support, take to oneself, take up, welcome

EMBRACE *(Encircle), verb*   begird, belt, cincture, circumscribe, compass, *complecti, comprehendere,* contain, cover, encincture, enclose, encompass, enfold, engird, envelop, gird, girdle, hold, include, incorporate, integrate, invest, involve, lap, receive, skirt, surround, take in

EMBROILMENT, noun   affray, agitation, brawl, breach, broil, chaos, clash, combat, commotion, complication, conflict, confusion, contention, contest, derangement, difference of opinion, disarrangement, disorder, disquiet, dissension, dissentience, disturbance, embranglement, encounter, engagement, entanglement, ferment, fracas, fray, imbroglio, involvement, mix-up, muddle, odds, outbreak, pandemonium, quarrel, riot, row, rupture, squabble, strife, struggle, tumult, turbulence, turmoil, unrest, uproar, violence

EMBRYO, noun   basis for development, beginning, bud, commencement, earliest stage, fetus, first stage, genesis, germ, immature stage, inchoation, incipience, incipient organism, origin, origination, *partus,* rudiment, rudimentary state, seed, source, start, starting point, undeveloped stage
ASSOCIATED CONCEPTS: abortion

EMEND, verb   adjust, alter, ameliorate, amend, better, change, correct, *corrigere,* do over, *emendare,* emendate, fix, help, improve, make better, make correc-

tions, make improvements, make repairs, meliorate, mend, put in order, put right, reconstruct, rectify, redo, refine, reform, remedy, remodel, remove errors, render better, reorganize, repair, restore, retouch, revamp, revise, rework, rewrite, rid of defects, right, set right, set straight, touch up, work over

EMERGE, verb   appear, arise, arrive, become apparent, become manifest, become plain, become visible, break through, burst forth, come forth, come forward, come into notice, come into view, come out, come out of hiding, come to light, crop up, dawn, emanate, *emergere,* enter the picture, exit, expose, issue, loom, make an appearance, manifest, materialize, put in an appearance, rise, show, show up, surface, turn up

EMERGENCY, noun   accident, *casus,* climacteric, condition of insufficiency, crisis, critical point, crucial period, difficulty, dilemma, *discrimen,* exigency, extremity, insufficiency of service, last minute need, necessitousness, need, need for action, needfulness, plight, predicament, pressing necessity, pressing need, strait, sudden peril, *tempus,* trouble, unexpected happening, unforeseen condition, unforeseen occurrence, urgency
ASSOCIATED CONCEPTS: Emergency Court of Appeals, Emergency Defense Act, emergency employment doctrine, Emergency Price Control Act, private necessity, public emergency, public necessity

EMINENCE, noun   aggrandizement, *amplissimus gradus,* authority, celebrity, consequence, dignity, distinction, elevated rank, elevation, esteem, exaltation, fame, *fastigium,* glory, grandeur, great station, greatness, height, high position, high rank, high station, honor, importance, important station, influence, loftiness, majesty, mark, mightiness, nobility, notability, note, noteworthiness, *praestantia,* preeminence, prestige, prominence, renown, repute, standing, supereminence, superiority, supremacy, weight

EMINENT DOMAIN, noun   annex for public use, assume for public use, take possession for public use, usurp for public use

EMIT, verb   beam, cast out, discharge, eject, *emittere,* eructate, erupt, exhale, exhaust, expel, expend, exude, give forth, give off, give out, gush, hurl, issue, jet, let out, pour forth, pour out, put forth, radiate, secrete, send forth, send out, shed, shoot, spurt, squirt, throw, throw off, throw out

EMOTION, noun   affect, agitation, *animi motus,* ardor, eagerness, ebullition, enthusiasm, ferment, fervor, furor, great feeling, mood, passion, reaction, response, sensation, sensitiveness, sentiment, spirit, stir, turmoil, verve, zeal

EMPANEL, verb   calendar, docket, enlist jurors, enroll, enter those names designated as jurors, insert names on a register, list for jury duty, list jurors, place upon a list, register, schedule, select jurors, sign in
ASSOCIATED CONCEPTS: empanel a jury

EMPHASIS, noun   accent, accentuation, attention, concentration, consequence, consideration, distinction, distinctness, eminence, *emphasis,* force, force of expression, force of voice, highlight, importance, impressiveness, intensity of expression, moment, most important point, notability, note, outstanding feature, primacy, prominence, salience, saliency, special attention, special concern, special intonation, special significance, strength, stress, thrust, underlining, underscoring, value, vigorous enunciation, weight, worth

EMPIRICAL, *adjective* analytical, based on evidence of the senses, based on observation, derived from experience, diagnostic, guided by experiment, provisional

EMPLOY *(Engage services), verb* add to the payroll, appoint, assign, authorize, commission, contract, delegate, *detineri,* empower, engage, enlist, enroll, entrust with a task, entrust with management, fill a position, fill a vacancy, fill an opening, find help, furnish occupation for, give a job to, give a position to, give a post to, give employment, give work to, hire, keep in service, *occupatum,* place, put to work, recruit, retain, retain the services of, secure, set to work, sign up, staff, take into employ, take into service, use another's services, use as an agent, *versari*
ASSOCIATED CONCEPTS: actual employment, customarily employed, dangerous employment, employed in hazardous work, employed in interstate commerce, lawfully employed, legally employed, permanently employed

EMPLOY *(Make use of), verb* apply, avail oneself of, capitalize upon, exercise, exploit, have recourse to, manipulate, mobilize, operate, ply, practice, profit by, put in action, put in operation, put to service, put to use, resort to, take advantage of, turn to account, turn to use, use, utilize, wield, work

EMPLOYEE, *noun* agent, apprentice, assistant, attache, factotum, hand, help, helper, hired hand, hireling, jobholder, laborer, mercenary, personnel, representative, salaried worker, servant, staff person, subordinate, toiler, wage earner, worker, workman
ASSOCIATED CONCEPTS: agent, bona fide employee, borrowed employee, casual employee, de facto employee, independent contractor, joint adventurer, loaned employee, part-time employee, permanent employee, provisional employee, servant, subcontractor

EMPLOYER, *noun* administrator, boss, chief, controller, director, executive, head, leader, management, manager, master, overseer, owner, patron, proprietor, superintendent, superior, supervisor, taskmaster
ASSOCIATED CONCEPTS: employers' liability acts

EMPLOYMENT, *noun* activity, appointment, assignment, avocation, berth, billet, business, calling, capacity, career, commission, craft, duty, employ, engagement, enterprise, field, function, incumbency, industry, job, labor, lifework, line, livelihood, living, means of livelihood, means of support, *negotium,* occupation, office, position, post, practice, profession, pursuit, retainment, service, situation, specialty, task, trade, vocation, work
ASSOCIATED CONCEPTS: abandonment of employment, arising out of and in course of employment, available for employment, casual employment, conditions of employment, contract of employment, course of employment, covered employment, dangerous employment, duration of employment, during term of employment, engaged in employment, exempt employment, extrahazardous employment, extraordinary employment,

general employment, grade of employment, injury arising in course of employment, permanent employment, place of employment, private employment, professional employment, public employment, scope of employment, seasonal employment, temporary employment, tenure of employment

EMPOWER, *verb* accredit, activate, aggrandize, allow, appoint, arm, assign, authorize, capacitate, commission, confer power on, delegate, depute, deputize, enable, endow, energize, entrust, franchise, give ability, give authority, give permission, give power, give right, grant, grant authority, grant power, *homini rei,* impart power to, implement, invest, license, make able, make capable, make potent, permit, potentiate, *potestatem facere,* privilege, qualify, render competent, sanction, strengthen, train, vest, warrant

EN BANC, *adverb* all together, as a unit, as a whole, collectively, *en bloc, en masse,* entirely, in a body, in a mass, in sum, *in toto,* one and all

EN MASSE, *adverb* all together, as a body, as a group, as a whole, as one, at the same time, collectively, *en bloc,* ensemble, in assembly, in mass, in the aggregate, together

EN ROUTE, *adverb* along the way, bound, during the journey, during travel, in passage, in progress, in transit, midway, on the journey, on the road, on the way

ENABLE, *verb* abet, aid, allow, approve, arm, assist, authorize, capacitate, confer, consent, emancipate, empower, endow, facilitate, *facultatem facere,* give ability, give authority, give means, give permission, give power, grant, help, *homini rei,* implement, indulge, invest, let, liberate, license, make able, make capable, make possible, make practicable, permit, privilege, provide, provide means, qualify, release, remove a disability, render assistance, render competent, sanction, strengthen, supply with means, support
ASSOCIATED CONCEPTS: enabling act, enabling legislation, enabling statute

ENACT, *verb* adopt a measure, appoint by act, codify, command, declare, decree, dictate, enjoin, establish, establish by law, give legislative sanction, institute by law, issue a command, legislate, make into a statute, make laws, ordain by law, order, pass, *perferre,* prescribe, put in force, put into effect
ASSOCIATED CONCEPTS: enacting clause
FOREIGN PHRASES: *Non obligat lex nisi promulgata.* A law is not obligatory unless it is promulgated. *Ejus est interpretari cujus est condere.* It is for him who enacts anything to give it interpretation.

ENACTMENT, *noun* act, bill, charter, codification, decree, dictate, edict, establishment, fiat, law, legislation, *lex,* measure, ordinance, *plebiscitum,* regulation, rule, ruling, *sanctio,* statute, statutory law
FOREIGN PHRASES: *Leges suum ligent latorem.* Laws should bind their own proposer. *Jus constitui oportet in his quae ut plurimum accidunt non quae ex inopi nato.* Laws ought to be made with a view to those cases which occur most frequently, and not to those which are of rare or accidental occurrence. *Leges figendi et refigendi consuetudo est periculosissima.* The practice of making and remaking the laws is a most dangerous one. *Quod populus postremum jussit, id jus ratum esto.* What the people have last enacted, let that be the settled law.

ENCLOSE, *verb*   blockade, bound, bracket, capture, *cingere,* circumscribe, circumvallate, close in, compass, confine, contain, embrace, encase, encincture, encircle, encompass, enfold, envelop, environ, fence in, gird, girdle, hem in, immure, impound, imprison, incarcerate, *includere,* insert in a wrapper, insert in an envelope, keep behind bars, keep in, keep in custody, limit, pen, put a barrier around, put into a receptacle, restrain, restrict, retain, ring, *saepire,* shut in, surround, take into custody, trammel, wall in

ENCLOSURE, *noun*   arena, barrier, blockade, border, boundary, bracket, cincture, circle, circumjacence, circumscription, circumvallation, confine, confinement, container, containment, custody, edge, embrace, encasement, encirclement, enclosed space, encompassment, enfoldment, envelopment, fence, fenced in area, girdle, immurement, impoundment, imprisonment, incarceration, insertion, limit, limitation, perimeter, pound, receptacle, restriction, trammel, walled in area, wrapper, zone

ENCOMPASS *(Include), verb*   adscribere, complecti, comprise, consist of, contain, *continere,* cover, embrace, hold, incorporate, span, subsume, take in
ASSOCIATED CONCEPTS: encompass a broad cross section of the law

ENCOMPASS *(Surround), verb*   be circumjacent, begird, belt, border, bound, cincture, *cingere,* circle, circuit, *circumcludere, circumplecti,* circumscribe, compass, corral, edge, encase, encincture, encircle, enclose, enclose on all sides, engird, enring, ensphere, envelop, enwrap, fence in, form a circle round, gird, girdle, hem in, immure, keep in, pen in, ring, shut in, wall in, wrap

ENCOURAGE, *verb*   back, back up, boost, embolden, endorse, hearten, inspire, support

ENCROACH, *verb*   breach, commit an infraction, enter by stealth, enter upon the domain of another, enter wrongfully, impinge, infiltrate, infringe, ingress wrongfully, interfere, interlope, intrude, intrude illegally, invade, invade unlawfully, *invadere,* irrupt, make an incursion, make inroads, obtrude, *occupare,* overstep, penetrate, raid, transgress, trespass, violate

ENCROACHMENT, *noun*   breach, entrance by stealth, entrance upon the domain of another, illegal intrusion, impingement, imposition, incursion, infiltration, infraction, infringement, *iniuria,* inroad, interference, interloping, intrusion, invasion, irruption, obtrusion, overlap, overstepping, penetration, prying, raid, real estate trespass, transgression, trespass, unlawful invasion, violation, wrongful entry, wrongful ingress
ASSOCIATED CONCEPTS: adverse possession, common nuissance, easements, public nuissance

ENCUMBER *(Financially obligate), verb*   assess, burden, charge, hold liable, *impedire,* impose a charge, impose a lien, make accountable for, make responsible for, mortgage, obligate, *onerare,* place a cloud on, *praegravare,* subject to a charge, subject to a liability
ASSOCIATED CONCEPTS: mortgage

ENCUMBER *(Hinder), verb*   block, block up, burden, charge, cramp, cumber, disadvantage, discommode, entangle, entrammel, frustrate, hamper, hinder movement, hold back action, hold up, impede, impose,

incommode, inconvenience, inflict, inhibit, interfere, interrupt, keep back, lade, limit, obstruct action, render difficult, retard, saddle, shackle, slow down, strain, tax, thwart, tie up, trammel, trouble, weaken, weigh down

ENCUMBRANCE, *noun*   burden, charge, claim, curb, difficulty, disadvantage, drawback, hampering, hindering, hindrance, hitch, hurdle, impediment, *impedimentum,* imposition, inconvenience, infliction, interference, liability, lien, lien on an estate, load, mortgage, obstacle, obstruction, *onus,* oppression, pressure, restriction, retardation, stay, stop, stoppage
ASSOCIATED CONCEPTS: easements, mortgage
FOREIGN PHRASES: *Transit terra cum onere.* Land passes subject to any encumbrances affecting it.

END *(Intent), noun*   aim, ambition, aspiration, bourn, *consilium,* desideration, desideratum, design, desire, desired result, destination, dream, expectation, goal, guiding principle, hope, idea, intended result, intendment, intention, mission, motivating idea, motivation, motive, object, objective, purpose, reason, target, wish
ASSOCIATED CONCEPTS: ends of justice

END *(Termination), noun*   accomplishment, achievement, adjournment, attainment, border, borderline, bound, boundary, cessation, close, closing piece, closure, completion, concluding part, conclusion, consummation, culmination, curtain, death, decease, decline, demise, denouement, departure, destination, destiny, determination, dissolution, edge, elimination, ending, estoppage, *exitus,* expiration, expiry, extinction, extinguishment, extreme, extreme point, extremity, fate, final event, final state, finale, finality, *finis,* finish, fulfillment, furthermost part, halt, last of a series, last part, limit, limitation, omega, outcome, point, pole, realization, remnant, result, resultant, retirement, stop, stoppage, tail, terminal, terminal point, termination, terminus, tip, upshot, wane

ENDANGER, *verb*   abuse, be careless with, be malevolent, bring into peril, bully, compromise, damage, dare, expose, expose to danger, expose to injury, expose to loss, harm, hazard, hurt, impair, imperil, *in discrimen, in periculum,* injure, jeopardize, leave defenseless, leave unprotected, make insecure, make liable to danger, make liable to injury, make unsafe, make vulnerable, maltreat, menace, misuse, molest, peril, persecute, prey upon, put in hazard, put in jeopardy, risk, risk exposure to harm, speculate with, stake, subject to loss, terrify, terrorize, threaten, torment, torture, victimize, violate
ASSOCIATED CONCEPTS: endanger life, endanger safety

ENDEAVOR, *noun*   achievement, aim, application, assiduity, attempt, bid, campaign, cause, *conatus, contentio,* deed, effort, emprise, enterprise, essay, exercise, exertion, experiment, exploit, feat, labor, *nisus,* pains, project, pursuance, pursuit, quest, scheme, search, strain, strenuous effort, struggle, sustained trial, task, toil, travail, trial, try, undertaking, venture, work

ENDEAVOR, *verb*   address oneself to, aim, apply oneself to, aspire, assay, assume, attempt, attempt strenuously, be resolute, bestir oneself, bid, compete for, *conari, contendere,* do all one can, do one's best, do one's utmost, engage in, *eniti,* essay, exert effort, exert oneself, experiment, labor, make a bid, make an attempt, make an effort, persevere, pursue, put oneself out, resolve, risk, seek, set about, spare no effort, spare no pains, strain, strive, struggle, tackle, take a crack at, take action, take on, take pains, take up, take upon oneself, test, toil, trouble oneself, try, undertake, venture, vie for, work at

ENDORSE, *verb*   approve, attest, authenticate, back, certify, commend, confirm, ratify, sanction, second, support, validate

ENDOW, *verb*   aid, allot, allow, award, bequeath, bestow, contribute, donate, endue, enrich, fund, furnish, give, grant, hand down, hand out, hand over, help, *hominem, instruere,* make pecuniary provision, pass down, present, provide, put in the hands of, subsidize, supply, supply with means

ENDOWMENT, *noun*   aid, allotment, allowance, appropriation, assistance, award, benefaction, benefit, bequeathal, bequest, bestowal, bestowment, boon, bounty, contribution, donation, dowry, enrichment, fund, funding, gift, grant, present, presentation, presentment, provision, stipend, subsidy
ASSOCIATED CONCEPTS: annuity, endowment fund, endowment policy in insurance

ENDUE, *verb*   accord, allot, allow, apportion, arm, assign, award, bestow, confer, dispense, donate, empower, enable, endow, enrich, entrust, fortify, furnish, give, grant, hand out, invest, invigorate, make provision for, present, provide, strengthen, supply

ENDURE *(Last), verb*   abide, be constant, be durable, be firm, be permanent, be preserved, be prolonged, be protracted, be timeless, carry on, continue, continue to be, continue to exist, *durare,* exist, exist uninterruptedly, exist without break, extend, forge ahead, go on, hang on, have duration, have no end, hold one's ground, hold out, keep, linger on, live on, maintain, move ahead, outlast, outlive, perdure, *permanere,* persevere, persist, press onward, prevail, progress, refuse to give up, refuse to yield, remain, remain alive, remain valid, stand, stand fast, stay, subsist, survive, sustain, wear, weather, withstand

ENDURE *(Suffer), verb*   accustom oneself to, be subjected to, bear, bear pain, bear up under, bear without resistance, bide, brave, brook, continue under pain, countenance, encounter, experience, experience unpleasantly, face, feel, forbear, go through, make the best of, meet, pass through, *perferre,* put up with, receive, resign oneself to, stand, stomach, submit to, suffer pain, sustain, *sustinere,* swallow, take, take patiently, *tolerare,* tolerate, undergo, weather, withstand

ENFORCE, *verb*   adminster, bring to pass, carry into effect, carry into execution, carry out, carry through, coerce, compel, compel obedience, *confirmare,* dictate, drive, effect, effectuate, employ force, exact, execute, *exsequi,* force, have executed, impel, implement, impose, insist on, insist upon, make compulsory, make effective, necessitate, obtain by compulsion, obtain by force, press, put in action, put in force, put in operation, put into effect, put into execution, put pressure on, require, strengthen, subject to pressure
ASSOCIATED CONCEPTS: enforce a contract, enforce a judgment, enforce a lien, enforce provisions of the law, enforce sanctions, enforcement proceedings

ENFORCEMENT, *noun*   administration, carrying into effect, carrying out, coaction, compulsion, compulsory execution, constraint, dictation, effectuation, exaction, execution, force, forcible urging, implementation, imposition, insistence, insistence upon, necessitation, necessity, obligation, obligement, pressure, requirement, strengthening, support
ASSOCIATED CONCEPTS: enforcement of a contract, enforcement of a judgment, enforcement of a lien, enforcement of a right, enforcement proceeding
FOREIGN PHRASES: *Pacta conventa quae neque contra leges neque dolo malo inita sunt omni modo observanda sunt.* Agreements which are not contrary to the laws nor entered into with a fraudulent design must be observed in all respects. *Executio juris non habet injuriam.* The execution of law does no injury. *Scire leges non hoc est verba earum tenere, sed vim ac potestatem.* To know the laws is not to observe their words alone, but their force and power. *Interest reipublicae ne maleficia remaneant impunita.* It concerns the state that crimes do not go unpunished. *Ex nudo pacto non oritur nascitur actio.* No action arises on a contract without a consideration. *Nemo jus sibi dicere potest.* No one can declare the law for himself.

ENFRANCHISE, *verb*   *accipere,* admit to citizenship, *adsciscere,* affranchise, allow, authorize, disenthrall, emancipate, empower, endow with political privilege, franchise, free, free from political disabilities, give liberty to, give political privileges to, give the right to vote, grant, liberate, license, manumit, permit, permit to vote, qualify, *recipere,* release, restore to liberty, sanction, set at liberty, set free

ENGAGE *(Hire), verb*   appoint, arrange for the services of, arrange for the use of, bind, book, charter, commission, *conducere,* contract for, employ, enlist, enlist in one's service, fill a position, give a job to, give a situation to, give employment to, lease, let, obtain, procure, put to work, put under contract, reserve, retain, secure, set to work, staff with, take into one's employ, take into service
ASSOCIATED CONCEPTS: engage the services of an employee

ENGAGE *(Involve), verb*   absorb, assail, associate, attack, battle, become involved, bring into conflict, busy, carry on hostilities, combat, compete, connect, contend, contest, draw in, encounter, engross, enmesh, entangle, enter into, enter into conflict with, entertain, fight with, fill one's time, gear with, hold the interest of, *incipere,* interest, interlock, join battle with, link, meet, mesh together, occupy, oppose, partake, participate, share, struggle, take on, take part, tangle, undertake, wage war, war with
ASSOCIATED CONCEPTS: doing business, engaged in agriculture, engaged in commerce, engaged in doing business, engaged in interstate commerce, engaged in manufacture, engaged in transacting business, primarily engaged, principally engaged

ENGENDER, *verb*   author, be the cause of, bear, beget, breed, bring about, bring forth, bring into being, bring into existence, call forth, call into being, cause, cause to exist, create, develop, effect, effectuate, excite, execute, furnish, *generare,* generate, *gignere,* give rise to, hatch, incite, induce, lead to, manufacture, occasion, originate, plant, produce, spawn, stir up, yield

ENHANCE, *verb*   add to, advance in value, aggrandize, *amplificare,* amplify, appreciate, *augere,* augment, better, boost, brighten, cultivate, deepen, develop, elaborate, elevate, emphasize, enlarge, enrich, escalate, exaggerate, expand, extend, heighten, improve, increase the value of, intensify, lift, magnify, make better, make improvements, make more attractive, make more valuable, maximize, perfect, polish, promote, raise, refine, reinforce, retouch, sharpen, strengthen, touch up, upgrade, uplift, upraise
ASSOCIATED CONCEPTS: enhanced in value

ENIGMA, *noun*   *aenigma, ambages,* ambiguous saying, arcanum, bewilderment, braintwister, complexity, confusing statement, confusion, difficulty, inexplicable statement, inscrutable person, knotty point, mystery, obscure question, obscure statement, paradox, perplexity, poser, problem, puzzle, puzzling problem, question, riddle, secret, stumper, teaser

ENIGMATIC, *adjective*   ambiguous, baffling, bewildering, bothering, confounding, confusing, conjectural, cryptic, disconcerting, esoteric, hard to understand, hidden, inexplicable, mysterious, mystifying, nebulous, obscure, of hidden meaning, perplexing, perturbing, puzzling, secret, veiled

ENJOIN, *verb*   abate, ban, bar, barricade, bid, block, blockade, bring to a standstill, cause to halt, charge, command, constrain, curb, decree, dictate, direct, disallow, disapprove, discountenance, embargo, exact, exhort, foil, forbid, forbid by law, forestall, frustrate, give orders, hamper, hinder, hold in check, impede, impose, impose a ban, impose a duty, impose a task, impose with authority, inhibit, insist on, instruct, interdict, issue an order, keep from happening, keep in bounds, lay under embargo, limit, make unlawful, not countenance, not permit, oblige, order, place under interdiction, place under the ban, positively direct, preclude, prevent, prohibit, prohibit by legal injunction, prompt, proscribe, put a stop to, put an end to, put under an injunction, put under an interdiction, put under embargo, put under the ban, quash, quell, repress, require, restrain, restrain by injunction, restrict, retard, rule, stem, stop, suppress, thwart
ASSOCIATED CONCEPTS: permanent injunction, preliminary injunction, temporary injunction

ENJOYMENT *(Pleasure), noun*   amusement, bliss, delectation, delight, diversion, ecstasy, entertainment, exhilaration, *fructus,* gaiety, *gaudium,* gratification, gusto, merriment, recreation, refreshment, rejoicing, relaxation, relish, satisfaction, thrill, treat, zest
FOREIGN PHRASES: *Omnis privatio praesupponit habitum.* Every privation presupposes a former enjoyment.

ENJOYMENT *(Use), noun*   avail, disposal, employment, habitation, occupancy, occupation, ownership, possession, prerogative, proprietorship, retention, seisin, tenancy, tenure, usuage, utilization
ASSOCIATED CONCEPTS: adverse enjoyment, covenant of quiet enjoyment

ENLARGE, *verb*   add to, aggrandize, *amplificare,* amplify, annex, *augere,* augment, broaden, build, build up, develop, *dilatare,* dilate, distend, elaborate, enhance, escalate, exaggerate, expatiate, extend, fatten, fill out, grow, increase, inflate, intensify, lengthen,

magnify, make greater, make larger, multiply, progress, protract, raise, spread, stretch, supplement, swell, widen
ASSOCIATED CONCEPTS: materially alter, repair

ENLIGHTEN, *verb*   account for, acquaint, apprise, clarify, disclose, divulge, edify, educate, elucidate, enable to comprehend, enable to see, enucleate, explain, explicate, expound, free from ignorance, free from prejudice, free from superstition, give reason for, illuminate, illumine, illustrate, impart, inform, *inluminare, inlustrare,* instruct, interpret, make aware, make clear, make known, notify, report, reveal, shed light upon, simplify, spell out, teach, tutor

ENROLL, *verb*   accept as a member, *adscribere,* book, catalogue, docket, draft, enlist, enter, enter on a list, enter on a record, enter on a register, file, induct, initiate, inscribe, join, list, make a member, make a record, record, recruit, register, sign up, subscribe

ENSCONCE, *verb*   blanket, camouflage, cloak, cloud, conceal, cover, cover up, curtain, disguise, eclipse, encase, enclose, enshield, enshroud, envelop, enwrap, guard, hide, hide away, hide from view, hide securely, keep from danger, keep guarded, keep hidden, keep safe, keep secret, keep under cover, mask, obscure, preserve, protect, safeguard, screen, seclude, secrete, secure, shade, shadow, sheathe, shelter, shield, shroud, suppress, veil, watch over, wrap

ENSHROUD, *verb*   blanket, camouflage, case, cloak, cloud, conceal, cover, curtain, disguise, eclipse, encase, enclose, ensconce, envelop, enwrap, guard, hide, hood, invest, keep clandestine, keep from notice, keep from view, keep hidden, keep out of sight, keep under cover, mantle, mask, obscure, obstruct the view of, prevent from being discovered, prevent from being seen, protect, render invisible, screen, seclude, secrete, shade, sheathe, shelter, shield, shroud, surround, swathe, veil, visor, wrap

ENSNARE, *verb*   allure, ambuscade, ambush, apprehend, bait, bamboozle, beguile, bilk, bluff, *capere,* capture, catch, catch unprepared, cheat, cozen, deceive, decoy, defraud, delude, dupe, enmesh, entangle, entice, entrap, fool, gull, hoax, hoodwink, hook, *inlicere, inretire,* lay a trap for, lead astray, lead on by artifice, lure, misdirect, misguide, mislead, net, outmaneuver, outwit, play one false, set a trap for, snare, take advantage of, take by craft, take by strategem, trap, trepan, trick, victimize, waylay
ASSOCIATED CONCEPTS: entrapment

ENSUE, *verb*   arise, attend as consequence, be caused by, be due to, be subsequent, be the effect of, come after, come afterward, come next, derive, develop, eventuate, flow, follow, follow as a consequence, follow in a train of events, grow out of, issue, occur, proceed, result, spring, succeed, supervene, transpire

ENSUING, *adjective*   after, following, later, next, posterior, resultant, resulting, subsequent, succeeding, successive, sequential

ENSURE, *verb*   ascertain, assure, certify, check, clinch, confirm, corroborate, dismiss doubt, endorse, give security, give surety, guarantee, indemnify against loss, insure, keep from harm, keep safe, make certain, make sure, offer collateral, promise, protect, safeguard, secure, underwrite, verify, warrant

ENTAIL, *verb* *adferre,* call for, demand, force, impel, include as a necessary consequence, *inferre,* involve, make essential, make incumbent, make inescapable, make necessary, make requisite, make unavoidable, necessitate, need, obligate, occasion, require

ENTANGLEMENT *(Confusion),* **noun** agitation, chaos, commotion, complexity, complication, confusedness, derangement, disarrangement, disarry, disorder, disorganization, embroilment, enmeshment, ferment, imbroglio, intricacy, irregularity, jumble, maze, mixup, snag, snarl, tumult

ENTANGLEMENT *(Involvement),* **noun** dilemma, entrapment, fix, *implicatio,* implication, incrimination, inculpation, predicament, scrape, strait

ENTER *(Go in),* **verb** arrive, board, come in, cross the threshold, effect an entrance, gain admittance, gain entry, go into, *inire, intrare, introire,* make an entrance, pass into, set foot in, step in, walk in
ASSOCIATED CONCEPTS: breaking and entering, forcible entry, immigration, lawful entry, open and peaceable entry, trespass

ENTER *(Insert),* **verb** implant, infuse, inject, intercalate, interject, interpose, introduce, intromit, place into, put in, stick in

ENTER *(Penetrate),* **verb** bore, cut into, cut through, drill, empierce, gore, impale, infiltrate, interpenetrate, invade, lance, perforate, pervade, pierce, prick, puncture, sink into, stab, transpierce

ENTER *(Record),* **verb** catalogue, check in, chronicle, enroll, file, inscribe, inscroll, jot down, list, log, make an entry, mark down, note, place in the record, post, put down, put in writing, put on record, *referre,* register, report, set down, tabulate, take down, transcribe, write down, write in
ASSOCIATED CONCEPTS: entered on the record, entry of a judgment

ENTERPRISE *(Economic organization),* **noun** business, business establishment, commercial establishment, company, concern, corporate body, corporation, firm, house, industry, syndicate
ASSOCIATED CONCEPTS: commercial enterprise, free enterprise, private enterprise

ENTERPRISE *(Undertaking),* **noun** activity, adventure, attempt, campaign, cause, effort, endeavor, engagement, *inceptum,* job, occupation, operation, *opus,* plan, program, project, pursuit, scheme, task, undertaking, venture
ASSOCIATED CONCEPTS: mutual enterprise

ENTICE, *verb* allure, bait, cajole, coax, decoy, divert, induce, inveigh, lure, seduce, tempt

ENTIRETY, *noun* accumulation, aggregate, all, amount, assemblage, collectiveness, collectivity, completeness, completion, comprehensiveness, congeries, ensemble, entire amount, entireness, everything, exhaustiveness, fullness, gross, gross amount, inclusiveness, indiscerptibility, indiscerptibleness, intactness,

lot, lump, mass, sum, total, totality, totalness, *totus,* undiminished quantity, undividedness, whole, wholeness
ASSOCIATED CONCEPTS: entirety clause, tenants by the entirety, tenants in common

ENTITLED, *adjective* allowed, authorized, deserved, deserving, desirable, due, earned, eligible, empowered, fit, having the right, justified, labeled, legalized, licensed, merited, ordained, permitted, privileged, qualified, sanctioned, suitable, warranted, worthy

ENTITY, *noun* actuality, being, body, character, corpus, creature, embodiment, existence, individual, item, life, living thing, matter, module, object, oneness, organism, separate existence, single item, single piece, specimen, tangible object, unit, unit of being
ASSOCIATED CONCEPTS: corporate entity, distinct entity, legal entity, separate entity

ENTRANCE, *noun* access, adit, *aditus,* admission, anteroom, approach, door, entry, entryway, foyer, gangway, gate, gateway, illapse, infiltration, influx, ingress, inlet, inroad, insertion, introgression, *introitus,* invasion, lobby, means of access, means of entering, mouth, opening, *ostium,* passage, passageway, penetration, place of entry, portal, reception, threshold, vestibule, way in
ASSOCIATED CONCEPTS: forcible entrance, public entrance

ENTRAP, *verb* allure, bait, beckon, befool, beguile, bring unawares into danger, bring unawares into evil, *capere,* catch, catch by artifice, deceive, decoy, draw as by a lure, draw by artful inducements, draw in, dupe, enmesh, ensnare, entangle, entice, fool, hold out allurement, hold out temptation, *inlicere, inretire,* inveigle, lay a snare for, lay a trap for, lead astray, lead by inducement, lead into danger by artifice, lead into temptation, lead on, lure, lure into a compromising act, set a snare for, set a trap for, snare, take in, tempt, trap, trip up
ASSOCIATED CONCEPTS: predisposition to commit a crime

ENTREATY, *noun* adjuration, appeal, beseechment, call, cry, earnest request, impetration, imploration, importunity, invocation, *obsecratio,* obsecration, *obtestatio,* petition, plea, prayer, *preces,* request, solicitation, suit, supplication

ENTRUST, *verb* appoint, assign, assign the care of, authorize, charge with a duty, charge with a trust, commit, *committere, concredere,* consign, delegate, depute, deputize, devolve, elect, empower, give a mandate, give a responsibility to, invest empower, license, make someone guardian of, *mandare,* place in the protection of, put in charge, trust, turn over for safekeeping
ASSOCIATED CONCEPTS: entrust goods, entrust personal property
FOREIGN PHRASES: *Securius expediuntur negotia commissa pluribus, et plus vident oculi quam oculus.* Matters which are entrusted to several persons are executed more surely, because eyes see more than an eye.

ENTRY *(Entrance),* **noun** access, adit, admission, entrance, immigration, ingress, ingression, passage
ASSOCIATED CONCEPTS: entry on land, forcible entry, lawful entry, trespass

ENTRY *(Record)*, **noun** account, bulletin, chronicle, deposition, file, information preserved in writing, inscription, item, memo, memorandum, minute, *nomen,* note, recorded item, registration, report, statement recorded in a book, writing, written record

ASSOCIATED CONCEPTS: entry by court, entry in regular course of business, entry of an appeal, entry of an appearance, entry of an order, entry of judgment, writ of entry

ENUMERATE, verb be specific, catalog, count, designate, detail, differentiate, enroll, *enumerare,* index, inventory, itemize, keep count, list, make a list, mention, mention one by one, mention specifically, name expressly, name one by one, number, numerate, point out, specify, tabulate

ASSOCIATED CONCEPTS: descriptive enumeration, enumerated counts, enumerated motions

FOREIGN PHRASES: *Enumeratio infirmat regulam in casibus non enumeratis.* Enumeration disaffirms the rule in cases which are not enumerated.

ENUNCIATE, verb accent, affirm, announce, annunciate, apprise, articulate, assert, asseverate, aver, declaim, declare, *edicere,* emit, enounce, explain, express, give expression, give utterance, *indicare,* inform, intonate, intone, make an announcement, mouth, notify, phonate, proclaim, profess, promulgate, pronounce, pronounce distinctly, pronounce in a distinct manner, *pronuntiare,* publish, put in words, say, speak, speak clearly, state, stress, tell, utter, verbalize, vocalize, voice

ENVELOP, verb beleaguer, beseige, beset, blanket, box, cage, *circumfundere,* circumscribe, cloak, cloister, close in, compass, conceal, confine, corral, cover, curtain, edge, embox, embrace, encapsulate, encase, encircle, enclose, encompass, enfold, enshroud, ensphere, environ, enwrap, fence in, frame, go around, hedge in, hem in, hide, *involvere,* mask, *obducere,* obscure, protect, screen, sheathe, shield, shroud, surround, swaddle, swathe, veil, wall in, wrap, wrap around

ENVIRONMENT, noun atmosphere, aura, circumstances, context, environs, locality, milieu, situation, surroundings

EPHEMERAL, adjective *brevis,* brief, caducous, *caducus,* continuing for a short time, deciduous, disappearing, elusive, enduring only a very short time, ephemerous, evanescent, existing for a short time, fleeting, fugacious, fugitive, hurried, impermanent, lasting a very short time, meteoric, meteorical, momentary, mortal, nondurable, not lasting, passing, perishable, short, short-lived, temporal, temporary, transient, transitory, unenduring, *unius diei,* unstable, vanishing, volatile

EPITOME, noun characteristic part, core, embodiment, essence, exemplification, model, representative, standard, *summarium,* typical component, typical part, typification

EQUAL, adjective abreast, *aequalis, aequus,* alike, balanced, coequal, coextensive, coordinate, democratic, equable, equalized, equally divided, equidistant, equilateral, equipollent, equitable, even, evenhanded, fair, fair-minded, homologous, identical in amount, identical in quantity, identical in size, identical in value, impartial, just, like, like in degree, like in quantity, matched, of the same degree, of the same rank, on a par, on even terms, on the same level, same, similar, symmetric, symmetrical, tantamount, tied, to the same degree, unbiased, unchanging, undeviating, unfluctuating, uniform, unprejudiced, unvaried, unvarying

ASSOCIATED CONCEPTS: equal before the law, equal in degree, equal in value, equal protection of laws, equal taxation, equally divided, separate but equal

EQUIPMENT, noun accouterment, apparatus, appointment, material, provisioning, supplies

ASSOCIATED CONCEPTS: equipment trust agreement, equipment trust certificate

EQUIPOISE, noun balance, counterbalance, counterpoise, counterweight, equal distribution of weight, equality of force, equality of weight, equilibration, equilibrium, equiponderance, even balance, evenness, match, offset, parity, stability, symmetry

EQUITABLE, adjective *aequus,* deserved, detached, disinterested, dispassionate, distributing justice, equal, evenhanded, exhibiting equity, existing in equity, fair, fair-minded, giving each his due, honest, honorable, impartial, incorrupt, incorruptible, *iustus,* just, merited, *meritus,* neutral, objective, principled, proper, reasonable, right, righteous, scrupulous, unbiased, unbigoted, unchallengeable, unprejudiced, upright

ASSOCIATED CONCEPTS: equitable assignment, equitable charge, equitable claim, equitable conversion, equitable counterclaim, equitable defenses, equitable estate, equitable estoppel, equitable interest, equitable lien, equitable life estate, equitable mortgage, equitable rate of interest, equitable recission, equitable recoupment, equitable relief, equitable remedy, equitable rights, equitable set-off, equitable title, fair and equitable value

EQUITY *(Justice)*, **noun** *aequitas, aequum,* chancery, evenhandedness, fair-mindedness, fair treatment, fairness, honesty, ideal justice, impartial justice, *iustitia,* justice, justice as distinguished from conformity to enactments or statutes, justice ascertained by natural reason, justice under the law, justness, natural right, quality of being equal and fair, reasonableness, recourse to the principles of natural justice, redress, remedial justice, right dealing, righteousness, rightfulness, spirit of the law, unwritten law, uprightness

ASSOCIATED CONCEPTS: balance of equities, chancery, equitable right, equity action, equity jurisdiction, existing equities, suit in equity

FOREIGN PHRASES: *Nihil tam conveniens est naturali aequitati quam unumquodque dissolvi eo ligamine quo ligatum est.* Nothing is so agreeable to natural equity as that a thing should be dissolved by the same means by which it was bound. *Lex aequitate gaudet; appetit perfectum; est norma recti.* The law delights in equity; it grasps at perfection; it is a rule of right. *In fictione juris semper aequitas existit.* In a fiction of law, equity is always present. *Equitas sequitur legem.* Equity follows the law. *Lex respicit aequitatem.* The law regards equity. *Ratio in jure aequitas integra.* Reason in law is impartial equity. *Nulli vendemus, nulli negabimus, aut differemus rectum vel justitian.* We will sell to none, we will deny to none, we will delay to none, either equity or justice. *Judex ante oculos aequitatem semper habere debet.* A judge ought always to have equity before his eyes. *Aequitas supervacua odit.* Equity abhors superfluous things. *Aequitas uxoribus, liberis, creditoribus maxime favet.* Equity favors wives and children, creditors most of all. *Aequitas est quasi aequalitas.* Equity is as it were equality. *Aequum et bonum est lex legum.* That which is equitable and right is the law of laws. *In omnibus quidem, maxime tamen injure, aequitas spectanda sit.* In all matters, but especially in law, equity should be regarded. *Prima pars aequitatis aequalitas.* The prime element of equity is equality. *Nemo allegans suam turpitudinem audien dus est.* No one should be permitted to testify as a witness to his own baseness or wickedness. *Nemo ex suo delicto meliorem suam conditionem facere potest.* No one can improve his condition by his own misdeed. *Jure naturae aequum est neminem cum alterius detrimento et injuria fieri locupletiorem.* According to the laws of nature, it is just that no one should be enriched by the detriment and injury of another. *Nihil iniquius quam aequitatem nimis intendere.* Nothing is more unjust than to extend equity too far. *Judex aequitatem semper spectare debet.* A judge ought always to regard equity. *Bonus judex secundum aequum et bonum judicat, et aequitatem stricto juri praefert.* Good judges decide according to what is just and right, and prefer equity to strict law. *Si aliquid ex solemnibus deficiat, cum aequitas poscit, subveniendum est.* If anything is deficient in formal requisites, where equity requires it, it should be supplied. *Aequitas nunquam contravenit legis.* Equity never counteracts the laws. *Aequitas non facit jus, sed juri auxiliatur.* Equity does not make law, but assists law. *Aequitas ignorantiae opitulatur, oscitantiae non item.* Equity assists ignorance, but not carelessness. *Vigilantibus et non dormientibus jura subveniunt.* The laws aid the vigilant and not those who slumber. *Aequitas agit in personam.* Equity acts upon the person. *Jure naturae aequum est neminem cum alterius detrimento et injuria fieri locupletiorem.* By natural law it is not just that any one should be enriched by the detriment or injury of another. *Hoc quidem perquam durum est, sed ita lex scripta est.* This indeed is exceedingly hard, but such is the written law. *Nemo debet aliena jactura locupletari.* No one ought to gain by another's loss. *Frustra legis auxilium quaerit qui in legem committit.* He vainly seeks the aid of the law who transgresses the law. *Commodum ex injuria sua non habere debet.* No person ought to derive any advantage by his own wrong. *Nemo ex proprio dolo consequitur actionem.* No one acquires a right of action from his own fraud.

EQUITY *(Share of ownership),* **noun** allotment, apportionment, claim, division, interest, investment, part, portion, right, stake, vested interest

EQUIVALENT, *adjective* alike, as good as, balancing, coequal, comparable, compensatory, equal, equal in effect, equal in force, equal in power, equal in significance, equal in value, equalized, equipollent, even, identical, identical in size, identical in value, interchangeable, like, of equal force, of equal value, of equal weight, on a par with, parallel, *pro re valere,* reciprocal, same, similar, substitutable, synonymous, tantamount, without difference
ASSOCIATED CONCEPTS: equivalent acts, fair equivalent, substantially equivalent

EQUIVOCAL, *adjective* ambiguous, *ambiguus,* ambivalent, amphibological, amphibolous, *anceps,* bewildering, cloudy, confusing, controversial, debatable, deceptive, dim, disputable, doubtful, dubious, *dubius,* enigmatic, enigmatical, equivocating, equivocatory, hard to understand, hazy, imperspicuous, imprecise, indecisive, indefinite, indeterminate, misleading, moot, nebulous, obscure, of doubtful meaning, of uncertain significance, open, open to question, perplexing, possessing double meaning, prevaricating, puzzling, questionable, recondite, shadowy, uncertain, unclarified, unclear, undecided, undefined, undetermined, unexplained, unintelligible, unplain, unresolved, unsolved, unsure, untransparent, vague, veiled
FOREIGN PHRASES: *Verba aequivoca, ac in dubio sensu posita, intelliguntur digniori et potentiori sensu.* Equivocal words and those which are used in a doubtful sense are to be understood in their more worthy and effective sense.

EQUIVOCATE, *verb* avoid a straight answer, be ambiguous, be false, be unclear, be untruthful, be vague, deceive, disguise, dissemble, dissimulate, dodge, elude, evade, fence, hedge, lie, misguide, misinform, mislead, misrepresent, misstate, mystify, palter, parry, prevaricate, quibble, shift, shuffle, *tergiversari,* tergiversate

ERADICATE, *verb* abolish, annihilate, annul, black out, blot out, cause to cease, deal destruction, delete, demolish, deracinate, destroy, destroy thoroughly, displace, dispose of, dissolve, do away with, do away with completely, efface, eject, eliminate, *eradere,* erase, *evellere, excidere,* expunge, expurgate, *exstirpare,* exterminate, extinguish, extirpate, extract, lay waste, leave no trace of, leave no vestige of, liquidate, obliterate, purge, remove, remove utterly, stamp out, strike out, subtract, sweep away, unroot, uproot, void, weed out

ERODE, *verb* abrade, break down, consume, decay, decrease, deteriorate, diminish, disintegrate, dissolve, file, gradually eat away, grind, lessen, lose, make thin, rasp, recede, reduce, rub away, scrape, shrink, strip, waste, weaken, wear, wear away, wear down, wear down by friction, weather
ASSOCIATED CONCEPTS: erode the credibility of a witness

EROSION, *noun* abrasion, attrition, breakdown, consumption, crumbling, decay, decrease, decrement, deterioration, detrition, diminishment, diminution, disappearance, disintegration, dissolution, gradual eating away, gradual wearing away, grinding, lessening, loss, recession, reduction, rubbing away, shrinkage, thinning out, waste, wear, wearing away, wearing down by friction

ERR, *verb* be deceived, be erroneous, be in the wrong, be misguided, be misled, be mistaken, blunder, cause error, commit an error, delude oneself, *errare,* fall into error, *falli,* go amiss, go astray, go wrong, labor under a misapprehension, make a mistake, misapprehend, miscalculate, miscompute, misconstrue, misinterpret, misjudge, misreckon, mistake, misunderstand, receive a false impression, slip, *vagari*

ERRANT, *adjective* aberrant, amiss, astray, at fault, awry, deviant, deviating, deviatory, erring, erroneous, fallacious, faultful, faulty, imperfect, incorrect, misdirected, mistaken, not right, peccant, wrong

ERRONEOUS, *adjective*   aberrant, amiss, blundering, containing error, counterfeit, devoid of truth, erring, fallacious, false, *falsus,* faulty, fictitious, groundless, illogical, inaccurate, incorrect, inexact, mistaken, spurious, unfounded, ungrounded, unreal, unsound, unsubstantial, unsustainable, untrue, wrong
ASSOCIATED CONCEPTS: erroneous assessment, erroneous decision, erroneous judgment, erroneous law, erroneous order, erroneous tax

ERROR, *noun*   aberrance, aberrancy, aberration, corrigendum, delusion, deviation, distorted conception, distortion, *erratum,* erroneous statement, *error,* false conception, false impression, fault, flaw, inaccuracy, incorrect belief, inexactness, injustice, lapse, malapropism, misbelief, miscalculation, miscarriage of justice, miscomputation, misconception, misconjecture, miscount, misguidance, misinterpretation, misjudgment, misprint, misreckoning, misstatement, mistake, mistaken belief, mistaken judgment, mistranslation, misunderstanding, misuse of words, oversight, *peccatum,* poor judgment, slip, unfactualness, wrong course, wrong impression, wrongness
ASSOCIATED CONCEPTS: assignment of error, clerical error, confession of error, coram nobis, cross-errors, error apparent on the record, error of fact, error of judgment, error of law, fatal errors, fundamental error, harmful error, immaterial error, judicial error, legal error, manifest error, obvious error, plain error, prejudicial error, presentation of error, reversible error, substantial error, technical error, writ of error
FOREIGN PHRASES: *De fide et officio judicis non recipitur quaestio, sed de scientia, sive sit error juris, sive facti.* The good faith and honesty of a judge are not to be questioned, but his knowledge, whether it be in error of law or fact, may be. *Praesentia corporis tollit errorem nominis; et veritas nominis tollit er rorem demonstrationis.* The presence of the body cures an error in the name; and the accuracy of the name cures an error of description. *Veritas nominis tollit errorem demonstrationis.* Correctness of the name cures error in the description. *Veritas demonstrationis tollit errorem nominis.* Correctness of the description cures the error of the name. *Error qui non resistitur approbatur.* An error which is not resisted or opposed is waived. *Error fucatus nuda veritate in multis est probabilior; et saepenumero rationibus vincit veritatem error.* Error artfully disguised is, in many instances, more probable than naked truth; and frequently error overwhelms truth by argumentation. *Non videntur qui errant consentire.* Those who err are not deemed to consent. *Falsa orthographia, sive falsa grammatica, non vitiat concessionem.* Bad spelling or grammar does not vitiate a deed. *Vitium clerici nocere non debet.* Clerical errors ought not to prejudice. *Communis error facit jus.* Common error makes the law. *Tutius erratur ex parte mitiori.* It is safer to err on the side of leniency. *In generalibus versatur error.* Error thrives on generalities. *Error juris nocet.* An error of law works an injury. *Nihil facit error nominis cum de corpore constat.* An error in the name is of no consequence when there is certainty as to the person. *Tutius semper est errare acquietando, quam in puniendo; ex parte miseric ordiae quam ex parte justitiae.* It is always safer to err in acquitting than in punishing; on the side of mercy

rather than on the side of justice. *Negatio conclusionis est error in lege.* The denial of a conclusion is error in law. *Errores ad sua principia referre, est refellere.* To refer errors to their sources is to refute them.

ESCAPE, *verb*   abscond, achieve liberty, avoid, avoid arrest, avoid capture, avoid peril, become free, bolt, break from prison, break loose, break out, circumvent, decamp, depart custody, depart unlawfully, desert, disappear, *elabi,* elude, evade, *evadere,* find freedom, flee, *fugere,* gain liberty, get to safety, levant, make a getaway, run away, slip away, sneak off, steal away, take flight
ASSOCIATED CONCEPTS: extradition, flight, forcible escape

ESCHEAT, *verb*   be forfeited back, cede back, go back, *hereditas caduca,* obstruct the course of descent, recede, regress, relapse, retrocede, retrovert, return, reverse, revert, revert to the state, slip back, turn back
ASSOCIATED CONCEPTS: forfeiture

ESCHEATMENT, *noun*   act of reverting, confiscation, conversion to the government, deprivation, descent by forfeiture, forfeiture, reversion to the government, reversion to the state

ESCHEW, *verb*   abstain, avoid, back away from, boycott, bypass, deny oneself, do without, elude, evade, flee from, forbear, forswear, give a wide berth, have nothing to do with, keep at a distance, keep away, keep clear of, keep out of the way, make unwelcome, neglect, recoil from, refrain, reject, shrink from, shun, stand aloof, stand clear, turn aside, turn away from, *vitare,* withdraw from

ESCROW, *noun*   conditional deed held in trust, conditional instrument, contingent deed held in trust, entrustment, instrument held until the performance of a condition, written instrument of contingency

ESOTERIC, *adjective*   abstruse, acroamatic, acroamatical, acroatic, arcane, cabalistic, cabalistical, concealed, confidential, confined to a select circle, covert, cryptic, deep, designed for the initiated, difficult to comprehend, enigmatic, enigmatical, esoterical, for a select few, hidden, involved, mysterious, mystic, mystical, obscure, occult, private, profound, puzzling, recondite, secret, shrouded, shrouded in mystery, understood by a select few, understood by the initiated, undisclosed, undivulged, untold, veiled

ESPIONAGE, *noun*   espial, intelligence, obtaining national defense secrets, obtaining of classified information, practice of spying on others, search made for useful military information, secret observation, secret watching, spying, subversive activity, surveillance, systematic secret observation of the words and conduct of others, undercover work
ASSOCIATED CONCEPTS: espionage act, treason

ESPOUSE, *verb*   abet, accept, adopt, advocate, aid, ally, argue for, assist, associate with, back, become a participator, become a partisan, champion, choose, contribute to, cooperate, defend, embrace, endorse, enter into, favor, help, join, lend oneself to, opt, participate, side with, sponsor, stand behind, stand up for, subscribe to, support, take part in, take up, uphold

ESQUIRE, *noun*   adviser, advocate, *armiger,* attorney, attorney-at-law, barrister, counsel, counselor, counselor-at-law, jurisconsult, jurisprudent, jurist, lawyer, legal adviser, legal practitioner, legist, member of the bar, member of the legal profession, officer of the court, practitioner, solicitor
ASSOCIATED CONCEPTS: advice of counsel, assigned counsel, assistance of counsel, attorney of record, attorney's fees, benefit of counsel, Code of Professional Responsibility, counsel of record, denial of counsel, effective counsel, of counsel, Sixth Amendment, waiver of counsel

ESSENCE, *noun*   basic part, core, embodiment, essential part, fundamental part, gist, heart, hypostasis, inmost nature, inner being, meaning, *natura,* nature, pith, quiddity, quintessence, soul, substance, *vis*
ASSOCIATED CONCEPTS: essence of a contract, essence of testimony by a witness

ESSENTIAL *(Inherent),* **adjective**   basal, basic, basilar, basilary, elemental, fundamental, immanent, implicit, integral, intrinsic, intrinsical, main, primary

ESSENTIAL *(Required),* **adjective**   basic, binding, called for, chief, compulsory, critical, crucial, demanded, exigent, fundamental, important, incumbent upon, indispensable, lacking, mandatory, material, necessary, needed, needful, obligatory, of vital importance, pressing, primary, *proprius,* requisite, urgent, *verus*
ASSOCIATED CONCEPTS: essential duties, essential governmental duties, essential parties, essential services, essential terms of a contract

ESTABLISH *(Entrench),* **verb**   cause to endure, *confirmare,* fix deeply, fix permanently, implant firmly, ingrain, make durable, make firm, make lasting, make permanent, make stable, make steadfast, perpetuate, plant, put on a firm basis, root, situate, solidify, *stabilire,* stabilitate, stabilize, steady, strengthen

ESTABLISH *(Launch),* **verb**   begin, bring about, bring into being, bring into existence, build, charter, *constituere,* constitute, construct, create, develop, form, found, give rise to, inaugurate, inchoate, initiate, *instituere,* institute, introduce, lay the foundations, open, organize, originate, prepare, put in motion, set going, set in operation, set up, start, *statuere*
FOREIGN PHRASES: *Cujus est instituere, ejus est abrogare.* Whoever may institute, his right it is to abrogate.

ESTABLISH *(Show),* **verb**   ascertain, attest, authenticate, certify, circumstantiate, cite evidence, confirm, corroborate, demonstrate, document, manifest, *probare,* prove, substantiate, testify to, uphold, uphold in evidence, validate, verify, *vincere*
ASSOCIATED CONCEPTS: conclusively establish, establish beyond a reasonable doubt, establish by a fair preponderance of the credible evidence, establish to a clear certainty, established by law, legally established

ESTATE *(Hereditament),* **noun**   bequest, birthright, devise, gift by succession, heritage, heritance, inheritance, legacy, patrimony
ASSOCIATED CONCEPTS: beneficial estate, charge against an estate, claim against an estate, distribution, estate tax, residue

ESTATE *(Property),* **noun**   acres, *ager,* assets, assets and liabilities, belongings, chattels, chattels real, chose in action, collective assets, earthly possessions, effects, equity, freehold, goods, grounds, hereditament, holdings, intangible assets, interest in land, land and buildings, lands, liquid assets, material assets, material things which are owned, personalty, piece of landed property, *possessio,* possessions, real estate, realty, resources, right, title and interest in land, tangible assets, tangibles, tenement, territory, valuables, *villa*
ASSOCIATED CONCEPTS: absolute estate, conditional estate, defeasible estate, equitable estate, estate at sufferance, estate at will, estate by entirety, estate by purchase, estate for life, estate for years, estate from period to period, estate from year to year, estate in common, estate in expectancy, estate in land, estate in remainder, estate in reversion, estate lands, estate on a conditional limitation, estate pour autre vie, estate tail, estate upon a limitation, executory estate, fee-simple estate, fee-tail estate, forfeiture of an estate, freehold, joint estate, landed estate, life estate, limited estate, next eventual estate, qualified estate, vested estate
FOREIGN PHRASES: *Post executionem status lex non patitur possibilitatem.* After the execution of the estate the law suffers not a possibility.

ESTIMATE *(Approximate cost),* **noun**   admeasurement, *aestimatio,* appraisal, appraisement, approximate calculation, approximate judgment of value, approximate value, approximation, assessment, calculation, charge, computation, considered guess, educated guess, estimation, evaluation, gauge, market price, measurement, quotation, rate, rating, reckoning, rough calculation, rough guess, statement of the costs, valuation, value, worth
ASSOCIATED CONCEPTS: fraudulent estimates

ESTIMATE *(Idea),* **noun**   assumption, belief, conjecture, consideration, deduction, determination, guess, guesswork, impression, *iudicium,* judgment, observation, opinion, perception, personal judgment, reaction, reckoning, speculation, supposal, supposition, surmisal, surmise, understanding, view

ESTIMATE, *verb*   *aestimare,* appraise, budget, calculate approximately, *censere,* conjecture, evaluate, figure, figure costs, form an opinion, gauge, give an approximate value, guess, judge, place a value on, put an approximate price on, rank, rate, reckon, set a price on, set a value on, suppose, survey, value, weigh
ASSOCIATED CONCEPTS: estimate tax, estimated cash value, estimated cost, estimated revenue, final estimate

ESTIMATION *(Calculation),* **noun**   admeasurement, appraisal, appraisement, approximate calculation, approximate judgment of value, approximation, assessment, assumption, computation, conjecture, considered guess, deduction, educated guess, estimate, evaluation, gauge, guess, guesswork, judgment, measurement, mensuration, opinion, rating, reckoning, rough calculation, rough guess, speculation, supposal, supposition, surmisal, surmise, valuation, weighing

ESTIMATION *(Esteem),* **noun**   admiration, appreciation, approbation, approval, commendation, credit, deference, favor, favorable opinion, favorable recognition, favorable repute, fondness, good opinion, good reputation, good standing, high opinion, high regard, homage, honor, praise, regard, respect, reverence, veneration

ESTOP, *verb*   avert, ban, bar, barricade, bind, block the way, block up, blockade, bring to a stop, create a stoppage, cut off, encumber, fend off, forbid, forestall, halt, hamper, handicap, hinder, impede, inhibit, interfere, interrupt, intervene, not allow, obstruct, obviate, preclude, prevent, prohibit, put a stop to, put an end to, restrain, restrict, shackle, stand in the way, stay, stop, stop the progress of, stop the way, stymie, thwart, turn aside, ward off
ASSOCIATED CONCEPTS: change in position

ESTOPPEL, *noun*   ban, bar, bar to an allegation, barrier, barring, blockage, disallowance, forbiddance, hindrance, impediment, inhibition, legal restraint, obstruction, preclusion, preclusion by act, preclusion by conduct, prohibition, restraint, restriction
ASSOCIATED CONCEPTS: agency by estoppel, collateral estoppel, equitable estoppel, estoppel by concealment, estoppel by conduct, estoppel by deed, estoppel by judgment, estoppel by laches, estoppel by matter in pais, estoppel by matter of accord, estoppel by recital, estoppel by record, estoppel by silence, estoppel by suppression, estoppel by verdict, estoppel letter, judicial estoppel, partnership by estoppel, ratification, stare decisis, waiver
FOREIGN PHRASES: *Nemo contra factum suum venire potest.* No man can contradict his own act or deed. *Un ne doit prise advantage de son tort demesne.* One ought not to take advantage of his own wrong.

ESTRANGE, *verb*   *abalienare,* alienate, avoid, be disjoined, break with, cut off, disaffect, disband, disconnect, dispart, dissever, dissociate, disunite, divert from original use, divert from the original possessor, divide, draw apart, drive apart, exclude, fall out, isolate, keep aloof, keep apart, keep at a distance, leave out, offend, part, part company, segregate, separate, set against, set apart, set at variance, sever, sunder
ASSOCIATED CONCEPTS: separation of spouses

ESTRANGEMENT, *noun*   abalienation, abandonment, *alienatio,* alienation, alienation of affection, breach, break, cleavage, conflict, detachment, difference, disaffection, disagreement, disassociation, *discidium,* disconnection, discord, disengagement, disfavor, disharmony, disjunction, disloyalty, disruption, dissevering, dissociation, dissonance, disunion, disunity, division, divorce, divorcement, dudgeon, enmity, hostility, ill will, incompatibility, loss of affection, parting, riddance, rift, rupture, schism, segregation, separate maintenance, separation, severance, severance of relations, split, sundering, termination of cohabitation, unfriendliness, variance, withdrawal

ET AL., *adverb*   and all, and everyone, and more of the same, and other parties, and other things, and others, and the rest

ETHICAL, *adjective*   above board, conforming to moral standards, conforming to professional conduct, decent, good, honest, honorable, idealistic, in accord with ethics, in accordance with the rules for right conduct, in accordance with the standards of a profession, just, law-abiding, legitimate, moral, *moralis,* principled, professional, relating to moral action, respectable, right, righteous, straight, uncorrupt, uncorrupted, unimpeachable, upright, virtuous

ASSOCIATED CONCEPTS: Code of Judicial Conduct, Code of Professional Responsibility

ETHICS, *noun*   casuistry, code, code of morals, code of right and wrong, conduct, good conduct, goodness, honesty, honor, ideals, integrity, justice, laws of a profession, moral behavior, moral conduct, moral judgment, moral obligation, moral philosophy, moral practice, moral principles, moral rectitude, moral strength, moral tone, morality, morals, *philosophia moralis,* principles, principles of morality, probity, professional standards, rectitude, righteousness, sense of right and wrong, standards, standards of conduct, standards of professional behavior, system of morals, uprightness, values, virtue, virtuous conduct, virtuousness
ASSOCIATED CONCEPTS: legal ethics, professional delinquency, professional ethics

EVACUATE, *verb*   abscond, absent oneself, break camp, clear out, decamp, depart, disappear, empty, escape, exit, flee, leave, leave empty, *locum vacuefacere,* make a departure, march out, move out, quit, remove, retreat, run away, send away, take flight, vacate, vanish, withdraw

EVADE *(Deceive),* *verb*   avoid, be evasive, beguile, circumvent, defraud, delude, dissemble, dodge, equivocate, falsify, fool, hedge, hoax, lie, mislead, misrepresent, outwit, palter, pretend, prevaricate, shuffle, sophisticate, trick

EVADE *(Elude),* *verb*   avoid, dodge, escape, escape notice, flee, get away from, hide from, keep clear of, slip out
ASSOCIATED CONCEPTS: evade execution of a judgment, evade the law

EVALUATE, *verb*   appraise, ascertain the amount of, assess, calculate, class, criticize, determine the worth of, estimate, express an opinion, figure costs, find the value of, form an opinion, gauge, give an estimate, give an opinion, judge, measure, place a value on, prepare an estimate, price, rank, rate, reckon, review, set a figure, set a price on, set a value on, value
ASSOCIATED CONCEPTS: evaluate the evidence

EVASION, *noun*   *ambages,* artful dodge, artifice, avoidance, camouflage, chicane, chicanery, circumvention, concealment, covering up, craftiness, cunningness, deceit, deceitfulness, deception, device, disingenuousness, distortion, dodge, elusiveness, equivocation, escape by cleverness, escape by trickery, fabrication, flight, guile, knavery, *latebra,* maneuver, masquerade, misrepresentation, obfuscation, partial truth, perversion of the truth, pretext, prevarication, ruse, secrecy, secretiveness, secretness, sham, slyness, sophistical excuse, stealth, stealthiness, subterfuge, subtlety, *tergiversatio,* tergiversation, trick, underhand dealing
ASSOCIATED CONCEPTS: evasion of taxation, evasive contempt, evasive pleading

EVASIVE, *adjective*   *ambiguus,* ambivalent, artful, avoiding, beguiling, clandestine, concealed, covert, covinous, crafty, deceitful, deceiving, deceptive, delusive, eluding, elusive, elusory, equivocating, feigned, fictitious, fictive, furtive, guileful, hedging, hypocritical, in disguise, misleading, misrepresentative, mysterious, perfidious, pretended, scheming, secluded, secretive, seeking to avoid, seeking to elude, seeking to

evade, shifty, sleightful, slippery, sneaky, stealthy, surreptitious, tending to evade, tricky, truthless, untruthful, unveracious, unwilling, using evasion, vague
ASSOCIATED CONCEPTS: evasive argument, evasive contempt, evasive pleading, evasive witness

EVENHANDED, *adjective* detached, disinterested, dispassionate, equal, equitable, fair, fair-minded, impartial, indifferent, just, neutral, objective, proper, scrupulous, unbiased, unbribed, unchallengeable, uncorrupt, uncorrupted, unprejudiced, upright, virtuous

EVENT, *noun* adventure, affair, development, episode, *eventus, exitus,* experience, *factum,* hap, happening, incident, marked occurrence, milestone, occasion, occurrence, proceeding, transaction
ASSOCIATED CONCEPTS: contingent event, fortuitous event, future event, person interested in the event, unforseen event, witness to an event
FOREIGN PHRASES: *Casus fortuitus non est sperandus, et nemo tenetur devinare.* A fortuitous event is not to be forseen, and no one is bound to expect it. *Casus fortuitus non est supponendus.* A fortuitous happening is not to be presumed.

EVICT, *verb* *depellere,* deprive of possession, *detrudere, deturbare,* dislodge, displace, dispossess, disturb, eject, expel, jettison, kick out, oust, put out of house by legal process, recover property, remove, take possession, thrust out, turn adrift, turn out, turn out of doors, turn out of house and home, uproot, wrest property from
ASSOCIATED CONCEPTS: actual eviction, constrictive eviction, partial eviction, total eviction, unlawful eviction

EVICTION, *noun* act of driving out, act of throwing out, deprivation of possession, dislodgment, dispossession, divestment, ejection, ejectment, entry under paramount title, *evictio,* expulsion, extrusion, forcible expulsion from property, intentional exclusion of lessee, ouster, ouster by paramount title, recovery of property from another's possession, removal, take-over of property
ASSOCIATED CONCEPTS: abandonment of possession, actual eviction, breach of covenant of quiet enjoyment, constructive eviction, eviction by paramount title, partial eviction, total eviction, unlawful eviction
FOREIGN PHRASES: *Sive tota res evincatur, sive pars, habet regressum emptor in venditorem.* The purchaser who has been evicted totally or in part has an action against the vendor.

EVIDENCE, *noun* admitted testimony, body of facts on which belief is based, circumstances in a case, confirmation, corroboration, document, documentation, documents, exhibit, exhibits, exhibits submitted to jury, facts, facts admitted at trial, facts judicially noted, facts which bear on the point in question, facts which establish the point in issue, factual matter, ground of proof, grounds for belief, *indicium,* instrument of proof, matter legally submitted to the jury, matters of fact, means of proof, means of proving a fact, medium of proof, persuasive facts, probative matter, proof, proof legally presented at trial, proof of facts, record, relevant fact, relevant material, species of proof, substantiation, *testimonium,* that which furnishes proof, that which tends to prove, validation, verification

ASSOCIATED CONCEPTS: acceptance of evidence, admission of evidence, affirmative evidence, after-discovered evidence, against the weight of the evidence, all the evidence favorable to the plaintiff, best evidence, burden of going forward, burden of persuasion, burden of proof, character evidence, circumstantial evidence, clear and convincing evidence, clear preponderance of the evidence, collateral evidence, competent evidence, conclusive evidence, conflicting evidence, corroborating evidence, credible evidence, cumulative evidence, demonstrative evidence, destruction of evidence, direct evidence, documentary evidence, evidence of title, exclusion of evidence, expert evidence, extrinsic evidence, fabricated evidence, fair preponderance of evidence, favorable evidence, foundation for evidence, hearsay evidence, immaterial evidence, impeaching evidence, incompetent evidence, incredible evidence, inculpatory evidence, independent evidence, indispensable evidence, insufficient evidence, intrinsic evidence, introduction of evidence, irrelevant evidence, judicial evidence, legal evidence, material evidence, newly discovered evidence, objection to evidence, offering in evidence, opinion evidence, parol evidence, persuasive evidence, positive evidence, preponderance of evidence, presumptive evidence, prima facie evidence, primary evidence, probative evidence, real evidence, rebutting evidence, receiving evidence into the record, record evidence, reliable evidence, res gestae, rules of evidence, satisfactory evidence, scintilla of evidence, secondary evidence, state's evidence, substantial evidence, substantive evidence, sufficient evidence, sufficient evidence to support the verdict, supporting evidence, suppression of evidence, sworn evidence, taking evidence, testimony, visible evidence, weight of evidence, written evidence
FOREIGN PHRASES: *Ponderantur testes, non numerantur.* Witnesses are weighed, not counted. *Principia probant, non probantur.* Principles prove, they are not proved. *Praesumptiones sunt conjecturae ex signo verisimili ad probandum assumptae.* Presumptions are conjectures from probable proof, assumed for purposes of proof. *Testimonia ponderanda sunt, non numeranda.* Evidence is to be weighed, not counted. *De non apparentibus, et non existentibus, eadem est ratio.* The law is the same respecting things which do not appear and those which do not exist. *Non potest probari quod probatum non relevat.* That may not be proved which, if proved is irrelevant.

EVIDENCE, *verb* attest, authenticate, avouch, bear out, bear witness to, bring to light, bring to view, certify, circumstantiate, confirm, declare to be genuine, declare to be true, demonstrate, denote, disclose, display, establish, evince, exemplify, expose, give indication of, illustrate, imply, indicate, *indicium,* infer, instance, lay bare, make obvious, make plain, manifest, reveal, signify, suggest, swear, tell of, tend to show, *testimonium,* uncover, unsheathe, verify
ASSOCIATED CONCEPTS: proof evidencing a crime occurred

EVIDENT, *adjective* *apertus,* apparent, appearing, axiomatic, axiomatical, bald, clear, conspicuous, discernible, disclosed, distinct, easily seen, easy to perceive, easy to see, *evidens,* explicit, exposed, express, glaring, in evidence, in full view, in sight, in view, indisputable, indubitable, lucid, manifest, *manifestus,* noticeable, obvious, open, open to the vision, open to

view, ostensible, overt, palpable, patent, perceivable, perceptible, perspicuous, plain, pronounced, revealed, salient, showing, standing out, standing out clearly, transparent, unconcealed, undeniable, undisguised, unequivocal, unhidden, unmistakable, unquestionable, visible
ASSOCIATED CONCEPTS: evident mistake, proof of guilt being evident

EVINCE, *verb*   bespeak, betoken, bring into view, demonstrate, denote, display, evidence, exhibit, furnish evidence, illustrate, indicate, make clear, make evident, make manifest, make plain, manifest, *ostendere,* point to, *praestare, probare,* prove, show, show signs

EVISCERATE, *verb*   cut out, damage, debilitate, deprive of essential parts, deprive of force, deprive of vital parts, devitalize, dig out, disembowel, dismantle, embowel, enervate, enfeeble, exenterate, exsect, extract, gut, harm, impair, injure, mar, pick out, pluck, pull out, remove an essential part, rip out, sap, spoil, take away an essential part, tear out, weaken

EVOKE, *verb*   accomplish, achieve, arouse, be the cause of, bring about, bring forth, bring out, bring to pass, call forth, call up, cause, cause to happen, draw forth, draw out, educe, effect, effectuate, *elicere,* elicit, *evocare,* excite, *excitare,* extract, generate, give rise to, hasten, incite, induce, initiate, inspire, instigate, motivate, obtain, occasion, precipitate, procure, produce, prompt, provoke, rouse, secure, stimulate, summon, summon forth, summon up

EVOLVE, *verb*   advance, arise from, become, change into, come from, come to be, derive from, descend from, develop, emerge, *evolvere, explicare,* follow, grow from, have a common origin, issue, originate from, progress, result, spring from, take form, take shape, turn into, undergo evolution, unfold

EVULSION, *noun*   avulsion, deracination, disengagement, displacement, drawing out, ejection, elicitation, elimination, eradication, excavation, exsection, extirpation, extraction, extrication, plucking out, pull, pulling out, removal, ripping out, separation, unravelment, unrooting, uprooting, withdrawal

EX OFFICIO, *adverb*   authoritarian, by divine right, by law, by right, de jure, duly, empowered, in authority, in charge, in control, in office, official

EX PARTE, *adjective*   by one party, done by one person, for one party, in behalf of one party, on one side only, on the application of one party, one-sided, unilateral
ASSOCIATED CONCEPTS: ex parte application, ex parte decree, ex parte hearing, ex parte motion, ex parte proceeding

EX PARTE, *adverb*   biased, in the interest of one party, one sided, partial, partisan, prejudiced, relating to one side only, unilateral
ASSOCIATED CONCEPTS: ex parte affidavit, ex parte appointment, ex parte certificate, ex parte commission, ex parte declaration, ex parte experiment, ex parte investigation, ex parte motion and order, ex parte petition, ex parte presentment, ex parte proceedings, ex parte settlement, ex parte statement

EX POST FACTO, *adjective*   affecting a previous act, after, after the act is committed, after the fact, afterward, at a later period, at a later time, at a subsequent period, at a succeeding time, directly after, following in time, later, later in time, retroactive, thereafter
ASSOCIATED CONCEPTS: ex post facto law

EXACERBATE, *verb*   aggravate, arouse, augment, deteriorate, enrage, *exacerbare,* excite, heighten, incense, incite, increase, inflame, infuriate, intensify, irritate, make more severe, make worse, provoke, render worse, worsen

EXACT, *adjective*   accurate, admitting of no deviation, allowing no departure from the standard, careful, clear cut, close, correct, defined, detailed, *diligens, exactus,* explicit, express, faithful, literal, meticulous, minute, particular, plain, precise, punctilious, punctual, right, rigid, scrupulous, specific, strict, *subtilis,* true to fact, undeviating, unerring, unexaggerated, verbatim, with no mistake, without error
ASSOCIATED CONCEPTS: exact copy

EXACT, *verb*   ask for, assess, call for, charge, claim, clamor for, coerce, compel, constrain, cry for, demand, demand payment, demand toll, draw from, dun, elicit, enforce, enjoin, extort, force, force payment, impel, impose, impose a duty, impose a tax, insist upon, lay a duty on, lay claim to, levy, make an authoritative request, make demands, make obligatory, make pay, make requisition, mulct, necessitate, obligate, oblige, order, press, require, require authoritatively, requisition, squeeze, task, tax, threaten, toll, urge, wrench, wrest, wring
ASSOCIATED CONCEPTS: certified copy, exact copy

EXAGGERATION, *noun*   addition, aggrandizement, augmentation, boast, brag, caricature, disproportion, distortion, embellishment, embroidery, enlargement, excess, excessiveness, exorbitance, exorbitancy, expansion, extravagance, extravagant statement, extremes, gasconade, histrionics, hyperbole, immoderacy, immoderateness, immoderation, inaccuracy, inexactitude, inexactness, inflation, inordinacy, inordinateness, intemperance, intemperateness, intensification, magnification, misleading enlargement, outrageousness, overassessment, overemphasis, overenthusiasm, overpraise, overstatement, overvaluation, rodomontade, sensationalism, stretch, superfluity, superfluousness, *superlatio,* superlative, *traiectio,* undueness, unreasonable amplification
ASSOCIATED CONCEPTS: deceit, fraud, misrepresentation

EXAMINATION *(Study),* *noun*   active study, analysis, audit, careful noting of details, check, close inquiry, close observation, consideration, deliberation, diligent attention, exhaustive inquiry, exploration, inquest, *inquisitio,* inquisition, inspection, *investigatio,* investigation, observation, perquisition, perusal, reconnaissance, research, review, scrutiny, search, strict inquiry, survey
ASSOCIATED CONCEPTS: cross-examination, direct examination of a witness, examination before trial, examination in chief, examination of records, examination of title

EXAMINATION *(Test)*, **noun** interrogation, interview, probation, questioning under oath, quiz, set of questions
ASSOCIATED CONCEPTS: blood tests, board of examiners, civil service examination, entrance examination, health examination, medical examiners, mental examination, motor vehicle examination, physical examination, professional examinations, title examination

EXAMINE *(Interrogate)*, **verb** catechize, challenge, inquire, *inquirere, inspicere,* interpellate, interview, *investigare,* probe, put questions to, query, question, question under oath, quiz, subject to questioning
ASSOCIATED CONCEPTS: examine a witness

EXAMINE *(Study)*, **verb** analyze, anatomize, audit, canvass, check, conduct research on, contemplate, delve into, dissect, explore, go over, inquire into, inspect, investigate, keep under surveillance, look for flaws, look into, look over, look through, make an analysis, monitor, observe, peer at, peruse, probe, pry into, reconnoiter, regard carefully, research, review, scrutinize, study systematically, subject to analysis, subject to scrutiny, survey, take stock of, watch closely
ASSOCIATED CONCEPTS: examine books and records

EXAMPLE, **noun** archetype, case, case in point, demonstration, *documentum,* exemplar, exemplification, *exemplum,* exponent, guide, ideal, illustration, instance, metaphor, model, norm, paradigm, pattern, point of comparison, representation, representative, representative selection, sample, simile, something to be imitated, specimen, standard, standard of comparison, typical instance
FOREIGN PHRASES: *Nil agit exemplum litem quod lite resolvit.* A precedent which settles a controversy with a question does no good. *Plus exempla quam peccata nocent.* Examples do more harm than crimes.

EXCEPT *(Exclude)*, **verb** count out, deduct, delete, differentiate, discount, discriminate, dismiss, disregard, eliminate, *excipere,* exempt, *eximere,* extract, leave out, make an exception, omit, pick out, put aside, remove, separate, set apart, single out, subduct, subtract, take out, treat as a special case

EXCEPT *(Object)*, **verb** be at variance, call in question, challenge, come in conflict with, contradict, contravene, cry out against, decry, demur, denounce, deplore, differ, disapprove, discountenance, dispute, dissent, entreat against, express disapproval, feel disapproval, find fault, gainsay, go contrary to, impeach, impugn, make objection, object to, oppose, protest, refuse to accept, repudiate, run counter to, take exception

EXCEPTION *(Exclusion)*, **noun** apartness, breach of practice, contrariety, defiance of custom, departure from usual, detachment, deviation, disconformity, disruption, *exceptio,* exemption, expulsion, inconsistency, infraction of rule, irregularity, nonconformity, noninclusion, nonuniformity, oddity, omission, preclusion, rarity, removal, segregation, separation, severance, special case, subtraction, unconformity, unconventionality, withdrawal
ASSOCIATED CONCEPTS: exception in a deed, proviso, reservation, statutory exception

EXCEPTION *(Objection)*, **noun** adverse criticism, challenge, charge, clamor, complaint, contradiction, contravention, criticism, demurrer, disapprobation, disapproval, discommendation, discontent, dislike, disparagement, displeasure, dispraise, dispute, dissatisfaction, dissent, grievance, improbation, impugnation, lack of agreement, lack of conformity, nonagreement, nonapproval, offense, opposition, outcry, protest, protest against a ruling, protestation, rebuke, rejection, remonstrance
ASSOCIATED CONCEPTS: bill of exceptions, formal objection, general exception, peremptory exception, special exception
FOREIGN PHRASES: *Exceptio firmat regulam in contrarium.* An exception affirms the rule to be the contrary. *Omnis regula suas patitur exceptiones.* Every rule is subject to its own exception. *Exceptio semper ultima ponenda est.* An exception is always to be placed last. *Exceptio quoque regulam declarat.* An exception also declares the rule. *Exceptio quae firmat legem, exponit legem.* An exception which confirms the law expounds the law. *Omnis exceptio est ipsa quoque regula.* Every exception is itself also a rule. *Ubi quid generaliter conceditur, inest haec exceptio, si non aliquid sit contra jus fasque.* Where anything is granted generally, this exception is implied: that nothing shall be contrary to law and right. *Exceptio firmat regulam in casibus non exceptis.* An exception confirms the rule in cases not excepted. *Exceptio probat regulam de rebus non exceptis.* The exception proves the rule concerning things not excepted.

EXCERPT, **noun** citation, clipping, excerption, extract, part, passage, passage taken from a book, portion, quotation, quote, quoted passage, reference, representative selection, select passage, selection
ASSOCIATED CONCEPTS: redact portions of a confession

EXCESS, **adjective** excessive, exorbitant, extra, extravagant, extreme, immoderate, inordinate, lavish, more than enough, needless, *nimium,* overabundant, overflowing, overmuch, profuse, recremental, recrementitial, recrementitious, redundant, spare, superabundant, supererogative, supererogatory, superfluous, supernumerary, surplus, undue, unnecessary, unneeded
ASSOCIATED CONCEPTS: excess fees, excess of jurisdiction, excess profits tax

EXCESSIVE, **adjective** characterized by excess, disproportionate, exaggerated, exceeding, exceeding what is usual, exorbitant, extra, extravagant, extreme, fanatical, fulsome, gross, immoderate, *immoderatus, immodicus,* inordinate, intemperate, needless, *nimius,* nonessential, out of bounds, outrageous, overflowing, overmuch, plethoric, preposterous, profuse, rank, redundant, spare, superabundant, supererogatory, superfluous, supernumerary, surplus, unbounded, uncalled for, unconscionable, undue, unnecessary, unneeded, unreasonable
ASSOCIATED CONCEPTS: excessive assessment, excessive bail, excessive damages, excessive sentence, excessive tax, excessive verdict

EXCHANGE, **noun** bargain, barter, bazaar, bourse, business intercourse, buying and selling, change, commerce, commutation, conversion, deal, interchange, intercourse, market, mart, merchantry, *permutatio,* permutation, rearrangement, reciprocation, reciprocity, replacement, reprisal, requital, retaliation,

shift, shuffle, stock market, substitute, substitution, supplanting, swap, trade, traffic, transaction, transfer, transposal, transposition
ASSOCIATED CONCEPTS: bill of exchange, exchange of property, reciprocal exchange, reciprocal transfers

EXCISE, noun   assessment, capitation, charge, custom, demand, duty, exaction, exactment, fee, imposition, impost, levy, liability, obligation, tariff, tax, taxation, toll
ASSOCIATED CONCEPTS: direct tax, excise tax, fee, gift tax, license tax, privilege tax

EXCISE (Cut away), verb   abscind, clip, cut, cut out, deduct, delete, detruncate, diminish, disjoin, dissever, divest, eradicate, expunge, expurgate, extract, pare, pluck out, remove, separate, sever, subduct, subtract, take away, take out, tear out, thin,n, truncate, weed, withdraw

EXCISE (Levy a tax), verb   appraise, assess, charge, charge duty, claim, collect, compel payment, demand, demand payment, demand toll, enforce payment, exact, force payment, impose a duty on, impost, lay a duty on, lay claim to, levy, levy an excise on, oblige, raise, require a tax, requisition, take, tax
ASSOCIATED CONCEPTS: direct tax, franchise tax, gift tax, indirect tax, privilege tax, succession tax

EXCLUDE, verb   avoid, ban, banish, bar, block, blockade, boycott, cast out, censor, count out, debar, deny entry, deport, deprive, disallow, disbar, discount, disdain, dismiss, disown, displace, disqualify, disregard, eject, eliminate, eradicate, except, excludere, excommunicate, excuse, exempt, exile, eximere, expatriate, expel, force out, forswear, have nothing to do with, ignore, impose a ban, isolate, keep from entering, keep out, lay aside, leave out, leave unregarded, liberate, make an exception, neglect, omit, ostracize, oust, outlaw, overlook, pass over, place out of bounds, preclude, prevent, prohibere, prohibit, proscribe, put aside, put out, quarantine, rebuff, refuse to admit, refuse to consider, refuse to include, refuse to see, reject, remove, renounce, repel, repudiate, repulse, restrict, rule out, scorn, segregate, sequester, set apart, set aside, shut out, spurn, taboo, take out, throw out, thrust out, treat as a special case, turn away, turn out, uproot, veto, weed
ASSOCIATED CONCEPTS: exclude from a will, exclude from employment

EXCLUSION, noun   apartheid, avoidance, ban, bar, blackball, boycott, debarment, denial, denial of entry, deportation, disbarment, discard, dislodgment, dismissal, disownment, displacement, ejection, exclusio, exemption, exile, expatriation, expulsion, immunity, intolerance, isolation, monopoly, nonacceptance, nonadmission, nonconsideration, noninclusion, omission, ostracism, preclusion, prejudice, privilege, prohibition, purge, refusal, rejection, removal, repudiation, riddance, seclusion, segregation, separation, voidance
ASSOCIATED CONCEPTS: Escobedo rule, exception, exclusion from a will, exclusion of a juror, exclusionary clause, exclusionary rule, Miranda rule, systematic exclusion
FOREIGN PHRASES: Inclusio unius est exclusio alterius. The inclusion of one is the exclusion of another. Expressio unius est exclusio alterius. The expression of one thing is the exclusion of another.

EXCLUSIVE (Limited), adjective   biased, bigoted, choice, clannish, cliquish, esoteric, exclusionary, exclusory, illiberal, preclusive, prejudiced, prohibitive, restricted, restrictive, select, selective, snobbish, snobby, uncharitable
ASSOCIATED CONCEPTS: exclusive agency, exclusive control, exclusive franchise, exclusive immunity, exclusive jurisdiction, exclusive license, exclusive ownership, exclusive possession, exclusive remedy, exclusive right, exclusive use

EXCLUSIVE (Singular), adjective   distinct, especial, isolated, lone, one, only, separate, single, sole, solitary, special, unique

EXCULPATE, verb   absolve, absolve of fault, absolve of wrongdoing, acquit, clear, clear from a charge, clear from alleged guilt, clear from imputation of fault, declare guiltless, declare not guilty, dismiss, excusare, excuse, exonerate, free, free from blame, give absolution to, justify, liberate, pardon, prove guiltless, prove not guilty, set free, vindicate, vindicate from unjust reproach
ASSOCIATED CONCEPTS: exculpatory clause, exculpatory evidence, exculpatory statement, mitigation of damages
FOREIGN PHRASES: Expurgare

EXCUSE, noun   alibi, allowance, defense, dispensation, exculpation, excusatio, exemption, exoneration, explanation for some delinquency, extenuation, justification, mitigation, ostensible reason, pretense, pretext, rationalization, reason, subterfuge
ASSOCIATED CONCEPTS: excusable assault, excusable homicide, excusable neglect, legal excuse
FOREIGN PHRASES: Impotentia excusat legem. The impossibility of performing a legal duty is an excuse from the performance. A l'impossible nul n'est tenu. No one is bound to do what is impossible.

EXCUSE, verb   absolve, acquit, allow for, bear with, clear, condone, discharge, exculpate, excusare, exempt, exonerate, expurgare, extenuate, forgive, free, give absolution to, give dispensation, grant amnesty to, judge with indulgence, justify, let off, liberate, make allowances for, overlook, pardon, pass over, pronounce innocent of wrong, provide with an alibi, regard indulgently, release, release from obligation, relieve, remit, reprieve, shrive, vindicate
ASSOCIATED CONCEPTS: affirmative defense, alibi, defense, just cause, justification, lawful excuse, legitimate excuse, reasonable excuse
FOREIGN PHRASES: Impotentia excusat legem. The impossibility of performing a legal duty is an excuse from the performance. Injuria non excusat injuriam. One wrong does not excuse another. Ignorantia excusator, non juris sed facti. Ignorance of fact may excuse, but not ignorance of law. Ignorantia eorum quae quis scire tenetur non excusat. Ignorance of those things which a person is deemed to know is no excuse. Vani timoris justa excusatio non est. A frivolous fear is not a lawful excuse. Ignorantia juris non excusat. Ignorance of the law is no excuse. Regula est, juris quidem ignorantiam cuique nocere, facti vero ignorantiam non nocere. The rule is that a person's ignorance of the law may prejudice him, but that his ignorance of fact will not.

EXECUTE (Accomplish), verb   achieve, act, act upon, attain, bring about, bring to pass, carry into ef-

fect, carry into execution, carry out, commit, complete, discharge, do, effect, effectuate, *efficere,* enact, fulfill, manage, perform, perpetrate, put in action, put in force, realize, see through, succeed, take action, transact
ASSOCIATED CONCEPTS: execute a contract, execute a note, execute a promise, execute a warrant, execute after entry of a judgment, execute an agreement, execute an instrument, execute an obligation, execute an order, execute the laws, executed consideration, executed contract, executed estate, executed fine, executed remainder, executed trust, execution creditor, execution debtor, execution lien, execution sales, garnishment, tax execution

EXECUTE *(Sentence to death), verb*   condemn, condemn to death, deprive of life, dispatch, end life, inflict capital punishment, kill, punish with death, put to death, put to death according to law, slay, *supplicium*
ASSOCIATED CONCEPTS: execute pursuant to a death sentence, execution of a sentence, sentence

EXECUTIVE, *adjective*   administrative, directing, high level, legislative, managing, ministerial, officiating, presiding
ASSOCIATED CONCEPTS: executive acts, executive branch, executive clemency, executive committee, executive council, executive department, executive director, executive duties, executive officer, executive order, executive powers, executive records, executive session

EXECUTIVE, *noun*   administrator, employer, industrialist, key man, key person, key woman, manager

EXECUTOR, *noun*   administrator, administrator of a will, administrator of the decedent's estate, administratrix, custodian, delegate, fiduciary, legal representative, person in charge, person in responsibility, person named to carry out the provisions of a will, personal representative, representative of the decedent, trustee
ASSOCIATED CONCEPTS: administor, administrix, ancillary executor, custodian, executor named in a will, executorship expenses, executrix, guardian, independent executors, probate court, surrogate's court

EXECUTORY, *adjective*   contingent, *imperfectus, infectus,* not yet carried into operation, unaccomplished, unadministered, uncompleted, unexecuted, unfinished, unfulfilled, unperformed
ASSOCIATED CONCEPTS: executory accord, executory bequest, executory consideration, executory contract, executory devise, executory estate, executory gift, executory instrument, executory interest, executory limitation, executory remainder, executory treaty, executory trust

EXEMPLAR, *noun*   apotheosis, archetype, example, *exemplum,* exponent, frame of reference, good example, guide, ideal, model, nonesuch, nonpareil, paradigm, paragon, pattern, prototype, shining example, standard, standard for comparison, standard for imitation, standard of perfection

EXEMPLARY, *adjective*   excellent, honorable, ideal, illustrative, in point, laudable, meritorious, model, normal, normative, paradigmatic, personifying, praiseworthy, precedential, representative, sample, serving as a deterrent, serving as a model, serving as a pattern, serving as a sample, serving as a warning, serving as an instance, typifying, used as a deterrent,

used as a model, used as a specimen, worthy, worthy of imitation
ASSOCIATED CONCEPTS: exemplary damages

EXEMPLIFY, *verb*   act the part of, actualize, be taken for, be the equivalent of, betoken, cite, connote, convey an impression, delineate, demonstrate, denote, depict, display, elucidate, embody, enucleate, evidence, evince, exhibit, explicate, express, give an example, give an instance, give concrete form to, illuminate, illustrate, indicate, instance, make clear by examples, make evident, make manifest, make obvious, make plain, manifest, picture, point to, portray, portray by example, produce an instance, render manifest, represent, show by example, signify, stand for, symbolize, typify
ASSOCIATED CONCEPTS: exemplified copies

EXEMPT, *adjective*   absolved, at liberty, cleared, discharged, excluded, excused, exempted, favored, free, free of binding obligation, freed from, immune, *immunis, liber,* liberated, not answerable, not liable, not responsible, not restricted, not subject to, outside, possessed of immunity, privileged, protected, released, relieved from liability, set apart, shielded, *solutus,* unaffected, unbound, unchecked, unconfined, uncontrolled, unencumbered, unimpeded, unrestrained, unrestricted, waived
ASSOCIATED CONCEPTS: exempt from attachment, exempt from execution, exempt from sale, exempt from taxation, exempt property

EXEMPTION, *noun*   allowance, discharge, disengagement, exception, freedom, freedom from duty, freedom from liability, freedom from obligation, freedom from requirements, freedom from service, *immunitas,* immunity, liberation, liberty, license, permit, privilege, release, release from liability, release from obligation, special privilege, *vacatio, vacuitas*
ASSOCIATED CONCEPTS: exemption from jury service, exemption from sale, exemption statute, homestead exemption, personal exemption, tax exemption

EXERCISE *(Discharge a function), verb*   act, administer, carry into execution, carry on, carry out, conduct, do duty, *efficere,* engage in, execute, *exercere, facere,* officiate, perform, practice, pursue, put in motion, put into action, put into effect, put into practice, serve as, translate into action, wage
ASSOCIATED CONCEPTS: authority exercised under the United States Constitution, exercise an option, exercise jurisdiction, exercise of judicial discretion
FOREIGN PHRASES: *Cui jurisdictio data est, ea quoque concessa esse videntur, sine quibus jurisdictio explicari non potest.* To whomsoever jurisdiction is given, those things also are supposed to be granted, without which the jurisdiction cannot be exercised. *Frustra est potentia quae nunquam venit in actum.* A power is a vain one if it is never exercised.

EXERCISE *(Use), verb*   apply, avail oneself of, bring into play, bring to bear, draw on, employ, make use of, manipulate, operate, practice, put in action, put in practice, put to use, put to work, turn to account, utilize, wield
ASSOCIATED CONCEPTS: exercise a right to vote, exercise an option, exercise discretion, exercise dominion, exercise due care, exercise of power

EXERT, *verb* apply, bring into operation, bring into play, bring to bear, *contendere,* employ, exercise, expend, *intendere,* make use of, manipulate, operate, put forth, put in action, set to work, spend, strain, strive, try, use, utilize, wield, work

EXHAUST *(Deplete), verb* *absumere, conficere,* consume, consume completely, *consumere,* debilitate, deflate, deprive of strength, devitalize, dissipate, drain, draw, draw out, empty, enervate, enfeeble, expend, fatigue, overtire, reach the end of, run through, sap, spend, strain, tax, tire, use, use up, waste, weaken, wear out, weary
ASSOCIATED CONCEPTS: exhaust all available assets

EXHAUST *(Try all possibilities), verb* carry to completion, complete, *exhaurire,* finish, follow through, litigate completely, treat thoroughly, use up available remedies
ASSOCIATED CONCEPTS: exhaustion of administrative remedies, exhaustion of remedies, exhaustion of state remedies

EXHIBIT, *noun* disclosure, display, document produced as evidence, evidence, exhibition, exposition, item of evidence, object produced as evidence, object submitted in proof of facts, presentation, revelation, showing

EXHIBIT, *verb* bring forward, bring to light, bring to notice, bring to view, demonstrate, disclose, display, evidence, evince, *exhibere, exponere,* expose, express, feature, illustrate, indicate, lay bare, lay open, make clear, make known, make obvious, make plain, manifest, offer for inspection, open up, point out, present, present for consideration, present to view, produce, *proponere,* reveal, reveal to public notice, set forth, show, submit in evidence, uncover, unveil
ASSOCIATED CONCEPTS: exhibit in evidence

EXHORT, *verb* *adhortari,* adjure, admonish, advise, advocate, animate, arouse, beg, beseech, caution, charge, coax, command, counsel, encourage, enjoin, entreat, goad, impel, implore, importune, incite, induce, influence, inspire, inspirit, instigate, instruct, offer advice, persuade, plead, press, prevail upon, prompt, push, recommend, rouse, spur, stimulate, talk into, urge, warn

EXIGENCY, *noun* crisis, critical situation, difficulty, exigence, imperativeness, necessity, need, press, pressing necessity, pressure, requirement, urgency, urgent need, want
ASSOCIATED CONCEPTS: public exigency

EXIGENT, *adjective* acute, badly needed, clamant, compelling, compulsory, critical, crucial, crying, demanding, essential, grave, high priority, imperative, important, indispensable, inescapable, insistent, mandatory, necessary, necessitous, needed, needful, not to be delayed, not to be overlooked, pressing, required, requiring immediate attention, requiring immediate care, requiring prompt action, serious, unavoidable, urgent, vital
ASSOCIATED CONCEPTS: exigent circumstances

EXIST, *verb* be, be alive, be in effect, be in present force, breathe, come into existence, continue, continue to be, continue to live, endure, *esse, exsistere, exstare,* go on, have being, have existence, have life, inhere, last, live, live on, persist, remain, remain alive, stay, stay alive, subsist, survive
ASSOCIATED CONCEPTS: corporate existence, existing creditors, existing debt, existing estate, existing law, existing liability, existing lien, existing rights, existing use

EXONERATE, *verb* absolve, absolve of a charge, acquit, clear, clear of an imputation of guilt, declare blameless, declare innocent, declare not guilty, discharge, discharge of responsibility, exculpate, excuse, forgive, free from accusation, free from blame, give absolution, grant a reprieve, grant amnesty, *liberare,* liberate, pardon, pronounce free from guilt, prove blameless, prove not guilty, purge, release from an obligation, release from liability, relieve, relieve from accusation, relieve of blame, relieve of liability, remit a penalty, set free, vindicate
ASSOCIATED CONCEPTS: indemnify

EXONERATION, *noun* absolution, absolution of a charge, acquittal, acquittance, act of indemnity, amnesty, bill of indemnity, clearance, clearing, discharge, dismissal of charges, dispensation, exculpation, excuse, forgiveness, freedom, freedom from accusation, freedom from guilt, freeing from blame, liberation, pardon, release, relief from, remission, reprieve, vindication, withdrawal of the charge
ASSOCIATED CONCEPTS: exoneration clause in a will, exoneration of bail, pardon

EXORBITANT, *adjective* dear, enormous, excessive, expensive, extortionate, extravagant, extreme, fabulous, greedy, gross, high-priced, huge, immense, immoderate, *immodicus,* inordinate, intemperate, outrageous, overmuch, preposterous, uncalled-for, unconscionable, undue, unreasonable, unwarranted

EXPAND, *verb* accumulate, add to, advance, aggrandize, aggravate, amplify, ascend, augment, balloon, be augmented, be distended, become broad, become greater, become larger, blow up, branch out, broaden, build up, burgeon, deepen, develop, develop in greater detail, *dilatare,* dilate, distend, elaborate, elevate, enhance, enlarge, enlarge on, enter into detail, escalate, exacerbate, exaggerate, expatiate on, express in fuller form, extend, *extendere,* fan out, fatten, fill out, further, gain, gain strength, go into detail, greaten, grow, grow larger, heighten, increase, increase in bulk, increase in extent, increase the capacity of, inflate, intensify, *lazare,* lengthen, magnify, make greater, make larger, make more comprehensive, maximize, multiply, outspread, outstretch, progress, prolong, raise, redouble, render broad, render larger, shoot upward, sprawl, spread, spread out, spread over, step up, stretch, stretch out, supplement, swell, unfold, wax, widen

EXPATRIATE, *verb* abandon nationality, banish, cast out, change national allegiance, deport, drive from one's native land, eject, exclude, exile, expel, leave one's country, outlaw, renounce citizenship, renounce rights of citizenship, send away, transport, withdraw from one's native land
ASSOCIATED CONCEPTS: aliens, citizenship, deportation

EXPECT *(Anticipate), verb* await, bargain for, be certain, be confident, be prepared, calculate upon, count on, *expectare,* have in prospect, look for, look forward to, plan on, prepare for, provide for, reckon on, *sperare*, wait for, watch for

ASSOCIATED CONCEPTS: contingent expectancy, expectancy of heir, expectant estate, expectant interest, expectant right, life expectancy

EXPECT *(Consider probable),* **verb** apprehend, assume, believe, conclude, conjecture, consider likely, divine, envision, fancy, forecast, foresee, gather, guess, have a hunch, have a presentiment, imagine, infer, judge, predict, presume, prognosticate, prophesy, regard likely, suppose, surmise, suspect, think, think likely

EXPECTATION, *noun* anticipation, assurance, awaiting, calculation, contemplation, expectance, expectancy, *exspectatio,* foreboding, forefeeling, foreknowledge, foresight, hope, intention, misgiving, *opinio,* preconception, presentiment, presumption, presurmise, prevenience, probability, promise, prospect, prospection, prospicience, *spes,* suspense, trust, waiting

ASSOCIATED CONCEPTS: expectant estates, expectant heir, expectant right, reasonal expectation

EXPEDIENCE, *noun* acceptability, advantageousness, appropriateness, aptness, commendableness, convenience, discrimination, expediency, favorableness, feasibility, felicitousness, fitness, fittingness, meetness, opportuneness, practicality, pragmatism, profitableness, propitiousness, propriety, prudence, reasonableness, rightness, seemliness, sense, sensibleness, sound judgment, suitability, suitableness, timeliness, usefulness, *utilitas,* utility, worthiness

EXPEDIENT, *noun* agency, alternative, apparatus, appliance, arrangement, artifice, auxiliary, campaign, *consilium,* contributing force, contrivance, convenience, course, design, device, equipment, formula, implement, instrument, invention, *machina,* machination, machine, makeshift, maneuver, material, means, means to an end, measure, mechanism, medium, method, mode of procedure, plan, practice, procedure, proceeding, process, *ratio,* resort, resource, ruse, scheme, shift, step, stopgap, stratagem, strategy, stroke, subterfuge, suggestion, tactic, technique, tool, treatment, trick, undertaking, utensil, vehicle, way, wherewithal

EXPEDITE, *verb* accelerate, accomplish promptly, advance, aid, assist, clear the way, dispatch, drive on, ease, encourage, *expedire,* facilitate, forward, foster, further, give a start, hasten, help, hurry, *maturare,* move up, pave the way, precipitate, promote, push ahead, push forward, push through, put into action, quicken, rush, set in motion, smoothe, speed, speed up, stimulate, support, urge forward, urge on

EXPEDITIOUS, *adjective* accelerated, accomplished efficiently, active, alacritious, brisk, *celer,* done quickly, done with expedition, efficient, express, fast, fleet, hasty, immediate, instant, *maturus,* prompt, *promptus,* punctual, quick, rapid, ready, snappy, speedy, spirited, swift, with alacrity, with dispatch, with speed

EXPEL, *verb* banish, cut out, deport, discard, discharge, dislodge, dismiss, disown, dispose of, dispossess, drive out, *eicere,* eject, eliminate, emit, evict, exclude, excommunicate, *exigere,* exile, expatriate, *expellere,* ex-

trude, force away, force out, get rid of, kick out, ostracize, oust, outlaw, purge, put out, reject, remove, rout out, throw out, thrust out, turn out, weed out

EXPEND *(Consume),* **verb** apply, avail oneself of, burn, deplete, devour, dissipate, employ, exert, exhaust, finish, lessen, reduce, spend, turn to account, use, use up, waste

EXPEND *(Disburse),* **verb** allocate, allot, apportion, assign, bear the cost of, bear the expense of, distribute, *erogare, expendere,* give money, *impendere,* incur an expense, incur costs, make an expenditure, make payment, meet the expense of, pay, pay out, render payment, spend, support the expense of

EXPENDABLE, *adjective* accessory, added, additional, auxiliary, dispensable, disposable, duplicate, excess, excessive, expletive, extra, extraneous, functionless, futile, gratuitous, impotent, inapplicable, inconsequential, ineffectual, inessential, inoperative, insignificant, inutile, irrelevant, leftover, needless, negligible, nonessential, nonfunctional, nugatory, of no account, overplus, peripheral, purposeless, redundant, replaceable, spare, substitutable, superabundant, supererogatory, superfluous, supernumerary, supplemental, supplementary, surplus, trifling, unavailing, uncalled-for, unessential, unimportant, unnecessary, unneeded, unprofitable, unrequired, unusable, unused, useless, valueless, worthless

EXPENDITURE, *noun* amount, cash paid, charge, cost, cost incurred, defrayal, defrayment, disbursement, discharge, expense, expenses, funds paid out, investment, money expended, outgo, outlay, payment, price, remittance, spendings, sum

ASSOCIATED CONCEPTS: actual expenditure, capital expenditure, extraordinary expenditure, good faith expenditure, lawful expenditure, legitimate expenditure, ordinary expenditure

EXPENSE *(Cost),* **noun** amount, appraisal, appraisement, assessment, budgeted items, buying price, charge, consideration, cost incurred, debit, defrayal, defrayment, discharge of a debt, *dispendium,* drain on resources, due, exaction, exactment, expenditure, fair value, fee, *impendium, impensa,* market price, monetary value, money expended, obligation, outgo, outlay, overhead, payment, price, rate, remittance, sum, sum charged, valuation, value, worth

ASSOCIATED CONCEPTS: accrued business expense, actual expenses, capital expense, collection expense, contingent expense, current expenses, deductible expense, disbursements, expenditures of an estate, expenses in bringing an action, expenses incurred, expenses of administration, expenses of condemnation, expenses of receivership, extraordinary expenses, general operating expense, incidental expenses, legitimate expense, maintenance expense, mandatory expense, necessary and regular expense, necessary business expense, nonbusiness expense, office expenses, operating expenses, ordinary expenses, personal expenses, proper expenses, reasonable expenses, unusual expenses, witness expenses

EXPENSE *(Sacrifice),* **noun** abandonment, casualty, cession, concession, consumption, costliness, damage, decline, deprival, deprivation, deterioration, detriment, disadvantage, disposal, dissipation, dissolution, drain, drain on resources, erosion, forfeit, forfeiture, harm, hurt, ill fortune, impairment, injury, loss, penalty, privation, relinquishment, renunciation, surrender

EXPERIENCE *(Background)*, *noun*   acquaintance, adroitness, apprenticeship, cognizance, competence, competency, cosmopolitanism, education, empiricism, enlightenment, *experientia,* expertise, expertness, familiarity, instruction, judgment, ken, know-how, knowledge, learning, mastery, maturity, *peritia,* perspicaciousness, practical knowledge, practical wisdom, practice, preparation, proficiency, qualification, schooling, seasoning, skill, skillfulness, sophistication, teaching, training, tuition, understanding, wisdom, worldliness

FOREIGN PHRASES: *Experientia per varios actus legem facit. magistra rerum experientia.* Experience by various acts makes law. experience is the mistress of things. *Per varios actus legem experientia facit.* By various acts experience makes the law.

EXPERIENCE *(Encounter)*, *noun*   adventure, befalling, circumstance, confrontation, episode, escapade, event, happening, incident, occasion, occurrence, pass, phenomenon, presentation, proceeding, situation, transpiration, venture

EXPERIMENT, *noun*   assay, attempt, dry run, endeavor, essay, examination, *experimentum,* first attempt, investigation, organized observation, *periculum,* research, search, test, testing program, trial, tryout, venture, verification

EXPERT, *adjective*   able, accomplished, acquainted, adept, adroit, all-knowing, apt, artful, *callidus,* capable, clever, cognizant, competent, conversant, deft, dexterous, effective, efficient, encyclopedic, experienced, facile, finished, handy, ingenious, knowing, knowledgeable, learned, masterful, masterly, omniscient, practiced, prepared, professional, proficient, qualified, *sciens,* seasoned, skilled, skillful, trained, tried, versed, veteran, well-qualified, wise

ASSOCIATED CONCEPTS: expert evidence, expert opinion, expert witness, handwriting expert

EXPERT, *noun*   authority, connoisseur, experienced hand, experienced person, experienced personnel, genius, knowing person, man of erudition, man of learning, master, master hand, mastermind, paragon, practiced hand, practitioner, professional, proficient person, qualified person, sage, savant, scholar, skilled hand, skilled practitioner, sophisticate, specialist, specializer, specially trained person, strategist, technician, trained person, trained personnel, veteran, virtuoso

ASSOCIATED CONCEPTS: expert testimony, expert witness

EXPIATION, *noun*   acknowledgement, adjustment, amends, apology, atonement, compensation, damages, *expiatio,* full satisfaction, guerdon, indemnification, indemnity, pacification, paying back, payment, *piaculum, poena,* propitiation, punishment, quittance, reckoning, recompense, reconciliation, recoupment, recovery, repayment, requital, restitution, satisfaction, settlement, solatium

EXPIRATION, *noun*   cessation, close, closing, closure, completion, conclusion, consummation, death, discontinuance, discontinuation, dissolution, dying, end, ending, expiry, *exspiratio,* finish, limit, period, retirement, running out, stop, stoppage, term, termination

ASSOCIATED CONCEPTS: expiration of a charter, expiration of a contract, expiration of a franchise, expiration of a grant, expiration of a lease, expiration of a license, expiration of a patent, expiration of a period of redemption, expiration of a sentence, expiration of a term of office, expiration of a trademark, expiration of an insurance policy, expiration of an option to buy, expiration of credit

EXPIRE, *verb*   *animam edere,* become void, cease, cease to be, close, come to a close, come to an end, conclude, decease, depart, die, die away, die out, disappear, discontinue, draw to a close, elapse, end, *exspirare,* fade away, finish, go, lapse, pass, pass away, perish, run out, stop, succumb, surcease, terminate, vanish, wear away, wind up

EXPLAIN, *verb*   account for, annotate, assign a meaning to, cause to be understood, clarify, clear of obscurity, clear up, decipher, define, demonstrate, describe, disentangle, elucidate, enlighten, enucleate, exemplify, *expedire, explanare,* explicate, *exponere,* expound, give reason for, illuminate, illustrate, increase clarity, interpret, make clear, make evident, make explicit, make manifest, make plain, manifest, offer an explanation, paraphrase, point out, popularize, put across, put in other words, rephrase, restate, reveal, shed light upon, show, simplify, solve, specify, spell out, teach, tell how, throw light upon, translate, unfold, unravel, unscramble, untangle

EXPLANATION, *noun*   amplification, annotation, clarification, commentary, deciphering, defense, definition, delineation, demonstration, description, elucidation, enucleation, exegesis, exemplification, *explanatio, explicatio,* explication, exposition, expounding, illumination, illustration, *interpretatio,* interpretation, justification, key, meaning, plain interpretation, rationale, rendering, rendition, showing, simplification, solution, strict interpretation, translation, unfolding

ASSOCIATED CONCEPTS: commentary to a statute, explanatory expressions in a will

EXPLETIVE, *noun*   addition, anathema, bad language, blaspheming, curse, denunciation, ecphonesis, embellishment, execration, foul invective, foul language, imprecation, injection, insertion, interjection, interpolation, irreverence, malediction, outcry, profane interjection, rhetorical phrase, rhetorical word, scurrility, strong language, swearing, unnecessary addition, unnecessary inclusion

EXPLICATE, *verb*   clarify, define, describe, detail, develop, elucidate, enlighten, *enodare,* enucleate, explain, *explicare,* expound, give a detailed explanation, illuminate, illustrate, interpret, *interpretari,* make clear, make explicit, make plain, render clear, reveal, shed light upon, simplify, spell out, throw light upon, translate, unfold, unfold the meaning of, unfold the sense of, unriddle, untangle

EXPLICIT, *adjective*   absolute, accurate, *apertus,* beyond doubt, categorical, certain, clear, clearly defined, clearly expressed, clearly formulated, clearly

stated, comprehensible, crystal-clear, decided, definite, *definitus*, determinate, direct, distinct, distinctly expressed, distinctly stated, easy to understand, evident, evincive, exact, explanatory, express, expressed outright, forthright, indisputable, intelligible, lucid, manifest, obvious, open, outspoken, patent, perspicuous, plain, pointed, positive, precise, recognizable, specific, straightforward, strict, sure, to the point, transparent, unambiguous, unconfusing, understandable, undisguised, unequivocal, unmistakable, well-developed
ASSOCIATED CONCEPTS: explicit notice, explicit power

EXPLOIT *(Make use of)*, **verb**   apply, avail oneself of, bring into play, capitalize on, consume, employ, exercise, fall back on, find useful, implement, make the most of, manipulate, operate, profit by, put in practice, put into action, put into operation, put to service, put to use, put to work, resort to, set in motion, set to work, take advantage of, turn to account, use, utilize, wield, work

EXPLOIT *(Take advantage of)*, **verb**   abuse, do an injustice to, ill-treat, ill-use, maltreat, manipulate, milk, misapply, misappropriate, misdirect, misemploy, misgovern, mishandle, mismanage, mistreat, misuse, oppress, overburden, overtask, overtax, overuse, overwork, persecute, put to wrong use, turn selfishly to one's own account, use badly, use improperly, use selfishly, use wrongly, victimize

EXPLOITATION, **noun**   employ, misapplication, misuse, overcharge, profiteering, turning to account, unethical use, use, usury, utilization, utilization for profit

EXPOSE, **verb**   advertise, air, bare, bring to light, cast out, *coarguere*, defame, denounce, denude, deprive of protection, descry, detect, *detegere*, dig up, disclose, discover, display, divest, divulge, endanger, evince, exhibit, *exponere*, feature, give away, hazard, hold up to public ridicule, hunt down, imperil, inform on, jeopardize, lay bare, lay open, lay open to harm, lay open to view, make liable, make visible, manifest, muckrake, open to view, present, publish, put in a conspicuous place, put in danger, put in peril, put in view, reveal, risk, shame, show, show off, smoke out, strip, strip of disguise, turn out, uncloak, unconceal, uncover, undrape, undress, unearth, unfold, unmask, unsheathe, unveil, unwrap, vent
ASSOCIATED CONCEPTS: expose to disease, expose to harm, expose to obloquy, expose to ridicule, expose to the elements

EXPOSIT, **verb**   account for, clarify, clear up, elucidate, enlighten, enucleate, explain, explicate, expound, give a lesson, give reason for, hold forth, illuminate, make clear, make lucid, make plain, make simple, make understandable, present, set forth, shed light upon, simplify, spell out, state, throw light upon, unfold

EXPOSTULATE, **verb**   admonish, advise against, animadvert upon, appeal against, argue, attempt to divert, cast reproach upon, castigate, caution, chastise, chide, convince to the contrary, correct, declaim against, dehort, deter, disapprove, discourage, disincline, dissuade, divert by appeal, divert by persuasion, enjoin, exclaim against, exhort against, find fault with, gainsay, give advice against, object, objurgate, oppose, premonish, protest, reason earnestly against, recom-

mend against, remonstrate, repugn, take exception, talk out of, turn aside, urge against, view with disfavor, withhold assent

EXPOUND, **verb**   clarify, clear of obscurity, clear up, comment upon, commentate, construe, define, delineate, develop, elucidate, enucleate, explain, explicate, exposit, illustrate, interpret, make clear, make plain, present the meaning of, reveal, set forth, simplify, solve, spell out, state fully, state in detail, unfold, unriddle
ASSOCIATED CONCEPTS: expound the law

EXPRESS, **adjective**   advised, aforethought, calculated, categorical, certain, clear, clearly indicated, clearly stated, conscious, decided, defined, definite, deliberate, determinate, direct, distinct, distinctly indicated, distinctly stated, emphatic, especially prepared, exact, explicit, fixed, intended, intended for a specific purpose, intentional, meant, not accidental, not by chance, outlined beforehand, outspoken, particular, peculiar, plain, planned, planned in advance, positive, prearranged, precise, predetermined, premeditated, purposeful, purposive, single, specially prepared, specific, specified, unambiguous, unequivocal, willful, with forethought
ASSOCIATED CONCEPTS: express abrogation, express agreement, express authority, express condition, express contract, express covenant, express malice, express notice, express permission, express promise, express terms, express trust, express warranty

EXPRESS, **verb**   affirm, air, allege, articulate, assert, asseverate, aver, breathe, comment, communicate, convey, couch in terms, *declarare*, declare, denote, describe, disclose, enumerate, enunciate, *exprimere*, find words for, formulate, give expression to, give vent to, give voice to, impart, indicate, make a statement, make an assertion, make explicit, make known, make plain, manifest directly, mouth, observe, phrase, predicate, present, proclaim, pronounce, put in words, remark, say, set down, set forth, set forth in words, show, *significare*, speak, state, state directly, state with conviction, tell, utter, vent, verbalize, voice
FOREIGN PHRASES: *Quoties in verbis nulla est ambiguitas, ibi nulla expositio contra verba fienda est.* Whenever there is no ambiguity in the words, then no exposition contrary to the words should be made. *Tacita quaedam habentur pro expressis.* Certain things, though unexpressed, are considered as explicit. *Expressio unius est exclusio alterius.* Expression of one thing is the exclusion of another. *Expressio eorum quae tacite insunt nihil operatur.* The expression of those things which are tacitly implied has no effect.

EXPRESSION *(Comment)*, **noun**   articulation, assertion, asseveration, cliche, communication, declaration, expressed opinion, formula, formulation, idiom, indication, locution, maxim, mention, motto, profession, remark, representation in language, saying, *sententia*, set phrase, setting forth in words, statement, verbalism, *verbum*, vocal embodiment of thought, voicing, *vox*
ASSOCIATED CONCEPTS: construction, interpretation
FOREIGN PHRASES: *Expressio unius est exclusio alterius.* The expression of one thing is the exclusion of another.

EXPRESSION (*Manifestation*), **noun**   appearance, demonstration, disclosure, display, emergence, evidence, evincement, exhibit, exhibition, exposition, exposure, illustration, indication, instance, mark, presentation, presentment, revealment, revelation, show, showing, sign, token, uncovering

EXPROPRIATION (*Divestiture*), **noun**   attachment, confiscation, deprivation, dislodgment, dispossession, disseisin, distraint, distress, divestment, ejection, eviction, expulsion, forcible seizure, foreclosure, removal, sequestration

EXPROPRIATION (*Right of eminent domain*), **noun** compulsory purchase, condemnation, condemnation for public use, government appropriation of private land, seizure of private property for public use, seizure of property by the government, seizure of property in the public interest, taking for public use, taking of private land by the government

EXPULSION, **noun**   ban, banishment, debarment, deportation, deprivation, detrusion, disbarment, discharge, disgorgement, dislodgment, dismissal, displacement, dispossession, disqualification, driving out, effusion, ejection, ejectment, elimination, enforced withdrawal, eruption, eviction, *exactio*, excision, exclusion, excommunication, exile, expatriation, expelling, *expulsio*, extradition, extrusion, isolation, ostracism, ouster, outlawing, permanent exclusion, purge, putting out, rejection, removal, segregation, separation, suspension, termination of membership, throwing out

EXPUNGE, **verb**   abrade, annul, black out, blot out, cancel, cause to disappear, censor, cross off, cross out, *delere*, delete, destroy, dispose of, do away with, edit out, efface, eradicate, erase, excise, extinguish, extirpate, *inducere*, leave no trace, nullify, obliterate, *oblitterare*, put an end to, quash, quell, raze, remove, remove all sign of, remove all trace of, render illegible, rub out, scratch out, strike out, take out, wipe away, wipe off, wipe out
ASSOCIATED CONCEPTS: expunge the record

EXPURGATE, **verb**   abridge, amend by removing, blue-pencil, bowdlerize, cancel, censor, clean up, cleanse, conceal, cross out, cut, cut out, delete, depurate, efface, eliminate, enforce censorship, erase, expunge, *expurgare*, free from objectionable content, make better, purge, purify, refine, strike out, suppress, weed

EXTANT, **adjective**   alive, current, currently existing, existent, existing, *exstare*, in being, in current use, in existence, living, not extinct, not lost, present, standing, still existing, still to be found, subsistent, surviving, undestroyed, visible

EXTEND (*Enlarge*), **verb**   add, aggrandize, amplify, *augere*, augment, broaden, build up, carry beyond the limit, carry further, cause to grow, continue, deepen, develop, dilate, distend, draw out, elongate, enlarge the scope of, expand, *extendere*, increase, increase the length of, inflate, lengthen, magnify, make larger, make more comprehensive, *propagare*, protract, spread out in area, stretch, stretch out, supplement, swell, widen
ASSOCIATED CONCEPTS: extended lease, extension of a contract, extension of credit, extension of time for good cause

EXTEND (*Offer*), **verb**   advance, give, hold out, introduce, place at one's disposal, present, present an opportunity, present for acceptance or rejection, proffer, propose, provide an opportunity, put forth, put forward, put forward for consideration, submit, tender

EXTENSION (*Expansion*), **noun**   addition, aggrandizement, amplification, augmentation, broadening, dilatation, dilation, distention, enlargement, growth, increase, increase of size, increment, magnification, *prolatio*, *propagatio*, spreading, stretching, supplementation, widening

EXTENSION (*Postponement*), **noun**   abeyance, added time, additional time, adjournment, break, continuance, continuation, deferment, deferral, delay, extra time, further time, intermission, moratorium, more time, pause, prolongation, recess, respite, rest, stall, stay, suspension, suspension of activity, temporary stop, temporary suspension
ASSOCIATED CONCEPTS: extension for good cause, extension of payment, extension of renewal of note, extension of time

EXTENSIVE, **adjective**   ample, *amplus*, big, branching, broad, broad-based, capacious, commodious, comprehensive, considerable, covering a wide area, deep, diffuse, diffusive, embracing a large area, encompassing a wide area, expanded, expansive, extended, extending, far-flung, far-ranging, far-reaching, great, inclusive, large, large-scale, *latus*, liberal, *magnus*, prevalent, spread-out, spreading, sweeping, vast, wide, wide-reaching, widely extended, widespread
ASSOCIATED CONCEPTS: extensive damage

EXTENT, **noun**   amount, area, borders, bounds, breadth, circuit, compass, comprehensiveness, coverage, degree, dimensions, distance, expanse, gauge, *hactenus*, length, limit, limitation, magnitude, measure, quantity, range, reach, scope, size, space, spaciousness, span, stretch, sweep, width
ASSOCIATED CONCEPTS: extent of injury, extent of loss

EXTENUATE, **verb**   absolve, acquit, allow for, attemper, attenuate, clear, condone, debilitate, deprive of strength, dilute, diminish, enervate, enfeeble, exculpate, excuse, exonerate, forgive, justify, lessen, *levare*, lighten, make allowance for, make excuses for, make less serious, *minuere*, *mitigare*, mitigate, moderate, palliate, pardon, qualify, reduce, reduce in strength, soften, temper, thin, vindicate, weaken

EXTENUATING CIRCUMSTANCES, **noun**   alleviating circumstances, consideration, exception, extenuation, mitigating circumstances, mitigation, palliation, palliative circumstances, partial excuse, qualification, qualifying reasons, softening circumstances

EXTINGUISH, **verb**   abolish, abort, annihilate, annul, assassinate, blot out, bring to an end, butcher, cancel, choke, crush, cut out, deaden, deal destruction, demolish, deracinate, destroy, devastate, dismantle, dispel, dispense with, do away with, drown out, efface, end, eradicate, erase, expunge, exterminate, *extinguere*, extirpate, finish off, hold down, keep down, kill, kill by suffocation, lay waste to, liquidate, murder, nullify, obliterate, put an end to, put out, put to death, quash, quell, quench, raze, reduce to nothing, repress, *restinguere*, ruin, shatter, slaughter, slay, smother,

squash, squelch, stifle, strangle, subdue, suffocate, suppress, terminate, wipe out
ASSOCIATED CONCEPTS: extinguish a debt, extinguish a legacy, extinguish a right
FOREIGN PHRASES: *Resoluto jure concedentis resolvitur jus concessum.* When the right of the grantor is extinguished the right granted is extinguished. *Extincto subjecto, tollitur adjunctum.* When the substance is extinguished, the incident ceases.

EXTIRPATE, *verb* abolish, annihilate, annul, blast, blot out, bring to ruin, cancel, consume, cut down, deal destruction, demolish, deracinate, desolate, destroy, devastate, devour, dissolve, do away with, efface, eliminate, end, *eradicare,* eradicate, erase, *excidere, exstirpare,* exterminate, extinguish, get rid of, gut, lay waste, level, liquidate, nullify, obliterate, overturn, pluck out, pull out, pull up by the roots, purge, put an end to, quash, quell, ravage, raze, remove, render null, rid, root out, rub out, sacrifice, shatter, smash, stamp out, tear out, tear to pieces, unmake, uproot, weed out, wipe out

EXTORT, *verb* blackmail, coerce, compel, compel by intimidation, compel by threat, constrain by force, draw out by compulsion, draw out by force, elicit by threat, exact, exact by force, *exprimere, extorquere,* force, gain by wrongful methods, gain wrongfully, obtain by compulsion, obtain in an unlawful manner, obtain unlawfully, victimize, wrest, wring
ASSOCIATED CONCEPTS: kidnapping
FOREIGN PHRASES: *Accipere quid ut justitiam facias, non est tam accipere quam extorquere.* The acceptance of anything as a reward for doing justice is extorting rather than accepting.

EXTORTION, *noun* blackmail, coercion, compulsion, corrupt demanding, exaction, exaction by oppression, illegal compulsion, obtaining by force, obtaining by threat, oppression, oppressive exaction, rapaciousness, rapacity, *res repetundae,* taking by undue exercise of power, unlawful taking, wrenching, wresting, wresting money by force, wringing, wrongful exaction
ASSOCIATED CONCEPTS: kidnapping
FOREIGN PHRASES: *Extortio est crimen quando quis colore officii extorquet quod non est debitum, vel supra debitum, vel ante tempus quod est debitum.* Extortion is a crime when anyone under color of office extorts that which is not due, or more than is due, or before the time when it is due.

EXTORTIONIST, *noun* blackmailer, compeller, corrupt demander, demander, exacter, illegal exacter, illegal taker, taker, unlawful obtainer, wrester
ASSOCIATED CONCEPTS: coercion, kidnapping, larceny

EXTRACT, *verb* abridge, abstract, bring forth, choose, cite, collect, cull, deduce, derive, dig out, distill, draw, draw forth, draw out, educe, elicit, epitomize, *evellere,* eviscerate, evoke, excavate, *excerpere,* excerpt, *extrahere,* gather, glean, make a selection, mine, obtain, pick, pick out, pull, pull out, quarry, quote, remove, select, separate, single out, summarize, take out, withdraw

EXTRADITION, *noun* apprehension and transfer, capture and deportation, change of place, deportation, seizure and transference, sending to another state for trial, surrender of an individual, transfer to another au-

thority, transference, translocation, turning over to a foreign state
ASSOCIATED CONCEPTS: habeas corpus, rendition

EXTRANEOUS, *adjective* additional, alien, *alienus,* aside from the point, coming from without, derived from without, dispensable, extra, *extraneus,* extrinsic, extrinsical, foreign, impertinent, inapplicable, inapposite, incidental, inconsequent, inconsequential, irrelative, irrelevant, needless, noncompulsory, nonessential, nonpertinent, optional, peripheral, pleonastic, redundant, strange, subsidiary, superfluous, supervenient, supplementary, unaffiliated, unallied, unassociated, uncalled for, unessential, unnecessary, unneeded, unrelated
ASSOCIATED CONCEPTS: extraneous evidence

EXTRAORDINARY, *adjective* above average, amazing, beyond the ordinary, curious, different, especial, exceeding the usual, exceptional, *extraordinarius,* infrequent, *inusitatus,* irregular, notable, noteworthy, *novus,* out of the ordinary, out of the regular order, outstanding, peculiar, phenomenal, rare, remarkable, singular, special, supernormal, unaccustomed, uncommon, uncustomary, unequalled, unexampled, unfamiliar, unheard of, unique, unordinary, unparalleled, unprecedented, unusual, worthy of attention, worthy of regard
ASSOCIATED CONCEPTS: extraordinary care, extraordinary circumstances, extraordinary expenses, extraordinary grand jury, extraordinary peril, extraordinary prerogative writ, extraordinary purpose, extraordinary remedy, extraordinary risks, extraordinary services, extraordinary session
FOREIGN PHRASES: *Ubi cessat remedium ordinarium, ibi decurritur ad extraordinarium.* Where an ordinary remedy fails, than resort must be made to an extraordinary one. *Recurrendum est ad extraordinarium quando non valet ordinarium.* Resort must be made to the extraordinary when the ordinary does not succeed. *Nunquam decurritur ad extraordinarium sed ubi deficit ordinarium.* Resort is never made to the extraordinary until the ordinary fails.

EXTREME *(Exaggerated),* *adjective* aggrandized, amplified, beyond the limit, drastic, enlarged, exceeding, exceeding the bounds of moderation, excessive, exorbitant, fanatical, flagrant, going to the utmost lengths, going too far, gross, hyperbolic, immoderate, inordinate, intemperate, magnified, out of bounds, out of proportion, outrageous, overboard, overdone, overstated, overzealous, rabid, radical, undue, unreasonable, unwarranted, violent

EXTREME *(Last),* *adjective* at the edge, at the utmost point, concluding, conclusive, definitive, determinative, ending, endmost, *extremus,* farthest, farthest removed, final, finishing, furthest, hindermost, hindmost, last, most distant, most remote, outermost, situated at the farthest limit, *summus,* terminal, terminative, ultimate, *ultimus,* utmost, uttermost
ASSOCIATED CONCEPTS: extreme cases
FOREIGN PHRASES: *Probatis extremis, praesumuntur media.* The extremes having been proved, those things which lie between are presumed.

EXTREMITY *(Death),* *noun* cessation of being, cessation of existence, cessation of life, close, completion, conclusion, demise, departure, discontinuance, discontinuation, dissolution, end, end of life, expiration, extinction, extinguishment, finish, passing, quietus, stoppage, termination

EXTREMITY *(Furthest point),* **noun** border, borderline, boundary, brink, edge, end, extreme limit, *extremitas,* farthest end, farthest point, farthest reach, final point, fringe, frontier, limit, margin, outer edge, outside, pole, tail end, terminal point, termination, terminus, tip, ultimate point, utmost point, verge

EXTRICATE, *verb* clear, cut loose, deliver, deobstruct, detach, disburden, discharge, disembarrass, disembroil, disencumber, disengage, disentangle, disenthrall, disjoin, dislodge, disprison, enlarge, exonerate, *expedire, exsolvere,* free, let loose, *liberare,* liberate, loosen, make free, ransom, redeem, release, release from restraint, relieve, rescue, save, set at large, set at liberty, set free, tear loose, unbind, unfetter, unhamper, unharness, unknot, unloose, unloosen, unravel, unshackle, untie

EXTRINSIC, *adjective* accessory, added, additional, alien, apart, applied from without, collateral, contingent, derived from without, exterior, external, extra, extraneous, extrinsical, foreign, incidental, irrelevant, nonessential, outside, peripheral, secondary, separate, strange, subordinate, subsidiary, supplemental, unessential

ASSOCIATED CONCEPTS: extrinsic agreements, extrinsic ambiguity, extrinsic circumstances, extrinsic evidence, extrinsic facts, extrinsic fraud, extrinsic mistake

EXUDE, *verb* bleed, discharge, disembogue, drain, drip, drop, effuse, eliminate, emit, escape, excrete, find outlet, find passage, find vent, flow out, give off, gush, issue, leak, *manare,* ooze, pass, release, run, secrete, seep, spout, trickle, vent, weep

EYEWITNESS, *noun* *arbiter,* attestant, attester, bystander, compurgator, corroborator, giver of evidence, identifier, informant, informer, looker-on, observer, one who obtains evidence first hand, one who personally observes an occurrence, one who testifies to what he has seen, onlooker, seer, spectator, *spectator et testis,* testifier, viewer, watcher

F

FABRICATE *(Construct),* **verb** assemble parts, bring into being, bring into existence, build, call into being, cast, cause to be, cause to exist, complete, compose, create, devise, erect, establish, execute, *fabricari,* fashion, form, generate, make, manufacture, mold, organize, piece together, produce, put together, set up, shape, structure, turn out

FABRICATE *(Make up),* **verb** be untruthful, beguile, counterfeit, deceive, delude, devise falsely, dissemble, dissimulate, distort, fake, falsify, feign, fictionalize, forswear, invent, lie, misguide, misinform, mislead, misrepresent, misstate, palter, perjure oneself, pretend, prevaricate, sham, stretch the truth, tell a falsehood, tell a lie, trump up

ASSOCIATED CONCEPTS: fabricated evidence

FACE AMOUNT, *noun* exact amount, precise amount, sum, sum shown, sum stated, total

FACE VALUE *(First blush),* **noun** appearance, emanation, manifestation, semblance, visual impact

FACE VALUE *(Price),* **noun** price charged, quoted price, sum, total, worth

FACILE, *adjective* accomplished, amenable, attainable, compliable, compliant, conquerable, deft, dexterous, docile, easily done, easily influenced, easily persuaded, easy, easygoing, effortless, *facilis,* flexible, flowing, fluent, impressionable, malleable, manageable, moldable, performable, pliable, pliant, practiced, quick, readily mastered, ready, simple, skilled, skillful, smooth, tractable, undemanding, within reach, yielding

FACILITATE, *verb* accelerate, advance, aid, assist, assist the progress, clear, clear the way, deobstruct, disburden, disencumber, disentangle, ease, enable, encourage, *expedire,* expedite, forward, foster, free from difficulty, free from hindrance, free from impediment, free from obstruction, further, give clearance, hasten, help, lend a hand, lessen the labor, lift a ban, lighten, make a path for, make easy, make possible, open the way for, pave the way, promote, push forward, quicken, *rem faciliorem reddere,* render a task easier, render assistance, render less difficult, simplify, smooth, speed up

ASSOCIATED CONCEPTS: accomplice, aiding and abetting, facilitation

FACILITY *(Easiness),* **noun** ability, adeptness, adroitness, capability, competence, deftness, dexterity, ease, effortlessness, expertise, expertness, *facilitas,* flexibility, fluency, freedom from difficulty, grace, gracefulness, proficiency, quickness, readiness, ready ability, skill, smoothness

FACILITY *(Institution)*, **noun**   agency, bureau, *conlegium*, establishment, foundation, institute, organization, organized society, *sodalitas*
ASSOCIATED CONCEPTS: reinsurance facility

FACILITY *(Instrumentality)*, **noun**   agency, apparatus, appliance, channel, *consilium*, contrivance, device, *facultas*, implement, instrument, machinery, manner, means, mechanism, medium, method, technique, tool, *via*, way

FACSIMILE, **noun**   copy, duplicate, exact copy, mold, molding, oneness, replica, reproduction, sameness, semblance

FACT, **noun**   absolute certainty, absolute reality, actual occurrence, actual reality, actuality, authenticated incident, certainty, documented event, established matter, established phenomenon, event, existent thing, experience, *factum*, incontrovertible incident, indisputable event, palpable episode, perceived happening, real episode, real experience, reality, *res*, substantiated incident, tangible proof, true incident, truth, verifiable happening
ASSOCIATED CONCEPTS: conceded facts, established fact, facts in issue, facts of a case, facts pleaded, facts presented, facts which constitute a cause of action, question of fact, stipulated facts, uncontroverted facts, undisputed facts
FOREIGN PHRASES: *Ubi factum nullum, ibi fortia nulla.* Where there is no principal fact, there can be no accessory. *Regula est, juris quidem ignorantiam cuique nocere, facti vero ignorantiam non nocere.* The rule is that a person's ignorance of the law may prejudice him, but that his ignorance of fact will not. *Ex facto jus oritur.* Law arises out of facts. *Ad quaestionem facti non respondent judices; ad quaestionem juris non respondent juratores.* Judges do not answer to a question of fact; jurors do not answer to a question of law. *Facta sunt potentiora verbis.* Facts are more powerful than words.

FACTION, **noun**   cabal, camarilla, clique, conspiracy, contentious group, disaccord, disagreeing party, discord, dissension, dissent, division, *factio, pars*, partisan conflict, partisanship, pressure group, side, splinter party, united body

FACTOR *(Commission merchant)*, **noun**   agent, broker, commercial agent, delegate, deputy, envoy, interagent, intermediary, manager, medium, middleman, one who sells for factorage, proctor, *procurator*, representative
ASSOCIATED CONCEPTS: consignee, factors' lien

FACTOR *(Ingredient)*, **noun**   additive, agent, aid, aspect, cause, component, constituent, constitutive element, content, contributing force, determinant, elementary unit, feature, integral part, part, portion, segment, unit

FACTUAL, **adjective**   accurate, actual, ascertained, attested, authentic, authoritative, correct, definite, definitive, dependable, disinterested, errorless, exact, faithful, genuine, honest, incontestable, incontrovertible, infallible, irrefutable, literal, objective, official, precise, real, realistic, reliable, right, rigid, scrupulous, strict, true, trustworthy, unbiased, uncolored, undeniable, undeviating, undisguised, undisputed, undistorted, unerring, unerroneous, unexaggerated, un-

fabricated, unimagined, unimpeachable, unmistakable, unprejudiced, unquestionable, unrefuted, unspurious, valid, veracious, veridical

FACULTY *(Ability)*, **noun**   ableness, adroitness, aptitude, capability, capacity, cleverness, competence, competency, cunning, deftness, dexterity, enablement, endowment, equipment, expertise, expertness, fitness, flair, gift, handiness, knack, know-how, potency, power, proficiency, qualification, readiness, skill, skillfulness, strength, talent, *vis*
ASSOCIATED CONCEPTS: the faculty to comprehend

FACULTY *(Teaching staff)*, **noun**   body of professors, instructional corps, instructional personnel, instructors, lecturers, literati, mentors, officers of instruction, professorate, professors, teachers, teaching body, teaching personnel, tutors

FAIL *(Lose)*, **verb**   be defeated, be demoted, be unsuccessful, become bankrupt, become insolvent, botch, bungle, *cadere*, collapse, come short, come to naught, come to nothing, *concidere*, crash, decline, *deficere*, deteriorate, disappoint, dishonor, err, fall short, flunk, fold, go out of business, go under, lose, miscarry, miss the mark, not succeed, prove inadequate, prove unsatisfactory, prove useless, succumb

FAIL *(Neglect)*, **verb**   abandon, avoid, break one's promise, break one's word, desert, evade, forsake, ignore, leave, let one down, mismanage, miss, miss an opportunity, omit, prove unreliable, shirk
ASSOCIATED CONCEPTS: fail to act, fail to appear, fail to comply

FAILURE *(Bankruptcy)*, **noun**   commercial failure, default, discontinuance of business, economic downfall, failure to maintain solvency, financial disaster, financial loss, financial ruin, inability to maintain solvency, inability to meet financial obligations, insolvency, insufficiency of funds, lack of funds, suspension of business
ASSOCIATED CONCEPTS: failure to meet one's obligations, insolvency

FAILURE *(Falling short)*, **noun**   *defectio*, defectiveness, deficiency, delinquency, dereliction, inability, insufficiency, lack, loss of strength, noncompletion, nonfulfillment, nonobservance, nonperformance, omission, oversight, pretermission, shortcoming, slip, want
ASSOCIATED CONCEPTS: failure of consideration, failure of evidence, failure of heirs, failure of issue, failure of proof, failure of purpose, failure of title, failure of trust, failure to act, failure to bargain collectively, failure to comply, failure to file a return, failure to give notice, failure to make delivery, failure to perform, failure to prosecute, law office failures, partial failure

FAILURE *(Lack of success)*, **noun**   aborted attempt, beating, botch, breakdown, collapse, debacle, defeat, disappointment, downfall, drubbing, error, fall, fiasco, fruitless effort, frustration, ineffectualness, labor in vain, loss, miscarriage, misfortune, mistake, ruin, unsuccessful attempt, vain attempt

FAIR *(Just)*, **adjective**   *aequus*, affording no undue advantage, appropriate, balanced, deserved, detached, dispassionate, equal, equitable, evenhanded, fairminded, fitting, honest, honorable, impartial, merited, objective, scrupulous, sporting, sportsmanlike, square, suitable, unbiased, uncolored, uncorrupted, uninfluenced, unprejudiced, unswayed, upright

ASSOCIATED CONCEPTS: fair and impartial trial, fair hearing, fair on its face, fair preponderance of evidence, fair representation, fair trade, fair trial, fair wages

FAIR (Satisfactory), **adjective**   acceptable, adequate, bearable, decent, good enough, mediocre, medium, middling, moderate, moderately good, passable, reasonable, reasonably good, respectable, *secundus,* sufficient, suitable, tolerable, unexceptional, unobjectionable

ASSOCIATED CONCEPTS: fair aggregate value, fair and equitable value, fair and reasonable compensation, fair and reasonable market value, fair and reasonable value, fair cash value, fair consideration, fair equivalent, fair market value, fair preponderance, fair return on investment, fair use, fair valuation, fair value

FAIRLY (Clearly), **adverb**   absolutely, *aperte,* certainly, *clare,* completely, conspicuously, decidedly, decisively, definitely, discernibly, *distincte,* distinctively, distinctly, distinguishable, doubtlessly, evidently, explicitly, fully, indubitably, intelligibly, irrefragably, irrefutably, legibly, lucidly, manifestly, markedly, noticeably, obviously, openly, palpably, perceptibly, plainly, pointedly, positively, prominently, recognizably, surely, tangibly, unambiguously, unconfusedly, undeniably, understandably, undoubtedly, unequivocally, unmistakably, unquestionably, visibly, vividly, with assurance, with certainty, with confidence

FAIRLY (Impartially), **adverb**   *aeque,* benevolently, disinterestedly, dispassionately, equably, equally, equitably, evenhandedly, evenly, free from prejudice, honestly, honorably, impersonally, in a fair manner, *iuste,* justly, lawfully, legally, morally, properly, righteously, rightfully, rightly, scrupulously, tolerantly, unbiasedly, with justice, without bias, without distinction, without favor, without prejudice

ASSOCIATED CONCEPTS: adjudicate a case fairly

FAIRLY (Moderately), **adverb**   acceptably, adequately, decently, *mediocriter,* mildly, modestly, not badly, passably, presentably, pretty well, rather well, satisfactorily, somewhat, to a degree, to a limited extent, to some extent, tolerably, up to standard, well enough, within bounds, within reason

FAIRNESS, noun   *aequitas,* appropriateness, balance, detachment, disinterestedness, dispassionateness, equality, equitable treatment, equitableness, equity, evenhanded justice, evenhandedness, fair-mindedness, fair play, fair treatment, honesty, impartiality, integrity, *iustitia,* just dealing, justice, justness, lack of corruption, lack of prejudice, objectivity, openmindedness, probity, reasonableness, rectitude, right, rightfulness, rightness, scrupulousness, unbiasedness, uprightness

FAIT ACCOMPLI, noun   accomplished fact, accomplishment, achievement, actuality, actualization, attainment, carrying through, certainty, completeness, completion, consummation, deed done, effectuation, execution, fact, finished product, fruition, fulfillment, implementation, matter of fact, reality, realization, undeniable fact, work done

FAITH, noun   acceptance, allegiance, assurance, assured expectation, belief, certainty, certitude, confidence, constancy, conviction, credence, deep-rooted belief, dependence, fidelity, *fides,* firm belief, freedom from doubt, hope, implicit belief, implicit confidence, loyalty, *opinio,* optimism, *persuasio,* reliance, sanguine expectation, sanguineness, staunch belief, staunch loyalty, steadfast belief, steadfastness, sureness, surety, troth, trust, unquestioning acceptance, unshakable trust

FOREIGN PHRASES: *Fides servanda est.* Faith must be observed. *Judiciis posterioribus fides est adhibenda.* Credit should be given to the more recent decisions. *Ligeantia est quasi legis essentia; est vinculum fidei.* Allegiance is the essence of law; it is the bond of faith.

FAITHFUL (Diligent), **adjective**   assiduous, attentive, careful, conscientious, constant, dogged, exacting, *fidelis, fidus,* indefatigable, industrious, laborious, meticulous, mindful, painstaking, particular, persevering, persistent, pertinacious, relentless, sedulous, thorough, tireless, unflagging, unrelenting, unremitting, untiring, unwavering

ASSOCIATED CONCEPTS: faithful discharge of duty, faithful performance bond, faithful service

FAITHFUL (Loyal), **adjective**   constant, dependable, devoted, devout, duteous, dutiful, firm, incorruptible, obedient, patriotic, reliable, resolute, sincere, singlehearted, staunch, steadfast, true, trustworthy, unfailing, unwavering, zealous

FAITHFUL (True to fact), **adjective**   accurate, adhering to an original, close, conformable, correct, corresponding, equivalent, exact, faultless, genuine, honest, like, literal, perfect, precise, real, realistic, strict, true

FAITHFULLY, adverb   absolutely, accurately, acquiescently, closely, compliantly, conscientiously, consistently, constantly, devotedly, diligently, duteously, dutifully, earnestly, exactly, expressly, *fideliter,* firmly, honestly, honorably, in every respect, in good faith, incorruptibly, literally, loyally, meticulously, obediently, observantly, precisely, punctiliously, reliably, religiously, resolutely, responsibly, rigidly, scrupulously, sincerely, stanchly, steadfastly, steadily, strictly, submissively, to the letter, truly, trustingly, trustworthily, truthfully, undeviatingly, unerringly, unswervingly, uprightly, veraciously, verbatim, virtuously, with allegiance, with constancy, with fealty, with fidelity, with good faith, word for word

ASSOCIATED CONCEPTS: faithfully discharge the duties of office, faithfully perform, perform duties faithfully, serve faithfully

FAITHLESS, adjective   apostatizing, changeable, corrupt, corruptible, deceitful, derelict, disaffected, dishonest, dishonorable, disloyal, double-dealing, false, falsehearted, fickle, fluctuating, hypocritical, inconstant, indifferent, *infidelis,* insincere, mutable, *perfidiosus,* perfidious, *perfidus,* recreant, shifting, traitorous, treacherous, treasonable, treasonous, trothless, two-faced, undependable, unfaithful, unloyal, unpatriotic, unreliable, unscrupulous, unstable, unsteadfast, untrue, untrustworthy, vacillating, variable, wavering

ASSOCIATED CONCEPTS: divorce

FAKE, noun   charlatan, copy, counterfeit copy, emulation, fabrication, facsimile, false representation,

falsehood, falsification, feigned copy, forged duplicate, forgery, fraud, fraudulent replica, hoax, imitation, imposter, pretender, quack, replica, reproduction, ruse, simulation, unauthorized reproduction
ASSOCIATED CONCEPTS: counterfeit, forgery

FAKE, *verb*   act, act falsely, adulterate, affect, alter with intent to deceive, be deceitful, beguile, belie, bluff, cheat, claim falsely, counterfeit, cover up, cozen, deceive, decoy, defraud, delude, disguise, dissemble, dissimulate, distort, dupe, fabricate, falsify, feign, foist off, forge, go through the motions, hoax, hoodwink, imitate, lie, make a show of, make believe, malinger, mislead, misrepresent, pass off, plagiarize, portray falsely, pose as, prepare something specious, pretend, put on an act, put up a front, render spurious, sham, simulate, swindle, trick
ASSOCIATED CONCEPTS: false pretenses

FALLACIOUS, *adjective*   abounding in error, beguiling, contrary to fact, deceitful, deceiving, deceptive, delusive, delusory, devoid of truth, distorted, erroneous, *fallax,* false, faultful, faulty, faulty in logic, fraudulent, groundless, guileful, illusive, illusory, in error, inaccurate, incorrect, invalid, miscalculated, misconstructed, misfigured, misleading, misrepresentative, mistaken, paralogistic, sophistical, truthless, unfounded, ungrounded, unsound, untrue, *vanus,* wrong

FALLACY, *noun*   *captio,* deception, deceptive belief, delusion, deviation from truth, distortion, erroneous reasoning, erroneousness, error, fallacious argument, false appearance, falseness, falsity, faultiness, faulty reasoning, flaw in reasoning, illusion, inaccuracy, misapprehension, misbelief, miscalculation, misconception, misconstruction, misinterpretation, misjudgment, misleading notion, mistake, mistaken idea, paralogism, sophism, sophistry, unsound argument, *vitium,* worthless argument

FALLIBLE, *adjective*   deficient, errable, errant, erring, *errori obnoxius,* faulty, flawed, imperfect, liable to be erroneous, liable to mistake, not perfect, prone to error, prone to inaccuracy, uncertain, undependable, unpredictable, unreliable, unstable, unsure, untrustworthy, weak

FALSE *(Disloyal), adjective*   apostatizing, corrupt, deceitful, disaffected, dishonest, dishonorable, double-dealing, double-tongued, faithless, false hearted, fickle, hypocritical, inconstant, insincere, knavish, perfidious, *perfidus,* recreant, roguish, tergiversating, traitorous, treacherous, treasonable, treasonous, trothless, two-faced, undependable, underhanded, unfaithful, unprincipled, unreliable, unscrupulous, unsteadfast, untrue, untrustworthy

FALSE *(Inaccurate), adjective*   abounding in error, concocted, contrary to fact, deceiving, deceptive, delusive, devoid of truth, distorted, erroneous, fallacious, faulty, fictitious, groundless, improper, in error, incorrect, invalid, mendacious, misleading, mistaken, truthless, unfounded, ungrounded, unreliable, unsound, untrue, unveracious, wrong
ASSOCIATED CONCEPTS: altered, false advertising, false and malicious, false and misleading, false arrest, false check, false entry, false imprisonment, false information, false instrument, false oath, false personation, false pretense, false reports, false representation, false

statement, false swearing, false testimony, a false writing, knowingly false, materially false

FALSE *(Not genuine), adjective*   artificial, assumed, beguiling, bogus, copied, counterfeit, deceitful, deceptive, delusory, designed to deceive, factitious, fake, feigned, *fictus,* forged, fraudulent, given to deceit, imitation, intentionally untrue, make believe, misrepresentative, mock, pretend, pseudo, sham, simulated, spurious, *subditus,* substitute, synthetic, unreal
ASSOCIATED CONCEPTS: false checks, false claim, false pretenses, false representation, false statement, false swearing, false witness

FALSE PRETENSE, *noun*   act, affectation, affectedness, artifice, artificiality, chicane, chicanery, circumvention, circumvention of truth, cozenage, deceit, deceitfulness, deceptive representation of fact, delusion, designed misrepresentation, device, disguise, dishonesty, dissemblance, dissimulation, dupery, duplicity, evasion of truth, fabrication, facade, fake, fakery, false representation of fact, falsehood, falseness, falsification, falsity, *falsus,* feint, *fictus,* forgery, fraud, fraudulence, fraudulency, guise, hoax, imposture, invention, lie, mask, masquerade, mendacity, misinformation, misrepresentation, misstatement, perfidy, perversion of truth, pettifoggery, pretense, pretext, prevarication, ruse, sham, simulation, *simulatus,* sleight, spuriousness, stratagem, subterfuge, suppression of truth, surreptitiousness, swindle, treacherousness, treachery, trick, underhandedness, unnaturalness, untruth, untruthfulness, unveracity, wile
ASSOCIATED CONCEPTS: cheating by false pretenses, deceit, false representation, fraud, larceny, obtaining property by false pretenses, under false pretenses

FALSEHOOD, *noun*   canard, *commentum,* deception, dissimulation, distortion, distortion of truth, equivocation, evasion, fabrication, false assertion, false statement, falsification, falsity, *falsum,* fiction, flam, fraud, fraudulence, inaccuracy, intentional misstatement, invention, inveracity, lie, *mendacium,* misrepresentation, misstatement, nonconformity to fact, perversion of truth, pretense, pretext, prevarication, story, tale, untrue declaration, untruth
FOREIGN PHRASES: *Lex punit mendacium.* The law punishes mendacity.

FALSIFICATION, *noun*   beguilement, *corrumpere,* counterfeit, deceit, deceitfulness, deception, disguise, dissimulation, distortion, dupery, duplicity, exaggeration, fabrication, fake, fibbing, flimflam, forgery, forswearing, fraud, hoax, imposture, indirection, insincerity, *interpolare,* invention, lying, mendacity, misconstruction, misquotation, misrepresentation, misstatement, mockery, perjury, phoniness, pretense, prevarication, trickery, trumpery, untruthfulness, *vitiare*
ASSOCIATED CONCEPTS: falsification of evidence, falsification of records, falsification of testimony, perjury

FALSIFY, *verb*   adulterate, alter, alter fraudulently, belie, camouflage, color, *corrumpere,* dissemble, distort, doctor, embellish, embroider, exaggerate, fabricate, fake, feign, garble, *interpolare,* lie, make false statements, miscite, miscolor, misquote, misreport, misrepresent, misstate, pervert, represent falsely, stretch, tamper with, tell a falsehood, twist, violate the truth, *vitiare*
ASSOCIATED CONCEPTS: falsify records

FAMILIAR *(Customary),* **adjective** accepted, accustomed, acknowledged, cliched, common, commonplace, consuetudinary, conventional, current, established, everyday, *familiaris,* frequent, general, generally seen, habitual, hackneyed, homely, household, humble, inveterate, natural, normal, *notus,* ordinary, popular, prevailing, prevalent, recognized, regular, regulation, routine, standard, stereotyped, stock, time-honored, traditional, typical, understood, unexceptional, universal, universally recognized, unoriginal, usual, well-known, well-trodden, widespread, wonted
ASSOCIATED CONCEPTS: custom and usage

FAMILIAR *(Informed),* **adjective** accomplished, acquainted, advised, apprised, aware of, briefed, capable, certified, closely acquainted, cognitive, cognizant, competent, conscious, conversant, counseled, deft, dexterous, educated, enlightened, erudite, experienced, expert, fit, fitted, *gnarus,* instructed, intimate, knowing, knowledgeable, learned, lettered, literate, mindful, on intimate terms, *peritus,* practiced, prepared, privy to, proficient, qualified, schooled, *sciens,* sensible, skilled, skillful, trained, tutored, used to, versed, well-acquainted, well-educated, well-versed
ASSOCIATED CONCEPTS: familiar with the facts sufficient to sign an affidavit

FAMILY *(Common ancestry),* **noun** ancestry, antecedents, birth, blood connection, clan, common extraction, common forebears, common lineage, common parentage, consanguinity, descent, dynasty, ethnic group, ethnicity, extraction, filiation, folk, genealogy, house, kin, kindred, kinship, kinsmen, line, line of ancestors, line of descent, lineage, origin, parentage, people, same line of descent, same strain, sept, stirps, stock, strain, tribe

FAMILY *(Household),* **noun** brood, domestic circle, domestic establishment, *familia,* family unit, home circle, issue, offspring, progeny
ASSOCIATED CONCEPTS: adoption, curtesy, dependent, domestic relation, dower, Family Court, family law, family purpose doctrine, head of household, heirs, next of kin, surving spouse

FAMOUS, **adjective** acclaimed, applauded, *celeber,* celebrated, celebrated in public, conspicuous, distinguished, elevated, eminent, esteemed, exalted, fabled, famed, foremost, glorified, glorious, held in high esteem, highly reputed, holding public interest, honored, illustrious, important, in the limelight, in the public eye, in the spotlight, *inlustris,* known, leading, legendary, memorable, notable, noted, noteworthy, notorious, outstanding, popular, preeminent, prominent, public, recognized, remarkable, renowned, sung, talked of, universally recognized, well-known
ASSOCIATED CONCEPTS: libel, public figure, right to privacy, slander

FANATICAL, **adjective** ardent, burning, devoted, dogmatic, enthusiastic, excessive, extreme, fanatic, *fanaticus,* fervent, immoderate, impassioned, inordinate, obsessed, obsessive, overemotional, overenthusiastic, overzealous, passionate, phrenetic, phrenetical, possessed, rabid, radical, resolute, ultrareligious, unreasonable, unreasonably resolute, unyielding, zealous

FAR REACHING, **adjective** boundless, comprehensive, considerable, endless, enormous, epidemic, extended, extensive, far-flung, far-ranging, great, having a significant impact, huge, immeasurable, immense, infinite, large scale, limitless, of great extent, of great scope, prodigious, spread out, substantial, sweeping, tremendous, uncircumscribed, unending, unlimited, vast, wide, widespread

FARE, **noun** carfare, charge, charge for carriage of passengers, charge for conveyance of a person, cost of commutation, cost of conveyance, cost of transportation, expense, expense of transportation, fee, hire, money paid for passage, *naulum,* passage, passage money, payment for the right of carriage, portage fee, price, price of a ticket, price of passage, sum paid for carrying a passenger, tariff, ticket, toll, transportation charge, transportation fee, *vectura*
ASSOCIATED CONCEPTS: rates, fares and charges of carrier

FATAL, **adjective** annihilative, calamitous, catastrophic, causing death, causing destruction, consumptive, deadly, death-dealing, deathly, deleterious, demolishing, destroying, destructive, devastating, dire, disastrous, eradicative, *exitialis,* exterminative, extirpative, fateful, fell, feral, *funestus,* harmful, hurtful, injurious, involving death, involving ruin, killing, lethal, lethiferous, malignant, mortiferous, murderous, noisome, noxious, *perniciosus,* pernicious, poisonous, ruining, ruinous, slaughterous, toxic, tragic, venomous, virulent, wasting
ASSOCIATED CONCEPTS: fatal consequences, fatal defect, fatal errors, fatal injury, fatal to a cause of action, fatal variance

FATALITY, **noun** accidental death, calamity, casualty, *casus,* cataclysm, catastrophe, deadliness, deadly accident, death, death by accident, destruction, disaster, downfall, fatal accident, fatal casualty, fatal mishap, lethality, liability to disaster, malignance, malignancy, malignity, mischance, misfortune, mortality, perniciousness, ruin, subjection to fate, sudden death, tragedy, violent death, virulence, virulency

FATUOUS, **adjective** absurd, absurdly foolish, addled, asinine, brainless, deficient in reason, destitute of reason, dumb, fatuitous, *fatuus,* foolish, idiotic, ill-advised, illogical, imbecilic, inane, incapable of managing one's own affairs, inept, *ineptus,* irrational, ludicrous, moronic, nonsensical, obtuse, ridiculous, scatter-brained, senseless, shallow, silly, simple, stupid, thoughtless, unintelligent, unreasoning, unthinking, unwise, vacuous, witless
ASSOCIATED CONCEPTS: fatuous claim

FAULT *(Mistake),* **noun** aberration, blunder, bungling, erratum, error, error of judgment, failing, false step, flaw, impropriety, inaccuracy, miscalculation, misjudgment, misstep, misunderstanding, omission, oversight, slip
FOREIGN PHRASES: *Imperitia culpae adnumeratur.* Unskillfulness is considered as negligence. *Quod quis ex culpa sua damnum sentit non intelligitur damnum sentire.* He who suffers a damage by his own fault is not considered to have suffered damage. *Culpa tenet suos auctores.* A fault binds its own authors. *Magna negligentia culpa est; magna culpa dolus est.* Gross negligence is fault; gross fault is equivalent to a fraud.

FAULT *(Responsibility),* **noun** accountability, answerability, blame, cause for blame, *culpa,* culpability, *delictum,* delinquency, dereliction, liability, malefaction, misbehavior, misconduct, misdeed, misfeasance, negligence, *peccatum,* transgression

ASSOCIATED CONCEPTS: comparative fault, contributory fault, contributory negligence, gross fault, with all faults, without fault

FOREIGN PHRASES: *Culpa est immiscere se rel ad se non pertinenti.* A person is at fault who intermeddles in matters not concerning him. *Ejus nulla culpa est, cui parere necesse sit.* No guilt attaches to a person who is compelled to obey. *In pari delicto potior est conditio possidentis, defendentis.* Where the parties are equally guilty of wrongdoing, the defendant holds the stronger position.

FAULT *(Weakness),* **noun** debility, defect, deficiency, delicacy, devitalization, drawback, emasculation, failing, feebleness, flaw, foible, frailty, impairment, imperfection, impotence, impuissance, inadequacy, incapacity, infirmity, instability, insufficiency, lack of strength, loss of strength, powerlessness, shortcoming, vitiation, vulnerable point, weak point

FAULT, *verb* *accusare,* accuse, admonish, animadvert, attack, berate, blame, bring into discredit, cast a slur upon, cast blame upon, castigate, censure, charge, chastise, chide, condemn, criticize, *culpare,* declaim against, decry, denigrate, denounce, deprecate, depreciate, disapprove, discommend, discountenance, disparage, dispraise, dress down, hold to blame, impeach, impugn, impute, remonstrate, reprehend, reprimand, reprove, scold, take to task, upbraid

FAULTY, *adjective* aberrant, amiss, awry, below par, blemished, damaged, defective, deficient, distorted, errant, erroneous, fallacious, false, flawed, found wanting, full of faults, impaired, imperfect, imprecise, improper, inaccurate, inadequate, incorrect, inferior, injured, invalid, lacking, less than perfect, malformed, *mendosus,* mistaken, not ideal, out of order, solecistic, solecistical, unfit, unprecise, unsatisfactory, unsound, *vitiosus,* wanting, warped, wrong

FAVOR *(Act of kindness),* **noun** accommodation, act of generosity, act of grace, benefaction, *beneficium,* benefit, benevolence, benignity, boon, bounty, charity, courtesy, friendly turn, good deed, good service, good turn, grace, indulgence, kind act, philanthropy

FAVOR *(Partiality),* **noun** approval, attachment, attraction, bent, bias, disposition, favoritism, fondness, inclination, kind regard, leaning, liking, partisanship, penchant, predilection, preference, preferential treatment, prejudice, proclivity, proneness, propensity

ASSOCIATED CONCEPTS: challenge to the favor, favored legislation, favored treatment

FAVOR *(Sanction),* **noun** abetment, advancement, advocacy, aegis, aid, approbation, approval, assistance, auspices, backing, benefaction, championship, cooperation, countenance, encouragement, endorsement, espousal, fosterage, furtherance, good opinion, help, leave, patronage, permission, sponsorship, subscription, support

FAVOR, *verb* advance, advocate, afford advantages, aid, approve, assist, back, be biased, be favorable to, be indulgent toward, be partial to, be prejudiced, befriend, benefit, bolster, boost, champion, countenance, deal with gently, ease, encourage, endorse, facilitate, fancy, *favere,* further, grant favors to, gratify, help, make easier, prefer, promote, regard with favor, regard with kindness, sanction, show consideration for, show favor to, show unfair bias, *studere,* succor, *suffragari,* support, treat differently, treat with partiality

ASSOCIATED CONCEPTS: favored beneficiary

FAVORABLE *(Advantageous),* **adjective** advisable, appropriate, auspicious, becoming, befitting, beneficial, *commodus,* conducive, convenient, desirable, encouraging, expedient, felicitous, fit, fitting, fortunate, full of promise, good, helpful, opportune, politic, profitable, promising, propitious, *prosperus,* providential, salutary, seasonable, suitable, timely, useful, wise

ASSOCIATED CONCEPTS: favorable decision

FAVORABLE *(Expressing approval),* **adjective** acclamatory, acquiescent, admiring, agreeable, approbative, approving, assenting, benign, commending, compliant, cooperative, encomiastic, encouraging, eulogistic, eulogistical, favorably prejudiced, favoring, generous, gracious, helpful, kind, laudatory, obliging, panegyrical, praising, reassuring, recommendatory, responsive, uncritical, willing

FAVORITISM, **noun** attachment, bias, discrimination, fondness, inequality, inequity, leaning, one-sidedness, partialism, partiality, partisanship, penchant, preference, prejudice, proclivity, proneness, slant

FEALTY, **noun** allegiance, compliance, constancy, deference, devotion, duteousness, duty, faith, faithfulness, fidelity, homage, humble service, loyalty, obedience, respect, reverence, servility, steadfastness, support, veneration

FEAR, **noun** affright, alarm, anxiety, apprehension, apprehension of danger, apprehension of harm, apprehension of injury, apprehension of punishment, apprehensiveness, awe, concern, consternation, cowardice, cowardliness, cravenness, diffidence, dismay, disquietude, dread, faintheartedness, fearfulness, foreboding, fright, horror, intimidation, *metus,* misgiving, panic, *pavor,* phobia, presentiment, pusillanimity, qualm, scare, state of anxiety, terror, timidity, *timor,* timorousness, trepidation, uneasiness, want of confidence

ASSOCIATED CONCEPTS: duress, mental anguish

FOREIGN PHRASES: *Nihil consensui tam contrarium est quam vis atque metus.* Nothing is so opposed to consent as force and fear. *Vani timoris justa excusatio non est.* A frivolous fear is not a lawful excuse. *Vani timores sunt aestimandi, qui non cadunt in constantem virum.* Those fears are to be regarded as groundless which do not affect an ordinary, steady man.

FEAR, *verb* anticipate danger, anticipate injury, apprehend, apprehend danger, apprehend harm, apprehend punishment, be a coward, be afraid, be alarmed, be anxious, be apprehensive, be concerned, be cowardly, be daunted, be fearful, be frightened, be horrified, be in awe, be intimidated, be nervous, be overawed, be petrified, be scared, be startled, be terrified, be timid, cower, dare not, dread, feel terror, fret, have qualms, live in terror, lose courage, *metuere,* stand aghast, stand in awe, take alarm, take fright, *timere, vereri,* worry

FEASIBILITY, noun achievability, advantageousness, attainability, expedience, expediency, feasibleness, likelihood, opportuneness, performability, possibility, potentiality, practicability, practicableness, practicality, profitableness, reasonableness, usefulness, utility, viability, workability, workableness
ASSOCIATED CONCEPTS: feasibility study

FEATURE (Appearance), noun aspect, countenance, external appearance, form, lineament, *lineamentum,* lines, look, outward appearance, physiognomy, shape, visage

FEATURE (Characteristic), noun aspect, attribute, component, constituent, detail, distinction, distinctive trait, element, factor, idiosyncrasy, individuality, ingredient, mark, notability, outstanding property, part, particular, peculiarity, point, *proprietas,* quality, salient point, salient quality, singularity, trait

FEATURE (Special attraction), noun featured attraction, highlight, lead item, main attraction, main item, outstanding item, principal item, special attraction, specialty, star

FEDERAL, adjective allied, associated, banded, central, combined, confederate, federate, federative, *foederatus, foedere sociatus,* governmental, joined in a union, joint, leagued, merged, national, united
ASSOCIATED CONCEPTS: federal aid, federal common law, federal Constitution, federal courts, federal government, federal jurisdiction, federal law, federal offense, federal question, federal regulation, federal rights

FEDERALIZE (Associate), verb act in concert, affiliate, ally, amalgamate, associate, band in a federation, band together, centralize, collaborate, combine, confederate, consociate, consolidate, cooperate, federate, form a cartel, form a union, go into partnership, incorporate, join, join forces, league, make a common cause with, merge, organize, participate, pool, syncretize, team up, unify, unionize, unite, unite in a league, work as a team, work together

FEDERALIZE (Place under federal control), verb assume authority, exercise federal authority over, exert authority, exert federal control, place under federal administration, place under federal rule, seize from private control, seize from state control, seize power, take command, take control

FEDERATE, verb act in concert, affiliate, ally, amalgamate, assemble, associate, band, collaborate, combine, concert, confederate, conjoin, consociate, join, join forces, league, merge, organize, participate, pool one's interests, unify, unionize, unite, unite by compact, unite in a federation, unite in a league

FEDERATION, noun affiliation, alliance, amalgamation, association, centralization, coalition, combination, combine, concert, confederacy, confederation, cooperation, federal union, integration, league, merger, organized body, pool, syndicate, unification, union
ASSOCIATED CONCEPTS: labor federation, unincorporated association

FEE (Charge), noun charge for services, compensation, compensation for labor, compensation for professional service, consideration, cost, disbursement, dues, emolument, exactment, expenditure, expense, fare, fixed charge, *merces,* payment, price, recompense, remuneration, reward, toll, wage
ASSOCIATED CONCEPTS: attorney's fee, counsel fees, reasonable fee, splitting a fee

FEE (Estate), noun absolute inheritance, absolute interest in realty, corporal hereditament, feod, feud, fief, freehold, hereditament, holding, interest, land, landed estate, landed property, lands, legal estate, property, real estate, real property, realty, right of possession, title, unconditional inheritance, unlimited inheritance, unrestricted inheritance, vested interest in land
ASSOCIATED CONCEPTS: absolute fee, base fee, conditional fee, contingent fee, defeasible estate, determinable fee, fee simple, fee tail, limited fee, qualified fee
FOREIGN PHRASES: **Feodum est quod quis tenet ex quacunque causa sive sit tenementum sive redditus.** A fee is that which any one holds from whatever cause, whether it be tenement or rent.

FEIGN, verb affect, beguile, belie, cheat, concoct, counterfeit, create a false appearance, deceive, delude, disguise, dissemble, dissimulate, distort the truth, fabricate, falsify, *fingere,* imagine, imitate deceptively, impersonate, lack candor, lie about, make a false show of, make believe, make up, mislead, misreport, misrepresent, misstate, palter, personate, pretend, prevaricate, represent fictitiously, sham, *simulare,* simulate, speak falsely
ASSOCIATED CONCEPTS: feigned accomplice, feigned disability, feigned dispute, feigned issue

FELICITOUS, adjective accordant, adapted, agreeing, applicable, apposite, appropriate, apropos, apt, becoming, befitting, concinnous, concordant, conformable, congruous, consonant, desirable, effective, excellent, fit, fitting, fortunate, germane, happy, harmonious, ideal, in place, inspired, joyful, joyous, meet, opportune, perfect, pertinent, relevant, rightful, seemly, successful, suitable, suiting, tasteful, timely, to the point, to the purpose, *venustus,* well-chosen, well-expressed, well-timed

FELON, noun convict, criminal, culprit, delinquent, evildoer, guilty person, lawbreaker, malefactor, *nefarius,* offender, outlaw, recidivist, recreant, reprobate, *sceleratus, scelestus,* transgressor, wrongdoer
ASSOCIATED CONCEPTS: convicted felon
FOREIGN PHRASES: **Nullus dicitur felo principalis nisi actor, aut qui praesens est, abettans aut auxilians ad feloniam faciendam.** No one is called a principal felon except the party actually committing the felony, or the person who is present, aiding and abetting in its commission.

FELONIOUS, adjective against the admonition of law, against the law, against the rules, base, condemnable, contrary to law, criminal, criminous, culpable, dishonest, dissolute, done with intent to commit crime, evildoing, extralegal, fraudulent, illegal, illegitimate, immoral, in violation of law, *inlicitus,* lawbreaking, lawless, malfeasant, malicious, nefarious, *non legitimus,* nonlegal, of the quality of a felon, offending, outlawed, outside the law, perfidious, transgressing, unallowed, unauthorized, unlawful, unlicensed, unpardonable, unwarrantable, *vetitus,* villainous, wicked, wrong, wrongful

ASSOCIATED CONCEPTS: felonious act, felonious arson, felonious assault, felonious homicide, felonious intent, felonious purpose, feloniously taking

FELONY, noun capital crime, crime graver than a misdemeanor, criminal activity, criminal offense, gross offense, heinous crime, heinous misconduct, illegality, indictable offense, misdeed punishable by imprisonment, offense, offense punishable by imprisonment, transgression, violation of law, wrongdoing

ASSOCIATED CONCEPTS: assault with intent to commit felony, capital felony, common law felony, compounding a felony, felonious intent, felony conviction, felony murder, substantive felony

FOREIGN PHRASES: *Felonia, ex vi termini significat quodlibet capitale crimen felleo animo perpetratum.* Felony by force of the term, signifies any capital crime perpetrated with a criminal mind. *Felonia implicatur in qualibet proditione.* Felony is implied in every treason.

FENCE, noun buyer of stolen goods, buyer of stolen property, disposer of stolen goods, purchaser of stolen goods, purchaser of stolen property, receiver, receiver of stolen goods, receiver of stolen property, recipient of stolen goods, recipient of stolen property, vendor of stolen goods, vendor of stolen property

ASSOCIATED CONCEPTS: burglary, robbery, theft

FEOFFEE, noun acceptor, assignee, devisee, donee, donee of a corporeal hereditament, grantee, legatee, one to whom a fee is conveyed, one to whom seisin passes, one to whom title is passed, one who is enfeoffed, receiver, recipient of a fee, transferee

FEOFFMENT, noun assignation of title, cession of a fee, conferral of a fee, conferrment of title, conveyance of realty, conveyancing, conveying title, delivery of title, gift of a freehold interest, investiture of title, livery of seisin, passing of seisin, transfer of property, transmission of title

FEOFFOR, noun assignor, bequeather, bestower, devisor, donor, giver, grantor, one who enfeoffs another, one who gives a corporeal hereditament, one who transfers property by deed, one who transfers real property to another, person making a feoffment, person who conveys a fee, transferor

FERRET, verb bring to light, dig out, discover, disinter, elicit, find, fish out, hunt, look for, *rimari,* root out, search, seek, trace, track down, unearth

ASSOCIATED CONCEPTS: ferret out a crime

FERTILE, adjective arable, bearing offspring freely, creative, fecund, *fecundus,* feracious, *ferax, fertilis,* flowering, fructiferous, fructuous, fruitful, imaginative, ingenious, inventive, lush, luxuriant, original, originative, parturient, philoprogenitive, procreant, procreative, productive, profitable, progenerative, prolific, rank, rich, yielding

ASSOCIATED CONCEPTS: fertile octogenarian rule, presumption of fertility

FERVENT, adjective active, animated, *ardens,* ardent, avid, devoted, eager, earnest, enthusiastic, excited, feeling, *fervens,* fervid, *fervidus,* fierce, fiery, hearty, impassioned, intense, keen, passionate, perfervid, sincere, spirited, vehement, zealous, zestful

ASSOCIATED CONCEPTS: testator's fervent desire

FETTER, noun bond, bridle, *catena,* chain, check, *compes,* confinement, constraint, control, curb, detention, deterrence, deterrent, disadvantage, encumbrance, gyve, hamper, handicap, hindrance, impediment, imprisonment, incarceration, inhibition, interference, iron, limitation, lock, manacle, means of restraint, obstacle, obstruction, prevention, prohibition, rein, repression, restraint, restriction, shackle, strap, suppression, tie, trammel, *vinculum,* yoke

FETTER, verb bind, *catenas,* chain, check, confine, curb, enchain, enclose, entrammel, gyve, hamper, handcuff, handicap, hinder, immobilize, impede, *impedire,* impose restraint, inhibit motion, inhibit movement, keep in check, lock up, make captive, make prisoner, manacle, paralyze, prohibit, put in irons, put under restraint, restrain, restrain motion, restrain movement, restrict, secure, secure with chains, shackle, shut in, suppress, tie, tie down, trammel, *vincula*

FEUD, noun alienation, altercation, animosity, animus, antagonism, bitterness, breach, clash, conflict, contention, controversy, difference, disaccord, disagreement, discord, dispute, dissension, enmity, estrangement, faction, grudge, hereditary enmity, hostility, ill will, incompatability, inimicality, *inimicitia,* intolerance, inveterate hatred, inveterate strife, malevolence, mutual aversion, odds, open breach, open quarrel, opposition, private war, quarrel, rancor, rupture, *simultas,* split, strain, strife, tension, variance, vendetta

FIAT, noun authoritative order, authorization, command, decree, decree having the force of law, dictate, direction, directive, edict, enactment, hest, *imperium,* imposition, injunction, instruction, *iussum,* judgment, mandamus, *mandatum,* order, prescript, prescription, pronouncement, regulation, rescript, rule, sanction, ukase, warrant

FICTION, noun canard, *commentum,* concoction, fable, fabrication, *fabula,* false statement, falsehood, falsification, fancy, fantasy, feigned story, figment, invention, legend, lie, myth, perjury, prevarication, product of imagination, *res ficta,* untruth, untruthful report

FOREIGN PHRASES: *Fictio legis inique operatur alieni damnum vel injuriam.* Fiction of law is wrongful if it works loss or harm to anyone. *Fictio juris non est ubi veritas.* A fiction of law will not exist where the fact appears. *Les fictions naissent de la loi, et non la loi des fictions.* Fictions arise from the law, and not law from fictions. *Fictio cedit veritati. fictio juris non est ubi veritas.* Fiction yields to truth. where truth is, fiction of law does not exist.

FICTITIOUS, adjective apocryphal, arbitrarily invented, artificial, chimerical, *commenticius,* concocted, counterfeit, deceiving, delusive, erroneous, fabled, fabricated, fake, faked, false, fancied, fanciful, feigned, fictional, fictive, *fictus,* figmental, forged, founded on fiction, illusive, illusory, imaginary, imagined, invented, legendary, make-believe, mendacious, misleading, misrepresentative, mythic, mythical, mythological, nonexistent, notional, phony, pretended, sham, spurious, trumped-up, unfounded, unhistorical, unreal, untrue

ASSOCIATED CONCEPTS: fictitious address, fictitious claims, fictitious corporation, fictitious debts, fictitious name, fictitious parties, fictitious payee, fictitious person, fictitious statements

FIDELITY, *noun* allegiance, conscientiousness, constancy, *constantia,* devotedness, devotion, dutiful adherence, dutifulness, faith, faithfulness, fealty, *fidelitas, fides,* good faith, homage, loyalty, stanchness, steadfastness, trueness, trustiness, trustworthiness
ASSOCIATED CONCEPTS: fidelity bond, fidelity guaranty, fidelity insurance

FIDUCIARY, *adjective* commanding belief, commanding confidence, confidential, deserving belief, fiducial, founded in confidence, reliable, sound, trusted, trustworthy, worthy of belief, worthy of credence
ASSOCIATED CONCEPTS: fiduciary bequest, fiduciary bond, fiduciary capacity, fiduciary relation

FIDUCIARY, *noun* agent, caretaker, custodian, executor, guardian, one who handles property for another, one who transacts business for another, person entrusted with property of another, trustee
ASSOCIATED CONCEPTS: escrow, trust

FIGHT *(Argument), noun* altercation, bickering, broil, *certamen,* clash, conflict, confrontation, contest, controversy, debate, difference, disagreement, discord, disputation, dispute, dissension, embroilment, estrangement, expression of contrary opinions, imbroglio, logomachy, oral contention, polemics, *pugna,* quarrel, row, schism, squabble, strife, variance, verbal contest, war of words, wrangle

FIGHT *(Battle), noun* action, affray, appeal to arms, armed action, assault, attack, bloodshed, bout, brawl, clash of arms, combat, contest, encounter, engagement, exchange of blows, fracas, fray, hostile encounter, *pugilatio,* rencounter, resistance, scuffle, skirmish, struggle, tussle, war, warfare

FIGHT *(Battle), verb* act in opposition, altercate, appeal to arms, assail, assault, assume the offensive, attack, bandy with, be violent, break the peace, campaign, carry on war, challenge, close with, combat, come to blows, commit hostilities, compete with, confront, contend, contest, declare war, dispute, duel, engage, exchange blows, exchange fisticuffs, face danger, go to war, grapple with, have words with, joust, make war, oppose, *proelium committere,* pummel, rebel, reluct, resist, resort to arms, revolt, scrimmage, scuffle, set to, skirmish, spar, squabble, stand up to, strike, struggle against, take on, take the offensive, take up arms, tourney, tussle, vie with, wage war, wrestle with

FIGHT *(Counteract), verb* act in opposition to, be at cross-purposes, be contrary, be obstructive, confound, confute, contradict, counter, countermine, counterpose, counterwork, cross, debar, defy, disapprove, foil, frustrate, hinder, impede, inhibit, interfere, make a stand against, negate, object, obstruct, oppose, preclude, prevent, protest, rebuff, reject, repulse, resist, run against, run counter to, side against, spurn, stand against, stand up to, thwart, traverse, vote down, work against
ASSOCIATED CONCEPTS: fight passage

FIGMENT, *noun* canard, chimera, concoction, creation of the mind, deception, delusion, fabrication, falsehood, falsification, fancy, fantasy, feigned story, fiction, fiction of the mind, flight of fancy, hallucination, idle fancy, illusion, imagined thought, inaccuracy, invention, lie, mirage, myth, product of the imagination, reverie, romance, story, unreality, untruth

FILE, *noun* archive, card index, catalogue, classified index, docket, dossier, entry, folder, information, list, notebook, orderly arrangement of papers, record, record of the court, recorded information, register, registry, report, roll
ASSOCIATED CONCEPTS: duly filed, file a brief, file a complaint, file a lien, file a mortgage, file a reply, file a reply brief, file a summons, file papers, filed in open court, filing fee, filing of a claim, reporting act

FILE *(Arrange), verb* align, arrange methodically, array, assign places to, bring into order, catalogue, categorize, class, classify, codify, collocate, coordinate, distribute, fix the order, grade, graduate, group, *limare,* line up, make orderly, marshal, organize, pigeonhole, place in order, position, put in array, put in order, range, rank, reduce to order, regulate, set in order, set to rights, sort, subdivide, systematize

FILE *(Place among official records), verb* book, calendar, chronicle, deliver an instrument, deposit among records of the court, docket, document, enroll, enter, inscribe, list, place an instrument in a place of deposit, place in official custody of the clerk, place on record, preserve permanently as a public record, put on record, receive an instrument officially, register, store in the archives
ASSOCIATED CONCEPTS: docket, filing fee, filing of a deed, filing of a suit, filing of claims, filing of papers, filing of pleadings, late filing, time to file

FILIATION, *noun* affiliation, assignment of paternity, blood relationship, cognation, determination of a child's paternity, family connection, fatherhood, fathership, kinship, lineage, parentage, paternity, relationship, ties of blood
ASSOCIATED CONCEPTS: filiation proceeding
FOREIGN PHRASES: *Semper praesumitur pro legitimatione puerorum.* The presumption always is in favor of the legitimacy of children. *Filiatio non potest probari.* Filiation cannot be proved. *Pater est quem nuptiae demonstrant.* He is the father whom the marriage points out.

FILIBUSTER, *noun* attempt to obstruct legislation, blockage, cunctation, delay, delay in legislation, dilatory obstruction, hindrance, impediment, interference, obstruction, obstruction to congressional action, prevention of congressional action, protraction, retardation, retardment, stalling, stoppage

FINAL, *adjective* closing, completing, concluding, conclusive, conclusory, crowning, decisive, definitive, determinative, end, ending, extreme, *extremus,* finishing, irrevocable, last, rearmost, supreme, terminal, terminating, terminational, terminative, ultimate, *ultimus,* unappealable, without appeal
ASSOCIATED CONCEPTS: final accounting, final adjudication, final and conclusive, final award, final conviction, final decision, final decree, final determination, final disposition, final finding, final hearing, final judgment, final offer, final order, final settlement, final submission

FINALITY, *noun* accomplishment, achievement, cessation, close, closure, completeness, completion, conclusion, consummation, definitiveness, denouement, determination, end, ending, entireness, entirety, execution, expiration, expiry, extremity, finish, fulfillment, fullness, halt, implementation, maturation, maturity, performance, stop, stoppage, term, terminal, termination, terminus, totality, wholeness

FINANCE, *noun*   accounts, *aerarium*, art of monetary relations, budget, business science, commercial theory, economics, exchange, expenditure, financial affairs, financial resources, *fiscus*, funds, income, investments, management of money, monetary theory, money, money dealings, money-making, money matters, *pecuniaria*, pecuniary management, public economy, public revenue, resources, revenue, science of monetary relations, science of wealth, theory of business, theory of fiscal relations, wealth, working capital

FINANCE, *verb*   advance, aid, assist, back, capitalize, float, fund, invest, lend, loan, patronize, pay for, provide capital, provide funds, provide money, provide subvention, put up the money, set up in business, sponsor, subsidize, supply money, support, sustain

FINANCIAL, *adjective*   *ad aerarium pertinens*, budgetary, bursal, fiscal, monetary, nummary, pecuniary, sumptuary
ASSOCIATED CONCEPTS: financial institution, financial loss, financial responsibility, financial worth

FIND *(Determine), verb*   adjudge, adjudicate, announce a conclusion, arrive at a conclusion, arrive at a verdict, ascertain, ascertain and declare, ascertain by judicial inquiry, calculate, come to a conclusion, compromise, conclude, decide, decide a question of fact, decide upon, declare a verdict, deduce, deliver judgment, determine a controversy, determine after judicial inquiry, determine an issue, draw a conclusion, establish as facts, give an opinion, give judgment, hold, judge, make a decision, pass an opinion, pass judgment, pronounce as an official act, resolve, rule, set a question at rest, sit in judgment
ASSOCIATED CONCEPTS: findings of fact

FIND *(Discover), verb*   acquire information about, answer, apprehend, ascertain, attain by effort, bare, become acquainted with, become apprised of, become informed, bring into the open, catch a glimpse of, chance upon, *cognoscere*, come upon, create, decipher, decode, detect, discern, disclose, disentangle, disinter, divine, divulge, elicit, encounter, explore, expose, fathom, ferret out, figure out, gather knowledge, get to the bottom of, glimpse, happen upon, hit upon, identify, *invenire*, invent, ken, know, learn, light upon, locate, make certain, meet with, notice, observe, obtain by search, perceive, realize, recognize, reveal, run across, solve, strike, stumble on, trace, uncloak, unconceal, uncover, understand, unearth, unfold, unlock, unmask, unravel, unscramble, unscreen, unshroud, unveil, verify

FINDING, *noun*   ascertainment, award, conclusion, decision, decree, determination, judgment, judicial conclusion, judicial outcome, judicial verdict, opinion, opinion of the court, order, outcome, precedent, pronouncement, report, resolution, resolution of the court, result, ruling, sentence, solution, verdict, verdict after judicial inquiry
ASSOCIATED CONCEPTS: administrative finding, erroneous finding, evidence sufficient to support a finding, evidentiary finding, finding of a referee, finding of fact, finding of guilt, general findings, implied findings, inconsistent findings, special finding, supplemental findings

FINE, *noun*   amercement, compulsory payment, forfeit, forfeiture, legal liability, liability, mulct, *multa*, payment for misconduct, pecuniary penalty, pecuniary punishment, penalty, prescribed punishment, sconce
ASSOCIATED CONCEPTS: excessive fine, forfeitures, penalties
FOREIGN PHRASES: *Quam rationabilis debet esse finis, non definitur, sed omnibus circumstantiis inspectis pendet ex justiciariorum discretione.* What a reasonable fine ought to be is not defined, but is left to the discretion of the judges, all the circumstances being considered. *Mulcta damnum famae non irrogat.* A fine does not impose a loss of reputation.

FINE, *verb*   amerce, exact a penalty, exact retribution, impose a forfeiture, impose a mulct, impose a penalty, impose payment for misconduct, impose pecuniary punishment, inflict a penalty upon, mulct, *multare*, penalize, punish, punish by pecuniary penalty, subject to a pecuniary penalty, tax

FINGERPRINTS, *noun*   identification, identification records, impression, impression of fingers, imprint, marks, marks left by a person's finger, means of identification, prints

FINISH, *verb*   accomplish, achieve, arrive at the end of, bring to a close, bring to an end, bring to completion, cap, carry out, carry through, cease, close, come to a close, come to an end, complete, conclude, *conficere*, *consummare*, consummate, discontinue, end, finalize, halt, perfect, put a stop to, put an end to, stop, *terminare*, terminate, wind up
FOREIGN PHRASES: *Extincto subjecto, tollitur adjunctum.* When the substance is extinguished, the incident ceases.

FIRM, *adjective*   anchored, balanced, confirmed, durable, established, fast, fastened, *firmus*, fixed, immobile, immotile, immovable, indissoluble, inflexible, irremovable, moored, motionless, rigid, rooted, secure, secured, securely fixed, set, settled, solid, *solidus*, sound, *stabilis*, stable, stanch, stationary, steadfast, steady, stout, strong, sturdy, substantial, taut, unalterable, unbending, unmovable, unmoving, unyielding
ASSOCIATED CONCEPTS: firm offer

FIRM, *noun*   association, bureau, business, business establishment, business house, commercial enterprise, commercial house, company, concern, enterprise, establishment, holding company, house, industry, institution, joint concern, office, organization, partnership
ASSOCIATED CONCEPTS: corporation, law firm, professional corporation

FIRST APPEARANCE, *noun*   appearance, debut, inauguration, initial, gambit, opening

FIRST OFFENSE, *noun*   first charge, first crime, first criminal violation, first violation

FISCAL, *adjective*   budgetary, bursal, economic, financial, *fiscalis*, monetary, pecuniary, pertaining to financial matters, pertaining to government finances, pertaining to monetary receipts and expenditures, pertaining to the public revenues, pertaining to the public treasury, relating to accounts, relating to money matters, relating to the management of revenue
ASSOCIATED CONCEPTS: fiscal affairs, fiscal year

FIT, *adjective* able, acceptable, accommodated, adapted, adequate, adjusted, advantageous, advisable, applicable, apposite, appropriate, apropos, apt, *aptus,* becoming, befitting, capable, *commodus,* compatible, competent, concordant, conformable, congruous, consistent, consonant, correspondent, eligible, fitted, fitting, harmonious, *idoneus,* in keeping, in place, legitimate, matched, opportune, pertinent, prepared, primed, proper, qualified, ready, relevant, right, seasonable, seemly, sortable, suitable, suited, tailor-made, tasteful, to the purpose, well-fitted, well-qualified, well-suited, well-timed, wise, workable, worthy
ASSOCIATED CONCEPTS: fit for use, fitness for a particular purpose, implied warranty of fitness, reasonably fit for the purpose intended

FITTING, *adjective* adapted, appropriate, auspicious, becoming, convenient, correct, desirable, expedient, favorable, geared to, likely, opportune, proper, propitious, providential, seasonable, seemly, suitable, suited, relevant, timely

FIX *(Arrange),* verb adjust, align, array, assign places to, assort, bring into order, catalogue, class, classify, codify, collocate, *constituere,* coordinate, distribute, divide, establish, file, form, grade, graduate, group, index, introduce order into, line up, list, marshal, methodize, *ordinare,* organize, place, place in order, prepare, put in order, put in proper order, range, rank, regulate, set in order, sort, sort out, sort systematically, straighten out, systematize, tabulate
ASSOCIATED CONCEPTS: fix prices

FIX *(Make firm),* verb attach, confirm, consolidate, embed, entrench, establish, fasten in position securely, fasten securely, ground, harden, implant, infix, ingraft, ingrain, lock, lodge, make fast, make rigid, pin, place permanently, plant, ratify, render solid, root, secure, set, solidify, stabilize, stiffen, tether
ASSOCIATED CONCEPTS: fix compensation, fix rates

FIX *(Repair),* verb adjust, alter, ameliorate, amend, correct, do repairs, emend, freshen, freshen up, heal, improve, improve upon, invigorate, make corrections, make over, make restoration, make sound, make whole, meliorate, mend, overhaul, patch, patch up, purify, put in condition, put in good condition, put in order, put in repair, put in shape, rebuild, reclaim, recondition, reconstruct, rectify, redintegrate, redress, refashion, *reficere,* refit, reform, refurbish, regenerate, rehabilitate, reinvigorate, rejuvenate, remake, remedy, remove the errors, renew, renovate, *reparare, restituere,* restore, retouch, return to the original state, revamp, revive, revivify, right, service, set aright, set right, straighten, touch up

FIX *(Settle),* verb agree, arrange, arrive at a conclusion, arrive at an agreement, ascertain, come to a determination, come to a resolution, come to an agreement, conclude, *constituere,* decide, *definire,* determine, establish, make a decision, resolve, seal, set, *statuere,* straighten out, work out

FIXED *(Securely placed),* adjective anchored, *certus,* fast, fastened, firm, firmly established, firmly implanted, firmly seated, firmly set, immovable, irremovable, made fast, permanent, rendered stable, rigid, secure, set, solid, sound, stable, steadfast, steady, tethered, tight

FIXED *(Settled),* adjective arranged, changeless, closed, decided, definite, determined, entrenched, established, not fluctuating, not varying, permanent, predetermined, prescribed, rooted, unchangeable, unchanging, unshifting, unvarying, unwavering, well established
ASSOCIATED CONCEPTS: fixed asset, fixed by law, fixed capital, fixed costs, fixed income, fixed liability, fixed salary, fixed term, fixed time

FIXTURE, *noun* addition to realty, affixed to realty, attachment to realty, permanent attachment to real property, something constructively affixed to real property, something immovable from realty, something physically annexed to realty
ASSOCIATED CONCEPTS: appurtenance, domestic fixtures, equipment, irremovable fixtures, machinery, permanent fixtures, removal of fixtures, trade fixtures

FLAGRANT, *adjective* aiming for effect, apparent, arrant, audacious, blatant, bold, brazen, clear, conspicuous, daring, done for effect, enormous, flagitious, flaming into notice, flashy, flaunting, glaring, gross, immodest, *impudens,* infamous, loud, manifest, *manifestus,* monstrous, nefarious, noticeable, notorious, obtrusive, obvious, open, outrageous, outstanding, plain, prominent, pronounced, scandalizing, scandalous, screaming, shameless, shocking, showy, striking, striving for effect, visible, wanton
ASSOCIATED CONCEPTS: flagrant abuse of the law

FLATULENT, *adjective* bombastic, bombastical, declamatory, fustian, garrulous, grandiloquent, highflown, inflated, long-winded, mouthy, oratorical, orotund, pompous, pretentious, prolix, rhetorical, talkative, tumid, turgid, verbose, wordy

FLAUNT, *verb* air, be conspicuous, be ostentatious, be showy, boast, brandish, display, display oneself boldly, display with effrontery, exhibit, exhibit boastfully, flash, flourish, *iactare,* make a gaudy display, make a show of, make a showy appearance, make a spectacle, *ostentare,* parade, parade conspicuously, put forward, show, show off, sport, strut, swagger, wave, wave brazenly, wave conspicuously, wave ostentatiously, wear

FLAW, *noun* blemish, blot, breach, crack, defacement, defect, deficiency, deformity, demerit, disfigurement, error, failing, failure, fault, foible, frailty, gap, imperfection, imperfectness, inferiority, infirmity, injury, limitation, loophole, maculation, marring feature, *mendum,* omission, patch, rift, shortcoming, stain, unevenness, vice, *vitium,* weak point, weak spot, weakness
ASSOCIATED CONCEPTS: latent defect

FLEE, *verb* abandon, abscond, absent oneself, clear out, decamp, desert, disappear, *effugere,* escape, evacuate, evade, fly, *fugam petere,* hasten away, hide, make an escape, make off, play truant, remove oneself, retire, retreat, run, run away, run off, take flight, take to one's heels, withdraw
ASSOCIATED CONCEPTS: flee from creditors, flee from justice, unlawful flight to avoid prosecution

FLEXIBLE, *adjective* adaptable, adjustable, bendable, bending, capable of conforming to new situations, capable of responding to changing situations, disposed to yield, ductile, easily bent, easily managed, elastic, *facilis, flexibilis,* flexile, formable, *lentus,* limber, lissome, lithe, malleable, manageable, moldable, plastic, pliable, pliant, responsive, responsive to change, soft, stretchable, supple, tractable, unexacting, unstrict, waxen, wieldy, willing to yield to influence of others, willowy, yielding

FLIGHT, noun absconding, avoidance, decampment, departing, departure, desertion, disappearance, *effugium,* elusion, escaping, evacuation, evasion, exodus, fleeing, *fuga,* hasty departure, hegira, leaving, removal, retreat, running away
ASSOCIATED CONCEPTS: flight from justice, fugitive from justice, unlawful flight to avoid prosecution

FLOUT, verb affront, be contemptuous of, be disrespectful, be scornful, care nothing for, *cavillari,* contemn, defy, deride, despise, disdain, disregard, esteem slightly, feel contempt for, fleer, gibe, hold in contempt, hold in derision, hold in disrespect, hold up to scorn, insult, jeer, laugh at, *ludificari,* mock, outrage, rail at, revile, ridicule, scoff, scorn, set no store by, show contempt for, slight, sneer, spurn, take no account of, treat with contempt, treat with disdain, view with a scornful eye

FLUCTUATE, verb alter, alternate, be changeful, be intermittent, be periodic, be unsteady, change, change continuously, *fluctuare,* intermit, move in waves, pendulate, rise and fall, shift, show variety, swing, vary, wave, waver

FLUVIAL, adjective along the river banks, coursing, diffluent, eddying, flowing, fluent, fluid, fluidic, fluviatic, fluviatile, fluvicoline, from the river, riparian, riverine, rivery, rolling, running, streaming, streamy, surging

FOCUS, noun arena, center, center of activity, center of attention, center of attraction, center of consciousness, center of interest, central point, centrality, convergence, converging point, focal point, gathering place, goal, heart, hub, objective, point of concentration, point of convergence
ASSOCIATED CONCEPTS: target of an investigation

FOCUS, verb attend, attend minutely, bring into focus, bring the mind to bear upon, bring together, center, centralize, come to a point, concenter, concentrate on, concentrate the mind, concentrate the thoughts, direct one's thoughts to, direct toward one object, examine closely, fix on, fix the thoughts upon, give attention, give the mind to, look to, meditate upon, occupy the thoughts with, regard carefully, render central
ASSOCIATED CONCEPTS: focus an investigation on a suspect

FOE, noun *adversarius,* adversary, adverse party, antagonist, armed enemy, assailant, attacker, belligerent, bitter enemy, combatant, competitor, contender, contestant, detractor, disputant, enemy, fighter, foeman, hostile person, *hostis, inimicus,* one who is unfriendly, one who opposes, open enemy, opponent, opposer, opposing party, opposite camp, opposite side, other side, outlaw, public enemy, public opponent, rival, sworn enemy

FOIBLE, noun blemish, defect, deficiency, demerit, failing, failure, fault, flaw, frailty, frailty of character,

human weakness, imperfection, lack, limitation, moral weakness, need, problem, room for improvement, shortcoming, vice, *vitium,* want, weak point, weak side, weakness, weakness of character

FOIL, verb baffle, balk, be obstructive, bring to naught, cause to be nugatory, check, confound, counter, counteract, countermine, cripple, crush, dash, dash one's hopes, defeat, disable, disappoint, disrupt, *eludere,* frustrate, get in the way of, hamper, hinder, impede, intercept, keep from being successful, nip, obstruct, override, prevent, render vain, restrain, retard, ruin, spoil, stultify, subdue, thwart, undermine, upset, vanquish
ASSOCIATED CONCEPTS: foil a crime

FOIST, verb apply pressure, beguile, coerce, compel, compel to accept, constrain, deceive, fob off on, force, force upon, gull, impose, impose by fraud, inflict, insert surreptitiously, palm off, palm off fraudulently, pass off as genuine, put in slyly, put in stealthily, *subdere, supponere,* thrust upon surreptitiously, trick

FOLLOW-UP, noun by-product, completion, consequence, result, sequel

FOLLOW-UP, verb be thorough, carry through, complete, follow through, go through with, prosecute to a conclusion, pursue, see through, trace, track, trail

FOMENT, verb abet, agitate, aid, arouse, awaken, call forth, encourage, engender, enkindle, excite, ferment, fire, foster, *fovere,* galvanize, goad, impassion, incite, infect, inflame, infuse life into, inspirit, instigate, kindle, promote, provoke, rouse, set astir, stimulate, stir, stir up, urge, wake up, waken, work up

FOR CAUSE, adverb for legitimate reason, for just reason, with cause, with justification

FORAY, noun aggression, armed attack, attack, brigandage, depredation, drive, hostile invasion, incursion, inimical descent, inroad, invasion, looting, maraud, offense, offensive, pillaging, plundering, predatory incursion, push, raid, ransack, razzia, sack, sudden attack, thrust

FORBEAR, verb abstain, be patient, be temperate, be tolerant, bear with, break off, cease, decline, delay enforcing rights, deny oneself, desist from, dispense with, do without, endure, forgo, hold back, hold in abeyance, hold off, keep back, keep from, leave off, not proceed with, *parcere,* put up with, refrain, refrain from action, renounce, restrain, sacrifice, stop, submit, submit without complaint, suffer, *supersedere, temperare,* tolerate, treat with indulgence, wait, waive, withhold, withhold action
ASSOCIATED CONCEPTS: forbearance as consideration

FORBID, verb ban, bar, block, check, command not to do, debar, declare illegal, deny, deny permission, deprive, deter, disallow, disapprove, discountenance, discourage, enjoin, exclude, forfend, hinder, impede, inhibit, *interdicere,* interdict, make forbidden, not allow, obstruct, oppose, order not to do, outlaw, preclude, prevent, prohibit, proscribe, put under an injunction, refuse, refuse approval, refuse consent, refuse to allow, refuse to authorize, refuse to give permission, refuse to permit, render impossible, restrain, restrict, stop, taboo, *vetare,* veto, withhold consent, withhold permission

ASSOCIATED CONCEPTS: disallow a claim, *mala prohibita,* prohibit by an administrative agency, prohibition

FOREIGN PHRASES: *Qui non prohibet id quod prohibere potest assentire videtur.* He who does not forbid what he is able to prevent, is deemed to assent.

FORCE (Compulsion), noun   arbitrary power, authority, coaction, coercion, command, compulsion, constraining power, constraint, constriction, control, demand, dictation, discipline, drive, duress, enforcement, exaction, impelling, imposition, impressment, inducement, insistence, martial law, necessitation, necessitude, necessity, need, oppression, persuasion, pressure, prevailing, repression, restraint, restriction, sanction, spur of necessity, stress, strict control, subjection, subjugation, urgency, vehemence

ASSOCIATED CONCEPTS: ejectment by force, forced merger, forced payment, forced sale

FOREIGN PHRASES: *Vis legibus est inimica.* Force is inimical to the laws. *Quod alias bonum et justum est, si per vim vel fraudem petatur, malum et injustum efficitur.* What otherwise is good and just, becomes bad and unjust if it is sought by force and fraud. *Non videtur vim facere, qui jure suo utitur et ordinaria actione experitur.* He is not considered to use force who exercises his own right, and proceeds by ordinary action. *Ejus nulla culpa est, cui parere necesse sit.* No guilt attaches to a person who is compelled to obey. *Nihil consensui tam contrarium est quam vis atque metus.* Nothing is so opposed to consent as force and fear.

FORCE (Legal efficacy), noun   authorized might, lawful power, lawful vigor, legal vitality, legitimate puissance, rightful strength, sanctioned effectiveness, sanctioned potency, statutory cogency, valid potentiality

FORCE (Strength), noun   ability, ableness, ascendancy, authoritativeness, brawn, capability, cogency, command, competence, consequence, control, domination, dominion, effectiveness, effectuality, efficacy, empowerment, enablement, endurance, energy, firmness, forcefulness, hardiness, impact, *impetus,* importance, influence, influentiality, intensity, *manus,* mastery, might, mightiness, omnipotence, physical power, potence, potency, power, powerfulness, predominance, pressure, primacy, proficiency, stamina, supremacy, sway, vigor, vigorousness, virulence, *vis,* vitality

ASSOCIATED CONCEPTS: armed force, constructive force, excessive force, intervening force, physical force, superior force, threats of force, unnecessary force, unreasonable force

FOREIGN PHRASES: *Vim vi repellere licet, modo fiat moderamine inculpatae tutelae, non ad sumendam vindictam, sed ad propulsandam injuriam.* It is lawful to repel force by force, provided it be done with the moderation of blameless defense, not for the purpose of taking revenge, but to repel injury.

FORCE (Break), verb   batter, breach, crack, disjoint, fissure, *inrumpere,* invade, pry, rend, rive, rupture, shatter, smash, split, strain, tear asunder, wrench

FORCE (Coerce), verb   apply pressure, cause to yield, command, compel, constrain, control, demand, enforce, enforce obedience, enjoin, enslave, enthrall, exercise power over, *exprimere, extorquere,* extort, impose, insist, make obligatory, necessitate, obligate, oblige, order, overpower, overwhelm, press, push, put under obligation, require, tax, urge, use violence

FORCIBLE, adjective   aggressive, authoritative, binding, brought about by force, coercive, commanding, compelling, compulsory, controlling, convincing, dominant, done by force, drastic, emphatic, energetic, enforced, forceful, full of power, full of strength, having a strong effect, having force, having great strength, impelling, impressive, incumbent, influential, intense, invincible, oppressive, *per vim factus,* powerful, predominant, prepotent, prevailing, producing a powerful effect, required, resistless, strong, vehement, vigorous, violent, wielding power

ASSOCIATED CONCEPTS: defilment, forcible detainer, forcible dispossession, forcible entry, forcible repossession, forcible trespass, rape, sodomy

FORECLOSURE, noun   confiscation, deprivation, disentitlement, dislodgment, dispossession, distraint, distress, divestment, enforcement of mortgage, eviction, expropriation, expulsion, forfeiture, legal enforcement of a lien, privation, process of extinguishment of rights, removal, suit to extinguish the equity of redemption

ASSOCIATED CONCEPTS: ejectment, foreclosure decree, foreclosure of a lien, foreclosure of a mortgage, foreclosure of collateral, foreclosure proceedings, foreclosure sale, redemption by purchaser

FOREGONE CONCLUSION, noun   forejudgment, foreordination, inevitable result, onesidedness, partiality, preconceived idea, preconclusion, predecision, predesigned conclusion, predetermination, predetermined conclusion, predilection, predisposition, prejudged conclusion, prejudgment, prejudice, prejudiced view, prenotion, preordination, prepossession, presentiment, presupposal, presupposition, presurmise

FOREIGN, adjective   *adventicius,* alien, attached to another jurisdiction, belonging to another country, detached, different, disconnected, dissociated, distant, *externus,* extraneous, extrinsic, independent, nonresident, not indigenous, not native, outside, peregrine, *peregrinus,* remote, separate, strange, subject to another jurisdiction, unaffiliated, unallied, unassociated, unconnected, unfamiliar, unrelated, unusual, without connection

ASSOCIATED CONCEPTS: foreign bills, foreign commerce, foreign corporation, foreign divorce, foreign judgment, foreign jurisdiction, foreign laws, foreign notes, foreign patents, foreign state

FOREJUDGE, verb   assume, be prejudiced, be rash, decide in advance, determine in advance, have a bias, have a prejudice, have a prepossession, judge beforehand, judge in advance, jump to a conclusion, preconceive, preconclude, predecide, predetermine, prejudge, prejudicate, prepossess, presume, presuppose, presurmise

FORENSIC, adjective   adapted to argumentation, arguable, argumentative, barristerial, belonging to courts of justice, belonging to debate, capable of being debated, concerning the law, contentious, contestable, controversial, controvertible, discursive, disputable, disputative, fitted for legal argumentation, fitted for public argumentation, *forensis,* in the field of public debate, *iudicialis, iuridicialis,* judicatory, judicial, jural,

juridic, juridical, jurisdictional, jurisprudential, juristic, lawful, learned in the law, legal, legalistic, litigious, open to discussion, pertaining to the courts, pertaining to the law, polemical, proper to public debate, solicitorial, statutory, subject to contention, subject to controversy
ASSOCIATED CONCEPTS: forensic medicine

FORERUNNER, noun ancestor, antecedent, antecessor, auspice, forebear, harbinger, herald, leader, messenger, omen, pioneer, portent, *praenuntius,* precedent, precursor, predecessor, preface, prefigurement, presage, progenitor, scout, sign, vanguard, warning

FORESEEABLE, adjective anticipatable, anticipated, calculable, contemplated, counted upon, expected, forecasted, foreknowable, foreseen, foretellable, known in advance, looked for, perceived, planned, *praesciens,* predictable, predicted, probable, prophesied, reasonably anticipated, to be expected, vaticinal
ASSOCIATED CONCEPTS: duty to anticipate, forseeability in considering proximate cause, forseeable dangers, forseeable injury, forseeable risk, last clear chance
FOREIGN PHRASES: *Nemo tenetur divinare.* No man is bound to foretell, or to have foreknowledge of, a future event. *Rerum progressus ostendunt multa, quae in initio praecaveri seu praevide ri non possunt.* In the course of events, many problems arise which at the beginning could not be guarded against or foreseen.

FORSEEN, adjective anticipated, awaited, expected, forecast, foretold, looked for, predicted, presaged, presumed, promised, prophesied

FORESTALL, verb act in advance, *antevertere,* anticipate, arrest, avert, avoid, await, be armed, be forewarned, bring to a standstill, cancel, censor, check, counteract, deter, disallow, enjoin, estop, filibuster, forbid, forfend, frustrate, halt, hinder, hold back, impede, inhibit, intercept, interfere, intervene, look forward to, make provisions, obstruct, obviate, *praecipere, praevenire,* preclude, prepare for, prevent, prohibit, provide against, stave off, stay, stifle, stop, stymie, suppress, suspend, take precautions, thwart, veto, wait for, ward off
ASSOCIATED CONCEPTS: forestall an action

FORETHOUGHT, noun advance planning, aim, anticipation, calculation, circumspection, consideration, consideration in advance, contemplation, deliberate intention, deliberation, design, direction, distinct purpose, fixed purpose, intent, intention, plan, planned course of action, planning ahead, plot, preconsideration, predeliberation, predetermination, premeditation, previous consideration, previous design, previous reflection, prior planning, prior thought, *providentia,* provision, purpose, resolution, resolve, scheme, shrewdness, strategy, thought beforehand, thoughtfulness, volition, will, willfulness
ASSOCIATED CONCEPTS: malice

FOREWARN, verb admonish beforehand, advise, advise against, advise beforehand, alarm, alert, alert to danger, augur, caution, caution against danger, caution beforehand, caution in advance, counsel, deter, discourage, dissuade, exhort, expostulate, forbid, forebode, forecast, foreshadow, foreshow, give fair warning, give intimation of impending evil, give notice, give previous notice to, give previous warning to, give warning of pos-

sible harm, inform, make acquainted with, make aware, notify, offer a word of caution, ominate, portend, *praemonere,* predict, prefigure, premonish, prepare, presage, preshow, prewarn, prognosticate, prophesy, put on guard, signal, threaten, urge against, urge to take heed, vaticinate, warn, warn beforehand, warn in advance
ASSOCIATED CONCEPTS: abandon a crime, forseeability, notice

FORFEIT, verb abandon, abdicate, abjure, alienate by breach of condition, be deprived of, capitulate, cede, concede, default, deliver up, demit, disgorge, escheat, fail to keep, fail to retain, forgo, forswear, give away, give up, give up claim to, give up the argument, give up the point, incur a loss, let go, let slip, lose, lose an opportunity, lose by breach of condition, lose by default, lose by failure to appear, meet with a loss, part with, put aside, quit, *re multari,* relinquish, *rem amittere,* renounce, repudiate, sacrifice, surrender, waive, withdraw, yield
ASSOCIATED CONCEPTS: forfeit a bond, forfeit a deposit, forfeit bail

FORFEITURE (Act of forfeiting), **noun** confiscation, deprivation, deprivation of a right, destruction of a right, disenfranchisement, disentitlement, dispossession, divestiture of property, divestment, eviction, exaction, expropriation, forcible seizure, foreclosure, involuntary loss of right, loss of right, punishment, seizure, seizure of a privilege
ASSOCIATED CONCEPTS: action for forfeiture, forfeiture clause, forfeiture of bail, forfeiture of bond, forfeiture of deposit, forfeiture of office, forfeiture provision, redemption of property forfeitured, relief from forfeiture, right of forfeiture, tax forfeiture
FOREIGN PHRASES: *Nullus jus alienum forisfacere potest.* No man can forfeit the right of another.

FORFEITURE (Thing forfeited), **noun** amercement, cost, fine, loss, loss consequent to a default, mulct, pecuniary penalty, penal retribution, penalization, penalty, punishment

FORGE (Counterfeit), **verb** commit forgery, copy fraudulently, fake, falsify, feign, imitate, imitate falsely, imitate fraudulently, issue counterfeit money, make a spurious copy of, produce counterfeit money, reproduce fraudulently, simulate, *subicere, supponere*
ASSOCIATED CONCEPTS: forged check, forged instrument

FORGE (Produce), **verb** actualize, bring into being, bring into existence, build, cause, compose, concoct, construct, contrive, create, develop, devise, efform, evolve, fabricate, fashion, form, formulate, frame, hammer out, invent, make, manufacture, model, mold, originate, put together, shape

FORGERY, noun copy, counterfeit, counterfeiting, deception, fake, false fabrication, falsification, fraud, fraudulence, fraudulent document, imitation, imposition, imposture, misrepresentation, sham, *subiectio*
ASSOCIATED CONCEPTS: alteration of instruments, false entry, forged check, forged instrument, fraud

FORGIVE, verb absolve, acquit, bear no malice, cancel, clear, *condonare,* condone, exculpate, excuse, exempt, exonerate, forget, give absolution, grant am-

nesty, grant pardon, *ignoscere*, overlook, palliate, pardon, reprieve, shrive, vindicate
ASSOCIATED CONCEPTS: executive pardon, forgiveness of debt

FORGO, *verb* abandon, abjure, abnegate, abstain from, avoid, bypass, cast aside, cast off, cease, decline, desist from, *dimittere*, discard, discontinue, dismiss, dispense with, dispose of, do without, eliminate, eschew, forbear, forsake, forswear, give up, give up claim to, give up the right to, keep aloof from, keep away from, keep from, lay aside, leave, let pass, omit, part with, pass, quit, refrain from, refuse, reject, relinquish, renounce, renounce claim to, resign, rid oneself of, shun, sign away, stop, surrender, swear off, throw aside, waive, withdraw from, yield

FORM *(Arrangement)*, ***noun*** array, ceremony, class, classification, custom, design, distribution, efformation, established practice, *facies*, fashion, *figura*, *forma*, formality, format, formation, formula, formulary, grouping, kind, manner, method, mode, model, order, organization, outline, pattern, plan, procedure, regimentation, regularity, rite, ritual, scheme, shape, sort, style, system, systematization, type, way
ASSOCIATED CONCEPTS: form of action, objections to form
FOREIGN PHRASES: *Si aliquid ex solemnibus deficiat, cum aequitas poscit, subveniendum est.* If anything is deficient in formal requisites, where equity requires it, it should be supplied. *Forma legalis forma essentialis.* Legal form is essential form. *Forma non observata, infertur adnullatio actus.* If form is not observed, it is inferred that the act is a nullity.

FORM *(Document)*, ***noun*** blank, card, copy, data sheet, information blank, instrument, muniment, questionary, questionnaire, record, reference form, register, registry, report, standard letter, written document
ASSOCIATED CONCEPTS: legal forms, standard form

FORM, *verb* arrange, assemble, build, compose, *conformare*, construct, contrive, create, design, devise, embody, establish, *fabricari*, fabricate, fashion, *figurare*, forge, formulate, frame, give shape to, initiate, make, manufacture, materialize, mold, organize, produce, put together, shape, structure
ASSOCIATED CONCEPTS: form a corporation

FORMAL, *adjective* accepted, according to established form, affected, approved, businesslike, ceremonial, ceremonious, confirmed, conventional, customary, decorous, fixed, following established custom, established form, following established rules, *formalis*, formalistic, in accordance with conventional requirements, inflexible, mannered, observant of form, official, polite, pompous, prescriptive, prim, proper, reserved, rigid, ritual, ritualistic, set, starched, stiff, stilted, systematic, traditional, unbending, uncompromising
ASSOCIATED CONCEPTS: formal acceptance, formal charges, formal defect, formal party

FORMALITY, *noun* ceremonial rite, ceremoniousness, ceremony, convention, conventionality, correctness, custom, decorum, established mode, etiquette, formalness, observance of form, outward form, prescribed form, propriety, punctilio, rigidity, rigidness, rite, rit-

ual, *ritus*, rule of proceeding, set form, settled method, solemnity, stiffness, stiltedness
ASSOCIATED CONCEPTS: formalities in executing a will

FORMALIZE, *verb* conventionalize, form, give form to, give formal approval to, give formal status to, legalize, legitimate, legitimatize, make formal, make official, make valid, ritualize, shape, solemnize, validate
ASSOCIATED CONCEPTS: formalize an agreement

FORMATION, *noun* arrangement, array, coinage, composition, concoction, configuration, *conformatio*, conformation, construction, creation, efformation, establishment, fabrication, figuration, *forma*, format, foundation, generation, genesis, institution, invention, layout, manufacture, order, organization, origination, production, structure, synthesis, systematization

FORMER, *adjective* antecedent, bygone, earlier, erstwhile, foregoing, late, past, preceding, preexistent, previous, prior, *pristinus*, quondam, retired, whilom
ASSOCIATED CONCEPTS: former adjudication, former conviction, former jeopardy, former marriage, former trial, former will

FORMIDABLE, *adjective* alarming, appalling, arduous, awe-inspiring, awesome, dangerous, deterring, difficult, disturbing, dreadful, exciting fear, fear-inspiring, fearful, fierce, *formidolosus*, frightening, frightful, hard to overcome, horrible, horrifying, huge, indomitable, menacing, overpowering, overwhelming, redoubtable, terrible, terrifying, threatening, unconquerable, unnerving, unyielding

FORMULATE, *verb* arrange, compose, devise, draft, draw up, efform, express in a formula, express in a systematic way, express in precise form, fabricate, fashion, forge, form, formularize, formulize, frame, give form to, hammer out, indite, produce, put into shape, put together, redact, reduce to a formula, set down, shape, state systematically, turn out

FORSWEAR, *verb* abandon, abhor, abjure, abnegate, avoid, break off, cast aside, cast away, cast off, decline, deny, desert, disaccustom, discard, disclaim, discontinue, discountenance, disdain, dispense with, divest oneself, do without, drop, eschew, forego, forsake, give up, lay aside, leave, let alone, omit, part with, proscribe, quit, refrain from, refuse, reject, relinquish, renounce, repel, repudiate, sacrifice, scorn, shun, spurn, toss aside, waive, withdraw from, yield

FORTHCOMING, *adjective* about to happen, advancing, anticipated, approaching, at hand, awaited, close at hand, coming, coming soon, destined, drawing near, due, ensuing, eventual, expected, fated, following, foreseeable, future, imminent, impending, inescapable, inevitable, in store, looming, near, nearing, nigh, on the agenda, on the docket, on the horizon, oncoming, pending, planned, predestined, predicted, projected, promised, prospective, scheduled, to come, ultimate, unavoidable, upcoming, yet to be
ASSOCIATED CONCEPTS: expectancy under a will

FORTHWITH, *adverb* as soon as can be reasonably expected, at once, immediately, instantaneously, instantly, promptly, quickly, straightaway, with all reasonable speed, with reasonable dispatch

FORTUITOUS, adjective   accidental, adventitious, casual, chance, circumstantial, coincidental, designless, *forte oblatus, fortuitus,* haphazard, happening by chance, involuntary, lucky, occurring by chance, providential, random, spontaneous, surprise, surprising, uncalculated, undesigned, undirected, unexpected, unforeseen, unintended, unintentional, unlooked for, unmeant, unmotivated, unplanned, unpredicted, unpremeditated, unrehearsed
ASSOCIATED CONCEPTS: fortuitous event

FORUM *(Court),* **noun**   assize, the bench, court of justice, court of law, courtroom, *forum,* judicatory, judicature, judicial tribunal, panel of judges, session of the court, tribunal
ASSOCIATED CONCEPTS: *forum non conveniens,* law of the forum

FORUM *(Medium),* **noun**   agency, agent, channel, instrument, intermediary, means, means of expression, mechanism, method of communication, method of expression, mode of communication, vehicle

FOSTER, verb   abet, advance, advocate, aid, *alere,* assist, befriend, breed, bring up, care for, cherish, coach, countenance, cultivate, encourage, favor, forward, further, harbor, help, hold dear, indulge, look after, minister to, nourish, nurse, nurture, *nutrire,* patronize, promote, protect, raise, rear, safeguard, stimulate, subserve, succor, support, sustain, take care of, tend, train, treasure, watch over, work for

FOUNDATION *(Basis),* **noun**   base, bedrock, beginning, cornerstone, frame, framework, *fundamenta,* fundamental principle, groundwork, keystone, origin, premise, root, rudiment, *sedes,* skeleton, substructure, support, supporting structure, underlying principle, underpinning
ASSOCIATED CONCEPTS: foundation for evidence, foundation of a claim, foundation of a lien, laying a foundation for a document

FOUNDATION *(Organization),* **noun**   association, charitable institution, charity, *conlegium,* eleemosynary corporation, endowed institution, endowment, establishment, fund invested for a charitable purpose, institute, institution, organization to aid the needy, organized body for charity, philanthropic institution, *sodalitas*
ASSOCIATED CONCEPTS: charitable foundation, not for profit organization

FRACAS, noun   affray, altercation, battle, bickering, blows, brawl, breach of the peace, broil, clash, commotion, conflict, contention, disagreement, discord, dispute, dissension, disturbance, fight, fray, fuss, jangle, jar, melee, noisy quarrel, outbreak, quarrel, riot, row, rowdiness, ruction, scramble, scuffle, set-to, squabble, squall, trouble, tumult, turmoil, tussle, uproar, wrangle
ASSOCIATED CONCEPTS: disorderly conduct, disturbing the peace

FRACTIOUS, adjective   apt to quarrel, badtempered, bearish, bickering, cantankerous, captious, carping, caviling, choleric, churlish, complaining, contentious, contrary, crabby, cranky, cross, cross-grained, crusty, *difficilis,* difficult, disposed to cavil, disputatious, exceptious, excitable, faultfinding, fretful, grouchy, hot-tempered, ill-tempered, impatient, inclined to anger, indocile, inflammable, irascible, irritable, moodish, moody, *morosus,* peevish, perverse, pettish, petulant, quarrelsome, querulous, rebellious, recalcitrant, refractory, restive, sharp-tempered, shorttempered, shrewish, snappish, spleenful, spleeny, splenetic, stubborn, surly, temperamental, testy, touchy, unmanageable, unruly, untractable, waspish

FRAILTY, noun   blemish, breakability, brittleness, debility, defect, defectiveness, deficiency, delicacy, demerit, destructibility, enervation, failing, failure, failure of strength, fallabity, fault, feebleness, flaw, flimsiness, foible, *fragilitas,* fragility, human weakness, imperfection, imperfectness, impotence, inadequacy, *infirmitas,* infirmity, instability, liability to err, loss of strength, peccability, proneness to error, shortcoming, unsoundness, unworthiness, vulnerability, vulnerableness, want of moral strength, weak point, weak side, weakness
ASSOCIATED CONCEPTS: human frailty

FRAME *(Mood),* **noun**   *animus,* attitude, bent, character, condition, constitution, cue, disposition, fiber, grain, heart, makeup, mental constitution, mettle, mind, nature, proclivity, proneness, propensity, spirit, state of feeling, state of mind, streak, temper, temperament

FRAME *(Structure),* **noun**   build, building, chassis, *compages,* construction, fabric, framework, groundwork, shell, skeleton, support

FRAME *(Charge falsely),* **verb**   accuse falsely, accuse unfairly, accuse unjustly, bear false witness, blame falsely, blame unfairly, blame unjustly, charge unfairly, charge unjustly, conspire against, criminate falsely, criminate unfairly, criminate unjustly, denounce falsely, denounce unfairly, denounce unjustly, fabricate evidence, fake charges against, falsely call to account, hatch a plot against, impeach falsely, impeach unfairly, impeach unjustly, implicate falsely, implicate unfairly, implicate unjustly, incriminate unjustly, inculpate falsely, inculpate unfairly, inculpate unjustly, lay a plot, lie against, make false statements, perjure oneself, prearrange fraudulently, swear falsely, tell falsehoods about, tell lies about, trump up a charge, unfairly call to account, unjustly call to account, unjustly involve

FRAME *(Construct),* **verb**   block out, build, carpenter, coin, compose, concoct, constitute, contrive, create, design, devise, draft, draw up, enframe, erect, fabricate, fashion, fit together, forge, form, formulate, hammer together, make, manufacture, map out, mold, organize, originate, piece together, plan, prepare, produce, put together, raise, set up, shape, sketch, systematize, write
ASSOCIATED CONCEPTS: frame an issue

FRAME *(Formulate),* **verb**   arrange, cast, *componere,* conceive, *concipere,* concoct, contrive, create, design, devise, draft, draw up, excogitate, express, fashion, forge, form, formalize, hatch, invent, lay plans, make arrangements, map out, organize, originate, plan, produce, pull into shape, put into shape, scheme, set up, shape, sketch, take measures, take steps, think up, work up
ASSOCIATED CONCEPTS: frame a complaint

FRAME *(Prearrange)*, *verb*   arrange, charge falsely, conspire against, contrive, contrive a result, ensure a result, fake, fake the evidence, incriminate unjustly, lie against, plan, plant the evidence, prearrange, prearrange fraudulently, predesign, predetermine, trump up, use false evidence

ASSOCIATED CONCEPTS: framed evidence, framed testimony, perjury

FRAME UP, *noun*   baseless charge, cabal, conspiracy, counterfeit evidence, faked charge, false charge, false evidence, false information, foul play, frame, hoax, intrigue, machination, perjured testimony, plant, trap, trickery, trumped-up charge, trumped-up story

ASSOCIATED CONCEPTS: perjury

FRANCHISE *(License)*, *noun*   allowance, assent, authorization, charter, concession, consent, dispensation, droit, exemption, favor, grace, grant, immunity, indulgence, leave, monopoly, pass, permission, permit, prerogative, privilege, recognition, right, sanction, sufferance, tolerance

ASSOCIATED CONCEPTS: corporate franchise, federal franchise, franchise tax, grant of a franchise, irrevocable franchise, license, municipal franchise, perpetual franchises, personal franchise, public franchise, secondary franchise, special franchise

FRANCHISE *(Right to vote)*, *noun*   ballot, choice, discretion, enfranchisement, freedom of choice, liberty of choice, liberty to vote, option, prerogative, privilege, right of choice, right of representation, suffrage, vote, voting power

FRAUD, *noun*   artfulness, artifice, beguilement, charlatanism, charlatanry, cheating, chicane, chicanery, *circumscriptio*, collusion, covin, cozenage, craftiness, crookedness, cunning, deceit, deceitful practice, deceitfulness, deception, deceptiveness, delusiveness, dishonesty, dissembling, dissimulation, double-dealing, dupery, duplicity, fabrication, *fallacia*, fallaciousness, false conduct, false representation, falseness, falsification, falsity, fraudulence, *fraus*, furtiveness, guile, improbity, insidiousness, intentional deception, intrigue, lack of probity, mendacity, misrepresentation, outwitting, perfidy, pretense, prevarication, quackery, ruse, sham, sneakiness, subreption, surreptitiousness, swindling, treachery, trickery, trickiness, underhandedness, unscrupulousness, untruthfulness, wiliness

ASSOCIATED CONCEPTS: action for fraud, actionable fraud, bad faith, collateral fraud, collusion, constructive fraud, debt created by fraud, deceit, discovery of fraud, extrinsic fraud, false representation, fraudulent misrepresentation, fraudulent representation, implied fraud, intrinsic fraud, mail fraud, material fraud, misrepresentation, positive fraud, presumptive fraud, public fraud, statute of frauds

FOREIGN PHRASES: *Qui per fraudem agit frustra agit.* What a man does fraudulently he does vainly. *Vendens eandem rem duobus falsarius est.* He is fraudulent who sells the same thing to two persons. *Dolus auctoris non nocet successori.* The fraud of a predecessor does not prejudice the successor. *Fraus latet in generalibus.* Fraud lies hidden in general expressions. *Fraus est odiosa et non praesumenda.* Fraud is odious and will not be presumed. *Fraus et jus nunquam cohabitant.* Fraud and justice never dwell together. *Nulla pactione effici potest ut dolus praestetur.* It cannot be provided in any contract that fraud can be practiced. *Nemo ex dolo suo proprio relevetur, aut auxilium capiat.* No one is relieved or gains an advantage by his own fraud. *Nemo videtur fraudare eos qui sciunt et consentiunt.* No one is considered as deceiving those who know and consent to his acts. *Lata culpa dolo aequiparatur.* Gross fault or negligence is equivalent to fraud. *Ex dolo malo non oritur actio.* No right of action can arise out of fraud. *Non decipitur qui scit se decipi.* A person is not deceived who knows he is being deceived. *Fraus et dolus nemini patrocinari debent.* Fraud and deceit should not excuse anyone. *Dolus et fraus nemini patrocinentur; patrocinari debent.* Deceit and fraud shall excuse or benefit no man; they themselves need to be excused. *Dolum ex indiciis perspicuis probari convenit.* Fraud should be established by clear showings of proof. *Aliud est celare, aliud tacere.* To conceal is one thing; to be silent is another. *Dolus circuitu non pergator.* Fraud is not purged by circuity. *Quod alias bonum et justum est, si per vim vel fraudem petatur, malum et injustum efficitur.* What otherwise is good and just, becomes bad and unjust if it is sought by force and fraud. *Megna negligentia culpa est; magna culpa dolus est.* Gross negligence is fault; gross fault is equivalent to a fraud. *Dolo malo pactumse non servaturum.* An agreement induced by fraud is not valid. *Fraus est celare fraudem.* It is fraud to conceal a fraud.

FRAUDULENT, *adjective*   beguiling, bogus, cheating, conniving, contrary to fact, corrupt, counterfeited, crafty, crooked, cunning, deceitful, deceiving, deceptive, delusive, delusory, designing, destitute of good faith, destitute of integrity, devoid of truth, discreditable, dishonest, dishonorable, disingenuous, disreputable, *dolosus*, double-dealing, fake, faked, fallacious, false, falsified, feigned, finagling, forsworn, *fraudulentus*, furtive, guileful, iniquitous, insidious, meretricious, misleading, not honest, not true, perfidious, perjured, phony, scheming, sham, shifty, sneaky, spurious, surreptitious, treacherous, trickish, tricky, truthless, unauthentic, underhanded, unethical, unfaithful, ungenuine, unreal, unreliable, unscrupulous, untrue, untrustworthy, untruthful, unveracious, unvirtuous, void of truth, wanting in probity, wily, without probity, without truth

ASSOCIATED CONCEPTS: fraudulent concealment, fraudulent conveyance, fraudulent intent, fraudulent misrepresentation, fraudulent practice, fraudulent preferences, fraudulent representation, fraudulent transfer

FOREIGN PHRASES: *Dolosus versatur in generalibus.* A fraudulent person takes refuge in generalities.

FRAY, *noun*   affray, battle, brabble, brawl, broil, clash, combat, commotion, contention, contest, disagreement, dispute, dissension, disturbance, fight, fracas, jangle, melee, *pugna*, quarrel, row, ruction, rumpus, scramble, scrimmage, scuffle, skirmish, strife, tumult, turmoil, uproar

FREE *(At no charge)*, *adjective*   complimentary, costing nothing, costless, expenseless, for nothing, given, given away, gratis, gratuitous, *gratuitus*, not charged for, provided without charge, unbought, uncharged, unpaid, untaxed, without cost

ASSOCIATED CONCEPTS: free on board

FREE *(Enjoying civil liberty)*, *adjective*   autonomic, autonomical, autonomous, democratic, emancipated, enfranchised, enjoying liberty, exempt from external authority, franchised, freed, independent, liberated, manumitted, not enslaved, not in bondage, not subject to regulation, removed from bondage, saved from bondage, self-directing, self-governing, self-ruling, sovereign, *sua sponte, sua voluntate,* unenslaved, unenthralled, unsubjected

ASSOCIATED CONCEPTS: free access, free press, free speech

FOREIGN PHRASES: *A piratis aut latronibus capti liberi permanent.* Persons taken by robbers remain free.

FREE *(Not restricted),* **adjective**   at large, at liberty, cast loose, clear from, disengaged, immune from restriction, independent, let out, *liber,* liberated, loose, privileged, *solutus,* unattached, unbound, unbridled, uncaught, unchained, unchecked, uncoerced, unconfined, uncurbed, unentangled, unfastened, unfettered, unfixed, unhampered, unhindered, unimpeded, unobstructed, unpent, unprevented, unqualified, unreined, unrestrained, unshackled, unstopped, untied, untrammeled

ASSOCIATED CONCEPTS: free and voluntary, free enterprise, free from encumbrances, free press, free speech

FREE *(Relieved from a burden),* **adjective**   absolved, acquitted, clear, cleared, delivered, disburdened, discharged, disembarrassed, disencumbered, disengaged, disentangled, dismissed, excused, exempted, exonerated, *immunis,* liberated, pardoned, paroled, quit of, ransomed, *re liber,* released, relieved, reprieved, rescued, rid, saved, set free, spared, unburdened, unencumbered, unimpeded, *vacuus*

ASSOCIATED CONCEPTS: free and clear, free from fault

FREE, *verb*   absolve, acquit, affranchise, clear, come to the rescue, deliver, deliver from bondage, disburden, discharge, disembroil, disencumber, disengage, disentangle, disenthrall, dismiss, emancipate, enfranchise, exculpate, excuse, exempt, *eximere,* exonerate, extricate, forgive, franchise, give a reprieve, give absolution, grant a reprieve, grant amnesty, grant pardon, let escape, let go, let loose, let out, let out of prison, *liberare,* liberate, manumit, pardon, parole, privilege, purge, ransom, redeem, release, release from restraint, relieve, remit, rescue, save, set at large, set at liberty, set free, *solvere,* turn loose, unbind, unburden, unchain, unfasten, unfetter, unfix, unimprison, unleash, unmanacle, unshackle, untie, vindicate

FREEDOM, *noun*   affranchisement, *arbitrium,* autonomy, civil liberty, decontrol, deliverance, discharge, disengagement, disenthrallment, disimprisonment, emancipation, empowerment, enfranchisement, entitlement, exemption, exemption from external control, exemption from restraint, extrication, franchise, franchisement, independence, latitude, leave, leeway, legal right, liberation, *libertas,* liberty, license, *licentia,* noninterference, permit, political independence, prerogative, privilege, redemption, relaxation of control, release, right to decide, room, self-determination, self-government, self-rule, unconstraint, unfettering, uninhibitedness, unrestraint

ASSOCIATED CONCEPTS: freedom from fault, freedom of action, freedom of assembly, freedom of conscience, freedom of contract, freedom of press, freedom of religion, freedom of speech, freedom of thought, freedom of trade, freedom of worship

FOREIGN PHRASES: *Impius et crudelis judicandus est qui libertati non favet.* He should be adjudged impious and cruel who does not favor liberty. *Libertas non recipit aestimationem.* Freedom does not admit a valuation. *Libertas est naturalis facultas ejus quod cuique facere libet, nisi quod de jure aut vi prohibetur.* Liberty is a person's natural power which permits one to do as he pleases. *Libertas inestimabilis res est.* Liberty is a thing of inestimable value.

FREEHOLD, *noun*   acres, domain, estate, estate for life, estate in fee, fee simple, feud, fief, hereditament, *immune,* interest in real property, land, landed estate, landed property, life estate, *praedium liberum,* property, real property, realty, territory, vested interest in land

FREIGHT, *noun*   article of commerce, cargo, carload, consignment, freightage, goods, lading, load, merchandise, *onus,* packages, pay load, shipment

FRENETIC, *adjective*   berserk, crazed, crazy, deranged, excited, feverish, frantic, frenzied, *furens,* furibund, hysterical, *insanus,* maniacal, overwrought, perturbed, possessed, raving, restless, unsettled, *vesanus,* worked up, wrought up

FREQUENCY, *noun*   common occurrence, commonness, continuity, *crebritas,* cycle, frequence, *frequentia,* periodicity, prevalence, rate, recurrence, regularity, regularity of recurrence, repetition, repetitiveness, succession, usualness

FREQUENT, *adjective*   accustomed, common, consuetudinal, consuetudinary, *creber,* customary, familiar, *frequens,* habitual, numberless, numerous, oft-repeated, often done, persistent, prevalent, reiterative, repeated, repetitive, usual

FRIGHT, *noun*   affright, agitation, alarm, anxiety, apprehension, consternation, cowardice, dismay, disquietude, dread, extreme fear, fear, fear of danger, horror, intimidation, misgiving, panic, *pavor,* phobia, scare, sudden terror, *terror,* trepidation

FRIGHTEN, *verb*   affright, alarm, browbeat, bully, bullyrag, cow, daunt, deter, disquiet, *exterrere,* fright, give cause for alarm, horrify, intimidate, menace, panic, petrify, raise apprehension, scare, shock, shock with sudden fear, startle, strike with overwhelming fear, terrify, terrorize, threaten, unnerve

FRISK, *verb*   check, conduct a search, examine, examine closely, examine intently, explore, hunt, hunt through, inspect, investigate, *lascivire,* look into, look over, look through, peer into, poke into, probe, pry into, rake through, review, *salire,* scan, scour, scrutinize, search one's pockets, search through, seek, subject to scrutiny

ASSOCIATED CONCEPTS: reasonable belief that safety requires a patting down, search, stop and frisk

FRIVOLOUS, *adjective*   childish, flighty, flimsy, flippant, giddy, immaterial, *inanis,* insignificant, *levis,* light, light-minded, meaningless, minor, *nugax,* of little weight, of no account, paltry, petty, senseless, shallow, silly, slight, superficial, trifling, trivial, unimportant, unserious, unworthy of serious notice, worthless

ASSOCIATED CONCEPTS: frivolous answer, frivolous appeal, frivolous cause of action, frivolous claims, frivolous pleading

FRONTIER, *noun*   ambit, border, borderland, bound, boundary, boundary line, circumjacencies, compass, *confinium,* demarcation line, edge, *faubourg, finis,* fringe, limit, limitations, line of demarcation, march, outer district, outer edge, outer part, outlines, outlying area, outlying borders, outlying districts, outpost, outskirts, perimeter, periphery, remote district, rim, termination

FROWARD, *adjective*   cantankerous, captious, contrary, contumacious, *contumax,* cross, crusty, *difficilis,* difficult, disobedient, fractious, headstrong, indocile, insubmissive, insubordinate, intractable, irascible, irritable, moody, obstinate, peevish, *pertinax,* perverse, petulant, querulous, rebellious, refractory, restive, splenetic, stubborn, surly, troublesome, unaccommodating, uncooperative, ungovernable, unmanageable, unruly, unyielding, wayward, willful, willfully contrary

FRUGAL, *adjective*   abstemious, careful, cautious, chary, cheap, conservative, economical, economy-minded, *frugi, parcus,* parsimonious, penny-conscious, provident, prudent, restrained, sparing, spartan, stinting, thrifty, unwasteful

FRUITION, *noun*   accomplishment, achievement, attainment, consummation, effectuation, execution, flowering, *fructus,* fulfillment, gratification, implementation, performance, production, realization, satisfaction, success
ASSOCIATED CONCEPTS: accrual of a cause of action, maturity of a debt

FRUSTRATE, *verb*   abort, *ad inritum redigere, ad vanum,* annul, baffle, balk, be obstructive, bring to nought, cancel, check, checkmate, confound, counter, counteract, cripple, defeat, disappoint, disconcert, discourage, foil, forestall, frustrari, hinder, invalidate, let down, mar, neutralize, nullify, obstruct, oppose, outwit, override, prevent, render invalid, render null and void, spoil, stultify, stymie, thwart, undermine, undo
ASSOCIATED CONCEPTS: frustrate performance of a contract, frustration of purpose

FRUSTRATION, *noun*   abortive attempt, defeat, failure, foil, futile effort, hindrance, impediment, inability of performance, inability to be completed, incapacity, interference, interruption, noncompletion, nonfulfillment, nonperformance, obstruction, prevention, prevention of accomplishment, thwarted expectation, thwarting, unsatisfied hopes, unsuccessfulness
ASSOCIATED CONCEPTS: commercial frustration, frustration of purpose, frustration under a contract, impossibility of performance

FUGITIVE, *noun*   absconder, avoider, defaulter, deserter, escaped prisoner, escapee, escaper, evader, fleer, *fugitivus,* hunted person, levanter, one who flees, person who flees justice, prisonbreaker, *profugus,* refugee prisoner, renegade, runagate, runaway
ASSOCIATED CONCEPTS: fugitive from justice, fugitive warrant

FULFILL, *verb*   abide by, accomplish, achieve, adhere to, answer, be faithful to, be sufficient, bring about, bring to completion, bring to pass, carry into effect, complete, comply with, consummate, discharge, do, effect, effectuate, *efficere,* execute, *explere,* fill, finish,

follow, heed, *implere,* keep, live up to, make good, meet, obey, observe, perfect, perform, realize, redeem, satisfy, serve, suffice
ASSOCIATED CONCEPTS: fulfillment of trust purpose

FULL, *adjective*   abounding, abundant, affluent, baggy, brimful, brimming over, charged, chock-full, cloyed, complete, comprehensive, crammed, detailed, entire, entirely occupied, exhaustive, filled, filled to utmost capacity, flowing, flush, fraught, glutted, gorged, imbued, *integer,* laden, loaded, mature, maximum, occupied, overflowing, packed, plenary, *plenus,* plethoric, replete, *repletus,* resonant, rich, sated, satiated, satisfied, saturated, soaked, stuffed, surfeited, swollen, teeming, total, unabridged, unstinted, well-provided, well-stocked, well-supplied, whole
ASSOCIATED CONCEPTS: full amount, full and true value, full cash value, full consideration, full control, full faith and credit, full hearing, full opportunity to be heard, full payment, full performance, full satisfaction, full settlement, full-time employment

FULLY EXECUTED *(Consummated), adjective* completed, discharged, fulfilled, realized

FULLY EXECUTED *(Signed), adjective*   authenticated, authorized, binding, completed, executed, legitimized

FULLY SECURED, *adjective*   backed-up, bonded, certified, covered, guaranteed, hypothecated, insured, pledged, mortgaged, warranted

FUNCTION, *noun*   appropriate activity, assignment, business, chore, design, duty, employment, exploitation, mission, *munus,* occupation, office, *officium,* performance, purpose, pursuit, responsibility, role, task, usage, use, utility, work
ASSOCIATED CONCEPTS: discretionary function, executive function, government function, judicial function, legislative function, political function, quasi-judicial function

FUNCTION, *verb*   achieve, act, act effectively, answer a purpose, avail, be effective, be in operation, be useful, benefit, carry on, carry out, effectuate, execute, have effect, manage, operate, perform, render a service, run, serve, work

FUNCTIONAL, *adjective*   adequate, advantageous, applicable, applied, convenient, effective, effectual, efficacious, efficient, employable, expedient, fit for use, gainful, handy, helpful, in action, in operation, in order, instrumental, invaluable, operable, operant, operational, operative, practicable, practical, pragmatic, profitable, sensible, serviceable, suitable for use, usable, useful, utile, utilitarian, utilizable, valuable, workable, working
ASSOCIATED CONCEPTS: functional claim, functional depreciation, functional disability

FUNCTIONARY, *noun*   administrator, bureaucrat, commissary, commissioner, delegate, dignitary, office holder, officer, official, representative, syndic

FUND, *noun*   accumulation, assets, capital, *copia,* endowment, foundation, fount, hoard, investment, mine, nest egg, *pecunia,* pool, reserve, reservoir, resources, savings, spring, stock, store, sum of money, supply, well

ASSOCIATED CONCEPTS: available fund, cash funds, commingling of funds, contingent fund, endowment fund, escrow fund, guaranty fund, insurance fund, joint fund, misapplication of funds, misappropriation of funds, permanent funds, reserve fund, residuary fund, trust fund

FUND, *verb* accommodate, accumulate, afford, allot, amass, apportion, bank, be a benefactor, bestow, cache, collect, conserve, contribute, deposit, dispense, dole, donate, endow, endue, equip, finance, furnish, garner, give, give money, grant, hand out, hoard, invest money, keep, keep in reserve, lay in store, lay up, maintain, pay, pay for, present, present money, preserve, provide, provide for, provide money, provide the wherewithal, provision, purvey, reserve, retain, save, save up, settle upon, spare, stock, stockpile, store, subsidize, supply, sustain, treasure, yield

FUNDAMENTAL, *adjective* basal, basic, basilar, basilary, cardinal, central, constitutional, elemental, elementary, essential, inchoative, indispensable, key, necessary, needed, organic, primary, *primus,* principal, *principalis,* required, requisite, rudimentary, structural, underlying, vital
ASSOCIATED CONCEPTS: fundamental change, fundamental error, fundamental issue, fundamental law, fundamental question, fundamental right

FURLOUGH, *noun* absence, *commeatus,* holiday, leave, leave of absence, leisure, liberty, recess, respite, rest, suspension of work, time off, vacation

FURNISH, *verb* accommodate, accouter, afford, appoint, apportion, arm, bestow, contribute, enable, endow, endue, equip, fit out, gear, give, grant, indulge, *instruere,* lavish, outfit, *praebere,* present, produce, provide, provision, purvey, rig, stock, *suppeditare,* supply, yield
ASSOCIATED CONCEPTS: furnish proof, labor furnished, material furnished, work furnished

FUROR, *noun* ado, agitation, broil, clamor, commotion, craze, disruption, disturbance, eruption, excitement, ferment, ferocity, fervency, fever, flare-up, fracas, fray, frenzy, fury, fuss, hysteria, madness, maelstrom, mania, outbreak, outburst, pandemonium, passion, pother, rabidity, rage, rumpus, stir, storm, tempest, tumult, turbulence, turmoil, upheaval, uproar, wildness

FURTHER, *adverb* additionally, besides, beyond, else, extra, furthermore, in addition, plus
ASSOCIATED CONCEPTS: further conveyance, further notice, further proceeding, further security, further waste, furtherance

FURTHER, *verb* advance, contribute to, facilitate, favor, forward, foster, impel, motivate, move, promote

FURTIVE, *adjective* backstair, catlike, clandestine, cloaked, concealed, covert, crafty, cunning, deceitful, evasive, feline, *furtivus,* hangdog, hidden, indirect, insidious, masked, mysterious, private, secret, secretive, shady, shifty, shrouded, sly, sneaking, sneaky, stealthy, subtle, surreptitious, thievish, undercover, underground, underhand, undisclosed, unobtrusive, unrevealed, unseen, veiled

FUSTIAN, *adjective* bombastic, declamatory, flatulent, *gausape,* grandiloquent, grandiose, high-flown, high-sounding, inflated, mouthy, orotund, pompous, pretentious, ranting, swollen, tumid, turgid

FUSTIAN, *noun* affectation, altiloquence, bombast, bombastic language, bombastry, declamation, empty talk, euphuism, *gausape,* high-sounding words, idle speech, inflated language, inflated speech, inflated style, magniloquence, orotundity, pomposity, pretentious speech, rant, rhetoric, rodomontade, sesquipedalianism, swollen language, turgid language, verbiage, verbosity, wordiness

FUTILE, *adjective* abortive, barren, bootless, feckless, fruitless, *futilis,* gainless, hopeless, *inanis,* ineffective, ineffectual, inefficacious, insignificant, inutile, nugatory, otiose, profitless, resultless, unavailing, unfruitful, unimportant, unproductive, unprofitable, unsubstantial, unsuccessful, useless, vain, valueless, *vanus,* wasted, worthless
ASSOCIATED CONCEPTS: failure to exhaust a futile remedy
FOREIGN PHRASES: ***Lex neminem cogit ad vana seu inutilia peragenda.*** The law compels no one to do futile or useless things. ***Lex nil facit frustra, nil jubet frustra.*** The law does not do anything nor commands anyone to do anything which would be futile.

FUTURE, *adjective* advancing, anticipated, approaching, arriving, close, close at hand, coming, designate, destined, ensuing, eventual, expected, fated, following, foreseeable, forthcoming, *futurus,* imminent, impending, inevitable, later, likely, looked toward, looming, near, near at hand, next, nigh, pending, planned, planned for, possible, *posterus,* predestined, predicted, probable, prospective, scheduled, sequent, subsequent, succeeding, to be, to come, ultimate, upcoming
ASSOCIATED CONCEPTS: after acquired property, future acquired property, future advances, future contingency, future damages, future debt, future earnings, future estates, future expectancy, future interests, future loss of earnings, future payments, future profits, future services

G

GAIN, *verb* accept, accomplish, achieve, acquire, adopt, advance, assume, attain, avail, bag, be better for, be improved by, benefit, *capere,* capture, cash in on, clear, collect, come by, come into, *consequi,* derive, draw, earn, extract, flourish, gather, get, get possession of, glean, grasp, harvest, improve, learn, *lucrari,* make, make a profit, make capital, make money, master, move forward, net, obtain, pick up, procure, profit, prosper, realize, reap, reap profits, reap rewards, reap the benefit of, receive, secure, succeed, take, thrive, turn to account, win, yield returns

ASSOCIATED CONCEPTS: accrued gain, activity for gain, annual gain, business gain, capital gains, economic gain, gainful employment, long term capital gain, net gain, pecuniary gain, private gain, short term capital gain

FOREIGN PHRASES: *Nemo debet aliena jactura locupletari.* No one ought to gain by another's loss.

GAINFUL, *adjective* advantageous, beneficial, fertile, fruitful, lucrative, *lucrosus,* money-making, paying, productive, profitable, *quaestuosus,* remunerative, rewarding, useful, valuable, well-paying, worthwhile

ASSOCIATED CONCEPTS: gainful employment

GAINSAY, *verb* act against, be contrary, conflict with, contest, contradict, contravene, controvert, counter, deny, disaffirm, disagree, disallow, disavow, disclaim, dispute, dissent, forbid, impugn, negate, oppose, oppugn, protest, rebut, refuse to admit, refute, reject, repudiate, speak against, take exception to, take issue with, traverse

GAMBLE, *verb* *alea ludere,* bet, chance, lay a wager, lay money on, play for money, play for stakes, practice gaming, risk, speculate, stake, take a chance, try one's luck, wager

ASSOCIATED CONCEPTS: bookmaking, gambling apparatus, gambling device, gambling houses

GAMUT, *noun* breadth, circuit, compass, complete sequence, complete series, extent, length, limit, progression, range, reach, scope, span, stretch, sweep, vastness, whole range, width

GARNER, *verb* accumulate, acquire, aggregate, amass, assemble, bank, bring together, cache, collect, compile, *condere,* deposit, fund, gather, group, hoard, keep in reserve, muster, reserve, save, stock, stockpile, store, stow, treasure

GARNISH, *verb* appropriate, attach, commandeer, confiscate, *decorare,* distrain, execute, *exornare,* impound, *instruere,* levy upon, seize, seize and appropriate, sequester, sequestrate

GARNISHMENT, *noun* annexation, appropriation, confiscation, dispossession, distraint, distress, divestiture, execution, expropriation, impoundment, levy, seizure

ASSOCIATED CONCEPTS: attachment, enforcement of judgments, equitable garnishment, execution, garnishment of a debt, lien

GAUGE, *verb* adjudge, appraise, appreciate, arrive at a conclusion, ascertain, assess, calculate, calibrate, class, compute, consider, decide, deduce, determine, draw an inference, estimate, evaluate, exercise judgment, fathom, form an estimate, form an opinion, imagine, judge, make an estimation, measure, *metiri,* opine, rank, rate, set a value on, size up, suppose, surmise, survey, valorize, valuate, value, weigh

GENERAL, *adjective* accepted, average, broad, catholic, characteristic, common, common to many, *communis,* customary, ecumenical, epidemic, extensive, *generalis,* habitual, illustrative, inclusive, not partial, not select, open to all, ordinary, pandemic, popular, prevailing, prevalent, regular, relevant to all, representative, rife, standard, sweeping, typical, undisputed, universal, unrestricted, usual, vast, widespread

ASSOCIATED CONCEPTS: general agency, general agent, general appearance, general applicability, general assignment for the benefit of creditors, general bequest, general brokerage, general circulation, general creditor, general damages, general denial, general election, general issue, general jurisdiction, general legacy, general lien, general obligation, general power of appointment, general release, general statute, general strike, general verdict, general welfare

FOREIGN PHRASES: *Generale tantum valet in generalibus, quantum singulare in singulis.* That which is general prevails in general matters, as that which is particular prevails in particular matters. *Generalibus specialia derogant.* Special words derogate from the meaning of general ones. *Generalis regula ge-*

239

neraliter est intelligenda. A general rule is to be understood generally. *Generalis clausula non porrigitur adea quaeantea specialiter sunt comprehensa.* A general clause is not extended to include those things that have been previously provided for specially. *Statutum generaliter est intelligendum quando verba statuti sunt specialia, ratio autem generalis.* When the words of a statute are special, but the reason general, the statute is to be understood generally. *Generalia praecedunt, specialia sequuntur.* General matters precede; special matters follow. *In generalibus versatur error.* Error thrives in generalities. *Fraus latet in generalibus.* Fraud lies hidden in general expressions.

GENERALITY *(Bulk)*, *noun* better part, biggest part, body, common run, greater part, greatest number, largest part, main body, main part, majority, mass, predominant part, preponderance, preponderancy, preponderation, principal part, universality

GENERALITY *(Vague statement)*, *noun* abstraction, broad statement, general law, general principle, general rule, general statement, generalization, imprecision, inexactitude, inexactness, loose statement, principle, simplistic statement

GENERALIZATION, *noun* appraisal, assumption, attitude, broad statement, conclusion, estimate, estimation, general statement, generality, guide, hypothesis, illation, imprecise statement, inexact statement, inference, observation, postulate, postulation, premise, presumption, presupposition, supposal, supposition, theorization, theory

GENERALIZE, *verb* assume, conclude, deal in generalities, discuss in the abstract, draw inferences, *generatim,* hypothesize, ignore distinctions, *loqui,* make a generalization, suppose, surmise, theorize, universalize, *universe*

GENERALLY, *adverb* as a rule, chiefly, commonly, customarily, extensively, for the most part, habitually, in general, in most cases, in the main, in the usual course of things, mainly, most frequently, most often, naturally, normally, on the whole, ordinarily, principally, regularly, usually, without particularizing

GENERALSHIP, *noun* administration, administratorship, authority, captainship, care, charge, command, direction, directorate, directorship, *ductus,* guidance, headship, intendance, intendancy, jurisdiction, lead, leadership, management, managership, mastership, stewardship, superintendency, supervision, supervisorship

GENERATE, *verb* animate, author, be the cause, beget, begin, breed, bring about, bring forth, bring into being, bring into existence, call into being, call into existence, cause, cause to be, conduce, construct, contrive, create, develop, do, effect, effectuate, elicit, engender, evoke, execute, fabricate, father, form, formulate, found, frame, *generare, gignere,* give life to, give rise to, inaugurate, induce, initiate, institute, invent, kindle, launch, lay the foundation of, make, manufacture, occasion, open, originate, *parere,* produce, provoke, set in motion, sire, start, undertake, vitalize, vivify

GENERIC, *adjective* applicable to a class, blanket, broad, collective, common, comprehensive, general, indeterminate, inexact, nonexclusive, nonspecific, not particular, not special, sweeping, universal, unspecified, wide
ASSOCIATED CONCEPTS: generic name, trade name, trademark

GENESIS, *noun* beginning, birth, commencement, cradle, creation, dawn, derivation, exordium, formation, foundation, inception, inchoation, incipience, incipiency, incunabula, initiation, introduction, launching, nativity, onset, origin, origination, outset, provenance, rise, root, source, start

GENETIC, *adjective* atavistic, congenital, hereditary, incarnate, ingrained, inherited, innate

GENUINE, *adjective* accurate, actual, ascertained, authentic, authenticated, bona fide, demonstrable, exact, factual, forthright, frank, *germanus,* guileless, honest, inartificial, legitimate, *merus,* natural, official, original, plain, pure, purebred, real, rightful, simple, sincere, *sincerus,* sterling, tested, true, unadulterated, unaffected, unalloyed, uncolored, uncounterfeited, undisguised, undistorted, unfabricated, unfaked, unfeigned, unfeigning, unfictitious, unimitated, unimpeachable, uninvented, unpretended, unpretending, unpretentious, unquestionable, unsimulated, unspurious, unsynthetic, unvarnished, valid, veridical, veritable
ASSOCIATED CONCEPTS: genuine issue

GERMANE, *adjective* accordant, *adfinis,* affinitive, allied, applicable, applying to, apposite, appropriate, appurtenant, apropos, apt, associated, bearing upon, belonging to, cognate, concerning, congruent, congruous, connected, correlated, correspondent, fitting, important, pertaining to, pertinent, referring, related, relating, relative, relevant, to the point

GERMINATE, *verb* become, bud, burgeon, develop, emerge, evolve, flourish, gemmate, generate, *germinare,* grow, produce, progress, pullulate, sprout, thrive, vegetate, yield

GIFT *(Flair)*, *noun* ability, adeptness, adroitness, aptitude, capability, capacity, cleverness, competence, cunning, deftness, dexterity, dextrousness, endowment, expertise, expertness, facility, faculty, felicity, forte, genius, handiness, inborn aptitude, ingeniousness, ingenuity, innate ability, innate quality, instinct, knack, mastery, *natura et ingenium,* natural ability, natural quality, proficiency, qualification, quality, readiness, skill, skillfulness, special ability, special endowment, talent, turn

GIFT *(Present)*, *noun* allowance, award, benefaction, bestowment, contribution, dispensation, donation, donative, *donum,* endowment, favor, grant, gratuity, legacy, *munus,* present, presentation, tribute
ASSOCIATED CONCEPTS: absolute gift, acceptance of a gift, bequest, charitable gift, class gift, conditional gift, contingent gift, delivery of a gift, devise, donative intent for a gift, executory gift, expectation of a gift, future gift, gift causa mortis, gift for a public purpose, gift in contemplation of death, gift in praesenti, gift to take effect at death, illusory gift, incomplete gift, intervivos gift, qualified gift, revocable gift, testamentary gift, unconditional gift, verbal gift
FOREIGN PHRASES: *Invito beneficium non datur.* A benefit is not conferred upon a person against his will. *Modus legem dat donationi.* Custom gives validity to

the gift. *Ubi et dantis et accipientis turpitudo versatur, non posse repeti dicimus; quotiens autem accipientis turpitudo versatur, repeti posse.* Where there is turpitude by both the giver and receiver, we say it cannot be recovered back; but whenever the turpitude is in the receiver only, it can be recovered. *Non valet donatio nisi subsequatur traditio.* A gift is invalid unless accompanied by possession. *Nemo dare potest quod non habet.* No one is able to give that which he has not. *Nemo praesumitur donare.* No one is presumed to have made a gift. *Inter alias causas acquisitionis, magna, celebris, et famosa est causa donationis.* Among other methods of acquiring property, there is a great, frequently used and famous means, that of gift. *Cujus per errorem dati repetitio est, ejus consulto dati donatio est.* That which, when given through mistake can be recovered back, when given deliberately is a gift. *Cujus est dare, ejus est disponere.* He who has a right to give, has the right to dispose of the gift. *Nul charter, nul vente, ne nul done vault perpetualment, si le donor n'est seise al temps de contracts de deux droits, sc. del droit de possession et del droit de propertie.* No grant, no sale, no gift, is valid forever, unless the donor, at the time of contract, has two rights, namely, the right of possession, and the right of property. *Sola ac per se senectus donationem testamentum aut transactionem non vitiat.* Old age alone and of itself will not vitiate a will or gift. *Qui sciens solvit indebitum donandi consilio id videtur fecisse.* One who knowingly pays what is not due is deemed to have done it with the intention of making a gift. *Legatum morte testatoris tantum confirmatur, sicut donatio inter vivos traditione sola.* A legacy is confirmed by the death of a testator, in the same manner as a gift, as between living persons is confirmed by delivery alone. *Donatio perficitur possessione accipientis.* A gift is perfected by the possession of the receiver. *Confirmatio est nulla ubi donum praecedens est invalidum.* A confirmation is a nullity, where the preceding gift is invalid. *Dans et retinens, nihil dat.* A person who gives and retains possession, gives nothing. *Donari videtur, quod nullo jure cogente conceditur.* That is considered to be given which is transferred under no legal compulsions. *Donator nunquam desinit possidere, antequam donatorius incipiat possidere.* A donor never ceases to possess until the donee begins to possess. *Donatio non praesumitur.* A gift is not presumed to have been made. *Dona clandestina sunt semper suspiciosa.* Clandestine gifts are always open to suspicion.

GIST *(Ground for a suit), noun*   alleged reason, base, basis, basis of argument, basis of litigation, cardinal point, cause, cause of action, essential ground, essential matter, essential part, focal point of the complaint, foundation of a suit, gravamen, gravamen of a charge, gravamen of the complaint, great point, ground, important point, keystone, main charge, main point, object of the action, outstanding feature, pith of a matter, point, principal part, principal point, reason, reason for which suit is commenced, salient point, substance, substantial part of a complaint, sum and substance, ultimate cause
ASSOCIATED CONCEPTS: gist of a cause of action, gist of an offense, gist of the complaint

GIST *(Substance), noun*   backbone, basis, broad meaning, connotation, core, drift, essence, essential meaning, essential part, fundamentals, general mean-

ing, idea conveyed, implication, import, *index,* intrinsic nature, marrow, matter, meaning, pith, primary meaning, purport, quiddity, quintessence, real content, reality, root, sense, spirit, substantial meaning, sum and substance, tenor, true meaning, vital principle

GIVE *(Grant), verb*   accord, adminster, afford, allot, assign, award, bequeath, bestow, cede, commit, concede, confer, consign, contribute, deal, deed, deliver, devise, devote, dispense, dispose of, distribute, donate, endow, entrust, equip, furnish, impart, indulge, leave, make a gift, make a presentation, pass, present, *prodere,* proffer, provide, remit, submit, supply, surrender, transfer, transmit, turn over, vouchsafe, will
ASSOCIATED CONCEPTS: bequeath, convey, deliver, devise, dispose, give judgment, give notice
FOREIGN PHRASES: *Praesentare nihil aliud est quam praesto dare seu offere.* To present is no more than to give or offer forthwith.

GIVE *(Yield), verb*   abate, become flexible, become less rigid, become pliant, collapse, compromise, concede, crumble, *deponere,* ease, loosen, retreat, sag, soften, surrender

GLEAN, *verb*   accumulate, aggregate, amass, assemble, batch together, bring together, collect, cull, cumulate, draw together, extract, *facere,* garner, gather, harvest, lay in store, obtain, pick up, procure, save, scrape together

GLUTTONOUS, *adjective*   crapulent, crapulous, debauched, edacious, excessive, greedy, immoderate, inabstinent, incontinent, indulgent, inordinate, insatiable, intemperate, omnivorous, orgiastic, ravenous, unrestrained, voracious

GO-BETWEEN, *noun*   agent, appeaser, arbiter, arbitrator, *conciliator,* connecting link, connection, dealer, diplomat, interagent, interceder, intermediary, intermediate, intermediate agent, intermediator, *interpres,* link, mediary, mediator, middleman, moderator, negotiator, pacifier, peacemaker, procurer, propitiator, reconciler, referee, spokesman, umpire, vehicle
ASSOCIATED CONCEPTS: conduit

GOAL, *noun*   aim, ambition, aspiration, design, destination, determination, end, fixed purpose, hope, intent, intention, mark, mission, object, objective, plan, predeliberation, predetermination, premeditation, purpose, resolution, resolve, scheme, set purpose, target

GOOD FAITH, *noun*   bona fide, goodness, honest effort, probity, rectitude, sanctity, uprightness
ASSOCIATED CONCEPTS: good faith attempt, good faith estimate, good faith purchaser, offer in good faith

GOOD SAMARITAN, *noun*   aide, aider, altruist, assistant, assister, befriender, benefactor, deliverer, donor, giver, helper, helping hand, humanitarian, kind person, one who gives assistance, one who helps another, one who renders aid, patron, philanthropist, redeemer, rescuer, succorer, unselfish person
ASSOCIATED CONCEPTS: Good Samaritan Law

GOODWILL, *noun*   altruism, amity, benefaction, beneficence, benevolence, brotherhood, charity, cheerful consent, cheerful willingness, commercial advantage, cordiality, countenance, customer approval, cus-

tomer encouragement, earnestness, established patronage, established popularity, established reputation, favor, favorable disposition, favorable regard, friendly disposition, geniality, good name, good nature, good reputation, helpfulness, humanity, kindness, known name, munificence, patronage, philanthropy, proven name, public favor, public support, sponsorship, support, sympathy, tolerance, willingness
ASSOCIATED CONCEPTS: impairment of good will, sale and transfer of good will

GOODS, noun appurtenances, articles of commerce, assets, belongings, chattels, commodities, consumer durables, durables, effects, items, materials, paraphernalia, personal estate, possessions, produce, products, property, resources, staples, stock, stock in trade, supplies, things for sale, vendibles
ASSOCIATED CONCEPTS: bulk sale, chattels, foreign goods, goods and chattels, goods sold and delivered, personalty, sale of goods, special goods, tangible goods

GOVERN, verb administer, administrate, assume command, be in power, *coercere,* command, conduct, control, dictate, direct, dominate, enact, exercise authority, exercise power over, exert authority, give orders, guide, have authority, have executive charge of, have jurisdiction over, head, hold authority, hold office, hold sway, lead, legislate, manage, officiate, order, oversee, pilot, prescribe, preside over, prevail on, *regere,* regulate, reign, restrain, rule, steer, superintend, supervise, take charge, take command, wield authority
ASSOCIATED CONCEPTS: governing authority, governing body, governing law
FOREIGN PHRASES: *Minor minorem custodire non debet, alios enim praesumitur male regere qui seipsum regere nescit.* A minor ought not to be guardian to a minor, for a person who knows not how to govern himself is presumed to be unfit to govern others. *Mitius imperanti melius paretur.* The more gently a person commands, the better he is obeyed.

GOVERNMENT (Administration), **noun** *administratio,* authorization, command, control, decision making, direction, dominion, governance, *gubernatio,* guidance, jurisdiction, management, power, *procuratio,* regnancy, regulation, reign, rule, rulership, state management, statecraft, statesmanship, stewardship, superintendence, sway

GOVERNMENT (Political administration), **noun** administration, agency of the state, authority, body of office holders, congress, delegates, *ii qui reipublicae praesunt,* lawgivers, lawmakers, legislators, ministers, *penes quos est reipublica,* political community, political leaders, political regime, politicians, politicos, polity, public servants, representatives, ruling power, sovereign, state managers, statemongers, statesmen
ASSOCIATED CONCEPTS: de facto government, de jure government, democratic government, federal government, governmental agency, governmental body, governmental function, governmental immunity, powers of government, provisional government
FOREIGN PHRASES: *Privilegium non valet contra rempublicam.* A privilege is of no avail against the state.

GRACE, noun absolution, clemency, concession, excuse, favor, forbearance, forgiveness, indulgence, pardon, reprieve

GRACE PERIOD, noun concession, exemption, leniency, pardon, period of allowance, period of indulgence, period of tolerance, reprieve

GRAFT, noun blackmail, bribery, corruption, exploitation, fraudulent income, hush money, illegal profit, illicit profit, illicit revenue, *inserere,* kickback, money illegally acquired, political corruption, profiteering, property illegally acquired, unjust acquisition, unlawful gain
ASSOCIATED CONCEPTS: bribery, corruption, official misconduct

GRANDIOSE, adjective affected, boastful, bombastic, enormous, exorbitant, flamboyant, flashy, flaunting, fustian, grandiloquent, high-sounding, huge, immense, inflated, lofty, magniloquent, mighty, ornate, orotund, ostentatious, pompous, pretentious, showy, stupendous, theatrical, tumid, turgid, vainglorious

GRANT, noun acknowledgment, allotment, allowance, appanage, award, benefaction, benefit, bequeathal, bequest, bestowal, boon, bounty, concession, devise, dispensation, donation, *donum,* douceur, endowment, favor, gift, gratuity, handsel, indulgence, lagniappe, largess, largesse, legacy, legal cession, libation, oblation, present, reward, subscription, subsidy, subvention
ASSOCIATED CONCEPTS: express grant, grant and convey, grant by implication, grant of power, legislative grant, license, private land grant, public grant
FOREIGN PHRASES: *Resoluto jure concedentis resolvitur jus concessum.* When the right of the grantor is extinguished the right granted is extinguished. *Ubi aliquid conceditur, conceditur et id sine quo res ipsa esse non potest.* When anything is granted, that also is granted without which it could not exist. *Quando aliquis aliquid concedit, concedere videtur et id sine quo res uti non potest.* When anyone grants anything, he is deemed to grant also that without which the thing cannot be used. *Quod sub certa forma concessum vel reservatum est non trahitur ad valorem vel compensationem.* That which is granted or reserved under a certain form, cannot be twisted into a valuation or compensation. *Qui concedit aliquid concedit omne id sine quo concessio est irrita.* He who grants anything is considered to grant everything without which the grant is worthless. *A gratia.* By grace, not by right. *Cuicunque aliquis quid concedit concedere videtur et id, sine quo res ipsa esse non potuit.* Whoever grants a thing is presumed also to grant that without which the grant of the thing itself would be of no use. *Quaelibet concessio fortissime contra donatorem interpretanda est.* Every grant is to be interpreted most strictly against the grantor. *Concessio versus concedentem latam interpretationem habere debet.* A grant ought to have a liberal interpretation against the grantor. *Nul charter, nul vente, ne nul done vault perpetualment, si le donor n'est seise al temps de contracts de deux droits, sc. del droit de possession et del droit de propertie.* No grant, no sale, no gift, is valid forever, unless the donor, at the time of the contract, has two rights, namely, the right of possession, and the right of property.

GRANT (Concede), **verb** accede, accept, accord, acknowledge, acquiesce, admit, agree, allow, approve, assent, authorize, be persuaded, cede, *concedere,* concur, confer a privilege, consent, *dare,* empower, enable, ex-

press concurrence, favor, give, give authority, give clearance, give consent, give leave, give permission, gratify, have no objection, indulge, let, license, permit, *permittere*, privilege, recognize, sanction, support, vouchsafe, warrant, yield, yield assent
ASSOCIATED CONCEPTS: grant a franchise, grant a mistrial, grant a motion, grant a right of way, grant a right to a jury trial, grant an adjournment, grant an easement, grant an injunction, grant or allowance, granting clause
FOREIGN PHRASES: *Cui jus est donandi, eidem et vendendi et concedendi jus est.* One who has a right to give has also a right to sell and to grant.

GRANT *(Transfer formally)*, **verb**   assign, award, bequeath, bestow, bestow voluntarily, cede, change ownership, *concedere*, confer, confer formally, confer ownership, consign, convey, convey by deed, deed, deliver, demise, devise, devolve upon, give, give away, give over to, impart, make a present, make conveyance of, make over, pass, pass over, *permittere*, present, put in possession, sign over, transfer, transfer by writing, transfer ownership, transmit
ASSOCIATED CONCEPTS: grant a license, grant a privilege, grant a right of way, grant of easement, grant by implication, grant by necessity, grant in gross, grant in praesenti, land grant, proprietary grant
FOREIGN PHRASES: *Quaelibet concessio fortissime contra donatorem interpretanda est.* Every grant is to be interpreted most strictly against the grantor.

GRANTEE, *noun*   acceptor, beneficiary, devisee, donee, recipient, taker
ASSOCIATED CONCEPTS: grantee of power

GRANTOR, *noun*   assignor, bequeather, bestower, conferrer, contributor, devisor, donator, giver, investor, presenter, rewarder, testator
ASSOCIATED CONCEPTS: grantor of a power

GRAPPLE, *verb*   attack, battle, clasp, clinch, close, close with, clutch, combat, come in conflict with, compete with, confront, contest, do battle with, encounter, engage with, fasten upon, fight, get hold of, grasp, grip, hang on, hold, hold fast, oppose, seize, struggle, tackle, take hold of, take on, tussle, vie with, wrestle

GRATIS, *adjective*   as a favor, complimentary, costless, expenseless, for nothing, free, free of charge, free of cost, free of expense, *gratiis, gratuito*, unbought, unpaid for, unrecompensed, voluntary, without charge, without consideration, without monetary inducement, without monetary reward, without pecuniary gain, without recompense, without reward

GRATUITOUS *(Given without recompense)*, **adjective** bestowed, by way of gift, chargeless, charitable, complimentary, contributory, costless, donated, expenseless, for nothing, free, free of cost, free of expense, given, given away, gratis, not charged, not charged for, not subject to a payment, provided without charge, unbought, unpaid, unpaid for, unrecompensed, voluntary, without charge, without compensation, without consideration
ASSOCIATED CONCEPTS: gratuitous agency, gratuitous allowance, gratuitous bailment, gratuitous contract, gratuitous guest, gratuitous invitee, gratuitous licensee, gratuitous service, gratuitous undertaking, gratuitous use

GRATUITOUS *(Unwarranted)*, **adjective**   additional, baseless, causeless, dispensable, excessive, extraneous, *gratuitus*, groundless, inapposite, inappropriate, inessential, irrelative, irrelevant, needless, nonpertinent, not fitting, not following, not necessitated, not pertinent, superfluous, uncalled for, unconnected, undesirable, undue, unessential, unfounded, unjustified, unnecessary, unneeded, unprovoked, unrelated, unsuitable, unsuited, without basis, without foundation
ASSOCIATED CONCEPTS: gratuitous remarks during an examination of a witness

GRATUITY *(Bribe)*, **noun**   corrupting gift, corruption, graft, hush money, illegal gain, influence by a gift, jobbery, kickback, price, price of corruption, protection, rakeoff, sop, subornation
ASSOCIATED CONCEPTS: bribe receiving, emolument, illegal gratuity, official misconduct, tampering with a witness

GRATUITY *(Present)*, **noun**   award, benefaction, bonus, charity, contribution, dispensation, dole, donative, extra, favor, gift, grant, handout, offering, perquisite, premium, presentation, reward, tip, unearned increment

GRAVAMEN, *noun*   cardinal point, center, central point, core, cornerstone, crux, essence, essence of a grievance, essential part, essential point, focal point, focus, fundamental, gist, gist of a charge, grievance, key, keystone, main point, material part, nucleus, pivotal point, principal part, root, salient point, spirit, substance, substantial cause, sum and substance, thrust

GRAVE *(Important)*, **adjective**   chief, consequential, critical, essential, exigent, *gravis*, imperative, indispensable, pressing, serious, *serius*, substantial, *tristis*, urgent, weighty

GRAVE *(Solemn)*, **adjective**   cheerless, dolorous, frowning, grim, heavy, humorless, joyless, pensive, sad, saturnine, serious, sober, somber, sorrowful, spiritless, uncheerful, uncheery, unlively
ASSOCIATED CONCEPTS: grave consequences for illegal acts

GRAVITATE, *verb*   approach, be attracted, be prone to, draw near, draw toward, have a proclivity for, have a propensity for, head toward, incline, lean, move toward, tend, tend toward, trend
ASSOCIATED CONCEPTS: gravitate to a life of crime

GREED, *noun*   acquisitiveness, appetency, avarice, avariciousness, *avaritia, aviditas*, avidity, covetousness, crapulence, *cupiditas*, cupidity, desire to hoard wealth, eagerness, edacity, excess, gluttonous appetite, gluttony, greediness, gulosity, incontinence, indulgence, inordinate desire, inordinate desire to gain, insatiability, insatiableness, intemperance, intense desire, lust for money, omnivorousness, overindulgence, possessiveness, ravenousness, selfishness, voraciousness, voracity

GRIEVANCE, *noun*   affliction, annoyance, burden, cause of sorrow, charge, complaint, criticism, discontent, disservice, foul play, grounds for complaint, hardship, iniquity, *iniuria*, injury, injustice, objection, oppression, problem, *querela, querimonia*, reason to complain, trial, trouble, unfairness, vexation, wrong

ASSOCIATED CONCEPTS: arbitration, exhaustion of contractual remedies, grievance committee

GROSS *(Flagrant), adjective* absolute, aggravated, atrocious, big, colossal, considerable, deplorable, dire, disgusting, dreadful, easily seen, egregious, enormous, evident, extreme, fulsome, gigantic, glaring, grave, great, grievous, heinous, horrible, huge, immense, indelicate, lamentable, large, manifest, massive, monstrous, obvious, odious, offensive, outrageous, reprehensible, shameful, shocking, terrible, unmitigated, utter
ASSOCIATED CONCEPTS: gross fraud, gross inadequacy, gross misconduct, gross neglect, gross negligence, gross unfairness

GROSS *(Total), adjective* aggregate, all-inclusive, complete, comprehensive, entire, exhaustive, full, inclusive, *incredibilis,* intact, inviolate, lacking nothing, *magnus, nimius,* plenary, unabridged, unbroken, uncut, undeducted from, undeleted, undiminished, undivided, unexpurgated, unreduced, unshorn, unshortened, whole, without deductions
ASSOCIATED CONCEPTS: easement in gross, gross earnings, gross estate, gross income, gross profit, gross receipts, gross sales, gross value

GROUND, *noun* assumption, backbone, base, basis, *causa,* cause, cause for complaint, cause for protest, complaint, criticism, data, evidence, fact, footing, foundation, grave injustice, gross wrong, inequity, infliction, iniquity, injury, injustice, justification, motive, objection, oppression, oppressive act, origin, outrage, premise, principle, proof, purpose, *ratio,* rationale, reason, resentment, root, support, supposition, unjust deed, unjustness, wrong
ASSOCIATED CONCEPTS: cause of action, general grounds, good and sufficient grounds, ground for complaint, ground of action, grounds of belief, meritorious grounds, reasonable grounds

GROWTH *(Evolution), noun* advancement, development, evolvement, expansion, flowering, fruition, germination, improvement, maturation, movement toward adulthood, movement toward maturity, progress, ripening, sprouting, unfolding

GROWTH *(Increase), noun* accumulation, addition, advancement, aggrandizement, amplification, *auctus,* augmentation, distention, enlargement, escalation, expansion, extension, heightening, increment, *incrementum,* inflation, intensification, multiplication, rise, spread, surge, swell, swelling

GUARANTEE, *verb* answer for, assume responsibility, assure, back, be responsible for, become liable, become surety for, certify, commit oneself, ensure, *fides,* give assurance, give one's word, guard, hypothecate, impignorate, insure, make oneself answerable for, obligate, pledge, promise, safeguard, secure, *sponsio,* sponsor, stake, support, underwrite, *vadimonium,* vouch for, warrant
ASSOCIATED CONCEPTS: guarantee a title, guarantee against breakage, guarantee payment

GUARANTY, *noun* assurance, backing, bond, certification, commitment, endorsement, gage, guard, hypothecation, indemnity, insurance, pact, pledge, promise to pay another's debt, recognizance, safeguard,

security, stake, support, surety, token, voucher, warrant, warranty
ASSOCIATED CONCEPTS: absolute guaranty, collateral guaranty, continuing guaranty, fidelity guaranty, guaranty company, guaranty fund, guaranty insurance, guaranty of payment, indemnity bond, limited guaranty, special guaranty, suretyship

GUARDED, *adjective* alert, attentive, awake, aware, careful, cautious, *cautus,* chary, circumspect, *circumspectus,* conservative, defended, discreet, fenced, heedful, in custody, noncommittal, protected, prudent, reserved, reticent, safe, safeguarded, secured, sheltered, shielded, shy, suspicious, under surveillance, vigilant, wary, watched over, watchful

GUARDIAN, *noun* argus, attendant, bodyguard, caretaker, champion, chaperon, conductor, conservator, curator, custodian, *custos,* defender, *defensor,* escort, gatekeeper, guard, keeper, overseer, patron, *praeses,* preserver, protector, safeguard, safekeeper, sentinel, sentry, sponsor, superintendent, supervisor, trustee, tutelar, warden, warder, watchman
ASSOCIATED CONCEPTS: de facto guardian, domestic guardian, general guardian, guardian ad litem, guardian by statute, guardian de son tort, guardian of the person, legal guardian, special guardian, testamentary guardian
FOREIGN PHRASES: *Tuta est custodia quae sibimet creditur.* That guardianship is secure which trusts to itself alone. *Lucrum facere ex pupilli tutela tutor non debet.* A guardian ought not to make money out of the guardianship of his ward. *Custos statum haeredis in custodia existentis meliorem, non deteriorem, facere potest.* A guardian can make the estate of an existing heir under his guardianship better, but not worse. *Minor minorem custodire non debet, alios enim praesumitur male regere qui seipsum regere nescit.* A minor ought not to be guardian to a minor, for a person who knows not how to govern himself is presumed to be unfit to govern others.

GUESS, *verb* assume, *augurari,* be of the opinion, believe, conjecture, deem, *divinare,* divine, estimate, forejudge, form an estimation, gather, have a hunch, hypothesize, imagine, infer, judge, judge at random, judge with uncertainty, *opinari,* opine, postulate, presume, presuppose, reckon, speculate, suppose, surmise, suspect, take for granted, theorize, think, think likely
ASSOCIATED CONCEPTS: speculative testimony

GUIDANCE, *noun* admonition, advice, advisement, advocacy, backing, bidding, briefing, coaching, *consilium,* consultation, counsel, criticism, cue, direction, directive, *ductus,* edification, education, encouragement, enlightenment, exhortation, expostulation, fosterage, help, hint, inculcation, indoctrination, information, instruction, lead, leadership, lesson, management, monition, opinion, orientation, patronage, pedagogy, persuasion, precept, prescription, prompting, recommendation, reference, schooling, sponsorship, steering, suggestion, supervision, teaching, training, tuition, tutelage, tutoring
ASSOCIATED CONCEPTS: advisory opinion, assistance of counsel, declaratory judgment

GUIDELINE, *noun* advisory limitation, boundary, guide, indication, limit, limitation, parameter, perimeter, restriction

GUILT, *noun*   blame, blameworthiness, breach of law, censurability, corruption, crime, criminal activity, criminal deed, criminal offense, criminality, criminousness, *culpa,* culpability, delict, delinquency, deviation from rectitude, dishonesty, fault, felonious conduct, ill conduct, immorality, impeachability, improbity, improper conduct, iniquity, law-breaking, malefaction, malfeasance, malpractice, malversation, misbehavior, misconduct, misdeed, misdemeanor, misdoing, misfeasance, misprision, *noxia,* offense, offense against the law, offensiveness, official misconduct, peccadillo, peccancy, reprehensibility, reproach, sin, sinfulness, transgression, turpitude, unlawful practice, unrighteousness, vice, viciousness, violation, violation of law, *vitium,* wrong, wrongdoing
ASSOCIATED CONCEPTS: admission of guilt, finding of guilt, guilt beyond a reasonable doubt, guilt by association, *nolo contendre,* presumption of innocense
FOREIGN PHRASES: *Cum par delictum est duorum, semper oneratur petitor et melior habetur possessoris causa.* When there is equal fault on both sides, the burden is always placed on the plaintiff, and the cause of the possessor is preferred. *Quae sunt minoris culpae sunt majoris infamiae.* Those things which are less culpable may be more infamous. *Poenae suos tenere debet*

actores et non alios. Punishment belongs to the guilty, and not others. *Excusat aut extenuat delictum in capitalibus quod non operatur idem in civilibus.* That excuses or extenuates a wrong in capital cases which would not have the same effect in civil suits.

GUILTY, *adjective*   at fault, blamable, blameworthy, censurable, chargeable, condemnable, convicted, criminal, criminous, culpable, delinquent, deserving of blame, deserving of punishment, deserving reproof, erring, imputable, in error, in the wrong, incriminated, indictable, peccant, reprehensible, reproachable, reprovable, *sceleratus,* to blame, transgressing
ASSOCIATED CONCEPTS: bail, conviction, find the defendant guilty, guilty as charged, guilty knowledge, guilty of the crime charged, guilty of wrongdoing, innocence, insanity, parole, plea of guilty, qualified plea of guilty, sentencing, verdict

GUN, *noun*   armament, arms, carbine, firearm, lethal instrument, munition, piece, pistol, repeater, revolver, rifle, shotgun, *tormentum,* weapon
ASSOCIATED CONCEPTS: concealed weapon, deadly weapon

H

HABEAS CORPUS, *noun*   appeal, application for discharge, application for liberty, collateral review of detention, collateral review, complaint to a higher court, examination, extraordinary remedy, extraordinary writ, judicial reexamination, petition for release, redress, remedy, review, writ, writ for deliverance from illegal confinement, writ to gain freedom
ASSOCIATED CONCEPTS: coram nobis, exhaustion of state remedies, federal writ of habeas corpus, prerogative writ, special proceeding, state writ of habeas corpus, writ of inquiry

HABIT, *noun*   acquired mode of behavior, attitude, characteristic behavior, characteristically repeated action, common practice, confirmed way, consuetude, *consuetudo,* convention, conventionality, course of conduct, custom, customary action, customary conduct, disposition, fashion, frequently repeated act, *habitus,* inclination, inveterate practice, leaning, mannerism, mode, *mos,* observance, particularity, pattern, peculiarity, practice, predisposition, proclivity, propensity, recurrence, repetition, routine, rule, second nature, style, tendency, tradition, trait, usual procedure, way
ASSOCIATED CONCEPTS: confirmed habits, continued habits, custom and usage, temperate habits

HABITABLE, *adjective*   adequate, appropriate for residence, capable of being inhabited, comfortable, fit for dwelling, fit for habitation, fit to be occupied, fit to live in, *habitabilis,* inhabitable, livable, occupiable, residential, suitable, suitable for living in, tenantable
ASSOCIATED CONCEPTS: warranty of habitability

HABITANT, *noun*   abider, boarder, denizen, domiciliary, dweller, *habitator, incola,* indweller, inhabitant, inhabiter, inmate, lodger, occupant, occupier, resident, residentiary, resider, settler, sojourner, squatter, tenant, townsman, villager
ASSOCIATED CONCEPTS: residency laws

HABITATION *(Act of inhabiting),* *noun*   abiding, continuance, dwelling, habitancy, inhabitance, inhabitancy, inhabitation, lodgment, occupancy, occupation, possession, remaining, residence, residing, settlement, sojourn, sojournment, tenancy

HABITATION *(Dwelling place),* *noun*   abiding place, abode, accommodations, address, domicile, *domicilium, domus,* dwelling, habitat, headquarters, home, homestead, house, housing, living quarters, lodging, lodgment, nest, place, place of abode, place of residence, quarters, residence, settlement, site, tabernacle, *tectum*

HABITUAL, *adjective* according to habit, accustomary, accustomed, automatic, chronic, common, commonplace, confirmed, constant, consuetudinary, continual, customary, daily, established, expected, familiar, fixed, frequent, general, ingrained, inveterate, *inveteratus,* natural, normal, ordinary, periodic, periodical, perpetual, prevalent, recurrent, recurring, regular, repeated, rooted, routine, set, standard, sustained, traditional, typical, *usitatus,* usual, wonted
ASSOCIATED CONCEPTS: habitual cohabitation, habitual criminal, habitual cruel and inhuman treatment, habitual insanity, habitual intemperance, habitual intoxication, habitual offender, habitual use, habitual violator, predicate felon, recidivist

HABITUATION, *noun* acclimation, acclimatization, accustoming, adaptation, adjustment, conditioning, confirmed habit, customariness, familiarization, inurement, inveteracy, inveterate habit, inveterateness

HAGGLE, *verb* argue, bargain, beat down, bid for, chaffer, deal, dicker, dispute, drive a bargain, higgle, make terms, negotiate, palter, quibble, stickle, underbid, wrangle
ASSOCIATED CONCEPTS: arms length bargaining, bickering over price

HALT, *noun* abandonment, abeyance, armistice, arrest, block, break, breathing spell, cessation, check, close, closing, deadlock, delay, desistance, detention, deterrent, discontinuance, discontinuation, end, ending, estoppage, estoppel, hesitation, impasse, impediment, inactivity, *intermissio,* intermission, interruption, lapse, lull, obstruction, pause, prevention, prohibition, recess, remission, respite, rest, shutdown, stalemate, standstill, stay, stop, stopover, stoppage, suspension, termination, time out, truce, wait
ASSOCIATED CONCEPTS: freeze, injunction, restraining order

HALT, *verb* adjourn, arrest, balk, bar, bar someone's way, barricade, block, blockade, break, break off, bring to a standstill, call a halt, cease, check, come to a stop, *consistere,* counteract, curb, cut short, dam, deadlock, debar, defeat, desist, deter, disallow, discontinue, end, estop, foil, forbid, frustrate, hamper, hinder, hold, impede, inhibit, interrupt, make inactive, obstruct, pause, preclude, prevent, prohibit, put an end to, quell, quit, remain, rest, restrain, restrict, stand, stand still, stay, stem, stop, stop an advance, stop short, subdue, *subsistere,* suspend, terminate, thwart, wait
ASSOCIATED CONCEPTS: abandon a crime, discontinue an action, injunction, stop and frisk laws

HAMPER, *verb* arrest, balk, bar, barricade, bind, block, brake, bridle, burden, check, choke, clog, confine, counteract, cramp, curb, debar, delay, deter, encumber, estop, fetter, foil, frustrate, handicap, hinder, hold back, impede, *impedire,* impedite, *implicare,* inhibit, intercept, interfere, interrupt, limit, manacle, muzzle, obstruct, oppose, preclude, prevent, rein, repress, resist, restrain, restrict, retard, shackle, smother, stymie, suppress, thwart, trammel, undermine, withhold
ASSOCIATED CONCEPTS: hamper a prosecution

HANDCUFF, *noun* bond, bridle, chain, collar, fastener, fetter, harness, manacle, *manicae,* padlock, pinion, shackle, trammel

HANDCUFF, *verb* belay, bind, bridle, chain, enchain, entrammel, fasten, fetter, gyve, hamper, hold, lash, leash, make fast, manacle, pinion, put in irons, render powerless, rope, secure, shackle, strap, string, tether, tie, tie one's hands, tie the hands of, tie up, trammel

HANDICAP, *noun* affliction, barrier, blemish, bridle, burden, defect, deficiency, detriment, difficulty, disability, disadvantage, discommodity, drawback, encumbrance, faultiness, hindrance, hurdle, impairment, impediment, *impedimentum,* imperfection, inconvenience, inferiority, insufficiency, interference, limitation, obstacle, obstruction, onus, remora, restraint, shortcoming, stumbling block

HANDLE *(Manage),* *verb* administer, be master of, command, conduct, control, deal with, direct, dominate, execute, exercise authority, exercise direction over, exercise power over, exert authority, govern, guide, have authority, have charge of, have the care of, have the direction of, have under control, hold authority, keep in order, keep order, keep under control, look after, manipulate, officiate, operate, possess authority, preside over, regulate, reign over, rule, see to, superintend, supervise, use, wield, wield authority

HANDLE *(Trade),* *verb* auction, barter, bring to market, carry, carry on a trade, carry on business, carry on commerce, carry on negotiations, chaffer, conduct business, deal in, do business, drive a bargain, effect a sale, exchange, exchange in commerce, have commerce, have for sale, hawk, interchange, make a bargain, make a sale, market, merchandise, offer for sale, peddle, put up for sale, sell, sell at the market, trade, trade in, traffic in, transact business, vend

HANDSEL, *noun* deposit, down payment, earnest money, first installment, first payment, first receipts, installment, payment, security, stake money

HANDWRITING, *noun* autography, calligraphy, *chirographum,* chirography, cursive writing, hand, longhand, *manus,* pencraft, penmanship, script, scription, style of penmanship, writing
ASSOCIATED CONCEPTS: forgery, handwriting expert, handwriting sample, holographic wills

HAPHAZARD, *adjective* accidental, adventitious, arbitrary, capricious, casual, chance, chaotic, confused, designless, desultory, determined by chance, disordered, disorderly, fitful, immethodical, indiscriminate, irregular, nonsystematic, orderless, planless, promiscuous, random, systemless, unaimed, unarranged, unconsidered, undirected, unforeseen, unguided, unintended, unintentional, unmethodical, unorganized, unplanned, unpredictable, unpremeditated, unsorted, unsystematic, without order

HAPPENING, *noun* action, affair, *casus,* chance event, course of events, development, episode, event, experience, incident, matter, occasion, occurrence, phenomenon, proceeding, transpiration, unfolding
ASSOCIATED CONCEPTS: unforeseen happening

HAPPENSTANCE, *noun* accident, accidental occurrence, casualty, chance, chance happening, circumstance, coincidence, fate, fortuitousness, fortuity, inexpectation, involuntariness, random luck, serendipity, unexpected occurrence, unforeseen occurrence, unpredictability

HARANGUE, noun abusive speech, bombast, *contio,* declamation, declamatory speech, diatribe, disquisition, effusion, exhortation, expatiation, invective, lecture, prelection, tirade, vehement speech
ASSOCIATED CONCEPTS: harassment

HARASS, verb afflict, agitate, agonize, anger, annoy, arouse, arrogate, assail, badger, be malevolent, bedevil, beset, besiege, bludgeon, bother, browbeat, burden, coerce, confound, convulse, discompose, dispirit, disquiet, distress, disturb, enrage, *exagitare,* excite, excruciate, goad, grieve, harbor a grudge, harrow, harry, haunt, heckle, ill-treat, ill-use, incense, incommode, infest, infuriate, injure persistently, intimidate, intrude upon, irritate, malign, maltreat, misuse, mock, obsess, oppress, outrage, overburden, overdrive, overrun, overstrain, overtax, overwork, pester, plague, prey upon, provoke, rankle, *sollicitare,* spite, strain, terrorize, torment, trouble, tyrannize, upbraid, vex, *vexare,* victimize, wear down, weigh on
ASSOCIATED CONCEPTS: barratry, harassing a witness

HARBINGER, noun announcer, annunciator, *antecursor,* augur, augury, auspice, courier, crier, forerunner, foretoken, forewarning, herald, informer, intelligencer, messenger, omen, portent, *praenuntius,* precursor, premonitory sign, presage, proclaimer, prognostic, publicizer, sign, teller, usher, warning

HARBOR, verb afford sanctuary, aid, cache, care for, cloak, conceal, cover, defend, ensconce, give refuge, grant asylum, guard, haven, hide, insure, keep, keep out of sight, keep safe, keep secret, lodge, look after, maintain, preserve, protect, provide refuge, provide safety, provide sanctuary, quarter, safeguard, screen, seclude, secrete, secure, shelter, shield, shroud, stow away, sustain, watch
ASSOCIATED CONCEPTS: accessory after the fact, alienation of affections, assisting escape, harbor and secrete, harboring a criminal, harboring a fugitive, harboring an animal

HARDSHIP, noun adversity, affliction, misfortune, suffering, travail

HARM, noun aggravation, balefulness, bedevilment, damage, *damnum,* deadliness, detriment, *detrimentum,* disablement, disservice, evil, hurt, hurtfulness, ill-consequence, ill-treatment, impairment, injury, malignance, malignancy, malignity, mischief, misfortune, mutilation, noxiousness, perniciousness, ruin, scathe, scourge, virulence
ASSOCIATED CONCEPTS: accidental harm, bodily harm, forseeable harm, irreparable harm, unreasonable risk of harm

HARM, verb abuse, adulterate, afflict, aggravate, attack, be malevolent, bruise, cause pain, corrode, corrupt, cripple, damage, debase, deface, demolish, devastate, disadvantage, disfigure, disserve, do evil, do mischief, do violence, endamage, exacerbate, hurt, ill-treat, ill-use, impair, incapacitate, infect, inflict injury, injure, *laedere,* maim, maltreat, mar, misuse, mutilate, *nocere,* pervert, plague, pollute, ravage, ruin, scathe, scourge, smite, spoil, subvert, worsen, wound, wrong

ASSOCIATED CONCEPTS: accidental harm, bodily harm, forseeable harm, irreparable harm, unreasonable harm
FOREIGN PHRASES: *Error scribentis nocere non debit.* An error made by a clerk ought not to prejudice. *Qui jure suo utitur, nemini facit injuriam.* One who exercises his legal rights, injures no one.

HARMFUL, adjective afflicting, bad, baleful, baneful, calamitous, cataclysmic, catastrophic, consuming, consumptive, corrosive, costly, crippling, cruel, crushing, damaging, dangerous, deleterious, destructive, detracting, detrimental, devouring, dire, disadvantageous, disastrous, disserviceable, evil, fell, fiendish, foul, hurtful, ill-intentioned, inexpedient, infectious, injurious, insalubrious, insidious, internecine, malefic, maleficent, malicious, malign, mephitic, merciless, miasmal, mischievous, morbific, nasty, *nocens,* nocent, nocuous, noisome, noxious, *noxius,* pernicious, pestiferous, pestilential, pitiless, poisonous, polluted, ruinous, spiteful, subversionary, subversive, toxic, treacherous, troublous, unfavorable, unfortunate, unhealthy, unlucky, unpropitious, unsafe, unwholesome, venomous, vicious, wicked, wounding
ASSOCIATED CONCEPTS: harmful consequences from an overt act, harmful products

HARMLESS, adjective benign, blunt, gentle, hurtless, impotent, *innocens,* innocent, innocuous, *innocuus,* innoxious, *innoxius,* inoffensive, nonmalignant, nonpoisonous, nontoxic, nonvenomous, nonviolent, nonvirulent, powerless, tame, trustworthy, unaggressive, unhazardous, uninjurious, unmilitant, unthreatening, weak, without risk
ASSOCIATED CONCEPTS: harmless beyond a reasonable doubt, harmless error, hold harmless

HARMONIOUS, adjective accordant, acquiescent, adapted, adjusted, agreeable, agreeing, allied, amicable, apposite, apt, arranged, assenting, becoming, blended, bonded, *canorus,* coexistent, coexisting, combined, compatible, concinnous, concordant, *concors,* conforming, congenial, *congruens,* congruent, congruous, consentaneous, consentient, consistent, consonant, cooperative, coordinated, correlative, correspondent, corresponding, equable, fraternal, frictionless, friendly, halcyon, joint, leagued, matching, pacific, peaceful, pleasant, pleasing, proportional, proportionate, sociable, suitable, suiting, unanimous, united, unstrained, untroubled

HARROW, verb aggrieve, agitate, alarm, annoy, appall, assail, badger, bedevil, beset, besiege, bother, browbeat, bully, chafe, chagrin, cross, discompose, disconcert, dismay, displease, disquiet, disturb, *excruciare,* fret, give pain, harass, harm, harry, hurt, ill-treat, illuse, inflict pain, injure, irritate, lacerate, lancinate, maltreat, misuse, molest, needle, outrage, persecute, perturb, pique, plague, provoke, spite, tease, torment, *torquere,* try, upset, vex, *vexare,* wrong

HARRY (Harass), verb aggrieve, annoy, badger, bait, be offensive, be rude, beleaguer, beset, bother, browbeat, bully, *cruciare,* deride, discompose, disconcert, displease, distress, disturb, fluster, fret, haze, heckle, hound, importune, irritate, needle, offend, oppress, persecute, pester, pique, plague, provoke, rile, ruffle, tease, torment, *torquere,* try, vex, *vexare,* worry

HARRY *(Plunder), verb*   assail, attack, create havoc, despoil, forage, foray, invade, lay waste, maraud, pillage, raid, ransack, ravage, rob, sack, seize, spoliate, strip

HARSH, *adjective*   acerb, acerbic, acid, acrid, acrimonious, ascetic, astringent, austere, biting, bitter, brusque, brutal, burning, caustic, corrosive, crude, cruel, despiteful, discordant, disrespectful, draconian, drastic, excessive, extreme, feral, ferine, ferocious, grating, grim, grueling, gruff, ill-natured, incisive, inclement, inharmonious, inhuman, inhumane, intense, merciless, mordacious, mordant, noisome, noxious, oppressive, piercing, pitiless, punishing, rancorous, rigorous, rough, ruthless, savage, scathing, severe, sharp, stern, stinging, strident, stridulous, stringent, surly, truculent, uncomforting, unconsoling, unfeeling, unflattering, ungentle, ungracious, unkind, unkindly, unmerciful, unmitigated, unpitying, unsympathetic, untender, virulent, vituperative, withering
ASSOCIATED CONCEPTS: cruel and unusual punishment, harsh penalty, harsh rule

HASTE, *noun*   acceleration, alacrity, briskness, celerity, dash, dispatch, eagerness to act quickly, expedition, expeditiousness, *festinatio,* flurry, frenzy, hurriedness, hurry, hustle, inability to wait, precipitance, precipitancy, precipitation, precipitousness, *properantia, properatio,* quickness, rapidity, rashness, rush, speed, swiftness, urgency, velocity
ASSOCIATED CONCEPTS: speedy trial
FOREIGN PHRASES: *Festinatio justitiae est noverca infortunii.* The hastening of justice is the stepmother of misfortune.

HASTEN, *verb*   *accelerare,* accelerate, advance, *contendere,* dash, dispatch, drive forward, expedite, facilitate, forward, help along, hurry, hurry along, hustle, incite, lose no time, make haste, *maturare,* move fast, move quickly, move speedily, precipitate, press, pressure, promote, *properare,* push on, put on speed, race, rouse, rush, rush through, speed along, spur, urge on

HATRED, *noun*   abhorrence, abomination, animosity, animus, antagonism, antipathy, aversion, defamation, detestation, dislike, enmity, hostility, ill feeling, ill will, intolerance, loathing, malevolence, odium, prejudice, revulsion

HAVEN, *noun*   anchorage, asylum, citadel, cove, harbor, hideout, landing, place of safety, port, *portus,* protection, refuge, resting place, retreat, sanctuary, shelter
ASSOCIATED CONCEPTS: diplomatic immunity

HAVOC, *noun*   anarchy, carnage, cataclysm, chaos, chaotic state, confusion, depredation, derangement, desolation, destruction, devastation, disorder, disorganization, dispersion, disruption, holocaust, overturning, pillage, plundering, ravage, ruin, ruination, sack, scattering, shambles, spoliation, *strages,* turmoil, upheaval, *vastatio,* violence, waste
ASSOCIATED CONCEPTS: disorderly conduct, disturbing the peace

HAZARD, *noun*   *casus,* cause for alarm, chance, danger, dangerous course, dangerous situation, endangerment, *fors,* gamble, imperilment, insecurity, jeopardy, liability to injury, menace, *periculum,* peril, pit-

fall, precariousness, risk, source of risk, threat, uncertainty, unsafe object, unsureness
ASSOCIATED CONCEPTS: dangerous hazard, extreme hazard, hazardous business, hazardous condition, hazardous employment, hazardous undertaking, inherent hazard, latent hazard, moral hazard, patent hazard, private hazard, public hazard, undue hazard

HEADING, *noun*   banner, caption, head, headline, label, proper title, section, superscription, title, topic

HEADQUARTERS, *noun*   base, base camp, base of authority, base of operations, center, center of authority, center of operations, central station, chief office, distributing center, home base, home office, main office, manager's office, *praetorium,* residence, seat, supply base
ASSOCIATED CONCEPTS: nerve center of a corporation

HEADWAY, *noun*   advance, ascent, betterment, climb, development, forward motion, furtherance, gain, ground gained, growth, improvement, momentum, progress, progression, promotion, upswing

HEALTH, *noun*   condition, fitness, freedom from ailment, freedom from disease, haleness, hardiness, heartiness, physical condition, robustness, ruggedness, salubriousness, salubrity, *salus, sanitas,* soundness, soundness of body, stamina, state of health, strength, sturdiness, *valetudo,* vigor, vitality, well-being, wholesomeness
ASSOCIATED CONCEPTS: bill of health, board of health, dangerous to health, department of health, health care, health education and welfare, health insurance, impairment of health, mental health, public health and safety, public health law, sanitary code

HEAR *(Give a legal hearing), verb*   adjudicate, *causam, cognoscere,* conduct a trial, decide, examine judicially, examine the witnesses, give a formal hearing to, give a judicial hearing to, give an official hearing to, hold court, inquire into, investigate judicially, judge, preside over, put on trial, referee, sit in judgment, try, try a case, try the cause
ASSOCIATED CONCEPTS: arbitrate, hear and report, mediate

HEAR *(Give attention to), verb*   accept advice, *accipere,* acknowledge, advert, attend to, audition, ausculate, be attentive, be guided by, *cognoscere,* comply, defer to, give audience, give way, heed, listen, mind, note, obey, pay attention, regard, submit, subscribe, succumb, yield

HEAR *(Perceive by ear), verb*   *auribus,* become aware of, become conscious of, detect, discern something audible, make out, notice, perceive something audible, *percipere,* receive information aurally, recognize, take cognizance of

HEARING, *noun*   action, case at law, close inquiry, *cognitio,* contest, examination, exhaustive inquiry, formal proceeding, formal questioning, inquest, inquiry, inquisition, interrogation, investigation, judicial examination, judicial investigation, legal proceedings, legal trial, litigation, presentation of arguments and evidence, presentation of testimony, probe, public inquest, public proceeding, searching inquiry, strict inquiry, trial, trial at the bar, trial by jury, trial in court

ASSOCIATED CONCEPTS: adjudicative hearing, adversary hearing, de novo hearing, default hearing, due process, fair and impartial hearing, fair hearing, final hearing, formal hearing, full hearing, hearing on damages, hearing on the merits, interlocutory hearing, judicial hearing, notice of hearing, preliminary hearing, public hearing, statutory hearing, suppression hearing, traverse

FOREIGN PHRASES: *Qui aliquid statuerit, parte inaudita altera, aequum licet dixerit, haud aequum fecerit.* He who decides anything without hearing both sides, although he may decide correctly, has by no means acted justly.

HEARSAY, *noun*   *auditio,* evidence from impersonal knowledge, gossip, groundless rumor, indirect evidence, popular report, report, *rumor,* secondary evidence, secondhand evidence, unconfirmed account, unconfirmed report, unverified comments, unverified news

ASSOCIATED CONCEPTS: admission, ancient writings, business records, declarations against pecuniary interest, declarations against penal interest, dying declarations, exceptions to hearsay rules, hearsay evidence, records of past recollection, reputation as to pedigree, res gestae, spontaneous declarations

HECTOR, *verb*   badger, bait, beset, bluster, bother, browbeat, bully, cow, distress, disturb, fret, gibe, goad, harass, harrow, harry, heckle, hound, insult, intimidate, irritate, jeer, menace, molest, nag, nettle, offend, persecute, pester, plague, pother, provoke, roil, tease, threaten, torment, treat with insolence, trouble, vex, worry

HEDGE, *verb*   be careful, be cautious, border, bound, circle, circumscribe, compass, conceal, cover, delimit, delimitate, delineate, demarcate, divide, dodge, edge, encircle, enclose, encompass, ensphere, evade, fence, flank, girdle, guard, hide, limit, mark off, outline, play safe, protect, render safe, ring, safeguard, screen, shelter, shield, surround

HEED, *verb*   attend to, be attentive, be aware, be careful, be cautious, be conscious of, be guided by, check, comply, consider, *curare,* follow, hark, hear, hearken to, listen to, look to, mark, mind, note, notice, obey, *observare,* observe, *parere,* pay attention, recognize, regard, respect, take care, take cognizance of, take into account, take note, take notice, watch

ASSOCIATED CONCEPTS: heed counsel's advice

HEEDLESS, *adjective*   blind, careless, deaf, disregardful, hasty, improvident, imprudent, impulsive, inattentive, incautious, *incautus,* insouciant, irresponsible, mindless, neglectful, *neglegens,* negligent, nonobservant, oblivious, off guard, precipitate, rash, reckless, *temerarius,* thoughtless, unaware, uncaring, unconcerned, undiscerning, unhearing, unheedful, unheeding, unmindful, unnoticing, unobservant, unperceiving, unseeing, unsolicitous, unthinking, unwary, unwatchful, without consideration

ASSOCIATED CONCEPTS: recklessness

HEGEMONY, *noun*   ascendance, ascendancy, authority, command, control, directorship, dominance, domination, dominion, governance, headship, importance, influence, lawful authority, leadership, lordship, mastery, paramountcy, power, predominance, predomi-

nating influence, prepollence, regency, reign, rule, superiority, supremacy, sway

HEIGHTEN *(Augment),* *verb*   add, advance, aggravate, *amplificare,* amplify, *augere,* build up, enhance, enlarge, exacerbate, *exaggerare,* expand, greaten, improve, increase, intensify, magnify, make higher, make larger, multiply, promote, raise, reinforce, strengthen, vivify

HEIGHTEN *(Elevate),* *verb*   *altior,* build up, hold up, lift up, make higher, pick up, raise, raise aloft, uplift, upraise

HEINOUS, *adjective*   abhorrent, abominable, arrant, atrocious, awful, bad, baleful, baneful, base, beastly, black, confounded, contemptible, damnable, deplorable, despicable, *detestabilis,* detestable, devilish, diabolic, dire, disgraceful, disgusting, distasteful, dreadful, egregious, evil, execrable, facinorous, flagitious, flagrant, foul, fulsome, ghastly, gross, hateful, hellish, horrendous, horrible, horrid, infamous, infernal, iniquitous, invidious, loathsome, low, malefic, mean, monstrous, *nafarius,* nasty, *nefandus,* nefarious, noisome, objectionable, obnoxious, odious, offensive, opprobrious, outrageous, pernicious, reprehensible, reptilian, repugnant, revolting, rotten, satanic, shameful, shocking, sickening, sinister, terrible, unprincipled, vicious, vile, villainous, wicked, wretched, wrong

ASSOCIATED CONCEPTS: heinous crime

HEIR, *noun*   acceptor, after-comer, after-generations, allottee, *bénéficiaire,* beneficiary, consignee, descendant, devisee, donee, inheritor, inheritrix, legatee, one who inherits, parcener, payee, possessor of descent, posterity, receiver, recipient, scion, successor, survivor, transferee

ASSOCIATED CONCEPTS: adopted heir, aggrieved heir, bodily heir, coheir, collateral heir, distributee, eligible heir, expectant heir, heir apparent, heirs at law, heirs in fee simple, illegitimate heir, immediate heir, intestate succession, issue, legal heir, legitimate heir, lineal heir, living heir, natural heir, natural offspring, next of kin, presumptive heir, pretermitted heir, Rule in Shelley's Case, surviving heir, unknown heir

FOREIGN PHRASES: *Haeres est aut jure proprietatis aut jure representationis.* A person is an heir either by right of property or by right of representation. *Haeredum appellatione veniunt haeredes haeredum in infinitum.* Under the name heirs come the heirs of heirs without limit. *Cohaeredes una persona censentur, propter unitatem juris quod habent.* Coheirs are regarded as one person because they own under unity of right. *In haeredes non solent transire actiones quae poenales ex maleficio sunt.* Actions which are penal and which arise out of anything of a criminal nature do not pass to the heirs. *Posthumus pro nato habetur.* A posthumous child is regarded as born before the death of the parent. *Nemo est haeres viventis.* No one can be the heir of a living person. *Haeres minor uno et viginti annis non respondebit, nisi in casu dotis.* A minor heir under twenty-one years of age is not answerable, except in the matter of dower. *Filius est nomen naturae, sed haeres nomen juris.* Son is the natural name, but heir is a name of law. *Nemo potest esse dominus et haeres.* No one can be both owner and heir. *Haeres est pars antecessoris.* An heir is a part of his ancestor.

HELP, *noun*   abetment, accommodation, advantage, advice, aid, assist, assistance, *auxilium,* avail, backing, benefaction, benefit, benevolence, boon, care, charity, contribution, cooperation, cure, deliverance, encouragement, expedient, facilitation, favor, fosterage, furtherance, good turn, guidance, hand, helpfulness, humanitarianism, kindness, ministration, patronage, philanthropy, redress, reinforcement, relief, remedy, rescue, resource, seconding, service, stead, strengthening, *subsidium,* subvention, succor, support, sustenance, use, utility

ASSOCIATED CONCEPTS: Good Samaritan

HELP, *verb*   abet, accommodate, advance, advise, aid, alleviate, ameliorate, apply a remedy, assist, avail, back, be benevolent, be of use, benefit, better, boost, come to the aid of, contribute, cooperate, correct, cure, do a service, ease, encourage, expedite, facilitate, fix, fortify, forward, furnish assistance, further, heal, improve, intercede for, lend a hand, lend aid, lend support, make easy, oblige, patronize, promote, prop, put right, rally, reinforce, relieve, remedy, render assistance, second, serve, smooth, speed, stand by, stead, strengthen, *subvenire,* succor, *succurrere,* support, sustain, work for

ASSOCIATED CONCEPTS: aid and abet, facilitation, rescue doctrine

HELPLESS *(Defenseless),* **adjective**   abandoned, aidless, conquerable, deserted, exposed, expugnable, forsaken, friendless, guardless, in danger, *inermis, inops,* open to attack, pregnable, resourceless, shelterless, unaided, unarmed, unarmored, unbefriended, uncovered, undefended, unfortified, unguarded, unprotected, unsheltered, unshielded, unstrengthened, unsupported, untenable, vincible, vulnerable, without aid, without succor

ASSOCIATED CONCEPTS: last clear chance

HELPLESS *(Powerless),* **adjective**   crippled, debilitated, dependent, disabled, enervated, feeble, impotent, incapable, incompetent, invalid, paralyzed, prostrate, strengthless, unable, weak, without force

ASSOCIATED CONCEPTS: disability, incompetency

HERALD, *verb*   advertise, air, announce, apprise, augur, betoken, blazon, circulate, communicate, cry, disseminate, enlighten, enunciate, forecast, forerun, foreshow, foretell, foretoken, gazette, give tidings, harbinger, inform, introduce, make known, notify, omen, presage, proclaim, prognosticate, promulgate, publicize, publish, report, spread, tell, tip, trumpet, usher in, warn

ASSOCIATED CONCEPTS: *nuntiare*

HEREAFTER *(Eventually),* **adverb**   at a fixed time, later, ultimately

ASSOCIATED CONCEPTS: hereafter acquired, hereafter built

HEREAFTER *(Henceforth),* **adverb**   afterwards, from here on, from now on, from this time on

HEREBY, *adverb*   by means of, by the aid of, by virtue of, through, through the medium of, whereby

HEREDITAMENT, *noun*   bequest, devise, heirloom, heritable, heritage, heritance, inheritable property, inheritance, patrimony, personal property capable of being inherited, property which may descend to an heir, real property capable of being inherited

ASSOCIATED CONCEPTS: corporeal hereditament, easement, incorporeal hereditament

HEREDITARY, *adjective*   ancestorial, ancestral, ancient, congenital, connatal, connate, constitutional, genealogical, genetic, hereditable, *hereditarius,* heritable, inborn, inbred, indigenous, ingenerate, inherited, innate, instinctive, instinctual, lineal, native, passed down, *paternus,* traditional, transmissible

ASSOCIATED CONCEPTS: hereditary disease, hereditary insanity, hereditary succession

HEREIN, *adverb*   in, inside, inwardly, therein, wherein, within

HERETIC, *noun*   apostate, dissenter, dissentient, dissident, *haereticus,* iconoclast, infidel, misbeliever, nonconformist, protestant, schismatic, sectarian, separatist, skeptic, unbeliever

HERETOFORE, *adverb*   before now, earlier, formerly, from the start, historically speaking, in the past, previous to, previously, prior to, retrospectively, up to this time

HERITABLE, *adjective*   alienable, assignable, bequeathable, bestowable, consignable, conveyable, devisable, exchangeable, givable, hereditable, hereditary, inheritable, negotiable, testamentary, transferable, transmissible

ASSOCIATED CONCEPTS: bequest, curtesy, devise, dower, intestate succession laws, legacy, testamentary gift

HERITAGE, *noun*   ancestry, bequest, birthright, descent, expectations, future possession, hereditament, *hereditas, heredium,* heritance, incorporeal hereditament, inheritance, inherited lot, inherited portion, legacy, lineage, *patrimonium,* patrimony, portion, reversion

ASSOCIATED CONCEPTS: descendants

HEROIC, *adjective*   bold, brave, courageous, daring, dauntless, doughty, fearless, *fortis, fortis et invictus,* gallant, herolike, intrepid, lionhearted, noble, resolute, soldierly, stalwart, stout, stouthearted, unblenching, undaunted, unflinching, unshrinking, valiant, valorous

ASSOCIATED CONCEPTS: Good Samaritan

HESITANT, *adjective*   averse, balking, balky, cautious, dallying, debating, deliberate, demurring, diffident, doubtful, doubting, equivocal, faltering, fluctuating, groping, halfhearted, hesitating, hesitative, indecisive, irresolute, lacking confidence, loath, pausing, qualmish, reluctant, shrinking, shy, slow, tentative, timid, unassured, uncertain, unconfident, undecided, unresolved, unsettled, unsure, vacillating, wavering

ASSOCIATED CONCEPTS: hestitant buyer, hestitant reluctant seller

HESITATE, *verb*   balk, be dilatory, be dubious, be irresolute, be tentative, be uncertain, *cunctari,* dally, delay, demur, doubt, *dubitare,* falter, *haerere,* have reservations, hold back, oscillate, pause, procrastinate, question, scruple, stop, think twice, vacillate, wait, waver

HESITATION, *noun*   caution, *cunctatio,* delay, diffidence, doubt, dubiety, *dubitatio,* dubitation, equivocation, faltering, fluctuation, *haesitatio,* hesitancy, holding back, incertitude, indecision, irresolution, nervousness, oscillation, overcaution, qualm, reluctance, scruple, second thoughts, slowness, tentativeness, uncertainness, uncertainty, unsureness, unwillingness, vacillation, wavering

HETEROGENEOUS, adjective   assorted, different, disparate, dissimilar, *dissimilis,* diverse, diversified, diversiform, *diversus,* incongruous, irrelative, miscellaneous, mixed, motley, multiform, nonuniform, unalike, unequal, unlike, unmatched, unrelated, variant, varied, variegated, variform, various, varying, without relation

HIATUS, noun   abeyance, adjournment, break, cessation, chasm, delay, disconnection, discontinuity, disjunction, disunion, fracture, gap, gulf, halt, *hiatus,* incompleteness, interference, interim, interlude, intermission, interregnum, interruption, interstice, interval, intervening period, lacuna, lapse, lull, moratorium, opening, pause, recess, respite, rest, rift, separation, spell, standstill, stop, stoppage, suspension, temporary stop

HIDDEN, adjective   *absconditus,* abstruse, ambushed, arcane, blind, buried, camouflaged, clandestine, cloaked, close, clouded, concealed, covered, covert, cryptic, dark, delitescent, disguised, eclipsed, enigmatical, enshrouded, esoteric, hieroglyphic, indiscernable, invisible, latent, lurking, masked, mysterious, mystic, mystical, obscure, obscured, occult, *occultus,* out of sight, out of view, perdu, puzzling, recondite, screened, secluded, secret, secreted, shrouded, suppressed, surreptitious, unapparent, uncomprehended, undeciphered, undercover, underground, underhanded, undetected, undisclosed, undivulged, unexplained, unexposed, unknown, unobserved, unperceived, unrevealed, unseen, untold, veiled
ASSOCIATED CONCEPTS: attractive nuisance, duty to discover, hidden assets, hidden danger, hidden defects, hidden traps, latent defects, patent defects

HIDE, verb   *abdere, abscondere,* bury, cache, camouflage, *celare,* cloak, closet, cloud, conceal, conceal from knowledge, conceal from sight, cover, cover up, curtain, deceive, disguise, dissemble, ensconce, envelop, harbor, hush up, keep out of sight, keep out of view, keep secret, keep to oneself, keep under cover, mask, obscure, put out of sight, render invisible, screen, seclude, secrete, shade, shadow, shelter, shroud, smuggle, stow away, suppress, veil, withhold, wrap
ASSOCIATED CONCEPTS: hide assets

HIERARCHY (*Arrangement in a series*), **noun**   arrangement, categorization, chain, classification, collocation, distribution, gradation, grouping, order, order of succession, progression, range, run, seriation, series, succession, system

HIERARCHY (*Persons in authority*), **noun**   administrators, authorities, bureaucracy, commanders, controllers, dictators, directors, government, heads, leadership power, management, managers, masters, officials, persons in power, powers, regency, regime, rulers, sovereignty

HIGH PROBABILITY, noun   almost certainly, favorable prospect, in all likelihood, in most instances, with a high degree of certainty

ASSOCIATED CONCEPTS: high probability of chance, high probability of risk, high probability of success

HIGH-MINDED, adjective   admirable, conscientious, estimable, ethical, fair, firm in principle, high-principled, honest, honorable, incorrupt, incorruptible, meritorious, moral, noble, principled, reputable, respectable, right-minded, righteous, scrupulous, sterling, trustworthy, uncorrupt, uncorrupted, upright, upstanding, virtuous, worthy

HIGHLIGHT, noun   central point, cynosure, distinctive feature, focal point, high spot, important event, keynote, memorable part, outstanding feature, prominent detail, prominent part, salient point, significant feature, striking part

HIJACK, verb   abduct, appropriate, arrogate, assume command, bear away, capture, carry away, carry off, commandeer, convey away, dispossess, expropriate, force, help oneself to, impress, intercept, lay hold of, make off with, make prisoner, overcome, overpower, overwhelm, pirate, plunder, secure, seize, snatch, take, take away, take by assault, take by force, take captive, take prisoner
ASSOCIATED CONCEPTS: air piracy

HINDER, verb   annoy, arrest, barricade, be an impediment, be an obstacle, block, bother, check, clog, constrain, cramp, cripple, curb, detain, discommode, discourage, encumber, fetter, get in the way, halt, hamper, hamstring, handicap, hold back, impair, impede, *impedire,* incommode, inconvenience, inhibit, intercept, interfere, interrupt, keep back, obstruct, occlude, prevent temporarily, *prohibere,* render difficult, restrain, restrict, retard, *retardare,* set back, shackle, slow down, stand in the way, trammel, traverse, work against
ASSOCIATED CONCEPTS: interference with a contract, interference with a lawful order, obstructing justice

HINDRANCE, noun   annoyance, arrest, barrier, blockade, bother, check, complication, constriction, detention, deterrent, detriment, difficulty, disadvantage, discouragement, drawback, embargo, encumbrance, hamper, handicap, holdback, impediment, *impedimentum,* inconvenience, inexpedience, inhibition, interference, interposition, interruption, obstacle, obstruction, preclusion, problem, restraint, restriction, retardation, retardment, setback, shackle, striction

HINDSIGHT, noun   act of looking backward, afterthought, consideration, contemplation, contemplation of past events, contemplation of the past, deliberation, later meditation, later thought, looking back, meditation, memory, musing, recall, recollection, reconsideration, reexamination, reflection, remembrance, retrospect, retrospection, review, review of things past, rumination, second thoughts, second view, subsequent meditation, subsequent reflection, survey of time past, thoughts of the past

HINT, noun   adumbration, allusion, clue, connotation, covert allusion, cue, faint outline, faint suggestion, foreshadowing, idea, implication, indication, indirect suggestion, inference, inkling, insinuation, intimation, *significatio,* slight indication, slight mention, suggestion, trace, vague impression, vague suggestion

HINT, *verb* adumbrate, advert, allude, clue, connote, cue, give an inkling, imply, indicate, infer, insinuate, intimate, make an allusion, prompt, refer, *significare,* signify, *subicere,* suggest
ASSOCIATED CONCEPTS: disclosure

HIRE, *verb* add to the payroll, appoint, assign to a position, authorize, commission, *conducere,* contract for, delegate, depute, designate to a post, employ, engage, enlist, fill a position, fill a vacancy, furnish occupation for, give a job to, give employment to, give work to, induct, install, place in office, procure, put on payroll, put to work, recruit, retain, secure the services of, set to work, staff, take into service, take on
ASSOCIATED CONCEPTS: bailee for hire, carriage, contract for hiring, discrimination in hiring, employment contract

HISTRIONIC, *adjective* affected, aiming for effect, artificial, dramatic, embroidered, exaggerated, exhibitionistic, insincere, mannered, melodramatic, orotund, ostentatious, overacted, pretentious, *scaenicus,* self-conscious, showy, stagy, stilted, striving for effect, theatric, theatrical, unnatural

HISTRIONICS, *noun* acting, affectation, affectedness, airs, *ars ludicra,* artificial behavior for effect, display, dramatic art, dramatic representation, dramaturgy, emotional display for effect, exaggeration, false show, fanfaronade, melodramatics, orotundity, ostentation, overacting, overemphasis, parade, performance, pretense, *scaenicus,* show, showmanship, stagecraft, theatrecraft, theatricalism, theatricality, theatricalness

HOARD, *noun* accumulation, *acervus,* aggregation, amassment, cache, collection, *copia,* cumulation, fund, heap, mass, repository, reserves, riches, saving, stack, stock, stockpile, store, supply, treasure

HOARD, *verb* accrue, accumulate, acquire, agglomerate, aggregate, aggroup, amalgamate, amass, augment, bank, batch together, bring together, build up, bunch, cache, cluster, *coacervare,* collect, *conligere, conquirere,* cumulate, deposit, draw together, garner, garner up, gather for oneself, gather in, gather up, get together, group, hang on to, have in store, heap, hide, hide away, hive, hold back, husband, husband one's resources, keep, keep back, keep in reserve, lay by, lay in store, lay up, load up, lump together, pack away, pile, pile up, preserve, provide, put aside, reposit, reserve, retain, save up, set apart, set aside, set by, stock up, stockpile, store, store secretly, store up, stow, stow away, treasure up, withhold

HOAX, *noun* artifice, beguilement, canard, cheat, chicanery, circumvention, counterfeit, cozenage, deceit, deception, defraudation, delusion, device, dupery, duplicity, fabrication, fake, false alarm, false report, falsification, fraud, fraudulence, fraudulency, guile, imposition, imposture, knavery, lie, *ludificatio,* machination, masquerade, misrepresentation, pettifogging, practical joke, pretense, ruse, scheme, sham, shift, stratagem, subterfuge, swindle, trick, trickery, wile
ASSOCIATED CONCEPTS: false representation, forgery, fraud, impersonation

HOLD *(Decide), verb* abjudge, abjudicate, ascertain, come to a conclusion, conclude, decide legally, de-

cree, determine, find, fix, judge, make a decision, pass judgment, propound, resolve, rule, settle

HOLD *(Possess), verb* assume authority, assume command, be accorded, be heir to, be in possession of, be master of, be offered, be possessed of, be proffered, be vouchsafed, bear the responsibility of, care for, cling to, collect, command, conserve, control, devolve upon, direct, dominate, exercise direction over, fill a post, gather, get control, get possession of, grasp, *habere,* have, have a firm grip on, have a title to, have absolute disposal of, have as property, have by inheritance, have by tenure, have claim upon, have in hand, have in one's possession, have inherited, have rights to, have the care of, have the charge of, have the direction of, have title to, have under control, hold fast, hold in one's grasp, impropriate, inherit, keep, keep as one's own, keep for, keep in hand, keep in readiness, keep in reserve, keep on, keep prepared, lay aside, lay away, not dispose of, not part with, occupy, own, *possidere,* preserve, receive, recover, retain, save, secure, set apart, set aside, take authority, take command, take over, *tenere,* wield restraint over
ASSOCIATED CONCEPTS: adverse holding, hold in due course, hostile holding

HOLD OUT *(Deliberate on an offer), verb* make overtures, offer, place at ones disposal, present, proffer, *promittere,* propone, propose, put forward, submit, suggest, urge, volunteer

HOLD OUT *(Resist), verb* balk, be unwilling, hold fast, hold ones own, make a resolute stand, not budge, not compromise, not give up, not submit, not weaken, not yield, offer resistance, oppugn, persevere, persist, refuse, refuse consent, remain firm, repel, *resistere,* stand fast, stand firm, withhold assent, withhold consent, withstand

HOLD UP *(Delay), verb* adjourn, arrest, arrest temporarily, be dilatory, block, brake, bring to a standstill, call a halt, call off, cause a stoppage, cause to arrive late, cause to move with undue slowness, cause to put off to a later time, check, contain, control, cumber, curb, decelerate, defer, detain, deter, *detinere,* encumber, filibuster, gain time, halt, hamper, hinder, hold in abeyance, impede, impede the progress of, incommode, inconvenience, inhibit, interfere, interrupt, intervene, keep one waiting, keep pending, lay aside, lay under restraint, obstruct, pigeonhole, postpone, procrastinate, prolong, protract, push aside, put a stop to, put aside, put off, put off to a future time, put under restraint, repress, reserve, resist, restrain, retard, *retinere,* set aside, set one back, shelve, slacken, slow up, stall, stand in the way, stave off, stop, suppress, suspend, table, *tardare,* thwart, undermine, upset, withhold

HOLD UP *(Rob), verb* abscond with, abstract, appropriate, carry away, carry off, commit robbery, *compilare,* deprecate, despoil, divert, *eripere, expilare,* impress, make off with, maraud, misappropriate, pickeer, pilfer, pillage, pirate, plunder, poach, purloin, reave, reive, remove, rob, run off with, sack, spirit away, spoil, stick up, take away, take by theft, take dishonestly, take feloniously, take possession of, take wrongfully, thieve, walk off with, withdraw

HOLDER, *noun* endorsee, individual in possession, keeper, owner, payee, person in possession, *possessor,* receiver, recipient

ASSOCIATED CONCEPTS: bona fide holder, holder for value, holder in due course, holder in good faith, holder of a lien, joint holder, legal holder, license holder, negotiable instruments, original holder, policyholder, property holder, shareholder, stockholder

HOLDING (*Property owned*), *noun*   asset, belonging, chattel, domain, effect, estate, exclusive possession, interest, land, landed estate, legal estate, *possessio*, possession, property, real estate, real property, realty, resource, seisin, share, stake
ASSOCIATED CONCEPTS: holding a lien, holding a position of authority, holding company, holding for value, holding in due course, holding office, holding over

HOLDING (*Ruling of a court*), *noun*   act of judgment, action, adjudication, ascertainment, conclusion, conclusion of the matter, considered opinion, decision, decree, *decretum,* deduction, deliverance, determination, dictate, final judgment, finding, *iudicium,* judgment, judgment on facts, judicial decision, law, law of the case, maxim, opinion, order, order of the court, outcome, precedent, precept, professional advice, professional decision, pronouncement, pronouncement by a court, recommendation, recorded expression of a formal judgment, report, resolution, result, sentence, *sententia,* settled decision, settlement by authoritative decision, that which is decided, upshot, verdict, written order
ASSOCIATED CONCEPTS: decision en banc, holding of the court, opinion per curiam

HOLDOVER, *noun*   carry over, individual who stays on, one who remains, one who stays on, relic, remainder, remaining portion
ASSOCIATED CONCEPTS: eviction, holdover tenant

HOLIDAY, *noun*   celebration, day of festivities, day off, *dies festus, feriae,* festival, fete, furlough, gala, jubilee, leave, leisure, lull, recess, rest, time off, vacation
ASSOCIATED CONCEPTS: general holiday, legal holiday

HOLOGRAPHIC, *adjective*   cursive, graphic, handwritten, in black and white, in longhand, in print, in writing, inscribed, inscriptional, longhand, manuscript, on paper, penned, printed, scribbled, scriptorial, scriptural, under one's hand, written
ASSOCIATED CONCEPTS: execution of a will, nuncapative will, Probate Court, Surrogates Court, will formalities

HOMAGE, *noun*   allegiance, attention, compliance, consideration, constancy, court, *cultus,* deference, devotedness, devotion, esteem, estimation, exaltation, faithfulness, fidelity, glorification, high regard, honor, humility, loyalty, obedience, obeisance, *observantia,* regard, respect, reverence, service, servility, servitude, subjection, submission, submissiveness, subservience, veneration, *verecundia*

HOME (*Domicile*), *noun*   abode, apartment, cottage, *domicilium, domus,* dormitory, dwelling, dwelling place, fireside, fixed residence, habitat, habitation, haven, homeland, homestead, house, household, living quarters, locality, lodging, lodging place, native environment, permanent legal address, place of abode, place of dwelling, place of existence, place of one's domestic affections, place of refuge, place of residence, place of rest, place to live in, place where one lives, quarters, refuge, residence, resting place

ASSOCIATED CONCEPTS: home office, home rule domicile, home site
FOREIGN PHRASES: *Constitutum esse eam domum unicuique nostrum debere existimari, ubi quisque sedes et tabulas haberet, suarumque rerum constitutionem fecisset.* It is established that the home of each of us is considered to be the place of his abode and books, and where he may have made an establishment of his business.

HOME (*Place of origin*), *noun*   birthplace, country, country of origin, fatherland, homeland, mother country, motherland, native ground, native hearth, native land, native soil, place of birth

HOME RULE, *noun*   autonomy, enfranchisement, franchise, freedom from domination, freedom from interference, freedom of action, freedom of choice, independence, individualism, noninterference, nonintervention, political independence, self-containment, self-derived power, self-determination, self-direction, self-government, self-legislation, self-reliance, self-subsistence, self-sufficiency, self-support, sovereignty, unlimited sovereignty

HOMESTEAD, *noun*   acreage, acres, country house, estate, farm, farm land, farmplace, farmstead, grounds, home, house, household, manor, messuage, place of settlement, residence
ASSOCIATED CONCEPTS: family homestead exemption, homestead interest, homestead tax, residential homestead, transfer of homestead, urban homestead

HOMICIDE, *noun*   annihilation, assassination, butchery, *caedes,* capital crime, capital murder, carnage, crime, destruction of life, elimination, extermination, felony, felony murder, killing, liquidation, manslaughter, massacre, murder, removal, slaughter, slaying, termination of life, violent death
ASSOCIATED CONCEPTS: assault with intent to murder, *corpus delicti,* criminally negligent homicide, culpable homicide, excusable homicide, felonious homicide, felony murder, infanticide, involuntary manslaughter, justifiable homicide, manslaughter, premeditated homicide, voluntary homicide
FOREIGN PHRASES: *Maihemium est homicidium inchoatum.* Mayhem is unfinished homicide.

HONEST, *adjective*   aboveboard, accurate, actual, artless, as represented, authentic, bald, blunt, candid, clean, conscientious, correct, creditable, decent, downright, earnest, equitable, erect, estimable, ethical, evenhanded, exact, factual, fair, fair-dealing, forthright, frank, free from fraud, genuine, guileless, historical, honorable, impartial, impeccable, inartificial, incapable of deceit, incorrupt, incorruptible, ingenuous, innocent, inviolate, irreproachable, just, laudable, law-abiding, legal, legitimate, licit, literal, moral, open, outspoken, plain-speaking, principled, *probus,* proper, pure, reliable, reputable, respectable, right, scrupulous, *simplex,* sincere, *sincerus,* sound, stainless, sterling, straightforward, true, true to the facts, truehearted, trustworthy, truthful, unadulterated, unaffected, unassumed, unassuming, unbiased, unbribable, uncolored, uncopied, uncounterfeited, undiluted, undisguised, undisguising, undissembling, undissimulating, undistorted, unembroidered, unexaggerated, unfabricated, unfaked, unfeigned, unfeigning, unfictitious, ungarbled, uninvented, unperjured, unpretended, unpretending, unpretentious, unsimulated, unsophisticated, unspecious, unspurious, unsynthetic, unvarnished, valid, veracious, veridical, veritable, well-principled

ASSOCIATED CONCEPTS: honest belief, honest claim, honest dispute

HONESTY, *noun* accuracy, artlessness, authenticity, baldness, bluntness, candidness, candor, conscientiousness, estimableness, exactitude, factualness, fairness, fidelity, *fides,* frankness, genuineness, guilelessness, high character, high-mindedness, high principles, honorableness, impartiality, inartificiality, incorruptibility, ingenuousness, integrity, legitimacy, openness, plainness, plainspeaking, principles, *probitas,* probity, reality, realness, reputability, repute, respectability, rightness, sanctity, scrupulosity, scrupulousness, simplicity, *sinceritas,* sincerity, soundness, stainlessness, trustworthiness, truth, truthfulness, unadulteration, unaffectedness, unconstraint, undeceitfulness, undeceptiveness, unreserve, unrestraint, unspeciousness, unspuriousness, unvarnished truth, uprightness, upstandingness, validity, veraciousness, veracity, veridicality, verity, virtue, worthiness

ASSOCIATED CONCEPTS: character evidence, reputation for honesty

HONOR *(Good reputation), **noun*** character, *dignitas, existimatio, fama,* good name, good opinion, goodness, high regard, incorruptibility, integrity, moral rectitude, principle, probity, purity, rectitude, regard, reliability, reputability, repute, respectability, righteousness, scrupulousness, sense of responsibility, standing, status, trustiness, trustworthiness, uprightness, virtue

ASSOCIATED CONCEPTS: reputation evidence

HONOR *(Outward respect), **noun*** acclaim, admiration, adulation, aggrandizement, appreciation, approbation, approval, commendation, consideration, courtesy, credit, deference, devotion, distinction, esteem, estimation, exaltation, favor, glorification, glory, high regard, homage, laud, laudation, obeisance, praise, prominence, regard, reverence, tribute, veneration, worship

HONOR, *verb* acclaim, accredit, advance, aggrandize, applaud, belaud, bepraise, canonize, *celebrare,* celebrate, cheer, cite, *colere,* commemorate, commend, compliment, confer distinction on, congratulate, consecrate, crown, *decorare,* decorate, defer to, distinguish, elevate, ennoble, esteem, eulogize, exalt, extol, glorify, hail, hold in esteem, idolize, laud, lionize, look up to, make important, memorialize, pay deference, pay homage, pay respects, pay tribute, praise, prize, promote, put on a pedestal, raise, raise to distinction, regard, respect, revere, reverence, salute, set store by, show respect, toast, value, venerate

ASSOCIATED CONCEPTS: honorary trust

HONORARIUM, *noun* acknowledgment, arrangement, compensation, consideration, earnings, emolument, fee, financial remuneration, gratuity, guerdon, income, indemnity, installment, meed, payment, quittance, recompense, reimbursement, remuneration, requital, retainer, reward for service, salary, settlement, stipend

HONORARY, *adjective* commemorative, commendatory, dedicatory, enshrining, hallowing, honorific, honorifical, in memory of, in tribute, kept in remembrance, memorial, perpetuating, recalling to mind, serving to commemorate

ASSOCIATED CONCEPTS: honorary degree, honorary officer, honorary trust

HOODLUM, *noun* agitator, bandit, blackguard, brigand, burglar, convict, criminal, embezzler, evildoer, felon, firebrand, gunman, holdup man, knave, larcener, larcenist, lawbreaker, malefactor, malevolent, malfeasant, malfeasor, miscreant, mobster, oppressor, outlaw, peculator, pickpocket, purloiner, rogue, roisterer, rough, ruffian, scoundrel, stealer, thief, villain, wrongdoer

ASSOCIATED CONCEPTS: juvenile delinquent, multiple offender, predicate felon, youthful offender

HOODWINK, *verb* be dishonest, befool, beguile, blind, blindfold, cheat, cozen, deceive, defraud, delude, dupe, *fallere,* hoax, *inludere,* inveigle, *ludificari,* make a fool of, misinform, mislead, mystify, outwit, puzzle, swindle, trick

ASSOCIATED CONCEPTS: deception, fraud, misrepresentation

HORNBOOK, *noun* abstract on the law, analysis, analyzation, annotated text, capitulation, capsule, commentary, compendium, condensation, desk book, digest of the law, discourse on the law, dissection, dissertation on the law, encyclopedia, excursus, exposition, manual, manual of instruction, pandect, primer, recapitulation, review, runthrough, study, study book, text, textbook, topical outline, treatise, treatise on the law

HORTATIVE, *adjective* admonitory, advising, advisory, consultative, didactic, exhortative, exhortatory, expostulative, expostulatory, full of exhortation, full of urgency, *hortans,* hortatory, *monens,* monitorial, persuading, persuasive, remonstrative, suasive, warning

HOSTAGE, *noun* bond, captive, collateral, guarantee, internee, *obses,* pledge, political prisoner, prisoner, real security, security

ASSOCIATED CONCEPTS: false imprisonment, kidnapping, ransom

HOSTILE, *adjective* abusive, acrimonious, actively opposed, adverse, aggressive, alienated, antagonistic, antipathetic, antipodal, antithetic, antithetical, antonymous, arguing, argumentative, assaulting, at odds, at variance, baneful, battling, besetting, bitter, bristling, calamitous, cantankerous, challenging, clashing, combative, competitive, conflicting, contentious, contesting, contradictory, contrariant, contrarious, contrary, counteracting, counteractive, destructive, disaffected, disagreeing, disastrous, discordant, disdainful, disloyal, disputatious, dissentient, dissenting, dissentious, dissident, divided, dreadful, embittered, estranged, factious, frictional, full of hate, full of malice, harmful, harsh, ill-disposed, ill-willed, in opposition, inacquiescent, incompatible, inconsistent with, *infensus, infestus,* inimical, *inimicus,* irreconcilable, malevolent, noncooperating, opposed, opposing, opposite, oppositional, oppugnant, polarized, pugnacious, rancorous, reactionary, refractory, renitent, reverse, schismatic, spiteful, truculent, unapproving, unconsonant, uncooperative, unharmonious, vicious, vis-à-vis, wrangling

ASSOCIATED CONCEPTS: hostile fire, hostile intent, hostile party, hostile possession of property, hostile witness

HOT-BLOODED, adjective aggressive, amorous, athirst, avid, barbarous, bold, brutal, burning, careless, danger-loving, daredevil, daring, desirous, desperate, eager, excessive, excitable, extreme, febrile, fervent, fervid, feverish, fiery, flaming, foolhardy, frantic, hasty, headstrong, heated, heedless, high-spirited, high-strung, hot-headed, hot-tempered, immoderate, impatient, impractical, imprudent, inattentive, incautious, inflamed, inflammatory, insuppressible, intemperate, intense, intent, irrepressible, lustful, madcap, oversensitive, passionate, piquant, quenchless, quick-tempered, rampant, rash, reckless, risk-taking, savage, sensitive, short-tempered, strong-willed, temerarious, thoughtless, torrid, turbulent, unadvised, unbridled, uncircumspect, uncontrollable, ungentle, ungovernable, unmitigable, unquelled, unquenched, unrepressed, unwary, vehement, venturesome, violent, wanton, willful, zealous
ASSOCIATED CONCEPTS: heat of passion, manslaughter, temporary insanity

HOUSE, noun abode, accommodations, *aedes,* business establishment, business firm, clan, commercial establishment, company, concern, domicile, *domicilium, domus,* dwelling, dwelling place, family, firm, habitation, home, homestead, household, kin, kindred, lineage, living place, living quarters, lodging, place of habitation, quarters, residence, shelter, tribe
ASSOCIATED CONCEPTS: House of Representatives

HOUSEBREAKING, noun appropriation, breaking and entering, burglarizing, burglary, felony, filching, forcible entry, larceny, looting, pilfering, plundering, raiding, robbery, stealing, theft, thievery, trespassing

HOUSEHOLD (Domestic), adjective at home, *domesticus,* domiciled, domiciliary, domiciliated, family, fond of home, having home interests, home, home-loving, home-owning, homemaking, housekeeping, in residence, *lares, penates,* pertaining to home, pertaining to the family, residential, residentiary
ASSOCIATED CONCEPTS: household articles, household effects, household goods, household servant, householder member

HOUSEHOLD (Familiar), adjective accustomed, celebrated, cognized, common, commonly known, commonplace, conventional, customary, everyday, famous, habitual, ordinary, plain, popular, prevalent, recognized, regular, renowned, simple, standard, stock, talked-about, talked-of, universally recognized, usual, well-known, well-recognized, widely known, widespread, workaday

HOUSEHOLD, noun domestic circle, domestic domicile, domestic establishment, *domus,* establishment, *familia,* family, family abode, family circle, family dwelling place, habitation, home, homestead, lodging, parents and children, place of abode, residence
ASSOCIATED CONCEPTS: homestead
FOREIGN PHRASES: **Domus sua cuique est tutissimum refugium.** Everyone's home is his safest refuge. **Debet sua cuique domus esse perfugium tutissimum.** Every man's home should be a perfectly safe refuge.

HUMANE, adjective altruistic, beneficent, benevolent, benign, bounteous, brotherly, charitable, *clemens,* clement, considerate, decent, fraternal, generous, helpful, hospitable, humanitarian, *humanus,* kind, kindhearted, kindly, merciful, *misericors,* philanthropic, unselfish, warmhearted
ASSOCIATED CONCEPTS: gift for a humane purpose

HUMANITY (Humaneness), noun altruism, beneficence, benevolence, benignancy, benignity, charitableness, clemency, *clementia,* compassion, feeling, gentleness, good will, *humanitas,* kindheartedness, kindness, lenience, leniency, lenity, mercifulness, mercy, mildness, *misericordia,* sympathy, understanding, unselfishness
ASSOCIATED CONCEPTS: crimes against humanity, humanitarian doctrine, humanitarian laws, last clear chance

HUMANITY (Mankind), noun generations of man, *gens humana, hominum generis,* homo sapiens, human beings, humankind, *humanum genus,* man, mortals, people, peoples of the earth, persons
ASSOCIATED CONCEPTS: crimes against humanity

HUMILIATE, verb abase, abash, affront, befool, bespatter, blackball, blacken, brand, bring shame upon, cast a slur upon, cast down, contemn, cow, crush, debase, defame, deflate, degrade, demean, demote, depreciate, deride, derogate, discredit, disgrace, dishonor, disparage, disrank, disrate, downgrade, embarrass, expose to infamy, fill with shame, give offense to, hold in derision, hold in disrespect, humble, incur blame, insult, laugh at, lower, make a fool of, make lowly, malign, misprize, mock, mortify, offend, put down, put out of countenance, put to shame, reduce to the ranks, render humble, ridicule, scoff, scorn, shame, show disrespect, slight, sneer, snub, spurn, stain, stigmatize, sully, taint, tarnish, treat with disrespect, treat with indignity, undervalue, vanquish, vilify
ASSOCIATED CONCEPTS: mental anguish

HUNT, verb burrow, chase, chase after, conduct a search, *consectari,* delve for, ensnare, explore, fasten oneself upon, ferret, follow, follow close upon, follow the trail, forage, give chase, go after, go in pursuit of, go in search of, grope for, gun for, hawk, hound, inquire for, look for, probe, prowl after, pry, pursue, quest, root, run after, search for, search out, seek, set a trap for, snare, stalk, trace, track down, trail, trap, try to find, *venari*
ASSOCIATED CONCEPTS: extradition, hunt for a fugitive, rendition, search and seizure, search warrant

HUSH MONEY, noun blackmail, blood money, bribe, corrupt money, enticement, graft, gratuity, inducement, prize, slush fund, temptation
ASSOCIATED CONCEPTS: bribery

HYPERBOLE, noun aggrandizement, amplification, enhancement, enlargement, exaggeration, extravagance, magnification, overemphasis, overenlargement, overstatement

HYPOCRISY, noun artfulness, charlatanism, charlatanry, deceit, deceitfulness, deception, dishonesty, dissembling, *dissimulatio,* double-dealing, duplicity, false profession, falsification, fraud, fraudulence, *fraus,* front, guile, hollow pretense, imposture, improbity, insincerity, perjury, pharisaism, pretense, pretense of virtue, pretension, quackery, sanctimoniousness, sanctimony, show, trickery

HYPOTHECATION, noun collateral, contract of mortgage, contract of pledge, creation of a lien, guarantee, lien, mortgage, pledge, security
ASSOCIATED CONCEPTS: hypothecated property

HYPOTHESIS, noun assertion, assignment of cause, assumption, conclusion drawn from accepted truths, *coniectura,* conjecture, deduction, guess, inference, postulate, postulation, speculation, suggestion, supposal, supposition, surmise, tentative explanation, tentative law, theory, thesis, unproved theory

HYPOTHETICAL, adjective assumed, conjectural, hypothetic, imaginary, make-believe, *opinabilis,* pretended, speculative, supposed, suppositional, suppositive, unreal, unverifiable
ASSOCIATED CONCEPTS: hypothetical controversy, hypothetical facts, hypothetical issue, hypothetical pleading, hypothetical question, speculation

I

IDEA, noun abstraction, aim, appraisal, apprehension, assessment, belief, calculation, *cogitatio,* conceit, concept, conception, conjecture, conviction, doctrine, dogma, estimate, estimation, evaluation, excogitation, fancy, guess, hypothesis, impression, inference, intent, intention, judgment, *notio,* notion, object, opinion, percept, perception, persuasion, plan, point of view, presupposition, product of imagination, purpose, reflection, sentiment, supposition, surmise, suspicion, tenet, theory, thought, train of thought, valuation, view, viewpoint

IDENTICAL, adjective alike, coequal, comparable, congeneric, congenerous, consimilar, consubstantial, duplicate, equal, equivalent, exact, exactly alike, exactly the same, faithful, homogeneous, *idem,* indistinguishable, interchangeable, like, matching, resembling, similar, synonymous, tantamount, twin, uniform, without distinction
ASSOCIATED CONCEPTS: identical issue, identical real estate

IDENTIFICATION, noun appellation, ascertainment, classification, cognizance, comparison, definition, delineation, denomination, designation, disclosure, identity classification, identity comparison, identity verification, label, proof of identity, recognition, recognizance, recollection
ASSOCIATED CONCEPTS: extrajudicial identification, lineup
FOREIGN PHRASES: *Nihil facit error nominis cum de corpore constat.* An error in the name is of no consequence when there is certainty as to the person. *Ex multitudine signorum, colligitur identitas vera.* The true identity of a thing is shown from a number of signs.

IDENTIFY, verb analyze, call, catalogue, classify, delineate, denominate, denote, describe, descry, designate, detect, determine, discriminate, distinguish, espy, give a name to, give an appellation to, know, label, name, perceive, place, provide with nomenclature, recognize, recollect, specify, style, term, verify
ASSOCIATED CONCEPTS: description of goods, identify a suspect, identify an assailant, identify handwriting, identify stolen property, line-up

IDENTITY (Individuality), noun being, characteristic, difference, dissimilarity, distinction, distinctive feature, distinctiveness, distinctness, distinguishing characteristic, distinguishing quality, idiosyncrasy, individualism, mannerism, oneness, originality, particularity, peculiarity, perceivable dissimilarity, personal characteristic, personality, personship, quality of being singular, self, selfhood, selfness, singleness, singularity, speciality, specialty, specific quality, specificity, uniqueness, unlikeness
ASSOCIATED CONCEPTS: duty to ascertain identity, proof of identity
FOREIGN PHRASES: *Nihil facit error nominis cum de corpore constat.* An error in the name is of no consequence when there is certainty as to the person. *Ex multitudine signorum, colligitur identitas vera.* The true identity of a thing is shown from a number of signs. *Nomina sunt mutabilia, res autem immobiles.* Names are mutable, but things are immutable.

IDENTITY (Similarity), noun agreement, alikeness, closeness, coequality, comparability, conformability, consimilarity, consimilitude, consimility, duplication, equality, equipollence, equipollency, equivalence, homogeneity, identicalness, interchangeability, likeness, match, oneness, parallelism, parity, resemblance, sameness, semblance, similarity, similitude, synonymity, uniformity, unity

IDLE, adjective disengaged, fallow, fruitless, futile, *ignavus,* inactive, indolent, inert, jobless, lazy, listless, motionless, *otiosus,* shiftless, slothful, still, uncultivated, unemployed, unoccupied, unprofitable, unused, vacant, *vacuus,* workless

IGNOBLE, *adjective* abject, base, baseborn, beggarly, below par, boorish, common, contemptible, corrupt, cowardly, craven, debased, degenerate, degraded, depraved, despicable, discreditable, disgraceful, dishonest, dishonorable, disreputable, humble, *humilis,* ignominious, indecent, infamous, inferior, inglorious, *inhonestus, inliberalis,* insignificant, low, lowborn, lowly, mean, menial, of humble birth, of low character, of low extraction, of low station, peasant, plebian, proletarian, raffish, reproachful, scandalous, scrubby, scurrilous, servile, shameful, sorry, subaltern, unchivalrous, uncouth, uncultivated, underbred, ungenteel, unmanly, unrespectable, untitled, unworthy, vile, vulgar, wicked, worthless

IGNOMINY, *noun* abasement, abjection, abjectness, attaint, bad name, bad reputation, bad repute, badge of infamy, blot, brand, chagrin, condemnation, contempt, contemptibility, contemptibleness, culpability, culpableness, debasement, dedecoration, degradation, demotion, denunciation, derision, derogation, despisedness, disapprobation, disapproval, discommendation, discredit, discreditableness, disesteem, disfavor, disgrace, dishonor, dishonorableness, dislike, disparagement, dispraise, disreputability, disreputableness, disreputation, disrepute, disvaluation, embarrassment, faded reputation, humiliation, ignobility, *ignominia,* ignomy, ill favor, ill repute, imputation, *infamia,* infamy, ingloriousness, irreverence, lack of respect, loss of honor, loss of reputation, loss of respect, low standing, mortification, obloquy, odium, opprobrium, ostracism, poor reputation, reproach, scandal, sense of disgrace, sense of shame, shame, slur, smirch, stain, stigma, taint, tarnish, tarnished honor, *turpitudo,* unrespectability

IGNORANCE, *noun* benightedness, bewilderment, blindness, darkness, denseness, fog, foolishness, greenness, haze, illiteracy, illiterateness, *imprudentia,* incapacity, incognizance, incomprehension, ineptitude, inerudition, inexperience, innocence, *inscientia, inscitia,* insensibility, lack of education, lack of knowledge, lack of learning, maze, nescience, obtuseness, perplexity, rawness, simpleness, simplicity, unacquaintance, unawareness, unconsciousness, unenlightenment, unfamiliarity, unintellectuality, unintelligence, unknowingness, unlearnedness, unscholarliness, untaught state, unworldliness, vagueness, want of knowledge

ASSOCIATED CONCEPTS: culpable ignorance, essential ignorance, ignorance of law, involuntary ignorance, plead ignornace, voluntary ignorance

FOREIGN PHRASES: *Ignorantia praesumitur ubi scientia non probatur.* Ignorance is presumed where knowledge is not proved. *Ignorantia legis neminem excusat.* Ignorance of the law excuses no one. *Regula est, juris quidem ignorantiam cuique nocere, facti vero ignorantiam non nocere.* The rule is that a person's ignorance of the law may prejudice him, but that his ignorance of fact will not. *Ignorantia juris sui non praejudicat juri.* Ignorance of one's right does not prejudice the right. *Ignorantia excusator, non juris sed facti.* Ignorance of fact may excuse, but not ignorance of law. *Ignorantia juris quod quisque tenetur scire, neminem excusat.* Ignorance of law, which everyone is bound to know, excuses no one. *Nemo tenetus informare qui nescit, sed quisquis scire quod informat.* No one who is ignorant of a thing is bound to give information about it, but everyone is bound to know that concerning which he gives information.

IGNORE, *verb* abstain from recognizing, be blind to, be inattentive, be rude, boycott, brush aside, bypass, cut, discard, disclaim, disdain, disregard, dodge, elude, evade, give the cold shoulder, hold in contempt, intentionally disregard, let slide, let slip, make unwelcome, miss, neglect, *neglegere,* omit, ostracize, overlook, pass by, pass over, pass without notice, pay no attention to, pay no heed to, *praeterire,* pretend not to see, push aside, refrain from noticing, refuse to acknowledge, refuse to admit, refuse to hear, refuse to notice, reject, repudiate, scorn, shrug off, skip, slight, slur over, snub, take no note, take no notice, treat rudely, turn a deaf ear to, turn one's back on, utterly overlook, willfully disregard

ILL-ADVISED, *adjective* disadvantageous, foolish, hasty, ill-considered, ill-judged, impolitic, imprudent, inadvisable, inappropriate, inconsiderate, *inconsultus,* inconvenient, inexpedient, infelicitous, injudicious, inopportune, irresponsible, misadvised, miscounseled, misguided, rash, reckless, senseless, shortsighted, *temerarius,* unconsidered, undesirable, unfit, unreasonable, unseemly, unsuitable, unwise

ILL-FOUNDED, *adjective* apocryphal, baseless, empty, erroneous, fallacious, false, fanciful, groundless, inaccurate, incorrect, insubstantial, sophistic, sophistical, suppositional, trumped up, unbased, unconfirmed, unfounded, ungrounded, unsubstantial, unsupportable, unsupported, unsustainable, untenable, unwarranted, without basis, without foundation, without sound basis, without substance

ILL-JUDGED, *adjective* acting without due consideration, against reason, blind, careless, hasty, headstrong, heedless, ill-advised, ill-chosen, ill-considered, ill-contrived, illogical, impatient, imprudent, inconsiderate, inept, inexact, inexpedient, injudicious, irrational, lacking discretion, misadvised, miscalculated, rash, reckless, shortsighted, showing poor judgment, thoughtless, unconsidered, undiscerning, unenlightened, unguided, unreasonable, unreasoning, unsensible, unsound, unthinking, unthoughtful, unwise, wild

ILL REPUTE, *noun* bad name, bad repute, baseness, contemptibility, contemptibleness, degradation, disapproval, disesteem, disfavor, disgrace, dishonor, dislike, disreputability, disreputation, disrespectability, improperness, impropriety, infamy, notoriety, questionability, questionableness, rascality, shadiness, shame, unpopularity

ILL USE, *verb* abuse, *abuti,* afflict, be hurtful, be malevolent, bruise, buffet, castigate, cause evil, damage, deal hard measure to, do an injustice to, do evil, do harm to, do violence, do wrong, flagellate, grind, harm, hurt, ill-treat, injure, knock about, malign, maltreat, manhandle, manipulate, mishandle, mistreat, misuse, oppress, overdrive, persecute, plague, show ill will, torment, torture, treat cruelly, treat unfairly, treat unkindly, use badly, use wrongly, vicitimize

ASSOCIATED CONCEPTS: contributory negligence, misuse of a product

ILL WILL, *noun* acerbity, acute dissatisfaction, adverseness, alienation, animosity, animus, antagonism, antipathy, aversion, bad intent, belligerency, bitter feelings, bitterness, chagrin, conflict, contrariety, coolness, deliberate malice, detestation, disaffection, discontent, dislike, disquiet, dissatisfaction, enmity, hard feelings, hostility, ill disposition, ill-feeling, ill-intent, incompatibility, inimicality, intolerance, malevolence, *malevolentia,* malice, maliciousness, malignance, malignancy, odium, opposition, rancor, resentment, spite, spitefulness, strain, tension, unfriendliness, unfriendly feeling, unkindness, unpopularity, wrath

ILLEGAL, *adjective*   actionable, against the law, banned, contrary to law, criminal, exceeding the law, felonious, forbidden, illegitimate, illicit, impermissible, improper, *inlicitus,* invalid, lawless, not according to law, not allowed, not approved, not authorized by law, not covered by law, not permitted, not valid, outlawed, outside the law, prohibited, prohibited by law, proscribed, punishable, *quod contra leges fit,* unauthorized, unchartered, unconstitutional, unjustified, unlawful, unsanctioned, unwarrantable, unwarranted, *vetitus,* without authority, wrongful
ASSOCIATED CONCEPTS: illegal acts, illegal business, illegal combination, illegal contract, illegal detention, illegal discrimination, illegal force, illegal operation, illegal picketing, illegal possession, illegal practice, illegal purpose, illegal restraint, illegal sale, illegal search and seizure, illegal statute, illegal taking, illegal tax, illegal trade, illegal transaction, illegal use, mala in se, mala prohibita

ILLEGALITY, *noun*   corruptness, criminality, illegitimacy, impropriety, infraction, infringement, lawlessness, malefaction, misdeed, transgression, unauthorization, underhandedness, unfitness, unlawfulness, violation of the law
ASSOCIATED CONCEPTS: *ultra vires*
FOREIGN PHRASES: *Pacta quae contra leges constitutionesque vel contra bonos mores fiunt nullam vim habere, indubitati juris est.* It is unquestionably the law that contracts which are made contrary to the laws or against good morals, have no force in law.

ILLEGALLY, *adverb*   contrary to law, criminally, feloniously, illegitimately, illicitly, impermissibly, improperly, in violation of law, tortiously, unlawfully, without legal authority, without legal sanction, wrongfully
ASSOCIATED CONCEPTS: acting illegally, illegally assessed, illegally obtained, illegally procured, illegally sold

ILLEGITIMATE *(Born out of wedlock), adjective* adulterine, base-born, bastard, misbegot, misbegotten, *nothus,* of illicit union, unlawfully begotten, unnatural
ASSOCIATED CONCEPTS: illegitimate children, legitimation, paternity proceeding, presumption of legitimacy
FOREIGN PHRASES: *Parentum est liberos alere atiam nothos.* It is the duty of parents to support their children even when illegitimate. ***Qui nascitur sine legitimo matrimonio, matrem sequitur.*** He who is born out of lawful matrimony succeeds to the condition of his mother. ***Non est justum aliquem antenatum post mortem facere bastardum qui toto tempore vitae suae pro legitimo habebatur.*** It is not just to make anyone a bastard after his death, who during his lifetime was regarded as legitimate. ***Justum non est aliquem antenatum mortuum facere bastardum, qui pro tota vita sua pro legitimo habetur.*** It is not just to make a bastard after his death one elder born who all his life

has been accounted legitimate. ***Qui ex damnato coitu nascuntur inter liberos non computentur.*** They who are born of an illicit union should not be reckoned among the children.

ILLEGITIMATE *(Illegal), adjective*   against the law, banned, contrary to law, criminal, forbidden, illicit, impermissible, improper, interdicted, lawbreaking, malfeasant, *non legitimus,* not according to law, not permitted, outlawed, outside the law, prohibited, prohibited by law, proscribed, unallowed, unauthorized, unlawful, unlicensed, unsanctioned, wrongful

ILLIBERAL, *adjective*   avaricious, *avarus,* biased, bigoted, churlish, close, closefisted, conservative, covetous, dogmatic, fanatical, grasping, greedy, grudging, hidebound, inhospitable, *inliberalis,* intolerant, mean, mercenary, miserly, narrow, narrow-minded, niggardly, one-sided, opinionated, parochial, parsimonious, partial, penurious, persecuting, petty, prejudiced, reactionary, selfish, *sordidus,* sparing, stingy, stinting, tight, tightfisted, uncharitable, unchivalrous, ungenerous, ungentlemanly

ILLICIT, *adjective*   accusable, actionable, against the law, banned, censored, contrary to law, criminal, exceeding the law, felonious, forbidden, forbidden by law, guilty, illegal, illegitimate, immoral, impermissible, improper, infamous, iniquitous, injudicial, *inlicitus,* interdicted, lawless, nonconstitutional, nonlegal, not according to law, not allowed, not approved, not covered by law, not permitted, out of bounds, outlawed, outside the law, prohibited, proscribed, punishable by law, *quod contra leges fit,* taboo, tortious, triable, unallowed, unauthorized, unconstitutional, under ban, unlawful, unlegalized, unlegislated, unprincipled, unsanctioned, unseemly, unwarrantable, unwarranted, *vetitus,* wicked, without authority, wrong, wrongful
ASSOCIATED CONCEPTS: illicit cohabitation, illicit relations, illicit relationship, illicit trade

ILLITERACY, *noun*   ineducation, inerudition, unintellectualism, unlearnedness, unscholarliness

ILLOGICAL, *adjective*   *absurdus,* contradictory, contrary to reason, contrary to the rules of logic, fallacious, faulty, groundless, inconsistent, indefensible, irrational, logically unsound, mistaken, nonscientific, paralogistic, self-contradictory, sophistic, sophistical, unfounded, ungrounded, unscientific, unsound, unsustainable, untenable, without basis, without foundation
ASSOCIATED CONCEPTS: arbitrary and capricious

ILLUDE, *verb*   be cunning, befool, beguile, cheat, chouse, circumvent, cozen, deceive, decoy, defraud, delude, deride, dupe, ensnare, fool, gerrymander, gull, hoax, inveigle, lead astray, lead into error, make a fool of, misdirect, misguide, misinform, mislead, mock, outmaneuver, outwit, play false, practice chicanery, put something over, ridicule, scorn, swindle, take advantage of, take in, trick, victimize

ILLUSORY, *adjective*   casuistic, casuistical, chimerical, conjuring, counterfeit, deceiving, deceptive, deluding, delusive, fabricated, fallacious, false, *falsus,* fancied, fanciful, fatuitous, feigned, fictitious, hatched, illusive, imaginary, imagined, insidious, insubstantial, invented, make-believe, misleading, mythic, mythological, not true, notional, phantasmal, pretended, sophistic, sophistical, suppositional, tenuous, tricky, unactual, unauthentic, unreal, unsubstantial, unsupportable, *vanus*, visionary

ASSOCIATED CONCEPTS: illusory agreement, illusory appointment, illusory contract, illusory promise, illusory transfer, illusory trust

FOREIGN PHRASES: *Judicium non debet esse illusorium; suum effectum habere debet.* A judgment ought not to be illusory; it ought to have its proper effect.

ILLUSTRATE, *verb*   cite, clarify, define, demonstrate, display, elucidate, enlighten, exemplify, exhibit, explain, expound, furnish an example, give an instance, illuminate, *inlustrare*, instance, interpret, make evident, make plain, make vivid, manifest, produce an example, represent, show, show by example, teach by examples

ASSOCIATED CONCEPTS: illustrative questions

ILLUSTRATION, *noun*   case in point, clarification, depiction, depictment, display, elucidation, enucleation, example, exemplar, exemplification, *exemplum*, explanation, explication, exponent, exposition, illumination, instance, manifestation, model, practical demonstration, relevant instance, representation, sample, showing, simplification, specimen

ILLUSTRIOUS, *adjective*   acclaimed, *amplus*, applauded, bright, brilliant, celebrated, conspicuous, distinguished, eminent, excellent, eximious, famed, famous, glorious, grand, great, heroic, honored, important, *inlustris*, known, memorable, noble, notable, noted, popular, prominent, radiant, remarkable, renowned, resplendent, shining, signal, splendid, *splendidus*, splendorous, sublime, talked of, time-honored, transplendent, well-known, widely known

IMBROGLIO, *noun*   babel, bedlam, broil, chaos, commotion, complexity, complicated misunderstanding, complication, confusing situation, confusion, difficult situation, difficulty, dilemma, disagreement, disorder, disturbance, embarrassing situation, embranglement, embroilment, entanglement, fracas, impasse, intricate involvement, intricate plot, involved situation, jam, jungle, labyrinth, maze, melee, mess, muddle, perplexing state of affairs, pickle, plight, predicament, quandary, riot, row, rumpus, scrape, stew, stymie, tight spot, tumult, turmoil, uproar, welter

IMBUE, *verb*   bathe, drench, fill, *imbuere*, implant, impress upon the mind, inculcate, indoctrinate, *inficere*, influence, infuse, inject, inspire, instill, leaven, permeate, pervade, pour in, saturate, soak, *tingere*

IMITATION, *adjective*   artificial, bogus, burlesque, copied, counterfeit, deceptive, dummy, *effigies*, ersatz, factitious, faked, false, feigned, imitated, imitative, make-believe, mock, phony, pretended, pseudo, quasi, sham, simulacrum, simulated, spurious, substitute, synthetic, unauthentic, ungenuine

ASSOCIATED CONCEPTS: forgery

IMMATERIAL, *adjective*   baseless, beside the point, beside the question, bodiless, chimerical, diminutive, ethereal, *expers corporis*, extraneous, groundless, impertinent, inapplicable, inappreciable, inappropriate, inconsequential, incorporeal, inessential, insignificant, insubstantial, intangible, irrelevant, lightweight, meaningless, minor, nominal, nonessential, nonphysi-

cal, not connected with, not important, not pertaining to, not pertinent, *nullius momenti*, of little account, of no consequence, of no essential consequence, of no importance, of no moment, of no significance, off the point, off the topic, other wordly, out of place, out-of-the-way, outside the question, pointless, remote, *sine corpore*, spectral, trivial, unessential, unimportant, unrelated, unsubstantial, vaporous, without depth, without substance, without weight, worthless

ASSOCIATED CONCEPTS: immaterial allegations, immaterial alteration, immaterial averment, immaterial breach, immaterial facts, immaterial issues, immaterial testimony, immaterial variance, incompetent evidence, irrelevant evidence

IMMATERIALITY, *noun*   inconsequence, incorporeality, inessentiality, insignificance, insubstantiality, insufficiency, intangibility, irrelevance, irrelevancy, lack of depth, lack of substance, lightness, meagerness, nonessentiality, otherworldliness, paltriness, pettiness, pointlessness, shallowness, spirituality, spiritualness, thinness, triviality, unimportance, unnoteworthiness, unsubstantiality, worthlessness

IMMEDIATE *(At once)*, *adjective*   flash, instant, instantaneous, *praesens*, prompt, quick, speedy, sudden, unhesitating, with reasonable dispatch, without delay

IMMEDIATE *(Imminent)*, *adjective*   about to happen, anticipated, approaching, at hand, close, close at hand, coming, drawing near, expected, following, foreseen, forthcoming, impendent, impending, in the offing, in view, looked for, momentary, near at hand, nearing, next, nigh, prospective, to come, upcoming

IMMEDIATE *(Not distant)*, *adjective*   abutting, adjacent, adjoining, at hand, bordering, bounding, close, close at hand, conjoining, conterminous, contiguous, handy, juxtapositional, near, near by, neighboring, next to, proximate, verging

ASSOCIATED CONCEPTS: immediate beneficiaries, immediate benefit, immediate cause, immediate consequences, immediate control, immediate damage, immediate delivery, immediate irreparable harm, immediate legatees, immediate need, immediate transferor

IMMERSE *(Engross)*, *verb*   absorb, attend, be attentive, bury, engage, enthrall, fascinate, grip, hold, hold spellbound, interest, involve, monopolize, occupy, overwhelm, preoccupy, submerge, take up

IMMERSE *(Plunge into)*, *verb*   bathe, cover with water, deluge, dip, douse, drench, drown, duck, dunk, engulf, flood, insert, inundate, place under a liquid, plunge into a liquid, put under water, send to the bottom, sink, soak, souse, steep, submerge, submerse, swamp, thrust under

IMMIGRATION, *noun*   admission of foreigners, *adventus*, change of national location, colonization, entry of aliens, establishment of foreign residence, expatriation, foreign influx, incoming population, ingress, migration, movement of population, transmigration

ASSOCIATED CONCEPTS: issuance of visas, passports

IMMINENT, *adjective*   about to be, about to happen, alarming, approaching, at hand, brewing, closing in, coming, destined, drawing near, expected, following,

forecasted, forthcoming, future, *imminere,* impendent, *impendere,* impending, in store, in the offing, in the wind, in view, instant, likely to happen, looming, menacing, minatorial, minatory, near, near at hand, nearing, next, ominous, on the way, oncoming, overhanging, portentous, *praesens,* predicted, prospective, threatening, threatening harm, upcoming
ASSOCIATED CONCEPTS: imminent danger, imminent irreparable harm, imminent peril

IMMORAL, *adjective* amoral, arrant, bad, base, conscienceless, corrupt, criminal, debauched, degenerate, depraved, dishonest, dishonorable, disreputable, dissipated, dissolute, evil, exploitative, false, flagitious, graceless, heinous, ignoble, illaudable, illegal, illicit, improper, impure, indecent, iniquitous, knavish, lacking morals, lecherous, lewd, libidinous, licentious, *male moratus,* miscreant, nefarious, objectionable, *perditus,* pernicious, perverted, pettifogging, *pravus,* profligate, promiscuous, prurient, reprobate, roguish, salacious, shameless, shocking, sinful, unchaste, unconscionable, unethical, unjustifiable, unlawful, unmoral, unprincipled, unrighteous, unscrupulous, unvirtuous, unwholesome, wicked, without integrity, wrong
ASSOCIATED CONCEPTS: immoral act, immoral agreement, immoral conduct, immoral consideration, immoral contract, obscenity
FOREIGN PHRASES: *Ex turpi causa non oritur actio.* No cause of action arises out of an immoral or illegal consideration.

IMMOVABLE, *noun* affixed property, fixed assets, fixed chattel, fixed property, fixture, *immobilis, immotus,* land, property permanently affixed to the realty, real estate, real property, *stabilis*

IMMUNE, *adjective* absolved, armored, clear, excused, exempt, free, granted amnesty, *immunis,* immunized, impregnable, inaccessible, inexpugnable, inviolable, invulnerable, not accountable, not answerable, not liable, not responsible, not subject, possessed of immunity, privileged, protected, released, safe, screened, sheltered, shielded, spared, unaccountable, unaffected by, unanswerable, unassailable, unattackable, under shelter, unencumbered, unexposed, unliable, unpunishable, unrestrained, unrestricted, unsubject, unsusceptible, unthreatened, untouchable, untouched, without risk
ASSOCIATED CONCEPTS: immune from prosecution

IMMUNITY, *noun* absolution, acquittal, charter, commutation, discharge, exception, exculpation, exemption, exemption from punishment, franchise, freedom, freedom from exemption, freedom from obligation, freedom from prosecution, *immunitas,* liberation, liberty, license, nonliability, privilege, protection, release, release from charge, release from duty, relief, reprieve, respite, safety from prosecution, special privilege, *vacatio*
ASSOCIATED CONCEPTS: absolute immunity, complete immunity, derivative immunity, full transactional immunity, full waiver, governmental immunity, immunity from arrest, immunity from prosecution, immunity from service of process, limited immunity, limited waiver, partial immunity, privileges and immunities, qualified immunity, state immunity, transactional immunity, use and derivative immunity, use immunity, waiver of immunity

IMMURE, *verb* cast into prison, commit to an institution, commit to prison, confine, constrain, detain, encage, enclose, enclose within walls, entomb, gate, hold, hold captive, hold in captivity, hold in check, hold within bounds, impound, imprison, incarcerate, *includere,* isolate, keep in, keep in captivity, keep in check, keep in custody, keep in detention, keep prisoner, keep under arrest, keep within bounds, lay under restraint, lead into captivity, lock in, lock up, make captive, put under arrest, quarantine, restrain, seal up, seclude, send to prison, shelter, shut up, take captive, take into custody, throw into prison, wall up

IMMUTABLE, *adjective* adamant, ageless, confirmed, *constans,* constant, continual, continuous, durable, eternal, firm, fixed, immovable, *immutabilis,* implacable, incontrovertible, indestructible, inexorable, inflexible, intractable, invariable, irremovable, irrevocable, never changing, never varying, nonelastic, not to be changed, not to be moved, obstinate, perennial, permanent, perpetual, persistent, relentless, riveted, rooted, settled, *stabilis,* static, steadfast, steady, stiff, unaging, unalterable, unbending, unchangeable, unchanging, uncompromising, undeviating, undying, unending, unmalleable, unpliable, unrelenting, untractable, unyielding, vested
ASSOCIATED CONCEPTS: immutable principle of law
FOREIGN PHRASES: *Nomina sunt mutabilia, res autem immobiles.* Names are mutable, but things are immutable.

IMPACT, *verb* compress, cram, crowd, drive, drive firmly in, fill, fill to capacity, force, force together, hammer in, inject, insert, jam, load, overburden, overcrowd, overload, pack, pack close, pack in, pack together, press, press together, push, push together, ram, shove, squeeze, strike, thrust in, wedge

IMPAIR, *verb* adulterate, affect injuriously, blight, blunt, contaminate, cripple, crumble, damage, *debilitare,* debilitate, decrease in excellence, demolish, deplete, deprive of power, desecrate, devalue, dilapidate, diminish, diminish in quality, dissipate, disturb, dull, enervate, enfeeble, erode, *frangere,* harm, hinder, hurt, *imminuere,* injure, lessen in power, lessen in value, make inroads on, make worse, mar, obtund, paralyze, pollute, put out of commission, reduce, relax, render feeble, ruin, sap, stifle, taint, undermine, unhinge, waste, weaken, wear out, worsen
ASSOCIATED CONCEPTS: impairing the obligation of contracts, impairment of capital, impairment of good will, impairment of memory, impairment of powers, impairment of security

IMPAIRMENT *(Damage),* ***noun*** detriment, disrepair, harm, hurt, injury, loss
ASSOCIATED CONCEPTS: impairment of vision

IMPAIRMENT *(Drawback),* ***noun*** detriment, disadvantage, inability, liability, limitation
ASSOCIATED CONCEPTS: impairment of funds, impairment of security

IMPALPABILITY, *noun* abstraction, bodilessness, flimsiness, immateriality, immaterialness, imperceptibility, inappreciability, incorporality, incorporealism, incorporeality, incorporeity, insubstantiality, intangibility, lack of substance, unconcreteness, unsolidity, unsubstantialness

IMPALPABLE, *adjective*   attenuated, barely seen, concealed, covered, covert, delicate, difficult to feel, difficult to perceive, difficult to see, doubtable, dubitable, equivocal, fine, hidden, immateriate, imperceptible, inappreciable, inapprehensible, incapable of being perceived, inconspicuous, incorporeal, indefinite, indistinct, infinitesimal, intangible, invisible, little, microscopic, minute, nonmaterial, not manifest, not readily discerned, obscure, *quod tangi non potest,* screened, shaded, shadowy, shrouded, slight, small, subtle, tiny, unapparent, unclear, undiscernable, unevident, unexplicit, unnoticeable, unobservable, unobvious, unpatent, unperceivable, unplain, unpronounced, unreal, unrecognizable, unrevealed, unsubstantial, untouchable, vague, veiled, very fine

IMPANEL, *verb*   catalog, enter, enumerate, itemize, list, record, register, schedule
ASSOCIATED CONCEPTS: impanel a jury

IMPART, *verb*   accord, acquaint, advise, apprise, be indiscreet, bestow, brief, *communicare,* communicate, confer, confide, convey, deliver, disclose, dispense, *donare,* educate, endow, enlighten, enrich, favor with, *impertire,* inform, instruct, issue, make known, mention, point out, present, provide, relate, reveal, teach, tell, transfer, transmit

IMPARTIAL, *adjective*   *aequabilis, aequus,* broadminded, detached, disinterested, dispassionate, equitable, even, evenhanded, evenly balanced, fair, fairminded, free from bias, free to choose, honest, honorable, impersonal, incorrupt, *incorruptus,* independent, indifferent, *integer,* judicious, just, lacking prejudice, neutral, nonpartisan, not biased, not partial, objective, open, open-minded, reasonable, scrupulous, unaffected, unbiased, unbigoted, unbought, unbribed, uncolored, uncommitted, uncompelled, uncorrupt, uncorrupted, undecided, uninfluenced, unjaundiced, unopinionated, unopinioned, unprejudiced, unprepossessed, unswayed, untouched, without a preference, without favoritism
ASSOCIATED CONCEPTS: fair and impartial, impartial hearing officer, impartial judge, impartial jury, impartial trial
FOREIGN PHRASES: *Nemo potest esse simul actor et judex.* No one can be at the same time judge and suitor. *Judex non potest injuriam sibi datam punire.* A judge cannot punish a wrong done to himself. *Judex non potest esse testis in propria causa.* A judge cannot be a witness in his own case.

IMPASSE, *noun*   abruption, bar, block, blockade, blockage, cessation, check, complete standstill, complexity, *cul-de-sac,* dead end, dead stop, deadlock, desistance, deterrence, difficulty, dilemma, discontinuance, discontinuance of activity, discontinuation, end, halt, hopelessness, impediment, impossibility, impossible task, inextricability, insoluble difference, insuperability, insuperable obstacle, nonresumption, obstacle, obstruction, perplexity, preclusion, predicament, problem, quagmire, quandary, stalemate, stall, standstill, state of inaction, state of no progress, stop
ASSOCIATED CONCEPTS: impasse in negotiations

IMPEACH, *verb*   *accusare,* accuse, accuse of maladministration, accuse of misconduct, admonish, animadvert, attack, attaint, blame, bring a charge, bring charges, bring into discredit, bring to account, bring to justice, bring up for investigation, call in question, call

to account, cast an imputation upon, cast blame upon, castigate, censure, challenge, challenge the credibility of, charge, charge to, charge with, complain against, condemn, confute, criticize, declaim against, decry, denigrate, denounce, denunciate, disapprove, discredit, disparage, dispute, expose, fault, file a claim, find an indictment against, hold at fault, implicate, impugn, impute fault to, inculpate, incur blame, indict, indict for maladministration, prefer a claim, prefer charges, put on trial, put the blame on, rebuff, recriminate, reprimand, reproach, reprove, ridicule, take to account, upbraid, vituperate
ASSOCIATED CONCEPTS: impeach a government official, impeach a witness

IMPEACHABILITY, *noun*   blame, blameworthiness, censurability, chargeability, culpability, discredit, dishonor, disrepute, grave culpability, guiltiness, liability, peccability

IMPEACHMENT, *noun*   accusal, *accusatio,* accusation, act of discrediting, admonition, animadversion, arraignment, attack, blame, castigation, censure, challenge, charge, complaint, condemnation, countercharge, criminal proceeding, crimination, criticism, denigration, denouncement, denunciation, disapproval, discommendation, exposure, hostile criticism, imputation of dereliction, imputation of fault, indictment, questioning integrity, questioning witness's veracity, rebuke, reprimand, reproach, reproof, vilification
ASSOCIATED CONCEPTS: articles of impeachment, character evidence, collateral impeachment, impeachment of a governmental officer, impeachment of a verdict, impeachment of a witness, impeachment of credibility, moral terpitude, prior inconsistent statement, reputation evidence

IMPECUNIOUS, *adjective*   bankrupt, beggared, beggarly, broke, cleaned out, destitute, distressed, embarrassed, flat, flat broke, hard up, impoverished, in need, in straitened circumstances, in the red, in want, indigent, insolvent, necessitous, needy, not well off, out of money, pauperized, penniless, penurious, pinched, poor, poorly off, poverty-stricken, short, short of cash, short of funds, short of money, strapped, unable to make ends meet, unmoneyed, unprosperous, without funds, without money

IMPEDE, *verb*   annul, arrest, barricade, be a drag on, be an obstacle to, be in the way, block, blockade, bolt, bother, brake, bring to a standstill, burden, cause to delay, check, circumscribe, confine, cramp, cumber, curb, dam up, deadlock, decelerate, delay, detain, deter, disable, drag, embarrass, encumber, erect a barrier, estop, fetter, foreclose, frustrate, hamper, handicap, hinder, hold back, hold in check, hold up, impair, *impedire,* incommode, inconvenience, inhibit, interfere, interrupt, keep back, keep in check, limit, load, mar, obstruct, paralyze, postpone, preclude, press, prevent, quell, restrain, restrict, retard, *retardare,* set one back, shackle, slacken, slow down, stalemate, stand in the way, stay, stop, stop in progress by hindrances, suffocate, suspend, thwart, trammel, turn aside
ASSOCIATED CONCEPTS: impede negotiations
FOREIGN PHRASES: *Ubi aliquid impeditur propter unum, eo remoto, tollitur impedimentum.* Where anything is impeded by one single cause with the removal of it, the impediment is removed.

IMPEDIMENT, noun bar, barrier, block, blockade, blockage, brake, burden, check, clog, counteraction, damper, deterrent, difficulty, disability, discouragement, drawback, encumbrance, estoppel, fetter, frustration, hamper, handicap, hindrance, holdback, *impedimentum,* inconvenience, inhibition, interference, interruption, limitation, obstacle, obstruction, opposition, prevention, resistance, restraint, restriction, retardation, retardment, setback, shackle, snag, stop, stoppage, trammel
ASSOCIATED CONCEPTS: absolute impediment, detrimental impediment, impediment to a legal remedy, legal impediment
FOREIGN PHRASES: *Non valet impedimentum quod de jure non sortitur effectum.* An impediment which has no effect in law is of no force. *Remoto impedimento, emergit actio.* The impediment being removed, the action comes to life.

IMPEL, verb actuate, agitate, arouse, catapult, cause, drive forward, drive onward, encourage, fling, give an impetus, heave, hurl, impart momentum, impart motion, *incitare,* incite, incite to action, induce, instigate, jaculate, launch, mobilize, motivate, move forward, precipitate, press on, prod, project, prompt, propel, push, put in motion, rouse, send headlong, set going, set in motion, set moving, shove, spur, start, stimulate, throw, urge, urge forward, *urgere*

IMPEND, verb approach, be at hand, be forthcoming, be imminent, be in store, be near, be near at hand, draw near, *imminere, impendere,* loom, menace, promise ill, threaten
ASSOCIATED CONCEPTS: impending danger, impending death, impending peril

IMPERATIVE, adjective compulsory, critical, crucial, demanding, essential, exigent, *impero,* indispensable, mandatory, necessary, needful, obligatory, pressing, required, requiring immediate attention, requisite, unavoidable, urgent
ASSOCIATED CONCEPTS: imperative power, imperative statute, imperative trust

IMPERFECT, adjective abortive, average, bad, below par, blemished, broken, corrupt, crippled, crude, damaged, decrepit, defective, deficient, deteriorated, disfigured, failing, fair, faulty, feeble, flawed, fragmentary, frail, garbled, harmed, hurt, impaired, *imperfectus,* inadequate, incomplete, indifferent, inelegant, inexact, inferior, infirm, injured, insufficient, lacking, lame, limited, marred, mediocre, middling, moderate, mutilated, ordinary, out of order, partial, passable, peccable, poor, raw, rickety, rough, ruined, scanty, short, tainted, tolerable, uncompleted, uncultured, undeveloped, unfinished, unpolished, unsatisfactory, unsound, unsuitable, wanting, warped, weak
ASSOCIATED CONCEPTS: imperfect description, imperfect grant, imperfect performance, imperfect title

IMPERMISSIBLE, adjective actionable, against the law, banned, black-market, contraband, contrary to law, criminal, disallowed, disapproved, felonious, forbidden, illegal, illegitimate, illicit, iniquitous, irregular, nonlegal, objectionable, out of bounds, outlawed, outside the law, prohibited, proscribed, punishable, unallowable, unauthorized, unchartered, unconstitutional, under ban, unentitled, unlawful, unlicensed, unsanctioned, vetoed, wicked, wrong, wrongful

ASSOCIATED CONCEPTS: impermissible grounds for divorce

IMPERSONATE, verb act a part, act out, act the part of, ape, assume a character, copy, double for, dress as, enact, *hominem imitari,* imitate, masquerade as, mime, mimic, mirror, parrot, *partes hominis agere,* pass for, personate, personify, portray, pose as, pretend to be, represent, represent oneself to be, take the part of
ASSOCIATED CONCEPTS: fraud, impersonation of a governmental officer

IMPERTINENT (Insolent), adjective abusive, arrogant, assuming, audacious, bellicose, bold, brash, brazen, cavalier, churlish, coarse, contempt, contemptuous, contumacious, contumelious, defiant, derisive, discourteous, disdainful, disrespectful, flippant, forward, fresh, haughty, hostile, ill-mannered, impolite, improper, impudent, *insolens,* insubordinate, insulting, intrusive, irreverent, malapert, offensive, pert, presumptuous, procacious, provocative, rebellious, rough, rude, saucy, scoffing, shameless, surly, unabashed, uncivil, uncouth, ungracious, unmannerly, unpolished, unrefined, vulgar

IMPERTINENT (Irrelevant), adjective alien, beside the mark, beside the point, beside the question, disconnected, extraneous, gratuitous, immaterial, inadmissible, inapplicable, inapposite, inappropriate, inapropos, incidental, incongruous, inconsequent, independent, irrelative, malapropos, off the subject, out of place, *quod nihil ad rem est,* remote, separate, unallied, unapt, unconnected, unrelated, without connection
ASSOCIATED CONCEPTS: impertinent questioning

IMPERVIOUS, adjective *adrogans,* airtight, blind to, blocked, buffered, callous, closed, deaf to, dense, detached, hard, hard to convince, hardened, hermetic, impassable, impassive, *impeditus, impenetrabilis,* impenetrable, imperforate, *imperiosus,* impermeable, impersuadable, impersuasible, imperturbable, imperviable, *impervious,* imporous, inaccessible, incapable of being affected, incapable of being impaired, incapable of being influenced, incapable of being injured, indifferent, indurate, indurated, insensate, insensitive, inured, invious, locked, not permitting passage, not permitting penetration, obstinate, obstructed, obtuse, opaque, pachydermatous, pathless, protected, safe, sealed, seared, shielded, shut, steeled, stubborn, thick, thick-skinned, tight, unaffected, unamenable, uninfluenceable, uninfluenced, unmovable, unmoved, unnavigable, unopened, unpassable, unperforated, unpierceable, unreachable, unreceptive, unresponsive, unswayable, unventilated, unyielding, waterproof, watertight

IMPETUS, noun actuation, boost, call, drive, encouragement, energy, force, goad, impellent, impelling force, impulse, impulsion, incentive, influence, instigation, jog, jolt, kick, momentum, motive, moving force, pressure, propellant, propulsion, propulsive force, purpose, push, reason, shove, spur, start, stimulus, thrust, urge, *vis*

IMPINGE, verb advance upon, aggress, attack, bang, barge in, break bounds, break in on, bump, butt against, collide, come into collision, contact, dash against, encroach, entrench on, fall against, foray, force oneself in, hit, *impingi,* impose, *incidere,* infringe, interlope, intrude, invade, knock, knock against, make impact, make inroads, obtrude, overrun, overstep, overstep boundaries, pommel, raid, run into, strike, tap, thrust, touch, transgress established bounds, trench upon, trespass, violate

IMPLACABLE, *adjective* adamant, immovable, *implacabilis, inexorabilis,* inexorable, inexpiable, inflexible, intransigent, irreconcilable, obdurate, obstinate, pitiless, relentless, unappeasable, unbending, uncompromising, unforgiving, unpacifiable, unpropitiating, unrelenting, unyielding, vindictive

IMPLAUSIBLE, *adjective* beyond belief, contrary to experience, doubtable, doubtful, dubitable, hard to believe, hardly possible, improbable, inconceivable, incredible, open to doubt, open to suspicion, questionable, suspicious, unbelievable, unconvincing, unheard of, unimaginable, unlikely, unsubstantiated, untenable, unthinkable

IMPLEAD, *verb* add as a third party, bring in as a third party, commence proceedings against a third party, *in ius vocare,* institute an action against a third party, join as a third party, make one a third party, plead a cause against a third party, sue a third party
ASSOCIATED CONCEPTS: counterclaim, crossclaim, third party defendant, third party plaintiff, third party practice

IMPLEMENT, *verb* accomplish, achieve, actualize, bring about, bring off, bring to pass, carry into effect, carry into execution, carry out, carry through, complete, consummate, discharge, do, effect, effectuate, enact, enforce, execute, fulfill, give force to, give validity to, make a reality, make active, make valid, perform, provide the means, put in force, put in practice, put into effect, realize, see through, set in motion, succeed, take action, work out
ASSOCIATED CONCEPTS: implement the agreement of the parties, implement the order of the court

IMPLICATE, *verb* accuse, *admiscere,* allege to be guilty, associate, brand, bring into connection with, charge, connect, criminate, delate, denounce, draw in, embroil, engage, enmesh, entangle, expose, hold responsible, *implicare,* impute, include, incriminate, inculpate, infer, inform against, *inligare,* interlace, intertwine, involve, link, lodge a complaint, make a party to, point to, suggest, tangle
ASSOCIATED CONCEPTS: implicate a codefendant, implicate an accomplice, implicate in a crime

IMPLICATION *(Incriminating involvement), noun* complicity, connection, crimination, culpability, enmeshment, entanglement, inculpation, link
ASSOCIATED CONCEPTS: implication of a codefendant

IMPLICATION *(Inference), noun* allusion, broad meaning, coloring, connotation, hidden meaning, hint, import, indication, innuendo, insinuation, intimation, overtone, signification, suggested meaning, suggestion, tacit inference
ASSOCIATED CONCEPTS: easement by implication, gift by implication, grant by implication, necessary implication
FOREIGN PHRASES: *Omissio eorum quae tacite insunt nihil operatur.* The omission of those things which are tacitly expressed is unimportant.

IMPLICIT, *adjective* absolute, allusive, basic, implied, implied rather than expressly stated, inherent, innate, intrinsic, not declared openly, not expressed, not plainly apparent, suggested, suggestive, tacit, *tacitus,* understood, unexpressed, unpronounced, unsaid, unspoken, unvoiced
ASSOCIATED CONCEPTS: implicit in the facts of a case, implicit powers

IMPLIED, *adjective* alluded to, allusive, assumed, connoted, expressed indirectly, implicit, indicated, inferential, inferred, insinuated, meant, signified, suggested, tacit, undeclared, understood, unspoken
ASSOCIATED CONCEPTS: implied acceptance, implied acquiescense, implied admission, implied agency, implied agreement, implied authority, implied contract, implied covenant, implied dedication, implied malice, implied notice, implied powers, implied promise, implied ratification, implied trust, implied warranty

IMPLY, *verb* advert, allude to, carry a suggestion, connote, denote, drop a hint, give a hint, give indirect information, hint at, include by implication, *indicare,* indicate, indirectly state, infer, insinuate, intimate, involve, leave an inference, make an allusion to, point to, show indirectly, *significare,* state in nonexplicit terms, suggest, whisper
ASSOCIATED CONCEPTS: implied acceptance, implied agency, implied authority, implied consent, implied contract, implied dedication, implied easement, implied in law, implied knowledge, implied license, implied malice, implied notice, implied permission, implied power, implied promise, implied ratification, implied trust, implied warranty
FOREIGN PHRASES: *In omnibus contractibus, sive nominatis sive innominatis, permutatio continetur.* In all contracts, whether nominate or innominate, there is implied an exchange. *Expressio eorum quae tacite insunt nihil operatur.* The expression of those things which are tacitly implied has no effect.

IMPOLITIC, *adjective* careless, foolish, harebrained, hasty, headlong, heedless, ill-advised, illconsidered, ill-judged, *imprudens,* imprudent, inadvisable, incautious, inconsiderate, *inconsultus,* indiscreet, inexpedient, injudicious, rash, reckless, senseless, stupid, temerarious, thoughtless, undiplomatic, unreasonable, unsensible, unsound, untactful, unthinking, unwary, unwise

IMPONDERABLE, *adjective* immaterial, immateriate, impalpable, imponderous, impossible to calculate, impossible to measure, impossible to weigh, incalculable, incapable of being evaluated, incomputable, inestimable, intangible, subtle, unsubstantial, unweighable, vague

IMPORT, *noun* connotation, consequence, drift, essence, gist, gravity, idea, importance, matter, meaning, meaningfulness, moment, pith, point, purport, sense, seriousness, significance, *significatio,* signification, substance, sum, tenor, *vis,* weight, weightiness

IMPORTANCE, *noun* concern, concernment, consequence, distinction, eminence, emphasis, essentiality, fame, grandeur, gravity, greatness, import, influence, irreplaceability, magnitude, mark, materiality, materialness, memorability, memorableness, merit, moment, momentousness, *momentum,* notability, note, noteworthiness, outstanding quality, paramountcy, *pondus,* precedence, prestige, primacy, priority, prominence, relevance, repute, salience, seriousness, significance, solemnity, substance, substantiality, superiority, supremacy, urgency, usefulness, value, *vis,* weight, weightiness

IMPORTANT *(Significant), adjective*   big, capital, chief, commanding, consequential, considerable, crucial, dignified, distinguished, esteemed, famous, far-reaching, first, foremost, formidable, grand, grave, *gravis,* high-level, illustrious, imposing, impressive, influential, leading, *magnus,* main, majestic, major, marked, material, mattering much, memorable, mighty, momentous, notable, noteworthy, of great consequence, of great magnitude, of great weight, of high standing, of high station, of importance, outstanding, overshadowing, paramount, portentous, powerful, preeminent, primary, prime, principal, prominent, relevant, remarkable, salient, serious, signal, solemn, substantial, superior, supreme, valuable, weighty, well-known

IMPORTANT *(Urgent), adjective*   acute, called for, clamant, clamorous, cogent, compelling, critical, crucial, crying, demanding attention, driving, essential, exigent, high-priority, impelling, imperative, importunate, in demand, indispensable, inescapable, instant, necessary, necessitous, needed, prerequisite, pressing, requested, required, requisite, unavoidable, vital, wanted

IMPORTUNE, *verb*   adjure, appeal, apply to, ask urgently, badger, beg, beseech, beset, besiege, bother, cajole, call upon, clamor for, coax, cry to, demand, dun, entreat persistently, *fatigare,* harass, hound, impetrate, implore, insist, inveigle, make bold to ask, nag, obsecrate, obtest, pester, petition, plague, plead, ply, pray, press, press by entreaty, push, *rem hominem flagitare,* request, requisition, solicit, solicit earnestly, solicit insistently, sue, supplicate, urge

IMPOSE *(Enforce), verb*   bid, bind, burden, charge, coerce, command, compel, conscript, constrain, decree, demand, dictate, direct, drive, enact, encumber, enjoin, exact, execute, extort, force upon, impel, *imponere, iniungere,* insist upon, lay upon, leave no option, make, make obligatory, necessitate, oblige, obtain by force, ordain, order, prescribe, press, put in force, require, require compliance, tax
ASSOCIATED CONCEPTS: impose by law

IMPOSE *(Intrude), verb*   encroach, enter unlawfully, entrench, force an entrance, force oneself in, impose, infringe, insinuate, intercede, interfere, interlope, interpose, intervene, invade, obtrude, overreach, overstep, poach, thrust oneself in, transgress, trespass, violate

IMPOSE *(Subject), verb*   bring under rule, coerce, compel, constrain, control, domineer, effect, enslave, force, make submissive, master, oblige, overcome, require, subdue, subject to authority, subject to control, subject to dependence, subject to influence, subjugate, subordinate

IMPOSITION *(Excessive burden), noun*   encroachment, encumbrance, excessive demand, extraordinarily burdensome requirement, hindrance, impediment, in-

fliction, infringement, interference, onus, unjust burden, unjust requirement

IMPOSITION *(Tax), noun*   charge, duty, excise, levy, penalty, tariff, toll

IMPOSSIBILITY, *noun*   difficulty, failure, futility, hopelessness, impossibleness, impracticability, impracticality, inaccessibility, inconceivability, infeasibility, inoperability, insuperability, insuperableness, insurmountability, lack of possibility, lack of potentiality, unachievability, unattainability, unfeasibility, unattainable, unavailability, unobtainability, unobtainableness, unperformability, unpracticability, unthinkability, unworkability
ASSOCIATED CONCEPTS: frustration of purpose, impossibility of performance, legal impossibility, recission, supervening impossibility
FOREIGN PHRASES: *Lex non intendit aliquid impossibile.* The law does not intend anything impossible. *Lex non cogit ad impossibilia.* The law does not require the performance of the impossible. *Impotentia excusat legem.* The impossibility of performing a legal duty excuses from the performance. *A l'impossible nul n'est tenu.* No one is bound to do what is impossible. *Argumentum ab impossibili valet in lege.* The argument from impossibility is of great force in law. *Impossibilium nulla obligatio est.* One cannot be obliged to perform impossible tasks.

IMPOSSIBLE, *adjective*   absurd, contrary to reason, hopeless, impassable, impracticable, improbable, inaccessible, incapable of being done, incapable of existing, incapable of happening, inconceivable, incredible, infeasible, innavigable, insuperable, insurmountable, *nullo modo fieri potest,* out of the question, paradoxical, preposterous, *quod fieri non potest,* self-contradictory, unachievable, unattainable, unbelievable, unfeasible, unimaginable, unlikely, unmanageable, unobtainable, unreasonable, unthinkable, unworkable, unyielding, visionary

IMPOSTURE, *noun*   cheat, chicane, counterfeit, craft, cunning, deceit, deception, dodge, duplicity, fake, *fallacia,* false conduct, forgery, fraud, fraudulence, *fraus,* guile, hoax, hollow pretense, imitation, knavery, pretense, ruse, sham, sleight, subterfuge, swindle, swindling, trap, trick, trickery, wile

IMPOTENCE, *noun*   debilitation, debility, defenselessness, failure, feebleness, forcelessness, helplessness, *imbecillitas,* impotency, impuissance, inability, inadequacy, incapability, incapacitation, incapacity, incompetence, incompetency, ineffectiveness, ineffectuality, ineffectualness, inefficaciousness, inefficacy, inefficiency, ineptitude, *infirmitas,* insufficiency, lack of power, lack of strength, powerlessness, strengthlessness, unfitness, weakness

IMPOUND, *verb*   appropriate, attach, confiscate, deprive of, distrain, hold in legal custody, remove, retain in custody, seize, sequester, sequestrate, take, take into custody, take into legal custody, take over, take possession of
ASSOCIATED CONCEPTS: impounding a jury, impounding property

IMPRACTICABLE, *adjective*   beyond control, difficult, hard to deal with, hopeless, impassable, impossible, impractical, inapplicable, incapable of being accomplished, inconceivable, inoperable, insuperable, insurmountable, out of the question, *quod fiere non potest,* thorny, too hard, unachievable, undoable, unemployable, unfeasible, unfunctional, unhandy, unmanageable, unperformable, unrealizable, unreasonable, unserviceable, unsuitable for practical use, unusable, unviable, unwieldy, unworkable, useless

IMPRECATION, *noun*   abuse, anathema, aspersion, bad wishes, blasphemy, commination, curse, damnation, denunciation, execration, expletive, *exsecratio,* foul language, fulmination, ill wishes, invocation of evil, malediction, malison, objuration, obsecration, *preces,* profanity, swearing, vilification, vindictive oath, vituperation

IMPRESS *(Affect deeply),* *verb*   absorb, amaze, arouse, astound, awe, electrify, galvanize, have a strong effect, hit, influence, inspire, intrigue, make an impact upon, make an impression on, move, move strongly, *movere,* penetrate, pierce, reach, rouse, smite, stir, strike, strike hard, strike home, stun, touch

IMPRESS *(Procure by force),* *verb*   acquire, appropriate, arrogate, attach, deprive, disentitle, disseise, expropriate, garnish, impound, impropriate, levy, seize, sequester, sequestrate, take, take possession of

IMPRESSION, *noun*   *animi motus,* apprehension, belief, concept, conception, consciousness, consideration, effect, feeling, general notion, guiding conception, image, image in the mind, impact, imprint, indirect influence, influence, inward perception, mark, mental attitude, mental image, mental view, notion, *opinio,* opinion, organizing conception, outward perception, perception, print, *putare,* reaction, reflection, remembrance, response, sensation, sense, sense perception, sensory perception, subconscious perception, trace, visible effect
ASSOCIATED CONCEPTS: case of first impression, impression on the minds of the jurors

IMPRISON, *verb*   bring into custody, cast into prison, circumscribe, commit to an institution, commit to prison, confine, constrain, deprive of freedom of movement, deprive of liberty, detain, detain in custody, enclose, entomb, hold captive, hold in captivity, hold in restraint, immure, *in carcerem, in custodiam,* incarcerate, *includere,* intern, jail, keep as captive, keep behind bars, keep in captivity, keep in custody, keep in detention, keep under arrest, lock in, lock up, mew, place in confinement, put behind bars, put in a cell, put in irons, put into a cage, put under lock and key, put under restraint, refuse bail, restrain, send to jail, send to prison
ASSOCIATED CONCEPTS: false imprisonment, habeas corpus, imprison at hard work, imprison for a term of years, parole, term of imprisonment

IMPROBABILITY, *noun*   bare possibility, doubt, doubtfulness, implausibility, impossibility, inexpectation, infrequency, little chance, long odds, *non verisimilis,* nonexpectation, poor chance, poor prospect, questionability, rare occurrence, rarity, small chance, small hope, uncertainty, unlikelihood, unlikeliness
ASSOCIATED CONCEPTS: inherently improbable evidence, inherently improbable testimony

IMPROBITY, *noun*   artfulness, breach of trust, corruption, craftiness, crookedness, deceit, deceitfulness,

deviousness, dishonesty, disingenuity, disingenuousness, duplicity, falsehood, falseness, falsity, fraud, fraudulence, fraudulency, furtiveness, graft, guile, indirection, insidiousness, insincerity, inveracity, jobbery, knavery, lack of conscience, lack of integrity, lack of principle, lying, mendaciousness, mendacity, obliquity, rascality, roguery, shadiness, surreptitiousness, treacherousness, trickiness, truthlessness, undependability, underhandedness, unreliability, unscrupulousness, unstraightforwardness, untrustworthiness, untruthfulness

IMPROPER, *adjective*   amiss, awkward, contrary to decency, contrary to good taste, discordant, discrepant, erroneous, false, forbidden, gross, ill-adapted, ill-founded, ill-timed, illicit, illogical, immodest, immoral, inaccurate, inadmissible, inapplicable, inapposite, inappropriate, inapt, incongruous, incorrect, indecent, indecorous, *indecorus,* indelicate, *indignus,* inept, inexact, infelicitous, inharmonious, inopportune, irrelevant, mistaken, naughty, not pertinent, not right, not suitable, objectionable, off-color, off the mark, out of place, prohibited, risque, unadapted, unallowable, unauthorized, unbecoming, unbefitting, uncharacteristic, undesirable, undue, unfit, unfitting, unmeet, unreasonable, unrefined, unseasonable, unseemly, unsound, unsuitable, unsuited, untimely, unwarrantable, wide of the mark, wrong, wrongful
ASSOCIATED CONCEPTS: improper act, improper conduct, improper discharge, improper influence, improper joinder of actions, improper motive, improper performance, improper practice, improper use

IMPROPRIATE, *verb*   accroach, adopt, annex, apply to one's own uses, appropriate, arrogate, assume, assume ownership, avail oneself of, bear away, carry away, claim, claim unduly, confer ownership on oneself, convert, disseise, embezzle, employ, help oneself to, lay hold of, make one's own, make use of, misappropriate, peculate, pirate, possess, purloin, rob, seize, steal, take as one's own, take for oneself, take over, take possession of, take to oneself, thieve, use, usurp

IMPROPRIETY, *noun*   bad taste, improper action, improper behavior, imprudence, inappropriate behavior, inappropriateness, incongruousness, incorrectness, indecency, indecorousness, indecorum, indelicacy, indiscretion, inelegance, inexpedience, inexpediency, inopportuneness, lack of good taste, misbehavior, peccadillo, *quod indecorum est,* tactlessness, unaptness, unfitness, unfittingness, unseemliness, unsuitability, unsuitable action, unsuitableness, untimeliness, want of caution, want of circumspection
ASSOCIATED CONCEPTS: crime, violation

IMPROVEMENT, *noun*   amelioration, betterment, change for the better, melioration, recovery, rehabilitation
ASSOCIATED CONCEPTS: improvement bond, improvement district

IMPROVIDENT, *adjective*   brash, careless, dissipated, extravagant, happy-go-lucky, hasty, headlong, heedless, *improvidus, imprudens,* imprudent, impulsive, incautious, *incautus,* indiscreet, injudicious, lacking foresight, lax, losel, neglectful, negligent, prodigal, profligate, rash, reckless, remiss, shiftless, spendthrift, squandering, temerarious, thoughtless, thriftless, uneconomical, unfrugal, unguarded, unpreparing, unproviding, unthrifty, unwary, wasteful, without foresight

IMPRUDENT, *adjective* adventurous, brash, careless, foolhardy, foolish, hasty, hazardous, heedless, hotheaded, ill-advised, ill-considered, ill-judged, impolitic, improvident, impulsive, inadvisable, incautious, inconsiderate, *inconsultus,* indiscreet, inexpedient, injudicious, inopportune, lacking caution, lacking judgment, lacking prudence, neglectful, overhasty, precipitate, rash, reckless, shortsighted, temerarious, *temerarius,* thoughtless, unadvised, uncalculated, uncircumspect, undesirable, unguarded, unwary, unwise, venturesome, venturous, wanting discretion, wanton
ASSOCIATED CONCEPTS: negligence

IMPUGN, *verb* assail, assail by argument, attack, attack by words, be skeptical, call in question, cast doubt, cast reflection upon, challenge as false, confute, contest, contradict, controvert, criticize, denounce, disbelieve, discredit, disprove, dispute, doubt the truth of, find fault with, impeach, *improbare, impugnare,* inveigh against, involve in suspicion, negate, oppose, oppose as false, *oppugnare,* overcome by argument, query, question, raise a hue and cry against, raise a question as to, raise one's voice against, raise questions, rebut, refuse credence, refute, render suspect, take issue with, throw doubt upon, undermine one's belief
ASSOCIATED CONCEPTS: defamation, impugn the integrity of a witness

IMPUGNATION, *noun* adverse comment, adverse criticism, animadversion, antagonism, attack, censure, challenge, condemnation, conflict, confrontation, contradiction, contrariety, contrariness, contravention, counteraction, counterwork, criticism, decrial, defiance, difference, disagreement, disapprobation, disapproval, discord, disfavor, disputation, dispute, dissent, faultfinding, gravamen, grievance, hostile attack, hostility, impugnment, lack of harmony, nonacceptance, nonagreement, noncompliance, nonconsent, noncooperation, obstruction, opposition, oppugnancy, protest, protestation, rejection, reprehension, reprobation, repudiation, resistance, rivalry, traversal, want of harmony

IMPUISSANCE, *noun* caducity, debility, decrepitude, disability, disablement, exhaustion, failure, feebleness, frailty, helplessness, impotence, inability, inaptitude, incapability, incapacity, incompetence, inefficacy, inefficiency, ineptitude, infirmity, invalidity, lack of force, lack of might, lack of power, lack of strength, lack of vigor, powerlessness, prostration, strengthlessness, weakness

IMPULSE, *noun* actuation, drive, encouragement, impelling force, *impetus, impulsio,* impulsion, *impulsus,* incentive, motivation, motive, pressure, push, spontaneity, spontaneous inclination, stimulant, sudden desire, sudden force, thrust
ASSOCIATED CONCEPTS: heat of passion, impulsive acts, irresistible impulse, uncontrollable impulse

IMPULSIVE *(Impelling),* adjective activating, actuating, animating, compelling, driving, dynamic, dynamical, energizing, impellent, kinetic, moving, prompting, propulsive, pushing, stimulating, urging

IMPULSIVE *(Rash),* adjective abrupt, adventurous, bold, breakneck, careless, daring, emotional, extemporaneous, extemporary, foolhardy, hasty, heedless, hotheaded, hurried, ill-considered, impetuous, impromptu, improvised, imprudent, incautious, indeliberate, injudicious, offhand, passionate, precipitant, precipitate, precipitous, quick, rapid, reckless, risk-taking, risky, snap, spontaneous, sudden, swift, temerarious, thoughtless, unadvised, unanticipated, uncalculating, unchary, uncircumspect, unconsidered, uncontrolled, unexpected, unmindful, unpremeditated, unprepared, unprompted, unthinking, venturesome, venturous, without prudence, without thought

IMPUNITY, *noun* absolution, acquittal, amnesty, condonation, dispensation, escape, exemption, exemption from judgment, exemption from penalty, exemption from punishment, freedom, freedom from judgment, freedom from penalty, freedom from punishment, immunity, *impunitas,* liberation, license, nonliability, nonprosecution, pardon, prerogative, privilege, protection, reprieve

IMPUTE, *verb* *adsignare,* apply, ascribe, *ascribere,* assign, attach, *attribuere,* attribute, attribute vicariously, blame, charge to, charge upon, credit, fix the burden of, fix the responsibility for, fix upon, place the blame on, place the responsibility for, put
ASSOCIATED CONCEPTS: imputed consent, imputed guilt, imputed intent, imputed knowledge, imputed liability, imputed negligence, imputed notice

IN CUSTODY, *adverb* behind bars, captive, confined, detained, held, imprisoned, in prison, incarcerated, jailed, kept in prison, maintained in prison, under arrest, under lock and key

IN DUE COURSE, *adverb* eventually, in good time, in the long run, in time, presently, shortly, soon, ultimately

IN EXTREMIS, *adjective* approaching death, at one's end, at the conclusion of life, at the last stage, at the point of death, at the termination of life, during the last moments of life, dying, expiring, in one's last moments, in the final moments of life, in the jaws of death, moribund, near death, near one's end, on one's deathbed, passing away, terminally ill, under a sense of impending death
ASSOCIATED CONCEPTS: dying declaration, gift causa mortis

IN FULL FORCE, *adjective* functioning, high powered, in full effect, mighty, omnipotent, operating, overpowering, potent, puissant, strong, with full effect, with full force

IN FURTHERANCE, *preposition* for, for the sake of, in favor of, in the name of, in the service of, on account of, on behalf of

IN GOOD FAITH, *adverb* bona fide, constantly, devotedly, fairly, faithfully, honestly, legitimately, steadily, truly
ASSOCIATED CONCEPTS: good faith effort, presented in good faith, written in good faith

IN LIEU OF, *preposition* as a substitute for, as an alternative, as proxy for, by proxy, for, in place of, instead of, on behalf of, rather than, representing
ASSOCIATED CONCEPTS: in lieu of payment

IN PART, *adverb*   in installments, in some measure, incompletely, not wholly, partially, partly, somewhat, to a certain extent, to a degree, to a limited extent

IN PERSON, *adverb*   bodily, in one's own person, individually, personally, privately

IN SOLIDO, *noun*   aggregate, each and every, in whole, joint and several, one and all, sum total, the entirety, total, totality

IN STRICT CONFORMITY, *adverb*   in accordance with, in keeping with, in line with, in obedience with, in strict compliance with, predominantly the same

IN TOTO, *adverb*   absolutely, all in all, altogether, as a whole, collectively, completely, comprehensively, entirely, fully, in all, in all respects, in full, in its entirety, in the aggregate, in the whole, *omnino,* on all counts, *plane, prorsus,* thoroughly, totally, unabridgedly, unanimously, undividedly, unreservedly, utterly, wholly, without omission

IN TRUST, *adverb*   held in pledge, held in trust, in escrow, under fiduciary control

IN WRITING, *adverb*   expressed in writing, in black and white, on paper, recorded, reduced to a writing, scriptory, stated in a writing, stated in writing

INABILITY, *noun*   disability, disablement, disqualification, failure, helplessness, impotence, impuissance, inadequacy, incapability, incapacitation, incapacity, incompetence, incompetency, ineffectualness, inefficacy, inefficiency, ineptitude, ineptness, *infirmitas,* infirmity, *inopia,* insufficiency, lack of ability, lack of competence, lack of power, powerlessness, shortcoming, undeftness, unfitness, unproficiency, unskillfulness, want of ability, want of capacity, want of power, want of skill
ASSOCIATED CONCEPTS: inability to meet an obligation, inability to pay a debt as it matures, inability to pay arrears, inability to work

INACCESSIBLE, *adjective*   beyond reach, distant, elusive, far, far away, far off, impossible to reach, *inaccessus,* inapproachable, out of reach, out of touch, *rari aditus,* remote, removed, separated, unaccessible, unachievable, unacquirable, unapproachable, unattainable, unavailable, unobtainable, unprocurable, unreachable, unrealizable, unsecurable
ASSOCIATED CONCEPTS: inaccessibility of property, inaccessible to service of process, inaccessible witness

INACCURATE, *adjective*   amiss, approximate, blundering, broad, careless, erring, erroneous, fallacious, false, *falsus,* faulty, garbled, general, generalized, groundless, imprecise, improper, incorrect, *indiligens,* inexact, loose, misreported, misstated, mistaken, slipshod, unconscientious, unfactual, unfounded, unfussy, unpainstaking, unreal, unsound, unstrict, untrue, untrustworthy, wrong

INACTION, *noun*   abeyance, abrogation, abstinence from action, *cessatio,* cessation, dormancy, failure to act, idleness, immobility, impotence, indolence, inertness, inoccupation, languor, latency, motionlessness, *otium,* paralysis, passiveness, passivity, *quies,* quiescence, rest, sloth, sluggishness, stagnation, stillness,

suspended animation, suspension, torpidity, torpor, unemployment, unprogressiveness, vegetation

INACTIVE, *adjective*   abeyant, abolished, abrogated, apathetic, canceled, comatose, destroyed, disabled, dormant, idle, *ignavus,* inanimate, indifferent, indolent, *iners,* inert, inoperative, insentient, invalid, languid, latent, lazy, lethargic, lethargical, listless, motionless, nugatory, null, obsolete, otiose, pococurante, powerless, *quietus,* recumbent, reposing, resting, sedentary, slothful, sluggish, spiritless, stagnant, static, supine, suspended, torpid, unbusied, unemployed, unexercised, unmoving, unspirited, unstirred, vegetative, void, weak
ASSOCIATED CONCEPTS: inactive account, inactive trust

INADEPT, *adjective*   artless, awkward, feckless, feeble, impotent, incapable, incompetent, ineffective, ineffectual, inefficacious, inefficient, inept, inexpert, insufficient, lacking, lame, poor, unable, unaccomplished, unadroit, unapt, unclever, undeft, undexterous, unendowed, unequal to, unfacile, unfit, unfitted, ungifted, unproficient, unqualified, unskillful, unsuccessful, untalented, wanting, without dexterity

INADEQUATE, *adjective*   assailable, deficient, depleted, disabled, disappointing, displeasing, emasculate, exhausted, feckless, feeble, helpless, impaired, *impar,* impotent, incapable, incompetent, incomplete, indefensible, ineffective, ineffectual, inefficacious, inept, inferior, inoperative, insubstantial, insufficient, lacking, not enough, not up to expectation, nugatory, perfunctory, poor, powerless, scant, short, unable, unapt, undeveloped, unempowered, unequal to, unfit, unfitted, unreplenished, unsatisfactory, unsufficing, untenable, useless, vincible, vulnerable, wanting, weak
ASSOCIATED CONCEPTS: inadequate consideration, inadequate damages, inadequate remedy at law, inadequate representation

INADMISSIBLE, *adjective*   banned, barred, disallowed, disapproved, excepted, excluded, improper, inapplicable, inapposite, inappropriate, incompetent, ineligible, *inlicitus,* irrelevant, not admitted, not allowed, not capable of being introduced as evidence, not included, not receivable as evidence, not receivable in evidence, not to be admitted, not to be allowed, not wanted, objectionable, prohibited, refused, rejected, suppressed, undue, unfit, unfitted, unqualified, unreceivable, unsuitable, wrong
ASSOCIATED CONCEPTS: inadmissible evidence, inadmissible statement, inadmissible testimony, incompetent testimony

INADVERTENT, *adjective*   accidental, blind, careless, disregardful, heedless, *imprudens,* inattentive, neglectful, negligent, oblivious, regardless, thoughtless, undesigned, undiscerning, unheedful, unheeding, unintended, unintentional, unmeant, unmindful, unnoticing, unobservant, unperceptive, unpremeditated, unseeing, unthinking
ASSOCIATED CONCEPTS: neglect, negligence

INADVISABLE, *adjective*   adverse, deleterious, detrimental, disadvantageous, disapproved, harmful, hurtful, ill-advised, ill-considered, ill-judged, impolitic, imprudent, inappropriate, inexpedient, infelicitous, injudicious, injurious, inopportune, insalubrious, misadvised, misguided, nocuous, objectionable, pernicious, undesirable, unfavorable, unfitting, unhealthy, unhelpful, unprofitable, unsatisfactory, unsensible, unsound, unsuitable, untoward, unwise, wrong

INALIENABLE, *adjective* incapable of being conveyed, incapable of being sold, incapable of being transferred, nontransferable, not able to be conveyed, *quod abalienari non potest,* secured by law, unable to be bought, unable to be disposed of, unforfeitable, untouchable

ASSOCIATED CONCEPTS: inalienable lands, inalienable rights

INAPPEALABLE, *adjective* absolute, beyond all dispute, beyond all question, beyond question, clear, conclusive, decided, decisive, definite, definitive, established, final, finally settled, fixed, impregnable, incapable of being reviewed, incontestable, incontrovertible, indisputable, irrefutable, irrevocable, not to be disputed, past dispute, peremptory, *quod refutari non potest,* unassailable, unchangeable, uncontroversial, unimpeachable, unrefutable, without power of appeal

INAPPLICABLE, *adjective* alien, at variance, clashing, disagreeing, discordant, discrepant, divergent, foreign, ill-adapted, impertinent, improper, inadmissible, inapposite, inappropriate, inapt, incommensurable, incompatible, incongruent, incongruous, inconsistent, infelicitous, irrelevant, jarring, malapropos, misapplied, mismatched, misplaced, *non valere,* out of keeping, out of place, unapt, uncalled for, unconformable, unconsonant, unfit, unfitted, unfitting, ungermane, unharmonious, unqualified, unsuitable, unsuited, unusable, wrong

INAPPOSITE, *adjective* alien, aside from the point, at variance, beside the mark, beside the point, clashing, disagreeing, discordant, discrepant, disproportionate, dissonant, extraneous, far-fetched, foreign, ill-adapted, ill-timed, illogical, immaterial, impertinent, improper, inaccordant, inadmissible, inapplicable, inappropriate, inapt, incidental, incompatible, incongruent, incongruous, inconsequent, inconsequential, inconsistent, inept, inessential, infelicitous, inharmonious, inopportune, insignificant, irreconcilable, irrelative, irrelevant, isolated, jarring, lacking importance, lacking relevance, malapropos, negligible, *non idoneus,* of little importance, pointless, remote, trivial, unallied, unapt, unbecoming, unbefitting, unconformable, uncongenial, unconnected, unconsonant, undue, unessential, unfavorable, unfit, unfitting, ungermane, unharmonious, unimportant, unnoteworthy, unrelated, unseasonable, unsuitable, unsuited, untimely, untoward, wrong

INAPPRECIABLE, *adjective* beneath consideration, beneath notice, disregarded, impalpable, imperceptible, inconsequential, inconsiderable, infinitesimal, insignificant, insubstantial, intangible, irrelevant, little, marginal, meager, mean, *minimus,* minor, negligible, of little account, of little importance, paltry, petty, scant, scanty, slight, small, trifling, unimportant, unworthy of consideration, unworthy of notice

INAPPREHENSIBLE, *adjective* abstruse, acroamatic, acroamatical, acroatic, ambiguous, beyond comprehension, beyond understanding, enigmatic, enigmatical, hidden, impenetrable, impossible to understand, incognizable, incomprehensible, indistinct, inexplicable, inexpressible, inscrutable, mysterious, mystic, mystical, obscure, opaque, past comprehension, puzzling, recondite, unaccountable, undecipherable, undefinable, undiscoverable, unexplainable, unfathomable, unintelligible, unknowable, unreadable, unrecognizable, vague

INAPPROPRIATE, *adjective* alien, amiss, clashing, disagreeing, discordant, discrepant, disproportionate, dissonant, divergent, forced, gratuitous, impertinent, impolitic, improper, in bad taste, inadmissible, inapplicable, inapposite, inapt, incompatible, incongruent, incongruous, inconsistent, indecorous, ineligible, inessential, inexpedient, infelicitous, inopportune, irrelevant, maladjusted, malapropos, misapplied, misbecoming, misdirected, misplaced, *non idoneus,* objectionable, odd, out of character, out of keeping, out of place, remote, unadvisable, unapt, unbecoming, unbefitting, uncalled for, uncommendable, unconformable, unconsonant, undesirable, undignified, undue, unfit, unfitted, unfitting, ungermane, unharmonious, unmeet, unseasonable, unseemly, unsuitable, unsuited, untimely, untoward, wrongly timed

INAPT, *adjective* at variance, clashing, discordant, discrepant, disproportionate, dissonant, ill-adapted, ill-suited, ill-timed, impolitic, improper, inaccordant, inadmissible, inadvisable, inapplicable, inapposite, inappropriate, incompatible, incongruent, incongruous, inconsistent, inexpedient, infelicitous, inharmonious, inopportune, irreconcilable, jarring, malapropos, mismatched, misplaced, objectionable, out of character, out of keeping, out of place, out of proportion, unapt, unbecoming, unbefitting, uncongenial, unconsonant, undesirable, undue, unfit, unfitting, unmeet, unqualified, unseasonable, unseemly, unsuitable, untimely, untoward, unwise

INARTICULATE, *adjective* close, guarded, inaudible, incommunicative, incomprehensible, inconversable, indistinct, indistinguishable, laconic, monosyllabic, mute, *parum distinctus,* reserved, reticent, silent, sparing of words, taciturn, tongue-tied, unclear, unfathomable, unintelligible, unplain, unvocal, vague, withdrawn

INAUSPICIOUS, *adjective* adverse, boding, disadvantageous, ill-timed, inadvisable, inexpedient, *infelix,* inopportune, mistimed, *nefastus,* ominous, presageful, problematic, problematical, unfavorable, unlucky, unpromising, unpropitious, untimely, untoward

INCAPABLE, *adjective* crippled, disabled, feeble, impuissant, inadequate, incompetent, ineffective, ineffectual, inept, *inhabilis,* insufficient, not equal to, unable, unempowered, unequipped, unfit, unpowerful, unqualified, unskillful, unsuitable, unsuited, useless, weak

ASSOCIATED CONCEPTS: incapable of conducting his own affairs, incapable of intended use, incapable party, legal incapacity, physically incapable, total incapacity

FOREIGN PHRASES: ***Contra non valentem agere nulla currit praescriptio.*** No prescription runs against a person who is unable to act. ***Nemo admittendus est inhabilitare seipsum.*** No one is allowed to incapacitate himself.

INCAPACITY, noun adynamy, anility, caducity, disability, disablement, disenablement, disqualification, dotage, failure, feebleness, helplessness, impotence, impuissance, inability, inadequacy, inaptitude, incapability, incapacitation, incompetence, incompetency, incomprehension, inefficacy, inefficiency, ineptitude, infirmity, *inscitia,* lack of capacity, lack of fitness, lack of power, morosis, unfitness, unproficiency, unskillfulness, weakness
ASSOCIATED CONCEPTS: disability, incapacity for work, incapacity to sue, legal incapacity, mental incapacity, permanent incapacity, physical incapacity, total incapacity

INCARCERATION, noun arrest, bondage, captivity, *carcer,* commitment, confinement, confinement by public authority, confinement in a jail, confinement in a penitentiary, confinement under legal process, constraint, *custodia,* custodianship, custody, detention, immurement, impoundment, imprisonment, internment, legal restraint, restraint, restriction, restriction on personal liberty, *vincula*
ASSOCIATED CONCEPTS: deterrence, habeas corpus, isolation, parole, rehabilitation, retribution, sentencing

INCENDIARY, adjective agitative, anarchistic, harmful, immoderate, inciting, incitive, inflammatory, instigative, intemperate, nihilistic, pernicious, poisonous, revolutionary, unbridled

INCENSE, verb *accendere,* aggravate, agitate, anger, antagonize, arouse, arouse ire, arouse resentment, cause dislike, cause loathing, cause resentment, chafe, discompose, disquiet, embitter, embroil, enkindle, enrage, envenom, exacerbate, exasperate, excite, excite hatred, excite indignation, harass, *incendere,* inflame, inflame with wrath, infuriate, irritate, kindle one's wrath, madden, make one lose one's temper, nettle, pique, provoke, provoke hatred, provoke ire, push too far, put into a temper, raise anger, rile, ruffle, vex, work into a passion
ASSOCIATED CONCEPTS: heat of passion, incense the jury, mistrial, prejudice, provocation

INCENTIVE, noun actuation, allure, allurement, appeal, attraction, bait, causality, causation, cause, cause of action, consideration, driving force, encouragement, enticement, goad, impetus, impulse, impulsion, *incitamentum,* incitement, inducement, influence, *inritamentum,* inspiration, instigation, lure, motivation, motive, persuasion, prompting, provocation, provocative, reason, spur, stimulant, stimulus, tantalization, temptation
ASSOCIATED CONCEPTS: incentive contract

INCEPTION, noun beginning, birth, commencement, dawn, debut, derivation, embarkation, exordium, genesis, inauguration, *inceptum,* inchoation, incipience, incipiency, initiation, *initium,* onset, opening, origin, origination, outbreak, outset, rise, source, start, starting point

INCERTITUDE, noun ambiguity, bewilderment, changeableness, dilemma, doubt, doubtfulness, dubiety, dubiosity, dubiousness, dubitancy, dubitation, fog, haze, hesitancy, hesitation, indecision, indetermination, insecurity, irresolution, misgiving, perplexity, quandary, question, uncertainness, uncertainty, unsureness, vacillation, vagueness

INCESSANT, adjective *adsiduus,* ceaseless, constant, continual, continuous, *continuus,* endless, eternal, everlasting, frequent, indefatigable, infinite, interminable, interminate, iterative, long-lasting, never-ending, nonstop, perennial, perpetual, *perpetuus,* persistent, recurrent, reiterative, repeated, repetitious, returning, steady, sustained, timeless, unbroken, unceasing, undying, unending, unintermittent, unintermitting, uninterrupted, unremitting, untiring, unwearying, without ceasing, without interruption, without stopping

INCHOATE, adjective beginning, begun but not completed, budding, elemental, elementary, embryonic, fragmentary, fundamental, half-begun, half-done, hardly begun, immature, imperfect, in its infancy, inceptive, incipient, *incohatus,* incomplete, infant, initial, introductory, just begun, nascent, not completely formed, not fully executed, partial, prefatory, preliminary, primary, rudimental, rudimentary, semiprocessed, sketchy, uncompleted, unexecuted, unfinalized, unfinished, unprocessed
ASSOCIATED CONCEPTS: inchoate contract, inchoate crimes, inchoate gift, inchoate interest, inchoate lien, inchoate right, inchoate title, inchoate will

INCIDENT, adjective accessory, affiliated, allied, appertaining to, apropos, associated, bearing upon, belonging, circumstantial, collateral, connected, contextual, contingent, correlative, dependent on, following upon, implicated in, in connection with, in relation to, inherent in, pertaining to, related to, relating to, relative to, subject to, subsidiary
ASSOCIATED CONCEPTS: customarily incident, necessary and incident to

INCIDENT, noun affair, case, *casus,* contingency, episode, event, experience, happening, occasion, occurrence, pass, proceeding

INCIDENTAL, adjective accessory, accidental, accompanying, added, additional, allied, associated, attendant, extrinsic, *forte oblatus,* minor, not vital, parenthetic, secondary, subordinate, subsidiary, supervenient, supplemental, supplementary
ASSOCIATED CONCEPTS: incidental authority, incidental benefits, incidental consequence, incidental damages, incidental expenses, incidental jurisdiction, incidental power, incidental relief, incidental to employment, incidental use, incidental work

INCIPIENT, adjective aboriginal, beginning, budding, commencing, elemental, elementary, embryonic, foundational, fundamental, immature, inceptive, inchoate, inchoative, incunabular, infant, initial, initiatory, introductory, maiden, nascent, original, precursory, prefatory, primal, primary, primeval, primitive, proemial, rudimental, rudimentary, starting, uncompleted

INCISIVE, adjective acute, biting, brisk, caustic, cutting, discerning, effective, electric, galvanic, harsh, keen, mordacious, mordant, *mordax,* moving, penetrating, piercing, piquant, pointed, powerful, pungent, sarcastic, sarcastical, satiric, satirical, scathing, sententious, severe, sharp, slashing, stinging, telling, trenchant, vehement

INCITE, *verb* advise, advocate, agitate, animate, arouse, arouse to action, awaken, bring about, bring on, call forth, cause, counsel, drive, encourage, energize, enthuse, excite, exert influence, exert pressure, exhort, foment, give advice, give impetus, goad, impart momentum, impassion, *incitare,* induce, influence, initiate, inspire, inspirit, *instigare,* instigate, kindle, launch, move, persuade, press, prevail upon, prompt, provoke, push, rally, recommend, rouse, set in motion, spur on, start, stimulate, stir, stir up, urge, wake
ASSOCIATED CONCEPTS: incite a riot

INCLINATION, *noun* affinity, aptitude, aptness, bent, bias, cast, direction, fondness, *inclinatio,* leaning, liking, partiality, penchant, predilection, predisposition, preference, prejudice, proclivity, proneness, propensity, readiness, slant, *studium,* tendency, *voluntas*
FOREIGN PHRASES: *Judicium redditur in invitum, in praesumptione legis.* In presumption of law, a judgment is given against one's inclination. *Favores ampliandi sunt; odia restringenda.* Favorable inclinations should be encouraged, animosities should be restrained.

INCLINED, *adjective* acquiescent, affected, agreeable, amenable, apt, assenting, bent, consenting, content, delighted, desirous, disposed, dispositioned, eager, favorable, glad, happy, leaning, liable, moved, partial to, pleased, predisposed, prepared, *proclivis,* prompted, prone, *propensus,* ready, receptive, slanted, stimulated, tending, trending, well-disposed, willing

INCLUDE, *verb* absorb, *adscribere,* be composed of, be formed of, be made up of, begird, boast, bound, bracket, circumscribe, classify, close in, combine, compass, *complecti,* comprehend, *comprehendere,* consist of, consolidate, contain, cover, embody, embrace, encircle, encompass, engird, envelop, girdle, hold, incorporate, involve, merge, put a barrier around, span, subsume, surround, take in, unify, unite
FOREIGN PHRASES: *In eo quod plus sit semper inest et minus.* The less is always included in the greater. *Inclusio unius est exclusio alterius.* The inclusion of one thing is the exclusion of another.

INCLUSIVE, *adjective* all-embracing, broad, comprehensive, comprising, consisting of, containing, embodying, embracing, encircling, enclosing, exhaustive, extensive, full, general, inclusory, sweeping, total, vast, wide

INCOGNIZANT, *adjective* benighted, blind, clueless, deaf, heedless, ignorant, insensible, mystified, nescient, oblivious, unacquainted, unadvised, unapprized, unaware, unconscious, unenlightened, unfamiliar, uninformed, uninstructed, unknowing, unmindful, unrealizing, unseeing, unsuspecting, unwitting

INCOHERENCE, *noun* absence of meaning, chaos, disconnection, discontinuity, disjunction, disorder, illegibility, imperspicuity, inapprehensibility, incomprehensibility, lack of clarity, meaninglessness, randomness, ranting, raving, unclearness, undecipherability, unevenness, unintelligibility, wandering
ASSOCIATED CONCEPTS: commitment to an institution, guardian, insanity, lack of capacity

INCOME, *noun* business profits, commercial profits, compensation, earnings, financial remuneration, financial resources, gain derived from capital, gain derived from labor, gains, gross return, increase in amount of wealth, money coming in, net return, pay, payment, *pecunia,* periodic returns from property or labor, proceeds, profit from conversion of assets, profit from sale, profits, profits of commerce, *quaestus,* receipts, remuneration, return in money, return on capital, revenue, salary, sale proceeds, something produced by capital, value received, *vectigal,* wage, wages, wealth
ASSOCIATED CONCEPTS: accumulated income, actual income, aggregate income, annual net income, current income, deferred income, division of income, estimated income, garnishment of income, gross income, income bearing property, income execution, income tax, income tax evasion, income yield, legacy, life income, net income

INCOMMENSURATE, *adjective* at variance, discordant, discrepant, disproportionate, inaccordant, incommensurable, inconsistent, mismatched, out of keeping, out of proportion, short, unconformable, unequal

INCOMPATIBILITY *(Difference),* *noun* animosity, antagonism, antipathy, clash, conflict, contradictoriness, contrariety, contrast, controversy, disaccord, disagreement, discord, discordance, dislike, dispute, dissension, dissent, dissidence, disunion, disunity, divergence, division, faction, fight, hatred, hostility, inimicality, intolerance, intransigence, intransigency, irreconcilability, irreconcilable difference, irreconcilableness, lack of agreement, misunderstanding, nonagreement, opposition, quarrel, repugnance, unfriendliness, variance, want of adaptation, want of agreement
ASSOCIATED CONCEPTS: divorce for incompatibility

INCOMPATIBILITY *(Inconsistency),* *noun* antithesis, clash, conflict, contrast, disagreement, disconformity, discongruity, discord, discordance, discordancy, discrepancy, disharmony, disparity, dissimilarity, dissimilitude, dissonance, divergence, incongruity, inconsonance, inequality, inharmoniousness, inharmony, lack of agreement, lack of harmony, nonconformity, nonuniformity, unconformity, unlikeness, unsuitableness, variance, want of agreement
ASSOCIATED CONCEPTS: incompatible use of land

INCOMPETENCE, *noun* illegitimacy, inadequacy, incapability, incapacity, inefficiency, inexpertness, insufficiency, mismanagement, negligence, undeftness, unendowment, unfitness, unprofessional conduct, unproficiency, unqualifiedness
ASSOCIATED CONCEPTS: incompetence of counsel, incompetence of representation, incompetent evidence

INCOMPETENT, *adjective* amateurish, awkward, bungling, clumsy, deficient, disqualified, floundering, gauche, gawky, ignorant, improficient, inadequate, incapable, incapacitated, ineffective, ineffectual, inefficient, inept, inexperienced, inexpert, *inhabilis, inscitus,* insufficient, *inutilis,* lacking qualification, maladroit, raw, stumbling, stupid, unable, unadapted, unapt, unequal, unequipped, unfit, unfitted, ungainly, unhandy, uninitiated, unqualified, unskilled, unskillful, unsuitable, untrained, useless, without adequate ability
ASSOCIATED CONCEPTS: incompetence of counsel, incompetent evidence, incompetent witness

INCOMPREHENSIBLE, *adjective* abstruse, acroamatic, acroamatical, acroatic, ambiguous, beyond comprehension, concealed, dark, deep, difficult to comprehend, dim, enigmatic, enigmatical, esoteric, fathomless, hard to understand, hidden, impenetrable, impossible to understand, inapprehensible, incalculable, incognoscible, incoherent, inconceivable, indefinite, inexplicable, inscrutable, insoluble, insolvable, *intellegi non potest,* intricate, meaningless, metaphysical, miraculous, mysterious, mystic, mystical, nebulousness, obscure, occult, puzzling, *quod comprehendi,* recondite, unaccountable, unclear, unfathomable, unimaginable, unintelligible, unknowable, unrecognizable, unthinkable, vague

INCONCLUSIVE, *adjective*   doubtful, flimsy, indecisive, ineffective, not final, *quo nihil efficitur,* subject to verification, unascertained, uncertain, unconfirmed, uncorroborated, undemonstrated, unestablished, unproved, unproven, unsettled, unsubstantiated, unsupported, unsupported by evidence, unsure, untested, untried, unverified, weak
ASSOCIATED CONCEPTS: inconclusive account, inconclusive evidence

INCONGRUITY, *noun*   abnormality, absurdity, absurdness, contradiction, contradictoriness, contrariety, contrariness, deviation, difference, disagreement, discordance, discordancy, discrepancy, disharmony, disparity, dissimilarity, dissimilitude, dissonance, impropriety, inapplicability, inappropriateness, incompatibility, incongruousness, inconsistency, inconsonance, inharmoniousness, lack of consonance, lack of harmony, ludicrousness, misalliance, mismatch, nonconformity, *repugnantia,* ridiculousness, unconformity, unfitness, unfittingness, unlikeness, unsuitability, variance

INCONGRUOUS, *adjective*   alien, *alienus,* at odds, at variance, clashing, conflicting, contradictory, contrary, disaccordant, disagreeing, discordant, discrepant, disharmonious, disproportionate, dissonant, divergent, ill-matched, illogical, improper, inaccordant, inapplicable, inapposite, inappropriate, incompatible, inconformable, *incongruens,* incongruent, inconsequent, inconsistent, inconsonant, inharmonious, irreconcilable, irregular, jarring, lacking agreement, lacking harmony, misjoined, mismatched, mismated, *non aptus,* out of character, out of keeping, out of place, strange, unbecoming, uncongenial, uncoordinated, unfit, unfitting, unsuitable

INCONSEQUENCE, *noun*   disassociation, disconnection, disjunction, dissociation, immateriality, impertinence, impertinency, inapplicability, inappositeness, inconsequentiality, inconsiderableness, inconsistence, inconsistency, insignificance, irrelevance, irrelevancy, negligibility, paltriness, smallness, triviality, unimportance, unnoteworthiness, unrelatedness

INCONSEQUENTIAL, *adjective*   dispensable, flimsy, frivolous, immaterial, impertinent, inapplicable, inappreciable, inappropriate, inconsequent, inconsiderable, inessential, insignificant, invalid, irrelevant, minor, niggling, nonessential, not vital, nugatory, of minor importance, of no account, of no consequence, paltry, petty, picayune, remote, slight, superficial, trifling, trivial, unconnected, unessential, ungermane, unimportant, unnecessary, unrelated, unsound, unwarranted, worthless
ASSOCIATED CONCEPTS: irrelevant evidence

INCONSIDERABLE, *adjective*   beneath notice, *exiguus,* immaterial, inappreciable, inconsequential, insignificant, insubstantial, irrelevant, *levis,* meager, mean, minor, minute, modest, negligible, nominal, nonessential, not worth considering, not worthy of notice, nugatory, of no consequence, of no moment, paltry, petty, piddling, slight, small, *tenuis,* trifling, trivial, unessential, unimportant, unworthy of consideration, unworthy of notice, worthless

INCONSIDERATION, *noun*   carelessness, cruelty, disregard, disrespect, disrespectfulness, foolhardiness, forgetfulness, hastiness, heedlessness, impetuosity, improvidence, imprudence, impulsiveness, inadvertence, inadvertency, inattention, inattention to consequences, incaution, incautiousness, incircumspection, inconsiderateness, indiscretion, injudiciousness, irresponsibility, lack of care, lack of caution, lack of consideration, lack of respect, lack of reverence, meanness, neglect, negligence, oversight, precipitance, precipitancy, prodigality, rashness, recklessness, regardlessness, thoughtlessness, unkindness, unpremeditation, unwariness

INCONSISTENCY, *noun*   antilogy, antinomy, capriciousness, changeableness, contradiction, contradictoriness, contrariety, deviation, difference, disaccord, disagreement, discord, discordance, discordancy, discrepancy, disparity, dissimilarity, dissimilitude, dissonance, divergence, diversity, fitfulness, flightiness, inapplicability, inappropriateness, incompatibility, incongruity, incongruousness, inconsonance, inconstancy, *inconstantia,* inequality, inharmony, instability, lack of accord, mercurialness, *mutabilitas,* nonconformity, unconformity, unlikeness, unsteadiness, unsuitableness, vacillation, variance, volatility, want of harmony

INCONSISTENT, *adjective*   at variance, capricious, changeable, conflicting, contradictory, *contrarius,* contrary, different, disagreeing, discordant, discrepant, dissonant, divergent, erratic, fickle, fitful, flighty, illogical, incompatible, incongruous, inconsonant, *inconstans,* inconstant, irreconcilable, jarring, lacking accord, lacking harmony, mercurial, moody, mutable, notional, paradoxical, unstable, unsteady, unsuitable, vacillating, variable, volatile
ASSOCIATED CONCEPTS: alternative pleadings, inconsistent causes of action, inconsistent defenses, inconsistent statements, inconsistent verdict

INCONSPICUOUS, *adjective*   barely seen, blurred, concealed, covert, dim, faint, feeble, hidden, ill-defined, imperceptible, indefinite, indiscernible, indistinct, invisible, misty, modest, nebulous, obscure, *obscurus,* out of sight, *parum insignis,* poorly defined, poorly seen, quiet, retiring, shadowy, shrouded, subtle, suppressed, unapparent, unassuming, unclear, undefined, undiscernible, unevident, unnoticeable, unnoticed, unobserved, unobtrusive, unobvious, unostentatious, unperceivable, unpretentious, unpronounced, unseeable, unseen, vague, veiled, viewless

INCONTESTABILITY, *noun*   impregnability, incontrovertibility, indefeasibility, indisputability, indubitableness, irrefragibility, irrefutability, unassailability, undeniability, unequivocalness, unimpeachability, unquestionability, unrefutability
ASSOCIATED CONCEPTS: incontestability clause, incontestable policy

INCONTESTABLE, *adjective*   absolutely clear, beyond all question, clear, conclusive, impregnable, inappealable, incontrovertible, indefeasible, indisputable, indubious, indubitable, irrefragable, irrefutable, noncontroversial, past dispute, unambiguous, unassailable, uncontradictable, undeniable, unequivocal, unimpeachable, unquestionable
ASSOCIATED CONCEPTS: incontestable claim

INCONTROVERTIBLE, *adjective*   absolute, apodictic, ascertained, assured, authoritative, beyond a shadow of a doubt, beyond contradiction, capable of proof, certain, clear-cut, conclusive, definite, demonstrable, established, factual, inappealable, incontestable, indisputable, indubious, indubitable, irrefragable, irrefutable, noncontroversial, past dispute, positive, questionless, *quod refutari non potest,* settled, sure, testable, true, unambiguous, unanswerable, unchallengeable, unconfutable, uncontradictable, undeniable, unequivocal, unimpeachable, unmistakable, unquestionable, unshakable, veracious
ASSOCIATED CONCEPTS: incontrovertible fact, incontrovertible proof

INCONVENIENCE, *verb*   annoy, be obstructive, be uncooperative, bother, disadvantage, discommode, displace, disturb, encumber, give trouble, hamper, hinder, impede, impose hardship, incommode, irritate, obstruct, stall, stand in the way, stymie, thwart, trouble, unsettle, vex
ASSOCIATED CONCEPTS: forum non conveniens, public inconvenience
FOREIGN PHRASES: *Privatum incommodum publico bono pensatur.* Private inconvenience is compensated by public benefit. *Argumentum ab inconvenienti est validum in lege; quia lex non permittit aliquod inconveniens.* An argument drawn from what is inconvenient is good in law, because the law will not permit any inconvenience. *Quod est inconveniens aut contra rationem non permissum est in lege.* What is inconvenient or contrary to reason is not permitted in the law.

INCONVINCIBLE, *adjective*   cynical, disbelieving, disposed to doubt, distrustful, doubtful, doubting, dubious, given to suspicion, hard to convince, inclined to suspect, incredulous, indisposed to believe, questioning, skeptical, slow to believe, suspecting, suspicious, unbelieving, uncertain, unwilling to accept, wary, without faith

INCORPORATE *(Form a corporation), verb*   affiliate, begin a corporation, charter, confer a corporate franchise upon, confer corporate status upon, create a corporation, establish a corporation, form a company, initiate a corporation, *inserere,* organize a corporation, start a corporation
ASSOCIATED CONCEPTS: certificate of incorporation

INCORPORATE *(Include), verb*   absorb, alloy, become a component, become an ingredient, bring together, centralize, coalesce, combine, compound, consolidate, contain, couple, cover, embody, embrace, encircle, encompass, fuse, interblend, interfuse, interlace, intermix, involve, join, meld, merge, mix, put together, take in, unite, weave, yoke
ASSOCIATED CONCEPTS: incorporate by reference

INCORPORATION *(Blend), noun*   aggregation, amalgamation, assimilation, centralization, coalescence, combination, commixtion, compound, consolidation, fusion, infusion, interfusion, interlacement, intermixture, minglement, mixture, unification, union
ASSOCIATED CONCEPTS: incorporation by reference
FOREIGN PHRASES: *Verba relata hoc maxime operantur per referentiam, ut in eis inesse videntur.* Words incorporated by reference have as great an effect through reference, as they are deemed to be inserted.

INCORPORATION *(Formation of a business entity), noun*   association, chartering, coalition, *coniunctio, cooptatio,* establishment of a firm, formation of a company, formation of a corporation, formation of an organization, organization of a commercial concern, organization of a company, unification, union
ASSOCIATED CONCEPTS: certificate of incorporation, dissolution of a corporation

INCORPOREAL, *adjective*   asomatous, bodiless, ethereal, immaterial, immateriate, impalpable, incorporal, intangible, nonphysical, not of material nature, spiritual, unbodied, unembodied, unfleshly, unsubstantial, unworldly, without body, without substance
ASSOCIATED CONCEPTS: incorporeal chattels, incorporeal hereditament
FOREIGN PHRASES: *Haereditas, alia corporalis, alia incorporalis; corporalis est, quae tan gi potest et videri; incorporalis quae tangi non potest nec videri.* An inheritance is either corporeal or incorporeal. Corporeal is that which can be touched and seen; incorporeal, that which can neither be touched nor seen.

INCORRECT, *adjective*   amiss, awry, erring, erroneous, fallacious, false, *falsus,* faulty, flawed, imperfect, imprecise, *improbus,* improper, inaccurate, inappropriate, inexact, miscalculated, misconstrued, misfigured, misjudged, misleading, mistaken, *perversus,* solecistic, solecistical, sophistic, sophistical, unfactual, ungrounded, unsound, untrue, unveracious, wrong

INCORRIGIBLE, *adjective*   beyond help, beyond reform, chronic, cureless, hardened, hopeless, impenitent, incapable of correction, incurable, intractable, intransigent, inveterate, irreclaimable, irrecoverable, irredeemable, irreformable, irremediable, irreparable, lost, obdurate, obstinate, past cure, past hope, *perditus,* recalcitrant, recidivous, refractory, remorseless, reprobate, stubborn, toughened, unapologizing, uncontrite, uncontrollable, ungovernable, unmanageable, unreformable, unregretful, unregretting, unrepentant, unsubmissive, wicked
ASSOCIATED CONCEPTS: incorrigible child, incorrigible juvenile delinquent, multiple offender

INCORRUPTIBLE, *adjective*   above suspicion, blameless, dependable, ethical, faultless, guiltless, having integrity, high-principled, honest, honorable, impeccable, *incorruptus,* inculpable, *integer,* irreproachable, just, meritorious, moral, reliable, reputable, respectable, *sanctus,* scrupulous, sinless, stanch, trustable, trustworthy, trusty, unable to be bought, unblemished, unbribable, uncorrupt, unerring, unimpeachable, untarnishable, untreacherous, unvenal, upright, virtuous

INCREASE, *verb*   abound, accrue, accumulate, add on, add to, aggrandize, *amplificare,* amplify, annex, appreciate, *augere,* augment, become larger, become

greater, boost, branch out, broaden, build, burgeon, *crescere,* develop, *dilatare,* dilate, enlarge, escalate, expand, extend, flourish, gain, gain ground, *gliscere,* greaten, grow, inflate, lengthen, make greater, make larger, maximize, mount, multiply, progress, proliferate, prolong, protract, pullulate, raise, rise, skyrocket, spread, step up, stretch, supplement, surge, swell, thrive, widen
ASSOCIATED CONCEPTS: increase in value, increased cost, increased hazard, increased risk, increased valuation

INCREDIBLE, *adjective*   absurd, beyond belief, doubtful, hard to believe, hardly credible, implausible, impossible, improbable, inconceivable, *incredibilis,* nonsensical, open to doubt, open to suspicion, preposterous, ridiculous, staggering, suspect, suspicious, unbelievable, unconvincing, unimaginable, unlikely, unthinkable
ASSOCIATED CONCEPTS: incredible statements, incredible testimony

INCREDULITY, *noun*   amazement, denial, disbelief, discredit, distrust, distrustfulness, doubt, doubtfulness, dubiety, dubiousness, faithlessness, inability to accept, inability to believe, inconvincability, incredulousness, indisposition to admit, indisposition to believe, lack of belief, lack of faith, mistrust, mistrustfulness, question, reluctance to believe, skepticalness, skepticism, suspicion, suspiciousness, uncertainty, unwillingness to believe, want of faith

INCREDULOUS, *adjective*   disposed to doubt, distrustful, doubtful, doubting, dubious, hard to convince, *incredulus,* indisposed to believe, mistrustful, questioning, skeptical, slow to believe, suspecting, suspicious, unbelieving, unconvinced, untrusting, unwilling to accept, without belief, without faith, wondering

INCREMENT, *noun*   accretion, addition, augmentation, boost, enlargement, expansion, extension, gain, growth, increase, *incrementum,* raise, rise, supplement, surge
ASSOCIATED CONCEPTS: unearned increment

INCRIMINATE, *verb*   accuse, ascribe blame, blame, bring accusation, bring charges against, bring proceedings against, bring up on charges, cast blame upon, charge, charge with an offense, complain against, condemn, connect with a crime, criminate, denounce, draw in, enmesh, entangle, expose, find fault with, hold accountable, *impedire, implicare,* implicate, impute guilt to, inculpate, indict, inform against, insinuate, involve, involve in criminal proceeding, involve in guilt, lay blame upon, lodge a complaint, make a party to, place the blame on, prefer charges, prosecute, stigmatize, *suspectum reddere*

INCRIMINATION, *noun*   accusal, accusation, assignation, attribution, blame, calling to account, censure, charge, complaint, crimination, decrial, denouncement, impeachment, implication, imputation, imputation of wrongdoing, inculpation, indictment, recrimination, reproach, reproachful accusation
ASSOCIATED CONCEPTS: Fifth Amendment, incriminating admission, incriminating circumstance, incriminating statement, privilege against self-incrimination, privileges and immunities, self-incrimination
FOREIGN PHRASES: *Accusare nemo se debet.* No one is bound to accuse himself.

INCRIMINATORY, *adjective*   accusatory, accusing, blaming, charging with guilt, condemnatory, condemning, convicting, criminative, criminatory, damaging, damnatory, damning, defamatory, denunciatory, disparaging, establishing guilt, harming, implicating, implicative, implicatory, imputative, imputing blame, inculpatory, involving in guilt
ASSOCIATED CONCEPTS: incriminatory admission, incriminatory statement, incriminatory testimony

INCULCATE, *verb*   convince, direct, discipline, educate, guide, imbue, implant, impress, impress by repeated statement, impress upon the mind, imprint, *inculcare,* indoctrinate, infix, infuse, inspire, instill, instruct, lecture, plant, preach, prelect, press, propagandize, sermonize, teach, train, urge

INCULPABLE, *adjective*   above suspicion, blameless, entirely defensible, exculpable, faultless, free from fault, free from guilt, guiltless, impeccable, *innocens,* innocent, *integer,* irreprehensible, irreproachable, not blamable, not guilty, pure, *sanctus,* sinless, unblamable, unblameworthy, uncorrupt, unerring, unimpeached, unreproached, unreproved, virtuous

INCULPATION, *noun*   accusation, blame, charging with fault, charging with guilt, condemnation, crimination, denunciation, faultfinding, implication, imputation, incrimination
ASSOCIATED CONCEPTS: confessions, exculpatory statements, inculpatory statements

INCULPATORY, *adjective*   accusative, accusatory, accusing, blaming, charging with guilt, condemnatory, condemning, convicting, criminative, criminatory, damaging, damnatory, damning, denouncing, denunciatory, disparaging, establishing guilt, implicating, implicative, implicatory, imputative, imputing blame, incriminating, incriminatory, inculpating, injuring, involving in guilt
ASSOCIATED CONCEPTS: inculpatory admission, inculpatory evidence, inculpatory facts, inculpatory statements

INCUMBENT, *noun*   bureaucrat, commissioner, dignitary, functionary, holder of an office, job holder, minister, occupant of an office, officebearer, officeholder, officer, official, person in authority
ASSOCIATED CONCEPTS: de facto incumbent, incumbent officer

INCUMBRANCE *(Burden), noun*   deadweight, disadvantage, handicap, impediment, load, millstone, onus, oppression, weight

INCUMBRANCE *(Lien), noun*   commitment, liability, imposition, obligation, restraint, title impairment
ASSOCIATED CONCEPTS: artisan's lien, encumbrance upon property, materialman's lien

INCUR, *verb*   acquire, assume, bargain for, become liable for, become responsible for, bring on, bring upon oneself, contract, enter into, expose onself to, fall into, get, *incurrere,* lay oneself open to, meet with, run the chance, *suscipere,* undertake
ASSOCIATED CONCEPTS: claim incurred, incur a debt, incur a liability, incur an obligation, incurred risk, incurring indebtedness, penalty incurred

INCURSION, *noun*   advancement, aggression, assault, attack, breach, encroachment, entrance, foray, forced entry, hostile entrance, *incursio,* infiltration, influx, infringement, ingress, ingression, inroad, introgression, intrusion, invasion, irruption, onslaught, overrun, overstepping, penetration, raid, rushing in, sortie, storm, violation

INDAGATION, *noun* analysis, audit, careful search, careful study, challenge, check, close inquiry, dissection, examination, exhaustive inquiry, exhaustive study, exploration, exploratory examination, inquest, inquiry, inquisition, inspection, interrogation, investigation, minute investigation, narrow search, observation, perquisition, perscrutation, perusal, probe, quest, questioning, research, review, rigorous search, scrutation, scrutiny, search, searching investigation, strict examination, strict inquiry, strict search, study, systematic search, test, trial

INDEBTED, *adjective* beholden, bound, bounden, devoted, encumbered, in arrears, in debt, legally obliged to repay, *obaeratus,* obligated, *obligatus,* obliged, owing, short of funds, thankful, unable to pay, under obligation
ASSOCIATED CONCEPTS: involuntary indebtedness, voluntary indebtedness

INDECENCY, *noun* impropriety, indecorousness, indelicacy, obnoxiousness, tastelessness, unseemingliness, untastefulness, vulgarity
ASSOCIATED CONCEPTS: indecent assault, indecent exposure, indecent liberties, indecent publications, lewd and lascivious conduct

INDECISION, *noun* changeableness, dilemma, doubt, doubtfulness, dubiety, dubiousness, dubitancy, *dubitatio,* dubitation, equivocalness, fickleness, fluctuation, *haesitatio,* hesitancy, hesitation, inability to decide, incertitude, *inconstantia,* indetermination, infirmity of purpose, instability, irresoluteness, irresolution, lack of certainty, lack of decision, oscillation, quandary, tendency to change the mind, tendency to waver, uncertainty, unsettled opinion, unsteadiness, unsureness, vacillation

INDEFEASIBLE, *adjective* binding, confirmed, entrenched, established, immutable, imperishable, imprescriptible, *in perpetuum ratus,* inalienable, incapable of being defeated, incapable of being revoked, incontestable, incontrovertible, indestructible, indissoluble, indubitable, ineradicable, inextinguishable, insusceptible of change, intransmutable, invariable, inviolable, irrefragable, irremovable, irreversible, irrevocable, nonreversible, not forfeitable, not to be abrogated, not to be annulled, not to be made void, permanent, reverseless, settled, unalterable, unchallengeable, unchangeable, undefeatable, undeniable, undisputable, unquestionable
ASSOCIATED CONCEPTS: indefeasible estate, indefeasible interest, indefeasible title, indefeasibly vested

INDEFENSIBLE, *adjective* accessible, assailable, capable of being conquered, capable of being overcome, conquerable, defenseless, exposed, helpless, inexcusable, inexpiable, insupportable, pregnable, *quod defendi non potest,* unfortified, unguarded, unjustifiable, unprotected, untenable, unwarrantable, vincible, vulnerable

INDEFINABLE, *adjective* abstruse, beyond expression, confusing, cryptic, difficult to explain, difficult to translate, difficult to understand, enigmatic, enigmatical, hard to explain, hard to translate, hard to understand, impenetrable, impossible to explain, impossible to translate, impossible to understand, incomprehensible, indescribable, inexplicable, inexpressible, inscrutable, mysterious, obscure, opaque, perplexing, puzzling, unaccountable, unclear, unfathomable, unplain, untranslatable

INDEFINITE, *adjective* alterable, ambiguous, *ambiguus,* amorphic, amorphous, barely seen, blurred, blurry, boundless, broad, changeable, cloudy, controvertible, cryptic, debatable, dim, doubtful, dubious, *dubius,* enigmatic, enigmatical, equivocal, evasive, faint, formless, ill-defined, imperspicuous, imprecise, in doubt, *incertus,* indecisive, indeterminate, indistinct, indistinguishable, inexact, inexplicit, mysterious, nondescript, nonspecific, not positive, not sharp, obscure, opaque, open to question, oracular, questionable, shapeless, subject to change, suppositional, theoretical, unascertained, unbounded, uncertain, unclear, undecided, undefined, undetermined, undiscernible, unexact, unintelligible, unlimited, unresolved, unsettled, unspecified, unstable, unsure, untold, vague
ASSOCIATED CONCEPTS: indefinite contract, indefinite failure of issue, indefinite liability, indefinite sentence

INDELIBLE, *adjective* changeless, durable, enduring, fadeless, fast, fixed, immovable, immutable, imperishable, incapable of being deleted, indefeasible, *indelibilis,* indestructible, ineffaceable, ineradicable, inerasable, inextinguishable, ingrained, irremovable, irreversible, irrevocable, lasting, nonperishable, permanent, persevering, persistent, persisting, reverseless, rooted, *sempiternus,* stable, steadfast, unalterable, unchangeable, undestroyable, unerasable, unfading, unforgettable, unforgotten, unyielding

INDEMNIFICATION, *noun* amends, compensation, indemnity, monetary remuneration, payment, recompense, redemption, reimbursement, remuneration, reparation, repayment, requital, requitement, restitution, restoration, return, satisfaction

INDEMNIFY, *verb* answer for, compensate, compensate for injury, compensate for loss, compensate for loss sustained, *damnum restituere, damnum sarcire,* give back, give satisfaction, grant monetary compensation, guarantee, insure, make good, make good against anticipated loss, make reparation, make restitution, make up, offer compensation, offer reparation, offer satisfaction, pay, pay back, pay compensation, pay reparations, recompense, recompense for past loss, redeem, refund, reimburse, remunerate, repay, requite, restore, return money paid out, save harmless, secure against damage, secure against loss
ASSOCIATED CONCEPTS: subrogate

INDEMNITY, *noun* act of holding harmless, amends, assurance against loss, compensation, full satisfaction, indemnification, *lex oblivionis,* payment, protection against loss, recompense, recoupment, redemption, refund, reimbursement, remuneration, repayment, requitement, restitution, restoration, return, security, security against damage, security against loss, setoff, vindication
ASSOCIATED CONCEPTS: contract of indemnity, covenant of indemnity, indemnity against liability, indemnity against loss, indemnity agreement, indemnity

bond, indemnity insurance, indemnity mortgage, indemnity policy, indemnity reinsurance, limitation of indemnity, subrogation

INDENTURE, *noun*   agreement, agreement to work, apprenticeship agreement, arrangement, commitment, compact, contract, contract to work, contractual obligation, contractual statement, covenant, deed of agreement, instrument, mutual agreement, mutual undertaking, pact, *pactum,* stipulation, undertaking

INDENTURED, *adjective*   apprenticed, articled, bound by agreement, bound by contract, contracted, engaged, enslaved, obligated, obliged, promised, tied down, under obligation
ASSOCIATED CONCEPTS: indentured apprentice

INDEPENDENT, *adjective*   autarkic, autonomous, detached, disconnected, dissociated, free, freelance, irrelative, *liber,* masterless, neutral, nonpartisan, self-governing, self-reliant, self-subsistent, self-supporting, *solutus,* sovereign, unaffiliated, unallied, unassociated, unattached, unbound, unbridled, unchecked, uncommitted, unconnected, unconquered, uncontrolled, uncurbed, unencumbered, unenslaved, unenthralled, unfettered, unhindered, uninfluenced, unreined, unshackled, unsubjected, unvanquished
ASSOCIATED CONCEPTS: independent advice, independent agreement, independent cause, independent contractor, independent covenant, independent duty, independent negligence, independent tortfeasor, independently established
FOREIGN PHRASES: *Illud quod alteri unitur extinguitur neque amplius per se vacare licet.* That which is united to another is extinguished, nor can it be independent.

INDESTRUCTIBILITY, *noun*   *aplomb,* ceaselessness, changelessness, constancy, continuance, continuity, durability, durableness, endlessness, endurance, eternalness, everlastingness, immortality, immutability, imperishability, indefeasibility, indelibility, indissolubility, ineradicableness, inerasableness, insusceptibility to change, interminability, lastingness, permanence, perpetuity, stability, steadiness, unalterability, unchangeability
ASSOCIATED CONCEPTS: indestructible trust

INDESTRUCTIBLE, *adjective*   abiding, durable, endless, enduring, everlasting, fadeless, hardy, imperishable, indefeasible, indelible, indissoluble, ineffaceable, inerasable, inextinguishable, insusceptible, invulnerable, irrevocable, lasting, nonperishable, perennial, permanent, perpetual, *perpetuus,* persevering, persisting, *quod everti non potest,* reliable, sturdy, tenacious, tough, undestroyable, undying, unfading, unyielding
ASSOCIATED CONCEPTS: indestructible trust

INDETERMINATE, *adjective*   ambiguous, *anceps,* boundless, cryptic, *dubius,* endless, equivocal, featureless, fluctuant, fluid, formless, hazy, ill-defined, immeasurable, in a state of uncertainty, in doubt, inarticulated, incalculable, *incertus,* inconclusive, indefinite, indistinct, infinite, interminable, limitless, measureless, nonspecific, not ascertained, not designated, not fixed, not fixed in extent, not made certain, not particularly designated, not precise, not settled, obscure, open, open to question, shapeless, speculative, termless, unbounded, uncertain, unclear, undecided, undefined, unfathomable, unfixed, unlimited, unmeasured, unor-

dered, unresolved, unsettled, unspecified, vague, without bound, without end, without limit, without measure
ASSOCIATED CONCEPTS: indeterminate damages, indeterminate penalty, indeterminate punishment, indeterminate sentence

INDEX *(Catalog), noun*   earmark, enumeration, indicant, indicator, list, listing, listing of contents, mark, sign

INDEX *(Docket), verb*   categorize, codify, file, submit

INDEX *(Gauge), noun*   measure, guide, scale

INDEX *(Relate), verb*   catalog, class, classify, document, enumerate, group, inventory, itemize, list, specify, record, supply or furnish with reference

INDICANT, *noun*   augury, auspice, badge, beacon, brand, caution, characteristic, cipher, clue, cue, diagnostic, emblem, ensign, example, exponent, figure, flag, foretoken, hint, implication, index, indication, indicator, landmark, manifestation, mark, note, omen, pointer, portent, presage, prognostic, representation, representative, sign, signal, signature, signboard, stamp, suggestion, symbol, symptom, token, trademark, visible token, watchword

INDICATE, *verb*   advert to, allude to, augur, be a sign of, be a token of, bespeak, betoken, brief, call attention to, connote, convey, direct, direct attention to, evidence, evince, express briefly, express generally, foretoken, give a signal, guide, highlight, hint, imply, index, *indicare,* insinuate, intimate, make necessary, make needed, mark out, point out, point to, portend, presage, show, signal, signalize, *significare,* signify, sketch, stand for, suggest, touch on

INDICATION, *noun*   allusion, augury, auspice, badge, brand, clue, connotation, cue, emblem, evidence, evincement, exponent, foretoken, guide, hint, implication, index, indicant, indicator, *indicium,* innuendo, insinuation, intimation, mark, marker, mention, monition, note, omen, pointer, portent, premonitor, premonitory sign, presage, prognostic, prompt, reference, sign, signal, *significatio,* signpost, suggestion, symbol, symptom, token, trace, *vestigium,* warning

INDICATOR, *noun*   attestant, attester, augury, auspice, badge, beacon, clue, cue, emblem, ensign, flag, foreshadowing, harbinger, herald, hint, index, informant, informer, landmark, mark, note, pointer, precursor, prognostic, semaphore, sign, stamp, symbol, symptom, token, warning, witness

INDICIA, *noun*   characteristic marks, characteristics, evidence, expressions, features, hints, indications, manifestations, marks, means of recognition, signs, symbols, tokens
ASSOCIATED CONCEPTS: indicia of ownership

INDICT, *verb*   *accusare,* accuse, blame, bring a formal accusation against, call to account, charge, charge with offense, charge with the commission of a crime, formally charge, formally charge with a crime, implicate, incriminate, inculpate, lodge a complaint, make formal accusation against, *nomen deferre,* prefer charges

INDICTMENT, noun accusal, *accusatio,* accusation, allegation, castigation, charge, complaint, *crimen,* delation, denunciation, formal accusation, grand jury's accusation, *libellus,* main charge, presentment, reproach, written accusation
ASSOCIATED CONCEPTS: arraignment, counts of an indictment, felony complaint, felony information, grand jury, indictable offense, motion to quash, no true bill, plea, presentment, true bill

INDIGENCE, noun bare subsistence, dearth, destitution, *egestas,* embarrassment, impecuniosity, impoverishment, *inopia,* insolvency, insufficiency, insufficient income, *mendicitas,* narrow means, necessitousness, need, neediness, needy circumstances, pauperism, pennilessness, penury, poor circumstances, poorness, poverty, privation, scarcity, want

INDIFFERENCE, noun aloofness, apathy, blankness, coldness, coolness, detachment, disinterestedness, disregard, impassiveness, imperturbability, inattention, inconsideration, insouciance, laxity, lukewarmness, neglect, negligence, nonchalance, nonobservance, unconcern

INDIRECT, adjective allusive, ambagious, backhanded, circuitous, circumambulating, circumlocutory, covert, crooked, desultory, deviating, deviatory, devious, *devius,* digressing, digressive, excursive, hidden, implicit, labyrinthine, meandering, *non rectus,* oblique, *obliquus,* out of the way, periphrastic, periphrastical, rambling, roundabout, serpentine, sidelong, sinuous, tacit, tortuose, turning, twisting, understood, unexpressed, vagrant, wandering, winding, zigzag
ASSOCIATED CONCEPTS: indirect benefit, indirect evidence, indirect interest, indirect notice, indirect result, indirect tax, indirect testimony

INDIRECTION *(Deceitfulness),* **noun** concealment of truth, cozenage, craft, craftiness, cunning, deceit, deception, deviousness, dishonesty, disingenuity, disingenuousness, dissimulation, duplicity, falsehood, falseness, fraud, fraudulency, guile, hypocrisy, improbity, insincerity, intrigue, lack of candidness, lack of conscience, lack of probity, mendaciousness, mendacity, obliqueness, obliquity, perfidiousness, perfidy, perversion of truth, pretense, prevarication, slyness, underhandedness, unstraightforwardness, untrustworthiness, untruthfulness

INDIRECTION *(Indirect action),* **noun** aberrance, aberrancy, circuitous action, circuitous route, circuitousness, circuity, circumflexion, circumlocution, crookedness, departure, deviation, deviousness, digression, divagation, obliquation, obliqueness, obliquity, periphrasis, roundabout action, roundaboutness, straying, swerve, unstraightforward action, zigzag

INDISCERNIBLE, adjective camouflaged, concealed, delitescent, disguised, evanescent, hidden, impalpable, imperceptible, inconspicuous, indistinguishable, invisible, screened, unapparent, unbeholdable, undiscoverable, unnoticeable, unperceivable, unrecognizable, unregarded, unseeable, veiled

INDISCRETION, noun blunder, carelessness, error, ill judgment, impoliticness, imprudence, *impudentia,* incaution, incautiousness, incircumspection, injudiciousness, lack of circumspection, lack of consideration, lack of judgment, misconduct, misjudgment, misstep, mistake, offense, *os impudens,* poor judgment, rashness, recklessness, slip, tactlessness, thoughtlessness, uncircumspection, unwariness, unwiseness

INDISCRIMINATE, adjective blanket, broad, comprehensive, designless, haphazard, immethodical, not choosy, not selective, orderless, promiscuous, *promiscuus,* random, systemless, unaimed, uncritical, undifferentiating, undirected, unmethodical, unorganized, unparticular, unspecific, unsystematic

INDISPENSABLE, adjective basic, called for, cardinal, central, compulsory, critical, crucial, dictated, essential, exigent, fundamental, high-priority, imperative, important, imposed, integral, irreplaceable, key, main, major, mandatory, *necessarius,* necessary, necessitated, needed, obligatory, of importance, pivotal, pressing, primary, required, requisite, significant, unavoidable, urgent, vital, wanted
ASSOCIATED CONCEPTS: indispensable evidence, indispensable parties

INDISTINCT, adjective ambiguous, blurred, blurry, cryptic, delitescent, dim, dusky, enigmatic, enigmatical, faded, faint, filmy, foggy, half-seen, hazy, ill-defined, illegible, imperceptible, inaudible, incomprehensible, indistinguishable, lacking clarity, lacking precision, misty, muffled, mysterious, nebulous, nubilous, *obscurus,* out of focus, *parum clarus, perplexus,* smoky, unclear, undecipherable, undefined, unintelligible, unplain, unrecognizable, vague, weak

INDISTINCTNESS, noun blur, blurriness, delitescence, delitescency, dimness, dullness, faintness, filminess, fog, fogginess, fuzziness, gloom, grayness, haziness, imperceptibility, inaudibility, indefiniteness, indistinguishability, mistiness, murkiness, mysteriousness, nebulosity, obscuration, obscurity, opacity, paleness, poor visiblity, shadow, shadowiness, smokiness, unclearness, unplainness, vagueness

INDIVIDUAL, adjective detached, deviating, different, differentiated, discrete, disjoined, disjunct, distinct, distinctive, distinguishable, exceptional, extracted, extraordinary, independent, individualized, isolated, nonconforming, nonuniform, particular, *proprius,* rare, separate, separated, single, singular, *singularis,* sole, solitary, special, unallied, unannexed, unassimilated, unassociated, unattached, unclassifiable, uncommon, unconnected, unconventional, unimitated, unique, unjoined, unrelated, unusual
ASSOCIATED CONCEPTS: individual capacity, individual causes of action, individual damages, individual debts, individual liability

INDIVIDUAL, noun autonomous being, being, body, character, distinct indivisible entity, human being, individuality, integer, monad, monas, one, organism, particular one, party, person, person full of character, personage, personality
ASSOCIATED CONCEPTS: individual capacity, individual liability, individual property, individual rights

INDIVISIBLE, adjective close, impartible, incapable of being divided, incapable of being separated, indiscerptible, *individuus,* inseparable, inseverable, nondivisible, one, tenacious, unbreakable, undividable, united, unsunderable

ASSOCIATED CONCEPTS: indivisible contract, indivisible injury, indivisible ownership of property

INDOLENT, *adjective* apathetic, cunctative, *deses,* dilatory, idle, *ignavus,* inactive, indifferent, indisposed to action, *iners,* lackadaisical, lacking vigor, laggard, languid, lax, lazy, leaden, lethargic, listless, loafing, motionless, negligent, otiose, passive, phlegmatic, procrastinative, shiftless, slack, slothful, sluggish, stagnant, supine, torpid, unenterprising

INDOMITABLE, *adjective* bold, brave, courageous, dauntless, defiant, determined, doughty, energetic, fearless, firm, forceful, forcible, formidable, hardy, impregnable, incapable of being subdued, indefatigable, indocile, *indomitus,* inextinguishable, insuperable, insurmountable, intractable, *invictus,* invincible, irrepressible, irresistible, masterful, omnipotent, overpowering, overwhelming, persevering, plucky, potent, powerful, puissant, quenchless, recalcitrant, redoubtable, refractory, resisting, resistless, resolute, resolved, solid, sound, stable, stalwart, stanch, stiff, stout, strong, stubborn, tough, unbeatable, unconquerable, undaunted, unflinching, ungovernable, unmanageable, unquenchable, unruly, unshrinking, unsubduable, unsubmissive, unwavering, unyielding, valiant, vigorous

INDORSE, *verb* accredit, acquiesce in, advocate, affirm, allow, assent to, assist, authenticate, authorize, certify, commend, concur in, confirm, confirm officially, consent to, *consignare,* cosign, countenance, countersign, encourage, guarantee, initial, inscribe one's signature, lend one's name to, make valid, *praestare,* ratify, recommend, sanction, second, sign, sign one's name on, stand by, subscribe to, support, sustain, undersign, underwrite, uphold, validate, vouch for
ASSOCIATED CONCEPTS: indorse a check, indorse a note, indorse a warrant, indorse an instrument

INDORSEMENT, *noun* acceptance, accord, acquiescence, *adfirmatio,* affirmance, agreement, approbation, approval, assent, authorization, backing, certification, championship, compliance, *comprobatio,* concurrence, *confirmatio,* confirmation, consent, encouragement, esteem, favor, liking, partisanship, permission, ratification, sanction, sponsorship, stamp of approval, support, warrant
ASSOCIATED CONCEPTS: conditional indorsement, indorsement for collection, indorsement in blank, indorsement in due course, indorsement of an instrument, indorsement without recourse, subsequent indorsement

INDUBIOUS, *adjective* absolute, ascertained, assured, attested, certain, confident, convinced, definite, demonstrable, demonstrated, doubtless, factual, foolproof, guaranteed, incontestable, irrefutable, official, past dispute, positive, safe, satisfied, sure, tested, tried, uncontested, undeniable, undoubtful, unequivocal, unshakable, verifiable, without doubt, without question

INDUCE, *verb* actuate, *adducere,* be responsible, bring about, bring on, bring to pass, call forth, cause, conduce, convince, create, effect, effectuate, exercise influence over, generate, hasten, *impellere,* incite, *inducere,* influence, instigate, kindle, lead one to, motivate, obtain, originate, persuade, precipitate, prevail upon, produce, prompt, stimulate, sway, talk into
ASSOCIATED CONCEPTS: fraud in inducement, inducing a breach of contract, inducing perjury, inducing trade, libel, material inducement, undue influence

INDUCEMENT, *noun* allurement, attraction, blandishment, *causa,* cause, consideration, drive, encouragement, enticement, exhortation, fillip, goad, *incitamentum,* incitation, incitement, influence, *inlecebra,* inspiration, instigation, persuasion, persuasiveness, pressure, prompting, provocation, provocative, stimulant, stimulater, stimulation, stimulative, stimulus, urging
ASSOCIATED CONCEPTS: fraud in the inducement, inducement to purchase, material inducement

INDUCT, *verb* admit, appoint, assign, bring in, call up, commission, conscript, delegate, employ, engage, give entrance to, impress, *inaugurare,* inaugurate, initiate, install, instate, introduce, introduce into office, invest, license, name, nominate, ordain, place in office, post, prepare, recruit, start up, usher in

INDULGENCE, *noun* accordance, acquiescence, allowance, approval, benevolence, *benignitas,* clearance, clemency, compassion, favor, forgiveness, generosity, generousness, grant, gratification, gratification of desire, humoring, inabstinence, *indulgentia,* leave, lenience, leniency, lenity, license, magnanimity, obligingness, pampering, pardon, patience, permission, quarter, sanction, sufferance, tolerance, toleration, *venia,* vouchsafement

INDUSTRIAL, *adjective* automated, commercial, engaged in business, engaged in traffic, factory-made, industrialized, machine-made, manufactural, manufactured, manufactured for sale, mass produced, mechanical, mechanized, mercantile, relating to traffic, standardized, technical, technological
ASSOCIATED CONCEPTS: industrial accident, industrial board, industrial commission, industrial disease, industrial dispute, industrial insurance, industrial uses

INDUSTRIOUS, *adjective* active, *adsiduus,* aggressive, ardent, assiduous, busily engaged, busy, dedicated, determined, devoted, diligent, eager, earnest, energetic, enthusiastic, hard working, indefatigable, *industrius,* intent, laborious, never idle, operose, painstaking, persevering, persistent, purposeful, sedulous, *sedulus,* sleepless, steadfast, steady, studious, tenacious, thorough, tireless, unceasing, undeviating, unfaltering, unflagging, unrelaxing, unremitting, unsleeping, unswerving, untiring, unwavering, unyielding, zealous

INDUSTRY *(Activity),* *noun* *adsiduitas,* alacrity, application, ardor, assiduity, assiduousness, attention, bustle, busyness, constancy, determination, devotedness, devotion, diligence, *diligentia,* drive, dynamism, eagerness, earnestness, effort, employment, endeavor, endurance, energy, enterprise, enthusiasm, exertion, hard work, indefatigability, *industria,* intentness, labor, laboriousness, occupation, perseverance, persistence, pursuance, pursuit, sedulity, sedulousness, steadfastness, stir, strenuousness, tenacity, toil, vigor, vim, work, zeal, zealousness

INDUSTRY *(Business),* *noun* enterprise, establishment, manufacture, mercantile business, metier, production, profession, pursuit, trade, undertaking, work
ASSOCIATED CONCEPTS: engage in industry, industry-wide contract

INEBRIATION, *noun* alcoholism, bacchanalianism, bibulosity, bibulousness, dipsomania, drunkenness, *ebrietas,* inebriety, influence of liquor, insobriety, intemperance, intoxication, potation
ASSOCIATED CONCEPTS: driving while intoxicated, drunken driving, under the influence of alcohol

INEFFABLE, *adjective* amazing, astounding, awe-inspiring, awesome, beyond expression, fearful, great, impossible to describe, impossible to express, incommunicable, inconceivable, *incredibilis,* indefinable, indescribable, inexpressible, *infandus,* marvelous, miraculous, mysterious, nameless, overwhelming, sacred, staggering, strange, unable to be expressed, unable to be spoken, undefinable, unheard, unimaginable, unmentionable, unnamable, unpronounceable, unspeakable, untranslatable, unutterable

INEFFECTIVE, *adjective* abortive, barren, disabled, effete, emasculated, feckless, feeble, figurehead, fruitless, futile, gainless, good for nothing, impotent, inadequate, incompetent, indecisive, ineffectual, inefficacious, inept, inoperative, insufficient, inutile, *inutilis,* invalid, *invalidus,* lame, neutralized, nugatory, null, powerless, profitless, sterile, unauthoritative, unavailing, unfruitful, uninfluential, unoperative, unproductive, unprofitable, unserviceable, unsuccessful, useless, vain, void, weak, withered, without effect, without weight, worthless
ASSOCIATED CONCEPTS: ineffective restriction

INEFFECTUAL, *adjective* abortive, barren, effete, emasculated, feckless, feeble, figurehead, fruitless, futile, gainless, good for nothing, idle, impotent, inadequate, incompetent, indecisive, ineffective, inefficacious, inept, inoperative, insufficient, inutile, *inutilis,* invalid, *invalidus,* lame, neutralized, nugatory, null, powerless, profitless, sterile, unauthoritative, unavailing, unempowered, unfruitful, uninfluential, unoperative, unproductive, unprofitable, unserviceable, unsuccessful, useless, vain, void, weak, withered, without effect, without weight, worthless

INEFFICACY, *noun* disability, disablement, failure, feebleness, forcelessness, helplessness, impotence, inability, inadequacy, incapability, incapacitation, incapacity, incompetence, incompetency, ineffectiveness, ineffectuality, ineffectualness, inefficaciousness, inefficiency, insufficiency, lack of power, lack of strength, powerlessness, unfruitfulness, unskillfulness, weakness

INELEGANT, *adjective* awkward, base, boorish, churlish, cloddish, coarse, common, crass, crude, earthy, graceless, gross, homely, homespun, ill-bred, ill-mannered, improper, in bad taste, indecorous, indelicate, *inelegans, inurbanus, invenustus,* lacking elegance, lacking good taste, lacking grace, lacking refinement, low, offensive, ribald, rough, rude, rustic, tasteless, uncourtly, uncouth, uncultivated, uncultured, undignified, ungainly, ungenteel, ungraceful, unkempt, unmannerly, unpolished, unrefined, unseemly, untasteful, vulgar, without taste

INELIGIBLE, *adjective* cast out, disallowed, disapproved, disentitled, disqualified, eliminated, excluded, expelled, improper, inadmissible, inappropriate, inapt, *inopportunus,* kept out, not considered, not eligible, objectionable, out of the question, outcast, rejected, unacceptable, unadapted, unchosen, undesirable, unentitled, unequipped, unfit, unfitted, unfitting, unqualified, unsuitable, unsuited, unwanted
ASSOCIATED CONCEPTS: disability, ineligible to run for political office

INEPT *(Inappropriate),* *adjective* absurd, at variance, bizarre, clashing, discordant, discrepant, disproportionate, dissonant, ill-adapted, ill-advised, ill-suited, ill-timed, illogical, impolitic, improper, imprudent, inaccordant, inadmissible, inadvisable, inapplicable, inapposite, inapt, incompatible, incongruent, incongruous, inconsistent, indecorous, inexpedient, infelicitous, inharmonious, injudicious, inopportune, insagacious, irreconcilable, jarring, ludicrous, malapropos, mismatched, misplaced, objectionable, out of character, out of keeping, out of place, out of proportion, outrageous, preposterous, ridiculous, silly, unapt, unbecoming, unbefitting, uncongenial, unconsonant, undesirable, undue, unfit, unfitting, unmeet, unqualified, unseasonable, unseemly, unsuitable, unsuited, untimely, untoward, unwise

INEPT *(Incompetent),* *adjective* awkward, blundering, bungling, clumsy, disqualified, foolish, ignorant, ill-qualified, impotent, inadept, inadequate, inapt, incapable, incompetent, ineffective, ineffectual, inefficacious, inefficient, *ineptus,* inexpert, lacking dexterity, lacking dexterousness, lacking skill, maladroit, powerless, puerile, raw, unable, unadroit, unapt, unclever, undeft, unfacile, ungainly, unhandy, unproductive, unproficient, unqualified, unskillful, useless
ASSOCIATED CONCEPTS: incompetency of counsel, incompetent to contract, insanity, under the age of majority

INEQUALITY, *noun* asymmetry, bias, contrast, deviation, difference, disaccord, disagreement, discrepance, discrepancy, disparity, disproportion, disproportionateness, dissimilarity, dissimilitude, *dissimilitudo,* dissonance, distinction, divergence, diversity, imbalance, imparity, *inaequalitas,* incompatibility, incongruity, incongruousness, inconsistency, inconsonance, injustice, irregularity, lack of equality, lack of symmetry, nonconformity, nonuniformity, partiality, prejudice, unbalance, unconformity, unevenness, unfairness, unlikeness, ununiformity, variance, variation

INEQUITABLE, *adjective* discriminatory, favoring, one sided, partial, partisan, prejudiced, unbalanced, uneven, unfair, unjust, weighted

INEQUITY, *noun* bias, biased judgment, bigotry, discrimination, disproportion, favor, favoritism, foregone conclusion, foul play, inequitableness, injustice, intolerance, leaning, miscarriage of justice, one-sidedness, partiality, partisanism, partisanship, preapprehension, preconceived idea, preconceived notion, preconception, predilection, preference, preferential treatment, prejudgment, prejudice, prenotion, prepossession, presentiment, presumption, undetachment, undispassionateness, undueness, unfairness, unjust decision, unjustness

INERTIA, *noun* apathy, dormancy, dullness, firmness, immobility, immobilization, immovability, inability to act, inaction, inactivity, indecision, indisposition to move, indolence, inertness, inexcitability, irresolution, lack of activity, lack of motion, lack of movement, languor, lassitude, laziness, lethargy, lifelessness, motionlessness, negligence, oscitancy, paralysis, passiveness, passivity, quiescence, resistance to change, rest, sloth, sluggishness, stagnation, stupor, supineness, torpor, vegetation, want of activity, weariness

INESTIMABLE, adjective above all price, above all value, above appraisal, beyond price, choice, costly, immeasurable, immensurable, *inaestimabilis*, incalculable, infinite, inimitable, invaluable, irreplaceable, matchless, measureless, peerless, precious, priceless, rare, select, unequalled, unique, unmatched, unparalleled, unsurpassable, valuable, without equal, without price

INEVITABLE, adjective about to happen, approaching, assured, at hand, brewing, certain, decided, definite, destined, determined, fated, fixed, following, foreordained, forthcoming, guaranteed, imminent, impending, in store, in the offing, ineluctable, ineludible, inescapable, inevasible, *inevitabilis*, looming, near, *necessarius*, next, ordained, predestined, preordained, sure, sure to happen, to come, unalterable, unavoidable, unchangeable, unfailing, unpreventable, unquestionable
ASSOCIATED CONCEPTS: inevitable accident, inevitable casualty, inevitable occurrence

INEXACT, adjective ambiguous, approximate, approximative, broad, careless, crude, erroneous, estimated, faulty, flawed, general, guessed, *haud accuratus*, hazy, imperfect, imprecise, inaccurate, incorrect, loose, miscalculated, misfigured, misinterpreted, misreported, misstated, mistranslated, more or less, nearly accurate, nearly correct, rough, surmised, unclear, unmeticulous, unrevised, unscientific, unspecified, vague, without precision

INEXCUSABLE, adjective atrocious, blameworthy, brutal, condemnable, cruel, disgraceful, flagitious, heinous, immoral, incapable of being justified, incorrigible, indefensible, inexpiable, irremissible, monstrous, objectionable, outrageous, *quod nihil excusationis habet*, reprehensible, reprobate, shameful, unallowable, unatonable, unforgivable, unjustifiable, unpardonable, unprincipled, unreasonable, unwarrantable, unwarranted, vicious, without defense, without excuse
ASSOCIATED CONCEPTS: inexcusable conduct, inexcusable delay, inexcusable neglect

INEXORABLE, adjective adamant, convinced, decided, determined, dogged, firm, headstrong, immovable, immutable, implacable, indomitable, *inexorabilis*, inflexible, intractable, merciless, obdurate, obstinate, opinionated, opinionative, persevering, persistent, persisting, pertinacious, pitiless, positive, relentless, resistant, resolute, resolved, set, severe, steadfast, steady, sternly just, strong-minded, strong-willed, stubborn, tenacious, unalterable, unbending, unchanging, uncompassionate, uncompromising, uncontrollable, unfaltering, unimpressible, unmanageable, unmerciful, unmovable, unmoved by entreaties, unpersuadable, unrelenting, unshaken, unwavering, unyielding, willful

INEXPEDIENCE, noun disadvantage, disadvantageousness, folly, foolishness, imprudence, inadvisability, inappropriateness, inexpediency, infelicity, injudiciousness, inopportuneness, *inutilitas*, ludicrous-

ness, rashness, senselessness, undesirability, undesirableness, unfitness, unfittingness, unprofitability, unsensibleness, unsoundness, unsuitability, unthoughtfulness, untimeliness, unwiseness

INEXPERIENCED, adjective amateur, artless, beardless, callow, green, *ignarus*, ignorant, ill-qualified, immature, *imperitus*, inapt, inept, inexpert, innocent, lacking experience, lacking proficiency, lacking skill, naive, new, poorly qualified, raw, *rudis*, sophomoric, unaccustomed, unacquainted, unadapted, unbusinesslike, unconversant, undeveloped, undisciplined, undrilled, unfamiliar, unfledged, unhabituated, uninformed, uninitiated, unlicensed, unpracticed, unqualified, unripe, unschooled, unseasoned, unskilled, unsophisticated, untrained, untried, untutored, unused, unversed, unworldly, verdant, without experience, without knowledge, young, youthful

INEXPIABLE, adjective base, blameworthy, censurable, condemnable, disgraceful, evil, facinorous, flagitious, heinous, indefensible, inexcusable, *inexplicabilis*, infamous, nefarious, reprehensible, scandalous, shameful, unallowable, unatonable, unforgivable, unjustifiable, unpardonable, unreasonable, vicious, villainous, virtueless, wicked, without defense, without excuse

INEXPLICABLE, adjective abstruse, acroamatic, acroamatical, acroatic, baffling, concealed, enigmatic, enigmatical, esoteric, hard to understand, hidden, impenetrable, inapprehensible, incapable of being explained, incomprehensible, indefinable, *inexplicabilis*, inscrutable, insoluble, insolvable, mysterious, mystic, mystical, obscure, occult, paradoxical, puzzling, recondite, shrouded in mystery, strange, unaccountable, undecipherable, undiscoverable, unexplainable, unfamiliar, unintelligible, unknowable, unknown, unrecognizable

INEXPRESSIVE, adjective apathetic, blank, characterless, cold, deadpan, devoid of expression, dim, dull, empty, enigmatic, enigmatical, expressionless, hardened, impassive, impenetrable, imperturbable, impervious, incomprehensible, inexplicable, inscrutable, lackluster, listless, meaningless, nebulous, nonsensical, obtuse, poker-faced, puzzling, senseless, spiritless, stupid, trite, unaffected, unanimated, undecipherable, unemotional, unfathomable, unintelligible, unmoved, vacant, vacuous, vague, void

INEXPUGNABLE, adjective defensible, formidable, hardy, immune, impenetrable, imperdible, impregnable, indomitable, *inexpugnabilis*, inextinguishable, insuperable, insurmountable, invincible, inviolable, invulnerable, irresistible, mighty, potent, powerful, protected, puissant, redoubtable, resistless, safe, secure, secure from capture, strong, sturdy, tenable, unassailable, unattackable, unbeatable, unbreakable, unchallengeable, unconquerable, unsubduable, unyielding

INEXTRICABLE, adjective adhering, attached, bound, cohesive, combined, complex, complicated, compounded, confused, conjunct, connected, convoluted, embrangled, entangled, fast, fixed, immovable, impacted, indissoluble, indivisible, *inexplicabilis, inextricabilis*, inseparable, inseverable, insoluble, intricate, involute, involuted, involved, irreducible, irremovable, jammed, joined, knotted, labyrinthine, matted, mazy, mixed, raveled, snarled, stuck, tangled, tangly, tied, turbid, twisted, wedged

INFALLIBLE, adjective   assured, *certus,* continuing, defectless, dependable, enduring, errorless, everlasting, exhaustless, faithful, faultless, flawless, foolproof, free from imperfection, free from mistake, *haud dubius,* imperishable, incapable of error, incontestable, incontrovertible, indefatigable, indefectible, indefective, indomitable, inerrable, inerrant, inexhaustible, irrefragable, irreproachable, lasting, never-failing, perfect, reliable, secure, stable, stainless, stanch, staying, steady, sure, tenacious, trustworthy, trusty, unassailable, unbeatable, unchanged, unchanging, unconquerable, undestroyable, undying, unerring, unfading, unfailing, unfaltering, unflagging, unimpeachable, unquestionable, unquestioned, unspotted, unstoppable, unsurpassed, untainted, unwavering, unyielding, without blemish

INFAMY, noun   abasement, aspersion, bad name, bad reputation, baseness, blot, brand, contempt, defamation, degradation, derision, detestableness, disapprobation, disapproval, discredit, disesteem, disfavor, disgrace, dishonor, disrepute, disrespect, evil fame, humiliation, ignobility, *ignominia,* ignominiousness, ignominy, ill repute, *infamia,* infamousness, ingloriousness, loss of reputation, notoriety, obloquy, odium, opprobrium, *probrum,* public reproach, reproach, scandal, scorn, shame, stain, stigma, taint, tarnish
ASSOCIATED CONCEPTS: infamous acts, infamous crime, infamous offense, infamous punishment, infamy from conviction of a crime
FOREIGN PHRASES: *Quae sunt minoris culpae sunt majoris infamiae.* Those things which are less culpable may be more infamous.

INFANT, noun   baby, child, *infans,* innocent, juvenile, little one, minor, nursling, one who has not come of age, one who has not reached his majority, person under the age of majority, person under 18 years old, person who is not of full age, toddler, tot, young person, youngster, youth
ASSOCIATED CONCEPTS: adoption, after-born child, age of minority, best interests of the child, child abuse, child labor, child support, custody, delinquent child, emancipation, filiation proceeding, foster child, guardian, guardian ad litem, illegitimate children, incompetency to contract, infanticide, juvenile delinquency, neglected child, pretermitted child, ratification of an infant's contract, visitation
FOREIGN PHRASES: *In omnibus poenalibus judiciis, et aetatl et imprudentiae succurritur.* In all penal judgments, allowance is made for youth and lack of prudence. *Infans non multum a furioso distat.* An infant does not differ much from an insane person. *In judiciis, minori aetati succurritur.* In judicial proceedings, infancy is aided. *Qui in utero est pro jam nato habetur, quoties de ejus commodo quaeritur.* He who is in the womb is regarded as already born, whenever a question arises for his benefit. *Pupillus pati posse non intelligitur.* An infant is not considered able to do an act to his own prejudice.

INFEASIBLE, adjective   absurd, impossible, impracticable, inaccessible, inconceivable, out of reach, out of the question, unachievable, unattainable, unimaginable, unlikely, unobtainable, unrealistic, unreasonable, unthinkable, unworkable, visionary

INFECT, verb   adulterate, befoul, besmirch, blight, canker, cause illness, *contaminare,* contaminate, corrupt, debase, defile, dirty, empoison, envenom, foul, harm, impair, make ill, make impure, pervert, poison, pollute, putrefy, render unclean, smirch, soil, spoil, stain, sully, taint, tarnish, transmit disease, vitiate, *vitiis inficere*

INFER, verb   conclude, conclude from evidence, *concludere,* conjecture, *conligere,* consider probable, construe, deduce, derive, derive by reasoning, draw a conclusion, draw an inference, extract, gather, glean, guess, hint, imply, indicate, insinuate, intimate, judge from premises, posit, postulate, presume, reach a conclusion, reason, reckon, suppose, surmise, suspect, understand
ASSOCIATED CONCEPTS: infer guilt from the evidence

INFERENCE, noun   allusion, assumption, *conclusio,* conclusion, *coniectura,* conjecture, deduction, guess, guesswork, hint, hypothesis, illation, implication, impression, inkling, judgment, observation, postulate, postulation, postulatum, premise, presupposal, presupposition, speculation, supposal, supposition, surmise, suspicion, theorem, theory, thesis, understanding
ASSOCIATED CONCEPTS: evidentiary inference, favorable inference, legal inference, legitimate inference, presumption
FOREIGN PHRASES: *Expressa nocent, non expressa non nocent.* Things expressed may be prejudicial; that which is not expressed will not.

INFERIOR *(Lower in position),* **adjective**   accessory, auxiliary, *deterior,* governed by, in the power of, insignificant, junior, less powerful, lesser, lower, lower in authority, lower in rank, lower in the scale, lowly, menial, minor, of less importance, puisne, reduced, secondary, subaltern, subject, subjugated to, subordinate, subservient, subsidiary, tributary, under, unimportant
ASSOCIATED CONCEPTS: inferior courts

INFERIOR *(Lower in quality),* **adjective**   adulterated, badly made, base, below par, blemished, cheap, contemptible, crude, damaged, defective, deficient, displeasing, faulty, flimsy, imperfect, inadequate, indifferent, inelegant, insipid, insufficient, less valuable, lesser, low-grade, malformed, mediocre, paltry, pedestrian, poor, second-rate, shabby, shoddy, trashy, unacceptable, undesirable, unsatisfactory
ASSOCIATED CONCEPTS: inferior bargaining position, inferior products, inferior quality

INFIDELITY, noun   abandonment of allegiance, apostasy, bad faith, betrayal, betrayal of oath, betrayal of trust, breach of faith, breach of promise, breach of trust, broken faith, broken word, cuckoldry, deceitfulness, defection, desertion, disaffection, dishonor, disloyalty, double-dealing, dutilessness, evasion of duty, faithlessness, falseheartedness, falsity, fickleness, inconstancy, *infidelitas,* lack of faith, lack of loyalty, mutiny, *perfidia,* perfidiousness, perfidy, rebellion, recreancy, revolt, sedition, seditiousness, traitorousness, treachery, treason, undutifulness, unfaithfulness, violation of oath
ASSOCIATED CONCEPTS: adultery

INFINITE, adjective   boundless, ceaseless, countless, endless, enduring, eternal, everlasting, exhaustless, illimitable, immeasurable, imperishable, incalculable, indestructible, inexhaustible, *infinitus,* innumerable, interminable, lasting, limitless, measureless, numberless, perdurable, permanent, perpetual, persistent, sempiternal, termless, timeless, unbounded, unceasing, undying, unending, unlimited, unmeasured, unnumbered, without end, without limit, without measure, without number

INFLATE, *verb* aggrandize, amplify, balloon, bloat, blow up, broaden, cause to bulge, dilate, distend, enlarge, escalate, exaggerate, expand, extend, fatten, fill out, fill with air, grow, increase, increase dimensions, *inflare,* magnify, make greater, make larger, make swollen, make tumid, pad, puff up, pump up, raise above the proper value, rise, spread, stretch, sufflate, surge, swell, upsurge, wax

INFLATED *(Bombastic),* **adjective** altiloquent, altisonant, artificial, declamatory, flatulent, fustian, grandiloquent, high-flown, high-sounding, *inflatus,* magniloquent, mouthy, oratorical, ostentatious, overblown, pedantic, pompous, pretentious, rhetorical, stilted, tumid, *tumidus,* turgid, vainglorious, verbose

INFLATED *(Enlarged),* **adjective** amplified, augmented, ballooned, bloated, blown up, dilated, distended, enlarged by swelling, expanded, extended, filled, *inflatus,* puffed, puffed up, puffy, spread, stretched, swelled, swollen, tumid, *tumidus,* turgid, *turgidus*

INFLATED *(Overestimated),* **adjective** aggrandized, amplified, embellished, enlarged, exaggerated, exaggerative, excessive, heightened, hyperbolic, magnified, miscalculated, overdrawn, overpraised, overpriced, overprized, overrated, overstated, overstressed, overvalued

INFLATED *(Vain),* **adjective** arrogant, boastful, braggart, bumptious, conceited, condescending, contemptuous, disdainful, egocentric, egoistic, egoistical, egotistic, egotistical, grandiose, haughty, immodest, impressed with oneself, lordly, overbearing, overproud, overweening, patronizing, pleased with oneself, pompous, pretentious, prideful, proud, scornful, self-applauding, self-centered, self-glorifying, self-important, self-lauding, self-satisfied, showy, strutting, superior, swaggering, vaporing, vauntful

INFLATION *(Decrease in value of currency),* **noun** boost in prices, currency devaluation, decrease in purchasing power, high prices, hike in prices, jump in prices, price increase, substantial rise of prices, undue expansion of currency, upturn in prices

INFLATION *(Increase),* **noun** aggrandizement, amplification, bloatedness, blowing up, dilation, distension, elevation, enlargement, escalation, exaggeration, expansion, extension, growth, increase, *inflatio,* rise, spread, sufflation, surge, swell, swelling, turgescence, turgidity, turgidness, upsurge, waxing
ASSOCIATED CONCEPTS: inflation of damages, inflation of value

INFLECTION, *noun* accent, accentuation, cadence, emphasis, expression, intonation, modulation, pitch, stress, tone, voice change
ASSOCIATED CONCEPTS: demeanor of a witness, polygraph test

INFLEXIBLE, *adjective* adamant, cantankerous, changeless, contumacious, decided, determined, dogged, firm, fixed, hard, hardened, headstrong, immobile, immovable, immutable, impersuadible, impersuasible, indocile, indomitable, inelastic, inexorable, intractable, intransigent, invariable, mulish, nonelastic, obdurate, obstinate, *obstinatus,* opinionated, opinionative, persevering, pertinacious, *pertinax,* refractory, relentless, resolute, resolved, rigid, *rigidus,* rigorous, solid, steadfast, stiff, strict, stringent, strong-willed, stubborn, tenacious, unalterable, unamenable, unbending, unchangeable, uncompromising, unmalleable, unmanageable, unmovable, unpliable, unpliant, unrelenting, unswayable, unyielding, willful
ASSOCIATED CONCEPTS: inflexible bargaining position

INFLICT, *verb* administer a penalty, administer punishment, agitate, agonize, apply, beset, bring about, bring upon, burden, cause, cause to suffer, coerce, commit, deal, disquiet, distress, enforce, force, force upon, give pain, harass, harm, hurt, *imponere,* impose, impose punishment, *inferre, infligere,* injure, maltreat, mete out, perform, produce injury, punish, put into force, strike, torment, torture, wound, wreak
ASSOCIATED CONCEPTS: inflict pain and suffering, inflict punishment

INFLICTION, *noun* abuse, application, blow, castigation, commission, commitment, execution, force, harassment, imposition, *incommodum,* injury, maltreatment, misfortune, oppression, ordeal, penalty, performance, perpetration, persecution, plague, punishment, torment, torture, trial, violence, wound

INFLOW, *noun* approach, arrival, coming in, entrance, entry, immigration, importation, incoming, incursion, induction, infiltration, influx, ingoing, ingress, ingression, initiation, inpour, inpouring, inroad, inrush, insertion, introduction, introgression, inundation, invasion, irruption, penetration, progress

INFLUENCE, *noun* ascendance, ascendancy, authority, command, consequence, control, dominance, domination, dominion, effect, effectiveness, effectuality, eminence, encouragement, forcefulness, governance, hegemony, hold, importance, incitation, incitement, inspiration, instigation, leadership, leverage, masterfulness, mastery, might, mightiness, omnipotence, paramountcy, *pondus,* potency, *potentia,* power, powerfulness, predominance, predominancy, prepollence, prepollency, prepotency, prestige, provocation, puissance, reign, rule, sovereignty, superiority, supremacy, sway, urging, *vis,* weight
ASSOCIATED CONCEPTS: coercion controlling influence, improper influence, influence peddling, political influence, undue influence

INFLUENCE, *verb* actuate, arouse, brainwash, bring pressure to bear, cajole, carry weight, convince, direct, form, guide, impel, *impellere,* impress, incite, induce, inspire, inveigle, lead, militate, modify, mold, motivate, move, *movere,* persuade, prejudice, pressure, prevail upon, prompt, pull strings, shape, stimulate, sway, talk into, urge, work upon
ASSOCIATED CONCEPTS: bribery, control, duress, improper influence, under the influence of alcohol, undue influence, wrong influence

INFLUENTIAL, adjective authoritative, cogent, commanding, consequential, controlling, convincing, determinative, distinguished, dominant, domineering, effective, effectual, efficacious, eminent, empowered, esteemed, foremost, governing, *gravis,* hegemonic, hegemonical, honored, illustrious, imperious, important, impressive, leading, mighty, multipotent, notable, noteworthy, omnipotent, paramount, *potens,* potent, powerful, predominant, preeminent, prepollent, preponderant, prepotent, prevailing, prevalent, prominent, puissant, recognized, reigning, renowned, reputable, respectable, respected, ruling, strong, supreme, well-known, well-recognized, well-regarded, worthy of notice

INFORM (Betray), verb accuse, announce, bear witness against, betray the secret, break faith, break trust, charge, communicate, confess, declare, denounce, disclose, disclose intentionally, disclose secrets, divulge, expose, give over to the foe, *hominis nomen deferre,* impart, impeach, implicate, incriminate, inculpate, lay bare, lay open, make known, report against, reveal, tell secrets, testify against, uncover, unmask, violate a confidence, violate the confidence of

INFORM (Notify), verb acquaint, advertise, advise, announce, annunciate, apprise, blazon, brief, carry tales, communicate, confide, describe, detail, disabuse, disclose, divulge, *docere,* educate, enlighten, explain, familiarize, give a report, give an account, give notice, give out information, give the facts, give tidings, herald, impart, instruct, keep posted, let know, level with, make known, mention, narrate, notify, *nuntiare,* orient, outline, point out, post, present information, proclaim, promulgate, publish, recite, recount, relate, report, reveal, send word, set right, set straight, signify, state, tattle, teach, tell, testify, tip, tout, trumpet, undeceive, warn

INFORMAL, adjective casual, common, congenial, cursory, extemporaneous, extempore, familiar, natural, nonchalant, offhand, ordinary, perfunctory, relaxed, spontaneous, unceremonial, unceremonious, unconventional, uncustomary, unmethodical, unofficial, unorthodox, unrestrained, unstereotyped, unstrict, without ceremony, without formality
ASSOCIATED CONCEPTS: informal charges, informal contract, informal hearing, informal proceeding

INFORMALITY, noun absence of ceremony, affability, casualness, ease, easiness, easygoingness, extemporaneousness, familiarity, fellowship, flexibility, freedom, freedom from affectation, friendliness, inexactitude, inexactness, informalness, ingenuousness, inobservance, irregularity, latitude, laxity, liberty, license, lightness, looseness, naturalness, noncompliance, nonconformity, nonobservance, offhandedness, plainness, relaxation, simplicity, slackness, unaffectedness, unassumingness, unceremoniousness, unconstraint, unconventionality, unorthodoxy, unrigorousness, want of formality

INFORMANT, noun accuser, adviser, announcer, annunciator, appriser, *auctor,* communicant, communicator, delator, dispatcher, divulger, enlightener, envoy, harbinger, herald, information giver, informer, intelligencer, narrator, notifier, proclaimer, relator, reporter, source, spy, stool pigeon, talebearer, tipper, tipster, witness

ASSOCIATED CONCEPTS: paid informant, reliable informants, undercover informant

INFORMATION (Charge), noun accusal, accusation, allegation, charge, criminal accusal, formal accusation, formal averment, formal charge, formal criminal charge, formal criminal complaint, official criminal charge, prosecutorial complaint, written accusation
ASSOCIATED CONCEPTS: felony information, misdemeanor information

INFORMATION (Facts), noun communique, data, exact data, figures, news, notice, notification, specifics, statistics

INFORMATION (Knowledge), noun acquired facts, acquired knowledge, available facts, book learning, collected writings, communication, communique, compilations, comprehension, education, enlightenment, erudition, experience, familiarity, grasp, intelligence, intelligent grip, knowledge, knowledge of facts, known facts, learning, lore, mental grasp, revelation, understanding, wisdom
ASSOCIATED CONCEPTS: duty to ascertain information, privileged information, upon information and belief, withholding information
FOREIGN PHRASES: *Nemo tenetur informare qui nescit, sed quisquis scire quod informat.* No one who is ignorant of a thing is bound to give information about it, but everyone is bound to know that concerning which he gives information.

INFORMATIVE, adjective advisory, communicative, communicatory, didactic, disclosing, edifying, educational, educative, enlightening, enriching, explanatory, explicative, explicatory, explicit, expositive, expository, expressive, homiletic, homiletical, hortative, hortatory, illuminating, instructional, instructive, newsy, pedogogic, preceptive, propaedeutic, propaedeutical, revealing, scholastic

INFORMATORY, adjective acquainting, admonitory, advising, advisory, chatty, clarifying, communicative, descriptive, disclosing, doctrinal, documentary, educational, elucidatory, enlightening, explanatory, explicative, explicatory, expositive, expository, gossipy, hortative, hortatory, illuminating, informational, informative, instructive, monitory, newsy, notifying, presenting information, reporting, revealing, revelatory, teaching, telling

INFORMED (Educated), adjective accomplished, conversant with, cultured, enlightened, erudite, expert, instructed, knowledgeable, learned, lettered, literate, prepared, proficient, schooled, taught, trained, versed, well-educated, well-grounded, well-read, well-rounded, well-versed, widely read

INFORMED (Having information), adjective abreast, acquainted, advised, apprized, briefed, enlightened, familiar, familiarized, forewarned, notified, posted, primed, set straight, tipped, told, undeceived, warned
ASSOCIATED CONCEPTS: informed decision, informed opinion

INFORMER (One providing criminal information), noun accuser, *auctor,* complainant, criminal information supplier, impeacher, indicter, informant, infor-

mation supplier, one who supplies criminal information to the police, police tipper, squealer, tipster, witness against
ASSOCIATED CONCEPTS: corroboration, reliable informer

INFORMER *(A person who provides information),* **noun**   adviser, announcer, annunciator, communicant, communicator, courier, crier, *delator,* divulger, envoy, harbinger, herald, intelligencer, messenger, notifier, proclaimer, relater, reporter, source, spokesman, teller, tipper, tipster, warner

INFRACTION, noun   breach, breach of faith, breach of law, breach of orders, breach of privilege, breach of promise, breach of the peace, breach of trust, breaking, contravention, crime, default, defiance, defiance of orders, disobedience, encroachment, evasion of duty, failure, failure of duty, *immunitio,* infringement, inobservance, noncompliance, nonobservance, nonobservance of rules, offense, omission, overstepping, refusal to obey, transgression, trespass, *violatio,* violation, violation of law, violation of orders, wrong
ASSOCIATED CONCEPTS: infraction of rules, infraction of the law, traffic infraction

INFRANGIBLE, adjective   cohesive, durable, everlasting, firm, hallowed, holy, indestructible, indiscerptible, indissoluble, indissolvable, indivisible, inseparable, insoluble, inviolable, invulnerable, lasting, perdurable, resistant, sacred, sacrosanct, secure, solid, strong, unbreakable, unchangeable, united, unshakeable, unshatterable

INFREQUENT, adjective   atypical, discontinuous, erratic, exceptional, extraordinary, few, inconstant, inhabitual, intermittent, irregular, limited, occasional, outstanding, periodic, phenomenal, rare, *rarus,* scarce, seldom happening, seldom occurring, seldom seen, singular, sparse, sporadic, uncommon, uncustomary, unfrequent, unsteady, untypical, unusual

INFRINGE, verb   abuse a privilege, abuse one's rights, advance stealthily, aggress, arrogate, breach, break, break bounds, break in upon, break into, commit a breach, *frangere,* impinge, impose, infract, interfere, interlope, intrude, invade, meddle, overstep, *rumpere,* seize wrongfully, take liberties, transgress, trespass, use wrongfully, usurp, *violare,* violate, violate a contract, violate a law, violate a privilege, violate a regulation
ASSOCIATED CONCEPTS: infringe on a copyright, infringe on a trademark

INFRINGEMENT, noun   abuse of privilege, aggression, arrogation, breach, contravention, disfranchisement, disobedience, dispossession, entrance upon domain of another, force, illegality, *immunitio,* incursion, infraction, injustice, interference, intrusion, invasion, invasion of a right, misdoing, misfeasance, nonobservance, repudiation, seizure, surpassing, transgression, transcendence, transcending, trespass, trespassing, usurpation, *violatio,* violation, violation of a contract, violation of a law, violation of a privilege, violation of a regulation, violence, wrong, wrong doing, wrongfulness
ASSOCIATED CONCEPTS: copyright infringement, license infringement, patent infringement, trademark infringement

INFUSE, verb   imbrue, imbue, implant, impregnate, inculcate, *incutere, infundere,* ingrain, *inicere,* inject, insert, inspire, inspirit, instill, introduce

INFUSION, noun   imbruement, imbuement, implantation, impregnation, inculcation, infiltration, *infusio,* injection, insertion, instillation, introduction, penetration, permeation

INGENUOUS, adjective   aboveboard, *apertus,* artless, blunt, candid, childlike, devoid of dissimulation, downright, forthright, frank, free from reserve, genuine, guileless, honest, honorable, inartificial, innocent, *liber,* naive, natural, open, outspoken, plain, rustic, simple, *simplex,* sincere, spontaneous, straightforward, transparent, trustworthy, truthful, unaffected, unconstrained, undesigning, undisguised, unforced, unreserved, unrestrained, unselfconscious, unsophisticated, unstudied, unsuspicious, veracious, with simplicity, without guile

INGRAINED, adjective   confirmed, deep, deep-seated, embedded, engrafted, entrenched, essential, established, firmly established, firmly fixed, fixed, habitual, implanted, inborn, inbred, indelible, indwelling, ineffaceable, infixed, ingrown, inherent, innate, *insitus,* intrinsic, inveterate, *inveteratus,* inwrought, permanent, rooted, set, settled, thorough, well-established

INGRATITUDE, adjective   *animus ingratus,* heedlessness, inappreciation, inconsiderateness, inconsideration, insensibility, lack of appreciation, lack of consideration, lack of gratitude, respectlessness, rudeness, thanklessness, thoughtlessness, unappreciativeness, unfeelingness, ungratefulness, unthankfulness, want of consideration

INGREDIENT, noun   aspect, component, component part, constituent, constituent part, content, element, essential part, factor, feature, fragment, fundamental part, integral part, member, *membrum, pars,* part, section, sector, unit, unit of composition, vital part

INGRESS, noun   access, admission, admittance, approach, entrance, entry, incoming, incursion, ingoing, ingression, *ingressus,* inlet, inroad, liberty to enter, means of access, means of entry, passage, power of entrance, right of entry, right to enter, way in, way to
ASSOCIATED CONCEPTS: easement, license, right of access

INHABIT, verb   abide, be established in, be resident in, board, colonize, domicile, dwell in, dwell permanently, *habitare,* have quarters, *incolere,* keep house, live, lodge, occupy, remain, reside in, room, sojourn, squat, stay, take up residence, tenant, visit

INHABITANT, noun   abider, addressee, boarder, citizen, cohabitant, denizen, dweller, habitant, *habitator, homo,* householder, *incola,* indweller, inhabiter, inmate, lodger, native, occupant, occupier, permanent resident, resident, residentiary, settler, sojourner, tenant
ASSOCIATED CONCEPTS: citizenry, residency

INHABITATION *(Act of dwelling in),* **noun**   dwelling, habitancy, habitation, inhabitancy, living, lodging, lodgment, occupancy, occupation, sojourn, stay, tenancy, tenantry

INHABITATION *(Place of dwelling),* **noun**   abode, ayslum, domicile, *domicilium,* dwelling, dwelling place, edifice, establishment, home, house, living quarters, living space, lodging, lodging place, lodgment, place, place of abode, place of residence, quarters, refuge, residence, residency, *sedes, tectum*

INHERENT, *adjective*   connate, deep-rooted, essential, fixed, immanent, implicit, inborn, inbred, ineffaceable, ingrained, ingredient, innate, *innatus, insitus,* instinctive, integral, internal, intrinsic, native, natural, *proprius,* subsistent
ASSOCIATED CONCEPTS: inherent defect, inherent power, inherently dangerous

INHERIT, *verb*   accede to, acquire, acquire from ancestors, be granted a legacy, be the heir of, come into possession as an heir, derive from, fall heir to, gain, have succession as an heir, obtain, receive, receive a legacy, receive an endowment, receive as right, receive by bequest, receive by devise, receive by law of descent, receive by succession, receive property as an heir, *rem hereditate accipere,* succeed to, take, take as an heir, take by descent, take by inheritance, take by succession

INHERITANCE, *noun*   appanage, benefaction, bequest, devise, dispensation, endowment, gift, *hereditas,* heritage, inherited property, legacy, presentation, property obtained by descent, property obtained by devise, provision, seisin, succession of property
ASSOCIATED CONCEPTS: coparcenary, curtesy, descent, distribution, dower, inheritance estate, inheritance tax, intestate succession, patrimony, wills
FOREIGN PHRASES: *Haereditas, alia corporalis, alia incorporalis; corporalis est, quae tangi potest et videri; incorporalis quae tangi non potest nec videri.* An inheritance is either corporeal or incorporeal. Corporeal is that which can be touched and seen; incorporeal, is that which can neither be touched nor seen. *Feodum simplex quia feodum idem est quod haereditas, et simplex idem est quod legitimum vel purum; et sic feodum simplex idem est quod haereditas legitima vel haereditas pura.* A fee-simple is so called because fee is the same as inheritance, and simple is the same as lawful or pure; and so fee-simple is the same as a lawful inheritance or pure inheritance. *Filius est nomen naturae, sed haeres nomen juris.* Son is the natural name, but heir is a name of law. *Haeredum appellatione veniunt haeredes haeredumin infinitum.* Under the name heirs come the heirs of heirs without limit. *Haereditas est successio in universum jus quod defunctus habuerit.* Inheritance is the succession to every right which the deceased had possessed. *Haereditas nihil aliud est, quam successio in universum jus, quod defunctus habuerit.* An inheritance is nothing other than the succession to all the rights which the deceased had. *Si quis praegnantem uxorem reliquit, non videtur sine liberis decessisse.* If a man dies, leaving his wife pregnant, he is considered as having died childless. *Major haereditas venit unicuique nostrum a jure et legibus quam a parentibus.* A greater inheritance comes to each one of us from justice and the laws than from our parents.

INHIBIT, *verb*   arrest, ban, bar, bridle, check, choke, constrain, control, curb, debar, delay, disallow, enjoin, estop, extinguish, forbid, frustrate, gag, govern, harness, hinder, hold back, hold in, impede, intercept, *interdicere,* interdict, interrupt, keep in, leash, muzzle, obstruct, paralyze, prevent, prohibit, proscribe, pull in, quench, refuse to allow, rein in, repress, restrain, restrict, retard, smother, stifle, stop, strangle, suppress, suspend, taboo, veto, withhold

INIMICAL, *adjective*   adverse, alienated, antagonistic, antipathetic, antipathetical, at variance, at war with, bellicose, belligerent, contrary, cool, cross, disaffected, estranged, harmful, hostile, hurtful, *inimicus,* irreconcilable, malevolent, mean, noxious, on bad terms, opposed, opposing, pernicious, repugnant, unfavorable, unfriendly, unpropitious, up in arms, warlike

INIQUITOUS, *adjective*   accursed, atrocious, bad, base, black, corrupt, criminal, culpable, depraved, dishonest, disreputable, dissolute, evil, facinorous, felonious, flagitious, foul, gross, heinous, immoral, *improbus,* improper, incorrigible, inequitable, infamous, *iniquus, iniustus,* irreclaimable, knavish, lawless, malevolent, miscreant, naughty, nefarious, objectionable, peccant, pernicious, profligate, recreant, reprehensible, reprobate, scandalous, scurvy, shameful, sinful, sinning, unfair, unjust, unjustifiable, unprincipled, unrighteous, vicious, vile, villainous, wicked, wrong
FOREIGN PHRASES: *Nullum iniquum est praesumendum in jure.* Nothing iniquitous is to be presumed in law.

INITIAL, *adjective*   basic, beginning, commencing, early, elementary, embryonic, first, fundamental, inaugural, inceptive, inchoate, incipient, initiative, initiatory, introductory, leading, maiden, nascent, opening, original, prefatory, premier, primal, primary, *primus,* pristine, rudimentary, starting
ASSOCIATED CONCEPTS: initial carrier, initial fault, initial license, initial loss, initial payment, initial pleading, initial stage of a proceeding

INITIATE, *verb*   admit, begin, break ground, bring into use, broach, commence, conceive, direct, discover, enlighten, enter upon, familiarize, found, give entrance to, *imbuere,* implant, inaugurate, inchoate, *incipere,* inculculate, indoctrinate, induct, inform, *initiare,* install, instill, institute, instruct, introduce, invent, launch, lay the foundation, lead, lead the way, open, originate, pioneer, plant, preinstruct, prepare, present, prime, prompt, propose, set afoot, set going, set up, start, take the initiative, take the lead, teach, think of, train, undertake, usher in
ASSOCIATED CONCEPTS: initiate an action

INJECT, *verb*   drive in, force in, imbed, imbue, implant, impregnate, infix, *infundere,* infuse, inoculate, insert, instill, interjaculate, interject, interpolate, interpose, introduce, intromit, pierce, place into, press in, put into, ram in, saturate, shoot, thrust in, transfuse, vaccinate

INJUDICIOUS, *adjective*   blind, disadvantageous, hasty, heedless, ill-advised, ill-judged, impolitic, impolitical, improvident, imprudent, inappropriate, incautious, inconsiderate, *inconsideratus, inconsultus,* indiscrete, inexpedient, inopportune, insufficiently considered, irrational, lacking discretion, misguided, needless, negligent, objectionable, precipitate, reckless, showing lack of judgment, showing poor judgment, temerarious, *temerarius,* thoughtless, unadvisable, uncalculating, unconsidered, undesirable, undiscerning, unfit, unprofitable, unreasoned, unsound, unsuitable, unwary, unwise

INJUNCTION, noun   ban, bidding, command, command to undo wrong, denial, enjoinder, imperative, *imperium,* interdiction, *iussum,* judicial order to refrain from an act, *mandatum,* order, precept, prescript, prohibition, proscription, restraining order, restraint, restriction, stay order, warrant
ASSOCIATED CONCEPTS: cease and desist order, dissolution of an injunction, interlocutory injunction, modification of injunction, order to show cause, permanent injunction, preliminary injunction, temporary injunction, temporary restraining order

INJURY, noun   abuse, adversity, bane, breakage, damage, *damnum,* deprivation, detriment, *detrimentum,* disservice, harm, harmful act, hurt, ill treatment, impairment, *incommodum,* invasion of a legal right, loss, offense, physical hurt, prejudice, privation, violence, wrong
ASSOCIATED CONCEPTS: accidental injury, cause of injury, comparative injury, compensable injury, contributory negligence, direct injury, efficient cause, future injury, indirect injury, indivisible injury, injury to business, injury to property, injury to reputation, intentional injury, irreparable injury, malicious injury, permanent injury, personal injury, previous injury, proof of injury, *res ipsa loquitur,* serious injury suffered, wanton injury
FOREIGN PHRASES: *Quid sit jus, et in quo consistit injuria, legis est definire.* What constitutes right, and what injury, it is the business of the law to define. *Non omne damnum inducit injuriam.* Not every loss produces an injury. *Neminem laedit qui jure suo utitur.* He who stands on his own rights injures no one. *Jus est norma recti; et quicquid est contra normam recti est injuria.* Law is the rule of right; and whatever is contrary to the rule of right is an injury. *Melius est in tempore occurrere, quam post causam vulneratum remedium quaerere.* It is better to meet a thing in time, than to seek a remedy after an injury has been inflicted. *Prohibetur ne quis faciat in suo quod nocere possit alieno.* It is forbidden for any one to do on his own property what may injure another's. *Lex nemini facit injuriam.* The law works injury to no one. *Paci sunt maxime contraria vis et injuria.* Violence and injury are especially hostile to peace. *Res inter alios judicatae nullum aliis praejudicium faciunt.* Transactions between strangers ought not to injure those who are not parties to them. *Volenti non fit injuria.* No injury is done where the person injured consents. *Corporalis injuria non recipit aestimationem de futuro.* A personal injury cannot be compensated for by later acts. *Fictio legis inique operatur alieni damnum vel injuriam.* Fiction of law is wrongful if it works loss or harm to anyone. *Privatis pactionibus non dubium est non laedi jus caeterorum.* There is no doubt that private contracts cannot prejudice the rights of others. *Damnum sine injuria esse potest.* There can be damage or injury inflicted without any act of injustice. *Ab assuetis non fit injuria.* No injury is done by things long acquiesced in. *Consuetudo neque injuria oriti neque tolli potest.* A custom can neither arise nor be abolished by an injury. *Aedificare in tuo proprio solo non licet quod alteri noceat.* It is not lawful to build upon one's own land what may injure another. *Factum unius alteri nocere non debet.* The act of one person should not prejudice

another. *Injuria non praesumitur.* A wrong is not presumed. *Lex nemini operatur iniquum, nemini facit injuriam.* The law never works an injury, or does a wrong.

INJUSTICE, noun   abuse, bias, denial of justice, encroachment, error of the court, fault of the court, favoritism, illegality, imposition, improbity, inequality, inequitable action, inequity, infringement, iniquity, *iniuria, iniustitia,* maltreatment, miscarriage of justice, mistake of the court, offense, omission of a court, oppression, partiality, partisanship, persecution, prejudice, transgression, tyranny, unfair action, unfairness, unjust action, unlawfulness, unrighteousness, violation of right, wrong, wrong verdict, wrongdoing
FOREIGN PHRASES: *Fictio legis inique operatur alicui damnum vel injuriam.* Fiction of law is wrongful if it works loss or harm to any one. *Lex nemini operatur iniquum, nemini facit injuriam.* The law never works an injury, or does a wrong.

INMATE, noun   captive, *captus,* convict, dweller, habitant, inhabitant, lawbreaker, occupant, occupier, prisoner, resident, roomer
ASSOCIATED CONCEPTS: inmate at a correctional institution

INNATE, adjective   basic, congenital, constitutional, derived from within, essential, existing from birth, fundamental, heriditary, immanent, inborn, inbred, indigenous, infixed, ingrained, inherent, inherited, *innatus, insitus,* instinctive, intrinsic, intuitive, involuntary, native, natural, *proprius*

INNOCENCE, noun   absence of guilt, blamelessness, exculpation, exoneration, freedom from blame, freedom from guilt, freedom from illegality, guiltlessness, incorruption, innocency, *innocentia, integritas,* sinlessness
ASSOCIATED CONCEPTS: presumption of innocence
FOREIGN PHRASES: *Omnis indemnatus pro innoxis legibus habetur.* Every uncondemned person is regarded by the law as innocent. *Quisquis praesumitur bonus; et semper in dubiis pro reo respondendum.* Everyone is presumed to be good; and in doubtful cases it should be resolved in favor of the accused. *In favorem vitae, libertatis, et innocentiae, omnia praesumuntur.* Every presumption is made in favor of life, liberty and innocence.

INNOCENT, adjective   blameless, *culpa vacuus,* faultless, free from guilt, guiltless, *innocens, insons,* sinless, unblamable, unoffending, upright, virtuous, without harm, without offense
ASSOCIATED CONCEPTS: innocent holder for value, innocent misrepresentation, innocent mistake, innocent purchaser, innocent third party, innocent trespass
FOREIGN PHRASES: *Minatur innocentibus qui parcit nocentibus.* He who spares the guilty threatens those who are innocent.

INNOCUOUS, adjective   harmless, hurtless, innocent, *innocuus,* innoxious, inoffensive, mild, nonirritating, nonmalignant, nontoxic, painless, safe, simple, uninjurious, unlikely to cause harm, unlikely to cause injury, unobjectionable, unobnoxious, unoffending, virtuous, without power to harm, without tendency to harm

INNOVATION, noun adaptation, alteration, breaking of precedent, change, change in method, departure, digression, divergence, diversification, exchange of obligations, invention, modernization, modification, *mutare,* neoterism, new device, new idea, new method, new phase, *novare,* novelty, radically new measure, revision, revolution, shift, variation

INNUENDO, noun accusation, allusion, aside, aspersion, charge, connotation, *denuntiatio,* hint, implication, implied indication, imputation, incrimination, indication, indirect allusion, inference, insinuation, mention, *nuntius,* oblique allusion, overtone, reference, reflection, *significatio,* suggestion
ASSOCIATED CONCEPTS: defamation, disparagement, libel, slander

INNUMERABLE, adjective boundless, countless, endless, exhaustless, frequent, immeasurable, immense, incalculable, incapable of being counted, incomprehensible, incomputable, inexhaustible, infinite, *innumerabilis, innumerus,* interminable, legionary, limitless, many, more than one can tell, much, multitudinous, myriad, numberless, sumless, uncountable, uncounted, unfathomable, unlimited, unmeasured, unnumbered, untold

INOPERABLE (Impracticable), adjective undoable, unfeasible, unworkable

INOPERABLE (Incurable), adjective cureless, hopeless, immedicable, remediless

INOPPORTUNE, adjective at the wrong time, badly calculated, badly timed, ill-chosen, ill-seasoned, ill-timed, inadvisable, inappropriate, inauspicious, inconvenient, inexpedient, *inopportunus,* malapropos, misjudged, mistimed, undesirable, unfavorable, unfit, unfortunate, unpropitious, unseasonable, unsuitable, unsuited, untimely, wrong

INORDINATE, adjective crammed, exaggerated, exceeding, excessive, exorbitant, extortionate, extraordinary, extravagant, extreme, fanatical, gluttonous, great, immoderate, *immoderatus, immodicus,* inabstinent, intemperate, lavish, monstrous, needless, nimious, out of bounds, out of limits, outrageous, overcharged, overflowing, overmuch, preposterous, prodigal, profuse, prohibitive, redundant, superabundant, supererogatory, superfluous, supersaturated, unbridled, uncalled-for, unconscionable, uncurbed, undue, unlimited, unnecessary, unreasonable, unrestrained, wasteful, without restraint

INQUEST, noun determination of damages, examination, hearing, inquiry, interrogation, investigation, judicial inquiry, legal investigation, *quaestio,* quest, questioning, review, search, search into facts
ASSOCIATED CONCEPTS: assessment of damages, civil inquest, coroner's inquest

INQUIRE, verb ask, catechize, conduct research, cross-examine, delve into, examine, explore, interrogate, investigate, look into, probe, propose a question, pry into, pursue, query, question, quiz, research, scrutinize, search, search into, seek information, solicit, sound out, study, subject to scrutiny, survey

INQUIRY (Request for information), noun examination, examination into facts or principles, explora-
tion, hearing, inquisition, *interrogatio,* interrogation, investigation, *percontatio,* poll, probe, query, question, scrutiny, search, search for information, survey
ASSOCIATED CONCEPTS: duty to inquire, inquiry into title, reasonable inquiry, speculative inquiry
FOREIGN PHRASES: *Quaerere dat sapere quae sunt legitima vere.* Inquiry is the way to know what things are truly lawful. *Quaeras de dubiis legem bene discere si vis.* Inquire into doubtful matters if you wish to understand the law well. *Quaere de dubiis, quia per rationes pervenitur ad legitimam rationem.* Inquire into doubtful matters, because by reasoning we arrive at legal reason.

INQUIRY (Systematic investigation), noun analyzation, asking, assay, canvassing, *cognitio,* conference, delving into evidence, disquisition, examination, exploration, fundamental research, hearing, hearing of evidence, inquest, *inquisitio,* inquisition, interrogation, investigation, legal trial, narrow search, overview, perusal, probe, pursuit, *quaestio,* question, research, scrutiny, search, study, survey, trial
ASSOCIATED CONCEPTS: grand jury inquiry, judicial inquiry, public inquiry

INQUISITIVE, adjective *audiendi, cupidus, curiosus,* curious, eager for knowledge, fond of investigation, given to research, inquiring, interested, interrogative, investigative, questioning, quizzical, scrutinizing, searching, seeking, speculative

INSALUBRIOUS, adjective baleful, baneful, calamitous, damaging, dangerous, deleterious, destructive, detrimental, disadvantageous, disastrous, fraught with danger, *gravis,* harmful, hazardous, hurtful, injurious, *insalubris,* lethal, lethiferous, malefic, maleficent, menacing, mephitic, miasmal, miasmatic, miasmatical, miasmic, morbific, morbifical, mortiferous, noisome, noxious, ominous, pathogenic, perilous, pernicious, pestiferous, *pestilens,* pestilent, pestilential, poisonous, risky, ruinous, threatening, toxic, unclean, unfavorable to health, unhealthful, unhealthy, unhygienic, unsafe, unsanitary, unwholesome, venomous, virulent

INSANITY, noun aberration, aberration of mind, abnormality, alienation, alienation of mind, amentia, brain damage, craziness, daftness, delirium, delusion, dementedness, *dementia,* deranged intellect, derangement, diseased mind, disordered intellect, disordered mind, disordered reason, disorientation, frenzy, hallucination, *insania,* loss of reason, lunacy, madness, mental abnormality, mental alienation, mental decay, mental deficiency, mental derangement, mental disease, mental incapacity, mental infirmities, mental instability, mental sickness, mental unsoundness, paranoia, raving, unbalanced mind, unsound mind, unsoundness of mind, *vecordia,* want of comprehension, want of reason
ASSOCIATED CONCEPTS: adjudication of insanity, diminished capacity, habitual insanity, incompetency, insane delusion, insane impulse to act, insanity defense, insanity plea, irresistible impulse
FOREIGN PHRASES: *Furiosus nullum negotium contrahere potest.* An insane person can make no contract. *Furiosus stipulare non potest nec aliquid negotium agere, qui non intelligit quid agit.* An insane person who knows not what he is doing, cannot contract nor transact any business. *Furiosi nulla voluntas est.* A

madman has no will. *Furiosus solo furore punitur.* A madman is punished by his madness alone. *Furor contrahi matrimonium non sinit, quia consensu opus est.* Insanity prevents a marriage from being contracted, because consent is required. *Ira furor brevis est.* Anger is short insanity. *Furiosus absentis loco est.* A madman is considered as a person who is absent. *Insanus est qui, abjecta ratione, omnia cum impetu et furore facit.* A person is insane who, deprived of reason, does everything with violence and rage.

INSATIABLE, *adjective*   acquisitive, avaricious, covetous, craving, discontented, gluttonous, grasping, greedy, hoggish, incapable of being satisfied, *inexplebilis, insatiabilis,* intemperate, piggish, quenchless, rapacious, selfish, unappeasable, unfilled, unquenchable, unsated, unsatisfied

INSCRIBE, *verb*   *ascribere,* commit to writing, *consignare,* engrave, enroll, enscroll, enter, imprint, *inscribere,* insert, letter, list, make an entry, mark, post, put in writing, put upon record, record, register, scribe, write

INSCRIPTION, *noun*   autograph, caption, dedication, engraving, entry, *index, inscriptio,* legend, mark, record, superscription, *titulus,* written matter
ASSOCIATED CONCEPTS: inscribed securities, registration of a deed

INSCRUTABLE, *adjective*   ambiguous, baffling, blank, cloudy, concealed, deadpan, enigmatic, expressionless, hidden, impassive, impenetrable, impossible to understand, inapprehensible, incognizable, incomprehensible, indiscernible, inexplicable, insoluble, mysterious, obscure, *obscurus,* occult, *occultus,* past comprehension, poker-faced, puzzling, secret, *tectus,* unable to be investigated, unaccountable, unclear, undiscoverable, unfathomable, unintelligible, unknowable, unrevealed, unsearchable, vague

INSECURE, *adjective*   adrift, borderline, changeable, changeful, dangerous, defenseless, dependent, endangered, exposed, exposed to risk, fragile, frail, fraught with danger, harborless, hazardous, helpless, *incertus,* infirm, *instabilis,* lacking stability, perilous, precarious, risky, shaky, slippery, speculative, subject to chance, subject to change, ticklish, tottering, treacherous, unassured, unbalanced, uncertain, unconfident, undependable, unfastened, unprotected, unreliable, unsafe, unsettled, unsheltered, unshielded, unsound, unstable, unsteadfast, unsteady, unsure, untrustworthy, venturesome, venturous, vulnerable
ASSOCIATED CONCEPTS: insecure obligation, insecurity clause

INSEMINATE, *verb*   embed, implant, impregnate, inject, insert, introduce, plant, pollinate, pollinize, seed, sow

INSENSIBLE, *adjective*   apathetic, benumbed, bewildered, blind, callous, clueless, comatose, dazed, deaf, deprived of sensation, dormant, drugged, dull, emotionless, exanimate, frigid, heedless, ignorant, imperceptive, impercipient, inanimate, incapable of feeling, incapable of perceiving, inexcitable, insensate, insensitive, insentient, *obdurescere,* passive, senseless, *sensu carere,* spiritless, stony, stupefied, supine, torporific, unacquainted, unaffected, unaroused, unaware, uncon-

scious, undiscerning, unenlightened, unfeeling, unhearing, unknowing, unmindful, unmoved, unperceptive, unrealizing, unresponsive, unseeing, unsuspecting, untouched, unwitting, vegetating, void of feeling

INSENTIENCE, *noun*   absence of feeling, absence of sensation, blackout, blankness, immobility, inability to act, inability to perceive, inaction, inactivity, inanimateness, inanimation, incognizance, incomprehension, indifference, *inertia,* inertness, insensateness, insensibility, insensibleness, insensitivity, lack of awareness, lack of comprehension, lack of knowledge, lack of perception, lifelessness, nonrecognition, powerlessness, senselessness, stillness, stupor, suspension of consciousness, trance, unawareness, unconsciousness, unfamiliarity, unfeelingness, want of sensibility

INSEPARABLE, *adjective*   attached, blended, cemented, close, combined, consolidated, constantly together, devoted, fast, firm, fused, glued, impartible, incapable of being parted, indiscerptible, indissoluble, indivisible, inextricable, infrangible, inseverable, insoluble, integrated, interdependent, intertwined, intimate, joined, locked, molded together, nondivisible, *perpetuo comitari,* tenacious, undissolvable, undividable, united, unsunderable, welded
ASSOCIATED CONCEPTS: inseparability of easement, inseparability of statutory provisions

INSERTION, *noun*   addendum, additament, addition, appendix, entry, extension, inclusion, inset, intercalation, interjection, interpolation, *interpositio,* introduction, parenthesis, penetration, plant, postscript, supplement, supplementation, transplantation
ASSOCIATED CONCEPTS: codicil, insertion of a clause to a contract, rider

INSIDIOUS, *adjective*   artful, beguiling, cheating, conniving, covinous, crafty, cunning, deceitful, deceiving, deceptive, designing, devious, dishonest, disloyal, *dolosus,* ensnaring, *fallax,* false, falsehearted, foxy, fraudulent, furtive, guileful, hypocritical, inconstant, indirect, *insidiosus,* intriguing, lying, perfidious, plotting, scheming, serpentine, sly, stealthy, subtle, surreptitious, treacherous, tricky, underhanded, unscrupulous, vulpine, wily

INSIGHT, *noun*   ability to understand, acuity, acumen, acuteness, apperception, astuteness, awareness, cleverness, *cognitio,* cognition, cognizance, comprehension, consciousness, discernment, discrimination, enlightenment, *intellegentia,* intuition, intuitiveness, *iudicium,* keenness, ken, noesis, penetration, perception, percipience, percipiency, perspicacity, realization, sagaciousness, sagacity, sensitivity, sharpness, shrewdness, understanding, wisdom

INSIGNIFICANCE, *noun*   *exiguitas,* immateriality, inconsequence, inconsequentiality, inessentiality, insubstantiality, irrelevance, irrelevancy, momentariness, nominalness, paltriness, paucity, scantiness, scarceness, shallowness, smallness, sparseness, transientness, triviality, unimportance, unnoteworthiness

INSINUATION, *noun*   allusion, aspersion, clue, hint, implication, indirect allusion, indirect comment, indirect implication, inference, innuendo, intimation, oblique hint, reference, *significatio,* suggestion, veiled observation, veiled remark

INSIPID, *adjective* banal, bloodless, boring, colorless, diluted, dreary, dull, feeble, flat, flavorless, *frigidus,* halfhearted, impotent, inactive, ineffective, *ineptus,* insubstantial, *insulsus,* irresolute, languid, limp, pointless, powerless, savorless, spiritless, tame, tasteless, torpid, unanimated, uncaptivating, undramatic, unelevated, unemphatic, unentertaining, unexciting, unimpassioned, uninspired, uninspiring, uninteresting, unsavory, unscintillating, unsparkling, unspiced, unspirited, unstrengthened, unvivid, vapid, void of taste, weak, without force, without taste

INSIST, *verb* accent, accentuate, argue, be obstinate, be peremptory, be resolute, bid, brook no denial, command, contend, demand, dictate, *efflagitare,* emphasize, enforce, enjoin, exact, exert pressure, exhort, *exposcere,* force upon, importune, impose, impress on, *instare,* lay stress on, order, override, persevere, persist, press, press earnestly, put pressure on, repeat, require, stand firm, stress, take no denial, underline, urge
ASSOCIATED CONCEPTS: insist on legal protections, insist on one's rights

INSISTENT, *adjective* argumentative, assertive, bent upon, clamorous, coactive, coercive, commanding, compelling, crying, demanding, disposed to insist, dogmatic, driving, emphatic, exigent, forceful, harping, impelling, imperative, importunate, incessant, insisting on notice, instant, intent upon, iterative, monotonous, peremptory, perseverant, persevering, persistent, persisting, pertinacious, pressing, recurrent, reiterative, repeated, repetitional, repetitionary, requesting, serious, striking, tenacious, urgent, vehement
ASSOCIATED CONCEPTS: coercion, improper influence, intimidation

INSOLENT, *adjective* abusive, arrogant, assuming, audacious, bellicose, bold, brazen, bumptious, contemptuous, contumacious, *contumax,* contumelious, defiant, derisive, discourteous, disdainful, disobedient, disobliging, disregardful, disrespectful, flippant, fresh, froward, haughty, hectoring, imperious, impertinent, impolite, *impudens,* impudent, *insolens,* insulting, intolerant, magisterial, malapert, nervy, offensive, opprobrious, outrageous, overbearing, pert, presumptuous, procacious, rude, sarcastic, saucy, shameless, supercilious, swaggering, toplofty, unabashed, unmannerly
ASSOCIATED CONCEPTS: contempt

INSOLVENT, *adjective* bankrupt, broke, defaulting, destitute, failed, impecunious, impoverished, in arrears, indebted, lacking funds, moneyless, out of funds, out of money, penniless, reduced, ruined, unable to pay

INSPECTION, *noun* appraisal, ascertainment, assessment, careful scrutiny, critical examination, critical viewing, critique, evaluation, examination, exploration, inquest, inquiry, inventory, observation, perusal, reconnaissance, review, scrutiny, study, surveillance, survey, trial, visual examination
ASSOCIATED CONCEPTS: audit, authority to inspect, inspection for patent or latent defects, inspection of premises, inspection of records, on sight inspection, subject to inspection

INSPIRE, *verb* actuate, animate, arouse, awaken, bring about, cause, convince, effect, effectuate, elicit, encourage, enkindle, enliven, evoke, *excitare,* exert influence, fill with enthusiasm, generate, give an impetus, imbue, impassion, impel, *incendere, incitare,* incite, induce, influence, instigate, kindle, launch, motivate, move, occasion, originate, persuade, precipitate, prevail upon, produce, prompt, provoke, set astir, stimulate, sway, underlie, urge, wake

INSTALLATION, *noun* admission, ceremony of induction into an office, establishment, inauguration, induction, initiation, installment, instatement, institution, introduction, investiture, launching, ordination, placement, presentation

INSTALLMENT, *noun* advance, allotment, contract payment, deposit, disbursement, dividend, division, down payment, fraction, one of several parts, one of several payments, one of successive parts, parcel, *pars,* part payment, part payment of a debt, partial payment, *pensio,* periodic payment, *portio,* portion, remittance, section, segment, successive portion, token payment
ASSOCIATED CONCEPTS: installment contract, installment note, installment payments, installment plan, installment sale

INSTANCE, *noun* case, case in point, clarification, demonstration, elucidation, embodiment, ensample, example, exemplar, exemplification, *exemplum,* frame of reference, illustration, model, paradigm, representative, representative selection, sample, specimen, type
ASSOCIATED CONCEPTS: first instance, special instance, specific instance

INSTANT, *adjective* approaching, at once, at the present time, at this moment, close, close at hand, current, early, existent, forthcoming, forthwith, imminent, impending, in process, looming, near, near at hand, punctual, *punctum temporis,* ready, simultaneous, speedy, upcoming, without delay
ASSOCIATED CONCEPTS: instant case, instant motion

INSTANTANEOUS, *adjective* abrupt, expeditious, hasty, hurried, immediate, instant, occurring in an instant, *praesens,* prompt, quick, rapid, simultaneous, speedy, *subitus,* swift, without delay, without perceptible time lapse

INSTANTLY, *adverb* anon, at once, directly, expeditiously, *extemplo,* fast, forthwith, hastily, hurriedly, immediately, instantaneously, now, presently, promptly, quickly, rapidly, right away, right now, shortly, soon, speedily, *statim,* straightway, swiftly, with speed, without a wait, without any lapse of time, without delay, without hesitation, without notice

INSTATE, *verb* admit, appoint, *confirmare, constituere,* designate, endow, enlist, enroll, ensconce, entrust, establish, establish in an office, found, give admittance to, give entrance to, *inaugurare,* inaugurate, induct, *initiare,* initiate, install, *instituere,* introduce, introduce into office, invest, launch, lay the foundations, lead the way, name, nominate, place, place in office, plant, put in possession, receive, seat, set, *stabilire, statuere,* take in

INSTIGATION, *noun* actuation, agitation, animation, cajolery, causation, coaxing, easement, encouragement, excitation, exhortation, fomentation, goading, helpfulness, hortation, impetus, impulsion, incentive,

incitation, incitement, inducement, influence, initiation, insistance, insistence, inspiration, invigoration, invitation, irritation, motivation, persuasion, perturbation, piquancy, pressure, prompting, provocation, solicitation, stimulation, *stimulus,* suasion, supporting, taunting, urging
ASSOCIATED CONCEPTS: accomplice, aiding and abetting a crime, instigation of a crime, promoting a crime
FOREIGN PHRASES: *Plus peccat author quam actor.* The originator or instigator of a crime is a worse offender than the actual perpetrator of it.

INSTILL, *verb*   direct, educate, familiarize with, ground, guide, impart, impart gradually, implant, impress upon the mind, inculcate, indoctrinate, infix, inform, infuse, inject, *instillare,* instruct, prepare, propagandize, qualify, school, teach, train, tutor

INSTINCT, *noun*   affinity, *appetitus,* aptitude, aptness, automatic reaction, bent, fitness, inborn proclivity, inclination, innate inclination, innate proclivity, intuition, involuntariness, native tendency, natural sense, natural tendency, predisposition, proclivity, proneness, propensity, reflex action, tendency, untutored intelligence

INSTITUTE, *noun*   academy, association, coalition, college, concern, *conlegium,* educational institution, establishment, firm, foundation, guild, house, institution, institution of learning, lyceum, organization, place of education, school, society, *sodalitas,* syndicate, system, union, university
ASSOCIATED CONCEPTS: business institution, charitable institution, educational institution, financial institution, lending institution, literary institution, penal institution, philanthropic institution, private institution, public institution

INSTRUCT *(Direct), verb*   advise, advocate, bid, brief, call upon, charge, coach, command, compel, counsel, decree, demand, dictate, enact, exact, give a directive, give a mandate, give an order, give authoritative instructions to, give the signal, give the word, give the word of command, guide, impose a duty, impose a task, issue a command, issue a decree, issue an order, lay down the law, make a decree, make an order, *mandare,* order, pass orders, *praecipere, praescribere,* prescribe, prescribe a task, prompt, promulgate a decree, promulgate an order, recommend, require, send an order, suggest, tell
ASSOCIATED CONCEPTS: instruct the jury

INSTRUCT *(Teach), verb*   acquaint, comment upon, convey information, direct one's attention, *docere,* edify, educate, elucidate, enlighten, *erudire,* explain, expound, familiarize, fill with information, give by way of information, give lessons in, give to understand, guide, guide the studies of, illumine, impart, implant, impress upon the memory, impress upon the mind, inculcate, indoctrinate, inform, instill, *instituere,* lecture, make known, point out, prepare, present, prime, provide with information, put before, qualify, school, show, train, tutor

INSTRUCTION *(Direction), noun*   advice, authoritative statement, bidding, categorical imperative, caveat, charge, command, commandment, commission, decree, edification, firm advice, guidance, jury charge, mandate, *mandatum,* order, *praescriptum,* precept, reg-

ulation, requirement, rule, word of command, written order
ASSOCIATED CONCEPTS: instruction to a jury, peremptory instruction, special instructions
FOREIGN PHRASES: *Matter en ley ne serra mise in bouche del jurors.* A matter of law shall not be put into the mouth of jurors.

INSTRUCTION *(Teaching), noun*   detailed statement, discourse, *doctrina,* edification, education, *eruditio,* explanation, exposition, guidance, inculcation, indoctrination, *institutio,* lecture, pedagogy, preaching, preparation, recital, recitation, schooling, sermon, training, tutelage, tutoring, upbringing

INSTRUMENT *(Document), noun*   bill, certificate, charter, deed, draft, evidential writing, executed and delivered writing, formal writing, official record, official writing, paper, record, solemn writing, *syngrapha, tabula,* writing, writing delivered as the evidence of an agreement, writing which gives formal expression to a legal act, written formal expression
ASSOCIATED CONCEPTS: allonge, instrument evidencing a debt, instrument of writing, negotiable instrument
FOREIGN PHRASES: *Mala grammatica non vitiat chartam. sed in expositione instrumentorum mala grammatica quoad fieri possit evitanda est.* Bad grammar does not vitiate a deed. but, in the drafting of instruments, bad grammar should, as far as possible, be avoided. *Ubi nulla est conjectura quae ducat alio, verba intelligenda sunt ex proprietate, non grammatica, sed populari ex usu.* Where there is nothing which calls for another construction, words are to be understood according to their proper sense, not according to their strict grammatical meaning, but according to their popular sense. *Qui haeret in litera haeret in cortice.* He who adheres to the letter of an instrument goes but skin deep into its meaning.

INSTRUMENT *(Tool), noun*   agency, agent, aid, apparatus, appliance, article, channel, contributing force, contrivance, device, equipment, facility, implement, *instrumentum,* machine, machinery, means, mechanical construction, mechanism, medium, utensil, utility, vehicle
ASSOCIATED CONCEPTS: instrument of fraud

INSTRUMENTAL, *adjective*   advantageous, aiding, assisting, auxiliary, beneficial, conducive, contributory, helpful, indispensable, serviceable, useful, valuable

INSTRUMENTALITY, *noun*   channel, device, equipment, expedient, implement, instrument, interagent, intermediary, intermediate, intermedium, machinery, manner, means, medium, method, mode, operation, process, resource, stratagem, technic, technique, tool, vehicle, way, wherewithal
ASSOCIATED CONCEPTS: dangerous instrumentality

INSUBORDINATE, *adjective*   contumacious, defiant, disloyal, disobedient, dissident, fractious, froward, indocile, insubmissive, insurgent, insurrectionary, intractable, lawless, mutinous, noncompliant, rebellious, recalcitrant, recusant, refractory, resistive, restive, revolutionary, sansculottic, *seditiosus,* treacherous, treasonous, *turbulentus,* uncomplying, ungovernable, unruly, wayward
ASSOCIATED CONCEPTS: contempt, discharge

INSUBSTANTIAL, *adjective*   airy, baseless, bodiless, chimerical, ephemeral, fanciful, feeble, flimsy, fragile, frail, groundless, hallucinatory, illusive, illusory, imaginary, imagined, immaterial, impalpable, inadequate, inconsequential, inconsiderable, incorporeal, infirm, insignificant, lacking firmness, lacking substance, lame, made poorly, modest, nonexistent, notional, of no consequence, paltry, petty, picayune, poor, powerless, scant, slender, slight, slim, spectral, superficial, tenuous, thin, trifling, trivial, unbased, unfirm, unfounded, ungrounded, unimportant, unreal, unsolid, unsound, unsubstantial, unsupportable, unsustainable, untenable, vague, visionary, weak, without basis, without foundation, without plausibility, without reality, wobbly, worthless

INSUFFERABLE, *adjective*   acute, agonizing, crushing, distressing, dreadful, excruciating, extreme, frightful, harrowing, harsh, hurtful, impossible, insupportable, *intolerabilis,* intolerable, *intolerandus,* painful, past bearing, past enduring, racking, searing, severe, torturous, unbearable, unendurable

INSUFFICIENCY, *noun*   absence, dearth, deficiency, deficit, depletion, emptiness, exhaustion, exiguity, exiguousness, falling short, fewness, inadequacy, inadequateness, incompetence, incompleteness, *inopia,* lack, meagerness, need, not enough, paucity, *penuria,* scantiness, scantness, scarcity, short fall, short measure, short supply, shortage, shortcoming, sparseness, stint, too few, want
ASSOCIATED CONCEPTS: insufficiency of evidence, insufficiency of law to support a verdict

INSUFFICIENT, *adjective*   bereft of, defective, deficient, denuded of, destitute of, devoid of, drained, failing, faint, feeble, *haud sufficiens, impar,* imperfect, in default, inadequate, incapable, incommensurate, incompetent, incomplete, inconsiderable, lacking, lean, meager, missing, negligible, not enough, not sufficient, paltry, poor, scant, scanty, scarce, short, shy, slender, slight, slim, spare, sparse, thin, too little, uncompleted, unequal, unfinished, unfit, unfitted, unqualified, unsound, unsufficing, unsuited, wanting, weak
ASSOCIATED CONCEPTS: insufficient evidence, insufficient funds, insufficient service, insufficient verdict

INSULAR, *adjective*   alone, apart, confined, detached, discrete, distinct, enisled, isolated, removed, self-sufficient, separate, solitary

INSULATE, *verb*   compartmentalize, cut off, detach, isolate, keep apart, quarantine, screen off, seclude, segregate, separate, sequester, set apart, zone

INSUPERABLE, *adjective*   beyond control, difficult, formidable, impassible, impervious, impossible, impracticable, impregnable, inaccessible, incapable of being overcome, incapable of being surmounted, indomitable, innavigable, insurmountable, *invictus,* invincible, invulnerable, out of reach, out of the question, unachievable, unassailable, unattackable, unattainable, unbeatable, unbridgeable, unconquerable, undefeatable, unfeasible, unmasterable, unobtainable, unovercomable

INSURANCE, *noun*   agreement to pay, assurance against loss, bond against risk, compensation for injury, compensation for loss, contract against future loss, contract against unknown contingencies, guarantee against loss, indemnification, indemnity against loss, pledge, promise, protection against loss, security against loss, stipulation to compensate for loss, warranty against loss
ASSOCIATED CONCEPTS: accident insurance, binder, casualty insurance, claim, coinsurance, contract of insurance, contributing insurance, controlled insurance, endowment insurance, excess insurance, fidelity insurance, fire insurance, group insurance, guaranty insurance, health insurance, insurance agent, insurance application, insurance broker, insurance carrier, insured, insurer, liability insurance, life insurance, loss, marine insurance, nonforfeitable insurance, occupational disability insurance, ordinary insurance, paid-up insurance, policy of insurance, premium, property insurance, reinsurance, surety insurance, term insurance, title insurance, valued insurance, vehicle insurance, whole life insurance

INSURE, *verb*   cover against loss, gain indemnity against loss, guarantee against loss, have underwritten, obtain insurance, protect against loss, reassure, secure against loss, underwrite against loss

INSURER, *noun*   assurer, compensator, guarantee, guarantor, indemnifier, indemnitor, insurance company, recompenser, remunerator, surety, underwriter
ASSOCIATED CONCEPTS: absolute insurer, accident and health insurer, agent, broker, casualty insurer, liability insurer, life insurer

INSURGENT, *noun*   agitator, anarchist, demagogue, disrupter, insubordinate, insurrectionary, insurrectionist, mutineer, nihilist, radical, rebel, *rebellis,* reformer, renegade, revolter, revolutionary, revolutionist, rioter, seditionary, subverter, traitor

INSURMOUNTABLE, *adjective*   beyond one's power, beyond one's reach, beyond the bounds of possibility, formidable, hardly possible, impassable, impenetrable, impossible, impracticable, impregnable, inaccessible, incapable of being done, incapable of being overcome, incapable of success, indomitable, inexpugnable, insoluble, insuperable, invincible, out of reach, out of the question, too difficult, too hard, unachievable, unassailable, unattackable, unattainable, unbeatable, unconquerable, undefeatable, unfeasible, unmasterable, unperformable, unrealizable, unsolvable, unsubduable, unsurmountable, unvanquishable, unviable, unworkable

INSURRECTION, *noun*   anarchy, defiance, disobedience, disorder, disturbance, insubordination, insurgence, insurgency, *motus,* mutineering, mutiny, noncompliance, outbreak, overthrow, political upheaval, *rebellio,* rebellion, resistance to government, revolt, revolution, riot, rising, *seditio,* sedition, uprising

INSUSCEPTIBLE (*Resistant*), *adjective*   able to withstand, capable of resisting, defended, fortified, having immunity, having resistance, immune, immunized, not sensitive to, protected, repellent, strengthened, strong, tough, unyielding

INSUSCEPTIBLE (*Uncaring*), *adjective*   aloof, apathetic, blind, callous, capable of resisting, capable of withstanding, cold, cool, deaf, detached, devoid of feeling, distant, frigid, hard, hardened, heartless, impassive, impervious, incapable of caring, indifferent, indurate, indurated, inflexible, insensate, insensible, insensitive, insolicitous, insouciant, insusceptire, lacking feeling, numb, obdurate, obstinate, pachydermatous, pococurante, recalcitrant, regardless, removed, renitent, *sensu carere,* stubborn, tough, toughened, unaffected, unaroused, unbending, unconcerned, unemotional, unfeeling, ungiving, unimpassioned, unimpressible, uninterested, unmoved, unresponsive, unstirred, unsympathetic, untouched, unwilling to care, unyielding, without regard

INTACT, *adjective*   complete, entire, faultless, flawless, free from imperfection, full, in good order, in one piece, in perfect condition, *intactus, integer,* inviolate, perfect, preserved, replete, safe, *salvus,* solid, sound, together, unabridged, unaffected by injury, unaltered, unblemished, unbroken, unbruised, uncensored, uncut, undamaged, undecayed, undefaced, undemolished, undestroyed, undiminished, undivided, unedited, unexpurgated, unfaded, unharmed, unhurt, unified, unimpaired, uninjured, unmarked, unmarred, unreduced, unscarred, unscathed, unscratched, unsevered, unshattered, unspoiled, untorn, untouched, unworn, whole, with nothing missing, without loss

INTANGIBLE, *adjective*   abstract, aerial, airy, amorphous, asomatous, bodiless, difficult to appraise, dim, discarnate, disembodied, ethereal, immaterial, impalpable, imperceptible, imponderable, inappreciable, inconspicuous, incorporal, incorporate, incorporeal, indefinite, indiscernible, infinitesimal, insensible, insubstantial, intactile, *intactilis,* invisible, nonphysical, nonsubstantial, not clear to the mind, not definite, shadowy, spiritual, theoretical, unapparent, unbeholdable, uncertain, unconcrete, undiscernible, unearthly, unfleshly, unperceivable, unphysical, unseeable, unsolid, unsubstantial, untouchable, vague, weightless, without form, without physical substance
ASSOCIATED CONCEPTS: intangible assets, intangible personalty, intangible property

INTANGIBLE, *noun*   assignable rights of action, chose in action, incorporeal entity, *intactilis,* personal chattels which are not in possession, personal right not reduced to possession, right, right to personal things, right to recovery
ASSOCIATED CONCEPTS: intangible assets, intangible personalty, intangible property, intangible trust property

INTEGRAL, *adjective*   basic, cardinal, central, component, constituent, elemental, essential, essential to completeness, fundamental, indispensable, integrant, irreplaceable, *necessarius,* necessary, needed, needful, prerequisite, primary, required, requisite, vital
ASSOCIATED CONCEPTS: integral part of a case

INTEGRATION *(Amalgamation),* *noun*   admixture, affiliation, alliance, association, blend, blending, coadunation, coalition, coexistence, combination, confederation, consolidation, federalization, fusion, incorporation, intermixture, medley, merger, mingling, mix, unification, union
ASSOCIATED CONCEPTS: integration of the terms into a contract

INTEGRATION *(Assimilation),* *noun*   agreement, alliance, association, coalition, coexistence, combination, confederation, consociation, cooperation, federation, fellowship, merger, mingling, participation, partnership, racial balance, racial harmonization, racial harmony, removal of discrimination, solidarity, togetherness, undividedness
ASSOCIATED CONCEPTS: Equal Protection, segregation

INTEGRITY, *noun*   character, estimableness, fairness, faithfulness, fidelity, good faith, goodness, high character, high-mindedness, honesty, honor, honorableness, incorruptibility, *innocentia, integritas,* justness, moral soundness, moral strength, morality, nobleness, principle, *probitas,* probity, propriety, purity, rectitude, reputability, responsibility, righteousness, scruples, scrupulousness, self-respect, sincerity, sound moral principle, strict honesty, trustworthiness, truthfulness, upright moral character, uprightness, uprightness of character, upstandingness, veridicality, virtue, virtuousness, worthiness
ASSOCIATED CONCEPTS: character evidence, impugning the integrity of a witness, want of integrity

INTELLECT, *noun*   ability to perceive, ability to reason, ability to understand, brain, brilliance, cerebration, cognition, cognitive faculty, comprehension, genius, intellectual powers, intellectuality, *intellegentia,* intelligence, *mens,* mental ability, mental acuteness, mental capacity, mental faculty, mentality, mind, power to reason, rational faculty, rationality, reach of mind, reason, reasoning faculty, reasoning power, sense, understanding

INTELLIGENCE *(Intellect),* *noun*   acumen, aptitude, astuteness, brains, brilliance, cleverness, cognition, cognitive faculty, comprehension, genius, insight, intellectional faculty, intellectual power, intellectuality, *intellegentia,* keenness, *mens,* mental ability, mental acuteness, mental capacity, mental faculty, mentality, mind, power to reason, quickness of perception, rational faculty, rationality, reach of mind, reason, reasoning faculty, reasoning power, sagacity, sense, understanding, wisdom

INTELLIGENCE *(News),* *noun*   account, acquired facts, aviso, communication, communique, data, details, dispatch, enlightenment, information, knowledge, known facts, message, monition, notice, *nuntius,* report, tidings, tip, warning, word

INTEMPERATE, *adjective*   exceeding, excessive, exorbitant, extravagant, extreme, immoderate, inabstinent, indulgent, inordinate, unbridled, unchecked, uncontrolled, uncurbed, uninhibited, unlimited, unmeasured, unreined, unrestrained, unruly, unsuppressed, untempered, wasteful

INTEND, *verb*   aim, aspire to, be determined to, calculate, *cogitare,* design, desire, determine upon, drive at, elect, endeavor, expect, fix the mind upon, harbor a design, have in mind, have in view, *intendere,* mean, plan, premeditate, presume, propose, purpose, resolve, scheme, set as a goal
ASSOCIATED CONCEPTS: intended design, intended destination, intended purpose, intended to take effect upon death, precatory words

INTENSE, *adjective*   *acer,* acute, *ardens,* ardent, close, concentrated, deep, diligent, dynamic, earnest, emotional, energetic, extreme, fervent, fierce, fiery, flaming, heightened, high-pressure, impassioned, intensified, intent, *intentus,* keen, passionate, perfervid, powerful, profound, purposeful, resolved, rigorous, severe, single-minded, strenuous, strict, strong, undeviating, unwavering, vehement, vigorous, vivid, zealous

INTENSIFY, *verb*   add to, aggravate, *amplificare, augere,* augment, boost, concentrate, deepen, emphasize, enhance, escalate, exacerbate, exaggerate, heighten, increase, inflame, magnify, redouble, sharpen, step up, strengthen

INTENSIVE, *adjective*   acute, ardent, concentrated, exhaustive, fervent, forceful, intense, *intentivus,* powerful, sharp, strenuous, strong, thorough, thoroughgoing, unmitigated, vehement, vigorous, zealous

INTENT, *noun*   aim, *attentus,* choice, contemplation, design, determination, end, *erectus, intentus,* meaning, mind, motive, object, objective, plan, point, predetermination, purport, purpose, resolution, resolve, scheme, scope, view, volition
ASSOCIATED CONCEPTS: charitable intent, corrupt intent, criminal intent, felonious intent, fraudulent intent, general intent, implied intent, intent of parties to contract, intent of testator, intent to defraud, larcenous intent, malice, mutual intent, premeditation, presumed intent, specific intent, testamentary intent, transferred intent
FOREIGN PHRASES: *Quod factum est, cum in obscuro sit, ex affectione cujusque capit interpretationem.* When there is doubt about an act, it receives interpretation from the feelings or disposition of the actor. *Impunitas continuum affectum tribuit delinquendi.* Impunity confirms the disposition of a delinquent. *Intentio mea imponit nomen operi meo.* My intent gives a name to my act. *Non aliter a significatione verborum recedi oportet quam cum manifestum est, aliud sensisse testatorem.* The ordinary meaning of the words ought not to be departed from unless it is evident that the testator intended otherwise. *Quicunque jussu judicis aliquid fecerit non videtur dolo malo fecisse, quia parere necesse est.* Whoever does anything by the command of a judge is not deemed to have done it with an evil intent, because it is necessary to obey. *Voluntas et propositum distinguunt maleficia.* The will and purpose distinguish offenses. *In criminalibus, sufficit generalis malitia intentionis, cum facto paris gradus.* In crimes, a general malicious intent suffices where there is an act of equal degree. *In criminalibus, voluntas reputabitur pro facto.* In criminal cases, the intent will be taken for the deed. *Voluntas facit quod in testamento scriptum valeat.* The will of the testator gives validity to what is written in the will. *Actus non facit reum, nisi mens sit rea.* An act does not render a person guilty, unless the mind is guilty. *Impunitas continuum affectum tribuit delinquendi.* Impunity confirms the disposition of a delinquent. *In atrocioribus delictis punitur affectus licet non sequatur effectus.* In the more atrocious crimes the intent is punished, although an effect does not follow. *Malitia est acida; est mali animi affectus.* Malice is sour; it is the quality of an evil mind. *Voluntas in delictis, non exitus spectatur.* In crimes, the intent, and not the result, is regarded.

INTENTION, *noun*   aim, ambition, *consilium,* design, desire, destination, determination, direction, earnestness, end in view, end intended, fixed direction, fixed purpose, goal, *institutum,* mark, object, objective, plan, *propositum,* purpose, resolution, resolve, set purpose, settled determination, target, ultimate purpose
ASSOCIATED CONCEPTS: donative intention, implied intention, the intention of the parties, malicious intention
FOREIGN PHRASES: *In testamentis plenius voluntates testantium interpretantur.* In wills, the intentions of the testators should be fully regarded. *Non efficit affectus nisi sequatur effectus.* The intention amounts to nothing unless some effect follows. *In conventionibus, contrahentium voluntas potius quam verba spectari placuit.* In contracts, it is the rule to regard the intention of the parties rather than the actual words. *Culpa lata dolo aequiparatur.* Gross negligence is held equivalent to malice. *In maleficiis voluntas spectatur, non exitus.* In offenses, the intention is regarded, not the result. *Intentio inservire debet legibus, non leges intentioni.* The intention of a party ought to be subservient to the laws, not the laws to intentions. *Benigne faciendae sunt interpretationes, propter simplicitatem laicorum, ut res magis valeat quam pereat; et verba intentioni, non e contra, debent inservire.* Interpretations should be liberal, because of the lack of training of laymen, so that the subject matter should be valid rather than void, and words should be subject to the intention, not the intention to the words.

INTENTIONAL, *adjective*   by design, calculated, *cogitatus,* conscious, *consideratus,* considered, contemplated, decided, deliberate, designed, determined, intended, knowing, *lentus,* meditated, outlined beforehand, planned, pondered, prearranged, preconsidered, predesigned, predetermined, premeditated, purposed, purposeful, reasoned, resolved, studied, thought out, thoughtful, willful
ASSOCIATED CONCEPTS: intentional act, intentional homicide, intentional neglect, intentional tort

INTER VIVOS, *noun*   conferment between the living, conveyance between the living, transfer among the living
ASSOCIATED CONCEPTS: inter vivos will

INTERAGENT, *noun*   agent, broker, go-between, instrument, intermediary, intermediate, intermediate agent, intermediator, intervener, intervening agent, mediating agency, mediator, medium, middleman, negotiator, spokesman, vehicle

INTERCEDE, *verb*   act as agent, act as go-between, act as mediator, arbitrate, bring into harmony, bring to an understanding, bring to terms, bring together, compose differences, conciliate, *deprecari,* interfere, intermeddle, intermediate, interpose, intervene, judge, make peace between, meddle, mediate, moderate, negotiate, petition for, plead, referee, settle, stand between, step in, umpire

INTERCESSION, *noun*   arbitrage, arbitration, conciliation, *deprecatio,* diplomacy, instrumentality, interference, interjection, intermeddling, intermediation, interposition, intervention, mediation, negotiation, peacemaking, reconcilement, reconciliation, supplication

INTERCHANGE, *noun*   alternation, barter, change, exchange, give and take, intercourse, *permutatio,* rearrangement, reciprocal exchange, reciprocation, requital, retaliation, swap, trade, transaction

INTERDICT, *verb*   arrest, bar, block, check, debar, declare illegal, deny, deter, disallow, embargo, enjoin, forbid, halt, hinder, impede, inhibit, *interdicere,* obstruct, preclude, prevent, prohibit, proscribe, refuse permission, repress, restrain, restrict, stop, thwart, veto

INTEREST *(Concern),* *noun*   absorption, admiration, anxiety, application, assiduity, attention, attention to detail, awe, care, close attention, concentration, conscientiousness, consequence, consideration, curiosity, curiousness, desire to know, diligent attention, disposition to inquire, eagerness, enthusiasm, esteem, excitement, gravity, heed, heedfulness, import, importance, inclination to ask questions, intentiveness, intentness, mark, meddling, meticulosity, mindfulness, minute attention, minuteness, moment, note, pertinence, preoccupation, prying, questioning, regard, regardfulness, relevance, reverence, salience, significance, solicitude, studiousness, *studium,* thoughtfulness, undivided attention, veneration, weight, weightiness, worry
ASSOCIATED CONCEPTS: conflict of interest, declaration against interest, direct interest, insurable interest, interest in the controversy, interested witness, legal interest, material interest, real party in interest, united in interest

INTEREST *(Ownership),* *noun*   assets, belongings, claim, dominion, droit, holding, lawful possession, part, participation, percentage of ownership, portion, possession, property, proprietorship, right, right of ownership, rightful possession, seisin, share, stake, title
ASSOCIATED CONCEPTS: accounts bearing interest, assignable interest, beneficial interest, common interest, contingent interest, continuity of interest, controlling interest, future interest, interest in land, joint interest, legal interest, legal rate of interest, life interest, person interested in a will, property interest, qualified interest, remainder interest, remaining interest, transfer of interest, undivided interest
FOREIGN PHRASES: *Nemo plus juris ad alienum transferre potest quam ipse habet.* No one can transfer to another any greater right than he himself has.

INTEREST *(Profit),* *noun*   accrual, advantage, dividend, earnings, *faenus,* gain, increment, monetary benefit, monetary gain, premium for the use of money, profit from money loaned, *usura*
ASSOCIATED CONCEPTS: legal rate of interest, usury

INTEREST, *verb*   absorb, affect, arouse, arouse notice, arouse one's enthusiasm, attract, attract notice, beguile, catch the eye, concern, *delectare,* divert one's attention, engage the attention, engage the mind, engage the thoughts, engross, engross the mind, engross the thoughts, entangle, entertain, enthrall, entice, excite, fascinate, grip, hold the attention, inspire, involve, move, occupy, occupy the attention, pique, *placere,* rouse, stir, tantalize, tempt, *tenere,* titillate, touch, whet one's interest

INTERESTED, *adjective*   affected, affiliated, associated, biased, concerned, connected, directly affected by the outcome of a controversy, having investments in, influenced, involved, one-sided, partial, partisan, prejudiced, prepossessed, solicitous, undetached
ASSOCIATED CONCEPTS: interested juror, interested party, interested witness

INTERFERE, *verb*   arrest, bar, be an obstacle, block, break in, burden, check, clog, counteract, countervail, cramp, cripple, cross, curb, deter, disallow, disturb, encroach, encumber, entrammel, fetter, foil, forbid, hamper, handicap, hinder, impede, infringe, inhibit, intercede, intercept, interject, intermeddle, intermit, *interpellare,* interpose, interrupt, intervene, *intervenire,* intrude, invade, meddle, obstruct, preclude, prevent, prohibit, retard, stop, thwart, work against
ASSOCIATED CONCEPTS: interference with business relations, interference with contract rights, interference with interstate commerce, unreasonable interference
FOREIGN PHRASES: *Forstellarius est pauperum depressor et totius communitatis et patriae publicus inimicus.* A forestaller is an enemy of the poor, and a public enemy of the country. *Nemo debet immiscere se rei ad se nihil pertinenti.* No one should interfere with a thing that in no respect concerns him.

INTERIM, *adjective*   impermanent, intermediate, makeshift, provisional, provisory, temporary, *temporis intervallum,* tenative, transient, unfinished, unofficial
ASSOCIATED CONCEPTS: interim relief, interim stay, provisional remedies

INTERIOR, *adjective*   inherent, innate, inner, innermost, internal, inward, private, secret

INTERIOR, *noun*   center, core, essence, inland, inner part, inside, middle

INTERJECT, *verb*   add, blurt, comment, exclaim, explain, express, force in, implant, include, incorporate, infiltrate, inject, insert, intercalate, *intericere,* interjaculate, intermingle, interpolate, *interponere,* interpose, interrupt, intervene, interweave, introduce, intromit, place into, put between, set forth, specify, state, thrust in, vociferate, work in

INTERLOCKING, *adjective*   connective, correlative, interacting, interlinking, meshing
ASSOCIATED CONCEPTS: interlocking defenses, interlocking instruments, interlocking signal systems

INTERLOCUTORY, *adjective*   interim, intermedial, intermediary, intervening, interventional, nonfinal, nonpermanent, not final, provisional, provisory, temporary, tentative, transient, transitory
ASSOCIATED CONCEPTS: interlocutory appeal, interlocutory costs, interlocutory decree, interlocutory injunction, interlocutory order, interlocutory rulings

INTERMEDIARY, *noun*   agent, *arbiter,* arbitrator, buffer, *conciliator,* connecting link, connection, delegate, *deprecator,* diplomat, emissary, go-between, interceder, intercessor, link, mediary, mediator, medium, middleman, moderator, negotiant, negotiator, peacemaker, pleader, propitiator, reconciler, referee, representative, vehicle

INTERMEDIATE, *adjective*   average, between, central, compromising, equidistant, halfway, inserted, instrumental, intercurrent, interjacent, intermediary, interposed, intervenient, intervening, mean, medial, median, mediatorial, mediatory, medium, *medius,* me-

sial, mesne, mid, middle, midmost, moderate, neutral, transitional
ASSOCIATED CONCEPTS: interlocutory order, intermediate appellate court, intermediate order
FOREIGN PHRASES: *Extremis probatis, praesumuntur media.* When the extremes have been proved, those things which are between them are presumed.

INTERMITTENT, *adjective*   alternate, broken, cyclic, cyclical, desultory, discontinuous, fitful, flickering, fluctuating, infrequent, intermitting, interrupted, irregular, nonuniform, occasional, periodic, recurrent, recurring, remittent, rhythmic, seasonal, serial, spasmodic, sporadic, termly, unregular, unsuccessive, wavering

INTERNAL, *adjective*   absorbed, domestic, *domesticus,* enclosed, implanted, infixed, ingrained, inmost, innate, inner, innermost, inside, *interior, intestinus,* private, under the surface, within boundary lines
ASSOCIATED CONCEPTS: internal affairs, Internal Revenue

INTERPOSE, *verb*   be an obstacle to, block, break into, come between, force in, hinder, impede, infiltrate, infringe, inject, insert, intercalate, intercede, intercept, interfere, *intericere,* interject, intermeddle, intermediate, *interponere,* interrupt, intervene, introduce, intrude, mediate, obstruct, obtrude, parenthesize, penetrate, place between, prevent, put in, stand in the way, thrust in
ASSOCIATED CONCEPTS: interpose a claim, interpose a defense, interpose an objection

INTERPRET, *verb*   annotate, characterize, clarify, clear up, *conicere,* construe, convey the meaning of, decipher, decode, deduce, define, delineate, depict, describe, diagnose, explain, explain the meaning, *explanare,* explicate, expound, figure out, give one an idea of, give one an impression of, illuminate, illustrate, *interpretari,* make clear, make plain, make sense of, offer an explanation of, reveal, set forth the meaning, simplify, solve, throw light upon, translate, translate orally, understand, unfold, unravel, unscramble
ASSOCIATED CONCEPTS: construction, interpret a contract, interpret a will

INTERPRETIVE, *adjective*   annotative, clarifying, constructive, definitive, elucidative, enlightening, explanatory, explicative, illuminating, interpretational

INTERRELATED, *adjective*   affiliated, affinitive, agnate, akin, allied, analogous, associated, cognate, conjugate, connatural, connected, consanguineous, consociate, correlated, correlative, enmeshed, fraternal, germane, interaffiliated, interallied, interassociated, interconnected, interlinked, interwoven, joined, kindred, linked, of the same family, pertinent, related, relevant, sib, tied, united

INTERROGATION, *noun*   catechization, cross-examination, examination, exploration, formal questioning, grilling, inquest, inquiry, inquisition, inspection, *interrogatio,* investigation, *percontatio,* probe, *quaestio,* query, questioning, scrutiny, search, taking information
ASSOCIATED CONCEPTS: grand jury inquiry, interrogation of a party to an action, interrogation of a witness

INTERROGATIVE, *adjective*   all-searching, diagnostic, exploratory, fact-finding, inquisitional, inquisitive, inquisitorial, interested, interrogational, *interrogativus,* investigative, penetrating, piercing, probing, prying, questioning, quizzical, scrutinizing, searching

INTERROGATORIES, *noun*   demands, inquiries, pre-trial inquiries, questioning, questions, written requests for information

INTERRUPT, *verb*   arrest, balk, barge in, break, break in, butt in, cause to cease, cause to delay, cease, check, chime in, clog, come between, cut, delay, desist, disconnect, discontinue, disjoin, dissever, dissolve, distract, disturb, disunite, divide, foil, frustrate, get in the way, hinder, inhibit, intercept, interfere, intermit, *intermittere, interpellare,* interpose, intrude, leave off, meddle, obstruct, punctuate, put a stop to, put an end to, retard, separate, sever, stop, sunder, suspend, thwart
ASSOCIATED CONCEPTS: interrupt a separation, interrupt possession

INTERRUPTION, *noun*   abeyance, armistice, arrest, bar, block, break, cessation, check, clog, deadlock, delay, disconnection, discontinuance, disjunction, dissolution, disunion, gap, halt, hiatus, hindrance, impediment, *intercapedo,* interception, interference, interim, interlude, *intermissio,* intermission, interstice, *intervallum,* intrusion, lull, obstacle, obstruction, pause, recess, respite, severance, standstill, stop, stoppage, sunderance, suspension, truce
ASSOCIATED CONCEPTS: business interruption insurance, interruption of adverse possession, interruption of service

INTERSECTION, *noun*   *bivium,* concourse, conjunction, connection, crossing, crossing point, crosspoint, crossroad, crosswalk, cruciation, *decussatio,* decussation, interconnection, intercrossing, joining place, joint, junction, juncture, meeting place, meeting point, traversal, union

INTERSPERSE, *verb*   diffuse, disseminate, distribute, *immiscere,* interfuse, interlard, intermingle, interpenetrate, interpolate, interpose, interweave, mix, pepper, put between, scatter, shake, sprinkle, work in

INTERTWINE, *verb*   braid, crisscross, cross, enlace, enmesh, entangle, entwine, form a network, *innectere,* inosculate, interknit, interlace, interlink, intermix, interthread, intertwist, interweave, inweave, knot, lace, mesh, plait, plat, *redimire,* reticulate, splice, tangle, tie together, twine together, twist, web, wreathe

INTERVAL, *noun*   abeyance, break, gap, halt, hiatus, interim, interlude, intermission, interregnum, interruption, interstice, *intervallum,* intervening time, lapse, lull, pause, recess, respite, rest, *spatium interiectum,* spell, truce

INTERVENE, *verb*   become a party to an action, break in, come between, encroach, infringe, intercede, *intercedere,* interfere, intermeddle, interpose, interrupt, *intervenire,* intrude, meddle, obtrude, step in, *supervenire*
ASSOCIATED CONCEPTS: intervening act, intervening agency, intervening cause, intervening efficient cause, intervening estate, intervening force, intervening par-

ties, intervening sufficient cause, intervening super-ceding cause, intervenor, intervention as of right, intervention by leave of court

INTERVENTION *(Imposition into a lawsuit),* **noun** entrance into a lawsuit, entrance of a third party, insertion, interference, interjection, interjection into a lawsuit, interposition, intrusion
ASSOCIATED CONCEPTS: intervention by leave of the court, intervention by right

INTERVENTION *(Interference),* **noun** intercalation, interception, intercession, interjacence, interjection, interloping, intermeddling, intermediation, interpolation, interposition, interruption, *interventus,* intrusion

INTERVIEW, noun audience, audition, colloquy, conference, *congressio, conloquium,* consultation, conversation, dialogue, discussion, exchange of views, hearing, meeting, mutual exchange, oral examination, question and answer, talk, verbal intercourse

INTIMATE, adjective allied, associated with, brotherly, close, closely acquainted, closely associated, confidential, confiding, *coniunctus,* consociated, faithful, familiar, *familiaris,* federate, fraternal, friendly, guarded, inmost, innermost, *intimus,* linked, on familiar terms, personal, private, secret, strongly attached, trusted
ASSOCIATED CONCEPTS: confidentiality, fiduciary relationship

INTIMATION, noun allusion, *denuntiatio,* hint, idea, implication, inference, inkling, innuendo, insinuation, mention, *nuntius,* overtone, reference, *significatio,* suggestion

INTIMIDATE, verb abash, affright, alarm, badger, browbeat, bully, coerce, cow, daunt, *deterrere,* dismay, dispirit, disquiet, duress, frighten, harass, hector, *incutere, inicere,* menace, overawe, petrify, put in fear, scare, shock, terrify, terrorize, threaten, unnerve
ASSOCIATED CONCEPTS: unlawful intimidation

INTOLERABLE, adjective impossible, insufferable, insupportable, unbearable, unendurable
ASSOCIATED CONCEPTS: intolerable cruelty, intolerable severity

INTOLERANCE, noun *acerbitas, adrogantia,* aversion, bias, bigotry, chauvinism, discrimination, dislike, hatred, illiberality, incapacity to endure, jaundice, jingoism, lack of toleration, narrow-mindedness, narrowness, one-sidedness, partiality, persecution, preconception, prejudgment, prejudice, racism, rejection, sectarianism, sectionalism, segregation, slant, subjectivity, *superbia,* want of forbearance, want of toleration
ASSOCIATED CONCEPTS: intolerable cruelty

INTONATION, noun accentuation, cadence, delivery, inflection, phonation, pitch, quality, resonance, sound, timbre, tonality, tone, tone of voice, vocalism, voice
ASSOCIATED CONCEPTS: demeanor

INTRACTABLE, adjective adamant, balky, beyond control, contrary, contumacious, defiant, *difficilis,* disobedient, dogged, firm, froward, headstrong, heed-less, incorrigible, indocile, *indocilis,* indomitable, inflexible, insubordinate, insuppressible, irrepressible, mulish, not easily governed, not pliable, obdurate, obstinate, obstreperous, pertinacious, perverse, pervicacious, rebellious, recalcitrant, refractory, resistive, restive, stubborn, tenacious, unbending, uncontrollable, uncurbed, undisciplined, ungovernable, unmalleable, unmanageable, unruly, unsubmissive, unwilling, unyielding, wayward, willful

INTRICATE, adjective complex, complicated, delicate, difficult, elaborate, involved, tangled, tricky

INTRINSIC *(Belonging),* **adjective** implicit, inherent, native, pertinent
ASSOCIATED CONCEPTS: intrinsic fraud, intrinsic jury, intrinsic value

INTRINSIC *(Deep down),* **adjective** deep seated, inner, internal, inward

INTRODUCE, verb bring in, enter, *inducere,* induct, inject, insert, interpose, *introducere, invehere,* offer, offer as an exhibit, place before, present, present formally, present to the court for acceptance, proffer, put, put forward, put forward for consideration, put in, submit, surrender, tender, usher in

INTRODUCTION, noun act of bringing in, admittance, formal presentation, *inductio,* induction, interposition, *introductio, invectio,* offering, offering as an exhibit, placing, presentation
ASSOCIATED CONCEPTS: introduction of evidence

INTROSPECTION, noun contemplation, innermost thoughts, introversion, *ipsum se inspicere,* looking within, meditation, musing, pensiveness, reflection, reverie, self-absorption, self-communion, self-counsel, self-examination, self-inspection, self-knowledge, self-scrutiny, self-study, thoughtfulness

INTRUDE, verb come uninvited, crash, encroach, enter uninvited, enter unlawfully, foist oneself, force oneself, horn in, impose, infringe, interfere, interlope, interrupt, invade, irrupt, obtrude, *se interponere,* thrust in, thrust oneself, trench on, trespass
ASSOCIATED CONCEPTS: invade privacy, trespass

INTRUSION, noun aggression, attack, encroachment, forced entrance, *importunitas,* imposition, incursion, infiltration, infringement, interference, interloping, interruption, invasion, irruption, meddling, obtrusion, overrunning, trespass, uninvited attendance, uninvited entry, unlawful entry, unwelcome suggestion
ASSOCIATED CONCEPTS: intrusion of rights, right of privacy, trespass

INTRUSIVE, adjective hindering, infringing, interfering, interloping, interruptive, invading, invasive, obtrusive, trespassing

INUNDATE, verb bury, deluge, drench, engulf, fill to superfluity, flood, flow over, glut, immerse, overflood, overflow, overspread, overwhelm, pour over, run over, rush upon, saturate, spill over, surge, swamp

INURE *(Accustom),* **verb** acclimate, acclimatize, accustom, acquaint, adjust, *adsuefacere,* condition, domesticate, familiarize, get used to, habituate, harden,n, make routine, naturalize, sanctify by custom, season, toughen

INURE *(Benefit), verb*   accumulate, advance, advantage, aid, assist, avail, be of use, be profitable, bolster, contribute, enhance, enrich, forward, furnish aid, further, gain, help, improve, pay, profit, promote, render useful, serve, subserve, supply aid, turn to account, upgrade, yield gain, yield profit

INVADE, *verb*   aggress, arrogate, assail, assault, attack, break in, encroach, enter hostilely, impinge, *incurrere, incursionem,* infringe, intrude, *invadere,* obtrude, overrun, overtake, penetrate, raid, run over, trespass, usurp, violate
ASSOCIATED CONCEPTS: invade the corpus of a trust, invade the province of the jury, invasion of privacy, invasion of property rights, invasion of rights

INVALID, *adjective*   abrogated, baseless, canceled, fallacious, faulty, futile, having no force, inadequate, ineffective, ineffectual, inefficacious, *infirmus,* inoperative, *inritus,* lacking authority, lacking force, lacking strength, not binding, *nugatorius,* nugatory, null, quashed, unauthentic, untenable, untrue, useless, vain, void, weak, without legal efficacy
ASSOCIATED CONCEPTS: invalid delegation, invalid gift, invalid transfer, invalid will
FOREIGN PHRASES: *Ab abusu ad usum non valet consequentia.* A conclusion as to the use of a thing from its abuse is invalid.

INVALIDATE, *verb*   abolish, abort, abrogate, annul, cancel, confute, deprive of legal effect, disannul, disprove, disqualify, erase, *inritum facere, labefactare,* make void, nullify, override, overrule, overthrow, quash, refute, repeal, repudiate, rescind, *rescindere,* retract, reverse, revoke, undermine, undo, vitiate, withdraw
ASSOCIATED CONCEPTS: invalidate a transfer, invalidate a will, invalidate an election

INVALIDITY, *noun*   annulment, cancellation, disqualification, erroneousness, fallaciousness, fallacy, falseness, falsity, inadequacy, incompetence, ineffectiveness, nullity, unsoundness, untenableness, vitiation, voidness
ASSOCIATED CONCEPTS: declaration of invalidity
FOREIGN PHRASES: *Pacta quae turpem causam continent non sunt observanda.* Contracts which are based on an unlawful consideration will not be enforced. *Pacta quae contra leges constitutionesque, vel contra bonos mores fiunt, nullam vim habere, indubitati juris est.* It is unquestionably the law that contracts which are made contrary to the laws or against good morals, have no force in law. *Quae ab initio non valent, ex post facto convalescere non possunt.* Things invalid from the beginning cannot be made valid by a subsequent act.

INVALUABLE, *adjective*   beyond price, costly, expensive, *inaestimabilis,* incalculable, incapable of being appraised, inestimable, matchless, of inestimable value, peerless, precious, *pretiosissimus,* priceless, unequalled, unparalleled, valuable, without price

INVARIABLY, *adverb*   always, as a rule, changelessly, commonly, constantly, conventionally, customarily, faithfully, fixedly, frequently, generally, habitually, immutably, in all cases, in every instance, normally, ordinarily, perpetually, regularly, repeatedly, rigidly, routinely, steadily, systematically, tradition-ally, unalterably, unchangeably, undeviatingly, uniformly, unvarying, usually, without exception

INVASION, *noun*   aggression, assault, attack, attack on rights, breach, disobedience, encroachment, foray, hostile entry, *incursio,* incursion, infiltration, infraction, infringement, inroad, *inruptio,* interference, interloping, intervention, intrusion, overstepping, raid, siege, transgression, trespass, violation
ASSOCIATED CONCEPTS: invasion of a corpus, invasion of principal, invasion of privacy, invasion of rights, wrongful invasion

INVEIGH, *verb*   attack, blast, cry out against, denounce, dispraise, exclaim against, fulminate, impugn, *incessere, increpare, insectari,* lash, protest against, rage against, rail, raise one's voice against, rate, revile, scold, score, storm against, thunder against, utter invective, vilify, vituperate

INVEIGLE, *verb*   allure, attract, bait, bamboozle, befool, beguile, blandish, cajole, cheat, chouse, coax, cozen, deceive, decoy, defraud, delude, draw, ensnare, entangle, entice, entrap, fool, gull, illaqueate, importune, induce, influence, lay a trap, lead astray, lead on, lure, maneuver, mislead, persuade, seduce, snare, suborn, sway, tempt, trap, trick, urge, victimize, wheedle, win

INVENT *(Falsify), verb*   *comminisci,* counterfeit, distort, embroider, exaggerate, fabricate, fake, falsify, feign, fib, fictionalize, humbug, lie, make believe, make up, misrepresent, misstate, pervert, pretend, prevaricate, sham, trump up, varnish

INVENT *(Produce for the first time), verb*   author, bring into being, build, coin, come upon, compose, conceive, concoct, construct, contrive, create, design, devise, discover, draft, dream up, envisage, *excogitare,* excogitate, fabricate, fashion, find, forge, form, imagine, improvise, initiate, introduce, *invenire,* manufacture, originate, produce, realize, *reperire,* think of, think up, visualize

INVENTION, *noun*   brain child, coinage, composition, concoction, contraption, contrivance, creation, creative effort, creative fabrication, discovery, fabrication, finding, formation, handiwork, improvisation, innovation, *inventum,* origination, product, *reperta*

INVENTORY, *noun*   catalogue, checklist, contents, enumeration, *index,* itemization, itemized list, list, list of properties, manifest, merchandise list, record, register, schedule of articles, stock book, stock list, stock sheet, *tabula,* tally sheet
ASSOCIATED CONCEPTS: inventory of assets

INVERSE, *adjective*   antipodal, antipodean, antithetical, contrary, converse, *conversus,* diametrically opposite, *inversus,* inverted, opposite, reverse, reversed, transposed, turned about
ASSOCIATED CONCEPTS: inverse condemnation, inverse discrimination

INVEST *(Fund), verb*   advance, back, buy into, buy stock, deal in futures, employ capital, finance, gamble, infuse funds, lay out, lend, lend on security, loan, make an investment, *occupare,* outlay, play the market, *ponere,* provide capital, provide money, put out at inter-

est, put up, risk, risk one's money, sink, speculate, sponsor, support, venture
ASSOCIATED CONCEPTS: invest capital

INVEST *(Vest), verb*   appoint, authorize, charge, charter, commission, confer power, *deferre,* delegate, depute, empower, enable, endow with authority, entrust, furnish with rank, give a mandate, give authority, give power, grant authority, grant power, inaugurate, induct, install, instate, institute, license, *mandare,* name, nominate, ordain, permit, privilege, put in commission, sanction

INVESTIGATE, *verb*   analyze, ask, *cognoscere,* collect facts, conduct an inquiry, consider, deliberate upon, delve into, dig into, discuss, dissect, examine, examine in detail, examine the particulars, examine with care and accuracy, explore, go into, hold an inquiry, inquire into, inquire into systematically, inspect, interrogate, look into, peer into, *perscrutari,* probe, pursue an inquiry, *quaerere,* question, reconnoiter, review, scan, scrutinize, search into, seek information regarding, study in detail, survey, take evidence, track, track mentally
ASSOCIATED CONCEPTS: investigate a crime, investigate charges, investigate the merits of a case

INVESTIGATION, *noun*   careful search, careful study, close inquiry, collection of facts, detailed examination, examination, exhaustive study, exploration, formal scrutiny, *indagatio,* inquire to ascertain facts, inquiry, *inquisitio,* interrogation, *investigatio,* legal inquiry, official inquiry, probe, questioning, research, scrutinization, scrutiny, search, searching inquiry, statistical inquiry, strict inquiry, systematic search
ASSOCIATED CONCEPTS: blanket investigation, criminal investigation, governmental investigation, judicial investigation, legislative investigation

INVESTMENT, *noun*   backing, capital invested, capital outlay, employment of capital, endowment, financial backing, financing, invested capital, invested money, invested property, loan, loan at interest, outlay, speculation, venture
ASSOCIATED CONCEPTS: investment broker, investment contract, investment security, investment trust

INVETERATE, *adjective*   accustomed, addicted, chronic, chronical, confirmed, customary, deep-rooted, entrenched, established, firmly established, fixed, frequent, habitual, habituated, hardened, ingrained, inured, *inveteratus,* long-standing, *penitus defixus, penitus insitus,* rooted, set, time-honored, wonted

INVIDIOUS, *adjective*   abominable, calculated to provoke resentment, disagreeable, disliked, disobliging, harmful, hateful, hurtful, injurious, *invidiosus,* irksome, likely to excite ill will, loathsome, malicious, objectionable, obnoxious, odious, offensive, plaguesome, rancorous, spiteful, troublesome, unacceptable, unaccommodating, ungracious, unkind, unpleasant, unwelcome, vexatious
ASSOCIATED CONCEPTS: invidious discrimination

INVINCIBLE, *adjective*   all-powerful, ever-victorious, impossible to defeat, impossible to vanquish, incapable of being overcome, indestructible, indomitable, ineradicable, inexpugnable, *inexsuperabilis,* inextinguishable, inpermeable, insuperable, insurmountable,

invictus, inviolable, invulnerable, irresistible, overpowering, overwhelming, resistless, secure from capture, unable to be overcome, unable to be quelled, unable to be subjugated, unassailable, unbeatable, unconquerable, unsubduable, unvanquishable, unyielding

INVIOLABILITY, *noun*   immunity from assault, impenetrability, impregnability, incorruptibility, indestructibility, inexpugnability, inviolableness, invulnerability, protection, safety, *sanctitas,* security, security against violence, unassailability
ASSOCIATED CONCEPTS: inviolability of Constitutional rights, inviolability of contracts

INVIOLATE, *adjective*   complete, consecrated, free from desecration, free from impairment, hallowed, intact, *intactus, integer, inviolatus,* pure, sacred, sanctified, scatheless, secure, sound, spotless, stainless, unaffected by injury, unaltered, unblemished, unbroken, uncorrupted, undefiled, undestroyed, undisturbed, unharmed, unhurt, unimpaired, uninjured, unpolluted, unprofaned, unscathed, unspotted, unstained, untouched, unviolated, whole

INVITATION, *noun*   advance, allurement, appeal, approach, attraction, bid, bidding, call, challenge, encouragement, enticement, incitement, inducement, *invitatio,* offer, overture, petition, plea, proffer, prompting, proposal, proposition, provocative, request, solicitation, summons, tender, urging
ASSOCIATED CONCEPTS: business invitation, invitation to bid, license by invitation

INVOICE *(Bill), noun*   account, account rendered, note, reckoning, statement, statement of account, statement of obligations, statement particularizing debts due, tab

INVOICE *(Itemized list), noun*   account of goods shipped, account of merchandise, bill of lading, check list, enumeration, inventory, itemized account, *libellus,* list of goods, list of items, list of items shipped, list of mercantile goods, merchandise specification, schedule, schedule of items and their respective prices
ASSOCIATED CONCEPTS: uniform commercial code

INVOKE, *verb*   ask solemnly for, beg for, bid, call on for a blessing, call on for help, call up, conjure, entreat, *implorare,* implore, *invocare,* invocate, raise spirits, recite a spell, recite an incantation, summon, summon by incantation
ASSOCIATED CONCEPTS: invoke the authority of the court, invoke the Fifth Amendment

INVOLUNTARY, *adjective*   against one's will, averse, *coactus,* coercive, compulsory, forced, independent of volition, *invitus,* mandatory, *non voluntarius,* obligatory, unassenting, unconscious, unintended, unintentional, unmeditated, unpremeditated, unthinking, unwilled, unwilling, without consent, without power of choice, without will
ASSOCIATED CONCEPTS: involuntary bailment, involuntary bankruptcy, involuntary confession, involuntary dismissal, involuntary manslaughter, involuntary payment, involuntary sale, involuntary servitude, involuntary statements, involuntary suretyship, involuntary trust, involuntary unemployment

INVOLUTION, *noun* complexity, complication, confusion, convolution, embroilment, entanglement, imbroglio, *implicatio,* intricacy, involvement, knot, labyrinth, maze, puzzle, sinuation, sinuosity, sleave, snarl, tangle, torsion, tortility, tortuosity, tortuousness, twist, web

INVOLVE *(Implicate),* **verb** accuse, ally, associate, blame, brand, bring accusation, bring charges, cast a slur on, charge, connect, consociate, *continere,* criminate, delate, denounce, draw in, entangle, incriminate, inculpate, interconnect, interrelate, lay the blame on, link together, lodge a complaint, make a party to, make participator, prefer charges, prove to be a participant in, relate, show to be an abettor, stigmatize, tie in with
ASSOCIATED CONCEPTS: involve a codefendant

INVOLVE *(Participate),* **verb** act in concert, associate, be a part of, be a party to, be in league with, collaborate, collude, confederate, connect, contribute, cooperate, enter into, have a hand in, join forces, join in, lend oneself to, make common cause with, partake, play a part, relate, share, side with, strike in with, support, take part, take sides, team up, unite, work together
ASSOCIATED CONCEPTS: involve a case or controversey, involve a Constitutional question, involve life or liberty, involve the merits of a case, involve title to real property, involve wrongdoing

IOTA, *noun* bit, crumb, dab, dash, drop, fragment, grain, jot, minute quantity, morsel, particle, scintilla, shred, small amount, small quantity, spark, tittle, trace, whit

IPSO FACTO, *adverb* absolutely, by the act itself, by the fact itself, by the mere fact, by the very fact, essentially, positively, truly

IRKSOME, *adjective* annoying, boresome, boring, bothersome, distressing, *gravis,* irritating, jejune, *molestus, odiosus,* tiresome, tiring, troublesome, weariful, wearing, wearisome, wearying

IRONCLAD, *adjective* covered, defended, difficult to alter, difficult to break, difficult to change, exacting, firm, immutable, impossible to alter, impossible to break, impossible to change, inexorable, inflexible, ironbound, irreversible, irrevocable, relentless, rigid, rigorous, strict, stringent, unalterable, unbending, unbreakable, unchangeable, unchanging, uncompromising, unmalleable, unpliant, unrelenting, unshakeable, unyielding

IRONIC, *adjective* cynical, ironical, paradoxical, quizzical, sarcastic, sarcastical, sardonic, satiric, satirical

IRONY, *noun* cynicism, *dissimulatio, ironia,* mockery, sarcasm, satire

IRRATIONAL, *adjective* absurd, *absurdus,* bizarre, brainless, contrary to reason, crazy, foolish, heedless, ill-advised, ill-considered, ill-judged, illogical, imprudent, injudicious, insensate, ludicrous, mindless, nonsensical, outrageous, preposterous, *rationis expers,* reasonless, ridiculous, senseless, *stultus,* stupid, thoughtless, unconsidered, unintelligent, unreasonable, unreasoned, unreasoning, unreflecting, unsensible, unsound, unthinking, unthoughtful, unwise, utterly illogical, void of reason, without judgment, without reason, without rhyme or reason, witless
ASSOCIATED CONCEPTS: irrational behavior

IRREBUTTABLE, *adjective* incontestable, indisputable, indubitable, irrefutable, unchallengeable, unimpeachable, unquestionable
ASSOCIATED CONCEPTS: irrebuttable evidence

IRRECONCILABLE, *adjective* adamant, alienated, antagonized, at variance, *contrariae,* estranged, firm, hostile, immovable, immutable, *implacabilis,* implacable, implacably opposed, *inexorabilis,* inexorable, inexpiable, inflexible, inimical, intransigent, refusing to agree, refusing to harmonize, rigid, unable to be pacified, unadjustable, unaffected, unalterable, unappeasable, unbending, unchangeable, uncompromising, unconformable, unforgiving, unmoved, unreconciled, unyielding
ASSOCIATED CONCEPTS: irreconcilable conflict, irreconcilable differences

IRRECOVERABLE, *adjective* beyond recall, incorrigible, irredeemable, irreparable, irretrievable, irreversible, past hope

IRREDEEMABLE, *adjective* beyond remedy, consumed, cureless, dissipated, expended, finished, gone, gone to waste, hopeless, immitigable, incapable of being bought back, inconvertible, incorrigible, incurable, irreclaimable, irrecoverable, irreformable, irreparable, irretrievable, irreversible, irrevocable, lost, past cure, past hope, past mending, past recall, remediless, ruined, spent, squandered, unchangeable, undone, unpayable, used up, wasted, without hope

IRREFUTABLE, *adjective* axiomatic, axiomatical, beyond doubt, certain, *certus,* demonstrable, *firmus,* inappealable, incontestable, incontrovertible, indisputable, indubious, indubitable, irrefragable, past dispute, positive, proven, questionless, sure, testable, unanswerable, unchallengeable, unconfutable, uncontestable, uncontroversial, undeniable, undoubtable, unequivocal, unimpeachable, unmistakable, unquestionable
ASSOCIATED CONCEPTS: irrebuttable presumption

IRREGULAR *(Improper),* **adjective** against the rules, condemnable, criminal, criminous, dishonest, foul, illegal, illegitimate, illicit, immoral, nefarious, open to objection, out of place, prohibited, unauthorized, unwarranted, wicked, wrong, wrongful
ASSOCIATED CONCEPTS: irregular conduct, irregular indorsement, irregularity in proceeding, jurisdictional irregularity

IRREGULAR *(Not usual),* **adjective** aberrant, abnormal, anomalistic, anomalous, asymmetric, asymmetrical, atypical, deviating from the general rule, deviating from the norm, deviating from the standard, deviative, divergent, eccentric, erratic, exceptional, extraordinary, freakish, heteroclite, *inaequabilis, inusitatus,* odd, out of order, out of place, out of the ordinary, peculiar, queer, singular, strange, unconformable, unconventional, unique, unnatural, unsymmetric, unsymmetrical, unusual
ASSOCIATED CONCEPTS: irregular incorporation, irregular judgment

IRREGULARITY, noun aberrance, aberrancy, aberration, abnormality, abnormity, anomaly, asymmetry, breach, changeableness, confusion, crookedness, desultoriness, deviation, disarrangement, discontinuity, disorder, disorderliness, distortion, divergence, eccentricity, exception, fitfulness, idiosyncrasy, illegality, imperfection, improperness, inconsistency, infringement, intermittence, jaggedness, lack of order, lack of propriety, lack of symmetry, lawlessness, lumpiness, malformation, malfunction, mutability, nonconformity, oddity, oddness, peculiarity, rarity, roughness, singularity, solecism, strangeness, turbulence, unconformity, unevenness, uniqueness, unnaturalness, unorthodoxy, unpunctuality, unruliness, unsmoothness, unsteadiness, ununiformity, unusualness, variability, variableness, variation, violation, want of method, wildness

IRRELATIVE, adjective alien, apart, detached, impertinent, inapplicable, inapposite, independent, irrelevant, removed, separate, separated, strange, unaffiliated, unallied, unassociated, unattached, unconnected, unrelated, without connection, without relation

IRRELEVANT, adjective alien, *alienus,* aside from the point, beside the mark, beside the point, beside the question, deviating, extraneous, far from the point, foreign, gratuitous, immaterial, impertinent, inapplicable, inapposite, inappropos, inappropriate, inapt, incongruous, inconsequent, inconsequential, inessential, insignificant, irrelative, malapropos, *nihil ad rem pertinet,* not applicable, not on point, not pertaining to, not pertinent, not significant, not to the point, not to the purpose, not vital, off the subject, off the topic, out of order, out of place, out of the way, remote, unallied, unapt, unconnected, unessential, unimportant, unrelated, unsuitable, unwarranted, without reference to
ASSOCIATED CONCEPTS: irrelevant evidence, irrelevant pleading, irrelevant statement, irrelevant testimony

IRREMEDIABLE, adjective beyond correction, beyond cure, beyond hope, beyond recall, beyond redress, beyond remedy, cureless, deadly, hopeless, immedicable, immitigable, impossible to better, incurable, inevitable, inexpiable, irrecoverable, irredeemable, irreparable, irretrievable, irreversible, irrevocable, past cure, past help, past mending, remediless, ruined, unable to be corrected, unable to be fixed, unable to be remedied, unfixable, unimprovable

IRREPARABLE, adjective incurable, irrecoverable, irredeemable, irreversible, remediless, ruined, undone
ASSOCIATED CONCEPTS: irreparable damage, irreparable harm, irreparable injury

IRREPREHENSIBLE, adjective above suspicion, aboveboard, blameless, circumspect, exalted, faultless, free from fault, free of guilt, guiltless, honest, impeccable, incorruptible, inculpable, *innocens,* innocent, innoxious, inoffensive, irreproachable, irreprovable, not guilty, *sanctus,* sinless, spotless, stainless, straightforward, unassailable, unblamable, unblameworthy, unblemished, uncensurable, unchallengeable, undeserving of censure, unerring, unexceptionable, unfallen, unimpeachable, uninvolved, unobjectionable, unoffending, unsullied, upright, virtuous

IRRESISTIBLE, adjective cogent, compelling, forceful, forcible, formidable, impossible to overcome, impossible to resist, impossible to withstand, indomitable, *insuperabilis, invictus,* invincible, mighty, omnipotent, overpowering, overwhelming, potent, powerful, puissant, resistless, strong, superior, unbeatable, unconquerable, vigorous
ASSOCIATED CONCEPTS: irresistible force, irresistible impulse

IRRESOLUTE, adjective capricious, changeable, changeful, doubtful, doubting, *dubius,* erratic, faltering, fickle, fluctuating, frivolous, hesitant, hesitating, *incertus,* indecisive, infirm of purpose, lukewarm, mercurial, mutable, oscillating, spineless, timid, uncertain, undecided, undetermined, unfixed, unresolved, unsettled, unsteadfast, unsteady, vacillant, vacillating, vacillatory, volatile, wavering

IRRESPECTIVE, adjective despite, in spite of, regardless of, without reference, without respect or regard to

IRRESPONSIBLE, adjective arbitrary, capricious, changeable, disloyal, disobedient, dutiless, flighty, fluctuating, frivolous, inconstant, infirm of purpose, lawless, mutinous, perfidious, rash, rebellious, shiftless, thoughtless, treacherous, trustless, uncontrolled, uncurbed, undependable, undisciplined, undutiful, unfaithworthy, unreliable, unrestrained, unstable, unsteady, untrustworthy, untrusty, vacillating, wavering
ASSOCIATED CONCEPTS: incompetence, irresponsible actions

IRRETRIEVABLE, adjective dissipated, dissolved, forfeited, given up, gone, hopelessly lost, *inreparabilis,* irreclaimable, irrecoverable, irredeemable, irreparable, lost, past recall, spent, unrecoverable, untraceable, vanished

IRREVERSIBLE, adjective beyond remedy, cureless, entrenched, hopeless, immutable, impossible to change, impossible to reverse, incommutable, incurable, indefeasible, indissoluble, indissolvable, ineradicable, inextinguishable, irreclaimable, irrecoverable, irredeemable, irreformable, irremedial, irremovable, irreparable, irrepealable, irretrievable, irrevocable, lasting, nonreversible, not capable of annulment, permanent, remediless, reverseless, unalterable, unchangeable, unrestorable, unreturnable
ASSOCIATED CONCEPTS: irreversible damage, irreversible detriment

IRREVOCABLE, adjective beyond recall, binding, changeless, definite, final, firm, fixed, immitigable, immovable, immutable, impossible to change, incapable of revocation, incommutable, indefeasible, indelible, indestructible, indissoluble, indissolvable, ineluctable, ineradicable, inescapable, inevasible, inevitable, inextinguishable, inflexible, *irrevocabilis,* intransmutable, irreclaimable, irredeemable, irremediable, irremovable, irreparable, irrepealable, irretrievable, irreversible, lasting, nonreversible, permanent, persisting, remediless, reverseless, settled, stable, unable to be annulled, unalterable, unavoidable, unchangeable, unmodifiable, unrepealable, unrestorable, without appeal
ASSOCIATED CONCEPTS: irrevocable dedication, irrevocable gift, irrevocable grant, irrevocable license, irrevo-

cable option, irrevocable pledge, irrevocable transfer, irrevocable trust

IRRITATE, *verb*   affront, aggravate, agitate, anger, annoy, badger, bother, bully, chafe, discompose, displease, disturb, enrage, exacerbate, exasperate, excite anger, excite impatience, fret, gall, give offense, grate, harass, hector, incense, inflame, infuriate, *irritare,* irk, jar, madden, molest, nag, needle, nettle, offend, pain, peeve, persecute, pester, pique, plague, provoke, put out of humor, rankle, rasp, rile, rub the wrong way, ruffle, sting, stir to anger, tease, torment, torture, vex

ISOLATE, *verb*   banish, blacklist, confine, cut off, detach, disconnect, disengage, disjoin, dislocate, dissever, dissociate, disunite, enisle, exclude, excommunicate, exile, insulate, island, keep apart, keep from contact with others, keep in solitude, maroon, ostracize, outlaw, part, place by itself, put aside, quarantine, refuse to associate with, rope off, *secernere,* seclude, segregate, *seiungere,* separate, sequester, set apart, set aside, sever, split, sunder
ASSOCIATED CONCEPTS: isolated occurrence, isolated transaction

ISSUANCE, *noun*   announcement, broadcast, bulletin, communication, communique, culmination, debouchment, decree, delivery, discharge, dispatch, effluence, effluency, effusion, egress, egression, emanation, emergence, emission, escape, exit, final result, fruit, gush, issue, manifesto, message, notice, notification, outcome, outflow, outgo, outlet, outpour, proclamation, promulgation, pronouncement, pronunciamento, prospectus, public announcement, publication, publicity, release, report, rescript, result, statement, ultimate result, upshot
ASSOCIATED CONCEPTS: issuance of an insurance policy, issuance of execution, issuance of order, issuance of process, issuance of subpoena, issuance of summons

ISSUE *(Matter in dispute), noun*   *causa,* cause, debatable point, disputed point of law, disputed question, fact put in controversy by the pleadings, field of inquiry, item on the agenda, material point, material point deduced by the pleadings, matter, matter in hand, matter in question, matter of contention, point, point in question, problem, proposition, question, question at issue, *res,* subject for inquiry, topic under consideration
ASSOCIATED CONCEPTS: bond issue, collateral issue, fundamental issue, genuine issue, immaterial issue, joining of issue, justiciable issue, labor issue, material issue, moot issue, note of issue, triable issue
FOREIGN PHRASES: *Placita negativa duo exitum non faciunt.* Two negative pleas do not make an issue.

ISSUE *(Progeny), noun*   child, children, descendants, family, heirs, *liberi,* lineage, lineal descendants, offspring, *progenies, stirps*
ASSOCIATED CONCEPTS: adopted children, die without issue, failure of issue, last issue, legitimate issue

FOREIGN PHRASES: *Si quis praegnantem uxorem reliquit, non videtur sine liberis decessisse.* If a man dies, leaving his wife pregnant, he is considered as having died childless.

ISSUE *(Publish), verb*   air, announce, assert formally, bring into the open, broadcast, call public attention to, circulate, communicate, declare, disclose, dispense, disperse, disseminate, distribute, divulge, *edere,* enunciate, expose, give out, give public notice of, inform, lay before the public, make a public announcement, make known, notify, notify publicly, offer to the public, post, print, proclaim, promulgate, pronounce, *pronuntiare, proponere,* propound, publicize, put forth, put forward, put into circulation, put out, release, reveal, send out, set forth, spread, state, utter with conviction
ASSOCIATED CONCEPTS: issue a decision of the court, issue a judgment, issue an order

ISSUE *(Send forth), verb*   break forth, burst forth, come forward, come onto the horizon, come out, come out in the open, *egredi,* egress, emanate, emerge, *erumpere, exire,* exit, exude, flow, flow out, make its appearance, manifest itself, pour forth, pour out, put in an appearance, spring up, stream, surface, surge, transmit
ASSOCIATED CONCEPTS: issue stock

ITEM, *noun*   article, asset, commodity, component, constituent, count, detail, effect, element, entity, entry, feature, gadget, good, ingredient, merchandise, object, *pars,* part, particular, piece, piece of information, piece of news, point, possession, product, *res,* salable commodity, separate paragraph, singleton, specification, staple, story, unit, vendible, ware
ASSOCIATED CONCEPTS: item of appropriation, item on deposit, itemization of damages, itemized account

ITEMIZE, *verb*   be specific, catalog, circumstantiate, count, designate, detail, document, enter into detail, enumerate, index, inventory, list, mention, mention in detail, note, number, particularize, point out, post, recapitulate, recount, register, set down, specify, state by items, tabulate
ASSOCIATED CONCEPTS: itemize an account, itemize damages, itemize expenses

ITERATIVE, *adjective*   duplicative, echoing, harping, recurrent, recurring, redundant, reiterant, repeated, repetitious, repetitive, tautological

ITINERANT, *adjective*   ambulant, ambulatory, passing, peripatetic, journeying, moving, travelling, wandering, wayfaring
ASSOCIATED CONCEPTS: itinerant dealer, itinerant merchant, itinerant trader, itinerant vendor

ITINERANT, *noun*   drifter, peripatetic, traveller, rambler, roamer, rover, runabout, voyager, wanderer

J

JACTATION, *noun* boast, boastfulness, brag, braggadocio, braggardism, conceit, fanfaronade, gasconade, jactitation, ostentation, pretension, rodomontade, self-glorification, swagger, swank, vainglory, vanity, vaunt, venditation

JAIL, *noun* *carcer,* cell, detention cell, detention center, detention station, house of correction, house of detention, inclosure, keep, penal institution, penitentiary, place of confinement, prison, prisonhouse, reformatory, stockade

JAIL, *verb* apprehend, capture, cast into prison, commit to an institution, commit to prison, confine, constrain, detain, hold captive, hold in captivity, hold in custody, immure, impound, imprison, *in carcerem, in custodiam,* incarcerate, institutionalize, isolate, lock in, lock up, place in confinement, put behind bars, put under restraint, restrain, restrict, send to prison, shut in, shut up, subjugate, take into custody

JAPE, *verb* bemock, burlesque, caricature, chaff, flout, fool, gibe at, imitate insultingly, jeer, jest, joke, lampoon, laugh at, make fun of, mimic, mock, parody, play tricks upon, poke fun at, ridicule, satirize, scoff, taunt, tease, travesty, twit

JARGON *(Technical language),* *noun* argot, cant, code, coined words, language of a particular profession, legalese, neologism, neology, private language, professional language, professional vocabulary, specialized language, specialized terminology, specialized vocabulary
ASSOCIATED CONCEPTS: legal jargon

JARGON *(Unintelligible language),* *noun* babble, blabber, blather, confused language, confused talk, confusion, double talk, empty talk, foolishness, gibberish, inanity, incoherence, incoherent discourse, jabber, jumble, nonsense, nonsensical language, nonsensical talk, nonsensicalness, prattle, rambling talk, senseless talk, silly talk, unintelligible talk

JEALOUS, *adjective* begrudging, competitive, covetous, desiring, desirous, discontented, disposed to envy, dissatisfied, distrustful, doubting, envious, greedy, grudging, *invidus, lividus,* longing, possessive, rival, suspicious

JEER, *verb* *cavillari,* deprecate, depreciate, deride, *deridere,* disparage, disregard, disrespect, gibe, have no regard for, hold in derision, *inridere,* insult, laugh at, make fun of, mock, ridicule, scoff, sneer, speak derisively, speak slightingly, taunt, treat with insolence, twit

JEJUNE *(Dull),* *adjective* bleak, boresome, boring, colorless, common, commonplace, drearisome, dreary, dry, flat, flavorless, hollow, indifferent, insipid, monotonous, ordinary, plain, ponderous, prosaic, prosy, stolid, tame, tasteless, tedious, thin, tiresome, torpid, undramatic, unenlivened, unentertaining, unexciting, unimpassioned, uninspired, uninspiring, unlively, unpointed, unspirited, usual, vacuous, vapid, weak, wearisome

JEJUNE *(Lacking maturity),* *adjective* adolescent, babyish, callow, childish, immature, inexperienced, infantile, infantine, juvenile, puerile, unfledged, unlearned

JEOPARDIZE, *verb* endanger, expose to danger, imperil, *in periculum,* leave unprotected, menace, peril, place in danger, risk, stake, threaten

JEOPARDY, *noun* crisis, danger, dangerous situation, dangerousness, endangerment, hazard, imperilment, insecurity, instability, menace, peril, perilousness, precariousness, risk, threat, uncertainty, unsafety, vulnerability
ASSOCIATED CONCEPTS: double jeopardy, former jeopardy, placed in jeopardy
FOREIGN PHRASES: *Nemo bis punitur pro eodem delicto.* No one can be punished twice for the same offense.

JETTISON, *verb* cast overboard, discard, dispense with, dispose of, eject, eliminate, expel, get rid of, part with, rid oneself of, slough, throw away, throw overboard, toss out, toss overboard

JOB, *noun* assignment, avocation, billet, business, calling, chore, duty, employment, function, labor, mission, obligation, occupation, position, profession, responsibility, role, task, trade, undertaking, vocation, work

JOCULAR, adjective amusing, arch, comic, diverting, facetious, frisky, frivolous, frolicsome, full of fun, funny, gamesome, gay, given to joking, gleeful, gleesome, hilarious, humorous, *iocosus, iocularis,* jesting, jocose, jocund, joking, jolly, joshing, jovial, joyful, joyous, laughing, light, merry, merrymaking, mirthloving, mirthful, playful, pleasant, *ridiculus,* roguish, rollicking, rompish, sportive, sprightly, tricksy, waggish, witty

JOIN (*Associate oneself with*), **verb** act in concert, affiliate, align, ally, associate, band together, be united, become a member, become connected with, belong to, combine, confederate, consociate, consort, cooperate, enlist, enroll, enter, fraternize, league together, make an agreement with, mingle, participate, pool, register, *se coniungere,* side with, sign on, subscribe, take part, take up membership, team up with, unite

JOIN (*Bring together*), **verb** accouple, accumulate, adhere, aggregate, aggroup, alloy, amalgamate, amass, annex, append, assemble, attach, band, bind, blend, bridge, bring in contact, coact, collect, colligate, collocate, combine, commingle, compound, concatenate, *conectere,* conglomerate, conglutinate, *coniungere,* conjoin, connect, consolidate, convene, *copulare,* couple, entwine, federalize, federate, fit together, fuse, gather, glue, group, harness, incorporate, inosculate, interlink, interlock, intertwine, intertwist, interweave, knit, link, marry, mass, match, meld, merge, mix, pair, piece together, pool, put together, rally, splice, subjoin, unify, unite, wed, weld, yoke
ASSOCIATED CONCEPTS: issue joined, joinder of parties

JOINDER, adjective assemblage, bringing together, coalescence, combination, concatenation, conjugation, conjunction, connection, coupling, joining, junction, linkage, linking, unification, union
ASSOCIATED CONCEPTS: fraudulent joinder, improper joinder, joinder of issue, joinder of parties, misjoinder, permissive joinder, severance

JOINT, adjective allied, amalgamated, associated, coadunate, coalitional, collaborative, collective, combined, common, communal, *communis,* community, concerted, concordant, concurrent, confederate, conjoint, conjugate, conjunct, consolidated, cooperative, coordinated, corporate, correal, harmonious, inseparable, joined, leagued, merged, mixed, mutual, shared, synergetic, unified, united
ASSOCIATED CONCEPTS: joint account, joint action, joint adventure, joint and several liability, joint enterprise, joint interest, joint liability, joint negligence, joint ownership, joint resolution, joint tenancy, joint tort feasors

JOSTLE (*Bump into*), **verb** bang into, buffet, bump, bump against, butt, collide, crash into, crowd, elbow, *fodicare,* graze against, hit against, hustle, jab, jar, jolt, knock, knock against, nudge, poke, press, prod, push, run against, shake, shove, strike against, strike together
ASSOCIATED CONCEPTS: disorderly conduct

JOSTLE (*Pickpocket*), **verb** abscond with, convey away, lift, loot, misappropriate, pick one's pockets, pilfer, purloin, run away with, run off with, steal, take away, walk off with, waylay
ASSOCIATED CONCEPTS: larceny

JOURNAL, noun *acta diurna,* biographical record, cashbook, chronicle, chronology, contemporary account, daily paper, daily register, daybook, diary, *ephemeris,* gazette, historical record, ledger, log, logbook, magazine, narrative, periodical, record, register, serial

JUDGE, noun adjudger, adjudicator, administrator of justice, arbiter, arbitrator, assessor, chancellor, the court, her honor, his honor, honorable justice, intercessor, interpreter, *iudex,* jurist, justice, justicer, magistrate, moderator, negotiator, one who dispenses justice, *praetor, quaesitor,* referee, surrogate, umpire, your honor
ASSOCIATED CONCEPTS: administrative judge, appellate judge, chief judge, County Court Judge, Court of Appeals Judge, Court of Claims Judge, District Court Judge, Family Court Judge, inferior court judge, judge de facto, judge of a court of record, justice of the peace, Justice of the Supreme Court, law clerk, lay judge, magistrates, presiding judge, removal of a judge, superior court judge, Surrogate, town judge
FOREIGN PHRASES: *In propria causa nemo judex.* No one can be a judge in his own case. *Ignorantia judicis est calamitas innocentis.* The ignorance of a judge is the misfortune of the innocent. *Judex bonus nihil ex arbitrio suo faciat, nec propositione domesticae voluntatis, sed juxta leges et jura pronunciet.* A good judge should do nothing of his own arbitrary will, nor on the dictate of his personal wishes, but should decide according to law and justice. *Veritas habenda est in juratore; justitia et judicium in judice.* Truth should be possessed by a juror; justice and judgment by a judge. *Judicium a non suo judice datum nullius est momenti.* A judgment rendered by one who is not the proper judge is of no force. *Quicquid judicis auctoritati subjicitur, novitati non subjicitur.* Whatever is subject to the authority of a judge is not subject to innovation. *Sententia a non judice lata nemini debet nocere.* A sentence or judgment rendered by a person who is not a judge ought not to harm anyone. *Respiciendum est judicanti ne quid aut durius aut remissius constituatur quam causa deposcit; nec enim aut severitatis aut clementiae gloria affectan da est.* It is a matter of import to a judge that nothing should be either more leniently or more severely construed than the cause itself demands; for the glory neither of severity nor clemency should be affected. *Judicis est in pronunciando sequi regulam, exceptione non probata.* The judge in his decision ought to follow the rule, the exception not having been proved. *Nemo potest esse simul actor et judex.* No one can be at the same time judge and suitor. *Praxis judicum est interpres legum.* The practice of judges is the interpreter of the laws. *Judex non potest injuriam sibi datam punire.* A judge cannot punish a wrong done to himself. *Boni judicis est ampliare justitiam.* It is the duty of a good judge to make precedents which amplify justice. *Quemadmodum ad quaestionem facti non respondent judices, ita ad quaestionem juris non respondent juratores.* Just as judges do not answer questions of fact, so jurors do not answer questions of law. *Boni judicis est judicium sine dilatione mandare executioni.* It is the duty of a good judge to issue judgments without delay. *De jure judices, de facto juratores, respondent.* Judges decide questions of law, jurors, questions of fact. *Ubi non est manifesta injustitia, judices habentur pro bonis viris, et judicatum pro veritate.* Where there is no manifest injustice, judges are to be regarded as honest men, and

their judgment as truth. *Judex damnatur cum nocens absolvitur.* A judge is condemned when a guilty person is acquitted. *Nemo sibi esse judex vel suis jus dicere debet.* No man ought to be his own judge, or to administer the law in cases involving his family. *Judici officium suum excedenti non paretur.* No obedience is to be given to a judge exceeding his office or jurisdiction. *Non refert quid notum sit judici, si notum non sit in forma judicii.* It matters not what is known to a judge, if it be not known in a judicial form. *Judex debet judicare secundum allegata et probata.* A judge ought to decide according to the allegations and the proofs. *Judex non potest esse testis in propria causa.* A judge cannot be a witness in his own case. *In re propria iniquum admodum est alicui licentiam tribuere sententiae.* It is unjust for anyone to assign to himself the privilege of deciding his own case. *De fide et officio judicis non recipitur quaestio, sed de scientia, sive sit error juris, sive facti.* The good faith and honesty of a judge are not to be questioned, but his knowledge, whether it be in error of law or fact, may be. *Judex ante oculos aequitatem semper habere debet.* A judge ought always to have equity before his eyes. *Judices non tenentur exprimere causam sententiae suae.* Judges are not bound to explain the reason for their sentences. *Judex aequitatem semper spectare debet.* A judge ought always to regard equity. *Bonus judex secundum aequum et bonum judicat, et aequitatem stricto juri praefert.* Good judges decide according to what is just and right, and prefer equity to strict law. *Ad questiones facti non respondent judices; ad questiones legis non respondent juratores.* Judges do not answer to a question of fact, jurors do not answer to a question of law. *Qui aliquid statuerit, parte inaudita altera, aequum licet dixerit, haud aequum fecerit.* He who decides anything without hearing both sides, although he may decide correctly, has by no means acted justly. *Judex habere debet duos sales,-salem sapientiae, ne sit insipidus; et salem conscientiae, ne sit diabolus.* A judge ought to have two salts,-the salt of wisdom, lest he be insipid; and the salt of conscience, lest he be devilish. *Optimam esse legem, quae minimum relinquit arbitrio judicis; id quod cer titudo ejus praestat.* That law is the best which leaves the least discretion to the judge; this is an advantage which results from its certainty. *Optima est lex quae minimum relinquit arbitrio judicis; optimus judex qui minimum sibi.* That is the best system of law which leaves the least to the discretion of the judge; that judge is the best who leaves the least to his own discretion. *Optimus judex, qui minimum sibi.* He is the best judge who leaves the least to his own discretion. *Judicis officium est opus diei in die suo perficere.* It is the duty of a judge to finish the day's work within that day. *Judicis est judicare secundum allegata et probata.* It is the duty of a judge to decide according to the allegations and proofs. *Quam rationabilis debet esse finis, non definitur, sed omnibus circumstantiis inspectis pendet ex justiciariorum discretione.* What a reasonable fine ought to be is not defined, but is left to the discretion of the judges, all the circumstances being considered.

JUDGE, *verb* adjudge, adjudicate, appraise, arbitrate, ascertain, assess, *censere,* conclude, condemn, consider, criticize, decide, decree, deduce, deem, derive, determine, discern, draw a conclusion, estimate, examine, find, hold, infer, interpret, *iudicare, iudicium exercere,* moderate, negotiate, pass sentence upon, pass under review, perceive, pronounce, reckon, referee, reprobate, resolve, review, rule on, sentence, settle, sit in judgment, try, try a case, umpire, value, weigh

FOREIGN PHRASES: *Judicis est jus dicere, non dare.* It is the duty of a judge to declare the law, not to make it. *Judex est lex loquens.* The judge is the law speaking; that is, he is the mouthpiece of the law. *Boni judicis est ampliare jurisdictionem.* It is the duty of a good judge to enlarge his remedial authority.

JUDGMENT (*Discernment*), *noun* ability to distinguish, acumen, acuteness, analysis, apperception, appraisal, assessment, astuteness, awareness, circumspection, close observation, cognitive faculties, cognitive powers, comprehension, conclusion, consideration, *consilium,* contemplation, critical faculty, critical spirit, criticalness, critique, decision, diagnosis, discrimination, discursive faculties, estimate, estimation, evaluation, examination, exhaustive inquiry, grasp, incisiveness, inquiry, insight, inspection, intellectual faculties, intellectual powers, intuition, *iudicium,* judiciousness, keenness, mental faculty, observation, opinion, penetration, perception, perceptiveness, percipience, perspicacity, perspicuousness, probing, quickness, ratiocination, rational faculty, rationality, reasoning, reasoning faculties, reasoning power, review, sagacity, sapience, sharpness of mind, understanding, weighing

ASSOCIATED CONCEPTS: failure to exercise reasonable judgment

FOREIGN PHRASES: *Incivile est, nisi tota lege perspecta, una aliqua particula ejus proposita, judicare, vel respondere.* Unless the entire law has been examined, it is improper to pass judgment upon a portion of it. *Judicia in deliberationibus crebro maturescunt, in accelerato processu nunquam.* Judgments frequently mature by deliberations, never by hurried process.

JUDGMENT (*Formal court decree*), *noun* adjudgment, adjudication, announcement, arbitrament, assessment, censure, conclusion, condemnation, consideration, decision, declaration, decree, determination, evaluation, finding, *iudicium,* judicature, judicial assertion, legal decision, opinion, order, precedent, pronouncement, recommendation, report, resolution, result, ruling, sentence

ASSOCIATED CONCEPTS: advisory judgment, collateral attack on a judgment, conditional judgment, confession by judgment, consent judgment, declaratory judgment, default judgment, deficiency judgment, docketing a judgment, enforcement of a judgment, execution of judgment, final judgment, foreign judgment, full faith and credit, interlocutory judgment, judgment by confession, judgment creditor, judgment debtor, judgment in rem, judgment lien, judgment non obstante veredicto, judgment roll, money judgment, opening a default judgment, personal judgment, relief from judgment, res judicata, satisfaction of a judgment, vacating a judgment

FOREIGN PHRASES: *Ubi eadem ratio ibi; idem jus; et de similibus idem est judicium.* Where there is the same reason, there is the same law; and where there are similar situations, the judgment is the same. *Respiciendum est judicanti ne quid aut durius aut remissius constituatur quam causa deposcit; nec enim aut severitatis aut clementiae gloria affectanda est.* It is a matter of import to a judge that nothing should be either more leniently or more severely construed than the cause itself demands; for the glory neither of severity nor clemency should be affected. *Non exemplis sed legibus judicandum est.* Judgment should not be rendered from examples, but by the law. *Res judicata pro veritate accipitur.* A thing which is adjudicated is accepted or received for the truth. *Judicium non debet esse illusorium; suum effectum habere debet.* A judgment ought not to be illusory; it ought to have its proper effect. *Judicium a non suo judice datum nullius est momenti.* A judgment by one who is not the proper judge is of no force. *Omnis conclusio boni et veri judicii sequitur ex bonis et veris praemissis et dictis juratorum.* Every conclusion of a good and true judgment arises from good and true premises, and the verdicts of jurors. *In praeparatoriis ad judicium favetur actori.* In those matters preceding judgment the plaintiff is favored. *Frustra agit qui judicium prosequi nequit cum effectu.* He sues vainly who cannot prosecute his judgment with effect. *Sacramentum habet in se tres comites,-veritatem, justitiam, et judicium; veritus habenda est in jurato; justitia et justicium in judice.* An oath has in it three components-truth, justice, and judgment; truth in the party swearing; justice and judgment in the judge administering the oath. *Veredictum, quasi dictum veritatis; ut judicium, quasi juris dictum.* A verdict is, as it were, the expression of the truth; as a judgment is the expression of the law. *Judicium semper pro veritate accipitur.* A judgment is always taken for truth. *Judiciis posterioribus fides est adhibenda.* Credit should be given in the more recent decisions. *Judex non reddit plus quam quod petens ipse requirit.* A judge should not render judgments for a larger sum than the plaintiff demands. *Parum est latam esse sententiam nisi mandetur executioni.* It is not enough that sentence should be given unless it be reduced to execution.

JUDICATORY, *noun*   bar of justice, bench, court, court of justice, court of law, forum, institution where justice is rendered, judicature, judiciary, law court, place where justice is administered, *ratio iudiciorum,* tribunal
ASSOCIATED CONCEPTS: inferior judicatory

JUDICATURE, *noun*   administration of justice, authority, bench, court, court of law, court's jurisdiction, extent of the court's authority, forum, *iurisdictio,* judicatory, jurisdiction, jurisdiction of the court, legal authority, legal power, tribunal

JUDICIAL, *adjective*   considerate, disinterested, equitable, fair, *forensis,* impartial, *iudicialis,* judgelike, judgmatic, judicative, judicious, juridical, juristic, juristical, just, knowing, politic, prudent, prudential, rational, reasonable, reasoned, sagacious, sage, sapient, sensible, thoughtful, unbiased, unbigoted, uninfluenced, unprejudiced, unswayed, wise
ASSOCIATED CONCEPTS: critical state in a judicial proceeding, judicial act, judicial business, judicial circuit, judicial decision, judicial district, judicial function, judicial inquiry, judicial notice, judicial office, judicial opinion, judicial power, judicial proceeding, judicial review, judicial separation, judicial sequestration, judicial tribunal
FOREIGN PHRASES: *Officia judicialia non concedantur antequam vacent.* Judicial offices are not to be granted or appointed before they become vacant.

JUDICIARY, *noun*   administration of justice, arm of the law, bar, bench, body of judges, courts, courts of justice, department of justice, explicators of the law, forum of justice, interpreters of the law, judicatory, judicature, judicial branch, judicial branch of government, judicial department, judicial forum, justices, law courts, legal forum, magistracy, tribunal
ASSOCIATED CONCEPTS: judiciary powers

JUDICIOUS, *adjective*   apperceptive, astute, calculating, careful, cautious, considerate, considered, deliberate, diplomatic, discerning, discreet, discretionary, discriminating, enlightened, heedful, judgmatic, mindful, moderate, perceptive, percipient, perspicacious, politic, provident, *prudens,* prudent, prudential, rational, reasonable, reflecting, regardful, sagacious, *sagax,* sage, *sapiens,* sapient, sensible, shrewd, sound, tactful, temperate, thorough, thoughtful, undaring, well-considered, wise

JURAL, *adjective*   according to law, *de jure,* founded in law, judicatory, judicial, judiciary, juridical, juristic, legal, of law, pertaining to law, recognized by law, sanctioned by law, within the law

JURAT, *noun*   accreditation, affirmation, asseveration, attestation, attesting statement, authentication, avouchment, avowal, certification, confirmation, documentation, endorsement, ratification, solemn declaration, statement which confirms information on an affidavit, substantiation, verification, verifying statement
ASSOCIATED CONCEPTS: affidavit, affirmation, notary public, oath

JURIDICAL, *adjective*   according to law, adjudged, advising, advisory, authoritative, authorized, concerning the law, conformable with the law, discerning, discretionary, discriminating, discriminative, enlightened, equitable, fair, forensic, impartial, in accordance with the law, in conformity to the law, *iuridicialis,* judgelike, judgmatic, judicative, judicatorial, judicatory, judicial, judiciary, judicious, jural, juridic, jurisprudential, juristic, just, justifiable, justified, lawful, legal, legalistic, legalized, magisterial, perceptive, percipient, perspicacious, politic, prescribed, principled, proper, provident, prudent, prudential, rational, reflecting, right, rightful, sagacious, sage, sanctioned, sapient, solicitorial, sound, unbiased, understanding, unprejudiced, warranted, well-advised, within the law

JURISDICTION, *noun*   authority, authority to hear and decide a case, capacity to decide the matter in issue, capacity to hear the controversy, command, control, decision-making power over the case, domain, domination, dominion, extent of authority, grasp, *iurisdictio,* legal authority, legal power, legal power to decide a case, legal right, power, province, purview, range, reach, realm, reign, sovereignty, sphere, superintendence, supervision, territorial range of authority, territory
ASSOCIATED CONCEPTS: basis jurisdiction, civil jurisdiction, concurrent jurisdiction, court of competent jurisdiction, equity jurisdiction, exclusive jurisdiction, forum non conveniens, in personam jurisdiction, in rem jurisdiction, inherent jurisdiction, jurisdiction of the court, jurisdiction over the person, jurisdictional amount, jurisdictional defect, jurisdictional dispute, jurisdictional facts, jurisdictional plea, jurisdictional requirement, jurisdictional statement, lack of jurisdic-

tion, limited jurisdiction, original jurisdiction, pendent jurisdiction, primary jurisdiction, quasi in rem jurisdiction, subject matter jurisdiction, submission to jurisdiction, venue, want of jurisdiction

FOREIGN PHRASES: *Est boni judicis ampliare jurisdictionem.* It is the duty of a good judge to extend the jurisdiction. *Extra territorium jus dicenti impune non paretur.* One exercising jurisdiction outside of his territorial limits cannot be obeyed with impunity. *Jurisdictio est potestas de publico introducta, cum necessitate juris dicendi.* Jurisdiction is a power introduced for the public good, on account of the necessity of administering justice. *Quaelibet jurisdictio cancellos suos habet.* Every jurisdiction has its own bounds. *Qui habet jurisdictionem absolvendi, habet jurisdictionem ligandi.* He who has jurisdiction to release, has jurisdiction to bind. *Rerum ordo confunditur si unicuique jurisdictio non servetur.* The order of things is confused if everyone does not give heed to his own jurisdiction. *Ubi est forum, ibi ergo est jus.* Where the forum is, there the law is accordingly. *Judici officium suum excedenti non paretur.* No obedience is to be given to a judge exceeding his office or jurisdiction. *Est boni judicis ampliare jurisdictionem.* It is the duty of a good judge to interpret his jurisdiction liberally. *In personam actio est, qua cum eo agimus qui obligatus est nobis ad faciendum aliquid vel dandum.* The action in personam is that in which we sue him who is under obligation to us to do something or give something. *In omni actione ubi duae concurrunt districtiones, videlicet, in rem et in personam, illa districtio tenenda est quae magis timetur et magis ligat.* In every action where two distresses concur, that is to say, in rem and in personam, that is to be chosen which is most dreaded, and which binds more firmly. *Cui jurisdictio data est, ea quoque concessa esse videntur, sine quibus jurisdictio explicari non potest.* Those things without which jurisdiction could not be exercised are held to be given to each to whom jurisdiction has been granted. *Debet quis juri subjacere ubi delinquit.* Everyone ought to be subject to the law of the place where he commits an offense. *Nihil habet forum ex scena.* The court has nothing to do with what is not before it. *Judicium a non suo judice datum nullius est momenti.* A judgment rendered by one who is not the proper judge is of no force.

JURISPRUDENCE, noun   body of laws, corpus juris, doctrines of lawmaking, *iuris prudentia,* knowledge of law, legal code, legal learning, legal philosophy, legal practice, legal precedent, legal science, nomography, nomology, philosophy of law, science of law, science of legal relations, system of laws

FOREIGN PHRASES: *Scire leges non hoc est verba earum tenere, sed vim ac potestatem.* To know the laws is not to observe their words alone, but their force and power. *Cessante ratione legis, cessat et ipsa lex.* Where the reason for a law ceases, the law itself also ceases. *Jurisprudentia est divinarum atque humanarum rerum notitia, justi atque injusti scientia.* Jurisprudence is the knowledge of things divine and human, the science of what is just and unjust.

JURIST, noun   advocate, attorney, attorney-at-law, barrister, bencher, counsel, counselor, counselor-at-law, intercessor, *iuris consultus, iuris peritus,* judge, jurisconsult, jurisprudent, justice, lawyer, learned counsel, legal adviser, legal expert, legal practitioner,

legal representative, legalist, legist, magistrate, master of jurisprudence, member of the bar, member of the legal profession, one called to the bar, pleader, practicing lawyer, practitioner of the law, procurator, prosecutor, public attorney, solicitor

FOREIGN PHRASES: *Natura appetit perfectum; ita et lex.* Nature seeks perfection, and so does the law. *Non verbis sed ipsis rebus. leges imponimus.* We do not impose laws upon words, but upon the things themselves. *Leges naturae perfectissimae sunt et immutabiles; humani vero juris conditio semper in infinitum decurrit, et nihil est in eo quod perpetuo stare possit.* The laws of nature are the most perfect and immutable, but the condition of human law is unending and there is nothing in it which can continue perpetually.

JUROR, noun   adjudger, adjudicator, appraiser, arbiter, assessor, assessor of liability and damages, estimator, evaluator, examiner, hearer, individual selected for jury service, *iudex,* jurat, juryman, member of a jury, one authorized to deliver a verdict, one of an adjudgment body, one sworn to deliver a verdict, reviewer, swearer, trier of fact

ASSOCIATED CONCEPTS: challenge for cause, competent juror, foreman, grand juror, peremptory challenge to the selection of a juror, petit juror

FOREIGN PHRASES: *Veritas habenda est in juratore; justitia et judicium in judice.* Truth should be possessed by a juror; justice and judgment by a judge. *Omnis conclusio boni et veri judicii sequitur ex bonis et veris praemissis et dictis juratorum.* Every conclusion of a good and true judgment arises from good and true premises, and the verdicts of jurors. *Triatio ibi semper debet fieri, ubi juratores meliorem possunt habere notitiam.* Trial ought always to be had where the jurors can have the best information. *Quemadmodum ad quaestionem facti non respondent judices, ita ad quaestionem juris non respondent juratores.* Just as judges do not answer questions of fact, so jurors do not answer questions of law.

JURY, noun   adjudgment body, adjudicators, arbiters, arbitrators, array, assessors, body of jurors, determiners, *iudices,* judges of the facts, jurymen, panel, reviewers of fact, talesmen, tribunal, triers of fact

ASSOCIATED CONCEPTS: acquittal by a jury, advisory jury, challenges, charge to the jury, empaneling a jury, fair and impartial jury, foreman of the jury, Grand Jury, hung jury, impartial jury, instructing the jury, invading the province of the jury, Petit Jury, polling a jury, right to trial by jury, Special Grand Jury, swearing of the jury

FOREIGN PHRASES: *Matter en ley ne serra mise in boutche del jurors.* A matter of law shall not be put into the mouth of jurors. *Paribus sententiis reus absolvitur.* When the opinions are equal, where the court is equally divided, the defendant is acquitted. *Nemo qui condemnare potest, absolvere non potest.* No one who can convict is unable to acquit. *Patria laboribus et expensis non debet fatigari.* A jury ought not to be troubled by labors and expenses. *De jure judices, de facto juratores, respondent.* Judges decide questions of law, jurors, questions of fact.

JUST, adjective   according to law, *aequus,* affording no undue advantage, befitting, condign, deserved, detached, disinterested, dispassionate, due, equable, equitable, ethical, evenhanded, fair, fair-minded, fit, fitting,

honest, honorable, impartial, incorruptible, *iustus,* justifiable, lawful, legal, licit, merited, *meritus,* moral, objective, principled, proper, reasonable, right, righteous, rightful, scrupulous, suitable, unbiased, unbigoted, unbought, unbribable, unbribed, unchallengeable, uncolored, uncorrupt, uncorrupted, unimpeachable, uninfluenced, unprejudiced, unswayed, upright, virtuous
ASSOCIATED CONCEPTS: just and reasonable grounds, just cause, just claim, just compensation, just debts, just decision, just terms, without just cause
FOREIGN PHRASES: *Ubi lex aliquem cogit ostendere causam, necesse est quod causa sit justa et legitima.* Where the law compels a man to show cause, it is necessary that the cause be just and legal.

JUSTICE, noun *aequitas,* equitableness, equity, fair-mindedness, fair play, fair treatment, fairness, freedom from bias, impartiality, *iustitia,* justness, objectivity, probity, propriety, reason, reasonableness, rectitude, reparation, retribution, right, righteousness, rightfulness, uprighteousness
ASSOCIATED CONCEPTS: due administration of justice, ends of justice, equity, fleeing from justice, fugitive from justice, in furtherance of justice, in the interests of justice, miscarriage of justice, obstructing justice, preventive justice, speedy justice, substantial justice
FOREIGN PHRASES: *Melior est justitia vere praeveniens quam severe puniens.* Truly preventive justice is better than severe punishment. *Justitia non est neganda non differenda.* Justice is neither to be denied nor delayed. *In re propria iniquum admodum est alicui licentiam tribuere sententiae.* It is unjust for anyone to assign to himself the privilege of deciding his own case. *Sacramentum habet in se tres comites,-veritatem, justitiam, et judicium; veritus habenda est in jurato; justitia et justicium in judice.* An oath has in it three components-truth, justice, and judgment; truth in the party swearing; justice and judgment in the judge administering the oath. *Justitia est constans et perpetua voluntas jus suum cuique tribuendi.* Justice is the constant and perpetual means to render to each one his rights. *Lex dilationes semper exhorret.* The law always abhors delays. *Boni judicis est ampliare justitiam.* It is the duty of a good judge to make precedents which amplify justice. *Discretio est scire per legem quid sit justum.* Discretion consists in knowing through the law what is just. *Justitia est duplex, viz., severe puniens et vere praeveniens.* Justice is double, that is to say punishing severely, and truly preventing. *Nulli vendemus, nulli negabimus, aut differemus rectum vel justitian.* We will sell to none, we will deny to none, we will delay to none, either equity or justice. *Justitia non novit patrem nec matrem; solum veritatem spectat justitia.* Justice knows neither father nor mother; justice looks to the truth alone. *Quod ad jus naturale attinet omnes homines aequales sunt.* All men are equal as far as the natural law is concerned. *Accipere quid ut justitiam facias, non est tam accipere quam extorquere.* The acceptance of a reward for doing justice is not so much an acceptance as an extortion. *Justitia nemini neganda est.* Justice is to be denied to no one. *Plena et celeris justitia fiat partibus.* Let full and speedy justice be done to the parties. *Jure naturae aequum est neminem cum alterius detrimento et injuria fieri locupletiorem.* According to the laws of nature, it is just that no one should be enriched by the detriment and injury of another. *Fiat justitia, ruat coelum.* Let right be done, though the heavens fall. *Nihil magis justum est quam*

quod necessarium est. Nothing is more just than what is necessary. *Lex non deficit in justitia exhibenda.* The law does not fail in dispensing justice. *Bonus judex secundum aequum et bonum judicat, et aequitatem stricto juri praefert.* Good judges decide according to what is just and right, and prefer equity to strict law. *Lex plus laudatur quando ratione probatur.* The law is most praiseworthy when it is consistent with reason. *Vigilantibus et non dormientibus jura subveniunt.* The laws aid the vigilant and not those who slumber. *Judex bonus nihil ex arbitrio suo faciat, nec propositione domesticae voluntatis, sed juxta leges et jura pronunciet.* A good judge should do nothing of his own arbitrary will, nor on the dictate of his personal wishes, but should decide according to law and justice. *Qui aliquid statuerit, parte inaudita altera, aequum licet dixerit, haud aequum fecerit.* He who decides anything without hearing both sides, although he may decide correctly, has by no means acted justly. *Fraus et jus nunquam cohabitant.* Fraud and justice never dwell together. *Festinatio justitiae est noverca infortunii.* The hastening of justice is the stepmother of misfortune. *Commodum ex injuria sua non habere debet.* No person ought to derive any advantage by his own wrong. *Veritas habenda est in juratore; justitia et judicium in judice.* Truth should be possessed by a juror; justice and judgment by a judge. *Jus est ars boni et aequi.* Law is the science of what is good and just. *Lex est dictamen rationis.* Law is the dictate of reason. *Lex est ratio summa, quae jubet quae sunt utilia et necessaria et contraria prohibet.* That which is law is the consummation of reason, which commands those things useful and necessary, while prohibiting the contrary. *Sequi debet potentia justitiam, non praecedere.* Power ought to follow justice, not precede it. *Summa caritas est facere justitiam singulis, et omni tempore quando necesse fuerit.* The greatest charity is to do justice to everyone, and at all time when it is necessary.

JUSTICIABLE, adjective actionable, amenable to law, arguable, capable of being decided by a court, cognizable, disputable, jurisdictional, liable to prosecution, litigable, proper for judicial examination, proper for judicial review, proper to be examined in courts of justice, ripe to submit for judicial review, subject to action of court of justice, triable
ASSOCIATED CONCEPTS: justiciable controversy

JUSTIFIABLE, adjective acceptable, admissible, allowable, condonable, defendable, defensible, excusable, exemptible, expiable, forgivable, inculpable, *iustus,* justified, lawful, legal, legalized, legitimate, *legitimus,* licit, maintainable, merited, meritorious, pardonable, permitted, plausible, practicable, proper, rational, reasonable, sanctioned, sensible, sound, suitable, vindicable, warrantable, warranted, well-grounded, worthy
ASSOCIATED CONCEPTS: defense of justification, justifiable controversy, justifiable homicide

JUSTIFICATION, noun adjustment, allowance, clarifying statement, clearance, compurgation, defense, exculpation, *excusatio,* excuse, exonerating circumstance, exonerating fact, exoneration, explanation, exposition, extenuation, good excuse, ground for excusing, legal defense, mitigating circumstance, mitigation, palliation, *purgatio,* rationalization, reason, reasonable excuse, reasoning, statement of defense, vindication

ASSOCIATED CONCEPTS: justification for committing an unlawful act, legal cause

JUSTIFY, *verb*   absolve, account for, allege in support, allege in vindication, answer for, argue for, back, be answerable for, be apologist for, bear out, bolster, champion, condone, contend for, countenance, declare guiltless, defend, defend as conformable to law, defend as conformable to right, endorse, espouse, espouse the cause of, exculpate, *excusare,* excuse, exonerate, explain, forgive, give as an excuse, legitimate, maintain, maintain as conformable to duty, maintain as conformable to justice, make defense for, make excuses for, make explanation of, make legitimate, mitigate, offer in defense, palliate, plead for, plead one's cause, pragmatize, prove the truth of, prove warranted, *purgare,* second, show to be just, speak in favor of, stand up for, strengthen, support, sustain, uphold, urge reasons for, vindicate, warrant

JUVENILE, *adjective*   callow, childish, childlike, immature, inexperienced, infantine, intended for youth, *iuvenilis,* minor, pubescent, *puerilis,* suited to youth, unadult, underage, undeveloped, unfledged, unseasoned, vernal, young, youthful

ASSOCIATED CONCEPTS: Juvenile Court, juvenile delinquent, Person in Need of Supervision, youthful offender

JUVENILE, *noun*   adolescent, child, fledgling, immature person, inexperienced person, *iuvenilis,* junior, juvenal, minor, person under legal age, puerile person, *puerilis,* stripling, teen, teenager, ward, young person, youngling, youngster, youth

ASSOCIATED CONCEPTS: Juvenile Court, juvenile delinquent

JUXTAPOSE, *verb*   abut, adjoin, align, annex, appose, arrange side by side, border, bring near, bring together, connect, coordinate, interconnect, join, line up, make contiguous, make even, make uniform, neighbor, osculate, place close together, place near, place next to, place side by side, position together, put alongside, put beside, put close together, put side by side, range together, set side by side

K

KEEP *(Continue), verb*   be constant, be steadfast, carry forward, carry on, endure, extend, forge ahead, go on, keep going, last, lengthen, live on, maintain, move ahead, never cease, perpetuate, *perseverare,* persevere, persist, press onward, progress, prolong, pursue, remain, run on, stay, stick to, support, survive, sustain, wear

KEEP *(Fulfill), verb*   abide by, acknowledge, adhere to, be faithful to, be true to, carry out, celebrate, commemorate, complete, comply with, conform to, discharge, follow, heed, honor, live up to, make good, meet, *observare,* observe, perform, regard, respect, *retinere,* satisfy, solemnize, stand by

KEEP *(Restrain), verb*   arrest, bar, block, cage, check, *cohibere,* confine, constrain, contain, control, curb, delay, deprive, detain, deter, enclose, foil, frustrate, halt, hamper, hinder, hold, hold back, hold in, hold up, impede, inhibit, obstruct, prevent, prohibit, restrict, retard, *retinere,* shut in, shut up, stay, stifle, stop, stymie, suppress, thwart, withhold

KEEP *(Shelter), verb*   accumulate, amass, bank, cache, care for, cause to endure, cause to last, cherish, cling to, *condere,* conserve, deposit, embrace, foster, guard, have, hold, husband, keep alive, keep safe, lay aside, lay away, look after, maintain, nurture, pile up, possess, preserve, protect, put aside, put away, reserve, retain, retard decay, safeguard, save, secure, shelter, spare, store, support, sustain, take care of, tend, treasure, watch over

KEY, *adjective*   critical, crucial, decisive, fateful, important, influential, major, momentous, significant, weighty

KEY *(Passport), noun*   bar, pass, permit, ticket

KEY *(Solution), noun*   answer, method, resolution, way

KEY MAN, *noun*   indispensable person, man of mark, officer, person of importance, person of repute, president, top person

KIDNAP, *verb*   abduct, bear off, capture, carry off, convey away, ensnare, hold for ransom, impress, put under duress, run away with, run off with, seize, shanghai, snatch, spirit away, steal away, take away, take by force, unlawfully seize, waylay

ASSOCIATED CONCEPTS: false imprisonment

FOREIGN PHRASES: *A piratis aut latronibus capti liberi permanent.* Persons captured by pirates or robbers remain free.

KILL *(Defeat), verb*   abolish, abrogate, annul, arrest, beat, block, cancel, check, *conficere,* counteract, crush, destroy, devitalize, dispatch, extinguish, *interficere,* invalidate, nullify, overthrow, overturn, prevail

over, put down, quash, quell, repress, repulse, revoke, squash, stop, surmount, thwart, triumph, *trucidare,* upset, vanquish
ASSOCIATED CONCEPTS: kill a legislative bill

KILL *(Murder), verb* assassinate, *conficere,* deprive of life, destroy, dispatch, execute, exterminate, injure fatally, *interficere,* liquidate, massacre, *occidere,* put to death, slaughter, slay, smite
ASSOCIATED CONCEPTS: deliberate killing, intent to kill, justifiable killing, malicious killing, premeditated killing

KILLING, *noun* annihilation, assassination, bloody murder, decimation, destruction, elimination, execution, extermination, homicide, liquidation, massacre, murder, murderous assault, slaughter, slaughtering, slaying, violent death
ASSOCIATED CONCEPTS: criminally negligent homicide, intent to kill, justifiable killing, malicious killing, premeditation, self-defense, wrongful death

KIND, *noun* breed, category, character, class, classification, denomination, designation, division, form, *forma,* generic class, *generis,* genre, genus, group, ilk, *modus,* nature, sort, species, type, variety
ASSOCIATED CONCEPTS: payment in kind

KINDRED, *noun* ancestor, ancestral relation, blood relations, blood relatives, brethren, clan, clansmen, *cognati, consanguinei,* descendant, family, folk, kin, kinsfolk, kinsmen, kinspeople, lineage, *necessarii,* next of kin, relation by birth, relation by blood, relation by consanguinity, relations, relatives, stock
ASSOCIATED CONCEPTS: collateral kindred, degree of kindred

KINSHIP, *noun* affiliation, affinity, association, bond, brotherhood, closeness, cognation, connection, consanguinity, family, family connection, kindredship, link, propinquity, relation, relationship, tie

KNAVERY, *noun* artfulness, artifice, beguilement, cheat, cheating, chicanery, circumvention, corruption, cozenage, craft, craftiness, criminality, cunning, cunningness, deceit, deceitfulness, deception, defraudation, deviousness, dishonesty, double-dealing, dupery, duplicity, foul play, fraud, fraudulence, *fraus,* guile, hoax, humbuggery, insincerity, knavishness, lack of principle, lack of probity, legerdemain, malfeasance, *malitia, nequitia,* pettifoggery, rascality, roguery, roguishness, scampishness, scoundrelism, shadiness, sharp practice, skulduggery, slyness, treachery, trick, trickery, tricki-

ness, turpitude, underhand dealing, unreliability, untrustworthiness, villainousness, villainy, wiles, wrongdoing

KNOWING, *adjective* acquainted, acute, apperceptive, apprehending, apprised, astute, aware, cognitive, cognizant, comprehending, conscious, deliberate, designed, educated, heedful, informed, instructed, intended, intentional, knowledgeable, meant, mindful, perceptive, percipient, planned, posted, *prudens,* purposeful, schooled, *sciens,* taught, understanding, well-informed, well-posted, well-versed
ASSOCIATED CONCEPTS: knowing or conscious, knowingly aid, knowingly and willfully, knowingly possess, knowingly receive, knowingly suffer or permit

KNOWINGLY, *adverb* advisedly, deliberately, designedly, intentionally, learnedly, pointedly, purposefully, with knowledge, wittingly
ASSOCIATED CONCEPTS: knowingly and willfully, knowingly permit, knowingly suffer •

KNOWLEDGE *(Awareness), noun* acquaintance, apperception, appreciation, appreciativeness, cognition, cognizance, comprehension, consciousness, discernment, enlightenment, familiarity, grasp, information, intellection, intelligence, ken, know-how, mindfulness, perception, perceptiveness, percipience, realization, recognition, understanding
ASSOCIATED CONCEPTS: actual knowledge, actual notice, common knowledge, constructive knowledge, discovery, full knowledge, guilty knowledge, implied knowledge, imputed knowledge, judicial notice, knowledge sufficient to form a belief, scienter

KNOWLEDGE *(Learning), noun* *cognitio,* command, *doctrina,* education, enlightenment, erudition, expertise, familiarity, familiarization, information, ken, know-how, mastery, proficiency, scholarship, *scientia,* skill, study, wisdom
FOREIGN PHRASES: *Idem est scire aut scire debet aut potuisse.* To be bound to know or to be able to know is the same as to know. *Lex neminem cogit ostendere quod nescire praesumitur.* The law compels no one to divulge that which he is presumed not to know. *Scienti et volenti non fit injuria.* A wrong is not done to a person who understands and consents. *Ignorantia praesumitur ubi scientia non probatur.* Ignorance is presumed where knowledge is not proved. *Ignorantia facti.* Ignorance of facts excuses; ignorance of law does not excuse. *Scientia utrimque par pares contrahentes facit.* Equal knowledge on both sides makes the contracting parties equal.

L

LABEL, *noun* brand, cachet, classification, description, docket, emblem, hallmark, identification, identification tag, insignia, mark, mark of identification, marker, sign, slip, stamp, sticker, superscription, tag, ticket

ASSOCIATED CONCEPTS: disclaimer on a label, misleading labels, trademark for a brand on a label, warning on a label

LABEL, *verb* betoken, brand, call, call by a distinctive title, characterize, classify, define, demarcate, denominate, denote, describe, designate, differentiate, distinguish by a mark, docket, earmark, entitle, identify, imprint, indicate, mark, name, provide with nomenclature, put a mark upon, set apart, single out, specify, stamp, tag, term, ticket, title

LABOR (*Exertion*), ***noun*** discipline, effort, endeavor, energy, enterprise, industry, mental toil, pains, strain, strife

LABOR (*Work*), ***noun*** advocation, assignment, calling, craft, duty, employ, employment, job, line of business, line of work, occupation, profession, pursuit, responsibility, task, toil, trade, undertaking, vocation

ASSOCIATED CONCEPTS: boycotts, closed shop, collective bargaining, labor arbitration, labor dispute, labor organization, labor relations, labor union, lockout, open shop, scope of employment, skilled labor, strikes, terms and conditions of employment, union labor, union shop, wildcat strike, workmen's compensation

LABOR, *verb* apply oneself, attend to business, be diligent, be employed, be industrious, *contendere*, devote oneself to, do a job, do work, drudge, endeavor, engage in, exercise, exert energy, exert oneself, follow one's vocation, *laborare*, plod, plug away, ply, ply one's trade, strain, strive, struggle, toil, travail, work, work hard

LABYRINTHINE, *adjective* ambagious, ambagitory, baffling, bewildering, chaotic, circuitous, complex, complicated, confounding, confusing, crooked, deviating, difficult, digressive, entangled, excursive, flexuous, full of curves, full of turns, *impeditus*, indirect, *inextricabilis*, intricate, involute, involuted, involved, jumbled, labyrinthian, labyrinthic, mazy, meandering, mixed up, muddled, mystifying, oblique, per-

plexing, *perplexus*, puzzling, rambling, raveled, roundabout, serpentine, sinuous, snarled, tangled, tortuous, twisted, twisting, wandering, winding

LACHES, *noun* delay, delay attended by change of position, delay that results in disadvantage, dereliction, dereliction of duty, failure of duty, failure to litigate within reasonable period, improvidence, inattention, inexcusable delay, inexcusable delay in assertion of rights, inobservance, lack of diligence, laggardness, laxity, laxness, laziness, neglect, neglectfulness, negligence, nonfeasance, nonperformance, omission, prejudicial delay, procrastination, remissness, unconscionable delay, undue delay, unexcused delay, unexplained delay, unnecessary prolongation, unreasonable delay, want of duty

ASSOCIATED CONCEPTS: equity, estoppel by laches, statute of limitations

FOREIGN PHRASES: *Tempus enim modus tollendi obligationes et actiones, quia tempus currit contra desides et sui juris contemptores.* For time is a means of dissipating obligations and actions, because time runs against the slothful and careless of their own rights. *Vigilantibus et non dormientibus jura subveniunt.* The laws relieve the vigilant and not those who sleep on their rights.

LACK, *verb* be bereft of, be deficient, be deprived of, be desirous, be destitute, be in need, be in want, be inadequate, be inferior, be insufficient, be needy, be poor, be wanting, be without, crave, desiderate, desire, fall short, feel a dearth, hunger for, long for, miss, need, require, suffer privation, want, wish for, yearn for

ASSOCIATED CONCEPTS: lack of capacity, lack of consideration, lack of due care, lack of good faith, lack of intent, lack of jurisdiction, lack of knowledge, lack of mutuality, lack of probable cause, lack of prosecution, lack of trustworthiness

LACONIC, *adjective* abbreviated, abridged, *adstrictus, brevis,* brief, brusque, closemouthed, compendious, compressed, concise, condensed, contracted, curt, economical of words, epigrammatic, exact, mum, pauciloquent, pithy, pointed, precise, quiet, reserved, reticent, secretive, sententious, short, sparing of words, succinct, summarized, taciturn, telegraphic, terse, to the point, uncommunicative, ungarrulous, unloquacious, untalkative

LAISSEZ FAIRE, noun abstinence from action, hands-off policy, nonhampering, noninfringement, noninterference, nonintermeddling, noninterruption, nonintervention, nonintrusion, nontampering, refraining from involvement, refusal to become involved

LAMENTABLE, adjective awful, comfortless, deplorable, depressing, depressive, disheartening, dismal, distressful, distressing, doleful, dreadful, *flebilis,* grave, grievous, horrible, horrid, joyless, *lamentabilis,* low, lugubrious, melancholy, miserable, mournful, painful, pathetic, piteous, pitiable, pitiful, poor, regrettable, rueful, sad, saddening, sorrowful, sorry, terrible, tragic, uncomfortable, unfavorable, unfortunate, unhappy, woeful, wretched

LANCINATE, verb break through, cleave, cut, cut into, discerp, divide, empierce, fractionalize, fragment, gash, gore, impale, incise, knife, lacerate, lance, make an incision, penetrate, perforate, pierce, prick, puncture, rend, rip, rive, slash, slit, stab, stick, sunder, tear, transpierce

LAND, noun property, real estate, seisin, terrain, tract
ASSOCIATED CONCEPTS: abutting land, adjacent land, agreement to sell land, alienation of land, appurtenance to land, common lands, condemnation of land, contiguous land, contract of sale of land, convey an interest in land, covenants running with the land, easement, easement running with the land, equitable interest in land, high land, improvements upon land, interest in land, land contract, land grant, land tax, lease of land, lien on land, raw land, right of way, subdivision of land, suit to recover land, survey of land, title in land, title in fee, trespass on land tract, undivided land, unimproved land, vacant land, waste lands

LANDHOLDER, noun estate owner, freeholder, holder of legal title, landlord, landowner, leaseholder, one who has land, owner of an estate in land, owner of the fee, owner of the fee simple absolute, property holder, property owner, proprietor, real property holder, real property owner, titleholder

LANDLORD, noun *agrorum possessor,* lessor, owner of an estate in land, owner of lands, owner of tenements, propietory owner, proprietor
ASSOCIATED CONCEPTS: ejectment proceeding, landlord's lien

LANDMARK *(Conspicuous object),* **noun** boundary marker, cairn, cynosure, direction post, familiar object, guidepost, *lapis,* marker, monument, prominent object, signpost, waymark
ASSOCIATED CONCEPTS: preservation of landmarks

LANDMARK *(Significant change),* **noun** cardinal point, critical happening, critical juncture, critical occasion, crucial point, decisive turn, event, high point, key point, material point, milestone, moment of change, salient point, significant event, significant occurrence
ASSOCIATED CONCEPTS: landmark decision

LANDOWNER, noun *agrorum possessor,* estate owner, freeholder, holder of legal title, landed proprietor, landholder, landlord, owner of an estate in land, owner of land, owner of real estate, owner of real property, owner of the fee, property holder, property owner, proprietor, real property holder, real property owner, titleholder
ASSOCIATED CONCEPTS: landowner's liability

LANGUAGE, noun communication, composition, dialect, expression, faculty of speech, folk speech, form of expression, formulation, idiom, jargon, *lingua,* linguistics, means of communication, oral, *oratio,* parlance, phrasing, phraseology, rhetoric, *sermo,* speech, spoken expression, spoken word, talk, terminology, tongue, verbal intercourse, verbiage, vernacular, vocabulary, wordage, wording, written expression, written word
ASSOCIATED CONCEPTS: abusive language, ambiguous language, obscene language, precatory language

LANGUID, adjective adynamic, anemic, apathetic, apathetical, asthenic, drooping, dry, dull, empty, exanimate, exhausted, faint, fatigued, feeble, flagging, hebetudinous, impotent, inactive, indifferent, ineffective, inert, lackadaisical, *languens,* languorous, *lassus,* leaden, lethargic, lethargical, lifeless, limp, listless, lukewarm, lustless, lymphatic, passionless, passive, phlegmatic, phlegmatical, pithless, pluckless, powerless, prosaic, *remissus,* sapless, sickly, sinewless, slack, slow, sluggish, spunkless, stagnant, stale, strengthless, supine, tired, torpid, unagressive, unanimated, unimpassioned, uninspired, uninterested, unrefreshed, unrestored, unspirited, unstrengthened, vapid, wan, weak, without animation, without force, without spirit

LANGUISH, verb ail, become disheartened, become ill, become weak, collapse, decay, decline, despair, despond, deteriorate, droop, drop, ebb, fade, fail, fail in health, fall ill, fall sick, flag, fret, go into a decline, grieve, grow weak, lament, *languere, languescere,* live under unfavorable conditions, lose heart, lose spirit, lose strength, pine, pine away, repine, sag, sicken, sink, slump, stagnate, succumb, suffer, *tabescere,* vegetate, waste away, weaken, wear away, wilt, wither

LANGUOR, noun apathy, debility, drowsiness, dullness, emasculation, enervation, fatigue, feebleness, heaviness, hebetude, helplessness, idleness, immobility, impotence, inaction, inactivity, indifference, indolence, inertness, inexcitability, lack of strength, *languor,* lassitude, laziness, lethargy, lifelessness, listlessness, oscitancy, passivity, phlegm, quiescence, sloth, slow motion, slow pace, slowness, sluggishness, somnolence, somnolency, stagnation, supineness, tiredness, torpidity, torpidness, torpor, vegetation, weakness, weariness

LAPSE *(Break),* **noun** *fuga,* hiatus, interlude, interruption, lull, pause, recess
ASSOCIATED CONCEPTS: devise, lapsed, legacy

LAPSE *(Expiration),* **noun** decline, default, delinquency, dereliction, *error,* error, expiry, failure, inconstancy, *lapsus,* misdeed, misstep, mistake, negligence, *peccatum,* recreancy, regression, relapse, retrogradation, retrogression, reversion, secession, shortcoming, slip, termination
ASSOCIATED CONCEPTS: lapsed bequest, lapsed devise, lapsed legacy, lapsed license, lapsed policy

LAPSE *(Cease),* **verb** abate, become forfeit, become void, come to an end, complete, conclude, discontinue, end, expire, pass to another, relinquish, *reverti,* run out, stop, terminate

FOREIGN PHRASES: *Accusator post rationabile tempus non est audiendus, nisi se bene de omissione excusaverit.* An accuser ought not to be heard after the lapse of a reasonable time, unless he can account satisfactorily for his delay.

LAPSE *(Fall into error), verb* be at fault, commit an error, deviate from the proper path, deviate from virtue, do wrong, err, *errare,* fail, fall from grace, go astray, go awry, misbehave, misstep, *peccare,* slip, slip from virtue, stray, transgress, trespass, weaken

LARCENOUS, *adjective* brigandish, burglarious, criminal, dishonest, felonious, fraudulent, lawbreaking, piratic, piratical, plundering, plunderous, predaceous, predatory, privateering, rapacious, ravaging, thieving, thievish
ASSOCIATED CONCEPTS: larcenous intent

LARCENY, *noun* abstraction, appropriation, brigandage, embezzlement, felonious stealing, fraudulent taking, *furtum,* misappropriation, peculation, pickpocketing, pilferage, rapacity, rapine, swindle, swindling, theft, thievery, unlawful acquisition, unlawful conversion, unlawful taking, wrongful taking
ASSOCIATED CONCEPTS: compound larceny, conversion, embezzlement, fraud, grand larceny, larceny by device, larceny by false pretenses, larceny by fraud, larceny by trick, petit larceny, receiving stolen goods, simple larceny

LARGESS *(Generosity), noun* aid, almsgiving, altruism, assistance, benefaction, beneficence, benignancy, benignity, bounteousness, bountifulness, bounty, charitableness, charity, *congiarium,* free giving, freehandedness, freeness, generosity, generousness, graciousness, help, helpfulness, hospitableness, hospitality, indulgence, kindliness, kindness, *largitio,* lavishment, lavishness, liberality, liberalness, magnanimity, magnanimousness, munificence, openhandedness, philanthropy, prodigality, readiness to give, selflessness, thoughtfulness, unselfishness

LARGESS *(Gift), noun* alms, assistance, award, benefaction, benefit, bestowment, bonus, boon, bounty, charity, contribution, dole, donation, donative, dotation, endowment, favor, grant, gratuity, handout, handsel, help, offering, present, presentation, presentment, vail, voluntary conveyance

LASCIVIOUS, *adjective* bawdy, carnal, coarse, concupiscent, corrupt, debauched, depraved, dissipated, dissolute, erotic, fleshly, goatish, immodest, immoral, improper, *impurus,* indecent, *lascivus,* lecherous, lewd, libertine, *libidinosus,* libidinous, lickerish, lubric, lubricous, lustful, obscene, Paphian, pornographic, promiscuous, prurient, ribald, salacious, satyric, satyrical, sensuous, sex-ridden, shameless, unblushing, unchaste, unregenerate, wanton
ASSOCIATED CONCEPTS: indecent and lascivious, lewd and lascivious cohabitation, obscenity

LASH *(Attack verbally), verb* admonish, animadvert upon, assail, berate, betongue, blackguard, cast reproach upon, castigate, chastise, chide, criticize severly, decry, excoriate, exprobrate, flay, fulminate against, impugn, increpate, inveigh, objurgate, rave against, rebuke, reprehend, reprimand, reproach, reprove, revile, scarify, scathe, slate, take to task, upbraid, vilify, vilipend, vituperate

LASH *(Strike), verb* bastinado, batter, beat, birch, bruise, cudgel, deal a blow to, deal a stroke, drub, *flagellare,* flagellate, flay, flog, fustigate, give a beating, give a thrashing, hit, larrup, maul, pelt, pound, pummel, scourge, slap, smite, switch, thrash, trounce, truncheon, *verberare,* whack

LAST *(Final), adjective* aftermost, climactic, climactical, closing, completive, completory, concluding, conclusive, conclusory, crowning, decisive, definitive, determinative, end, ending, endmost, extreme, farthest, final, finishing, furthest, hindermost, hindmost, outermost, permanent, rear, terminal, terminating, terminational, terminative, ultimate
ASSOCIATED CONCEPTS: last clear chance, last known address, last residence, last will and testament

LAST *(Preceding), adjective* above, above-cited, above-mentioned, above-named, above-stated, aforegoing, aforementioned, aforesaid, *antecedens,* antecedent, anterior, before mentioned, earlier, fore, foregoing, former, freshest, introductory, most recent, newest, past, precedent, precursory, prefatory, preliminary, preludial, preludious, prelusive, prelusory, previous, *prior*

LAST, *verb* be long-lived, be stable, be timeless, be unconsumed, be unexhausted, bide, carry on, continue, *durare,* endure, exist, hang on, hold on, hold out, hold up, keep up, linger, live on, outlive, perdure, *permanere,* persevere, persist, prevail, prolong, protract, remain, stand firm, stay, stay on, subsist, survive, sustain, wait, withstand

LASTING, *adjective* abiding, continuing, enduring, lingering, maintained, perpetuated, perseverant, persistent, persisting, preserved, remaining, standing, staying, surviving, sustained, undestroyed, uneradicated, unerased, unfailing, unremoved, unrepealed

LATE *(Defunct), adjective* dead, deceased, demised, *demortuus,* departed, erstwhile, former, once, one-time, passed on, perished, previous, then

LATE *(Tardy), adjective* after time, behind time, belated, deferred, delayed, detained, held up, lagging, moratory, overdue, past due, postponed, retarded, slow, unpunctual, unready
ASSOCIATED CONCEPTS: late filing

LATENT, *adjective* *abditus, absconditus,* arcane, behind the scenes, below the surface, camouflaged, concealed, covered, covert, delitescent, hidden from view, imperceptible, indiscernible, *occultus,* screened, submerged, unapparent, under the surface, underlying, undetected, undeveloped, undiscovered, unexposed, unmanifested, unnoticed, unrevealed, unseen, unspied, unsuspected, veiled
ASSOCIATED CONCEPTS: latent ambiguity, latent danger, latent defect, latent injury, latent liability

LATITUDE, *noun* absence of restraint, accommodation, amplitude, autonomy, carte blanche, choice, discretion, ease of movement, exemption from control, expanse, expansion, extension, field, free course, free decision, free hand, free play, free thought, free will, freedom, freedom of action, full play, independence, indiscipline, largeness, leverage, liberalism, *libertas,* liberty, license, *licentia,* maneuverability, margin, noninterference, nonintervention, openness, opportunity, option, play, power of choice, power to choose, range, range of choice, right of choice, room, scope, space, unconstraint, uninhibitedness, unrestraint, unstrictness, will

LAUDABLE, adjective admirable, approvable, commendable, creditable, deserving, estimable, excellent, exemplary, hallowed, *laudabilis, laudatus, laude dignus,* matchless, meritorious, model, noble, peerless, praiseworthy, saintly, sterling, uncensurable, unimpeachable, virtuous, worthwhile, worthy, worthy of estimation

LAUDATION, noun benediction, blessing, doxology, encomium, eulogy, exaltation, glorification, honor, idolatry, invocation, magnification, praise

LAUNCH *(Initiate), verb* activate, begin, embark, establish, found, generate, handsel, inaugurate, induce, institute, introduce, lay the foundations, make active, open, originate, put in motion, set going, set in motion, start, take the first step, take the lead, touch off, trigger, undertake

LAUNCH *(Project), verb* cast, catapult, *contorquere,* eject, fling, heave, hurl, *immittere,* impel forward, jaculate, lance, pitch, precipitate, propel, push, send flying, send forth, send headlong, send off, set in motion, shoot, throw, thrust, toss

LAW, noun act, article, body of rules, canon, charter, code, command, decree, decree absolute, dictum, enactment, established rule, expressed command, fiat, firm principle, instruction, *ius,* jurisprudence, legal code, *lex,* mandate, maxim, norm, order, ordinance, precedent, precept, prescribed form, prescription, principle, pronouncement, *regula,* regulation, rescript, rubric, rule, rule of conduct, set of rules, settled principle, standard, standing order, statute, tenet

ASSOCIATED CONCEPTS: action at law, adequate remedy at law, adjective law, administrative law, allowed by law, amendatory law, antitrust laws, application of the law, appropriation law, arising under laws of the united states, at law and in equity, attorney-at-law, authorized by law, aviation law, bankruptcy law, blue sky law, breach of the law, by operation of law, change in the law, civil law, civil rights law, civil service law, color of law, color of state law, commercial law, common law, common-law marriage, common-law trust, compliance with laws, conclusion of law, constitutional law, contrary to law, controversy arising under the laws of the United States, corporate law, court of law, criminal law, declare the law, domestic relations law, due process of law, duties and liabilities imposed by law, election law, enjoined by law, entertainment law, environmental law, equal protection of the law, error of law, established by law, ex post facto, executed in accordance with law, existing laws, federal law, fixed by law, foreign laws, fundamental law, general law, governed by law, homestead law, ignorance of law, implied by law, inconsistent with law, instructions on the law, insufficient in law, insurance law, international law, issue of law, judgment founded upon a matter of law, knowledge of the law, labor law, law and equity, law enforcement, law of the case, law of the land, limited by law, local law, maritime law, martial law, matter of law, military law, mistake of law, municipal law, natu-

ral heirs at law, not in accordance with law, obligation imposed by law, omnibus law, operation of law, ordinary course of law, organic law, patent and trademark law, penal law, practice of law, preexisting law, prescribed by law, presumption of law, procedural law, process of law, prospective law, provided by law, provided by state law, question of law, question of local law, question of state law, real estate law, regulated by law, remedy at law, securities law, session laws, special law, specially prescribed by law, specific law, standing laws, state law, substantive law, sufficient as a matter of law, suits at law, supreme law, surrender by operation of law, tax law, terminate by limitation of law, under color of law, unemployment compensation law, uniform operation of laws, unwritten law, without due process of law

FOREIGN PHRASES: *Ubi lex est specialis, et ratio ejus generalis, generaliter accipienda est.* Where the law is special, and the reason of it general, it ought to be construed generally. *Praxis judicum est interpres legum.* The practice of the judges is the interpreter of the laws. *Lex nemini operatur iniquum, nemini facit injuriam.* The law never works an injury, or does a wrong. *Lex est norma recti.* Law is the rule of right. *Lex est sanctio sancta, jubens honesta, et prohibens contraria.* Law is a sacred santion, commanding that which is right, and prohibiting the contrary. *Lex est tutissima cassis; sub clypeo legis nemo decipitur.* Law is the safest helmet; under the shield of the law no one is deceived. *Lex fingit ubi subsistit aequitas.* The laws feigns where equity subsists. *Lex intendit vicinum vicini facta scire.* The law presumes that one neighbor is cognizant of the acts of his neighbor. *Non est certandum de regulis juris.* There is no disputing about rules of the law. *Receditur a placitis juris, potius quam injuriae et delictamaneant impunita.* In order that crimes not go unpunished, the law will be departed from. *Res est misera ubi jus est vagum et incertum.* It is a sorry state of affairs when law is vague and mutable. *Salus populi est suprema lex.* The welfare of the people is the supreme object of the law. *Si a jure discedas, vagus eris, et erunt omniaomnibus incerta.* If you depart from the law, you will go astray, and everything will be in a state of uncertainty to everyone. *Ubi lex non distinguit, nec nos distinguere debemus.* Where the law does not distinguish, we ought not to distinguish. *Ubi non est lex, ibi non est transgressio, quo ad mundum.* Where there is no law, there is no transgression, so far as worldly concerns and matters. *Firmior et potentior est operatio legis quam dispositio hominis.* The operation of the law is more firm and more powerful than the will of man. *Non jus ex regula, sed regula ex jure.* The law does not arise from the rule but the rule comes from the law. *Non verbis sed ipsis rebus, leges imponimus.* We do not impose laws upon words, but upon the things themselves. *Quando abest provisio partis, adest provisio legis.* When a provision of the party is lacking, the provision of the law supplies it. *Quod naturalis ratio inter omnes homines constituit, vocatur jus gentium.* The rule which natural reason has established among all men is called the law of nations. *Ratio est legis anima; mutata legis ratione mutatur et lex.* Reason is the soul of law; the reason of law being changed, the law is also changed. *Ratio potest allegari deficiente lege; sed ratio vera et legaliset non apparens.* Where the law is deficient, the reason can be alleged, but it must be true and lawful and not merely apparent. *Non in legendo sed in intelligendo legis consistunt.* The laws consist not in being read, but in being understood. *Lex semper intendit quod convenit rationi.* The law always intends what is agreeable to reason. *Lex spectat naturae ordinem.* The law regards the order of nature. *Lex succurrit ignoranti.* The laws assist the ignorant. *Lex succurrit minoribus.* The law assists minors. *Melius est jus deficiens quam jus incertum.* A deficient law is better than an uncertain one. *Multa in jure communi contra rationem disputandi, procommuni utilitate introducta sunt.* Many things have been introduced into the common law, which are contrary to the public good, which are inconsistent with sound reason. *Non exemplis sed legibus judicandum est.* Judgment should not be rendered from examples, but by the law. *Id possumus quod de jure possumus.* We may do only that which we are able to do lawfully. *Idem est non probari et non esse; non deficit jus, sed probatio.* What is not proved, and what is not, are the same; it is not a defect of the law, but a want of proof. *Jus civile et quod sibi populus constituit.* The civil law is that law which the people establish for themselves. *Lex prospicit, non respicit.* The law looks forward, not backward. *Lex rejicit superflua, pugnantia, incongrua.* The law rejects those matters which are superfluous, repugnant, or incongruous. *Lex semper dabit remedium.* The law always furnishes a remedy. *Contra legem facit qui id facit quod lex prohibit; in fraudem vero qui, salvis verbis legis, sententiam ejus circumvenit.* He who does what the law prohibits, acts in fraud of the law, the letter of the law being inviolate, cheats the spirit of it. *Les fictions naissent de la loi, et non la loi des fictions.* Fictions arise from the law, and not law from fictions. *Legem enim contractus dat.* The contract makes the law. *Ubi non est directa lex, standum est arbitrio judicis, vel procedendum ad similia.* Where there is no direct law, the decision of the judge is to be taken, or references to be made to similar cases. *Consuetudo ex certa causa rationabili usitata privatcommunem legem.* A custom, based on a certain and reasonable cause, supersedes the common law. *Jus vendit quod usus approbavit.* The law recommends what use or custom has approved. *La ley favour la vie d'un homme.* The law favors human life. *Actus legis nemini est damnosus.* The act of the law shall prejudice no one. *Matter en ley ne serra mise in bouche del jurors.* A matter of law shall not be put into the mouth of jurors. *Equitas sequitur legem.* Equity follows the law. *Non obligat lex nisi promulgata.* A law is not obligatory unless it is promulgated. *Lex respicit aequitatem.* The law regards equity. *Ignorantia juris non excusat.* Ignorance of the law is no excuse. *Executio juris non habet injuriam.* The execution of law does no injury. *Ignorantia excusatur, non juris sed facti.* Ignorance of fact may excuse, but not ignorance of law. *Scire leges non hoc est verba earum tenere. sed vim ac potestatem.* To know the laws is not to observe their words alone, but their force and power. *Perpetua lex est nullam legem humanam ab positivam perpetuamesse, et clausula quae abrogationem excludit ab initio non valet.* It is a perpetual law that no human and positive law can be perpetual, and a clause in a law which precludes the power of abrogationor repeal is void from the beginning. *Experientia per varios actus legem facit. magistra rerum experientia.* Experience by various acts makes law. experience is the mistress of things. *Nemo jus sibi dicere potest.* No one can declare the law for himself. *Lex aequitate gaudet; appetit perfectum; est norma recti.* The law delights in equity; it grasps at perfection; it is a rule of right. *In fictione juris semper aequitas existit.* In a fiction of

law, equity is always present. *Optima est lex quae minimum relinquit arbitrio judicis; optimus judex qui minimum sibi.* That is the best system of law which leaves the least to the discretion of the judge; that judge is the best who leaves the least to his own discretion. *Jus quo universitates utuntur est idem quod habent privati.* The law which governs corporations is the same as that which governs individuals. *Ignorantia facti excusat, ignorantia juris non excusat.* Ignorance of fact excuses; ignorance of the law does not excuse. *Regula est, juris quidem ignorantiam cuique nocere, facti vero ignorantiam non nocere.* The rule is that a person's ignorance of the law may prejudice him, but that his ignorance of fact will not. *Per varios actus legem experientia facit.* By various acts experience makes the law. *Juris affectus in executione consistit.* The effectiveness of a law lies in its execution. *Cessante ratione legis, cessat et ipsa lex.* Where the reason for a law ceases, the law itself also ceases. *Fortior et potentior est dispositio legis quam hominis.* The disposition of the law has greater force and stronger effect than that of man. *Lex non curat de minimis.* The law does not regard small matters. *Hominum causa jus constitutum est.* Law is established for the benefit of mankind. *Judicis est jus dicere, non dare.* It is the duty of a judge to declare the law, not to make it. *Lex est dictamen rationis.* Law is the dictate of reason. *Lex est ratio summa, quae jubet quae sunt utilia et necessaria, et contraria prohibet.* That which is law is the consummation of reason, which commands those things useful and necessary, while prohibiting the contrary. *Nemo est supra leges.* No one is above the law. *Ubi jus incertum, ibi jus nullum.* Where the law is uncertain, there is no law. *Lex neminem cogit ad vana seu inutilia peragenda.* The law compels no one to do futile or useless things. *Ex facto jus oritur.* Law arises out of facts. *Ad quaestionem facti non respondent judicis; ad quaestionem juris non respondent juratores.* Judges do not answer to a question of fact; jurors do not answer to a question of law. *Constructio legis non facit injuriam.* A law properly interpreted creates no wrong. *Argumentum ab inconvenienti est validum in lege; quia lex non permittit aliquod inconveniens.* An argument drawn from what is inconvenient is good in law, because the law will not permit any inconvenience. *Injustum est, nisi tota lege inspecta, de una aliqua ejus particula proposita judicare vel respondere.* It is unjust to give judgement or advice concerning any particular clause of a law without having examined the whole law. *Cuilibet licet juri pro se introducto renunciare.* Any one may waive or renounce the benefit of a principle or rule of law that exists only for his protection. *Ignorantia legis neminem excusat.* Ignorance of law excuses no one. *Ipsae leges cupiunt ut jure regantur.* The laws themselves are desirous of being governed by what is right. *Exempla illustrant non restringunt legem.* Examples illustrate, but do not restrain, the law. *Obedientia est legis essentia.* Obedience is the essence of the law. *Consuetudo est altera lex.* Custom is another law. *Consuetudo vincit communem legem.* Custom overrules common law. *Consuetudo praescripta et legitima vincit legem.* A prescriptive and legitimate custom prevails over the law. *Consuetudo et communis assue tudo vincit legem non scriptam, si sitspecialis; et interpretatur legem scriptam, si lex sit generalis.* Custom and common usage override the unwritten law, if it be special; and interpret the written law, if the law be general. *Consuetudo est optimus interpres legum.* Custom is the best interpreter of the laws. *Conventio privatorum non potest publico juri derogare.* The agreement of private persons cannot derogate from public right. *Conventio vincit legem.* The express agreement of parties overcomes the law. *Quamvis lex generaliter loquitur, restringenda tamen est, ut, cessante ratione, ipsa cessat.* Although a law speaks generally, yet it is to be restrained, so that when its reason fails, it should cease also. *Processus legis est gravis vexatio, executio legis coronat opus.* The process of the law is a grave vexation; the execution of the law crowns the work. *Ubi eadem ratio, ibi idem jus; et de similibus idem est judicium.* Where there is the same reason, there is the same law; and where there are similar situations, the judgment is the same. *Lex nil frustra facit.* The law does nothing in vain. *Lex non deficit in justitia exhibenda.* The law does not fail in dispensing justice. *Lex plus laudatur quando ratione probatur.* The law is most praiseworthy when it is consistent with reason. *Ubi lex aliquem cogit ostendere causam, necesse est quod causa sit justa et legitima.* Where the law compels a man to show cause, it is necessary that the cause be just and legal. *Ita semper fiat relatio ut valeat dispositio.* Let the interpretation be so made that the disposition stands. *Judex est lex loquens.* The judge is the law speaking; that is, he is the mouthpiece of the law. *Natura appetit perfectum; ita et lex.* Nature seeks perfection, and so does the law. *A verbis legis non est recedendum.* The words of the law must not be departed from. *Apices juris non sunt jura.* Legal niceties are not law. *Communis error facit jus.* A common error makes law. *Casus omissus et oblivioni datus dispositioni communis juris relinquitur.* A case omitted and forgotten is left to the disposal of the common law. *Contemporanea expositio est optima et fortissima in lege.* Contemporaneous exposition is the best and most powerful in the law. *Neque leges neque senatus consulta ita scribi possunt ut omnis casus qui quandoque in sediriunt comprehendatur; sed sufficit ea quae plaerumque accidunt contineri.* Neither laws nor acts of a legislature can be so written as to include all actual or possible cases; it is sufficient if they provide for those things which frequently or ordinarily may happen. *Jura eodem modo destituuntur quo constituuntur.* Laws are abrogated by the same means by which they are enacted. *Jura naturae sunt immutabilia.* The laws of nature are unchangeable. *Leges humanae nascuntur, vivunt, et moriuntur.* Human laws are born, live, and die. *Legibus sumptis desinentibus, lege naturae utendum est.* When laws imposed by the state fail, the laws of nature must be invoked. *Tortura legum pessima.* The torture or wresting of laws is the worst kind of torture. *Leges suum ligent latorem.* Laws should bind their own proposer. *Jus constitui oportet in his quae ut plurimum accidunt non quae ex inopinato.* Laws ought to be made with a view to those cases which occur most frequently and not to those which are of rare or accidental occurrence. *Nova constitutio futuris formam imponere debet, non praeteritis.* A new law ought to affect the future, not what is past. *Ad ea quae frequentius accidunt jura adaptantur.* Laws are adapted to those cases which most commonly occur. *Inde datae leges ne fortior omnia posset.* Laws were made lest the stronger might become all-powerful. *Ex malis moribus bonae leges natae sunt.* Good laws arise from evil morals. *Quando lex est specialis, ratio autem generalis, generaliter lex est intelligenda.* When a law is special, but its reason general, the law is to be under-

stood generally. *Intentio inservire debet legibus, non legesintentioni.* The intention ought to be subservient to the laws, not the laws to intentions. *Legislatorum est viva vox, rebus etnon verbis, legem imponere.* The voice of the legislators is the living voice, to impose laws upon things, and not on words. *Optimam esse legem, quae minimum relinquit arbitrio judicis; id quod certitudo ejus praestat.* That law is best which leaves the least to the decision of the judge; this being an advantage which results from its certainty. *Leges posteriores priores contrariasabrogant.* Subsequent laws repeal prior laws that are repugnant to them. *Jus est ars boni et aequi.* Law is the science of what is good and just. *Nihil infra regnum subditos magis conservatin tranquilitate et concordia quam debitalegum administratio.* Nothing better preserves in tranquillity and concord those subjected to the same government better than one due administration of the laws. *Aequum et bonum est lex legum.* That which is equitable and good is the law of laws.

LAW-ABIDING, *adjective*   according to law, acquiescent, *bene moratus*, complying, conforming, dutiful, ethical, evenhanded, high-minded, high-principled, honest, honorable, incorrupt, incorruptible, inviolate, irrepproachable, law-revering, licit, moral, noble, obedient, obsequious, observant, principled, reputable, respectable, right-minded, righteous, scrupulous, statutable, statutory, straightforward, trustworthy, trusty, unbribable, uncorrupted, unimpeachable, upright, upstanding, virtuous, well-principled, within the law

LAWBREAKER, *noun*   arsonist, convict, criminal, defrauder, delinquent, felon, guilty person, hoodlum, *legis violator*, malefactor, malfeasor, misdemeanant, misfeasor, murderer, offender, thief, transgressor, wrongdoer

LAWFUL, *adjective*   according to fiat, according to law, allowable, allowed, authorized by law, conformable to law, conformable with the law, constitutional, established, in accordance with the law, in conformity to the law, inviolable, juridic, law-abiding, legal, legalized, legitimate, *legitimus,* licit, nomothetic, obedient, permissible, permitted, prescribed by law, proper, sanctioned, sanctioned by law, statutable, statutory, unprohibited, valid, warranted by law, within the law

ASSOCIATED CONCEPTS: lawful act, lawful age, lawful beneficiary, lawful business, lawful command, lawful custody, lawful damages, lawful entry, lawful heirs, lawful interest, lawful issue, lawful order, lawful possession, lawful process, lawful purpose, lawful representative, lawful use

LAWLESS, *adjective*   against the law, anarchic, anarchical, arrant, *audax,* capricious, contrarious, contumacious, corrupt, criminal, degenerate, difficult, disobedient, disobeyed, disobeying, disorderly, disreputable, *effrenatus,* felonious, heedless, ill-disciplined, illegal, immoral, in defiance of the law, incorrigible, insidious, insolent, insubordinate, intemperate, intractable, irresponsible, knavish, lawbreaking, licensed, mutinous, nonconformist, nonlegal, nonobservant, not observant of the law, outlaw, profligate, rascally, rebellious, recalcitrant, recreant, recusant, refractory, reinless, restive, revolutionary, riotous, seditious, subversive, transgressive, unaccountable, unbidden, uncompliant, uncomplying, unconformable, unconstrained, uncontrolled, uncurbed, undisciplined, unfettered, ungovernable, ungoverned, unprincipled, unreined, unrighteous, unscrupulous, unsubmissive, unsuppressed, untamed, untoward, unwarrantable, unwarranted, venal, violative, wayward, without law, wrongful

LAWMAKER, *noun*   alderman, alderwoman, assemblyman, assemblywoman, bill drafter, congressman, congresswoman, councilman, councilwoman, formulator of laws, lawgiver, legislative draftsman, legislator, member of a legislature, member of Congress, member of the Assembly, member of the House, member of the Senate, politician, politico, proposer of a law, proposer of legistation, representative, representative in Congress, senator
ASSOCIATED CONCEPTS: Assembly, Congress, House of Representatives, Senate

LAWSUIT, *noun*   action, action at law, case, case for decision, cause in court, claim, contention, contest, *controversia,* controversy, controversy before a court, court action, dispute, judicial contest, legal action, legal argument, legal contest, legal controversy, legal dispute, legal proceedings, *lis,* litigation, matter for judgment, proceeding, suit at law, suit in equity, trial

LAWYER, *noun*   avocat, advocate, attorney, attorney-at-law, barrister, barrister-at-law, counsel, counselor, counselor-at-law, *iurisconsultus, iurisperitus,* jurisconsult, jurisprudent, jurist, legal advisor, legal advocate, legal consultant, legal practitioner, legist, member of the legal profession, solicitor
ASSOCIATED CONCEPTS: admission to bar, attorney-client privilege, bar association, character and fitness committee, code of professional conduct, grievance committee, work product

LAX, *adjective*   absentminded, apathetic, careless, casual, derelict, disorganized, disregarding, *dissolutus,* feckless, forgetful, halfhearted, heedless, idle, imprecise, improvident, imprudent, inaccurate, inadvertent, inattentive, incautious, indifferent, indolent, inexact, lackadaisical, lazy, loose, mindless, neglectful, *neglegens,* negligent, nonaggressive, oblivious, perfunctory, pococurante, regardless, remiss, *remissus,* slack, slipshod, slothful, slovenly, sluggish, temerarious, thoughtless, unambitious, unapprehensive, unaspiring, unaware, uncaring, uncircumspect, unconcerned, undemanding, unenterprising, unguarded, unheeding, uninterested, unmindful, unobservant, unobserving, unprepared, unstrict, unthinking, unthorough, unthoughtful, untidy, unwary, unwatchful

LAXITY, *noun*   amorality, apathy, carelessness, dereliction, disregard, heedlessness, imprecision, improvidence, inaccuracy, inadvertence, inadvertency, inattention, inattentiveness, indifference, indolence, inexactitude, inexactness, inobservance, lack of control, lack of interest, lack of thoroughness, laziness, looseness, neglect, neglectfulness, *neglegentia,* negligence, noncompletion, nonfeasance, nonfulfillment, nonperformance, oversight, perfunctoriness, remissness, slackness, sloppiness, sloth, slovenliness, thoughtlessness, unconcern, unpreparedness, unrigorousness, untidiness, unwatchfulness

LAYMAN, *noun*   amateur, civilian, laic, nonprofessional, nonspecialist, one who has no specialized training, unskilled practitioner, untrained person
ASSOCIATED CONCEPTS: lay witness

LAYOFF, *noun*   banishment, cashiering, cessation, desistance, discarding, discharge, discontinuance, discontinuation, disemployment, dismissal, displacement, ejection, ejectment, elimination, expulsion, firing, halt, idling, interruption, letting go, ouster, rejection, release, removal, retirement, riddance, stoppage, suspension of employment, temporary deprivation, temporary discharge, temporary suspension, termination, termination of employment
ASSOCIATED CONCEPTS: suspension, temporary layoff

LEADING *(Guiding),* **adjective**   controlling, directing, implicational, implicative, implicatory, inferential, insinuating, insinuative, instructional, instructive, referential, regulating, steering, suggestive, supervising, supervisory
ASSOCIATED CONCEPTS: leading a witness, leading question

LEADING *(Ranking first),* **adjective**   beyond compare, capital, cardinal, central, chief, dominant, dominating, finest, first, foremost, greatest, main, most influential, outstanding, paramount, predominant, preeminent, prevailing, *primarius,* primary, prime, *princeps,* principal, prominent, stellar, supreme, top, topmost, unequaled, unexcelled, unmatched, unparalleled, unrivalled, unsurpassed

LEAGUE, *noun*   accord, affiliation, agreement, alignment, alliance, association, axis, band, bloc, cartel, club, coalition, collaboration, combination, combine, compact, complicity, concord, concordat, concurrence, confederacy, confederation, conjunction, cooperation, copartnership, corporation, covenant, deal, federation, fellowship, *foedus,* fusion, gang, group, guild, mutual undertaking, network, organization, pact, *pactum,* participation, partnership, pool, ring, *societas,* society, sodality, treaty, trust, understanding, unification, union

LEARNED, *adjective*   accomplished, acquainted with, acroatic, apprised of, aware, bibliophilic, bookish, cognizant, conversant, *doctus,* educated, enlightened, erudite, *eruditus,* experienced, expert, familiar, informed, instructed, knowing, knowledgeable, lettered, literate, *litteratus,* omniscient, pansophic, pedantic, pedantical, professional, professorial, proficient, profound, recondite, sagacious, sage, sapient, scholarly, schooled, skilled, studious, versant, versed, well-educated, well-informed, well-read, well-rounded, well-taught, well-trained, widely read, wise

LEASE, *noun*   agreement, *conductio,* contract, contract for exclusive possession of lands, contract for possession and profits, conveyance in consideration of recompense, conveyance of interest in real property, conveyance of land for a designated period, grant, grant of realty, grant of use and possession, instrument, instrument granting possession of premises, legal agreement, permission to rent, tenant-landlord agreement, written agreement
ASSOCIATED CONCEPTS: assignment of lease, building lease, cancellation of a lease, concurrent lease, divisible lease, forfeiture of lease, implied lease, let premises, long-term lease, option to lease, parol lease, perpetual lease, renewal of lease, rent, sublease, term of lease, termination of lease, voidable lease

LEASE, *verb*   allow the use of, charter, contract for exclusive possession, contract for possession of land, contract for use and occupation, convey for a designated period, convey real property for a specified period, demise, engage, engage premises for a designated period, grant exclusive possession for a designated period, grant use and possession, lend on security, let, let premises for a designated period, *locare,* rent, rent out, sublet, subrent

ASSOCIATED CONCEPTS: assignment of a lease, cancellation of a lease, commencement of a lease, extension of a lease, forfeiture of a lease, joint lease, lease at will, lease for years, lease of premises, month to month tenacy, perpetual lease, renewable lease, sublease, tenacy, tenacy at sufferance, tenacy at will, term of a lease, termination of a lease, voidable lease

LEASEHOLD, *noun*   estate for a fixed term, estate for a fixed term of years, estate in realty, freehold, interest in real estate, interest of a lessee, land held by lease, land leased, property leased, real property subject to a lease, tenure by lease

LEAVE *(Absence), noun*   absentation, break, *commeatus,* departure, freedom from duty, furlough, holiday, inactivity, interlude, intermission, interval of rest, leisure, liberty, nonappearance, nonattendance, parting, pause, recess, recreation time, relaxation, removal, repose, respite, rest, retirement, retreat, suspension of work, vacation

ASSOCIATED CONCEPTS: leave of absence, sick leave

LEAVE *(Permission), noun*   accordance, acquiescence, agreement, allowance, approbation, approval, assent, authorization, certification, concurrence, consent, countenance, dispensation, endorsement, exemption, favor, grace, grant, imprimatur, indorsement, indulgence, legalization, liberty, license, *licentia, permissio,* permittance, sanction, sufferance, tolerance, vouchsafement, warrant

ASSOCIATED CONCEPTS: leave of court

LEAVE *(Allow to remain), verb*   cease, deposit, desist, discard, disuse, drop, forbear, forget, give up, let be, let continue, let go, let stand, neglect, permit, relinquish, renounce, repudiate, set aside, shun, stop, supersede, surrender, suspend, waive

ASSOCIATED CONCEPTS: leave no issue, leave the scene of an accident

LEAVE *(Depart), verb*   abandon, abdicate, abjure, abscond, be off, bid farewell, break away, decamp, defect, desert, disappear, *discedere,* drop out, embark, emigrate, escape, evacuate, *excedere,* exit, flee, fly, forsake, go, go away, go forth, migrate, move on, part, *proficisci,* pull out, quit, resign, retire, retreat, run away, secede, set out, slip away, take leave, tergiversate, vacate, vanish, withdraw

LEAVE *(Give), verb*   accord, allot, apportion, assign, award, bequeath, bestow, confer, consign, demise, devise, donate, endow, entrust, give by will, grant, hand down, impart, *legare,* make a bequest, make a testamentary disposition, present, *relinquere,* settle upon, transmit, will

LECHEROUS, *adjective*   addicted to lewdness, bawdy, concupiscent, corrupt, debauched, depraved, desirous, dissipated, dissolute, erotic, erotical, fleshly, gluttonous, goatish, immoral, inclined to lewdness, lascivious, lewd, libertine, libidinous, licentious, lickerish,

loose, lubric, lubricous, lustful, profligate, prurient, rakish, reprobate, ruttish, salacious, sexually indulgent, unbridled, unchaste, unregenerate, unrestrained, unspiritual, wanton

LEDGER, *noun*   account book, account of transactions, accounts, balance sheet, bankbook, book of accounts, book of records, books, calculation, cashbook, *codex accepti et expensi,* computation, daybook, diary, entries, file, index, log, logbook, passbook, profit and loss statement, record, record book, record of credits and debits, record of money transactions, register, registry, running account, statement

LEERY, *adjective*   afraid, apprehensive, careful, cautious, chary, circumspect, distrustful, doubtful, doubting, dubious, entertaining suspicion, frightened, guarded, heedful, hesitant, hesitating, in doubt, mistrustful, questioning, shy of, skeptical, suspect, suspecting, suspicious, unbelieving, uncertain, unconvinced, unsure, vigilant, wary, watchful, without belief, without faith

LEGACY, *noun*   bequeathal, bequest, bestowal, conferment, dispensation, disposition, disposition of personalty, dotation, endowment, gift by will, gift of property by will, grant, heritance, impartment, inheritance, *legatum,* testamentary gift

ASSOCIATED CONCEPTS: absolute legacy, alternate legacy, charitable legacy, conditional legacy, contingent legacy, cumulative legacy, demonstrative legacy, general legacy, indefinite legacy, lapsed legacy, pecuniary legacy, residuary legacy, special legacy, specific legacy

LEGAL, *adjective*   according to the law, allowable, allowed, approved, authorized, authorized by law, cognizable in courts of law, constitutional, decreed, enforceable in a court of law, established by law, good and effectual in law, governed by law, in conformity with law, lawful, legalized, legitimate, *legitimus,* licit, permissible, permitted by law, prescribed, prescribed by law, proper, *quod ex lege,* recognized by the law, required by law, rightful, sanctioned, *secundum leges fit,* statutory, sufficient in law, valid, warranted, within the law

ASSOCIATED CONCEPTS: legal action, legal age, legal arrest, legal beneficiaries, legal capacity to sue, legal cause, legal claim, legal consideration, legal damages, legal detriment, legal disability, legal duty, legal entity, legal heir, legal notice, legal obligation, legal presumption, legal proceedings, legal process, legal remedy, legal representative, legal tender, legal title

FOREIGN PHRASES: *Id possumus quod de jure possumus.* We may do only that which we are able to do lawfully.

LEGALITY, *noun*   accordance with law, allowableness, authorization, conformity to law, conformity with the law, constitutionality, lawfulness, legalism, legitimacy, legitimateness, permissibleness, rightfulness, sanction, sanctionableness, validity, warrantableness

ASSOCIATED CONCEPTS: legality of consideration, legality of contract, legality of obligation, legality of purpose

LEGALIZATION, *noun*   affirmation, approval, authorization, codification, confirmation, legislative sanction, legitimatization, passing into law, ratification, regulation by statute, sanction, validation

LEGALIZE, *verb*   approve, authorize, bring into conformity with law, confirm, confirm by law, decree by law, enact by law, *ferre,* legislate, legitimate, legitimatize, make lawful, make legal, order by law, permit by law, pronounce legal, sanction, sanction by law, validate

LEGATEE, *noun*   beneficiary, devisee, distributee, donee, feoffee, grantee, heir apparent, heir at law, heiress, inheritor, legal heir, legatary, one who inherits, recipient, transferee
ASSOCIATED CONCEPTS: pecuniary legatee, remainderman, residuary legatee, sole legatee, specific legatee

LEGISLATE, *verb*   authorize, codify, *constituere,* create by law, decree, dictate, effect, enact, enact laws, establish, establish by law, exercise the function of legislation, formulate, institute, *leges facere,* make into law, make laws, make legal, order, originate, pass, pass laws, prescribe laws, put in force, rule, sanction, *scribere,* vote in

LEGISLATION (*Enactments*), *noun*   acts, bills, body of laws enacted, canon, canons, codes, dictates, laws, measures, ordinances, prescripts, provisions of a law, regulations, rulings, statutes

LEGISLATION (*Lawmaking*), *noun*   codification of laws, enacting laws, formulating rules for the future, legislative process, preparation of laws
FOREIGN PHRASES: *Leges figendi et refigendi consuetudo est periculosissima.* The practice of making and remaking the laws is a most dangerous one. *Jura eodem modo destituuntur quo constituuntur.* Laws are abrogated by the same means by which they are enacted. *Legislatorum est viva vox, rebus et non verbis, legem imponere.* The voice of the legislators is the living voice, to impose laws upon things, and not on words. *Neque leges neque senatus consulta ita scribi possunt ut omnis casus qui quandoque in sediriunt comprehendatur; sed sufficit ea quae plaerumque accidunt contineri.* Neither laws nor acts of a legislature can be so written as to include all actual or possible cases; it is sufficient if they provide for those things which frequently or ordinarily may happen.

LEGISLATIVE, *adjective*   congressional, decreeing, enacting, lawgiving, lawmaking, legislating, ordained by legislation, ordaining, prescriptive, statutory
ASSOCIATED CONCEPTS: legislative enactment

LEGISLATOR, *noun*   congressman, lawgiver, lawmaker, member of a governmental body, member of a legislative body, member of parliament, officer of state, official representative, one who formulates laws, one who gives or makes laws, one who helps to pass laws, parliamentarian, politician, public servant, representative, senator

LEGISLATURE, *noun*   assembly, body of persons who formulate laws, congress, house of representatives, law-making body, law-making branch of government, lawgivers, lawmakers, legislative body, parliament, senate

LEGITIMACY, *noun*   authorization, conformity to law, genuineness, justifiability, lawfulness, legality, legitimateness, legitimation, legitimization, licitness, originality, permissibility, realness, rightfulness, soundness, validity

ASSOCIATED CONCEPTS: illegitimacy, paternity proceeding
FOREIGN PHRASES: *Semper praesumitur pro legitimatione puerorum.* The presumption always is in favor of the legitimacy of children. *Cum legitimae nuptiae factae sunt, patrem liberi sequuntur.* Children of a lawful marriage follow the condition of the father. *Praesumitur pro legitimatione.* There is a presumption in favor of legitimacy. *Non est justum aliquem antenatum post mortem facere bastardum qui toto tempore vitae suae pro legitimo habebatur.* It is not just to make anyone a bastard after death, who during his lifetime was regarded as legitimate. *Pater est quem nuptiae demonstrant.* He is the father whom the marriage points out.

LEGITIMATE (*Lawfully conceived*), *adjective*
born in wedlock, born of parents legally married, conceived of parents legally married, natural, of lawful parentage, sired in wedlock
ASSOCIATED CONCEPTS: legitimate issue

LEGITIMATE (*Rightful*), *adjective*   according to law, allowed, authorized, constitutional, enacted, genuine, in accordance with law, in accordance with legal provisions, juristic, law-abiding, lawful, legal, legalized, legislated, licensed, licit, mandated, official, real, recognized by law, rightful, sanctioned, sanctioned by custom, sanctioned by law, sanctioned by legal authority, sound, statutable, statutory, valid, well-founded, well-grounded, within the law
ASSOCIATED CONCEPTS: legitimate business, legitimate heirs, legitimate purpose, legitimate title

LEGITIMATE, *verb*   approve, authorize, certify, declare lawful, legalize, legitimatize, make lawful, make legal, make legitimate, sanction, validate

LEND, *verb*   accommodate with, advance, afford, aid, allow credit, assist, *commodare,* entrust, extend credit, finance, furnish, furnish credit, give, give credit, give money over, grant, invest, loan, permit to borrow, provide, provide with, put up the money, sign over, supply, supply aid, turn over
ASSOCIATED CONCEPTS: lend credit, lend funds

LENIENCE, *noun*   acceptance, benevolence, charity, clemency, compassion, condonation, consideration, disposition to mercy, endurance, favor, flexibility, forbearance, forgiveness, forgivingness, freedom from vindictiveness, generousness, gentleness, grace, humanity, indulgence, kindness, lack of strictness, leniency, lenity, liberality, longanimity, mercifulness, mercy, mildness, moderation, pampering, patience, pity, placability, placableness, quarter, ruth, softheartedness, softness, sympathy, tolerance, toleration, understanding

LENIENT, *noun*   allowing, benevolent, charitable, *clemens,* clement, compassionate, condoning, considerate, easy, easygoing, enduring, exorable, favoring, forbearing, forgiving, free from vindictiveness, generous, gentle, humane, humoring, indulgent, indulging, kind, kindhearted, *lenis,* liberal, long-suffering, longanimous, magnanimous, merciful, mild, *mitis,* moderate, pampering, pardoning, patient, pitying, placable, soft, softhearted, sparing, sympathetic, tolerant, undemanding, unstrict, willing to forgive, yielding

FOREIGN PHRASES: *Cum confitente sponte mitius est agendum.* One confessing voluntarily should be dealt with more leniently.

LESSEE, *noun* boarder, *conductor,* holder of an estate by virtue of a lease, leaseholder, lodger, occupant, occupier, person in possession, possessor, property holder, rent payer, rentee, renter, resident, roomer, tenant

LESSEN, *verb* abate, abbreviate, abridge, abstract, adulterate, allay, alleviate, assuage, attenuate, bate, belittle, boil down, calumniate, censure, check, compress, condense, contract, curb, curtail, cut, cut down, decimate, decline, decrease, decry, deduct, defame, deflate, degenerate, deliquesce, *deminuere,* deplete, depreciate, dequantitate, deride, derogate, deteriorate, detract, devaluate, die away, dilute, diminish, discommend, discount, discredit, disparage, dispraise, disvalue, dock, drop off, dull, dwarf, dwindle, ease, ebb, erode, evaporate, extenuate, *imminuere,* let up, lighten, lower, malign, melt away, minify, minimize, mitigate, moderate, modulate, palliate, pare, qualify, reduce, remit, run down, set at naught, shorten, shrink, slacken, slight, soothe, speak slightingly, stigmatize, stunt, subdue, subside, subtract, summarize, take away, taper, temper, thin, thin out, traduce, trim, underestimate, underrate, undervalue, vilify, vilipend, wane, waste away, water down, weaken, wear away, weed out

LESSOR, *noun* business owner, landlord, owner, property owner

LET *(Lease), **verb*** allow the use of, charter, contract, convey, demise, grant, grant the occupancy of, hire, hire out, lend, loan, make available, rent, rent out

LET *(Permit), **verb*** affranchise, allow, approve, assent, authorize, certify, commission, concede, *concedere,* consent, empower, enable, endorse, enfranchise, entitle, entrust, favor, franchise, give leave, give permission, grant, have no objection, indulge, liberate, license, make possible, oblige, *pati,* privilege, release, sanction, *sinere,* suffer, support, tolerate, vouchsafe, warrant, yield

LETHAL, *adjective* annihilative, baleful, baneful, dangerous, deadly, death-bringing, death-dealing, deathly, destructive, evil, *exitialis,* fatal, fell, feral, *funestus,* harmful, hurtful, injurious, internecine, internecive, killing, lethiferous, malefic, maleficent, maleficial, malign, malignant, mortal, *mortifer,* mortiferous, murderous, nocent, nocuous, noxious, pernicious, pestiferous, pestilent, pestilential, poisonous, slaughtering, toxic, toxiferous, unhealthy, venomous, virulent
ASSOCIATED CONCEPTS: lethal weapon

LETTER OF CREDIT, *noun* credit account, credit note, guaranty, negotiable instrument, paper credit, security
ASSOCIATED CONCEPTS: financial guarantee, letter of delegation, letter of exchange, letter of introduction, letter of license, letters testamentary

LEVERAGE, *noun* advantage, force, influence, potency, pressure, purchase, vantage

LEVY, *noun* assessment, attachment, collection, confiscation, duty, exaction, exactment, excise, gather-ing, impost, impressment, seizure, setting aside of specific property, tariff, tax, taxation, toll

LEVY, *verb* affix, assess, attach, charge, collect, confiscate, conscript, demand, disseise, distrain, divest, enlist, exact, execute, force, garnish, gather, impose, inflict, lay on, muster, place, put on, raise, require, seize, set, take by force, take up, tax, usurp, wrest
ASSOCIATED CONCEPTS: levy a tax, levy an assessment, wrongful levy

LEWD, *adjective* bawdy, carnal, concupiscent, corrupt, depraved, dissolute, exhibiting lust, immodest, immoral, *impudicus,* impure, *impurus, incestus,* indecent, indelicate, lascivious, lecherous, libertine, libidinous, licentious, lubricous, lustful, morally impure, morally unrestrained, obscene, offensive, pornographic, profligate, prurient, publicly indecent, questionable, reprobate, ribald, risque, ruttish, rutty, salacious, scandalous, scarlet, scurrilous, sexually impure, sexually indecent, shameless, suggestive, unchaste, unclean, unvirtuous, vulgar, wanton
ASSOCIATED CONCEPTS: lewd and lascivious cohabitation, obscenity

LIABILITY, *noun* accountability, accountableness, amenability, amenableness, answerability, aptness, bounden duty, burden, contract obligation, debit, debt, disadvantage, drawback, due, duty, duty to pay, encumbrance, handicap, hindrance, indebtedness, legal obligation, legal responsibility, obligation, onus, proclivity, proneness, responsibility, unliquidated claim, vulnerability
ASSOCIATED CONCEPTS: absolute liability, admission of liability, civil liability, contingent liability, criminal liability, denial of liability, existing liability, fixed liability, incurring a liability, joint liability, known liability, legal liability, liability imposed by law, liability insurance, liability without fault, limited liability, manufacturer's liability, original liability, pecuniary liability, potential liability, primary liability, secondary liability, several liability, statutory liability, strict liability, tort liability
FOREIGN PHRASES: *Quando de una et eadem re duo onerabiles existunt, unus pro insufficientia alterius, de integro, onerabitur.* When two persons are chargeable with one and the same thing, one of them is chargeable with the whole thing, upon the failure of the other.

LIABLE, *adjective* accountable, amenable, answerable, bound in equity, bound in law, bound to, bound to respond, chargeable, exposed to, exposed to penalty, in danger, justly responsible, legally bound, legally responsible, obligated, obliged, obliged in law, *obnoxius,* responsible, subject to, susceptible, under legal obligation, under obligation, vulnerable
ASSOCIATED CONCEPTS: jointly liable, liable for debts, liable in tort, liable to forfeiture, liable to penalty, liable to prosecution, liable to punishment, party liable, personally liable, secondarily liable

LIAISON, *noun* administrator, agent, bond, connection, contact, delegate, deputy, emissary, envoy, go-between, interagent, intercessor, intermediary, intermedium, lieutenant, link, linkage, manger, mediating agency, mediator, messenger, negotiant, negotiator, nexus, representative, spokesman, spokesperson, substitute, tie

LIBEL, noun accusation, aspersion, calumny, *carmen famosum,* censorious writing, defamation, defamatory writing, degradation, denigration, denunciation, disparagement, false accusation, false publication, false statement, falsehood, falseness, falsification, impairment of reputation, impeachment of virtue, injury to character, injury to one's reputation, invective, *libellus famosus,* malicious defamation, malicious falsehood, malicious publication, revilement, slur, smear, vilification, writing that discredits, written accusation

ASSOCIATED CONCEPTS: actionable libel, libel per quod, libel per se, publication of libel, slander

LIBEL, verb accuse falsely, accuse in writing, asperse, besmirch, calumniate, censure, condemn, debase, decry, defame, defame by a published writing, degrade, denigrate, denounce, derogate, discredit, discredit in writing, disparage, expose to public contempt, impair one's reputation, incriminate, injure another's reputation, injure by a published writing, injure one's reputation, maliciously defame, malign, publish a falsehood, revile, ridicule, scandalize, slander, slur, smear, traduce, vilify

ASSOCIATED CONCEPTS: absolute privilege, actionable libel, actual malice, criminal libel, defamation, defense of truth, disparagement, First Amendment, libel per quod, libel per se, privileged communication, publication, qualified privileged, republication, slander, trade libel

LIBELOUS, adjective abusive, acrimonious, aspersive, calumnious, condemnatory, contemptuous, damaging, damnatory, defamatory, denunciatory, derogatory, detracting, detractive, discreditable, discrediting, disgracing, dishonorable, dishonoring, disparaging, false and injurious, humiliating, ignominious, ill-willed, improficient, injurious, insulting, malevolent, malicious, malignant, odious, pejorative, scandalous, scurrile, scurrilous, traducing, vilifying, vituperative

LIBERAL (Broad minded), **adjective** adaptable to change, advanced, emancipated, fair-minded, flexible, freethinking, impartial, *liberalis,* liberated, neutral, nonpartisan, not narrow-minded, objective, open, open-minded, progressive, receptive, tolerant, unbiased, unbigoted, uninfluenced, unopinionated, unprejudiced, unswayed

LIBERAL (Generous), **adjective** abundant, almsgiving, altruistic, ample, beneficent, benevolent, bounteous, bountiful, charitable, copious, free, freely giving, generous, handsome, hospitable, humane, humanitarian, lavish, magnanimous, munificent, *munificus,* openhanded, openhearted, philanthropic, plentiful, princely, prodigal, profuse, selfless, stintless, ungrudging, unselfish, unsparing, unstinting

LIBERAL (Not literal), **adjective** broad, enlarged, extended, free from narrowness, general, imprecise, inexact, loose, open, unprecise, unrigorous, unstrict, wide, with license

ASSOCIATED CONCEPTS: liberal construction, liberal interpretation

LIBERATE, verb acquit, affranchise, bail out, deliver, discharge, disembroil, disengage, disenthrall, disimprison, dislodge, dismiss, emancipate, enfranchise, exculpate, exonerate, extract, franchise, free, give freedom, give liberty to, let go, let loose, let out, *liberare,* loose, manumit, *manumittere,* open up, pardon, parole, redeem, release, release from custody, rescue, separate, set at large, set at liberty, set free, turn loose, unbind, unchain, undo, unfasten, unfetter, unloose, unshackle, untie, vindicate

LIBERATION, noun absolution, achievement of liberty, acquittal, acquittance, affranchisement, deliverance, delivery, discharge, disembroiling, disengagement, disenthrallment, disimprisonment, dislodgment, dismissal, emancipation, enfranchisement, exculpation, exoneration, franchisement, freedom, freeing, *liberatio, manumissio,* manumission, pardon, parole, redemption, release, releasing from custody, rescue, separation, unbinding, unchaining, unfettering, unshacking, untying, vindication

LIBERTY, noun absence of foreign rule, absence of restraint, absence of servitude, affranchisement, autonomy, choice, clearance, deliverance, emancipation, enfranchisement, exemption from control, exemption from external control, exemption from restraint, franchise, free will, freedom, freedom from captivity, freedom of action, freedom of choice, grant, independence, latitude, leave, *liber,* liberation from foreign restraint, *libertas,* license, *licentia,* noninterference, permission, political independence, power of choice, power to choose, prerogative, privilege, right, right of choice, sanction, self-determination, self-direction, self-government, unconstraint, uninhibitedness

ASSOCIATED CONCEPTS: abuse of liberty, civil liberty, deprivation of liberty, individual liberties, liberty of contract, liberty of free press, liberty of speech, personal liberty, political liberty, religious liberty

FOREIGN PHRASES: *Favorabilia in lege sunt fiscus, dos, vita, libertas.* Favorites of the law are the treasury, dower, life, and liberty. *Libertas inaestimabilis res est.* Liberty is a thing of inestimable value. *Libertas est naturalis facultas ejus quod, cuique facere libet, nisi quod de jure aut vi prohibetur.* Liberty is a person's natural power which permits one to do as he pleases. *Libertas non recipit aestimationem.* Freedom does not admit a valuation.

LICENSE, noun accordance, allowance, approbation, approval, assurance, authority, authorization, canation, certification, charter, clearance, confirmation, consent, *copia,* empowerment, endorsement, enfranchisement, entitlement, exception, fiat, formal permission, franchise, freedom, grant, imprimatur, leave, liberty, permission, permit, *potestas,* power, prerogative, privilege, right, sanction, special privilege, vouchsafement, warrant, written permission

ASSOCIATED CONCEPTS: assignment of a license, cancellation of license, easement, issuance of license, patent license, permanent license, renewal of a license, revocation of license, suspension of license

LICENSEE, noun appointee, assignee, assignee in fact, consignee, donee, nominee, selectee, transferee

LICENSOR, noun appointer, assignor, consignor, nominator, releasor, selector, transferor

LICENTIOUS, adjective abandoned, aberrant, bawdy, concupiscent, debauched, disorderly, dissipated, dissolute, *dissolutus,* free, freethinking, immoral, *impudicus,* impure, indecent, indelicate, lascivious, lewd, libertine, *libidinosus,* loose, lubricous, lurid, nonconforming, obscene, profligate, promiscuous, rakish, riotous, ruttish, scandalous, scarlet, unchaste, uncontrolled, unconventional, uncurbed, undisciplined, ungoverned, unreined, unrestrained, unruly, vulgar, wanton, wild

LICIT, *adjective* according to edict, according to law, admissible, allowable, allowed, authorized, chartered, constitutional, in accordance with the law, judicatory, judicial, juridic, jurisprudent, jurisprudential, just, law-abiding, lawful, lawlike, legal, legalized, legislated, legitimate, *legitimus,* licensed, mandated, obedient, permissible, permitted, prescribed, proper, *quod ex lege,* right, rightful, sanctionable, sanctioned, sound, statutable, statutory, unprohibited, upright, valid, warrantable, warranted, within the law

LIE, *noun* calumny, deceit, deception, distortion, fabrication, false statement, falsehood, falsification, falsity, *falsum,* fiction, fraud, intentional distortion, intentional exaggeration, intentional misstatement, intentional untruth, invention, mendacity, *mendacium,* misrepresentation, misstatement, perversion, prevarication, untruth
ASSOCIATED CONCEPTS: defamation, libel, perjury, polygraph test, slander

LIE *(Be sustainable), verb* be allowable, be appropriate, be available, be established, be evident, be fitting, be permissible, be permitted, be possible, be proper, be suitable, be suited, be supportable, be warranted, exist, extend, stand

LIE *(Falsify), verb* be dishonest, be untruthful, bear false witness, belie, commit perjury, concoct, counterfeit, deceive, delude, deviate from the truth, dissimulate, equivocate, fable, fabricate, falsify, fib, fool, forswear, invent, *mentiri,* misguide, misinform, mislead, misrepresent, misstate, palter, perjure oneself, pervert, pretend, prevaricate, represent falsely, swear falsely, tell a falsehood, tell an untruth
ASSOCIATED CONCEPTS: false testimony, lie detector, perjury

LIEN, *noun* charge, charge imposed on specific property, claim, claim on property, debt, hold on property, hold upon the property of another, incumbrance, indebtedness, indebtment, liability, obligation, pledge, property right, real security, right to enforce charge upon property, security, security on property, stake
ASSOCIATED CONCEPTS: agricultural lien, artisan's lien, attorney's lien, builder's lien, carrier's lien, common-law lien, concurrent lien, contractor's lien, discharge of lien, equitable lien, factor's lien, general lien, judgment lien, junior lien, landlord's lien, mechanic's lien, possessory lien, prior lien, priority of a lien, statutory lien, superior lien, vendor's lien

LIFE *(Period of existence), noun* *anima,* continuance, cycle, duration, endurance, existence, lastingness, lifetime, period, period of survival, span, survival, term, term of activity, term of effectiveness, time, time from birth to death, *vita*
ASSOCIATED CONCEPTS: life annuity, life estate, life expectancy, life imprisonment, life insurance company, life interest, life tenant
FOREIGN PHRASES: *Non nasci, et natum mori, paria sunt.* Not to be born, and to be born dead, are the same. *La ley favour la vie d'un homme.* The law favors human life.

LIFE *(Vitality), noun* activeness, activity, *alacritas,* alertness, animation, ardor, breeziness, briskness, drive, dynamic quality, dynamism, eagerness, effervescence, energy, enthusiasm, exuberance, fieriness, fire, impassionedness, intensity, jocularity, jocundity, joviality, liveliness, lustiness, spirit, spiritedness, sprightliness, verve, vigor, vim, *vis,* vivacity, zeal, zest, zestfulness

LIFELESS *(Dead), adjective* abrogated, annihilated, annulled, at rest, bereft of life, breathless, cadaveric, cadaverous, canceled, deceased, defunct, demised, departed, destitute of life, devoid of life, ended, exanimate, *exanimus,* expired, extinct, gone, impercipient, inanimate, insensate, insensient, irrecoverable, late, null, passed away, passed on, perished, pulseless, quashed, repealed, unanimated, unfeeling, unrevived, void, without life

LIFELESS *(Dull), adjective* apathetic, arid, banal, barren, benumbing, boring, characterless, colorless, commonplace, deactivated, deadened, debilitated, dismal, dormant, drearisome, dreary, dronish, dry, empty, *exsanguis,* feeble, flat, *frigidus,* hebetudinous, inactive, indolent, inert, inexcitable, insensible, insipid, insulse, lackadaisical, lackluster, laggard, languid, languourness, lazy, leaden, lethargic, lethargical, listless, lumpish, lusterless, monotonous, oscitant, passionless, passive, phlegmatic, pococurante, producing boredom, producing ennui, prosaic, quiescent, quiet, slothful, sluggish, somber, spiritless, stagnant, stale, stodgy, stupefied, supine, tame, tedious, tired, tiresome, torpescent, torpid, trite, unactivated, unaroused, uncaptivating, unenlivened, unenterprising, unentertaining, unenthusiastic, unfeeling, unfertile, unimaginative, unimpassioned, uninspired, uninspiring, uninteresting, uninventive, unlively, unoriginal, unresponsive, unsparkling, unspirited, unvivid, usual, vapid, vegatating, vegetative, weak, wearisome, wearying

LIFETIME, *noun* *aetas, aevum,* age, duration of life, epoch, era, generation, life, life span, life's duration, period of existence, period of life, period of survival, season, span, span of years, term, time, years of existence
ASSOCIATED CONCEPTS: life estate, per otra vie, rule against perpetuities

LIKELIHOOD, *noun* anticipation, chance, conceivability, conceivableness, confident expectation, excellent prospect, expectance, expectancy, expectation, fair chance, fair prospect, favorable chance, favorable prospect, good chance, good prospect, likeliness, plausibility, possibility, possibleness, potential, potentiality, *probabilitas,* probability, prospect, reasonable chance, reasonable ground, reasonable presumption, reasonable prospect, *veri similitudo,* well-grounded hope, well-grounded possibility

LIMIT, *noun* ambit, border, bound, boundary, boundary line, *circumscriptio,* circumscription, extreme boundary, final point, *finis,* fringe, frontier, furthest point, line of demarcation, outer edge, outer line, outer point, perimeter, rim, *terminus,* verge
ASSOCIATED CONCEPTS: jurisdictional limit, territorial limit

LIMIT, *verb* bind, bridle, check, circumscribe, *circumscribere,* confine, constrain, constrict, contain, curb, deter, enclose, *finire,* hamper, hem in, hinder, hold back, impede, leash, modulate, narrow, proscribe, repress, restrain, restrict, set bounds, suppress, *terminare*

LIMITATION, noun   barrier, block, *circumscriptio,* circumscription, clause, condition, constraint, curb, demarcation, *determinatio,* disallowance, prohibition, proscription, provision, qualification, reservation, restraint, restriction, specific confinement, specific curtailment, specification
ASSOCIATED CONCEPTS: alternative limitations, collateral limitation, conditional limitation, contingent limitation, conveyance upon a limitation, estate upon a limitation, executory limitation, limitation of actions, limitation of damages, limitation of liability, limitation of time, limitation of warranties, limitation over, public debt limitation, special limitation, statute of limitations, tax limitation, words of limitation

LIMITED, adjective   *angustus,* bounded, *brevis,* checked, circumscribed, circumscriptive, confined, confining, constricted, controlled, cramped, curbed, definite, enclosed, fixed, hampered, impeded, insular, narrow, *parvus,* prescribed, restrained, restricted, stinted
ASSOCIATED CONCEPTS: limited agency, limited by law, limited guaranty, limited jurisdiction, limited partnership, limited waiver of immunity, limited warranty

LIMITING, adjective   checking, circumscribing, close-fitting, confining, constricting, containing, curbing, hampering, hindering, impeding, repressing, restraining, restricting, restrictive, stinting, suppressing

LINEAGE, noun   ancestors, ancestry, antecedents, blood relatives, bloodline, clan, descent, extraction, family, folk, forebears, forefathers, genealogy, gens, *genus,* line, line of descent, origin, *origo,* parentage, progenitors, *stirps*

LINEUP, noun   arrangement, file, formation, grouping, order, parade, queue, showing, showing of criminal defendants, showing of criminals for inspection and identification, showing of possible suspects, showing of suspected criminals
ASSOCIATED CONCEPTS: prejudicial and overly suggestive lineup, show-up

LIQUIDATE *(Convert into cash),* **verb**   cash in, change into cash, change into money, conclude, distribute assets, exchange for money, finish, realize in cash, redeem, sell, sell assets, terminate, terminate business affairs, turn into money
ASSOCIATED CONCEPTS: liquidated account, liquidating trust, liquidation of assets, trustees in liquidation

LIQUIDATE *(Determine liability),* **verb**   adjust, ascertain liability, ascertain the amount of indebtedness, ascertain the balance due, assemble and apportion assets, cancel debts, determine the amount of indebtedness, discharge, discharge a liability, discharge debts, dispose of, extinguish indebtedness, make restitution, meet payments, pay, pay and settle, pay debts, satisfy, settle, settle accounts with the debtors and creditors
ASSOCIATED CONCEPTS: liquidated claim, liquidated damages, liquidated debt, liquidated demand

LIS PENDENS, noun   filed notice, notice of an action, notice of pending suit, notice of right, notice on file

LITERAL, adjective   accurate, authentic, careful, close, correct, exact, factual, faithful, faultless, meticulous, precise, rigid, scrupulous, strict, textual, to the letter, true, true to fact, truthful, unchanged, uncorrupted, undeviating, undistorted, unembroidered, unerring, unexaggerated, unfigurative, ungarbled, unmetaphorical, unvaried, unvarnished, veracious, verbatim, without exaggeration, word for word
ASSOCIATED CONCEPTS: literal interpretation

LITERATE, adjective   accomplished, apprised, aware, conversant, cultivated, cultured, disciplined, educated, enlightened, enriched, erudite, having formal education, informed, intellectual, knowing, knowledgeable, learned, lettered, literary, polished, practiced, proficient, qualified, sapient, scholarly, scholastic, schooled, skilled, studied, studious, trained, well-educated, well-informed, well-read, well-taught, widely read

LITIGABLE, adjective   actionable, appealable, arguable, argumentative, capable of being debated, confutable, contestable, controversial, controvertible, disputable, in dispute, justiciable, refutable

LITIGANT, noun   adversary, adverse party, appellant, appellee, claimant, complainant, contender, contestant, controversialist, correspondent, defendant, the defense, disputant, intervenor, legal adversary, legal opponent, litigationist, litigator, opponent, opponent in a lawsuit, party, party to a suit, petitioner, plaintiff, respondent, suitor

LITIGATE, verb   altercate, appeal to the law, assert in court, bring action against, bring an action, bring suit, bring to the bar, bring to trial, carry on a lawsuit, contend, contest in court, contest in law, go into litigation, institute legal proceedings, *litigare,* prefer a claim, press in court, pursue in court, seek legal redress, start a lawsuit, start an action, sue, take to court, urge in court

LITIGIOUS, adjective   actionable, aggressive, antagonistic, arguing, argumental, argumentative, at variance, bellicose, belligerent, combative, conflicting, contentious, contested, contrary, controversial, controvertible, debatable, disagreeing, discordant, disposed to controversy, disputable, disputatious, disputative, dissentious, eristic, eristical, exceptious, fighting, given to disputation, hostile, inimical, irreconcilable, litigatory, *litigiosus,* militant, offensive, open to debate, open to question, opposing, polemic, polemical, pugnacious, quarrelsome, querulous, unpeaceful, warlike
ASSOCIATED CONCEPTS: barratry

LITTORAL, adjective   beach, beachfront, coastal, coastland, lakeside, riparian, seaboard, seacoast, seashore, seaside, tidewater, waterfront, waterside

LIVE *(Conscious),* **adjective**   animate, animated, breathing, endowed with life, existent, existing, full of life, growing, imbued with life, incarnate, living, mortal, quick, viable, vital

LIVE *(Existing),* **adjective**   abiding, continued, continuing, enduring, existent, extant, intact, lasting, ongoing, perduring, persevering, persisting, progressing, remaining, staying, surviving, sustained, unceasing,

unchecked, undestroyed, unended, unfading, unfailing, unreversed, unrevoked, unstopped
ASSOCIATED CONCEPTS: live cause of action

LIVELIHOOD, *noun* business, calling, career, craft, employment, enterprise, job, keep, line of work, living, maintenance, means, occupation, position, profession, pursuit, resources, situation, source of income, subsistence, support, sustainment, sustenance, trade, undertaking, venture, *victus,* vocation, work

LOAD, *verb* burden, cram, cumber, fill, fill up, flood, freight, inundate, lade, make heavy, mass, *onerare, onus imponere,* pack, pile, put aboard, put goods in, put on board, saddle, shower upon, stack, steeve, store, stow, stuff, take on cargo, weigh down, weight

LOAN, *noun* accommodation, advance, advancement, aid, allotment, assistance, backing, *commodare,* credit, dole, entrustment, extension of credit, financing, funding, grant, imprest, moneys borrowed, *mutuum,* pledge, *res commodata,* stake, stipend, subsidy, sum entrusted, sum of money borrowed, sum of money lent, temporary accommodation, time payment, trust
ASSOCIATED CONCEPTS: bond, building loan, construction loan, continuing loan, discount, excessive loan, forbearance, gratuitous loan, loan association, loan broker, loan value of a policy, mortgage, secured loan, simple loan, stock loan, temporary loan, unpaid loan, usurious loan, usury laws
FOREIGN PHRASES: *Creditorum appellatione non hi tantum accipiuntur qui pecuniam crediderunt, sed omnes quibus ex qualibet causa debetur.* Under the head of "creditors" are included, not only those who have lent money, but all to whom from any cause a debt is owing.

LOAN, *verb* accommodate, advance, allow, extend credit, furnish funds, give, lend, permit to borrow, supply funds

LOATHSOME, *adjective* abhorrent, abject, abominable, accursed, annoying, appalling, atrocious, base, below contempt, beneath contempt, blameworthy, contemptible, deplorable, despicable, detestable, disagreeable, disgusting, disliked, dissatisfactory, distasteful, distressing, dreadful, execrable, *foedus,* forbidding, foul, frightful, fulsome, ghastly, hateful, heinous, hellish, hideous, horrible, horrid, insufferable, intolerable, invidious, irritating, loathful, mean, nasty, nauseating, nauseous, objectionable, obnoxious, odious, offensive, opprobrious, painful, putrid, rancid, rank, repellent, repelling, reprehensible, repugnant, repulsive, revolting, shocking, sickening, *taeter,* terrible, ugly, unbearable, undesirable, unendurable, unpalatable, unpleasant, unsavory, vile

LOBBY, *noun* active partisans, active reformers, active supporters, activists, advocates, agitators, influencers, influential persons, persuaders, petitioners, pressure group, reformers, special interest group, special interests, zealous advocates

LOBBY, *verb* actively represent, actuate, advance, arouse, bring pressure to bear, defend, effect, encourage, enlist, espouse, exercise influence, exert influence, exert pressure, incline, induce, influence, inspirit, instigate, motivate, negotiate, personally solicit, persuade,

press, pressure, procure, promote, provoke, pull strings, put pressure on, represent, request, solicit, solicit votes, sway, urge, use one's influence, work on
ASSOCIATED CONCEPTS: lobbyists, registration laws, special interest groups

LOCAL, *adjective* adjacent, adjoining, civic, close, district, divisional, domestic, limited, localized, municipal, native, near, nearby, neighborhood, provincial, regional, restricted, sectional, subdivisional, surrounding, territorial
ASSOCIATED CONCEPTS: local act, local action, local agent, local application, local assessment, local authorities, local bill, local concern, local improvement, local law, local rules

LOCALITY, *noun* address, area, bearings, demesne, district, domain, environment, environs, habitat, locale, location, *locus,* neighborhood, pale, place, position, province, purlieus, quarter, region, scene, seat, section, sector, site, situation, *situs,* spot, station, surroundings, terrain, territory, venue, vicinage, vicinity, whereabouts, zone

LOCATE, *verb* ascertain a position, assign to a place, bring to light, come upon, define limits, define location, delineate, demarcate, deposit, designate a place, detect, discern, discover, discover by search, discover by survey, discover the location of, discover the place of, establish, expose, ferret out, find, fix the position, house, install, lodge, make a place for, map out, move to, park, pinpoint, place, position, put, put in place, quarter, reveal, search out, select boundaries, set, set in place, settle, situate, station, stumble on, take up abode, trace, track down, uncover, unearth

LOCATION, *noun* area, demesne, district, environment, fixation, locale, locality, locus, neighborhood, place, placement, plot, point, position, post, purlieus, quarter, region, scene, section, site, spot, station, territory, vicinage, vicinity, zone
ASSOCIATED CONCEPTS: domicile, residency, venue

LOCK, *verb* arrest, attach, band, bar, barricade, block, blockade, bolt, cage, catch, cement, check, cinch, clasp, close, close fast, *concludere,* confine, connect, couple, curb, cut off, dam, encircle, enclose, enthrall, entwine, fasten, fuse, glue, grapple, hamper, hinder, hold, immobilize, immure, impede, impound, imprison, incarcerate, inhibit, intern, jail, join, link, lock up, make fast, make inseperable, *obserere,* obstruct, occlude, padlock, pen, prohibit, put behind bars, restrain, restrict, seal, secure, shackle, shut out, shut up, stop, trap, unite, weld, yoke
ASSOCIATED CONCEPTS: lockout

LOCKOUT, *noun* barring out, cessation of employment, cessation of the furnishing of work, close-out, coercive refusal to furnish work, employer work stoppage, exclusion of workers, nonadmission of employees, preclusion of work, refusal to furnish work, repudiation of employment, stoppage of work, temporary closing, work stoppage
ASSOCIATED CONCEPTS: strike

LOCO PARENTIS, *adverb* as a substitute for a parent, as an alternative for a parent, in place of a parent, instead of a parent

LODGE *(Bring a complaint)*, **verb**   accuse, bring a case, bring a suit, bring accusation, bring an action against, bring charges against, bring proceedings against, bring to justice, bring to the bar, bring to trial, bring up on charges, call to account, cast blame upon, charge with, file a claim, file a suit, fix the blame for, incriminate, inculpate, place the blame for, prefer charges, prosecute
ASSOCIATED CONCEPTS: lodge a criminal complaint

LODGE *(House)*, **verb**   afford sanctuary, assign to lodgings, bed, berth, domicile, find a place for, find room for, furnish room for, furnish with quarters, garrison, harbor, *hospitio excipere,* hostel, install, locate, make a place for, park, place, put, quarter, screen, shield, situate, station, supply accommodations for

LODGE *(Reside)*, **verb**   abide, board, camp, *deversari, devertere,* domicile, dwell, encamp, establish oneself, inhabit, live, locate oneself, make one's home at, place, quarter, remain, reside, rest, set up housekeeping, settle, sleep at, sojourn, squat, station, stay, stop, take lodgings, take rooms, take up quarters, take up residence in, tarry, tenant

LODGER, **noun**   addressee, boarder, denizen, *deversor,* dweller, habitant, indweller, inhabitant, inhabiter, inmate, *inquilinus,* leaseholder, lessee, occupant, occupier, possessor, rent payer, renter, resident, residentiary, resider, roomer, sojourner, tenant, termor, transient

LODGING, **noun**   abode, accommodation, address, apartment, asylum, berth, billet, chambers, *deversorium, deverticulum,* domicile, dormitory, dwelling, dwelling place, habitat, habitation, harbor, home, housing, inhabitance, inhabitancy, living place, lodging place, lodgment, *meritoria,* place of residence, place of rest, protection, quarters, refuge, residence, rooms, shelter

LOGICAL, **adjective**   analytic, analytical, cogent, coherent, consistent, deductive, dialectic, dialectical, inductional, inductive, philosophical, ratiocinative, ratiocinatory, rational, reasonable, reasoned, sound

LOITER, **verb**   be idle, be vagrant, *cessare,* hang around, idle, linger, move aimlessly, pass time in idleness, poke, stand around, tarry, wander aimlessly
ASSOCIATED CONCEPTS: vagrancy

LONGANIMITY, **noun**   composure, control, endurance, forbearance, forgiveness, forgivingness, fortitude, imperturbation, indulgence, inexcitability, lenience, leniency, magnanimity, optimism, pardon, patience, patient endurance, perseverance, placability, placidity, refusal to be provoked, resignation, self-control, stamina, steadiness, stoicism, submission, sufferance, temperance, tenacity, tolerance, toleration, tranquility, understanding

LONGEVITY, **noun**   advancement, age, continuance, continuation, durability, durableness, duration, elderliness, endurance, furtherance, great span of life, lastingness, length of life, long life, longlivedness, maintenance, old age, oldness, perpetuation, persistence, prolongation, protraction, seniority, surviviorship, survival, survivance, years

LOOPHOLE, **noun**   alternative, aperture, contrivance, device, escape clause, escape hatch, escape valve, evasion, exception, excuse, expedient, *foramen,* means of escape, mechanism for evasion, opening, outlet, saving clause, uncommunicativeness, vehicle for escape, way of escape, way out

LOOT, **verb**   abscond with, appropriate, break into, burglarize, carry off, defalcate, depredate, despoil, embezzle, forage, harry, lay waste, make off with, maraud, peculate, pilfer, pillage, pirate, plunder, prey upon, purloin, raid, ransack, ravage, rifle, rob, sack, seize, spoil, spoliate, steal, strip, take, thieve

LOQUACIOUS, **adjective**   babbling, blabbing, chattering, chatty, communicative, copious in speech, disposed to talk freely, effusive, exuberant, flatulent, fluent, gabby, garrulous, *garrulus,* glib, gushy, informative, jabbering, long-winded, longiloquent, *loquax,* noisy, prattling, profuse, prolix, rambling, talkative, talking, tonguey, verbal, verbose, *verbosus,* vociferous, voluble, windy, wordy

LOSE *(Be deprived of)*, **verb**   *amittere,* be deprived of, be impoverished, be without, become poorer by, experience a loss, fail to find, fail to keep, forfeit, forget, incur a loss, meet with a loss, mislay, misplace, miss, part with, *perdere,* sacrifice, squander, suffer a deprivation, suffer loss, waste

LOSE *(Undergo defeat)*, **verb**   be confounded, be defeated, be destroyed, be disappointed, be foiled, be frustrated, be humbled, be left behind, be outdistanced, be outvoted, be overthrown, be ruined, be thwarted, be unsuccessful, come in last, fail, fail to win, forfeit, go down in defeat, succumb, suffer by comparison, suffer defeat, take a beating, yield
ASSOCIATED CONCEPTS: lose a case

LOSS, **noun**   calamity, catastrophe, cost, *damnum,* decline, decrement, deprivation, *detrimentum,* disaster, failure, forfeit, forfeiture, *iactura,* ill fortune, ill luck, misfortune, privation, removal, ruin, sacrifice, waste
ASSOCIATED CONCEPTS: actual loss, allowable loss, business loss, capital loss, cause of loss, consequential loss, constructive total loss, damages, deductible, direct loss, financial loss, guaranty funds, indemnification, involuntary losses, irreparable loss, loss of bargain, loss of earnings, loss of life, loss of profits, loss of services, loss payable clause, loss reserves, measure of damages, net loss, operating loss, out-of-pocket loss, pecuniary loss, permanent loss, profit and loss, recovery of losses from bad debts, salvage loss
FOREIGN PHRASES: *Nemo debet locupletari ex alterius incommodo.* No one ought to gain by another's loss. *Fictio legis inique operatur alieni damnum vel injuriam.* Fiction of law is wrongful if it works loss or harm to anyone. *Non omne damnum inducit injuriam.* Not every loss produces an injury. *Lex citius tolerare vult privatum damnum quam publicum malum.* The law would rather tolerate a private loss than a public evil. *Officium nemini debet esse damnosum.* An office ought to be injurious to no one. *Non videntur rem amittere quibus propria non fuit.* Persons to whom a thing did not belong are not considered to have lost it.

LOST *(Disoriented)*, **adjective**   adrift, astray, baffled, befogged, befuddled, bemuddled, bewildered, confused, mystified, obfuscated, perplexed, puzzled, strayed, unable to find the way, wandering, without bearings

LOST *(Taken away),* **adjective** absent, annihilated, confiscated, depleted, destroyed, dissipated, effaced, eliminated, eradicated, exhausted, exterminated, extinguished, extirpated, forfeited, gone, gone to waste, hidden, irreclaimable, irrecoverable, irredeemable, irretrievable, irrevocable, mislaid, misplaced, missing, nowhere to be found, obliterated, obscured, out of sight, perished, sacrificed, squandered, taken, thrown away, vanished, wasted

LOT, *noun* parcel, part, piece, piece of ground, plot, portion, small parcel of land, subdivision, tract **ASSOCIATED CONCEPTS:** adjacent lots, block, building lot, contiguous lots, partition of lots, vacant lot

LOTTERY, *noun* allotment by chance, bet, chance, draw, drawing, gamble, game of chance, lot, raffle, *sors, sortitio,* sweepstake, wager

LOYAL, *adjective* allegiant, beholden, biddable, bound, bounden, committed, compliant, conscientious, constant, dedicated, dependable, devoted, duteous, dutiful, faithful, fast, *fidelis, fidus,* filial, firm, honorable, incorrupt, incorruptible, indebted, obedient, patriotic, pledged, reliable, resolute, slavish, staunch, steadfast, steady, tried, true, truehearted, trustworthy, trusty, unbetraying, unbought, unbribed, unchangeable, unchanging, undeviating, unfailing, unimpeachable, uninfluenced, unperfidious, unswayed, unswerving, untreacherous, unwavering, worthy of confidence **ASSOCIATED CONCEPTS:** duty of loyalty, faithful performance, loyalty oath, undivided loyalty

LOYALTY, *noun* adherence, adherency, allegiance, attachment, bond, compliance, constancy, dedication, dependability, devotedness, devotion, duty, faithfulness, fealty, *fidelitas,* fidelity, *fides,* good faith, group feeling, incorruptibility, obedience, reliability, singlemindedness, singleness of heart, stanchness, steadfastness, submissiveness, support, troth, trueness, trustworthiness, zeal

LUCID, *adjective* apparent, articulate, certain, clear, clear-cut, clear-minded, clear-thinking, clearwitted, clearheaded, comprehending, comprehensible, crystalline, diaphanous, discerning, discriminating, distinct, effulgent, evident, explicit, express, fulgid, illuminated, illumined, indisputable, intelligible, limpid, lucent, *lucidus,* luculent, manifest, nitid, obvious, overt, palpable, patent, pellucid, *pellucidus,* perceptive, perspicacious, perspicuous, *perspicuus,* plain, pronounced, rational, refulgent, responsible, sagacious, sage, sane, sensible, simple, sober, sound, straightforward, transparent, unambiguous, undeniable, understandable, understood, undisguised, unequivocal, unmistakable, unquestionable

LUCRATIVE, *adjective* accumulative, advantageous, bearing revenue, beneficial, compensating, compensatory, contributive, fertile, fruitful, gainful, highpaying, invaluable, *lucrosus,* moneymaking, paying, productive, profitable, *quaestuosus,* remunerative, rewardful, rewarding, successful, useful, valuable, well-paying, worthwhile

LUDICROUS, *adjective* absurd, amusing, asinine, at variance with the facts, barely possible, beyond belief, bizarre, comical, contrary to common sense, contrary to reason, crazy, derisible, doubtable, dubitable, eccentric, fallacious, fantastic, fantastical, farcical, fatuous, foolish, funny, hard to believe, humorous, idiotic, implausible, impossible, inane, incongruous, inconsistent, incredible, irrational, laugh-provoking, laughable, nonsensical, odd, open to doubt, outlandish, peculiar, preposterous, queer, questionable, ridiculous, risible, senseless, silly, staggering belief, strange, suspect, unbelievable, unconvincing, unheard of, unreasonable, untenable, unthinkable, wild, without reason

LUGUBRIOUS, *adjective* cheerless, crestfallen, dark, dejected, depressing, despondent, disconsolate, discouraged, disheartened, dismal, dispirited, doleful, dolorous, downcast, dreary, elegiac, *flebilis,* forbidding, forlorn, funereal, gloomy, glum, grieving, heavyhearted, joyless, low-spirited, *lugubris,* melancholy, miserable, morose, mournful, piteous, plaintive, sad, saturnine, somber, sorrowful, tearful, unhappy, weary, woebegone, woeful, wretched

LULL, *noun* abatement, armistice, break, breather, breathing spell, breathing time, brief silence, calm, calmness, cessation, cessation of activity, cessation of sound, desistance, discontinuance, discontinuation, halt, hush, idleness, inactivity, interlude, intermission, interregnum, interruption, pause, peace, period of rest, quiescence, quiescency, quiet, recess, remission, repose, respite, rest, silence, soundlessness, standstill, stay, stillness, stop, stoppage, subsidence, suspension, temporary quiet, temporary stillness, tranquillity, truce

LULL, *verb* allay, alleviate, assuage, calm, cause to relax, compose, cradle, dulcify, ease, encourage repose, hush, induce forgetfulness, make calm, mitigate, pacify, palliate, placate, put to rest, put to sleep, quell, quiet, quiet down, quieten, relax, remit, remove one's anxieties, remove one's fears, rock, *sedare,* settle, silence, soothe, still, stupefy, subdue, tranquilize

LUNACY, *noun* craziness, delusion, dementia, derangement, disordered mind, folly, foolishness, frenzy, impairment of mental faculties, insaneness, insanity, instability of mental powers, madness, mania, mental aberration, mental abnormality, mental dissociation, mental illness, mental imbalance, mental sickness, unsoundness of mind

LUNATIC, *adjective* absurd, bereft of reason, crazed, crazy, daft, dementate, demented, deranged, disordered, foolish, frenetic, frenzied, insane, insensate, irrational, mad, maniacal, manic, mentally aberrant, mentally ill, mentally unbalanced, nonsensical, obsessed, of unsound mind, out of one's mind, out of one's senses, possessed, raging, ranting, raving, reasonless, senseless, touched, unhinged, unsettled, wandering, wild

LURE, *verb* *adlicere,* allure, attract, bait, beguile, bewitch, bribe, cajole, captivate, charm, coax, court, decoy, draw on, entice, hold out allurement, hold out temptation, induce, *inlicere,* inveigle, *pellicere,* provoke desire, seduce, tantalize, tempt

LURID, *adjective* appalling, *caliginosus,* coarse, disgusting, exaggerated, extreme, fulsome, ghastly, glaringly vivid, graphic, gross, gruesome, harsh, horrible, horrifying, indelicate, *luridus, obscurus,* offensive, overwhelming, racy, repulsive, revolting, risque, salacious, scabrous, scrofulous, sensational, shocking, startling, uncensored, unexpurgated, unusual, vulgar

LURK, *verb*   ambuscade, be stealthy, be unseen, conceal oneself, crouch, *delitescere,* ensconce oneself, escape detection, escape notice, escape observation, escape recognition, hide, keep out of sight, *latere, latitare,* lie concealed, lie hidden, lie in ambush, lie in wait, lie low, move furtively, prowl, seclude oneself, secrete oneself, skulk, slink, sneak, steal

LUXATE, *verb*   break, detach, disconnect, disengage, disjoin, disjoint, dislocate, dispart, displace, dissever, dissociate, disunite, eject, expel, part, put out of joint, put out of place, rend, rive, separate, sever, sunder, throw out of gear, unhinge, unjoint, wrench

LYING, *adjective*   bluffing, covinous, cunning, deceitful, deceptive, delusive, delusory, devoid of truth, dishonest, disingenuous, dissembling, double-dealing, equivocating, fabricating, faithless, faked, false, feigned, fictitious, forsworn, fraudulent, mendacious, misleading, misrepresentative, perfidious, perjured, sneaky, spurious, treacherous, tricky, trumped up, truthless, uncandid, unfactual, untrue, untruthful, unveracious
ASSOCIATED CONCEPTS: perjury

LYNCH LAW, *noun*   anarchy, blatant violation of law, breakdown of administration, disorderliness, flagrant abuse of the law, illegal infliction of punishment, lack of due process, lack of justice, lack of legal sanction, lawlessness, misgovernment, misrule, mob rule, mobocracy, nihilism, ochlocracy, outlawry, paralysis of authority, punishment without trial, reign of terror, summary punishment by mob, taking the law in one's own hands, terrorism, unruliness

M

MACHIAVELLIAN, *adjective*   arch, artful, base, cagey, calculating, canny, cheating, clever, collusive, collusory, conniving, conscienceless, contriving, corrupt, covinous, crafty, crooked, cunning, deceitful, deceiving, deceptive, delusive, designing, devious, dirty, dishonest, dishonorable, disingenuous, double-crossing, double-dealing, double-tongued, evasive, faithless, falsehearted, feline, foxy, fraudulent, guileful, hypocritical, ignoble, immoral, infamous, insidious, insincere, intriguing, knavish, mean, misdealing, opportunist, perfidious, plotting, rascally, roguish, scheming, shady, shameless, sharp, shifty, shrewd, slick, slippery, sly, smooth, sneaking, sneaky, stealthy, subdolous, tortuous, treacherous, trickish, tricky, two-faced, undependable, underhand, underhanded, unethical, unprincipled, unscrupulous, untrustworthy, untruthful, venal, vile, vulpine, wily

MACHINATION, *noun*   artful dodge, artifice, cabal, collusion, conspiracy, contrivance, covin, crafty design, crafty device, crafty plan, design, dodge, *dolus,* foul play, intrigue, jugglery, *machina,* maneuver, manipulation, plot, ploy, ruse, scheme, stratagem, strategy, subterfuge, tactic, treachery, trick, underplot, wile, wily device

MAGISTRATE, *noun*   arbitrator, assessor, judge, jurist, justice, legist, *magistratus,* moderator, officer, official

MAGNANIMOUS, *adjective*   above meanness, above pettiness, altruistic, beneficent, charitable, chivalrous, elevated, exalted, forgiving, free of pettiness, gallant, generous, great, handsome, high-minded, honorable, illustrious, kind, largehearted, liberal, lofty, *magnanimus,* noble, noble-minded, philanthropic, princely, ungrudging, unselfish

MAGNIFY, *verb*   add to, aggrandize, *amplificare,* amplify, *augere,* augment, balloon, boost, broaden, build up, cause growth, deepen, emphasize, enhance, enlarge, *exaggerare,* exaggerate, exalt, expand, extend, glorify, heighten, idealize, increase, increase the size of, inflate, intensify, make great, make larger, make more important, maximize, overestimate, overprize, overrate, overstate, overstress, overvalue, play up, raise, spread, strengthen, stretch, stretch a point, swell, widen

MAGNITUDE, *noun*   amplitude, *amplitudo,* bearing, concern, consequence, consideration, degree, dimension, effect, eminence, enormity, essentiality, extension, extent, gauge, gravity, immensity, import, importance, *magnitudo,* mark, materiality, materialness, measure, measurement, momentousness, precedence, primacy, priority, proportions, range, reach, scale, scope, seriousness, significance, size, span, *spatium,* stature, stretch, value, vastness, volume, weight, weightiness, worth

MAIM, *verb*   cripple, damage, deface, disable, hobble, hurt, impair, incapacitate, injure, lame, make useless, mutilate, wound

MAIN FORCE, *noun* aggressiveness, brute force, compulsion, controlling force, controlling power, dominant strength, duress, effort, energy, forcefulness, full force, intensity, matchless effort, maxim effort, might, potence, potency, power, powerfulness, pressure, puissance, push, sheer force, sheer power, strength, toughness, unrivaled effort, utter force, vigor

MAIN POINT, *noun* backbone, basis, *caput,* cardinal feature, cardinal point, central idea, chief feature, chief issue, chief part, chief point, core, cream, critical feature, critical point, crucial feature, crucial point, crux, drift, elixir, essence, essential matter, essential part, essential point, essentialness, force, fundamental feature, fundamental part, fundamental point, gist, gravamen, heart, implication, import, important feature, important part, important point, kernel, key, keynote, keystone, lifeblood, main idea, main thing, major part, marrow, material point, meaning, nucleus, outstanding feature, pith, pivotal point, prime constituent, prime ingredient, principal point, prominent aspect, prominent point, purport, quiddity, quintessence, *res summa,* salient feature, salient point, sense, significance, substance, tenor, vital concern

MAINSTAY, *noun* anchor, assurance, backbone, backer, bastion, brace, bulwark, buttress, champion, chief reliance, cornerstone, crutch, deliverance, dependence, foundation, help, keystone, maintainer, nucleus, pillar, principal backer, principal maintainer, principal support, principal supporter, principal sustainer, prop, rampart, reinforcement, reliance, right arm, right hand, salvation, security, staff, stay, strength, stronghold, support, sustainer, sustenance, tower of strength, upholder

MAINTAIN *(Carry on),* *verb* *adfirmare, confirmare, contendere,* continue, follow up, go on, keep alive, keep going, keep on, keep up, perpetuate, persevere, persist, proceed with, prolong, pursue, shore up, stick to

MAINTAIN *(Commence),* *verb* activate, begin, embark upon, initiate, institute, introduce, launch, originate, set in motion, set in operation, start, undertake
ASSOCIATED CONCEPTS: maintain an action

MAINTAIN *(Sustain),* *verb* abet, adhere, advocate, aid, assist, attend, be firm, be firmly fixed, bear up against, bolster, buttress, care for, champion, come to the defense of, conserve, countenance, cover, defend, espouse the cause of, feed, finance, guard, hold up, justify, look after, make provision, make safe, nourish, nurse, nurture, oversee, preserve, protect, provide for, rally to, safeguard, save, screen, secure, see to, service, shelter, shield, shoulder, side with, stand by, stand firm, stand one's ground, stick to, subscribe to, subsidize, substantiate, supply, support, take care of, take charge of, uphold, vindicate, watch over, weather

MAINTENANCE *(Support of spouse),* *noun* aid, alimony, allowance, assistance, financial backing, financing, legal assistance, legal support, means of subsistence, monetary help, necessaries, necessities of life, preservation, provisions, subsidy, subsistence, sustenance, upkeep, *victus*
ASSOCIATED CONCEPTS: separate maintenance, support and maintenance

MAINTENANCE *(Upkeep),* *noun* care, carrying charge, *conservatio,* conservation, cost, disbursement, drain on resources, expenditure, expense, outlay, overhead, repair, running expenses, *salus,* service
ASSOCIATED CONCEPTS: ordinary maintenance and repair, reasonable maintenance

MAJOR, *adjective* big, chief, comprehensive, consequential, considerable, crucial, decisive, distinguished, enormous, essential, extensive, extraordinary, far-reaching, fateful, goodly, grave, great, high-level, important, imposing, impressive, intense, key, large, leading, massive, matchless, material, memorable, meritorious, moderately large, momentous, notable, noteworthy, outstanding, paramount, ponderous, pressing, prime, principal, remarkable, serious, significant, sizable, sober, solemn, substantial, supreme, top, top-level, tremendous, unparalleled, vital, weighty, worthy of consideration, worthy of remark

MAJORITY *(Adulthood),* *noun* age of discretion, age of majority, age of responsibility, full age, full legal age, legal age, legal competence, legal maturity, manhood, matureness, maturity, voting age, womanhood
FOREIGN PHRASES: *Minor ante tempus agere non potest in casu proprietatis nec etiam convenire.* A minor under age cannot act in a case of property.

MAJORITY *(Greater part),* *noun* better part, biggest share, body, bulk, generality, greater number, larger number, larger part, lion's share, main body, main part, *maior numerus, maior pars,* major part, mass, more than half, most, plurality, predominance, predominant part, preponderance, preponderation, principal part, weight of numbers
ASSOCIATED CONCEPTS: majority rule, majority vote, plurality, quorum, requisite majority

MAKE, *verb* accomplish, achieve, actualize, assemble, attain, author, beget, bring about, bring forth, bring into being, bring into existence, bring to effect, bring to pass, build, call into being, call into existence, carry into effect, carry into execution, cast, cause, cause to exist, coin, compel, complete, compose, compound, concoct, constitute, constrain, construct, contrive, *creare,* create, develop, devise, draft, draw up, effect, effectuate, efform, enact, enforce, engender, erect, establish, evolve, execute, *fabricari,* fabricate, *facere,* fashion, force, forge, form, formulate, frame, generate, give birth to, give origin to, give rise to, hammer out, hatch, have in production, improvise, initiate, institute, invent, kindle, machine, manufacture, model, mold, organize, originate, pattern, perform, piece together, prepare, produce, provide, put together, set up, shape, synthesize, think up, turn out, yield results
ASSOCIATED CONCEPTS: make a decision, make a demand, make a motion, make an agreement, make an offer

MAKER, *noun* author, devisor, donor, initiator, producer
ASSOCIATED CONCEPTS: maker of a note, maker of an instrument

MALADMINISTRATION, *noun* bad job, blunder, botchery, bungling, default, dereliction of duty, evasion of duty, failure of duty, incompetency, inefficiency, inefficient management, malfeasance, malversation, misadministration, misapplication, misconduct, misdirection, misfeasance, misgovernment, misguidance, mishandling, mismanagement, misrule, neglect, negligence, poor administration, *prava rerum administratio,* unproficiency, want of duty

MALCONTENT, *noun*   agitator, anarchist, ardent champion of change, brawler, caviler, censurer, complainant, complainer, critic, crusader, demonstrator, detractor, diehard, disputer, dissenter, dissentient, dissident, extremist, fanatic, faultfinder, fighter, fretter, griper, grumbler, heretic, *homo rerum novarum cupidus,* instigator, insubordinate, insurgent, insurrectionist, kicker, mutineer, nihilist, nonconformist, noncooperator, objector, obstructionist, petitioner, political agitator, protester, rabble-rouser, radical, reactionary, reactionist, rebel, recusant, reformer, renegade, repiner, resister, revisionist, revolter, revolutionary, revolutionist, rioter, seditionary, seditionist, traitor, troublemaker, whiner, wrangler

MALEDICTION, *noun*   abusive speech, anathema, curse, damnation, defamation, denunciation, *dirae,* dispraise, evil-speaking, execration, *exsecratio,* foul language, fulmination, ill wishes, imprecation, invective, malevolence, malison, obloquy, revilement, tongue-lashing, verbal abuse, verbal assault, verbal attack, vilification, vituperation

MALEFACTOR, *noun*   bandit, brigand, convict, criminal, culprit, delinquent, desperado, evildoer, felon, gangster, hardened criminal, *homo maleficus, homo sceleratus,* hoodlum, hooligan, lawbreaker, lawless individual, mischief-maker, miscreant, misdemeanant, offender, offender against the law, outlaw, racketeer, rapscallion, rascal, recidivist, reprobate, rogue, ruffian, scamp, scoundrel, transgressor, trespasser, villain, violator of laws, wrongdoer

MALEVOLENT, *adjective*   acrimonious, actively opposed, adverse, aggressive, antagonistic, antipathetic, antipathetical, baleful, baneful, barbarous, bellicose, belligerent, bilious, bitter, bloodthirsty, brutal, churlish, cold, cold-blooded, conspiratorial, cruel, damaging, deadly, deleterious, demoniac, demoniacal, demonial, despiteful, devilish, diabolic, diabolical, disaffected, disobliging, embittered, envenomed, evil, evil-minded, faithless, ferocious, feuding, fiendish, full of hate, full of malice, full of revenge, full of spite, galling, grim, grudgeful, grudging, hardhearted, harmful, harsh, hateful, heinous, hellish, hostile, hurtful, ill-disposed, ill-intentioned, ill-natured, ill-wishing, implacable, infamous, infernal, iniquitous, injurious, invidious, lethal, malefic, maleficent, *malevolus,* malicious, malign, malignant, mean, merciless, mischievous, oppugnant, perfidious, pernicious, pitiless, plotting, poisonous, rancorous, repugnant, resentful, retaliative, retaliatory, revengeful, ruinous, ruthless, satanic, savage, scatheful, sinister, snaky, spiteful, spleenful, treacherous, truculent, unamicable, unfeeling, unfriendly, unkind, venomous, vicious, villainous, vindictive, viperous, virulent, vitriolic, warlike, wicked

MALFEASANCE, *noun*   bad conduct, corruption, dereliction, deviation from rectitude, ill conduct, illegal action, infringement, injurious action, misbehavior, misdeed, misdoing, misgovernment, mismanagement, overstepping, peccadillo, peccancy, transgression, unjust performance, unlawful action, wrongful action, wrongful conduct

ASSOCIATED CONCEPTS: malfeasance in office, malfeasance of a public officer, misconduct, misfeasance, nonfeasance

MALICE, *noun*   acrimony, active ill will, animosity, animus, antagonism, antipathy, aversion, bad intent, bad intention, bitter animosity, conscious violation of law, contempt, culpable recklessness, detestation, disaffection, dislike, enmity, evil disposition, evil intent, hard feelings, hardheartedness, harmful desire, hate, hatred, hostility, ill feeling, ill will, intentional wrongdoing, *invidia,* invidiousness, loathing, malevolence, *malevolentia,* maliciousness, *malignitas,* malignity, odium, personal hatred, pique, pitilessness, rancor, rankling, repugnance, repulsion, resentment, spite, spitefulness, umbrage, venom, viciousness, violent animosity, wanton disregard, wrath

ASSOCIATED CONCEPTS: actual malice, constructive malice, implied malice, legal malice, malice aforethought, malice in fact, malice in law, malicious abandonment, malicious abuse of process, malicious arrest, malicious injury, malicious intent, malicious mischief, malicious prosecution, malicious use, malicious wrong, universal malice

FOREIGN PHRASES: ***In criminalibus, sufficit generalis malitia intentionis, cum facto paris gradus.*** In crimes, a general malicious intent suffices where there is an act of equal degree. ***Malitia est acida; est mali animi affectus.*** Malice is sour; it is the quality of an evil mind. ***Maleficia propositis distinguuntur.*** Evil deeds are distinguished by their evil purposes. ***Malitiis hominum est obviandum.*** The malicious designs of men must be thwarted. ***Eum qui nocentem infamat, non est aequum et bonum ob eam rem condemnari; delicta enim nocentium nota esse oportet et expedit.*** It is not just and proper that he who speaks ill of a bad man should be condemned on that account; for it is fitting and expedient that the crimes of bad men be made known. ***Malum non praesumitur.*** Evil is not presumed.

MALICIOUS, *adjective*   acrimonious, antagonistic, brutal, cruel, demoniac, demoniacal, destructive, diabolic, diabolical, evil, evil-minded, feral, ferocious, harmful, hateful, hostile, ill-disposed, ill-natured, invidious, *invidus,* malefic, maleficent, maleficial, malevolent, *malevolus,* malignant, merciless, mischievous, ornery, pernicious, relentless, resentful, ruthless, savage, spiteful, treacherous, truculent, unfeeling, venemous, vicious, vindictive, virulent, wanton, wicked

ASSOCIATED CONCEPTS: malicious mischief, malicious prosecution

FOREIGN PHRASES: ***Malitiis hominum est obviandum.*** The malicious designs of men must be thwarted.

MALIGN, *verb*   abuse, anathematize, asperse, attack, attack the reputation of, besmirch, blaspheme, bring into discredit, calumniate, cast a slur upon, cast aspersions, curse, decry, defame, defile, denigrate, denounce, deprecate, derogate, disesteem, dishonor, dishonor by false reports, disparage, dispraise, falsify, fulminate against, impugn, libel, revile, ridicule, slander, slur, smear, smirch, speak evil of, speak ill of, spread an evil report, stain one's reputation, traduce, vilify, vilipend, vituperate

MALIGNANT, *adjective*   atrocious, baleful, baneful, barbarous, bitter, blackhearted, bloodthirsty, brutal, brutish, cancerous, caustic, cold-blooded, cold-hearted, consuming, corrosive, cruel, damaging, dangerous, deadly, death-bringing, death-dealing, deathly, deleterious, demoniacal, despiteful, destructive, detrimental, devilish, diabolical, envenomed, evil, evil-minded, execrable, fatal, fell, feral, ferocious, fiendish, fiendlike, flint-hearted, foul, hard of heart, harmful, hateful, heinous, hellish, hostile, hurtful, ill-intentioned, infernal, inhuman, iniquitous, injurious, insalubrious, invidious, lethal, malefic, maleficent, malevolent, malicious, malign, marble-hearted, mephitic, miasmal, miasmatic, miasmatical, monstrous, morbid, morbiferous, morbific, morbifical, mordacious, murderous, nasty, nefarious, nocuous, noisome, noxious, oppressive, peccant, pernicious, persecuting, pestiferous, pestilential, poisonous, rancorous, resentful, revengeful, ruinous, ruthless, satanic, savage, scatheful, scurrilous, sinful, sinister, spiteful, spleenful, stonyhearted, tending to cause death, toxic, toxiferous, treacherous, truculent, unmerciful, venomous, vicious, vile, villainous, vindictive, violent, virulent, virulently inimical, vitriolic, wicked

MALLEABLE, *adjective* accommodating, acquiescent, adaptable, adjustable, agreeable, amenable, amiable, bendable, bending, compliant, conformable, conforming, controllable, deferential, docile, ductile, *ductilis,* easily bent, easily influenced, easily persuaded, easy, easygoing, elastic, flexible, flexile, following, formable, governable, impressionable, *lentus,* limber, lissome, lithe, lithesome, manageable, meek, moldable, *mollis,* obliging, pliable, pliant, soft, softened, stretchable, submissive, supple, tame, teachable, tractable, twistable, usable, well-behaved, willing, yielding

MALPRACTICE, *noun* breach of practice, breach of profession, carelessness, culpable professional neglect, dereliction of duty, improper professional action, improper professional conduct, injudicious treatment, injurious treatment by a professional, misconduct, professional error of judgment, professional laxness, professional misconduct, professional neglect, professional negligence, unprofessional conduct, unprofessional treatment, violation of professional code, violation of professional duty

ASSOCIATED CONCEPTS: legal malpractice, medical malpractice, professional malpractice

MALTREAT, *verb* abuse, assail, ill-treat, ill-use, mishandle, mistreat, oppress, persecute

MANAGE, *verb* administer, *administrare,* administrate, be in power, boss, care for, carry on, command, conduct, control, cope with, dictate, direct, disburse, dominate, engineer, execute, exercise authority, govern, guide, handle, have control, have under command, head, keep in order, lead, look after, maneuver, manipulate, master, mastermind, occupy the chair, officiate, operate, order, oversee, pilot, preside, preside over, *regere,* regiment, regulate, rule, run, see to, steer, subjugate, superintend, supervise, sway, take charge of, take over, *tractare,* transact, treat, wield authority, work

MANAGEMENT *(Directorate), **noun*** administration, administrators, advisers, authority, board, board of directors, bureau, bureaucracy, caretakers, central office, chair, chairmen, command, committee, controllers, custodians, decision-making body, directors, directorship, executive committee, executive office, executives, front office, generals, governing body, government, headmen, headquarters, leaders, leadership, officers, officials, party in power, power, presidency, presidium, regime, steering committee, stewards, strategists, superintendents, supervisors

MANAGEMENT *(Judicious use), **noun*** conduct, cunning practice, dealing, disposal, economic use, employment, finesse, frugality, handling, manipulation, operation, prudent conduct, running, skillful treatment, steerage, thrifty use, treatment, usage, utilization

MANAGEMENT *(Supervision), **noun*** *administratio,* administration, administrators, authority, board of directors, care, charge, command, control, controllers, *cura,* direction, directorate, directors, directorship, executive arm, executives, generalship, governance, guidance, leadership, managers, managership, oversight, pilotage, protectorship, regulation, steering, stewardship, superintendence, surveillance, *tractatio,* wardship

ASSOCIATED CONCEPTS: exclusive management, fraud in management, general management, management of one's affairs, management of property

MANDAMUS, *noun* charge, command, decree, dictate, direct, legislate, order, rule

ASSOCIATED CONCEPTS: writ of mandamus

MANDATE, *noun* authoritative command, authoritative order, behest, bid, canon, charge, command, command by the court, commandment, decree, decretal, dictate, dictation, direction, directive, edict, enactment, fiat, imperative, instruction, judicial command, judicial decree, judicial order, *mandatum,* order, precept, prescript, prescription, proscription, regulation, request, requirement, requisition, rule, ruling, ultimatum, written order

ASSOCIATED CONCEPTS: judicial mandate, legislative mandate, mandate of the court

FOREIGN PHRASES: *Rei turpis nullum mandatum est.* The mandate of an immoral thing is void. *Cui jurisdictio data est, ea quoque concessa esse videntur, sine quibus jurisdictio explicari non potest.* To whom jurisdiction is given, those things also are held to be granted, without which the jurisdiction cannot be exercised.

MANDATORY, *adjective* binding, bounden, called for, coercive, commanded, commanding, compulsory, crucial, decreed, demanded, essential, exigent, imperative, incumbent on, indispensable, involuntary, necessary, necessitated, necessitous, obligatory, ordained, peremptory, prerequisite, prescribed, pressing, required, requisite, unavoidable, urgent, vital, without appeal, without choice

ASSOCIATED CONCEPTS: mandatory injunction, mandatory relief, mandatory sentence, mandatory statutory provisions

MANEUVER *(Tactic), **noun*** approach, course of conduct, *decursio, decursus,* device, line of action, management, manipulation, mode of procedure, move, operation, plan of attack, planned campaign, procedure, scheme, stratagem, strategy, stroke, undertaking

MANEUVER *(Trick), **noun*** artful dodge, artifice, *artificium,* chicanery, circumvention, cozenage, crafty device, cunning contrivance, deception, decoy, design, device, dodge, *dolus,* feint, fraud, fraudulent expedient, hoax, legerdemain, machination, plot, ruse, scheme, sharp practice, sleight, stratagem, subterfuge, trap, underhanded act, wile

MANEUVER, *verb*   arrange, be in collusion, brew, cabal, cheat, collude, complot, concoct, connive, conspire, contrive, countermine, counterplot, deploy, design, devise, engineer, *evagari,* form a plot, frame, intrigue, jockey, lay plans, machinate, make a plan, make arrangements, manage, move, plan, plan strategy, plot, prearrange, proceed by stratagem, scheme, shift, take steps, trick, work out

MANIFEST, *adjective*   *apertus,* apparent, avowed, bald, bare, beholdable, blatant, clear, clear-cut, conspicuous, crying, crystal clear, defined, discernible, disclosed, distinct, easy to see, *evidens,* evident, explicit, exposed, express, eye-catching, flagrant, glaring, gross, identifiable, in bold relief, in evidence, in focus, in full view, in sight, in the foreground, in view, indisputable, indubitable, insuppressible, lucid, marked, naked, not concealed, not obscure, notable, noticeable, observable, obvious, open, ostensible, overt, palpable, patent, perceivable, perceptible, perspicuous, *perspicuus,* plain, prominent, pronounced, public, recognizable, revealed, salient, seeable, showable, standing out, sticking out, striking, tangible, transparent, unclouded, unconcealed, uncontestable, undisguised, unhidden, unmistakable, unquestionable, visible, well-defined, well-marked, well-seen
ASSOCIATED CONCEPTS: manifest danger, manifest error, manifest necessity, manifest peril

MANIFEST, *verb*   air, *aperire,* attest, bare, be evidence of, bespeak, betoken, bring forth, bring forward, bring into the open, bring out, bring to light, bring to notice, bring to the front, bring to view, certify, *declarare,* declare, demonstrate, denote, designate, disclose, discover, display, divulge, evidence, evince, exhibit, explain, expose, expose to view, express, hold up, hold up to view, illuminate, illustrate, impart, indicate, lay bare, lay open, lay out, make clear, make conspicuous, make evident, make known, make obvious, make plain, make visible, mark, open, open up, *patefacere,* point out, present, proclaim, prove, publish, represent, reveal, set forth, set out, show, signify, speak out, testify, throw open, unconceal, uncover, uncurtain, undrape, unearth, unfold, unmask, unscreen, unshroud, unveil
FOREIGN PHRASES: *In rebus manifestis, errat qui auctoritates legum allegat; quia perspicua vera non sunt probanda.* In clear cases, he mistakes who cites legal authorities; for obvious truths are not to be proved. *Manifesta probatione non indigent.* Manifest facts do not require proof.

MANIFESTATION, *noun*   appearance, badge, *declaratio, demonstratio,* demonstration, disclosure, discovery, display, divulgence, emblem, emergence, evidence, evincement, exhibit, exhibition, expose, exposition, exposure, expression, indication, *indicium,* mark, materialization, production, representation, revelation, show, showing, sign, signal, signification, symbol, symptom, uncovering, unfolding, unmasking, unveiling
ASSOCIATED CONCEPTS: manifestation of intent

MANIFOLD, *adjective*   assorted, considerable, divers, diverse, diversified, innumerable, many, miscellaneous, multifarious, multifold, multiform, multiple, *multiplex,* multiplicate, multitudinous, myriad, numerous, populous, profuse, several, sundry, teeming, variegated, various, *varius*

MANIPULATE *(Control unfairly),* *verb*   dominate, exploit, influence, manage, misuse, pull strings, pull wires, rig, rule, take advantage of, use

MANIPULATE *(Utilize skillfully),* *verb*   apply, command, conduct, control, direct, drive, employ, engineer, govern, guide, handle, lead, make use of, maneuver, operate, pilot, ply, put in action, put into operation, regulate, run, set in motion, set to work, steer, *tractare,* use, utilize, wield, work

MANNER *(Behavior),* *noun*   actions, acts, address, air, appearance, approach, aspect, attitude, bearing, behavior pattern, carriage, comportment, conduct, consuetude, course of action, course of conduct, custom, customary procedure, decorum, demeanor, deportment, distinctive social attitude, etiquette, fashion, guise, habit, habitual practice, line of action, line of conduct, look, method, method of action, mien, mode, mode of proceeding, observance, operation, pattern, personal bearing, personal style, port, posture, practice, praxis, presence, procedure, proceeding, routine, stance, style, tactics, tone, usage, way, wise, wont

MANNER *(Kind),* *noun*   brand, categorization, category, class, classification, denomination, description, designation, division, fashion, form, grouping, ilk, kind, make, order, selection, sort, species, style, type, variety

MANSLAUGHTER, *noun*   accidental homocide, homicide, *homicidium, hominis caedes,* killing, murder, reckless homocide, unintentional homocide, unintentional murder, unpremeditated murder
ASSOCIATED CONCEPTS: involuntary manslaughter, killing in the heat of passion, second degree manslaughter, voluntary manslaughter

MANUFACTURE, *noun*   assemblage, assembly, composition, construction, creation, development, execution, *fabrica,* fabrication, fashioning, forging, formation, forming, making, molding, origination, preparation, production, synthesis

MANUFACTURE, *verb*   assemble, build, compose, construct, contrive, create, devise, engineer, evolve, *fabricari,* fabricate, fashion, forge, form, formulate, generate, invent, make, make by mechanical industry, make up, mass produce, mold, originate, process, produce, put in production, put together, turn out, turn out by industrial process
ASSOCIATED CONCEPTS: manufacture goods, products liability involved in manufactured goods

MARGIN *(Outside limit),* *noun*   bank, border, boundary, bounds, brim, brink, circumference, curb, edge, frame, fringe, hem, ledge, limit, lip, outskirt, perimeter, periphery, portal, rim, shore, skirt, threshold, verge

MARGIN *(Spare amount),* *noun*   amount reserved, clearance, elbowroom, extra amount for contingencies, extra amount for emergencies, headway, latitude, lee-

way, opening, reserve, reserved amount, room, room to spare, space
ASSOCIATED CONCEPTS: margin of profit

MARGINAL, adjective average, bare, barely acceptable, barely adequate, below par, borderline, fair, humble, *in margine positus, in margine scriptus,* inappreciable, indifferent, low-quality, meager, mediocre, mere, middling, moderate, modest, passable, poor, scant, scanty, skimpy, tenuous, tolerable, trifling, undistinguished, wanting, weak

MARGINALIA, noun commentary, entry, footnote, inscription, notation, note, memorandum, record, register

MARKET *(Business),* **noun** agora, bazaar, bourse, concern, department store, emporium, establishment, exchange, fair, financial center, general store, house, *macellum,* mart, *mercatus, nundinae,* open mart, place of business, place of buying and selling, place of commerce, place of trade, place of traffic, retail store, rialto, shop, shopping center, store, trade fair, trading house, trading post, variety store
ASSOCIATED CONCEPTS: actual market value, fair market price, market conditions, market place, market price, market value

MARKET *(Demand),* **noun** call, call for, consumer demand, desire, desire to buy, desire to obtain, earnest seeking, essentiality, heavy demand, indispensability, inquiry, insufficiency, interest, lack, mania, necessity, need, outlet, pressing requirement, pursuit, request, requirement, requisition, run, search, steady demand, strong demand, vogue, want, willingness to purchase, wish

MARKET PLACE, noun agora, emporium, exchange, exposition, financial center, *forum,* open market, place of business, place of business traffic, place of buying and selling, place of commerce, place of trade, plaza, shopping center, square, trading place
ASSOCIATED CONCEPTS: public markets

MARKETABLE, adjective commercial, exchangeable, fit for sale, merchantable, salable, tradable, *venalis,* vendible
ASSOCIATED CONCEPTS: marketable title

MARRED, adjective blemished, blighted, bruised, cankered, contaminated, corrupted, crippled, damaged, defaced, defective, deformed, despoiled, disabled, discolored, disfigured, faulty, flawed, fouled, garbled, hamstrung, harmed, hurt, impaired, imperfect, impure, infected, injured, lamed, maimed, mangled, marked, mutilated, no longer in perfect condition, pitted, rotten, ruined, scarred, scathed, scratched, speckled, spoiled, spotted, stained, sullied, tainted, tarnished, wounded

MARRIAGE *(Intimate relationship),* **noun** accouplement, alliance, bond, close relationship, closeness, cohabitation, couplement, coupling, intimacy, joining, linkage, linking, tie, union
ASSOCIATED CONCEPTS: common-law marriage

MARRIAGE *(Wedlock),* **noun** bond of matrimony, cohabitation, *coniugium,* conjugal union, conjugality, connubiality, espousal, espousement, marriage tie, married life, married state, married status, *matri-*

monium, matrimony, *nuptiae,* nuptial bond, nuptial tie, spousal, wedded state, wedding
ASSOCIATED CONCEPTS: adultery, annulment, bigamous marriage, consensual marriage, consummation of marriage, contract of marriage, coverture, curtesy, divorce, dower, marriage ceremony, marriage license, marriage promise, polygamous marriage, solemnize a marriage, void marriage, voidable marriage
FOREIGN PHRASES: *Nuptias non concubitus sed consensus facit.* Not cohabitation but consent makes the valid marriage. *Pater est quem nuptioe demonstrant.* He is the father whom the marriage points out. *Semper praesumitur pro matrimonio.* The presumption is always in favor of the validity of a marriage. *Subsequens matrimonium tollit peccatum praecedens.* A subsequent marriage removes a previous fault.

MARSHAL, noun arm of the law, bailiff, county officer, court officer, *dux,* federal officer, law enforcement agent, minor officer of the law, officer, officer of the law, officer who carries out orders of the court, peace officer

MARSHAL, verb allocate, allot, apportion, arrange, array, assign, bring to order, collocate, compose, coordinate, deal out, *disponere,* distribute, fix, form into ranks, group, guide, index, *instruere,* introduce order, lead, line up, manage, muster, organize, parcel out, place, place in order, position, put in order, rank, regiment, regulate, set in order, set up, systematize
ASSOCIATED CONCEPTS: marshaling assets, marshaling liens, marshaling remedies, marshaling securities

MASS *(Body of persons),* **noun** aggregate, assemblage, body, cluster, congregation, crowd, drove, flock, gathering, host, mob, multitude, *multitudo,* phalanx, plurality, swarm, throng, *vulgus*
ASSOCIATED CONCEPTS: mass market, mass picketing

MASS *(Weight),* **noun** amplitude, bigness, body, bulk, density, dimension, extent, fullness, gauge, greatness, immensity, largeness, magnitude, measure, measurement, sizableness, size

MASTER, adjective arch, authoritative, capital, central, chief, commanding, controlling, crowning, dictating, dominant, eminent, foremost, governing, great, head, hegemonic, hegemonical, incomparable, influential, leading, main, most important, outstanding, paramount, predominating, preeminent, prepotent, prevailing, prevalent, primary, prime, ranking, recognized, regnant, reigning, ruling, sovereign, star, stellar, supereminent, supreme, top-flight, well-known
ASSOCIATED CONCEPTS: agency, master and servant

MASTERMIND, noun authority, creative genius, creator, expert, genius, intellect, intellectual, intellectual prodigy, leader, learned person, luminary, master, mental giant, mentor, person of intellect, prodigy, pundit, qualified person, sage, savant, specialist, strategist, tactician, thinker, wise man

MATERIAL *(Important),* **adjective** basic, capital, cardinal, central, compelling, consequential, considerable, critical, crucial, decisive, effective, essential, extensive, far-reaching, fundamental, indispensable, influential, key, leading, main, major, memorable, momentous, necessary, paramount, pertinent, pivotal, prevalent, primary, principal, relevant, remarkable,

salient, signal, significant, substantial, valuable, vital, weighty, worth considering
ASSOCIATED CONCEPTS: material allegation, material alteration, material amendment, material change in circumstances, material defect, material defendant, material departure from the truth, material error, material evidence, material fact, material false representation, material misrepresentation, material witness

MATERIAL *(Physical)*, **adjective**   actual, bodily, concrete, corporeal, *corporeus, de facto,* earthly, mundane, nonspiritual, palpable, real, secular, solid, substantial, tactile, tangible, temporal, unspiritual, worldly
ASSOCIATED CONCEPTS: material furnished

MATERIALITY *(Consequence)*, **noun**   caliber, distinction, eminence, gravity, greatness, import, importance, magnitude, materialness, matter, memorability, momentousness, notability, notableness, priority, prominence, purport, rank, relevance, salience, significance, substantiality, sum and substance, value, weight, weightiness, worth

MATERIALITY *(Physical existence)*, **noun**   bodiliness, bodily existence, body, concreteness, corporality, corporeity, embodiment, entity, essential nature, existence, mass, material existence, materialness, matter, palpability, physical being, physical nature, physicalness, reality, solidity, substance, substantiality, substantialness, tangibility

MATERIALMAN, noun   artificer, builder, constructor, contractor, designer, deviser, engineer, outfitter, provider, supplier
ASSOCIATED CONCEPTS: materialman's lien

MATERNITY, noun   fertility, motherhood, motherliness, parenthood, propagation, reproduction

MATRIMONY, noun   alliance, cohabitation, conjugality, connubiality, consortium, espousal, espousement, joining, marriage, marriage tie, married life, married state, married status, match, mating, *matrimonium,* nuptial bond, nuptial state, nuptial tie, partnership, sacrament of marriage, spousal, union, wedded state, wedlock
ASSOCIATED CONCEPTS: matrimonial action, matrimonial cohabitation, matrimonial domicile, matrimonial res

MATTER *(Case)*, **noun**   action, *causa,* cause, cause in court, claim, court action, dispute, inquiry, lawsuit, legal action, legal proceedings, litigation, pleadings, proceedings, suit, suit at law, trial
ASSOCIATED CONCEPTS: matter of record

MATTER *(Subject)*, **noun**   business on hand, case, case in question, claim, concern, debatable point, dispute, field of inquiry, *institutum,* issue, item on the agenda, point, point at issue, point in question, problem, proposition, *propositum,* question, *res,* subject for inquiry, subject matter, topic, topic for discussion
ASSOCIATED CONCEPTS: immaterial matter, matter in controversy, matter in dispute, matter in issue, matter in pais, matter of fact, matter of form, matter of law, matter of record, matter of substance, matters pending
FOREIGN PHRASES: *Certa debet esse intentio, et narratio, et certum fundamentum, et certa res quae deducitur in judicium.* The intention, declaration,

foundation, and matter brought to judgment ought to be certain. *Eventus varios res nova semper habet.* A new matter always holds the possibility of a different result. *Culpa est immiscere se rel ad se non pertinenti.* It is a fault for anyone to meddle in matters which do not concern him.

MATTER OF COURSE, noun   common practice, common run, common state of affairs, customary procedure, general run, natural state, ordinary run of things, ordinary state, prescribed form, procedure, regular procedure, routine, routine event, routine happening, rule, set form, usual custom, usual occurrence, usual practice, usual procedure, usual thing

MATURE, verb   accrue, advance toward perfection, age, attain majority, attain maturity, become due, become fully developed, become payable, become perfected, become prime, become ripe, bring to full development, bring to its peak, bring to maturity, bring to perfection, come of age, consummate, *coquere,* culminate, develop, evolve, fall due, finish, grow up, *maturare,* maturate, nurture, perfect, ripen, season
ASSOCIATED CONCEPTS: matured account

MATURITY, noun   adulthood, completion, consummation, culmination, due date, evolution, falling due, fulfillment, full age, full development, full growth, majority, matureness, *maturitas,* perfected condition, perfection, preparedness, readiness
ASSOCIATED CONCEPTS: maturity of a debt, maturity of an obligation

MAXIM, noun   adage, aphorism, aphoristic expression, axiom, byword, canon, established principle, expression, gnomic saying, moralism, pithy saying, postulate, *praeceptum,* precept, principium, principle, proverb, proverbial saying, *regula,* rule, sage reflection, saw, saying, sententious saying, sententious utterance, statement of general truth, teaching, truth, wise saying

MAXIMUM *(Amplitude)*, **noun**   ampleness, capacity, fullness, greatest, peak, plentitude, saturation, size, total, utmost

MAXIMUM *(Pinnacle)*, **noun**   crown, culmination, limit, most, ne plus ultra, upper extremity

MEANING, noun   acceptation, connotation, content, definition, denotation, drift, explanation, idea, import, interpretation, purport, semantics, semasiology, sense, *sententia,* significance, *significatio,* signification, substance, tenor, text, *vis*
ASSOCIATED CONCEPTS: plain meaning, secondary meaning
FOREIGN PHRASES: *Primo excutienda est verbi vis, ne sermonis vitio obstruatur oratio, sive lex sine argumentis.* The force of a word should be ascertained in the beginning, lest the sentence be destroyed by the fault of expression, or the law be without reason. *Sensus verborum est anima legis.* The meaning of words is the spirit of the law. *In testamentis ratio tacita non debet considerari, sed verba solum spectari debent; adeo per divinationem mentis a verbis recedere durum est.* In wills an unexpressed intention ought not to be considered, but the words alone ought to be regarded; for it is difficult to recede from the words by guessing at their intention.

MEANS *(Funds),* **noun**   assets, finances, resource, resources, wealth, wherewithal
ASSOCIATED CONCEPTS: means doctrine, means of knowledge, means of satisfaction, means of support

MEANS *(Opportunity),* **noun**   application, capacity, devices, employment, fashion, form, guise, handiness, manner, measures, method, mode, serviceability, style, system, tone, usage, use, ways, wherewithal

MEASURE, *noun*   act, bill, caveat, declaration, decree, dictate, edict, enactment, law, legislation, legislative enactment, legislative mandate, legislative proclamation, mandate, piece of legislation, prescript, prescription, proposal, proposed act, proposition, regulation, rubric, rule, ruling, statute
ASSOCIATED CONCEPTS: appropriate measures, measure of benefit, measure of damages, measure of value, regulatory measure, remedial measures

MEASURE, *verb*   admeasure, appraise, ascertain dimensions, ascertain size, assess, bring into comparison, calculate, calibrate, compare, compute, correlate, *demetiri,* determine size, determine value, estimate, evaluate, fathom, form an estimate, form an opinion, gauge, grade, graduate, graph, judge, liken, make a comparison, make an estimate, mark off, match, *metari,* mete, meter, pace off, *permetiri,* portion out, quantify, rank, rate, reckon, rule, set a value on, size, span, survey, value, weigh
ASSOCIATED CONCEPTS: appropriate measure of damages

MEASUREMENT, *noun*   admeasurement, amount, analysis, appraisal, appraisement, assessment, bulk, calculation, capaciousness, capacity, computation, dimensions, estimate, estimation, extent, gauge, girth, greatness, largeness, limit, magnitude, mass, measure, *mensio, mensura,* mensuration, metage, meterage, quantification, quantity, rating, reckoning, size, span, survey, valuation, vastness
ASSOCIATED CONCEPTS: measurement of damages, measurement of liability

MECHANICS LIEN, *noun*   charge, charge imposed on specific property, claim on property, hold on property, right to enforce charge on property, security on property

MEDIATE, *verb*   adjust, adjust difficulties, arbitrate, arrange differences, bring to an understanding, bring to terms, bring together, compromise, conciliate, effect an agreement, intercede, interfere, intervene, moderate, negotiate, *pacem conciliare,* parley, reconcile, referee, restore harmony, *se interponere,* settle, settle a dispute, settle by conciliation, settle differences, umpire, work out differences
ASSOCIATED CONCEPTS: arbitrate

MEDIATION, *noun*   adjustment, adjustment of difficulties, arbitration, conciliation, finding a middle course, intercession, interference, intervention, intervention to facilitate a compromise, negotiation, negotiation process, parley, reconciliation, settlement of difficulties, settlement of dispute
ASSOCIATED CONCEPTS: fact finding, mediation board

MEDICINAL, *adjective*   Aesculapian, alexipharmic, alleviative, analeptic, anodyne, antidotal, an-

tifebrile, assuasive, balmy, beneficial, cleansing, corrective, curative, demulcent, depurative, emollient, febrifugal, healing, health-giving, helpful, invigorating, lenitive, medical, medicative, palliative, purifying, recuperative, recuperatory, reformative, remedial, restitutive, restorative, roborant, salubrious, salutary, salutiferous, sanative, sanatory, soothing, therapeutic, therapeutical, tonic, vulnerary

MEDIOCRE, *adjective*   acceptable, adequate, all right, average, banal, colorless, common, commonplace, decent, everyday, fair, fairish, good enough, inconsequential, indifferent, inferior, inglorious, insignificant, lesser, lifeless, low-class, low-grade, low-quality, meager, mean, *mediocris,* medium, middle, middling, moderate, modest, normal, ordinary, passable, poor, prosaic, prosaical, run of the mill, satisfactory, second-rate, so-so, standard, tolerable, trite, trivial, typical, undistinguished, unexceptionable, unexciting, unimportant, uninspiring, uninteresting, unnoteworthy, unobjectionable, unremarkable, usual

MEDIOCRITY, *noun*   acceptability, adequateness, average, averageness, baseness, common lot, commonness, commonplaceness, deficiency, fairness, inconsiderableness, inferiority, inferiorness, insignificance, low grade, low quality, mean, meanness, *mediocritas,* middle state, ordinariness, passableness, poorness, satisfactoriness, standardness, tolerability, tolerableness, triviality, unexceptionality, unimportance, unnoteworthiness, unremarkableness, unsatisfactoriness

MEDIUM, *noun*   agency, agent, broker, channel, delegate, deputy, emissary, envoy, expedient, go-between, instrument, instrumentality, interagency, interagent, intermediary, intermediate, intermediate agent, intervener, link, machinery, means, mechanism, mediating agency, mediator, middleman, mouthpiece, negotiant, negotiator, spokesperson, tool, vehicle

MEET, *verb*   amass, assemble, associate, band together, center around, cluster, collect, collide, come face to face, come together, concur, *concurrere, confluere,* congregate, convene, converge, convoke, encounter, flock, forgather, gather together, get together, group, hold a convocation, hold a meeting, hold a session, huddle, *inter se congredi,* join, mass, muster, parley, rally, rejoin, reunite, swarm, throng, unite

MEETING *(Conference),* **noun**   assembly, caucus, colloquy, conclave, *concursus, congressio,* consistory, consultation, convention, *conventus,* convocation, discussion, encounter, exchange of views, forum, gathering, interchange of views, negotiation, open discussion, panel, parley, plenum, reunion, seminar, session, summit, symposium, synod
ASSOCIATED CONCEPTS: annual meeting of shareholders, meeting of creditors, organizational meeting, public meeting, regular meeting, special meeting

MEETING *(Encounter),* **noun**   appulsion, clash, collision, *concours,* confrontation, contact, convergence, convergency, engagement, fusion, intersection, joining, junction, juncture, merger, rendezvous, unification, union
ASSOCIATED CONCEPTS: meeting of minds

MELANGE, *noun*   admixture, amalgam, assortment, blend, cento, combination, commixture, composition, compound, confused mass, conglomeration, far-rago, gallimaufry, hash, hodgepodge, intermixture, jumble, medley, minglement, miscellaneous collection, miscellany, mixture, olio, pastiche, patchwork, pot-pourri, union

MELIORATE, *verb*   adorn, advance, ameliorate, amend, assuage, beautify, better, correct, cultivate, cure, doctor, elaborate, elevate, embellish, emend, en-hance, enrich, forward, have a good influence, improve, invigorate, lard, make better, make improvements, mend, mitigate, modernize, palliate, polish, purify, raise, reclaim, rectify, reface, refine, reform, refresh, re-furbish, regenerate, rehabilitate, reinvigorate, relieve, render better, renew, renovate, reorganize, repair, re-store, revive, touch up, transfigure, transform, upgrade, uplift

MEMBER *(Constituent part),* *noun*   article, branch, category, component, department, division, element, factor, feature, fraction, ingredient, integral part, item, link, part, piece, portion, section, segment, share, small part, subdivision, subordinate part, unit

MEMBER *(Individual in a group),* *noun*   affiliate, associate, belonger, cardholder, committeeperson, com-rade, confederate, constituent, cooperator, copartner, cosharer, enlistee, enrolled person, fellow, follower, guildsman, insider, participator, partner, patron, regis-tered person, shareholder, sharer, stockholder, team-mate

MEMORANDUM, *noun*   aide-memoir, annotation, brief, chronicle, memoir, notation, note, postnote, rec-ord, report
ASSOCIATED CONCEPTS: memorandum of law

MEMORY *(Commemoration),* *noun*   celebration, remembrance, writing

MEMORY *(Retention),* *noun*   mind, recalling, recol-lection, reflection

MENACE, *noun*   commination, danger, dangerous situation, hazard, imminent danger, imperilment, in-timidating force, intimidation, minacious force, min-acity, peril, prognostic, threat

MENACE, *verb*   affright, alarm, cause alarm, com-minate, direct a threat against, disconcert, disquiet, disturb, exhibit hostile intentions, frighten, impend, in-spire fear, intimidate, put in bodily fear, put in fear, raise apprehensions, scare, show hostility, startle, strike with overwhelming fear, terrify, threaten, un-nerve

MENDACIOUS, *adjective*   artful, clever in decep-tion, collusive, concocted, counterfeit, covinous, cun-ning, deceitful, deceiving, devoid of truth, dishonest, distorted, embroidered, fabricated, false, falsified, feigned, fictitious, fraudulent, given to lying, incorrect, insincere, invented, lacking truth, lying, made up, make-believe, *mendax,* misrepresentative, misrepre-sented, misstated, not straightforward, perfidious, per-jured, perverted, pretended, prevaricating, sham, sly, spurious, truthless, uncandid, ungenuine, untrue, un-truthful, unveracious, unveridical, varnished, void of truth, wrong

MENS REA, *noun*   criminal design, criminal guilt, criminal intent, criminal purpose, criminality, culpa-bility, vice, wrong, wrongdoing

MENTION *(Reference),* *noun*   allegation, allusion, assertion, *commemoratio,* comment, communication, enlightenment, expression, hint, implication, indica-tion, indirect hint, inference, insinuation, intimation, *mentio,* note, passing word, recital, recitation, referent, relation, remark, report, statement, suggestion

MENTION *(Tribute),* *noun*   acclaim, acclamation, adulation, applause, appreciation, approbation, ap-proval, blandishment, celebration, citation, commenda-tion, compliment, credit, decoration, esteem, eulogistic speech, eulogy, exaltation, expression of merit, flattery, glorification, high opinion, homage, honor, laud, lauda-tion, mark of honor, official recognition, panegyric, plaudit, praise, public recognition, regard, respect

MENTION, *verb*   acquaint, adduce, advert to, af-firm, allude to, announce, annunciate, apprise, assert, bring word, broach, cite, comment upon, communicate, confide to, convey information, convey knowledge, de-clare incidentally, denominate, direct the attention to, disclose, discuss, divulge, enlighten, enumerate, ex-press, give a hint, give notice, give utterance, hint at, impart, indicate, inform, insinuate, intimate, let know, make allusion to, make known, name, note, notify, ob-serve, point out, point to, recite, recount, refer to, re-mark on, report, reveal, speak of, specify, state, stipu-late, suggest, talk about, tell, touch upon, utter, voice

MERCANTILE, *adjective*   business, commercial, economic, exchange, financial, fiscal, industrial, mar-ket, merchandising, monetary, trade
ASSOCIATED CONCEPTS: mercantile law, mercantile paper

MERCENARY, *adjective*   accessible to bribery, ac-quisitive, avaricious, bribable, *conductus,* corrupt, cor-ruptible, covetous, exacting, exploitative, grasping, greedy, hired, hireling, leased, materialistic, *mer-cenarius,* money conscious, money hungry, motivated by a desire for money, motivated by greed, opportunis-tic, paid, possessive, profiteering, purchasable, rapa-cious, selfish, simoniacal, unidealistic, usurious, venal, *venalis*

MERCHANDISE, *noun*   articles, articles of com-merce, assets, belongings, capital goods, cargo, chattel, commodities, consumer durables, consumer goods, con-tents, effects, freight, goods, goods for sale, items for sale, line, line of goods, manufactured goods, material assets, materials, *merx,* movables, possessions, produce, property, provisions, *res venales,* salable commodities, shop goods, specialty, staples, stock, stock in trade, store, supplies, tangible assets, vendibles, wares

MERCHANT, *noun*   businessperson, chandler, con-signer, dealer, distributer, distributor, entrepreneur, handler, hawker, huckster, *mercator,* merchandiser, middleman, monger, peddler, retailer, salesperson, seller, shopkeeper, shopman, storekeeper, trader, tradesperson, vendor
FOREIGN PHRASES: *Jus accrescendi inter mercatores, pro beneficio commercii, locum non habet.* The right of survivorship does not exist between merchants for the benefit of commerce.

MERE, *adjective*   bare, just, nothing but, only, plain, sheer, simple
ASSOCIATED CONCEPTS: mere assumption of title, mere glimmering of reason, mere license, mere possibility

MERETRICIOUS, *adjective*   artificial, bedizened, brummagem, cheap, counterfeit, deceitful, deceptive, delusive, fake, false, fraudulent, garish, gaudy, imitation, misleading, mock, ornate, sham, showy, speciously attractive, spurious, tawdry, theatrical, tinsel, vulgar
ASSOCIATED CONCEPTS: adultery, meretricious relationship

MERGE, *verb*   absorb, ally, amalgamate, associate, band together, be one with, be swallowed up, blend, cement, combine, compound, conglomerate, conjoin, consolidate, entwine, fuse, harmonize, incorporate, intermingle, intermix, intertwine, join, join forces, lose identity, lose individuality, melt into one, mix, piece together, unify, unite, weld

MERGER, *noun*   absorption, affiliation, alliance, amalgamation, assimilation, association, centralization, coalescence, coalition, combination, confederation, conflation, consolidation, federation, fellowship, fusion, incorporation, integration, joinder, joint concern, loss of identity, mixture, partnership, solidarity, syndicate, unification, union, united front, voluntary association
ASSOCIATED CONCEPTS: compulsory merger, conglomerate merger, consolidation, forced merger, horizontal merger, merger of estates, vertical merger

MERIT, *noun*   character, credit, desert, deservedness, *dignitas,* distinction, excellence, good actions, good behavior, goodness, greatness, honor, meritoriousness, *meritum,* praiseworthy quality, quality, rectitude, righteousness, superiority, uprightness, value, virtue, *virtus,* worth, worthiness
ASSOCIATED CONCEPTS: affidavit of merits, dismissal on the merits, merit system

MERITORIOUS, *adjective*   above par, acceptable, admirable, approvable, approved, august, benevolent, better, charitable, chivalric, chivalrous, choice, commendable, commendatory, conscientious, creditworthy, creditable, dazzling, decent, deserving, deserving of commendation, deserving of compliment, deserving of praise, deserving of reward, desirable, dignified, distinctive, distinguished, duteous, dutiful, edifying, elevated, eminent, entitled, enviable, estimable, ethical, excellent, exemplary, extraordinary, fine, first-rate, generous, glorious, good, good-quality, gracious, great, greathearted, guiltless, heroic, high-minded, high-principled, honest, honorable, idealistic, impeccable, incorrupt, incorruptible, irreproachable, just, *laudabilis,* laudable, laudatory, *laude dignus,* lofty, magnanimous, magnificent, marvelous, moral, noble, perfect, philanthropic, popular, possessing merit, praiseworthy, preeminent, prime, princely, principled, proper, quality, rare, refined, reliable, remarkable, reputable, rightminded, righteous, select, solid, sound, splendid, stainless, sterling, sublime, substantial, superb, superior, superlative, supreme, terrifc, tested, uncensurable, unimpeachable, unselfish, upright, valuable, virtuous, well-done, well-intentioned, wonderful, worth imitating, worthwhile, worthy, worthy of fame, worthy of praise

ASSOCIATED CONCEPTS: meritorious cause, meritorious cause of action, meritorious claim, meritorious defense, meritorious grounds

MESNE, *adjective*   coming between, interfering, interjacent, intermediary, intermediate, intervenient, intervening, mean, median, middle, transitional
ASSOCIATED CONCEPTS: mesne attachment, mesne grant, mesne process, mesne profits

METE, *noun*   barrier, border, borderland, borderline, bound, boundary, boundary line, boundary mark, bounds, circumscription, confine, division line, end, limit, limitation, line of circumvallation, line of demarcation, margin, measure, outline, perimeter, periphery, rim, terminal, terminus
ASSOCIATED CONCEPTS: legal description, metes and bounds

METE, *verb*   admeasure, administer, allocate, allot, apportion, apportion by measure, appropriate, assess, assign, bestow, consign, deal out, dispense, distribute, divide, dole out, give, give out, hand out, issue, measure, measure out, parcel out, pay out, present, ration, share out, split, weigh out

METHOD, *noun*   arrangement, blueprint, classification, consistency, course, course of action, custom, discipline, established order, fixed order, formula, habit, layout, logical order, manner, master plan, means, mode, *modus,* operation, order, orderliness, orderly arrangement, orderly disposition, organization, plan, practice, procedure, process, program, program of action, *ratio,* reduction to order, regular arrangement, regularity, regularity of action, routine, rule, scheme of arrangement, sequence, settled procedure, setup, system, tactic, technique, uniformity, *via,* way, working plan
ASSOCIATED CONCEPTS: business methods, method of operations

METICULOUS, *adjective*   alert, assiduous, attentive, careful, circumspect, clean, conscientious, considered, correct, *diligens,* diligent, exact, exacting, faithful, fastidious, finical, finicking, finicky, fussy, gingerly, heedful, industrious, mindful, minutely careful, neat, orderly, overcareful, painstaking, particular, precise, punctilious, regardful, rigid, rigorous, scrupulous, strict, thorough, thoroughgoing, tidy, vigilant, watchful

MIGRANT, *noun*   colonist, gypsy, nomad, ranger, rover, settler, trekker, wanderer

MILITATE, *verb*   act on, affect, agitate, bring about change, carry on, *contra rem facere,* contrive, control, deal with, direct, engineer, handle, have effect on, have influence on, influence, interfere, manage, maneuver, manipulate, meddle, mold, operate, perform on, *rei adversari, rei obstare,* shape, steer, take action, wield, work

MINIMAL, *adjective*   abbreviated, abridged, below the mark, brief, cut, deficient, diminished, diminutive, exiguous, fragmentary, impalpable, inappreciable, inconsiderable, infinitesimal, insufficient, lean, least, lesser, light, Lilliputian, limited, little, low, meager, minimum, minor, minute, moderate, modest, narrow, paltry, reduced, rudimentary, scant, scanty, scarce,

short, shortened, slender, slight, slim, small, smallest, thin, tiny, under par, under the mark, undersized, unimportant
ASSOCIATED CONCEPTS: minimal jurisdictional contacts, minimal standards

MINIMIZE, verb abbreviate, abridge, attach little importance to, attenuate, bedwarf, belittle, cheapen, clip, criticize, curtail, cut down, cut down to size, cut short, decimate, decrease, decry, deduct, deflate, degrade, demote, depreciate, derogate, detract, diminish, discount, disparage, disprize, dwarf, lessen, lower, make brief, make less, make little of, make smaller, make thin, misprize, overshadow, pare, pay little attention to, pay little heed to, prune, reduce, render less, ridicule, run down, scale down, scorn, set at naught, shave, shorten, show no respect, shrink, slash, slight, slur over, sneer at, strip, subtract, thin, think little of, think nothing of, underestimate, underpraise, underprice, underrate, underreckon, understate, undervalue
ASSOCIATED CONCEPTS: minimize damage

MINIMUM, noun bit, dash, drop, fragment, iota, jot, least amount, least part, least quantity, lowest quantity, minim, modicum, morsel, mote, *pars minima*, particle, piece, quorum, scantling, scintilla, shade, sliver, small amount, small quantity, sprinkling, sufficiency, sufficient amount, tincture, tinge, tittle, touch, trace, whit
ASSOCIATED CONCEPTS: minimum age, minimum charge, minimum fee schedule, minimum price, minimum wage

MINISTERIAL, adjective administrative, agential, attendant, attending, auxiliary, bureaucratic, effectual, functional, helpful, helping, implemental, instrumental, intermedial, intermediary, intermediate, intervening, managing, officiating, operative, practical, serviceable, useful
ASSOCIATED CONCEPTS: ministerial act, ministerial duty, ministerial officer

MINOR, adjective accessory, cursory, dispensable, expendable, futile, immaterial, inappreciable, inconsequential, inconsiderable, ineffectual, inessential, inferior, insignificant, insubstantial, irrelevant, junior, less important, lesser, little, low-level, lower, meaningless, mere, minimal, minimum, minute, modest, negligible, nonessential, not vital, not worth mentioning, nugatory, obscure, of no account, of second rank, paltry, peripheral, petty, picayune, scant, secondary, slight, small, smaller, subaltern, subordinate, subsidiary, superficial, trifling, trivial, unessential, unimportant, uninfluential, unnecessary, unnoteworthy, unnoticeable
ASSOCIATED CONCEPTS: minor breach, minor defect, minor dispute, minor subdivision

MINOR, noun adolescent, baby, child, dependent, *filius familias,* individual under age, individual under the age of majority, infant, junior, juvenile, one not legally competent, person under legal age, person under 18 years of age, person who is not of full age, pubescent, teenager, underage person, ward, young person, youngling, youngster, youth
ASSOCIATED CONCEPTS: emancipation of a minor, minor dependent, unemancipated minor
FOREIGN PHRASES: *Minor minorem custodire non debet, alios enim praesumitur male regere qui seipsum*

regere nescit. A minor ought not to be guardian to a minor, for a person who knows not how to govern himself is presumed to be unfit to govern others. *Meliorem conditionem suam facere potest minor, deteriorem nequaquam.* A minor can make his own condition better, but by no means worse. *Succurritur minori; facilis est lapsus juventutis.* A minor is to be favored; youth errs easily. *Minor non tenetur respondere durante minori aetati, nisi, in causa dotis, propter favorem.* A minor is not held responsible during his minority, unless, by reason of favor, in the matter of dower.

MINORORITY (Infancy), **noun** childhood, immaturity, inexperience, infant status, legal immaturity, legal incapacity, legal incompetence, nonage, period of being under legal age, period of being under statutory age, puerility, unripeness, youth, youthfulness
ASSOCIATED CONCEPTS: age of minority, incapacity to contract, voidable contracts
FOREIGN PHRASES: *Haeres minor uno et viginti annis non respondebit, nisi in casu dotis.* A minor heir under twenty-one years of age is not answerable, except in the matter of dower. *Minor ante tempus agere non potest in casu proprietatis nec etiam convenire.* A minor under age cannot act in a case of property.

MINORITY (Outnumbered group), **noun** insignificant number, lesser group, lesser part, the outvoted, paltry few, peripheral group, powerless group, secondary group, small group, small number, small percentage, small proportion, small quantity, smaller group, smaller part, subordinate group, subsidiary group, uninfluential group, weak group
ASSOCIATED CONCEPTS: minority group, minority member, minority party, minority stockholders

MISADVISED, adjective badly advised, fatuous, ill-advised, ill-considered, ill-judged, illogical, impolitic, imprudent, in error, inadvisable, incautious, indiscreet, inexpedient, infelicitous, injudicious, irrational, irresponsible, misconducted, misdirected, misguided, misinformed, misinstructed, misled, mistaken, poorly advised, reasonless, reckless, senseless, shortsighted, thoughtless, unconsidered, unreasonable, unreflecting, unsensible, unsound, unthinking, unthoughtful, unwary, unwise, wrongly advised

MISAPPLICATION, noun abuse, corrupt use, dishonest application, dishonest use, distortion, errancy, error, extravagance, false construction, fraudulent application, idle expenditure, illegal application, improper use, impropriety, incorrect application, incorrect usage, incorrect use, irregularity, malapropism, malpractice, misappropriation, misconception, misconstruction, misemployment, misexplanation, misexplication, mishandling, misinterpretation, misjudgment, mismanagement, mistake, mistranslation, misunderstanding, misusage, misuse, misuse of funds, misuse of words, perversion, poor usage, prodigality, reckless expenditure, squandering, useless expenditure, *usus perversus*, waste, wasteful expenditure, wastefulness, wrong application, wrong interpretation, wrong usage, wrong use, wrongful use
ASSOCIATED CONCEPTS: misapplication of funds

MISAPPREHEND, verb be deceived, be in error, be misled, be mistaken, blunder, confuse, distort, err, fail to understand, have the wrong impression, miscalculate, miscomprehend, misconceive, misconstrue, misdeem, misinterpret, misjudge, misreckon, mistake, misunderstand, receive a false impression, take amiss, take wrongly

MISAPPROPRIATION, _noun_ abuse, appropriation for a dishonest use, appropriation for a wrongful use, arrogation, breach of trust, conversion, defalcation, defraudation, diversion, embezzlement, fraud, fraudulent conversion, illegal use of property, larceny, malversation, misapplication, misemployment, misusage, misuse, peculation, pilferage, stealing, swindle, theft, thievery, wrongful conversion of property, wrongful use
ASSOCIATED CONCEPTS: conversion, misappropriation of funds

MISCALCULATE, _verb_ be erroneous, be in error, be misguided, be misled, be mistaken, be wrong, blunder, calculate wrongly, commit an error, deceive oneself, deviate, err, _errare,_ estimate incorrectly, fall into error, _falli,_ go amiss, go astray, go awry, have the wrong impression, labor under a misapprehension, labor under an error, make a mistake, _male computare,_ miscompute, misconceive, misconjecture, misconstrue, miscount, misdeem, misestimate, misjudge, misreckon, mistake, receive a false impression, slip, slip up, stray, stumble, understand incorrectly

MISCARRIAGE, _noun_ abortion, abortive attempt, abortive effort, bad behavior, breakdown, _cadere,_ collapse, default, defeat, disappointment, downfall, failure, fiasco, frustration, futile effort, hopeless failure, ineffectiveness, ineffectual attempt, loss, lost labor, misadventure, misbehavior, mischance, misconduct, misfire, mistake, negative result, noncompletion, nonfulfillment, nonperformance, nonsuccess, overthrow, _parum procedere,_ perdition, rout, ruin, _secus procedere,_ stoppage, successlessness, total loss, unlawful act, unproductivity, vain attempt, vain effort
ASSOCIATED CONCEPTS: miscarriage of justice

MISCELLANEOUS, _adjective_ admixed, aggregated, amalgamated, assorted, blended, collected, combined, commingled, commixed, composite, disparate, diverse, diversified, diversiform, _diversus,_ eclectic, heterogeneous, inconsistent, indiscriminate, intermixed, jumbled, manifold, many, medley, merged, mixed, mosaic, motley, multifarious, multiform, multiplex, nonuniform, of every description, of mixed character, of various kinds, _promiscuus,_ scrambled, sundry, unclassified, unselected, unsorted, varied, variegated, variform, various, _varius_

MISCHIEF, _noun_ annoyance, criminality, cruelty, damage, _damnum,_ danger, detriment, devilment, deviltry, disservice, evil, evil conduct, fault, foul play, frolicsomeness, harm, harmful action, hurt, ill consequence, impishness, _incommodum,_ infliction, injurious conduct, injuriousness, injury, injustice, knavery, _maleficium,_ malicious action, malignity, maltreatment, meanness, misbehavior, misconduct, misdoing, misusage, molestation, nastiness, naughtiness, nuisance, outrage, playfulness, prankishness, puckishness, rascality, roguery, roguishness, ruin, transgression, trouble, vice, villainy, waggery, waggishness, wickedness, wrong, wrongdoing
ASSOCIATED CONCEPTS: malicious mischief

MISCONCEIVE, _verb_ be deceived, be misguided, be misinformed, be misled, be mistaken, blunder, deceive oneself, delude oneself, distort the meaning, err,

estimate incorrectly, fail to understand, fall into error, guess wrong, interpret incorrectly, labor under a misapprehension, make a mistake, misapprehend, miscalculate, misconjecture, misconstrue, misdeem, misestimate, misinterpret, misjudge, misreckon, misunderstand, _perperam accipere,_ pervert, put a false construction on, receive a false impression, receive a wrong impression, value incorrectly

MISCONDUCT, _noun_ bad conduct, bad management, crime, _delictum,_ delinquency, dereliction, deviation from rectitude, dishonest management, disorderly conduct, error, failing, failure, fault, guilty act, ill management, illegality, improper conduct, impropriety, indiscretion, infamous conduct, maladministration, malfeasance, malpractice, malversation, misadministration, misbehavior, misdeed, misdemeanor, misdoing, misfeasance, misgovernment, misguidance, mismanagement, misprision, negligence, nonfeasance, offense, peccadillo, _peccatum,_ tort, transgression, turpitude, unprofessional conduct, wrong, wrongdoing
ASSOCIATED CONCEPTS: discharge for misconduct, gross misconduct, misconduct in office, official misconduct

MISCONSTRUE, _verb_ be confused, be in error, be misled, be wrong, blunder, confuse, construe wrongly, distort, fail to understand, garble, get wrong, have an incorrect impression, make a mistake, misapprehend, misconceive, misinterpret, misjudge, misread, mistake, misunderstand, pervert, put a false sense on, receive a false idea, receive a false impression, twist the words, understand improperly

MISCUE, _noun_ bad idea, blunder, botch, bungle, clumsy performance, corrigendum, deviation, erratum, error, flaw, fumble, impropriety, inadvertence, inadvertency, irregularity, miscalculation, misjudgment, miss, misstatement, misstep, mistake, misunderstanding, omission, oversight, slip, stumble

MISDEED, _noun_ abomination, atrocity, bad behavior, blunder, crime, cruel act, culpable omission, delict, _delictum,_ delinquency, dereliction, dutilessness, evil deed, fault, felony, guilty act, illegality, improper behavior, impropriety, infamous conduct, infraction, infringement, iniquity, injury, injustice, lapse, lawlessness, malefaction, _maleficium,_ malfeasance, malpractice, malversation, misbehavior, misconduct, misdemeanor, misdoing, misfeasance, mistake, offense, outrageous act, peccadillo, peccancy, _peccatum,_ scrape, sin, slip, transgression, trespass, villainy, violation, wicked action, wicked deed, wrong, wrongdoing

MISDEMEANOR, _noun_ act committed in violation of law, act of lawbreaking, breach of law, crime committed, criminal act, criminal activity, criminal offense, _delictum,_ dereliction, guilty act, illegality, improbity, impropriety, indiscretion, infamous conduct, malfeasance, malversation, misdeed, misdoing, misfeasance, offense, offense against the law, peccadillo, punishable offense, transgression, violation of law, wicked deed, wrong
ASSOCIATED CONCEPTS: felony, high crimes and misdemeanors, misdemeanor complaint, petit misdemeanor, violation

MISDIRECT, _verb_ confound, confuse, create a false impression, give a false impression, instruct badly, involve in error, lead astray, lead into error, misaddress, misadvise, miseducate, misguide, misinform, misinstruct, mislead, misteach, put off the scent, throw into confusion

MISDOING, noun   badness, blunder, bungle, crime, cruel act, culpability, delinquency, deviation from rectitude, dishonesty, disorderly conduct, dutilessness, error, evildoing, fault, foul play, guilty act, illegality, immorality, improbity, impropriety, incorrectness, indiscretion, inexcusability, infamous conduct, injustice, irregularity, knavery, lawlessness, maladministration, malefaction, malpractice, malversation, misapplication, misbehavior, mischief, misconduct, misdeed, misdemeanor, misfeasance, mismanagement, misprision, offense, outrage, peccadillo, rascality, roguery, ruffianism, scrape, sharp practice, slip, transgression, trespass, turpitude, unrighteousness, unsuitability, vice, villainy, violation, wicked deed, wickedness, wrong, wrongfulness

MISDOUBT, verb   be apprehensive, be doubtful, be irresolute, be nervous, be skeptical, be uncertain, be undetermined, challenge, cherish doubts, disbelieve, distrust, doubt, entertain doubts, entertain suspicions, give no credence to, give no credit to, harbor suspicions, have doubts about, have fears, have no confidence in, have no faith in, have questions, have reservations, have suspicions, hesitate, hold questionable, lack confidence, lack conviction, lack faith, misbelieve, misgive, mistrust, pause, question, scruple, suspect, waver, withhold judgment

MISEMPLOY, verb   abuse, *abuti*, corrupt, defile, desecrate, dissipate, distort, divert, employ improperly, ill treat, ill use, maltreat, manipulate improperly, misapply, misappropriate, misconduct, misdirect, misdo, mishandle, mismanage, misrule, misspend, mistreat, misuse, molest, overtax, overwork, pervert, pollute, prostitute, ruin, spoil, squander, taint, use wrongly, violate, waste, wear out

MISESTIMATION, noun   bad judgment, distorted idea, distorted impression, erroneousness, error, fallaciousness, false idea, false impression, inaccuracy, inaccurateness, incorrect appraisal, incorrect evaluation, incorrect valuation, inexactitude, inexactness, misapprehension, miscalculation, miscomputation, misconception, misconjecture, misinterpretation, misjudgment, misreckoning, misstatement, mistake, misunderstanding, poor judgment, uncorrectness, unpreciseness, warped idea, warped impression, warped judgment, wrong impression

MISFEASANCE, noun   breach of law, civil wrong, dereliction, deviation from rectitude, improper action, improper performance, infringement, injurious exercise of lawful authority, injurious exercise of authority, misconduct, misdeed, misdoing, offense, offense against the law, official misconduct, peccadillo, transgression, unlawful use of power, violation of law, wrong, wrong arising from affirmative action, wrongdoing, wrongful performance of a normally legal act, wrongfulness
ASSOCIATED CONCEPTS: malfeasance, negligence, nonfeasance

MISFORTUNE, noun   accident, adverse event, adverse fortune, adverse lot, adverse luck, adversity, affliction, backset, bad fortune, bad luck, bale, blow,

calamitas, calamity, casualty, cataclysm, catastrophe, comedown, destruction, disadvantage, disappointment, disaster, evil fortune, *fortuna adversa,* hardship, ill fortune, ill luck, *incommodum,* infelicity, misadventure, mischance, mishap, problem, reverse, ruin, setback, suffering, tragedy, trial, tribulation, trouble, unforeseen adversity, unfortunate occurrence, unlucky accident, unlucky happening, visitation
FOREIGN PHRASES: *Festinatio justitiae est noverca infortunii.* The hastening of justice is the stepmother of misfortune. *Negligentia semper habet infortunium comitem.* Negligence always has misfortune for a companion.

MISGIVING, noun   anxietude, anxiety, anxious concern, anxiousness, apprehension, apprehensiveness, concern, critical attitude, disquiet, distrust, doubt, doubtfulness, dubiety, fear, fearfulness, forbodement, foreboding, gaingiving, hesitation, inquietude, lack of certainty, lack of confidence, *metus timor,* mistrust, mistrustfulness, nervousness, objection, perturbation, *praesagium,* prediction of misfortune, premonition, presage, presentiment, qualm, reluctance, reservation, reserve, skepticalness, skepticism, *sollicitudo,* trepidation, uncertainty, uneasiness

MISGOVERN, verb   administer badly, administer improperly, administer poorly, govern badly, maladminister, *male administrare, male regere,* manage badly, misadminister, misdirect, misguide, mismanage, misrule, rule dishonestly

MISGUIDE, verb   befool, beguile, bewilder, cause a mistake, cause error, conceal, corrupt, create a false impression, deceive, delude, dissemble, distort, falsify, fool, *in errorum inducere,* lead astray, lead into error, lie, maladminister, misadvise, misconduct, misdirect, miseducate, mishandle, misinform, misinstruct, mislead, mismanage, misrepresent, misstate, misteach, pervert, tell a falsehood, tell a lie, tell an untruth, trip

MISHANDLE *(Maltreat), verb*   abuse, assail, assault, batter, defile, handle badly, ill treat, ill use, impose upon, injure, manhandle, maul, misemploy, misuse, molest, overburden, persecute, ravish, rough, treat abusively, treat ill, treat improperly, tyrannize, use dispiteously, use wrongly, victimize, violate, wrong

MISHANDLE *(Mismanage), verb*   abuse, administer improperly, conduct dishonestly, conduct without efficiency, conduct without honesty, handle badly, maladminister, manage badly, misconduct, misdirect, misuse, squander, use wrongly, waste

MISINFORM, verb   conceal, create a false impression, deceive, delude, distort, exaggerate, *falsa docere,* falsify, give a false impression, misadvise, miscolor, misdirect, miseducate, misguide, misinstruct, mislead, misrepresent, misstate, misteach, propagandize, report inaccurately

MISINTERPRET, verb   be misled, blunder, confuse, distort, err, explain incorrectly, fail to understand, garble, jumble, make a mistake, make an error, *male interpretari,* misapprehend, miscalculate, misconceive, misconjecture, misconstrue, misdeem, misjudge, misread, misreckon, misrepresent, mistake, mistranslate, misunderstand, place a false construction on, place a wrong construction on, place an erroneous construction on, receive a false impression, receive a wrong idea, receive an incorrect impression, twist the meaning, understand incorrectly

ASSOCIATED CONCEPTS: bilateral mistake, mistake of fact, mistake of law, recission, reformation, unilateral mistake

MISJOINDER, *noun*   bad match, incongruity, misalliance, misfit, mismatch

ASSOCIATED CONCEPTS: misjoinder of causes, misjoinder of parties

MISJUDGE, *verb*   be bewildered, be perplexed, blunder, err, err in judgment, estimate incorrectly, fail to recognize, have a wrong impression, judge erroneously, judge inaccurately, judge wrongly, make a mistake, make an error, *male iudicare,* misapprehend, miscalculate, miscompute, misconceive, misconstrue, misdeem, misesteem, misestimate, misinterpret, misread, misreckon, mistake, misthink, misunderstand, rate incorrectly

MISJUDGMENT, *noun*   bad judgment, error, fallacy, grave injustice, gross injustice, imposition, inaccuracy, inaccurateness, inequitableness, inequity, inexactitude, inexactness, injustice, misapprehension, miscalculation, miscarriage of justice, miscomputation, misconception, misconstruction, misestimation, misinterpretation, mistake, misunderstanding, poor judgment, unfair judgment, unfairness, unjust opinion, unpreciseness, wrong estimation

MISLABEL, *verb*   brand incorrectly, classify incorrectly, deceive, defraud, describe incorrectly, designate incorrectly, docket incorrectly, falsely characterize, identify incorrectly, label incorrectly, lead astray, lead into error, mark incorrectly, misbrand, mischaracterize, misclassify, misdenominate, misdescribe, misdesignate, misdirect, misguide, misidentify, misinform, mislead, mismark, misname, misrepresent, misstate, misticket, mistitle, name incorrectly, represent incorrectly, stamp incorrectly, tag incorrectly, ticket incorrectly, title incorrectly

ASSOCIATED CONCEPTS: fraud

MISLEAD, *verb*   bait, be dishonest, befool, beguile, cause error, cheat, corrupt, counterfeit, cozen, create a false impression, cully, deceive, *decipere,* decoy, defraud, delude, dissemble, distort, double-cross, dupe, ensnare, entrap, *fallere,* falsify, fib, fool, give a false idea, give a false impression, guide astray, guide into error, guide wrongly, *in errorem inducere,* lead astray, lead into error, lie, misadvise, misdescribe, misdirect, miseducate, misguide, misinform, misinstruct, misrepresent, misstate, misteach, pervert, practice deception, prevaricate, seduce, snare, sophisticate, swindle, take advantage of, take in, tell a falsehood, tell an untruth, trap, trick, varnish

MISMANAGE, *verb*   act foolishly, act improperly, administer improperly, administer inefficiently, administer poorly, blunder, boggle, botch, bungle, confound, derange, disarrange, fail, flounder, fumble, illmanage, maladminister, manage poorly, manage unskillfully, misadminister, misapply, misappropriate, misconduct, misdirect, misdo, misemploy, misgovern, misguide, mishandle, misrule, missend, misuse, neglect, pervert, reduce to chaos, spoil, violate rules

ASSOCIATED CONCEPTS: mismanage trust assets

MISNOMER, *Noun*   error in naming, misapplied name, miscalling, misnaming, misterm, wrong designation, wrong name

MISPRISION, *noun*   contempt, delinquency, deviation from rectitude, malefaction, malfeasance, malpractice, malversation, misconduct, misdeed, misfeasance, neglect, negligence, obstruction of justice, offense, transgression, violation, wrongful action of a public official

ASSOCIATED CONCEPTS: clerical misprision, misprision of felony, misprision of treason

MISPRIZE, *verb*   be contemptuous of, belittle, contemn, deprecate, depreciate, despise, disdain, disesteem, disparage, disprize, disregard, feel contempt for, hold cheap, hold in contempt, look down upon, make little of, make nothing of, minimize, misjudge, overlook, push aside, ridicule, run down, scorn, set at naught, slight, sneer at, speak slightingly of, underestimate, underprize, underrate, underreckon, undervalue

MISREAD, *verb*   be deceived, be erroneous, be mistaken, blunder, confuse, distort, err, fall into error, garble, interpret incorrectly, make a mistake, misapprehend, misconstrue, misdeem, misidentify, misinterpret, mistake, mistranslate, misunderstand, pervert, put a false construction on, put a wrong construction on, read incorrectly, receive a false impression, receive a wrong impression, receive an incorrect impression, translate incorrectly, twist the meaning of, understand incorrectly

MISREPRESENT, *verb*   assert incorrectly, be false, bear false witness, beguile, belie, betray, break faith, *calumniari,* camouflage, color, contort, deceive, defraud, delude, *depravare,* disguise, dissemble, dissimulate, distort, distort intentionally, dupe, embroider, equivocate, exaggerate, explain wrongly, fabricate, fake, falsify, feign, fool, give a false coloring, give a false representation, hoax, lie, malign, miscite, miscolor, misdescribe, misexplain, misguide, mislead, misquote, misreport, misrepresent, misstate, misteach, mock, overstate, palter, pass off for, perjure oneself, pervert, pretend, prevaricate, put a false appearance on, put a false construction on, represent falsely, represent fraudulently, represent incorrectly, sham, simulate, slant, speak falsely, state an untruth, state falsely, tell a falsehood, tell lies, trick, trump up, twist the meaning of, understate, utter a falsehood

ASSOCIATED CONCEPTS: fraud, knowingly misrepresent, misrepresent a material fact

MISREPRESENTATION, *noun*   deceitfulness, deception, deceptive statement, deceptiveness, distortion, exaggeration, fabrication, false representation, false statement, falsehood, falsification, falsity, fraud, inaccuracy, incorrect assertion, intentional misstatement, lie, misapplication, misconstruction, misguidance, misquotation, misreport, misstatement, misstatement of fact, overstatement, untrue statement, untruth, untruthfulness, unveracity

ASSOCIATED CONCEPTS: actionable misrepresentation, deceit, false misrepresentation, fraudulent misrepresentation, innocent misrepresentation, material misrepresentation, misrepresentation of a material fact, negligent misrepresentation

MISRULE, *noun* anarchism, anarchy, breakdown of administration, chaos, confusion, disorder, disorganization, impolicy, lawlessness, maladministration, malfeasance, misconduct, misdirection, misgovernment, misguidance, mishandling, mismanagement, turmoil, unruliness

MISSION, *noun* aim, appointment, assignment, business, calling, charge, commission, concern, delegation, design, duty, embassy, errand, goal, job, legation, mandate, objective, office, profession, purpose, pursuit, task, trust, undertaking, venture, vocation, work

MISSTATE, *verb* be deceptive, be erroneous, deceive, delude, dissemble, distort, falsify, give a false impression, give a wrong idea, lead astray, lead into error, lie, misguide, misinform, mislead, misreport, misrepresent, pervert, prevaricate, state incorrectly, state misleadingly, tell a falsehood, tell a lie, tell an untruth, twist the meaning

MISSTATEMENT, *noun* bad reporting, blunder, deceit, deception, deviation from truth, distortion, duplicity, erratum, error, false statement, falsehood, falsification, fiction, imprecision, inaccuracy, incorrect statement, inexactitude, inexactness, insincerity, lie, mendacity, *mendacium,* misinformation, misrepresentation, mistake, perjury, perversion, pretense, slip, subreption, suppression of truth, untruth, untruthfulness, wrong statement
ASSOCIATED CONCEPTS: misstatement of fact

MISTAKE, *verb* be deceived, be erroneous, be in the wrong, be misguided, be misled, be mistaken, blunder, bungle, commit an error, confuse, err, fall into error, get wrong, go amiss, go astray, go wrong, identify incorrectly, *ignorare,* labor under a misapprehension, misapprehend, miscalculate, misconceive, misconstrue, misidentify, misinterpret, misjudge, misread, misunderstand, name inaccurately, put a false sense on, receive a false impression, receive a wrong impression, slip up, stumble
ASSOCIATED CONCEPTS: excusable mistake, harmless error, mistake of fact, mistake of law, mistaken identity, mutual mistake, unilateral mistake

MISTREAT, *verb* abuse, afflict, aggrieve, annoy, assail, assault, attack, badger, be hurtful, be malevolent, be offensive, be pitiless, be rude, be violent, bear malice, berate, bother, bruise, bully, burden, cause evil, cause pain, create havoc, debase, desecrate, destroy, disoblige, distress, disturb, do an injustice to, do violence to, do wrong, force, give pain, harass, harm, harrow, harry, heckle, hurt, ill treat, ill use, impair, induce pain, inflict evil, inflict pain, injure, lay waste, lead into trouble, make mischief, malign, maltreat, manhandle, maul, misemploy, misgovern, mishandle, mismanage, misrule, misuse, molest, offend, oppress, overburden, overtask, overtax, overwork, persecute, pervert, plague, pollute, prostitute, provoke, run down, savage, show ill will, spite, strain, strike, torment, torture, trample on, tread on, treat badly, tyrannize, use dispiteously, use hard, use wrongly, vex, victimize, violate, waste, wear out, work evil, worry, wound, wrong

MISTRIAL, *noun* abrogation, annulment, cancellation, collapse, disannulment, erroneous trial, failure, fruitless trial, ineffective trial, invalid trial, nonfulfillment, nonsuccess, nugatory trial, nullification, nullity,

revocation, terminated trial, unproductive trial, unsuccessful trial, useless trial, void trial, worthless trial
ASSOCIATED CONCEPTS: deadlocked jury, declaration of a mistrial, prejudicial error

MISTRUST, *verb* apprehend, be anxious, be apprehensive, be cautious, be doubtful, be dubious, be loath, be nervous, be skeptical, be uncertain, cherish doubts, distrust, doubt, dread, entertain doubts, entertain suspicions, fear, give no credit to, harbor doubts, harbor suspicions, have anxiety, have doubts, have fears, have misgivings, have no faith in, have no trust in, have qualms, have reservations, have suspicions, hesitate, hold back, lack belief in, lack confidence in, lack faith in, lack trust in, misdoubt, misgive, question, regard with suspicion, shrink from, shy from, suspect, treat with reserve

MISUNDERSTAND, *verb* be confused, be ignorant, be in the wrong, be misguided, be misled, be mistaken, blunder, commit an error, confuse, delude oneself, distort, err, fail to understand, fall into error, jumble, labor under a misapprehension, lack information, make a mistake, misapprehend, miscalculate, misconceive, misconstrue, misdeem, misinterpret, misjudge, misperceive, misread, misreckon, mistake, *perperam,* pervert, put a false construction on, put a wrong construction on, put an erroneous construction on, receive a wrong impression, twist the meaning, understand wrongly

MISUSAGE, *noun* abuse, bad treatment, corruption, debasement, defilement, degradation, desecration, distortion, diversion, exploitation, force, ill treatment, ill usage, improper usage, improper use, impropriety, maladministration, malapropism, malpractice, malversation, misapplication, misappropriation, misemployment, mismanagement, mispronunciation, misuse, peculation, perversion, pollution, prostitution, violation, wrong use

MISUSE, *noun* abuse, degradation, erroneous use, ill treatment, ill usage, ill use, improper usage, improper use, incorrect usage, incorrect use, maladministration, malpractice, maltreatment, misapplication, misappropriation, misemployment, mishandling, mismanagement, mistreatment, misusage, perversion, solecism, *usus,* violation, wrong use
ASSOCIATED CONCEPTS: misuse of a product, misuse of an easement, misuse of funds, misuse of powers, misuse of property, patent misuse
FOREIGN PHRASES: *Expedit reipublicae ne sua re quis male utatur.* It is for the interest of the state that no one should make ill use of his property.

MITIGATE, *verb* abate, abate in intensity, adjust, allay, alleviate, ameliorate, appease, assuage, check, control, curb, cushion, decrease, diminish, ease, give relief, *lenire,* lessen, lessen in force, lighten, make less severe, meliorate, *mitigare, mitiorem facere,* moderate, moderate in severity, mollify, palliate, reduce, regulate, relieve, restrain, soften, temper, unburden
ASSOCIATED CONCEPTS: duty to mitigate

MITIGATING, *adjective* abating, alleviating, ameliorative, assuaging, calmative, diminishing, discounting, easing, exculpatory, excusing, extenuating, lessening, limiting, meliorative, modifying, palliative,

qualifying, reducing, relieving, softening, subduing, tempering
ASSOCIATED CONCEPTS: duty to mitigate damages, mitigating circumstances

MITIGATION, noun abatement, abridgment, adjustment, alleviation, assuagement, attenuation, comforting, decrease, diminishment, diminution, easing, lessening, *levamentum, levatio,* lightening, *mitigatio,* moderation, palliation, reduction, relaxation, relief, softening, soothing, weakening
ASSOCIATED CONCEPTS: mitigation of damages, mitigation of sentence

MITTIMUS, noun authorization, command, command to incarcerate, court order of imprisonment, decree, decretal, direction to imprison, edict, legal order, mandate, official order, order, transcript of minutes of commitment, warrant of commitment, written precept of imprisonment
ASSOCIATED CONCEPTS: commitment

MOCK *(Deride), verb* chaff, *deridere,* disparage, fleer, flout, gibe, heckle, hold in derision, hold up to ridicule, hoot, *inridere,* insult, jeer, joke about, lampoon, laugh at, *ludibrio,* make a butt of, make a fool of, make fun of, poke fun at, rag, ridicule, satirize, scoff, scorn, sneer, snicker, snigger, spurn, taunt, tease, treat with contempt, treat with derision, treat with disrespect, treat with scorn, trifle with, twit

MOCK *(Imitate), verb* act, ape, assume the appearance of, burlesque, caricature, copy, counterfeit, do likewise, duplicate, echo, emulate, fake, feign, follow, follow suit, follow the example of, impersonate, mime, mimic, mirror, model after, pantomine, parody, parrot, pattern after, personate, play a part, portray, pretend, repeat, reproduce, satirize, simulate, take after, take off on, travesty

MODE, noun convention, course, craze, custom, design, fad, fashion, form, formula, guise, habit, manner, means, method, *modus,* outline, practice, precedent, prevailing style, prevailing taste, prevalence, procedure, process, protocol, rage, *ratio,* regulations, routine, rule, rules, scheme, shape, style, system, taste, technique, tendency, tenor, trend, usage, *via,* vogue, way

MODEL, noun antetype, archetype, copy, copy in miniature, design, example, *exemplar, exemplum,* facsimile, gauge, guide, ideal, image, imitation, miniature, mold, paradigm, paragon, pattern, plan, precedent, prototype, replica, representation, sample, specimen, standard
ASSOCIATED CONCEPTS: Model Code

MODERATE *(Preside over), verb* act as chairman, act as moderator, act as president, administer, be at the head of, be in authority, chair, command, control, direct, discipline, govern, have charge of, head, hold in check, hold sway over, hold the chair, lead, manage, master, officiate, oversee, pilot, police, regulate, run, stand over, steer, supervise, take charge of

MODERATE *(Temper), verb* abate, allay, alleviate, appease, assuage, attemper, blunt, calm, chasten, check, constrain, cool, curb, dampen, decelerate, decrease, diminish, dull, ease, hush, keep within bounds, lessen, lighten, limit, make less, mitigate, modify, mol-

lify, mute, narrow, pacify, palliate, qualify, quell, quiet, reduce, repress, restrain, season, slacken, slow down, smooth, sober, soften, soothe, still, subdue, suppress, tame, tone down, tranquilize, weaken

MODERATION, noun abstemiousness, abstinence, alleviation, assuagement, avoidance of extremes, balance, calmness, composure, conservatism, constraint, continence, *continentia,* control, coolness, deliberateness, diminution, dispassionateness, economy, equanimity, fairness, forbearance, frugality, gentleness, innocuousness, justice, lack of excess, lenience, leniency, lenity, limitation, mean, mildness, mitigation, moderateness, moderatism, *modus,* nonviolence, palliation, patience, quiet, reasonableness, reduction, regulation, restraint, restriction, sedateness, self-control, sobriety, steadiness, temperance, *temperantia,* temperateness, thrift, thriftiness

MODICUM, noun fraction, fragment, grain, insignificant amount, iota, minimum, minor amount, mite, particle, *paululum, paulum,* small amount, small quantity, trifle amount

MODIFICATION, noun adaptation, adjustment, alteration, change, correction, exception, limitation, partial change, qualification, reservation, restriction, slight change, variation
ASSOCIATED CONCEPTS: amendment, material modification, modification of a contract, modification of a decree, modification of a will, modification of an order, modification of judgment, reformation

MODIFY *(Alter), verb* adapt, adjust, affect, ameliorate, amend, change, *commutare,* convert, correct, effect a change, emend, emendate, give a new form to, improve, improve upon, introduce changes, make adjustments, make corrections, make improvements, meliorate, metamorphose, modernize, *mutare,* overhaul, qualify, readjust, rearrange, recast, reconstruct, rectify, refine, reform, regularize, remodel, remold, render in a better form, reshape, revamp, revise, rework, rewrite, touch up, transfigure, transform, transmute, transubstantiate, vamp, vary, work over
ASSOCIATED CONCEPTS: modify a contract, modify a decision, modify an order

MODIFY *(Moderate), verb* abate, allay, assuage, blunt, check, condition, curb, cushion, decrease, ease, extenuate, lessen, lighten, limit, lower, make less extreme, make less intense, make less severe, mitigate, *moderari,* mollify, qualify, reduce, regulate, restrict, soften, subdue, temper, *temperare,* tone down

MODUS OPERANDI, noun approach, behavior, conduct, course, course of conduct, definite procedure, line of conduct, manner, manner of operating, means, method, methodology, mode, mode of operation, mode of procedure, operation, order, pattern, procedure, process, routine, standard procedure, style, system, tactics, technique, way, ways and means

MODUS VIVENDI, noun interim agreement, manner of living, method of living, mode of living, nonpermanent agreement, nonpermanent arrangement, provisional settlement, temporary agreement, temporary arrangement, temporary settlement, transient arrangement, way of life, way of living, working arrangement

MOIETY, *noun*   allotment, division, equal part, equal share, fifty percent, fraction, fragment, half, indefinite portion, indefinite share, measure, parcel, part, percentage, piece, portion, ration, section, segment, share

MOLEST *(Annoy),* *verb*   anger, arouse, badger, bother, discommode, disquiet, disturb, harass, harm, harry, hound, hurt, incense, incommode, inconvenience, inflame, injure, interfere with, interrupt, irk, irritate, misuse, perturb, pester, pique, plague, provoke, ruffle, *sollicitare,* tease, torment, trouble, vex, *vexare,* worry

MOLEST *(Subject   to   indecent   advances),* *verb* abuse, assault, attack, defile, rape, ravish, sexually abuse, sexually assault, violate

MOLESTATION, *noun*   abuse, aggravation, annoyance, bother, disturbance, ill treatment, ill usage, inconvenience, interference, interruption, intrusion, irritation, maltreatment, meddling, mistreatment, nuisance, oppression, persecution, *vexatio,* vexation

MOLLIFICATION, *noun*   abatement, allayment, alleviation, amelioration, appeasement, assuagement, calmness, check, conciliation, curb, deadening, decrease, diminishment, diminution, dulcification, easement, easing, lessening, lightening, lull, mediation, melioration, mitigation, pacification, palliation, placation, propitiation, reconciliation, reduction, relaxation, relief, slackening, softening, softness, soothing, tranquilization

MOLLIFY, *verb*   abate, allay, alleviate, ameliorate, appease, assuage, attemper, blunt, calm, check, compose, conciliate, cool, curb, deaden, decrease, diminish, dulcify, dull, ease, give relief, hush, improve, *lenire,* lessen, lull, make better, mediate, meliorate, mellow, milden, *mitigare,* mitigate, moderate, *mollire,* pacificate, pacify, palliate, placate, propitiate, quell, quiet, reconcile, reduce, relax, relieve, restrain, smooth, soften, soothe, still, subdue, temper, tone down, tranquilize, weaken

MOMENTOUS, *adjective*   big, consequential, critical, crucial, earthshaking, far-reaching, fateful, grand, grave, great, important, impressive, *magni momenti,* major, marked, material, memorable, notable, noteworthy, outstanding, prominent, remarkable, serious, signal, significant, special, stirring, substantial, uncommon, unordinary, unusual, weighty

MONETARY, *adjective*   capital, financial, fiscal, minted, numismatical, nummulary, pecuniary, stamped
ASSOCIATED CONCEPTS: monetary damages, monetary relief

MONEY, *noun*   *aes,* affluence, assets, bank note, bankroll, buying power, capital, cash, change, coin, coinage, currency, finances, fortune, funds, greenback, hard cash, income, legal tender, means, measure of value, medium of exchange, mintage, *nummus, pecunia,* property, resources, revenue, riches, specie, standard of value, substance, token, treasure, wealth, wherewithal, working capital
ASSOCIATED CONCEPTS: money award, money damages, money decree, money demand, money due and owing, money had and received, money judgment, money paid into court, moneyed corporation

MONITION *(Legal summons),* *noun*   authoritative citation to appear, authoritative command, bidding, call, citation, command, commandment, decree, dictate, direction, edict, fiat, invitation, legal notice, mandate, notice to appear, notification, official call, official notice, order, requisition, rescript, subpoena, summons, summons to appear and answer, warrant, writ

MONITION *(Warning),* *noun*   admonishment, admonition, advice, alarm, alert, caution, caveat, dehortation, enlightenment, exhortation, forewarning, hint, indication, information, notice, notification, prediction of danger

MONITOR, *verb*   *admonitor,* attend, audit, check, conduct an inquiry, control, eavesdrop, examine, guard, inquire into, inspect, investigate, keep in sight, keep in view, listen, observe, overlook, oversee, review, scan, scrutinize, study, subject to examination, subject to scrutiny, survey, watch

MONOPOLIZE, *verb*   absorb, appropriate, control, control market supply, control prices, control trade, corner, corner the market, dominate, engage, engross, enthrall, exercise exclusive rights, grip, have all to oneself, hold spellbound, hold the interest of, involve, keep entirely to oneself, obtain exclusive possession, occupy, own exclusively, retain exclusive control, retain exclusive possession, secure exclusive control, secure exclusive possession, stifle competition, suppress competition
ASSOCIATED CONCEPTS: conspiracy to monopolize, restraint of trade

MONOPOLY, *noun*   control, control of the market, control of trade, domination, exclusive control, exclusive possession, exclusive privilege to carry on a traffic, exclusive right, *monopolium,* oligopoly, sole control of a commodity
ASSOCIATED CONCEPTS: antitrust laws, combination in restraint of trade, exemptions from antitrust laws, price fixing, trust
FOREIGN PHRASES: *Commercium jure gentium commune esse debet, et non in monopolium et privatum paucorum quaestum convertendum.* By the law of nations, commerce ought to be common and not converted into a monopoly and the private gain of a few persons. *Monopolia dicitur, cum unus solus aliquod genus mercaturae universum emit, pretium ad suum libitum statuens.* A monopoly is said to exist when one person alone buys up the whole of one kind of commodity, fixing a price at his own pleasure.

MONUMENT, *noun*   achievement, cairn, cenotaph, cromlech, dolmen, lasting reminder, mark, memorial, *monumentum,* permanent structure, remembrance, reminder, shrine, testimonial

MOOT, *adjective*   abstract, academic, actionable, arguable, contentious, contestable, contested, controversial, controvertible, debatable, disputable, disputatious, disputed, doubtful, dubious, hypothetical, in dispute, in issue, in question, open to discussion, open to question, problematical, questionable, questioned, speculative, subject to controversy, suppositional, theoretical, uncertain, undecided, under discussion, undetermined, unsettled, untried

ASSOCIATED CONCEPTS: academic question, moot appeal, moot case, moot controversy, moot court, moot question

MORAL, *adjective* aboveboard, *bene moratus,* bound by duty, commendable, conscientious, correct, creditable, decent, deserving, duteous, dutiful, estimable, ethical, exemplary, good, high-minded, high-principled, honest, *honestus,* honorable, idealistic, incorrupt, incorruptible, innocent, just, laudable, law-abiding, meritorious, noble, praiseworthy, principled, *probus,* proper, pure, reputable, respectable, responsible, right-minded, righteous, *sanctus,* scrupulous, spotless, truehearted, trustworthy, uncorrupt, uncorrupted, unerring, upright, upstanding, virtuous, well-conducted, worthy
ASSOCIATED CONCEPTS: moral certainty, moral character, moral consideration, moral dereliction, moral duty, moral obligation, moral turpitude

MORATORIUM, *noun* abeyance, break, cessation, close, deferral, delay, desistance, discontinuance, end, ending, halt, hold, interim, interval, leaving off, lull, pause, period, period of obligatory delay, postponement, recess, respite, rest, standstill, stop, stoppage, suspension, temporary halt, temporary relief, termination, wait, waiting period
ASSOCIATED CONCEPTS: moratorium acts, moratorium on repayment of debt

MORDACIOUS, *adjective* acerbic, acid, acrid, acrimonious, acute, biting, bitter, caustic, corrosive, cutting, harsh, incisive, knifelike, malicious, mordant, penetrating, piercing, pointed, pungent, rancorous, raw, rough, scathing, severe, sharp, slashing, spiteful, stinging, trenchant, uncharitable, unkind, virulent, vitriolic

MORTALITY, *noun* *condicio mortalis,* death, destruction, evanescence, extinction, fatality, fugaciousness, fugacity, human race, humanity, humanness, impermanence, man, mankind, *mortalitas,* mortalness, subjection to death, temporary existence, transientness, transitoriness
ASSOCIATED CONCEPTS: mortality tables

MORTGAGE, *noun* charge, collateral security, conditional conveyance of land, conditional property transfer, contractual obligation, encumbrance, engagement, indebtedness, loan transaction, obligation, *pignus,* pledge, pledge for the payment of a debt, pledge of security, real security, security, security for a debt, something owing, state of indebtedness, transfer of property as security for a debt, transfer of security
ASSOCIATED CONCEPTS: amortization of a mortgage, assignment of a mortgage, assumption of a mortgage, chattel mortgage, constructive mortgage, equitable mortgage, first mortgage, foreclosure of a mortgage, holder of a mortgage, lien, maturity of a mortgage, mortgage commitment, mortgagee in possession, mortgagee of record, mortgagor, purchase money mortgage, recording of a mortgage, redemption of a mortgage, second mortgage, subject to a mortgage

MOTIF, *noun* adornment, arrangement, beautification, composition, construction, decoration, design, detail, dominant theme, embellishment, figuration, figure, form, format, garnishment, illumination, main feature, ornament, ornamentation, overall theme, pattern, plan, prevailing idea, recurring theme, shape, structure, style, theme

MOTION, *noun* application, application for a ruling, application for an order, application for proposed relief, claim, demand, petition, proposal, proposed measure, proposition, request, *rogatio, sententia*
ASSOCIATED CONCEPTS: alternative motions, costs of a motion, ex parte motion, interlocutory motion, motion for a more definite statement, motion for a new trial, motion for a nonsuit, motion for a decree, motion for judgment, motion for judgment notwithstanding verdict, motion for reargument, motion for summary judgment, motion papers, motion to dismiss, motion to quash, motion to set aside judgment, motion to strike, motion to vacate a judgment, omnibus motion, premature motion, renewal of a motion, withdrawal of a motion

MOTIVATE, *verb* activate, actuate, adjure, advise, affect, allure, animate, appeal, arouse desire, attract, captivate, carry weight, cause, challenge, charge, command, compel, convince, direct, draw, encourage, exert influence, exhort, fill with longing, fire up, goad, guide, impel, incite, incline, induce, infect, inflame, influence, inspire, inspirit, instigate, interest, invite, lead, move, move to action, persuade, press, prevail upon, promote, prompt, provide with a motive, provoke desire, rouse, set in motion, spirit, spur, stimulate, stir up, sway, talk into, tempt, urge, work upon

MOTIVE, *noun* aim, *causa,* causation, compulsion, consideration, design, determination, driving force, encouragement, end, goal, impelling power, impulse, incentive, inducement, influence, inner drive, inspiration, moving cause, moving power, moving spirit, object, objective, personal reasons, persuasion, plan, point, proposal, prospect, provocation, purpose, *ratio,* rationale, reason, reason for action, stimulant, stimulation, stimulus
ASSOCIATED CONCEPTS: corrupt motive, intent

MOVABLE, *noun* *agilis,* chattels personal, effects, goods, *mobilis,* personal effects, personal property, personalty, possessions, transportables, transportable property
ASSOCIATED CONCEPTS: fixtures, movable goods, movable machinery
FOREIGN PHRASES: **Mobilia non habent situm.** Movables have no situs or local habitation.

MOVE (*Alter position*), ***verb*** abscond, alter the position, break camp, carry, change an abode, change place, change residence, come away, *commovere,* convey, depart, disperse, emigrate, exit, flee, go, go away, go forth, go from home, go on, go one's way, journey, leave, leave a place, migrate, move out, part company, progress, propel, push on, put in motion, remove, slip away, slip off, take flight, transfer, translocate, transport, transpose, vacate, walk away, walk off

MOVE (*Judicially request*), ***verb*** apply, ask for, introduce, make a demand, make a motion, make a petition, make a request, make a requisition, make application, make formal application, make one's submission, offer for consideration, petition, propose, propose a motion, propose an action formally, put forth, put forward, put up a petition, *referre,* request, requisition, submit, submit a formal request

ASSOCIATED CONCEPTS: motion practice, move the court

MOVING *(Evoking emotion),* **adjective** absorbing, affecting, agitating, animating, arousing, arresting, astonishing, awakening, breathtaking, captivating, charming, dramatic, electrifying, enchanting, encouraging, evocative, exciting, excitive, expressive, glowing, gripping, impelling, imposing, impressive, inciting, inflaming, influencing, inspiriting, instigating, interesting, *miserabilis,* overpowering, overwhelming, persuading, piquant, poignant, prompting, provocative, provoking, rousing, sensational, sensitive, stimulating, stimulative, stirring, thrilling, touching, warm

MOVING *(In motion),* **adjective** active, ambulant, ambulative, ambulatory, changing, conveyable, detachable, drifting, fugitive, itinerant, journeying, kinetic, locomotive, meandering, mercurial, migratory, mobile, motile, motive, mundivagant, nomadic, passing, peripatetic, removable, restless, roaming, roving, separable, shifting, touring, transient, transitional, transmigratory, traveling, unattached, unfastened, unsettled, unstaid, unstationary, vacillating, vagabond, vagrant, voyaging, wandering, wavering, wayfaring
ASSOCIATED CONCEPTS: moving papers, moving party, moving violation

MUDDLE, *verb* addle, baffle, becloud, befog, befuddle, bewilder, botch, bungle, cloud, complicate, confound, *confundere,* confuse, daze, derange, disarrange, discompose, disconcert, disorder, disorganize, disturb, embrangle, entangle, fluster, fog, fuddle, ignore distinctions, jumble, make a mess of, make havoc, mismanage, mix up, obfuscate, *permiscere,* puzzle, scramble, stupefy, throw into confusion, throw out of order, *turbare,* unsettle, upset

MULCT *(Defraud),* **verb** cheat, deceive, embezzle, fudge, peculate, practice fraud, sharp, steal, swindle, trick

MULCT *(Fine),* **verb** amerce, deprive, distrain, exact a fine, impose a fine, penalize, punish

MULTIFARIOUS, *adjective* different, disparate, dissimilar, diverse, diversified, heterogeneous, irregular, manifold, many, miscellaneous, mixed, motley, multiform, multigenerous, multiplex, nonuniform, numerous, varied, variegated, various, *varius*

MULTIFOLD, *adjective* diversified, diversiform, manifold, many, multifarious, multiform, multigenerous, multiple, multiplex, multiplicate, multitudinous, numerous, varied, variegated, variform

MULTIPLE, *adjective* abundant, aggregate, ample, assorted, composed of several elements, considerable, different, divergent, diverse, diversified, generous, innumerable, many, miscellaneous, mixed, more than one, multifarious, multifold, multiplex, multitudinous, myriad, numerous, plenteous, plural, profuse, several, sundry, superabundant, uncounted, unnumbered, untold, varied, various
ASSOCIATED CONCEPTS: multiple claims, multiple damages, multiple dwelling, multiple offender, multiplicity of suits

MULTIPLICITY, *noun* many sidedness, multitudinous, numerousness, plurality

MUNDANE, *adjective* accustomary, average, banal, bodily, carnal, common, commonplace, conventional, corporeal, customary, earthly, everyday, familiar, fleshly, frequent, habitual, hackneyed, homespun, irreligious, material, nonsacred, nonspiritual, ordinary, pedestrian, physical, plain, profane, prosaic, prosy, regular, routine, secular, sensual, simple, stale, standard, stereotyped, sublunar, sublunary, tedious, tellurian, telluric, temporal, terrene, terrestrial, trite, typical, undistinguished, uneventful, unexalted, ungodly, unhallowed, unholy, unimaginative, uninspired, uninteresting, unpoetical, unsacred, unsanctified, unspiritual, usual, wearisome, well-known, well-trodden, workday, worldly, worldly-minded

MURDER, *noun* act of killing, act of slaying, act of taking life, assassination, *caedes,* destruction, destruction of human life, destruction of life, destructiveness, elimination, genocide, homicide, intentional killing, killing, liquidation, massacre, *occisio,* taking of human life, unlawful killing, violent death
ASSOCIATED CONCEPTS: assault with intent to murder, attempted murder, felonious homicide, felony murder, first-degree murder, premeditated murder, second-degree murder, voluntary manslaughter, willful murder

MUSE, *verb* be abstracted, be distracted, be in a reverie, be inattentive, be occupied in concentration, be occupied in study, bestow thought upon, brood, cerebrate, cogitate, comment, commune with oneself, concentrate, consider, contemplate, daydream, debate, deliberate, digest, disregard, examine, intellectualize, introspect, meditate, mull, note, ponder, reflect, remark, review, revolve, ruminate, speculate, study in silence, study quietly, take into consideration, take stock of, think, think about, think over, turn over, weigh

MUTABLE, *adjective* alterable, capricious, changeable, changeful, commutable, fickle, fluctuating, *inconstans,* inconstant, irresolute, *mutabilis,* protean, subject to change, transient, uncertain, undecided, unreliable, unsettled, unstable, unsteadfast, unsteady, vacillating, variable, versatile, volatile, wavering
FOREIGN PHRASES: *Nomina sunt mutabilia, res autem immobiles.* Names are mutable, but things are immutable. *Res est misera ubi jus est vagum et incertum.* It is a sorry state of affairs when law is vague and mutable.

MUTE, *adjective* close-lipped, closemouthed, dumb, hushed, inarticulate, incapable of speech, incommunicative, indisposed to talk, *mutus,* noiseless, pauciloquent, quiescent, quiet, refraining from utterance, reserved, reticent, silent, soundless, speechless, still, taciturn, tight-lipped, tongue-tied, unable to speak, unable to utter articulate sound, uncommunicative, unexpressive, unloquacious, untalkative, unvocal, unvocalizing, voiceless, wordless

MUTILATE, *verb* amputate, batter, blemish, bruise, butcher, cripple, cut, damage, debilitate, deface, deform, deprive of an important part, disable, disfigure, dismantle, dismember, distort, gash, impair, incapacitate, injure, knock out of shape, lacerate, maim, mangle, mar, *mutilare,* render a document imperfect, render imperfect, tear, tear apart, *truncare,* truncate, twist, unshape, warp, wound, wreck

MUTINY, *noun*   defiance, disloyalty, disobedience, insubordination, insurgence, insurgency, insurrection, *motus,* opposition, oppugnancy, outbreak, rebellion, refusal to comply, resistance, revolt, revolution, *seditio,* sedition, subversion, treason, upheaval, uprising

MUTUAL *(Collective), adjective*   coadjutant, coadjutive, coadjuvant, coadunate, coalitional, collaborated, collaborative, combined, common, communal, communalistic, commutual, confederated, conjoint, cooperant, cooperative, federal, federate, federated, federative, general, in common, interdependent, joint, leagued, participatory, shared, unified, united
ASSOCIATED CONCEPTS: mutual benefit association, mutual enterprise, mutual insurance company, mutual savings bank

MUTUAL *(Reciprocal), adjective*   bilateral, commutative, complemental, complementary, concurrent, correlative, correspondent, corresponding, done reciprocally, equivalent, interactive, interchanged, interrelated, *mutuus,* parallel, reciprocating, reciprocative, two-sided, two-way
ASSOCIATED CONCEPTS: mutual consent, mutual covenants, mutual easements, mutual mistake, mutual promise, mutual wills

MUTUAL UNDERSTANDING, *noun*   accord, agreement, alliance, amity, bilateral contract, common agreement, common understanding, communion, compact, concordance, concurrence, contract, correlative agreement, entente, interchangeable commitment, joint agreement, joint pact, meeting of minds, mutual promise, pact, reciprocal agreement, reciprocal commitment, treaty

MUTUALITY, *noun*   coequality, commonality, commutability, commutation, correlation, correlativeness, correlativity, correspondence, dependence, exchange, interaffiliation, interassociation, interchange, interchangeability, interconnection, interdependence, intermutation, interplay, interrelation, mutual dependence, mutual relation, permutation, reciprocality, reciprocalness, reciprocation, reciprocity

ASSOCIATED CONCEPTS: mutuality of consent, mutuality of contract, mutuality of obligation, mutuality of remedy

MYRIAD, *adjective*   boundless, countless, endless, illimitable, immense, incalculable, inexhaustible, infinite, innumerable, innumerous, limitless, manifold, many, measureless, multitudinous, numberless, numerous, *sescenti,* sumless, uncountable, uncounted, unending, unfathomable, unlimited, unnumberable, unnumbered, untold, without number

MYSTERIOUS, *adjective*   abstruse, arcane, *arcanus,* baffling, cabalistic, clandestine, cloaked, coded, concealed, covert, cryptic, dark, disguised, enigmatic, enigmatical, esoteric, furtive, hidden, impenetrable, incomprehensible, ineffable, inexplicable, inscrutable, magical, masked, mystic, mystical, mystifying, obscure, occult, *occultus,* oracular, perplexing, preternatural, privy, puzzling, recondite, runic, screened, secret, secretive, *secretus,* shadowy, sphinxian, sphinx-like, stealthy, strange, supernatural, supernormal, surreptitious, transcendental, umbrageous, unaccountable, uncanny, undeciphered, undercover, underhand, undisclosed, unexplainable, unexplained, unfathomable, unintelligible, unknown, unrevealed, untold, veiled, weird

MYSTERY, *noun*   abstruseness, arcanum, cabala, cabalism, concealment, enigma, hidden meaning, inexplicableness, inscrutability, inscrutableness, mysticism, obscurity, occultism, occultness, puzzle, *res occulta,* riddle, secrecy, secret, secretiveness, thaumaturgy, undiscoverability, unexplored ground, unfathomability, unfathomableness

MYTH, *noun*   absurd story, concoction, doubtful narrative, fable, fabrication, *fabula,* false story, falsehood, fantasy, fiction, fictitious story, figment, folklore, folktale, invention, legend, legendary story, story, tale, tall story, tradition, trumped up story, unreality, untrue story, untruth, yarn
ASSOCIATED CONCEPTS: legal fiction

N

NAIVE, *adjective*   believing, callow, childish, childlike, credulous, deceivable, deludable, dupable, exploitable, foolable, green, gullible, immature, inexperienced, innocent, natural, open, plain, provincial, simple, *simplex,* trusting, unaffected, unfeigned, unschooled, unsophisticated, unsuspecting, unsuspicious, unworldly, void of suspicion

NAKED *(Lacking embellishment), adjective*   bare, basal, basic, devoid of consideration, elementary, fundamental, laid bare, mere, plain, sheer, simple, stark, straight, unadorned, unadulterated, uncomplicated, undecorated, undisguised, unembellished, unexaggerated, unmasked, unornamented, unvarnished, unveiled
ASSOCIATED CONCEPTS: naked promise

NAKED *(Perceptible),* **adjective**   apparent, brought to light, clear, cognizable, conspicuous, discernible, disclosed, discoverable, distinct, distinguishable, easy to see, evident, explicit, exposed, express, in plain view, made public, manifest, not obscure, noticeable, observable, obvious, open, ostensible, overt, patent, perceivable, plain, prominent, recognizable, revealed, unconcealed, unmistakable, visible

NARCOTIC, *adjective*   anesthetic, anodyne, anodynous, assuaging, assuasive, calmant, calmative, deadening, depressant, dulling, hypnotic, mitigating, narcotical, opiate, pain-killing, palliative, paregoric, sedative, slumberous, somniferous, somnific, soothing, soporiferous, soporific, stupefactive, torporifc, tranquilizing

NARCOTIC, *noun*   alleviative, alleviator, anesthetic, anodyne, assuasive drug, barbiturate, calmative, depressant, dope, drug, hypnotic, lenitive, medication, medicine, mitigative, opiate, pain reliever, painkiller, palliative, sedative, somnifacient, soother, soporific, stupefacient, tranquilizer

NARRATION, *noun*   account, chronicle, delineation, depiction, depictment, description, descriptive account, discourse, disquisition, *expositio,* exposition, iteration, *narratio,* narrative, portrayal, recapitulation, recital, recitation, recountal, recounting, reiteration, relation, rendition, repetition, report, representation, restatement, retelling, review, setting forth, sketch, storytelling, summarization, summary, tale, tale telling

NARRATIVE, *adjective*   anecdotal, communicative, declarative, declaratory, descriptive, detailed, disquisitional, epic, exegetic, exegetical, explanatory, explicative, explicatory, expositive, expository, graphic, illuminating, illuminative, illustrative, informational, informative, *narrare,* recounted, reported, sequential, storylike, told
ASSOCIATED CONCEPTS: narrative testimony

NARROW, *adjective*   attenuated, bigoted, circumscribed, compressed, confined, contracted, *contractus,* cramped, defined, dogmatic, exact, fanatical, fine, illiberal, incapacious, intolerant, limited, literal, narrow-minded, opinionated, parochial, pinched, precise, provincial, restricted, rigid, simple, strict, tapering, thin
ASSOCIATED CONCEPTS: narrow interpretation

NASCENCY, *noun*   beginning, birth, commencement, creation, debut, development, emergence, entrance, entry, evolution, evolvement, first appearance, first stage, first step, formation, foundation, founding, genesis, inauguration, inception, inchoation, incipience, incipiency, incunabula, induction, infancy, initiation, introduction, invention, launching, nascence, nativity, onset, origin, origination, outset, rise, start, starting

NATIONAL, *adjective*   affecting the nation as a whole, common, country-wide, domestic, established by the federal government, federal, general, government, government-owned, governmental, public, publicly owned, societal, sovereign

NATIONALITY, *noun*   allegiance, birth, body politic, citizenry, commonwealth, country, fatherland, habitancy, homeland, inhabitancy, inhabitation, nation, national group, national status, native land, nativity, origin, people, polity, populace, society, sovereign state, statehood, stock
ASSOCIATED CONCEPTS: immigration and naturalization

NATIONALIZE, *verb*   appropriate for federal use, appropriate for government use, make national, make national in character, place under government control, remove from private ownership, seize for public use, seize for the government, socialize, transfer control to the government, transfer ownership to the government

NATIVE *(Domestic),* **adjective**   aboriginal, autochthonal, autochthonic, autochthonous, domestic, enchorial, enchoric, endemic, endemical, home-grown, indigenous, local, locally born, not alien, not foreign, original, regional, unborrowed, vernacular

NATIVE *(Inborn),* **adjective**   basic, born, congenital, connate, connatural, essential, fundamental, genetic, hereditary, inbred, indigenous, ingenerate, ingenit, ingrained, inherent, inherited, innate, instinctive, instinctual, intrinsic, natal, natural, organic, original

NATURAL, *adjective*   artless, authentic, characteristic, connate, consistent, crude, free from affectation, fundamental, genuine, inborn, inbred, indigenous, ingenerate, ingrained, innate, *innatus,* instinctive, instinctual, lifelike, native, *nativus,* normal, organic, original, pure, real, realistic, regular, true to life, typical, unadulterated, unartificial, uncultivated, unsynthetic, untouched
ASSOCIATED CONCEPTS: natural law

NATURALIZE *(Acclimate),* **verb**   accommodate, accustom, adapt, adjust, assimilate, become habituated, cultivate a habit, familiarize, fit the pattern, get used to, habituate, harmonize, inure, learn a habit, make easy, make natural, normalize, regularize

NATURALIZE *(Make a citizen),* **verb**   accept as a citizen, admit citizenship, adopt, adopt as a citizen, adopt into a nation, assimilate, citizenize, confer privileges of a native citizen, confer rights of citizenship, denizenize, endow with rights of citizenship, extend citizenship to an alien, *homini civitatem dare,* nationalize, place in the condition of natural born subjects

NEBULOUS, *adjective*   abstruse, ambiguous, bleared, blurred, blurry, clouded, cloudy, confused, dim, dusky, faint, foggy, hazy, ill-defined, imperspicuous, indeterminate, indistinct, lacking clarity, nebulose, *nebulosus,* not clear, obfuscated, obscure, out of focus, pale, recondite, shadowed, shadowy, uncertain, unclear, undefined, undiscernible, unintelligible, vague
ASSOCIATED CONCEPTS: nebulous contract

NECESSARY *(Inescapable),* **adjective**   avoidless, certain, choiceless, compelling, constraining, decided, decreed, designated, destined, expected, fated, fateful, fixed, foreordained, imminent, impending, ineluctable, ineludible, inevitable, inexorable, irresistible, irrevocable, ordained, sealed, settled, sure, unalterable, unavoidable, uncontrollable, undeniable, unevasible, unpreventable

ASSOCIATED CONCEPTS: necessary damages, necessary expenses, necessary implication, necessary inference, necessary injury

NECESSARY *(Required), adjective*   all-important, basic, binding, bounden, chief, coercive, compelling, compulsory, critical, crucial, demanded, dictated, essential, exigent, expedient, fundamental, imperative, important, imposed, incumbent, indispensable, integral, key, mandatory, necessitated, necessitous, needed, obligatory, paramount, prerequisite, prescribed, prime, principal, requisite, requisitioned, significant, strategic, strategical, substantive, urgent, vital
ASSOCIATED CONCEPTS: necessary parties

NECESSARY, *noun*   essence, essential, essentiality, indispensable thing, *necessitas,* necessities, necessitousness, necessitude, necessity, need, prerequirement, prerequisite, qualification, requirement, requisite, vitals
ASSOCIATED CONCEPTS: duty to provide necessaries, necessaries of life

NECESSITATE, *verb*   call for, clamor for, coerce, *cogere,* compel, concuss, create a need, decree, demand, dictate, enjoin, exact, force, impel, impose, insist upon, leave no choice, leave no option, make indispensable, make inevitable, make necessary, make unavoidable, obligate, oblige, ordain, predetermine, raise a demand, render necessary, require

NECESSITY, *noun*   absolute requisite, basic ingredient, central element, characteristic feature, compelling quality, compulsory detail, crucial part, *egestas,* elementary detail, essential, essential element, exigency, fundamental, fundamental principle, fundamental unit, highly important detail, imperative, indispensable, indispensable provision, inevitable, integral part, irreplaceable feature, irresistible compulsion, main ingredient, mandatory factor, necessary attribute, necessary component, *necessitas,* need, precondition, prerequirement, prerequisite, primary constituent, qualification, recognized condition, required item, requirement, requisite, rudiment, significant detail, strategic item, urgency, urgent requirement, vital part, vitals
ASSOCIATED CONCEPTS: compelling necessity, economic necessity, finding of necessity, prescription by necessity, public necessity, strict necessity
FOREIGN PHRASES: *Quod est necessarium est licitum.* That which is necessary is lawful. *Necessitas excusat aut extenuat delictum in capitalibus, quod non operatur idem in civilibus.* Necessity excuses or extenuates an offense in capital cases, but not in civil cases. *Necessitas est lex temporis et loci.* Necessity is the law of a particular time and place. *Lex judicat de rebus necessario faciendis quasi re ipsa factis.* The law judges of things which must necessarily be done as if they were actually done. *Necessitas inducit privilegium quoad jura privata.* Necessity gives a privilege with reference to private rights. *Necessitas publica major est quam privata.* Public necessity is greater than private.

NECTARIOUS, *adjective*   candied, cloying, delectable, delicious, dulcet, honeyed, luscious, melliferous, oversweet, rich, saccharine, sugary, sweet, tasty

NEED *(Deprivation), noun*   absence, dearth, deficiency, deficit, demand, exigency, extremity, inadequacy, incompleteness, indigence, insufficiency, lack,

necessitousness, necessitude, necessity, paucity, penury, privation, scantiness, scarcity, shortage, shortness of supply, thirst, vacuum, want, wantage

NEED *(Requirement), noun*   compulsion, compulsory detail, crucial part, demand, desideration, desideratum, essential element, essentiality, essentialness, fundamental, highly important detail, indispensability, indispensable provision, integral part, irreplaceability, irreplaceable feature, mandatory factor, necessary, necessary attribute, necessary component, necessity, obligation, precondition, preliminary condition, prequisiteness, prerequirement, proviso, required item, requisite, requisiteness, strategic item, urgency, urgent requirement, vital part, vitalness

NEED, *verb*   claim, clamor for, crave, cry for, demand, desire, exact, feel the necessity for, feel the want of, find indispensable, find necessary, have an urge for, have need for, have occasion for, have use of, hunger for, long for, lust for, miss, require, thirst for, want, yearn for

NEEDLESS, *adjective*   avoidable, beside the point, causeless, dispensable, excess, excessive, exorbitant, expendable, expletive, extra, extraneous, fruitless, futile, gratuitous, groundless, inordinate, irrelevant, *non necessarius,* noncompulsory, nonessential, optional, overabundant, overmuch, overplentiful, oversufficient, pleonastic, prodigal, redundant, spare, superabundant, supererogatory, superfluous, supernumerary, supervenient, surplus, unavailing, uncalled-for, undesirable, unessential, unnecessary, unneeded, unprofitable, unrequired, unrewarding, unwanted, useless, valueless, wanton, wasteful, worthless

NEFARIOUS, *adjective*   abominable, arrant, bad, base, confounded, contemptible, corrupt, criminal, degenerate, deplorable, depraved, despicable, detestable, devilish, diabolical, discreditable, disgraceful, dishonorable, dissolute, dreadful, evil, execrable, felonious, flagitious, flagrant, foul, gross, hateful, heinous, horrible, ignoble, immoral, impious, improper, indecent, infamous, infernal, iniquitous, malignant, miscreant, monstrous, *nefarius,* obnoxious, odious, outrageous, peccant, pernicious, profligate, reprehensible, reprobate, scandalous, shameful, sinful, sinister, terrible, treacherous, unrighteous, vile, villainous, wicked, wrong

NEGATE, *verb*   abnegate, abolish, abort, abrogate, annihilate, annul, cancel, confound, confute, contradict, contravene, controvert, counter, counteract, countermand, counterpoise, declare invalid, declare null and void, defeat, demur, deny, deprive of force, destroy, disaffirm, disallow, disavow, disclaim, discontinue, discredit, disprove, dispute, disregard, explain away, falsify, impugn, invalidate, negative, neutralize, nullify, object, obliterate, offset, oppose, override, overrule, overthrow, prohibit, protest, prove the contrary, quash, rebut, recant, refute, render null and void, renounce, repeal, repudiate, rescind, retract, reverse, revoke, rule out, set aside, suppress, suspend, traverse, vacate, veto

NEGATION, *noun*   abjuration, abnegation, abolishment, abolition, abrogation, annulment, cancellation, cassation, confutation, contradiction, contravention, declination, declinature, defiance, denial, disaffirmation, disagreement, disapprobation, disapproval, disavowal, disclaimer, disproof, dissent, forswearing, gainsay, gainsaying, *infitiatio,* invalidation, *negatio,* nonacceptance, nonagreement, noncompliance, nonconsent, noncorroboration, nullification, objection, opposition, protest, protestation, recantation, refusal, refutation, rejection, repeal, repudiation, rescission, resistance, retractation, retraction, reversal, revocation, revokement, traversal

ASSOCIATED CONCEPTS: negation of warranty

NEGATIVE, *adjective* acrimonious, antagonistic, antipathetic, antipathetical, argumentative, at odds with, attacking, averse, belligerent, bickering, cantankerous, clashing, conflicting, confutative, contentious, contesting, contradictory, contrary, contrasted, contrasting, contravening, converse, counteractive, countering, demurring, denying, disaccordant, disavowing, discordant, disobliging, disputing, dissentient, dissident, factious, fractious, gainsaying, hostile, ill-willed, impugning, incompatible, inimical, inverse, *negans,* negatory, opposed, opposing, opposite, quarrelsome, rancorous, rebuffing, rebutting, refuting, rejecting, repudiating, repugnant, resistive, reverse, spurning, traversing, unaffirmative, unconverted, unconvinced

ASSOCIATED CONCEPTS: negative covenant, negative easement, negative evidence, negative testimony

NEGLECT, *noun* abandonment, absentmindedness, breach, bungling, careless abandon, carelessness, default, delinquency, dereliction, disregard, failure, heedlessness, idleness, improvidence, imprudence, inaction, inadvertence, inattention, inattentiveness, *incuria,* indifference, indiligence, *indiligentia,* inexecution, inexertion, laches, laxity, laxness, misprision, *neglegentia,* negligence, noncompletion, noncompliance, nonfeasance, nonfulfillment, nonobservance, nonperformance, omission, oversight, procrastination, prodigality, rashness, recklessness, remissness, slackness, slight, sloth, slovenliness, thoughtlessness, unactivity, unalertness, unconcern, unconscientiousness, unheedfulness, unmindfulness, unobservance, unwariness, unwatchfulness

ASSOCIATED CONCEPTS: culpable neglect, neglect of duty, neglect to act, neglect to prosecute, willful neglect
FOREIGN PHRASES: *Magna culpa dolus est.* Gross neglect is the equivalent of fraud.

NEGLECT, *verb* be careless, be inattentive, be lax, *deserere,* disdain, disregard, fail, forget, gloss over, ignore, *intermittere,* lay aside, leave alone, lose sight of, *neglegere,* not care for, not use, omit, overlook, pass by, pass over, pay no attention, pay no heed to, pay no regard to, pretermit, procrastinate, refuse to recognize, shirk, shun, skip, slight, take no note, take no notice

NEGLIGENCE, *noun* abandonment, breach of duty, carelessness, culpa, delinquency, dereliction, disregard, failure, heedlessness, improvidence, imprudence, inadvertence, inadvertency, inattention, inattentiveness, incautiousness, incircumspection, inconsideration, *incuria,* indifference, *indiligentia,* inobservance, irresponsibility, lack of attention, lack of diligence, laxity, laxness, neglectfulness, *neglegentia,* obliviousness, omission, oversight, recklessness, regardlessness, remissness, slackness, unalertness, unconcern, unmindfulness, unobservance, unwariness, unwatchfulness, want of thought

ASSOCIATED CONCEPTS: actionable negligence, active negligence, assumption of risk, causal negligence, comparative negligence, concurrent negligence, contributory negligence, criminal negligence, culpable negligence, estoppel by negligence, gross negligence, imputed negligence, last clear chance doctrine, malpractice, negligence per se, ordinary negligence, passive negligence, *res ipsa loquitur,* standard of care, supervening negligence, wanton negligence, willful negligence
FOREIGN PHRASES: *Magna negligentia culpa est; magna culpa dolus est.* Gross negligence is fault; gross fault is equivalent to a fraud. *Culpa lata dolo aequiparatur.* Gross negligence is equivalent to intentional wrong.

NEGLIGENT, *adjective* bungling, careless, delinquent, derelict, disregardant, disregardful, heedless, ill-considered, improvident, imprudent, inadvertent, inattentive, incautious, indifferent, *indiligens,* injudicious, inobservant, irresponsible, lax, mindless, neglectful, *neglegens,* oblivious, off guard, rash, reckless, regardless, remiss, *remissus,* slack, slipshod, slothful, slovenly, temerarious, temerous, thoughtless, unalert, uncalculating, uncircumspect, unconcerned, undiligent, unheedful, unheeding, unmindful, unthinking, unthorough, unwary, unwatchful

ASSOCIATED CONCEPTS: negligent act, negligent conduct, negligent injury

NEGLIGIBLE, *adjective* beneath notice, dispensable, expendable, immaterial, imperceptible, inappreciable, inconsequential, inconsiderable, insignificant, insubstantial, irrelevant, *levis,* light, little, meager, minor, minute, moderate, modest, nominal, nugatory, of little account, of little consequence, of little importance, of no moment, of no significance, paltry, picayune, poor, puny, scant, scanty, slight, small, *tenuis,* trifling, trivial, unessential, unimportant, unnoteworthy, unsubstantial, unworthy of regard, valueless
FOREIGN PHRASES: *De minimis non curat lex.* The law pays no attention to insignificant things.

NEGOTIABLE, *adjective* alienable, assignable, capable of being transferred, consignable, conveyable, exchangeable, interchangeable, maneuverable, marketable, salable, transferable, transmissible, transmittible, vendible

ASSOCIATED CONCEPTS: commercial paper, negotiable contract, negotiable instruments, promissory note

NEGOTIATE, *verb* accommodate, arbitrate, arrange for, bargain, bid for, bring to terms, come to terms, dicker, haggle, hurdle, intercede, intermediate, make peace, make terms, mediate, meet halfway, parley, referee, settle, settle disputes, straighten out, surmount, transact, umpire, work out

NEGOTIATION, *noun* arbitrament, arbitration, bargaining, compromise, conference, *conloquium,* consultation, contract talks, deliberation, dickering, diplomacy, discussion, exchange of views, haggling, mediation, parley, summitry, treaty-making

ASSOCIATED CONCEPTS: collective bargaining, preliminary negotiation

NEOPHYTE, *noun* abecedarian, amateur, apprentice, beginner, catechumen, debutant, entrant, fledgling, freshman, learner, newcomer, novice, prentice, pupil, student, tenderfoot, trainee, tyro

NEPOTISM, *noun* bias, corruptibility, corruption, family patronage, favor, favoritism, inequitableness, inequity, injustice, interest, leaning, partiality, partisanism, partisanship, patronage, preferential treatment, undetachment, unfairness, unjustness

NESCIENCE, *noun* blindness, darkness, greenness, ignorance, ignoration, incognizance, inexperience, lack of awareness, lack of knowledge, lack of learning, naivete, rawness, unawareness, uncomprehension, unenlightenment, uninformedness, unintelligence, unknowingness, unlearnedness

NET, *adjective* clear, irreducible, leftover, remaining, residual, residuary, surplus, surviving, unexpended, unspent
ASSOCIATED CONCEPTS: net assets, net balance, net capital stock, net earnings, net estate, net income, net loss, net premium, net price, net proceeds, net profit, net rents, net revenues, net value, net worth

NEUTRAL, *adjective* disengaged, disinterested, dispassionate, equitable, fair, fair-minded, impartial, impersonal, independent, indifferent, isolationist, *medius, neutrius partis,* nonaligned, nonbelligerent, noncombatant, noncommittal, noninterfering, noninterventionist, nonparticipant, nonparticipating, nonpartisan, objective, pacific, pacifistic, peaceable, peaceful, unaffected, unbiased, unbigoted, uncommitted, unconcerned, uninfluenced, uninvolved, unjaundiced, unprejudiced, unprepossessed, unswayed
ASSOCIATED CONCEPTS: neutral property

NEUTRALITY, *noun* aloofness, detachment, disinterest, disinterestedness, dispassionateness, impartiality, indifference, moderateness, neutralism, nonbelligerence, noncombatance, noninterference, nonintervention, nonparticipance, nonparticipation, nonpartisanship

NEUTRALIZE, *verb* annul, balance, cancel, cancel out, counterbalance, counterpoise, countervail, deactivate, deaden, demagnetize, destroy the effect of, disable, disenable, equalize, incapacitate, invalidate, make ineffective, negate, nullify, offset, render inert, render inoperative, render neutral, vitiate

NEXT OF KIN, *noun* blood kindred, blood relation, blood relative, close relative, collateral relative, consanguineal relations, family, family connection, family tie, individual's nearest relative, kin, kindred, kinsman, kinspeople, near relation, nearest blood relation, nearest relative by blood, related by affinity, relation by blood, relations, relatives
ASSOCIATED CONCEPTS: decedent's estate, heirs

NEXUS, *noun* affiliation, alliance, association, attachment, bond, bridge, connecting link, connection, connective, coupling, interconnection, intermedium, interrelation, kinship, liaison, link, privity, relation, relationship, thread, tie, union, vinculum

NOISE, *noun* ado, blare, blatancy, cacophony, charivari, clamor, clamorousness, clangor, clatter, cry, detonation, din, discord, fanfare, fracas, harsh sound, hubbub, hullabaloo, jangle, loudness, outcry, pandemonium, racket, ruckus, ruction, *sonitus,* sound, stir, *strepitus,* tumult, unpleasant sound, uproar, uproariousness, vociferance, vociferation

ASSOCIATED CONCEPTS: disturbing the peace, noise pollution, nuisance

NOLLO CONTENDERE, *noun* acceptance of penalty, admission of the facts, plea, settlement

NOLLO PROSEQUI, *noun* abrogation, cancellation, counter order, countermand, reversal, reversion

NOMINAL, *adjective* cheap, cut-rate, hardly worth mention, honorary, in name only, inconsiderable, inexpensive, insignificant, little, low, low-priced, meager, meaningless, minimum, minute, moderate, modest, negligible, *nomine,* petty, reduced, scanty, simple, slight, small, superficial, symbolic, titular, titulary, token, trifling, trivial, unactual, unimportant, unsubstantial
ASSOCIATED CONCEPTS: nominal capital, nominal consideration, nominal damages, nominal defendant, nominal owner, nominal parties, nominal plaintiff, nominal value

NOMINATE, *verb* appoint, assign, call, choose, commission, constitute, denominate, *designare,* designate, designate for appointment, designate for election, *dicere,* draft, engage, entitle, install, label, name, name for office, *nominare,* ordain, ordinate, place in authority, place in command, place in office, propose, propose as a candidate, put up, select, specify, style, suggest, tag, title, vote into office

NOMINATION, *noun* appointment, assignment, authorization, choice, choosing, delegation, denomination, deputization, *designatio,* designation, election, naming, *nominatio,* ordainment, ordination, proposal, selection

NOMINEE *(Candidate), noun* chosen representative, flag bearer, named representative, political representative, selection

NOMINEE *(Delegate), noun* appointee, consignee, licensee, representative, selectee, trustee

NON COMPOS MENTIS, *adjective* abnormal, bereft of reason, crazed, crazy, declared insane, defective, demented, deprived of one's wits, deranged, dim-witted, diseased in mind, disoriented, distraught, dull-witted, feeble-minded, idiotic, insane, insanely deluded, lunatic, mad, maddened, manic, maniacal, mental, mentally deficient, mentally diseased, mentally ill, mentally sick, mentally unsound, mindless, moronic, of unsound mind, out of one's mind, out of one's senses, out of one's wits, psychologically abnormal, psychopathic, psychotic, raving, senseless, simple-minded, unbalanced, unsettled, unsettled in one's mind, unsound, unstable, utterly senseless
ASSOCIATED CONCEPTS: insanity, lack of capacity

NON SEQUITUR, *noun* anacoluthon, bad logic, circular reasoning, contradiction of terms, disconnectedness, discontinuity, fallacious argument, fallacious reasoning, fallacy, false reasoning, flaw in the argument, illogical conclusion, illogical deduction, illogical result, inconsequence, irrational conclusion, irrelevancy, loose thinking, lost connection, nonsensicality, nonsensicalness, paralogism, sophism, sophistry, specious argument, specious reasoning, unfounded conclusion, unwarranted conclusion, wrong reasoning

NONAGE, *noun*   adolescence, childhood, early stage, immaturity, infancy, legal immaturity, legal minority, minority, period of legal immaturity, period of legal minority, tender age, youth

NONAPPEARANCE, *noun*   absence without leave, absentation, absenteeism, concealment, default, failure to appear, hiding, imperceptibility, indiscernibility, inexistence, invisibility, invisibleness, nonattendance, nonpresence, obscurity, truancy, unperceivability, unseeableness, vanishment

NONCANCELLABLE, *adjective*   abiding, durable, indelible, ineffaceable, irrepealable, irreversible, lasting, nonabolishable, nonannullable, nonerasable, nonrescindable, nonretractable, nonreversible, permanent, unchangeable, undestroyable, unquashable, unvoidable
ASSOCIATED CONCEPTS: noncancellable clause

NONCHALANT, *adjective*   *aequo animo,* apathetic, blase, calm, carefree, casual, collected, composed, cool, dispassionate, easygoing, impassive, imperturbable, indifferent, insouciant, inured, lacking enthusiasm, lacking interest, lacking warmth, lukewarm, offhand, passionless, pococurante, self-controlled, spiritless, studied, unaffected, unaroused, unblushing, uncaring, unconcerned, unenthusiastic, unexcited, unfeeling, unflappable, unimpassioned, unimpressed, uninterested, unmindful, unmoved, unruffled, unshocked, unspirited, unstirred, untouched, unworried

NONCOMMITTAL, *adjective*   careful, cautious, changeable, close, discreet, evasive, faltering, guarded, hedging, heedful, hesitant, hesitating, incommunicative, inconstant, indecisive, infirm of purpose, irresolute, irresolved, laconic, lukewarm, mutable, neutral, on guard, precautionary, precautious, prudent, reserved, reticent, secretive, silent, taciturn, unassured, uncertain, uncommitted, uncommunicative, undaring, undecided, unforthcoming, uninvolved, unresolved, unresponsive, unsettled, unsteadfast, unsteady, unsure, vacillating, vague, wary, watchful, wavering

NONCOMPLIANCE *(Improper completion),* *noun* deficient work, faulty work, inadequate final work, poor quality work, shabby work, wrong implementation
ASSOCIATED CONCEPTS: noncompliance with a judicial order

NONCOMPLIANCE *(Nonobservance),* *noun*   defiance, disloyalty, disregard of orders, non occurrence, nonconformity, refusal

NONCONFORMING, *adjective*   aberrant, alien, at odds with, at variance with, Bohemian, contrary, defiant, deviating, different, differing, disagreeing, disapproved, discordant, disobedient, dissentient, dissenting, dissident, dissimilar, distinct, distinguished, diversified, eccentric, exotic, heretical, incongruous, independent, irregular, lawless, nonadhering, noncompliant, nonobservant, nonuniform, original, out of line, out of step, peculiar, quaint, rare, remarkable, singular, solitary, special, unaccountable, unaccustomed, unadaptable, unadjustable, unclassifiable, uncommon, unconformable, unconventional, uncustomary, unexpected, unfashionable, unique, unordinary, unorthodox, unparalleled, unprecedented, unsubmissive, unusual, unwonted
ASSOCIATED CONCEPTS: nonconforming use

NONCONFORMITY, *noun*   aberration, abnormality, abnormity, anomalousness, anomaly, apostasy, bizarreness, Bohemianism, change, contrast, defiance, departure, deviation, difference, disagreement, disconformity, disobedience, disparity, dispute, dissent, dissidence, dissimilarity, distinctness, divergence, diverseness, diversity, eccentricity, exception, exceptionality, heresy, heterodoxy, heterogeneity, idiosyncrasy, incongruity, inconsistency, independence, individuality, irregularity, lack of agreement, nonagreement, nonconcurrence, nonuniformity, objection, originality, otherness, peculiarity, protest, protestation, recusancy, rejection, separateness, separatism, singularity, strangeness, unconformity, unconventionality, uniqueness, unlikeness, unorthodoxness, unorthodoxy, variance, variation, variety, veto

NONCONSENTING, *adjective*   critical, declinatory, defiant, disapproving, discontented, disobedient, disparaging, dissentient, dissenting, dissident, faultfinding, hostile, inacquiescent, insubordinate, intractable, nonconformant, noncontent, objecting, overcritical, protesting, recalcitrant, recusant, refusing, resistant, seditious, unapproving, uncomplying, unconsenting, unsubmissive, unwilling

NONCONTESTABLE, *adjective*   nonchallengeable, noncontrovertible, nondebatable, nondisputable, nonproblematical, nonquestionable, nonrefutable, undeniable, undoubtable, unquestionable
ASSOCIATED CONCEPTS: noncontestable clause

NONDESCRIPT, *adjective*   average, boring, characteristic, common, commonplace, conventional, difficult to classify, difficult to describe, dull, everyday, familiar, hackneyed, homely, indescribable, insipid, mediocre, middling, not extraordinary, not odd, not singular, not special, not unique, ordinary, pedestrian, plain, prosaic, stock, trite, typical, unadorned, unclassifiable, undistinguished, unenlivened, unexceptional, unexciting, unidentifiable, uninteresting, unremarkable, usual

NONENTITY, *noun*   blank, cipher, existenceless, figurehead, inexistence, insignificance, insignificancy, insubstantiality, matter of no consequence, matter of no importance, *nihil,* no one, nobody, nonbeing, nonexistence, nothing, nothingness, nought, nullity, *terrae filius,* unsubstantiality, unsubstantialness

NONESSENTIAL, *adjective*   accessory, added, additional, adscititious, auxiliary, avoidable, beside the point, beside the question, dispensable, excess, expendable, extra, extraneous, extrinsic, extrinsical, frivolous, gratuitous, incidental, inconsequential, inessential, insignificant, minor, needless, negligible, of little consequence, of little importance, of no account, of no concern, of no consequence, of no importance, of no significance, of small importance, optional, parenthetic, parenthetical, peripheral, redundant, spare, supererogatory, superfluous, supervenient, supplemental, supplementary, trifling, trivial, uncalled for, unessential, ungermane, unimportant, unnecessary, unneeded, unnoteworthy, unrequired, unwarranted
ASSOCIATED CONCEPTS: nonessential services

NONEXISTENT, *adjective*   chimerical, fancied, fantastic, fantastical, hallucinatory, hypothetical, ideal, illusory, imaginary, imagined, inexistent, leg-

endary, notional, theoretical, unborn, uncreated, unexisting, unreal, visionary

NONFEASANCE, noun delinquency, dereliction,
disregard, disregard of duty, failure, inattention, indifference, laxity, misprision, neglect of duty, negligence,
nonfulfillment, nonperformance, omission

NONMILITANT, adjective accommodative, agreeable, amicable, appeasable, conciliable, conciliative,
conciliatory, concordant, forgiving, gentle, halcyon,
irenic, irenical, meek, neutral, nonaggresive, noncombatant, noncombative, nonviolent, pacificatory, pacifistic, peace-loving, peaceable, peaceful, placable, placative, propitiable, propitiatory, tolerant, unaggressive,
unbellicose, unbelligerent, uncontentious, unhostile,
unmilitant, unpugnacious, unwarlike

NONPARTISAN, adjective autonomous, broad-
minded, detached, disengaged, equitable, evenhanded,
fair, fair-minded, impartial, independent, judicious,
latitudinarian, moderate, neutral, nonaligned, objective, self-determined, self-directing, self-governing,
sovereign, unbiased, unbigoted, uncommitted, uncompelled, unforced, uninduced, uninfluenced, unprejudiced, unswayed, unwarped

NONPAYMENT, noun bad debt, balance due, default, deferred payment, delinquency, dishonor, dishonored bill, evasion, failure, failure to pay, lapse, neglect,
outstanding debt, oversight, refusal to pay, repudiation,
unpaid dues
ASSOCIATED CONCEPTS: nonpayment of rent

NONPERFORMANCE, noun avoidance, breach of
promise, default, delinquency, dereliction of duty, disregard, dutilessness, evasion, evasion of duty, failure to
perform, idleness, inactivity, inexecution, laxity, neglect, negligence, noncompletion, noncompliance, noncooperation, nonfeasance, nonfulfillment, nonpractice,
omission, truancy, unduteousness, undutifulness, unfulfillment
ASSOCIATED CONCEPTS: nonperformance of a contract,
nonperformance of a duty

NONPROFIT, adjective altruistic, beneficent, benevolent, charitable, eleemosynary, humanitarian, munificent, philanthropic, public service
ASSOCIATED CONCEPTS: nonprofit corporation

NONRESIDENCE, noun absence, nondomicile,
nonhabitancy, nonhabitation, noninhabitance, noninhabitancy, nonoccupance, nonoccupancy, nonoccupation, nonpresence, nontenancy

NONSECTARIAN, adjective all-comprehensive,
all-embracing, all-including, all-inclusive, broad,
broad-based, collective, comprehensive, ecumenical,
general, global, interdenominational, mixed, undenominational, universal, unspecified, world-wide

NONSUBSTANTIAL *(Not sturdy)*, **adjective** adynamic, asthenic, attenuated, below par, breakable, brittle, defective, deficient, delicate, destructible, enervated, ephemeral, fallacious, feeble, flimsy, fragile,
frail, frangible, ghostly, illogical, inadequate, infirm,
intangible, lame, limp, mediocre, perishable, powerless,
slight, sorry, strengthless, tenuous, unearthly, ungrounded, unsolid, unsound, unstable, unsturdy, unsubstantial, untenable, weak, weakly, without force,
without foundation, wobbly

NONSUBSTANTIAL *(Not sufficient)*, **adjective**
deficient, depleted, deprived, disappointing, drained,
inadequate, incomplete, insignificant, insubstantial,
lacking, low, meager, niggardly, paltry, scant, scanty,
scarce, stingy, thin, too little, too small, unacceptable,
ungratifying, unsatisfactory, unsatisfying, unsufficing,
wanting

NONSUIT, noun defeat, directed verdict, failure to
establish a cause of action, failure to make a case, failure to meet the burden of proof, failure to present sufficient evidence, hostile verdict, insufficiency as a matter
of law, insufficient evidence, judgment for the defendant as a matter of law, termination of an action
ASSOCIATED CONCEPTS: compulsory nonsuit, discontinuance, dismissal, involuntary nonsuit, motion for
nonsuit, voluntary nonsuit

NONTOXIC, adjective benign, harmless, hurtless,
innocent, innocuous, innoxious, inoffensive, nonfatal,
nonirritating, nonlethal, nonmalignant, nonpoisonous,
nonvenomous, nonvirulent, not baneful, not dangerous,
not deadly, not deleterious, not pernicious, not toxiferous, safe, undestructive, unhazardous, uninjurious, unobjectionable, without risk

NONUSE, noun abeyance, absence, abstinence,
desuetude, disusage, disuse, forebearance, neglect, nonemployment, nonutilization, suspension

NORM, noun average, general performance, generality, habit, median, midpoint, model, mold, ordinary
run, pattern, point of comparison, regular performance,
rule, standard, typical performance

NORMAL *(Regular)*, **adjective** according to rule,
average, common, commonplace, conforming, conventional, customary, established, everyday, habitual, natural, orderly, ordinary, representative, routine, standard, standardized, true to form, typical, unexceptional,
unvarying, usual
ASSOCIATED CONCEPTS: normal conditions, normal
course of business, normal use

NORMAL *(Sane)*, **adjective** fit, logical, lucid, mentally sound, of sound judgment, rational, reasonable,
responsible, sensible, sound, temperate

NOSCITUR A SOCIIS, adverb comprehended
from accompanying words, perceived from accompanying words, realized from accompanying words, recognized from accompanying words, understood from accompanying words

NOT GUILTY, adjective above suspicion, blameless, clean-handed, exculpable, faultless, free from
guilt, guilt-free, guiltless, impeccable, incorrupt, inculpable, innocent, not responsible, sinless, unblemished,
unimpeachable, uninvolved
ASSOCIATED CONCEPTS: plea of not guilty

NOTABLE, adjective above par, acclaimed, astonishing, atypical, awe-inspiring, awesome, celebrated,
conspicuous, distinguished, eminent, exceptional, extraordinary, famed, famous, foremost, illustrious, important, impressive, leading, luminous, marked, memorable, momentous, momumental, newsworthy, *notabilis,* noted, noteworthy, outstanding, preeminent,
prime, prominent, rare, remarkable, rememberable, renowned, salient, signal, significant, singular, special,

striking, superior, talked of, top-rank, transcendent, unforgettable, worthy of notice, worthy of remark

NOTARIZE, *verb* accord one's approval, accredit, affirm, affix a legal signature, affix one's signature to, approve, attach a legal signature, attest to, authenticate, authorize, bear witness, certify, confirm, confirm officially, evidence, legalize, make valid, pronounce legal, seal, set one's hand and seal, sign, sign and seal, sign legally, subscribe, undersign, validate, witness

NOTARY PUBLIC, *noun* attestor of documents, clerk of the court, commissioner of oaths, functionary, indorser, notary, official, recorder, register, registerer, registrar, *scriba,* scribe, scrivener, subscriber

NOTATION, *noun* annotation, chronicle, comment, commentary, entry, footnote, inscription, marginalia, memorandum, minute, note, record, register

NOTE *(Brief comment),* **noun** abstract, *adnotatio,* annotation, billet, brief, *codicilli,* comment, commentary, communication, dispatch, entry, *epistula,* exegesis, explanatory comment, explanatory remark, footnote, gloss, marginal annotation, memorandum, message, minute, missive, record, reminder, scholium, short letter, statement, word of explanation
ASSOCIATED CONCEPTS: note of issue

NOTE *(Written promise to pay),* **noun** bond, check, debenture, draft, money order, negotiable instrument, negotiable paper, voucher
ASSOCIATED CONCEPTS: accommodation note, bank note, bearer notes, cognovit note, commercial paper, negotiable note, promissory note, treasury note

NOTE *(Notice),* **verb** acknowledge, advert to, apperceive, appreciate, attend, be attentive, become aware, become conscious, cognize, direct attention to, discern, discover, fix attention on, give attention to, hearken to, heed, look at, make out, mark, mind, observe, pay attention to, pay heed to, perceive, realize, regard, see, take account of, take cognizance of, take notice, turn attention to, watch, witness

NOTE *(Record),* **verb** *adnotare,* annotate, calendar, catalogue, chronicle, commit to writing, docket, document, enregister, enter, jot down, keep accounts, log, make a memorandum, make an entry, mark, mark down, pen, put in writing, put on paper, put on record, scribe, set down, take down, write, write down

NOTEWORTHY, *adjective* above par, amazing, anomalous, astonishing, astounding, atypical, bizarre, breathtaking, celebrated, choice, commanding, considerable, conspicuous, curious, different, distinctive, distinguished, egregious, eminent, especial, excellent, exceptional, extraordinary, extreme, famous, fantastic, foremost, idiosyncratic, illustrious, important, impressive, incredible, individual, individualistic, infrequent, leading, main, marked, material, memorable, momentous, monumental, newsworthy, notable, noticeable, novel, odd, original, out of the ordinary, outstanding, paramount, peculiar, peerless, pertinent, phenomenal, preeminent, principal, prodigious, prominent, queer, rare, remarkable, renowned, salient, signal, significant, singular, special, standing out, stirring, strange, surprising, telling, uncommon, uncustomary, unequaled, unfamiliar, unforgettable, unheard of, un-

imitated, unique, unparalleled, unprecedented, unusual, wonderful, wondrous, worthy of notice, worthy of remark

NOTICE *(Announcement),* **noun** bulletin, circular, communication, communique, declaration, decree, *denuntiatio,* disclosure, dispatch, enlightenment, enunciation, flier, information, memorandum, mention, message, news, note, notification, presentation, proclamation, *promulgatio,* pronouncement, publicity, release, reminder, report, revelation, statement
ASSOCIATED CONCEPTS: legal notice, notice of appeal, notice of appearance, notice of claim, notice of motion, notice of protest, public notice
FOREIGN PHRASES: *Notitia dicitur a noscendo; et notitia non debet claudicare.* Notice is named from a knowledge being had; and notice ought not to be imperfect.

NOTICE *(Heed),* **noun** absorption, advertence, advertency, alertness, *animadversio,* attention, attentiveness, care, careful attention, carefulness, cautel, caution, cautiousness, circumspection, cognizance, consideration, discernment, engrossment, guard, heedfulness, mindfulness, *notatio,* observance, observation, recognition, regard, regardfulness, scrutiny, surveillance, thought, vigil, vigilance, wariness, watch, watchfulness
ASSOCIATED CONCEPTS: judicial notice
FOREIGN PHRASES: *De minimis non curat lex.* The law is not concerned with trifling matters.

NOTICE *(Warning),* **noun** admonishment, admonition, caution, caveat, commination, communication, counsel, dehortation, *denuntiatio,* forewarning, monition, premonishment, prenotification, ultimatum
ASSOCIATED CONCEPTS: absence of notice, actual notice, adequate notice, constructive notice, due notice, explicit notice, express notice, implied notice, imputed notice, notice of disallowance, notice to appear, notice to vacate, proper notice, reasonable notice, requisite notice, timely notice, verified notice, written notice

NOTICE *(Give formal warning),* **verb** address a warning to, advise, apprise, communicate, convey knowledge to, *denuntiatio,* direct attention to, disclose, divulge, entrust with information, forewarn, formally advise, give fair warning, give information, give warning, impart knowledge of, impart to, inform, instruct, make a formal proclamation, make acquainted with, make an announcement, make known, make mention of, make public, notify, offer a word of caution, pass on information, *promulgatio,* publish, put on one's guard, reveal, warn
ASSOCIATED CONCEPTS: notice a deposition, notice a hearing

NOTICE *(Observe),* **verb** acknowledge, *animadvertere,* appreciate, ascertain, assess, attend to, be attentive, be conscious of, become aware of, become conscious of, behold, call attention to, cognize, comment, detect, discern, discover, distinguish, elucidate, examine closely, examine intently, give heed to, glance at, hear, heed, inspect, investigate, look, look at, mark, mention, *notatio,* note, observe, occupy oneself with, pass under review, pay attention, perceive, pore over, realize, recognize, regard, review, scrutinize, see, sight, spot, take cognizance, take into account, take into consideration, take stock of, view, watch, witness

NOTIFICATION, noun announcement, annunciation, aviso, bulletin, caution, communication, communique, declaration, *denuntiatio,* disclosure, dispatch, dissemination, divulgation, enlightenment, enunciation, evulgation, information, intelligence, intercommunication, knowledge, legal notice, mention, message, monition, news, notice, proclamation, *promulgatio,* promulgation, pronouncement, publicity, release, report, revelation, statement, transmission of knowledge, warning
ASSOCIATED CONCEPTS: due process, process of service, proper notification

NOTIFY, verb acquaint, advertise, advise, alert, announce, annunciate, apprise, break the news, brief, bring word, call attention to, caution, communicate, confide, contact, convey, counsel, declare, disclose, disseminate, divulge, enlighten, enunciate, exhort, forewarn, give notice, give the facts, give to understand, give warning, herald, impart, indicate, inform, instruct, issue a proclamation, issue a pronouncement, let know, make an announcement, make known, make public, mention, post, proclaim, promote, promulgate, propagate, publicize, publish, recount, relate, remind, report, reveal, serve notice, signal, signify, state, tell, tip off, transmit, warn
ASSOCIATED CONCEPTS: notify a defendant of charges pending, notify of an action pending

NOTION, noun abstraction, apprehension, belief, caprice, concept, conception, conviction, desire, estimation, fancy, feeling, humor, idea, impression, inclination, inkling, judgment, mental image, *notio,* opinion, sentiment, suggestion, supposition, *suspicio,* thought, understanding, vagary, view, whim

NOTORIETY, noun attaint, bad report, bad reputation, bad repute, bruit, celebrity, censure, conspicuousness, dedecoration, degradation, denunciation, disapprobation, discredit, disesteem, disfavor, disgrace, dishonor, disparagement, disreputability, disreputableness, disrepute, disrespect, distinction, eclat, eminence, *fama,* fame, famousness, flagrancy, ignominy, ignomy, ill repute, imputation, indignity, *infamia,* infamousness, infamy, ingloriousness, loss of honor, loss of reputation, name, notability, notedness, obloquy, odium, opprobrium, popular repute, popularity, prominence, public notice, publicity, recognition, renown, reproach, reputation, repute, scandal, shame, significance, slur, stigma, stigmatization, taint, unrespectability

NOTORIOUS, adjective arrant, blameworthy, celebrated, conspicuous, contemptible, degraded, deplorable, despised, discreditable, disgraceful, dishonorable, disreputable, disrespectable, egregious, famed, famous, flagrant, generally known, glaring, held in contempt, ignoble, ignominious, infamous, inglorious, *nobilis,* noted, *notus,* odious, of ill fame, of ill repute, opprobrious, outcast, outrageous, prominent, publicized, renowned, scandalous, shameful, shameless, shocking, unfavorably known, unrespectable, unseemly, unworthy of respect, villainous, without repute
ASSOCIATED CONCEPTS: notorious easement, notorious possession, open and notorious use

NOTWITHSTANDING, preposition all the same, although, despite, even, however, in any case, in any event, in spite of, nevertheless, none the less, still, yet

NOVATION, noun complete substitution, exchange, replacement, substitution
ASSOCIATED CONCEPTS: novation of a contract

NOVEL, adjective alien, anomalous, bizarre, different, distinctive, eccentric, exceptional, extraordinary, foreign, fresh, innovative, inusitate, irregular, modern, neoteric, neoterical, new, newly come, nonconformist, *novus,* odd, original, peculiar, quaint, rare, recent, singular, strange, uncharacteristic, uncommon, unconventional, uncustomary, unfamiliar, unheard of, unique, unordinary, unorthodox, unprecedented, untested, untried, unused, unusual, up-to-date, up-to-the-minute
ASSOCIATED CONCEPTS: novel question of law

NOVICE, noun amateur, apprentice, aspirant, beginner, catechumen, disciple, entrant, fledgling, freshman, hopeful, inexperienced person, initiate, learner, neophyte, new arrival, newcomer, probationer, pupil, recruit, rookie, *rudis,* student, trainee, tyro, unskilled person, untrained individual

NOW AND FOREVER, adverb evermore, for ever and ever, forever, forevermore

NOXIOUS, adjective adverse, bad, baleful, baneful, brutal, causing danger, contaminated, corrupting, damaging, dangerous, deleterious, destructive, detrimental, disadvantageous, fatal, fraught with danger, harmful, hazardous, hurtful, impairing, injurious, insalubrious, internecine, jeopardous, lethal, malefic, malicious, malignant, menacing, mischievous, nocent, noisome, offensive, perilous, pernicious, pestiferous, pestilent, poisonous, precarious, risky, ruinous, scatheful, threatening, toxic, unfavorable, unhealthy, unsafe, unwholesome, vicious, virulent

NUANCE, noun cast, degree, delicacy, difference, differentiation, discrimination, distinction, hidden meaning, implication, nicety, shade, shade of difference, shade of meaning, shadow, subtle difference, subtlety, suggestion, touch, variance

NUGATORY, adjective fatuous, frivolous, frothy, futile, immaterial, inadequate, inane, inapt, incompetent, inconsequential, ineffective, ineffectual, inefficacious, inept, inoperative, insignificant, insubstantial, inutile, invalid, irrelevant, jejune, *nugatorius,* null, null and void, otiose, paltry, petty, purposeless, slight, superficial, trifling, trivial, unavailing, unfruitful, unimportant, unproductive, unprofitable, unserviceable, useless, vain, valueless, void, worthless

NUISANCE, noun affliction, aggravation, annoyance, anxiety, bedevilment, bother, burden, cause of distress, devilment, difficult situation, difficulty, discomfort, displeasure, disturbance, grievance, handicap, harassment, hardship, hindrance, imposition, inconvenience, infliction, infringement, injurious interference, interference, intrusion, irritation, molestation, obstacle, ordeal, pain, pest, pestilence, plague, problem, scourge, trial, trouble, unlawful obstruction, unwarrantable intrusion, vexation, worry
ASSOCIATED CONCEPTS: abatement of a nuisance, attractive nuisance, common nuisance, continuing nuisance, nuisance at law, nuisance in fact, nuisance per se, public nuisance

FOREIGN PHRASES: *Aedificare in tuo proprio solo non licet quod alteri noceat.* It is not lawful to build upon one's own land what may injure another.

NULL *(Insignificant), adjective* beneath notice, dispensable, disregarded, empty, expendable, immaterial, impuissant, inappreciable, inconsequential, inconsiderable, inessential, inferior, insubstantial, insufficient, irrelevant, meaningless, minor, negligible, nominal, nugatory, of no account, of no effect, of no moment, of no value, paltry, peripheral, petty, pointless, powerless, puny, secondary, small, superficial, tenuous, token, trifling, trivial, unavailing, unessential, unimportant, uninfluential, unmeaningful, unnecessary, unsubstantial, useless, valueless, without consequence, without meaning, without significance, without substance, worthless

NULL *(Invalid), adjective* abolished, abrogated, annulled, canceled, dead, defeated, defunct, deleted, disannulled, disestablished, effectless, extinct, extinguished, forceless, gone, impotent, ineffective, ineffectual, inefficacious, inoperative, *inritus,* negated, no longer law, not valid, nugatory, nullified, obliterated, of no binding force, of no effect, of no validity, of no weight, omitted, overruled, powerless, quashed, repealed, rescinded, reversed, revoked, set aside, strengthless, superseded, suspended, unauthorized, unsanctioned, useless, vacated, valueless, void, withdrawn, without authority, without legal effect, without legal force, without potency, without value, worthless

NULL AND VOID, *adjective* abolished, abrogated, annulled, canceled, defeated, defunct, disannulled, disestablished, effectless, extinct, extinguished, forceless, impotent, ineffective, ineffectual, inefficacious, inoperative, invalid, negated, no longer law, not valid, nugatory, nullified, obliterated, of no binding force, of no effect, of no legal weight, of no validity, omitted, overruled, quashed, repealed, rescinded, reversed, revoked, set aside, strengthless, superseded, suspended, unauthorized, unsanctioned, useless, vacated, valueless, void, withdrawn, without authority, without legal effect, without legal force, without potency, without value, worthless

NULLIFY, *verb* abolish, abrogate, *ad inritum redigere,* annul, cancel, cast aside, counteract, countermand, declare null and void, deprive of efficacy, deprive of legal force, disannul, dissolve, invalidate, make useless, make valueless, make void, negate, neutralize, obliterate, offset, outweigh, override, overrule, overturn, quash, recall, recant, render invalid, renege, repeal, repudiate, rescind, retract, reverse, revoke, suspend, vacate, vitiate, void

NULLITY, *noun* blankness, *inanitas,* inefficacy, inexistence, insignificance, invalidity, naught, nihility, nonbeing, nonentity, nonexistence, nothing, nothingness, oblivion, vacuity, *vanitas,* void
ASSOCIATED CONCEPTS: decision to overrule decision

NUNC PRO TUNC, *noun* acknowledged, operative with respect to the past, ratified, reaffirmed, reconfirmed, reendorsed, reestablished, retroactive effect, retrospective effect, revalidated
ASSOCIATED CONCEPTS: nunc pro tunc order

NUNCUPATIVE, *adjective* articulated, conversational, conveyed orally, declared, dictated, enunciated, expressed in words, not written, oral, oral declaration, oral testimony, oratorical, parol, phonic, pronounced, spoken, stated, unwritten, uttered, verbal, vocal, voiced
ASSOCIATED CONCEPTS: nuncupative will

NUPTIAL, *adjective* allied, betrothed, bridal, conjugal, connubial, coupled, espoused, *genialis,* marital, married, mated, matrimonial, *nuptialis,* united, wedded
ASSOCIATED CONCEPTS: antenuptial agreement

NURTURE, *verb* advance, aid, assist, back, bolster, bring to maturity, bring up, care for, cherish, coach, cultivate, develop, direct, educate, encourage, enrich, feed, fortify, forward, foster, further, give aid, harbor, help, improve, instruct, invigorate, maintain, make provisions for, make strong, mold, nourish, nurse, *nutrire,* patronize, prepare, promote, provide for, rear, render better, render strong, sponsor, strengthen, succor, supply aid, support, sustain, teach, train, tutor, victual

O

OATH, *noun* adjuration, affirmation, affirmation of truth, affirmation of truth of a statement, asseveration, attestation, avouchment, avowal, avowance, guarantee, *iusiurandum,* open declaration, pledge, promise, solemn affirmation, solemn avowal, solemn declaration, solemn invocation, swearing, sworn pledge, sworn promise, sworn statement, vow

FOREIGN PHRASES: *Repellitur a sacramento infamis.* An infamous person is denied the right to make an oath. *Sacramentum habet in se tres comites, -veritatem, justitiam, et judicium; veritus habenda est in jurato; justitia et justicium in judice.* An oath has in it three components-truth, justice, and judgment; truth in the party swearing; justice and judgment in the judge administering the oath. *Juramentum est indivisibile; et non est admittendum in parte verum et in parte falsam.* An oath is indivisible; it is not to be held as partly true and partly false. *Jusjurandum inter alios factum nec nocere nec prodesse debet.* An oath made between other parties ought neither to hurt nor profit. *Non est arctius vinculum inter homines quam jusjurandum.* There is no stronger bond between men than an oath. *Jurato creditur in judicio.* He who makes an oath is to be believed in a judicial proceeding. *Jusjurandi forma verbis differt, re convenit; hunc enim sensum habere debet: ut Deus invocetur.* The form of taking an oath differs in language, agrees in meaning; for it ought to have this meaning: that the deity is invoked. *Perjuri sunt qui servatis verbis juramenti decipiunt aures eorum qui accipiunt.* They are perjured, who, preserving the words of an oath, deceive the ears of those who receive it. *Omne sacramentum debet esse de certa scientia.* Every oath ought to be founded on certain knowledge. *Sacramentum si fatuum fuerit, licet falsum, tamen non committit perjurium.* A foolish oath, although false, does not give rise to perjury.

OBDURATE, *adjective*   callous, cold, decided, determined, dogged, dogmatic, dogmatical, firm, hard, hard-bitten, hardened, hardhearted, harsh, headstrong, heartless, immovable, immutable, impervious, impossible to influence, incorrigible, indifferent, indurate, indurated, inexorable, inflexible, insensitive, intractable, intransigent, invariable, iron-hearted, irreclaimable, merciless, mulish, obstinate, opinionated, opinionative, pertinacious, pervicacious, pig-headed, positive, recalcitrant, refractory, relentless, remorseless, resolute, stony, strong-minded, strong-willed, stubborn, tenacious, unalterable, unbending, uncaring, unchangeable, uncompassionate, uncompromising, unconcerned, uncontrollable, unfeeling, unforgiving, ungovernable, unmalleable, unmanageable, unmerciful, unpitying, unrelenting, unresponsive, unstirred, unsusceptible, unsympathetic, untouched, unyielding, willful

OBEDIENT, *adjective*   acquiescent, amenable, attentive, behaved, biddable, complaisant, compliable, compliant, complying, conformable, conforming, controllable, dedicated, deferential, devoted, *dicto audiens,* docile, ductile, duteous, dutiful, faithful, governable, honoring, law-abiding, loyal, manageable, meek, obeisant, obliging, *oboediens,* observant, *obtemperans,* passive, pliant, regardful, respectful, reverential, rule-abiding, servile, submissive, subservient, supple, tame, tractable, unresisting, venerating, well-behaved, willing, yielding

FOREIGN PHRASES: *Ubi non est condendi auctoritas, ibi non est parendi necessitas.* Where there is no authority for establishing a rule, there is no need of obeying it. *Ejus nulla culpa est cui parere necesse sit.* No guilt attaches to a person who is compelled to obey. *Quicunque jussu judicis aliquid fecerit non videtur dolo malo fecisse, quia parere necesse est.* Whoever does anything by the command of a judge is not deemed to have done it with an evil intent, because it is necessary to obey. *Prudenter agit qui praecepto legis obtemperat.* He acts prudently who obeys the precept of the law. *Obedientia est legis essentia.* Obedience is the essence of the law. *Legitime imperanti parere necesse est.* One who commands lawfully must be obeyed.

OBEISANT, *adjective*   affable, amiable, civil, complaisant, compliant, conciliatory, courteous, decorous,
deferential, deferring, duteous, dutiful, eager to please, good-humored, good-natured, gracious, helpful, honorable, humble, meek, nonresisting, obedient, obliging, pliant, polite, respectful, reverent, reverential, self-abasing, showing homage, submissive, subservient, surrendering, unresisting, willing, yielding

OBEY, *verb*   abide by, accede, accept, accommodate, acquiesce, act in accordance with orders, act on, adhere to, agree, answer to, assent, attend to, attend to orders, be devoted to, be faithful to, be governed by, be guided by, be loyal to, be obedient, be regulated by, be subject, behave, bend to, be ruled by, bow to, carry out, come at call, comply, conform, consent, defer to, do the will of, execute, fall in with, follow, follow orders, fulfill, fulfill the commands of, give allegiance to, give way, heed, humble oneself to, keep, kneel to, listen, live by, mind, *oboedire, obsequi,* observe, *parere,* perform, please, respect, respond, satisfy, serve, submit, succumb, surrender, take orders, yield

FOREIGN PHRASES: *Ejus nulla culpa est cui parere necesse sit.* No guilt attaches to a person who is compelled to obey.

OBFUSCATE, *verb*   addle, adumbrate, baffle, becloud, bedim, befuddle, begloom, bemist, bewilder, blacken, blind, blur, cloak, cloud, complicate, conceal, confound, confuse, cover, curtain, darken, daze, dim, disconcert, disturb, dull, eclipse, fluster, fog, hide, keep one guessing, mist, mix up, muddle, mystify, nonplus, obscure, obumbrate, occult, overshadow, perplex, perturb, put off the track, puzzle, screen, shade, shield, shroud, stupefy, throw into confusion, throw off the scent, unsettle, upset, veil

OBJECT, *noun*   aim, butt, commodity, concern, *consilium,* corporeal body, design, destination, end, final cause, *finis,* goal, item, material product, material substance, matter, point, *propositum,* purpose, subject, substance, target, ultimate purpose

OBJECT, *verb*   attack, be at variance, be averse, call in question, challenge, complain, *contra dicere recusare,* contravene, controvert, criticize, demur, disagree, disapprove, dispute, dissent, enter a demurrer, enter a protest, except, express an objection, express disapproval, find fault, oppose, protest, put forward in opposition, quarrel, *repugnare,* resist, state by way of objection, state opposition, take exception

OBJECTION, *noun*   adverse argument, adverse charge, adverse comment, adverse reason, challenge, *contradictio,* counterargument, countercharge, criticism, denunciation, difference, disagreement, disapprobation, disapproval, dissatisfaction, dissent, exception, expostulation, grievance, opposition, protest, *quod contra dicitur,* reason for disapproval, rebuke, rejection, remonstrance, reservation

ASSOCIATED CONCEPTS: frivolous objection, general objection, grounds for an objection, oral objection, overrule an objection, preservation of an objection, specific objection, sustain an objection, technical objection, waiver, written objection

OBJECTIONABLE, *adjective*   abhorrent, abominable, annoying, antipathetic, base, deplorable, despicable, detestable, disagreeable, disgusting, dislikable, displeasing, distasteful, evil, exceptionable, execrable, filthy, foul, fulsome, gross, hateful, heinous, horrid, illaudable, impalatable, improper, inadvisable, inappropriate, inexpedient, insufferable, intolerable, invidious, loathsome, nasty, nefarious, noisome, noxious, obnoxious, obscene, odious, offensive, opprobrious, peccant, pernicious, repugnant, repulsive, revolting, scurvy, sickening, unacceptable, unappealing, unbearable, unbecoming, uncommendable, undesirable, unendurable, uninviting, unlikable, unpalatable, unpleasant, unpleasing, unsatisfactory, unsavory, unseemly, unsuitable, vile, wrong

ASSOCIATED CONCEPTS: objectionable conduct, objectionable material, objectionable question

OBJECTIVE, adjective actual, broad-minded, candid, concrete, corporeal, desired, detached, disinterested, dispassionate, equitable, factual, fair, fairminded, impartial, impersonal, judicial, just, material, neutral, nonpartisan, nonsubjective, open-minded, real, reasonable, scientific, sober, unbiased, unbigoted, uncolored, uninfluenced, unjaundiced, unprejudiced, unslanted, unswayed, unwarped

OBJECTIVE, noun achievement, aim, ambition, aspiration, design, desire, desired object, destination, dream, end, expectation, final point, fixed purpose, formulated intention, goal, height of one's ambition, hope, idea, intent, intention, *locus qui petitur,* mark, mission, point, purpose, pursuit, set purpose, settled purpose, target, terminal point

ASSOCIATED CONCEPTS: lawful objectives

OBJECTIVITY, noun *aequitas,* broadmindedness, detachment, disinterest, disinterestedness, dispassion, dispassionateness, equitableness, equity, fair-mindedness, fair play, fairness, immovability, impartiality, impersonality, justice, justness, lack of bias, lack of jaundice, lack of prejudice, neutrality, noninvolvement, nonpartisanship, nonsubjectivity, open-mindedness

OBJURGATION, noun accusation, admonishment, admonition, berating, castigation, chiding, denunciation, expostulation, lecture, rebuke, reprehension, reprimand, reproach, reproof, reproval, scolding, sermon, upbraiding

OBLIGATION (Duty), noun agreement, burden, charge, commitment, compulsion, contract, covenant, debt, duty owed, *homini gratiam debere,* legal responsibility, moral responsibility, necessity, oath, obligement, *officium,* pact, performance owed, promise, responsibility, social responsibility, that which a person owes to another, that which is due from a person

ASSOCIATED CONCEPTS: alternative obligation, antecedent obligation, community obligation, conditional obligation, contingent obligation, contractual obligation, existing obligation, fiduciary obligation, impairment of obligation, joint obligation, legal obligation, moral obligation, mutual obligations, parental obligation, pecuniary obligation, personal obligation, privity of obligation, secured obligation, several obligations, statutory obligations, voluntary obligation

FOREIGN PHRASES: *Fides est obligatio conscientiae alicujus ad intentionem alterius.* A truth is an obligation of conscience of one to the wishes of another. *Nihil tam naturale est, quam eo genere quidque dissolvere, quo colligatum est; ideo verborum obligatio verbis tollitur; nudi consensus obligatio contrario consensu dissolvitur.* Nothing is so natural as to dissolve anything in the way in which it was made binding. *In om-*

nibus obligationibus in quibus dies non ponitur, praesenti die debetur. In all obligations in which no time is fixed for their fulfillment, the obligation is due immediately. *Eisdem modis dissolvitur obligatio quae nascitur ex contractu, vel quasi, quibus contrahitur.* An obligation which arises in contract, or quasi contract, is dissolved in the same ways in which it is contracted. *Idem est scire aut scire debet aut potuisse.* To be bound to know or to be able to know is the same as to know. *Nuda pactio obligationem non parit.* A naked agreement does not effect an otherwise binding obligation. *Impossibilium nulla obligatio est.* One cannot be obliged to perform impossible tasks. *Unumquodque dissolvitur eodem ligamine quo ligatur.* Every obligation is dissolved by the same manner with which it is created. *Omnia quae jure contrahuntur, contrario jure pereunt.* All contracts which are entered into under a law, become void under a contrary law. *Ignorantia eorum quae quis scire tenetur non excusat.* Ignorance of those things which a person is deemed to know is no excuse. *L'obligation sans cause, ou sur une fausse cause, ou sur cause illicite, ne peut avoir aucun effet.* An obligation without consideration, or upon a false consideration, or upon unlawful consideration, cannot have any effect. *Nudum pactum est ubi nulla subest causa praeter conventionem; sed ubi subest causa, fit obligatio, et parit actionem.* A naked contract is where there is no consideration except the agreement; but, where there is a consideration, an obligation is created and gives rise to a right of action.

OBLIGATION (Liability), noun accountability, amount due, charge, debit, debt, duty to pay money, indebtedness, indenture, outstanding debt, that which is owing, unliquidated claim, unpaid debt

OBLIGATORY, adjective binding, coactive, coercive, commanded, compelling, compulsatory, compulsive, compulsory, constrained, dictated, enforced, essential, exigent, forced, forcible, imperative, importunate, imposed, incumbent on, indispensable, inescapable, involuntary, leaving no choice, mandatory, necessary, necessitated, not to be avoided, not to be evaded, prerequisite, pressing, required, requisite, unavoidable, unforgoable, urgent, vital, with force of law, without appeal, without choice

ASSOCIATED CONCEPTS: obligatory advance, obligatory payment, obligatory writing

OBLIGEE, noun bestower, financier, grantor, lender, lessor, mortgage holder, mortgagee

OBLIGOR, noun borrower, debtor, drawee, loan applicant, loanee, mortgagor, pledgor

ASSOCIATED CONCEPTS: obligor on a note

OBLIQUE (Evasive), adjective ambivalent, backhanded, circuitous, circumlocutory, cloaked, concealed, devious, disingenuous, elusive, elusory, equivocal, equivocating, furtive, indeterminate, indirect, inexact, lacking clarity, prevaricating, recondite, roundabout, secretive, sinuous, unclear, underhand, underhanded, unstraightforward, vague, veiled

OBLIQUE (Slanted), adjective angled, askew, aslant, awry, diagonal, inclined, inclining, leaning, *obliquus,* slanting, sloping, steep, tilted, tipped, tipping

OBLITERATE, *verb* *abolere,* abolish, annihilate, annul, blot out, bring to nothing, cancel, conceal, consume, cover, cover up, defeat, *delere,* delete, demolish, deracinate, desolate, destroy, devastate, devour, disintegrate, dispel, dissipate, dissolve, efface, eliminate, erase, expunge, exterminate, extinguish, extirpate, gut, invalidate, level, liquidate, mask, mow down, nullify, obscure, omit, pull up by the roots, quash, quell, ravage, raze, remove, remove the traces, render illegible, render imperceptible, rub off, rub out, ruin, rule out, scratch out, screen, shroud, smash, snuff out, squash, stamp out, strike out, suppress, swallow up, sweep away, tear down, topple, unmake, wipe out, wreck, write off

OBLIVIOUS, *adjective* absent, absentminded, absorbed, abstracted, blank, careless, distracted, dreamy, faraway, forgetful, heedless, *immemor,* inattentive, inconsiderate, indifferent, insensible, mindless, neglectful, negligent, *obliviosus,* overlooking, preoccupied, remiss, thoughtless, unaware, uncaring, unconscious, undiscerning, unheeding, unmindful, unnoticing, unobservant, unrecognizing, without consideration

OBLOQUY, *noun* abasement, abuse, abusive language, accusation, animadversion, aspersion, berating, blame, castigation, censure, chastisement, chiding, contempt, criticism, debasement, defamation, degradation, denunciation, derision, derogation, diatribe, disapprobation, discredit, disesteem, disfavor, disgrace, dishonor, disparagement, disrepute, disrespect, dressing down, execration, exprobration, faultfinding, humiliation, ignominy, ill favor, ill repute, infamy, ingloriousness, invective, lashing, *maledictum,* objurgation, odium, opprobrium, reproach, revilement, scolding, shame, slur, stigma, stricture, tirade, tongue-lashing, traducement, verbal abuse, vilification, *vituperatio,* vituperation
ASSOCIATED CONCEPTS: defamation

OBNOXIOUS, *adjective* abhorrent, abominable, annoying, antagonizing, antipathetic, base, beastly, blameworthy, censurable, contemptible, deplorable, despicable, detestable, disagreeable, disgusting, displeasing, execrable, faulty, foul, fulsome, gross, hateful, heinous, hellish, horrible, horrid, impalatable, insufferable, intolerable, invidious, *invisus,* loathful, loathsome, nasty, nauseating, nefarious, noisome, noxious, *noxius,* objectionable, odious, offensive, opprobrious, pernicious, poisonous, rank, repellent, reprehensible, repugnant, repulsive, revolting, unbearable, unendurable, unpleasant, unpleasing, unwholesome, vile, villainous, vulgar, wretched

OBNUBILATE, *verb* adumbrate, becloud, bedim, blacken, blind, blur, cast a shadow, cloak, cloud, cloud over, conceal, cover, cover up, curtain, darken, dim, disguise, dull, eclipse, encompass with gloom, enshroud, fog, haze, hide, make indistinct, mask, obfuscate, obscure, occult, overcast, overcloud, overshadow, screen, shade, shadow, shroud, veil, wrap

OBSCENE, *adjective* bawdy, broad, debauched, foul, immodest, immoral, impure, indecent, indelicate, *inquinatus,* lascivious, lecherous, lewd, libidinous, licentious, lubricous, lurid, lustful, *obscenus,* offensive, offensive to decency, offensive to modesty, patently offensive, pornographic, profane, profligate, ribald, risque, salacious, scabrous, sensual, sexy, shameful, shameless, spicy, tending to excite lustful desires, *turpis,* unchaste, unwholesome, vile, vulgar, wanton

OBSCENITY, *noun* bawdiness, coarseness, dirtiness, immodesty, immorality, impropriety, indecency, indecorum, indelicacy, lechery, lewdness, lubricity, *obscenitas,* offensiveness, pornography, ribaldry, salaciousness, salacity, scurrillity, smut, smuttiness, *turpitudo,* unchastity, vileness, vulgarity

OBSCURATION, *noun* adumbration, blackout, blur, cloud, concealment, darkening, darkness, dimming, dimness, disappearance, faintness, fogginess, fuzziness, gloom, gloominess, indistinctness, obfuscation, obliteration, obscurity, occultation, opacity, opaqueness, overshadowing, privacy, retirement, seclusion, secrecy, shade, shading, shadowing, unclearness, unintelligibleness, vagueness

OBSCURE *(Abstruse),* *adjective* complex, cryptic, cryptical, deep, difficult, difficult to understand, enigmatic, enigmatical, esoteric, hidden, impalpable, incomprehensible, intricate, involved, mysterious, profound, recondite, transcendental, unapparent, unintelligible

OBSCURE *(Faint),* *adjective* blurred, blurry, concealed, dim, hard to see, hidden, impalpable, imperceptible, inconspicuous, indefinite, indiscernible, indistinct, invisible, murky, nebulous, pale, shadowy, subtle, unapparent, unclear, undistinguished, unplain, vague, veiled, weak

OBSCURE *(Remote),* *adjective* alien, distant, far, foreign, isolated, private, rare, removed, secluded, strange, unconnected, unknown, unrenowned
ASSOCIATED CONCEPTS: obscure meaning

OBSCURE, *verb* adumbrate, becloud, bedim, befog, begloom, benight, blacken, blind, blur, cast a shadow, cloak, cloud, conceal, cover, cover up, curtain, darken, darkle, dim, disguise, dull, dusk, eclipse, encloud, enshroud, fog, haze, hide, keep in the dark, make dim, make indistinct, mask, mislead, obfuscate, occult, overcast, overcloud, overshadow, screen, shade, shroud, suppress, veil, wrap
FOREIGN PHRASES: *Semper in obscuris quod minimum est sequimur.* In obscure matters the construction which is least obscure should always be applied.

OBSEQUIOUS, *adjective* compliable, compliant, concessive, crawling, cringing, crouching, deferential, docile, enslaved, fawning, flattering, groveling, humble, ingratiating, obedient, scraping, servile, slavish, spineless, submissive, subordinate, subservient, sycophantic, toadying, unassertive, yielding

OBSERVATION, *noun* advertence, advertency, annotation, ascertainment, assertion, attention, attentiveness, check, cognition, cognizance, comment, commentary, concentration, conclusion, consideration, declaration, detection, *dictum,* discovery, espial, espionage, estimation, examination, expression of opinion, finding, heed, heedfulness, inspection, intentness, investigation, look, mention, mindfulness, *notatio,* note, notice, *observatio,* opinion, pronouncement, reconnaissance, reflection, regard, remark, report, scrutiny, statement, study, supervision, surveillance, survey, utterance, view, watch, watchfulness, witnessing

ASSOCIATED CONCEPTS: observation of the demeanor of a witness

OBSERVE *(Obey), verb*   abide by, acquiesce, adhere to, attend, be faithful to, be guided by, be regulated by, be submissive to, bow to, carry out, cling to, comply with, conform, *conservare,* cooperate, discharge, do the will of, execute, follow, fulfill, heed, honor, keep, obey, *observare,* pay attention to, perform, respect, satisfy, show regard for, yield to
ASSOCIATED CONCEPTS: observe the laws

OBSERVE *(Remark), verb*   announce, articulate, assert, aver, comment, communicate, couch in terms, declare, exclaim, express, give expression to, give tongue to, give utterance to, give voice to, impart, make a remark, make mention of, mention, muse, phrase, proclaim, put into words, say, state, tell, utter, vocalize, voice

OBSERVE *(Watch), verb*   *animadvertere,* attend, be a spectator, be a witness, be attentive, be aware, be conscious, be vigilant, behold, command a view, descry, devote attention to, direct the eyes to, espy, examine, eye, follow, gaze at, give attention to, give heed to, have in sight, heed, hold in view, inspect, keep an eye on, keep in sight, keep in view, lay eyes on, look, look at, mark, mind, note, notice, *observare,* pay attention, pay heed, peer at, perceive, peruse, reconnoiter, regard, review, scan, scout, scrutinize, see, *spectare,* spy, survey, take cognizance of, take note, take notice, take stock, turn the attention to, turn the eyes on, view
ASSOCIATED CONCEPTS: eyewitness

OBSESS, *verb*   agitate, annoy, bedevil, beset, besiege, bewitch, compel, control, craze, dement, derange, discompose, disconcert, distress, dominate, drive, enthrall, gnaw, haunt, hold captive, hound, infatuate, madden, nag, overpower, pervade, plague, possess, preoccupy, prey on the mind, seize, torment, trouble, unbalance, unhinge, vex, weigh on the mind

OBSESSION, *noun*   absorption, application, attraction, compulsion, craze, crotchet, dominating action, engrossment, exclusive attention, fanaticism, fancy, fascination, fetish, fixation, fixed idea, immersion, infatuation, irresistible impulse, mania, monomania, passion, preoccupation, rapt attention, ruling passion, ruling whim, single-mindedness, undivided attention, whole attention

OBSOLETE, *adjective*   abandoned, anachronistic, anachronous, ancient, antediluvian, antiquated, antique, archaic, archaistic, bygone, dated, dead, discarded, discontinued, dismissed, disused, early, expired, extinct, fallen into desuetude, fallen into disuse, no longer in use, obsolescent, *obsoletus,* old, old-fashioned, out-of-date, out of use, outdated, outmoded, outworn, past, primitive, rejected, retired, stale, timeworn, unfashionable, unmodern
ASSOCIATED CONCEPTS: obsolete covenant, obsolete records, obsolete restrictions

OBSTACLE, *noun*   arrest, balk, barricade, barrier, block, bridle, catch, check, constraint, curb, dam, delay, detainment, difficulty, disallowance, drawback, embargo, enjoining, estoppel, fence, forbiddance, hamper, handicap, hindrance, hurdle, impediment, *impedimentum,* inconvenience, inhibition, injunction, limitation,

obstruction, preclusion, prohibition, proscription, remora, restraint, restriction, snag, stop, stoppage, stopper, stumbling block, suppression, trammel

OBSTRUCT, *verb*   bar, barricade, block, brake, bridle, bring to a standstill, check, choke, circumscribe, congest, countervail, cramp, cripple, curb, debar, delay, disable, embar, encumber, estop, forbid, frustrate, halt, hamper, hamstring, handicap, hinder, impede, impedite, inhibit, interfere with, interrupt, intervene, limit, occlude, oppilate, preclude, prevent, prohibit, restrain, retard, slow down, snag, stall, stand in the way, stay, stem, stop, stop up, stymie, suppress, suspend, terminate, thwart, trammel, trap
ASSOCIATED CONCEPTS: obstruct a lawful authority, obstruct an investigation, obstruct justice, obstructing governmental administration

OBSTRUCTION, *noun*   balk, ban, bar, barricade, barrier, block, blockade, blockage, bridle, catch, check, clog, closure, congestion, constraint, constriction, cork, curb, dam, difficulty, disallowance, embargo, embarrassment, enjoining, fence, forbiddance, hamper, hindrance, hitch, hurdle, impediment, *impedimentum,* impedition, injunction, interference, interruption, limitation, obstacle, *obstructio,* obstruent, obturation, occlusion, plug, preclusion, prevention, prohibition, proscription, remora, restraint, restriction, shackle, snag, stop, stopper, stricture, trammel
FOREIGN PHRASES: *Forstellarius est pauperum depressor, et totius communitatis et patriae publicus inimicus.* A forestaller is an enemy of the poor, and a public enemy of the county.

OBTAIN, *verb*   accumulate, achieve, acquire, *adipisci,* appropriate, arrive at, attain, be in receipt of, capture, collect, come into possession, *consequi,* earn, enter into possession, gain, gain possession, gather, get, get hold of, get possession of, grab, hold, lay hands upon, *nancisci,* pick up, pocket, possess, procure, reach, realize, receive, recover, secure, seize, take, take over, take possession, win
ASSOCIATED CONCEPTS: obtain a judgment, obtain a search warrant

OBTRUDE, *verb*   accroach, break in, burst in, butt in, encroach, force, impose, *inculcare,* infringe, *ingerere,* interfere, interlope, intermeddle, interpose, interrupt, intervene, intrude, invade, meddle, trespass

OBTRUSIVE, *adjective*   aggressive, assuming, bold, brash, brazen, encroaching, forward, impertinent, insolent, interfering, interrupting, interruptive, intruding, intrusive, invasive, malapert, meddlesome, meddling, officious, presuming, presumptuous, prominent, protruding, protrusive, protuberant, prying, pushy, rude, saucy, self-assertive, unmannerly

OBTUND, *verb*   abate, allay, alleviate, anesthetize, assuage, benumb, blunt, calm, deaden, desensitize, dull, ease, impair the force of, make blunt, make less violent, mitigate, moderate, modulate, numb, palliate, quell, quiet, reduce the edge, reduce the violence, soften, take the edge off, weaken

OBTURATE, *verb*   block, clog, close, cork, hinder, interfere, obstruct, prevent, shut, stop up, stopper

OBTUSE, *adjective*   asinine, blockish, blunt, blunt-witted, callous, dense, doltish, dronish, dull, dull-witted, *hebes,* idiotic, ignorant, imbecilic, imperceptive, impercipient, insensitive, lumpish, moronic, oafish, *obtusus,* opaque, phlegmatic, *retusus,* senseless, simple, simple-minded, slow, stupid, thick, thickheaded, torporific, uncaring, uncomprehending, undiscerning, unfeeling, unimaginative, unintelligent, witless

OBVIATION, *noun*   abolition, abrogation, arresting, bar, blockage, cancellation, check, deterrent, elimination, forestalling, interdiction, prevention, removal, stoppage, turning aside

OBVIOUS, *adjective*   accessible, *apertus,* apparent, axiomatic, axiomatical, bald, bright, clear, comprehensible, conspicuous, discernible, discoverable, distinct, distinguishable, evident, exoteric, exoterical, explicit, exposed, glaring, in evidence, in view, indisputable, intelligible, lucid, manifest, *manifestus,* notable, noticeable, observable, open, overt, palpable, patent, perceivable, perceptible, perspicuous, *perspicuus,* plain, prominent, pronounced, recognizable, revealed, standing out, striking, transparent, uncamouflaged, unconcealed, undeniable, understandable, undisguised, unhidden, unmasked, unmistakable, unquestionable, unscreened, visible, well-defined
ASSOCIATED CONCEPTS: obvious danger, obvious defect, obvious error, obvious risks

OCCASION, *noun*   advent, affair, chance, conjuncture, episode, event, experience, happening, incident, instance, juncture, moment, *occasio,* occurrence, opening, opportunity, point, situation, suitable time, *tempus,* time

OCCASION, *verb*   breed, bring about, cause, create, effect, generate, give cause for, induce, make, produce, provoke

OCCLUDE, *verb*   arrest, bar, barricade, block, blockade, check, choke off, close, cork, cover, dam up, debar, deter, fasten, hamper, hedge in, hem in, hinder, impede, inhibit, intercept, interclude, interrupt, lock, obstruct, obturate, oppilate, plug, preclude, prevent, prohibit, restrain, restrict, retard, seal, shut, shut in, shut off, stanch, stop, stop up, throttle, thwart, trammel, trap

OCCUPANCY, *noun*   actual possession, control, dominion, enjoyment, habitation, holding, inhabitancy, occupation, ownership, *possessio,* possession, proprietorship, residence, retention, temporary possession, tenure
ASSOCIATED CONCEPTS: certificate of occupancy, continuous occupancy, illegal occupancy, partial occupancy, physical occupancy, principal occupation, residency laws, right of occupancy

OCCUPANT, *noun*   addressee, denizen, dweller, freeholder, habitant, householder, inhabitant, inmate, leaseholder, lessee, lodger, occupier, possessor, renter, resident, residentiary, resider, roomer, sojourner, tenant
ASSOCIATED CONCEPTS: bona fide occupant, illegal occupancy, lawful occupant, right of occupancy, tenant in occupancy

OCCUPATION *(Possession),* *noun*   ascendancy, authority, charge, command, control, direction, domination, dominion, influence, inhabitation, jurisdiction, mastery, occupancy, *occupatio,* ownership, power, predominance, predominancy, proprietary rights, proprietorship, residence, retention, right to retain, rule, seizure, superintendence, tenure

OCCUPATION *(Vocation),* *noun*   activity, avocation, business, calling, capacity, career, chosen work, craft, employment, enterprise, field, industry, job, line, livelihood, mission, *negotium,* office, position, profession, pursuit, situation, specialty, trade, undertaking, venture, work

OCCUPY *(Engage),* *verb*   absorb, absorb the attention, absorb the mind, absorb the thoughts, address oneself to, amuse, apply oneself to, apply the attention to, apply the mind to, arrest the attention, attract the attention, attract the mind, attract the thoughts, be active with, be at work on, be concerned with, be employed, busy oneself with, captivate, catch the attention, claim one's thoughts, concentrate on, concern oneself with, devote, direct the attention to, direct the mind to, engage the attention, engage the mind, engage the thoughts, engross, engross the mind, engross the thoughts, entertain, enthrall, entrance, excite the attention, fascinate, go about, immerse, *in re versari,* interest, invite the attention, involve, keep busy, monopolize, monopolize the thoughts, obsess, *occupare,* plunge into, ply, preoccupy, rivet the attention, rivet the mind, rivet the thoughts, set about, set to work, specialize in, spend one's time in, tackle, take employment, take on, take part, take up, *tenere,* turn the attention to, turn the mind to, undertake, work at

OCCUPY *(Take possession),* *verb*   abide, acquire, annex, appropriate, assume, assume ownership, be possessed of, *capere,* capture, claim, colonize, command, conquer, control, denizen, dominate, dwell, dwell in, expropriate, have possession of, have rights to, have title to, help oneself to, hold, indwell, inhabit, invade, keep, keep hold of, keep house, live, live in, lodge, make one's home at, move into, obtain, *occupare,* own, possess, procure, recover, reside in, retain, seize, settle in, stay, take from, take over, take up residence in
ASSOCIATED CONCEPTS: actually occupy, lawfully occupy

OCCUR *(Come to mind),* *verb*   be uppermost in the mind, become aware, become visible, come into view, conjure up, crop up, cross one's mind, emerge, enter the mind, enter the picture, manifest itself, pass in the mind, present itself, present itself to the mind, remember, reveal itself, show itself, *subit,* suggest itself

OCCUR *(Happen),* *verb*   arise, become a fact, become known, come about, come into being, come into existence, come to pass, develop, emerge, *fieri, incidere,* materialize, proceed, recur, result, take effect, take its course, take place, transpire

OCCURRENCE, *noun*   affair, *casus,* circumstance, contingency, episode, event, eventuality, experience, fortuity, happening, happenstance, incident, instance, occasion, phenomenon, predicament, proceeding, realization, *res,* situation, transaction, turn, venture
FOREIGN PHRASES: **Casus fortuitus.** A chance occurrence.

ODIOUS, *adjective* abject, abominable, accursed, annoying, base, beastly, blameworthy, coarse, confounded, contemptible, corrupt, cursed, damnable, despicable, detestable, diabolic, dirty, disagreeable, disgraceful, disgusting, displeasing, evil, execrable, forbidding, foul, frightening, fulsome, grotesque, hateful, heinous, hideous, horrible, horrid, ignoble, ignominious, infamous, infernal, insufferable, intolerable, *invidiosus,* invidious, *invisus,* loathsome, low, mean, monstrous, nasty, objectionable, obnoxious, *odiosus,* offensive, rank, repellent, reprehensible, repugnant, repulsive, revolting, rotten, scurvy, shocking, sickening, sinister, tainted, ugly, unbearable, unendurable, unlovable, unpalatable, unpleasant, unpopular, unworthy, vile, vulgar

ODIUM, *noun* abhorrence, alienation, animosity, animus, antipathy, aversion, avoidance, bad feeling, blame, censure, contempt, criticism, debasement, degradation, derision, despite, detestation, disaffection, disapproval, disesteem, disfavor, disgrace, disgust, dishonor, dislike, displeasure, disrepute, distaste, dudgeon, enmity, execration, hate, hatred, horror, hostility, humiliation, ignobility, ignominy, ill will, infamy, inimicalness, loathing, malevolence, malice, maliciousness, obloquy, odiousness, opprobrium, rancor, rebuke, reproach, repugnance, repulsiveness, resentment, revulsion, scandal, scorn, shame, strong aversion, unpopularity, venom

OFFEND *(Insult), **verb*** abuse, affront, anger, annoy, be discourteous, be impolite, chagrin, displease, distress, disturb, embarrass, enrage, gall, horrify, hurt, incense, inflame, infuriate, injure, irk, irritate, *laedere,* madden, make angry, mortify, nettle, *offendere,* outrage, pain, pique, provoke, ridicule, rile, slight, snub, taunt, tease, treat with discourtesy, treat with indignity, vex, wound

OFFEND *(Violate the law), **verb*** break a law, break the law, commit a breach of the law, commit a crime, commit a fault, commit an infraction, commit offense, commit sin, contravene, disobey the law, disregard the law, err, infringe, infringe a law, misconduct oneself, *peccare,* transgress, trespass, *violare*

OFFENDER, *noun* aggressor, assailant, criminal, delinquent, evildoer, felon, lawbreaker, malefactor, malfeasant, one implicated in the commission of a crime, one who breaks the law, one who commits a crime, *peccans,* sinner, transgressor, violator, wrongdoer
ASSOCIATED CONCEPTS: first offender, multiple offender, youthful offender

OFFENSE, *noun* aggression, assault, attack, breach, breach of the law, breaking of the law, crime, criminal act, criminal deed, criminality, delict, *delictum,* delinquency, disobedience, encroachment, evil behavior, evil deed, failure, felony, illegal act, illegal conduct, illegality, impropriety, infraction, infringement, injury, inobservance, lawbreaking, lawlessness, malefaction, malfeasance, malpractice, malversation, misconduct, misdeed, misdemeanor, misdoing, misfeasance, misprision, noncompliance, nonobservance, *offensio,* official misconduct, omission, outrage, pecability, *peccatum,* transgression, umbrage, unlawful act, unrighteousness, violation, violation of law, violation of orders, wrong, wrongdoing, wrongfulness

ASSOCIATED CONCEPTS: bailable offense, capital offense, charged with an offense, compound offense, continuing offense, degree of offense, grave offense, lesser offense, minor offense, offense against public decency, offense at common law, petty offense, prior offense, public offense
FOREIGN PHRASES: *Peccata contra naturam sunt gravissima.* Crimes against nature are the most heinous.

OFFENSIVE *(Offending), **adjective*** abhorrent, abominable, abusive, annoying, antipathetic, beneath contempt, biting, blasphemous, coarse, contemptible, contumelious, detestable, disagreeable, discourteous, disdainful, disgusting, displeasing, disrespectful, distasteful, execrable, foul, *gravis,* harsh, hateful, heinous, hideous, horrible, horrid, ignoble, ill-bred, impertinent, impious, impudent, inaffable, indecent, inharmonious, insolent, insulting, intolerable, invidious, irritating, loathsome, low, malignant, monstrous, nasty, nauseating, noxious, objectionable, obnoxious, *odiosus molestus,* odious, offending, opprobrious, outrageous, peccant, putrid, reeking, repellent, repelling, reprehensible, repugnant, repulsive, revolting, ribald, rude, sarcastic, saucy, shocking, sickening, stinging, truculent, unbearable, uncivil, uncongenial, unendurable, ungracious, unmannered, unmannerly, unpalatable, unpleasant, unpleasing, unsavory, unspeakable, vile, wounding

OFFENSIVE *(Taking the initiative), **adjective*** aggressive, agitational, antagonistic, assailant, assailing, attacking, battling, bellicose, combative, contentious, disruptive, exciting, fighting, hostile, inciting, incursive, inflammatory, instigating, instigative, invading, invasive, militant, militaristic, provocative, provoking, unpacific, unpeaceful, warlike

OFFER *(Propose), **verb*** bid, bring forward, hold forth, hold out, invite, lay before, make a bid, make a proposition, make an overture, *offerre,* pose, proffer, *profiteri,* propound, put forth, put forth for acceptance, put forth for consideration, put forward, put forward for consideration, recommend, submit, suggest, urge upon, venture

OFFER *(Tender), **verb*** advance, cede, extend, offer performance, pay, present, present for acceptance, produce, proffer, proffer payment, remit, render, submit, tender performance
FOREIGN PHRASES: *Praesentare nihil aliud est quam praesto dare seu offere.* To present is no more than to give or offer forthwith.

OFFICE, *noun* appointment, assigned task, berth, billet, bureau, business, capacity, charge, duty, employment, function, incumbency, job, *munus,* occupation, *officium, partes,* place of business, place of employment, position, post, profession, role, service, situation, station, trade, trust, work, work place
ASSOCIATED CONCEPTS: impeachment from public office, malfeasance in office, misconduct in office, misfeasance in office, neglect of duty, nonfeasance in office, removal from office, vacancy in office
FOREIGN PHRASES: *Officium nemini debet esse damnosum.* An office ought to be injurious to no one. *Nemo duobus utatur officiis.* No one should hold two offices at the same time. *Officia judicialia non concedantur antequam vacent.* Judicial offices are not to be granted or appointed before they become vacant.

OFFICER, *noun*   elected representative, functionary, named representative, officeholder, official
ASSOCIATED CONCEPTS: officer of the court, officer of the law

OFFICIAL, *adjective*   accredited, approved, assured, attested, authenticated, authoritative, ceremonious, certain, certified, conclusive, correct, decided, definite, dependable, endorsed, established, formal, guaranteed, indisputable, insured, legitimate, licensed, magisterial, officiary, proper, proven, *publicus,* reliable, sanctioned, to be depended on, to be trusted, trustworthy, undeniable, unequivocal, unimpeachable, valid, verified, worthy of confidence
ASSOCIATED CONCEPTS: official act, official bond, official business, official misconduct, official notice, official proceeding, official record

OFFICIAL, *noun*   administrative head, administrator, bureaucrat, executive, executive officer, functionary, head of government, leader, leader of affairs, office bearer, officeholder, officer, overseer, person in authority, person responsible, *praefectus,* public office holder, superintendent, supervisor
ASSOCIATED CONCEPTS: public official

OFFICIATE, *verb*   act, administer, carry out, command, conduct, direct, discharge a function, do duty, execute, exercise, fill an office, function, govern, guide, head, hold an office, lead, manage, minister, moderate, occupy the chair, *officio fungi,* oversee, perform, pilot, preside, regulate, run, serve, steer, superintend, supervise, take the chair

OFFSET, *noun*   allowance, balance, compensation, contrast, counter, counteractant, counteragent, counterbalance, counterblast, counterpoise, counterweight, equalization, equivalent, hedge, impedance, neutralizer, nullifier, opposite, opposition, preventative, satisfaction, set off, substitute

OFFSHOOT, *noun*   addition, annex, branch, byproduct, derivative, descendant, development, division, extension, issue, member, offspring, outgrowth, satellite, scion, subdivision, subsidiary, supplement

OFFSPRING, *noun*   brood, cadet, child, children, descendants, family, heir, issue, lineage, next generation, offshoots, posterity, *progenies,* progeny, *proles,* scion, spawn, *stirps,* successor, younger generation
ASSOCIATED CONCEPTS: illegitimate offspring, natural offspring

OLD, *adjective*   advanced in years, ancient, antiquated, antique, archaic, crumbling, decadent, decayed, declining, decrepit, deteriorated, dilapidated, discontinued, disintegrated, early, elderly, enfeebled, hoary, *inveteratus,* matured, no longer young, not modern, obsolete, olden, original, past, preceding, preexisting, run down, rusty, stale, superannuated, timeworn, used, *vetus, vetustus,* vintage, waning, weakened, weathered, worn, worn out
ASSOCIATED CONCEPTS: ancient records doctrine

OMINOUS, *adjective*   adverse, alarming, augurial, auspicial, baleful, bodeful, dangerous, dark, depressing, dire, direful, disastrous, dismaying, dispiriting, disquieting, disturbing, divinatory, fatidic, fatidical, fear-inspiring, fearful, forbidding, foreboding, frightful, gloomy, grim, hapless, haunting, hopeless, ill-boding, ill-fated, ill-omened, ill-starred, inauspicious, luckless, menacing, minacious, minatory, monitory, morbid, perilous, pessimistic, portending evil, portentous, precursive, precursory, premonitory, presageful, presaging, presentient, pythonic, sinister, somber, threatening, threatful, unfortunate, unlucky, unpromising, unpropitious, vatic, vaticinal

OMISSION, *noun*   breach, carelessness, default, default in performance, delinquency, dereliction, disregard, excluding, exclusion, failure, failure to perform, inadvertence, laxity, laxness, leaving out, neglect, neglect to perform, negligence, nonfeasance, noninclusion, oversight, passing over, *praetermissio,* pretermission, remissness, slip
ASSOCIATED CONCEPTS: material omission, negligent omission, omission of duty, omission to act, willful omission
FOREIGN PHRASES: *Omissio eorum quae tacite insunt nihil operatur.* The omission of those things which are tacitly expressed is unimportant.

OMIT, *verb*   abstain from inserting, bypass, cast aside, count out, cut out, delete, discard, dodge, drop, exclude, fail to do, fail to include, fail to insert, fail to mention, leave out, leave undone, let go, let pass, let slip, miss, neglect, *omittere,* pass by, pass over, *praetermittere,* skip, slight, *transire*
FOREIGN PHRASES: *Casus omissus et oblivioni datus dispositioni communis juris relinquitur.* A case omitted and forgotten is left to the disposal of the common law.

OMNIBUS, *adjective*   all-embracing, all-inclusive, blanket, broad, catholic, collective, compendious, complete, composite, comprehensive, encyclopedic, encyclopedical, exhaustive, expansive, extensive, general, generic, generical, inclusive, inclusory, indiscriminate, limitless, miscellaneous, of great scope, overall, pandemic, sweeping, unlimited, unqualified, unrestricted, wide-reaching, widespread
ASSOCIATED CONCEPTS: omnibus law

OMNIPOTENT, *adjective*   able, all-powerful, almighty, capable, dominant, dominating, effective, effectual, godlike, Herculean, illimitable, infinitely powerful, irresistible, mighty, *omnipotens,* overwhelming, plenipotent, plenipotentiary, possessing unlimited power, potent, powerful, predominant, prepotent, puissant, ruling, sovereign, strong, supreme, uncircumscribed, unlimited in power

OMNISCIENT, *adjective*   all-knowing, all-seeing, all-wise, apperceptive, comprehending, deific, deifical, discerning, encyclopedic, farseeing, foreseeing, godlike, infinitely wise, informed, knowing, knowledgeable, oracular, Palladian, pansophic, pansophical, perceptive, percipient, predicting, prescient, sagacious, sapient, smart, understanding, well-informed, wise

ON OR ABOUT, *adverb*   approximately, in the general time frame, in the immediate vicinity of, in the neighborhood of, more or less, somewhere about

ONE-SIDED, *adjective*   biased, colored, discriminatory, exparte, *impar, inaequalis,* influenced, *iniquus,* interested, jaundiced, narrow, narrow-minded, partial, partisan, prejudiced, prepossessed, sectarian, slanted, swayed, undetached, undispassionate, uneven, unfair, unjust, warped

ASSOCIATED CONCEPTS: one-sided contract

ONEROUS, *adjective* arduous, backbreaking, burdensome, crushing, cumbersome, difficult, exacting, excessive, fatiguing, formidable, *gravis,* grinding, grueling, hard, harrowing, harsh, heavy, Herculean, intolerable, laborious, oppressive, overbearing, overpowering, overtaxing, pressing, rigorous, severe, strenuous, taxing, tedious, toilsome, trying, unbearable, unwieldy, wearisome, weighty

ONLY *(No more than),* **adjective** bare, mere, plain, simple

ONLY *(Sole),* **adjective** exclusive, first and last, individual, lone, singular, solitary, unique

ONLY *(Unrepeated),* **adjective** unmatched, unparalleled

ONLY, *adverb* alone, apart, at least, at the very least, exclusively, merely, plainly, purely, simply, singly, solely

ONLY, *conjunction* but, but for the fact that, excepting that, if it were not that

ONSET *(Assault),* **noun** advance, aggression, assailment, attack, barrage, blitzkrieg, bombardment, charge, dragonnade, encounter, foray, forced entrance, fusillade, incursion, intrusion, invasion, maraud, offense, offensive, onrush, onslaught, raid, seizure, siege, storm, strike, thrust

ONSET *(Commencement),* **noun** aurora, beginning, birth, coming, dawn, embarkation, entrance, establishment, exordium, fashioning, first appearance, first move, first step, forging, forming, foundation, genesis, inauguration, inception, inchoation, incipience, incunabula, infancy, initiation, introduction, launching, making, oncoming, opening, origin, origination, outbreak, outset, rise, source, start, starting point, threshold

ONUS *(Blame),* **noun** accusation, blameworthiness, charge, culpability, error, fault, flaw, guiltiness, misdeed, reprehension, responsibility, shortcoming, transgression

ONUS *(Burden),* **noun** affliction, burdensome requirement, charge, drawback, encumbrance, handicap, hindrance, impediment, inescapable duty, interference, load, obstruction, responsibility, struggle, unusual task, weary load, weight

ONUS *(Stigma),* **noun** badge, blemish, blot, blotch, brand, censure, condemnation, degradation, denunciation, discredit, disgrace, dishonor, dispraise, imputation, infamy, mark of Cain, reproach, scar, shame, slur, smirch, smudge, smutch, soil, spot, stain, taint, tarnish

OPACITY, *noun* asininity, blockishness, confusion, darkness, denseness, density, dimness, doltishness, dull-wittedness, dullness, fatuity, hebetude, impenetrability, imperceptibility, inapprehensibility, incomprehensibility, indiscernibility, indistinctness, indistinguishability, inscrutability, lack of understanding, lumpishness, nebulosity, oafishness, obfuscation, obscuration, obscurity, obtuseness, opaqueness, simplicity, slow-wittedness, slowness, stolidity, stolidness, stupidity, stupidness, thickheadedness, thick-wittedness, thickness, unclarity, unclearness, unfathomableness, unintelligibility, unplainness, unsearchableness, vacuity, vagueness, vapidity, want of transparency

OPAQUE, *adjective* addlebrained, addleheaded, addlepated, ambiguous, asinine, benighted, bewildering, birdbrained, blind, blockish, boeotian, brainless, cloddish, clouded, cloudy, concealed, confused, confusing, cryptic, dark, dense, difficult, difficult to comprehend, difficult to understand, dim, dimwitted, doltish, dull, dull-witted, duncelike, duncical, enigmatic, fatuitous, fatuous, featherbrained, foggy, hard to comprehend, hard to understand, hazy, ignorant, ill-defined, imbecilic, impenetrable, imperceptive, imperspicuous, impervious, incomprehensible, indistinct, inscrutable, lacking clarity, loutish, lumpish, mindless, misty, moronic, muddleheaded, muddy, nebulous, nescient, nontranslucent, oafish, obfuscated, obscure, obtuse, purblind, puzzling, recondite, senseless, shadowy, simple, simple-minded, slow in understanding, stolid, stupid, thick, thick-headed, thick-witted, turbid, unclarified, unclear, uncomprehending, unenlightened, unfathomable, unintelligent, unintelligible, unplain, unreasoning, unthinking, untransparent, vacuous, vague, witless

OPEN *(Accessible),* **adjective** allowable, allowed, approachable, attainable, available, defenseless, fit for travel, free of access, free to all, insecure, navigable, obtainable, *patere,* permitted, pregnable, procurable, public, reachable, securable, susceptible, unbarred, unblocked, undefended, unenclosed, unfenced, unfortified, unguarded, unlocked, unobstructed, unoccupied, unrestricted, unsealed, unshielded, vacated, vulnerable, within reach

ASSOCIATED CONCEPTS: open account, open market, open shop

OPEN *(In sight),* **adjective** *apertus,* apparent, bare, beholdable, blatant, *clarus,* clear, conspicuous, discernible, discoverable, distinct, evident, exposed, exposed to view, eye-catching, glaring, in full view, manifest, *manifestus,* marked, noticeable, observable, obvious, outstanding, overt, patent, perceivable, perceptible, perspicuous, plain, prominent, pronounced, recognizable, revealed, salient, seeable, striking, transparent, unclouded, unconcealed, uncovered, undisguised, unhidden, unmistakable, unobstructed, unprotected, unsecluded, unsheltered, unshielded, visible

ASSOCIATED CONCEPTS: open and notorious possession, open court

OPEN *(Persuasible),* **adjective** acquiescent, amenable, *apertus, candidus,* flexible, impressible, impressionable, inducible, influenceable, malleable, movable, open-minded, persuadable, pervious, receptive, respondent, responsive, sensitive, *simplex,* suasible, suggestible, susceptible, swayable, sympathetic, tractable

OPEN *(Unclosed),* **adjective** *adapertus,* agape, ajar, coverless, dehiscent, gaping, lidless, *patens, patulous, patulus,* spacious, spread out, unclogged, uncorked, uncovered, unfastened, unfurled, unlatched, unlocked, unsealed, unshut, unstoppered, wide, yawning

OPEN-ENDED, *adjective* boundless, ceaseless, changing, continued, continuing, expansive, going on, illimitable, illimited, indecisive, indefinite, indeterminable, inexact, infinite, interminable, limitless, loose, measureless, modifiable, not particular, not specific, ongoing, termless, unbounded, unbridled, unceasing, unconfined, unconstrained, uncontrolled, undefined, unending, unlimited, unmeasured, unrestricted, vague, variable, wide-open, without limits, without specified limits

OPEN-MINDED, *adjective* accessible, amenable, broad-minded, detached, disinterested, dispassionate, equitable, evenhanded, fair, fair-minded, impartial, independent, indifferent, judicial, just, latitudinarian, liberal, neutral, objective, open, persuadable, persuasible, reasonable, receptive, responsive, tolerant, unbiased, unbigoted, uncolored, undogmatic, unimpassioned, uninfluenced, unjaundiced, unprepossessed, unswayed, unwarped

OPENING STATEMENT, *noun* opening argument, presentation of basics, presentation of data, presentation of essentials, presentation of the documentation, presentation of the evidence, presentation of the facts

OPERATE, *verb* accomplish, achieve, act, act upon, administer, administrate, assume responsibility, attain, bring about, caretake, carry into execution, carry on, carry out, cause, command, conduct, control, deal with, direct, discharge, do, drive, effect, effectuate, enforce, engage in, engineer, execute, exercise, exercise power over, exert, fulfill, function, govern, handle, have charge of, impel, implement, lead, look after, manage, maneuver, manipulate, mastermind, militate, minister, move, officiate, oversee, perform, perpetrate, pilot, practice, preside over, prevail over, put into effect, put into practice, regulate, rule, run, steer, superintend, supervise, take care of, take charge of, work
ASSOCIATED CONCEPTS: operate to the detriment of a party

OPERATION, *noun* act, action, campaign, course of action, crusade, *effectio,* enterprise, execution, exploit, function, handling, management, move, movement, performance, practice, procedure, proceeding, process, production, pursuit, routine, step, stratagem, stroke, task, thrust, transaction, undertaking, venture

OPERATIVE, *adjective* acting, active, adequate, advantageous, ample, applicable, at work, beneficial, capable, competent, effective, effectual, *efficax,* efficient, employed, fruitful, functional, functioning, helpful, in action, in effect, in force, in harness, in operation, in play, instrumental, on duty, operational, performing, potent, productive, serviceable, successful, sufficient, useable, useful, valid, workable, working, yielding

OPEROSE, *adjective* arduous, backbreaking, bothersome, burdensome, crushing, demanding, difficult, effortful, emasculating, embittering, enervating, exacting, exhausting, fagging, fatiguing, formidable, grinding, grueling, hard, hard to cope with, Herculean, irksome, laborious, onerous, painstaking, plodding, pressing, Sisyphean, straining, strenuous, tiresome, tiring, toilsome, troublesome, trying, uphill, vexatious, weakening, wearing, wearisome, wearying

OPINE, *verb* adjudge, appraise, *arbitrari,* assume, be convinced, be persuaded, be satisfied, believe, cherish a belief, conclude, conjecture, consider, dare say, deem, determine, diagnose, esteem, estimate, express an opinion, fancy, feel, guess, have a hunch, have an idea, have an opinion, have faith, have no doubt, hold, hypothesize, imagine, infer, judge, look upon, nurture a belief, *opinari,* postulate, preconceive, prejudge, presume, presuppose, pronounce judgment, reckon, regard, rest assured, speculate, stand, suppose, surmise, suspect, theorize, think, view, ween

OPINION *(Belief),* *noun* assumption, attitude, conclusion, conjecture, consideration, conviction, determination, estimate, estimation, evaluation, fancy, feeling, guess, hypothesis, idea, impression, *iudicium,* judgment, notion, outlook, perspective, persuasion, point of view, position, posture, preconception, presumption, presupposition, reaction, reflection, sentiment, speculation, stance, stand, supposition, surmise, suspicion, theory, thesis, thinking, thought, view, viewpoint
FOREIGN PHRASES: *Incivile est, nisi tota lege perspecta, una aliqua particula ejus proposita, judicare, vel respondere.* Unless the entire law has been examined, it is improper to pass judgement upon a portion of it. *Incivile est, nisi tota sententia inspecta, de aliqua parte judicare.* It is improper to pass an opinion on any part without examining the entire sentence. *Nullius hominis auctoritas apud nos valere debet, ut meliora non sequeremur si quis attulerit.* No man's influence ought to prevail upon us, that we should not follow better opinions, should any one present them. *Opinio est duplex, scilicet, opinio vulgaris, orta inter graves et discretos, et quae vultum veritatis habet; et opinio tantum orta inter leves et vulgares homines absque specie veritatis.* Opinion is of two fold, namely, common opinion, which springs up among grave and discreet persons, and which has the appearance of truth, and opinion which arises among foolish and ordinary men. *Opinio quae favet testamento est tenenda.* An opinion which favors a will is to be followed.

OPINION *(Judicial decision),* *noun* adjudication, ascertainment, assessment, authoritative statement, conclusion, conclusion of the matter, consideration, decision, declaration, decree, decreement, determination, final judgment, finding, formal statement, judgment, judgment on facts, order, position, pronouncement, report, resolution, rule, ruling, sentence, *sententia,* settlement by authoritative decision, solution
ASSOCIATED CONCEPTS: advisory opinion, concurring opinion, dissenting opinion, expert opinion, judicial opinion, legal opinion, majority opinion, memorandum opinion, minority opinion, opinion evidence, opinion of the court, per curiam opinion, professional opinion, written opinion
FOREIGN PHRASES: *Ubi non est directa lex, standum est arbitrio judicis, vel procedendum ad similia.* Where there is no direct law, the decision of the judge is to be taken, or references to be made to similar cases. *Judices non tenentur exprimere causam sententiae suae.* Judges are not bound to explain the reason for their sentences.

OPPONENT, *noun* *adversarius,* adversary, adverse party, challenger, combatant, contender, corrival, disputant, one who opposes, opposer, opposing litigant, opposing party, opposite, opposite side, opposition, other side

OPPORTUNE, *adjective* advantageous, appropriate, apt, auspicious, befitting, *commodus,* convenient, due, expedient, fit, fitting, *idoneus, opportunus,* propitious, providential, seasonable, suitable, suited, timely, well-timed

OPPORTUNITY, *noun* auspiciousness, chance, convenience, *copia,* fair chance, favorable chance, favorable time, fit time, fitting occasion, fitting time, fortuity, good chance, good fortune, hap, liberty, luck, *occasio,* occasion, opening, opportune moment, opportune time, possibility, *potestas,* proper occasion, proper time, propitiousness, prospect, readiness, reasonable chance, right time, ripeness, scope, suitable circumstance, suitable occasion, suitable time, time, turn
ASSOCIATED CONCEPTS: earliest practicable opportunity, opportunity to appear, opportunity to be heard

OPPOSE, *verb* act in opposition to, argue against, balk, battle, be at cross purposes, be contrary to, block, buck, challenge, collide, combat, come in conflict with, confront, confute, contend, contest, contradict, contravene, controvert, counter, counteract, counterattack, counterbalance, countermine, counterpoise, countervail, counterweigh, counterwork, debate, defy, demur, deny, disaffirm, disagree, disapprove, dispute, encounter, fight, go against, go contrary to, join issue, negate, not submit, not yield, object, obstruct, offer resistance, oppugn, prevent, prohibit, protest, put in opposition, rebut, recalcitrate, refute, reject, remonstrate, repel, repugn, repulse, resist, set against, stand firm against, strive, strive against, take a stand against, take exception to, take issue with, tourney
ASSOCIATED CONCEPTS: oppose a motion, opposing counsel, opposing interest, opposing parties
FOREIGN PHRASES: *Error qui non resistitur approbatur.* An error which is not resisted or opposed is waived.

OPPOSITE, *adjective* absonant, *adversarius,* adverse, antagonistic, antipodal, antipodean, antithetic, antithetical, clashing, conflicting, contradictive, contradictory, *contrarius,* contrary, contrasted, contrasting, converse, counter, diametrically opposed, disagreeing, discordant, facing, hostile, incompatible, inconsistent, inharmonious, inimical, inverse, inverted, mismated, mutually opposed, negative, opposed, opposing, oppugnant, perverse, resisting, resistive, reverse, reversed, wayward

OPPOSITION, *noun* antinomy, challenge, conflict, confutation, contention, contrariety, contrary action, contravention, counteraction, counterattack, counterplot, counterworking, denial, disagreement, disapprobation, disapproval, dissension, enmity, impugnation, impugnment, interference, objection, oppugnancy, oppugnation, protest, protestation, recalcitration, refutation, remonstrance, remonstration, resistance, running counter to, struggle, traversal, want of harmony

OPPRESSION, *noun* abuse, abusiveness, brutality, brute force, coercion, compulsion, cruelty, despotism, dictatorship, domination, enslavement, force, harassment, harshness, ill treatment, inhumanity, *iniuria,* injustice, iron rule, liberticide, maltreatment, misrule, mistreatment, misuse of power, persecution, reign of terror, repression, rule of might, ruthlessness, severity, subjection, subjugation, suppression, torment, totalitarianism, tyranny, *vexatio,* victimization

OPPRESSIVE, *adjective* afflictive, arduous, burdensome, confining, cruel, crushing, cumbersome, cumbrous, depressing, detrimental, devouring, difficult, difficult to bear, distressing, engulfing, exacting, exhausting, fatiguing, formidable, galling, grievous, grinding, hard, harmful, harsh, heavy, hurtful, imperious, inhuman, *iniquus,* intolerable, irksome, laborious, *molestus,* onerous, operose, overbearing, overpowering, overwhelming, painful, pernicious, ponderous, rigorous, severe, stifling, strenuous, suffocating, taxing, tiring, toilsome, troublesome, trying, tyrannical, unbearable, uncomfortable, unendurable, unreasonable, unyielding, upsetting, vexatious, wearing, wearisome, weighty

OPPROBRIUM, *noun* abasement, attaint, bad light, bad name, blot, brand, contempt, culpability, debasement, *dedecus,* defamation, degradation, derogation, disapprobation, discredit, disesteem, disgrace, dishonor, disrepute, disrespect, humiliation, ignobility, ignominiousness, ignominy, ill fame, ill repute, imputation, indignity, infamousness, infamy, ingloriousness, loss of honor, loss of reputation, loss of standing, notoriety, obloquy, odium, reproach, scandal, shady reputation, shame, slur, smirch, stain, stigma, taint, tarnish, vilification

OPPUGN, *verb* aggress, assault, attack, be contrary, buck, call in question, challenge, clash, combat, conflict, confront, contend, contradict, contravene, controvert, counter, countervail, counterwork, criticize adversely, cross, deal a blow, defy, denounce, descend upon, disagree, dispute, dissent, fall upon, fight, foil, gainsay, go against, hinder, hold out against, interfere with, militate against, object, obstruct, oppose, outface, pounce upon, protest, reason against, recalcitrate, refute, reluct, reluctate, remonstrate, resist, run against, run counter to, set upon, side against, stand against, stand up to, strike at, strive against, take exception, take the offensive, thrust at, thwart, traverse, wrangle

OPTION *(Choice),* *noun* alternate choice, alternative, choice, discretion, election, free decision, free selection, free will, freedom, freedom of choice, leave, liberty, opportunity, pick, power to choose, preference, right of choice, selection
ASSOCIATED CONCEPTS: election between options, exercise of option, options after default

OPTION *(Contractual provision),* *noun* acquired right, agreement, allowance, approval, authorization, consent, continuing offer, continuing offer to buy, favor, grant, guaranty, license, power, prerogative, privilege, proviso, right, right to buy or sell, sanction, stipulation, term, understanding
ASSOCIATED CONCEPTS: conditional option, continuing option, exercise of an option, first option, irrevocable option, option to buy, option to lease, option to purchase, option to renew, option to sell

OPULENT, *adjective* abounding in riches, affluent, comfortable, flourishing, flush, moneyed, *opulentus,* pecunious, propertied, prosperous, rich, richly endowed, rolling in riches, substantial, well-fixed, well-off, well provided for, well-situated, well-to-do, with means, worth a great deal

ORACULAR, *adjective* cryptic, divinatory, enigmatic, fatidic, fatidical, foreknowing, foretelling, knowing, mysterious, mystical, obscure, ominous, portentous, precursive, precursory, predicting, predictive, presaging, prognostic, prophetic, sage, sapient, sibylline, vatic, vaticinal, wise

ORAL, *adjective* announced, articulated, audible, by word of mouth, communicated, enunciated, expressed, expressed in words, phonic, said, said aloud, sounded, spoken, spoken out loud, told, unwritten, uttered, verbal, vocal, vocalized, voiced
ASSOCIATED CONCEPTS: nuncupative will, oral contract, oral testimony, statute of frauds

ORCHESTRATE, *verb* adapt, adjust, allot the parts, arrange, assemble, assign the parts, bring into order, bring together, compose, concert, conduct, construct, coordinate, harmonize, lay out, methodize, order, organize, preconcert, predetermine, put in order, put into a systematic form, reduce to order, regiment, regulate, set in order, set to music, standardize, symphonize, systematize

ORDER *(Arrangement),* ***noun*** adjustment, allocation, allotment, apportionment, array, catalogue, categorization, chronology, classification, composition, design, disposal, distribution, form, formation, gradation, grouping, layout, lineup, methodology, *ordo,* organization, pattern, placement, plan, procession, progression, rotation, sequence, setup, stratification, structure, system, systematization
ASSOCIATED CONCEPTS: order of creditors, order of priorities, order of proof

ORDER *(Judicial directive),* ***noun*** authoritative command, behest, command, commandment, court commandment, court instruction, declaration, decree, dictate, direction, directive, edict, *edictum,* fiat, imperative, instruction, *iussum,* judicial command, judicial instruction, mandate, *mandatum,* precept, prescript, prescription, proclamation, pronouncement, rescript, rule, ruling, ukase
ASSOCIATED CONCEPTS: appealable order, charging order, confinement order, decision, decretal order, entry of order, final order, interlocutory order, motion, nonappealable order, nunc pro tunc order, order granting a new trial, order of dismissal, order of the court, order staying execution, order to show cause, preliminary order, restraining order, self-executing order, settle order, suspension order

ORDER, *verb* adjure, call forth, call upon, cite, command, compel, decree, demand, dictate, direct, *edicere, imperare,* impose, impose a duty, impose a task, insist on, instruct, issue a decree, issue one's fiat, *iubere,* make a requisition, make demands on, oblige, ordain, prescribe, proscribe, require, rule, serve, tell, warrant
ASSOCIATED CONCEPTS: administrative order, amended order, appealable order, charging order, confinement order, contempt order, entry of judgment and order of the court, ex parte order, final order, interlocutory order, nunc pro tunc order, order granting a new trial, order of discontinuance, order of probate, order of proof, order of the court, order to show cause, restraining order, reviewable order, special order, stay order, suspension order, vacation of an order
FOREIGN PHRASES: *Quando aliquid mandatur, mandatur et omne per quod pervenitur ad illud.* When something is commanded, everything by which it can be accomplished is also ordered.

ORDINANCE, *noun* authoritative rule, canon, charter, code, command, decree, *decretum,* direction, edict, *edictum,* enactment, fiat, imperative, law, legal command, legislation, legislative decree, legislative edict, local law, local legislation, local rule, mandate, maxim, municipal code, municipal regulation, ordainment, order, ordination, prescript, proclamation, regulation, requirement, rule, statute
ASSOCIATED CONCEPTS: city ordinance, criminal ordinance, local ordinance, municipal ordinance, regulatory ordinance, traffic ordinance, violation of an ordinance, zoning ordinance

ORDINARY, *adjective* accepted, accustomary, accustomed, average, banal, boring, bourgeois, bromidic, characteristic, colloquial, commonplace, *communis,* consuetudinary, conventional, customary, daily, drab, established, expected, familiar, fixed, frequent, general, generally practiced, habitual, hackneyed, homely, homespun, household, humdrum, insipid, known, mediocre, middling, normal, oft-repeated, pedestrian, philistine, platitudinous, plebeian, plentiful, popular, prevailing, prevalent, prosaic, prosaical, *quotidianus,* recognized, regular, regulation, repeated, representative, rife, simple, stale, standard, stereotyped, stock, taken for granted, traditional, *translaticius,* trite, typical, unassuming, undistinguished, unexceptional, unexciting, unimaginative, unoriginal, unvaried, usual, vernacular, wearisome, well-trodden, well-worn, widespread, wonted, workaday
ASSOCIATED CONCEPTS: necessary expenses, ordinary care and skill, ordinary course of business, ordinary course of trade, ordinary duty, ordinary expenses, ordinary income, ordinary loss, ordinary meaning, ordinary negligence, ordinary prudent person, ordinary reasonable man, ordinary risk, ordinary standard of care, ordinary use, ordinary wear and tear
FOREIGN PHRASES: *Recurrendum est ad extraordinarium quando non valet ordinarium.* Resort must be made to the extraordinary when the ordinary does not succeed.

ORGAN, *noun* affiliate, agency, annex, appendage, arm, associate, branch, branch office, bureau, chapter, component, department, division, extension, instrument, instrumentality, local, lodge, means, member, newspaper, office, offshoot, part, periodical, post, ramification, section, subdivision, subsidiary, unit, wing

ORGANIC, *adjective* anatomical, basal, basic, constitutional, deep-rooted, derived from within, elemental, fundamental, implanted, inborn, inbred, indigenous, ingrained, inherent, innate, instinctive, intrinsic, intrinsical, native, natural, original, primary, primitive, rooted, rudimentary, structural, substantial, substantive, underlying

ORGANIZATION *(Association),* ***noun*** affiliation, aggregation, alliance, bloc, club, coalition, combination, community, company, corps, coterie, establishment, faction, federation, foundation, group, institute, institution, joint concern, league, *reipublicae forma,* school, sodality, syndicate, troupe
ASSOCIATED CONCEPTS: charitable organization, de facto organization, domestic organization, labor organization, nonprofit organization, political organization

ORGANIZATION *(Structure),* ***noun*** arrangement, build, classification, composition, configuration, conformation, constitution, construction, *descriptio,* design, figuration, figure, form, formation, framework, grouping, interrelation of parts, makeup, manner of construction, order, placement, plan, regularity, scheme, shape, style of arrangement, systematization, *temperatio*

ORGANIZE *(Arrange), verb*   adjust, align, assort, catalogue, categorize, class, classify, combine, *componere,* correlate, establish guide lines, establish parameters, file, form into classes, get in formation, grade, group, introduce a system, introduce order, lay down guide lines, list, marshal, methodize, order, *ordinare,* place, place in order, put in array, put in order, put into shape, rank, rate, reduce to order, regiment, regulate, separate into categories, set guidelines, set in array, set in order, sort, standardize, straighten, systematize
ASSOCIATED CONCEPTS: organize a corporation, organized labor

ORGANIZE *(Unionize), verb*   affiliate, amalgamate, associate, band together, cement a union, centralize, collaborate, combine, confederate, consolidate, create, enlist employees in a labor union, enlist in a labor union, enter into a league, establish, federate, form, form a labor union, form into a body, formulate, incorporate, institute, join, join together, merge, mold, set up, unify, unite, unite for a common purpose
ASSOCIATED CONCEPTS: organized labor

ORGULOUS, *adjective*   affected, aloof, arrogant, assuming, blustering, boastful, boasting, bragging, conceited, condescending, contemptuous, disdainful, egocentric, egoistic, egoistical, egotistic, egotistical, fanfaronading, flaunting, gasconading, grand, grandiose, haughty, immodest, imperious, inflated, insolent, intolerant, lofty, lordly, narcissistic, overbearing, overproud, overweening, patronizing, pompous, presumptuous, prideful, scornful, self-applauding, self-centred, self-flattering, self-glorifying, self-important, self-lauding, self-magnifying, self-praising, self-satisfied, supercilious, thrasonical, vain, vainglorious, vaunting

ORIGIN *(Ancestry), noun*   ancestral descent, birth, bloodline, derivation, descent, dynasty, extraction, family, filiation, genealogical tree, genealogy, heritage, kith and kin, line, line of ancestors, line of descent, lineage, *origo,* parentage, parenthood, pedigree, race, stock, tribe
FOREIGN PHRASES: *Origine propria neminem posse voluntate sua eximi manifestum est.* It is evident that no one by his own will can renounce his own origin.

ORIGIN *(Source), noun*   beginning, birth, birthplace, cause, commencement, cradle, creation, dawn, derivation, *fons,* font, foundation, fountainhead, genesis, inception, initiation, nascency, nativity, onset, *origo, principium,* root, starting point, wellspring
FOREIGN PHRASES: *Ex facto jus oritur.* Law arises out of facts. *Causa et origo est materia negotii.* The cause and origin are the substance of the transaction.

ORIGINAL *(Creative), adjective*   artful, clever, daring, demiurgic, demiurgical, different, eccentric, envisioning, exceptional, fanciful, fecund, fertile, fictive, fresh, gifted, imaginal, imaginative, individual, ingenious, inimitable, inspired, inventive, nonconformist, novel, odd, originative, out of the ordinary, poetic, productive, rare, resourceful, singular, unborrowed, un-

common, unconformable, unconventional, uncopied, uncustomary, underived, unexampled, unexpected, unfashionable, unheard of, unimitated, unique, unmatched, unordinary, unorthodox, unparalleled, unusual, unwonted, visioned, visualizing, whimsical

ORIGINAL *(Initial), adjective*   antecedent, authentic, basal, basic, basilar, beginning, commencing, earliest, elemental, elementary, embryonic, first, formative, foundational, fundamental, germinal, inaugural, inauguratory, inchoate, inchoative, incipient, incunabular, infant, initial, initiative, initiatory, introductory, maiden, nascent, natal, native, nonimitative, opening, precursory, preliminary, prelusive, prelusory, primal, primary, prime, primeval, primigenial, primitive, primordial, pristine, proemial, pure, rudimental, rudimentary, seminal, starting, underlying
ASSOCIATED CONCEPTS: best evidence rule, original action, original decree, original evidence, original holder, original issue, original jurisdiction, original stock, original undertaking, original writing

ORIGINATE, *verb*   activate, arouse, author, awaken, beget, begin, break ground, breed, bring about, bring into existence, bring on, bring to pass, cause, coin, commence, compose, conceive, concoct, contrive, create, devise, draft, effect, elicit, engender, engineer, establish, evoke, fabricate, father, forge, form, formulate, found, frame, generate, get going, get up, give birth to, give impulse to, give origin to, give rise to, handsel, improvise, inaugurate, induce, initiate, inspire, institute, introduce, invent, kindle, launch, lay the foundation for, lead, make, make up, manufacture, motivate, mount, open, pioneer, plan, precipitate, prepare, produce, promote, prompt, propagate, provoke, raise, set afloat, set going, set in motion, set up, sire, start, stimulate, take the first step, take the initiative, take the lead, think up, trigger, undertake, usher in

ORIGINATION, *noun*   ancestry, beginning, birth, causation, cause, coinage, commencement, composition, cradle, creation, dawn, derivation, discovery, emergence, etymology, exordium, fabrication, fomentation, font, foundation, fountain, fountainhead, genesis, inauguration, inception, inchoation, incipience, incipiency, incunabula, infancy, initiation, instigation, introduction, invention, motivation, motive, nascency, nativity, onset, opening, outset, parentage, production, provenance, provenience, rise, root, source, spring, start, starting point, stimulation, stimulus, wellspring

OROTUND, *adjective*   affected, artificial, blustering, bombastic, clear, declamatory, elocutionary, flatulent, forceful, full, fustian, grandiloquent, grandiose, high-flown, histrionic, inflated, magniloquent, mellow, oratorical, pompous, presumptuous, pretentious, resonant, rhetorical, showy, sonorous, stilted, strong, stuffy, swelling, swollen, theatrical, tumid, turgescent, turgid, vainglorious, windy

ORPHAN, *noun*   abandoned child, abandoned infant, bereaved child, castaway, child without parents, foundling, homeless child, *orbus,* orphaned child, orphaned infant, parentless child, twice-bereaved child, waif, ward

ORTHODOX, *adjective*   accepting, according to custom, according to regulation, according to rule, according to the book, accustomed, acknowledged, approved, believing, bound by convention, canonical, common, commonplace, compliant, conformable, conforming, conservative, conventional, correct, customary, devoted to convention, doctrinal, established, formal, habitual, inflexible, literal, ordinary, *orthodoxus,* prescriptive, prevailing, proper, recognized, rigid, scrupulous, strict, traditional, typical, unbending, unchangeable, uncompromising, unheterodox, usual, wonted

OSCILLATE, *verb* *agitari,* agitate, alternate, be doubtful, be indecisive, be irresolute, be uncertain, be undecided, be undetermined, be unresolved, be unsteady, be unsure, beat, bounce, debate, deliberate, falter, flap, fluctuate, flutter, fret, hesitate, librate, lurch, move in waves, move to and fro, pendulate, rock, rotate, seesaw, shift, sway, swerve, swing, turn, undulate, vacillate, vary, waver

OSMOSIS, *noun* absorption, assimilation, diffusion, digestion, engulfment, infiltration, ingress, interpenetration, introgression, passage, penetration, permeation, saturation, seepage, transmission

OSSIFIED, *adjective* bony, calcified, calloused, congealed, crystallized, dense, firm, fossilized, hard, hardened, incrassate, incrassated, indurated, lapidified, petrified, solid, solidified, stiff, stiffened, stony, thick, thickened, tough, toughened, turned to bone

OSTENSIBLE, *adjective* able to be seen, apparent, appearing, assumable, assumed, avowed, believable, claimed, clear, colorable, conjecturable, credible, deceiving, deceptive, declared, deluding, delusional, delusive, delusory, discernible, evident, explicit, express, *fictus,* illusional, illusionary, illusive, illusory, indubitable, likely, manifest, misleading, noticeable, observable, obvious, outward, overt, patent, perceivable, perceptible, perspicuous, plain, plausible, presumable, pretended, professed, purported, reasonable, seeable, seeming, self-evident, shown, *simulatus,* so-called, specious, supposable, supposed, surface, surmisable, visible

OSTRACISM, *noun* avoidance, ban, banishment, blackball, blacklist, blame, blockade, censure, condemnation, coventry, criticism, decrial, deportation, disbarment, dislodgment, dismissal, displacement, dissociability, distance, ejection, elimination, eviction, exclusion, excommunication, exile, exilement, expatriation, expulsion, extrusion, hostility, inhospitality, intolerance, isolation, lockout, nonadmission, noninclusion, obloquy, omission, preclusion, prejudice, prohibition, proscription, quarantine, refusal, rejection, reprobation, reproof, segregation, separation, shame, snub, stricture, suspension, unfriendliness, unsociableness

OTIOSE, *adjective* abortive, apathetic, arid, barren, bootless, dallying, dilatory, disengaged, dispensable, disused, dormant, dried up, effete, exhausted, expendable, faineant, fallow, feckless, fruitless, futile, idle, impotent, impracticable, impractical, inactive, indolent, ineffective, ineffectual, inefficacious, inefficient, inert, infertile, inoperative, invalid, issueless, jejune, jobless, lackadaisical, laggard, lagging, lame, languorous, lazy, leaden, lethargic, lethargical, lifeless, listless, lymphatic, motionless, neglectful, nonfunctional, nonfunctioning, nonparticipating, nugatory, null and void, oscitant, passive, phlegmatic, powerless, resultless,

slack, slothful, slow, sluggish, spiritless, stagnating, sterile, supine, torpescent, torpid, unable, unadaptable, unavailing, uncalled-for, unemployed, unfertile, unfruitful, unnecessary, unneeded, unoccupied, unpersevering, unproductive, unprofitable, unprolific, unserviceable, unsubstantial, unsuccessful, unusable, unwanted, unworkable, useless, vain, valueless, wasted, weary, worthless

OUST, *verb* banish, cast out, chase out, depose, deprive of office, dislodge, dismiss, displace, dispossess, divest of office, drive out, eject, expel, force out, purge, put out, remove, remove from office, repudiate, throw out, thrust out, turn out, unseat
ASSOCIATED CONCEPTS: impeachment, removal from public office

OUSTER, *noun* deprivation, dislodgment, dispossession, ejection, elimination, eviction, exclusion, permanent exclusion, removal, repudiation

OUT OF POCKET, *adverb* compensation, costs, damages, expenses, just compensation, payment, recovery, remuneration, reparation for loss, repayment, restitution, restoration, retrieval, satisfaction
ASSOCIATED CONCEPTS: pocket expenses

OUTBALANCE, *verb* be greater in value, be greater in weight, be superior, better, compensate, counteract, counterbalance, counterpoise, countervail, counterweigh, cover, dominate, eclipse, equalize, equiponderate, exceed, gain the ascendancy, get ahead of, have the advantage, have the edge on, hedge, indemnify, make compensation, make leeway, make up for, neutralize, offset, outdo, outpoint, outrival, outstrip, outvie, outweigh, overbalance, overcome, overmatch, overtop, overweigh, pass, predominate, preponderate, prevail, recoup, redeem, rise above, rival, set off, surpass, top, transcend, trump

OUTBREAK, *noun* affray, aggression, agitation, assault, attack, bloodshed, blow up, brawl, breach, breach of the peace, burst, cataclysm, commotion, conflict, convulsion, declaration of war, disruption, disturbance, ebullition, eruption, explosion, ferocity, fit, flare-up, foment, fomentation, fracas, fray, fury, insurgence, insurrection, invasion, irruption, mayhem, mutinousness, mutiny, onslaught, outburst, overthrow of authority, paroxysm, proruption, quarrel, rage, raid, rebellion, revolt, revolution, riot, rising, rush, siege, spasm, strife, throe, thunder, torrent, unruliness, uprising, uproar, violent behavior, warfare

OUTBURST, *noun* affray, agitation, attack, blast, blaze, blowout, blowup, bluster, breach of the peace, burst, clamor, commotion, convulsion, detonation, discharge, disgorgement, disquiet, disquietude, disruption, disturbance, ebullition, ejaculation, emission, eruption, explosion, expulsion, fit, flare up, flurry, foment, fomentation, fray, frenzy, furor, fury, fuss, gush, hysteria, hysterical state, hysterics, impetuosity, insurgence, insurrection, irascibility, irascibleness, irruption, jet, mayhem, outbreak, outpour, paroxysm, proruption, rage, rampage, rebellion, restlessness, revolt, revolution, rising, rush, sally, spasm, spurt, stir, strife, sudden excursion, tempest, throe, thunder, torrent, unruliness, upheaval, uproar, vehemence, violence, volcano

OUTCOME, noun achievement, aftereffect, aftermath, answer, attainment, close, completion, consequence, consummation, creation, culmination, decision, denouement, development, effect, end, end product, ending, eventuality, eventuation, finding, finish, fruit, fruition, fulfillment, issue, judgment, offspring, outgrowth, product, production, realization, resolution, result, resultant, sequence, sequent, settlement, solution, upshot, yield
ASSOCIATED CONCEPTS: outcome-determinative test

OUTCRY, noun accusation, blame, brawl, broken silence, bruit, burst of sound, castigation, censure, charge, chiding, chorus, clamor, clamorousness, complaint, condemnation, *convicium,* criticism, cry, denunciation, diatribe, din, disapprobation, disapproval, discontent, dislike, dissatisfaction, dissent, disturbance, execration, explosion, fracas, furor, grievance, howl, hullabaloo, invective, lament, loud noise, loud protest, noise, objection, opposition, pandemonium, philippic, plaint, protest, protestation, racket, raised voice, rebuke, reprimand, reproach, reprobation, revilement, scolding, scream, shout, stricture, tumult, turmoil, upbraiding, uproar, vilification, vituperation, *voces, vociferatio,* vociferation, wail, weeping, yell

OUTDATED, adjective anachronistic, anachronous, ancient, antediluvian, antiquated, antique, archaic, behind the age, behind the times, bygone, dated, defunct, demode, discarded, disused, expired, extinct, fallen into desuetude, fallen into disuse, forgotten, former, gone by, gone out, grown old, no longer customary, no longer fashionable, no longer in style, no longer prevailing, no longer prevalent, no longer stylish, not current, not in vogue, not modern, obsolescent, obsolete, of a previous fashion, of a previous style, of great age, of old, of the old order, of the old school, old, old-fashioned, old-time, old-world, olden, out-of-date, out-of-fashion, out-of-use, outmoded, outworn, passe, past, primitive, quaint, rejected, stale, styleless, superannuated, superseded, unaccepted, uncontemporary, uncurrent, unfashionable, unpracticed, unstylish

OUTFLOW, noun abatement, current, defluxion, discharge, disemboguement, drain, drainage, ebb, effluence, efflux, effusion, egression, emanation, emergence, emersion, emigration, eruption, escape, evacuation, exodus, expenditure, expense, export, exportation, expulsion, extravasation, extrusion, exudation, flood, flux, gush, issue, jet, leakage, movement, ooze, outburst, outgush, outpour, outstream, outward flow, outward sweep, overflow, recession, refluence, reflux, runoff, seep, shipments, spill, spout, spurt, stream, tide, transudation, wane, withdrawal

OUTGROWTH, noun aftereffect, aftermath, development, effect, end result, eventuality, eventuation, excrescence, fruit, issue, offshoot, offspring, repercussion, result, resultance, resultant, sequel, sprout, yield

OUTLAW, noun bandit, brigand, convict, criminal, delinquent, evildoer, felon, fugitive, fugitive from the law, habitual criminal, habitual offender, hardened criminal, lawbreaker, lawless individual, malefactor, miscreant, notorious criminal, offender, offender against society, *proscriptus,* public enemy, racketeer, recidivist, robber, swindler, thief, transgressor, underworld character, violator of the law

OUTLAW, verb *aqua et igni interdicere,* banish, bar, declare illegal, declare unlawful, exclude, expel, forbid by law, make unlawful, place outside the protection of the law, proscribe, *proscribere,* put beyond the protection of the law, reject, repel

OUTLAY, noun amount expended, budgeted items, charge, cost, disbursement, expenditure, expense, *impensa,* outgo, payment, spending, *sumptus*

OUTLET, noun access, aperture, avenue, channel, chute, conduit, demand, door, egress, *egressus, emissarium,* exhaust, exit, *exitus,* floodgate, gate, gateway, hatch, hole, market, means of escape, opening, passage out, path, portal, spout, vent, way out

OUTLINE (Boundary), noun ambit, border, bounds, bourn, brink, circuit, circumference, circumscription, compass, confine, contour, demarcation, edge, edging, external form, *extrema lineamenta,* extremity, frame, fringes, frontier, limitations, limits, line of demarcation, lineaments, margin, metes, pale, perimeter, periphery, profile, rim, skirt, threshold, tracing, verge

OUTLINE (Synopsis), noun abbreviation, abridgment, abstract, *adumbratio,* agenda, brief, compend, compendium, compression, condensation, conspectus, contents, contraction, core, digest, epitome, essence, minute, note, pandect, recapitulation, report, skeleton, sketch, summation, syllabus

OUTLOOK, noun angle, aspect, attitude, emotional tone, field of view, frame of mind, frame of reference, observation, perspective, point of observation, point of view, position, posture, regard, slant, stand, standpoint, viewpoint, way of thinking

OUTMODED, adjective anachronistic, anachronous, ancient, antediluvian, antiquated, antique, archaic, behind the age, behind the times, bygone, dated, demoded, desuete, disapproved, discarded, disused, expired, extinct, fallen into desuetude, fallen into disuse, forgotten, former, gone out, grown old, neglected, no longer conventional, no longer customary, no longer prevailing, not in vogue, obsolescent, obsolete, of a previous fashion, of a previous style, of the old school, old, old-fashioned, old-world, out-of-date, out of fashion, out of use, outdated, outworn, passe, past, primitive, quaint, rejected, retired, stale, styleless, superannuated, superseded, unaccepted, uncurrent, unfashionable, unpracticed, unstylish

OUTPOUR, verb be effusive, be prolix, cascade, cast forth, decant, detrude, discharge, discourse at length, disembogue, disgorge, drain, effuse, eject, emit, empty, enlarge upon, eruct, eructate, evacuate, exhaust, expel, extravasate, harangue, inundate, let fall, pour forth, pour out, rant, send forth, send out, shed, spill, spout, spurt, stream, vent

OUTPUT, noun accomplishment, achievement, amount produced, avail, benefit, creation, crop, discharge, earnings, effectuation, emanation, end, end product, fruit, gain, harvest, issuance, issue, manufactured product, merchandise, outcome, proceeds, produce, product, production, profit, quantity produced, result, return, yield
ASSOCIATED CONCEPTS: output contract

OUTRAGEOUS, adjective abominable, absurd, abusive, acrimonious, affronting, arrant, atrocious, barefaced, base, black, brazen, conspicuous, contemptible, *contumeliosus,* contumelious, corrupt, cruel, deplorable, despicable, despiteful, dire, disgraceful, dishonorable, disobliging, disrespectful, drastic, egregious, enormous, exaggerated, excessive, execrable, exorbitant, extreme, fanatic, fanatical, ferocious, flagitious, flagrant, foul, fulsome, galling, glaring, gross, grossly offensive, harmful, hateful, heinous, horrifying, hotheaded, hyperbolical, ignoble, *immanis,* immense, immoderate, *immoderatus,* infamous, infuriating, iniquitous, injurious, inordinate, insolent, insulting, intolerable, low, mad, madcap, malevolent, malicious, malign, malignant, maniacal, monstrous, nefarious, notorious, odious, offensive, opprobrious, overdone, perfidious, preposterous, questionable, rabid, radical, raging, reprehensible, scandalous, shameless, shocking, sinful, spiteful, tempestuous, unconscionable, undue, unpleasant, unreasonable, unwarranted, villainous, wanton, wicked, wild, wrongful
ASSOCIATED CONCEPTS: outrageous conduct

OUTRIGHT, adjective absolute, all-out, altogether, complete, comprehensive, consummate, downright, entire, exhaustive, flagrant, full, full-fledged, obvious, out-and-out, sheer, straightforward, straight out, sweeping, thorough, through and through, total, unconditional, undiminished, undivided, unequivocal, unmitigated, unqualified, utter
ASSOCIATED CONCEPTS: outright grant

OUTSET, noun beginning, birth, commencement, dawn, embarkation, entrance, exordium, first move, first step, foundation, genesis, inauguration, inception, inchoation, incipience, incipiency, induction, infancy, initiation, *initium,* introduction, launching, onset, opening, origin, origination, outbreak, rise, start, starting point, threshold

OUTSTANDING (Prominent), adjective august, celebrated, chief, consequential, conspicuous, distinctive, distinguished, elevated, eminent, especial, esteemed, exalted, excellent, excelling, exceptional, eximious, extraordinary, famed, famous, far-famed, foremost, great, honorable, honored, illustrious, important, imposing, impressive, incomparable, influential, known, luminous, lustrous, majestic, marked, memorable, nonpareil, notable, noted, noteworthy, paramount, peerless, preeminent, prestigious, princely, principal, ranking, recognized, remarkable, renowned, reputable, respected, revered, royal, salient, significant, special, starring, sublime, substantial, supereminent, superior, superlative, supreme, transcendent, unforgettable, unparalleled, venerable

OUTSTANDING (Unpaid), adjective delinquent, due, in arrears, overdue, owing, past due, payable, surviving, uncollected, ungathered, unliquidated, unrecompensed, unrequited, unsatisfied, unsettled

OUTSTANDING (Unresolved), adjective in suspense, incomplete, indefinite, irresolved, open, pending, unadjusted, unascertained, unconcluded, undecided, undetermined, unfinished, unsettled

OUTWEIGH, verb be of greater significance, beat, better, come first, dominate, eclipse, exceed, exceed in importance, exceed in value, excel, get ahead of, go be-yond, outbalance, outdo, outrank, outrival, overbalance, overpoise, overpower, overshadow, overtop, overweigh, *potiorem,* predominate, preponderate, prevail, rise above, *superare,* surpass, take precedence over, top, transcend, *vincere,* weigh more than

OVERAGE, noun avalanche, balance, deluge, excess, extra, glut, inundation, leftover, overabundance, overflow, overmeasure, overplus, oversupply, plenty, profusion, redundance, redundancy, remainder, remnant, repletion, residue, spare, supersaturation, surfeit, surplus, surplusage, too many, too much, undue amount

OVERCOME (Overwhelm), verb astonish, awestrike, bewilder, bowl over, break down, burden, confound, crush, daze, deluge, discomfit, drown, encumber, engulf, flood, get the upper hand, glut, hamper, immerse, inundate, overlay, overload, overpower, overtax, prostrate, saddle, shatter, stagger, stun, submerge, swallow up, swamp, weigh down, whelm

OVERCOME (Surmount), verb beat, command, conquer, defeat, destroy, dominate, drub, eclipse, get the better of, get the upper hand, master, outdo, outrival, outshine, outstrip, overmatch, overpower, overshadow, overthrow, prevail over, quash, quell, rise above, rout, subdue, subjugate, tower above, transcend, triumph over, vanquish
ASSOCIATED CONCEPTS: overcome a presumption

OVERDRAW, verb *aes alienum contrahere,* be debited with, be in debt, be prodigal, become bankrupt, become insolvent, deplete, dissipate, exhaust, incur a debt, overcharge, overextend, overspend, overstrain, overstretch, owe, owe money, run into debt, spend more than one has, squander
ASSOCIATED CONCEPTS: overdraw an account

OVERDUE, adjective behind time, belated, *debitus,* delayed, delinquent, due, in arrears, late, long-delayed, more than due, not on time, outstanding, past due, past the time for payment, remiss, tardy, unpaid, untimely

OVERESTIMATE, verb adulate, aggrandize, attach too much importance to, enlarge, estimate too highly, exaggerate, exalt, exceed, expand, extol, flatter, glorify, inflate, magnify, make too much of, maximize, misestimate, misjudge, misrepresent, overassess, overcalculate, overcount, overdo, overjudge, overlaud, overmeasure, overpraise, overprize, overrate, overstate, overvalue, set too high an estimate

OVEREXTEND, verb develop too fast, develop too much, distend, go too far, grow too fast, grow too much, overcommit, overdevelop, overexpand, spread too far, spread too thin, strain, stretch, stretch too far

OVERHEAD, noun budget, business expenses, charges, cost, cost incurred, cost of living, current expenses, disbursement, drain on resources, expenditures, expense, general expenses, liabilities, living expenses, money expended, operating expenses, outlay, payments, spendings, upkeep
ASSOCIATED CONCEPTS: overhead expenses

OVERHEAR, verb attend, become aware of, catch, detect, eavesdrop, *exaudire, excipere,* find out, glean knowledge of, hear, intercept, listen in on, listen

stealthily, monitor, obtain knowledge of, pick up, receive information, receive knowledge of, *subauscultare*
ASSOCIATED CONCEPTS: eavesdropping, wiretapping

OVERINDULGE, *verb*   be gluttonous, be greedy, be intemperate, be selfish, be voracious, carry to excess, carry too far, cater to excessively, coddle excessively, eat excessively, favor excessively, gratify to excess, humor excessively, lack self-control, overdo, overeat, overgorge, overgratify, pamper excessively, satiate to excess, satisfy to excess, spoil excessively

OVERLAP, *verb*   adjoin, cover, encroach, exceed, extend beyond, go beyond, imbricate, *imminere, impendere,* impinge, infringe, invade, lap over, lie over, make contact, overgrow, overhang, overlay, overlie, override, overrun, overspread, project, protrude, reach over, run over, spread over, superimpose, touch

OVERLOAD, *verb*   burden, choke, congest, cram, crowd, cumber, deluge, drench, encumber, flood, force, glut, gorge, inundate, load to excess, make heavy, oppress, overabound, overburden, overdo, overdose, overexert, overfeed, overfill, overstrain, overstuff, overtask, overtax, overuse, overweigh, overwhelm, overwork, pack, saddle, saturate, soak, strain, supercharge, supersaturate, surcharge, surfeit, weigh down, work to excess

OVERLOOK (*Disregard*), *verb*   fail to appreciate, fail to observe, fail to see, forget, leave out, leave undone, let ride, miss, neglect, omit, pass over, take no notice

OVERLOOK (*Excuse*), *verb*   condone, disregard, excuse, forgive, pardon

OVERLOOK (*Superintend*), *verb*   administer, be at the helm, be inattentive to, command, command a view of, *condonare,* conduct, control, direct, examine, govern, guide, have charge of, hold the reins, ignore, *ignoscere,* inspect, look after, look out, look over, oversee, pilot, *praeterire,* preside, review, scrutinize, steer, study, supervise, survey, watch over

OVERREACH, *verb*   accroach, annul, cheat, *circumscribere, circumvenire,* circumvent, deceive, defeat one's own purpose, defeat oneself by overdoing matters, defraud, dupe, encroach, exceed, extend beyond, extend over, fool, get the better of, have one's plans backfire, mislead, nullify one's gains, offset, outsmart, outwit, overact, overdo, overextend, overshoot, reach beyond, reach over, reach too far, thwart, trick, trip, undermine, undo
ASSOCIATED CONCEPTS: undue influence

OVERRIDE, *verb*   act despite, annul, cancel, counteract, countermand, crush, defeat, discard, dismiss, disregard, do away with, dominate, flout, fly in the face of, ignore, invalidate, make ineffectual, make null and void, make void, neglect, nullify, outweigh, overcome, overpower, overrule, overturn, pass over, prevail over, quell, reverse, revoke, set aside, subdue, supersede, surpass, take no account of, take precedence, thwart, upset
ASSOCIATED CONCEPTS: override a veto, overriding state interest

OVERRULE, *verb*   abrogate, annul, cancel, countermand, decide against, *gubernare,* invalidate, make null, make void, nullify, obviate, override, overturn, re-

fuse to sustain, reject, reject by subsequent action, reject by subsequent decision, renounce, repeal, repudiate, rescind, retract, reverse, revoke, rule against, rule out, set aside, supersede, undo, upset, *vincere,* void
ASSOCIATED CONCEPTS: overrule a decision, overrule a motion, overrule an objection

OVERSEE, *verb*   administer, attend to, be at the helm, be the guiding force, carry on, coach, command, conduct, control, dictate, direct, dominate, engineer, examine, execute, govern, guide, handle, have authority over, have charge of, have the direction of, head, instruct, lead, look after, manage, master, mastermind, navigate, officiate, pay attention to, pilot, *procurare,* reconnoiter, regiment, regulate, rein, rule, scrutinize, steer, superintend, supervise, watch, watch over
ASSOCIATED CONCEPTS: master servant relationship, principal agent relationship, respondeat superior

OVERSIGHT (*Carelessness*), *noun*   blunder, careless mistake, careless omission, *erratum,* error, failure, failure to notice, heedlessness, inadvertency, inattention, *incuria,* lapse, laxity, laxness, mistake, neglect, negligence, nonobservance, remissness, slip, supervision, thoughtlessness, unintentional mistake, unintentional omission
ASSOCIATED CONCEPTS: negligence

OVERSIGHT (*Control*), *noun*   management, overlooking, superintendence, supervision, watchful care, watchfulness

OVERSTATEMENT, *noun*   aggrandizement, amplification, boasting, coloring, distortion, elaboration, embroidery, enlargement, exaggerated statement, exaggeration, expansion, extravagance, extravagancy, falsification, hyperbole, hyperbolism, inflated statement, inflation, magnification, magniloquence, misjudgment, misrepresentation, misstatement, overestimation, puffery

OVERSTEP, *verb*   accroach, advance beyond proper limits, break in upon, encroach, entrench, exceed, go beyond, go over, go too far, impinge, infringe, interfere, intrude, invade, meddle, not observe, obtrude, overpass, overrun, run over, strain, stretch, transcend, transgress, trench on, trespass, usurp, violate

OVERT, *adjective*   *apertus,* apparent, clear, definite, disclosed, distinct, easily seen, evident, explicit, exposed, express, glaring, in full view, in plain sight, manifest, *manifestus,* noticeable, notorious, obvious, open, ostensible, palpable, patent, perceptible, perspicuous, plain, public, revealed, unconcealed, uncovered, undisguised, unhidden, visible

OVERT ACT, *noun*   action, beginnings, commencement, criminal act, dealings, deed, doings, intentional act, maneuver, manifest act, open act, outward act, start
ASSOCIATED CONCEPTS: conspiracy

OVERTHROW, *verb*   abolish, *adfligere,* be victorious over, break up, bring down, cast down, conquer, defeat, *deicere,* dethrone, *diruere,* disrupt, eradicate, exterminate, extirpate, fell, invert, master, nullify, obliterate, obviate, overmaster, overpower, overrun, overset, overturn, overwhelm, prostrate, quash, quell, ravage, refute, remove, reverse, revolt, revolutionize, shatter, subdue, subjugate, subvert, suppress, surmount, terminate, throw down, throw over, topple, turn upside down, uncrown, unseat, upend, uproot, upset

OVERTURE, noun advance, approach, beginning, bid, *condicio,* exordium, foreword, initiative, introduction, invitation, motion, offer, opening of negotiations, preamble, preface, preliminary, preliminary negotiation, prelude, presentation, proem, proffer, proposal, proposition, tender

OVERTURN, verb abolish, annihilate, conquer, crush, defeat, demolish, destroy, *evertere,* foil, invert, obliterate, overcome, overpower, overset, overthrow, overwhelm, quell, repress, reverse, ruin, subdue, subvert, *subvertere,* suppress, topple, upend, uproot, upset, vanquish

ASSOCIATED CONCEPTS: overturn a decision

OVERWHELM, verb astonish, beat, besiege, bewilder, bury, confound, confuse, conquer, daze, defeat, deluge, *demergere,* destroy, discomfit, immerse, impress, inundate, master, *obruere, opprimere,* overcome, overpower, overrun, overthrow, quash, quell, shock, stun, subdue, subjugate, submerge, suppress, surmount, surprise, triumph over, vanquish, weigh down

OWE, verb be beholden, be bound, be due, be in debt, be indebted, be liable, be obligated, be under obli-

gation, contract a debt, *debere,* have a loan, have an obligation, incur a debt

ASSOCIATED CONCEPTS: debt owed, debtor-creditor laws, legally owed, taxes owed

OWN, verb be in possession of, be in receipt of, be master of, be possessed of, claim, command, contain, control, dominate, enjoy, *habere,* have, have a deed for, have a title to, have claim upon, have hold of, have in hand, have rights to, have to one's name, hold, keep, maintain, occupy, possess, *possidere,* retain, *tenere*

FOREIGN PHRASES: *Id solum nostrum quod debitis deductis nostrum est.* That only is ours which remains to us after deduction of our debts.

OWNERSHIP, noun claim, control, dominion, *dominium,* holding, mastery, occupancy, possessorship, proprietary, proprietorship, right of possession, seisin, tenancy, tenure, title, use

ASSOCIATED CONCEPTS: absolute ownership, apparent ownership, certificate of ownership, change of ownership, exclusive ownership, incident of ownership, individual ownership, joint ownership, occupation, ownership rights, possession, proprietary interest, qualified ownership, silent partner, sole ownership, sole proprietor, tenancy by the entirety, transfer of ownership, unconditional ownership, undisclosed interest, unqualified ownership

P

PACIFY, verb accommodate, alleviate, appease, assuage, becalm, bring to terms, calm, *componere,* conciliate, dulcify, ease, *lenire,* make peace, mediate, mellow, mollify, pacificate, *placare,* placate, please, propitiate, quell, quiet, reconcile, relieve, restore harmony, restore to a state of peace, restore to a state of tranquillity, reunite, salve, satiate, satisfy, settle, settle differences, smooth, soothe, still, subdue, tranquilize

PACT, noun agreement, alliance, arrangement, assurance, bargain, bond, charter, coalition, compact, compromise, concord, concordance, concordat, consentaneity, consortium, contract, convention, cooperation, covenant, deal, entente, *foedus,* guarantee, indenture, league, mutual agreement, mutual pledge, mutual promise, *pactio,* paction, *pactum,* pledge, promise, reconciliation, settlement, stipulation, treaty, understanding, union, warranty

PAIN, noun ache, adversity, affliction, aggravation, agony, ailment, anguish, blight, calamity, disability, discomfort, disease, displeasure, distress, *dolor,* grief, grievous trouble, hurt, ill, infliction, injury, mal-

ady, malaise, misery, ordeal, pang, sickness, sore, soreness, sorrow, strong discomfort, suffering, torment, unease, woe, worry

ASSOCIATED CONCEPTS: pain and suffering

PAINFUL, adjective aching, afflictive, agonizing, anguishing, arduous, beset with difficulties, difficult, difficult to endure, discomforting, distressful, distressing, disturbing, excruciating, grievous, grueling, hard to endure, harmful, harrowing, hurtful, hurting, inflamed, insufferable, intolerable, irksome, irritating, laborious, smarting, sore, throbbing, tiresome, tormenting, torturous, troublesome, troubling, trying, unbearable, uncomfortable, unendurable, unpleasant, unsufferable, wearisome

PAINSTAKING, adjective assiduous, attentive, careful, conscientious, diligent, earnest, elaborate, energetic, exacting, hardworking, heedful, industrious, labored, laborious, meticulous, never-tiring, operose, *operosus,* particular, persevering, plodding, precise, punctilious, regardful, scrupulous, sedulous, *sedulus,* sparing no pains, strenuous, strict, thorough, untiring, zealous

PALATABLE, *adjective* acceptable, agreeable, ambrosial, ambrosian, amenable, appetizing, becoming, causing pleasure, cibarious, comestible, congenial, delectable, delicate, delicious, delightful, drinkable, dulcet, *dulcis,* eatable, edible, enjoyable, epicurean, esculent, flavorful, flavorous, flavorsome, good, good-tasting, good to eat, gratifying, inviting, *iucundus,* likable, luscious, meeting standards, nectareous, nice, piquant, pleasant, pleasing, pleasurable, potable, prepossessing, refreshing, relishable, sapid, satisfactory, savory, scrumptious, *suavis,* succulent, tangy, tasteful, tasty, tempting, toothsome, unobjectionable, up to par, welcome

PALLIATE (*Abate*), *verb* allay, alleviate, appease, arrest, assuage, attemper, bate, bound, bring to a standstill, cease, check, circumscribe, curb, curtail, deactivate, decelerate, decrease, desist, diminish, discontinue, ease, eliminate, lenify, lessen, limit, make less severe, make mild, minimize, mitigate, moderate, modulate, obtund, pacify, qualify, quell, quiet, reduce, regulate, relieve, soften, still, stop, subdue, suppress, suspend, temper, terminate

PALLIATE (*Excuse*), *verb* absolve, acquit, adjudge innocent, allow for, assoil, be lenient, clear, condone, declare guiltless, defend, discharge, disculpate, dismiss charges, exculpate, exempt, exonerate, extenuate, forbear, forgive, give amnesty, give dispensation, grant absolution, grant amnesty, grant exemption, grant immunity, judge innocent, justify, let go, let off, liberate, license, make allowance for, overlook, pardon, permit, privilege, provide justification, release, release from obligation, remit the penalty, reprieve, rescue, set free, show mercy, shrive, spare, support, tolerate, vindicate

PALLIATIVE (*Abating*), *adjective* allaying, alleviating, alleviative, assuaging, assuasive, beneficial, calmative, consolatory, corrective, curative, easeful, helpful, lenient, drudge, mitigating, mitigative, modifying, modulatory, mollifying, pacifying, quelling, quieting, relieving, restorative, sedative, softening, soothing, stilling, subduing, tempering, therapeutic, tranquilizing

PALLIATIVE (*Excusing*), *adjective* apologetic, condonable, condoning, excepting, exculpable, exculpating, excusatory, exempting, expiating, extenuating, extenuative, forgiving, justificatory, justifying, pardoning, qualifying, vindicating, vindicative, vindicatory

PALPABLE, *adjective* able to be felt, able to be handled, able to be touched, apparent, bold, certain, clear, clear-cut, conspicuous, crystal clear, definite, detectable, discernible, disclosed, discoverable, distinct, easily perceived, easily seen, *evidens,* evident, exhibited, explicit, glaring, identifiable, in evidence, indisputable, indubitable, lucid, manifest, *manifestus,* marked, notable, noticeable, observable, obvious, overt, patent, perceivable, perceptible, perspicuous, plain, prominent, pronounced, readily perceived, readily seen, recognizable, revealed, salient, seeable, self-evident, stark, striking, tactile, tangible, touchable, *tractabilis,* unconcealed, uncontestable, uncovered, uncurtained, undisguised, undoubtable, unequivocal, unhidden, unmasked, unmistakable, unobscure, unobscured, un-

questionable, unscreened, unshrouded, unveiled, visible

PALTER, *verb* act, act insincerely, be deceitful, be deceptive, be dishonest, be evasive, be false, be fraudulent, be hypocritical, be inconstant, be insincere, be mendacious, be perfidious, be uncandid, be untruthful, bear false witness, beguile, betray, bluff, break faith, cant, cheat, concoct, counterfeit, cozen, deal crookedly, deceive, defraud, delude, deviate, disguise, dissemble, dissimulate, distort, doctor, dodge, dupe, equivocate, evade, evade the truth, fabricate, fake, falsify, feign, fence, fool, forswear, gammon, hoax, inveigle, invent, lack candor, lead astray, lie, make false pretenses, make false statements, manufacture, masquerade, misdirect, misguide, misinform, mislead, misrender, misreport, misrepresent, misstate, perjure, pervert, playact, pose, pretend, prevaricate, profess, render lip service, represent falsely, shift, shuffle, talk insincerely, tergiversate, trifle, trump up, twist, use trickery, utter a falsehood, victimize

PALTRY, *adjective* below par, beneath contempt, beneath notice, cheap, contemptible, deficient, despicable, diminutive, humble, inadequate, incomplete, inconsequential, inconsiderable, insignificant, irrelevant, lacking, little, meager, mean, measly, mediocre, minute, *minutus,* miserable, modest, negligible, niggardly, nugatory, of little consequence, of little value, of no account, of small value, pathetic, petty, piddling, pitiful, poor, puny, *pusillus,* scant, scanty, scarce, shameful, slight, small, sorry, trifling, trivial, unappreciable, unimportant, unsatisfactory, unworthy of serious consideration, useless, valueless, vile, *vilis,* wanting, worthless, wretched

PANACEA, *noun* answer, assistance, balm, catholicon, correction, corrective, curative, cure, cure-all, cure for all ills, healing agent, improvement, medicament, medicine, palliative, relief, remedy, restorative, restorative agent, solution, solution to difficulties, tonic, universal cure, universal remedy

PANDECT (*Code of laws*), *noun* body of law, canon, canon of laws, charter, code, codification, codified law, collection of laws, complete body of laws, digest, digest of law, enactment, legal code, principles, statute book

PANDECT (*Treatise*), *noun* analysis, article, commentary, compendium, complete digest, comprehensive digest, conspectus, data paper, digest, discourse, discussion, disquisition, dissertation, essay, excursus, exhaustive tract, explanation, exposition, formal discourse, formal essay, handbook, lucubration, manual, outline, paper, position paper, publication, study, summary, survey, syllabus, synopsis, tract, tractate, treatment

PANDEMONIUM, *noun* affray, agitation, anarchy, bedlam, chaos, clamor, commotion, confusedness, confusion, convulsion, derangement, din, disarrangement, disarray, discomposure, disharmony, disorder, disorganization, disquietude, disruption, disturbance, embroilment, entanglement, ferment, fracas, frenzy, imbroglio, inquietude, jumble, lack of order, melee, mixup, noise, outcry, panic, racket, rampage, riot, roar, row, ruction, rumpus, stir, storm, trouble, tumult, turbulence, turmoil, unruliness, uproar, uproariousness, vociferation, want of method, wild uproar, wildness

PANDER, *verb*   assist, attend, be instrumental, be of service, be servile, be subservient, be useful, cater, court favor, do service, furnish, give, gratify, help, humor, indulge, ingratiate oneself, make contented, make oneself useful, minister, obey, oblige, pamper, please, procure, provide, purvey, render service, satisfy, satisfy desires, serve, subserve, supply, tend, toady, truckle to, wait on, work in the service of

PANEL *(Discussion group),* **noun**   advisory body, caucus, conference, *consilium,* council, deliberative body, exchange of views, forum, joint discussion, open discussion, open forum, round table, seminar, summit, symposium

PANEL *(Jurors),* **noun**   body of jurors, body of persons summoned as jurors, body of persons sworn to render a verdict, group of jurors, jury, list of jurors, persons summoned to attend the court as jurymen, triers of fact
ASSOCIATED CONCEPTS: grand jury, panel en banc, petit jury

PANIC, *noun*   affright, agitation, alarm, anxiety, awe, confusedness, confusion, consternation, cowardice, despair, discomposure, disorder, disquietude, disturbance, dread, fear, fearfulness, flutter, frenzy, fright, great fear, horror, hysteria, hystericalness, inquietude, irrational terror, nervousness, outcry, overpowering fright, pandemonium, *pavor,* perturbance, perturbation, phobia, sheer terror, stampede, state of terror, sudden fear, terror, trepidation, turmoil, unreasoning fear
ASSOCIATED CONCEPTS: heat of passion, manslaughter, temporary insanity

PANOPLY, *noun*   armature, armor, armored protection, barrier, brigandine, buffer, covering, cuirass, defense, defensive arms, defensive clothing, defensive equipment, deterrent, envelopment, fender, fortification, full array, guard, means of protection, precaution, preservation, preventive measure, protection, protective covering, protective outfit, safeguard, screen, shelter, shield, targe

PAR *(Equality),* **noun**   *aequalis, aequus,* balance, equal footing, equal value, equal worth, equality, equalness, equipollence, equivalence, evenness, identicalness, identity, interchangeableness, likeness, sameness, similarity
ASSOCIATED CONCEPTS: above par value, at par value, par value of stock

PAR *(Face amount),* **noun**   amount, appraisal, appraisement, evaluation, face value, market price, price, rate, valuation, value, value in exchange, worth

PARADIGM, *noun*   archetype, example, exemplar, guide, ideal, model, norm, original, *paradigma,* pattern, prototype, sample, standard

PARADOX, *noun*   antilogy, antinomy, contradiction, contrariety, disagreement, discrepancy, dissonance, enigma, incompatibility, incongruity, inconsistency, inconsonance, irreconcilability, lack of agreement, lack of harmony, perplexity, puzzle, *quod est ad-*

mirabile contraque opinionem omnium, seeming contradiction, self-contradiction

PARAGON, *noun*   acme of perfection, champion, eminent person, example, exceller, exemplar, good example, great person, height of perfection, hero, ideal, man of mark, model, model of virtue, nonesuch, nonpareil, person of repute, prize, *specimen,* standard, standard for comparison, summit, superior individual

PARAMOUNT, *adjective*   arch, beyond compare, beyond comparison, cardinal, champion, chief, crowning, distinguished, extraordinary, first, foremost, grand, great, greatest, head, hegemonic, hegemonical, highest, incomparable, inimitable, leading, main, master, matchless, memorable, model, notable, peerless, preeminent, prepollent, prepotent, primary, prime, principal, prominent, regnant, reigning, remarkable, salient, second to none, significant, sovereign, *summus,* supereminent, superior, superlative, supreme, top, transcendent, transcendental, unapproached, unequaled, unexcelled, unmatched, unparalleled, unrivaled, unsurpassed, without parallel, worthy of notice, worthy of remark

PARANOIA, *noun*   delusional insanity, delusions, diseased mind, disordered reason, insanity, lunacy, madness, mania, mental aberration, mental disease, phobia, unreasonable fear, unreasonable fright

PARAPHERNALIA *(Apparatus),* **noun**   accessories, accompaniments, accouterments, apparatus, appliances, articles, attachments, contrivances, conveniences, equipage, equipment, gear, impedimenta, implements, instruments, material, supplies, tools, utensils

PARAPHERNALIA *(Personal   belongings),* **noun**   accessories, appointments, assets, chattels, effects, estate, goods, holdings, merchandise, movables, parcels, perquisites, personal effects, personal estate, personal property, personalty, possessions, property, resources, seisin, trappings

PARAPHRASE, *noun*   abridgment, brief, citation, condensation, description, elucidation, enucleation, equivalent meaning, explanation, explication, free translation, free wording, indirect quotation, *interpretatio,* interpretation, loose rendering, loose translation, meaning, minute, nonliteral translation, *paraphrasis,* recapitulation, rendering, rendition, representation, restatement, rewording, simplification, summary, synopsis, translation, version

PARASITE, *noun*   *adsecula,* barnacle, beggar, bloodsucker, borrower, burden, cadger, destructive agency, follower, leech, loafer, mendicant, nonworker, panhandler, scrounger, sponge, sycophant

PARCEL, *noun*   acreage, area, block, district, enclave, enclosure, estate, field, ground, land, lot, property, patch, piece, piece of land, plot, plot of ground, plot of land, portion, real estate, region, section, sector, segment, square, terrain, territory, tract
ASSOCIATED CONCEPTS: conveyance, partition

PARCEL, *verb*   administer, allocate, allot, appoint, apportion, appropriate, assign, award, bestow, carve, deal out, dispense, dispose of, *distribuere,* distribute, divide, divide into shares, *dividere,* dole out, give away, give out, grant, measure, mete, part with, *partiri*, partition, pass out, portion out, prorate, ration, sectionalize, segment, split up, subdivide

PARDON, *noun* absolution, acquittal, amnesty, clearance, clemency, compurgation, discharge, dismissal, dispensation, exemption from punishment, exoneration, forgiveness, leniency, obliteration of grievances, release, release from penalty, release from punishment, relinquishment, reprieve, *venia*, vindication
ASSOCIATED CONCEPTS: amnesty, commutation, conditional pardon, parole, relief from disabilities, suspended sentence, unconditional pardon
FOREIGN PHRASES: *Veniae facilitas incentivum est delinquendi.* Facility of pardon is an encouragement to crime.

PARDON, *verb* acquit, cancel a punishment, cancel an offense, condone, deliver, discharge, emancipate, excuse, exonerate, expunge the record of, fail to exact a penalty, forgive, give absolution, grant amnesty, grant clemency, grant forgiveness, grant remission, let loose, liberate, overlook, purge, redeem, release, release from punishment, remission of guilt, reprieve, set at liberty, set free, suspend charges, vindicate

PARDONABLE, *adjective* admissible, allowable, blameless, condonable, defensible, *excusabilis*, excusable, expiable, faultless, forgivable, guiltless, innocent, inoffensive, justifiable, justified, passable, permitted, slight, unblamable, unculpable, understandable, unobjectionable, vindicable

PARENTAGE, *noun* ancestry, antecedents, birth, bloodline, derivation, descent, extraction, family, family connection, family tree, filiation, forebears, forefathers, foreparents, former generations, genealogical tree, genealogy, genesis, *genus,* house, line, line of ancestors, lineage, origin, paternity, pedigree, primogenitors, progenitors, source, stem, *stirps,* stock, tribe
ASSOCIATED CONCEPTS: determination of parentage, illegitimacy, legitimacy, paternity proceeding

PARENTS, *noun* ancestor, begetter, creator, father, forebear, founder of the family, genitor, head of the household, immediate forebear, matriarch, mother, *parens,* patriarch, precursor, predecessor, procreator, progenitor
ASSOCIATED CONCEPTS: abandonment of child, adoptive parent, custody of children, duty to support, fitness of parent, foster parent, in loco parentis, natural parent, paternity proceeding, sole surviving parent
FOREIGN PHRASES: *Parentum est liberos alere etiam nothos.* It is the duty of parents to support their children even when illegitimate.

PARI MATERIA, *noun* in consonance, in harmony, on the same matter, read as one, read in tandem, read with respect of another, read together

PARIAH, *noun* castaway, deportee, derelict, exile, expatriate, fugitive, heretic, offender, outcast, outlaw, outsider, proscribed person, rebel, renegade, scab, sectarist, sectary, tergiversator

PARITY, *noun* alikeness, analogy, approximation, balance, close correspondence, coequality, comparability, comparison, correlation, correspondence, equability, equality, equation, equilibrium, equipoise, equivalence, equivalency, identical value, identicalness, likeness, parallelism, resemblance, sameness, semblance, similarity, similtude, state of being equal, symmetry, uniformity
ASSOCIATED CONCEPTS: wage parity

PARLANCE, *noun* address, allocution, choice of words, command of idiom, command of language, command of words, conference, conversation, delivery, diction, discourse, elocution, eloquence, expression, fashion, flow of language, flow of words, fluency, formulation, idiom, interlocution, locution, manner, manner of speaking, mode, oral communication, oratory, phraseology, recitation, rhetoric, sense of language, speech, spoken word, style, talk, terminology, tone, use of words, utterance, verbal intercourse, vocabulary, vocalization, wordage

PARLAY (*Bet*), *verb* ante, back, bet on, gamble, hazard, lay a wager, lay money on, make a bet, make book, play, risk, speculate, stake, take a chance, trust to chance, venture, wager

PARLAY (*Exploit successfully*), *verb* boost, broaden, build up, develop, elevate, escalate, exalt, expand, further, maximize, pyramid, raise, use

PARLEY, *noun* assembly, collocution, colloquy, communication, conclave, conference, congress, *conloqui*, consultation, convention, conversation, council, debate, deliberation, dialogue, diplomacy, *disceptare*, discussion, exchange of views, hearing, intercommunication, interlocution, interview, meeting, negotiation, oral communication, seminar, summit, summit conference, summit talk, symposiac, symposium, talk, verbal intercourse

PAROCHIAL, *adjective* biased, dogmatic, fanatical, hidebound, illiberal, insular, intolerant, jaundiced, limited, literal, narrow, narrow-minded, one-sided, opinionated, opinionative, orthodox, *parochialis*, partial, partisan, predisposed, prejudiced, prepossessed, provincial, regional, restricted to a small area, restricted to a small scope, sectarian, small-minded, unbending, uncatholic, unimaginative, unliberal, untolerating

PARODY, *noun* amphigory, apery, buffoonery, burlesque, caricature, cartoon, comical representation, distortion, exaggeration, farce, imitation, lampoon, ludicrous imitation, mime, mimicry, mockery, mummery, pasquinade, *ridicula imitatio*, ridicule, satire, squib, travesty

PAROL, *adjective* evidenced solely by speech, expressed solely by speech, lingual, not committed to writing, not expressed by writing, not written, nuncupative, oral, outspoken, told, unwritten, uttered, verbal, vocal, voiced
ASSOCIATED CONCEPTS: extrinsic evidence, parol agreement, parol assignment, parol contract, parol evidence rule, parol gift, parol lease

PAROLE, *noun* affirmation, conditional deliverance, conditional discharge, conditional disenthrallment, conditional disimprisonment, conditional emancipation, conditional freedom, conditional freedom from confinement, conditional independence, conditional liberation, conditional liberty, conditional release, condi-

tional reprieve, declaration, deliverance, discharge, emancipation, freedom, freeing from prison, granting freedom, liberation, liberty, release, release from prison, reprieve, setting free
ASSOCIATED CONCEPTS: commutation of sentence, conditions of parole, pardon, parole board, probation, release from dissabilities

PAROLE, *verb* cast loose, conditionally release, conditionally release from imprisonment, deliver, discharge, disimprison, emancipate, free, let go free, let out of jail, let out of prison, liberate, make free, release, release conditionally, release from imprisonment, set at liberty, set free, turn loose, unbolt, uncage, unchain, unfetter, unharness, unshackle
ASSOCIATED CONCEPTS: commutation, commute, pardon, Parole Board, probation

PARRY, *verb* avert, avoid, beat off, block, brush off, chase away, chase off, confute, counter, *defendere,* deflect, dodge, drive away, drive back, elude, escape, evade, fence, fend off, fight off, foil, force back, hedge, hold at bay, hold back, hold off, intercept, interfere, intervene, keep at bay, keep away, keep clear of, keep off, offer resistance, oppose, outface, prevent, *propulsare,* push away, put up a struggle, rebuff, refute, reluct, reluctate, repel, *repellere,* repulse, resist, sidestep, stave off, stop, stymie, take evasive action, thwart, turn aside, turn away, turn back, ward off, withstand

PARSIMONIOUS, *adjective* acquisitive, avaricious, chary, cheap, close, closefisted, curmudgeonly, economical, excessively frugal, frugal, grasping, grudging, illiberal, mean, mercenary, miserly, niggardly, *parcus,* penny-pinching, penurious, petty, *restrictus,* scrimping, selfish, small-minded, sparing, stingy, stinting, *tenax,* thrifty, tight, uncharitable, ungenerous, unwilling to give, unyielding

PART *(Place), noun* area, division, locale, location, premises, purlieus, quarter, room, section, site, spot
ASSOCIATED CONCEPTS: part in a courthouse

PART *(Portion), noun* allocation, allowance, amount, bit, chip, chunk, collop, component, constituent, cutting, detachment, detail, division, excerpt, factor, fraction, fragment, helping, ingredient, interest, lump, measure, particle, percentage, piece, quantity, section, segment, serving, share, slab, slice, subdivision, subgroup
ASSOCIATED CONCEPTS: principal part

PART *(Role), noun* burden, character, charge, chore, concern, function, impersonation, job, mimesis, *partes,* performance, portrayal, province, realm, representation, responsibility, task, undertaking

PART *(Leave), verb* be gone, break away, defect, depart, escape, evacuate, get away from, go, go away, go forth, march off, migrate, move away, move out, quit, remove, retire, retreat, separate oneself from, set off, set out, take leave, take one's departure, tear oneself away, withdraw

PART *(Separate), verb* be severed, be sundered, bifurcate, break, carve, compartmentalize, cut in two, detach, disassociate, disconnect, disengage, disentangle, disjoin, dismember, dissever, dissociate, dissolve, disunite, divide, *dividere,* fissure, halve, isolate, keep

apart, parcel, *partiri,* partition, portion, section, *separare,* sever, sort out, split, stand between, subdivide, sunder, tear assunder, undo, unloose

PARTAKE, *verb* accept, be a party to, experience, have a hand in, have a portion of, have a share of, lend oneself to, participate, receive, sample, savor, share, share in, take, take a share of, take an active part in, take part in, taste

PARTIAL *(Biased), adjective* bigoted, *cupidus,* discriminatory, favorably disposed, inclined, influenced, *iniquus,* interested, jaundiced, narrow-minded, one-sided, partisan, predisposed, prejudiced, prepossessed, prone, restricted, *studiosus,* subjective, swayed, unbalanced, unequal, uneven, unfair, unjust, unjustified, unreasonable
ASSOCIATED CONCEPTS: partial acceptance, partial delivery, partial performance, partial restraint, partial summary judgment

PARTIAL *(Part), adjective* apart, confined, divided, divisible, factional, fragmentary, incomplete, limited, narrow, not complete, not completed, *partim,* sectional, split, uncompleted, unfinished, unperformed, wanting

PARTIAL *(Relating to a part), adjective* abridged, deficient, divided, divisible, fractional, fragmentary, imperfect, incomplete, inexact, insufficient, limited, *partim,* scanty, sectional, segmental, sketchy, uncompleted, undeveloped, unfinalized, unfinished, unperfected, unthorough, wanting
ASSOCIATED CONCEPTS: partial payment, partial summary judgment

PARTIALITY, *noun* affinity, attachment, attraction, bent, bias, biased judgment, discrimination, favor, favoritism, fondness, inclination, *iniquitas,* injustice, intolerance, leaning, liking, one-sidedness, partisanship, penchant, preconception, predilection, predisposition, preference, preferential treatment, prejudgment, prejudice, prepossession, proclivity, propensity, taste

PARTICIPANT, *noun* abettor, accessory, accomplice, adjuvant, aid, ally, assistant, associate, attendant, auxiliary, coadjutor, collaborator, colleague, comate, companion, comrade, confederate, cooperator, copartner, coworker, fellow, fellow worker, helper, mate, partaker, *particeps,* participator, partner, party, shareholder, sharer
ASSOCIATED CONCEPTS: participant in a crime

PARTICIPATE, *verb* act in concert, act together, affiliate with, aid, associate, be a party to, be in league with, be involved, become involved with, collaborate, compete, confederate, *consortem,* contribute, cooperate, engage, engage in, enter into, *esse participem,* get in the act, go along with, have a hand in, have a part in, have a part of, have a share of, join, join forces, join in, join in partnership with, partake, play a part in, share, share in, take a part in, take a part of, take an active part in, take an interest in, take part, undertake, unite efforts with, unite with, work together
ASSOCIATED CONCEPTS: participate in a business venture, participate in a conspiracy, participate in a crime, participate in a labor dispute

PARTICULAR *(Exacting)*, **adjective**   accurate, astringent, attentive, attentive to detail, careful, choosy, conscientious, critical, *delicatus,* demanding, difficult to please, discriminating, discriminative, *elegans,* epicurean, excessively critical, exigent, fastidious, faultfinding, finical, finicky, fussy, hairsplitting, hard to please, heedful, hypercritical, inflexible, meticulous, mindful, overconscientious, overcritical, overfastidious, overmeticulous, painstaking, persnickety, picky, precise, punctilious, quality-minded, querulous, regardful, rigid, rigorous, scrupulous, selective, stern, strict, stringent, thorough, thoroughgoing, uncompromising, unyielding

PARTICULAR *(Individual)*, **adjective**   characteristic, definite, distinct, distinctive, distinguished, especial, exclusive, original, own, peculiar, personal, respective, separate, single, singular, special, specific, unique, unusual
ASSOCIATED CONCEPTS: particular gift, particular purpose
FOREIGN PHRASES: *Generale tantum valet in generalibus, quantum singulare in singulis.* That which is general prevails in general matters, as that which is particular prevails in particular matters.

PARTICULAR *(Specific)*, **adjective**   characteristic, chosen, differential, differentiated, distinct, distinctive, distinguishable, distinguished, eccentric, especial, exceptional, express, extraordinary, idiosyncratic, individual, marked, noteworthy, odd, outstanding, peculiar, prominent, *proprius,* select, selected, separate, *separatus,* signal, single, singular, special, striking, uncommon, unique, unmistakable, unusual

PARTICULAR, *noun*   article, aspect, case, circumstance, detail, event, experience, fact, feature, incident, incidental, instance, item, item of information, matter, minutia, occasion, occurrence, particularity, piece of information, point, punctilio, respect, single case, special point, specific, specification
ASSOCIATED CONCEPTS: bill of particulars

PARTICULARITY, *noun*   care, carefulness, characteristic, characteristic quality, circumstantiality, conscientiousness, criticalness, detail, discriminatingness, discrimination, distinctive feature, exactingness, exactitude, exactness, fastidiousness, feature, finicality, finicalness, fussiness, individuality, item, lineament, mark, meticulousness, minute circumstance, minuteness, particularness, perfectionism, preciseness, precision, punctiliousness, rigidness, scrupulosity, scrupulousness, selectiveness, singleness, singularity, special point, specific quality, strictness, trait, uniqueness

PARTICULARLY, *adverb*   above all, chiefly, distinctly, eminently, especially, expressly, extraordinally, individually, inordinately, mainly, markedly, *maxime,* notably, observably, peculiarly, *praecipue, praesertim,* preeminently, primarily, principally, prominently, remarkably, signally, singularly, specially, specifically, strikingly, supremely, uncommonly, uncustomarily, unfamiliarly, uniquely, unusually

PARTISAN, *adjective*   biased, clannish, cliquish, denominational, devoted, factional, factionary, fanatic, *fautor, homo studiosus,* influenced, leagued, partial, predisposed, sectarian, swayed, undetached, undispassionate

PARTISAN, *noun*   adherent, advocate, ally, apostle, backer, believer, champion, comrade, confederate, copartner, coworker, defender, devotee, disciple, encourager, enthusiast, favorer, fellow worker, follower, friend, hanger on, mainstay, maintainer, participant, partner, party-liner, party member, patron, promoter, proselyte, satellite, seconder, sectarian, sectary, sponsor, support, supporter, sustainer, sympathizer, upholder, votary, zealot, zealotist
ASSOCIATED CONCEPTS: discrimination, partisan motives

PARTITION, *verb*   allocate, allot, apportion, break up, carve, compartmentalize, cut up, dissect, distribute, divide, divide into distinct portions, divide into portions, divide into shares, divide proportionately, divide up, dole out, form into classes, group, mete, mete out, parcel out, pigeonhole, place in a category, portion, portion out, prorate, section, sectionalize, segment, sever, sever the unity of possession, share, split up, subdivide
ASSOCIATED CONCEPTS: partition property

PARTNER, *noun*   abettor, accessory, accomplice, adjutant, adjutor, adjuvant, aid, aider, ally, assistant, associate, coadjutant, coadjutor, cohelper, collaborator, colluder, comate, companion, compeer, confederate, consociate, cooperator, coowner, copartner, coworker, fellow worker, helper, member of a partnership, partaker, *particeps,* participant, participator, sharer, *socius,* teammate, teamworker, workfellow
ASSOCIATED CONCEPTS: equal partner, general partner, limited partner, managing partner, nominal partner, partner in crime, silent partner, surviving partner
FOREIGN PHRASES: *Cum aliquis renunciaverit societati, solvitur societas.* When any partner renounces the partnership, the partnership is dissolved. *Socii mei socius meus socius non est.* The partner of my partner is not my partner.

PARTNERSHIP, *noun*   alliance, association, coalition, combination, concord, confederacy, confederation, conjunction, connection, consociation, *consortio,* consortium, cooperation, cooperative society, copartnership, federation, fellowship, firm, guild, joint interest, league, legal entity, mutual company, participation, pool, *societas,* sodality, syndicate
ASSOCIATED CONCEPTS: commercial partnership, copartnership, corporation, dissolution of partnership, general partnership, joint enterprise, joint venture, limited partnership, partnership agreement, partnership assets, partnership at will, partnership debts, partnership for a single transaction, partnership property, professional partnership, silent partner, special partnership, voluntary association
FOREIGN PHRASES: *Nemo debet in communione invitus teneri.* No one should be retained in a partnership against his will. *Si alicujus rei societas sit et finis negotio impositus est, finitus societas.* If there is a partnership in any matter, and the business is concluded, the partnership is ended.

PARTY *(Litigant)*, **noun**   adversary, appellant, appellee, challenger, charger, claimant, complainant, contender, contestant, controversialist, defendant, disputant, intervener, libelant, opposing party, petitioner, plaintiff, respondent, suitor
ASSOCIATED CONCEPTS: adverse party, defect in parties, disinterested party, indispensable party, jurisdic-

tion of parties, material party, mutuality of parties, necessary parties, nominal party, nonjoinder of parties, opposing party, party-in practice, prevailing party, proper party, real party in interest, substantial party
FOREIGN PHRASES: *Saepe constitutum est, res inter alios judicatas aliis non praejudicare.* It has often been decided that matters adjudged between others ought not to prejudice those who are not parties.

PARTY *(Participant),* **noun** attendant, cooperator, member, partaker, participator, partisan, partner, sharer
ASSOCIATED CONCEPTS: accommodation party, competent party, guilty party, injured party, innocent party, real party in interest, third party

PARTY *(Political organization),* **noun** association, body, caucus, club, coalition, combine, confederation, faction, group, league, lobby, organized group, party machine, political machine

PASS *(Advance),* **verb** *abalienatio,* award, bequeath, cede, change, change ownership, communicate, confer ownership, continue, convey, cross, deliver over, devolve, endow, flow, go, go by, go on, go past, *praetervehi,* proceed, progress, relay, remise, transfer ownership, transfer title, *transgredi, transire,* transmit, transpire
ASSOCIATED CONCEPTS: pass by will, pass title

PASS *(Approve),* **verb** accede to, accept, acquiesce, adopt, advocate, affirm, agree to, allow, approbate, assent, authorize, be in favor of, carry, confirm, consent, declare lawful, decree, dictate, enact, endorse, establish, establish by law, favor, give approval, give legislative sanction to, institute, institute by law, *iubere,* legalize, legislate, legitimize, make into law, make legal, ordain, ordain by law, prescribe, put in force, put into effect, put through, ratify, sanction, support, sustain, uphold, validate, vote favorably, vote in
ASSOCIATED CONCEPTS: pass a law

PASS *(Determine),* **verb** announce, decide, declare, decree, deliver, deliver a judgment, determine, enunciate, give an opinion, impart, ordain, present, pronounce, pronounce judgment, put forth, render a decision, render a judgment, rule, set forth
ASSOCIATED CONCEPTS: pass judgment

PASS *(Satisfy requirements),* **verb** accomplish, achieve, *approbare,* attain, be accepted, be graduated, be promoted, be successful, be victorious, come up to the standard, conform to, conquer, do well, earn, finish, fulfill, get by, get through, make one's mark, master, meet requirements, prevail, qualify, reach, realize, satisfy requirements, stand the test, succeed, triumph

PASSABLE, *adjective* acceptable, accessible, achievable, admissible, allowable, approachable, bearable, beaten, broad, capable of passing, clear, crossable, easy, fair, fit for travel, fordable, free, mediocre, middling, moderate, navigable, open, ordinary, penetrable, pervious, presentable, pretty good, reachable, realizable, receivable, serviceable, tolerable, travelable, traveled, traversable, unimpeded, unobstructed, usable, within reach

PASSION, *noun* agitation, anger, ardency, ardor, avidity, craze, desire, eagerness, ecstasy, emotion, eruption, excitability, excitement, explosion, fanaticism, feeling, ferment, fervency, fervor, fierceness, fire, frenzy, furor, fury, glow, gusto, heat, hunger, impetuosity, impulse, infatuation, intensity, intoxication, ire, irresistible urge, itch, lust, mania, rabidity, rage, rampage, rampancy, rapture, storm, strong feeling, temper, thrill, transport, vehemence, vehement desire, verve, violence, violent anger, wrath, zeal
ASSOCIATED CONCEPTS: heat of passion

PASSIVE, *adjective* acquiescent, amenable, apathetic, calm, compliable, compliant, complying, concessive, conformable, docile, dormant, duteous, dutiful, enduring, feeble, flexible, forbearant, heedless, indifferent, indolent, influenced, irresolute, lamblike, languorous, malleable, nonresistant, nonresisting, obedient, obeisant, obsequious, otiose, phlegmatic, pliable, pliant, quiescent, receptive, recumbent, resigned, resistless, restrained, sequacious, servile, subdued, subject, submissive, subordinate, subservient, supine, supple, tame, tractable, unassertive, undemonstrative, unopposing, unresistant, unresisting, yielding
ASSOCIATED CONCEPTS: passive negligence, passive tortfeasor

PAST DUE, *adverb* in arrears, in debt, in default, outstanding, overdrawn, overdue

PATENT, *adjective* *apertus,* apparent, *clarus,* clear, conspicuous, disclosed, discoverable, easy to be seen, evident, exposed, exposed to view, free to all, glaring, in full view, in view, individual, manifest, *manifestus,* noticeable, observable, obvious, open, ostensible, overt, perceivable, perceptible, perspicuous, plain, plain to be seen, prominent, public, published, revealed, standing out, uncamouflaged, unconcealed, undisguised, unhidden, unmasked, unobstructed, unshaded, unusual, visible, wide-open
ASSOCIATED CONCEPTS: patent ambiguity, patent danger, patent defect, patent error

PATENT, *noun* certificate of invention, *diplomatis,* exclusive license, exclusive privilege, exclusive right, exclusive title, governmental grant, grant, grant of authority, legal right, license, permit, privilege, right, right to profits accruing, use and title
ASSOCIATED CONCEPTS: assignment of a patent, infringement of a patent, patent license, patent right

PATERNAL, *adjective* ancestral, benevolent, benign, family, fatherlike, fatherly, kindly, parental, *paternus,* patriarchal, patrimonial, *patrius,* protective

PATERNITY, *noun* ancestry, derivation, descent, fatherhood, fathership, lineage, male parentage, origin, parentage, paternal parentage, progenitorship
ASSOCIATED CONCEPTS: paternity proceeding
FOREIGN PHRASES: *Filiatio non potest probari.* Filiation cannot be proved. *Pater est quem nuptiae demonstrant.* He is the father whom the marriage points out.

PATIENT, *adjective* acquiescent, agreeable, assiduous, calm, compliant, composed, constant, continuing, controlled, decided, determined, diligent, docile, dogged, dutiful, easygoing, enduring, firm, forbearing, forgiving, hard working, imperturbable, indefatigable, indulgent, lamblike, levelheaded, long-suffering, longanimous, meek, mild, mild-tempered, nonresisting, pacific, passive, *patiens,* peaceable, perseverant, persevering, persistent, persisting, pertinacious, philosophic, placid, pliant, plodding, quiescent, quiet, quietly persevering, reconciled, relentless, resigned, resolute, resolved, restrained, sedulous, self-controlled, serene, steadfast, steady, stoic, stoical, submissive, sympathetic, tenacious, *tolerans,* tolerant, tractable, tranquil, unceasing, unchangeable, uncomplaining, uncompromising, undaunted, understanding, undeviating, undiscouraged, undisturbed, unfaltering, unflagging, unflinching, unmurmuring, unperturbed, unrelaxing, unrelenting, unremitting, unresisting, unruffled, unshaken, unswerving, untiring, unvexed, unwavering, unwearied, unwearying, unyielding, yielding

PATIENT, *noun*　　*aeger, aegrotus,* case, convalescent, convalescent case, hospital case, hospitalized person, ill individual, inmate, invalid, medical case, one seeking cure, one seeking relief, one undergoing therapy, one undergoing treatment, shut-in, sick individual, sick person, sickling, victim
ASSOCIATED CONCEPTS: doctor-patient privilege

PATROL, *verb*　　attend, be on the alert, be on the lookout, be on the watch, *circumire,* cover, cover a beat, go the rounds, guard, inspect, keep an eye on, keep guard, keep in view, keep vigil, keep watch, look out, march, monitor, observe, overlook, pace, perform sentry duty, police, protect, reconnoiter, safeguard, scan, scout, stand guard, stand sentinel, superintend, sweep through, traverse, walk, walk a beat, watch

PATRON *(Influential supporter),* *noun*　　advocate, backer, benefactor, champion, defender, endorser, favorer, financer, friend, guardian, helper, influential sponsor, investor, leader, *patronus,* philanthropist, promoter, sponsor, supporter, upholder

PATRON *(Regular customer),* *noun*　　business contact, buyer, client, *consultor,* consumer, customer, *emptor,* frequenter, patronizer, prospective buyer, purchaser, shopper, supporter, vendee

PATRONAGE *(Power to appoint jobs),* *noun*　　advantage, assistance, *auctoritas,* authority, backing, choice, control, controlling power, directing agency, dominance, domination, *favor,* good offices, *gratia, indulgentia,* influence, influentiality, *patrocinium,* persuasion, position of influence, power, *praesidium,* predominance, preference, right of choice, selection, sway

PATRONAGE *(Support),* *noun*　　aid, assistance, backing, care, commendation, commercial backing, cordial assistance, countenance, encouragement, favor, friendly interest, friendship, guardianship, guidance, help, influence, interest, protection, protectorship, recommendation, special privileges, sponsorship, support, tutelage

PATRONIZE *(Condescend toward),* *verb*　　assume a lofty bearing, deign, favor, grant, indulge, look down on, lower oneself, oblige, talk down to, treat in a condescending way, vouchsafe

PATRONIZE *(Trade with),* *verb*　　be a customer of, buy from, deal with, do business with, *favere,* favor with one's patronage, frequent, frequent as a customer, have dealings with, purchase from, shop at, shop with, support, traffic with, transact business with, transact with, use

PATTERN, *noun*　　antetype, archetype, basis, criterion, design, die, draft, example, *exemplar, exemplum,* form, guide, ideal, impression, layout, matrix, model, mold, norm, original, outline, paradigm, paragon, plan, precedent, prototype, rule, sample, shape, specifications, *specimen,* standard, standard of criticism, standard of judgment, template, tracing
ASSOCIATED CONCEPTS: pattern jury instructions

PAUCITY, *noun*　　absence, bare subsistence, dearth, deficiency, deprivation, destitution, drought, exigency, exiguity, famine, fewness, finite quantity, fraction, inadequacy, infrequency, insufficiency, lack, limited amount, minimum, minority, modicum, need, *paucitas,* pittance, poverty, privation, rareness, scantiness, scantness, scarceness, scarcity, shortage, small number, small quantity, sparseness, sparsity, thinness, trickle, trifle, uncommonness, want

PAUSE, *noun*　　abeyance, armistice, break, breather, breathing spell, cessation, deferment, delay, demur, demurral, disconnection, gap, halt, hesitance, hesitancy, hesitation, *intercapedo,* interim, interlude, *intermissio,* intermission, interruption, interval, *intervallum,* intervening period, lag, letup, lull, moratorium, procrastination, recess, relaxation, remission, respite, rest, rest period, space, standstill, stay, stillness, stoppage, suspension, time out, truce, vacation

PAUSE, *verb*　　be dubious, be irresolute, be uncertain, bide time, break, breathe, cast anchor, cease, come to a standstill, consider, dally, dawdle, delay, deliberate, demur, desist, discontinue, dwell, forbear, halt, hang back, hesitate, hold back, hold off, intermit, *intermittere,* interrupt, linger, loiter, mark time, *morari,* put off, reflect, repose, rest, slacken, stall, stand still, stay, stop and consider, straddle, suspend, take a breather, take time out, tarry, think over, think twice, vacillate, wait, waver, weigh

PAWN, *verb*　　bond, deposit, deposit as collateral, deposit as security, give as security, give in earnest, guarantee, hypothecate, impignorate, mortgage, offer collateral, oppignerare, *pignerare,* pledge, post, put at hazard, put at stake, put in pledge, risk, stake, wager

PAY, *noun*　　allowance, award, compensation, consideration, defrayal, defrayment, earnings, emolument, fee, grant, hire, income, indemnity, meed, *merces,* monetary return, payment, perquisite, profit, reckoning, recompense, reimbursement, remittance, remuneration, repayment, return, revenue, reward, salary, settlement, solatium, stipend, *stipendium,* support, wages

PAY, *verb*　　acquit, adjust, award, be a good investment, be profitable, bear the cost, clear, compensate, contribute, defray, deposit, disburse, discharge a debt, expend, *exsolvere,* finance, foot, give payment, hand over, honor, indemnify, liquidate, make a good return, make compensation, make good, make payment, make restitution, meet, *numerare, pendere,* present, quit, ransom, reckon with, recompense, reimburse, remunerate, render, reward, satisfy, settle, spend, square, square accounts, subsidize, support, tender

PAYABLE, *adjective*　　collectable, due, justly claimable, mature, maturing, outstanding, owing, redeemable, uncollected, unpaid, unsatisfied, unsettled

ASSOCIATED CONCEPTS: accounts payable, bills payable, due and payable, payable to bearer, payable upon demand, sum payable

PAYEE, noun acceptor, assignee, consignee, devisee, donee, drawer, endorsee, grantee, recipient, taker, transferee

PAYMENT *(Act of paying)*, **noun** acquittal, acquittance, amortization, amortizement, clearance, compensation, defrayal, defrayment, disbursement, discharge of a debt, expenditure, liquidation, outlay, quittance, receipt in full, reckoning, recompense, reimbursement, remittance, restitution, return, satisfaction, settlement, spending, subsidy

PAYMENT *(Remittance)*, **noun** allotment, allowance, amount, charge, compensation, consideration, earnings, emolument, expenditure, expense, fee, gratuity, guerdon, honorarium, indemnification, indemnity, money, pay, premium, quittance, recompense, reimbursement, remittance, remuneration, reparation, restitution, salary, solatium, stipend, tribute, wage

FOREIGN PHRASES: *In satisfactionibus non permittitur amplius fieri quam semel factum est.* In settlements, more must not be received than was received once for all. *Reprobata pecunia liberat solventem.* Money refused releases the debtor. *Quicquid solvitur, solvitur secundum modum solventis; quicquid recipitur, recipitur secundum modum recipientis.* Whatever money is paid, is paid according to the direction of the payor, whatever money is received, is received according to that of the recipient. *Qui ignorat quantum solvere debeat, non potest improbus videre.* He who does not know how much he ought to pay, cannot seem dishonest. *Jus non patitur ut idem bis solvatur.* Law does not suffer the same thing to be twice paid. *Bona fides non patitur ut bis idem exigatur.* Good faith does not allow us to demand the payment of the same thing twice.

PAYOFF *(Payment in full)*, **noun** discharge, payout, satisfaction in full, settlement

PAYOFF *(Result)*, **noun** closure, conclusion, consummation, determination, end, finale, finish

PAYROLL, noun allowance, compensation, disbursement of salary, employees' earnings, employees' salaries, labor expense, list of paid employees, list of salaried employees, list of wages to be paid out, payment, payment for services, recompense, remuneration, salary, stipend, wages

ASSOCIATED CONCEPTS: certification payroll, payroll check-off system, payroll deduction, payroll tax

PEACE, noun accord, adjustment of differences, agreement, alliance, amity, armistice, brotherhood, calm, calmness, coexistence, community of interests, conciliation, concord, concordance, concordancy, *concordia,* consentaneity, consentaneousness, cooperation, end of hostilities, fellowship, fraternalism, freedom from war, friendliness, friendship, good will, harmoniousness, harmony, hush, law and order, lull, neutrality, oneness, order, orderliness, *otium,* pacification, pact, *pax,* quiescence, quiet, quietness, rapport, reconciliation, repose, serenity, silence, stillness, suspension of hostilities, tranquility, treaty, truce, unanimity, unity

ASSOCIATED CONCEPTS: breach of the peace, disturbing the peace, peace officer

FOREIGN PHRASES: *Paci sunt maxime contraria vis et injuria.* Violence and injury are especially hostile to peace.

PEACE OFFICER, noun arm of the law, civil officer, constable, custodian of the law, detective, guard, guardian of the peace, law enforcement agent, law officer, member of the police force, officer, officer of the law, patrolman, police, police constable, police officer, policeman, policewoman, protector, security officer, sheriff

PEACEABLE, adjective agreeable, amiable, amicable, bloodless, calm, composed, contented, disposed to peace, easygoing, equable, forgiving, free from war, friendly, gentle, good-tempered, halcyon, halcyonian, imperturbable, inoffensive, kindly, lamblike, mild, moderate, neutral, noncombative, orderly, pacific, pacificatory, pacifistic, patient, peace-loving, peaceful, peacelike, *placabilis,* placid, *placidus,* quiescent, quiet, reasonable, restrained, satisfied, sedate, serene, slow to take offense, sober, still, tame, temperate, tolerant, tranquil, unagitated, unanxious, unbellicose, unbelligerent, uncontentious, undisturbed, unexcitable, unexcited, unmilitant, unmoved, unpugnacious, unresisting, unruffled, untroubled, well-disposed

PECCABLE, adjective bad, below par, blamable, blameworthy, censurable, culpable, defective, erring, exceptionable, fallen, fallible, faulty, flawed, guilty, illaudable, imperfect, inadequate, iniquitous, lacking, lax, less than perfect, liable to err, liable to sin, objectionable, recreant, reprehensible, reprobate, tainted, twisted, unchaste, uncommendable, unheroic, unprincipled, unrighteous, unsound, unstable, unvirtuous, virtueless, warped, wayward

PECCANT *(Culpable)*, **adjective** aberrant, accursed, accusable, amoral, astray, bad, base, blameful, blameworthy, censurable, chargeable, criminal, criminous, debauched, dishonest, erroneous, evil, execrable, faultful, fiendish, foul, full of mischief, guilty, guilty of transgression, heinous, illegal, immoral, impious, incorrigible, inexcusable, inexpiable, infamous, iniquitous, intolerable, maleficent, maleficial, meriting blame, mischievous, naughty, nefarious, offensive, *peccans,* reprehensible, reprobate, scandalous, shameful, sinful, transgressing, trespassing, unforgivable, unjust, unjustifiable, unpardonable, unprincipled, unrighteous, unscrupulous, unvirtuous, unworthy, vicious, vile, villainous, wicked, without excuse, wretched, wrong, wrongful

PECCANT *(Unhealthy)*, **adjective** afflicting, contaminated, corroding, corrosive, dangerous, deadly, deleterious, detrimental, disadvantageous, diseased, disserviceable, envenomed, *gravis,* harmful, injurious, insalubrious, *insalubris,* lethal, malefic, maleficent, malignant, miasmal, morbid, morbific, nocuous, noisome, noxious, perilous, pestilent, poisoned, poisonous, septic, tainted, toxic, unfavorable to health, unhygienic, unwholesome, venomous, virulent

PECULATE, verb appropriate criminally, appropriate dishonestly, appropriate illegally, appropriate wrongfully, bilk, cheat, cozen, deceive, defraud, divert, embezzle, misappropriate, mulct, obtain money on false pretenses, obtain under false pretenses, pilfer, purloin, rob, steal, swindle

PECULIAR *(Curious)*, *adjective* aberrant, abnormal, abnormous, alien, anomalistic, anomalistical, anomalous, astonishing, bizarre, breaking with tradition, eccentric, foreign, inexplicable, irregular, little-known, mysterious, mystifying, odd, out of place, out of the ordinary, out of the way, outlandish, perplexing, preternatural, puzzling, queer, rare, remarkable, signal, singular, startling, strange, supernatural, surprising, unaccountable, unaccustomed, unclassified, unconformable, unconventional, uncustomary, unexampled, unexpected, unfamiliar, unheard of, unimaginable, unnatural, unorthodox, weird

PECULIAR *(Distinctive)*, *adjective* atypical, characteristic, contrasted, contrasting, contrastive, deviating, different, differentiated, differing, disagreeing, discordant, discrepant, disparate, dissimilar, dissonant, distinct, distinguishable, distinguished, divergent, exceptional, extraordinary, idiosyncratic, in a different class, inconformable, incongruent, incongruous, individual, marked, noteworthy, original, out of the ordinary, particular, separated, singular, special, uncommon, unconformable, unconforming, unequal, unimitated, unique, unlike, unusual, variant

PECUNIARY, *adjective* budgetary, economic, economical, fiducial, fiduciary, financial, fiscal, monetary, numismatical, nummary, *pecuniarius*, sumptuary
ASSOCIATED CONCEPTS: pecuniary advantage, pecuniary damages, pecuniary gain, pecuniary injury, pecuniary interest, pecuniary legacy, pecuniary loss, pecuniary profit

PEDAGOGUE, *noun* academician, adviser, classmaster, don, educator, expounder, faculty member, governor, guide, headmaster, inculcator, instructor, learned man, lecturer, *magister*, man of letters, master, preceptor, professor, sage, scholar, schoolman, schoolmaster, schoolteacher, teacher, trainer, tutor

PEDANT, *noun* affecter, bluffer, closed-minded person, dogmatist, narrow-minded person, opinionated person, philosophaster, pretender, sciolist

PEDESTRIAN, *adjective* arid, banal, barren, boresome, boring, characterless, cold, colorless, commonplace, dead, deadly, diffuse, drab, drearisome, dreary, dry, dull, flat, graceless, hackneyed, heavy, humorless, inelegant, inferior, insipid, jejune, lifeless, meaningless, mediocre, monotonous, ordinary, plain, platitudinous, plodding, pointless, ponderous, prosaic, prosy, soporific, spiritless, stale, stodgy, stuffy, tame, tasteless, tedious, tiresome, trite, unamusing, uncaptivating, uncharming, unenlivened, unentertaining, unimaginative, uninspiring, uninteresting, uninventive, unlively, unoriginal, unpoetical, unreadable, unscintillating, unsparkling, unvaried, unvivid, unwitty, usual, wearisome

PEDESTRIAN, *noun* ambulator, foot passenger, foot traveler, marcher, peripatetic, roamer, rover, traveler afoot, walker

PEER, *noun* associate, coequal, companion, compeer, competitor, comrade, contemporary, contender, corrival, equal, equivalent, fellow, likeness, match, mate, opposite number, *par*, parallel, rival

PEJORATIVE, *adjective* abusive, acrimonious, belittling, blackening, calumnious, castigatory, censorious, critical, cynical, damaging, decrying, defamatory, denigrating, denunciatory, depreciative, depreciatory, derisive, derogative, derogatory, detracting, disapproving, discourteous, disdainful, disparaging, disrespectful, faultfinding, harsh, injurious, insulting, irreverent, scornful, severe, slighting, smearing, spiteful, uncomplimentary, underestimating, unflattering, venomous, vilifying, vituperative

PELLUCID, *adjective* apparent, clear, clear-cut, comprehensible, crystalline, diaphanous, disclosed, easy to understand, exoteric, explicit, express, hyaline, intelligible, limpid, lucid, manifest, obvious, overt, palpable, patent, *pellucidus*, plain, pure, recognizable, revealed, simple, straightforward, transparent, unambiguous, unconcealed, understandable, undisguised, unhidden, unquestionable

PENAL, *adjective* castigatory, containing a penalty, corrective, disciplinary, enacting punishment, inflictive, mulctuary, *poenalis*, prohibiting, punishing, punitive, punitory, relating to a penalty, retaliatory, retributive
ASSOCIATED CONCEPTS: penal action, penal bond, penal law, penal ordinances, penal statute
FOREIGN PHRASES: *In haeredes non solent transire actiones quae poenales ex maleficio sunt.* Actions which are penal and which arise out of anything of criminal nature do not pass to the heirs.

PENALIZE, *verb* amerce, avenge, bring to account, call to account, carry out a sentence, castigate, chastise, confiscate, correct, discipline, exact a penalty, exact retribution, execute a sentence, execute judgment, fine, forfeit, harm, hurt, impose a penalty, inflict a penalty, inflict punishment, mulct, punish, put at a disadvantage, rebuke, reprimand, reprove, retaliate, revenge, sentence, subject to a handicap, subject to penalty, subject to punishment, visit punishment

PENALTY, *noun* amercement, castigation, compulsory payment, cost, deprivation, disadvantage, disciplinary action, fine, forefeiture, forfeit, handicap, infliction, liability, loss, *multa*, onus, penal retribution, penance, *poena*, prescribed punishment, punishment, punishment fixed by law, punishment prescribed by law, reprisal, retributive justice, sconce, sentence
ASSOCIATED CONCEPTS: action for penalty, civil penalty, confiscatory penalty, criminal penalty, excessive penalty, penalty clause, penalty for forfeiture, subject to penalty
FOREIGN PHRASES: *Quod a quoque poenae nomine exactum est id eidem restituere nemo cogitur.* No one is compelled to restore that which has been exacted as a penalty.

PENCHANT, *noun* affinity, appetite, ardor, attachment, attraction, bent, bias, capacity, competence, direction, disposition, eagerness, enthusiasm, fancy, fondness, gravitation, inborn ability, *inclinatio*, inclination, innate ability, leaning, liking, partiality, particular aptitude, passion, polarity, predilection, predisposition, preference, prejudice, proclivity, proneness, *propensio*, propension, propensity, relish, specialty, specific aptness, specific quality, talent, tendency, weakness

PENDENCY, noun abeyance, adjournment, break, cessation, continuance, discontinuity, halt, hiatus, interim, interlude, intermediate time, intermission, interregnum, interruption, interval, intervening period, lapse, lull, moratorium, pause, postponement, recess, respite, suspense, suspension, temporary stop

ASSOCIATED CONCEPTS: pendency of an action, pendency of an appeal

PENDENT, adjective additional, adjunct, adscititious, affinitive, allied to, ancillary, appurtenant, auxiliary, close, closely connected, cognate, collateral, complementary, congeneric, congenerical, congenerous, connatural, correspondent, corresponding, equivalent, *instar omnium,* matching, much the same, *quasi,* secondary, similar, something like, subsidiary, supplemental

ASSOCIATED CONCEPTS: pendent claim, pendent jurisdiction

PENDING *(Imminent),* **adjective** about to happen, anticipated, approaching, at hand, close, close at hand, coming, eventual, expectant, fearful, foreseen, foreshadowing, forthcoming, immediate, impending, instant, looming, minacious, momentary, near, ominous, on the horizon, oncoming, overhanging, prospective, threatening, upcoming

ASSOCIATED CONCEPTS: pending action, pending case, pending cause, pending claim, pending proceeding

PENDING *(Unresolved),* **adjective** in a state of uncertainty, in abeyance, in question, indefinite, indeterminate, open to discussion, open to question, still in debate, suspenseful, unascertained, uncertain, unclear, unconcluded, undecided, under consideration, undetermined, unfixed, unsettled, unsolved

PENETRABLE, adjective able to be pierced, absorbent, accessible, agape, ajar, assailable, attackable, conquerable, dehiscent, foraminated, foraminous, gaping, open, opened, passable, *penetrabilis,* perforable, perforated, permeable, pervious, *pervius,* porous, pregnable, receptive, riddled, susceptible, unclosed, vincible, vulnerable, wide open, yawning

PENETRATE, verb absorb, bore, break into, burst in upon, cut through, empierce, enter, erupt, fill, filter in, flow in, force a passage, give entrance to, go through, gore, imbrue, impale, impregnate, infiltrate, inflow, inject, insert, interfuse, lance, leak into, leaven, make a passage, osmose, overspread, pass, *penetrare,* perforate, permeate, pervade, *pervadere,* pierce, pour in, prick, probe, puncture, riddle, run through, saturate, seep in, sink in, skewer, slip into, soak through, spear, spike, stab, suffuse, tincture, transpierce, tunnel

PENITENT, adjective apologetic, atoning, awakened, chastened, compunctious, conciliatory, conscience-smitten, conscience-stricken, contrite, expiatory, full of regrets, humble, making amends, penitential, piacular, plagued by conscience, propiatory, purgatorial, reformed, regenerate, regretful, remorseful, repentant, rueful, self-accusing, self-condemned, self-convicted, self-reproachful, sobered, sorrowful, sorry

PENITENT, noun confessor, conscience-smitten person, conscience-stricken person, contrite person, penance doer, reformed character, remorseful person, repentant person, shriver

ASSOCIATED CONCEPTS: priest-penitent privilege

PENITENTIARY, noun cell, detention camp, detention center, house of correction, house of detention, jail, jailhouse, lockup, penal colony, penal institution, penal settlement, place of confinement, place of detention, place of imprisonment, prison, prisonhouse, reformatory

PENSION, noun allotment, allowance, *annua,* annual allowance, annuity, compensation, emolument, endowment, fee, financial remuneration, grant, grant for support, grant in aid, payment, pecuniary aid, remittance, remuneration, retirement benefits, retirement income, specified income payable for life, stated maintenance, stipend, subsidization, subsidy, subvention, support

ASSOCIATED CONCEPTS: pension act, pension and benefit fund, pension benefits

PENSIVE, adjective absorbed, abstracted, attentive, calculating, concentrating, contemplative, deliberative, dreaming, dreamy, engrossed, full of thought, given to thought, *in cogitatione defixus,* introspective, meditative, museful, musing, obsessed, occupied, rapt, ratiocinative, ratiocinatory, reasoning, reflective, ruminant, ruminative, self-communing, serious, sober, speculative, studious, thoughtful, wistful

PENUMBRA, noun brink, cover, edge, fringe, margin, outskirt, reflection, shade, shadow

ASSOCIATED CONCEPTS: penumbra of a Constitutional Amendment

PENURIOUS, adjective chary, cheap, churlish, close, close-fisted, close-handed, frugal, greedy, grudging, illiberal, impoverished, in distress, in need, in want, indigent, mean, mercenary, miserly, needy, niggard, niggardly, nonpaying, parsimonious, penniless, petty, poverty-stricken, saving, selfish, shabby, sordid, sparing, stingy, *tenax,* ungenerous, unwilling to pay, venal

PER ANNUM, adverb annually, at a fixed interval, on the anniversary, on the basis of a year, yearly

PER CAPITA, adverb allocated, an equal percentage, each to each, per head, percentage, pro rata, proportionately, respectively, share and share alike, to each according to his share

PER DIEM, preposition per day, for each and every day, for each day, for every day

PERAMBULATE, verb amble, circle, circumambulate, course, cover, cross, go around, go for a walk, go on an outing, go on foot, hike, jaunt, journey, make rounds, march, meander, pace, pass, pass through, patrol, pedestrianize, *peragrare,* peregrinate, *perlustrare, pervagari,* promenade, prowl, ramble, range, reconnoiter, roam, rove, saunter, scour, stalk, step, stride, stroll, strut, sweep through, take a constitutional, take a walk, take an airing, tour, tramp, travel, traverse, tread, trek, trudge, walk, walk through, wander

PERCEIVABLE, adjective apparent, appearing, appreciable, apprehensible, before one's eyes, beholdable, bold, clear, cognizable, detectable, discernible, disclosed, discoverable, distinct, distinguishable, easy to see, evident, exoteric, explicit, exposed, exposed to view, express, glaring, in evidence, in full view, in plain sight, in sight, in view, knowable, macroscopic, mani-

fest, naked, notable, noticeable, observable, obvious, open, open to view, overt, palpable, patent, perceptible, perspicuous, plain, plain to be seen, prominent, recognizable, remarkable, revealed, salient, seeable, showing, sighted, tangible, transparent, unclouded, unconcealed, unhidden, unmistakable, viewable, visible, visual, well-defined, well-marked
ASSOCIATED CONCEPTS: last clear chance, latent defect, patent defect

PERCEIVE, *verb*   apperceive, appreciate, apprehend, awaken, be acquainted with, be apprized of, be attentive to, be aware of, be cognizant of, be conscious of, be informed of, be sensitive to, become aware of, become conscious of, cognize, *cognoscere,* come to know, comprehend, detect, discern, discover, discriminate, distinguish, espy, experience, externalize, familiarize oneself, feel, gain insight into, give attention to, have cognizance of, have knowledge of, ken, know, learn, make out, mark, note, notice, observe, *percipere,* react, realize, recognize, regard, see, sense, *sentire,* take notice, understand, witness
ASSOCIATED CONCEPTS: perceive a product defect, perceive danger

PERCEPTIBLE, *adjective*   apparent, apprehensible, ascertainable, beholdable, clear, clearly defined, clearly marked, cognizable, comprehensible, defined, detectable, discernible, disclosed, discoverable, distinct, distinguishable, easy to be seen, evident, explicit, exposed, exposed to view, express, glaring, in bold relief, in evidence, in full view, in plain sight, in sight, in view, indubitable, knowable, macroscopic, manifest, *manifestus,* marked, naked, notable, noticeable, observable, obvious, open, open to view, overt, palpable, patent, perceivable, perspicuous, plain, prominent, recognizable, revealed, salient, seeable, showing, shown, sighted, tangible, unconcealed, understandable, unhidden, unmistakable, viewable, visible, visual, well-defined, well-marked

PERCEPTION, *noun*   ability to make distinctions, acuity, acumen, acuteness, apperception, appraisal, appreciation, apprehension, ascertainment, assessment, astuteness, attention, awareness, clear sight, cleverness, cognition, cognizance, comprehension, consciousness, deduction, detection, determination, discernment, discovery, discriminating judgment, discrimination, espial, estimate, evaluation, field of vision, finding, grasp, idea, image, impression, inkling, insight, *iudicium,* judgment, keen sight, keeness, mental image, mental impression, *mentis acies,* mindfulness, noesis, note, notice, notion, observation, penetration, percipience, perspicaciousness, perspicacity, point of view, quick sense, realization, recognition, regard, sagaciousness, *sagacitas,* sagacity, scrutiny, sense, sensibility, sensory experience, sharp sight, sharpness, shrewdness, sight, smartness, supposition, surmise, theory, understanding, view, viewpoint, visualization

PERCEPTIVE, *adjective*   acute, apperceptive, apprehensive, astute, aware, cognitive, cognizant, comprehending, conscious, discerning, discriminating, discriminative, easily affected, feeling, impressible, impressionable, keen, knowing, mindful, percipient, perspicacious, quick of apprehension, receptive, responsive, *sagax,* sensible, sensitive, sentient, sharp, shrewd, understanding, wise

PEREMPTORY *(Absolute),* *adjective*   actual, axiomatic, certain, complete, decided, decisive, definite, determinate, determined, express, final, imperious, implicit, incontrovertible, independent, overbearing, perfect, positive, real, resolute, resolved, self-existent, total, unalterable, unconditional, unconditioned, unequivocal, unlimited, unqualified, unquestionable, unrestricted, without limitation
ASSOCIATED CONCEPTS: peremptory adjournment, peremptory challenge, peremptory exception, peremptory plea, peremptory writ

PEREMPTORY *(Imperative),* *adjective*   assertive, authoritative, commanding, compulsory, crucial, decisive, demanding, despotic, dictatorial, domineering, essential, exigent, firm, imperious, important, inexorable, inflexible, iron-handed, mandatory, necessary, obligatory, paramount, pressing, unavoidable, urgent
ASSOCIATED CONCEPTS: peremptory instruction

PERFECT, *verb*   *absolvere,* accomplish, bring to a conclusion, bring to an end, bring to completion, bring to fullness, carry out, complete, conclude, consummate, correct, culminate, *cumulare,* effectuate, execute, finish, follow to a conclusion, *perficere,* refine
ASSOCIATED CONCEPTS: perfect a security interest, perfect an appeal, perfect title

PERFERVID, *adjective*   burning, exceedingly ardent, impassioned, on fire, overly passionate, too zealous

PERFIDIOUS, *adjective*   base, betraying, cheating, conniving, corrupt, deceitful, deceiving, designing, dishonest, dishonorable, disloyal, disobedient, dissembling, double-crossing, double-dealing, faithless, false, falsehearted, fraudulent, guileful, hypocritical, inconstant, insidious, intriguing, knavish, lying, *perfidiosus, perfidus,* perjured, plotting, scheming, shifty, slippery, sneaking, sneaky, traitorous, treacherous, treasonable, treasonous, tricky, trothless, unconscionable, undependable, unfaithful, unprincipled, unreliable, unscrupulous, untrue, untrustworthy, untruthful, without honor

PERFORM *(Adhere to),* *verb*   abide by, achieve, be faithful to, carry into execution, carry out, cling to, complete, comply with, conclude, consummate, enact, end, enforce, execute, finish, fulfill, keep, keep one's word, observe, obtain, practice, put in force, put in practice, respect, satisfy, transact
ASSOCIATED CONCEPTS: perform a contract

PERFORM *(Execute),* *verb*   accomplish, achieve, bring into operation, bring to pass, carry into execution, complete, discharge, discharge a duty, do, effect, effectuate, employ oneself, enact, function, *perficere,* perpetrate, pursue a course, put in force, serve, serve in the capacity of, take action, take steps, work

PERFORMANCE *(Execution),* *noun*   accomplished fact, accomplishment, achievement, act, action, attainment, carrying into effect, carrying through, commission, completion, consummation, culmination, deed, enactment, finished product, fulfilment, implementation, operation, perpetration, production, realization, rendition, work
ASSOCIATED CONCEPTS: full performance, impossibility of performance, partial performance, performance bond, prevention of performance

FOREIGN PHRASES: *Non quod dictum est, sed quod factum est inspicitur.* Not what is said, but what is done, is to be regarded. *Lex non cogit ad impossibilia.* The law does not require the performance of the impossible.

PERFORMANCE *(Workmanship),* **noun** ability, accomplishment, achievement, action, aptitude, aptness, *ars,* art, artfulness, *artificium,* attainment, caliber, capability, capacity, competence, competency, composition, construction, craft, craftsmanship, creation, dexterity, effort, endowment, exhibition, expertness, faculty, finesse, formation, forte, handicraft, handiness, handiwork, ingenuity, manipulation, manufacture, mastership, mastery, operation, *opus,* play, preparation, production, proficiency, qualification, quality of execution, quality of work, representation, show, skill, skillfulness, talent, technique, virtuosity, work, working ability

PERFUNCTORY, *adjective* absent-minded, abstracted, apathetic, below par, careless, casual, cursory, deficient, disinterested, dispassionate, disregardful, failing, formal, halfhearted, hasty, heedless, hollow, hurried, ill-done, imperfect, inadequate, inattentive, incautious, incomplete, indifferent, inexact, insubstantial, lacking, lax, lenient, lukewarm, mechanical, mindless, needing, neglectful, negligent, offhand, omitting, passionless, poor, poorly done, quick, regardless, remiss, requiring, routine, rushed, short, sketchy, speedy, substandard, superficial, thoughtless, unattended to, uncaring, unconcerned, undiscerning, unenthusiastic, unexamined, unfeeling, unguarded, unheeded, unheedful, unheeding, uninspired, uninterested, uninvolved, unmindful, unobservant, unregarded, unresponsive, unstudied, unthinking, unthorough, unthought of, unwatchful, unweighed, wanting, without concern, without enthusiasm

PERIL, *noun* approach of danger, crisis, danger, dangerous situation, desperate situation, emergency, endangerment, exposure to danger, exposure to destruction, exposure to harm, exposure to injury, exposure to loss, hazard, helplessness, hopelessness, imperilment, insecurity, jeopardy, liability to injury, parlous state, precariousness, predicament, risk, source of danger, source of risk, susceptibility, susceptibleness, susceptivity, threat, uncertainty, unhealthy situation, unsafety, unsureness, vulnerability, vulnerable point
ASSOCIATED CONCEPTS: common peril, discovered peril, doctrine of discovered peril, doctrine of last clear chance, manifest peril, unforseen peril

PERIOD, *noun* age, bout, continuance, course, diuturnity, duration, eon, epoch, era, hitch, interval, juncture, length of time, limited time, point, season, shift, span, spell, stage, stint, stretch, tenure, term, time, time interval, time stretch, tour, while
ASSOCIATED CONCEPTS: period of redemption

PERIODIC, *adjective* cadenced, cadent, continual, cyclic, cyclical, erratic, fluctuating, frequent, habitual, intermittent, measured, occasional, occurring again, oft-repeated, oftentime, patterned, perpetual, reappearing, recurrent, recurring, regular, regulated, remittent, repeated, returning, returning at intervals, rhythmic, rhythmical, seasonal, serial, *sollemnis,* spasmodic, sporadic, successive, systematic, variable

PERIPHERAL, *adjective* beside the point, circumferential, collateral, exterior, external, extraneous, farthest, fringe, impertinent, inconsequential, inessential, irrelevant, on the edge, outer, outermost, outland, outlying, outmost, outside, perimetric, perimetrical, secondary, trivial, ungermane, unimportant, without

PERIPHERY, *noun* ambit, border, borderland, bound, boundary line, circuit, circumambiency, circumference, circumscription, compass, confine, contour, delimitation, demarcation, edge, end, exterior, extreme edge, fringe, frontier, limit, limitation, line of demarcation, march, margin, mete, outer boundary, outer part, outline, outpost, outside, outside surface, outskirts, pale, perimeter, *perimetros,* purlieu, rim, skirts, surrounding area, surrounding space, terminus, verge

PERISH, *verb* be annihilated, be destroyed, be eradicated, be extinguished, be null and void, be ruined, become extinct, cease, cease living, cease to be, cease to exist, cease to live, come to an end, come to naught, come to ruin, crumble, depart, die, die away, die out, disappear, evanesce, evaporate, expire, fade, fade away, fade out, fail, go, *interire,* leave no trace, lose life, meet death, melt away, *occidere,* pass, pass away, pass on, *perire,* peter out, relinquish life, render null, sink away, succumb, surrender, vanish, wilt, wither

PERJURE, *verb* be false, be untruthful, bear false witness, break one's oath, break one's word, deviate from the truth, falsify, falsify testimony, feign, forswear, hide the truth, lie, misrepresent, palter, *periurare, periurium facere,* put a false construction upon, say less than the truth, speak falsely, strain the truth, stretch the truth, swear falsely, tell a falsehood, tell a lie, trump up, utter a falsehood

PERJURY, *noun* act of oath-breaking, distortion of the truth, false statement, false swearing, falsehood, falseness, falsification, intentional misstatement, invention of lies, misrepresentation, misstatement, *periurium,* perversion of truth, prevarication, untruth, violation of an oath, willful distortion of the truth, willful falsehood, willful telling of a falsehood, willful telling of a lie
ASSOCIATED CONCEPTS: subornation of perjury
FOREIGN PHRASES: *Lex punit mendacium.* The law punishes mendacity. *Perjuri sunt qui servatis verbis juramenti decipiunt aures eorum qui accipiunt.* They are perjured, who, preserving the words of an oath, deceive the ears of those who receive it. *Sacramentum si fatuum fuerit, licet falsum, tamen non committit perjurium.* A foolish oath, although false, does not give rise to perjury. *Qui non libere veritatem pronunciat proditor est veritatis.* He who does not freely speak the truth is a betrayer of the truth.

PERMANENT, *adjective* abiding, ageless, ceaseless, changeless, chronic, confirmed, constant, continued, continuing, dateless, deep-seated, durable, endless, enduring, engrafted, entrenched, established, eternal, everlasting, fast, fixed, immortal, immutable, imperishable, incommutable, indefatigable, indefeasible, indelible, indestructible, ineradicable, inextinguishable, infinite, ingrained, insusceptible to change, interminable, intransient, intransmutable, invulnerable, irremovable, irreversible, irrevocable, lasting, long-lasting, never-ceasing, never-ending, never-stopping, nonreversible, perdurable, perduring, perennial, *perennis,* perpetual, perpetuated, persevering, persistent, persisting, preserved, radicated, remaining, reverseless, rooted, secure, sempiternal, set, *stabilis*, stable, static, stationary, staying, steadfast, steady, surviving, sustained, tenacious, unalterable, unceasing, unchangeable, unchanging, unchecked, undestroyable, undying, unending, unerasable, unfading, unfailing, unflagging, uninterrupted, unmodifiable, unmovable, unrepealable, unshifting, unvarying, unwavering, unyielding, without end

PERMEATE, *verb* bathe, diffuse, drench, fill, go through, imbue, impregnate, infiltrate, infuse, inject, interpenetrate, leaven, osmose, overrun, overspread, pass through, penetrate, percolate, pervade, run through, saturate, seep, soak, souse, spread through, steep, suffuse, transfuse, wash, waterlog

PERMISSIBLE, *adjective* according to law, admissible, allowable, allowed, amenable to law, approvable, approved, authorized, constitutional, empowered, fitting, franchised, granted, lawful, legal, legally sound, legitimate, licensed, *licet*, licit, *licitus,* permitted, proper, sanctioned, sanctioned by law, stamped with approval, sufferable, tolerable, unchallenged, unforbidden, unprohibited, viable, warrantable, within the law

PERMISSION, *noun* acquiescence, allowance, approval, assent, authority, authorization, blessing, concurrence, consent, *copia*, countenance, *facultas*, formal consent, full authority, grace, leave, license, *potestas*, sanction, tolerance, visa
ASSOCIATED CONCEPTS: explicit permission, implied permission, permission of the court
FOREIGN PHRASES: *Tout ce que la loi ne defend pas est permis.* Everything which the law does not prohibit is allowed.

PERMISSIVE, *adjective* acquiescent, allowing, broad-minded, complaisant, discretional, granting, indulgent, lenient, liberal, mild, nonprohibitive, tolerant, tolerating, volitive, yielding
ASSOCIATED CONCEPTS: permissive counterclaim, permissive joinder, permissive statute, permissive use

PERMIT, *noun* affirmation, approbation, approval, authority, authorization, *carte blanche*, certificate, charter, confirmation, document granting permission, fiat, grant, leave, legalization, license, pass, passport, patent, permission, privilege, sanction, ticket of leave, visa, voucher, warrant
ASSOCIATED CONCEPTS: license

PERMIT, *verb* accord one's approval, agree to, allow, approve, approve of, assent, authorize, award assent, be in favor of, be indulgent of, confer a privilege, consent, empower, enable, entitle, facilitate, give clearance, give consent, give leave, give opportunity for, give permission, give power, grant permission, have no objection, let, license, make possible, remove the obstacles, sanction, suffer, tolerate, warrant, yield assent

PERNICIOUS, *adjective* adverse, afflicting, baleful, baneful, brutal, calamitous, catastrophic, corrosive, crippling, cruel, damaging, deadly, death-bringing, death-dealing, deathful, deathly, deleterious, destructive, detrimental, devouring, diabolic, dire, disadvantageous, disastrous, disserviceable, distressing, envenomed, evil, *exitiosus,* extirpative, fatal, fell, fiendish, fraught with evil, fraught with harm, harmful, hurtful, inimical, injurious, insalubrious, insidious, killing, lethal, malefic, maleficent, maleficial, malevolent, malign, malignant, menacing, mephitic, mischievous, morbiferous, morbific, mortal, murderous, nocent, noisome, noxious, *noxius,* painful, *perniciosus,* pestiferous, pestilential, poisonous, ruinous, serious, sinister, tending to cause death, toxic, toxicant, toxiferous, treacherous, unhealthful, unhealthy, unkind, unpropitious, unwholesome, venomous, vicious, violent, virulent, wicked

PERORATION, *noun* address, bombast, declamation, discourse, *epilogus,* formal speech, grandiloquence, homily, lecture, magniloquence, monologue, oration, oratorical display, orotundity, *peroratio,* prelection, prepared speech, public address, recitation, rhetorical discourse, sermon, soliloquy, speech, talk

PERPETRATE, *verb* accomplish, achieve, be guilty of, bring about, bring to pass, carry into execution, carry off, carry on, carry out, carry through, commit, *committere,* do, effect, effectuate, execute, follow through, fulfill, implement, impose, inflict, maneuver, manipulate, perform, produce, put into action, put into effect, take measures, transact, work, work out
ASSOCIATED CONCEPTS: perpetrate a crime

PERPETUAL, *adjective* *adsiduus,* amaranthine, ceaseless, chronic, constant, continuous, deathless, endless, enduring, eternal, ever-abiding, everlasting, fixed, having no limit, immortal, imperishable, impossible to stop, incessant, indelible, indestructible, ineradicable, inexhaustible, infinite, interminable, intransient, lasting, never-ceasing, never-dying, never-fading, never-failing, never-stopping, perdurable, *perennis,* permanent, perpetuated, persistent, sempiternal, *sempiternus,* stable, surviving, unceasing, undestroyable, unending, unerasable, unfading, unfailing, uninterrupted, unlimited, unrepealable, without end
ASSOCIATED CONCEPTS: perpetual easement, perpetual franchise, perpetual injunction, perpetual lease, perpetual lien, perpetual succession
FOREIGN PHRASES: *Perpetua lex est nullam legem humanam ac positivam perpetuam esse, et clausula quae abrogationem excludit ab initio non valet.* It is a perpetual law that no human and positive law can be perpetual, and a clause in a law which precludes the power of abrogation or repeal is void from the beginning.

PERPETUATE, *verb* carry forward, carry on, cause to be continued, cause to endure, cause to last, eternize, immortalize, keep alive, keep in existence, maintain, make eternal, make everlasting, make last, make permanent, make perpetual, preserve, prolong, render deathless, retain, save, sustain
ASSOCIATED CONCEPTS: perpetuate testimony

PERPETUITY, *noun* boundlessness, ceaselessness, constancy, constant progression, continualness, continuance, continuation, continued existence, continuous time, continuousness, endless duration, endless time, endlessness, eternalness, eternity, everlasting, forever, incessancy, indefiniteness, infinite duration, infiniteness, infinity, interminability, never-endingness, perenniality, permanence, perpetualness, perpetuation, *perpetuitas,* time without end, timelessness, unintermitted continuance, uninterrupted existence, uninterruptedness

ASSOCIATED CONCEPTS: after-born children, in perpetuity, lives in being, period of perpetuities, restraint on alienation, rule against perpetuities

PERPLEX, *verb* baffle, bedevil, bemuse, beset, bewilder, bother, complicate, confound, confuse, corner, discompose, disconcert, disorient, disquiet, *distrahere,* disturb, embarrass, encumber, entangle, fill with doubt, fog, involve, make difficult, make intricate, mix up, muddle, mystify, nonplus, perturb, pose, pother, puzzle, rattle, render uncertain, snarl, *sollicitare,* tangle, tease, trouble, unsettle, upset, vex, worry

PERQUISITE, *noun* allowance, annuity, benefaction, bonus, compensation, consideration, donation, emolument, endowment, fee, financial remuneration, financial reward, gain, gift, gratuity, incidental profits, payment, premium, present, profit, recompense, remuneration, return, revenue, reward, reward for service, stipend, subsidy, tip, token, wage

PERSECUTE, *verb* abuse, afflict, aggrieve, agonize, annoy, assail, attack, badger, be intolerant, be malevolent, be malicious, be offensive, be ruthless, bedevil, beset, bother, browbeat, bully, carp at, chevy, crucify, damage, distress, disturb, do an injustice to, do harm, do mischief, do violence, do wrong to, dragoon, endamage, enrage, harass, ill treat, ill use, inflict evil, injure, maltreat, manhandle, misemploy, mishandle, mistreat, misuse, offend, oppress, outrage, overburden, overtax, overwork, plague, provoke, refuse to tolerate, scathe, scourge, show no mercy, show no pity, torment, treat poorly, trouble, use dispiteously, *vexare,* victimize, wrong

PERSEVERE, *verb* adhere, apply oneself, be constant, be determined, be obstinate, be resolute, be steadfast, be steady, be stubborn, be tenacious, be unyielding, carry on, cling, cling tenaciously, *constare,* continue, endure, exert oneself, follow up, go forward, go on, hang on, hold fast, hold on, hold out, keep driving, keep going, keep on, keep up, labor, last, maintain, maintain a course, outlast, perpetuate, persist, *persistere, perstare,* plod, plug away, prevail, prolong, pursue, refuse to give up, refuse to yield, remain, resist change, run on, spare no effort, stand fast, stand firm, stay, stick to, stop at nothing, struggle, survive, sustain, take no denial, toil, work unceasingly, work unflaggingly

PERSIST, *verb* abide, be determined, be obstinate, be resolute, be steadfast, be steady, be tenacious, be unyielding, bide, carry on, cling to, continue, drag on, endure, go forward, go on, hold fast, hold on, hold out, insist, keep at, keep on, last, linger, live on, maintain, make headway, never cease, outlast, perdure, persevere, *persistere, perstare,* plod, plug away, prevail, progress, pursue relentlessly, refuse to give up, remain, remain unchanged, stay, stick to, survive, sustain, take no denial, toil unceasingly, work unceasingly, work unflaggingly

PERSISTENT, *adjective* abiding, adamant, assiduous, chronic, continued, continuing, continuous, determined, diligent, dogged, durable, enduring, everlasting, faithful, indefatigable, insistent, lasting, obstinate, patient, perdurable, perseverant, persevering, pertina-

cious, purposeful, refusing to relent, relentless, remaining, repeated, resolute, resolved, sedulous, serious, set upon, staying, steadfast, steady, strong-willed, stubborn, sustained, tenacious, tireless, unallayed, unceasing, unchanging, unchecked, undaunted, undeviating, undiscouraged, undying, unfailing, unfaltering, unflagging, unrelaxing, unremitting, unstopping, unswerving, untiring, unvarying, unwavering, unwearying, unyielding

PERSON, *noun* autonomous being, being, *caput,* chap, character, fellow, *homo,* human, human being, human creature, individual, living being, living soul, member of the human race, mortal, mortal body, *mortalis,* party, personage, somebody, someone, soul

ASSOCIATED CONCEPTS: adult person, artificial person, competent person, credible person, disorderly person, fictitious person, injured person, natural person, person aggrieved, person in need of supervision, poor person, third person, unauthorized person

PERSONAL *(Individual),* *adjective* characteristic, differentiating, discriminative, distinct, distinguishing, idiosyncratic, own, particular, peculiar, private, select, specific

ASSOCIATED CONCEPTS: personal action, personal appearance, personal communication, personal covenant, personal effects, personal estate, personal exemption, personal expenses, personal goods, personal injury, personal judgment, personal jurisdiction, personal liability, personal obligation, personal privilege, personal property, personal representative, personal rights, personal safety, personal service of process, personal services, personal transaction, personally responsible

PERSONAL *(Private),* *adjective* buried, clandestine, closed, concealed, confidential, covert, cryptic, hidden, intimate, *privatus,* privy, restricted, secret, singular, subjective, undisclosed, unrevealed, unshared, untold, veiled

ASSOCIATED CONCEPTS: personal articles, personal belongings

PERSONALITY, *noun* attributes, being, character, characteristics, disposition, distinction, distinctiveness, egohood, identity, individualism, individuality, *ingenium,* makeup, nature, oneness, originality, particularity, peculiarities, personal identity, personal mark, predisposition, selfhood, selfness, singularity, soul, style, temperament, traits, type, uniqueness

PERSONALTY, *noun* assets, available means, belongings, chattels, effects, funds, holdings, investments, personal property, personal resources, possessions, property, resources, wealth

PERSONIFY, *verb* ascribe personal qualities to, be the embodiment, characterize, copy, embody, embrace, exemplify, humanize, incarnate, manifest, *orationem attribuere,* symbolize, treat as human, typify

PERSONNEL, *noun* assistants, band of employees, body of employees, cast, clerical staff, company, corps of employees, coworkers, crew, employees, factotums, fellow workers, help, labor supply, laborers, laboring force, manpower, members, office force, servantry, servants, staff, team of employees, work force, work party, workers, working people

PERSPECTIVE, *noun*   angle of vision, attitude, conception, distance, eyereach, feeling, field of view, field of vision, framework, impression, inclination, leaning, line of sight, mental view, orientation, outlook, point of observation, point of view, position, range of view, range of vision, scope of vision, sense of proportion, situation, slant, standpoint, thought, vantage point, view, viewpoint, way of thinking

PERSPICACIOUS, *adjective*   *acutus,* alert, apperceptive, argute, artful, astute, bright, canny, clear-sighted, clearheaded, clever, crafty, cunning, dioristic, discerning, discriminating, discriminative, farseeing, farsighted, foresighted, forethoughtful, hardheaded, informed, intelligent, judicious, keen, keen-eyed, keen-sighted, keen-witted, knowing, longsighted, nimble-witted, observant, penetrating, perceptive, percipient, *perspicax,* piercing, quick, quick-witted, sagacious, *sagax,* sage, sapient, sensible, sharp, sharp-sighted, sharp-witted, shrewd, understanding, wise

PERSUADE, *verb*   actuate, advise, align, bend to one's will, blandish, bring a person to his senses, bring around, bring over, bring to reason, cajole, coax, compel, convert, convince, counsel, enlist, exercise influence, exert influence, exhort, gain the confidence of, impel, importune, impress, indoctrinate, induce, influence, inveigle, lead, lead to believe, lure, make one's point, make oneself felt, motivate, move, prevail upon, prompt, propagandize, proselyte, proselytize, rouse, satisfy by evidence, satisfy by proof, seduce, sell, suborn, sway, urge, win over, woo

PERSUASION, *noun*   actuation, advocacy, alignment, argument, blandishment, cajolement, cajolery, cajoling, coaxing, conversion, dissuasion, encouragement, enlistment, enticement, exhortation, incitation, incitement, inducement, influence, insistence, inveiglement, motivation, pleading, pressure, prompting, propaganda, proselytism, salesmanship, solicitation, suasion, winning over

PERSUASIVE, *adjective*   actuating, arousing, authoritative, coaxing, cogent, compelling, convictive, convincing, credible, effective, eloquent, forceful, hortative, hortatory, impelling, impressive, inductive, influential, inspiring, inviting, logical, moving, persuasory, plausible, pointed, potent, powerful, propagandistic, provocative, provoking, rousing, sound, strong, suasive, subornative, swaying, telling, tempting, tenable, touching, valid, weighty
ASSOCIATED CONCEPTS: persuasive arguments, persuasive authority, persuasive legal testimony

PERTAIN, *verb*   appertain, be appropriate, be associated with, be concerned with, be connected to, be suitable, bear upon, befit, behoove, belong, concern, have implications for, have interrelationship with, have reference to, have relation to, have relevance, have significance for, refer, relate, stand in relation to, tie in with, touch upon

PERTINACIOUS, *adjective*   adamant, adhering to a purpose, assiduous, bent, bullheaded, certain, continuing, decided, determined, diligent, dogged, earnest, enduring, exhibiting purpose, faithful, firm, hard to get rid of, headstrong, holding to a purpose, immovable, immutable, implacable, indefatigable, indomitable, industrious, inexorable, inflexible, insistent, intent, intracta-

ble, inveterate, mulish, never-tiring, never-wearying, obdurate, obstinate, *obstinatus,* painstaking, patient, persevering, persistent, persisting, *pertinax,* pervicacious, *pervicax,* pigheaded, plodding, purposeful, relentless, resolute, resolved, rigid, sedulous, self-willed, serious, set, single-minded, stalwart, stanch, steadfast, steady, strong-willed, stubborn, sure, tough, unbending, uncompromising, undaunted, undeviating, undistracted, undoubting, unfaltering, unflagging, unflinching, unmovable, unrelaxing, unrelenting, unremitting, unshakable, unshaken, unshrinking, unswerving, untiring, unwavering, unwearying, unyielding, willful, zealous

PERTINENT, *adjective*   adapted, affinitive, appertaining, applicable, apposite, appropriate, appurtenant, apropos, apt, associated, associative, bearing on the question, belonging, concerning, connected, fit, fitting, germane, having direct bearing, having to do with, material, opposite, pertaining, referrential, referring, regarding, related, relating, relational, relevant, suitable, to the point, to the purpose, with reference to
ASSOCIATED CONCEPTS: pertinent testimony, relevant evidence

PERTURB, *verb*   abash, agitate, alarm, annoy, arouse, badger, baffle, bewilder, bother, bring into disorder, cause a fuss, cause agitation, cause alarm, cause confusion, cause disorder, cause upset, churn, complicate, confound, confuse, derange, disarrange, discomfit, discompose, disconcert, dismay, disorder, disquiet, distract, distress, disturb, embarrass, entangle, exasperate, excite, ferment, flurry, fluster, fret, frustrate, gall, give cause for alarm, grieve, harass, harry, inflame, infuriate, irk, irritate, jar, jolt, madden, make havoc, make uneasy, nonplus, outrage, pain, perplex, perturbate, *perturbo,* pester, pique, plague, pother, provoke, put out, rouse, ruffle, shake, shake up, shock, snarl, stir, stir up, throw into confusion, trouble, unnerve, unsettle, upset, vex, work up, worry

PERUSE, *verb*   analyze, browse, check, con, conduct research on, consider, contemplate, delve into, devote oneself to, examine, explore, feel out, glance over, glean information, go over, inquire into, inspect, investigate, look over, observe, overlook, pass under review, peer into, *perlegere,* pore over, probe, pry into, read, regard studiously, research, review, scan, scrutinize, search, study, subject to scrutiny, survey, take note of, take stock of, thumb, turn one's gaze upon, turn the leaves of, watch

PERVADE, *verb*   affect entirely, bathe, be rife, diffuse, disseminated, drench, enter, extend through, fill, filter through, flow into, force a passage, go through, imbrue, imbue, implant, impregnate, infiltrate, infuse, inject, instill, interfuse, interpenetrate, intrude, invade, make an entrance, overspread, pass through, penetrate, perforate, permeate, pierce, radiate, run into, run through, saturate, seep in, soak, spread, spread through, steep, suffuse, transfuse

PERVERSE, *adjective*   bad, bad-natured, bad-tempered, base, bellicose, belligerent, boorish, bumptious, cantankerous, captious, churlish, contemptible, contrary, contumacious, contumelious, corrupt, corrupted, crabbed, cranky, cross, crusty, debauched, degenerate, depraved, deviating, difficult, discourteous, disobedient, disorderly, evil, evil-minded, fractious, froward, hard to deal with, hard to manage, headstrong, ill-behaved, ill-natured, ill-tempered, impolite, improper, impudent, inaffable, incorrigible, inimical, insubordinate, insulting, intractable, irascible, mean, nasty, naughty, negative, negativistic, noncompliant, obstinate, obstreperous, peevish, persisting in error, persisting in fault, *perversus,* perverted, petulant, pugnacious, refractory, reprobate, resistive, rude, self-willed, snappish, snarling, spiteful, spleenful, spleeny, splenetic, stubborn, surly, testy, thoughtless, touchy, troublesome, truculent, unaccommodating, uncivil, uncomplaisant, uncompliant, uncooperative, unfriendly, ungallant, ungovernable, ungracious, unhelpful, unmanageable, unmannerly, unpolite, unreasonable, unruly, untoward, unyielding, venomous, vexatious, waspish, wayward, wicked, wrong, wrongheaded

PERVERSION, *noun*   abasement, aberrance, aberrancy, aberration, abnormality, abomination, abuse, baseness, contamination, *corruptio,* corruption, debasement, debauchery, defilement, degradation, demoralization, *depravatio,* depravation, depravity, evil behavior, foulness, immorality, infraction, lewdness, looseness of morals, malefaction, misuse, pollution, prostitution, sophistication, turpitude, unnatural habit, violation, vitiation, want of principle, wickedness
ASSOCIATED CONCEPTS: deviant sexual behavior

PERVERT, *verb*   abuse, canker, contaminate, *corrumpere,* corrupt, debauch, degenerate, demoralize, *depravare,* deprave, divert, falsify, infect, lead astray, lower, make corrupt, misapply, mislead, misrepresent, misuse, poison, pollute, prostitute, render evil, ruin, soil, sophisticate, spoil, stain, subvert, taint, tamper with, teach wickedness, vitiate, warp
FOREIGN PHRASES: *Quae ad unum finem loquuta sunt, non debent ad alium detorqueri.* Those words which are spoken to one end ought not to be perverted to another.

PESSIMISM, *noun*   blighted hope, cheerlessness, cynicism, dashed hopes, defeatism, dejectedness, dejection, depression, despair, desperation, despondence, despondency, disconsolation, discouragement, disheartenment, dispiritedness, dolefulness, downcastness, downheartedness, faint hope, forlorn hope, gloom, gloominess, gloomy outlook, glumness, heaviness of heart, heaviness of spirit, hopelessness, joylessness, lack of enthusiasm, lack of expectation, low-spiritedness, low spirits, melancholia, melancholy, misery, sorrowfulness, uncheerfulness, unhappiness, wretchedness

PESSIMISTIC, *adjective*   cheerless, crushed, cynical, defeatist, dejected, depressed, despairing, desperate, despondent, disconsolate, discouraged, disheartened, dismayed, dispirited, distrustful, downcast, downhearted, foreboding, forlorn, gloomy, glum, grieved, heavyhearted, hopeless, joyless, low-spirited, melancholic, melancholy, miserable, morbid, morose, sad, sorrowful, troubled, uncheerful, uncheery, unhappy, unjoyful, unpromising, wretched

PESTILENT, *adjective*   baleful, baneful, contagious, damaging, dangerous, deadly, death-dealing, deathly, deleterious, destructive, disastrous, disease-ridden, diseased, epidemic, evil, fatal, feral, foul, harmful, hurtful, infectious, injurious, insalubrious, killing, lethal, lethiferous, malefic, maleficent, malign, malignant, mephitic, morbid, morbiferous, morbific, morbifical, mortal, murderous, nocent, nocuous, noisome, nox-

ious, pernicious, *pestilens,* pestilential, plagueful, poisonous, tending to cause death, terrible, threatening, toxic, toxicant, toxiferous, unhealthful, unhealthy, venomous, violent, virulent

PETITION, *noun*   adjuration, application, bid, call for aid, demand, earnest request, entreaty, formal writing embodying a request, formal written plea, formal written request, invocation, *libellus,* motion, plea, prayer, request, request for relief, requisition, solemn request, written application for relief
ASSOCIATED CONCEPTS: affidavit, cross-petition, ex parte petition, filing of petition, order dismissing a petition, petition for a name change, petition for divorce, verified petition, voluntary petition in bankruptcy

PETITION, *verb*   adjure, advocate, appeal for, apply for, apply to, ask for, beseech, bid, call upon, clamor for, entreat, entreat earnestly, file for, formally urge, *implorare,* implore, make a requisition, make application, make demands, make written application, obtest, *petere,* plead, pray for, prefer a request to, request, requisition, *rogare,* seek, solemnly request, solicit, urge
ASSOCIATED CONCEPTS: petition for a rehearing, petition for a writ of certiorari, petition for a writ of mandamus, petition for a writ of prohibition, petition for redress, petition for removal, petition for review

PETITIONER, *noun*   applicant, asker, litigant, movant, one who applies for relief, one who files an application for relief, one who requests relief, party, pleader, solicitant, solicitor, *supplex,* supplicant
ASSOCIATED CONCEPTS: aggrieved party

PETTIFOG, *verb*   beguile, bluff, cavil, circumvent, connive, deceive, dodge, dupe, ensnare, evade, fence, mislead, outmaneuver, palter, prevaricate, split hairs, trick, trifle

PETTIFOGGERY, *noun*   artfulness, artifice, bamboozlement, cheating, chicane, chicanery, circumvention, corruption, cozenage, craft, craftiness, cunning, deceit, deception, dishonesty, dodgery, duplicity, equivocation, evasion, foul play, fraud, fraudulence, fraudulency, fraudulent practice, guile, humbug, indirection, intrigue, jobbery, jugglery, juggling, knavery, petty dishonesty, sharp practice, treachery, trickery, trickiness, underhand dealing, underhand practice

PETTY, *adjective*   beggarly, contemptible, diminutive, dispensable, expendable, fribble, frivolous, inappreciable, inconsequential, inconsiderable, insignificant, limited, little, marginal, meager, mean, minor, minute, *minutus,* negligible, nonessential, nugatory, of small account, of small moment, paltry, petit, picayune, piddling, puny, scant, scanty, skimpy, slight, small, sparse, *tenuis,* trifling, trivial, unessential, unimportant, unnotable, unworthy of regard, worthless
ASSOCIATED CONCEPTS: petty larceny, petty misdemeanor, petty offense

PETULANT, *adjective*   acrimonious, annoyed, argumentative, bad-tempered, bearish, cantankerous, captious, carping, cavilling, censorious, choleric, churlish, contentious, crabbed, crabby, cranky, cross, cross-tempered, crusty, curmudgeonly, difficult, disagreeable, disputatious, fractious, fretful, froward, grouchy, growling, grumbling, grumbly, grumpy, hot-headed, hot-tempered, huffy, ill-humored, ill-tempered, impatient, indocile, iracund, irascible, irritable, liverish, mean, mean-tempered, moody, nagging, out of humor, out of sorts, peevish, perverse, pettish, *petulans,* piqued, pugnacious, quarrelsome, querulous, short, short-tempered, shrewish, snappish, snappy, snarling, sour, sour-tempered, spiteful, spleenful, splenetic, spleneti-cal, surly, testy, touchy, vixenish, waspish, whiny

PHANTOM, *noun*   airy spirit, apparition, appear-ance, banshee, chimera, creation of the imagination, creation of the mind, delusion, disembodied spirit, dream, eidolon, fiction, fictive creation, figment, fig-ment of the imagination, ghost, ghostly form, halluci-nation, illusion, image, *imago,* incorporeal being, men-tal image, mirage, phantasm, poltergeist, revenant, shade, specter, spirit, sprite, unreality, vapor, vision, wraith

PHASE *(Aspect),* **noun**   angle, consideration, facet, feature, part, point, portion, *ratio,* section, side, *status*

PHASE *(Period),* **noun**   age, continuance, duration, epoch, era, measured time, moment, period of time, point, point of time, season, session, shift, space of time, span, spell, stage, state, step, stretch, tenure, term, time, tour

PHENOMENON *(Manifestation),* **noun**   appari-tion, appearance, display, feature, figure, form, image, materialization, presence, realization, shape, show, sight, sign, spectacle, vision

PHENOMENON *(Unusual   occurrence),* **noun** amazement, amazing thing, astonishing thing, aston-ishment, curiosity, exception, experience, freak occur-rence, marvel, miracle, nonesuch, nonpareil, *ostentum,* portent, *prodigium,* rare occurrence, rarity, *res mira,* sight, special occurrence, spectacle, unusual circum-stance, unusual happening, unusual incident, wonder, wonderment, wonderwork

PHILANTHROPIC, *adjective*   accommodating, almsgiving, altruistic, beneficent, benevolent, benign, benignant, bighearted, bounteous, bountiful, brotherly, charitable, civic-minded, considerate, devoted to others, eleemosynary, free, freehanded, generous, giving, good-natured, good-hearted, gracious, helpful, hospitable, humane, humanitarian, *humanus,* indulgent, kind, kindhearted, kindly, lavish, liberal, magnanimous, mu-nificent, obliging, open-handed, princely, public-spir-ited, selfless, ungrudging, unselfish, unsparing, un-stinting

PHILANTHROPY, *noun*   almsgiving, altruism, beneficence, benevolence, *benevolentia,* benignancy, be-nignity, bounteousness, bountifulness, bounty, brother-hood, brotherliness, brotherly love, charitableness, charity, considerateness, consideration, devotion to oth-ers, fellow feeling, free giving, free-handedness, gener-osity, good-heartedness, good nature, good will, good works, graciousness, helpfulness, hospitableness, hos-pitality, humaneness, humanitarianism, *humanitas,* indulgence, kindliness, kindness, largess, lavishness, liberality, love of mankind, magnanimity, munificence, open-handedness, princeliness, public spirit, self-sacri-fice, selflessness, ungrudgingness, unselfishness, un-sparingness

PHILISTINE, *noun*   artless person, conformist, conventionalist, nouveau riche, social climber, tradi-tionalist

PHILLIPIC, *noun*   abusive language, acrimony, as-persion, bitter language, bitter words, castigation, cen-sure, chastisement, commination, contumely, defama-tion, denunciation, detraction, diatribe, disparagement, execration, harangue, invective, malediction, obloquy, reprobation, revilement, screed, tirade, tongue-lashing, verbal abuse, vilification, vituperation

PHLEGMATIC, *adjective*   aloof, apathetic, blood-less, bovine, callous, calm, cold, coldblooded, comatose, cool, detached, disinterested, dispassionate, distant, dull, frigid, halfhearted, hebetudinous, impassive, im-perturbable, indifferent, inert, insensible, lackadaisi-cal, languid, languorous, lazy, *lentus,* lethargic, lethar-gical, lifeless, listless, lymphatic, oscitant, passionless, passive, *patiens,* phlegmatical, pluckless, sedate, se-rene, slow, sluggish, sober, spiritless, spunkless, staid, stoical, stolid, stony, stupefied, supine, tame, *tardus,* torpid, unagitated, unanxious, unapprehensive, uncar-ing, uncommunicative, unconcerned, undemonstrative, undisturbed, unemotional, unexcitable, unexcited, un-feeling, unflustered, unimpassioned, unperturbed, un-responsive, unruffled, unsusceptible, untroubled, un-worried

PHOBIA, *noun*   abhorrence, abject fear, alarm, an-tipathy, anxiety, apprehension, aversion, awe, detesta-tion, dislike, distaste, disturbance, dread, fear, fright, horror, loathing, obsession, panic, repugnance, terror, trepidation, unreasoned alarm, unreasoned fear

PHRASE, *noun*   adage, aphorism, apothegm, by-word, caption, clause, dictum, figure of speech, formula, idiom, inscription, motto, peculiar expression, proverb, saw, saying, slogan, trite expression, turn of expression, utterance, watchword, word group

PHRASE, *verb*   articulate, call, clothe in words, come out with, comment, communicate, convey, couch, declare, deliver, denominate, describe, designate, dub, entitle, enunciate, express, find words to express, for-mulate, give expression to, give tongue to, give utter-ance, give voice to, give words to, impart, make known, mouth, name, observe, present, pronounce, put, put into language, put into words, recite, relate, remark, say, sound, speak, state, style, talk, tell, term, utter, verbal-ize, vocalize, voice, word

PHRASEOLOGY, *noun*   argot, cant, choice of lan-guage, choice of words, command of idiom, command of language, composition, dialect, *dicendi genus,* diction, expression, expression of ideas, formulation, idiom, jar-gon, language, lingo, literary artistry, literary style, *locutio,* locution, manner of expression, mode of expres-sion, mode of speech, oratory, parlance, patois, pattern of words, peculiarity of phrasing, phrasing, rhetoric, se-lection of words, speech, style, terminology, text, tone, turn of expression, usage, use of words, vein, vocabu-lary, wording

PHYSICAL, *adjective*   actual, bodily, carnal, con-crete, corporal, corporeal, corporeous, earthly, embod-ied, external, flesh and blood, fleshly, human, incar-nate, material, materiate, mundane, natural, nonspir-itual, organic, palpable, real, sensible, sensual, sensuous, somatic, substantial, substantive, systemic, tangible, temporal, unspiritual, worldly

ASSOCIATED CONCEPTS: physical assets, physical condition, physical contact, physical control, physical damage, physical delivery, physical depreciation, physical disability, physical force, physical impairment, physical injury, physical loss, physical property

PICKET, verb avoid, blackball, blockade, boycott, demonstrate, demonstrate against, demonstrate protest, dissuade from entering, persuade not to work, protest, repudiate, restrict access, take part in a demonstration

ASSOCIATED CONCEPTS: informational picketing, lawful picketing, mass picketing, organizational picketing, peaceful picketing, primary picketing, recognitional picketing, retaliatory picketing, secondary boycotts, situs picketing, sympathy strikes, unlawful picketing, violent picketing

PIECEMEAL, adverb by degrees, drop by drop, gradually, in installments, in small doses, in small quantities, inch by inch, little by little, partially

ASSOCIATED CONCEPTS: piecemeal zoning

PIERCE (Discern), verb appreciate, apprehend, be acquainted with, be apprized of, be aware of, be conscious of, be informed, behold, cognize, comprehend, descry, detect, discover, distinguish, fathom, glimpse, grasp, have in sight, have knowledge of, know, lay eyes on, make out, make sensible, note, notice, observe, perceive, realize, recognize, see, understand, view, witness

PIERCE (Lance), verb bore, *confodere*, cut through, drive into, empierce, gore, impale, insert, knife, penetrate, *perforare*, perforate, plunge in, poniard, prick, puncture, run through, skewer, spear, spike, spit, stab, stick, *transfigere*, transfix, transpierce

ASSOCIATED CONCEPTS: pierce the corporate veil

PIGEONHOLE, verb allocate, allot, arrange, assort, bracket, break down, catalogue, categorize, class, collocate, divide, docket, file, form into classes, grade, group, index, label, list, methodize, name, order, organize, place, place in a category, put in order, rank, rate, reduce to order, section, sort, subdivide, subsume, systematize, tabulate, tag, ticket, type

PILFER, verb abscond with, appropriate illegally, bilk, commit larceny, convert, deprive illegally, embezzle, filch, *furari*, loot, make off with, misappropriate, pillage, poach, purloin, rob, seize, steal, *surripere*, take, thieve

PILLAGE, noun appropriation, booty, brigandage, depredation, deprivation, despoilment, despoliation, destruction, devestation, *direptio, expilatio,* foray, havoc, maraud, piracy, plunder, plunderage, prey, raid, ransack, rapacity, *rapina,* rapine, ravage, razzia, sack, spoliation, vandalism

PILLAGE, verb bring to ruin, burglarize, damage, depopulate, depredate, desolate, despoil, destroy, devastate, lay in ashes, lay in ruins, lay waste, level, loot, make a shambles, make havoc, maraud, pirate, plunder, raid, ransack, reave, rob, ruin, ruinate, sabotage, sack, spoil, spoliate, steal, strip, thieve, waste, wreck

ASSOCIATED CONCEPTS: larceny

PILLORY, verb accuse, asperse, attaint, befoul, belittle, berate, besmear, besmirch, bespatter, blacken, blot, brand, bring shame upon, calumniate, cast a slur upon, cast aspersions on, cause a scandal, damage a reputation, debase, defame, defile, degrade, denigrate, denounce, destroy a reputation, discredit, disgrace, dishonor, disparage, expose to infamy, gibbet, give a bad name, hold up to ridicule, hold up to shame, impute shame to, lampoon, laugh at, lower, make fun of, malign, mock, put in a bad light, put to shame, ridicule, run down, scandalize, scorn, smear, smirch, soil, spatter, speak ill of, stain, stigmatize, sully, taint, tarnish, traduce, vilify, vituperate

PINNACLE, noun acme, apex, apogee, cap, ceiling, climax, consummation, crest, crown, crowning point, culmination, extremity, head, height, highest degree, highest point, meridian, peak, point, summit, tip, top, upper extremity, utmost extent, utmost height, zenith

PINPOINT, verb be specific, enumerate, fix in, focus, locate, place, quantify, site, situate, specify

ASSOCIATED CONCEPTS: pinpoint rule

PIONEER, noun adventurer, colonist, colonizer, discoverer, establisher, explorer, forerunner, founder, founding father, frontiersman, innovator, inventor, lead, leader, modernist, pacesetter, pathfinder, precursor, predecessor, ringleader, scout, settler, trail blazer, vanguard

PIQUE, verb affront, agitate, anger, annoy, arouse resentment, bait, bedevil, beset, bother, bully, bullyrag, cause resentment, discompose, disgust, dismay, displease, disquiet, distemper, disturb, enrage, exasperate, fret, gall, give offense, give umbrage, gnaw, goad, harass, harry, heckle, hurt, incense, incite, incommode, inflame, infuriate, instigate, insult, irk, irritate, kindle wrath, madden, make wrathful, molest, needle, nettle, offend, pain, persecute, perturb, pester, plague, pother, provoke, put out of countenance, rile, roil, rouse, ruffle, *sollicitare,* sting, stir up, taunt, tease, torment, torture, trouble, try the patience, upset, vex, *vexare,* work up, worry

PIRATE (Reproduce without authorization), verb adopt and pass off as one's own, appropriate, borrow dishonestly, copy, counterfeit, crib, help oneself to, make use of without permission, plagiarize, purloin, steal, take illegally

PIRATE (Take by violence), verb commit piracy, commit robbery, despoil, lay hold of, loot, pillage, plunder, ransack, rifle, rob, sack, seize, spoil, spoilate, steal, take by force, thieve

PITFALL, noun abyss, catch, chasm, danger, dangerous spot, exposure to danger, exposure to harm, *fovea,* hazard, imminent danger, obstacle, peril, predicament, problem, quagmire, risk, risks, snare, threat, trap

PITHY, adjective brief, compact, compendious, compressed, concise, condensed, epigrammatic, full of meaning, gnomic, incisive, juicy, laconic, meaningful, meaty, *medullosus,* packed, pointed, sententious, substantial, succinct, summary, terse, trenchant

PITY, noun commiseration, compassion, condolement, condolence, consolation, feeling, fellow feel-

ing, fellow suffering, fellowship in sorrow, kindliness, lenience, leniency, lenity, mercifulness, mercy, *misericordia,* quarter, ruth, sympathy
ASSOCIATED CONCEPTS: amnesty, clemency, pardon

PLACABLE, *adjective*   appeasable, benevolent, capable of being appeased, capable of being pacified, charitable, clement, compassionate, conciliatory, disposed to mercy, *exorabilis,* exorable, forbearant, forbearing, forgiving, generous, gracious, indulgent, lenient, longanimous, magnanimous, merciful, mild, pacifiable, *placabilis,* reasonable, reconcilable, reluctant to punish, ruthful, satisfiable, softhearted, sparing, understanding, unresentful, unrevengeful, unvindictive, willing to forgive

PLACATE, *verb*   allay, appease, assuage, bring to terms, calm, conciliate, disarm, dulcify, heal the breach, humor, hush, make peace, mollify, pacificate, pacify, patch up a quarrel, *placare,* please, propitiate, quiet, reconcile, restore harmony, salve, satisfy, silence, smooth, soothe, still, tranquilize, win over

PLACID, *adjective*   at peace, balmy, calm, calmative, collected, composed, cool, easeful, easygoing, equable, even, gentle, halcyon, halcyonian, imperturable, irenic, irenical, meek, mild, motionless, pacific, paradisiacal, pastoral, patient, peaceable, peaceful, *placidus,* quiescent, quiet, *quietus,* reposeful, restful, serene, smooth, soothing, still, stormless, subdued, tame, tranquil, *tranquillus,* unagitated, undemonstrative, undisturbed, unexcited, unimpassioned, unmoved, unruffled, unstirring, untroubled

PLAGIARISM, *noun*   appropriation, appropriation of a literary composition, copying, copyright infringement, duplication, forgery, imitation, imitation of an original, infringement, literary forgery, literary piracy, literary theft, misappropriation, pilfering, reproducing, reproduction, simulation, stealing, taking, thievery, unauthorized borrowing
ASSOCIATED CONCEPTS: copyright

PLAGIARIZE, *verb*   adopt as one's own, apply to one's own uses, appropriate, avail oneself of, borrow dishonestly, copy from, counterfeit, duplicate, expropriate, fabricate, falsify, follow as a model, forge, imitate, infringe, misappropriate, paraphrase, pass off another's ideas as one's own, pass off another's writings as one's own, pirate, reduplicate, steal

PLAGUE, *verb*   afflict, aggravate, aggrieve, annoy, badger, bait, bedevil, beset, bother, browbeat, bullyrag, cross, devil, discommode, discompose, displease, disquiet, distress, disturb, *exagitare,* exasperate, *exercere,* fret, gall, gibe, grate, harry, haunt, heckle, hector, incommode, inflict pain on, irk, irritate, macerate, molest, mortify, nag, needle, nettle, offend, oppress, pain, persecute, pester, pique, pother, prey on, provoke, rack, roil, ruffle, scourge, smite, spite, taunt, tease, torment, torture, trouble, try the patience, vex, *vexare,* worry

PLAIN LANGUAGE, *noun*   accepted language, clear language, conventional language, correct English, plain English, plain speaking, plain speech, plain words, understandable language
ASSOCIATED CONCEPTS: plain language laws

PLAINT, *noun*   agony, anguish, complaint, cry, dirge, discontent, displeasure, dissatisfaction, distress,

expression of discontent, expression of grief, expression of pain, grief, grieving, groan, lament, *lamenta,* lamentation, moan, outcry, *querela, querimonia,* sigh, sorrow, wail, whine, woe

PLAINTIFF, *noun*   accuser, adversary, claimant, complainant, individual who brings a lawsuit, litigant, one who brings an action, opponent, party to the suit, party who sues, petitioner, *petitor,* suitor
ASSOCIATED CONCEPTS: indispensable party plaintiff, nominal plaintiff, proper plaintiff, real plaintiff, third party plaintiff
FOREIGN PHRASES: *Reus excipiendo fit actor.* The defendant by pleading may make himself a plaintiff. *Melior est conditio possidentis ubi neuter jus habet.* The condition of the possessor and that of the defendant is better than that of the plaintiff. *Cum par delictum est duorum, semper oneratur petitor, et melior habetur possessoris causa.* When there is equal fault on both sides, the burden is always placed on the plaintiff, and the cause of the possessor is preferred. *In praeparatoriis ad judicium favetur actori.* In those matters preceding judgment the plaintiff is favored.

PLAN, *noun*   agenda, alternative, ambition, arrangement, cabal, campaign, complot, conspiracy, course of action, curriculum, design, draft, expedient, forethought, hope, intendment, intent, intention, itinerary, plot, predeliberation, preparation, program, projection, proposal, proposed action, proposition, prospectus, readiness, resolve, schedule, scheme, strategem, strategy, suggestion, syllabus, tactic, undertaking
ASSOCIATED CONCEPTS: ecological plan, feasibility plan, plan for reorganization, planning board

PLAN, *verb*   aim, arrange, block out, cabal, calculate, collude, complot, concoct, connive, conspire, contrive, counterplot, design, determine upon, devise, engineer, establish guidelines for, expect, figure, frame, harbor a design, have a policy, intend, intrigue, lay out, lay the foundation, look ahead, machinate, make arrangements, make preparations, make ready, map out, mark out a course, organize, outline, plot, prearrange, preconcert, precontrive, predesign, predetermine, premeditate, prepare, project, propose, provide for, purpose, resolve, schedule, scheme, set up, shape a course, take measures, think ahead, work out

PLANT *(Covertly place),* *verb*   bury, cache, camouflage, cloak, cover up, disguise, hide away, keep clandestine, keep hidden, keep secret, mantle, mask, obscure, put in concealment, put out of sight, render invisible, screen, secrete, shade, shroud, veil, wrap
ASSOCIATED CONCEPTS: entrapment

PLANT *(Place firmly),* *verb*   base, bed, deposit, embed, engraft, ensconce, establish, fix, ground, implant, impregnate, infix, inject, inlay, insert, inset, install, instill, lay the foundation, locate, make a place for, place, put, root, set, set firmly, set up, settle, situate, sow, station, stick in, thrust in

PLATFORM, *noun*   assumed position, attitude, body of principles, campaign promises, course, course of action, declaration, declaration of policy, doctrine, line of conduct, outlook, party line, party planks, plan, plan of action, point of view, policy, position, precepts, principles, program, proposal, proposed action, proposition, rule of action, scheme, tenets, view

PLATITUDE, *noun* absence of meaning, banality, cliche, commonplace expression, commonplace idea, commonplace phrase, dearth of ideas, dull comment, flat saying, hackneyed expression, hackneyed idea, hackneyed phrase, hackneyed saying, inanity, insipid remark, meaningless saying, nonsense, reiteration, senseless prate, stale comment, stereotyped saying, threadbare phrase, trite expression, trite phrase, trite remark, trite saying, triviality, truism, vapid expression, want of originality

PLAUSIBLE, *adjective* accepted, apparent, arguable, believable, cogitable, colorable, commanding belief, conceivable, conjecturable, convincing, credible, defensible, demanding belief, deserving belief, feasible, grantable, imaginable, justifiable, legitimate, logical, maintained, ostensible, possible, presumable, *probabilis,* putative, rational, reasonable, seeming, seemingly worthy of acceptance, sensible, sound, supposed, suppositional, thinkable, *verisimilis,* within the realm of possibility, worthy of credence

PLEA, *noun* allegation, answer, arguments at the bar, assertion, claim, counterstatement, defendant's answer to charges, defense, *exceptio, excusatio,* legal argument, legal defense, *petitio,* pleading, pleadings, rebuttal, refutation, reply, response, retort, statement alleged in defense, statement alleged in justification, statement of defense, statement which answers the charges, statements on behalf of the defense
ASSOCIATED CONCEPTS: entering a plea, plea in abatement, plea in bar, plea in equity, plea of estoppel, plea of guilty, plea of insanity, plea of nolo contendere, plea of not guilty, plea of payment, plea of recoupment, plea of release, plea of self-defense, plea of setoff
FOREIGN PHRASES: *Ambiguum placitum interpretari debet contra proferentem.* An ambiguous plea ought to be interpreted against the party entering it. *Exceptio falsi omnium ultima.* A false plea is the worst of all. *Interdum evenit ut exceptio quae prima facie justa videtur, tamen inique noceat.* It sometimes happens that a plea which on its face seems just, nevertheless is injurious and inequitable.

PLEAD *(Allege in a legal action), verb* advance, affirm, affirm explicitly, allege, assert, assert formally, assert positively, attest to, bring forward, contend, emphasize, enunciate, maintain, make an affidavit, make an assertion, present, proclaim, put forth, put forward, put in an affidavit, reaffirm, reassert, set forth, state, state emphatically, stress, swear
ASSOCIATED CONCEPTS: plead a cause of action, responsive pleading

PLEAD *(Argue a case), verb* advocate, argue at the bar, argue the point, bring into court, *causam agere,* contend for, defend a case, maintain by arguments, prosecute one's case, put one's case, speak for, speak up for, stand up for, state one's case, urge reasons for, use arguments

PLEAD *(Implore), verb* address a request, beseech, call upon, charge, clamor for, entreat, importune, make a request, *obsecrare, orare,* petition, prefer a request, press, put up a request, request, solicit, supplicate, urge

PLEADING, *noun* accusation, allegation, allegation of facts, answer, argument, claim, complaint, counterstatement, defendant's answer to charges, defense,

denial, formal assertion, formal averment, plaintiff's allegations, plea, rebuttal, reply, responsive allegations, statement of defense, written statement of defense, written statements of accusation
ASSOCIATED CONCEPTS: alternative pleading, amendment to a pleading, amplication of the pleadings, argumentative pleading, blind pleading, clarification of the pleading, defect in the pleading, demurrer, failure to state a cause of action, failure to state a claim, formal pleading, frivolous pleading, inconsistent pleadings, liberal construction of pleadings, motion to correct pleadings, motion to dismiss the pleading, petition, prejudicial pleading, privileged pleadings, responsive pleading, scandalous pleading, sham pleading, supplemental pleading, verified pleading
FOREIGN PHRASES: *Placita negativa duo exitum non faciunt.* Two negative pleas do not make an issue. *Qui non negat fatetur.* He who does not deny, admits. *Ambigua responsio contra proferentem est accipienda.* An ambiguous answer is to be taken against him who offers it.

PLEBISCITE, *noun* ballot, choice, election, mandate, poll, referendum, vote

PLEDGE *(Binding promise), noun* act of giving one's word, agreement, assurance, attestation, avowal, avowance, commitment, compact, contract, covenant, guarantee, oath, obligation, promise, promissory oath, *promissum,* solemn declaration, solemn word, statement on oath, undertaking, vow, warranty, word, word of honor

PLEDGE *(Security), noun* collateral, deposit, earnest, earnest payment, guarantee, installment, personal security, *pignus,* real security, security, stake, stake money, token payment
ASSOCIATED CONCEPTS: assignment, collateral security, pledge of securities, pledged personalty, pledged property, secured transactions

PLEDGE *(Deposit), verb* bond, give as a guarantee, give as security for a debt, give as security for an obligation, give as surety, give one's signature, give security, guarantee, hypothecate, impignorate, indorse, insure, offer collateral, post, put in pawn, put up, stake

PLEDGE *(Promise the performance of), verb* assert solemnly, assure, avow, be answerable for, become bound to, bind, bind oneself, commit oneself, contract an obligation, covenant, engage solemnly, engage to give, give a guarantee, give assurance, give one's word, guarantee, make a promise, *obligare, oppignerare,* promise solemnly, take upon oneself, undertake, warrant, vow

PLENARY, *adjective* absolute, complete, comprehensive, entire, exhaustive, full, full-blown, full-charged, fully constituted, fully furnished, limitless, thorough, total, unconfined, undiminished, unlimited, unqualified, unrestricted, whole
ASSOCIATED CONCEPTS: plenary action

PLENIPOTENTIARY, *noun* advocate, agent, ambassador, assistant, broker, chancellor, coagent, consul, delegate, deputy, diplomat, diplomatic agent, emissary, envoy, factor, internuncio, legate, lieutenant, messenger, official representative, proctor, provost, proxy, regent, representative, secondary, speaker, spokesman, spokesperson, substitute, surrogate, viceroy

PLETHORA, noun abundance, accumulation, amplitude, congestion, deluge, engorgement, excess, exorbitance, exorbitancy, flood, full measure, fullness, glut, great quantity, heap, impletion, inundation, load, margin, nimiety, overabundance, overflow, overload, overplus, oversupply, plentifulness, plenty, profuseness, profusion, repleteness, repletion, richness, satiation, satiety, saturation, spate, superabundance, superfluity, superfluousness, supersaturation, surfeit, surplus, surplusage, swelling, turgescence, undue amount

PLIABLE, adjective accommodating, acquiescent, adaptable, adaptive, adjustable, alterable, amenable, assenting, bendable, biddable, changeable, compliant, conformable, conforming, controllable, docile, ductile, easily bent, easily influenced, easily persuaded, easygoing, elastic, facile, fictile, *flexibilis,* flexible, flexile, formable, formative, governable, impressionable, inclined, lamblike, *lentus,* limber, lissome, lithe, lithesome, malleable, manageable, manipulable, meek, modifiable, moldable, mutable, nonresisting, obedient, obliging, persuadable, persuasible, pervious, plastic, pliant, protean, proteiform, receptive, responsive, sequacious, servile, slavish, stretchable, suasible, submissive, supple, swayable, teachable, tractable, tractile, variable, versatile, willing, yielding

PLIANT, adjective accommodating, acquiescent, adaptable, agreeable, bendable, compliable, compliant, concessive, conformable, conforming, deferential, docile, ductile, easily bent, easily persuaded, elastic, flexible, formable, impressible, impressionable, indecisive, indulgent, influenceable, irresolute, *lentus,* limber, lithe, malleable, manageable, meek, moldable, *mollis,* movable, nonresisting, obedient, obeisant, passive, plastic, pliable, readily influenced, receptive, responsive, sequacious, servile, slavish, soft, submissive, subordinate, subservient, suggestible, supple, susceptible, susceptive, swayable, tractable, tractile, unassertive, undecided, willing, yielding

PLIGHT, noun adverse circumstance, adversity, awkward situation, case, circumstance, condition, corner, crisis, critical situation, difficulty, dilemma, embarrassing position, embarrassing situation, emergency, footing, hardship, imbroglio, lot, misfortune, muddle, pass, pinch, position, predicament, problem, quagmire, quandary, reverse, scrape, setback, situation, state, state of affairs, station, strait, trial, trouble

PLOT (Land), noun acreage, *agellus,* block, division, field, ground, lot, parcel of land, patch, piece of land, plat, property, tract

PLOT (Secret plan), noun cabal, chicane, collusion, complicity, complot, *coniuratio,* conspiracy, *conspiratio,* counterplot, deception, design, intrigue, manipulation, ploy, ruse, scheme, stratagem, tactic, trick

PLOT, verb act in collusion, arrange, be in collusion, cabal, collude, *coniurare,* connive, *consentire, conspirare,* conspire, deal secretly, devise, engineer, form a plan, frame, have designs, intrigue, machinate, make a plan, make arrangements, make preparations, maneuver, organize, outline, plan mischief, plan secretly, pre-

arrange, preconcert, premeditate, prepare, scheme, take measures, take steps, undermine, work out

PLOY, noun action, artifice, contrivance, device, maneuver, mechanism, plan, ruse, scheme, stratagem, trick, way, wile

PLUNDER, noun booty, depredation, devastation, foray, haul, ill-gotten goods, illicit gains, loot, maraud, pillage, *praeda,* raid, *rapina,* rapine, ravin, razzia, robbery, sack, seizure, spoils, spoliation, stolen articles, stolen goods, take, theft

PLUNDER, verb buccaneer, carry off, *compilare,* deplume, depredate, desolate, despoil, displume, divest, *expilare,* flay, impoverish, lay in ruins, lay waste, loot, maraud, overthrow, pillage, pirate, *praedari,* prey on, purloin, raid, ransack, ravage, raze, reave, rifle, rob, ruin, sack, seize, spoliate, steal, strip, take away, thieve

PLURALITY, noun advantage in votes cast, bulk, great number, host, large amount, large number, large quantity, lead, main part, majority, multitude, *multitudo,* preponderance, preponderancy, shoal, superiority in number, weight of numbers
ASSOCIATED CONCEPTS: majority, quorum

PLY, verb busy oneself with, carry on, devote oneself to, do work with, employ, engage in, *exercere,* exercise, exploit, handle, make use of, manipulate, occupy oneself with, operate, persevere at, practice, pursue, put in practice, put into effect, tackle, take up, undertake, use, utilize, wage, wield, work

POACH, verb appropriate, carry off, filch, *furtim feras intercipere,* make off with, misappropriate, peculate, pilfer, pirate, plunder by stealth, purloin, rifle, run off with, snatch, steal, take by illegal methods, take by unfair methods, take illegally, walk off with

POINT (Item), noun argument, *caput,* consideration, designated ground, detail, feature, ground, issue, matter, particular, reason, *res,* specific, thought
ASSOCIATED CONCEPTS: point of law, point of order

POINT (Period of time), noun conjuncture, exact moment, hour, instant, interval, juncture, moment, occasion, precise moment, second, specific moment, stage, time

POINT (Purpose), noun aim, core, design, end, essence, goal, import, intent, intention, motive, object, objective, purport, reason, significance, substance

POLARIZE, verb break up into opposing factions, contrapose, contrast, oppose, pit against one another, put in opposition

POLEMIC, adjective argumental, argumentative, conflicting, contentious, contestable, contradictory, controversial, debatable, dialectic, dialectical, discordant, discrepant, disputatious, dissentient, dissonant, divided, eristic, eristical, factious, inharmonious, open to debate, open to discussion, open to question, polemical, pugnacious, quarrelsome, schismatic, subject to controversy, unreconciled

POLICE, noun arm of the law, constabulary, custodians of the law, detective force, forces of law and order,

government officers, law enforcement agency, law enforcement agents, law enforcement body, officers, officers of the law, peace officers, police force, police officers
ASSOCIATED CONCEPTS: police action, police brutality, police power

POLICE, *verb*   care for, check, control, exercise authority, exert authority, have authority, have charge of, invigilate, keep guard, keep in order, keep in view, keep order, keep orderly, keep under control, keep vigil, keep watch, observe, overlook, oversee, patrol, preserve public order, preserve public tranquility, prevent crime, prevent offenses against the state, promote public health and safety, protect, regulate, render safe, restrain, restrict access, rule, safeguard, secure, stand guard, stand sentinel, superintend, supervise, systematize, use one's authority, watch, watch diligently

POLICY *(Contract),* *noun*   agreement, arrangement, contractual obligation, contractual statement, insurance contract, legal document, mutual agreement, mutual undertaking, obligation, pact, schedule, understanding
ASSOCIATED CONCEPTS: insurance policy

POLICY *(Plan of action),* *noun*   approach, *consilium,* course, course of action, course of conduct, doctrine, established order, fundamental principles, general guidelines, general principles, governing course of action, governing plan, governing principle, line, line of action, line of conduct, management, manner of proceeding, method, mode of management, party line, plan, plan of campaign, platform, polity, prescribed form, principles, procedure, program, proposal, proposed action, proposition, rule of action, scheme, stratagem, ways
ASSOCIATED CONCEPTS: public policy

POLITIC, *adjective*   acute, artful, artfully contrived, astute, *astutus,* brilliant, calculating, canny, careful, cautious, circumspect, clever, considerate, contemplative, crafty, cunning, deceitful, diplomatic, discreet, effective, efficacious, enlightened, expedient, farsighted, feline, foxy, guarded, heedful, ingenious, judicial, judicious, knowing, mindful, perceptive, practical, provident, *prudens,* prudent, prudential, prudently contrived, regardful, sagacious, sensible, sharp, shrewd, subtle, tactful, thoughtful, well-adapted, well-advised, well-devised, well-informed, well-judged, wily, wise

POLITICAL, *adjective*   administrative, bureaucratic, civic, *civilis,* governmental, partisan, public, *publicus*
ASSOCIATED CONCEPTS: political question

POLITICIAN, *noun*   campaigner, candidate, governmental leader, lawgiver, lawmaker, legislator, office seeker, officeholder, officer of state, official, partisan, party member, politico, public servant, representative, statesman

POLITICS, *noun*   campaigning, *civilis ratio,* electioneering, governance, government, matters of state, partisanship, party leadership, party politics, party system, political affairs, political influence, political involvement, political maneuvers, political methods, political partisanship, political process, political strategy, public service, state affairs, statesmanship

ASSOCIATED CONCEPTS: campaign financing laws, disclosure laws, election laws, lobbying laws, reporting laws
FOREIGN PHRASES: *Politiae legibus non leges, politiis adaptandae.* Politics should be adapted to the laws, not the laws to politics.

POLITY, *noun*   body politic, civil constitution, commonwealth, constitution, country, course, form of government, fundamental principles of government, line, nation, nationality, plan of action, platform, policy, principles, procedure, program, recognized principles, *reipublicae forma,* republic, sovereignty, state, system of government

POLL *(Canvass),* *noun*   capitation, catalogue of persons, census, census report, census return, count, enumeration, evaluation, inquiry, numbering, numeration, public opinion, questionary, questionnaire, register, registration, return, statistic, survey, tabulation, tally

POLL *(Casting of votes),* *noun*   ballot, casting of ballots, choice, consensus, decision, determination, election, elective privilege, expression of will, formal expression of choice, plebiscite, popular decision, preference, referendum, selection, voice, vote
ASSOCIATED CONCEPTS: electioneering at poll, polling place

POLL, *verb*   ballot, call the roll, canvass, collect the vote, compute, conduct research on, count, enumerate, keep count of, keep score, list, make a survey, record the vote, register, run checks on, sample, score, survey, tabulate, take a census, take a roll call, tally, total

POLLUTE, *verb*   adulterate, alloy, befoul, begrime, bemire, besmirch, bespatter, contaminate, corrupt, debase, debauch, defile, degrade, denaturalize, deprave, desecrate, destroy, dirty, dishonor, filthify, foul, grime, impair, infect, maculate, make foul, mess, mire, muck, muddy, pervert, poison, profane, prostitute, render filthy, smirch, soil, spatter, spoil, stain, sully, taint, tarnish, undermine, unhallow, violate, vitiate
ASSOCIATED CONCEPTS: ecology, environmental conservation, environmental protection, nuissance

POLYGAMOUS, *adjective*   engaging in bigamy, engaging in unlawful marriage, having multiple husbands, having multiple wives, having plurality of wives or husbands, practicing plural marriage
ASSOCIATED CONCEPTS: bigamy, monogamy

PONDER, *verb*   analyze, apply the mind, appraise, brood over, cerebrate, cogitate, commune with oneself, concentrate upon, consider, *considerare,* contemplate, debate, deliberate, devote thought to, digest, evaluate, examine, excogitate, give thought to, intellectualize, introspect, meditate, mull over, muse, occupy the thoughts with, *ponderare,* premeditate, puzzle over, rack the brains, ratiocinate, rationalize, reason, reflect upon, review, revolve in the mind, ruminate, speculate, study, take account of, take under consideration, theorize, think deeply, think on, turn over in the mind, view from all sides, view with deliberation, weigh, wonder about

PONDERABLE, *adjective*   appreciable, ascertainable, cognizable, comprehensible, considerable, discernible, discoverable, distinguishable, knowable, palpable, perceptible, real, recognizable, substantive, understandable, weighable

PONDEROUS, *adjective* awkward, big, boring, bulky, burdensome, clumsy, corpulent, cumbersome, cumbrous, dense, drearisome, dreary, droning, dull, elephantine, enormous, forced, *gravis,* hard to lift, heavy, hulking, labored, large, leaden, lifeless, lumbering, lumpish, lusterless, lymphatic, massive, monotonous, onerous, oppressive, overweight, *ponderosus,* prosaic, slow-moving, sluggish, stiff, stolid, stout, supine, tedious, unlively, unmanageable, unwieldy, wearisome, wearying, weighty

POOL, *noun* alliance, amalgamation, bank, cartel, coalition, collaboration, collective, collectivism, combination, combination of funds, combine, common fund, common ownership, community of possession, confederacy, confederation, consolidation, consortium, cooperation, copartnership, cosharing, federation, joint concern, joint ownership, joint possession, league, mutual ownership, partnership, syndicate, trust, unification, union
ASSOCIATED CONCEPTS: insolvency pool, involuntary market pool, mortgage pool, stock pool

POOL, *verb* affiliate with, ally, amalgamate, associate, band together, blend, collaborate, combine, confederate, conjoin, connect, consolidate, coordinate, enter into partnership with, federate, involve together, league, merge, mix, share, unify, unite
ASSOCIATED CONCEPTS: pooling of assets

POOR (*Inferior in quality*), ***adjective*** bad, badly made, barely passable, base, beggarly, below par, below standard, cheap, coarse, common, contemptible, crude, defective, deficient, dubious, faulty, flimsy, gimcrack, imperfect, inadequate, inartistic, indifferent, inferior, lacking in quality, low, low-grade, marred, meager, mean, mediocre, *mediocris,* miserable, ordinary, paltry, pitiful, rejected, scant, scrub, scrubby, scurvy, second best, second-rate, seedy, shabby, shoddy, sleazy, sordid, sorry, subgrade, substandard, tawdry, *tenuis,* trashy, under average, undergrade, unimpressive, unsatisfactory, unsightly, unworthy, valueless, vulgar, wanting, weak, worthless, wretched
ASSOCIATED CONCEPTS: poor condition

POOR (*Underprivileged*), ***adjective*** bankrupt, beggared, bereft of funds, depleted, deprived, destitute, dispossessed, distressed, drained, *egens,* embarrassed, empty-handed, fortuneless, hard up, ill-provided for, impecunious, impoverished, in distress, in embarrassed circumstances, in narrow circumstances, in need, in penury, in pinched circumstances, in reduced circumstances, in straitened circumstances, in want, indigent, *inops,* insolvent, *mendicus,* moneyless, necessitous, needful, needy, out of cash, out of money, pauperized, penniless, penurious, poverty-stricken, reduced, reduced to beggary, ruined, short, short of money, starved, straitened, strapped, suffering privation, unable to make ends meet, unmoneyed, unprosperous, unprovided for, with meager funds, with scanty funds, without a penny
ASSOCIATED CONCEPTS: petition to proceed as a poor person

POPULACE, *noun* body politic, canaille, citizenry, common folk, common people, commonage, commonalty, commoners, community, crowd, folk, folks, general public, habitants, humanity, individuals, inhabitants, masses, multitude, nation, people, persons, *plebs,* population, proletariat, public, residents, society

POPULAR, *adjective* accepted, accredited, admired, asked for, attractive, beloved, celebrated, conventional, coveted, current, customary, demanded, desirable, desired, doted on, enjoyed, esteemed, estimable, fair-haired, famous, fashionable, favored, favorite, highly thought of, in demand, in favor, in high esteem, in high favor, in vogue, liked, loved, noted, orthodox, palatable, pet, pleasing, praised, preferred, prevailing, prevalent, received, requested, respected, sought after, stamped with approval, standard, stylish, venerable, wanted, well-liked, well-received, well thought of, winning
ASSOCIATED CONCEPTS: popular election, popular name, popular name for a statute, popular sense

POPULATION, *noun* body politic, citizenry, citizens, *civium,* commonalty, community, dwellers, folk, general public, habitancy, habitants, humanity, *incolarum numerus,* inhabitants, masses, nation, natives, number of people, people, persons, populace, populacy, public, residents, society

POPULOUS, *adjective* *celeber,* close, closely packed, compact, crammed, crawling with people, crowded, dense, *frequens,* full, inhabited, massed, multitudinous, numerous, occupied, packed, peopled, populated, rife, swarming, teeming, tenanted, thick, thickly settled, thronged, well-populated

PORNOGRAPHY, *noun* bawdiness, curiosa, erotica, filth, indecency, lewdness, lubricity, obscene art, obscene literature, obscenity, prurience, salaciousness, salacity, smut, vulgarity
ASSOCIATED CONCEPTS: censorship, First Amendment rights

PORTAL, *noun* access, aperture, approach, corridor, door, doorway, entrance, entranceway, entry, gate, gateway, ingress, inlet, means of access, opening, passageway, postern, pylon

PORTEND, *verb* adumbrate, announce, augur, augurate, auspicate, be an omen, be harbinger, betoken, bode, caution, divine, forebode, forecast, foreshadow, foreshow, foretell, foretoken, forewarn, give token, herald, indicate, indicate beforehand, menace, notify, omen, ominate, *portendere,* precurse, predict, prefigurate, prefigure, preindicate, premonish, premonstrate, presage, preshow, presignify, prognosticate, prophesy, put on guard, show promise, *significare,* signify, threaten, vaticinate, warn

PORTENTOUS (*Eliciting amazement*), ***adjective*** amazing, astonishing, breathtaking, exceptional, extraordinary, great, inconceivable, incredible, indescribable, marvelous, memorable, miraculous, notable, noteworthy, novel, out of the ordinary, outstanding, phenomenal, prodigal, prodigious, rare, remarkable, shocking, singular, staggering, startling, stirring, striking, stupendous, superb, superlative, surprising, tremendous, uncustomary, unexampled, unheard of, unique, unparalleled, unprecedented, unusual, wonderful, wondrous

PORTENTOUS (*Ominous*), **adjective**   alarming, augural, augurous, baleful, black, bodeful, boding, cautionary, dark, dire, direful, divinatory, doomful, dread, dreadful, dreary, fateful, fatiloquent, fearful, forbidding, foreboding, foretelling, forewarning, forthcoming, frightening, frightful, gloomy, grim, haunting, heralding, ill-boding, ill-fated, ill-starred, inauspicious, indicative, intimidating, mantic, menacing, minacious, minatorial, minatory, monitory, ominous, oracular, perilous, portending evil, premonitive, premonitory, presageful, presaging, presentient, prophetic, prophetical, pythonic, sibylline, sinister, somber, suggestive, threatening, unpropitious

PORTFOLIO, **noun**   futures, holdings, investments, negotiables, *scrinium,* securities, stocks, stocks and bonds

PORTRAY, **verb**   act, adumbrate, characterize, convey a verbal image, convey an impression, delineate, depict, depicture, *depingere,* describe, detail, draw, express, give words to, illustrate, limn, outline, paint, particularize, picture, present, recreate, report, represent, represent in words, reproduce, set forth, show, sketch, specify, stage, tell vividly

POSE (*Impersonate*), **verb**   act as, act the part of, ape, assume the character of, assume the role of, copy, counterfeit, double for, emulate, imitate, masquerade as, mimic, mock, model oneself after, parody, pass for, personate, play a part, portray, pretend to be, simulate, take the part of

POSE (*Propound*), **verb**   advance, ask, assert, broach, declare, interrogate, introduce, lay before, lay down, make a motion, moot, move, offer, posit, postulate, predicate, present, proffer, propose, put forward, put to, puzzle, query, question, set before, state, submit, suggest, tender, throw out, volunteer
ASSOCIATED CONCEPTS: pose a question

POSIT, **verb**   acknowledge, advance, advocate, affirm, allege, announce, argue, assert, asseverate, assume, attest, aver, avouch, avow, bring forward, certify, cite, claim, contend, declare, enunciate, express, hypothesize, inform, insist, issue a statement, lay down, maintain, moot, pose, postulate, predicate, proclaim, profess, promulgate, pronounce, propose, propound, put forth, put forward, say, set forth, state, stipulate, submit, take a stand, tell, testify, utter with conviction, vouch

POSITION (*Business status*), **noun**   appointment, assignment, avocation, business, calling, career, concern, duty, echelon, employment, function, incumbency, job, line of business, line of work, means of livelihood, occupation, office, post, practice, profession, pursuit, responsibility, role, situation, specialty, sphere, station, trade, vocation, walk of life, work

POSITION (*Point of view*), **noun**   apprehension, attitude, bearing, bent, bias, conclusion, feeling, frame of mind, inclination, judgment, leaning, mental outlook, mind set, opinion, outlook, pose, posture, predilection, predisposition, preference, presumption, proclivity, proneness, propensity, sentiment, slant, standpoint, tendency, turn of mind, view, viewpoint, way of thinking

POSITION (*Situation*), **noun**   circumstances, condition, footing, ground, *locus,* place, plight, posture, predicament, spot, state, station, *status*

POSITIVE (*Confident*), **adjective**   assured, believing, certain, *certus,* convinced, decided, decisive, definite, determined, fully convinced, insistent, perfectly sure, persuaded, reassured, satisfied, secure, self-assured, self-confident, sure, trusting, undoubting, unhesitating, unquestioning, unshaken, untroubled, unwavering
ASSOCIATED CONCEPTS: positive identification

POSITIVE (*Incontestable*), **adjective**   absolute, ascertained, authentic, axiomatic, axiomatical, beyond all question, beyond doubt, categorical, certain, clear, conclusive, decided, definite, determinate, evident, explicit, final, inappealable, incontestable, incontrovertible, indisputable, indubitable, inescapable, infallible, irrefragable, irrefutable, past dispute, precise, reliable, sound, sure, true, trustworthy, unanswerable, unchallengeable, unconfutable, undeniable, unequivocal, unerring, unimpeachable, unmistakable, unqualified, unquestionable, unrefutable
ASSOCIATED CONCEPTS: positive proof

POSITIVE (*Prescribed*), **adjective**   assigned, binding, commanded, compulsory, decreed, demanded, dictated, enacted, enjoined, established, exacted, fixed, imperative, imposed, instituted, issued, laid down, legislated, mandatory, obligatory, ordained, required, requisite, ruled, set, stated authoritatively
ASSOCIATED CONCEPTS: positive law

POSSE, **noun**   arm of the law, armed band, band, band of armed men, band of men armed with legal authority, body of men armed with legal process, body of men summoned by a sheriff, civilian police, custodians of the law, detachment of police, detail, force armed with legal authority, group of deputies, group of persons organized with legal authorization, law enforcement body

POSSESS, **verb**   acquire, *adfirmatio,* assume ownership, be in possession of, be in receipt of, be seized of, come into possession of, command, control, devolve upon, enjoy, enter into possession, gain, gain for oneself, get, get as one's own, *habere,* have, have a deed for, have a title to, have absolute disposal of, have as property, have at one's command, have at one's disposal, have for one's own, have in hand, have rights to, hold, keep, maintain, monopolize, obtain, occupy, own, receive, retain, secure, seize, take possession, *tenere*
ASSOCIATED CONCEPTS: lawfully possess, seized or possessed
FOREIGN PHRASES: *Aliud est possidere, aliud esse in possessione.* It is one thing to possess; it is another to be in possession.

POSSESSION (*Ownership*), **noun**   authority, custody, demesne, domination, dominion, exclusive right, lordship, occupancy, *possessio,* proprietorship, right, right of retention, seisin, supremacy, tenancy, title
ASSOCIATED CONCEPTS: action to recover possession, actual possession, adverse possession, chain of possession, constructive possession, continuity of possession, continuous possession, debtor in possession, estate in possession, holder in possession, hostile possession,

lawful possession, mortgagee in possession, naked possession, notorious possession, open and notorious possession, party in possession, peaceable possession, person in possession, physical possession, purchaser in possession, quiet possession, right of possession, tenant in possession, undisturbed possession, uninterrupted possession, unlawful possession, wrongful possession
FOREIGN PHRASES: *Traditio nihil amplius transferre debet vel potest, ad eum qui accipit, quam est apud eum qui tradit.* Delivery ought to, and can, transfer nothing more to him who receives than is in possession of him who makes the delivery. *Jus triplex est, -propietatis, possessionis, et possibilitatis.* Right is threefold,-of property, of possession, and of possibility. *In aequali jure melior est conditio possidentis.* In a case of equal right the condition of the party in possession is the better. *Pro possessione praesumitur de jure.* A presumption of law arises from possession. *Nihil praescribitur nisi quod possidetur.* There is no prescription for that which is not possessed. *Privatio praesupponit habitum.* A deprivation presupposes something held or possessed. *Duorum in solidum dominium vel possessio esse non potest.* Sole ownership or possession cannot be in two persons. *Cum de lucro duorum quaeritur, melior est causa possidentis.* When the question of gain lies between two persons, the cause of the possessor is the better. *Longa possessio parit jus possidendi, et tollit actionem vero domino.* Long possession creates the right of possession, and deprives the true owner of his right of action. *Aliud est possidere, aliud esse in possessione.* It is one thing to possess; it is another to be in possession. *Quod meum est sine facto meo vel defectu meo amitti vel in alium transferri non potest.* That which is mine cannot be transferred to another without my act or my default. *Quod meum est sine me auferri non potest.* What is mine cannot be taken away without my consent. *Nul charter, nul vente, ne nul done vault perpetualment, si le donor n'est seise al temps de contracts de deux droits, sc. del droit de possession et del droit de propertie.* No grant, no sale, no gift, is valid forever, unless the donor, at the time of the contract, has two rights, namely, the right of possession, and the right of property. *Donatio perficitur possessione accipientis.* A gift is perfected by the possession of the receiver. *Melior est conditio possidentis, et rei quam actoris.* The condition of the possessor and that of the defendant is better than that of the plaintiff. *In pari delicto melior est conditio possidentis.* When the parties are equally in the wrong, the condition of the possessor is the preferable one. *Longa possessio jus parit.* Long possession begets right. *Donator nunquam desinit possidere, antequam donatorius incipiat possidere.* A donor never ceases to possess until the donee begins to possess. *Non valet donatio nisi subsequatur traditio.* A gift is invalid unless accompanied by possession. *Nemo dare potest quod non habet.* No one is able to give that which he has not. *Terra manens vacua occupanti conceditur.* Land remaining vacant is given to the occupant. *Non potest videri desisse habere qui nunquam habuit.* A person who has never had cannot be deemed to have ceased to have it. *In pari causa possessor potior haberi debet.* In an equal cause he who has the possession has the advantage. *Cum par delictum est duorum, semper oneratur petitor et melior habetur possessoris causa.* When there is equal fault on both sides, the burden is always placed on the plaintiff, and the cause of the possessor is preferred.

POSSESSION *(Property), noun* asset, belonging, *bona,* chattel, effect, goods, holding, item, item of personalty, money, movable, *possessio, res,* resource, treasure, valuable
FOREIGN PHRASES: *Non possessori incumbit necessitas probandi possessiones ad se pertinere.* It is not incumbent on the possessor of property to prove that his possessions belong to him.

POSSESSIONS, *noun* assets, belongings, *bonorum,* capital, chattels, colonies, domain, dominions, earnings, effects, equity, estate, fortune, funds, goods, holdings, items of personalty, material wealth, movables, pecuniary resources, personal property, personalty, *possessio,* private property, property, *res,* resources, stock, stock in trade, territory, treasure, wealth, worldly belongings

POSSIBILITY, *noun* achievability, anticipation, attainability, availability, chance, conceivability, conceivableness, expectance, expectancy, expectation, *facultas,* favorable opportunity, favorable prospect, feasibility, gamble, hope, likelihood, opportunity, plausibility, *posse,* potential, potentiality, *potestas,* probability, promise, prospect, suggestion, uncertainty, viability, viableness
FOREIGN PHRASES: *Jus triplex est-propietatis, possessionis, et possibilitatis.* Right is threefold-of property, of possession, and of possibility. *Ultra posse non potest esse, et vice versa.* What is beyond possibility cannot exist, and the reverse, what cannot exist is not possible.

POSSIBLE, *adjective* achievable, anticipated, apt, attainable, believable, capable, cogitable, conceivable, credible, feasible, grantable, imaginable, liable, likely, obtainable, performable, plausible, potential, probable, promising, rational, realizable, reasonable, superable, supposable, surmountable, thinkable, unrealized, viable, within reach, within the range of possibility, within the realm of possibility, workable

POST, *noun* appointment, berth, billet, business, capacity, career, charge, commission, department, employment, field, function, incumbency, job, line, *locus,* means of livelihood, *munus,* occupation, office, place, position, profession, pursuit, service, situation, station, task, undertaking, vocation, work

POST, *verb* advertise, announce publicly, bestow, call public attention to, circulate, communicate, convey, deliver, dispose of, distribute, give away, give forth, give out, give public notice of, impart, issue, issue a statement, make known, make public, offer to the public, pay, present, print, proclaim, publish, put up a sign, report, spread, spread abroad
ASSOCIATED CONCEPTS: post a notice, post bail

POSTERITY, *noun* bloodline, children, descendants, descent, family, future relatives, heirs, issue, later generations, line, lineage, offspring, *posteritas,* progeny, scion, seed, stock, succeeding generations, successors

POSTHUMOUS, *adjective* after death, continuing after death, following death, occurring after death, post mortem
ASSOCIATED CONCEPTS: posthumous child

POSTPONE, verb adjourn, arrest temporarily, defer, delay, *differre*, extend, gain more time, hold off, keep for future action, lay aside, pigeonhole, *proferre*, prorogate, prorogue, push aside, put aside, put off, reprieve, set aside, shelve, stall, stave off, stay, suspend, table
ASSOCIATED CONCEPTS: postpone a case

POSTULATE, noun assertion, assumed truth, assumption, axiom, conjecture, foundation, hypothesis, premise, speculation, starting point, statement, suggestion, *sumptio*, supposal, supposition, surmise, theorem, thesis, truism

POSTULATE, verb advance, assume, conjecture, consider, contend, determine, guess, hazard a supposition, hypothesize, infer, posit, predicate, premise, presume, presuppose, propound, put forth, put forward, reason, regard as axiomatic, specify, speculate, start, suggest, surmise, take as an axiom, take for granted, theorize, venture a conjecture, venture a supposition

POSTURE *(Attitude)*, **noun** air, aspect, bearing, bent, cast, demeanor, disposition, disposition of mind, feeling, inclination, leaning, lie, manner, nature, opinion, outlook, partisan outlook, philosophy, point of view, pose, position, presence, sentiment, standpoint, temper, temperament, view, viewpoint, way of thinking

POSTURE *(Situation)*, **noun** circumstance, *condicio*, condition, conjuncture, context, existing state, footing, juncture, lot, pass, plight, point, position, predicament, setting, shape, standing, state, state of affairs, station, *status*, terms, turn

POTENT, adjective able, active, affecting, capable, cogent, commanding, compelling, convincing, dominant, dramatic, dynamic, effective, effectual, efficacious, efficient, energetic, forceful, forcible, formidable, generative, impelling, important, impressive, indefatigable, indomitable, influential, inspiring, inspiriting, intense, invincible, manly, masterful, mighty, moving, operative, penetrating, powerful, predominant, prepotent, prevailing, productive, puissant, ruling, stiff, strong, telling, trenchant, useful, valid, vigorous, virile, weighty

POTENTIAL, adjective accessible, achievable, allowable, allowed, anticipated, attainable, concealed, conceivable, covert, doable, dormant, expected, feasible, future, imaginable, latent, likely, obtainable, performable, permissible, permitted, possible, *potentialis*, practicable, realizable, thinkable, unapparent, undetected, undisclosed, undiscovered, unexposed, unexpressed, unmanifested, unrealized, unseen, workable
ASSOCIATED CONCEPTS: potential existence, potential interest

POTENTIAL, noun ability, aptitude, capability, capacity, chance, competence, dormant energy, endowment, feasibility, force, latent power, might, mightiness, possibility, possibleness, potency, *potentialis*, power, powerfulness, practicability, proficiency, promise, prospect, puissance, qualification, skill, strength, talent, workability
ASSOCIATED CONCEPTS: potential damages, potential loss

POVERTY, noun absence, bare subsistence, beggarliness, beggary, dearth, deficiency, deficit, depletion, destitution, difficulty, distress, embarrassed circumstances, exigency, famine, humbleness, impecuniosity, impecuniousness, impoverishment, indigence, insolvency, lack, leanness, loss of fortune, meagerness, mendicancy, mendicity, moneylessness, narrow means, necessitousness, necessity, need, neediness, needy circumstances, paucity, pauperism, *paupertas*, pennilessness, penury, poor circumstances, poorness, privation, reduced circumstances, scantiness, scantity, scantness, scarceness, scarcity, shortage, slender means, sparseness, starvation, straitened circumstances, straits, subsistence level, *tenuitas*, unprosperousness, want
ASSOCIATED CONCEPTS: proceed in forma pauperus

POWER, noun auspices, authority, command, competence, control, controlment, dominance, domination, dominion, eminence, facility, force, hold, importance, influence, jurisdiction, mastership, mastery, potency, *potestas*, predominance, prepollence, prepollency, pressure, prestige, primacy, puissance, reign, rule, supremacy, supremeness, sway, *vis*, warrant, weight
ASSOCIATED CONCEPTS: apparent power, appointing power, arbitrary power, capacity, concurrent power, contingent power, continuing power, delegated power, discretionary power, equitable power, exercise of power, extinguishment of power, extraordinary power, general power, implicit power, implied power, inchoate power, incidental power, inherent power, legislative power, limited power, mandatory power, necessary power, nonexclusive power of appointment, power coupled with an interest, power of alienation, power of appointment, power of attorney, power of disposition, power of sale, power of termination, release of power, retention of power, revocation of power, special power, taxing power, testamentary power
FOREIGN PHRASES: *Nemo potest facere per obliquum quod non potest facere per directum.* No man can do indirectly that which he cannot do directly. *Sequi debet potentia justitiam, non praecedere.* Power ought to follow justice, not precede it. *Potentia non est nisi ad bonum.* Power is not conferred but for the good. *Fortior et potentior est dispositio legis quam hominis.* The disposition of the law has greater force and stronger effect than that of man. *Frustra est potentia quae nunquam venit in actum.* A power is a vain one if it is never exercised. *Potestas stricte interpretatur.* Power should be strictly interpreted. *Delegatus non potest delegare.* A representative cannot delegate his authority.

POWERFUL, adjective able, able-bodied, armipotent, authoritative, autocratic, autocratical, brawny, cogent, commanding, compelling, consequential, controlling, deafening, dominant, dominating, dynamic, effective, effectual, efficacious, empowered, forceful, forcible, great, hard, hearty, hegemonic, hegemonical, Herculean, high-potency, impelling, imperious, important, impregnable, indomitable, influential, intense, invincible, irresistible, leonine, loud, lusty, magisterial, mighty, multipotent, muscular, obeyed, omnipotent, overpowering, overwhelming, physically strong, plenipotent, potent, powerpacked, prevailing, puissant, regnant, reigning, resounding, rugged, ruling, sinewy, sovereign, stalwart, stentorian, stout, strapping, striking, strong, telling, trenchant, unconquerable, unquenchable, unweakened, vehement, vigorous, weighty

POWERLESS, adjective abrogated, adynamic, asthenic, canceled, crippled, debilitated, decrepit, defenseless, deposed, disabled, disqualified, drooping, droopy, effete, emasculated, exhausted, faint, faintish, feeble, figurehead, flaccid, forceless, fragile, frail, futile, harmless, helpless, impotens, impotent, impuissant, inactive, inadequate, inapt, incapable, incapacitated, incompetent, indefensible, ineffective, ineffectual, inefficacious, inept, infirm, infirmus, inoperative, invalidus, languid, languishing, listless, lustless, marrowless, mightless, nerveless, nugatory, null and void, palsied, paralytic, paralyzed, pithless, pregnable, sapless, sickly, sinewless, spent, spineless, strengthless, submissive, superannuated, torpid, unable, unapt, unarmed, unavailing, unempowered, unendowed, unequipped, unfit, unfortified, uninfluential, unnerved, unqualified, unsteady, unstrengthened, unstrung, unsupported, useless, vigorless, vincible, weak, weaponless, without authority, without force, without vitality, yielding

PRACTICABLE, adjective achievable, attainable, capable of being done, doable, effectible, feasible, not too difficult, obtainable, operable, performable, possible, practical, realizable, reasonable, within reach, within the bounds of possiblity, workable
ASSOCIATED CONCEPTS: as soon as practicable

PRACTICAL, noun adaptable, advantageous, aiding, all-purpose, applicable, assisting, beneficial, commodious, conducive, convenient, effective, effectual, efficacious, efficient, employable, expedient, expediential, fitting, functional, handy, helpful, implemental, instrumental, invaluable, of general utility, operational, operative, practicable, profitable, serviceable, suitable, to the purpose, useful, utilitarian, utilizable, valuable, workable

PRACTICE (Custom), noun behavior, common course, confirmed habit, consuetude, conventionality, course of action, course of conduct, customary course, established order, fixed ways, frequent repetition, general course, habit, habitual course, habituation, habitude, inveterate habit, line of action, line of proceeding, manner, matter of course, method, mode, mode of procedure, natural course, order of the day, ordinary course, pattern, prescription, procedure, routine, settled disposition, style, usage, use, usual custom, usual method, way
ASSOCIATED CONCEPTS: custom and usage, practice in the industry
FOREIGN PHRASES: Cursus curiae est lex curiae. The practice of the court is the law of the court. Multa multo exercitatione facilius quam regulis percipies. You will perceive many things much more easily by practice than by rule.

PRACTICE (Procedure), noun approach, arrangement, conduct, consuetudo, course, course of action, course of conduct, established order, exercitatio, form, general guidelines, governing course of action, governing plan, line of action, line of conduct, manner of proceeding, method, mode, mode of management, mos, observance, operation, order of the day, organization, outline, plan of action, policy, prescribed form, prescribed usage, process, program, protocol, required manner,

routine, rule, rules of business, scheme, stratagem, strategy, system, tactics, treatment, usual way, usus, way, way of doing things
ASSOCIATED CONCEPTS: civil practice, criminal practice

PRACTICE (Professional business), noun avocation, business, calling, career, chosen career, chosen field, chosen profession, employment, life, life's work, line of business, line of work, occupation, pursuit, specialty, trade, undertaking, vocation
ASSOCIATED CONCEPTS: practice of law, practice of profession

PRACTICE (Engage in), verb be employed, carry on business, devote oneself to, employ, employ one's professional skill, employ oneself in, engage in, exercere, facere, factitare, follow a calling, follow a profession, follow as an occupation, labor at one's vocation, perform the duties of, perform the functions of, pursue, specialize, specialize in, undertake, work at
ASSOCIATED CONCEPTS: practice law

PRACTICE (Train by repetition), verb acquire the habit, apply one's self to, become familiar with, condition, cultivate a habit, discipline, do repeatedly, drill, exercise, familiarize with, learn a habit, meditari, perfect a routine, perform repeatedly, prepare, rehearse, school, take training, work at

PRACTICED, adjective able, accomplished, adept, adroit, apt, artful, canny, capable, clever, competent, conversant, crafty, deft, dextrous, efficient, effortless, equipped, experienced, expert, facile, gifted, habituated, handy, informed, initiated, knowing, learned, masterful, masterly, panurgic, prepared, proficient, qualified, resourceful, seasoned, shrewd, skilled, skillful, smooth, sophisticated, talented, trained, veteran, well-qualified

PRACTITIONER, noun artificer, artisan, artist, attorney, counselor, craftsman, creative worker, journeyman, lawyer, master worker, professional, solicitor, specialist, trained person
ASSOCIATED CONCEPTS: legal practitioner, single practitioner, sole practitioner

PRAGMATIC, adjective clear-thinking, expedient, feasible, matter-of-fact, practical, rational, realistic, reasonable, sensible, serviceable, sound, straight-thinking, unidealistic, unromantic, unsentimental, useful, utilitarian

PRAGMATISM, noun expedience, expediency, matter of factness, practical attitude, practicality, practicalness, rationality, realism, realistic attitude, realisticness, reasonableness, sensibility, sensibleness, sound thinking, unidealism, unsentimentality

PRATTLE, noun blather, gabble, nonsensical talk, twaddle, verbiage

PRATTLE, verb babble, blather, chatter, gab, jabber, prate, prattle, talk nonsense

PRAY, verb address a request, adjure, appeal to, apply to, ask earnestly, beseech, bid, call upon, clamor for, cry for help, entreat, entreat persistently, impetrate, implore, importune, make a request, make earnest petition for, make supplication, obtest, orare, petition, plead, *precari,* prefer a petition, prefer a request, press, put up petitions, raise up one's voice, requisition, *rogare,* solicit, supplicate, urge, urge persistently, urge repeatedly

ASSOCIATED CONCEPTS: pray for relief in a complaint

PRAYER, noun application, application for relief, beseechment, call, claim, earnest entreaty, earnest request, entreaty, humble entreaty, *imploratio,* imploration, importunity, invocation, motion, petition, plea, *precatio,* request, request for relief, request for the aid of the court, requisition, solemn entreaty, supplication, urgent request, *votum*

ASSOCIATED CONCEPTS: prayer for relief

PREAMBLE, noun beginning, *exordium,* foreword, foundation, introduction, introductory part, introductory statement, lead, opening, preface, prefatory note, prelude, prelusion, proem, prolegomenon, prologue

ASSOCIATED CONCEPTS: preamble to a constitution

PREARRANGE, verb agree to beforehand, arrange beforehand, arrange in advance, concoct, consider beforehand, ensure a result, forearm, foreordain, lay down a plan, map out, plan, plot, preconcert, precontrive, predesign, predestinate, predestine, predetermine, preestablish, premeditate, preorder, prepare, preresolve, project, resolve beforehand

PRECARIOUS, adjective alarming, chancy, changeable, critical, crumbling, dangerous, defenseless, delicate, doubtful, dubious, *dubius,* equivocal, exposed, fraught with danger, full of risk, guardless, hazardous, impermanent, *incertus,* infirm, insecure, jeopardous, menacing, perilous, riskful, risky, shaky, slippery, thorny, threatening, ticklish, tottering, treacherous, unassured, uncertain, undependable, unfaithworthy, unprotected, unreliable, unsafe, unsettled, unsheltered, unshielded, unsound, unstable, unsteadfast, unsteady, unsubstantial, unsure, untrustworthy, vulnerable

PRECATORY, adjective advisory, appealing, asking, beseeching, entreating, expressing entreaty, imploratory, imploring, importunate, pleading, suggesting, suggestive

ASSOCIATED CONCEPTS: precatory words

PRECAUTION, noun alertness, anticipation, attention, care, carefulness, caution, circumspection, forearming, foresight, forethought, guarantee, guardedness, heed, heedfulness, premunition, preventive measures, prior measure, protection, providence, provision, prudence, safeguard, security, solicitude, surveillance, timely care, vigil, vigilance, wariness, warning, watch, watchfulness

ASSOCIATED CONCEPTS: last clear chance doctrine, precautions to guard against injury, standard of care

PRECEDE, verb antecede, *antecedere,* antedate, *antegredi, anteire,* anticipate, be ahead of, come before, come first, forerun, go ahead of, go before, go in advance, go in front of, harbinger, herald, introduce, lead, lead the way, pave the way, pioneer, preexist, prepare the ground, scout, take the lead, usher in

PRECEDENCE, noun advantage, antecedence, authority, elevation, exaltation, importance, predomi-

nance, preeminence, preference, prestige, primacy, priority, rank, seniority, status, superiority, supremacy

ASSOCIATED CONCEPTS: recording statute

PRECEDENT, noun archetype, authoritative example, authoritative rule, authority, authortative decision, authortative principle of law, basis, criterion, example, *exemplum,* foundation, frame of reference, guide, judicial antecedent, justification, maxim, model, model instance, point of comparison, preceding instance, precept, precursor, predecessor, prior instance, rule, rule for future determinations, rule for future guidance, standard

ASSOCIATED CONCEPTS: collateral estoppel, condition precedent, controlling authority, precedent sub silentio, res judicata, stare decisis

PRECEPT, noun axiom, canon, charge, code, command, commandment, decree, dictate, direction, doctrine, dogma, edict, fiat, guide, injunction, instruction, law, legal order, mandate, order, ordinance, *praeceptum, praescriptum,* prescript, principle, regulation, requirement, rubric, rule, statute, teaching, tenet, warrant, writ

ASSOCIATED CONCEPTS: legal precept

PRECIPITATE, adjective abrupt, breakneck, foolhardy, harebrained, hasty, headlong, headstrong, heady, hellbent, hot-headed, hurried, immediate, impetuous, imprudent, impulsive, *inconsultus,* indiscreet, injudicious, madcap, overconfident, overly hasty, *praeceps,* precipitant, precipitous, quick, rapid, rash, reckless, rushed, speedy, sudden, swift, *temerarius,* thoughtless, uncalculating, unexpected, unprepared for, violent, wild

PRECIPITATE (*Hasten*), **verb** *accelerare,* accelerate, advance, bring on, expedite, forward, further, hurry, make haste, *maturare, praecipitare,* quicken, rush, speed, speed up, spur, urge forward

PRECIPITATE (*Throw down violently*), **verb** catapult, chuck, *deicere,* discharge, drop, ejaculate, expel, fell, fling, fling downward, heave, hurl headlong, jaculate, launch, let fall, let fly, pitch, *praecipitare,* project, propel, send flying, send forth, send headlong, shoot, shy, throw down, throw headlong, toss

PRECISE, adjective accurate, careful, clean-cut, clear-cut, close, correct, critical, defined, definite, detailed, determinate, *diligens,* distinct, *elegans,* even, exact, explicit, express, faithful, fastidious, faultless, finical, finicky, flawless, fussy, inflexible, literal, methodical, meticulous, narrow, painstaking, particular, precisian, proper, punctilious, punctual, rigid, rigorous, scientific, scrupulous, severe, sharply defined, specific, stiff, strict, thorough, truthful, unambiguous, unbending, uncompromising, unequivocal, unerring, watchful, well-defined

PRECLUDE, verb ban, bar, bar from access, block, check, choke, control, cramp, cripple, curb, cut off, debar, defeat, detain, deter, discourage, encumber, estop, exclude, foil, forbid, foreclose, frustrate, handicap, hinder, impede, interfere with, interrupt, make impossible, obstruct, oppose, override, preempt, prevent, *prohibere,* prohibit, regulate, restrain, restrict, retard, stay, stop, thwart

ASSOCIATED CONCEPTS: estoppel, preclude from introducing into evidence

PRECOGNITION, *noun* clairvoyance, foreboding, foreknowledge, foresight, forethought, perception, prenotion, presage, prescience, presentiment

PRECONCEIVE, *verb* anticipate, assume, be biased, be jaundiced, be prejudiced, forejudge, foresee, have a bias, have foreknowledge, incline, intuit, judge beforehand, jump to a conclusion, *praeiudicare,* preapprehend, precognize, preconclude, predecide, predetermine, predict, predispose, prejudge, prepossess, presume, presuppose, presurmise, surmise

PRECONCEPTION, *noun* anticipation, assumption, bent, bias, fixed idea, foregone conclusion, forejudgment, inclination, leaning, partiality, *praeiudicata opinio,* preapprehension, preconceived idea, preconclusion, predetermination, preestimate, prejudgment, prejudication, prejudice, prejudiced view, prenotion, prepossession, presentiment, presumption, presupposal, presupposition, presurmise

PRECURSOR, *noun* advance guard, ancestor, announcer, antecedent, augury, avant-courier, forebearer, forefather, foregoer, forerunner, guide, harbinger, herald, omen, parent, pathfinder, patriarch, pioneer, portent, *praecursor, praenuntius,* precedent, predecessor, preparation, preparer, presage, preview, prodrome, prognostic, scout, sign, token, usher, vanguard, warning

PRECURSORY, *adjective* advance, antecedent, beginning, earlier, exploratory, first, foregoing, forerunning, foreshadowing, forewarning, foundational, inaugural, inauguratory, initiatory, introductory, leading, *praecurrentia,* precedent, preceding, precursive, prefatory, preliminary, preludial, preludious, prelusive, prelusory, preparatory, prevenient, previous, prior, prognosticative

PREDATORY, *adjective* bloodthirsty, carnivorous, depredatory, devouring, greedy, living by prey, lupine, pillaging, plundering, *praedabundus, praedatorius,* predacious, predative, raiding, rapacious, raptorial, ravaging, ravening, ravenous, spoliatory, voracious, vulturine, vulturish, vulturous, wolfish

PREDECESSOR, *noun* ancestor, antecedent, antecessor, elder, forebearer, forefather, foregoer, foreparent, forerunner, former incumbent, former officeholder, founder, originator, patriarch, precursor, procreator, progenitor

PREDETERMINATION, *noun* aim, bias, closedmindedness, conclusion beforehand, conclusion in advance, decision beforehand, decision in advance, destined lot, destiny, fate, fixed future, force of circumstances, foredoom, foregone conclusion, forejudgment, foreordainment, forethought, fortune, goal, inevitability, inevitableness, inexorable fate, intention, jaundice, kismet, lot, object, objective, one-sidedness, partiality, preapprehension, preconception, preconclusion, predecision, predeliberation, predestination, predetermined course of events, prejudgment, prejudice, premeditation, prenotion, prepossession, preresolution, presumption, presupposal, presupposition, presurmise, purpose, resolve, undetachment, will

PREDETERMINE, *verb* agree beforehand, be biased, be influenced, be jaundiced, be prejudiced, be prepossessed, be swayed, contrive a result, decide beforehand, decide in advance, destinate, destine, determine beforehand, determine in advance, doom, fate, forecast, forejudge, foreordain, foreordinate, intend, jump to a conclusion, map out, ordain, plan, *praefinire, praestituere,* prearrange, preconceive, preconclude, preconsider, predecide, predestinate, predestine, predispose, preestablish, prejudge, premeditate, preordain, preresolve, presume, presuppose, presurmise, project, reserve, resolve beforehand

PREDICAMENT, *noun* adverse circumstances, adversity, *angustiae,* barrier, case, circumstance, complication, condition, conjuncture, corner, crisis, critical situation, danger, dangerous condition, *difficultas,* difficulty, dilemma, embarrassing position, embarrassment, emergency, entanglement, exigency, fix, hole, imbroglio, impasse, impediment, intricacy, jeopardy, mess, misfortune, obstacle, obstruction, occurrence, pass, perplexity, pinch, plight, position, posture, precariousness, pressure, quandary, scrape, situation, sorry plight, state, straits, tight situation, tight spot, trial, trouble, trying situation

PREDICT, *verb* adumbrate, advise, announce in advance, anticipate, augur, auspicate, betoken, bode, divine, envision, forebode, forecast, foreknow, foresee, foreshadow, foreshow, forespeak, foretell, foretoken, forewarn, give notice, herald, indicate, indicate beforehand, make a prediction, make a prognosis, notify, omen, ominate, point to, portend, *praedicere,* preannounce, preindicate, premonish, premonstrate, presage, presignify, prognose, prognosticate, promise, prophesy, read, read the future, signify, soothsay, tell fortunes, tell the future, *vaticinari,* vaticinate, warn

PREDILECTION, *noun* affection, affinity, appetence, appetency, appetite, attachment, bent, bias, choice, desire, disposition, fancy, favor, fondness, inclination, infatuation, leaning, liking, love, partiality, partisanship, penchant, predisposition, preference, prejudgment, prejudice, prepossession, proneness, propensity, *studium,* taste, tendency

PREDISPOSITION, *noun* affection, appetence, appetency, appetite, aptitude, aptness, ardor, attachment, attraction, bent, bias, cast, character, desire, disposition, fancy, favor, favoritism, fondness, foregone conclusion, *inclinatio,* inclination, keenness, leaning, liking, longing, natural tendency, nature, partiality, penchant, preapprehension, preconception, preconclusion, preconsideration, predecision, predetermination, predilection, preference, prejudice, prepossession, *proclivitas,* proclivity, proneness, propenseness, propension, propensity, readiness, *studium,* susceptibility, taste, temperament, tendency, turn, warp, weakness, willingness, wish, yearning, zeal

PREDOMINANCE, *noun* almightiness, ascendency, authority, command, control, controlling influence, dominance, domination, dominion, imperium, influence, jurisdiction, lead, leadership, mastery, mightiness, omnipotence, paramountcy, *potentia,* power, predominancy, predomination, prepollence, prepollency, prepotency, *principatus,* puissance, pull, regency, reign, rule, seniority, sovereignty, strength, superiority, supremacy, supreme authority, sway, upper hand, weight

PREDOMINANT, *adjective* abundant, all-powerful, almighty, ascendant, authoritative, cogent, commanding, common, controlling, dominant, dominating, effective, efficacious, epidemic, extensive, forceful, foremost, general, governing, important, influential, mighty, omnipotent, overpowering, overruling, pandemic, paramount, *potens,* potent, powerful, *praepollens,* preponderant, prevailing, prevalent, principal, puissant, rampant, recognized, regnant, reigning, rife, ruling, sovereign, strong, superior, supervisory, supreme, weighty, widely recognized, widespread

PREDOMINATE *(Command), verb* administer, be sovereign, be supreme, carry weight, command, determine, direct, dominate, gain the upper hand, govern, guide, have influence, have sway, have the upper hand, hold dominion, hold office, influence, lead, manage, master, mastermind, override, overrule, oversee, overshadow, play a leading part, *praepollere,* prevail, pull the strings, reign, rule, rule over, *superare,* supervise, sway, take the lead, *vincere*

PREDOMINATE *(Outnumber), verb* be in the majority, be rife, be superior in number, eclipse, exceed, go beyond, outrank, outrival, outstrip, outweigh, overtop, *plures esse,* preponderate, rise above, surpass

PREEMPT, *verb* acquire beforehand, annex, appropriate, appropriate for use, arrogate to oneself, assume, capture, catch, exclude, force from, gain possession, impropriate, invade, obtain, occupy, preclude, preoccupy, seize, take, take over, take possession of, usurp
ASSOCIATED CONCEPTS: doctrine of federal preemption, preemption in filing, preemptive right, preemptive right of shareholders, right of preemption

PREEMPTION, *noun* appropriation, displacement, exclusion, preclusion, replacement, substitution, supersedence, supersession, supervention, supplanting
ASSOCIATED CONCEPTS: federal preemption, preemption doctrine

PREEXISTING, *adjective* antecedent, anterior, earlier, preexistent, previous, prior
ASSOCIATED CONCEPTS: preexisting condition, preexisting debt

PREFACE, *noun* beginning, commencement, exordium, foreword, introduction, introductory part, opening, overture, *praefatio,* preamble, prefatory note, preliminary comment, preliminary statement, prelude, prelusion, proem, prolegomenon, prolusion, *prooemium*

PREFACE, *verb* advance, begin, commence, head, herald, inaugurate, initiate, institute, introduce, launch, lead in, lead the way, make a start, open, place before, *praefari,* preamble, precede, prelude, put first, say in advance, set in motion, start, usher in

PREFER, *verb* adopt, advance, *anteponere,* approve, be fond of, be partial to, bring forward, choose, cling to, dignify, elect, elevate, embrace, espouse, fancy, favor, fix upon, further, graduate, grant favors to, have a fancy for, indulge one's fancy, lean toward, like better, move up, patronize, pick, pick out, play favorites, *praeoptare, praeponere,* prize, promote, pull strings for, put forward, raise, recommend, sanction, select, set

above others, show preference, single out, take a fancy to, take to, tend, think better, treat with partiality, value

PREFERABLE, *adjective* above par, better, choice, chosen, deserving of preference, enjoyable, excellent, excelling, favorite, good, likable, *melior,* more advantageous, more desirable, more in demand, more pleasing, more popular, more select, picked, *potior,* preferred, relishable, selected, superior, surpassing, worthy of choice

PREFERENCE *(Choice), noun* bias, discretion, disposition, election, fancy, favorite, inclination, leaning, liking, option, partiality, preconceived liking, predilection, prejudice, proclivity, proneness, propensity, selection
ASSOCIATED CONCEPTS: preferred risk

PREFERENCE *(Priority), noun* advancement, advantage, benefit, favored treatment, front position, *praepositio,* precedence, preeminence, preferment, preferred standing, seniority
ASSOCIATED CONCEPTS: calendar preference, fraudulent conveyances, fraudulent preference, preferred stock, unlawful preference, voidable preference
FOREIGN PHRASES: **Qui prior est tempore potior est jure.** He who is first in time is first in right. **Prior tempore potior jure.** First in time, superior in right.

PREFERENTIAL, *adjective* advantageous, better, biased, choice, desired, discriminating, discriminative, distinguished, elite, exceptional, exclusive, extraordinary, favored, first-rate, high-grade, marked, outstanding, paramount, partial, partisan, preferred, priority, privileged, prize, recommended, select, selected, selective, special, superb, superior
ASSOCIATED CONCEPTS: preferential treatment

PREFERRED *(Favored), adjective* adopted, approved, choice, chosen, decided upon, elected, endorsed, especially liked, fancied, favorite, handpicked, liked, picked out, preferable, preferential, selected, set apart, settled upon, singled out, special, taken

PREFERRED *(Given priority), adjective* first, given preference, having priority, having seniority, placed in advance, preceding, prior
ASSOCIATED CONCEPTS: preferred stock, voidable preference

PREJUDGE, *verb* condemn beforehand, forejudge, judge before hearing, judge beforehand, judge in advance, jump to a conclusion, *praeiudicare,* preconceive, preconclude, precondemn, preconsider, predecide, predetermine, preestimate, prejudicate, presume, presuppose, presurmise, resolve beforehand, rush to conclusion

PREJUDICE *(Injury), noun* damage, detriment, *detrimentum,* disadvantage, harm, hurt, impairment, injustice, irreversible damage, loss, unfairness, wrong
ASSOCIATED CONCEPTS: absence of prejudice, dismissal with prejudice, dismissal without prejudice, prejudice to a party's rights, prejudicial error

PREJUDICE *(Preconception), noun* bent, bias, discrimination, favoritism, forejudgment, inclination, intolerance, leaning, narrow-mindedness, one-sidedness, *opinio praeiudicata,* partiality, partisanship, personal

bias, preconceived idea, preconceived notion, preconception, predetermination, predilection, predisposition, preference, prejudgment, prepossession, provincialism, slant, subjectivity, unreasonable bias
ASSOCIATED CONCEPTS: disqualification for bias

PREJUDICE (*Influence*), *verb*　　affect, bear upon, bend to one's will, bias, bring pressure to bear, carry weight, color, convince, distort, exercise influence over, exercise influence upon, exert influence, gain over, give an inclination, have influence over, have influence upon, influence against, jaundice, persuade, predetermine, predispose, prejudge, prepossess unfavorably, present with bias, prevail over, slant, sway, turn, twist, warp, win over
ASSOCIATED CONCEPTS: prejudice the trier of fact

PREJUDICE (*Injure*), *verb*　　affect detrimentally, cause damage to, cause detriment, cause pain, damage, demolish, destroy, devastate, disadvantage, disservice, exacerbate, harm, hurt, impair, inflict injury, maim, mar, play havoc with, ravage, ruin, spoil, taint, weaken, wound, wreck, wrong
ASSOCIATED CONCEPTS: prejudicial error

PREJUDICIAL, *adjective*　　biased, colored, damaging, *damnosus*, deleterious, destructive, detrimental, directed against, disadvantageous, disserviceable, harmful, hostile, hurtful, inimical, injurious, *nocens*, *noxius*, opinionated, partisan, pernicious, preconceived, preconceptual, predecisive, predispositional, prepossessed, slanted, tending to impair, tending to obstruct, unfavorable, unjust
ASSOCIATED CONCEPTS: prejudicial error

PRELIMINARY, *adjective*　　aforementioned, antecedent, anterior, beginning, coming before, early, exordial, foregoing, former, inaugural, incipient, initial, initiatory, introductory, opening, original, preceding, precursive, precursory, preexisting, prefatory, preludial, prelusive, prelusory, preparative, preparatory, prevenient, previous, primary, prior, proemial, starting, trial
ASSOCIATED CONCEPTS: preliminary agreement, preliminary hearing, preliminary injunction, preliminary notice, preliminary plea, preliminary relief, preliminary restraining order

PRELUDE, *noun*　　beginning, commencement, exordium, foreword, inauguration, inception, induction, initiation, introduction, opening, outset, overture, preamble, preface, preliminary part, prelusion, preparation, proem, prologue, *prooemium*, start

PREMATURE, *adjective*　　ahead of time, anticipatory, before time, embryonic, green, hasty, ill-considered, ill-timed, *immaturus*, inchoate, inopportune, mistimed, overhasty, *praematurus*, precipitate, rash, raw, sooner than due, sooner than intended, too early, too soon, unanticipated, underripe, undeveloped, unformed, unmatured, unprepared, unready, unripe, unseasonable, untimely
ASSOCIATED CONCEPTS: exhaustion of remedies, premature action

PREMEDITATED, *adjective*　　aforethought, calculated, conscious, considered, deliberate, deliberately intended, foreordained, intended, intentional, maturely considered, outlined beforehand, planned, planned beforehand, planned in advance, plotted, prearranged, preconsidered, precontrived, predeliberated, predesigned, predeterminated, predetermined, predevised, preresolved, reasoned, studied, thought out, well-considered, well-devised, willful, with forethought
ASSOCIATED CONCEPTS: intent, malice aforethought, premeditated crime, premeditated murder

PREMEDITATION, *noun*　　advance planning, aforethought, deliberate intent, deliberate intention, design, distinct purpose, forethought, machination, *praemeditatio*, prearrangement, preconsideration, predeliberation, predetermination, preresolution, previous deliberation, previous reflection, prior determination
ASSOCIATED CONCEPTS: intent

PREMISES (*Buildings*), *noun*　　*aedificium*, bounds, domiciles, *domus*, dwellings, edifices, grounds, homes, house with the grounds belonging to it, land, limits, lodgings, piece of land, place, property, quarters, real estate, residences, structures, tract of land
ASSOCIATED CONCEPTS: premises liability

PREMISES (*Hypotheses*), *noun*　　affirmations, assertions, assumed positions, axioms, bases, foundations, grounds, positions, postulates, *principia*, terms, theorems, theses

PREMIUM, *adjective*　　best, capital, choice, desirable, elect, estimable, excellent, fine, finest, first-class, first-rate, grade A, high-grade, high-quality, incomparable, inimitable, matchless, peerless, precious, prime, quality, second to none, select, specially selected, splendid, superb, superfine, superior, superlative, top-notch, unbeatable, unequaled, unmatched, unparalleled, unrivaled, unsurpassed, very fine, worthy

PREMIUM (*Excess value*), *noun*　　amount over par, bonus, bounty, charge beyond normal, charge to excess, excessive charge, extra, incentive, increased value, overcharge, prize

PREMIUM (*Insurance payment*), *noun*　　amount paid periodically, annual commitment, annual encumbrance, annual fee, annual installment, annual liability, annual obligation, annual payment, annual rate of insurance, annual remittance, contract payment, periodic payment, yearly payment
ASSOCIATED CONCEPTS: assessment of a premium, earned premiums, gross premium, net premium, reduction of premium

PREMONITION, *noun*　　augury, auspice, boding, caution, divination, evil adumbration, feeling, foreboding, forefeeling, foreshadowing, foretoken, forewarning, hunch, intimation, misgiving, *monitio, monitum*, omen, portent, prediction, premonishment, prenotification, presage, presentiment, presurmise, prevision, prewarning, sign, warning

PREOCCUPATION, *noun*　　absorbed interest, absorption, abstraction, attentiveness, concentration, daydreaming, deep study, depth of thought, devotion, distraction, dreaminess, engrossment, enthrallment, fascination, fixation, fixed idea, *idée fixe*, immersion, intentness, involvement, musing, obsession, pensiveness, *praeoccupatio*, prepossession, profound thought, rapt attention, reverie, study, trance

PREORDAIN, *verb* appoint beforehand, appoint in advance, decide in advance, decree beforehand, destine, determine beforehand, enact beforehand, establish beforehand, fix beforehand, foredoom, forejudge, foreshadow, preconceive, preconclude, preconsider, predecide, predeliberate, predestine, predetermine, preestablish, prejudge, preresolve, resolve beforehand

PREPARATION, *noun* anticipation, apprenticeship, arrangement, background, basis, building, development, education, equipment, establishment, evolution, foresight, forethought, foundation, groundwork, initiation, instruction, making ready, neophytism, novitiate, plan, precaution, preliminaries, preliminary step, premunition, prior measure, probation, providence, provision, prudence, qualification, readiness, readying, rehearsal, safeguard, teaching, training
ASSOCIATED CONCEPTS: preparation for trial, preparation of a crime

PREPARATORY, *adjective* anticipatory, beginning, early, expectant, foundational, inaugural, inceptive, incipient, initial, initiative, initiatory, introductory, opening, precautionary, precedent, preceding, precursory, prefatory, preliminary, preludial, prelusive, prelusory, preparative, prepositional, prior, proemial, provident, qualifying, starting
ASSOCIATED CONCEPTS: preparatory acts

PREPAY, *verb* defray in advance, discharge in advance, give compensation for in advance, make payment in advance, meet the bill ahead of time, pay in advance, presettle, satisfy in advance, settle in advance, tender in advance
ASSOCIATED CONCEPTS: prepayment clause

PREPONDERANCE, *noun* dominance, domination, majority, outweighing, paramountcy, plurality, predominance, predomination, preeminence, prepollence, prepollency, preponderancy, preponderation, prevalence, superiority
ASSOCIATED CONCEPTS: preponderance of the credible evidence

PREREQUISITE, *noun* condition, demand, essential desideratum, exigency, fundamental, groundwork, indispensable item, necessary condition, necessary item, necessity, need, needed item, precondition, preliminary condition, pressing need, prior condition, proviso, requirement, requisite, specification, stipulation, vital part
ASSOCIATED CONCEPTS: condition precedent, jurisdictional prerequisite

PREROGATIVE, *noun* advantage, authority, authorization, benefit, charter, claim, droit, due, exclusive privilege, exclusive right, franchise, freedom, grant, inalienable right, legal power, liberty, license, perquisite, power, preference, prior right, priority, privilege, right, rightful power, sanction, special right, title, vested right, warrant
ASSOCIATED CONCEPTS: managerial prerogative, prerogative writ

PRESAGE, *verb* adumbrate, advise, announce in advance, anticipate, augur, *augurari,* augurate, auspicate, betoken, bode, divine, envision, forebode, forecast, foreknow, foresee, foreshadow, foreshow, foretell, foretoken, forewarn, have a presentiment, impend, indicate beforehand, indicate in advance, judge the future, make a prediction, omen, ominate, point to, portend, *portendere, praesagire,* predict, prefigurate, prefigure, preindicate, premonstrate, preshow, presignify, prewarn, prognosticate, promise, prophesy, signify, soothsay, threaten, vaticinate, warn

PRESAGEFUL, *adjective* augural, augurial, auspicial, foreboding, monitory, ominous, portentous

PRESCRIBE, *verb* administer, advocate, bid, charge, command, conduct, control, decide, decree, demand, designate, dictate, direct, enjoin, exact, exercise authority, give a directive, give a mandate, give an order, give directions, guide, impose, instruct, issue an order, lay out, lead, mandate, mark out, ordain, order, pilot, *praescribere,* prevail over, proclaim, regulate, require, set, steer, superintend, write a prescription
ASSOCIATED CONCEPTS: prescribe remedies, prescribed by law

PRESCRIPTION *(Claim of title),* *noun* authority, claim, inalienable right, interest, license, prerogative, right, vested interest, vested right
ASSOCIATED CONCEPTS: adverse possession, easement by prescription, right by prescription, title by prescription
FOREIGN PHRASES: *Praescriptio et executio non pertinent ad valorem contractus, set ad tempus et modum actionis instituendae.* Prescription and execution do not affect the validity of the contract, but the time and manner of instituting an action. *Usucapio constituta est ut aliquis litium finis esset.* Prescription was established so that there be an end to lawsuits. *Nihil praescribitur nisi quod possidetur.* There is no prescription for that which is not possessed. *Interruptio multiplex non tollit praescriptionem semel obtentam.* Frequent interruptions do not defeat a prescription once obtained. *Praescriptio est titulus ex usu et tempore substantiam capiens ab auctoritate legis.* Prescription is a title by authority of law, deriving its force from use and time.

PRESCRIPTION *(Custom),* *noun* convention, conventional usage, fashion, habit, institution, observance, practice, precedent, tradition, usage, use

PRESCRIPTION *(Directive),* *noun* act, authority, axiom, canon, charge, command, decree, dictate, direction, doctrine, edict, enactment, formula, formulary, injunction, instruction, law, maxim, measure, order, ordinance, precept, prescript, principle, proposal, regulation, rubric, rule, ruling, statute, theorem

PRESCRIPTIVE, *adjective* accepted, acknowledge, acknowledge through possession, acknowledge through use, admitted, binding, commanded by long use, commanding, compulsory, customary, decretal, determined, dictated, established, fixed, legalized, long-established, longstanding, obligatory, ordained by custom, popular, preceptive, prescribed, recognized, recognized because of continued possession, recognized through use, required by custom, rooted, set, settled, time-honored, traditional, traditive, understood, unwritten, usual, vested, wonted
ASSOCIATED CONCEPTS: prescriptive rights

PRESENCE *(Attendance),* *noun* being, nearness, *praesentia,* proximity, sojournment, visitation

PRESENCE *(Poise)*, **noun**　　air, appearance, aspect, bearing, behavior, carriage, comportment, conduct, decorum, demeanor, deportment, gentility, guise, image, look, manner, mien, ostent, outward show, personality, posture, presentation, refinement, semblance, style, visage, way, ways
ASSOCIATED CONCEPTS: demeanor of a witness

PRESENT *(Attendant)*, **adjective**　　accessible, accounted for, adjacent, at close quarters, at hand, available, close, close at hand, close by, convenient, handy, in attendance, in the company of, in the presence of, in the vicinity, in view, near at hand, nearby, nigh, on hand, on the spot, *praesens,* proximate, unremoved, vicinal, within reach

PRESENT *(Current)*, **adjective**　　at hand, at this moment, at this time, attendant, available, contemporaneous, contemporary, current, existent, existing, extant, going on, here, immediate, in view, instant, latest, living, modern, near, near in time, nigh, on the spot, *praesens,* present-day, present-time, prevalent, ready, recent, topical, ubiquitary, ubiquitous, unremoved, up-to-date, up-to-the-minute
ASSOCIATED CONCEPTS: clear and present danger, present ability, present consideration, present controversy, present enjoyment, present gift, present interest, present transfer

PRESENT *(Introduce)*, **verb**　　demonstrate, disclose, display, exhibit, expose to view, give an introduction, *introducere,* make acquainted, make an introduction, make known, offer, offer evidence, open to view, propose, put forth, set forth, show, suggest, uncover, unveil
ASSOCIATED CONCEPTS: present a case, present evidence

PRESENT *(Make a gift)*, **verb**　　accord, allot, award, bequeath, bestow, confer, contribute, convey, deed, deliver, dispense, dole out, *donare,* donate, endow, extend, furnish, give, give as a gift, give over, grant, hand, hand over, impart, let have, make over, mete out, *munerari,* offer, place at one's disposal, proffer, provide, remit, render, supply, tender, vouchsafe

PRESENT *(Prefer charges)*, **verb**　　accuse, blame, charge, cite, criminate, fix the responsibility, implicate, impute, incriminate, lodge a complaint, prefer charges
ASSOCIATED CONCEPTS: present an indictment

PRESENTMENT, **noun**　　accusation, arraignment, charge, citation, imputation, indictment, information

PRESERVATION, **noun**　　care, cherishing, *conservatio,* conservation, curing, custody, defense, eternization, freedom from danger, guardianship, guarding, immortalization, maintenance, nourishment, nurture, perpetuation, protection, protective custody, safeguarding, safekeeping, safety, salvation, sanctuary, saving, security, shielding, storage, support, *tuitio,* upkeep, ward, wardship

PRESERVE, **verb**　　attend to, bolster, care for, champion, cherish, *condire, conservare,* conserve, continue, cure, defend, economize, ensconce, ensure, favor, foster, give support, guard, harbor, haven, hoard, house, husband, insure, keep, keep alive, keep from harm, keep intact, keep safe, keep sound, keep under cover, keep up, keep watch over, lend support, look

after, maintain, mind, minister to, nourish, patronize, perpetuate, prolong, promote, protect, protect from injury, provide for, provide sanctuary, put away, reinforce, rescue, safeguard, save, screen, secure, *servare,* shelter, shield, shield from danger, shield from injury, spare, stand behind, support, sustain, *sustinere,* take care of, tend, treasure, *tueri,* uphold, watch, watch over
ASSOCIATED CONCEPTS: preserve one's rights, preserve records, preserve the peace

PRESIDE, **verb**　　act as chairman, act as president, administer, administrate, assume command, be at the head of, be in authority, be in charge, be in the chair, be the chairman, chair, command, control, direct, exercise supervision, govern, guide, have authority over, have control, head, hold a position of authority, hold authority, hold sway, hold the chair, keep order, lead, manage, occupy the chair, officiate, overlook, oversee, pilot, *praesidere,* regulate, reign, rule, steer, superintend, supervise, sway, take care of, take charge, take over, wield authority
ASSOCIATED CONCEPTS: preside over a hearing, preside over court, presiding justice, presiding officer

PRESS, **noun**　　authors, columnists, commentators, contributors, correspondents, editors, interviewers, journalistic writers, journalists, literary publications, media, members of the media, members of the press, news business, news gatherers, newsmen, newspaper world, newspaperman, newspapers, newswriters, publicists, publishers, reporters
ASSOCIATED CONCEPTS: censorship, First Amendment, freedom of speech, freedom of the press

PRESS *(Beseech)*, **verb**　　adjure, appeal, ask earnestly, beg, call upon, enjoin, entreat, exhort, impetrate, implore, importune, petition, plead, request, supplicate, urge, *urgere*

PRESS *(Constrain)*, **verb**　　bear down on, bind, bring pressure to bear, coerce, command, compel, decree, demand, drive, enforce, exact, extort, force, impel, impose, insist, make, make necessary, necessitate, obligate, oblige, order, put pressure on, put under obligation, require, take no denial, urge forward, wring

PRESS *(Goad)*, **verb**　　aggravate, agonize, annoy, badger, beset, bother, browbeat, carp at, disquiet, drive, harry, heckle, hector, hound, incite, *instigare,* instigate, irritate, molest, persecute, pester, plague, prod, provoke, put pressure on, stir up, taunt, tease, torment, trouble, vex, worry

PRESSURE, **noun**　　anxiety, anxiousness, brunt, brute force, burden, coercion, compulsion, constraining force, constraint, controlling power, crisis, drive, duress, encumbrance, exertion, exhortation, exigency, force, hardship, heaviness, hindrance, imperativeness, importunateness, influence, influentiality, insistence, intensity, intimidation, load, necessity, need, obligation, oppression, persuasion, *pondus,* power, power of directing, power of impelling, press, pull, push, strain, stress, sway, tension, undue influence, urgency, *vis,* weight
ASSOCIATED CONCEPTS: undue influence

PRESSURE, **verb**　　adjure, advocate, bear down, beg, beseech, blandish, cajole, coax, coerce, command, compel, constrain, drive, entreat, exhort, force, goad, implore, induce, influence, insist, intimidate, oppress, persuade, plead, press, prod, push, request, solicit, stress, urge

ASSOCIATED CONCEPTS: coercion, duress, intimidation, undue influence

PRESTIDIGITATION, *noun*   conjuring, deluding, illusion, juggling, legerdemain, magic, palming, sleight of hand, sorcery, trickery

PRESTIGE, *noun*   ascendance, ascendency, aura, authority, celebrity, consequence, control, credit, dazzle, degree, dignity, distinction, *éclat,* eclat, eminence, esteem, estimation, exaltation, *fama,* fame, famousness, favor, force, glamor, *gloria,* glory, good repute, grandeur, greatness, high honor, high repute, honor, illustriousness, import, importance, influence, influentiality, luster, majesty, mark, name, nobility, *nomen,* notability, note, noteworthiness, notoriety, paramountcy, place, position, potency, power, precedence, predominance, predomination, preeminence, primacy, prominence, public favor, rank, regard, renown, reputation, repute, respect, significance, splendor, standing, station, status, superiority, sway, weight, worth

PRESUME, *verb*   anticipate, apprehend, assume, believe, come to a hasty conclusion, conceive, conclude, conjecture, consider as true, consider probable, contemplate, count upon, *credere,* dare say, deduce, deem, derive, divine, estimate, expect, forejudge, form an opinion, gather, guess, hazard a guess, hypothesize, infer, judge, jump to conclusions, opine, perceive as true, posit, postulate, preconceive, prejudge, presuppose, presurmise, regard as axiomatic, speculate, *sumere,* suppose, surmise, suspect, take for granted, take without proof, theorize, think, think likely, understand, venture

ASSOCIATED CONCEPTS: presume innocence

PRESUMPTION, *noun*   anticipation, assumption, belief, conception, *coniectura,* conjecture, deduction, ground for believing, hypothesis, inference, likelihood, *opinio,* opinion, postulate, predilection, predisposition, premise, presupposition, probability, reasonable supposition, required assumption, required legal assumption, speculation, strong probability, supposition, surmise

ASSOCIATED CONCEPTS: conclusive presumption, disputable presumption, presumption against suicide, presumption of authority, presumption of constitutionality, presumption of continuance, presumption of death, presumption of delivery, presumption of innocence, presumption of knowledge, presumption of law, presumption of legitimacy, presumption of regularity, rebuttable presumption, statutory presumption

FOREIGN PHRASES: *Cuicunque aliquis quid concedit concedere videtur et id, sine quo res ipsa esse non potuit.* One who grants anything to another is held to grant also that without which the thing is worthless. *Lex judicat de rebus necessario faciendis quasi re ipsa factis.* The law judges of things which must necessarily be done as if they were actually done. *Novatio non praesumitur.* A novation is not presumed. *Nemo praesumitur malus.* No one is presumed to be wicked. *Nemo praesumitur ludere in extremis.* No one is presumed to be jesting while at the point of death. *Nihil nequam est praesumendum.* Nothing wicked should be presumed. *Semper praesumitur pro legitimatione puerorum.* The presumption always is in favor of the

legitimacy of children. *Stabit praesumptio donec probetur in contrarium.* A presumption stands until the contrary is proven. *Praesumptiones sunt conjecturae exsigno verisimili ad probandum assumptae.* Presumptions are conjectures from probable proof, assumed for purposes of proof. *Fraus est odiosa et non praesumenda.* Fraud is odious and will not be presumed. *Donatio non praesumitur.* A gift is not presumed to have been made. *Nemo praesumitur donare.* No one is presumed to have made a gift. *Favorabiliores rei, potius quam actores, habentur.* The condition of the defendant is to be favored rather than that of the plaintiff. *Nobiliores et benigniores praesumptiones in dubiis sunt praeferendae.* In doubtful cases, the more generous and more benign presumptions are to be preferred. *Nullum iniquum est praesumendum in jure.* Nothing iniquitous is to be presumed in law. *Quisquis praesumitur bonus; et semper in dubiis pro reo respondendum.* Everyone is presumed to be good; and in doubtful cases it should be resolved in favor of the accused. *Praesumitur pro legitimatione.* There is a presumption in favor of legitimacy. *Semper praesumitur pro matrimonio.* The presumption is always in favor of the validity of a marriage. *Malum non praesumitur.* Evil is not presumed. *Pro possessione praesumitur de jure.* A presumption of law arises from possession. *Praesumptio violenta, plena probatio.* Strong presumption is full proof. *Semper qui non prohibet pro se intervenire, mandare creditur.* He who does not prohibit the intervention of another in his behalf is deemed to have authorized it. *Probatis extremis, praesumuntur media.* The extremes having been proved, those things which lie between are presumed. *In favorem vitae, libertatis, et innocentiae, omnia praesumuntur.* Every presumption is made in favor of life, liberty and innocence. *Nulla impossibilia aut inhonesta sunt praesumenda; vera autem et honesta et possibilia.* No things that are impossible or dishonorable are to be presumed; but things that are true and honorable and possible. *Omnia praesumuntur legitime facta donec probetur in contrarium.* All things are presumed to be lawfully done, until the contrary is proven. *Lex neminem cogit ostendere quod nescire praesumitur.* The law compels no one to divulge that which he is presumed not to know. *Injuria non praesumitur.* A wrong is not presumed.

PRESUMPTIVE, *adjective*   anticipated, apparent, assumed, assumptive, believable, circumstantial, conceivable, conjecturable, conjectural, conjectured, credible, easy to believe, evidential, feasible, hypothesized, imagined, inferable, inferred, likely, plausible, possible, postulated, postulational, presumable, presumed, presupposed, probable, putative, seeming, speculative, speculatory, supposed, suppositional, supposititious, suppositive, surmisable, suspect, theoretical, well-founded, well-grounded

ASSOCIATED CONCEPTS: presumptive damages, presumptive evidence, presumptive grant, presumptive notice, presumptive ownership, presumptive possession

PRESUMPTUOUS, *adjective*   *adrogans,* arrogant, assuming, audacious, bold, brash, brazen, cavalier, conceited, contumelious, daring, dictatorial, discourteous, disdainful, disrespectful, domineering, egoistic, egotistic, egotistical, excessively bold, excessively confident, familiar, flippant, foolhardy, forward, haughty, ill-bred, ill-mannered, imperious, impertinent, impolite, impudent, insolent, insulting, intrusive, irreverent, lacking respect, lofty, lordly, magisterial, malapert, offensive, outrageous, overbearing, overconfident, overfamiliar, overly bold, overly confident, overweening, pert, pompous, presuming, provocative, rash, rude, saucy, shameless, supercilious, unabashed, unceremonious, uncourtly, ungenteel, vain

PRESUPPOSE, *verb*   assume, be biased, be inclined to think, be jaundiced, be prejudiced, believe, conjecture, count upon, decide beforehand, decide in advance, deduce, deem, determine beforehand, determine in advance, divine, draw an inference, estimate, expect, forejudge, gather, guess, have a bias, hypothesize, imagine, infer, intuit, judge, judge in advance, jump to a conclusion, opine, persuade oneself, posit, postulate, preconceive, preconclude, predecide, predetermine, preestimate, prefigurate, prefigure, prejudge, presume, presurmise, reckon, regard, rush to a conclusion, speculate, suppose, surmise, suspect, take for granted, theorize, think, trow, understand
ASSOCIATED CONCEPTS: presuppose a fact not in evidence

PRETEND, *verb*   act, affect, assume, be deceitful, be hypocritical, beguile, bemask, bluff, cheat, claim falsely, counterfeit, cozen, deceive, delude, disguise, dissemble, *dissimulare,* dissimulate, dupe, fake, falsify, feign, *fingere,* fool, give a false appearance, hide under a mask, hoodwink, imagine, imitate, impersonate, lie, make a pretext of, make a show, make believe, malinger, mask, masquerade, mimic, mislead, misrepresent, pass off, perform, play, play act, play false, portray, present falsely, prevaricate, profess, purport, put on, put on a false front, seem, sham, *simulare,* simulate, twist the truth

PRETENSE *(Ostentation),* **noun**   affectation, affectedness, airs, artificiality, blatancy, bravado, demonstration, display, empty show, false appearance, false show, fanfaronade, flagrancy, flashiness, flourish, fuss, garishness, gaudiness, glare, glitter, grandiosity, histrionics, impressive effect, inflation, insincerity, loftiness, mockery, obtrusiveness, *ostentatio,* ostentatiousness, outward show, panache, parade, pomp, pomposity, pompousness, pose, pretension, pretentiousness, sham, show, showiness, splash, splurge, theatricality, unnaturalness, window-dressing

PRETENSE *(Pretext),* **noun**   appearance, beguilement, bluff, camouflage, cheat, claim, cloak, color, cover, deceit, deception, disguise, duplicity, empty words, excuse, fabrication, false appearance, false plea, false show, falsehood, falseness, falsification, feint, forgery, fraud, fraudulence, guise, hoax, hypocrisy, imitation, invention, lie, mask, mendacity, misrepresentation, ostensible purpose, ostensible reason, plea, *postulatio,* professed purpose, ruse, semblance, sham, show, simulation, *simulatione,* subterfuge, trick, trickery, untruth
ASSOCIATED CONCEPTS: false pretense, fraudulent pretense, larceny by false pretense

PRETENTIOUS *(Ostentatious),* **adjective**
adorned, artificial, bespangled, brassy, conspicuous, decorated, embellished, flamboyant, flashy, fulgent, fulgid, garish, gaudy, *iactans,* meretricious, ornamented, ornate, *ornatus,* overly decorated, showy, superficial, tawdry

PRETENTIOUS *(Pompous),* **adjective**   affected, arrogant, boastful, boasting, bombastic, braggardly, braggart, conceited, extravagant, full of affectation, *gloriosus,* grandiloquent, grandiose, haughty, *iactans,* immodest, inflated, *inflatus,* opinionated, overdramatized, prideful, prim, self-admiring, self-applauding, self-esteeming, self-glorifying, self-important, self-satisfied, smug, snobbish, stilted, swollen, *theatralis,* tumid, *tumidus,* turgescent, turgid, vain, vainglorious

PRETERMIT, *verb*   abandon, avoid, bypass, cast aside, disregard, forget, gloss over, ignore, lay aside, leave, leave out, leave undone, let pass, miss, neglect, not care for, omit, overlook, pass, pass over, pay no attention to, pay no regard to, put aside, put off, shelve, skip, slight, suspend
ASSOCIATED CONCEPTS: pretermitted heir

PRETEXT, *noun*   affectation, alibi, alleged purpose, alleged reason, camouflage, charade, claim, cover, deception, defense, disguise, evasion, excuse, fabrication, false appearance, false ground, false motive, false pretense, false reason, false show, falsification, feint, fraud, guise, insincerity, invention, justification, lie, make-believe, mask, misrepresentation, misstatement, obfuscation, ostensible motive, ostensible purpose, ostensible reason, *praetextum,* pretense, pretension, professed purpose, profession, ruse, semblance, sham, shift, show, *simulatio,* simulation, *species,* stratagem, subterfuge, trick, trickery, untruth, wile
FOREIGN PHRASES: *Praetextu liciti non debet admitti illicitum.* That which is illegal ought not to be permitted under a pretext of legality.

PREVAIL *(Be in force),* **verb**   be in general use, control, dictate, direct, dominate, domineer, exist widely, govern, guide, have authority over, have charge of, have dominion over, have force, have superiority over, predominate, preponderate
ASSOCIATED CONCEPTS: prevailing rate of interest, prevailing rate of wages

PREVAIL *(Persuade),* **verb**   actuate, argue into, bring around, cajole, carry weight with, coax, convert, convince, enlist, gain the confidence of, guide, have effect, impel, incite, indoctrinate, induce, influence, inspire, inveigle, lure, motivate, move, *persuadere,* prompt, propagandize, seduce, sway, urge, wear down, win over, woo

PREVAIL *(Triumph),* **verb**   be a winner, be effective, be efficacious, be in control, be in general use, be in the ascendant, be prevalent, be successful, be the victor, be triumphant, be victorious, carry authority, command, conquer, control, dominate, exceed, excel, gain a victory, gain the advantage, gain the upper hand, get the upper hand, have mastery, have superiority, lead, master, meet with success, overcome, predominate, preponderate, prosper, quell, reign, rule, subdue, succeed, *superare,* suppress, surmount, surpass, take over, thrive, transcend, *vincere,* win
ASSOCIATED CONCEPTS: prevail in a court of law, prevailing party

PREVAIL UPON, *verb*   affect, be influential, beseech, bring over, bring to reason, carry weight with, coax, convince, encourage, enlist, entice, entreat, exercise influence over, exercise influence upon, exercise influence with, exhort, *exorare,* have influence over, have influence upon, have influence with, impel, importune, induce, influence, lead, motivate, move, move by persuasion, overcome another's resistence, persuade, *persuadere,* predispose, spur, sway, talk into, urge, wield influence, win over

PREVAILING *(Current), adjective* abundant, accepted, accustomary, accustomed, all-embracing, bourgeois, catholic, characteristic, colloquial, common, commonplace, comprehensive, conformable, contemporary, conventional, current, customary, diffuse, dominant, epidemic, established, everyday, extensive, familiar, frequent, general, generally accepted, global, habitual, in vogue, latest, natural, normal, pandemic, popular, predominant, prevalent, rampant, regular, rife, stock, sweeping, typical, universal, up-to-date, usual, vernacular, well-known, widely accepted, widespread, wonted, workaday, worldwide
ASSOCIATED CONCEPTS: prevailing conditions, prevailing rate, prevailing rate of interest

PREVAILING *(Having superior force), adjective* ascendant, authoritative, chief, commanding, conquering, controlling, defeating, determining, directing, dominant, dominating, effective, effectual, efficacious, forceful, governing, heading, hegemonic, hegemonical, influential, leading, mighty, moving, operative, overcoming, overruling, paramount, persuasive, potent, powerful, predominant, predominating, preponderant, preponderating, *puissant, régnant,* ruling, strong, successful, supreme, triumphal, triumphant, unvanquished, victorious, weighty, winning
ASSOCIATED CONCEPTS: prevailing party

PREVALENT, *adjective* abundant, accepted, accustomary, accustomed, all-embracing, ascendant, catholic, characteristic, chief, colloquial, common, commonplace, conformable, conventional, current, customary, dominant, epidemic, established, everyday, extensive, familiar, frequent, frequently met, general, generally accepted, global, habitual, household, normal, ordinary, pandemic, pedestrian, *pervulgatus,* popular, predominant, preponderant, prevailing, rampant, regular, rife, run of the mill, set, standard, stock, sweeping, typical, universal, vernacular, well-known, widely accepted, widely known, widespread, worldwide

PREVARICATE, *verb* be dishonest, be evasive, be untruthful, bear false witness, beg the question, belie, conceal the truth, concoct, counterfeit, deceive, defraud, delude, deviate, deviate from the truth, dissemble, dissimulate, distort, dodge, dupe, elude, equivocate, evade, evade the truth, fabricate, falsify, feign, fence, fergiversate, fib, forswear, gloss over, hedge, hoodwink, invent, lie, make believe, mince the truth, misguide, misinform, mislead, misrepresent, misstate, palter, parry, perjure, pervert, pretend, put on, quibble, sham, shift, shuffle, sophisticate, speak falsely, stretch the truth, tell a falsehood, tell a lie, tell an untruth, *tergiversari,* tergiversate, twist the truth
ASSOCIATED CONCEPTS: false swearing, perjury

PREVENT, *verb* arrest, avert, avoid, baffle, balk, bar, block, check, checkmate, circumvent, contest, counter, counteract, countercheck, cut off, debar, defeat, deflect, delay, detain, deter, discourage, estop, fend off, foil, forbid, foreclose, forestall, forfend, frustrate, halt, hamper, handicap, hinder, hold back, impede, *impedire,* inhibit, intercept, interfere, interrupt, keep

from, keep from happening, limit, muzzle, neutralize, *obstare,* obstruct, obviate, oppose, override, overrule, paralyze, parry, preclude, *prohibere,* prohibit, repress, restrain, restrict, retard, rule out, stave off, stay, stop, thwart, tie, turn aside, turn away, veto, ward off
ASSOCIATED CONCEPTS: prevent competition, prevent waste, prevented by law, prevention of performance
FOREIGN PHRASES: *Qui non prohibet id quod prohibere potest assentire videtur.* He who does not forbid what he is able to prevent, is deemed to assent.

PREVENTIVE, *adjective* alert, antidotal, antiseptic, arresting, aseptic, averting, blocking, careful, cautious, checking, counteractant, counteracting, defensive, deterrent, deterring, disinfectant, forestalling, germicidal, guarded, guarding, hindering, hygienic, impedimental, impeding, impeditive, inhibitive, inhibitory, interfering, judicious, neutralizing, obstructive, opposing, precautionary, preclusive, preservative, preventative, prohibitive, prophylactic, protecting, protective, provident, regardful, resistive, restraining, restrictive, retardant, safeguarding, shielding, thwarting, warding off, watchful

PREVIOUS, *adjective* above-cited, above-mentioned, above-named, aforementioned, aforesaid, already indicated, antecedent, anterior, earlier, early, erstwhile, first, fore, foregoing, foregone, forementioned, forerunning, former, initial, initiatory, introductory, one-time, past, precedent, preceding, precursive, precursory, preexistent, prefatorial, prefatory, preliminary, prelusive, prelusory, preparatory, prevenient, previously mentioned, prior
ASSOCIATED CONCEPTS: previous conviction, previous disability, previous injury, previous order, previously considered, previously determined, prior conduct, prior conviction, prior injury

PREY, *verb* commit violence, consume, depredate, despoil, destroy, devour, eat, extort, fatten upon, feast upon, feed upon, fleece, forage, foray, grab, gut, harass, harrow, hunt, kill, loot, maraud, oppress, parasitize, pillage, pirate, plague, plunder, *praedari,* profit by cheating, profit by swindling, raid, ransack, ravage, raven, ravish, rob, seize, spoil, spoliate, strip, torment, torture, victimize, waste

PRICE, *noun* amount, appraisal, appraisement, charge, compensation, cost, disbursement, due, estimate, estimation, exaction, exchange value, expenditure, expense, fare, fee, figure, outlay, payment, premium, *pretium,* purchase money, quotation, rate, recompense, selling price, toll, valuation, value, worth
ASSOCIATED CONCEPTS: abatement of price, contract price, established price, fair price, inadequacy of price, market price, market value, price adjustment, price control fee schedules, price discrimination, price fixing, reasonable price, retail price, stipulated price
FOREIGN PHRASES: *Emptor emit quam minimo potest, venditor vendit quam maximo potest.* The buyer purchases for the least he can; the seller sells for the most he can.

PRICELESS, *adjective* beyond price, commanding a high price, costly, dear, expensive, extraordinary, high, high-priced, *inaestimabilis,* incalculable, incomparable, inestimable, invaluable, irreplaceable, matchless, peerless, precious, *pretiosissimus,* rare, sterling, unequaled, valuable, without price

PRIDE, noun affectation, affected manner, affectedness, airs, boastfulness, braggadocio, braggartism, cockiness, condescension, coxcombry, dandyism, egoism, egotism, foppishness, haughtiness, hubris, immodesty, lordliness, narcissism, pomposity, satisfaction, self-admiration, self-applause, self-approval, self-esteem, self-exaltation, self-glorification, self-importance, self-satisfaction, smugness, snobbery, superciliousness, superiority, swagger, toploftiness, vain pretensions, vainglory, vanity

PRIMA FACIE *(Legally sufficient),* **adjective** adequate, lawfully sufficient, legally adequate, satisfactory, sufficient on its face, sufficient on the pleadings, sufficient to make out a case, sufficiently strong, suitable
ASSOCIATED CONCEPTS: prima facie case, prima facie claim, prima facie evidence, prima facie negligence, prima facie nuisance, prima facie proof, prima facie tort

PRIMA FACIE *(Self-evident),* **adjective** apparently, at first glance, at first sight, at first view, at sight, before further examination, by all appearances, on presentation, on the face of the matter, on the first view, ostensibly, presumably, seemingly, to all appearances

PRIMACY, noun ascendancy, authority, command, consequence, control, domination, dominion, eminence, excellency, first place, greatness, headship, hegemony, height, high position, hold, importance, influence, jurisdiction, lead, leadership, paramountcy, power, predominancy, predomination, preeminence, prestige, rule, seniority, sovereignty, supereminence, superiority, supremacy, supremeness, sway, weight

PRIMARY, adjective basal, basic, central, chief, constitutive, determining, dominant, earliest, elemental, elementary, essential, first, formative, fundamental, greatest, highest, important, inaugural, initial, key, leading, main, nascent, necessary, nonpareil, original, overriding, overruling, paramount, predominant, preeminent, prime, *primus,* principal, *principalis,* prominent, requisite, ruling, second to none, supereminent, supreme, topmost, transcendent, underlying, unsurpassed, uppermost, utmost, vital
ASSOCIATED CONCEPTS: primary boycott, primary evidence, primary insurance, primary jurisdiction, primary liability, primary picketing, primary purpose, primary right, primary surety, primary tort feasor

PRIMARY, noun ballot, choice, contest, contestation, election, election contest, exclusive competition, exclusive contest, exclusive election, exclusive political competition, exclusive political contest, first competition, first contest, first election, first political competition, first political contest, inaugural competition, inaugural contest, inaugural election, inaugural political competition, inaugural political contest, nomination contest, nominative competition, nominative contest, nominative election, partisan competition, partisan contest, partisan election, party competition, party contest, party election, political competition, political contention, political election, political rivalry, poll, preference, selection, vote
ASSOCIATED CONCEPTS: primary evidence, primary responsibility

PRIME *(Most valuable),* **adjective** best, beyond all praise, beyond compare, capital, cardinal, champion, chief, choice, crowning, dominant, eminent, excelling, exceptional, exemplary, exquisite, finest, first-class, first in quality, first-rate, foremost, front, greatest, head, highest, important, leading, matchless, nonpareil, of highest excellence, of the best quality, *optimas,* paramount, peerless, predominant, preeminent, preponderant, prevailing, priceless, principal, prize, prominent, remarkable, select, specially selected, splendid, superb, supereminent, superior, superlative, supreme, top, transcendant, unequaled, unmatched, unparalleled, unrivaled, unsurpassable, unsurpassed, utmost, without comparison

PRIME *(Original),* **adjective** aboriginal, authentic, basal, basic, beginning, dawning, earliest, early, elemental, elementary, embryonic, first, formative, fossil, fundamental, generative, genuine, germinal, inaugural, inceptive, incipient, initial, institutive, introductory, native, oldest, originative, primal, primary, primeval, primitive, primordial, *primus,* rudimentary, starting

PRIMOGENITOR, noun ancestor, ancestral relation, ancestral relative, antecedent, ascendant, elder, father, forebear, forefather, forerunner, founder of the family, grandsire, *origo,* parent, patriarch, precursor, predecessor, procreator

PRIMORDIAL, adjective aboriginal, archetypal, basal, basic, beginning, creative, elemental, elementary, first, fundamental, original, primal, primary, prime, primeval, primigenial, primitive, pristine, protogenic, prototypal, rudimentary, underived

PRINCIPAL, adjective cardinal, chief, controlling, dominant, essential, first, foremost, hegemonic, hegemonical, highest, leading, main, most considerable, most important, most powerful, outstanding, paramount, predominant, preeminent, prevailing, primal, primary, prime, *primus, princeps, principalis,* prominent, ruling, stellar, supereminent, supreme
ASSOCIATED CONCEPTS: principal activity, principal contract, principal contractor, principal obligation, principal place of business, principal sum, principal wrongdoing
FOREIGN PHRASES: *Omne principale trahit ad se accessorium.* Every principal thing draws the accessory to itself. *Quae accessionum locum obtinent, extinguuntur cum principales res peremptae fuerint.* When the principal thing is destroyed, those things which are accessory to it are also destroyed. *Sublato principali, tollitur adjunctum.* By the removal of the principal thing, the adjunct is also taken.

PRINCIPAL *(Capital sum),* **noun** assets, assets in hand, capital, *caput,* circulating capital, economic resources, fixed capital, fund, funds, gross amount, holdings, invested sum, main body, material assets, money, *nummi,* original sum, principal part, property, resources, *sors,* sum, sum total, tangible assets, totality, wealth, whole, working capital

PRINCIPAL *(Director),* **noun** boss, chief, chief actor, chief authority, chief executive, chief party, chieftain, commandant, commander, controller, directing head, director, employer, engager of services, executive, executive officer, foreperson, governor, head, headperson, *magister,* manager, master, overlooker, overseer, owner, person in authority, person in charge, proprietor, senior, superintendent, superior, supervisor, taskmaster

ASSOCIATED CONCEPTS: partially disclosed principal, principal in the first degree, undisclosed principal

FOREIGN PHRASES: *Nullus dicitur accessorius post feloniam, sed ille qui novit principalem feloniam fecisse, et illum receptavit et comfortavit.* No one is called an "accessory" after the fact but the one who knew the principal had committed a felony, and who received and comforted him. *Nullus dicitur felo principalis nisi actor, aut qui praesens est, abettans aut auxilians ad feloniam faciendam.* No one is called a principal felon except the party actually committing the felony, or the person who is present, aiding and abetting in its commission. *Res accessoria sequitur rem principalem.* An accessory follows the principal. *Qui per alium facit per seipsum facere videtur.* He who acts through another is deemed as having acted himself. *Ubi non est principalis, non potest esse accessorius.* Where there can be no principal, there cannot be an accessory.

PRINCIPLE *(Axiom), noun*   accepted belief, adage, admitted maxim, article of belief, article of faith, assertion, assurance, basic doctrine, basic law, basic rule, basic truth, belief, canon, conviction, credo, declaration of faith, *decretum,* doctrine, dogma, established rule, form, formula, formulated belief, foundation, fundamental doctrine, fundamental law, fundamental rule, gospel, *institutum,* instruction, intuitive truth, law, law of conduct, maxim, model, philosophy, policy, position, postulate, postulate of reason, precept, professed belief, profession of faith, proposition, provision, received maxim, recognized maxim, *regula,* regulation, reliance on, rubric, rule, rule of action, sage maxim, self-evident proposition, self-evident truth, settled principle, standard, statement of belief, statement of position, tenet, theorem, truism, way of thinking

ASSOCIATED CONCEPTS: equitable principle, legal principle

FOREIGN PHRASES: *Principia data sequuntur concomitantia.* Given principles are followed by their concomitants. *Principia probant, non probantur.* Principles prove, they are not proved. *Unumquodque principiorum est sibimetipsi fides; et perspicua vera non sunt probanda.* Every general principle is its own evidence, and plain truths need not be proved.

PRINCIPLE *(Virtue), noun*   character, conviction, ethics, goodness, honesty, honor, honorableness, incorruptibility, *integritas,* integrity, justice, moral excellence, moral rectitude, morality, nobleness, probity, rectitude, righteousness, rightfulness, scrupulousness, trustworthiness, truth, uprightness, virtuousness

PRIOR, *adjective*   antecedent, anterior, earlier, first, foregoing, former, inaugural, introductory, late, lead, leading, old, past, precedent, preceding, precursory, preexistent, prefatory, preliminary, preludial, prelusive, preparatory, prevenient, previous, proemial, quondam, *superior*

ASSOCIATED CONCEPTS: prior approval, prior conviction, prior lien, prior restraint

PRIORITY, *noun*   advantage, antecedence, commanding position, essential status, exigency, first place, importance, necessity, needfulness, precedence,

preeminence, preference, primacy, prior right, requisiteness, right-of-way, right to precedence, right to preference, seniority, superiority, supremacy, urgency, vitalness

ASSOCIATED CONCEPTS: priority of claim, priority of lien, priority statute

FOREIGN PHRASES: *Qui prior est tempore potior est jure.* He who is first in time is first in right. *Prior tempore potior jure.* First in time, superior in right.

PRISON, *noun*   bastille, *carcer,* cell, facility, house of correction, house of detention, house of reform, incarceration facility, jail, penal colony, penal institution, penitentiary, prison house, reformatory

ASSOCIATED CONCEPTS: prison term

FOREIGN PHRASES: *Carcer ad homines custodiendos, non ad puniendos, dari debet.* A prison should be used for the custody of men, and not for their punishment.

PRISONER, *noun*   captive, confined individual, convict, criminal, detainee, felon, hostage, incarcerated person, individual held in custody, individual jailed, inmate, internee, jailed person, person under arrest

PRIVACY, *noun*   concealment, confidentiality, confidentialness, delitescence, disassociation, dissociation, evasion, evasiveness, intimacy, isolation, obscurity, penetralia, privateness, quietude, retirement, retreat, seclusion, secrecy, secretiveness, separateness, separation, solitariness, solitude, *solitudo,* voluntary exile, withdrawal

ASSOCIATED CONCEPTS: invasion of privacy, right of privacy

PRIVATE *(Confidential), adjective*   abstruse, arcane, *arcanus,* clandestine, closet, concealed, covert, cryptic, cryptical, dark, esoteric, esoterical, hidden, intimate, inviolable, mysterious, off-the-record, personal, privy, recondite, secret, undercover, undisclosable, undivulgable, unrevealable

ASSOCIATED CONCEPTS: private papers, private writings

PRIVATE *(Not public), adjective*   closed, confined, exclusive, individual, individualized, limited, nonofficial, nonpublic, not open, personalized, *privatus,* reserved, restricted, select, unofficial

ASSOCIATED CONCEPTS: private action, private agreement, private bill, private carrier, private corporation, private detective, private dwelling, private employment, private enterprise, private grant, private institution, private investigator, private nuissance, private property, private purposes, private sale, private statute, private trust, private use

FOREIGN PHRASES: *Privatum incommodum publico bono pensatur.* Private inconvenience is compensated for by public benefit. *Pactis privatorum juri publico non derogatur.* Private contracts do not derogate from public law. *Jura publica anteferenda privatis.* Public rights are to be preferred to private rights.

PRIVATE *(Secluded), adjective*   apart, cloistered, hidden, inaccessible, insular, isolated, out-of-the-way, quiet, remote, removed, seclusive, separate, solitary, unfrequented

PRIVATION, *noun*   absence, attachment, bad fortune, bad luck, bankruptcy, beggary, bereavement, confiscation, dearth, deprivation, deprivement, destitution, dispossession, dissipation, distress, divestment, *egestas,* exhaustion, famine, financial straits, hardship, impecuniosity, impecuniousness, indigence, *inopia,* insufficiency, lack, loss, loss of fortune, mendicancy, mendicity, narrow means, necessitude, necessity, need, neediness, pauperism, penury, pinch, poverty, reduced circumstances, riddance, sequestration, starvation, straitened means, want

PRIVILEGE, noun advantage, affranchisement, allowance, authority, authorization, *beneficium,* benefit, chance, charter, dispensation, enfranchisement, entitlement, exemption, favor, franchise, freedom, grant, honor, *immunitas,* immunity, indulgence, liberty, license, opportunity, permission, perquisite, prerogative, priority, release, right, sanction, title, tolerance, vouchsafement, warrant
ASSOCIATED CONCEPTS: executive privilege, immunity, privilege against self-incrimination, privileged communications, privileged statement, privileges and immunities, qualified privilege
FOREIGN PHRASES: *Privilegium est beneficium personale, et extinguitur cum persona.* A privilege is a personal benefit, and is extinguished with the death of the person. *Privilegium non valet contra rempublicam.* A privilege is of no avail against the state. *Necessitas inducit privilegium quo ad jura privata.* Necessity gives a privilege with reference to private rights.

PRIVILEGED, adjective allowed, authorized, chartered, empowered, entitled, excepted, excluded, excused, exempt, exempted, favored, franchised, free of, immune, *immunis,* immunized, licensed, not accountable, not subject, permitted, sanctioned, specially provided for, unrestrained
ASSOCIATED CONCEPTS: privileged communications, privileged information, privileged matter

PRIVITY, noun affiliation, attachment, connecting medium, connection, contractual bond, derivative interest, interconnection, legal relationship, link, mutual relationship, mutuality of interest, nexus, relation, relationship, successive relationship, tie
ASSOCIATED CONCEPTS: privity of contract, privity of estate, privity of possession

PRIVY, adjective acquainted with, arcane, auricular, buried, clandestine, cognizant of, concealed, confidential, covert, cryptic, cryptical, dark, exclusive, furtive, hidden, inmost, limited, murky, mysterious, nonpublic, obscure, personal, private, recondite, reserved, restricted, secret, sequestered, stealthy, surreptitious, undisclosed, unrevealed

PRIVY, noun contracting party, interested party, partaken, participant, party
ASSOCIATED CONCEPTS: parties and privies

PRIZE, noun accolade, advantage, award, blue ribbon, bonus, booty, bounty, capture, catch, cordon, cup, decoration, distinction, find, first place, gain, guerdon, honor, inducement, jackpot, loot, medal, meed, payment, pillage, plum, plunder, *praemium,* premium, prey, privilege, recompense, reward, spoil, title, token, trophy, winning

PRO FORMA, adjective as a matter of form, by course of conduct, by custom, by habit, by past practice, by trade and usage, by usage, ceremoniously, common, customary, for the sake of appearances, for the sake of form, formally, in due form, in set form, ritualistically, ritually, standard, superficially, usual
ASSOCIATED CONCEPTS: pro forma decree, pro forma judgment, pro forma order

PRO RATA, adjective alloted, apportioned, appropriately, distributed, equivalently, in proportion, on even terms, proportionate
ASSOCIATED CONCEPTS: apportionment, pro rata share

PRO RATA, adverb each to each, in equal shares, proportionately, respectively, to each according to his share

PRO TEMPORE, adverb briefly, for a time, for the moment, for the present occasion, for the time being, momentarily, pro tem, provisionally, temporarily, transitorily

PROBABILITY, noun anticipation, appearance of truth, believability, chance, conceivability, credibility, credibleness, expectation, fair chance, fair expectation, favorable chance, liability, liableness, likelihood, likeliness, odds, ostensibility, plausibility, possibility, presumption, promise, prospect, reasonable chance, reasonableness, susceptibility, tendency, *veri similitudo,* verisimilitude

PROBABLE, adjective apparent, apt, believable, conceivable, conjecturable, credible, feasible, foreseeable, full of promise, indubitable, liable, likely, logical, ostensible, plausible, possible, practicable, presumable, presumptive, promising, reasonable, seeming, supposed, surmisable, to be expected, unquestionable, *veri similis,* verisimilar, verisimilous
ASSOCIATED CONCEPTS: probable cause

PROBATE, noun authentication of a will, authentication proceeding, judicial validation of a will, proof of the validity of a will, proof of the will, validation of a testament, validity proceedings, will validation proceeding, will verification proceeding

PROBATE, verb adjudge the validity of a will, adjudicate the validity of a will, authenticate a will, certify a will, confirm the validity of a will, establish the authenticity of a will, establish the genuineness of a will, establish the validity of a will, prove the validity of a will, substantiate, validate a will, verify a testament
ASSOCIATED CONCEPTS: probate a will, probate court, probate proceeding

PROBATION, noun conditional suspension of sentence, exemption, freedom, liberation, parole, period of testing, period of trial, *probatio,* release
ASSOCIATED CONCEPTS: parole, probation term, probationary employee, revocation of probation

PROBATIONER *(One being tested),* **noun** apprentice, beginner, candidate, entrant, initiate, learner, neophyte, newcomer, novice, novitiate, *tiro*

PROBATIONER *(Released offender),* **noun** criminal released at large, criminal under suspension of sentence, lawbreaker under suspension of sentence, malefactor under suspension of sentence, offender under suspension of sentence, parolee, released convict, released criminal, released felon, released lawbreaker, released malefactor, released prisoner, released transgressor, released wrongdoer, wrongdoer released from prison

PROBATIVE, *adjective* demonstrative, empiric, empirical, evidential, evidentiary, experimental, exploratory, offering evidence, probatory, providing evidence, providing proof, verificative
ASSOCIATED CONCEPTS: probative evidence, probative facts, probative value, probative weight

PROBE, *noun* analysis, careful search, critical examination, deep study, examination, exhaustive study, exploration, exploratory examination, indagation, inquiry, inspection, investigation, perquisition, perscrutation, pursuit, quest, research, review, rigorous search, *rimari, scrutari,* scrutiny, search, searching examination, strict examination

PROBE, *verb* check over, conduct an inquiry, conduct research on, consider attentively, delve into, dig into, dissect, examine, explore, follow up, indagate, inquire into, inspect, institute an inquiry, interrogate, investigate, look into, make an examination, make inquiries, observe, peruse, plumb, poke into, pry into, pursue an inquiry, put to the test, question, review, *rimari,* run checks on, scan, *scrutari,* scrutinize, search into, seek, seek information regarding, study, study in detail, subject to scrutiny, take up an inquiry, unearth

PROBITY, *noun* candidness, candor, conscience, dependability, deservingness, equitableness, equity, fair play, fairness, faith, frankness, good faith, goodness, guilelessness, high principles, honesty, honor, honorableness, impartiality, incorruptibility, ingenuousness, integrity, justice, merit, moral excellence, morality, morals, principle, *probitas,* rectitude, reputability, righteousness, scrupulousness, sincerity, straightforwardness, trustiness, trustworthiness, truth, truthfulness, undeceptiveness, uprightness, veraciousness, veracity, virtue

PROBLEM, *noun* anxiety, bafflement, bone of contention, care, cause for concern, complexity, complication, crisis, difficulty, dilemma, enigma, exercise, matter in dispute, moot point, mystery, obstacle, plight, point in dispute, point to be settled, predicament, puzzle, quandary, question, riddle, source of perplexity, stumper, subject of dispute, tight situation, trouble, vexed question

PROBLEMATIC, *adjective* ambiguous, complex, complicated, contestable, controversial, controvertible, cryptic, cryptical, debatable, difficult, disputable, doubtful, dubious, *dubius,* enigmatic, enigmatical, equivocal, imperspicuous, *incertus,* insoluble, involved, knotty, moot, mysterious, open to doubt, paradoxical, perplexing, problematical, puzzling, questionable, raveled, shrouded in mystery, snarled, tangled, tentative, troublesome, uncertain, unconvincing, undecided, undemonstrable, undetermined, unsettled, vague, worrisome

PROCEDURAL, *adjective* adjective, directive, functional, methodical, operative, relating to method, relating to the mechanics of a lawsuit, relative to the manner of proceeding, systematic
ASSOCIATED CONCEPTS: procedural defect, procedural due process, procedural law, procedural matter, procedural question, procedural right, procedural rule of law, procedural statute

PROCEDURE, *noun* act, action, adjective law, behavior, common practice, conduct, course, course of action, custom, established method, habit, line of action, manner of proceeding, manner of working, matter of course, measure, method, methodology, mode, mode of operation, mode of use, modus operandi, motion, order, particular course of action, plan, plan of action, policy, practice, proceeding, process, program, proscribed form, routine, rule, scheme, set form, set format, step, strategy, system, tactics, usage, way, way of operation
ASSOCIATED CONCEPTS: civil procedure, criminal procedure, judicial procedure, pretrial procedure, rule of procedure
FOREIGN PHRASES: *Cursus curiae est lex curiae.* The practice of the court is the law of the court.

PROCEED *(Continue), verb* begin again, begin where one left off, carry on, get back to work, get on, recommence, reinstate, renew, resume, return, take up again

PROCEED *(Go forward), verb* act, advance, arise, emanate, ensue, extend, flow, follow, follow a course, gain ground, get ahead, get on, go, go ahead, go forth, issue, keep going, keep moving, make headway, make progress, make rapid strides, move ahead, move forward, pass on, press on, progress, propel oneself, push ahead, push on, roll on, spring, take steps
ASSOCIATED CONCEPTS: proceed with a case, proceed with due diligence

PROCEEDING, *noun* *actio,* action, action at law, case, cause, conduct of a lawsuit, course of an action at law, dispute, hearing, lawsuit, legal action, legal procedure, litigation, matter, performance, prescribed method of action, prescribed mode of action, procedure, process, prosecution, series of events, step, steps in the prosecution of an action, suit, suit at law, transaction, trial, undertaking
ASSOCIATED CONCEPTS: abandonment of a proceeding, annulment proceeding, arbitration proceeding, bankruptcy proceeding, bastardy proceeding, certiorari proceeding, commencement of a proceeding, condemnation proceeding, contempt proceeding, criminal proceeding, custody proceeding, discontinuance of a proceeding, enforcement proceeding, equitable proceeding, extraordinary proceeding, filiation proceeding, garnishment proceeding, guardianship proceeding, habeas corpus proceeding, in personam proceeding, in rem proceeding, judicial proceeding, lawful proceeding, legal proceeding, liquidation proceeding, mandamus proceeding, official proceeding, partition proceeding, pending proceeding, plenary proceeding, probate proceeding, public proceeding, quasi in rem proceeding, special proceeding, supplementary proceeding, testamentary proceeding, void proceeding

PROCEEDS, *noun* avails, balance, benefit, earnings, effect, end result, gain, gross profit, income, money coming in, net profit, produce, product, profit, receipts, *reditus,* renumeration, result, returns, revenue, sum derived from a sale, value received, yield
ASSOCIATED CONCEPTS: proceeds of a crime, proceeds of a sale, proceeds of an insurance policy

PROCESS *(Course), noun* action, conduct, continued movement, continuing development, handling, line of action, manner, means, method, methodology, mode of operation, operation, performance, plan, policy, procedure, progressive course, *ratio,* regular proceeding, ritual, routine, scheme, series of measures, strategy, system, tactics, transaction, treatment, way, ways and means

ASSOCIATED CONCEPTS: due process, judicial process

PROCESS *(Summons),* **noun**   authoritative citation to appear before a court, authoritative command, behest, bidding, citation, command, direction, instruction to appear, legal call, *lis,* official call, official notice, requirement to appear, signal by which one is summoned, subpoena, writ

ASSOCIATED CONCEPTS: abuse of process, compulsory process, defective process, irregular process, return of process, service of process

PROCLAIM, verb   advertise, air, announce, annunciate, assert, asseverate, blare, blaze abroad, broach, broadcast, bruit, call out, circulate, communicate, cry, *declarare,* declare, disseminate, divulge, enounce, exclaim, gazette, give notice of, give out, hawk about, herald, inform, make a proclamation, make known, make public, noise abroad, *praedicare,* promulgate, *pronuntiare,* propagate, publicize, publish, release, report, set forth, sing out, sound forth, spread abroad, state, tell, thunder forth, trumpet, utter, ventilate

PROCLAMATION, noun   announcement, annunciation, declaration, decree, decretal, edict, *edictum,* exclamation, fiat, mandate, manifesto, message, notification, official publication, promulgation, pronouncement, public announcement, public avowal, public notice, publication, recitation, rescript, statement

PROCLIVITY, noun   ability, appetence, appetency, aptitude, aptness, bent, bias, disposition, facility, gift, gravitation, inclination, inherent ability, innate disposition, innate sense, instinct, leaning, liking, natural sense, partiality, penchant, predilection, predisposition, prejudice, *proclivitas,* proneness, propensity, readiness, talent, tendency, turn

PROCRASTINATE, verb   adjourn, be dilatory, be idle, be inert, be neglectful, block, dally, dawdle, defer, delay, *differre,* dilly dally, do nothing, filibuster, gain time, hang back, hesitate, hold back, hold up, idle, keep one waiting, kill time, lag, let slide, let slip, let the matter stand, linger, loaf, loiter, neglect, pause, pigeonhole, play for time, postpone, *procrastinare,* prolong, prorogue, protract, push aside, put off, retard, shelve, stall, stave off, suspend, table, tarry, wait, waste time

PROCTOR, noun   advocate, agent, appointee, broker, caretaker, delegate, deputy, functionary, instrument, lawyer, lieutenant, manager, minister, monitor, officer, procurator, proxy, representative, second, steward, surrogate, vicar

PROCURATOR, noun   administrator, adviser, agent, appointee, assistant, broker, business representative, caretaker, conductor, *curator,* delegate, deputy, director, emissary, envoy, executor, factor, go-between, intendant, intermediary, intermediate, intermedium, *legatus,* lieutenant, manager, middleman, *moderator,* monitor, overseer, proctor, prolocutor, proxy, representative, solicitor, spokesman, steward, substitute, superintendent, supervisor, syndic, viceregent

PROCURE, verb   accomplish, accumulate, achieve, acquire, appropriate, attain, bag, bring, buy, capture, cause, come by, commandeer, *comparare,* dig up, earn, effect, enlist, fetch, find, force from, gain, gather, get, glean, help oneself to, hire, lay hands on, make a purchase, obtain, pick up, provide, purchase, realize, reap, receive, secure, seize, take, take possession of

PRODIGAL, adjective   careless, dissipated, dissipative, excessive, extravagant, heedless, immoderate, improvident, imprudent, intemperate, lavish, liberal, profligate, reckless, spendthrift, squandering, thriftless, unbridled, uncurbed, uneconomical, unfrugal, unrestrained, unthrifty, wanton, wasteful

PRODIGIOUS *(Amazing),* **adjective**   abnormal, anomalous, astonishing, astounding, bizarre, curious, dumbfounding, exceptional, extraordinary, fantastic, freakish, grotesque, impressive, inconceivable, incredible, indescribable, marvelous, miraculous, noteworthy, out of the common run, out of the ordinary, outlandish, overwhelming, peculiar, phenomenal, queer, remarkable, renowned, singular, startling, strange, striking, supernormal, surprising, unaccountable, unaccustomed, uncommon, unconventional, uncustomary, unexampled, unfamiliar, unheard of, unimaginable, unique, unprecedented, unthinkable, weird, wonderful, wondrous

PRODIGIOUS *(Enormous),* **adjective**   astronomical, big, colossal, cyclopean, elephantine, gargantuan, giant, gigantic, grand, great, Herculean, huge, *immanis,* immense, *ingens,* large, leviathan, mammoth, massive, mighty, monster, monstrous, monumental, sizable, stupendous, substantial, terrific, thumping, titanic, towering, tremendous, vast, whopping

PRODUCE *(Manufacture),* **verb**   accomplish, achieve, assemble, bear, beget, breed, bring about, bring forth, bring into being, bring into existence, bring to pass, build, coin, compose, conceive, concoct, construct, contrive, create, devise, draw up, effect, effectuate, engender, erect, execute, fabricate, fashion, form, formulate, furnish, generate, give birth to, give rise to, hatch, institute, invent, make, make up, originate, prepare, procreate, propagate, provide, raise, realize, result in, turn out, yield

ASSOCIATED CONCEPTS: producing cause

PRODUCE *(Offer to view),* **verb**   air, bring forward, bring into view, bring out, bring to light, bring to the fore, bring to the front, demonstrate, disclose, display, divulge, dramatize, evidence, evince, exhibit, expose, give a performance, hold up to view, impart, lay bare, lay out, make known, make visible, manifest, parade, present, put on display, put on the stage, reveal, set out, show, uncover, unfold, unmask, unscreen, unveil

ASSOCIATED CONCEPTS: failure to produce, notice to produce, produce a witness, produce evidence

PRODUCT, noun   accomplishment, article, article of merchandise, article of trade, commodity, creation, crop, effect, emanation, end result, final outcome, fruit, handiwork, harvest, invention, issue, item, merchandise, offspring, *opus,* outcome, output, proceeds, produce, result, salable commodity, stock in trade, yield

ASSOCIATED CONCEPTS: product defect, product patent, products liability

PRODUCTIVE, *adjective*   advantageous, causative, constructive, creational, creative, demiurgic, demiurgical, efficient, fecund, *ferax,* fertile, formative, fructiferous, fructuous, fruitful, gainful, imaginative, industrial, inventive, life-giving, luxuriant, manufacturing, original, originative, paying, potent, pregnant, profitable, proliferative, proliferous, prolific, rank, remunerative, resourceful, rich, teeming, *uber,* useful, valuable, worthwhile, yielding

PROFANE, *adjective*   bad, blasphemous, coarse, common, damnatory, dirty, disrespectful, evil, execrative, faithless, foul-spoken, foulmouthed, godless, impious, *impius,* imprecative, imprecatory, improper, impure, indelicate, irreligious, irreverant, laic, laical, lay, maledictive, maledictory, miscreant, mundane, peccable, peccant, polluted, *profanus,* sacrilegious, secular, shameless, sinful, smutty, temporal, transient, transitory, unblest, unconsecrated, undevout, ungodly, unhallowed, unholy, unprintable, unreligious, unsacred, unsaintly, unsanctified, unspeakable, unvirtuous, vice-ridden, virtueless, vulgar, wicked, worldly

PROFANITY, *noun*   billingsgate, blasphemy, cursing, denunciation, derisive language, desecration, disparagement, disrespect, execration, foul language, foul talk, *impietas,* invective, malediction, obloquy, profanation, profane language, profaneness, swearing, vilification, vituperation, vulgarity
ASSOCIATED CONCEPTS: censorship, obscenity

PROFESS *(Avow),* *verb*   acknowledge, admit, advocate, affirm, announce, assert, asseverate, assure, attest, aver, avouch, contend, declare, disclose, divulge, hold out, lay bare, lay open, maintain, make a statement, make an assertion, make clear, make evident, make known, own, pledge, proclaim, pronounce, put forth, put forward, reveal, set forth, state, subscribe to, tell, utter

PROFESS *(Pretend),* *verb*   affect, claim, concoct, counterfeit, create a false impression, disguise, dissemble, dissimulate, fabricate, feign, give a false impression, imagine, make a show of, make believe, pass for, posture, practice chicanery, put a false construction upon, represent fictitiously, sham, simulate

PROFESSION *(Declaration),* *noun*   affirmation, announcement, assertion, assurance, attestation, averment, avowal, claim, confession, declaration of faith, disclosure, enunciation, notification, oath, pledge, presentation, *professio,* pronouncement, representation, statement, troth, vow, word, word of honor

PROFESSION *(Vocation),* *noun*   association, avocation, business, calling, career, chosen work, concern, craft, employment, endeavor, engagement, field, job, learned profession, lifework, line of work, *manus,* occupation, office, position, practice, pursuit, role, specialty, trade, undertaking, vocation, walk of life, work
ASSOCIATED CONCEPTS: professional corporation

PROFESSIONAL *(Stellar),* *adjective*   admirable, businesslike, choice, commendable, excellent, exemplary, foremost, highest quality, illustrious, incomparable, laudable, model, paramount, praiseworthy, preeminent, prime, principal, sterling, superb, superior, unequaled, unexcelled, unrivaled, unsurpassed, well done

PROFESSIONAL *(Trained),* *adjective*   able, adept, career, competent, established, experienced, expert, learned, proficient, qualified, skilled, skillful, specialized, trained, well-qualified
ASSOCIATED CONCEPTS: professional capacity, professional corporation, professional ethics, professional misconduct, professional opinion, professional skill and judgment

PROFESSIONAL, *noun*   accomplished practitioner, adept practitioner, adroit practitioner, authority, competent practitioner, experienced person, expert, master, practiced individual, practitioner, proficient practitioner, qualified practitioner, skilled practitioner, skilled technician, specialist, trained person
ASSOCIATED CONCEPTS: professional opinion

PROFFER, *verb*   adduce, advance, advertise, bid, bring forward, donate, extend, give, hold out, invite, lay before, make a bid, make a motion, make an offer, make an overture, make possible, move, offer, prefer, present, promise, *promittere,* propose, propound, put forward, put up, render, set forth, submit, suggest, tender, volunteer

PROFICIENT, *adjective*   able, accomplished, adept, adequate, adroit, advanced, capable, clever, competent, conversant, cunning, deft, dexterous, effective, efficacious, efficient, equal to, excellent, experienced, expert, facile, good, habilitated, handy, ingenious, knowing, masterful, *peritus,* practiced, qualified, quick, ready, *sciens,* skilled, skillful, talented, trained, up to, well-qualified, well-versed

PROFIT, *noun*   accruance, accumulation, acquisition, advancement, advantage, augmentation, avails, benefaction, benefit, clearance, compensation, dividend, earnings, emolument, financial reward, *fructus,* fruits, gain, growth, harvest, improvement, incentive, income, increase, increment, interest, *lucrum,* meed, output, pay, payment, premium, prize, proceeds, produce, *quaestus,* realization, receipts, remuneration, return, revenue, reward, service, take, utility, value received, windfall, winnings, yield
ASSOCIATED CONCEPTS: accumulated profits, anticipated profits, capital, carrying on business for profit, distributable profits, excessive profits, excess profits tax, gross profit, loss of profits, margin of profit, net profit, not for profit, pecuniary profits, profit a prendre, profit sharing, prospective profit, remote profits, secret profits, speculative profits, surplus profits, underwriting profits, undistributed profits
FOREIGN PHRASES: *Ubi periculum, ibi et lucrum collocatur.* He who risks a thing, should receive the profits arising from it.

PROFIT, *verb*   acquire, advance, assist, avail, be better for, be improved by, be of use, benefit, cash in on, clear, confer a benefit on, contribute, draw profit from, edify, gain, gain advantage, harvest, help, improve, learn a lesson from, make capital out of, make good use of, make improvement, make money by, make use of, obtain a return, produce a good effect, produce a good result, *proficere,* put to use, realize, reap, reap the fruits, turn to account, use, utilize, yield returns

PROFITABLE, *adjective*   advantageous, advisable, aiding, assisting, beneficial, desirable, edifying, emolumental, expedient, favorable, *fructuosus, frugifer,* fruitful, gainful, helpful, invaluable, lucrative, money-making, paying, productive, remunerative, rewarding, salutary, serviceable, successful, *utilis,* valuable, well-paying, worthwhile

PROFLIGATE *(Corrupt),* **adjective**   abandoned to vice, base, corrupted, debauched, degenerate, depraved, disgraceful, disreputable, dissipated, dissipative, dissolute, evil, evil-minded, fallen, flagitious, foul, heinous, immoral, indecent, infamous, iniquitous, lacking decency, lacking principle, lacking shame, lawless, lost to principle, lost to virtue, morally evil, nefarious, offensive, peccant, *perditus,* rascally, rotten, scampish, shameful, shameless, sinful, unethical, unprincipled, unredeemable, unregenerate, unrepentant, vice-ridden, vicious, vile, vitiated, wicked

PROFLIGATE *(Extravagant),* **adjective**   economically imprudent, immoderate, improvident, intemperate, overly liberal, prodigal, *profligatus,* reckless, spendthrift, squandering, thriftless, unrestrained, unthrifty, wasteful

PROFOUND *(Esoteric),* **adjective**   abstruse, acroamatic, acroamatical, acroatic, astute, complicated, erudite, esoteric, gnostic, intellectual, intellectually deep, knowing, learned, oracular, penetrating, perceptive, philosophical, recondite, reflective, sagacious, sage, scholarly, thoughtful, wise

PROFOUND *(Intense),* **adjective**   abysmal, acute, bottomless, deep, deeply felt, fathomless, great, heart-stirring, heartfelt, heavy, impressive, indelible, intense, moving, penetrating, piercing, sharp, soul-stirring, strong, touching, unfathomable, vivid

PROFUSE, **adjective**   abounding, abundant, affluent, ample, boundless, bounteous, bountiful, copious, countless, crowded, diffuse, discursive, *effusus,* endless, excessive, exorbitant, extravagant, exuberant, flush, full, garrulous, generous, illimitable, immeasurable, immoderate, improvident, incalculable, inexhaustible, infinite, innumerable, inordinate, intemperate, interminable, lavish, liberal, limitless, long-winded, loquacious, luxuriant, measureless, multitudinary, multitudinous, munificent, myriad, numberless, numerous, overabounding, overflowing, overgenerous, padded, plentiful, prodigal, profligate, *profusus,* prolific, prolix, protracted, rambling, reckless, redundant, replete, rich, rife, spendthrift, squandering, sumptious, superfluous, surplus, swarming, teeming, thriftless, unbridled, uncurbed, unnumbered, unsparing, unstinted, unstinting, unthrifty, unwarranted, verbose, wanton, wasteful, without bound, without end, without limit, without stint, wordy

PROGENITOR, **noun**   ancestor, antecedent, antecessor, begettor, forebear, forefather, foregoer, forerunner, genitor, origin, *parens,* parent, precursor, predecessor, primogenitor, procreator, sire, source

PROGENY, **noun**   bloodline, brood, children, descendants, family, fruit, heirs, issue, line, lineage, offspring, posterity, *progenies,* scions, seed, sons, stock, succeeding generations, tribe, young

PROGNOSIS, **noun**   conjecture, estimate, foreboding, forecast, foreknowledge, foresight, foretelling, guess, opinion, preannouncement, prediction, pre-figuration, prefigurement, premonition, prenotice, presage, presagement, presumption, prognostication, promise, prophesy, supposition, vaticination

PROGNOSTICATE, **verb**   advise, augur, augurate, auspicate, betoken, bode, conjecture, counsel, divine, forebode, forecast, foresee, foresee the future, foreshadow, foreshow, foretell, foretoken, herald, indicate beforehand, indicate in advance, look ahead to, look forward to, make a prediction, ominate, portend, preannounce, predict, premonish, premonstrate, presage, presignify, presume, promise, prophesy, signify, soothsay, speculate, spell, surmise, tell fortunes, theorize, vaticinate

PROGRAM, **noun**   agenda, arrangement, blueprint, calendar, campaign, catalogue, course, curriculum, design, docket, draft, list, order, outline, plan, policy, presentation, project, proposal, prospectus, schedule, series of events, set of tactics, strategy, syllabus, system

PROGRAM, **verb**   arrange, block out, book, budget, calendar, design, determine, devise, direct, docket, draft, engineer, *excogitare,* form a plan, frame, lay a plan, lay out, list, make an agenda, make arrangements, manage, map out, organize, outline, plan, plot, preconcert, predetermine, preestablish, project, register, schedule, scheme, sketch, slate, work out

PROGRESS, **noun**   accomplishment, achievement, advance, advancement, amelioration, augmentation, betterment, change, development, emendation, enhancement, enrichment, flow, furtherance, gain, growth, headway, improvement, increase, increment, march, melioration, movement, movement forward, onward motion, passage, perfection, preferment, progression, *progressus,* promotion, reclamation, recovery, redemption, reform, rehabilitation, reorganization, restoration, rise, steady advance, success

PROGRESS, **verb**   advance, ameliorate, approach, ascend, become better, climb, continue onward, convalesce, develop, enhance, enrich, expand, forge ahead, gain, gain ground, get ahead, go ahead, go forward, go on, grow, grow better, grow up, improve, increase, keep going, keep moving, make headway, make progress, maturate, mature, meliorate, mend, mount, move ahead, move on, move onward, press on, press onward, proceed, *proficere, progredi,* prosper, push on, recuperate, ripen, rise

PROGRESSIVE *(Advocating   change),* **adjective** advanced, corrective, emendatory, enterprising, forward looking, improvement-minded, liberal, modern, open-minded, reformational, reformative, reformatory, remedial, up to date

PROGRESSIVE *(Going   forward),* **adjective**   advancing, consecutive, continuous, dynamic, endless, forward, forward moving, growing, moving, ongoing, proceeding, profluent, rising, serial, successive, transitional, traveling, uninterrupted

PROHIBIT, **verb**   ban, banish, bar, block, check, circumscribe, control, counteract, curb, debar, deny, disallow, disqualify, embargo, enjoin, exclude, forbid, foreclose, forfend, gainsay, halt, hamper, hinder, impede, inhibit, interdict, interfere, limit, make illegal, negate, negative, obstruct, omit, oppose, preclude, prevent, proscribe, protest, quash, quell, refuse, refuse permission, regulate, reject, repress, repudiate, restrain, restrict, revoke, shut out, smother, stay, stop, suppress, suspend, thwart, traverse, veto

ASSOCIATED CONCEPTS: prohibited action, prohibited by law, prohibited form, prohibited practice

FOREIGN PHRASES: *Contra legem facit qui id facit quod lex prohibit; in fraudem vero qui, salvis verbis legis, sententiam ejus circumvenit.* He who does what the law prohibits, acts in fraud of the law; the letter of the law being inviolate, cheats the spirit of it. *Cui licet quod majus, non debet quod minus est non licere.* He who is allowed to do the greater ought not to be prohibited from doing the less. *Idem est facere, et nolle prohibere cum possis.* It is the same thing to commit an act as not to prohibit it when it is in your power.

PROHIBITION, noun ban, banishment, bar, barrier, block, check, circumscription, constraint, counterorder, curb, debarment, denial, determent, deterrence, deterrent, disallowance, discouragement, disqualification, elimination, embargo, enforced abstention, enjoining, eradication, estoppel, exclusion, forbiddance, hindrance, illegality, illegitimacy, impediment, inhibition, injunction, interdict, interdiction, *interdictum,* interference, limit, limitation, negation, nonadmission, noninclusion, obstacle, obstruction, ostracism, outlawry, preclusion, prevention, proscription, refusal, rejection, repression, repudiation, restraint, restriction, stay, stop, stoppage, suppression, taboo, traversal, unconstitutionality, unlawfulness, veto

ASSOCIATED CONCEPTS: injunctions, restraining orders, statutory prohibition, writ of prohibition

FOREIGN PHRASES: *Semper qui non prohibet pro se intervenire, mandare creditur.* He who does not prohibit the intervention of another in his behalf is deemed to have authorized it. *Quando aliquid prohibetur ex directo, prohibetur et per obliquum.* When anything is prohibited directly, it is also prohibited indirectly.

PROHIBITIVE *(Costly), adjective* exorbitant, expensive, extortionate, extravagant, high-priced, immoderate, inordinate, preposterous, unconscionable, undue, unreasonable, unwarranted

PROHIBITIVE *(Restrictive), adjective* deterrent, disallowing, disqualifying, exclusive, exclusory, hindering, impeding, impossible, inhibitive, inhibitory, injunctive, interdictive, interdictory, interfering, limitative, limiting, obstructive, preclusive, preventing, preventive, prohibitory, proscriptive, repressive, restraining, suppressive

PROJECT, noun activity, aim, ambition, assignment, attempt, *consilium,* contrivance, deal, design, determination, device, employment, end, endeavor, engagement, enterprise, essay, fixed intention, goal, idea, *inceptum,* intent, intention, job, object, objective, occupation, outline, plan, projected campaign, projected scheme, proposal, proposition, *propositum,* purpose, pursuit, resolution, scheme, set purpose, task, undertaking, venture

PROJECT *(Extend beyond), verb* arch, bulge, hang over, jut, jut out, lengthen, overhang, protrude, protuberate, stand out, stick out, widen

PROJECT *(Impel forward), verb* cast, discharge, drive, eject, emit, expel, fling, hurl, launch, let fly, propel, push, send, send off, shoot forward, sling, throw, thrust, traject

PROLEPSIS, noun apriorism, assumption, hypothesis, postulation, presupposition

PROLIFERATE, verb abound, be fruitful, be numerous, be plentiful, blossom, breed, bud, burgeon, fecundate, fecundify, flourish, flower, grow, grow in number, have offspring, have progeny, increase the number of, make manifold, *multiplicare,* multiply, mushroom, produce rapidly, propagate, reproduce, reproduce in kind, reproduce rapidly, spawn, spread, sprout, swell, thrive, wax

PROLIFIC, adjective abundant, breedy, copious, creative, fecund, feracious, fertile, fruitbearing, fruitful, generative, philoprogenitive, procreative, productive, profuse, progenitive, proliferative, proliferous, rich, teeming, verbose, wordy, yielding

PROLIX, adjective bombastic, boresome, boring, circumlocutory, copious, diffuse, discursive, drearisome, extended, full of verbiage, lengthy, long, longspun, long-winded, *longus,* maundering, monotonous, padded, pleonastic, pleonastical, prolonged, prosy, protracted, rambling, redundant, repetitive, spread out, spun out, tedious, tiresome, unconcise, uneconomical, verbose, *verbosus,* wandering, wearisome, wordy

PROLIXITY, noun effusion, long windedness, loquacity, redundancy, verbiage, verbosity, wordiness

PROLONG, verb be steadfast, continue, drag out, draw out, extend, *extendere,* hold over, increase, keep, lengthen, linger, maintain, make longer, perpetuate, persevere, preserve, *prorogare,* protract, retain, slow down, spin out, stretch, sustain, tarry, *trahere*

PROMINENT, adjective apparent, bold, brilliant, celebrated, consequential, conspicuous, credited, dignified, discernible, distinct, distinctive, distinguished, elevated, eminent, evident, exalted, extended, famous, flagrant, foremost, glaring, honored, illustrious, important, imposing, influential, jutting, known, leading, lofty, main, manifest, marked, memorable, noble, notable, noticeable, notorious, obtrusive, obvious, outstanding, powerful, predominent, preeminent, principal, projecting, *prominens,* pronounced, protruding, protrusive, protuberant, raised, recognizable, relieved, remarkable, renowned, respected, rising, salient, showy, significant, striking, upmost, visible, weighty, well-known, well-marked, well-seen

PROMISCUOUS, adjective alloyed, amalgamated, blended, carnal, casual, chaotic, commingled, composite, confused, conjoined, crossbred, crossed, debauched, dissolute, diverse, easy, free, fused, heterogeneous, immodest, immoral, incontinent, indiscriminate, indiscriminative, indistinguishable, intemperate, interlarded, intermixed, interwoven, joined, jumbled, lax, lewd, licentious, loose, mingled, miscellaneous, mixed, profligate, *promiscuus,* scrambled, unchaste, uncritical, undiscerning, undiscriminating, unselective, unvirtuous, variegated, wanton, wild

PROMISE, noun affirmation, agreement, asseveration, assurance, avowal, bond, commitment, com-

pact, consent, contract, covenant, declaration, engagement, *fides*, guarantee, oath, obligation, pact, paction, pledge, *promissum*, stipulation, treaty, understanding, vadium, vow, warranty, word
ASSOCIATED CONCEPTS: bilateral promises, consideration, contract, gift, unilateral promise
FOREIGN PHRASES: *Ea quae, commendandi causa, in venditionibus dicuntur, si palam appareant, venditorem non obligant.* Those things which are said as praise of the things sold, if they are openly apparent do not bind the seller. *Nudum pactum est ubi nulla subest causa praeter conventionem; sed ubi subest causa, fit obligatio, et parit actionem.* A naked contract is where there is no consideration except the agreement; but where there is a consideration, an obligation is created and gives rise to a right of action. *Nuda pactio obligationem non parit.* A naked agreement does not effect an otherwise binding obligation. *Nuda ratio et nuda pactio non ligant aliquem debitorem.* Naked intention and naked promise do not bind any debtor.

PROMISE *(Raise expectations), verb*   augur well, betoken, bid fair, cheer, embolden, encourage, enhearten, excite expectation, forebode, forecast, foreshadow, foreshow, foretell, forewarn, foster hope, give expectation, give hope, inspirit, lead one to expect, make a prediction, portend, predict, presage, prognosticate, prophesy, quicken, raise hopes, set astir, show signs of, signify, stimulate, suggest, threaten

PROMISE *(Vow), verb*   accept a liability, accept an obligation, accept responsibility, adjure, affirm, affirm positively, agree, assert, assert an oath, assert positively, assert solemnly, assert under oath, asseverate, assure, attest, aver, avouch, avow, be answerable for, bear witness, become bound, bind, bind by a pledge, bind oneself, bind oneself by oath, certify, commit oneself, consent, contract, contract an obligation, covenant, declare, engage, engage in solemn manner, give assurance, give one's honor, give one's word, give one's word of honor, give security, guarantee, hypothecate, incur a duty, insure, make a solemn resolution, make an avowal, make an engagement, make an oath, make oneself answerable, obligate oneself, pledge, pledge one's credit, pledge one's honor, pledge one's word, pledge oneself, plight, plight one's honor, plight one's word, *polliceri*, stake one's credit, stipulate, swear, swear an oath, take a vow, take an oath, take upon oneself, testify, undertake, underwrite, vouch, vow, warrant
ASSOCIATED CONCEPTS: breach of promise, nude promise, promise to answer for the debt of another, promise to pay

PROMISSORY, *adjective*   committed to payment, consisting of a guarantee, consisting of a pledge, containing a pledge, containing an assurance, guaranteed, on oath, on one's word, on one's word of honor, promising, promising to underwrite, under oath, vouched for
ASSOCIATED CONCEPTS: promissory estoppel, promissory note

PROMOTE *(Advance), verb*   advocate, advance in rank, aggrandize, better, dignify, elevate, encourage, exalt, favor, forward, further, graduate, help, magnify, move up, pass, prefer, *producere, promovere, provehere,* push up, raise, upgrade

PROMOTE *(Organize), verb*   abet, advertise, advocate, aid in organizing, assist, avail, back, befriend, benefit, bestead, bolster, build up, carry on, champion, come to the aid of, contribute to, cooperate, cultivate, develop, encourage, facilitate, foster, further, help, hold up, lend a hand, maintain, nourish, nurse, nurture, patronize, propagandize, push, render a service to, sanction, second, serve, speak for, speed, sponsor, stir up, subscribe to, subserve, support, sustain, uphold, urge

PROMOTER, *noun*   *adiutor*, advocate, aider, *auctor*, backer, benefactor, encourager, enterpriser, *fautor*, financial backer, financier, founder, organizer, organizer of business enterprises, organizer of commercial enterprises, patron, planner, prime mover, publicist, sponsor, supporter

PROMOTION *(Advancement), noun*   advance, amelioration, betterment, elevation, elevation in rank, exaltation, forwarding, graduation, headway, improvement, increase, lift, passing, preferment, progress, progression, raise, rise, uplift

PROMOTION *(Encouragement), noun*   abetting, advertising, aid, *amplificatio*, assistance, backing, benefit, boosting, campaign, cultivation, fostering, furtherance, help, maintenance, publicity, service, sponsorship, upkeep

PROMPT, *adjective*   businesslike, eager, early, efficient, expeditious, immediate, instant, instantaneous, on time, precise, *promptus*, punctual, quick, ready, seasonable, speedy, spontaneous, summary, swift, timely, unhesitating, without delay
ASSOCIATED CONCEPTS: prompt judicial action

PROMPT, *verb*   activate, actuate, advise, alert, animate, arouse, cause, dispose, encourage, excite, exhort, goad, hint, hound, impel, incite, incline, induce, influence, initiate, inspire, instigate, lead, motivate, move, occasion, persuade, press, prod, promote, provoke, push, recommend, remind, rouse, spur on, stimulate, stir, suggest, tempt, urge
ASSOCIATED CONCEPTS: leading a witness, subornation

PROMULGATE, *verb*   air, announce, annunciate, blaze, blazon, bring into the open, broadcast, bruit, circulate, communicate, declare, disclose, disseminate, divulge, emit, enounce, give currency, give notice of, give publicity to, hawk about, herald, issue, make known, notify, proclaim, *promulgare*, propagate, publicize, publish, report, reveal, set forth, spread, spread abroad, vent
ASSOCIATED CONCEPTS: promulgate a law, promulgate a rule
FOREIGN PHRASES: *Non obligat lex nisi promulgata.* A law is not obligatory unless it is promulgated.

PRONE, *adjective*   agreeable, apt, bent, biased, compliant, disposed, eager, easily persuaded, favorable, given, inclined, liable, likely, minded, partial, predisposed, *proclivis, pronus,* propense, ready, tending, well-disposed, willing

PRONOUNCE *(Pass judgment), verb*   adjudge, adjudicate, announce authoritatively, conclude, decide, declare to be, decree, deliver judgment, determine, find, give a ruling, give an opinion, give judgment, judge, officially utter, pass sentence upon, prescribe punishment, *pronuntiare,* rule, utter formally, utter judicial sentence

PRONOUNCE *(Speak), verb*   accent, accentuate, announce, announce authoritatively, announce officially, articulate, assert, break silence, communicate, declare, deliver, deliver an address, deliver formally, *dicere,* emit, emphasize, enounce, enunciate, *enuntiare,* express, form, frame, present, proclaim, recite, say, sound, speak formally, state, stress, tell, utter, utter formally, utter forth, verbalize, vocalize, voice

PRONOUNCEMENT, *noun*   affirmation, announcement, annunciation, assertion, asseveration, authoritative statement, averment, comment, decision, declaration, decree, deliverance, dictum, edict, enunciation, expression, fiat, formal statement, imperative, judgment, manifesto, notice, notification, observation, opinion, predication, profession, promulgation, pronunciamento, publication, remark, report, ruling, statement, utterance

PROOF, *noun*   *argumentum,* assurance, attestation, averment, certainty, certification, clear demonstration, clear indication, conclusiveness, confirmation, data, demonstration, documentation, establishment, evidence, evident demonstration, facts, *indicium,* manifestation, process of proving, proved strength, ratification, records, satisfaction, satisfactory evidence, showing, substantiation, sufficient evidence, *testimonium,* testimony, verification, warrant
ASSOCIATED CONCEPTS: adequate proof, affirmative proof, burden of proof, clear and convincing proof, collateral proof, failure of proof, final proof, furnish proof, legal proof, positive proof, proof beyond a reasonable doubt, proof evident, proof of claim, proof of death, proof of disability, proof of payment, proof positive, quantum of proof, satisfactory proof
FOREIGN PHRASES: *Semper necessitas probandi incumbit ei qui agit.* The burden of proof always lies upon the claimant. *Non possessori incumbit necessitas probandi possessiones ad se pertinere.* It is not incumbent on the possessor of property to prove that his possessions belong to him. *Affirmanti, non neganti incumbit probatio.* The burden of proof is on the party who affirms, not upon one who denies. *Facultas probationum non est angustanda.* The right of offering proof is not to be narrowed. *In criminalibus, probationes debent esse luce clariores.* In criminal cases, the proofs ought to be clearer than light. *Quod per recordum probatum, non debet esse negatum.* That which is proved by record ought not to be denied. *Quod constat curiae opere testium non indiget.* That which is clear to the court needs not the help of witnesses. *Qui melius probat melius habet.* He who proves most recovers most. *Praesumptio violenta, plena probatio.* Strong presumption is full proof. *Perspicua vera non sunt probanda.* Evident facts need not be proved. *Per rerum naturam factum negantis nulla probatio est.* It is in the nature of things that a person who denies a fact is not bound to give proof. *Probandi necessitas incumbit illi qui agit.* The necessity of proving lies with the person who sues. *Frustra probatur quod probatum non relevat.* It is useless to prove that which when proved is irrelevant. *Principia probant, non probantur.* Principles prove, they are not proved. *Praesumptiones sunt conjecturae ex signo verisimili ad probandum assumptae.* Presumptions are conjectures from pro-

bable proof, assumed for purposes of proof. *Reus excipiendo fit actor.* The defendant by pleading may make himself a plaintiff. *Idem est non probari et non esse: non deficit jus, sedprobatio.* What is not proved, and what is not, are the same; it is not a defect of the law, but a want of proof. *Factum negantis nulla probatio sit.* No proof is required of him who denies a fact. *Quod constat clare non debet verificari.* What is clearly apparent is not required to be proved. *Semper necessitas probandi incumbit ei qui agit.* The claimant is always bound to prove; the burden of proof lies on the actor. *Ei incumbit probatio, qui dicit, non qui negat; cum per rerum naturam factum negantis probatio nulla sit.* The burden of proof lies upon him who asserts it, not upon him who denies; since, by the nature of things, he who denies a fact cannot produce any proof of it.

PROPAGANDA, *noun*   *arrière pensée,* brainwashing, conditioning, conversion, distortion, false teaching, implantation, inculcation, indoctrination, initiation, inoculation, misinstruction, misleading, persuasion, preaching, promotion, teaching

PROPAGATE *(Increase), verb*   be fruitful, bear, beget, breed, bring into being, continue, create, engender, father, fecundate, generate, *gignere,* give birth, multiply, originate, *procreare,* procreate, produce, progenerate, proliferate, pullulate, reproduce, sire, spawn, teem

PROPAGATE *(Spread), verb*   advertise, air, blaze, blazon, broadcast, circulate, diffuse, disseminate, enunciate, evulgate, hawk about, herald, issue, make known, make public, noise abroad, notify, proclaim, promote, promulgate, publicize, publish, repeat, report, *serere,* spread abroad, tell, transmit, trumpet, vent, ventilate, *vulgare*

PROPENSITY, *noun*   ability, affinity, aptitude, aptness, art, attraction, bent, bias, capacity, deftness, dexterity, disposition, facility, fancy, favor, felicity, fondness, forte, genius, gift, inclination, knack, leaning, liking, mind, partiality, passion, penchant, ply, predilection, predisposition, preference, *proclivitas,* proclivity, proneness, *pronus,* propenseness, propension, *propensus,* qualification, readiness, relish, sharpness, skill, talent, taste, tendency, warp, weakness
ASSOCIATED CONCEPTS: propensity to commit a crime, viscous propensities

PROPER, *adjective*   acceptable, accurate, adapted, apposite, appropriate, apt, *aptus,* becoming, befitting, condign, conventional, correct, decorous, ethical, fitting, formal, free of error, honest, *idoneus,* legitimate, moral, opportune, orthodox, particular, precise, *rectus,* relevant, respectable, right, righteous, seasonable, seemly, suitable, suited, tasteful, true, unmistaken, virtuous, well-bred
ASSOCIATED CONCEPTS: proper party
FOREIGN PHRASES: *Non solum quid licet, sed quid est conveniens, est considerandum; quia nihil quod est inconveniens est licitum.* Not only that which is lawful, but that which is convenient is to be considered, because nothing which is inconvenient is lawful.

PROPERTY *(Distinctive attribute), noun*   aspect, attitude, attribute, character, characteristic, disposition, distinction, distinguishing quality, distinguishing trait, earmark, feature, individuality, mark, marked feature, marked quality, particularity, peculiarity, personality, point, *proprietas,* quality, singularity, specific quality, style, temperament, tone, trait

PROPERTY *(Land), noun*   acreage, acres, demesne, domain, dominions, estate, freehold, ground, grounds, holding, homestead, household, land, landed interests, landed property, leasehold, lot, parcel, plot, premises, real estate, real property, realty, territory, tract

ASSOCIATED CONCEPTS: abandoned property, absolute property, accretions to property, acquisition of property, after-acquired property, assessable property, assessed valuation of taxable property, base property, commercial property, community property, corporate property, damage to property, devising property, distributable property, encumbrance on property, estate, execution against property, freehold, homestead, individual property, joint property, lien on property, market value, property tax, public property, purchase of property, separate and distinct properties, similar property, special property, specific property, suit affecting property, suit concerning property, taking of property for private purposes, taking of property for public use without just compensation, taxable property, title to real property, transfer of interest in property, transfer of property intended to take effect at death, unplatted land, urban property, value of the property

FOREIGN PHRASES: *Transit terra cum onere.* Land passes subject to any encumbrances affecting it. *Jus descendit, et non terra.* The right descends, not the land. *Regulariter non valet pactum de re mea non alienanda.* It is a rule that an agreement not to alienate my property is not binding. *Cujus est solum, ejus est usque ad coelum et ad inferos.* He who owns the soil owns also up to the sky above it, and to the center of the earth beneath it.

PROPERTY *(Possessions), noun*   accessories, appointments, assets, available means, belongings, *bona,* chattels, effects, estate, financial resources, funds, goods, hereditaments, holdings, immovables, investments, material assets, movables, ownership, pecuniary resources, personal effects, personal resources, possessions, resources, substance, tangible assets, tangibles, valuables

ASSOCIATED CONCEPTS: appurtenance, articles of personalty, bequeathing property, fixtures, intangibles, moveables, proceeds of property, receiving stolen property, tangible property, trust property

FOREIGN PHRASES: *Nemo cogitur rem suam vendere, etiam justo pretio.* No one is compelled to sell his own property, even for a just price. *Quae ab hostibus capiuntur, statim capientium fiunt.* Things taken from enemies immediately become the property of the captors. *Duorum in solidum dominium vel possessio esse non potest.* Sole ownership of possessions cannot be in two persons. *Jus triplex est,-propietatis, possessionis, et possibilitatis.* Right is threefold,-of property, of possession, and of possibility. *Nemo alienae rei, sine satisdatione, defensor idoneus intelligitur.* No one is considered a competent defender of another's property, without security. *Nul charter, nul vente, ne nul done vault perpetualment, si le donor n'est seise al temps de contracts de deux droits, sc. del droit de possession et del droit de propertie.* No grant, no sale, no gift, is valid forever, unless the donor, at the time of the contract,

has two rights, namely, the right of possession, and the right of property. *Prohibetur ne quis faciat in suo quod nocere possit alieno.* It is forbidden for any one to do on his own property what may injure another's. *Proprietas verborum est salus proprietatum.* Propriety of words is the salvation of property. *In re communi neminem dominorum jure facere quicquam, invito altero posse.* One of the owners of common property may not exercise any authority over it against the will of another of them. *Expedit reipublicae ne sua re quis male utatur.* It is for the interest of the state no one should make ill use of his property. *Mobilia non habent situm.* Movables have no situs or local habitation. *Catalla juste possessa amitti non possunt.* Chattels cannot be deprived of when they are lawfully possessed. *Interest reipublicae ne sua quis male utatur.* It concerns the state that people do not misuse their property. *Rerum suarum quilibet est moderator et arbiter.* Every one is the manager and master of his own affairs or his property. *In re pari potiorem causam esse prohibentis constat.* Where a thing is owned in common, it is clear that the cause of the party prohibiting its use is the stronger. *In re communi potior est conditio prohibentis.* In relation to property held in common, the position of the one who prohibits is the more favorable.

PROPHETIC, *adjective*   alarming, augural, bodeful, clairvoyant, divinatory, *divinus,* farseeing, farsighted, fateful, fatidic, fatidical, *fatidicus,* fatiloquent, foreboding, forecasting, foreknowing, foreseeing, foresighted, foretelling, forewarning, haruspical, indicative, mantic, menacing, minacious, minatorial, minatory, monitorial, monitory, ominous, oracular, portentous, precognitive, precursive, predictive, predictory, prefigurative, preindicative, premonitory, presageful, presaging, prescient, presentient, prognostic, prognosticative, prophetical, pythonic, sibylic, sibylline, vatic, vaticinal

PROPHYLACTIC, *adjective*   preservative, preventative, preventive, protective, safeguarding, salutary

ASSOCIATED CONCEPTS: prophylactic rule

PROPINQUITY *(Kinship), noun*   affiliation, affinity, agnation, alliance, association, bond, close association, cognation, common ancestry, connection, consanguinity, family connection, filiation, kindred, link, nearness of blood, nearness of relation, relationship, tie

PROPINQUITY *(Proximity), noun*   adjacency, apposition, closeness, contiguity, juxtaposition, nearness, vicinage

PROPINQUITY *(Similarity), noun*   accord, affinity, affinity of nature, alikeness, comparison, compatibility, concert, concord, congeniality, correspondence, equivalence, harmony, homogeneity, likeness, parallelism, proximity, resemblance, semblance, similitude, synonymity, unity

PROPITIATE, *verb*   accommodate, appeal to, appease, beguile, calm, conciliate, content, disarm, gain the favor of, humor, ingratiate, make amends, make favorably inclined, make peace, mollify, offer sacrifice, pacificate, pacify, *placare,* placate, please, *propitiare,* reconcile, satisfy, soften, soothe, tranquilize, win over

PROPITIOUS, adjective accommodating, advantageous, approving, auspicious, beneficial, benevolent, benign, benignant, cheering, clear, clement, cloudless, conducive, disposed to bestow favors, encouraging, expedient, favorable, favorably inclined, felicitous, fortunate, friendly, full of promise, generous, golden, gracious, happy, heartening, heaven sent, helpful, helping, hopeful, indulgent, inspiriting, kind, kindhearted, kindly, lucky, merciful, obliging, opportune, presenting favorable conditions, promising, *propitius,* providential, reassuring, roseate, seasonable, supporting, sympathetic, timely, unhostile, well-disposed, well-intentioned, well-meaning

PROPONENT, noun abettor, advocate, ally, apologist, backer, benefactor, champion, defender, endorser, enthusiast, espouser, exponent, friend, justifier, partisan, patron, pleader, protector, seconder, spokesman, sponsor, subscriber, supporter, sympathizer, upholder, vindicator, votary, well-wisher
ASSOCIATED CONCEPTS: proponent of a will

PROPORTION, noun allotment, apportionment, commensuration, comparative size, comparison, concinnity, correlation, distribution, eurhythmy, factional part, fraction, grace, harmony, interrelation, measure, *pars,* part, percent, percentage, portion, quantum, quotum, ratio, relation, relationship, relative estimate, relativity, share, symmetry

PROPORTIONATE, adjective agreeing, analogous, balanced, commeasurable, commensurate, comparable, comparative, compatible, consistent, correlative, corresponding, distributional, equivalent, even, harmonious, proportionable, proportional, relative, scaled, uniform, well-balanced
ASSOCIATED CONCEPTS: per capita, per stirpes, pro rata

PROPOSAL *(Report),* **noun** analysis, appraisal, commentary, critical analysis, examination, in-depth analysis, plan, summary, writing

PROPOSAL *(Suggestion),* **noun** design, draft, exhortation, idea, measure, motion, offer, overture, plan, possibility, presentation, proffer, proposition, recommendation, scheme, submission, suggestion, tender, thought

PROPOSE, verb advance, advise, advocate, contend, counsel, declare, introduce, lay before, make a motion, make a suggestion, move, nominate, offer, plan, *ponere,* pose, postulate, present, proffer, propound, put forward, recommend, set forth, submit, suggest, tender, voice

PROPOSITION, noun approach, arrangement, assertion, assumption, bid, *condicio,* conjecture, course of action, declaration, declared intention, design, formulated intention, hypothesis, idea, offer, overture, plan, position, postulate, premise, presentation, program of action, project, proposal, *propositio,* prospectus, provisional hypothesis, recommendation, resolution, *rogatio,* scheme, strategy, submission, suggestion, supposition, tender, tentative approach, tentative statement, terms proposed, theory, thesis

PROPOUND, verb advance, advocate, allege, argue, aver, contend, exhibit, hypothesize, introduce, lay before, maintain, make a motion, moot, move, offer,

pose, posit, postulate, predicate, present, proffer, project, propose, put forth, put forward, recommend, set forth, submit, suggest, tender, throw out, voice
ASSOCIATED CONCEPTS: propound the law

PROPRIETARY, adjective entailed, exclusive, holding property, landed, pertaining to ownership, pertaining to property, praedial, restrictive
ASSOCIATED CONCEPTS: proprietary function, proprietary interest, proprietary lease, proprietary right

PROPRIETOR, noun *dominus,* householder, landlord, landowner, manager, master, owner, possessor, proprietary

PROPRIETY *(Appropriateness),* **noun** accordance, adaptation, admissibility, advisability, agreeableness, applicability, aptitude, aptness, becomingness, compatibility, conformity, congruity, consonance, correspondence, dueness, equity, expedience, expediency, felicity, fitness, harmony, justness, pertinence, properness, reasonableness, relevance, right, rightness, seemliness, suitability, suitableness, utility

PROPRIETY *(Correctness),* **noun** convention, conventional conduct, conventionalities, correctitude, correctness, courteousness, courtesy, decency, decorousness, decorum, delicacy, demureness, dignity, discrimination, elegance, ethicality, etiquette, good behavior, good breeding, good manners, grace, manners, modesty, morality, politeness, proper formality, properness, rectitude, refinement, respectability, restraint, ritual, taste, tradition
FOREIGN PHRASES: *Proprietates verborum observandae sunt.* The proper meanings of words are to be observed.

PRORATE, verb allocate, allot, apportion, apportion pro rata, assess pro rata, assess proportionally, distribute, distribute proportionally, divide, divide proportionally, dole, mete out, parcel out, portion, split up
ASSOCIATED CONCEPTS: prorate taxes

PROSAIC, adjective boresome, boring, colorless, common, commonplace, dry, dull, everyday, flat, *frigidus,* hackneyed, humdrum, *ieiunus,* jejune, matter of fact, mediocre, monotone, monotonous, mundane, ordinary, pedestrian, plain, platitudinous, prolix, prosaical, prosy, spiritless, stale, stock, tame, tedious, tiresome, trite, unentertaining, unimaginative, unimpassioned, uninspiring, uninteresting, unoriginal, unpoetic, unpoetical, unvaried, usual, vapid, wearisome

PROSCRIBE *(Denounce),* **verb** accuse, anathematize, banish, blame, castigate, censure, charge, condemn, criticize, curse, damn, denunciate, execrate, incriminate, ostracize, outlaw, reject

PROSCRIBE *(Prohibit),* **verb** abrogate, ban, bar, circumscribe, disallow, embargo, enjoin, exclude, forbid, halt, oppose, outlaw, prevent, *proscribere,* refuse, refuse permission, repudiate, restrain, restrict, revoke, taboo

PROSCRIPTION, noun ban, banishment, boycott, censure, condemnation, countermand, denial, denunciation, disallowance, disfavor, elimination, embargo, eviction, exclusion, forbiddance, inhibition, injunction, interdict, interdiction, intolerance, prohibition, *proscriptio,* rejection, relegation

PROSECUTE *(Carry forward)*, **verb**   advance, be resolute in, be steadfast, bring about, bring to pass, carry on, carry out, conduct, continue, follow up, go after, maintain, *persequi*, persevere in, persist, proceed with, pursue, put through
ASSOCIATED CONCEPTS: dismissal for want of prosecution, failure to prosecute, prosecute a claim, prosecute an action

PROSECUTE *(Charge)*, **verb**   *accusare*, arraign, bring action against, bring before a court, bring suit, bring to justice, file a charge, file a claim, prefer a claim, prefer charges, proceed against civilly, proceed against criminally, sue, summon, take one to court
ASSOCIATED CONCEPTS: prosecute for a criminal offense, prosecuting attorney

PROSECUTION *(Criminal trial)*, **noun**   action, bringing to trial, legal action, legal process, legal trial, litigation, pursuit by a law enforcement agency, suit, trial, undertaking
ASSOCIATED CONCEPTS: criminal prosecution, lawful prosecution, pending prosecution, want of prosecution

PROSECUTION *(Government agency)*, **noun**   the government, the people, the prosecuting attorney, the state, state's attorney
ASSOCIATED CONCEPTS: the prosecution

PROSECUTOR, **noun**   *accusator*, attorney general, criminal trial lawyer for the people, district attorney, government attorney, prosecuting attorney, prosecution, public prosecutor, state's attorney
ASSOCIATED CONCEPTS: public prosecutor, special prosecutor

PROSPECT *(Outlook)*, **noun**   ambition, anticipation, assurance, calculation, certainty, chance, coming events, confidence, contemplation, destiny, expectance, expectancy, expectation, fair chance, faith, fate, forecast, fortune, futurity, good chance, hope, intention, likelihood, likeliness, plan, possibility, prediction, presumption, probability, promise, reasonable chance, reliance, speculation, time ahead, trust, well-grounded hope

PROSPECT *(Prospective patron)*, **noun**   applicant, candidate, interested party, likely client, likely customer, likely patron, likely person, possibility, possible client, possible customer, possible patron, prospective client, prospective customer, recruit

PROSPECTIVE, **adjective**   abeyant, about to be, anticipated, approaching, arranged, awaited, close at hand, coming, conceivable, considered, destined, earmarked, eventual, expectant, expected, foreseen, forthcoming, future, *futurus,* hoped for, imaginable, immediate, imminent, impending, in prospect, in store, in view, intended, likely, looked for, looming, on the horizon, planned, possible, potential, preparing, projected, promised, scheduled, soon to be, soon to happen, subsequent, to be, to come, ultimate, upcoming
ASSOCIATED CONCEPTS: prospective contract, prospective liabilities, prospective relief, prospective rights
FOREIGN PHRASES: *Nova constitutio futuris formam imponere debet non praeteritis.* A new law ought to affect the future, not what is past. *Lex prospicit, non respicit.* The law looks forward, not backward.

PROSPECTUS, **noun**   analysis, announcement, blueprint, bulletin, catalogue, description, outline, plan, platform, program, scheme, sketch, statement, summary, syllabus, synopsis

PROSPERITY, **noun**   abundance, achievement, affluence, blessings, boom, booming economy, comfort, comfortable circumstances, ease, expansion, felicity, fortunate condition, full purse, good fortune, good luck, good times, heyday, luck, luxury, opulence, palmy days, plenty, profit, *prosperitas*, prosperousness, *res secundae*, riches, richness, run of luck, success, successfulness, thriving condition, weal, wealth, well being

PROSPEROUS, **adjective**   abounding in riches, affluent, ascendant, blooming, booming, comfortable, established, *florens,* flourishing, flush, fortunate, happy, in clover, in easy circumstances, lucky, moneyed, palmy, pecunious, profiting, *prosperus,* providential, rich, rising, *secundus,* successful, thriving, unbeaten, undefeated, wealthy, well off, well-situated, well to do

PROSTRATION, **noun**   abasement, bow, breakdown, cataclysm, collapse, consumption, debility, decay, decrepitude, defeat, dejection, demolition, depression, desolation, despair, despondency, destruction, distress, downfall, downthrow, enervation, exhaustion, extinction, extremity, faint, fall, fatigue, feebleness, genuflection, helplessness, horizontality, illness, impotence, kneeling, lassitude, loss of power, lowliness, misery, obeisance, overset, overthrow, overturn, ravage, recumbency, repose, rout, ruin, ruination, sickness, stupor, subjection, submission, suffering, surrender, swoon, tiredness, undoing, upset, vanquishment, waste, weakness, weariness, wrack, wreck, wretchedness

PROTAGONIST, **noun**   agent, champion, hero, lead, leader, leading character, main character, most important character, mouthpiece, prime mover, principal, principal character

PROTEAN, **adjective**   alterable, assuming different forms, changeable, changeful, everchanging, fluid, kaleidoscopic, metamorphic, mobile, modifiable, movable, multiform, multiphase, mutable, nonuniform, omniform, permutable, polymorphic, polymorphous, proteiform, transformable, unsettled, variable, varying, versatile

PROTECT, **verb**   arm, armor, attend, barricade, bulwark, care for, champion, chaperone, cherish, conduct, conserve, convoy, cover, cushion, *custodire,* defend, *defendere,* ensure, escort, fight for, flank, fortify, foster, garrison, guard, harbor, haven, house, immunize, inoculate, insulate, keep, look after, maintain, mount guard, nurse, patrol, patronize, preserve, safeguard, save, screen, seclude, secure, sentinel, shade, sheathe, shelter, shepherd, shield, shroud, shutter, sponsor, support, sustain, take care of, treasure, *tutari,* veil, ward, watch over
ASSOCIATED CONCEPTS: self-defense

PROTECTION, **noun**   aegis, armor, asylum, barricade, buckler, bulwark, citadel, conservation, covering, covert, coverture, custody, defense, fortification, freedom from danger, guarantee, guard, guardianship, haven, hedge, immunity, invulnerability, oversight, palladium, panoply, patronage, *praesidium,* preservation, preserve, refuge, safe conduct, safeguard, safekeeping, safety, salvation, sanctuary, security, shelter, shield, strength, stronghold, supervision, support, *tutela*, tutelage, wardship, wing

FOREIGN PHRASES: *Inde datae leges ne fortior omnia posset.* Laws were make lest the stronger might become all-powerful.

PROTECTIVE, *adjective*   armored, conservational, conservative, conservatory, covering, custodial, defensive, fortified, guardian, heedful, preservative, preventive, prophylactic, safeguarding, screening, sheltering, shielding, solicitous, strengthened, tutelary, vigilant, watchful

ASSOCIATED CONCEPTS: protective custody, protective order

PROTÉGÉ, *noun*   adherent, apprentice, charge, dependent, disciple, follower, initiate, learner, novice, pensioner, pupil, student, trainee, trust, ward

PROTEST, *noun*   challenge, clamor, complaint, counteraction, criticism, declaration of disapproval, declaration of dissent, declaration of opposition, defiance, demonstration, disapproval, dissent, dissidence, formal criticism, formal declaration, formal declaration of dissent, hostile demonstration, opposition, outcry, *recusatio,* remonstrance, remonstration, repudiation, resistance

ASSOCIATED CONCEPTS: file a protest

PROTEST, *verb*   announce, attack, challenge, complain, contradict, contravene, cry out against, dehort, demur, denounce, deny, disaffirm, disagree, disapprove, disclaim, discountenance, dispute, dissent, exclaim against, exhort against, express opposition, go contrary to, impugn, *intercedere,* inveigh, negate, oppose, raise objections, *recusare,* refuse, remonstrate, reprehend, repudiate, revolt, speak against, take exception, traverse, veto, vote against

ASSOCIATED CONCEPTS: payment under protest, protest a will, protest an election, written notice of protest

PROTOCOL *(Agreement), noun*   arrangement, charter, compact, concord, concordat, contract, covenant, diplomatic agreement, pact, stipulation, treaty, understanding

PROTOCOL *(Etiquette), noun*   behavior, ceremony, code, code of behavior, conventional practice, conventionalities, correct behavior, correctitude, correctness, courtesy, customs, decorum, dictates, diplomatic code, form, formalities, good behavior, good form, good manners, manners, politeness, practice, prevailing form, proper behavior, proprieties, punctilio, regulations, rules, set of rules, set of standards, system of rules

PROTOTYPE, *noun*   archetype, example, *exemplar, exemplum,* first, guide, ideal, model, mold, original, paradigm, paragon, pattern, precedent, protoplast, sample, source, standard

PROTRACT *(Prolong), verb*   delay, drag out, filibuster, gain time, hold up, procrastinate, retard

PROTRACT *(Stall), verb*   continue, elongate, extend, lengthen out, shelve, string out

PROTRACTED, *adjective*   continuing, dragged out, drawn out, elongated, extended, lengthened,

lengthy, lingering, long, long-continued, long-drawn, meandering, never-ending, ongoing, prolix, prolonged, unending

PROUD *(Conceited), adjective*   affected, aloof, arrogant, assuming, boastful, braggart, condescending, contemptuous, defiant, disdainful, egoistic, egoistical, flaunting, haughty, imperious, insolent, lordly, obstinate, orgulous, overweening, overbearing, patronizing, pompous, presumptuous, prideful, puffed up, self-applauding, self-important, self-satisfied, supercilious, swollen, turgescent, turgid, uppish, uppity, vain, vainglorious, without modesty

PROUD *(Self-respecting), adjective*   content, contented, delighted, dignified, grand, gratified, happy, honored, imposing, impressive, lofty, magnificent, majestic, noble, pleased, satisfied, splendid, stately, thrilled, well-pleased, well-satisfied

PROVABLE, *adjective*   ascertainable, capable of being demonstrated, capable of being proven, capable of being shown, capable of positive proof, capable of proof, confirmable, deducible, demonstrable, determinable, discoverable, establishable, incontestable, indisputable, inferable, irrefutable, supportable, susceptible of proof, sustainable, unimpeachable, verifiable, verificatory, well-founded, well-grounded

ASSOCIATED CONCEPTS: provable claim

PROVE, *verb*   ascertain, ascertain as truth, authenticate, confirm, corroborate, *declarare,* demonstrate, establish, establish as truth, establish the genuineness of, establish the validity of, evince, manifest, *ostendere, probare,* put to the proof, put to the test, show, show clearly, substantiate, support, uphold, validate, verify

FOREIGN PHRASES: *In rebus manifestis, errat qui auctoritates legum allegat; quia perspicua vera non sunt probanda.* In clear cases, he makes mistakes who cites legal authorities; for obvious truths are not to be proved.

PROVERBIAL, *adjective*   acknowledged, aphoristic, axiomatic, common, commonly known, commonplace, epigrammatic, familiar, general, known, legendary, notorious, oft repeated, popular, prevalent, recognized, sententious, succinct, traditional, universal, unquestioned, well-known, widely known

PROVIDE *(Arrange for), verb*   anticipate needs, appoint, care for, *consulere,* contract, direct, engage, get ready, look after, make allowance for, make preparations, make provision, make ready, manage, organize, pave the way, plan, prepare, *providere,* ready, serve, take into account, take measures, take steps

PROVIDE *(Supply), verb*   accommodate, accord, administer, afford, allow, award, bestow, confer, contribute, deliver, donate, endow, equip, feed, fund, furnish, give, grant, impart, maintain, *ornare, praebere,* present, produce, purvey, replenish, stock, *suppeditare,* sustain

PROVIDED, *adverb*   assuming that, on condition that, provisionally, subject to, with the understanding, with the stipulation, with this proviso

ASSOCIATED CONCEPTS: as provided by law

PROVIDENT *(Frugal), adjective*   careful, economical, money conscious, parsimonious, penurious, prudent, saving, sparing, stingy, thrifty, unlavish

PROVIDENT *(Showing foresight), adjective*   alert, anticipating, calculating, careful, cautious, chary, circumspect, discerning, discreet, equipped, farseeing, forecasting, forehanded, foreseeing, heedful, judicious, on guard, politic, precautionary, precautious, predictive, prepared, prognostic, prudent, prudential, ready, thoughtful, vigilant, wary, watchful

PROVINCE, *noun*   appointment, area, assigned task, assignment, business, canton, capacity, charge, circuit, colony, compass, county, demesne, department, district, division, domain, dominion, duty, field, function, job, jurisdiction, occupation, office, orbit, part, precinct, *provincia,* realm, region, scope, section, specialty, sphere, subdivision, territory, tract

PROVINCIAL, *adjective*   annexed, backwood, boorish, bucolic, churlish, closed-minded, colonial, divisional, dogmatic, fanatical, gauche, gawky, hayseed, ill-mannered, illiberal, inflexible, ingrown, insular, intolerant, inurbane, local, loutish, narrow, narrow-minded, oafish, outlying, parochial, petty, regional, rigid, rough, rude, sectional, small-minded, straitlaced, unbroadened, uncourtly, uncouth, ungraceful, unpolished, unrefined, unsophisticated, untraveled

PROVISION *(Act of supplying), noun*   accommodation, arrangement, catering, donation, endowment, furnishing, preparation, procurement, providence, purveyance, servicing, serving

PROVISION *(Clause), noun*   article of agreement, *condicio,* condition, limitation, obligation, proviso, qualification, requirement, reservation, restriction, specification, stipulation, term
ASSOCIATED CONCEPTS: damages provision, express provision, forfeiture provision, mandatory provision, penal provision, procedural provision, restrictive provision, self-executing provision, statutory provision, substantive provision, technical provision
FOREIGN PHRASES: *Quando abest provisio partis, adest provisio legis.* When a provision of the party is lacking, the provision of the law supplies it.

PROVISION *(Something provided), noun*   cache, cumulation, fund, hoard, maintenance, ration, reserve, resources, staples, stock, stockpile, store, supply

PROVISIONAL, *adjective*   alterable, conditional, contingent, dependent on circumstances, equivocal, for a time, in a state of uncertainty, *in tempus,* indefinite, indeterminate, interim, limited, makeshift, modifiable, nonpermanent, of short duration, passing, provisory, subject to change, subject to terms, substitute, temporarily established, temporary, tentative, transient, transitional, transitory, unascertained, unassured, unconfirmed, undecided, undetermined, unsettled
ASSOCIATED CONCEPTS: provisional appointment, provisional court, provisional employee, provisional government, provisional receiver, provisional remedy

PROVOCATION, *noun*   abuse, actuation, affront, aggression, agitation, angering, annoyance, causation, cause, defiance, exasperation, excitation, excitement, fomentation, goad, grievance, impulsion, incentive, incitement, inducement, inflammation, inspiration, instigation, insult, invitation, irritation, motivation, motive, offense, pressure, prick, prodding, prompting, provocative, spur, stimulant, stimulation, stimulus, taunt, temptation, urge, vexation
ASSOCIATED CONCEPTS: defense of provocation, extreme provocation, just provocation, legal provocation

PROVOCATIVE, *adjective*   aggravating, alluring, annoying, arousing, attractive, bellicose, captivating, challenging, defiant, desirable, electric, electrifying, enchanting, entrancing, exasperating, exciting, galling, galvanic, galvanical, grating, inciting, inflaming, inflammatory, influential, inspirational, interesting, intoxicating, intriguing, invidious, inviting, irksome, irresistible, irritating, motivating, persuasive, piquant, provoking, ravishing, seductive, stimulating, stimulative, stirring, suggestive, tantalizing, tempting, thrilling, titillating, urgent, vexatious, vexing

PROVOKE, *verb*   actuate, affront, aggravate, agitate, anger, animate, annoy, antagonize, arouse, awaken, badger, bait, begin, beset, bother, bring about, call forth, cause, challenge, defy, discompose, displease, disquiet, distress, drive, effect, egg on, elicit, enkindle, enrage, envenom, evoke, exacerbate, exasperate, excite, fire, fret, gall, generate, give offense, give origin, give rise, grate, harass, heckle, hector, hound, impel, incense, incite, induce, inflame, infuriate, instigate, insult, irk, irritate, kindle, madden, motivate, move, move to anger, nettle, occasion, offend, originate, persecute, perturb, pique, plague, promote, prompt, propel, push, put out, put out of humor, rally, roil, rouse, spur, stimulate, sting, stir, stir up, taunt, tease, torment, try one's patience, vex, work into a passion, work up, wound

PROWESS *(Ability), noun*   adeptness, adroitness, cleverness, competence, competency, craft, deftness, dexterity, excellence, expertise, expertness, facility, finesse, know-how, mastership, mastery, proficiency, skill, skillfulness, virtuosity, wizardry

PROWESS *(Bravery), noun*   absence of fear, backbone, boldness, braveness, constancy, contempt of danger, courage, courageous deeds, courageousness, daring, dauntlessness, defiance of danger, derringdo, doggedness, doughtiness, fearlessness, fiber, firmness, gallant acts, gallantness, gallantry, grit, hardihood, hardiness, heroic achievement, heroism, intrepidity, lustiness, manliness, mettle, might, nerve, perseverance, pluck, resoluteness, sinew, spirit, stability, stamina, stout heart, strength, sturdiness, valiancy, valor, valorousness, vigor, *virtus,* vitality

PROWL, *verb*   be stealthy, creep, cruise, drift, gad, go about stealthily, gumshoe, hover, lie in ambush, lie in wait, loiter, lurk, meander, move secretly, move under cover, *peragrare,* peregrinate, ramble, range, roam, rove, scavenge, skulk, slink, sneak, stay incognito, steal, stray, stroll, tramp, *vagari,* wander about

PROXIMATE, *adjective*   about to happen, abutting, adjacent, adjoining, approaching, at hand, attached, bordering, bordering upon, close, close at hand, close by, closest, connected, connecting, contactual, conterminal, conterminous, contiguous, edging, expected, following, forthcoming, fringing, immediate, imminent, impendent, impending, in close proximity, juxtaposed, near, nearest, neighboring, next, nigh, prospective, proximal, *proximus,* sequent, subsequent, succeeding, tangent, tangential, touching, upcoming, verging, vicinal

ASSOCIATED CONCEPTS: proximate cause

PROXY, *noun* agency, agent, authority to act for another, broker, delegate, deputy, dummy, emissary, envoy, lieutenant, messenger, *procurator,* representation, representative, substitute, substitution, surrogate, *vicarius,* written authorization

ASSOCIATED CONCEPTS: proxy statement, solicitation of proxy

PRUDENCE, *noun* attention, calculation, care, careful budgeting, carefulness, *cautio,* caution, *circumspectio,* circumspection, close watch, common sense, concern, conservation, conservatism, considerateness, consideration, cunning, deliberation, discretion, discrimination, economy, forethought, foresight, frugality, heed, heedfulness, husbandry, judgment, judiciousness, precaution, preparedness, presence of mind, providence, *prudentia,* regard, sense, shrewdness, tact, temperance, thrift, vigilance, watchfulness

PRUDENT, *adjective* advertent, calculating, canny, careful, cautious, *cautus,* chary, circumspect, *circumspectus,* considerate, discreet, discriminating, economical, farsighted, forearmed, foreseeing, foresighted, frugal, guarded, heedful, judicious, levelheaded, mindful, politic, precautionary, precautious, prepared, provident, *prudens,* prudential, regardful, sagacious, sage, sapient, saving, sensible, shrewd, sober, sparing, thoughtful, thrifty, wary, well-advised, wise

ASSOCIATED CONCEPTS: prudent person, reasonable man

FOREIGN PHRASES: *Prudenter agit qui praecepto legis obtemperat.* He acts prudently who obeys the precept of the law. *Sapiens omnia agit cum consilio.* A wise man does everything deliberately.

PRURIENT, *adjective* bawdy, carnal, coarse, concupiscent, cyprian, debauched, dirty, dissipated, dissolute, erotic, fleshly, foul, immodest, impure, indecent, lascivious, lecherous, lewd, *libidinosus,* libidinous, licentious, lickerish, lubricious, lustful, obscene, pornographic, ribald, salacious, satyric, shameless, smutty, suggestive, unchaste, unclean, unvirtuous, wanton

ASSOCIATED CONCEPTS: pornography, prurient interests

PUBLIC *(Affecting people),* **adjective** civic, civil, collective, common, communal, country-wide, federal, general, government, governmental, municipal, national, nationwide, social, societal, state

ASSOCIATED CONCEPTS: public authorities, public benefit, public benefit corporation, public business, public charge, public charity, public convenience, public corporation, public document, public function, public funds, public good, public improvements, public interest, public necessity, public notice, public nuisance, public office, public policy, public purpose, public safety, public sector, public service commission, public use, public utilities, public welfare, public works

FOREIGN PHRASES: *Pacta privata juri publico derogare non possunt.* Private contracts cannot derogate from public right. *Necessitas publica major est quam privata.* Public necessity is greater than private. *Jura publica anteferenda privatis.* Public rights are to be preferred to private parts. *Privatum commodum publico cedit.* Private good yields to public good. *Privatum incommodum publico bono pensatur.* Private inconvenience is compensated for by public benefit. *Lex citius tolerare vult privatum damnum quam publicum malum.* The law would rather tolerate a private loss than a public evil.

PUBLIC *(Known),* **adjective** acknowledged, aired, announced, apparent, broadcast, bruited about, circulated, commonly known, disclosed, disseminated, divulged, encyclic, encyclical, evident, exoteric, familiar, manifest, notorious, obvious, overt, popular, proclaimed, promulgated, propagated, *publicus,* published, recognized, released, renowned, reported, revealed, spread abroad, ventilated, well-known, widely known

PUBLIC *(Open),* **adjective** accessible, approachable, attainable, available, community, free to all, not private, permitted, reachable, unbarred, unprohibited, unreserved, unrestricted

ASSOCIATED CONCEPTS: public accommodations, public documents, public domain, public hearing, public institutions, public place, public property, public records, public sale

PUBLIC, *noun* body politic, citizenry, commonalty, commonwealth, community, folk, general public, *homines,* laymen, nation, persons, polity, populace, population, *populus,* social group, society

ASSOCIATED CONCEPTS: public good, public use, public utility, public welfare

PUBLICATION *(Disclosure),* **noun** advertisement, announcement, broadcast, circulation, communication, currency, dissemination, enlightenment, *expositio,* issuance, notice, notification, *praedicatio,* presentation to the public, proclamation, promulgation, pronouncement, *pronuntiatio,* propagation, public announcement, release, report, revealment, revelation, statement, transmission

ASSOCIATED CONCEPTS: defamation, libel, slander

PUBLICATION *(Printed matter),* **noun** book, *editio libri,* edition, folio, issue, literary magazine, literature, magazine, organ, periodical, printing, reading matter, tome, volume, work, writing, written discourse

PUBLICITY, *noun* advertisement, advertising, airing, announcement, billing, broadcast, bulletin, common knowledge, disclosure, dissemination, divulgation, divulgement, divulgence, enunciation, evulgation, exposure, fame, famousness, information, issuance, limelight, news, notice, notification, notoriety, presentation, press agentry, press notice, proclamation, promotion, promulgation, propagation, public distribution, public notice, public relations, publication, release, report, revealment, revelation, spotlight, utterance, ventilation, write-up

PUBLISH, *verb* advertise, air, announce, blazon, bring before the public, bring out, broadcast, call public attention to, circulate, communicate, cover, declare, deliver, diffuse, disclose, disseminate, distribute, *divulgare,* divulge, emit, expose, express, give out, give public notice of, go to press, have printed, herald, impart, inform, issue, issue a statement, issue for distribution, issue for public sale, lay before the public, make known, make public, *praedicare,* print, proclaim, *proferre,* publicize, put forth, put into circulation, put out, put to press, report, reveal, run off, spread, state, tell, trumpet, utter, ventilate

ASSOCIATED CONCEPTS: publish libel, publish slander

PUERILE, *adjective* asinine, callow, childish, childishly foolish, fatuous, foolish, green, immature, inadequate, inane, infantile, infantine, injudicious, jejune, juvenile, kiddish, naive, nonsensical, petty, piddling, *puerilis,* raw, senseless, shallow, silly, simple, unwise, unworthy of serious consideration

PUERILITY, *noun* babyishness, boyishness, childishness, childlike, girlishness, infantilism

PUGNACIOUS, *adjective* aggressive, antagonistic, argumentative, bellicose, belligerent, bickering, combative, contentious, defiant, disposed to fight, disputatious, dissentious, factious, fighting, fractious, given to fighting, hostile, inimical, militant, militaristic, offensive, quarrelsome, rebellious, rowdy, stubborn, threatening, unfriendly, unpacific, unpeaceful, warlike

PUISSANCE, *noun* authoritativeness, brawn, dint, dominance, energy, force, lustiness, masterfulness, might, mightiness, potence, potency, power, predominance, robustness, stamina, stoutness, strength, vigor, vitality

PULLULATE, *verb* be fruitful, be productive, bloom, blossom, breed, bud, burgeon, burst forth, come forth, develop, flourish, flower, generate, germinate, increase, luxuriate, multiply, open, procreate, produce, proliferate, *pullalare,* put forth, reproduce, rise, shoot forth, spring up, sprout, teem, vegetate, wax

PUNCTILIOUS, *adjective* accurate, attentive, careful, ceremonious, conscientious, correct, *diligens,* dutiful, exact, exacting, faithful, fastidious, finical, finicking, finicky, formal, fussy, methodical, meticulous, minutely correct, observant, observant of decorum, particular, precise, refined, rigid, rigorous, scrupulous, starched, stiff, strict, systematic, thorough, uncompromising

PUNCTUAL, *adjective* accurate, *ad tempus advenire,* attentive, conscientious, dependable, diligent, early, exact, exacting, expeditious, fussy, meticulous, minutely correct, never late, on schedule, on time, precise, prompt, properly timed, ready, regular, scrupulous, seasonable, steady, strict, systematic, timed, timely, well-timed

PUNISH, *verb* amerce, bring to retribution, call to account, *castigare,* castigate, chasten, chastise, condemn, correct, discipline, exact retribution, flog, inflict penalty, lash, penalize, reprimand, retaliate, scourge, sentence, slate, smite, subject to penalty, take to task, take vengeance on, teach a lesson to, torture, trounce, *ulcisci,* whip

ASSOCIATED CONCEPTS: cruel and excessive punishment, cruel and inhuman punishment, cruel and unusual punishment, excessive punishment

FOREIGN PHRASES: *In quo quis delinquit, in eo de jure est puniendus.* In whatever the offense, he is to be punished by the law.

PUNISHMENT, *noun* amercement, avengement, *castigatio,* castigation, censure, chastening, chastisement, compulsory payment, correction, damages, depri-

vation, disciplinary action, discipline, forfeiture, infliction, mulct, nemesis, penal retribution, penalization, penalty, penalty imposed on an offender, penance, *poena,* punition, reprimand, retribution, retributive justice, talion, vengeance

ASSOCIATED CONCEPTS: capital punishment, corporal punishment, cruel and inhuman punishment, excessive punishment

FOREIGN PHRASES: *Nulla curia quae recordum non habet potest imponere finem neque aliquem mandare carceri; quia ista spectant tantummodo ad curias de recordo.* No court which has not a record can impose a fine nor commit any person to prison; because those powers belong only to courts of record. *Poena ad paucos, metus ad omnes perveniat.* If punishment is inflicted on a few, a fear comes to all. *Nemo prudens punit ut praeterita revocentur, sed ut futura praeveniantur.* No wise man punishes in order that past things may be revoked, but that future wrongs may be prevented. *Ubi damna dantur, victus victori in expensis condemnari debet.* Where damages are given, the losing party ought to be condemned to pay costs to the victor. *Interest reipublicae ne maleficia remaneant impunita.* It concerns the state that crimes do not go unpunished. *Tutius semper est errare acquietando, quam in puniendo, ex parte misericordiae quam ex parte justitiae.* It is always safer to err in acquitting than in punishing, on the side of mercy rather than on the side of justice. *In omnibus poenalis judiciis, et aetati et imprudentiae succurritur.* In all penal judgments, allowance is made for youth and lack of prudence. *Qui peccat ebrius luat sobrius.* He who offends when drunk shall be punished when sober. *Melior est justitia vere praeveniens quam severe puniens.* Truly preventative justice is better than severe punishment. *Justitia est duplex, viz., severe puniens et vere praeveniens.* Justice is double, that is to say punishing severely, and truly preventing. *Qui parcit nocentibus innocentes punit.* He who spares those who are guilty punishes those who are innocent. *Reus laesae majestatis punitur ut pereat unus ne pereant omnes.* A traitor is punished that one may die lest all perish. *Poena non potest, culpa perennis erit.* Punishment cannot be everlasting but error or sin will be. *Judex damnatur cum nocens absolvitur.* The judge is condemned when a guilty person is acquitted. *Lubricum linguae non facile trahendum est in poenam.* A slip of the tongue ought not readily be subjected to punishment. *In atrocioribus delictis punitur affectus licet non sequatur effectus.* In the more atrocious crimes the intent is punished, although an effect does not follow. *Judex non potest injuriam sibi datam punire.* A judge cannot punish a wrong done to himself. *Nemo bis punitur pro eodem delicto.* No one can be punished twice for the same offense. *Transgressione multiplicata, crescat poenae inflictio.* Upon the multiplication of transgression, let the infliction of punishment be increased. *Poena suos tenere debet actores et non alios.* Punishment belongs to the guilty, and not others. *Nemo cogitationis poenam patitur.* No one suffers punishment on account of his thoughts. *Receditur a placitis juris, potius quam injuriae et delicta maneant impunita.* In order that crimes not go unpunished, the law will be departed from.

PUNITIVE, *adjective* avenging, castigatory, disciplinary, mulctuary, penal, penalizing, punishing, punitory, retaliatory, retributive, talionic, vindictive

ASSOCIATED CONCEPTS: punitive action, punitive damages

PURCHASE, *verb*   acquire, acquire ownership of, assume ownership, buy, buy up, collect, gain, invest in, make payment for, obtain, order, pay for, pick up, procure, procure title to, redeem, secure, secure for a consideration
ASSOCIATED CONCEPTS: words of purchase

PURE, *adjective*   absolute, chaste, clean, clear, complete, disinfected, entire, expurgated, faultless, flawless, guileless, guiltless, homogeneous, honorable, immaculate, incorrupt, innocent, *integer,* perfect, positive, *purus,* real, righteous, sheer, simple, sincere, sinless, spotless, stainless, sterilized, taintless, total, true, unadulterated, unblemished, unclouded, uncontaminated, uncorrupt, uncorrupted, undefiled, unmarred, unmingled, unmitigated, unmixed, unpolluted, unspotted, unstained, unsullied, untainted, untarnished, untouched, upright, utter, virtuous, whole
ASSOCIATED CONCEPTS: pure comparative negligence

PURELY (Positively), *adverb*   absolutely, decidedly, downright, entirely, essentially, fundamentally, in all respects, in truth, perfectly, really, seriously, thoroughly, totally, unconditionally, unequivocally, utterly
ASSOCIATED CONCEPTS: purely charitable institution, purely charitable purpose, purely manufacturing purposes, purely public charity

PURELY (Simply), *adverb*   barely, essentially, merely, mostly, plainly

PURGE (Purify), *verb*   clarify, clean, cleanse, clear, depurate, deterge, discharge, edulcorate, eliminate, elutriate, empty, eradicate, evacuate, excrete, expel, expurgate, filter, free from impurity, get rid of, rectify, refine, rout out, sanctify, scour, separate, strain, sublimate, sweep out, wash away

PURGE (Wipe out by atonement), *verb*   absolve, acquit, clear, exculpate, excuse, exempt, forgive, grant absolution, pardon, reclaim, redeem, shrive
ASSOCIATED CONCEPTS: purge of contempt

PURLOIN, *verb*   appropriate dishonestly, appropriate fraudulently, *avertere,* burglarize, cheat, commit larceny, defalcate, defraud, embezzle, filch, *furari,* misapply, misappropriate, misuse, peculate, pilfer, poach, rob, seize, snatch, spirit away, steal, *surripere,* swindle, take, take by fraud, take dishonestly, take feloniously, take wrongfully, thieve, unlawfully deprive

PURPORT, *verb*   allege, allude, claim, connote, convey, declare, declare with positiveness, denote, express, imply, *indicare,* indicate, infer, insinuate, intend, intimate, mean, pose as, pretend, profess, represent, say, show, *significare,* signify, state, suggest

PURPORTED, *adjective*   alleged, assumed, avowedly, claimed, in name only, ostensible, pretended, pretexed, professed, specious, so-called

PURPOSE, *noun*   aim, ambition, application, aspiration, avail, basis, constancy, deliberation, design, desire, desired result, destination, determination, direction, doggedness, drive, eagerness, end, expectation, final cause, firmness, force, function, goal, guiding

principle, hope, idea, *institutum,* intended result, intent, intention, *mens,* mission, motivating idea, motive, object, objective, perseverance, persistence, plan, point, *propositum,* resolution, resolve, service, significance, singleness, target, tenacity, use, volition, voluntariness, will, wish, zeal
ASSOCIATED CONCEPTS: business purpose, charitable purpose, intent, malice, unlawful purpose
FOREIGN PHRASES: *Lex neminem cogit ad vana seu inutilia peragenda.* The law compels no one to do futile or useless things. *Lex nil facit frustra, nil jubet frustra.* The law does not do anything nor commands anyone to do anything which would be futile. *Impunitas continuum affectum tribuit delinquendi.* Impunity confirms the disposition of a delinquent. *Benigne faciendae sunt interpretationes, propter simplicitatem laicorum, ut res magis valeat quam pereat; et verba intentioni, non e contra, debent inservire.* Interpretations should be liberal, because of the lack of training of laymen, so that the subject matter should be valid rather than void, and words should be subject to the intention, not the intention to the words. *Frustra fit per plura, quod fieri potest per pauciora.* That is needlessly done by many which can be done by fewer. *Potentia inutilis frustra est.* Useless power is vain.

PURPOSEFUL, *adjective*   advantageous, beneficial, bound, calculated, contributory, decided, dedicated, deliberate, designed, determined, devoted, dogged, earnest, firm, helpful, inexorable, intended, intense, intent, intentional, intransigent, meant, obstinate, persevering, persistent, pertinacious, planned, practical, productive, purposive, resolute, resolved, sedulous, serious, single-minded, stalwart, staunch, steadfast, steady, strong-minded, strong-willed, stubborn, studied, telic, tenacious, uncompromising, undeviating, unfaltering, unflagging, unflinching, unhesitating, unshrinking, unswerving, unwavering, useable, useful, utilitarian, valuable, willful, worthwhile, zealous

PURPOSELY, *adverb*   according to plan, by choice, by design, by will, calculatedly, consciously, deliberately, designedly, expressly, intentionally, knowingly, on purpose, pointedly, purposefully, studiously, volitionally, voluntarily, willfully, willingly, with forethought, with free will, with intent, with premeditation, wittingly
ASSOCIATED CONCEPTS: intent, malice

PURSUANT TO, *preposition*   according to, agreeable to, agreeing to, commensurate with, compatible to, conforming to, consistent with, consonant with, in accord with, in accordance with, in harmony with
ASSOCIATED CONCEPTS: pursuant to the law

PURSUE (Carry on), *verb*   adhere to, cling to, conduct, continue, cultivate, enact, engage, execute, follow, go in for, keep on, keep up, maintain, perform, *permanere,* persevere, persist, *persistere,* practice, proceed, prosecute, stick to

PURSUE (Chase), *verb*   *consectari,* ferret out, follow, follow a trail, go after, go in pursuit of, hunt, *prosequi,* prowl, quest, run after, run down, search, seek, *sequi,* trace, track, trail

PURSUE (Strive to gain), *verb*   aim, aspire to, attempt, be bent upon, be determined to get, be intent upon, bid for, *consectari,* contrive to gain, court, covet, desire, endeavor to gain, exert oneself for, intend, labor for, progress, push toward, seek, seek to attain, *sequi*, set as a goal, solicit, steer for, strive for, struggle for, try for, try one's best, try to obtain, work for

PURSUIT *(Chase)*, **noun** chase, *consectatio*, effort to secure, hunt, inquest, inquiry, inquisition, investigation, probe, prosecution, quest, search, stalk, *studium*
ASSOCIATED CONCEPTS: hot pursuit doctrine

PURSUIT *(Effort to secure)*, **noun** attempt, campaign, *consectatio*, effort, endeavor, exertion, hunt, investigation, laborious application, probe, quest, search, strenuous effort, struggle, sustained trial, try, undertaking, venture
ASSOCIATED CONCEPTS: hot pursuit doctrine

PURSUIT *(Goal)*, **noun** aim, ambition, destination, end, object, objective, purpose, target

PURSUIT *(Occupation)*, **noun** activity, appointment, *artificium*, avocation, business, calling, capacity, career, chosen work, concern, craft, department, em-
ployment, endeavor, engagement, enterprise, field, function, job, lifework, line, living, means of livelihood, metier, *negotium, occupatio,* office, position, post, practice, profession, project, province, regular employment, situation, specialization, specialty, sphere, task, trade, undertaking, venture, vocation, work

PURVIEW, noun ambit, area, arena, borderline, boundary, bounds, breadth, circumscription, compass, concern, confine, contemplation, delimitation, department, design, extent, latitude, *latitudo,* limit, limitation, limits, *locus,* magnitude, meaning, orbit, perimeter, plan, province, purpose, range, reach, scope, span, sphere, stretch, term, territory, view, zone
ASSOCIATED CONCEPTS: purview of a statute

PUTATIVE, adjective acknowledged, alleged, assumed, attributed, avowed, believed, claimed, commonly considered, conjectured, deemed, *falsus,* ostensible, presumed, presumptive, professed, purported, recognized, reported, reputed, speculative, supposed
ASSOCIATED CONCEPTS: putative father, putative parent

Q

QUAGMIRE, noun complication, crisis, critical situation, dead end, deadlock, difficulty, dilemma, distress, emergency, entanglement, exigency, imbroglio, impasse, involvement, mess, misfortune, muddle, nonplus, perplexity, pinch, plight, predicament, problem, quandary, scrape, spot, state, strait, tight situation, trial, tribulation, trouble

QUALIFICATION *(Condition)*, **noun** *condicio, exceptio*, exception, exemption, limitation, modification, provision, proviso, requirement, requisite, reservation, restriction, specification, stipulation, term

QUALIFICATION *(Fitness)*, **noun** ability, acceptability, admissibility, applicability, appositeness, appropriateness, aptitude, aptness, capability, capacity, compatibility, competency, correctness, desirability, efficiency, eligibility, endowment, entitlement, expedience, fittingness, occasion, pertinence, preparation, preparedness, propriety, readiness, relevance, right, rightness, skill, suitability, suitableness, suitedness, worthiness

QUALIFIED *(Competent)*, **adjective** able, acceptable, accomplished, adapted, adept, adequate, apt, capable, deft, efficacious, eligible, entitled, equal to, equipped, experienced, expert, fit, knowing, licensed, practiced, proficient, skilled, skillful, suitable, trained, versed, well-suited, worthy, worthy of choice

ASSOCIATED CONCEPTS: qualified applicant, qualified elector

QUALIFIED *(Conditioned)*, **adjective** *accommodatus,* checked, circumscribed, circumstanced, conditional, contingent upon, controlled, curbed, decreased, defined, delimited, dependent, diminished, *idoneus,* limitary, limited, moderated, modified, not absolute, prerequisite, prescribed, provisional, provisionary, provisory, restricted, stipulatory, subject to terms
ASSOCIATED CONCEPTS: qualified acceptance, qualified endorsement, qualified privilege, qualified right

QUALIFY *(Condition)*, **verb** alter, attemper, bound, *circumscribere,* confine, control, correct, *extenuare,* govern, introduce changes, introduce new conditions, keep within limits, limit, modify, narrow, regulate, restrict, revise, specify, temper
ASSOCIATED CONCEPTS: qualified acceptance, qualified fee, qualified gift, qualified endorsement, qualified privilege

QUALIFY *(Meet standards)*, **verb** accredit, allow, *aptum,* authorize, certify, confer a right, empower, enable, endorse, entitle, give a permit, give a warrant, have the qualifications, have the requisites, license, make capable, make competent, make suitable, measure up, meet the demands, meet the specifications, permit, practice, prepare, sanction

ASSOCIATED CONCEPTS: failure to qualify, qualify for appointment

QUALITY *(Attribute),* **noun**   characteristic, endowment, feature, idiocrasy, idiosyncrasy, individualism, nature, particularity, peculiarity, property, singularity, trait

QUALITY *(Excellence),* **noun**   ability, ableness, aptness, caliber, character, class, competency, fineness, goodness, grade, merit, might, potency, potentiality, power, puissance, rank, soundness, standing, status, superiority, validity, value, worth

QUALITY *(Grade),* **noun**   ability, ableness, aptness, character, condition, distinction, earmark, endowment, feature, merit, nature, particularity, property, standing, tendency, worth
ASSOCIATED CONCEPTS: inferior quality, warranty as to quality

QUALM, **noun**   anxiety, apprehension, apprehensiveness, compunction, concern, diffidence, disquiet, distrust, doubt, doubtfulness, dubiety, dubiousness, equivocalness, feeling of uncertainty, foreboding, hesitance, hesitancy, hesitation, incertitude, lack of certainty, lack of confidence, lack of conviction, misgiving, mistrust, nervousness, pause, question, scruple, skepticism, suspicion, twinge of conscience, uncertainty, undecidedness, uneasiness, want of confidence, worry

QUANDARY, **noun**   bafflement, bewilderment, confoundment, confusedness, confusion, difficulty, dilemma, disconcertion, doubt, doubtfulness, dubiety, dubiosity, dubiousness, dubitation, incertitude, indecision, indetermination, irresolution, nonplus, perplexity, perturbation, plight, predicament, puzzlement, quagmire, state of doubt, uncertainness, uncertainty

QUANTITY, **noun**   abundance, aggregate, allotment, amount, amplitude, apportionment, batch, bulk, bunch, crowd, fullness, heap, host, large number, legion, lot, mass, measure, measurement, mess, muchness, multiplicity, multitude, multitudinousness, myriads, number, *numerus,* pack, plenty, portion, profusion, *quantitas,* quantum, store, sum, sum total, supply, totality, volume

QUARANTINE, **noun**   confinement, custody, detachment, medical segregation, period of detention, period of isolation, restraint of movement, sanitary cordon, seclusion, segregation, separation, strict isolation

QUASH, *verb*   abate, abolish, annul, cancel, countermand, declare null and void, destroy, disannul, discard, disestablish, dismiss, dispel, dissolve, end, eradicate, extinguish, extirpate, *infirmare, inritum facere,* invalidate, make void, nullify, obliterate, overrule, overthrow, overturn, overwelm, put an end to, put down, quell, quench, repeal, repress, rescind, *rescindere,* reverse, squelch, stop, subdue, suppress, terminate, vacate, withdraw
ASSOCIATED CONCEPTS: motion to quash, quash a subpoena

QUASI, *adjective*   almost, imitation, mock, mostly, near, not entirely, pseudo, pseudonymous
ASSOCIATED CONCEPTS: quasi civil action, quasi contract, quasi corporation, quasi crime, quasi criminal,

quasi criminal proceeding, quasi derelict, quasi easement, quasi estoppel, quasi fee, quasi guardian, quasi in rem, quasi individual, quasi judicial officer, quasi jurisdictional facts, quasi legislative agency, quasi lien, quasi municipal corporation, quasi partnership, quasi party, quasi powers, quasi proceedings, quasi public corporation, quasi remainder, quasi trustee

QUASI, *adverb*   almost as, apparently, as if, as though, as though it were, in a certain sense, in a manner, in name only, just as, seemingly but not actually, to a certain extent

QUERULOUS, *adjective*   bewailing, canting, captious, carping, censorious, clamorous, complaining, contentious, cross, difficult, difficult to please, discontented, disputatious, dissatisfied, exceptious, faultfinding, fractious, fretful, grouchy, grumbling, hard to please, hypercritical, hypersensitive, irritable, lamentative, lamenting, maledicent, mournful, nagging, overcritical, peevish, pettish, petulant, plaintful, plaintive, pugnacious, puling, quarrelsome, *queribundus,* querimonious, *querulus,* shrewish, splenetic, tearful, testy, touchy, vixenish, wailful, waspish, whimpering, whining, whiny

QUEST, **noun**   chase, crusade, expedition, exploration, hunt, inquiry, journey, perquisition, pursuit, research, search, searching, seeking

QUESTION *(Inquiry),* **noun**   asking, essay, examination, exploration, inquisition, interpellation, interrogation, interrogatory, investigation, probe, *quaestio,* query, *rogatio,* scrutiny, search, subject of inquiry, survey, test, theme of inquiry
ASSOCIATED CONCEPTS: leading question
FOREIGN PHRASES: *Rogationes, quaestiones, et positiones debent esse simplices.* Demands, questions, and claims ought to be simple. *Multiplex et indistinctum parit confusionem; et quaestiones quo simpliciores, eo lucidiores.* Multiplicity and indistinctness produce confusion; and the more simple the questions, the more lucid they are.

QUESTION *(Issue),* **noun**   bone of contention, case, enigma, mystery, point in dispute, problem, proposition, puzzle, subject, theme, topic
ASSOCIATED CONCEPTS: mixed question of law and fact, political question, question of fact, question of law

QUID PRO QUO, **noun**   agreement, counterbalance, counterpoise, equipoise, exchange, express agreement, give and take, interchange, measure for measure, mutual agreement, mutual consideration, mutual understanding, one thing in return for another, reciprocality, reciprocation, reciprocity, something equivalent, something for something, substitute, understanding

QUIRK *(Accident),* **noun**   accidental occurrence, casualty, chance, circumstance, fate, fortuitous event, fortuity, freak, hap, inadvertence, luck, misadventure, mischance, mishap, nonintentional occurrence, turn, twist, undesigned occurrence, unforeseen event, unforeseen occurrence, unintentionality, unplanned happening, unpremeditation

QUIRK *(Idiosyncrasy),* **noun**   aberration, abnormality, abnormity, anomaly, bizarreness, defiance of custom, departure, deviation, divergence, eccentricity, exception, fancy, habit, idiocrasy, individuality, infringement of custom, irregularity, kink, mannerism, nonconformity, oddity, outlandishness, particularity, peculiarity, queerness, singularity, strange behavior, strange occurrence, strangeness, twist, unconformity, unconventionality, unorthodoxy, unusualness, vagary

QUIT (*Discontinue*), *verb*   abandon, abdicate, abjure, abort, acknowledge defeat, admit defeat, apostatize, arrest, back out, become inactive, break off, bring to an end, call a halt, capitulate, cause a stoppage, cause to halt, cease, cease progress, cease to use, cease work, check, come to a standstill, cut out, desist from, drop, finish, forgo, forsake, forswear, give up, go into retirement, go out of business, halt, have done with, intermit, lay aside, leave off, leave unfinished, make an end of, nol-pros, put a stop to, put an end to, relinquish, renounce, resign, retire, secede, stand aside, step down, stop, succumb, suffer defeat, surcease, surrender, suspend, tergiversate, terminate, withdraw, yield

QUIT (*Evacuate*), *verb*   abandon, abscond, beat a retreat, decamp, defect, depart from, desert, disappear, egress, emigrate, escape, exit, flee, forsake, get out, go, go away, go forth, go out, hurry away, leave, make a departure, make an exit, move away, part, pull out, remove oneself, retire, retreat, run away, separate from, set forth, set out, take flight, take leave, take leave of, take oneself away, turn one's back on, vacate, vanish, walk away, walk out, withdraw
ASSOCIATED CONCEPTS: notice to quit, quit

QUIT (*Free of*), *verb*   absolve, acquit, clear, deliver, discharge, disembroil, disencumber, disengage, disentangle, emancipate, exonerate, extricate, grant amnesty to, liberate, lift controls, manumit, pardon, release, render free, rescue, set at liberty, set free

QUIT (*Repay*), *verb*   balance accounts, be even with, clear a debt, clear accounts, compensate, discharge a debt, indemnify, make compensation, make payment, make reparation, make restitution, pay a debt, pay an indemnity, pay back, pay in full, pay off, pay old debts, recompense, refund, reimburse, remunerate, restore, return, settle a debt, settle an account

QUITCLAIM, *noun*   acquittance, deed exculpating the transferor, deed of release, quittance, receipt, waiver
ASSOCIATED CONCEPTS: quitclaim and convey, quitclaim deed, quitclaim sales

QUIXOTIC, *adjective*   chimerical, dreamy, fanciful, idealistic, illusory, impracticable, impractical, mad, notional, quixotical, romantic, unrealistic, utopian, visionary

QUORUM, *noun*   abundance, adequacy, adequateness, ampleness, completeness, enough, full measure, legal minimum, plentifulness, plenty, plenum, quota, sufficience, sufficiency, sufficient number, sufficient quantity
ASSOCIATED CONCEPTS: absence of quorum, full quorum

QUOTA, *noun*   allocation, allotment, allowance, apportionment, appropriation, assignment, check, circumscription, constraint, containment, contingent, control, curb, dispensation, extent, inhibition, limit, limitation, measure, number, percentage, portion, proportion, quantity, quantum, ratio, ration, regulation, restraint, restriction, share, suppression
ASSOCIATED CONCEPTS: quota system, racial quota

QUOTE, *verb*   adduce, *adferre*, circumstantiate, cite, cite a holding of a case, corroborate, detail, document, duplicate, establish, excerpt, extract, give word for word, go into detail, instance, make reference, paraphrase, point out, produce an instance, *proferre*, recapitulate, recite, recount, refer, reiterate, repeat, rephrase, report, reproduce, restate, retell, reword, specify, substantiate, support, validate, verify

R

RACE, *noun*   ancestry, birth, breed, class, cultural group, culture, descent, ethnic group, ethnic stock, extraction, family, folk, genealogy, genus, group, kind, line, parentage, people, phylum, stem, stirps, stock, strain
ASSOCIATED CONCEPTS: discrimination, race, creed, and color

RACE, *verb*   accelerate, bolt, chase, compete, dart, dash, engage in a contest of speed, enter a competition, fly, gallop, hasten, hie, hurry, hustle, move at an accelerated rate of speed, plunge ahead, pursue, run, run a race, run swiftly, rush, scamper, scramble, scud, speed, sprint, spurt, tear, whiz
ASSOCIATED CONCEPTS: assumption of risk, race to the recording office, racing commission

RACKET, *noun*   conspiracy, corruption, criminal activity, criminality, dishonesty, fraud, fraudulence, illegitimate undertaking, illicit business, illicit scheme, improbity, lawbreaking, lawlessness, misdealing, organized illegal activity, scheme, thievery, trick, underworld activity

RACKETEER, *noun* contrabandist, criminal, dealer in illicit goods, extorter, gangleader, gangster, illicit dealer, malefactor, member of organized crime, miscreant, mobster, offender, underworld character, underworld gangster

RADIATE, *verb* beam, branch out, coruscate, diffuse, disperse, emanate in rays, emit heat, emit rays, exude, *fulgere,* irradiate, issue rays, overspread, *radiare,* ramify, reflect, scatter, send, send forth, shed, splay, spread, throw off heat, throw out, transmit

RADICAL *(Extreme),* **adjective** absolute, altogether, complete, comprehensive, entire, exhaustive, intensive, maximal, plenary, sweeping, thorough, thoroughgoing, total, whole

RADICAL *(Favoring drastic change),* **adjective** advocating change, fanatical, freethinking, iconoclastic, insurgent, insurrectionary, militant, mutinous, progressive, rebellious, recusant, revolutionary, ultraist, uncompromising

RAISE *(Advance),* **verb** aggrandize, augment, boost, bring up, dignify, elevate, enhance, enlarge, ennoble, exalt, further, glorify, heighten, honor, increase, lift, move up, prize, promote, propose, *provehere,* put, suggest, uplift, upraise
ASSOCIATED CONCEPTS: raise an objection

RAISE *(Collect),* **verb** accumulate, assemble, bring together, *conligere,* gather together, get, levy, muster, obtain, procure

RAMPANT, *adjective* dominant, everywhere, excessive, extravagant, exuberant, *ferox,* flourishing, growing, irrepressible, overabundant, prevalent, prolific, rife, spreading, *superbire,* unchecked, uncontrolled, unrestrained, unstopped, widespread, wild

RANCOR, *noun* acerbity, acrimony, animosity, antagonism, antipathy, aversion, bitter feelings, bitterness, enmity, grudge, harshness, hate, hatred, hostility, ill feeling, ill will, *invidia,* malevolence, malice, malignity, *odium,* resentment, revenge, revengefulness, ruthlessness, spite, spitefulness, uncharitableness, unfriendliness, vendetta, vengeance, vengefulness, venom, venomousness, vindictiveness, virulence

RANDOM, *adjective* accidental, aimless, blind, casual, chance, cursory, designless, desultory, done without reason, fortuitous, haphazard, immethodical, incidental, indiscriminate, irregular, orderless, promiscuous, purposeless, stray, unaimed, unarranged, uncoordinated, undesigned, undirected, unguided, unorganized, unpremeditated

RANGE, *noun* ambit, area, arena, boundaries, bounds, breadth, compass, distance, earshot, extent, field, gamut, *genus,* hearing, limit, line, perimeter, power, reach, scope, space, span, sphere, stretch, sweep

RANSOM, *noun* cost of reclamation, cost of recovery, deliverance, extrication, *pretium,* price of redemption, price of retaking, price of retrieval, redemption, rescue

RAPACIOUS, *adjective* avaricious, *avidus,* cormorant, depredatory, devouring, grasping, greedy, insatiable, insatiate, living on prey, lupine, marauding, pillaging, piratical, plundering, predacious, predatory, preying, *rapax,* ravening, ravenous, voracious, vulturine, vulturous, wolfish

RAPE, *noun* abuse, assault, constupration, defilement, defloration, depredation, despoliation, forcible violation, pillage, plunder, plunderage, *rapere,* rapine, ravage, ravishment, seduction, sexual assault, spoliation, stupration, violation
ASSOCIATED CONCEPTS: criminal assault, statutory rape

RAPID, *adjective* accelerated, active, bustling, expeditious, express, fast, feverish, fleet, galloping, hasty, hurried, instant, light-footed, lively, nimble, posthaste, quick, *rapidus,* rushing, smart, speedy, swift, *velox,* winged

RAPPORT, *noun* accord, accordance, affinity, agreement, alliance, closeness, compatibility, concord, concordance, concurrence, congruity, consonance, empathy, harmonious relation, harmony, intimacy, mutual appreciation, mutuality, relationship, understanding

RAPPROCHEMENT, *noun* accord, accordance, agreement, alliance, amiability, amicability, amity, concord, concordance, cordial relations, cordiality, fellow feeling, fellowship, fraternization, friendliness, friendship, harmony, improved relations, mutual friendliness, mutuality, neighborliness, rapport, reciprocity, reconcilement, reconciliation, reunion, unanimity, understanding, unison, unity

RARE, *adjective* choice, curious, different, excellent, exceptional, exquisite, extraordinary, fine, incomparable, inconceivable, infrequent, *inusitatus,* matchless, noteworthy, out of circulation, out of the ordinary, peerless, precious, priceless, *rarus,* scarce, seldom seen, select, singular, *singularis,* special, strange, superlative, uncommon, uncustomary, unequaled, unexampled, unfamiliar, unique, unparalleled, unusual

RATE, *noun* amount, assessment, charge, cost, expense, fare, fee, hire, *magno,* obligation, pace, *parvo emere,* payment, price, quotation, standard, tempo, valuation, value, velocity, worth
ASSOCIATED CONCEPTS: legal rate of interest, rate of exchange

RATE, *verb* *aestimare,* appraise, apprize, assess, calculate, class, classify, compute, determine, esteem, estimate, evaluate, figure, fix the price of, gauge, grade, judge, measure, merit, price, quantify, rank, reckon, set a value on, tag, value, weigh

RATIFICATION, *noun* acceptance, acknowledgment, approbation, approval, assent, certification, confirmation, consent, corroboration, endorsement, *sanctio,* sanction, stamp of approval, substantiation, validation
ASSOCIATED CONCEPTS: implied ratification, ratification of a contract, ratification of unauthorized acts
FOREIGN PHRASES: *Ratihabitio mandato aequiparatur.* Ratification is equivalent to an express command. *Omnis ratihabitio retrotrahitur et mandato priori*

aequiparatur. Every ratification relates back and is taken to be the equal of prior authority. **In maleficio, ratihabitio mandato comparatur.** In tort, a ratification is regarded as a command.

RATING, noun analysis, appraisal, assessment, classification, determination, estate, estimation, evaluation, grade, grading, grouping, measurement, placement, quantification, rank, ranking, status, valorization, valuation

RATIOCINATION, noun analysis, argumentation, cerebration, cogitation, deduction, dialectics, intellection, intellectualization, logic, *ratiocinatio,* rationality, rationalization, reasoning, thinking, thought

RATION, noun allotment, allowance, apportionment, appropriation, assignment, *demensum,* dispensation, distribution, division, dole, helping, measure, parcel, part, percentage, piece, pittance, portion, proportion, provision, quantity, quota, serving, share, slice

RATIONAL, adjective agreeable to reason, analytical, balanced, cerebral, clearheaded, cognitive, *consentaneus,* discerning, discriminating, endowed with reason, enlightened, exercising reason, intelligent, judicious, justifiable, knowing, legitimate, levelheaded, logical, lucid, objective, plausible, ratiocinative, *ratione praeditus,* reasonable, reasoning, reflective, sagacious, sage, sane, sensible, sober, sound, stable, thinking, thoughtful, understanding, well-grounded, wise
ASSOCIATED CONCEPTS: rational basis

RATIONALE, noun account, basis, cause, elucidation, explanation, explication, exposition, fundamental reason, ground, logical reasoning, motivation, motive, presumption, proposition, reason, reasoning, speculation, surmise, theory

RATIONALIZE, verb account for, adduce, analyze, cogitate, construe, excogitate, excuse, explain, explain away, justify, make acceptable, make allowances, make excuses, reason, reconcile, reflect, theorize, think, think logically, vindicate

REACH, verb accomplish, achieve, amount to, approach, arrive, attain, catch up, come to, communicate with, contact, equal, extend to, gain, get, get at, get in touch with, get through to, impress, influence, keep pace with, meet, move, obtain, overtake, strike, succeed, touch, triumph
ASSOCIATED CONCEPTS: overreaching

REACTION (Opposition), noun backfire, backlash, challenge, clash, conflict, contradiction, contrariety, countertendency, differences, disagreement, disapprobation, discountenance, expression of disapproval, objection, offset, polarity, protest, rebound, rebuff, recalcitration, renitence, renitency, reprisal, resistance, retaliation, retroaction

REACTION (Response), noun answer, attitude, effect, emotion, feeling, impact, impression, perception, reciprocal action, rejoinder, repercussion, reply, return, reverberation, sensation, sense, sentiment, view
ASSOCIATED CONCEPTS: allergic reaction

READ, verb apprehend, collect, con, conclude, consider probable, decipher, deduce, derive, digest, discern, draw a conclusion, gather, glean, grasp, guess, infer, interpret, know, leaf through, make out, perceive, peruse, pore over, presume, reason, scan, skim, study, thumb through, understand

READILY, adverb eagerly, easily, effortlessly, enthusiastically, freely, gladly, graciously, heartily, lief, *prompte,* promptly, quickly, smoothly, voluntarily, willingly

READY (Prepared), adjective able, accessible, armed, arranged, at hand, available, equipped, expectant, fit, groomed, in harness, in order, in position, in readiness, in working order, loaded, mature, mobilized, on call, *paratus,* primed, prompt, *promptus,* quick, ripe, set, speedy, standing by, swift, waiting

READY (Willing), adjective acquiescent, agreeable, alacritous, alert, animated, anxious, ardent, assenting, available, avid, cheerful, compliant, consenting, delighted, disposed, eager, enthusiastic, expeditious, favorably minded, fervent, given, glad, happy, inclined, keen, predisposed, prone, propense, zealous, zestful

REAFFIRM, verb accent, accentuate, buttress, confirm, emphasize, fortify, go over, insist, iterate, punctuate, reassert, reiterate, repeat, restate, retell, stress, sustain, underline

REAL, adjective accurate, actual, ascertained, authentic, bonafide, conformable to fact, correct, dependable, factual, genuine, *germanus,* inartificial, incontestable, indisputable, irrefutable, legitimate, natural, right, scientific, *sincerus,* sure, true, trustworthy, truthful, undeniable, undoubtable, unerroneous, unfallacious, unfeigned, unimagined, unimpeachable, unmistaken, unquestionable, unsimulated, unspurious, unsynthetic, valid, veracious, veritable, *verus*
ASSOCIATED CONCEPTS: real estate, real party interest, real property, real servitude

REAL ESTATE, noun acreage, block, chattels real, domain, estate, fee, freehold, ground, hereditament, land, landed estate, lot, parcel, plot, property, real property, realty

REALISTIC, adjective actual, authentic, depictive, exact, faithful, genuine, graphic, lifelike, natural, naturalistic, practical, pragmatic, real, representational, representative, truthful, undisguised, undistorted, unidealistic, unromantic, veracious

REALITY, noun actual existence, actuality, authenticity, being, existence, factualness, genuineness, legitimacy, realness, substance, substantiality, substantialness, truth, veracity, *veritas,* verity

REALIZATION, noun accomplishment, achievement, acquirement, acquisition, actualization, apperception, appreciation, apprehension, attainment, awareness, cognition, cognizance, completion, comprehension, consciousness, consummation, discernment, discovery, effectuation, *effectus,* execution, fruition, fulfilment, illumination, implementation, ken, knowledge, materialization, mindfulness, perception, performance, production, profit, receipt, recognition, sensibility, substantiation, understanding

REALIZE (Make real), verb accomplish, achieve, actualize, bring about, bring to pass, carry into effect, carry out, carry through, complete, consummate, do, effect, effectuate, *efficere,* engineer, *facere,* implement, materialize, perform, produce, substantiate

REALIZE *(Obtain as a profit),* **verb**   achieve, acquire, attain, benefit, clear, come by, earn, enjoy, gain, get, make, net, obtain, obtain a return, *pecuniam redigere,* procure, produce, profit, reap, receive, turn into cash, turn into money

REALIZE *(Understand),* **verb**   absorb, appreciate, apprehend, assimilate, become aware, become conscious, cognize, comprehend, *comprehendere,* digest, discern, fathom, grasp, *intellegere,* know, learn, make out, perceive, recognize, see, take in

REALM, noun   area, authority, bailiwick, country, demesne, department, domain, dominion, empire, field, jurisdiction, kingdom, land, monarchy, orbit, perimeters, power, province, region, *respublica,* sphere, territory

REALTY, noun   acres, estate, grounds, holdings, land, land owned, property, real estate, real property
ASSOCIATED CONCEPTS: conveyance of realty, description of realty, interest in realty, sale of realty, title to realty

REAP, verb   achieve, acquire, attain, be rewarded, benefit, clear, collect, cull, cut, *demetere,* derive, draw, earn, gain, gather, get, glean, harvest, obtain, pick, pick up, procure, profit, realize, receive, recover, retrieve, secure, take, take in, take the yield, win

REAPPORTION, verb   allot again, apportion anew, deal out anew, dispense, distribute again, distribute anew, dole out, parcel, portion out, ration, reallocate, reallot, reappoint, rearrange, reassign, reassort, reclassify, redisperse, redistribute, redistrict, redivide, remeasure, repartition, rezone, split again
ASSOCIATED CONCEPTS: reapportion a legislature

REARREST, verb   catch again, constrain again, legally restrain again, make captive again, place in custody again, recapture, recommit, reconfine, redetain, reimprison, rejail, seize again, take prisoner again

REASON *(Basis),* **noun**   account, actuation, aim, argument, *causa,* causation, cause, consideration, defense, derivation, design, end, excuse, explanation, extenuation, foundation, genesis, goal, ground, impetus, incentive, incitation, inducement, inspiration, instigation, intent, intention, mainspring, motivation, motive, object, origin, prime mover, principle, provocation, purpose, *ratio,* rationale, root, sake, source, spring, stimulation, vindication, wherefore
ASSOCIATED CONCEPTS: reason for classification
FOREIGN PHRASES: Causa patet. The reason is apparent. **Eadem est ratio, eadem est lex.** The reason being the same, the law is the same. **Vitium est quod fugi debet, ne, si rationem non invenias, mox legem sine ratione esse clames.** It is a fault which ought to be avoided, that if you cannot discover the reason you presently exclaim that the law is without reason. **Ratio potest allegari deficiente lege; sed vera et legalis et non apparens.** Where the law is deficient, the reason can be alleged, but it must be true and lawful and not merely apparent.

REASON *(Sound judgment),* **noun**   ability to know, acumen, apperception, awareness, clearheadedness, cognition, cognizance, common sense, comprehension, *consilium,* discernment, discretion, discrimination, good sense, insight, intellect, intelligence, judiciousness, knowledge, logic, logicalness, lucidity, *mens,* mental capacity, mind, perception, percipiency, rationality, recognition, sagacity, sanity, sense, sensibility, sensibleness, sobriety, thinking, thought, understanding, wisdom
ASSOCIATED CONCEPTS: business reason, rule of reason
FOREIGN PHRASES: Quaere de dubiis, quia per rationes pervenitur ad legitimam rationem. Inquire into doubtful matters, because by reasoning we arrive at legal reason. **Lex est dictamen rationis.** Law is the dictate of reason. **Lex est ratio summa, quae jubet quae sunt utilia et necessaria, et contraria prohibet.** That which is law is the consummation of reason, which commands those things useful and necessary, while prohibiting the contrary. **Nihil quod est contra rationem est licitum.** Nothing is lawful which is contrary to reason. **Lex plus laudatur quando ratione probatur.** The law is most praiseworthy when it is consistent with reason. **Ratio non clauditur loco.** Reason is not confined to any place. **Ratio et auctoritas duo clarissima mundi lumina.** Reason and authority are the two brightest lights in the world. **Ratio legis est anima legis.** The reason of the law is the spirit of the law. **Ratio in jure aequitas integra.** Reason in law is impartial equity. **Ratio est formalis causa consuetudinis.** Reason is the source and cause of custom. **Lex semper intendit quod convenit rationi.** The law always intends what is agreeable to reason. **Quod naturalis ratio inter omnes homines constituit, vocatur jus gentium.** The rule which natural reason has established among all men is called the law of nations. **Ratio est legis anima; mutata legis ratione mutatur et lex.** Reason is the soul of law; the reason of law being changed, the law is also changed.

REASON *(Conclude),* **verb**   analyze, cerebrate, cogitate, conclude, consider, contemplate, deduce, deliberate, derive, draw inferences, examine, excogitate, figure out, gather, hypothesize, infer, intellectualize, judge, make deductions, philosophize, ponder, *ratiocinari,* ratiocinate, rationalize, reflect, resolve, study, suppose, theorize, think, think through, try conclusions, turn over in the mind, weigh

REASON *(Persuade),* **verb**   advise, argue, bring to reason, coax, contend, convince, debate, demonstrate, discuss, dissuade, establish, explain, expostulate, expound, join issue, justify, move, persuade, plead, point out, prevail upon, prove, remonstrate, set forth, speak logically, talk over, urge, ventilate a question, win over

REASONABLE *(Fair),* **adjective**   *aequus,* conscionable, equitable, fit, fitting, judicious, just, *modicus,* not excessive, not extreme, proper, *rationi consentaneus,* restrained, suitable, temperate, tempered, tolerable, unextravagant, unextreme
ASSOCIATED CONCEPTS: reasonable agreement, reasonable allowance, reasonable attorney's fees, reasonable market value, reasonable notice, reasonable opportunity to cure, reasonable restraint, reasonable return, reasonable time, reasonable value
FOREIGN PHRASES: Quam rationabilis debet esse finis, non definitur, sed omnibus circumstantiis inspectis pendet ex justiciariorum discretione. What a reason-

able fine ought to be is not defined, but is left to the discretion of the judges, all the circumstances being considered. *Quam longum debet esse rationabile tempus non definitur in lege, sed pendet ex discretione justiciariorum.* How long a reasonable time ought to be is not defined by law, but is left to the discretion of the judges.

REASONABLE *(Rational), adjective* amenable to reason, broad-minded, capable of reason, clearheaded, cognitive, credible, discerning, fit, intelligent, judicious, justifiable, logical, lucid, perceiving, percipient, persuable, plausible, probable, proper, *prudens,* ratiocinative, rational, *rationis particeps,* realistic, right, sagacious, sapient, sensible, sound, tenable, understandable, unjaundiced, unprejudiced, valid, warrantable, well-advised, well-founded, wise
ASSOCIATED CONCEPTS: reasonable care, reasonable cause, reasonable certainty, reasonable degree of care, reasonable diligence, reasonable doubt, reasonable excuse, reasonable ground, reasonable inference, reasonable injury, reasonable interpretation, reasonable judgment, reasonable notice, reasonable person, reasonable probability, reasonable use

REASSESS, *verb* reappraise, reappreciate, reapprise, recalculate, recharge, reclass, reestimate, reevaluate, regauge, rejudge, relevy, remeasure, rerank, retax, revalue
ASSOCIATED CONCEPTS: reassessed tax

REASSIGN, *verb* assign again, change, commit again, consign again, deal again, portion out again, reallocate, reallot, reappoint, reappropriate, recommission, redistribute, redivide, reengage, reinstall, rezone, transfer
ASSOCIATED CONCEPTS: reassign a case

REASSURE, *verb* affirm, approve, assure again, bolster up, buoy up, certify, cheer, comfort, confirm, *confirmare,* convince, dismiss doubt, ease, embolden, encourage, enhearten, give confidence, give hope, guarantee, hearten, help, hold out hope, infuse courage, inspire, inspirit, nerve, rally, *recreare,* refresh, remove doubt, remove fear, restore courage to, restore to assurance, restore to confidence, sanction, satisfy, solace, strengthen, support, sustain, uphold, uplift, warrant

REBATE, *noun* allowance, cut, decrease, deduction, diminution, discount, lessening of price, markdown, reduction, refund, reimbursement, repayment

REBATE, *verb* allow, allow as a discount, cut, deduct, diminish, discount, give back, lessen, make allowance, mark down, offer a discount, pare, pay back, reduce, refund, reimburse, render, repay, replace, restore, return, slash, strike off, subtract, take off

REBEL, *verb* arise, be disloyal, be insubordinate, be treasonable, betray, break with, *concitare,* defy, denounce, dethrone, disobey, insurrect, mutiny, oppose, overthrow, recalcitrate, refuse to conform, refuse to support, renounce, resist, resist lawful authority, revolt, revolutionize, riot, rise, rise in arms, *seditionem,* strike, take up arms, tergiversate, turn against, undermine

REBELLION, *noun* breach of orders, contumacy, defiance, disobedience, indiscipline, insubordination, insurgence, insurgency, insurrection, lack of discipline, lese majesty, *motus,* mutiny, opposition, outbreak, overthrow, overturn, resistance, resistance movement, revolt, revolution, riot, rising, *seditio,* sedition, strike, subversion, treason, upheaval, uprising, upset, violation

REBUFF, *noun* admonition, censure, check, chiding, cold shoulder, condemnation, counteraction, criticism, defeat, defiance, disapproval, discouragement, discourtesy, disregard, flat refusal, insult, opposition, peremptory refusal, rebuke, recoil, refusal, rejection, renouncement, renunciation, reprimand, reproach, reproof, repudiation, *repulsa,* repulse, resistance, rudeness, scolding, slight, snub, spurn

REBUFF, *verb* affront, brush aside, cast aside, check, chide, decline, despise, disallow, discard, disdain, dismiss, disown, disregard, drive back, ignore, insult, jilt, keep at a distance, neglect, rebuke, refuse, *reicere,* reject, renounce, repel, *repellere,* reprobate, reprove, repudiate, repulse, resist, scorn, send away, set aside, slight, snub, spurn, turn away

REBUKE, *verb* accuse, admonish, animadvert on, berate, blame, bring to book, call down, call to account, call to task, castigate, censure, charge, chastise, chide, correct, criminate, criticize, disapprove, exprobrate, find fault with, judge, lecture, objurgate, rate, remonstrate with, reprehend, *reprehendere,* reprimand, reproach, reprove, revile, scold, slate, take to task, tax, upbraid, *vituperare,* vituperate

REBUT, *verb* answer, argue, argue against, conflict, confute, contradict, contravene, controvert, countercharge, counterclaim, deny, disagree, disprove, dispute, explode, join issue, negate, negative, oppose, parry, prove false, rebuff, *redarguere,* refute, rejoin, *repellere,* reply, repudiate, respond, retaliate, retort, surrebut, surrejoin, take a stand against
ASSOCIATED CONCEPTS: rebut a presumption, rebut an argument

RECALCITRANT, *adjective* balky, callous, contrary, contumacious, defiant, disobedient, fractious, hardened, headstrong, immovable, insubordinate, intractable, mulish, mutinous, noncooperative, obstinate, obstreperous, opposing, oppugnant, pervicacious, rebellious, recusant, refractory, relentless, renitent, resistant, resistive, restive, stubborn, uncompliant, uncomplying, uncontrollable, uncooperative, ungovernable, unmanageable, unrelenting, unsubmissive, unwilling, unyielding, willful
ASSOCIATED CONCEPTS: recalcitrant witness

RECALL *(Call back), verb* abolish, abrogate, annul, cancel, disannul, dismiss, disqualify, invalidate, nullify, reanimate, reassemble, reconvene, repudiate, rescind, resuscitate, revive, revivify, *revocare,* revoke, summon back, take back, unsay, void, withdraw

RECALL *(Remember), verb* be reminded of, call up, commemorate, conjure up, dwell upon, evoke, fix in the mind, have memories of, keep in mind, know again, know by heart, look back upon, memorialize, memorize, place, recognize, recollect, *recordari,* recover knowledge of, refresh one's memory, relive, reminisce, retain, retrace, retrospect, review, revive, see in retrospect, summon up, think back to

RECANT, *verb* abjure, abrogate, annul, cancel, contradict, countermand, disaffirm, disannul, disavow, disclaim, disenact, disown, negate, nullify, recall, *recantare,* renounce, repudiate, rescind, retract, *retractare,* reverse, revoke, take back, tergiversate, unsay, vacate, void, withdraw
ASSOCIATED CONCEPTS: recant a confession, recant prior testimony

RECAPITULATE, *verb* *commemorare,* enumerate, give a summary of, go over, ingeminate, paraphrase, recite, recount, *referre,* reiterate, relate, repeat, rephrase, restate, retell, retrospect, reutter, review, reword, run over, say again, sum up, summarize, tell again

RECEIPT *(Act of receiving),* **noun** acceptance, *acceptio,* accession, acquirement, acquisition, admittance, assumption, attainment, gain, income, intake, obtainment, possession, reception, recipience
ASSOCIATED CONCEPTS: receipt of dividend, receipt of letters
FOREIGN PHRASES: *Quicquid recipitur, recipitur secundum modum recipientis.* Whatever is received is received in accordance with the intention of the recipient.

RECEIPT *(Proof of receiving),* **noun** acknowledgment of payment, acquittance, *apocha,* certificate of deposit, discharge, proof of delivery, proof of payment, quittance, release, signed notice, slip, stub, voucher
ASSOCIATED CONCEPTS: receipt in full, receipt of goods, receipt of letters, receipt of message, receipt of payment, rent receipt, warehouse receipt

RECEIPT *(Voucher),* **noun** assumption, bill, payment, reimbursement

RECEIVABLE, *adjective* due, due to be paid, in arrears, mature, outstanding, owed, owing, payable, redeemable, unpaid

RECEIVE *(Acquire),* **verb** accept, *accipere,* assume, be given, *capere,* catch, collect, come by, derive, draw, earn, gain, gather, get, inherit, make, obtain, pick up, pocket, procure, realize, reap, secure, seize, take, take in, take possession, win
ASSOCIATED CONCEPTS: contructively received, receive process, receive stolen property

RECEIVE *(Permit to enter),* **verb** absorb, accept, admit, adopt, allow, allow entrance, approve, embrace, entertain, give entrance, grant asylum, include, induct, initiate, install, let in, let through, permit, shelter, show in, take in, tolerate, usher in
ASSOCIATED CONCEPTS: receive into evidence, receive into the record

RECEIVER, **noun** accepter, assignee, benefactor, beneficiary, collector, consignee, depositary, fence, grantee, holder, receptacle, *receptor,* recipient, trustee
ASSOCIATED CONCEPTS: ancillary receiver, appointment of a receiver, equitable receiver, general receiver, joint receivers, legal receiver, principal receiver, provisional receiver, receiver in bankruptcy, receiver of stolen property, receivership, statutory receiver, temporary receiver

RECENT, *adjective* fresh, lately, new, newly arrived, not long past, novel, of recent occurrence, up-to-date

ASSOCIATED CONCEPTS: in recent memory, recent possession, recently

RECEPTIVE, *adjective* accessible, admissive, admitting, affectible, alert, amenable, aware, broadminded, cognitive, compassionate, comprehending, conscious, cordial, disposed, favorable, flexible, friendly, gracious, hospitable, impartial, impressible, impressionable, inclined, influenceable, interested, keen, movable, observant, open, open-minded, open to suggestion, perceptive, persuadable, reasonable, receiving, recipient, responsive, sensitive, susceptible, sympathetic, tolerant, tractable, unbiased, understanding, unjaundiced, unprejudiced, unswayed, welcoming, willing

RECESS, **noun** break, cessation, halt, hiatus, interim, interlude, intermission, interruption, interval, intervening period, lull, pause, repose, respite, rest, spell, stop, stoppage, time out, vacation, withdrawal

RECESS, *verb* adjourn, break, break up, dissolve, halt, hesitate, intermit, interrupt, lay off, pause, postpone, prorogue, relax, rest, retire, stop, suspend, take a recess, take a rest, take time out, vacation, withdraw
ASSOCIATED CONCEPTS: recess the court

RECIDIVATE, *verb* backslide, degenerate, deteriorate, relapse, regress, retrograde, slip back

RECIDIVISM, **noun** backsliding, degeneration, deterioration, habitual relapse into crime, recreancy, regression, relapse, repeated relapse into crime, retrogradation, retrogression, reversion

RECIDIVIST, **noun** convict, criminal, delinquent, guilty person, habitual criminal, hardened offender, lawbreaker, malefactor, malfeasant, malfeasor, offender, outlaw, repeat offender, reprobate, transgressor, wrongdoer

RECIPIENT, **noun** accepter, assignee, beneficiary, consignee, devisee, donee, grantee, heir, holder, inheritor, legatee, liquidator, object, payee, receiver, repository, transferee

RECIPROCAL, *adjective* alternating, bilateral, common, commutual, complemental, complementary, contingent, correlative, corresponding, give and take, interchangeable, interconnected, interdependent, interrelated, mutual, *mutuus,* parallel, reciprocative, requited, responded to, retaliative, retaliatory, retributive, returned, two-sided
ASSOCIATED CONCEPTS: reciprocal agreements, reciprocal promises, reciprocal wills

RECIPROCATE, *verb* act interchangeably, alternate, cooperate, exchange, follow successively, give and take, give in return, *inter se dare,* interchange, pay back, perform by turns, perform responsively, recompense, refund, reimburse, repay, requite, respond, retaliate, return, share, switch, take a turn, trade

RECIPROCITY, **noun** concord, cooperation, correspondence, exchange, give and take, interchange, interplay, mutuality, reciprocality, reciprocalness, reciprocation, return, *vicissitudo*
ASSOCIATED CONCEPTS: reciprocity of enforcement of laws between states

RECITAL, noun account, depiction, description, detailed statement, discourse, dissertation, *enumeratio,* explanation, exposition, graphic account, iteration, lecture, *narratio,* narration, narrative, oration, reaffirmation, reassertation, recapitulation, recitation, recountal, recounting, reiteration, relation, rendition, report, representation, restatement, retelling, review, statement, story, summary, summing up, telling
ASSOCIATED CONCEPTS: recital in a deed, recital of consideration

RECITE, verb address, articulate, chant, communicate, declaim, delineate, deliver, detail, *dicere,* discourse, divulge, dramatize, enact, *enumerare,* enumerate, *exponere,* express, give a verbal account, give expression, hold forth, interpret, lecture, list, make a speech, mouth, narrate, orate, parrot, perform, portray, preach, prelect, present, pronounce, quote, recapitulate, recount, reel off, rehearse, reiterate, relate, render, repeat, repeat by rote, repeat from memory, report, retell, say by heart, set forth, soliloquize, speak, spout, state, talk, tell, utter, voice

RECKLESS, adjective careless, disregardful, foolhardy, foolish, hasty, heedless, impetuous, improvident, imprudent, impulsive, inattentive, incautious, *incautus,* inconsiderate, *inconsideratus,* indifferent, indiscreet, injudicious, insensible, irrational, irresponsible, mindless, neglectful, *neglegens,* negligent, overconfident, overhasty, precipitate, temerous, thoughtless, unaware, uncircumspect, unconcerned, unheeding, unmindful, unobservant, unthinking, unwary, unwatchful, unwise, wanton, wild, without caution, without prudence
ASSOCIATED CONCEPTS: reckless abandon, reckless conduct, reckless disregard, reckless driving, reckless endangerment, reckless indifference

RECLAIM, verb appropriate, develop, get back, reacquire, rebuild, recall, recover, redeem, reestablish, regain, regenerate, reinstate, reoccupy, replevin, replevy, repossess, retake, retrieve
ASSOCIATED CONCEPTS: reclaim land

RECLASSIFICATION, noun change, changed ordering of priorities, changed priorities, reallocation, reallotment, reanalysis, reapportionment, rearrangement, reassignment, reassorting, reassortment, reconstitution, redistributing, redistribution, reestablishment, regradation, regrouping, reordering, reorganization, retabulating
ASSOCIATED CONCEPTS: reclassification of job titles

RECOGNITION, noun acceptance, acknowledgment, admission, apperception, appreciation, approval, attention, audition, avowal, award, awareness, citation, cognition, cognizance, commemoration, comprehension, consciousness, consideration, detection, diagnosis, discovery, distinguishment, divination, espial, finding, floor, gratitude, identification, insight, insite, knowledge, memory, nod, notice, perception, prize, realization, recall, recollection, regard, remembrance, reward, thanks, tribute
ASSOCIATED CONCEPTS: identification of a defendent

RECOGNIZANCE, noun acknowledgment, assurance, avowal, bond, commitment, guaranty, obligation, promise, security, *sponsio,* surety, warranty

RECOGNIZE *(Acknowledge),* **verb** accept, admit, allow, appreciate, avow, cite, commemorate, concede, confess, consent, defer to, dignify, exalt, give the floor to, give the nod to, grant, greet, honor, *noscere,* own, permit, realize, salute, suffer, tolerate, yield to

RECOGNIZE *(Perceive),* **verb** *agnoscere,* apprehend, ascertain, be aware of, be familiar with, call to mind, catch sight of, *cognoscere,* comprehend, conceive, descry, diagnose, discern, discover, distinguish, espy, identify, know, make out, mark, *noscitare,* notice, place, recall, recollect, recover knowledge, reidentify, remember, retain the impression of, see, sight, spy, understand, verify, view

RECOLLECT, verb be reminded of, bring to mind, call to mind, *commeminisse,* conjure up, go back, know again, look back upon, place, recall, recognize, *recordari,* relive, remember, reminisce, *reminisci,* renew, retrospect, review, revive, summon up, think of

RECOLLECTION, noun afterthought, consciousness, contemplation of the past, memoir, *memoria,* memory, mental image, mental picture, mindfulness, recall, recognition, *recordatio,* remembrance, reminiscence, retrospection
ASSOCIATED CONCEPTS: past recollection recorded, present recollection revived

RECOMMEND, verb acclaim, advance, advise, advocate, applaud, approbate, approve, back, be satisfied with, celebrate, commend, *commendare,* compliment, counsel, countenance, direct, endorse, esteem, exalt, exhort, extol, favor, give credit, glorify, guarantee, guide, instruct, laud, lend approval, lend support, make desirable, make preferable, move, persuade, praise, prescribe, present as worthy, prize, *probare,* promote, prompt, propose, ratify, sanction, second, speak highly of, speak well of, stand by, suggest, support, think highly of, uphold, urge, value, vouch for

RECOMMENDATION, noun admonition, advice, advocacy, advocation, approbation, approval, boost, celebration, certificate, *commendatio,* commendation, counsel, credential, encouragement, endorsement, esteem, exhortation, good opinion, guidance, injunction, instruction, judgment, *laudatio,* laudation, motion, opinion, praise, precept, prescription, proposal, proposition, reference, sanction, suggestion, support, testimonial, tip, tribute
FOREIGN PHRASES: *Simplex commendatio non obligat.* A mere recommendation is not binding. *Liberum est cuique apud se explorare an expediat sibi consilium.* Everyone is free to determine for himself whether a recommendation is advantageous to his interests.

RECOMMIT, verb call back, commit again, commit anew, give back, order back, refer back, remand, remit, return, send back

RECOMPENSE, noun amends, compensation, consideration, damages, defrayment, deserts, earnings, emolument, fee, gratuity, guerdon, income, indemnification, indemnity, meed, *merces,* payment, *praemium,* price, quittance, recoupment, recovery, redress, reimbursement, *remuneratio,* remuneration, reparation, repayment, requital, requitement, restitution, return, reward, salary, satisfaction, settlement, solatium, substitution, wage

RECONCILE, *verb* accustom, adapt, adjust, appease, arbitrate, bring into harmony, bring to acquiescence, bring to terms, bring together, conciliate, dictate peace, harmonize, heal the breach, intercede, make compatible, make consistent, make contented, make peace, make up, mediate, mend, mollify, negotiate, pacify, placate, propitiate, render concordant, resign, restore harmony, restore to friendship, reunite, settle, unite, win over

RECONCILIATION, *noun* accord, adjustment, agreement, amnesty, appeasement, arbitration, conciliation, concord, concordance, forgiveness, harmony, improved relations, mediation, mollification, mutual forgiveness, pacification, peace, peacemaking, propitiation, rapprochement, reconcilement, restoration of harmony, reunion, settlement, understanding, union
ASSOCIATED CONCEPTS: reconciliation of contradictory clauses

RECONDITE, *adjective* abstract, abstruse, arcane, cabalistic, complex, complicated, concealed, convoluted, covert, crabbed, cryptic, cryptical, dark, deep, difficult, elusive, enigmatic, esoteric, *exquisitus,* hidden, impenetrable, imperspicuous, intricate, involved, knotty, little-known, mysterious, mystic, mystical, nebulous, obscure, occult, orphic, perdu, perplexing, profound, puzzling, *reconditus,* secret, subtle, tangled, transcendental, unfamiliar, unintelligible

RECONFIRM, *verb* make certain, make sure again, reacknowledge, reaffirm, reapprove, reauthenticate, recertify, recheck, reendorse, reenforce, reestablish, resanction, resubstantiate, revalidate, verify again

RECONSIDER, *verb* amend, consider again, consult again, *denuo,* go over, have second thoughts, redeliberate, reevaluate, reexamine, reflect again, rehear, rejudge, reponder, *reputare,* rethink, retry, review, revise one's thoughts, reweigh, rework, think better of, think over
ASSOCIATED CONCEPTS: reconsider a judicial decision

RECONSTITUTE, *verb* bring back, make over, put back, reactivate, rebuild, recondition, reconstruct, reconvert, redo, reestablish, reform, regenerate, reintegrate, remake, remodel, remold, renew, renovate, reorganize, replace, restore

RECONSTRUCT, *verb* duplicate, make over, modernize, rearrange, rebuild, recast, reclaim, recompose, recondition, reconstitute, recreate, redo, reestablish, refashion, *reficere,* reform, refresh, refurbish, regenerate, rehabilitate, remake, remodel, remold, renew, renovate, reorganize, *restituere,* restore, revamp, rework
ASSOCIATED CONCEPTS: reconstruct the scene of a crime

RECONVERSION, *noun* change, change over, demilitarization, disarmament, palingenesis, passage, readjustment, rebirth, redintegration, reestablishment, regenerateness, regeneration, regenesis, rehabilitation, renaissance, reorganization, restoration, retrogression, retroversion, return, reversal, reversion, shift, transformation, transit, transition

RECORD, *noun* account, affidavit, annal, archive, attestation, catalogue, certificate, chronicle, contract, diurna, docket, documentation, dossier, entry, evidence, file, history, journal, list, log, memorandum, minute, note, proceedings, recording, register, roll, roster, transcript, transcription, *urbana,* written material
ASSOCIATED CONCEPTS: courts of record, judicial record, liens of record, matter of record, public record, record of convictions, record of encumbrances, Recording Acts

RECORD, *verb* book, calendar, catalogue, chronicle, copy, docket, document, enroll, enter, file, formalize, historify, historize, *in tabulas referre,* index, inscribe, insert, jot down, journalize, keep accounts, list, log, make a memorandum, make a note, make an entry, mark, note, *perscribere,* post, preserve, put in writing, put on paper, put on record, register, report, set down, tabulate, take down, take minutes, tally, write, write down
ASSOCIATED CONCEPTS: record a deed, record a lien, record a mortgage

RECOUNT, *verb* articulate, *commemorare,* communicate, convey, delineate, depict, describe, detail, divulge, *enarrare,* give an account, give the facts, give the particulars, hold forth, impart, iterate, particularize, picture, portray, recapitulate, recite, *referre,* reiterate, relate, render, repeat, report, retail, retell, reword, set forth, state, summarize, talk, tell, tell in detail, unfold

RECOUP *(Regain),* *verb* gain anew, get back, reacquire, reassume, recapture, reclaim, recover, redeem, reobtain, replace, replevin, replevy, repossess, retake, retrieve, take back, win back

RECOUP *(Reimburse),* *verb* compensate, give back, indemnify, make amends, make good, make reparations, make restitution, make up for, pay, pay back, quit, recompense, refund, remunerate, repay, replace, requite, restitute, restore, return, satisfy, settle

RECOURSE, *noun* avail, benefit, *confugere,* corrective device, corrective measure, device, disposal, legal redress, means, redress, remedy, resource, *se applicare, se conferre*
FOREIGN PHRASES: *Electa una via, non datur recursus ad alteram.* He who has chosen one course cannot have recourse to another.

RECOVER, *verb* achieve, acquire, attain, carry back, confer again, devolve again, *emergere,* gain anew, gain possession, get back, get by judgment, grant again, obtain, obtain by course of law, pass on again, procure, reacquire, realize, reassign, recapture, rechannel, reclaim, recoup, *recuperare,* redeem, regain, reobtain, *reparare,* replevy, repossess, resell, retake, retransmit, retrieve, salvage, secure, transfer again, transfer back, transport back, win back

RECOVERY *(Award),* *noun* compensation, damages, defrayal, discharge, financial remuneration, indemnification, indemnity, reckoning, reclamation, recompense, recoupment, redress, remittal, remuneration, reparation, repayment, restitution, satisfaction
ASSOCIATED CONCEPTS: primary recovery, recovery from an adversary
FOREIGN PHRASES: *Frustra agit qui judicium prosequi nequit cum effectu.* He sues vainly who cannot prosecute his judgment with effect. *Qui melius probat melius habet.* He who proves most recovers most.

RECOVERY (*Repossession*), *noun*   acquisition, *evictio*, obtainment, procuration, procurement, recapture, reclamation, recouping, redemption, regaining, regainment, replevin, replevy, rescue, restoration, retrieval, return, reversion, revindication, salvage, trover

ASSOCIATED CONCEPTS: recovery of chattels

RECREANT, *adjective*   afraid, apostate, apostatic, apostatical, base, betraying, caitiff, conniving, corrupt, cowardly, cowering, craven, dastardly, deceitful, derelict, designing, disaffected, disgraceful, dishonest, dishonorable, disloyal, dissembling, double-dealing, fainthearted, faithless, false, falsehearted, fearful, frightened, guileful, hesitant, inglorious, insidious, knavish, lilylivered, perfidious, pigeonhearted, poltroon, pusillanimous, renegade, reprobate, scheming, sham, skulking, sneaking, spiritless, timid, timorous, traitorous, treacherous, treasonable, two-faced, unconscienced, uncourageous, undependable, unfaithful, unmanly, unreliable, unscrupulous, untrue, untrustworthy, villainous, without honor, yellow

RECREATE, *verb*   create anew, duplicate, fascimile, heal, invigorate, make over, mend, reanimate, rebuild, recast, reconstruct, redo, reestablish, refashion, refocillate, reform, refresh, regenerate, rehabilitate, rejuvenate, remake, remodel, renew, *renovare*, renovate, reorganize, reproduce, restore, revamp, revive

RECRIMINATE, *verb*   accuse, bring a countercharge, come back at, countercharge, get even with, give in kind, have revenge, hit back, lash back, match, pay back, requite, retaliate, retort, retort a charge, return an accusation, return the charge, shift the blame, strike back, turn on, turn the tables on

RECRUDESCENCE, *noun*   backsliding, eruption, fresh outbreak, lapse, new outbreak, reactivation, reanimation, reappearance, recidivation, recrudescency, recurrence, regression, reinfection, relapse, renewal, resumption, resurgence, return, reversal, reverse, reversion, revival, revivification, reviviscence, reviviscency

RECRUIT, *verb*   add, augment, call up, collect, *conscribere*, conscript, draft, employ, enlarge, enlist, enroll, find manpower, gain, gather, increase, induct, muster, obtain, provide, raise, raise troops, reinvigorate, replenish, select, sign up, strengthen, supply, swell the ranks, take in

RECTIFY, *verb*   adjust, alter, ameliorate, amend, better, correct, *corrigere*, cure, emend, *emendare*, emendate, improve, make corrections, make right, meliorate, mend, perfect, put to rights, redress, reform, rehabilitate, remedy, renovate, repair, restore, revise, right, set right, set to rights, straighten, untangle

RECTITUDE, *noun*   character, conscientiousness, correctness, equity, fairness, faithfulness, faultlessness, fidelity, goodness, honesty, honor, honorableness, impartiality, impeccability, *integritas*, integrity, justice, justness, loyalty, merit, morality, principle, *probitas*, probity, propriety, purity, reputability, responsibility, right, righteousness, scrupulousness, straight course, straightforwardness, straightness, trustworthiness, uncorruptibility, uprightness, upstandingness, veracity, virtue, worthiness

RECUR, *verb*   be persistent, come again, come back, continue, crop up again, happen again, haunt, intermit, keep on, occur again, persevere, persist, reappear, recrudesce, renew, reoccur, repeat, resume, return, revert

RECUSANT, *adjective*   abjuratory, antagonistic, apostate, contrary, contumacious, differing, disagreeing, discordant, disobedient, dissentient, dissenting, dissident, heretic, heterodox, hostile, iconoclastic, impenitent, inflexible, inimical, insubordinate, negative, nonconformist, nonjuring, nonobservant, obdurate, obstinate, oppugnant, protestant, rebellious, recalcitrant, resistant, restive, schismatic, uncompliant, unconformable, unconforming, unconsenting, unfriendly, unrepentant, unresigned, unsubmissive, unwilling

REDACT, *verb*   blot out, censor, cut out, delete, edit, edit out, erase, excise, expunge, extirpate, make deletions, redraft, revamp, rework, rewrite, strike out, work over

ASSOCIATED CONCEPTS: censorship, redact testimony

REDEEM (*Repurchase*), *verb*   buy back, deliver, emancipate, get back, liberate, obtain, ransom, recall, recapture, reclaim, recoup, recover, regain, release, replevin, replevy, repossess, rescue, retrieve

ASSOCIATED CONCEPTS: right to redeem

REDEEM (*Satisfy debts*), *verb*   absolve, atone, compensate, do penance, expiate, give satisfaction, make amends, make up for, offset bad debts, propitiate, reform, satisfy, set straight, shrive, turn from sin

REDEMPTION, *noun*   deliverance, indemnification, reclamation, recovery, release, reparation, replevin, repossession, repurchase, rescue, restoration, retrieval, return, salvation

ASSOCIATED CONCEPTS: right of redemption

REDIRECT, *verb*   change course, change direction, direct again, forward, mail again, post on, readdress, remail, reship, send forward, send on, transmit

REDISTRIBUTE, *verb*   allot again, deal out again, dole out again, give out again, hand out again, parcel out again, readminister, reallot, reapportion, rearrange, reassign, reassort, reclass, reclassify, redivide, regroup, reissue, repartition, replace

REDOUND, *verb*   accrue, arise, cause, conduce, contribute, effect, ensue, flow from, follow, germinate from, influence, lead, proceed, *redundare*, result, spring, sprout from, yield

REDRESS, *verb*   adjust, aid, allay, alleviate, appease, atone, change, *compensare*, compensate, correct, cure, ease, expiate, fix, heal, help, improve, make amends, make good, make reparation, make up for, mend, pacify, palliate, propitiate, put right, readjust, rectify, relieve, remedy, repair, *restituere*, restore, right, satisfy, set right

ASSOCIATED CONCEPTS: legal redress

REDUCE, *verb*   abate, abbreviate, abridge, attenuate, bring low, compact, compress, condense, contract, curtail, cut down, decimate, decrease, demean, diminish, disgrace, downgrade, humble, *imminuere*, lessen, lower, make less, make smaller, minimize, narrow, shorten, shrink, thin

ASSOCIATED CONCEPTS: reduce a sentence, reduce damages

REDUNDANCY, noun duplication, excess, excessiveness, immoderation, inordinacy, inordinate amount, needlessness, nimiety, overplus, oversupply, pleonasm, recurrence, redundance, *redundantia,* reiteration, repetition, restatement, retelling, superabundance, superfluity, surplus, tautology

REDUNDANT, adjective excessive, inordinate, needless, otiose, overmuch, periphrastic, pleonastic, repetitive, repititious, superabundant, superfluous, supernumerary, *supervacaneus,* surplus, tautologic, tautological, uncalled-for, undue, unnecessary, unrequired, useless, verbose, wordy

REEXAMINE, verb check upon again, crossexamine, cross-question, go back over, reanalyze, recheck, reconsider, reinquire, reinvestigate, reprobe, requestion, rescrutinize, restudy, retrace, review

REFER (Direct attention), verb adduce, allude, appertain, apply, assign, bear upon, cite, concern, connect, connote, denote, hint at, indicate, mention, *perstringere,* pertain, point, quote, relate, signify, suggest, touch on

REFER (Send for action), verb ask help of, assign, call in, call on, consign, consult, deliver, entrust, recommend, *referre,* seek advice, send, submit, transfer

REFEREE, noun adjudicator, arbiter, arbitrator, compromiser, conciliator, interceder, intercessor, intermediary, intermediate, intermediator, internuncio, intervener, judge, judicator, mediator, moderator, peacemaker, propitiator, reconciler, settler, umpire
ASSOCIATED CONCEPTS: appointment of referee, referee in bankruptcy, referee's findings, special referee, trial before referee

REFERENCE (Allusion), noun attribution, clue, connotation, cue, hint, implication, implied indication, imputation, incidental mention, indication, indirect implication, inference, inkling, innuendo, insinuation, intimation, mention, *ratio,* referment, subtle communication, suggestion

REFERENCE (Citation), noun ascription, assignation, assignment, authority, citing, connecting, credit, data, derivation from, designation, documentation, enumeration, indicating, mention, mentioning, pointing out, quotation, quoted passage, quoting, recitation, referment, referral, relating, source, source material, substantiation
ASSOCIATED CONCEPTS: incorporation by reference
FOREIGN PHRASES: *Verba relata hoc maxime operantur per referentiam, ut in eis inesse videntur.* Words incorporated by reference have as great an effect through reference, as they are deemed to be inserted.

REFERENCE (Recommendation), noun affirmation, assurance, attestation, attesting declaration, authenticated confirmation, averment, avouchment, avowal, avowance, certificate of character, certification, commendation, confirmation, declaration, endorsement, laudation, letter in support, letter of introduction, letter of recommendation, substantiation, testification, testimony, validification, verification, voucher, vouching, witnessing

REFERENDUM, noun ballot, decision, determination, discretion, election, expression of choice, mandate, plebiscite, poll, popular choice, popular decision, popular vote, preference, say, selection, voice, vote

REFERRAL, noun allusion, implication, inference, innuendo, insinuation, making reference, mention, reference, referment

REFINANCE, verb back again, contribute to again, finance again, fund again, invest in again, lend to again, loan to again, provide capital again, provide funds for again, reinvest, sponsor again, subsidize again, support again, underwrite again

REFLECT (Mirror), verb bounce back, cast back, copy, ditto, emulate, give back, give forth, imitate, *ostendere,* rebound, repeat, reproduce, send back, show an image, simulate, throw back

REFLECT (Ponder), verb analyze, brood over, cerebrate, *cogitare,* cogitate, commune with oneself, conceive, concentrate, consider, *considerare,* contemplate, deduce, deliberate, dream, dwell upon, excogitate, give thought to, meditate, mull over, muse, pore over, puzzle over, reason, revolve in the mind, ruminate, speculate, study, theorize, think, turn over, weigh, wonder

REFLECTION (Image), noun counterpart, double, duplicate, echo, *imago,* impression, likeness, semblance, specter

REFLECTION (Thought), noun absorption, analysis, cerebration, *cogitatio,* cogitation, concentration, *consideratio,* consideration, contemplation, deliberation, excogitation, exercise of the intellect, intellection, meditation, mentation, musing, pondering, *ratio,* reasoning, reverie, rumination, self-communing, self-counsel, speculation, study, thinking, weighing
FOREIGN PHRASES: *Nemo cogitationis poenam patitur.* No one suffers punishment on account of his thoughts.

REFORM, noun advancement, alteration, amelioration, amendment, betterment, change, *correctio,* correction, development, elevation, *emendatio,* enhancement, enrichment, improvement, innovation, melioration, progress, progression, progressivism, recast, reclamation, reconstitution, reconstruction, recovery, recreation, rectification, refinement, reformation, regeneration, remaking, renewal, renovation, repair, revision

REFORM, verb ameliorate, amend, better, change, convert, correct, *corrigere,* cure, emend, enhance, fix, form anew, improve, make better, make over, meliorate, mend, modify, rearrange, recast, reclaim, reconstitute, reconstruct, rectify, redeem, redo, redress, reestablish, refashion, refine, regenerate, rehabilitate, remake, remedy, remodel, renew, renovate, reorganize, repair, repent, reshape, restore, revise, revolutionize, rework, set straight, uplift
ASSOCIATED CONCEPTS: reform a contract, reform a deed, reform a lease, reform a will, reform an instrument

REFORMATORY, noun bridewell, correction facility, house of correction, house of detention, jail, penal institution, penitentiary, prison, reform school

REFRAIN, verb abstain, avoid, be temperate, break off, cease, check, contain oneself, curb oneself, decline, desist, discontinue, dispense with, do without, eschew, evade, exercise self-control, forbear, forestall, forgo, forsake, halt, have nothing to do with, hold back, keep from, leave off, refuse, renounce, *se abstinere, se continere,* shun, stop, swear off, take no part in, waive, withdraw, withhold

REFUGE, *noun*   ark, asylum, citadel, covert, coverture, harbor, haven, hiding place, lee, *perfugium,* place of protection, place of safety, protection, *receptaculum, refugium,* resort, retreat, safe place, safety, sanctuary, security, shelter, stronghold
ASSOCIATED CONCEPTS: flight
FOREIGN PHRASES: *Domus sua cuique est tutissimum refugium.* Everyone's home is his safest refuge. *Debet sua cuique domus esse perfugium tut issimum.* Everyman's home should be a perfectly safe refuge.

REFUND, *noun*   compensation, cut, discount, indemnification, money back, payment for expenses, rebate, recompense, recoupment, reduction, refundment, reimbursement, repayment, replacement, restitution, return, satisfaction, settlement

REFUND, *verb*   adjust, compensate, *dissolvere,* give back, honor a claim, indemnify, make amends, make compensation, make good, make restitution, pay back, rebate, recompense, *reddere,* redeem, reimburse, repay, replace, requite, restore, return, satisfy, settle, square

REFUSAL, *noun*   abjuration, abnegation, ban, debarment, declination, declinature, defiance, denial, disallowance, disapprobation, disapproval, disavowal, disclaimer, discountenance, enjoinment, exclusion, incompliance, interdiction, negation, negative answer, nonacceptance, noncompliance, nonconsent, prohibition, proscription, rebuff, *recusatio,* regrets, rejection, renouncement, renunciation, repudiation, repulse, resistance, unwillingness, veto
ASSOCIATED CONCEPTS: refusal to answer, refusal to bargain, refusal to proceed, refusal to testify, right of first refusal
FOREIGN PHRASES: *Reprobata pecunia liberat solventem.* Money refused releases the debtor.

REFUSE, *verb*   abjure, abnegate, abstain, balk, bar, be obstinate, be unwilling, beg to be excused, cast aside, debar, decline, demur, deny, disaccord with, disallow, disapprove, disavow, disclaim, discountenance, discredit, dismiss, disown, dispense with, dissent, exclude, forswear, grudge, hesitate, hold back, negative, object to, oppose, pass up, prohibit, protest, rebuff, recoil, regret, reject, renege, renounce, repel, repudiate, resist, revoke, scruple, send regrets, shirk, shun, shy at, spurn, stick at, stickle, traverse, turn down, turn from, veto, withdraw, withhold consent

REFUTE, *verb*   abnegate, belie, cancel, confute, contend, contradict, contravene, controvert, crush, debate, defeat, demolish, deny, destroy, disaffirm, disclaim, discredit, dispose of, disprove, explode, falsify, gainsay, impugn, invalidate, negate, oppose, oppugn, overthrow, parry, prove false, quash, rebut, *redarguere, refellere,* repel, repudiate, retort, squelch, tear down, traverse

REGARD *(Attention),* **noun**   advertence, advertency, alertness, application, attentiveness, care, concentration, concern, consideration, examination, heed,

heedfulness, intentness, interest, mindfulness, notice, observation, scrutiny, vigilance, watch, watchfulness

REGARD *(Esteem),* **noun**   admiration, affection, appreciation, approbation, approval, attachment, awe, celebrity, consideration, credit, deference, devotion, distinction, eminence, estimation, fame, famousness, favor, fondness, good name, honor, interest, judgment, liking, loyalty, note, opinion, reputability, reputation, repute, respect, *respectus,* reverence, *studium,* valuation, value, veneration

REGARD *(Hold in esteem),* **verb**   admire, adore, appreciate, approve, be fond of, be impressed, be in awe, care for, cherish, defer to, esteem, exalt, extol, glorify, have a liking for, have regard for, hold a high opinion of, hold dear, hold in affection, hold in regard, honor, idolize, look up to, pay homage to, pay tribute, praise, prize, respect, *respicere,* revere, reverence, think highly of, think well of, treasure, value, venerate, worship

REGARD *(Pay attention),* **verb**   advert to, attend, be attentive, be aware of, be conscious of, be mindful, bear in mind, behold, consider, contemplate, deem, *ducere,* gaze, give heed to, heed, keep in sight, look, look at, look upon, mark, mind, note, notice, *observare,* observe, perceive, peruse, scan, scrutinize, see, survey, take cognizance of, take notice, think about, view, watch, witness
ASSOCIATED CONCEPTS: due regard

REGARDLESS, *adverb*   albeit, all the same, although, anyhow, anyway, anywise, at any rate, by any means, despite, even though, however, in any case, in any event, in spite of, *incuriosus,* irrespective of, *neglegens,* nevertheless, nonetheless, notwithstanding, still, though, without regard to, without respect to

REGIME, *noun*   administration, authority, command, directorship, dominion, governance, government, incumbency, management, political system, power, primacy, regency, regimen, reign, rule, sovereignty, supervision, supremacy

REGION, *noun*   area, circle, circuit, clime, compass, confines, country, county, demesne, diocese, district, division, domain, environs, field, land, latitude, limited area, locale, locality, location, *locus,* neighborhood, part, place, portion, precinct, province, purlieus, quarter, range, realm, *regio,* scene, scope, section, sector, situation, space, sphere, spot, terrain, territory, *tractus,* vicinage, vicinity, ward, zone

REGIONAL, *adjective*   circumscribed, district, divisional, geographical, insular, local, localized, native, neighborhood, parochial, provincial, restricted, sectional, specific, subdivisional, territorial, vernacular, zonal

REGISTER, *noun*   agenda, *album,* almanac, archive, arrangement, balance sheet, calendar, catalogue, chronicle, chronology, day book, diary, docket, ephemeris, file, invoice, journal, ledger, *liber,* list, log, log book, memorandum, minutes, notes, proceedings, record, registration book, roll, roster, schedule, *tabulae,* written record
ASSOCIATED CONCEPTS: register a complaint, register to vote

REGISTER, *verb*　　book, calendar, catalogue, check in, chronicle, engage, enlist, enroll, enter, file, *in album,* index, inscribe, join, matriculate, note down, order, *perscribere,* post, program, record, reserve, schedule, sign in, sign up, subscribe, *tabulas referre,* tabulate
ASSOCIATED CONCEPTS: register to vote

REGISTRATION, *noun*　　booking, bookkeeping, cataloguing, certification, chronicling, enlistment, enrolling, enrollment, filing, inscribing, installing, listing, matriculation, noting down, record keeping, recording, registry, reservation, signing up, tabulation

REGRESS, *verb*　　backslide, fall again into, fall back, fall behind, go back, move backward, pass back, recede, relapse, retrocede, retrograde, retrogress, return, reverse, revert, turn back

REGRESSIVE, *adjective*　　atavistic, backsliding, backward, decadent, degenerate, ill-advised, lapsing, on the decline, receding, recessive, recidivistic, recidivous, refluent, relapsing, retrocedent, retrograde, retrogressive, reverse, reversed, reversional, reversionary, tergiversating, withering
ASSOCIATED CONCEPTS: regressive tax

REGRET, *verb*　　apologize, be disturbed over, be penitent, be remorseful, be sorry for, bemoan, bewail, blame oneself, cry over, deplore, disapprove of, feel conscience stricken, feel uneasy about, fret, grieve at, have a bad conscience, have qualms about, lament, mourn for, repent, repine, reproach oneself, rue, sorrow for, weep over

REGRETTABLE, *adjective*　　adverse, calamitous, catastrophic, deplorable, dire, disadvantageous, disastrous, dreadful, grievous, ill-boding, ill-fated, ill-omened, inauspicious, inopportune, lamentable, *paenitendus,* regretted, ruinous, sad, scandalous, terrible, unfavorable, unfortunate, unhappy, unlucky, unpropitious, unsuccessful, untimely, untoward, woeful

REGULAR *(Conventional), adjective*　　according to rule, accustomed, average, classic, common, commonplace, conformable, consuetudinal, consuetudinary, conventional, customary, everyday, expected, familiar, general, habitual, *iustus,* natural, normal, *ordinarius,* ordinary, popular, predictable, prevailing, prevalent, routine, run of the mill, standard, stock, traditional, typical, unchanged, undeviating, unexceptional, usual, wonted, workaday
ASSOCIATED CONCEPTS: regular employment, regular interest

REGULAR *(Orderly), adjective*　　balanced, *certus, constans,* controlled, cyclic, established, even, fixed, invariable, measured, methodical, patterned, periodic, periodical, recurring, regulated, rhythmic, seasonal, stable, steady, successive, symmetrical, systematic, uniform, unvarying, well-regulated
ASSOCIATED CONCEPTS: presumption of regularity, regular course of business, regular election

REGULARITY, *noun*　　balance, clockwork precision, conformity, congruity, consistency, *constantia,* even tenor, evenness, exactness, harmony, homogeneity, invariability, levelness, method, methodicalness, order, orderliness, *ordo,* periodicity, precision, proportion, punctuality, recurrence, regular recurrence, regular return, regularness, rhythm, sameness, steadiness, symmetry, uniformity
ASSOCIATED CONCEPTS: presumption of regularity

REGULATE *(Adjust), verb*　　*administrare,* allocate, arrange, balance, coordinate, correct, dispose, level, make right, make uniform, methodize, moderate, modulate, normalize, order, organize, put in order, rectify, reduce to method, regularize, remedy, render accordant, restore equilibrium, set right, square, standardize, straighten out, systematize, temper

REGULATE *(Manage), verb*　　administer, conduct, control, determine, direct, discipline, govern, guide, handle, have authority over, have charge of, head, lead, order, oversee, police, preside over, rule, steer, superintend, supervise
ASSOCIATED CONCEPTS: regulate commerce, regulated by law

REGULATION *(Management), noun*　　adjustment, *administratio,* administration, arrangement, conduct, coordination, disposal, disposition, economy, government, guidance, handling, lawmaking, moderation, organization, regimentation, steerage, superintendence, supervision, systematization

REGULATION *(Rule), noun*　　act, bylaw, canon, code, command, commandment, decree, dictate, direction, directive, discipline, edict, enactment, injunction, instruction, *iussum,* law, legislation, mandate, measure, order, ordinance, *praeceptum,* precept, prescript, prescription, regimen, statute
ASSOCIATED CONCEPTS: municipal regulation, reasonable regulation, zoning regulation

REHABILITATE, *verb*　　ameliorate, amend, bring back, fix, furbish, improve, make over, meliorate, mend, readjust, rebuild, reclaim, recondition, reconstitute, reconstruct, reconvert, rectify, redeem, redintegrate, reestablish, refashion, refit, refurbish, reintegrate, reinvigorate, remake, renew, renovate, repair, reproduce, *restituere,* restore, revamp, revive, revivify, salvage
ASSOCIATED CONCEPTS: rehabilitate an offender, rehabilitate an insurance company

REHABILITATION, *noun*　　adjustment, alteration, amelioration, development, improvement, instauration, melioration, readjustment, rebuilding, reclamation, reconstitution, reconstruction, recreation, recuperation, redemption, redintegration, reeducation, reestablishment, reformation, regeneration, reindoctrination, reinstatement, reinvigoration, remaking, remodeling, renewal, renovation, reorganization, repair, reparation, restitution, restoration, resurrection, resuscitation, return, revival, revivement, revivification, salvation
ASSOCIATED CONCEPTS: company rehabilitation

REHEARING, *noun*　　new hearing, reassessment, reexamination, reinquiry, retrial

REIMBURSE, *verb*　　compensate, indemnify, make good, make reparation, make restitution, pay back, rebate, recompense, *reddere,* redress, refund, remit, remunerate, repay, replace, requite, restore, satisfy, settle

REIMBURSEMENT, *noun*　　compensation, damages, defrayal, disbursement, giving back, indemnification, indemnity, paying back, payment, rebate, recompense, recoupment, redress, refund, remuneration, reparation, repayment, replacement, restitution, restoration

FOREIGN PHRASES: *Frustra petis quod statim alteri reddere cogeris.* You ask in vain that which you will immediately be compelled to restore to another.

REINFORCE, *verb* augment, bolster, boost, brace, buttress, *confirmare,* energize, fortify, intensify, reconstitute, redouble, reestablish, refurbish, reinvigorate, reorganize, replenish, strengthen, supplement, support

REINFORCEMENT, *noun* addition, additional strength, aid, assistance, augmentation, auxiliary, backing, boost, buttress, fresh supply, furtherance, help, helping hand, increase, prop, protection, relief, replenishment, strengthener, supplement, *supplementum,* support

REINSTATE, *verb* bring back, place in a former state, put back, put back into service, reappoint, reconstitute, reestablish, rehabilitate, rehire, reinaugurate, reinstall, reinvest, remit, replace, reseat, *restituere,* restore, restore to office, restore to power, return, revest, revive

ASSOCIATED CONCEPTS: reinstate to a job

REITERATE, *verb* duplicate, echo, go over, harp upon, ingeminate, *iterare,* iterate, reaffirm, reassert, recapitulate, redouble, repeat, rephrase, reproduce, restate, retell, reutter, review, reword, say again, say repeatedly, state again

REJECT, *verb* abandon, abhor, abjure, abnegate, banish, blackball, boycott, brush aside, cashier, cast aside, cast away, cast off, challenge, contravene, controvert, decline, demur, deny, despise, detest, disaffirm, disallow, disapprove, disavow, disbelieve, discard, disclaim, discount, discredit, disdain, disinherit, dismiss, disown, dispute, disregard, dissent, dodge, eject, eliminate, eradicate, excise, exclude, expel, extirpate, extract, forbid, forswear, gainsay, get rid of, hold in contempt, ignore, impugn, jeer, jettison, jilt, keep out, lay aside, leave out, neglect, object, oppose, ostracize, oust, overrule, pass by, pass over, preclude, prohibit, proscribe, protest, rebuff, refuse, refuse to accept, refuse to consider, *reicere,* remove, renounce, repel, reprobate, *repudiare,* repudiate, repulse, revolt, scoff at, scout, scrap, screen out, set aside, shun, slight, snub, spurn, take exception to, throw aside, throw out, traverse, uproot, veto, vote against, waive, weed out

REJECTION, *noun* abandonment, abhorrence, abjuration, abnegation, averseness, ban, banishment, cashiering, contempt, contravention, debarment, declension, declination, declinature, defeat, denial, deportation, deposal, disaffirmation, disagreement, disallowance, disapprobation, disapproval, disbelief, discardure, discharge, discrediting, disdain, disfavor, disinheritance, dislike, dislodgment, dismissal, disownment, dissent, distrust, dubiety, dubiousness, elimination, eradication, erasure, eviction, excision, exclusion, excommunication, exile, exilement, expatriation, expulsion, extirpation, firing, gainsaying, hatred, intolerance, intoleration, mistrust, negation, neglect, nonacceptance, noninclusion, objection, omission, opposition, ostracism, ouster, overruling, prohibition, proscription, rebuff, recantation, refusal, *reiectio,* relegation, removal,

renunciation, reprobation, *repudiatio,* repudiation, repulse, revilement, revolt, riddance, scorn, slight, snub, spurning, uprooting, veto, waiver

ASSOCIATED CONCEPTS: rejection of claim

REJOINDER, *noun* answer, counteraccusation, counterargument, countercharge, counterstatement, defense, plea in rebuttal, reply, response, retort

RELAPSE, *noun* backsliding, declension, declination, decline, degeneration, deterioration, escheat, fall, lapse, *recidere,* recidivation, recidivism, recrudescence, recrudescency, recurrence, regress, regression, reoccurrence, repetition, retrocession, retrogradation, retrogression, retroversion, return, reversal, reverse, reversion, setback, sinking, weakening

RELAPSE, *verb* backslide, decline, degenerate, deteriorate, fall, fall back, *recidere,* recidivate, recrudesce, regress, *relabi,* renew, retrocede, retrograde, retrogress, retrovert, return, reverse, revert, sink back, slide back, slip back, start again, start fresh, suffer a relapse, wane, weaken

RELATE (Establish a connection), *verb* affect, affiliate, ally, appertain to, apply, associate, bear upon, bracket, concern, connect, consociate, correlate, draw a parallel, filiate, group, have a bearing on, identify, integrate, interconnect, interrelate, link, parallel, pertain, *pertinere,* tie, unite

RELATE (Tell), *verb* acquaint, advise, air, announce, apprise, broadcast, communicate, convey, declare, describe, detail, disclose, divulge, elucidate, *enarrare,* express, give a report, give an account, impart, inform, make known, mention, narrate, notify, observe, particularize, phrase, portray, put into words, recite, recount, repeat, report, represent in words, retell, reveal, say, set forth, speak, state, utter, vent, ventilate, verbalize

RELATED, *adjective* affiliated, affined, affinitive, agnate, akin, allied, analogous, applicable, apposite, appropriate, appurtenant, associated, cognate, *cognatus,* collateral, commutual, complementary, congeneric, congenerical, congenerous, connate, connatural, connected, consanguine, consanguineous, consociate, contingent, correlated, correlative, correspondent, dependent, enmeshed, germane, implicated, interconnected, interdependent, interrelated, intertwined, interwoven, kindred, knit, like, linked, mutual, pertinent, *propinquus, proximus,* reciprocal, relative, relevant, tied

RELATION (Connection), *noun* affiliation, affinity, alliance, analogy, applicability, appositeness, apposition, association, bearing, bond, closeness, cognation, comparableness, connation, connaturalness, *connexion,* correlation, correspondence, homology, indentification, interconnection, interrelationship, liaison, likeness, link, mutuality, nearness, nexus, pertinence, propinquity, reference, relationship, relative position, relevance, resemblance, similarity, similitude, tie, tie-in

RELATION (Kinship), *noun* blood relative, blood tie, *cognatus,* common ancestry, common descent, common lineage, common stock, consanguinity, family connection, family tie, kin, kindred, kinsman, *propinquus,* relationship, relative

RELATIONSHIP *(Connection),* **noun** alignment, amalgamation, analogy, appositeness, association, bearing, bond, coaction, coalition, *cognatio,* cognation, combination, confederacy, *coniunctio,* connecting link, consociation, correlation, interconnection, interdependence, interrelation, interrelationship, involvement, likeness, link, linkage, mutuality, nearness, pertinence, rapport, reciprocity, relation, relevance, relevancy, tie, unification, union, unity
ASSOCIATED CONCEPTS: privity

RELATIONSHIP *(Family tie),* **noun** affinity, blood relation, blood ties, consanguinity, extraction, family connection, filiation, kindredship, kinship, lineage, *propinquitas,* relation
ASSOCIATED CONCEPTS: blood relationship, intestate succession, paternity proceeding
FOREIGN PHRASES: *Affinis mei affinis non est mihi affinis.* One who is a relative of my relative by marriage is not my relative.

RELATIVE *(Comparative),* **adjective** analogous, commensurable, commensurate, *comparare,* compared, contrastive, correlative, correspondent, corresponding, proportional, proportionate
ASSOCIATED CONCEPTS: dependent relative revocation, relative fault

RELATIVE *(Relevant),* **adjective** affinitive, allied, applicable, apposite, appositional, appropriate, appurtenant, apropos, apt, associated, bearing on, cognate, collateral, compatible, concerning, connected, connective, correlated, fit, fitting, germane, interconnected, kindred, material, pertaining, pertinent, referring, related, relating, relational, respecting, suitable

RELATIVE, **noun** blood relation, clansman, cognate, *cognatus,* connection, family, kin, kindred, kinsman, kith, member of the family, *propinquus,* relation, sib

RELAX, **verb** abate, allay, assuage, be lenient, bend, diminish, ease, give, lenify, lessen, milden, mitigate, moderate, modify, modulate, reduce, relent, remit, show clemency, show pity, slacken, soften, temper, weaken, yield
ASSOCIATED CONCEPTS: relax a restriction

RELEASE, **noun** abandonment, absolution, acquittal, acquittance, amnesty, casting away, cession, clearance, compurgation, deliverance, disbanding, discarding, discharge, disculpation, disengagement, disentanglement, disenthrallment, dismissal, dispensation, disposal, emancipation, exculpation, excusal, excuse, exemption, exoneration, extrication, forgiveness, freeing, immunity, laying aside, *liberatio,* liberation, manumission, *missio,* pardon, pardonment, quietus, relinquishment, salvation, setting free, sparing, unchaining, unfettering, unharnessing, untying, waiver, yielding
ASSOCIATED CONCEPTS: binding release
FOREIGN PHRASES: *Eodem modo quo oritur, eodem modo dissolvitur.* It is discharged in the same manner in which it was created. *Quodque dissolvitur eodem modo quo ligatur.* A thing is unbound in the same manner that it is made binding.

RELEASE, **verb** clear, deliver, discharge, disengage, disenthrall, dismiss, emancipate, enfranchise, exculpate, excuse, exempt, exonerate, *exsolvere,* extricate,

forgive, free, give clearance, give up, *laxare,* let go, let out, *liberare,* liberate, manumit, relieve, relinquish, remit, reprieve, save, set at large, set at liberty, set free, set loose, spare, unburden, unfetter, yield
ASSOCIATED CONCEPTS: release a claim, release a lien

RELEGATE, **verb** allocate, assign, ban, banish, bar, cast out, consign, convey, delegate, deport, depute, discard, dislodge, dismiss, dispatch, displace, elide, eliminate, entrust, eradicate, exclude, excommunicate, exile, expatriate, expel, isolate, omit, ostracize, oust, outlaw, proscribe, push aside, refer, reject, remand, remove, segregate, send away, separate, set apart, shut out, throw out, transfer, transport, turn over to

RELENT, **verb** abate severity, accede, acquiesce, be assuaged, be compassionate, be compliant, be forgiving, be merciful, be mollified, be placated, be pliant, be submissive, be tolerant, bend, defer to, feel compassion, feel for, forgive, give, give in, give quarter, give way, grow lenient, grow less severe, have mercy, have sympathy, *iram remittere, molliri,* pity, relax, remit, resign, show mercy, soften, spare, succumb, sympathize, unbend, yield

RELENTLESS, **adjective** assiduous, bowelless, brutish, cold, cold-blooded, cold-hearted, continuous, cruel, determined, dictatorial, endless, hard, hard of heart, hardhearted, harsh, heedless, *immisericors,* impenitent, imperious, implacable, inclement, indefatigable, *inexorabilis,* inexorable, inflexible, insensitive, insistent, intolerant, intransigent, iron, merciless, obdurate, obstinate, perseverant, persevering, persistent, pertinacious, pitiless, pressing, rancorous, remorseless, resolute, rigid, ruthless, sedulous, severe, steadfast, stern, stony-hearted, stringent, stubborn, tenacious, truculent, tyrannical, unappeasable, unbending, uncompassionate, uncompromising, undaunted, undeviating, unfaltering, unfeeling, unflinching, unforgiving, unintermitting, unmerciful, unmitigable, unmoved by pity, unpitying, unrelenting, unremitting, unshrinking, unsparing, unswerving, unsympathetic, unyielding, vindictive, without regrets

RELEVANCE, **noun** affinity, applicability, application, appositeness, appropriateness, aptness, association, bearing, compatibility, concern, congruence, congruency, congruity, connection, correlation, correspondence, importance, materiality, pertinence, reference, relation, relationship, significance, suitability, suitableness, tie-in
ASSOCIATED CONCEPTS: objection as to relevance

RELEVANT, **adjective** *ad rem spectare,* admissible, affinitive, allied, applicable, apposite, appropriate, appurtenant, apropos, apt, associated, cognate, compatible, concerning, conformant, conforming, congruent, congruous, connected, consentaneous, consistent, consonant, correlated, correspondent, felicitous, fit, fitting, germane, important, material, pertaining to, pertinent, proper, referring to, related, relative, seasonable, suitable, tied in with, to the point, to the purpose
ASSOCIATED CONCEPTS: relevant evidence, relevant question

RELIABLE, **adjective** accurate, assured, authentic, believable, certain, competent, conclusive, conscientious, constant, credible, definite, dependable, devoted, evidential, exact, faithful, genuine, guaranteed, honest,

honorable, incontestable, incontrovertible, indisputable, indubitable, inerrable, inerrant, infallible, irrefutable, legitimate, loyal, proved, real, reputable, respectable, responsible, safe, scrupulous, secure, sincere, sound, stable, stanch, steadfast, steady, strong, sure, tried, true, trustworthy, trusty, truthful, undeniable, unequivocal, unerring, unfailing, unhazardous, unperilous, unquestionable, upright, veracious, veridical, worthy of trust
ASSOCIATED CONCEPTS: reliable evidence, reliable testimony, reliable witness

RELIANCE, *noun*   acceptance, affiance, assurance, assuredness, belief, certainty, certitude, confidence, conviction, credence, credulity, dependability, dependence, expectation, faith, *fides, fiducia,* security, support, sureness, troth, trust

RELIEF *(Aid), noun*   accommodation, assistance, attention, *auxilium,* avail, backing, care, cooperation, encouragement, help, ministration, ministry, promotion, reinforcement, rescue, respite, salvation, *subsidium,* succor, support, sustenance, treatment

RELIEF *(Legal redress), noun*   award, compensation, correction, decision, indemnification, judgment, payment, recompense, rectification, remedy, reparation, restitution, restoration, retribution, satisfaction
ASSOCIATED CONCEPTS: affirmative relief, bill of discovery and relief, complete relief, declaratory relief, further relief, primary relief, supplemental relief
FOREIGN PHRASES: **Judex non reddit plus quam quod petens ipse requirit.** A judge should not render judgments for a larger sum than the plaintiff demands.

RELIEF *(Release), noun*   abatement, alleviation, amelioration, assuagement, deliverance, diminishment, diminution, discharge, disencumberance, easement, liberation, mitigation, palliation, reduction, *remedium,* remission, reprieve, respite, rest, *sublevatio*

RELIEVE *(Free from burden), verb*   abate, allay, assuage, deliver, disburden, disencumber, disengage, emancipate, exempt, extricate, free, liberate, lighten, manumit, mitigate, moderate, relax, release, rid, set free, unburden, unload

RELIEVE *(Give aid), verb*   aid, alleviate, ameliorate, assist, better, calm, comfort, cure, ease, give help, give relief, heal, help, improve, medicate, meliorate, minister to, palliate, reenforce, remedy, render assistance, salve, soothe, succor, treat

RELINQUISH, *verb*   abandon, abdicate, abjure, cast off, cease, cede, deliver, demit, desert, disclaim, discontinue, dismiss, do without, drop, eliminate, forgo, forsake, forswear, give over, give up, give up claim to, go without, hand over, jettison, lay aside, leave, let go, part with, pull out, quit, reject, release, *relinquere,* renounce, resign, rid, sacrifice, secede from, sign away, spare, surrender, throw away, turn one's back on, vacate, waive, withdraw, yield
ASSOCIATED CONCEPTS: relinquish a claim

RELISH, *verb*   appreciate, bask in, be fond of, be pleased with, delight in, derive pleasure from, enjoy, fancy, feel gratification, feel joy, feel pleasure, gloat over, like, luxuriate in, prefer, rejoice in, revel in, savor, take pleasure in

RELOCATE, *verb*   reassign, reestablish, replace, reposition, rereside, resettle, resite, restation

RELUCTANCE, *noun*   antipathy, averseness, aversion, *coactus,* deprecation, diffidence, disaffection, disapproval, disfavor, disinclination, dislike, dissent, distaste, doubt, hesitance, hesitancy, hesitation, indisposedness, indisposition, indocility, *invitus,* misgiving, nolition, objection, obstinacy, qualms, recoiling, renitence, renitency, repugnance, reservations, resistance, scruples, shyness, skepticism, squeamishness, uncertainty, unwillingness

RELUCTANT, *adjective*   adverse, averse, avoiding, begrudging, diffident, discontented, disinclined, dissenting, dissentious, evasive, grudging, hesitant, hesitating, hesitative, inacquiescent, indisposed, involuntary, irreconcilable, not disposed, not inclined, opposed, protestant, querulous, recalcitrant, refusing, rejective, renitent, shrinking, shunning, squeamish, uncertain, uncomplaisant, uncomplying, unconsenting, uncooperated, uninclined, unwilling
ASSOCIATED CONCEPTS: reluctant witness

RELY, *verb*   bank on, be confident, be dependent on, believe in, confide, *confidere,* count upon, depend, entrust, feel sure, have confidence in, have faith in, lean on, look to, place trust in, put confidence in, put faith in, rely on, trust

REMAIN *(Continue), verb*   adhere, be constant, be permanent, be steadfast, be tenacious, carry on, continue, endure, exist, extend, go on, hang on, hold out, keep, keep going, keep on, last, linger, maintain, outlast, outlive, perdure, perpetuate, persevere, persist, prevail, proceed, progress, prolong, pursue, stand fast, stand firm, stay, subsist, survive, sustain

REMAIN *(Occupy), verb*   be present, dwell, enjoy, have, have possession, hold, hold possession, inhabit, live in, lodge, maintain, own, possess, reside, retain

REMAIN *(Stay), verb*   adhere, await, be anchored, be dormant, be immobile, be immovable, be inert, be motionless, be sedentary, be stationary, be transfixed, come to stay, delay, *durare,* hold, last, linger, lodge, pause, *remanere,* repose, rest, set in, stand, stand fast, wait
ASSOCIATED CONCEPTS: remain in possession after the expiration of a lease, remain on premises

REMAINDER *(Estate in property), noun*   estate, excess, expectancy, interest, property, residual estate, reversionary estate, surplus
ASSOCIATED CONCEPTS: contingent remainder, vested remainder

REMAINDER *(Remaining part), noun*   balance, carry-over, excess, leftover, overplus, *quod restat, reliquum,* remaining portion, remains, residuals, residue, *residuum,* rest, reversion, superfluity, surplus

REMAND, *verb*   command back, commit, commit to an institution, consign, delegate, entrust, imprison again, order back, reassign, recommit, reincarcerate, reinstitutionalize, relegate, remit, *remittere,* replace, restore, return, return to prison, send, send back, transfer
ASSOCIATED CONCEPTS: general remand, reversed and remanded

REMARK, *noun*   animadversion, assertion, averment, comment, commentary, declaration, *dictum,* exclamation, expression, interjection, mention, note, observation, point, pronouncement, recitation, reflection, saying, speech, statement, thought, utterance, word

REMARK, *verb*   affirm, animadvert, articulate, assert, asseverate, aver, come out with, comment, communicate, convey, dare say, declare, deliver, *dicere,* discuss, emit, expound, express, give utterance, let fall, make mention, make note of, mention, note, observe, present, recite, relate, respond, say, speak, state, suggest, talk about, tell, utter, verbalize, vocalize, voice

REMARKABLE, *adjective*   amazing, astonishing, astounding, celebrated, consequential, conspicuous, *conspicuus,* curious, distinct, distinctive, distinguished, egregious, exceptional, extraordinary, eye-catching, fabulous, flagrant, great, important, imposing, impressive, incredible, lofty, marked, marvelous, memorable, miraculous, momentous, monumental, notable, noteworthy, outstanding, overwhelming, peculiar, predominent, prominent, rare, salient, signal, significant, singular, *singularis,* special, strange, striking, stupendous, surprising, unbelievable, uncommon, unforgettable, unique, unparalleled, unspeakable, unusual, visible, wonderful, wondrous, worthy of note

REMEDIAL, *adjective*   alleviating, alleviative, alterative, amendatory, analeptic, anodyne, antidotal, assuasive, balmy, beneficial, benign, bracing, calmative, cleansing, compensatory, corrective, counteracting, curative, curing, easing, emollient, healing, healthgiving, healthful, invigorating, lenitive, medical, medicative, medicinal, palliative, prophylactic, purifying, recuperative, reformative, reparative, reparatory, restitutive, restorative, revivifying, roborant, salubrious, *salutaris,* salutary, salutiferous, sanative, sanatory, sanitary, soothing, stimulating, strengthening, therapeutic, tonic, wholesome
ASSOCIATED CONCEPTS: remedial act, remedial laws

REMEDIAL STATUTE, *noun*   correction, corrective measure, cure, legislative cure, legislative redress, rectification, relief, remedial measure, remedy
ASSOCIATED CONCEPTS: remedial act, remedial action, remedial cases, remedial legislation, remedial right, remedial statute, remedial writ

REMEDY *(Legal means of redress),* *noun*   aid, alleviation, amelioration, assistance, compensation, corrective measure, counteraction, effective help, help, recompense, rectification, rehabilitation, relief, remedial measure, reparation, reparative measure, restitution, solution
ASSOCIATED CONCEPTS: adequate remedy at law, ancillary relief, appropriate relief, equitable remedy, exclusive remedy, exhaustion of administrative remedies, extraordinary remedy, inadequate remedy, legal remedy, mutuality of remedy, provisional remedy, statutory remedy

REMEDY *(That which corrects),* *noun*   aid, antidote, assistance, correction, corrective measure, cure, help, *medicina,* palliative, relief, remedial measure, *remedium,* restorative

REMEDY, *verb*   adjust, aid, alleviate, ameliorate, amend, assist, assuage, attend, calm, change, correct,

cure, ease, fix, heal, help, improve, indemnify, make amends, make better, make sound, *medicamentum,* medicate, *medicina,* meliorate, mend, minister to, mitigate, mollify, neutralize, overhaul, palliate, put into condition, put into shape, readjust, rectify, redress, reinvigorate, relieve, *remedium,* renew, repair, restore, resuscitate, retrieve, revise, revive, revivify, right, satisfy, save, set straight, solve, soothe, succor, treat, work a cure

REMEMBER, *verb*   be reminded of, bear in memory, bear in mind, bring to mind, call to mind, call up, commemorate, conjure up, fix in the mind, keep in mind, know again, know by heart, look back, master, memorialize, memorize, not forget, place, preserve a memory, recall, recognize, recollect, *recordari,* recover knowledge of, reidentify, relive, remind oneself, reminisce, *reminisci,* retain, review, summon up, think back

REMEMBRANCE *(Commemoration),* *noun*   acclaim, aggrandizement, celebration, ceremony, commendation, consecration, dignification, elevation, enshrinement, exaltation, glorification, holiday, homage, honoring, immortalization, keepsake, memento, memorial, memorialization, monument, observance, perpetuation, praise, ritual, salutation, solemnization, souvenir, testimonial, token, tribute

REMEMBRANCE *(Recollection),* *noun*   *memoria,* memory, mental image, recall, recognition, recognizance, reconstruction, reidentification, reminiscence, retention, retrospect, retrospection, revival in the mind

REMIND, *verb*   *admonere,* advise, awaken memories, bring back, bring to recollection, bring up, cause to recollect, cause to remember, *commonere,* cue, drop a hint, give notice, haunt, hint, jog the memory, make an allusion to, note, point out, prod, prompt, refresh the memory, renew memories, state, stress, suggest, tell, warn

REMINDER, *noun*   allusion, commemoration, cue, hint, jog, keepsake, memento, memo, memorandum, memorial, mnemonic, mnemonic device, notation, note, phylactery, prod, prompt, reference, relic, remembrance, shrine, souvenir, suggestion, testimonial

REMISE, *verb*   cede, give back, give up, grant, quit, quitclaim, release, relinquish, remit, resign, surrender

REMISS, *adjective*   careless, delinquent, derelict, dilatory, disregardant, disregardful, dutiless, forgetful, heedless, idle, improvident, imprudent, inattentive, inconsiderate, indifferent, indolent, injudicious, lackadaisical, late, lax, lazy, loafing, neglectful, *neglegens,* negligent, omissive, procrastinative, reckless, shiftless, slack, slothful, tardy, temerarious, thoughtless, uncircumspect, unconcerned, unheeding, unmindful, unsolicitous, unthinking, unwatchful, unwilling

REMISSION, *noun*   abatement, absolution, acquittal, acquittance, allayment, alleviation, amnesty, assuagement, break, cancellation, cessation, check, clearance, condonation, decrease, diminution, discharge, discontinuance, exculpation, exemption, exoneration, forbearance, forgiveness, grace, halt, indulgence, intermission, interruption, interval, lapse, lessening, letup, liberation, lull, mitigation, moderation, modulation, pardon, pause, quietus, quittance, recess, reduction, relaxation, release, relief, relinquishment, *remissio,* reprieve, respite, rest, standstill, stay, stop, stoppage, subsidence, suspense, suspension, tranquilization, *venia*

REMIT *(Relax), verb*   abate, alleviate, assuage, attemper, brake, calm, check, *condonare,* decrease, diminish, ease, give up, halt, hold up, lenify, lessen, let slacken, let up, loosen, make less violent, minimize, mitigate, moderate, palliate, quell, quiet, reduce, relinquish, *remittere,* soften, soothe, stall, stop, suspend, tranquilize, weaken

REMIT *(Release from penalty), verb*   absolve, acquit, amnesty, assoil, cancel, clear, condone, discharge, dismiss, disregard, drop charges, exculpate, excuse, exempt, exonerate, forgive, free, give amnesty, let go, let out, liberate, overlook, pardon, pass over, reinstate, release, reprieve, respite, show clemency, show mercy, spare, vindicate, waive

REMIT *(Send payment), verb*   compensate, defray, disburse, discharge, forward payment, make payment, *mittere,* pay, recompense, remunerate, render, repay, requite, satisfy, send money, send payment, settle, tender, transmit payment

REMIT *(Submit for consideration), verb*   advance, commit, consign, forward, offer, present, proffer, propose, refer, relegate, remand, send, tender, transmit

REMITTANCE, *noun*   acquittal, defrayal, defrayment, disbursement, expenditure, money sent, payment, *pecunia,* quittance, recompense, reimbursement, remuneration, reparation, transmittal

REMONSTRANCE, *noun*   admonishment, *admonitio,* admonition, animadversion, argument, castigation, censure, challenge, chastisement, correction, criticism, dehortation, demur, determent, discouragement, dissuasion, exception, exhortation, expostulation, exprobration, gainsaying, objection, objurgation, opposition, protest, protestation, rebuke, *reclamatio,* reprimand, reproach, reprobation, reproof, reproval, warning

REMONSTRATE, *verb*   admonish, advise, advise against, altercate, animadvert, argue against, berate, castigate, censure, challenge, chastise, correct, counsel, counsel against, criticize, cry out against, decry, demur, deprecate, deter, disapprove, discourage, disparage, dispute, dissuade, exhort, expostulate, express disapproval, exprobate, find fault, find flaws, frown upon, make objections, object, objurgate, oppose, protest, raise objections, rebuke, *reclamare,* reprehend, reproach, reprove, scold, stickle, take exception, upbraid, urge against, warn

REMONSTRATIVE, *adjective*   admonitive, admonitory, argumentative, censorious, contentious, corrective, critical, dehortative, dehortatory, demurring, deprecative, deprecatory, discouraging, disputatious, dissuasive, enjoining, expostulatory, exprobrative, exprobratory, objecting, objurgatory, protesting, rebuking, remonstrant, reprimanding, reproachful, reprobative, reprobatory, reproving, warning

REMORSE, *noun*   anguish, chagrin, compunction, concern, conscience, *conscientia mala,* contriteness, contrition, disquiet, feelings of guilt, grief, pangs of con-

science, penitence, regret, regretfulness, remorsefulness, repentance, rue, self-accusation, self-condemnation, self-conviction, self-criticism, self-reproach, self-reproof, sorriness, sorrow

REMORSEFUL, *adjective*   apologetic, compunctious, conscience-smitten, conscience-stricken, contrite, full of regret, lamenting, penitent, penitential, regretful, repentant, repenting, rueful, sad, self-accusatory, self-condemnatory, self-reproaching, sorrowful, sorry

REMORSELESS, *adjective*   cruel, dispiteous, hardened, heartless, *immisericors,* impenitent, implacable, indurate, indurated, insensitive, intolerant, lacking remorse, merciless, obdurate, pitiless, relentless, ruthless, shameless, unappeasable, uncompassionate, unforgiving, unmerciful, unpitying, unregenerate, unrelenting, unremorseful, unrepentant

REMOTE *(Not proximate), adjective*   at a great distance, distant, far, far-off, far removed, indirect, not immediate, *remotus,* removed
ASSOCIATED CONCEPTS: remote cause, remote damages
FOREIGN PHRASES: *Id quod est magis remotum, non trahit ad se quod est magis junctum, sed e contrario in omni casu.* That which is more remote does not draw to itself that which is more proximate but the contrary in every case.

REMOTE *(Secluded), adjective*   alone, apart, curtained, detached, disassociated, distant, far, far-off, faraway, hidden, inaccessible, insular, isolated, not close, not near, not nearby, out of the way, private, remote, removed, seclusive, segregated, separated, sequestered, shut away, solitary, unapproachable, unassociated, unconnected, unfrequented

REMOTE *(Small), adjective*   diminutive, faint, in small amount, inappreciable, inconsequential, inconsiderable, insignificant, insubstantial, little, minimal, minute, scant, slight, slim, small, superficial, tiny, trivial, unessential, unimportant

REMOVAL, *noun*   abatement, abolition, *amotio,* amotion, banishment, cashiering, change of place, conveyance, debarment, deduction, demission, demotion, departure, deportation, deposal, deposition, deprivation of office, detachment, discard, discharge, disemployment, dislocation, dislodgment, dismissal, displacement, divestment, ejection, elimination, eradication, erasure, evacuation, evulsion, exception, excision, exclusion, exile, expulsion, extermination, extirpation, extraction, extrication, isolation, layoff, noninclusion, obliteration, omission, ousting, purge, reallocation, rejection, relegation, remotion, retirement, retreat, riddance, segregation, separation, sequestration, shift, sublation, subtraction, suppression, taking away, transfer, transference, transhipment, translocation, transplacement, transplantation, transportation, unseating, withdrawal
ASSOCIATED CONCEPTS: removal from office, removal of cloud from title, removal to federal court

REMOVE *(Dismiss from office), verb*   cashier, depose, disassociate, disbar, discharge, dismiss, displace, dissociate, divest, eject, expel, fire, get rid of, impeach, oust, put out, relieve, replace, suspend, turn out
ASSOCIATED CONCEPTS: removal proceeding, remove from office

REMOVE *(Eliminate), verb*   abolish, annihilate, bar, cancel, clear, confiscate, debar, deduct, delete, delocalize, detach, deterge, detruncate, disassociate, disconnect, disjoin, dislocate, dislodge, displace, disroot, dissociate, disturb, divest, drain, eliminate, eradicate, except, exclude, exhume, export, expunge, exterminate, extirpate, extract, extricate, isolate, kill, liquidate, obliterate, obviate, omit, part, purge, reject, segregate, separate, sequester, sequestrate, set apart, strip, subtract, take away, take out, truncate, unattach, unbind, unfasten, unload, untie, uproot, withdraw
ASSOCIATED CONCEPTS: remove a cloud on title, remove disabilities, remove obstructions

REMOVE *(Transfer), verb*   *amovere,* change address, change place, change venue, convey to, deliver to, forward, move, relocate, *removere,* send, send forth, shift, switch, transmit
ASSOCIATED CONCEPTS: removal from the state, remove a case to federal court, remove a cause of action

REMUNERATE, *verb*   acquit, award, compensate, defray, disburse, discharge, give payment, indemnify, make payment, make up for, pay, recompense, reimburse, remit, *remunerari,* repay, requite, reward, satisfy, settle
ASSOCIATED CONCEPTS: legal fees

REMUNERATION, *noun*   award, compensation, defrayal, defrayment, indemnification, indemnity, money, pay, payment, *praemium,* quittance, recompense, reimbursement, *remuneratio,* requital, restitution, return, reward, satisfaction, settlement

RENASCENT, *adjective*   awakened, overhauled, reanimated, reappearing, reborn, reclaimed, reconditioned, reconstituted, reconstructed, recreated, redintegrated, redivivus, reestablished, refashioned, reformed, refreshed, regenerated, rehabilitated, rejuvenated, remade, renewed, renovated, repaired, reproduced, restored, resurgent, resurrected, resuscitated, revived, revivified, salvaged

REND, *verb*   break, burst, cleave, crack, cut, dilacerate, discerp, *disscindere,* dissect, dissever, disunite, divide, fracture, lacerate, lancinate, rip, rive, rupture, sever, shatter, shiver, slash, slice, snap, splinter, split, sunder, tear, tear asunder

RENDER *(Administer), verb*   accomplish, accord, administrate, bring about, conduct, contribute, dispense, execute, furnish, give, mete out, perform, preside over, provide, provide with, put into effect

RENDER *(Deliver), verb*   communicate, confer, convey, execute, give, give back, hand down, hand over, impart, pass down, present, *reddere, referre,* set down, submit, surrender, *tribuere*
ASSOCIATED CONCEPTS: render a judgment, render a verdict, render an accounting

RENDER *(Depict), verb*   characterize, construe, define, delineate, describe, detail, elucidate, illustrate, interpret, outline, picture, portray, record, represent, reproduce, set forth, show, sketch, translate

RENDEZVOUS, *noun*   appointment, assembly, assignation, concourse, confluence, congregation, congress, date, encounter, engagement, gathering, gathering place, get-together, ingathering, meeting, meeting place, muster, place of assignation, place of meeting, tryst

RENDEZVOUS, *verb*   assemble, be closeted with, become acquainted, come together, congregate, convene, encounter, forgather, gather, keep a date, keep an appointment, meet, muster

RENDITION *(Explication), noun*   account, construction, definition, delineation, explanation, interpretation, reading, rendering, report, representation, rewording, statement, translation

RENDITION *(Restoration), noun*   compensation, indemnification, recommitment, rehabilitation, reparation, restitution, return, submission, surrender

RENEGE, *verb*   abandon, abolish, abrogate, annul, back out, bolt, break a promise, call back, contradict, counterorder, countermand, desert, disannul, dissolve, go back on a commitment, go back on a promise, invalidate, nullify, pull out, quit, recall, refuse to honor a commitment, refuse to honor a promise, repeal, rescind, retract, retreat, reverse, revoke, secede, vacate, withdraw

RENEW *(Begin again), verb*   continue, *iterare,* launch again, progress, put back, readmit, recommence, *redintegrare,* reembark, reenter, regenerate, reinstall, reinstate, reinstitute, reintroduce, reopen, reorganize, repeat, *repetere,* resume, return to, revive, set going again, start again, stimulate, transform
ASSOCIATED CONCEPTS: leave to renew, renew a motion, renew an objection

RENEW *(Refurbish), verb*   ameliorate, amend, bring up to date, cure, enhance, fix, freshen, give new life to, improve, invigorate, make over, make perfect, make sound, make well, make whole, meliorate, mend, modernize, overhaul, patch up, perfect, put into shape, reanimate, reawaken, rebuild, reclaim, *reconcinnare,* recondition, reconstitute, reconstruct, reconvert, recover, recreate, rectify, redesign, redintegrate, redo, redress, refashion, *reficere,* refinish, refit, refresh, refurbish, regenerate, rehabilitate, reintegrate, reinvigorate, rejuvenate, rekindle, remake, remodel, *renovare,* renovate, repair, replace, replenish, reproduce, restore, resurge, resurrect, resuscitate, retouch, revamp, revise, revitalize, revive, rework, salvage, save

RENEWAL, *noun*   amelioration, comeback, continuance, enhancement, fixing, improvement, instauration, making over, melioration, mending, modernization, new start, readjustment, reanimation, rearrangement, rebirth, recharging, reclamation, recommencement, reconstitution, reconstruction, recrudescence, recrudescency, recurrence, redoubling, reestablishment, refitting, reformation, refreshment, regeneration, rehabilitation, reinstatement, reinvigoration, reissue, rejuvenation, relapse, renaissance, renascence, *renovatio,* renovation, reopening, repair, repetition, replenishment, reproduction, restoration, resumption, resurrection, resuscitation, return, revamping, revision, revival, revivification, salvage
ASSOCIATED CONCEPTS: motion to renew, renewal of a claim, renewal of a license, renewal of a motion

RENITENT, *adjective*   adverse, antagonistic, antipathetic, antipathetical, conflicting, counteracting, counteractive, demurring, disapproving, disgusted, disinclined, dissenting, firm, indisposed, indocile, insurrectional, intractable, intransigent, loath, mutinous, opposed, opposing, reactionary, recalcitrant, reluctant, resistant, resisting, rigid, stiff, unsubmissive, unwilling

RENOUNCE, verb   abandon, abdicate, abhor, abjure, abnegate, banish, break with, cast aside, cast off, cease, decline, demit, deny, deprive oneself, desert, desist from, despise, detest, disagree, disapprove, disavow, discard, disclaim, discountenance, disdain, dismiss, disown, dissent, divorce oneself from, drop, eliminate, exclude, forbear, forbid, forgo, forsake, forswear, give away, give up, give up claim to, go without, interdict, lay aside, leave, let go, oppose, ostracize, part with, proscribe, protest, quit, rebuff, recant, refuse, reject, relinquish, renege, repel, repudiate, repulse, resign, rid oneself of, scorn, spurn, surrender, swear off, take exception to, turn from, waive
ASSOCIATED CONCEPTS: renounce a will
FOREIGN PHRASES: *Cuilibet licet juri pro se introducto renunciare.* Anyone may renounce the benefit of a legal right that exists only for his protection.

RENOVATE, verb   ameliorate, amend, convert, fix, improve, make better, make new, make over, make sound, make whole, meliorate, mend, modernize, perfect, readjust, reanimate, rebuild, recondition, reconstitute, reconstruct, reconvert, recreate, redeem, redintegrate, reestablish, refashion, *reficere*, refit, refresh, refurbish, regenerate, rehabilitate, reinvigorate, rejuvenate, remake, remodel, renew, renovize, reorganize, repair, replace, restore, resurrect, revamp, revive, revivify, salvage

RENOWNED, adjective   acclaimed, applauded, celebrated, *clarus,* consequential, conspicuous, distinguished, eminent, exalted, extraordinary, famed, famous, far-famed, foremost, great, honored, illustrious, important, *inlustris,* known, leading, matchless, much touted, notable, noted, noteworthy, notorious, outstanding, popular, preeminent, prominent, recognized, remarkable, reputable, singular, talked about, top-flight, unexampled, unique, unparalled, unprecedented, well-known

RENT, noun   assessment, compensation, cost, fee, income, income from real estate, land revenue, *merces,* payment, proceeds, *reditus,* remuneration, rental, return, revenue
ASSOCIATED CONCEPTS: action for rent, assignment of rent, ejectment, fair rent, fair rental value, holdover, month-to-month rental, prepayment of rent, reasonable rent, rent strike, rents and proceeds, security, suit for rent, tenancy by will, unaccrued rent

RENT, verb   allow residency, allow the use of, charter, *conducere,* contract, demise, enjoy the use of premises, engage, give occupation, grant a lease, hire out, lease, lend, let, let out, *locare,* make available, sublease, sublet, subrent, take a lease, underlease, underlet, use premises
ASSOCIATED CONCEPTS: option to rent

RENUNCIATION, noun   abandonment, *abdicatio,* abdication, abjuration, abnegation, cancellation, cession, declination, demission, denial, disaffirmation, disallowance, disapprobation, disapproval, disavowal, disavowment, discard, disclaimer, discontinuance, disinheritance, dismissal, disownment, elimination, exclusion, forswearing, giving up, negation, omission, proscription, rebuff, recantation, refusal, *reiectio,* rejection, relinquishment, renouncement, reprobation, *repudiatio,* repudiation, repulsion, resignation, retraction, sacrifice, shutting out, spurning, swearing off, veto, waiver, withdrawal, yielding
ASSOCIATED CONCEPTS: renunciation of a contract, renunciation of a will

REOPEN, verb   *aperire,* begin again, carry on, come back to, commence again, continue, *iterum,* open again, proceed, recommence, reembark, reestablish, reinstitute, renew, repeat, resume, return to, revive, start over
ASSOCIATED CONCEPTS: motion to reopen, reopen a case, reopen a hearing, reopen an investigation

REORGANIZATION, noun   alteration, amelioration, betterment, change, conversion, improvement, melioration, overhauling, readjustment, rearrangement, rebuilding, recasting, reconstitution, reconstruction, rectification, reestablishment, reformation, rehabilitation, remaking, remodeling, restoration, restructuring, revising, revision, transformation
ASSOCIATED CONCEPTS: bankruptcy, corporate reorganization

REPAIR, noun   adjustment, alteration, amelioration, betterment, correction, cure, fixing, improvement, melioration, mending, overhaul, patching, reanimation, reassembling, reconditioning, reconstruction, recovery, rectification, redintegration, refitting, reform, reformation, rehabilitation, remedy, remodeling, renewal, renovation, reorganization, reparation, restoration, resurrection, retouching, revival
ASSOCIATED CONCEPTS: duty to repair, failure to keep in repair, opportunity to make repairs

REPAIR, verb   adjust, ameliorate, amend, brush up, condition, correct, cure, darn, fix, improve, make better, make good, make improvements, meliorate, mend, overhaul, patch, piece, put in order, put into shape, put right, readjust, rebuild, recondition, reconstruct, rectify, redress, *reficere,* refit, reform, refresh, refurbish, rehabilitate, remedy, render better, renew, *reparare,* reshape, restore, resurrect, retouch, retread, revamp, revive, right, salvage, service, tinker, touch up, vamp
ASSOCIATED CONCEPTS: duty to repair

REPARATION (Indemnification), noun   adjustment, amends, atonement, compensation, conscience money, correction, damages, expiation, financial remuneration, indemnity, payment, peace offering, penalty, quittance, recompense, redress, reimbursement, relief, remedy, repayment, restitution, restoration, return, *satisfactio,* satisfaction, settlement, wergild

REPARATION (Keeping in repair), noun   correction, instauration, overhaul, readjustment, rebuilding, reconditioning, reconstruction, rectification, refurbishment, rehabilitation, rejuvenation, remedy, renewal, renovation, repair, replacement, restoral, restoration, revamping, salvage, service

REPAY, verb   avenge, compensate, get even, give back, give in exchange, indemnify, make amends, make payment, make reparation, make requital, make restitution, pay back, pay in kind, punish, rebate, reciprocate, recompense, *reddere,* refund, reimburse, remunerate, replace, *reponere,* requite, restore, retaliate, return, revenge, reward, satisfy, square accounts

REPEAL, *verb*   abolish, *abrogare,* abrogate, annul, avoid, cancel, countermand, declare null and void, delete, eliminate, formally withdraw, invalidate, make void, negate, nullify, obliterate, officially withdraw, override, overrule, quash, recall, render invalid, rescind, *rescindere,* retract, reverse, revoke, set aside, vacate, void, withdraw

ASSOCIATED CONCEPTS: repeal a bylaw, repeal a law, repeal a statute, repeal by implication

FOREIGN PHRASES: *Leges posteriores priores contrarias abrogant.* Subsequent laws repeal prior laws that are repugnant to them. *Jura eodem modo destituuntur quo constituuntur.* Laws are abrogated by the same means by which they are enacted. .

REPEAT *(Do again), verb*   backslide, copy, do over, duplicate, give an encore, imitate, ingeminate, *iterare,* persist, reconstruct, recreate, recur, redo, reduplicate, reenact, regenerate, reinstitute, relapse, remake, renew, replicate, reproduce, resume, retrace, return, revert

REPEAT *(State again), verb*   chant, drum, dwell on, echo, emphasize, harp on, insist upon, iterate, paraphrase, parrot, quote, read back, reaffirm, reassert, recapitulate, recite, recount, rehash, reiterate, relate, rephrase, report, restate, retell, review, reword, run over, say again, say over, sum up, summarize, tell again, tell over, utter again

REPEATED, *adjective*   common, commonplace, consuetudinal, consuetudinary, copied, customary, done again, done over, duplicated, echoed, everyday, frequent, habitual, imitated, incessant, monotonous, multiple, paraphrased, periodic, persistent, recited, recurrent, recurring, redone, redoubled, redundent, reduplicated, reduplicative, regular, rehearsed, reiterated, renewed, repetitional, repetitionary, repetitious, repetitive, reproduced, restated, retold, reuttered, reworded, said again, standard, stock, successive, twice-told, uniform

ASSOCIATED CONCEPTS: repeated wrongdoing

REPEL *(Disgust), verb*   alienate, appall, be unpalatable, cause aversion, cause dislike, displease, excite dislike, fill with loathing, frighten, give offense, grate, horrify, incense, irritate, make one shudder, make one sick, make unwelcome, nauseate, offend, repulse, revolt, scandalize, shock, sicken, vex

REPEL *(Drive back), verb*   avert, beat back, cast aside, challenge, chase away, check, checkmate, confound, confront, deflect, dispel, disperse, divert, drive away, drive back, fend off, fight off, foil, forbid, force back, forestall, frustrate, *fugare,* keep at bay, make a stand against, oppose, parry, prevent, prohibit, push back, put to flight, rebuff, renounce, *repellere,* repercuss, repudiate, repulse, resist, retrude, rout, scatter, spurn, stave off, strive against, throw off, thrust back, traverse, ward off, withstand

REPENT, *verb*   apologize, atone for, be conscience striken, be penitent, be sorry for, beg pardon, bemoan, bewail, cry over, deplore, do penance, expiate, feel con-

trition, feel regret, feel remorse, grieve, have a guilty conscience, have qualms, humble oneself, lament, make amends, make up for, mourn, pay the penalty, plead guilty, recant, redress, reform, regret, remember with sorrow, rue, show regret for, think better of, weep over

REPENTANT, *adjective*   apologetic, atoning, compunctious, confessing, conscience-smitten, conscience-stricken, contrite, full of regrets, humble, lamenting, *paenitens,* penitent, penitential, reclaimed, reformative, reformatory, reformed, regretful, regretting, remorseful, rueful, self-abasing, self-accusatory, self-condemnatory, self-convicted, self-denouncing, self-reproachful, self-reproving, sorrowful, sorry, weeping

REPERCUSSION, *noun*   backfire, backlash, blast, counteraction, echo, explosion, force, impact, reaction, rebound, reciprocal action, recoil, reflection, reflex, report, response, retroaction, reverberation, ricochet, shock

REPETITIOUS, *adjective*   duplicative, echoic, echoing, harping, incessant, invariable, monotonous, pleonastic, pleonastical, recapitulatory, recurrent, recurring, redundant, reduplicative, reechoed, reiterant, reiterative, repeated, repeating, repetitional, repetitionary, repetitive, stale, tedious

REPLACE, *verb*   act for, alternate, change, commute, compensate, cover for, depute, deputize, duplicate, exchange, fill in for, interchange, make amends, pay back, put back, refund, reimburse, reinstall, reinstate, repay, *reponere,* represent, restitute, stand for, subrogate, *substituere,* substitute, succeed, supersede, supplant, supply an equivalent, surrogate, swap, switch, symbolize, understudy, vary

REPLACEMENT, *noun*   alternate, alternative, change, commutation, compensation, counterfeit, delegate, deputy, dislocation, displacement, envoy, equivalent, exchange, fill in, interchange, makeshift, proxy, reclamation, reconstitution, reconstruction, recovery, refund, reinstatement, relief, removal, renewal, renovation, reorganization, reparation, representative, reproduction, restitution, restoration, second, secondary, shift, stand in, subrogation, substitute, substitution, successor, supersedure, supersession, supplantation, supplanter, surrogate, surrogation, swap, switch, temporary expedient, transfer, transposition, understudy

ASSOCIATED CONCEPTS: replacement cost

REPLENISH, *verb*   build up, complete, contribute, deposit, enrich, fill, fill in, fill up, furnish, give, make complete, make full, make up, make up a lack, make whole, present, provender, provide, provision, purvey, recharge, refill, refresh, refuel, reload, renew, replace, *replere,* restock, resupply, saturate, stock, store, supplement, *supplere,* supply, supply deficiencies

REPLETE, *adjective*   abounding, abundant, affluent, ample, bounteous, bountiful, brimfull, brimming, chock-full, closely packed, cloyed, complete, completely full, copious, crammed, crammed solid, filled, filled to repletion, flush, fraught, full, fully supplied, gorged, jam-packed, jammed, laden, lavish, loaded, luxurious, overflowing, packed, plenitudinous, plenteous, plentiful, plethoric, pregnant, profuse, refilled, replenished, rife, satiated, satisfied, saturated, stocked, stuffed, surfeited, teeming, well-provided, well-stocked

REPLEVIN, noun acquisition, delivery back, reclamation, recoupment, recovery, recovery of property, redelivery, redemption, repossession, retaking, retrieval, salvage
ASSOCIATED CONCEPTS: detinue, replevin bond

REPLY, noun answer, counterstatement, reaction, rebuttal, reciprocation, rejoinder, remonstrance, replication, response, *responsio, responsum,* retort, return, surrebuttal
ASSOCIATED CONCEPTS: reply brief, sham reply, surreply
FOREIGN PHRASES: *Ambigua responsio contra proferentem est accipienda.* An ambiguous answer is to be taken against him who offers it.

REPLY, verb acknowledge, answer, come back at, confute, counter, make rejoinder, parry, react, rebut, refute, rejoin, respond, *respondere,* retort, return, riposte, surrebut, surrejoin
ASSOCIATED CONCEPTS: reply to a counterclaim, reply to new matter contained in an answer, surreply

REPORT *(Detailed account),* **noun** account, address, article, brief, broadcast, bulletin, chronicle, communication, criticism, description, digest, disclosure, dissemination, exposition, history, information, intelligence, manifesto, message, minute, narration, news, news story, note, notice, notification, proclamation, propagation, recapitulation, recital, recitation, record, recounting, *relatio,* relation, release, *renuntiatio,* revelation, review, saga, specification, statement, summary, talk, tidings, ventilation
ASSOCIATED CONCEPTS: accident report, grand jury report

REPORT *(Rumor),* **noun** bruit, *fama,* gossip, grapevine, hearsay, hint, intimation, scuttlebutt, talk, tattle, unconfirmed report, unverified news, whisper

REPORT *(Disclose),* **verb** acquaint, *adferre,* advise, air, announce, annunciate, apprise, broadcast, bruit, circulate publicly, communicate, declare, deliver information, describe, detail, disseminate, divulgate, divulge, enlighten, expose, expound, express, give an account of, give the facts, herald, impart, inform, make an announcement, make known, mention, notify, outline, proclaim, promulgate, publish, recite, recount, *referre, renuntiare,* report, reveal, set forth, speak about, specify, state, tell, testify to, unmask, voice, write up

REPORT *(Present oneself),* **verb** announce one's presence, answer, answer a summons, appear, appear for duty, arrive, attend, be at hand, be in attendance, check in, come, *comparere,* fulfill an engagement, meet, present oneself, put in an appearance, reveal oneself, show oneself

REPOSE *(Place),* **verb** deposit, establish, fix, invest, lodge, plant, put, reposit, set, settle, store, vest in

REPOSE *(Rest),* **verb** be calm, be serene, be tranquil, compose oneself, lie down, recline, relax, rest, settle, sleep, slumber

REPOSITORY, noun arsenal, bank, bursary, cache, chest, coffer, conservatory, container, depository, depot, garner, promptuary, receptacle, *receptaculum,* reservatory, reservoir, safe, storehouse, storeroom, treasurehouse, treasury, warehouse

REPOSSESS, verb capture, foreclose, obtain again, reacquire, recall, recapture, reclaim, recoup, recover, redeem, regain, replevy, retrieve, secure, seize, take back, take possession of
ASSOCIATED CONCEPTS: attachment, security interest

REPREHEND, verb accuse, admonish, animadvert, berate, betongue, blame, bring to book, call down, call to account, cast blame upon, castigate, censure, charge, chastise, chide, condemn, correct, criticize, decry, denounce, disapprove, dress down, expostulate, exprobate, find fault with, impeach, impugn, increpate, lash, lay blame upon, lecture, object, objurgate, protest, punish, rate, rebuke, recriminate, *reprehendere,* reprimand, reproach, reprobate, reprove, run down, scold, slate, take exception, take to task, trounce, upbraid, voice disapproval

REPREHENSIBLE, adjective accusable, bad, base, blamable, blameful, blameworthy, censurable, chargeable, condemnable, convictable, criminal, *culpa dignus,* culpable, delinquent, deserving censure, deserving reproof, discreditable, disgraceful, disgusting, dishonorable, disreputable, evil, exceptionable, flagitious, flagrant, foul, guilty, hateful, heinous, horrendous, ignoble, illaudable, immoral, impeachable, incorrigible, indefensible, inexcusable, inexpiable, infamous, iniquitous, monstrous, naughty, nefarious, objectionable, obnoxious, odious, offensive, open to criticism, opprobrious, peccable, peccant, rebukable, recreant, *reprehendendus,* reproachable, reprobate, reprovable, shameful, shocking, sinful, uncommendable, unjustifiable, unpardonable, unprincipled, unrighteous, unworthy, vicious, villainous, wicked, wrong

REPRESENT *(Portray),* **verb** adumbrate, characterize, connote, delineate, denote, depict, designate, evoke, exemplify, *exprimere,* illustrate, image, indicate, mean, outline, picture, show, signify, stand for, symbolize, typify

REPRESENT *(Substitute),* **verb** act, act as broker, act as delegate, act for, act in place of, act on behalf of, act vicariously, appear for, be ambassador for, be an agent for, be attorney for, be deputy for, be proxy for, be spokesman for, factor, replace, speak for, stand in the place of, take the part of
ASSOCIATED CONCEPTS: agency, represent a client's interests, represent a defendant, represent a principal

REPRESENTATION *(Acting for others),* **noun** acting as attorney for, advocacy, agency, agentship, body of delegates, body of deputies, deputation, rendering legal advice, rendering legal assistance, speaking for another, substitution, supplying another's place

REPRESENTATION *(Statement),* **noun** account, assertion of facts, asseveration, declaration, depiction, description, *effigies,* explanation, illustration, *imago,* indication, narration, narrative, portraiture, portrayal, presentation, relation, report, setting forth
ASSOCIATED CONCEPTS: false representation, material representation, misrepresentation, public representation

REPRESENTATIVE, adjective   acting, adumbrative, agential, characteristic, connotative, delegated, denotative, depictive, deputative, deputed, distinctive, emblematic, exemplary, faithful, figurative, graphic, graphical, illustrational, illustrative, indicative, indicatory, representational, sample, standard, symbolic, symbolical, typical, typifying
ASSOCIATED CONCEPTS: representative action, representative capacity, representative suit

REPRESENTATIVE *(Example)*, **noun**   exemplar, model, paragon, sample, specimen, symbol, typical example, typical instance

REPRESENTATIVE *(Proxy)*, **noun**   agent, barrister, broker, counsel, delegate, deputy, emissary, envoy, go-between, lawyer, messenger, middle man, solicitor, spokesman, substitute, substitution, trustee, *vicarius*
ASSOCIATED CONCEPTS: lawful representative, legal representative

REPRESS, verb   allay, bottle up, bridle, censor, check, choke, *comprimere*, control, cork, crush, curb, damp, dampen, deaden, domineer, dull, enchain, gag, hinder, hobble, hold back, hold in, hush, inhibit, keep down, keep in, keep in check, keep under control, kill, leash, limit, master, muffle, mute, muzzle, *opprimere*, overbear, overcome, overmaster, overpower, pen up, press back, prohibit, put down, quell, quench, quiet, reduce to subjection, rein in, restrain, restrict, seal up, shackle, silence, smother, squash, stay, stifle, still, strangle, subdue, subjugate, suffocate, suppress, trammel, vanquish, withhold

REPRIEVE, noun   day of grace, deferment, delay, delay in execution, delay in punishment, dispensation, interval of ease, moratorium, pause, postponement, postponement of penalty, quittance, respite, respite from impending punishment, stay, stay of execution, stop, suspension of execution, suspension of punishment, temporary escape, temporary relief, temporary suspension of the execution of a sentence, withdrawal of a sentence
ASSOCIATED CONCEPTS: executive reprieve, judicial reprieve, pardon

REPRIMAND, noun   admonishment, admonition, animadversion, blame, castigation, censure, chiding, condemnation, correction, criticism, denunciation, derogation, disapprobation, disapproval, displeasure, dispraise, dressing down, exception, exprobration, improbation, increpation, jobation, lecture, objection, objurgation, rating, rebuke, remonstrance, *reprehensio*, reprehension, reproach, reprobation, reproof, reproval, revilement, scolding, sermon, sharp censure, sharp words, stricture, trimming, upbraiding, *vituperatio*, warning
ASSOCIATED CONCEPTS: reprimand issued by the grievance committee of the bar association

REPRIMAND, verb   accuse, admonish, animadvert on, asperse, berate, blame, call to account, call to task, castigate, censure formally, chastise, chide, condemn, correct, criminate, decry, denounce, deprecate, disapprove, discommend, disparage, dispraise, dress down, execrate, exprobrate, find fault, flay, fulminate against, impeach, impugn, inveigh against, lash, lecture, objurgate, rail at, rant, rebuke, recriminate, remonstrate, reprehend, *reprehendere*, reproach, reprobate, reprove,

revile, run down, scold, thunder against, trounce, upbraid, vilify, vilipend, *vituperare*, vituperate, warn
ASSOCIATED CONCEPTS: reprimand by the grievance committee

REPRISAL, noun   avengement, counterattack, counterblast, counterplot, counterstroke, desert, disciplinary action, discipline, due, due punishment, getting even, measure for measure, nemesis, penalty, punishment, punition, punitive action, reaction, reciprocation, repayment, requital, retaliation, retribution, retributive justice, return, revenge, revengefulness, talion, vendetta, vengeance, vengefulness, vindictiveness

REPROACH, noun   accusation, animadversion, blame, castigation, censure, chastisement, chiding, complaint, condemnation, contempt, *contumelia*, contumely, correction, degradation, denouncement, denunciation, derogation, disapprobation, disapproval, discredit, disgrace, dishonor, disparagement, disrepute, dressing down, exprobration, *exprobratio*, impeachment, increpation, incrimination, inculpation, indignity, jobation, objection, objurgation, obloquy, opprobrium, *probrum*, rating, rebuke, reprehension, reprimand, reprobation, reproof, revilement, scolding, shame, sharp criticism, slur, stigma, taint, tarnish, upbraiding, vilification

REPROACH, verb   abuse, accuse, admonish, animadvert, asperse, berate, blame, brand, call to account, castigate, censure, chide, complain, condemn, criminate, criticize, decry, defame, denounce, denunciate, deprecate, disapprove, discredit, disgrace, dishonor, disparage, excoriate, express displeasure, exprobrate, find fault with, flay, frown upon, increpate, *increpitare*, incriminate, inculpate, *incusare*, inveigh against, lecture, malign, objurgate, protest against, put to shame, rail at, rant at, rebuke, reprehend, reprimand, reprobate, reprove, revile, scold, slate, speak ill of, take to task, tax, tongue lash, traduce, upbraid, vilify, vilipend, vituperate

REPROBATE, adjective   accusable, bad, base, blameworthy, corrupt, criminal, culpable, degenerate, depraved, disgusting, disreputable, dissolute, evil-minded, facinorous, felonious, flagitious, flagrant, hardened, heinous, immoral, incorrigible, infamous, iniquitous, irreclaimable, irredeemable, irreverent, knavish, lost, morally abandoned, naughty, nefarious, obdurate, peccant, *perditus*, profligate, *profligatus*, rascally, recidivous, recreant, roguish, shameless, sinful, unconscionable, unprincipled, unregenerate, unrighteous, vicious, vile, vitiated, wicked, worthless

REPRODUCE, verb   beget, breed, bring forth, conceive, copy, create, do again, double, duplicate, engender, father, fecundate, fructify, generate, give birth to, imitate, make again, manifold, mirror, multiply, parallel, portray, procreate, progenerate, proliferate, propagate, rebuild, reconstitute, reconstruct, recreate, redo, reduplicate, refashion, reform, *regignere*, remake, renew, repeat, replicate, sire, spawn
ASSOCIATED CONCEPTS: copyright, reproduce a record on appeal

REPUDIATE, verb   abandon, abdicate, abjure, abnegate, abolish, abrogate, cancel, change sides, contradict, contravene, countermand, declare null and void, decline, default, demur, deny, disallow, disannul, dis-

avow, disbar, discard, disclaim, dishonor, dissent, dissolve, exclude, forswear, negate, neglect, nullify, override, overrule, proscribe, protest, recant, refuse to accept, refuse to acknowledge, *reicere,* reject, renounce, repeal, *repudiare,* retract, reverse, revoke, set aside, spurn, withdraw
ASSOCIATED CONCEPTS: repudiate a cause of action, repudiate a contract

REPUDIATION, *noun*   abjuration, abolition, abrogation, annulment, breach, cancellation, confutation, contradiction, counterorder, countermand, declination, defeasance, defection, denial, deposition, disaffirmation, disagreement, disallowance, disapproval, disavowal, disclaimer, disclamation, disproof, disproval, dissent, dissociation, exclusion, forswearing, negation, nonobservance, nullification, recantation, refusal, refutation, rejection, renouncement, renunciation, repeal, repellence, *repudiatio,* rescission, retractation, retraction, reversal, revocation, setting aside, veto, voidance, withdrawal
ASSOCIATED CONCEPTS: repudiation of a contract

REPUGNANT *(Exciting aversion),* **adjective**   abhorrent, abominable, detestable, disagreeable, disgustful, disgusting, disliked, displeasing, distasteful, *diversus,* forbidding, fulsome, hateful, inedible, insufferable, loathsome, nauseating, noisome, objectionable, obnoxious, odious, offending, offensive, out of favor, painful, repellent, repelling, *repugnans,* repulsive, revolting, unacceptable, unappetizing, undesirable, unpalatable, unpleasant, unpopular, unsavory

REPUGNANT *(Incompatible),* **adjective**   adverse, alien, antagonistic, at odds, at variance, clashing, conflicting, contradictory, contrary, different, disagreeing, discordant, hostile, inaccordant, incongruous, inconsistent, inharmonious, inimical, irreconcilable, jarring, opposed, opposing, unconformable
ASSOCIATED CONCEPTS: repugnant to the Constitution

REPULSE, *verb*   beat back, beat off, chase, check, counteract, countervail, defeat, dispel, drive away, drive back, eschew, fend off, frustrate, gainsay, grapple with, hinder, impede, keep at bay, make a stand, obstruct, oppose, oppugn, overthrow, *propulsare,* push back, put to flight, rebuff, reject, repel, *repellere,* repercuss, repudiate, resist, retrude, rout, scorn, send away, shun, snub, spurn, stem, throw back, thwart, turn away, ward off, withstand

REPULSIVE, *adjective*   abhorrent, abominable, appalling, arousing aversion, beastly, contemptible, despicable, detestable, dirty, disagreeable, disgusting, disliked, displeasing, distasteful, dreadful, execrable, fearful, feculent, filthy, *foedus,* forbidding, foul, frightful, ghastly, grim, grisly, gross, hateful, hideous, horrible, horrid, horrifying, insufferable, loathsome, misshapen, monstrous, nasty, nauseating, nauseous, noisome, noxious, objectionable, obnoxious, obscene, *odiosus,* odious, offensive, rank, repellent, repelling, repugnant, revolting, rotten, shocking, sickening, sloppy, squalid, ugly, unbearable, unclean, uninviting, unpalatable, unpleasant, unprepossessing, unsavory, unsightly, vile

REPUTABLE, *adjective*   acclaimed, celebrated, conscientious, creditable, dependable, dignified, distinguished, eminent, esteemed, estimable, ethical, faithful, famed, held in esteem, held in good repute, highprincipled, honest, *honestus,* honorable, honored, illustrious, incorruptible, known, meritorious, moral, noble, notable, principled, prominent, reliable, renowned, respectable, respected, revered, reverenced, righteous, scrupulous, trustworthy, uncorrupt, unimpeachable, upright, venerated, virtuous, well-known, well thought of, worthy

REPUTATION, *noun*   acclaim, celebration, celebrity, consequence, credit, distinction, eminence, esteem, estimation, *fama,* fame, famousness, glory, good name, illustriousness, importance, luster, mark, name, notability, note, notoriety, *opinio,* popular favor, position, position in society, precedence, preeminence, prestige, prominence, rank, regard, renown, report, repute, respect, respectability, standing, station, status
ASSOCIATED CONCEPTS: character witness, reputation evidence

REPUTEDLY, *adverb*   according to general belief, according to reputation, allegedly, assumedly, assumptively, presumably, reportedly, rumored, seemingly, supposedly

REQUEST, *noun*   appeal, application, asking, begging, behest, beseechment, bid, call, claim, demand, desideratum, entreaty, exaction, expressed desire, impetration, imploration, importunity, insistence, invitation, invocation, motion, obsecration, order, petition, plea, *postulatio,* postulation, prayer, *preces,* proposal, requirement, requisition, *rogatio,* solicitation, suggestion, supplication, wish

REQUEST, *verb*   adjure, appeal, apply for, ask for, beckon, beg for, beseech, bid, cadge, call for, canvass, claim, clamor for, command, cry for, demand, desire, dun, enjoin, entreat, exact, impetrate, *implorare,* implore, importune, invite, make application, mendicate, nag, *obsecrare,* obtest, order, petition, petition for, plead for, pray, put in for, require, requisition, *rogare,* seek, send for, solicit, sue for, summon, supplicate, urge, want

REQUIRE *(Compel),* **verb**   assess, call for, cause, coerce, command, constrain, decree, demand, dictate, direct, draft, drive, enact, enforce, enjoin, entail, exact, *exigere,* force, impose, insist on, issue a command, levy, make, necessitate, obligate, oblige, ordain, order, *poscere,* postulate, prescribe, requisition, subject, summon, tax
ASSOCIATED CONCEPTS: required by law

REQUIRE *(Need),* **verb**   crave, demand, *desiderare,* desire, *egere,* fall short, feel the necessity for, have an insufficiency, lack, miss, necessitate, request, *requirere,* stand in need of, want

REQUIREMENT, *noun*   adjuration, behest, bidding, call, claim, command, commandment, compulsion, conscription, constraint, decree, decretal, demand, dictate, direction, directive, edict, enforcement, enjoinment, essential, essential desideratum, exaction, exigency, extremity, fiat, imperative, imposition, indispensable item, injunction, mandate, matter of necessity, must, necessitation, necessity, need, obligation, obsession, onus, order, precondition, prerequisite, prescript, prescription, pressing concern, pressure, proviso, regulation, request, requisite, requisition, rescript, re-

sponsibility, ruling, specification, ukase, ultimatum, urgency, vital part, want, warrant
ASSOCIATED CONCEPTS: requirement contract

REQUISITE, adjective basic, binding, called for, compulsory, crying, demanded, entailed, essential, exigent, expedient, imperative, important, in demand, incumbent on, indispensable, ineluctable, inevasible, instant, mandatory, must, *necessarius*, necessary, necessitated, needed, needful, obligatory, postulated, prerequisite, pressing, required, requisitory, urgent, vital, wanted

REQUISITION, noun application, behest, bidding, call, claim, compulsory acquisition, demand, direction, exaction, forcible demand, formal request, indent, injunction, levy, mandate, necessitation, necessity, need, order, petition, *postulatio,* request, requirement, requisite, want

REQUITAL, noun acknowledgment, *compensare,* compensation, consideration, desert, emolument, guerdon, indemnification, indemnity, meed, pay, payment, quittance, recompense, redress, remuneration, reparation, repayment, reprisal, requitement, restitution, retaliation, return, reward, satisfaction

RES IPSA LOQUITUR, noun automatic lack of due diligence, automatic negligence, breach of duty, certain dereliction, definite carelessness, imprudence, irresponsibility, lack of attention

RES JUDICATA, noun accommodated, adjudication, adjusted, agreed, arranged, brought to termination, came to determination, concluded, decided, decision, decree, determination, judgment, negotiated, resolved

RESCIND, verb abolish, *abrogare,* abrogate, annul, call back, cancel, countermand, counterorder, cut off, cut short, declare null and void, disannul, discard, disestablish, dismiss, dissolve, do away with, end, erase, invalidate, negate, nullify, obliterate, override, overrule, quash, recall, recant, remove, render invalid, renege, renounce, repeal, repudiate, *rescindere,* retract, reverse, revoke, set aside, sweep aside, take back, vacate, void, wipe out, withdraw
ASSOCIATED CONCEPTS: rescind a contract, rescind an offer

RESCISION, noun abandonment, abjuration, abnegation, abolishment, abolition, abrogation, annulment, cancellation, change of mind, countermand, counterorder, defeasance, deletion, destruction, disannulment, disavowal, disclaimer, dissolution, eradication, invalidation, negation, nullification, overruling, overthrow, quashing, recall, recantation, renunciation, repeal, repudiation, rescindment, retraction, reversal, revocation, revokement, suspension, termination, vitiation, voidance, withdrawal
ASSOCIATED CONCEPTS: rescision and restriction

RESCUE, verb aid, deliver, disenthrall, disimprison, emancipate, *exsolvere,* extricate, free, free from confinement, free from danger, let escape, let out, *liberare,* liberate, manumit, preserve, ransom, recapture, reclaim, recover, redeem, release, retake, retrieve, safeguard, salvage, save, set free, set loose, take to safety, unbind, unchain, unfetter, unloose, unshackle, untrammel

ASSOCIATED CONCEPTS: Good Samaritan laws, rescue doctrine

RESEARCH, noun analysis, careful search, close inquiry, *eruditio,* examination, experimentation, exploration, factfinding, indagation, inquest, inquiry, inquisition, inspection, investigation, observation, probe, pursuit, quest, questioning, reconnaissance, scrutiny, search, study, survey, testing program

RESEARCH, verb analyze, burrow, chase after, check on, delve into, dissect, examine, experiment, explore, go in quest of, hunt, indagate, inquire, inspect, investigate, look into, probe into, pry, pursue, pursue an inquiry, quest, read up on, scan, scrutinize, search, seek, sleuth, study, test, trace, track, unearth

RESEMBLANCE, noun affinity, agreement, alikeness, analogy, approximation, closeness, conformance, conformity, correspondence, counterpart, ditto, double, duplication, effigy, equality, fascimile, fellow, homogeneity, identicalness, identity, image, imitation, kinship, likeness, match, mate, mold, parallel, parity, reflection, replica, representation, reproduction, sameness, selfsameness, semblance, similarity, similitude, *similitudo,* type, uniformity

RESENT, verb be angry, be indignant, be insulted, be offended, be piqued, be provoked, be revengeful, be vengeful, be vexed, bear malice, bridle, bristle, chafe, dislike, express annoyance, express ill will, feel annoyance, feel displeasure, feel hurt, feel ill will, feel resentment, find intolerable, harbor a grudge, hate, *moleste ferre,* show indignation, take amiss, take exception to, take offense, take poorly, take umbrage, view with dissatisfaction

RESENTFUL, adjective acrimonious, angry, bitter, bristling, choleric, churlish, discontented, displeased, distrustful, embittered, envious, furious, galled, grouchy, grudging, grumpy, huffy, hurt, illdisposed, implacable, in a huff, in high dudgeon, indignant, infuriated, *iracundus,* jealous, malevolent, malicious, malignant, miffed, mistrustful, moody, offended, outraged, pained, peevish, piqued, querulous, resentive, revengeful, sore, spiteful, splenetic, sulky, sullen, surly, suspicious, touchy, umbrageous, unforgiving, up in arms, vengeful, venomous, vindictive, waspish

RESENTMENT, noun acrimony, affront, anger, animosity, animus, antagonism, bile, bitterness, choler, dander, disaffection, discontent, displeasure, dissatisfaction, dudgeon, enmity, envy, fury, gall, grudge, hatred, huff, ill will, indignation, *ira,* ire, jealousy, malice, malignity, offense, pique, rankling, resentfulness, soreness, spite, spleen, *stomachus,* umbrage, vengefulness, venom, vindictiveness, wounded pride, wrath

RESERVATION *(Condition),* **noun** condition, *exceptio,* exception, exemption, limitation, provision, proviso, qualification, requisite, restriction, salvo, saving clause, specification, stipulation
ASSOCIATED CONCEPTS: conditional contracts, reservation contained in acceptance, reservation contained in grant, reservation in deed, reservation in insurance policy

RESERVATION *(Engagement),* **noun** booking, preengagement, promise to set aside, registration, retaining, retainment, retention, saving, withholding

ASSOCIATED CONCEPTS: reservation of interest, reservation of life estate, reservation of rights, reservation of title

FOREIGN PHRASES: *Quod sub certa forma concessum vel reservatum est non trahitur ad valorem vel compensationem.* That which is granted or reserved under a certain form, cannot be twisted into a valuation or compensation.

RESERVE, *noun*   assets, cache, conservation, *copia,* depository, fund, means, provision, resource, resources, savings, stock, store, storehouse, supply

ASSOCIATED CONCEPTS: accumulated reserve, held in reserve, insurance reserve, legal reserve, minimum reserves, premium reserve, reserve funds, reserve valve, reserved powers

RESERVE, *verb*   accumulate, amass, bank, bespeak, cache, create a fund, deposit, earmark, except, garner, hide, hoard, hold, hold back, keep, keep back, keep in reserve, keep on hand, lay away, maintain, preselect, preserve, put aside, *reponere,* retain, save, set apart, set aside, shelve, stock pile, store, store away, store up, withhold

ASSOCIATED CONCEPTS: reserve an interest, reserve one's rights

RESIDE, *verb*   abide, be located, be quartered, be situated, become a citizen, bide, domicile, domiciliate, dwell, establish oneself, *habitare,* have an address, *incolere,* indwell, inhabit, *inhabitare,* live, live at, lodge, occupy, remain, settle, sojourn, squat, stay, take up abode, take up residence, tarry, tenant

RESIDENCE, *noun*   abode, accommodations, address, billet, commorance, commorancy, domicile, domiciliation, *domicilium, domus,* dwelling, habitancy, habitat, habitation, home, housing, inhabitancy, inhabitation, living place, living quarters, lodgings, lodgment, place, place of residence, quarters, residency, *sedes*

ASSOCIATED CONCEPTS: domicile, legal residence, residency requirement

RESIDENT, *noun*   addressee, boarder, burgess, denizen, dweller, habitant, *habitator,* indweller, inhabitant, inhabiter, inmate, lodger, native, occupant, occupier, oppidan, residentiary, resider, settler, sojourner, tenant, townsman, villager

RESIDENTIAL, *adjective*   domestic, domiciliary, fit for habitation, home, household, inhabited, living, not commercial, not public, occupied, private

ASSOCIATED CONCEPTS: residential area, residential property, residential purposes, residential use

RESIDUAL, *noun*   balance, excess, leftover, remainder, remains, residuary, residue, residuum, surplus

RESIDUARY, *adjective*   excess, excessive, left over, outstanding, remaining, residual, resultant, spare, surplus, unspent

ASSOCIATED CONCEPTS: residuary bequest, residuary clause, residuary devise, residuary estate, residuary fund, residuary interest, residuary legacy, residuary legatee

RESIGN, *verb*   abandon, abdicate, *abire,* abjure, capitulate, cease work, cede, *cedere,* demit, depart, *deponere,* desist from, disclaim, divest oneself of, drop out, forego, forsake, give notice, give up, leave, quit, reject, relinquish, renounce, repudiate, retreat, stand aside, step down, surrender, tender one's resignation, vacate, withdraw, yield

RESIGNATION *(Passive acceptance),* *noun*   acquiescence, *animus submissus,* capitulation, deference, docility, endurance, fatalism, forbearance, fortitude, lack of complaint, lack of resistance, longanimity, meekness, nonresistance, obedience, passiveness, passivity, patience, stoicism, submission, submissiveness, sufferance, surrender, tolerance, toleration, yeilding

RESIGNATION *(Relinquishment),* *noun*   abandonment, *abdicatio,* abdication, abjuration, abjurement, cession, demission, departure, evacuation, forsaking, giving up, leaving, quitting, renouncement, renunciation, retirement, secession, surrender, termination, vacation, withdrawal, yielding

FOREIGN PHRASES: *Resignatio est juris proprii spontanea refutatio.* Resignation is a spontaneous relinquishment of one's own right.

RESIGNED, *adjective*   adapted, adjusted, agreeable, biddable, defeatist, easily managed, enduring, forbearant, forbearing, long-suffering, manageable, meek, nonresistant, passive, patient, reconciled, resistless, stoic, stoical, submissive, surrendered, tame, tolerant, tractable, unassertive, uncomplaining, unrepining, unresisting, willing, yielding

RESILIENT, *adjective*   able to endure, adaptable, adaptive, adjustable, bendable, bouncing, buoyant, durable, elastic, flexible, flexile, jaunty, malleable, *mollis,* pliable, pliant, recoiling, responsive, responsive to change, rubbery, sequacious, spongy, sprightly, springy, strong, tractable, wiry, yielding

RESIST *(Oppose),* *verb*   assail, assault, bar, beat back, block, breast, check, combat, confront, contradict, contravene, counter, counteract, cross, defy, dissent, fight, hinder, impugn, make a stand against, obstruct, offer resistance, oppugn, parry, prevent, protest, rebel, rebuff, recalcitrate, refuse to yield, reluctate, repel, repulse, retaliate, rival, stem, stop, strike, strike back, strive against, thwart

FOREIGN PHRASES: *Error qui non resistitur approbatur.* An error which is not resisted or opposed is waived.

RESIST *(Withstand),* *verb*   be immune, be strong, be unsusceptible, bear, bear up, challenge, continue, cope with, disregard, endure, fend off, hold off, hold out, hold up, last, maintain, persevere, persist, prevail against, refuse to submit, remain, stand, stand fast, stand firm, stand up to, stay, tolerate, weather

ASSOCIATED CONCEPTS: resisting arrest

RESISTANCE, *noun*   antagonism, assault, attack, battle, blocking, check, combat, confrontation, contention, contrariety, contrariness, contravention, contumacy, counteraction, defiance, disobedience, fight, hindrance, immunity, imperviousness, insubordination, insurgence, insurrection, interference, mutiny, noncompliance, nonconformance, obstinacy, obstruction, oppugnance, oppugnation, protest, rebellion, rebuff, recalcitrance, recusancy, refusal, reluctance, renitence, repugnance, repulsion, revolt, revolution, sedition, stand, strife, strike, struggle, unalterableness, unsusceptibility, unwillingness, unyieldingness, uprising, withstanding

RESOLUTE, adjective adamant, bent, *constans,* constant, decided, determined, diligent, dogged, earnest, faithful, firm, *firmus,* fixed, *fortis,* immutable, indefatigable, indomitable, industrious, inexorable, inflexible, intent upon, intransigent, obdurate, obstinate, persevering, persistent, pertinacious, purposeful, relentless, resolved, sedulous, serious, set, settled, stanch, steadfast, steady, strong-willed, stubborn, tenacious, unalterable, unbending, unchanging, uncompromising, undaunted, undeviating, unfaltering, unflinching, unrelenting, unshaken, unswerving, untiring, unwavering, unyielding, vigorous, zealous

RESOLUTION *(Decision),* **noun** application, constancy, *decretum,* determination, earnestness, firmness, indefatigability, intention, obduracy, obstinacy, perseverance, persistence, purpose, resoluteness, resolve, *scitum, sententia,* spunk, staying power, steadfastness, steadiness, tenacity, will, will power, zealotry

RESOLUTION *(Formal statement),* **noun** declaration, deliverance, formal expression, plan, presentation, pronouncement, proposal, proposition, statement, written announcement

RESOLVE *(Decide),* **verb** arrive at a conclusion, arrive at a decision, ascertain, be firm, be settled in opinion, come to a determination, *constituere, decernere,* determine, devote oneself to, fix in purpose, make a choice, make a decision, make up one's mind, plan, propose, purpose, settle on by deliberate will, settle upon, *statuere,* take a stand, will

RESOLVE *(Solve),* **verb** clarify, clear up, decipher, disentangle, dispel misunderstanding, elucidate, enucleate, figure out, find a solution, find the answer, hit upon a solution, illuminate, interpret, make clear, make plain, provide the answer, remove misunderstanding, reveal, reveal the answer, shed light upon, throw light upon, understand, unravel, unscramble, untangle

RESORT, verb administer, adopt, apply, avail oneself of, bring into play, call forth, employ, enlist, exercise, fall back upon, have recourse, look to, make use of, practice, press into service, put to use, try, turn to for help, turn to for support, use, utilize

RESOUNDING, adjective absolute, booming, certain, clear, decided, definite, echoing, emphatic, explicit, forceful, incontestable, incontrovertible, intensive, loud, marked, overwhelming, pealing, positive, rebounding, repercussive, reverberant, reverberating, reverberatory, rich, ringing, sonorous, sounding, strong, thunderous, undisputed, vigorous

RESOURCE, noun accumulation, asset, available means, capital, contrivance, dependence, device, essential, estate, expedient, *facultates,* fund, income, instrument, material, means, property, provision, reserve, reserve fund, resort, revenue, source, stock, stock in trade, store, supply, support, tool, wealth, wherewithal

RESOURCEFUL, adjective able, able to meet situations, accomplished, adroit, apt, artful, bright, *callidus,* capable, clever, competent, conversant, crafty,

creative, cunning, deft, dexterous, efficient, endowed, enterprising, experienced, facile, felicitous, fertile, gifted, habile, handy, imaginative, *ingeniosus,* ingenious, inventive, original, practiced, prepared, proficient, sagacious, sharp, shrewd, skillful, smart, *sollers,* talented, trained, venturesome, versatile

RESPECT, noun admiration, adoration, appreciation, approbation, approval, attention, awe, civility, commendation, consideration, courtesy, courtliness, credit, deference, devoirs, dignity, esteem, estimation, etiquette, favor, good manners, good will, homage, honor, humbleness, humility, idolization, laudation, note, obeisance, *observantia,* ovation, polite regard, politeness, praise, prestige, recognition, regard, repute, reverence, testimonial, tribute, veneration, worship, worth

RESPECTFULLY, adverb compliantly, courteously, decorously, deferentially, dutifully, humbly, obediently, politely, regardfully, *reverenter,* reverently, submissively, *summisse,* unassumingly, *verecunde,* with all respect, with compliance, with deference, with due deference, with due respect, with the highest respect
ASSOCIATED CONCEPTS: respectfully submitted to the court

RESPECTIVELY, adverb apiece, each, each in turn, in turn, independently, individually, one at a time, one by one, separately, severally, singly

RESPITE *(Interval of rest),* **noun** abeyance, break, breathing spell, breathing time, cessation, halt, interim, interlude, intermediate time, intermission, interruption, lapse, letup, lull, pause, recess, relaxation, rest, spell, stay, stop, suspension, temporary stoppage, wait

RESPITE *(Reprieve),* **noun** acquittal, amnesty, clearance, deliverance, discharge, exemption, grace, immunity, pardon, release, stay of execution

RESPOND, verb acknowledge, answer, counterclaim, debate, discuss, exchange opinions, explain, give an answer, join issue, make a rejoinder, parry, plead, provide an answer, react, rebut, rejoin, reply, retort, return an answer

RESPONDENT, noun answerer, appellant, corespondent, defendant, party answering a summons or bill, replier, responder

RESPONSE, noun acknowledgment, answer, antiphon, countercharge, counterstatement, explanation, plea, reaction, rebuttal, rejoinder, replication, reply, respondence, responsal, retort, return, riposte, surrebutter, surrejoinder

RESPONSIBILITY *(Accountability),* **noun** accountableness, amenability, answerability, bounden duty, boundness, burden, chargeability, commitment, compulsion, culpability, duty, encumbrance, engagement, imperative duty, liability, obligation, obligatoriness, pledge, promise, *rationem rei,* subjection to, that which is owing
ASSOCIATED CONCEPTS: diminished responsibility

RESPONSIBILITY *(Conscience),* **noun** claims of conscience, compunction, conscientiousness, dependability, ethical judgment, faithfulness, feeling of obligation, incorruptibility, inviolability, inward monitor, moral consciousness, moral faculty, moral obligation, moral sense, morality, scruples, scrupulousness, sense of duty, sense of obligation, sense of right and wrong, stability, trustworthiness, unperfidiousness, untreacherousness, uprightness

RESPONSIVE, *adjective*   accessible, active, acute, admissive, alert, alive, answering, communicative, discerning, keen, perceptive, prudent, reacting, reactive, receptive, reciprocative, rejoining, replying, respondent, sensible, sensitive, sentient, sharp, susceptible
ASSOCIATED CONCEPTS: responsive answers, responsive pleading

REST *(Be supported by), verb*   couch, lay, lean, lie, lounge, perch, prop, recline, squat

REST *(Cease from action), verb*   abstain, be at ease, be peaceful, be quiet, be still, be tranquil, calm down, cease, come to a standstill, desist, discontinue, end, halt, idle, keep quiet, lounge, pause, recess, relax, repose, retire, settle, stand still, stay, stop, stop work, take a break, take time out, terminate

REST *(End a legal case), verb*   cease to litigate, complete prosecution, conclude proceeding, end the introduction of evidence, end the presentation of evidence, finish litigation, submit the case, terminate a trial
ASSOCIATED CONCEPTS: rest a case

RESTATEMENT, *noun*   abridgment, abstract, brief, compendium, condensation, *collectio,* conspectus, digest, *enumeratio,* epitome, explanation, going over, iteration, paraphrase, reaffirmation, reassertion, recapitulation, recital, recountal, recounting, rehash, reiteration, repetition, rephrasing, replay, retelling, review, rewording, summary, synopsis, translation

RESTITUTION, *noun*   adjustment, amends, atonement, compensation, damages, emolument, expiation, giving back, indemnification, paying back, payment, quittance, rebate, reclamation, recompense, recoupment, recovery, reddition, redemption, redress, refund, reimbursement, reinstatement, remitter, remuneration, reparation, repayment, replacement, requital, requitement, restoration, retrieval, return, reversion, satisfaction, settlement
ASSOCIATED CONCEPTS: order of restitution, partial restitution, *quantum meruit,* writ of restitution
FOREIGN PHRASES: *In restitutionibus benignissima interpretatio facienda est.* The most favorable construction is to be adopted in restitutions.

RESTIVE, *adjective*   averse, balking, balky, cantankerous, contumacious, crossgrained, crotchety, deaf to reason, demurring, difficult, discontented, disinclined, disobedient, exceptious, excitable, excited, fidgety, fractious, fretful, grumpy, headstrong, humorsome, ill at ease, impatient, incorrigible, inflexible, insubordinate, insurgent, intractable, intransigent, irreconcilable, lawless, loath, moody, mulish, mutinous, obdurate, obstinate, on edge, out-of-sorts, peevish, perverse, pervicacious, rebellious, recalcitrant, recusant, refractory, reluctant, renitent, resentful, resisting control, restiff, restless, revolutionary, seditious, skittish, splenetic, stickling, stubborn, sulky, sullen, unaccommodating,

uncomplaisant, uncompliant, uncomplying, unconsenting, uncontrollable, uneasy, ungovernable, unmanageable, unquiet, unrestful, unruly, unsettled, unsubmissive, unwilling, unyielding, wayward, willful

RESTORE *(Renew), verb*   ameliorate, amend, correct, cure, doctor up, energize, fix, heal, improve, make better, make whole, meliorate, mend, patch, patch up, put in order, put in repair, put right, reanimate, rearrange, rebuild, recondition, reconstitute, reconstruct, recreate, rectify, redintegrate, redo, refashion, refit, reform, refresh, regenerate, rehabilitate, reinvigorate, rejuvenate, remake, remedy, remodel, renovate, reorganize, repair, restitute, resuscitate, retouch, revive, revivify

RESTORE *(Return), verb*   atone, bring back, give back, hand back, indemnify, make amends, make good, make reparation, make restitution, put back, recompense, recoup, *reddere,* redeem, redress, reestablish, *referre,* refund, reimburse, reinstall, reinstate, reinvest with, remit, render up, repay, replace, revest, satisfy, send back
ASSOCIATED CONCEPTS: restore to one's former position, restored to possession
FOREIGN PHRASES: *Reddere, nil aliud est quam acceptum restituere; seu, reddere est quasi retro dare, et redditur dicitur a redeundo, quia retro it.* To render is nothing more than to restore that which has been received; or, to render is as it were to give back, and it is called "rendering" from "returning", because it goes back again.

RESTRAIN, *verb*   arrest, bar, bind, blockade, bridle, call a halt, check, confine, constrain, contain, control, cramp, curb, curtail, debar, delimit, deprive of liberty, detain, deter, disallow, discountenance, enchain, enclose, enjoin, fasten, fetter, forbid, govern, hamper, handcuff, handicap, harness, hinder, hold, hold back, hold in check, hold in custody, immure, impound, imprison, incarcerate, inhibit, interdict, jail, keep, keep under control, keep within bounds, limit, lock up, manacle, moderate, obstruct, oppose, prevent, prohibit, proscribe, quell, repress, *reprimere,* restrict, *retinere,* shackle, stifle, stop, subdue, subjugate, suppress, take into custody, take prisoner, *tenere,* tie, trammel, vanquish, wall in, withhold
ASSOCIATED CONCEPTS: restraining order, restraining statute
FOREIGN PHRASES: *Exempla illustrant non restrigunt legem.* Examples illustrate, but do not restrain, the law.

RESTRAINT, *noun*   arrest, ban, bar, barricade, blockade, bondage, brake, bridle, captivity, caution, censure, check, circumscription, confinement, constraint, containment, control, curb, custody, damper, deprivation of liberty, detention, determent, deterrence, deterrent, disallowance, discipline, dissuasion, durance, embargo, forbearance, forbiddance, guardianship, hamper, hindrance, holdback, impediment, *impedimentum,* imprisonment, incarceration, inhibition, injunction, interception, interference, limitation, *moderatio,* moderation, obstacle, obstruction, opposition, prevention, prohibition, proscription, repression, reserve, restriction, retardation, self-control, self-denial, servitude, shackle, slavery, stay, stop, stoppage, suppression, taboo, temperance, veto

ASSOCIATED CONCEPTS: combination in restraint of trade, conspiracy in restraint of trade, prior restraint, restraint on alienation

RESTRICT, *verb* astrict, bar, bind, bound, bridle, cage, censor, chain, check, circumscribe, *circumscribere,* cloister, *coercere,* confine, constrain, control, coop, cramp, curb, debar, define, delimit, delimitate, demarcate, diminish, disallow, enchain, encumber, entrammel, exclude, fetter, forbid, frustrate, hamper, handcuff, handicap, hedge in, hem in, hobble, hold back, immure, inhibit, interdict, keep within limits, limit, localize, manacle, modify, muzzle, narrow, obstruct, pen, pin down, pinion, preclude, prevent, prohibit, proscribe, put under restraint, qualify, reduce, repress, restrain, restringe, secure, shackle, shut out, specialize, stifle, stop, suppress, taboo, tether, tie up, trammel, veto, wall in
ASSOCIATED CONCEPTS: restricted allotment, restricted assets

RESTRICTION, *noun* *angustiae,* bonds, boundary, bounds, check, circumscription, condition, confinement, constraint, constriction, containment, curb, demarcation, distinction, *finis,* impediment, interdiction, limitation, *modus,* obligation, prohibition, qualification, regulation, reservation, restraint
ASSOCIATED CONCEPTS: restriction on alienation

RESTRICTIVE, *adjective* circumscriptive, clannish, cliquish, conditional, contingent, defining, deterrent, exclusive, hindering, impeditive, inflexible, interdictive, interdictory, limitary, limitative, limiting, modificatory, modifying, narrow, preclusive, preventative, preventive, prohibitionary, prohibitive, prohibitory, proscriptive, provisional, provisory, qualifying, repressive, restraining, select, selective, stiff, straitlaced, suppressive
ASSOCIATED CONCEPTS: restrictive covenant, restrictive endorsement, restrictive interpretation, restrictive provisions, restrictive title

RESULT, *noun* aftermath, conclusion, consequence, *consequentia,* decision, denouement, determination, development, effect, end, eventuality, *exitus,* finding, *fructus,* fruit, fruition, harvest, judgment, outcome, outgrowth, output, product, resolution, resultant, termination, turnout, upshot, verdict, yield

RESULT, *verb* accrue, arise, be due to, be the effect, be the outcome, come forth, come from, conclude, *consequi,* derive from, develop, emanate, emerge, end, ensue, *evenire,* eventuate, *fieri,* flow, follow, issue, originate, proceed, proceed from, redound, rise, spring, terminate, turn out
ASSOCIATED CONCEPTS: causation, direct result, necessary result, probable result, proximate result, result in damages suffered

RESUME, *verb* advance, begin again, carry on, continue, follow, forge ahead, get a fresh start, go on, move ahead, proceed, progress, pursue, *recolere,* recommence, renew, *repetere,* return to, start afresh, start again, start forward again, take up again

RESURGENCE, *noun* come back, fresh spurt, new energy, reanimation, reappearance, rebirth, recovery, recuperation, recurrence, reestablishment, regeneration, regenesis, rejuvenation, renaissance, renascence,

renewal, restoration, resumption, resurgence, resurrection, resuscitation, reversion, revival, revivification

RESURRECT, *verb* bring back, bring to, call back, reanimate, rebuild, recall to life, recondition, regenerate, reincarnate, rejuvenate, rekindle, renew, reorganize, restore, resuscitate, revitalize, revive, revivify

RETAIL, *adjective* by the piece, commercial, engaged in commerce, marketing, mercantile, singly

RETAIN *(Employ), verb* book, commission, contract for, engage, enlist, give a job, hire, keep, keep in pay, maintain, put to work, recruit, reserve, secure

RETAIN *(Keep in possession), verb* bear in mind, call up, cause to be remembered, cling to, clutch, *conservare,* continue to hold, detain, grasp, have, hold, hold fast, hold in possession, impress upon the memory, keep, keep hold of, keep in mind, maintain, possess, preserve, put away, recall, recollect, remember, reserve, save, secure, sustain, *tenere,* withhold

RETAINER, *noun* *arrhabo,* compensation, employment fee, engaging fee, fee contingent on future legal services, fee paid to secure legal services, income, payment, professional fee, recompense, remuneration, retaining fee
ASSOCIATED CONCEPTS: attorney's retainer

RETALIATE, *verb* answer back, avenge, counter, exchange blows, get back, get even, give measure for measure, match, pay back, rebut, reciprocate, repay, repay in kind, requite, return, revenge, strike back, take retribution, take revenge, take vengeance, *ulcisci*

RETENTION, *noun* *conservatio,* constraint, control, custodianship, grasp, hold, holding action, holding power, keeping, memory, *possessio,* reservation, restraint, retainment, *retentio,* tenacity
ASSOCIATED CONCEPTS: retention of benefits

RETIRE *(Conclude a career), verb* abdicate, demit, drop out, give notice, give up office, give up work, leave, quit, relinquish, resign, stand aside, take leave, tender one's resignation, vacate

RETIRE *(Retreat), verb* abandon, *abire, concedere,* decamp, depart, discharge, fall back, go back, leave, part, recede, *recedere,* remove, retrocede, seclude oneself, separate oneself, shelve, take leave, turn in, vacate, withdraw

RETORT, *verb* answer, answer back, come back, counter, countercharge, counterclaim, make a rebuttal, parry, rebut, rejoin, replicate, reply, requite, respond, *respondere,* return, riposte, say in reply, snap back, surrebut, surrejoin

RETRACTION, *noun* abjuration, abolishment, annulment, cancellation, contradiction, countermand, counterorder, disannulment, disavowal, gainsaying, negation, nullification, palinode, recall, recantation, recision, renunciation, repeal, repudiation, rescindment, retractation, reversal, revocation, taking back, unsaying, voidance, withdrawal
ASSOCIATED CONCEPTS: retraction of erroneous or defamatory statements

RETREAT, verb abandon, back away, back out, backtrack, bolt, decamp, depart, desert, disengage, draw back, ebb, escape, evacuate, fall back, fall to the rear, flee, *fugere,* give way, go away, go back, leave, lose ground, make oneself scarce, move back, *pedem referre,* pull back, quit, recede, recoil, regrade, remove oneself, retire, retrocede, reverse, run away, rusticate, *se recipere,* seclude oneself, shrink, slip away, take flight, turn tail, vacate, withdraw

RETRENCH, verb abridge, be economical, be frugal, *circumcidere,* clip, confine, *contrahere,* curtail, cut, cut down, cut short, decrease, deduct, delete, diminish, economize, lessen, limit, lop, pare, pinch, practice economy, prune, reduce, reduce expenses, remove, shorten, subduct, subtract, *sumptus minuere*

RETRIBUTION, noun amends, atonement, avengement, compensation, counterstroke, desert, due, indemnification, justice, measure for measure, nemesis, payment, penalty, *poena,* punishment, punitive action, reciprocation, reparation, repayment, reprisal, requital, requitement, retaliation, retributive justice, return, revenge, reward, satisfaction, vengeance, vengefulness, vindictiveness

RETROACTIVE, adjective affecting the past, beginning before, commencing before, effective before, having prior application, having prior effect, operational before, starting before, taking effect before
ASSOCIATED CONCEPTS: ex post facto, retroactive effect

RETROSPECT, noun afterthought, contemplation of the past, hindsight, looking back, memory, recall, recapitulation, recollection, reconsideration, reexamination, remembrance, rememoration, reminiscence, *respectus,* retentive memory, review, survey, thoughts of the past
ASSOCIATED CONCEPTS: ex post facto

RETURN (Go back), verb backslide, come again, come back, double back, reappear, rebound, recidivate, *redire,* reenter, reestablish, relapse, resume, retrace one's steps, retreat, retrograde, reverse direction, revert, *reverti,* revisit

RETURN (Refund), verb compensate, give back, indemnify, make compensation, make good, make reparation, make restitution, pay back, *reddere,* reimburse, repay, restore, satisfy, settle

RETURN (Respond), verb acknowledge, answer, answer back, counter, countercharge, exchange, field questions, give an answer, interchange, make a rebuttal, make a rejoinder, make acknowledgment, react, rebut, reciprocate, recriminate, rejoin, reply, *respondere,* retaliate, retort, riposte, say in reply, surrebut, surrejoin

REVEAL, verb acknowledge, admit, advise, affirm, announce, apprise, bare, blazon, blurt out, break the news, bring to light, bruit, circulate, communicate, concede, confess, confide, confirm, debunk, declare, describe, disabuse, disclose, display, disseminate, divulgate, divulge, enlighten, evince, *evulgare,* evulgate, explain, expose, give inside information, give out, grant, impart, indicate, inform, make known, make public, make publicly known, manifest, mention, notify, open, *patefacere,* promulgate, publish, set right, tell, uncloak,

uncover, uncurtain, undeceive, unearth, unfold, unmask, unseal, unshroud, unveil, utter, vent, verify, voice
ASSOCIATED CONCEPTS: disclosure of grand jury secrets, disclosure of secret, scientific information

REVENGE, noun avengement, counterblast, counterstroke, desert, feud, implacability, nemesis, punishment, punitive action, quittance, reciprocation, repayment, reprisal, requital, retaliation, retaliatory punishment, retribution, retributive punishment, revengefulness, satisfaction, *ultio,* vendetta, vengeance, vengefulness, *vindicta,* vindictiveness

REVENUE, noun compensation, dividends, earnings, emolument, gain, hire, income, intake, interest, livelihood, pay, payment, perquisites, proceeds, profit, receipts, recompense, *reditus,* remuneration, return, reward, salary, *vectigal,* wages, yield
ASSOCIATED CONCEPTS: appropriation law, internal revenue, revenue bills, revenue law, revenue-producing income, revenue tax

REVERSAL, noun abolishment, abolition, about-face, abrogation, annulment, backslide, cancellation, change, change of mind, check, countermandment, counterorder, disavowal, invalidation, inversion, nonapproval, nullification, overriding, overruling, overthrowing, rebuff, rebuke, recantation, rejection, renouncement, renunciation, repeal, repudiation, rescission, retraction, reversion, revocation, revokement, tergiversation, turnabout, undoing, voidance, voiding
ASSOCIATED CONCEPTS: reversal of a lower court's decision

REVERSION (Act of returning), noun about-face, backslide, recidivism, regress, regression, relapse, retroaction, retrocession, retrogradation, retrogression, retroversion, return, reversal, reverse, reverting, throwback, turnabout, turnaround

REVERSION (Remainder of an estate), noun future interest, future possession, *hereditas,* remainder over, residue, right of future enjoyment, right of future possession, right of succession
ASSOCIATED CONCEPTS: equitable reversion, life estate, partial reversion, reversionary interest, right of reversion

REVERT, verb backslide, change back, lapse, recede, recoil, regress, retreat, retrograde, retrogress, retrovert, return, reverse, turn back

REVIEW (Critical evaluation), noun account, analysis, appraisal, comment, commentary, critical article, critical discussion, criticism, critique, editorial, essay, exposition, report
ASSOCIATED CONCEPTS: law review

REVIEW (Official reexamination), noun investigation, judicial reconsideration, recapitulation, reconsideration, reinquiry, scrutiny, second examination, study, survey
ASSOCIATED CONCEPTS: administrative review, judicial review, scope of review

REVIEW, verb abstract, analyze, brood over, check thoroughly, comment upon, *contemplari,* criticize, critique, deliberate, describe, digest, epitomize, examine, explain, go over, inspect, *inspicere,* interpret, investigate, look over, make corrections, make improvements, mull over, notice critically, overlook, recapitulate, recheck, reconsider, reexamine, rehearse, reiterate, remember, restate briefly, retell, retrace, revise, reword, run over, scrutinize, skim, study, sum up, summarize, survey, view retrospectively, weigh

REVILEMENT, *noun*   abuse, affront, animadversion, aspersion, berating, billingsgate, bitter words, castigation, censure, condemnation, contumely, criticism, cursing, denunciation, depreciation, detraction, diatribe, discommendation, disparagement, execration, exprobration, increpation, insult, invective, *maledictio,* malediction, objurgation, obloquy, opprobrium, philippic, reprehension, reproach, reprobation, reproof, stricture, tirade, traducement, upbraiding, verbal abuse, vilification, vituperation

REVISE, *verb*   alter, amend, bring up to date, change, correct, develop, doctor, edit, examine, exchange, improve, modify, overhaul, polish, recast, reconsider, reconstruct, rectify, redact, reexamine, remold, *retractare,* revamp, review, rework, rewrite, touch up, work over
ASSOCIATED CONCEPTS: revise a statute

REVISION *(Corrected version), noun*   corrected edition, current edition, *emendatio,* improved version, improvement, new edition, rescript, revised edition, rewrite, updated version

REVISION *(Process of correcting), noun*   alteration, change, correcting, editing, elaboration, overhauling, rectification, refining, reform, removal of errors, restyling, review, revisal, rewriting
ASSOCIATED CONCEPTS: law revision commission, revision of a statute

REVIVAL, *noun*   awakening, comeback, convalescence, freshening, improvement, invigoration, new version, palingenesis, phoenix, quickening, reanimation, reappearance, reawakening, rebirth, reclamation, recovery, recreation, recuperation, recurrence, redintegration, reestablishment, refreshment, regeneracy, regeneration, regenesis, reincarnation, rejuvenation, rejuvenescence, renaissance, renascence, renewal, reproduction, restoration, resumption, resurgence, resurrection, resuscitation, return, revivification, reviviscence, vivification
ASSOCIATED CONCEPTS: abatement and revival, revival of a cause of action

REVOCATION, *noun*   abolishment, abolition, *abrogatio,* abrogation, annulment, cancellation, cancelling, countermand, counterorder, defeasance, disavowal, disownment, invalidation, negation, nullification, recall, recantation, recission, renouncement, repeal, repudiation, rescindment, retractation, retraction, reversal, *revocatio,* revokement, revoking, vacatur, withdrawal
ASSOCIATED CONCEPTS: dependent relative revocation, express revocation, implied revocation, power of revocation, presumption of revocation, revocation of a contract, revocation of a license, revocation of a will
FOREIGN PHRASES: *Non refert verbis an factis fit revocatio.* It matters not whether a revocation is made by words or by acts. *Quod inconsulto fecimus, consultius revocemus.* That which we have done without due consideration, we should revoke upon further consideration.

REVOKE, *verb*   abjure, abolish, *abrogare,* abrogate, annul, cancel, countermand, counterorder, declare null and void, disannul, discard, disclaim, dismiss, dissolve, expunge, invalidate, make void, negate, nullify, override, prohibit, quash, recall, recant, remove, renege, renounce, *renuntiare,* repeal, repudiate, rescind, *rescindere,* retract, reverse, revert, suppress, suspend, vacate, vitiate, void, wipe out, withdraw
ASSOCIATED CONCEPTS: dependent relative revocation, revoke a license, revoke a will

REVOLT, *noun*   agitation, apostasy, change of sides, contrariety, counteraction, defection, *defectio,* defiance, desertion, disobedience, dissension, faithlessness, inconstancy, insubordination, insurgency, insurrection, *motus,* mutiny, noncompliance, opposition, outbreak, overthrow, overturn, political upheaval, rebellion, recalcitrance, resistance, revolution, rising, secession, *seditio,* sedition, strife, strike, subversion, tergiversation, *tumultus,* uprising

REVOLUTION, *noun*   anarchy, *débâcle,* general uprising, insurrection, lawlessness, outbreak, overthrow, overthrow of authority, overturn of authority, overturn of government, political upheaval, public uprising, rebellion, resistance to government, revolt, sweeping change, tumult, turbulence, upheaval, uprising, violent change

REWARD, *noun*   acknowledgment, award, benefit, bonus, booty, bounty, compensation, consideration, donation, emolument, fee, gift, grant, gratuity, guerdon, honorarium, incentive, indemnification, indemnity, meed, pay, payment, perquisite, *praemium proponere,* premium, presentation, prize, purse, quittance, recognition, recompense, remembrance, remuneration, requital, requitement, return, solatium, tip, tribute

RHETORIC *(Insincere language), noun*   affectation, artificial eloquence, bombastic speech, declamation, euphuism, grandiloquence, grandiosity, inflated language, loftiness, magniloquence, pomposity, pompous speech, pompousness, pretension, pretentiousness

RHETORIC *(Skilled speech), noun*   address, allocution, appeal, *ars dicendi,* art of composition, art of discourse, art of prose, command of words, compositional skill, delivery, diction, discourse, elocution, eloquence, exhortation, expression, flowery language, forensic oratory, language, oratory, parlance, phraseology, phrasing, public speaking, recitation, *rhetorica,* science of oratory, speech-making, wording

RIDER, *noun*   accompaniment, addendum, additament, addition, additional clause, adjunct, affix, amendment, appendage, appendant, appendix, appurtenance, attachment, augmentation, complement, continuation, endorsement, extension, insertion, postscript, subjunction, subscript, supplement
ASSOCIATED CONCEPTS: codicil, rider to a contract

RIDICULE, *noun*   buffoonery, burlesque, caricature, chaff, contempt, derision, derisiveness, disdain, disparagement, disrespect, game, gibe, jeer, lampoonery, ludicrous representation, mimicry, mockery, pasquinade, raillery, *ridiculum,* sarcasm, satire, scorn, scornful imitation, sneer, sniggering, sport, squib, taunt, travesty

RIFE, *adjective* abundant, accustomed, bristling, catholic, common, considerable, crowded, current, customary, dense, dominant, endless, epidemic, extensive, far-reaching, galore, general, manifold, many, multitudinous, numerous, pandemic, plenteous, plentiful, popular, populous, predominant, prevailing, prevalent, profuse, rampant, regnant, reigning, replete, swarming, teeming, thick, unending, universal, usual, well-supplied, widespread, worldwide

RIFT *(Disagreement),* *noun* argument, break, clash, contention, controversy, difference, disceptation, dispute, estrangement, fight, misunderstanding, parting, split, variance

RIFT *(Gap),* *noun* aperture, breach, break, chasm, chink, cleft, crack, cranny, crevice, disjunction, fault, fissure, fracture, gash, hiatus, interstice, opening, parting, rent, *rima,* rupture, scissure, separation, split

RIGHT *(Correct),* *adjective* aboveboard, accurate, equitable, ethical, fair, honest, honorable, in accordance with duty, in accordance with justice, in accordance with morality, in accordance with truth, legitimate, reasonable, righteous, rightful, scrupulous, truthful, unswerving, upright, upstanding, valid, veracious, virtuous

RIGHT *(Direct),* *adjective* absolute, exact, immediate, straight, straightaway, straightforward, undeviating, unswerving

RIGHT *(Suitable),* *adjective* accepted, admissible, allowable, appropriate, apt, conventional, customary, fit, fitting, orderly, perfect, proper, reasonable, recognized, satisfactory, seemly, suitable, valid, virtuous, well-done, well-performed, well-regulated

RIGHT *(Entitlement),* *noun* authority, authorization, due, fair claim, heritage, inalienable interest, *ius,* *iusta,* just claim, justification, legal claim, legal power, legal title, ownership, power, prerogative, privilege, sanction, stake, title, vested interest, warrant
ASSOCIATED CONCEPTS: absolute right, accrued rights, Bill of Rights, claim of right, color of right, Constitutional right, contingent right, established right, exclusive right, future right, inchoate right, incorporeal right, inherent right, marital rights, material rights, mineral rights, natural rights, permissive right, preemptive right, preferential right, prescriptive right, prima facie right, proprietary right, prospective right, reciprocal rights, right of action, right of entry, right of privacy, right of redemption, right of way, right to bear arms, right to counsel, right to jury trial, right to vote, right-to-work laws, riparian rights, substantive right, vested rights
FOREIGN PHRASES: *Assignatus utitur jure auctoris.* An assignee is clothed with the right of his principal. *Nul charter, nul vente, ne nul done vault perpetualment, si le donor n'est seise al temps de contracts de deux droits, sc. del droit de possession et del droit de propertie.* No grant, no sale, no gift, is valid forever, unless the donor, at the time of contract, has two rights, namely, the right of possession, and the right of property. *Non videtur vim facere, qui jure suo utitur et ordinaria actione experitur.* He is not considered to use force who exercises his own right, and proceeds by ordinary action. *Nemo plus juris ad alienum transferre potest*

quam ipse habet. No one can transfer to another any greater right than he himself has. *Cui jus est donandi, eidem et vendendi et concedendi jus est.* He who has the right to give has also the right to sell and to grant. *L'ou le ley done chose, la ceo done remedie a vener a ceo.* Where the law gives a right, it gives a remedy to recover. *Ubi jus, ibi remedium.* Where there is a right, there is a remedy. *Non debeo melioris conditionis esse, quam auctor meus a quo jus in me transit.* I ought not to be in better condition than he to whose rights I succeed. *Nemo potest plus juris ad alium transferre quam ipse habet.* No one can transfer a greater right to another than he himself has. *Jus publicum privatorum pactis mutari non potest.* A public right cannot be changed by agreement of private persons. *Nullus jus alienum forisfacere potest.* No man can forfeit the right of another. *Neminem laedit qui jure suo utitur.* He who stands on his own rights injures no one. *Cujus est instituere, ejus est abrogare.* Whose right it is to institute anything, may also abrogate it. *Qui jure suo utitur, nemini facit injuriam.* One who exercises his legal rights, injures no one. *Ignorantia juris sui non praejudicat juri.* Ignorance of one's right does not prejudice the right. *Jus triplex est,-propietatis, possessionis, et possibilitatis.* Right is threefold,-of property, of possession, and of possibility. *Nullus videtur dolo facere qui suo jure utitur.* No one is considered to have committed a wrong who exercises his legal rights. *Cuilibet licet juri pro se introducto renunciare.* Any one may wave the benefit of a legal right that exists only for his protection. *Qui prior est tempore potior est jure.* He who is first in time is first in right.

RIGHT *(Righteousness),* *noun* correctness, due, duty, equitableness, equity, evenhanded justice, excellence, fair treatment, fairness, good actions, good behavior, goodness, honor, integrity, justice, justness, merit, morality, morals, nobleness, principle, probity, propriety, rectitude, *rectus,* straight course, truth, uprightness, *verus,* virtue, worthiness
FOREIGN PHRASES: *Fiat justitia, ruat coelum.* Let right be done, though the heavens fall. *Ipsae leges cupiunt ut jure regantur.* The laws themselves are desirous of being governed by what is right. *Jus et fraus nunquam cohabitant.* Right and fraud never dwell together. *Jus naturale est quod apud homines eandem habet potentiam.* Natural right is that which has the same force among all mankind. *Pacta privata juri publico derogare non possunt.* Private compacts cannot derogate from public right. *Jus est norma recti; et quicquid estcontra normam recti est injuria.* Law is the rule of right; and whatever is contrary to the rule of right is an injury. *Lex est norma recti.* Law is the rule of right. *Quid sit jus, et in quo consistit injuria, legis est definire.* What constitutes right, and what injury, it is the business of the law to define. *Jus ex injuria non oritur.* A right does not arise from a wrong.

RIGHTFUL, *adjective* according to law, allowable, allowed, appropriate, authentic, authorized, becoming, befitting, chartered, constitutional, correct, deserved, due, enfranchised, equitable, fair, fitting, genuine, honest, inalienable, *iustus,* just, justifiable, lawful, legal, legalized, legitimate, licit, meet, merited, ordained, permitted, prescriptive, privileged, proper, real, reasonable, right, sanctioned, seemly, square, statutory, suitable, true, valid, warranted, within the law

RIGID, *adjective* austere, dour, *durus,* exact, exacting, firm, firmly set, fixed, flinty, formal, hard, harsh, hidebound, indurate, indurated, indurative, inelastic, inexorable, inflexible, intractable, motionless, obdurate, obstinate, orthodox, precise, punctilious, puritanical, relentless, renitent, resistant, *rigidus,* rigorous, set, severe, *severus,* starched, starchy, static, steely, stern, stiff, stony, straitlaced, strict, stringent, stubborn, taut, tense, tough, unadaptable, unalterable, unbending, uncompromising, unconformable, undeviating, unmalleable, unmitigated, unmoving, unpliant, unrelaxed, unrelenting, unyielding, wooden

RIGOR, *noun* accuracy, asperity, austerity, care, carefulness, conscientiousness, discipline, *duritia,* exactitude, exactness, firmness, force, freedom from deviation, intensity, keenness, meticulousness, preciseness, precision, relentlessness, rigidity, rigidness, rigorousness, scrupulousness, *severitas,* sharpness, sternness, strictness, stringency, tenacity, uncompromisingness, unyieldingness

RIOT, *noun* affray, bedlam, brawl, breach of the peace, broil, commotion, confusion, disorder, disorderliness, disturbance, ferment, fracas, fray, furor, hubbub, insurgence, insurrection, lawlessness, melee, outbreak, outburst, pandemonium, rebellion, revolt, row, rumpus, shindy, tumult, *tumultus, turba,* turmoil, unruliness, uprising, uproar, wild confusion
ASSOCIATED CONCEPTS: disturbing the peace, inciting a riot

RIPE, *adjective* adult, advanced, brought to perfection, complete, consummate, filled out, finished, fit, full, full-blown, full-grown, fully developed, fully grown, grown, ideal, mature, *maturus,* mellow, perfect, prepared, prime, primed, ready, seasoned, *tempestivus,* usable, well-developed
ASSOCIATED CONCEPTS: ripe for adjudication

RISK, *noun* *alea,* bet, chance, danger, *discrimen,* endangerment, exposure, exposure to harm, gamble, gaming, hazard, imperilment, insecurity, instability, jeopardy, *periculum,* peril, plunge, possibility, possibility of injury, possibility of loss, precariousness, speculation, stake, uncertainty, venture, vulnerability, wager
ASSOCIATED CONCEPTS: acceptance of risk, assumption of risk, extraordinary risk, forseeable risk, incurred risk, insurance risk, limitation of risk, mutuality of risk, risk of loss, shifting of risk, unreasonable risk
FOREIGN PHRASES: *Periculum rei venditae, nondum traditae, est emptoris.* The risk of a thing sold, but not yet delivered, is the purchaser's. *Ubi periculum, ibi et lucrum collocatur.* He who risks a thing, should receive the profits arising from it. *Cujus est dominium ejus est periculum.* He who has the ownership should bear the risk.

RIVAL, *noun* adversary, *aemulus,* antagonist, aspirant, bidder, candidate, challenger, combatant, competition, competitor, contender, contestant, corrival, disputant, enemy, entrant, foe, litigant, opponent, opposition

ROB, *verb* appropriate illegally, burglarize, commit robbery, *despoliare, exspoliare,* hold up, loot, misappropriate, peculate, pilfer, pillage, plunder, purloin, seize, steal, take by force, take unlawful possession

ROBBERY, *noun* depredation, felonious taking, felonious taking of the property of another, holdup, larceny by force, *latrocinium,* piracy, plundering, *rapina, spoliatio,* stealing, theft, thievery

RODOMONTADE, *noun* bluster, boastfulness, boasting, brag, braggadocio, braggartism, bragging, bunkum, embroidery, empty talk, exaggeration, extravagance, fanfaronade, gasconade, hyperbole, inflation, jactitation, ostentation, pretense, pretension, pretentious talk, puffery, rant, swagger, swashbuckling, tall talk, turgescence, vainglorious boasting, vainglory, vaporing

ROLE, *noun* act, assignment, billet, capacity, character, characterization, department, false show, function, guise, impersonation, job, mission, part, *partes,* performance, place, pose, position, post, posture, presentation, pretense, province, representation, sham, task, undertaking, work

ROLL, *noun* account, *album,* catalogue, census, chronicle, directory, docket, document, enumeration, index, inventory, ledger, list, membership, muster, record, register, registry, roster, schedule, *tabula*

ROUTINE, *adjective* accustomed, automatic, common, commonplace, conventional, customary, established, everyday, expected, familiar, fixed, frequent, general, habitual, ingrained, mechanical, normal, popular, prevalent, recurrent, recurring, regular, repeated, ritual, set, standard, stereotyped, stock, uniform, usual, *usus,* well-trodden

RUBRIC *(Authoritative rule),* ***noun*** act, bylaw, canon, code, convention, dictate, enactment, institution, law, legislation, measure, ordinance, precept, prescription, regulation, rule, ruling, statute

RUBRIC *(Title),* ***noun*** caption, classification, denomination, designation, division, genus, grouping, head, heading, headline, label, superscription

RUDIMENTARY, *adjective* abecedarian, basal, basic, beginning, crude, elemental, elementary, embryonic, essential, formative, fundamental, germinal, germinative, immature, inceptive, inchoate, *incohatus,* incomplete, initial, initiative, initiatory, original, originative, primal, primary, primitive, primordial, protomorphic, rudimental, simple, starting, uncompleted, underlying, undeveloped, unfinished

RULE *(Guide),* ***noun*** code, course, criterion, custom, direction, formula, habit, matter of course, method, model, norm, *norma,* order, pattern, policy, practice, procedure, protocol, prototype, *regula,* routine, standard, standing order, system

RULE *(Legal dictate),* ***noun*** act, bylaw, canon, charge, code, command, commandment, decree, dictate, direction, doctrine, dogma, edict, enactment, formula, formulary, formulation, law, legislation, maxim, order, ordinance, *praeceptum, praescriptum,* precept, prescription, principle, regulation, standing order, statute, tenet
ASSOCIATED CONCEPTS: administrative rule, court rule, cy-pres rule, discriminatory rule, home rule, parol evidence rule, rule against perpetuities, Rule in Shelley's Case, rules of construction, rules of evidence, rules of procedure

FOREIGN PHRASES: *Ubi non est condendi auctoritas, ibi non est parendi necessitas.* Where there is no authority for establishing a rule, there is no need of obeying it. *Exceptio probat regulam de rebus non exceptis.* The exception proves the rule in matters not excepted. *Exceptio firmat regulam in contrarium.* An exception affirms the rule to be the contrary. *Non est certandum de regulis juris.* There is no disputing about rules of the law. *Regula est, juris quidem ignorantiam cuique nocere, facti vero ignorantiam non nocere.* The rule is that a person's ignorance of the law may prejudice him, but that his ignorance of fact will not. *Non jus ex regula, sed regula ex jure.* The law does not arise from the rule but the rule comes from the law. *Omnis regula suas patitur exceptiones.* Every rule is subject to its own exceptions. *Exceptio firmat regulam in casibus non exceptis.* An exception confirms the rule in cases not excepted.

RULE *(Decide), verb*   adjudge, adjudicate, ascertain, come to a conclusion, come to a determination, conclude, decide by judicial sentence, declare, declare authoritatively, decree, deliver judgment, determine, draw a conclusion, establish, exercise judgment, find, fix conclusively, give an opinion, give judgment, hold, make a decision, make a resolution, pass judgment, pass sentence, pass upon, pronounce, pronounce judgment, reach an official decision, resolve, settle, settle by decree, umpire

ASSOCIATED CONCEPTS: rule from the bench

RULE *(Govern), verb*   administer, be in power, command, compel, conduct, control, decree, dictate, direct, dispose, domineer, enact, enforce obedience, exercise authority, exert authority, give orders, guide, have authority, have control, have jurisdiction over, have predominating influence, have responsibility, hold authority, hold dominion, hold office, keep in order, manage,

manipulate, master, officiate, order, oversee, police, possess authority, predominate, prescribe, preside over, *regnare,* regulate, reign, restrain, run, serve the people, superintend, supervise

RULING, *noun*   adjudication, award, command, conclusion, court's finding, decision, decree, determination, edict, finding, findings of fact and conclusions of law, holding, judgment, judicial determination, judicial proclamation, judicial pronouncement, opinion of the court, order, order of the court, pronouncement, resolution, rule, sentence, verdict

ASSOCIATED CONCEPTS: judicial ruling, ruling from the bench

RUSE, *noun*   art, artifice, bait, blind, camouflage, cheat, chicane, chicanery, chouse, circumvention, craft, crafty device, deceit, deception, decoy, delusion, design, disguise, dodge, *dolus,* duplicity, evasion, feint, fetch, finesse, flimflam, fraud, guile, hoax, humbug, imposture, jugglery, machination, maneuver, mask, masquerade, plot, pretext, scheme, sham, sharp practice, shift, snare, stratagem, strategy, subterfuge, trick, trickery, wile

RUTHLESS, *adjective*   atrocious, barbarous, bloodthirsty, brutal, brutish, callous, cold, cold-blooded, coldhearted, cruel, deadly, demoniac, devilish, diabolical, dispiteous, fell, feral, ferine, ferocious, fiendish, grim, hard, hardhearted, harsh, heartless, *immisericors,* implacable, inclement, *inexorabilis,* inexorable, inflexible, inhuman, inhumane, *inhumanus,* insensitive, lethal, maleficent, malevolent, malign, malignant, marblehearted, merciless, murderous, obdurate, pitiless, poisonous, rancorous, relentless, remorseless, retaliative, revengeful, sadistic, sanguinary, savage, stonyhearted, treacherous, truculent, uncompassionate, unfeeling, unforgiving, unkind, unmerciful, unpitying, unrelenting, unsparing, unsympathetic, vengeful, venomous, vicious, vindictive, virulent, without pity

S

SACROSANCT, *adjective*   anointed, awesome, blessed, ceremonial, consecrated, dedicated, devotional, divine, elevated, enshrined, godly, hallowed, heavenly, holy, ineffable, inviolable, inviolate, mystical, purified, religious, revered, reverend, sacramental, sacred, sainted, sanctified, set apart, solemn, spiritual, theistic, theologic, theological, transcedent, venerable, venerated, worshiped

SAFE, *adjective*   armed, armored, benign, cared for, certain, covered, defended, dependable, ensconced, entrenched, *fidus,* foolproof, free from danger, free from harm, free from hurt, free from injury, free from risk, guaranteed, guarded, harmless, impervious, impregnable, insured, intact, invulnerable, looked after, maintained, on guard, out of danger, panoplied, preserved, proof, protected, prudent, regulated, reliable, safeguarded, salubrious, scatheless, screened, screened from danger, secure, *securus,* sheltered, shielded, sound, sure, sustained, tested, trustworthy, *tutus,* unadventurous, unassailable, unattackable, unbroken, undamaged, undaring, under cover, unendangered, unexposed, unharmed, unhazarded, unhurt, unimpaired, uninjured, unmolested, unscathed, unshakable, unthreatened, whole, without risk

SAFEGUARD, *noun*   armor, assurance, buffer, bulwark, cover, defense, fortification, insurance, *munimentum,* palladium, precaution, preventive measure, *propugnaculum,* protection, provision, screen, security, shield, surety

SAFEKEEPING, *noun*   aegis, auspices, care, charge, conservation, custody, defense, guard, guardianship, keeping, lee, patronage, preservation, protection, protective custody, salvation, security, shelter, superintendence, supervision, support, tutelage, upkeep, wardship, watch
ASSOCIATED CONCEPTS: bailment

SAGACITY, *noun*   acuity, acumen, acuteness, apperception, arguteness, astuteness, awareness, brilliance, clear thinking, clear thought, cleverness, comprehension, discernment, discrimination, excellent judgment, farsightedness, foresight, genius, good judgment, incisiveness, insight, intelligence, intuition, judgment, keenness, keensightedness, levelheadedness, mentality, penetration, perception, percipience, perspicaciousness, *perspicacitas,* perspicacity, profundity, prudence, *prudentia,* quickness, rationality, reason, reasoning power, sagaciousness, *sagacitas,* sapience, sapiency, sense, sharpness, shrewdness, smartness, sobriety, understanding, vision, wisdom

SAID, *adjective*   above-mentioned, aforegoing, aforenamed, aforesaid, already indicated, before mentioned, earlier, exact, foregoing, forementioned, named, preceding, prevenient, previous, previously mentioned, previously named, previously referred to, prior, specific

SALACIOUS, *adjective*   bawdy, carnal, coarse, concupiscent, corrupt, debauched, dirty, dissolute, erotic, Fescennine, filthy, foul, free, goatish, gross, immoral, impure, incontinent, indecent, lascivious, lecherous, lewd, libertine, libidinous, licentious, lickerish, lickerous, loose, lurid, lustful, obscene, offensive, Paphian, polluted, pornographic, profligate, provocative, prurient, ribald, risque, ruttish, satyric, satyrical, scabrous, scarlet, scrofulous, scurrile, scurrilous, sensual, sexy, shameful, shameless, sinful, smutty, spicy, suggestive, titillating, unblushing, unbowdlerized, unchaste, unclean, unexpurgated, unprintable, unvirtuous, virtueless, wanton

SALE, *noun*   disposal, exchange, trade, transaction, transfer, vendition
ASSOCIATED CONCEPTS: sales and exchange, sale and return, sale at auction, sale by commercial broker, sale by sample, sale confirmed, sale for payment, sale of debt, sale of office, sale on credit, sale on return, sale on trial

SALIENT, *adjective*   bold, capital, cardinal, chief, clear, commanding, conspicuous, distinct, distinguished, dominant, dominating, eminent, evident, exalted, explicit, extraordinary, flagrant, foremost, glar-

ing, illustrious, important, imposing, indubitable, leading, main, marked, memorable, notable, noticeable, obvious, outstanding, overt, paramount, plain, *praecipuus,* predominant, primary, prime, principal, prominent, pronounced, protrudent, protruding, protrusive, protuberant, recognized, remarkable, showing, significant, standing out, striking, towering, unconcealed, unmistakable, visible, well-known, worthy of notice, worthy of remark

SALUBRIOUS, *adjective*   advantageous, analeptic, beneficial, corrective, corroborant, curative, favorable to health, healing, health-promoting, healthful, healthy, invigorating, life-giving, medicinal, nourishing, nutritious, nutritive, recuperative, remedial, reparative, restorative, reviviscent, roborant, salutary, salutiferous, sanatory, stimulating, sustentative, therapeutic, therapeutical, tonic, wholesome

SALUTARY, *adjective*   advantageous, aidant, analeptic, beneficial, benign, bracing, constitutional, corrective, corroborant, curative, edifying, favorable, good, harmless, healing, health-giving, health-preserving, healthful, healthy, helpful, hurtless, hygienic, innocuous, innoxious, invigorating, medicinal, nourishing, nutritious, nutritive, palliative, preventive, profitable, promoting health, prophylactic, protective, remedial, reparative, reparatory, restorative, roborant, safe, salubrious, *salutaris,* salutiferous, sanative, sanatory, sanitary, sustaining, sustentative, therapeutic, tonic, uninjurious, useful, *utilis,* wholesome

SALVAGE, *noun*   conservation, deliverance, extrication, property saved, recapture, reclaimed materials, reclamation, recoupment, recovery, redemption, remains, reoccupation, repossession, rescue, retrieval, return, salvation, scrap
ASSOCIATED CONCEPTS: equitable salvage, net salvage, salvage charges, salvage loss, salvage service

SALVO, *noun*   condition, defense, escape clause, evasion, exception, exemption, explosion, fusillade, general discharge, proviso, qualification, quibbling excuse, reservation, restriction, salute, saving clause, simultaneous discharge of shots, volley

SAMARITAN, *noun*   aid, aider, altruist, assister, befriender, benefactor, champion, defender, friend, good neighbor, help, helper, helping hand, kind person, ministering angel, ministrant, patron, philanthropist, protector, savior, succorer, sympathizer, well-wisher
ASSOCIATED CONCEPTS: Good Samaritan laws, rescue doctrine

SAME, *adjective*   alike, cognate, duplicate, equal, equivalent, exactly like, identical, one and the same, parallel, similar, synonymous, twin, uniform, without difference
ASSOCIATED CONCEPTS: same act or transaction, same as, same cause, same cause of action, same character of work, same class of subject, same compensation, same condition(s), same descriptive properties, same direction, same extent, same fees, same fund, same general business, same grade of employment, same grantor, same manner, same offense, same parties, same punishment, same rate of interest, same right

SAME, *noun*   consistency, counterpart, double, equal, equivalent, idem, identical, match, mate, reciprocal, resemblance, similarity, synonym

SAMPLE, noun archetype, case in point, cross section, *documentum,* ensample, example, exemplar, exemplification, *exemplum,* guide, illustration, instance, model, original, paradigm, prototype, representation, representative, representative selection, showpiece, *specimen,* standard of comparison, swatch, typical example

SANCTION *(Permission),* **noun** acceptance, acquiescence, affirmance, affirmation, agreement, allowance, approbation, approval, assent, *auctoritas,* authorization, charter, *confirmatio,* consent, cooperation, countenance, empowerment, encouragement, endorsement, favor, grant, homologation, immunity, indulgence, legality, license, permission, permit, ratification, seal, stamp of approval, subscription, sufferance, support, tolerance, toleration, validation, vouchsafement, willingness
FOREIGN PHRASES: *Multa conceduntur per obliquum quae non conceduntur de directo.* Many things are allowed indirectly which are not allowed directly.

SANCTION *(Punishment),* **noun** condemnation, denunciation, deprivation, disciplinary action, discipline, imposition, infliction, penal retribution, penalty, retributive action, suffering

SANCTION, verb accede, accept, acquiesce, agree to, allow, approbate, approve, assent to, authenticate, authorize, charter, confer a privilege, confer a right, *confirmare,* consent to, countenance, empower, enable, endorse, entitle, foster, give approval, give permission, go along with, grant, gratify, homologate, indulge, legitimate, legitimatize, legitimize, license, permit, privilege, promote, ratify, *ratum facere, sancire,* stand behind, subscribe to, suffer, support, tolerate, uphold, validate, vouchsafe
ASSOCIATED CONCEPTS: civil sanctions, criminal sanctions, penal sanctions

SANE, adjective *animi,* balanced, clearheaded, competent, coolheaded, judicious, legitimate, levelheaded, logical, lucid, mentally sound, *mentis compos,* normal, rational, realistic, reasonable, responsible, *sanus,* sensible, sober, sober-minded, sound, understanding, undisturbed

SANGUINE, adjective anticipative, assured, bright, buoyant, cheerful, confident, encouraged, enthusiastic, expectant, full of hope, hopeful, in good spirits, inspirited, optimistic, reassured, sanguineous, trustful, trusting, undespairing, undoubting

SANITY, noun balance, clear thinking, clearmindedness, comprehension, health of mind, healthy mind, levelheadedness, lucidity, mental balance, mental equilibrium, mental health, normalcy, normality, rationality, reason, reasonableness, saneness, sense, sensibleness, sound understanding, soundmindedness, soundness, understanding
ASSOCIATED CONCEPTS: competency hearing, presumption of sanity

SAPID, adjective acceptable, affecting, agreeable, alluring, ambrosial, amusing, appealing, appetizing, arresting, attractive, bewitching, captivating, challenging, charming, delectable, delicious, delightful, dulcet, enchanting, engaging, entertaining, enthralling, enticing, entrancing, exciting, fascinating, fine,

flavorful, flavorous, flavorsome, flavory, full-bodied, full-flavored, good, good-tasting, gratifying, gustable, gustful, impressive, inspiring, interesting, intriguing, inviting, likable, lovely, luscious, nectareous, palatable, piquant, pleasant, pleasing, pleasurable, popular, prepossessing, provocative, provoking, refreshing, relishable, saporous, satisfying, savory, scrumptious, seasoned, stirring, succulent, sweet, tantalizing, tasty, tempting, thought-provoking, titallative, titillating, welcome, winning, winsome

SAPIENT, adjective acute, astute, bright, clearheaded, clever, deep, discerning, discriminating, farsighted, intellectual, intelligent, judicious, keen, knowing, learned, perceptive, perspicacious, profound, quick of apprehension, quick-witted, rational, sagacious, sage, *sapiens,* sensible, sharp, shrewd, thinking, wise

SATISFACTION *(Discharge of debt),* **noun** acquitment, acquittal, acquittance, amortizement, clearance, compensation, damages, defrayal, defrayment, discharge, guerdon, indemnification, indemnity, payment, quittance, receipted payment, recompense, recoupment, redress, reimbursement, release from debt, remuneration, reparation, repayment, requital, requitement, restitution, return, settlement, solatium
ASSOCIATED CONCEPTS: accord and satisfaction, ademption, reasonable satisfaction, satisfaction of lien, satisfaction piece

SATISFACTION *(Fulfilment),* **noun** accomplishment, achievement, appeasement, attainment, consummation, content, contentedness, contentment, enjoyment, *expletio,* fruition, gratification, pleasure, realization, reparation, success, sufficiency
ASSOCIATED CONCEPTS: satisfaction of judgment

SATISFY *(Discharge),* **verb** arrange a settlement, carry into execution, carry out, clear, compensate, fulfill an obligation, make compensation, make good, make payment, meet an obligation, pay, pay in full, pay off, pay up, recompense, reimburse, remit, remunerate, render, repay, requite, settle, settle accounts, tender
ASSOCIATED CONCEPTS: satisfy a debt, satisfy a judgment

SATISFY *(Fulfill),* **verb** answer the purpose, appease, avail, be agreeable, be sufficient, carry out, comply with, conform to, content, fill, fit, gratify, meet requirements, please, prove acceptable, qualify, quench, sate, satiate, serve the purpose, set at ease, slake, suffice, suit, surfeit
ASSOCIATED CONCEPTS: satisfy to a moral certainty

SAVE, conjunction bar, barring, besides, but for, deducting, excepting, lacking, leaving out, not including, short of, without

SAVE, preposition but, except, exclusive of, less, minus, omitting

SAVE *(Conserve),* **verb** hold, keep safe, preserve, redeem, salvage

SAVE *(Hold back),* **verb** economize, hoard, keep, reserve, retain

SAVE *(Rescue),* **verb** avert, defend, fend off, give salvation, help, liberate, protect, safeguard, shield

SAVORY, adjective agreeable, ambrosiac, ambrosial, ambrosian, appetizing, *conditus,* delectable, delicious, delightful, flavor, flavored, flavorous, flavorsome, full-bodied, full-flavored, good, good-tasting, gustable, gustative, likable, luscious, nectarean, nectareous, palatable, piquant, pleasant, pleasing, rich, sapid, sweet, tasty, tempting

SCANDAL, noun aspersion, attaint, bad name, bad reputation, bad repute, baseness, brand, censure, damaging report, dedecoration, defamation, degradation, disapprobation, disapproval, discredit, disesteem, disgrace, dishonor, disrepute, humiliation, ignominy, ill repute, imputation, infamy, ingloriousness, loss of honor, loss of reputation, malicious gossip, notoriety, obloquy, odium, opprobrium, reproach, shame, slur, stain, stigma, taint, talk, tarnish, tarnished honor, vilification
ASSOCIATED CONCEPTS: defamatory reports, deformatory rumors

SCANDALOUS, adjective arrant, atrocious, base, black, condemnatory, corrupt, damnatory, dastardly, defamatory, denunciatory, deplorable, despicable, discreditable, disgraceful, dishonorable, disreputable, disrespectable, execrable, facinorous, flagitious, flagrant, fulsome, heinous, horrifying, ignoble, ignominious, illaudable, immodest, immoral, indecent, infamous, inglorious, iniquitous, lewd, licentious, low, mean, nefarious, notorious, objurgatory, odious, offensive, opprobrious, outrageous, *probrosus,* profligate, reprehensible, scurrilous, shameful, shocking, thersitical, *turpis,* ugly, uncommendable, unworthy, wicked
ASSOCIATED CONCEPTS: motion to strike scandalous matter, scandalous allegations, scandalous pleading

SCARCE, adjective at a premium, dear, deficient, few, inadequate, incomplete, inconsiderable, insufficient, limited, little, low, meager, minute, not abundant, not plentiful, out of the way, paltry, rare, *rarus,* scant, seldom met with, short, skimpy, sparing, sparse, thinly scattered, unavailable, uncommon, unique, unobtainable, unplentiful, unusual, wanting

SCATHING, adjective *acerbus,* acrimonious, *aculeatus,* biting, brutal, burning, cruel, cutting, damaging, envenomed, excoriating, harmful, harsh, hurtful, insulting, maleficent, malevolent, malicious, malignant, mordacious, *mordax,* rancorous, scatheful, searing, severe, sharp, spiteful, stinging, trenchant, unbenevolent, uncharitable, uncompromising, ungentle, unkind, venemous, virulent, vitriolic, withering

SCENARIO, noun abstract, analysis, brief, capsule, compression, condensation, contents, digest, essence, narrative, outline, plot, recap, recapitulation, report, review, script, sketch, story, sum and substance, summary, synopsis, text

SCENE, noun act, arena, background, display, episode, eyereach, eyeshot, field, landscape, locale, locality, location, *locus,* panorama, place, range, *scaena,* scope, setting, sight, site, spectacle, sphere, stage, stage setting, surroundings, theater, view, vista, whereabouts
ASSOCIATED CONCEPTS: scene of an accident

SCHEDULE, noun agenda, calendar, check list, docket, enumeration, index, inventory, *libellus,* list, outline, plan, program, roll, *tabula,* timetable

ASSOCIATED CONCEPTS: payment schedule, schedule of assets

SCHEME, noun arrangement, cabal, *consilium,* contrivance, course of action, delineation, design, device, enterprise, machination, maneuver, method, operation, order, organization, plan, plot, policy, procedure, program of action, project, *ratio,* schedule, stratagem, strategy, subterfuge, system, tactics
ASSOCIATED CONCEPTS: conspiracy

SCHEME, verb arrange, be cunning, cabal, calculate, chart, collude, complot, compose, concoct, connive, conspire, contrive, design, devise, diagram, engineer, excogitate, fabricate, fashion, frame, hatch, have designs, improvise, intrigue, invent, lay a plan, machinate, make arrangements, maneuver, manipulate, map, map out, organize, outline, plan, plot, predesign, predetermine, premeditate, prepare, project, *ratio,* think ahead, think out, weave a plot, work out, work up
ASSOCIATED CONCEPTS: collude, conspire

SCHISM, noun breach, break, cabal, desertion, difference, disassociation, disconnection, discord, dissension, dissent, disunion, division, faction, falling out, nonconformity, partition, recusancy, rent, rift, rupture, *schisma,* secession, sectarianism, sectarism, separation, severance, split, withdrawal

SCIENCE *(Study),* **noun** body of fact, branch of knowledge, data, discipline, facts, information, knowledge, learning, organized knowledge, *scientia,* system of knowledge

SCIENCE *(Technique),* **noun** ability, adroitness, aptitude, aptness, capacity, competence, competency, dexterity, expertness, facility, finesse, genius, highly developed skill, know-how, mastery, method, proficiency, skill, skillfulness

SCIENTER, noun appreciation, apprehension, awareness, cognition, cognizance, comprehension, consciousness, discernment, familiarity, intent, intention, knowledge, perception, recognition, understanding

SCIENTIAL, adjective able, accomplished, adapted, adept, adequate, capable, competent, deft, educated, efficacious, fitted, gifted, intelligent, knowing, knowledgeable, learned, proficient, qualified, schooled, skillful, suitable, suited, trained, up to, well-suited

SCINTILLA, noun bit, corpuscle, grain, insignificant amount, iota, minim, modicum, particle, small amount, small quantity, spark, tittle, trace, trifle, whit
ASSOCIATED CONCEPTS: scintilla of evidence

SCOPE, noun ambit, amplitude, area, boundary, bounds, circle, circuit, compass, confines, demesne, expanse, extent, field, latitude, limit, *locus,* margin, orbit, purview, range, reach, realm, region, room, space, span, sphere, spread, stretch, sweep, territory, zone
ASSOCIATED CONCEPTS: scope of a patent, scope of authority, scope of employment, scope of jurisdiction, scope of review

SCREEN *(Guard),* **verb** camouflage, cloak, conceal, cover, defend, disguise, fence, harbor, haven, hide, mask, protect, safeguard, shade, shelter, shield, shroud, veil

SCREEN *(Select), verb*   choose, class, classify, discard, discriminate, eliminate, evaluate, exclude, filter, grade, group, keep out, pick, prefer, segregate, separate, sieve, sift, single out, sort, strain, weed, winnow
ASSOCIATED CONCEPTS: screen prospective jurors

SCRIPT, *noun*   book, calligraphy, characters, cursive hand, dialogue, handwriting, jottings, libretto, lines, longhand, manuscript, penmanship, penscript, playbook, printing, scrawl, scription, text, writing, written characters, written matter

SCRUPLE, *noun*   anxiety, apprehension, apprehensiveness, compunction, concern, *cunctatio,* doubt, doubtfulness, drawback, dubiety, dubiousness, *dubitatio,* fear, fearfulness, *haesitatio,* hesitancy, hesitation, misgiving, objection, qualm, question, reluctance, uncertainty, unease, uneasiness, unwillingness

SCRUPULOUS, *adjective*   aboveboard, *accuratus,* admirable, careful, choosy, *diligens,* discriminating, discriminative, equitable, ethical, fair, forthright, honest, honorable, laudable, legitimate, moral, noble, principled, reliable, *religiosus,* reputable, sincere, sound, thorough, trustworthy, truthful, upright, worthy

SCRUTABLE, *adjective*   apprehensible, beholdable, cognizable, comprehensible, conspicuous, discoverable, easily observed, easily seen, easily understood, evident, explicable, explicit, fathomable, intelligible, knowable, manifest, noticeable, observable, obvious, open, overt, penetrable, perceptible, plain, seeable, unconcealed, understandable, unhidden, unmasked, unveiled

SCRUTINIZE, *verb*   analyze, anatomize, audit, canvass, check, contemplate, delve into, dissect, examine, explore, eye, give close attention, inquire into, inspect, *inspicere, investigare,* investigate, keep under surveillance, look at closely, look into, look over, observe, overhaul, peer into, *perscrutari,* peruse, probe, pry into, question, regard carefully, research, review, scan, search, search into, sift, stare, study, survey, view, watch

SCRUTINY, *noun*   analysis, attention, careful examination, close investigation, close look, close search, consideration, critical examination, examination, exploration, indagation, inquest, inquiry, inquisition, inspection, investigation, minute attention, observance, observation, *perscrutatio,* perusal, probe, research, review, scrutation, search, study, surveillance, survey

SCURRILOUS, *adjective*   abusive, coarse, *contumeliosus,* disgusting, disrespectful, foul, gross, indecent, indelicate, insulting, lascivious, lewd, libidinous, licentious, low, mean, obscene, offensive, opprobrious, *probrosus,* ribald, risque, salacious, scabrous, scurrile, *scurrilis,* shameless, vile, vulgar

SEAL *(Close), verb*   bar, block off, bolt, close up, cover, keep from public view, keep in confidence, keep in secrecy, lock, occlude, secret, secure
ASSOCIATED CONCEPTS: sealed case, sealed grand jury report, sealed indictment, sealed instrument, sealed verdict

SEAL *(Solemnize), verb*   accept, accredit, approve, attest, authenticate, authorize, bear witness, certify, confirm, endorse, enstamp, impress with mark, imprint, inscribe, legalize, license, ratify, sanction, sign, stamp, substantiate, support, undersign, validate, verify, vouch

SEARCH, *verb*   chase after, closely examine, comb, delve, examine, examine by inspection, explore, ferret, follow the trail of, go through, hunt, indagate, inquire into, inspect, investigate, look into, look over, look through, probe, pry into, pursue, scan, scour, scout, scrutinize, seek, trace, track, track down, trail
ASSOCIATED CONCEPTS: illegal search by law enforcement officers, searching premises, unlawful search, unreasonable search and seizure

SEARCH WARRANT, *noun*   authority to search, bench warrant, court order, judicial order to search, judicial process, legal document to search, legal order, legal process, order authorizing a search, process, writ
ASSOCIATED CONCEPTS: illegal search warrant, probable cause to issue search warrant

SEASONABLE, *adjective*   acceptable, apposite, appropriate, auspicious, befitting, convenient, due, expedient, favorable, fit, opportune, *opportunus,* proper, properly timed, propitious, seemly, suitable, *tempestivus,* timeful, timely, towardly, well-timed

SEAT, *noun*   base, berth, capital, center, *domicilium,* headquarters, home, locale, locality, location, perch, place, position, post, region, residence, *sedes,* site, spot, station, vital center
ASSOCIATED CONCEPTS: county seat

SECEDE, *verb*   abandon, *abire,* apostatize, break away, *decedere,* depart, desert, disaffiliate, dissent, evacuate, insurrect, leave, mutiny, pull out, quit, rebel, refuse to support, relinquish, remove oneself, repudiate, resign, retire, retract, revolt, separate, sever one's connections, tergiversate, vacate, walk out, withdraw

SECERN, *verb*   differentiate, discern, discriminate, distinguish, note the distinctions, perceive differences

SECLUDE, *verb*   banish, blockade, bury, conceal, confine, cover, cut off, deport, disassociate, dissociate, embargo, exclude, excommunicate, exile, expatriate, hide, imprison, insulate, isolate, keep apart, keep in detention, keep in private, keep out, maroon, ostracize, outlaw, quarantine, relegate, remove, *removere,* retire, retire from sight, retreat, rope off, screen out, *secludere, segregare,* segregate, separate, sequester, set apart, set aside, shut out, withdraw

SECONDARY, *adjective*   accessory, alternative, ancillary, auxiliary, collateral, contingency, derived, following, indirect, inferior, junior, less important, lesser, minor, *secundarius,* subaltern, subordinate, subsequent, subsidiary, substitute, unessential, unimportant, vicarious
ASSOCIATED CONCEPTS: secondary boycott, secondary evidence, secondary liability

SECRET, *adjective*   abstruse, acroamatic, acroamatical, arcane, *arcanus,* clandestine, close, concealed, confidential, covert, cryptic, dark, esoteric, furtive, hidden, latent, mysterious, not public, obscure, occult, *occultus,* private, privy, recondite, secluded, *secretus,* shrouded, sly, surreptitious, undisclosed, undivulged,

unknown, unpublished, unrevealed, unseen, untold, veiled
ASSOCIATED CONCEPTS: secret lien, undisclosed principal

SECRET, noun abstruse knowledge, *arcana,* cabal, classified information, concealed knowledge, confidence, confidential communication, confidential matter, enigma, hidden knowledge, inside information, intimacy, intrigue, mystery, obscure information, personal matter, private affair, private communication, private matter, privileged communication, privileged information, puzzle, recondite knowledge, *res arcana, res occulta,* unknown information, veiled information

SECTION *(Division), noun* category, class, compartment, component, department, detachment, fraction, fragment, group, grouping, part, segment, separate part, separation, subdivision, subgroup

SECTION *(Vicinity), noun* area, block, clime, demesne, environs, field, locale, locality, location, *locus,* milieu, neighborhood, parcel of land, part, plot, plot of ground, plot of land, province, purlieus, *regio,* region, surroundings, territory, tract, vicinage, *vicinitas*
ASSOCIATED CONCEPTS: block, plot, and section

SECURE *(Confident), adjective* assured, carefree, certain, convinced, not nervous, not scared, positive, reassured, sure, unafraid, unanxious, unconcerned, undisturbed, unfrightened, unhesitating, unshaken, unsuspecting

SECURE *(Free from danger), adjective* armored, defended, dependable, guaranteed, guarded, impregnable, in safety, insured, inviolable, invulnerable, protected, safe, sheltered, stable, unassailable, unattackable, unharmable, unimperiled, unthreatened
ASSOCIATED CONCEPTS: secured transactions

SECURE *(Sound), adjective* dependable, fast, fastened, firm, fixed, immovable, infallible, reliable, solid, sound, stable, strong, substantial, trustworthy, trusty, unerring, unfailing, unimpeachable

SECURITIES, noun assets, bonds, capital, evidences of debts, evidences of obligations, holdings, invested property, investment, negotiables, property, shares, stocks
ASSOCIATED CONCEPTS: corporate securities, investment securities, sale of securities

SECURITY *(Pledge), noun* bail, bond, collateral, debenture, deposit, earnest, gage, guarantee, indemnity, insurance, lien, pawn, pignoration, promise, promissory note, stipulation, surety, token, vadium, voucher, warranty
ASSOCIATED CONCEPTS: collateral security, investment securities, issuing securities, public securities, real security, sale of securities, security agreement, security deposit, security interest, treasury securities, valuable securities

SECURITY *(Safety), noun* anchor, assurance, asylum, bastion, bulwark, certainty, defense, dependability, faith, freedom from danger, freedom from harm, guard, immovability, immunity, impregnability, *incolumitas,* invulnerability, maintenance, palladium, preservation, protection, rampart, reliance, safe conduct, safeguard, safeness, *salus,* salvation, sanctuary, secureness, shelter, stability, support, trust, unassailability, unattackability
ASSOCIATED CONCEPTS: national security

SECURITY *(Stock), noun* assets, bill of exchange, capital, *cautio,* certificate of debt, certificate of indebtedness, coupon, funds, indenture, invested property, investment, money invested, negotiable instrument, negotiable paper, obligation, *pignus,* secured debenture

SEDITION, noun apostasy, defection, defiance, desertion, disloyalty, disobedience, dissidence, infidelity, infraction, insubordination, insurgence, insurrection, *motus,* mutiny, noncompliance, overthrow, rebellion, recreance, recreancy, recusancy, resistance to authority, revolt, revolution, riot, rising, *seditio,* seditiousness, subversion, tergiversation, treachery, treason, underground activity, uprising, violation
ASSOCIATED CONCEPTS: alien and sedition acts, seditious libel

SEDUCTION, noun allure, allurement, attraction, bait, bewitchment, blandishment, cajolery, captivation, coaxing, *corruptela,* corruption, defilement, enchantment, enticement, fascination, inducement, inveiglement, invitation, lure, persuasion, seducement, solicitation, *stuprum,* tantalization, temptation

SEDULOUS, adjective active, *adsiduus,* alert, ardent, assiduous, attentive, avid, brisk, busily engaged, busy, conscientious, constant, diligent, dogged, eager, energetic, firm, hardworking, indefatigable, industrious, keen, laborious, painstaking, patient, perseverant, persevering, persistent, pertinacious, relentless, resolute, resolved, *sedulus,* stalwart, steadfast, tenacious, uncompromising, undeviating, unfaltering, unflagging, unrelenting, unremitting, unswerving, untiring, unwearying, unyielding, zealous

SEGMENT, noun bit, branch, cantle, cantlet, chapter, chunk, component, constituent, detached part, detail, division, element, fraction, fractional part, fragment, *fragmentum,* ingredient, installment, measure, moiety, *pars,* part, piece, portion, section, sector, *segmentum,* share, slice, small part, subdivision

SEGREGATION *(Isolation by races), noun* apartheid, discrimination, division by races, ostracism, prejudice, racial prejudice, racialism, racism, separation by races
ASSOCIATED CONCEPTS: equal protection clause

SEGREGATION *(Separation), noun* classification, detachment, differentiation, disassociation, disconnection, disengagement, dissociation, distinguishment, disunion, division, grouping, isolation, partition, *seiunctio,* setting apart
ASSOCIATED CONCEPTS: segregation of trust funds

SEISIN, noun control, hold, mastery, occupancy, occupation, ownership, possession, possessorship, tenancy, tenure, title
ASSOCIATED CONCEPTS: actual seisin, constructive seisin, covenant of seisin, equitable seisin, seisin in deed, seisin in fact, seisin in law

SEIZE *(Apprehend), verb* *apprehendere,* arrest, arrest with authority, capture, catch, *comprehendere,* detain by criminal process, imprison, incarcerate, jail, put in duress, *rapere,* take, take in, take into custody, take prisoner

SEIZE *(Confiscate)*, **verb**   annex, appropriate, arrogate, assume, capture, cause to be forfeited, commandeer, deprive of, dispossess, disseise, distrain, expropriate, grasp, impound, impress, mulct, pillage, pirate, pounce upon, put in possession, sequester, sequestrate, take, take possession of, usurp, wrest
ASSOCIATED CONCEPTS: attachment, execution on property, garnishment, seize property

SELECT, *adjective*   accepted, adopted, appointed, best, capital, choice, chosen, culled, designated, elected, *electus*, elite, embraced, excellent, exceptional, exclusive, *exquisitus*, first-rate, good, handpicked, matchless, named, picked, popular, preferable, preferred, prime, quality, rare, selected, superior, top-notch, unequaled, unexcelled
ASSOCIATED CONCEPTS: select committee

SELECT, *verb*   abstract, adopt, appoint, assign, be jaundiced, be prejudiced, champion, choose, collect, cull, decide, designate, determine, differentiate, discriminate, distinguish between, draft, elect, *eligere*, eliminate, excerpt, exclude, extract, fix upon, glean, have a bias, isolate, lay aside, lean, *legere*, make a choice, make a distinction, make a selection, mark, name, nominate, pick, point out, prefer, prize, put aside, reject, segregate, seperate, set apart, shut out, sift, single out, sort out, specialize, specify, stipulate, take out, weed out, winnow
ASSOCIATED CONCEPTS: select a jury

SELECTION *(Choice)*, **noun**   adoption, appointment, appropriation, assignment, compilation, cooptation, decision, *delectus*, denomination, designation, determination, *electio*, election, extraction, indication, naming, nomination, ordainment, ordination, preference, reservation, segregation, separation, specification, stipulation
ASSOCIATED CONCEPTS: jury selection

SELECTION *(Collection)*, **noun**   accumulation, aggregation, anthology, arrangement, array, assemblage, assembly, assortment, batch, bunch, cluster, collectanea, combination, compilation, conglomeration, cumulation, examples, gathering, group, hoard, mass, pile, quantity, samples, treasury, variety

SELL, *verb*   auction, barter, bring to market, deal in, dispense, dispose of for profit, *divendere*, drive a trade, effect a sale, exchange, furnish, give title to, handle, hawk, huckster, make a sale, market, merchandise, offer for sale, peddle, provide, put on sale, put up for sale, trade in, traffic in, transfer for a consideration, vend, *vendere*

SEMBLANCE, *noun*   air, appearance, aspect, bearing, closeness, copy, counterpart, effect, example, exterior, guise, identity, illusion, image, *imago*, likeness, look, mien, outward form, replica, representation, resemblance, sameness, show, similarity, similitude, simulacrum, *species*, uniformity, visage

SEMI, *adjective*   fractional, fragmentary, half, half finished, not whole, partial, unfinished
ASSOCIATED CONCEPTS: semi annually

SEND, *verb*   *ablegare*, advance, broadcast, cast, circulate, convey, direct, discharge, dismiss, dispatch, displace, drive, ejaculate, eject, emit, *emittere*, export,

fling, forward, freight, give, give forth, hurl, impel, issue, jaculate, launch, mail, *mittere*, post, project, propel, relay, route, send forth, send out, ship, shoot, throw, toss, transfer, transmit

SENSE *(Feeling)*, **noun**   apperception, apprehension, awareness, consciousness, discernment, idea, impression, instinct, mental image, mindfulness, notion, opinion, perception, realization, sensation, *sensus*, speculation, understanding

SENSE *(Intelligence)*, **noun**   acumen, astuteness, awareness, brightness, brilliance, cleverness, cognition, cognitive faculties, cognitive powers, comprehension, depth, enlightenment, foresight, genius, good judgment, grasp, insight, intellect, intellectual ability, intellectuality, *iudicium*, judgment, judiciousness, mentality, observation, perception, perspicacity, prudence, *prudentia*, rational faculty, rationality, reason, recognition, sagaciousness, sagacity, sapience, shrewdness, smartness, talent, understanding, wisdom, wiseness

SENSIBILITY, *noun*   acuteness, affectibility, alertness, appreciation, attentiveness, awareness, comprehension, consciousness, delicacy, delicacy of feeling, discernment, discrimination, emotion, feeling, fineness, impressibility, judgment, keenness, mindfulness, perception, perceptivity, response, responsiveness, sensation, sensitiveness, sensitivity, sharpness, susceptibility, sympathy, taste
ASSOCIATED CONCEPTS: peculiar sensibilities

SENSIBLE, *adjective*   advisable, apprised, astute, conscious, cool-headed, discerning, discreet, discriminating, enlightened, farsighted, informed, intelligent, judicious, justifiable, knowing, knowledgeable, levelheaded, logical, observant, palpable, perceptive, politic, *prudens*, prudent, ratiocinative, rational, reasonable, sagacious, sage, sane, sapient, sapiential, shrewd, sober, sound, thinking, thoughtful, understanding, well-advised, wise

SENSITIVE *(Discerning)*, *adjective*   aesthetic, alert, alive to, apperceptive, appercipient, astute, attentive, awake to, aware, cognizant, conscious, critical, discriminating, discriminative, fastidious, heedful, keen, mindful, observant, penetrating, perceptive, percipient, perspicacious, quick of apprehension, responsive, *sensilis*, sentient, understanding

SENSITIVE *(Easily affected)*, *adjective*   easily excited, easily offended, emotive, feeling, high-strung, hypercritical, impassionable, impressible, impressionable, irritable, merciful, *mollis*, moving, overemotional, peevish, perceptive, quick-tempered, reactive, sentimental, softhearted, susceptible, susceptive, sympathetic, temperamental, tenderhearted, touchy, uncontrolled

SENTENCE, *noun*   adjudication, award of punishment, censure, conviction, decision, declaration of penalty, decree of punishment, *decretum*, determination, determined punishment, doom, edict, formally pronounced judgment, *iudicium*, order of penalty, order of the court, penalty, prescribed punishment, pronouncement, punishment, ruling, verdict
ASSOCIATED CONCEPTS: concurrent sentences, consecutive sentences, cumulative sentences, excessive sentence, indeterminative sentence, life sentence, presentence hearing, suspended sentence

SENTENCE, verb   adjudge, bring in a verdict, commit, condemn, *condemnare,* convict, *damnare,* decide, declare guilty of an offense, decree, determine, find, find guilty, hold, immure, impose penalty, imprison, inflict penalty, *multare,* order, pass judgment upon, prescribe punishment, pronounce guilty, pronounce judgment, proscribe, reprobate
ASSOCIATED CONCEPTS: presentence report

SENTENTIOUS, adjective   abridged, aphoristic, apothegmatic, blunt, commatic, compact, compressed, concise, condensed, direct, economical of words, epigrammatic, epigrammatical, expressive, full of meaning, gnomic, laconic, meaningful, meaty, packed with meaning, pithy, pointed, precise, *sententiosus,* sparing of words, succinct, summarized, telegraphic, terse, to the point

SEPARABLE, adjective   breakable, cleavable, detachable, divisible, partible, severable
ASSOCIATED CONCEPTS: joint and separable liability, separability of arbitration, separable controversy, separable interest, separate provision

SEPARATE, adjective   alone, apart, asunder, departing, detached, different, disassociated, disconnected, *disiunctus,* disjoined, disjointed, disjunct, disparate, disrelated, dissimilar, dissociated, distinct, disunited, divergent, diverse, divided, divorced, independent, individual, insular, isolated, lone, loose, parted, removed, secluded, *secretus,* segregated, separated, *separatus,* set apart, severed, solitary, split, sundered, unaccompanied, unaffiliated, unallied, unassociated, unattached, unattended, unconnected
ASSOCIATED CONCEPTS: separate action, separate cause of action, separate maintenance

SEPARATE, verb   alienate, break, break off, break up, cleave, come apart, come between, cut adrift, cut off, detach, disassociate, disband, disconnect, disengage, *disiungere,* disjoin, dismember, dispart, disperse, dissever, dissociate, dissolve, disunite, divide, exclude, fractionize, hold apart, intersect, keep apart, part, part company, part ways, rend, rive, rupture, section, sectionalize, segment, segregate, *separare,* set apart, sever, splinter, split, split up, sunder, tear, unbind, uncouple, unloose, unmarry, unravel, untie, unyoke, winnow
ASSOCIATED CONCEPTS: annul, divorce

SEPARATION, noun   alienation, breach, break, cleavage, detachment, disassociation, *disiunctio,* disseverance, dissociation, dissolution, dissolution of marriage, disunion, division, divorce, divorcement, estrangement, legal dissolution of marriage, parting, rending, rupture, *separatio,* severance, split, sundering, tearing, termination of marital cohabitation, uncoupling
ASSOCIATED CONCEPTS: judgment of separation, judicial separation, just cause for separation, legal separation, separation agreement, separation by consent, separation decree, separation of powers, separation order, voluntary separation

SEQUACIOUS, adjective   accommodating, acquiescent, adaptable, amenable, bendable, bending, compliant, deferential, dependent, docile, ductile, easily influenced, easily led, easily taught, easygoing, elastic, facile, fictile, flexible, flexile, giving, governable, impressible, impressionable, lacking individuality, malleable, manageable, meek, moldable, obedient, obeisant, obliging, obsequious, passive, plastic, pliable, pliant, reverential, servile, slavish, submissive, subordinate, sycophantic, teachable, toadying, tractable, unassertive, undeviating, unimaginative, without originality, yielding

SEQUENCE, noun   alternation, arrangement, array, catenation, chain, classification, concatenation, consecution, continuum, cycle, flow, gradation, group, list, logical order, nexus, order, *ordo,* procession, progression, rotation, serialization, *series,* string, succession

SEQUESTER (Seclude), verb   cloister, closet, conceal, confine, exclude, isolate, quarantine, remove, retire, secret, segregate, separate, withdraw
ASSOCIATED CONCEPTS: sequester a jury, sequester a witness

SEQUESTER (Seize property), verb   annex, appropriate, arrogate, attach, confiscate, dispossess, distrain, impound, impress, levy, preempt, replevy, separate, sequestrate, set apart, set aside, take, take hold of, wrest
ASSOCIATED CONCEPTS: sequester assets

SEQUESTRATION, noun   annexation, appropriation, attachment, confiscation, deprivation, displacement, distraint, distress, divestment, execution, garnishment, impoundage, impoundment, impressment, levy, seizure, take-over

SERIAL, noun   consecution, fascicle, issue, periodical, procession, progression, series, successive portion

SERIOUS (Devoted), adjective   ardent, assiduous, decided, dedicated, determined, devout, dogged, dutiful, eager, earnest, faithful, fervent, firm, fixed, intent, loyal, passionate, purposeful, relentless, resolute, resolved, settled, sincere, steadfast, steady, tenacious, true, uncompromising, unfaltering, unswerving, unyielding, zealous
ASSOCIATED CONCEPTS: serious crime, serious wrongdoing

SERIOUS (Grave), adjective   *austerus,* consequential, critical, crucial, dangerous, dire, dreadful, fatal, *gravis,* great, grim, highly serious, important, intense, momentous, pensive, pressing, *serius,* severe, *severus,* sober, solemn, stern, weighty
ASSOCIATED CONCEPTS: serious and willful misconduct, serious bodily injury, serious crime, serious harm, serious wrongdoing

SERVE (Assist), verb   accommodate, administer to, advance, afford aid, aid, assist, attend, be of use, care for, come to the aid of, *commodare,* comply, confer a benefit, contribute to, cooperate, *deservire,* discharge one's duty, do a service, do one's bidding, fill an office, forward, furnish aid, furnish assistance, give help, help, lend aid, minister to, promote, render help, *servire,* submit, succor, supply aid, take care of, tend, wait on, work for

SERVE (Deliver a legal instrument), verb   afford notice, deliver, deliver a summons and complaint, deliver over, forward, give notice to, hand over, issue, make delivery of legal process, present, subpoena, summon, turn over
ASSOCIATED CONCEPTS: serve with process

SERVICE *(Assistance)*, **noun**   abetment, accommodation, advice, aid, attendance, backing, benefit, care, cooperation, favor, guidance, help, helping hand, *ministerium,* ministration, *opera,* relief, succor, support, useful office, usefulness
ASSOCIATED CONCEPTS: essential service, professional service, public service, service contract, service mark

SERVICE *(Delivery of legal process)*, **noun**   commencement of an action, delivery of a writ, delivery of process, handing over legal papers, institution of proceedings, notification of legal action
ASSOCIATED CONCEPTS: actual service of process, constructive service of process, personal service, service by mail, service by publication, service of notice, service of subpoena, service of summons, service rendered, special service, substituted service of process

SERVILE, *adjective*   *abiectus,* abject, compliant, deferential, downtrodden, fawning, groveling, harnessed, humble, *humilis,* ingratiating, low, mean, meek, menial, obedient, obeisant, obsequious, passive, prostrate, respectful, *servilis,* slavish, subject, submissive, subordinate, supple, sycophantic, tractable, truckling, unassertive, unresisting, vernile

SERVITUDE, **noun**   bonds, burden, captivity, charge, compulsion, enslavement, enthrallment, fetters, helotism, helotry, indenture, obedience, oppression, restraint, service, *servitium, servitus,* slavery, subjection, subjugation, submission, subordination, subservience, suppression, thrall, thralldom
ASSOCIATED CONCEPTS: involuntary servitude, penal servitude, real servitude

SESQUIPEDALIAN, *adjective*   grandiloquent, lengthy, long, magniloquent, multisyllabic, pedantic, sonorous

SESSION, **noun**   assembly, audience, caucus, conclave, conference, congregation, congress, consultation, convention, *conventus,* convocation, council, diet, forgathering, forum, gathering, hearing, meeting, parley, plenum, rendezvous, round table, sitting, synod, term, union
ASSOCIATED CONCEPTS: general sessions, joint session, regular session, session laws, special sessions

SET ASIDE *(Annul)*, **verb**   abandon, abjure, abnegate, abrogate, accumulate, amass, cast off, discard, dispense with, dispose of, disuse, drop, omit, reject, relegate, relinquish, renounce, repudiate, shunt, spurn
ASSOCIATED CONCEPTS: set aside a verdict

SET ASIDE *(Reserve)*, **verb**   keep in reserve, lay aside, pigeonhole, pile up, put aside, put away, save up, set apart, shelve, store up

SET DOWN, *verb*   book, calender, chronicle, commit to writing, docket, enter, jot down, line up, list, note, place, plan, post, program, put on record, record, register, schedule, slate
ASSOCIATED CONCEPTS: set down for trial

SETOFF, **noun**   counter, counterbalance, counterdebt, counterdemand, counterpoise, counterweight, debt owed, equivalent claim, money due, offset, offsetting claim, recoupment
ASSOCIATED CONCEPTS: counterclaim, cross-claim

SETTLE, *verb*   settle order on notice, accommodate, adjust, agree, agree upon, approve, arrange, arrange matters, arrange matters in dispute, ascertain, bring to terms, bring together, clear up, come to a determination, come to an agreement, come to an understanding, come to terms, compromise, conclude, *conficere, constituere,* decide, determine, determine once for all, dispose of, end, even the score, harmonize, make a compact, mend, negotiate, put in order, reach a compromise, reconcile, rectify, resolve, restore harmony, set at rest, set in place, settle, solve, stabilize, straighten out, strike a bargain, work out
ASSOCIATED CONCEPTS: settle a bill of exceptions, settle a claim, settle a judgment, settle an account, settle an estate, settle an order, settle issues, settle property, settled account

SETTLEMENT, **noun**   accommodation, adjustment, agreement, arrangement, arrangement of difficulties, bargain, *compositio,* composure of differences, composure of doubts, compromise, conciliation, concordat, *constitutio,* contract, determination by agreement, discharge, disposition, final terms, negotiation, pact, *pactum,* payment, reconciliation, release, satisfaction, set of terms, terms, understanding
ASSOCIATED CONCEPTS: deed of settlement, final settlement, settlement of a case, voluntary settlement

SEVER, *verb*   break apart, break off, cleave, cut, cut adrift, detach, *dirimere,* disband, disconnect, disengage, disjoin, dismember, dispair, dispart, dissever, dissociate, dissolve, disunite, divide, *dividere,* divorce, fissure, isolate, keep apart, lacerate, lop off, part, partition, rend, rend asunder, rive, rupture, segment, segregate, *separare,* separate, set apart, slit, splinter, split, subdivide, sunder, tear, unbind, uncouple, unfasten, untie, wrench
ASSOCIATED CONCEPTS: sever a claim, sever a party, sever an action, severable cause of action, severable contract

SEVERABLE, *adjective*   apportionable, cleavable, detachable, dissoluable, dividual, *dividuus,* divisible, fissile, fissionable, fractional, partible, scissile, *separabilis,* separable
ASSOCIATED CONCEPTS: severable contract, severable statute

SEVERAL *(Plural)*, *adjective*   assorted, certain, diverse, few, more than one, some, sundry

SEVERAL *(Separate)*, *adjective*   appropriate, certain, chosen, definite, different, distinctive, distinguishable, exclusive, fixed, independent, marked, peculiar, personal, private, proper, representative, singular, unique
ASSOCIATED CONCEPTS: several defendants, several liability, several ownership, several tracts, several trusts, several transactions, severally

SEVERANCE, **noun**   bifurcation, cleavage, demarcation, detachment, differentiation, disassociation, discrimination, distinction, distinguishment, division, divorce, fission, isolation, scission, segregation, separation, sunderance, withdrawal
ASSOCIATED CONCEPTS: severance damages, severance of statute, severance pay, severance tax

SEVERE, *adjective* acrimonious, afflictive, agonizing, astringent, austere, *austerus,* bearish, brutal, censorious, churlish, coercive, cold, condemnatory, critical, cruel, despotic, difficult, domineering, dour, drastic, *durus,* exacting, excruciating, exigent, faultfinding, fierce, firm, forbidding, furious, grievous, grim, gruff, hard, hard to endure, harsh, hypercritical, ill-natured, ill-tempered, immovable, implacable, inclement, inexorable, inflexible, insufferable, intense, intractable, ironclad, ironhanded, mordant, nasty, obdurate, oppressive, overbearing, overpowering, painful, peremptory, pitiless, punitive, puritan, puritanical, raging, relentless, rigid, rigorous, rough, rugged, ruthless, savage, *severus,* sharp, sour, stark, stern, stiff, stinging, stony, stony-hearted, stormy, strait-laced, strict, stringent, stubborn, tempestuous, tough, trying, tyrannical, unbending, uncompromising, unfeeling, ungentle, ungracious, unjust, unkind, unmerciful, unmitigated, unrelenting, unsparing, unyielding, vicious, vindictive, violent
ASSOCIATED CONCEPTS: severe penalties

SEVERITY, *noun* *acerbitas,* acerbity, acrimony, asperity, austerity, causticity, cruel treatment, cruelty, ferity, ferociousness, ferocity, fierceness, force, fury, *gravitas,* gravity, grimness, harshness, inclemency, inexorability, inflexibility, inhumanity, intensity, might, relentlessness, rigor, rigorousness, ruthlessness, savagery, seriousness, *severitas,* sharpness, sternness, strictness, stringency, turbulence, tyranny, unkindness, venom, violence, virulence

SHALL, *verb* as required will, by compulsion will, by imperative will, mandatorily will, obligatorily will
ASSOCIATED CONCEPTS: shall be lawful, shall be legal, shall become, shall give, shall have, shall not, shall perform, shall work

SHAM, *noun* chicanery, counterfeit, deception, delusion, *dolus,* fabrication, fake, *fallacia,* false show, feint, forgery, fraud, *fraus,* guise, imitation, impersonation, impostor, imposture, masquerade, misrepresentation, mock, pretense, reproduction, simulacrum, simulation, trick, trickery
ASSOCIATED CONCEPTS: sham defense, sham pleading

SHAMBLES, *noun* cataclysm, chaos, confusion, destruction, disorder, disorganization, disruption, havoc, holocaust, jumble, *laniena,* madhouse, maelstrom, mayhem, mess, pandemonium, scene of destruction, scene of disorder, state of violence, turmoil, upheaval, uproar, welter

SHAME, *noun* abasement, abjectness, abuse, aspersion, attaint, bad name, baseness, blot, contempt, debasement, defamation, defilement, degradation, discredit, disesteem, disfavor, disgrace, dishonor, disrepute, disrespect, humiliation, *ignominia,* ignominy, ill repute, *infamia,* infamy, loss of honor, loss of reputation, obloquy, odium, opprobrium, reproach, scandal, scorn, smirch, stain, stigma, taint, tarnish, tarnished honor, turpitude, vileness

SHARE *(Interest), noun* allocation, allotment, apportioned lot, commission, dole, measure, *pars,* part, percent, percentage, *portio,* portion, proportion, quotum, ratio, ration, right, section, segment, slice
ASSOCIATED CONCEPTS: distributive share, equal share, share and share alike, share of capital, similiar share

SHARE *(Stock), noun* asset, capital, corporate interest, holding, invested property, investment, property, security, stockholding
ASSOCIATED CONCEPTS: bank shares, corporate shares, share of corporate stock, shareholder, treasury shares

SHAREHOLDER, *noun* investor, owner, property owner, stockholder, stockholder of record, stockowner
ASSOCIATED CONCEPTS: shareholder action, shareholder's derivative suit

SHELTER *(Protection), noun* aid, *asylum,* care, cover, covering, coverture, defense, habitation, harbor, haven, home, house, lodging, place of refuge, preservation, *receptaculum,* refuge, retreat, roof, safety, sanctuary, screen, security, shield, stronghold, support

SHELTER *(Tax benefit), noun* advantage, gain, hedge, refuge, security, tax haven, tax sanctuary
ASSOCIATED CONCEPTS: tax shelter

SHIELD, *noun* aegis, buckler, buffer, bulwark, *clipeus,* cover, covert, coverture, defense, guard, protection, protector, rampart, refuge, safeguard, sanctuary, screen, *scutum,* security, shelter

SHIFTING, *adjective* alternating, changeable, changing, deviating, digressive, discursive, drifting, fluctuating, inconstant, interim, roaming, roving, straying, transient, transitory, uncertain, vacillating, varying, wandering, wavering
ASSOCIATED CONCEPTS: shifting risk, shifting the burden of proof, shifting trust, shifting use

SHIRK, *verb* abstain, avoid, cheat, *detrectare,* dodge, duck, elude, escape from, evade, funk, ignore, keep away from, leave undone, malinger, neglect, quit, refuse, run from, shrink, shun, slink away, stay away, steer clear

SHOW CAUSE, *verb* present a case, present argument, present cause, present reason, show grounds for
ASSOCIATED CONCEPTS: order to show cause

SHROUD, *verb* adumbrate, becloud, befog, blanket, bury, cloak, closet, conceal, cover, curtain, darken, eclipse, encase, ensconce, envelop, enwrap, hide, mask, muffle, obscure, overshadow, protect, render invisible, screen, seclude, sheathe, shelter, suppress, *tegere,* veil, *velare,* wrap

SHUN, *verb* abhor, abstain, avoid, back away, boycott, bypass, circumvent, cold-shoulder, *defugere,* deliberately avoid, disregard, dodge, draw back, elude, escape, eschew, evade, give a wide berth to, have no part of, have nothing to do with, hide from, ignore, keep away from, keep clear of, keep one's distance, leave, let alone, malinger, neglect, rebuff, recoil from, refrain, shirk, shrink from, shy away from, snub, spurn, stay away from, steer clear of, turn aside, turn away from, *vitare,* ward off

SHUT, *verb* bar, barricade, block, block off, block up, blockade, bound, bung, button, cease, choke off, clasp, *claudere,* cloister, close, close down, *coercere,* cork, corral, cover, dam, discontinue, encase, enclose, end, envelop, enwrap, fasten, fence in, finish, halt, hem in, *includere,* intern, latch, lock, obstruct, occlude, plug, prevent passage, retard flow, seal, secure, shut down, stop, stop up, stopper, terminate, throttle, turn off

SIDE, noun affiliation, angle, aspect, body of partisans, cause, coalition, conception, direction, facet, faction, outlook, *pars,* party, point of view, position, sect, slant, standpoint, surface, verge, view, viewpoint

SIDE, verb advocate, aid, assist, back up, befriend, bolster, brace, buttress, champion, defend, encourage, endorse, favor, further, help, plead for, promote, protect, rally around, reinforce, second, stand behind, stand by, stick up for, strengthen, support, sustain, take the part of, unite with, uphold, vote for, vouch for

SIGN, verb accept, accredit, acknowledge, affix a signature, affix one's name, affix one's signature to, agree to, approve, authenticate, authorize, autograph, certify, confirm, *consignare,* covenant, enter into a contract, execute, indorse, initial, inscribe one's name, inscribe one's signature, license, paraph, ratify, sanction, seal, set one's name to, subscribe, *subscribere,* undersign, underwrite, validate
ASSOCIATED CONCEPTS: countersign

SIGNIFICANCE, noun bearing, concern, concernment, consequence, distinction, eminence, essentiality, excellence, force, gist, gravity, greatness, import, importance, interest, mark, materiality, materialness, matter, meaning, merit, moment, momentousness, notability, note, paramountcy, pith, portent, precedence, preeminence, primacy, priority, prominence, relevance, salience, salient point, seriousness, *significatio,* signification, substance, substantiality, supremacy, value, *vis,* weight, weightiness, worth

SIGNIFICATION, noun acceptation, aim, connotation, designation, drift, effect, essence, explanation, force, gist, impact, implication, import, importance, indication, inference, intent, intention, interpretation, meaning, meat, moral, object, pith, point, purport, purpose, sense, significance, *significatio,* substance, tenor, value, *vis,* worth

SIGNIFY *(Denote), verb* betoken, connotate, connote, delineate, demonstrate, depict, evidence, evince, exemplify, hint, illustrate, imply, indicate, insinuates, intimate, manifest, mark, mean, point out, portray, purport, represent, reveal, show, stand for, suggest, symbolize, tell of, typify

SIGNIFY *(Inform), verb* acquaint, advance, advise, air, announce, apprise, assert, bruit, caution, communicate, convey, convey knowledge, declare, demonstrate, designate, direct the attention to, disclose, disseminate, divulge, enlighten, enumerate, express, give notice, give sign, impart, instruct, issue, make known, make obvious, make plain, make public, mention, notify, proclaim, promulgate, publish, report, reveal, set forth, specify, state, stipulate, tell, vent, voice

SILENCE, noun absolute quiet, hush, lack of sound, noiselessness, quiescence, quiescency, quiet, quietness, quietude, *silentium,* soundlessness, speechlessness, stillness, suppression of sound, *taciturnitas,* wordlessness
ASSOCIATED CONCEPTS: estopped by silence, silence as an admission
FOREIGN PHRASES: *Qui tacet, consentire videtur.* He who is silent is deemed to consent. *Qui tacet consentire videtur, ubi tractatur de ejus commodo.* He who is silent is deemed to consent, when his interest is at stake.

SIMILAR, adjective agreeing, allied, analogous, approximate, close, cognate, collateral, companion, comparable, conformable, congeneric, congenerical, congruent, connatural, consimilar, consubstantial, correspondent, corresponding, equivalent, homogeneous, identical, indistinguishable, kindred, like, matching, *par,* parallel, related, resembling, same, *similis,* synonymous, twin, uniform
FOREIGN PHRASES: *Ubi eadem ratio, ibi idem jus; et de similibus idem est judicium.* Where there is the same reason, there is the same law; and where there are similar situations, the judgment is the same.

SIMPLE, adjective artless, bare, basal, basic, clear, crude, downright, elemental, elementary, frank, free of duplicity, fundamental, guileless, homespun, homogeneous, inartificial, incomplex, *inconditus,* ingenuous, inornate, intelligible, irreducible, mere, natural, open, plain, primary, pure, rudimentary, rustic, simpleminded, *simplex,* simplified, sincere, *sincerus,* single, straightforward, unadorned, unadulterated, unaffected, unalloyed, unblended, uncombined, uncomplicated, uncompounded, unconstrained, undecorated, understandable, undesigning, unembellished, uninvolved, unmingled, unmixed, unpretentious, unsophisticated, unstudied, unvarnished, without confusion
ASSOCIATED CONCEPTS: simple assault, simple battery, simple contract, simple larceny, simple will

SIMPLIFY *(Clarify), verb* clear up, elucidate, explain, make clear, make plain, unfold, untwist

SIMPLIFY *(Make easier), verb* disentangle, make plain, streamline, uncomplicate, unravel

SIMULATE, verb act, copy, counterfeit, fabricate, feign, imitate, make believe, mock, play-act, pretend, represent
ASSOCIATED CONCEPTS: simulated conveyance, simulated sale, simulation

SIMULTANEOUS, adjective accompanying, at the same time, coetaneous, coeval, coexistent, coexisting, coincident, coinstantaneous, concomitant, concurrent, contemporaneous, contemporary, cotemporary, *eodem tempore,* in concert, *simul,* synchronal, synchronic, synchronical, synchronistic, synchronistical, synchronous
ASSOCIATED CONCEPTS: simultaneous death

SINE DIE, adverb at no period, at no time, never, never again, on no occasion, without date

SINE QUA NON, noun absolute condition, absolute prerequisite, antecedent, condition, contingency, essential clause, essential condition, essential matter, essential part, essential qualification, indispensable condition, indispensable item, necessity, precondition, prerequisite, prime constituent, prime ingredient, qualification, requirement, vital concern

SINECURE, noun easily managed job, easy chore, easy employment, easy job, easy labor, effortless assignment, effortless employment, effortless undertaking, effortless work, light labor, light work, simple job, soft job, undemanding chore, undemanding job, undemanding task

SINEW, noun brawn, brawniness, effectiveness, endurance, energy, force, forcefulness, grit, lustiness, might, muscle, *nervus,* potence, potency, power, powerfulness, robustness, stamina, staying power, strength, thews, vigor, vigorousness

SINGULAR, adjective different, distinct, eccentric, *egregius,* eminent, especial, exceptional, exclusive, extraordinary, individual, isolated, lone, matchless, nonpareil, odd, out of the ordinary, particular, peculiar, peerless, queer, rare, remarkable, separate, single, *singularis,* sole, special, unaccompanied, uncommon, uncustomary, unequaled, unexampled, *unicus,* unique, unparalleled, unprecedented, unusual

SINISTER, adjective alarming, baleful, baneful, blameworthy, censurable, cold-blooded, comminatory, conscienceless, contemptible, corrupt, creepy, cruel, culpable, dangerous, demoniac, demoniacal, deserving of condemnation, designing, despiteful, destructive, detrimental, diabolic, diabolical, dishonest, disingenuous, dismaying, disquieting, disreputable, disturbing, dreadful, eerie, envenomed, evil, exceptionable, facinorous, fear-inspiring, fearsome, fiendish, flagitious, flawed, frightening, ghoulish, harmful, heartless, heinous, horrible, horrid, hurtful, ignoble, ill-disposed, illaudable, immeritorious, immoral, impious, inauspicious, infamous, injurious, iniquitous, insidious, intimidating, lawless, malefic, maleficent, maleficial, malevolent, malicious, malign, malignant, menacing, minatory, mischievous, miscreant, murderous, nefarious, nocuous, noisome, noxious, obliquitous, peccable, peccant, pernicious, perverse, portending evil, *pravus,* presageful, rascally, remorseless, reprehensible, satanic, scatheful, scheming, scoundrelly, sinful, spiteful, tainted, terrible, threatening, treacherous, truculent, unbenevolent, uncommendable, unfair, unfavorable, unjustifiable, unprincipled, unpromising, unpropitious, unrighteous, untrustworthy, unwholesome, venomous, villainous, virulent, wicked, worthy of blame, wrong

SINUOUS, adjective ambagious, ambagitory, anfractuous, circuitous, coiled, complex, complicated, convolute, convoluted, convolutional, crooked, curved, curvilinear, deviating, deviative, devious, entangled, flexuous, indirect, intricate, involute, involuted, involutional, involutionary, involved, labyrinthian, labyrinthine, mazy, meandering, meandrous, oblique, plexiform, rambling, reticular, roundabout, serpentine, sinuate, *sinuosus,* snaky, spiral, tangled, tortile, tortuous, turning, twisted, twisting, volute, winding, zigzag

SITE, noun address, base, environs, habitat, locale, locality, location, neighborhood, place, position, setting, situation, situs, stead, territory, vicinity

SITE, verb arrange, assign, base, center, localize, locate, place, position, situate

SITUATED, adjective anchored, bestead, *conlocatus,* embedded, ensconced, established, fixed, found, housed, implanted, installed, laid, located, lodged, occupying, placed, planted, posited, positioned, *positus,* posted, proximate to, put, quartered, rooted, seated, set, settled, *situs,* stationed
ASSOCIATED CONCEPTS: similarly situated

SITUATION, noun arrangement, case, circumstance, circumstances, condition, crisis, environment, exigency, happening, incidence, instance, juncture, lot, mishap, occurrence, plight, position, post, posture, predicament, *situs,* standing, state, station, status

SITUS, noun locale, locality, location, locus, place, placement, point, position, site, situation
ASSOCIATED CONCEPTS: situs of a crime

SKEPTICAL, adjective agnostic, cynical, disbelieving, distrustful, distrusting, doubting, dubious, faithless, freethinking, heretical, heterodox, iconoclastic, incredulous, questioning, quizzical, scoffing, suspecting, suspicious, unbelieving, uncertain, unorthodox, unsure, untrusting, wary

SKILL, noun ability, adeptness, adroitness, aptitude, aptness, art, artistry, cleverness, command, competence, craft, cunning, deftness, dexterity, ease, endowment, excellence, experience, expertness, facility, felicity, finesse, fluency, gift, handiness, ingeniousness, ingenuity, knack, knowledge, mastery, *peritia,* proficiency, prowess, quickness, *scientia, sollertia,* talent

SLANDER, noun abusive language, accusation, aspersion, *calumnia,* calumniation, calumny, censure, character assassination, *criminatio,* damaging report, defamation, defamatory words, denigration, denunciation, disparagement, execration, false report, imprecation, insinuation, invective, libel, *maledictio,* malicious report, obloquy, opprobrium, reproach, revilement, scandal, scurrility, slur, smear, stricture, traducement, vilification
ASSOCIATED CONCEPTS: malice, publication, slander of title, slander per quod, slander per se

SLANT, verb angle, bias, color, distort, doctor, embroider, exaggerate, falsify, incline, interpret falsely, misapply, miscolor, misconstrue, misdirect, misinterpret, misquote, misrender, misrepresent, misstate, overstate, pervert, predispose, prejudice, prepossess, stretch, turn, twist, varnish, veer, warp, wrest

SLAY, verb annihilate, assassinate, deprive of life, destroy, dispatch, dispose of, execute, exterminate, *interficere, interimere,* kill, liquidate, massacre, murder, *occidere,* put to death, slaughter, take a life, terminate, victimize
ASSOCIATED CONCEPTS: homicide

SLIGHT, adjective ancillary, auxiliary, diminutive, exiguous, *exiguus,* immaterial, inappreciable, inconsequential, inconsiderable, inferior, insignificant, *levis,* light, limited, little, meager, mean, minor, minute, modest, negligible, niggardly, nonessential, nugatory, of small account, of small importance, paltry, petty, scant, secondary, slender, slim, small, stinted, subaltern, subordinate, subsidiary, *tenuis,* tenuous, thin, trifling, trivial, unessential, unimportant, unsubstantial
ASSOCIATED CONCEPTS: slight care, slight evidence, slight fault, slight negligence

SLIPSHOD, adjective careless, disordered, disorderly, disorganized, haphazard, heedless, imprecise, improper, inaccurate, indifferent, inexact, lackadaisical, lax, negligent, offhand, orderless, poor, remiss, shabby, sloppy, slovenly, thoughtless, uncareful, uncaring, uncoordinated, unmeticulous, unneat, unorganized, unseemly, untidy

SLOTH, noun acedia, apathy, *desidia,* disinclination to action, disinclination to labor, dullness, faineance, idleness, *ignavia,* inaction, inactivity, indifference, indolence, inertia, inertness, inexertion, languidness, laxness, laziness, leadenness, lethargy, listlessness, lumpishness, neglectfulness, otiosity, passivity, phlegm, *segnitia,* shiftlessness, slackness, sluggishness, stupor, supineness, torpescence, torpidity, torpor, unconcern

SLY, adjective arch, artful, astute, *astutus,* calculating, clandestine, conniving, covert, covinous, crafty, crooked, cunning, deceitful, deceiving, deceptious, deceptive, delusive, designing, devious, dishonest, dishonorable, disingenuous, double-dealing, evasive, feline, foxy, furtive, guileful, hidden, insidious, intriguing, keen, obreptitious, plotting, scheming, secret, secretive, sharp, shifty, shrewd, skulking, slippery, sneaking, sneaky, stealthy, *subdolus,* subtle, surreptitious, treacherous, tricky, uncandid, undercover, underhand, underhanded, unscrupulous, *vafer,* vulpine, wily

SMEAR, verb asperse, attack, attaint, belittle, besmear, besmirch, besmut, blacken, blemish, brand, calumniate, cast a slur, contaminate, decry, defame, defile, degrade, denigrate, denounce, depreciate, derogate, destroy one's reputation, detract, discredit, dishonor, disparage, disrate, expose to infamy, hold up to shame, humiliate, *inlinere,* libel, make scandal, malign, mar, mark, *oblinere,* pillory, pollute, render unclean, ridicule, slander, slur, smirch, soil, speak evil of, stain, stigmatize, sully, taint, tarnish, traduce, undermine, vilify, vilipend
ASSOCIATED CONCEPTS: defamation

SNARL, noun complexus, complication, confusion, disarray, disorder, entanglement, *gannitus,* imbroglio, involute, kink, knot, labyrinth, mat, maze, mess, ravel, snag, tangle, twist

SOBRIQUET, noun byname, cognomen, fanciful name, fictitious, nickname, nom de plume, pseudonym

SOCIETY, noun alliance, aristocracy, association, bloc, body, brethren, brotherhood, circle, citizenry, civilization, class, clique, club, coalition, colleagueship, combine, commonwealth, community, companionship, comradeship, confederacy, confederation, confraternity, consociation, culture, denomination, faction, federation, fellowship, fold, folk, fraternal order, fraternity, fraternization, gentility, group, guild, higher class, *homines,* institute, league, order, organization, organized group, patriciate, peerage, polity, population, privileged class, religious order, sect, set, sodality, tribe, union, upper class

SODALITY, noun alignment, alliance, amity, association, bond, brotherhood, brotherliness, camaraderie, clique, club, colleagueship, combination, communion, community, community of interest, companionship, compatibility, comradeship, concord, confederacy, confederation, confraternity, consolidation, copartnership, faction, federation, fellowship, fraternity, fraternization, friendliness, friendly relations, friendship, group, guild, intercourse, league, order, organization, partnership, social group, society, sorosis, unification, union

SODOMY, noun buggery, degeneration, depravity, deviation, indecency, pederasty, perversion, sexual deviation, unlawful sexual intercourse, unnatural carnal intercourse, unnatural sexual intercourse, vice

SOLACE, noun abatement, allayment, alleviation, amelioration, cheer, comfort, commiseration, condolence, *consolatio,* consolation, ease, easement, encouragement, help, kindliness, melioration, mitigation, palliation, reassurance, refreshment, relief, *solatium,* sympathy, tranquility

SOLE, adjective individual, insular, isolated, lone, one, only, separate, single, singular, solitary, *solus,* unaccompanied, unattended, *unicus,* unique, *unus*
ASSOCIATED CONCEPTS: sole actor, sole and exclusive cause, sole and unconditional owner, sole proprietor, sole surviving heir

SOLELY (Purely), adverb barely, merely, plainly, purely, simply

SOLELY (Singly), adverb alone, entirely, exclusively, only, wholly

SOLEMN, adjective august, awe-inspiring, awesome, ceremonial, ceremonious, devotional, devout, earnest, formal, funereal, gloomy, grave, *gravis,* grim, hallowed, holy, imposing, impressive, majestic, meditative, mirthless, mournful, pensive, quiet, reflective, religious, reverential, ritual, sacramental, sacred, sanctified, sedate, serious, *severus,* sober, somber, spiritual, staid, stately, stern, stirring, subdued, *tristis,* venerable, worshipful

SOLEMNITY, noun awesomeness, ceremoniousness, ceremony, dignity, graveness, *gravitas,* gravity, impressiveness, pomp, seriousness, *severitas,* soberness, sobriety, solemn feeling, stateliness, tradition, *tristitia*

SOLICIT, verb appeal for, appeal to, apply, ask, ask earnestly, beseech, call for, canvass, *captare,* clamor for, coax, demand, entreat, *flagitare,* implore, importune, induce, make a request, obsecrate, obtest, *petere,* petition, plead, press, request, supplicate, urge

SOLICITOUS, adjective ambitious, anxious, *anxius,* apprehensive, aspiring, bent on, beseeching, caring, concerned, craving, desirous, eager, hopeful, inclined, intent on, keen, optative, petitionary, *sollicitus,* supplicatory, wanting, willing, yearning

SOLID (Compact), adjective bunched, close, coagulated, compressed, concentrated, condensed, congealed, consolidated, dense, firm, grumose, hard, hardened, impenetrable, impermeable, incompressible, indiscerptible, indivisible, inflexible, insecable, inseparable, massed, massive, monolithical, nonporous, ossified, packed, packed together, pressed together, rigid, serried, solidified, stiff, thick, tight, undissolved, united, unyielding

SOLID (Sound), adjective able to pay, assured, considered, convincing, dependable, durable, enduring, established, faithworthy, fast, firm, *firmus,* guaranteed, incontestable, incontrovertible, irrefutable, judicious, just, lasting, logical, politic, precautional, precautionary, precautious, prudent, prudential, rational, reasonable, reliable, responsible, rugged, safe, sagacious, sage, sapient, secure, sensible, *solidus,* solvent, *stabilis,* stable, stanch, steadfast, steady, strong, sturdy, substantial, substantive, true, trustworthy, trusty, unconfutable, unerring, unfailing, unimpeachable, unquestionable, unrefutable, valid, weighty, well-built, well-constructed, well-established, well-founded, well-grounded, well-made, wise

SOLITARY, adjective abandoned, aloof, anchoretic, anchoretical, avoiding the society of others, celibate, cloistered, companionless, deserted, desolate, detached, disjoined, disjunct, enisled, eremetical, eremitic, eremitish, estranged, fellowless, forsaken, friendless, hermitic, hermitical, homeless, insular, isolated, kithless, lone, lonely, lonesome, orphaned, private, reclusive, remote, removed, rootless, secluded, separate, separated, single, sole, solo, *solus,* unabetted, unaccompanied, unaided, unassisted, unattended, unconnected, unescorted, uninhabited, unmatched, unoccupied, unpaired, unseconded, unshared, unsupported, unvisited, without companions, without company
ASSOCIATED CONCEPTS: solitary confinement

SOLUTION *(Answer),* **noun** clarification, decipherment, determination, elucidation, explanation, *explicatio,* explication, exposition, finding, illumination, interpretation, key, reason, resolution, right answer, *solutio*
ASSOCIATED CONCEPTS: equitable solution

SOLUTION *(Substance),* **noun** admixture, amalgam, blend, combination, commixture, composite, composition, compound, *dilutum,* emulsion, intermixture, mix, mixture, solvent, suspension

SOLVABLE, adjective ascertainable, cognizable, decipherable, decodable, determinable, discoverable, exegetical, explainable, explicative, explicatory, expository, fathomable, intelligible, recognizable, resolvable, scrutable, soluble, workable

SOLVE, verb account for, answer, arrive at the truth, ascertain, bring out, clear up, crack, decipher, decode, deduce, discover, disentangle, disinter, *dissolvere,* educe, elucidate, *enodare,* enucleate, *expedire,* explain, fathom, ferret out, figure out, find out, find the cause, find the key, find the solution, guess correctly, guess right, interpret, learn the answer, make out, make plain, penetrate, piece together, puzzle out, realize, reason out, render intelligible, resolve, root out, shed light upon, think out, throw light upon, trace, understand, unearth, unfold, unlock, unravel, unriddle, unscramble, untangle, work out
ASSOCIATED CONCEPTS: solve a crime

SOLVENT, adjective able to pay, clear of encumbrance, creditworthy, financially sound, in good financial condition, moneyed, not owing, out of debt, owing nothing, pecunious, unindebted, with funds, with good credit
ASSOCIATED CONCEPTS: solvent debt
FOREIGN PHRASES: *Id solum nostrum quod debitis deductis nostrum est.* That only is ours which remains to us after deduction of our debts.

SOOTHE, verb allay, alleviate, ameliorate, appease, assuage, attemper, balm, becalm, blunt, calm, comfort, compose, deaden, dulcify, dull, ease, free from anxiety, free from pain, give relief, humor, hush, lenify, *lenire,* lessen, lull, mitigate, moderate, mollify, *mulcere,* obtund, pacificate, pacify, palliate, *placare,* placate, propitiate, quell, quench, quiet, relax, relieve, relieve pressure, render less painful, salve, slake, smooth, soften, still, succor, tame, temper, tranquilize

SOPHISTIC, adjective *captiosus,* captious, casuistic, casuistical, contrary to reason, erroneous, fallacious, false, faulty in logic, groundless, ill-reasoned, illogical, inconsequent, inconsistent, incorrect, invalid, irrational, misleading, paralogical, sophistical, specious, tricky, unfounded, ungrounded, unreasonable, unsound, untenable, unwarranted, wrong

SOPHISTICATED, adjective advanced, avant garde, complex, contemporary, forward looking, innovative, knowledgeable, modern, new, progressive, ultramodern, up to date, up to the minute, urbane

SOPHISTRY, noun casuistry, cavil, chicanery, deception, distortion, equivocation, evasion, evasive reasoning, fallacious reasoning, false logic, misrepresentation, specious reasoning

SORDID, adjective *abiectus,* abject, abominable, base, corrupt, debased, decayed, defiled, degraded, deteriorated, dilapidated, disgusting, foul, fouled, fulsome, fusty, grimy, gruesome, *inliberalis,* mucky, odious, repellent, slatternly, slovenly, *sordidus,* squalid, undesirable

SORT, verb allocate, allot, apportion, arrange, array, assign places to, assort, catalogue, categorize, class, classify, collocate, deal, *digerere,* disentangle, distribute, divide, file, grade, graduate, group, methodize, order, organize, parcel out, place in order, put in order, range, rank, reduce to order, screen, segregate, separate, sieve, sift, size, split, subdivide, systematize, tabulate

SOUND, adjective accurate, acknowledged, admitted, cogent, compelling, convincing, correct, credible, effective, effectual, efficacious, factual, forceful, incontrovertible, irrefutable, justified, legitimate, persuasive, potent, powerful, proven, right, rightful, scientific, solid, strong, substantial, true, truthful, unanswerable, unchallengeable, unconfutable, undisputable, undistorted, unexaggerated, unimagined, unimpeachable, veracious, veritable, weighty, well-founded, well-grounded
ASSOCIATED CONCEPTS: sound discretion, sound value

SOURCE, noun ancestry, authority, basis, beginning, *caput,* cause, cradle, derivation, *fons,* font, foundation, fount, fountain, fountainhead, generator, genesis, germ, headspring, incunabula, informant, inspiration, lineage, motive, origin, original, origination, *origo,* parent, parentage, place, provenance, provenience, root, spring, springhead, stem, well, wellhead, wellspring
ASSOCIATED CONCEPTS: source of income, source of information

SOVEREIGN *(Absolute),* **adjective** authoritative, chief, commanding, controlling, dominant, governing, hegemonic, hegemonical, imperial, influential, leading, master, most powerful, paramount, potent, powerful, predominant, prepollent, prepotent, regent, regnant, reigning, royal, ruling, supreme

SOVEREIGN *(Independent),* **adjective** at liberty, autonomous, enjoying liberty, enjoying political independence, exempt from external authority, free, liberated, politically independent, removed from bondage, self-determined, self-directing, self-governed, self-ruling, *sui iuris,* unattached, unbound, unconquered, uncontrolled, unenslaved, unrestricted, unsubjected, unvanquished

ASSOCIATED CONCEPTS: sovereign right, sovereign states

SPACE, noun   accommodation, acreage, area, capaciousness, capacity, compass, distance, expanse, extent, field, footage, gap, interstice, interval, latitude, *locus,* margin, mileage, range, room, scope, size, spaciousness, span, *spatium,* stretch, sweep, territory, vastness, yardage

SPARTAN, adjective   aggressive, *audax,* bellicose, bold, brave, courageous, daring, dauntless, determined, disciplined, doughty, fearless, fierce, firm, formidable, *fortis,* hardy, hero-like, heroic, highly disciplined, indomitable, intrepid, iron-hearted, lionhearted, manly, martial, mighty, militant, plucky, pugnacious, resisting, resolute, resolved, self-reliant, severe, soldier-like, soldierly, stalwart, stoic, stoical, stout, stout-hearted, *strenuus,* strong, unafraid, unapprehensive, unblenching, unconquerable, undaunted, unflinching, unshrinking, valiant, valorous, virile, warlike, well-disciplined

SPATE, noun   abundance, cataract, deluge, flood, outburst, profusion, rush, torrent

SPEAK, verb   address, air, announce, annunciate, apprise, articulate, aver, badinage, bandy words, bear witness, break silence, carry on a conversation, colloque, communicate with, converse, declaim, declare, deliver, deliver an address, denote, *dicere,* disclose, discourse, divulge, engage in a conversation, engage in a dialogue, enunciate, exchange opinions, explain, expound, express, give a talk, give expression, give indication of, give voice, give words to, have a dialogue, hold a conversation, hold a discussion, indicate, inform, issue a statement, join in a conversation, make a speech, make a statement, make mention, make oral communication, make oral mention, make solemn affirmation, make solemn declaration, murmur, mutter, palaver, parley, phrase, pour forth, proclaim, pronounce, publish, put into words, recite, remark, render an account of, repeat, report, reveal, say, sermonize, state, state emphatically, state one's case, state with conviction, talk, tell, utter, utter forth, utter with conviction, utter words

FOREIGN PHRASES: *Idem est nihil dicere et insufficienter dicere.* It is the same thing to say nothing, and to say a thing insufficiently.

SPECIAL, adjective   amazing, astonishing, astounding, atypical, awe-inspiring, awesome, certain, conspicuous, different, distinctive, distinguished, *egregius,* endemic, esoteric, especial, exceptional, *eximius,* extraordinary, fabulous, fantastic, gala, important, imposing, incredible, individualistic, infrequent, marked, marvelous, memorable, miraculous, notable, noteworthy, outstanding, particular, *praecipuus,* prodigious, rare, remarkable, significant, singular, specific, striking, stupendous, superior, unaccustomed, uncommon, uncustomary, unexampled, unfamiliar, unforgettable, unimitative, unique, unparalleled, unprecedented, unusual, wonderful

ASSOCIATED CONCEPTS: special act, special appearance, special assessment, special benefits, special case, special circumstances, special damages, special election, special interest, special law, special legislation, special proceeding, special remedy, special tax, special verdict

FOREIGN PHRASES: *Statutum generaliter est intelligendum quando verba statuti sunt specialia, ratio autem generalis.* When the words of a statute are special, but the reason general, the statute is to be understood generally. *Generalia praecedunt, specialia sequuntur.* General matters precede, special matters follow.

SPECIAL INTEREST, noun   advocate, appealer, aspirant, influencer, instigator, lobby, lobbyist, mover, petitioner, pressure group, prompter, seeker, solicitor, suggester, suitor, suppliant

SPECIALIST, noun   authority, connoisseur, consultant, degreeholder, devotee, experienced person, expert, *homo peritus,* knowing person, learned person, master, practiced hand, practitioner, professional, professor, proficient, proficient person, qualified person, savant, scholar, skilled hand, skilled person, skilled practitioner, skilled worker, specializer, technician, trained person, veteran, virtuoso

SPECIALITY, noun   badge, character, distinction, distinctive characteristic, distinctive mark, distinctive quality, distinctiveness, feature, identification, individual characteristic, individual trait, individuality, mark, oddity, particularity, peculiarity, quality, quirk, singularity, specialness, stamp

SPECIALIZE, verb   address oneself to, apply oneself, bound, concentrate on, concern oneself with, dedicate oneself to, devote oneself to, focus attention on, give attention to, limit, narrow, practice exclusively, pursue, qualify, restrict, select, take up, train

SPECIALTY *(Contract),* **noun**   agreement, arrangement, bargain under seal, bond, commitment, compact, concordat, contractual obligation, contractual statement, covenant, covenant of indemnity, debenture, engagement, guaranty, hypothecation, indenture, legal agreement, obligation, pact, pledge, pledged word, promise under seal, recognizance, security, stipulation, understanding, undertaking, warranty

ASSOCIATED CONCEPTS: specialty debts, suit upon a specialty

SPECIALTY *(Distinctive mark),* **noun**   attribute, badge, brand, character, characteristic, definiteness, disconformity, dissimilarity, distinction, distinctive feature, distinctiveness, distinctness, dominant characteristic, earmark, eccentricity, feature, idiosyncrasy, impress, inconsistency, individualism, mannerism, mark, oddity, particular characteristic, particular item, particular matter, particular point, particularity, peculiar idiom, peculiar temperament, peculiarity, personal characteristic, point of difference, property, quality, quirk, rarity, singularity, special characteristic, special item, special matter, special point, specific quality, specificness, stamp, token, trait, uniqueness, unlikeness

SPECIALTY *(Special aptitude),* **noun**   ability, accomplishment, adeptness, aptness, artistry, calling, capability, career, competence, craft, dexterity, endowment, expertise, expertness, faculty, forte, function, genius, handicraft, inborn aptitude, ingenuity, innate ability, knowledge, main interest, mastership, mastery, natural ability, object of study, occupation, particular object of pursuit, professionalism, proficiency, pursuit, qualification, skill, skillfulness, special line of work, special project, special skill, special study, specialization, strong point, talent, task, technique, virtuosity, vocation

SPECIFIC, *adjective* appropriate, categorical, certain, characteristic, definite, denominational, determinate, determined, different, *disertus,* distinctive, divisional, endemic, endemical, esoteric, especial, exact, exceptional, exclusive, explicit, express, idiomatic, idiosyncratic, idiosyncratical, indigenous, individual, individualistic, limited, marked, narrow, out of the ordinary, particular, peculiar, *peculiaris,* precise, precisely formulated, *proprius,* respective, restricted, sectarian, select, special, uncommon, unique, unusual
ASSOCIATED CONCEPTS: specific bequest, specific denial, specific devise, specific legacy, specific performance

SPECIFICATION, *noun* assignment, condition, definition, delimitation, description, designation, detail, detailed statement, determination, distinction, enumeration, item, itemization, minute account, nicety, particular, particularization, proviso, recital, special point, statement of particulars, stipulation, written requirement

SPECIFY, *verb* advert to, circumscribe, cite, clearly define, demarcate, *denotare,* designate, detail, differentiate, disclose, *enumerare,* enumerate, explain, express, give full particulars, go into detail, indicate, instance, itemize, list, mark out, mention, name, particularize, point out, refer to, represent, select, show, state in detail, state precisely, stipulate

SPECIMEN, *noun* case in point, *documentum,* ensample, example, *exemplum,* exponent, guide, illustration, instance, model, paradigm, pattern, representative, representative selection, sample

SPECIOUS, *adjective* affected, apparent, appearing, artificial, assumed, believable, bogus, casuistic, casuistical, colorable, colored, convincing, counterfeit, credible, deceiving, deceptive, deluding, delusive, delusory, erroneous, exterior, external, fake, fallacious, false, hypocritical, illusional, illusive, illusory, misleading, ostensible, outward, persuasive, phony, plausible, posed, pretend, pretended, professed, purported, put on, resembling truth, seeming, simulated, so-called, sophistic, sophistical, *speciosus,* spurious, unfounded, would-be
ASSOCIATED CONCEPTS: specious argument, specious defense

SPECTER, *noun* apparition, appearance, eidolon, form, illusion, presence, revenant, shadow, shape, spirit, sprite

SPECULATE *(Chance),* *verb* assume a risk, bet, chance, dare, deal in futures, gamble, hazard, invest, lay money on, play the market, plunge, risk, stake, take a chance, try one's luck, venture, wager

SPECULATE *(Conjecture),* *verb* assume, *cogitare,* consider, dare say, debate, deliberate, guess, have a theory, hypothesize, judge, muse, philosophize, ponder, puzzle over, *quaerere,* reckon, ruminate, suppose, sur-

mise, theorize, think, turn over in the mind, venture, weigh, wonder about
ASSOCIATED CONCEPTS: speculative damages

SPECULATION *(Conjecture),* *noun* assumption, *coniectura,* contemplation, deliberation, guesswork, hypothesis, inference, presumption, reasoning, rumination, supposition, surmise, suspicion, theorization, theory
ASSOCIATED CONCEPTS: speculative damages, speculative testimony

SPECULATION *(Risk),* *noun* bet, calculated risk, chance, fortuity, fortune, gamble, gambling, gaming, hazard, uncertainty, venture, wager

SPECULATIVE, *adjective* abstract, academic, aleatory, assumptive, chancy, cogitative, *coniecturalis,* conjectural, contemplative, contestable, controvertible, debatable, deliberative, doubtful, dubious, experimental, hazardous, hypothetical, imaginary, impractical, indefinite, indistinct, insecure, irresolute, meditative, presumptive, projected, provisional, questionable, risky, speculatory, suppositional, tentative, theoretical, uncertain, unconfirmed, undemonstrated, undetermined, unproven, unsafe, unsettled
ASSOCIATED CONCEPTS: speculative testimony

SPECULATOR, *noun* adventurer, backer, bettor, entrepreneur, experimenter, gambler, hazarder, prospector, risk taker, trader, venturer, wagerer

SPEECH, *noun* address, allocution, articulation, audible expression, colloquy, confabulation, conversation, declamation, declaration, delivery, dialect, diction, discourse, enunciation, expression, idiom, interlocution, language, lecture, lingo, locution, oral communication, oral expression, *oratio,* oration, oratory, palaver, parlance, phonation, phraseology, prattle, pronouncement, pronunciation, recital, recitation, rhetoric, say, sermon, spoken language, spoken word, statement, talk, tongue, utterance, verbal expression, verbal intercourse, vocalization, words
ASSOCIATED CONCEPTS: First Amendment, freedom of speech
FOREIGN PHRASES: **Lubricum linguae non facile trahendum est in poenam.** A slip of the tongue ought not readily be subjected to punishment.

SPEECHLESS, *adjective* agape, aghast, amazed, aphonic, astonished, awe-struck, bewildered, dumb, dumb-struck, *elinguis,* gagged, inarticulate, incapable of utterance, indisposed to words, mum, mute, *mutus,* noiseless, open-mouthed, quiet, silent, soundless, stunned, stupefied, *tacere,* thunderstruck, tongue-tied, unable to speak, unvocal, voiceless, wordless

SPEND, *verb* apply, bestow, consume, *consumere,* contribute, deplete, devote, disburse, dispense, dispose of, donate, drain, employ, empty, exhaust, expend, give, go through, impoverish, incur expense, *insumere,* invest, lay out money, make expenditure, outlay, part with, pay, run through, splurge, use, use up, wear away, wear out
ASSOCIATED CONCEPTS: spendthrift

SPHERE, *noun* ambit, arena, ball, bounds, capacity, circle, circuit, demesne, department, domain, field, field of activity, field of operation, function, globe, globoid, globular mass, influence, office, orb, orbit, pale, province, *provincia,* range, realm, region, round body, scope, *sphaera,* spheroid

SPIRIT, *noun* angel, *anima,* animation, apparition, ardor, boldness, bravery, character, characteristic quality, cheer, cheerfulness, complexion, courage, daring, dash, disposition, earnestness, energy, enterprise, enthusiasm, essence, essential part, fire, firmness, force, fortitude, frame of mind, gist, humor, hypostasis, immaterial substance, immortal part, *ingenium,* intent, life, liveliness, meaning, mettle, mood, nature, passion, psyche, purport, quintessence, resoluteness, resolution, sense, sentiment, significance, soul, sparkle, specter, spice, substance, supernatural being, temper, temperament, tenor, turn of mind, verve, vigor, vim, vital essence, vitality, vivacity, zeal
ASSOCIATED CONCEPTS: spirit of the law

SPIRIT, *verb* actuate, animate, arouse, encourage, enliven, *excitare,* excite, exhilarate, exhort, impassion, impel, *incitare,* incite, inspire, inspirit, instigate, kindle, motivate, move, press, prod, prompt, propel, provoke, push, rouse, spur, *stimulare,* stimulate, stir up, urge on

SPITE, *noun* acrimoniousness, acrimony, animosity, animus, antagonism, bitterness, cattiness, contempt, defiance, despite, enmity, gall, grudge, harsh feeling, hate, hatred, hostility, ill feeling, ill nature, ill will, inimicality, intolerance, *livor,* malevolence, *malevolentia,* malice, maliciousness, malignance, malignancy, *malignitas,* malignity, rancor, resentment, revengefulness, spitefulness, vengeance, venom, viciousness, vindictiveness, virulence, virulency

SPITEFUL, *adjective* acrimonious, antagonistic, antipathetic, belligerent, caustic, contrary, despiteful, envenomed, evil-minded, froward, harsh, hateful, hostile, ill-disposed, ill-intentioned, ill-natured, inimical, invidious, *lividus,* malevolent, *malevolus,* malicious, malign, malignant, *malignus,* mean, rancorous, resentful, revengeful, testy, venemous, vicious, vindictive, viperous, virulent

SPLIT, *noun* aperture, bifurcation, bisection, breach, break, chasm, chink, cleavage, cleft, crack, crater, crevice, cut, detachment, dichotomy, difference, dilaceration, dimidiation, diremption, disagreement, disassociation, discerption, disconnection, disengagement, disjunction, dismemberment, disruption, dissection, dissension, disseverance, disunion, divarication, divergence, division, divorce, divulsion, faction, *fissura,* fissure, fork, fracture, furrow, gap, gash, gulf, hiatus, incision, interruption, lacuna, partage, partition, perforation, quarrel, rent, rift, *rima,* rip, scission, *scissura,* scissure, sect, segmentation, segregation, separation, severance, slit, slot, subdivision, sunderance, variance
ASSOCIATED CONCEPTS: split among the Circuit Courts, split in authority, split sentence, splitting a cause of action

SPLIT, *verb* abscind, allocate, allot, apportion, assign, bisect, break, break with, carve, chop, cleave, crack, cut, deal, detach, dichotomize, *diffindere,* disconnect, disjoin, dispense, dissect, dissever, distribute, disunite, divide, dole, fissure, fracture, give way, hack, halve, hew, incise, intersect, isolate, lance, mete, open, parcel out, part, part company, partition, rend, rift, rip,

rive, rupture, *scindere,* section, segment, segregate, separate, sever, share, shiver, slash, slice, slit, snap, splinter, subdivide, sunder, tear, unbind, untie
ASSOCIATED CONCEPTS: split a cause of action

SPOIL *(Impair),* *verb* addle, blemish, blight, botch, break, bungle, butcher, *corrumpere,* corrupt, damage, damage irreparably, debase, decay, decompose, deface, defile, deform, demolish, destroy, deteriorate, dilapidate, disable, disfigure, go bad, harm, hurt, impair, injure, lay waste, mangle, mar, mess up, mutilate, *perdere,* putrefy, rot, ruin, ruinate, sabotage, smash, sour, turn, vitiate, wreck

SPOIL *(Pillage),* *verb* despoil, forage, foray, loot, maraud, pirate, plunder, raid, ransack, ravage, rob, *spoliare,* spoliate, steal, waste

SPOILAGE, *noun* blight, corrosion, corruption, decay, decomposition, decrement, deterioration, dilapidation, disintegration, dissolution, erosion, putrefaction, putrescence, rot, wastage, waste

SPOILS, *noun* booty, gains, grab, graft, haul, ill-gotten gains, loot, pelf, pickings, pillage, plunder, plunderage, prize, ravin, *spolia,* stolen goods, swag, take, takings, winnings

SPOKESMAN, *noun* advocate, agent, ambassador, attorney, *auctor,* broker, delegate, deputy, emissary, envoy, go-between, interlocutor, mediary, mediator, messenger, mouthpiece, negotiator, *patronus,* plenipotentiary, prolocutor, representative, speaker, speechmaker, *suasor,* vicar, voice

SPOLIATION, *noun* attack, brigandage, buccaneering, depredation, deprivation, desolation, despoliation, destruction, devastation, *direptio,* direption, *expilatio,* foray, looting, marauding, pilfering, pillage, pillaging, piracy, plunder, plunderage, plundering, raid, ransack, rapine, robbery, sack, theft, thievery

SPONSOR, *noun* advocate, *auctor,* backer, benefactor, champion, favorer, guarantor, guardian, insurer, patron, promoter, protector, succorer, surety, sympathizer
ASSOCIATED CONCEPTS: sponsor of legislation

SPONSOR, *verb* accept responsibility for, act as surety for, answer for, assure, back, be responsible for, befriend, certify, champion, defend, endorse, ensure, favor, finance, financier, guarantee, insure, patronize, pay for, promote, protect, provide for, put up the money, secure, stand behind, subscribe to, support, sustain, sympathize, take responsibility for, underwrite, uphold, vouch for, warrant
ASSOCIATED CONCEPTS: sponsor a bill

SPONTANEOUS, *adjective* discretional, discretionary, elective, extemporal, extemporaneous, extemporary, extempore, free, free-willed, impetuous, impromptu, improvisatorial, improvised, impulsive, indeliberate, independent, natural, optional, rash, self-acting, self-determined, snap, *spontaneus,* sudden, unbidden, uncompelled, unconstrained, uncontrived, uncontrolled, unforced, unintentional, unplanned, unpremeditated, unprepared, unprompted, unrehearsed, unstudied, untaught, unthinking, volitient, volitional, volitive, *voluntarius,* voluntary, willful
ASSOCIATED CONCEPTS: res gestae, spontaneous declaration

SPORADIC, *adjective* appearing at intervals, casual, changeable, desultory, disconnected, discontinuous, disjunct, dispersed, erratic, fitful, fluctuating, immethodical, inconstant, indefinite, infrequent, intermittent, intermitting, *inusitatus,* irregular, isolated, nonuniform, now and then, occasional, periodic, periodical, rare, *rarus,* recurrent, recurring, remittent, scattered, scrappy, separate, shifting, single, sparse, spasmodic, sporadical, spotty, stray, uncertain, uneven, unsteady, unsuccessive, unsystematic, variable, wavering

SPOUSE, *noun* *coniunx,* consort, espouse, helpmate, helpmeet, husband, marital partner, marriage partner, mate, wife

SPREAD, *verb* advertise, bestrew, bloat, branch, broadcast, broaden, bruit, circulate, cover, deploy, diffuse, dilate, disperse, disseminate, distribute, divaricate, *divulgare,* divulge, emanate, expand, *explicare,* extend, fan, fill out, flow, fork, inflate, irradiate, lengthen, make known, make public, mantle, open, outspread, overrun, overspread, penetrate, permeate, pervade, promulgate, propagate, publicize, publish, radiate, ramify, roll out, rumor, scatter, smear, sow, *spargere,* splay, sprawl, sprinkle, straggle, stretch, stretch out, strew, suffuse, swell, uncoil, unfold, unfurl, unravel, unroll, unwind, vent, widen

SPURIOUS, *adjective* apocryphal, artificial, bogus, counterfeit, deceitful, deceptive, delusive, ersatz, fabricated, fake, faked, false, feigned, fictitious, forged, fraudulent, illegitimate, imitation, misrepresented, mock, pinchbeck, pretend, pseudo, quasi, sham, simulated, synthetic, unauthentic, ungenuine, unreal, untrue
ASSOCIATED CONCEPTS: spurious claim

SPURN, *verb* *aspernari,* belittle, boot, brush aside, cast aside, cast out, censure, contemn, decline, depreciate, despise, disapprove, discard, disdain, disparage, disregard, drive away, drive back, elude, evade, *fastidire,* flout, frown upon, have nothing to do with, hold in contempt, ignore, jilt, kick, laugh at, look down upon, neglect, ostracize, rebuff, refuse, refuse to accept, reject, renounce, repel, reprobate, repudiate, repulse, scorn, scout, set at nought, shun, slight, slur, sneer, snub, trample, tread on, treat with disdain, turn down

SPY, *noun* agent, detective, *emissarius, explorator,* informant, informer, intelligence agent, intelligencer, investigator, lookout, observer, reconnoiterer, reporter, scout, secret agent, sleuth, snoop, snooper, source, *speculator,* undercover agent, undercover man, watcher
ASSOCIATED CONCEPTS: espionage

SPY, *verb* behold, catch sight of, descry, detect, discern, discover, discover by artifice, distinguish, eavesdrop, espy, examine secretely, *explorare,* follow, glimpse, inspect secretely, look at, look for, make a reconnaissance, make out, make secret observations, observe, peep, peer, perceive, pry, recognize, reconnoiter, scrutinize, search out, see, shadow, sight, snoop, *speculari,* spy upon, take note, trail, view, watch, watch secretely

STABILIZE, *verb* balance, clinch, counterbalance, establish, firm up, round, secure, set, settle, steady

STABLE, *adjective* abiding, anchored, chronic, *constans,* constant, continuing, deep-rooted, diligent, durable, endless, enduring, established, everlasting, faithful, fast, fastened, firm, *firmus,* fixed, grounded, immovable, immutable, indissoluble, indomitable, industrious, inert, inexorable, intact, invariable, inveterate, irremovable, irreversible, irrevocable, lasting, long-lasting, long-lived, long-standing, moored, motionless, perdurable, permanent, perpetual, persistent, plodding, relentless, reliable, riveted, rooted, secure, sedulous, settled, solid, sound, stabile, *stabilis,* stalwart, stanch, stationary, steadfast, steady, strong, sturdy, substantial, sure, tenacious, unalterable, unchangeable, unchanging, uncompromising, undeviating, unfailing, unfaltering, unflagging, unflinching, unhesitating, unremitting, unshakeable, unshaken, unswerving, untiring, unwavering, unyielding, well-built, well-grounded

STAFF, *noun* *adiutores,* aides, assistants, associates, body of employees, cadre, clerical staff, complement, corps, council, crew, deputies, employees, faculty, force, help, *legatio,* management, personnel, professional force, professional staff, servants, staff members, workers

STAGNANT, *adjective* apathetic, dormant, dull, hebetudinous, idle, immobile, inactive, indolent, inert, lacking activity, lazy, *lentus,* lethargic, lifeless, listless, lumpish, motionless, otiose, passive, phlegmatic, phlegmatical, *piger,* quiescent, sluggish, *stagnans,* stagnating, standing, static, stationary, still, supine, torpid, torporific, unflowing, unmoving, unstirring, without current, without motion

STAIN, *verb* attaint, bedaub, befoul, besmear, besmirch, blacken, blemish, blot, blotch, bring reproach upon, color, contaminate, corrupt, damage, daub, debase, defame, defile, detract from, dirty, discolor, discredit, disgrace, dishonor, dye, grime, impair, *inquinare, maculare,* maculate, malign, mar, mark, *polluere,* pollute, ruin, smear, smirch, smudge, soil, spatter, splotch, spoil, spot, stigmatize, sully, taint, tarnish, tinge, tint

STAKE *(Award), **noun*** ante, bet, pot, prize, purse, spoils, wager, winnings

STAKE *(Interest), **noun*** claim, equity, holding, ownership, right, share, title
ASSOCIATED CONCEPTS: interpleader stake deposited in court

STALE, *adjective* banal, boring, common, commonplace, decayed, declining, dull, effete, faded, fetid, flat, flavorless, fusty, hackneyed, humdrum, insipid, jejune, mildewed, moldy, monotonous, musty, *obsoletus,* off, old, pedestrian, prosaic, prosy, rancid, rotten, savorless, shopworn, sour, soured, spoiled, tasteless, timeworn, trite, unimaginative, uninteresting, unvaried, vapid, *vetus,* vitiated, wasted, wilted, withered, without novelty, worn out
ASSOCIATED CONCEPTS: stale cause of action, stale check

STALL, *verb* arrest, avert, bar, block, bog, break down, bring to a standstill, check, dally, dawdle, defer, delay, detain, dillydally, disable, filibuster, halt, hamper, hinder, hold up, impede, incapacitate, inhibit, in-

terrupt, keep back, lag, linger, obstruct, paralyze, postpone, procrastinate, put off, render powerless, retard, *stabulare,* stalemate, still, stop, take time, temporize, ward off
ASSOCIATED CONCEPTS: dilatory motions

STAMP, *noun*   attestation, authentication, brand, cast, certification, die, endorsement, engraving, form, hallmark, identification, impress, impression, imprint, intaglio, mark, *nota,* pattern, print, ratification, seal, sigil, signit, *signum,* validation
ASSOCIATED CONCEPTS: tax stamps

STAND *(Position),* *noun*   attitude, belief, bent, bias, *consistere,* inclination, leaning, opinion, outlook, point of view, position, slant, standpoint, vantage point, view, viewpoint

STAND *(Witness' place in court),* *noun*   booth, box, corner, place, platform, position, post, stall, station, witness box, witness stand

STANDARD, *noun*   archetype, basis of comparison, canon, comparison, criterion, example, exemplar, frame of reference, gauge, grade of excellence, guide, ideal, level of excellence, measure, model, norm, *norma,* paradigm, paragon, pattern, precedent, prototype, *regula,* touchstone
ASSOCIATED CONCEPTS: standard established by law, standard of care, standard of conduct, standard of proof

STANDING, *adjective*   constant, continued, continuing, conventional, enduring, established, fixed, lasting, permanent, perpetual, perpetuated, settled, stationary, still, traditional, unceasing, unchanging
ASSOCIATED CONCEPTS: standing committee

STANDPOINT, *noun*   angle, aspect, attitude, belief, bent, conviction, direction, disposition, inclination, judgment, leaning, location, observation post, opinion, orientation, outlook, perspective, persuasion, point, point of view, position, post, predilection, proclivity, propensity, seat, *sententia,* situation, spot, station, tendency, vantage point, view, viewpoint, vision

STARE DECISIS, *noun*   authoritative example, basis, foundation, precedent, principle of law, rule, standard
ASSOCIATED CONCEPTS: *stare decisis et non quieta movere, stare in judicio*

STARK, *adjective*   absolute, bald, bare, complete, conspicuous, decided, downright, entire, glaring, gross, obvious, outright, plain, positive, pure, *rigidus,* sheer, simple, staring, total, unmitigated, unqualified, utter, very

START, *noun*   beginning, birth, commencement, dawn, derivation, embarkation, emergence, evolution, exordium, first step, foundation, genesis, inauguration, inception, inchoation, incipience, incipiency, infancy, initiation, *initium,* onset, opening, origin, origination, outbreak, outset, *profectio,* rise, scare, source, threshold

STATE *(Condition),* *noun*   appearance, aspect, circumstance, class, complexion, disposition, grade, mien, mood, plight, position, posture, predicament, shape, situation, standing, station, *status,* way
ASSOCIATED CONCEPTS: state of mind

STATE *(Political unit),* *noun*   body politic, civil community, *civitas,* commonwealth, governmental unit, mandated territory, nation, political division, polity, sovereign unit
ASSOCIATED CONCEPTS: state's evidence, state's rights
FOREIGN PHRASES: *Privilegium non valet contra rempublicam.* A privilege is of no avail against the state.

STATED, *adjective*   aforementioned, aforesaid, arranged, ascertained, decided, defined, detailed, determined, established, expressed, fixed, prearranged, predetermined, prescribed, reported, said, set forth, settled, specified, stipulated, told, uttered, voiced
ASSOCIATED CONCEPTS: stated capital, stated term

STATEMENT, *noun*   account, affidavit, affirmation, announcement, assertion, asseveration, averment, avowal, claim, comment, declaration, deposition, detailed account, dictum, enumeration, exclamation, explanation, exposition, manifesto, narrative, observation, prepared announcement, prepared text, pronouncement, recapitulation, recital, recitation, remark, report, story, summary, testimony, utterance
ASSOCIATED CONCEPTS: statement of claim, statement of defense, statement of particulars

STATIC, *adjective*   changeless, dormant, fixed, immobile, *immobilis, immotus,* inactive, inert, motionless, passive, permanent, quiescent, quiet, resting, rigid, stable, stagnant, standing, statical, stationary, still, suspended, torpid, unmoving, unprogressive

STATUS, *noun*   caliber, caste, circumstance, class, condition, dignity, elevation, eminence, esteem, footing, grade, importance, notability, place, position, posture, prestige, prominence, quality, rank, rating, situation, standing, state, station, superiority
ASSOCIATED CONCEPTS: proof of status, status of purchaser, status of trustee

STATUS QUO, *noun*   absence of change, conservation of the same situation, equilibrium, existing conditions, existing state, maintenance of regularity, preservation of the same conditions, same conditions, stable state, static condition, things as they are

STATUTE, *noun*   act, canon, code, codified law, commandment, decree, dictate, edict, enactment, *ius,* law, legislation, legislative enactment, *lex,* mandate, measure, order, ordinance, provision of the law, regulation, rubric, rule, written law
ASSOCIATED CONCEPTS: affirmative statute, criminal statute, declaratory statute, enabling statute, penal statute, private statute, remedial statute, statute of frauds, statute of limitations
FOREIGN PHRASES: *Quae communi lege derogant stricte interpretantur.* Statutes which derogate from the common law are to be strictly construed. *Optima statuti interpretatrix est ipsum statutum.* The best interpreter of a statute is the statute itself. *Ex malis moribus bonae leges natae sunt.* Good laws arise from evil morals. *Casus omissus et oblivioni datus dispositioni communis juris relinquitur.* A case omitted and forgotten is left to the disposal of the common law. *Statutum generaliter est intelligendum quando verba statuti sunt specialia ratio autem generalis.* When the words of a statute are special, but the reason general, the statute is to be understood generally. *Constructio*

legis non facit injuriam. The interpretation of the law works no injury. *Ad ea quae frequentius accidunt jura adaptantur.* Laws are adapted to those cases which occur. *Jus constitui oportet in his quae ut plurimum accidunt non quae ex inopinato.* Laws ought to be made with a view to those cases which occur most frequently, and not to those which are of rare or accidental occurrence. *Nova constitutio futuris formam imponere debet non praeteritis.* A new law ought to affect the future, not what is past. *A verbis legis non est recendendum.* From the words of a statute there must be no departure. *Lex posterior derogat priori.* A later law takes away the effect of a prior one. *Leges posteriores priores contrarias abrogant.* Subsequent laws repeal prior laws that are repugnant to them. *Non est novum ut priores leges ad posteriores trahantur.* It is not novel that prior statutes should give way to later ones. *In rebus quae sunt favorabilia animae, quamvis sunt damnosa rebus, fiat aliquando extensio statuti.* In matters that are favorable to the spirit, though injurious to things, an extension of a statute should sometimes be made. *Est ipsorum legislatorum tanquam viva vox; rebus et non verbis legem imponimus.* The voice of the lawmakers is like the living voice; we impose law upon things and not upon words. *Statutum speciale statuto speciali non derogat.* One special statute does not derogate from another special statute. *Statutum affirmativum non derogat communi legi.* An affirmative statute does not derogate from the common law.

STATUTORY, *adjective*   according to law, authorized, established, fixed, lawful, legal, legalized, legislative, legislatorial, licit, sanctioned, within the law
ASSOCIATED CONCEPTS: statutory crime

STAUNCH, *adjective*   *certus,* constant, dependable, devoted, faithful, fast, *fidus,* firm, *firmus,* inflexible, iron, loyal, reliable, resolute, solid, sound, stable, stalwart, steadfast, steady, strong, substantial, sure, tried, true, trustworthy, trusty, unfailing, unfaltering, unshakeable, unwavering, unyielding

STAVE, *verb*   avert, avoid, beat off, block, check, deflect, drive away, fend off, *fugare,* hamper, hinder, hold off, impede, inhibit, intercept, keep at bay, keep off, obstruct, prevent, *propulsare,* push away, put off, repel, *repellere,* shun, turn aside, ward off

STAY, *noun*   abeyance, abeyancy, bar, cessation, check, curb, delay, desistance, discontinuance, halt, hindrance, interruption, *mansio,* obstacle, obstruction, prevention, reprieve, respite, restraint, stop, stoppage, suspension, wait
ASSOCIATED CONCEPTS: judicial stay, stay of enforcement, stay of execution, stay of proceedings, stay pending appeal

STAY *(Halt), verb*   arrest, bar, block, check, *cohibere,* constrain, curb, delay, *demorari,* desist, detain, deter, *detinere,* discontinue, forbid, foreclose, forestall, frustrate, hamper, hinder, hold, impede, intercept, interrupt, obstruct, obviate, preclude, prevent, prohibit, put an end to, quell, reprieve, respite, restrain, stem, stop, stymie, suppress, thwart
ASSOCIATED CONCEPTS: permanent injunction, stay enforcement, stay of execution, stay order, stay proceedings, temporary injunction, temporary restraining order

STAY *(Continue), verb*   endure, extend, keep on, last, persevere, persist, prolong, remain, subsist
ASSOCIATED CONCEPTS: stay in occupancy

STAY *(Rest), verb*   await, be anchored, be dormant, be fixed, be immobile, be inert, be inmovable, be motionless, be riveted, be sedentary, be stationary, be transfixed, halt, lodge, park, pause, remain, repose, stand, stop, wait

STEADFAST, *adjective*   abiding, anchored, assiduous, *constans,* constant, decided, dedicated, dependable, determined, devoted, diligent, enduring, established, faithful, fast, firm, firmly established, *firmus,* fixed, gritty, indissoluble, indomitable, industrious, inexorable, inflexible, intransigent, lasting, long-lasting, loyal, obstinate, patient, perseverant, persevering, persistent, pertinacious, plodding, relentless, reliable, resolute, resolved, riveted, rooted, secure, sedulous, serious, settled, single-minded, *stabilis,* stable, stationary, staunch, steady, strong, strong-willed, tenacious, tried, true, trustworthy, unalterable, unchanging, uncompromising, undaunted, undeviating, undistracted, unfailing, unfaltering, unflagging, unflinching, unhesitating, unmoved, unshaken, unswerving, untiring, unvarying, unwavering, unyielding, zealous

STEAL, *verb*   abscond with, abstract, burglarize, depredate, despoil, embezzle, filch, fleece, *furari,* hold up, lift, mulct, nim, peculate, pilfer, pillage, pirate, plagiarize, plunder, poach, pocket, prig, purloin, rifle, rob, shoplift, snatch, *subducere, surripere,* take unlawfully, thieve, usurp

STEALTHY, *adjective*   arcane, artful, catlike, clandestine, *clandestinus,* cloaked, concealed, covert, crafty, elusive, evasive, feline, furtive, *furtivus,* hidden, masked, obreptitious, obscure, *occultus,* privy, prowling, secret, secretive, shrouded, silent, skulking, sly, sneaking, sneaky, stealthful, surreptitious, thievish, undercover, underhand, undisclosed, unrevealed, unseen, veiled

STELLAR, *adjective*   astral, capital, celebrated, celestial, chief, crowning, distinguished, dominant, eminent, eventful, extraordinary, famous, first, foremost, grand, heavenly, impressive, leading, main, marked, memorable, momentous, noteworthy, outstanding, paramount, predominant, primary, principal, prominent, sidereal, starlike, starry, uranic

STEM *(Check), verb*   arrest, balk, bear up against, block, bung, checkmate, choke, clog, *coercere, cohibere,* cork, counteract, curb, dam up, deadlock, deter, foil, frustrate, halt, hamper, hinder, hold back, impede, intercept, interrupt, keep at bay, keep in, obstruct, oppose, plug, prevent, quell, rein in, repel, repulse, resist, restrain, retard, scotch, stall, stanch, stay, stop, suppress, thwart, veto

STEM *(Originate), verb*   arise, begin, branch off, come, commence, derive, descend, emanate, ensue, flow, follow, germinate, grow, issue, originate, proceed, result, rise, spring, sprout, start, trail

STEP, *noun*   achievement, act, action, advance, advancement, deed, degree, expedient, footpace, footstep, gait, gradation, grade, maneuver, milestone, move, pace, procedure, proceeding, process, progression, rundle, rung, stride, tramp, tread

STERLING, *adjective* authentic, bona fide, *bonus,* consummate, costly, creditable, excellent, exceptional, exemplary, extraordinary, genuine, good, high-grade, high-quality, honest, honorable, matchless, meritorious, noble, peerless, precious, prime, pure, quality, real, splendid, superb, superior, superlative, true, unadulterated, unalloyed, unmingled, unsynthetic, upright, valuable, *verus,* virtuous, worthy

STIFLE, *verb* annihilate, arrest, balk, bar, block, check, choke, conceal, constrain, contain, control, crush, damp, deaden, destroy, drown, dull, extinguish, frustrate, gag, hush, inhibit, kill, mask, muffle, mute, muzzle, obstruct, *opprimere,* prevent, put down, quell, quench, repress, *reprimere,* restrain, silence, smother, snuff out, squash, squelch, still, stop, strangle, strangulate, stymie, subdue, suffocate, suppress, throttle, withhold

STIGMA, *noun* badge of infamy, blemish, blot, brand, defect, disgrace, dishonor, disrepute, flaw, imputation, infamousness, infamy, mark of disgrace, mark of shame, *nota,* notoriety, notoriousness, reproach, *scandalum magnatum,* scar, shame, slur, smear, smirch, spot, stain, taint, tarnish

STIMULATE, *verb* activate, actuate, animate, arouse, awaken, brace, drive, egg on, encourage, energize, enkindle, enliven, *excitare,* excite, fan, fillip, fire, foment, goad, impel, *incitare,* incite, inflame, initiate, *inritare,* inspire, inspirit, instigate, invigorate, jog, kindle, motivate, move, move to action, pique, prod, prompt, propel, provoke, rally, rouse, spur, stir up, vitalize, vivify, whet, work up

STIMULUS, *noun* activator, animator, arouser, *calcar,* catalyst, catalytic agent, cause, drive, encouragement, excitant, fillip, goad, impetus, impulse, incentive, *incitamentum,* incitement, inducement, influence, *inritamentum,* motivating force, motive, needle, prod, provocation, push, reason, shock, spur, stimulant, stimulation, stimulative, stimulator, sting, urge, whet

STIPULATE, *verb* adjust, agree, arrange, assent, bargain, become bound, clarify, contract, covenant, decide, designate, engage, guarantee, include in an agreement, lay down, make a condition, make clear, make definite, name, pledge, promise, provide, settle, settle terms, specify, state, *stipulari*
ASSOCIATED CONCEPTS: stipulated damages, stipulated fact

STIPULATION, *noun* agreement, arrangement, article of agreement, bargain, bond, compact, concordat, *condicio,* condition, contract, convention, covenant, deal, engagement, pact, *pactum,* promise, provise, specification, *stipulatio,* treaty, understanding
ASSOCIATED CONCEPTS: stipulated facts, stipulation of settlement

STOCK *(Shares), noun* assets, capital, fund, holdings, invested property, investment, negotiables, property, security
ASSOCIATED CONCEPTS: bank stock, bonus stock, capital stock, common stock, debenture stock, ordinary stock, original stock, outstanding stock, preferred stock, prepaid stock, sale of stock, shares of stock, special stock, stock certificate, subscription to stock, treasury stock, value of stock, watered stock

STOCK *(Store), noun* accumulation, *copia,* effects, hoard, inventory, provision, reserve, reservoir, supply, *vis*

STOCK IN TRADE, *noun* articles of commerce, available assets, contents, equipment, goods, line, merchandise, products, provisions, resources, staple, stock, store, supply, supply on hand, vendibles, wares

STOICAL, *adjective* apathetic, ascetic, controlled, dispassionate, impassive, imperturbable, indifferent, long-suffering, passionless, passive, patient, philosophic, placid, repressing emotion, resigned, self-controlled, self-disciplined, spartan, tolerant, undemonstrative, undisturbed, unimpassioned, unimpressible, unmoved, unresisting, unruffled

STOP, *verb* abandon, abolish, arrest, bar, barricade, block, block up, blockade, brake, break off, bring to a close, bring to a standstill, bring to naught, cease, check, checkmate, choke, clog, close, come to a standstill, conclude, counteract, countermand, crush, cut short, dam up, delay, desist, detain, deter, die away, disallow, discontinue, drop, end, expire, finish, foil, forbear, forbid, forestall, freeze, halt, hamper, hinder, hold, hold back, impede, *inhibere,* intercept, interrupt, lapse, lay an embargo on, leave off, obstruct, occlude, pause, plug, preclude, prevent, *prohibere,* prohibit, put an end to, quell, quit, refrain, render impassable, repress, rest, restrain, silence, sojourn, stall, stanch, stay, stem, stifle, stopper, stopple, stymie, suppress, suspend, tarry, terminate, thwart, ward off, wipe out, withdraw from
ASSOCIATED CONCEPTS: stop and frisk

STOPGAP, *noun* alternate, alternative, auxiliary, expedient, impermanent fixture, makeshift, means, measure, provisional measure, replacement, reserve, resort, substitute, substitution, succedaneum, temporary arrangement, temporary expedient, temporary substitute

STORE *(Business), noun* booth, business house, concern, emporium, establishment, exchange, market, market place, mart, outlet, shop, stall

STORE *(Depository), noun* abundance, *abundantia,* accumulation, amassment, assets, backlog, cache, collection, conservatory, *copia,* deposit, depository, fund, great quantity, hoard, inventory, nest egg, plenty, profusion, provisions, reserve, reservoir, savings, stack, stock, stockpile, storehouse, sufficiency, supplies, supply, treasure, treasury, wealth

STORE, *verb* accumulate, acquire, amass, assemble, bank, cache, collect, conserve, *copia,* cumulate, deposit, garner, gather, hoard, hold, husband, keep, lay away, maintain, mass, pile up, put by, reposit, reserve, retain, save, stock, stockpile, stow away, treasure, warehouse

STORY *(Falsehood), noun* canard, concoction, deceit, deception, deliberate falsification, dissemblance, dissimulation, distortion, duplicity, evasion, fabrication, faithlessness, false statement, falsification, falsity, fantasy, fib, fiction, figment, inaccuracy, incorrectness, insincerity, intentional misstatement, intentional untruth, invention, inveracity, lie, *mendacium,* misrepresentation, misstatement, myth, perversion of truth, pretense, prevarication, suppression of truth, untrue statement, untruth, want of fidelity

STORY *(Narrative)*, **noun** account, adventures, article, chronicle, conte, description, dispatch, epic, *fabula,* historiette, history, legend, memoir, *narratio,* narration, news, news article, news item, newspaper report, particulars, piece, portrayal, press notice, publicity, recapitulation, recital, recitation, record, recountal, relation, report, saga, sketch, summary of facts, tale, tidings

STRAIGHTFORWARD, adjective aboveboard, *apertus,* artless, candid, direct, forthright, frank, guileless, honest, honorable, ingenuous, legitimate, open, outspoken, plain-spoken, scrupulous, *simplex,* sincere, straight, truth-speaking, truthful, unaffected, uncontrived, uncorrupt, undesigning, undeviating, undissembling, undistorted, unfeigned, unperjured, unswerving, unturned, unwavering, upright, veracious, veridical

STRANGER, noun *advena,* alien, foreign person, foreigner, *hospes,* newcomer, outsider, strange person, tramontane, unknown person

STRANGLE, verb arrest, block, check, choke off, crush, extinguish, hush, inhibit, keep back, keep down, mask, muzzle, put a stop to, quell, quiet, repress, reserve, restrain, silence, smother, snuff out, squelch, still, stop, *strangulare,* subdue, suppress, withhold

STRATAGEM, noun *ars,* artful contrivance, artifice, blind, cheat, chicane, contrivance, crafty device, cunning, deceit, deception, device, dodge, *dolus,* evasion, excuse, expedient, feint, finesse, gimmick, intrigue, machination, maneuver, manipulation, plan, plot, ploy, pretext, ruse, scheme, shift, strategy, subterfuge, tactic, trap, trick, wile

STRATEGIC, adjective calculated, clever, consequential, contrived, critical, crucial, decisive, designed, diplomatic, diplomatical, important, key, momentous, planned, politic, pregnant, significant, strategical, tactical, telling, tricky, turning, vital, well thought out

STRATEGY, noun approach, arrangement, art of war, artifice, battle maneuver, campaign, careful methods, careful plans, *consilium,* contrivance, course, course of action, cunning, design, devices, engineering, forethought, intrigue, intriguery, invention, machination, management, maneuvering, maneuvers, manipulation, method, military evolutions, military science, mode of operation, plan, plan of action, plan of attack, planned campaign, platform, policy, procedure, proceedings, program, proposal, proposed action, proposition, *propositum,* rules of war, scheme, schemery, set of maneuvers, skillful management, soldiership, system, tactics, technique
ASSOCIATED CONCEPTS: trial strategy

STRENGTH, noun brawn, cogency, concentration, durability, efficacy, emphasis, endurance, energy, fervor, firmness, force, hardiness, health, impregnability, intensity, main, mainstay, might, mightiness, muscle, *opes,* potency, power, proof, puissance, *robur,* robustness, solidity, soundness, stalwartness, stamina, stoutness, sturdiness, substantiality, substantialness, superiority, tenaciousness, tenacity, toughness, validity, vigor, *vires,* virility, vitality, vividness, willpower

STRESS *(Accent)*, **noun** accentuation, attention, beat, distinction, emphasis, force, import, importance, inflection, insistence, intonation, paramountcy, primacy, prominence, pronunciation, significance, superiority, tone, urgency, weight

STRESS *(Strain)*, **noun** adversity, affliction, agony, alarm, anxiety, apprehension, apprehensiveness, burden, coercion, compulsion, cross, demand, disquiet, disquietude, distention, dread, duress, exertion, exigency, extension, fear, fearfulness, ferment, fluster, force, fright, load, misgiving, *momentum,* need, nervousness, overexertion, pinch, *pondus,* pressure, pull, stretch, tautness, tenseness, tension, tensity, tightness, traction, trepidation, trial, urgency

STRICT, adjective absolute, accurate, austere, authoritarian, authoritative, autocratic, careful, close, conscientious, despotic, dictatorial, *diligens,* disciplined, exact, exacting, extreme, faithful, fastidious, formal, hard, harsh, high-principled, imperious, inexorable, inflexible, limited, literal, meticulous, obdurate, obligatory, orthodox, particular, positive, precise, principled, punctilious, puritanical, rigid, *rigidus,* rigorous, scrupulous, severe, *severus,* stern, stiff, straitlaced, stringent, tyrannical, unbending, uncompromising, unconditional, unerring, unyielding, veracious
ASSOCIATED CONCEPTS: strict construction, strict interpretation, strict necessity

STRICTURE, noun accusation, adverse comment, adverse criticism, *animadversio,* animadversion, aspersion, blame, castigation, censure, critical remark, criticism, denunciation, deprecation, depreciation, diatribe, disapprobation, disapproval, exception, faultfinding, objection, objurgation, obloquy, philippic, rebuke, *reprehensio,* reprehension, reproach, reprobation, reproof, tirade, unfavorable remark, vituperation

STRIFE, noun agitation, altercation, animosity, battle, belligerency, broil, *certamen, certatio,* clash, combat, competition, conflict, contention, contest, contestation, contrariety, controversy, counteraction, disaccord, disaggreement, discord, disputation, dispute, disquiet, dissension, dissent, dissidence, encounter, engagement, eruption, faction, factionalism, fight, fighting, fray, friction, imbroglio, incompatibility, match, opposition, outbreak, outburst, polemics, quarrel, race, rift, rivalry, row, squabble, struggle, trouble, unrest, upheaval, variance, violence, war, warfare, wrangle

STRIKE, noun boycott, collective refusal to work, concerted refusal to work, group refusal to work, job action, labor dispute, organized refusal to work, shutdown, stoppage, suspension of work, walkout, work stoppage
ASSOCIATED CONCEPTS: lockout, mass strike, picketing, secondary strike

STRIKE *(Assault)*, **verb** afflict, aggress, assail, attack, bat, batter, beat, besiege, damage, deal a blow, fall upon, harm, hit, hurt, inflict harm, inflict injury, lunge at, pound, slap, smash, smite, storm

STRIKE *(Collide)*, **verb** butt, come in contact, come into collision, come together, *conlidere,* crash, encounter, hit, hit against, jar, jolt, knock into, meet, smash

STRIKE *(Refuse to work)*, **verb**   blockade, boycott, cease work, discontinue work, halt work, interrupt work, leave the job, obstruct work, quit work, rebel, refrain from working, revolt, stop work, suspend work, terminate work, walk out
ASSOCIATED CONCEPTS: economic strike, general strike, wildcat strike

STRINGENT, *adjective*   authoritative, binding, compelling, compulsory, despotic, dictatorial, draconian, exact, exacting, exigent, forceful, hard, harsh, inescapable, inflexible, ironhanded, precise, puritanical, rigid, rigorous, rough, stern, stiff, strait-laced, strict, tyrannical, uncompromising, unyielding

STRIVE, *verb*   aim, aspire, attempt, bestir oneself, bid for, carry into execution, compete, *conari,* contend, *contendere,* contest, do all one can, do one's best, do one's utmost, drive at, drudge, employ one's time, employ oneself, endeavor, endeavor to accomplish, endeavor to effect, *eniti,* exert one's energies, exert oneself, fight, go after, labor for, make a bid, make an attempt, make an effort, point at, pursue, put forth an effort, seek, strain, struggle, tackle, take action, take pains, take steps, take trouble, tax one's energies, toil, travail, trouble oneself, try, try for, try one's best, undertake, venture, vie, work, work hard

STRONG, *adjective*   able, brawny, burly, clear, compelling, concentrated, crushing, determined, durable, effective, enduring, energetic, firm, forceful, forcible, formidable, *fortis,* hard, hardy, harsh, healthy, Herculean, husky, inflexible, intense, lasting, lusty, manly, mighty, omnipotent, overpowering, overwhelming, perseverant, persevering, persistent, persuasive, potent, powerful, puissant, reinforced, reliable, resolute, rich, robust, *robustus,* rugged, secure, solid, sound, stable, stalwart, staunch, steadfast, steady, stiff, stout, strapping, strengthful, sturdy, tenacious, titanic, tough, unflimsy, unmixed, unpliant, unremitting, unyielding, *valens,* vibrant, vigorous, violent, virile, vivid, well-built, well-made, wiry
ASSOCIATED CONCEPTS: strong case, strong evidence, strong probability

STRUCTURE *(Composition)*, **noun**   arrangement, configuration, constitution, design, disposition, essence, fabric, form, formation, layout, make up, organization, pattern, plan, set up, shape, style, substance

STRUCTURE *(Edifice)*, **noun**   building, establishment, erection, location, premises
ASSOCIATED CONCEPTS: corporate structure

STRUGGLE, *noun*   affray, agitation, attempt, battle, broil, *certamen,* clash, combat, competition, conflict, confrontation, contention, contestation, controversy, disagreement, dissension, effort, encounter, endeavor, engagement, essay, exertion, feud, fight, force, fracas, grind, haul, labor, *luctatio,* opposition, pains, pursuit, push, quarrel, rencounter, resistance, scrimmage, scuffle, strain, striving, tussle, work

STUDY, *verb*   acquire knowledge, analyze, apply the mind, attend, audit, cerebrate, consider, contemplate, devote oneself to, dissect, do research, educate oneself, examine, excogitate, explore, eye, *incumbere,* inquire into, inspect, intellectualize, investigate, learn, meditate, mull over, muse, note, observe, peruse, pon-der, pore over, probe, pursue, read, reconnoiter, reflect upon, research, review, revolve in the mind, ruminate, scan, school oneself, scrutinize, search into, sift, specialize, *studere,* survey, think about, train in, view, weigh

STYLE, *noun*   appearance, artistry, aspect, cast, character, class, custom, denomination, description, expression, fashion, form, genre, *genus,* guise, habit, individual method, kind, make, manner, manner of presentation, method, mode, model, *modus,* pattern, presentation, rage, *ratio,* school, shape, taste, technique, tone, trend, type, vogue, way

SUASIBLE, *adjective*   accessible, amenable, convincible, docile, easily convinced, easily persuaded, easygoing, facile, flexible, inducible, influenceable, movable, open, open-minded, persuadable, persuasible, pervious, pliable, pliant, receptive, responsive, swayable, tractable

SUBALTERN, *adjective*   baser, humble, inferior, junior, less, lesser, low, lower, lower in rank, lowly, minor, of lower rank, secondary, servile, subalternate, *subcenturio,* subordinate, subsidiary, under

SUBDIVIDE, *verb*   apportion, bisect, break down, categorize, classify, cleave, cut, dissect, dissever, distribute, divide, divide into parcels, divide up, graduate, group, parcel, partition, portion, redistribute, redivide, separate, sever, share, split, sunder

SUBDIVISION, *noun*   bisection, categorization, category, class, classification, compartment, component, division, fraction, fragment, group, grouping, *pars,* part, partition, section, sector, segment, separation, subcategory, subclass, subgroup, subheading
ASSOCIATED CONCEPTS: political subdivision, subdivision of a statute

SUBDUE, *verb*   abate, allay, beat, beat down, bend, best, break, bring under rule, calm, captivate, capture, choke, conquer, control, crush, curb, deaden, defeat, discipline, discomfit, *domare,* dominate, dull, enthrall, foil, get the better of, harness, humble, inhibit, lessen, lower, make docile, make submissive, make tractable, master, moderate, mollify, muffle, mute, obtund, oppress, overbear, overcome, overpower, overwhelm, put down, quell, quiet, reduce, rein, repress, restrain, silence, slacken, smash, smother, soften, *subiungere,* subject, subjugate, suppress, tame, temper, tone down, tranquilize, triumph over, vanquish, worst
ASSOCIATED CONCEPTS: subdue an assailant

SUBHEADING, *noun*   article, categorization, chapter, classification, clause, division, heading, paragraph, section, segment, subdivision, subgroup, subsection, title

SUBJECT *(Conditional)*, *adjective*   contingent, dependent, dependent on circumstances, depending upon, incident to, incidental, provisional, relying upon, *subiectus,* subordinate, uncertain
ASSOCIATED CONCEPTS: subject to approval, subject to defeasance, subject to review

SUBJECT *(Exposed)*, *adjective*   accountable, answerable, at the mercy of, chargeable, liable, open, prone, susceptible, unexempt from, vulnerable

SUBJECT *(Object),* **noun**   case, experimentee, liegeman, recipient, testee, victim
ASSOCIATED CONCEPTS: subject of an investigation

SUBJECT *(Topic),* **noun**   affair, *argumentum,* content, course, gist, issue, material, matter, motif, pith, point, point at issue, *quaestio,* study, text, theme, thesis
ASSOCIATED CONCEPTS: interest in subject matter, subject of agreement, subject of bailment, subject of commerce, subject of statute, subject of tax

SUBJECT, verb   bring under domination, bring under rule, cause to undergo, conquer, control, crush, defeat, disfranchise, dominate, enslave, enthrall, expose, get the better of, govern, hold down, hold in bondage, hold in subjection, humble, keep down, make liable, make submissive, make subordinate, make subservient, master, *obnoxium reddere,* oppress, overcome, overmaster, overthrow, quell, repress, rule, subdue, *subicere,* subjugate, subordinate, suppress, tame, triumph over, vanquish, worst

SUBJECTION, noun   bondage, captivity, conquest, control, disenfranchisement, disfranchisement, duress, enslavement, enthrall, force, helotry, inferior rank, involuntary servitude, loss of freedom, *officium,* servitude, *servitus,* slavery, subdual, subjugation, submission, subordination, subserviency, thrall, yielding, yoke

SUBJECTIVE, adjective   biased, colored by bias, emotional, individual, individualized, internal, introspective, nonobjective, personal, personalized, prejudiced, unrealistic

SUBJUGATE, verb   beat, bring to terms, command, conquer, control, crush, defeat, dominate, enslave, enthrall, govern, hold captive, hold in bondage, hold sway over, humble, master, overbear, overcome, overpower, overrule, overthrow, overwhelm, put down, quash, quell, reduce, restrain, rob of freedom, rout, rule over, sell into slavery, subdue, subject, suppress, tame, trample, triumph over, vanquish

SUBLEASE, verb   allow the use of, demise, grant a demise, grant a lease, hire, let out, make available for rent, rent, rent out, sublet, subrent, underlet

SUBLET, verb   allow the use of, contract to lease, lease, let out, relet, rent, rent out, sublease, subrent, underlet
ASSOCIATED CONCEPTS: assignment, covenant against subletting, restriction against subletting

SUBMIT *(Give),* **verb**   advance, commit, extend, hold out, introduce, make a motion, make a suggestion, present, propose, propound, put, put forth, put forward, refer, *referre,* suggest, tender
ASSOCIATED CONCEPTS: submit to arbitration, submit to the court, submit to the jury

SUBMIT *(Yield),* **verb**   accede, accept, acknowledge defeat, acquiesce, admit defeat, bear with, bend, bow to, capitulate, cease resistance, comply, endure, give in, give up, give way to, heed, listen to, make the best of, mind, obey, put up with, reconcile oneself to, relent, resign, succumb, surrender, tolerate
ASSOCIATED CONCEPTS: submit to the jurisdiction of the court

SUBORDINATE, adjective   subordinate position, accessory, ancillary, auxiliary, collateral, humble, inferior, junior, less important, less significant, lesser, low-level, lower, lower in rank, lowly, minor, secondary, subaltern, subject, subjected, submissive, subservient, subsidiary
ASSOCIATED CONCEPTS: subordinate interest, subordinate lien

SUBORN, verb   bribe, bribe to take a false oath, buy off, corrupt, fraudulently induce, induce, induce another to commit perjury, induce by illegal gratuity, instigate, offer an inducement, procure another to commit perjury, procure indirectly, seduce, *subornare,* tamper with
ASSOCIATED CONCEPTS: suborn perjury

SUBPOENA, noun   call, citation, command, command to appear, demand, *denuntiatio testimonii,* directive, imperative, instruction, invocation, judicial imperative, legal mandate, legal process, mandate, notification, order, order to appear, order to appear in court, process, request, requirement to attend, summons, writ
ASSOCIATED CONCEPTS: information subpoena, judicial subpoena, *subpoena ad testificandum, subpoena duces tecum*

SUBPOENA, verb   beckon, call for the presence of, call forth, call out, call to witness, call with authority, command to appear, compel attendence, demand, *denuntiatio testimonii,* direct, direct the attendance of, issue a command, issue a court directive, issue a writ, issue process, notify to appear, order, order to appear, require compliance, require to attend, send for, summon, summon to court
ASSOCIATED CONCEPTS: subpoena a witness, subpoena before a jury, subpoena records, subpoena to a Grand Jury

SUBREPTION, noun   deception, deliberate misrepresentation, fabrication, false swearing, falsehood, falsification, guile, invention, lying, mendacity, misrepresentation, perjury, prevarication, untruth

SUBROGATION, noun   change, commutation, displacement, exchange, interchange, replacement, replacing, substitution, succession, supersedure, supersession, supplantation, supplanting, surrogation, switch, transfer, transference
ASSOCIATED CONCEPTS: conventional subrogation, legal subrogation, rights of subrogation

SUBSCRIBE *(Promise),* **verb**   advocate, agree, assent, consent, donate to, enroll, guarantee, patronize, pledge, promise to contribute, register, support, warrant

SUBSCRIBE *(Sign),* **verb**   acknowledge, affix one's signature, approve, attest, certify, confirm, endorse, inscribe, mark, ratify, seal, set a name to, sign a name to, undersign, underwrite, witness, write

SUBSCRIPTION, noun   acceptance, affirmation, agreement, approval, assent, authentication, certification, confirmation, consent, endorsement, enrollment, ratification, registration, sanction, signature, validation

SUBSEQUENT, *adjective*   coming, ensuing, eventual, following, future, *insequens,* later, latter, next, *posterior,* sequent, sequential, succeeding, trailing
ASSOCIATED CONCEPTS: subsequent condition, subsequent creditor

SUBSERVIENT, *adjective*   abject, accessory, adjuvant, aidful, aiding, ancillary, auxiliary, base, contributory, cringing, deferential, dependent, enslaved, fawning, helpful, inferior, ingratiating, junior, lesser, lower, menial, ministrant, obedient, obeisant, *obsequens,* obsequious, prostrate, secondary, serviceable, servile, slavish, subaltern, subject, submissive, subordinate, subsidiary, sycophantic, toadying, tractable, truckling, unassertive, unctious, useful, utilitarian, valuable

SUBSIDE, *verb*   abate, become less active, calm, *considere,* decline, decrease, descend, die away, diminish, dip, drop, dwindle, ebb, fall, fall away, fall off, grow less, lapse, lessen, let up, lull, melt away, mitigate, moderate, peter out, quiet, recede, relax, remit, *residere,* settle, shrink, sink, slack off, slacken, taper off, wane

SUBSIDIARY, *noun*   adjuvant, aiding, assistant, auxiliary, cooperating, helping, secondary, subordinate, subservient, *subsidiarius,* supplemental, supplementary
ASSOCIATED CONCEPTS: subsidiary corporation

SUBSIDIZE, *verb*   abet, *adiuvare,* advance, afford aid, afford support, aid, assist, back, befriend, bestow, bolster, contribute, endow, finance, foster, furnish aid, furnish support, further, give, give a grant to, give aid, give support to, help, help with money, keep, lend one's aid, lend support, maintain, patronize, pay, pay for, pay towards, promote, provide capital for, provide financing, provide for, provide funds for, provide money for, render assistance, stand behind, stand by, subscribe, subserve, subventionize, supply aid, supply support, support, sustain, underwrite, uphold

SUBSIDY, *noun*   allotment, allowance, backing, bounty, contribution, gift, grant, grant-in-aid, stipend, subsistence, subvention
ASSOCIATED CONCEPTS: government subsidy

SUBSIST, *verb*   abide, be, be nurtured, be supported, be sustained, *constare,* continue, endure, *esse,* exist, go on, hold on, last, live, maintain, outlast, outlive, perdure, persist, prevail, remain, remain alive, stand fast, stay, stay alive, survive

SUBSTANCE (*Essential nature*), *noun*   actuality, backbone, basis, body, content, core, drift, essence, essential part, force, gist, heart, hypostasis, idea, import, marrow, material, meaning, pith, principle, purport, reality, *res,* sense, significance, signification, soul, sum, tenor, vital part

SUBSTANCE (*Material possessions*), *noun*   assets, capital, command of money, *corpus,* estate, fortune, income, means, money, ownership, property, resources, revenue, riches, treasure, wealth, wherewithal

SUBSTANTIAL, *adjective*   abundant, ample, concrete, consequential, considerable, established, existent, existing, *firmus,* flush, genuine, *gravis,* great, important, large, plentiful, real, significant, sizable, strong, substantive, valid

ASSOCIATED CONCEPTS: substantial breach, substantial claim, substantial compliance, substantial controversy, substantial damages, substantial error, substantial evidence, substantial factor, substantial impairment, substantial injury, substantial interest, substantial issue, substantial justice, substantial performance, substantial question, substantial right, substantial use

SUBSTANTIATE, *verb*   actualize, affirm, attest, authenticate, bear out, bear witness, certify, circumstantiate, confirm, corroborate, demonstrate, embody, establish by proof, evidence, make good, materialize, objectify, prove, ratify, realize, reify, substantialize, support, uphold, validate, verify, vindicate
ASSOCIATED CONCEPTS: substantiate a claim, substantiate charges

SUBSTANTIVE, *adjective*   actual, appreciable, basic, concrete, considerable, constituent, elemental, essential, existent, existing, fundamental, important, independent, main, material, not subordinate, objective, palpable, positive, primary, principal, real, requisite, separate, solid, substantial, tangible, underlying, vital
ASSOCIATED CONCEPTS: substantive law, substantive right, substantive statute of limitations

SUBSTITUTE, *noun*   agent, alternate, alternative, auxiliary, delegate, deputy, double, emissary, envoy, factor, lieutenant, pinch hitter, plenipotentiary, proxy, regent, relief, replacement, representation, representative, stand-in, steward, stopgap, substitution, supplanter, surrogate, symbol, temporary expedient, trustee, understudy

SUBTERFUGE, *noun*   artifice, camouflage, chicane, chicanery, concealment, counterfeit, deception, *deverticulum,* device, dodge, duplicity, elusion, evasion, excuse, fabrication, falsehood, fib, fiction, finesse, forgery, guise, imposture, jugglery, *latebra,* lie, loophole, machination, maneuver, mask, plan, pretense, pretext, prevarication, ruse, sham, shift, smoke screen, sophistry, strategem, subtlety, trick, untruth

SUBTLE (*Insidious*), *adjective*   canny, contriving, crafty, cunning, deceitful, deceptive, designing, feline, guileful, illusive, implied, indistinct, inferred, insinuated, intriguing, serpentine, shifty, shrewd, sly, sophistical, stealthy, tricky, underhand, vulpine, wily

SUBTLE (*Refined*), *adjective*   accomplished, airy, apt, artful, artistic, astute, clever, deft, delicate, diplomatic, discerning, discreet, discriminating, exact, expert, keen, light, masterly, meticulous, perceptive, politic, precise, sagacious, sharp, skillful, slender, sophisticated, strategic, subtile, superfine, tactful

SUBVERSION, *noun*   abolition, annihilation, breakup, debacle, defeat, demolition, destruction, devastation, disestablishment, disruption, *eversio,* extinction, extirpation, incendiarism, inversion, overset, overthrow, overturn, perdition, rebellion, revolt, revolution, ruin, ruination, sabotage, sedition, subversive activities, upheaval, uprising, upset

SUBVERT, *verb*   annihilate, confound, corrupt, defeat, demolish, demoralize, despoil, destroy, devastate, disestablish, dismantle, disrupt, *evertere,* extinguish, extirpate, impair, injure, lay waste, level, overset, overthrow, overturn, pervert, pull down, put an end to, ruin,

spy against, *subvertere*, throw down, topple, tumble, turn over, undermine, undo, upset, vitiate
ASSOCIATED CONCEPTS: subvert the laws

SUCCEDANEUM, *noun*   change, ersatz, exchange, replacement, secondary, substitute, substitution

SUCCEED (*Attain*), *verb*   accomplish, achieve, acquire, advance, be victorious, bear fruit, bloom, capture, come through, conquer, do well, earn, fare well, flourish, fulfill, gain, gain a victory, make a hit, manage, master, meet with success, obtain, prevail, profit, progress, prosper, reach, realize, reap, *rem bene,* score a success, secure, surmount obstacles, thrive, triumph, vanquish, win, wrest

SUCCEED (*Follow*), *verb*   arise, be subsequent, come after, come subsequently, derive, develop, displace, ensue, *excipere,* follow after, follow in order, give place to, go after, go next, outmode, postdate, relieve, remove, replace, serve as a substitute, set aside, subrogate, substitute for, *succedere,* supersede, supervene, supplant, take over, take the place of

SUCCESSFUL, *adjective*   affluent, auspicious, blooming, blossoming, booming, champion, comfortable, effective, efficacious, felicitous, *felix,* flourishing, fortunate, *fortunatus,* fruitful, gainful, prevailing, profitable, prospering, prosperous, rich, satisfied, thriving, triumphant, unbeaten, undefeated, unvanquished, victorious, wealthy, well-off, well-situated, well-to-do, winning

SUCCESSION, *noun*   chain, concatenation, consecution, consecutive order, *continuatio,* cycle, descent, devolution, family, issue, lineage, offspring, order, posterity, procession, progeny, progression, sequence, series, successorship, train
ASSOCIATED CONCEPTS: hereditary succession, intestate succession, legal succession, line of succession, natural succession, successor employer, successor interest, testamentary succession
FOREIGN PHRASES: *Haereditas est successio in universum jus quod defunctus habuerit.* Inheritance is the succession to every right which the deceased had possessed. *Haereditas nihil aliud est, quam successio in universum jus, quod defunctus habuerit.* An inheritance is nothing other than the succession to all the rights which the deceased had. *Qui in jus dominiumve alterius succedit jure ejus uti debet.* One who succeeds to the ownership rights of another, should enjoy the rights of the other. *Non debeo melioris conditionis esse, quam auctor meus a quo jus in me transit.* I ought not to be in better condition than he to whose rights I succeed.

SUCCESSIVE, *adjective*   after, consecutive, ensuing, following, later, subsequent, succeeding, sequent, sequential
ASSOCIATED CONCEPTS: successive application, successive continuance, successive proceeding, successive term of imprisonment, successive writ

SUCCESSOR, *noun*   beneficiary, descendant, follower, grantee, newcomer, next in line, replacement, scion
ASSOCIATED CONCEPTS: successor in estate, successor in interest, successor in office, successor in trust

SUCCINCT, *adjective*   abbreviated, *brevis,* brief, compact, compendious, concise, condensed, curt, epigrammatic, expressed in few words, irreducible, laconic, pauciloquent, pithy, sententious, short, summary, synoptic, terse, to the point, trenchant

SUCCUMB, *verb*   accede, acquiesce, be defeated, bend, bow, break down, capitulate, cave in, cease, collapse, come to naught, come to terms, comply, concede, die, droop, drop, end, expire, fail, fall, flag, give in, give way, go down, go under, knuckle under, lose, perish, relent, resign, stoop, submit, *succumbere,* surrender, tire, yield

SUE, *verb*   appeal to the law, apply for, ask for relief, beseech, bring a legal action, bring an action, bring to justice, bring to the bar, claim, commence a suit, contest, entreat, file a legal claim, file suit, implore, initiate a civil action, institute a legal proceeding, institute process, legally pursue, litigate against, make appeal to, *orare,* petition, plead, prefer a claim, press a claim, pursue a claim, put on trial, *rogare,* seek by request, supplicate, take to court
ASSOCIATED CONCEPTS: power to sue, right to sue, standing to sue
FOREIGN PHRASES: *Nemo alieno nomine lege agere potest.* No one can sue in the name of another.

SUFFER (*Permit*), *verb*   abide, accede, accept, acquiesce, allow, assent, authorize, be reconciled, be resigned, bear with, brook, comply, concede, consent, empower, give consent, give leave, give permission, grant, grant permission, indulge, let, license, oblige, *pati, permittere,* put up with, *sinere,* tolerate

SUFFER (*Sustain loss*), *verb*   agonize, ail, anguish, be afflicted, be impaired, be injured, be racked, be stricken, be subjected to, be wounded, bear, endure, experience loss, feel pain, hurt, incur loss, languish, lose, *minui,* sacrifice, sustain damage
ASSOCIATED CONCEPTS: suffer harm, suffer loss

SUFFERANCE, *noun*   allowance, authorization, calmness, capacity to endure, composure, concession, control, countenance, forbearance, fortitude, imperturbation, indulgence, leave, license, longanimity, patience, patient endurance, *patientia,* permission, resignation, sanction, self-control, self-possession, self-restraint, stoicism, submission, suffering, tolerance, *toleratio,* toleration

SUFFICIENCY, *noun*   abundance, accumulation, adequacy, adequate resources, affluence, ample stock, ampleness, amplitude, cache, capacity, competence, competency, copiousness, cornucopia, enough, fill, full measure, fullness, fund, glut, hoard, large amount, plenitude, plenty, plethora, profuseness, profusion, *quod satis est,* redundance, repletion, reservoir, satiety, satisfactoriness, saturation, shower, store, sufficientness, superabundance, supply, surfeit, treasure, wealth, wherewithal
ASSOCIATED CONCEPTS: legal sufficiency, sufficiency of the evidence

SUFFRAGE, *noun*   affranchisement, autonomy, choice, emancipation, enfranchisement, exemption from control, exemption from restraint, franchise, freedom, freedom of choice, liberation, liberty, license, manumission, option, popular decision, prerogative,

right to vote, say, self-determination, self-government, *suffragium,* voice, vote
ASSOCIATED CONCEPTS: election law, voters' rights

SUGGESTION, noun   *admonitio,* advancement, advice, allusion, breath, clue, *consilium,* counsel, cue, exhortation, glimmer, hint, idea, implication, indication, inference, inkling, innuendo, insinuation, intimation, lead, motion, outline, overtone, pointer, possibility, prompting, prompture, proposal, proposition, recommendation, reminder, representation, resolution, scheme, slight trace, statement, suggested plan, suspicion, symbol, tentative statement, thought, tip, touch, trace, whisper
ASSOCIATED CONCEPTS: suggestion of error, suggestive interrogation

SUGGESTIVE (Evocative), adjective   allusive, commemorative, commemoratory, connotative, demonstrative, expressive, graphic, graphical, implicative, indicant, indicative, indicatory, inferential, insinuative, insinuatory, intriguing, lifelike, meaningful, ominous, pictorial, provocative, recollective, redolent, referential, remindful, reminiscent, reminiscential, symbolic, thought-provoking, vivid
ASSOCIATED CONCEPTS: suggestive lineup

SUGGESTIVE (Risqué), adjective   bawdy, carnal, coarse, erotic, improper, indecent, indelicate, lascivious, lecherous, lewd, libidinous, lickerish, loose, lurid, lustful, obscene, off-color, pornographic, provocative, racy, ribald, salacious, seductive, sexy, shameless, smutty, spicy, titillating, wanton

SUIT, noun   *actio,* action, action at law, action to serve justice, case, *causa,* cause, cause in court, judicial contest, lawsuit, legal action, legal proceeding, legal remedy, *lis,* litigation, petition, proceeding, suit in law, trial
ASSOCIATED CONCEPTS: class suits, nonsuit, suit against state
FOREIGN PHRASES: *Secta est pugna civilis; sicut actores armantur actionibus, et, quasi, accinguntur gladiis, ita rei muniuntur exceptionibus, et defenduntur, quasi, clypeis.* A suit is a civil battle; for as the plaintiffs are armed with actions, and, as it were, girded with swords, so the defendants are fortified with pleas, and are defended, as it were, with shields. *Frustra agit qui judicium prosequi nequit cum effectu.* He sues vainly who cannot prosecute his judgment with effect. *Nemo alieno nomine lege agere potest.* No one can sue in the name of another.

SUITABLE, adjective   acceptable, accommodating, accordant, adapted, adequate, admissible, advantageous, advisable, applicable, apposite, appropriate, apropos, apt, *aptus,* becoming, befitting, commensurate, commodious, compatible, condign, conformable, congenial, congruent, congruous, consentaneous, *consentaneus,* consistent, consonant, convenient, correct, correspondent, decent, decorous, deserved, desirable, due, eligible, expedient, favorable, feasible, felicitous, fit, fitting, germane, harmonious, idoneous, *idoneus,* just, likely, meet, merited, opportune, pat, pertinent, practicable, proper, proportionate, qualified, reasonable, reconcilable, relevant, right, rightful, satisfactory, seasonable, seemly, sufficient, suited, timely, valid, worthy
ASSOCIATED CONCEPTS: suitable for a particular purpose

SUITOR, noun   appellant, applicant, claimant, litigant, litigator, party to a suit, petitioner, plaintiff, pleader, seeker, solicitor, suppliant, supplicant

SULLY, verb   asperse, attaint, bedim, begrime, belittle, bemire, besmear, blacken, blemish, blot, blur, brand, contaminate, corrupt, daub, debase, decry, deface, defame, defile, degrade, denigrate, denounce, deprecate, depreciate, dirty, discredit, disgrace, dishonor, disparage, dispraise, drabble, dull, foul, gibbet, impeach, impugn, injure, *inquinare,* knock, *maculare,* make unclean, malign, mar, pollute, put to shame, run down, shame, slur, smear, smirch, smudge, soil, spatter, speak ill of, splash, spoil, spot, stain, stigmatize, taint, tarnish, traduce, vilify, vilipend, vitiate

SUM (tally), noun   compendium, essence, figure, gist, idea conveyed, meaning, score, substance, summary

SUM (total), noun   aggregate amount, all, entirety, everything, gross amount, sum total, the whole, totality, wholeness
ASSOCIATED CONCEPTS: sum paid, sum and substance, sum in controversy, sum certain, sum demanded, sum in question

SUM, verb   add, compute, count up, figure up, reckon up, summate, total

SUMMARY, adjective   *brevis,* concise, direct, done without delay, expeditious, hasty, hurried, immediate, instantaneous, prompt, quick, quickly executed, quickly performed, rapid, speedy, sudden, swift
ASSOCIATED CONCEPTS: summary action, summary contempt, summary conviction, summary hearing, summary judgment, summary proceeding, summary process, summary punishment

SUMMARY, noun   abbreviation, abridgment, abstract, analysis, brief, compend, compendium, compilation, compressed statement, conspectus, core, digest, *epitoma,* epitome, minute, note, outline, pandect, recap, recapitulation, report, restatement, review, short version, skeleton, *summarium,* syllabus, synopsis

SUMMON, verb   *advocare, appellare,* beckon, bid, call for, call for the presence of, call forth, call into action, call to witness, call with authority, charge, cite, command, command to appear, compel attendance, demand, give orders, issue a command, issue a court directive, issue process, notify to appear, order, order to appear, require compliance, require to attend, send for, subpoena
ASSOCIATED CONCEPTS: summon to appear in court

SUMMONS, noun   authoritative citation to appear before a court, authoritative command, bid, calling to court, citation, command to appear, commandment, direction, invocation, legal process, mandate, notification to appear, official call, official court order, official notice, official order, order to appear, request to appear, writ, written notification to appear in court

SUPERANNUATE, verb   antiquate, cancel, dismiss, make extinct, make obsolete, make outdated, remove, replace, retire, shelve, withdraw

SUPERCILIOUS, adjective   arrogant, assumptive, bumptious, cavalier, condescending, contemptuous, contumelious, derisive, dictatorial, disdainful, disrespectful, domineering, egotistic, *fastidiosus,* haughty, imperious, insolent, intolerant, irreverent, lofty, lordly, magisterial, overbearing, overweening, patronizing, peremptory, pompous, presumptuous, prideful, proud, puffed up, scornful, *superbus,* swollen, toplofty, uppish, uppity, vainglorious, withering

SUPERFICIAL, *adjective* careless, cursory, depthless, desultory, empty, exterior, external, frivolous, hasty, hurried, inane, insubstantial, lax, *levis,* outward, perfunctory, sciolistic, shallow, shoal, silly, skindeep, slapdash, slight, surface, trifling, trivial, unthinking

SUPERFLUOUS, *adjective* additional, adscititious, dispensable, duplicate, excess, excrescent, expendable, extra, extravagant, inessential, inordinate, lavish, luxuriant, luxurious, more than enough, more than sufficient, needless, overflowing, overmuch, prodigal, profuse, redundant, remaining, remanent, residual, residuary, spare, superabundant, supererogative, supererogatory, supernumerary, supervacaneous, *supervacaneus, supervacuus,* supplemental, surplus, uncalled-for, unessential, unnecessary, useless, wasteful
ASSOCIATED CONCEPTS: superfluous lands

SUPERINTEND, *verb* administer, *administrare,* administrate, boss, caretake, command, control, direct, exercise charge over, exercise supervision over, govern, guide, handle, have charge of, head, instruct, keep in order, lead, look after, manage, overlook, oversee, pilot, *praeesse, procurare,* regulate, rule, see to, steer, supervise, watch

SUPERINTENDENT, *noun* administrator, agent, captain, caretaker, chief, controller, curator, custodian, director, foreman, governor, guardian, intendant, leader, manager, master, monitor, overseer, *praefectus,* proctor, steward, supervisor, taskmaster, warden

SUPERIOR *(Excellent),* *adjective* above average, above par, better, choice, deluxe, distinguished, exceptional, finer, first-rate, foremost, greater, high-class, high-grade, high-quality, illustrious, incomparable, matchless, *melior,* noble, nonpareil, peerless, *praestantior,* preferable, preferred, second to none, superexcellent, superlative, supreme, topping, transcendent, unequaled, unexcelled, unparalleled, unrivalled, unsurpassed

SUPERIOR *(Higher),* *adjective* chief, greater, more elevated, of greater influence, of higher rank, paramount, senior
ASSOCIATED CONCEPTS: respondeat superior, superior court, superior force

SUPERLATIVE, *adjective* best, champion, chief, consummate, crowning, excellent, excessive, *eximius,* extreme, first-rate, foremost, greatest, highest, immoderate, incomparable, inflated, inimitable, matchless, most eminent, nonpareil, *optimus,* paramount, peerless, prime, principal, second to none, sovereign, super, superexcellent, superfine, superior, supreme, surpassing, tiptop, transcendent, unequaled, unexcelled, unmatched, unparalleled, unrivaled, unsurpassed, utmost, without parallel

SUPERSEDE, *verb* abolish, annul, discard, displace, make obsolete, make void, nullify, obviate, oust, override, overrule, preclude, put in the place of, remove, repeal, replace, set aside, stand in stead of, subrogate, substitute, *succedere,* succeed, supplant, take the place of, void
ASSOCIATED CONCEPTS: superseding cause

SUPERVENE, *verb* arise, be subsequent, bechance, befall, come to pass, crop up, ensue, eventuate, follow, happen, issue, occur, result, spring up, succeed, *supervenire,* take place

SUPERVISION, *noun* administration, care, charge, command, control, direction, government, gubernation, guidance, inspection, jurisdiction, management, oversight, *procuratio,* proctorage, regulation, steerage, stewardship, superintendence, surveillance
ASSOCIATED CONCEPTS: direct supervision, general supervision, person in need of supervision, personal supervision, right of supervision, supervision and control, supervisory powers

SUPPLANT, *verb* abolish, act for, bring low, cashier, cause the downfall of, depose, deracinate, dethrone, discharge, dismiss, displace, drive away, drive out, eject, eradicate, expel, extirpate, fire, force out, oust, overthrow, overpower, remove, replace, retire, subrogate, substitute, subvert, succeed, supersede, take over, take the place of, transfer, turn out, undermine, unseat, uproot, upset, usurp

SUPPLEMENT, *verb* add, add to, amend, amplify, augment, bolster, broaden, buttress, complement, contribute to, enhance, enlarge, enrich, expand, fortify, improve, increase, lengthen, magnify, reinforce, strengthen, subsidize, superadd, widen

SUPPLEMENTARY, *adjective* accessory, additional, additive, adjunct, adscititious, ancillary, attendant, augmentative, auxiliary, collateral, concomitant, extra, incidental, nonessential, secondary, spare, subordinate, subsidiary, supervenient, supplemental, suppletive, suppletory, unessential
ASSOCIATED CONCEPTS: supplementary proceedings

SUPPLIER, *noun* caterer, chandler, commissary, contractor, furnisher, giver, merchant, provider, provisioner, purveyor, seller, steward, trader, victualer

SUPPLY, *verb* accommodate with, accouter, administer, afford, bestow, cater, contribute, deal out, deliver, distribute, endow, endue, equip, feed, fill up, fit out, furnish, give, grant, invest, lavish, maintain, minister, *ministrare,* oblige, outfit, present, provide, provision, purvey, recruit, refill, render, replenish, satisfy, serve, stock, *suppeditare,* suppeditate, sustain, victual, yield

SUPPORT *(Assistance),* *noun* accommodation, *adiumentum,* aid, assist, assistance, *auxilium,* backing, comfort, contribution, cooperation, defense, encouragement, endowment, help, helping hand, lift, livelihood, mainstay, maintenance, patronage, preservation, promotion, protection, relief, subsistence, succor, *subsidium,* sustenance, upkeep
ASSOCIATED CONCEPTS: alimony, child support, failure to provide support, inadequate support, maintenance

SUPPORT *(Corroboration)*, **noun**　　affirmation, approval, attestation, authentication, backing, certification, circumstantiation, confirmation, documentation, endorsement, fortification, justification, ratification, strengthening, substantiation, validation, verification, vindication

SUPPORT *(Assist)*, **verb**　　accommodate, *adesse*, aid, back, bolster, champion, come to the defense of, come to the help of, contribute, cooperate with, defend, endorse, facilitate, feed, finance, furnish funds, further, help, lend money to, maintain, minister to, nourish, patronize, promote, protect, provide for, reinforce, second, subsidize, *suffragari*, supply the necessities of, sustain, take care of, take the part of, uphold
FOREIGN PHRASES: *Parentum est liberos alere atiam nothos.* It is the duty of parents to support their children even when illegitimate.

SUPPORT *(Corroborate)*, **verb**　　accredit, affirm, attest, authenticate, back up, bear out, buttress, certify, circumstantiate, confirm, establish, make absolute, make good, make more certain, prove, ratify, reinforce, strengthen, substantiate, sustain, uphold in evidence, validate, verify, vindicate, vouch for

SUPPORT *(Justify)*, **verb**　　account for, approve, defend, defend successfully, explain, give grounds for, make defense for, make legitimate, provide justification, say in defense, stand up for, vindicate

SUPPOSITION, *noun*　　assumption, belief, conception, *coniectura*, conjecture, guess, hypothesis, likelihood, likeliness, *opinio*, opinion, position, postulate, premise, presumption, probability, speculation, supposal, surmise, suspicion, theorem, theory, thesis
FOREIGN PHRASES: *In claris non est locus conjecturis.* In matters which are obvious there is no room for conjecture.

SUPPRESS, *verb*　　arrest, ban, burke, bury, cancel, censor, check, choke, choke back, cloak, conceal, cover up, crush, delete, end, *exstinguere*, extinguish, gag, hush up, inhibit, keep back, keep down, keep out of sight, keep secret, mask, muffle, obstruct, overcome, overpower, overthrow, overwhelm, prevent, prohibit, quash, quell, quench, repress, *reprimere*, restrain, screen, shroud, silence, smother, stifle, still, stop, strangle, subdue, *supprimere*, vanquish, veil
ASSOCIATED CONCEPTS: motion to suppress evidence

SUPREMACY, *noun*　　ascendancy, authority, championship, chieftaincy, command, control, direction, *dominatio*, domination, dominion, governance, headship, highest position, importance, influence, leadership, lordship, management, masterdom, mastership, mastery, omnipotence, paramountcy, power, precedence, predominance, predominancy, predomination, preeminence, primacy, *principatus*, regulation, rule, scepter, sovereignty, superintendence, superiority, supervision, supreme authority, supremeness, sway, transcendence, transcendency, triumph, upperhand, victory
ASSOCIATED CONCEPTS: Supremacy Clause

SURCHARGE, *noun*　　added charge, additional charge, excessive burden, excessive charge, extra charge, extra fee, overassessment, overburden, overcharge, overload, penalty

ASSOCIATED CONCEPTS: identifiable surcharge, surcharge for services

SURETY *(Certainty)*, **noun**　　absolute confidence, absoluteness, affirmance, affirmation, aplomb, ascertainment, asseveration, assurance, assuredness, averment, avowal, avowance, certain knowledge, certification, certitude, complete conviction, confirmation, contract, conviction, convincement, declaration, definiteness, determination, earnest averment, earnest avowal, earnest declaration, firmness, guaranty, hardihood, persuasion, positiveness, pronouncement, reassurance, reliance on, self-assurance, self-conviction, solemn averment, solemn avowal, solemn declaration, sureness, unequivocalness, unmistakableness, unquestionableness, vow, warrant

SURETY *(Guarantor)*, **noun**　　attester, backer, certifier, confirmer, consignee, endorser, financer, indemnitor, insurer, promisor, ratifier, signatory, signer, sponsor, subscriber, supporter, underwriter, voucher, warrantor
ASSOCIATED CONCEPTS: surety bond, surety company, surety insurance, surety of the peace
FOREIGN PHRASES: *In veram quantitatem fidejussor teneatur, nisi pro certa quantitate accessit.* A surety should be held for the true quantity, unless he agreed for a certain quantity. *Natura fide jussionis sit strictissimi juris et non durat vel extendatur de re ad rem, de persona ad personam, de tempore ad tempus.* The nature of a suretyship is one of strictest law and cannot endure or be extended from one thing to another, from one person to another, or from one time to another.

SURFEIT, *noun*　　avalanche, deluge, excess, excessive amount, fullness, glut, inundation, nimiety, overabundance, overdose, overflow, overfullness, overload, oversupply, plenty, profuseness, profusion, redundance, repletion, satiation, *satietas*, satiety, satisfaction, saturation, superabundance, superfluity, supersaturation, surplus, surplusage

SURMISE, *verb*　　apprehend, assume, *augurari*, be of the opinion, believe, conceive, conclude, conjecture, count, deduce, deem, divine, esteem, fancy, feel, gather, guess, have an idea, hazard a guess, hypothesize, imagine, infer, judge, opine, posit, predicate, presume, presuppose, regard, speculate, suppose, suspect, *suspicari*, theorize, think, trow, understand, view, ween

SURMOUNT, *verb*　　beat, clear, climb, command, conquer, crest, crown, defeat, dominate, exceed, excel, *exsuperare*, get the better of, go beyond, master, outdo, outmaneuver, outrival, overcome, overpass, overpower, overthrow, overturn, pass, prevail over, rise above, rout, scale, subdue, subjugate, surpass, top, transcend, *transcendere*, triumph over, upset, vanquish, vault

SURPASS, *verb*　　*antecellere*, be greater, be superior, beat, better, break the record, cap, come first, distance, eclipse, exceed, excel, *excellere*, get ahead, go beyond, go one better, have the upper hand, improve upon, leave behind, outmaneuver, outclass, outdo, outmatch, outnumber, outplay, outrank, outrival, outrun, outshine, outstrip, outvie, outweigh, overshadow, pass, predominate, prevail, rank first, reach a new high, rise above, rival, supererogate, take prprecedence, top, tower over, transcend, triumph over

SURPLUS, noun   balance, bonus, excess, expletive, glut, leavings, margin, nimiety, overabundance, overage, overflow, overmeasure, overplus, overrun, oversupply, redundance, redundancy, remainder, residue, *residuum,* spare, superabundance, superfluity, superplus, supersaturation, surfeit, surplusage
ASSOCIATED CONCEPTS: accumulated surplus, distribution of surplus, surplus after sale, surplus goods, surplus income, surplus of proceeds, transfer to surplus

SURPRISE, noun   *admiratio,* amazement, astonishment, astoundment, bafflement, bewilderment, consternation, lack of warning, *miratio,* shock, unexpected event, unexpected occurrence, unforeseen contingency, unforeseen event, unforeseen occurrence, unsuspected event, unusual occurrence, wonder, wonderment
ASSOCIATED CONCEPTS: take an opposing party by surprise

SURRENDER *(Give back),* **verb**   abdicate, abjure, abnegate, cede, disclaim, disown, forego, forfeit, forsake, forswear, hand over, let go, part with, reinstate, relinquish, render up, renounce, resign, restore, return, waive

SURRENDER *(Yield),* **verb**   acquiesce, agree to, back down, be submissive, capitulate, concede, *dedere,* give in, obey, relent, submit, succumb, *tradere*

SURREPTITIOUS, adjective   artful, clandestine, *clandestinus,* concealed, conniving, covert, crafty, cunning, deceitful, deceptive, delitescent, disguised, done by stealth, evasive, faked, fraudulently introduced, furtive, *furtivus,* guileful, hidden, indirect, insidious, lurking, mysterious, obreptitious, private, secret, secretive, sneaky, stealthy, subdolous, subtle, tricky, uncommunicative, undercover, underground, underhand, undisclosed, unknown, unseen, unspied, unsuspected, veiled, vulpine, wily

SURROGATE, adjective   acting, alternate, delegated, deputy, foster, imitation, makeshift, provisional, proxy, pseudo, representative, simulated, stand-in, substitute, substitutional, vicarial, vicarious, *vicarius*

SURVEILLANCE, noun   care, charge, circumspection, examination, guard, heed, inspection, lookout, observation, oversight, protection, scrutiny, stewardship, superintendence, supervision, vigil, vigilance, watch, watchfulness

SURVEY *(Examine),* **verb**   analyze, appraise, consider, *considerare, contemplari,* evaluate, inspect, keep an eye upon, keep watch, look at, observe, overlook, oversee, peruse, reconnoiter, review, scan, scrutinize, search, *spectare,* study, view, watch, weigh

SURVEY *(Poll),* **verb**   canvass, compute, count, count ballots, count votes, enroll, enumerate, estimate, list, register, review, tabulate, take stock, test, total

SURVIVAL, noun   being, continuance, continuation, continuation of life, durability, duration, endurance, existence, extension, life, maintenance, permanence, prolongation

SUSCEPTIBLE *(Responsive),* **adjective**   compassionate, easily affected, flexible, impressible, impressionable, influenceable, *mollis,* movable, persuadable, pliant, reactive, readily impressed, receptive, sensitive, susceptive, swayable, sympathetic

SUSCEPTIBLE *(Unresistent),* **adjective**   exposed, helpless, in danger, liable, nonresistant, open, predisposed, resistless, sensitive, undefended, unprotected, unsafe, vulnerable, yielding

SUSPECT, noun   accused, accused person, alleged malfeasor, alleged offender, alleged transgressor, alleged wrongdoer, individual under suspicion, one suspected of a crime, person accused of crime, presumed wrongdoer, suspected criminal
ASSOCIATED CONCEPTS: defendant

SUSPECT *(Distrust),* **verb**   be doubtful, be dubious, be skeptical, be suspicious, disbelieve, doubt, feel distrust, harbor suspicious, have no confidence in, lack confidence in, misdoubt, misgive, mistrust, question, without reliance in
ASSOCIATED CONCEPTS: suspect of wrongdoing

SUSPECT *(Think),* **verb**   assume, be of the opinion, believe, conclude, conjecture, consider, deduce, deem, divine, fancy, gather, guess, have the idea, hold, hypothesize, imagine, infer, judge, opine, posit, presume, presuppose, reckon, speculate, suppose, surmise, *suspicari, suspicionem habere,* take for granted, theorize, understand, view

SUSPEND, verb   arrest, break off, bring to a standstill, bring to a stop, cease, check, defer, delay, desist, *differre,* discharge, discontinue, halt, hinder, hold in abeyance, interfere with, intermit, *intermittere,* interrupt, lay aside, lay off, leave off, postpone, put off, remit, remove, shelve, stall, stay, stop, table, temporize
ASSOCIATED CONCEPTS: suspend a license, suspend a sentence, suspend an employee, suspend payment, suspend the power of alienation, suspend the writ of habeas corpus

SUSPICION *(Mistrust),* **noun**   apprehension, cynicism, disbelief, distrust, doubt, doubtfulness, dubiety, dubiousness, fear, fearfulness, incredulity, lack of faith, lack of trust, misdoubt, misgiving, qualm, skepticism, *suspicio,* suspiciousness, trepidation, unbelief
ASSOCIATED CONCEPTS: suspicious circumstances, suspicious origin
FOREIGN PHRASES: **Dona clandestina sunt semper suspiciosa.** Clandestine gifts are always open to suspicion.

SUSPICION *(Uncertainty),* **noun**   chance, conjecture, doubtfulness, guess, hint, impression, incertitude, inconclusiveness, inference, inkling, insecurity, intimation, notion, postulate, postulation, question, speculation, suggestion, supposition, surmise, trace, unsureness

SUSPICIOUS *(Distrustful),* **adjective**   apprehensive, cautious, concerned, disposed to doubt, doubting, dubious, fearful, hard to convince, hesitant, inconvincible, jealous, leery, mistrustful, nervous, quizzical, skeptical, suspecting, *suspiciosus,* untrustful, untrusting, untrustworthy, wary, watchful

SUSPICIOUS *(Questionable),* **adjective**   abnormal, cryptic, doubtful, dubious, enigmatic, equivocal, farfetched, hard to believe, irregular, open to doubt, open to question, peculiar, strange, suspect, unbelievable,

uncertain, unconvincing, unplausible, unworthy of belief
ASSOCIATED CONCEPTS: suspicious circumstances, suspicious origin

SUSTAIN *(Confirm), verb* affirm, approve, assent to, attest, authenticate, bear out, buttress, certify, circumstantiate, consent to, corroborate, defend, document, endorse, establish, evidence, justify, make firm, prove, ratify, reinforce, sanction, settle, strenghten, substantiate, support, uphold, uphold in evidence, validate, verify, vindicate
ASSOCIATED CONCEPTS: sustain a lower court's decision

SUSTAIN *(Prolong), verb* attentuate, bolster, conserve, continue, contribute to, elongate, extend, fortify, guard, keep going, keep up, lengthen, maintain, nourish, perpetuate, preserve, promote, protect, protract, reinforce, save, spare, strengthen, stretch, *sustentare, sustinere,* uphold

SUSTENANCE, *noun* aliment, alimentation, *alimentum,* food, keep, living, maintenance, means of sustaining life, necessities, nourishment, nutriment, nutrition, provisions, subsistence, supplies, support, sustentation, upkeep, victuals, *victus*

SWEAR, *verb* adjure, affirm, allege under oath, assert as true, assure, authenticate, aver, avow, bear witness, bind oneself by oath, certify, confirm, declare, declare solemnly, declare true, give a promise, give evidence, give one's word, guarantee, *iurare, iureiurando adfirmare,* maintain under oath, promise, put one's trust in, state, state under oath, utter an oath, vouch, vow
ASSOCIATED CONCEPTS: false swearing, public swearing
FOREIGN PHRASES: *In judicio non creditur nisi juratis.* In a court of justice no one is given credence who is not sworn.

SYMBOL, *noun* abbreviation, badge, clue, connotation, cue, delineation, depiction, emblem, enactment, ensign, exponent, gesture, image, index, indication, manifestation, mark, model, notation, note, picture, portrayal, representation, seal, sign, signal, signification, *signum, symbolum,* symptom, token, trademark, visible sign
ASSOCIATED CONCEPTS: trademark

SYMPATHIZE, *verb* be compassionate, be moved, be sorry for, be touched, be understanding, comfort, commiserate, condole, *congruere,* console, *eadem sentire,* empathize, express sympathy, feel for, grieve with, have pity, identify with, lament with, *misereri,* mourn with, pity, share grief, share sorrow, show mercy, show tenderness, solace, soothe, understand

SYMPTOM, *noun* alarm, augury, characteristic, clue, danger signal, diagnostic, evidence, evincement, feature, forewarning, guide, index, indicant, indication, indicator, indice, *indicium,* intimation, manifestation, mark, means of recognition, monition, monitor, *nota,* notice, preindication, premonitor, premonitory sign, prognostic, sign, signal, token, trait, warning, warning sign

SYNCHRONISM, *noun* accompaniment, accord, *aequalitas temporum,* agreement, attunement, coexistence, coincidence, compatibility, concord, concurrence, conformity, consistency, harmony, simultaneity, simultaneousness, unison

SYNDICATE, *noun* alliance, association, cartel, coalition, combine, company, consortium, council, federation, guild, league, machine, merger, organization, partnership, pool, ring, *societas,* union

SYNERGETIC, *adjective* coacting, coactive, collaborative, concurrent, concurring, co-operant, cooperative, coworking, in agreement, in concord

SYNERGY, *noun* coaction, coincidence, collaboration, combined action, combined effect, combined operation, concert, concurrence, cooperation, cooperative action, joint effect, synergism, united action

SYNOPSIS, *noun* abridgment, abstract, brief, compend, compendium, condensation, conspectus, digest, *epitome,* minute, outline, recapitulation, review, *summarium,* summary, summation

SYNTHETIC, *adjective* artificial, counterfeit, ersatz, factitious, illegitimate, man-made, manufactured, mock, not genuine, not natural, pretended, pseudo, quasi, spurious, unnatural

SYSTEM, *noun* arrangement, *artificium,* classification, design, *formula,* logical process, manner, means, method, mode of management, operation, order, orderliness, orderly combination, organization, pattern, plan, policy, practice, procedure, process, program, recipe, regime, regimen, regularity, routine, scheme, settled procedure, state of order, strategy, technique, way
ASSOCIATED CONCEPTS: commercial system, governmental system, judicial system, legal system, retirement system

SYSTEMATIC, *adjective* according to rule, *accuratus,* arranged, businesslike, classified, disciplined, exact, habitual, in order, methodical, ordered, orderly, organized, precise, regular, regulated, routine, standardized, systematical, thorough, thoroughgoing, under control, uniform, well-ordered, well-organized, well-regulated

T

TABULATE, *noun* alphabetize, allocate, arrange, assign places to, catalogue, chart, chronicle, codify, coordinate, docket, enumerate, file, grade, graduate, group, index, inventory, itemize, list, marshal, methodize, organize, rank, register, sort, systematize

TACIT, *adjective* allusive, assumed, connoted, implicit, implied, indicated, inferential, inferred, not openly expressed, silent, suggested, symbolized, *tacitus,* taken for granted, undeclared, understood, unexpressed, unmentioned, unpronounced, unsaid, unspoken, unstated, untold, unvoiced, wordless
ASSOCIATED CONCEPTS: tacit approval, tacit consent

TACITURN, *adjective* brusque, close, closemouthed, curt, dumb, guarded, habitually silent, inarticulate, laconic, mum, mute, pauciloquent, quiet, reserved, restrained, reticent, secretive, silent, sparing of words, speechless, *taciturnus,* uncommunicative, ungarrulous, unloquacious, unsociable, untalkative, unvocal, withdrawn

TACTICAL, *adjective* aimed, artful, *astutus,* blueprinted, calculated, *cautus,* considered, contrived, crafty, cunning, deliberate, designed, devised, diplomatic, diplomatical, engineered, intended, intriguing, knowing, maneuvering, organized, planned, plotted, politic, prepared, *prudens,* purposed, purposeful, skillful, strategic, strategical, studied, systematized, weighed, well-planned, well-thought-out

TAINT *(Contaminate), verb* adulterate, alloy, befoul, besmirch, blemish, blight, *contaminare,* decay, defile, degrade, dirty, disease, envenom, foul, *imbuere,* infect, make noxious, make putrid, poison, pollute, putrefy, render impure, rot, soil, spoil, sully
ASSOCIATED CONCEPTS: tainted evidence

TAINT *(Corrupt), verb* cause to be dishonest, debase, debauch, defile, degenerate, demoralize, deprave, despoil, destroy the integrity of, lower morally, misuse, pervert, suborn, tarnish, violate, vitiate

TAINTED *(Contaminated), adjective* adulterated, befouled, blighted, defiled, dirtied, dirty, diseased, envenomed, foul, impaired, impure, infected, noxious, poisoned, polluted, putrefied, putrid, rancid, rotten, smirched, soiled, spoiled, stained, sullied, unclean

ASSOCIATED CONCEPTS: Fruit of the Poisonous Tree Doctrine, tainted evidence

TAINTED *(Corrupted), adjective* abandoned, criminal, debased, debauched, degenerate, degraded, demoralized, depraved, dishonest, dissolute, evil, immoral, low, perverted, profligate, reprobate, rotten, shameless, vicious, vitiated, warped, wicked

TAKEOVER, *noun* acquisition, obtainment, procurement, purchase, transference
ASSOCIATED CONCEPTS: corporate raider, corporate takeover

TAKEOVER, *verb* arrogate, assume, command, seize, take command, take charge, take possession, usurp

TAKING, *noun* abduction, *acceptio,* acquisition, ademption, appropriation, capture, confiscation, deprivation, dispossession, distraint, divestment, expropriation, foreclosure, impoundage, impoundment, *occupatio,* preemption, seizure, sequestration
ASSOCIATED CONCEPTS: attachment, eminent domain

TAMPER, *verb* alter, change, convert, corrupt, debase, hinder, interfere, intermeddle, intervene, manipulate, meddle
ASSOCIATED CONCEPTS: tamper with a jury, tamper with evidence

TANGENTIAL, *adjective* akin, associated, attendant, connected, correlated, dependent on, digressive, excursive, extraneous, germane, incidental, interrelated, nonessential, pertinent, related, subordinate, tangent, touching

TANGIBLE, *adjective* actual, certain, clear-cut, concrete, corporal, corporeal, definite, discernible by touch, embodied, evident, manifest, material, not elusive, not vague, obvious, palpable, perceivable, perceptible, physical, plain, positive, real, solid, somatic, substantial, substantive, tactile, tactual, touchable, *tractabilis,* verifiable, visible, well-defined
ASSOCIATED CONCEPTS: tangible object, tangible property, tangible value

TANTAMOUNT, *adjective*   analogous, comparable, corresponding to, ditto, equal, equivalent, identical, parallel, similar, synonymous

TARGET, *noun*   aim, ambition, aspiration, butt, center, contemplation, design, desired object, destination, end, goal, hope, intention, mark, motive, object, objective, plan, point

TARIFF *(Bill), noun*   account, itemized account, list, list of items, money's worth, quoted price, price list, scale of prices, table of charges

TARIFF *(Duties), noun*   assessment, duty, excise, impost, levy, schedule of duties, tax

TARNISH, *verb*   asperse, befoul, blacken, blemish, blot, brand, cloud, contaminate, corrode, darken, deface, defame, degrade, denigrate, desecrate, dim, dirty, discolor, discredit, disgrace, dishonor, dull, fade, foul, *inquinare,* lose luster, maculate, pollute, shame, slander, slur, smear, smirch, smudge, soil, spot, stain, stigmatize, sully, taint, vilify
ASSOCIATED CONCEPTS: defamation

TARTUFFISH, *adjective*   affected, dissembling, false, feigned, hypocritical, insincere, pious, pretended, puritanical, sanctimonious, two-faced

TAUTOLOGY, *noun*   battology, duplication, loquacity, pleonasm, profuseness, redundancy, repetition, superfluousness, surfeit, verbiage, verbosity

TAWDRY, *adjective*   baroque, bedizened, blatant, brummagem, catchpenny, cheap, common, crass, crude, flashy, garish, gaudy, glaring, glittering, inelegant, loud, meretricious, ostentatious, pretentious, shoddy, showy, sleazy, tasteless, tinsel, vulgar

TAX, *noun*   assessment, capitation, charge, dues, duty, exaction, exactment, excise, imposition, impost, levy, pollage, *portorium,* scot, tariff, taxation, tithe, toll, tribute, *vectigal*
ASSOCIATED CONCEPTS: action for taxes, *ad valorem tax,* apportionment of taxes, back taxes, collection of taxes, current tax, delinquent tax, direct tax, discriminatory tax, double taxation, estate tax, evasion of taxation, excess profits tax, excessive tax, excise tax, federal estate tax, federal taxes, franchise tax, general tax, graduated tax, income tax, indirect tax, inheritance tax, land tax, levy a tax, personal tax, power of taxation, power to tax, progressive tax, property tax, proportional tax, regulatory tax, retroactive tax, sales tax, tax anticipation note, tax assessor, tax deed, tax district, tax lien, tax roll, tax sale, tax title, tax warrants, taxpayer, transfer tax, withholding taxes

TAX *(Levy), verb*   assess, collect, exact, lay a duty, require

TAX *(Overwork), verb*   burden, cumber, debilitate, deplete, deprive of strength, disable, drain, encumber, enervate, exact, fatigue, load, make excessive demands, oppress, overexercise, overexert, overfatigue, overload, overstrain, overtire, overuse, push too far, require, saddle with, strain, task, tire out, tyrannize, use hard, weaken, wear down, wear out, weary, weigh down

TECHNICAL, *adjective*   abstruse, difficult to understand, highly specialized, highly specific, industrial, mechanical, occupational, professional, scientific, special, specialized, specific, trained, vocational

TECHNICALITY, *noun*   aspect, detail, distinctive feature, fact, feature, fine point, inessentiality, item, method, minor point, minutiae, nuance, particular, particularity, peculiarity, petty detail, point, precept, rule, singularity, special point, speciality, specific, specification, subtlety, technical term, term, trifle, triviality

TEMERITY, *noun*   audacity, boldness, carelessness, daring, effrontery, foolhardiness, foolishness, gall, hastiness, heedlessness, impetuosity, improvidence, imprudence, impudence, incautiousness, inconsiderateness, indiscretion, injudiciousness, nerve, overconfidence, presumptuousness, procacity, rashness, recklessness, rudeness, shamelessness, *temeritas,* thoughtlessness, unthoughtfulness, venturesomeness, want of caution

TEMPERAMENT, *noun*   aptitude, attitude, carriage, character, composition, constitution, demeanor, disposition, ethos, makeup, mentality, nature, patience, personality, qualities, structure, style, tendency, tenor, way

TEMPERANCE, *noun*   abnegation, abstemiousness, abstention, abstinence, calmness, control, forbearance, frugality, indulgence, moderateness, *moderatio,* moderation, patience, prohibition, prudence, restraint, self-control, self-denial, self-restraint, soberness, sobriety, sparing use, teetotalism, *temperantia,* temperateness, tolerance, toleration, unexcessiveness

TEMPERED, *adjective*   adapted, adjusted, altered, changed, corrected, indurate, indurated, moderated, modified, recast, reconstructed, remolded, reshaped, revised, transformed, treated

TEMPORARY, *adjective*   acting, *ad tempus,* brief, changeable, deciduous, elusive, ephemeral, evanescent, fleeting, fugacious, fugitive, impermanent, interim, limited, makeshift, momentary, monohemerous, nondurable, passing, perishable, provisional, shifting, short-lived, stopgap, temporal, transient, transitional, transitive, transitory, unenduring, unstable, volatile
ASSOCIATED CONCEPTS: temporary restraining order

TENABLE, *adjective*   acceptable, befitting, believable, capable of being maintained, defendable, defensible, dependable, deserving, fitting, immune, imperdible, impregnable, inviolable, invulnerable, justifiable, legitimate, logical, maintainable, plausible, proper, rational, reasonable, reliable, strong, supportable, trustworthy, unassailable, unattackable, unchallengeable, unquestionable, vindicable, warrantable, wellfounded, well-grounded

TENACITY, *noun*   ability to pursue, adhesiveness, backbone, cohesiveness, constancy, courage, determination, diligence, doggedness, endurance, firmness, grip, grit, immovability, indefatigability, intransigence, iron will, obduracy, obstinacy, perseverance, persistence, persistency, *pertinacia,* pertinaciousness, pertinacity, recalcitrance, resoluteness, resolution, stamina, steadfastness, strength, stubbornness, tenaciousness, *tenacitas,* toughness, unyieldingness, will

TENANCY, *noun*   holding, holding by title, leasing, occupancy, occupation, ownership, possession, posses-

sorship, proprietorship, renting, residency, temporary possession, tenure
ASSOCIATED CONCEPTS: joint tenancy, month to month tenancy, tenancy at sufferance, tenancy at will, tenancy by the entirety, tenancy for years, tenancy in common

TENANT, *noun* border, *conductor,* dweller, holder, householder, *incola,* inhabitant, *inquilinus,* landholder, landowner, leaseholder, lessee, lodger, occupant, occupier, one holding land of another, one occupying another's land, one occupying real property, one using real property, owner, paying guest, possessor, proprietor, rent payer, renter, resident
ASSOCIATED CONCEPTS: disorderly tenant, eviction, holdover tenant, joint tenant, life tenant, objectionable tenant, subtenant, tenant at sufferance, tenant at will, tenant by the entirety, tenant for a fixed term, tenant from month to month, tenant in common, tenant per autre vie

TENDENCY, *noun* aptitude, aptness, bearing, bent, bias, character, direction, disposition, facility, gift, gravitation, idiosyncrasy, *inclinatio,* inclination, instinct, leaning, natural disposition, nature, partiality, penchant, predisposition, prejudice, *proclivitas,* proclivity, proneness, propensity, slant, susceptibility, temperament, trend, turn, twist, warp

TENDER, *verb* advance, *deferre,* deliver, extend, furnish, give, grant, hold out, issue, lay before, offer, pay, present, present for payment, proffer, propose, put forward, render, submit, urge upon, volunteer
ASSOCIATED CONCEPTS: tender payment, tender performance
FOREIGN PHRASES: *Reprobata pecunia liberat solventem.* Money refused releases the debtor.

TENOR, *noun* cast, character, content, course, cut, direction, drift, *exemplum,* feeling, form, gist, idea, import, manner, meaning, mode, mood, nature, purport, sense, *sententia,* significance, signification, spirit, stamp, subject matter, tendency, tone, trend, vein

TENTATIVE, *adjective* cautious, conditional, contingent, dependent, experimental, exploratory, groping, interim, probationary, probative, proposed, provisional, provisory, questionable, speculative, temporary, trial, undecided, unsettled
ASSOCIATED CONCEPTS: tentative agreement

TENUOUS, *adjective* airy, attenuated, delicate, diminutive, fine, flimsy, illusory, inconsequential, infinitesimal, insignificant, little, miniature, minute, narrow, paltry, petty, scant, slender, slight, small, thin, tiny, trifling, trivial, unimportant, unsubstantial

TENURE, *noun* duration, holding, occupancy, occupation, period, *possessio, possidere,* regime, term
ASSOCIATED CONCEPTS: tenure in office
FOREIGN PHRASES: *Tenura est pactio contra communem feudi naturam ac rationem, in contractu interposita.* Tenure is a compact contrary to the common nature and reason of the fee, put into a contract.

TERGIVERSATE, *verb* apostatize, avoid, be uncertain, be unsure, change one's mind, change sides, desert, dodge, equivocate, evade, hedge, quibble, recant, renege, renounce, shift, straddle, turn renegade, use evasions, use subterfuge, vacillate

TERM (*Duration*), **noun** age, course, era, incumbency, interval, lifetime, period, reign, season, session, span, *spatium temporis,* spell, stage, tenancy, tenure, time
ASSOCIATED CONCEPTS: term for years, term insurance, term of a lease, term of confinement, term of court, term of office
FOREIGN PHRASES: *Terminus annorum certus debet esse et determinatus.* A term of years ought to be certain and determinate.

TERM (*Expression*), **noun** appellation, appellative, cognomen, denomination, designation, epithet, heading, idiom, locution, name, phrase, title, verbalism, *verbum,* vocable, *vocabulum,* word
ASSOCIATED CONCEPTS: definition of terms

TERM (*Provision*), **noun** agreement, arrangement, article of agreement, bargain, clause, *condicio,* condition, covenant, item, *lex,* limitation, particular, point, proviso, qualification, specification, stipulation, understanding
ASSOCIATED CONCEPTS: terms and conditions of a contract, terms of a policy, terms of payment, terms of sale

TERMINABLE, *adjective* capable of being bounded, capable of being completed, capable of being concluded, capable of being conditioned, capable of being ended, capable of being fixed, capable of being limited, capable of being made definite, conditional, defeasible, finite, limitable
ASSOCIATED CONCEPTS: terminable at will, terminable fee, terminable interest, terminable trust, terminable upon a condition subsequent

TERMINATE, *verb* abolish, annul, bring to an end, bring to completion, cancel, cease, close, come to an end, complete, conclude, culminate, die, discontinue, drop, eliminate, end, expire, finish, fire from employment, halt, let go, put an end to, release, run out, stop, wind up
ASSOCIATED CONCEPTS: notice to terminate, terminate a contract, terminate a lease, terminate an action, terminate an agreement, terminate employment

TERRITORY, *noun* *ager,* area, beat, circuit, clime, demesne, district, division, domain, dominion, environs, expanse, field, land, latitude, locale, place, precinct, property, province, quarter, realm, *regio,* region, scene, section, terrain, tract, zone

TEST, *noun* analysis, audit, check, checkup, effort, endeavor, examination, experience, experiment, exploration, inquest, inquiry, inquisition, inspection, interrogation, investigation, observation, questioning, quiz, research, review, scrutiny, search, study, survey, trial, try, tryout
ASSOCIATED CONCEPTS: blood test, clear and present danger test, compelling state interest test, prudent man test, right from wrong test, substantial evidence test

TESTAMENT, *noun* agreement, binding agreement, contract, covenant, engagement, expression of conviction, formal declaration, legal will, promise, solemn agreement, solemn promise, testamentary declaration, testamentary decree, *testamentum,* will, writing
ASSOCIATED CONCEPTS: codicil, last will and testament, testamentary capacity, testamentary devise, testamentary trust

FOREIGN PHRASES: *Omne testamentum morte consummatum est.* Every will or testament is consummated by death.

TESTAMENTARY, *adjective*   by way of a will, bequeathed by will, contained in a will, devised by will, distributed by will, given by testament, hereditary, patrimonial, set forth in a will, transferred by a legacy, transferred by bequest, transferred by devise
ASSOCIATED CONCEPTS: letters testamentary, testamentary assets, testamentary capacity, testamentary condition, testamentary devise, testamentary disposition, testamentary gifts, testamentary guardian, testamentary guardianship, testamentary instrument, testamentary intent, testamentary inventory, testamentary power, testamentary succession, testamentary trust, testamentary trustee

TESTATE, *adjective*   having left a will, having written a testament, relating to a will, with a valid will, with an executed will
ASSOCIATED CONCEPTS: intestate succession

TESTIFY, *verb*   acknowledge openly, affirm, affirm under oath, allege, assert, asseverate, attest, aver, avow, be sworn, bear witness, declare, depone, depose, establish, express, give evidence, give one's word, indicate, make solemn declaration, profess, prove, show, state, state a fact, state a truth, swear, take one's oath, take the stand, *testari, testificari,* verify
ASSOCIATED CONCEPTS: compulsion to testify, privilege against self-incrimination, testify in one's own defense, testify under oath

TESTIMONY, *noun*   affidavit, affirmation, assertion, asseveration, attestation, averment, avowal, declaration, declaration of facts, deposition, disclosure, evidence, evidence by a competent witness, evidence in support of, expression, profession, proof, proof by a witness, revelation, statement, statement of facts, *testimonium*
ASSOCIATED CONCEPTS: circumstantial testimony, compelled testimony, corroborative testimony, cross-examination, deposition, direct examination, expert testimony, impeachment of testimony, incompetent testimony, involuntary testimony, oral testimony, perjured testimony, preservation of testimony, testimony under oath

THEFT, *noun*   burglary, embezzlement, felonious taking, filchery, fraudulent taking, *furtum,* larceny, looting, misappropriation, peculation, pilferage, pilfering, purloining, purloinment, robbery, stealing, swindling, thievery, wrongful taking
ASSOCIATED CONCEPTS: theft of services
FOREIGN PHRASES: *Contrectatio rei alienae animo furando, est furtum.* The touching or removing of another's property, with an intention of stealing, is theft.

THEORETICAL, *adjective*   abstract, academic, assumed, conjectural, *doctrina,* doctrinaire, hypothetical, ideational, ideative, ideological, impractical, open to proof, philosophical, postulated, postulatory, presumed, presumptive, pure, *ratio,* speculative, speculatory, stated as a premise, supposable, suppositional, suppositive, unapplied, unproved, unproven, unsubstantiated, visionary

THEORY, *noun*   assumption, belief, conjecture, *doctrina,* doctrine, dogma, guesswork, hypothesis, ideology, opinion, philosophy, postulate, presupposition, proposition, *ratio,* speculation, supposition, surmise, thesis, thought, untested opinion, view
ASSOCIATED CONCEPTS: conflicts of law theory, contract theory, inconsistent theories, rescue theory, theory of the case

THEREBY, *adverb*   by means of, by use of, by virtue of, in consequence of, per, through, through the medium of, whereby, with the aid of

THEREAFTER, *adverb*   after, afterwards, at a later period, from that time, later, next, since, subsequently

THERETOFORE, *adverb*   before, earlier, formerly, heretofore, previous to, prior to

THESIS, *noun*   affirmation, argument, belief, claim, conjecture, debatable issue, debatable point, doctrine, dogma, hypothesis, issue, moot point, position, postulate, postulation, premise, principle, problem, proposition, question, speculation, stand, subject, supposition, tenet, theme, theory, topic, tract

THIEF, *noun*   bandit, contrabandist, criminal, defalcator, defaulter, defrauder, depredator, embezzler, lawbreaker, lifter, marauder, outlaw, peculator, pilferer, pillager, pirate, purloiner, robber, stealer, swindler
ASSOCIATED CONCEPTS: burglary, larceny, robbery

THOROUGH, *adjective*   absolute, accurate, all-inclusive, assiduous, careful, complete, comprehensive, consummate, definitive, detailed, diligent, downright, entire, exhaustive, extensive, full, fully executed, inclusive, intensive, meticulous, painstaking, perfect, plenary, sheer, sound, sweeping, systematic, thoroughgoing, total, trustworthy, unabridged, uncompromising, unmitigated, unqualified, utter, zealous

THOUGHTLESS, *adjective*   absent-minded, abstracted, blank, blockish, careless, casual, dazed, disregardful, distracted, distrait, dull, flighty, foolhardy, giddy, harebrained, headlong, heedless, ill-advised, improvident, *imprudens,* imprudent, impulsive, inadvertent, inane, inattentive, incogitant, inconsiderate, *inconsultus,* indelicate, indifferent, indiscreet, insensate, irrational, irresponsible, neglectful, *neglegens,* negligent, precipitate, rash, reckless, regardless, remiss, scatterbrained, selfish, stupid, tactless, unaccommodating, unconcerned, unmindful, unobliging, unobservant, unreasoning, unreflecting, unreflective, unthinking, unthoughtful, unwatchful, vacant, vacuous, without consideration

THRALL, *noun*   bondage, captivity, confinement, custody, durance, enslavement, enthrallment, helotry, oppression, servitude, *servitus,* slavery, subjection, subjugation, submission, thralldom, tyranny, vassalage, yoke

THREAT, *noun*   alarm, augury, auspice, commination, danger, *denuntiatio,* foreboding, fulmination, hazard, imminence, impendence, impendency, insecurity, intimidation, jeopardy, menace, *minae,* omen, peril, portent, presage, risk, sign, warning
ASSOCIATED CONCEPTS: coercion

FOREIGN PHRASES: *Non videtur consensum retinuisse si quis ex praescripto minantis aliquid immutavit.* He does not appear to have retained consent, who has changed anything at the command of a threatening party.

THREATEN, *verb* admonish, augur, be near at hand, blackmail, bode, browbeat, coerce, *comminari,* comminate, forebode, foreshadow, forewarn, frighten, fulminate, hector, intimidate, menace, portend, presage, terrorize, use threats

THRESHOLD *(Commencement),* **noun** beginning, foreword, inception, onset, outbreak, overture, preamble, prelude, prologue, start

THRESHOLD *(Entrance),* **noun** door, entrance way, entry, gateway, sill

THRESHOLD *(Verge),* **noun** brink, edge
ASSOCIATED CONCEPTS: monetary threshold

THROUGH, *adjective* completed, concluded, decided, done, done with, ended, finished, set at rest, settled, terminated

THROUGH *(By means of),* **adverb** by means of, by the hand of, by way of, using, using the help of

THROUGH *(From beginning to end),* **adverb** all along, all the way, by way of, via

THROUGH *(Until now),* **adverb** to this day

THROUGHOUT *(All over),* **adverb** all over, every bit, extensively, from beginning to end, from first to last, from the ground up, from the word go, inside and out, over all, to the end

THROUGHOUT *(During),* **adverb** for the duration, for the period of, in the course of, until the conclusion of

THWART, *verb* avert, baffle, balk, bar, blight, bring to naught, check, contravene, counteract, countermine, counterwork, cripple, cross, damp, debar, defeat, foil, forestall, frustrate, hamper, hinder, impede, inhibit, intercept, interfere, interrupt, nip, obstruct, oppose, outmaneuver, override, preclude, prevent, restrain, retard, ruin, spoil, stave off, stifle, stop, stultify, stymie, traverse, turn aside, undermine, ward off

TIES, *noun* adherences, adhesions, attachments, bands, bonds, chains, commitments, connections, engagements, interconnections, knots, liaisons, links, pledges, unions, vincula

TIME, *noun* age, chronology, duration, end of the matter, era, extent, interlude, interim, interval, period, tenancy, tenure, term
ASSOCIATED CONCEPTS: time being of the essence, time certificate, time deposit, time fixed by agreement, time of absence, time of adjudication, time of bankruptcy, time of injury, time of memory, time option, time policy, time studies, timetables

TIMELINESS, *noun* appropriateness, aptness, auspiciousness, climacteric, compliance, convenient time, felicitousness, fitness, matureness, opportuneness, proper time, seasonableness, suitability, suitable time, time, within appropriate time provided

ASSOCIATED CONCEPTS: laches, notice, statute of limitations

TIP *(Clue),* **noun** advice, aviso, communication, confidential information, cue, enlightenment, forewarning, guidance, head, hint, indication, inside information, insinuation, instruction, intimation, key, lead, mention, point, pointer, prenotification, recommendation, report, suggestion, warning, whisper

TIP *(Gratuity),* **noun** award, benefaction, bestowment, bonus, compensation, consideration, contribution, donation, donative, gift, guerdon, meed, offering, payment, perquisite, reward
ASSOCIATED CONCEPTS: unreported income

TITLE *(Designation),* **noun** appellation, caption, denomination, heading, inscription, label, name, rubric, sign, signification, superscription, tag
ASSOCIATED CONCEPTS: title of statute

TITLE *(Division),* **noun** article, branch, chapter, clause, item, paragraph, part, portion, provision, section, statement, term

TITLE *(Position),* **noun** employment, office, post, rank, situation, station, status

TITLE *(Right),* **noun** authority, authorization, claim, deed, domain, droit, entitlement, equity, interest, legal title, ownership, permission, possession, power, prerogative, prescription, proprietorship, right, sanction, stake, tenure, vested interest
ASSOCIATED CONCEPTS: absolute title, abstract of title, acquisition of title, apparent title, chain of title, claim of title, clear title, cloud on title, color of title, defeasible title, disparagement of title, documents of title, equitable title, failure of title, good title, imperfect title, marketable title, merchantable title, nominal title, paramount title, perfection of title, prima facie title, quieting title, reservation of title, superior title, title by adverse possession, title by deeds, title by prescription, title insurance, title search, title to property, unmarketable title, warranty of title, worthier title
FOREIGN PHRASES: *Praescriptio est titulus ex usu et tempore substantiam capiens ab auctoritate legis.* Prescription is a title by authority of law, deriving its force from use and time. *A piratis et latronibus capta dominum non mutant.* Things captured by pirates and robbers do not change title.

TOKEN, *noun* augury, auspice, chip, device, emblem, evidence, expression, favor, figurehead, indicant, indicator, keepsake, manifestation, memento, omen, portent, proof, relic, remembrance, sign, souvenir, symbol

TOLERANCE, *noun* abiding, ability to bear, ability to endure, ability to tolerate, ability to withstand, allowance, bravery, broad-mindedness, capacity to endure, capacity to stand suffering, capacity to take pain, charter, compassion, constancy, courage, durability, endurance, fortitude, franchise, freedom, freedom from bigotry, freedom from prejudice, good will, humanity, immunity, immunization, impunity, indulgence, *indulgentia,* lack of bias, liberality, license, patience, perseverance, persistence, resignation, stamina, stoicism, strength, submission, sufferance, sustainment, sympathy, *tolerantia,* toleration, understanding

TOLERATE, verb abide, accept, acquiesce, allow, be lenient, bear, bear with, brook, carry on, consent, endure, forbear, indulge, make the best of, oblige, permit, put up with, receive, sanction, stand, stomach, submit to, suffer, swallow, take patiently, *tolerare*, undergo

TOLL (Effect), noun casualties, consequence, cost, damage, distress, effect, exaction, forfeit, grievous price, loss, payment, result, ruinous price, setback, suffering

TOLL (Tax), noun assessment, charge, exaction, excise, fare, fee, impost, levy, payment, *portorium*, tithe, *vectigal*
ASSOCIATED CONCEPTS: collection of tolls, toll bridges, toll roads

TOLL (Exact payment), verb collect payment, exact tribute, extort, levy, raise taxes, tax

TOLL (Stop), verb arrest, block, check, cut off, embar, estop, frustrate, halt, hinder, hold back, impede, inhibit, interrupt, limit, obstruct, put a stop to, restrain, restrict, stay, suspend, thwart
ASSOCIATED CONCEPTS: toll a statute of limitations

TOOL, noun agent, apparatus, channel, contrivance, device, implement, instrument, machine, means, mechanism, medium, recourse, resource, utensil, vehicle

TORPID, adjective apathetic, benumbed, comatose, dead, disinterested, dormant, drowsy, dull, heavy, idle, impervious, inactive, inanimate, indifferent, indolent, *iners*, inert, inexcitable, insensate, insensible, languid, languorous, lazy, leaden, *lentus*, lethargic, lifeless, listless, motionless, numb, otiose, passive, phlegmatic, sedentary, sleepy, slow, sluggish, somnolent, spiritless, stagnant, static, stupefied, stuperous, stupid, supine, torpescent, torporific, unconcerned, unconscious, unfeeling

TORT, noun breach of legal duty, civil wrong, dereliction of duty, error, fault, invasion of a legal right, legal wrong, malfeasance, misdeed, misdoing, misfeasance, negligent act, personal wrong, private wrong, transgression, violation of a legal duty, wrong, wrongdoing, wrongful act
ASSOCIATED CONCEPTS: action founded in tort, comparative negligence, continuing tort, contributory negligence, foreseeable consequences, intentional tort, prima facie tort, proximate cause, standard of care, strict liability in tort, successive torts, tort feasor, tortious act, tortious conduct

TORTIOUS ACT, noun actionable act, criminal act, felonious act, illegitimate act, improper act, incorrect act, nefarious act, punishable act, triable act, unlawful act, wrongful act

TORTUOUS (Bending), adjective anfractuous, circuitous, complicated, conniving, contorted, convoluted, curved, curvilinear, indirect, involved, irregular, labyrinthine, mazy, meandering, roundabout, serpentine, sinuate, sinuated, sinuous, snakelike, torsional, tortile, turning, twisted, twisting, undulatory, vermicular, vermiculate, vermiculated, winding, wreathed, zigzag

TORTUOUS (Corrupt), adjective crafty, crooked, deceitful, devious, dishonest, dishonorable, disingenu-

ous, fraudulent, immoral, knavish, perfidious, treacherous, unscrupulous

TOTAL, adjective absolute, aggregate, all, complete, downright, entire, full, global, gross, inclusive, integral, *omnis*, outright, radical, thorough, thoroughgoing, *totus*, undivided, universal, *universus*, unqualified, utter, whole, with no exception, without omission

TOTALITY, noun aggregate, aggregation, allness, collectivity, completeness, comprehensiveness, entireness, entirety, entity, everything, gross, integration, lump, mass, sum, totalness, unity, whole
ASSOCIATED CONCEPTS: totality of the circumstances

TOXIC, adjective damaging, deadly, deleterious, fatal, festering, harmful, injurious, insalubrious, lethal, malign, noxious, pestilent, pernicious, poisonous, purulent, risky, unsafe, venomous, virulent
ASSOCIATED CONCEPTS: toxic chemicals, toxic dementia, toxic ingredients, toxic psychosis, toxic torts

TRACE (Delineate), verb copy, define, describe, *designare*, detail, draw, duplicate, explain, go over, mark out, reproduce, set forth, sketch

TRACE (Follow), verb chase, detect, ensue, ferret out, hound, hunt out, inquire, *investigare*, investigate, *odorari*, probe, pursue, scent, search, seek, shadow, track, track down, trail, unearth

TRACTABLE, adjective acquiescent, adaptable, amenable, bendable, compliant, conformable, controllable, docile, *docilis*, ductile, easily l lead, easily managed, easily taught, easygoing, elastic, facile, *facilis*, flexible, flexile, formable, governable, guidable, impressionable, leadable, malleable, manageable, obedient, plastic, pliable, pliant, readily wrought, submissive, teachable, *tractabilis*, tractile, willing, yielding

TRADE (Commerce), noun barter, business, business affairs, business intercourse, buying and selling, commercial enterprise, deal, exchange, exchange of commodities, interchange, marketing, mercantile business, mercantile relations, *mercatus*, merchandising, merchantry, negotiation, nundination, open market, patronage, purchase, sale, sales, swap, traffic, transaction, truck
ASSOCIATED CONCEPTS: combination in restraint of trade, hazardous trade, in the ordinary course of trade or business, restraint of trade, stock in trade, unfair trade

TRADE (Occupation), noun *ars*, assignment, avocation, berth, business, calling, concern, craft, duty, employment, engagement, function, handicraft, job, line, line of work, livelihood, living, metier, office, position, post, practice, profession, pursuit, situation, specialty, task, vocation

TRADE, verb bargain, barter, buy, buy and sell, carry on commerce, chaffer, *commercari*, deal, do business, drive a bargain, exchange, huckster, interchange, *mercaturam*, merchandise, negotiate, purchase, scorse, sell, shop, traffic, transact
ASSOCIATED CONCEPTS: combination in restraint of trade, trade acceptance, trade in interstate commerce

TRADEMARK, noun badge, brand, countermark, countersign, hallmark, identification, imprint, label, mark, signet, symbol, ticket, trade sign

TRADITIONAL, *adjective* accepted, acknowledged, ancestral, classic, classical, common, confirmed, conformable, consuetudinal, consuetudinary, conventional, customary, established, fixed, habitual, handed down, historic, historical, ingrained, inherited, inveterate, long-established, long-standing, old, orthodox, prescribed, prescriptive, regular, rooted, sanctioned, time-honored, traditionary, traditive
ASSOCIATED CONCEPTS: custom and usage, past practices, prior conduct between the parties

TRAGEDY, *noun* accident, adversity, affliction, bale, blow, calamity, casualty, cataclysm, catastrophe, disaster, doom, dreadful event, fatal affair, hardship, misadventure, misfortune, mishap, reverse, sorrow, *tragoedia,* woe

TRAIT, *noun* attribute, characteristic, detail, differentia, distinguished quality, feature, habit, idiosyncrasy, individualism, item, lineament, manner, mannerism, mark, nature, *nota,* oddity, particularity, peculiarity, property, *proprietas,* quality, singularity, specialty, temperament

TRAMMEL, *verb* bind, bridle, check, clog, confine, constrain, control, cramp, cumber, curb, debar, discommode, enchain, encumber, entangle, entrammel, fasten, fetter, frustrate, hamper, handicap, hinder, hobble, hold back, impede, incommode, inconvenience, keep within bounds, manacle, obstruct, oppose, pinion, put in irons, repress, restrain, restrict, retard, shackle, suppress, tether, thwart, tie, tie up

TRANSACT, *verb* accomplish, achieve, carry on, carry on business, carry out, conduct, consummate, deal, deal with, discharge, do business, execute, fulfill, *gerere,* make terms, manage, negotiate, operate, perform, proceed with, put into practice, render, *transigere*
ASSOCIATED CONCEPTS: transact business

TRANSACTION, *noun* accomplishment, achievement, act, action, activity, administration, adventure, affair, business, commission, completion, consummation, deal, dealing, deed, direction, effectuation, enactment, enterprise, execution, exercise, exploit, management, measure, negotiation, *negotium,* operation, performance, proceeding, process, purchase, sale, undertaking
ASSOCIATED CONCEPTS: arms length transaction, transacting business, transactional immunity
FOREIGN PHRASES: *Res inter alios judicatae nullum aliis praejudicium faciunt.* Transactions between strangers ought not to injure those who are not parties to them.

TRANSCEND, *verb* be better, be superior, best, better, eclipse, exceed, excel, *excellere, exsuperare,* go beyond, outdistance, outdo, outrank, outrival, outshine, outstrip, outvie, outweigh, overpass, overshadow, overstep, overtop, pass, predominate, prevail, rise above, rival, surmount, surpass, take precedence, top, tower above

TRANSCRIPT, *noun* apograph, copy, *exemplar, exemplum,* fascimile, minutes, record, recording, reprint, reproduction, rescript, stenographic copy, transcription, written copy
ASSOCIATED CONCEPTS: stenographic transcript, transcript of proceedings, transcript on appeal, trial transcript

TRANSFER, *verb* assign, bequeath, bestow, carry, confer, consign, deed, deliver, deliver over, demise, devolve, forward, grant, hand on, pass, pass on, remove, send, shift, *traducere, transferre,* transmit, *transmittere,* transport
ASSOCIATED CONCEPTS: transfer an interest

TRANSFEREE, *noun* acceptor, allottee, assignee, beneficiary, consignee, devisee, donee, grantee, heir, inheritor, legatee, licensee, payee, recipient, successor, trustee

TRANSFEROR, *noun* allotter, assignor, consignor, devisor, donor, grantor, lessor, licensor, payor

TRANSFORM, *verb* adjust, alter, change, commute, convert, denature, do over, make over, metamorphose, modify, mutate, recast, recondition, reconstruct, reconvert, redo, reform, regenerate, remake, remodel, remold, render different, renovate, reorganize, restyle, revamp, revise, revolutionize, shift, substitute, switch, tailor, transfigure, translate, transmogrify, transmute, transshape, transubstantiate, turn, vary

TRANSGRESSION, *noun* abuse, breach, contravention, crime, *delictum,* delinquency, dereliction, disobedience, encroachment, error, fault, guilty act, illegal action, illegality, infraction, infringement, iniquity, misbehavior, misconduct, misdeed, misdoing, misfeasance, noncompliance, nonobservance, offense, *peccatum,* sin, slip, transcursion, trespass, violation, wrong, wrongdoing
FOREIGN PHRASES: *Frustra legis auxilium quaerit qui in legem committit.* He vainly seeks the aid of the law who transgresses the law.

TRANSIENT, *adjective* *brevis,* brief, caducous, deciduous, elusive, ephemeral, ephemerous, evanescent, fading, fleeting, *fluxus,* fugacious, *fugax,* fugitive, hasty, impermanent, inconstant, interim, meteoric, migratory, momentary, passing, perishable, provisional, provisory, roaming, roving, short, short-lived, temporal, temporary, transitory, unenduring, unstable, vanishing, volatile

TRANSITION, *noun* alteration, break, change, change-over, conversion, development, flux, graduation, growth, jump, leap, metastasis, modification, motion, movement, passage, passing, phase, progress, realignment, shift, transference, transformation, transit, *transitio,* transmigration, transmutation, turn

TRANSITORY, *adjective* brief, cursory, ephemeral, evanescent, fleeting, flitting, fugacious, impermanent, momentary, not permanent, passing away, provisional, short lived, temporal, temporary, transient, unenduring, unstable, volatile
ASSOCIATED CONCEPTS: transitory actions, transitory causes of action, transitory possession of property, transitory seizen, transitory trade name, transitory use and occupation, transitory work

TRANSMIT, *verb* bear, carry, cede, communicate, conduct, consign, convey, deliver, dispatch, forward, give, hand on, hand over, impart, issue, pass, pass on, provide, radiate, remit, send, send a message, send on, ship, transfer, *transmittere,* transport

TRANSMITTAL, *noun* circulation, communication, conveyance, deliverance, delivery, direction, dispatch, forwarding, impartation, letter, movement, note, passage, propagation, remittance, sending, transfer, transference, translocation, transmission, transmittance, transplantation, transportation

TRANSPORT, *verb* banish, bear, bring, carry, cart, conduct, consign, convey, deliver, deport, dispatch, drive out, exile, expel, extradite, fetch, imprison, move, ostracize, remove, send, ship, take, tote, transfer, transmit, *transmittere,* transplant, *transportare*
ASSOCIATED CONCEPTS: transport across state lines, transport contraband, transport illegal goods, transport in interstate commerce

TRAP, *noun* ambush, artifice, bait, catch, catch-all, lure, maneuver, net, pitfall, snare, stratagem

TRAP, *verb* bait, catch, ensnare, entangle, entrap, hook, inveigle, snare, snatch

TRAVERSE, *verb* course, crisscross, cross, cross in opposition, cross in traveling, cut across, ford, go across, intersect, march, over pass, pass, pass from point to point, pass through, patrol, probe, survey carefully, tramp, travel over, trek

TRAVESTY, *noun* burlesque, burlesque translation, caricature, crude presentation, distortion, exaggeration, farce, imitation, lampoon, low comedy, ludicrous presentation, mimicry, mockery, parody, perversion, ridicule, take-off

TREASON, *noun* betrayal, betrayal of a trust, breach of allegiance, breach of faith, disloyalty, infidelity, insurgence, insurrection, *maiestas,* mutiny, *perfidia,* perfidy, rebellion, rebellion against the government, revolt, revolution, sedition, subversion, treachery, violation of allegiance
FOREIGN PHRASES: *Felonia implicatur in qualibet proditione.* Felony is implied in every treason. *Reus laesae majestatis punitur ut pereat unus ne pereant omnes.* A traitor is punished that one may die lest all perish. *Crimen laesae majestatis omnia alia crimina excedit quoad poenam.* The crime of high treason exceeds all other crimes in its punishment. *In alta proditione nullus potest esse accessorius sed principalis solummodo.* In high treason each one is a principal. *Qui molitur insidias in patriam id facit quod insanus nauta perforans navem in qua vehitur.* He who betrays his country is like the insane sailor who bores a hole in the ship which carries him.

TREASURY, *noun* accumulation, *aerarium,* bank, bursary, cache, capital, central money office, coffer, conservatory, deposit, depository, depot, exchequer, *fiscus,* fund, place of deposit, purse, receptacle, repertory, repository, reservatory, reserve, reserve fund, safe, store, storehouse, strongbox, thesaurus, till, treasure house, vault

TREAT, *noun* amusement, delight, diversion, festival, pleasure, refreshment, repast, revelry

TREAT (Process), *verb* act on, analyze, attend, bargain with, behave towards, comment upon, confer, correct, deal with, debate, deliberate, discuss, edit, entertain, examine, handle, heal, investigate, modify, negotiate, parley, reason, reason about, revise, use, work on, write about

TREAT (Remedy), *verb* ameliorate, better, cure, improve

TREATMENT, *noun* adjustment, analysis, arrangement, consideration, cure, design, examination, execution, handling, investigation, management, modification, process, processing, study, technique, therapy, transaction, way
ASSOCIATED CONCEPTS: inhuman treatment, medical treatment

TREATY, *noun* accord, agreement, agreement between nations, alliance, armistice, arrangement, bargain, bond, cartel, charter, compact, concordance, concordat, contract, *conventio,* convention, covenant, deal, entente, formal contract, international compact, negotiation, pact, *pactio,* protocol, settlement, truce, understanding
ASSOCIATED CONCEPTS: insurance treaty

TRENCHANT, *adjective* acrimonious, acute, biting, brisk, caustic, clear-cut, cutting, distinct, dynamic, energetic, explicit, forceful, incisive, intense, keen, mordant, penetrating, penetrative, piercing, pointed, powerful, pungent, sarcastic, scathing, severe, sharp, spirited, stinging, telling, thoroughgoing, unsparing, vigorous

TREPIDATION, *noun* affright, agitation, alarm, apprehension, awe, consternation, disconcertion, dismay, disquiet, disquietude, dread, fear, flutter, fret, fright, funk, horror, jitteriness, jumpiness, nervousness, oscillation, panic, perturbation, quaking, quivering, restlessness, scare, shaking, terror, trembling, tremor, tremulousness, *trepidatio,* trepidity, uneasiness, unrest

TRESPASS, *verb* advance upon, breach, break in, break the law, contravene, deviate from rectitude, disobey, disobey the law, disregard, encroach, enter unlawfully, exceed, go astray, ignore limits, *in alienum fundum ingredi,* infringe, intrude, invade, offend, overrun, overstep, sin, transgress, usurp, violate
ASSOCIATED CONCEPTS: action of trespass, constructive trespass, continuing trespass, forcible trespass, innocent trespass, malicious trespass, technical trespass, willful and deliberate trespass
FOREIGN PHRASES: *Aedificare in tuo proprio solo non licet quod alteri noceat.* It is not lawful to build upon one's own land what may injure another. *Prohibetur ne quis faciat in suo quod nocere possit alieno.* It is forbidden for anyone to do on his own property what may injure another's.

TRIABLE, *adjective* actionable, cognizable, justiciable, legally enforceable

TRIAL (Experiment), *noun* analysis, attempt, check, endeavor, evaluation, examination, experimental method, *experimentum,* exploration, in-depth analysis, inquiry, inspection, probe, review, scrutiny, study, test, testing
ASSOCIATED CONCEPTS: trial period

TRIAL (Legal proceeding), *noun* action, action at law, case, cause, contest, court action, examination, formal examination by a court of law, formal examination of facts by a court, hearing, *iudicium,* inquest, inquiry, inquisition, judicial contest, lawsuit, legal dispute, litigation, proceeding, *quaestio,* suit, suit at law

ASSOCIATED CONCEPTS: appeal from a trial, close of a trial, examination before trial, fair trial, former trial, impartial trial, joint trial, jury trial, mistrial, new trial, order of trial, post-trial evidence, pretrial evidence, proceed to trial, public trial, retrial, separate trial, speedy trial, trial by jury, trial by the court, trial court, trial de novo, trial judge

FOREIGN PHRASES: *Triatio ibi semper debet fieri, ubi juratores meliorem possunt habere notitiam.* Trial ought always to be had where the jurors can have the best information.

TRIBUNAL, *noun*   bench, chancery, court, court of justice, court of law, forum, *iudicium,* judges, judgment seat, judiciary, law court, panel of judges

ASSOCIATED CONCEPTS: administrative tribunal, appellate tribunal, fair tribunal, inferior tribunal, tribunal of limited jurisdiction

TRITE, *adjective*   banal, boring, bromidic, common, commonplace, conventional, dull, familiar, hackneyed, known, much used, oft repeated, old, ordinary, overused, *pervulgatus,* platitudinous, prosaic, proverbial, routine, run of the mill, shopworn, stale, stereotyped, stock, tedious, threadbare, too familiar, *tritus,* uncreative, unexciting, unimaginative, unoriginal, used, wearisome, well-known, widely known, worn, worn out

TRIVIAL, *adjective*   cursory, empty, foolish, frivolous, inane, inappreciable, inconsiderable, indifferent, idle, immaterial, inconsequential, inferior, insignificant, *levis,* light, little, meager, meaningless, mediocre, minute, negligible, nominal, nonessential, nugatory, of little consequence, petty, picayune, scanty, shallow, slight, slim, small, superficial, trashy, trifling, unimportant, useless, worthless

ASSOCIATED CONCEPTS: trivial defect rule, trivial matter

TROUBLE, *noun*   ado, adversity, affliction, ailment, annoyance, bane, blow, bother, burden, calamity, catastrophe, cause of distress, commotion, difficulty, discomfort, discontent, discord, dissatisfaction, distress, disturbance, fuss, grievance, hardship, hindrance, ill, inconvenience, misfortune, obstruction, ordeal, pitfall, plague, problem, reverse, row, setback, snag, *sollicitudo,* suffering, torment, trial, tribulation

TROVER, *noun*   atonement, award, compensation, damages, fine, forfeiture, indemnification, indemnity, mulct, payment, penalty, quittance, recompense, recoupment, recovery, redress, reparation, requital, requitement, restitution, retrieval, retrievement, return, satisfaction, solatium

TRUANT, *adjective*   absent, apathetic, dilatory, errant, flown, fugitive, idle, inattentive, indifferent, indolent, laggard, lazy, loitering, missing, neglectful, nonattendant, remiss, shiftless, shirking, slack, slothful, straying, unconcerned, unemployed, unpersevering, wandering

TRUCKLE, *verb*   crawl, cringe, fawn, grovel, toady, yield to the wishes of others

TRUE *(Authentic),* *adjective*   according to the facts, accurate, actual, as represented, authenticated, certain, correct, creditable, dependable, exact, factual, *fidelis, fidus,* founded on fact, genuine, honest, legitimate, literal, not false, not faulty, not fictitious, original, precise, pure, real, realistic, reliable, right, rightful, sound, trustworthy, truthful, unadulterated, unaffected, uncolored, undisguised, undisputed, undistorted, unexaggerated, unfabricated, unfallacious, unfeigned, unfictitious, unimagined, unimpeachable, unmistaken, unperjured, unpretended, unquestionable, unspurious, unvarnished, valid, veracious, veridical, verifiable, veritable, *verus,* well-based, well-founded, well-grounded

ASSOCIATED CONCEPTS: true bill, true copy, true value, true verdict

TRUE *(Loyal),* *adjective*   ardent, assiduous, compliant, complying, conscientious, constant, dedicated, dependable, devoted, duteous, dutiful, earnest, faithful, fervent, firm in adherence, firm in allegiance, incorruptible, obedient, reliable, resolute, responsible, sincere, stanch, steadfast, steady, sure, tried, truehearted, trustworthy, trusty, unbetraying, unfailing, unfalse, unperfidious, unswerving, untreacherous, unwavering, zealous

TRUST *(Combination of businesses),* *noun*   association, cartel, combination of companies, combine, consortium, corporation, merger, monopolistic organization, monopoly, pool, syndicate

ASSOCIATED CONCEPTS: antitrust laws, combination in restraint of trade

TRUST *(Confidence),* *noun*   assurance, belief, certainty, confident expectation, conviction, credence, credulity, dependence, faith, *fides, fiducia,* reassurance, reliance, sureness, trustworthiness

ASSOCIATED CONCEPTS: breach of trust, office of trust, public trust

TRUST *(Custody),* *noun*   care, charge, control, duty, guardianship, holding, keeping, management, obligation, possession and control, power over, protection, responsibility, safety

ASSOCIATED CONCEPTS: beneficiary of trust, business trust, *cestui que trust,* charitable trust, constructive trust, continuing trust, corpus of trust, de facto trust, declaration of trust, discretionary trust, dormant trust, dry trust, execution of trust, executory trust, express trust, implied trust, parol trust, presumptive trust, principal of a trust, private trust, residuary trust, resultant trust, revocable trust, shifting trust, special trust, spendthrift trust, totten trust, trust agreement, trust certificate, trust company, trust deed, trust estate, trust funds, trust mortgage, trust receipts

FOREIGN PHRASES: *Fides est obligatio conscientiae alicujus ad intentionem alterius.* A trust is an obligation of conscience of one to the wishes of another.

TRUST, *verb*   accept, accredit, assume, be confident, confide, *confidere,* count upon, *credere,* credit, depend upon, expect, feel sure, give credence to, give credit to, have faith in, have no doubt, have no reservations, hope, lean on, *mandare,* place reliance in, presume, put confidence in, rely on, swear by, take, take for granted

TRUSTEE, *noun*   administrator, agent, appointee, caretaker, curator, custodian, *custos,* depositary, fiduciary, financier, functionary, guardian, holder of the legal estate, one to whom something is entrusted, person appointed to administer affairs, recipient

ASSOCIATED CONCEPTS: acting trustee, appointment of trustee, bare trustee, change of trustee, corporate trustee, cotrustees, de facto trustee, designation of trustee, disinterested trustee, duty of trustee, fiduciary responsibility, interested trustee, involuntary trustee, liability of trustee, nominal trustee, public trustee, qualification of trustees, quasi trustee, removal of trustee, successor trustee, testamentary trustee, trustee by deed, trustee of an estate, trustee ex maleficio, trustee in bankruptcy

TRUSTWORTHINESS, *noun*   dependability, faithfulness, honesty, integrity, loyalty, probity, rectitude, reliability, uprightness

TRUTH, *noun*   accuracy, actuality, authenticity, candor, conformity to fact, correctness, exactness, fact, genuineness, honesty, integrity, precision, probity, realism, reality, right, sincerity, veracity, *veritas,* verity
ASSOCIATED CONCEPTS: credibility of a witness, reputation for truth, truth in lending laws
FOREIGN PHRASES: *Error fucatus nuda veritate in multis, est probabilior; et saepenumero rationibus vincit veritatem error.* Error artfully disguised is, in many instances, more probable than naked truth; and frequently error overwhelms truth by argumentation. *Veritas nimium altercando amittitur.* Truth is lost by too much altercation. *Sacramentum habet in se tres comites,-veritatem, justitiam, et judicium; veritus habenda est in jurato; justitia et justicium in judice.* An oath has in it three components,-truth, justice, and judgment; truth in the party swearing; justice and judgment in the judge administering the oath. *Fictio cedit veritati. fictio juris non est ubi veritas.* Fiction yields to truth. where truth is, fiction of law does not exist. *Qui non libere veritatem pronunciat proditor est veritatis.* He who does not freely speak the truth is a betrayer of the truth. *Veritas, quae minime defensatur opprimitur; et qui non improbat, approbat.* Truth which is not sufficiently defended is overpowered; and he who does not disapprove, approves. *Veritas nihil veretur nisi abscondi.* Truth fears nothing but concealment.

TRY *(Attempt),* *verb*   aim, aspire, *conari,* endeavor, exert oneself, make an effort, put forth effort, seek, strain, strive, tackle, take a chance, *temptare,* test, undertake, venture

TRY *(Conduct a trial),* *verb*   adjudge, adjudicate, *cognoscere,* consider, decide, deliberate, examine, examine judicially, hear a case, hear a cause, *iudicare,* judge, legally determine, pronounce, rule, sit in judgment
ASSOCIATED CONCEPTS: try a case before a judge, try a case before a jury

TURGID, *adjective*   bombastic, circumlocutory, declamatory, diffuse, digressive, euphuistic, flowery, fustian, grandiloquent, high-flown, inflated, long-winded, magniloquent, orotund, periphrastic, pleonastic, plethoric, pompous, prolix, puffed up, redundant, rhetorical, sesquipedalian, stilted, swelled, swollen, tumid, turgent, wordy

TURMOIL, *noun*   activity, ado, agitation, bedlam, bustle, chaos, commotion, confusion, convulsion, discord, disorder, disquiet, distraction, disturbance, excitement, ferment, fracas, fuss, havoc, huddle, imbroglio, jumble, melee, muddle, pandemonium, perturbation, pother, row, rumpus, stir, storm, tempest, trouble, tumult, *turba,* turbulence, turbulency, unrest, upheaval, uproar, welter

TURPITUDE, *noun*   bad character, bad name, baseness, character, corruption, decadence, degeneracy, degradation, depravity, disrepute, ill repute, immorality, infamy, obscenity, perfidy, shady reputation, vileness, wickedness, wrongdoing

TYPICAL, *adjective*   according to custom, according to routine, accustomed, average, characteristic, common, commonplace, conformable, conformable to rule, consistent, conventional, current, customary, everyday, exemplifying a class, familiar, habitual, illustrative, in character, indicative, indicatory, model, normal, of everyday occurrence, of frequent occurrence, oft-repeated, ordinary, orthodox, popular, prevailing, prevalent, *proprius,* prosaic, recurrent, regular, representative, *solitus,* standard, standardized, stereotyped, stock, traditional, true to type, *typicus,* unexceptional, usual

TYRANNOUS, *adjective*   arbitrary, brutal, despotic, domineering, grinding, hard, harsh, high-handed, imperious, lordly, masterful, oppressive, overbearing, peremptory, severe, strict, tyrannical, uncompromising, unjustly severe

U

UBIQUITOUS, *adjective* ever-present, omnipresent, permeative, pervading, pervasive, ubiquitary, universal, world-wide

ULTERIOR, *adjective* concealed, hidden, not manifest, obscure, secret, unadvertised, unavowed, undisclosed, undivulged, unevident, unexpressed, unknown, unmentioned, unobvious, unperceived, unrevealed, unseen
ASSOCIATED CONCEPTS: ulterior motive

ULTIMATE, *adjective* basic, conclusive, conclusory, crowning, elemental, elementary, end, ending, essential, eventual, extreme, *extremus,* farthest, final, fundamental, furthermost, furthest, greatest possible, last, maximum, most distant, most remote, primary, rudimental, rudimentary, supreme, terminal, terminative, *ultimus*
ASSOCIATED CONCEPTS: ultimate facts

ULTIMATUM, *noun* condition, demand, exaction, *extrema condicio,* final condition, final offer, final proposal, final proposition, last offer, notice, proposition, provision, proviso, requirement, requisite, specification, stipulation, threat, warning

ULTRA VIRES, *adjective* illegitimate, unallowed, unauthorized, unchartered, unlicensed, unsanctioned, unwarranted
ASSOCIATED CONCEPTS: *ultra vires* act, *ultra vires* doctrine

UMBRAGE, *noun* acrimony, alienation, anger, animosity, annoyance, bad blood, bile, bitterness, choler, disaffection, discord, dislike, displeasure, dissatisfaction, dudgeon, enmity, estrangement, grudge, hatred, hostility, ill humor, ill will, indignation, irritation, offense, pique, rancor, resentment, soreness, spleen, wrath

UMPIRE, *noun* adjudicator, arbiter, arbitrator, compromiser, *disceptator,* go-between, interagent, intercessor, intermediary, intermediator, intermedium, intervenor, judge, mediator, moderator, peacemaker, reconciler, referee

UNABASHED, *adjective* aweless, barefaced, bold, brazen, forward, hardened, immodest, *impudens,* not

ashamed, not disconcerted, shameless, unafraid, unapprehensive, unashamed, unawed, unblushing, unconcerned, uncringing, undaunted, undismayed, unembarrassed, unfearing, unflinching, unshaken, unshrinking, without shame

UNABLE, *adjective* defenseless, disabled, feckless, forceless, helpless, impotent, inadequate, incapable, incompetent, ineffective, inefficient, inept, inoperative, insufficient, lame, not able, powerless, unfit, unqualified, useless, worthless

UNACCEPTABLE, *adjective* displeasing, distasteful, exceptionable, impossible, inadmissable, inappropriate, *ingratus, iniucundus,* intolerable, not fitting, objectionable, offensive, repugnant, unappealing, unattractive, undesirable, undesired, uninviting, unpleasant, unpleasing, unpopular, unsatisfactory, unsuitable, unwanted, unwelcome

UNACCUSTOMED, *adjective* aberrant, abnormal, amazing, anomalous, astonishing, bizarre, curious, different, eccentric, exceptional, exotic, extraordinary, foreign, freakish, green, inexperienced, *insolitus, insuetus,* inusitate, irregular, naive, new, novel, odd, out of the ordinary, outlandish, peculiar, queer, rare, raw, remarkable, singular, strange, surprising, unacquainted, uncommon, unconventional, unconversant, uncustomary, unfamiliar, unhabituated, uninitiated, uninured, unique, unnatural, unordinary, unpracticed, unseasoned, unskilled, untrained, untried, unusual, unversed

UNACQUAINTED, *adjective* *ignarus,* ignorant, inexperienced, *inscius,* new, strange, unaccustomed, unapprized, unaware, unconversant, unenlightened, unfamiliar, uninformed, unknowing, unversed

UNADULTERATED, *adjective* genuine, *integer, merus,* neat, pure, simple, *sincerus,* straight, true, unalloyed, uncombined, uncompounded, uncontaminated, uncorrupted, undebased, undefiled, undiluted, undistorted, unmingled, unmixed, unsophisticated, untouched, unvarnished, virgin

UNAFFECTED (Sincere), *adjective* aboveboard, artless, candid, *candidus,* childlike, direct, downright, forthright, frank, free from affectation, guileless, honest, inartificial, ingenuous, innocent, modest, naive, natural, open, outspoken, plain, plainspoken, simple, *simplex,* spontaneous, straightforward, truthful, unassuming, uncounterfeited, undeceptive, undesigning, unfeigning, unpretending, unpretentious, unreserved, unsimulated, unsophisticated, unsynthetic, upright, wholesome

UNAFFECTED *(Uninfluenced), adjective*   aweless, callous, calm, *constans,* disdainful, frigid, hardhearted, heartless, icy, *immotus,* impassive, impervious, implacable, indifferent, inflexible, insensitive, insentient, inured, obdurate, obtuse, pitiless, remorseless, steely, stoic, stoical, stony, unaltered, uncaring, unchanged, uncompassionate, unconcerned, unexcited, unfeeling, unimpressed, uninspired, unmoved, unresponsive, unstirred, unstruck, unswayed, unsympathetic, untouched, unyielding

UNALIENABLE, *adjective*   absolute, actual, certain, conclusive, definite, fixed, imprescriptible, inalienable, incapable of being surrendered, indefeasible, inviolable, lawful, prescriptive, privileged, rightful, unalterable, unchallengeable, unimpeachable, untransferable
ASSOCIATED CONCEPTS: unalienable rights

UNALTERABLE, *adjective*   adamant, changeless, constant, definite, determined, fated, firm, fixed, *immutabilis,* immutable, inalterable, incommutable, inevitable, inflexible, invariable, irreversible, obdurate, permanent, relentless, resolute, rigid, settled, stable, unbending, unchangeable, undeviating, unmodifiable, unpliant, unwavering, unyielding

UNAMBIGUOUS, *adjective*   *apertus,* articulate, certain, *clarus,* clear, clear-cut, clearly defined, comprehensible, defined, definite, *definitus,* distinct, distinguishable, evident, exact, explicit, express, intelligible, lucid, not vague, obvious, perspicuous, plain, precise, recognizable, sure, transparent, unconfused, understandable, unequivocal, univocal, unmistakable, well-defined
ASSOCIATED CONCEPTS: plain language

UNANTICIPATED, *adjective*   abrupt, *improvisus, inexspectatus, insperatus,* startling, sudden, surprising, uncontemplated, unexpected, unforeseen, unlooked for, unthought of

UNAPPROACHABLE, *adjective*   aloof, austere, beyond reach, distant, far-off, faraway, forbidding, formidable, impregnable, inaccessible, inaffable, incomparable, inimitable, matchless, nongregarious, out of reach, out-of-the-way, peerless, *rari aditus,* remote, removed, reserved, secluded, separated, standoffish, stern, superior, superlative, supreme, unattainable, unequaled, unexcelled, unique, unobtainable, unparalleled, unreachable, unsociable, unsurpassed, withdrawn

UNATTAINABLE, *adjective*   impossible, impracticable, impractical, inaccessible, infeasible, insuperable, insurmountable, out of reach, out of the question, unachievable, unacquirable, unapproachable, unavailable, unfeasible, ungettable, unobtainable, unperformable, unprocurable, unreachable, unsecurable

UNAUTHORIZED, *adjective*   disallowed, forbidden, inappropriate, incorrect, illegal, illegitimate, improper, prohibited, proscribed, unaccredited, unaffirmed, unapproved, uncertified, unchartered, uncommanded, uncommissioned, unconstitutional, undue, unempowered, unendorsed, unentitled, unjustified, unlawful, unlicensed, unpermitted, unratified, unsanctioned, unsuitable, unsupported, unwarranted, wrongful
ASSOCIATED CONCEPTS: unauthorized conduct, unauthorized use

UNAVAILABILITY, *noun*   inaccessibility, unacquirability, unapproachability, unattainability, unobtainability

UNAVAILING, *adjective*   abortive, barren, bootless, empty, fruitless, futile, *futilis,* idle, impotent, inadequate, incompetent, ineffective, ineffectual, inefficacious, inefficient, inoperative, *inritus,* inutile, invalid, nugatory, of no avail, pointless, profitless, purposeless, successless, to no end, to no purpose, uneventful, unproductive, unprofitable, unserviceable, unsuccessful, useless, vain, valueless, *vanus,* wasted, wasteful, worthless

UNAVOIDABLE *(Inevitable), adjective*   avoidless, certain, coercive, compelling, compulsory, fated, fixed, impending, imperative, inavertible, ineluctable, ineludible, inescapable, inevasible, *inevitabilis,* inexorable, involuntary, irresistible, irrevocable, mandatory, *necessarius,* necessary, obligatory, resistless, sure, uncontrollable, unpreventable
ASSOCIATED CONCEPTS: unavoidable accident, unavoidable casualty, unavoidable cause, unavoidable consequences, unavoidable dangers

UNAVOIDABLE *(Not voidable), adjective*   binding, fixed, indefeasible, *inrevocabilis,* irrebuttable, irrefutable, irrevocable, mandatory, settled, unable to be annulled, unchangeable

UNAWARE, *adjective*   blinded, heedless, *ignarus,* ignorant, inattentive, incognizant, inexpectant, *inscius,* insensible, mindless, nescient, *nescius,* oblivious, off guard, surprised, unacquainted, unadvised, unapprised, unconscious, undiscerning, unenlightened, unfamiliar with, unforewarned, unguarded, unheeding, uninformed, unknowing, unmindful, unobservant, unprepared, unrealizing, unsuspecting, unversed, unwarned, unwary, without notice

UNBECOMING, *adjective*   awkward, degrading, dishonorable, disreputable, graceless, improper, in bad taste, inapposite, inappropriate, incongruous, incorrect, indecent, indecorous, *indecorus,* indelicate, *indignus,* infelicitous, offensive, out of keeping, out of place, unapt, unbefitting, unbeseeming, uncomely, undignified, unfit, unfitted, ungenteel, unhandsome, unladylike, unmeet, unpraiseworthy, unseemly, unsuitable, unsuited, untasteful, vulgar

UNBELIEVABLE, *adjective*   absurd, difficult to accept, difficult to believe, disbelieved, distrusted, doubtful, dubious, farfetched, hard to believe, implausible, improbable, inconceivable, incredible, open to doubt, open to suspicion, palpably false, questionable, staggering, suspect, suspicious, unconvincing, unimaginable, unlikely, untenable, unthinkable

UNBENDING, *adjective* adamant, *durus,* firm, fixed, hard, immobile, immovable, implacable, inflexible, intractable, intransigent, narrow-minded, obdurate, obstinate, relentless, renitent, resistant, resolute, rigid, *rigidus,* stern, stiff, straight, straitlaced, strict, strong-minded, stubborn, unchangeable, uncompromising, unpliant, unrelenting, unyielding, willful

UNBIASED, *adjective* broad-minded, detached, disinterested, dispassionate, equitable, fair, fairminded, impartial, impersonal, independent, indifferent, just, liberal, neutral, nonpartisan, objective, open, open-minded, tolerant, unbigoted, uncolored, uninfluenced, unjaundiced, unprejudiced, unslanted, unswayed, unwarped

UNBLEMISHED, *adjective* clear, faultless, flawless, free from imperfection, guiltless, immaculate, impeccable, innocent, intact, *integer,* perfect, pure, *purus,* sinless, sound, spotless, taintless, undefiled, unerring, uninjured, unmarred, unsoiled, unspotted, unsullied, untainted, untarnished, without defect, without stain
ASSOCIATED CONCEPTS: unblemished record

UNBOUND, *adjective* disunited, exempt, free, liberated, limitless, manumitted, paroled, released, set free, uncaught, unchained, unchecked, unconfined, unconstrained, uncontrolled, unencumbered, unfastened, unfettered, unfixed, unhindered, unlimited, unobstructed, unprevented, unrestrained, unrestricted, untied, untrammeled

UNCANNY, *adjective* astonishing, exceptional, inconceivable, incredible, intuitional, magical, mysterious, mystifying, noteworthy, odd, peculiar, preternatural, rare, remarkable, secret, singular, strange, supernatural, unaccountable, unbelievable, uncommon, unearthly, unfamiliar, unheard of, unnatural, weird

UNCERTAIN (*Ambiguous*), ***adjective*** amphibolic, cryptic, enigmatical, inconclusive, indeterminate, indistinct, mistakable, mysterious, mystifying, nebulous, not certain, not clear, not plain, obscure, occult, open to various interpretations, perplexing, puzzling, unclear, unintelligible, vague
FOREIGN PHRASES: *Ubi jus incertum, ibi jus nullum.* Where the law is uncertain, there is no law. *Res est misera ubi jus est vagum et incertum.* It is a sorry state of affairs when law is vague and mutable. *Incerta pro nullis habentur.* Uncertain things are regarded as nothing.

UNCERTAIN (*Questionable*), ***adjective*** arguable, conjectural, contestable, contingent, controvertible, debatable, disputable, doubtful, dubious, equivocal, insecure, liable to question, not sure, open to discussion, open to question, precarious, problematic, problematical, provisional, suspect, suspicious, tentative, unconfirmed, undecided, undetermined, unreliable, unsettled, unsure, untrustworthy

UNCLAIMED, *adjective* forgotten, unallocated, unapplied, unappropriated, unasked for, uncalled-for, undemanded, unexacted, unpossessed, unrequisitioned, unsought, untaken
ASSOCIATED CONCEPTS: last property, unclaimed property

UNCLEAR, *adjective* ambiguous, blurred, blurry, clouded, cloudy, confused, difficult to comprehend, difficult to understand, dim, equivocal, faint, foggy, fuzzy, hazy, ill-defined, illegible, imperspicuous, incomprehensible, inconspicuous, indistinct, indistinguishable, misty, muddy, murky, obscure, out of focus, poorly defined, poorly seen, shadowy, sketchy, turbid, uncertain, undefined, unevident, unexplicit, unintelligible, unobvious, unplain, unreadable, unrecognizable, vague

UNCOMMON, *adjective* aberrant, abnormal, anomalous, bizarre, curious, different, distinctive, eccentric, exceptional, exotic, extraordinary, infrequent, *insolitus,* inusitate, *inusitatus,* marked, noteworthy, novel, occasional, odd, out of the way, outstanding, peculiar, rare, *rarus,* remarkable, scarce, seldom met with, singular, special, startling, strange, surprising, unaccustomed, unconventional, uncustomary, unexampled, unfamiliar, unheard of, unimitated, unique, unorthodox, unparalleled, unprecedented, unusual

UNCOMPROMISING, *adjective* adamant, austere, conservative, determined, difficult, exacting, exigent, fanatic, fanatical, firm, hard, immovable, implacable, incorruptible, inexorable, inflexible, intransigent, irreconcilable, narrow, obdurate, obstinate, orthodox, puritanic, puritanical, relentless, resolute, resolved, rigid, ruthless, severe, steadfast, strict, stringent, unbending, unchangeable, unrelenting, unremitting, unyielding

UNCONDITIONAL, *adjective* absolute, categorical, complete, not limited by conditions, *purus, simplex,* unbounded, unchecked, unconfined, unqualified, unrestricted, utter, without conditions, without reservations
ASSOCIATED CONCEPTS: unconditional claim, unconditional guaranty, unconditional pardon, unconditional payment, unconditional promise, unconditional refusal

UNCONFIRMED, *adjective* inconclusive, indecisive, unascertained, unattested, unauthenticated, uncertain, uncertified, unchecked, uncorroborated, undemonstrated, unestablished, unproved, unproven, unratified, unsettled, unshown, unsubstantiated, unsupported, untried, unvalidated, unverified, unwitnessed

UNCONSCIONABLE, *adjective* blackguard, conniving, conscienceless, corrupt, criminal, designing, dishonest, dishonorable, disingenuous, excessive, exorbitant, extreme, immoderate, inordinate, intemperate, intriguing, knavish, monstrous, outrageous, preposterous, rascally, scheming, tricky, unconscienced, unequal, unethical, unfair, unjust, unprincipled, unreasonable, unscrupulous, unwarranted
ASSOCIATED CONCEPTS: unconscionable bargain, unconscionable conduct, unconscionable contract

UNCONTESTED, *adjective* accepted, admitted, axiomatic, believed, incontestable, incontrovertible, indubitable, irrefragable, irrefutable, not argued over, not challenged, not disputed, *sine certamine,* unchallengeable, unchallenged, uncontradicted, uncontroversial, uncontroverted, undeniable, undisputed, undoubted, unquestionable, unquestioned
ASSOCIATED CONCEPTS: uncontested action, uncontested divorce, uncontested election

UNCONTROLLABLE, *adjective* bullheaded, carried away, disobedient, disorderly, fractious, frenzied,

headstrong, hysterical, impetuous, *impotens,* incorrigible, indocile, indomitable, insuppressible, insurgent, intractable, irrepressible, irresistable, lawless, mulish, obdurate, obstinate, obstreperous, opinionated, out of control, rampageous, rampant, recalcitrant, refractory, restive, riotous, rowdy, stubborn, troublesome, unappeasable, ungovernable, unmalleable, unmanageable, unrestrainable, unruly, unsubmissive, untoward, violent, wild, willful
ASSOCIATED CONCEPTS: uncontrollable impulse

UNCONTROVERTED, *adjective* beyond doubt, doubtless, indubious, past dispute, unchallenged, uncontested, uncontradicted, undisputed, undoubted, unquestioned
ASSOCIATED CONCEPTS: uncontroverted fact, uncontroverted truth

UNCORROBORATED, *adjective* unattested, unauthenticated, unauthorative, unconfirmed, undemonstrated, unofficial, unproven, unratified, unsubstantiated, unsupported, unvalidated, unverified
ASSOCIATED CONCEPTS: uncorroborated evidence, uncorroborated fact

UNCOUTH, *adjective* *agrestis,* awkward, barbaric, barbarous, boorish, brutish, callow, churlish, clownish, clumsy, coarse, crass, crude, discourteous, doltish, gawky, graceless, gross, heavy-handed, ill-bred, ill-mannered, impolite, *incultus,* indelicate, inelegant, loutish, plebeian, rough, rude, *rudis,* rustic, strange, uncivil, uncourteous, uncourtly, uncultivated, uncultured, ungainly, ungentlemanly, unmannerly, unpolished, unrefined, unseemly, vulgar

UNCURBED, *adjective* abandoned, *effrenatus, effusus,* incontinent, *infrenatus,* irresponsible, lawless, lax, licentious, out of control, out of hand, reinless, unaccountable, unanswerable, unbound, unbridled, unchained, unchecked, unconfined, unconstrained, uncontrolled, undisciplined, ungoverned, unhindered, unimpeded, uninhibited, unmuzzled, unobstructed, unprevented, unreined, unrepressed, unrestrained, unruly, unshackled, unsuppressed

UNDAUNTED, *adjective* bold, brave, courageous, daring, dauntless, doughty, dreadless, fearless, firm, gallant, gritty, heroic, *impavidus,* indefatigable, indomitable, *interritus,* intrepid, *intrepidus,* mettlesome, perseverant, persevering, persistent, persisting, resolute, stalwart, steady, stouthearted, tireless, unafraid, unalarmed, unapprehensive, unblenched, unconcerned, undiscouraged, undismayed, unfaltering, unfearing, unflinching, unfrightened, unrelenting, unshaken, unshrinking, unsubdued, unterrified, untimid, valiant, valorous

UNDECIDED, *adjective* ambiguous, *ambiguus,* changeful, contestable, debatable, disputable, doubtful, doubting, drawn, dubious, *dubius,* hesitant, *incertus,* indecisive, indefinite, irresolute, moot, open, pending, problematical, questionable, speculative, tentative, unascertained, uncertain, unconvinced, undetermined, unfixed, unresolved, unsettled, unsure, vacillating, vacillatory, vague, wavering

UNDEFINABLE, *adjective* esoteric, indefinable, indescribable, indeterminate, indistinct, ineffable, inexplicable, inexpressible, unexplainable, untranslatable, vague

UNDENIABLE, *adjective* axiomatic, axiomatical, beyond a doubt, beyond all question, beyond dispute, certain, clear, compelling, conclusive, convincing, demonstrable, established, *evidens,* evident, firm, *haud dubius,* inappealable, incontestable, incontrovertible, indisputable, indubitable, inescapable, infallible, irrefragable, irrefutable, obvious, past dispute, proven, sound, unanswerable, unavoidable, unimpeachable, unquestionable

UNDEPENDABLE, *adjective* capricious, careless, changeable, deceitful, dishonest, double-dealing, erratic, fickle, fluctuating, frivolous, inconstant, irresponsible, mercurial, open to error, perfidious, shifty, slippery, tergiversating, timeserving, treacherous, two-faced, uncertain, unpredictable, unreliable, unstable, unsteadfast, unsteady, unsure, untrustworthy, vacillating, variable, wavering

UNDERESTIMATE, *verb* belittle, deprecate, depreciate, detract from, discredit, disesteem, disparage, do scant justice to, make light of, minimize, *minoris aestimare, minoris facere,* misjudge, misprize, rate below the true value, rate too low, run down, set at naught, set little store by, slight, think too little of, underprice, underprize, underrate, underreckon, undervalue

UNDERLYING, *adjective* based on, basic, built on, deep-rooted, elemental, elementary, essential, fundamental, latent, not evident, obscure, original, primal, primary, rudimentary, supporting, undermost, unseen
ASSOCIATED CONCEPTS: underlying contract, underlying fact, underlying obligation

UNDERSIGNED, *noun* attestant, attester, author, covenanter, endorser, petitioner, ratifier, signatory, signer, subscriber, supporter

UNDERSTAND, *verb* absorb, apperceive, appreciate, apprehend, assimilate, be apprised, be informed, cognize, comprehend, conceive, conclude, conjecture, deduce, digest, discern, fathom, gather, glean, grasp, infer, *intellegere,* internalize, know, learn, master, perceive, retain, take to mean
ASSOCIATED CONCEPTS: express understanding, want of understanding

UNDERSTANDING (Agreement), *noun* accord, accordance, alliance, arrangement, common view, compact, compliance, concord, concordance, congruence, consentaneity, contract, cooperation, covenant, harmony, likemindedness, meeting of minds, mutual pledge, pact, rapport, unanimity
ASSOCIATED CONCEPTS: express understanding, understanding of the parties
FOREIGN PHRASES: *Conventio facit legem.* An agreement creates the law, i.e. the parties to a binding contract will be held to their promises.

UNDERSTANDING (Comprehension), *noun* apperception, apprehension, assimilation, awareness, conception, discernment, grasp, *ingenium,* insight, intelligence, knowledge, *mens,* mental ability, perception, power to understand, prehension, realization, reason, recognition, sense, wisdom
ASSOCIATED CONCEPTS: intent, want of understanding
FOREIGN PHRASES: *Sermones semper accipiendi sunt secundum subjectam materiam, et conditionem per-*

sonarum. Language is always to be understood according to its subject-matter and the condition of the person. *Probationes debent esse evidentes, id est, perspicuae et faciles intelligi.* Proofs ought to be evident, that is, clear and easily understood. *Quod tacite intelligitur deesse non videtur.* What is tacitly understood does not appear to be wanting.

UNDERSTANDING *(Tolerance),* **noun**   acceptance, altruism, benevolence, charitableness, compassion, condonation, consideration, empathy, good will, humanity, indulgence, kindliness, lack of prejudice, mercy, patience, sensitivity, sufferance, sympathy, toleration

UNDERSTATEMENT, *noun*   conservative estimate, grossly inadequate representation, minimization, misrepresentation, underestimation, undervaluation

UNDERTAKE, *verb*   accept, address oneself to, agree, answer for, apply oneself to, assume, attempt, be answerable for, begin, carry on, carry out, commence, commit, commit oneself to, contract, covenant, devote oneself to, embark upon, endeavor, engage in, enter into, enter upon, execute, go in for, guarantee, *in se recipere,* incur a duty, indent, indenture, initiate, launch, make an effort, obligate oneself, pledge, pledge one's word, promise, pursue, set about, set in motion, start, strive, *suscipere,* tackle, take in hand, take up, take upon oneself, try, venture, vow
ASSOCIATED CONCEPTS: overt act

UNDERTAKING *(Attempt),* **noun**   design, effort, plan, purpose, quest, search, task undertaken, trial

UNDERTAKING *(Bond),* **noun**   pledge, security

UNDERTAKING *(Business),* **noun**   engagement, enterprise, project, pursuit, task, transaction, venture

UNDERTAKING *(Commitment),* **noun**   agreement, contract, obligation, pledge

UNDERTAKING *(Enterprise),* **noun**   adventure, affair, attempt, business, *coeptum,* concern, effort, emprise, endeavor, engagement, essay, exercise, *inceptum,* job, move, occupation, operation, plan, program, project, pursuit, quest, search, task, trial, venture
ASSOCIATED CONCEPTS: joint undertaking

UNDERTAKING *(Pledge),* **noun**   agreement, assurance, avowal, commitment, compact, contract, covenant, engagement, guarantee, insurance, oath, obligation, parole, pledged word, promise, security, stipulation, troth, vow, warrant, word
ASSOCIATED CONCEPTS: bail undertaking, insufficiency of undertaking, statutory undertaking, undertaking

UNDERWRITE, *verb*   agree to support, assume a risk, assure, back, consent to support, countersign, endorse, finance, fund, guarantee, guaranty, insure, pledge, promise, secure, shoulder, sponsor, support, take responsibility, undertake, uphold, vouch for

UNDESIRABLE, *adjective*   abominable, annoying, bothersome, defective, disadvantageous, disagreeable, disliked, displeasing, distasteful, dreaded, exceptionable, improper, inadvisable, inappropriate, incom-

modious, inconvenient, ineligible, inexpedient, insufferable, intolerable, loathed, loathsome, objectionable, obnoxious, out of character, out of keeping, outcast, rejected, repellent, repulsive, scorned, shunned, thankless, troublesome, unacceptable, unalluring, unappealing, unapprovable, unattractive, unbecoming, unbefitting, unfit, uninviting, unlikable, unmeet, unpalatable, unpleasant, unpleasing, unpopular, unsatisfactory, unseemly, unsought, unsuitable, unwanted, unwelcome, unwished, unworthy

UNDIMINISHED, *adjective*   in full force, *indelibatus, inlibatus,* intact, *integer,* not decreased, not lessened, unabated, unallayed, unceasing, uncut, undamaged, undivided, unfaded, unimpaired, unincreased, unlessened, unreduced, unretarded, unsevered, unweakened, unworn, whole, without loss

UNDISCLOSED, *adjective*   concealed, covert, hidden, invisible, latent, mysterious, occult, sealed, secret, suppressed, tacit, ulterior, unaired, unannounced, unapparent, unbreathed, uncommunicated, unconveyed, undeclared, undetected, undivulged, unexplained, unexposed, unexpressed, unheralded, unimparted, unknown, unmentioned, unproclaimed, unpronounced, unpublicized, unpublished, unrevealed, unsaid, unseen, untalked of, untold, unvoiced
ASSOCIATED CONCEPTS: undisclosed interest, undisclosed principal

UNDISPUTED, *adjective*   absolute, accepted, acknowledged, assured, axiomatic, believed, beyond doubt, beyond question, certain, *certus,* conclusive, doubtless, *haud dubius,* incontestable, incontrovertible, indisputable, indubitable, irrefragable, irrefutable, past dispute, positive, questionless, trusted, unanswerable, unchallengeable, unchallenged, uncontroversial, undebatable, undeniable, undoubted, unquestioned, without doubt, without question
ASSOCIATED CONCEPTS: undisputed fact

UNDISTORTED, *adjective*   authentic, direct, exact, faithful, genuine, natural, original, right, scrupulous, straight, true, true to nature, truthful, unbiased, undeviating, undisguised, unembroidered, unexaggerated, unfaked, unfictitious, unjaundiced, unperverted, unprejudiced, unswerving, unwarped, veracious

UNDUE *(Excessive),* **adjective**   disproportionate, exceeding propriety, excessive, exorbitant, extravagant, extreme, ill-advised, immoderate, *immodicus,* improper, inappropriate, indecorous, inordinate, needless, *nimius,* objectionable, out of bounds, outrageous, overmuch, profuse, superfluous, unbecoming, unbefitting, uncalled-for, undeserved, unfit, unjustified, unmerited, unnecessary, unneeded, unreasonable, unseemly, unsuitable, unwarranted
ASSOCIATED CONCEPTS: undue influence

UNDUE *(Not owing),* **adjective**   not mature, not yet due, not yet payable, premature, unowed, unseasonable, untimely

UNDULY, *adverb*   excessively, exorbitantly, extremely, immoderately, inordinately, intemperately, overly
ASSOCIATED CONCEPTS: unduly harsh criminal sanctions

UNEMPLOYED, *adjective*   disengaged, disused, doing nothing, idle, inactive, jobless, leisured, not em-

ployed, not working, *otiosus,* out of employment, out of work, unengaged, unoccupied, unused, *vacuus,* without employment, workless
ASSOCIATED CONCEPTS: unemployment insurance

UNENDURABLE, *adjective*   displeasing, excessive, extreme, impalatable, impossible, insufferable, intolerable, objectionable, obnoxious, offensive, past bearing, past enduring, unacceptable, unbearable, undesirable, unpalatable, unpleasant, unsavory

UNEQUAL *(Unequivalent), adjective*   different, differing, *dispar,* disparate, disproportionate, dissimilar, *impar, inaequalis,* irregular, unbalanced, uneven, unlike, unmatched
ASSOCIATED CONCEPTS: unequal bargaining powers

UNEQUAL *(Unjust), adjective*   biased, inequitable, influenced, jaundiced, one-sided, partial, prejudiced, prepossessed, unfair, unjustifiable

UNEQUIVOCAL, *adjective*   absolute, categorical, certain, clear, clear-cut, decided, defined, definite, downright, evident, explicit, forthright, inappealable, incontestable, incontrovertible, indisputable, indubitable, irrefragable, irrefutable, outright, peremptory, plain, positive, straightforward, sure, unambiguous, unanswerable, unchallenged, undeniable, undisputed, unmistakable, unqualified, unquestionable, utter

UNESSENTIAL, *adjective*   *adventicius,* dispensable, extraneous, extrinsic, immaterial, inapposite, incidental, inconsequential, inconsiderable, insignificant, irrelevant, meaningless, minor, needless, negligible, nonessential, of no account, of no consequence, secondary, superfluous, trifling, trivial, uncalled-for, unimportant, unnecessary, unneeded
ASSOCIATED CONCEPTS: *minimis*

UNETHICAL, *adjective*   corrupt, corruptible, dishonest, dishonorable, disreputable, ignoble, immoral, inglorious, questionable, shady, uncommendable, unconscionable, underhanded, unfair, unprincipled, unprofessional, unscrupulous, unworthy, wrong

UNEXPECTED, *adjective*   abrupt, accidental, astonishing, chance, extemperaneous, extempore, fortuitous, impetuous, impromptu, impulsive, *inexpectatus, insperatus,* instantaneous, precipitate, shocking, startling, subitaneous, sudden, surprising, unannounced, unanticipated, unawaited, uncontemplated, undesigned, unforeseen, unheralded, unintended, unintentional, unlooked for, unpredicted, unpremeditated, unprepared for, unthought of, untimely, unusual

UNEXPIRED TERM, *noun*   remaining period, remaining time, residual time, surplus time, unelapsed period

UNFAIR, *adjective*   biased, fraudulent, inequitable, iniquitous, jaundiced, not equitable, one-sided, prejudiced, unequal, uneven, unjust, unprincipled, unreasonable, unsporting, weighted
ASSOCIATED CONCEPTS: unfair advantage, unfair claim practices, unfair competition, unfair labor practices, unfair proceedings, unfair trade

UNFAVORABLE, *adjective*   adverse, *adversus,* antagonistic, bad, calamitous, contrary, damaging, derogatory, deterrent, disadvantageous, disapprobatory,

discouraging, disparaging, foul, hopeless, hostile, ill-boding, ill-disposed, ill-omened, impedimental, impedimentary, impedimentive, inadvisable, inappropriate, inauspicious, inclement, inconvenient, indisposed, inexpedient, infelicitous, inhibitive, inimical, *iniquus,* inopportune, malapropos, malign, misfortunate, noxious, ominous, opposed, poor, prejudicial, repugnant, sinister, unfortunate, unfriendly, unlucky, unpromising, unpropitious, unsatisfactory, unsuited, untimely, untoward

UNFIT, *adjective*   badly qualified, foolish, ill-adapted, ill-advised, impertinent, improper, inadequate, inadvisable, inapplicable, inapposite, inappropriate, inapt, incapable, *incommodus,* incompetent, incongruous, inconvenient, *indignus,* ineligible, inept, inexpedient, inexpert, injudicious, inopportune, inutile, *inutilis,* irrelevant, maladjusted, malapropros, objectionable, out of keeping, out of place, unable, unadapted, unbecoming, unbefitting, undesirable, undue, unequipped, unfitting, unlikely, unprepared, unpromising, unqualified, unseemly, unsuitable, unsuited, unusable, unwise, unworthy, useless, valueless, wrong
ASSOCIATED CONCEPTS: unfit for consumption, unfit for occupancy, unfit parent

UNFORESEEABLE, *adjective*   contrary to expectations, improbable, startling, subitaneous, sudden, surprise, unaccountable, unanticipated, uncertain, unexpected, unintended, unlooked for, unplanned, unprecedented, unpredictable, unpredicted, unprepared for, unthought of, unusual, unwonted
ASSOCIATED CONCEPTS: unforseeable consequences, unforseeable events

UNFORESEEN, *adjective*   accidental, sudden, surprise, unanticipated, undesigned, unexpected, unheralded, unintended, unpredicted, unthought of
ASSOCIATED CONCEPTS: unforeseen cause, unforeseen difficulties, unforeseen event, unforeseen peril

UNFOUNDED, *adjective*   baseless, empty, erroneous, fabricated, fallacious, false, fictitious, *fictus,* fraudulent, groundless, idle, illogical, insubstantial, invented, spurious, suppositional, supposititious, trumped up, unattested, unauthenticated, unestablished, ungrounded, unproven, unsubstantial, unsupportable, unsupported, untenable, untrue, unwarranted, *vanus,* without basis, without foundation, without reality, without substance

UNIFORM, *adjective*   *aequabilis,* alike, compatible, conformable, consistent, consonant, *constans,* constant, conventional, correspondent, equable, equal, even, harmonious, homogeneous, identical, invariable, matched, orderly, orthodox, regular, same, similar, standard, steady, systematic, unaltered, unchanging, undeviating, undiversified, universal, unswerving, unvaried, unvarying, well-matched
ASSOCIATED CONCEPTS: uniform accounting system, uniform act, uniform commercial code, uniform fiduciary act, uniform laws, uniformity of laws, uniform operation of laws, uniform rate of taxation, uniform rates, uniform rule of taxation, uniform sales, uniform taxation

UNIFORMITY, *noun*   absence of diversity, absence of variation, conformity, consistency, constancy, continuity, equability, evenness, homogeneity, levelness, order, persistence, regularity, singleness, smoothness, stability, standardization, symmetry, unity

UNILATERAL, *adjective* independent, lone, not reciprocal, one-sided, single, singular, unaided
ASSOCIATED CONCEPTS: unilateral action, unilateral contract, unilateral mistake

UNIMPEACHABLE, *adjective* above reproach, approved, believable, beyond reproach, blameless, commendable, credible, creditable, excellent, faultless, guiltless, ideal, impeccable, incontestable, incontrovertible, inculpable, indefeasible, innocent, irrefragable, irrefutable, irreprehensible, irreproachable, laudable, *locuples,* meritorious, noncontroversial, perfect, questionless, reputable, *sanctus,* sinless, spotless, stainless, unable to be discredited, unassailable, unblamable, unblameworthy, unblemished, uncensurable, unchallengeable, unconfutable, undeniable, undisputed, undoubted, unexceptionable, unmarred, unobjectionable, unquestionable, unrefutable, untainted, upright, worthy

UNINTENTIONAL, *adjective* accidental, adventitious, casual, chance, fortuitous, inadvertent, *insciens,* involuntary, purposeless, spontaneous, uncalculated, unconscious, undeliberate, undesigned, unexpected, unforeseen, unintended, unknowing, unmeant, unpremeditated, unpurposeful, unthinking, unwitting
ASSOCIATED CONCEPTS: unintentional act

UNION *(Labor organization),* **noun** affiliation, alliance of workers, amalgamation, association, brotherhood, confederacy, consociation, council, federation, fellowship, fraternity, guild, league, organization, organized labor, sodality, trade association
ASSOCIATED CONCEPTS: anti-union animus, craft union, international union, labor union, local union, trade union, union membership, union shop

UNION *(Unity),* **noun** accord, accordance, agreement, coalition, coherence, combination, concert, concord, concurrence, *congregatio,* connection, consensus, *consociatio,* consolidation, cooperation, coupling, fusion, harmony, homogeneity, joining, junction, oneness, unification, uniformity, unison

UNIQUE, *adjective* anomalous, atypical, beyond comparison, bizarre, curious, different, dissimilar, exceptional, extraordinary, incomparable, individual, matchless, nonpareil, nonuniform, novel, odd, original, peculiar, peerless, rare, single, singular, *singularis,* sole, special, uncommon, unconformable, unequaled, unexampled, *unicus,* unimitated, unmatched, unparalleled, unprecedented, unrepeated, unrivaled, unusual

UNIT *(Department),* **noun** branch, division, group, staff

UNIT *(Item),* **noun** ace, component, constituent, element, formation, integral, measure, monad, one, part, piece, quantity

UNITE, *verb* act in concert, add, affiliate, agglomerate, agree, ally, amalgamate, amass, assemble, assimilate, associate, be one, become one, blend, bring together, cement, centralize, cluster, coact, coalesce, collect, combine, come together, commingle, concur, confederate, conglomerate, congregate, *coniungere,* conjoin, connect, consolidate, consubstantiate, converge,

cooperate, coordinate, *copulare,* couple, cowork, entwine, fall in with, form a league, form a single unit, form an alliance, fuse, gather together, group, grow together, harmonize, incorporate, interfuse, join, join forces, league, link, marry, mass, meet, meld, merge, mingle, *miscere,* mix, pool, pull together, reconcile, side with, solidify, syncretize, unify, wed
ASSOCIATED CONCEPTS: join in an action, united in interest

UNJUST, *adjective* biased, crooked, dishonorable, heinous, immoral, improper, inequitable, influenced, iniquitous, *iniquus, iniurius, iniustus,* interested, jaundiced, partial, prejudiced, prepossessed, undeserved, unequal, unfair, unjustifiable, unmerited, unprincipled, unreasonable, unwarranted, venal, warped, wicked, wrong, wrongful
ASSOCIATED CONCEPTS: unjust decision, unjust enrichment, unjust penalty, unjust sentence

UNJUSTIFIABLE, *adjective* accusable, blameworthy, censurable, chargeable, culpable, discreditable, dishonorable, groundless, impeachable, indefensible, inexcusable, *iniquus, iniurius, iniustus,* irremissible, objectionable, reprehensible, unallowable, unforgivable, unjust, unjustified, unpardonable, unreasonable, vicious, wicked, without excuse, wrong
ASSOCIATED CONCEPTS: unjustifiable cause, unjustifiable claim, unjustifiable deviation

UNKNOWINGLY, *adverb* adventitiously, fortuitously, ignorantly, inadvertently, innocently, insensibly, unawares, unconsciously, unintentionally, unmindfully, unsuspectingly, unwittingly, witlessly

UNLAWFUL, *adjective* actionable, against the law, contraband, criminal, forbidden, illegal, illegitimate, illicit, *inlicitus,* lawless, *non legitimus,* not allowed by law, outlawed, prohibited, transgressive, unallowed, unauthorized, unconstitutional, unlicensed, unsanctioned, unwarranted, *vetitus,* wrongful, wrongous
ASSOCIATED CONCEPTS: unlawful accumulation, unlawful act, unlawful assembly, unlawful combination, unlawful contract, unlawful detainer, unlawful detention, unlawful enrichment, unlawful entrapment, unlawful entry, unlawful flight, unlawful force, unlawful picketing
FOREIGN PHRASES: *Ex pacto illicito non oritur actio.* From an unlawful agreement, no action will lie.

UNLESS, *preposition* except, excepting, however, precluding, save, without

UNLIMITED, *adjective* boundless, endless, free, immeasurable, *immensus,* incalculable, indefinite, inexhaustible, infinite, *infinitus,* interminable, limitless, measureless, perpetual, termless, unbounded, unchecked, unconditional, unconfined, uncontrolled, unending, unfathomable, universal, unrestrained, unrestricted, untold, vast, without number
ASSOCIATED CONCEPTS: unlimited liability

UNMARKETABLE, *adjective* not readily salable, non salable, unsalable, unvendible
ASSOCIATED CONCEPTS: unmarketable title

UNMISTAKABLE, *adjective* apparent, autoptic, autoptical, bald, certain, clear, conclusive, conspicuous, decided, defined, distinct, distinguishable, evident, explicit, express, glaring, identifiable, indubitable, intelligible, known, lucid, manifest, notorious, obvious, open, overt, palpable, patent, perspicuous, plain, positive, pronounced, recognizable, sure, unambiguous, unconcealed, unconfusing, uncontestable, undeniable, undisguised, undoubted, unequivocal, unquestionable, visible, well-defined

UNMITIGATED, *adjective*   absolute, complete, consummate, downright, exhaustive, full, intensive, plenary, rank, rigid, severe, sheer, stark, thorough, unbounded, unconditional, unqualified, unsoftened, unsuppressed, untamed, untempered, unyielding, utter

UNNECESSARY, *adjective*   auxiliary, avoidable, dispensable, excess, excessive, expendable, expletive, extra, extraneous, extrinsic, gratuitous, inessential, irrelevant, needless, *non necessarius,* noncompulsory, optional, overmuch, redundant, spare, supererogative, supererogatory, superfluous, *supervacaneus, supervacuus,* supplemental, supplementary, surplus, uncalled-for, uncritical, unessential, unimportant, unneeded, unrequired
ASSOCIATED CONCEPTS: unnecessary force

UNOBJECTIONABLE, *adjective*   acceptable, adequate, admissible, allowable, condonable, defensible, harmless, inoffensive, irreprehensible, irreproachable, irreprovable, passable, satisfactory, tolerable, unblameworthy, uncensurable, unexceptionable, unimpeachable, vindicable

UNOBTRUSIVE, *adjective*   clandestine, covert, humble, meek, modest, natural, passive, quiet, reserved, restrained, reticent, retiring, self-effacing, shrinking, simple, subdued, surreptitious, unassuming, unconspicuous, undercover, underground, unimposing, unostentatious, unseen

UNOFFICIAL, *adjective*   casual, informal, not to be quoted, off the record, personal, unauthoritative, unauthorized, unendorsed, without authority, without ceremony
ASSOCIATED CONCEPTS: unofficial ruling

UNORTHODOX, *adjective*   *a ceteris dissentire,* aberrant, anomalous, deviative, different, divergent, eccentric, heretical, heterodox, irregular, lawless, out of step, unaccepted, unapproved, uncanonical, uncommon, unconformable, unconventional, unfashionable, unobservant, unusual

UNPAID, *adjective*   due, free, given, gratis, gratuitous, in arrears, outstanding, owing, payable, uncollected, uncompensated, undischarged, unrecompensed, unremunerated, unrequited, unrewarded, unsalaried, unsettled, volunteer

UNPOLITIC, *adjective*   careless, clumsy, foolish, harebrained, hasty, heedless, ill-advised, ill-judged, impolitic, improvident, imprudent, incautious, inconsiderate, indiscreet, inexpedient, injudicious, rash, reckless, senseless, stupid, tactless, temerarious, undiplomatic, unsagacious, unshrewd, untactful, unwary, unwise

UNPRECEDENTED, *adjective*   anomalous, exceptional, extraordinary, first, *inauditus,* incomparable, initial, miraculous, modern, new, newfangled, novel, *novus,* original, rare, singular, uncustomary, un-

equaled, unexampled, unexpected, unfamiliar, unheard of, unique, unknown, unmatched, unparalleled, unrivaled, untraditional, unusual

UNPREDICTABLE, *adjective*   aberrant, arbitrary, capricious, causeless, changeable, changeful, deviative, eccentric, erratic, fanciful, fickle, fitful, incalculable, inconstant, irregular, mercurial, mutable, random, spasmodic, speculative, unaccountable, uncertain, undependable, uneven, unexpected, unforeseeable, unmethodical, unreliable, unstable, unsteadfast, unsteady, unsure, unsystematic, variable, vicissitudinous, wavering

UNPREJUDICED, *adjective*   broadminded, detached, disinterested, dispassionate, equitable, evenhanded, fair, fairminded, impartial, independent, *integer,* judicial, just, neutral, nonpartisan, objective, open, openminded, proper, reasonable, tolerant, unbiased, unbigoted, uncolored, uninfluenced, unjaundiced, unprepossessed, unslanted, unswayed, unwarped
ASSOCIATED CONCEPTS: right to fair trial

UNPREMEDITATED, *adjective*   extemporaneous, extempore, hasty, impromptu, improvisate, improvised, impulsive, indeliberate, not intended, offhand, rash, snap, spontaneous, thoughtless, uncalculated, unconsidered, undesigned, unintended, unintentional, unmeant, unplanned, unprepared, unpurposeful, unrehearsed, unstudied, unthinking
ASSOCIATED CONCEPTS: manslaughter, unpremeditated murder

UNPRETENTIOUS, *adjective*   artless, humble, *inadfectatus,* informal, matter of fact, meek, modest, *modicus,* natural, plain, quiet, retiring, simple, *simplex,* unaffected, unassuming, undistinguished, unelaborate, unobtrusive, unostentatious, without airs

UNPRODUCTIVE, *adjective*   abortive, arid, barren, doomed, dry, effete, exhausted, fallow, fruitless, futile, impotent, ineffectual, inefficacious, inefficient, infecund, *infecundus,* infertile, inoperative, issueless, jejune, nugatory, otiose, profitless, sterile, *sterilis,* unavailing, unfruitful, unprofitable, unprolific, unremunerative, unrewarding, unsuccessful, unyielding, useless, wasteful, without results, worthless

UNPROFESSIONAL, *adjective*   amateurish, contrary to professional ethics, improper, imprudent, inappropriate, indiscreet, injudicious, nonexpert, not of high standards, unbefitting, unbusinesslike, undignified, unethical, unfitting, unscholarly, unseemly, unsuitable
ASSOCIATED CONCEPTS: Code of Professional Responsibility, disbarment, grievance committee, unprofessional conduct

UNPROPITIOUS, *adjective*   adverse, hopeless, illdisposed, ill-omened, ill-timed, inauspicious, minatory, ominous, sinister, threatening, unfavorable, unfortunate, unpromising, untoward

UNQUALIFIED *(Not competent), adjective*   deficient, disqualified, ill-qualified, inadequate, incapable, incompetent, ineffective, inefficient, ineligible, inept, inexperienced, inexpert, unable, unadapted, uneffective, unequipped, unfit, unprepared, unready, unsuited
ASSOCIATED CONCEPTS: unqualified opinion

UNQUALIFIED *(Unlimited)*, **adjective** absolute, all-encompassing, boundless, complete, consummate, downright, full, illimitable, immoderate, limitless, measureless, not modified, outright, plenary, *summus,* sweeping, total, unbound, unchecked, unconditional, unconstrained, uncontrolled, unmitigated, unmodified, unreserved, unrestrained, unrestricted, unsparing, unstinted, utter
ASSOCIATED CONCEPTS: unqualified acceptance, unqualified ownership

UNREASONABLE, adjective absurd, asinine, capricious, contorted, contrary, exaggerated, excessive, exorbitant, extravagant, extreme, foolish, groundless, ill-advised, ill-judged, illogical, immoderate, *iniquus,* indefensible, injudicious, inordinate, intemperate, irrational, ludicrous, nonsensical, pervicacious, pointless, preposterous, recalcitrant, ridiculous, senseless, twisted, undue, unfair, unjust, unjustifiable, unsensible, unsound, untenable, unwarranted, unwise
ASSOCIATED CONCEPTS: arbitrary and capricious action, unreasonable delay, unreasonable force, unreasonable rate of interest, unreasonable restraint, unreasonable restraint on alienation, unreasonable search, unreasonable use

UNREFUTABLE, adjective accurate, certain, demonstrated, doubtless, factual, inappealable, incontestable, incontrovertible, indisputable, indubitable, irrefragable, irrefutable, positive, proved, proven, sure, true, unanswerable, unconfutable, uncontroversial, undeniable, unequivocal, unimpeachable, unquestionable, valid, veracious, veritable

UNRELATED, adjective alien, different, differing, discrepant, disparate, dissimilar, diverse, extraneous, foreign, heterogeneous, incomparable, incompatible, incongruous, independent, irrelative, irrelevant, mismatched, separate, strange, unaffiliated, unallied, unassociated, unattached, unconformable, unconnected, ungermane, unlike, unmatched
ASSOCIATED CONCEPTS: unrelated claims

UNRELENTING, adjective adamant, austere, ceaseless, constant, continual, continuous, cruel, determined, diligent, endless, enduring, hard, *immitis,* implacable, incessant, inclement, indefatigable, *inexorabilis,* inexorable, inflexible, merciless, obdurate, perseverant, persevering, persistent, pertinacious, pitiless, relentless, remorseless, resolved, rigid, rigorous, ruthless, sedulous, severe, steadfast, stern, stubborn, tenacious, unappeasable, unbending, uncompassionate, uncompromising, undeviating, unforgiving, unmerciful, unpitying, unsoftening, unsparing, unsympathetic, unwavering, unyielding

UNRELIABLE, adjective capricious, changeful, deceitful, faithless, fallible, false, fickle, inconstant, insecure, irresponsible, perfidious, precarious, shifty, tergiversating, treacherous, two-faced, undependable, unpredictable, unsound, unstable, unsteady, untrue, untrustworthy, vacillating, wavering
ASSOCIATED CONCEPTS: unreliable evidence, unreliable testimony, unreliable witness

UNREMITTING, adjective *adsiduus,* assiduous, ceaseless, constant, continual, continuous, *continuus,* diligent, durable, enduring, incessant, indefatigable, perennial, perpetual, perseverant, persevering, persis-

tent, pertinacious, sedulous, tenacious, unabated, unbroken, unceasing, unchanging, unfailing, unintermittent, uninterrupted, unshifting, unswerving, untiring, unvarying, unwearied

UNREQUITED, adjective thankless, unacknowledged, unanswered, uncompensated, unrecompensed, unremunerated, unrepaid, unreturned, unrewarded

UNRESPONSIVE, adjective aloof, cold, cool, dispassionate, elusive, emotionless, evasive, impassive, inattentive, indifferent, insensitive, irresponsive, laconic, mum, mute, pitiless, reserved, reticent, secretive, taciturn, unanswering, uncommunicative, uncompassionate, unconcerned, unconversable, uncooperative, unemotional, unfeeling, unimpressible, unimpressionable, uninfluenceable, uninterested, unmoved, unreacting, unreplying, unresponding, unsociable, unsympathetic
ASSOCIATED CONCEPTS: evasive contempt, unresponsive answer, unresponsive testimony

UNRESTRAINED *(Not in custody)*, **adjective** free, independent, unbounded, unbridled, unchecked, unconfined, unconstrained, uncurbed, unencumbered, unfettered, unhampered, unhindered, unimpeded, unlimited, unobstructed, unprevented, unshackled, unsuppressed, untrammeled

UNRESTRAINED *(Not repressed)*, **adjective** dissolute, effusive, excessive, extravagant, immoderate, incontinent, intemperate, lawless, lewd, libertine, licentious, loose, prodigal, rampant, spirited, unbridled, unchecked, unconstrained, uncontrolled, uncurbed, undisciplined, unfettered, ungoverned, unhampered, unhindered, unlimited, unreined, unrepressed, unreserved, unsuppressed, wanton, wild

UNRESTRICTED, adjective boundless, *effrenatus,* free, immoderate, independent, limitless, open, permitted, unbound, unbounded, unbridled, unchecked, unconditional, unconfined, unconstrained, uncontained, uncontrolled, unfettered, unforbidden, unlimited, unobstructed, unqualified, unrestrained, unshackled, untrammeled, without strings
ASSOCIATED CONCEPTS: unrestricted use

UNRULY, adjective chaotic, contrary, contumacious, disobedient, disorderly, *effrenatus, ferox,* fractious, froward, hard to control, headstrong, incorrigible, indocile, insubordinate, intractable, irrepressible, lawless, mutinous, obstinate, obstreperous, out of control, perverse, rampant, rebellious, recalcitrant, refractory, resistive, restive, riotous, rowdy, stormy, stubborn, troublesome, turbulent, unbridled, uncompliant, uncomplying, uncontrollable, uncurbed, ungovernable, unmanageable, unrestrained, unsubmissive, untoward, unyielding, wanton, wayward, wild, willful

UNSATISFACTORY, adjective deficient, disagreeable, disappointing, disapproved, displeasing, disquieting, distressing, disturbing, faulty, feeble, imperfect, inadequate, inappropriate, inapt, inept, inexpedient, inferior, insufficient, intolerable, lame, *non idoneus,* not up to par, objectionable, offensive, poor, rejected, unacceptable, unapt, unbefitting, undesirable, unfavorable, unfit, ungratifying, unpleasant, unsatisfying, unseemly, unsuitable, untoward, unwelcome, unworthy, upsetting, useless, vexing, wanting, weak
ASSOCIATED CONCEPTS: unsatisfactory testimony

UNSAVORY, *adjective* disagreeable, disgusting, disliked, distasteful, intolerable, loathsome, mawkish, nasty, nauseating, nauseous, objectionable, obnoxious, offensive, repelling, repugnant, revolting, sickening, unalluring, unappetizing, unattractive, undelectable, undesirable, uninviting, unpalatable, unpleasant, unpleasing

UNSCRUPULOUS, *adjective* base, conscienceless, corrupt, crooked, deceitful, dishonest, dishonorable, disingenuous, faithless, false, fraudulent, immoral, inequitable, iniquitous, lawless, perfidious, profligate, questionable, roguish, ruthless, shifty, sly, treacherous, two-faced, underhand, unethical, unfair, unjust, unlawful, unprincipled, unrestrained, vicious, villainous, wanton, wicked, without integrity, without scruples, wrongful

UNSEEMLY, *adjective* base, boorish, coarse, crude, discreditable, disreputable, distasteful, gross, ignoble, improper, in bad taste, inappropriate, incongruous, incorrect, indecent, indecorous, *indecorus,* indelicate, inelegant, offensive, out of character, out of place, preposterous, reprehensible, rude, shameful, unapt, unbecoming, unbefitting, undignified, undue, unfit, unfitting, ungenteel, unhandsome, unmanly, unmeet, unpraiseworthy, unpresentable, unrefined, unsightly, unsuitable, untasteful, vulgar, wrong

UNSETTLED, *adjective* adrift, afloat, agitated, capricious, changeable, changing, conjectural, deranged, desolate, disarranged, disputable, disturbed, doubtful, dubious, due, fickle, *incertus, inconstans,* inconstant, migratory, mutable, nervous, new, open, outstanding, owing, pending, perturbed, restless, speculative, tentative, transient, troubled, unadjusted, unattached, unbalanced, uncertain, unchartered, uncollected, undecided, undetermined, uneasy, unessayed, unexplored, unfixed, uninhabited, unnerved, unoccupied, unpaid, unresolved, unrooted, unstable, unstaid, unsteady, untried, untrodden, unventured, upset, vacillating, *varius,* wandering, wavering

UNSOLICITED, *adjective* complimentary, free, gratuitous, offered, proffered, unasked, unbidden, uncalled-for, undesired, uninvited, unrequested, unsought, unwanted, unwelcome, unwished, voluntary, volunteered
ASSOCIATED CONCEPTS: unsolicited response, unsolicited sale

UNSOUND *(Fallacious),* **adjective** absurd, defective, disputable, erroneous, false, faulty, groundless, illfounded, illogical, improbable, incongruous, incorrect, insubstantial, invalid, irrational, mistaken, questionable, senseless, sophistical, speculative, unauthentic, ungrounded, unreal, unreasonable, unreasoned, unsubstantial, untenable, untrue, unwarranted, worthless, wrong

UNSOUND *(Not strong),* **adjective** below par, broken, decayed, decrepit, defective, deficient, deranged, deteriorated, diseased, disturbed, exhausted, faulty, feeble, ill, impaired, imperfect, infirm, insecure, insolvent, precarious, sickly, tainted, unbacked, unhealthy, unreliable, unsafe, unsettled, unstable, unsteady, unsubstantial, untrustworthy, unwell, warped, wasted, weak, worn

UNSPECIFIED, *adjective* anonymous, general, generic, indefinable, indefinite, indeterminate, indistinct, non specific, obscure, unacknowledged, unclear, undefined, undesignated, unfixed, unnamed, unsettled, vague

UNSUITABLE, *adjective* absurd, *alienus,* amiss, awkward, conflicting, contrary, discordant, discrepant, disparate, dissonant, disturbing, divergent, ill-adapted, impertinent, improper, imprudent, in bad taste, inadequate, inadmissible, inadvisable, inapplicable, inapposite, inappropriate, inapt, incommodious, *incommodus,* incompatible, incongruous, inconvenient, indecorous, inexpedient, infelicitous, inharmonious, inopportune, intolerable, irrelevant, malapropos, mismatched, objectionable, out of character, out of keeping, out of place, poorly adapted, unacceptable, unapt, unbecoming, unbeseeming, uncongenial, undesirable, unfavorable, unfit, unfitting, unfortunate, unsatisfactory, unsatisfying, unseasonable, unseemly, unsuited, untimely, untoward
ASSOCIATED CONCEPTS: unsuitable for consumption

UNSUPPORTED, *adjective* based on conjecture, baseless, groundless, not authenticated, not established, not substantiated, suppositional, supposititious, unabetted, unaided, unassisted, unattested, unauthenticated, unbacked, uncertified, uncollaborated, unconfirmed, uncorroborated, undemonstrated, unfounded, unproved, unproven, unseconded, unsubstantiated, unsustained, untenable, unvalidated, unverified, without basis, without foundation
ASSOCIATED CONCEPTS: unsupported by a preponderance of the evidence

UNSUSPECTING, *adjective* believing, credulous, easily deceived, gullible, *incautus,* innocent, *minime suspicax,* naive, off guard, simple, trustful, trusting, unaware, unconscious, undoubting, unexpectant, unguarded, unquestioning, unsuspecting, unsuspicious, unwarned, without suspicion

UNSUSTAINABLE, *adjective* baseless, controvertible, doubtful, erroneous, false, groundless, incorrect, insupportable, questionable, unauthentic, unconfirmable, undemonstrable, unmaintainable, unprovable, untenable, untrue, untrustworthy, unverifiable, wrong

UNTENABLE, *adjective* accessible, baseless, controvertible, defenseless, erroneous, exposed, fallacious, false, faulty, groundless, hollow, illogical, implausible, incapable of being defended, incapable of being held, incapable of being maintained, incorrect, indefensible, insupportable, invalid, irrational, powerless, pregnable, questionable, refutable, ridiculous, specious, undefended, undemonstrable, unfortified, unguarded, unjustifiable, unmaintainable, unprotected, unreasonable, unsound, unsustainable, unwarrantable, vincible, vulnerable, weak, wrong

UNTIL, *adverb* as far as, by the time that, down to, pending, til, to, to the time when, up to, up to the time of

UNTIMELY, *adjective* anachronic, anachronistic, anachronous, badly timed, erroneous in date, illadvised, ill-considered, ill-timed, *immaturus,* improper, imprudent, inapposite, inappropriate, inappropriately timed, inauspicious, inconvenient, infelicitous, inopportune, *intempestivus,* malapropos, misjudged, mistimed, out of keeping, out of place, poorly timed, unfavorable, unpromising, unpropitious, unpunctual, unseasonable, unsuitably timed

UNTRUE, *adjective*   apocryphal, contrary to fact, counterfeit, deceitful, deceptive, delusive, dishonest, disingenuous, disloyal, disobedient, erroneous, faithless, fake, fallacious, false, *falsus,* fictitious, forged, fraudulent, groundless, hypocritical, inaccurate, inconstant, incorrect, insidious, insincere, invented, lying, mendacious, misleading, mock, perfidious, prevaricating, recreant, scheming, shifty, spurious, traitorous, treacherous, treasonable, trumped up, truthless, two-faced, uncandid, undutiful, unfaithful, unfounded, unreal, unsubstantial, untrustworthy, untruthful, unveracious, wrong

UNTRUSTWORTHY, *adjective*   capricious, changeable, conniving, deceitful, deceptive, dishonest, dishonorable, disloyal, double-dealing, faithless, fallible, false, fickle, fly-by-night, fraudulent, frivolous, illusive, inconstant, insecure, insidious, irresponsible, mercurial, perfidious, precarious, questionable, shifty, slippery, tergiversating, treacherous, two-faced, unauthenticated, uncertain, undependable, unfaithful, unreliable, unsafe, unsound, unstable, unsteadfast, untrue, unworthy of confidence, unworthy of trust, variable, wavering

UNUSUAL, *adjective*   aberrant, abnormal, alien, amazing, anomalous, astonishing, astounding, atypical, bizarre, choice, conspicuous, curious, different, distinctive, distinguished, exceptional, extraordinary, extreme, fantastic, fresh, important, incomparable, inconceivable, inconsistent, incredible, indescribable, individual, infrequent, inusitate, irregular, little-known, marked, marvelous, matchless, memorable, modern, new, newfangled, nonpareil, notable, noteworthy, novel, occasional, odd, offbeat, original, out of the ordinary, outlandish, outstanding, particular, peculiar, peerless, phenomenal, portentous, prodigious, prominent, radical, rare, refreshing, remarkable, scarce, significant, singular, special, startling, strange, striking, supernormal, surprising, unaccustomed, unclassifiable, uncommon, unconventional, uncustomary, unequaled, unexpected, unfamiliar, unhabitual, unheard of, unique, unmatched, unnatural, unorthodox, unparalleled, unprecedented, unprevalent, unrivaled, unroutine, untraditional, untypical, unwonted
ASSOCIATED CONCEPTS: cruel and unusual punishment

UNVEIL, *verb*   *aperire,* bare, begin, bring to light, demonstrate, denude, *detegere,* disclose, display, divest, divulge, exhibit, expose, extract, lay open, make known, make plain, make visible, manifest, open up, originate, present, reveal, show, start, strip, uncase, uncloak, unconceal, uncover, uncurtain, undrape, undress, unfold, unmask, unrobe, unseal, unwrap

UNVERSED, *adjective*   ignorant, illiterate, *imperitus,* inexperienced, inexpert, raw, *rudis,* unacquainted, unclever, unconversant, undisciplined, undrilled, uneducated, unexcercised, unfamiliar, unindoctrinated, uninformed, uninitiated, unknowing, unknowledgeable, unlearned, unlettered, unpracticed, unprepared, unproficient, unqualified, unread, unschooled, unskilled, unstudied, untaught

UNWARRANTED, *adjective*   arbitrary, baseless, excessive, fulsome, groundless, immoderate, improper, indefensible, inexcusable, inordinate, needless, objectionable, outrageous, overmuch, superabundant, superfluous, supernumerary, unauthorized, uncalled-for, unconscionable, undue, unentitled, unfair, unfounded, unjust, unjustifiable, unjustified, unlawful, unnecessary, unreasonable, unsanctioned, unwarrantable, wrongful

UNWILLINGLY, *adverb*   adversely, demurringly, indisposedly, involuntarily, recalcitrantly, reluctantly, unconsentingly, without assent, without consent
ASSOCIATED CONCEPTS: unknowingly

UNWITTING, *adjective*   accidental, adventitious, aimless, blind, chance, fortuitous, ignorant, inadvertent, *insciens, inscius,* involuntary, purposeless, thoughtless, unapprized, unaware, unconscious, undesigned, unexpected, uninformed, unintended, unintentional, unknowing, unmeant, unmindful, unpremeditated, unpurposed, unsuspecting, unthinking

UNWORTHY, *adjective*   base, contemptible, inferior, lacking worth, meager, meritless, not fit, undeserving, unfit, unqualified, worthless

UNYIELDING, *adjective*   adamant, adamantine, constant, decided, dedicated, determined, devoted, enduring, faithful, firm, fixed, hard, headstrong, immobile, immovable, impliant, indomitable, inductile, inexorable, inflexible, intractable, intransigent, invariable, obdurate, obstinate, opinionated, perseverant, persevering, persistent, pertinacious, perverse, pervicacious, recalcitrant, refractory, relentless, renitent, resisting, resolute, resolved, rigid, sedulous, set, settled, solid, stable, stanch, steadfast, steady, stern, stiff, strong, stubborn, tenacious, tough, true, unbending, unchangeable, uncompromising, uncontrollable, undeviating, ungovernable, unimpressible, uninfluenceable, unmanageable, unpliable, unwavering, wayward, willful, zealous

UPHOLD, *verb*   accept, acknowledge, advocate, affirm, agree with, aid, approve, assert, assist, authenticate, back, back up, bear up, bolster, brace, buttress, carry, champion, confirm, corroborate, countenance, decide in favor of, defend, elevate, encourage, endorse, espouse, favor, guard, help, hold up, justify, keep, maintain, perpetuate, preserve, prop, protect, raise, sanction, second, speak for, stand by, stand up for, stay, substantiate, support, sustain, *sustentare, sustinere,* upraise, vindicate, warrant
ASSOCIATED CONCEPTS: uphold a decision, uphold the law

UPRIGHT, *adjective*   aboveboard, candid, circumspect, conscientious, erect, estimable, ethical, fair, forthright, good, guileless, highly principled, honest, *honestus,* honorable, incorruptible, *integer,* just, laudable, legitimate, moral, *probus,* pure, reasonable, reputable, respectable, righteous, scrupulous, square, straightforward, trustworthy, truthful, uncorrupt, unimpeachable, upstanding, veracious, virtuous, worthy

UPSET, *verb*   agitate, beat, bother, capsize, confuse, conquer, crush, defeat, demolish, derange, destroy, disarrange, discomfit, discompose, disconcert, disorganize, displace, disquiet, distress, disturb, embarrass, enrage, *evertere,* fluster, invert, overpower, overthrow, overturn, overwhelm, perturb, put out of order, quash, re-

verse, ruin, shock, startle, subvert, *subvertere,* supersede, tip over, topple, tumble, turn upside down, undo, unnerve, unsettle, upend, vanquish, worst
ASSOCIATED CONCEPTS: upset a lower court's ruling

URGE, *verb* activate, adjure, advance, advise, advocate, appeal to, beg, beseech, coax, drive, encourage, entreat, evoke, exhort, expostulate, goad, hurry, impel, *impellere,* implore, importune, *incitare,* incite, insist, instigate, invite, motivate, move, persuade, prescribe, press, prevail upon, prod, promote, prompt, propel, provoke, push, recommend, request, rouse, solicit, spur, stimulate, *urgere*

URGENT, *adjective* clamant, compelling, compulsory, critical, crucial, crying, demanding, earnest, essential, exigent, grave, *gravis,* impelling, imperative, important, importunate, indispensable, insistent, instant, *necessarius,* necessary, necessitous, pressing, required, serious, vital, weighty

USAGE, *noun* application, conduct, consuetude, *consuetudo,* convention, custom, customary use, disposition, employment, established custom, established practice, fashion, fixed procedure, form, formula, habit, habitual use, habitude, management, manner, method, mode, *mos,* operation, practice, prescription, prevalence, routine, service, style, system, tradition, treatment, use, utilization, vogue, wear, wont
ASSOCIATED CONCEPTS: common usage, custom and usage, general usage
FOREIGN PHRASES: *Consuetudo ex certa causa rationabili usitata privat communem legem.* A custom, based on a certain and reasonable cause, supersedes the common law. *Optimus interpres rerum usus.* Usage is the best interpreter of things. *In contractibus, tacite insunt quae sunt moris et consuetudinis.* In contracts, matters of custom and usage are tacitly implied. *Non ex opinionibus singulorum, sed ex communi usu, nomina exaudiri debent.* The names of things ought to be understood, not according to individual opinions, but according to common usage. *Obtemperandum est consuetudini rationabili tanquam legi.* A reasonable custom is to be obeyed like law. *Quae praeter consuetudinem et morem majorum fiunt neque placent neque recta videntur.* Things which are done contrary to the custom and manner of our ancestors neither please nor appear right.

USE, *noun* adhibition, adoption, application, avail, benefit, convenience, disposal, disposition, employment, enjoyment, exercitation, exploitation, function, means, practice, purpose, service, serviceability, suitability, usage, usefulness, *usus, utilitas,* utility, utilization
ASSOCIATED CONCEPTS: actual use, apparent use, beneficial use, best and highest use, business use, charitable use, common use, contingent use, convenient use, corporate use, customary use, declared use, domestic use, dominent use, exclusive use, existing use, forseeable use, hostile use, lawful use, mutual use, nonconforming use, nonpublic use, normal use, offensive use, official use, ordinary use, permissive use, personal use, primary use, principal use, private use, reasonable use, resulting use, secondary use, shifting use, Statute of Uses, suitable use, unfit for use, use and derivate use

USUAL, *adjective* abundant, accepted, accustomed, acknowledged, average, banal, casual, charac-

teristic, characterless, colorless, common, commonplace, conformable, conforming, consistent, consuetudinal, consuetudinary, conventional, current, customary, daily, established, everyday, expected, familiar, frequent, general, habitual, humdrum, inconspicuous, indifferent, insignificant, known, mediocre, middling, moderate, monotonous, natural, nondescript, normal, ordinary, orthodox, pat, pedestrian, plain, plentiful, popular, prevailing, prevalent, prosaic, prosy, recurrent, regular, repeated, representative, rife, routine, set, stale, standard, stereotyped, stock, tedious, traditional, trivial, typical, undistinctive, undistinguished, unexceptional, unimaginitive, unimpressive, uninteresting, universal, unmarked, unmemorable, unoriginal, unremarkable, unsophisticated, unsurprising, unvaried, vernacular, well-known, well-trodden, wonted, workaday
ASSOCIATED CONCEPTS: usual conduct, usual course of conduct, usual place of abode, usual terms

USURIOUS, *adjective* criminal interest, excessive, exorbitant, extortionate, illegal, immoderate, improper rate of interest, inordinate, unconscionable, undue, unreasonable

USURP, *verb* accroach, appropriate unlawfully, arrogate, assume, assume command, assume without authority, commandeer, encroach, help oneself to, hold by force, lay hold of, seize, seize power, *sibi adsumere,* squat, steal, take, take charge, take possession, wrest

USURY, *noun* criminal rate of interest, excessive interest, excessive rate, exorbitant interest, exploitation, *faeneratio,* high interest, illegal interest, overcharge, unconscionable rate of interest

UTILITY *(Public service),* *noun* public business, public company, public corporation, public industry

UTILITY *(Usefulness),* *noun* adequacy, advantage, advantageousness, applicability, avail, benefit, convenience, efficacy, employability, fruitfulness, function, helpfulness, practicality, productiveness, productivity, profit, profitability, service, serviceability, suitability, usability, use, value
FOREIGN PHRASES: *Omne magnum exemplum habet aliquid ex iniquo, quod publica utilitate compensatur.* Every great example has some unfairness, which is compensated by the public utility.

UTILIZATION, *noun* applicability, employability, practicality, serviceability, usability, usefulness

UTMOST, *adjective* extreme, furthest, greatest, highest, maximal, maximum, most, superlative, supreme
ASSOCIATED CONCEPTS: utmost care

UTMOST, *noun* best, degree, extreme limit, extremity, farthest reach, furthest point, greatest amount, greatest degree, highest, maximum, optimum, the most possible

UTTER, *verb* air, announce, articulate, assert, asseverate, aver, breathe, broach, circulate, come out with, communicate, declaim, declare, deliver, *dicere,* disclose, divulge, emit, enunciate, express, give expression to, give forth, impart, issue, make known, mouth, proclaim, pronounce, propound, publicize, publish, recite, reveal, sound, speak, spread, state, talk, tell, vent, voice

V

VACANT, *adjective*   bare, blank, clear, depleted, deserted, devoid, disengaged, empty, exhausted, free, hollow, idle, not in use, not occupied, open, unemployed, unfilled, uninhabited, unoccupied, unpossessed, untenanted, unused, unutilized, vacuous, *vacuus,* void

VACATE *(Leave), verb*   abandon, cease, depart, depart from, desert, empty, evacuate, exit, forgo, go away, move, move out, quit, relinquish, remove, retreat, surrender, *vacuefacere,* withdraw
ASSOCIATED CONCEPTS: vacate premises

VACATE *(Void), verb*   abandon, abdicate, abolish, abrogate, annul, cancel, countermand, deprive of force, disannul, do away with, eliminate, evacuate, invalidate, make void, negate, nullify, overrule, quash, recant, relinquish, render inoperative, repeal, rescind, retract, reverse, revoke, set aside
ASSOCIATED CONCEPTS: vacate a default, vacate a judgment, vacate an award, vacate an order, vacate occupancy, vacate office

VACILLATE, *verb*   alternate, be capricious, be inconstant, be irresolute, be uncertain, be unsettled, be unsteady, be unsure, change, debate, demur, equivocate, falter, feel uncertain, fluctuate, hesitate, hover, librate, move to and fro, oscillate, rock, seesaw, shift, show indecision, stagger, sway, swing, totter, undulate, *vacillare,* vibrate, waver

VACUOUS, *adjective*   absent, barren, blank, depleted, devoid, drained, dull, empty, empty-headed, exhausted, expressionless, fatuous, foolish, hollow, idle, inadequate, inane, incogitative, insufficient, lacking content, missing, null, purposeless, senseless, silly, stupid, thoughtless, unfilled, unintelligent, unoccupied, unreasoning, unthinking, vacant, void, wanting

VAGRANCY, *noun*   evagation, hoboism, indolence, itinerancy, pererration, roaming, roving, shiftlessness, vagabondage, vagabondism, wandering, wayfaring
ASSOCIATED CONCEPTS: common-law vagrancy, loitering

VAGUE, *adjective*   ambiguous, *ambiguus,* amorphous, blurred, blurry, broad, cloudy, confused, cryptic, dim, doubtful, dubious, *dubius,* enigmatic, equivocal, evasive, faint, general, ill-defined, impalpable, impre-

cise, *incertus,* incomprehensible, indecisive, indefinite, indeterminate, indistinct, indistinguishable, inexplicit, intangible, misunderstood, mysterious, nebulous, obscure, perplexing, poorly defined, problematical, questionable, shadowy, uncertain, unclear, undefined, undetermined, unsettled, unspecified, unsure
ASSOCIATED CONCEPTS: void for vagueness
FOREIGN PHRASES: *Res est misera ubi jus est vagum et incertum.* It is a sorry state of affairs when law is vague and mutable.

VALID, *adjective*   accurate, attested, authentic, authoritative, authorized, binding, bona fide, canonic, canonical, conclusive, confirmed, constitutional, correct, credible, effective, effectual, enforceable, executed with proper formalities, factual, *firmus,* forcible, good, *gravis,* having legal force, having legal strength, *iustus,* lawful, legal, legalized, legally binding, legitimate, licit, logical, official, potent, powerful, proved, sanctioned, scientific, solid, sound, statutory, strong, substantial, supportable by law, sustainable in law, true, truthful, veritable, warranted, well-grounded
ASSOCIATED CONCEPTS: valid argument, valid case, valid claim, valid commitment, valid consideration, valid contract, valid delivery, valid existing marriage, valid gift, valid judgment, valid obligation, valid reasoning, valid reasons, valid statute

VALIDATE, *verb*   accept, affirm, approve, attest, authorize, certify, circumstantiate, confirm, corroborate, declare legal, declare valid, endorse, give legal force, legalize, legitimatize, legitimize, make binding, make legal, make valid, prove, qualify, ratify, sanction, seal, stamp, substantiate, verify, warrant
ASSOCIATED CONCEPTS: validate a sale, validate records

VALIDITY, *noun*   authenticity, authority, correctness, force, forcefulness, genuineness, *gravitas,* lawfulness, legal force, legality, legitimacy, legitimateness, meritoriousness, *pondus,* potency, power, puissance, reality, realness, significance, soundness, strength, trueness, truth, veracity, verity
ASSOCIATED CONCEPTS: validity of a statute
FOREIGN PHRASES: *Quod in minori valet valebit in majori; et quod in majori non valet nec valebit in minori.* That which is valid in the greater shall be valid

512

in the less; and that which is not valid in the greater shall neither be valid in the less. *Nul charter, nul vente, ne nul done vault perpetualment, si le donor n'est seise al temps de contracts de deux droits, sc. del droit de possession et del droit de propertie.* No grant, no sale, no gift, is valid forever, unless the donor, at the time of the contract, has two rights, namely, the right of possession, and the right of property. *Quae ab initio non valent, ex post facto convalescere non possunt.* Things invalid from the beginning cannot be made valid by a subsequent act. *Semper praesumitur pro matrimonio.* The presumption is always in favor of the validity of a marriage. *Quod initio vitiosum est non potest tractu temporis convalescere.* That which is void from the beginning cannot become valid by lapse of time. *Pacta conventa quae neque contra leges neque dolo malo inita sunt omni modo observanda sunt.* Agreements which are not contrary to the laws nor entered into with a fraudulent design must be observed in all respects. *Quod initio non valet, tractu temporis non valet.* That which is void at the beginning does not become valid by lapse of time.

VALUABLE, *adjective*   above par, advantageous, beneficial, choice, commanding a good price, costly, dear, desirable, edifying, effective, effectual, efficacious, esteemed, estimable, excellent, expensive, favorable, fine, gainful, good, helpful, important, in demand, inestimable, invaluable, marketable, operative, precious, *pretiosus,* prizable, profitable, rare, relevant, remunerative, rewarding, salable, select, serviceable, significant, suitable, superior, treasured, useful, utilitarian, worthy
ASSOCIATED CONCEPTS: valuable consideration

VALUE, *noun*   advantage, *aestimatio,* amount, appraisal, assessment, benefit, caliber, consequence, cost, desirability, effect, equivalent, esteem, estimate, estimation, excellence, expense, force, impact, importance, merit, price, purport, quality, quotation, significance, substance, superiority, use, usefulness, utility, valuation, worth, worthiness
ASSOCIATED CONCEPTS: acquisition value, actual cash value, actual market value, appraised value, assessed value, book value, cash market value, cash surrender value, current market value, face value, fair and reasonable value, fair market value, fair value, full cash value, good faith purchaser for value, gross value, highest market value, holder for value, instrument of value, insurable value, intrinsic value, market value, negotiable instrument, nominal value, nuisance value, par value, pecuniary value, present value, probative value, prospective value, purchaser for value, real value, reasonable value, relative value, rental value, reserve value, residual value, retention value, substantial value, sufficient value, surrender value, tangible value, taxable value, transfer for value, true value, value received
FOREIGN PHRASES: *Libertas non recipit aestimationem.* Freedom does not admit a valuation. *Tantum bona valent, quantum vendipossunt.* Goods are worth as much as they are sold for. *Res per pecuniam aestimatur, et non pecunia per rem.* The value of a thing is estimated according to its worth in money, but the value of money is not estimated by reference to property. *Sapientia legis nummario pretio non est aestimanda.* The wisdom of the law cannot be computed in money value.

VANDAL, *noun*   criminal, defacer, demolisher, destroyer, evildoer, lawbreaker, pillager, plunderer, raider, ravager, reprobate, robber, ruiner, spoiler, transgressor, wrecker

VANWARD, *adverb*   forward, frontward, headward, in advance, in front, in the lead, onward

VARIABLE, *adjective*   aberrant, alterable, capricious, changeable, changeful, erratic, faithless, fanciful, fast and loose, fickle, fitful, fluctuating, inconstant, irregular, irresponsible, mercurial, modifiable, oscillating, protean, shifting, spasmodic, uneven, unreliable, unsettled, unstable, unsteadfast, unsteady, vagrant, variant, volatile, wavering, wayward

VARIANCE *(Disagreement), noun*   alienation, altercation, breach, contention, contrariety, controversy, difference, disaccord, discongruity, discord, *discordia,* discrepancy, disharmony, disparity, dispute, *dissensio,* dissension, dissent, dissidence, disunity, divergence, diversity, division, incompatibility, nonagreement, odds, opposition, quarrel, rupture, split, strife, unconformity

VARIANCE *(Exemption), noun*   anomaly, deviation, divergence, exception, leave, special dispensation

VARY, *verb*   alter, alternate, assort, be inconstant, be unlike, change, contrast, depart, deviate, differ, diverge, diversify, exchange, fluctuate, give variety, innovate, interchange, make a change, make different, modify, *mutare,* mutate, reorganize, rotate, shift, show variety, transfigure, transform, transmute, turn into, vacillate, *variare,* variegate, veer, waver
ASSOCIATED CONCEPTS: vary the terms of an agreement

VEHEMENT, *adjective*   agitated, angry, ardent, boisterous, burning, clamorous, demonstrative, eager, earnest, emphatic, enthusiastic, excited, explosive, fanatical, *fervens,* fervent, fervid, fierce, fiery, forceful, forcible, frenzied, furious, glowing, headstrong, heated, hot, impassioned, impetuous, impulsive, *incitatus,* inflamed, insistent, intense, lusty, mighty, passionate, perfervid, powerful, rabid, rampant, strong, tempestuous, turbulent, unequivocal, urgent, violent, volcanic, wild, zealous

VEIL, *noun*   camouflage, cloak, cloud, concealment, cover, covering, curtain, guise, *involucrum, integumentum,* mantle, mask, pall, protection, screen, shade, shelter, shield, shroud, visor, vizard
ASSOCIATED CONCEPTS: pierce the corporate veil

VENAL, *adjective*   avaricious, bribable, corrupt, corruptible, dishonorable, extortionate, grasping, greedy, mercenary, *nummarius,* purchasable, self-seeking, *venalis*

VEND, *verb*   auction, deal in, dispense, make a sale, market, offer for sale, peddle, put up for sale, retail, sell, trade, unload
ASSOCIATED CONCEPTS: vendee, vendor, vendor's lien

VENDOR, *noun*   businessman, chapman, dealer, hawker, huckster, merchant, monger, peddler, retailer, salesman, seller, trader, tradesman
ASSOCIATED CONCEPTS: good faith vendor, vendor's liability, vendor's lien, vendor's title

VENGEANCE, *noun*   avengement, enmity, implacability, malevolence, nemesis, punishment, rancor, repayment, reprisal, retaliation, retribution, retributive punishment, revenge, revengefulness, *ultio,* vendetta, vengefulness, *vindicta,* vindictiveness

VENIRE, *noun*   authoritative citation to appear before a court, command to appear, notification to appear, required to attend, subpoena, summons

VENTURE, *noun*   adventure, *alea,* attempt, business, campaign, chance, crusade, danger, dangerous undertaking, endeavor, enterprise, essay, experiment, *facinus,* gamble, hazard, investment, jeopardy, move, *periculum,* peril, plunge, project, quest, risk, risky undertaking, speculation, step, task, test, trial, uncertainty, wager
ASSOCIATED CONCEPTS: business venture, joint venture, private venture

VENUE, *noun*   county, jurisdiction, locale, locality, location, neighborhood, place of jurisdiction, political subdivision, position, seat, site, station, territory
ASSOCIATED CONCEPTS: *forum non conveniens*
FOREIGN PHRASES: *Triatio ibi semper debet fieri, ubi juratores meliorem possunt habere notitiam.* Trial ought always to be had where the jurors can have the best information.

VERACITY, *noun*   accuracy, actuality, artlessness, authenticity, candidness, candor, conformity to fact, correctness, credibility, exactitude, exactness, factualness, faithfulness, frankness, genuiness, guilelessness, honesty, ingenuousness, integrity, precision, principle, probity, rectitude, sincerity, trustworthiness, truth, truthfulness, veraciousness, veridicality, *veritas,* verity, virtue
ASSOCIATED CONCEPTS: reputation for veracity, veracity of a witness

VERBAL, *adjective*   audible, expressed, nuncupative, oral, parole, pronounced, recited, spoken, stated, unwritten, uttered, *verbum,* voiced, *vox*
ASSOCIATED CONCEPTS: Statute of Frauds, verbal acts, verbal agreements, verbal contracts, verbal gift, verbal no fault threshold

VERBATIM, *adjective*   exact, following the letter, literal, precise, true to the letter, word for word

VERBATIM, *adverb*   chapter and verse, in the same words, literally, literatim, strictly to the letter, to the letter, word for word

VERDICT, *noun*   adjudication, answer, assessment, award, conclusion, decision, decision of a jury, declaration of a jury, decree of a jury, definitive answer, determination, finding, *iudicium,* judgment, opinion of the jury, pronouncement of a jury, resolution by a jury, ruling, sentence, *sententia*
ASSOCIATED CONCEPTS: adverse verdict, arbitrary verdict, compromise verdict, directed verdict, estoppel by verdict, excessive verdict, final verdict, general verdict, incongruous verdict, informal verdict, judgment notwithstanding verdict, open verdict, partial verdict, quotient verdict, recorded verdict, rendering of a verdict, special verdict, unanimous verdict, void verdict
FOREIGN PHRASES: *Veredictum, quasi dictum veritatis; ut judicium, quasi juris dictum.* A verdict is, as it were, the expression of the truth; as a judgment is, as it were, the expression of the law. *Non obstante veredicto.* Notwithstanding the verdict.

VERIDICAL, *adjective*   authentic, bona fide, genuine, honest, inartificial, legitimate, natural, real, sincere, true, truth-telling, truthful, uncounterfeited, unfaked, unficticious, unperjured, unpretending, unsynthetic, veracious, verifiable

VERIFY *(Confirm), verb*   accredit, assure, attest, bear out, certify, check, circumstantiate, *confirmare,* corroborate, document, establish, establish the truth of, give evidence, make certain, make sure, *probare,* produce evidence, prove, substantiate, support, validate
ASSOCIATED CONCEPTS: verified copy

VERIFY *(Swear), verb*   affirm, asseverate, attest, avouch, avow, declare, evidence, guarantee, state, testify, vouch for, vow, warrant, witness
ASSOCIATED CONCEPTS: verify pleadings

VEST, *verb*   authorize, bestow upon, clothe, confer, consign, empower, enable, endow, entrust, establish, furnish, give authority, give control, invest, place authority, place control, put in possession, sanction
ASSOCIATED CONCEPTS: contingently vested, estate vested subject to being divested, indefeasibly vested, vested estate, vested future estate, vested gift, vested in possession, vested interest, vested legacy, vested property right, vested remainder, vested remainder subject to open, vested right, vesting of title

VETERAN, *adjective*   adept, adroit, apt, capable, deft, dexterous, disciplined, experienced, expert, facile, finished, knowing, practiced, proficient, qualified, seasoned, skilled, sophisticated, talented, trained, tried, world-wise

VETERAN, *noun*   dean, expert, knowing person, old campaigner, old soldier, person of experience, practiced hand, senior statesman, sophisticate

VETO, *noun*   ban, bar, denial, disallowance, embargo, forbiddance, inhibition, injunction, *intercessio,* interdict, interdiction, interference, negative, prevention, prohibition, proscription, refusal of approval, refusal to sanction, rejection, restraint, restriction, taboo

VEXATIOUS, *adjective*   aggravating, annoying, bothersome, disturbing, exasperating, galling, harassing, irksome, irritating, maddening, pestering, provocative, provoking, syncophantic, tiresome, troublesome, trying, wearisome

VIABLE, *adjective*   acceptable, actable, alive, appropriate, apt, capable of development, capable of growth, conceivable, doable, effective, effectual, efficacious, encouraging, expedient, favorable, feasible, functional, imaginable, legitimate, likely, living, logical, operative, performable, plausible, possible, potential, practicable, practical, promising, propitious, reasonable, sensible, sound, suitable, thinkable, usable, useful, valid, vital, workable

VICARIOUS *(Delegated), adjective*   acting, acting as a substitute, commissioned, deputed, empathic, intermediary, mental, perceptive, procuratory, sympathetic, sympathizing, taking the place of another, understanding

VICARIOUS *(Substitutional)*, **adjective** alternate, alternative, equivalent, ersatz, makeshift, provisional, representational, temporary, tentative
ASSOCIATED CONCEPTS: vicarious liability

VICE, **noun** atrocity, bad habit, blemish, corruption, debauchery, defect, deficiency, degeneracy, delinquency, depravation, depravity, dereliction, dissipation, dissoluteness, evil, excess, failing, failure, fault, flaw, foible, fraility, immoral habit, immorality, imperfection, impurity, inadequacy, incontinence, indecency, indulgence, infamy, infirmity, iniquity, lack, lewdness, libertinism, licentiousness, looseness, mar, maleficence, malignance, misconduct, misdeed, obliquity, outrage, perversion, profligacy, shortcoming, sin, sinfulness, transgression, turpitude, unchastity, vileness, wantonness, weak point, weakness, wickedness, wrong, wrongdoing

VICINITY, **noun** area, confines, environs, neighborhood, outskirts, precincts, propinquity, proximity, purlieu, region, scene, setting, suburbs, surroundings, territory, zone

VICIOUS, **adjective** abandoned, acrimonious, atrocious, barbarous, beastly, blameworthy, brutal, censurable, contrary, corrupt, criminal, cruel, dangerous, debased, degenerate, demoralized, depraved, devilish, diabolical, disgraceful, evil, evil-minded, ferocious, fierce, flawed, foul, frightful, given to vice, guilty, hateful, heinous, horrid, ill-disposed, ill-natured, immoral, imperfect, improper, impure, incorrigible, inhuman, inimical, iniquitous, malevolent, malicious, malign, malignant, mean, merciless, mischievous, nasty, offensive, pernicious, perverse, profligate, recalcitrant, refractory, reprehensible, reprobate, savage, scandalous, shameless, spiteful, steeped in vice, treacherous, *turpis,* uncivilized, unfriendly, unprincipled, unrighteous, unruly, untamed, venomous, vile, villainous, virulent, *vitiosus,* wicked, wrong
ASSOCIATED CONCEPTS: vicious propensity

VICISSITUDES, **noun** alteration, alternating conditions, alternation, changes, fluctuations, interchanges, modifications, successions, successive phases, transformations, ups and downs, variations

VICTIM, **noun** casualty, complainant, complaining witness, *hostia,* injured, prey, quarry, sufferer, target, unfortunate person, unlucky person, *victima*

VIGILANT, **adjective** alert, apprehensive, attentive, canny, careful, cautious, circumspect, guarded, heedful, *intentus,* judicious, keenly aware, observant, on guard, precautious, prescient, provident, *providus,* prudent, regardful, scrupulous, searching, sharp, suspicious, unsleeping, unslumbering, *vigilans,* wakeful, wary, watchful, wide awake

VILIFICATION, **noun** abuse, abusive language, blackening, calumniation, calumny, contemptuous language, contumely, defamation, denigration, denunciation, detraction, impugnment, invective, malediction, opprobrium, revilement, scorn, slander, smear, traducement, verbal attack, vituperation

VINDICATE, **verb** absolve, account for, acquit, clear, declare innocent, discharge, dismiss, exculpate, excuse, exonerate, give good reasons for, justify, par-

don, *probare,* pronounce not guilty, *purgare,* release, relieve of burden, reprieve, set free

VINDICTIVE, **adjective** angry, avenging, grudgeful, implacable, inclined to vengeance, malevolent, malicious, malignant, punitive, punitory, rancorous, resentful, retaliative, retaliatory, retributive, revengeful, spiteful, *ulciscendi cupidus,* unforgiving, unrelenting, vengeful, vindicatory

VIOLATE, **verb** act illegally, break, constuprate, contravene, defy, desecrate, dishonor, disobey, disregard, disrespect, do violence to, encroach upon, fail to keep, fail to observe, infringe, injure, invade, offend against the law, *rumpere,* trample on, transgress, treat improperly, treat without reverence, trespass, *violare*
ASSOCIATED CONCEPTS: violate the law

VIOLATION, **noun** abuse, breach, *contra leges,* dereliction, desecration, disturbance, encroachment, illegality, impiety, infraction, infringement, interruption, invasion, irreverence, lawbreaking, misbehavior, mistreatment, misuse, nonobservance, offense, recusancy, transgression, trespass, wrong
ASSOCIATED CONCEPTS: crime, felony, misdemeanor
FOREIGN PHRASES: *Mulcta damnum famae non irrogat.* A fine does not impose a loss of reputation.

VIOLENCE, **noun** assault, attack, brutality, clash, convulsion, disorder, eruption, explosion, ferocity, force, fracas, furiousness, fury, inclemency, *manus,* onslaught, outburst, rage, rampage, ruthlessness, savagery, severity, unlawful force, vehemence, *violentia,* wildness
FOREIGN PHRASES: *Insanus est qui, abjecta ratione, omnia cum impetu et furore facit.* A person is insane who, deprived of reason, does everything with violence and rage. *Paci sunt maxime contraria vis et injuria.* Violence and injury are especially hostile to peace. *Est autem vis legem simulans.* Violence may also be masquerading as the law.

VIRTUAL, **adjective** basic, capable, constructive, deep down, deep rooted, deep seated, equivalent, essential, fundamental, implicit, indirect, inherent, intrinsic, material, potent, potential, powerful, practical, substantive, tantamount to, underlying, viable
ASSOCIATED CONCEPTS: virtual adoption, virtual representation

VIRULENT, **adjective** *acerbus,* acrid, acrimonious, antagonistic, baleful, baneful, bitter, deadly, deleterious, despiteful, destructive, envenomed, *gravis,* harmful, hateful, hostile, hurtful, injurious, lethal, malevolent, malicious, malign, malignant, mordacious, noxious, pernicious, poison, poisonous, rancorous, spiteful, toxic, treacherous, unfriendly, venomous, violent

VISIBLE *(In full view)*, **adjective** clear, distinct, in focus, in full view, in plain sight, in sight, in view, manifest, perceptible, plain, seeable, showing, viewable, well defined

VISIBLE *(Noticeable)*, **adjective** apparent, conspicuous, detectable, discernible, observable, perceivable, recognizable
ASSOCIATED CONCEPTS: visible easements, visible mark, visible means of support, visible possession, visible property, visible risk, visible sign of injury

VISION *(Dream),* **noun** abstraction, apparition, appearance, concept, conception, discernment, fantasy, form, glance, glimpse, illusion, image, look, perception, perspective, phenomenon, picture, presence, revelation, shape, spectacle, specter

VISION *(Sight),* **noun** field of view, vista

VITAL, *adjective* basic, cardinal, chief, critical, essential, extremely important, fundamental, important, indispensable, irreplaceable, life-supporting, main, necessary to life, needed, paramount, pressing, primary, principal, radical, required, requisite, urgent, vitalic, *vitalis*

VITIATE, *verb* abolish, abrogate, annul, blight, cancel, counteract, damage, *depravare,* destroy, disannul, impair, injure, invalidate, make faulty, make imperfect, make impure, make ineffective, make void, mar, negate, negative, neutralize, nullify, overturn, pervert, poison, pollute, quash, render defective, render inefficacious, rescind, reverse, spoil, sully, tamper with, undo, *vitiare,* weaken
FOREIGN PHRASES: *Crimen omnia ex se nata vitiat.* Crime vitiates all that is born of it.

VOID *(Empty),* *adjective* abandoned, bare, barren, blank, deserted, desolate, destitute, devoid, forsaken, free, hollow, *inanis,* lacking, unfilled, unfurnished, uninhabited, unoccupied, unsupplied, untenanted, vacant, vacuous, *vacuus,* wanting, without contents

VOID *(Invalid),* *adjective* cancelled, ineffective, ineffectual, inoperative, *inritus,* insubstantial, meaningless, not binding, not in force, nugatory, null, null and void, unenforceable, useless, *vanus,* without legal force
ASSOCIATED CONCEPTS: void act, void contract, void in part, void in toto, void judgment, void marriage, void on its face, void process, voidable
FOREIGN PHRASES: *Quae ab initio non valent, ex post facto convalescere non possunt.* Things invalid from the beginning cannot be made valid by a subsequent act. *Judicium a non suo judice datum nullius est momenti.* A judgment rendered by one who is not the proper judge is of no force. *Quod initio non valet, tractu temporis non valet.* That which is void at the beginning does not become valid by lapse of time. *Quod initio vitiosum est non potest tractu temporis convalescere.* That which is void from the beginning cannot become valid by lapse of time.

VOIDABLE, *adjective* capable of being adjudged invalid, capable of being adjudged void, capable of being annulled, capable of being declared ineffectual, capable of being declared void, defeasible, liable to be annulled, nullifiable, revocable, subject to being revoked, subject to cancellation
ASSOCIATED CONCEPTS: voidable contract, voidable judgment, voidable marriage, voidable preference

VOIR DIRE, *noun* examination for qualification for jury service, hearing before the court, hearing without jury's presence, inquiry, judicial examination

VOLATILE, *adjective* active, animated, brief, brisk, buoyant, capricious, changeable, cometary, deciduous, desultory, effervescent, elastic, elusive, ephemeral, erratic, evanescent, evaporable, excitable, explosive, fickle, fleeting, flighty, full of spirit, giddy, humorsome, inconstant, instable, irresolute, *levis,* lively, mercurial, *mobilis,* momentary, passing, precarious, quick, shallow, short-lived, spirited, sprightly, transient, transitory, unstable, unsteady, vacillating, vaporable, vaporizable, vaporous, *volaticus,* wavering

VOLITION, **noun** accord, choice, decision, desire, determination, discretion, election, elective preference, exercise of will, free agency, free will, intent, option, pick, power of choice, preference, purpose, resolution, selection, *voluntas,* will, willingness, wish

VOLUBLE, *adjective* copious, declamatory, discursive, eloquent, effusive, expansive, fluent, garrulous, glib, long-winded, loquacious, multiloquent, profuse, rambling, ready-tongued, rhetorical, talkative, verbose, wordy

VOLUNTARY, *adjective* conative, deliberate, designed, discretionary, effected by choice, elective, facultative, free, intended, intentional, offered, optional, purposeful, self-willed, unaccidental, unbidden, uncoerced, uncompelled, unconstrained, unforced, unprompted, unrestrained, *volens,* volitient, volitional, volitionary, *voluntarius,* willful, without compulsion, without constraint
ASSOCIATED CONCEPTS: voluntary abandonment, voluntary acceptance, voluntary act, voluntary agreement, voluntary appearance, voluntary assignment, voluntary confession, voluntary conveyance, voluntary discontinuance, voluntary dismissal, voluntary exposure, voluntary gift, voluntary grant, voluntary homocide, voluntary manslaughter, voluntary partition, voluntary payment, voluntary petition in bankruptcy, voluntary retirement, voluntary separation, voluntary statement, voluntary suspension, voluntary testimony, voluntary trust, voluntary waste

VOLUNTEER, *noun* amateur, enlisted man, enlisted person, enlistee, freewill worker, gratuitous worker, nonprofessional, recruit, taker, unpaid worker, voluntary worker
ASSOCIATED CONCEPTS: Good Samaritan

VOTE, *noun* ballot, chirotony, choice, choosing, decision, determination, election, formal expression of choice, judgment, option, pick, poll, predilection, preference, *punctum,* selection, *sententia, suffragium*

VOTE, *verb* approve, ballot, be counted, cast a ballot, cast a vote, choose, elect, exercise the right of suffrage, judge, poll, *suffragium ferre*

VOUCH, *verb* acknowledge, *adseverare,* affirm, assererate, assure, attest, authenticate, aver, avouch, back, bear witness, certify, confirm, corroborate, declare, depone, depose, endorse, give assurance, give evidence, give one's word, guarantee, maintain by affirmation, pledge, promise, *rem praestare,* secure, support, sustain, swear to, testify, underwrite, uphold, warrant, witness

VOUCHSAFE, *verb* accord, acquiesce, admit, allow, assent, bear with, bestow, comply with, concede, *concedere,* condescend, condescend to grant, consent, deign to give, deign to grant, favor with, give in, grant, grant by favor, gratify, humor, indulge, let, permit, satisfy, show favor, stoop, suffer, tolerate, yield

VOW, *noun* affirmation, asseveration, assurance, aver, avow, covenant, *devotio,* endorsement, *fides,* formal guaranty, oath, pledge, promise, *promissum,* solemn assertion, solemn declaration, solemn promise, subscription, undertaking, vouch, warrant, word, word of honor, written assurance

VULNERABLE, *adjective* accessible, approachable, assailable, attainable, beatable, capable of receiving injuries, defenseless, exposed, fallible, guardless, indefensible, insecure, liable to attack, obtainable, open, penetrable, precarious, pregnable, *qui vulnerari potest,* reachable, risky, susceptible, unguarded, unprepared, unprotected, unsafe, unshielded, untenable, vincible, weak, woundable

W

WAGE, *noun* allowance, compensation, earnings, emolument, fee, hire, income, meed, *merces,* pay, payment, quittance, rate of pay, recompense, remuneration, revenue, reward for service, salary, stipend
ASSOCIATED CONCEPTS: minimum wage, wage rate

WAIVE, *verb* cast off, cease, *de re decedere,* desist from, disclaim, dismiss, disown, dispense with, forgo, give up, give up claim to, not retain, not use, put aside, refrain from, refuse, reject, relinquish, *rem concedere,* renounce, repudiate, sacrifice, set aside, surrender, yield
ASSOCIATED CONCEPTS: election of remedy, waive a jury trial, waive jurisdictional requirements, waive objections, waive rights, waive rights to payment under a contract

WAIVER, *noun* abandonment, abandonment of a known right, abdication, abrogation, absolution, acquittal, act of relinquishing a right, clearance, deed of release, discharge, excusal, forgoing, giving up, intentional relinquishment, loss of right, release, relinquishment, renunciation, surrender, voluntary relinquishment
ASSOCIATED CONCEPTS: express waiver, implied waiver, waiver of immunity
FOREIGN PHRASES: *Omnis consensus tollit errorem.* Every consent removes error. *Potest quis renunciare pro se et suis juri quod pro se introductum est.* One may relinquish for himself and his successors a right which was introduced for his own benefit. *Cuilibet licet juri pro se introducto renunciare.* Anyone may waive a legal right which is for his protection. *Ab assuetis non fit injuria.* No legal injury is done by things long acquiesced in. *Omnes licentiam habere his quae pro se indulta sunt, renunciare.* All are free to renounce those privileges which have been allowed for their benefit.

WANT OF JURISDICTION, *adverb* beyond the jurisdiction of the court, improper jurisdiction, not legitimate, want of authority, without judicial authority

WANTON, *adjective* careless, dissolute, froward, groundless, heedless, immoral, *impudicus,* intemper-ate, *lascivus,* lewd, libidinous, licentious, lustful, luxuriant, reckless, unjustifiable, unmanageable, unprovoked
ASSOCIATED CONCEPTS: wanton act, wanton disregard, wanton indifference, wanton injury, wanton misconduct, wanton negligence

WARD, *noun* care, charge, custody, defense, guard, guardianship, keeping, preservation, protection, safeguard, safekeeping, security, trusteeship, tutelage, vigilance, watch, watchfulness
ASSOCIATED CONCEPTS: ward of the state

WARDEN, *noun* chaperon, claviger, custodian, *custos,* gatekeeper, guard, guardian, jailer, overseer, patrolman, protector, sentry, superintendent, supervisor, supervisory official, turnkey, warder, watchman

WARNING, *noun* *admonitio,* admonition, alarm, alert, augury, caution, caveat, commination, contraindication, foreboding, foreshadow, monition, *monitus,* notice of danger, omen, portent, presage, prognostic, symptom, threat, ultimatum
ASSOCIATED CONCEPTS: adequate warning, ample warning, duty to warn, failure to warn, proper warning, sufficient warning, timely warning, warning attached to a products label

WARRANT (*Authorization*), *noun* *auctoritas,* authority, brevet, charter, commission, credentials, license, *mandatum,* permission, permit, *potestas,* power, sanction, voucher
ASSOCIATED CONCEPTS: warrant of attorney

WARRANT (*Guaranty*), *noun* agreement, assurance, authentication, covenant, pledge, promise, security, surety, warranty

WARRANT (*Judicial writ*), *noun* certificate, decree, edict, judicial authorization, judicial order, legal process, mandate of a court, order, process, subpoena, summons
ASSOCIATED CONCEPTS: arrest warrant, bench warrant, dispossess warrant, fugitive warrant, search war-

rant, tax warrant, warrant of attachment, warrant of commitment

WARRANTY, *noun*　assurance, certificate, contractual assurance, contractual promise, contractual representation, covenant, guarantee, guaranty, pledge, promise, *satisdatio,* voucher
ASSOCIATED CONCEPTS: affirmative warranty, breach of warranty, disclaimer of warranty, express warranty, implied warranty, limited warranty, material warranty, prospective warranty, warranty deed, warranty of fitness, warranty of merchantability, warranty of title
FOREIGN PHRASES: *Ea quae, commendandi causa, in venditionibus dicuntur, si palam appareant, venditorem non obligant.* Those things which are said as praise of the things sold, if they are openly apparent do not bind the seller.

WASTE, *noun*　careless loss, consumption, depletion, diminution, *dispendium,* dispersion, dissipation, *effusio,* excessive use, exhaustion, expenditure, extravagance, ill-usage, improvidence, intemperance, lavishness, misapplication, misemployment, misusage, misuse, prodigality, profusion, ruination, squandering, *sumptus,* unnecessary loss, unthriftiness, useless consumption, wanton destruction, wastage, wastefulness, wasting
ASSOCIATED CONCEPTS: economic waste, permissive waste, voluntary waste, waste of public property, wasting assets

WAY *(Channel), noun*　alley, artery, avenue, custom, direction, lane, mode, path, pathway, plan, road, roadway, route, throughway

WAY *(Manner), noun*　behavior, fashion, habit, means, progression, ritual
ASSOCIATED CONCEPTS: way appurtenant, way by dedication, way of necessity, way reserved, wayfarer, waylay

WEAPONS, *noun*　armaments, *armorum,* arms, deadly devices, deadly weapons, instruments of combat, lethal instruments, lethal weapons, munitions
ASSOCIATED CONCEPTS: concealed weapons, deadly weapons, possession of a weapon
FOREIGN PHRASES: *Arma in armatos sumere jura sinunt.* The laws permit the use of arms against those who are armed.

WEAR AND TEAR, *noun*　corrosion, damage, decay, depletion, depreciation, deterioration, dissolution, dilapidation, diminution, erosion, exhaustion, impairment, ravage, ruination, wastage
ASSOCIATED CONCEPTS: award with wear and tear excepted

WEIGH, *verb*　balance, bear heavily, burden, cogitate, consider, *considerare,* contemplate, cumber, deliberate, determine the heaviness of, encumber, estimate, evaluate, examine, find the weight of, gauge, load down, measure according to weight, meditate upon, mull over, ponder, press, put on the scale, reflect upon, *reputare,* ruminate, study
ASSOCIATED CONCEPTS: weigh the evidence

WEIGHT *(Burden), noun*　care, cumbrance, duty, encumbrance, incubus, liability, load, mass, obligation, onus, oppression, ponderousness, pressure, responsibility

WEIGHT *(Credibility), noun*　belief, certainty, confidence, credence, credibleness, credit, faith, impressiveness, likelihood, positiveness, reliance, trustworthiness, validity

WEIGHT *(Importance), noun*　authority, consequence, degree of importance, effect, efficacy, eminence, emphasis, enormity, force, import, impressiveness, influence, interest, magnitude, merit, moment, potency, power, prominence, quality, seriousness, significance, value
ASSOCIATED CONCEPTS: weight of the evidence
FOREIGN PHRASES: *Ponderantur testes, non numerantur.* Witnesses are weighed, not counted. *Testimonia ponderanda sunt, non numeranda.* Evidence is to be weighed, not counted.

WELFARE, *noun*　advantage, affluence, benefit, *commodis consulere,* fortune, good, haleness, happiness, health, *hominis,* interest, luck, prosperity, prosperousness, soundness, success, weal, well-being
ASSOCIATED CONCEPTS: public welfare

WELL-GROUNDED, *adjective*　firm, legitimate, positive, solid, sound, steady, strong, well based, well founded

WHATEVER, *adverb*　at all, of any description, of any kind or sort, whatsoever, whichever

WHENEVER, *adverb*　at whatever time, at which time, no matter when, once, when

WHEREIN, *adverb*　concerning, herein, in regard to which, inwardly, of which, regarding, respecting, therein, touching, whereon, whereupon, within

WHOEVER, *noun*　any individual, any person, anybody, anyone, no matter who, whomever, whomsoever, whosoever

WHOLE *(Undamaged), adjective*　aggregate, all, complete, entire, gross, intact, solid, total, undiminished, unhurt, unimpaired, unreduced, without loss
ASSOCIATED CONCEPTS: whole capital, whole estate, whole quantity, whole truth

WHOLE *(Unified), adjective*　holistic, indivisible, one, single, total, undivisible, universal

WHOLE, *noun*　aggregate, all, allness, assemblage, collectiveness, collectivity, completeness, entirety, everything, gross amount, indivisibility, intactness, integer, integrity, sum total, totality, undividedness, universality, wholeness

WHOLLY, *adverb*　altogether, as a whole, collectively, completely, entirely, fully, in all respects, in the aggregate, in the main, in the mass, in toto, outright, roundly, throughout, totally, utterly
ASSOCIATED CONCEPTS: wholly dependant, wholly liable

WIELD, *verb*　avail oneself of, brandish, carry, command, control, direct, employ, exercise, exert, govern, handle, make use of, manage, manipulate, operate, ply, rule, sway, swing, *tractare,* use, utilize, work

WILL *(Desire)*, **noun**   *animus*, aspiration, backbone, choice, command, decision, desideration, determination, disposition, grit, hankering, hope, inclination, intent, longing, mind, pleasure, power of choosing, power of determination, preference, purpose, resoluteness, resolution, self-control, self-discipline, velleity, volition, *voluntas*, want, wish, yearning

FOREIGN PHRASES: *Voluntas donatoris in charta doni sui manifeste expressa observetur.* The will of the donor which is clearly expressed in his deed of gift should be observed. *Furiosi nulla voluntas est.* A madman has no will.

WILL *(Testamentary instrument)*, **noun**   bequeathal, bestowal, document, dispensation, disposition, instrument, legacy, testament, *testamentum*

ASSOCIATED CONCEPTS: absolute will, alienation, alteration, ambulatory will, appointment of an administrator, attempt to defeat will, bequest, cancellation, challenge to a will, codicil, commercial will, conditional will, conjoint will, contested will, contractual wills, counter wills, devise, election, execute a will, executor named in a will, existence of a will, forgery of a will, gift inter vivos, holographic will, incorporation by reference, instructions, joint wills, mutual wills, nuncupative will, precatory words, probate, property which passes by will, pursuant to terms of will, reciprocal wills, revocation of a will, suit for construction of a will, suit to annul or suspend a will, unconditional will, validity of a will, voidable will, witness to a will, written instrument

FOREIGN PHRASES: *Da tua dum tua sunt, post mortem tunc tua non sunt.* Give that which is yours while it is yours; after death it is not yours. *Haereditas est successio in universum jus quod defunctus habuerit.* Inheritance is the succession to every right which the deceased had possessed. *Sola ac per se senectus donationem testamentum aut transactionem non vitiat.* Old age does not alone and of itself vitiate a will, gift, or transaction. *Haereditas nihil aliud est, quam successio in universum jus, quod defunctus habuerit.* An inheritance is nothing other than the succession to all the rights which the deceased had. *In testamentis plenius testatoris intentionem scrutamur.* In wills, the intentions of the testators should be fully regarded. *In testamentis ratio tacita non debet considerari, sed verba solum spectari debent; adeo per divinationem mentis a verbis recedere durum est.* In wills an unexpressed intention ought not to be considered, but the words alone ought to be regarded; for it is difficult to recede from the words by guessing at their intention. *In dubiis, non praesumitur pro testamento.* In doubtful cases, there is no presumption in favor of the will. *Interest reipublicae suprema hominum testamenta rata haberi.* It concerns the state that men's last wills be held valid. *Quae in testamento ita sunt scripta ut intelligi non possint, perinde sunt ac si scripta non essent.* Things which are so written in a will that they cannot be understood, are the same as if they had not been written at all. *Testatoris ultima voluntas est perimplenda secundum veram intentionem suam.* The last will of a testator is to be thoroughly fulfilled according to his true intention. *Non aliter a significatione verborum recedi oportet quam cum manifestum est, aliud sensisse testatorem.* The ordinary meaning of the words ought not to be departed from unless it is evident that the testator intended otherwise. *Ubi pugnantia inter se in testamento juberentur, neutrum ratum est.*

When two directions conflicting with each other are given in a will, neither is held valid. *Cum in testamento ambigue aut etiam perperam scriptum est benigne interpretari et secundum id quod credibile est cogitatum credendum est.* When an ambiguous, or even an incorrectly written, expression is found in a will, it should be interpreted liberally and according to what is the probable intention of the testator. *Omne testamentum morte consummatum est.* Every will or testament is consummated by death. *Nemo plus commodi haeredi suo relinquit quam ipse habuit.* No one leaves a greater advantage for his heir than he himself had. *Ambulatoria est voluntas defunctiusque ad vitae supremum exitum.* The will of a deceased person is revocable until the last moment of life. *Relatio semper fiat ut valeat dispositio.* Reference should always be made that a testamentary disposition may be effective. *Cum duo inter se pugnantia reperiuntur in testamento, ultimum ratum est.* When two repugnant matters are found in a will, the last one will be confirmed. *Voluntas facit quod in testamento scriptum valeat.* The will of the testator gives validity to what is written in the will. *Opinio quae favet testamento est tenenda.* An opinion which favors a will is to be followed.

WILLFUL, **adjective**   conscious, contemplated, *contumax*, deliberate, designed, inflexible, intended, intentional, intractable, intransigent, obdurate, obstinate, *obstinatus, pertinax*, planned, premeditated, purposed, purposeful, restive, retractory, studied, tenacious, uncompromising, unconstrained, unyielding, volitional, volitive, voluntary

ASSOCIATED CONCEPTS: willful acts

WILLING *(Desirous)*, **adjective**   assenting, disposed, eager, earnest, enthusiastic, partial to, ready, volitional, zealous

WILLING *(Not averse)*, **adjective**   acquiescent, agreeable, amenable, compliant, content, consenting, fain, favorably inclined, favorable, genial, receptive, responsive, susceptible, tractable, unreluctant, voluntary, yielding

WILLING *(Uncompelled)*, **adjective**   gratuitous, unbidden, unforced

WITHDRAW, **verb**   abandon, abdicate, abjure, abolish, abscond, absent oneself, abstract, back out, backtrack, cease, deduct, depart, desert, disappear, disassociate, disavow, disengage, disestablish, dissociate, draw out, evacuate, extract, invalidate, keep apart, leave, nullify, overrule, pull back, quash, quit, recall, recant, recede, relinquish, remove, renege, repeal, rescind, resign, retire, retract, retreat, reverse, revoke, secede, separate, sequester, sequestrate, subduce, subduct, subtract, surrender, take away, take back, unsheathe, vacate, wean

WITHHOLD, **verb**   abstain, begrudge, block, censor, check, *comprimere*, conceal, constrain, curb, debar, deny, disallow, forbear, forbid, hide, hinder, hold, hold back, hold in, hold out, hush up, inhibit, keep, keep back, keep in, keep secret, muzzle, prohibit, refrain, refuse, refuse to disclose, rein in, repress, reserve, restrain, restrict, *retinere*, smother, stifle, suppress, *supprimere*

WITHOUT RECOURSE, *adverb* conditional endorsement, qualified endorsement, restricted, subject to terms
ASSOCIATED CONCEPTS: endorsement without recourse

WITHSTAND, *verb* block, breast, challenge, check, confront, contravene, cope with, counteract, countercheck, countervail, defy, endure, face, face danger, face up to, fight, foil, hamper, hinder, hold out, impede, inhibit, interrupt, last, *obsistere, obstare,* obstruct, offer resistance, oppose, preclude, prevail against, prevent, refuse to submit, repel, repulse, resist, *resistere,* retard, stand fast, stand firm, stand up to, stave off, stay, stem, stop, thwart, weather
ASSOCIATED CONCEPTS: withstand a challenge on appeal

WITNESS, *noun* attestant, attestor, beholder, bystander, compurgator, corroborator, deponent, informant, informer, looker, looker-on, observer, one who gives testimony, onlooker, person affording evidence, reporter, swearer, testifier, *testis*
ASSOCIATED CONCEPTS: adverse witness, attestation, attesting witness, available witness, call as a witness, compel the attendance of witnesses, competent disinterested witness, competent witness, confronting a witness, credible witness, cross-examination, discredited witness, disinterested witness, expert witness, eyewitness, hostile witness, impeachment of a witness, material witness, nonexpert witness, prosecution witness, res gestae witness, skilled witness, specially qualified witness, state witness, subscribing witness, tampering with a witness, voluntary witness
FOREIGN PHRASES: *Habemus optimum testem, confitentem reum.* We have the best witness, a confessing defendant. *Nemo allegans suam turpitudinem audien dus est.* No one should be permitted to testify as a witness to his own baseness or wickedness. *Nullus idoneus testis in re sua intelligitur.* No person is deemed to be a competent witness in his own behalf. *Judex non potest esse testis in propria causa.* A judge cannot be a witness in his own case. *Jurato creditur in judicio.* He who makes an oath is to be believed in a judicial proceeding. *Quod constat curiae opere testium non indiget.* That which is clear to the court needs not the help of witnesses. *Nemo tenetur edere instrumenta contra se.* No one is bound to produce writings against himself. *Nemo tenetur jurare in suam turpitudinem.* No one is bound to testify to his own turpitude. *Nemo tenetur prodere seipsum.* No one is bound to betray himself. *Testis nemo in sua causa esse potest.* No one can be a witness in his own cause. *Testis de visu praeponderat aliis.* An eyewitness is preferred to others. *Nemo in propria causa testis esse debet.* No one ought to be a witness in his own cause.

WITNESS *(Attest to),* *verb* acknowledge, affirm, authenticate, bear out, bear witness, certify, confirm, corroborate, cosign, countersign, endorse, give evidence, give testimony, say under oath, sign, substantiate, sustain, swear, take one's oath, *testari, testificari,* testify to, *testimonium dicere,* undersign, uphold, validate, verify, vouch for, warrant
ASSOCIATED CONCEPTS: witness a crime, witness a document, witness a will

WITNESS *(Have direct knowledge of),* *verb* be a spectator, be present and note, behold, mark, note, no-

tice, observe, recognize, see, sight, *spectare,* spot, take cognizance of, *videre,* view, watch

WORK *(Effort),* *noun* application, attempt, campaign, chore, diligence, drudgery, endeavor, enterprise, essay, exercise, exertion, grind, industry, labor, *opus,* strain, stress, strife, struggle, toil, undertaking

WORK *(Employment),* *noun* assignment, avocation, business, calling, charge, craft, duty, engagement, function, incumbency, industry, job, line, metier, occupation, office, position, post, profession, pursuit, specialty, task, trade, vocation

WORTH, *noun* account, advantage, *aestimatio,* appraisal, appraisement, avail, benefit, caliber, charge, cost, credit, desert, esteem, estimation, excellence, expense, importance, merit, par, *pretium,* price, profit, profitableness, quality, quotation, rate, regard, respect, service, serviceableness, use, utility, valuation, value, *virtus,* worthiness
FOREIGN PHRASES: *Tantum bona valent, quantum vendi possunt.* Goods are worth as much as they are sold for.

WRIT, *noun* bid, bidding, command, commandment, decree, decretal, dictate, direction, directive, fiat, mandate, order, ordinance, precept, regulation, requirement
ASSOCIATED CONCEPTS: concurrent writ, judicial writ, original writ, preemptory writ, prerogative writ, writ of attachment, writ of certiorari, writ of covenant, writ of detinue, writ of error, writ of error coram nobis, writ of execution, writ of habeas corpus, writ of inquiry, writ of mandemus, writ of prohibition, writ of protection, writ of quo warranto, writ of replevin, writ of right

WRONG, *noun* abomination, abuse, atrocity, crime, delinquency, dereliction, evil, grievance, harm, illegality, immorality, improbity, infraction, iniquity, *iniuria,* injury, injustice, lawlessness, malfeasance, malpractice, miscreancy, misdeed, misdoing, mistake, mistreatment, obliquity, offense, outrage, sin, transgression, trespass, turpitude, unfairness, unrighteousness, vice, villainy, violation, violation of right, wickedness
FOREIGN PHRASES: *Scienti et volenti non fit injuria.* A wrong is not done to a person who understands and consents. *Peccatum peccato addit qui culpae quam facit patrocinium defensionis adjungit.* He adds one offense to another who connects a wrong which he has committed with his defense. *Nemo ex suo delicto meliorem suam conditionem facere potest.* No one can improve his condition by his own misdeed. *Nemo ex proprio dolo consequitur actionem.* No one acquires a right of action from his own fraud. *Un ne doit prise advantage de son tort demesne.* One ought not to take advantage of his own wrong. *Nemo damnum facit, nisi qui id fecit quod facere jus non habet.* No one is considered as doing damage, except he who does that which he has no right to do. *Jus ex injuria non oritur.* A right does not arise from a wrong. *Injuria non excusat injuriam.* One wrong does not excuse another. *Ubi et dantis et accipientis turpitudo versatur, non posse repeti dicimus; quotiens autem accipientis turpitudo versatur, repeti posse.* Where there is turpitude by both giver and receiver, we say it cannot be recovered back; but whenever the turpitude is in the receiver only, it can be recovered. *Ubicunque est injuria, ibi damnum sequitur.*

Wherever there is a wrong, there damage follows. *Nullum iniquum est praesumendum in jure.* Nothing iniquitous is to be presumed in law. *Nullus videtur dolo facere qui suo jure utitur.* No one is considered to have committed a wrong who exercises his legal rights. *Aliquid conceditur ne injuria remaneat impunita, quod alias non concederetur.* Something is conceded, lest a wrong remain unredressed, which otherwise would not be conceded.

WRONGDOER, *noun*   criminal, debauchee, delinquent, evildoer, *homo maleficus,* lawbreaker, *malefactor,* malfeasant, miscreant, misdemeanant, misdoer, offender, outlaw, profligate, reprobate, scoundrel, sinner, transgressor, villain
FOREIGN PHRASES: *In pari delicto potior est conditio possidentis, defendentis.* Where the parties are equally guilty of wrongdoing, the defendant holds the stronger position. *Nullus videtur dolo facere qui suo jure utitur.* No one is considered to have committed a wrong who exercises his legal rights.

WRONGFUL, *adjective*   against the law, bad, criminal, felonious, illegal, illegitimate, illicit, improper, incorrect, iniquitous, *iniuriosus, iniustus,* lawless, malicious, mischievous, unauthorized, undue, unfair, unjust, unlawful, unseemly, unsuitable, wrong
ASSOCIATED CONCEPTS: wrongful act, wrongful conversion, wrongful death, wrongful detention, wrongful discharge, wrongful interference
FOREIGN PHRASES: *Fictio legis inique operatur alieni damnum vel injuriam.* Fiction of law is wrongful if it works loss or harm to anyone.

Y

YIELD *(Produce a return),* **verb**   accord, accrue, afford, bear, bestow, bring, bring about, bring forth, bring in, fetch, furnish, generate, give, provide, render, return, supply

YIELD *(Submit),* **verb**   abandon, abdicate, accede, accept, acquiesce, admit, agree to, allow, assent, back down, be submissive, bend, bow, capitulate, cede, comply, concede, *concedere,* consent, *dedere,* forgo, give in, give up, give way, grant, leave, let go, make way, obey, pay homage to, permit, quit, relent, relinquish, renounce, resign, sacrifice, succumb, suffer defeat, surrender, waive

YIELDING, *adjective*   accommodating, acquiescent, alterable, amenable, complaisant, compliant, docile, easy, easygoing, elastic, facile, *facilis,* flexible, impressible, impressionable, malleable, manageable, obedient, obliging, *obsequens,* obsequious, passive, pliable, pliant, soft, submissive, supple, tractable, unresistant, unresisting
ASSOCIATED CONCEPTS: confessions

Z

ZEALOUS, *adjective*   active, ardent, assiduous, attentive, bent upon, dedicated, desirous, devoted, devout, eager, earnest, enthusiastic, fanatical, fervent, fervid, fiery, hearty, impassioned, impetuous, industrious, infatuated, keen, loving, passionate, perfervid, perseverant, persistent, pious, rabid, raving, ready, sedulous, solicitous, *studiosus,* willing
ASSOCIATED CONCEPTS: overly zealous representation of a client

ZONE, *noun*   area, band, circumference, compartment, hemisphere, latitude, orb, perimeter, periphery, region, sphere, terrain, territory
ASSOCIATED CONCEPTS: zone of employment

INDEX

A

a ceteris dissentire unorthodox

a commanding portion bulk

a fortiori discursive *(analytical)*

a good deal of considerable

a posteriori discursive *(analytical)*

a priori axiomatic

a priori discursive *(analytical)*

à propos admissible, applicable

a.k.a. alias

ab origine ab initio

ab ovo ab initio

ab re desistere abandon *(withdraw)*

ab re discrepare contradict

abalienare alienate *(estrange)*, alienate *(transfer title)*, estrange

abalienate alienate *(transfer title)*, assign *(transfer ownership)*, cede, consign, convey *(transfer)*

abalienatio alienation *(transfer of title)*, pass *(advance)*

abalienation alienation *(transfer of title)*, assignment *(transfer of ownership)*, cession, demise *(conveyance)*, estrangement

abandon betray *(lead astray)*, cede, disclaim, disinherit, disown *(refuse to acknowledge)*, fail *(neglect)*, flee, forfeit, forgo, forswear, leave *(depart)*, pretermit, quit *(discontinue)*, quit *(evacuate)*, reject, relinquish, renege, renounce, repudiate, resign, retire *(retreat)*, retreat, secede, set aside *(annul)*, stop, vacate *(leave)*, vacate *(void)*, withdraw, yield *(submit)*

abandon allegiance defect

abandon nationality expatriate

abandoned dissolute, helpless *(defenseless)*, licentious, obsolete, solitary, tainted *(corrupted)*, uncurbed, vicious, void *(empty)*

abandoned child orphan

abandoned infant orphan

abandoned to vice profligate *(corrupt)*

abandoning cancellation

abandonment abdication, abjuration, absence *(nonattendance)*, cancellation, capitulation, cessation *(termination)*, cloture, dereliction, desertion, desuetude, disclaimer, disuse, estrangement, expense *(sacrifice)*, halt, neglect, negligence, rejection, release, renunciation, rescision, resignation *(relinquishment)*, waiver

abandonment of a known right waiver

abandonment of allegiance desertion, infidelity

abase adulterate, betray *(lead astray)*, damage, debase, demean *(make lower)*, demote, denigrate, depress, derogate, disgrace, dishonor *(deprive of honor)*, humiliate

abasement attaint, bad repute, degradation, deterioration, disgrace, dishonor *(shame)*, disrepute, ignominy, infamy, obloquy, opprobrium, perversion, prostration, shame

abash browbeat, confound, confuse *(bewilder)*, disconcert, disgrace, disorient, dissuade, embarrass, humiliate, intimidate, perturb

abashed diffident

abashment embarrassment

abasing contemptuous

abate abolish, allay, alleviate, assuage, cease, check *(restrain)*, commute, curtail, decrease, deduct *(reduce)*, diminish, discount *(minimize)*, discount *(reduce)*, ease, enjoin, give *(yield)*, lapse *(cease)*, lessen, mitigate, moderate *(temper)*, modify *(moderate)*, mollify, obtund, quash, reduce, relax, relieve *(free from burden)*, remit *(relax)*, subdue, subside

abate in intensity mitigate

abate severity relent

abatement abridgment *(disentitlement)*, curtailment, decline, decrease, decrement, deduction *(diminution)*, diminution, discount, lull, mitigation, mollification, outflow, relief *(release)*, remission, removal, solace

abatement of differences adjustment, arrangement *(understanding)*, collective bargaining, compromise, conciliation

abating mitigating

abbreviate abridge *(shorten)*, abstract *(summarize)*, commute, condense, constrict *(compress)*, curtail, decrease, digest *(summarize)*, dilute, diminish, discount *(minimize)*, lessen, minimize, reduce

abbreviated brief, compact *(pithy)*, concise, laconic, minimal, succinct

abbreviation abridgment *(condensation)*, abstract, capsule, compendium, curtailment, decrease, digest, diminution, outline *(synopsis)*, summary, symbol

abbreviatory compact *(pithy)*

abbreviature abridgment *(condensation)*, abstract, curtailment

abdere hide

abdicate abandon *(withdraw)*, cede, defect, demit, forfeit, leave *(depart)*, quit *(discontinue)*, relinquish, renounce, repudiate, resign, retire *(conclude a career)*, surrender *(give back)*, vacate *(void)*, withdraw, yield *(submit)*

abdicatio abdication, renunciation, resignation *(relinquishment)*

abdication abandonment *(discontinuance)*, renunciation, resignation *(relinquishment)*, waiver

abditus latent

abduce carry away

abduct carry away, hijack, kidnap

abduction taking

abecedarian elementary, neophyte, rudimentary

aberrance deviation, error, indirection *(indirect action)*, irregularity, perversion

aberrancy deviation, digression, error, indirection *(indirect action)*, irregularity, perversion

aberrant anomalous, astray, atypical, deviant, devious, disordered, disorderly, disparate, dissimilar, divergent, eccentric, errant, erroneous, faulty, irregular *(not usual)*, licentious, nonconforming, peccant *(culpable)*, peculiar *(curious)*, unaccustomed, uncommon, unorthodox, unpredictable, unusual, variable

aberrare detour, deviate, digress

aberration deviation, digression, discrepancy, error, fault *(mistake)*, insanity, irregularity, nonconformity, perversion, quirk *(idiosyncrasy)*

aberration of mind insanity

abet aid, assist, bear *(support)*, conduce, conspire, contribute *(assist)*, countenance, enable, espouse, foment, foster, help, maintain *(sustain)*, promote *(organize)*, subsidize

abetment aid *(help)*, auspices, collusion, conspiracy, contribution *(participation)*, favor *(sanction)*, help, service *(assistance)*

abetting ancillary *(auxiliary)*, concerted, concurrent *(united)*, promotion *(encouragement)*

abettor accessory, accomplice, advocate *(espouser)*, assistant, backer, benefactor, catalyst, coactor, coadjutant, coconspirator, cohort, colleague, confederate, consociate, conspirator, conspirer, contributor *(contributor)*, copartner *(coconspirator)*, participant, partner, proponent

abeyance cessation *(interlude)*, check *(bar)*, cloture, desuetude, discontinuance *(act of discontinuing)*, extension *(postponement)*, halt, hiatus, inaction, interruption, interval, moratorium, nonuse, pause, pendency, respite *(interval of rest)*, stay

abeyancy stay

abeyant dormant, inactive, prospective

abhor blame, condemn *(ban)*, contemn, disdain, forswear, reject, renounce, shun

abhorrence alienation *(estrangement)*, contempt *(disdain)*, disapprobation, disapproval, disdain, hatred, odium, phobia, rejection

abhorrent antipathetic *(distasteful)*, bad *(offensive)*, contemptible, heinous, loathsome, objectionable, obnoxious, offensive *(offending)*, repugnant *(exciting aversion)*, repulsive

abide adhere *(persist)*, allow *(endure)*, bear *(tolerate)*, continue *(persevere)*, dwell *(reside)*, endure *(last)*, inhabit, lodge *(reside)*, occupy *(take possession)*, persist, reside, subsist, suffer *(permit)*, tolerate

abide by accede *(concede)*, adhere *(maintain loyalty)*, comply, concede, conform, defer *(yield in judgment)*, fulfill, keep *(fulfill)*, obey, observe *(obey)*, perform *(adhere to)*

abide together cohabit

abider habitant, inhabitant

abiding constant, continuance, durable, habitation *(act of inhabiting)*, indestructible, lasting, live *(existing)*, noncancellable, permanent, persistent, stable, steadfast, tolerance

abiding place building *(structure)*, domicile, habitation *(dwelling place)*

abiding together cohabitation *(living together)*

abiectus contemptible, servile, sordid

ability aptitude, caliber *(mental capacity)*, capacity *(aptitude)*, efficiency, facility *(easiness)*, force *(strength)*, gift *(flair)*, performance *(workmanship)*, potential, proclivity, propensity, qualification *(fitness)*, quality *(excellence)*, quality *(grade)*, science *(technique)*, skill, specialty *(special aptitude)*

ability to bear tolerance

ability to distinguish judgment *(discernment)*

ability to endure tolerance

ability to get along with others discretion *(quality of being discreet)*

ability to know comprehension, reason *(sound judgment)*

ability to make distinctions perception

ability to perceive intellect

ability to pursue tenacity

ability to reason intellect

ability to tolerate tolerance

ability to understand insight, intellect

ability to withstand tolerance

abire disappear, resign, retire *(retreat)*, secede

abject base *(inferior)*, blameful, blameworthy, caitiff, contemptible, contemptuous, ignoble, loathsome, odious, servile, sordid, subservient

abject fear phobia

abject slavery bondage

abjection bad faith, bad repute, degradation, dishonor *(shame)*, ignominy

abjectness bad faith, bad repute, disgrace, dishonor *(shame)*, disrepute, ignominy, shame

abjudge hold *(decide)*

abjudicate hold *(decide)*

abjuration abdication, denial, desertion, disclaimer, disdain, negation, refusal, rejection, renunciation, repudiation, rescision, resignation *(relinquishment)*, retraction

abjuratory contradictory, recusant

abjure abandon *(relinquish)*, abrogate *(annul)*, cede, controvert, disaffirm, disallow, disown *(deny the validity)*, disown *(refuse to acknowledge)*, forfeit, forgo, forswear, leave *(depart)*, quit *(discontinue)*, recant, refuse, reject, relinquish, renounce, repudiate, resign, revoke, set aside *(annul)*, surrender *(give back)*, withdraw

abjurement confutation, disclaimer, resignation *(relinquishment)*

able adequate, artful, capable, competent, deft, effective *(efficient)*, efficient, expert, fit, omnipotent, potent, powerful, practiced, professional *(trained)*, proficient, qualified *(competent)*, ready *(prepared)*, resourceful, sciential, strong

able to be altered ambulatory

able to be confirmed deductible *(provable)*

able to be felt palpable

able to be handled palpable

able to be pierced penetrable

able to be seen apparent *(perceptible)*, ostensible

able to be shown deductible *(provable)*

able to be subducted deductible *(capable of being deducted from taxes)*

able to be subtracted for tax purposes deductible *(capable of being deducted from taxes)*

able to be touched palpable

able to contain a great deal capacious

able to endure resilient

able to improve corrigible

able to meet situations resourceful

able to pay solid *(sound)*, solvent

able to recognize conscious *(awake)*

able to withstand insusceptible *(resistant)*

able-bodied powerful

ablegare send

ableness ability, caliber *(mental capacity)*, capacity *(aptitude)*, dint, efficiency, faculty *(ability)*, force *(strength)*, quality *(excellence)*, quality *(grade)*

ablude conflict, discaccord

abnegate abrogate *(annul)*, adeem, annul, condemn *(ban)*, controvert, countercharge, decline *(reject)*, deny *(refuse to grant)*, disaffirm, disallow, disapprove *(reject)*, disavow, disclaim, disown *(deny the validity)*, forgo, forswear, negate, refuse, refute, reject, renounce, repudiate, set aside *(annul)*, surrender *(give back)*

abnegation abandonment *(repudiation)*, ademption, declination, denial, disdain, negation, refusal, rejection, renunciation, rescision, temperance

abnegative contrary

abnormal anomalous, atypical, deviant, disordered, irregular *(not usual)*, non compos mentis, peculiar *(curious)*, prodigious *(amazing)*, suspicious *(questionable)*, unaccustomed, uncommon, unusual

abnormality deviation, incongruity, insanity, irregularity, nonconformity, perversion, quirk *(idiosyncrasy)*

abnormity irregularity, nonconformity, quirk *(idiosyncrasy)*

abnormous peculiar *(curious)*

abode address, base *(place)*, building *(structure)*, domicile, dwelling, habitation *(dwelling place)*, home *(domicile)*, house, inhabitation *(place of dwelling)*, lodging, residence

abolere abolish, annul, obliterate

abolish abate *(extinguish)*, abrogate *(annul)*, abrogate *(rescind)*, adeem, annul, cancel, destroy *(void)*, disaffirm, discharge *(release from obligation)*, discontinue *(abandon)*, eliminate *(eradicate)*, eradicate, extinguish, extirpate, invalidate, kill *(defeat)*, negate, nullify, obliterate, overthrow, overturn, quash, recall *(call back)*, remove *(eliminate)*, renege, repeal, repudiate, rescind, revoke, stop, supersede, supplant, terminate, vacate *(void)*, vitiate, withdraw

abolish the organization of disorganize

abolished inactive, null *(invalid)*, null and void

abolishing cancellation

abolishment abolition, ademption, annulment, cancellation, countermand, defeasance, discharge *(annulment)*, discontinuance *(act of discontinuing)*, dissolution *(termination)*, disuse, negation, rescision, retraction, reversal, revocation

abolition abatement *(extinguishment)*, ademption, annulment, cancellation, censorship, countermand, defeasance, destruction, discharge *(annulment)*, discharge *(release from obligation)*, discontinuance *(act of discontinuing)*, dissolution *(termination)*, disuse, negation, obviation, removal, repudiation, rescision, reversal, revocation, subversion

abominable bad *(offensive)*, contemptible, contemptuous, depraved, disgraceful, disreputable, heinous, invidious, loathsome, nefarious, objectionable, obnoxious, odious, offensive *(offending)*, outrageous, repugnant *(exciting aversion)*, repulsive, sordid, undesirable

abominableness disrepute

abominari deprecate

abominate contemn

abomination alienation *(estrangement)*, atrocity, bad repute, contaminate, contempt *(disdain)*, defilement, disgrace, hatred, misdeed, perversion, wrong

aboriginal incipient, native *(domestic)*, prime *(original)*, primordial

abort cancel, conclude *(complete)*, destroy *(efface)*, discontinue *(abandon)*, dissolve *(terminate)*, extinguish, frustrate, invalidate, negate, quit *(discontinue)*

aborted attempt failure *(lack of success)*

aborticide abortion *(feticide)*

abortio abortion *(feticide)*

abortion miscarriage

abortive futile, imperfect, ineffective, ineffectual, otiose, unavailing, unproductive

abortive attempt frustration, miscarriage

abortive effort miscarriage

abound increase, proliferate

abounding ample, copious, full, profuse, replete

abounding in error fallacious, false *(inaccurate)*

abounding in riches opulent, prosperous

about to be imminent, prospective

about to happen forthcoming, immediate *(imminent)*, imminent, inevitable, pending *(imminent)*, proximate

about-face reversal, reversion *(act of returning)*

aboutir abut

above before mentioned, last *(preceding)*

above all a fortiori, particularly

above all price inestimable

above all value inestimable

above appraisal inestimable

above average extraordinary, superior *(excellent)*

above board ethical

above meanness magnanimous

above par meritorious, notable, noteworthy, preferable, superior *(excellent)*, valuable

above pettiness magnanimous

above reproach blameless, unimpeachable

above suspicion blameless, clean, incorruptible, inculpable, irreprehensible, not guilty

above the average best

above-cited before mentioned, last *(preceding)*, previous

above-mentioned aforesaid, before mentioned, last *(preceding)*, previous, said

above-named before mentioned, last *(preceding)*, previous

above-stated before mentioned, last *(preceding)*

aboveboard bona fide, candid, direct *(forthright)*, honest, ingenuous, irreprehensible, moral, right *(correct)*, scrupulous, straightforward, unaffected *(sincere)*, upright
abrade diminish, erode, expunge
abrasion deterioration, erosion
abrasive caustic
abreaction catharsis
abreast equal, informed *(having information)*
abrégé capsule
abri cache *(hiding place)*
abridge abstract *(summarize)*, commute, condense, constrict *(compress)*, curtail, decrease, digest *(summarize)*, diminish, discount *(minimize)*, expurgate, extract, lessen, minimize, reduce, retrench
abridged brief, compact *(pithy)*, concise, laconic, minimal, partial *(relating to a part)*, sententious
abridgment abstract, brief, capsule, censorship, compendium, curtailment, decrease, decrement, deduction *(diminution)*, denial, deterrence, digest, mitigation, outline *(synopsis)*, paraphrase, restatement, summary, synopsis
abrogare abrogate *(annul)*, annul, discredit, repeal, rescind, revoke
abrogate abate *(extinguish)*, abolish, adeem, annul, ban, bear false witness, cancel, cease, condemn *(ban)*, contradict, controvert, countervail, debar, disallow, discharge *(release from obligation)*, disclaim, discontinue *(abandon)*, disinherit, dissolve *(terminate)*, invalidate, kill *(defeat)*, negate, nullify, overrule, proscribe *(prohibit)*, recall *(call back)*, recant, renege, repeal, repudiate, rescind, revoke, set aside *(annul)*, vacate *(void)*, vitiate
abrogated defunct, inactive, invalid, lifeless *(dead)*, null *(invalid)*, null and void, powerless
abrogatio revocation
abrogation abandonment *(desertion)*, abandonment *(discontinuance)*, abatement *(extinguishment)*, abolition, ademption, annulment, avoidance *(cancellation)*, cancellation, condemnation *(seizure)*, countermand, default, defeasance, desuetude, discharge *(annulment)*, discharge *(release from obligation)*, dissolution *(termination)*, inaction, mistrial, negation, nollo prosequi, obviation, repudiation, rescision, reversal, revocation, waiver
abrupt caustic, impulsive *(rash)*, instantaneous, precipitate, unanticipated, unexpected
abruption impasse
abruptness disrespect
abscind break *(violate)*, excise *(cut away)*, split
abscission cancellation
abscond abandon *(physically leave)*, defect, depart, disappear, elude, escape, evacuate, flee, leave *(depart)*, move *(alter position)*, quit *(evacuate)*, withdraw
abscond with hold up *(rob)*, jostle *(pickpocket)*, loot, pilfer, steal
abscondence bad faith
absconder fugitive
abscondere hide

absconding flight
absconditus hidden, latent
absence blank *(emptiness)*, dearth, deficiency, deficit, desuetude, furlough, insufficiency, need *(deprivation)*, nonresidence, nonuse, paucity, poverty, privation
absence of authority anarchy
absence of ceremony informality
absence of change status quo
absence of diversity uniformity
absence of doubt certainty
absence of fear prowess *(bravery)*
absence of feeling insentience
absence of foreign rule liberty
absence of guilt innocence
absence of meaning incoherence, platitude
absence of restraint latitude, liberty
absence of sensation insentience
absence of servitude liberty
absence of variation uniformity
absence without leave desertion, nonappearance
absent lost *(taken away)*, oblivious, truant, vacuous
absent oneself abandon *(physically leave)*, abscond, depart, evacuate, flee, withdraw
absent-minded perfunctory, thoughtless
absentation leave *(absence)*, nonappearance
absenteeism nonappearance
absentia absence *(nonattendance)*
absentminded lax, oblivious
absentmindedness neglect
absinthal bitter *(acrid tasting)*
absinthian bitter *(acrid tasting)*
absolute actual, affirmative, arbitrary and capricious, axiomatic, cardinal *(outstanding)*, categorical, certain *(fixed)*, certain *(positive)*, clear *(certain)*, compelling, complete *(all-embracing)*, conclusive *(determinative)*, convincing, decisive, definite, definitive, demonstrable, dogmatic, explicit, gross *(flagrant)*, implicit, inappealable, incontrovertible, indubious, outright, plenary, positive *(incontestable)*, pure, radical *(extreme)*, resounding, right *(direct)*, stark, strict, thorough, total, unalienable, unconditional, undisputed, unequivocal, unmitigated, unqualified *(unlimited)*
absolute assertion affirmance *(legal affirmation)*, affirmation
absolute certainty certification *(certainness)*, certitude, fact
absolute condition sine qua non
absolute confidence certainty, certification *(certainness)*, surety *(certainty)*
absolute difference antipode, antithesis
absolute inheritance fee *(estate)*
absolute interest in realty fee *(estate)*
absolute leader dictator
absolute prerequisite sine qua non
absolute quiet silence
absolute reality fact
absolute requisite necessity
absolute right birthright
absolute ruler dictator
absolutely de facto, fairly *(clearly)*, faithfully, in toto, ipso facto, purely

(positively)
absolutely clear incontestable
absoluteness belief *(state of mind)*, certainty, certitude, surety *(certainty)*
absolutio acquittal
absolution acquittal, amnesty, clemency, compurgation, condonation, discharge *(liberation)*, discharge *(release from obligation)*, dispensation *(exception)*, exoneration, grace, immunity, impunity, liberation, pardon, release, remission, waiver
absolution of a charge exoneration
absolutistic dictatorial
absolutus absolute *(complete)*
absolve acquit, clear, condone, discharge *(liberate)*, discharge *(release from obligation)*, exculpate, excuse, exonerate, extenuate, forgive, free, justify, palliate *(excuse)*, purge *(wipe out by atonement)*, quit *(free of)*, redeem *(satisfy debts)*, remit *(release from penalty)*, vindicate
absolve of a charge exonerate
absolve of fault exculpate
absolve of wrongdoing exculpate
absolved blameless, clear *(free from criminal charges)*, exempt, free *(relieved from a burden)*, immune
absolvere absolve, acquit, dispatch *(dispose of)*, perfect
absonant contradictory, opposite
absorb comprehend *(understand)*, conceive *(comprehend)*, concern *(involve)*, digest *(comprehend)*, engage *(involve)*, immerse *(engross)*, impress *(affect deeply)*, include, incorporate *(include)*, interest, merge, monopolize, occupy *(engage)*, penetrate, realize *(understand)*, receive *(permit to enter)*, understand
absorb the attention occupy *(engage)*
absorb the mind occupy *(engage)*
absorb the thoughts occupy *(engage)*
absorbed internal, oblivious, pensive
absorbed interest preoccupation
absorbent penetrable
absorbing moving *(evoking emotion)*
absorption centralization, contemplation, interest *(concern)*, merger, notice *(heed)*, obsession, osmosis, preoccupation, reflection *(thought)*
absorption of mind diligence *(care)*
abstain abandon *(relinquish)*, decline *(reject)*, defer *(yield in judgment)*, desist, discontinue *(abandon)*, eschew, forbear, refrain, refuse, rest *(cease from action)*, shirk, shun, withhold
abstain from avoid *(evade)*, cease, forgo
abstain from inserting omit
abstain from recognizing ignore
abstainment abstention, continence
abstemious frugal
abstemiousness abstention, austerity, moderation, temperance
abstention absence *(nonattendance)*, continence, desuetude, temperance
abstention from buying boycott
abstention from using boycott
absterge decontaminate
absterrere deter
abstinence abstention, continence, disuse, moderation, nonuse, temperance
abstinence from action abstention, inaction, laissez faire

abstract abridgment *(condensation)*, capsule, compendium, condense, delineation, digest, digest *(summarize)*, extract, hold up *(rob)*, intangible, lessen, moot, note *(brief comment)*, outline *(synopsis)*, recondite, restatement, review, scenario, select, speculative, steal, summary, synopsis, theoretical, withdraw

abstract idea concept

abstract on the law hornbook

abstracted compact *(pithy)*, concise, disconnected, oblivious, pensive, perfunctory, thoughtless

abstraction concept, generality *(vague statement)*, idea, impalpability, larceny, notion, preoccupation, vision *(dream)*

abstruse ambiguous, complex, elusive, esoteric, hidden, inapprehensible, incomprehensible, indefinable, inexplicable, mysterious, nebulous, private *(confidential)*, profound *(esoteric)*, recondite, secret, technical

abstruse knowledge secret

abstruseness ambiguity, mystery

absumere consume, exhaust *(deplete)*

absurd egregious, fatuous, impossible, incredible, inept *(inappropriate)*, infeasible, irrational, ludicrous, lunatic, outrageous, unbelievable, unreasonable, unsound *(fallacious)*, unsuitable

absurd story myth

absurdity incongruity

absurdly foolish fatuous

absurdness incongruity

absurdus illogical, irrational

abundance boom *(prosperity)*, bulk, plethora, prosperity, quantity, quorum, spate, store *(depository)*, sufficiency

abundant ample, considerable, copious, full, liberal *(generous)*, multiple, predominant, prevailing *(current)*, prevalent, profuse, prolific, replete, rife, substantial, usual

abundantia store *(depository)*

abuse aspersion, atrocity, attack, badger, beat *(strike)*, contumely, criticism, damage, debauch, defamation, diatribe, dissipate *(expend foolishly)*, endanger, exploit *(take advantage of)*, harm, ill use, imprecation, infliction, injury, injustice, malign, maltreat, misapplication, misappropriation, misemploy, mishandle *(maltreat)*, mishandle *(mismanage)*, mistreat, misusage, misuse, molest *(subject to indecent advances)*, molestation, obloquy, offend *(insult)*, oppression, persecute, perversion, pervert, provocation, rape, reproach, revilement, shame, transgression, vilification, violation, wrong

abuse a privilege infringe

abuse of privilege infringement

abuse of public trust corruption

abuse one's rights infringe

abused aggrieved *(harmed)*

abusive calumnious, contemptuous, hostile, impertinent *(insolent)*, insolent, libelous, offensive *(offending)*, outrageous, pejorative, scurrilous

abusive harangue diatribe

abusive language diatribe, obloquy, phillipic, slander, vilification

abusive speech harangue, malediction

abusiveness oppression

abut contact *(touch)*, juxtapose

abut on adjoin

abut upon border *(approach)*, border *(bound)*

abuti abuse *(misuse)*, ill use, misemploy

abutment bulwark, contact *(touching)*

abuttal connection *(abutment)*, contact *(touching)*

abutting adjacent, coalescence, contiguous, immediate *(not distant)*, proximate

abysmal profound *(intense)*

abyss pitfall

academic didactic, disciplinary *(educational)*, moot, speculative, theoretical

academic honor degree *(academic title)*

academician pedagogue

academy institute

accede acknowledge *(respond)*, admit *(concede)*, agree *(comply)*, allow *(endure)*, assent, cede, coincide *(concur)*, concede, confirm, conform, consent, defer *(yield in judgment)*, grant *(concede)*, obey, relent, sanction, submit *(yield)*, succumb, suffer *(permit)*, yield *(submit)*

accede to accept *(admit as sufficient)*, accept *(assent)*, approve, bear *(tolerate)*, certify *(approve)*, comply, concur *(agree)*, countenance, inherit, pass *(approve)*

accedence acceptance, acquiescence, compliance, consent

accedere approach

accedere ad approximate

accelerare hasten, precipitate *(hasten)*

accelerate expedite, facilitate, hasten, precipitate *(hasten)*, race

accelerated expeditious, rapid

accelerated decision accelerated judgment

accelerating cumulative *(intensifying)*

acceleration boom *(increase)*, haste

acceleration lane causeway

accendere incense

accent consequence *(significance)*, dwell *(linger over)*, emphasis, enunciate, inflection, insist, pronounce *(speak)*, reaffirm

accentuate dwell *(linger over)*, insist, pronounce *(speak)*, reaffirm

accentuation emphasis, inflection, intonation, stress *(accent)*

accept abide, accede *(concede)*, accommodate, accredit, acquire *(receive)*, admit *(concede)*, adopt, agree *(comply)*, allow *(endure)*, approve, assent, assume *(undertake)*, bear *(tolerate)*, certify *(approve)*, coincide *(concur)*, collect *(recover money)*, comply, concede, conceive *(comprehend)*, concur *(agree)*, condone, conform, consent, defer *(yield in judgment)*, espouse, gain, grant *(concede)*, obey, partake, pass *(approve)*, receive *(acquire)*, receive *(permit to enter)*, recognize *(acknowledge)*, sanction, seal *(solemnize)*, sign, submit *(yield)*, suffer *(permit)*, tolerate, trust, undertake, uphold, validate, yield *(submit)*

accept a liability promise *(vow)*

accept advice hear *(give attention to)*

accept an obligation assume *(undertake)*, promise *(vow)*

accept an offer close *(agree)*, contract

accept as a citizen naturalize *(make a citizen)*

accept as a member enroll

accept responsibility promise *(vow)*

accept responsibility for sponsor

accept the loan of borrow

acceptability admissibility, expedience, mediocrity, qualification *(fitness)*

acceptable adequate, admissible, allowable, allowed, applicable, commensurate, convenient, conventional, desirable *(qualified)*, eligible, fair *(satisfactory)*, fit, justifiable, mediocre, meritorious, palatable, passable, proper, qualified *(competent)*, sapid, seasonable, suitable, tenable, unobjectionable, viable

acceptable evidence admissible evidence

acceptably fairly *(moderately)*

acceptance acquiescence, acquisition, affirmance *(judicial sanction)*, approval, assent, assumption *(adoption)*, charter *(sanction)*, compliance, concession *(compromise)*, confirmation, consent, credence, faith, indorsement, lenience, ratification, receipt *(act of receiving)*, recognition, reliance, sanction *(permission)*, subscription, understanding *(tolerance)*

acceptance bill draft

acceptance of penalty nollo contendere

acceptation acquisition, meaning, signification

accepted allowable, allowed, assumed *(inferred)*, boiler plate, common *(customary)*, conventional, customary, familiar *(customary)*, formal, general, ordinary, plausible, popular, prescriptive, prevailing *(current)*, prevalent, right *(suitable)*, select, traditional, uncontested, undisputed, usual

accepted belief principle *(axiom)*

accepted fact common knowledge

accepted language plain language

accepted meaning content *(meaning)*

acceptedly admittedly

accepter disciple, receiver, recipient

accepting orthodox

acceptio acceptance, receipt *(act of receiving)*, taking

acceptor bearer, customer, devisee, donee, feoffee, grantee, heir, payee, transferee

access admission *(entry)*, admittance *(means of approach)*, entrance, entry *(entrance)*, ingress, outlet, portal

access road causeway

accesses approaches

accessibility access *(opening)*

accessible amenable, available, convenient, destructible, indefensible, obvious, open-minded, passable, penetrable, potential, present *(attendant)*, public *(open)*, ready *(prepared)*, receptive, responsive, suasible, untenable, vulnerable

accessible to all competitive *(open)*

accessible to bribery mercenary

accessibleness amenability

accessio accession *(annexation)*, addition, appendix *(supplement)*, augmentation

accession acceptance, acknowledgment *(acceptance)*, acquiescence, addition, appurtenance, arrogation, collection *(accumulation)*, cumulation, receipt *(act of receiving)*

accessories paraphernalia *(apparatus)*, paraphernalia *(personal belongings)*, property *(possessions)*

accessory abettor, accomplice, addition, additional, adjunct, ancillary *(auxiliary)*, appendix *(accession)*, appliance, appurtenance, appurtenant, assistant, attachment *(thing affixed)*, augmentation, circumstantial, clerical, coactor, coadjutant, coconspirator, codicil, cohort, collateral *(accompanying)*, colleague, confederate, consociate, conspirer, contributor *(contributor)*, contributory, copartner *(coconspirator)*, expendable, extrinsic, incident, incidental, inferior *(lower in position)*, minor, nonessential, participant, partner, secondary, subordinate, subservient, supplementary

accessory after the fact accomplice, coactor, coconspirator, conspirer, copartner *(coconspirator)*

accessory before the fact accomplice, coactor, coconspirator, conspirer, copartner *(coconspirator)*

accessus access *(right of way)*

accident act of god, casualty, catastrophe, contingency, emergency, happenstance, misfortune, tragedy

accidental coincidental, fortuitous, haphazard, inadvertent, incidental, random, unexpected, unforeseen, unintentional, unwitting

accidental death fatality

accidental homocide manslaughter

accidental occurrence happenstance, quirk *(accident)*

accipere accept *(take)*, construe *(comprehend)*, enfranchise, hear *(give attention to)*, receive *(acquire)*

accipient assignee

acclaim honor *(outward respect)*, honor, mention *(tribute)*, recommend, remembrance *(commemoration)*, reputation

acclaimed famous, illustrious, notable, renowned, reputable

acclamation consensus, mention *(tribute)*

acclamatory favorable *(expressing approval)*

acclimate inure *(accustom)*

acclimated accustomed *(familiarized)*

acclimation compatibility, habituation

acclimatization habituation

acclimatize adapt, attune, conform, inure *(accustom)*

acclimatized accustomed *(familiarized)*

accolade prize

accommodare accommodate, adjust *(regulate)*

accommodate adjust *(regulate)*, agree *(comply)*, assist, attune, comply, compromise *(settle by mutual agreement)*, conform, contribute *(assist)*, fund, furnish, help, loan, naturalize *(acclimate)*, negotiate, obey, pacify, propitiate, provide *(supply)*, serve *(assist)*, settle, support *(assist)*

accommodate oneself adapt, condescend *(deign)*

accommodate with lend, supply

accommodated fit, res judicata

accommodating benevolent, charitable *(lenient)*, civil *(polite)*, consenting, malleable, philanthropic, pliable, pliant, propitious, sequacious, suitable, yielding

accommodatio adjustment

accommodation accord, accordance *(compact)*, accordance *(understanding)*, adjustment, advance *(allowance)*, advancement *(loan)*, advantage, aid *(help)*, amenity, arrangement *(understanding)*, assistance, benefit *(betterment)*, comity, compatibility, compliance, conciliation, condonation, conformity *(agreement)*, consideration *(recompense)*, consideration *(sympathetic regard)*, consortium *(marriage companionship)*, coverage *(scope)*, dispensation *(act of dispensing)*, favor *(act of kindness)*, help, latitude, loan, lodging, provision *(act of supplying)*, relief *(aid)*, service *(assistance)*, settlement, space, support *(assistance)*

accommodations domicile, habitation *(dwelling place)*, house, residence

accommodative concordant, nonmilitant

accommodativeness amenability

accommodatus adequate, appropriate, convenient, qualified *(conditioned)*

accompanied composite

accompanier colleague, consort, copartner *(coconspirator)*

accompaniment appurtenance, attendance, codicil, rider, synchronism

accompaniments paraphernalia *(apparatus)*

accompany coincide *(correspond)*, concur *(coexist)*

accompanying coincidental, concomitant, concurrent *(at the same time)*, incidental, simultaneous

accompanying events circumstances

accomplice abettor, accessory, assistant, coactor, coadjutant, coconspirator, cohort, colleague, confederate, consociate, conspirer, contributor *(contributor)*, copartner *(coconspirator)*, participant, partner

accomplice in crime abettor, accessory, coactor, conspirer, copartner *(coconspirator)*

accomplish attain, avail *(bring about)*, carry *(succeed)*, commit *(perpetrate)*, complete, compose, consummate, culminate, discharge *(perform)*, dispatch *(dispose of)*, effectuate, evoke, finish, fulfill, gain, implement, make, operate, pass *(satisfy requirements)*, perfect, perform *(execute)*, perpetrate, procure, produce *(manufacture)*, reach, realize *(make real)*, render *(administer)*, succeed *(attain)*, transact

accomplish promptly expedite

accomplished capable, cognizant, competent, complete *(ended)*, deft, expert, facile, familiar *(informed)*, informed *(educated)*, learned, literate, practiced, proficient, qualified *(competent)*, resourceful, sciential, subtle *(refined)*

accomplished efficiently expeditious

accomplished fact fait accompli, performance *(execution)*

accomplished practitioner professional

accomplishment act *(undertaking)*, action *(performance)*, boom *(prosperity)*, commission *(act)*, development *(outgrowth)*, discharge *(performance)*, effect, end *(termination)*, fait accompli, finality, fruition, output, performance *(execution)*, performance *(workmanship)*, product, progress, realization, satisfaction *(fulfilment)*, specialty *(special aptitude)*, transaction

accomplishments civilization, education

accord accede *(concede)*, accordance *(compact)*, adjust *(resolve)*, adjustment, administer *(tender)*, agree *(comply)*, agreement *(concurrence)*, allow *(endure)*, approval, arbitrate *(conciliate)*, arrangement *(understanding)*, ascribe, assent, assent, attune, authorize, bargain, bestow, cartel, certify *(approve)*, cohere *(be logically consistent)*, coincide *(concur)*, comity, compatibility, compliance, concert, concession *(compromise)*, conciliation, concordance, concur *(agree)*, condescend *(deign)*, confer *(give)*, confirm, confirmation, conform, conformity *(agreement)*, consensus, consent, consent, contact *(association)*, contract, contribute *(supply)*, correspondence *(similarity)*, defer *(yield in judgment)*, delegate, endue, give *(grant)*, grant *(concede)*, impart, indorsement, league, leave *(give)*, mutual understanding, peace, present *(make a gift)*, propinquity *(similarity)*, provide *(supply)*, rapport, rapprochement, reconciliation, render *(administer)*, synchronism, treaty, understanding *(agreement)*, union *(unity)*, volition, vouchsafe, yield *(produce a return)*

accord one's approval certify *(approve)*, notarize, permit

accord recognition to accept *(recognize)*

accord superiority to defer *(yield in judgment)*

accord with comport *(agree with)*

accordance acceptance, accommodation *(adjustment)*, accord, acquiescence, adjustment, arrangement *(understanding)*, assent, bargain, capacity *(authority)*, cartel, coalescence, compatibility, compliance, concert, conciliation, concordance, confirmation, conformity *(agreement)*, contract, indulgence, leave *(permission)*, license, propriety *(appropriateness)*, rapport, rapprochement, understanding *(agreement)*, union *(unity)*

accordance with law legality

accordant agreed *(harmonized)*, apposite, appropriate, commensurate, concerted, concordant, concurrent *(united)*, congruous, consensual, consenting, consistent, consonant, contractual, correlative, felicitous, germane, harmonious, suitable

accordant with the facts authentic

according to pursuant to

according to contract as agreed upon

according to custom orthodox, typi-

cal
according to desires arbitrary
according to edict licit
according to established form formal
according to fiat lawful
according to general belief reputedly
according to habit habitual
according to law choate lien, de jure, due *(regular)*, jural, juridical, just, law-abiding, lawful, legitimate *(rightful)*, licit, permissible, rightful, statutory
according to plan purposely
according to regulation orthodox
according to reputation reputedly
according to routine typical
according to rule normal *(regular)*, orthodox, regular *(conventional)*, systematic
according to the agreement as agreed upon
according to the bargain as agreed upon
according to the book orthodox
according to the contract as agreed upon
according to the facts authentic, true *(authentic)*
according to the law legal
according to usage customary
according to value ad valorem
accordingly a fortiori, a priori, consequently
accost approach, assail, assault, confront *(encounter)*
accost bellicosely assault
accoster assailant
account amount *(sum)*, behalf, bill *(invoice)*, brief, calculate, census, computation, deem, delineation, description, distinction *(reputation)*, entry *(record)*, intelligence *(news)*, invoice *(bill)*, narration, rationale, reason *(basis)*, recital, record, rendition *(explication)*, report *(detailed account)*, representation *(statement)*, review *(critical evaluation)*, roll, statement, story *(narrative)*, tariff *(bill)*, worth
account book ledger
account debtor debtor
account for enlighten, explain, exposit, justify, rationalize, solve, support *(justify)*, vindicate
account of goods shipped invoice *(itemized list)*
account of merchandise invoice *(itemized list)*
account of transactions ledger
account outstanding debt
account owing debt
account rendered invoice *(bill)*
accountability blame *(respononsibility)*, burden, charge *(lien)*, charge *(responsibility)*, commitment *(responsibility)*, duty *(obligation)*, fault *(responsibility)*, liability, obligation *(liability)*
accountable actionable, bound, cognizable, determinable *(ascertainable)*, liable, subject *(exposed)*
accountableness charge *(responsibility)*, commitment *(responsibility)*, liability, responsibility *(accountability)*
accountancy budget, computation
accountant comptroller

accounted detailed
accounted for present *(attendant)*
accounting attribution, computation
accounts budget, finance, ledger
accounts collectable due
accounts outstanding due
accounts payable bill *(invoice)*
accouple cement, join *(bring together)*
accouplement marriage *(intimate relationship)*
accouter clothe, furnish, supply
accouterment equipment
accouterments paraphernalia *(apparatus)*
accredit allow *(authorize)*, ascribe, authorize, bestow, certify *(approve)*, concur *(agree)*, confirm, cosign, countenance, delegate, empower, honor, indorse, notarize, qualify *(meet standards)*, seal *(solemnize)*, sign, support *(corroborate)*, trust, verify *(confirm)*
accredit with attribute
accreditation jurat
accredited authentic, documentary, official, popular
accreted coherent *(joined)*
accretion accession *(enlargement)*, boom *(increase)*, collection *(accumulation)*, compilation, cumulation, development *(progression)*, increment
accretive coherent *(joined)*
accroach annex *(arrogate)*, assume *(seize)*, condemn *(seize)*, impropriate, obtrude, overreach, overstep, usurp
accroachment appropriation *(taking)*
accrual accession *(enlargement)*, additive, appreciation *(increased value)*, augmentation, boom *(increase)*, interest *(profit)*
accruance profit
accrue accumulate *(enlarge)*, arise *(originate)*, bear *(yield)*, compound, develop, hoard, increase, mature, redound, result, yield *(produce a return)*
accruement appreciation *(increased value)*, augmentation, boom *(increase)*, cumulation
accruing cumulative *(increasing)*
accumulare accumulate *(amass)*
accumulate accrue *(increase)*, aggregate, codify, collect *(gather)*, compile, concentrate *(consolidate)*, congregate, conjoin, consolidate *(unite)*, convene, crystallize, cull, expand, fund, garner, glean, hoard, increase, inure *(benefit)*, join *(bring together)*, keep *(shelter)*, obtain, procure, raise *(collect)*, reserve, set aside *(annul)*, store
accumulated accrued, collective, conglomerate
accumulation accession *(enlargement)*, agglomeration, appreciation *(increased value)*, arsenal, assemblage, augmentation, boom *(increase)*, boom *(prosperity)*, bulk, compilation, conglomeration, cumulation, deposit, development *(progression)*, entirety, fund, growth *(increase)*, hoard, plethora, profit, resource, selection *(collection)*, stock *(store)*, store *(depository)*, sufficiency, treasury
accumulative collective, cumulative *(increasing)*, lucrative
accuracy honesty, rigor, truth, veracity

accurate absolute *(conclusive)*, actual, appropriate, authentic, bona fide, definite, definitive, detailed, documentary, exact, explicit, factual, faithful *(true to fact)*, genuine, honest, literal, particular *(exacting)*, precise, proper, punctilious, punctual, real, reliable, right *(correct)*, sound, strict, thorough, true *(authentic)*, unrefutable, valid
accurately duly, faithfully
accuratus careful, circumstantial, scrupulous, systematic
accursed arrant *(onerous)*, diabolic, iniquitous, loathsome, odious, peccant *(culpable)*
accusable bad *(offensive)*, blameful, blameworthy, culpable, delinquent *(guilty of a misdeed)*, illicit, peccant *(culpable)*, reprehensible, reprobate, unjustifiable
accusal accusation, blame *(culpability)*, complaint, denunciation, impeachment, incrimination, indictment, information *(charge)*
accusant accuser, claimant, complainant
accusare accuse, arraign, charge *(accuse)*, complain *(charge)*, fault, impeach, indict, prosecute *(charge)*
accusatio accusation, charge *(accusation)*, denunciation, impeachment, indictment
accusation arraignment, blame *(culpability)*, claim *(legal demand)*, complaint, condemnation *(blame)*, count, criticism, denunciation, diatribe, disparagement, impeachment, incrimination, inculpation, indictment, information *(charge)*, innuendo, libel, objurgation, obloquy, onus *(blame)*, outcry, pleading, presentment, reproach, slander, stricture
accusation in court arraignment
accusative inculpatory
accusator prosecutor
accusatory contemptuous, incriminatory, inculpatory
accusatrix accuser
accuse arraign, blame, book, complain *(charge)*, complain *(criticize)*, condemn *(blame)*, contemn, defame, denigrate, denounce *(inform against)*, fault, impeach, implicate, incriminate, indict, inform *(betray)*, involve *(implicate)*, lodge *(bring a complaint)*, pillory, present *(prefer charges)*, proscribe *(denounce)*, rebuke, recriminate, reprehend, reprimand, reproach
accuse falsely defame, frame *(charge falsely)*, libel
accuse in writing libel
accuse of maladministration impeach
accuse of misconduct impeach
accuse of wrong arraign
accuse unfairly frame *(charge falsely)*
accuse unjustly frame *(charge falsely)*
accused convict, suspect
accused litigant defendant
accused party defendant
accused person convict, suspect
accuser claimant, complainant, district attorney, informant, informer *(one providing criminal information)*, plain-

tiff

accusing critical *(faultfinding)*, incriminatory, inculpatory

accustom discipline *(train)*, inure *(accustom)*, naturalize *(acclimate)*, reconcile

accustom oneself to endure *(suffer)*

accustomary habitual, mundane, ordinary, prevailing *(current)*, prevalent

accustomed addicted, conventional, customary, daily, familiar *(customary)*, frequent, habitual, household *(familiar)*, inveterate, ordinary, orthodox, prevailing *(current)*, prevalent, regular *(conventional)*, rife, routine, typical, usual

accustoming habituation

ace unit *(item)*

acedia sloth

acer acute, intense

acerb harsh

acerbate aggravate *(annoy)*, annoy, bitter *(acrid tasting)*

acerbic bitter *(acrid tasting)*, harsh, mordacious

acerbitas intolerance, severity

acerbity ill will, rancor, severity

acerbus bitter *(acrid tasting)*, caustic, scathing, virulent

acervation assemblage, collection *(accumulation)*, cumulation

acervus collection *(accumulation)*, hoard

ache pain

achievability feasibility, possibility

achievable passable, possible, potential, practicable

achieve accomplish, acquire *(receive)*, attain, build *(construct)*, carry *(succeed)*, commit *(perpetrate)*, complete, compose, consummate, discharge *(perform)*, dispatch *(dispose of)*, earn, effectuate, evoke, execute *(accomplish)*, finish, fulfill, function, gain, implement, make, obtain, operate, pass *(satisfy requirements)*, perform *(adhere to)*, perform *(execute)*, perpetrate, procure, produce *(manufacture)*, reach, realize *(make real)*, realize *(obtain as a profit)*, reap, recover, succeed *(attain)*, transact

achieve by continued effort earn

achieve liberty escape

achieved complete *(ended)*

achievement act *(undertaking)*, action *(performance)*, boom *(prosperity)*, commission *(act)*, development *(outgrowth)*, discharge *(performance)*, effect, end *(termination)*, endeavor, fait accompli, finality, fruition, monument, objective, outcome, output, performance *(execution)*, performance *(workmanship)*, progress, prosperity, realization, satisfaction *(fulfilment)*, step, transaction

achievement of liberty liberation

aching painful

acid astringent, bitter *(acrid tasting)*, harsh, mordacious

acidulous bitter *(acrid tasting)*

acidus bitter *(acrid tasting)*

acknowledge abide, accede *(concede)*, accept *(recognize)*, admit *(concede)*, agree *(comply)*, allow *(authorize)*, answer *(reply)*, appreciate *(comprehend)*, assent, avouch *(avow)*, avow, bear *(adduce)*, betray *(disclose)*, certify *(approve)*, certify *(attest)*, comply, concede, concur *(agree)*, confess, confirm, correspond *(communicate)*, corroborate, defer *(yield in judgment)*, disclose, grant *(concede)*, hear *(give attention to)*, keep *(fulfill)*, note *(notice)*, notice *(observe)*, posit, prescriptive, profess *(avow)*, reply, respond, return *(respond)*, reveal, sign, subscribe *(sign)*, uphold, vouch, witness *(attest to)*

acknowledge defeat quit *(discontinue)*, submit *(yield)*

acknowledge one's guilt confess

acknowledge openly bear *(adduce)*, testify

acknowledge through possession prescriptive

acknowledge through use prescriptive

acknowledged alleged, allowed, customary, familiar *(customary)*, nunc pro tunc, orthodox, proverbial, public *(known)*, putative, sound, traditional, undisputed, usual

acknowledged elsewhere as alias

acknowledged judgment cognovit

acknowledgement disclosure *(something disclosed)*, expiation

acknowledgment acceptance, acquiescence, admission *(disclosure)*, adoption *(acceptance)*, affirmance *(authentication)*, affirmation, answer *(reply)*, approval, assent, asseveration, attribution, avouchment, avowal, charter *(sanction)*, common knowledge, concession *(compromise)*, confession, confirmation, consensus, consent, corroboration, grant, honorarium, ratification, recognition, recognizance, requital, response, reward

acknowledgment of guilt confession

acknowledgment of payment receipt *(proof of receiving)*

acme ceiling, culmination, pinnacle

acme of perfection paragon

acolyte coactor

acquaint apprise, communicate, convey *(communicate)*, disabuse, disclose, divulge, enlighten, impart, inform *(notify)*, instruct *(teach)*, inure *(accustom)*, mention, notify, relate *(tell)*, report *(disclose)*, signify *(inform)*

acquaintance cognition, experience *(background)*, knowledge *(awareness)*

acquaintanceship contact *(association)*

acquainted accustomed *(familiarized)*, cognizant, expert, familiar *(informed)*, informed *(having information)*, knowing

acquainted with conscious *(aware)*, learned, privy

acquainting informatory

acquest demesne

acquiesce abide, accede *(concede)*, accept *(admit as sufficient)*, accept *(assent)*, admit *(concede)*, agree *(comply)*, allow *(endure)*, assent, bear *(tolerate)*, coincide *(concur)*, concede, concur *(agree)*, confirm, consent, defer *(yield in judgment)*, grant *(concede)*, obey, observe *(obey)*, pass *(approve)*, relent, sanction, submit *(yield)*, succumb, suffer *(permit)*, surrender *(yield)*, tolerate, vouchsafe, yield *(submit)*

acquiesce in approve, authorize, comply, countenance, indorse

acquiesced in consensual

acquiescence acceptance, acknowledgment *(acceptance)*, affirmance *(judicial sanction)*, affirmation, amenability, approval, assent, capitulation, charter *(sanction)*, compliance, concession *(compromise)*, confession, confirmation, conformity *(agreement)*, consent, deference, discipline *(obedience)*, dispensation *(exception)*, indorsement, indulgence, leave *(permission)*, permission, resignation *(passive acceptance)*, sanction *(permission)*

acquiescent amenable, charitable *(lenient)*, concurrent *(united)*, congruous, consensual, consenting, favorable *(expressing approval)*, harmonious, inclined, law-abiding, malleable, obedient, open *(persuasible)*, passive, patient, permissive, pliable, pliant, ready *(willing)*, sequacious, tractable, willing *(not averse)*, yielding

acquiescently faithfully

acquiescing consenting

acquire accept *(take)*, accrue *(arise)*, accrue *(increase)*, aggregate, appropriate, attain, collect *(gather)*, collect *(recover money)*, condemn *(seize)*, derive *(receive)*, gain, garner, hoard, impress *(procure by force)*, incur, inherit, obtain, occupy *(take possession)*, possess, procure, profit, purchase, realize *(obtain as a profit)*, reap, recover, store, succeed *(attain)*

acquire beforehand preempt

acquire by purchase buy

acquire by service earn

acquire currency circulate

acquire from ancestors inherit

acquire information ascertain

acquire information about find *(discover)*

acquire intelligence about ascertain

acquire knowledge study

acquire ownership of buy, purchase

acquire the habit practice *(train by repetition)*

acquired facts information *(knowledge)*, intelligence *(news)*

acquired knowledge civilization, information *(knowledge)*

acquired mode of behavior habit

acquired right option *(contractual provision)*

acquirement acquisition, distress *(seizure)*, edification, realization, receipt *(act of receiving)*

acquirements education

acquisition accession *(enlargement)*, adverse possession, appropriation *(taking)*, assumption *(adoption)*, boom *(prosperity)*, collection *(accumulation)*, cumulation, distress *(seizure)*, profit, realization, receipt *(act of receiving)*, recovery *(repossession)*, replevin, takeover, taking

acquisition by right of eminent domain condemnation *(seizure)*

acquisition of knowledge discovery, education

acquisitive confiscatory, insatiable, mercenary, parsimonious

acquisitiveness greed

acquit absolve, clear, comport *(behave)*, demean *(deport oneself)*, deport *(conduct oneself)*, discharge *(liberate)*, exculpate, excuse, exonerate, extenuate, forgive, free, liberate, palliate *(excuse)*, pardon, pay, purge *(wipe out by atonement)*, quit *(free of)*, remit *(release from penalty)*, remunerate, vindicate

acquitment acquittal, discharge *(payment)*, satisfaction *(discharge of debt)*

acquittal absolution, compurgation, condonation, discharge *(liberation)*, discharge *(payment)*, discharge *(release from obligation)*, emancipation, exoneration, immunity, impunity, liberation, pardon, payment *(act of paying)*, release, remission, remittance, respite *(reprieve)*, satisfaction *(discharge of debt)*, waiver

acquittance acquittal, amnesty, collection *(payment)*, compurgation, discharge *(payment)*, exoneration, liberation, payment *(act of paying)*, quitclaim, receipt *(proof of receiving)*, release, remission, satisfaction *(discharge of debt)*

acquitted blameless, clean, clear *(free from criminal charges)*, free *(relieved from a burden)*

acreage homestead, parcel, plot *(land)*, property *(land)*, real estate, space

acres estate *(property)*, freehold, homestead, property *(land)*, realty

acrid astringent, bitter *(acrid tasting)*, caustic, harsh, mordacious, virulent

acrimonious astringent, bitter *(penetrating)*, bitter *(reproachful)*, caustic, cruel, cynical, harsh, hostile, libelous, malevolent, malicious, mordacious, negative, outrageous, pejorative, petulant, resentful, scathing, severe, spiteful, trenchant, vicious, virulent

acrimoniousness spite

acrimony alienation *(estrangement)*, malice, phillipic, rancor, resentment, severity, spite, umbrage

acroamatic esoteric, inapprehensible, incomprehensible, inexplicable, profound *(esoteric)*, secret

acroamatical esoteric, inapprehensible, incomprehensible, inexplicable, profound *(esoteric)*, secret

acroatic esoteric, inapprehensible, incomprehensible, inexplicable, learned, profound *(esoteric)*

act amendment *(legislation)*, canon, codification, commit *(perpetrate)*, comport *(behave)*, constitution, course, demean *(deport oneself)*, deport *(conduct oneself)*, dictate, enactment, execute *(accomplish)*, exercise *(discharge a function)*, fake, false pretense, function, law, measure, mock *(imitate)*, officiate, operate, operation, palter, performance *(execution)*, portray, prescription *(directive)*, pretend, procedure, proceed *(go forward)*, regulation *(rule)*, represent *(substitute)*, role, rubric *(authoritative rule)*, rule *(legal dictate)*, scene, simulate, statute, step, transaction

act a part impersonate

act against counter, gainsay

act against with equal force compensate *(counterbalance)*, countervail

act as assume *(simulate)*, pose *(impersonate)*

act as agent intercede

act as assistant to assist

act as broker represent *(substitute)*

act as chairman moderate *(preside over)*, preside

act as delegate represent *(substitute)*

act as go-between intercede

act as mediator intercede

act as moderator moderate *(preside over)*

act as one combine *(act in concert)*

act as president moderate *(preside over)*, preside

act as surety for sponsor

act committed in violation of law misdemeanor

act contrary disoblige

act demanded by social custom decorum

act despite override

act dishonestly cheat

act effectively function

act falsely fake

act foolishly mismanage

act for displace *(replace)*, replace, represent *(substitute)*, supplant

act illegally disobey, violate

act improperly mismanage

act in accordance with orders obey

act in advance forestall

act in collusion plot

act in combination conspire

act in concert concur *(agree)*, connive, conspire, cooperate, federalize *(associate)*, federate, involve *(participate)*, join *(associate oneself with)*, participate, unite

act in harmony conspire

act in opposition fight *(battle)*

act in opposition to antagonize, confront *(oppose)*, counter, counteract, cross *(disagree with)*, fight *(counteract)*, oppose

act in place of represent *(substitute)*

act in response to answer *(reply)*

act in support adhere *(maintain loyalty)*

act insincerely palter

act interchangeably alternate *(take turns)*, reciprocate

act jointly combine *(act in concert)*, cooperate

act of bearing witness attestation

act of believing credence

act of berating diatribe, disparagement

act of bribing corruption

act of bringing in introduction

act of coming together chain *(nexus)*

act of compassing coverage *(scope)*

act of comprehending coverage *(scope)*

act of containing coverage *(scope)*

act of copying counterfeit

act of coupling chain *(nexus)*

act of crumbling decline

act of despising disdain

act of discrediting disdain, impeachment

act of dissembling color *(deceptive appearance)*

act of driving out eviction

act of dwelling together cohabitation *(living together)*

act of dwindling decline

act of embracing coverage *(scope)*

act of encircling coverage *(scope)*

act of encompassing coverage *(scope)*

act of engrossing coverage *(scope)*

act of facing confrontation *(act of setting face to face)*

act of falling away decline

act of ferocity atrocity

act of forestalling constraint *(restriction)*

act of forsaking desertion

act of generosity favor *(act of kindness)*

act of giving one's word pledge *(binding promise)*

act of God calamity

act of grace amnesty, favor *(act of kindness)*

act of hampering constraint *(restriction)*

act of hardening congealment

act of holding harmless indemnity

act of hostility assault

act of indemnity exoneration

act of inhumanity brutality

act of joining chain *(nexus)*

act of judgment adjudication, award, choice *(decision)*, holding *(ruling of a court)*

act of keeping in constraint *(imprisonment)*

act of killing dispatch *(act of putting to death)*, murder

act of lawbreaking misdemeanor

act of lessening decline

act of living together as husband and wife cohabitation *(married state)*

act of loathing disdain

act of looking backward hindsight

act of losing ground decline

act of maneuvering connivance

act of mercy amnesty

act of oath-breaking perjury

act of pairing cohabitation *(married state)*

act of profiteering corruption

act of promise-making coverage *(insurance)*

act of protecting custody *(supervision)*

act of pursuing course

act of quelling constraint *(restriction)*

act of relinquishing a right waiver

act of reverting escheatment

act of running down disparagement

act of scheming connivance

act of scorning disdain

act of setting forth delineation

act of shrinking decline

act of shunning disdain

act of slaying dispatch *(act of putting to death)*, murder

act of slipping back decline

act of spanning coverage *(scope)*

act of spurning disdain

act of stifling constraint *(restriction)*

act of strangling constraint *(restriction)*

act of subsuming coverage *(scope)*

act of surrounding coverage *(scope)*

act of taking life murder

act of taunting disdain

act of throwing out eviction

act of thwarting constraint *(restriction)*

act of uniting chain *(nexus)*
act of wasting away decline
act of weakening decline
act of working together collusion
act of worsening decline
act on affect, award, commit *(perpetrate)*, discharge *(perform)*, militate, obey, treat *(process)*
act on behalf of represent *(substitute)*
act on one's own authority choose
act out impersonate
act prohibited by law crime
act the part of displace *(replace)*, exemplify, impersonate, pose *(impersonate)*
act together cooperate, participate
act upon execute *(accomplish)*, operate
act vicariously represent *(substitute)*
acta diurna journal
actable viable
acte act *(enactment)*
acting histrionics, operative, representative, surrogate, temporary, vicarious *(delegated)*
acting as a substitute vicarious *(delegated)*
acting as attorney for representation *(acting for others)*
acting in conjunction concurrent *(united)*
acting out catharsis
acting with force drastic
acting without due consideration ill-judged
actio action *(proceeding)*, delivery, proceeding, suit
action act *(undertaking)*, award, campaign, case *(lawsuit)*, cause *(lawsuit)*, cause of action, contest *(dispute)*, controversy *(lawsuit)*, course, day in court, fight *(battle)*, happening, hearing, holding *(ruling of a court)*, lawsuit, matter *(case)*, operation, overt act, performance *(execution)*, performance *(workmanship)*, ploy, procedure, proceeding, process *(course)*, prosecution *(criminal trial)*, step, suit, transaction, trial *(legal proceeding)*
action at law action *(proceeding)*, cause of action, lawsuit, proceeding, suit, trial *(legal proceeding)*
action in court cause *(lawsuit)*
action to defeat plaintiff's demand counterclaim
action to serve justice suit
actionable illegal, illicit, impermissible, justiciable, litigable, litigious, moot, triable, unlawful
actionable act tortious act
actions behavior, conduct, dealings, deportment, manner *(behavior)*
activate empower, launch *(initiate)*, maintain *(commence)*, motivate, originate, prompt, stimulate, urge
activating impulsive *(impelling)*
activator catalyst, stimulus
active alert *(vigilant)*, conscious *(awake)*, effective *(operative)*, expeditious, fervent, industrious, moving *(in motion)*, operative, potent, rapid, responsive, sedulous, volatile, zealous
active application diligence *(care)*
active attention diligence *(care)*
active discouragement deterrence

active element catalyst
active espousal advocacy
active giving charity
active ill will malice
active partisan catalyst
active partisans lobby
active reformer catalyst
active reformers lobby
active study diligence *(care)*, examination *(study)*
active supporters lobby
active thought diligence *(care)*
actively opposed hostile, malevolent
actively represent lobby
activeness life *(vitality)*
activism campaign
activists lobby
activities affairs, dealings
activity agency *(legal relationship)*, business *(affair)*, business *(occupation)*, calling, campaign, career, course, employment, enterprise *(undertaking)*, life *(vitality)*, occupation *(vocation)*, project, pursuit *(occupation)*, transaction, turmoil
actor actor
acts conduct, dealings, legislation *(enactments)*, manner *(behavior)*
actual absolute *(conclusive)*, accurate, authentic, bona fide, certain *(positive)*, clear *(certain)*, corporeal, de facto, definite, documentary, factual, genuine, honest, material *(physical)*, objective, peremptory *(absolute)*, physical, real, realistic, substantive, tangible, true *(authentic)*, unalienable
actual existence reality
actual occurrence fact
actual possession occupancy
actual reality fact
actuality entity, fact, fait accompli, reality, substance *(essential nature)*, truth, veracity
actualization commission *(act)*, embodiment, fait accompli, realization
actualize compose, consummate, embody, exemplify, forge *(produce)*, implement, make, realize *(make real)*, substantiate
actually de facto
actuate agitate *(activate)*, bait *(lure)*, constrain *(compel)*, impel, induce, influence, inspire, lobby, motivate, persuade, prevail *(persuade)*, prompt, provoke, spirit, stimulate
actuating impulsive *(impelling)*, persuasive
actuation commission *(act)*, impetus, impulse, incentive, instigation, persuasion, provocation, reason *(basis)*
actuator abettor, catalyst
acuity insight, perception, sagacity
aculeatus scathing
acumen caliber *(mental capacity)*, common sense, discrimination *(good judgment)*, insight, intelligence *(intellect)*, judgment *(discernment)*, perception, reason *(sound judgment)*, sagacity, sense *(intelligence)*
acuminate acute
acute artful, caustic, conscious *(awake)*, critical *(crucial)*, crucial, exigent, important *(urgent)*, incisive, insufferable, intense, intensive, knowing, mordacious, perceptive, politic, profound *(intense)*, responsive, sapient,

trenchant
acute alcoholism dipsomania
acute dissatisfaction ill will
acuteness caliber *(mental capacity)*, discretion *(quality of being discreet)*, discrimination *(good judgment)*, insight, judgment *(discernment)*, perception, sagacity, sensibility
acutus acute, perspicacious
ad administrationem pertimens clerical
ad aerarium pertinens financial
ad captandum colorable *(plausible)*
ad hominem confugere apply *(request)*
ad inritum redigere frustrate, nullify
ad persuadendum accommodatus convincing
ad pugnam provocare challenge
ad rem apposite
ad rem spectare relevant
ad sententiam adopt
ad tempus temporary
ad tempus advenire punctual
ad vadimonium non venire default *(noun)*, default *(verb)*
ad vanum frustrate
adage catchword, maxim, phrase, principle *(axiom)*
adamant callous, immutable, implacable, inexorable, inflexible, intractable, irreconcilable, persistent, pertinacious, resolute, unalterable, unbending, uncompromising, unrelenting, unyielding
adamantine callous, unyielding
adapertus open *(unclosed)*
adapt accommodate, adjust *(regulate)*, agree *(comply)*, alter, apply *(put in practice)*, arrange *(methodize)*, attune, change, conform, modify *(alter)*, naturalize *(acclimate)*, orchestrate, reconcile
adapt to correspond *(be equivalent)*
adaptability ability, amenability, compliance, conciliation
adaptable applicable, corrigible, disposable, flexible, malleable, pliable, pliant, practical, resilient, sequacious, tractable
adaptable to change liberal *(broad minded)*
adaptation accommodation *(adjustment)*, adjustment, compromise, habituation, innovation, modification, propriety *(appropriateness)*
adapted accustomed *(familiarized)*, agreed *(harmonized)*, apposite, congruous, consonant, correlative, effective *(efficient)*, felicitous, fit, fitting, harmonious, pertinent, proper, qualified *(competent)*, resigned, sciential, suitable, tempered
adapted to applicable, appropriate
adapted to argumentation forensic
adapted to teach didactic
adapted to the understanding coherent *(clear)*
adaption arrangement *(ordering)*
adaptive pliable, resilient
add affix, append, attach *(join)*, conjoin, contribute *(supply)*, extend *(enlarge)*, heighten *(augment)*, interject, recruit, sum, supplement, unite
add as a third party implead
add as an accessory attach *(join)*
add details embellish
add on accrue *(increase)*, increase
add strength to confirm

add to accumulate *(enlarge)*, aggravate *(exacerbate)*, amend, amplify, build *(augment)*, collect *(gather)*, compound, conjoin, consolidate *(strengthen)*, elaborate, enhance, enlarge, expand, increase, intensify, magnify, supplement
add to the payroll employ *(engage services)*, hire
add together aggregate
add up to consist
add water dilute
add weight to aggravate *(exacerbate)*
added additional, ancillary *(auxiliary)*, attached *(annexed)*, expendable, extrinsic, incidental, nonessential
added charge surcharge
added monetary worth appreciation *(increased value)*
added protection buffer zone
added time extension *(postponement)*
added to accrued
added together cumulative *(increasing)*
addend addition
addendum addition, additive, adjunct, allonge
addendum appendix *(supplement)*
addendum appurtenance, attachment *(thing affixed)*, codicil, insertion, rider
addere append, appendix *(supplement)*
addicere adjudge, allot, award
addicted accustomed *(familiarized)*, inveterate
addicted to lewdness lecherous
addictedness dipsomania
addiction dipsomania
adding augmentation, computation
additament addendum, addition, adjunct, allonge, appendix *(accession)*, appurtenance, boom *(increase)*, codicil, insertion, rider
addition accession *(annexation)*, accession *(enlargement)*, accretion, addendum, additive, adjunct, allonge, appendix *(supplement)*, appreciation *(increased value)*, appurtenance, boom *(increase)*, codicil, collection *(accumulation)*, continuation *(prolongation)*, corollary, cumulation, exaggeration, expletive, extension *(expansion)*, growth *(increase)*, increment, insertion, offshoot, reinforcement, rider
addition to adjoiner
addition to a will codicil
addition to realty fixture
additional ancillary *(auxiliary)*, circumstantial, collateral *(accompanying)*, contributory, cumulative *(increasing)*, expendable, extraneous, extrinsic, gratuitous *(unwarranted)*, incidental, nonessential, pendent, superfluous, supplementary
additional charge surcharge
additional clause rider
additional strength reinforcement
additional time extension *(postponement)*
additionally also, further
additive addition, additional, bonus, codicil, cumulative *(increasing)*, factor *(ingredient)*, supplementary
additory boom *(increase)*, cumulative *(increasing)*
additum attachment *(thing affixed)*, codicil
additus additional

addle confuse *(bewilder)*, decay, discompose, muddle, obfuscate, spoil *(impair)*
addlebrained opaque
addled fatuous
addleheaded opaque
addlepated opaque
address abode, accost, bestow, building *(structure)*, call *(appeal)*, conduct, converse, declaim, declamation, deportment, discourse, discourse, dispatch *(send off)*, domicile, habitation *(dwelling place)*, locality, lodging, manner *(behavior)*, parlance, peroration, recite, report *(detailed account)*, residence, rhetoric *(skilled speech)*, site, speak, speech
address a petition call *(appeal to)*
address a request call *(appeal to)*, plead *(implore)*, pray
address a warning to admonish *(warn)*, notice *(give formal warning)*
address oneself to call *(appeal to)*, endeavor, occupy *(engage)*, specialize, undertake
address to dedicate
address to the jury charge *(statement to the jury)*
addressee inhabitant, lodger, occupant, resident
addriri assault
adduce allege, depose *(testify)*, mention, proffer, quote, rationalize, refer *(direct attention)*
adduce evidence corroborate
adduced alleged
adducere adduce, induce
adeem assume *(seize)*, attach *(seize)*, confiscate
adeemed attached *(seized)*
ademption taking
adept artful, capable, competent, deft, diplomatic, expert, practiced, professional *(trained)*, proficient, qualified *(competent)*, sciential, veteran
adept practitioner professional
adeptness ability, efficiency, facility *(easiness)*, gift *(flair)*, prowess *(ability)*, skill, specialty *(special aptitude)*
adequacy ability, caliber *(mental capacity)*, competence *(ability)*, quorum, sufficiency, utility *(usefulness)*
adequate ample, capable, commensurate, competent, effective *(efficient)*, fair *(satisfactory)*, fit, functional, habitable, mediocre, operative, prima facie *(legally sufficient)*, proficient, qualified *(competent)*, sciential, suitable, unobjectionable
adequate resources sufficiency
adequately fairly *(moderately)*
adequately perceive appreciate *(value)*
adequateness admissibility, mediocrity, quorum
adesse appear *(attend court proceedings)*, support *(assist)*
adeundi copiam admit *(give access)*
adferre entail, quote, report *(disclose)*
adficere affect
adfigere affix, attach *(join)*
adfinis germane
adfirmare affirm *(uphold)*, assert, contend *(maintain)*, maintain *(carry on)*
adfirmatio affirmation, allegation, assertion, indorsement, possess

adfligere overthrow
adgredi assail, assault, attack
adherance concrescence
adhere abide, affix, attach *(join)*, cement, confirm, join *(bring together)*, maintain *(sustain)*, persevere, remain *(continue)*, remain *(stay)*
adhere to bear *(tolerate)*, comply, conform, fulfill, keep *(fulfill)*, obey, observe *(obey)*, pursue *(carry on)*
adherence accession *(annexation)*, adhesion *(affixing)*, adhesion *(loyalty)*, allegiance, coalescence, coherence, compliance, conformity *(obedience)*, continuation *(prolongation)*, loyalty
adherence to duty adhesion *(loyalty)*, allegiance
adherences ties
adherency loyalty
adherent addict, advocate *(espouser)*, backer, coadunate, coherent *(joined)*, cohesive *(sticking)*, consociate, disciple, partisan, protégé
adhering coadunate, coherent *(joined)*, cohesive *(sticking)*, inextricable
adhering to a purpose pertinacious
adhering to an original faithful *(true to fact)*
adhesion accession *(annexation)*, coalescence, coherence, contact *(touching)*
adhesions ties
adhesive coadunate, coherent *(joined)*, cohesive *(sticking)*
adhesiveness adhesion *(affixing)*, coherence, tenacity
adhibition use
adhortari exhort
adiacere adjoin, border *(bound)*
adiectio addition
adiectus additional
adipisci acquire *(receive)*, obtain
adit access *(right of way)*, entrance, entry *(entrance)*
aditus access *(right of way)*, entrance
adiudicare adjudge, award
adiumentum assistance, support *(assistance)*
adiungere append, appendix *(accession)*
adiutor assistant, promoter
adiutores staff
adiutrix assistant
adiuvare abet, contribute *(assist)*, cooperate, subsidize
adjacency conjunction, contact *(touching)*, propinquity *(proximity)*
adjacent close *(near)*, contiguous, immediate *(not distant)*, local, present *(attendant)*, proximate
adjective procedural
adjective law procedure
adjoin abut, affix, attach *(join)*, border *(approach)*, border *(bound)*, contact *(touch)*, juxtapose, overlap
adjoining accession *(annexation)*, adjacent, close *(near)*, contiguous, immediate *(not distant)*, local, proximate
adjourn cease, conclude *(complete)*, defer *(put off)*, delay, discontinue *(break continuity)*, halt, hold up *(delay)*, postpone, procrastinate, recess
adjournal adjournment, cloture
adjourned arrested *(checked)*
adjournment cessation *(interlude)*, close *(conclusion)*, cloture, deferment,

discontinuance *(act of discontinuing)*, end *(termination)*, extension *(postponement)*, hiatus, pendency

adjournment of a cause continuance

adjournment of a proceeding continuance

adjudge adjudicate, ascertain, award, condemn *(punish)*, confer *(give)*, criticize *(evaluate)*, decide, decree, deem, determine, find *(determine)*, gauge, judge, opine, pronounce *(pass judgment)*, rule *(decide)*, sentence, try *(conduct a trial)*

adjudge innocent absolve, palliate *(excuse)*

adjudge the validity of a will probate

adjudge to be due award

adjudged juridical

adjudger judge, juror

adjudgment adjudication, arbitration, award, conviction *(finding of guilt)*, decree, determination, judgment *(formal court decree)*

adjudgment body jury

adjudicate adjudge, arbitrate *(adjudge)*, award, decide, decree, determine, find *(determine)*, hear *(give a legal hearing)*, judge, pronounce *(pass judgment)*, rule *(decide)*, try *(conduct a trial)*

adjudicate the validity of a will probate

adjudication award, cognovit, conclusion *(determination)*, conviction *(finding of guilt)*, decree, determination, direction *(order)*, holding *(ruling of a court)*, judgment *(formal court decree)*, opinion *(judicial decision)*, res judicata, ruling, sentence, verdict

adjudicator arbiter, arbitrator, judge, juror, referee, umpire

adjudicators jury

adjunct addendum, addition, additive, allonge, ancillary *(auxiliary)*, appendix *(supplement)*, appliance, appurtenance, appurtenant, associate, attachment *(thing affixed)*, backer, coactor, codicil, colleague, confederate, consociate, copartner *(coconspirator)*, corollary, pendent, rider, supplementary

adjunct in crime coconspirator

adjunction addition, attachment *(act of affixing)*

adjuration affirmance *(legal affirmation)*, asseveration, assurance, attestation, averment, avouchment, call *(appeal)*, charge *(statement to the jury)*, claim *(legal demand)*, entreaty, oath, petition, requirement

adjure attest, bear *(adduce)*, call *(appeal to)*, command, direct *(order)*, exhort, importune, motivate, order, petition, pray, press *(beseech)*, pressure, promise *(vow)*, request, swear, urge

adjurement affirmation, averment, avowal

adjust accommodate, adapt, alter, amend, apply *(put in practice)*, arrange *(methodize)*, attune, change, check *(restrain)*, compromise *(settle by mutual agreement)*, conform, coordinate, decide, defray, discharge *(pay a debt)*, discharge *(perform)*, emend, fix *(arrange)*, fix *(repair)*, inure *(accustom)*, liquidate *(determine liability)*, mediate, mitigate,

modify *(alter)*, naturalize *(acclimate)*, orchestrate, organize *(arrange)*, pay, reconcile, rectify, redress, refund, remedy, repair, settle, stipulate, transform

adjust differences agree *(comply)*, agree *(contract)*, arbitrate *(conciliate)*, dicker

adjust difficulties mediate

adjust oneself to countenance

adjustable flexible, malleable, pliable, resilient

adjusted accustomed *(familiarized)*, fit, harmonious, res judicata, resigned, tempered

adjustment accord, accordance *(compact)*, accordance *(understanding)*, amendment *(correction)*, arbitration, arrangement *(understanding)*, collection *(payment)*, collective bargaining, compatibility, compromise, conciliation, conformity *(agreement)*, correction *(change)*, disposition *(determination)*, disposition *(final arrangement)*, expiation, habituation, justification, mediation, mitigation, modification, order *(arrangement)*, reconciliation, regulation *(management)*, rehabilitation, repair, reparation *(indemnification)*, restitution, settlement, treatment

adjustment by agreement arrangement *(understanding)*

adjustment of differences peace

adjustment of difficulties mediation

adjutant abettor, acting, assistant, backer, coactor, coadjutant, colleague, confederate, consociate, conspirer, copartner *(coconspirator)*, partner

adjutant in crime coconspirator

adjutor partner

adjuvancy assistance

adjuvant ancillary *(auxiliary)*, assistant, backer, coactor, coadjutant, colleague, confederate, copartner *(business associate)*, copartner *(coconspirator)*, participant, partner, subservient, subsidiary

adjuvant in crime coconspirator

adlevare alleviate

adlicere lure

adligare affix, attach *(join)*, connect *(join together)*

admeasure distribute, divide *(distribute)*, dole, measure, mete

admeasurement estimate *(approximate cost)*, estimation *(calculation)*, measurement

administer allocate, allot, apportion, bestow, commit *(perpetrate)*, conduct, confer *(give)*, contribute *(supply)*, control *(regulate)*, direct *(supervise)*, disburse *(distribute)*, discharge *(perform)*, discipline *(control)*, dispense, disperse *(disseminate)*, distribute, divide *(distribute)*, dominate, drug, exercise *(discharge a function)*, govern, handle *(manage)*, manage, mete, moderate *(preside over)*, officiate, operate, overlook *(superintend)*, oversee, parcel, predominate *(command)*, prescribe, preside, provide *(supply)*, regulate *(manage)*, resort, rule *(govern)*, superintend, supply

administer a penalty inflict

administer a rebuke admonish *(warn)*, blame, censure

administer badly misgovern

administer correction condemn *(punish)*, discipline *(punish)*

administer improperly misgovern, mishandle *(mismanage)*, mismanage

administer inefficiently mismanage

administer poorly misgovern, mismanage

administer punishment inflict

administer to accommodate, assist, bequeath, care *(regard)*, concern *(care)*, serve *(assist)*

administrare conduct, direct *(supervise)*, manage, regulate *(adjust)*, superintend

administrate administer *(conduct)*, conduct, control *(regulate)*, direct *(supervise)*, govern, manage, operate, preside, render *(administer)*, superintend

administrating clerical

administratio administration, government *(administration)*, management *(supervision)*, regulation *(management)*

administration act *(enactment)*, action *(performance)*, agency *(commission)*, apportionment, authorities, bureau, bureaucracy, charge *(custody)*, control *(supervision)*, custody *(supervision)*, direction *(guidance)*, dispensation *(act of dispensing)*, disposition *(final arrangement)*, economy *(economic system)*, enforcement, generalship, government *(political administration)*, management *(directorate)*, management *(supervision)*, regime, regulation *(management)*, supervision, transaction

administration of economics economy *(economic system)*

administration of justice judicature, judiciary

administration of resources economy *(economic system)*

administrative clerical, executive, ministerial, political

administrative head administrator, official

administrative unit bureau

administrator caretaker *(one fulfilling the function of office)*, director, employer, executive, executor, functionary, liaison, official, procurator, superintendent, trustee

administrator of a will executor

administrator of justice judge

administrator of the decedent's estate executor

administrators hierarchy *(persons in authority)*, management *(directorate)*, management *(supervision)*

administratorship generalship

administratrix executor

adminster enforce, give *(grant)*

admirable high-minded, laudable, meritorious, professional *(stellar)*, scrupulous

admiratio surprise

admiration affection, estimation *(esteem)*, honor *(outward respect)*, interest *(concern)*, regard *(esteem)*, respect

admire regard *(hold in esteem)*

admired popular

admirer disciple

admiring favorable *(expressing approval)*

admiscere implicate

admissibility propriety *(appropriateness)*, qualification *(fitness)*

admissible allowable, allowed, appropriate, justifiable, licit, pardonable, passable, permissible, relevant, right *(suitable)*, suitable, unobjectionable

admission access *(right of way)*, acknowledgment *(avowal)*, admittance *(acceptance)*, admittance *(means of approach)*, adoption *(acceptance)*, charter *(sanction)*, concession *(compromise)*, confession, confirmation, consent, declaration, disclosure *(act of disclosing)*, disclosure *(something disclosed)*, entrance, entry *(entrance)*, ingress, installation, recognition

admission of fault confession

admission of foreigners immigration

admission of guilt confession

admission of postponement continuance

admission of the facts nollo contendere

admissive receptive, responsive

admit accede *(concede)*, acknowledge *(declare)*, acknowledge *(verify)*, adopt, authorize, avow, bare, bear *(adduce)*, betray *(disclose)*, certify *(approve)*, confess, disclose, grant *(concede)*, induct, initiate, instate, profess *(avow)*, receive *(permit to enter)*, recognize *(acknowledge)*, reveal, vouchsafe, yield *(submit)*

admit a right acknowledge *(verify)*

admit as satisfactory accept *(admit as sufficient)*

admit citizenship naturalize *(make a citizen)*

admit defeat quit *(discontinue)*, submit *(yield)*

admit frankly avow

admit guilt confess

admit the charge acknowledge *(verify)*

admit to citizenship enfranchise

admittance access *(right of way)*, acknowledgment *(acceptance)*, admission *(entry)*, ingress, introduction, receipt *(act of receiving)*

admitted allowed, prescriptive, sound, uncontested

admitted judgment cognovit

admitted maxim principle *(axiom)*

admitted testimony evidence

admittere admit *(give access)*

admitting concession *(compromise)*, receptive

admitting of decision determinable *(ascertainable)*

admitting of doubt debatable, disputable

admitting of no deviation exact

admix amalgamate, combine *(join together)*, commingle, desegregate

admixed composite, miscellaneous

admixture coalescence, integration *(amalgamation)*, melange, solution *(substance)*

admonere admonish *(advise)*, remind

admonish blame, castigate, caution, censure, charge *(instruct on the law)*, complain *(criticize)*, decry, disabuse, disapprove *(condemn)*, exhort, expostulate, fault, impeach, lash *(attack verbally)*, rebuke, remonstrate, reprehend, reprimand, reproach, threaten

admonish beforehand forewarn

admonishment admonition, caveat, deterrent, disapprobation, disparage-

ment, monition *(warning)*, notice *(warning)*, objurgation, remonstrance, reprimand

admonitio remonstrance, suggestion, warning

admonition caution *(warning)*, caveat, charge *(statement to the jury)*, criticism, deterrence, deterrent, diatribe, direction *(guidance)*, guidance, impeachment, monition *(warning)*, notice *(warning)*, objurgation, rebuff, recommendation, remonstrance, reprimand, warning

admonitive remonstrative

admonitor monitor

admonitory hortative, informatory, remonstrative

admovere apply *(put in practice)*

adnectere affix

adnotare note *(record)*

adnotatio note *(brief comment)*

adnuere assent

ado furor, noise, trouble, turmoil

adolescence nonage

adolescent child, jejune *(lacking maturity)*, juvenile, minor

adolescere develop

adopt accept *(embrace)*, acquire *(receive)*, agree *(comply)*, apply *(put in practice)*, appropriate, approve, assume *(seize)*, choose, copy, embrace *(accept)*, espouse, gain, impropriate, naturalize *(make a citizen)*, pass *(approve)*, prefer, receive *(permit to enter)*, resort, select

adopt a measure enact

adopt an opinion deem

adopt and pass off as one's own pirate *(reproduce without authorization)*

adopt as a citizen naturalize *(make a citizen)*

adopt as one's own plagiarize

adopt into a nation naturalize *(make a citizen)*

adoptare adopt

adopted assumed *(feigned)*, preferred *(favored)*, select

adoptio adoption *(affiliation)*

adoption acceptance, appropriation *(taking)*, approval, arrogation, consent, distress *(seizure)*, selection *(choice)*, use

adoptivus adoptive

adorable attractive

adoration affection, respect

adore regard *(hold in esteem)*

adoriri accost, assail, attack

adorn embellish, meliorate

adorned pretentious *(ostentatious)*

adornment motif

adquirere acquire *(secure)*

adrift astray, derelict *(abandoned)*, disconnected, insecure, lost *(disoriented)*, unsettled

adrogans impervious, presumptuous

adrogantia intolerance

adroit artful, capable, competent, deft, efficient, expert, practiced, proficient, resourceful, veteran

adroit practitioner professional

adroitness competence *(ability)*, efficiency, experience *(background)*, facility *(easiness)*, faculty *(ability)*, gift *(flair)*, prowess *(ability)*, science *(technique)*, skill

adsciscere enfranchise

adscititius circumstantial, nonessential, pendent, superfluous, supplemen-

tary

adscribere encompass *(include)*, enroll, include

adsecula parasite

adsensio assent

adsensus acquiescence, assent

adsentari assent

adsentire consent

adsequi attain

adseverare vouch

adsiduitas continuance, continuation *(prolongation)*, diligence *(care)*, industry *(activity)*

adsiduus continual *(perpetual)*, incessant, industrious, perpetual, sedulous, unremitting

adsignare allot, apportion, ascribe, attribute, impute

adsignatio allotment

adstrictorius astringent

adstrictus laconic

adstringere bind *(obligate)*

adsuefacere inure *(accustom)*

adsuetus accustomed *(customary)*

adsumere assume *(seize)*

adulate overestimate

adulation doxology, honor *(outward respect)*, mention *(tribute)*

adulescentia adolescence

adult ripe

adulterare adulterate

adulterate contaminate, corrupt, debase, denature, deteriorate, fake, falsify, harm, impair, infect, lessen, pollute, taint *(contaminate)*

adulterated inferior *(lower in quality)*, tainted *(contaminated)*

adulteration contaminate, defilement, detriment, dissolution *(disintegration)*

adultered bad *(inferior)*

adulterine artificial, bastard, illegitimate *(born out of wedlock)*

adulterium adultery

adulthood maturity

adultus adult

adumbrare delineate

adumbrate blind *(obscure)*, camouflage, hint, obfuscate, obnubilate, obscure, portend, portray, predict, presage, represent *(portray)*, shroud

adumbratio delineation, outline *(synopsis)*

adumbration hint, obscuration

adumbrative representative

advance abet, accession *(enlargement)*, accretion, accrue *(increase)*, adduce, advancement *(loan)*, aid *(help)*, aid, allege, ameliorate, appreciate *(increase)*, approach, argue, assert, augmentation, bid, boom *(increase)*, boom *(prosperity)*, capitalize *(provide capital)*, certify *(attest)*, cite *(state)*, compound, conduce, contend *(maintain)*, contribute *(assist)*, course, credit *(delayed payment)*, cultivate, declare, develop, development *(progression)*, elevate, evolve, expand, expedite, extend *(offer)*, facilitate, favor, finance, foster, further, gain, hasten, headway, heighten *(augment)*, help, honor, installment, inure *(benefit)*, invest *(fund)*, invitation, lend, loan, loan, lobby, meliorate, nurture, offer *(tender)*, onset *(assault)*, overture, plead *(allege in a legal action)*, pose *(propound)*, posit, postulate, precipitate *(hasten)*, precursory, preface, prefer, proceed *(go forward)*, proffer, profit, progress, progress, promotion *(advancement)*, propose, propound, prosecute *(carry forward)*, recommend, remit *(submit for consideration)*, resume, send, serve *(assist)*, signify *(inform)*, step, submit *(give)*, subsidize, succeed *(attain)*, tender, urge

advance against assail

advance beyond proper limits overstep

advance guard precursor

advance in rank promote *(advance)*

advance in successive gradation develop

advance in value enhance

advance in worth appreciation *(increased value)*

advance near to approximate

advance notice admonition, caveat

advance planning forethought, premeditation

advance stealthily infringe

advance toward perfection mature

advance upon assail, attack, impinge, trespass

advanced alleged, liberal *(broad minded)*, proficient, progressive *(advocating change)*, ripe, sophisticated

advanced in years elderly, old

advancement advocacy, application, augmentation, boom *(increase)*, boom *(prosperity)*, civilization, development *(progression)*, edification, elevation, favor *(sanction)*, growth *(evolution)*, growth *(increase)*, incursion, loan, longevity, preference *(priority)*, profit, progress, reform, step, suggestion

advancement of knowledge civilization

advancing cumulative *(increasing)*, forthcoming, future, progressive *(going forward)*

advantage behalf, benefit *(betterment)*, chance *(fortuity)*, dividend, edification, help, interest *(profit)*, inure *(benefit)*, leverage, patronage *(power to appoint jobs)*, precedence, preference *(priority)*, prerogative, priority, privilege, prize, profit, shelter *(tax benefit)*, utility *(usefulness)*, value, welfare, worth

advantage in land easement

advantage in votes cast plurality

advantageous ancillary *(auxiliary)*, beneficial, constructive *(creative)*, convenient, disposable, effective *(efficient)*, fit, functional, gainful, instrumental, lucrative, operative, opportune, practical, preferential, productive, profitable, propitious, purposeful, salubrious, salutary, suitable, valuable

advantageous position edge *(advantage)*

advantageousness expedience, feasibility, utility *(usefulness)*

advena alien, stranger

advent occasion

adventare approach

adventicius foreign, unessential

adventitious fortuitous, haphazard, unintentional, unwitting

adventitiously unknowingly

adventitiousness accident *(chance occurrence)*

adventure bet, enterprise *(undertaking)*, event, experience *(encounter)*, transaction, undertaking *(enterprise)*, venture

adventurer pioneer, speculator

adventures story *(narrative)*

adventurous aleatory *(perilous)*, imprudent, impulsive *(rash)*

adventus appearance *(emergence)*, immigration

adversarius adversary, foe, opponent, opposite

adversary contender, contestant, disputant, foe, litigant, opponent, party *(litigant)*, plaintiff, rival

adversative contradictory, contrary

adverse antipathetic *(oppositional)*, averse, competitive *(antagonistic)*, contradictory, contrary, deleterious, detrimental, disadvantageous, discordant, disinclined, hostile, inadvisable, inauspicious, inimical, malevolent, noxious, ominous, opposite, pernicious, regrettable, reluctant, renitent, repugnant *(incompatible)*, unfavorable, unpropitious

adverse argument objection

adverse charge objection

adverse circumstance disadvantage, plight

adverse circumstances adversity, predicament

adverse comment criticism, diatribe, disapprobation, disapproval, impugnation, objection, stricture

adverse criticism disparagement, exception *(objection)*, impugnation, stricture

adverse event misfortune

adverse fortune adversity, calamity, misfortune

adverse lot misfortune

adverse luck misfortune

adverse party adversary, contender, contestant, disputant, foe, litigant, opponent

adverse reason objection

adverse to contra, contra, deviant

adversely unwillingly

adversely affected aggrieved *(victimized)*

adverseness antipode, antithesis, conflict, contradiction, difference, ill will

adversity accident *(misfortune)*, burden, calamity, casualty, catastrophe, damage, debacle, detriment, disadvantage, disaster, hardship, injury, misfortune, pain, plight, predicament, stress *(strain)*, tragedy, trouble

adversus adverse *(opposite)*, antipode, contrary, unfavorable

advert allude, hear *(give attention to)*, hint, imply

advert to consider, indicate, mention, note *(notice)*, regard *(pay attention)*, specify

advertence diligence *(care)*, notice *(heed)*, observation, regard *(attention)*

advertency consideration *(contemplation)*, diligence *(care)*, notice *(heed)*, observation, regard *(attention)*

advertent prudent

advertise communicate, divulge, expose, herald, inform *(notify)*, notify, post, proclaim, proffer, promote *(organize)*, propagate *(spread)*, publish, spread

advertisement publication *(disclosure)*, publicity

advertising promotion *(encouragement)*, publicity

advice admonition, advocacy, charge *(statement to the jury)*, direction *(guidance)*, guidance, help, instruction *(direction)*, monition *(warning)*, recommendation, service *(assistance)*, suggestion, tip *(clue)*

advisability propriety *(appropriateness)*

advisable favorable *(advantageous)*, fit, profitable, sensible, suitable

advise advocate, alert, annunciate, apprise, charge *(instruct on the law)*, communicate, confer *(consult)*, contribute *(assist)*, converse, convey *(communicate)*, counsel, disabuse, disclose, exhort, forewarn, help, impart, incite, inform *(notify)*, instruct *(direct)*, motivate, notice *(give formal warning)*, notify, persuade, predict, presage, prognosticate, prompt, propose, reason *(persuade)*, recommend, relate *(tell)*, remind, remonstrate, report *(disclose)*, reveal, signify *(inform)*, urge

advise against admonish *(warn)*, caution, discourage, dissuade, expostulate, forewarn, remonstrate

advise beforehand forewarn

advise together deliberate

advise with consult *(ask advice of)*, deliberate

advised acquainted, deliberate, express, familiar *(informed)*, informed *(having information)*

advisedly knowingly

advisement advice, caveat, consideration *(contemplation)*, deliberation, disclosure *(act of disclosing)*, guidance

adviser advocate *(counselor)*, counsel, esquire, informant, informer *(a person who provides information)*, pedagogue, procurator

advisers management *(directorate)*

advising hortative, informatory, juridical

advisor accessory, accomplice, arbiter, counselor

advisory hortative, informative, informatory, juridical, precatory

advisory board council *(assembly)*

advisory body congress, panel *(discussion group)*

advisory group commission *(agency)*, committee

advisory limitation guideline

advocacy advice, aid *(help)*, assistance, behalf, direction *(guidance)*, favor *(sanction)*, guidance, persuasion, recommendation, representation *(acting for others)*

advocare call *(summon)*, summon

advocate abet, abettor, adhere *(maintain loyalty)*, admonish *(advise)*, advise, amicus curiae, apologist, approve, assistant, attorney, authorize, backer, barrister, benefactor, certify *(attest)*, claim *(maintain)*, coactor, colleague, conduit *(intermediary)*, corroborate, council *(consultant)*, counsel, counsel, counselor, countenance, defend, disciple, embrace *(accept)*, espouse, esquire, exhort, favor, foster, incite, indorse, instruct *(direct)*, jurist, lawyer, maintain *(sustain)*, partisan, pass *(approve)*, patron *(influential supporter)*, petition, plead *(argue a case)*, plenipotentiary, posit, prescribe, pressure, proctor, profess *(avow)*, promote *(advance)*, promote *(organize)*, promoter, proponent, propose, propound, recommend, side, special interest, spokesman, sponsor, subscribe *(promise)*, uphold, urge

advocated alleged

advocates bar *(body of lawyers)*, lobby

advocating change radical *(favoring drastic change)*

advocation labor *(work)*, recommendation

adynamic languid, nonsubstantial *(not sturdy)*, powerless

adynamy incapacity

aedes house

aedificatio building *(business of assembling)*

aedificium building *(structure)*, premises *(buildings)*

aeger patient

aegis auspices, custody *(supervision)*, favor *(sanction)*, protection, safekeeping, shield

aegrotus patient

aemulus contestant, rival

aenigma enigma

aeonian constant, durable

aequabilis impartial, uniform

aequalis coequal, equal, par *(equality)*

aequalitas temporum synchronism

aeque fairly *(impartially)*

aequiperare compare

aequitas equity *(justice)*, fairness, justice, objectivity

aequo animo nonchalant

aequum equity *(justice)*

aequus admissible, equal, equitable, fair *(just)*, impartial, just, par *(equality)*, reasonable *(fair)*

aequus animus composure

aerarium finance, treasury

aerial intangible

aes money

aes alienum debt

aes alienum contrahere overdraw

Aesculapian medicinal

aesthetic elegant, sensitive *(discerning)*

aesthetic judgment discretion *(quality of being discreet)*

aestimare appreciate *(value)*, assess *(appraise)*, estimate, rate

aestimatio assessment *(estimation)*, estimate *(approximate cost)*, value, worth

aetas age, lifetime

aetate provectus elderly

aevum lifetime

affability comity, courtesy, informality

affable amicable, benevolent, civil *(polite)*, obeisant

affair event, happening, incident, occasion, occurrence, subject *(topic)*, transaction, undertaking *(enterprise)*

affairs case *(set of circumstances)*, dealings

affect appertain, apply *(pertain)*, concern *(involve)*, dispose *(incline)*, emotion, fake, feign, interest, militate, modify *(alter)*, motivate, prejudice *(influence)*, pretend, prevail upon, profess

(pretend), relate *(establish a connection)*

affect detrimentally prejudice *(injure)*

affect dishonorably disgrace

affect entirely pervade

affect injuriously impair

affectation bombast, color *(deceptive appearance)*, false pretense, fustian, histrionics, pretense *(ostentation)*, pretext, pride, rhetoric *(insincere language)*

affected bogus, formal, grandiose, histrionic, inclined, interested, orgulous, orotund, pretentious *(pompous)*, proud *(conceited)*, specious, tartuffish

affected manner pride

affectedness false pretense, histrionics, pretense *(ostentation)*, pride

affecter pedant

affectibility sensibility

affectible receptive

affecting moving *(evoking emotion)*, potent, sapid

affecting a previous act ex post facto

affecting the nation as a whole national

affecting the past retroactive

affection affinity *(regard)*, benevolence *(disposition to do good)*, predilection, predisposition, regard *(esteem)*

affiance confidence *(faith)*, reliance

affiant declarant, deponent

affidavit certificate, confirmation, record, statement, testimony

affiliate adopt, ascribe, chapter *(branch)*, connect *(relate)*, consolidate *(unite)*, corporate *(associate)*, corporation, correlate, correlative, embrace *(accept)*, federalize *(associate)*, federate, incorporate *(form a corporation)*, join *(associate oneself with)*, member *(individual in a group)*, organ, organize *(unionize)*, relate *(establish a connection)*, unite

affiliate with combine *(act in concert)*, participate, pool

affiliated akin *(germane)*, akin *(related by blood)*, allied, apposite, associated, cognate, collateral *(accompanying)*, conjoint, consanguineous, correlative, incident, interested, interrelated, related

affiliates constituency

affiliation affinity *(family ties)*, ancestry, association *(alliance)*, bloodline, cartel, chain *(nexus)*, coalescence, coalition, combination, compatibility, confederacy *(compact)*, connection *(relation)*, consolidation, consortium *(marriage companionship)*, contact *(association)*, corporation, degree *(kinship)*, federation, filiation, integration *(amalgamation)*, kinship, league, merger, nexus, organization *(association)*, privity, propinquity *(kinship)*, relation *(connection)*, side, union *(labor organization)*

affined cognate, correlative, related

affinitive allied, apposite, correlative, germane, interrelated, pendent, pertinent, related, relative *(relevant)*, relevant

affinity analogy, blood, chain *(nexus)*, conformity *(agreement)*, consortium

(marriage companionship), inclination, instinct, kinship, partiality, penchant, predilection, propensity, propinquity *(kinship)*, propinquity *(similarity)*, rapport, relation *(connection)*, relationship *(family tie)*, relevance, resemblance

affinity of nature propinquity *(similarity)*

affirm accept *(assent)*, accredit, acknowledge *(declare)*, admit *(concede)*, allege, annunciate, approve, argue, assert, assure *(insure)*, attest, authorize, avouch *(avow)*, avow, bear *(adduce)*, certify *(attest)*, claim *(maintain)*, concede, concur *(agree)*, consent, contend *(maintain)*, convey *(communicate)*, corroborate, countenance, declare, depose *(testify)*, enunciate, express, indorse, mention, notarize, pass *(approve)*, plead *(allege in a legal action)*, posit, profess *(avow)*, promise *(vow)*, reassure, remark, reveal, substantiate, support *(corroborate)*, sustain *(confirm)*, swear, testify, uphold, validate, verify *(swear)*, vouch, witness *(attest to)*

affirm explicitly certify *(attest)*, plead *(allege in a legal action)*

affirm in an official capacity certify *(attest)*

affirm positively promise *(vow)*

affirm the contrary bear false witness, contradict, disown *(deny the validity)*

affirm under oath depose *(testify)*, testify

affirm with confidence avouch *(avow)*

affirmance affirmation, approval, assent, asseveration, averment, avouchment, avowal, certification *(certification of proficiency)*, confirmation, consensus, consent, indorsement, sanction *(permission)*, surety *(certainty)*

affirmant declarant

affirmation acknowledgment *(avowal)*, adjuration, approval, assent, assertion, asseveration, assurance, attestation, attribution, averment, avouchment, avowal, certification *(attested copy)*, claim *(assertion)*, confirmation, consensus, consent, corroboration, declaration, declaratory judgment, disclosure *(something disclosed)*, jurat, legalization, oath, parole, permit, profession *(declaration)*, promise, pronouncement, reference *(recommendation)*, sanction *(permission)*, statement, subscription, support *(corroboration)*, surety *(certainty)*, testimony, thesis, vow

affirmation of truth oath

affirmation of truth of a statement oath

affirmation under oath affidavit

affirmations premises *(hypotheses)*

affirmatory affirmative

affirmed agreed *(promised)*, alleged, alleged

affirmer affirmant

affix addendum, allonge, annex *(add)*, append, attach *(join)*, cement, cohere *(adhere)*, combine *(join together)*, levy, rider

affix a date to date

affix a legal signature notarize

affix a signature sign

affix an earlier date antedate

affix an impost assess *(tax)*

affix one's name sign

affix one's signature subscribe *(sign)*

affix one's signature to notarize, sign

affixation accession *(annexation),* attachment *(act of affixing),* codicil

affixed attached *(annexed),* conjoint

affixed property immovable

affixed to realty fixture

affixture attachment *(thing affixed),* codicil

afflicting pernicious

afflict affront, badger, bait *(harass),* beat *(strike),* discommode, discompose, distress, harass, harm, ill use, mistreat, persecute, plague, strike *(assault)*

afflicted aggrieved *(harmed),* deplorable, disconsolate

afflicting detrimental, harmful, peccant *(unhealthy)*

affliction accident *(misfortune),* adversity, burden, calamity, casualty, catastrophe, damage, detriment, disability *(physical inability),* disaster, disease, disorder *(abnormal condition),* grievance, handicap, hardship, misfortune, nuisance, onus *(burden),* pain, stress *(strain),* tragedy, trouble

afflictive adverse *(negative),* bitter *(penetrating),* oppressive, painful, severe

affluence boom *(prosperity),* money, prosperity, sufficiency, welfare

affluent full, opulent, profuse, prosperous, replete, successful

afford administer *(tender),* allow *(endure),* bear *(yield),* bequeath, bestow, contribute *(supply),* fund, furnish, give *(grant),* lend, provide *(supply),* supply, yield *(produce a return)*

afford advantages favor

afford aid abet, assist, capitalize *(provide capital),* contribute *(assist),* serve *(assist),* subsidize

afford notice serve *(deliver a legal instrument)*

afford proof of bear *(adduce)*

afford sanctuary harbor, lodge *(house)*

afford support capitalize *(provide capital),* subsidize

affording no undue advantage fair *(just),* just

affording proof demonstrative *(illustrative)*

affranchise enfranchise, free, let *(permit)*

affranchisement freedom, liberation, liberty, privilege, suffrage

affray altercation, belligerency, collision *(dispute),* commotion, conflict, confrontation *(altercation),* disaccord, disturbance, embroilment, fight *(battle),* fracas, fray, outbreak, outburst, pandemonium, riot, struggle

affreightment carriage

affright consternation, discourage, fear, fright, frighten, intimidate, menace, panic, trepidation

affront accost, annoy, aspersion, bait *(harass),* challenge, contumely, defiance, defy, discommode, disoblige, disparage, disregard *(lack of respect),* disrespect, flout, humiliate, irritate, offend

(insult), pique, provocation, provoke, rebuff, resentment, revilement

affront hostilely assault

affronting outrageous

afield astray

afloat unsettled

aforecited aforesaid

aforedescribed aforesaid

aforegiven aforesaid

aforegoing aforesaid, last *(preceding),* said

aforehand before mentioned

aforementioned aforesaid, last *(preceding),* preliminary, previous, stated

aforenamed aforesaid, before mentioned, said

aforesaid before mentioned, last *(preceding),* previous, said, stated

aforestated aforesaid, before mentioned

aforethought express, premeditated, premeditation

afraid caitiff, leery, recreant

afresh anew, de novo

after ensuing, ex post facto, successive, thereafter

after death posthumous

after the act is committed ex post facto

after the fact ex post facto

after the same pattern boiler plate

after time dilatory, late *(tardy)*

after-comer heir

after-generations heir

aftereffect consequence *(conclusion),* outcome, outgrowth

aftergrowth consequence *(conclusion),* development *(outgrowth)*

aftermath consequence *(conclusion),* development *(outgrowth),* effect, outcome, outgrowth, result

aftermost last *(final)*

afterthought hindsight, recollection, retrospect

afterward ex post facto

afterwards hereafter *(henceforth),* thereafter

agacerie catalyst

again anew, de novo

against contiguous, contra, contra, disinclined

against fair trade antitrust act

against free commerce antitrust act

against free mercantilism antitrust act

against free trade antitrust act

against one's will compulsory, involuntary

against open business antitrust act

against open markets antitrust act

against reason ill-judged

against the admonition of law felonious

against the law felonious, illegal, illegitimate *(illegal),* illicit, impermissible, lawless, unlawful, wrongful

against the rules deviant, felonious, irregular *(improper)*

agape open *(unclosed),* penetrable, speechless

age annum, cycle, duration, lifetime, longevity, mature, period, phase *(period),* term *(duration),* time

age of discretion majority *(adulthood)*

age of majority majority *(adulthood)*

age of responsibility majority *(adulthood)*

aged elderly

ageless durable, immutable, permanent

agellus plot *(land)*

agency bureau, bureaucracy, committee, conduit *(channel),* delegation *(assignment),* department, expedient, facility *(institution),* facility *(instrumentality),* forum *(medium),* instrument *(tool),* medium, organ, proxy, representation *(acting for others)*

agency of the state government *(political administration)*

agenda calendar *(list of cases),* calendar *(record of yearly periods),* docket, outline *(synopsis),* plan, program, register, schedule

agent assistant, broker, cause *(reason),* conduit *(intermediary),* dealer, deputy, detective, determinant, employee, factor *(commission merchant),* factor *(ingredient),* fiduciary, forum *(medium),* go-between, instrument *(tool),* interagent, intermediary, liaison, medium, plenipotentiary, proctor, procurator, protagonist, proxy, representative *(proxy),* spokesman, spy, substitute, superintendent, tool, trustee

agent provocateur catalyst

agent provocateur conspirer

agential ministerial, representative

agents deputation *(delegation)*

agentship delegation *(assignment),* representation *(acting for others)*

ager district, estate *(property),* territory

agger causeway

agglomerate accumulate *(amass),* agglomeration, aggregate, aggregate, cement, coadunate, cohere *(adhere),* compile, composite, concentrate *(consolidate),* conglomerate, corporation, cumulation, desegregate, hoard, unite

agglomeration adhesion *(affixing),* arsenal, assemblage, coalescence, collection *(accumulation),* compilation, conglomeration, cumulation

agglutinate adhere *(fasten),* affix, attach *(join),* cement, cohere *(adhere),* coherent *(joined),* cohesive *(sticking),* combine *(join together)*

agglutinated attached *(annexed)*

agglutination adhesion *(affixing),* agglomeration, coalescence

agglutinative coherent *(joined),* cohesive *(sticking)*

aggrandize accrue *(increase),* accumulate *(enlarge),* bear *(yield),* build *(augment),* compound, elevate, empower, enhance, enlarge, expand, extend *(enlarge),* honor, increase, inflate, magnify, overestimate, promote *(advance),* raise *(advance)*

aggrandized extreme *(exaggerated),* inflated *(overestimated)*

aggrandizement accession *(enlargement),* advancement *(improvement),* augmentation, boom *(prosperity),* elevation, eminence, exaggeration, extension *(expansion),* growth *(increase),* honor *(outward respect),* hyperbole, inflation *(increase),* overstatement, remembrance *(commemoration)*

aggravate alienate *(estrange),* annoy,

badger, bait *(harass)*, compound, deteriorate, discommode, discompose, distress, exacerbate, expand, harm, heighten *(augment)*, incense, intensify, irritate, plague, press *(goad)*, provoke

aggravated gross *(flagrant)*

aggravating provocative, vexatious

aggravation complication, damage, detriment, harm, molestation, nuisance, pain

aggravative cumulative *(intensifying)*

aggregate accumulate *(amass)*, agglomeration, amount *(quantity)*, coadunate, collect *(gather)*, collection *(accumulation)*, collective, combination, compile, complex *(development)*, composite, compound, comprise, concentrate *(consolidate)*, conglomerate, conglomeration, congregate, congregation, corpus, cumulation, entirety, garner, glean, gross *(total)*, hoard, in solido, join *(bring together)*, mass *(body of persons)*, multiple, quantity, total, totality, whole *(undamaged)*, whole

aggregate amount sum *(total)*

aggregated coadunate, collective, composite, compound, miscellaneous

aggregation adhesion *(affixing)*, affiliation *(amalgamation)*, agglomeration, aggregate, assemblage, assembly, body *(collection)*, centralization, chamber *(body)*, collection *(accumulation)*, collection *(assembly)*, combination, company *(assemblage)*, compilation, complex *(development)*, conglomeration, congregation, consolidation, corpus, cumulation, hoard, incorporation *(blend)*, organization *(association)*, selection *(collection)*, totality

aggress antagonize, assail, assault, attack, impinge, infringe, invade, oppugn, strike *(assault)*

aggression assault, belligerency, foray, incursion, infringement, intrusion, invasion, offense, onset *(assault)*, outbreak, provocation

aggressive contentious, disorderly, forcible, hostile, hot-blooded, industrious, litigious, malevolent, obtrusive, offensive *(taking the initiative)*, pugnacious, spartan

aggressive action assault

aggressive argument dispute

aggressiveness belligerency, main force

aggressor assailant, offender

aggrieve affront, aggravate *(annoy)*, badger, bait *(harass)*, distress, harrow, harry *(harass)*, mistreat, persecute, plague

aggrieved despondent

aggrieved party actor, appellant, complainant

aggroup aggregate, congregate, convene, hoard, join *(bring together)*

aghast speechless

agile deft

agilis movable

agio brokerage

agitare discuss

agitari oscillate

agitate bait *(harass)*, bicker, debate, discommode, discompose, disconcert, dislocate, disorganize, disrupt, distress, disturb, foment, harass, harrow, impel, incense, incite, inflict, irritate, militate,

obsess, oscillate, perturb, pique, provoke, upset

agitate against counter, counteract, countervail

agitated disordered, disorderly, unsettled, vehement

agitating moving *(evoking emotion)*

agitatio commotion

agitation affray, aggravation *(exacerbation)*, apprehension *(fear)*, commotion, consternation, distress *(anguish)*, disturbance, embroilment, emotion, entanglement *(confusion)*, fright, furor, instigation, outbreak, outburst, pandemonium, panic, passion, provocation, revolt, strife, struggle, trepidation, turmoil

agitational offensive *(taking the initiative)*

agitative incendiary

agitator catalyst, demagogue, hoodlum, insurgent, malcontent

agitators lobby

agnate associated, cognate, consanguineous, correlate, correlative, interrelated, related

agnation affiliation *(bloodline)*, blood, propinquity *(kinship)*

agnoscere recognize *(perceive)*

agnostic skeptical

agonize bait *(harass)*, brood, distress, harass, inflict, persecute, press *(goad)*, suffer *(sustain loss)*

agonizing cruel, insufferable, painful, severe

agony distress *(anguish)*, pain, plaint, stress *(strain)*

agora market *(business)*, market place

agree abide, accommodate, acknowledge *(respond)*, admit *(concede)*, allow *(endure)*, assent, bond *(secure a debt)*, certify *(approve)*, cohere *(be logically consistent)*, coincide *(concur)*, compromise *(settle by mutual agreement)*, concede, conform, consent, conspire, contract, correspond *(be equivalent)*, decide, defer *(yield in judgment)*, fix *(settle)*, grant *(concede)*, obey, promise *(vow)*, settle, stipulate, subscribe *(promise)*, undertake, unite

agree beforehand predetermine

agree in principle concede

agree to accede *(concede)*, accept *(admit as sufficient)*, accept *(assent)*, approve, authorize, certify *(approve)*, confirm, countenance, embrace *(accept)*, pass *(approve)*, permit, sanction, sign, surrender *(yield)*, yield *(submit)*

agree to beforehand prearrange

agree to indemnify for loss assure *(insure)*

agree to support underwrite

agree upon settle

agree with comply, confirm, uphold

agreeability compliance

agreeable amenable, attractive, benevolent, concordant, congruous, consensual, consenting, convenient, favorable *(expressing approval)*, harmonious, inclined, malleable, nonmilitant, palatable, patient, peaceable, pliant, prone, ready *(willing)*, resigned, sapid, savory, willing *(not averse)*

agreeable manner amenity

agreeable to pursuant to

agreeable to reason rational

agreeable way amenity

agreeableness amenability, amenity, benevolence *(disposition to do good)*, comity, propriety *(appropriateness)*

agreed concerted, congruous, conjoint, contractual, res judicata

agreed to contractual

agreed upon consensual

agreeing coequal, coextensive, commensurate, concerted, concordant, concurrent *(united)*, consenting, consistent, consonant, correlative, felicitous, harmonious, proportionate, similar

agreeing to pursuant to

agreement acceptance, accommodation *(adjustment)*, accord, accordance *(compact)*, accordance *(understanding)*, acknowledgment *(acceptance)*, acquiescence, adjustment, analogy, approval, arrangement *(understanding)*, assent, attornment, bargain, cartel, coherence, collusion, commitment *(responsibility)*, compact, compatibility, compliance, composition *(agreement in bankruptcy)*, compromise, concert, concession *(compromise)*, conciliation, concordance, conformity *(agreement)*, conjunction, consensus, consent, contract, correspondence *(similarity)*, covenant, deal, identity *(similarity)*, indenture, indorsement, integration *(assimilation)*, league, lease, leave *(permission)*, mutual understanding, obligation *(duty)*, option *(contractual provision)*, pact, peace, pledge *(binding promise)*, policy *(contract)*, promise, quid pro quo, rapport, rapprochement, reconciliation, resemblance, sanction *(permission)*, settlement, specialty *(contract)*, stipulation, subscription, synchronism, term *(provision)*, testament, treaty, undertaking *(commitment)*, undertaking *(pledge)*, union *(unity)*, warrant *(guaranty)*

agreement as to time and place of meeting appointment *(meeting)*

agreement before marriage antenuptial agreement

agreement between nations treaty

agreement between parties compact

agreement for fraud collusion

agreement to accomplish an unlawful end conspiracy

agreement to commit a crime conspiracy

agreement to pay insurance

agreement to work indenture

agressive eager

agrestis uncouth

agrorum possessor landlord, landowner

ahead of time premature

aid abet, accommodate, accomplice, advantage, advocacy, assist, assistance, associate, avail *(be of use)*, bear *(support)*, behalf, benefactor, benefit *(conferment)*, bolster, capitalize *(provide capital)*, charity, coactor, coadjutant, conduce, confederate, conspire, conspirer, contribute *(assist)*, contribution *(participation)*, copartner *(coconspirator)*, countenance, enable, endow, endowment, espouse, expedite, facilitate, factor *(ingredient)*, favor

(sanction), favor, finance, foment, foster, harbor, help, help, instrument *(tool)*, inure *(benefit)*, largess *(generosity)*, lend, loan, maintain *(sustain)*, maintenance *(support of spouse)*, nurture, participant, participate, partner, patronage *(support)*, promotion *(encouragement)*, redress, reinforcement, relieve *(give aid)*, remedy *(legal means of redress)*, remedy *(that which corrects)*, remedy, rescue, samaritan, serve *(assist)*, service *(assistance)*, shelter *(protection)*, side, subsidize, support *(assistance)*, support *(assist)*, uphold
aid a judge clerk
aid in organizing promote *(organize)*
aid with a subsidy capitalize *(provide capital)*
aidance aid *(help)*, behalf
aidant salutary
aide abettor, assistant, coadjutant, consociate, contributor *(contributor)*, good samaritan
aide in crime coconspirator
aide in wrongdoing coconspirator
aide-de-camp assistant
aide-de-camp associate, coactor, copartner *(coconspirator)*
aide-memoir memorandum
aider abettor, accessory, accomplice, assistant, backer, benefactor, coactor, coadjutant, confederate, conspirer, donor, good samaritan, partner, promoter, samaritan
aider and abettor accomplice, coactor, cohort, colleague, conspirer, copartner *(coconspirator)*
aider in wrongdoing coconspirator
aides staff
aidful ancillary *(auxiliary)*, beneficial, subservient
aiding ancillary *(auxiliary)*, beneficial, concurrent *(united)*, contributory, donative, instrumental, practical, profitable, subservient, subsidiary
aiding and abetting concerted
aidless helpless *(defenseless)*
ail languish, suffer *(sustain loss)*
ailment disability *(physical inability)*, disease, disorder *(abnormal condition)*, pain, trouble
aim cause *(reason)*, contemplation, content *(meaning)*, desideratum, design *(intent)*, destination, direction *(course)*, end *(intent)*, endeavor, endeavor, forethought, goal, idea, intend, intent, intention, mission, motive, object, objective, plan, point *(purpose)*, predetermination, project, purpose, pursue *(strive to gain)*, pursuit *(goal)*, reason *(basis)*, signification, strive, target, try *(attempt)*
aim at attempt
aimed deliberate, direct *(straight)*, tactical
aiming for effect flagrant, histrionic
aiming to destroy deadly
aiming to kill deadly
aimless casual, discursive *(digressive)*, disjointed, random, unwitting
air appearance *(look)*, atmosphere, bare, behavior, betray *(disclose)*, conduct, deportment, disabuse, disclose, discuss, divulge, expose, express, flaunt, herald, issue *(publish)*, manifest, manner *(behavior)*, posture *(atti-*

tude), presence *(poise)*, proclaim, produce *(offer to view)*, promulgate, propagate *(spread)*, publish, relate *(tell)*, report *(disclose)*, semblance, signify *(inform)*, speak, utter
aired public *(known)*
airfreight carriage
airing publicity
airs disdain, histrionics, pretense *(ostentation)*, pride
airspace atmosphere
airtight impervious
airy insubstantial, intangible, subtle *(refined)*, tenuous
airy spirit phantom
ajar open *(unclosed)*, penetrable
akin allied, analogous, associated, cognate, comparable *(capable of comparison)*, congruous, consanguineous, correlative, interrelated, related, tangential
alacritas life *(vitality)*
alacritious expeditious
alacritous eager, ready *(willing)*
alacrity dispatch *(promptness)*, haste, industry *(activity)*
alarm admonition, agitate *(perturb)*, alert, apprehension *(fear)*, caution *(warning)*, consternation, disconcert, disturb, fear, forewarn, fright, frighten, harrow, intimidate, menace, monition *(warning)*, panic, perturb, phobia, stress *(strain)*, symptom, threat, trepidation, warning
alarming dangerous, formidable, imminent, ominous, portentous *(ominous)*, precarious, prophetic, sinister
albeit regardless
album register, roll
alcoholic addiction dipsomania
alcoholic beverage alcohol
alcoholism dipsomania, inebriation
alcove chamber *(compartment)*
alderman lawmaker
alderwoman lawmaker
alea risk, venture
alea ludere gamble
aleatory speculative
alere develop, foster
alert acute, admonish *(advise)*, advise, apprise, careful, caution *(warning)*, caveat, circumspect, cognizant, conscious *(awake)*, forewarn, guarded, meticulous, monition *(warning)*, notify, perspicacious, preventive, prompt, provident *(showing foresight)*, ready *(willing)*, receptive, responsive, sedulous, sensitive *(discerning)*, vigilant, warning
alert to danger forewarn
alertness comprehension, diligence *(care)*, life *(vitality)*, notice *(heed)*, precaution, regard *(attention)*, sensibility
alexipharmic medicinal
alias call *(title)*
alias dictus alias
alibi compurgation, excuse, pretext
alien antipathetic *(oppositional)*, apart, different, extraneous, extrinsic, foreign, impertinent *(irrelevant)*, inapplicable, inapposite, inappropriate, incongruous, irrelative, irrelevant, nonconforming, novel, obscure *(remote)*, peculiar *(curious)*, repugnant *(incompatible)*, stranger, unrelated, unusual
alienable heritable, negotiable
alienate antagonize, assign *(transfer*

ownership), cede, convey *(transfer)*, disaffect, disown *(refuse to acknowledge)*, estrange, repel *(disgust)*, separate
alienate by breach of condition forfeit
alienated antipathetic *(oppositional)*, hostile, inimical, irreconcilable
alienatio alienation *(estrangement)*, estrangement
alienation assignment *(transfer of ownership)*, conveyance, demise *(conveyance)*, disposition *(transfer of property)*, estrangement, feud, ill will, insanity, odium, separation, umbrage, variance *(disagreement)*
alienation of affection estrangement
alienation of mind insanity
alienation of property conveyance
alienigena alien
alienus averse, extraneous, incongruous, irrelevant, unsuitable
align conform, convert *(persuade)*, file *(arrange)*, fix *(arrange)*, join *(associate oneself with)*, juxtapose, organize *(arrange)*, persuade
align convergently border *(approach)*
aligned coextensive, concerted, concomitant, concordant
alignment affiliation *(connectedness)*, confederacy *(compact)*, league, persuasion, relationship *(connection)*, sodality
alike akin *(germane)*, analogous, approximate, cognate, comparable *(capable of comparison)*, consistent, consonant, equal, equivalent, identical, same, uniform
alikeness comparison, identity *(similarity)*, parity, propinquity *(similarity)*, resemblance
aliment sustenance
alimentation sustenance
alimentum sustenance
alimony maintenance *(support of spouse)*
alius different, diverse
alive alert *(agile)*, alert *(vigilant)*, conscious *(awake)*, extant, responsive, viable
alive to sensitive *(discerning)*
all complete *(all-embracing)*, entirety, sum *(total)*, total, whole *(undamaged)*, whole
all along through *(from beginning to end)*
all gone defunct
all in all in toto
all over throughout *(all over)*
all over with defunct
all right mediocre
all the more a fortiori
all the same notwithstanding, regardless
all the time always *(forever)*
all the way through *(from beginning to end)*
all the while always *(forever)*
all together en banc, en masse
all-comprehending complete *(all-embracing)*
all-comprehensive complete *(all-embracing)*, nonsectarian
all-covering complete *(all-embracing)*, comprehensive
all-destroying disastrous
all-embracing composite, comprehensive, inclusive, nonsectarian, omnibus,

prevailing (*current*), prevalent

all-encompassing unqualified (*unlimited*)

all-important necessary (*required*)

all-including nonsectarian

all-inclusive complete (*all-embracing*), comprehensive, detailed, gross (*total*), nonsectarian, omnibus, thorough

all-knowing expert, omniscient

all-out outright

all-pervading complete (*all-embracing*), comprehensive

all-powerful cardinal (*outstanding*), invincible, omnipotent, predominant

all-purpose practical

all-searching interrogative

all-seeing omniscient

all-sufficing complete (*all-embracing*)

all-wise omniscient

allay alleviate, ameliorate, assuage, commute, decrease, discount (*minimize*), lessen, lull, mitigate, moderate (*temper*), modify (*moderate*), mollify, obtund, palliate (*abate*), placate, redress, relax, relieve (*free from burden*), repress, soothe, subdue

allay fears disarm (*set at ease*)

allay mistrust disarm (*set at ease*)

allaying palliative (*abating*)

allayment mollification, remission, solace

allegation accusation, assertion, attestation, bad repute, charge (*accusation*), claim (*assertion*), color (*deceptive appearance*), complaint, contention (*argument*), count, indictment, information (*charge*), mention (*reference*), plea, pleading

allegation of criminal wrongdoing arraignment

allegation of facts bill (*formal declaration*), pleading

allege adduce, argue, avouch (*avow*), bear (*adduce*), certify (*attest*), cite (*accuse*), claim (*maintain*), comment, express, plead (*allege in a legal action*), posit, propound, purport, testify

allege as a fact avouch (*avow*), avow

allege in support advocate, assert, defend, justify

allege in vindication justify

allege to be guilty implicate

allege to belong ascribe

allege under oath swear

alleged colorable (*plausible*), purported, putative

alleged malfeasor suspect

alleged motive color (*deceptive appearance*)

alleged offender suspect

alleged purpose pretext

alleged reason cover (*pretext*), gist (*ground for a suit*), pretext

alleged transgressor suspect

alleged wrongdoer suspect

allegedly reputedly

allegiance adherence (*devotion*), adhesion (*loyalty*), charge (*responsibility*), commitment (*responsibility*), duty (*obligation*), faith, fealty, fidelity, homage, loyalty, nationality

allegiant loyal

allegorical demonstrative (*illustrative*)

alleviate abate (*lessen*), allay, as-

suage, commute, diminish, disencumber, ease, help, lessen, lull, mitigate, moderate (*temper*), mollify, obtund, pacify, palliate (*abate*), redress, relieve (*give aid*), remedy, remit (*relax*), soothe

alleviating mitigating, palliative (*abating*), remedial

alleviating circumstances extenuating circumstances

alleviation abatement (*reduction*), decrease, mitigation, moderation, mollification, relief (*release*), remedy (*legal means of redress*), remission, solace

alleviative corrigible, medicinal, narcotic, palliative (*abating*), remedial

alleviator narcotic

alley way (*channel*)

alliance adhesion (*loyalty*), affiliation (*amalgamation*), agreement (*contract*), band, cartel, centralization, chain (*nexus*), coaction, coalescence, coalition, cohabitation (*living together*), collusion, committee, concert, confederacy (*compact*), conformity (*agreement*), conjunction, connection (*relation*), connivance, consortium (*marriage companionship*), contact (*association*), contribution (*participation*), cooperative, corporation, federation, integration (*amalgamation*), integration (*assimilation*), league, marriage (*intimate relationship*), matrimony, merger, mutual understanding, nexus, organization (*association*), pact, partnership, peace, pool, propinquity (*kinship*), rapport, rapprochement, relation (*connection*), society, sodality, syndicate, treaty, understanding (*agreement*)

alliance of workers union (*labor organization*)

allied affiliated, akin (*germane*), analogous, apposite, associated, close (*intimate*), coadunate, cognate, coherent (*joined*), concomitant, concordant, concurrent (*united*), conjoint, consanguineous, corporate (*associate*), correlative, federal, germane, harmonious, incident, incidental, interrelated, intimate, joint, nuptial, related, relative (*relevant*), relevant, similar

allied to pendent

allness totality, whole

allocate allot, apportion, arrange (*methodize*), assign (*allot*), classify, delegate, demarcate, detail (*assign*), disburse (*distribute*), dispense, disperse (*disseminate*), distribute, divide (*distribute*), dole, expend (*disburse*), marshal, mete, parcel, partition, pigeonhole, prorate, regulate (*adjust*), relegate, sort, split, tabulate

allocated per capita

allocation allotment, appointment (*act of designating*), apportionment, appropriation (*allotment*), assignment (*allotment*), budget, circulation, classification, consignment, coupon, dispensation (*act of dispensing*), distribution (*apportionment*), division (*act of dividing*), order (*arrangement*), part (*portion*), quota, share (*interest*)

allocute converse

allocution declamation, discourse, parlance, rhetoric (*skilled speech*), speech

allot allocate, apportion, attorn, bear (*yield*), bestow, classify, commit (*entrust*), contribute (*supply*), delegate, delimit, demarcate, devise (*give*), devote, disburse (*distribute*), dispense, distribute, divide (*distribute*), dole, endow, endue, expend (*disburse*), fund, give (*grant*), leave (*give*), marshal, mete, parcel, partition, pigeonhole, present (*make a gift*), prorate, sort, split

allot again reapportion, redistribute

allot the parts orchestrate

alloted pro rata

alloting disbursement (*act of disbursing*)

allotment alimony, annuity, appointment (*act of designating*), apportionment, budget, circulation, classification, commission (*fee*), consignment, disbursement (*act of disbursing*), dispensation (*act of dispensing*), distribution (*apportionment*), dividend, division (*act of dividing*), dower, endowment, equity (*share of ownership*), grant, installment, loan, moiety, order (*arrangement*), payment (*remittance*), pension, proportion, quantity, quota, ration, share (*interest*), subsidy

allotment by chance lottery

allottee assignee, heir, transferee

allotter transferor

allow accept (*admit as sufficient*), accept (*assent*), accept (*recognize*), agree (*comply*), approve, assent, authorize, bear (*tolerate*), bequeath, bestow, certify (*approve*), concede, concur (*agree*), condone, consent, countenance, deign, dole, empower, enable, endow, endue, enfranchise, grant (*concede*), indorse, let (*permit*), loan, pass (*approve*), permit, provide (*supply*), qualify (*meet standards*), rebate, receive (*permit to enter*), recognize (*acknowledge*), sanction, suffer (*permit*), tolerate, vouchsafe, yield (*submit*)

allow a margin discount (*reduce*)

allow as a discount rebate

allow credit lend

allow entrance admit (*give access*), receive (*permit to enter*)

allow for compensate (*counterbalance*), compensate (*remunerate*), excuse, extenuate, palliate (*excuse*)

allow residency rent

allow the use of lease, let (*lease*), rent, sublease, sublet

allow with condescension deign

allowable admissible, allowed, deductible (*capable of being deducted from taxes*), due (*regular*), justifiable, lawful, legal, licit, open (*accessible*), pardonable, passable, permissible, potential, right (*suitable*), rightful, unobjectionable

allowableness admissibility, legality

allowance acceptance, acquiescence, advancement (*loan*), alimony, annuity, apportionment, appropriation (*allotment*), approval, assignment (*allotment*), budget, capacity (*authority*), cession, charter (*sanction*), commission (*fee*), concession (*authorization*), concession (*compromise*), condonation, consent, disbursement (*funds paid out*), discount, dispensation (*exception*), dower, endowment, excuse, exemption, franchise (*license*), gift (*present*), grant, indulgence, justification, leave (*permission*), license, maintenance (*support of spouse*), offset, option (*contractual provision*), part (*portion*), pay, payment (*remittance*), payroll, pension, permission, perquisite, privilege, quota, ration, rebate, sanction (*permission*), subsidy, sufferance, tolerance, wage

allowed admissible, choate lien, definite, entitled, lawful, legal, legitimate (*rightful*), licit, open (*accessible*), permissible, potential, privileged, rightful

allowedly admittedly

allowing consenting, lenient, permissive

allowing no departure from the standard exact

alloy commingle, incorporate (*include*), join (*bring together*), pollute, taint (*contaminate*)

alloyed composite, promiscuous

allude adduce, hint, purport, refer (*direct attention*)

allude to appertain, bear (*adduce*), connote, disclose, imply, indicate, mention

alluded to implied

allure amenity, bait (*lure*), cajole, coax, convince, decoy, ensnare, entice, entrap, incentive, inveigle, lure, motivate, seduction

allurement bribery, cause (*reason*), decoy, incentive, inducement, invitation, seduction

alluring attractive, provocative, sapid

allusion attribution, connotation, hint, implication (*inference*), indication, inference, innuendo, insinuation, intimation, mention (*reference*), referral, reminder, suggestion

allusive implicit, implied, indirect, suggestive (*evocative*), tacit

allusory allusive

alluvion cataclysm

ally affiliate, backer, bear (*support*), benefactor, coactor, coadjutant, cohort, colleague, combine (*act in concert*), confederate, confirm, conjoin, connect (*relate*), consociate, consolidate (*unite*), contributor (*contributor*), cooperate, correlate, disciple, espouse, federalize (*associate*), federate, involve (*implicate*), join (*associate oneself with*), merge, participant, partisan, partner, pool, proponent, relate (*establish a connection*), unite

ally in crime coconspirator

ally in wrongdoing coconspirator

almanac calendar (*record of yearly periods*), register

almightiness predominance

almighty omnipotent, predominant

almoner contributor (*giver*)

almost approximate, quasi

almost as quasi

almost certainly high probability

alms contribution (*donation*), donation, largess (*gift*)

almsgiver contributor (*giver*), donor

almsgiving charitable (*benevolent*), charity, largess (*generosity*), liberal (*generous*), philanthropic, philanthropy

alodium domain (*land owned*)

alone apart, insular, only, remote (*secluded*), separate, solely (*singly*)

along in years elderly

along the river banks fluvial

along the way en route

alongside adjacent

aloof cold-blooded, controlled (*restrained*), disdainful, dispassionate, insusceptible (*uncaring*), orgulous, phlegmatic, proud (*conceited*), solitary, unapproachable, unresponsive

aloofness disinterest (*lack of interest*), disregard (*lack of respect*), indifference, neutrality

alphabetize tabulate

already indicated previous, said

already mentioned aforesaid

already said aforesaid

also alias

also acknowledged as alias

also acknowledging the name of alias

also answering to alias

also called alias

also known as alias

also known by alias

also known under the name of alias

also recognized as alias

alter adapt, amend, change, commute, convert (*change use*), countervail, denature, edit, emend, falsify, fix (*repair*), fluctuate, qualify (*condition*), rectify, revise, tamper, transform, vary

alter course deviate, digress

alter ego counterpart (*complement*)

alter fraudulently falsify

alter one's course detour

alter the appearance of camouflage, disguise

alter the position move (*alter position*)

alter with intent to deceive fake

alterable aleatory (*uncertain*), conditional, indefinite, mutable, pliable, protean, provisional, variable, yielding

alterant drug

alteration conversion (*change*), correction (*change*), deviation, digression, diversification, innovation, modification, reform, rehabilitation, reorganization, repair, revision (*process of correcting*), transition, vicissitudes

alterative ambulatory, corrigible, remedial

altercari dispute (*contest*)

altercate bicker, brawl, collide (*clash*), contend (*dispute*), contest, debate, disaccord, dispute (*contest*), fight (*battle*), litigate, remonstrate

altercatio altercation, controversy (*argument*), dispute

altercation affray, argument (*contention*), belligerency, brawl, collision (*dispute*), commotion, conflict, contest (*dispute*), controversy (*argument*), disagreement, dispute, feud, fight (*argument*), fracas, strife, variance (*disagreement*)

altered different, tempered

altered for the worse dilapidated

alternare alternate (*take turns*)

alternate agent, alter ego, attorney in fact, beat (*pulsate*), cover (*substitute*), deputy, disjunctive (*alternative*), fluctuate, intermittent, oscillate, reciprocate, replace, replacement, stopgap, substitute, surrogate, vacillate, vary, vicarious (*substitutional*)

alternate choice alternative (*option*), option (*choice*)

alternate route detour

alternating reciprocal, shifting

alternating conditions vicissitudes

alternation cycle, interchange, sequence, vicissitudes

alternative call (*option*), cover (*substitute*), elective (*selective*), expedient, loophole, option (*choice*), plan, replacement, secondary, stopgap, substitute, vicarious (*substitutional*)

alterner alternate (*take turns*)

although notwithstanding, regardless

altiloquence fustian

altiloquent inflated (*bombastic*)

altior heighten (*elevate*)

altisonant inflated (*bombastic*)

altitude ceiling, elevation

altogether in toto, outright, radical (*extreme*), wholly

altruism benevolence (*disposition to do good*), charity, goodwill, humanity (*humaneness*), largess (*generosity*), philanthropy, understanding (*tolerance*)

altruist benefactor, contributor (*giver*), donor, good samaritan, samaritan

altruistic benevolent, charitable (*benevolent*), humane, liberal (*generous*), magnanimous, nonprofit, philanthropic

always invariably

amalgam melange, solution (*substance*)

amalgamate cement, collect (*gather*), combine (*join together*), commingle, connect (*join together*), consolidate (*unite*), cooperate, crystallize, desegregate, federalize (*associate*), federate, hoard, join (*bring together*), merge, organize (*unionize*), pool, unite

amalgamated collective, composite, compound, concerted, concurrent (*united*), conglomerate, conjoint, correlative, joint, miscellaneous, promiscuous

amalgamating concrescence

amalgamation association (*alliance*), building (*business of assembling*), cartel, centralization, coalescence, coalition, combination, consolidation, federation, incorporation (*blend*), merger, pool, relationship (*connection*), union (*labor organization*)

amalgamative coadunate, coherent (*joined*)

amaranthine durable, perpetual

amass accrue (*increase*), aggregate, collect (*gather*), compile, concentrate (*consolidate*), congregate, conjoin, consolidate (*strengthen*), consolidate (*unite*), convene, cull, fund, garner, glean, hoard, join (*bring together*), keep (*shelter*), meet, reserve, set aside (*annul*), store, unite

amassed collective, composite, conglomerate

amassing centralization

amassment agglomeration, assemblage, collection (*accumulation*), conglomeration, congregation, corpus, cumulation, hoard, store (*depository*)

amateur inexperienced, layman, neophyte, novice, volunteer

amateurish incompetent, unprofessional

amaze impress (*affect deeply*)

amazed speechless

amazement incredulity, phenomenon *(unusual occurrence)*, surprise

amazing extraordinary, ineffable, noteworthy, portentous *(eliciting amazement)*, remarkable, special, unaccustomed, unusual

amazing thing phenomenon *(unusual occurrence)*

ambages enigma, evasion

ambagious circuitous, devious, indirect, labyrinthine, sinuous

ambagitory labyrinthine, sinuous

ambassador deputy, plenipotentiary, spokesman

ambassadorial function embassy

ambassadorial office embassy

ambassadorial residence embassy

ambience atmosphere

ambigere dispute *(debate)*

ambiguitas ambiguity

ambiguity doubt *(indecision)*, incertitude

ambiguous aleatory *(uncertain)*, allusive, debatable, disputable, dubious, enigmatic, equivocal, inapprehensible, incomprehensible, indefinite, indeterminate, indistinct, inexact, inscrutable, nebulous, opaque, problematic, unclear, undecided, vague

ambiguous saying enigma

ambiguus ambiguous, equivocal, evasive, indefinite, undecided, vague

ambire canvass

ambit border, capacity *(sphere)*, circuit, contour *(outline)*, coverage *(scope)*, frontier, limit, outline *(boundary)*, periphery, purview, range, scope, sphere

ambition desideratum, design *(intent)*, desire, end *(intent)*, goal, intention, objective, plan, project, prospect *(outlook)*, purpose, pursuit *(goal)*, target

ambitious eager, solicitous

ambivalent ambiguous, equivocal, evasive, oblique *(evasive)*

amble perambulate

ambrosiac savory

ambrosial palatable, sapid, savory

ambrosian palatable, savory

ambulant itinerant, moving *(in motion)*

ambulative moving *(in motion)*

ambulator pedestrian

ambulatory itinerant, moving *(in motion)*

ambuscade cache *(hiding place)*, ensnare, lurk

ambush accost, decoy, ensnare, trap

ambushed hidden

ameliorable corrigible

ameliorate amend, commute, cure, ease, emend, fix *(repair)*, help, meliorate, mitigate, modify *(alter)*, mollify, progress, rectify, reform, rehabilitate, relieve *(give aid)*, remedy, renew *(refurbish)*, renovate, repair, restore *(renew)*, soothe, treat *(remedy)*

amelioration amendment *(correction)*, boom *(prosperity)*, correction *(change)*, development *(progression)*, improvement, mollification, progress, promotion *(advancement)*, reform, rehabilitation, relief *(release)*, remedy *(legal means of redress)*, renewal, reorganization, repair, solace

ameliorative mitigating

amenability decorum, liability, responsibility *(accountability)*

amenable actionable, corrigible, facile, inclined, liable, malleable, obedient, open *(persuasible)*, open-minded, palatable, passive, pliable, receptive, sequacious, suasible, tractable, willing *(not averse)*, yielding

amenable to law justiciable, permissible

amenable to measurement determinable *(ascertainable)*

amenable to reason reasonable *(rational)*

amenableness decorum, liability

amend adjust *(resolve)*, alter, convert *(change use)*, edit, emend, fix *(repair)*, meliorate, modify *(alter)*, reconsider, rectify, reform, rehabilitate, remedy, renew *(refurbish)*, renovate, repair, restore *(renew)*, revise, supplement

amend by removing expurgate

amendable ambulatory, corrigible

amendatory ambulatory, remedial

amending correction *(change)*

amendment correction *(change)*, reform, rider

amends collection *(payment)*, compensation, damages, expiation, indemnification, indemnity, recompense, reparation *(indemnification)*, restitution, retribution

amenities decorum

amenity comity, courtesy

amentia insanity

amerce fine, mulct *(fine)*, penalize, punish

amercement correction *(punishment)*, cost *(penalty)*, discipline *(punishment)*, fine, forfeiture *(thing forfeited)*, penalty, punishment

amercing disciplinary *(punitory)*

amiability benevolence *(disposition to do good)*, comity, courtesy, rapprochement

amiable amenable, amicable, benevolent, civil *(polite)*, malleable, obeisant, peaceable

amicability rapprochement

amicable benevolent, harmonious, nonmilitant, peaceable

amicableness benevolence *(disposition to do good)*

amicire clothe

amid among

amidst among

amiss astray, defective, disordered, errant, erroneous, faulty, improper, inaccurate, inappropriate, incorrect, unsuitable

amittere lose *(be deprived of)*

amity accordance *(understanding)*, agreement *(concurrence)*, comity, compatibility, concordance, goodwill, mutual understanding, peace, rapprochement, sodality

ammassment arsenal

ammount accrued cumulation

ammunition bomb

amnesty absolution, acquittal, clear, clemency, condonation, dispensation *(exception)*, exoneration, impunity, pardon, reconciliation, release, remission, remit *(release from penalty)*, respite *(reprieve)*

amoenitas amenity

amoral bad *(offensive)*, diabolic, immoral, peccant *(culpable)*

amoralism bad repute

amoralistic diabolic

amorality bad repute, laxity

amorous hot-blooded

amorousness affection

amorphic indefinite

amorphous indefinite, intangible, vague

amortization discharge *(payment)*, payment *(act of paying)*

amortize discharge *(pay a debt)*

amortizement discharge *(payment)*, payment *(act of paying)*, satisfaction *(discharge of debt)*

amotio removal

amotion removal

amount aggregate, bulk, caliber *(measurement)*, compound, degree *(magnitude)*, entirety, expenditure, expense *(cost)*, extent, measurement, par *(face amount)*, part *(portion)*, payment *(remittance)*, price, quantity, rate, value

amount accrued collection *(accumulation)*

amount assessed as payable assessment *(levy)*

amount computed computation

amount deducted discount

amount due bill *(invoice)*, debit, debt, obligation *(liability)*

amount expended outlay

amount for which anything is insured coverage *(insurance)*

amount of surface area *(surface)*

amount over par premium *(excess value)*

amount owing debt

amount paid periodically premium *(insurance payment)*

amount payable debit

amount produced output

amount reserved margin *(spare amount)*

amount to aggregate, comprise, consist, reach

amovere avert, remove *(transfer)*

amphibolic uncertain *(ambiguous)*

amphibological equivocal

amphibolous equivocal

amphigory parody

ample adequate, broad, capacious, considerable, copious, extensive, liberal *(generous)*, multiple, operative, profuse, replete, substantial

ample notice adequate notice

ample stock sufficiency

ampleness capacity *(maximum)*, maximum *(amplitude)*, quorum, sufficiency

ampliare adjourn, compound

ampliation development *(progression)*, discontinuance *(interruption of a legal action)*

amplificare compound, enhance, enlarge, heighten *(augment)*, increase, intensify, magnify

amplificatio augmentation, promotion *(encouragement)*

amplification accession *(enlargement)*, advance *(increase)*, advancement *(improvement)*, aggravation *(exacerbation)*, augmentation, boom *(increase)*, clarification, development *(progression)*, explanation, extension *(expansion)*, growth *(increase)*, hyperbole, inflation *(increase)*, overstatement

amplified extreme *(exaggerated)*, inflated *(enlarged)*, inflated *(overestimated)*

amplify accrue *(increase)*, accumulate *(enlarge)*, aggravate *(exacerbate)*, build *(augment)*, detail *(particularize)*, develop, elaborate, enhance, enlarge, expand, extend *(enlarge)*, heighten *(augment)*, increase, inflate, magnify, supplement

amplifying cumulative *(intensifying)*

amplissimus gradus eminence

amplitude boom *(increase)*, boom *(prosperity)*, caliber *(measurement)*, capacity *(maximum)*, degree *(magnitude)*, latitude, magnitude, mass *(weight)*, plethora, quantity, scope, sufficiency

amplitudinous broad

amplitudo bulk, magnitude

amplus broad, extensive, illustrious

amputate mutilate

amuse occupy *(engage)*

amusement enjoyment *(pleasure)*, treat

amusing jocular, ludicrous, sapid

an equal percentage per capita

anabasis development *(progression)*

anachronic untimely

anachronistic obsolete, outdated, outmoded, untimely

anachronize antedate

anachronous obsolete, outdated, outmoded, untimely

anacoluthon non sequitur

analagous coextensive, commensurable, commensurate, comparable *(capable of comparison)*

analagous to comparative

analagousness balance *(equality)*

analect abstract

analeptic curative, medicinal, remedial, salubrious, salutary

analgesic drug

analogical analogous, cognate, commensurable, comparable *(capable of comparison)*, congruous

analogical procedure collation, comparison

analogize compare

analogous akin *(germane)*, coequal, cognate, congruous, correlative, interrelated, proportionate, related, relative *(comparative)*, similar, tantamount

analogue correlate, counterpart *(complement)*

analogy collation, comparison, connection *(relation)*, correspondence *(similarity)*, parity, relation *(connection)*, relationship *(connection)*, resemblance

analysis capsule, choice *(decision)*, classification, criticism, deliberation, diagnosis, digest, discretion *(power of choice)*, discrimination *(differentiation)*, examination *(study)*, hornbook, indagation, judgment *(discernment)*, measurement, pandect *(treatise)*, probe, proposal *(report)*, prospectus, rating, ratiocination, reflection *(thought)*, research, review *(critical evaluation)*, scenario, scrutiny, summary, test, treatment, trial *(experiment)*

analytic deductive, discursive *(analytical)*, logical

analytical clinical, deductive, demonstrative *(illustrative)*, empirical, logical, rational

analyzation hornbook, inquiry *(systematic investigation)*

analyze canvass, classify, consider, construe *(comprehend)*, construe *(translate)*, deliberate, detail *(particularize)*, diagnose, digest *(comprehend)*, discuss, examine *(study)*, identify, investigate, peruse, ponder, rationalize, reason *(conclude)*, reflect *(ponder)*, research, review, scrutinize, study, survey *(examine)*, treat *(process)*

anamorphosis distortion

anarchic disorderly, lawless

anarchical disordered, disorderly, lawless

anarchism disorder *(lack of order)*, misrule

anarchist insurgent, malcontent

anarchistic contumacious, disorderly, incendiary

anarchy confusion *(turmoil)*, disorder *(lack of order)*, havoc, insurrection, lynch law, misrule, pandemonium, revolution

anathema denunciation, expletive, imprecation, malediction

anathematize blame, condemn *(blame)*, defame, denounce *(condemn)*, malign, proscribe *(denounce)*

anatomical organic

anatomize analyze, examine *(study)*, scrutinize

anatomy body *(person)*, configuration *(form)*, content *(structure)*

anceps critical *(crucial)*, dubious, equivocal, indeterminate

ancestor ascendant, derivation, forerunner, kindred, parents, precursor, predecessor, primogenitor, progenitor

ancestorial hereditary

ancestors lineage

ancestral consanguineous, hereditary, paternal, traditional

ancestral descent origin *(ancestry)*

ancestral relation kindred, primogenitor

ancestral relative primogenitor

ancestry affiliation *(bloodline)*, affinity *(family ties)*, birth *(lineage)*, birthright, blood, bloodline, derivation, descent *(lineage)*, family *(common ancestry)*, heritage, lineage, origination, parentage, paternity, race, source

anchor adhere *(fasten)*, mainstay, security *(safety)*

anchorage haven

anchored firm, fixed *(securely placed)*, situated, stable, steadfast

anchoretic solitary

anchoretical solitary

ancient antique, hereditary, obsolete, old, outdated, outmoded

ancillary appurtenant, collateral *(accompanying)*, dependent, pendent, secondary, slight, subordinate, subservient, supplementary

and all et al.

and everyone et al.

and more of the same et al.

and other parties et al.

and other things et al.

and others et al.

and the rest et al.

anecdotal narrative

anemic languid

anent correlative

anesthetic drug, narcotic, narcotic

anesthetic agent drug

anesthetize drug, obtund

anew de novo

anfractuous circuitous, sinuous, tortuous *(bending)*

angel spirit

angelic clean

anger bait *(harass)*, harass, incense, irritate, molest *(annoy)*, offend *(insult)*, passion, pique, provoke, resentment, umbrage

angering provocation

angle outlook, phase *(aspect)*, side, slant, standpoint

angle of vision perspective

angle off deviate

angled oblique *(slanted)*

angry resentful, vehement, vindictive

angry disagreement dissension

angry dispute altercation

anguilliform circuitous

anguine circuitous

anguish pain, plaint, remorse, suffer *(sustain loss)*

anguished aggrieved *(harmed)*, disconsolate

anguishing painful

angustiae predicament, restriction

angustus limited

anility incapacity

anima life *(period of existence)*, spirit

animadversio correction *(punishment)*, notice *(heed)*, stricture

animadversion admonition, bad repute, comment, condemnation *(blame)*, correction *(punishment)*, criticism, diatribe, disapprobation, disapproval, discredit, impeachment, impugnation, obloquy, remark, remonstrance, reprimand, reproach, revilement, stricture

animadvert blame, comment, complain *(criticize)*, condemn *(blame)*, criticize *(find fault with)*, denounce *(condemn)*, disapprove *(condemn)*, fault, impeach, remark, remonstrate, reprehend, reproach

animadvert on rebuke, reprimand

animadvert upon censure, expostulate, lash *(attack verbally)*

animadvertere notice *(observe)*, observe *(watch)*

animalism bestiality

animam edere expire

animans animal

animate conscious *(awake)*, exhort, generate, incite, inspire, live *(conscious)*, motivate, prompt, provoke, spirit, stimulate

animated alert *(agile)*, born *(alive)*, fervent, live *(conscious)*, ready *(willing)*, volatile

animating impulsive *(impelling)*, moving *(evoking emotion)*

animation birth *(beginning)*, instigation, life *(vitality)*, spirit

animator catalyst, stimulus

animi sane

animi motus emotion, impression

animosity alienation *(estrangement)*, belligerency, conflict, contempt *(disdain)*, disaccord, discord, feud, hatred, ill will, incompatibility *(difference)*, malice, odium, rancor, resentment, spite, strife, umbrage

animum attendere concentrate *(pay attention)*

animum frangere discourage

animus character *(personal quality)*

animus design *(intent)*, feud

animus frame *(mood)*

animus hatred, ill will, malice, odium, resentment, spite

animus will *(desire)*

animus ingratus ingratitude

animus submissus resignation *(passive acceptance)*

annal record

annals calendar *(record of yearly periods)*, documentation

annex accrue *(increase)*, acquire *(secure)*, addendum, addition, adopt, affix, append, appropriate, appurtenance, assume *(seize)*, attach *(join)*, attach *(seize)*, attachment *(thing affixed)*, cement, codicil, combine *(join together)*, compound, confiscate, conjoin, connect *(join together)*, contact *(touch)*, distrain, enlarge, impropriate, increase, join *(bring together)*, juxtapose, occupy *(take possession)*, offshoot, organ, preempt, seize *(confiscate)*, sequester *(seize property)*

annex for public use eminent domain

annexation accretion, addendum, addition, appendix *(accession)*, appropriation *(taking)*, appurtenance, assumption *(seizure)*, attachment *(act of affixing)*, attachment *(seizure)*, boom *(increase)*, coalescence, codicil, distraint, distress *(seizure)*, garnishment, sequestration

annexe addendum, appurtenance

annexed accrued, appurtenant, attached *(seized)*, provincial

annexing accession *(annexation)*, coalescence

annexion attachment *(act of affixing)*

annihilate abolish, annul, cancel, consume, destroy *(efface)*, eliminate *(eradicate)*, eradicate, extinguish, extirpate, negate, obliterate, overturn, remove *(eliminate)*, slay, stifle, subvert

annihilated lifeless *(dead)*, lost *(taken away)*

annihilating deadly, destructive

annihilation abolition, assassination, demise *(death)*, destruction, dissolution *(termination)*, homicide, killing, subversion

annihilative dire, disastrous, fatal, lethal

annotate comment, describe, edit, elucidate, explain, interpret, note *(record)*

annotated detailed

annotated text hornbook

annotation caption, comment, explanation, memorandum, notation, note *(brief comment)*, observation

annotative demonstrative *(illustrative)*, interpretive

announce allege, annunciate, apprise, assert, bare, circulate, communicate, convey *(communicate)*, declare, disabuse, disclose, disseminate, enunciate, herald, inform *(betray)*, inform *(notify)*, issue *(publish)*, mention, notify, observe *(remark)*, pass *(determine)*, por-

tend, posit, proclaim, profess *(avow)*, promulgate, pronounce *(speak)*, protest, publish, relate *(tell)*, report *(disclose)*, reveal, signify *(inform)*, speak, utter

announce a conclusion find *(determine)*

announce authoritatively pronounce *(pass judgment)*, pronounce *(speak)*

announce in advance anticipate *(prognosticate)*, predict, presage

announce officially pronounce *(speak)*

announce one's presence report *(present oneself)*

announce publicly post

announced alleged, oral, public *(known)*

announcement assertion, averment, caveat, charter *(declaration of rights)*, common knowledge, communication *(statement)*, declaration, declaratory judgment, dictum, disclosure *(act of disclosing)*, disclosure *(something disclosed)*, issuance, judgment *(formal court decree)*, notification, proclamation, profession *(declaration)*, pronouncement, prospectus, publication *(disclosure)*, publicity, statement

announcer harbinger, informant, informer *(a person who provides information)*, precursor

annoy aggravate *(annoy)*, badger, bait *(harass)*, discommode, discompose, disconcert, disrupt, distress, disturb, embarrass, harass, harrow, harry *(harass)*, hinder, inconvenience, irritate, mistreat, obsess, offend *(insult)*, persecute, perturb, pique, plague, press *(goad)*, provoke

annoy excessively badger

annoyance dissatisfaction, disturbance, grievance, hindrance, mischief, molestation, nuisance, provocation, trouble, umbrage

annoyed petulant

annoying irksome, loathsome, objectionable, obnoxious, odious, offensive *(offending)*, provocative, undesirable, vexatious

annua pension

annua pecunia annuity

annual allowance annuity, pension

annual commitment premium *(insurance payment)*

annual encumbrance premium *(insurance payment)*

annual fee premium *(insurance payment)*

annual installment premium *(insurance payment)*

annual liability premium *(insurance payment)*

annual obligation premium *(insurance payment)*

annual payment premium *(insurance payment)*

annual rate of insurance premium *(insurance payment)*

annual remittance premium *(insurance payment)*

annually per annum

annuciative declaratory

annuity allotment, pension, perquisite

annul abate *(extinguish)*, abolish, abrogate *(rescind)*, adeem, avoid *(cancel)*, cancel, cease, contradict, counteract,

destroy *(void)*, disable, discharge *(release from obligation)*, disclaim, discontinue *(abandon)*, disinherit, disown *(deny the validity)*, divorce, eradicate, expunge, extinguish, extirpate, frustrate, impede, invalidate, kill *(defeat)*, negate, neutralize, nullify, obliterate, overreach, override, overrule, quash, recall *(call back)*, recant, renege, repeal, rescind, revoke, supersede, terminate, vacate *(void)*, vitiate

annul a marriage divorce

annulled defunct, lifeless *(dead)*, null *(invalid)*, null and void

annulling avoidance *(cancellation)*, cancellation

annulment abatement *(extinguishment)*, abolition, ademption, avoidance *(cancellation)*, cancellation, countermand, defeasance, disclaimer, dismissal *(termination of a proceeding)*, dissolution *(termination)*, invalidity, mistrial, negation, repudiation, rescision, retraction, reversal, revocation

annulment of debt discharge *(payment)*

annulment of marriage divorce

annunciate allege, assert, convey *(communicate)*, disseminate, enunciate, inform *(notify)*, mention, notify, proclaim, promulgate, report *(disclose)*, speak

annunciation common knowledge, communication *(statement)*, declaration, notification, proclamation, pronouncement

annunciator harbinger, informant, informer *(a person who provides information)*

annunciatory declaratory

annus annum

anodyne beneficial, drug, medicinal, narcotic, narcotic, remedial

anodynous narcotic

anoint drug

anointed sacrosanct

anomalistic anomalous, irregular *(not usual)*, peculiar *(curious)*

anomalistical peculiar *(curious)*

anomalous atypical, disordered, eccentric, irregular *(not usual)*, noteworthy, novel, peculiar *(curious)*, prodigious *(amazing)*, unaccustomed, uncommon, unique, unorthodox, unprecedented, unusual

anomalousness deviation, nonconformity

anomaly deviation, discrepancy, irregularity, nonconformity, quirk *(idiosyncrasy)*, variance *(exemption)*

anon instantly

anonymous unspecified

another additional

another addressee cotenant

another denizen cotenant

another dweller cotenant

another inhabitant cotenant

another inhabiter cotenant

another leaseholder cotenant

another lessee cotenant

another lodger cotenant

another occupant cotenant

another occupier cotenant

another paying guest cotenant

another possessor cotenant

another renter cotenant

another resident cotenant
another residentiary cotenant
another time anew, de novo
answer acknowledge *(respond)*, acknowledgment *(acceptance)*, appear *(attend court proceedings)*, appearance *(coming into court)*, controvert, converse, counterargument, countercharge, disclosure *(something disclosed)*, find *(discover)*, fulfill, key *(solution)*, outcome, panacea, plea, pleading, reaction *(response)*, rebut, rejoinder, reply, reply, report *(present oneself)*, respond, response, retort, return *(respond)*, solve, verdict
answer a purpose function
answer a summons report *(present oneself)*
answer back contradict, countercharge, retaliate, retort, return *(respond)*
answer conclusively controvert
answer for assure *(insure)*, cosign, displace *(replace)*, guarantee, indemnify, justify, sponsor, undertake
answer the purpose correspond *(be equivalent)*, satisfy *(fulfill)*
answer to obey
answerability duty *(obligation)*, fault *(responsibility)*, liability, responsibility *(accountability)*
answerable accountable *(responsible)*, actionable, ascertainable, blameworthy, bound, consonant, liable, subject *(exposed)*
answerer respondent
answering contrary, responsive
antagonism alienation *(estrangement)*, argument *(contention)*, bad repute, belligerency, collision *(dispute)*, conflict, contention *(opposition)*, contest *(dispute)*, contradistinction, contraposition, contravention, controversy *(argument)*, disaccord, discord, feud, hatred, ill will, impugnation, incompatibility *(difference)*, malice, rancor, resentment, resistance, spite
antagonist adversary, aggressor, assailant, contender, contestant, disputant, foe, rival
antagonistic adverse *(hostile)*, antipathetic *(oppositional)*, averse, contradictory, different, discordant, disinclined, dissident, hostile, inimical, litigious, malevolent, malicious, negative, offensive *(taking the initiative)*, opposite, pugnacious, recusant, renitent, repugnant *(incompatible)*, spiteful, unfavorable, virulent
antagonistic to contrary
antagonistical adverse *(hostile)*
antagonize affront, alienate *(estrange)*, collide *(clash)*, counter, counteract, disaffect, disoblige, incense, provoke
antagonized irreconcilable
antagonizing obnoxious
ante bet, parlay *(bet)*, stake *(award)*
ante up bet
antecede precede
antecedence precedence, priority
antecedens antecedent, last *(preceding)*
antecedent aforesaid, ascendant, before mentioned, derivation, forerunner, former, last *(preceding)*, original *(ini-*

tial), precursor, precursory, predecessor, preexisting, preliminary, previous, primogenitor, prior, progenitor, sine qua non
antecedents family *(common ancestry)*, lineage, parentage
antecedere precede
antecellere surpass
antecessor forerunner, predecessor, progenitor
antechamber chamber *(compartment)*
antecursor harbinger
antedate antecede, precede
antedeluvian antique
antediluvian obsolete, outdated, outmoded
antegredi precede
anteire precede
anteponere prefer
anterior aforesaid, antecedent, before mentioned, last *(preceding)*, preexisting, preliminary, previous, prior
anteroom chamber *(compartment)*, entrance
antetype model, pattern
antevertere anticipate *(expect)*, forestall
anthologize compile
anthology compilation, digest, selection *(collection)*
antibiotic drug
anticipatable foreseeable
anticipate forestall, precede, preconceive, predict, presage, presume
anticipate danger fear
anticipate injury fear
anticipate needs provide *(arrange for)*
anticipated foreseeable, forseen, forthcoming, future, immediate *(imminent)*, pending *(imminent)*, possible, potential, presumptive, prospective
anticipated loan advance *(allowance)*
anticipating provident *(showing foresight)*
anticipation advancement *(loan)*, expectation, forethought, likelihood, possibility, precaution, preconception, preparation, presumption, probability, prospect *(outlook)*
anticipation of adversity apprehension *(fear)*
anticipative sanguine
anticipatory premature, preparatory
antidotal medicinal, preventive, remedial
antidote cure, remedy *(that which corrects)*
antifebrile medicinal
antilogy contrary, inconsistency, paradox
antimony antipode
antinomy inconsistency, opposition, paradox
antipathetic averse, bitter *(reproachful)*, contrary, disinclined, hostile, inimical, malevolent, negative, objectionable, obnoxious, offensive *(offending)*, renitent, spiteful
antipathetical discordant, disinclined, inimical, malevolent, negative, renitent
antipathy alienation *(estrangement)*, antipode, conflict, contradiction, deviation, difference, hatred, ill will, incompatibility *(difference)*, malice, odium, phobia, rancor, reluctance

antiphon response
antipodal adverse *(opposite)*, hostile, inverse, opposite
antipode antithesis, contra, contrary
antipodean adverse *(opposite)*, antipathetic *(oppositional)*, inverse, opposite
antipodes antipode
antipoison cure
antipole antipode
antipollution project ecology
antiquate superannuate
antiquated obsolete, old, outdated, outmoded
antique obsolete, old, outdated, outmoded
antiseptic preventive
antisepticize decontaminate
antithesis antipode, contra, contradiction, contradistinction, contraposition, contrary, deviation, difference, distinction *(difference)*, incompatibility *(inconsistency)*
antithetic antipathetic *(oppositional)*, contrary, different, hostile, opposite
antithetical adverse *(opposite)*, antipathetic *(oppositional)*, contradictory, contrary, discordant, hostile, inverse, opposite
antitheticalness difference
antitoxin cure
antonomasia call *(title)*
antonym contra
antonymous adverse *(opposite)*, discordant, hostile
anxietude disturbance, misgiving
anxiety apprehension *(fear)*, burden, concern *(interest)*, consternation, distress *(anguish)*, disturbance, doubt *(indecision)*, fear, fright, interest *(concern)*, misgiving, nuisance, panic, phobia, pressure, problem, qualm, scruple, stress *(strain)*
anxious eager, ready *(willing)*, solicitous
anxious concern consternation, misgiving
anxiousness consternation, distress *(anguish)*, disturbance, misgiving, pressure
anxius solicitous
any individual whoever
any person whoever
anybody whoever
anyhow regardless
anyone whoever
anyway regardless
anywise regardless
apart alone *(solitary)*, bipartite, disconnected, discrete, extrinsic, insular, irrelative, only, partial *(part)*, private *(secluded)*, remote *(secluded)*, separate
apartheid exclusion, segregation *(isolation by races)*
apartment chamber *(compartment)*, home *(domicile)*, lodging
apartness exception *(exclusion)*
apathetic casual, cursory, inactive, indolent, inexpressive, insensible, insusceptible *(uncaring)*, languid, lax, lifeless *(dull)*, nonchalant, otiose, passive, perfunctory, phlegmatic, stagnant, stoical, torpid, truant
apathetical languid
apathy disinterest *(lack of interest)*, indifference, inertia, languor, laxity,

sloth

ape copy, impersonate, mock *(imitate)*, pose *(impersonate)*

aperçu abridgment *(condensation)*

aperire betray *(disclose)*, disclose, manifest, reopen, unveil

aperte fairly *(clearly)*

aperture loophole, outlet, portal, rift *(gap)*, split

apertus evident, explicit, ingenuous, manifest, obvious, open *(in sight)*, open *(persuasible)*, overt, patent, straightforward, unambiguous

apertus sincerus candid

apery caricature, parody

apex ceiling, culmination, pinnacle

aphonic speechless

aphorism maxim, phrase

aphoristic axiomatic, brief, compact *(pithy)*, proverbial, sententious

aphoristic expression maxim

aphoristical compact *(pithy)*

apical cardinal *(basic)*

apiece respectively

aplomb composure, confidence *(faith)*

aplomb indestructibility

aplomb surety *(certainty)*

apocha receipt *(proof of receiving)*

apocryphal assumed *(feigned)*, disputable, fictitious, ill-founded, spurious, untrue

apodictic axiomatic, categorical, incontrovertible

apodosis denouement

apogee ceiling, culmination, pinnacle

apograph transcript

apologetic contrite, palliative *(excusing)*, penitent, remorseful, repentant

apologist advocate *(counselor)*, advocate *(espouser)*, proponent

apologize regret, repent

apology expiation

apostasize abandon *(relinquish)*, defect, discontinue *(abandon)*

apostasy abandonment *(desertion)*, bad faith, blasphemy, desertion, disloyalty, dissent *(difference of opinion)*, infidelity, nonconformity, revolt, sedition

apostate heretic, recreant, recusant

apostatic recreant

apostatical recreant

apostatize bear false witness, quit *(discontinue)*, secede, tergiversate

apostatizing disobedient, faithless, false *(disloyal)*

apostil clarification

apostle disciple, partisan

apotheca depository

apothegm phrase

apothegmatic compact *(pithy)*, sententious

apothegmatical compact *(pithy)*

apotheosis exemplar

appall discompose, disconcert, harrow, repel *(disgust)*

appalling deplorable, dire, disastrous, egregious, formidable, loathsome, lurid, repulsive

appanage addendum, adjunct, appurtenance, codicil, dower, grant, inheritance

apparatus appliance, device *(mechanism)*, equipment, expedient, facility *(instrumentality)*, instrument *(tool)*, paraphernalia *(apparatus)*, tool

apparatus belli ammunition

apparent axiomatic, blatant *(conspicuous)*, candid, circumstantial, coherent *(clear)*, colorable *(plausible)*, conclusive *(determinative)*, conspicuous, constructive *(inferential)*, demonstrable, discernible, distinct *(clear)*, elementary, evident, flagrant, lucid, manifest, naked *(perceptible)*, obvious, open *(in sight)*, ostensible, overt, palpable, patent, pellucid, perceivable, perceptible, plausible, presumptive, probable, prominent, public *(known)*, specious, unmistakable, visible *(noticeable)*

apparent character color *(complexion)*, complexion

apparent right color *(deceptive appearance)*

apparent state complexion

apparentation affiliation *(bloodline)*

apparently prima facie *(self-evident)*, quasi

apparently right colorable *(plausible)*

apparere appear *(materialize)*

apparition phantom, phenomenon *(manifestation)*, specter, spirit, vision *(dream)*

appeal address *(petition)*, amenity, call *(appeal to)*, challenge, coax, entreaty, habeas corpus, importune, incentive, invitation, motivate, press *(beseech)*, request, request, rhetoric *(skilled speech)*

appeal against expostulate

appeal for petition, solicit

appeal to bait *(lure)*, pray, propitiate, solicit, urge

appeal to a higher court certiorari

appeal to arms fight *(battle)*, fight *(battle)*

appeal to the law litigate, sue

appealable litigable

appealer appellant, special interest

appealing attractive, precatory, sapid

appealing conclusively cogent

appealing forcibly cogent

appealing to reason disputable

appear bare, comport *(behave)*, demean *(deport oneself)*, emerge, report *(present oneself)*

appear for represent *(substitute)*

appear for duty report *(present oneself)*

appearance aspect, color *(deceptive appearance)*, complexion, condition *(state)*, configuration *(form)*, demeanor, deportment, expression *(manifestation)*, face value *(first blush)*, first appearance, manifestation, manner *(behavior)*, phantom, phenomenon *(manifestation)*, presence *(poise)*, pretense *(pretext)*, semblance, specter, state *(condition)*, style, vision *(dream)*

appearance of truth credibility, probability

appearing apparent *(presumptive)*, colorable *(specious)*, evident, ostensible, perceivable, specious

appearing at intervals sporadic

appeasable nonmilitant, placable

appease allay, assuage, disarm *(set at ease)*, mitigate, moderate *(temper)*, mollify, pacify, palliate *(abate)*, placate, propitiate, reconcile, redress, satisfy *(fulfill)*, soothe

appeased agreed *(harmonized)*

appeasement conciliation,

mollification, reconciliation, satisfaction *(fulfilment)*

appeaser go-between

appelare appeal

appelation cognomen

appellant claimant, contender, contestant, litigant, party *(litigant)*, respondent, suitor

appellare summon

appellate review appeal

appellatio appeal

appellation call *(title)*, denomination, designation *(naming)*, identification, term *(expression)*, title *(designation)*

appellative call *(title)*, cognomen, term *(expression)*

appellator appellant

appellee litigant, party *(litigant)*

append affix, annex *(add)*, attach *(join)*, combine *(join together)*, compound, connect *(join together)*, join *(bring together)*

appendage accession *(annexation)*, addendum, adjoiner, adjunct, allonge, appendix *(accession)*, appendix *(supplement)*, appurtenance, attachment *(thing affixed)*, codicil, organ, rider

appendant appurtenance, attached *(annexed)*, rider

appended additional, appurtenant, attached *(annexed)*

appendix addendum, allonge, appurtenance, attachment *(thing affixed)*, codicil, insertion, rider

apperceive note *(notice)*, perceive, understand

apperception appreciation *(perception)*, cognition, insight, judgment *(discernment)*, knowledge *(awareness)*, perception, realization, reason *(sound judgment)*, recognition, sagacity, sense *(feeling)*, understanding *(comprehension)*

apperceptive cognizant, conscious *(aware)*, judicious, knowing, omniscient, perceptive, perspicacious, sensitive *(discerning)*

appercipient sensitive *(discerning)*

appertain correspond *(be equivalent)*, pertain, refer *(direct attention)*

appertain to concern *(involve)*, connect *(relate)*, relate *(establish a connection)*

appertaining akin *(germane)*, applicable, appurtenant, cognate, collateral *(accompanying)*, pertinent

appertaining to incident

appetence predilection, predisposition, proclivity

appetency desire, greed, predilection, predisposition, proclivity

appetent eager

appetere assault

appetite desire, penchant, predilection, predisposition

appetitio desire

appetitus instinct

appetizing palatable, sapid, savory

applaud honor, recommend

applauded famous, illustrious, renowned

applause mention *(tribute)*

appliable applicable

appliance device *(mechanism)*, expedient, facility *(instrumentality)*, instrument *(tool)*

appliances paraphernalia *(apparatus)*

applicability admissibility, aptitude, connection *(relation)*, propriety *(appropriateness)*, qualification *(fitness)*, relation *(connection)*, relevance, utility *(usefulness)*, utilization

applicable admissible, akin *(germane)*, apposite, appropriate, congruous, constructive *(creative)*, convenient, correlative, felicitous, fit, functional, germane, operative, pertinent, practical, related, relative *(relevant)*, relevant, suitable

applicable to a class generic

applicant candidate, claimant, contender, petitioner, prospect *(prospective patron)*, suitor

application arrogation, assignation, call *(appeal)*, call *(title)*, connection *(relation)*, connotation, diligence *(care)*, diligence *(perseverance)*, endeavor, industry *(activity)*, infliction, interest *(concern)*, means *(opportunity)*, motion, obsession, petition, prayer, purpose, regard *(attention)*, relevance, request, requisition, resolution *(decision)*, usage, use, work *(effort)*

application for a ruling motion

application for an order motion

application for discharge habeas corpus

application for liberty habeas corpus

application for proposed relief motion

application for relief prayer

application for retrial appeal, certiorari

application for review by a higher tribunal appeal

application of force compulsion *(coercion)*

applied functional

applied energy effort

applied from without extrinsic

applied logic dialectic

apply ascribe, concern *(involve)*, devote, employ *(make use of)*, exercise *(use)*, exert, expend *(consume)*, exploit *(make use of)*, impute, inflict, manipulate *(utilize skillfully)*, move *(judicially request)*, refer *(direct attention)*, relate *(establish a connection)*, resort, solicit, spend

apply a closure complete

apply a remedy cure, drug, help

apply dishonestly convert *(misappropriate)*

apply for desire, petition, request, sue

apply for a loan borrow

apply for a reexamination of a case appeal

apply for a retrial appeal

apply for a review of a case to a higher tribunal appeal

apply one's self to practice *(train by repetition)*

apply oneself labor, persevere, specialize

apply oneself to address *(direct attention to)*, commit *(perpetrate)*, endeavor, occupy *(engage)*, undertake

apply pressure coerce, constrain *(compel)*, foist, force *(coerce)*

apply reason deduce, deduct *(conclude by reasoning)*

apply the attention to occupy *(engage)*

apply the closure close *(terminate)*

apply the mind concentrate *(pay attention)*, ponder, study

apply the mind to occupy *(engage)*

apply to appertain, call *(appeal to)*, importune, petition, pray

apply to one's own uses impropriate, plagiarize

applying to apposite, germane

appoint allocate, allot, assign *(designate)*, authorize, bestow, charge *(empower)*, choose, clothe, delegate, designate, detail *(assign)*, dispense, employ *(engage services)*, empower, engage *(hire)*, entrust, furnish, hire, induct, instate, invest *(vest)*, nominate, parcel, provide *(arrange for)*, select

appoint as agent delegate

appoint as representative delegate

appoint beforehand preordain

appoint by act enact

appoint by vote elect *(select by a vote)*

appoint in advance preordain

appoint the time of date

appointed select

appointed group commission *(agency)*, committee

appointee agent, deputy, licensee, nominee *(delegate)*, proctor, procurator, trustee

appointer licensor

appointing deputation *(selection of delegates)*

appointive adoptive, elective *(voluntary)*

appointment agency *(legal relationship)*, allotment, assignment *(designation)*, charge *(responsibility)*, delegation *(assignment)*, deputation *(selection of delegates)*, designation *(naming)*, dispensation *(act of dispensing)*, election *(choice)*, employment, equipment, mission, nomination, office, position *(business status)*, post, province, pursuit *(occupation)*, rendezvous, selection *(choice)*

appointment by vote election *(selection by vote)*

appointments paraphernalia *(personal belongings)*, property *(possessions)*

apportion allocate, allot, arrange *(methodize)*, assign *(allot)*, bestow, classify, demarcate, devote, dichotomize, disburse *(distribute)*, dispense, disperse *(disseminate)*, divide *(distribute)*, dole, endue, expend *(disburse)*, fund, furnish, leave *(give)*, marshal, mete, parcel, partition, prorate, sort, split, subdivide

apportion anew reapportion

apportion by measure mete

apportion pro rata prorate

apportionable divisible, severable

apportioned pro rata

apportioned lot share *(interest)*

apportioning disbursement *(act of disbursing)*

apportionment allotment, appropriation *(allotment)*, arbitration, assignment *(allotment)*, classification, decentralization, disbursement *(act of disbursing)*, dispensation *(act of dispensing)*, division *(act of dividing)*, equity

(share of ownership), order *(arrangement)*, proportion, quantity, quota, ration

appose adjoin, border *(bound)*, contrast, juxtapose

apposite appropriate, congruous, correlative, felicitous, fit, germane, harmonious, pertinent, proper, related, relative *(relevant)*, relevant, seasonable, suitable

appositeness admissibility, affiliation *(connectedness)*, collation, qualification *(fitness)*, relation *(connection)*, relationship *(connection)*, relevance

apposition affiliation *(connectedness)*, propinquity *(proximity)*, relation *(connection)*

appositional relative *(relevant)*

appraisable appreciable, determinable *(ascertainable)*

appraisal account *(evaluation)*, appreciation *(perception)*, arbitration, assessment *(estimation)*, choice *(decision)*, computation, concept, cost *(price)*, determination, discretion *(power of choice)*, discrimination *(differentiation)*, estimate *(approximate cost)*, estimation *(calculation)*, expense *(cost)*, generalization, idea, inspection, judgment *(discernment)*, measurement, par *(face amount)*, perception, price, proposal *(report)*, rating, review *(critical evaluation)*, value, worth

appraise calculate, charge *(assess)*, consider, criticize *(evaluate)*, diagnose, estimate, evaluate, excise *(levy a tax)*, gauge, judge, measure, opine, ponder, rate, survey *(examine)*

appraised ad valorem

appraisement ad valorem, appraisal, assessment *(estimation)*, determination, estimate *(approximate cost)*, estimation *(calculation)*, expense *(cost)*, measurement, par *(face amount)*, price, worth

appraiser juror

appraising discriminating *(judicious)*

appraisment appreciation *(perception)*

appreciable corporeal, determinable *(ascertainable)*, perceivable, ponderable, substantive

appreciate accrue *(increase)*, apprehend *(perceive)*, comprehend *(understand)*, conceive *(comprehend)*, digest *(comprehend)*, discern *(detect with the senses)*, enhance, gauge, increase, note *(notice)*, notice *(observe)*, perceive, pierce *(discern)*, realize *(understand)*, recognize *(acknowledge)*, regard *(hold in esteem)*, relish, understand

appreciation accession *(enlargement)*, augmentation, boom *(increase)*, cognition, comprehension, computation, concept, determination, discretion *(quality of being discreet)*, discrimination *(differentiation)*, estimation *(esteem)*, honor *(outward respect)*, knowledge *(awareness)*, mention *(tribute)*, perception, realization, recognition, regard *(esteem)*, respect, scienter, sensibility

appreciation of differences diagnosis

appreciative conscious *(aware)*

appreciativeness discretion *(quality of being discreet)*, knowledge *(awareness)*

apprehend appreciate *(comprehend)*,

capture, comprehend *(understand)*, conceive *(comprehend)*, construe *(comprehend)*, detain *(hold in custody)*, discern *(detect with the senses)*, ensnare, expect *(consider probable)*, fear, find *(discover)*, jail, mistrust, perceive, pierce *(discern)*, presume, read, realize *(understand)*, recognize *(perceive)*, surmise, understand
apprehend clearly discern *(detect with the senses)*
apprehend danger fear
apprehend harm fear
apprehend punishment fear
apprehendere seize *(apprehend)*
apprehending attachment *(seizure)*, conscious *(aware)*, knowing
apprehensibility coherence
apprehensible cognizable, coherent *(clear)*, comprehensible, perceivable, perceptible, scrutable
apprehension appropriation *(taking)*, arrest, cloud *(suspicion)*, cognition, comprehension, concept, consternation, constraint *(imprisonment)*, detection, dialectic, doubt *(indecision)*, doubt *(suspicion)*, fear, fright, idea, impression, misgiving, notion, perception, phobia, position *(point of view)*, qualm, realization, scienter, scruple, sense *(feeling)*, stress *(strain)*, suspicion *(mistrust)*, trepidation, understanding *(comprehension)*
apprehension and transfer extradition
apprehension of danger fear
apprehension of harm fear
apprehension of injury fear
apprehension of punishment fear
apprehensive cognizant, leery, perceptive, solicitous, suspicious *(distrustful)*, vigilant
apprehensiveness apprehension *(fear)*, cloud *(suspicion)*, consternation, doubt *(indecision)*, fear, misgiving, qualm, scruple, stress *(strain)*
apprentice amateur, assistant, coadjutant, disciple, employee, neophyte, novice, probationer *(one being tested)*, protégé
apprenticed indentured
apprenticeship experience *(background)*, preparation
apprenticeship agreement indenture
apprisal disclosure *(act of disclosing)*
apprise advise, annunciate, caution, communicate, convey *(communicate)*, disabuse, disclose, disseminate, divulge, enlighten, enunciate, herald, impart, inform *(notify)*, mention, notice *(give formal warning)*, notify, relate *(tell)*, report *(disclose)*, reveal, signify *(inform)*, speak
apprised acquainted, cognizant, conscious *(aware)*, familiar *(informed)*, knowing, literate, sensible
apprised of learned
apprisement determination
appriser informant
apprize assess *(appraise)*, rate
apprized informed *(having information)*
apprizement determination
apprizer affirmant, bystander, deponent
approach access *(right of way)*, ac-

cost, address *(direct attention to)*, admittance *(means of approach)*, approximate, avenue *(means of attainment)*, avenue *(route)*, bid, confrontation *(act of setting face to face)*, converge, correspond *(be equivalent)*, course, design *(intent)*, direction *(course)*, entrance, gravitate, impend, inflow, ingress, invitation, maneuver *(tactic)*, manner *(behavior)*, modus operandi, overture, policy *(plan of action)*, portal, practice *(procedure)*, progress, proposition, reach, strategy
approach closely approximate
approach in amount approximate
approach of danger peril
approach one another converge
approach road causeway
approachability access *(opening)*
approachable available, open *(accessible)*, passable, public *(open)*, vulnerable
approaching approximate, close *(near)*, forthcoming, future, immediate *(imminent)*, imminent, inevitable, instant, pending *(imminent)*, prospective, proximate
approaching an end determinable *(liable to be terminated)*
approaching death in extremis
approaching the finish determinable *(liable to be terminated)*
approbare approve, countenance, pass *(satisfy requirements)*
approbate approve, concur *(agree)*, countenance, pass *(approve)*, recommend, sanction
approbatio approval
approbation acceptance, adoption *(acceptance)*, advocacy, approval, assent, consent, estimation *(esteem)*, favor *(sanction)*, honor *(outward respect)*, indorsement, leave *(permission)*, license, mention *(tribute)*, permit, ratification, recommendation, regard *(esteem)*, respect, sanction *(permission)*
approbative favorable *(expressing approval)*
appropinquare approach
appropriate accroach, acquire *(secure)*, admissible, adopt, allocate, annex *(arrogate)*, applicable, apposite, ascribe, assign *(allot)*, assume *(seize)*, attach *(seize)*, certain *(specific)*, collect *(recover money)*, commensurate, condemn *(seize)*, condign, confiscate, congruous, consonant, convenient, correlative, devote, dispense, distrain, distribute, divide *(distribute)*, dole, due *(regular)*, eligible, fair *(just)*, favorable *(advantageous)*, felicitous, fit, fitting, garnish, germane, hijack, hold up *(rob)*, impound, impress *(procure by force)*, impropriate, loot, mete, monopolize, obtain, occupy *(take possession)*, opportune, parcel, pertinent, pirate *(reproduce without authorization)*, plagiarize, poach, preempt, procure, proper, reclaim, related, relative *(relevant)*, relevant, right *(suitable)*, rightful, seasonable, seize *(confiscate)*, sequester *(seize property)*, several *(separate)*, specific, suitable, viable
appropriate activity function
appropriate behavior decorum
appropriate criminally peculate

appropriate dishonestly peculate, purloin
appropriate for federal use nationalize
appropriate for government use nationalize
appropriate for residence habitable
appropriate for use preempt
appropriate fraudulently bilk, embezzle, purloin
appropriate illegally peculate, pilfer, rob
appropriate to one's own use defalcate, embezzle
appropriate to public use confiscate
appropriate unlawfully usurp
appropriate wrongfully convert *(misappropriate)*, peculate
appropriated attached *(seized)*
appropriately pro rata
appropriateness admissibility, decorum, expedience, fairness, qualification *(fitness)*, relevance, timeliness
appropriating confiscatory
appropriation acquisition, adverse possession, allotment, arrogation, assignment *(allotment)*, assumption *(seizure)*, budget, condemnation *(seizure)*, consignment, conversion *(misappropriation)*, distraint, distress *(seizure)*, distribution *(apportionment)*, embezzlement, endowment, garnishment, housebreaking, larceny, pillage, plagiarism, preemption, quota, ration, selection *(choice)*, sequestration, taking
appropriation for a dishonest use misappropriation
appropriation for a wrongful use misappropriation
appropriation of a literary composition plagiarism
approvable admissible, allowable, allowed, laudable, meritorious, permissible
approval acceptance, adoption *(acceptance)*, advantage, advocacy, affirmation, assent, charter *(sanction)*, confirmation, consent, designation *(naming)*, dispensation *(exception)*, estimation *(esteem)*, favor *(partiality)*, favor *(sanction)*, honor *(outward respect)*, indorsement, indulgence, leave *(permission)*, legalization, license, mention *(tribute)*, option *(contractual provision)*, permission, permit, ratification, recognition, recommendation, regard *(esteem)*, respect, sanction *(permission)*, subscription, support *(corroboration)*
approve accede *(concede)*, accredit, advocate, affirm *(uphold)*, agree *(comply)*, allow *(authorize)*, allow *(endure)*, appoint, assent, authorize, bear *(tolerate)*, coincide *(concur)*, concur *(agree)*, confirm, conform, consent, cosign, countenance, enable, endorse, favor, grant *(concede)*, legalize, legitimate, let *(permit)*, notarize, permit, prefer, reassure, receive *(permit to enter)*, recommend, regard *(hold in esteem)*, sanction, seal *(solemnize)*, settle, sign, subscribe *(sign)*, support *(justify)*, sustain *(confirm)*, uphold, validate, vote
approve of countenance, permit
approved agreed *(promised)*, allowable, allowed, conventional, eligible, formal, legal, meritorious, official, or-

thodox, permissible, preferred *(favored)*, unimpeachable

approving consensual, consenting, ecstatic, favorable *(expressing approval)*, propitious

approximate border *(approach)*, close *(near)*, comparable *(capable of comparison)*, copy, correspond *(be equivalent)*, inaccurate, inexact, similar

approximate calculation estimate *(approximate cost)*, estimation *(calculation)*

approximate judgment of value estimate *(approximate cost)*, estimation *(calculation)*

approximate value estimate *(approximate cost)*

approximately almost, on or about

approximation estimate *(approximate cost)*, estimation *(calculation)*, parity, resemblance

approximative inexact

appulsion meeting *(encounter)*

appurtenance additive, appliance, attachment *(thing affixed)*, augmentation, boom *(increase)*, corollary, droit, rider

appurtenances goods

appurtenant apposite, cognate, germane, pendent, pertinent, related, relative *(relevant)*, relevant

apriorism prolepsis

apropos akin *(germane)*, apposite, appropriate, felicitous, fit, germane, incident, pertinent, relative *(relevant)*, relevant, suitable

apt acute, applicable, apposite, appropriate, artful, consonant, deft, expert, felicitous, fit, germane, harmonious, inclined, opportune, pertinent, possible, practiced, probable, prone, proper, qualified *(competent)*, relative *(relevant)*, relevant, resourceful, right *(suitable)*, subtle *(refined)*, suitable, veteran, viable

apt to change suddenly capricious

apt to distrust cynical

apt to flee elusive

apt to quarrel fractious

aptare adapt, adjust *(regulate)*

aptitude ability, caliber *(mental capacity)*, chance *(possibility)*, competence *(ability)*, disposition *(inclination)*, faculty *(ability)*, gift *(flair)*, inclination, instinct, intelligence *(intellect)*, performance *(workmanship)*, potential, predisposition, proclivity, propensity, propriety *(appropriateness)*, qualification *(fitness)*, science *(technique)*, skill, temperament, tendency

aptness ability, admissibility, capacity *(aptitude)*, expedience, inclination, instinct, liability, performance *(workmanship)*, predisposition, proclivity, propensity, propriety *(appropriateness)*, qualification *(fitness)*, quality *(excellence)*, quality *(grade)*, relevance, science *(technique)*, skill, specialty *(special aptitude)*, tendency, timeliness

aptum qualify *(meet standards)*

aptus adequate, appropriate, attached *(annexed)*, capable, fit, proper, suitable

aqua et igni interdicere outlaw

arable fertile

arbiter arbiter

arbiter arbitrator

arbiter eyewitness

arbiter go-between

arbiter intermediary

arbiter judge, juror, referee, umpire

arbiters jury

arbitrage adjudication, arbitration, collective bargaining, intercession

arbitrament adjudication, collective bargaining, conclusion *(determination)*, judgment *(formal court decree)*, negotiation

arbitrari opine

arbitrarily invented fictitious

arbitrary contemptuous, dictatorial, disobedient, haphazard, irresponsible, tyrannous, unpredictable, unwarranted

arbitrary power force *(compulsion)*

arbitrate adjudge, adjudicate, decide, intercede, judge, mediate, negotiate, reconcile

arbitrate terms dicker

arbitrated agreed *(harmonized)*

arbitrater adjuster

arbitration adjudication, collective bargaining, intercession, mediation, negotiation, reconciliation

arbitrator arbiter, go-between, intermediary, judge, magistrate, referee, umpire

arbitrators jury

arbitrium arbitration, determination, freedom

arca coffer

arcana secret

arcane clandestine, confidential, esoteric, hidden, latent, mysterious, private *(confidential)*, privy, recondite, secret, stealthy

arcanum enigma, mystery

arcanus confidential, mysterious, private *(confidential)*, secret

arch jocular, machiavellian, master, paramount, project *(extend beyond)*, sly

archaic antique, obsolete, old, outdated, outmoded

archaism desuetude, disuse

archaistic obsolete

archetypal primordial

archetype example, exemplar, model, paradigm, pattern, precedent, prototype, sample, standard

architect author *(originator)*, contractor

architectural monument edifice

architecture building *(business of assembling)*

architectus architect

archive dossier, file, record, register

archives depository

archivist caretaker *(one caring for property)*, clerk

ardency ardor, passion

ardens fervent, intense

ardent eager, fanatical, fervent, industrious, intense, intensive, ready *(willing)*, sedulous, serious *(devoted)*, true *(loyal)*, vehement, zealous

ardent admirer addict

ardent champion of change malcontent

ardent impulse desire

ardor ardor

ardor adhesion *(loyalty)*, affection, compulsion *(obsession)*, desire, diligence *(perseverance)*, emotion, industry *(activity)*, life *(vitality)*, passion, penchant, predisposition, spirit

arduous difficult, formidable, onerous, operose, oppressive, painful

arduousness effort

area area *(province)*

area bailiwick, caliber *(measurement)*, capacity *(sphere)*, circuit, department, dimension, district, division *(administrative unit)*, extent, locality, location, parcel, part *(place)*, province, purview, range, realm, region, scope, section *(vicinity)*, space, territory, vicinity, zone

area of disagreement contention *(argument)*

area of education discipline *(field of study)*

area of learning discipline *(field of study)*

arena area *(province)*, bailiwick, capacity *(sphere)*, enclosure, focus, purview, range, scene, sphere

argot jargon *(technical language)*, phraseology

arguable controversial, debatable, disputable, doubtful, dubious, forensic, justiciable, litigable, moot, plausible, uncertain *(questionable)*

argue bear *(adduce)*, bespeak, bicker, challenge, collide *(clash)*, conflict, contend *(dispute)*, contend *(maintain)*, contest, contradict, controvert, cross *(disagree with)*, debate, differ *(vary)*, disaccord, disagree, dispute *(debate)*, dissent *(differ in opinion)*, expostulate, haggle, insist, posit, propound, reason *(persuade)*, rebut

argue a case dispute *(debate)*

argue a point dispute *(debate)*

argue against confront *(oppose)*, discourage, dispute *(contest)*, dissuade, oppose, rebut, remonstrate

argue at the bar plead *(argue a case)*

argue for adhere *(maintain loyalty)*, advocate, assert, defend, espouse, justify

argue for and against discuss

argue in opposition dispute *(debate)*

argue into convince, prevail *(persuade)*

argue price dicker

argue pros and cons debate

argue the case controvert, discuss

argue the point controvert, discuss, plead *(argue a case)*

argue to no purpose bicker

argue vehemently dispute *(contest)*

argued alleged

arguer contender

arguer in defense apologist

arguere accuse, charge *(accuse)*

argufy dispute *(debate)*

arguing disputable, dissenting, hostile, litigious

argument altercation, brief, conflict, confrontation *(altercation)*, contest *(dispute)*, contravention, disaccord, disagreement, discourse, disparity, dispute, dissent *(difference of opinion)*, dissidence, persuasion, pleading, point *(item)*, reason *(basis)*, remonstrance, rift *(disagreement)*, thesis

argument at the bar argument *(pleading)*

argumental litigious, polemic

argumentari argue

argumentation conflict, contention *(argument)*, controversy *(argument)*, dialectic, disaccord, disagreement, discord, discourse, dissension, ratiocination

argumentative contentious, discursive *(analytical)*, disputable, dissenting, forensic, hostile, insistent, litigable, litigious, negative, petulant, polemic, pugnacious, remonstrative

argumentative person disputant

arguments at the bar plea

argumentum context, proof, subject *(topic)*

argus guardian

argute perspicacious

arguteness caliber *(mental capacity)*, sagacity

arid barren, lifeless *(dull)*, otiose, pedestrian, unproductive

arise appear *(materialize)*, commence, disobey, emerge, ensue, occur *(happen)*, proceed *(go forward)*, rebel, redound, result, stem *(originate)*, succeed *(follow)*, supervene

arise from develop, emanate, evolve

aristocracy elite, society

ark refuge

arm affiliate, clothe, cudgel, empower, enable, endue, furnish, organ, protect

arm of the law judiciary, marshal, peace officer, police, posse

arma homini adimere disarm *(divest of arms)*

armament ammunition, bomb, gun

armaments weapons

armature ammunition, panoply

armatus armed

armed defensible, ready *(prepared)*, safe

armed action fight *(battle)*

armed attack foray

armed band posse

armed enemy foe

armiger esquire

armipotent powerful

armistice cessation *(interlude)*, halt, interruption, lull, pause, peace, treaty

armor panoply, protect, protection, safeguard

armored immune, protective, safe, secure *(free from danger)*

armored protection panoply

armorum weapons

arms ammunition, gun, weapons

army band

arouse abet, agitate *(activate)*, alert, bait *(harass)*, discommode, disturb, elicit, evoke, exacerbate, exhort, foment, harass, impel, impress *(affect deeply)*, incense, incite, influence, inspire, interest, lobby, molest *(annoy)*, originate, perturb, prompt, provoke, spirit, stimulate

arouse desire motivate

arouse ire incense

arouse notice interest

arouse one's enthusiasm interest

arouse resentment incense, pique

arouse to action incite

arouser cannabis, stimulus

arousing moving *(evoking emotion)*, persuasive, provocative

arousing aversion repulsive

arraign blame, charge *(accuse)*, complain *(charge)*, denounce *(inform against)*, prosecute *(charge)*

arraigned accused *(charged)*

arraignment charge *(accusation)*, impeachment, presentment

arrange accommodate, adapt, adjust *(resolve)*, allocate, arbitrate *(adjudge)*, arbitrate *(conciliate)*, classify, codify, compile, compose, contrive, coordinate, devise *(invent)*, disentangle, dispose *(incline)*, distribute, edit, fix *(settle)*, form, formulate, frame *(formulate)*, frame *(prearrange)*, maneuver, marshal, orchestrate, pigeonhole, plan, plot, program, regulate *(adjust)*, scheme, settle, site, sort, stipulate, tabulate

arrange a settlement satisfy *(discharge)*

arrange beforehand prearrange

arrange by mutual concession compromise *(settle by mutual agreement)*

arrange differences mediate

arrange for negotiate

arrange for the services of engage *(hire)*

arrange for the use of engage *(hire)*

arrange in advance prearrange

arrange in succession continue *(prolong)*

arrange itself crystallize

arrange materials for publication compile

arrange matters settle

arrange matters in dispute settle

arrange methodically file *(arrange)*

arrange side by side juxtapose

arrange terms dicker

arranged agreed *(harmonized)*, agreed *(promised)*, consonant, contractual, fixed *(settled)*, harmonious, prospective, ready *(prepared)*, res judicata, stated, systematic

arranged within a small space compact *(dense)*

arrangement accommodation *(adjustment)*, accord, accordance *(compact)*, adjustment, agreement *(concurrence)*, agreement *(contract)*, allotment, array *(order)*, attornment, bargain, building *(business of assembling)*, case *(set of circumstances)*, classification, combination, compact, compilation, composition *(agreement in bankruptcy)*, composition *(makeup)*, conciliation, configuration *(form)*, contract, covenant, creation, deal, digest, disposition *(final arrangement)*, expedient, formation, hierarchy *(arrangement in a series)*, honorarium, indenture, lineup, method, motif, organization *(structure)*, pact, plan, policy *(contract)*, practice *(procedure)*, preparation, program, proposition, protocol *(agreement)*, provision *(act of supplying)*, register, regulation *(management)*, scheme, selection *(collection)*, sequence, settlement, situation, specialty *(contract)*, stipulation, strategy, structure *(composition)*, system, term *(provision)*, treatment, treaty, understanding *(agreement)*

arrangement for disposal disposition *(transfer of property)*

arrangement of difficulties settlement

arrangement of laws codification

arrangement of parts content *(structure)*

arrangement of rules codification

arrangement of statutes code, codification

arrangements dealings

arrangment course

arrant bad *(offensive)*, blameworthy, disreputable, egregious, flagrant, heinous, immoral, lawless, nefarious, notorious, outrageous, scandalous

array assemblage, band, chain *(series)*, clothe, composition *(makeup)*, conglomeration, disposition *(final arrangement)*, distribute, embellish, file *(arrange)*, fix *(arrange)*, form *(arrangement)*, formation, jury, marshal, order *(arrangement)*, selection *(collection)*, sequence, sort

arraying arrangement *(ordering)*

arrear default

arrearage arrears, debt, delinquency *(shortage)*

arrears debit, debt, deficit, delinquency *(shortage)*, due

arrest abeyance, apprehension *(act of arresting)*, avert, block, bondage, book, capture, cease, cessation *(interlude)*, check *(bar)*, check *(restrain)*, clog, cloture, commit *(institutionalize)*, confine, constrain *(imprison)*, constraint *(imprisonment)*, constrict *(inhibit)*, contain *(restrain)*, control *(restrain)*, curb, custody *(incarceration)*, debar, defer *(put off)*, delay, desist, desuetude, detain *(hold in custody)*, detain *(restrain)*, detention, discontinue *(abandon)*, discontinue *(break continuity)*, durance, forestall, halt, halt, hamper, hinder, hindrance, hold up *(delay)*, impede, incarceration, inhibit, interdict, interfere, interrupt, interruption, keep *(restrain)*, kill *(defeat)*, lock, obstacle, occlude, palliate *(abate)*, prevent, quit *(discontinue)*, restrain, restraint, seize *(apprehend)*, stall, stay *(halt)*, stem *(check)*, stifle, stop, strangle, suppress, suspend, toll *(stop)*

arrest temporarily continue *(adjourn)*, delay, hold up *(delay)*, postpone

arrest the attention occupy *(engage)*

arrest with authority seize *(apprehend)*

arresting moving *(evoking emotion)*, obviation, preventive, sapid

arrestment custody *(incarceration)*

arrêt arrest *(apprehend)*

arrhabo retainer

arrière pensée propaganda

arrival birth *(beginning)*, birth *(emergence of young)*, inflow

arrival into view appearance *(emergence)*

arrive emerge, enter *(go in)*, reach, report *(present oneself)*

arrive at attain, obtain

arrive at a conclusion arbitrate *(adjudge)*, ascertain, deduce, deduct *(conclude by reasoning)*, determine, find *(determine)*, fix *(settle)*, gauge, resolve *(decide)*

arrive at a decision resolve *(decide)*

arrive at a judgment decide

arrive at a price dicker

arrive at a settlement agree *(contract)*

arrive at a verdict find *(determine)*

arrive at an agreement close *(agree)*, coincide *(concur)*, concede, fix *(settle)*

arrive at an understanding coincide *(concur)*

arrive at terms coincide *(concur)*, conform

arrive at the end of finish

arrive at the truth solve

arriving future

arrogance contempt *(disdain)*, contumely, disdain, disrespect

arrogant brazen, contemptuous, cynical, dictatorial, disdainful, dogmatic, impertinent *(insolent)*, inflated *(vain)*, insolent, orgulous, presumptuous, pretentious *(pompous)*, proud *(conceited)*, supercilious

arrogate accroach, adopt, appropriate, assume *(seize)*, attach *(seize)*, collect *(recover money)*, condemn *(seize)*, demand, deprive, harass, hijack, impress *(procure by force)*, impropriate, infringe, invade, seize *(confiscate)*, sequester *(seize property)*, takeover, usurp

arrogate to oneself preempt

arrogated attached *(seized)*

arrogation assignation, assumption *(seizure)*, condemnation *(seizure)*, disseisin, distress *(seizure)*, infringement, misappropriation

arrondissement circuit

ars performance *(workmanship)*, stratagem, trade *(occupation)*

ars dicendi rhetoric *(skilled speech)*

ars ludicra histrionics

arsenal repository

arsonist lawbreaker

art performance *(workmanship)*, propensity, ruse, skill

art of composition rhetoric *(skilled speech)*

art of discourse rhetoric *(skilled speech)*

art of monetary relations finance

art of negotiating discretion *(quality of being discreet)*

art of prose rhetoric *(skilled speech)*

art of speaking declamation

art of war strategy

arterial causeway

arterial highway causeway

artery causeway, conduit *(channel)*, way *(channel)*

artful collusive, colorable *(specious)*, competent, delusive, devious, diplomatic, disingenuous, evasive, expert, insidious, machiavellian, mendacious, original *(creative)*, perspicacious, politic, practiced, resourceful, sly, stealthy, subtle *(refined)*, surreptitious, tactical

artful contrivance artifice, stratagem

artful dodge evasion, machination, maneuver *(trick)*

artful management discretion *(quality of being discreet)*

artfully contrived politic

artfulness artifice, discretion *(quality of being discreet)*, fraud, hypocrisy, improbity, knavery, performance *(workmanship)*, pettifoggery

article chapter *(division)*, clause, condition *(contingent provision)*, instrument *(tool)*, item, law, member *(constituent part)*, pandect *(treatise)*, particular, product, report *(detailed account)*, story *(narrative)*, subheading, title *(division)*

article of agreement provision *(clause)*, stipulation, term *(provision)*

article of belief principle *(axiom)*

article of commerce freight

article of faith dogma, principle *(axiom)*

article of merchandise product

article of trade product

articled indentured

articles commodities, merchandise, paraphernalia *(apparatus)*

articles of agreement contract

articles of commerce commodities, goods, merchandise, stock in trade

articles of merchandise commodities

articles of trade commodities

articulate avow, clarify, coherent *(clear)*, communicate, comprehensible, converse, convey *(communicate)*, eloquent, enunciate, express, lucid, observe *(remark)*, phrase, pronounce *(speak)*, recite, recount, remark, speak, unambiguous, utter

articulated nuncupative, oral

articulation conversation, expression *(comment)*, speech

artifex artisan

artifice bad faith, contrivance, deception, device *(contrivance)*, disguise, duplicity, evasion, expedient, false pretense, fraud, hoax, knavery, machination, maneuver *(trick)*, pettifoggery, ploy, ruse, stratagem, strategy, subterfuge, trap

artificer architect, artisan, contractor, materialman, practitioner

artificial bogus, deceptive, disingenuous, false *(not genuine)*, fictitious, histrionic, imitation, inflated *(bombastic)*, meretricious, orotund, pretentious *(ostentatious)*, specious, spurious, synthetic

artificial behavior for effect histrionics

artificial eloquence rhetoric *(insincere language)*

artificial entity corporation

artificial person corporation

artificiality artifice, false pretense, pretense *(ostentation)*

artificiosus artificial

artificium maneuver *(trick)*, performance *(workmanship)*, pursuit *(occupation)*, system

artillery fire barrage

artisan practitioner

artist practitioner

artistic aesthetic, artful, subtle *(refined)*

artistic effort creation

artistic judgment discretion *(quality of being discreet)*

artistry skill, specialty *(special aptitude)*, style

artless honest, inadept, inexperienced, ingenuous, natural, simple, straightforward, unaffected *(sincere)*, unpretentious

artless person philistine

artlessness honesty, veracity

as a body en masse

as a consequence a priori, consequently

as a favor gratis

as a group en masse

as a matter of course as a rule, con-

sequently

as a matter of fact de facto

as a matter of form pro forma

as a result consequently

as a result of a priori

as a rule generally, invariably

as a start ab initio

as a substitute for in lieu of

as a substitute for a parent loco parentis

as a unit en banc

as a whole en banc, en masse, in toto, wholly

as agreed to as agreed upon

as an alternative in lieu of

as an alternative for a parent loco parentis

as arranged by the agreement as agreed upon

as contained as so defined

as contained in the statutes as provided by law

as contracted for as agreed upon

as delineated as so defined

as explained as so defined

as far as until

as good as equivalent

as great as another coequal

as if quasi

as is a priori

as it is as is

as it stands as is

as matters stand consequently

as near as may be cy pres

as near as possible cy pres

as near as practicable cy pres

as negotiated for as agreed upon

as offered as is

as one en masse

as pledged as agreed upon

as presented as is

as promised as agreed upon

as proxy for in lieu of

as represented actual, as is, authentic, bona fide, honest, true *(authentic)*

as required duly

as required will shall

as seen as is

as set forth as so defined

as set forth by law as provided by law

as settled upon as agreed upon

as shown as is

as soon as can be reasonably expected forthwith

as soon as possible as soon as feasible

as soon as reasonably possible as soon as feasible

as specified as so defined

as specified in the law as provided by law

as the case may be consequently

as things are as is

as though quasi

as though it were quasi

as well also

ascend expand, progress

ascendance dominance, hegemony, influence, prestige

ascendancy advantage, dominance, dominion *(supreme authority)*, force *(strength)*, hegemony, influence, occupation *(possession)*, primacy, supremacy

ascendant ancestor, dominant, predominant, prevailing *(having superior* *force),* prevalent, primogenitor, prosperous

ascendants ancestry

ascendency predominance, prestige

ascent headway

ascertain assess *(appraise),* bear *(adduce),* decide, deduce, deduct *(conclude by reasoning),* determine, discern *(detect with the senses),* discover, distinguish, elucidate, ensure, establish *(show),* find *(determine),* find *(discover),* fix *(settle),* gauge, hold *(decide),* judge, notice *(observe),* prove, recognize *(perceive),* resolve *(decide),* rule *(decide),* settle, solve

ascertain a position locate

ascertain after reasoning arbitrate *(adjudge)*

ascertain and declare find *(determine)*

ascertain as truth prove

ascertain by judicial inquiry find *(determine)*

ascertain dimensions measure

ascertain liability liquidate *(determine liability)*

ascertain mathematically calculate

ascertain size measure

ascertain the amount of evaluate

ascertain the amount of indebtedness liquidate *(determine liability)*

ascertain the balance due liquidate *(determine liability)*

ascertain the meaning of construe *(comprehend)*

ascertain the time of date

ascertainable appreciable, cognizable, comprehensible, deductible *(provable),* perceptible, ponderable, provable, solvable

ascertained actual, axiomatic, certain *(positive),* certain *(specific),* clear *(certain),* cognizable, common *(customary),* conclusive *(determinative),* conclusive *(settled),* definite, definitive, factual, genuine, incontrovertible, indubious, positive *(incontestable),* real, stated

ascertained fact certification *(certainness),* certitude

ascertained principle conviction *(persuasion)*

ascertainment analysis, certification *(certainness),* collation, conclusion *(determination),* detection, determination, discovery, finding, holding *(ruling of a court),* identification, inspection, observation, opinion *(judicial decision),* perception, surety *(certainty)*

ascetic dispassionate, harsh, stoical

asceticism continence

ascribable derivative

ascribe acknowledge *(declare),* assign *(designate),* attribute, impute

ascribe blame incriminate

ascribe personal qualities to personify

ascribe to blame

ascribere ascribe, impute, inscribe

ascription accusation, arrogation, assignation, attribution, blame *(responsibility),* citation *(attribution),* condemnation *(blame),* reference *(citation)*

aseptic preventive

aside innuendo

aside from the point extraneous, inapposite, irrelevant

asinine fatuous, ludicrous, obtuse, opaque, puerile, unreasonable

asininity opacity

ask apply *(request),* call *(appeal to),* canvass, consult *(ask advice of),* demand, desire, inquire, investigate, pose *(propound),* solicit

ask advice consult *(ask advice of)*

ask an opinion consult *(ask advice of)*

ask earnestly canvass, pray, press *(beseech),* solicit

ask for call *(appeal to),* claim *(demand),* delve, desire, exact, move *(judicially request),* petition, request

ask for credit borrow

ask for recommendations consult *(ask advice of)*

ask for relief sue

ask for suggestions consult *(ask advice of)*

ask for with authority call *(demand),* demand

ask help of refer *(send for action)*

ask questions cross-examine

ask solemnly for invoke

ask to come call *(summon)*

ask urgently importune

asked for popular

asker petitioner

askew disordered, oblique *(slanted)*

asking inquiry *(systematic investigation),* precatory, question *(inquiry),* request

asking for what is due demand

asking price cost *(price)*

asking questions cross-examination

aslant oblique *(slanted)*

asleep dormant

asomatous incorporeal, intangible

aspect appearance *(look),* characteristic, complexion, component, condition *(state),* conduct, demeanor, deportment, detail, factor *(ingredient),* feature *(appearance),* feature *(characteristic),* ingredient, manner *(behavior),* outlook, particular, posture *(attitude),* presence *(poise),* property *(distinctive attribute),* semblance, side, standpoint, state *(condition),* style, technicality

aspects character *(personal quality),* color *(complexion)*

aspectus appearance *(look),* aspect

asper bitter *(acrid tasting)*

asperity rigor, severity

aspernari disdain, spurn

asperse brand *(stigmatize),* complain *(criticize),* condemn *(blame),* contemn, defame, denigrate, denounce *(condemn),* deprecate, derogate, discommend, discredit, dishonor *(deprive of honor),* disparage, libel, malign, pillory, reprimand, reproach, smear, sully, tarnish

aspersion bad repute, contempt *(disdain),* contumely, conviction *(finding of guilt),* criticism, defamation, denunciation, disapprobation, discredit, dishonor *(shame),* disparagement, imprecation, infamy, innuendo, insinuation, libel, obloquy, phillipic, revilement, scandal, shame, slander, stricture

aspersive libelous

aspirant amateur, applicant *(candidate),* candidate, contender, novice, rival, special interest

aspiration desideratum, design *(intent),* desire, destination, end *(intent),* goal, objective, purpose, target, will *(desire)*

aspire desire, endeavor, strive, try *(attempt)*

aspire to intend, pursue *(strive to gain)*

aspirer candidate

aspiring eager, solicitous

assail accost, ambush, assault, attack, badger, censure, complain *(criticize),* confront *(oppose),* defame, denounce *(condemn),* despoil, engage *(involve),* fight *(battle),* harass, harrow, harry *(plunder),* impugn, invade, lash *(attack verbally),* maltreat, mishandle *(maltreat),* mistreat, persecute, resist *(oppose),* strike *(assault)*

assail by argument impugn

assail with censure condemn *(blame),* denounce *(condemn)*

assailability danger

assailable dangerous, destructible, inadequate, indefensible, penetrable, vulnerable

assailant aggressor, disputant, foe, offender, offensive *(taking the initiative)*

assailer aggressor, assailant

assailing offensive *(taking the initiative)*

assailment assault, onset *(assault)*

assassinate dispatch *(put to death),* extinguish, kill *(murder),* slay

assassination aberemurder, dispatch *(act of putting to death),* homicide, killing, murder

assault accost, ambush, assail, attack, barrage, battery, belligerency, denounce *(condemn),* fight *(battle),* fight *(battle),* incursion, invade, invasion, mishandle *(maltreat),* mistreat, molest *(subject to indecent advances),* offense, oppugn, outbreak, rape, resist *(oppose),* resistance, violence

assault belligerently accost, assail, assault

assaulter aggressor, assailant

assaulting hostile

assay analysis, attempt, diagnosis, endeavor, experiment, inquiry *(systematic investigation)*

assemblage agglomeration, aggregate

assemblage assemblage

assemblage assembly, body *(collection),* caucus, coalescence, collection *(assembly),* combination, compilation, congregation, congress, consolidation, corpus, cumulation, distribution *(arrangement),* entirety, joinder, manufacture, mass *(body of persons),* selection *(collection),* whole

assemble accumulate *(amass),* aggregate, attach *(join),* build *(construct),* call *(summon),* codify, collect *(gather),* commingle, compile, concentrate *(consolidate),* congregate, conjoin, connect *(join together),* convene, converge, federate, form, garner, glean, join *(bring together),* make, manufacture, meet, orchestrate, produce *(manufacture),* raise *(collect),* rendezvous, store, unite

assemble and apportion assets liquidate *(determine liability)*

assemble by summons call *(sum-*

mon)

assemble parts fabricate (construct)
assemble the facts document
assembled coadunate, collective, composite, conglomerate
assembled body company (assemblage)
assemblée caucus, chamber (body), company (assemblage)
assembling building (business of assembling), centralization
assembly aggregate, assemblage, caucus, chamber (body), company (assemblage), conference, conglomeration, congregation, congress, cumulation, legislature, manufacture, meeting (conference), parley, rendezvous, selection (collection), session
assembly of persons congregation
assemblyman lawmaker
assemblywoman lawmaker
assent abide, accede (concede), acceptance, accordance (understanding), acknowledgment (acceptance), acquiescence, admit (concede), affirmance (judicial sanction), agree (comply), agreement (concurrence), allow (endure), approval, bear (adduce), capitulation, certify (approve), charter (sanction), coincide (concur), compliance, concede, concession (compromise), concordance, confirm, confirmation, conformity (agreement), consent, consent, corroborate, defer (yield in judgment), deference, franchise (license), grant (concede), indorsement, leave (permission), let (permit), obey, pass (approve), permission, permit, ratification, sanction (permission), stipulate, subscribe (promise), subscription, suffer (permit), vouchsafe, yield (submit)
assent to approve, authorize, certify (approve), comply, concur (agree), countenance, indorse, sanction, sustain (confirm)
assented consensual
assentient consenting
assenting concerted, concordant, concurrent (united), congruous, consenting, favorable (expressing approval), harmonious, inclined, pliable, ready (willing), willing (desirous)
assentive concordant, consenting
assererate vouch
assert acknowledge (declare), adduce, advocate, affirm (claim), allege, annunciate, argue, attest, avouch (avow), avow, bear (adduce), cast (register), certify (attest), claim (maintain), comment, communicate, contend (maintain), convey (communicate), declare, enunciate, express, mention, observe (remark), plead (allege in a legal action), pose (propound), posit, proclaim, profess (avow), promise (vow), pronounce (speak), remark, signify (inform), testify, uphold, utter
assert a right to call (demand), demand
assert absolutely bear (adduce)
assert an oath promise (vow)
assert as one's own claim (demand)
assert as one's right claim (demand)
assert as true swear
assert formally certify (attest), issue (publish), plead (allege in a legal ac-

tion)

assert in court litigate
assert incorrectly misrepresent
assert on oath avow
assert one's rights demand
assert oneself certify (attest), constrain (compel)
assert peremptorily avouch (avow), avow
assert positively avouch (avow), certify (attest), plead (allege in a legal action), promise (vow)
assert solemnly pledge (promise the performance of), promise (vow)
assert the contrary contradict
assert the opposite contradict
assert under oath avouch (avow), avow, certify (attest), promise (vow)
assertative declaratory
asserted alleged
asserted formally alleged
asserter claimant
asserting the contrary contradictory
asserting the opposite contradictory
assertion accusation, acknowledgment (avowal), admission (disclosure), affirmance (authentication), affirmation, allegation, asseveration, attestation, averment, avouchment, avowal, comment, confession, confirmation, count, declaration, dictum, disclosure (act of disclosing), disclosure (something disclosed), expression (comment), hypothesis, mention (reference), observation, plea, postulate, principle (axiom), profession (declaration), pronouncement, proposition, remark, statement, testimony
assertion against the plaintiff counterclaim
assertion of facts representation (statement)
assertion of legal right demand
assertion of the contrary contradiction
assertion of the opposite contradiction
assertions premises (hypotheses)
assertive certain (positive), compelling, declaratory, dogmatic, insistent, peremptory (imperative)
assertment averment
assertory dogmatic
assertory oath affidavit, affirmance (legal affirmation), affirmation, averment
assess arbitrate (adjudge), calculate, consider, criticize (evaluate), encumber (financially obligate), evaluate, exact, excise (levy a tax), gauge, judge, levy, measure, mete, notice (observe), rate, require (compel), tax (levy)
assess a tax upon charge (assess)
assess pro rata charge (assess), prorate
assess proportionally prorate
assessable ad valorem, appreciable, determinable (ascertainable)
assessment account (evaluation), ad valorem, appraisal, appreciation (perception), arbitration, charge (cost), choice (decision), computation, concept, conclusion (determination), cost (price), determination, discretion (power of choice), discrimination (differentiation), duty (tax), estimate (approximate cost),

estimation (calculation), excise, expense (cost), idea, inspection, judgment (discernment), judgment (formal court decree), levy, measurement, opinion (judicial decision), perception, rate, rating, rent, tariff (duties), tax, toll (tax), value, verdict
assessment of damages additur
assessor judge, juror, magistrate
assessor of liability and damages juror
assessors jury
asset advantage, chattel, holding (property owned), item, possession (property), resource, share (stock)
assets capital, commodities, effects, estate (property), fund, goods, interest (ownership), means (funds), merchandise, money, paraphernalia (personal belongings), personalty, possessions, principal (capital sum), property (possessions), reserve, securities, security (stock), stock (shares), store (depository), substance (material possessions)
assets and liabilities estate (property)
assets in hand principal (capital sum)
assever assert
asseverate acknowledge (declare), affirm (claim), affirm (declare solemnly), allege, assert, assure (insure), avouch (avow), avow, bear (adduce), certify (attest), claim (maintain), contend (maintain), declare, depose (testify), enunciate, express, posit, proclaim, profess (avow), promise (vow), remark, testify, utter, verify (swear)
asseverated alleged
asseveration acknowledgment (avowal), affirmance (legal affirmation), affirmation, assertion, attestation, averment, avouchment, avowal, claim (assertion), expression (comment), jurat, oath, promise, pronouncement, representation (statement), statement, surety (certainty), testimony, vow
assidous pertinacious
assiduity diligence (perseverance), effort, endeavor, industry (activity), interest (concern)
assiduous active, circumspect, close (rigorous), conscientious, diligent, eager, earnest, faithful (diligent), industrious, meticulous, painstaking, patient, persistent, relentless, sedulous, serious (devoted), steadfast, thorough, true (loyal), unremitting, zealous
assiduousness diligence (perseverance), effort, industry (activity)
assign abalienate, adduce, alienate (transfer title), allocate, allot, appoint, apportion, ascribe, attorn, attribute, authorize, bear (yield), cede, charge (assess), charge (empower), commit (entrust), contribute (supply), convey (transfer), delegate, demarcate, designate, devise (give), devote, direct (supervise), disburse (distribute), dispense, disperse (disseminate), distribute, divide (distribute), dole, employ (engage services), empower, endue, entrust, expend (disburse), give (grant), grant (transfer formally), impute, induct, leave (give), marshal, mete, nominate, parcel, refer (direct attention), refer

(send for action), relegate, select, site, split, transfer

assign a duty delegate

assign a meaning to construe *(translate)*, explain

assign a time to date

assign again reassign

assign dower bequeath

assign one's share to charge *(assess)*

assign places to distribute, file *(arrange)*, fix *(arrange)*, sort, tabulate

assign power of attorney to delegate

assign the care of entrust

assign the parts orchestrate

assign to blame, consign

assign to a place locate

assign to a position delegate, hire

assign to an earlier date antedate

assign to battle stations deploy

assign to lodgings lodge *(house)*

assign to positions deploy

assignable heritable, negotiable

assignable rights of action intangible

assignation alienation *(transfer of title)*, arrogation, assignment *(allotment)*, assignment *(transfer of ownership)*, attribution, blame *(responsibility)*, consignment, conveyance, incrimination, reference *(citation)*, rendezvous

assignation of title feoffment

assigned certain *(specific)*, positive *(prescribed)*

assigned task office, province

assigned time date

assignee deputy, feoffee, licensee, payee, receiver, recipient, transferee

assignee in fact licensee

assigning designation *(naming)*

assigning by lot disbursement *(act of disbursing)*

assignment activity, agency *(legal relationship)*, alienation *(transfer of title)*, allotment, appointment *(act of designating)*, apportionment, arrogation, assignation, attribution, blame *(responsibility)*, burden, capacity *(job)*, cession, charge *(responsibility)*, citation *(attribution)*, classification, commitment *(responsibility)*, consignment, conveyance, deed, department, deputation *(selection of delegates)*, designation *(naming)*, devolution, dispensation *(act of dispensing)*, disposition *(transfer of property)*, distribution *(apportionment)*, duty *(obligation)*, employment, function, job, labor *(work)*, mission, nomination, position *(business status)*, project, province, quota, ration, reference *(citation)*, role, selection *(choice)*, specification, trade *(occupation)*, work *(employment)*

assignment by share allotment

assignment in proportion apportionment

assignment of cause hypothesis

assignment of paternity filiation

assignor contributor *(giver)*, donor, feoffor, grantor, licensor, transferor

assimilate adopt, comprehend *(understand)*, conceive *(comprehend)*, conform, construe *(comprehend)*, coordinate, desegregate, digest *(comprehend)*, naturalize *(acclimate)*, naturalize *(make a citizen)*, realize *(understand)*, understand, unite

assimilated compound, conjoint

assimilation adoption *(acceptance)*, conformity *(obedience)*, incorporation *(blend)*, merger, osmosis, understanding *(comprehension)*

assist abet, accommodate, aid, avail *(be of use)*, bear *(support)*, conduce, contribute *(assist)*, countenance, enable, espouse, expedite, facilitate, favor, finance, foster, help, help, indorse, inure *(benefit)*, lend, maintain *(sustain)*, nurture, pander, profit, promote *(organize)*, relieve *(give aid)*, remedy, serve *(assist)*, side, subsidize, support *(assistance)*, uphold

assist a judge clerk

assist in accomplishing a purpose avail *(be of use)*

assist substantially contribute *(assist)*

assist the progress facilitate

assistance accommodation *(backing)*, advantage, advocacy, aid *(help)*, auspices, behalf, benefit *(betterment)*, benevolence *(act of kindness)*, charity, consortium *(marriage companionship)*, contribution *(donation)*, contribution *(participation)*, endowment, favor *(sanction)*, help, largess *(generosity)*, largess *(gift)*, loan, maintenance *(support of spouse)*, panacea, patronage *(power to appoint jobs)*, patronage *(support)*, promotion *(encouragement)*, reinforcement, relief *(aid)*, remedy *(legal means of redress)*, remedy *(that which corrects)*, support *(assistance)*

assistant abettor, accessory, accomplice, affiliate, agent, ancillary *(auxiliary)*, associate, clerical, coactor, coadjutant, coconspirator, cohort, colleague, confederate, consociate, conspirer, contributor *(contributor)*, copartner *(coconspirator)*, employee, good samaritan, participant, partner, plenipotentiary, procurator, subsidiary

assistants personnel, staff

assister backer, benefactor, good samaritan, samaritan

assisting clerical, contributory, instrumental, practical, profitable

assize bar *(court)*, forum *(court)*

associate abettor, accomplice, affiliate, affiliate, appertain, assistant, chapter *(branch)*, coactor, coadjutant, cohort, colleague, combine *(act in concert)*, commingle, confederate, connect *(relate)*, consociate, consort, conspire, conspirer, constituent *(member)*, contributor *(contributor)*, cooperate, copartner *(business associate)*, copartner *(coconspirator)*, corporation, correlate, desegregate, engage *(involve)*, federalize *(associate)*, federate, implicate, involve *(implicate)*, involve *(participate)*, join *(associate oneself with)*, meet, member *(individual in a group)*, merge, organ, organize *(unionize)*, participant, participate, partner, peer, pool, relate *(establish a connection)*, unite

associate in crime accomplice, coconspirator

associate in guilt accomplice, coconspirator

associate with accompany, espouse

associated affiliated, akin *(germane)*, allied, analogous, apposite, coadunate,

cognate, collateral *(accompanying)*, collective, comparable *(capable of comparison)*, compound, concomitant, concurrent *(at the same time)*, conjoint, corporate *(joint)*, correlative, federal, germane, incident, incidental, interested, interrelated, joint, pertinent, related, relative *(relevant)*, relevant, tangential

associated with intimate

associates constituency, staff

associating concurrent *(united)*

association adhesion *(loyalty)*, affiliation *(amalgamation)*, affiliation *(connectedness)*, assemblage, attribution, band, cartel, centralization, chain *(nexus)*, coaction, coalescence, coalition, collection *(assembly)*, collusion, committee, company *(enterprise)*, comparison, complex *(development)*, confederacy *(compact)*, conformity *(obedience)*, congregation, conjunction, connection *(relation)*, connivance, consolidation, consortium *(business cartel)*, consortium *(marriage companionship)*, contribution *(participation)*, cooperative, corporation, denomination, federation, firm, foundation *(organization)*, incorporation *(formation of a business entity)*, institute, integration *(amalgamation)*, integration *(assimilation)*, kinship, league, merger, nexus, partnership, party *(political organization)*, profession *(vocation)*, propinquity *(kinship)*, relation *(connection)*, relationship *(connection)*, relevance, society, sodality, syndicate, trust *(combination of businesses)*, union *(labor organization)*

associative apposite, correlative, pertinent

assoil condone, palliate *(excuse)*, remit *(release from penalty)*

assonance accordance *(understanding)*, consensus

assonant concurrent *(united)*

assort allocate, apportion, classify, codify, distribute, fix *(arrange)*, organize *(arrange)*, pigeonhole, sort, vary

assorted composite, diverse, heterogeneous, manifold, miscellaneous, multiple, several *(plural)*

assortment class, classification, conglomeration, diversification, diversity, melange, selection *(collection)*

assuage allay, alleviate, diminish, disarm *(set at ease)*, lessen, lull, meliorate, mitigate, moderate *(temper)*, modify *(moderate)*, mollify, obtund, pacify, palliate *(abate)*, placate, relax, relieve *(free from burden)*, remedy, remit *(relax)*, soothe

assuagement mitigation, moderation, mollification, relief *(release)*, remission

assuager cure

assuaging mitigating, narcotic, palliative *(abating)*

assuasive medicinal, narcotic, palliative *(abating)*, remedial

assuasive drug narcotic

assumable constructive *(inferential)*, ostensible

assume accede *(succeed)*, accroach, acquire *(secure)*, adopt, annex *(arrogate)*, anticipate *(expect)*, appropriate, collect *(recover money)*, condemn *(seize)*, confiscate, copy, deduce, deduct *(conclude by reasoning)*, deem, embrace *(accept)*,

endeavor, expect *(consider probable)*, forejudge, gain, generalize, guess, impropriate, incur, occupy *(take possession)*, opine, posit, postulate, preconceive, preempt, presume, presuppose, pretend, receive *(acquire)*, seize *(confiscate)*, speculate *(conjecture)*, surmise, suspect *(think)*, takeover, trust, undertake, usurp
assume a character impersonate
assume a fighting attitude defy
assume a lofty bearing patronize *(condescend toward)*
assume a mask camouflage
assume a patronizing air condescend *(patronize)*
assume a pattern crystallize
assume a risk speculate *(chance)*, underwrite
assume authority federalize *(place under federal control)*, hold *(possess)*
assume command govern, hijack, hold *(possess)*, preside, usurp
assume definite characteristics crystallize
assume for public use eminent domain
assume ownership acquire *(secure)*, annex *(arrogate)*, appropriate, condemn *(seize)*, distrain, impropriate, occupy *(take possession)*, possess, purchase
assume responsibility conduct, guarantee, operate
assume responsibility for avouch *(guarantee)*
assume the appearance of mock *(imitate)*
assume the character of pose *(impersonate)*
assume the offensive attack, fight *(battle)*
assume the role of pose *(impersonate)*
assume unlawful rights of ownership convert *(misappropriate)*
assume without authority usurp
assumed artificial, false *(not genuine)*, hypothetical, implied, ostensible, presumptive, purported, putative, specious, tacit, theoretical
assumed position platform
assumed positions premises *(hypotheses)*
assumed truth postulate
assumedly reputedly
assuming brazen, impertinent *(insolent)*, insolent, obtrusive, orgulous, presumptuous, proud *(conceited)*
assuming different forms protean
assuming ownership disseisin
assuming that provided
assumption acquisition, adoption *(acceptance)*, adverse possession, appropriation *(taking)*, arrogation, basis, concept, condemnation *(seizure)*, conjecture, conviction *(persuasion)*, deduction *(conclusion)*, distress *(seizure)*, estimate *(idea)*, estimation *(calculation)*, generalization, ground, hypothesis, inference, opinion *(belief)*, postulate, preconception, presumption, prolepsis, proposition, receipt *(act of receiving)*, receipt *(voucher)*, speculation *(conjecture)*, supposition, theory
assumptive apparent *(presumptive)*, presumptive, speculative, supercilious

assumptively reputedly
assurance acceptance, accommodation *(backing)*, affirmance *(authentication)*, approval, avouchment, bail, belief *(state of mind)*, binder, bond, certainty, certification *(attested copy)*, certification *(certainness)*, certitude, commitment *(responsibility)*, confidence *(faith)*, confirmation, consent, contract, conviction *(persuasion)*, corroboration, coverage *(insurance)*, credence, expectation, faith, guaranty, license, mainstay, pact, pledge *(binding promise)*, principle *(axiom)*, profession *(declaration)*, promise, proof, prospect *(outlook)*, recognizance, reference *(recommendation)*, reliance, safeguard, security *(safety)*, surety *(certainty)*, trust *(confidence)*, undertaking *(pledge)*, vow, warrant *(guaranty)*, warranty
assurance against loss indemnity, insurance
assurance of secrecy confidence *(relation of trust)*
assure avouch *(guarantee)*, bear *(adduce)*, bond *(secure a debt)*, certify *(attest)*, contend *(maintain)*, convince, corroborate, cosign, declare, disarm *(set at ease)*, ensure, guarantee, pledge *(promise the performance of)*, profess *(avow)*, promise *(vow)*, sponsor, swear, underwrite, verify *(confirm)*, vouch
assure again reassure
assure oneself ascertain
assured agreed *(promised)*, alleged, axiomatic, categorical, certain *(fixed)*, certain *(positive)*, conclusive *(determinative)*, convincing, credible, decisive, definite, demonstrable, dependable, dogmatic, incontrovertible, indubious, inevitable, infallible, official, positive *(confident)*, reliable, sanguine, secure *(confident)*, solid *(sound)*, undisputed
assured belief conviction *(persuasion)*
assured expectation faith
assuredly admittedly
assuredness assurance, belief *(state of mind)*, certainty, certification *(certainness)*, certitude, reliance, surety *(certainty)*
assurer insurer
assuring convincing
assymetrical disproportionate
asthenic languid, nonsubstantial *(not sturdy)*, powerless
astir conscious *(awake)*
astonish confound, confuse *(bewilder)*, overcome *(overwhelm)*, overwhelm
astonished speechless
astonishing moving *(evoking emotion)*, notable, noteworthy, peculiar *(curious)*, portentous *(eliciting amazement)*, prodigious *(amazing)*, remarkable, special, unaccustomed, uncanny, unexpected, unusual
astonishing thing phenomenon *(unusual occurrence)*
astonishment bombshell, phenomenon *(unusual occurrence)*, surprise
astound confound, discommode, discompose, disconcert, impress *(affect deeply)*
astounding ineffable, noteworthy, prodigious *(amazing)*, remarkable, special, unusual
astoundment surprise

astral stellar
astray errant, lost *(disoriented)*, peccant *(culpable)*
astrict clog, constrict *(inhibit)*, debar, disadvantage, restrict
astriction constraint *(restriction)*
astringe constrict *(compress)*
astringent bitter *(penetrating)*, caustic, harsh, particular *(exacting)*, severe
astronomical prodigious *(enormous)*
astute acute, artful, circumspect, cognizant, discreet, discriminating *(judicious)*, judicious, knowing, perceptive, perspicacious, politic, profound *(esoteric)*, sapient, sensible, sensitive *(discerning)*, sly, subtle *(refined)*
astuteness common sense, insight, intelligence *(intellect)*, judgment *(discernment)*, perception, sagacity, sense *(intelligence)*
astutus artful, politic, sly, tactical
asunder apart, disconnected, discrete, disperse *(scatter)*, separate
asylum bulwark, haven, lodging, protection, refuge, security *(safety)*
asylum shelter *(protection)*
asymmetric irregular *(not usual)*
asymmetrical dissimilar, irregular *(not usual)*
asymmetry difference, discrepancy, disparity, inequality, irregularity
at a fixed interval per annum
at a fixed time hereafter *(eventually)*
at a great distance remote *(not proximate)*
at a later period ex post facto, thereafter
at a later time ex post facto
at a premium scarce
at a subsequent period ex post facto
at a succeeding time ex post facto
at all whatever
at all times always *(forever)*
at an end complete *(ended)*
at any rate regardless
at close quarters contiguous, present *(attendant)*
at cross purposes contra, contrary, discordant
at cross-purposes antipathetic *(oppositional)*, dissenting
at ease complacent
at fault blameful, blameworthy, culpable, delinquent *(guilty of a misdeed)*, errant, guilty
at first ab initio
at first glance prima facie *(self-evident)*
at first sight prima facie *(self-evident)*
at first view prima facie *(self-evident)*
at hand available, close *(near)*, forthcoming, immediate *(imminent)*, immediate *(not distant)*, imminent, inevitable, pending *(imminent)*, present *(attendant)*, present *(current)*, proximate, ready *(prepared)*
at home household *(domestic)*
at issue arguable, competitive *(antagonistic)*, contestable, contrary, controversial, debatable, disputable, dissenting, doubtful
at large free *(not restricted)*
at least only
at liberty autonomous *(self governing)*, clear *(free from criminal charges)*, exempt, free *(not restricted)*, sovereign

(independent)

at loggerheads dissenting

at no period sine die

at no time sine die

at odds contradictory, controversial, disproportionate, dissenting, hostile, incongruous, repugnant *(incompatible)*

at odds with dissident, negative, nonconforming

at once forthwith, instant, instantly

at one concordant, consonant

at one with consensual

at one's disposal available

at one's end in extremis

at one's own risk caveat emptor

at other times known as alias

at peace placid

at peril at risk

at rest dead, dormant, lifeless *(dead)*

at sight prima facie *(self-evident)*

at the beginning ab initio

at the conclusion of life in extremis

at the edge extreme *(last)*

at the first opportunity as soon as feasible

at the first possible moment as soon as feasible

at the last stage in extremis

at the mercy of subject *(exposed)*

at the point of death in extremis

at the present time instant

at the same instant concurrent *(at the same time)*

at the same time ad interim, coincidental, en masse, simultaneous

at the start ab initio

at the termination of life in extremis

at the utmost point extreme *(last)*

at the very least only

at the wrong time inopportune

at this moment instant, present *(current)*

at this time present *(current)*

at variance adverse *(opposite)*, competitive *(antagonistic)*, contradictory, contrary, controversial, discordant, disproportionate, dissenting, hostile, inapplicable, inapposite, inapt, incommensurate, incongruous, inconsistent, inept *(inappropriate)*, inimical, irreconcilable, litigious, repugnant *(incompatible)*

at variance with dissident, nonconforming

at variance with the facts ludicrous

at war with inimical

at whatever time whenever

at which time whenever

at work active, effective *(operative)*, operative

atavistic genetic, regressive

athirst eager, hot-blooded

athwart contra

atmosphere climate, environment

atomization dissolution *(disintegration)*

atomize dissolve *(disperse)*

atone compensate *(counterbalance)*, redeem *(satisfy debts)*, redress, restore *(return)*

atone for repent

atonement compensation, expiation, reparation *(indemnification)*, restitution, retribution, trover

atoning compensatory, penitent, repentant

atrabilious deplorable, disconsolate

atrocious arrant *(onerous)*, bad *(offensive)*, brutal, contemptible, cruel, deplorable, disgraceful, gross *(flagrant)*, heinous, inexcusable, iniquitous, loathsome, malignant, outrageous, ruthless, scandalous, vicious

atrocious crime atrocity

atrocitas atrocity

atrocity abuse *(physical misuse)*, cruelty, delinquency *(misconduct)*, misdeed, vice, wrong

atrophy decay, decline, degenerate, depreciate, deteriorate, deterioration, detriment, dissolution *(disintegration)*

attach abridge *(divest)*, abut, adhere *(fasten)*, affiliate, affix, annex *(add)*, append, ascribe, bond *(hold together)*, border *(bound)*, cement, cohere *(adhere)*, combine *(join together)*, condemn *(seize)*, confiscate, conjoin, connect *(join together)*, contact *(touch)*, deprive, distrain, divest, fix *(make firm)*, garnish, impound, impress *(procure by force)*, impute, join *(bring together)*, levy, lock, sequester *(seize property)*

attach a legal signature notarize

attach little importance to minimize

attach oneself to adopt

attach too much importance to overestimate

attache employee

attached addicted, appurtenant, cohesive *(sticking)*, conjoint, inextricable, inseparable, proximate

attached to another jurisdiction foreign

attaching attachment *(act of affixing)*, confiscatory

attachment accession *(annexation)*, addendum, addition, additive, adherence *(adhesion)*, adherence *(devotion)*, adhesion *(affixing)*, adhesion *(loyalty)*, adjoiner, affection, affinity *(regard)*, allegiance, allonge, appendix *(accession)*, appendix *(supplement)*, appliance, appurtenance, arrogation, boom *(increase)*, chain *(nexus)*, coalescence, codicil, coherence, connection *(fastening)*, consortium *(marriage companionship)*, disseisin, distraint, distress *(seizure)*, expropriation *(divestiture)*, favor *(partiality)*, favoritism, levy, loyalty, nexus, partiality, penchant, predilection, predisposition, privation, privity, regard *(esteem)*, rider, sequestration

attachment to adoption *(acceptance)*

attachment to realty fixture

attachments paraphernalia *(apparatus)*, ties

attack accost, accuse, ambush, assail, assault, assault, bait *(harass)*, barrage, battery, beat *(strike)*, belligerency, cavil, censure, charge *(accusation)*, charge *(accuse)*, condemn *(blame)*, condemnation *(blame)*, controvert, course, denigrate, denounce *(condemn)*, despoil, discommend, disease, engage *(involve)*, fault, fight *(battle)*, fight *(battle)*, foray, grapple, harm, harry *(plunder)*, impeach, impeachment, impinge, impugn, impugnation, incursion, intrusion, invade, invasion, inveigh, malign, mistreat, molest *(subject to indecent advances)*, object, offense, onset *(assault)*, oppugn, outbreak, outburst, persecute,

protest, resistance, smear, spoliation, strike *(assault)*, violence

attack by words impugn

attack from a concealed position ambush

attack on rights invasion

attack physically assault

attack the reputation of malign

attackable penetrable

attacked accused *(attacked)*

attacker aggressor, assailant, foe

attacking negative, offensive *(taking the initiative)*

attain accede *(succeed)*, accomplish, acquire *(secure)*, carry *(succeed)*, consummate, discharge *(perform)*, dispatch *(dispose of)*, earn, effectuate, execute *(accomplish)*, gain, make, obtain, operate, pass *(satisfy requirements)*, procure, reach, realize *(obtain as a profit)*, reap, recover

attain by effort find *(discover)*

attain majority mature

attain maturity mature

attain the goal consummate

attainability chance *(possibility)*, feasibility, possibility

attainable available, facile, open *(accessible)*, possible, potential, practicable, public *(open)*, vulnerable

attainment accession *(enlargement)*, acquisition, adverse possession, boom *(prosperity)*, caliber *(mental capacity)*, commission *(act)*, development *(outgrowth)*, discharge *(performance)*, edification, end *(termination)*, fait accompli, fruition, outcome, performance *(execution)*, performance *(workmanship)*, realization, receipt *(act of receiving)*, satisfaction *(fulfilment)*

attaint bad repute, brand *(stigmatize)*, convict, denigrate, discredit, disgrace, disgrace, dishonor *(shame)*, dishonor *(deprive of honor)*, ignominy, impeach, notoriety, opprobrium, pillory, scandal, shame, smear, stain, sully

attemper adjust *(regulate)*, assuage, attune, check *(restrain)*, denature, extenuate, moderate *(temper)*, mollify, palliate *(abate)*, qualify *(condition)*, remit *(relax)*, soothe

attempt assume *(undertake)*, conatus, effort, endeavor, endeavor, enterprise *(undertaking)*, experiment, project, pursue *(strive to gain)*, pursuit *(effort to secure)*, strive, struggle, trial *(experiment)*, undertake, undertaking *(enterprise)*, venture, work *(effort)*

attempt strenuously endeavor

attempt to disprove debate

attempt to divert dissuade, expostulate

attempt to equal competition

attempt to obstruct legislation filibuster

attempt to prevent dissuade

attempt violence to assault

attend care *(regard)*, concentrate *(pay attention)*, concern *(care)*, devote, focus, immerse *(engross)*, maintain *(sustain)*, monitor, note *(notice)*, observe *(obey)*, observe *(watch)*, overhear, pander, patrol, protect, regard *(pay attention)*, remedy, report *(present oneself)*, serve *(assist)*, study, treat *(process)*

attend as consequence ensue

attend minutely concentrate *(pay attention)*, focus

attend to assume *(undertake)*, care *(regard)*, concern *(care)*, hear *(give attention to)*, heed, notice *(observe)*, obey, oversee, preserve

attend to business labor

attend to instructions conform

attend to orders comply, obey

attendance service *(assistance)*

attendant ancillary *(auxiliary)*, caretaker *(one caring for property)*, clerical, coactor, coadjutant, cohort, collateral *(accompanying)*, colleague, concomitant, concurrent *(at the same time)*, consociate, copartner *(coconspirator)*, guardian, incidental, ministerial, participant, party *(participant)*, present *(current)*, supplementary, tangential

attendant conditions circumstances

attended by obstacles difficult

attended with death deadly

attended with risk dangerous

attending circumspect, clerical, concomitant, concurrent *(at the same time)*, ministerial

attention adhesion *(loyalty)*, caution *(vigilance)*, concern *(interest)*, consideration *(contemplation)*, contemplation, diligence *(care)*, discretion *(quality of being discreet)*, emphasis, homage, industry *(activity)*, interest *(concern)*, notice *(heed)*, observation, perception, precaution, prudence, recognition, relief *(aid)*, respect, scrutiny, stress *(accent)*

attention to detail diligence *(care)*, interest *(concern)*

attentive alert *(vigilant)*, careful, circumspect, close *(rigorous)*, conscientious, conscious *(aware)*, deliberate, diligent, faithful *(diligent)*, guarded, meticulous, obedient, painstaking, particular *(exacting)*, pensive, punctilious, punctual, sedulous, sensitive *(discerning)*, vigilant, zealous

attentive to detail particular *(exacting)*

attentiveness caution *(vigilance)*, comprehension, consideration *(contemplation)*, consideration *(sympathetic regard)*, notice *(heed)*, observation, preoccupation, regard *(attention)*, sensibility

attentuate deduct *(reduce)*, sustain *(prolong)*

attentus careful, economical, intent

attenuare attenuate

attenuate alleviate, decrease, depreciate, dilute, disarm *(divest of arms)*, discount *(minimize)*, extenuate, lessen, minimize, reduce

attenuated deficient, impalpable, narrow, nonsubstantial *(not sturdy)*, tenuous

attenuation decrease, deduction *(diminution)*, mitigation

attest affirm *(declare solemnly)*, affirmation, allege, assert, assure *(insure)*, attestation, averment, avouch *(avow)*, avouchment, avow, bear *(adduce)*, bespeak, certify *(attest)*, cite *(state)*, claim *(maintain)*, confirm, contend *(maintain)*, corroborate, depose *(testify)*, endorse, establish *(show)*, evidence, manifest, posit, profess *(avow)*, promise *(vow)*, seal *(solemnize)*, subscribe *(sign)*, substantiate, support *(corroborate)*, sus-

tain *(confirm)*, testify, validate, verify *(confirm)*, verify *(swear)*, vouch

attest to acknowledge *(declare)*, converse, notarize, plead *(allege in a legal action)*

attestable convincing

attestant affiant, affirmant, bystander, deponent, eyewitness, indicator, undersigned, witness

attestation adjuration, admission *(disclosure)*, affirmance *(authentication)*, affirmance *(legal affirmation)*, affirmation, assertion, asseveration, assurance, averment, avouchment, avowal, certificate, certification *(attested copy)*, certitude, confirmation, corroboration, declaration, jurat, oath, pledge *(binding promise)*, profession *(declaration)*, proof, record, reference *(recommendation)*, stamp, support *(corroboration)*, testimony

attestator affirmant, deponent

attested agreed *(promised)*, authentic, certain *(fixed)*, certain *(positive)*, definite, documentary, factual, indubious, official, valid

attested statement affidavit

attester affiant, affirmant, bystander, deponent, eyewitness, indicator, surety *(guarantor)*, undersigned

attesting declaration attestation, certification *(attested copy)*, reference *(recommendation)*

attesting statement jurat

attestor deponent, witness

attestor of documents notary public

attinere concern *(involve)*

attingere adjoin, allude, border *(bound)*

attire oneself clothe

attitude conduct, conviction *(persuasion)*, demeanor, deportment, frame *(mood)*, generalization, habit, manner *(behavior)*, opinion *(belief)*, outlook, perspective, platform, position *(point of view)*, property *(distinctive attribute)*, reaction *(response)*, stand *(position)*, standpoint, temperament

attollere elevate

attonement consensus

attorney advocate *(counselor)*, barrister, counsel, counselor, esquire, jurist, lawyer, practitioner, spokesman

attorney for the people district attorney

attorney general prosecutor

attorney representing the state's interest district attorney

attorney-at-law advocate *(counselor)*, attorney, barrister, counsel, counselor, esquire, jurist, lawyer

attorneys bar *(body of lawyers)*

attorneys-at-law bar *(body of lawyers)*

attract bait *(lure)*, coax, interest, inveigle, lure, motivate

attract notice interest

attract the attention occupy *(engage)*

attract the mind occupy *(engage)*

attract the thoughts occupy *(engage)*

attracting attractive

attraction affinity *(regard)*, chain *(nexus)*, decoy, desire, favor *(partiality)*, incentive, inducement, invitation, obsession, partiality, penchant, predisposition, propensity, seduction

attractive popular, provocative, sapid

attractive feature amenity

attractive quality amenity

attractiveness amenity, draw *(attraction)*

attrahent attractive

attribuere ascribe, assign *(allot)*, bestow, impute

attributable derivative

attribute ascribe, assign *(designate)*, caliber *(quality)*, character *(personal quality)*, characteristic, color *(complexion)*, differential, feature *(characteristic)*, impute, property *(distinctive attribute)*, specialty *(distinctive mark)*, trait

attribute to blame

attribute vicariously impute

attributed putative

attributed to contingent

attributes personality

attribution accusation, arrogation, assignation, blame *(responsibility)*, incrimination, reference *(allusion)*

attrition erosion

attroupement caucus, company *(assemblage)*, cumulation

attune accommodate, comport *(agree with)*, conform

attuned consonant

attuned to acquainted, consensual

attunement adjustment, compatibility, synchronism

atypical anomalous, deviant, different, disordered, disparate, dissimilar, infrequent, irregular *(not usual)*, notable, noteworthy, peculiar *(distinctive)*, special, unique, unusual

atypicality difference

auctio auction

auction handle *(trade)*, sell, vend

auctione vendere auction

auctor advocate *(espouser)*, author *(originator)*, informant, informer *(one providing criminal information)*, promoter, spokesman, sponsor

auctor esse authorize

auctor generis ancestor

auctor gentis ancestor

auctorem esse advise

auctoritas authority *(power)*, consequence *(significance)*, credibility, patronage *(power to appoint jobs)*, sanction *(permission)*, warrant *(authorization)*

auctus development *(progression)*, growth *(increase)*

audacia audacity

audacious brazen, bumptious, disdainful, flagrant, impertinent *(insolent)*, insolent, presumptuous

audaciousness audacity

audacity contempt *(disobedience to the court)*, disrespect, temerity

audax lawless, spartan

audi alteram partem counterargument

audible coherent *(clear)*, oral, verbal

audible expression speech

audience assemblage, bystander, collection *(assembly)*, confrontation *(act of setting face to face)*, congregation, interview, session

audiendi inquisitive

audit analysis, analyze, bill *(invoice)*, canvass, check *(inspect)*, computation, examination *(study)*, examine *(study)*, indagation, monitor, scrutinize, study, test

auditing accounting

auditio hearsay

audition hear *(give attention to)*, interview, recognition

auditor comptroller

auditor disciple

augere compound, enhance, enlarge, extend *(enlarge)*, heighten *(augment)*, increase, intensify, magnify

augeri develop

augment accrue *(increase)*, accumulate *(enlarge)*, aggravate *(exacerbate)*, aid, amplify, append, bear *(yield)*, boom *(increase)*, conduce, develop, elaborate, enhance, enlarge, exacerbate, expand, extend *(enlarge)*, hoard, increase, intensify, magnify, raise *(advance)*, recruit, reinforce, supplement

augmentation accession *(enlargement)*, accretion, addition, additive, adjunct, advance *(increase)*, aggravation *(exacerbation)*, boom *(increase)*, boom *(prosperity)*, codicil, continuation *(prolongation)*, cumulation, exaggeration, extension *(expansion)*, growth *(increase)*, increment, profit, progress, reinforcement, rider

augmentative cumulative *(intensifying)*, supplementary

augmented inflated *(enlarged)*

augur anticipate *(prognosticate)*, forewarn, harbinger, herald, indicate, portend, predict, presage, prognosticate, threaten

augur well promise *(raise expectations)*

augural portentous *(ominous)*, presageful, prophetic

augurari guess, presage, surmise

augurate portend, presage, prognosticate

augurial ominous, presageful

augurous portentous *(ominous)*

augury caution *(warning)*, caveat, harbinger, indicant, indication, indicator, precursor, premonition, symptom, threat, token, warning

august meritorious, outstanding *(prominent)*, solemn

aura atmosphere, climate, environment, prestige

aura popularis distinction *(reputation)*

auribus hear *(perceive by ear)*

auricular confidential, privy

aurora onset *(commencement)*

ausculate hear *(give attention to)*

auspicate anticipate *(prognosticate)*, commence, embark, portend, predict, presage, prognosticate

auspice forerunner, harbinger, indicant, indication, indicator, premonition, threat, token

auspices advocacy, aid *(help)*, behalf, charge *(custody)*, control *(supervision)*, custody *(supervision)*, direction *(guidance)*, favor *(sanction)*, power, safekeeping

auspicial ominous, presageful

auspicious favorable *(advantageous)*, fitting, opportune, propitious, seasonable, successful

auspiciousness boom *(prosperity)*, opportunity, timeliness

auspicium auspices

austere astringent, bitter *(penetrat-*

ing), bleak *(severely simple)*, caustic, draconian, harsh, rigid, severe, strict, unapproachable, uncompromising, unrelenting

austeritas austerity

austerity cruelty, rigor, severity

austerus serious *(grave)*, severe

autarch dictator

autarchic autonomous *(self governing)*

autarkic independent

authentic accurate, actual, convincing, de facto, definitive, documentary, factual, genuine, honest, literal, natural, original *(initial)*, positive *(incontestable)*, prime *(original)*, real, realistic, reliable, rightful, sterling, undistorted, valid, veridical

authentically admittedly

authenticate accredit, affirm *(uphold)*, approve, attest, avouch *(guarantee)*, avow, bear *(adduce)*, certify *(attest)*, cite *(state)*, confirm, corroborate, demonstrate *(establish)*, document, endorse, establish *(show)*, evidence, indorse, notarize, prove, sanction, seal *(solemnize)*, sign, substantiate, support *(corroborate)*, sustain *(confirm)*, swear, uphold, vouch, witness *(attest to)*

authenticate a will probate

authenticated actual, definitive, fully executed *(signed)*, genuine, official, true *(authentic)*

authenticated confirmation certification *(attested copy)*, reference *(recommendation)*

authenticated incident fact

authentication acknowledgment *(avowal)*, affirmation, approval, attestation, avowal, certificate, confirmation, consent, corroboration, deed, documentation, jurat, stamp, subscription, support *(corroboration)*, warrant *(guaranty)*

authentication of a will probate

authentication proceeding probate

authenticity honesty, reality, truth, validity, veracity

authentification certification *(attested copy)*

author architect, compose, derivation, elicit, engender, generate, invent *(produce for the first time)*, make, maker, originate, undersigned

authoritarian dictatorial, dogmatic, ex officio, strict

authoritative arbitrary and capricious, assertive, authentic, categorical, certain *(positive)*, clear *(certain)*, cogent, compelling, compulsory, consequential *(substantial)*, decisive, definite, definitive, determinative, dictatorial, documentary, dogmatic, dominant, factual, forcible, incontrovertible, influential, juridical, master, official, peremptory *(imperative)*, persuasive, powerful, predominant, prevailing *(having superior force)*, sovereign *(absolute)*, strict, stringent, valid

authoritative assertion dictum

authoritative attestation certification *(attested copy)*

authoritative citation to appear monition *(legal summons)*

authoritative citation to appear before a court process *(summons)*, summons, venire

authoritative command edict, mandate, monition *(legal summons)*, order *(judicial directive)*, process *(summons)*, summons

authoritative decision adjudication, award, decree

authoritative estimate determination

authoritative example authority *(documentation)*, precedent, stare decisis

authoritative law codification

authoritative opinion conclusion *(determination)*, determination

authoritative order fiat, mandate

authoritative power clout

authoritative request demand

authoritative rule ordinance, precedent

authoritative rule for future similar cases authority *(documentation)*

authoritative statement instruction *(direction)*, opinion *(judicial decision)*, pronouncement

authoritative stoppage of trade embargo

authoritative suggestion dictate

authoritatively admittedly

authoritativeness authority *(power)*, certainty, certification *(certainness)*, force *(strength)*, puissance

authorities bureaucracy, hierarchy *(persons in authority)*

authority advantage, agency *(commission)*, agency *(legal relationship)*, auspices, bailiwick, basis, bureau, certification *(certification of proficiency)*, charter *(license)*, charter *(sanction)*, clout, concession *(authorization)*, consent, control *(supervision)*, copyright, derivation, determinant, dint, documentation, dominance, dominion *(supreme authority)*, droit, eminence, expert, force *(compulsion)*, generalship, government *(political administration)*, hegemony, influence, judicature, jurisdiction, license, management *(directorate)*, management *(supervision)*, mastermind, occupation *(possession)*, patronage *(power to appoint jobs)*, permission, permit, possession *(ownership)*, power, precedence, precedent, predominance, prerogative, prescription *(claim of title)*, prescription *(directive)*, prestige, primacy, privilege, professional, realm, reference *(citation)*, regime, right *(entitlement)*, source, specialist, supremacy, title *(right)*, validity, warrant *(authorization)*, weight *(importance)*

authority to act for another proxy

authority to hear and decide a case jurisdiction

authority to search search warrant

authorization appointment *(act of designating)*, approval, assent, assignment *(designation)*, brevet, capacity *(authority)*, certificate, certification *(certification of proficiency)*, charter *(sanction)*, concession *(authorization)*, confirmation, consent, copyright, credentials, delegation *(assignment)*, deputation *(selection of delegates)*, designation *(naming)*, dispensation *(exception)*, droit, fiat, franchise *(license)*, government *(administration)*, indorsement, leave *(permission)*, legality, legalization, legitimacy, license, mittimus, nomination, option (*contractual provision*), permission, permit, prerogative, privilege, right (*entitlement*), sanction (*permission*), sufferance, title (*right*)

authorize accept (*assent*), accredit, appoint, approve, assent, assign (*designate*), bestow, certify (*approve*), charge (*empower*), command, commit (*entrust*), confirm, consent, consign, cosign, delegate, designate, detail (*assign*), employ (*engage services*), empower, enable, enfranchise, entrust, grant (*concede*), hire, indorse, invest (*vest*), legalize, legislate, legitimate, let (*permit*), notarize, pass (*approve*), permit, qualify (*meet standards*), sanction, seal (*solemnize*), sign, suffer (*permit*), validate, vest

authorize formally charge (*empower*), delegate

authorize to represent delegate

authorized admissible, allowable, allowed, de jure, due (*regular*), entitled, fully executed (*signed*), juridical, legal, legitimate (*rightful*), licit, permissible, privileged, rightful, statutory, valid

authorized by law de jure, lawful, legal

authorized might force (*legal efficacy*)

authorizing deputation (*selection of delegates*)

authorless anonymous

authors press

authorship creation

authortative decision precedent

authortative principle of law precedent

autochthonal native (*domestic*)

autochthonic native (*domestic*)

autochthonous native (*domestic*)

autocrat dictator

autocratic dictatorial, powerful, strict

autocratic master dictator

autocratical powerful

autograph brand (*mark*), inscription, sign

autography handwriting

automated industrial

automatic habitual, routine

automatic lack of due diligence res ipsa loquitur

automatic negligence res ipsa loquitur

automatic reaction instinct

autonomic autonomous (*self governing*), free (*enjoying civil liberty*)

autonomical free (*enjoying civil liberty*)

autonomous free (*enjoying civil liberty*), independent, nonpartisan, sovereign (*independent*)

autonomous being individual, person

autonomy freedom, home rule, latitude, liberty, suffrage

autoptic unmistakable

autoptical unmistakable

auxiliari assist

auxiliary abettor, additional, adjunct, affiliate, appurtenance, appurtenant, associate, backer, clerical, coactor, coadjutant, cohort, collateral (*accompanying*), colleague, confederate, consociate, contributor (*contributor*), contributory, copartner (*business associate*), expedient, expendable, inferior (*lower in position*), instrumental, ministerial, nones-

sential, participant, pendent, reinforcement, secondary, slight, stopgap, subordinate, subservient, subsidiary, substitute, supplementary, unnecessary

auxiliary in crime coconspirator

auxilium assistance, help, relief (*aid*), support (*assistance*)

avail advantage, aid, behalf, benefit (*betterment*), edification, enjoyment (*use*), function, gain, help, help, inure (*benefit*), output, profit, promote (*organize*), purpose, recourse, relief (*aid*), satisfy (*fulfill*), use, utility (*usefulness*), worth

avail against countervail

avail oneself of adopt, capitalize (*seize the chance*), employ (*make use of*), exercise (*use*), expend (*consume*), exploit (*make use of*), impropriate, plagiarize, resort, wield

availability access (*opening*), possibility

available amenable, convenient, disposable, open (*accessible*), present (*attendant*), present (*current*), public (*open*), ready (*prepared*), ready (*willing*)

available assets stock in trade

available facts information (*knowledge*)

available means assets, capital, cash, personalty, property (*possessions*), resource

availing adequate, beneficial

avails boom (*prosperity*), proceeds, profit

avalanche cataclysm, overage, surfeit

avant garde sophisticated

avant-courier precursor

avarice greed

avaricious illiberal, insatiable, mercenary, parsimonious, rapacious, venal

avariciousness greed

avaritia greed

avarus illiberal

avenge penalize, repay, retaliate

avengement conviction (*finding of guilt*), punishment, reprisal, retribution, revenge, vengeance

avenging punitive, vindictive

avenue admission (*entry*), admittance (*means of approach*), causeway, conduit (*channel*), outlet, way (*channel*)

avenues approaches

aver adduce, affirm (*claim*), affirm (*declare solemnly*), allege, annunciate, assert, assure (*insure*), attest, avouch (*avow*), avow, bear (*adduce*), certify (*attest*), claim (*maintain*), contend (*maintain*), convey (*communicate*), corroborate, declare, depose (*testify*), enunciate, express, observe (*remark*), posit, profess (*avow*), promise (*vow*), propound, remark, speak, swear, testify, utter, vouch, vow

average cross section, customary, general, imperfect, intermediate, marginal, mediocre, mediocrity, mundane, nondescript, norm, normal (*regular*), ordinary, regular (*conventional*), typical, usual

average out calculate

averageness mediocrity

averment adjuration, affidavit, affirmance (*legal affirmation*), affirmation, allegation, assertion, asseveration,

assurance, attestation, avouchment, avowal, claim (*assertion*), comment, confirmation, corroboration, count, disclosure (*something disclosed*), profession (*declaration*), pronouncement, proof, reference (*recommendation*), remark, statement, surety (*certainty*), testimony

averred alleged

averse antipathetic (*oppositional*), contrary, disinclined, disobedient, hesitant, involuntary, negative, reluctant, restive

averseness disincentive, rejection, reluctance

aversion alienation (*estrangement*), consternation, contempt (*disdain*), hatred, ill will, intolerance, malice, odium, phobia, rancor, reluctance

aversus averse, disinclined

avert arrest (*stop*), avoid (*evade*), balk, bar (*hinder*), block, counter, deter, discourage, estop, forestall, parry, prevent, repel (*drive back*), save (*rescue*), stall, stave, thwart

avertere alienate (*estrange*), avert, divert, embezzle, purloin

averting preventive

aveu avowal

avid eager, fervent, hot-blooded, ready (*willing*), sedulous

aviditas greed

avidity desire, greed, passion

avidus eager, rapacious

aviso dispatch (*message*), intelligence (*news*), notification, tip (*clue*)

avocare disengage

avocat lawyer

avocation business (*occupation*), career, employment, job, occupation (*vocation*), position (*business status*), practice (*professional business*), profession (*vocation*), pursuit (*occupation*), trade (*occupation*), work (*employment*)

avoid abscond, adeem, annul, avert, cancel, default, deter, detour, discriminate (*treat differently*), disdain, disfavor, elude, escape, eschew, estrange, evade (*deceive*), evade (*elude*), exclude, fail (*neglect*), forestall, forgo, forswear, parry, picket, pretermit, prevent, refrain, repeal, shirk, shun, stave, tergiversate

avoid a straight answer equivocate

avoid arrest escape

avoid capture escape

avoid doing circumvent

avoid peril escape

avoid using conserve

avoidable needless, nonessential, unnecessary

avoidance absence (*nonattendance*), abstention, boycott, default, evasion, exclusion, flight, nonperformance, odium, ostracism

avoidance of extremes moderation

avoidance of waste economy (*frugality*)

avoided derelict (*abandoned*)

avoider fugitive

avoiding evasive, reluctant

avoiding extravagance economical

avoiding the society of others solitary

avoidless certain (*positive*), necessary (*inescapable*), unavoidable (*inevitable*)

avouch affirm *(declare solemnly)*, allege, assert, assure *(insure)*, avow, bear *(adduce)*, certify *(attest)*, claim *(maintain)*, corroborate, depose *(testify)*, evidence, posit, profess *(avow)*, promise *(vow)*, verify *(swear)*, vouch

avouched alleged

avouchment adjuration, affidavit, affirmance *(legal affirmation)*, affirmation, assertion, asseveration, attestation, averment, avowal, certification *(attested copy)*, claim *(assertion)*, confirmation, contract, corroboration, jurat, oath, reference *(recommendation)*

avow acknowledge *(declare)*, affirm *(declare solemnly)*, agree *(comply)*, assert, assurance, assure *(insure)*, bear *(adduce)*, betray *(disclose)*, certify *(attest)*, claim *(maintain)*, confirm, contend *(maintain)*, convey *(communicate)*, declare, depose *(testify)*, pledge *(promise the performance of)*, posit, promise *(vow)*, recognize *(acknowledge)*, swear, testify, verify *(swear)*, vow

avowal adjuration, admission *(disclosure)*, affidavit, affirmance *(legal affirmation)*, affirmation, assertion, asseveration, assurance, attestation, averment, avouchment, claim *(assertion)*, contract, conviction *(persuasion)*, covenant, disclosure *(something disclosed)*, jurat, oath, pledge *(binding promise)*, profession *(declaration)*, promise, recognition, recognizance, reference *(recommendation)*, statement, surety *(certainty)*, testimony, undertaking *(pledge)*

avowal of guilt confession

avowance acknowledgment *(avowal)*, adjuration, affidavit, assurance, avouchment, avowal, common knowledge, oath, pledge *(binding promise)*, reference *(recommendation)*, surety *(certainty)*

avowed agreed *(promised)*, alleged, manifest, ostensible, putative

avowedly admittedly, purported

avulsion evulsion

await expect *(anticipate)*, forestall, remain *(stay)*, stay *(rest)*

awaited forseen, forthcoming, prospective

awaiting expectation

awake guarded

awake a suspicion doubt *(distrust)*

awake to discern *(detect with the senses)*, discover, sensitive *(discerning)*

awaken disabuse, elicit, foment, incite, inspire, originate, perceive, provoke, stimulate

awaken memories remind

awakened acquainted, penitent, renascent

awakening moving *(evoking emotion)*, revival

award adjudge, adjudicate, adjudication, apportion, benefit *(conferment)*, bestow, bounty, cession, confer *(give)*, contribute *(supply)*, contribution *(donation)*, convey *(transfer)*, decide, decree, decree, dedicate, degree *(academic title)*, delegate, demise, determination, determine, dole, dower, endow, endowment, endue, finding, gift *(present)*, give *(grant)*, grant, grant *(transfer formally)*, gratuity *(present)*, largess *(gift)*,

leave *(give)*, parcel, pass *(advance)*, pay, pay, present *(make a gift)*, prize, provide *(supply)*, recognition, relief *(legal redress)*, remunerate, remuneration, reward, ruling, tip *(gratuity)*, trover, verdict

award assent permit

award judgment adjudicate

award of punishment sentence

awarding donative

aware acute, artful, cognizant, guarded, knowing, learned, literate, perceptive, receptive, sensitive *(discerning)*

aware of acquainted, familiar *(informed)*

awareness appreciation *(perception)*, cognition, comprehension, insight, judgment *(discernment)*, perception, realization, reason *(sound judgment)*, recognition, sagacity, scienter, sense *(feeling)*, sense *(intelligence)*, sensibility, understanding *(comprehension)*

awareness of comprehension

awe fear, impress *(affect deeply)*, interest *(concern)*, panic, phobia, regard *(esteem)*, respect, trepidation

awe-inspiring formidable, ineffable, notable, solemn, special

awe-strike overcome *(overwhelm)*

awe-struck speechless

aweless brazen, unabashed, unaffected *(uninfluenced)*

awesome formidable, ineffable, notable, sacrosanct, solemn, special

awesomeness solemnity

awestricken diffident

awestruck diffident

awful dire, heinous, lamentable

awkward difficult, improper, inadept, incompetent, inelegant, inept *(incompetent)*, ponderous, unbecoming, uncouth, unsuitable

awkward predicament dilemma

awkward situation dilemma, embarrassment, plight

awkwardness embarrassment

AWOL desertion

awry anomalous, astray, defective, disordered, errant, faulty, incorrect, oblique *(slanted)*

axiom dogma, maxim, postulate, precept, prescription *(directive)*

axiomatic absolute *(conclusive)*, certain *(positive)*, definite, evident, irrefutable, obvious, peremptory *(absolute)*, positive *(incontestable)*, proverbial, uncontested, undeniable, undisputed

axiomatical evident, irrefutable, obvious, positive *(incontestable)*, undeniable

axioms premises *(hypotheses)*

axis center *(central position)*, league

ayslum inhabitation *(place of dwelling)*

B

babble jargon *(unintelligible language)*, prattle

babbling loquacious

babel imbroglio

babies children

baby infant, minor

babyish jejune *(lacking maturity)*

babyishness puerility

bacchanalia debauchery

bacchanalianism inebriation

back abet, adhere *(maintain loyalty)*, advocate, assist, avouch *(guarantee)*, bear *(support)*, bolster, capitalize *(provide capital)*, cosign, countenance, delinquent *(overdue)*, document, encourage, endorse, espouse, favor, finance, guarantee, help, invest *(fund)*, justify, nurture, parlay *(bet)*, promote *(organize)*, recommend, sponsor, subsidize, support *(assist)*, underwrite, uphold, vouch

back again refinance

back away retreat, shun

back away from eschew

back down abandon *(withdraw)*, accede *(concede)*, disavow, surrender *(yield)*, yield *(submit)*

back off abandon *(withdraw)*

back out abandon *(physically leave)*, abandon *(withdraw)*, defect, disavow, quit *(discontinue)*, renege, retreat, withdraw

back payments arrears

back up bear *(support)*, capitalize *(provide capital)*, encourage, side, support *(corroborate)*, uphold

back-up data

backbiting denunciation, diatribe

backbone cornerstone, gist *(substance)*, ground, main point, mainstay, prowess *(bravery)*, substance *(essential nature)*, tenacity, will *(desire)*

backbreaking onerous, operose

backed-up fully secured

backer abettor, advocate *(espouser)*, assistant, benefactor, colleague, creditor, disciple, donor, mainstay, partisan, patron *(influential supporter)*, promoter, proponent, speculator, sponsor, surety *(guarantor)*

backfire reaction *(opposition)*, repercussion

background atmosphere, basis, case *(set of circumstances)*, context, determinant, preparation, scene

backhanded indirect, oblique *(evasive)*

backing advocacy, aid *(help)*, auspices, charity, coverage *(insurance)*, favor *(sanction)*, guaranty, guidance, help, indorsement, investment, loan, patronage *(power to appoint jobs)*, patronage *(support)*, promotion *(encouragement)*, reinforcement, relief *(aid)*, service *(assistance)*, subsidy, support *(assistance)*, support *(corroboration)*

backlash reaction *(opposition)*, repercussion

backlog store *(depository)*

backroom cache *(hiding place)*

backset casualty, damper *(depressant)*, misfortune

backslide recidivate, regress, relapse, repeat *(do again)*, return *(go back)*, reversal, reversion *(act of returning)*, revert

backsliding recidivism, recrudescence, regressive, relapse

backstair furtive

backtrack retreat, withdraw

backward back *(in reverse)*, regressive

backward step decline

backwood provincial

baculum cudgel

bad deleterious, delinquent *(guilty of a misdeed)*, deplorable, depraved, detrimental, disastrous, disreputable, harmful, heinous, immoral, imperfect, iniquitous, nefarious, noxious, peccable, peccant *(culpable)*, perverse, poor *(inferior in quality)*, profane, reprehensible, reprobate, unfavorable, wrongful

bad behavior miscarriage, misdeed

bad blood umbrage

bad character bad repute, disgrace, dishonor *(shame)*, disrepute, turpitude

bad conduct malfeasance, misconduct

bad debt nonpayment

bad example convict

bad faith dishonesty, infidelity

bad favor dishonor *(shame)*

bad feeling odium

bad fortune calamity, casualty, misfortune, privation

bad habit vice

bad idea miscue

bad influence bad repute

bad intent ill will, malice

bad intention malice

bad job maladministration

bad judgment misestimation, misjudgment

bad language expletive

bad light opprobrium

bad logic non sequitur

bad luck misfortune, privation

bad management misconduct

bad manners disregard *(lack of respect)*

bad match misjoinder

bad name attaint, bad character, bad repute, disgrace, dishonor *(shame)*, ignominy, ill repute, infamy, opprobrium, scandal, shame, turpitude

bad report disgrace, notoriety

bad reporting misstatement

bad reputation attaint, bad character, disgrace, dishonor *(shame)*, disrepute, ignominy, infamy, notoriety, scandal

bad repute attaint, bad character, disgrace, dishonor *(shame)*, disrepute, ignominy, ill repute, notoriety, scandal

bad review disparagement

bad taste impropriety

bad treatment abuse *(physical misuse)*, misusage

bad turn disservice

bad wishes imprecation

bad-hearted diabolic

bad-natured perverse

bad-tempered fractious, perverse, petulant

badge brand, designation *(symbol)*, indicant, indication, indicator, manifestation, onus *(stigma)*, speciality, specialty *(distinctive mark)*, symbol, trademark

badge of infamy disgrace, dishonor *(shame)*, ignominy, stigma

badge of office device *(distinguishing mark)*

badger annoy, bait *(harass)*, browbeat, discommode, discompose, disturb, harass, harrow, harry *(harass)*, hector, importune, intimidate, irritate, mistreat, molest *(annoy)*, persecute, perturb, plague, press *(goad)*, provoke

badinage speak

badly advised misadvised

badly calculated inopportune

badly made inferior *(lower in quality)*, poor *(inferior in quality)*

badly needed exigent

badly qualified unfit

badly timed inopportune, untimely

badness delinquency *(misconduct)*, misdoing

baffle balk, confound, confuse *(bewilder)*, dilemma, disadvantage, disorient, elude, embarrass, foil, frustrate, muddle, obfuscate, perplex, perturb, prevent, thwart

baffled lost *(disoriented)*

bafflement ambiguity, complication, confusion *(ambiguity)*, dilemma, embarrassment, problem, quandary, surprise

baffling debatable, elusive, enigmatic, inexplicable, inscrutable, labyrinthine, mysterious

bag gain, procure

baggage cargo

baggy full

bail security *(pledge)*

bail out discharge *(liberate)*, disenthrall, liberate

bailiff marshal

bailiwick domain *(sphere of influence)*, realm

bait badger, bilk, cajole, coax, decoy, ensnare, entice, entrap, harry *(harass)*, hector, incentive, inveigle, lure, mislead, pique, plague, provoke, ruse, seduction, trap, trap

bait a trap ambush

baiting bribery

balance adjust *(regulate)*, collation, comparison, compatibility, compensate *(counterbalance)*, composure, coordinate, countervail, earnings, equipoise, fairness, moderation, neutralize, offset, overage, par *(equality)*, parity, proceeds, regularity, regulate *(adjust)*, remainder *(remaining part)*, residual, sanity, stabilize, surplus, weigh

balance accounts check *(inspect)*, quit *(repay)*

balance against compare

balance due arrears, bill *(invoice)*, nonpayment

balance owed debt

balance sheet budget, ledger, register

balance statement budget

balance to pay debt, deficit, due

balanced agreed *(harmonized)*, coextensive, consonant, equal, fair *(just)*, firm, proportionate, rational, regular *(orderly)*, sane

balanced contrast antithesis

balanced judgment common sense

balances capital

balancing compensatory, equivalent

bald evident, honest, manifest, obvious, stark, unmistakable

baldness honesty

bale adversity, assemblage, disaster, misfortune, tragedy

baleful bad *(offensive)*, dangerous, deadly, deleterious, destructive, dire, disadvantageous, harmful, heinous, insalubrious, lethal, malevolent, malignant, noxious, ominous, pernicious, pestilent, portentous *(ominous)*, sinister, virulent

balefulness harm

balk bar *(obstruction)*, contravene, disadvantage, discontinue *(break continuity)*, disoblige, foil, frustrate, halt, hamper, hesitate, hold out *(resist)*, interrupt, obstacle, obstruction, oppose, prevent, refuse, stem *(check)*, stifle, thwart

balk at avoid *(evade)*

balking disinclined, hesitant, restive

balky hesitant, intractable, recalcitrant, restive

ball sphere

ballistics ammunition

balloon expand, inflate, magnify

ballooned inflated *(enlarged)*

ballot cast *(register)*, franchise *(right to vote)*, plebiscite, poll *(casting of votes)*, poll, primary, referendum, vote, vote

balloter constituent *(part)*

balloting election *(selection by vote)*

balm cure, panacea, soothe

balmy medicinal, placid, remedial

bamboozle bait *(lure)*, betray *(lead astray)*, bilk, ensnare, inveigle

bamboozlement bunko, pettifoggery

ban bar *(obstruction)*, bar *(exclude)*, block, boycott, censor, constrain *(restrain)*, countermand, debar, deter, disapprobation, eliminate *(exclude)*, embargo, enjoin, estop, estoppel, exclude, exclusion, expulsion, forbid, inhibit, injunction, obstruction, ostracism, preclude, prohibit, prohibition, proscribe *(prohibit)*, proscription, refusal, rejection, relegate, restraint, suppress, veto

banal insipid, lifeless *(dull)*, mediocre, mundane, ordinary, pedestrian, stale, trite, usual

banality platitude

band assemblage, cabal, commingle, connect *(join together)*, consolidate *(unite)*, denomination, desegregate, federate, join *(bring together)*, league, lock, posse, zone

band in a federation federalize *(associate)*

band of armed men posse

band of employees personnel

band of men armed with legal authority posse

band of union affiliation *(connectedness)*

band together adhere *(fasten)*, combine *(act in concert)*, concur *(agree)*, connect *(join together)*, federalize *(associate)*, join *(associate oneself with)*, meet, merge, organize *(unionize)*, pool

banded corporate *(associate)*, federal

banded together concordant, concurrent *(united)*, conjoint

bandit burglar, criminal, hoodlum, malefactor, outlaw, thief

bands ties

bandy circulate, debate

bandy with fight *(battle)*

bandy words bicker, communicate, discuss, dispute *(debate)*, speak

bane detriment, disaster, injury, trouble

baneful bad *(offensive)*, dangerous, deleterious, disadvantageous, disastrous, harmful, heinous, hostile, insalubrious, lethal, malevolent, malignant, noxious, pernicious, pestilent, sinister, virulent

bang impinge

bang into jostle *(bump into)*

banish ban, condemn *(ban)*, dislodge, dispel, displace *(remove)*, eliminate *(exclude)*, exclude, expatriate, expel, isolate, oust, outlaw, prohibit, proscribe *(denounce)*, reject, relegate, renounce, seclude, transport

banishment deportation, disqualification *(rejection)*, expulsion, layoff, ostracism, prohibition, proscription, rejection, removal

bank coffer, deposit *(submit to a bank)*, edge *(border)*, fund, garner, hoard, keep *(shelter)*, margin *(outside limit)*, pool, repository, reserve, store, treasury

bank annuities capital

bank check draft

bank note draft, money

bank notes currency

bank on rely

bank paper check *(instrument)*, draft

bank robber burglar

bankbook ledger

banker comptroller

banknote check *(instrument)*

bankroll money

bankrupt destitute, impecunious, insolvent, poor *(underprivileged)*

bankruptcy default, privation

banned barred, illegal, illegitimate *(illegal)*, illicit, impermissible, inadmissible

banned goods contraband

banner caption, heading

banner head caption

banner line caption

banning boycott

banshee phantom

bantling bastard

baptism call *(title)*

bar abrogate *(rescind)*, balk, ban, barrier, bench, block, blockade *(barrier)*, censor, censorship, clog, condemn *(ban)*, constrain *(restrain)*, constraint *(restriction)*, court, cudgel, damper *(stopper)*, debar, deport *(banish)*, deter, disable, disapprobation, disqualify, eliminate *(exclude)*, embargo, enjoin, estop, estoppel, exclude, exclusion, forbid, halt, hamper, impasse, impediment, inhibit, interdict, interfere, interruption, judiciary, keep *(restrain)*, key *(passport)*, lock, obstruct, obstruction, obviation, occlude, outlaw, preclude, prevent, prohibit, prohibition, proscribe *(prohibit)*, refuse, relegate, remove *(eliminate)*, resist *(oppose)*, restrain, restraint, restrict, save, seal *(close)*, shut, stall, stay, stay *(halt)*, stifle, stop, thwart, veto

bar from access preclude

bar of justice bench, court, judicatory

bar someone's way halt

bar to an allegation estoppel

barbaric disorderly, uncouth

barbarity atrocity, bestiality, brutality, cruelty

barbarize brutalize

barbarous brutal, cold-blooded, cruel, disorderly, hot-blooded, malevolent, malignant, ruthless, uncouth, vicious

barbarousness bestiality, cruelty

barbiturate narcotic

bare barren, betray *(disclose)*, bleak *(exposed and barren)*, brief, clarify, confess, convey *(communicate)*, denude, devoid, disclose, disinter, divulge, expose, find *(discover)*, manifest, manifest, marginal, mere, naked *(lacking embellishment)*, only *(no more than)*, open *(in sight)*, reveal, simple, stark, unveil, vacant, void *(empty)*

bare possibility chance *(possibility)*, improbability

bare subsistence austerity, indigence, paucity, poverty

barefaced brazen, outrageous, unabashed

barely purely *(simply)*, solely *(purely)*

barely acceptable marginal

barely adequate marginal

barely passable poor *(inferior in quality)*

barely possible ludicrous

barely seen impalpable, inconspicuous, indefinite

bargain adjustment, agree *(contract)*, agreement *(contract)*, barter, close *(agree)*, compact, compromise, compromise *(settle by mutual agreement)*, contract, deal, deal, dicker, discount, exchange, haggle, negotiate, pact, settlement, stipulate, stipulation, term *(provision)*, trade, treaty

bargain for buy, expect *(anticipate)*, incur

bargain under seal specialty *(contract)*

bargain with treat *(process)*

bargainer customer

bargaining collective bargaining, commerce, negotiation

bargaining agent broker

barge in impinge, interrupt

barnacle parasite

barometer criterion

baroque elaborate, tawdry

barrage onset *(assault)*

barratry disloyalty

barred blind *(impassable)*, inadmissible

barren bleak *(exposed and barren)*, deficient, devoid, futile, ineffective, ineffectual, lifeless *(dull)*, otiose, pedestrian, unavailing, unproductive, vacuous, void *(empty)*

barrenness blank *(emptiness)*

barricade bar *(obstruction)*, bar *(hinder)*, barrier, block, blockade *(barrier)*, bulwark, check *(bar)*, clog, confine, constrict *(inhibit)*, contain *(restrain)*, damper *(stopper)*, debar, deter, enjoin, estop, halt, hamper, hinder, impede, lock, obstacle, obstruct, obstruction, occlude, protect, protection, restraint, shut, stop

barricaded blind *(impassable)*

barrier bar *(obstruction)*, bulwark, check *(bar)*, complication, damper *(stopper)*, deterrence, deterrent, enclosure, estoppel, handicap, hindrance, impediment, limitation, mete, obstacle, obstruction, panoply, predicament, prohibition

barring deterrent, estoppel, save

barring out lockout

barrister advocate *(counselor)*, attorney, counsel, counselor, esquire, jurist, lawyer, representative *(proxy)*

barrister-at-law advocate *(counselor)*, counsel, counselor, lawyer

barristerial forensic

barristers bar *(body of lawyers)*

barter alienate *(transfer title)*, business *(commerce)*, commerce, deal, dealings, dicker, exchange, handle *(trade)*, interchange, sell, trade *(commerce)*, trade

bartering commerce

basal cardinal *(basic)*, central *(essential)*, elementary, essential *(inherent)*, fundamental, naked *(lacking embellishment)*, organic, original *(initial)*, primary, prime *(original)*, primordial, rudimentary, simple

base arrant *(onerous)*, bad *(inferior)*, bad *(offensive)*, basis, caitiff, cause *(reason)*, center *(essence)*, consequence *(significance)*, contemptible, contemptuous, cornerstone, depraved, derivation, determinant, disgraceful, disreputable, felonious, foundation *(basis)*, gist *(ground for a suit)*, ground, headquarters, heinous, ignoble, immoral, inelegant, inexpiable, inferior *(lower in quality)*, iniquitous, loathsome, machiavellian, nefarious, objectionable, obnoxious, odious, outrageous, peccant *(culpable)*, perfidious, perverse, plant *(place firmly)*, poor *(inferior in quality)*, profligate *(corrupt)*, recreant, reprehensible, reprobate, scandalous, seat, site, site, sordid, subservient, unscrupulous, unseemly, unworthy

base camp headquarters

base conduct bad faith

base of authority headquarters

base of operations headquarters

base-born illegitimate *(born out of wedlock)*

base-minded depraved, dissolute

baseborn caitiff, ignoble

based on underlying

based on conjecture unsupported

based on evidence deductible *(provable)*

based on evidence of the senses empirical

based on observation empirical

based on proof deductible *(provable)*

baseless arbitrary and capricious, gratuitous *(unwarranted)*, ill-founded, immaterial, insubstantial, invalid, unfounded, unsupported, unsustainable, untenable, unwarranted

baseless charge frame up

baseness abuse *(corrupt practice)*, bad character, corruption, degradation, delinquency *(misconduct)*, discredit, disgrace, dishonor *(shame)*, disrepute, ill repute, infamy, mediocrity, perversion, scandal, shame, turpitude

baser subaltern

bases circumstances, premises *(hypotheses)*

bashful diffident

basic central *(essential)*, elementary, essential *(inherent)*, essential *(required)*, fundamental, implicit, indispensable, initial, innate, integral, material *(important)*, naked *(lacking embellishment)*, native *(inborn)*, necessary *(required)*, organic, original *(initial)*, primary, prime *(original)*, primordial, requisite, rudimentary, simple, sub-

stantive, ultimate, underlying, virtual, vital
basic doctrine principle *(axiom)*
basic ingredient necessity
basic law principle *(axiom)*
basic part essence
basic rule principle *(axiom)*
basic substance component
basic truth principle *(axiom)*
basilar essential *(inherent)*, fundamental, original *(initial)*
basilary essential *(inherent)*, fundamental
basilica court
basis assumption *(supposition)*, base *(foundation)*, cause *(reason)*, center *(essence)*, consequence *(significance)*, content *(meaning)*, criterion, derivation, determinant, documentation, gist *(ground for a suit)*, gist *(substance)*, ground, main point, pattern, precedent, preparation, purpose, rationale, source, stare decisis, substance *(essential nature)*
basis for development embryo
basis for relief cause of action
basis of argument gist *(ground for a suit)*
basis of comparison standard
basis of litigation gist *(ground for a suit)*
bask in relish
bastard illegitimate *(born out of wedlock)*
bastardism bar sinister
bastardization bar sinister
bastardize debase
bastardy bar sinister
baste beat *(strike)*
bastille prison
bastinado beat *(strike)*, cudgel, lash *(strike)*
bastion bulwark, mainstay, security *(safety)*
bat cudgel, strike *(assault)*
batch assemblage, body *(collection)*, bulk, congregation, quantity, selection *(collection)*
batch together glean, hoard
bate abridge *(shorten)*, attenuate, check *(restrain)*, commute, decrease, deduct *(reduce)*, dilute, diminish, ease, lessen, palliate *(abate)*
bathe imbue, immerse *(plunge into)*, permeate, pervade
baton bar sinister
batter beat *(strike)*, force *(break)*, lash *(strike)*, mishandle *(maltreat)*, mutilate, strike *(assault)*
battering ram cudgel
battle affray, bicker, collision *(dispute)*, compete, conflict, confrontation *(altercation)*, contend *(dispute)*, contest *(dispute)*, contest, defy, disagree, engage *(involve)*, fracas, fray, grapple, oppose, resistance, strife, struggle
battle maneuver strategy
battle verbally debate
battlement bulwark
battler contestant
battling belligerency, hostile, offensive *(taking the initiative)*
battology tautology
batture alluvion
bawdiness obscenity, pornography
bawdy lascivious, lecherous, lewd, li-

centious, obscene, prurient, salacious, suggestive *(risqué)*
bazaar exchange, market *(business)*
be exist, subsist
be a benefactor fund
be a candidate compete
be a coward fear
be a customer of patronize *(trade with)*
be a drag on impede
be a drunkard carouse
be a factor concern *(involve)*
be a feature constitute *(compose)*
be a good investment pay
be a name for denote
be a part of involve *(participate)*
be a participator in commit *(perpetrate)*
be a party to commit *(perpetrate)*, connive, contribute *(assist)*, cooperate, involve *(participate)*, partake, participate
be a reproach to disgrace
be a sign of denote, indicate
be a sound argument cohere *(be logically consistent)*
be a spectator observe *(watch)*, witness *(have direct knowledge of)*
be a suppliant call *(appeal to)*
be a token of indicate
be a winner prevail *(triumph)*
be a witness observe *(watch)*
be absorbed in devote
be abstracted muse
be accepted pass *(satisfy requirements)*
be accordant agree *(comply)*, cohere *(be logically consistent)*, coincide *(concur)*, comport *(agree with)*, correspond *(be equivalent)*
be accorded hold *(possess)*
be accountable answer *(be responsible)*
be acquainted comprehend *(understand)*
be acquainted with apprehend *(perceive)*, perceive, pierce *(discern)*
be active with occupy *(engage)*
be adjacent to abut, adjoin, border *(bound)*
be afflicted suffer *(sustain loss)*
be afraid fear
be after desire
be against confront *(oppose)*, disapprove *(reject)*
be agreeable satisfy *(fulfill)*
be ahead of precede
be akin appertain, correspond *(be equivalent)*
be alarmed fear
be alive exist
be all over cease
be allowable lie *(be sustainable)*
be ambassador for represent *(substitute)*
be ambiguous equivocate
be an accomplice commit *(perpetrate)*
be an agent for represent *(substitute)*
be an impediment constrict *(inhibit)*, hinder
be an indication of denote
be an obstacle constrict *(inhibit)*, hinder, interfere
be an obstacle to impede, interpose
be an omen portend

be anchored remain *(stay)*, stay *(rest)*
be angry resent
be annihilated perish
be answerable allow *(endure)*, answer *(be responsible)*
be answerable for avouch *(guarantee)*, justify, pledge *(promise the performance of)*, promise *(vow)*, undertake
be antagonistic collide *(clash)*
be anxious fear, mistrust
be apologist for justify
be applicable appertain, apply *(pertain)*, comport *(agree with)*
be applicable to concern *(involve)*
be apposite comport *(agree with)*
be apprehensive doubt *(distrust)*, fear, misdoubt, mistrust
be apprised understand
be apprized comprehend *(understand)*
be apprized of apprehend *(perceive)*, perceive, pierce *(discern)*
be appropriate comport *(agree with)*, lie *(be sustainable)*, pertain
be apt comport *(agree with)*
be armed forestall
be associated with attend *(accompany)*, pertain
be assuaged relent
be at an end cease
be at cross purposes conflict, counter, counteract, differ *(vary)*, dispute *(contest)*, oppose
be at cross-purposes collide *(clash)*, confront *(oppose)*, fight *(counteract)*
be at ease rest *(cease from action)*
be at fault lapse *(fall into error)*
be at hand impend, report *(present oneself)*
be at loggerheads bicker
be at one with agree *(comply)*, coincide *(concur)*, conform
be at the head of moderate *(preside over)*, preside
be at the helm overlook *(superintend)*, oversee
be at variance bicker, collide *(clash)*, conflict, demurrer, deviate, differ *(vary)*, disaccord, disagree, dispute *(contest)*, dissent *(differ in opinion)*, except *(object)*, object
be at work attempt
be at work on occupy *(engage)*
be attendant on attend *(take care of)*
be attentive consider, devote, hear *(give attention to)*, heed, immerse *(engross)*, note *(notice)*, notice *(observe)*, observe *(watch)*, regard *(pay attention)*
be attentive to attend *(heed)*, perceive
be attorney for represent *(substitute)*
be attracted gravitate
be augmented compound, expand
be auxiliary to aid
be available lie *(be sustainable)*
be averse object
be aware comprehend *(understand)*, heed, observe *(watch)*
be aware of appreciate *(comprehend)*, apprehend *(perceive)*, construe *(comprehend)*, perceive, pierce *(discern)*, recognize *(perceive)*, regard *(pay attention)*
be banded together conspire
be beholden owe
be benevolent help

be bent upon desire, pursue *(strive to gain)*
be bereft of lack
be better transcend
be better for gain, profit
be bewildered misjudge
be biased favor, preconceive, predetermine, presuppose
be blind to ignore
be born arise *(originate)*
be bound answer *(be responsible)*, avow, owe
be calm repose *(rest)*
be capable of holding accommodate
be capricious vacillate
be careful beware, hedge, heed
be careless neglect
be careless with endanger
be caused by ensue
be cautious beware, care *(be cautious)*, hedge, heed, mistrust
be censorious denounce *(condemn)*
be certain expect *(anticipate)*
be changeful fluctuate
be characteristic of appertain
be chargeable answer *(be responsible)*
be chary beware
be circumjacent encompass *(surround)*
be circumjacent to border *(bound)*
be circumspect beware
be clear cohere *(be logically consistent)*
be closeted with rendezvous
be cognizant comprehend *(understand)*
be cognizant of appreciate *(comprehend)*, apprehend *(perceive)*, perceive
be coherent cohere *(be logically consistent)*
be compassionate relent, sympathize
be compelled answer *(be responsible)*
be complemental correspond *(be equivalent)*
be compliant relent
be composed of comprehend *(include)*, comprise, consist, contain *(comprise)*, include
be compounded of contain *(comprise)*
be comprised of comprehend *(include)*, consist
be concealed camouflage, elude
be concerned care *(be cautious)*, care *(regard)*, fear
be concerned for care *(regard)*
be concerned with appertain, apply *(pertain)*, occupy *(engage)*, pertain
be concomitant coincide *(correspond)*
be concomittant concur *(coexist)*
be confident expect *(anticipate)*, rely, trust
be confounded lose *(undergo defeat)*
be confused misconstrue, misunderstand
be congruent appertain, coincide *(correspond)*, correspond *(be equivalent)*
be congruous cohere *(be logically consistent)*
be connected to pertain
be connected with appertain, apply *(pertain)*, attend *(accompany)*
be conscience striken repent
be conscious comprehend *(understand)*, observe *(watch)*

be conscious of appreciate *(comprehend)*, apprehend *(perceive)*, detect, heed, notice *(observe)*, perceive, pierce *(discern)*, regard *(pay attention)*
be consistent comport *(agree with)*
be consonant comport *(agree with)*
be conspicuous flaunt
be constant adhere *(persist)*, endure *(last)*, keep *(continue)*, persevere, remain *(continue)*
be constituted of contain *(comprise)*
be consumed decrease
be contained in consist
be contemporaneous coincide *(correspond)*, concur *(coexist)*
be contemporary concur *(coexist)*
be contemptuous condescend *(patronize)*
be contemptuous of contemn, disdain, flout, misprize
be conterminous border *(bound)*
be contiguous abut, border *(bound)*, contact *(touch)*
be continuous to adjoin
be contrary collide *(clash)*, conflict, counter, counteract, countervail, differ *(vary)*, disagree, disapprove *(reject)*, dispute *(debate)*, dissent *(differ in opinion)*, fight *(counteract)*, gainsay, oppugn
be contrary to contravene, oppose
be conversant with comprehend *(understand)*
be converted change
be convinced opine
be convivial carouse
be counted vote
be courteous condescend *(deign)*
be cowardly fear
be critical complain *(criticize)*
be cunning cheat, circumvent, delude, illude, scheme
be daunted fear
be debited with overdraw
be deceitful bear false witness, fake, palter, pretend
be deceived err, misapprehend, misconceive, misread, mistake
be deceptive misstate, palter
be defeated fail *(lose)*, lose *(undergo defeat)*, succumb
be deficient default, lack
be dejected brood
be delinquent default
be demoted fail *(lose)*
be dense cohere *(adhere)*
be dependent on rely
be dependent upon appertain
be deprived of forfeit, lack, lose *(be deprived of)*
be deputy for represent *(substitute)*
be derelict break *(violate)*, default, disobey
be derived accrue *(arise)*, arise *(originate)*
be derogatory derogate
be deserving earn
be desirous lack
be destitute lack
be destroyed degenerate, lose *(undergo defeat)*, perish
be determined persevere, persist
be determined to intend
be determined to get pursue *(strive to gain)*
be devoid of truth bear false witness
be devoted adhere *(maintain loyalty)*,

adhere *(persist)*
be devoted to obey
be different conflict, deviate
be diffuse digress
be dilatory defer *(put off)*, delay, hesitate, hold up *(delay)*, procrastinate
be diligent labor
be disappointed lose *(undergo defeat)*
be disclosed bare
be discordant bicker, collide *(clash)*, conflict, contend *(dispute)*, differ *(disagree)*, disagree
be discourteous offend *(insult)*
be dishonest bear false witness, betray *(lead astray)*, cheat, hoodwink, lie *(falsify)*, mislead, palter, prevaricate
be disjoined estrange
be disloyal defect, disobey, rebel
be disposed to choose
be disrespectful flout
be dissatisfied complain *(criticize)*
be dissimilar differ *(vary)*
be distended expand
be distinct differ *(vary)*
be distinguished from deviate, differ *(vary)*
be distracted muse
be disturbed over regret
be disunited disagree
be dormant remain *(stay)*, stay *(rest)*
be doubtful disbelieve, doubt *(distrust)*, misdoubt, mistrust, oscillate, suspect *(distrust)*
be drunk carouse
be dubious doubt *(distrust)*, hesitate, mistrust, pause, suspect *(distrust)*
be due owe
be due to ensue, result
be durable continue *(persevere)*, endure *(last)*
be eager desire
be economical retrench
be effaced disappear
be effective function, prevail *(triumph)*
be efficacious prevail *(triumph)*
be effusive outpour
be employed labor, occupy *(engage)*, practice *(engage in)*
be engaged in commit *(perpetrate)*
be engrossed in commit *(perpetrate)*, concentrate *(pay attention)*, devote
be entitled to as a matter of right, earn
be equivalent compensate *(counterbalance)*
be eradicated perish
be erased disappear
be erroneous bear false witness, err, miscalculate, misread, misstate, mistake
be established lie *(be sustainable)*
be established in inhabit
be evasive evade *(deceive)*, palter, prevaricate
be even with quit *(repay)*
be evidence of manifest
be evident lie *(be sustainable)*
be extinguished perish
be extravagant dissipate *(expend foolishly)*
be faithful adhere *(maintain loyalty)*
be faithful to comply, fulfill, keep *(fulfill)*, obey, observe *(obey)*, perform *(adhere to)*

be faithless bear false witness, default

be fallacious bear false witness

be false bear false witness, equivocate, misrepresent, palter, perjure

be false to betray *(lead astray)*

be familiar with recognize *(perceive)*

be favorable to authorize, bestow, favor

be fearful fear

be firm endure *(last)*, maintain *(sustain)*, resolve *(decide)*

be firmly fixed maintain *(sustain)*

be fitting lie *(be sustainable)*

be fixed stay *(rest)*

be foiled lose *(undergo defeat)*

be fond of prefer, regard *(hold in esteem)*, relish

be forewarned beware, forestall

be forfeited back escheat

be forgiving relent

be formed of comprise, consist, contain *(comprise)*, include

be forsworn bear false witness

be forthcoming impend

be fraudulent bear false witness, palter

be frightened fear

be frugal retrench

be fruitful proliferate, propagate *(increase)*, pullulate

be frustrated lose *(undergo defeat)*

be given acquire *(receive)*, collect *(recover money)*, receive *(acquire)*

be given to understand construe *(comprehend)*

be gluttonous overindulge

be gone abandon *(physically leave)*, depart, part *(leave)*

be good to avail *(be of use)*

be governed by obey

be gracious condescend *(deign)*

be graduated pass *(satisfy requirements)*

be granted a legacy inherit

be greater surpass

be greater in value outbalance

be greater in weight outbalance

be greedy overindulge

be guarded beware

be guided by hear *(give attention to)*, heed, obey, observe *(obey)*

be guilty of perpetrate

be guilty of infraction break *(violate)*

be handed down to devolve

be handed over devolve

be harbinger portend

be harmonious attune

be hateful alienate *(estrange)*

be heir to hold *(possess)*

be helpful contribute *(assist)*

be horrified fear

be humbled lose *(undergo defeat)*

be hurtful ill use, mistreat

be hypocritical palter, pretend

be identical coincide *(correspond)*

be idle loiter, procrastinate

be ignorant misunderstand

be imminent impend

be immobile remain *(stay)*, stay *(rest)*

be immoderate carouse, dissipate *(expend foolishly)*

be immovable remain *(stay)*

be immune resist *(withstand)*

be impaired suffer *(sustain loss)*

be impolite offend *(insult)*

be impoverished lose *(be deprived of)*

be impressed regard *(hold in esteem)*

be improved by gain, profit

be in a quandary doubt *(hesitate)*

be in a reverie muse

be in accordance with comport *(agree with)*

be in action attempt

be in antagonism collide *(clash)*

be in arrears default

be in attendance appear *(attend court proceedings)*, report *(present oneself)*

be in authority moderate *(preside over)*, preside

be in awe fear, regard *(hold in esteem)*

be in charge preside

be in collusion maneuver, plot

be in collusion with connive

be in conflict with contravene

be in conjunction with border *(bound)*

be in contact with border *(bound)*

be in control prevail *(triumph)*

be in debt default, overdraw, owe

be in effect exist

be in error misapprehend, miscalculate, misconstrue

be in favor of approve, authorize, consent, countenance, embrace *(accept)*, pass *(approve)*, permit

be in general use prevail *(be in force)*, prevail *(triumph)*

be in harmony conform

be in harmony with agree *(comply)*

be in keeping comport *(agree with)*, conform

be in league with involve *(participate)*, participate

be in need lack

be in operation function

be in opposition disagree

be in possession of hold *(possess)*, own, possess

be in possession of the facts comprehend *(understand)*

be in power govern, manage, rule *(govern)*

be in present force exist

be in proximity approach

be in receipt of obtain, own, possess

be in sight appear *(materialize)*

be in sight of approach

be in store impend

be in the ascendant prevail *(triumph)*

be in the chair preside

be in the majority predominate *(outnumber)*

be in the neighborhood of approach

be in the running compete

be in the vicinity of approach, approximate, border *(approach)*

be in the way impede

be in the wrong err, mistake, misunderstand

be in tune with comport *(agree with)*

be in unison agree *(comply)*

be in want lack

be inadequate lack

be inattentive ignore, muse, neglect

be inattentive to overlook *(superintend)*

be incident to appertain

be inclined to think assume *(suppose)*, deem, presuppose

be incompatible collide *(clash)*

be incongruent differ *(disagree)*

be inconsistent conflict

be inconstant change, palter, vacillate, vary

be incredulous disbelieve, doubt *(distrust)*

be incurious disregard

be indebted owe

be indecisive oscillate

be indifferent disregard

be indifferent to discount *(disbelieve)*

be indignant resent

be indiscreet impart

be indulgent of allow *(endure)*, permit

be indulgent toward favor

be industrious labor

be inert procrastinate, remain *(stay)*, stay *(rest)*

be inferior lack

be influenced predetermine

be influential prevail upon

be informed comprehend *(understand)*, pierce *(discern)*, understand

be informed of perceive

be inharmonious conflict, differ *(disagree)*, differ *(vary)*

be inherent constitute *(compose)*

be inimical collide *(clash)*, counter

be injured suffer *(sustain loss)*

be inmovable stay *(rest)*

be insensitive disregard

be insincere bear false witness, palter

be insolent disparage

be instrumental pander

be insubordinate disobey, rebel

be insufficient lack

be insulted resent

be intelligible cohere *(be logically consistent)*

be intemperate carouse, debauch, dissipate *(expend foolishly)*, overindulge

be intent upon pursue *(strive to gain)*

be interdependent with concern *(involve)*

be intermittent fluctuate

be intimate cohabit

be intimidated fear

be intolerant persecute

be intrinsic appertain

be involved concern *(involve)*, participate

be irresolute change, doubt *(hesitate)*, hesitate, misdoubt, oscillate, pause, vacillate

be jaundiced preconceive, predetermine, presuppose, select

be joined conjoin

be joined to adjoin

be juxtaposed border *(bound)*

be lax neglect

be left behind lose *(undergo defeat)*

be lenient bear *(tolerate)*, condone, palliate *(excuse)*, relax, tolerate

be liable answer *(be responsible)*, owe

be loath disfavor, mistrust

be located dwell *(reside)*, reside

be logical cohere *(be logically consistent)*

be long-lived last

be lost to view disappear

be loyal adhere *(maintain loyalty)*

be **loyal to** obey

be **lucid** cohere *(be logically consistent)*

be **made of** comprise, consist

be **made up of** comprehend *(include)*, consist, include

be **malevolent** bait *(harass)*, endanger, harass, harm, ill use, mistreat, persecute

be **malicious** persecute

be **manifest** appear *(attend court proceedings)*, appear *(materialize)*

be **master** direct *(supervise)*

be **master of** handle *(manage)*, hold *(possess)*, own

be **mendacious** bear false witness, palter

be **merciful** condone, relent

be **mindful** concern *(care)*, regard *(pay attention)*

be **misguided** err, miscalculate, misconceive, mistake, misunderstand

be **misinformed** misconceive

be **misled** err, misapprehend, miscalculate, misconceive, misconstrue, misinterpret, mistake, misunderstand

be **mistaken** err, misapprehend, miscalculate, misconceive, misread, mistake, misunderstand

be **mixed** desegregate

be **mollified** relent

be **more specific** elaborate

be **motionless** remain *(stay)*, stay *(rest)*

be **moved** sympathize

be **mutinous** disobey

be **mutually opposed** collide *(clash)*

be **near** approach, approximate, border *(approach)*, impend

be **near at hand** impend, threaten

be **needy** lack

be **neglectful** default, procrastinate

be **negligent** default, disobey

be **nervous** doubt *(distrust)*, fear, misdoubt, mistrust

be **no more** die

be **noisy** brawl

be **null and void** perish

be **numerous** compound, proliferate

be **nurtured** subsist

be **obedient** obey

be **obligated** answer *(be responsible)*, owe

be **obliged** answer *(be responsible)*

be **oblique** deviate

be **obstinate** adhere *(persist)*, insist, persevere, persist, refuse

be **obstructive** balk, clog, counter, fight *(counteract)*, foil, frustrate, inconvenience

be **occupied in concentration** muse

be **occupied in study** muse

be **occupied with** address *(direct attention to)*

be **of contrary sentiment** dissent *(differ in opinion)*

be **of different opinions** disagree

be **of greater significance** outweigh

be **of help** assist

be **of service** aid, avail *(be of use)*, contribute *(assist)*, pander

be **of the opinion** assume *(suppose)*, deem, guess, surmise, suspect *(think)*

be **of the same mind** coincide *(concur)*

be **of use** assist, help, inure *(benefit)*, profit, serve *(assist)*

be **of value** avail *(be of use)*

be **off** abandon *(physically leave)*, leave *(depart)*

be **offended** resent

be **offensive** affront, bait *(harass)*, harry *(harass)*, mistreat, persecute

be **offered** hold *(possess)*

be **on one's guard** beware

be **on the alert** beware, patrol

be **on the lookout** beware, patrol

be **on the watch** beware, patrol

be **one** unite

be **one of** concern *(involve)*

be **one with** coincide *(concur)*, merge

be **opposed** conflict, disagree

be **opposed to** conflict, cross *(disagree with)*, disapprove *(reject)*

be **opposite** confront *(oppose)*, differ *(vary)*

be **ostentatious** flaunt

be **outdistanced** lose *(undergo defeat)*

be **outvoted** lose *(undergo defeat)*

be **overawed** fear

be **overbearing** condescend *(patronize)*

be **overthrown** lose *(undergo defeat)*

be **paid** collect *(recover money)*

be **parallel** concur *(coexist)*

be **part of** appertain, constitute *(compose)*

be **partial** discriminate *(treat differently)*

be **partial to** favor, prefer

be **partisan** adhere *(maintain loyalty)*

be **patent** appear *(seem to be)*

be **patient** bear *(tolerate)*, forbear

be **peaceful** rest *(cease from action)*

be **penitent** regret, repent

be **peremptory** insist

be **perfidious** bear false witness, disobey, palter

be **periodic** alternate *(fluctuate)*, fluctuate

be **perjured** bear false witness

be **permanent** continue *(persevere)*, endure *(last)*, remain *(continue)*

be **permissible** lie *(be sustainable)*

be **permitted** lie *(be sustainable)*

be **perplexed** misjudge

be **persistent** recur

be **persuaded** concede, grant *(concede)*, opine

be **pertinent** appertain, apply *(pertain)*

be **pertinent to** concern *(involve)*

be **petrified** fear

be **piqued** resent

be **pitiless** brutalize, mistreat

be **placated** relent

be **pleased with** relish

be **plentiful** proliferate

be **pliant** relent

be **poor** lack

be **possessed of** hold *(possess)*, occupy *(take possession)*, own

be **possible** lie *(be sustainable)*

be **precise** detail *(particularize)*

be **predisposed** discriminate *(treat differently)*

be **prejudiced** favor, forejudge, preconceive, predetermine, presuppose, select

be **prepared** beware, expect *(anticipate)*

be **prepossessed** predetermine

be **present** appear *(attend court proceedings)*, dwell *(reside)*, remain *(occupy)*

be **present and note** witness *(have direct knowledge of)*

be **present to answer** appear *(attend court proceedings)*

be **preserved** endure *(last)*

be **prevalent** prevail *(triumph)*

be **prewarned** beware

be **prodigal** bestow, dissipate *(expend foolishly)*, overdraw

be **productive** pullulate

be **proffered** hold *(possess)*

be **profitable** avail *(be of use)*, inure *(benefit)*, pay

be **prolix** outpour

be **prolonged** endure *(last)*

be **promoted** pass *(satisfy requirements)*

be **prone to** gravitate

be **proper** lie *(be sustainable)*

be **proper to** apply *(pertain)*

be **protracted** endure *(last)*

be **provoked** fear

be **proxy for** represent *(substitute)*

be **prudent** beware

be **public** bare, circulate

be **published** circulate

be **puzzled** doubt *(hesitate)*

be **quartered** reside

be **quiescent** desist

be **quiet** rest *(cease from action)*

be **racked** suffer *(sustain loss)*

be **rash** forejudge

be **rationally connected** cohere *(be logically consistent)*

be **ready for** anticipate *(expect)*

be **reasonable** cohere *(be logically consistent)*

be **recalcitrant** disobey

be **reconciled** condone, suffer *(permit)*

be **recusant** disobey

be **reduced in worth** decay, degenerate

be **regulated by** conform, obey, observe *(obey)*

be **related** correspond *(be equivalent)*

be **related to** concern *(involve)*

be **relevant** apply *(pertain)*, concern *(involve)*

be **reminded of** recall *(remember)*, recollect, remember

be **remiss** default

be **remorseful** regret

be **resident in** inhabit

be **resigned** suffer *(permit)*

be **resolute** choose, endeavor, insist, persevere, persist

be **resolute in** prosecute *(carry forward)*

be **respondent** countercharge

be **responsible** cause, compose, create, induce

be **responsible for** guarantee, sponsor

be **responsive** acknowledge *(respond)*, answer *(reply)*, countercharge

be **revengeful** resent

be **rewarded** reap

be **rife** pervade, predominate *(outnumber)*

be **riveted** stay *(rest)*

be **rude** affront, disparage, harry *(harass)*, ignore, mistreat be ruined lose *(undergo defeat)*, perish

be ruled by obey

be ruthless persecute

be satisfied opine

be satisfied with approve, recommend

be scared fear

be scornful flout

be sedentary remain *(stay)*, stay *(rest)*

be seized of possess

be selfish overindulge

be sensitive to perceive

be serene repose *(rest)*

be servile pander

be settled dwell *(reside)*

be settled in opinion resolve *(decide)*

be severe castigate

be severed part *(separate)*

be showy flaunt

be silent cease

be simultaneous coincide *(correspond)*

be situated dwell *(reside)*, reside

be skeptical disbelieve, doubt *(distrust)*, impugn, misdoubt, mistrust, suspect *(distrust)*

be sly circumvent

be so good as to deign

be so minded choose

be solid crystallize

be sorry for deplore, regret, repent, sympathize

be sovereign predominate *(command)*

be specific describe, designate, enumerate, itemize, pinpoint

be spokesman for represent *(substitute)*

be spurious bear false witness

be stable last

be startled fear

be stationary remain *(stay)*, stay *(rest)*

be stationed dwell *(reside)*

be steadfast adhere *(maintain loyalty)*, adhere *(persist)*, keep *(continue)*, persevere, persist, prolong, prosecute *(carry forward)*, remain *(continue)*

be steady adhere *(persist)*, persevere, persist

be stealthy conspire, lurk, prowl

be still rest *(cease from action)*

be stricken suffer *(sustain loss)*

be strong resist *(withstand)*

be stubborn persevere

be subject answer *(be responsible)*, obey

be subjected to bear *(tolerate)*, endure *(suffer)*, suffer *(sustain loss)*

be submissive relent, surrender *(yield)*, yield *(submit)*

be submissive to observe *(obey)*

be subsequent ensue, succeed *(follow)*, supervene

be subservient pander

be successful attain, earn, pass *(satisfy requirements)*, prevail *(triumph)*

be sufficient fulfill, satisfy *(fulfill)*

be suitable comport *(agree with)*, lie *(be sustainable)*, pertain

be suited lie *(be sustainable)*

be sundered part *(separate)*

be superior beat *(defeat)*, outbalance, surpass, transcend

be superior in number predominate

(outnumber)

be supportable lie *(be sustainable)*

be supported subsist

be supreme beat *(defeat)*, predominate *(command)*

be surety answer *(be responsible)*

be surety for avouch *(guarantee)*, cosign

be suspicious doubt *(distrust)*, suspect *(distrust)*

be sustained subsist

be swallowed up merge

be swayed predetermine

be sworn certify *(attest)*, testify

be tacked together cohere *(adhere)*

be taken for exemplify

be temperate forbear, refrain

be tenacious persevere, persist, remain *(continue)*

be tentative hesitate

be terrified fear

be the agent compose, create

be the author create

be the author of cause

be the cause generate

be the cause of compose, create, engender, evoke

be the chairman preside

be the effect result

be the effect of ensue

be the embodiment personify

be the equivalent of exemplify

be the guiding force oversee

be the heir of inherit

be the outcome result

be the reason compose, create

be the victor prevail *(triumph)*

be thorough follow-up

be thwarted lose *(undergo defeat)*

be timeless endure *(last)*, last

be timid fear

be tolerant condone, forbear, relent

be touched sympathize

be tranquil repose *(rest)*, rest *(cease from action)*

be transferred devolve

be transfixed remain *(stay)*, stay *(rest)*

be treasonable rebel

be treasonous disobey

be triumphant prevail *(triumph)*

be true adhere *(maintain loyalty)*

be true to keep *(fulfill)*

be unable to respect decry, disgrace

be unaccommodating disoblige

be uncandid palter

be uncertain confound, doubt *(distrust)*, doubt *(hesitate)*, hesitate, misdoubt, mistrust, oscillate, pause, tergiversate, vacillate

be unclear equivocate

be unconsumed last

be unconvinced disbelieve

be uncooperative inconvenience

be undecided doubt *(hesitate)*, oscillate

be under legal obligation answer *(be responsible)*

be under obligation owe

be under the impression apprehend *(perceive)*, deem

be understandable cohere *(be logically consistent)*

be understanding sympathize

be undetermined doubt *(hesitate)*, misdoubt, oscillate

be undisciplined disobey

be unexhausted last

be unfaithful default

be unfriendly alienate *(estrange)*

be unique differ *(vary)*

be united join *(associate oneself with)*

be unlike differ *(vary)*, vary

be unpalatable repel *(disgust)*

be unresolved oscillate

be unruly disobey

be unseen lurk

be unsettled alternate *(fluctuate)*, vacillate

be unsteady fluctuate, oscillate, vacillate

be unsuccessful fail *(lose)*, lose *(undergo defeat)*

be unsure oscillate, tergiversate, vacillate

be unsusceptible resist *(withstand)*

be untruthful bear false witness, equivocate, fabricate *(make up)*, lie *(falsify)*, palter, perjure, prevaricate

be unwilling conflict, disoblige, dissent *(withhold assent)*, hold out *(resist)*, refuse

be unyielding adhere *(persist)*, persevere, persist

be uppermost in the mind occur *(come to mind)*

be useful avail *(be of use)*, function, pander

be vagrant loiter

be vague equivocate

be vengeful resent

be vexed resent

be vicious to brutalize

be victorious carry *(succeed)*, pass *(satisfy requirements)*, prevail *(triumph)*, succeed *(attain)*

be victorious over beat *(defeat)*, overthrow

be vigilant caution, concern *(care)*, observe *(watch)*

be violent fight *(battle)*, mistreat

be voracious overindulge

be vouchsafed hold *(possess)*

be wanting lack

be warned beware

be warranted lie *(be sustainable)*

be wary beware

be watchful concern *(care)*

be wicked to brutalize

be willing agree *(comply)*, comply, consent

be willing to bear assume *(undertake)*

be without lack, lose *(be deprived of)*

be worse degenerate

be worthy earn

be wounded suffer *(sustain loss)*

be wrong miscalculate, misconstrue

beach littoral

beachfront littoral

beacon indicant, indicator

beam emit, radiate

bear allow *(endure)*, carry *(transport)*, demean *(deport oneself)*, endure *(suffer)*, engender, produce *(manufacture)*, propagate *(increase)*, resist *(withstand)*, suffer *(sustain loss)*, tolerate, transmit, transport, yield *(produce a return)*

bear a grudge against discriminate *(treat differently)*

bear a part contribute *(assist)*

bear away distrain, hijack,

impropriate

bear down coerce, pressure
bear down against compel
bear down on press *(constrain)*
bear down upon attack
bear false witness frame *(charge falsely)*, lie *(falsify)*, misrepresent, palter, perjure, prevaricate
bear fruit avail *(bring about)*, succeed *(attain)*
bear hard upon compel
bear heavily weigh
bear in memory remember
bear in mind care *(be cautious)*, regard *(pay attention)*, remember, retain *(keep in possession)*
bear malice alienate *(estrange)*, discriminate *(treat differently)*, mistreat, resent
bear no malice forgive
bear no resemblance deviate, differ *(vary)*
bear off deviate, kidnap
bear on appertain
bear oneself deport *(conduct oneself)*
bear out attest, certify *(attest)*, corroborate, document, evidence, justify, substantiate, support *(corroborate)*, sustain *(confirm)*, verify *(confirm)*, witness *(attest to)*
bear pain endure *(suffer)*
bear resemblance correspond *(be equivalent)*
bear the cost bear the expense, defray, pay
bear the cost of disburse *(pay out)*, expend *(disburse)*
bear the expense defray
bear the expense of disburse *(pay out)*, expend *(disburse)*
bear the responsibility of hold *(possess)*
bear up resist *(withstand)*, uphold
bear up against maintain *(sustain)*, stem *(check)*
bear up under endure *(suffer)*
bear upon affect, apply *(pertain)*, based on, pertain, prejudice *(influence)*, refer *(direct attention)*, relate *(establish a connection)*
bear with condone, excuse, forbear, submit *(yield)*, suffer *(permit)*, tolerate, vouchsafe
bear without resistance endure *(suffer)*
bear witness acknowledge *(declare)*, avouch *(avow)*, avow, certify *(attest)*, corroborate, notarize, promise *(vow)*, seal *(solemnize)*, speak, substantiate, swear, testify, vouch, witness *(attest to)*
bear witness against betray *(disclose)*, denounce *(inform against)*, inform *(betray)*
bear witness to attest, certify *(attest)*, depose *(testify)*, evidence
bearable fair *(satisfactory)*, passable
beard defy
beardless inexperienced
bearing behavior, color *(complexion)*, conduct, connection *(relation)*, connotation, content *(meaning)*, demeanor, deportment, direction *(course)*, magnitude, manner *(behavior)*, position *(point of view)*, posture *(attitude)*, presence *(poise)*, relation *(connection)*, relationship *(connection)*, relevance, semblance,

significance, tendency
bearing good will benevolent
bearing no name anonymous
bearing offspring freely fertile
bearing on relative *(relevant)*
bearing on the question pertinent
bearing out corroboration
bearing revenue lucrative
bearing the cost collection *(payment)*
bearing upon apposite, cognate, germane, incident
bearings locality
bearish brutal, fractious, petulant, severe
beast animal
beast of burden animal
beast of the field animal
beastliness bestiality, disrepute
beastly brutal, disreputable, heinous, obnoxious, odious, repulsive, vicious
beat attack, defeat, kill *(defeat)*, lash *(strike)*, oscillate, outweigh, overcome *(surmount)*, overwhelm, stress *(accent)*, strike *(assault)*, subdue, subjugate, surmount, surpass, territory, upset
beat a retreat quit *(evacuate)*
beat back repel *(drive back)*, repulse, resist *(oppose)*
beat down browbeat, haggle, subdue
beat off parry, repulse, stave
beatable vulnerable
beaten despondent, passable
beatific ecstatic
beatify elevate
beating battery, defeat, failure *(lack of success)*
beauteous attractive
beautification motif
beautified elaborate
beautiful attractive, elegant
beautify embellish, meliorate
becalm pacify, soothe
becalmed dormant
because consequently
because of this a priori
bechance supervene
beckon call *(summon)*, entrap, request, subpoena, summon
beckoning attractive
becloud blind *(obscure)*, camouflage, confound, cover *(conceal)*, disguise, muddle, obfuscate, obnubilate, obscure, shroud
become arise *(originate)*, comport *(agree with)*, convert *(change use)*, develop, evolve, germinate
become a citizen reside
become a component incorporate *(include)*
become a fact occur *(happen)*
become a member join *(associate oneself with)*
become a participator espouse
become a partisan espouse
become a party to an action intervene
become a reality crystallize
become acquainted rendezvous
become acquainted with ascertain, discern *(detect with the senses)*, find *(discover)*
become added accrue *(increase)*
become an ingredient incorporate *(include)*
become apparent develop, emerge
become apprised of find *(discover)*

become apprized discern *(detect with the senses)*
become aware note *(notice)*, occur *(come to mind)*, realize *(understand)*
become aware of apprehend *(perceive)*, detect, discern *(detect with the senses)*, hear *(perceive by ear)*, notice *(observe)*, overhear, perceive
become bankrupt fail *(lose)*, overdraw
become better progress
become bound promise *(vow)*, stipulate
become bound to pledge *(promise the performance of)*
become broad expand
become connected with join *(associate oneself with)*
become conscious note *(notice)*, realize *(understand)*
become conscious of hear *(perceive by ear)*, notice *(observe)*, perceive
become definite crystallize
become delineated crystallize
become depraved degenerate
become detached disengage
become deteriorated degenerate, depreciate
become disheartened languish
become due accrue *(arise)*, mature
become enfeebled decay, degenerate
become enforceable accrue *(arise)*
become extinct disappear, perish
become familiar with practice *(train by repetition)*
become firm crystallize
become flexible give *(yield)*
become forfeit lapse *(cease)*
become free escape
become fully developed mature
become greater accrue *(increase)*, appreciate *(increase)*, compound, expand, increase
become habituated naturalize *(acclimate)*
become heir to accede *(succeed)*
become ill languish
become impaired degenerate
become imperceptible disappear
become inactive quit *(discontinue)*
become informed discern *(detect with the senses)*, discover, find *(discover)*
become insolvent fail *(lose)*, overdraw
become involved care *(regard)*, engage *(involve)*
become involved with participate
become known convey *(communicate)*, occur *(happen)*
become larger accrue *(increase)*, compound, expand, increase
become less active subside
become less rigid give *(yield)*
become liable guarantee
become liable for incur
become like conform
become lower in quality decay, degenerate
become manifest arise *(appear)*, emerge
become more numerous appreciate *(increase)*
become notably worse degenerate
become noticeable arise *(appear)*
become of greater value appreciate

(increase)

become of less worth depreciate

become one consolidate *(unite)*, unite

become operative arise *(occur)*

become payable mature

become perfected mature

become perverted degenerate

become plain emerge

become pliant give *(yield)*

become poorer by lose *(be deprived of)*

become present accrue *(arise)*

become prime mature

become public circulate

become putrescent decay

become responsible for assume *(undertake)*, incur

become ripe mature

become settled crystallize

become similar conform

become smaller decrease, diminish

become solid cohere *(adhere)*, crystallize

become surety for guarantee

become tainted degenerate

become unable to meet obligations default

become visible appear *(materialize)*, arise *(appear)*, crystallize, emerge, occur *(come to mind)*

become void cease, expire, lapse *(cease)*

become weak languish

become worse degenerate, deteriorate

becoming attractive, consonant, favorable *(advantageous)*, felicitous, fit, fitting, harmonious, palatable, proper, rightful, suitable

becoming greater cumulative *(increasing)*

becoming larger cumulative *(increasing)*

becoming more intense cumulative *(intensifying)*

becomingness propriety *(appropriateness)*

becripple disable

becurtain blind *(obscure)*, camouflage

bed lodge *(house)*, plant *(place firmly)*

bedaub stain

bedazzle discompose, disconcert

bedeck clothe, embellish

bedecked elaborate

bedevil annoy, discompose, disconcert, disorganize, distress, disturb, embarrass, harass, harrow, obsess, perplex, persecute, pique, plague

bedevilment detriment, harm, nuisance

bedim blind *(obscure)*, camouflage, obfuscate, obnubilate, obscure, sully

bedizen embellish

bedizened meretricious, tawdry

bedlam imbroglio, pandemonium, riot, turmoil

bedraggled disordered

bedrape clothe

bedridden disabled *(made incapable)*

bedrock center *(essence)*, foundation *(basis)*

bedwarf minimize

befall supervene

befalling accident *(chance occurrence)*, chance *(fortuity)*, contingency, experience *(encounter)*

befit applicable, comport *(agree with)*, pertain

befitting applicable, apposite, appropriate, condign, convenient, due *(regular)*, eligible, favorable *(advantageous)*, felicitous, fit, just, opportune, proper, rightful, seasonable, suitable, tenable

befog blind *(obscure)*, camouflage, confuse *(bewilder)*, cover *(conceal)*, disorganize, muddle, obscure, shroud

befogged lost *(disoriented)*

befool bait *(lure)*, betray *(lead astray)*, bilk, cheat, deceive, defraud, delude, dupe, entrap, hoodwink, humiliate, illude, inveigle, misguide, mislead

before theretofore

before further examination prima facie *(self-evident)*

before mentioned last *(preceding)*, said

before now heretofore

before one's eyes perceivable

before time premature

before-mentioned aforesaid

beforehand aforethought

beforesaid aforesaid

befoul contaminate, corrupt, debase, infect, pillory, pollute, stain, taint *(contaminate)*, tarnish

befouled tainted *(contaminated)*

befoulment contaminate

befriend favor, foster, promote *(organize)*, side, sponsor, subsidize

befriender good samaritan, samaritan

befuddle confuse *(bewilder)*, discompose, disorganize, disorient, disturb, muddle, obfuscate

befuddled lost *(disoriented)*

befuddlement confusion *(ambiguity)*

beg exhort, importune, press *(beseech)*, pressure, urge

beg a favor call *(appeal to)*, desire

beg for invoke, request

beg leave call *(appeal to)*

beg pardon repent

beg the question prevaricate

beg to be excused refuse

beg to differ demur

beget create, elicit, engender, generate, make, originate, produce *(manufacture)*, propagate *(increase)*, reproduce

begetter architect, author *(originator)*, derivation, parents

begettor progenitor

beggar deplete, parasite

beggared impecunious, poor *(underprivileged)*

beggarliness poverty

beggarly destitute, ignoble, impecunious, petty, poor *(inferior in quality)*

beggary poverty, privation

begging request

begin arise *(originate)*, assume *(undertake)*, commence, conceive *(invent)*, embark, establish *(launch)*, generate, initiate, launch *(initiate)*, maintain *(commence)*, originate, preface, provoke, stem *(originate)*, undertake, unveil

begin a corporation incorporate *(form a corporation)*

begin again continue *(resume)*, proceed *(continue)*, reopen, resume

begin from develop

begin hostilities against attack

begin over continue *(resume)*

begin where one left off proceed *(continue)*

beginner amateur, apprentice, neophyte, novice, probationer *(one being tested)*

beginning causative, creation, derivation, elementary, embryo, foundation *(basis)*, genesis, inception, inchoate, incipient, initial, nascency, onset *(commencement)*, origin *(source)*, original *(initial)*, origination, outset, overture, preamble, precursory, preface, preliminary, prelude, preparatory, prime *(original)*, primordial, rudimentary, source, start, threshold *(commencement)*

beginning before retroactive

beginnings overt act

begird circumscribe *(surround by boundary)*, embrace *(encircle)*, encompass *(surround)*, include

begloom obfuscate, obscure

begotten born *(alive)*

begrime deface, pollute, sully

begrudge withhold

begrudging jealous, reluctant

beguile bait *(lure)*, betray *(lead astray)*, bilk, cheat, circumvent, cloak, deceive, defraud, delude, disarm *(set at ease)*, dupe, ensnare, entrap, evade *(deceive)*, fabricate *(make up)*, fake, feign, foist, hoodwink, illude, interest, inveigle, lure, misguide, mislead, misrepresent, palter, pettifog, pretend, propitiate

beguilement artifice, deceit, deception, falsification, fraud, hoax, knavery, pretense *(pretext)*

beguiling attractive, collusive, deceptive, delusive, dishonest, evasive, fallacious, false *(not genuine)*, fraudulent, insidious

begun but not completed inchoate

behave demean *(deport oneself)*, deport *(conduct oneself)*, obey

behave towards treat *(process)*

behaved obedient

behavior conduct, demeanor, deportment, modus operandi, practice *(custom)*, presence *(poise)*, procedure, protocol *(etiquette)*, way *(manner)*

behavior pattern conduct, manner *(behavior)*

behaviorism casuistry

behest canon, demand, dictate, directive, mandate, order *(judicial directive)*, process *(summons)*, request, requirement, requisition

behind back *(in arrears)*, delinquent *(overdue)*

behind bars in custody

behind the age outdated, outmoded

behind the scenes clandestine, latent

behind the times outdated, outmoded

behind time back *(in arrears)*, dilatory, late *(tardy)*, overdue

behindhand delinquent *(overdue)*

behold detect, discern *(detect with the senses)*, discover, notice *(observe)*, observe *(watch)*, pierce *(discern)*, regard *(pay attention)*, spy, witness *(have direct knowledge of)*

beholdable discernible, manifest, open *(in sight)*, perceivable, perceptible, scrutable

beholden accountable *(responsible)*, bound, indebted, loyal

beholder bystander, witness

behoof advantage, behalf, benefit *(betterment)*

behoove pertain

being character *(an individual)*, entity, identity *(individuality)*, individual, person, personality, presence *(attendance)*, reality, survival

being analyzed at issue

being done current

being in ill repute disreputable

being in two corresponding parts bipartite

being of no importance collateral *(immaterial)*

bejewel embellish

belated back *(in arrears)*, dilatory, late *(tardy)*, overdue

belaud honor

belay handcuff

beleaguer attack, contain *(enclose)*, envelop, harry *(harass)*

belie bear false witness, cloak, deceive, disguise, disprove, fake, falsify, feign, lie *(falsify)*, misrepresent, prevaricate, refute

belief assumption *(supposition)*, concept, conjecture, credence, credulity, doctrine, dogma, estimate *(idea)*, faith, idea, impression, notion, presumption, principle *(axiom)*, reliance, stand *(position)*, standpoint, supposition, theory, thesis, trust *(confidence)*, weight *(credibility)*

beliefs behavior

believability credibility, probability

believable convincing, credible, defensible, ostensible, plausible, possible, presumptive, probable, reliable, specious, tenable, unimpeachable

believableness credibility

believe deem, expect *(consider probable)*, guess, opine, presume, presuppose, surmise, suspect *(think)*

believe in confide *(trust)*, rely

believe on consideration deem

believed convincing, putative, uncontested, undisputed

believer addict, disciple, partisan

believing convincing, credulous, naïve, orthodox, positive *(confident)*, unsuspecting

belittle cavil, condescend *(patronize)*, contemn, decry, defame, demean *(make lower)*, demote, denigrate, denounce *(condemn)*, deprecate, depreciate, derogate, dilute, diminish, disapprove *(condemn)*, discommend, discount *(disbelieve)*, disdain, disparage, lessen, minimize, misprize, pillory, smear, spurn, sully, underestimate

belittlement disparagement, disregard *(lack of respect)*

belittling derogatory, disparagement, pejorative

bellicose contentious, disorderly, impertinent *(insolent)*, inimical, insolent, litigious, malevolent, offensive *(taking the initiative)*, perverse, provocative, pugnacious, spartan

bellicosity belligerency

belligerance belligerency

belligerant inimical

belligerency argument *(contention)*, conflict, ill will, strife

belligerent aggressor, argumentative,

contentious, contestant, disputant, foe, litigious, malevolent, negative, perverse, pugnacious, spiteful

bellowing blatant *(obtrusive)*

belong comport *(agree with)*, constitute *(compose)*, correspond *(be equivalent)*, pertain

belong as a part appertain

belong as an attribute appertain

belong intrinsically constitute *(compose)*

belong to affiliate, apply *(pertain)*, join *(associate oneself with)*

belonger member *(individual in a group)*

belonging applicable, appurtenant, chattel, cognate, collateral *(accompanying)*, correlative, holding *(property owned)*, incident, pertinent, possession *(property)*

belonging equally to common *(shared)*

belonging to apposite, germane

belonging to all common *(shared)*

belonging to another country foreign

belonging to courts of justice forensic

belonging to debate forensic

belonging to many common *(shared)*

belonging to the house domestic *(household)*

belonging to the time current

belongings assets, capital, effects, estate *(property)*, goods, interest *(ownership)*, merchandise, personalty, possessions, property *(possessions)*

beloved popular

below a savoir

below contempt loathsome

below par defective, deficient, faulty, ignoble, imperfect, inferior *(lower in quality)*, marginal, nonsubstantial *(not sturdy)*, paltry, peccable, perfunctory, poor *(inferior in quality)*, unsound *(not strong)*

below standard poor *(inferior in quality)*

below standards defective

below the mark minimal

below the surface latent

belt circumscribe *(surround by boundary)*, contain *(enclose)*, embrace *(encircle)*, encompass *(surround)*

bemask blind *(obscure)*, camouflage, disguise, pretend

bemingle denature

bemire pollute, sully

bemist obfuscate

bemoan deplore, regret, repent

bemock disparage, jape

bemuddle confuse *(bewilder)*

bemuddled disordered, lost *(disoriented)*

bemuse perplex

ben trovato colorable *(plausible)*

bench bar *(court)*, chamber *(body)*, court, judicatory, judicature, judiciary, tribunal

bench of judges chamber *(body)*

bench warrant search warrant

bencher jurist

bend conform, contort, dispose *(incline)*, distort, relax, relent, subdue, submit *(yield)*, succumb, yield *(submit)*

bend out of shape contort

bend to obey

bend to one's will persuade, prejudice *(influence)*

bendable flexible, malleable, pliable, pliant, resilient, sequacious, tractable

bending flexible, malleable, sequacious

bene moratus law-abiding, moral

beneath consideration inappreciable

beneath contempt blameworthy, loathsome, offensive *(offending)*, paltry

beneath notice inappreciable, inconsiderable, negligible, null *(insignificant)*, paltry

beneath one's dignity disgraceful

beneath standards defective

benediction laudation

benefaction aid *(subsistence)*, appropriation *(donation)*, behalf, benefit *(betterment)*, benefit *(conferment)*, benevolence *(act of kindness)*, boom *(prosperity)*, bounty, charity, clemency, contribution *(donation)*, donation, endowment, favor *(act of kindness)*, favor *(sanction)*, gift *(present)*, goodwill, grant, gratuity *(present)*, help, inheritance, largess *(generosity)*, largess *(gift)*, perquisite, profit, tip *(gratuity)*

benefactor backer, contributor *(giver)*, donor, good samaritan, patron *(influential supporter)*, promoter, proponent, receiver, samaritan, sponsor

benefactress donor

beneficence benevolence *(act of kindness)*, benevolence *(disposition to do good)*, clemency, consideration *(sympathetic regard)*, goodwill, humanity *(humaneness)*, largess *(generosity)*, philanthropy

beneficent beneficial, charitable *(benevolent)*, charitable *(lenient)*, donative, humane, liberal *(generous)*, magnanimous, nonprofit, philanthropic

beneficent friend benefactor

beneficentia charity

bénéficiaire heir

beneficial ancillary *(auxiliary)*, contributory, convenient, corrigible, favorable *(advantageous)*, gainful, instrumental, lucrative, medicinal, operative, palliative *(abating)*, practical, profitable, propitious, purposeful, remedial, salubrious, salutary, valuable

beneficial interest claim *(right)*

bènèficiare beneficiary

beneficiary devisee, donee, grantee, heir, legatee, receiver, recipient, successor, transferee

beneficence benefit *(conferment)*

beneficient benevolent

beneficium favor *(act of kindness)*, privilege

beneficus charitable *(benevolent)*

benefit accommodate, advantage, aid *(help)*, aid *(subsistence)*, aid, assistance, avail *(be of use)*, behalf, bonus, capitalize *(seize the chance)*, contribution *(donation)*, dividend, edge *(advantage)*, edification, endowment, favor *(act of kindness)*, favor, function, gain, grant, help, help, largess *(gift)*, output, preference *(priority)*, prerogative, privilege, proceeds, profit, profit, promote *(organize)*, promotion *(encouragement)*, realize *(obtain as a profit)*, reap, recourse, reward, service *(assistance)*, use, utility

(usefulness), value, welfare, worth
benefit of doubt compurgation
benefiter benefactor
benefits consideration *(recompense)*
benevolence assistance, behalf, benefit *(conferment)*, bounty, charity, clemency, comity, consideration *(sympathetic regard)*, favor *(act of kindness)*, goodwill, help, humanity *(humaneness)*, indulgence, lenience, philanthropy, understanding *(tolerance)*
benevolent charitable *(lenient)*, donative, humane, lenient, liberal *(generous)*, meritorious, nonprofit, paternal, philanthropic, placable, propitious
benevolentia benevolence *(act of kindness)*, philanthropy
benevolently fairly *(impartially)*
benevolentness charity
benevolus benevolent
benight blind *(obscure)*, obscure
benighted blind *(not discerning)*, incognizant, opaque
benightedness ignorance
benign beneficial, benevolent, charitable *(lenient)*, favorable *(expressing approval)*, harmless, humane, nontoxic, paternal, philanthropic, propitious, remedial, safe, salutary
benign favor auspices
benignancy benevolence *(disposition to do good)*, humanity *(humaneness)*, largess *(generosity)*, philanthropy
benignant beneficial, charitable *(lenient)*, philanthropic, propitious
benignitas indulgence
benignity clemency, consideration *(sympathetic regard)*, favor *(act of kindness)*, humanity *(humaneness)*, largess *(generosity)*, philanthropy
benignus charitable *(benevolent)*
bent animus, aptitude, character *(personal quality)*, design *(intent)*, desire, direction *(course)*, disposition *(inclination)*, favor *(partiality)*, frame *(mood)*, inclination, inclined, instinct, partiality, penchant, pertinacious, position *(point of view)*, posture *(attitude)*, preconception, predilection, predisposition, prejudice *(preconception)*, proclivity, prone, propensity, resolute, stand *(position)*, standpoint, tendency
bent on solicitous
bent upon eager, earnest, insistent, zealous
benumb drug, obtund
benumbed insensible, torpid
benumbing chilling effect, lifeless *(dull)*
bepraise honor
bequeath abalienate, bestow, cede, contribute *(supply)*, convey *(transfer)*, demise, descend, devise *(give)*, devolve, endow, give *(grant)*, grant *(transfer formally)*, leave *(give)*, pass *(advance)*, present *(make a gift)*, transfer
bequeathable heritable
bequeathal bequest, demise *(conveyance)*, devolution, endowment, grant, legacy, will *(testamentary instrument)*
bequeathed by will testamentary
bequeather donor, feoffor, grantor
bequest benefit *(conferment)*, contribute *(supply)*, contribution *(donation)*, devolution, donation, dower, endowment, estate *(hereditament)*, grant, her-

editament, heritage, inheritance, legacy
berate blame, castigate, censure, complain *(criticize)*, condemn *(blame)*, criticize *(find fault with)*, decry, defame, denounce *(condemn)*, deprecate, disapprove *(condemn)*, fault, lash *(attack verbally)*, mistreat, pillory, rebuke, remonstrate, reprehend, reprimand, reproach
berating contumely, objurgation, obloquy, revilement
bereave deprive, despoil
bereaved disconsolate
bereaved child orphan
bereavement cost *(penalty)*, privation
bereft bankrupt, destitute
bereft of devoid, insufficient
bereft of funds poor *(underprivileged)*
bereft of life dead, deceased, lifeless *(dead)*
bereft of reason deranged, lunatic, non compos mentis
beribbon embellish
berserk frenetic
berth employment, lodge *(house)*, lodging, office, post, seat, trade *(occupation)*
beseech call *(appeal to)*, exhort, importune, petition, plead *(implore)*, pray, pressure, prevail upon, request, solicit, sue, urge
beseeching precatory, solicitous
beseechment call *(appeal)*, entreaty, prayer, request
beseige dun, envelop
beset accost, assail, attack, badger, bait *(harass)*, discommode, dun, embarrass, envelop, harass, harrow, harry *(harass)*, hector, importune, inflict, obsess, perplex, persecute, pique, plague, press *(goad)*, provoke
beset with danger dangerous
beset with difficulties painful
beset with difficulty difficult
beset with perils aleatory *(perilous)*
besetting hostile
besetting idea compulsion *(obsession)*
beside adjacent, contiguous
beside oneself ecstatic
beside the mark impertinent *(irrelevant)*, inapposite, irrelevant
beside the point immaterial, impertinent *(irrelevant)*, inapposite, irrelevant, needless, nonessential, peripheral
beside the question immaterial, impertinent *(irrelevant)*, irrelevant, nonessential
besides also, further, save
besiege assault, attack, bait *(harass)*, harass, harrow, importune, obsess, overwhelm, strike *(assault)*
besiegement assault
besieger aggressor
besmear brand *(stigmatize)*, defame, denigrate, denounce *(condemn)*, disgrace, dishonor *(deprive of honor)*, disparage, pillory, smear, stain, sully
besmirch brand *(stigmatize)*, contemn, defame, denigrate, denounce *(condemn)*, derogate, discredit, dishonor *(deprive of honor)*, infect, libel, malign, pillory, pollute, smear, stain, taint *(contaminate)*
besmirched blemished
besmirching defilement
besmut smear

bespangle embellish
bespangled pretentious *(ostentatious)*
bespatter brand *(stigmatize)*, defame, denigrate, derogate, disparage, humiliate, pillory, pollute
bespeak call *(appeal to)*, denote, evince, indicate, manifest, reserve
bespread diffuse
besprinkle diffuse
best absolute *(ideal)*, cardinal *(outstanding)*, premium, prime *(most valuable)*, select, subdue, superlative, transcend, utmost
best behavior decorum
best of taste decorum
best part elite
best people elite
bestead avail *(be of use)*, promote *(organize)*, situated
bestial brutal
bestiality brutality
bestir oneself endeavor, strive
bestow bear *(yield)*, confer *(give)*, contribute *(supply)*, dedicate, delegate, descend, devise *(give)*, dispel, dispense, dole, endow, endue, fund, furnish, give *(grant)*, grant *(transfer formally)*, impart, leave *(give)*, mete, parcel, post, present *(make a gift)*, provide *(supply)*, spend, subsidize, supply, transfer, vouchsafe, yield *(produce a return)*
bestow by judicial decree award
bestow by will demise
bestow in shares disperse *(disseminate)*
bestow on administer *(tender)*
bestow thought upon muse
bestow upon bequeath, dispense, vest
bestow voluntarily grant *(transfer formally)*
bestowable heritable
bestowal appropriation *(donation)*, benefit *(conferment)*, cession, charity, concession *(authorization)*, contribution *(donation)*, conveyance, dedication, dispensation *(act of dispensing)*, dower, endowment, grant, legacy, will *(testamentary instrument)*
bestowed gratuitous *(given without recompense)*
bestowed by ballot elective *(selective)*
bestower contributor *(giver)*, donor, feoffor, grantor, obligee
bestowing donative
bestowment conveyance, dispensation *(act of dispensing)*, donation, dower, endowment, gift *(present)*, largess *(gift)*, tip *(gratuity)*
bestowment of a share contribution *(donation)*
bestrew cast *(throw)*, diffuse, dispel, disperse *(disseminate)*, dissipate *(spread out)*, spread
bet gamble, lottery, risk, speculate *(chance)*, speculation *(risk)*, stake *(award)*
bet on parlay *(bet)*
betoken anticipate *(prognosticate)*, denote, evince, exemplify, herald, indicate, label, manifest, portend, predict, presage, prognosticate, promise *(raise expectations)*, signify *(denote)*
betokening success auspicious
betongue lash *(attack verbally)*, rep-

rehend

betray bear false witness, bilk, cheat, defect, disobey, misrepresent, palter, rebel

betray the secret inform *(betray)*

betrayal bad faith, bad repute, disloyalty, infidelity, treason

betrayal of a trust treason

betrayal of oath infidelity

betrayal of trust disloyalty, infidelity

betraying perfidious, recreant

betrayment bad faith

betrothed conjugal, nuptial

better ameliorate, amend, bettor, embellish, emend, enhance, help, meliorate, meritorious, outbalance, outweigh, preferable, preferential, promote *(advance)*, rectify, reform, relieve *(give aid)*, superior *(excellent)*, surpass, transcend, treat *(remedy)*

better part generality *(bulk)*, majority *(greater part)*

betterment advancement *(improvement)*, amendment *(correction)*, behalf, correction *(change)*, development *(progression)*, edification, headway, improvement, progress, promotion *(advancement)*, reform, reorganization, repair

bettor speculator

between among, intermediate

bevy assemblage, band

bewail deplore, regret, repent

bewailing querulous

beware care *(be cautious)*

bewilder confound, discompose, disorganize, disorient, disturb, embarrass, misguide, muddle, obfuscate, overcome *(overwhelm)*, overwhelm, perplex, perturb

bewildered insensible, lost *(disoriented)*, speechless

bewildering complex, enigmatic, equivocal, labyrinthine, opaque

bewilderment ambiguity, bombshell, confusion *(ambiguity)*, enigma, ignorance, incertitude, quandary, surprise

bewitch lure, obsess

bewitching attractive, sapid

bewitchment seduction

beyond further

beyond a doubt definitive, undeniable

beyond a question demonstrable

beyond a shadow of a doubt clear *(certain)*, incontrovertible

beyond a shadow of doubt categorical, certain *(positive)*

beyond all dispute certain *(positive)*, clear *(certain)*, decisive, definite, definitive, inappealable

beyond all doubt demonstrable

beyond all praise prime *(most valuable)*

beyond all question axiomatic, categorical, certain *(positive)*, decisive, definite, inappealable, incontestable, positive *(incontestable)*, undeniable

beyond belief implausible, incredible, ludicrous

beyond compare absolute *(ideal)*, best, leading *(ranking first)*, paramount, prime *(most valuable)*

beyond comparison paramount, unique

beyond comprehension inapprehen-

sible, incomprehensible

beyond contradiction incontrovertible

beyond control impracticable, insuperable, intractable

beyond correction irremediable

beyond cure irremediable

beyond dispute axiomatic, conclusive *(settled)*, undeniable

beyond doubt absolute *(conclusive)*, explicit, irrefutable, positive *(incontestable)*, uncontroverted, undisputed

beyond expression indefinable, ineffable

beyond help incorrigible

beyond hope irremediable

beyond one's power insurmountable

beyond one's reach difficult, insurmountable

beyond price inestimable, invaluable, priceless

beyond question inappealable, undisputed

beyond reach inaccessible, unapproachable

beyond recall irrecoverable, irremediable, irrevocable

beyond redress irremediable

beyond reform incorrigible

beyond remedy irredeemable, irremediable, irreversible

beyond reproach unimpeachable

beyond the bounds of possibility insurmountable

beyond the jurisdiction of the court want of jurisdiction

beyond the limit extreme *(exaggerated)*

beyond the ordinary extraordinary

beyond understanding inapprehensible

bhang cannabis

bi-facial bilateral

bias bait *(lure)*, discrimination *(bigotry)*, dispose *(incline)*, disposition *(inclination)*, favor *(partiality)*, favoritism, inclination, inequality, inequity, injustice, intolerance, nepotism, partiality, penchant, position *(point of view)*, preconception, predetermination, predilection, predisposition, preference *(choice)*, prejudice *(preconception)*, prejudice *(influence)*, proclivity, propensity, slant, stand *(position)*, tendency

biased disadvantageous, ex parte, exclusive *(limited)*, illiberal, interested, one-sided, parochial, partisan, preferential, prejudicial, prone, subjective, unequal *(unjust)*, unfair, unjust

biased judgment inequity, partiality

bibacity dipsomania

bibliophilic learned

bibulosity inebriation

bibulousness inebriation

bicameral bipartite

bicker brawl, contend *(dispute)*, dicker, differ *(disagree)*, disaccord, disagree, dispute *(debate)*, dissent *(differ in opinion)*

bickering altercation, argument *(contention)*, contest *(dispute)*, discord, dispute, dissension, dissidence, fight *(argument)*, fracas, fractious, negative, pugnacious

bid appeal, appeal, application, call *(appeal)*, command, detail *(assign)*, dic-

tate, direct *(order)*, endeavor, endeavor, enjoin, impose *(enforce)*, insist, instruct *(direct)*, invitation, invoke, mandate, offer *(propose)*, overture, petition, petition, pray, prescribe, proffer, proposition, request, request, summon, summons, writ

bid against counter, counteract

bid come call *(summon)*

bid defiance to challenge

bid fair promise *(raise expectations)*

bid farewell leave *(depart)*

bid for attempt, dicker, haggle, negotiate, pursue *(strive to gain)*, strive

biddable loyal, obedient, pliable, resigned

bidder applicant *(candidate)*, customer, rival

bidding demand, directive, guidance, injunction, instruction *(direction)*, invitation, monition *(legal summons)*, process *(summons)*, requirement, requisition, writ

bide continue *(persevere)*, defer *(put off)*, endure *(suffer)*, last, persist, reside

bide time pause

bienséance decorum

bifurcate dichotomize, divergent, part *(separate)*

bifurcated bicameral, bipartite, divergent

bifurcation dichotomy, severance, split

bifurcous bipartite

big capacious, extensive, gross *(flagrant)*, important *(significant)*, major, momentous, ponderous, prodigious *(enormous)*

big-hearted benevolent

biggest part generality *(bulk)*

biggest share majority *(greater part)*

bighearted philanthropic

bigness mass *(weight)*

bigoted exclusive *(limited)*, illiberal, narrow, partial *(biased)*

bigotry bias, inequity, intolerance

bilateral mutual *(reciprocal)*, reciprocal

bilateral contract mutual understanding

bile resentment, umbrage

bileful bilious

bilious bitter *(penetrating)*, dyseptic, malevolent

bilk defraud, dupe, ensnare, peculate, pilfer

bilked aggrieved *(harmed)*

bill act *(enactment)*, amendment *(legislation)*, cash, charge *(assess)*, check *(instrument)*, codification, debt, draft, enactment, instrument *(document)*, measure, receipt *(voucher)*

bill drafter lawmaker

bill of accounts dun

bill of complaint allegation, claim *(legal demand)*

bill of costs dun

bill of exchange check *(instrument)*, draft, security *(stock)*

bill of indemnity exoneration

bill of indictment accusation, complaint

bill of lading invoice *(itemized list)*

billet domicile, dwell *(reside)*, employment, job, lodging, note *(brief comment)*, office, post, residence, role

billing publicity

billingsgate profanity, revilement

bills currency, debit, legislation (*enactments*)

billy cudgel

bind affix, amalgamate, annex (*add*), attach (*join*), cement, combine (*join together*), confine, connect (*join together*), consolidate (*strengthen*), constrain (*imprison*), constrict (*compress*), contain (*enclose*), contain (*restrain*), detain (*restrain*), engage (*hire*), estop, fetter, hamper, handcuff, impose (*enforce*), join (*bring together*), limit, pledge (*promise the performance of*), press (*constrain*), promise (*vow*), restrain, restrict, trammel

bind by a pledge promise (*vow*)

bind oneself pledge (*promise the performance of*), promise (*vow*)

bind oneself by oath promise (*vow*), swear

bind together commingle

binder connection (*fastening*)

binding accession (*annexation*), attachment (*act of affixing*), choate lien, coalescence, coalition, compelling, compulsory, concurrent (*united*), contractual, decretal, essential (*required*), forcible, fully executed (*signed*), indefeasible, irrevocable, mandatory, necessary (*required*), obligatory, positive (*prescribed*), prescriptive, requisite, stringent, unavoidable (*not voidable*), valid

binding agreement adjustment, contract, covenant, testament

binding promise agreement (*contract*)

bioecology ecology

biographical record journal

bionomics ecology

bipartisanship conciliation, consensus

bipartite bicameral

bipartition dichotomy

birch lash (*strike*)

birdbrained opaque

birth bloodline, creation, derivation, descent (*lineage*), family (*common ancestry*), genesis, inception, nascency, nationality, onset (*commencement*), origin (*ancestry*), origin (*source*), origination, outset, parentage, race, start

birth out of wedlock bar sinister

birthplace derivation, home (*place of origin*), origin (*source*)

birthright bequest, descent (*lineage*), droit, estate (*hereditament*), heritage

bisect bifurcate, cross (*intersect*), dichotomize, divide (*separate*), split, subdivide

bisectable divisible

bisected bicameral, bipartite, divisive

bisection dichotomy, split, subdivision

bit iota, minimum, part (*portion*), scintilla, segment

biting bitter (*acrid tasting*), bitter (*penetrating*), bitter (*reproachful*), caustic, harsh, incisive, mordacious, offensive (*offending*), scathing, trenchant

bitter antipathetic (*distasteful*), astringent, dyseptic, harsh, hostile, malevolent, malignant, mordacious, resentful, virulent

bitter animosity malice

bitter enemy foe

bitter feelings ill will, rancor

bitter harangue diatribe

bitter language phillipic

bitter words diatribe, phillipic, revilement

bitterness alienation (*estrangement*), feud, ill will, rancor, resentment, spite, umbrage

bivium intersection

bizarre eccentric, egregious, inept (*inappropriate*), irrational, ludicrous, noteworthy, novel, peculiar (*curious*), prodigious (*amazing*), unaccustomed, uncommon, unique, unusual

bizarreness nonconformity, quirk (*idiosyncrasy*)

blabber jargon (*unintelligible language*)

blabbing loquacious

black deplorable, heinous, iniquitous, outrageous, portentous (*ominous*), scandalous

black marketeer bootlegger

black out eradicate, expunge

black-listing boycott

black-market impermissible

blackball condemn (*ban*), denounce (*condemn*), exclusion, humiliate, ostracism, picket, reject

blackballing boycott

blacken brand (*stigmatize*), deface, defame, denigrate, denounce (*condemn*), derogate, disgrace, disparage, humiliate, obfuscate, obnubilate, obscure, pillory, smear, stain, sully, tarnish

blacken one's good name denigrate

blackening calumnious, defilement, pejorative, vilification

blackguard criminal, hoodlum, lash (*attack verbally*), unconscionable

blackhearted malignant

blackjack cudgel

blacklist bar (*exclude*), denounce (*condemn*), isolate, ostracism

blackmail coercion, compel, extort, extortion, graft, hush money, threaten

blackmailer extortionist

blackout censorship, insentience, obscuration

blamable blameful, blameworthy, culpable, delinquent (*guilty of a misdeed*), guilty, peccable, reprehensible

blame accuse, arraign, assignation, censure, charge (*accusation*), charge (*accuse*), cite (*accuse*), complain (*charge*), complain (*criticize*), conviction (*finding of guilt*), criticism, criticize (*find fault with*), culpability, denounce (*inform against*), denunciation, diatribe, disparagement, fault (*responsibility*), fault, guilt, impeach, impeachability, impeachment, impute, incriminate, incrimination, inculpation, indict, involve (*implicate*), obloquy, odium, ostracism, outcry, present (*prefer charges*), proscribe (*denounce*), rebuke, reprehend, reprimand, reprimand, reproach, reproach, stricture

blame falsely frame (*charge falsely*)

blame oneself regret

blame unfairly frame (*charge falsely*)

blame unjustly frame (*charge falsely*)

blameful blameworthy, delinquent

(*guilty of a misdeed*), peccant (*culpable*), reprehensible

blameless clean, incorruptible, inculpable, innocent, irreprehensible, not guilty, pardonable, unimpeachable

blamelessness innocence

blameworthiness blame (*culpability*), culpability, guilt, impeachability, onus (*blame*)

blameworthy blameful, contemptible, culpable, delinquent (*guilty of a misdeed*), disgraceful, guilty, inexcusable, inexpiable, loathsome, notorious, obnoxious, odious, peccable, peccant (*culpable*), reprehensible, reprobate, sinister, unjustifiable, vicious

blameworthy conduct criminality

blaming critical (*faultfinding*), incriminatory, inculpatory

blandish coax, inveigle, persuade, pressure

blandishment bribery, inducement, mention (*tribute*), persuasion, seduction

blank bleak (*exposed and barren*), devoid, form (*document*), inexpressive, inscrutable, nonentity, oblivious, thoughtless, vacant, vacuous, void (*empty*)

blanked blind (*impassable*)

blanket absolute (*complete*), blind (*obscure*), broad, camouflage, complete (*all-embracing*), cover (*protection*), ensconce, enshroud, envelop, generic, indiscriminate, omnibus, shroud

blankness indifference, insentience, nullity

blare barrage, noise, proclaim

blase casual

blasé dispassionate

blase nonchalant

blaspheme malign

blaspheming expletive

blasphemous offensive (*offending*), profane

blasphemy imprecation, profanity

blast barrage, destroy (*efface*), discharge (*shot*), discharge (*shoot*), extirpate, inveigh, outburst, repercussion

blasting blasphemy, discharge (*shot*)

blatancy noise, pretense (*ostentation*)

blatant brazen, flagrant, manifest, open (*in sight*), tawdry

blatant violation of law lynch law

blather jargon (*unintelligible language*), prattle, prattle

blaze brand (*mark*), burn, conflagration, deflagrate, outburst, promulgate, propagate (*spread*)

blaze abroad proclaim

blazon disclose, embellish, herald, inform (*notify*), promulgate, propagate (*spread*), publish, reveal

bleak devoid, jejune (*dull*)

bleakness damper (*depressant*)

blear blind (*obscure*)

bleared nebulous

bleed deplete, exude

blemish damage, deface, defacement, defame, defect, denigrate, detriment, disgrace, dishonor (*shame*), flaw, foible, frailty, handicap, mutilate, onus (*stigma*), smear, spoil (*impair*), stain, stigma, sully, taint (*contaminate*), tarnish, vice

blemished defective, deficient, faulty, imperfect, inferior (*lower in quality*), marred

blend amalgamate, attune, bond
(*hold together*), combine (*join together*),
commingle, conjoin, connect (*join together*), consolidate (*strengthen*), converge, denature, desegregate, integration (*amalgamation*), join (*bring together*), melange, merge, pool, solution
(*substance*), unite
blended composite, compound, concerted, concurrent (*united*), conglomerate, conjoint, harmonious, inseparable,
miscellaneous, promiscuous
blending coherence, concordant, concrescence, integration (*amalgamation*)
blessed sacrosanct
blessing laudation, permission
blessings prosperity
blight calamity, casualty, damage,
decay, destroy (*efface*), disaster, distress
(*anguish*), impair, infect, pain, spoil
(*impair*), spoilage, taint (*contaminate*),
thwart, vitiate
blight one's optical powers blind
(*deprive of sight*)
blighted marred, tainted (*contaminated*)
blighted hope pessimism
blighting disastrous
blind camouflage, cloak, deceive, deception, decoy, heedless, hidden, hoodwink, ill-judged, inadvertent,
incognizant, injudicious, insensible, insusceptible (*uncaring*), obfuscate,
obnubilate, obscure, opaque, random,
ruse, stratagem, unwitting
blind chance accident (*chance occurrence*)
blind faith credulity
blind to impervious
blind zeal discrimination (*bigotry*)
blinded unaware
blindfold hoodwink
blindness ignorance, nescience
bliss enjoyment (*pleasure*)
blissful ecstatic
blister burn
blistered blemished
blitz barrage
blitzkrieg onset (*assault*)
bloat inflate, spread
bloated inflated (*enlarged*)
bloatedness inflation (*increase*)
bloc cartel, league, organization (*association*), society
block arrest (*stop*), balk, ban, bar (*obstruction*), bar (*hinder*), bind (*restrain*),
blockade (*barrier*), bulk, censorship,
check (*bar*), check (*restrain*), clog, condemn (*ban*), constrain (*restrain*), constrict (*inhibit*), contain (*restrain*),
damper (*stopper*), deadlock, debar, defeat, delay, deter, deterrence, deterrent,
disadvantage, disqualify, encumber
(*hinder*), enjoin, exclude, forbid, halt,
halt, hamper, hinder, hold up (*delay*),
impasse, impede, impediment, interdict,
interfere, interpose, interruption, keep
(*restrain*), kill (*defeat*), limitation, lock,
obstacle, obstruct, obstruction,
obturate, occlude, oppose, parcel, parry,
plot (*land*), preclude, prevent, procrastinate, prohibit, prohibition, real estate, resist (*oppose*), section (*vicinity*),
shut, stall, stave, stay (*halt*), stem
(*check*), stifle, stop, strangle, toll (*stop*),

withhold, withstand
block off seal (*close*), shut
block out delineate, frame (*construct*), plan, program
block the way estop
block up clog, encumber (*hinder*),
estop, shut, stop
blockade bar (*hinder*), block, contain
(*enclose*), control (*restriction*), deterrence, disadvantage, eliminate (*exclude*), enclose, enclosure, enjoin, estop,
exclude, halt, hindrance, impasse, impede, impediment, lock, obstruction, occlude, ostracism, picket, restrain, restraint, seclude, shut, stop, strike (*refuse to work*)
blockaded blind (*impassable*)
blockage bar (*obstruction*), blockade
(*barrier*), censorship, check (*bar*),
damper (*stopper*), deadlock, disadvantage, estoppel, filibuster, impasse, impediment, obstruction, obviation
blockbuster bomb
blocked arrested (*checked*), blind (*impassable*), impervious
blocking preventive, resistance
blockish obtuse, opaque, thoughtless
blockishness opacity
blood ancestry, bloodline, descent
(*lineage*)
blood connection family (*common
ancestry*)
blood kindred next of kin
blood money hush money
blood related consanguineous
blood relation affiliation (*bloodline*),
degree (*kinship*), next of kin, relationship (*family tie*), relative
blood relations kindred
blood relationship affiliation (*bloodline*), ancestry, degree (*kinship*), filiation
blood relative affinity (*family ties*),
next of kin, relation (*kinship*)
blood relatives kindred, lineage
blood tie ancestry, relation (*kinship*)
blood ties relationship (*family tie*)
blood-thirsty cruel
bloodless clean, insipid, peaceable,
phlegmatic
bloodline ancestry, birth (*lineage*),
descent (*lineage*), lineage, origin (*ancestry*), parentage, posterity, progeny
bloodshed dispatch (*act of putting to
death*), fight (*battle*), outbreak
bloodsucker parasite
bloodthirstiness bestiality, cruelty
bloodthirsty malevolent, malignant,
predatory, ruthless
bloody brutal
bloody murder killing
bloom pullulate, succeed (*attain*)
blooming prosperous, successful
blossom proliferate, pullulate
blossoming successful
blot brand (*stigmatize*), deface, defacement, defect, derogate, disgrace, disgrace, dishonor (*shame*), dishonor (*deprive of honor*), disparage, flaw, ignominy, infamy, onus (*stigma*), opprobrium, pillory, shame, stain, stigma,
sully, tarnish
blot out censor, condone, deface, delete, destroy (*efface*), eliminate (*eradicate*), eradicate, expunge, extinguish,
extirpate, obliterate, redact

blotch deface, defacement, onus
(*stigma*), stain
blotting out defacement
blow bombshell, debacle, detriment,
infliction, misfortune, tragedy, trouble
blow up expand, inflate, outbreak
blowing up inflation (*increase*)
blown up inflated (*enlarged*)
blowout outburst
blows fracas
blowup outburst
bludgeon coerce, cudgel, harass
bludgeon man assailant
blue ribbon prize
blue-pencil expurgate
blue-penciling censorship
blueprint agenda, arrange (*plan*), delineate, delineation, design (*construction plan*), direction (*course*), method,
program, prospectus
blueprinted tactical
bluff betray (*lead astray*), bilk, brazen, cloak, deception, delude, ensnare,
fake, palter, pettifog, pretend, pretense
(*pretext*)
bluffer pedant
bluffing lying
blunder abortion (*fiasco*), disaster,
err, fault (*mistake*), indiscretion, maladministration, misapprehend, miscalculate, misconceive, misconstrue, miscue, misdeed, misdoing, misinterpret,
misjudge, mismanage, misread, misstatement, mistake, misunderstand,
oversight (*carelessness*)
blundering erroneous, inaccurate,
inept (*incompetent*)
blunt allay, alleviate, assuage, candid, clear (*apparent*), decrease, deter,
direct (*forthright*), harmless, honest,
impair, ingenuous, moderate (*temper*),
modify (*moderate*), mollify, obtund, obtuse, sententious, soothe
blunt-witted obtuse
bluntness candor (*straightforwardness*), disrespect, honesty
blur blind (*obscure*), deface, indistinctness, obfuscate, obnubilate, obscuration, obscure, sully
blur the outline blind (*obscure*)
blurred inconspicuous, indefinite, indistinct, nebulous, obscure (*faint*), unclear, vague
blurriness indistinctness
blurry indefinite, indistinct, nebulous,
obscure (*faint*), unclear, vague
blurt interject
blurt out divulge, reveal
blushful diffident
blushing diffident
bluster hector, outburst, rodomontade
blustering disorderly, orgulous,
orotund
blustery disorderly
board bench, bureau, chamber (*body*),
commission (*agency*), committee, council (*assembly*), enter (*go in*), inhabit,
lodge (*reside*), management (*directorate*)
board of directors management (*directorate*), management (*supervision*)
board of inquiry commission
(*agency*)
boarder habitant, inhabitant, lessee,
lodger, resident
boardinghouse building (*structure*)

boast bluster *(speech)*, exaggeration, flaunt, include, jactation

boastful grandiose, inflated *(vain)*, orgulous, pretentious *(pompous)*, proud *(conceited)*

boastfulness bombast, jactation, pride, rodomontade

boasting bombast, orgulous, overstatement, pretentious *(pompous)*, rodomontade

boatload cargo

bode portend, predict, presage, prognosticate, threaten

bodeful ominous, portentous *(ominous)*, prophetic

bodement caveat

bodiless immaterial, incorporeal, insubstantial, intangible

bodilessness impalpability

bodiliness materiality *(physical existence)*

bodily concrete, corporal, corporeal, in person, material *(physical)*, mundane, physical

bodily deviation from health disease

bodily existence materiality *(physical existence)*

bodily presentation embodiment

bodily representation embodiment

boding consternation, inauspicious, portentous *(ominous)*, premonition

body aggregate, assemblage, assembly, band, character *(an individual)*, committee, community, confederacy *(compact)*, configuration *(form)*, content *(structure)*, cornerstone, corporation, corpse, corpus, entity, generality *(bulk)*, individual, majority *(greater part)*, mass *(body of persons)*, mass *(weight)*, materiality *(physical existence)*, party *(political organization)*, society, substance *(essential nature)*

body corporate cartel, company *(enterprise)*, corporation

body of commissioners commission *(agency)*

body of consultants committee

body of delegates commission *(agency)*, delegation *(envoy)*, deputation *(delegation)*, representation *(acting for others)*

body of deputies commission *(agency)*, representation *(acting for others)*

body of employees personnel, staff

body of fact science *(study)*

body of facts on which belief is based evidence

body of judges chamber *(body)*, judiciary

body of jurors array *(jury)*, jury, panel *(jurors)*

body of knowledge education

body of law constitution, pandect *(code of laws)*

body of laws code, jurisprudence

body of laws enacted legislation *(enactments)*

body of members constituency

body of men armed with legal process posse

body of men summoned by a sheriff posse

body of office holders government *(political administration)*

body of partisans caucus, side

body of persons summoned as jurors panel *(jurors)*

body of persons sworn to render a verdict panel *(jurors)*

body of persons who formulate laws legislature

body of principles platform

body of professors faculty *(teaching staff)*

body of representatives delegation *(envoy)*, deputation *(delegation)*

body of rules law

body of rules of government constitution

body politic community, nationality, polity, populace, population, public, state *(political unit)*

bodyguard guardian

boeotian opaque

bog stall

boggle mismanage

bogus assumed *(feigned)*, counterfeit, deceptive, delusive, dishonest, false *(not genuine)*, fraudulent, imitation, specious, spurious

Bohemian nonconforming

Bohemianism nonconformity

boil down abridge *(shorten)*, distill, lessen

boisterous blatant *(obtrusive)*, disorderly, vehement

boisterousness bluster *(commotion)*

bold brazen, flagrant, heroic, hot-blooded, impertinent *(insolent)*, impulsive *(rash)*, indomitable, insolent, obtrusive, palpable, perceivable, presumptuous, prominent, salient, spartan, unabashed, undaunted

bold front audacity

boldfaced brazen

boldness audacity, confidence *(faith)*, prowess *(bravery)*, spirit, temerity

bolster bear *(support)*, favor, inure *(benefit)*, justify, maintain *(sustain)*, nurture, preserve, promote *(organize)*, reinforce, side, subsidize, supplement, support *(assist)*, sustain *(prolong)*, uphold

bolster up corroborate, reassure

bolt abscond, assemblage, bar *(hinder)*, escape, impede, lock, race, renege, retreat, seal *(close)*

bombard attack

bombardment barrage, discharge *(shot)*, onset *(assault)*

bombast fustian, harangue, peroration

bombastic flatulent, fustian, grandiose, orotund, pretentious *(pompous)*, prolix, turgid

bombastic language fustian

bombastic speech rhetoric *(insincere language)*

bombastical flatulent

bombastry fustian

bombings barrage

bombshell bomb

bona assets, effects, possession *(property)*, property *(possessions)*

bona fide accurate

bona fide actual, adherence *(devotion)*, adhesion *(loyalty)*

bona fide authentic, convincing

bona fide corporeal, de facto

bona fide genuine, good faith, in

good faith, sterling, valid, veridical

bonafide real

bonanza bounty

bond adherence *(adhesion)*, adherence *(devotion)*, adhesion *(loyalty)*, affiliation *(connectedness)*, agreement *(contract)*, association *(connection)*, attachment *(act of affixing)*, bail, chain *(nexus)*, charge *(lien)*, coalescence, coalition, connection *(fastening)*, contact *(association)*, contract, coverage *(insurance)*, debenture, fetter, guaranty, handcuff, hostage, kinship, liaison, loyalty, marriage *(intimate relationship)*, nexus, note *(written promise to pay)*, pact, pawn, pledge *(deposit)*, promise, propinquity *(kinship)*, recognizance, relation *(connection)*, relationship *(connection)*, security *(pledge)*, sodality, specialty *(contract)*, stipulation, treaty

bond against risk insurance

bond of matrimony cohabitation *(married state)*, marriage *(wedlock)*

bond of slavery bondage

bond of union chain *(nexus)*

bondage captivity, coercion, constraint *(imprisonment)*, custody *(incarceration)*, durance, duress, incarceration, restraint, subjection, thrall

bonded allied, concerted, concordant, concurrent *(united)*, fully secured, harmonious

bondman captive

bonds bondage, constraint *(imprisonment)*, durance, restriction, securities, servitude, ties

bondsman captive

bone of contention problem, question *(issue)*

bonfire conflagration

boni bonus

bonorum possessions

bonus benefit *(conferment)*, bounty, commission *(fee)*, contribution *(donation)*, gratuity *(present)*, largess *(gift)*, perquisite, premium *(excess value)*, prize, reward

bonus sterling

bonus surplus, tip *(gratuity)*

bony ossified

book document, engage *(hire)*, enroll, file *(place among official records)*, program, publication *(printed matter)*, record, register, retain *(employ)*, script, set down

book learning information *(knowledge)*

book of accounts ledger

book of records ledger

booking registration, reservation *(engagement)*

bookish learned

bookkeeper accountant, comptroller

bookkeeping accounting, computation, registration

bookkeeping expert comptroller

books ledger

boom barrage, prosperity

booming prosperous, resounding, successful

booming economy boom *(prosperity)*, prosperity

boon behalf, benefit *(conferment)*, benevolence *(act of kindness)*, bonus, bounty, contribution *(donation)*, endowment, favor *(act of kindness)*, grant,

help, largess *(gift)*
boorish ignoble, inelegant, perverse, provincial, uncouth, unseemly
boost boom *(increase)*, elevate, encourage, enhance, favor, help, impetus, increase, increment, intensify, magnify, parlay *(exploit successfully)*, raise *(advance)*, recommendation, reinforce, reinforcement
boost in prices inflation *(decrease in value of currency)*
boosting cumulative *(intensifying)*, promotion *(encouragement)*
boot spurn
booth stand *(witness' place in court)*, store *(business)*
bootlegged commerce contraband
bootlegged goods contraband
bootlegged trade contraband
bootlegged traffic contraband
bootless futile, otiose, unavailing
booty pillage, plunder, prize, reward, spoils
border ambit, boundary, circumscribe *(define)*, circumscribe *(surround by boundary)*, connection *(abutment)*, contact *(touch)*, contain *(enclose)*, demarcate, enclosure, encompass *(surround)*, end *(termination)*, extremity *(furthest point)*, frontier, hedge, juxtapose, limit, margin *(outside limit)*, mete, outline *(boundary)*, periphery, tenant
border on abut, adjoin, approximate, contact *(touch)*, correspond *(be equivalent)*
bordering adjacent, close *(near)*, contiguous, immediate *(not distant)*, proximate
bordering upon proximate
borderland border, frontier, mete, periphery
borderline boundary, end *(termination)*, extremity *(furthest point)*, insecure, marginal, mete, purview
borders configuration *(confines)*, confines, extent
bore enter *(penetrate)*, penetrate, pierce *(lance)*
boredom disinterest *(lack of interest)*
boresome irksome, jejune *(dull)*, pedestrian, prolix, prosaic
boring insipid, irksome, jejune *(dull)*, lifeless *(dull)*, nondescript, ordinary, pedestrian, ponderous, prolix, prosaic, stale, trite
born native *(inborn)*
born in wedlock legitimate *(lawfully conceived)*
born of parents legally married legitimate *(lawfully conceived)*
borough community
borrow adopt, appropriate, copy
borrow dishonestly pirate *(reproduce without authorization)*, plagiarize
borrower debtor, obligor, parasite
bosom close *(intimate)*
boss chief, direct *(supervise)*, director, employer, manage, principal *(director)*, superintend
botch fail *(lose)*, failure *(lack of success)*, miscue, mismanage, muddle, spoil *(impair)*
botchery maladministration
bother aggravate *(annoy)*, annoy, badger, bait *(harass)*, burden, care *(regard)*, discommode, disorganize, dis-

tress, disturb, embarrass, harass, harrow, harry *(harass)*, hector, hinder, hindrance, impede, importune, inconvenience, irritate, mistreat, molest *(annoy)*, molestation, nuisance, perplex, persecute, perturb, pique, plague, press *(goad)*, provoke, trouble, upset
botheration burden
bothering enigmatic
bothersome difficult, irksome, operose, undesirable, vexatious
bottle up repress
bottleneck blockade *(barrier)*
bottomless baseless, profound *(intense)*
boulevard avenue *(route)*
bounce oscillate
bounce back reflect *(mirror)*
bouncing resilient
bound abut, accountable *(responsible)*, actionable, attached *(annexed)*, barrier, boundary, circumscribe *(surround by boundary)*, confine, definite, delimit, demarcate, detain *(restrain)*, diminish, en route, enclose, encompass *(surround)*, end *(termination)*, frontier, hedge, include, indebted, inextricable, limit, loyal, mete, palliate *(abate)*, periphery, purposeful, qualify *(condition)*, restrict, shut, specialize
bound by agreement indentured
bound by contract indentured
bound by convention orthodox
bound by duty moral
bound in equity liable
bound in law liable
bound to liable
bound to respond liable
bound together conjoint
boundaries capacity *(sphere)*, confines, dimension, range
boundary ambit, barrier, border, configuration *(confines)*, edge *(border)*, enclosure, end *(termination)*, extremity *(furthest point)*, frontier, guideline, limit, margin *(outside limit)*, mete, purview, restriction, scope
boundary line ambit, frontier, limit, mete, periphery
boundary lines confines
boundary mark mete
boundary marker landmark *(conspicuous object)*
bounded certain *(specific)*, limited
bounded with precision definite
bounden indebted, loyal, mandatory, necessary *(required)*
bounden duty allegiance, burden, liability, responsibility *(accountability)*
bounding contiguous, immediate *(not distant)*
boundless continual *(perpetual)*, far reaching, indefinite, indeterminate, infinite, innumerable, myriad, open-ended, profuse, unlimited, unqualified *(unlimited)*, unrestricted
boundlessly ad infinitum
boundlessness perpetuity
boundness responsibility *(accountability)*
bounds ambit, area *(province)*, border, capacity *(sphere)*, circuit, configuration *(confines)*, confines, constraint *(imprisonment)*, contour *(outline)*, coverage *(scope)*, custody *(incarceration)*, edge *(border)*, extent, margin *(outside*

limit)*, mete, outline *(boundary)*, premises *(buildings)*, purview, range, restriction, scope, sphere
bounteous benevolent, charitable *(benevolent)*, humane, liberal *(generous)*, philanthropic, profuse, replete
bounteousness charity, largess *(generosity)*, philanthropy
bountiful ample, benevolent, copious, donative, liberal *(generous)*, philanthropic, profuse, replete
bountifulness benevolence *(disposition to do good)*, boom *(prosperity)*, charity, largess *(generosity)*, philanthropy
bounty bonus, consideration *(recompense)*, contribution *(donation)*, donation, endowment, favor *(act of kindness)*, grant, largess *(generosity)*, largess *(gift)*, philanthropy, premium *(excess value)*, prize, reward, subsidy
bourgeois ordinary, prevailing *(current)*
bourn destination, end *(intent)*, outline *(boundary)*
bourse exchange, market *(business)*
bout competition, confrontation *(altercation)*, contest *(competition)*, fight *(battle)*, period
bout of sickness disease
bovine phlegmatic
bow prostration, succumb, yield *(submit)*
bow to obey, observe *(obey)*, submit *(yield)*
bowdlerization censorship
bowdlerize censor, expurgate
bowelless relentless
bowing compliance
bowl over overcome *(overwhelm)*
box chamber *(compartment)*, envelop, stand *(witness' place in court)*
box number address
boy child
boycott condemn *(ban)*, disapprove *(reject)*, eschew, exclude, exclusion, ignore, picket, proscription, reject, shun, strike, strike *(refuse to work)*
boyishness puerility
brabble affray, bicker, disaccord, fray
brace bear *(support)*, mainstay, reinforce, side, stimulate, uphold
bracing remedial, salutary
bracket class, connect *(relate)*, enclose, enclosure, include, pigeonhole, relate *(establish a connection)*
brag exaggeration, jactation, rodomontade
braggadocio jactation, pride, rodomontade
braggardism jactation
braggardly pretentious *(pompous)*
braggart inflated *(vain)*, pretentious *(pompous)*, proud *(conceited)*
braggartism pride, rodomontade
braggery bombast
bragging bluster *(speech)*, orgulous, rodomontade
braid cross *(intersect)*, intertwine
brain intellect
brain child invention
brain damage insanity
brainless fatuous, irrational, opaque
brains intelligence *(intellect)*
braintwister enigma
brainwash convert *(persuade)*, influ-

ence

brainwashing propaganda
brainwork dialectic
brake control *(restriction)*, curb, hamper, hold up *(delay)*, impede, impediment, obstruct, remit *(relax)*, restraint, stop
branch adjunct, affiliate, bifurcate, bureau, class, denomination, department, dichotomize, division *(administrative unit)*, member *(constituent part)*, offshoot, organ, segment, spread, title *(division)*, unit *(department)*
branch member chapter *(branch)*
branch of instruction discipline *(field of study)*
branch of knowledge discipline *(field of study)*, science *(study)*
branch off bifurcate, stem *(originate)*
branch office chapter *(branch)*, organ
branch organization affiliate
branch out accrue *(increase)*, bifurcate, compound, deploy, deviate, digress, expand, increase, radiate
branching divergent, extensive
branching off deviation
branching out circulation, decentralization
brand arraign, attaint, burn, class, classify, defame, denigrate, denounce *(condemn)*, derogate, disapprove *(condemn)*, discredit, disgrace, disgrace, dishonor *(shame)*, dishonor *(deprive of honor)*, disparagement, disrepute, earmark, humiliate, ignominy, implicate, indicant, indication, infamy, involve *(implicate)*, label, label, manner *(kind)*, onus *(stigma)*, opprobrium, pillory, reproach, scandal, smear, specialty *(distinctive mark)*, stamp, stigma, sully, tarnish, trademark
brand incorrectly mislabel
brand with reproach arraign
brandish display, flaunt, wield
brangle bicker, brawl, brawl, disaccord
brash brazen, caustic, impertinent *(insolent)*, improvident, imprudent, obtrusive, presumptuous
brashness disrespect
brassy pretentious *(ostentatious)*
bravado audacity, pretense *(ostentation)*
brave bear *(tolerate)*, confront *(encounter)*, defy, endure *(suffer)*, heroic, indomitable, spartan, undaunted
brave face audacity
braveness prowess *(bravery)*
bravery spirit, tolerance
bravura audacity
brawl affray, bicker, bluster *(commotion)*, commotion, confrontation *(altercation)*, contend *(dispute)*, contest *(dispute)*, controversy *(argument)*, disaccord, embroilment, fight *(battle)*, fracas, fray, outbreak, outcry, riot
brawler malcontent
brawn force *(strength)*, puissance, sinew, strength
brawniness sinew
brawny powerful, strong
braying blatant *(obtrusive)*
braze cement
brazen contemptuous, flagrant, impertinent *(insolent)*, insolent, obtrusive,

outrageous, presumptuous, unabashed
brazenness disrespect
breach alienation *(estrangement)*, argument *(contention)*, break *(violate)*, conflict, default, delinquency *(failure of duty)*, dereliction, difference, disassociation, disloyalty, embroilment, encroach, encroachment, estrangement, feud, flaw, force *(break)*, incursion, infraction, infringe, infringement, invasion, irregularity, neglect, offense, omission, outbreak, repudiation, rift *(gap)*, schism, separation, split, transgression, trespass, variance *(disagreement)*, violation
breach of a promise delinquency *(failure of duty)*
breach of allegiance treason
breach of duty negligence, res ipsa loquitur
breach of faith bad faith, bribery, corruption, dishonor *(nonpayment)*, disloyalty, infidelity, infraction, treason
breach of law crime, guilt, infraction, misdemeanor, misfeasance
breach of legal duty tort
breach of orders default, disregard *(omission)*, infraction, rebellion
breach of peace disorder *(lack of order)*
breach of practice deviation, exception *(exclusion)*, malpractice
breach of privilege infraction
breach of profession malpractice
breach of promise dishonor *(nonpayment)*, disloyalty, infidelity, infraction, nonperformance
breach of the law delinquency *(misconduct)*, offense
breach of the peace brawl, fracas, infraction, outbreak, outburst, riot
breach of trust abuse *(corrupt practice)*, corruption, disloyalty, embezzlement, improbity, infidelity, infraction, misappropriation
breach the agreement default
breadth caliber *(measurement)*, capacity *(maximum)*, extent, gamut, purview, range
break adjournment, alienation *(estrangement)*, breach, cessation *(interlude)*, cloture, controversy *(argument)*, damage, digression, disable, disassociation, discontinue *(abandon)*, discontinue *(break continuity)*, estrangement, extension *(postponement)*, halt, halt, hiatus, infringe, interrupt, interruption, interval, leave *(absence)*, lull, luxate, moratorium, part *(separate)*, pause, pause, pendency, recess, recess, remission, rend, respite *(interval of rest)*, rift *(disagreement)*, rift *(gap)*, schism, separate, separation, split, split, spoil *(impair)*, subdue, transition, violate
break a law disobey, offend *(violate the law)*
break a promise renege
break a rule disobey
break apart disband, disjoint, disrupt, dissolve *(separate)*, sever
break away defect, elude, leave *(depart)*, part *(leave)*, secede
break bounds accroach, deviate, impinge, infringe
break camp evacuate, move *(alter position)*

break down classify, codify, damage, decay, erode, overcome *(overwhelm)*, pigeonhole, stall, subdivide, succumb
break faith bear false witness, cheat, inform *(betray)*, misrepresent, palter
break faith with betray *(lead astray)*
break fealty defect
break forth issue *(send forth)*
break from prison escape
break ground initiate, originate
break in discipline *(train)*, interfere, interrupt, intervene, invade, obtrude, trespass
break in on impinge
break in upon infringe, overstep
break into infringe, interpose, loot, penetrate
break loose elude, escape
break news divulge
break off alienate *(estrange)*, close *(terminate)*, conclude *(complete)*, detach, discontinue *(abandon)*, discontinue *(break continuity)*, forbear, forswear, halt, quit *(discontinue)*, refrain, separate, sever, stop, suspend
break one's oath perjure
break one's promise betray *(lead astray)*, fail *(neglect)*
break one's promise to disappoint
break one's trust default
break one's word fail *(neglect)*, perjure
break out escape
break silence pronounce *(speak)*, speak
break the association of disband
break the connection with disengage
break the contract default
break the law disobey, offend *(violate the law)*, trespass
break the news notify, reveal
break the pattern deviate
break the peace brawl, fight *(battle)*
break the record surpass
break through emerge, lancinate
break to pieces destroy *(efface)*
break trust inform *(betray)*
break up decay, degenerate, destroy *(void)*, diffuse, disband, disintegrate, disjoint, dispel, dissipate *(spread out)*, dissociate, dissolve *(separate)*, dissolve *(terminate)*, overthrow, partition, recess, separate
break up into opposing factions polarize
break with defect, disaccord, disagree, estrange, rebel, renounce, split
breakability frailty
breakable destructible, divisible, nonsubstantial *(not sturdy)*, separable
breakage injury
breakdown debacle, decentralization, defeat, diagnosis, disassociation, disaster, disease, erosion, failure *(lack of success)*, miscarriage, prostration
breakdown of administration anarchy, lynch law, misrule
breaking division *(act of dividing)*, infraction
breaking an obligation contravention
breaking and entering burglary, housebreaking
breaking down decadent, destruction
breaking of precedent innovation

breaking of the law offense
breaking off discontinuance (act of discontinuing)
breaking up dissolution (disintegration), dissolution (termination)
breaking with tradition anomalous, peculiar (curious)
breakneck dangerous, impulsive (rash), precipitate
breakup defeasance, division (act of dividing), subversion
breast confront (encounter), defy, resist (oppose), withstand
breath suggestion
breathe communicate, divulge, exist, express, pause, utter
breathe one's last die
breather lull, pause
breathing born (alive), conscious (awake), live (conscious)
breathing spell halt, lull, pause, respite (interval of rest)
breathing time lull, respite (interval of rest)
breathless dead, lifeless (dead)
breathtaking moving (evoking emotion), noteworthy, portentous (eliciting amazement)
breed bear (yield), blood, cause, class, descent (lineage), engender, foster, generate, kind, occasion, originate, produce (manufacture), proliferate, propagate (increase), pullulate, race, reproduce
breeding conduct, deportment
breedy prolific
breeziness life (vitality)
brethren affinity (family ties), blood, kindred, society
brevet warrant (authorization)
breviary compendium
brevis ephemeral, laconic, limited, succinct, summary, transient
brew maneuver
brewing imminent, inevitable
bribable mercenary, venal
bribe coax, corrupt, hush money, lure, suborn
bribe to take a false oath suborn
bribery corruption, graft
bribing bribery
bridal conjugal, nuptial
bridewell reformatory
bridge chain (nexus), connect (join together), connect (relate), connection (fastening), contact (touch), join (bring together), nexus
bridle bar (hinder), block, clog, constrain (imprison), constrain (restrain), contain (restrain), damper (stopper), disadvantage, discipline (control), fetter, hamper, handcuff, handcuff, handicap, inhibit, limit, obstacle, obstruct, obstruction, repress, resent, restrain, restraint, restrict, trammel
bridled arrested (checked)
brief abridgment (condensation), abstract, account (report), apprise, capsule, compact (pithy), compendium, concise, cursory, digest, disabuse, dossier, edify, educate, ephemeral, impart, indicate, inform (notify), instruct (direct), laconic, memorandum, minimal, note (brief comment), notify, outline (synopsis), paraphrase, pithy, report (detailed account), restatement, scenario, succinct, summary, synopsis, temporary,

transient, transitory, volatile
brief silence lull
briefed acquainted, familiar (informed), informed (having information)
briefing guidance
briefly pro tempore
brigand hoodlum, malefactor, outlaw
brigandage foray, larceny, pillage, spoliation
brigandine panoply
brigandish larcenous
bright illustrious, obvious, perspicacious, resourceful, sanguine, sapient
brighten enhance
brightness sense (intelligence)
brilliance distinction (reputation), intellect, intelligence (intellect), sagacity, sense (intelligence)
brilliant illustrious, politic, prominent
brim border, edge (border), margin (outside limit)
brimful full
brimfull replete
brimming replete
brimming over full
bring carry (transport), cause, commence, procure, transport, yield (produce a return)
bring a case lodge (bring a complaint)
bring a charge accuse, cite (accuse), impeach
bring a countercharge recriminate
bring a formal accusation against indict
bring a legal action sue
bring a person to his senses persuade
bring a suit complain (charge), lodge (bring a complaint)
bring about accomplish, attain, bear (yield), cause, commit (perpetrate), compose, conduce, constitute (establish), create, discharge (perform), dispatch (dispose of), elicit, engender, establish (launch), evoke, execute (accomplish), fulfill, generate, implement, incite, induce, inflict, inspire, make, occasion, operate, originate, perpetrate, produce (manufacture), prosecute (carry forward), provoke, realize (make real), render (administer), yield (produce a return)
bring about by force constrain (compel)
bring about by legislation constitute (establish)
bring about change militate
bring accusation accuse, arraign, charge (accuse), denounce (inform against), incriminate, involve (implicate), lodge (bring a complaint)
bring action against litigate, prosecute (charge)
bring aid capitalize (provide capital), contribute (assist)
bring an action cite (accuse), complain (charge), litigate, sue
bring an action against lodge (bring a complaint)
bring around convert (persuade), disarm (set at ease), persuade, prevail (persuade)
bring back reconstitute, rehabilitate, reinstate, remind, restore (return), resurrect

bring before a court arraign, prosecute (charge)
bring before the public circulate, publish
bring charges complain (charge), denounce (inform against), impeach, involve (implicate)
bring charges against incriminate, lodge (bring a complaint)
bring discredit on decry
bring disgrace upon discredit
bring disrepute upon defame
bring down cause, demean (make lower), demote, depress, derogate, disgrace, dispatch (put to death), overthrow
bring forth avail (bring about), bear (yield), develop, educe, elicit, engender, evoke, extract, generate, make, manifest, produce (manufacture), reproduce, yield (produce a return)
bring forward bear (adduce), certify (attest), cite (state), elicit, exhibit, manifest, offer (propose), plead (allege in a legal action), posit, prefer, produce (offer to view), proffer
bring from obscurity into view disinter
bring in induct, introduce, yield (produce a return)
bring in a supply bear (yield)
bring in a true bill accuse
bring in a verdict award, determine, sentence
bring in as a third party implead
bring in contact join (bring together)
bring in contact with commingle, connect (join together)
bring in question canvass, dispute (contest)
bring into a small compass concentrate (consolidate)
bring into accord attune
bring into agreement arbitrate (conciliate), attune
bring into being compose, conceive (invent), create, develop, engender, establish (launch), fabricate (construct), forge (produce), generate, invent (produce for the first time), make, produce (manufacture), propagate (increase)
bring into close connection affiliate
bring into close relation affiliate
bring into comparison compare, contrast, measure
bring into concord agree (contract)
bring into conflict engage (involve)
bring into conformity with law legalize
bring into connection with implicate
bring into consistency accommodate
bring into court plead (argue a case)
bring into custody imprison
bring into danger compromise (endanger)
bring into discredit brand (stigmatize), censure, condemn (blame), denounce (condemn), derogate, discommend, disgrace, dishonor (deprive of honor), fault, impeach, malign
bring into disfavor discredit
bring into disorder confound, discompose, perturb
bring into disrepute decry, demean (make lower)

bring into effect compose
bring into existerce cause, compose, conceive *(invent)*, engender, establish *(launch)*, fabricate *(construct)*, forge *(produce)*, generate, make, originate, produce *(manufacture)*
bring into focus converge, focus
bring into harmony arbitrate *(conciliate)*, intercede, reconcile
bring into meaningful relation with compare
bring into operation exert, perform *(execute)*
bring into order arrange *(methodize)*, codify, file *(arrange)*, fix *(arrange)*, orchestrate
bring into peril endanger
bring into play exercise *(use)*, exert, exploit *(make use of)*, resort
bring into question audit
bring into relation compare
bring into relation with correspond *(be equivalent)*
bring into the open betray *(disclose)*, disclose, find *(discover)*, issue *(publish)*, manifest, promulgate
bring into use initiate
bring into view bare, disclose, evince, produce *(offer to view)*
bring low demean *(make lower)*, demote, depress, derogate, reduce, supplant
bring near converge, juxtapose
bring new evidence appeal
bring off dispatch *(dispose of)*, implement
bring off successfully attain
bring on cause, conduce, create, incite, incur, induce, originate, precipitate *(hasten)*
bring out circulate, comment, create, disclose, disinter, educe, elicit, evoke, manifest, produce *(offer to view)*, publish, solve
bring out in evidence bare
bring out more clearly elucidate
bring over disarm *(set at ease)*, persuade, prevail upon
bring pressure to bear coerce, influence, lobby, prejudice *(influence)*, press *(constrain)*
bring pressure to bear upon compel, constrain *(compel)*
bring proceedings against complain *(charge)*, incriminate, lodge *(bring a complaint)*
bring reproach upon discredit, disgrace, disparage, stain
bring shame upon derogate, disgrace, dishonor *(deprive of honor)*, humiliate, pillory
bring suit litigate, prosecute *(charge)*
bring the mind to bear upon focus
bring to resurrect
bring to a close complete, conclude *(complete)*, consummate, discontinue *(abandon)*, finish, stop
bring to a common center collect *(gather)*
bring to a complete condition develop
bring to a conclusion dispatch *(dispose of)*, perfect
bring to a more advanced state develop
bring to a point of union collect

(gather)
bring to a standstill arrest *(stop)*, check *(restrain)*, delay, discontinue *(break continuity)*, enjoin, forestall, halt, hold up *(delay)*, impede, obstruct, palliate *(abate)*, stall, stop, suspend
bring to a state of obedience discipline *(control)*
bring to a stop arrest *(stop)*, estop, suspend
bring to account condemn *(punish)*, denounce *(condemn)*, impeach, penalize
bring to acquiescence reconcile
bring to agreement adjust *(resolve)*
bring to an end cease, close *(terminate)*, complete, conclude *(complete)*, determine, discontinue *(abandon)*, dispatch *(dispose of)*, dissolve *(terminate)*, extinguish, finish, perfect, quit *(discontinue)*, terminate
bring to an understanding intercede, mediate
bring to attention address *(direct attention to)*
bring to bear avail *(be of use)*, exercise *(use)*, exert
bring to book rebuke, reprehend
bring to completion finish, fulfill, perfect, terminate
bring to conclusion complete, dissolve *(terminate)*
bring to effect consummate, create, make
bring to full development mature
bring to fullness perfect
bring to its peak mature
bring to justice convict, determine, impeach, lodge *(bring a complaint)*, prosecute *(charge)*, sue
bring to light bare, bear *(adduce)*, betray *(disclose)*, clarify, denude, detect, disclose, discover, display, divulge, educe, evidence, exhibit, expose, ferret, locate, manifest, produce *(offer to view)*, reveal, unveil
bring to light by degrees develop
bring to market handle *(trade)*, sell
bring to maturity complete, effectuate, mature, nurture
bring to mind allude, recollect, remember
bring to naught destroy *(void)*, foil, stop, thwart
bring to nothing obliterate
bring to notice address *(direct attention to)*, exhibit, manifest
bring to nought frustrate
bring to order marshal
bring to pass attain, carry *(succeed)*, cause, commit *(perpetrate)*, create, discharge *(perform)*, dispatch *(dispose of)*, effectuate, enforce, evoke, execute *(accomplish)*, fulfill, implement, induce, make, originate, perform *(execute)*, perpetrate, produce *(manufacture)*, prosecute *(carry forward)*, realize *(make real)*
bring to perfection complete, mature
bring to reason convince, persuade, prevail upon, reason *(persuade)*
bring to recollection remind
bring to rest conclude *(complete)*
bring to retribution discipline *(punish)*, punish
bring to ruin destroy *(efface)*, extirpate, pillage

bring to terms accommodate, arbitrate *(conciliate)*, arrange *(methodize)*, beat *(defeat)*, intercede, mediate, negotiate, pacify, placate, reconcile, settle, subjugate
bring to the bar litigate, lodge *(bring a complaint)*, sue
bring to the fore adduce, produce *(offer to view)*
bring to the front manifest, produce *(offer to view)*
bring to trial arraign, litigate, lodge *(bring a complaint)*
bring to view evidence, exhibit, manifest
bring together accumulate *(amass)*, aggregate, annex *(add)*, arbitrate *(conciliate)*, collect *(gather)*, compile, congregate, conjoin, consolidate *(strengthen)*, consolidate *(unite)*, convene, converge, crystallize, focus, garner, glean, hoard, incorporate *(include)*, intercede, juxtapose, mediate, orchestrate, raise *(collect)*, reconcile, settle, unite
bring together in a crowd congregate
bring toward a central point concentrate *(consolidate)*
bring unawares into danger entrap
bring unawares into evil entrap
bring under domination subject
bring under rule impose *(subject)*, subdue, subject
bring under subjection discipline *(control)*
bring up bear *(adduce)*, discipline *(train)*, educate, foster, nurture, raise *(advance)*, remind
bring up for investigation arraign, impeach
bring up on charges arraign, complain *(charge)*, incriminate, lodge *(bring a complaint)*
bring up to date renew *(refurbish)*, revise
bring upon inflict
bring upon oneself incur
bring word communicate, mention, notify
bringing forth creation
bringing to trial prosecution *(criminal trial)*
bringing together centralization, combination, cumulation, joinder
brink border, edge *(border)*, extremity *(furthest point)*, margin *(outside limit)*, outline *(boundary)*, penumbra, threshold *(verge)*
brisk brief, expeditious, incisive, sedulous, trenchant, volatile
briskness dispatch *(promptness)*, haste, life *(vitality)*
bristle resent
bristling hostile, resentful, rife
bristling with arms armed
brittle nonsubstantial *(not sturdy)*
brittleness frailty
broach assume *(undertake)*, commence, initiate, mention, pose *(propound)*, proclaim, utter
broad capacious, collective, comprehensive, extensive, general, generic, inaccurate, inclusive, indefinite, indiscriminate, inexact, liberal *(not literal)*, nonsectarian, obscene, omnibus, passa-

ble, vague

broad enough ample

broad guage caliber *(measurement)*

broad meaning connotation, gist *(substance)*, implication *(inference)*

broad statement generality *(vague statement)*, generalization

broad-based complete *(all-embracing)*, extensive, nonsectarian

broad-minded impartial, nonpartisan, objective, open-minded, permissive, reasonable *(rational)*, receptive, unbiased

broad-mindedness disinterest *(lack of prejudice)*, tolerance

broadcast circulate, communicate, convey *(communicate)*, diffuse, dispel, disseminate, divulge, issuance, issue *(publish)*, proclaim, promulgate, propagate *(spread)*, public *(known)*, publication *(disclosure)*, publicity, publish, relate *(tell)*, report *(detailed account)*, report *(disclose)*, send, spread

broaden accrue *(increase)*, accumulate *(enlarge)*, deploy, develop, enlarge, expand, extend *(enlarge)*, increase, inflate, magnify, parlay *(exploit successfully)*, spread, supplement

broadening accession *(enlargement)*, augmentation, boom *(increase)*, cumulative *(increasing)*, extension *(expansion)*

broadminded unprejudiced

broadmindedness objectivity

broadness caliber *(measurement)*

broadside barrage

broil altercation, brawl, brawl, controversy *(argument)*, disaccord, embroilment, fight *(argument)*, fracas, fray, furor, imbroglio, riot, strife, struggle

broke bankrupt, impecunious, insolvent

broken bankrupt, defective, desultory, disconnected, disjunctive *(tending to disjoin)*, imperfect, intermittent, unsound *(not strong)*

broken faith bad faith, infidelity

broken in spirit contrite

broken marriage divorce

broken off disconnected

broken promise bad faith, disloyalty

broken silence outcry

broken thread anacoluthon

broken word infidelity

brokenhearted disconsolate

broker dealer, deputy, factor *(commission merchant)*, interagent, medium, plenipotentiary, proctor, procurator, proxy, representative *(proxy)*, spokesman

bromidic ordinary, trite

brood blood, children, deliberate, family *(household)*, muse, offspring, progeny

brood over deplore, dwell *(linger over)*, ponder, reflect *(ponder)*, review

brooding contemplation, deliberation

brook allow *(endure)*, endure *(suffer)*, suffer *(permit)*, tolerate

brook no denial insist

brother colleague, counterpart *(complement)*

brotherhood denomination, goodwill, kinship, peace, philanthropy, society, sodality, union *(labor organization)*

brotherliness benevolence *(disposition to do good)*, philanthropy, sodality

brotherly close *(intimate)*, humane, intimate, philanthropic

brotherly love philanthropy

brought about by force forcible

brought charges accused *(charged)*

brought to a conclusion complete *(ended)*

brought to fruition choate lien

brought to light naked *(perceptible)*

brought to perfection best, ripe

brought to termination res judicata

brought together collective, conglomerate

brouillerie dissension

browbeat bait *(harass)*, discompose, frighten, harass, harrow, harry *(harass)*, hector, intimidate, persecute, plague, press *(goad)*, threaten

browse peruse

bruise beat *(strike)*, damage, harm, ill use, lash *(strike)*, mistreat, mutilate

bruised blemished, defective, marred

bruit declare, disseminate, notoriety, outcry, proclaim, promulgate, report *(rumor)*, report *(disclose)*, reveal, signify *(inform)*, spread

bruit abroad circulate

bruited about public *(known)*

brummagem meretricious, tawdry

brunt burden, pressure

brush affray, confrontation *(altercation)*

brush aside discount *(disbelieve)*, disdain, dismiss *(put out of consideration)*, ignore, rebuff, reject, spurn

brush off parry

brush up repair

brusque harsh, laconic, taciturn

brusqueness disrespect

brutal bitter *(penetrating)*, callous, cold-blooded, cruel, diabolic, disorderly, harsh, hot-blooded, inexcusable, malevolent, malicious, malignant, noxious, pernicious, ruthless, scathing, severe, tyrannous, vicious

brutality bestiality, cruelty, oppression, violence

brutalized diabolic

brutalness brutality, cruelty

brute animal

brute creation animal

brute force coercion, main force, oppression, pressure

brute-like brutal

brutify brutalize

brutilization brutality

brutish brutal, caitiff, cold-blooded, malignant, relentless, ruthless, uncouth

brutishness bestiality, brutality, cruelty

brutum fulmen disaster

buccaneer criminal, plunder

buccaneering spoliation

buck defy, oppose, oppugn

buckler protection, shield

bucolic provincial

bud embryo, germinate, proliferate, pullulate

budding inchoate, incipient

budget appropriation *(allotment)*, estimate, finance, overhead, program

budgetary financial, fiscal, pecuniary

budgeted items expense *(cost)*, outlay

budgeting appropriation *(allotment)*

buffer bulwark, intermediary, panoply, safeguard, shield

buffered impervious

buffet beat *(strike)*, ill use, jostle *(bump into)*

buffoonery parody, ridicule

buggery sodomy

build accrue *(increase)*, compose, create, enlarge, establish *(launch)*, fabricate *(construct)*, forge *(produce)*, form, frame *(structure)*, frame *(construct)*, increase, invent *(produce for the first time)*, make, manufacture, organization *(structure)*, produce *(manufacture)*

build up accrue *(increase)*, accumulate *(enlarge)*, aggregate, compound, consolidate *(strengthen)*, cumulation, develop, elevate, enlarge, expand, extend *(enlarge)*, heighten *(augment)*, heighten *(elevate)*, hoard, magnify, parlay *(exploit successfully)*, promote *(organize)*, replenish

build-up augmentation

builder architect, contractor, developer, materialman

building creation, edifice, frame *(structure)*, preparation, structure *(edifice)*

building entrepeneur developer

building of imposing appearance edifice

built on based on, underlying

bulge project *(extend beyond)*

bulk amount *(quantity)*, assemblage, cargo, corpus, cumulation, majority *(greater part)*, mass *(weight)*, measurement, plurality, quantity

bulkhead buffer zone, bulwark

bulky ponderous

bulletin declaration, dispatch *(message)*, entry *(record)*, issuance, notice *(announcement)*, notification, prospectus, publicity, report *(detailed account)*

bullheaded pertinacious, uncontrollable

bully badger, browbeat, brutalize, endanger, frighten, harrow, harry *(harass)*, hector, intimidate, irritate, mistreat, persecute, pique

bullyrag frighten, pique, plague

bulwark barrier, bear *(support)*, buffer zone, mainstay, protect, protection, safeguard, security *(safety)*, shield

bump collide *(crash against)*, impinge, jostle *(bump into)*

bump against jostle *(bump into)*

bump into collide *(crash against)*

bumptious contemptuous, disdainful, inflated *(vain)*, insolent, perverse, supercilious

bunch assemblage, compile, congregate, hoard, quantity, selection *(collection)*

bunch together compile

bunched compact *(dense)*, solid *(compact)*

bundle assemblage

bung shut, stem *(check)*

bungle fail *(lose)*, miscue, misdoing, mismanage, mistake, muddle, spoil *(impair)*

bungling fault *(mistake)*, incompetent, inept *(incompetent)*, maladministration, neglect, negligent

bunk dwell *(reside)*

bunker depository

bunkum rodomontade

buoy up assure *(give confidence to)*,

bear *(support)*, bolster, reassure
buoyant resilient, sanguine, volatile
burden bind *(obligate)*, charge *(lien)*, charge *(responsibility)*, clog, cloud *(incumbrance)*, commitment *(responsibility)*, compel, constrain *(compel)*, disadvantage, disadvantage, duty *(obligation)*, duty *(tax)*, embarrass, encumber *(financially obligate)*, encumber *(hinder)*, encumbrance, grievance, hamper, handicap, harass, impede, impediment, impose *(enforce)*, inflict, interfere, liability, load, mistreat, nuisance, obligation *(duty)*, overcome *(overwhelm)*, overload, parasite, part *(role)*, pressure, responsibility *(accountability)*, servitude, stress *(strain)*, tax *(overwork)*, trouble, weigh
burdened disadvantaged, disconsolate
burdensome difficult, onerous, operose, oppressive, ponderous
burdensome requirement onus *(burden)*
bureau agency *(commission)*, board, chapter *(branch)*, commission *(agency)*, committee, department, facility *(institution)*, firm, management *(directorate)*, office, organ
bureaucracy hierarchy *(persons in authority)*, management *(directorate)*
bureaucrat functionary, incumbent, official
bureaucratic ministerial, political
burgeon compound, expand, germinate, increase, proliferate, pullulate
burgeoning accession *(enlargement)*, boom *(increase)*, boom *(prosperity)*
burgess resident
burgher denizen
burglar criminal, hoodlum
burglarious larcenous
burglarize loot, pillage, purloin, rob, steal
burglarizing housebreaking
burglary housebreaking, theft
buried blind *(concealed)*, dead, hidden, personal *(private)*, privy
burke suppress
burlesque imitation, jape, mock *(imitate)*, parody, ridicule, travesty
burlesque translation travesty
burly strong
burn deflagrate, destroy *(efface)*, expend *(consume)*
burn fiercely deflagrate
burn to a cinder burn
burn up consume, deflagrate, dissipate *(expend foolishly)*
burning bitter *(penetrating)*, caustic, fanatical, harsh, hot-blooded, perfervid, scathing, vehement
burrow delve, hunt, research
bursal financial, fiscal
bursar comptroller
bursary bank, repository, treasury
burst barrage, break *(fracture)*, discharge *(shot)*, discharge *(shoot)*, outbreak, outburst, rend
burst forth emerge, issue *(send forth)*, pullulate
burst in obtrude
burst in upon penetrate
burst into flame burn, deflagrate
burst of sound outcry
bury camouflage, cloak, cover *(conceal)*, embed, hide, immerse *(engross)*,

inundate, overwhelm, plant *(covertly place)*, seclude, shroud, suppress
busily employed active
busily engaged active, industrious, sedulous
busily intent diligent
business agenda, assignment *(task)*, calling, career, commerce, commercial, company *(enterprise)*, concern *(business establishment)*, corporation, dealings, employment, enterprise *(economic organization)*, firm, function, job, livelihood, mercantile, mission, occupation *(vocation)*, office, position *(business status)*, post, practice *(professional business)*, profession *(vocation)*, province, pursuit *(occupation)*, trade *(commerce)*, trade *(occupation)*, transaction, undertaking *(enterprise)*, venture, work *(employment)*
business affairs agenda, commerce, trade *(commerce)*
business agreement consortium *(business cartel)*
business association corporation
business combine consortium *(business cartel)*
business contact client, customer, patron *(regular customer)*
business deals commerce
business entente consortium *(business cartel)*
business establishment company *(enterprise)*, corporation, enterprise *(economic organization)*, firm, house
business expense cost *(expenses)*
business expenses overhead
business firm house
business house firm, store *(business)*
business intercourse commerce, dealings, exchange, trade *(commerce)*
business manager comptroller
business on hand agenda, matter *(subject)*
business owner lessor
business profits income
business representative procurator
business science finance
business transaction deal, dealings
business transactions commerce
businesslike commercial, diligent, formal, professional *(stellar)*, prompt, systematic
businessman dealer, vendor
businessperson dealer, merchant
bustle dispatch *(promptness)*, industry *(activity)*, turmoil
bustling rapid
busy active, diligent, engage *(involve)*, industrious, sedulous
busy oneself with occupy *(engage)*, ply
busyness industry *(activity)*
but only, save
but for save
but for the fact that only
butcher extinguish, mutilate, spoil *(impair)*
butchery homicide
butt abut, border *(bound)*, jostle *(bump into)*, object, strike *(collide)*, target
butt against collide *(crash against)*, contact *(touch)*, impinge
butt in interrupt, obtrude
button shut

buttress bear *(support)*, bulwark, corroborate, document, mainstay, maintain *(sustain)*, reaffirm, reinforce, reinforcement, side, supplement, support *(corroborate)*, sustain *(confirm)*, uphold
buy procure, purchase, trade
buy and sell barter, deal, trade
buy back redeem *(repurchase)*
buy from patronize *(trade with)*
buy into invest *(fund)*
buy off suborn
buy stock invest *(fund)*
buy up purchase
buyer consumer, customer, patron *(regular customer)*
buyer of labor client, consumer, customer
buyer of stolen goods fence
buyer of stolen property fence
buying and selling business *(commerce)*, commerce, dealings, exchange, trade *(commerce)*
buying power money
buying price expense *(cost)*
by a stronger reason a fortiori
by all appearances prima facie *(self-evident)*
by and large as a rule
by and large each and every time always *(without exception)*
by any means regardless
by choice purposely
by circumstance coincidental
by compulsion will shall
by course of conduct pro forma
by custom pro forma
by degrees piecemeal
by design intentional, purposely
by divine right ex officio
by habit pro forma
by imperative will shall
by inference a fortiori, circumstantial
by law de jure, ex officio
by means of hereby, thereby, through *(by means of)*
by one party ex parte
by order de jure
by past practice pro forma
by proxy in lieu of
by reason of a priori, consequently
by right as a matter of right, ex officio
by right of law de jure
by statute de jure
by the act itself ipso facto
by the aid of hereby
by the fact itself ipso facto
by the hand of through *(by means of)*
by the mere fact ipso facto
by the piece retail
by the same sign consequently
by the same token consequently
by the time that until
by the very fact ipso facto
by trade and usage pro forma
by usage pro forma
by use of thereby
by virtue of hereby, thereby
by vote elective *(selective)*
by way of through *(by means of)*, through *(from beginning to end)*
by way of a will testamentary
by way of gift gratuitous *(given without recompense)*

by will purposely
by word of mouth oral
by-pass detour, detour
by-passage causeway, detour
by-product development *(outgrowth),* follow-up
bygone antique, former, obsolete, outdated, outmoded
bylaw code, regulation *(rule),* rubric *(authoritative rule),* rule *(legal dictate)*
bylaws codification
byname cognomen, sobriquet
bypass avoidance *(evasion),* circumvent, eschew, forgo, ignore, omit, pretermit, shun
byproduct offshoot
bystander eyewitness, witness
byword call *(title),* catchword, cognomen, maxim, phrase

C

cabal band, collusion, confederacy *(conspiracy),* conspire, cooperate, faction, frame up, machination, maneuver, plan, plan, plot *(secret plan),* plot, scheme, scheme, schism, secret
cabala mystery
cabalism mystery
cabalistic esoteric, mysterious, recondite
cabalistical esoteric
cabinet bench, board, chamber *(body),* commission *(agency),* committee
cache depository, fund, garner, harbor, hide, hoard, hoard, keep *(shelter),* plant *(covertly place),* provision *(something provided),* repository, reserve, reserve, store *(depository),* store, sufficiency, treasury
cachet earmark, label
cacoethes dipsomania
cacophonous discordant
cacophony noise
cadaver body *(person)*
cadaver corpse
cadaveric lifeless *(dead)*
cadaverous dead, lifeless *(dead)*
cadeau bounty
cadence inflection, intonation
cadenced periodic
cadent periodic
cadere abate *(extinguish),* fail *(lose),* miscarriage
cadet offspring
cadge request
cadger parasite
cadre division *(administrative unit),* staff
caducity deterioration, impuissance, incapacity
caducous ephemeral, transient
caducus ephemeral
caecus blind *(sightless)*
caedere beat *(strike)*
caedes assassination, homicide, murder
caelum climate
caerimonia ceremony
cage cell, confine, contain *(restrain),* envelop, keep *(restrain),* lock, restrict
cagey machiavellian
cairn landmark *(conspicuous object),* monument
caitiff recreant
cajole coax, entice, importune, influ-

ence, inveigle, lure, persuade, pressure, prevail *(persuade)*
cajolement bribery, persuasion
cajolery bribery, instigation, persuasion, seduction
cajoling persuasion
calamitas adversity, calamity, catastrophe, disaster, misfortune
calamitosus disastrous
calamitous adverse *(negative),* deadly, deplorable, dire, disastrous, fatal, harmful, hostile, insalubrious, pernicious, regrettable, unfavorable
calamity accident *(misfortune),* adversity, casualty, catastrophe, debacle, disaster, fatality, loss, misfortune, pain, tragedy, trouble
calcar stimulus
calcified ossified
calculable appreciable, foreseeable
calculate arrange *(plan),* assess *(appraise),* conspire, deduce, deduct *(conclude by reasoning),* devise *(invent),* evaluate, find *(determine),* gauge, intend, measure, plan, rate, scheme
calculate approximately estimate
calculate on anticipate *(expect)*
calculate upon expect *(anticipate)*
calculate wrongly miscalculate
calculated aforethought, cold-blooded, deliberate, express, intentional, premeditated, purposeful, strategic, tactical
calculated risk speculation *(risk)*
calculated to give a false impression deceptive
calculated to provoke resentment invidious
calculated to stir eloquent
calculatedly purposely
calculating artful, cold-blooded, collusive, discreet, judicious, machiavellian, pensive, politic, provident *(showing foresight),* prudent, sly
calculation appraisal, assessment *(estimation),* census, computation, contemplation, deduction *(conclusion),* deliberation, estimate *(approximate cost),* expectation, forethought, idea, ledger, measurement, prospect *(outlook),* prudence
calculator accountant
calculator of insurance risks actuary
calendar agenda, date, docket, empanel, file *(place among official records),* note *(record),* program, program, record, register, register, schedule
calender set down
caliber degree *(magnitude),* materiality *(consequence),* performance *(workmanship),* quality *(excellence),* status, value, worth
calibrate adjust *(regulate),* assess *(appraise),* gauge, measure
caliginosus lurid
call bespeak, charge *(command),* contact *(communicate),* convene, deem, demand, denominate, detail *(assign),* entreaty, identify, impetus, invitation, label, market *(demand),* monition *(legal summons),* nominate, phrase, prayer, request, requirement, requisition, summons
call a halt check *(restrain),* close *(terminate),* condemn *(ban),* halt, hold

up *(delay),* quit *(discontinue),* restrain
call attention to address *(direct attention to),* admonish *(advise),* indicate, notice *(observe),* notify
call back annul, disavow, recommit, renege, rescind, resurrect
call before a court arraign
call by a distinctive title label
call by name denominate
call down rebuke, reprehend
call for command, demand, desire, entail, exact, market *(demand),* necessitate, request, require *(compel),* solicit, summon
call for aid call *(appeal to),* petition
call for help call *(appeal to)*
call for the presence of subpoena, summon
call forth educe, elicit, engender, evoke, foment, incite, induce, order, provoke, resort, subpoena, summon
call in consult *(ask advice of),* refer *(send for action)*
call in question disown *(deny the validity),* dispute *(contest),* except *(object),* impeach, impugn, object, oppugn
call into action summon
call into being compose, engender, fabricate *(construct),* generate, make
call into existence compose, generate, make
call names defame, denigrate
call of duty allegiance, burden, commitment *(responsibility)*
call off desist, discontinue *(abandon),* dissolve *(terminate),* hold up *(delay)*
call on refer *(send for action)*
call on for a blessing invoke
call on for help invoke
call out challenge, proclaim, subpoena
call public attention to issue *(publish),* post, publish
call the roll poll
call to account arraign, blame, castigate, cite *(accuse),* condemn *(blame),* convict, denounce *(condemn),* disapprove *(condemn),* discipline *(punish),* impeach, indict, lodge *(bring a complaint),* penalize, punish, rebuke, reprehend, reprimand, reproach
call to answer challenge, contest
call to mind bear *(adduce),* conjure, recognize *(perceive),* recollect, remember
call to notice address *(direct attention to)*
call to task rebuke, reprimand
call to witness corroborate, subpoena, summon
call together convene
call up convene, evoke, induct, invoke, recall *(remember),* recruit, remember, retain *(keep in possession)*
call upon address *(petition),* call *(appeal to),* command, delegate, direct *(order),* importune, instruct *(direct),* order, petition, plead *(implore),* pray, press *(beseech)*
call with authority subpoena, summon
called by duty bound
called for essential *(required),* important *(urgent),* indispensable, mandatory, requisite
callidus artful, expert, resourceful

calligraphy handwriting, script
calling business *(occupation)*, career, designation *(naming)*, employment, job, labor *(work)*, livelihood, mission, occupation *(vocation)*, position *(business status)*, practice *(professional business)*, profession *(vocation)*, pursuit *(occupation)*, specialty *(special aptitude)*, trade *(occupation)*, work *(employment)*
calling to account incrimination
calling to court summons
callosus callous
callous cold-blooded, diabolic, impervious, insensible, insusceptible *(uncaring)*, obdurate, obtuse, phlegmatic, recalcitrant, ruthless, unaffected *(uninfluenced)*
calloused ossified
callousness disinterest *(lack of interest)*, disregard *(lack of respect)*
callow inexperienced, jejune *(lacking maturity)*, juvenile, naive, puerile, uncouth
calm allay, alleviate, composure, controlled *(restrained)*, dispassionate, ease, lull, lull, moderate *(temper)*, mollify, nonchalant, obtund, pacify, passive, patient, peace, peaceable, phlegmatic, placate, placid, propitiate, relieve *(give aid)*, remedy, remit *(relax)*, soothe, subdue, subside, unaffected *(uninfluenced)*
calm before a storm crossroad *(turning point)*
calm down rest *(cease from action)*
calmant narcotic
calmative mitigating, narcotic, narcotic, palliative *(abating)*, placid, remedial
calme dispassionate
calmness common sense, composure, lull, moderation, mollification, peace, sufferance, temperance
calumnia aspersion, slander
calumniari cavil, defame, misrepresent
calumniate contemn, defame, denigrate, denounce *(condemn)*, derogate, disparage, lessen, libel, malign, pillory, smear
calumniating contemptuous
calumniation aspersion, bad repute, defamation, slander, vilification
calumniatory calumnious, contemptuous, derogatory
calumnious contemptuous, derogatory, libelous, pejorative
calumny aspersion, bad repute, defamation, denunciation, dishonor *(shame)*, libel, lie, slander, vilification
camarade copartner *(coconspirator)*
camaraderie comity, contact *(association)*, sodality
camarilla cabal, faction
came to determination res judicata
camera chamber *(compartment)*
camouflage blind *(obscure)*, cloak, conceal, concealment, cover *(pretext)*, cover *(conceal)*, deceit, deception, decoy, disguise, disguise, distort, distortion, ensconce, enshroud, evasion, falsify, hide, misrepresent, plant *(covertly place)*, pretense *(pretext)*, pretext, ruse, screen *(guard)*, subterfuge, veil
camouflaged blind *(concealed)*, clandestine, deceptive, hidden, indiscernible, latent

camp dwelling, lodge *(reside)*
campaign activity, course, endeavor, enterprise *(undertaking)*, expedient, fight *(battle)*, operation, plan, program, promotion *(encouragement)*, pursuit *(effort to secure)*, strategy, venture, work *(effort)*
campaign promises platform
campaigner contender, politician
campaigning politics
canaille populace
canard falsehood, fiction, figment, hoax, story *(falsehood)*
canation license
cancel abate *(extinguish)*, abolish, abrogate *(annul)*, abrogate *(rescind)*, adeem, annul, cease, censor, condemn *(ban)*, countervail, debar, delete, disable, discharge *(release from obligation)*, disclaim, discontinue *(abandon)*, dissolve *(terminate)*, eliminate *(eradicate)*, expunge, expurgate, extinguish, extirpate, forestall, forgive, frustrate, invalidate, kill *(defeat)*, negate, neutralize, nullify, obliterate, override, overrule, quash, recall *(call back)*, recant, refute, remit *(release from penalty)*, remove *(eliminate)*, repeal, repudiate, rescind, revoke, superannuate, suppress, terminate, vacate *(void)*, vitiate
cancel a punishment pardon
cancel an offense pardon
cancel debts liquidate *(determine liability)*
cancel out annul, counteract, countervail, neutralize
canceled inactive, invalid, lifeless *(dead)*, null *(invalid)*, null and void, powerless
canceling defeasance, discharge *(annulment)*
cancellation abandonment *(repudiation)*, abatement *(extinguishment)*, abolition, ademption, annulment, censorship, condonation, countermand, defeasance, desuetude, discharge *(annulment)*, discharge *(release from obligation)*, discontinuance *(act of discontinuing)*, dismissal *(termination of a proceeding)*, dissolution *(termination)*, invalidity, mistrial, negation, nollo prosequi, obviation, remission, renunciation, repudiation, rescision, retraction, reversal, revocation
cancellation of a legacy ademption
cancelled defunct, void *(invalid)*
cancelling avoidance *(cancellation)*, discontinuance *(act of discontinuing)*, dissolution *(termination)*, revocation
cancerous malignant
candid bona fide, direct *(forthright)*, honest, ingenuous, objective, straightforward, unaffected *(sincere)*, upright
candidate contender, contestant, politician, probationer *(one being tested)*, prospect *(prospective patron)*, rival
candidate under consideration applicant *(candidate)*
candidatus candidate
candidness candor *(straightforwardness)*, honesty, probity, veracity
candidus candid, open *(persuasible)*, unaffected *(sincere)*
candied nectarious
candor disinterest *(lack of prejudice)*, honesty, probity, truth, veracity

cane cudgel
canker decay, degenerate, infect, pervert
cankered decadent, marred
cannabis sativa cannabis
cannonade barrage
canny artful, deft, machiavellian, perspicacious, politic, practiced, prudent, subtle *(insidious)*, vigilant
canon article *(precept)*, belief *(something believed)*, bylaw, code, codification, constitution, direction *(order)*, doctrine, dogma, edict, law, legislation *(enactments)*, mandate, maxim, ordinance, pandect *(code of laws)*, precept, prescription *(directive)*, principle *(axiom)*, regulation *(rule)*, rubric *(authoritative rule)*, rule *(legal dictate)*, standard, statute
canon of laws pandect *(code of laws)*
canonic valid
canonical dogmatic, orthodox, valid
canonization elevation
canonize elevate, honor
canons legislation *(enactments)*
canons regarding securities blue sky law
canorus harmonious
cant jargon *(technical language)*, palter, phraseology
cantankerous contentious, fractious, froward, hostile, inflexible, negative, perverse, petulant, restive
canting querulous
cantle element, segment
cantlet segment
canton division *(administrative unit)*, province
canvass analyze, check *(inspect)*, debate, examine *(study)*, poll, request, scrutinize, solicit, survey *(poll)*
canvassing analysis, inquiry *(systematic investigation)*
cap culminate, culmination, finish, pinnacle, surpass
capability ability, caliber *(mental capacity)*, caliber *(quality)*, capacity *(aptitude)*, competence *(ability)*, competence *(sanity)*, comprehension, efficiency, facility *(easiness)*, faculty *(ability)*, force *(strength)*, gift *(flair)*, performance *(workmanship)*, potential, qualification *(fitness)*, specialty *(special aptitude)*
capable adequate, artful, competent, deft, effective *(efficient)*, efficient, eligible, expert, familiar *(informed)*, fit, omnipotent, operative, possible, potent, practiced, proficient, qualified *(competent)*, resourceful, sciential, veteran, virtual
capable of being adjudged invalid voidable
capable of being adjudged void voidable
capable of being annulled voidable
capable of being appeased placable
capable of being bounded terminable
capable of being completed terminable
capable of being concluded terminable
capable of being conditioned terminable
capable of being conquered indefensible

capable of being debated debatable, forensic, litigable

capable of being decided by a court justiciable

capable of being declared ineffectual voidable

capable of being declared void voidable

capable of being deducted deductible *(capable of being deducted from taxes)*

capable of being demonstrated provable

capable of being divided divisible

capable of being done practicable

capable of being ended terminable

capable of being examined cognizable

capable of being exchanged convertible

capable of being figured out deductible *(provable)*

capable of being fixed terminable

capable of being inhabited habitable

capable of being limited terminable

capable of being made definite terminable

capable of being maintained tenable

capable of being overcome indefensible

capable of being pacified placable

capable of being perceived appreciable

capable of being proved deductible *(provable)*

capable of being proven provable

capable of being rebated deductible *(capable of being deducted from taxes)*

capable of being shown provable

capable of being transferred negotiable

capable of being tried in the court cognizable

capable of conforming to new situations flexible

capable of decision determinable *(ascertainable)*

capable of development viable

capable of growth viable

capable of holding much capacious

capable of loss at risk

capable of passing passable

capable of positive proof provable

capable of proof certain *(positive)*, incontrovertible, provable

capable of reason reasonable *(rational)*

capable of receiving injuries vulnerable

capable of resisting insusceptible *(resistant)*, insusceptible *(uncaring)*

capable of responding to changing situations flexible

capable of withstanding insusceptible *(uncaring)*

capableness caliber *(mental capacity)*, capacity *(aptitude)*, efficiency

capacious ample, complete *(all-embracing)*, comprehensive, extensive

capaciousness measurement, space

capacitate empower, enable

capacity ability, appointment *(position)*, caliber *(mental capacity)*, cargo, competence *(ability)*, coverage *(scope)*, employment, faculty *(ability)*, gift *(flair)*, maximum *(amplitude)*, means *(opportunity)*, measurement, occupation *(vocation)*, office, penchant, performance *(workmanship)*, post, potential, propensity, province, pursuit *(occupation)*, qualification *(fitness)*, role, science *(technique)*, space, sphere, sufficiency

capacity to decide the matter in issue jurisdiction

capacity to endure sufferance, tolerance

capacity to hear the controversy jurisdiction

capacity to stand suffering tolerance

capacity to take pain tolerance

capacity to understand comprehension

capere capture, contain *(comprise)*, ensnare, entrap, gain, occupy *(take possession)*, receive *(acquire)*

capital assets, cardinal *(basic)*, cash, central *(essential)*, deadly, fund, important *(significant)*, leading *(ranking first)*, master, material *(important)*, monetary, money, possessions, premium, prime *(most valuable)*, principal *(capital sum)*, resource, salient, seat, securities, security *(stock)*, select, share *(stock)*, stellar, stock *(shares)*, substance *(material possessions)*, treasury

capital crime felony, homicide

capital gains boom *(prosperity)*

capital goods merchandise

capital invested investment

capital murder homicide

capital outlay investment

capitalize finance

capitalize on exploit *(make use of)*

capitalize upon employ *(make use of)*

capitation assessment *(levy)*, duty *(tax)*, excise, poll *(canvass)*, tax

capitulary code, codification

capitulate accede *(concede)*, defer *(yield in judgment)*, forfeit, quit *(discontinue)*, resign, submit *(yield)*, succumb, surrender *(yield)*, yield *(submit)*

capitulation capsule, concession *(compromise)*, hornbook, resignation *(passive acceptance)*

caprice notion

capricious aleatory *(uncertain)*, arbitrary, disordered, haphazard, inconsistent, irresolute, irresponsible, lawless, mutable, undependable, unpredictable, unreasonable, unreliable, unsettled, untrustworthy, variable, volatile

capriciousness inconsistency

capsize upset

capsule abridgment *(condensation)*, abstract, brief, compendium, concise, digest, hornbook, scenario

capsulize abridge *(shorten)*, abstract *(summarize)*, condense, constrict *(compress)*, digest *(summarize)*

capsulized concise

captain chief, superintendent

captainship generalship

captare solicit

captio fallacy

caption apprehension *(act of arresting)*, call *(title)*, denomination, heading, inscription, phrase, rubric *(title)*, title *(designation)*

captiosus sophistic

captious contentious, contrary, critical *(faultfinding)*, fractious, froward, perverse, petulant, querulous, sophistic

captivate coax, lure, motivate, occupy *(engage)*, subdue

captivating attractive, moving *(evoking emotion)*, provocative, sapid

captivation seduction

captive convict, hostage, in custody, inmate, prisoner

captivitas captivity

captivity bondage, constraint *(imprisonment)*, custody *(incarceration)*, detention, durance, duress, incarceration, restraint, servitude, subjection, thrall

captivus captive

capture apprehend *(arrest)*, apprehension *(act of arresting)*, appropriate, appropriation *(taking)*, arrest, arrest *(apprehend)*, carry away, confine, deprive, detain *(hold in custody)*, disseisin, distraint, distress *(seizure)*, enclose, ensnare, gain, hijack, jail, kidnap, obtain, occupy *(take possession)*, preempt, prize, procure, repossess, seize *(apprehend)*, seize *(confiscate)*, subdue, succeed *(attain)*, taking

capture and deportation extradition

captured arrested *(apprehended)*

captured goods contraband

captured person captive

capturing confiscatory

captus captive, inmate

caput article *(precept)*, capital, chapter *(division)*, chief, clause, main point, person, point *(item)*, principal *(capital sum)*, source

carbine gun

carbon counterpart *(parallel)*, duplicate

carbon copy counterpart *(parallel)*, duplicate

carcass body *(person)*, cadaver, corpse

carcer custody *(supervision)*, incarceration, jail, prison

card coupon, form *(document)*

card index file

cardholder member *(individual in a group)*

cardinal central *(essential)*, considerable, dominant, fundamental, indispensable, integral, leading *(ranking first)*, material *(important)*, paramount, prime *(most valuable)*, principal, salient, vital

cardinal feature main point

cardinal point center *(essence)*, content *(meaning)*, cornerstone, gist *(ground for a suit)*, gravamen, landmark *(significant change)*, main point

care administration, agency *(legal relationship)*, alimony, apprehension *(fear)*, auspices, burden, caution *(vigilance)*, charge *(custody)*, concern *(interest)*, consideration *(sympathetic regard)*, constraint *(imprisonment)*, control *(supervision)*, custody *(supervision)*, direction *(guidance)*, discretion *(quality of being discreet)*, generalship, help, interest *(concern)*, maintenance *(upkeep)*, management *(supervision)*, notice *(heed)*, particularity, patronage *(support)*, precaution, preservation, problem, prudence, regard *(attention)*, relief *(aid)*, rigor, safekeeping, service *(assistance)*, shelter *(protection)*, supervision, surveillance, trust (custody), ward, weight (burden)

care for attend (take care of), cover (guard), foster, harbor, hold (possess), keep (shelter), maintain (sustain), manage, nurture, police, preserve, protect, provide (arrange for), regard (hold in esteem), serve (assist)

care nothing for condescend (patronize), disdain, flout

cared for safe

career business (occupation), calling, employment, livelihood, occupation (vocation), position (business status), post, practice (professional business), profession (vocation), professional (trained), pursuit (occupation), specialty (special aptitude)

carefree complacent, convenient, nonchalant, secure (confident)

careful accurate, circumspect, close (rigorous), conscientious, deliberate, discreet, economical, exact, faithful (diligent), frugal, guarded, judicious, leery, literal, meticulous, noncommittal, painstaking, particular (exacting), politic, precise, preventive, provident (frugal), provident (showing foresight), prudent, punctilious, scrupulous, strict, thorough, vigilant

careful appreciation diagnosis

careful attention notice (heed)

careful budgeting prudence

careful consideration deliberation

careful examination scrutiny

careful management economy (frugality)

careful methods strategy

careful noting of details examination (study)

careful plans strategy

careful scrutiny inspection

careful search indagation, investigation, probe, research

careful study indagation, investigation

carefully considered deliberate

carefully weighed deliberate

carefulness caution (vigilance), deliberation, diligence (care), discretion (quality of being discreet), economy (frugality), notice (heed), particularity, precaution, prudence, rigor

carefulness in outlay economy (frugality)

careless blind (not discerning), cursory, derelict (negligent), disorderly, heedless, hot-blooded, ill-judged, impolitic, improvident, imprudent, impulsive (rash), inaccurate, inadvertent, inexact, lax, negligent, oblivious, perfunctory, prodigal, reckless, remiss, slipshod, superficial, thoughtless, undependable, unpolitic, wanton

careless abandon neglect

careless loss waste

careless mistake oversight (carelessness)

careless omission oversight (carelessness)

carelessness delinquency (failure of duty), dereliction, disinterest (lack of interest), disregard (unconcern), inconsideration, indiscretion, laxity, malpractice, neglect, negligence, omission, temerity

caretake operate, superintend

caretaker custodian (warden), fiduciary, guardian, proctor, procurator, superintendent, trustee

caretakers management (directorate)

careworn disconsolate

carfare fare

cargo freight, merchandise

caricature copy, disguise, distort, distortion, exaggeration, jape, mock (imitate), parody, ridicule, travesty

caring solicitous

caritas dearth

carload cargo, freight

carmen famosum libel

carnage aberemurder, havoc, homicide

carnal bodily, dissolute, lascivious, lewd, mundane, physical, promiscuous, prurient, salacious, suggestive (risqué)

carnivorous predatory

carp blame, cavil, complain (criticize)

carp at discompose, persecute, press (goad)

carpenter build (construct), frame (construct)

carpere cavil, cull

carping critical (faultfinding), criticism, denunciation, diatribe, fractious, petulant, querulous

carriage behavior, complexion, conduct, demeanor, deportment, manner (behavior), presence (poise), temperament

carried consensual

carried away ecstatic, uncontrollable

carried through complete (ended)

carrier bearer

carrion body (person), corpse

carry bear (support), convey (transfer), deliver, demean (deport oneself), handle (trade), move (alter position), pass (approve), transfer, transmit, transport, uphold, wield

carry a report disseminate

carry a suggestion connote, imply

carry authority dominate, prevail (triumph)

carry away abduct, capture, displace (remove), distrain, hijack, hold up (rob), impropriate

carry back recover

carry beyond the limit extend (enlarge)

carry conviction convince

carry forward keep (continue), perpetuate

carry further extend (enlarge)

carry into effect comply, consummate, discharge (perform), effectuate, enforce, execute (accomplish), fulfill, implement, make, realize (make real)

carry into execution abide, commit (perpetrate), comply, compose, discharge (perform), effectuate, enforce, execute (accomplish), exercise (discharge a function), implement, make, operate, perform (adhere to), perform (execute), perpetrate, satisfy (discharge), strive

carry off carry away, dislodge, distrain, hijack, hold up (rob), kidnap, loot, perpetrate, plunder, poach

carry on adhere (persist), attempt, bear (tolerate), commit (perpetrate), conduct, continue (resume), endure (last), exercise (discharge a function), func-

tion, keep (continue), last, manage, militate, operate, oversee, perpetrate, perpetuate, persevere, persist, ply, proceed (continue), promote (organize), prosecute (carry forward), remain (continue), reopen, resume, tolerate, transact, undertake

carry on a conversation converse, discuss, speak

carry on a lawsuit litigate

carry on a trade handle (trade)

carry on an argument contend (dispute), dispute (debate)

carry on an inquiry canvass

carry on business handle (trade), practice (engage in), transact

carry on commerce handle (trade), trade

carry on hostilities engage (involve)

carry on intensive research delve

carry on negotiations deal, handle (trade)

carry on under allow (endure)

carry on war fight (battle)

carry oneself deport (conduct oneself)

carry out administer (conduct), apply (put in practice), commit (perpetrate), complete, comply, conduct, consummate, discharge (perform), dispatch (dispose of), enforce, execute (accomplish), exercise (discharge a function), finish, function, implement, keep (fulfill), obey, observe (obey), officiate, operate, perfect, perform (adhere to), perpetrate, prosecute (carry forward), realize (make real), satisfy (discharge), satisfy (fulfill), transact, undertake

carry out a sentence condemn (punish), discipline (punish), penalize

carry over continue (resume), holdover

carry tales inform (notify)

carry through attain, commit (perpetrate), complete, consummate, discharge (perform), dispatch (dispose of), effectuate, enforce, finish, follow-up, implement, perpetrate, realize (make real)

carry to completion complete, conclude (complete), consummate, dispatch (dispose of), exhaust (try all possibilities)

carry to excess carouse, overindulge

carry too far overindulge

carry weight influence, motivate, predominate (command), prejudice (influence)

carry weight with prevail (persuade), prevail upon

carry-over balance (amount in excess), remainder (remaining part)

carrying carriage

carrying charge cost (price), maintenance (upkeep)

carrying into effect enforcement, performance (execution)

carrying on continuation (resumption)

carrying out action (performance), commission (act), enforcement

carrying through discharge (performance), fait accompli, performance (execution)

cart carry (transport), deliver, transport

cart away dislodge, displace (remove)

cartage carriage

carte blanche dispensation *(exception)*
carte blanche latitude
carte blanche permit
cartel business *(commercial enterprise)*, coalition, compact, confederacy *(compact)*, consortium *(business cartel)*, league, pool, syndicate, treaty, trust *(combination of businesses)*
cartload cargo
cartoon caricature, copy, parody
cartridges ammunition
carve create, disjoint, divide *(distribute)*, parcel, part *(separate)*, partition, split
carve up apportion
cascade outpour
case action *(proceeding)*, cause *(lawsuit)*, check *(inspect)*, complaint, controversy *(lawsuit)*, day in court, enshroud, example, incident, instance, lawsuit, matter *(subject)*, particular, patient, plight, predicament, proceeding, question *(issue)*, situation, subject *(object)*, suit, trial *(legal proceeding)*
case at law controversy *(lawsuit)*, hearing
case for decision lawsuit
case for the prosecution complaint, count
case history dossier
case in point example, illustration, instance, sample, specimen
case in question matter *(subject)*
case of conscience allegiance
cases ready for argument calendar *(list of cases)*
cash currency, money
cash box bank
cash in liquidate *(convert into cash)*
cash in on gain, profit
cash paid expenditure
cash payment advance *(allowance)*, collection *(payment)*
cash supplies capital
cashbook journal, ledger
casher bearer
cashier comptroller, demote, discharge *(dismiss)*, dislodge, dismiss *(discharge)*, eliminate *(exclude)*, reject, remove *(dismiss from office)*, supplant
cashier's check draft
cashiering dismissal *(discharge)*, layoff, rejection, removal
cassation cancellation, defeasance, negation
cast allocate, build *(construct)*, characteristic, configuration *(form)*, copy, discharge *(dismiss)*, disposition *(inclination)*, fabricate *(construct)*, frame *(formulate)*, inclination, launch *(project)*, make, nuance, personnel, posture *(attitude)*, predisposition, project *(impel forward)*, send, stamp, style, tenor
cast a ballot vote
cast a reproach censure
cast a shadow obnubilate, obscure
cast a slur smear
cast a slur on blame, dishonor *(deprive of honor)*, involve *(implicate)*
cast a slur upon brand *(stigmatize)*, censure, denounce *(condemn)*, derogate, disgrace, fault, humiliate, malign, pillory
cast a vote vote
cast accounts calculate
cast adrift dispel

cast an imputation upon impeach
cast anchor pause
cast aside abandon *(relinquish)*, condemn *(ban)*, derelict *(abandoned)*, forgo, forswear, nullify, omit, pretermit, rebuff, refuse, reject, renounce, repel *(drive back)*, spurn
cast aspersions complain *(criticize)*, contemn, denigrate, denounce *(condemn)*, deprecate, derogate, dishonor *(deprive of honor)*, malign
cast aspersions at brand *(stigmatize)*
cast aspersions on defame, disapprove *(condemn)*, discredit, pillory
cast away abandon *(relinquish)*, depose *(remove)*, disown *(refuse to acknowledge)*, forswear, reject
cast back reflect *(mirror)*
cast blame upon censure, condemn *(blame)*, convict, disapprove *(condemn)*, fault, impeach, incriminate, lodge *(bring a complaint)*, reprehend
cast dishonor upon disgrace
cast doubt impugn
cast doubt upon debunk
cast down disconsolate, discourage, humiliate, overthrow
cast eyes on discern *(detect with the senses)*
cast forth diffuse, disperse *(disseminate)*, dissipate *(spread out)*, eject *(expel)*, outpour
cast into prison arrest *(apprehend)*, immure, imprison, jail
cast light upon elucidate
cast loose discharge *(dismiss)*, free *(not restricted)*, parole
cast lots bet
cast off abandon *(physically leave)*, abandon *(relinquish)*, defect, derelict *(abandoned)*, disencumber, disown *(refuse to acknowledge)*, dispel, disperse *(disseminate)*, forgo, forswear, reject, relinquish, renounce, set aside *(annul)*, waive
cast out condemn *(ban)*, deport *(banish)*, depose *(remove)*, disinherit, dislocate, dislodge, dismiss *(discharge)*, dispel, displace *(remove)*, eject *(evict)*, eject *(expel)*, eliminate *(exclude)*, emit, exclude, expatriate, expose, ineligible, oust, relegate, spurn
cast overboard jettison
cast reflection upon censure, denounce *(condemn)*, impugn
cast reproach upon denounce *(condemn)*, disgrace, dishonor *(deprive of honor)*, expostulate, lash *(attack verbally)*
cast shame upon discredit
cast the majority of ballots for elect *(select by a vote)*
castaway derelict *(abandoned)*, discard, orphan, pariah
caste bloodline, class, status
castigare castigate, punish
castigate blame, censure, complain *(criticize)*, condemn *(blame)*, criticize *(find fault with)*, denounce *(condemn)*, disapprove *(condemn)*, discipline *(punish)*, expostulate, fault, ill use, impeach, lash *(attack verbally)*, penalize, proscribe *(denounce)*, punish, rebuke, remonstrate, reprehend, reprimand, reproach
castigating critical *(faultfinding)*

castigatio correction *(punishment)*, punishment
castigation bad repute, blame *(culpability)*, charge *(accusation)*, condemnation *(blame)*, contumely, correction *(punishment)*, denunciation, diatribe, discipline *(punishment)*, discredit, disparagement, impeachment, indictment, infliction, objurgation, obloquy, outcry, penalty, phillipic, punishment, remonstrance, reprimand, reproach, revilement, stricture
castigatory calumnious, disciplinary *(punitory)*, pejorative, penal, punitive
casting away release
casting of ballots poll *(casting of votes)*
casting out deportation
castoff discard
casual careless, coincidental, cursory, fortuitous, haphazard, informal, lax, nonchalant, perfunctory, promiscuous, random, sporadic, thoughtless, unintentional, unofficial, usual
casualness informality
casualties toll *(effect)*
casualty accident *(misfortune)*, corpse, damage, disaster, expense *(sacrifice)*, fatality, happenstance, misfortune, quirk *(accident)*, tragedy, victim
casuistic artificial, illusory, sophistic, specious
casuistical illusory, sophistic, specious
casuistry duplicity, ethics, sophistry
casus accident *(chance occurrence)*, chance *(fortuity)*, contingency, emergency, fatality, happening, hazard, incident, occurrence
casus foederis counteroffer
cataclysm calamity, catastrophe, debacle, disaster, fatality, havoc, misfortune, outbreak, prostration, shambles, tragedy
cataclysmal disastrous
cataclysmic deadly, dire, disastrous, harmful
catalog codify, docket, enumerate, impanel, index *(relate)*, itemize
catalogue classify, detail *(particularize)*, digest *(summarize)*, directory, enroll, enter *(record)*, file, file *(arrange)*, fix *(arrange)*, identify, inventory, note *(record)*, order *(arrangement)*, organize *(arrange)*, pigeonhole, program, prospectus, record, record, register, register, roll, sort, tabulate
catalogue of persons poll *(canvass)*
cataloguing classification, registration
catalyst stimulus
catalytic agent catalyst, stimulus
catapult cast *(throw)*, impel, launch *(project)*, precipitate *(throw down violently)*
cataract spate
catastrophe adversity, calamity, casualty, debacle, disaster, fatality, loss, misfortune, tragedy, trouble
catastrophic adverse *(negative)*, deplorable, dire, disastrous, fatal, harmful, pernicious, regrettable
catastrophical dire
catch apprehend *(arrest)*, apprehension *(act of arresting)*, arrest *(apprehend)*, capture, connection *(fastening)*,

ensnare, entrap, lock, obstacle, obstruction, overhear, pitfall, preempt, prize, receive *(acquire)*, seize *(apprehend)*, trap, trap

catch a glimpse of find *(discover)*

catch again rearrest

catch by artifice entrap

catch by perfidy ambush

catch fire burn

catch phrase catchword

catch sight of discern *(detect with the senses)*, recognize *(perceive)*, spy

catch the attention occupy *(engage)*

catch the eye interest

catch unprepared ensnare

catch up reach

catch-all trap

catchall depository

catching attractive, contagious

catchpenny tawdry

catchy attractive

catechization interrogation

catechize cross-examine, examine *(interrogate)*, inquire

catechumen neophyte, novice

categorical absolute *(conclusive)*, actual, affirmative, axiomatic, certain *(specific)*, clear *(certain)*, compelling, conclusive *(determinative)*, convincing, decisive, definite, dogmatic, explicit, express, positive *(incontestable)*, specific, unconditional, unequivocal

categorical imperative conscience, instruction *(direction)*

categorically true actual, candid

categorization classification, denomination, department, designation *(naming)*, diagnosis, distribution *(arrangement)*, hierarchy *(arrangement in a series)*, manner *(kind)*, order *(arrangement)*, subdivision, subheading

categorization of laws codification

categorize classify, codify, file *(arrange)*, index *(docket)*, organize *(arrange)*, pigeonhole, sort, subdivide

category class, classification, denomination, department, diagnosis, division *(administrative unit)*, kind, manner *(kind)*, member *(constituent part)*, section *(division)*, subdivision

catena chain *(series)*, fetter

catenas fetter

catenation chain *(series)*, connection *(fastening)*, sequence

cater bestow, pander, supply

cater to excessively overindulge

caterer supplier

catering provision *(act of supplying)*

catholic general, omnibus, prevailing *(current)*, prevalent, rife

catholicity disinterest *(lack of prejudice)*

catholicon cure, panacea

catlike furtive, stealthy

cattiness spite

caucas company *(assemblage)*

caucus assemblage, assembly, chamber *(body)*, meeting *(conference)*, panel *(discussion group)*, party *(political organization)*, session

caught arrested *(apprehended)*

causa cause *(reason)*, cause, ground, inducement, issue *(matter in dispute)*, matter *(case)*, motive, reason *(basis)*, suit

causal causative

causality derivation, incentive

causam hear *(give a legal hearing)*

causam agere plead *(argue a case)*

causation building *(business of assembling)*, cause *(reason)*, creation, derivation, incentive, instigation, motive, origination, provocation, reason *(basis)*

causative causal, constructive *(creative)*, productive

cause action *(proceeding)*, activity, answer *(solution)*, avail *(bring about)*, base *(foundation)*, basis, bear *(yield)*, campaign, case *(lawsuit)*, catalyst, cause of action, compel, compose, conduce, contention *(argument)*, contrive, controversy *(lawsuit)*, create, derivation, effectuate, elicit, endeavor, engender, enterprise *(undertaking)*, evoke, factor *(ingredient)*, forge *(produce)*, generate, gist *(ground for a suit)*, ground, impel, incentive, incite, induce, inducement, inflict, inspire, issue *(matter in dispute)*, make, matter *(case)*, motivate, occasion, operate, origin *(source)*, originate, origination, proceeding, procure, prompt, provocation, provoke, rationale, reason *(basis)*, redound, require *(compel)*, side, source, stimulus, suit, trial *(legal proceeding)*

cause a discontinuance discontinue *(abandon)*

cause a fuss perturb

cause a mistake misguide

cause a rift disaffect

cause a scandal pillory

cause a stoppage check *(restrain)*, close *(terminate)*, hold up *(delay)*, quit *(discontinue)*

cause against an opposing party counterclaim

cause agitation perturb

cause alarm menace, perturb

cause aversion repel *(disgust)*

cause chaos disrupt

cause confusion disrupt, embarrass, perturb

cause damage to prejudice *(injure)*

cause detriment damage, prejudice *(injure)*

cause discomfort embarrass

cause discontent disappoint, disconcert, discourage

cause dislike affront, alienate *(estrange)*, antagonize, disaffect, discourage, incense, repel *(disgust)*

cause disorder perturb

cause displeasure disoblige

cause doubt discourage, dissuade

cause error delude, err, misguide, mislead

cause evil ill use, mistreat

cause for alarm hazard

cause for blame fault *(responsibility)*

cause for complaint ground

cause for concern problem

cause for protest ground

cause growth magnify

cause hostility disaffect

cause illness infect

cause in court action *(proceeding)*, lawsuit, matter *(case)*, suit

cause injury damage

cause loathing alienate *(estrange)*, incense

cause mischief damage

cause of action claim *(legal de-*

mand), gist *(ground for a suit)*, incentive

cause of action in favor of defendants counterclaim

cause of distress nuisance, trouble

cause of reproach disgrace

cause of shame disgrace

cause of sorrow grievance

cause offense affront, antagonize

cause pain aggravate *(annoy)*, harm, mistreat, prejudice *(injure)*

cause problems disadvantage

cause resentment bait *(harass)*, incense, pique

cause scission disrupt

cause suffering distress

cause the downfall of supplant

cause to constrain *(compel)*

cause to alter affect

cause to arrive late hold up *(delay)*

cause to be compose, fabricate *(construct)*, generate

cause to be continued perpetuate

cause to be dishonest corrupt, taint *(corrupt)*

cause to be forfeited confiscate, seize *(confiscate)*

cause to be nugatory foil

cause to be remembered retain *(keep in possession)*

cause to be smaller diminish

cause to be still allay

cause to be understood explain

cause to bend divert

cause to bulge inflate

cause to cease eradicate, interrupt

cause to contract constrict *(compress)*

cause to curve divert

cause to delay impede, interrupt

cause to descend demote

cause to deviate divert

cause to diminish decrease

cause to disappear expunge

cause to endure establish *(entrench)*, keep *(shelter)*, perpetuate

cause to exist compose, create, engender, fabricate *(construct)*, make

cause to expand develop

cause to feel certain assure *(give confidence to)*

cause to feel ill at ease embarrass

cause to forfeit dispossess

cause to grow develop, extend *(enlarge)*

cause to halt cease, enjoin, quit *(discontinue)*

cause to happen carry *(succeed)*, effectuate, evoke

cause to last keep *(shelter)*, perpetuate

cause to move with undue slowness hold up *(delay)*

cause to pass to another devolve

cause to put off to a later time hold up *(delay)*

cause to recollect remind

cause to relax lull

cause to remember remind

cause to rise elevate

cause to sink demote, depress

cause to subside allay

cause to suffer inflict

cause to taper diminish

cause to turn from divert

cause to undergo subject

cause to vary affect
cause to yield force (coerce)
cause umbrage antagonize
cause upset perturb
caused causative, derivative
causeless casual, gratuitous (unwarranted), needless, unpredictable
causer author (originator)
causerie conversation
causey causeway
causidical actionable
causing danger dangerous, noxious
causing death fatal
causing destruction fatal
causing disagreement divisive
causing disassociation divisive
causing disjunction divisive
causing pleasure palatable
causing separation divisive
caustic astringent, bitter (acrid tasting), bitter (reproachful), calumnious, critical (faultfinding), cynical, harsh, incisive, malignant, mordacious, spiteful, trenchant
causticity severity
cautel notice (heed)
cauterize burn
cautio caution (vigilance), prudence, security (stock)
caution admonish (warn), admonition, advise, alert, castigate, caveat, charge (instruct on the law), counsel, deliberation, deter, deterrent, diligence (care), discourage, discretion (quality of being discreet), dissuade, exhort, expostulate, forewarn, hesitation, indicant, monition (warning), notice (heed), notice (warning), notification, notify, portend, precaution, premonition, prudence, restraint, signify (inform), warning
caution against danger forewarn
caution beforehand forewarn
caution in advance forewarn
caution money bail, binder
cautionary advisory, portentous (ominous)
cautious careful, circumspect, deliberate, diffident, discreet, frugal, guarded, hesitant, judicious, leery, noncommittal, politic, preventive, provident (showing foresight), prudent, suspicious (distrustful), tentative, vigilant
cautious in dealing diplomatic
cautiousness deliberation, discretion (quality of being discreet), notice (heed)
cautus circumspect, discreet, guarded, prudent, tactical
cavalier cynical, disdainful, impertinent (insolent), presumptuous, supercilious
cavalierness disrespect
cave in break (fracture), succumb
caveat admonition
caveat caution (warning), deterrence, deterrent, instruction (direction), measure, monition (warning), notice (warning), warning
cavil bicker, blame, complain (criticize), denounce (condemn), differ (disagree), disagree, disapprove (condemn), disparage, pettifog, sophistry
caviler disputant, malcontent
caviling contentious, critical (faultfinding), criticism, disaccord, disapprobation, dissension, dissent (differ-

ence of opinion), dissenting, fractious
cavillari flout, jeer
cavilling petulant
cease abandon (relinquish), close (terminate), cloture, conclude (complete), desist, discontinue (abandon), dissipate (spread out), dissolve (terminate), expire, finish, forbear, forgo, halt, interrupt, leave (allow to remain), palliate (abate), pause, perish, quit (discontinue), refrain, relinquish, renounce, rest (cease from action), shut, stop, succumb, suspend, terminate, vacate (leave), waive, withdraw
cease existing decease
cease living decease, die, perish
cease progress quit (discontinue)
cease resistance comply, submit (yield)
cease to be decease, dissipate (spread out), expire, perish
cease to exist decease, die, perish
cease to litigate rest (end a legal case)
cease to live decease, perish
cease to use quit (discontinue)
cease using discontinue (abandon)
cease work quit (discontinue), resign, strike (refuse to work)
ceaseless chronic, continual (perpetual), continuous, durable, incessant, infinite, open-ended, permanent, perpetual, unrelenting, unremitting
ceaselessness indestructibility, perpetuity
ceasing cessation (interlude)
cede abandon (relinquish), attorn, bequeath, bestow, confer (give), contribute (supply), convey (transfer), defer (yield in judgment), devolve, disown (refuse to acknowledge), forfeit, give (grant), grant (concede), grant (transfer formally), offer (tender), pass (advance), relinquish, remise, resign, surrender (give back), transmit, yield (submit)
cede back escheat
cedere resign
ceiling cap, pinnacle
celare hide
celeber famous, populous
celebrare honor
celebrate carouse, honor, keep (fulfill), recommend
celebrated blatant (conspicuous), famous, household (familiar), illustrious, notable, noteworthy, notorious, outstanding (prominent), popular, prominent, remarkable, renowned, reputable, stellar
celebrated in public famous
celebration ceremony, dedication, holiday, memory (commemoration), mention (tribute), recommendation, remembrance (commemoration), reputation
celebrity character (reputation), distinction (reputation), eminence, notoriety, prestige, regard (esteem), reputation
celer expeditious
celerity dispatch (promptness), haste
celestial stellar
celibate solitary
cell chamber (compartment), jail, penitentiary, prison
cella cell

cement adhere (fasten), bond (hold together), cohere (adhere), conjoin, connect (join together), crystallize, lock, merge, unite
cement a union affiliate, organize (unionize)
cementation accession (annexation), adherence (adhesion), adhesion (affixing)
cemented concordant, concurrent (united), conjoint, inseparable
cementitious cohesive (sticking)
cenotaph monument
censeo comment
censere comment, estimate, judge
censor assessor
censor ban, bowdlerize
censor censor
censor condemn (ban), constrain (restrain), delete, eliminate (exclude), exclude, expunge, expurgate, forestall, redact, repress, restrict, suppress, withhold
censored illicit
censorious blameful, calumnious, critical (faultfinding), cynical, derogatory, dictatorial, pejorative, petulant, querulous, remonstrative, severe
censorious writing libel
censoriousness bad repute
censurability blame (culpability), guilt, impeachability
censurable blameful, blameworthy, contemptible, culpable, delinquent (guilty of a misdeed), disgraceful, guilty, inexpiable, obnoxious, peccable, peccant (culpable), reprehensible, sinister, unjustifiable, vicious
censurableness blame (culpability), culpability
censure admonish (warn), admonition, aspersion, bad repute, blame (culpability), blame, charge (accusation), charge (accuse), cite (accuse), complain (charge), complain (criticize), condemnation (blame), contemn, convict, conviction (finding of guilt), correction (punishment), criticism, criticize (find fault with), decry, defame, denounce (condemn), denunciation, depreciate, diatribe, disapprobation, disapproval, disapprove (condemn), discommend, discredit, disparage, fault, impeach, impeachment, impugnation, incrimination, judgment (formal court decree), lessen, libel, notoriety, obloquy, odium, onus (stigma), ostracism, outcry, phillipic, proscribe (denounce), proscription, punishment, rebuff, rebuke, remonstrance, remonstrate, reprehend, reprimand, reproach, reproach, restraint, revilement, scandal, sentence, slander, spurn, stricture
censure as faulty decry
censure bitterly castigate
censure formally reprimand
censure frivolously cavil
censured blameful
censurer malcontent
censuring critical (faultfinding)
census assessment (levy), census
census poll (canvass), roll
census report poll (canvass)
census return poll (canvass)
center average (midmost), base (place), central (situated near center),

concentrate *(consolidate)*, focus, focus, gravamen, headquarters, interior, seat, site, target
center around   meet
center of activity   focus
center of attention   focus
center of attraction   focus
center of authority   headquarters
center of consciousness   focus
center of gravity   center *(central position)*
center of interest   focus
center of operations   headquarters
center upon   converge
centering   centralization
centermost   average *(midmost)*, central *(situated near center)*
cento   melange
central   cardinal *(basic)*, cardinal *(outstanding)*, federal, fundamental, indispensable, integral, intermediate, leading *(ranking first)*, master, material *(important)*, primary
central element   necessity
central headquarters   base *(place)*
central idea   main point
central money office   treasury
central nature   center *(essence)*
central office   management *(directorate)*
central point   center *(central position)*, focus, gravamen, highlight
central station   headquarters
centralism   centralization
centrality   focus
centralization   affiliation *(amalgamation)*, coalescence, consolidation, federation, incorporation *(blend)*, merger
centralize   amalgamate, concentrate *(consolidate)*, consolidate *(unite)*, converge, federalize *(associate)*, focus, incorporate *(include)*, organize *(unionize)*, unite
centralized   coadunate, concurrent *(united)*
centric   central *(situated near center)*
centrical   central *(situated near center)*
cerebral   rational
cerebrate   consider, deliberate, muse, ponder, reason *(conclude)*, reflect *(ponder)*, study
cerebration   contemplation, deliberation, dialectic, intellect, ratiocination, reflection *(thought)*
ceremonial   formal, sacrosanct, solemn
ceremonial rite   formality
ceremonious   formal, official, punctilious, solemn
ceremoniously   pro forma
ceremoniousness   formality, solemnity
ceremony   custom, form *(arrangement)*, formality, protocol *(etiquette)*, remembrance *(commemoration)*, solemnity
ceremony of induction into an office   installation
certain   absolute *(conclusive)*, actual, affirmative, axiomatic, conclusive *(determinative)*, concrete, constant, convincing, corporeal, de facto, decisive, definite, dependable, dogmatic, explicit, express, incontrovertible, indubious, inevitable, irrefutable, lucid, necessary

(inescapable), official, palpable, peremptory *(absolute)*, pertinacious, positive *(confident)*, positive *(incontestable)*, reliable, resounding, safe, secure *(confident)*, several *(plural)*, several *(separate)*, special, specific, tangible, true *(authentic)*, unalienable, unambiguous, unavoidable *(inevitable)*, undeniable, undisputed, unequivocal, unmistakable, unrefutable
certain dereliction   res ipsa loquitur
certain knowledge   certification *(certainness)*, surety *(certainty)*
certainly   a fortiori, admittedly, fairly *(clearly)*
certainness   certitude
certainty   belief *(state of mind)*, certification *(certainness)*, certitude, confidence *(faith)*, constant, conviction *(persuasion)*, credence, fact, fait accompli, faith, proof, prospect *(outlook)*, reliance, security *(safety)*, trust *(confidence)*, weight *(credibility)*
certainty of meaning   certitude
certamen   contest *(competition)*, fight *(argument)*, strife, struggle
certare   compete
certatio   contest *(competition)*, strife
certifiable   ascertainable, determinable *(ascertainable)*
certificate   charter *(license)*, check *(instrument)*, coupon, deed, degree *(academic title)*, document, instrument *(document)*, permit, recommendation, record, warrant *(judicial writ)*, warranty
certificate of character   reference *(recommendation)*
certificate of debt   bond, security *(stock)*
certificate of deposit   receipt *(proof of receiving)*
certificate of exemption   dispensation *(exception)*
certificate of indebtedness   bond, security *(stock)*
certificate of invention   copyright, patent
certificate of permission   charter *(license)*
certificates   credentials
certification   acknowledgment *(avowal)*, affirmance *(authentication)*, affirmation, appointment *(act of designating)*, asseveration, attestation, capacity *(authority)*, certainty, certificate, confirmation, consent, copyright, corroboration, credentials, documentation, droit, guaranty, indorsement, jurat, leave *(permission)*, license, proof, ratification, reference *(recommendation)*, registration, stamp, subscription, support *(corroboration)*, surety *(certainty)*
certified   alleged, allowed, certain *(fixed)*, certain *(positive)*, definite, documentary, familiar *(informed)*, fully secured, official
certified public accountant   accountant
certifier   comaker, surety *(guarantor)*
certify   accredit, acknowledge *(declare)*, affirm *(uphold)*, allow *(authorize)*, approve, ascertain, assert, assure *(insure)*, attest, audit, authorize, avouch *(avow)*, avouch *(guarantee)*, avow, bear *(adduce)*, bond *(secure a*

debt), cite *(state)*, claim *(maintain)*, corroborate, cosign, countersign, depose *(testify)*, endorse, ensure, establish *(show)*, evidence, guarantee, indorse, legitimate, let *(permit)*, manifest, notarize, posit, promise *(vow)*, qualify *(meet standards)*, reassure, seal *(solemnize)*, sign, sponsor, subscribe *(sign)*, substantiate, support *(corroborate)*, sustain *(confirm)*, swear, validate, verify *(confirm)*, vouch, witness *(attest to)*
certify a will   probate
certitude   belief *(state of mind)*, certainty, certification *(certainness)*, confidence *(faith)*, conviction *(persuasion)*, faith, reliance, surety *(certainty)*
certus   authentic, certain *(particular)*, certain *(positive)*, certainty, conclusive *(settled)*, definite, fixed *(securely placed)*, infallible, irrefutable, positive *(confident)*, regular *(orderly)*, staunch, undisputed
cess   assessment *(levy)*
cessare   loiter
cessatio   delay, inaction
cessation   abandonment *(discontinuance)*, abeyance, avoidance *(cancellation)*, check *(bar)*, close *(conclusion)*, cloture, conclusion *(outcome)*, defeasance, desuetude, discharge *(annulment)*, discontinuance *(act of discontinuing)*, discontinuance *(interruption of a legal action)*, dissolution *(termination)*, end *(termination)*, expiration, finality, halt, hiatus, impasse, inaction, interruption, layoff, lull, moratorium, pause, pendency, recess, remission, respite *(interval of rest)*, stay
cessation of activity   lull
cessation of being   extremity *(death)*
cessation of employment   lockout
cessation of existence   extremity *(death)*
cessation of life   death, demise *(death)*, extremity *(death)*
cessation of sound   lull
cessation of the furnishing of work   lockout
cessation of use   disuse
cession   abandonment *(desertion)*, alienation *(transfer of title)*, assignment *(transfer of ownership)*, consignment, demise *(conveyance)*, expense *(sacrifice)*, release, renunciation, resignation *(relinquishment)*
cession of a fee   feoffment
chafe   affront, aggravate *(annoy)*, annoy, badger, bait *(harass)*, discommode, discompose, harrow, incense, irritate, resent
chaff   jape, mock *(deride)*, ridicule
chaffer   haggle, handle *(trade)*, trade
chaffering   commerce
chagrin   disconcert, dissatisfaction, distress, embarrass, embarrassment, harrow, ignominy, ill will, offend *(insult)*, remorse
chain   constrain *(imprison)*, constrain *(restrain)*, contain *(restrain)*, detain *(restrain)*, fetter, fetter, handcuff, handcuff, hierarchy *(arrangement in a series)*, restrict, sequence, succession
chain of reasoning   dialectic
chains   bondage, ties
chair   chairman, management *(directorate)*, moderate *(preside over)*, preside

chairman chief
chairmen management *(directorate)*
chairperson chief
chalk out compose
challenge argue, charge *(accuse)*, cite *(accuse)*, claim *(legal demand)*, compete, competition, complain *(charge)*, conflict, confront *(oppose)*, confutation, contend *(dispute)*, contention *(opposition)*, contest *(competition)*, contest *(dispute)*, contest, contradict, counter, counterargument, cross-examination, cross-examine, defiance, defy, demonstrate *(protest)*, demur, demurrer, denial, denounce *(condemn)*, disaccord, disaffirm, disagree, disagreement, disbelieve, disown *(deny the validity)*, dispute, dispute *(contest)*, dissent *(difference of opinion)*, dissent *(withhold assent)*, doubt *(distrust)*, examine *(interrogate)*, except *(object)*, exception *(objection)*, fight *(battle)*, impeach, impeachment, impugnation, indagation, invitation, misdoubt, motivate, object, objection, oppose, opposition, oppugn, protest, protest, provoke, reaction *(opposition)*, reject, remonstrance, remonstrate, repel *(drive back)*, resist *(withstand)*, withstand
challenge as false impugn
challenge the credibility of impeach
challenge to the sufficiency of the pleading demurrer
challenger accuser, candidate, complainant, contender, contestant, opponent, party *(litigant)*, rival
challenging competitive *(antagonistic)*, contemptuous, dissident, hostile, provocative, sapid
chamber bench, cell
chambers lodging
chambre chamber *(compartment)*
champain bar sinister
champion absolute *(ideal)*, adhere *(maintain loyalty)*, advocate *(counselor)*, advocate *(espouser)*, advocate, amicus curiae, apologist, assistant, backer, bear *(support)*, benefactor, colleague, custodian *(protector)*, defend, espouse, favor, guardian, justify, mainstay, maintain *(sustain)*, paragon, paramount, partisan, patron *(influential supporter)*, preserve, prime *(most valuable)*, promote *(organize)*, proponent, protagonist, protect, samaritan, select, side, sponsor, sponsor, successful, superlative, support *(assist)*, uphold
championing accommodation *(backing)*
championship advocacy, assistance, favor *(sanction)*, indorsement, supremacy
chance access *(opening)*, bet, coincidental, contingency, fortuitous, gamble, haphazard, happenstance, hazard, likelihood, lottery, occasion, opportunity, possibility, potential, privilege, probability, prospect *(outlook)*, quirk *(accident)*, random, risk, speculate *(chance)*, speculation *(risk)*, suspicion *(uncertainty)*, unexpected, unintentional, unwitting, venture
chance event happening
chance happening happenstance
chance occurrence act of god
chance the odds bet

chance to borrow money on time credit *(delayed payment)*
chance upon discover, find *(discover)*
chancellor judge, plenipotentiary
chancery equity *(justice)*, tribunal
chancy dubious, precarious, speculative
chandler dealer, merchant, supplier
change adapt, adjust *(resolve)*, affect, alter, alternative *(substitute)*, amend, amendment *(correction)*, commute, conflict, convert *(change use)*, denature, development *(progression)*, difference, digression, diversification, emend, exchange, fluctuate, innovation, interchange, modification, modify *(alter)*, money, nonconformity, pass *(advance)*, progress, reassign, reclassification, reconversion, redress, reform, reform, remedy, reorganization, replace, replacement, reversal, revise, revision *(process of correcting)*, subrogation, succedaneum, tamper, transform, transition, vacillate, vary
change address remove *(transfer)*
change an abode move *(alter position)*
change back revert
change by alternation alternate *(take turns)*
change continuously fluctuate
change course redirect
change direction detour, deviate, digress, redirect
change for displace *(replace)*
change for the better ameliorate, improvement
change for the worse adulterate
change from higher to lower descent *(declination)*
change from one to another devolve
change hands bequeath, circulate
change in method innovation
change into convert *(change use)*, develop, evolve
change into cash liquidate *(convert into cash)*
change into money liquidate *(convert into cash)*
change national allegiance expatriate
change of direction deviation
change of hands devolution
change of mind rescision, reversal
change of national location immigration
change of place extradition, removal
change of position deviation
change of sides revolt
change one's mind tergiversate
change out of recognition distort
change over convert *(change use)*, reconversion
change ownership devolve, grant *(transfer formally)*, pass *(advance)*
change penalties commute
change place move *(alter position)*, remove *(transfer)*
change places circulate
change residence move *(alter position)*
change sides defect, repudiate, tergiversate
change the appearance of disguise
change the bearing detour
change the course of avert, divert

change the face of camouflage, disguise, distort
change the guise of disguise
change the place of displace *(remove)*
change venue remove *(transfer)*
change-over devolution, transition
changeable aleatory *(uncertain)*, ambulatory, capricious, conditional, convertible, debatable, disordered, faithless, inconsistent, indefinite, insecure, irresolute, irresponsible, mutable, noncommittal, pliable, precarious, protean, shifting, sporadic, temporary, undependable, unpredictable, unsettled, untrustworthy, variable, volatile
changeableness incertitude, inconsistency, indecision, irregularity
changed different, tempered
changed ordering of priorities reclassification
changed priorities reclassification
changeful aleatory *(uncertain)*, capricious, disordered, insecure, irresolute, mutable, protean, undecided, unpredictable, unreliable, variable
changeless certain *(fixed)*, certain *(positive)*, constant, durable, fixed *(settled)*, indelible, inflexible, irrevocable, permanent, static, unalterable
changelessly invariably
changelessness indestructibility
changer dealer
changes circumstances, vicissitudes
changing capricious, moving *(in motion)*, open-ended, shifting, unsettled
channel avenue *(route)*, facility *(instrumentality)*, forum *(medium)*, instrument *(tool)*, instrumentality, medium, outlet, tool
channels approaches
chant recite, repeat *(state again)*
chaos anarchy, confusion *(turmoil)*, disorder *(lack of order)*, embroilment, entanglement *(confusion)*, havoc, imbroglio, incoherence, misrule, pandemonium, shambles, turmoil
chaotic complex, disordered, haphazard, labyrinthine, promiscuous, unruly
chaotic state havoc
chap person
chaperon guardian, warden
chaperonage charge *(custody)*
chaperone protect
chapman vendor
chapter affiliate, article *(distinct section of a writing)*, constituency, department, division *(administrative unit)*, organ, segment, subheading, title *(division)*
chapter and verse verbatim
char burn
character animus, behavior, caliber *(quality)*, color *(complexion)*, complexion, condition *(state)*, configuration *(form)*, disposition *(inclination)*, entity, frame *(mood)*, honor *(good reputation)*, individual, integrity, kind, merit, part *(role)*, person, personality, predisposition, principle *(virtue)*, property *(distinctive attribute)*, quality *(excellence)*, quality *(grade)*, rectitude, role, speciality, specialty *(distinctive mark)*, spirit, style, temperament, tendency, tenor, turpitude
character assassination slander

characteristic certain (specific), customary, demonstrative (illustrative), differential, disposition (inclination), distinct (distinguished from others), distinctive, general, identity (individuality), indicant, natural, nondescript, ordinary, particular (individual), particular (specific), particularity, peculiar (distinctive), personal (individual), prevailing (current), prevalent, property (distinctive attribute), quality (attribute), representative, specialty (distinctive mark), specific, symptom, trait, typical, usual
characteristic behavior habit
characteristic difference distinction (difference)
characteristic feature necessity
characteristic marks indicia
characteristic mood character (personal quality), disposition (inclination)
characteristic part epitome
characteristic quality particularity, spirit
characteristic way custom
characteristically repeated action habit
characteristics color (complexion), indicia, personality
characterization caption, caricature, cross section, denomination, description, role
characterize call (title), construe (translate), define, depict, describe, designate, differentiate, discriminate (distinguish), distinguish, interpret, label, personify, portray, render (depict), represent (portray)
characterize precisely construe (translate), define
characterized by argument argumentative
characterized by art artful
characterized by decision decisive
characterized by excess excessive
characterized by reflection deliberate
characterizing descriptive
characterless arrant (onerous), disreputable, inexpressive, lifeless (dull), pedestrian, usual
characters script
charade pretext
charge accusation, ad valorem, admonish (advise), agency (commission), agency (legal relationship), allegation, allege, ammunition, appoint, arraign, assessment (levy), assign (designate), assignation, assignment (task), attack, auspices, authorize, bad repute, bind (obligate), blame (responsibility), blame, bomb, brevet, brokerage, burden, cargo, cite (accuse), claim (maintain), cloud (incumbrance), command, commit (entrust), commitment (responsibility), complaint, condemn (blame), condemnation (blame), consign, constrain (compel), constraint (imprisonment), control (supervision), conviction (finding of guilt), cost (expenses), cost (price), count, criticism, custody (supervision), decree, defame, delegate, delegation (assignment), denigrate, denounce (inform against), denunciation, dependent, deprecate, detail (assign), dictate, dictate, direct (order), direction

(guidance), direction (order), directive, due, duty (obligation), duty (tax), encumber (financially obligate), encumber (hinder), encumbrance, enjoin, estimate (approximate cost), exact, exception (objection), excise, excise (levy a tax), exhort, expenditure, expense (cost), fare, fault, generalship, grievance, impeach, impeachment, implicate, impose (enforce), imposition (tax), incriminate, incrimination, indict, indictment, inform (betray), information (charge), innuendo, instruct (direct), instruction (direction), invest (vest), involve (implicate), levy, lien, management (supervision), mandamus, mandate, mechanics lien, mission, mortgage, motivate, obligation (duty), obligation (liability), occupation (possession), office, onset (assault), onus (blame), onus (burden), outcry, outlay, part (role), payment (remittance), plead (implore), post, precept, prescribe, prescription (directive), present (prefer charges), presentment, price, proscribe (denounce), protégé, province, rate, rebuke, reprehend, rule (legal dictate), safekeeping, servitude, summon, supervision, surveillance, tax, toll (tax), trust (custody), ward, work (employment), worth
charge beyond normal premium (excess value)
charge duty excise (levy a tax)
charge falsely frame (prearrange)
charge for carriage of passengers fare
charge for conveyance of a person fare
charge for services fee (charge)
charge imposed on specific property lien, mechanics lien
charge levied assessment (levy)
charge to impeach, impute
charge to excess premium (excess value)
charge unfairly frame (charge falsely)
charge unjustly frame (charge falsely)
charge upon impute
charge with accuse, ascribe, attribute, commit (entrust), complain (charge), impeach, lodge (bring a complaint)
charge with a duty entrust
charge with a trust entrust
charge with an errand delegate
charge with an offense incriminate
charge with offense indict
charge with one's share assess (tax)
charge with the commission of a crime indict
chargeability blame (culpability), impeachability, responsibility (accountability)
chargeable accountable (responsible), actionable, ad valorem, blameful, blameworthy, bound, culpable, delinquent (overdue), due (owed), guilty, liable, peccant (culpable), reprehensible, subject (exposed), unjustifiable
chargeableness culpability
charged accused (charged), ad valorem, full
charged party defendant
chargeless gratuitous (given without

recompense)
charger assessor, complainant, contender, party (litigant)
charges bill (invoice), brokerage, overhead
chargeship appointment (position)
charging with fault inculpation
charging with guilt incriminatory, inculpation, inculpatory
chariness austerity, discretion (quality of being discreet), doubt (suspicion), economy (frugality)
charismatic leader demagogue
charitable benevolent, donative, gratuitous (given without recompense), humane, lenient, liberal (generous), magnanimous, meritorious, nonprofit, philanthropic, placable
charitable effort benevolence (act of kindness)
charitable institution foundation (organization)
charitableness benevolence (disposition to do good), humanity (humaneness), largess (generosity), philanthropy, understanding (tolerance)
charity aid (subsistence), benefit (conferment), benevolence (act of kindness), benevolence (disposition to do good), clemency, condonation, contribution (donation), donation, favor (act of kindness), foundation (organization), goodwill, gratuity (present), help, largess (generosity), largess (gift), lenience, philanthropy
charivari noise
charlatan fake
charlatanism fraud, hypocrisy
charlatanry artifice, deception, fraud, hypocrisy
charm lure
charming attractive, moving (evoking emotion), sapid
chart delineation, design (construction plan), scheme, tabulate
charter allow (authorize), appoint, appointment (act of designating), authorize, bestow, brevet, bylaw, capacity (authority), certificate, certify (approve), code, confirm, constitute (establish), constitution, contract, countenance, deed, delegate, enactment, engage (hire), establish (launch), franchise (license), immunity, incorporate (form a corporation), instrument (document), invest (vest), law, lease, let (lease), license, ordinance, pact, pandect (code of laws), permit, prerogative, privilege, protocol (agreement), rent, sanction (permission), sanction, tolerance, treaty, warrant (authorization)
chartered allowed, licit, privileged, rightful
chartered accountant accountant, comptroller
chartering incorporation (formation of a business entity)
chary circumspect, discreet, frugal, guarded, leery, parsimonious, penurious, provident (showing foresight), prudent
chary of expense economical
chase embellish, hunt, pursuit (chase), quest, race, repulse, trace (follow)
chase after hunt, research, search

chase away parry, repel *(drive back)*
chase off parry
chase out oust
chasm hiatus, pitfall, rift *(gap)*, split
chassis frame *(structure)*
chaste pure
chasten assuage, castigate, discipline *(punish)*, moderate *(temper)*, punish
chastened contrite, penitent
chastening condemnation *(blame)*, correction *(punishment)*, disciplinary *(punitory)*, discipline *(punishment)*, punishment
chastise blame, castigate, censure, complain *(criticize)*, denounce *(condemn)*, disapprove *(condemn)*, discipline *(punish)*, expostulate, fault, lash *(attack verbally)*, penalize, punish, rebuke, remonstrate, reprehend, reprimand
chastisement condemnation *(blame)*, correction *(punishment)*, discipline *(punishment)*, obloquy, phillipic, punishment, remonstrance, reproach
chastity continence
chat conversation
chattel holding *(property owned)*, merchandise, possession *(property)*
chattel property effects
chattels assets, commodities, effects, estate *(property)*, goods, paraphernalia *(personal belongings)*, personalty, possessions, property *(possessions)*
chattels personal movable
chattels real demesne, estate *(property)*, real estate
chatter bombast, prattle
chattering loquacious
chatty informatory, loquacious
chauvinism intolerance
cheap base *(inferior)*, disreputable, economical, frugal, inferior *(lower in quality)*, meretricious, nominal, paltry, parsimonious, penurious, poor *(inferior in quality)*, tawdry
cheapen damage, debase, deduct *(reduce)*, demean *(make lower)*, denature, depreciate, depress, dilute, diminish, disparage, minimize
cheapening decline
cheapness of operation economy *(frugality)*
cheat betray *(lead astray)*, bilk, copy, deceive, deception, defalcate, defraud, delude, dupe, ensnare, fake, feign, hoax, hoodwink, illude, imposture, inveigle, knavery, maneuver, mislead, mulct *(defraud)*, overreach, palter, peculate, pretend, pretense *(pretext)*, purloin, ruse, shirk, stratagem
cheat out of money defraud
cheated aggrieved *(victimized)*
cheater embezzler
cheating artifice, bunko, deceit, deceptive, dishonest, dishonesty, embezzlement, fraud, fraudulent, insidious, knavery, machiavellian, perfidious, pettifoggery
check abeyance, allay, alleviate, arrest *(stop)*, assuage, audit, avert, balk, ban, barrier, bill *(invoice)*, bind *(restrain)*, block, cease, cloture, collation, concern *(care)*, condemn *(ban)*, constrain *(restrain)*, constrict *(inhibit)*, contain *(restrain)*, control *(restriction)*, control *(regulate)*, countervail, coupon,

cross-examine, curb, damper *(stopper)*, deadlock, debar, desist, detain *(restrain)*, deter, deterrence, disadvantage, disadvantage, discipline *(control)*, discontinue *(abandon)*, discontinue *(break continuity)*, disincentive, disqualify, draft, ensure, examination *(study)*, examine *(study)*, fetter, fetter, foil, forbid, forestall, frisk, frustrate, halt, halt, hamper, heed, hinder, hindrance, hold up *(delay)*, impasse, impede, impediment, indagation, inhibit, interdict, interfere, interrupt, interruption, keep *(restrain)*, kill *(defeat)*, lessen, limit, lock, mitigate, moderate *(temper)*, modify *(moderate)*, mollification, mollify, monitor, note *(written promise to pay)*, observation, obstacle, obstruct, obstruction, obviation, occlude, palliate *(abate)*, peruse, police, preclude, prevent, prohibit, prohibition, quit *(discontinue)*, quota, rebuff, rebuff, refrain, remission, remit *(relax)*, repel *(drive back)*, repress, repulse, resist *(oppose)*, resistance, restrain, restraint, restrict, restriction, reversal, scrutinize, stall, stave, stay, stay *(halt)*, stifle, stop, strangle, suppress, suspend, test, thwart, toll *(stop)*, trammel, trial *(experiment)*, verify *(confirm)*, withhold, withstand
check a reference consult *(seek information from)*
check a source consult *(seek information from)*
check holder bearer
check in enter *(record)*, register, report *(present oneself)*
check list invoice *(itemized list)*, schedule
check on audit, research
check over probe
check thoroughly review
check up check *(inspect)*
check upon again reexamine
check-up diligence *(care)*
checked broken *(interrupted)*, limited, qualified *(conditioned)*
checking collation, cross-examination, discovery, limiting, preventive
checklist inventory
checkmate beat *(defeat)*, check *(bar)*, clog, deadlock, defeat, frustrate, prevent, repel *(drive back)*, stem *(check)*, stop
checkup test
cheer assure *(give confidence to)*, honor, promise *(raise expectations)*, reassure, solace, spirit
cheerful ready *(willing)*, sanguine
cheerful consent goodwill
cheerful giver donor
cheerful willingness goodwill
cheerfulness spirit
cheering propitious
cheerless bleak *(severely simple)*, disconsolate, grave *(solemn)*, lugubrious, pessimistic
cheerlessness damper *(depressant)*, pessimism
chemical substance drug
cheque coupon
cherish foster, keep *(shelter)*, nurture, preserve, protect, regard *(hold in esteem)*
cherish a belief opine

cherish doubts misdoubt, mistrust
cherishing preservation
chest repository
chevy persecute
chic elegant
chicane deceive, deception, dishonesty, evasion, false pretense, fraud, imposture, pettifoggery, plot *(secret plan)*, ruse, stratagem, subterfuge
chicanery artifice, bunko, collusion, connivance, deception, dishonesty, duplicity, evasion, false pretense, fraud, hoax, knavery, maneuver *(trick)*, pettifoggery, ruse, sham, sophistry, subterfuge
chide blame, browbeat, castigate, censure, complain *(criticize)*, condemn *(blame)*, criticize *(find fault with)*, denounce *(condemn)*, disapprove *(condemn)*, expostulate, fault, lash *(attack verbally)*, rebuff, rebuke, reprehend, reprimand, reproach
chiding condemnation *(blame)*, critical *(faultfinding)*, criticism, denunciation, diatribe, disapprobation, objurgation, obloquy, outcry, rebuff, reprimand, reproach
chief best, cardinal *(basic)*, cardinal *(outstanding)*, central *(essential)*, critical *(crucial)*, director, dominant, employer, essential *(required)*, grave *(important)*, important *(significant)*, leading *(ranking first)*, major, master, necessary *(required)*, outstanding *(prominent)*, paramount, prevailing *(having superior force)*, prevalent, primary, prime *(most valuable)*, principal, principal *(director)*, salient, sovereign *(absolute)*, stellar, superintendent, superior *(higher)*, superlative, vital
chief accounting officer comptroller
chief actor principal *(director)*
chief authority principal *(director)*
chief constituent content *(meaning)*
chief controller chief
chief executive administrator, principal *(director)*
chief feature main point
chief issue main point
chief office headquarters
chief part bulk, center *(essence)*, content *(meaning)*, corpus, main point
chief party principal *(director)*
chief point main point
chief reliance mainstay
chiefly a fortiori, ab initio, as a rule, generally, particularly
chieftain chief, principal *(director)*
chieftaincy supremacy
child dependent, descendant, infant, issue *(progeny)*, juvenile, minor, offspring
child born before marriage bastard
child born out of wedlock bastard
child without parents orphan
child-stealing abduction
childbirth birth *(emergence of young)*
childhood minority *(infancy)*, nonage
childish frivolous, jejune *(lacking maturity)*, juvenile, naive, puerile
childishly foolish puerile
childishness puerility
childless barren
childlike ingenuous, juvenile, naive, puerility, unaffected *(sincere)*
children blood, issue *(progeny)*, off-

spring, posterity, progeny
chill damper *(depressant)*, deter
chime in interrupt
chime in with comport *(agree with)*
chimera figment, phantom
chimerical delusive, fictitious, illusory, immaterial, insubstantial, nonexistent, quixotic
chink rift *(gap)*, split
chip part *(portion)*, token
chipped blemished
chirographum bond, handwriting
chirography handwriting
chirotony vote
chisel bilk, create
chivalric civil *(polite)*, meritorious
chivalrous civil *(polite)*, magnanimous, meritorious
chivalry consideration *(sympathetic regard)*, courtesy
chock-full full, replete
choice adoption *(acceptance)*, advantage, alternative *(option)*, appointment *(act of designating)*, best, call *(option)*, certain *(specific)*, conatus, decision *(judgment)*, discretion *(power of choice)*, exclusive *(limited)*, franchise *(right to vote)*, inestimable, intent, latitude, liberty, meritorious, nomination, noteworthy, option *(choice)*, patronage *(power to appoint jobs)*, plebiscite, poll *(casting of votes)*, predilection, preferable, preferential, preferred *(favored)*, premium, primary, prime *(most valuable)*, professional *(stellar)*, rare, select, suffrage, superior *(excellent)*, unusual, valuable, volition, vote, will *(desire)*
choice between alternatives election *(choice)*
choice group elite
choice of language phraseology
choice of words parlance, phraseology
choiceless necessary *(inescapable)*
choke bar *(hinder)*, block, clog, constrict *(inhibit)*, extinguish, hamper, inhibit, obstruct, overload, preclude, repress, stem *(check)*, stifle, stop, subdue, suppress
choke back suppress
choke off bar *(hinder)*, occlude, shut, strangle
choler resentment, umbrage
choleric bilious, bitter *(penetrating)*, critical *(faultfinding)*, dyseptic, fractious, petulant, resentful
choose adopt, appoint, conclude *(decide)*, cull, decide, delegate, designate, determine, edit, espouse, extract, nominate, prefer, screen *(select)*, select, vote
choose a course of action decide
choose an alternative decide
choose an option decide
choose for office elect *(select by a vote)*
choosing adoptive, decision *(election)*, designation *(naming)*, elective *(selective)*, nomination, vote
choosing by vote election *(selection by vote)*
choosy particular *(exacting)*, scrupulous
chop split
chore assignment *(task)*, burden, duty *(obligation)*, function, job, part *(role)*, work *(effort)*

chorus outcry
chose in action estate *(property)*, intangible
chosen particular *(specific)*, preferable, preferred *(favored)*, select, several *(separate)*
chosen career practice *(professional business)*
chosen few elite
chosen field practice *(professional business)*
chosen profession practice *(professional business)*
chosen representative nominee *(candidate)*
chosen work calling, career, occupation *(vocation)*, profession *(vocation)*, pursuit *(occupation)*
chouse bait *(lure)*, illude, inveigle, ruse
christen call *(title)*, denominate
chronic constant, durable, habitual, incorrigible, inveterate, permanent, perpetual, persistent, stable
chronic alcoholism dipsomania
chronic disability disease
chronical inveterate
chronicle book, calendar *(record of yearly periods)*, detail *(particularize)*, enter *(record)*, entry *(record)*, file *(place among official records)*, journal, memorandum, narration, notation, note *(record)*, record, record, register, register, report *(detailed account)*, roll, set down, story *(narrative)*, tabulate
chronicled documentary
chronicler clerk
chronicling registration
chronological consecutive
chronologize date
chronology calendar *(record of yearly periods)*, journal, order *(arrangement)*, register, time
chuck precipitate *(throw down violently)*
chunk part *(portion)*, segment
churlish brutal, caitiff, disorderly, fractious, illiberal, impertinent *(insolent)*, inelegant, malevolent, penurious, perverse, petulant, provincial, resentful, severe, uncouth
churn disturb, perturb
chute outlet
cibarious palatable
cinch lock
cincture border *(bound)*, embrace *(encircle)*, enclosure, encompass *(surround)*
cingere enclose, encompass *(surround)*
cipher blank *(emptiness)*, calculate, designation *(symbol)*, indicant, nonentity
ciphering census
circle bailiwick, contour *(outline)*, cycle, enclosure, encompass *(surround)*, hedge, perambulate, region, scope, society, sphere
circonvenir circumvent
circuit bench, circulate, circumscribe *(surround by boundary)*, contour *(outline)*, cycle, detour, district, encompass *(surround)*, extent, gamut, outline *(boundary)*, periphery, province, region, scope, sphere, territory
circuitous astray, complex, devious, discursive *(digressive)*, indirect, labyrinthine, oblique *(evasive)*, sinuous, tor-

tuous *(bending)*
circuitous action indirection *(indirect action)*
circuitous route detour, indirection *(indirect action)*
circuitousness indirection *(indirect action)*
circuitus circuit
circuity digression, indirection *(indirect action)*
circular dispatch *(message)*, notice *(announcement)*
circular reasoning non sequitur
circularize circulate
circulate diffuse, disburse *(distribute)*, disclose, disperse *(disseminate)*, disseminate, herald, issue *(publish)*, post, proclaim, promulgate, propagate *(spread)*, publish, reveal, send, spread, utter
circulate publicly report *(disclose)*
circulated public *(known)*
circulating capital principal *(capital sum)*
circulating medium currency
circulation coverage *(scope)*, publication *(disclosure)*, transmittal
circulus circuit, cycle
circumagere circulate, circulation
circumambience atmosphere
circumambiency climate, periphery
circumambulate detour, perambulate
circumambulating circuitous, indirect
circumcidere abridge *(shorten)*, retrench
circumcludere encompass *(surround)*
circumduction cancellation
circumference ambit, border, contour *(outline)*, margin *(outside limit)*, outline *(boundary)*, periphery, zone
circumferential peripheral
circumflexion indirection *(indirect action)*
circumfluent circuitous
circumfluous circuitous
circumfundere envelop
circumfuse diffuse
circumire patrol
circumjacence blockade *(enclosure)*, border, enclosure
circumjacencies frontier
circumlocution indirection *(indirect action)*
circumlocutory circuitous, indirect, oblique *(evasive)*, prolix, turgid
circumplecti encompass *(surround)*
circumpose border *(bound)*
circumscribe bar *(exclude)*, comprehend *(include)*, confine, constrain *(imprison)*, delimit, delineate, demarcate, detain *(restrain)*, deter, disadvantage, embrace *(encircle)*, enclose, encompass *(surround)*, envelop, hedge, impede, imprison, include, limit, obstruct, palliate *(abate)*, prohibit, proscribe *(prohibit)*, restrict, specify
circumscribed arrested *(checked)*, certain *(specific)*, limited, narrow, qualified *(conditioned)*, regional
circumscribere circumscribe *(define)*, circumvent, define, defraud, limit, overreach, qualify *(condition)*, restrict
circumscribing limiting
circumscriptio fraud, limit, limitation
circumscription bar *(obstruction)*, blockade *(enclosure)*, boundary, configu-

ration *(confines)*, constraint *(restriction)*, contour *(outline)*, coverage *(scope)*, custody *(incarceration)*, delineation, detention, enclosure, limit, limitation, mete, outline *(boundary)*, periphery, prohibition, purview, quota, restraint, restriction

circumscriptive limited, restrictive

circumspect careful, discreet, guarded, irreprehensible, leery, meticulous, politic, provident *(showing foresight)*, prudent, upright, vigilant

circumspectio prudence

circumspection caution *(vigilance)*, deliberation, diligence *(care)*, discretion *(quality of being discreet)*, discrimination *(good judgment)*, forethought, judgment *(discernment)*, notice *(heed)*, precaution, prudence, surveillance

circumspective circumspect

circumspectness discretion *(quality of being discreet)*

circumspectus guarded, prudent

circumstance accident *(chance occurrence)*, case *(set of circumstances)*, chance *(fortuity)*, condition *(state)*, context, contingency, detail, experience *(encounter)*, happenstance, occurrence, particular, plight, posture *(situation)*, predicament, quirk *(accident)*, situation, state *(condition)*, status

circumstanced qualified *(conditioned)*

circumstances environment, position *(situation)*, situation

circumstances in a case evidence

circumstantial coincidental, descriptive, fortuitous, incident, presumptive

circumstantial event contingency

circumstantiality detail, particularity

circumstantiate bear *(adduce)*, cite *(state)*, corroborate, demonstrate *(establish)*, detail *(particularize)*, document, establish *(show)*, evidence, itemize, quote, substantiate, support *(corroborate)*, sustain *(confirm)*, validate, verify *(confirm)*

circumstantiation corroboration, documentation, support *(corroboration)*

circumvalate border *(bound)*

circumvallate circumscribe *(surround by boundary)*, enclose

circumvallation blockade *(enclosure)*, enclosure

circumvenire circumvent, overreach

circumvent betray *(lead astray)*, bilk, border *(bound)*, deceive, dupe, escape, evade *(deceive)*, illude, overreach, pettifog, prevent, shun

circumvention artifice, deception, device *(contrivance)*, evasion, false pretense, hoax, knavery, maneuver *(trick)*, pettifoggery, ruse

circumvention of truth false pretense

cista coffer

citadel bulwark, haven, protection, refuge

citare accuse, arraign

citation accusation, canon, certification *(certification of proficiency)*, charge *(accusation)*, complaint, count, direction *(order)*, excerpt, mention *(tribute)*, monition *(legal summons)*, paraphrase, presentment, process *(summons)*, recognition, subpoena, summons

cite accuse, allege, allude, arraign, bear *(adduce)*, blame, charge *(accuse)*, complain *(charge)*, denounce *(condemn)*, exemplify, extract, honor, illustrate, mention, order, posit, present *(prefer charges)*, quote, recognize *(acknowledge)*, refer *(direct attention)*, specify, summon

cite a holding of a case quote

cite evidence establish *(show)*

cited alleged

citing reference *(citation)*

citizen denizen, domiciliary, inhabitant

citizenize naturalize *(make a citizen)*

citizenry community, nationality, populace, population, public, society

citizens population

city community

civic civil *(public)*, local, political, public *(affecting people)*

civic-minded philanthropic

civicus civic

civil civic, obeisant, public *(affecting people)*

civil code code

civil community state *(political unit)*

civil constitution polity

civil law constitution

civil liberty freedom

civil officer peace officer

civil wrong misfeasance, tort

civilian civil *(public)*, layman

civilian police posse

civilis civic, political

civilis ratio politics

civility amenity, comity, consideration *(sympathetic regard)*, courtesy, decorum, respect

civilization community, society

civilize educate

civilized civil *(polite)*

civilized behavior decorum

civilized life civilization

civilized society civilization

civis citizen

civitas community, state *(political unit)*

civitatis constitution

civium population

clades calamity, disaster

claim adduce, allegation, allege, appeal, appropriate, argue, assert, bear *(adduce)*, bill *(formal declaration)*, call *(demand)*, case *(lawsuit)*, cause of action, certify *(attest)*, cloud *(incumbrance)*, contend *(maintain)*, count, cover *(pretext)*, declare, demand, demand, dominion *(absolute ownership)*, droit, due, dun, encumbrance, equity *(share of ownership)*, exact, excise *(levy a tax)*, impropriate, interest *(ownership)*, lawsuit, lien, matter *(case)*, matter *(subject)*, motion, need, occupy *(take possession)*, own, ownership, plea, pleading, posit, prayer, prerogative, prescription *(claim of title)*, pretense *(pretext)*, pretext, profess *(pretend)*, profession *(declaration)*, purport, request, request, requirement, requisition, stake *(interest)*, statement, sue, thesis, title *(right)*

claim a victory beat *(defeat)*

claim advanced by defendant counterclaim

claim as a right call *(demand)*

claim as one's due demand

claim falsely fake, pretend

claim for damages ad damnum clause

claim for relief cause of action

claim for relief by defendant counterclaim

claim on property charge *(lien)*, cloud *(incumbrance)*, lien, mechanics lien

claim one's thoughts occupy *(engage)*

claim presented by defendant counterclaim

claim to know contend *(maintain)*

claim unduly impropriate

claimable due *(owed)*

claimant applicant *(petitioner)*, complainant, contender, contestant, litigant, party *(litigant)*, plaintiff, suitor

claimed alleged, ostensible, purported, putative

claimer claimant

claims of conscience responsibility *(conscience)*

clairvoyance precognition

clairvoyant prophetic

clamant exigent, important *(urgent)*, urgent

clamare call *(appeal to)*

clamor barrage, brawl, commotion, confusion *(turmoil)*, demonstrate *(protest)*, exception *(objection)*, furor, noise, outburst, outcry, pandemonium, protest

clamor against decry, discommend

clamor for call *(demand)*, desire, exact, importune, necessitate, need, petition, plead *(implore)*, pray, request, solicit

clamor for payment dun

clamorous blatant *(obtrusive)*, important *(urgent)*, insistent, querulous, vehement

clamorousness noise, outcry

clamp adhere *(fasten)*

clan affinity *(family ties)*, blood, descent *(lineage)*, family *(common ancestry)*, house, kindred, lineage

clandestine allusive, collusive, covert, evasive, furtive, hidden, mysterious, personal *(private)*, private *(confidential)*, privy, secret, sly, stealthy, surreptitious, unobtrusive

clandestinus clandestine, stealthy, surreptitious

clangor noise

clannish exclusive *(limited)*, partisan, restrictive

clansman relative

clansmen kindred

clap together conjoin

claque assemblage

clare fairly *(clearly)*

clarification clarification, comment, construction, definition, explanation, illustration, instance, solution *(answer)*

clarified clear *(apparent)*

clarify adjust *(resolve)*, comment, construe *(translate)*, define, demonstrate *(establish)*, describe, detail *(particularize)*, distill, elucidate, enlighten, explain, explicate, exposit, expound, illustrate, interpret, purge *(purify)*, resolve *(solve)*, stipulate

clarifying demonstrative *(illustrative)*, informatory, interpretive

clarifying statement justification

clarus conspicuous, distinct *(clear)*, open *(in sight)*, patent, renowned, unambiguous

clash affray, bicker, collision *(dispute)*, commotion, compete, conflict, conflict, confrontation *(altercation)*, contend *(dispute)*, contest *(competition)*, contest *(dispute)*, contradict, contravene, contravention, counter, counteract, deviate, differ *(disagree)*, disaccord, disagree, discrepancy, dispute *(contest)*, dissent *(difference of opinion)*, dissent *(differ in opinion)*, embroilment, feud, fight *(argument)*, fracas, fray, incompatibility *(difference)*, incompatibility *(inconsistency)*, meeting *(encounter)*, oppugn, reaction *(opposition)*, rift *(disagreement)*, strife, struggle, violence

clash of arms conflict, fight *(battle)*

clash of opinions dispute

clash of temperament difference

clash with deviate

clashing argument *(contention)*, belligerency, competitive *(antagonistic)*, contention *(opposition)*, contradictory, contradistinction, controversy *(argument)*, deviant, difference, different, disaccord, discord, discordant, disparate, dissension, dissenting, dissidence, dissident, dissimilar, hostile, inapplicable, inapposite, inappropriate, inapt, incongruous, inept *(inappropriate)*, negative, opposite, repugnant *(incompatible)*

clasp adhere *(fasten)*, cohere *(adhere)*, grapple, lock, shut

clasp together conjoin

class allocate, classification, classify, denomination, department, distribute, division *(administrative unit)*, evaluate, file *(arrange)*, fix *(arrange)*, form *(arrangement)*, gauge, index *(relate)*, kind, manner *(kind)*, organize *(arrange)*, pigeonhole, quality *(excellence)*, race, rate, screen *(select)*, section *(division)*, society, sort, state *(condition)*, status, style, subdivision

class prejudice discrimination *(bigotry)*

classic regular *(conventional)*, traditional

classical conventional, traditional

classification array *(order)*, chain *(series)*, class, compilation, degree *(station)*, denomination, department, diagnosis, distribution *(arrangement)*, division *(administrative unit)*, form *(arrangement)*, hierarchy *(arrangement in a series)*, identification, kind, label, manner *(kind)*, method, order *(arrangement)*, organization *(structure)*, rating, rubric *(title)*, segregation *(separation)*, sequence, subdivision, subheading, system

classificatory descriptive

classificatory description diagnosis

classified confidential, systematic

classified communication confidence *(relation of trust)*

classified index file

classified information secret

classify allocate, apportion, call *(title)*, characterize, codify, denominate, diagnose, differentiate, digest *(summarize)*, discriminate *(distinguish)*, distinguish, distribute, file *(arrange)*, fix *(ar-*

range), identify, include, index *(relate)*, label, organize *(arrange)*, rate, screen *(select)*, sort, subdivide

classify as classify, constitute *(compose)*

classify incorrectly mislabel

classis class

classmaster pedagogue

clatter noise

claudere close *(terminate)*, shut

clause amendment *(legislation)*, article *(distinct section of a writing)*, caption, chapter *(division)*, condition *(contingent provision)*, limitation, phrase, subheading, term *(provision)*, title *(division)*

claviger warden

clean blameless, decontaminate, honest, meticulous, pure, purge *(purify)*

clean up expurgate

clean-cut precise

clean-handed not guilty

cleaned out impecunious

cleanhanded clean

cleanminded clean

cleanse decontaminate, expurgate, purge *(purify)*

cleansing medicinal, remedial

clear absolute *(conclusive)*, absolve, acquit, apparent *(perceptible)*, arrant *(definite)*, blameless, blatant *(conspicuous)*, certain *(positive)*, clean, cognizable, comment, comprehensible, conclusive *(settled)*, condone, conspicuous, decisive, definite, demonstrable, descriptive, direct *(forthright)*, discharge *(liberate)*, discharge *(pay a debt)*, disencumber, disentangle, earn, evident, exculpate, excuse, exonerate, explicit, express, extenuate, extricate, facilitate, flagrant, forgive, free *(relieved from a burden)*, free, gain, immune, inappealable, incontestable, lucid, manifest, naked *(perceptible)*, net, obvious, open *(in sight)*, orotund, ostensible, overt, palliate *(excuse)*, palpable, passable, patent, pay, pellucid, perceivable, perceptible, positive *(incontestable)*, profit, propitious, pure, purge *(purify)*, purge *(wipe out by atonement)*, quit *(free of)*, realize *(obtain as a profit)*, reap, release, remit *(release from penalty)*, remove *(eliminate)*, resounding, salient, satisfy *(discharge)*, simple, strong, surmount, unambiguous, unblemished, undeniable, unequivocal, unmistakable, vacant, vindicate, visible *(in full view)*

clear a debt quit *(repay)*

clear accounts quit *(repay)*

clear away disencumber, displace *(remove)*

clear cut exact

clear demonstration proof

clear from free *(not restricted)*

clear from a charge exculpate

clear from alleged guilt exculpate

clear from imputation of fault exculpate

clear from obscurity ascertain

clear indication proof

clear language plain language

clear of an imputation of guilt exonerate

clear of doubt ascertain

clear of encumbrance solvent

clear of obscurity ascertain, elucidate, explain, expound

clear out eliminate *(eradicate)*, evacuate, flee

clear perception appreciation *(perception)*

clear sight perception

clear the mind disabuse

clear the way expedite, facilitate

clear thinking common sense, sagacity, sanity

clear thought sagacity

clear to the mind distinct *(clear)*

clear to the senses distinct *(clear)*

clear up clarify, construe *(translate)*, elucidate, explain, exposit, expound, interpret, resolve *(solve)*, settle, simplify *(clarify)*, solve

clear-cut accurate, categorical, certain *(positive)*, certain *(specific)*, clear *(apparent)*, coherent *(clear)*, comprehensible, conspicuous, definite, demonstrable, distinct *(clear)*, incontrovertible, lucid, manifest, palpable, pellucid, precise, tangible, trenchant, unambiguous, unequivocal

clear-headed sapient

clear-minded lucid

clear-sighted acute, cognizant, discriminating *(judicious)*, perspicacious

clear-thinking lucid, pragmatic

clear-witted lucid

clearance absolution, acquittal, amortization, collection *(payment)*, composition *(agreement in bankruptcy)*, compurgation, concession *(authorization)*, condonation, discharge *(liberation)*, discharge *(payment)*, dispensation *(exception)*, exoneration, indulgence, justification, liberty, license, margin *(spare amount)*, pardon, payment *(act of paying)*, profit, release, remission, respite *(reprieve)*, satisfaction *(discharge of debt)*, waiver

cleared acquitted, clear *(free from criminal charges)*, exempt, free *(relieved from a burden)*

clearheaded lucid, perspicacious, rational, reasonable *(rational)*, sane

clearheadedness reason *(sound judgment)*

clearing exoneration

clearly define specify

clearly defined absolute *(conclusive)*, certain *(specific)*, decisive, distinct *(clear)*, explicit, perceptible, unambiguous

clearly expressed explicit

clearly formulated explicit

clearly indicated express

clearly known certain *(positive)*

clearly marked perceptible

clearly stated certain *(specific)*, explicit, express

clearmindedness competence *(sanity)*, sanity

cleavable divisible, divisive, separable, severable

cleavage coherence, disaccord, division *(act of dividing)*, estrangement, separation, severance, split

cleave bifurcate, break *(separate)*, cohere *(adhere)*, detach, disjoint, divide *(separate)*, lancinate, rend, separate, sever, split, subdivide

cleave in two dichotomize

cleaving coherent *(joined)*, cohesive *(sticking)*
cleaving together coherent *(joined)*
cleft rift *(gap)*, split
clemency benevolence *(disposition to do good)*, charity, condonation, consideration *(sympathetic regard)*, grace, humanity *(humaneness)*, indulgence, lenience, pardon
clemens humane, lenient
clement charitable *(lenient)*, humane, lenient, placable, propitious
clementia clemency, humanity *(humaneness)*
clementness clemency
clench constrict *(compress)*
clerical staff personnel, staff
clerk accountant, amanuensis, assistant
clerk of the court notary public
clever artful, deft, expert, machiavellian, original *(creative)*, perspicacious, politic, practiced, proficient, resourceful, sapient, strategic, subtle *(refined)*
clever in deception mendacious
cleverness artifice, discretion *(quality of being discreet)*, faculty *(ability)*, gift *(flair)*, insight, intelligence *(intellect)*, perception, prowess *(ability)*, sagacity, sense *(intelligence)*, skill
clew catchword
cliché catchword
cliche expression *(comment)*, platitude
cliched familiar *(customary)*
click comport *(agree with)*
cliens client
client consumer, customer, patron *(regular customer)*
clientele consumer
climacteric critical *(crucial)*, crossroad *(turning point)*, crucial, emergency, timeliness
climactic critical *(crucial)*, last *(final)*
climactical last *(final)*
climate atmosphere
climatic condition atmosphere
climax ceiling, cessation *(termination)*, conclude *(complete)*, consequence *(conclusion)*, crossroad *(turning point)*, culminate, culmination, denouement, pinnacle
climb headway, progress, surmount
climb down alight
clime climate, region, section *(vicinity)*, territory
clinch complete, ensure, grapple, stabilize
clinch an argument convince
cling cohere *(adhere)*, persevere
cling tenaciously adhere *(persist)*, persevere
cling to adhere *(fasten)*, hold *(possess)*, keep *(shelter)*, observe *(obey)*, perform *(adhere to)*, persist, prefer, pursue *(carry on)*, retain *(keep in possession)*
clinging adhesion *(affixing)*, coadunate, coherent *(joined)*, cohesive *(sticking)*
clip curtail, excise *(cut away)*, minimize, retrench
clipeus shield
clipping excerpt
clique cabal, denomination, faction, society, sodality
cliquish exclusive *(limited)*, partisan, restrictive

cloak blind *(obscure)*, camouflage, circumvent, clothe, color *(deceptive appearance)*, conceal, cover *(conceal)*, disguise, disguise, ensconce, enshroud, envelop, harbor, hide, obfuscate, obnubilate, obscure, plant *(covertly place)*, pretense *(pretext)*, screen *(guard)*, shroud, suppress, veil
cloaked clandestine, covert, furtive, hidden, mysterious, oblique *(evasive)*, stealthy
clockwork precision regularity
cloddish inelegant, opaque
clog block, damper *(stopper)*, hamper, hinder, impediment, interfere, interrupt, interruption, obstruction, obturate, stem *(check)*, stop, trammel
cloister circumscribe *(surround by boundary)*, envelop, restrict, sequester *(seclude)*, shut
cloistered private *(secluded)*, solitary
close approximate, block, brief, cease, cessation *(termination)*, clog, cognate, coherent *(joined)*, cohesive *(compact)*, compact *(dense)*, comparable *(capable of comparison)*, complete, conclude *(complete)*, conclusion *(outcome)*, constrict *(inhibit)*, contestable, contiguous, culminate, defeasance, denouement, discontinue *(abandon)*, dispatch *(dispose of)*, dissolution *(termination)*, end *(termination)*, exact, expiration, expire, extremity *(death)*, faithful *(true to fact)*, finality, finish, future, grapple, halt, hidden, illiberal, immediate *(imminent)*, immediate *(not distant)*, inarticulate, indivisible, inseparable, instant, intense, intimate, literal, local, lock, moratorium, noncommittal, obturate, occlude, outcome, parsimonious, pendent, pending *(imminent)*, penurious, populous, precise, present *(attendant)*, proximate, secret, shut, similar, solid *(compact)*, stop, strict, taciturn, terminate
close application diligence *(care)*
close around circumscribe *(surround by boundary)*
close association propinquity *(kinship)*
close at hand close *(near)*, forthcoming, future, immediate *(imminent)*, immediate *(not distant)*, instant, pending *(imminent)*, present *(attendant)*, prospective, proximate
close attention deliberation, diligence *(care)*, interest *(concern)*
close by close *(near)*, present *(attendant)*, proximate
close contact adhesion *(affixing)*
close correspondence parity
close down shut
close fast lock
close identification adhesion *(loyalty)*
close in border *(bound)*, circumscribe *(surround by boundary)*, contain *(enclose)*, enclose, envelop, include
close in upon converge
close inquiry analysis, cross-questioning, examination *(study)*, hearing, indagation, investigation, research
close investigation scrutiny
close look scrutiny
close observance conformity *(obedi-*

ence)
close observation examination *(study)*, judgment *(discernment)*
close off clog
close on border *(approach)*
close relation analogy
close relationship marriage *(intimate relationship)*
close relative next of kin
close resemblance analogy
close search scrutiny
close study deliberation, diligence *(care)*
close the curtain camouflage
close thought diligence *(care)*
close to almost
close together compact *(dense)*
close union contact *(association)*
close up seal *(close)*
close watch prudence
close with fight *(battle)*, grapple
close-fisted penurious
close-fitting limiting
close-handed penurious
close-knit compact *(dense)*
close-lipped mute
close-out lockout
close-set compact *(dense)*
closed blind *(impassable)*, complete *(ended)*, fixed *(settled)*, impervious, personal *(private)*, private *(not public)*
closed purse austerity
closed-minded provincial
closed-minded person pedant
closed-mindedness predetermination
closefisted illiberal, parsimonious
closely faithfully
closely acquainted familiar *(informed)*, intimate
closely allied affiliated, associated, cognate, consanguineous
closely associated intimate
closely connected pendent
closely examine search
closely packed populous, replete
closely related affiliated, akin *(germane)*, associated, cognate, collateral *(accompanying)*, consanguineous
closely resemble approximate
closely united compact *(dense)*
closemouthed laconic, mute, taciturn
closeness affection, affinity *(regard)*, coalescence, consortium *(marriage companionship)*, density, identity *(similarity)*, kinship, marriage *(intimate relationship)*, propinquity *(proximity)*, rapport, relation *(connection)*, resemblance, semblance
closest proximate
closet chamber *(compartment)*, hide, private *(confidential)*, sequester *(seclude)*, shroud
closing cessation *(termination)*, close *(conclusion)*, cloture, conclusive *(settled)*, definitive, denouement, dissolution *(termination)*, expiration, final, halt, last *(final)*
closing in imminent
closing piece end *(termination)*
closure cessation *(termination)*, close *(conclusion)*, cloture, conclusion *(outcome)*, denouement, end *(termination)*, expiration, finality, obstruction, payoff *(result)*
clot cohere *(adhere)*
clothe vest

clothe in words phrase
cloture cessation *(interlude)*
cloud blind *(obscure)*, camouflage, cloak, damper *(depressant)*, ensconce, enshroud, hide, muddle, obfuscate, obnubilate, obscuration, obscure, tarnish, veil
cloud over obnubilate
clouded hidden, nebulous, opaque, unclear
cloudless propitious
cloudy equivocal, indefinite, inscrutable, nebulous, opaque, unclear, vague
clownish uncouth
cloyed full, replete
cloying nectarious
club beat *(strike)*, cudgel, league, organization *(association)*, party *(political organization)*, society, sodality
clue catchword, hint, hint, indicant, indication, indicator, insinuation, reference *(allusion)*, suggestion, symbol, symptom
clueless incognizant, insensible
clump aggregate, assemblage, bulk
clumsiness abortion *(fiasco)*
clumsy incompetent, inept *(incompetent)*, ponderous, uncouth, unpolitic
clumsy performance miscue
cluster agglomeration, aggregate, assemblage, bulk, compile, concentrate *(consolidate)*, congregate, hoard, mass *(body of persons)*, meet, selection *(collection)*, unite
clustered compact *(dense)*, composite
clutch grapple, retain *(keep in possession)*
clutter complex *(entanglement)*, confuse *(create disorder)*, confusion *(turmoil)*, disorganize
co-existent contemporary
co-obligor comaker
co-operant synergetic
co-opt adopt, choose
co-optation adoption *(acceptance)*
co-respondent respondent
coacervare accumulate *(amass)*, hoard
coach advise, counsel, direct *(supervise)*, discipline *(train)*, edify, educate, foster, instruct *(direct)*, nurture, oversee
coaching direction *(guidance)*, discipline *(training)*, education, guidance
coact combine *(act in concert)*, consolidate *(unite)*, conspire, cooperate, join *(bring together)*, unite
coacting concerted, concurrent *(at the same time)*, concurrent *(united)*, synergetic
coaction affiliation *(connectedness)*, concert, concordance, contribution *(participation)*, duress, enforcement, force *(compulsion)*, relationship *(connection)*, synergy
coactive associated, compulsory, concerted, concurrent *(at the same time)*, concurrent *(united)*, insistent, obligatory, synergetic
coactor accomplice, confederate, conspirer
coactor in crime coconspirator
coactus involuntary, reluctance
coaddressee cotenant
coadjument concert
coadjutant associate, backer, coactor, colleague, concerted, confederate,

conspirer, copartner *(business associate)*, copartner *(coconspirator)*, mutual *(collective)*, partner
coadjutive mutual *(collective)*
coadjutor abettor, assistant, associate, backer, coactor, coadjutant, coconspirator, cohort, colleague, confederate, consociate, conspirer, contributor *(contributor)*, copartner *(coconspirator)*, participant, partner
coadjutorship combination
coadjutress colleague, copartner *(coconspirator)*
coadjutrix colleague
coadjuvancy affiliation *(connectedness)*, aid *(help)*, association *(connection)*, cartel, collusion, concert
coadjuvant ancillary *(auxiliary)*, associate, backer, colleague, concerted, mutual *(collective)*
coadjuvate consolidate *(unite)*
coadunate amalgamate, associated, coherent *(joined)*, joint, mutual *(collective)*
coadunation adhesion *(affixing)*, coalescence, consolidation, integration *(amalgamation)*
coagency collusion, concert, connivance
coagent plenipotentiary
coagulate bond *(hold together)*, cement, cohere *(adhere)*, coherent *(joined)*, crystallize
coagulated coadunate, coherent *(joined)*, solid *(compact)*
coagulation adhesion *(affixing)*, agglomeration, coalescence, congealment
coagulative coadunate
coaid assistant, colleague, copartner *(coconspirator)*
coaider in crime coconspirator
coalesce adhere *(fasten)*, amalgamate, bond *(hold together)*, cement, cohere *(adhere)*, combine *(join together)*, commingle, concentrate *(consolidate)*, conjoin, connect *(join together)*, consolidate *(strengthen)*, consolidate *(unite)*, converge, desegregate, incorporate *(include)*, unite
coalesced coadunate
coalescence centralization, combination, concrescence, conspiracy, incorporation *(blend)*, joinder, merger
coalescent coadunate, coherent *(joined)*, concerted, conjoint
coalescing centralization
coalition affiliation *(amalgamation)*, affiliation *(connectedness)*, association *(alliance)*, association *(connection)*, band, cabal, cartel, centralization, coaction, coalescence, combination, company *(assemblage)*, concert, confederacy *(compact)*, connection *(relation)*, consortium *(business cartel)*, conspiracy, contact *(association)*, contribution *(participation)*, corporation, federation, incorporation *(formation of a business entity)*, institute, integration *(amalgamation)*, integration *(assimilation)*, league, merger, organization *(association)*, pact, partnership, party *(political organization)*, pool, relationship *(connection)*, side, society, syndicate, union *(unity)*
coalitional concurrent *(united)*, conjoint, joint, mutual *(collective)*
coapplicant comaker

coaptation adjustment
coarct constrict *(compress)*
coarctate decrease
coarctation bondage
coarguere expose
coarse blatant *(obtrusive)*, brutal, disreputable, impertinent *(insolent)*, inelegant, lascivious, lurid, odious, offensive *(offending)*, poor *(inferior in quality)*, profane, prurient, salacious, scurrilous, suggestive *(risqué)*, uncouth, unseemly
coarsen debase
coarseness obscenity
coartare curtail
coastal littoral
coastland littoral
coating cover *(protection)*
coax agitate *(activate)*, cajole, entice, exhort, importune, inveigle, lure, persuade, pressure, prevail *(persuade)*, prevail upon, reason *(persuade)*, solicit, urge
coaxing instigation, persuasion, persuasive, seduction
coborrower comaker
cockiness pride
cocksureness confidence *(faith)*
coconspirator accessory, accomplice
coddle excessively overindulge
code act *(enactment)*, bylaw, canon, conduct, criterion, digest, ethics, jargon *(technical language)*, law, ordinance, pandect *(code of laws)*, precept, protocol *(etiquette)*, regulation *(rule)*, rubric *(authoritative rule)*, rule *(guide)*, rule *(legal dictate)*, statute
code of behavior protocol *(etiquette)*
code of duty conscience
code of honor conscience
code of laws constitution
code of morals ethics
code of right and wrong ethics
code of what is fitting decorum
coded mysterious
codefendant accomplice
codenizen cotenant
codes legislation *(enactments)*
codex accepti et expensi ledger
codicil addendum, appendix *(supplement)*
codicilli note *(brief comment)*
codification classification, code, compilation, constitution, enactment, legalization, pandect *(code of laws)*
codification of laws legislation *(lawmaking)*
codified law code, constitution, pandect *(code of laws)*, statute
codify classify, constitute *(establish)*, digest *(summarize)*, enact, file *(arrange)*, fix *(arrange)*, index *(docket)*, legislate, tabulate
codirector accessory, accomplice, colleague
codweller cotenant
coefficiency concert
coemptor consumer
coeptum undertaking *(enterprise)*
coequal analogous, coextensive, commensurable, commensurate, comparable *(equivalent)*, counterpart *(complement)*, equal, equivalent, identical, peer
coequality identity *(similarity)*, mutuality, parity
coerce compel, constrain *(compel)*, enforce, exact, extort, foist, harass, im-

pose *(enforce)*, impose *(subject)*, inflict, intimidate, necessitate, press *(constrain)*, pressure, require *(compel)*, threaten

coercere coerce, confine, control *(regulate)*, govern, restrict, shut, stem *(check)*

coercion constraint *(restriction)*, duress, extortion, force *(compulsion)*, oppression, pressure, stress *(strain)*

coercitio coercion

coercive binding, compelling, compulsory, forcible, insistent, involuntary, mandatory, necessary *(required)*, obligatory, severe, unavoidable *(inevitable)*

coercive refusal to furnish work lockout

coetaneous concurrent *(at the same time)*, simultaneous

coetus company *(enterprise)*, congregation

coeval concerted, concurrent *(at the same time)*, contemporaneous, simultaneous

coexist accompany, coincide *(correspond)*

coexistence compatibility, integration *(amalgamation)*, integration *(assimilation)*, peace, synchronism

coexistent coincidental, concerted, concordant, concurrent *(at the same time)*, congruous, contemporaneous, harmonious, simultaneous

coexisting coincidental, concerted, concordant, concurrent *(at the same time)*, congruous, contemporaneous, harmonious, simultaneous

coextending coextensive

coextensive coequal, commensurable, commensurate, equal

coffer bank, depository, repository, treasury

cofunction cooperate

cog deceive

cogency force *(strength)*, strength

cogent clear *(certain)*, coherent *(clear)*, convincing, important *(urgent)*, influential, irresistible, logical, persuasive, potent, powerful, predominant, sound

cogere compel, constrain *(compel)*, necessitate

cogitable plausible, possible

cogitare intend, reflect *(ponder)*, speculate *(conjecture)*

cogitate brood, consider, deliberate, muse, ponder, rationalize, reason *(conclude)*, reflect *(ponder)*, weigh

cogitatio idea, reflection *(thought)*

cogitation consideration *(contemplation)*, contemplation, deliberation, dialectic, ratiocination, reflection *(thought)*

cogitative deliberate, speculative

cogitatus deliberate, intentional

cognate analogous, apposite, comparable *(capable of comparison)*, consanguineous, correlate, correlative, germane, interrelated, pendent, related, relative *(relevant)*, relative, relevant, same, similar

cognati kindred

cognatio affinity *(family ties)*, relationship *(connection)*

cognation affinity *(family ties)*, ancestry, blood, degree *(kinship)*, filiation, kinship, propinquity *(kinship)*, relation

(connection), relationship *(connection)*

cognatus related, relation *(kinship)*, relative

cognitio cognition, hearing, inquiry *(systematic investigation)*, insight, knowledge *(learning)*

cognition appreciation *(perception)*, apprehension *(perception)*, comprehension, insight, intellect, intelligence *(intellect)*, knowledge *(awareness)*, observation, perception, realization, reason *(sound judgment)*, recognition, scienter, sense *(intelligence)*

cognitive cognizant, familiar *(informed)*, knowing, perceptive, rational, reasonable *(rational)*, receptive

cognitive faculties judgment *(discernment)*, sense *(intelligence)*

cognitive faculty intellect, intelligence *(intellect)*

cognitive powers judgment *(discernment)*, sense *(intelligence)*

cognitive process cognition

cognitus acquainted

cognizable appreciable, ascertainable, coherent *(clear)*, comprehensible, concrete, determinable *(ascertainable)*, discernible, justiciable, naked *(perceptible)*, perceivable, perceptible, ponderable, scrutable, solvable, triable

cognizable in courts of law legal

cognizance appreciation *(perception)*, apprehension *(perception)*, cognition, comprehension, experience *(background)*, identification, insight, knowledge *(awareness)*, notice *(heed)*, observation, perception, realization, reason *(sound judgment)*, recognition, scienter

cognizant certain *(positive)*, circumspect, conscious *(aware)*, expert, familiar *(informed)*, knowing, learned, perceptive, sensitive *(discerning)*

cognizant of acquainted, privy

cognize apprehend *(perceive)*, comprehend *(understand)*, construe *(comprehend)*, digest *(comprehend)*, discern *(detect with the senses)*, note *(notice)*, notice *(observe)*, perceive, pierce *(discern)*, realize *(understand)*, understand

cognized household *(familiar)*

cognomen call *(title)*, sobriquet, term *(expression)*

cognomination call *(title)*

cognoscere ascertain, discover, find *(discover)*, hear *(give a legal hearing)*, hear *(give attention to)*, investigate, perceive, recognize *(perceive)*, try *(conduct a trial)*

cognoscible comprehensible

cohabitant inhabitant

cohabitation marriage *(intimate relationship)*, marriage *(wedlock)*, matrimony

cohaerens coherent *(clear)*, coherent *(joined)*

cohaerere cohere *(adhere)*, cohere *(be logically consistent)*

cohelper associate, coactor, cohort, colleague, consociate, conspirer, contributor *(contributor)*, copartner *(business associate)*, copartner *(coconspirator)*, partner

cohere adhere *(fasten)*, adjoin, affix, attach *(join)*, bond *(hold together)*, cement, combine *(join together)*, comport *(agree with)*, conjoin, connect *(join to-*

gether), connect *(relate)*, consolidate *(strengthen)*, conspire, contact *(touch)*, correspond *(be equivalent)*, crystallize

coherence adherence *(adhesion)*, adhesion *(affixing)*, coalescence, competence *(sanity)*, connection *(relation)*, contact *(touching)*, continuity, union *(unity)*

coherency coherence, connection *(relation)*

coherent agreed *(harmonized)*, cohesive *(sticking)*, commensurable, consensual, consistent, consonant, convincing, logical

cohering coadunate, coherent *(joined)*, cohesive *(sticking)*, consistent

cohesion accession *(annexation)*, adherence *(adhesion)*, adhesion *(affixing)*, attachment *(act of affixing)*, coaction, coalescence, coherence, congealment, connection *(fastening)*

cohesive coadunate, coherent *(joined)*, compact *(dense)*, concerted, concurrent *(united)*, conjoint, inextricable, infrangible

cohesiveness adherence *(adhesion)*, adhesion *(affixing)*, coalescence, coherence, tenacity

cohibere confine, keep *(restrain)*, stay *(halt)*, stem *(check)*

cohibit block

cohors cohort

cohort associate, consociate, copartner *(coconspirator)*

cohouseholder cotenant

coiled sinuous

coin cash, conceive *(invent)*, currency, denominate, frame *(construct)*, invent *(produce for the first time)*, make, money, originate, produce *(manufacture)*

coin of the realm cash

coinage cash, formation, invention, money, origination

coincide agree *(comply)*, certify *(approve)*, comport *(agree with)*, concur *(coexist)*, correspond *(be equivalent)*

coincidence concordance, conformity *(agreement)*, connivance, contingency, happenstance, synchronism, synergy

coincident coequal, coincidental, concerted, concomitant, concurrent *(at the same time)*, congruous, consonant, contemporaneous, corporate *(joint)*, simultaneous

coincident with consensual

coincidental contingent, fortuitous

coinciding coincidental, concerted, concordant, congruous, contemporaneous, correlative

coined words jargon *(technical language)*

coinhabitant cotenant

coinhabiter cotenant

coinstantaneous coincidental, concurrent *(at the same time)*, contemporaneous, simultaneous

coire converge

cojugate conjugal

cold bleak *(exposed and barren)*, bleak *(severely simple)*, callous, cold-blooded, cruel, disdainful, dispassionate, inexpressive, insusceptible *(uncaring)*, malevolent, obdurate, pedestrian, phlegmatic, relentless, ruthless, severe, unresponsive

cold of heart callous
cold shoulder rebuff
cold-blooded cruel, dispassionate, malevolent, malignant, relentless, ruthless, sinister
cold-hearted cold-blooded, cruel, dispassionate, relentless
cold-shoulder shun
coldblooded callous, phlegmatic
coldhearted callous, malignant, ruthless
coldness indifference
coleaseholder cotenant
colere cultivate, honor
colessee cotenant
collaborate aid, combine *(act in concert)*, cooperate, federalize *(associate)*, federate, involve *(participate)*, organize *(unionize)*, participate, pool
collaborated mutual *(collective)*
collaborating concerted, consensual
collaboration bad faith, coaction, collusion, concert, conformity *(agreement)*, connivance, contribution *(participation)*, league, pool, synergy
collaborationist coactor, conspirer
collaborative concurrent *(united)*, joint, mutual *(collective)*, synergetic
collaborator abettor, accessory, accomplice, assistant, associate, coactor, coadjutant, coconspirator, cohort, colleague, confederate, consociate, conspirer, contributor *(contributor)*, copartner *(business associate)*, copartner *(coconspirator)*, participant, partner
collapse catastrophe, debacle, decline, defeat, destruction, deteriorate, detriment, disaster, disease, disrepair, fail *(lose)*, failure *(lack of success)*, give *(yield)*, languish, miscarriage, mistrial, prostration, succumb
collar handcuff
collared arrested *(apprehended)*
collateral additional, akin *(germane)*, ancillary *(auxiliary)*, bail, binder, circumstantial, coextensive, concurrent *(at the same time)*, consanguineous, correlative, deposit, downpayment, extrinsic, hostage, hypothecation, incident, pendent, peripheral, pledge *(security)*, related, relative *(relevant)*, secondary, security *(pledge)*, similar, subordinate, supplementary
collateral relative next of kin
collateral review of detention habeas corpus
collateral security binder, deposit, mortgage
collateral review habeas corpus
colleague affiliate, assistant, associate, coactor, coadjutant, cohort, confederate, consociate, consort, conspirer, contributor *(contributor)*, copartner *(business associate)*, participant
colleague in crime coconspirator
colleagueship affiliation *(connectedness)*, association *(connection)*, cartel, coaction, society, sodality
collect accrue *(increase)*, accumulate *(amass)*, aggregate, codify, compile, concentrate *(consolidate)*, congregate, conjoin, convene, cull, excise *(levy a tax)*, extract, fund, gain, garner, glean, hoard, hold *(possess)*, join *(bring together)*, levy, meet, obtain, purchase, read, reap, receive *(acquire)*, recruit,

select, store, tax *(levy)*, unite
collect evidence document
collect facts investigate
collect into a focus congregate
collect into a mass accumulate *(amass)*, aggregate
collect knowledge discover
collect payment collect *(recover money)*, toll *(exact payment)*
collect the vote poll
collect together accumulate *(amass)*
collectable due *(owed)*, payable
collectanea selection *(collection)*
collected composite, conglomerate, dispassionate, miscellaneous, nonchalant, placid
collected writings information *(knowledge)*
collection agglomeration, aggregate, assemblage, assembly, band, code, combination, compilation, conglomeration, congregation, corpus, cumulation, depository, digest, hoard, levy, store *(depository)*
collection of facts investigation
collection of laws code, constitution, pandect *(code of laws)*
collection of statutes code, codification
collective broad, common *(shared)*, composite, conjoint, cooperative, generic, joint, nonsectarian, omnibus, pool, public *(affecting people)*
collective action coaction
collective agreement bargain, contract, covenant
collective assets estate *(property)*
collective members constituency
collective refusal to work strike
collectively en banc, en masse, in toto, wholly
collectively agreed contractual
collectiveness entirety, whole
collectivism pool
collectivity complex *(development)*, corpus, entirety, totality, whole
collectivized conglomerate
collector assessor, caretaker *(one fulfilling the function of office)*, receiver
college institute
collegiate distinction degree *(academic title)*
collide conflict, counter, counteract, cross *(disagree with)*, disagree, dispute *(contest)*, dissent *(differ in opinion)*, impinge, jostle *(bump into)*, meet, oppose
collide with contact *(touch)*
colliding competitive *(antagonistic)*, discordant
colligate accumulate *(amass)*, aggregate, combine *(join together)*, join *(bring together)*
colligation assemblage, body *(collection)*, collection *(assembly)*, compilation, corpus
collision antipode, conflict, confrontation *(altercation)*, meeting *(encounter)*
collocate allocate, arrange *(methodize)*, classify, file *(arrange)*, fix *(arrange)*, join *(bring together)*, marshal, pigeonhole, sort
collocation arrangement *(ordering)*, array *(order)*, building *(business of assembling)*, chamber *(body)*, collection *(assembly)*, compilation, distribution *(arrangement)*, hierarchy *(arrangement*

in a series)
collocution communication *(discourse)*, conversation, parley
collop part *(portion)*
colloque speak
colloquial ordinary, prevailing *(current)*, prevalent
colloquial discourse conversation
colloquialism catchword
colloquy communication *(discourse)*, conference, confrontation *(act of setting face to face)*, conversation, interview, meeting *(conference)*, parley, speech
collude combine *(act in concert)*, connive, conspire, contrive, cooperate, involve *(participate)*, maneuver, plan, plot, scheme
colluder coactor, coconspirator, confederate, conspirator, conspirer, copartner *(coconspirator)*, partner
colluding concerted
collusion bad faith, bribery, cabal, coaction, confederacy *(conspiracy)*, connivance, conspiracy, contribution *(participation)*, contrivance, deceit, fraud, machination, plot *(secret plan)*
collusive clandestine, deceptive, machiavellian, mendacious
collusory machiavellian
colonial provincial
colonies possessions
colonist migrant, pioneer
colonization immigration
colonize inhabit, occupy *(take possession)*
colonizer pioneer
colony province
colophon brand
color camouflage
color complexion
color falsify, misrepresent, prejudice *(influence)*, pretense *(pretext)*, slant, stain
colorable ostensible, plausible, specious
colored one-sided, prejudicial, specious
colored by bias subjective
coloring connotation, context, implication *(inference)*, overstatement
colorless insipid, jejune *(dull)*, lifeless *(dull)*, mediocre, pedestrian, prosaic, usual
colossal capacious, gross *(flagrant)*, prodigious *(enormous)*
colporteur dealer
column chapter *(division)*
columnists press
comate accomplice, associate, cohort, colleague, confederate, consociate, consort, copartner *(business associate)*, copartner *(coconspirator)*, participant, partner
comatose inactive, insensible, phlegmatic, torpid
comb search
combat affray, attack, belligerency, collision *(dispute)*, compete, competition, conflict, conflict, confrontation *(altercation)*, contend *(dispute)*, contention *(opposition)*, contest *(dispute)*, contest, dispute *(contest)*, embroilment, engage *(involve)*, fight *(battle)*, fight *(battle)*, fray, grapple, oppose, oppugn, resist *(oppose)*, resistance, strife, struggle
combat an opinion challenge

combatant aggressor, competitive *(antagonistic)*, contender, contestant, disputant, foe, opponent, rival
combative argumentative, competitive *(antagonistic)*, contentious, hostile, litigious, offensive *(taking the initiative)*, pugnacious
combativeness belligerency
combatting competitive *(antagonistic)*
combination accession *(annexation)*, affiliation *(amalgamation)*, affiliation *(connectedness)*, assemblage, association *(alliance)*, association *(connection)*, band, cabal, cartel, centralization, coalescence, coalition, company *(enterprise)*, compilation, composition *(makeup)*, concert, confederacy *(compact)*, connection *(fastening)*, consolidation, consortium *(business cartel)*, conspiracy, contact *(association)*, content *(structure)*, contribution *(participation)*, corporation, federation, incorporation *(blend)*, integration *(amalgamation)*, integration *(assimilation)*, joinder, league, melange, merger, organization *(association)*, partnership, pool, relationship *(connection)*, selection *(collection)*, sodality, solution *(substance)*, union *(unity)*
combination for fraud collusion
combination of companies trust *(combination of businesses)*
combination of financial institutions consortium *(business cartel)*
combination of funds pool
combinative concordant, concurrent *(united)*
combine accumulate *(amass)*, affix, amalgamate, annex *(add)*, association *(alliance)*, attach *(join)*, bond *(hold together)*, business *(commercial enterprise)*, cartel, cement, coalition, cohere *(adhere)*, commingle, compile, concentrate *(consolidate)*, confederacy *(compact)*, conjoin, connect *(join together)*, connive, consolidate *(strengthen)*, consolidate *(unite)*, conspire, cooperate, coordinate, corporation, crystallize, federalize *(associate)*, federate, federation, include, incorporate *(include)*, join *(associate oneself with)*, join *(bring together)*, league, merge, organize *(arrange)*, organize *(unionize)*, party *(political organization)*, pool, pool, society, syndicate, trust *(combination of businesses)*, unite
combine for some evil design conspire
combine forces cooperate
combine operations conspire
combine racially desegregate
combine with desegregate
combine with water dilute
combined associated, coadunate, coherent *(joined)*, collective, composite, compound, concerted, concurrent *(united)*, conglomerate, conjoint, federal, harmonious, inextricable, inseparable, joint, miscellaneous, mutual *(collective)*
combined action concert, synergy
combined effect synergy
combined effort coaction, concert
combined operation collusion, conformity *(agreement)*, connivance, conspiracy, synergy

combining accession *(annexation)*, concerted, concrescence, congruous
come accrue *(arise)*, report *(present oneself)*, stem *(originate)*
come about arise *(occur)*, occur *(happen)*
come across confront *(encounter)*
come after accede *(succeed)*, ensue, succeed *(follow)*
come afterward ensue
come again recur, return *(go back)*
come and go beat *(pulsate)*
come apart separate
come at call obey
come away move *(alter position)*
come back recur, resurgence, retort, return *(go back)*
come back at recriminate, reply
come back to reopen
come before precede
come between alienate *(estrange)*, disaffect, interpose, interrupt, intervene, separate
come by attain, gain, procure, realize *(obtain as a profit)*, receive *(acquire)*
come clean betray *(disclose)*
come close border *(approach)*
come close in estimation approximate
come close to approximate
come closer converge
come down decline *(fall)*, degenerate
come down by transmission descend
come down lineally descend
come face to face meet
come face to face with confront *(encounter)*
come first outweigh, precede, surpass
come formally before a tribunal appear *(attend court proceedings)*
come forth arise *(appear)*, confess, emanate, emerge, pullulate, result
come forward approach, emerge, issue *(send forth)*
come from arise *(originate)*, emanate, evolve, result
come gradually into existence develop
come in enter *(go in)*
come in conflict with confront *(oppose)*, contradict, counter, counteract, disapprove *(reject)*, except *(object)*, grapple, oppose
come in contact collide *(crash against)*, confront *(encounter)*, congregate, strike *(collide)*
come in last lose *(undergo defeat)*
come in sight arise *(appear)*
come in view arise *(appear)*
come into gain
come into action arise *(originate)*
come into being arise *(originate)*, occur *(happen)*
come into collision collide *(crash against)*, conflict, impinge, strike *(collide)*
come into court appear *(attend court proceedings)*
come into existence arise *(originate)*, commence, exist, occur *(happen)*
come into notice emerge
come into possession derive *(receive)*, obtain
come into possession as an heir inherit

come into possession of acquire *(receive)*, possess
come into sight appear *(materialize)*
come into the world commence
come into view appear *(materialize)*, emerge, occur *(come to mind)*
come near approach, approximate
come near in position approximate
come next accede *(succeed)*, ensue
come of age mature
come onto the horizon issue *(send forth)*
come out circulate, declare, emerge, issue *(send forth)*
come out in the open issue *(send forth)*
come out of hiding emerge
come out with phrase, remark, utter
come round conform
come short fail *(lose)*
come subsequently succeed *(follow)*
come through succeed *(attain)*
come to attain, reach
come to a close cease, expire, finish
come to a conclusion ascertain, decide, deduce, deduct *(conclude by reasoning)*, determine, find *(determine)*, hold *(decide)*, rule *(decide)*
come to a decision determine
come to a determination conclude *(decide)*, determine, fix *(settle)*, resolve *(decide)*, rule *(decide)*, settle
come to a focus converge
come to a hasty conclusion presume
come to a point border *(approach)*, converge, focus
come to a resolution fix *(settle)*
come to a standstill cease, pause, quit *(discontinue)*, rest *(cease from action)*, stop
come to a stop close *(terminate)*, halt
come to an agreement agree *(contract)*, arrange *(methodize)*, coincide *(concur)*, compromise *(settle by mutual agreement)*, concur *(agree)*, decide, fix *(settle)*, settle
come to an arrangement close *(agree)*
come to an end cease, close *(terminate)*, decease, expire, finish, lapse *(cease)*, perish, terminate
come to an understanding agree *(comply)*, agree *(contract)*, close *(agree)*, coincide *(concur)*, compromise *(settle by mutual agreement)*, concur *(agree)*, settle
come to be arise *(originate)*, develop, evolve
come to blows fight *(battle)*
come to know apprehend *(perceive)*, ascertain, discover, perceive
come to light appear *(materialize)*, arise *(appear)*, emerge
come to maturity develop
come to naught fail *(lose)*, perish, succumb
come to nothing fail *(lose)*
come to notice arise *(appear)*
come to pass arise *(occur)*, occur *(happen)*, supervene
come to pieces disorganize
come to ruin perish
come to stay remain *(stay)*
come to terms agree *(comply)*, agree *(contract)*, arrange *(methodize)*, close *(agree)*, coincide *(concur)*, compromise

(settle by mutual agreement), concede, concur *(agree)*, consent, decide, dicker, negotiate, settle, succumb

come to the aid of assist, help, promote *(organize)*, serve *(assist)*

come to the defense of maintain *(sustain)*, support *(assist)*

come to the help of support *(assist)*

come to the rescue free

come to understand comprehend *(understand)*

come together cohere *(adhere)*, collide *(crash against)*, concur *(agree)*, congregate, contact *(touch)*, converge, crystallize, meet, rendezvous, strike *(collide)*, unite

come uninvited intrude

come up to the standard pass *(satisfy requirements)*

come upon discover, find *(discover)*, invent *(produce for the first time)*, locate

comeback renewal, revival

comedown descent *(declination)*, disgrace, misfortune

comely attractive

comes consort, count

comestible palatable

cometary brief, volatile

comfort accommodate, assuage, assure *(give confidence to)*, benefit *(betterment)*, consortium *(marriage companionship)*, ease, prosperity, reassure, relieve *(give aid)*, solace, soothe, support *(assistance)*, sympathize

comfortable habitable, opulent, prosperous, successful

comfortable circumstances prosperity

comforting mitigation

comfortless bleak *(severely simple)*, disconsolate, lamentable

comic jocular

comical ludicrous

comical representation parody

coming appearance *(emergence)*, close *(near)*, forthcoming, future, immediate *(imminent)*, imminent, onset *(commencement)*, pending *(imminent)*, prospective, subsequent

coming after consecutive

coming before preliminary

coming between mesne

coming down descent *(declination)*

coming events prospect *(outlook)*

coming from derivative

coming from another land alien *(foreign)*

coming from without extraneous

coming in inflow

coming soon forthcoming

coming to an end determinable *(liable to be terminated)*

coming together coalition, confrontation *(act of setting face to face)*

comissari carouse

comitas courtesy

comity compatibility, courtesy

command agency *(commission)*, agency *(legal relationship)*, call *(demand)*, canon, claim *(legal demand)*, coerce, coercion, compel, conduct, constrain *(compel)*, control *(supervision)*, control *(regulate)*, decree, decree, demand, demand, detail *(assign)*, dictate, dictate, direct *(order)*, direct *(super-*

vise), direction *(order)*, directive, discipline *(control)*, dominate, dominion *(supreme authority)*, edict, efficiency, enact, enjoin, exhort, fiat, force *(compulsion)*, force *(strength)*, force *(coerce)*, generalship, govern, government *(administration)*, handle *(manage)*, hegemony, hold *(possess)*, impose *(enforce)*, influence, injunction, insist, instruct *(direct)*, instruction *(direction)*, jurisdiction, knowledge *(learning)*, law, manage, management *(directorate)*, management *(supervision)*, mandamus, mandate, manipulate *(utilize skillfully)*, mittimus, moderate *(preside over)*, monition *(legal summons)*, motivate, occupation *(possession)*, occupy *(take possession)*, officiate, operate, order *(judicial directive)*, order, ordinance, overcome *(surmount)*, overlook *(superintend)*, oversee, own, possess, power, precept, predominance, predominate *(command)*, prescribe, prescription *(directive)*, preside, press *(constrain)*, pressure, prevail *(triumph)*, primacy, process *(summons)*, regime, regulation *(rule)*, request, require *(compel)*, requirement, rule *(legal dictate)*, rule *(govern)*, ruling, skill, subjugate, subpoena, summon, superintend, supervision, supremacy, surmount, takeover, wield, will *(desire)*, writ

command a view observe *(watch)*

command a view of discern *(detect with the senses)*, overlook *(superintend)*

command back remand

command by the court mandate

command influence constrain *(compel)*

command not to do forbid

command of idiom parlance, phraseology

command of language parlance, phraseology

command of money substance *(material possessions)*

command of one's faculties composure

command of temper composure

command of thought comprehension

command of words parlance, rhetoric *(skilled speech)*

command to appear call *(summon)*, citation *(charge)*, subpoena, subpoena, summon, summons, venire

command to incarcerate mittimus

command to undo wrong injunction

commandant chief, principal *(director)*

commanded compulsory, decretal, mandatory, obligatory, positive *(prescribed)*

commanded by long use prescriptive

commandeer assume *(seize)*, carry away, deprive, garnish, hijack, procure, seize *(confiscate)*, usurp

commandeering condemnation *(seizure)*, confiscatory, disseisin

commander chief, principal *(director)*

commanders authorities, hierarchy *(persons in authority)*

commanding cardinal *(outstanding)*, cogent, compelling, considerable, convincing, critical *(crucial)*, decisive, decretal, dictatorial, dominant, forcible,

important *(significant)*, influential, insistent, mandatory, master, noteworthy, peremptory *(imperative)*, potent, powerful, predominant, prescriptive, prevailing *(having superior force)*, salient, sovereign *(absolute)*

commanding a good price valuable

commanding a high price priceless

commanding belief credible, fiduciary, plausible

commanding confidence credible, fiduciary

commanding position priority

commandment canon, charge *(command)*, codification, decree, dictate, direction *(order)*, directive, instruction *(direction)*, mandate, monition *(legal summons)*, order *(judicial directive)*, precept, regulation *(rule)*, requirement, rule *(legal dictate)*, statute, summons, writ

commatic sententious

commeasurable commensurate, proportionate

commeatus furlough, leave *(absence)*

commeminisse recollect

commemorare recapitulate, recount

commemorate honor, keep *(fulfill)*, recall *(remember)*, recognize *(acknowledge)*, remember

commemoratio mention *(reference)*

commemoration ceremony, recognition, reminder

commemorative honorary, suggestive *(evocative)*

commemoratory suggestive *(evocative)*

commence embark, initiate, originate, preface, stem *(originate)*, undertake

commence a suit sue

commence again reopen

commence proceedings against a third party implead

commencement birth *(beginning)*, derivation, embryo, genesis, inception, nascency, origin *(source)*, origination, outset, overt act, preface, prelude, start

commencement of an action service *(delivery of legal process)*

commencing incipient, initial, original *(initial)*

commencing before retroactive

commend advocate, confirm, counsel, countenance, endorse, honor, indorse, recommend

commendable congruous, laudable, meritorious, moral, professional *(stellar)*, unimpeachable

commendableness expedience

commendare recommend

commendatio recommendation

commendation consent, credit *(recognition)*, estimation *(esteem)*, honor *(outward respect)*, mention *(tribute)*, patronage *(support)*, recommendation, reference *(recommendation)*, remembrance *(commemoration)*, respect

commendatory honorary, meritorious

commending favorable *(expressing approval)*

commensurability balance *(equality)*

commensurable commensurate, comparable *(capable of comparison)*, correlative, relative *(comparative)*

commensurate adequate, coequal,

cognate, commensurable, comparable *(equivalent)*, congruous, consonant, correlative, proportionate, relative *(comparative)*, suitable

commensurate notice adequate notice

commensurate with pursuant to

commensuration proportion

comment construction, convey *(communicate)*, discourse, discuss, express, interject, mention *(reference)*, muse, notation, note *(brief comment)*, notice *(observe)*, observation, observe *(remark)*, phrase, pronouncement, remark, remark, review *(critical evaluation)*, statement

comment on converse, edit

comment upon clarify, discuss, elucidate, expound, instruct *(teach)*, mention, review, treat *(process)*

commentary clarification, comment, construction, criticism, discourse, explanation, hornbook, marginalia, notation, note *(brief comment)*, observation, pandect *(treatise)*, proposal *(report)*, remark, review *(critical evaluation)*

commentate elucidate, expound

commentators press

commenticius fictitious

commentum falsehood, fiction

commercari trade

commerce contact *(association)*, deal, dealings, exchange

commerce with communicate

commercial industrial, marketable, mercantile, retail

commercial advantage goodwill

commercial agent factor *(commission merchant)*

commercial backing patronage *(support)*

commercial building development *(building)*

commercial enterprise company *(enterprise)*, corporation, dealings, firm, trade *(commerce)*

commercial establishment enterprise *(economic organization)*, house

commercial failure failure *(bankruptcy)*

commercial house firm

commercial instrument check *(instrument)*

commercial intercourse business *(commerce)*, commerce, dealings

commercial paper check *(instrument)*, draft

commercial profits income

commercial theory finance

commercial transaction deal

commercialize deal

commercium commerce, commercial

comminari threaten

comminate denounce *(condemn)*, menace, threaten

commination denunciation, disapprobation, imprecation, menace, notice *(warning)*, phillipic, threat, warning

comminatory calumnious, critical *(faultfinding)*, sinister

commingle accompany, amalgamate, combine *(join together)*, desegregate, diffuse, join *(bring together)*, unite

commingled miscellaneous, promiscuous

comminisci invent *(falsify)*

comminute break *(fracture)*

commiscere commingle

commiserate sympathize

commiseration pity, solace

commissaries deputation *(delegation)*

commissary deputy, functionary, supplier

commission act *(undertaking)*, agency *(legal relationship)*, allow *(authorize)*, appoint, assign *(designate)*, assignment *(designation)*, assignment *(task)*, authorize, bestow, board, brokerage, bureau, charge *(command)*, charge *(empower)*, commit *(entrust)*, committee, constitute *(establish)*, delegate, delegation *(assignment)*, delegation *(envoy)*, deputation *(delegation)*, deputation *(selection of delegates)*, designate, detail *(assign)*, dictate, discharge *(performance)*, duty *(obligation)*, earnings, embassy, employ *(engage services)*, employment, empower, engage *(hire)*, hire, induct, infliction, instruction *(direction)*, invest *(vest)*, let *(permit)*, mission, nominate, performance *(execution)*, post, retain *(employ)*, share *(interest)*, transaction, warrant *(authorization)*

commission agent broker, dealer

commission man dealer

commission merchant broker

commissioned allowed, vicarious *(delegated)*

commissioner caretaker *(one fulfilling the function of office)*, deputy, functionary, incumbent

commissioner of oaths notary public

commissioning delegation *(assignment)*, designation *(naming)*

commit apprehend *(arrest)*, arrest *(apprehend)*, confide *(trust)*, confine, consign, constrain *(imprison)*, contribute *(supply)*, delegate, deliver, deposit *(submit to a bank)*, detain *(hold in custody)*, entrust, execute *(accomplish)*, give *(grant)*, inflict, perpetrate, remand, remit *(submit for consideration)*, sentence, submit *(give)*, undertake

commit a breach infringe

commit a breach of the law offend *(violate the law)*

commit a crime disobey, offend *(violate the law)*

commit a debauch carouse

commit a fault offend *(violate the law)*

commit again reassign, recommit

commit an error err, lapse *(fall into error)*, miscalculate, mistake, misunderstand

commit an infraction encroach, offend *(violate the law)*

commit anew recommit

commit breach of trust cheat, defraud

commit forgery forge *(counterfeit)*

commit hostilities attack, fight *(battle)*

commit larceny embezzle, pilfer, purloin

commit murder dispatch *(put to death)*

commit offense offend *(violate the law)*

commit oneself assume *(undertake)*, avow, cast *(register)*, decide, guarantee,

pledge *(promise the performance of)*, promise *(vow)*

commit oneself to undertake

commit oneself to a course choose

commit perjury lie *(falsify)*

commit piracy pirate *(take by violence)*

commit powers to another assign *(designate)*, delegate

commit robbery hold up *(rob)*, pirate *(take by violence)*, rob

commit sin offend *(violate the law)*

commit to an institution arrest *(apprehend)*, constrain *(imprison)*, immure, imprison, jail, remand

commit to another's trust assign *(transfer ownership)*, consign

commit to prison arrest *(apprehend)*, confine, constrain *(imprison)*, contain *(restrain)*, immure, imprison, jail

commit to the hands of delegate

commit to writing inscribe, note *(record)*, set down

commit violence prey

commitment adhesion *(loyalty)*, agreement *(contract)*, allegiance, assurance, attornment, captivity, charge *(lien)*, charge *(responsibility)*, cloud *(incumbrance)*, compact, constraint *(imprisonment)*, contract, covenant, custody *(incarceration)*, debit, detention, durance, duty *(obligation)*, guaranty, incarceration, incumbrance *(lien)*, indenture, infliction, obligation *(duty)*, pledge *(binding promise)*, promise, recognizance, responsibility *(accountability)*, specialty *(contract)*, undertaking *(pledge)*

commitments ties

committal captivity, commitment *(confinement)*, detention

committed agreed *(promised)*, arrested *(apprehended)*, bound, contractual, loyal

committed to payment promissory

committee agency *(commission)*, assemblage, bureau, caucus, chamber *(body)*, council *(assembly)*, delegation *(envoy)*, deputation *(delegation)*, management *(directorate)*

committeeperson member *(individual in a group)*

committere consign, delegate, entrust, perpetrate

commix amalgamate, combine *(join together)*, commingle, desegregate

commixed composite, compound, concerted, miscellaneous

commixtion incorporation *(blend)*

commixture coalescence, melange, solution *(substance)*

commodare lend, loan, serve *(assist)*

commodious ample, capacious, convenient, extensive, practical, suitable

commodis consulere welfare

commodities cargo, goods, merchandise

commodity appliance, chattel, item, object, product

commodus favorable *(advantageous)*, fit, opportune

common accustomed *(customary)*, average *(standard)*, base *(inferior)*, blatant *(obtrusive)*, boiler plate, civic, cognate, competitive *(open)*, concurrent *(united)*, conjoint, conventional, customary, daily, familiar *(customary)*, frequent, general, generic, habitual, household *(familiar)*, ignoble, inelegant, informal, jejune *(dull)*, joint, mediocre, mundane, mutual *(collective)*, national, nondescript, normal *(regular)*, orthodox, poor *(inferior in quality)*, predominant, prevailing *(current)*, prevalent, pro forma, profane, prosaic, proverbial, public *(affecting people)*, reciprocal, regular *(conventional)*, repeated, rife, routine, stale, tawdry, traditional, trite, typical, usual

common agreement mutual understanding

common ancestry affinity *(family ties)*, blood, propinquity *(kinship)*, relation *(kinship)*

common assent agreement *(concurrence)*, concordance

common consent agreement *(concurrence)*, cartel, consensus

common course practice *(custom)*

common denominator connection *(relation)*

common derivation affiliation *(bloodline)*

common descent relation *(kinship)*

common effort coaction

common extraction family *(common ancestry)*

common feature analogy

common folk populace

common forebears family *(common ancestry)*

common fund pool

common knowledge publicity

common lineage family *(common ancestry)*, relation *(kinship)*

common lot mediocrity

common occurrence frequency

common ownership pool

common parentage family *(common ancestry)*

common people populace

common practice habit, matter of course, procedure

common reference connection *(relation)*

common run generality *(bulk)*, matter of course

common saying catchword

common sense prudence, reason *(sound judgment)*

common state of affairs matter of course

common stock relation *(kinship)*

common to many general

common understanding mutual understanding

common usage custom

common view accordance *(understanding)*, agreement *(concurrence)*, compatibility, understanding *(agreement)*

commonage populace

commonality mutuality

commonalty community, populace, population, public

commonere admonish *(warn)*, remind

commoners populace

commonition admonition

commonly as a rule, generally, invariably

commonly considered putative

commonly known household *(famil-*

iar), proverbial, public *(known)*

commonly observed customary

commonly practiced customary

commonness frequency, mediocrity

commonplace accustomed *(customary)*, average *(standard)*, boiler plate, common *(customary)*, customary, familiar *(customary)*, habitual, household *(familiar)*, jejune *(dull)*, lifeless *(dull)*, mediocre, mundane, nondescript, normal *(regular)*, ordinary, orthodox, pedestrian, prevailing *(current)*, prevalent, prosaic, proverbial, regular *(conventional)*, repeated, routine, stale, trite, typical, usual

commonplace expression platitude

commonplace idea platitude

commonplace phrase platitude

commonplaceness mediocrity

commonwealth community, nationality, polity, public, society, state *(political unit)*

commorance residence

commorancy residence

commotion affray, altercation, brawl, confusion *(turmoil)*, disorder *(lack of order)*, disturbance, embroilment, entanglement *(confusion)*, fracas, fray, furor, imbroglio, outbreak, outburst, pandemonium, riot, trouble, turmoil

commovere affect, disturb, move *(alter position)*

communal civic, civil *(public)*, common *(shared)*, concurrent *(united)*, joint, mutual *(collective)*, public *(affecting people)*

communal business establishment cooperative

communal society cooperative

communalistic mutual *(collective)*

commune communicate, community, cooperative

commune with converse, discourse

commune with oneself muse, ponder, reflect *(ponder)*

communicable contagious

communicant deponent, informant, informer *(a person who provides information)*

communicare communicate, impart

communicate advise, annunciate, apprise, bestow, circulate, connote, declare, deliver, depict, disabuse, disclose, disseminate, divulge, express, herald, impart, inform *(betray)*, inform *(notify)*, issue *(publish)*, mention, notice *(give formal warning)*, notify, observe *(remark)*, pass *(advance)*, phrase, post, proclaim, promulgate, pronounce *(speak)*, publish, recite, recount, relate *(tell)*, remark, render *(deliver)*, report *(disclose)*, reveal, signify *(inform)*, transmit, utter

communicate orally discourse

communicate to caution

communicate with converse, reach, speak

communicated oral

communicatio communication *(discourse)*

communication admission *(disclosure)*, caveat, contact *(association)*, conversation, correspondence *(communication by letters)*, disclosure *(act of disclosing)*, disclosure *(something disclosed)*, dispatch *(message)*, expression

(comment), information *(knowledge)*, intelligence *(news)*, issuance, language, mention *(reference)*, note *(brief comment)*, notice *(announcement)*, notice *(warning)*, notification, parley, publication *(disclosure)*, report *(detailed account)*, tip *(clue)*, transmittal

communication of knowledge advice, declaration

communicative declaratory, demonstrative *(expressive of emotion)*, eloquent, informative, informatory, loquacious, narrative, responsive

communicator deponent, informant, informer *(a person who provides information)*

communicatory advisory, informative

communion accordance *(understanding)*, concordance, mutual understanding, sodality

communiqué communication *(discourse)*, declaration, dispatch *(message)*

communique information *(facts)*, information *(knowledge)*, intelligence *(news)*, issuance, notice *(announcement)*, notification

communis common *(shared)*, general, joint, ordinary

community body *(collection)*, civic, coalition, constituency, contact *(association)*, denomination, joint, organization *(association)*, populace, population, public *(open)*, public, society, sodality

community of interest cartel, sodality

community of interests agreement *(concurrence)*, peace

community of possession pool

commutability mutuality

commutable convertible, mutable

commutare alter, modify *(alter)*

commutation clemency, compensation, compromise, exchange, immunity, mutuality, replacement, subrogation

commutative convertible, mutual *(reciprocal)*

commute alter, convert *(change use)*, replace, transform

commutual common *(shared)*, concurrent *(united)*, conjoint, correlative, mutual *(collective)*, reciprocal, related

compact abstract *(summarize)*, adjustment, agreement *(contract)*, arrangement *(understanding)*, attornment, bargain, brief, cartel, coadunate, composition *(agreement in bankruptcy)*, concentrate *(consolidate)*, conciliation, concise, concordance, conjoint, consensus, consolidate *(strengthen)*, consolidation, consortium *(marriage companionship)*, conspiracy, constrict *(compress)*, contract, corporate *(joint)*, covenant, crystallize, decrease, indenture, league, mutual understanding, pact, pithy, pledge *(binding promise)*, populous, promise, protocol *(agreement)*, reduce, sententious, specialty *(contract)*, stipulation, succinct, treaty, understanding *(agreement)*, undertaking *(pledge)*

compact to govern constitution

compacted compact *(dense)*, concise

compacting centralization

compactness congealment, density

compages complex *(development)*, corpus

compages frame *(structure)*

companion associate, cohort, colleague, complement, confederate, consociate, consort, copartner *(business associate)*, copartner *(coconspirator)*, correlate, participant, partner, peer, similar

companion in crime coconspirator

companionless solitary

companionship compatibility, consortium *(marriage companionship)*, contact *(association)*, society, sodality

company assemblage, assembly, association *(alliance)*, body *(collection)*, business *(commercial enterprise)*, collection *(assembly)*, concern *(business establishment)*, corporation, enterprise *(economic organization)*, firm, house, organization *(association)*, personnel, syndicate

comparabilis comparable *(capable of comparison)*

comparability analogy, balance *(equality)*, collation, correspondence *(similarity)*, identity *(similarity)*, parity

comparable analogous, apposite, approximate, coequal, coextensive, cognate, commensurable, commensurate, comparative, correlative, equivalent, identical, proportionate, similar, tantamount

comparableness balance *(equality)*, relation *(connection)*

comparare compare, contrast, procure, relative *(comparative)*

comparatio comparison

comparative cognate, correlative, proportionate

comparative estimate collation, comparison

comparative size proportion

comparativeness balance *(equality)*

comparativus comparative

compare correspond *(be equivalent)*, discriminate *(distinguish)*, measure

compare by observing differences contrast

compare critically diagnose

compare opinions confer *(consult)*

compare to contrast

compare with approximate, contrast

compared cognate, relative *(comparative)*

comparere appear *(attend court proceedings)*, report *(present oneself)*

comparison analogy, collation, correlate, identification, parity, propinquity *(similarity)*, proportion, standard

compartment cell, section *(division)*, subdivision, zone

compartmentalize insulate, part *(separate)*, partition

compass blockade *(enclosure)*, boundary, caliber *(measurement)*, capacity *(maximum)*, circumscribe *(surround by boundary)*, comprehend *(include)*, demarcate, embrace *(encircle)*, enclose, encompass *(surround)*, envelop, extent, frontier, gamut, hedge, include, outline *(boundary)*, periphery, province, purview, range, region, scope, space

compassion benevolence *(disposition to do good)*, clemency, condonation, consideration *(sympathetic regard)*, humanity *(humaneness)*, indulgence,

lenience, pity, tolerance, understanding *(tolerance)*

compassionate lenient, placable, receptive, susceptible *(responsive)*

compatibility accordance *(understanding)*, concert, conformity *(agreement)*, consensus, propinquity *(similarity)*, propriety *(appropriateness)*, qualification *(fitness)*, rapport, relevance, sodality, synchronism

compatible apposite, concordant, concurrent *(united)*, congruous, conjoint, consensual, consistent, consonant, correlative, fit, harmonious, proportionate, relative *(relevant)*, relevant, suitable, uniform

compatible to pursuant to

compeer associate, colleague, consort, contributor *(contributor)*, copartner *(business associate)*, partner, peer

compel bait *(harass)*, bait *(lure)*, bind *(obligate)*, bind *(restrain)*, cause, coerce, command, constrain *(compel)*, convince, detail *(assign)*, dictate, dominate, enforce, exact, extort, foist, force *(coerce)*, impose *(enforce)*, impose *(subject)*, instruct *(direct)*, make, motivate, necessitate, obsess, order, persuade, press *(constrain)*, pressure, rule *(govern)*

compel attendance summon

compel attendence subpoena

compel belief convince

compel by intimidation extort

compel by threat extort

compel obedience enforce

compel payment excise *(levy a tax)*

compel to accept foist

compellare accost

compellation call *(title)*

compelled bound

compeller extortionist

compellere compel, constrain *(compel)*

compelling binding, causal, cogent, compulsory, considerable, convincing, decisive, dictatorial, eloquent, exigent, forcible, important *(urgent)*, impulsive *(impelling)*, insistent, irresistible, material *(important)*, necessary *(inescapable)*, necessary *(required)*, obligatory, persuasive, potent, powerful, sound, stringent, strong, unavoidable *(inevitable)*, undeniable, urgent

compelling quality necessity

compend capsule, compendium, outline *(synopsis)*, summary, synopsis

compendious brief, compact *(pithy)*, comprehensive, concise, laconic, omnibus, pithy, succinct

compendium abridgment *(condensation)*, abstract, brief, capsule, codification, digest, hornbook, outline *(synopsis)*, pandect *(treatise)*, restatement, sum *(tally)*, summary, synopsis

compensare compensate *(counterbalance)*, redress, requital

compensate bear the expense, contribute *(indemnify)*, defray, disburse *(pay out)*, indemnify, outbalance, pay, quit *(repay)*, recoup *(reimburse)*, redeem *(satisfy debts)*, redress, refund, reimburse, remit *(send payment)*, remunerate, repay, replace, return *(refund)*, satisfy *(discharge)*

compensate for cover *(provide for)*

compensate for injury indemnify

compensate for loss indemnify

compensate for loss sustained indemnify

compensating compensatory, disbursement *(act of disbursing)*, lucrative

compensatio collection *(payment)*, compensation

compensation advance *(allowance)*, aid *(subsistence)*, benefit *(conferment)*, brokerage, collection *(payment)*, commission *(fee)*, consideration *(recompense)*, contribution *(indemnification)*, damages, disbursement *(funds paid out)*, discharge *(payment)*, earnings, expiation, fee *(charge)*, honorarium, income, indemnification, indemnity, offset, out of pocket, pay, payment *(act of paying)*, payment *(remittance)*, payroll, pension, perquisite, price, profit, recompense, recovery *(award)*, refund, reimbursement, relief *(legal redress)*, remedy *(legal means of redress)*, remuneration, rendition *(restoration)*, rent, reparation *(indemnification)*, replacement, requital, restitution, retainer, retribution, revenue, reward, satisfaction *(discharge of debt)*, tip *(gratuity)*, trover, wage

compensation for delay demurrage

compensation for injury insurance

compensation for labor fee *(charge)*

compensation for loss insurance

compensation for professional service fee *(charge)*

compensation owed due

compensative compensatory

compensator insurer

compensatory equivalent, lucrative, remedial

comperire ascertain, discover

compes fetter

compete contend *(dispute)*, dispute *(contest)*, engage *(involve)*, participate, race, strive

compete for endeavor

compete with antagonize, counter, fight *(battle)*, grapple

competence ability, caliber *(mental capacity)*, capacity *(aptitude)*, discretion *(quality of being discreet)*, efficiency, experience *(background)*, facility *(easiness)*, faculty *(ability)*, force *(strength)*, gift *(flair)*, penchant, performance *(workmanship)*, potential, power, prowess *(ability)*, science *(technique)*, skill, specialty *(special aptitude)*, sufficiency

competency ability, capacity *(aptitude)*, efficiency, experience *(background)*, faculty *(ability)*, performance *(workmanship)*, prowess *(ability)*, qualification *(fitness)*, quality *(excellence)*, science *(technique)*, sufficiency

competent adequate, capable, deft, effective *(efficient)*, efficient, expert, familiar *(informed)*, fit, operative, practiced, professional *(trained)*, proficient, reliable, resourceful, sane, sciential

competent practitioner professional

competere competent

competing competitive *(antagonistic)*, contestable

competition conflict, contention *(opposition)*, rival, strife, struggle

competitive contentious, hostile, jealous

competitiveness contention *(opposition)*

competitor adversary, candidate, contender, foe, peer, rival

competitory competitive *(antagonistic)*

compilare hold up *(rob)*, plunder

compilation abstract, assemblage, body *(collection)*, building *(business of assembling)*, centralization, code, codification, collection *(accumulation)*, composition *(makeup)*, conglomeration, corpus, cumulation, digest, selection *(choice)*, selection *(collection)*, summary

compilation of law code, constitution

compilation of laws code

compilations information *(knowledge)*

compile accumulate *(amass)*, aggregate, build *(construct)*, codify, collect *(gather)*, compose, congregate, garner

compiled collective

compiler author *(writer)*

compiler of tables of mortality actuary

complacence composure

complacent benevolent

complain cite *(accuse)*, criticize *(find fault with)*, deplore, object, protest, reproach

complain against accuse, arraign, blame, charge *(accuse)*, denounce *(inform against)*, impeach, incriminate

complain frivolously cavil

complain publicly demonstrate *(protest)*

complainant accuser, actor, claimant, contender, contestant, declarant, informer *(one providing criminal information)*, litigant, malcontent, party *(litigant)*, plaintiff, victim

complained of accused *(charged)*

complainer malcontent

complaining criticism, diatribe, disapproval, fractious, querulous

complaining party complainant

complaining witness victim

complaint allegation, charge *(accusation)*, claim *(legal demand)*, condemnation *(blame)*, criticism, denunciation, disapprobation, disapproval, disorder *(abnormal condition)*, disparagement, dissatisfaction, exception *(objection)*, grievance, ground, impeachment, incrimination, indictment, outcry, plaint, pleading, protest, reproach

complaint to a higher court habeas corpus

complaint to a superior court appeal

complaisance consideration *(sympathetic regard)*, courtesy, deference

complaisant complacent, obedient, obeisant, permissive, yielding

complecti embrace *(encircle)*, encompass *(include)*, include

complement addendum, addition, adjunct, allonge, appendix *(accession)*, boom *(increase)*, codicil, component, content *(structure)*, corollary, correlate, correspond *(be equivalent)*, rider, staff, supplement

complemental concomitant, correlative, mutual *(reciprocal)*, reciprocal

complemental term correlate

complementary cognate, concordant, concurrent *(united)*, convertible, correlative, mutual *(reciprocal)*, pendent, reciprocal, related

complementing ancillary *(subsidiary)*

complementum complement

complete accomplish, adjust *(resolve)*, arrant *(definite)*, attain, cap, carry *(succeed)*, categorical, close *(terminate)*, commit *(perpetrate)*, comply, comprehensive, conclusive *(settled)*, consummate, culminate, definitive, detailed, discharge *(perform)*, discontinue *(abandon)*, dispatch *(dispose of)*, effectuate, execute *(accomplish)*, exhaust *(try all possibilities)*, fabricate *(construct)*, finish, follow-up, fulfill, full, gross *(total)*, implement, intact, inviolate, keep *(fulfill)*, lapse *(cease)*, make, omnibus, outright, peremptory *(absolute)*, perfect, perform *(adhere to)*, perform *(execute)*, plenary, pure, radical *(extreme)*, realize *(make real)*, replenish, replete, ripe, stark, terminate, thorough, total, unconditional, unmitigated, unqualified *(unlimited)*, whole *(undamaged)*

complete a purchase buy

complete body of laws pandect *(code of laws)*

complete conviction certainty, certification *(certainness)*, surety *(certainty)*

complete digest pandect *(treatise)*

complete lawsuit day in court

complete prosecution rest *(end a legal case)*

complete report accounting

complete sequence gamut

complete series gamut

complete standstill impasse

complete substitution novation

complete trust credence

completed complete *(ended)*, conclusive *(settled)*, definitive, fully executed *(consummated)*, fully executed *(signed)*, through

completely fairly *(clearly)*, in toto, wholly

completely end destroy *(void)*

completely full replete

completeness conclusion *(outcome)*, entirety, fait accompli, finality, quorum, totality, whole

completing ancillary *(auxiliary)*, conclusive *(settled)*, final

completion cessation *(termination)*, close *(conclusion)*, commission *(act)*, complement, conclusion *(outcome)*, consequence *(conclusion)*, course, denouement, discharge *(performance)*, dissolution *(termination)*, end *(termination)*, entirety, expiration, extremity *(death)*, fait accompli, finality, follow-up, maturity, outcome, performance *(execution)*, realization, transaction

completive complete *(ended)*, comprehensive, conclusive *(settled)*, last *(final)*

completory last *(final)*

complex composite, compound, conglomerate, difficult, elaborate, inextricable, intricate, labyrinthine, obscure *(abstruse)*, problematic, recondite, sinuous, sophisticated

complexion appearance *(look)*, condition *(state)*, spirit, state *(condition)*

complexity complication, confusion *(turmoil)*, enigma, entanglement *(confusion)*, imbroglio, impasse, involution, problem

complexness complication

complexus complex *(entanglement)*

complexus complication

complexus corpus, snarl

compliable complacent, consenting, consistent, facile, obedient, obsequious, passive, pliant

compliance acceptance, accordance *(understanding)*, acknowledgment *(acceptance)*, acquiescence, adherence *(devotion)*, amenability, assent, capitulation, comity, compatibility, conciliation, conduct, conformity *(obedience)*, conjunction, consent, consortium *(marriage companionship)*, conspiracy, deference, discipline *(obedience)*, fealty, homage, indorsement, loyalty, timeliness, understanding *(agreement)*

compliancy amenability, compliance

compliant amenable, charitable *(lenient)*, complacent, concordant, consensual, consenting, facile, favorable *(expressing approval)*, loyal, malleable, obedient, obeisant, obsequious, orthodox, passive, patient, pliable, pliant, prone, ready *(willing)*, sequacious, servile, tractable, true *(loyal)*, willing *(not averse)*, yielding

compliantly faithfully, respectfully

complicate aggravate *(exacerbate)*, confound, dislocate, disorganize, muddle, obfuscate, perplex, perturb

complicated circuitous, complex, compound, difficult, elaborate, inextricable, intricate, labyrinthine, problematic, profound *(esoteric)*, recondite, sinuous, tortuous *(bending)*

complicated misunderstanding imbroglio

complicated state complication

complication aggravation *(annoyance)*, complex *(entanglement)*, confusion *(ambiguity)*, embroilment, entanglement *(confusion)*, hindrance, imbroglio, involution, predicament, problem, quagmire, snarl

complicity bad faith, bribery, cabal, coaction, collusion, concert, confederacy *(conspiracy)*, connivance, conspiracy, contribution *(participation)*, contrivance, corruption, implication *(incriminating involvement)*, league, plot *(secret plan)*

compliment belaud, doxology, honor, mention *(tribute)*, recommend

complimentary free *(at no charge)*, gratis, gratuitous *(given without recompense)*, unsolicited

complot cabal, collusion, confederacy *(conspiracy)*, connivance, connive, maneuver, plan, plan, plot *(secret plan)*, scheme

complotter conspirator

comply abide, accede *(concede)*, accept *(admit as sufficient)*, accept *(assent)*, adhere *(maintain loyalty)*, assent, concur *(agree)*, conform, consent, defer *(yield in judgment)*, discharge *(perform)*, hear *(give attention to)*, heed, obey, serve *(assist)*, submit *(yield)*, succumb, suffer *(permit)*, yield *(submit)*

comply with adapt, agree *(comply)*, concede, correspond *(be equivalent)*, fulfill, keep *(fulfill)*, observe *(obey)*, perform *(adhere to)*, satisfy *(fulfill)*, vouchsafe

complying law-abiding, obedient, passive, true *(loyal)*

component adjunct, affiliate, chapter *(branch)*, chapter *(division)*, color *(complexion)*, constituent *(part)*, detail, element, factor *(ingredient)*, feature *(characteristic)*, ingredient, integral, item, member *(constituent part)*, organ, part *(portion)*, section *(division)*, segment, subdivision, unit *(item)*

component part component, constituent *(part)*, detail, element, ingredient

components contents

componere agree *(comply)*, arrange *(methodize)*, compare, compile, compose, constitute *(compose)*, frame *(formulate)*, organize *(arrange)*, pacify

comport demean *(deport oneself)*

comport oneself deport *(conduct oneself)*

comport with cohere *(be logically consistent)*, correspond *(be equivalent)*

comportment behavior, conduct, demeanor, deportment, manner *(behavior)*, presence *(poise)*

compose accommodate, allay, alleviate, assuage, build *(construct)*, compile, conceive *(invent)*, contrive, create, devise *(invent)*, fabricate *(construct)*, forge *(produce)*, form, formulate, frame *(construct)*, invent *(produce for the first time)*, lull, make, manufacture, marshal, mollify, orchestrate, originate, produce *(manufacture)*, scheme, soothe

compose differences intercede

compose oneself repose *(rest)*

composed complacent, dispassionate, nonchalant, patient, peaceable, placid

composed of several elements multiple

composer architect, author *(originator)*

composer of a literary work author *(writer)*

composite coherent *(joined)*, collective, complex *(development)*, compound, concerted, conglomerate, conjoint, content *(structure)*, miscellaneous, omnibus, promiscuous, solution *(substance)*

composite representation cross section

compositio accommodation *(adjustment)*, arrangement *(ordering)*, composition *(makeup)*, settlement

composition adjustment, arrangement *(ordering)*, array *(order)*, building *(business of assembling)*, combination, compromise, configuration *(form)*, conspiracy, content *(structure)*, coverage *(scope)*, creation, formation, invention, language, manufacture, melange, motif, order *(arrangement)*, organization *(structure)*, origination, performance *(workmanship)*, phraseology, solution *(substance)*, temperament

composition of differences accommodation *(adjustment)*

compositional skill rhetoric *(skilled speech)*

compositus composite, compound

composure common sense, longanimity, moderation, sufferance

composure of differences settlement

composure of doubts settlement

compound adhere *(fasten)*, close *(enclosed area)*, coalescence, collective, combination, combine *(join together)*, commingle, complex *(development)*,

composite, confines, conglomerate, conjoin, consolidate *(strengthen)*, consolidate *(unite)*, desegregate, incorporate *(include)*, incorporation *(blend)*, join *(bring together)*, make, melange, merge, solution *(substance)*

compounded composite, conglomerate, inextricable

compounding building *(business of assembling)*, composition *(makeup)*

comprehend apprehend *(perceive)*, discern *(detect with the senses)*, include, perceive, pierce *(discern)*, realize *(understand)*, recognize *(perceive)*, understand

comprehendable comprehensible

comprehended from accompanying words noscitur a sociis

comprehendere apprehend *(arrest)*, apprehend *(perceive)*, arrest *(apprehend)*, capture, comprehend *(understand)*, contain *(comprise)*, embrace *(encircle)*, include, realize *(understand)*, seize *(apprehend)*

comprehending cognizant, conscious *(aware)*, knowing, lucid, omniscient, perceptive, receptive

comprehensibility coherence

comprehensible cognizable, coherent *(clear)*, explicit, lucid, obvious, pellucid, perceptible, ponderable, scrutable, unambiguous

comprehensio comprehension

comprehension appreciation *(perception)*, apprehension *(perception)*, caliber *(mental capacity)*, cognition, connotation, coverage *(scope)*, discrimination *(differentiation)*, information *(knowledge)*, insight, intellect, intelligence *(intellect)*, judgment *(discernment)*, knowledge *(awareness)*, perception, realization, reason *(sound judgment)*, recognition, sagacity, sanity, scienter *(intelligence)*, sensibility

comprehensive absolute *(complete)*, ample, broad, capacious, collective, competitive *(open)*, complete *(all-embracing)*, detailed, extensive, far reaching, full, generic, gross *(total)*, inclusive, indiscriminate, major, nonsectarian, omnibus, outright, plenary, prevailing *(current)*, radical *(extreme)*, thorough

comprehensive digest pandect *(treatise)*

comprehensively in toto

comprehensiveness capacity *(maximum)*, corpus, coverage *(scope)*, entirety, extent, totality

compress abridge *(shorten)*, abstract *(summarize)*, cohere *(adhere)*, concentrate *(consolidate)*, condense, consolidate *(strengthen)*, consolidate *(unite)*, crystallize, decrease, diminish, impact, lessen, reduce

compressed brief, coherent *(joined)*, cohesive *(compact)*, compact *(dense)*, concise, laconic, narrow, pithy, sententious, solid *(compact)*

compressed statement summary

compression abridgment *(condensation)*, abstract, blockade *(limitation)*, capsule, centralization, curtailment, outline *(synopsis)*, scenario

comprimere repress, withhold

comprisal composition *(makeup)*, cov-

erage *(scope)*

comprise comprehend *(include)*, consist, constitute *(compose)*, encompass *(include)*

comprising comprehensive, inclusive

comprobare approve, confirm, corroborate

comprobatio acceptance, approval, indorsement

compromisable convertible

compromise accommodation *(adjustment)*, accord, adjustment, agree *(contract)*, arrangement *(understanding)*, bargain, collective bargaining, compact, conciliation, contract, deal, denigrate, endanger, find *(determine)*, give *(yield)*, mediate, negotiation, pact, settle, settlement

compromise agreement composition *(agreement in bankruptcy)*

compromised agreed *(harmonized)*

compromiser referee, umpire

compromising calumnious, contemptuous, disgraceful, intermediate

compromittere compromise *(settle by mutual agreement)*

compte rendu account *(evaluation)*

compulsatory obligatory

compulsion coercion, constraint *(restriction)*, deterrence, dipsomania, duress, enforcement, extortion, force *(compulsion)*, main force, motive, need *(requirement)*, obligation *(duty)*, obsession, oppression, pressure, requirement, responsibility *(accountability)*, servitude, stress *(strain)*

compulsive compelling, obligatory

compulsorily acquire condemn *(seize)*, confiscate, distrain

compulsory binding, choate lien, compelling, essential *(required)*, exigent, forcible, imperative, indispensable, involuntary, mandatory, necessary *(required)*, obligatory, peremptory *(imperative)*, positive *(prescribed)*, prescriptive, requisite, stringent, unavoidable *(inevitable)*, urgent

compulsory acquisition condemnation *(seizure)*, disseisin, requisition

compulsory detail necessity, need *(requirement)*

compulsory execution enforcement

compulsory payment fine, penalty, punishment

compulsory purchase expropriation *(right of eminent domain)*

compulsory service bondage

compunction conscience, qualm, remorse, responsibility *(conscience)*, scruple

compunctious blameful, contrite, penitent, remorseful, repentant

compurgate acquit, confess

compurgation acquittal, deposition, justification, pardon, release

compurgator deponent, eyewitness, witness

computable appreciable, determinable *(ascertainable)*

computare calculate

computation accounting, appraisal, census, estimate *(approximate cost)*, estimation *(calculation)*, ledger, measurement

compute assess *(appraise)*, calculate, charge *(assess)*, gauge, measure, poll, rate, sum, survey *(poll)*

comrade cohort, colleague, confederate, consociate, consort, contributor *(contributor)*, copartner *(coconspirator)*, member *(individual in a group)*, participant, partisan, peer

comrade in crime coconspirator

comrade in wrongdoing coconspirator

comradeship consortium *(marriage companionship)*, contribution *(participation)*, society, sodality

con contra, deception, peruse, read

con game bunko

conari attempt, endeavor, strive, try *(attempt)*

conation conatus

conative discretionary, voluntary

conative will conatus

conatus effort, endeavor

concatenate combine *(join together)*, consolidate *(strengthen)*, join *(bring together)*

concatenation chain *(series)*, conjunction, connection *(fastening)*, joinder, sequence, succession

conceal blind *(obscure)*, camouflage, circumvent, cloak, clothe, disguise, distort, ensconce, enshroud, envelop, expurgate, harbor, hedge, hide, misguide, misinform, obfuscate, obliterate, obnubilate, obscure, screen *(guard)*, seclude, sequester *(seclude)*, shroud, stifle, suppress, withhold

conceal from knowledge hide

conceal from sight blind *(obscure)*, hide

conceal oneself lurk

conceal the truth cloak, prevaricate

concealed clandestine, confidential, covert, esoteric, evasive, furtive, hidden, impalpable, incomprehensible, inconspicuous, indiscernible, inexplicable, inscrutable, latent, mysterious, oblique *(evasive)*, obscure *(faint)*, opaque, personal *(private)*, potential, private *(confidential)*, privy, recondite, secret, stealthy, surreptitious, ulterior, undisclosed

concealed knowledge secret

concealment artifice, color *(deceptive appearance)*, confidence *(relation of trust)*, disguise, evasion, mystery, nonappearance, obscuration, privacy, subterfuge, veil

concealment of truth indirection *(deceitfulness)*

concede abandon *(relinquish)*, acknowledge *(verify)*, agree *(comply)*, allow *(endure)*, assent, authorize, bear *(tolerate)*, bestow, cede, compromise *(settle by mutual agreement)*, confess, confirm, conform, forfeit, give *(grant)*, give *(yield)*, let *(permit)*, recognize *(acknowledge)*, reveal, succumb, suffer *(permit)*, surrender *(yield)*, vouchsafe, yield *(submit)*

conceded agreed *(harmonized)*, allowed, consensual

conceded judgment cognovit

concededly admittedly

concedere admit *(concede)*, cede, comply, concede, grant *(concede)*, grant *(transfer formally)*, let *(permit)*, retire *(retreat)*, vouchsafe, yield *(submit)*

conceit idea, jactation

conceited inflated *(vain)*, orgulous, presumptuous, pretentious *(pompous)*

conceivability chance *(possibility)*, likelihood, possibility, probability

conceivable believable, colorable *(plausible)*, comprehensible, constructive *(inferential)*, plausible, possible, potential, presumptive, probable, prospective, viable

conceivableness chance *(possibility)*, likelihood, possibility

conceive appreciate *(comprehend)*, compose, comprehend *(understand)*, conjure, contrive, create, deem, devise *(invent)*, frame *(formulate)*, initiate, invent *(produce for the first time)*, originate, presume, produce *(manufacture)*, recognize *(perceive)*, reflect *(ponder)*, reproduce, surmise, understand

conceive of apprehend *(perceive)*, construe *(comprehend)*

conceived of parents legally married legitimate *(lawfully conceived)*

concent consensus

concenter concentrate *(consolidate)*, converge, focus

concentralization centralization

concentralize converge

concentrate accumulate *(amass)*, border *(approach)*, collect *(gather)*, congregate, consolidate *(strengthen)*, consolidate *(unite)*, constrict *(compress)*, converge, decrease, devote, distill, draw *(extract)*, intensify, muse, reflect *(ponder)*

concentrate on focus, occupy *(engage)*, specialize

concentrate the mind focus

concentrate the thoughts focus

concentrate upon ponder

concentrated cohesive *(compact)*, collective, compact *(dense)*, intense, intensive, solid *(compact)*, strong

concentrating cumulative *(intensifying)*, earnest, pensive

concentration assemblage, barrage, centralization, collection *(accumulation)*, contemplation, corpus, cumulation, density, emphasis, interest *(concern)*, observation, preoccupation, reflection *(thought)*, regard *(attention)*, strength

concentric coextensive

concentus consensus

concept conviction *(persuasion)*, idea, impression, notion, vision *(dream)*

conception apprehension *(perception)*, arrangement *(plan)*, cognition, comprehension, concept, conviction *(persuasion)*, design *(construction plan)*, idea, impression, notion, perspective, presumption, side, supposition, understanding *(comprehension)*, vision *(dream)*

conceptualize conceive *(comprehend)*, conjure

concern affinity *(regard)*, agitate *(perturb)*, appertain, apply *(pertain)*, apprehension *(fear)*, business *(affair)*, business *(commercial enterprise)*, calling, caution *(vigilance)*, charge *(custody)*, company *(enterprise)*, consideration *(sympathetic regard)*, corporation, devote, diligence *(care)*, discretion *(quality of being discreet)*, enterprise *(economic organization)*, fear, firm,

house, importance, institute, interest, magnitude, market *(business)*, matter *(subject)*, misgiving, mission, object, part *(role)*, pertain, position *(business status)*, profession *(vocation)*, prudence, pursuit *(occupation)*, purview, qualm, refer *(direct attention)*, regard *(attention)*, relate *(establish a connection)*, relevance, remorse, scruple, significance, store *(business)*, trade *(occupation)*, undertaking *(enterprise)*

concern oneself with address *(direct attention to)*, discharge *(perform)*, occupy *(engage)*, specialize

concerned careful, interested, solicitous, suspicious *(distrustful)*

concerning correlative, germane, pertinent, relative *(relevant)*, relevant, wherein

concerning the law forensic, juridical

concernment concern *(interest)*, importance, significance

concerns affairs

concert affiliation *(connectedness)*, cartel, coherence, collusion, combine *(act in concert)*, conciliation, concordance, conformity *(agreement)*, conjunction, connivance, connive, consensus, consolidate *(unite)*, conspiracy, conspire, contribution *(participation)*, cooperate, federate, federation, orchestrate, propinquity *(similarity)*, synergy, union *(unity)*

concert of action coaction

concertare dispute *(contest)*

concerted associated, coadunate, collective, concurrent *(at the same time)*, concurrent *(united)*, conjoint, consonant, joint

concerted refusal to work strike

concessio admission *(disclosure)*, concession *(authorization)*

concession accord, acknowledgment *(acceptance)*, acquiescence, admission *(disclosure)*, advancement *(loan)*, appropriation *(allotment)*, cession, compliance, compromise, conciliation, consent, consignment, copyright, disclosure *(act of disclosing)*, disclosure *(something disclosed)*, expense *(sacrifice)*, franchise *(license)*, grace, grace period, grant, sufferance

concessive obsequious, passive, pliant

concidere fail *(lose)*

concierge caretaker *(one caring for property)*

conciliable nonmilitant

conciliate arbitrate *(adjudge)*, compromise *(settle by mutual agreement)*, disarm *(set at ease)*, intercede, mediate, mollify, pacify, placate, propitiate, reconcile

conciliated agreed *(harmonized)*

conciliatio conciliation

conciliation accordance *(compact)*, amnesty, arbitration, collective bargaining, condonation, intercession, mediation, mollification, peace, reconciliation, settlement

conciliative nonmilitant

conciliator go-between, intermediary

conciliator referee

conciliatory nonmilitant, obeisant, penitent, placable

concinere agree *(comply)*

concinnity accordance (*understanding*), conformity (*agreement*), consensus, proportion
concinnous felicitous, harmonious
concipere conceive (*invent*), frame (*formulate*)
concise brief, coherent (*clear*), cohesive (*compact*), compact (*pithy*), laconic, pithy, sententious, succinct, summary
concise treatment compendium
concitare rebel
conclave assemblage, assembly, caucus, company (*assemblage*), conference, congregation, council (*assembly*), meeting (*conference*), parley, session
conclude adjudge, adjudicate, adjust (*resolve*), ascertain, assume (*suppose*), award, cap, cease, close (*terminate*), complete, construe (*comprehend*), consummate, culminate, decide, deduce, deduct (*conclude by reasoning*), deem, derive (*deduce*), determine, discharge (*perform*), discontinue (*abandon*), dispatch (*dispose of*), dissolve (*terminate*), expect (*consider probable*), expire, find (*determine*), finish, fix (*settle*), generalize, hold (*decide*), infer, judge, lapse (*cease*), liquidate (*convert into cash*), opine, perfect, perform (*adhere to*), presume, pronounce (*pass judgment*), read, reason (*conclude*), result, rule (*decide*), settle, stop, surmise, suspect (*think*), terminate, understand
conclude from evidence construe (*comprehend*), infer
conclude proceeding rest (*end a legal case*)
concluded complete (*ended*), res judicata, through
concludere conclude (*decide*), infer, lock
concluding dialectic, extreme (*last*), final, last (*final*)
concluding part end (*termination*)
conclusible deductible (*provable*)
conclusio close (*conclusion*), conclusion (*determination*), conclusion (*outcome*), inference
conclusion adjudication, alternative (*option*), amount (*result*), belief (*something believed*), belief (*state of mind*), cessation (*termination*), choice (*decision*), concept, consequence (*conclusion*), conviction (*persuasion*), defeasance, denouement, destination, determination, development (*outgrowth*), diagnosis, discharge (*performance*), disposition (*determination*), dissolution (*termination*), divorce, end (*termination*), expiration, extremity (*death*), finality, finding, generalization, holding (*ruling of a court*), inference, judgment (*discernment*), judgment (*formal court decree*), observation, opinion (*belief*), opinion (*judicial decision*), payoff (*result*), position (*point of view*), result, ruling, verdict
conclusion beforehand predetermination
conclusion drawn from accepted truths hypothesis
conclusion in advance predetermination
conclusion of a proceeding dismissal (*termination of a proceeding*)
conclusion of an action dismissal

(*termination of a proceeding*)
conclusion of the matter holding (*ruling of a court*), opinion (*judicial decision*)
conclusive categorical, certain (*fixed*), certain (*positive*), clear (*certain*), cogent, complete (*ended*), convincing, crucial, decisive, definite, definitive, demonstrable, determinative, extreme (*last*), final, inappealable, incontestable, incontrovertible, last (*final*), official, positive (*incontestable*), reliable, ultimate, unalienable, undeniable, undisputed, unmistakable, valid
conclusive evidence corroboration
conclusive proof certification (*certainness*), corroboration
conclusiveness certainty, certification (*certainness*), certitude, proof
conclusory conclusive (*settled*), decisive, definitive, final, last (*final*), ultimate
concoct conceive (*invent*), contrive, create, feign, forge (*produce*), frame (*construct*), frame (*formulate*), invent (*produce for the first time*), lie (*falsify*), make, maneuver, originate, palter, plan, prearrange, prevaricate, produce (*manufacture*), profess (*pretend*), scheme
concoct a plot conspire
concocted artificial, false (*inaccurate*), fictitious, mendacious
concoction arrangement (*plan*), composition (*makeup*), creation, fiction, figment, formation, invention, myth, story (*falsehood*)
concomitance conjunction
concomitant addendum, appurtenance, coincidental, collateral (*accompanying*), concurrent (*at the same time*), conjoint, consensual, contemporaneous, simultaneous, supplementary
concord accord, accordance (*compact*), affirmance (*judicial sanction*), agree (*comply*), agreement (*concurrence*), arrangement (*understanding*), assent, bargain, cartel, collusion, comity, compact, compatibility, compliance, concert, conciliation, concordance, condonation, conformity (*agreement*), conjunction, connivance, consensus, consent, cooperate, league, pact, partnership, peace, propinquity (*similarity*), protocol (*agreement*), rapport, rapprochement, reciprocity, reconciliation, sodality, synchronism, understanding (*agreement*), union (*unity*)
concord before marriage antenuptial agreement
concordance acceptance, accord, accordance (*compact*), acquiescence, affirmance (*judicial sanction*), agreement (*concurrence*), approval, assent, bargain, cartel, compatibility, concert, consensus, consent, consortium (*marriage companionship*), mutual understanding, pact, peace, rapport, rapprochement, reconciliation, treaty, understanding (*agreement*)
concordancy peace
concordant agreed (*harmonized*), appropriate, commensurable, commensurate, concerted, concurrent (*united*), congruous, consensual, consenting, consistent, consonant, correlative, felici-

tous, fit, harmonious, joint, nonmilitant
concordat agreement (*contract*), bargain, cartel, compact, contract, covenant, league, pact, protocol (*agreement*), settlement, specialty (*contract*), stipulation, treaty
concordia agreement (*contract*), peace
concors concordant, harmonious
concours meeting (*encounter*)
concourse assemblage, assembly, caucus, causeway, coaction, intersection, rendezvous
concredere entrust
concrescence coalescence
concrete actual, appreciable, cement, certain (*positive*), certain (*specific*), cohesive (*compact*), corporeal, distinct (*clear*), material (*physical*), objective, physical, substantial, substantive, tangible
concrete expression embodiment
concrete results action (*performance*)
concreteness congealment, materiality (*physical existence*)
concretion adherence (*adhesion*), adhesion (*affixing*), congealment, corpus, density
concupiscence desire
concupiscent dissolute, lascivious, lecherous, lewd, licentious, prurient, salacious
concur abide, accede (*concede*), acknowledge (*respond*), admit (*concede*), agree (*comply*), assent, certify (*approve*), comply, comport (*agree with*), confirm, conform, consent, conspire, cooperate, correspond (*be equivalent*), grant (*concede*), meet, unite
concur in approve, certify (*approve*), countenance, embrace (*accept*), indorse
concurred in consensual
concurrence accordance (*compact*), accordance (*understanding*), acknowledgment (*acceptance*), acquiescence, adjustment, approval, assent, cartel, charter (*sanction*), coaction, coalescence, coalition, collusion, compatibility, compliance, concert, concession (*compromise*), conciliation, concordance, confederacy (*compact*), conformity (*agreement*), conjunction, connivance, consensus, consent, indorsement, league, leave (*permission*), mutual understanding, permission, rapport, synchronism, synergy, union (*unity*)
concurrence in opinions concordance
concurrency concert
concurrent coextensive, cognate, coincidental, collateral (*accompanying*), collective, commensurable, concerted, concomitant, concordant, congruous, conjoint, consensual, consonant, contemporaneous, corporate (*joint*), correlative, current, joint, mutual (*reciprocal*), simultaneous, synergetic
concurrent effort cooperative
concurrent opinion conformity (*agreement*), conjunction, connivance
concurrere coincide (*correspond*), meet
concurring concerted, concordant, concurrent (*united*), contemporaneous, synergetic
concursio collision (*dispute*)
concursus collision (*dispute*), meeting (*conference*)

concuss beat *(strike)*, necessitate
concussion collision *(accident)*
condemn blame, cavil, censure, charge *(accuse)*, complain *(criticize)*, confiscate, convict, criticize *(find fault with)*, decry, defame, denigrate, discommend, disparage, execute *(sentence to death)*, fault, impeach, incriminate, judge, libel, proscribe *(denounce)*, punish, reprehend, reprimand, reproach, sentence
condemn after judicial investigation convict
condemn as worthless decry
condemn beforehand prejudge
condemn openly denounce *(condemn)*
condemn to death execute *(sentence to death)*
condemn to public use confiscate
condemnable blameful, blameworthy, contemptible, culpable, delinquent *(guilty of a misdeed)*, felonious, guilty, inexcusable, inexpiable, irregular *(improper)*, reprehensible
condemnare condemn *(blame)*, disapprove *(reject)*, sentence
condemnatio condemnation *(blame)*
condemnation aspersion, bad repute, blame *(culpability)*, charge *(accusation)*, confutation, contempt *(disdain)*, conviction *(finding of guilt)*, correction *(punishment)*, count, criticism, denunciation, diatribe, disapprobation, disapproval, discredit, disparagement, expropriation *(right of eminent domain)*, ignominy, impeachment, impugnation, inculpation, judgment *(formal court decree)*, onus *(stigma)*, ostracism, outcry, proscription, rebuff, reprimand, reproach, revilement, sanction *(punishment)*
condemnation for public use expropriation *(right of eminent domain)*
condemnatory blameworthy, calumnious, contemptible, critical *(faultfinding)*, cynical, derogatory, incriminatory, inculpatory, libelous, scandalous, severe
condemned blameful, blameworthy, dilapidated
condemned person convict
condemned prisoner convict
condemning critical *(faultfinding)*, incriminatory, inculpatory
condensation abstract, adhesion *(affixing)*, brief, capsule, centralization, compendium, congealment, curtailment, digest, hornbook, outline *(synopsis)*, paraphrase, restatement, scenario, synopsis
condense abridge *(shorten)*, abstract *(summarize)*, concentrate *(consolidate)*, consolidate *(strengthen)*, constrict *(compress)*, crystallize, decrease, digest *(summarize)*, discount *(minimize)*, distill, draw *(extract)*, lessen, reduce
condensed brief, compact *(dense)*, compact *(pithy)*, concise, laconic, pithy, sententious, solid *(compact)*, succinct
condere garner, keep *(shelter)*
condescend deign, vouchsafe
condescend to grant vouchsafe
condescending disdainful, inflated *(vain)*, orgulous, proud *(conceited)*, supercilious

condescension disrespect, pride
condicio article *(precept)*, condition *(contingent provision)*, condition *(state)*, contract, overture, posture *(situation)*, proposition, provision *(clause)*, qualification *(condition)*, stipulation, term *(provision)*
condicio mortalis mortality
condign appropriate, due *(owed)*, just, proper, suitable
condire preserve
condisciple disciple
condition aspect, attornment, case *(set of circumstances)*, clause, climate, discipline *(train)*, disease, disorder *(abnormal condition)*, frame *(mood)*, health, inure *(accustom)*, limitation, modify *(moderate)*, plight, position *(situation)*, posture *(situation)*, practice *(train by repetition)*, predicament, prerequisite, provision *(clause)*, quality *(grade)*, repair, reservation *(condition)*, restriction, salvo, sine qua non, situation, specification, status, stipulation, term *(provision)*, ultimatum
condition of a married woman coverture
condition of infamy disgrace
condition of insufficiency emergency
conditional circumstantial, dependent, doubtful, dubious, provisional, qualified *(conditioned)*, restrictive, tentative, terminable
conditional conveyance of land mortgage
conditional deed held in trust escrow
conditional deliverance parole
conditional discharge parole
conditional disenthrallment parole
conditional disimprisonment parole
conditional emancipation parole
conditional endorsement without recourse
conditional event contingency
conditional freedom parole
conditional freedom from confinement parole
conditional independence parole
conditional instrument escrow
conditional liberation parole
conditional liberty parole
conditional property transfer mortgage
conditional release parole
conditional reprieve parole
conditional suspension of sentence probation
conditionally release parole
conditionally release from imprisonment parole
conditioned accustomed *(familiarized)*, conditional, contingent, controlled *(restrained)*, dependent
conditioning discipline *(training)*, habituation, propaganda
conditions circumstances
conditiosine qua non clause
conditus savory
condole sympathize
condolement pity
condolence pity, solace
condolent benevolent
condonable blameless, defensible, justifiable, palliative *(excusing)*, par-

donable, unobjectionable
condonare forgive, overlook *(superintend)*, remit *(relax)*
condonation amnesty, impunity, lenience, remission, understanding *(tolerance)*
condone bear *(tolerate)*, concur *(agree)*, excuse, extenuate, forgive, justify, overlook *(excuse)*, palliate *(excuse)*, pardon, remit *(release from penalty)*
condoned clear *(free from criminal charges)*
condoning charitable *(lenient)*, lenient, palliative *(excusing)*
conduce affect, avail *(bring about)*, contribute *(assist)*, generate, induce, redound
conduce to cause
conducere conduce, engage *(hire)*, hire, rent
conducive ancillary *(auxiliary)*, beneficial, contributory, convenient, favorable *(advantageous)*, instrumental, practical, propitious
conduct administration, agency *(legal relationship)*, behavior, comport *(behave)*, control *(regulate)*, course, decorum, demean *(deport oneself)*, demeanor, deportment, direct *(show)*, direct *(supervise)*, direction *(guidance)*, discipline *(training)*, ethics, exercise *(discharge a function)*, govern, handle *(manage)*, manage, management *(judicious use)*, manipulate *(utilize skillfully)*, manner *(behavior)*, modus operandi, officiate, operate, orchestrate, overlook *(superintend)*, oversee, practice *(procedure)*, prescribe, presence *(poise)*, procedure, process *(course)*, prosecute *(carry forward)*, protect, pursue *(carry on)*, regulate *(manage)*, regulation *(management)*, render *(administer)*, rule *(govern)*, transact, transmit, transport, usage
conduct a search frisk, hunt
conduct a trial hear *(give a legal hearing)*
conduct an inquiry analyze, audit, canvass, delve, investigate, monitor, probe
conduct business handle *(trade)*
conduct dishonestly mishandle *(mismanage)*
conduct involving graft corruption
conduct of a lawsuit proceeding
conduct of affairs agency *(legal relationship)*
conduct research inquire
conduct research on examine *(study)*, peruse, poll, probe
conduct without efficiency mishandle *(mismanage)*
conduct without honesty mishandle *(mismanage)*
conductio contract, lease
conductive causal
conductor chairman, guardian
conductor lessee
conductor procurator
conductor tenant
conductus mercenary
conduit dealer, outlet
conectere join *(bring together)*
confabulate communicate, converse, discourse, discuss
confabulation conference, conversa-

tion, speech

confectio consumption

confederacy affiliation *(amalgamation)*, association *(alliance)*, cabal, chamber *(body)*, coaction, coalescence, collusion, committee, company *(enterprise)*, connivance, consortium *(business cartel)*, conspiracy, corporation, federation, league, partnership, pool, relationship *(connection)*, society, sodality, union *(labor organization)*

confederate abettor, accessory, accomplice, affiliate, allied, assistant, associate, coactor, coadjutant, coconspirator, cohort, colleague, collective, combine *(act in concert)*, conjoint, consociate, consolidate *(unite)*, conspirator, conspire, conspirer, contributor *(contributor)*, cooperate, copartner *(coconspirator)*, desegregate, federal, federalize *(associate)*, federate, involve *(participate)*, join *(associate oneself with)*, joint, member *(individual in a group)*, organize *(unionize)*, participant, participate, partisan, partner, pool, unite

confederate for an unlawful purpose conspire

confederated affiliated, associated, concurrent *(united)*, conjoint, mutual *(collective)*

confederation affiliation *(amalgamation)*, association *(alliance)*, band, cartel, chamber *(body)*, coalescence, committee, concert, confederacy *(compact)*, consolidation, contribution *(participation)*, federation, integration *(amalgamation)*, integration *(assimilation)*, league, merger, partnership, party *(political organization)*, pool, society, sodality

confer administer *(tender)*, attorn, bear *(yield)*, bestow, cede, consider, consult *(ask advice of)*, contribute *(supply)*, counsel, dedicate, devise *(give)*, discourse, discuss, dispense, enable, endue, give *(grant)*, grant *(transfer formally)*, impart, leave *(give)*, present *(make a gift)*, provide *(supply)*, render *(deliver)*, transfer, treat *(process)*, vest

confer a benefit serve *(assist)*

confer a benefit on avail *(be of use)*, profit

confer a corporate franchise upon incorporate *(form a corporation)*

confer a privilege authorize, bestow, grant *(concede)*, permit, sanction

confer a right authorize, qualify *(meet standards)*, sanction

confer a trust commit *(entrust)*

confer again recover

confer an honor elevate

confer by will demise

confer corporate status upon incorporate *(form a corporation)*

confer distinction bestow

confer distinction on honor

confer formally deliberate, grant *(transfer formally)*

confer honor on dedicate

confer on price dicker

confer ownership attorn, devolve, grant *(transfer formally)*, pass *(advance)*

confer ownership on oneself impropriate

confer power invest *(vest)*

confer power on charge *(empower)*, delegate, empower

confer privileges of a native citizen naturalize *(make a citizen)*

confer rights of citizenship naturalize *(make a citizen)*

confer with advise, converse, debate, discuss

conference assembly, caucus, collective bargaining, communication *(discourse)*, company *(assemblage)*, confrontation *(act of setting face to face)*, congregation, council *(assembly)*, discourse, inquiry *(systematic investigation)*, interview, negotiation, panel *(discussion group)*, parlance, parley, session

conferment alienation *(transfer of title)*, assignment *(transfer of ownership)*, bounty, concession *(authorization)*, contribution *(donation)*, conveyance, demise *(conveyance)*, deputation *(selection of delegates)*, dispensation *(act of dispensing)*, legacy

conferment between the living inter vivos

conferral alienation *(transfer of title)*, assignment *(transfer of ownership)*, concession *(authorization)*, demise *(conveyance)*, dispensation *(act of dispensing)*

conferral of a fee feoffment

conferre bestow, collect *(gather)*, compare, confer *(give)*, contribution *(donation)*, converse

conferrer donor, grantor

conferring donative

conferment of title feoffment

confess acknowledge *(verify)*, admit *(concede)*, avow, bare, betray *(disclose)*, certify *(attest)*, disclose, inform *(betray)*, recognize *(acknowledge)*, reveal

confessed judgment cognovit

confessedly admittedly

confessing repentant

confessio acknowledgment *(avowal)*, avowal

confession acknowledgment *(avowal)*, admission *(disclosure)*, avowal, disclosure *(act of disclosing)*, disclosure *(something disclosed)*, profession *(declaration)*

confessor penitent

conficere conclude *(complete)*, consummate, dispatch *(dispose of)*, exhaust *(deplete)*, finish, kill *(defeat)*, kill *(murder)*, settle

confidant confederate, consociate

confidante associate

confide commit *(entrust)*, convey *(communicate)*, delegate, divulge, impart, inform *(notify)*, notify, rely, reveal, trust

confide for care delegate

confide for use delegate

confide in confer *(consult)*

confide to mention

confidence assurance, belief *(state of mind)*, certification *(certainness)*, certitude, credence, credit *(delayed payment)*, faith, prospect *(outlook)*, reliance, secret, weight *(credibility)*

confidence in one's powers audacity

confidence trick bunko

confident assertive, categorical, certain *(fixed)*, certain *(positive)*, definite, dogmatic, indubious, sanguine

confident expectation likelihood, trust *(confidence)*

confidential clandestine, close *(intimate)*, collusive, esoteric, fiduciary, intimate, personal *(private)*, privy, secret

confidential communication confidence *(relation of trust)*, secret

confidential information tip *(clue)*

confidential matter confidence *(relation of trust)*, secret

confidentiality privacy

confidentialness privacy

confidentness assurance, certainty, certitude, confidence *(faith)*

confidere rely, trust

confiding intimate

configuration boundary, construction, content *(structure)*, contour *(outline)*, contour *(shape)*, delineation, formation, organization *(structure)*, structure *(composition)*

configurattion dimension

confine apprehend *(arrest)*, arrest *(apprehend)*, bind *(restrain)*, border, border *(bound)*, boundary, capture, circumscribe *(surround by boundary)*, close *(enclosed area)*, commit *(institutionalize)*, conceal, constrain *(imprison)*, contain *(enclose)*, contain *(restrain)*, control *(restrain)*, debar, delimit, demarcate, detain *(hold in custody)*, detain *(restrain)*, enclose, enclosure, envelop, fetter, hamper, immure, impede, imprison, isolate, jail, keep *(restrain)*, limit, lock, mete, outline *(boundary)*, periphery, purview, qualify *(condition)*, restrain, restrict, retrench, seclude, sequester *(seclude)*, trammel

confine forcibly constrain *(imprison)*

confined arrested *(apprehended)*, in custody, insular, limited, narrow, partial *(part)*, private *(not public)*

confined individual prisoner

confined room cell

confined to a select circle esoteric

confinement apprehension *(act of arresting)*, arrest, blockade *(limitation)*, bondage, boundary, cache *(hiding place)*, captivity, cell, concealment, constraint *(imprisonment)*, custody *(incarceration)*, detention, durance, duress, enclosure, fetter, incarceration, quarantine, restraint, restriction, thrall

confinement by public authority incarceration

confinement in a jail incarceration

confinement in a penitentiary incarceration

confinement under legal process incarceration

confinements confines

confines area *(province)*, barrier, circuit, edge *(border)*, region, scope, vicinity

confining binding, commitment *(confinement)*, limited, limiting, oppressive

confinis contiguous

confinium frontier

confirm accept *(admit as sufficient)*, accept *(assent)*, accredit, acknowledge *(verify)*, admit *(concede)*, affirm *(uphold)*, agree *(comply)*, appoint, approve, ascertain, assent, assure *(insure)*, attest, authorize, avouch *(avow)*, avow, bind *(obligate)*, bond *(secure a debt)*, certify *(approve)*, certify *(attest)*, corroborate, cosign, countenance, countersign, demonstrate *(establish)*, determine, document, endorse, ensure, establish *(show)*, evidence, fix *(make firm)*, indorse, legalize, notarize, pass *(approve)*, prove, reaffirm, reassure, reveal, seal *(solemnize)*, sign, subscribe *(sign)*, substantiate, support *(corroborate)*, swear, uphold, validate, vouch, witness *(attest to)*

confirm as correct certify *(attest)*

confirm by law legalize

confirm by oath avouch *(avow)*

confirm in conviction assure *(give confidence to)*

confirm officially authorize, certify *(approve)*, indorse, notarize

confirm the validity of a will probate

confirmable ascertainable, convincing, provable

confirmare affirm *(uphold)*, assert, certify *(attest)*, contend *(maintain)*, enforce, establish *(entrench)*, instate, maintain *(carry on)*, reassure, reinforce, sanction, verify *(confirm)*

confirmatio assurance, indorsement, sanction *(permission)*

confirmation acknowledgment *(avowal)*, admittance *(acceptance)*, affirmance *(authentication)*, affirmation, approval, assent, asseveration, averment, avowal, certification *(attested copy)*, certification *(certification of proficiency)*, charter *(sanction)*, collation, confession, consent, contract, corroboration, disclosure *(something disclosed)*, document, documentation, evidence, indorsement, jurat, legalization, license, permit, proof, ratification, reference *(recommendation)*, subscription, support *(corroboration)*, surety *(certainty)*

confirmation under oath affidavit

confirmative affirmative, definitive, demonstrative *(illustrative)*

confirmatory affirmative, convincing, demonstrative *(illustrative)*

confirmed accustomed *(customary)*, agreed *(promised)*, arrant *(definite)*, certain *(fixed)*, chronic, customary, firm, formal, habitual, immutable, indefeasible, ingrained, inveterate, permanent, traditional, valid

confirmed habit habituation, practice *(custom)*

confirmed judgment cognovit

confirmed opposition dissent *(difference of opinion)*

confirmed way habit

confirmer surety *(guarantor)*

confirming conclusive *(settled)*, consensual, convincing, demonstrative *(illustrative)*

confirmist affirmant

confiscate annex *(arrogate)*, assume *(seize)*, attach *(seize)*, condemn *(seize)*, deprive, distrain, divest, garnish, impound, levy, penalize, remove *(eliminate)*, sequester *(seize property)*

confiscated attached *(seized)*, lost *(taken away)*

confiscated goods contraband

confiscated property contraband

confiscation appropriation *(taking)*,

attachment *(seizure)*, condemnation *(seizure)*, disseisin, distraint, distress *(seizure)*, escheatment, expropriation *(divestiture)*, foreclosure, forfeiture *(act of forfeiting)*, garnishment, levy, privation, sequestration, taking

confiteri avow, confess

confixation attachment *(act of affixing)*

conflagrate burn, deflagrate

conflate amalgamate

conflation merger

conflict affray, altercation, antipode, antithesis, argument *(contention)*, belligerency, bicker, collision *(dispute)*, commotion, competition, confrontation *(altercation)*, contend *(dispute)*, contention *(argument)*, contention *(opposition)*, contest, contradict, contradiction, contrary, contravention, controversy *(argument)*, disaccord, disaccord, disagree, disagreement, discord, discrepancy, dispute, dispute *(contest)*, dissension, dissent *(difference of opinion)*, dissent *(differ in opinion)*, dissidence, embroilment, estrangement, feud, fight *(argument)*, fracas, ill will, impugnation, incompatibility *(difference)*, incompatibility *(inconsistency)*, opposition, oppugn, outbreak, reaction *(opposition)*, rebut, strife, struggle

conflict of interest disagreement

conflict of opinion conflict, controversy *(argument)*, difference, disaccord, disagreement, disparity, dispute, dissension, dissent *(difference of opinion)*

conflict with antagonize, collide *(clash)*, contravene, counter, counteract, countervail, cross *(disagree with)*, defy, deviate, differ *(disagree)*, disaffirm, gainsay

conflicting adverse *(opposite)*, antipathetic *(oppositional)*, competitive *(antagonistic)*, contradictory, contrary, discordant, disparate, disproportionate, dissenting, hostile, incongruous, inconsistent, litigious, negative, opposite, polemic, renitent, repugnant *(incompatible)*, unsuitable

conflicting evidence contradiction

conflictive adverse *(opposite)*, dissenting

conflictory discordant, dissenting

confligere collide *(crash against)*

confluence assemblage, coalescence, coalition, company *(assemblage)*, corpus, crossroad *(intersection)*, rendezvous

confluent coadunate

confluere meet

conflux assemblage, chamber *(body)*, collection *(assembly)*, company *(assemblage)*

confodere pierce *(lance)*

conform abide, accede *(concede)*, adapt, adhere *(maintain loyalty)*, adjust *(resolve)*, cohere *(be logically consistent)*, comport *(agree with)*, copy, correspond *(be equivalent)*, obey, observe *(obey)*

conform to adopt, assent, coincide *(concur)*, coincide *(correspond)*, comply, defer *(yield in judgment)*, keep *(fulfill)*, pass *(satisfy requirements)*, satisfy *(fulfill)*

conform with concur *(agree)*

conformability amenability, compli-

ance, conciliation, identity *(similarity)*

conformable appropriate, commensurable, concerted, concordant, congruous, consistent, consonant, conventional, correlative, faithful *(true to fact)*, felicitous, fit, malleable, obedient, orthodox, passive, pliable, pliant, prevailing *(current)*, prevalent, regular *(conventional)*, similar, suitable, tractable, traditional, typical, uniform, usual

conformable to fact real

conformable to law lawful

conformable to rule typical

conformable with the law juridical, lawful

conformance accordance *(understanding)*, adjustment, agreement *(concurrence)*, compliance, concordance, conduct, conformity *(agreement)*, conformity *(obedience)*, consensus, resemblance

conformant relevant

conformare form

conformatio formation

conformation adjustment, arrangement *(ordering)*, building *(business of assembling)*, composition *(makeup)*, configuration *(form)*, conformity *(agreement)*, conformity *(obedience)*, consensus, construction, content *(structure)*, contour *(shape)*, dimension, formation, organization *(structure)*

conforming agreed *(harmonized)*, concerted, concordant, concurrent *(united)*, congruous, consonant, conventional, harmonious, law-abiding, malleable, normal *(regular)*, obedient, orthodox, pliable, pliant, relevant, usual

conforming to consensual, pursuant to

conforming to accepted standards conventional

conforming to moral standards ethical

conforming to professional conduct ethical

conformist philistine

conformity accordance *(understanding)*, adjustment, compatibility, compliance, conciliation, concordance, conjunction, consensus, constant, correspondence *(similarity)*, decorum, propriety *(appropriateness)*, regularity, resemblance, synchronism, uniformity

conformity to fact truth, veracity

conformity to law legality, legitimacy

conformity with the law legality

confound confuse *(bewilder)*, defeat, discompose, disconcert, dislocate, disorganize, disorient, disturb, fight *(counteract)*, foil, frustrate, harass, misdirect, mismanage, muddle, negate, obfuscate, overcome *(overwhelm)*, overwhelm, perplex, perturb, repel *(drive back)*, subvert

confounded heinous, nefarious, odious

confounded meaning ambiguity

confounding enigmatic, labyrinthine

confoundment confusion *(ambiguity)*, dilemma, quandary

confraternity confederacy *(compact)*, society, sodality

confrère accessory, accomplice, assistant

confrere associate
confrère colleague
confrere confederate, consociate
confrère consort
confrere contributor *(contributor)*
confrère copartner *(business associate)*, copartner *(coconspirator)*
confront accost, approach, challenge, collide *(clash)*, contrast, cross *(disagree with)*, defy, fight *(battle)*, grapple, oppose, oppugn, repel *(drive back)*, resist *(oppose)*, withstand
confrontation contraposition, contravention, disaccord, experience *(encounter)*, fight *(argument)*, impugnation, meeting *(encounter)*, resistance, struggle
confrontment confrontation *(altercation)*, contraposition
confugere recourse
confundere confound, confuse *(bewilder)*, disorganize, muddle
confuse circumvent, confound, discompose, disconcert, dislocate, disorganize, disrupt, disturb, embarrass, misapprehend, misconstrue, misdirect, misinterpret, misread, mistake, misunderstand, muddle, obfuscate, overwhelm, perplex, perturb, upset
confused ambiguous, complex, deranged, disjointed, disordered, disorderly, haphazard, inextricable, lost *(disoriented)*, nebulous, opaque, promiscuous, unclear, vague
confused language jargon *(unintelligible language)*
confused mass melange
confused meaning ambiguity
confused talk jargon *(unintelligible language)*
confusedness confusion *(ambiguity)*, entanglement *(confusion)*, pandemonium, panic, quandary
confusing dubious, enigmatic, equivocal, indefinable, labyrinthine, opaque
confusing situation imbroglio
confusing statement enigma
confusio confusion *(turmoil)*
confusion ambiguity, anarchy, commotion, complex *(entanglement)*, complication, dilemma, disorder *(lack of order)*, disturbance, doubt *(indecision)*, embarrassment, embroilment, enigma, havoc, imbroglio, involution, irregularity, jargon *(unintelligible language)*, misrule, opacity, pandemonium, panic, quandary, riot, shambles, snarl, turmoil
confutable contestable, controversial, debatable, defeasible, disputable, dubious, litigable
confutation answer *(judicial response)*, bad repute, contradiction, counterargument, defeat, defense, demurrer, denial, disparagement, negation, opposition, repudiation
confutative contradictory, contrary, negative
confute answer *(reply)*, argue, challenge, contradict, controvert, counter, counteract, countercharge, countervail, cross *(disagree with)*, debate, disagree, disapprove *(reject)*, disown *(deny the validity)*, disprove, dispute *(contest)*, dispute *(debate)*, dissent *(differ in opinion)*, fight *(counteract)*, impeach, im-

pugn, invalidate, negate, oppose, parry, rebut, refute, reply
confuting contradictory, contrary
congé dispensation *(exception)*
congeal cement, cohere *(adhere)*, consolidate *(strengthen)*, consolidate *(unite)*
congealed coherent *(joined)*, ossified, solid *(compact)*
congelation adhesion *(affixing)*, congealment
congener complement, correlate, counterpart *(complement)*
congeneric apposite, cognate, comparable *(capable of comparison)*, correlative, identical, pendent, related, similar
congenerical pendent, related, similar
congenerous apposite, cognate, consanguineous, correlative, identical, pendent, related
congenial apposite, cognate, consonant, harmonious, informal, palatable, suitable
congeniality compatibility, concordance, conformity *(agreement)*, propinquity *(similarity)*
congenital born *(innate)*, genetic, hereditary, innate, native *(inborn)*
congerere collect *(gather)*
congeries agglomeration, assemblage, body *(collection)*, entirety
congest concentrate *(consolidate)*, obstruct, overload
congestion confusion *(turmoil)*, obstruction, plethora
congestus collection *(accumulation)*
congiarium largess *(generosity)*
conglomerate agglomeration, aggregate, assemblage, coadunate, coalition, coherent *(joined)*, collect *(gather)*, collection *(accumulation)*, combine *(join together)*, commingle, compile, complex *(development)*, composite, compound, concentrate *(consolidate)*, congregate, consolidate *(unite)*, corporation, corpus, crystallize, cumulation, desegregate, join *(bring together)*, merge, unite
conglomeratic coadunate, coherent *(joined)*
conglomeration adhesion *(affixing)*, agglomeration, aggregate, arsenal, assemblage, body *(collection)*, centralization, coalescence, collection *(accumulation)*, compilation, complex *(development)*, cumulation, melange, selection *(collection)*
conglutemate bond *(hold together)*
conglutinare cement
conglutinate cement, combine *(join together)*, join *(bring together)*
conglutination adherence *(adhesion)*, adhesion *(affixing)*, coalescence
conglutinative cohesive *(sticking)*
congratulate honor
congregari congregate
congregate collective, concentrate *(consolidate)*, conglomerate, convene, converge, meet, rendezvous, unite
congregated coadunate, compound, conglomerate
congregated body congregation
congregatio union *(unity)*
congregation assemblage, assembly, band, centralization, collection *(assembly)*, combination, committee, company *(assemblage)*, cumulation, mass *(body*

of persons), rendezvous, session
congregational collective
congregative collective
congress assemblage, chamber *(body)*, coalition, company *(assemblage)*, government *(political administration)*, legislature, parley, rendezvous, session
congressio interview, meeting *(conference)*
congressional legislative
congressman lawmaker, legislator
congresswoman lawmaker
congruence adjustment, agreement *(concurrence)*, coherence, concordance, conformity *(agreement)*, consensus, correspondence *(similarity)*, relevance, understanding *(agreement)*
congruency agreement *(concurrence)*, concordance, conformity *(agreement)*, relevance
congruens appropriate, coherent *(clear)*, coherent *(joined)*, consonant, harmonious
congruent coequal, coextensive, commensurate, concerted, concordant, congruous, conjoint, consensual, consonant, correlative, germane, harmonious, relevant, similar, suitable
congruent with consistent
congruentia correspondence *(similarity)*
congruere agree *(comply)*, coincide *(correspond)*, correspond *(be equivalent)*, sympathize
congruity adjustment, agreement *(concurrence)*, analogy, coherence, compatibility, conformity *(agreement)*, consortium *(marriage companionship)*, correspondence *(similarity)*, propriety *(appropriateness)*, rapport, regularity, relevance
congruous appropriate, commensurable, commensurate, concerted, concordant, consistent, consonant, correlative, felicitous, fit, germane, harmonious, relevant, suitable
congruousness compatibility, consortium *(marriage companionship)*
conicere cast *(throw)*, interpret
coniectio discharge *(shot)*
coniectura hypothesis, inference, presumption, speculation *(conjecture)*, supposition
coniecturalis speculative
coniectus discharge *(shot)*
coniugalis conjugal
coniugium marriage *(wedlock)*
coniunctio affinity *(family ties)*, combination, incorporation *(formation of a business entity)*, relationship *(connection)*
coniunctus intimate
coniungere combine *(join together)*, join *(bring together)*, unite
coniunx spouse
coniurare conspire, plot
coniuratio confederacy *(conspiracy)*, conspiracy, plot *(secret plan)*
coniuratus conspirator
conjacent cohesive *(compact)*
conjecturable colorable *(plausible)*, debatable, ostensible, plausible, presumptive
conjectural apparent *(presumptive)*, circumstantial, debatable, disputable,

doubtful, enigmatic, hypothetical, presumptive, speculative, theoretical, uncertain *(questionable)*, unsettled

conjecture anticipate *(prognosticate)*, assume *(suppose)*, assumption *(supposition)*, concept, deduce, deduct *(conclude by reasoning)*, estimate *(idea)*, estimate, estimation *(calculation)*, expect *(consider probable)*, guess, hypothesis, idea, infer, inference, opine, opinion *(belief)*, postulate, postulate, presume, presumption, presuppose, prognosis, prognosticate, proposition, supposition, surmise, suspect *(think)*, suspicion *(uncertainty)*, theory, thesis, understand

conjectured assumed *(inferred)*, presumptive, putative

conjoin abut, adjoin, affix, annex *(add)*, append, attach *(join)*, border *(bound)*, cement, cohere *(adhere)*, combine *(join together)*, commingle, concentrate *(consolidate)*, connect *(join together)*, consolidate *(strengthen)*, consolidate *(unite)*, conspire, contact *(touch)*, cooperate, correspond *(be equivalent)*, desegregate, federate, join *(bring together)*, merge, pool, unite

conjoined attached *(annexed)*, coadunate, coherent *(joined)*, collateral *(accompanying)*, concerted, concordant, concurrent *(united)*, promiscuous

conjoiner adjoiner

conjoining accession *(annexation)*, coalition, conjunction, contiguous, immediate *(not distant)*

conjoint associated, coadunate, common *(shared)*, composite, compound, concerted, concomitant, consolidate *(strengthen)*, corporate *(joint)*, correlative, joint, mutual *(collective)*

conjugal nuptial

conjugal bliss cohabitation *(married state)*

conjugal partner consort

conjugal union marriage *(wedlock)*

conjugality cohabitation *(married state)*, coverture, marriage *(wedlock)*, matrimony

conjugate coadunate, cohabit, compound, interrelated, joint

conjugation coalescence, combination, joinder

conjunct associated, coadunate, coherent *(joined)*, cohesive *(compact)*, composite, compound, concerted, conjoint, consensual, contiguous, corporate *(joint)*, correlative, inextricable, joint

conjunctio coalition

conjunction adhesion *(affixing)*, affiliation *(connectedness)*, association *(connection)*, attachment *(act of affixing)*, building *(business of assembling)*, cartel, chain *(nexus)*, coalescence, coalition, coherence, collusion, combination, concert, concordance, conformity *(agreement)*, connection *(fastening)*, connivance, consolidation, contact *(association)*, intersection, joinder, league, partnership

conjunctional coincidental, concomitant, concordant

conjunctive composite, concomitant, concurrent *(at the same time)*, conjoint, correlative

conjuncture case *(set of circumstances)*, coalition, consolidation, cross-

road *(intersection)*, crossroad *(turning point)*, occasion, point *(period of time)*, posture *(situation)*, predicament

conjure invoke

conjure up conceive *(comprehend)*, occur *(come to mind)*, recall *(remember)*, recollect, remember

conjuring illusory, prestidigitation

conlatio collation, comparison

conlectio restatement

conlega colleague

conlegium association *(alliance)*, association *(connection)*, board, corporation, facility *(institution)*, foundation *(organization)*, institute

conlidere strike *(collide)*

conligere argue, concentrate *(consolidate)*, conclude *(decide)*, hoard, infer, raise *(collect)*

conlocatio arrangement *(ordering)*, disposition *(final arrangement)*

conlocatus situated

conlocutio discourse

conloqui discourse, parley

conloquium conversation, discourse, interview, negotiation

conlusio collusion

connatal hereditary

connate akin *(related by blood)*, associated, born *(innate)*, correlative, hereditary, inherent, native *(inborn)*, natural, related

connation degree *(kinship)*, relation *(connection)*

connatural apposite, born *(innate)*, consanguineous, correlative, interrelated, native *(inborn)*, pendent, related, similar

connaturalness relation *(connection)*

connect abut, adjoin, affiliate, affix, annex *(add)*, append, attach *(join)*, bond *(hold together)*, border *(bound)*, cement, combine *(join together)*, commingle, conjoin, consolidate *(strengthen)*, consolidate *(unite)*, contact *(touch)*, desegregate, engage *(involve)*, implicate, involve *(implicate)*, involve *(participate)*, join *(bring together)*, juxtapose, lock, pool, refer *(direct attention)*, relate *(establish a connection)*, unite

connect with ascribe, attribute

connect with a crime incriminate

connected affiliated, akin *(germane)*, allied, apposite, appurtenant, associated, attached *(annexed)*, coadunate, cognate, coherent *(joined)*, cohesive *(sticking)*, collateral *(accompanying)*, composite, compound, concurrent *(united)*, conjoint, consecutive, contiguous, correlative, direct *(uninterrupted)*, germane, incident, inextricable, interested, interrelated, pertinent, proximate, related, relative *(relevant)*, relevant, tangential

connected series chain *(series)*

connected with comparative

connectedness adherence *(adhesion)*, association *(connection)*, chain *(nexus)*, coherence, continuity

connectere connect *(join together)*

connecting proximate, reference *(citation)*

connecting link chain *(nexus)*, go-between, intermediary, nexus, relationship *(connection)*

connecting medium chain *(nexus)*, privity

connection adhesion *(affixing)*, adjoiner, affiliation *(connectedness)*, affinity *(family ties)*, ancestry, attachment *(act of affixing)*, attribution, chain *(nexus)*, coalescence, coalition, coherence, conjunction, contact *(association)*, contact *(touching)*, context, continuity, degree *(kinship)*, go-between, implication *(incriminating involvement)*, intermediary, intersection, joinder, kinship, liaison, nexus, partnership, privity, propinquity *(kinship)*, relative, relevance, union *(unity)*

connections ties

connective concerted, contact *(touching)*, correlative, interlocking, nexus, relative *(relevant)*

connexion relation *(connection)*

connivance artifice, bad faith, bribery, cabal, collusion, confederacy *(conspiracy)*, conspiracy, contrivance

connivant collusive

connive conspire, contrive, cooperate, maneuver, pettifog, plan, plot, scheme

conniver conspirator

conniving collusive, concerted, dishonest, fraudulent, insidious, machiavellian, perfidious, recreant, sly, surreptitious, tortuous *(bending)*, unconscionable, untrustworthy

connoisseur expert, specialist

connote signify *(denote)*

connotation context, gist *(substance)*, hint, implication *(inference)*, import, indication, innuendo, meaning, reference *(allusion)*, signification, symbol

connotative allusive, demonstrative *(illustrative)*, representative, suggestive *(evocative)*

connote allude, bespeak, construe *(translate)*, depict, exemplify, hint, imply, indicate, purport, refer *(direct attention)*, represent *(portray)*, signify *(denote)*

connoted assumed *(inferred)*, constructive *(inferential)*, implied, tacit

connubial conjugal, nuptial

connubiality cohabitation *(married state)*, marriage *(wedlock)*, matrimony

conprehensible ascertainable

conquer beat *(defeat)*, defeat, demean *(make lower)*, occupy *(take possession)*, overcome *(surmount)*, overthrow, overturn, overwhelm, pass *(satisfy requirements)*, prevail *(triumph)*, subdue, subject, subjugate, succeed *(attain)*, surmount, upset

conquerable facile, helpless *(defenseless)*, indefensible, penetrable

conqueri de rem complain *(criticize)*

conquering confiscatory, prevailing *(having superior force)*

conquest subjection

conquirere hoard

consanguine akin *(related by blood)*, cognate, consanguineous, related

consanguineal relations next of kin

consanguinean akin *(related by blood)*

consanguinei kindred

consanguineous akin *(related by blood)*, cognate, interrelated, related

consanguineus akin *(related by blood)*

consanguinitas affinity *(family ties)*

consanguinity affiliation *(bloodline)*, affinity *(family ties)*, ancestry, blood, connection *(relation)*, contact *(association)*, degree *(kinship)*, family *(common ancestry)*, kinship, propinquity *(kinship)*, relation *(kinship)*, relationship *(family tie)*

conscendere embark

conscience commitment *(responsibility)*, probity, remorse

conscience money reparation *(indemnification)*

conscience-smitten contrite, penitent, remorseful, repentant

conscience-smitten person penitent

conscience-stricken contrite, penitent, remorseful, repentant

conscience-stricken person penitent

conscienceless brazen, delinquent *(guilty of a misdeed)*, diabolic, dishonest, disingenuous, disreputable, immoral, machiavellian, sinister, unconscionable, unscrupulous

conscientia conscience

conscientia mala remorse

conscientious accurate, circumspect, close *(rigorous)*, dependable, diligent, earnest, faithful *(diligent)*, high-minded, honest, loyal, meritorious, meticulous, moral, painstaking, particular *(exacting)*, punctilious, punctual, reliable, reputable, sedulous, strict, true *(loyal)*, upright

conscientiously faithfully

conscientiousness adhesion *(loyalty)*, caution *(vigilance)*, conscience, fidelity, honesty, interest *(concern)*, particularity, rectitude, responsibility *(conscience)*, rigor

conscionable reasonable *(fair)*

conscious circumspect, cognizant, deliberate, express, familiar *(informed)*, intentional, knowing, perceptive, premeditated, receptive, sensible, sensitive *(discerning)*, willful

conscious of acquainted

conscious purpose deliberation

conscious violation of law malice

consciously purposely

consciousness appreciation *(perception)*, cognition, comprehension, impression, insight, knowledge *(awareness)*, perception, realization, recognition, recollection, scienter, sense *(feeling)*, sensibility

conscius accessory, accomplice, cognizant, conscious *(aware)*

conscribere recruit

conscript bind *(obligate)*, coerce, impose *(enforce)*, induct, levy, recruit

conscription requirement

consecrare dedicate, devote

consecrate dedicate, devote, elevate, honor

consecrated inviolate, sacrosanct

consecration adhesion *(loyalty)*, dedication, elevation, remembrance *(commemoration)*

consectari hunt, pursue *(chase)*, pursue *(strive to gain)*

consectatio pursuit *(chase)*, pursuit *(effort to secure)*

consecutio consequence *(conclusion)*, effect

consecution chain *(series)*, continuity, cycle, sequence, serial, succession

consecutive continuous, direct *(uninterrupted)*, progressive *(going forward)*, successive

consecutive order succession

consecutiveness continuity

consensual concerted, concordant, congruous, contractual

consensus accordance *(understanding)*, concordance, conformity *(agreement)*

consensus consent

consensus poll *(casting of votes)*, union *(unity)*

consensus omnium compatibility

consent accede *(concede)*, acceptance, acquiescence, advocate, agree *(comply)*, agree *(contract)*, agreement *(concurrence)*, allow *(endure)*, approval, assent, assent, bestow, capacity *(authority)*, capitulation, certify *(approve)*, charter *(sanction)*, close *(agree)*, coincide *(concur)*, compatibility, compliance, concede, concordance, concur *(agree)*, confirm, conformity *(agreement)*, conformity *(obedience)*, contribution *(participation)*, defer *(yield in judgment)*, dispensation *(exception)*, enable, franchise *(license)*, grant *(concede)*, indorsement, leave *(permission)*, let *(permit)*, license, obey, option *(contractual provision)*, pass *(approve)*, permission, permit, promise, promise *(vow)*, ratification, recognize *(acknowledge)*, sanction *(permission)*, subscribe *(promise)*, subscription, suffer *(permit)*, tolerate, vouchsafe, yield *(submit)*

consent to approve, authorize, comply, countenance, embrace *(accept)*, indorse, sanction, sustain *(confirm)*

consent to support underwrite

consentaneity agreement *(concurrence)*, assent, compatibility, concert, concordance, consensus, pact, peace, understanding *(agreement)*

consentaneous concerted, concordant, concurrent *(united)*, congruous, consensual, consenting, consonant, correlative, harmonious, relevant, suitable

consentaneousness agreement *(concurrence)*, concordance, consensus, peace

consentaneus consonant, rational, suitable

consented allowed

consentience accordance *(understanding)*, agreement *(concurrence)*, consensus

consentient concerted, congruous, consensual, consenting, consonant, contractual, harmonious

consenting concerted, concordant, inclined, ready *(willing)*, willing *(not averse)*

consentire agree *(contract)*, consent, plot

consenus cartel

consequence amount *(result)*, clout, concern *(interest)*, conclusion *(outcome)*, degree *(magnitude)*, development *(outgrowth)*, effect, eminence, emphasis, follow-up, force *(strength)*, import, importance, influence, interest *(concern)*, magnitude, outcome, prestige, primacy, reputation, result, significance, toll *(effect)*, value, weight *(importance)*

consequent conclusion *(outcome)*,

consecutive, consonant, derivative, development *(outgrowth)*

consequentia result

consequential considerable, contingent, crucial, decisive, derivative, grave *(important)*, important *(significant)*, influential, major, material *(important)*, momentous, outstanding *(prominent)*, powerful, prominent, remarkable, renowned, serious *(grave)*, strategic, substantial

consequently a fortiori, a priori

consequi attain, gain, obtain, result

conservare conserve, observe *(obey)*, preserve, retain *(keep in possession)*

conservatio maintenance *(upkeep)*, preservation, retention

conservation ecology, maintenance *(upkeep)*, preservation, protection, prudence, reserve, safekeeping, salvage

conservation of the same situation status quo

conservational protective

conservatism continence, moderation, prudence

conservative frugal, guarded, illiberal, orthodox, protective, uncompromising

conservative estimate understatement

conservator guardian

conservatory protective, repository, store *(depository)*, treasury

conserve fund, hold *(possess)*, keep *(shelter)*, maintain *(sustain)*, preserve, protect, store, sustain *(prolong)*

consider analyze, assess *(appraise)*, assume *(suppose)*, brood, calculate, care *(be cautious)*, concern *(care)*, contrive, criticize *(evaluate)*, debate, deem, deliberate, digest *(comprehend)*, discuss, gauge, heed, investigate, judge, muse, opine, pause, peruse, ponder, postulate, reason *(conclude)*, reflect *(ponder)*, regard *(pay attention)*, speculate *(conjecture)*, study, survey *(examine)*, suspect *(think)*, try *(conduct a trial)*, weigh

consider again reconsider

consider again with a view to a change or action appeal

consider as belonging to attribute

consider as true accept *(embrace)*, presume

consider attentively deliberate, probe

consider beforehand prearrange

consider beneath notice condescend *(patronize)*, disdain

consider beneath oneself disdain

consider carefully deliberate

consider closely concentrate *(pay attention)*

consider implausible disbelieve

consider in advance anticipate *(expect)*

consider likely expect *(consider probable)*

consider not to be true disbelieve

consider pro and con deliberate

consider probable deduce, deduct *(conclude by reasoning)*, infer, presume, read

consider unproven disbelieve

consider untrue disbelieve

consider unworthy of regard disdain

considerable appreciable, consequential *(substantial)*, copious, critical *(crucial)*, extensive, far reaching, gross *(flagrant)*, important *(significant)*, major, manifold, material *(important)*, multiple, noteworthy, ponderable, rife, substantial, substantive

considerare consider, deliberate, ponder, reflect *(ponder)*, survey *(examine)*, weigh

considerate benevolent, charitable *(lenient)*, circumspect, humane, judicial, judicious, lenient, philanthropic, politic, prudent

considerateness charity, comity, consideration *(sympathetic regard)*, discretion *(quality of being discreet)*, philanthropy, prudence

consideratio consideration *(contemplation)*, reflection *(thought)*

consideration advancement *(loan)*, analysis, benevolence *(disposition to do good)*, cause *(reason)*, caution *(vigilance)*, charity, clemency, comity, commission *(fee)*, compensation, concept, concern *(interest)*, conclusion *(determination)*, contemplation, conviction *(persuasion)*, cost *(price)*, courtesy, credit *(recognition)*, decorum, deference, deliberation, determinant, determination, dialectic, diligence *(care)*, discretion *(power of choice)*, discretion *(quality of being discreet)*, discrimination *(differentiation)*, emphasis, estimate *(idea)*, examination *(study)*, expense *(cost)*, extenuating circumstances, fee *(charge)*, forethought, hindsight, homage, honor *(outward respect)*, honorarium, impression, incentive, inducement, interest *(concern)*, judgment *(discernment)*, judgment *(formal court decree)*, lenience, magnitude, motive, notice *(heed)*, observation, opinion *(belief)*, opinion *(judicial decision)*, pay, payment *(remittance)*, perquisite, phase *(aspect)*, philanthropy, point *(item)*, prudence, reason *(basis)*, recognition, recompense, reflection *(thought)*, regard *(attention)*, regard *(esteem)*, requital, respect, reward, scrutiny, tip *(gratuity)*, treatment, understanding *(tolerance)*

consideration in advance forethought

consideratus deliberate, discreet, intentional

considere subside

considered deliberate, intentional, judicious, meticulous, premeditated, prospective, solid *(sound)*, tactical

considered decision choice *(decision)*

considered guess estimate *(approximate cost)*, estimation *(calculation)*

considered opinion determination, holding *(ruling of a court)*

considered together collective

considered true assumed *(inferred)*

consign alienate *(transfer title)*, allocate, assign *(transfer ownership)*, attorn, authorize, cede, commit *(entrust)*, commit *(institutionalize)*, confide *(trust)*, contribute *(supply)*, convey *(transfer)*, delegate, detail *(assign)*, disperse *(disseminate)*, divide *(distribute)*, entrust, give *(grant)*, grant *(transfer formally)*, leave *(give)*, mete, refer *(send for action)*, relegate, remand,

remit *(submit for consideration)*, transfer, transmit, transport, vest

consign again reassign

consignable assignable, heritable, negotiable

consignare indorse, inscribe, sign

consignation alienation *(transfer of title)*, assignment *(transfer of ownership)*, consignment, conveyance

consignee heir, licensee, nominee *(delegate)*, payee, receiver, recipient, surety *(guarantor)*, transferee

consigner dealer, merchant

consignify construe *(comprehend)*

consigning delegation *(assignment)*

consignment alienation *(transfer of title)*, apportionment, assignment *(transfer of ownership)*, cargo, delegation *(assignment)*, freight

consignor donor, licensor, transferor

consiliari advise

consilium advice, assembly, committee, counsel, design *(intent)*, determination, direction *(guidance)*, end *(intent)*, expedient, facility *(instrumentality)*, guidance, intention, judgment *(discernment)*, object, panel *(discussion group)*, policy *(plan of action)*, project, reason *(sound judgment)*, scheme, strategy, suggestion

consilium dare advise

consimilar identical, similar

consimilarity identity *(similarity)*

consimilitude identity *(similarity)*

consimility identity *(similarity)*

consist of comprehend *(include)*, comprise, constitute *(compose)*, contain *(comprise)*, encompass *(include)*, include

consistence congealment

consistency adjustment, coherence, compatibility, concordance, conformity *(obedience)*, consensus, constant, continuity, method, regularity, same, synchronism, uniformity

consistent apposite, appropriate, certain *(positive)*, cohesive *(sticking)*, commensurable, commensurate, concordant, consonant, constant, fit, harmonious, logical, natural, proportionate, relevant, suitable, typical, uniform, usual

consistent with concerted, congruous, consensual, pursuant to

consistent with the agreement as agreed upon

consistently faithfully

consistere consist, halt, stand *(position)*

consisting of inclusive

consisting of a guarantee promissory

consisting of a pledge promissory

consistory board, meeting *(conference)*

consociare combine *(join together)*

consociate accessory, accomplice, affiliate, coactor, coadjutant, cohort, colleague, confederate, connect *(relate)*, conspirer, contact *(communicate)*, copartner *(business associate)*, copartner *(coconspirator)*, correlative, federalize *(associate)*, federate, interrelated, involve *(implicate)*, join *(associate oneself with)*, partner, relate *(establish a connection)*, related

consociate in crime coconspirator

consociated intimate

consociatio union *(unity)*

consociation affiliation *(connectedness)*, association *(connection)*, cartel, coalescence, coalition, company *(enterprise)*, connection *(relation)*, consortium *(marriage companionship)*, contact *(association)*, corporation, integration *(assimilation)*, partnership, relationship *(connection)*, society, union *(labor organization)*

consolatio solace

consolation pity, solace

consolatory palliative *(abating)*

console alleviate, assure *(give confidence to)*, ease, sympathize

consolidate amalgamate, annex *(add)*, attach *(join)*, bond *(hold together)*, cement, cohere *(adhere)*, collect *(gather)*, combine *(join together)*, commingle, condense, conjoin, connect *(join together)*, constrict *(compress)*, convene, converge, crystallize, desegregate, federalize *(associate)*, fix *(make firm)*, include, incorporate *(include)*, join *(bring together)*, merge, organize *(unionize)*, pool, unite

consolidated coadunate, coherent *(joined)*, cohesive *(compact)*, collective, compact *(dense)*, concerted, concurrent *(united)*, conjoint, inseparable, joint, solid *(compact)*

consolidation abridgment *(condensation)*, abstract, accession *(annexation)*, adhesion *(affixing)*, agglomeration, centralization, coalescence, coalition, coherence, combination, compilation, concrescence, confederacy *(compact)*, congealment, conglomeration, connection *(fastening)*, consortium *(business cartel)*, corporation, digest, incorporation *(blend)*, integration *(amalgamation)*, merger, pool, sodality, union *(unity)*

consonance accordance *(compact)*, accordance *(understanding)*, agreement *(concurrence)*, assent, coherence, compatibility, compliance, concert, conciliation, concordance, conformity *(agreement)*, consensus, propriety *(appropriateness)*, rapport

consonancy accordance *(understanding)*, cartel, compliance

consonant apposite, appropriate, boiler plate, commensurable, concerted, concordant, concurrent *(united)*, congruous, consistent, correlative, felicitous, fit, harmonious, relevant, suitable, uniform

consonant with pursuant to

consort accompany, cartel, coactor, colleague, consociate, contributor *(contributor)*, copartner *(business associate)*, join *(associate oneself with)*, spouse

consort with commingle

consortem participate

consortio partnership

consortium affiliation *(amalgamation)*, cartel, coalition, consolidation, contact *(association)*, matrimony, pact, partnership, pool, syndicate, trust *(combination of businesses)*

consortship consortium *(marriage companionship)*

conspecific correlative

conspectus abridgment *(condensation)*, abstract, brief, capsule, compendium, digest, outline *(synopsis)*, pandect *(treatise)*, restatement, summary, synopsis

conspici appear *(materialize)*

conspicuous apparent *(perceptible)*, appreciable, arrant *(definite)*, conclusive *(determinative)*, distinct *(clear)*, distinctive, evident, famous, flagrant, illustrious, manifest, naked *(perceptible)*, notable, noteworthy, notorious, obvious, open *(in sight)*, outrageous, outstanding *(prominent)*, palpable, patent, pretentious *(ostentatious)*, prominent, remarkable, renowned, salient, scrutable, special, stark, unmistakable, unusual, visible *(noticeable)*

conspicuously fairly *(clearly)*

conspicuousness notoriety

conspicuus conspicuous, remarkable

conspiracy cabal, collusion, connivance, faction, frame up, machination, plan, plot *(secret plan)*, racket

conspirare conspire, plot

conspiratio coalition, plot *(secret plan)*

conspirational collusive

conspirative collusive

conspirator abettor, coactor, confederate, conspirer

conspiratorial collusive, malevolent

conspire combine *(act in concert)*, connive, contrive, cooperate, maneuver, plan, plot, scheme

conspire against frame *(charge falsely)*, frame *(prearrange)*

conspirer coactor, confederate, copartner *(coconspirator)*

conspiring clandestine, collusive

constable peace officer

constabulary police

constancy adherence *(devotion)*, adhesion *(loyalty)*, allegiance, constant, continuity, diligence *(perseverance)*, discipline *(obedience)*, faith, fealty, fidelity, homage, indestructibility, industry *(activity)*, loyalty, perpetuity, prowess *(bravery)*, purpose, resolution *(decision)*, tenacity, tolerance, uniformity

constans consistent, constant, constant, immutable, regular *(orderly)*, resolute, stable, steadfast, unaffected *(uninfluenced)*, uniform

constant chronic, continual *(connected)*, continuous, dependable, diligent, durable, faithful *(diligent)*, faithful *(loyal)*, habitual, immutable, incessant, loyal, patient, permanent, perpetual, reliable, resolute, sedulous, stable, standing, staunch, steadfast, true *(loyal)*, unalterable, uniform, unrelenting, unremitting, unyielding

constant flow chain *(series)*

constant progression perpetuity

constantia fidelity, regularity

constantly faithfully, in good faith, invariably

constantly recurring continual *(connected)*

constantly together inseparable

constare persevere, subsist

consternation apprehension *(fear)*, bombshell, cloud *(suspicion)*, confusion *(ambiguity)*, doubt *(suspicion)*, fear, fright, panic, surprise, trepidation

constituency chamber *(body)*, constituent *(member)*, district

constituent component, element, factor *(ingredient)*, feature *(characteristic)*, ingredient, integral, item, member *(individual in a group)*, part *(portion)*, segment, substantive, unit *(item)*

constituent part component, ingredient

constituents constituency, contents

constituere adopt, agree *(contract)*, appoint, arrange *(methodize)*, constitute *(establish)*, decide, determine, establish *(launch)*, fix *(arrange)*, fix *(settle)*, instate, legislate, resolve *(decide)*, settle

constitute comprehend *(include)*, comprise, consist, create, embody, establish *(launch)*, frame *(construct)*, make, nominate

constituting creation

constituting a difference differential

constitutio settlement

constitution building *(business of assembling)*, character *(personal quality)*, characteristic, charter *(declaration of rights)*, code, color *(complexion)*, composition *(makeup)*, configuration *(form)*, construction, content *(structure)*, disposition *(inclination)*, frame *(mood)*, organization *(structure)*, polity, structure *(composition)*, temperament

constitutional fundamental, hereditary, innate, lawful, legal, legitimate *(rightful)*, licit, organic, permissible, rightful, salutary, valid

constitutionally legality

constitutionally opposed antipathetic *(oppositional)*

constitutive causal, causative, primary

constitutive element determinant, factor *(ingredient)*

constitutive principle center *(essence)*

constitutus definite

constrain allay, apprehend *(arrest)*, arrest *(apprehend)*, bind *(obligate)*, bind *(restrain)*, check *(restrain)*, coerce, command, commit *(institutionalize)*, compel, confine, constrict *(inhibit)*, contain *(restrain)*, control *(restrain)*, debar, detain *(restrain)*, disadvantage, enjoin, exact, foist, force *(coerce)*, hinder, immure, impose *(enforce)*, impose *(subject)*, imprison, inhibit, jail, keep *(restrain)*, limit, make, moderate *(temper)*, pressure, require *(compel)*, restrain, restrict, stay *(halt)*, stifle, trammel, withhold

constrain again rearrest

constrain by force extort

constrained arrested *(apprehended)*, bound, controlled *(restrained)*, obligatory

constraining binding, compelling, compulsory, necessary *(inescapable)*

constraining force pressure

constraining power force *(compulsion)*

constraint bar *(obstruction)*, bondage, captivity, coercion, commitment *(confinement)*, composure, compulsion *(coercion)*, control *(restriction)*, custody *(incarceration)*, detention, deterrence, deterrent, discipline *(obedience)*, disincentive, duress, embarrassment, enforcement, fetter, force *(compulsion)*, incarceration, limitation, moderation, obstacle, obstruction, pressure, prohibition, quota, requirement, restraint, restriction, retention

constraint by force bondage, coercion

constraint to obedience compulsion *(coercion)*

constrict attenuate, block, clog, concentrate *(consolidate)*, decrease, deter, limit

constricted compact *(dense)*, limited

constricting limiting

constriction compulsion *(coercion)*, constraint *(restriction)*, curtailment, decrease, deterrence, deterrent, force *(compulsion)*, hindrance, obstruction, restriction

constringe attenuate, constrict *(compress)*, decrease

constringed compact *(dense)*

constringent bitter *(penetrating)*

construability construction

construable accountable *(explainable)*, circumstantial, determinable *(ascertainable)*

construal construction

construct build *(construct)*, compose, create, devise *(invent)*, establish *(launch)*, forge *(produce)*, form, generate, invent *(produce for the first time)*, make, manufacture, orchestrate, produce *(manufacture)*

construct a figure delineate

construction building *(business of assembling)*, building *(structure)*, composition *(makeup)*, configuration *(form)*, connotation, content *(structure)*, creation, development *(building)*, edifice, formation, frame *(structure)*, manufacture, motif, organization *(structure)*, performance *(workmanship)*, rendition *(explication)*

constructional constructive *(inferential)*

constructive beneficial, causative, interpretive, productive, virtual

constructive criticism advocacy

constructor architect, contractor, materialman

construe characterize, clarify, deduce, deduct *(conclude by reasoning)*, define, derive *(deduce)*, elucidate, expound, infer, interpret, rationalize, render *(depict)*

construe falsely cloak

construe wrongly misconstrue

constuprate violate

constupration rape

consubstantial congruous, identical, similar

consubstantiate unite

consuescere cohabit

consuetude behavior, custom, habit, manner *(behavior)*, practice *(custom)*, usage

consuetudinal accustomed *(customary)*, frequent, regular *(conventional)*, repeated, traditional, usual

consuetudinary accustomed *(customary)*, customary, familiar *(customary)*, frequent, habitual, ordinary, regular *(conventional)*, repeated, traditional, usual

consuetudo habit, practice *(procedure)*, usage

consul plenipotentiary

consulate deputation (*delegation*), embassy

consulere provide (*arrange for*)

consult consider, counsel, deliberate, discuss, refer (*send for action*)

consult again reconsider

consult with advise, confer (*consult*), converse, debate

consultant specialist

consultants commission (*agency*)

consultare confer (*consult*), consult (*ask advice of*), deliberate

consultatio deliberation

consultation caucus, conference, confrontation (*act of setting face to face*), conversation, guidance, interview, meeting (*conference*), negotiation, parley, session

consultation meeting conference

consultative hortative

consultative body board

consulting advisory

consultive body congress

consulto design (*intent*)

consultor client, patron (*regular customer*)

consultum edict

consumable disposable

consume burn, decay, deflagrate, degenerate, deplete, despoil, destroy (*efface*), diminish, dissipate (*expend foolishly*), eliminate (*eradicate*), erode, exhaust (*deplete*), exploit (*make use of*), extirpate, obliterate, prey, spend

consume completely exhaust (*deplete*)

consume one's substance dissipate (*expend foolishly*)

consumed irredeemable

consumer client, customer, patron (*regular customer*)

consumer demand market (*demand*)

consumer durables goods, merchandise

consumer goods merchandise

consumere consume, exhaust (*deplete*), spend

consuming deadly, deleterious, harmful, malignant

consummare consummate, finish

consummate absolute (*ideal*), accomplish, arrant (*definite*), attain, cease, close (*terminate*), commit (*perpetrate*), complete (*all-embracing*), complete, comprehensive, conclude (*complete*), culminate, definitive, discharge (*perform*), discontinue (*abandon*), dispatch (*dispose of*), finish, fulfill, implement, mature, outright, perfect, perform (*adhere to*), realize (*make real*), ripe, sterling, superlative, thorough, transact, unmitigated, unqualified (*unlimited*)

consummated choate lien, complete (*ended*)

consummation action (*performance*), cessation (*termination*), close (*conclusion*), commission (*act*), conclusion (*outcome*), consequence (*conclusion*), denouement, destination, discharge (*performance*), end (*termination*), expiration, fait accompli, finality, fruition, maturity, outcome, payoff (*result*), performance (*execution*), pinnacle, realization, satisfaction (*fulfilment*), transaction

consumptio consumption

consumption decline, destruction, deterioration, erosion, expense (*sacrifice*), prostration, waste

consumptive fatal, harmful

contact coalescence, collision (*accident*), connection (*abutment*), convey (*communicate*), correspond (*communicate*), impinge, liaison, meeting (*encounter*), notify, reach

contactual proximate

contactus contact (*touching*), contact (*communicate*)

contagion contaminate, disease

contagious pestilent

contain accommodate, border (*bound*), circumscribe (*surround by boundary*), comprehend (*include*), comprise, confine, consist, constitute (*compose*), detain (*hold in custody*), detain (*restrain*), embrace (*encircle*), enclose, encompass (*include*), hold up (*delay*), include, incorporate (*include*), keep (*restrain*), limit, own, restrain, stifle

contain oneself refrain

contained arrested (*checked*)

contained in a will testamentary

container catchall, coffer, depository, enclosure, repository

containing comprehensive, inclusive, limiting

containing a penalty penal

containing a pledge promissory

containing an assurance promissory

containing error erroneous

containing power capacity (*maximum*)

containing stipulations conditional

containment blockade (*enclosure*), constraint (*imprisonment*), enclosure, quota, restraint, restriction

contaminare infect, taint (*contaminate*)

contaminate adulterate, corrupt, damage, debase, impair, infect, pervert, pollute, smear, stain, sully, tarnish

contaminated marred, noxious, peccant (*unhealthy*)

contaminating contagious

contamination air pollution, defilement, detriment, perversion

contankerous contumacious

conte story (*narrative*)

contemn condescend (*patronize*), decry, denounce (*condemn*), depreciate, discommend, disdain, dishonor (*deprive of honor*), disparage, flout, humiliate, misprize, spurn

contemned blameworthy, contemptible

contemnendus contemptible

contemplari review, survey (*examine*)

contemplate anticipate (*expect*), brood, concentrate (*pay attention*), conjure, consider, deliberate, devote, digest (*comprehend*), examine (*study*), muse, peruse, ponder, presume, reason (*conclude*), reflect (*ponder*), regard (*pay attention*), scrutinize, study, weigh

contemplated apparent (*presumptive*), deliberate, foreseeable, intentional, willful

contemplatio contemplation

contemplation deliberation, design (*intent*), dialectic, diligence (*care*), discretion (*power of choice*), discrimination (*differentiation*), expectation, fore-

thought, hindsight, intent, introspection, judgment (*discernment*), prospect (*outlook*), purview, reflection (*thought*), speculation (*conjecture*), target

contemplation of past events hindsight

contemplation of the past hindsight, recollection, retrospect

contemplative circumspect, cogitative, deliberate, pensive, politic, speculative

contemplativeness deliberation

contemporaneous coincidental, concomitant, concurrent (*at the same time*), current, present (*current*), simultaneous

contemporary concomitant, concurrent (*at the same time*), contemporaneous, current, peer, present (*current*), prevailing (*current*), simultaneous, sophisticated

contemporary account journal

contempt contumely, disdain, disgrace, dishonor (*shame*), disparagement, disregard (*lack of respect*), disrespect, ignominy, impertinent (*insolent*), infamy, malice, misprision, obloquy, odium, opprobrium, rejection, reproach, ridicule, shame, spite

contempt of danger prowess (*bravery*)

contemptibility bad repute, disrepute, ignominy, ill repute

contemptible bad (*offensive*), base (*bad*), blameful, blameworthy, contemptuous, depraved, disgraceful, disreputable, heinous, ignoble, inferior (*lower in quality*), loathsome, nefarious, notorious, obnoxious, odious, offensive (*offending*), outrageous, paltry, perverse, petty, poor (*inferior in quality*), repulsive, sinister, unworthy

contemptibleness ignominy, ill repute

contemptio disdain

contemptousness disregard (*lack of respect*)

contemptuous blameful, blameworthy, calumnious, contumacious, cynical, disdainful, impertinent (*insolent*), inflated (*vain*), insolent, libelous, orgulous, proud (*conceited*), supercilious

contemptuous language vilification

contemptuous resistance contempt (*disobedience to the court*)

contemptuous treatment contumely

contemptuousness contempt (*disdain*), contumely, disdain, disrespect

contemptus contempt (*disdain*), contemptible

contend allege, answer (*reply*), argue, assert, avouch (*avow*), avow, bear (*adduce*), bicker, claim (*maintain*), collide (*clash*), compete, conflict, contest, counter, counteract, cross (*disagree with*), debate, declare, dicker, differ (*disagree*), disaccord, dispute (*contest*), engage (*involve*), fight (*battle*), insist, litigate, oppose, oppugn, plead (*allege in a legal action*), posit, postulate, profess (*avow*), propose, propound, reason (*persuade*), refute, strive

contend against antagonize, confront (*oppose*)

contend against in discussion controvert

contend for advocate, dispute (*con-

test), justify, plead *(argue a case)*
contend in argument argue, dispute *(debate)*
contend in words discuss
contend with confront *(oppose)*
contended alleged
contender adversary, aggressor, appellant, candidate, contestant, disputant, foe, litigant, opponent, party *(litigant)*, peer, rival
contendere contend *(dispute)*, contend *(maintain)*, contest, endeavor, exert, hasten, labor, maintain *(carry on)*, strive
contending competitive *(antagonistic)*
content complacent, component, composure, disarm *(set at ease)*, element, factor *(ingredient)*, inclined, ingredient, meaning, propitiate, proud *(self-respecting)*, satisfaction *(fulfilment)*, satisfy *(fulfill)*, subject *(topic)*, substance *(essential nature)*, tenor, willing *(not averse)*
contented complacent, peaceable, proud *(self-respecting)*
contentedness satisfaction *(fulfilment)*
contentio antithesis, competition, effort, endeavor
contention avowal, case *(lawsuit)*, collision *(dispute)*, conflict, confrontation *(altercation)*, contest *(dispute)*, contravention, controversy *(argument)*, disaccord, disagreement, discord, dispute, dissension, embroilment, feud, fracas, fray, lawsuit, opposition, resistance, rift *(disagreement)*, strife, struggle, variance *(disagreement)*
contentious argumentative, competitive *(antagonistic)*, debatable, dissenting, forensic, fractious, hostile, litigious, moot, negative, offensive *(taking the initiative)*, petulant, polemic, pugnacious, querulous, remonstrative
contentious group faction
contentiousness argument *(contention)*, belligerency, conflict, contention *(opposition)*
contentment composure, satisfaction *(fulfilment)*
contents capsule, cargo, composition *(makeup)*, effects, inventory, merchandise, outline *(synopsis)*, scenario, stock in trade
conterminal proximate
conterminous adjacent, contiguous, immediate *(not distant)*, proximate
contest answer *(reply)*, answer *(respond legally)*, appeal, argue, bicker, compete, competition, conflict, conflict, contend *(dispute)*, contention *(argument)*, contention *(opposition)*, contravene, contravention, controversy *(argument)*, controversy *(lawsuit)*, controvert, cross *(disagree with)*, debate, disagree, discuss, disown *(deny the validity)*, embroilment, engage *(involve)*, fight *(argument)*, fight *(battle)*, fight *(battle)*, fray, gainsay, grapple, hearing, impugn, lawsuit, oppose, prevent, primary, strife, strive, sue, trial *(legal proceeding)*
contest a case by asking for review appeal
contest in court litigate
contest in law litigate

contestability cloud *(suspicion)*
contestable arguable, controversial, debatable, disputable, doubtful, dubious, dubitative, forensic, litigable, moot, polemic, problematic, speculative, uncertain *(questionable)*, undecided
contestant adversary, candidate, contender, disputant, foe, litigant, party *(litigant)*, rival
contestation affray, altercation, belligerency, confrontation *(altercation)*, contention *(opposition)*, controversy *(argument)*, primary, strife, struggle
contested litigious, moot
contester adversary, contender, contestant
contesting hostile, negative
context case *(set of circumstances)*, connotation, environment, posture *(situation)*
contextual incident
contexture content *(structure)*
contextus coherence, coherent *(joined)*
contiguity border, contact *(touching)*, propinquity *(proximity)*
contiguous adjacent, close *(near)*, immediate *(not distant)*, proximate
contiguousness connection *(abutment)*, contact *(touching)*
contiguus adjacent
continence moderation
continens consecutive, contiguous
continentia continence, moderation
continere contain *(enclose)*, control *(restrain)*, encompass *(include)*, involve *(implicate)*
contingence contact *(touching)*, contingency
contingency chance *(possibility)*, incident, occurrence, secondary, sine qua non
contingent circumstantial, contingency, correlative, dependent, dubious, executory, extrinsic, incident, provisional, quota, reciprocal, related, restrictive, subject *(conditional)*, tentative, uncertain *(questionable)*
contingent deed held in trust escrow
contingent event contingency
contingent interest claim *(right)*
contingent on conditional
contingent upon based on, qualified *(conditioned)*
continual chronic, consecutive, constant, continuous, direct *(uninterrupted)*, durable, habitual, immutable, incessant, periodic, unrelenting, unremitting
continually increasing cumulative *(increasing)*
continually recurring constant
continualness continuity, perpetuity
continuance continuation *(prolongation)*, continuation *(resumption)*, continuity, diligence *(perseverance)*, duration, extension *(postponement)*, habitation *(act of inhabiting)*, indestructibility, life *(period of existence)*, longevity, pendency, period, perpetuity, phase *(period)*, renewal, survival
continuance in time duration
continuatio continuance, continuation *(prolongation)*, continuity, succession
continuation adjournment, appendix *(supplement)*, continuance, continuity,

extension *(postponement)*, longevity, perpetuity, rider, survival
continuation in time duration
continuation of life survival
continue adhere *(persist)*, adjourn, bear *(tolerate)*, dwell *(linger over)*, endure *(last)*, exist, extend *(enlarge)*, last, maintain *(carry on)*, pass *(advance)*, persevere, persist, preserve, prolong, propagate *(increase)*, prosecute *(carry forward)*, protract *(stall)*, pursue *(carry on)*, recur, remain *(continue)*, renew *(begin again)*, reopen, resist *(withstand)*, resume, subsist, sustain *(prolong)*
continue onward progress
continue to be endure *(last)*, exist
continue to exist endure *(last)*
continue to hold retain *(keep in possession)*
continue to live exist
continue under pain endure *(suffer)*
continued continual *(connected)*, live *(existing)*, open-ended, permanent, persistent, standing
continued existence perpetuity
continued movement process *(course)*
continuing chronic, consecutive, constant, continual *(connected)*, continuous, durable, infallible, lasting, live *(existing)*, open-ended, patient, permanent, persistent, pertinacious, protracted, stable, standing
continuing after death posthumous
continuing development process *(course)*
continuing for a short time ephemeral
continuing offer option *(contractual provision)*
continuing offer to buy option *(contractual provision)*
continuity chain *(series)*, coherence, frequency, indestructibility, uniformity
continuous adjacent, chronic, consecutive, constant, continual *(perpetual)*, direct *(uninterrupted)*, immutable, incessant, perpetual, persistent, progressive *(going forward)*, relentless, unrelenting, unremitting
continuous time perpetuity
continuousness continuity, perpetuity
continuum continuity, sequence
continuum of days annum
continuus continual *(connected)*, incessant, unremitting
contio assembly, harangue
contorquere launch *(project)*
contort distort, misrepresent
contorted circuitous, tortuous *(bending)*, unreasonable
contortion distortion
contour ambit, boundary, circumscribe *(surround by boundary)*, complexion, configuration *(confines)*, configuration *(form)*, delineate, delineation, outline *(boundary)*, periphery
contra dicere recusare object
contra leges violation
contra rem facere militate
contraband impermissible, unlawful
contrabandist bootlegger, racketeer, thief
contract abridge *(shorten)*, abstract

(summarize), accordance *(compact)*, adjustment, arrangement *(understanding)*, assume *(undertake)*, attenuate, bargain, bond *(secure a debt)*, buy, cartel, clause, commitment *(responsibility)*, compact, composition *(agreement in bankruptcy)*, condense, consolidate *(strengthen)*, constrict *(compress)*, covenant, deal, decrease, diminish, employ *(engage services)*, incur, indenture, lease, lessen, let *(lease)*, mutual understanding, obligation *(duty)*, pact, pledge *(binding promise)*, promise, promise *(vow)*, protocol *(agreement)*, provide *(arrange for)*, record, reduce, rent, settlement, stipulate, stipulation, surety *(certainty)*, testament, treaty, understanding *(agreement)*, undertake, undertaking *(commitment)*, undertaking *(pledge)*

contract a debt owe
contract against future loss insurance
contract against unknown contingencies insurance
contract an obligation pledge *(promise the performance of)*, promise *(vow)*
contract before marriage antenuptial agreement
contract for assume *(undertake)*, engage *(hire)*, hire, retain *(employ)*
contract for exclusive possession lease
contract for exclusive possession of lands lease
contract for possession and profits lease
contract for possession of land lease
contract for use and occupation lease
contract obligation liability
contract of mortgage hypothecation
contract of pledge hypothecation
contract payment installment, premium *(insurance payment)*
contract talks negotiation
contract to lease sublet
contract to work indenture
contracted agreed *(promised)*, brief, compact *(dense)*, compact *(pithy)*, concise, indentured, laconic, narrow
contracting party privy
contraction abridgment *(condensation)*, abstract, blockade *(limitation)*, compendium, curtailment, decline, decrease, decrement, digest, diminution, outline *(synopsis)*
contractor materialman, supplier
contracts dealings
contractual assurance warranty
contractual bond privity
contractual clause article *(distinct section of a writing)*
contractual obligation bill *(formal declaration)*, compact, covenant, indenture, mortgage, policy *(contract)*, specialty *(contract)*
contractual promise warranty
contractual representation warranty
contractual statement agreement *(contract)*, compact, covenant, indenture, policy *(contract)*, specialty *(contract)*
contractual terms condition *(contin-*

gent provision), counteroffer
contractus narrow
contradicere contradict
contradict abrogate *(annul)*, annul, answer *(reply)*, bear false witness, challenge, collide *(clash)*, conflict, confront *(oppose)*, contend *(dispute)*, contest, contravene, controvert, counter, counteract, countercharge, countervail, cross *(disagree with)*, demur, differ *(disagree)*, disaccord, disagree, disallow, disapprove *(reject)*, disown *(deny the validity)*, dispute *(contest)*, dispute *(debate)*, dissent *(differ in opinion)*, except *(object)*, fight *(counteract)*, gainsay, impugn, negate, oppose, oppugn, protest, rebut, recant, refute, renege, repudiate, resist *(oppose)*
contradict absolutely controvert
contradicting contradictory, contrary, dissenting
contradictio objection
contradiction antipode, antithesis, collision *(dispute)*, conflict, confutation, contradistinction, contraposition, contrary, contravention, counterargument, denial, difference, disaccord, disagreement, disapproval, discrepancy, disparity, dissidence, exception *(objection)*, impugnation, incongruity, inconsistency, negation, paradox, reaction *(opposition)*, repudiation, retraction
contradiction of terms non sequitur
contradictive opposite
contradictoriness contradistinction, incompatibility *(difference)*, incongruity, inconsistency
contradictory adverse *(opposite)*, antipathetic *(oppositional)*, contrary, different, discordant, disparate, hostile, illogical, incongruous, inconsistent, negative, opposite, polemic, repugnant *(incompatible)*
contradictory evidence answer *(judicial response)*
contradistinct adverse *(opposite)*, antipathetic *(oppositional)*, contradictory, contrary, different, discordant, discriminating *(distinguishing)*
contradistinction antipode, antithesis, contradiction, contraposition, contrary, difference, disparity
contradistinctive different
contradistinguish demarcate, distinguish
contrahere abridge *(shorten)*, concentrate *(consolidate)*, contract, retrench
contraindicate discourage
contraindicating contradictory, contrary
contraindication admonition, antipode, contradiction, deterrence, deterrent, warning
contrapose confront *(oppose)*, polarize
contraposition antipode, antithesis, conflict, contradiction, difference, disagreement, disparity, dissent *(difference of opinion)*
contrapositive adverse *(opposite)*, antipathetic *(oppositional)*, contradictory, contrary
contraption invention
contraremonstrance counterargument, counterclaim
contrariae irreconcilable
contrariant adverse *(opposite)*, hostile

contraries contradiction
contrariety admonition, antipode, antithesis, collision *(dispute)*, conflict, confutation, contention *(opposition)*, contradiction, contradistinction, contraposition, difference, disaccord, disagreement, dissent *(nonconcurrence)*, dissidence, distinction *(difference)*, exception *(exclusion)*, ill will, impugnation, incompatibility *(difference)*, incongruity, inconsistency, opposition, paradox, reaction *(opposition)*, resistance, revolt, strife, variance *(disagreement)*
contrarily contra
contrariness antipode, conflict, contradiction, difference, disaccord, disagreement, impugnation, incongruity, resistance
contrarious adverse *(opposite)*, contradictory, discordant, hostile, lawless
contrarium antithesis
contrarius adverse *(opposite)*, contradictory, contrary, inconsistent, opposite
contrariwise contra, contrary
contrary adverse *(opposite)*, antipathetic *(oppositional)*, antipode, antithesis, competitive *(antagonistic)*, contentious, contra, contradictory, deviant, different, discordant, disinclined, disobedient, dissident, dissimilar, eccentric, fractious, froward, hostile, incongruous, inconsistent, inimical, intractable, inverse, litigious, negative, nonconforming, opposite, perverse, recalcitrant, recusant, repugnant *(incompatible)*, spiteful, unfavorable, unreasonable, unruly, unsuitable, vicious
contrary action opposition
contrary advice admonition
contrary assertion confutation, contradiction, denial
contrary to common sense ludicrous
contrary to decency improper
contrary to expectations unforeseeable
contrary to experience implausible
contrary to fact dishonest, fallacious, false *(inaccurate)*, fraudulent, untrue
contrary to good business antitrust act
contrary to good taste improper
contrary to law felonious, illegal, illegally, illegitimate *(illegal)*, illicit, impermissible
contrary to professional ethics unprofessional
contrary to reason arbitrary, contradictory, disproportionate, illogical, impossible, irrational, ludicrous, sophistic
contrary to the rules of logic illogical
contrast antipode, antithesis, collation, compare, comparison, conflict, conflict, contradict, contradiction, contradistinction, contraposition, contrary, deviate, deviation, differ *(vary)*, difference, differentiate, discrepancy, discriminate *(distinguish)*, disparity, distinction *(difference)*, diversification, incompatibility *(difference)*, incompatibility *(inconsistency)*, inequality, nonconformity, offset, polarize, vary
contrast with collide *(clash)*, confront *(oppose)*
contrastable adverse *(opposite)*

contrasted antipathetic *(oppositional)*, contradictory, contrary, dissimilar, distinct *(distinguished from others)*, negative, opposite, peculiar *(distinctive)*

contrasting contrary, different, discriminating *(distinguishing)*, discrimination *(differentiation)*, disparate, dissimilar, distinct *(distinguished from others)*, distinctive, negative, opposite, peculiar *(distinctive)*

contrasting quality differential

contrastive comparative, different, diverse, peculiar *(distinctive)*, relative *(comparative)*

contravene abrogate *(annul)*, annul, answer *(reply)*, circumvent, collide *(clash)*, complain *(criticize)*, confront *(oppose)*, contest, contradict, controvert, counter, countervail, cross *(disagree with)*, defeat, demonstrate *(protest)*, demur, deny *(contradict)*, disaccord, disaffirm, disagree, disallow, disapprove *(reject)*, discommode, disobey, disown *(deny the validity)*, disprove, dispute *(contest)*, except *(object)*, gainsay, negate, object, offend *(violate the law)*, oppose, oppugn, protest, rebut, refute, reject, repudiate, resist *(oppose)*, thwart, trespass, violate, withstand

contravened broken *(unfulfilled)*

contravening contradictory, negative

contravention ademption, annulment, breach, conflict, confutation, contention *(opposition)*, contradiction, counterargument, crime, criticism, denial, disagreement, disapproval, exception *(objection)*, impugnation, infraction, infringement, negation, opposition, rejection, resistance, transgression

contraway contrary

contrawise contra

contretemps accident *(misfortune)*, adversity

contretemps casualty, catastrophe, debacle

contretemps deterrence, disaster

contribuere contribution *(donation)*

contribute abet, bear *(yield)*, bequeath, bestow, capitalize *(provide capital)*, convey *(transfer)*, cooperate, create, defray, dole, endow, fund, furnish, give *(grant)*, help, inure *(benefit)*, involve *(participate)*, participate, pay, present *(make a gift)*, profit, provide *(supply)*, redound, render *(administer)*, replenish, spend, subsidize, supply, support *(assist)*

contribute to bear *(support)*, cause, compound, espouse, further, promote *(organize)*, serve *(assist)*, supplement, sustain *(prolong)*

contribute to again refinance

contribute toward conduce, conspire

contributing concerted, concurrent *(united)*, contributory, donative

contributing force determinant, expedient, factor *(ingredient)*, instrument *(tool)*

contribution appropriation *(donation)*, behalf, benefit *(conferment)*, charity, collection *(payment)*, donation, endowment, gift *(present)*, gratuity *(present)*, help, largess *(gift)*, subsidy, support *(assistance)*, tip *(gratuity)*

contributive beneficial, constructive *(creative)*, lucrative

contributor benefactor, determinant, donor, grantor

contributors press

contributory ancillary *(auxiliary)*, beneficial, donative, gratuitous *(given without recompense)*, instrumental, purposeful, subservient

contrite penitent, remorseful, repentant

contrite person penitent

contriteness remorse

contrition remorse

contrivance appliance, arrangement *(plan)*, artifice, collusion, conduit *(channel)*, connivance, conspiracy, expedient, facility *(instrumentality)*, instrument *(tool)*, invention, loophole, machination, ploy, project, resource, scheme, stratagem, strategy, tool

contrivances paraphernalia *(apparatus)*

contrive arrange *(plan)*, build *(construct)*, cause, circumvent, compose, conceive *(invent)*, conspire, create, devise *(invent)*, forge *(produce)*, form, frame *(construct)*, frame *(formulate)*, frame *(prearrange)*, generate, invent *(produce for the first time)*, make, maneuver, manufacture, militate, originate, plan, produce *(manufacture)*, scheme

contrive a result frame *(prearrange)*, predetermine

contrive to gain pursue *(strive to gain)*

contrived aforethought, assumed *(feigned)*, controlled *(automatic)*, strategic, tactical

contrived in advance aforethought

contriver accomplice, architect, author *(originator)*, coactor, conspirer

contriving artful, building *(business of assembling)*, collusion, creation, machiavellian, subtle *(insidious)*

control administer *(conduct)*, administration, agency *(commission)*, agency *(legal relationship)*, allay, authority *(power)*, capacity *(authority)*, censor, censorship, charge *(custody)*, check *(bar)*, check *(restrain)*, coercion, compel, composure, conduct, confine, constrain *(restrain)*, constraint *(imprisonment)*, constrict *(inhibit)*, contain *(restrain)*, curb, custody *(supervision)*, damper *(stopper)*, detain *(hold in custody)*, detain *(restrain)*, detention, deterrence, dint, direct *(supervise)*, discipline *(obedience)*, disposition *(final arrangement)*, dominance, dominate, dominion *(absolute ownership)*, dominion *(supreme authority)*, duress, fetter, force *(compulsion)*, force *(strength)*, force *(coerce)*, govern, government *(administration)*, handle *(manage)*, hegemony, hold *(possess)*, hold up *(delay)*, impose *(subject)*, influence, inhibit, jurisdiction, keep *(restrain)*, longanimity, manage, management *(supervision)*, manipulate *(utilize skillfully)*, militate, mitigate, moderate *(preside over)*, moderation, monitor, monopolize, monopoly, obsess, occupancy, occupation *(possession)*, occupy *(take possession)*, operate, overlook *(superintend)*, oversee, own, ownership, patronage *(power to appoint jobs)*, police, possess, power, preclude, predomi-

nance, prescribe, preside, prestige, prevail *(be in force)*, prevail *(triumph)*, primacy, prohibit, qualify *(condition)*, quota, regulate *(manage)*, repress, restrain, restraint, restrict, retention, rule *(govern)*, seisin, stifle, subdue, subject, subjection, subjugate, sufferance, superintend, supervision, supremacy, temperance, trammel, trust *(custody)*, wield

control market supply monopolize

control of the market monopoly

control of trade embargo, monopoly

control prices monopolize

control the flow of news censor

control trade monopolize

controllable corrigible, malleable, obedient, pliable, tractable

controlled arrested *(checked)*, deliberate, dispassionate, limited, patient, qualified *(conditioned)*, regular *(orderly)*, stoical

controlled by dependent

controller caretaker *(one fulfilling the function of office)*, employer, principal *(director)*, superintendent

controllers hierarchy *(persons in authority)*, management *(directorate)*, management *(supervision)*

controlling cardinal *(basic)*, cardinal *(outstanding)*, dictatorial, dominant, forcible, influential, leading *(guiding)*, master, powerful, predominant, prevailing *(having superior force)*, principal, sovereign *(absolute)*

controlling factors circumstances

controlling force main force

controlling influence predominance

controlling power clout, main force, patronage *(power to appoint jobs)*, pressure

controlment power

controversia controversy *(argument)*, dispute, lawsuit

controversial arguable, contestable, debatable, disputable, dubious, dubitative, equivocal, forensic, litigable, litigious, moot, polemic, problematic

controversialist contender, disputant, litigant, party *(litigant)*

controversion contest *(dispute)*, contradiction, contravention, counterargument

controversus controversial

controversy altercation, argument *(contention)*, belligerency, case *(lawsuit)*, conflict, contention *(argument)*, contention *(opposition)*, contest *(dispute)*, contradiction, difference, disaccord, disagreement, discord, disparity, dispute, dissension, dissidence, feud, fight *(argument)*, incompatibility *(difference)*, lawsuit, rift *(disagreement)*, strife, struggle, variance *(disagreement)*

controversy before a court lawsuit

controvert answer *(reply)*, answer *(respond legally)*, argue, bicker, challenge, collide *(clash)*, conflict, confront *(oppose)*, contest, contradict, cross *(disagree with)*, debate, demonstrate *(protest)*, demur, deny *(contradict)*, disaccord, disaffirm, disagree, disallow, disapprove *(reject)*, disown *(deny the validity)*, disprove, dispute *(contest)*, dispute *(debate)*, gainsay, impugn, negate, object, oppose, oppugn, rebut, refute, reject

controvertibility cloud *(suspicion)*
controvertible actionable, arguable, contestable, controversial, debatable, disputable, doubtful, dubious, dubitative, forensic, indefinite, litigable, litigious, moot, problematic, speculative, uncertain *(questionable)*, unsustainable, untenable
controverting dissenting
controvertist disputant
contumacious contentious, disobedient, disorderly, froward, impertinent *(insolent)*, inflexible, insolent, insubordinate, intractable, lawless, perverse, recalcitrant, recusant, restive, unruly
contumaciousness contempt *(disobedience to the court)*, dissidence
contumacy contempt *(disobedience to the court)*, defiance, disloyalty, disrespect, rebellion, resistance
contumax contumacious, froward, insolent, willful
contumelia contumely, reproach
contumeliosus outrageous, scurrilous
contumelious blameworthy, bumptious, calumnious, contemptible, contemptuous, cynical, derogatory, disdainful, impertinent *(insolent)*, insolent, offensive *(offending)*, outrageous, perverse, presumptuous, supercilious
contumeliousness disdain
contumely aspersion, bad repute, contempt *(disdain)*, contempt *(disobedience to the court)*, denunciation, disapprobation, discredit, dishonor *(shame)*, disregard *(lack of respect)*, disrespect, phillipic, reproach, revilement, vilification
contund beat *(strike)*
conturbare disturb, embarrass
contuse beat *(strike)*
convalesce progress
convalescence revival
convalescent patient
convalescent case patient
convenance decorum
convenant certify *(attest)*
convene call *(summon)*, collect *(gather)*, congregate, converge, join *(bring together)*, meet, rendezvous
convenience accommodate, advantage, appliance, benefit *(betterment)*, easement, expedience, expedient, opportunity, use, utility *(usefulness)*
conveniences paraphernalia *(apparatus)*
conveniens consistent, consonant
convenient available, beneficial, constructive *(creative)*, effective *(efficient)*, favorable *(advantageous)*, fitting, functional, opportune, practical, present *(attendant)*, seasonable, suitable
convenient time timeliness
convenientia coherence, conformity *(agreement)*
convenire coincide *(correspond)*
conventicle collection *(assembly)*
conventio contract, covenant, treaty
convention agreement *(contract)*, assemblage, assembly, bargain, caucus, collection *(assembly)*, compact, company *(assemblage)*, conference, conformity *(agreement)*, congregation, constant, covenant, custom, decorum, formality,

habit, meeting *(conference)*, mode, pact, parley, prescription *(custom)*, propriety *(correctness)*, rubric *(authoritative rule)*, session, stipulation, treaty, usage
conventional accustomed *(customary)*, average *(standard)*, boiler plate, common *(customary)*, customary, familiar *(customary)*, formal, household *(familiar)*, mundane, nondescript, normal *(regular)*, ordinary, orthodox, popular, prevailing *(current)*, prevalent, proper, regular *(conventional)*, right *(suitable)*, routine, standing, traditional, trite, typical, uniform, usual
conventional conduct propriety *(correctness)*
conventional language plain language
conventional practice protocol *(etiquette)*
conventional usage prescription *(custom)*
conventionalism custom
conventionalist philistine
conventionalities propriety *(correctness)*, protocol *(etiquette)*
conventionality ceremony, conformity *(obedience)*, custom, decorum, formality, habit, practice *(custom)*
conventionalize conform, formalize
conventionally invariably
conventions decorum
conventions of society decorum
conventus assembly, collection *(assembly)*, compact, congregation, meeting *(conference)*, session
converge adjoin, border *(approach)*, collide *(crash against)*, concentrate *(consolidate)*, congregate, contact *(touch)*, convene, meet, unite
converge upon approach
convergence adjoiner, caucus, center *(central position)*, centralization, coalescence, coalition, collection *(accumulation)*, collision *(accident)*, company *(assemblage)*, congregation, contact *(touching)*, focus, meeting *(encounter)*
convergency meeting *(encounter)*
convergent adjacent, concurrent *(at the same time)*, contiguous
converging centralization, coalescence, concerted, concurrent *(at the same time)*
converging point center *(central position)*, focus
conversance competence *(ability)*
conversant cognizant, competent, expert, familiar *(informed)*, learned, literate, practiced, proficient, resourceful
conversant with acquainted, informed *(educated)*
conversation communication *(discourse)*, discourse, interview, parlance, parley, speech
conversational nuncupative
conversations conference
converse adverse *(opposite)*, antipathetic *(oppositional)*, antipode, antithesis, communicate, contra, contradictory, contraposition, contrary, contrary, discourse, discuss, inverse, negative, opposite, speak
conversely contra
conversing conversation
conversion appropriation *(taking)*, exchange, misappropriation, persua-

sion, propaganda, reorganization, transition
conversion to the government escheatment
conversus inverse
convert adapt, alter, annex *(arrogate)*, change, convince, denature, deprive, impropriate, modify *(alter)*, persuade, pilfer, prevail *(persuade)*, reform, renovate, tamper, transform
convert to use apply *(put in practice)*, capitalize *(seize the chance)*
convertere convert *(change use)*
convertere in change
convertible terms call *(title)*
convey abalienate, advise, alienate *(transfer title)*, allude, annunciate, assign *(transfer ownership)*, attorn, bear *(yield)*, bespeak, bestow, carry *(transport)*, cede, circulate, commit *(entrust)*, communicate, confer *(give)*, connote, consign, construe *(translate)*, contribute *(supply)*, dedicate, delegate, deliver, demise, depict, devise *(give)*, devolve, disabuse, disperse *(disseminate)*, displace *(remove)*, disseminate, express, grant *(transfer formally)*, impart, indicate, let *(lease)*, move *(alter position)*, notify, pass *(advance)*, phrase, post, present *(make a gift)*, purport, recount, relate *(tell)*, relegate, remark, render *(deliver)*, send, signify *(inform)*, transmit, transport
convey a meaning denote
convey a verbal image portray
convey an impression exemplify, portray
convey an impression of delineate
convey away abduct, carry away, hijack, jostle *(pickpocket)*, kidnap
convey by deed grant *(transfer formally)*
convey for a designated period lease
convey information instruct *(teach)*, mention
convey knowledge apprise, mention, signify *(inform)*
convey knowledge to notice *(give formal warning)*
convey real property for a specified period lease
convey the impression appear *(seem to be)*, demean *(deport oneself)*
convey the meaning of interpret
convey to remove *(transfer)*
conveyable assignable, contagious, heritable, moving *(in motion)*, negotiable
conveyance alienation *(transfer of title)*, assignment *(transfer of ownership)*, cargo, carriage, cession, consignment, deed, delivery, devolution, disposition *(transfer of property)*, removal, transmittal
conveyance between the living inter vivos
conveyance in consideration of recompense lease
conveyance of interest in real property lease
conveyance of land for a designated period lease
conveyance of realty feoffment
conveyancing alienation *(transfer of title)*, assignment *(transfer of owner-*

ship), consignment, delivery, demise *(conveyance)*, disposition *(transfer of property)*, feoffment

conveyed orally nuncupative

conveying donative

conveying title feoffment

conveyor carrier

convicium outcry

convict captive, condemn *(punish)*, criminal, felon, hoodlum, inmate, lawbreaker, malefactor, outlaw, prisoner, recidivist, sentence

convictable culpable, reprehensible

convicted blameworthy, guilty

convicting incriminatory, inculpatory

conviction belief *(something believed)*, belief *(state of mind)*, certainty, certification *(certainness)*, certitude, condemnation *(punishment)*, confidence *(faith)*, credence, determination, dogma, faith, idea, notion, opinion *(belief)*, principle *(axiom)*, principle *(virtue)*, reliance, sentence, standpoint, surety *(certainty)*, trust *(confidence)*

convictive convincing, persuasive

convince assure *(give confidence to)*, coax, convert *(persuade)*, inculcate, induce, influence, inspire, motivate, persuade, prejudice *(influence)*, prevail *(persuade)*, prevail upon, reason *(persuade)*, reassure

convince to the contrary discourage, dissuade, expostulate

convinced affirmative, categorical, certain *(positive)*, definite, indubious, inexorable, positive *(confident)*, secure *(confident)*

convincement surety *(certainty)*

convincible suasible

convincing believable, categorical, cogent, colorable *(plausible)*, credible, determinative, eloquent, forcible, influential, persuasive, plausible, potent, solid *(sound)*, sound, specious, undeniable

convocare call *(summon)*, collect *(gather)*, convene

convocate call *(summon)*, congregate, converge

convocation assemblage, assembly, caucus, chamber *(body)*, commission *(agency)*, company *(assemblage)*, conference, congregation, meeting *(conference)*, session

convoke call *(summon)*, convene, meet

convolute sinuous

convoluted circuitous, complex, compound, difficult, inextricable, recondite, sinuous, tortuous *(bending)*

convolution complex *(entanglement)*, digression, distortion, involution

convolutional circuitous, sinuous

convoy accompany, caretaker *(one caring for property)*, carry *(transport)*, protect

convulse agitate *(shake up)*, beat *(pulsate)*, churn, discompose, harass

convulsion cataclysm, commotion, outbreak, outburst, pandemonium, turmoil, violence

cooccupant cotenant

cooccupier cotenant

cool controlled *(restrained)*, inimical, insusceptible *(uncaring)*, moderate *(temper)*, mollify, nonchalant, phlegmatic, placid, unresponsive

cool-headed dispassionate, sensible

coolheaded sane

coolness disinterest *(lack of interest)*, ill will, indifference, moderation

coop restrict

cooperancy coaction

cooperant associated, mutual *(collective)*

cooperate abide, agree *(comply)*, agree *(contract)*, combine *(act in concert)*, concur *(agree)*, conduce, connive, consolidate *(unite)*, conspire, contribute *(assist)*, espouse, federalize *(associate)*, help, involve *(participate)*, join *(associate oneself with)*, observe *(obey)*, participate, promote *(organize)*, reciprocate, serve *(assist)*, unite

cooperate with abet, aid, assist, comply, support *(assist)*

cooperate with secretly connive

cooperating concerted, consonant, subsidiary

cooperation accommodation *(backing)*, agreement *(concurrence)*, aid *(help)*, assistance, cartel, coaction, coalition, collusion, compatibility, compliance, concert, conciliation, concordance, conformity *(agreement)*, conjunction, connivance, consensus, contact *(association)*, contribution *(participation)*, favor *(sanction)*, federation, help, integration *(assimilation)*, league, pact, partnership, peace, pool, reciprocity, relief *(aid)*, sanction *(permission)*, service *(assistance)*, support *(assistance)*, synergy, understanding *(agreement)*, union *(unity)*

cooperation for fraud collusion

cooperative ancillary *(auxiliary)*, associated, beneficial, benevolent, coadunate, common *(shared)*, concerted, concurrent *(united)*, consensual, constructive *(creative)*, favorable *(expressing approval)*, harmonious, joint, mutual *(collective)*, synergetic

cooperative action synergy

cooperative society partnership

cooperativeness coaction

cooperator abettor, accessory, accomplice, assistant, associate, coactor, coadjutant, cohort, colleague, confederate, consociate, conspirer, contributor *(contributor)*, copartner *(business associate)*, copartner *(coconspirator)*, member *(individual in a group)*, participant, partner, party *(participant)*

cooperator in crime coconspirator

cooptatio incorporation *(formation of a business entity)*

cooptation election *(choice)*, selection *(choice)*

cooptive elective *(selective)*

coordinate adjust *(regulate)*, arrange *(methodize)*, centralization, classify, codify, coequal, coextensive, cognate, combine *(act in concert)*, commensurable, complement, concordant, conform, correlate, correlative, correspond *(be equivalent)*, counterpart *(complement)*, equal, file *(arrange)*, fix *(arrange)*, juxtapose, marshal, orchestrate, pool, regulate *(adjust)*, tabulate, unite

coordinated harmonious, joint

coordination adjustment, compatibility, contribution *(participation)*, regulation *(management)*

coowner partner

copartner accessory, assistant, associate, coactor, consociate, consort, contributor *(contributor)*, member *(individual in a group)*, participant, partisan, partner

copartner in crime coconspirator, copartner *(coconspirator)*

copartnership affiliation *(connectedness)*, association *(connection)*, company *(enterprise)*, league, partnership, pool, sodality

cope with manage, resist *(withstand)*, withstand

copia fund, hoard, license, opportunity, permission, reserve, stock *(store)*, store *(depository)*, store

copied false *(not genuine)*, imitation, repeated

copiosus copious

copious ample, comprehensive, liberal *(generous)*, profuse, prolific, prolix, replete, voluble

copious in speech loquacious

copiousness boom *(prosperity)*, sufficiency

copossessor cotenant

copula connection *(fastening)*

copulare join *(bring together)*, unite

copulate cohabit

copy certification *(certification of proficiency)*, correspond *(be equivalent)*, counterfeit, counterpart *(parallel)*, duplicate, facsimile, fake, forgery, form *(document)*, impersonate, mock *(imitate)*, model, personify, pirate *(reproduce without authorization)*, pose *(impersonate)*, record, reflect *(mirror)*, repeat *(do again)*, reproduce, semblance, simulate, trace *(delineate)*, transcript

copy fraudulently forge *(counterfeit)*

copy from plagiarize

copy in miniature model

copying plagiarism

copyist clerk

copyright infringement plagiarism

copyright label brand

coquere mature

coratifier comaker

cordial amicable, benevolent, civil *(polite)*, receptive

cordial assistance patronage *(support)*

cordial relations rapprochement

cordiality benevolence *(disposition to do good)*, comity, consideration *(sympathetic regard)*, courtesy, goodwill, rapprochement

cordon blockade *(barrier)*, chain *(series)*, prize

core body *(main part)*, center *(central position)*, center *(essence)*, consequence *(significance)*, content *(structure)*, cornerstone, corpus, epitome, essence, gist *(substance)*, gravamen, interior, main point, outline *(synopsis)*, point *(purpose)*, substance *(essential nature)*, summary

corenter cotenant

coresident cotenant

coresidentiary cotenant

corival adversary

cork damper *(stopper)*, obstruction, obturate, occlude, repress, shut, stem *(check)*

cormorant rapacious

corner edge *(border)*, monopolize, perplex, plight, predicament, stand *(witness' place in court)*

corner the market monopolize

cornerstone corpus, foundation *(basis)*, gravamen, mainstay

cornucopia boom *(prosperity)*, sufficiency

corollary adjunct

coronation elevation

corporal bodily, corporeal, physical, tangible

corporal hereditament fee *(estate)*

corporality body *(person)*, corpus, materiality *(physical existence)*

corporalness body *(person)*

corporate collective, conjoint, joint

corporate body company *(enterprise)*, corporation, enterprise *(economic organization)*

corporate interest share *(stock)*

corporation affiliation *(amalgamation)*, association *(alliance)*, business *(commercial enterprise)*, company *(enterprise)*, concern *(business establishment)*, enterprise *(economic organization)*, league, trust *(combination of businesses)*

corporeal bodily, corporal, material *(physical)*, mundane, objective, physical, tangible

corporeal body object

corporeality body *(person)*

corporealize embody

corporeity corpus, embodiment, materiality *(physical existence)*

corporeous bodily, physical

corporeus bodily, material *(physical)*

corps assemblage, band, organization *(association)*, staff

corps of employees personnel

corpse body *(person)*, cadaver, dead

corpulent ponderous

corpus body *(main part)*, body *(person)*

corpus bulk, cornerstone, corpse, entity

corpus substance *(material possessions)*

corpus delecti cadaver

corpus juris code

corpus juris jurisprudence

corpuscle scintilla

corral border *(bound)*, encompass *(surround)*, envelop, shut

correal corporate *(joint)*, joint

correct accurate, actual, adjust *(resolve)*, admonish *(advise)*, ameliorate, amend, appropriate, certain *(positive)*, cure, definite, disabuse, discipline *(punish)*, documentary, due *(regular)*, edit, emend, exact, expostulate, factual, faithful *(true to fact)*, fitting, fix *(repair)*, help, honest, literal, meliorate, meticulous, modify *(alter)*, moral, official, orthodox, penalize, perfect, precise, proper, punctilious, punish, qualify *(condition)*, real, rebuke, rectify, redress, reform, regulate *(adjust)*, remedy, remonstrate, repair, reprehend, reprimand, restore *(renew)*, revise, rightful, sound, suitable, treat *(process)*, true *(authentic)*, valid

correct behavior protocol *(etiquette)*

correct English plain language

correct valuation appreciation *(perception)*

correctable corrigible

corrected tempered

corrected edition revision *(corrected version)*

correcting revision *(process of correcting)*

correctio amendment *(correction)*, correction *(change)*, reform

correction adjustment, discipline *(punishment)*, modification, panacea, punishment, reform, relief *(legal redress)*, remedial statute, remedy *(that which corrects)*, remonstrance, repair, reparation *(indemnification)*, reparation *(keeping in repair)*, reprimand, reproach

correction facility reformatory

correctitude propriety *(correctness)*, protocol *(etiquette)*

corrective curative, cure, disciplinary *(punitory)*, medicinal, palliative *(abating)*, panacea, penal, progressive *(advocating change)*, remedial, remonstrative, salubrious, salutary

corrective device recourse

corrective measure correction *(punishment)*, recourse, remedial statute, remedy *(legal means of redress)*, remedy *(that which corrects)*

correctly as a matter of right, duly

correctness conduct, decorum, formality, propriety *(correctness)*, protocol *(etiquette)*, qualification *(fitness)*, rectitude, right *(righteousness)*, truth, validity, veracity

correlate adapt, classify, compare, complement, conform, connect *(relate)*, correspond *(be equivalent)*, counterpart *(complement)*, measure, organize *(arrange)*, relate *(establish a connection)*

correlated apposite, cognate, collateral *(accompanying)*, concordant, germane, interrelated, related, relative *(relevant)*, relevant, tangential

correlation analogy, chain *(nexus)*, collation, comparison, connection *(relation)*, corollary, correspondence *(similarity)*, counterpart *(complement)*, mutuality, parity, proportion, relation *(connection)*, relationship *(connection)*, relevance

correlative agreed *(harmonized)*, akin *(germane)*, analogous, apposite, coequal, coextensive, cognate, comparable *(capable of comparison)*, comparative, concomitant, concordant, congruous, convertible, counterpart *(complement)*, harmonious, incident, interlocking, interrelated, mutual *(reciprocal)*, proportionate, reciprocal, related, relative *(comparative)*

correlative agreement mutual understanding

correlativeness mutuality

correlativity mutuality

correspond agree *(comply)*, cohere *(be logically consistent)*, coincide *(concur)*, communicate, compensate *(counterbalance)*, comport *(agree with)*, conform, contact *(communicate)*

correspondence analogy, balance *(equality)*, coherence, communication *(discourse)*, concordance, conformity *(agreement)*, consensus, consortium *(marriage companionship)*, corollary, dispatch *(message)*, mutuality, parity,

propinquity *(similarity)*, propriety *(appropriateness)*, reciprocity, relation *(connection)*, relevance, resemblance

correspondency coherence

correspondent agreed *(harmonized)*, akin *(germane)*, analogous, apposite, appropriate, coequal, coextensive, cognate, collateral *(accompanying)*, commensurable, complement, concomitant, concordant, congruous, consistent, consonant, contemporaneous, correlate, correlative, counterpart *(complement)*, fit, germane, harmonious, litigant, mutual *(reciprocal)*, pendent, related, relative *(comparative)*, relevant, similar, suitable, uniform

correspondents press

corresponding akin *(germane)*, analogous, apposite, coequal, coextensive, cognate, coincidental, collateral *(accompanying)*, commensurate, concerted, concomitant, concordant, congruous, consonant, contemporaneous, correlative, faithful *(true to fact)*, harmonious, mutual *(reciprocal)*, pendent, proportionate, reciprocal, relative *(comparative)*, similar

corresponding part complement, counterpart *(parallel)*

corresponding to comparative, tantamount

corresponding to the contract as agreed upon

corridor avenue *(route)*, portal

corrigendum error, miscue

corrigere ameliorate, amend, emend, rectify, reform

corrival contender, contestant, opponent, peer, rival

corrivalry competition, conflict, contest *(competition)*

corroborant salubrious, salutary

corroborate attest, bear *(adduce)*, certify *(attest)*, confirm, countenance, countersign, demonstrate *(establish)*, document, ensure, establish *(show)*, prove, quote, substantiate, sustain *(confirm)*, uphold, validate, verify *(confirm)*, vouch, witness *(attest to)*

corroborating convincing, demonstrative *(illustrative)*

corroboration avowal, certainty, certification *(attested copy)*, confirmation, consent, documentation, evidence, ratification

corroborative convincing, deductible *(provable)*

corroborative excuse alibi

corroborative statement confirmation

corroborator bystander, eyewitness, witness

corrode corrupt, decay, depreciate, destroy *(efface)*, deteriorate, harm, tarnish

corroding caustic, deleterious, peccant *(unhealthy)*

corrosion decline, deterioration, detriment, disrepair, dissolution *(disintegration)*, spoilage, wear and tear

corrosive adverse *(negative)*, bitter *(penetrating)*, caustic, decadent, deleterious, disadvantageous, harmful, harsh, malignant, mordacious, peccant *(unhealthy)*, pernicious

corrumpere adulterate, corrupt, de-

base, debauch, deteriorate, falsification, falsify, pervert, spoil *(impair)*
corrupt adulterate, bad *(offensive)*, betray *(lead astray)*, blameful, blameworthy, brand *(stigmatize)*, brutalize, contaminate, contemptible, damage, debase, debauch, decadent, decay, degenerate, delinquent *(guilty of a misdeed)*, denature, depraved, deteriorate, disgrace, dishonest, disreputable, dissolute, distort, faithless, false *(disloyal)*, fraudulent, harm, ignoble, immoral, imperfect, infect, iniquitous, lascivious, lawless, lecherous, lewd, machiavellian, mercenary, misemploy, misguide, mislead, nefarious, odious, outrageous, perfidious, perverse, pervert, pollute, recreant, reprobate, salacious, scandalous, sinister, sordid, spoil *(impair)*, stain, suborn, subvert, sully, tamper, unconscionable, unethical, unscrupulous, venal, vicious
corrupt agreement connivance, conspiracy
corrupt collusion connivance
corrupt consent connivance
corrupt consenting connivance
corrupt cooperation connivance
corrupt demander extortionist
corrupt demanding extortion
corrupt inducement bribery, corruption
corrupt money bribe, hush money
corrupt offering bribe
corrupt payment bribery
corrupt person degenerate
corrupt use misapplication
corrupted dissolute, marred, perverse, profligate *(corrupt)*
corruptela corruption, seduction
corruptibility bribery, corruption, nepotism
corruptible dishonest, faithless, mercenary, unethical, venal
corrupting detrimental, noxious
corrupting gift gratuity *(bribe)*
corruptio corruption, perversion
corruption bad repute, bribery, crime, decline, defilement, delict, delinquency *(misconduct)*, deterioration, detriment, dishonesty, dissolution *(disintegration)*, graft, gratuity *(bribe)*, guilt, improbity, knavery, malfeasance, misusage, nepotism, perversion, pettifoggery, racket, seduction, spoilage, turpitude, vice
corruption of purity defilement
corruptness criminality, dishonesty, illegality
coruscate radiate
cosh cudgel
cosharer member *(individual in a group)*
cosharing pool
cosign indorse, witness *(attest to)*
cosignatory comaker
cosigner comaker
cosmopolitanism experience *(background)*
cost bill *(invoice)*, detriment, expenditure, fee *(charge)*, forfeiture *(thing forfeited)*, loss, maintenance *(upkeep)*, outlay, overhead, penalty, price, rate, rent, toll *(effect)*, value, worth
cost effective economic
cost incurred expenditure, expense

(cost), overhead
cost of commutation fare
cost of conveyance fare
cost of living overhead
cost of reclamation ransom
cost of recovery ransom
cost of transportation fare
cost reducing economic
cost-reducing economical
costing nothing free *(at no charge)*
costless free *(at no charge)*, gratis, gratuitous *(given without recompense)*
costliness expense *(cost)*, expense *(sacrifice)*
costly harmful, inestimable, invaluable, priceless, sterling, valuable
costs damages, disbursement *(funds paid out)*, out of pocket
costume clothe
cotemporary simultaneous
coterie association *(alliance)*, band, confederacy *(compact)*, denomination, organization *(association)*
cottage home *(domicile)*
couch camouflage, cloak, phrase, rest *(be supported by)*
couch in terms express, observe *(remark)*
council bench, board, cabal, caucus, chamber *(body)*, commission *(agency)*, committee, congress, panel *(discussion group)*, parley, session, staff, syndicate, union *(labor organization)*
council meeting caucus
councilman lawmaker
councilwoman lawmaker
counsel admonish *(advise)*, admonition, advice, advise, advocate, apprise, attorney, bar *(body of lawyers)*, barrister, caution, charge *(instruct on the law)*, confer *(consult)*, counselor, deliberation, direction *(guidance)*, esquire, exhort, forewarn, guidance, incite, instruct *(direct)*, jurist, lawyer, notice *(warning)*, notify, persuade, prognosticate, propose, recommend, recommendation, remonstrate, representative *(proxy)*, suggestion
counsel against admonish *(warn)*, remonstrate
counsel learned in the law advocate *(counselor)*
counseled familiar *(informed)*
counselling advisory
counselor attorney, barrister, council *(consultant)*, counsel, esquire, jurist, lawyer, practitioner
counselor-at-law advocate *(counselor)*, attorney, barrister, counsel, counselor, esquire, jurist, lawyer
counselors bar *(body of lawyers)*
counselors-at-law bar *(body of lawyers)*
count amount *(quantity)*, amount *(sum)*, assess *(appraise)*, calculate, canvass, census, charge *(accusation)*, complaint, computation, enumerate, item, itemize, poll *(canvass)*, poll, surmise, survey *(poll)*
count against confront *(oppose)*
count ballots survey *(poll)*
count for displace *(replace)*
count on anticipate *(expect)*, expect *(anticipate)*
count out eliminate *(exclude)*, except *(exclude)*, exclude, omit

count up sum
count upon presume, presuppose, rely, trust
count votes survey *(poll)*
countable appreciable, determinable *(ascertainable)*
counted upon foreseeable
countenance advocacy, aid *(help)*, allow *(endure)*, approval, approve, auspices, authorize, behalf, certify *(approve)*, charter *(sanction)*, concur *(agree)*, condone, consent, demeanor, embrace *(accept)*, endure *(suffer)*, favor *(sanction)*, favor, feature *(appearance)*, foster, goodwill, indorse, justify, leave *(permission)*, maintain *(sustain)*, patronage *(support)*, permission, recommend, sanction *(permission)*, sanction, sufferance, uphold
countenancer advocate *(espouser)*
counter adverse *(opposite)*, answer *(reply)*, antipathetic *(oppositional)*, balk, collide *(clash)*, condemn *(ban)*, contest, contra, contra, contra, contradict, contradictory, contrary, controvert, counteract, countercharge, countervail, demonstrate *(protest)*, discordant, disinclined, fight *(counteract)*, foil, frustrate, gainsay, negate, offset, oppose, opposite, oppugn, parry, prevent, reply, resist *(oppose)*, retaliate, retort, return *(respond)*, setoff
counter order nollo prosequi
counter to deviant
counteraccusation contradiction, counterargument, rejoinder
counteract antagonize, avert, balk, circumvent, collide *(clash)*, compensate *(counterbalance)*, conflict, confront *(oppose)*, contradict, contravene, counter, countervail, demonstrate *(protest)*, discommode, disprove, disqualify, foil, forestall, frustrate, halt, hamper, interfere, kill *(defeat)*, negate, nullify, oppose, outbalance, override, prevent, prohibit, repulse, resist *(oppose)*, stem *(check)*, stop, thwart, vitiate, withstand
counteractant contradictory, cure, disadvantageous, offset, preventive
counteracting contrary, hostile, preventive, remedial, renitent
counteraction antipode, collision *(dispute)*, conflict, contention *(opposition)*, contradiction, contravention, counterattack, counterclaim, deterrent, impediment, impugnation, opposition, protest, rebuff, remedy *(legal means of redress)*, repercussion, resistance, revolt, strife
counteractive adverse *(opposite)*, competitive *(antagonistic)*, hostile, negative, renitent
counteragent offset
counterapplication counterclaim
counterargument contradiction, defense, objection, rejoinder
counterassault counterattack
counterattack confront *(oppose)*, oppose, opposition, reprisal
counterbalance counteract, cover *(provide for)*, equipoise, neutralize, offset, oppose, outbalance, quid pro quo, setoff, stabilize
counterbalanced agreed *(harmonized)*
counterbid counteroffer

counterblast answer (respond legally), counterattack, offset, reprisal, revenge

counterblow counterattack

counterchangeable convertible

countercharge answer (judicial response), answer (respond legally), charge (accusation), confutation, contradiction, count, counterargument, counterclaim, diatribe, impeachment, objection, rebut, recriminate, rejoinder, response, retort, return (respond)

countercheck arrest (stop), balk, check (restrain), counter, prevent, withstand

counterclaim answer (judicial response), answer (reply), answer (respond legally), claim (legal demand), counterargument, rebut, respond, retort

counterclause counteroffer

counterconditions counteroffer

counterdebt setoff

counterdeclaration counterclaim

counterdemand counterclaim, setoff

counterevidence answer (judicial response), confutation, contradiction

counterexception counteroffer

counterfeit assume (simulate), assumed (feigned), bogus, copy, deception, deceptive, disguise, disguise, dishonest, disingenuous, dupe, erroneous, fabricate (make up), fake, false (not genuine), falsification, feign, fictitious, forgery, hoax, illusory, imitation, imposture, invent (falsify), lie (falsify), mendacious, meretricious, mislead, mock (imitate), palter, pirate (reproduce without authorization), plagiarize, pose (impersonate), pretend, prevaricate, profess (pretend), replacement, sham, simulate, specious, spurious, subterfuge, synthetic, untrue

counterfeit copy fake

counterfeit evidence frame up

counterfeited artificial, fraudulent

counterfeiting forgery

countering negative

counterlimitation counteroffer

countermand abrogate (rescind), annul, cancel, cancellation, counter, counteract, debar, disown (deny the validity), negate, nollo prosequi, nullify, override, overrule, proscription, quash, recant, renege, repeal, repudiate, repudiation, rescind, rescision, retraction, revocation, revoke, stop, vacate (void)

countermandment reversal

countermark trademark

countermeaning antipode

countermeasure counterattack, counteroffer

countermine connive, conspiracy, conspire, counteract, fight (counteract), foil, maneuver, oppose, thwart

countermotion counterclaim

countermovement counterattack

counteroath contradiction

counteroffensive counterattack

counterorder annul, cancel, cancellation, countermand, prohibition, renege, repudiation, rescind, rescision, retraction, reversal, revocation, revoke

counterpart alter ego, antipode, antithesis, complement, conspirer, contraposition, copy, correlate, reflection (image), resemblance, same, semblance

counterpetition counterclaim

counterplan counteroffer

counterplot collusion, connive, conspiracy, conspire, contrive, counterattack, maneuver, opposition, plan, plot (secret plan), reprisal

counterpoint contradistinction, difference

counterpoise cancel, compensate (counterbalance), counteract, countervail, equipoise, negate, neutralize, offset, oppose, outbalance, quid pro quo, setoff

counterpole antipode, antithesis

counterpose fight (counteract)

counterpostulation counterclaim

counterpresentation counteroffer

counterpressure deterrent

counterproposal counterclaim, counteroffer

counterproposition counteroffer

counterprotest counterargument

counterprovision counteroffer

counterpush counterattack

counterqualification counteroffer

counterreclamation counterclaim

counterrecommendation counteroffer

counterreply answer (judicial response), counterargument

counterrequest counterclaim, counteroffer

counterreservation counteroffer

countersign certify (attest), confirm, corroborate, cosign, indorse, trademark, underwrite, witness (attest to)

countersignature affirmance (authentication), affirmance (judicial sanction)

counterstatement answer (judicial response), argument (pleading), confutation, contradiction, counterargument, plea, pleading, rejoinder, reply, response

counterstipulation counteroffer

counterstrike counterattack

counterstroke counterattack, reprisal, retribution, revenge

countersuggestion counteroffer

countersuit counterclaim

countertendency reaction (opposition)

counterthrust counterattack

countervail collide (clash), compensate (counterbalance), contradict, contravention, counter, counteract, disprove, interfere, neutralize, obstruct, oppose, oppugn, outbalance, repulse, withstand

countervailing contradictory, contrary

counterweigh compensate (counterbalance), oppose, outbalance

counterweight equipoise, offset, setoff

counterwork circumvent, collide (clash), confront (oppose), contradict, counteract, fight (counteract), impugnation, oppose, oppugn, thwart

counterworking contradictory, opposition

counting census, computation

countless copious, infinite, innumerable, myriad, profuse

country home (place of origin), na-

tionality, polity, realm, region

country house homestead

country of origin home (place of origin)

country-wide national, public (affecting people)

county province, region, venue

county officer marshal

coup de bec denunciation, diatribe

coup de grâce dispatch (put to death)

couple affix, attach (join), bond (hold together), cement, cohabit, combine (join together), commingle, connect (join together), connection (fastening), consolidate (unite), incorporate (include), join (bring together), lock, unite

coupled affiliated, associated, coherent (joined), composite, concomitant, concurrent (at the same time), concurrent (united), conjoint, conjugal, contiguous, nuptial

coupled with along, collateral (accompanying)

couplement marriage (intimate relationship)

coupling accession (annexation), coalescence, joinder, marriage (intimate relationship), nexus, union (unity)

coupon security (stock)

courage confidence (faith), prowess (bravery), spirit, tenacity, tolerance

courageous heroic, indomitable, spartan, undaunted

courageous deeds prowess (bravery)

courageousness prowess (bravery)

courier harbinger, informer (a person who provides information)

course access (right of way), act (undertaking), admission (entry), admittance (means of approach), array (order), avenue (means of attainment), avenue (route), behavior, conduit (channel), cycle, discipline (field of study), duration, expedient, method, mode, modus operandi, perambulate, period, platform, policy (plan of action), polity, practice (procedure), procedure, program, rule (guide), strategy, subject (topic), tenor, term (duration), traverse

course of action arrangement (plan), avenue (means of attainment), campaign, design (intent), direction (course), manner (behavior), method, operation, plan, platform, policy (plan of action), practice (custom), practice (procedure), procedure, proposition, scheme, strategy

course of an action at law proceeding

course of behavior conduct

course of business custom

course of conduct action (performance), behavior, campaign, habit, maneuver (tactic), manner (behavior), modus operandi, policy (plan of action), practice (custom), practice (procedure)

course of events case (set of circumstances), circumstances, happening

course of law certiorari

course of life behavior

course of proceeding campaign

course of reasoning argument (pleading)

coursing fluvial

court bench, board, chamber (body), chamber (compartment), close (enclosed *area),* courtroom, curtilage, homage, judicatory, judicature, lure, pursue *(strive to gain),* tribunal

court action case *(lawsuit),* lawsuit, matter *(case),* trial *(legal proceeding)*

court commandment order *(judicial directive)*

court decision determination

court employee clerk

court favor pander

court instruction order *(judicial directive)*

court of appellate jurisdiction appellate court

court of justice bar *(court),* bench, forum *(court),* judicatory, tribunal

court of law bar *(court),* bench, forum *(court),* judicatory, judicature, tribunal

court of review appellate court

court officer marshal

court official clerk

court order search warrant

court order of imprisonment mittimus

court proceeding action *(proceeding)*

court rule authority *(documentation)*

court scribe clerk

court's finding ruling

court's jurisdiction judicature

court's log calendar *(list of cases)*

courteous civil *(polite),* obeisant

courteous conduct courtesy

courteously respectfully

courteousness consideration *(sympathetic regard),* courtesy, propriety *(correctness)*

courtesy benefit *(conferment),* benevolence *(disposition to do good),* comity, consideration *(sympathetic regard),* decorum, deference, favor *(act of kindness),* honor *(outward respect),* propriety *(correctness),* protocol *(etiquette),* respect

courtliness consideration *(sympathetic regard),* courtesy, respect

courtly civil *(polite)*

courtly politeness comity

courtroom forum *(court)*

courts judiciary

courts of justice judiciary

courtyard close *(enclosed area),* curtilage

cove haven

coven assemblage

covenant adjustment, agree *(contract),* agreement *(contract),* assurance, bargain, bond *(secure a debt),* cartel, certificate, clause, commitment *(responsibility),* compact, contract, contract, coverage *(insurance),* deed, indenture, league, obligation *(duty),* pact, pledge *(binding promise),* pledge *(promise the performance of),* promise, promise *(vow),* protocol *(agreement),* sign, specialty *(contract),* stipulate, stipulation, term *(provision),* testament, treaty, understanding *(agreement),* undertake, undertaking *(pledge),* vow, warrant *(guaranty),* warranty

covenant of indemnity specialty *(contract)*

covenanted agreed *(promised)*

covenanter undersigned

coventry ostracism

cover artifice, blind *(obscure),* camou-

flage, circumvent, cloak, clothe, comprehend *(include),* conceal, concealment, consist, disguise, disguise, embrace *(encircle),* encompass *(include),* ensconce, enshroud, envelop, harbor, hedge, hide, include, incorporate *(include),* maintain *(sustain),* obfuscate, obliterate, obnubilate, obscure, occlude, outbalance, overlap, patrol, penumbra, perambulate, pretense *(pretext),* pretext, protect, publish, safeguard, screen *(guard),* seal *(close),* seclude, shelter *(protection),* shield, shroud, shut, spread, veil

cover a beat patrol

cover against loss insure

cover for replace

cover up blind *(obscure),* camouflage, cloak, clothe, conceal, deface, ensconce, fake, hide, obliterate, obnubilate, obscure, plant *(covertly place),* suppress

cover with water immerse *(plunge into)*

coverage extent

covered blind *(concealed),* covert, fully secured, hidden, impalpable, ironclad, latent, safe

covering cover *(protection),* disguise, panoply, protection, protective, shelter *(protection),* veil

covering a wide area extensive

covering all cases broad

covering fire barrage

covering up evasion

coverless open *(unclosed)*

covert allusive, asylum *(hiding place),* blind *(concealed),* clandestine, esoteric, evasive, furtive, hidden, impalpable, inconspicuous, indirect, latent, mysterious, personal *(private),* potential, private *(confidential),* privy, protection, recondite, refuge, secret, shield, sly, stealthy, surreptitious, undisclosed, unobtrusive

covert allusion hint

coverture cohabitation *(married state),* cover *(protection),* protection, refuge, shelter *(protection),* shield

covet desire, pursue *(strive to gain)*

coveted popular

covetous eager, illiberal, insatiable, jealous, mercenary

covetousness desire, greed

covey band

covin collusion, fraud, machination

covinous collusive, deceptive, evasive, insidious, lying, machiavellian, mendacious, sly

cow browbeat, deter, frighten, hector, humiliate, intimidate

cowardice fear, fright, panic

cowardliness fear

cowardly base *(bad),* ignoble, recreant

cower fear

cowering recreant

cowork consolidate *(unite),* conspire, cooperate, unite

coworker accessory, accomplice, assistant, associate, coactor, coadjutant, cohort, colleague, confederate, consociate, contributor *(contributor),* copartner *(business associate),* participant, partisan, partner

coworker in crime coconspirator

coworkers personnel

coworking affiliation *(connectedness),* associated, association *(connection),* coaction, concerted, concurrent *(united),* conjoint, synergetic

coxcombry pride

cozen bait *(lure),* betray *(lead astray),* bilk, cheat, deceive, defraud, delude, dupe, ensnare, fake, hoodwink, illude, inveigle, mislead, palter, peculate, pretend

cozenage artifice, bad faith, deceit, deception, dishonesty, false pretense, fraud, hoax, indirection *(deceitfulness),* knavery, maneuver *(trick),* pettifoggery

crabbed perverse, petulant, recondite

crabby fractious, petulant

crack break *(separate),* deface, defacement, flaw, force *(break),* rend, rift *(gap),* solve, split, split

cradle bear *(support),* genesis, lull, origin *(source),* origination, source

craft business *(occupation),* calling, career, contrivance, deception, device *(contrivance),* discretion *(quality of being discreet),* employment, imposture, indirection *(deceitfulness),* knavery, labor *(work),* livelihood, occupation *(vocation),* performance *(workmanship),* pettifoggery, profession *(vocation),* prowess *(ability),* pursuit *(occupation),* ruse, skill, specialty *(special aptitude),* trade *(occupation),* work *(employment)*

craftiness artifice, deceit, deception, evasion, fraud, improbity, indirection *(deceitfulness),* knavery, pettifoggery

craftsman artisan, practitioner

craftsmanship building *(business of assembling),* performance *(workmanship)*

craftworker artisan

crafty artful, colorable *(specious),* deceptive, delusive, devious, disingenuous, evasive, fraudulent, furtive, insidious, machiavellian, perspicacious, politic, practiced, resourceful, sly, stealthy, subtle *(insidious),* surreptitious, tactical, tortuous *(corrupt)*

crafty design machination

crafty device artifice, machination, maneuver *(trick),* ruse, stratagem

crafty plan machination

cram constrict *(compress),* impact, load, overload

crammed compact *(dense),* full, inordinate, populous, replete

crammed solid replete

cramp block, constrict *(compress),* deter, disadvantage, encumber *(hinder),* hamper, hinder, impede, interfere, obstruct, preclude, restrain, restrict, trammel

cramped limited, narrow

cranky fractious, perverse, petulant

cranny rift *(gap)*

crapulence dipsomania, greed

crapulent gluttonous

crapulous gluttonous

crash cataclysm, collision *(accident),* debacle, discharge *(shot),* fail *(lose),* intrude, strike *(collide)*

crash into collide *(crash against),* jostle *(bump into)*

crash together collide *(crash against)*

crasis condition *(state)*

crass blatant *(obtrusive),* disreputable, inelegant, tawdry, uncouth

crater split
crave desire, lack, need, require (*need*)
craven caitiff, ignoble, recreant
cravenness fear
craving desire, eager, insatiable, solicitous
craving for drink dipsomania
crawl truckle
crawling obsequious
crawling with people populous
craze compulsion (*obsession*), furor, mode, obsess, obsession, passion
crazed frenetic, lunatic, non compos mentis
craziness insanity, lunacy
crazy frenetic, irrational, ludicrous, lunatic, non compos mentis
cream main point
cream of society elite
creare appoint, create, elect (*choose*), make
create appoint, bear (*yield*), build (*construct*), cause, conceive (*invent*), conjure, constitute (*compose*), constitute (*establish*), devise (*invent*), engender, establish (*launch*), fabricate (*construct*), find (*discover*), forge (*produce*), form, frame (*construct*), frame (*formulate*), generate, induce, invent (*produce for the first time*), make, manufacture, occasion, organize (*unionize*), originate, produce (*manufacture*), propagate (*increase*), reproduce
create a corporation incorporate (*form a corporation*)
create a disturbance brawl, disrupt
create a false appearance feign
create a false impression delude, dupe, misdirect, misguide, misinform, mislead, profess (*pretend*)
create a fund reserve
create a need necessitate
create a riot brawl
create a stoppage estop
create an opening admit (*give access*), capitalize (*seize the chance*)
create anew recreate
create by law constitute (*establish*), legislate
create disorder disrupt
create havoc harry (*plunder*), mistreat
create strife disagree
create the impression appear (*seem to be*), demean (*deport oneself*)
created being animal
creating building (*business of assembling*)
creating dissension divisive
creating disunity divisive
creating hostility divisive
creation birth (*beginning*), composition (*makeup*), formation, genesis, invention, manufacture, nascency, origin (*source*), origination, outcome, output, performance (*workmanship*), product
creation of a lien hypothecation
creation of housing project development (*building*)
creation of the imagination phantom
creation of the mind figment, phantom
creational productive
creative causal, causative, fertile, pri-

mordial, productive, prolific, resourceful
creative effort invention
creative fabrication invention
creative genius mastermind
creative worker practitioner
creator architect, author (*originator*), derivation, developer, mastermind, parents
creature animal, entity
creature of habit addict
creber frequent
crebritas frequency
credal convincing
credence belief (*state of mind*), confidence (*faith*), conviction (*persuasion*), faith, reliance, trust (*confidence*), weight (*credibility*)
credendum doctrine, dogma
credential believable, certification (*certification of proficiency*), recommendation
credentials certificate, certification (*certification of proficiency*), degree (*academic title*), warrant (*authorization*)
credere delegate, presume, trust
credibilis credible
credibility probability, veracity
credible authentic, believable, colorable (*plausible*), competent, convincing, defensible, ostensible, persuasive, plausible, possible, presumptive, probable, reasonable (*rational*), reliable, sound, specious, unimpeachable, valid
credibleness credibility, probability, weight (*credibility*)
credit advance (*allowance*), authorize, character (*reputation*), citation (*attribution*), coupon, credence, degree (*academic title*), distinction (*reputation*), estimation (*esteem*), honor (*outward respect*), impute, loan, mention (*tribute*), merit, prestige, reference (*citation*), regard (*esteem*), reputation, respect, trust, weight (*credibility*), worth
credit account letter of credit
credit check coupon
credit note letter of credit
credit with ascribe
credit-worthy meritorious
creditable believable, convincing, honest, laudable, meritorious, moral, reputable, sterling, true (*authentic*), unimpeachable
creditable evidence admissible evidence
credited prominent
credits capital
creditworthy candid, credible, solvent
credo belief (*something believed*), doctrine, dogma, principle (*axiom*)
credulitas credulity
credulity belief (*state of mind*), confidence (*faith*), reliance, trust (*confidence*)
credulous certain (*positive*), naive, unsuspecting
credulousness credulity
credulus credulous
creed belief (*something believed*), conviction (*persuasion*), doctrine, dogma
creedal dogmatic
creep prowl
creepy sinister
cremate burn, deflagrate

crescere develop, increase
crest culmination, pinnacle, surmount
crestfallen disappointed, disconsolate, lugubrious
crevice rift (*gap*), split
crew band, personnel, staff
crib pirate (*reproduce without authorization*)
crier harbinger, informer (*a person who provides information*)
crime bribery, burglary, corruption, delict, delinquency (*misconduct*), guilt, homicide, infraction, misconduct, misdeed, misdoing, offense, transgression, wrong
crime committed misdemeanor
crime graver than a misdemeanor felony
crimen accusation, charge (*accusation*), indictment
criminal aggressor, assailant, blameful, blameworthy, burglar, convict, culpable, delinquent (*guilty of a misdeed*), delinquent, embezzler, felon, felonious, guilty, hoodlum, illegal, illegitimate (*illegal*), illicit, immoral, impermissible, iniquitous, irregular (*improper*), larcenous, lawbreaker, lawless, malefactor, nefarious, offender, outlaw, peccant (*culpable*), prisoner, racketeer, recidivist, reprehensible, reprobate, tainted (*corrupted*), thief, unconscionable, unlawful, vandal, vicious, wrongdoer, wrongful
criminal ablation asportation
criminal accusal information (*charge*)
criminal act misdemeanor, offense, overt act, tortious act
criminal activity crime, felony, guilt, misdemeanor, racket
criminal agreement confederacy (*conspiracy*)
criminal attitude criminality
criminal conduct criminality
criminal deed guilt, offense
criminal design mens rea
criminal guilt mens rea
criminal imitation counterfeit
criminal information supplier informer (*one providing criminal information*)
criminal intent mens rea
criminal interest usurious
criminal offense crime, felony, guilt, misdemeanor
criminal proceeding impeachment
criminal purpose mens rea
criminal rate of interest usury
criminal released at large probationer (*released offender*)
criminal remotion asportation
criminal removement asportation
criminal setting of fires arson
criminal transmission asportation
criminal trial lawyer for the people prosecutor
criminal unchastity adultery
criminal under suspension of sentence probationer (*released offender*)
criminality bad repute, bribery, conviction (*finding of guilt*), corruption, culpability, delinquency (*misconduct*), guilt, illegality, knavery, mens rea, mischief, offense, racket
criminally illegally

criminate accuse, arraign, blame, charge *(accuse)*, complain *(charge)*, denounce *(condemn)*, implicate, incriminate, involve *(implicate)*, present *(prefer charges)*, rebuke, reprimand, reproach

criminate falsely frame *(charge falsely)*

criminate unfairly frame *(charge falsely)*

criminate unjustly frame *(charge falsely)*

criminatio accusation, slander

crimination accusation, allegation, bad repute, blame *(culpability)*, charge *(accusation)*, complaint, count, impeachment, implication *(incriminating involvement)*, incrimination, inculpation

crimination through law enforcement arraignment

criminative critical *(faultfinding)*, incriminatory, inculpatory

criminatory calumnious, critical *(faultfinding)*, incriminatory, inculpatory

criminologist detective

criminosus calumnious

criminous blameful, blameworthy, culpable, felonious, guilty, irregular *(improper)*, peccant *(culpable)*

criminousness guilt

cringe truckle

cringing obsequious, subservient

cripple damage, debilitate, disable, disarm *(divest of arms)*, foil, frustrate, harm, hinder, impair, interfere, maim, mutilate, obstruct, preclude, thwart

crippled defective, disabled *(made incapable)*, helpless *(powerless)*, imperfect, incapable, marred, powerless

crippling detriment, detrimental, disabling, harmful, pernicious

crisis crossroad *(turning point)*, danger, emergency, exigency, jeopardy, peril, plight, predicament, pressure, problem, quagmire, situation

crisp compact *(pithy)*

crisscross cross *(intersect)*, intertwine, traverse

criterion canon, pattern, precedent, rule *(guide)*, standard

critic malcontent

critical acute, crucial, cynical, decisive, discriminating *(judicious)*, essential *(required)*, exigent, grave *(important)*, imperative, important *(urgent)*, indispensable, key, material *(important)*, momentous, necessary *(required)*, nonconsenting, particular *(exacting)*, pejorative, precarious, precise, remonstrative, sensitive *(discerning)*, serious *(grave)*, severe, strategic, urgent, vital

critical analysis proposal *(report)*

critical appraisal diagnosis

critical article review *(critical evaluation)*

critical attitude doubt *(suspicion)*, misgiving

critical discussion review *(critical evaluation)*

critical examination analysis, criticism, inspection, probe, scrutiny

critical faculty judgment *(discernment)*

critical feature main point

critical happening landmark *(signif-icant change)*

critical juncture landmark *(significant change)*

critical moment crossroad *(turning point)*

critical occasion landmark *(significant change)*

critical period crossroad *(turning point)*

critical point cornerstone, crossroad *(turning point)*, emergency, main point

critical remark stricture

critical remarks criticism

critical scrutiny diagnosis

critical situation exigency, plight, predicament, quagmire

critical spirit judgment *(discernment)*

critical viewing inspection

criticalness judgment *(discernment)*, particularity

criticism bad repute, blame *(culpability)*, complaint, condemnation *(blame)*, denunciation, diatribe, disapprobation, disapproval, discredit, disparagement, exception *(objection)*, grievance, ground, guidance, impeachment, impugnation, objection, obloquy, odium, ostracism, outcry, protest, rebuff, remonstrance, report *(detailed account)*, reprimand, review *(critical evaluation)*, revilement, stricture

criticize blame, comment, condemn *(blame)*, contemn, decry, defame, denigrate, denounce *(condemn)*, disapprove *(condemn)*, discommend, disparage, evaluate, fault, impeach, impugn, judge, minimize, object, proscribe *(denounce)*, rebuke, remonstrate, reprehend, reproach, review

criticize adversely oppugn

criticize frivolously cavil

criticize severely castigate, denounce *(condemn)*

criticize severly lash *(attack verbally)*

criticized blameful, blameworthy

criticizing severely critical *(faultfinding)*

critique analysis, criticism, diagnosis, inspection, judgment *(discernment)*, review *(critical evaluation)*, review

cromlech monument

crook convict, embezzler

crooked circuitous, devious, fraudulent, indirect, labyrinthine, machiavellian, sinuous, sly, tortuous *(corrupt)*, unjust, unscrupulous

crookedness criminality, fraud, improbity, indirection *(indirect action)*, irregularity

crop output, product

crop up emerge, occur *(come to mind)*, supervene

crop up again recur

cross annoy, antagonize, bitter *(reproachful)*, conflict, confront *(oppose)*, contentious, contravene, counter, counteract, countervail, discompose, disobey, fight *(counteract)*, fractious, froward, harrow, inimical, interfere, intertwine, oppugn, pass *(advance)*, perambulate, perverse, petulant, plague, querulous, resist *(oppose)*, stress *(strain)*, thwart, traverse

cross dimension caliber *(measurement)*

cross fire barrage, counterattack

cross in opposition traverse

cross in traveling traverse

cross interrogate cross-examine

cross interrogation cross-examination

cross measurement caliber *(measurement)*

cross off delete, expunge

cross one's mind occur *(come to mind)*

cross out deface, delete, edit, expunge, expurgate

cross purposes contention *(opposition)*

cross question cross-examine

cross questioning cross-examination

cross section sample

cross the threshold enter *(go in)*

cross with commingle

cross-action counterclaim

cross-bill counterclaim

cross-check collation

cross-examination cross-questioning, interrogation

cross-examine inquire, reexamine

cross-grained fractious

cross-interrogation cross-questioning

cross-purposes argument *(contention)*, disaccord

cross-question reexamine

cross-tempered petulant

cross-way crossroad *(intersection)*

crossable passable

crossbred promiscuous

crosscut cross *(intersect)*

crossed promiscuous

crossgrained restive

crossing crossroad *(intersection)*, intersection

crossing point intersection

crosspoint intersection

crossroad causeway, intersection

crosswalk intersection

crossways crossroad *(intersection)*, crossroad *(turning point)*

crotchet obsession

crotchety restive

crouch lurk

crouching obsequious

crowd assembly, collection *(assembly)*, company *(assemblage)*, congregation, constrict *(compress)*, impact, jostle *(bump into)*, mass *(body of persons)*, overload, populace, quantity

crowd together concentrate *(consolidate)*, congregate

crowded compact *(dense)*, populous, profuse, rife

crown culminate, culmination, honor, maximum *(pinnacle)*, pinnacle, surmount

crowning absolute *(ideal)*, best, cardinal *(outstanding)*, definitive, final, last *(final)*, master, paramount, prime *(most valuable)*, stellar, superlative, ultimate

crowning point crossroad *(turning point)*, pinnacle

crowning touch culmination

crucial acute, central *(essential)*, decisive, essential *(required)*, exigent, imperative, important *(significant)*, important *(urgent)*, indispensable, key, major, mandatory, material *(important)*, momentous, necessary *(required)*, peremptory *(imperative)*, serious *(grave)*, strategic, urgent

crucial feature main point
crucial moment crossroad *(turning point)*
crucial part necessity, need *(requirement)*
crucial period emergency
crucial point cornerstone, landmark *(significant change)*, main point
cruciare harry *(harass)*
cruciation intersection
crucify persecute
crude blatant *(obtrusive)*, elementary, harsh, imperfect, inelegant, inexact, inferior *(lower in quality)*, natural, poor *(inferior in quality)*, rudimentary, simple, tawdry, uncouth, unseemly
crude presentation travesty
crudelis cruel
crudelitas cruelty
cruel bad *(offensive)*, brutal, caustic, cold-blooded, diabolic, harmful, harsh, inexcusable, malevolent, malicious, malignant, oppressive, outrageous, pernicious, relentless, remorseless, ruthless, scathing, severe, sinister, unrelenting, vicious
cruel act cruelty, misdeed, misdoing
cruel conduct cruelty
cruel hearted cold-blooded
cruel treatment severity
cruelness brutality
cruelty bestiality, brutality, inconsideration, mischief, oppression, severity
cruise prowl
crumb iota
crumble decay, degenerate, disintegrate, ebb, give *(yield)*, impair, perish
crumbled broken *(fractured)*
crumbling decadent, dissolution *(disintegration)*, erosion, old, precarious
crusade activity, campaign, operation, quest, venture
crusader malcontent
crush beat *(defeat)*, constrict *(compress)*, damage, defeat, demean *(make lower)*, disable, extinguish, foil, humiliate, kill *(defeat)*, overcome *(overwhelm)*, override, overturn, refute, repress, stifle, stop, strangle, subdue, subject, subjugate, suppress, upset
crushed disconsolate, pessimistic
crushed spirits damper *(depressant)*
crushing disastrous, harmful, insufferable, onerous, operose, oppressive, strong
crushing reverse disaster
crusty fractious, froward, perverse, petulant
crutch mainstay
crux cornerstone, gravamen, main point
cry call *(appeal)*, call *(appeal to)*, entreaty, herald, noise, outcry, plaint, proclaim
cry down decry, denounce *(condemn)*
cry for call *(demand)*, exact, need, request
cry for help pray
cry out against challenge, decry, demonstrate *(protest)*, denounce *(condemn)*, except *(object)*, inveigh, protest, remonstrate
cry out for desire
cry over deplore, regret, repent
cry to call *(appeal to)*, importune
crying blatant *(obtrusive)*, exigent,

important *(urgent)*, insistent, manifest, requisite, urgent
cryptic covert, debatable, disputable, enigmatic, esoteric, hidden, indefinable, indefinite, indeterminate, indistinct, mysterious, obscure *(abstruse)*, opaque, oracular, personal *(private)*, private *(confidential)*, privy, problematic, recondite, secret, suspicious *(questionable)*, uncertain *(ambiguous)*, vague
cryptical covert, obscure *(abstruse)*, private *(confidential)*, privy, problematic, recondite
crystal clear distinct *(clear)*, manifest, palpable
crystal-clear explicit
crystalline lucid, pellucid
crystallization congealment
crystallize cement, consolidate *(strengthen)*
crystallized ossified
cubicle cell, chamber *(compartment)*
cubiculum cell, chamber *(compartment)*
cuckoldry adultery, infidelity
cudgel beat *(strike)*, lash *(strike)*
cue frame *(mood)*, guidance, hint, hint, indicant, indication, indicator, reference *(allusion)*, remind, reminder, suggestion, symbol, tip *(clue)*
cue word catchword
cuff beat *(strike)*
cuirass panoply
cul-de-sac impasse
cull choose, compile, extract, glean, reap, select
culled select
cully bilk, delude, dupe, mislead
culminate carry *(succeed)*, cease, conclude *(complete)*, discharge *(perform)*, mature, perfect, terminate
culminated complete *(ended)*
culminating conclusive *(settled)*, decisive
culmination ceiling, conclusion *(outcome)*, consequence *(conclusion)*, crossroad *(turning point)*, discharge *(performance)*, end *(termination)*, issuance, maturity, maximum *(pinnacle)*, outcome, performance *(execution)*, pinnacle
culpa blame *(culpability)*
culpa dereliction
culpa fault *(responsibility)*, guilt
culpa negligence
culpa dignus reprehensible
culpa vacuus innocent
culpability conviction *(finding of guilt)*, criminality, delinquency *(misconduct)*, fault *(responsibility)*, guilt, ignominy, impeachability, implication *(incriminating involvement)*, mens rea, misdoing, onus *(blame)*, opprobrium, responsibility *(accountability)*
culpable at fault, blameful, blameworthy, contemptible, delinquent *(guilty of a misdeed)*, disobedient, felonious, guilty, iniquitous, peccable, reprehensible, reprobate, sinister, unjustifiable
culpable conduct criminality
culpable omission misdeed
culpable professional neglect malpractice
culpable recklessness malice
culpableness blame *(culpability)*, ignominy

culpae socius accessory, accomplice
culpandus culpable
culpare blame, condemn *(blame)*, criticize *(find fault with)*, fault
culprit convict, delinquent, embezzler, felon, malefactor
cultivate ameliorate, cause, develop, discipline *(train)*, educate, enhance, foster, meliorate, nurture, promote *(organize)*, pursue *(carry on)*
cultivate a habit naturalize *(acclimate)*, practice *(train by repetition)*
cultivated civil *(polite)*, literate
cultivated taste decorum
cultivation civilization, development *(progression)*, discipline *(training)*, education, promotion *(encouragement)*
cultural disciplinary *(educational)*
cultural group race
culture civilization, education, race, society
cultured aesthetic, informed *(educated)*, literate
cultus homage
cum homine contendere compete
cumber clog, deter, disadvantage, encumber *(hinder)*, hold up *(delay)*, impede, load, overload, tax *(overwork)*, trammel, weigh
cumbersome onerous, oppressive, ponderous
cumbrance burden, weight *(burden)*
cumbrous oppressive, ponderous
cumulare perfect
cumulate accumulate *(amass)*, aggregate, compile, glean, hoard, store
cumulated conglomerate
cumulation agglomeration, assemblage, collection *(accumulation)*, conglomeration, corpus, hoard, provision *(something provided)*, selection *(collection)*
cumulative collective, consecutive
cumulative effect augmentation
cumulativeness augmentation
cunctari hesitate
cunctatio delay, hesitation, scruple
cunctation deferment, delay, filibuster
cunctative indolent
cunning artful, artifice, clandestine, collusive, color *(deceptive appearance)*, deceit, deception, deceptive, deft, delusive, devious, diplomatic, dishonest, disingenuous, faculty *(ability)*, fraud, fraudulent, furtive, gift *(flair)*, imposture, indirection *(deceitfulness)*, insidious, knavery, lying, machiavellian, mendacious, perspicacious, pettifoggery, politic, proficient, prudence, resourceful, skill, sly, stratagem, strategy, subtle *(insidious)*, surreptitious, tactical
cunning contrivance maneuver *(trick)*
cunning practice management *(judicious use)*
cunningness artifice, evasion, knavery
cup prize
cupere desire
cupiditas desire, greed
cupidity desire, greed
cupidus inquisitive, partial *(biased)*
cura caution *(vigilance)*, management *(supervision)*

curable corrigible

curare care *(be cautious)*, care *(regard)*, charge *(custody)*, concern *(care)*, heed

curative correction *(change)*, medicinal, palliative *(abating)*, panacea, remedial, salubrious, salutary

curative preparation drug

curator administrator, caretaker *(one caring for property)*, custodian *(protector)*, director, guardian

curator procurator

curator superintendent, trustee

curb adjust *(resolve)*, allay, arrest *(stop)*, assuage, balk, bar *(obstruction)*, bar *(hinder)*, block, blockade *(barrier)*, censorship, check *(bar)*, check *(restrain)*, constrain *(restrain)*, constraint *(restriction)*, constrict *(inhibit)*, contain *(restrain)*, control *(restriction)*, damper *(stopper)*, debar, delay, detain *(restrain)*, deterrence, deterrent, diminish, disadvantage, disadvantage, discipline *(obedience)*, discipline *(control)*, disincentive, encumbrance, enjoin, fetter, fetter, halt, hamper, hinder, hold up *(delay)*, impede, inhibit, interfere, keep *(restrain)*, lessen, limit, limitation, lock, margin *(outside limit)*, mitigate, moderate *(temper)*, modify *(moderate)*, mollification, mollify, obstacle, obstruct, obstruction, palliate *(abate)*, preclude, prohibit, prohibition, quota, repress, restrain, restraint, restrict, restriction, stay, stay *(halt)*, stem *(check)*, subdue, trammel, withhold

curb oneself refrain

curbed arrested *(checked)*, limited, qualified *(conditioned)*

curbing limiting

curbs confines

cure correction *(change)*, drug, help, help, meliorate, panacea, preserve, rectify, redress, reform, relieve *(give aid)*, remedial statute, remedy *(that which corrects)*, remedy, renew *(refurbish)*, repair, repair, restore *(renew)*, treat *(remedy)*, treatment

cure for all ills panacea

cure-all panacea

cureless incorrigible, inoperable *(incurable)*, irredeemable, irremediable, irreversible

curia bar *(court)*, board

curing preservation, remedial

curiosa pornography

curiosity interest *(concern)*, phenomenon *(unusual occurrence)*

curiosus inquisitive

curious eccentric, extraordinary, inquisitive, noteworthy, prodigious *(amazing)*, rare, remarkable, unaccustomed, uncommon, unique, unusual

curiousness interest *(concern)*

curmudgeonly parsimonious, petulant

currency cash, money, publication *(disclosure)*

currency devaluation inflation *(decrease in value of currency)*

current common *(customary)*, extant, familiar *(customary)*, instant, outflow, popular, present *(current)*, prevailing *(current)*, prevalent, rife, typical, usual

current edition revision *(corrected version)*

current expenses overhead

currently existing extant

currently perceived common *(customary)*

curricular didactic

curriculum career

curriculum discipline *(field of study)*, plan, program

currish caitiff

curse expletive, imprecation, malediction, malign, proscribe *(denounce)*

cursed diabolic, odious

cursing blasphemy, profanity, revilement

cursive holographic

cursive hand script

cursive writing handwriting

cursory brief, careless, casual, informal, minor, perfunctory, random, superficial, transitory, trivial

cursus career, direction *(course)*

curt caustic, compact *(pithy)*, laconic, succinct, taciturn

curtail abate *(lessen)*, abridge *(shorten)*, allay, arrest *(stop)*, attenuate, bowdlerize, commute, condense, decrease, diminish, discount *(minimize)*, lessen, minimize, palliate *(abate)*, reduce, restrain, retrench

curtailed brief, concise

curtailment abatement *(reduction)*, abridgment *(condensation)*, abridgment *(disentitlement)*, decrease, decrement

curtain blind *(obscure)*, camouflage, cessation *(termination)*, cloak, conceal, cover *(conceal)*, disguise, end *(termination)*, ensconce, enshroud, envelop, hide, obfuscate, obnubilate, obscure, shroud, veil

curtained remote *(secluded)*

curtate concise

curtilages confines

curtness disrespect

curved circuitous, sinuous, tortuous *(bending)*

curvilinear sinuous, tortuous *(bending)*

cushion bear *(support)*, ease, mitigate, modify *(moderate)*, protect

custodia charge *(custody)*, custody *(supervision)*, detention, incarceration

custodial protective

custodial detention arrest

custodian administrator, caretaker *(one caring for property)*, executor, fiduciary, guardian, superintendent, trustee, warden

custodian of the law peace officer

custodians management *(directorate)*

custodians of the law police, posse

custodianship bondage, constraint *(imprisonment)*, custody *(supervision)*, detention, incarceration, retention

custodire protect

custody adoption *(affiliation)*, auspices, bondage, captivity, constraint *(imprisonment)*, control *(supervision)*, detention, durance, enclosure, incarceration, possession *(ownership)*, preservation, protection, quarantine, restraint, safekeeping, thrall, ward

custom criterion, decorum, excise, form *(arrangement)*, formality, habit, manner *(behavior)*, method, mode, procedure, rule *(guide)*, style, usage, way *(channel)*

customarily as a rule, generally, invariably

customariness habituation

customary boiler plate, conventional, current, formal, frequent, general, habitual, household *(familiar)*, inveterate, mundane, normal *(regular)*, ordinary, orthodox, popular, prescriptive, prevailing *(current)*, prevalent, pro forma, regular *(conventional)*, repeated, rife, right *(suitable)*, routine, traditional, typical, usual

customary action habit

customary conduct habit

customary course practice *(custom)*

customary manner of procedure course

customary procedure manner *(behavior)*, matter of course

customary use usage

customary way avenue *(means of attainment)*

customer client, consumer, patron *(regular customer)*

customer approval goodwill

customer encouragement goodwill

customers' man broker

customs protocol *(etiquette)*

customs documents bill *(formal declaration)*

custos guardian, trustee, warden

cut bowdlerize, break *(fracture)*, censor, commute, curtail, decrease, decrement, deduct *(reduce)*, deduction *(diminution)*, delete, depreciate, discontinue *(break continuity)*, discount *(reduce)*, divide *(separate)*, division *(act of dividing)*, edit, excise *(cut away)*, expurgate, ignore, interrupt, lancinate, lessen, minimal, mutilate, reap, rebate, rebate, refund, rend, retrench, sever, split, split, subdivide, tenor

cut across cross *(intersect)*, traverse

cut adrift dissociate, separate, sever

cut apart disconnected

cut back decrease, diminish

cut down abridge *(shorten)*, curtail, decrease, deduct *(reduce)*, digest *(summarize)*, diminish, dispatch *(put to death)*, extirpate, lessen, minimize, reduce, retrench

cut down to size minimize

cut in halves dichotomize

cut in two bifurcate, dichotomize, disconnected, part *(separate)*

cut into enter *(penetrate)*, lancinate

cut loose disengage, extricate

cut off border *(bound)*, check *(restrain)*, decrease, disband, discrete, disengage, disinherit, disown *(refuse to acknowledge)*, dissociate, estop, estrange, insulate, isolate, lock, preclude, prevent, rescind, seclude, separate, toll *(stop)*

cut off from inheritance disinherit

cut out bowdlerize, delete, eliminate *(eradicate)*, eviscerate, excise *(cut away)*, expel, expurgate, extinguish, omit, quit *(discontinue)*, redact

cut out of one's will disinherit, disown *(refuse to acknowledge)*

cut short brief, condense, curtail, decrease, discontinue *(break continuity)*, halt, minimize, rescind, retrench, stop

cut through enter *(penetrate)*, penetrate, pierce *(lance)*

cut up disjoint, partition
cut-back curtailment
cut-rate nominal
cutback decrease
cutting acute, bitter *(acrid tasting)*, bitter *(penetrating)*, caustic, division *(act of dividing)*, incisive, mordacious, part *(portion)*, scathing, trenchant
cutting down curtailment
cutting off curtailment
cutting words diatribe
cycle annum, frequency, life *(period of existence)*, sequence, succession
cyclic intermittent, periodic, regular *(orderly)*
cyclical chronic, intermittent, periodic
cyclopean prodigious *(enormous)*
cynical critical *(faultfinding)*, disdainful, inconvincible, ironic, pejorative, pessimistic, skeptical
cynicism irony, pessimism, suspicion *(mistrust)*
cynosure highlight, landmark *(conspicuous object)*
cyprian prurient

D

dab iota
daedal elaborate
daft lunatic
daftness insanity
daily habitual, ordinary, usual
daily paper journal
daily register journal
dalliance deferment, delay
dally hesitate, pause, procrastinate, stall
dallying hesitant, otiose
dam block, clog, constrict *(inhibit)*, halt, lock, obstacle, obstruction, shut
dam up discontinue *(break continuity)*, impede, occlude, stem *(check)*, stop
damage abuse *(physical misuse)*, cost *(penalty)*, countervail, decrement, deface, defacement, defect, detriment, disable, disadvantage, disadvantage, disrepair, disservice, drawback, endanger, eviscerate, expense *(sacrifice)*, harm, harm, ill use, impair, injury, maim, mischief, mutilate, persecute, pillage, prejudice *(injury)*, prejudice *(injure)*, spoil *(impair)*, stain, strike *(assault)*, toll *(effect)*, vitiate, wear and tear
damage a reputation pillory
damage irreparably spoil *(impair)*
damage one's reputation defame
damaged aggrieved *(victimized)*, blemished, broken *(fractured)*, defective, dilapidated, faulty, imperfect, inferior *(lower in quality)*, marred
damages amercement, compensation, cost *(penalty)*, expiation, out of pocket, punishment, recompense, recovery *(award)*, reimbursement, reparation *(indemnification)*, restitution, satisfaction *(discharge of debt)*, trover
damaging calumnious, chilling effect, contemptuous, deleterious, destructive, detrimental, disabling, disadvantageous, disastrous, disgraceful, harmful, incriminatory, inculpatory, insalubrious, libelous, malevolent, malignant, noxious, pejorative, pernicious, pestilent, prejudicial, scathing, toxic,

unfavorable
damaging report scandal, slander
damn proscribe *(denounce)*
damnable contemptible, heinous, odious
damnare condemn *(punish)*, sentence
damnatio conviction *(finding of guilt)*
damnation blame *(culpability)*, conviction *(finding of guilt)*, denunciation, disapprobation, disparagement, imprecation, malediction
damnatory blameful, blameworthy, calumnious, critical *(faultfinding)*, incriminatory, inculpatory, libelous, profane, scandalous
damnified aggrieved *(harmed)*
damning incriminatory, inculpatory
damnosus prejudicial
damnum detriment, harm, injury, loss, mischief
damnum restituere indemnify
damnum sarcire indemnify
damp repress, stifle, thwart
damp down diminish
dampen alleviate, decrease, depress, deter, diminish, discourage, moderate *(temper)*, repress
damper check *(bar)*, deterrent, disincentive, impediment, restraint
dander resentment
dandify embellish
dandyism pride
danger hazard, jeopardy, menace, mischief, peril, pitfall, predicament, risk, threat, venture
danger signal symptom
danger-loving hot-blooded
dangerous aleatory *(perilous)*, deadly, formidable, harmful, insalubrious, insecure, lethal, malignant, noxious, ominous, peccant *(unhealthy)*, pestilent, precarious, serious *(grave)*, sinister, vicious
dangerous condition predicament
dangerous course hazard
dangerous person delinquent
dangerous situation hazard, jeopardy, menace, peril
dangerous spot pitfall
dangerous to life deadly
dangerous undertaking venture
dangerousness jeopardy
dangle before the eyes brandish
dare defiance, defy, endanger
dare grant *(concede)*
dare speculate *(chance)*
dare not fear
dare say opine, presume, remark, speculate *(conjecture)*
daredevil hot-blooded
daring audacity, brazen, defiance, flagrant, heroic, hot-blooded, impulsive *(rash)*, original *(creative)*, presumptuous, prowess *(bravery)*, spartan, spirit, temerity, undaunted
dark bleak *(not favorable)*, covert, hidden, incomprehensible, lugubrious, mysterious, ominous, opaque, portentous *(ominous)*, private *(confidential)*, privy, recondite, secret
darken depress, obfuscate, obnubilate, obscure, shroud, tarnish
darkening obscuration
darkle obscure
darkness ignorance, nescience, obscuration, opacity

darn repair
dart race
dash beat *(defeat)*, dispatch *(promptness)*, foil, haste, hasten, iota, minimum, race, spirit
dash against impinge
dash one's expectation disappoint
dash one's hopes foil
dashed disappointed
dashed hopes pessimism
dastardly caitiff, recreant, scandalous
data clue, documentation, dossier, ground, information *(facts)*, intelligence *(news)*, proof, reference *(citation)*, science *(study)*
data paper pandect *(treatise)*
data sheet blank *(form)*, form *(document)*
date age, appointment *(meeting)*, rendezvous
date back antedate
date before the true date antedate
date before the true time antedate
date earlier than the fact antedate
dated obsolete, outdated, outmoded
dateless permanent
daub stain, sully
daughter child
daunt browbeat, discourage, dissuade, frighten, intimidate
dauntless heroic, indomitable, spartan, undaunted
dauntlessness prowess *(bravery)*
dawdle pause, procrastinate, stall
dawn emerge, genesis, inception, onset *(commencement)*, origin *(source)*, origination, outset, start
dawning prime *(original)*
day date
day book register
day of festivities holiday
day of grace reprieve
day of the week date
day off holiday
daybook calendar *(record of yearly periods)*, journal, ledger
daydream muse
daydreaming preoccupation
daze confuse *(bewilder)*, discompose, disorganize, muddle, obfuscate, overcome *(overwhelm)*, overwhelm
dazed insensible, thoughtless
dazzle delude, discompose, prestige
dazzling meritorious
de facto actual
de facto bodily
de facto material *(physical)*
de jure ex officio
de jure jural
de re decedere waive
de re disserere argue
de rigueur binding
déabacle disaster
deactivate counteract, disable, disarm *(divest of arms)*, disband, disorganize, neutralize, palliate *(abate)*
deactivated dormant, lifeless *(dull)*
deactivation deterrent
dead deceased, defunct, late *(defunct)*, null *(invalid)*, obsolete, pedestrian, torpid
dead body cadaver, corpse
dead certainty certitude
dead end deadlock, impasse, quagmire
dead heat deadlock, draw *(tie)*

dead man decedent
dead person corpse, decedent
dead stop impasse
dead-end blind (impassable)
deaden allay, drug, extinguish, mollify, neutralize, obtund, repress, soothe, stifle, subdue
deadened lifeless (dull)
deadening abatement (extinguishment), mollification, narcotic
deadliness fatality, harm
deadlock abeyance, check (bar), clog, draw (tie), halt, halt, impasse, impede, interruption, quagmire, stem (check)
deadly dangerous, deleterious, diabolic, dire, disastrous, fatal, irremediable, lethal, malevolent, malignant, peccant (unhealthy), pedestrian, pernicious, pestilent, ruthless, toxic, virulent
deadly accident fatality
deadly device cudgel
deadly devices weapons
deadly weapon cudgel
deadly weapons weapons
deadpan inexpressive, inscrutable
deadstop check (bar)
deadweight incumbrance (burden)
deaf heedless, incognizant, insensible, insusceptible (uncaring)
deaf to impervious
deaf to reason restive
deafening powerful
deafening row brawl
deal agreement (contract), allocate, allot, attornment, barter, bestow, compact, compromise, contract, dicker, dispense, disperse (disseminate), distribute, dole, exchange, give (grant), haggle, inflict, league, pact, project, sort, split, stipulation, trade (commerce), trade, transact, transaction, treaty
deal a blow assault, oppugn, strike (assault)
deal a blow to lash (strike)
deal a death blow dispatch (put to death)
deal a stroke lash (strike)
deal again reassign
deal crookedly palter
deal destruction destroy (efface), eradicate, extinguish, extirpate
deal hard measure to ill use
deal in handle (trade), sell, vend
deal in futures invest (fund), speculate (chance)
deal in generalities generalize
deal out administer (tender), allocate, apportion, assign (allot), diffuse, disburse (distribute), dispel, disperse (disseminate), dispose (apportion), disseminate, marshal, mete, parcel, supply
deal out again redistribute
deal out anew reapportion
deal retributive justice castigate, condemn (punish), discipline (punish)
deal secretly plot
deal to dispense
deal with appertain, apply (pertain), communicate, concern (involve), conduct, correspond (be equivalent), handle (manage), militate, operate, patronize (trade with), transact, treat (process)
deal with definitely dispatch (dispose of)
deal with gently favor
dealer broker, go-between, merchant,

vendor
dealer in illicit goods racketeer
dealing act (undertaking), commerce, management (judicious use), transaction
dealing death aberemurder, capital punishment
dealing out disbursement (act of disbursing), distribution (apportionment)
dealings business (commerce), conduct, contact (association), overt act
deals dealings
dean veteran
dear close (intimate), exorbitant, priceless, scarce, valuable
dearth deficiency, deficit, delinquency (shortage), indigence, insufficiency, need (deprivation), paucity, poverty, privation
dearth of ideas platitude
death capital punishment, dissolution (termination), end (termination), expiration, fatality, mortality
death by accident fatality
death by violence dispatch (act of putting to death)
death sentence capital punishment
death-bringing deadly, lethal, malignant, pernicious
death-dealing deadly, fatal, lethal, malignant, pernicious, pestilent
deathblow dispatch (act of putting to death)
deathful deadly, pernicious
deathless perpetual
deathly deadly, fatal, lethal, malignant, pernicious, pestilent
débâcle casualty
debacle cataclysm
débâcle catastrophe
debacle failure (lack of success)
débâcle revolution
debacle subversion
debar bar (exclude), block, condemn (ban), constrain (restrain), disable, disqualify, eliminate (exclude), exclude, fight (counteract), forbid, halt, hamper, inhibit, interdict, obstruct, occlude, preclude, prevent, prohibit, refuse, remove (eliminate), restrain, restrict, thwart, trammel, withhold
debarkation point destination
debarment embargo, exclusion, expulsion, prohibition, refusal, rejection, removal
debarred barred
debarring blockade (limitation), boycott
debase adulterate, brand (stigmatize), contaminate, contemn, corrupt, damage, debauch, degenerate, demean (make lower), demote, depreciate, derogate, deteriorate, disapprove (condemn), discredit, disgrace, dishonor (deprive of honor), disoblige, disparage, harm, humiliate, infect, libel, mistreat, pillory, pollute, spoil (impair), stain, sully, taint (corrupt), tamper
debase in quality degenerate
debased depraved, dissolute, ignoble, sordid, tainted (corrupted), vicious
debased person degenerate
debasement abuse (physical misuse), attaint, bad faith, bad repute, contempt (disdain), corruption, defilement, degradation, depression, deterioration, dis-

credit, disgrace, dishonor (shame), disrepute, ignominy, misusage, obloquy, odium, opprobrium, perversion, shame
debatable arguable, contestable, controversial, disputable, doubtful, dubious, equivocal, indefinite, litigious, moot, polemic, problematic, speculative, uncertain (questionable), undecided
debatable issue thesis
debatable point issue (matter in dispute), matter (subject), thesis
debate answer (reply), argue, argument (contention), challenge, conflict, conflict, consider, contention (argument), contention (opposition), contest (dispute), contest, contravention, controversy (argument), controvert, converse, cross (disagree with), deliberate, deliberation, disaccord, disaccord, disagree, disagreement, discourse, discuss, dispute, doubt (hesitate), fight (argument), muse, oppose, oscillate, parley, ponder, reason (persuade), refute, respond, speculate (conjecture), treat (process), vacillate
debater contender
debating dissenting, hesitant
debauch abuse (violate), betray (lead astray), carouse, contemn, corrupt, debase, degenerate, deteriorate, dishonor (deprive of honor), pervert, pollute, taint (corrupt)
débauche delineation
debauched bad (offensive), decadent, depraved, dissolute, gluttonous, immoral, lascivious, lecherous, licentious, obscene, peccant (culpable), perverse, profligate (corrupt), promiscuous, prurient, salacious, tainted (corrupted)
debauchee degenerate, wrongdoer
debauchery perversion, vice
debauchment debauchery, defilement
debenture bond, charge (lien), check (instrument), draft, note (written promise to pay), security (pledge), specialty (contract)
debere owe
deberi due
debilitare disable, impair
debilitate adulterate, attenuate, depreciate, deteriorate, disable, disarm (divest of arms), eviscerate, exhaust (deplete), extenuate, impair, mutilate, tax (overwork)
debilitated disabled (made incapable), helpless (powerless), lifeless (dull), powerless
debilitating disabling
debilitation disability (physical inability), impotence
debility disability (physical inability), fault (weakness), frailty, impotence, impuissance, languor, prostration
debit arrears, charge (cost), debt, due, expense (cost), liability, obligation (liability)
debitus condign, due (owed), overdue
debouch emanate
debouchment issuance
debris discard
debt arrears, cloud (incumbrance), debit, delinquency (shortage), due, duty (obligation), liability, lien, obligation (duty), obligation (liability)
debt owed setoff
debt unpaid though due arrears

debtee creditor

debtor obligor

debunk disabuse, disapprove *(reject)*, disgrace, reveal

debut birth *(beginning)*, first appearance, inception, nascency

debutant neophyte

decadence caducity, degradation, delinquency *(misconduct)*, deterioration, detriment, disrepair, turpitude

decadency decline, degradation, disrepair

decadent dissolute, old, regressive

decadent person degenerate

decamp abandon *(physically leave)*, abduct, abscond, depart, disappear, escape, evacuate, flee, leave *(depart)*, quit *(evacuate)*, retire *(retreat)*, retreat

decampment abandonment *(desertion)*, flight

decant outpour

decay caducity, consumption, corrupt, decline, decline *(fall)*, degenerate, depreciate, deteriorate, deterioration, detriment, disintegrate, disrepair, dissolution *(disintegration)*, disuse, ebb, erode, erosion, languish, prostration, spoil *(impair)*, spoilage, taint *(contaminate)*, wear and tear

decayed old, sordid, stale, unsound *(not strong)*

decaying bad *(inferior)*, decadent

decease death, demise *(death)*, die, end *(termination)*, expire

deceased corpse, dead, decedent, defunct, late *(defunct)*, lifeless *(dead)*

deceased person decedent

decedent dead

decedere secede

deceit artifice, bad faith, canard, collusion, color *(deceptive appearance)*, deception, dishonesty, evasion, false pretense, falsification, fraud, hoax, hypocrisy, imposture, improbity, indirection *(deceitfulness)*, knavery, lie, misstatement, pettifoggery, pretense *(pretext)*, ruse, story *(falsehood)*, stratagem

deceitful collusive, colorable *(specious)*, deceptive, delusive, devious, dishonest, disingenuous, evasive, faithless, fallacious, false *(disloyal)*, false *(not genuine)*, fraudulent, furtive, insidious, lying, machiavellian, mendacious, meretricious, perfidious, politic, recreant, sly, spurious, subtle *(insidious)*, surreptitious, tortuous *(corrupt)*, undependable, unreliable, unscrupulous, untrue, untrustworthy

deceitful agreement collusion

deceitful compact collusion

deceitful practice fraud

deceitfulness bad faith, collusion, concealment, deceit, dishonesty, duplicity, evasion, false pretense, falsification, fraud, hypocrisy, improbity, infidelity, knavery, misrepresentation

deceivability credulity

deceivable credulous, naive

deceive bait *(lure)*, betray *(lead astray)*, bilk, camouflage, cheat, circumvent, cloak, defraud, delude, disguise, dupe, ensnare, entrap, equivocate, fabricate *(make up)*, fake, feign, foist, hide, hoodwink, illude, inveigle, lie *(falsify)*, misguide, misinform, mislabel, mislead, misrepresent, misstate,

mulct *(defraud)*, overreach, palter, peculate, pettifog, pretend, prevaricate

deceive by treachery betray *(lead astray)*

deceive oneself miscalculate, misconceive

deceiver conspirator

deceiving colorable *(specious)*, deceptive, delusive, dishonest, disingenuous, evasive, fallacious, false *(inaccurate)*, fictitious, fraudulent, illusory, insidious, machiavellian, mendacious, ostensible, perfidious, sly, specious

decelerate decrease, diminish, hold up *(delay)*, impede, moderate *(temper)*, palliate *(abate)*

deceleration decrease, delay

decencies decorum

decency clemency, decorum, propriety *(correctness)*

decent benevolent, clean, ethical, fair *(satisfactory)*, honest, humane, mediocre, meritorious, moral, suitable

decently fairly *(moderately)*

decentralize diffuse, disperse *(scatter)*, dissolve *(separate)*, distribute

deception artifice, bad faith, canard, collusion, color *(deceptive appearance)*, contrivance, corruption, counterfeit, deceit, decoy, disguise, dishonesty, distortion, duplicity, evasion, fallacy, falsehood, falsification, figment, forgery, fraud, hoax, hypocrisy, imposture, indirection *(deceitfulness)*, knavery, lie, maneuver *(trick)*, misrepresentation, misstatement, pettifoggery, plot *(secret plan)*, pretense *(pretext)*, pretext, ruse, sham, sophistry, story *(falsehood)*, stratagem, subreption, subterfuge

deceptious sly

deceptive artificial, assumed *(feigned)*, collusive, colorable *(specious)*, delusive, dishonest, disingenuous, equivocal, evasive, fallacious, false *(inaccurate)*, false *(not genuine)*, fraudulent, illusory, imitation, insidious, lying, machiavellian, meretricious, ostensible, sly, specious, spurious, subtle *(insidious)*, surreptitious, untrue, untrustworthy

deceptive belief fallacy

deceptive check bad check

deceptive covering color *(deceptive appearance)*, disguise

deceptive representation of fact false pretense

deceptive statement misrepresentation

deceptiveness deceit, fraud, misrepresentation

decernere contend *(dispute)*, decide, determine, resolve *(decide)*

decerpere cull

decessio discount, discount *(disbelieve)*

decide adjudge, adjudicate, arbitrate *(adjudge)*, ascertain, award, choose, deem, determine, dispose *(incline)*, elect *(choose)*, find *(determine)*, fix *(settle)*, gauge, hear *(give a legal hearing)*, judge, pass *(determine)*, prescribe, pronounce *(pass judgment)*, select, sentence, settle, stipulate, try *(conduct a trial)*

decide a question of fact find *(determine)*

decide against overrule

decide beforehand predetermine, presuppose

decide between opposing parties arbitrate *(adjudge)*

decide by judicial sentence rule *(decide)*

decide in advance forejudge, predetermine, preordain, presuppose

decide in favor of uphold

decide legally hold *(decide)*

decide upon conclude *(decide)*, determine, find *(determine)*

decided absolute *(conclusive)*, actual, affirmative, axiomatic, categorical, certain *(fixed)*, certain *(positive)*, complete *(ended)*, conclusive *(settled)*, definite, definitive, demonstrable, dogmatic, explicit, express, fixed *(settled)*, inappealable, inevitable, inexorable, inflexible, intentional, necessary *(inescapable)*, obdurate, official, patient, peremptory *(absolute)*, pertinacious, positive *(confident)*, positive *(incontestable)*, purposeful, res judicata, resolute, resounding, serious *(devoted)*, stark, stated, steadfast, through, unequivocal, unmistakable, unyielding

decided by competition vying competitive *(antagonistic)*

decided upon preferred *(favored)*

decidedly fairly *(clearly)*, purely *(positively)*

decidedly different distinct *(distinguished from others)*

deciding critical *(crucial)*, crucial, determinative

deciduous ephemeral, temporary, transient, volatile

decimate destroy *(efface)*, diminish, disarm *(divest of arms)*, eliminate *(eradicate)*, lessen, minimize, reduce

decimation aberemurder, catastrophe, destruction, killing

decipere mislead

decipher ascertain, clarify, construe *(comprehend)*, construe *(translate)*, detect, elucidate, explain, find *(discover)*, interpret, read, resolve *(solve)*, solve

decipherable ascertainable, cognizable, coherent *(clear)*, comprehensible, determinable *(ascertainable)*, solvable

deciphering clarification, explanation

decipherment definition, solution *(answer)*

decision adjudication, alternative *(option)*, animus, arbitration, authority *(documentation)*, award, call *(option)*, cognovit, conclusion *(determination)*, consequence *(conclusion)*, conviction *(finding of guilt)*, decree, determination, dilemma, discretion *(power of choice)*, disposition *(determination)*, election *(choice)*, finding, holding *(ruling of a court)*, judgment *(discernment)*, judgment *(formal court decree)*, opinion *(judicial decision)*, outcome, poll *(casting of votes)*, pronouncement, referendum, relief *(legal redress)*, res judicata, result, ruling, selection *(choice)*, sentence, verdict, volition, vote, will *(desire)*

decision beforehand predetermination

decision in advance predetermination

decision making government *(administration)

decision of a jury verdict
decision-making body management (directorate)
decision-making power over the case jurisdiction
decisive absolute (conclusive), axiomatic, categorical, certain (fixed), certain (positive), compelling, conclusive (settled), convincing, critical (crucial), crucial, definite, definitive, determinative, final, inappealable, key, last (final), major, material (important), peremptory (absolute), peremptory (imperative), positive (confident), strategic
decisive factor determinant
decisive moment crossroad (turning point)
decisive turn landmark (significant change)
decisively fairly (clearly)
decivilize brutalize
deck embellish
declaim enunciate, recite, speak, utter
declaim against censure, complain (charge), condemn (blame), decry, denounce (condemn), disapprove (condemn), expostulate, fault, impeach
declaimer demagogue
declamatio bluster (speech), declamation
declamation bombast, charge (statement to the jury), discourse, fustian, harangue, peroration, rhetoric (insincere language), speech
declamatory flatulent, fustian, inflated (bombastic), orotund, turgid, voluble
declamatory speech harangue
declarare declare, express, manifest, proclaim, prove
declaratio declaration, manifestation
declaration acknowledgment (avowal), adjudication, adjuration, admission (disclosure), affirmance (authentication), affirmation, alibi, allegation, assertion, asseveration, assurance, attestation, averment, avouchment, avowal, brevet, certificate, certification (attested copy), certification (certification of proficiency), claim (assertion), claim (legal demand), cognovit, common knowledge, communication (statement), conclusion (determination), confession, confirmation, count, declaratory judgment, decree, determination, dictum, directive, disclosure (act of disclosing), disclosure (something disclosed), discovery, edict, expression (comment), judgment (formal court decree), measure, notice (announcement), notification, observation, opinion (judicial decision), order (judicial directive), parole, platform, proclamation, promise, pronouncement, proposition, reference (recommendation), remark, representation (statement), resolution (formal statement), speech, statement, surety (certainty), testimony
declaration of a jury verdict
declaration of disapproval protest
declaration of dissent protest
declaration of facts testimony
declaration of faith conviction (persuasion), dogma, principle (axiom), pro-

fession (declaration)
declaration of opposition protest
declaration of penalty sentence
declaration of policy platform
declaration of war outbreak
declaration under oath affidavit, deposition
declarative declaratory, demonstrative (illustrative), narrative
declaratory narrative
declare adduce, admit (concede), allege, annunciate, assert, attest, avouch (avow), avow, bare, bear (adduce), betray (disclose), claim (maintain), comment, communicate, conclude (decide), confess, contend (maintain), convey (communicate), designate, determine, disclose, enact, enunciate, express, inform (betray), issue (publish), manifest, notify, observe (remark), pass (determine), phrase, pose (propound), posit, proclaim, profess (avow), promise (vow), promulgate, pronounce (speak), propose, publish, purport, relate (tell), remark, report (disclose), reveal, rule (decide), signify (inform), speak, swear, testify, utter, verify (swear), vouch
declare a verdict find (determine)
declare authoritatively rule (decide)
declare blameless exonerate
declare forfeit dispossess
declare guiltless exculpate, justify, palliate (excuse)
declare guilty of an offense convict, sentence
declare illegal ban, forbid, interdict, outlaw
declare incidentally mention
declare innocent acquit, exonerate, vindicate
declare invalid cancel, negate
declare lawful authorize, constitute (establish), legitimate, pass (approve)
declare legal validate
declare not guilty exculpate, exonerate
declare not to be true disavow
declare null and void abolish, abrogate (annul), abrogate (rescind), adeem, cancel, discharge (release from obligation), disclaim, negate, nullify, quash, repeal, repudiate, rescind, revoke
declare one's right claim (demand)
declare openly avouch (avow), avow
declare opposition demonstrate (protest)
declare positively avow
declare solemnly affirm (declare solemnly), swear
declare the truth of attest, avow, certify (attest)
declare to be pronounce (pass judgment)
declare to be fact affirm (claim), bear (adduce)
declare to be false deny (contradict)
declare to be forfeited condemn (seize)
declare to be genuine evidence
declare to be true certify (attest), evidence
declare to be untrue deny (contradict)
declare true swear
declare under oath depose (testify)

declare unlawful outlaw
declare valid validate
declare war fight (battle)
declare with positiveness avouch (avow), purport
declared agreed (promised), alleged, nuncupative, ostensible
declared insane non compos mentis
declared intention proposition
déclassé discard
declension curtailment, decrease, decrement, degradation, deterioration, rejection, relapse
declinare deviate
declinatio deviation
declination abandonment (repudiation), abatement (reduction), damage, decrease, degradation, deterioration, disdain, dishonor (nonpayment), negation, refusal, rejection, relapse, renunciation, repudiation
declinatory nonconsenting
declinature negation, refusal, rejection
decline abate (lessen), abatement (reduction), avoid (evade), caducity, curtailment, damage, decay, decrease, decrease, deduction (diminution), degenerate, degradation, depreciate, depress, depression, deteriorate, disavow, disdain, dismiss (put out of consideration), disoblige, dissent (withhold assent), ebb, end (termination), expense (sacrifice), fail (lose), forbear, forgo, forswear, languish, lapse (expiration), lessen, loss, rebuff, refrain, refuse, reject, relapse, relapse, renounce, repudiate, spurn, subside
decline and fall decrease
decline to agree dissent (withhold assent)
decline to pay dishonor (refuse to pay)
decline to redeem dishonor (refuse to pay)
decline to sanction disapprove (reject)
declining decadent, old, stale
declining to agree dissenting
decoct distill
decoctor bankrupt
decodable solvable
decode construe (comprehend), construe (translate), elucidate, find (discover), interpret, solve
decoding definition
decompose decay, degenerate, deteriorate, disintegrate, disorganize, dissolve (disperse), spoil (impair)
decomposed dilapidated
decomposing decadent
decomposition consumption, destruction, deterioration, dissolution (disintegration), spoilage
decompound decay
decontrol disengage, freedom
decorare embellish, garnish, honor
decorate embellish, honor
decorated elaborate, pretentious (ostentatious)
decoration mention (tribute), motif, prize
decorous formal, obeisant, proper, suitable
decorously respectfully
decorousness decorum, propriety

(correctness)
decorum behavior, conduct
decorum decorum
decorum deportment, formality, manner *(behavior)*, presence *(poise)*, propriety *(correctness)*, protocol *(etiquette)*
decoy bait *(lure)*, betray *(lead astray)*, cloak, deceive, deception, delude, ensnare, entice, entrap, fake, illude, inveigle, lure, maneuver *(trick)*, mislead, ruse
decrease abate *(lessen)*, abatement *(reduction)*, abridge *(shorten)*, allay, attenuate, attrition, curtail, curtailment, decline, decrement, deduct *(reduce)*, deduction *(diminution)*, deplete, depreciate, depress, deteriorate, diminish, diminution, discount, discount *(reduce)*, ebb, erode, erosion, lessen, minimize, mitigate, mitigation, moderate *(temper)*, modify *(moderate)*, mollification, mollify, palliate *(abate)*, rebate, reduce, remission, remit *(relax)*, retrench, subside
decrease a punishment commute
decrease in excellence impair
decrease in importance demote
decrease in purchasing power inflation *(decrease in value of currency)*
decreased qualified *(conditioned)*
decree adjudge, adjudicate, adjudication, appointment *(act of designating)*, arbitrate *(adjudge)*, arbitration, award, award, brevet, canon, charter *(declaration of rights)*, citation *(charge)*, codification, cognovit, command, compel, conclude *(decide)*, conclusion *(determination)*, constitute *(establish)*, constrain *(compel)*, conviction *(finding of guilt)*, decide, decision *(judgment)*, declaration, detail *(assign)*, determination, determine, dictate, dictate, direct *(order)*, direction *(order)*, directive, edict, enact, enactment, enjoin, fiat, finding, hold *(decide)*, holding *(ruling of a court)*, impose *(enforce)*, instruct *(direct)*, instruction *(direction)*, issuance, judge, judgment *(formal court decree)*, law, legislate, mandamus, mandate, measure, mittimus, monition *(legal summons)*, necessitate, notice *(announcement)*, opinion *(judicial decision)*, order *(judicial directive)*, order, ordinance, pass *(approve)*, pass *(determine)*, precept, prescribe, prescription *(directive)*, press *(constrain)*, proclamation, pronounce *(pass judgment)*, pronouncement, regulation *(rule)*, require *(compel)*, requirement, res judicata, rule *(legal dictate)*, rule *(decide)*, rule *(govern)*, ruling, sentence, statute, warrant *(judicial writ)*, writ
decree absolute law
decree authoritatively arbitrate *(adjudge)*
decree beforehand preordain
decree by deliberate judgment award
decree by judicial authority conclude *(decide)*, determine
decree by law legalize
decree having the force of law fiat
decree of a jury verdict
decree of nullity annulment, divorce
decree of punishment sentence
decree to be merited award

decreed decretal, legal, mandatory, necessary *(inescapable)*, positive *(prescribed)*
decreeing legislative
decreement declaration, opinion *(judicial decision)*
decrement abatement *(reduction)*, consumption, damage, decline, decrease, deduction *(diminution)*, discount, erosion, loss, spoilage
decremental drawback
decrepit decadent, dilapidated, disabled *(made incapable)*, imperfect, old, powerless, unsound *(not strong)*
decrepitude decline, deterioration, disrepair, impuissance, prostration
decreptitude caducity
decrescence curtailment, decrease, decrement, deduction *(diminution)*
decrescere abate *(lessen)*
decretal declaratory, determinative, directive, mandate, mittimus, prescriptive, proclamation, requirement, writ
decretive compulsory, declaratory, decretal
decretory declaratory, decretal
decretum decree, edict, holding *(ruling of a court)*, ordinance, principle *(axiom)*, resolution *(decision)*, sentence
decrial bad repute, blame *(culpability)*, conviction *(finding of guilt)*, denunciation, disapprobation, dishonor *(shame)*, disparagement, impugnation, incrimination, ostracism
decried blameful
decry brand *(stigmatize)*, cavil, censure, complain *(criticize)*, condemn *(blame)*, contemn, criticize *(find fault with)*, debunk, defame, denigrate, denounce *(condemn)*, deprecate, depreciate, derogate, disapprove *(condemn)*, discommend, discredit, disdain, disparage, except *(object)*, fault, impeach, lash *(attack verbally)*, lessen, libel, malign, minimize, remonstrate, reprehend, reprimand, reproach, smear, sully
decrying calumnious, contemptuous, cynical, pejorative
decurrence decline
decursio maneuver *(tactic)*
decursus maneuver *(tactic)*
decussatio intersection
decussation intersection
dedecorare disgrace, dishonor *(deprive of honor)*
dedecorate demote
dedecoration ignominy, notoriety, scandal
dedecori esse disgrace
dedecus degradation, discredit, opprobrium
dedere deliver, devote, surrender *(yield)*, yield *(submit)*
dedicare dedicate
dedicate devote
dedicate oneself to specialize
dedicated industrious, loyal, obedient, purposeful, sacrosanct, serious *(devoted)*, steadfast, true *(loyal)*, unyielding, zealous
dedication adherence *(devotion)*, inscription, loyalty
dedicatory honorary
deditum esse adhere *(maintain loyalty)*
deduce ascertain, assume *(suppose)*,

conclude *(decide)*, construe *(comprehend)*, deduct *(conclude by reasoning)*, detect, determine, discover, educe, extract, find *(determine)*, gauge, infer, interpret, judge, presume, presuppose, read, reason *(conclude)*, reflect *(ponder)*, solve, surmise, suspect *(think)*, understand
deduce by interpretation construe *(comprehend)*
deduce the meaning of construe *(comprehend)*
deduced circumstantial
deducere derive *(deduce)*, divert
deducible accountable *(explainable)*, convincing, deductible *(provable)*, deductive, determinable *(ascertainable)*, provable
deducibly a priori
deducing dialectic
deduct construe *(comprehend)*, decrease, deduce, depreciate, diminish, except *(exclude)*, excise *(cut away)*, lessen, minimize, rebate, remove *(eliminate)*, retrench, withdraw
deduct from discount *(reduce)*
deducting save
deductio deduction *(diminution)*, discount, discount *(disbelieve)*
deduction computation, concept, conclusion *(determination)*, consequence *(conclusion)*, construction, corollary, decrease, decrement, dialectic, diminution, discount, estimate *(idea)*, estimation *(calculation)*, holding *(ruling of a court)*, hypothesis, inference, perception, presumption, ratiocination, rebate, removal
deductive discursive *(analytical)*, logical
deductively a priori
deed act *(enactment)*, act *(undertaking)*, alienate *(transfer title)*, cede, contribute *(supply)*, convey *(transfer)*, descend, dominion *(absolute ownership)*, endeavor, give *(grant)*, grant *(transfer formally)*, instrument *(document)*, overt act, performance *(execution)*, present *(make a gift)*, step, title *(right)*, transaction, transfer
deed done fait accompli
deed exculpating the transferor quitclaim
deed of agreement indenture
deed of release quitclaim, waiver
deed of savagery atrocity
deeding alienation *(transfer of title)*, demise *(conveyance)*
deeds conduct, dealings
deem adjudge, adjudicate, conclude *(decide)*, deduce, deduct *(conclude by reasoning)*, guess, judge, opine, presume, presuppose, regard *(pay attention)*, surmise, suspect *(think)*
deem true assume *(suppose)*
deem unbecoming disdain
deem unsuitable disdain
deemed putative
deep broad, capacious, esoteric, extensive, incomprehensible, ingrained, intense, obscure *(abstruse)*, profound *(intense)*, recondite, sapient
deep application diligence *(care)*
deep attention diligence *(care)*
deep down virtual
deep rooted virtual

deep seated intrinsic *(deep down)*, virtual

deep study diligence *(care)*, preoccupation, probe

deep thought diligence *(care)*

deep-rooted chronic, inherent, inveterate, organic, stable, underlying

deep-rooted belief faith

deep-seated chronic, ingrained, permanent

deepen aggravate *(exacerbate)*, enhance, expand, extend *(enlarge)*, intensify, magnify

deepening aggravation *(exacerbation)*, boom *(increase)*, cumulative *(intensifying)*

deeply felt profound *(intense)*

deescalate disarm *(divest of arms)*

deface damage, destroy *(efface)*, harm, maim, mutilate, spoil *(impair)*, sully, tarnish

defaced blemished, marred

defacement flaw

defacer vandal

defalcate cheat, embezzle, loot, purloin

defalcation bad faith, embezzlement, misappropriation

defalcator embezzler, thief

defamation aspersion, denunciation, dishonor *(shame)*, hatred, infamy, libel, malediction, obloquy, opprobrium, phillipic, scandal, shame, slander, vilification

defamatory calumnious, contemptuous, critical *(faultfinding)*, cynical, derogatory, incriminatory, libelous, pejorative, scandalous

defamatory words slander

defamatory writing libel

defame brand *(stigmatize)*, denigrate, denounce *(condemn)*, depreciate, derogate, disgrace, dishonor *(deprive of honor)*, disparage, expose, humiliate, lessen, libel, malign, pillory, reproach, smear, stain, sully, tarnish

defame by a published writing libel

defamed accused *(attacked)*

default arrears, breach, defeat, defect, deficit, delinquency *(failure of duty)*, delinquency *(shortage)*, dereliction, dishonor *(nonpayment)*, disregard *(omission)*, failure *(bankruptcy)*, forfeit, infraction, lapse *(expiration)*, maladministration, miscarriage, neglect, nonappearance, nonpayment, nonperformance, omission, repudiate

default in performance omission

defaultant delinquent *(overdue)*

defaulter convict, fugitive, thief

defaulting bankrupt, bankruptcy, delinquent *(overdue)*, insolvent

defeasance abolition, countermand, discharge *(annulment)*, discharge *(release from obligation)*, discontinuance *(act of discontinuing)*, dissolution *(termination)*, repudiation, rescision, revocation

defeasible terminable, voidable

defeat abate *(extinguish)*, abatement *(extinguishment)*, answer *(reply)*, avoid *(cancel)*, balk, circumvent, contravene, controvert, counteract, debacle, failure *(lack of success)*, foil, frustrate, frustration, halt, miscarriage, negate, nonsuit, obliterate, overcome *(surmount)*, over-

ride, overthrow, overturn, overwhelm, preclude, prevent, prostration, rebuff, refute, rejection, repulse, subdue, subject, subjugate, subversion, subvert, surmount, thwart, upset

defeat of the prosecution compurgation

defeat one's own purpose overreach

defeat oneself by overdoing matters overreach

defeated despondent, disappointed, null *(invalid)*, null and void

defeating prevailing *(having superior force)*

defeatism pessimism

defeatist cynical, despondent, pessimistic, resigned

defect abandon *(physically leave)*, defacement, deficiency, disadvantage, disease, disqualification *(factor that disqualifies)*, drawback, fault *(weakness)*, flaw, foible, frailty, handicap, leave *(depart)*, part *(leave)*, quit *(evacuate)*, stigma, vice

defect-free accurate

defectio failure *(falling short)*, revolt

defection abandonment *(desertion)*, abjuration, absence *(nonattendance)*, bad faith, dereliction, desertion, disloyalty, infidelity, repudiation, revolt, sedition

defective bad *(inferior)*, blemished, broken *(fractured)*, deficient, faulty, imperfect, inferior *(lower in quality)*, insufficient, marred, non compos mentis, nonsubstantial *(not sturdy)*, peccable, poor *(inferior in quality)*, undesirable, unsound *(fallacious)*, unsound *(not strong)*

defective check bad check

defectiveness failure *(falling short)*, frailty

defectless absolute *(ideal)*, infallible

defend adhere *(maintain loyalty)*, advocate, answer *(reply)*, answer *(respond legally)*, corroborate, countercharge, cover *(guard)*, espouse, harbor, justify, lobby, maintain *(sustain)*, palliate *(excuse)*, preserve, protect, save *(rescue)*, screen *(guard)*, side, sponsor, support *(assist)*, support *(justify)*, sustain *(confirm)*, uphold

defend a case plead *(argue a case)*

defend as conformable to law justify

defend as conformable to right justify

defend successfully support *(justify)*

defendable defensible, justifiable, tenable

defendant convict, litigant, party *(litigant)*, respondent

defendant's answer to charges plea, pleading

defended guarded, insusceptible *(resistant)*, ironclad, safe, secure *(free from danger)*

defender advocate *(counselor)*, advocate *(espouser)*, apologist, backer, benefactor, custodian *(protector)*, guardian, partisan, patron *(influential supporter)*, proponent, samaritan

defendere parry, protect

defense advocacy, alibi, ammunition, answer *(judicial response)*, argument *(pleading)*, behalf, bulwark,

compurgation, counterargument, excuse, explanation, justification, panoply, plea, pleading, preservation, pretext, protection, reason *(basis)*, rejoinder, safeguard, safekeeping, salvo, security *(safety)*, shelter *(protection)*, shield, support *(assistance)*, ward

defenseless disabled *(made incapable)*, indefensible, insecure, open *(accessible)*, powerless, precarious, unable, untenable, vulnerable

defenselessness danger, impotence

defensible inexpugnable, justifiable, pardonable, plausible, tenable, unobjectionable

defensio assertion

defensive preventive, protective

defensive arms panoply

defensive clothing panoply

defensive equipment panoply

defensive evidence alibi

defensive plea alibi

defensor apologist, guardian

defer accommodate, adjourn, continue *(adjourn)*, delay, discontinue *(break continuity)*, hold up *(delay)*, postpone, procrastinate, stall, suspend

defer to acknowledge *(verify)*, comply, concur *(agree)*, hear *(give attention to)*, honor, obey, recognize *(acknowledge)*, regard *(hold in esteem)*, relent

deference allegiance, character *(reputation)*, comity, consideration *(sympathetic regard)*, courtesy, discipline *(obedience)*, estimation *(esteem)*, fealty, homage, honor *(outward respect)*, regard *(esteem)*, resignation *(passive acceptance)*, respect

deferential civil *(polite)*, malleable, obedient, obeisant, obsequious, pliant, sequacious, servile, subservient

deferentially respectfully

deferment adjournment, delay, extension *(postponement)*, pause, reprieve

deferral deferment, extension *(postponement)*, moratorium

deferre devolve, invest *(vest)*, tender

deferred arrested *(checked)*, back *(in arrears)*, late *(tardy)*

deferred payment arrears, bill *(invoice)*, debit, debt, nonpayment

deferring dilatory, obeisant

defiance conflict, contradiction, disrespect, impugnation, infraction, insurrection, mutiny, negation, noncompliance *(nonobservance)*, nonconformity, protest, provocation, rebellion, rebuff, refusal, resistance, revolt, sedition, spite

defiance of custom deviation, exception *(exclusion)*, quirk *(idiosyncrasy)*

defiance of danger audacity, prowess *(bravery)*

defiance of orders contempt *(disobedience to the court)*, infraction

defiance of precedent creation

defiant brazen, contemptuous, contumacious, disobedient, disorderly, impertinent *(insolent)*, indomitable, insolent, insubordinate, intractable, nonconforming, nonconsenting, proud *(conceited)*, provocative, pugnacious, recalcitrant

deficere fail *(lose)*

deficiency absence *(omission)*, dearth, defect, deficit, delinquency *(shortage)*, disadvantage, failure *(falling short)*, fault *(weakness),* flaw, foible, frailty, handicap, insufficiency, mediocrity, need *(deprivation),* paucity, poverty, vice

deficient defective, delinquent *(overdue),* devoid, fallible, faulty, imperfect, inadequate, incompetent, inferior *(lower in quality),* insufficient, minimal, nonsubstantial *(not sturdy),* nonsubstantial *(not sufficient),* paltry, partial *(relating to a part),* perfunctory, poor *(inferior in quality),* scarce, unqualified *(not competent),* unsatisfactory, unsound *(not strong)*

deficient in reason fatuous

deficient work noncompliance *(improper completion)*

deficit arrears, debt, decrement, deficiency, delinquency *(shortage),* due, insufficiency, need *(deprivation),* poverty

defile abuse *(violate),* adulterate, betray *(lead astray),* brand *(stigmatize),* contaminate, contemn, damage, debase, deteriorate, disgrace, dishonor *(deprive of honor),* infect, malign, misemploy, mishandle *(maltreat),* molest *(subject to indecent advances),* pillory, pollute, smear, spoil *(impair),* stain, sully, taint *(contaminate),* taint *(corrupt)*

defiled sordid, tainted *(contaminated)*

defilement abuse *(physical misuse),* air pollution, attaint, bad repute, contaminate, contempt *(disdain),* debauchment, disgrace, dishonor *(shame),* misusage, perversion, rape, seduction, shame

definability construction

definable accountable *(explainable),* ascertainable, determinable *(ascertainable)*

define border *(bound),* call *(title),* clarify, comment, construe *(translate),* delimit, delineate, demarcate, describe, designate, distinguish, elucidate, explain, explicate, expound, illustrate, interpret, render *(depict),* restrict, trace *(delineate)*

define limits locate

define location locate

defined actual, coherent *(clear),* comprehensible, exact, express, manifest, narrow, perceptible, precise, qualified *(conditioned),* stated, unambiguous, unequivocal, unmistakable

defining restrictive

definire circumscribe *(define),* define, fix *(settle)*

definite absolute *(conclusive),* actual, apparent *(perceptible),* axiomatic, categorical, certain *(fixed),* certain *(positive),* certain *(specific),* clear *(certain),* cogent, cognizable, coherent *(clear),* conclusive *(determinative),* concrete, conspicuous, corporeal, decisive, definitive, demonstrable, distinct *(clear),* dogmatic, explicit, express, factual, fixed *(settled),* inappealable, incontrovertible, indubious, inevitable, irrevocable, limited, official, overt, palpable, particular *(individual),* peremptory *(absolute),* positive *(confident),* positive *(incontestable),* precise, reliable, resounding, several *(separate),* specific, tangible, unalienable, unalterable, unambiguous, unequivocal

definite carelessness res ipsa

loquitur

definite form embodiment

definite procedure avenue *(means of attainment),* modus operandi

definitely fairly *(clearly)*

definiteness belief *(state of mind),* certainty, certitude, specialty *(distinctive mark),* surety *(certainty)*

definition clarification, construction, description, explanation, identification, meaning, rendition *(explication),* specification

definitional descriptive

definitions on the law charge *(statement to the jury)*

definitive absolute *(conclusive),* categorical, clear *(certain),* cogent, complete *(ended),* conclusive *(settled),* crucial, decisive, descriptive, determinative, dogmatic, extreme *(last),* factual, final, inappealable, interpretive, last *(final),* thorough

definitive answer verdict

definitiveness finality

definitus categorical, definite, explicit, unambiguous

deflagrate burn

deflagration conflagration

deflate attenuate, browbeat, debunk, decrease, deduct *(reduce),* demean *(make lower),* demote, denounce *(condemn),* depreciate, depress, diminish, disable, discount *(minimize),* disgrace, disparage, exhaust *(deplete),* humiliate, lessen, minimize

deflated disgraceful

deflation decline, decrease, depression, diminution, disgrace

deflect avert, counter, deter, detour, deviate, discourage, divert, parry, prevent, repel *(drive back),* stave

deflection alienation *(estrangement),* detour

deflere deplore

defloration debauchment, rape

deflower dishonor *(deprive of honor)*

deflowering debauchment, defilement

defluxion outflow

defoliate denude

deform camouflage, contort, damage, deface, denature, disorganize, distort, mutilate, spoil *(impair)*

deform one's character brutalize

deformare deface

deformation defacement, detriment, distortion

deformed blemished, defective, marred

deformity defacement, defect, distortion, flaw

defraud betray *(lead astray),* bilk, cheat, circumvent, corrupt, deceive, defalcate, delude, dupe, embezzle, ensnare, evade *(deceive),* fake, hoodwink, illude, inveigle, mislabel, mislead, misrepresent, overreach, palter, peculate, prevaricate, purloin

defraudare defraud

defraudation bunko, conversion *(misappropriation),* deception, hoax, knavery, misappropriation

defrauded aggrieved *(victimized)*

defrauder criminal, embezzler, lawbreaker, thief

defrauding collusive

defraudment deception

defray bear the expense, compensate *(remunerate),* disburse *(pay out),* pay, remit *(send payment),* remunerate

defray expenses bear the expense

defray in advance prepay

defray the cost bear the expense, disburse *(pay out)*

defrayal amortization, collection *(payment),* compensation, disbursement *(funds paid out),* discharge *(payment),* expenditure, expense *(cost),* pay, payment *(act of paying),* recovery *(award),* reimbursement, remittance, remuneration, satisfaction *(discharge of debt)*

defrayment advance *(allowance),* amortization, collection *(payment),* commission *(fee),* compensation, consideration *(recompense),* disbursement *(funds paid out),* discharge *(payment),* expenditure, expense *(cost),* pay, payment *(act of paying),* recompense, remittance, remuneration, satisfaction *(discharge of debt)*

defrock disgrace

deft artful, capable, competent, diplomatic, efficient, expert, facile, familiar *(informed),* practiced, proficient, qualified *(competent),* resourceful, sciential, subtle *(refined),* veteran

deftness discretion *(quality of being discreet),* efficiency, facility *(easiness),* faculty *(ability),* gift *(flair),* propensity, prowess *(ability),* skill

defugere shun

defunct dead, deceased, lifeless *(dead),* null *(invalid),* null and void, outdated

defy break *(violate),* challenge, complain *(criticize),* conflict, confront *(oppose),* contest, contravene, counter, counteract, cross *(disagree with),* disaffirm, disagree, disobey, dissent *(withhold assent),* fight *(counteract),* flout, oppose, oppugn, provoke, rebel, resist *(oppose),* violate, withstand

defying contemptuous

defying lawful authority contumacious

degeneracy bad repute, caducity, decline, delinquency *(misconduct),* turpitude, vice

degenerare degenerate

degenerate bad *(offensive),* contaminate, corrupt, debauch, decadent, decay, decline *(fall),* depraved, depreciate, deteriorate, dissolute, ebb, ignoble, immoral, lawless, lessen, nefarious, perverse, pervert, profligate *(corrupt),* recidivate, regressive, relapse, reprobate, taint *(corrupt),* tainted *(corrupted),* vicious

degenerateness decline

degeneratess degradation

degenerating decadent

degeneration decline, degradation, detriment, disrepair, recidivism, relapse, sodomy

degenerative bad *(inferior)*

degradation attaint, bad repute, defilement, deterioration, discredit, disgrace, dishonor *(shame),* disrepute, ignominy, ill repute, infamy, libel, misusage, misuse, notoriety, obloquy, odium, onus *(stigma),* opprobrium, perversion, reproach, scandal, shame, turpitude

degrade abuse *(violate)*, adulterate, contaminate, damage, debase, debauch, decry, defame, degenerate, demean *(make lower)*, demote, denigrate, denounce *(condemn)*, depreciate, deteriorate, discredit, disgrace, dishonor *(deprive of honor)*, disoblige, disparage, humiliate, libel, minimize, pillory, pollute, smear, sully, taint *(contaminate)*, tarnish

degraded bad *(inferior)*, bad *(offensive)*, depraved, disreputable, dissolute, ignoble, notorious, sordid, tainted *(corrupted)*

degraded person degenerate

degrading disgraceful, unbecoming

degredi deviate

degree caliber *(measurement)*, extent, magnitude, nuance, prestige, step, utmost

degree of importance weight *(importance)*

degreeholder specialist

dehiscent open *(unclosed)*, penetrable

dehonestare disgrace, dishonor *(deprive of honor)*

dehort admonish *(warn)*, discourage, expostulate, protest

dehortari dissuade

dehortation admonition, monition *(warning)*, notice *(warning)*, remonstrance

dehortative remonstrative

dehortatory remonstrative

dehumanize brutalize, debase

dehumanized diabolic

deicere disappoint, dislodge, eject *(evict)*, overthrow, precipitate *(throw down violently)*

deific omniscient

deifical omniscient

deification elevation

deify elevate

deign accede *(concede)*, bestow, patronize *(condescend toward)*

deign to give vouchsafe

deign to grant vouchsafe

deject depress, discourage

dejected despondent, disappointed, disconsolate, lugubrious, pessimistic

dejectedness pessimism

dejection depression, dissatisfaction, pessimism, prostration

delate complain *(charge)*, denigrate, implicate, involve *(implicate)*

delatio denunciation

delation accusation, blame *(culpability)*, charge *(accusation)*, count, denunciation, indictment

delation by criminal charges arraignment

delator accuser, appellant, complainant, informant

delator informer *(a person who provides information)*

delay abeyance, adjourn, arrest *(stop)*, balk, block, cessation *(interlude)*, check *(bar)*, check *(restrain)*, constrict *(inhibit)*, continue *(adjourn)*, curb, damper *(stopper)*, defer *(put off)*, deferment, detain *(restrain)*, discontinue *(break continuity)*, doubt *(hesitate)*, extension *(postponement)*, filibuster, halt, hamper, hesitate, hesitation, hiatus, impede, inhibit, interrupt, interruption, keep *(restrain)*, laches, moratorium, obstacle,

obstruct, pause, pause, postpone, prevent, procrastinate, protract *(prolong)*, remain *(stay)*, reprieve, stall, stay, stay *(halt)*, stop, suspend

delay attended by change of position laches

delay enforcing rights forbear

delay in execution reprieve

delay in legislation filibuster

delay in punishment reprieve

delay that results in disadvantage laches

delayed arrested *(checked)*, back *(in arrears)*, dilatory, late *(tardy)*, overdue

delaying dilatory

dele delete, edit

delectable nectarious, palatable, sapid, savory

delectare interest

delectation enjoyment *(pleasure)*

delectus choice *(alternatives offered)*, choice *(decision)*, selection *(choice)*

delegare delegate

delegate agent, appoint, assign *(designate)*, charge *(empower)*, commit *(entrust)*, conduit *(intermediary)*, deliver, deputy, detail *(assign)*, employ *(engage services)*, empower, entrust, executor, factor *(commission merchant)*, functionary, hire, induct, intermediary, invest *(vest)*, liaison, medium, plenipotentiary, proctor, procurator, proxy, relegate, remand, replacement, representative *(proxy)*, spokesman, substitute

delegate authority to charge *(empower)*

delegate to authorize

delegate upon another devolve

delegated representative, surrogate

delegated authority bureaucracy

delegates delegation *(envoy)*, deputation *(delegation)*, government *(political administration)*

delegating delegation *(assignment)*, designation *(naming)*

delegation agency *(commission)*, agency *(legal relationship)*, appointment *(act of designating)*, assignment *(designation)*, charter *(sanction)*, commission *(agency)*, committee, constituency, decentralization, deputation *(delegation)*, deputation *(selection of delegates)*, designation *(naming)*, devolution, embassy, mission, nomination

delegation of duties devolution

delere abolish, cancel, expunge, obliterate

delete abolish, bowdlerize, censor, deface, diminish, edit, eliminate *(eradicate)*, eradicate, except *(exclude)*, excise *(cut away)*, expunge, expurgate, obliterate, omit, redact, remove *(eliminate)*, repeal, retrench, suppress

deleted null *(invalid)*

deleterious adverse *(negative)*, bad *(inferior)*, detrimental, disadvantageous, disastrous, fatal, harmful, inadvisable, insalubrious, malevolent, malignant, noxious, peccant *(unhealthy)*, pernicious, pestilent, prejudicial, toxic, virulent

deletion annulment, cancellation, rescision

deliberare deliberate

deliberate aforethought, circumspect, cogitative, cold-blooded, confer *(con-

sult)*, consider, consult *(ask advice of)*, debate, discreet, doubt *(hesitate)*, express, hesitant, intentional, judicious, knowing, muse, oscillate, pause, ponder, premeditated, purposeful, reason *(conclude)*, reflect *(ponder)*, review, speculate *(conjecture)*, tactical, treat *(process)*, try *(conduct a trial)*, voluntary, weigh, willful

deliberate application diligence *(care)*

deliberate attention diligence *(care)*

deliberate burning of property arson

deliberate choice election *(choice)*

deliberate determination adjudication

deliberate falsification story *(falsehood)*

deliberate intent premeditation

deliberate intention forethought, premeditation

deliberate malice cruelty, ill will

deliberate misrepresentation subreption

deliberate omission dispensation *(exception)*

deliberate over brood

deliberate study diligence *(care)*

deliberate thought diligence *(care)*

deliberate upon discuss, investigate

deliberately knowingly, purposely

deliberately avoid shun

deliberately intended premeditated

deliberately slow dilatory

deliberateness animus, contemplation, moderation

deliberatio deliberation

deliberation conference, contemplation, conversation, council *(consultant)*, dialectic, discretion *(quality of being discreet)*, examination *(study)*, forethought, hindsight, negotiation, parley, prudence, purpose, reflection *(thought)*, speculation *(conjecture)*

deliberative circumspect, cogitative, deliberate, pensive, speculative

deliberative body panel *(discussion group)*

deliberative group commission *(agency)*

delicacy consideration *(sympathetic regard)*, decorum, discretion *(quality of being discreet)*, fault *(weakness)*, frailty, nuance, propriety *(correctness)*, sensibility

delicacy of feeling sensibility

delicate destructible, impalpable, intricate, nonsubstantial *(not sturdy)*, palatable, precarious, subtle *(refined)*, tenuous

delicate distinction differential

delicatus particular *(exacting)*

delicious nectarious, palatable, sapid, savory

delict crime, guilt, misdeed, offense

delictum crime, delict, delinquency *(misconduct)*, fault *(responsibility)*, misconduct, misdeed, misdemeanor, offense, transgression

deligere choose, elect *(choose)*

delight enjoyment *(pleasure)*, treat

delight in relish

delighted ecstatic, inclined, proud *(self-respecting)*, ready *(willing)*

delightful attractive, palatable, sapid,

savory
delightfulness amenity
delimit allot, apportion, border
(bound), circumscribe *(define)*, demarcate, determine, hedge, restrain, restrict
delimitate border *(bound)*, demarcate, hedge, restrict
delimitation boundary, definition, periphery, purview, specification
delimited qualified *(conditioned)*
delineate amplify, analyze, border
(bound), characterize, circumscribe *(define)*, circumscribe *(surround by boundary)*, clarify, construe *(translate)*, define, depict, describe, detail
(particularize), draw *(depict)*, exemplify, expound, hedge, identify, interpret, locate, portray, recite, recount, render
(depict), represent *(portray)*, signify
(denote)
delineated detailed
delineation analysis, boundary, clarification, configuration *(confines)*, construction, contour *(outline)*, definition, description, design *(construction plan)*, explanation, identification, narration, rendition *(explication)*, scheme, symbol
delineation lines ambit
delineative descriptive
delineatory demonstrative *(illustrative)*
delinquence default
delinquency arrears, bad repute, blame *(culpability)*, breach, crime, culpability, default, dereliction, dishonor
(nonpayment), disregard *(omission)*, failure *(falling short)*, fault *(responsibility)*, guilt, lapse *(expiration)*, misconduct, misdeed, misdoing, misprision, neglect, negligence, nonfeasance, nonpayment, nonperformance, offense, omission, transgression, vice, wrong
delinquent blameful, blameworthy, broken *(unfulfilled)*, convict, culpable, derelict *(negligent)*, disobedient, due
(owed), felon, guilty, lawbreaker, malefactor, negligent, offender, outlaw, outstanding *(unpaid)*, overdue, recidivist, remiss, reprehensible, wrongdoer
deliquare clarify
deliquesce lessen
delirious with joy ecstatic
delirium insanity
delitescence indistinctness, privacy
delitescency indistinctness
delitescent covert, hidden, indiscernible, indistinct, latent, surreptitious
delitescere abscond, lurk
deliver assign *(transfer ownership)*, attorn, bear *(yield)*, bestow, cede, clear, confer *(give)*, consign, contribute *(supply)*, convey *(transfer)*, delegate, devolve, discharge *(liberate)*, disengage, disenthrall, dole, extricate, free, give
(grant), grant *(transfer formally)*, impart, liberate, pardon, parole, pass *(determine)*, phrase, post, present *(make a gift)*, pronounce *(speak)*, provide *(supply)*, publish, quit *(free of)*, recite, redeem *(repurchase)*, refer *(send for action)*, release, relieve *(free from burden)*, relinquish, remark, rescue, serve
(deliver a legal instrument), speak, supply, tender, transfer, transmit, transport, utter
deliver a charge discharge *(shoot)*
deliver a judgment pass *(determine)*
deliver a speech discourse
deliver a summons and complaint
serve *(deliver a legal instrument)*
deliver a talk address *(talk to)*, discourse
deliver an address discourse, pronounce *(speak)*, speak
deliver an instrument file *(place among official records)*
deliver as one's act and deed certify *(attest)*
deliver formally consign, pronounce
(speak)
deliver from a hindrance disencumber
deliver from bondage disenthrall, free
deliver from uncertainty assure
(give confidence to)
deliver in trust delegate
deliver information report *(disclose)*
deliver into custody commit *(institutionalize)*
deliver judgment adjudge, adjudicate, award, conclude *(decide)*, decree, determine, find *(determine)*, pronounce
(pass judgment), rule *(decide)*
deliver oratorically declaim
deliver over alienate *(transfer title)*, consign, convey *(transfer)*, delegate, demise, pass *(advance)*, serve *(deliver a legal instrument)*, transfer
deliver over to a successor devolve
deliver to bequeath, remove *(transfer)*
deliver to the care of confide *(trust)*
deliver up betray *(lead astray)*, forfeit
deliverable assignable
deliverance absolution, alienation
(transfer of title), catharsis, delivery, demise *(conveyance)*, devolution, discharge *(liberation)*, discharge *(release from obligation)*, disposition *(transfer of property)*, emancipation, freedom, help, holding *(ruling of a court)*, liberation, liberty, mainstay, parole, pronouncement, ransom, redemption, relief *(release)*, resolution *(formal statement)*, respite *(reprieve)*, salvage, transmittal
deliverance from bondage emancipation
delivered clear *(free from criminal charges)*, free *(relieved from a burden)*
deliverer donor, good samaritan
delivering to consignment
delivery alienation *(transfer of title)*, assignment *(transfer of ownership)*, birth *(emergence of young)*, cession, conveyance, course, demise *(conveyance)*, devolution, discharge *(release from obligation)*, disposition *(transfer of property)*, intonation, issuance, liberation, parlance, rhetoric *(skilled speech)*, speech, transmittal
delivery back replevin
delivery of a writ service *(delivery of legal process)*
delivery of process service *(delivery of legal process)*
delivery of title feoffment
delocalization asportation
delocalize dislodge, displace *(remove)*, remove *(eliminate)*

deludable naive
delude bait *(lure)*, betray *(lead astray)*, bilk, circumvent, deceive, defraud, dupe, ensnare, evade *(deceive)*, fabricate *(make up)*, fake, feign, hoodwink, illude, inveigle, lie *(falsify)*, misguide, misinform, mislead, misrepresent, misstate, palter, pretend, prevaricate
delude oneself err, misconceive, misunderstand
deluded blind *(not discerning)*
deludere delude
deluding delusive, illusory, ostensible, prestidigitation, specious
deluge cataclysm, immerse *(plunge into)*, inundate, overage, overcome
(overwhelm), overload, overwhelm, plethora, spate, surfeit
delusion artifice, bad faith, deception, error, fallacy, false pretense, figment, hoax, insanity, lunacy, phantom, ruse, sham
delusional ostensible
delusional insanity paranoia
delusions paranoia
delusive assumed *(feigned)*, colorable
(specious), deceptive, dishonest, disingenuous, evasive, fallacious, false *(inaccurate)*, fictitious, fraudulent, illusory, lying, machiavellian, meretricious, ostensible, sly, specious, spurious, untrue
delusiveness bad faith, deceit, fraud
delusory colorable *(specious)*, deceptive, delusive, dishonest, disingenuous, fallacious, false *(not genuine)*, fraudulent, lying, ostensible, specious
deluxe elaborate, elegant, superior
(excellent)
delve search
delve for hunt
delve into analyze, canvass, examine
(study), inquire, investigate, peruse, probe, research, scrutinize
delving into evidence inquiry *(systematic investigation)*
demagnetize neutralize
demagogue insurgent
demand call *(demand)*, canon, cause of action, coerce, command, compel, compulsion *(coercion)*, constrain *(compel)*, detail *(assign)*, dictate, direct *(order)*, direction *(order)*, directive, dun, dun, entail, exact, excise, excise
(levy a tax), force *(compulsion)*, force
(coerce), importune, impose *(enforce)*, insist, instruct *(direct)*, levy, motion, necessitate, need *(deprivation)*, need
(requirement), need, order, outlet, petition, prerequisite, prescribe, press *(constrain)*, request, request, require *(compel)*, require *(need)*, requirement, requisition, solicit, stress *(strain)*, subpoena, subpoena, summon, ultimatum
demand a payment assess *(tax)*
demand and obtain payment collect
(recover money)
demand for payment bill *(invoice)*
demand made on a stock holder
call *(option)*
demand payment charge *(assess)*, dun, exact, excise *(levy a tax)*
demand toll assess *(tax)*, exact, excise
(levy a tax)
demand with threats dun

demanded compulsory, decretal, essential *(required)*, mandatory, necessary *(required)*, popular, positive *(prescribed)*, requisite

demanded damages ad damnum clause

demander extortionist

demanding exigent, imperative, insistent, operose, particular *(exacting)*, peremptory *(imperative)*, urgent

demanding attention important *(urgent)*

demanding belief plausible

demands interrogatories

demarcate allot, apportion, border *(bound)*, circumscribe *(define)*, delimit, differentiate, distinguish, divide *(separate)*, hedge, label, locate, restrict, specify

demarcation definition, discrimination *(differentiation)*, limitation, outline *(boundary)*, periphery, restriction, severance

demarcation line edge *(border)*, frontier

demark circumscribe *(define)*, demarcate

dematerialize disappear, dissipate *(spread out)*

demean comport *(behave)*, demote, deprecate, derogate, disgrace, humiliate, reduce

demeaning disgraceful

demeanor appearance *(look)*, behavior, complexion, conduct, decorum, deportment, manner *(behavior)*, posture *(attitude)*, presence *(poise)*, temperament

démêlé dispute

demens deranged

demensum ration

dement discompose, disorient, obsess

dementate lunatic

demented deranged, lunatic, non compos mentis

dementedness insanity

dementia insanity

dementia lunacy

demergere overwhelm

demerit defect, flaw, foible, frailty

demesne area *(province)*, domain *(land owned)*, dominion *(absolute ownership)*, locality, location, possession *(ownership)*, property *(land)*, province, realm, region, scope, section *(vicinity)*, sphere, territory

demetere reap

demetiri measure

demilitarization reconversion

demilitarize disarm *(divest of arms)*

deminuere decrease, diminish, lessen

deminutio abatement *(reduction)*, decline, decrease, deduction *(diminution)*

demise abalienate, alienate *(transfer title)*, alienation *(transfer of title)*, assignment *(transfer of ownership)*, attorn, bequeath, bequest, contribute *(supply)*, convey *(transfer)*, conveyance, death, decease, descend, devolution, die, dissolution *(termination)*, end *(termination)*, extremity *(death)*, grant *(transfer formally)*, lease, leave *(give)*, let *(lease)*, rent, sublease, transfer

demised dead, deceased, decedent, defunct, late *(defunct)*, lifeless *(dead)*

demission abandonment *(desertion)*, abdication, deterioration, removal, renunciation, resignation *(relinquishment)*

demit abandon *(relinquish)*, defect, discontinue *(abandon)*, forfeit, relinquish, renounce, resign, retire *(conclude a career)*

demiurgic original *(creative)*, productive

demiurgical original *(creative)*, productive

demobilize disarm *(divest of arms)*, disband, dismiss *(discharge)*, disorganize, dissociate, dissolve *(separate)*

democratic equal, free *(enjoying civil liberty)*

demode outdated

demoded outmoded

demography census

demolish consume, damage, defeat, destroy *(efface)*, devastate, eliminate *(eradicate)*, eradicate, extinguish, extirpate, harm, impair, obliterate, overturn, prejudice *(injure)*, refute, spoil *(impair)*, subvert, upset

demolisher vandal

demolishing dire, disastrous, fatal

demolishment debacle, destruction, detriment

demolition debacle, destruction, dissolution *(disintegration)*, prostration, subversion

demoniac cold-blooded, diabolic, malevolent, malicious, ruthless, sinister

demoniacal cruel, malevolent, malicious, malignant, sinister

demonial malevolent

demonic diabolic

demonstrability corroboration

demonstrable actual, ascertainable, certain *(positive)*, cogent, concrete, convincing, corporeal, de facto, deductible *(provable)*, definite, genuine, incontrovertible, indubious, irrefutable, provable, undeniable

demonstrate bear *(adduce)*, clarify, communicate, construe *(translate)*, disagree, display, document, elucidate, establish *(show)*, evidence, evince, exemplify, exhibit, explain, illustrate, manifest, picket, present *(introduce)*, produce *(offer to view)*, prove, reason *(persuade)*, signify *(denote)*, signify *(inform)*, substantiate, unveil

demonstrate against picket

demonstrate protest picket

demonstrated actual, authentic, certain *(positive)*, conclusive *(determinative)*, indubious, unrefutable

demonstrating cogent

demonstratio manifestation

demonstration argument *(pleading)*, case *(example)*, clarification, corroboration, example, explanation, expression *(manifestation)*, instance, manifestation, pretense *(ostentation)*, proof, protest

demonstrative clear *(apparent)*, declaratory, probative, suggestive *(evocative)*, vehement

demonstrator malcontent

demoralization bad repute, confusion *(turmoil)*, defilement, perversion

demoralize brutalize, debase, deteriorate, discompose, discourage, disgrace, pervert, subvert, taint *(corrupt)*

demoralized bad *(offensive)*, tainted *(corrupted)*, vicious

demoralizing deplorable, disgraceful, disreputable

demorari stay *(halt)*

demortuus late *(defunct)*

demote depose *(remove)*, derogate, dislodge, humiliate, minimize

demotion degradation, ignominy, removal

demulcent medicinal

demur demonstrate *(protest)*, disaffirm, disagree, disapprove *(reject)*, disoblige, disown *(deny the validity)*, dissent *(difference of opinion)*, dissent *(withhold assent)*, doubt *(hesitate)*, except *(object)*, hesitate, negate, object, oppose, pause, pause, protest, refuse, reject, remonstrance, remonstrate, repudiate, vacillate

demure diffident

demureness propriety *(correctness)*

demurral delay, disagreement, pause

demurrer disapproval, exception *(objection)*

demurring disapproval, disinclined, dissenting, hesitant, negative, remonstrative, renitent, restive

demurringly unwillingly

den chamber *(compartment)*

denaturalize contaminate, denature, pollute

denature adulterate, convert *(change use)*, debilitate, deteriorate, transform

deniability cloud *(suspicion)*

deniable contestable, debatable, disputable, dubitative

denial abandonment *(repudiation)*, abjuration, answer *(judicial response)*, answer *(reply)*, contravention, counterargument, declination, disapproval, disclaimer, disdain, embargo, exclusion, incredulity, injunction, negation, opposition, pleading, prohibition, proscription, refusal, rejection, renunciation, repudiation, veto

denial of entry exclusion

denial of justice injustice

denial of the allegations demurrer

denial of the pleading demurrer

denial of the statements demurrer

denigrate cavil, censure, condemn *(blame)*, contemn, decry, defame, denounce *(condemn)*, deprecate, depreciate, derogate, discommend, discredit, dishonor *(deprive of honor)*, disoblige, disparage, fault, impeach, libel, malign, pillory, smear, sully, tarnish

denigrating pejorative

denigration aspersion, bad repute, condemnation *(blame)*, contempt *(disdain)*, defamation, defilement, denunciation, disparagement, impeachment, libel, slander, vilification

denigratory calumnious, contemptuous

dénigrement disparagement

denizen citizen, domiciliary, dwell *(reside)*, habitant, inhabitant, lodger, occupant, occupy *(take possession)*, resident

denizenize adopt, naturalize *(make a citizen)*

denominare denominate

denominate call *(title)*, define, denote, designate, identify, label, mention, nominate, phrase

denomination class, classification, cognomen, color *(complexion)*, designation *(naming)*, identification, kind, manner *(kind)*, nomination, rubric *(title)*, selection *(choice)*, society, style, term *(expression)*, title *(designation)*

denominational partisan, specific

denotare specify

denotate denote

denotation connotation, content *(meaning)*, designation *(naming)*, meaning

denotative representative

denote bear *(adduce)*, bespeak, connote, construe *(translate)*, denominate, designate, evidence, evince, exemplify, express, identify, imply, label, manifest, purport, refer *(direct attention)*, represent *(portray)*, speak

dénouement cessation *(termination)*

denouement conclusion *(outcome)*, consequence *(conclusion)*

dénouement denouement

denouement end *(termination)*, finality, outcome, result

denounce accuse, arraign, blame, cavil, censure, challenge, charge *(accuse)*, cite *(accuse)*, complain *(charge)*, complain *(criticize)*, condemn *(blame)*, contemn, convict, decry, defame, demonstrate *(protest)*, denigrate, deprecate, depreciate, disapprove *(condemn)*, discommend, dishonor *(deprive of honor)*, disoblige, except *(object)*, expose, fault, impeach, implicate, impugn, incriminate, inform *(betray)*, inveigh, involve *(implicate)*, libel, malign, oppugn, pillory, protest, rebel, reprehend, reprimand, reproach, smear, sully

denounce falsely frame *(charge falsely)*

denounce unfairly frame *(charge falsely)*

denounce unjustly frame *(charge falsely)*

denouncement blame *(culpability)*, charge *(accusation)*, complaint, conviction *(finding of guilt)*, denunciation, disapprobation, disapproval, disparagement, impeachment, incrimination, reproach

denouncer accuser, complainant, contender

denouncing inculpatory

dense cohesive *(compact)*, impervious, obtuse, opaque, ossified, ponderous, populous, rife, solid *(compact)*

denseness ignorance, opacity

densified compact *(dense)*

densify concentrate *(consolidate)*, consolidate *(strengthen)*

density mass *(weight)*, opacity

dented blemished

denudate denude

denude abduct, bare, deprive, despoil, expose, unveil

denuded of devoid, insufficient

denunciate arraign, censure, charge *(accuse)*, complain *(charge)*, convict, denounce *(condemn)*, disapprove *(condemn)*, impeach, proscribe *(denounce)*, reproach

denunciation allegation, aspersion, bad repute, blame *(culpability)*, charge

(accusation), complaint, condemnation *(blame)*, contempt *(disdain)*, contradiction, conviction *(finding of guilt)*, count, criticism, diatribe, disapprobation, disapproval, discredit, disparagement, expletive, ignominy, impeachment, imprecation, inculpation, indictment, libel, malediction, notoriety, objection, objurgation, obloquy, onus *(stigma)*, outcry, phillipic, profanity, proscription, reprimand, reproach, revilement, sanction *(punishment)*, slander, stricture, vilification

denunciatory calumnious, contemptuous, critical *(faultfinding)*, cynical, derogatory, incriminatory, inculpatory, libelous, pejorative, scandalous

denuntiatio innuendo, intimation, notice *(announcement)*, notice *(warning)*, notice *(give formal warning)*, notification, threat

denuntiatio testimonii subpoena, subpoena

denuo reconsider

deny adeem, annul, answer *(reply)*, ban, bar *(exclude)*, bear false witness, cancel, condemn *(ban)*, confront *(oppose)*, constrain *(restrain)*, contradict, contravene, controvert, demur, disaccord, disaffirm, disagree, disallow, disapprove *(reject)*, disavow, disclaim, dismiss *(put out of consideration)*, disown *(deny the validity)*, disprove, dispute *(contest)*, disqualify, forbid, forswear, gainsay, interdict, negate, oppose, prohibit, protest, rebut, refuse, refute, reject, renounce, repudiate, withhold

deny absolutely disavow, disown *(deny the validity)*, dispute *(contest)*

deny access deter

deny any knowledge of disclaim

deny connection with disavow

deny emphatically disavow, dispute *(contest)*

deny entirely disavow, dispute *(contest)*

deny entry exclude

deny flatly dispute *(contest)*

deny oneself eschew, forbear

deny oneself nothing dissipate *(expend foolishly)*

deny peremptorily disavow, disown *(deny the validity)*, dispute *(contest)*

deny permission forbid

deny respect decry, disfavor, disgrace

deny responsibility for disavow

deny the genuineness of dispute *(contest)*

deny the possibility disown *(deny the validity)*

deny wholly disavow, disown *(deny the validity)*

denying contradictory, contrary, dissenting, negative

deobstruct extricate, facilitate

deontology casuistry

depart abscond, alight, decease, defect, die, digress, disagree, disperse *(scatter)*, evacuate, expire, move *(alter position)*, part *(leave)*, perish, resign, retire *(retreat)*, retreat, secede, vacate *(leave)*, vary, withdraw

depart custody escape

depart from abandon *(physically leave)*, avoid *(evade)*, conflict, detour, deviate, differ *(vary)*, quit *(evacuate)*,

vacate *(leave)*

depart from life decease

depart from one's course detour, deviate

depart unlawfully escape

departed corpse, dead, deceased, decedent, defunct, late *(defunct)*, lifeless *(dead)*

departed this life dead

departing divergent, flight, separate

departing from deviant, disparate, distinct *(distinguished from others)*

departing from the usual course eccentric

department agency *(commission)*, bailiwick, board, bureau, chapter *(branch)*, district, division *(administrative unit)*, domain *(sphere of influence)*, member *(constituent part)*, organ, post, province, pursuit *(occupation)*, purview, realm, role, section *(division)*, sphere

department of justice judiciary

department store market *(business)*

departmentalization bureaucracy, division *(act of dividing)*

departure abandonment *(desertion)*, abdication, demise *(death)*, desertion, detour, deviation, difference, digression, discrepancy, egress, end *(termination)*, extremity *(death)*, flight, indirection *(indirect action)*, innovation, leave *(absence)*, nonconformity, quirk *(idiosyncrasy)*, removal, resignation *(relinquishment)*

departure from contradistinction, difference

departure from life death

departure from usage deviation

departure from usual exception *(exclusion)*

dépêche dispatch *(promptness)*

depellere dislodge, evict

depend rely

depend upon appertain, trust

dependability adhesion *(loyalty)*, certification *(certainness)*, loyalty, probity, reliance, responsibility *(conscience)*, security *(safety)*, trustworthiness

dependable accurate, authentic, believable, certain *(positive)*, constant, credible, demonstrable, diligent, factual, faithful *(loyal)*, incorruptible, infallible, loyal, official, punctual, real, reliable, reputable, safe, secure *(free from danger)*, secure *(sound)*, solid *(sound)*, staunch, steadfast, tenable, true *(authentic)*, true *(loyal)*

dependence faith, mainstay, mutuality, reliance, resource, trust *(confidence)*

dependence on credence

dependency appurtenance

dependent ancillary *(subsidiary)*, contingent, correlative, dubious, helpless *(powerless)*, insecure, minor, protégé, qualified *(conditioned)*, related, sequacious, subject *(conditional)*, subservient, tentative

dependent event contingency

dependent on appurtenant, based on, conditional, contingent, incident, tangential

dependent on circumstances contingent, provisional, subject *(conditional)*

depending aleatory *(uncertain)*, contingent

depending on conditional

depending on a future event conditional

depending upon subject *(conditional)*

depict characterize, construe *(translate)*, copy, delineate, denote, describe, detail *(particularize)*, exemplify, interpret, portray, recount, represent *(portray)*, signify *(denote)*

depict the essential qualities of define

depiction brief, caricature, delineation, description, design *(construction plan)*, illustration, narration, recital, representation *(statement)*, symbol

depiction of essential features delineation

depictive demonstrative *(illustrative)*, realistic, representative

depictment illustration, narration

depicture denote, portray

depingere delineate, depict, describe, portray

depletable destructible

deplete deduct *(reduce)*, dissipate *(expend foolishly)*, expend *(consume)*, impair, lessen, overdraw, spend, tax *(overwork)*

depleted deficient, destitute, inadequate, lost *(taken away)*, nonsubstantial *(not sufficient)*, poor *(underprivileged)*, vacant, vacuous

depletion consumption, decrement, delinquency *(shortage)*, insufficiency, poverty, waste, wear and tear

deplorable arrant *(onerous)*, bad *(inferior)*, bad *(offensive)*, blameful, blameworthy, contemptible, disgraceful, disreputable, gross *(flagrant)*, heinous, lamentable, loathsome, nefarious, notorious, objectionable, obnoxious, outrageous, regrettable, scandalous

deplorare deplore

deplore blame, deprecate, except *(object)*, regret, repent

deplored blameful

deploy maneuver, spread

deplume despoil, plunder

depone acknowledge *(declare)*, affirm *(declare solemnly)*, attest, bear *(adduce)*, certify *(attest)*, depose *(testify)*, testify, vouch

deponent affiant, affirmant, witness

deponere deposit *(place)*, give *(yield)*, resign

depopulate devastate, diminish, pillage

deport comport *(behave)*, dislodge, displace *(remove)*, eliminate *(exclude)*, exclude, expatriate, expel, relegate, seclude, transport

deportation banishment, exclusion, expulsion, extradition, ostracism, rejection, removal

deportee pariah

deportment behavior, conduct, demeanor, manner *(behavior)*, presence *(poise)*

deposal abolition, disqualification *(rejection)*, rejection, removal

deposcere call *(demand)*

depose acknowledge *(declare)*, affirm *(declare solemnly)*, assert, attest, avouch *(avow)*, avow, bear *(adduce)*, certify *(attest)*, demote, discharge *(dismiss)*, dislodge, dismiss *(discharge)*,

dispossess, divest, oust, remove *(dismiss from office)*, supplant, testify, vouch

deposed powerless

deposit alluvion, binder, downpayment, embed, fund, garner, handsel, hoard, installment, keep *(shelter)*, leave *(allow to remain)*, locate, pawn, pay, plant *(place firmly)*, pledge *(security)*, replenish, repose *(place)*, reserve, security *(pledge)*, store *(depository)*, store, treasury

deposit among records of the court file *(place among official records)*

deposit as collateral pawn

deposit as security pawn

deposit formally cast *(register)*

deposit with consign, delegate

depositary comptroller, receiver, trustee

deposition abdication, affirmation, alluvion, confirmation, disclosure *(something disclosed)*, dismissal *(discharge)*, entry *(record)*, removal, repudiation, statement, testimony

depository arsenal, bank, cache *(storage place)*, catchall, coffer, repository, reserve, store *(depository)*, treasury

depositum deposit

depot depository, repository, treasury

depravare contort, corrupt, debauch, deteriorate, misrepresent, pervert, vitiate

depravatio corruption, perversion

depravation damage, defilement, perversion, vice

deprave corrupt, debase, debauch, degenerate, pervert, pollute, taint *(corrupt)*

depraved bad *(offensive)*, blameworthy, contemptible, decadent, dissolute, ignoble, immoral, iniquitous, lascivious, lecherous, lewd, nefarious, perverse, profligate *(corrupt)*, reprobate, salacious, tainted *(corrupted)*, vicious

depraved person degenerate

depravity bad repute, delinquency *(misconduct)*, dishonor *(shame)*, perversion, sodomy, turpitude, vice

deprecari intercede

deprecate admonish *(warn)*, blame, cavil, censure, complain *(criticize)*, condemn *(blame)*, criticize *(find fault with)*, decry, denounce *(condemn)*, disapprove *(condemn)*, disapprove *(reject)*, discommend, discourage, discredit, disoblige, fault, jeer, malign, misprize, remonstrate, reprimand, reproach, sully, underestimate

deprecating diffident, disdainful

deprecatio intercession

deprecation admonition, bad repute, condemnation *(blame)*, contempt *(disdain)*, contempt *(disobedience to the court)*, criticism, denunciation, diatribe, disapprobation, disapproval, disparagement, reluctance, stricture

deprecative diffident, remonstrative

deprecator intermediary

deprecatory adverse *(hostile)*, calumnious, derogatory, remonstrative

depreciate adulterate, blame, censure, contemn, criticize *(find fault with)*, debase, decay, decrease, decry, deduct *(reduce)*, defame, demean *(make lower)*, demote, denigrate, denounce

(condemn), depress, derogate, deteriorate, dilute, diminish, discommend, discount *(disbelieve)*, discount *(reduce)*, discredit, disparage, fault, humiliate, jeer, lessen, minimize, misprize, smear, spurn, sully, underestimate

depreciate publicly decry

depreciating contemptuous

depreciation contempt *(disdain)*, criticism, damage, decline, decrease, denunciation, depression, deterioration, diatribe, disapprobation, disparagement, disregard *(lack of respect)*, disrespect, revilement, stricture, wear and tear

depreciative calumnious, contemptuous, derogatory, pejorative

depreciatory calumnious, derogatory, pejorative

depredate despoil, devastate, hold up *(rob)*, loot, pillage, plunder, prey, steal

depredation foray, havoc, pillage, plunder, rape, robbery, spoliation

depredator thief

depredatory predatory, rapacious

deprehendere arrest *(apprehend)*

depress debase, decrease, depreciate, derogate, diminish, discourage, disgrace

depressant narcotic (adjective), narcotic (noun)

depressed despondent, disconsolate, pessimistic

depressing bleak *(not favorable)*, bleak *(severely simple)*, deplorable, lamentable, lugubrious, ominous, oppressive

depressing influence damper *(depressant)*

depression curtailment, decrease, distress *(anguish)*, pessimism, prostration

depressive deplorable, lamentable

deprival expense *(sacrifice)*

deprival of honor degradation

deprivation abridgment *(disentitlement)*, absence *(omission)*, attachment *(seizure)*, censorship, condemnation *(seizure)*, constraint *(restriction)*, conversion *(misappropriation)*, curtailment, defeasance, deficiency, detriment, discipline *(punishment)*, disqualification *(rejection)*, disseisin, distress *(seizure)*, escheatment, expense *(sacrifice)*, expropriation *(divestiture)*, expulsion, foreclosure, forfeiture *(act of forfeiting)*, injury, loss, ouster, paucity, penalty, pillage, privation, punishment, sanction *(punishment)*, sequestration, spoliation, taking

deprivation of a right forfeiture *(act of forfeiting)*

deprivation of liberty restraint

deprivation of office removal

deprivation of possession disseisin, eviction

deprivative confiscatory

deprive abduct, condemn *(ban)*, confiscate, demote, derogate, despoil, diminish, disfranchise, disinherit, dispossess, divest, exclude, forbid, impress *(procure by force)*, keep *(restrain)*, mulct *(fine)*

deprive dishonestly defraud

deprive illegally pilfer

deprive of abridge *(divest)*, adeem, confiscate, distrain, impound, seize *(confiscate)*

deprive of advantage disadvantage
deprive of an important part mutilate
deprive of arms disarm *(divest of arms)*
deprive of corporal possession condemn *(seize)*
deprive of courage discourage
deprive of credit discredit
deprive of dishonestly cheat
deprive of efficacy nullify
deprive of essential parts eviscerate
deprive of force abolish, cancel, dismiss *(discharge)*, eviscerate, negate, vacate *(void)*
deprive of form deface
deprive of freedom of movement imprison
deprive of hereditary succession disinherit, disown *(refuse to acknowledge)*
deprive of legal effect invalidate
deprive of legal force nullify
deprive of liberty arrest *(apprehend)*, imprison, restrain
deprive of life dispatch *(put to death)*, execute *(sentence to death)*, kill *(murder)*, slay
deprive of means of defense disarm *(divest of arms)*
deprive of occupancy dispossess
deprive of office discharge *(dismiss)*, oust
deprive of organization disorganize
deprive of ownership condemn *(seize)*
deprive of possession evict
deprive of power abrogate *(rescind)*, disable, disarm *(divest of arms)*, disqualify, impair
deprive of protection expose
deprive of rank depose *(remove)*
deprive of strength debilitate, disable, disarm *(divest of arms)*, exhaust *(deplete)*, extenuate, tax *(overwork)*
deprive of the right to inherit disown *(refuse to acknowledge)*
deprive of vital parts eviscerate
deprive of weapons disarm *(divest of arms)*
deprive oneself renounce
deprived destitute, disadvantaged, nonsubstantial *(not sufficient)*, poor *(underprivileged)*
deprived of devoid
deprived of legal rights aggrieved *(harmed)*
deprived of life dead, deceased
deprived of one's wits non compos mentis
deprived of sensation insensible
deprived of sight blind *(sightless)*
deprived of strength disabled *(made incapable)*
deprivement abridgment *(disentitlement)*, attachment *(seizure)*, denial, distress *(seizure)*, privation
depriving confiscatory
depth caliber *(mental capacity)*, sense *(intelligence)*
depth of thought preoccupation
depthless superficial
depurate decontaminate, expurgate, purge *(purify)*
depurative medicinal
deputation agency *(legal relation-*

ship), appointment *(act of designating)*, assignment *(designation)*, delegation *(assignment)*, designation *(naming)*, embassy, representation *(acting for others)*
deputative acting, representative
depute appoint, assign *(designate)*, authorize, delegate, detail *(assign)*, empower, entrust, hire, invest *(vest)*, relegate, replace
deputed representative, vicarious *(delegated)*
deputies delegation *(envoy)*, staff
deputization delegation *(assignment)*, deputation *(selection of delegates)*, nomination
deputize charge *(empower)*, empower, entrust, replace
deputy acting, assistant, broker, coadjutant, conduit *(intermediary)*, factor *(commission merchant)*, liaison, medium, plenipotentiary, proctor, procurator, proxy, replacement, representative *(proxy)*, spokesman, substitute, surrogate
dequantitate lessen
deracinate disinter, dislodge, eliminate *(eradicate)*, eradicate, extinguish, extirpate, obliterate, supplant
deracination evulsion
derail dislocate
derange confuse *(create disorder)*, degenerate, discompose, dislocate, disorganize, disorient, disrupt, disturb, mismanage, muddle, obsess, perturb, upset
deranged anomalous, broken *(interrupted)*, disjointed, disorderly, frenetic, lunatic, non compos mentis, unsettled, unsound *(not strong)*
deranged intellect insanity
derangement complex *(entanglement)*, disorder *(lack of order)*, embroilment, entanglement *(confusion)*, havoc, insanity, lunacy, pandemonium
derelict broken *(unfulfilled)*, degenerate, delinquent *(guilty of a misdeed)*, discard, disobedient, faithless, lax, negligent, pariah, recreant, remiss
derelictio abandonment *(discontinuance)*, desertion
dereliction abandonment *(desertion)*, abortion *(fiasco)*, bad faith, blame *(culpability)*, breach, contempt *(disobedience to the court)*, crime, culpability, default, delinquency *(misconduct)*, failure *(falling short)*, fault *(responsibility)*, laches, lapse *(expiration)*, laxity, malfeasance, misconduct, misdeed, misdemeanor, misfeasance, neglect, negligence, nonfeasance, omission, transgression, vice, violation, wrong
dereliction of allegiance disloyalty
dereliction of duty bad faith, default, delict, delinquency *(failure of duty)*, disregard *(omission)*, laches, maladministration, malpractice, nonperformance, tort
deride bait *(harass)*, brand *(stigmatize)*, cavil, contemn, decry, denigrate, depreciate, discommend, disdain, disgrace, dishonor *(deprive of honor)*, disparage, flout, harry *(harass)*, humiliate, illude, jeer, lessen
deridere jeer, mock *(deride)*
derisible ludicrous
derision aspersion, bad repute, con-

tempt *(disdain)*, contumely, disdain, disrespect, ignominy, infamy, obloquy, odium, ridicule
derisive calumnious, caustic, contemptuous, cynical, disdainful, impertinent *(insolent)*, insolent, pejorative, supercilious
derisive language profanity
derisiveness disrespect, ridicule
derisory caustic, contemptuous
derivable deductible *(provable)*
derivare divert
derivate derivative
derivation ancestry, birth *(lineage)*, blood, bloodline, cause *(reason)*, citation *(attribution)*, connotation, consequence *(conclusion)*, corollary, descent *(lineage)*, development *(outgrowth)*, genesis, inception, origin *(ancestry)*, origin *(source)*, origination, parentage, paternity, reason *(basis)*, source, start
derivation from reference *(citation)*
derivational ancillary *(subsidiary)*, derivative
derivative ancillary *(subsidiary)*, consequence *(conclusion)*, consequential *(deducible)*, dependent, offshoot
derivative authority agency *(legal relationship)*
derivative interest privity
derivatively a priori
derive acquire *(receive)*, ascertain, deduce, deduct *(conclude by reasoning)*, draw *(extract)*, educe, ensue, extract, gain, infer, judge, presume, read, reap, reason *(conclude)*, receive *(acquire)*, stem *(originate)*, succeed *(follow)*
derive by reasoning construe *(comprehend)*, infer
derive from ascribe, develop, emanate, evolve, inherit, result
derive pleasure from relish
derived derivative, secondary
derived from dependent
derived from experience empirical
derived from within innate, organic
derived from without extraneous, extrinsic
derived principle conclusion *(determination)*, corollary
deriving derivative, dialectic
derogare derogate, discredit
derogate brand *(stigmatize)*, condemn *(blame)*, contemn, debunk, decry, demean *(make lower)*, denounce *(condemn)*, deprecate, diminish, discommend, disgrace, disparage, humiliate, lessen, libel, malign, minimize, smear
derogate from depreciate, discredit
derogation attaint, bad repute, condemnation *(blame)*, contempt *(disdain)*, criticism, defamation, denunciation, disapprobation, discredit, disgrace, dishonor *(shame)*, disparagement, ignominy, obloquy, opprobrium, reprimand, reproach
derogation of religion blasphemy
derogative contemptuous, cynical, pejorative
derogatory bad *(offensive)*, calumnious, contemptuous, critical *(faultfinding)*, cynical, disgraceful, libelous, pejorative, unfavorable
derogatory criticism aspersion
derring-do audacity

derringdo prowess *(bravery)*

descant censure, comment, converse, declaim

descend alight, condescend *(deign)*, deign, demean *(make lower)*, stem *(originate)*, subside

descend by inheritance devolve

descend from develop, emanate, evolve

descend on attack

descend to particulars characterize

descend upon devolve, oppugn

descendant derivative, heir, kindred, offshoot, successor

descendants children, issue *(progeny)*, offspring, posterity, progeny

descended derivative

descendere alight, condescend *(deign)*, descend

descension decline

descent affiliation *(bloodline)*, ancestry, birth *(lineage)*, blood, bloodline, decline, derivation, family *(common ancestry)*, heritage, lineage, origin *(ancestry)*, parentage, paternity, posterity, race, succession

descent by forfeiture escheatment

descrial discovery

describable accountable *(explainable)*

describe apprise, characterize, construe *(translate)*, convey *(communicate)*, define, delineate, depict, detail *(particularize)*, disclose, draw *(depict)*, elucidate, explain, explicate, express, identify, inform *(notify)*, interpret, label, phrase, portray, recount, relate *(tell)*, render *(depict)*, report *(disclose)*, reveal, review, trace *(delineate)*

describe incorrectly mislabel

describe the properties of define

described detailed, documentary

describere delineate, depict, describe

descriptio delineation, description, design *(construction plan)*, organization *(structure)*

description account *(report)*, brief, call *(title)*, caption, character *(personal quality)*, clarification, color *(complexion)*, construction, definition, delineation, denomination, designation *(naming)*, explanation, label, manner *(kind)*, narration, paraphrase, prospectus, recital, report *(detailed account)*, representation *(statement)*, specification, story *(narrative)*, style

descriptive demonstrative *(illustrative)*, detailed, informatory, narrative

descriptive account narration

descry ascertain, comprehend *(understand)*, detect, discern *(detect with the senses)*, discover, expose, identify, observe *(watch)*, pierce *(discern)*, recognize *(perceive)*, spy

desecrate contaminate, contemn, debase, dishonor *(deprive of honor)*, impair, misemploy, mistreat, pollute, tarnish, violate

desecration blasphemy, defilement, misusage, profanity, violation

desensitize drug, obtund

deserere neglect

desert abandon *(physically leave)*, abandon *(relinquish)*, abscond, default, defect, depart, disclaim, escape, fail *(neglect)*, flee, forswear, leave *(depart)*, merit, quit *(evacuate)*, relinquish, re-

nege, renounce, reprisal, requital, retreat, retribution, revenge, secede, tergiversate, vacate *(leave)*, withdraw, worth

deserted bleak *(exposed and barren)*, derelict *(abandoned)*, devoid, helpless *(defenseless)*, solitary, vacant, void *(empty)*

deserter fugitive

desertion absence *(nonattendance)*, dereliction, disloyalty, flight, infidelity, revolt, schism, sedition

deserts recompense

deserve earn

deserved condign, due *(owed)*, entitled, equitable, fair *(just)*, just, rightful, suitable

deservedly duly

deservedness merit

deserving entitled, laudable, meritorious, moral, tenable

deserving belief credible, fiduciary, plausible

deserving blame culpable

deserving censure culpable, reprehensible

deserving of blame guilty

deserving of commendation meritorious

deserving of compliment meritorious

deserving of condemnation sinister

deserving of confidence credible

deserving of praise meritorious

deserving of preference preferable

deserving of punishment guilty

deserving of reward meritorious

deserving reproach disgraceful

deserving reproof guilty, reprehensible

deservingness probity

deservire serve *(assist)*

deses indolent

desiderare desire, require *(need)*

desiderate desire, lack

desideration desideratum, end *(intent)*, need *(requirement)*, will *(desire)*

desideratum condition *(contingent provision)*, end *(intent)*, need *(requirement)*, request

desiderium desire

desidia sloth

design animus, arrange *(plan)*, array *(order)*, artifice, blueprint, building *(business of assembling)*, cabal, calculate, campaign, cause *(reason)*, composition *(makeup)*, conceive *(invent)*, configuration *(form)*, conspire, contemplation, content *(meaning)*, content *(structure)*, contrivance, contrive, course, criterion, delineation, device *(contrivance)*, device *(distinguishing mark)*, devise *(invent)*, direction *(course)*, direction *(guidance)*, end *(intent)*, expedient, forethought, form *(arrangement)*, form, frame *(construct)*, frame *(formulate)*, function, goal, intend, intent, intention, invent *(produce for the first time)*, machination, maneuver *(trick)*, maneuver, mission, mode, model, motif, motive, object, objective, order *(arrangement)*, organization *(structure)*, pattern, plan, plan, plot *(secret plan)*, point *(purpose)*, premeditation, program, program, project, proposal *(suggestion)*, proposition, purpose, purview, reason

(basis), ruse, scheme, scheme, strategy, structure *(composition)*, system, target, treatment, undertaking *(attempt)*

designare allude, characterize, constitute *(establish)*, denote, designate, nominate, trace *(delineate)*

designate allocate, allot, appoint, call *(title)*, connote, define, delegate, denominate, denote, detail *(assign)*, direct *(show)*, discriminate *(distinguish)*, enumerate, future, identify, instate, itemize, label, manifest, nominate, phrase, prescribe, represent *(portray)*, select, signify *(inform)*, specify, stipulate

designate a place locate

designate for appointment nominate

designate for election nominate

designate for office by vote elect *(select by a vote)*

designate incorrectly mislabel

designate to a post delegate, hire

designated certain *(specific)*, necessary *(inescapable)*, select

designated ground point *(item)*

designating descriptive

designatio designation *(naming)*, nomination

designation admittance *(acceptance)*, allotment, call *(title)*, caption, choice *(decision)*, citation *(attribution)*, class, classification, cognomen, color *(complexion)*, delegation *(assignment)*, denomination, department, deputation *(selection of delegates)*, device *(distinguishing mark)*, diagnosis, discretion *(power of choice)*, earmark, election *(choice)*, identification, kind, manner *(kind)*, nomination, reference *(citation)*, rubric *(title)*, selection *(choice)*, signification, specification, term *(expression)*

designation of use appropriation *(allotment)*

designation to office appointment *(act of designating)*

designed aforethought, deliberate, intentional, knowing, purposeful, strategic, tactical, voluntary, willful

designed for the initiated esoteric

designed misrepresentation false pretense

designed to deceive false *(not genuine)*

designedly knowingly, purposely

designee candidate

designer architect, contractor, developer, materialman

designing collusive, creation, deceptive, devious, dishonest, disingenuous, fraudulent, insidious, machiavellian, perfidious, recreant, sinister, sly, subtle *(insidious)*, unconscionable

designing power contrivance

designless casual, fortuitous, haphazard, indiscriminate, random

desinere cease, desist

desirability qualification *(fitness)*, value

desirable attractive, constructive *(creative)*, convenient, eligible, entitled, favorable *(advantageous)*, felicitous, fitting, meritorious, popular, premium, profitable, provocative, suitable, valuable

desirable feature amenity

desire choose, conatus, desideratum,

design *(intent)*, end *(intent)*, intend, intention, lack, market *(demand)*, need, notion, objective, passion, predilection, predisposition, purpose, pursue *(strive to gain)*, request, require *(need)*, volition

desire the presence of call *(summon)*

desire to buy market *(demand)*

desire to hoard wealth greed

desire to know interest *(concern)*

desire to obtain market *(demand)*

desired objective, popular, preferential

desired object objective, target

desired result end *(intent)*, purpose

desirer candidate

desiring jealous

desirous eager, hot-blooded, inclined, jealous, lecherous, solicitous, zealous

desirous of forgiveness contrite

desist abandon *(relinquish)*, cease, discontinue *(abandon)*, dissolve *(terminate)*, halt, interrupt, leave *(allow to remain)*, palliate *(abate)*, pause, refrain, rest *(cease from action)*, stay *(halt)*, stop, suspend

desist from discontinue *(abandon)*, forbear, forgo, quit *(discontinue)*, renounce, resign, waive

desistance abandonment *(discontinuance)*, abeyance, cessation *(interlude)*, cloture, desuetude, discontinuance *(act of discontinuing)*, discontinuance *(interruption of a legal action)*, halt, impasse, layoff, lull, moratorium, stay

desistere cease, desist

desk book hornbook

desolate barren, bleak *(exposed and barren)*, derelict *(abandoned)*, despoil, despondent, destroy *(efface)*, devastate, devoid, disconsolate, eliminate *(eradicate)*, extirpate, obliterate, pillage, plunder, solitary, unsettled, void *(empty)*

desolating disastrous

desolation catastrophe, consumption, distress *(anguish)*, havoc, prostration, spoliation

despair brood, consternation, distress *(anguish)*, languish, panic, pessimism, prostration

despairing despondent, disconsolate, pessimistic

despatch delegate

desperado convict, malefactor

desperate drastic, hot-blooded, pessimistic

desperate criminal convict

desperate situation peril

desperation pessimism

despicability bad repute, disrepute

despicable bad *(offensive)*, base *(bad)*, blameful, blameworthy, caitiff, contemptible, deplorable, disgraceful, disreputable, heinous, ignoble, loathsome, nefarious, objectionable, obnoxious, odious, outrageous, paltry, repulsive, scandalous

despicableness bad repute, disrepute

despicere disdain

despise contemn, decry, disdain, disfavor, dishonor *(deprive of honor)*, flout, misprize, rebuff, reject, renounce, spurn

despised base *(bad)*, contemptible, disreputable, notorious

despisedness ignominy

despising cynical, disdainful

despite contumely, irrespective, notwithstanding, odium, regardless, spite

despiteful bitter *(reproachful)*, harsh, malevolent, malignant, outrageous, sinister, spiteful, virulent

despiteful treatment contumely

despoil debauch, deface, deprive, devastate, divest, harry *(plunder)*, hold up *(rob)*, loot, pillage, pirate *(take by violence)*, plunder, prey, spoil *(pillage)*, steal, subvert, taint *(corrupt)*

despoiled marred

despoiler burglar

despoilment defilement, pillage

despoliare rob

despoliation pillage, rape, spoliation

despond brood, languish

despondence depression, pessimism

despondency depression, distress *(anguish)*, pessimism, prostration

despondent disappointed, disconsolate, lugubrious, pessimistic

despot dictator

despotic brutal, dictatorial, peremptory *(imperative)*, severe, strict, stringent, tyrannous

despotic commander dictator

despotic master dictator

despotism oppression

destillare distill

destinare appoint

destinate predetermine

destination design *(intent)*, end *(intent)*, end *(termination)*, goal, intention, object, objective, purpose, pursuit *(goal)*, target

destine allocate, predetermine, preordain

destined bound, forthcoming, future, imminent, inevitable, necessary *(inescapable)*, prospective

destined lot predetermination

destiny destination, end *(termination)*, predetermination, prospect *(outlook)*

destituere abandon *(physically leave)*

destitute bankrupt, impecunious, insolvent, poor *(underprivileged)*, void *(empty)*

destitute of devoid, insufficient

destitute of good faith dishonest, fraudulent

destitute of integrity dishonest, fraudulent

destitute of life dead, deceased, lifeless *(dead)*

destitute of reason fatuous

destituteness bankruptcy

destitution bankruptcy, dearth, deficiency, indigence, paucity, poverty, privation

destroy abate *(extinguish)*, abolish, abrogate *(rescind)*, annul, break *(fracture)*, consume, countervail, damage, deface, denounce *(condemn)*, devastate, discontinue *(abandon)*, dispatch *(put to death)*, dissolve *(terminate)*, eliminate *(eradicate)*, eradicate, expunge, extinguish, extirpate, kill *(defeat)*, kill *(murder)*, mistreat, negate, obliterate, overcome *(surmount)*, overturn, overwhelm, pillage, pollute, prejudice *(injure)*, prey, quash, refute, slay, spoil *(impair)*, stifle, subvert, upset, vitiate

destroy a reputation pillory

destroy confidence discourage

destroy form deface

destroy good will antagonize

destroy goodwill alienate *(estrange)*

destroy one's perception blind *(deprive of sight)*

destroy one's reputation defame, smear

destroy the affection of disaffect

destroy the effect of counteract, neutralize

destroy the efficacy of avoid *(cancel)*

destroy the form of disorganize

destroy the integrity of taint *(corrupt)*

destroy thoroughly eradicate

destroyable destructible

destroyed broken *(fractured)*, inactive, lost *(taken away)*

destroyer vandal

destroying deadly, destructive, dire, disastrous, fatal

destruct destroy *(efface)*

destructibility frailty

destructible nonsubstantial *(not sturdy)*

destruction abatement *(extinguishment)*, abolition, assassination, calamity, catastrophe, consumption, damage, debacle, defacement, defeat, deterioration, detriment, dispatch *(act of putting to death)*, dissolution *(termination)*, fatality, havoc, killing, misfortune, mortality, murder, pillage, prostration, rescision, shambles, spoliation, subversion

destruction of a right forfeiture *(act of forfeiting)*

destruction of human life murder

destruction of life aberemurder, homicide, murder

destruction of property by fire arson

destructive adverse *(negative)*, bad *(offensive)*, dangerous, deadly, detrimental, dire, disadvantageous, disastrous, disorderly, fatal, harmful, hostile, insalubrious, lethal, malicious, malignant, noxious, pernicious, pestilent, prejudicial, sinister, virulent

destructive agency parasite

destructive criticism disparagement

destructive fire conflagration

destructiveness murder

destruere destroy *(efface)*

desuete outmoded

desuetude abolition, disuse, nonuse

desuetudo desuetude

desultoriness irregularity

desultory broken *(interrupted)*, casual, cursory, deviant, discursive *(digressive)*, disjointed, disjunctive *(tending to disjoin)*, haphazard, indirect, intermittent, random, sporadic, superficial, volatile

detach abstract *(separate)*, alienate *(estrange)*, break *(separate)*, dichotomize, disband, disengage, disentangle, disjoint, displace *(remove)*, dissociate, dissolve *(separate)*, divide *(separate)*, divorce, extricate, insulate, isolate, luxate, part *(separate)*, remove *(eliminate)*, separate, sever, split

detachable divisible, moving *(in motion)*, separable, severable

detachable part of a certificate coupon

detachable portion coupon

detached alien *(unrelated)*, alone *(solitary)*, apart, autonomous *(independent)*, bipartite, clinical, controlled *(restrained)*, disconnected, discrete, disjunctive *(tending to disjoin)*, dispassionate, equitable, evenhanded, fair *(just)*, foreign, impartial, impervious, independent, individual, insular, insusceptible *(uncaring)*, irrelative, just, nonpartisan, objective, open-minded, phlegmatic, remote *(secluded)*, separate, solitary, unbiased, unprejudiced

detached part segment

detachment candor *(impartiality)*, disassociation, disinterest *(lack of interest)*, disinterest *(lack of prejudice)*, division *(act of dividing)*, estrangement, exception *(exclusion)*, fairness, indifference, neutrality, objectivity, part *(portion)*, quarantine, removal, section *(division)*, segregation *(separation)*, separation, severance, split

detachment of police posse

detail allocate, assign *(designate)*, band, characterize, convey *(communicate)*, delegate, delineate, depict, describe, designate, develop, dispatch *(send off)*, dispense, elaborate, element, elucidate, enumerate, explicate, feature *(characteristic)*, inform *(notify)*, item, itemize, motif, part *(portion)*, particular, particularity, point *(item)*, portray, posse, quote, recite, recount, relate *(tell)*, render *(depict)*, report *(disclose)*, segment, specification, specify, technicality, trace *(delineate)*, trait

detail the law charge *(instruct on the law)*

detailed descriptive, elaborate, exact, full, narrative, precise, stated, thorough

detailed account statement

detailed examination investigation

detailed plan blueprint

detailed statement instruction *(teaching)*, recital, specification

details circumstances, contents, description, intelligence *(news)*

details now to be provided a savoir

details on the law charge *(statement to the jury)*

detain apprehend *(arrest)*, arrest *(apprehend)*, arrest *(stop)*, balk, check *(restrain)*, clog, confine, constrain *(imprison)*, constrict *(inhibit)*, contain *(restrain)*, curb, debar, defer *(put off)*, delay, hinder, hold up *(delay)*, immure, impede, imprison, jail, keep *(restrain)*, preclude, prevent, restrain, retain *(keep in possession)*, stall, stay *(halt)*, stop

detain by criminal process arrest *(apprehend)*, seize *(apprehend)*

detain by legal process apprehend *(arrest)*

detain in custody imprison

detained arrested *(apprehended)*, back *(in arrears)*, in custody, late *(tardy)*

detainee prisoner

detainment check *(bar)*, constraint *(imprisonment)*, constraint *(restriction)*, delay, detainer, detention, deterrence, disadvantage, obstacle

detect apprehend *(perceive)*, comprehend *(understand)*, discern *(detect with the senses)*, discover, disinter, expose, find *(discover)*, hear *(perceive by ear)*, identify, locate, notice *(observe)*, overhear, perceive, pierce *(discern)*, spy, trace *(follow)*

detect differences discern *(discriminate)*

detectable apparent *(perceptible)*, appreciable, discernible, palpable, perceivable, perceptible, visible *(noticeable)*

detectible determinable *(ascertainable)*

detection discovery, observation, perception, recognition

detective peace officer, spy

detective force police

detegere betray *(disclose)*, disclose, expose, unveil

detention apprehension *(act of arresting)*, bondage, captivity, check *(bar)*, commitment *(confinement)*, constraint *(imprisonment)*, custody *(incarceration)*, delay, durance, fetter, halt, hindrance, incarceration, restraint

detention camp penitentiary

detention cell jail

detention center jail, penitentiary

detention of ships embargo

detention station jail

deter arrest *(stop)*, avert, check *(restrain)*, constrict *(inhibit)*, debar, discourage, divert, expostulate, forbid, forestall, forewarn, frighten, halt, hamper, hold up *(delay)*, impede, interdict, interfere, keep *(restrain)*, limit, occlude, preclude, prevent, remonstrate, restrain, stay *(halt)*, stem *(check)*, stop

deter from one's purpose dissuade

deterge decontaminate, purge *(purify)*, remove *(eliminate)*

deterimental inadvisable

deterior inferior *(lower in position)*

deterior condicio deterioration

deteriorate adulterate, aggravate *(exacerbate)*, debase, decay, decline *(fall)*, degenerate, depreciate, depress, disorganize, ebb, erode, exacerbate, fail *(lose)*, languish, lessen, recidivate, relapse, spoil *(impair)*

deteriorated bad *(inferior)*, blemished, decadent, depraved, imperfect, old, sordid, unsound *(not strong)*

deteriorating decadent

deterioration caducity, damage, decline, decrease, degradation, detriment, disability *(physical inability)*, disease, disrepair, dissolution *(disintegration)*, erosion, expense *(sacrifice)*, recidivism, relapse, spoilage, wear and tear

determent constraint *(restriction)*, damper *(stopper)*, deterrent, disadvantage, disincentive, prohibition, remonstrance, restraint

determinable accountable *(explainable)*, appreciable, ascertainable, provable, solvable

determinant causal, causative, decisive, derivation, factor *(ingredient)*

determinate absolute *(conclusive)*, actual, axiomatic, certain *(fixed)*, certain *(specific)*, concrete, de facto, definite, definitive, demonstrable, explicit, express, peremptory *(absolute)*, positive *(incontestable)*, precise, specific

determinatio limitation

determination adjudication, alternative *(option)*, animus, appraisal, assessment *(estimation)*, award, cessation *(termination)*, choice *(decision)*, cognovit, collation, conatus, consequence *(conclusion)*, contemplation, conviction *(finding of guilt)*, decision *(judgment)*, denouement, design *(intent)*, diligence *(perseverance)*, discretion *(power of choice)*, election *(choice)*, end *(termination)*, estimate *(idea)*, finality, finding, goal, holding *(ruling of a court)*, industry *(activity)*, intent, intention, judgment *(formal court decree)*, motive, opinion *(belief)*, opinion *(judicial decision)*, payoff *(result)*, perception, poll *(casting of votes)*, project, purpose, rating, referendum, res judicata, resolution *(decision)*, result, ruling, selection *(choice)*, sentence, solution *(answer)*, specification, surety *(certainty)*, tenacity, verdict, volition, vote, will *(desire)*

determination by agreement settlement

determination of a child's paternity filiation

determination of damages inquest

determination of issues adjudication

determination prepense deliberation

determinative causal, cause *(reason)*, cogent, decisive, definitive, extreme *(last)*, final, influential, last *(final)*

determine adjudge, adjudicate, arbitrate *(adjudge)*, arrange *(methodize)*, ascertain, assess *(appraise)*, award, calculate, call *(title)*, choose, circumscribe *(define)*, complete, conclude *(decide)*, constitute *(establish)*, construe *(comprehend)*, decide, deduce, deduct *(conclude by reasoning)*, deem, delimit, delineate, demarcate, designate, detect, discover, dispose *(incline)*, elucidate, fix *(settle)*, gauge, hold *(decide)*, identify, judge, opine, pass *(determine)*, postulate, predominate *(command)*, program, pronounce *(pass judgment)*, rate, regulate *(manage)*, resolve *(decide)*, rule *(decide)*, select, sentence, settle

determine a controversy arbitrate *(adjudge)*, find *(determine)*

determine a point at issue arbitrate *(adjudge)*

determine after judicial inquiry find *(determine)*

determine an issue find *(determine)*

determine beforehand predetermine, preordain, presuppose

determine boundaries circumscribe *(surround by boundary)*, demarcate

determine exactly construe *(comprehend)*

determine finally adjudicate

determine in advance forejudge, predetermine, presuppose

determine in favor elect *(choose)*

determine once for all settle

determine size measure

determine the amount of indebtedness liquidate *(determine liability)*

determine the essential qualities of define

determine the essentials discriminate *(distinguish)*

determine the heaviness of weigh

determine the worth of evaluate
determine upon choose, intend, plan
determine value measure
determine with precision define
determined certain *(fixed)*, definite, deliberate, earnest, fixed *(settled)*, indomitable, industrious, inevitable, inexorable, inflexible, intentional, obdurate, patient, peremptory *(absolute)*, persistent, pertinacious, positive *(confident)*, prescriptive, purposeful, relentless, resolute, serious *(devoted)*, spartan, specific, stated, steadfast, strong, unalterable, uncompromising, unrelenting, unyielding
determined by conditional
determined by chance haphazard
determined by no principle arbitrary
determined punishment sentence
determiner arbiter, arbitrator
determiners jury
determining conclusive *(settled)*, contributory, critical *(crucial)*, crucial, decisive, definitive, prevailing *(having superior force)*, primary
determining circumstance determinant
determining element determinant
determining influence determinant
determining of a controversy arbitration
deterred arrested *(checked)*
deterrence control *(restriction)*, deterrent, disadvantage, disincentive, fetter, impasse, prohibition, restraint
deterrent ammunition, control *(restriction)*, cudgel, damper *(stopper)*, deterrence, disadvantage, disincentive, fetter, halt, hindrance, impediment, obviation, panoply, preventive, prohibition, prohibitive *(restrictive)*, restraint, restrictive, unfavorable
deterrere deter, discourage, dissuade, intimidate
deterring chilling effect, formidable, preventive
detersion catharsis
detest contemn, disdain, reject, renounce
detestabilis heinous
detestable contemptible, contemptuous, disgraceful, disreputable, heinous, loathsome, nefarious, objectionable, obnoxious, odious, offensive *(offending)*, repugnant *(exciting aversion)*, repulsive
detestableness infamy
detestation contempt *(disdain)*, disdain, disgrace, hatred, ill will, malice, odium, phobia
dethrone demote, depose *(remove)*, dislodge, overthrow, rebel, supplant
dethronement abdication, disqualification *(rejection)*
detinere delay, hold up *(delay)*, stay *(halt)*
detineri employ *(engage services)*
detonate discharge *(shoot)*
detonation discharge *(shot)*, noise, outburst
detonator bomb
detorquere contort
detour avoidance *(evasion)*, deter, deviation, digress, digression
detract bait *(harass)*, blame, debunk, decry, denounce *(condemn)*, deprecate,

derogate, diminish, discommend, discount *(minimize)*, discount *(reduce)*, disparage, lessen, minimize, smear
detract from decrease, decry, demean *(make lower)*, depreciate, dilute, diminish, stain, underestimate
detracting abusive, contemptuous, derogatory, harmful, libelous, pejorative
detraction aspersion, bad repute, contempt *(disdain)*, criticism, defamation, denunciation, detriment, disapprobation, disapproval, disdain, dishonor *(shame)*, disparagement, disrespect, phillipic, revilement, vilification
detractive libelous
detractor foe, malcontent
detractory calumnious, derogatory
detrahere derogate
detrectare depreciate, disparage, shirk
detriment damage, disadvantage, disservice, expense *(sacrifice)*, handicap, harm, hindrance, impairment *(damage)*, impairment *(drawback)*, injury, mischief, prejudice *(injury)*
detrimental adverse *(negative)*, bad *(inferior)*, bad *(offensive)*, destructive, disadvantageous, disastrous, harmful, insalubrious, malignant, noxious, oppressive, peccant *(unhealthy)*, pernicious, prejudicial, sinister
detrimentum detriment, disservice, harm, injury, loss, prejudice *(injury)*
detrition erosion
detritus discard
detrude dislodge, eject *(expel)*, outpour
detrudere evict
detruncate condense, excise *(cut away)*, remove *(eliminate)*
detrusion expulsion
deturbare dispossess, evict
deuterogamy digamy
devaluate deduct *(reduce)*, depreciate, depress, lessen
devaluation decline, decrease
devalue adulterate, corrupt, damage, denature, depreciate, depress, deteriorate, disable, impair
devastate damage, despoil, destroy *(efface)*, extinguish, extirpate, harm, obliterate, pillage, prejudice *(injure)*, subvert
devastating dire, disastrous, fatal
devastation catastrophe, conflagration, consumption, debacle, defilement, destruction, disaster, havoc, plunder, spoliation, subversion
develop accrue *(arise)*, ameliorate, amplify, bear *(yield)*, build *(augment)*, cause, compose, compound, conceive *(invent)*, constitute *(establish)*, convert *(change use)*, create, crystallize, cultivate, elaborate, engender, enhance, enlarge, ensue, establish *(launch)*, evolve, expand, explicate, expound, extend *(enlarge)*, forge *(produce)*, generate, germinate, increase, mature, nurture, occur *(happen)*, parlay *(exploit successfully)*, progress, promote *(organize)*, pullulate, reclaim, result, revise, succeed *(follow)*
develop a course contrive
develop in greater detail expand
develop too fast overextend
develop too much overextend
developed complete *(all-embracing)*

developed minutely elaborate
development accession *(enlargement)*, advancement *(improvement)*, augmentation, boom *(increase)*, boom *(prosperity)*, building *(business of assembling)*, complication, consequence *(conclusion)*, creation, denouement, discipline *(training)*, effect, event, growth *(evolution)*, happening, headway, manufacture, nascency, offshoot, outcome, outgrowth, preparation, progress, reform, rehabilitation, result, transition
development of industrial sites development *(building)*
developmental constructive *(creative)*, corrigible
deversari lodge *(reside)*
deversor lodger
deversorium lodging
devertere lodge *(reside)*
deverticulum lodging, subterfuge
devestation pillage
deviant eccentric, errant
deviate alter, change, conflict, depart, detour, digress, disaccord, disagree, disobey, divert, miscalculate, palter, prevaricate, vary
deviate from differ *(vary)*
deviate from a direct course detour
deviate from rectitude trespass
deviate from the proper path lapse *(fall into error)*
deviate from the truth bear false witness, lie *(falsify)*, perjure, prevaricate
deviate from virtue lapse *(fall into error)*
deviating astray, circuitous, desultory, deviant, devious, different, discursive *(digressive)*, disordered, disparate, dissimilar, divergent, eccentric, errant, indirect, individual, irrelevant, labyrinthine, nonconforming, peculiar *(distinctive)*, perverse, shifting, sinuous
deviating from the common rule anomalous
deviating from the general rule irregular *(not usual)*
deviating from the norm irregular *(not usual)*
deviating from the standard irregular *(not usual)*
deviation avoidance *(evasion)*, defect, detour, difference, digression, discrepancy, disparity, diversification, error, exception *(exclusion)*, incongruity, inconsistency, indirection *(indirect action)*, inequality, irregularity, miscue, nonconformity, quirk *(idiosyncrasy)*, sodomy, variance *(exemption)*
deviation from a direct course detour
deviation from probity dishonesty
deviation from rectitude abuse *(corrupt practice)*, attaint, bad faith, bad repute, blame *(culpability)*, corruption, crime, disgrace, dishonor *(shame)*, guilt, malfeasance, misconduct, misdoing, misfeasance, misprision
deviation from truth fallacy, misstatement
deviation from virtue bad repute
deviative anomalous, devious, discursive *(digressive)*, divergent, diverse, eccentric, irregular *(not usual)*, sinuous, unorthodox, unpredictable

deviatory circuitous, divergent, errant, indirect

device appliance, artifice, color *(deceptive appearance)*, conduit *(channel)*, contrivance, deception, evasion, expedient, facility *(instrumentality)*, false pretense, hoax, instrument *(tool)*, instrumentality, loophole, maneuver *(tactic)*, maneuver *(trick)*, ploy, project, recourse, resource, scheme, stratagem, subterfuge, token, tool

devices means *(opportunity)*, strategy

devil plague

devil-like diabolic

devilish cold-blooded, cruel, diabolic, heinous, malevolent, malignant, nefarious, ruthless, vicious

devilishness delinquency *(misconduct)*

devilment mischief, nuisance

deviltry cruelty, mischief

devious artful, blameworthy, circuitous, discursive *(digressive)*, disingenuous, disreputable, indirect, insidious, machiavellian, oblique *(evasive)*, sinuous, sly, tortuous *(corrupt)*

deviousness bad faith, bad repute, corruption, improbity, indirection *(deceitfulness)*, indirection *(indirect action)*, knavery

devisable assignable, heritable

devisal bequest

devise arrange *(methodize)*, arrange *(plan)*, attorn, benefit *(conferment)*, bequeath, bequest, build *(construct)*, calculate, circumvent, compose, conceive *(invent)*, conjure, conspire, constitute *(establish)*, contrive, conveyance, create, demise, devolution, estate *(hereditament)*, fabricate *(construct)*, forge *(produce)*, form, formulate, frame *(construct)*, frame *(formulate)*, give *(grant)*, grant, grant *(transfer formally)*, hereditament, inheritance, invent *(produce for the first time)*, leave *(give)*, make, maneuver, manufacture, originate, plan, plot, produce *(manufacture)*, program, scheme

devise falsely fabricate *(make up)*

devise treachery conspire

devised controlled *(automatic)*, tactical

devised by will testamentary

devisee donee, feoffee, grantee, heir, legatee, payee, recipient, transferee

deviser architect, author *(originator)*, coactor, contractor, materialman

devising building *(business of assembling)*, creation

devisor donor, feoffor, grantor, maker, transferor

devitalization fault *(weakness)*

devitalize adulterate, attenuate, debilitate, disable, disarm *(divest of arms)*, eviscerate, exhaust *(deplete)*, kill *(defeat)*

devitalized disabled *(made incapable)*

devius devious, indirect

devoid deficient, vacant, vacuous, void *(empty)*

devoid of insufficient

devoid of consideration naked *(lacking embellishment)*

devoid of dissimulation ingenuous

devoid of expression inexpressive

devoid of feeling insusceptible *(un-*

caring)

devoid of life dead, deceased, defunct, lifeless *(dead)*

devoid of truth dishonest, erroneous, fallacious, false *(inaccurate)*, fraudulent, lying, mendacious

devoir burden

devoir commitment *(responsibility)*

devoirs respect

devolution conveyance, delegation *(assignment)*, deputation *(selection of delegates)*, succession

devolve alienate *(transfer title)*, cede, convey *(transfer)*, detail *(assign)*, entrust, pass *(advance)*, transfer

devolve again recover

devolve on delegate

devolve upon assign *(transfer ownership)*, attorn, bequeath, demise, grant *(transfer formally)*, hold *(possess)*, possess

devolvement assignment *(transfer of ownership)*

devolving on accountable *(responsible)*

devote contribute *(supply)*, dedicate, give *(grant)*, occupy *(engage)*, spend

devote attention to consider, observe *(watch)*

devote oneself adhere *(maintain loyalty)*

devote oneself to address *(direct attention to)*, concern *(care)*, discharge *(perform)*, labor, peruse, ply, practice *(engage in)*, resolve *(decide)*, specialize, study, undertake

devote thought to ponder

devoted close *(intimate)*, dependable, earnest, faithful *(loyal)*, fanatical, fervent, indebted, industrious, inseparable, loyal, obedient, partisan, purposeful, reliable, staunch, steadfast, true *(loyal)*, unyielding, zealous

devoted to convention orthodox

devoted to others philanthropic

devotedly faithfully, in good faith

devotedness adherence *(devotion)*, adhesion *(loyalty)*, allegiance, diligence *(perseverance)*, fidelity, homage, industry *(activity)*, loyalty

devotee addict, disciple, partisan, specialist

devotio vow

devotion adhesion *(loyalty)*, affection, affinity *(regard)*, allegiance, dedication, diligence *(perseverance)*, discipline *(obedience)*, fealty, fidelity, homage, honor *(outward respect)*, industry *(activity)*, loyalty, preoccupation, regard *(esteem)*

devotion to others philanthropy

devotional sacrosanct, solemn

devour consume, despoil, destroy *(efface)*, eliminate *(eradicate)*, expend *(consume)*, extirpate, obliterate, prey

devouring harmful, oppressive, pernicious, predatory, rapacious

devouring element conflagration

devout faithful *(loyal)*, serious *(devoted)*, solemn, zealous

devoutness adhesion *(loyalty)*

devovere devote

dexterity competence *(ability)*, efficiency, facility *(easiness)*, faculty *(ability)*, gift *(flair)*, performance *(workmanship)*, propensity, prowess *(ability)*, science *(technique)*, skill, specialty *(special*

aptitude)

dexterous artful, competent, deft, diplomatic, efficient, expert, facile, familiar *(informed)*, proficient, resourceful, veteran

dexterousness efficiency

dextrous practiced

dextrousness gift *(flair)*

diabolic bad *(offensive)*, cold-blooded, heinous, malevolent, malicious, odious, pernicious, sinister

diabolical cruel, malevolent, malicious, malignant, nefarious, ruthless, sinister, vicious

diacritical discriminating *(distinguishing)*, distinctive

diagnose decide, detect, discover, interpret, opine, recognize *(perceive)*

diagnosis construction, determination, judgment *(discernment)*, recognition

diagnostic empirical, indicant, interrogative, symptom

diagnosticate detect

diagonal oblique *(slanted)*

diagram blueprint, characterize, contour *(outline)*, delineate, delineation, depict, design *(construction plan)*, scheme

dialect language, phraseology, speech

dialectic controversial, discursive *(analytical)*, logical, polemic

dialectical argumentative, logical, polemic

dialectics ratiocination

dialogize discuss

dialogue communication *(discourse)*, conference, confrontation *(act of setting face to face)*, conversation, discourse, interview, parley, script

diameter caliber *(measurement)*

diameter of a cylindrical body caliber *(measurement)*

diametric different

diametrically opposed opposite

diametrically opposite adverse *(opposite)*, antipathetic *(oppositional)*, contradictory, contrary, inverse

diaphanous lucid, pellucid

diary calendar *(record of yearly periods)*, journal, ledger, register

diatribe bombast, denunciation, disapprobation, harangue, obloquy, outcry, phillipic, revilement, stricture

dicendi genus phraseology

dicere appoint, assert, call *(title)*, nominate, pronounce *(speak)*, recite, remark, speak, utter

dichotomize bifurcate, split

dichotomous bipartite

dichotomy disassociation, split

dicio dominion *(supreme authority)*

dicker barter, haggle, negotiate

dickering negotiation

dictate act *(enactment)*, canon, charge *(command)*, citation *(charge)*, coerce, compel, constitution, decree, decree, detail *(assign)*, direct *(order)*, direction *(order)*, directive, dominate, edict, enact, enactment, enforce, enjoin, fiat, govern, holding *(ruling of a court)*, impose *(enforce)*, insist, instruct *(direct)*, legislate, manage, mandamus, mandate, measure, monition *(legal summons)*, necessitate, order *(judicial directive)*, order, oversee, pass *(approve)*,

precept, prescribe, prescription *(directive)*, prevail *(be in force)*, regulation *(rule)*, require *(compel)*, requirement, rubric *(authoritative rule)*, rule *(legal dictate)*, rule *(govern)*, statute, writ
dictate of conscience duty *(obligation)*
dictate peace reconcile
dictated boiler plate, indispensable, necessary *(required)*, nuncupative, obligatory, positive *(prescribed)*, prescriptive
dictated term article *(precept)*
dictates legislation *(enactments)*, protocol *(etiquette)*
dictates of society custom, decorum
dictating master
dictation canon, coercion, compulsion *(coercion)*, enforcement, force *(compulsion)*, mandate
dictatorial arbitrary and capricious, dogmatic, peremptory *(imperative)*, presumptuous, relentless, strict, stringent, supercilious
dictatorial mogul dictator
dictatorius dictatorial
dictators hierarchy *(persons in authority)*
dictatorship oppression
dictio delivery
diction parlance, phraseology, rhetoric *(skilled speech)*, speech
dicto audiens obedient
dicto oboediens amenable
dictum canon, comment
dictum declaration
dictum dogma, law
dictum observation
dictum phrase, pronouncement
dictum remark
dictum statement
didactic disciplinary *(educational)*, hortative, informative
didactical disciplinary *(educational)*
die decease, expire, pattern, perish, stamp, succumb, terminate
die away expire, lessen, perish, stop, subside
die down decrease
die out expire, perish
die-hard bigot
diehard malcontent
dies date
dies festus holiday
diet session
differ bicker, challenge, collide *(clash)*, complain *(criticize)*, conflict, contend *(dispute)*, contradict, contrast, demur, depart, deviate, disaccord, disaffirm, disagree, dispute *(contest)*, dispute *(debate)*, dissent *(differ in opinion)*, except *(object)*, vary
differ in opinion collide *(clash)*, conflict, disaccord, disagree
differ in sentiment dissent *(differ in opinion)*
differ violently collide *(clash)*
difference conflict, contention *(opposition)*, contradistinction, deviation, disaccord, disagreement, disapproval, discord, discrepancy, disparity, dispute, dissidence, diversification, estrangement, feud, fight *(argument)*, identity *(individuality)*, impugnation, incongruity, inconsistency, inequality, nonconformity, nuance, objection, rift *(dis-*

agreement), schism, split, variance *(disagreement)*
difference of degree differential
difference of opinion argument *(contention)*, contest *(dispute)*, contradiction, controversy *(argument)*, disagreement, disapproval, dispute, dissension, embroilment
differences dissension, reaction *(opposition)*
different alien *(unrelated)*, contrary, discrete, disparate, dissimilar, distinct *(distinguished from others)*, distinctive, divergent, diverse, eccentric, extraordinary, foreign, heterogeneous, inconsistent, individual, multifarious, multiple, nonconforming, noteworthy, novel, original *(creative)*, peculiar *(distinctive)*, rare, repugnant *(incompatible)*, separate, several *(separate)*, singular, special, specific, unaccustomed, uncommon, unequal *(unequivalent)*, unique, unorthodox, unrelated, unusual
differentia characteristic, distinction *(difference)*, trait
differential characteristic, discrepancy, distinction *(difference)*, particular *(specific)*
differentiate call *(title)*, characterize, compare, contrast, define, demarcate, discern *(discriminate)*, discriminate *(distinguish)*, distinguish, enumerate, except *(exclude)*, label, secern, select, specify
differentiated disparate, individual, particular *(specific)*, peculiar *(distinctive)*
differentiating discriminating *(distinguishing)*, distinctive, personal *(individual)*
differentiating trait differential
differentiation collation, denomination, diagnosis, difference, discrepancy, distinction *(difference)*, diversification, nuance, segregation *(separation)*, severance
differentiative discriminating *(distinguishing)*, distinctive
differing discordant, discriminating *(distinguishing)*, disparate, dissenting, dissident, dissimilar, distinct *(distinguished from others)*, distinctive, divergent, diverse, eccentric, nonconforming, peculiar *(distinctive)*, recusant, unequal *(unequivalent)*, unrelated
differre defer *(put off)*, postpone, procrastinate, suspend
difficile difficult
difficilis difficult, fractious, froward, intractable
difficult complex, elusive, formidable, fractious, froward, impracticable, insuperable, intricate, labyrinthine, lawless, obscure *(abstruse)*, onerous, opaque, operose, oppressive, painful, perverse, petulant, problematic, querulous, recondite, restive, severe, uncompromising
difficult choice dilemma
difficult situation imbroglio, nuisance
difficult to accept unbelievable
difficult to alter ironclad
difficult to appraise intangible
difficult to bear oppressive
difficult to believe unbelievable

difficult to break ironclad
difficult to catch elusive
difficult to change ironclad
difficult to classify nondescript
difficult to comprehend ambiguous, elusive, esoteric, incomprehensible, opaque, unclear
difficult to describe nondescript
difficult to endure painful
difficult to explain indefinable
difficult to feel impalpable
difficult to perceive impalpable
difficult to please particular *(exacting)*, querulous
difficult to see impalpable
difficult to translate indefinable
difficult to understand elusive, indefinable, obscure *(abstruse)*, opaque, technical, unclear
difficultas predicament
difficulty adversity, aggravation *(annoyance)*, bar *(obstruction)*, burden, complex *(entanglement)*, complication, confusion *(ambiguity)*, confusion *(turmoil)*, damper *(stopper)*, dilemma, disadvantage, distress *(anguish)*, emergency, encumbrance, enigma, exigency, handicap, hindrance, imbroglio, impasse, impediment, impossibility, nuisance, obstacle, obstruction, plight, poverty, predicament, problem, quagmire, quandary, trouble
diffidence fear, hesitation, qualm, reluctance
diffidens diffident
diffident hesitant, reluctant
diffindere split
diffiteri disavow
diffluent fluvial
diffundere diffuse
diffundi diffuse
diffuse broad, circulate, deploy, desultory, disburse *(distribute)*, disintegrate, dispel, disperse *(scatter)*, disseminate, dissipate *(spread out)*, dissolve *(disperse)*, extensive, intersperse, pedestrian, permeate, pervade, prevailing *(current)*, profuse, prolix, propagate *(spread)*, publish, radiate, spread, turgid
diffusion circulation, decentralization, osmosis
diffusive extensive
dig down into delve
dig into canvass, delve, investigate, probe
dig out disinter, eviscerate, extract, ferret
dig up disinter, expose, procure
dig up out of the earth disinter
digerere arrange *(methodize)*, codify, sort
digest abridgment *(condensation)*, abstract, brief, capsule, code, compendium, conceive *(comprehend)*, condense, consider, muse, outline *(synopsis)*, pandect *(code of laws)*, pandect *(treatise)*, ponder, read, realize *(understand)*, report *(detailed account)*, restatement, review, scenario, summary, synopsis, understand
digest of law pandect *(code of laws)*
digest of the law hornbook
digested compact *(pithy)*
digestion osmosis
dignification degree *(academic title)*,

elevation, remembrance *(commemoration)*

dignified civil *(polite),* elegant, important *(significant),* meritorious, prominent, proud *(self-respecting),* reputable

dignify bestow, elevate, prefer, promote *(advance),* raise *(advance),* recognize *(acknowledge)*

dignitary functionary, incumbent

dignitas distinction *(reputation),* honor *(good reputation),* merit

dignity decorum, deportment, distinction *(reputation),* eminence, prestige, propriety *(correctness),* respect, solemnity, status

dignus eligible

digredi detour, digress

digress depart, detour, deviate, differ *(vary)*

digressing indirect

digressio deviation, digression

digression detour, indirection *(indirect action),* innovation

digressive alien *(unrelated),* circuitous, desultory, disparate, indirect, labyrinthine, shifting, tangential, turgid

diiudicare decide, discriminate *(distinguish)*

dijudicare arbitrate *(adjudge)*

dilacerate rend

dilaceration damage, split

dilapidate decay, degenerate, deteriorate, impair, spoil *(impair)*

dilapidated base *(inferior),* decadent, old, sordid

dilapidation decline, deterioration, detriment, disrepair, dissolution *(disintegration),* spoilage, wear and tear

dilatare compound, deploy, enlarge, expand, increase

dilatation extension *(expansion)*

dilate compound, declaim, discourse, enlarge, expand, extend *(enlarge),* increase, inflate, spread

dilate upon comment

dilated inflated *(enlarged)*

dilatio adjournment

dilation extension *(expansion),* inflation *(increase)*

dilatoriness deferment, delay

dilatory indolent, otiose, remiss, truant

dilatory obstruction filibuster

dilemma complication, confusion *(ambiguity),* deadlock, emergency, entanglement *(involvement),* imbroglio, impasse, incertitude, indecision, plight, predicament, problem, quagmire, quandary

diligence caution *(vigilance)*

diligence dispatch *(promptness)*

diligence industry *(activity),* tenacity, work *(effort)*

diligens careful, diligent, economical, exact, meticulous, precise, punctilious, scrupulous, strict

diligent circumspect, close *(rigorous),* conscientious, eager, earnest, industrious, intense, meticulous, painstaking, patient, persistent, pertinacious, punctual, resolute, sedulous, stable, steadfast, thorough, unrelenting, unremitting

diligent application diligence *(care)*

diligent attention diligence *(care),* examination *(study),* interest *(concern)*

diligent exercise discipline *(training)*

diligent practice discipline *(training)*

diligent study diligence *(care)*

diligent thought diligence *(care)*

diligentia diligence *(care),* industry *(activity)*

diligently faithfully

dilly dally procrastinate

dillydally stall

diluere dilute

dilute commute, deduct *(reduce),* denature, depreciate, diminish, disarm *(divest of arms),* extenuate, lessen

diluted insipid

dilutum solution *(substance)*

dim blind *(concealed),* blind *(obscure),* equivocal, incomprehensible, inconspicuous, indefinite, indistinct, inexpressive, intangible, nebulous, obfuscate, obnubilate, obscure *(faint),* obscure, opaque, tarnish, unclear, vague

dim-sighted blind *(sightless)*

dim-witted non compos mentis

dimension degree *(magnitude),* magnitude, mass *(weight)*

dimensions area *(surface),* caliber *(measurement),* configuration *(confines),* extent, measurement

dimidiate bifurcate

dimidiation split

diminish abate *(lessen),* abridge *(shorten),* allay, alleviate, assuage, attenuate, check *(restrain),* commute, curtail, damage, decrease, deduct *(reduce),* demean *(make lower),* demote, depress, derogate, discount *(minimize),* disgrace, erode, excise *(cut away),* extenuate, impair, lessen, minimize, mitigate, moderate *(temper),* mollify, palliate *(abate),* rebate, reduce, relax, remit *(relax),* restrict, retrench, subside

diminish in effect attenuate

diminish in quality impair

diminish the price of depreciate

diminish the value of depreciate

diminished minimal, qualified *(conditioned)*

diminishing abatement *(reduction),* decline, mitigating

diminishment consumption, curtailment, decrease, decrement, diminution, erosion, mitigation, mollification, relief *(release)*

diminution abatement *(reduction),* consumption, curtailment, damage, decrease, decrement, discount, erosion, mitigation, moderation, mollification, rebate, relief *(release),* remission, waste, wear and tear

diminutive immaterial, minimal, paltry, petty, remote *(small),* slight, tenuous

dimissio discharge *(dismissal),* dismissal *(discharge)*

dimittere disband, discharge *(dismiss),* dispense, forgo

dimming obscuration

dimness indistinctness, obscuration, opacity

dimwitted opaque

din brawl, noise, outcry, pandemonium

dint puissance

diocese region

dioristic perspicacious

dip immerse *(plunge into),* subside

diploma degree *(academic title),* document

diplomacy consideration *(sympathetic regard),* discretion *(quality of being discreet),* intercession, negotiation, parley

diplomat go-between, intermediary, plenipotentiary

diplomatic civil *(polite),* discreet, judicious, politic, strategic, subtle *(refined),* tactical

diplomatic agent plenipotentiary

diplomatic agreement protocol *(agreement)*

diplomatic code protocol *(etiquette)*

diplomatic corps embassy

diplomatical strategic, tactical

diplomatis patent

dipsomania inebriation

dirae malediction

dire adverse *(negative),* bad *(offensive),* deplorable, disastrous, drastic, fatal, gross *(flagrant),* harmful, heinous, ominous, outrageous, pernicious, portentous *(ominous),* regrettable, serious *(grave)*

direct accurate, administer *(conduct),* advise, appoint, arrange *(methodize),* candid, cause, charge *(instruct on the law),* clear *(apparent),* coherent *(clear),* command, compact *(pithy),* conduct, control *(regulate),* counsel, decree, demand, determine, dictate, discipline *(control),* discipline *(train),* dispatch *(send off),* edify, educate, enjoin, explicit, express, govern, handle *(manage),* hold *(possess),* impose *(enforce),* inculcate, indicate, influence, initiate, instill, manage, mandamus, manipulate *(utilize skillfully),* militate, moderate *(preside over),* motivate, nurture, officiate, operate, order, overlook *(superintend),* oversee, predominate *(command),* prescribe, preside, prevail *(be in force),* program, provide *(arrange for),* recommend, regulate *(manage),* require *(compel),* rule *(govern),* send, sententious, straightforward, subpoena, summary, superintend, unaffected *(sincere),* undistorted, wield

direct a threat against menace

direct affairs conduct

direct again redirect

direct approach access *(right of way)*

direct attention devote

direct attention to indicate, note *(notice),* notice *(give formal warning)*

direct imperatively command

direct one's attention instruct *(teach)*

direct one's thoughts to focus

direct opposite antipode, antithesis, contradiction

direct the attendance of subpoena

direct the attention to concern *(care),* convey *(communicate),* disabuse, mention, occupy *(engage),* signify *(inform)*

direct the eyes to observe *(watch)*

direct the mind to occupy *(engage)*

direct the mind upon concentrate *(pay attention)*

direct to address *(direct attention to)*

direct toward one object focus

directed against prejudicial

directed verdict nonsuit

directing advisory, determinative, executive, leading *(guiding),* prevailing *(having superior force)*

directing agency patronage *(power to appoint jobs)*

directing head chief, principal *(director)*

directing power clout

direction administration, advice, agency *(legal relationship),* canon, caveat, charge *(command),* charge *(statement to the jury),* conatus, control *(supervision),* course, custody *(supervision),* decree, design *(intent),* dictate, directive, disposition *(final arrangement),* edification, education, fiat, forethought, generalship, government *(administration),* guidance, inclination, intention, management *(supervision),* mandate, monition *(legal summons),* occupation *(possession),* order *(judicial directive),* ordinance, penchant, precept, prescription *(directive),* process *(summons),* purpose, regulation *(rule),* requirement, requisition, rule *(guide),* rule *(legal dictate),* side, standpoint, summons, supervision, supremacy, tendency, tenor, transaction, transmittal, way *(channel),* writ

direction post landmark *(conspicuous object)*

direction to imprison mittimus

directive causative, decretal, direction *(order),* fiat, guidance, mandate, order *(judicial directive),* procedural, regulation *(rule),* requirement, subpoena, writ

directly instantly

directly affected by the outcome of a controversy interested

directly after ex post facto

directness candor *(straightforwardness)*

director administrator, caretaker *(one fulfilling the function of office),* chairman, chief, employer, principal *(director),* procurator, superintendent

directorate board, generalship, management *(supervision)*

directorial administrative

directors authorities, hierarchy *(persons in authority),* management *(directorate),* management *(supervision)*

directorship board, direction *(guidance),* generalship, hegemony, management *(directorate),* management *(supervision),* regime

directory roll

direful dire, ominous, portentous *(ominous)*

diremption split

direptio pillage, spoliation

direption spoliation

dirge plaint

dirigere direct *(supervise)*

dirimere sever

dirtied tainted *(contaminated)*

dirtiness defilement, obscenity

dirty base *(inferior),* brand *(stigmatize),* infect, machiavellian, odious, pollute, profane, prurient, repulsive, salacious, stain, sully, taint *(contaminate),* tainted *(contaminated),* tarnish

diruere destroy *(efface),* overthrow

disability detriment, disadvantage, disease, disorder *(abnormal condition),* disqualification *(factor that disquali-*

---

fies), handicap, impediment, impuissance, inability, incapacity, inefficacy, pain

disable damage, disarm *(divest of arms),* disqualify, foil, impede, maim, mutilate, neutralize, obstruct, spoil *(impair),* stall, tax *(overwork)*

disabled helpless *(powerless),* inactive, inadequate, incapable, ineffective, marred, powerless, unable

disablement abortion *(fiasco),* detriment, disability *(legal disqualification),* disability *(physical inability),* disadvantage, disqualification *(factor that disqualifies),* harm, impuissance, inability, incapacity, inefficacy

disabuse debunk, inform *(notify),* reveal

disaccommodate disadvantage, discommode, disoblige

disaccord alteration, argument *(contention),* bicker, collide *(clash),* conflict, contend *(dispute),* contention *(opposition),* contest *(dispute),* contradiction, controversy *(argument),* deviation, differ *(vary),* difference, disagreement, discord, discrepancy, disparity, dispute, dissension, dissent *(difference of opinion),* dissidence, distinction *(difference),* division *(act of dividing),* faction, feud, incompatibility *(difference),* inconsistency, inequality, strife, variance *(disagreement)*

disaccord with differ *(vary),* disapprove *(reject),* refuse

disaccordance deviation, discord

disaccordant discordant, disproportionate, dissenting, incongruous, negative

disaccustom forswear

disadvantage damper *(stopper),* detriment, discommode, drawback, encumber *(hinder),* encumbrance, expense *(sacrifice),* fetter, handicap, harm, hindrance, impairment *(drawback),* inconvenience, incumbrance *(burden),* inexpedience, liability, misfortune, penalty, prejudice *(injury),* prejudice *(injure)*

disadvantageous adverse *(negative),* deleterious, detrimental, harmful, ill-advised, inadvisable, inauspicious, injudicious, insalubrious, noxious, peccant *(unhealthy),* pernicious, prejudicial, regrettable, undesirable, unfavorable

disadvantageousness inexpedience

disaffect alienate *(estrange),* antagonize, discourage, disfavor, estrange

disaffected faithless, false *(disloyal),* hostile, inimical, malevolent, recreant

disaffection abandonment *(desertion),* alienation *(estrangement),* bad faith, contempt *(disobedience to the court),* desertion, disaccord, dissatisfaction, dissension, estrangement, ill will, infidelity, malice, odium, reluctance, resentment, umbrage

disaffiliate disaffirm, disown *(refuse to acknowledge),* secede

disaffirm contest, controvert, deny *(contradict),* disaccord, disallow, disavow, disclaim, disinherit, disown *(deny the validity),* gainsay, negate, oppose, protest, recant, refute, reject

disaffirmation abjuration, denial, disclaimer, negation, rejection, renunciation, repudiation

---

disaffirming contrary

disaggreement strife

disagree argue, bicker, challenge, collide *(clash),* complain *(criticize),* conflict, contend *(dispute),* contest, contradict, contravene, debate, demur, deny *(contradict),* deviate, differ *(vary),* disaccord, disaffirm, disallow, disown *(deny the validity),* dispute *(debate),* dissent *(differ in opinion),* gainsay, object, oppose, oppugn, protest, rebut, renounce

disagree in opinion dissent *(differ in opinion)*

disagree with confront *(oppose),* controvert, disapprove *(reject),* dispute *(contest)*

disagreeable adverse *(hostile),* antipathetic *(distasteful),* bitter *(acrid tasting),* deplorable, disorderly, invidious, loathsome, objectionable, obnoxious, odious, offensive *(offending),* petulant, repugnant *(exciting aversion),* repulsive, undesirable, unsatisfactory, unsavory

disagreeing contradictory, contrary, discordant, disparate, dissenting, dissident, dissimilar, diverse, hostile, inapplicable, inapposite, inappropriate, incongruous, inconsistent, litigious, nonconforming, opposite, peculiar *(distinctive),* recusant, repugnant *(incompatible)*

disagreeing party faction

disagreement antipode, antithesis, argument *(contention),* belligerency, collision *(dispute),* conflict, confrontation *(altercation),* contention *(opposition),* contest *(dispute),* contradiction, contraposition, contravention, controversy *(argument),* deviation, difference, disaccord, disapprobation, disapproval, discord, discrepancy, disparity, dispute, dissatisfaction, dissension, dissent *(difference of opinion),* dissent *(nonconcurrence),* dissidence, distinction *(difference),* division *(act of dividing),* estrangement, feud, fight *(argument),* fracas, fray, imbroglio, impugnation, incompatibility *(difference),* incompatibility *(inconsistency),* incongruity, inconsistency, inequality, negation, nonconformity, objection, opposition, paradox, reaction *(opposition),* rejection, repudiation, split, struggle

disallow ban, bar *(exclude),* censor, condemn *(ban),* constrain *(restrain),* controvert, debar, deny *(contradict),* disaffirm, disapprove *(reject),* dismiss *(put out of consideration),* disown *(deny the validity),* disown *(refuse to acknowledge),* dissent *(withhold assent),* eliminate *(exclude),* enjoin, exclude, forbid, forestall, gainsay, halt, inhibit, interdict, interfere, negate, prohibit, proscribe *(prohibit),* rebuff, refuse, reject, repudiate, restrain, restrict, stop, withhold

disallow payment dishonor *(refuse to pay)*

disallowance abjuration, constraint *(restriction),* control *(restriction),* countermand, defeasance, denial, disapproval, disclaimer, estoppel, limitation, obstacle, obstruction, prohibition, proscription, refusal, rejection, renuncia-

tion, repudiation, restraint, veto
disallowance of trade embargo
disallowed barred, impermissible, inadmissible, ineligible, unauthorized
disallowing prohibitive *(restrictive)*
disannul abolish, abrogate *(annul)*, abrogate *(rescind)*, disclaim, disown *(deny the validity)*, invalidate, nullify, quash, recall *(call back)*, recant, renege, repudiate, rescind, revoke, vacate *(void)*, vitiate
disannulled null *(invalid)*, null and void
disannulment mistrial, rescision, retraction
disappear abandon *(physically leave)*, abscond, consume, depart, dissipate *(spread out)*, escape, evacuate, expire, flee, leave *(depart)*, perish, quit *(evacuate)*, withdraw
disappearance absence *(omission)*, concealment, erosion, flight, obscuration
disappearing ephemeral
disappoint fail *(lose)*, foil, frustrate
disappointing deficient, inadequate, nonsubstantial *(not sufficient)*, unsatisfactory
disappointment defeat, dissatisfaction, failure *(lack of success)*, miscarriage, misfortune
disapprobation abandonment *(repudiation)*, attaint, bad repute, charge *(accusation)*, condemnation *(blame)*, conflict, constraint *(restriction)*, contempt *(disdain)*, denunciation, disapproval, discredit, disdain, disgrace, dishonor *(shame)*, disparagement, disqualification *(rejection)*, dissatisfaction, exception *(objection)*, ignominy, impugnation, infamy, negation, notoriety, objection, obloquy, opposition, opprobrium, outcry, reaction *(opposition)*, refusal, rejection, renunciation, reprimand, reproach, scandal, stricture
disapprobatory derogatory, unfavorable
disapproval abandonment *(repudiation)*, blame *(culpability)*, condemnation *(blame)*, contempt *(disdain)*, criticism, denunciation, disapprobation, discredit, disdain, disgrace, disparagement, dissatisfaction, dissent *(nonconcurrence)*, exception *(objection)*, ignominy, ill repute, impeachment, impugnation, infamy, negation, objection, odium, opposition, outcry, protest, rebuff, refusal, rejection, reluctance, renunciation, reprimand, reproach, repudiation, scandal, stricture
disapprove abrogate *(annul)*, blame, cavil, censor, censure, challenge, complain *(criticize)*, condemn *(ban)*, condemn *(blame)*, conflict, confront *(oppose)*, contemn, counter, criticize *(find fault with)*, decry, demur, denounce *(condemn)*, deprecate, disaccord, disagree, disallow, discommend, disfavor, dissent *(withhold assent)*, enjoin, except *(object)*, expostulate, fault, fight *(counteract)*, forbid, impeach, object, oppose, protest, rebuke, refuse, reject, remonstrate, renounce, reprehend, reprimand, reproach, spurn
disapprove of decry, discriminate *(treat differently)*, regret

disapproved blameful, disadvantageous, impermissible, inadmissible, inadvisable, ineligible, nonconforming, outmoded, unsatisfactory
disapproving calumnious, contemptuous, critical *(faultfinding)*, cynical, derogatory, disdainful, dissenting, nonconsenting, pejorative, renitent
disarm disable, disqualify, placate, propitiate
disarmament reconversion
disarmed disabled *(made incapable)*
disarrange agitate *(shake up)*, confuse *(create disorder)*, discompose, dislocate, disorganize, disorient, disrupt, disturb, mismanage, muddle, perturb, upset
disarranged anomalous, broken *(interrupted)*, deranged, desultory, disjointed, disordered, disorderly, unsettled
disarrangement complex *(entanglement)*, confusion *(turmoil)*, disorder *(lack of order)*, disturbance, embroilment, entanglement *(confusion)*, irregularity, pandemonium
disarray complex *(entanglement)*, confuse *(create disorder)*, confusion *(turmoil)*, disorder *(lack of order)*, pandemonium, snarl
disarry entanglement *(confusion)*
disarticulate disjoint
disarticulated disjunctive *(tending to disjoin)*
disassemble disable, disjoint
disassembly dissolution *(disintegration)*
disassociate depart, disjoint, dissociate, part *(separate)*, remove *(dismiss from office)*, remove *(eliminate)*, seclude, separate, withdraw
disassociated disconnected, discrete, disjointed, distinct *(distinguished from others)*, remote *(secluded)*, separate
disassociation division *(act of dividing)*, estrangement, inconsequence, privacy, schism, segregation *(separation)*, separation, severance, split
disaster abortion *(fiasco)*, accident *(misfortune)*, adversity, calamity, casualty, cataclysm, catastrophe, debacle, fatality, loss, misfortune, tragedy
disastrous adverse *(negative)*, bad *(offensive)*, dangerous, deadly, deplorable, detrimental, dire, fatal, harmful, hostile, insalubrious, ominous, pernicious, pestilent, regrettable
disavow controvert, defect, demur, deny *(contradict)*, disaccord, disaffirm, disallow, disapprove *(reject)*, disclaim, disdain, dismiss *(put out of consideration)*, disown *(deny the validity)*, gainsay, negate, recant, refuse, reject, renounce, repudiate, withdraw
disavowal abandonment *(desertion)*, abandonment *(repudiation)*, abjuration, bad faith, confutation, declination, denial, disclaimer, disdain, dissent *(nonconcurrence)*, negation, refusal, renunciation, repudiation, rescision, retraction, reversal, revocation
disavowing contrary, negative
disavowment renunciation
disband break *(separate)*, degenerate, diffuse, disintegrate, disjoint, disorganize, disperse *(scatter)*, dissociate, dis-

solve *(separate)*, dissolve *(terminate)*, estrange, separate, sever
disbanding dissolution *(disintegration)*, release
disbandment decentralization, division *(act of dividing)*
disbar discharge *(dismiss)*, disgrace, dislodge, eliminate *(exclude)*, exclude, remove *(dismiss from office)*, repudiate
disbarment disqualification *(rejection)*, exclusion, expulsion, ostracism
disbelief cloud *(suspicion)*, discredit, doubt *(suspicion)*, incredulity, rejection, suspicion *(mistrust)*
disbelieve disavow, disclaim, disown *(deny the validity)*, doubt *(distrust)*, impugn, misdoubt, reject, suspect *(distrust)*
disbelieved unbelievable
disbelieving doubtful, inconvincible, skeptical
disbench disbar
disburden alleviate, clear, disencumber, disentangle, ease, extricate, facilitate, free, relieve *(free from burden)*
disburden one's conscience confess
disburdened clear *(free from criminal charges)*, clear *(unencumbered)*, free *(relieved from a burden)*
disburse administer *(tender)*, defray, manage, pay, remit *(send payment)*, remunerate, spend
disbursement advance *(allowance)*, amortization, appropriation *(donation)*, charge *(cost)*, collection *(payment)*, commission *(fee)*, consideration *(recompense)*, cost *(expenses)*, expenditure, fee *(charge)*, installment, maintenance *(upkeep)*, outlay, overhead, payment *(act of paying)*, price, reimbursement, remittance
disbursement of salary payroll
discard abandon *(relinquish)*, cancel, delete, depose *(remove)*, disavow, discharge *(dismiss)*, disclaim, discontinue *(abandon)*, disdain, disinherit, displace *(remove)*, eject *(expel)*, eliminate *(exclude)*, exclusion, expel, forgo, forswear, ignore, jettison, leave *(allow to remain)*, omit, override, quash, rebuff, reject, relegate, removal, renounce, renunciation, repudiate, rescind, revoke, screen *(select)*, set aside *(annul)*, spurn, supersede
discarded derelict *(abandoned)*, obsolete, outdated, outmoded
discarding desuetude, layoff, release
discardure rejection
discarnate intangible
discedere depart, leave *(depart)*
discept contend *(dispute)*, debate, differ *(vary)*, disaccord, dispute *(debate)*
disceptare arbitrate *(conciliate)*, discuss, dispute *(debate)*, parley
disceptatio controversy *(argument)*, dispute
disceptation contest *(dispute)*, controversy *(argument)*, rift *(disagreement)*
disceptator arbiter, arbitrator, umpire
discern appreciate *(comprehend)*, apprehend *(perceive)*, comprehend *(understand)*, conceive *(comprehend)*, construe *(comprehend)*, detect, diagnose, discover, distinguish, find *(discover)*, judge, locate, note *(notice)*, notice *(observe)*, perceive, read, realize *(under-*

stand), recognize *(perceive)*, secern, spy, understand

discern between differentiate

discern something audible hear *(perceive by ear)*

discernere discriminate *(distinguish)*

discernible apparent *(perceptible)*, appreciable, ascertainable, blatant *(conspicuous)*, cognizable, coherent *(clear)*, conspicuous, determinable *(ascertainable)*, evident, manifest, naked *(perceptible)*, obvious, open *(in sight)*, ostensible, palpable, perceivable, perceptible, ponderable, prominent, visible *(noticeable)*

discernible by touch tangible

discernibly fairly *(clearly)*

discerning acute, circumspect, cognizant, conscious *(aware)*, discreet, discriminating *(judicious)*, incisive, judicious, juridical, lucid, omniscient, perceptive, perspicacious, provident *(showing foresight)*, rational, reasonable *(rational)*, responsive, sapient, sensible, subtle *(refined)*

discernment alternative *(option)*, appreciation *(perception)*, apprehension *(perception)*, caliber *(mental capacity)*, cognition, comprehension, conclusion *(determination)*, diagnosis, discovery, discretion *(quality of being discreet)*, discrimination *(good judgment)*, insight, knowledge *(awareness)*, notice *(heed)*, perception, realization, reason *(sound judgment)*, sagacity, scienter, sense *(feeling)*, sensibility, understanding *(comprehension)*, vision *(dream)*

discerp lancinate, rend

discerpted disjointed

discerption disassociation, split

discharge absolution, absolve, accomplish, acquit, acquittal, action *(performance)*, amnesty, amortization, banishment, bear the expense, clear, collection *(payment)*, commission *(act)*, commit *(perpetrate)*, complete, composition *(agreement in bankruptcy)*, conclude *(complete)*, condonation, conduct, defeasance, defray, depose *(remove)*, disband, disburse *(distribute)*, disclaim, disenthrall, dislodge, dispel, displace *(remove)*, disqualification *(rejection)*, divest, egress, eject *(expel)*, emancipation, emit, excuse, execute *(accomplish)*, exemption, exonerate, exoneration, expel, expenditure, expulsion, extricate, exude, free, freedom, fulfill, immunity, implement, issuance, keep *(fulfill)*, layoff, liberate, liberation, liquidate *(determine liability)*, observe *(obey)*, operate, outburst, outflow, outpour, output, palliate *(excuse)*, pardon, pardon, parole, parole, payoff *(payment in full)*, perform *(execute)*, precipitate *(throw down violently)*, project *(impel forward)*, purge *(purify)*, quit *(free of)*, receipt *(proof of receiving)*, recovery *(award)*, rejection, release, release, relief *(release)*, remission, remit *(release from penalty)*, remit *(send payment)*, removal, remove *(dismiss from office)*, remunerate, respite *(reprieve)*, retire *(retreat)*, satisfaction *(discharge of debt)*, send, settlement, supplant, suspend, transact, vindicate, waiver

discharge a debt compensate *(remu-*

nerate), pay, quit *(repay)*

discharge a duty perform *(execute)*

discharge a function officiate

discharge a liability liquidate *(determine liability)*

discharge debts liquidate *(determine liability)*

discharge from accusation acquit

discharge from employment dismissal *(discharge)*

discharge from office depose *(remove)*

discharge in advance prepay

discharge of a debt expense *(cost)*, payment *(act of paying)*

discharge of emotions catharsis

discharge of responsibility exonerate

discharge one's duty serve *(assist)*

discharge the duties of commit *(perpetrate)*

discharged clear *(free from criminal charges)*, exempt, free *(relieved from a burden)*, fully executed *(consummated)*

discidium divorce, estrangement

disciple addict, amateur, novice, partisan, protégé

disciplina discipline *(obedience)*

disciplinarian dictator

disciplinary penal, punitive

disciplinary action condemnation *(punishment)*, correction *(punishment)*, penalty, punishment, reprisal, sanction *(punishment)*

discipline castigate, comport *(behave)*, condemn *(punish)*, control *(supervision)*, correction *(punishment)*, criterion, edify, educate, force *(compulsion)*, inculcate, labor *(exertion)*, method, moderate *(preside over)*, penalize, practice *(train by repetition)*, punish, punishment, regulate *(manage)*, regulation *(rule)*, reprisal, restraint, rigor, sanction *(punishment)*, science *(study)*, subdue

disciplined controlled *(restrained)*, literate, spartan, strict, systematic, veteran

discipulus disciple

disclaim answer *(reply)*, cancel, contradict, controvert, deny *(contradict)*, deprecate, disaccord, disaffirm, disallow, disapprove *(reject)*, disavow, disdain, disinherit, disown *(deny the validity)*, disown *(refuse to acknowledge)*, forswear, gainsay, ignore, negate, protest, recant, refuse, refute, reject, relinquish, renounce, repudiate, resign, revoke, surrender *(give back)*, waive

disclaim the responsibility for disown *(refuse to acknowledge)*

disclaimer abjuration, declination, denial, dissent *(nonconcurrence)*, negation, refusal, renunciation, repudiation, rescision

disclaiming contradictory

disclamation abjuration, ademption, denial, disclaimer, disdain, repudiation

disclose acknowledge *(declare)*, adduce, admit *(concede)*, apprise, bare, communicate, confess, confide *(divulge)*, construe *(translate)*, convey *(communicate)*, declare, denude, disabuse, display, divulge, enlighten, evidence, exhibit, expose, express, find *(discover)*, impart, inform *(betray)*, inform *(notify)*,

issue *(publish)*, manifest, mention, notice *(give formal warning)*, notify, present *(introduce)*, produce *(offer to view)*, profess *(avow)*, promulgate, publish, relate *(tell)*, reveal, signify *(inform)*, speak, specify, unveil, utter

disclose intentionally inform *(betray)*

disclose secrets inform *(betray)*

disclose something secret confide *(divulge)*

disclosed comprehensible, evident, manifest, naked *(perceptible)*, overt, palpable, patent, pellucid, perceivable, perceptible, public *(known)*

disclosed judgment cognovit

disclosing disclosure *(act of disclosing)*, informative, informatory

disclosure assertion, common knowledge, communication *(statement)*, confession, denouement, deposition, detection, discovery, divulgation, exhibit, expression *(manifestation)*, identification, manifestation, notice *(announcement)*, notification, profession *(declaration)*, publicity, report *(detailed account)*, testimony

disclosure of fault confession

disclosure proceedings discovery

discolor stain, tarnish

discoloration defacement

discolored blemished, marred

discomfit beat *(defeat)*, discompose, disconcert, disturb, embarrass, overcome *(overwhelm)*, overwhelm, perturb, subdue, upset

discomfiture confusion *(ambiguity)*, disturbance, embarrassment

discomfort agitate *(perturb)*, badger, discompose, disconcert, disease, dissatisfaction, distress *(anguish)*, embarrass, embarrassment, nuisance, pain, trouble

discomforting painful

discommend blame, denounce *(condemn)*, deprecate, disapprove *(condemn)*, fault, lessen, reprimand

discommendable blameful

discommendation bad repute, criticism, defamation, denunciation, diatribe, disapprobation, disapproval, exception *(objection)*, ignominy, impeachment, revilement

discommode annoy, badger, bait *(harass)*, condemn *(ban)*, deter, disadvantage, discompose, disoblige, encumber *(hinder)*, hinder, inconvenience, molest *(annoy)*, plague, trammel

discommodious detrimental

discommodity disadvantage, handicap

discompose annoy, badger, confuse *(bewilder)*, disconcert, disorganize, disorient, disrupt, distress, disturb, embarrass, harass, harrow, harry *(harass)*, incense, irritate, muddle, obsess, perplex, perturb, pique, plague, provoke, upset

discomposed disordered, disorderly

discomposure disorder *(lack of order)*, distress *(anguish)*, disturbance, embarrassment, pandemonium, panic

disconcert affront, agitate *(perturb)*, badger, confuse *(bewilder)*, counteract, discommode, discompose, disorganize, disorient, disturb, embarrass, frustrate, harrow, harry *(harass)*, menace, muddle, obfuscate, obsess, perplex, perturb,

upset
disconcerted deranged
disconcerting enigmatic
disconcertion ambiguity, confusion *(ambiguity)*, disturbance, quandary, trepidation
disconformity exception *(exclusion)*, incompatibility *(inconsistency)*, nonconformity, specialty *(distinctive mark)*
discongruity controversy *(argument)*, deviation, difference, disaccord, discord, discrepancy, dissidence, distinction *(difference)*, diversity, incompatibility *(inconsistency)*, variance *(disagreement)*
disconnect break *(separate)*, detach, dichotomize, disband, discontinue *(abandon)*, discontinue *(break continuity)*, disengage, disentangle, disjoint, dislocate, dissociate, dissolve *(separate)*, divide *(separate)*, estrange, interrupt, isolate, luxate, part *(separate)*, remove *(eliminate)*, separate, sever, split
disconnectable divisible
disconnected alien *(unrelated)*, apart, bipartite, broken *(interrupted)*, desultory, discrete, discursive *(digressive)*, disjunctive *(tending to disjoin)*, foreign, impertinent *(irrelevant)*, independent, separate, sporadic
disconnectedness anacoluthon, non sequitur
disconnection difference, disassociation, division *(act of dividing)*, estrangement, hiatus, incoherence, inconsequence, interruption, pause, schism, segregation *(separation)*, split
disconsolate despondent, lugubrious, pessimistic
disconsolation pessimism
discontent disapprobation, disparagement, dissatisfaction, dissent *(nonconcurrence)*, exception *(objection)*, grievance, ill will, outcry, plaint, resentment, trouble
discontented disappointed, dissident, insatiable, jealous, nonconsenting, querulous, reluctant, resentful, restive
discontentedness dissatisfaction
discontenting deficient
discontentment dissatisfaction
discontinu discrete
discontinuance abatement *(extinguishment)*, abeyance, abolition, ademption, annulment, cancellation, cessation *(interlude)*, close *(conclusion)*, cloture, defeasance, desuetude, discharge *(annulment)*, dismissal *(termination of a proceeding)*, dissolution *(termination)*, disuse, expiration, extremity *(death)*, halt, impasse, interruption, layoff, lull, moratorium, remission, renunciation, stay
discontinuance of activity impasse
discontinuance of business failure *(bankruptcy)*
discontinuation abandonment *(discontinuance)*, abeyance, adjournment, avoidance *(cancellation)*, cessation *(interlude)*, close *(conclusion)*, cloture, disassociation, discontinuance *(act of discontinuing)*, discontinuance *(interruption of a legal action)*, disuse, expiration, extremity *(death)*, halt, impasse, layoff, lull
discontinue abandon *(relinquish)*, abate *(extinguish)*, abolish, annul, can-

cel, cease, close *(terminate)*, conclude *(complete)*, continue *(adjourn)*, defer *(put off)*, desist, discharge *(release from obligation)*, disrupt, dissolve *(terminate)*, expire, finish, forgo, forswear, halt, interrupt, lapse *(cease)*, negate, palliate *(abate)*, pause, refrain, relinquish, rest *(cease from action)*, shut, stay *(halt)*, stop, suspend, terminate
discontinue work strike *(refuse to work)*
discontinued obsolete, old
discontinuity anacoluthon, deviation, difference, disturbance, hiatus, incoherence, irregularity, non sequitur, pendency
discontinuous broken *(interrupted)*, desultory, disconnected, discrete, disordered, disorderly, infrequent, intermittent, sporadic
discord anarchy, argument *(contention)*, belligerency, collision *(dispute)*, conflict, confrontation *(altercation)*, confusion *(turmoil)*, contend *(dispute)*, contention *(argument)*, contention *(opposition)*, contest *(dispute)*, contradiction, contravention, controversy *(argument)*, deviation, difference, disaccord, disagree, disagreement, discrepancy, disparity, dispute, dissension, dissent *(difference of opinion)*, dissidence, division *(act of dividing)*, estrangement, faction, feud, fight *(argument)*, fracas, impugnation, incompatibility *(difference)*, incompatibility *(inconsistency)*, inconsistency, noise, schism, strife, trouble, turmoil, umbrage, variance *(disagreement)*
discordance conflict, controversy *(argument)*, difference, disaccord, disagreement, disapproval, discord, discrepancy, disparity, dissension, dissent *(difference of opinion)*, dissidence, incompatibility *(difference)*, incompatibility *(inconsistency)*, incongruity, inconsistency
discordancy disaccord, disagreement, dissidence, incompatibility *(inconsistency)*, incongruity, inconsistency
discordant adverse *(hostile)*, argumentative, competitive *(antagonistic)*, contentious, contradictory, contrary, deviant, different, disjointed, disparate, disproportionate, dissenting, dissident, dissimilar, divisive, harsh, hostile, improper, inapplicable, inapposite, inappropriate, inapt, incommensurate, incongruous, inconsistent, inept *(inappropriate)*, litigious, negative, nonconforming, opposite, peculiar *(distinctive)*, polemic, recusant, repugnant *(incompatible)*, unsuitable
discordia discord, dissension, variance *(disagreement)*
discors discordant
discount brokerage, deduct *(reduce)*, deduction *(diminution)*, depreciate, discredit, disparage, drawback, except *(exclude)*, exclude, lessen, minimize, rebate, rebate, refund, reject
discountable deductible *(capable of being deducted from taxes)*
discountenance bad repute, blame, censor, condemn *(ban)*, condemn *(blame)*, condemnation *(blame)*, denounce *(condemn)*, denunciation, deter, disapprobation, disapproval, disapprove

(condemn), disclaim, disconcert, discount *(disbelieve)*, discourage, disfavor, dismiss *(put out of consideration)*, enjoin, except *(object)*, fault, forbid, forswear, protest, reaction *(opposition)*, refusal, refuse, renounce, restrain
discountenancing disdain
discounting mitigating
discourage browbeat, check *(restrain)*, debar, depress, deter, disappoint, dissuade, expostulate, forbid, forewarn, frustrate, hinder, preclude, prevent, remonstrate
discouraged arrested *(checked)*, disappointed, disconsolate, lugubrious, pessimistic
discouragement damper *(depressant)*, damper *(stopper)*, deterrence, deterrent, disadvantage, disincentive, dissatisfaction, hindrance, impediment, pessimism, prohibition, rebuff, remonstrance
discouraging chilling effect, remonstrative, unfavorable
discourse address *(talk to)*, charge *(statement to the jury)*, conversation, converse, declaim, declamation, discuss, instruction *(teaching)*, narration, pandect *(treatise)*, parlance, peroration, recital, recite, rhetoric *(skilled speech)*, speak, speech
discourse about deliberate, discuss
discourse at length outpour
discourse designed to convince argument *(pleading)*
discourse on the law hornbook
discourse upon comment
discourse with communicate
discourteous contemptuous, disdainful, disorderly, impertinent *(insolent)*, insolent, offensive *(offending)*, pejorative, perverse, presumptuous, uncouth
discourteousness disrespect
discourtesy contumely, disparagement, disregard *(lack of respect)*, disrespect, rebuff
discover ascertain, detect, discern *(detect with the senses)*, disinter, educe, expose, ferret, initiate, invent *(produce for the first time)*, locate, manifest, note *(notice)*, notice *(observe)*, perceive, pierce *(discern)*, recognize *(perceive)*, solve, spy
discover by artifice spy
discover by observation apprehend *(perceive)*
discover by search locate
discover by survey locate
discover the location of locate
discover the place of locate
discoverable appreciable, ascertainable, cognizable, conspicuous, determinable *(ascertainable)*, naked *(perceptible)*, obvious, open *(in sight)*, palpable, patent, perceivable, perceptible, ponderable, provable, scrutable, solvable
discoverer author *(originator)*, pioneer
discovery detection, disclosure *(something disclosed)*, invention, manifestation, observation, origination, perception, realization, recognition
discredit attaint, bad character, bad repute, brand *(stigmatize)*, cavil, cite *(accuse)*, condemnation *(blame)*, contemn, debase, decry, defame, degradation, demean *(make lower)*, denounce

(condemn), deprecate, depreciate, derogate, disaccord, disallow, disapprove *(condemn),* disavow, disbelieve, discommend, discount *(disbelieve),* disfavor, disgrace, disgrace, dishonor *(shame),* dishonor *(deprive of honor),* disparage, disprove, doubt *(suspicion),* doubt *(distrust),* humiliate, ignominy, impeach, impeachability, impugn, incredulity, infamy, lessen, libel, negate, notoriety, obloquy, onus *(stigma),* opprobrium, pillory, refuse, refute, reject, reproach, reproach, scandal, shame, smear, stain, sully, tarnish, underestimate

discredit in writing libel

discreditable arrant *(onerous),* blameful, blameworthy, calumnious, contemptible, culpable, disgraceful, dishonest, disreputable, fraudulent, ignoble, libelous, nefarious, notorious, reprehensible, scandalous, unjustifiable, unseemly

discreditableness bad character, disrepute, ignominy

discredited blameful, blameworthy, blemished, disreputable

discrediting derogatory, libelous, rejection

discreet careful, circumspect, diplomatic, guarded, judicious, noncommittal, politic, provident *(showing foresight),* prudent, sensible, subtle *(refined)*

discreetness discretion *(quality of being discreet),* discrimination *(good judgment)*

discrepance inequality

discrepancy conflict, deviation, difference, disaccord, disagreement, discord, disparity, distinction *(difference),* incompatibility *(inconsistency),* incongruity, inconsistency, inequality, paradox, variance *(disagreement)*

discrepans different, discordant

discrepant contradictory, deviant, different, discordant, disparate, disproportionate, dissenting, dissident, dissimilar, distinct *(distinguished from others),* divergent, diverse, divisive, improper, inapplicable, inapposite, inappropriate, inapt, incommensurate, incongruous, inconsistent, inept *(inappropriate),* peculiar *(distinctive),* polemic, unrelated, unsuitable

discrepantia contradiction, difference, disagreement, diversity

discrepare conflict, contrast, differ *(vary),* disagree

discrete disconnected, disjunctive *(tending to disjoin),* distinct *(distinguished from others),* individual, insular

discretion alternative *(option),* call *(option),* choice *(alternatives offered),* diagnosis, discrimination *(good judgment),* franchise *(right to vote),* latitude, option *(choice),* preference *(choice),* prudence, reason *(sound judgment),* referendum, volition

discretional adoptive, discreet, discretionary, disjunctive *(alternative),* permissive, spontaneous

discretionary circumspect, discreet, disjunctive *(alternative),* elective *(voluntary),* judicious, juridical, spontane-

ous, voluntary

discretionary order call *(option)*

discretive discrete

discrimen danger, discrimination *(differentiation),* distinction *(difference),* emergency, risk

discriminate call *(title),* choose, contrast, demarcate, designate, differentiate, discreet, discriminating *(distinguishing),* distinct *(distinguished from others),* distinguish, except *(exclude),* identify, perceive, screen *(select),* secern, select

discriminate between choose, compare

discriminating circumspect, cognizant, discreet, distinctive, judicious, juridical, lucid, particular *(exacting),* perceptive, perspicacious, preferential, prudent, rational, sapient, scrupulous, sensible, sensitive *(discerning),* subtle *(refined)*

discriminating judgment diagnosis, perception

discriminating taste discretion *(quality of being discreet)*

discriminatingness particularity

discrimination alternative *(option),* caliber *(mental capacity),* choice *(alternatives offered),* decorum, diagnosis, difference, discretion *(power of choice),* discretion *(quality of being discreet),* distinction *(difference),* expedience, favoritism, inequity, insight, intolerance, judgment *(discernment),* nuance, partiality, particularity, perception, prejudice *(preconception),* propriety *(correctness),* prudence, reason *(sound judgment),* sagacity, segregation *(isolation by races),* sensibility, severance

discriminative aesthetic, circumspect, discreet, discretionary, juridical, particular *(exacting),* perceptive, personal *(individual),* perspicacious, preferential, scrupulous, sensitive *(discerning)*

discriminatory inequitable, one-sided, partial *(biased)*

discriminatory powers discretion *(quality of being discreet)*

discrown demote

disculpate palliate *(excuse)*

disculpated clear *(free from criminal charges)*

disculpation amnesty, release

discursive circuitous, comprehensive, desultory, forensic, profuse, prolix, shifting, voluble

discursive faculties judgment *(discernment)*

discursive reasoning dialectic

discuss address *(talk to),* canvass, comment, confer *(consult),* consult *(ask advice of),* controvert, converse, counsel, debate, deliberate, discourse, investigate, mention, reason *(persuade),* remark, respond, treat *(process)*

discuss in the abstract generalize

discuss private affairs confide *(divulge)*

discussant disputant

discussion caucus, conference, confrontation *(act of setting face to face),* conversation, deliberation, discourse, interview, meeting *(conference),* negotiation, pandect *(treatise),* parley

discutere breach, dispel

disdain affront, condemn *(blame),* condemnation *(blame),* condescend *(patronize),* contemn, contumely, criticism, debunk, decry, deprecate, disapprobation, disapproval, disavow, discount *(disbelieve),* disfavor, disinterest *(lack of interest),* disoblige, disown *(refuse to acknowledge),* disregard *(lack of respect),* disrespect, eliminate *(exclude),* exclude, flout, forswear, ignore, misprize, neglect, rebuff, reject, rejection, renounce, ridicule, spurn

disdainful blameworthy, contemptuous, cynical, derogatory, hostile, impertinent *(insolent),* inflated *(vain),* insolent, offensive *(offending),* orgulous, pejorative, presumptuous, proud *(conceited),* supercilious, unaffected *(uninfluenced)*

disdainfulness contempt *(disdain),* contumely

disease contaminate, disorder *(abnormal condition),* pain, taint *(contaminate)*

disease-ridden pestilent

diseased peccant *(unhealthy),* pestilent, tainted *(contaminated),* unsound *(not strong)*

diseased in mind non compos mentis

diseased mind insanity, paranoia

disembark alight

disembarrass extricate

disembarrassed free *(relieved from a burden)*

disembodied disconnected, intangible

disembodied spirit phantom

disembody disband

disembogue exude, outpour

disemboguement outflow

disembowel eviscerate

disembroil clear, disencumber, disengage, disentangle, extricate, free, liberate, quit *(free of)*

disembroiling liberation

disemploy depose *(remove),* discharge *(dismiss),* dislodge, dismiss *(discharge)*

disemployment dismissal *(discharge),* layoff, removal

disenable disable, disarm *(divest of arms),* disqualify, neutralize

disenabled disabled *(deprived of legal right),* disabled *(made incapable)*

disenablement incapacity

disenact recant

disenchant debunk, deter, disaffect, disappoint, discourage, dissuade

disenchanted disappointed

disencourage deter

disencumber clear, disengage, disentangle, dissociate, ease, extricate, facilitate, free, quit *(free of),* relieve *(free from burden)*

disencumberance relief *(release)*

disencumbered clear *(unencumbered),* free *(relieved from a burden)*

disendow deprive, disinherit, disown *(refuse to acknowledge),* dispossess, divest

disendowment defeasance, disseisin

disenfranchise disable

disenfranchisement forfeiture *(act of forfeiting),* subjection

disengage abstract *(separate),* break *(separate),* depart, detach, disband, discontinue *(break continuity),* disencumber, disentangle, disenthrall, disjoint, dissociate, dissolve *(separate)*, divide *(separate)*, extricate, free, isolate, liberate, luxate, part *(separate)*, quit *(free of)*, release, relieve *(free from burden)*, retreat, separate, sever, withdraw

disengaged apart, bipartite, controlled *(restrained)*, discrete, dispassionate, free *(not restricted)*, free *(relieved from a burden)*, idle, neutral, nonpartisan, otiose, unemployed, vacant

disengagement disassociation, division *(act of dividing)*, estrangement, evulsion, exemption, freedom, liberation, release, segregation *(separation)*, split

disengaging divisive

disentail disencumber

disentangle ascertain, break *(separate)*, clarify, clear, construe *(comprehend)*, detach, disencumber, disengage, elucidate, explain, extricate, facilitate, find *(discover)*, free, part *(separate)*, quit *(free of)*, resolve *(solve)*, simplify *(make easier)*, solve, sort

disentangled free *(relieved from a burden)*

disentanglement denouement, release

disenthrall disengage, enfranchise, extricate, free, liberate, release, rescue

disenthrallment discharge *(liberation)*, freedom, liberation, release

disenthrone dislodge

disentitle condemn *(seize)*, confiscate, depose *(remove)*, deprive, disinherit, dispossess, disqualify, divest, impress *(procure by force)*

disentitled ineligible

disentitlement denial, disqualification *(rejection)*, foreclosure, forfeiture *(act of forfeiting)*

disentomb disinter

disequalization discrimination *(differentiation)*

disequilibrium difference, disparity

disertus eloquent, specific

disestablish abolish, annul, cancel, depose *(remove)*, dislodge, quash, rescind, subvert, withdraw

disestablished null *(invalid)*, null and void

disestablishment annulment, defeasance, subversion

disesteem attaint, bad character, bad repute, contemn, contempt *(disdain)*, decry, depreciate, disapprobation, disapproval, discount *(disbelieve)*, discredit, disdain, disgrace, dishonor *(shame)*, disparage, disparagement, disregard *(lack of respect)*, disrepute, disrespect, dissatisfaction, ignominy, ill repute, infamy, malign, misprize, notoriety, obloquy, odium, opprobrium, scandal, shame, underestimate

disfavor alienation *(estrangement)*, bad character, bad repute, condemn *(ban)*, condemnation *(blame)*, contempt *(disdain)*, deprecate, disaffect, disapprobation, disapproval, disapprove *(condemn)*, discommend, discredit, discriminate *(treat differently)*, disdain, disgrace, dishonor *(shame)*, disparage, disparagement, disqualification *(rejection)*, disregard *(lack of respect)*, dissatisfaction, estrangement, ignominy, ill re-

pute, impugnation, infamy, notoriety, obloquy, odium, proscription, rejection, reluctance, shame

disfiguration defacement

disfigure damage, deface, harm, mutilate, spoil *(impair)*

disfigured blemished, imperfect, marred

disfigurement defacement, flaw

disfranchise disable, disqualify, subject

disfranchisement disqualification *(rejection)*, infringement, subjection

disfurnish denude

disgorge eject *(expel)*, forfeit, outpour

disgorgement expulsion, outburst

disgrace attaint, bad character, bad repute, brand, brand *(stigmatize)*, corruption, debase, defame, defilement, degradation, demean *(make lower)*, depreciate, derogate, discredit, discredit, dishonor *(shame)*, dishonor *(deprive of honor)*, disparage, humiliate, ignominy, ill repute, infamy, notoriety, obloquy, odium, onus *(stigma)*, opprobrium, pillory, reduce, reproach, reproach, scandal, shame, stain, stigma, sully, tarnish

disgraced bad *(offensive)*, blemished, disreputable

disgraceful arrant *(onerous)*, contemptible, disorderly, disreputable, heinous, ignoble, inexcusable, inexpiable, nefarious, notorious, odious, outrageous, profligate *(corrupt)*, recreant, reprehensible, scandalous, vicious

disgracefulness bad repute, disrepute

disgracing libelous

disgruntle disappoint, discourage

disgruntled disappointed

disgruntlement dissatisfaction

disguise artifice, camouflage, cloak, clothe, conceal, concealment, cover *(pretext)*, cover *(conceal)*, deception, decoy, denature, distort, distortion, ensconce, enshroud, equivocate, fake, false impression, falsification, feign, hide, misrepresent, obnubilate, obscure, palter, plant *(covertly place)*, pretend, pretense *(pretext)*, pretext, profess *(pretend)*, ruse, screen *(guard)*

disguised assumed *(feigned)*, blind *(concealed)*, clandestine, covert, deceptive, hidden, indiscernible, mysterious, surreptitious

disguisement concealment

disgust contempt *(disdain)*, dissatisfaction, distress, odium, pique

disgusted renitent

disgustful repugnant *(exciting aversion)*

disgusting antipathetic *(distasteful)*, bad *(offensive)*, contemptible, gross *(flagrant)*, heinous, loathsome, lurid, objectionable, obnoxious, odious, offensive *(offending)*, reprehensible, reprobate, repugnant *(exciting aversion)*, repulsive, scurrilous, sordid, unsavory

disharmonious dissenting, divergent, incongruous

disharmonize disaccord

disharmony conflict, contention *(opposition)*, contest *(dispute)*, controversy *(argument)*, deviation, difference, disaccord, disagreement, discord, discrepancy, disorder *(lack of order)*, disparity, dissension, dissent *(difference of opin-*

ion), dissidence, distinction *(difference)*, division *(act of dividing)*, estrangement, incompatibility *(inconsistency)*, incongruity, pandemonium, variance *(disagreement)*

dishearten deter, disappoint, discommode, discourage, dissuade

disheartened disconsolate, lugubrious, pessimistic

disheartener damper *(depressant)*

disheartening bleak *(not favorable)*, deplorable, disastrous, lamentable

disheartenment depression, pessimism

disherit deprive, disinherit

dishevel agitate *(shake up)*, discompose, disorganize, disrupt, disturb

disheveled disordered, disorderly

dishevelment disorder *(lack of order)*, disturbance

dishonest culpable, deceptive, delinquent *(guilty of a misdeed)*, disgraceful, disingenuous, disreputable, faithless, false *(disloyal)*, felonious, fraudulent, ignoble, immoral, iniquitous, insidious, irregular *(improper)*, larcenous, lying, machiavellian, mendacious, peccant *(culpable)*, perfidious, recreant, sinister, sly, tainted *(corrupted)*, tortuous *(corrupt)*, unconscionable, undependable, unethical, unscrupulous, untrue, untrustworthy

dishonest application misapplication

dishonest management misconduct

dishonest use misapplication

dishonesty abuse *(corrupt practice)*, bad faith, corruption, deception, false pretense, fraud, guilt, hypocrisy, improbity, indirection *(deceitfulness)*, knavery, misdoing, pettifoggery, racket

dishonor abuse *(physical misuse)*, abuse *(violate)*, aspersion, attaint, bad character, bad faith, bad repute, brand *(stigmatize)*, browbeat, contemn, contumely, corruption, debase, defame, default, defilement, degradation, demean *(make lower)*, denigrate, denounce *(condemn)*, derogate, discredit, discredit, disfavor, disgrace, disgrace, dishonesty, disoblige, disparage, disparagement, disregard *(lack of respect)*, disrepute, disrespect, fail *(lose)*, humiliate, ignominy, ill repute, impeachability, infamy, infidelity, malign, nonpayment, notoriety, obloquy, odium, onus *(stigma)*, opprobrium, pillory, pollute, reproach, reproach, repudiate, scandal, shame, smear, stain, stigma, sully, tarnish, violate

dishonor by false reports malign

dishonorable bad *(offensive)*, blameful, blameworthy, contemptible, contemptuous, disgraceful, dishonest, disreputable, faithless, false *(disloyal)*, fraudulent, ignoble, immoral, libelous, machiavellian, nefarious, notorious, outrageous, perfidious, recreant, reprehensible, scandalous, sly, tortuous *(corrupt)*, unbecoming, unconscionable, unethical, unjust, unjustifiable, unscrupulous, untrustworthy, venal

dishonorableness bad character, bad repute, disrepute, ignominy

dishonored blemished

dishonored bill bad debt, nonpayment

dishonoring abuse *(physical misuse)*, contemptuous, default, derogatory, libelous

disillusion debunk, disabuse, disaffect, disappoint, discourage, dissuade

disillusioned cynical, disappointed

disillusionize disappoint

disillusionment disparagement

disimprison liberate, parole, rescue

disimprisonment freedom, liberation

disincentive deterrence, deterrent

disinclination bias, disincentive, reluctance

disinclination to action sloth

disinclination to labor sloth

disincline deter, discourage, expostulate

disinclined adverse *(hostile)*, averse, dissident, reluctant, renitent, restive

disinfect decontaminate

disinfectant preventive

disinfected pure

disingenuity improbity, indirection *(deceitfulness)*

disingenuous deceptive, dishonest, fraudulent, lying, machiavellian, oblique *(evasive)*, sinister, tortuous *(corrupt)*, unconscionable, unscrupulous, untrue

disingenuousness bad faith, color *(deceptive appearance)*, dishonesty, evasion, improbity, indirection *(deceitfulness)*

disingeuous sly

disinherit adeem, confiscate, deprive, disown *(refuse to acknowledge)*, reject

disinheritance rejection, renunciation

disinhume disinter

disintegrate break *(separate)*, decay, degenerate, destroy *(efface)*, diffuse, disorganize, dispel, disperse *(scatter)*, dissipate *(spread out)*, dissolve *(disperse)*, erode, obliterate

disintegrated broken *(fractured)*, old

disintegrating decadent

disintegration attrition, decentralization, deterioration, detriment, erosion, spoilage

disinter detect, ferret, find *(discover)*, solve

disinterest discourage, disregard *(unconcern)*, neutrality, objectivity

disinterested dispassionate, equitable, evenhanded, factual, impartial, judicial, just, neutral, objective, openminded, perfunctory, phlegmatic, torpid, unbiased, unprejudiced

disinterestedly fairly *(impartially)*

disinterestedness candor *(impartiality)*, disinterest *(lack of interest)*, disregard *(unconcern)*, fairness, indifference, neutrality, objectivity

disinterestness candor *(impartiality)*

disinvigorate disarm *(divest of arms)*

disinvolve disentangle

disiunctio separation

disiunctus separate

disiungere detach, divide *(separate)*, separate

disjoin abstract *(separate)*, break *(separate)*, depart, detach, dichotomize, disband, discontinue *(abandon)*, discontinue *(break continuity)*, disencumber, disengage, disentangle, disjoint, dislocate, disorganize, disperse *(scatter)*, disrupt, dissociate, dissolve *(separate)*, di-

vide *(separate)*, divorce, excise *(cut away)*, extricate, interrupt, isolate, luxate, part *(separate)*, remove *(eliminate)*, separate, sever, split

disjoined alien *(unrelated)*, apart, bipartite, desultory, disconnected, discrete, disjunctive *(tending to disjoin)*, divisive, individual, separate, solitary

disjoining decentralization

disjoint apart, disband, discrete, disjunctive *(tending to disjoin)*, dislocate, force *(break)*, luxate

disjointed apart, bipartite, deranged, disconnected, disjunctive *(tending to disjoin)*, disorderly, separate

disjointure disassociation

disjunct anomalous, apart, bipartite, broken *(interrupted)*, desultory, disconnected, discrete, disordered, individual, separate, solitary, sporadic

disjunction abandonment *(discontinuance)*, decentralization, difference, disassociation, division *(act of dividing)*, estrangement, hiatus, incoherence, inconsequence, interruption, rift *(gap)*, split

disjunctive disconnected, disjointed, divisive, elective *(selective)*

disjuncture division *(act of dividing)*

dislikable contemptuous, objectionable

dislike conflict (noun), conflict (verb), contempt *(disdain)*, deprecate, disapprobation, disapproval, disapprove *(condemn)*, disdain, disfavor, disparagement, dissatisfaction, exception *(objection)*, hatred, ignominy, ill repute, ill will, incompatibility *(difference)*, intolerance, malice, odium, outcry, phobia, rejection, reluctance, resent, umbrage

disliked disreputable, invidious, loathsome, repugnant *(exciting aversion)*, repulsive, undesirable, unsavory

disliking averse

dislocate break *(separate)*, contort, disband, discompose, disjoint, dislodge, disorient, displace *(remove)*, disturb, isolate, luxate, remove *(eliminate)*

dislocated anomalous, deranged, disordered

dislocation deportation, disturbance, removal, replacement

dislodge deport *(banish)*, depose *(remove)*, disengage, dislocate, disorient, displace *(remove)*, dispossess, disturb, divest, eject *(evict)*, evict, expel, extricate, liberate, oust, relegate, remove *(eliminate)*

dislodgment dismissal *(discharge)*, disqualification *(rejection)*, eviction, exclusion, expropriation *(divestiture)*, expulsion, foreclosure, liberation, ostracism, ouster, rejection, removal

disloyal broken *(unfulfilled)*, disobedient, faithless, hostile, insidious, insubordinate, irresponsible, perfidious, recreant, untrue, untrustworthy

disloyalty bad faith, corruption, desertion, estrangement, infidelity, mutiny, noncompliance *(nonobservance)*, sedition, treason

dismal bleak *(not favorable)*, bleak *(severely simple)*, deplorable, despondent, dire, disconsolate, lamentable, lifeless *(dull)*, lugubrious

dismantle break *(separate)*, destroy

(void), disable, disjoint, disorganize, dissolve *(separate)*, eviscerate, extinguish, mutilate, subvert

dismantlement dissolution *(disintegration)*

dismask disclose

dismay aggravate *(annoy)*, agitate *(perturb)*, consternation, deter, discompose, disconcert, discourage, disturb, doubt *(suspicion)*, fear, fright, harrow, intimidate, perturb, pique, trepidation

dismayed pessimistic

dismaying ominous, sinister

dismember disband, disjoint, divide *(separate)*, mutilate, part *(separate)*, separate, sever

dismembered broken *(fractured)*, disjunctive *(tending to disjoin)*

dismemberment disassociation, division *(act of dividing)*, split

dismiss cancel, cede, clear, condone, controvert, decry, deport *(banish)*, depose *(remove)*, disband, discharge *(release from obligation)*, discontinue *(abandon)*, dislodge, dispel, displace *(remove)*, disregard, eject *(expel)*, eliminate *(exclude)*, except *(exclude)*, exclude, exculpate, expel, forgo, free, liberate, oust, override, quash, rebuff, recall *(call back)*, refuse, reject, release, relegate, relinquish, remit *(release from penalty)*, remove *(dismiss from office)*, renounce, rescind, revoke, send, superannuate, supplant, vindicate, waive

dismiss all doubt assure *(give confidence to)*

dismiss charges palliate *(excuse)*

dismiss doubt ensure, reassure

dismiss from favor demote, disgrace

dismiss from service disband

dismiss from the bar disbar

dismiss from the legal profession disbar

dismissal abandonment *(repudiation)*, absolution, acquittal, avoidance *(cancellation)*, banishment, cancellation, compurgation, condonation, deportation, discharge *(release from obligation)*, discontinuance *(act of discontinuing)*, discontinuance *(interruption of a legal action)*, disqualification *(rejection)*, dissolution *(termination)*, exclusion, expulsion, layoff, liberation, ostracism, pardon, rejection, release, removal, renunciation

dismissal from office degradation

dismissal of an accusation absolution

dismissal of charges exoneration

dismissed clear *(free from criminal charges)*, free *(relieved from a burden)*, obsolete

dismissible defeasible

dismount alight

disobedience anarchy, bad faith, breach, contempt *(disobedience to the court)*, defiance, disloyalty, disregard *(lack of respect)*, disrespect, infraction, infringement, insurrection, invasion, mutiny, nonconformity, offense, rebellion, resistance, revolt, sedition, transgression

disobedient adverse *(hostile)*, broken *(unfulfilled)*, contumacious, disorderly, dissident, froward, insolent, insubordinate, intractable, irresponsible, lawless, nonconforming, nonconsenting, perfidious, perverse, recalcitrant, recusant, restive, uncontrollable, unruly, untrue

disobey break *(violate)*, defect, defy, rebel, trespass, violate

disobey the law offend *(violate the law)*, trespass

disobeyed lawless

disobeying lawless

disoblige affront, disaffect, discommode, mistreat

disobliging insolent, invidious, malevolent, negative, outrageous

disorder agitate *(shake up)*, anarchy, commotion, complex *(entanglement)*, confuse *(create disorder)*, confusion *(turmoil)*, degenerate, detriment, disability *(physical inability)*, discompose, disease, dislocate, disorganize, disorient, disrupt, disturb, disturbance, embroilment, entanglement *(confusion)*, havoc, imbroglio, incoherence, insurrection, irregularity, misrule, muddle, pandemonium, panic, perturb, riot, shambles, snarl, turmoil, violence

disordered anomalous, broken *(interrupted)*, deranged, disjointed, haphazard, lunatic, slipshod

disordered intellect insanity

disordered mind insanity, lunacy

disordered reason insanity, paranoia

disorderliness anarchy, commotion, confusion *(turmoil)*, irregularity, lynch law, riot

disorderly culpable, disjointed, disobedient, haphazard, lawless, licentious, perverse, slipshod, uncontrollable, unruly

disorderly conduct disorder *(lack of order)*, misconduct, misdoing

disorganization anarchy, commotion, complex *(entanglement)*, confusion *(turmoil)*, disorder *(lack of order)*, dissolution *(disintegration)*, disturbance, entanglement *(confusion)*, havoc, misrule, pandemonium, shambles

disorganize confuse *(create disorder)*, disband, discompose, dislocate, disorient, disrupt, disturb, muddle, upset

disorganized anomalous, deranged, disjointed, disordered, disorderly, lax, slipshod

disorient dislocate, perplex

disorientate disorganize, disturb

disorientation insanity

disoriented non compos mentis

disown condemn *(ban)*, defect, deny *(contradict)*, deprive, disaffirm, disallow, disavow, disclaim, disdain, disinherit, exclude, expel, rebuff, recant, refuse, reject, renounce, surrender *(give back)*, waive

disowned blameful, derelict *(abandoned)*

disownment abandonment *(repudiation)*, abjuration, ademption, attachment *(seizure)*, disclaimer, disdain, exclusion, rejection, renunciation, revocation

dispair sever

dispar dissimilar, diverse, unequal *(unequivalent)*

disparage blame, brand *(stigmatize)*, censure, complain *(criticize)*, condemn *(blame)*, condescend *(patronize)*, contemn, criticize *(find fault with)*, dam-

age, debunk, decry, defame, demean *(make lower)*, denounce *(condemn)*, deprecate, depreciate, derogate, disapprove *(condemn)*, discommend, discount *(disbelieve)*, discredit, disdain, dishonor *(deprive of honor)*, disoblige, fault, humiliate, impeach, jeer, lessen, libel, malign, minimize, misprize, mock *(deride)*, pillory, remonstrate, reprimand, reproach, smear, spurn, sully, underestimate

disparage frivolously cavil

disparagement aspersion, bad repute, blame *(culpability)*, condemnation *(blame)*, contempt *(disdain)*, criticism, defamation, denunciation, diatribe, disapprobation, disapproval, discredit, disgrace, dishonor *(shame)*, disrepute, disrespect, exception *(objection)*, ignominy, libel, notoriety, obloquy, phillipic, profanity, reproach, revilement, ridicule, slander

disparaging calumnious, contemptuous, cynical, derogatory, incriminatory, inculpatory, libelous, nonconsenting, pejorative, unfavorable

disparate different, disconnected, disproportionate, dissimilar, divergent, diverse, heterogeneous, miscellaneous, multifarious, peculiar *(distinctive)*, separate, unequal *(unequivalent)*, unrelated, unsuitable

disparity contradistinction, contraposition, deviation, difference, disaccord, discord, discrepancy, dissent *(difference of opinion)*, distinction *(difference)*, distortion, incompatibility *(inconsistency)*, incongruity, inconsistency, inequality, nonconformity, variance *(disagreement)*

dispart break *(separate)*, detach, disengage, disjoint, disperse *(scatter)*, dissociate, dissolve *(separate)*, divide *(separate)*, estrange, luxate, separate, sever

dispassion disinterest *(lack of prejudice)*, objectivity

dispassionate clinical, cold-blooded, deliberate, discriminating *(judicious)*, equitable, evenhanded, fair *(just)*, impartial, just, neutral, nonchalant, objective, open-minded, perfunctory, phlegmatic, stoical, unbiased, unprejudiced, unresponsive

dispassionately fairly *(impartially)*

dispassionateness candor *(impartiality)*, disinterest *(lack of prejudice)*, fairness, moderation, neutrality, objectivity

dispatch acceleration, accomplish, close *(terminate)*, commission *(act)*, complete, conduct, delegate, discharge *(performance)*, discharge *(perform)*, dismiss *(discharge)*, displace *(remove)*, eliminate *(eradicate)*, execute *(sentence to death)*, expedite, haste, hasten, intelligence *(news)*, issuance, kill *(defeat)*, kill *(murder)*, note *(brief comment)*, notice *(announcement)*, notification, relegate, send, slay, story *(narrative)*, transmit, transmittal, transport

dispatch news annunciate, disseminate

dispatcher carrier, informant

dispatches correspondence *(communication by letters)*

dispatching assassination

dispatchment consignment

dispel disband, disorganize, disperse *(scatter)*, disprove, dissolve *(disperse)*, extinguish, obliterate, quash, repel *(drive back)*, repulse

dispel misunderstanding resolve *(solve)*

dispellere dispel, disperse *(scatter)*

dispendium expense *(cost)*, waste

dispensable disposable, expendable, extraneous, gratuitous *(unwarranted)*, inconsequential, minor, needless, negligible, nonessential, null *(insignificant)*, otiose, petty, superfluous, unessential, unnecessary

dispensation administration, alimony, allotment, appointment *(act of designating)*, appropriation *(allotment)*, assignment *(allotment)*, benefit *(conferment)*, capacity *(authority)*, charter *(license)*, circulation, contribution *(donation)*, discharge *(release from obligation)*, disposition *(final arrangement)*, disposition *(transfer of property)*, distribution *(apportionment)*, donation, excuse, exoneration, franchise *(license)*, gift *(present)*, grant, gratuity *(present)*, impunity, inheritance, leave *(permission)*, legacy, pardon, privilege, quota, ration, release, reprieve, will *(testamentary instrument)*

dispense adjudge, administer *(tender)*, allocate, allot, apportion, assign *(allot)*, bear *(yield)*, bequeath, bestow, confer *(give)*, contribute *(supply)*, convey *(transfer)*, disburse *(distribute)*, dispense, disperse *(disseminate)*, disseminate, distribute, divide *(distribute)*, dole, endue, fund, give *(grant)*, impart, issue *(publish)*, mete, parcel, present *(make a gift)*, reapportion, render *(administer)*, sell, spend, split, vend

dispense judgment adjudge

dispense with abandon *(relinquish)*, abolish, censor, disavow, disclaim, dismiss *(discharge)*, disown *(refuse to acknowledge)*, extinguish, forbear, forgo, forswear, jettison, refrain, refuse, set aside *(annul)*, waive

dispensed with derelict *(abandoned)*

dispensing circulation, donative

dispergere circulate, circulation, disperse *(scatter)*, disseminate

dispersal circulation, decentralization, disbursement *(act of disbursing)*, dispensation *(act of dispensing)*, dissolution *(disintegration)*, division *(act of dividing)*

disperse administer *(tender)*, allocate, allot, break *(separate)*, circulate, diffuse, disband, disintegrate, disorganize, dispel, dispense, displace *(remove)*, disseminate, dissipate *(spread out)*, dissociate, divide *(distribute)*, issue *(publish)*, move *(alter position)*, radiate, repel *(drive back)*, separate, spread

disperse completely dispel

dispersed desultory, sporadic

dispersion circulation, decentralization, dispensation *(act of dispensing)*, division *(act of dividing)*, havoc, waste

dispertire apportion, distribute

dispirit depress, discourage, dissuade, harass, intimidate

dispirited despondent, disconsolate, lugubrious, pessimistic

dispiritedness depression, pessimism

dispiriting ominous

dispiteous remorseless, ruthless

displace accede (succeed), change, confuse (create disorder), deport (banish), depose (remove), discharge (dismiss), discompose, disjoint, dislocate, dislodge, dismiss (discharge), dispossess, dissociate, disturb, divest, eject (evict), eradicate, evict, exclude, inconvenience, luxate, oust, relegate, remove (dismiss from office), remove (eliminate), send, succeed (follow), supersede, supplant, upset

displaced deranged

displaced person derelict

displacement banishment, deportation, discharge (dismissal), dismissal (discharge), disqualification (rejection), disturbance, evulsion, exclusion, expulsion, layoff, ostracism, preemption, removal, replacement, sequestration, subrogation

displacement of rightful owner disseisin

displacency bad repute

displant disengage, dislodge, disturb

display bare, bear (adduce), brandish, color (deceptive appearance), complexion, demonstrate (establish), disinter, evidence, evince, exemplify, exhibit, exhibit, expose, expression (manifestation), flaunt, histrionics, illustrate, illustration, manifest, manifestation, phenomenon (manifestation), present (introduce), pretense (ostentation), produce (offer to view), reveal, scene, unveil

display line caption

display oneself boldly flaunt

display with effrontery flaunt

displease agitate (perturb), annoy, antagonize, bait (harass), disappoint, discommode, disturb, harrow, harry (harass), irritate, offend (insult), pique, plague, provoke, repel (disgust)

displeased disappointed, resentful

displeasing antipathetic (distasteful), deplorable, inadequate, inferior (lower in quality), objectionable, obnoxious, odious, offensive (offending), repugnant (exciting aversion), repulsive, unacceptable, undesirable, unendurable, unsatisfactory

displeasure disapprobation, disapproval, disparagement, dissatisfaction, exception (objection), nuisance, odium, pain, plaint, reprimand, resentment, umbrage

displume plunder

disponere marshal

disposable assignable, expendable

disposal administration, allotment, cession, conveyance, disbursement (act of disbursing), dismissal (termination of a proceeding), dispatch (act of putting to death), dispensation (act of dispensing), disposition (determination), disposition (final arrangement), disposition (transfer of property), distribution (apportionment), enjoyment (use), expense (sacrifice), management (judicious use), order (arrangement), recourse, regulation (management), release, sale, use

dispose abolish, allocate, allot, bait (lure), classify, convince, disperse (disseminate), divide (distribute), prompt,

regulate (adjust), rule (govern)

dispose of abandon (relinquish), administer (conduct), assign (transfer ownership), attorn, bequeath, bestow, close (terminate), complete, conclude (complete), contribute (supply), debar, decide, discharge (perform), dispatch (put to death), dispense, dissolve (terminate), eliminate (eradicate), eradicate, expel, expunge, forgo, give (grant), jettison, liquidate (determine liability), parcel, post, refute, set aside (annul), settle, slay, spend

dispose of for profit sell

disposed eager, inclined, prone, ready (willing), receptive, willing (desirous)

disposed of complete (ended)

disposed to believe credulous

disposed to bestow favors propitious

disposed to cavil fractious

disposed to cheat dishonest

disposed to controversy litigious

disposed to doubt cynical, inconvincible, incredulous, suspicious (distrustful)

disposed to envy jealous

disposed to fight pugnacious

disposed to good benevolent

disposed to insist insistent

disposed to mercy placable

disposed to peace peaceable

disposed to question debatable, doubtful

disposed to talk freely loquacious

disposed to yield flexible

disposer of stolen goods fence

dispositio disposition (final arrangement)

disposition adjudication, adjustment, administration, allotment, animus, apportionment, array (order), assignment (transfer of ownership), bias, cession, character (personal quality), choice (decision), classification, complexion, conatus, dispensation (act of dispensing), distribution (arrangement), favor (partiality), frame (mood), habit, legacy, penchant, personality, posture (attitude), predilection, predisposition, preference (choice), proclivity, propensity, property (distinctive attribute), regulation (management), settlement, spirit, standpoint, state (condition), structure (composition), temperament, tendency, usage, use, will (desire), will (testamentary instrument)

disposition of mind posture (attitude)

disposition of personalty legacy

disposition to believe credulity

disposition to deceive dishonesty

disposition to defraud dishonesty

disposition to inquire interest (concern)

disposition to lie dishonesty

disposition to mercy clemency, lenience

disposition to pardon clemency, condonation

disposition to please comity

disposition to resist contempt (disobedience to the court)

dispositioned inclined

dispossess assume (seize), condemn (seize), confiscate, demote, depose (re-

move), deprive, despoil, dislodge, dismiss (discharge), disown (refuse to acknowledge), displace (remove), divest, eject (evict), evict, expel, hijack, oust, seize (confiscate), sequester (seize property)

dispossess of abridge (divest)

dispossess of hereditary right disinherit, disown (refuse to acknowledge)

dispossess of right disqualify

dispossess oneself of abandon (relinquish)

dispossessed poor (underprivileged)

dispossession abridgment (disentitlement), appropriation (taking), assumption (seizure), attachment (seizure), condemnation (seizure), disqualification (rejection), disseisin, distraint, distress (seizure), eviction, expropriation (divestiture), expulsion, foreclosure, forfeiture (act of forfeiting), garnishment, infringement, ouster, privation, taking

disposure array (order), distribution (arrangement)

dispraise blame (culpability), blame, censure, condemn (blame), condemnation (blame), contempt (disdain), criticism, criticize (find fault with), decry, defame, denounce (condemn), denunciation, deprecate, depreciate, derogate, diatribe, disapprobation, disapprove (condemn), discommend, discredit, exception (objection), fault, ignominy, inveigh, lessen, malediction, malign, onus (stigma), reprimand, reprimand, sully

dispraised blameful

dispread diffuse

disprison extricate

disprize contemn, decry, derogate, minimize, misprize

disproof confutation, contradiction, counterargument, negation, repudiation

disproportion difference, distort, distortion, exaggeration, inequality, inequity

disproportionate disparate, excessive, inapposite, inappropriate, inapt, incommensurate, incongruous, inept (inappropriate), undue (excessive), unequal (unequivalent)

disproportionateness inequality

disprovable defeasible

disproval repudiation

disprove answer (reply), contradict, controvert, disown (deny the validity), impugn, invalidate, negate, rebut, refute

disputability cloud (suspicion)

disputable actionable, arguable, contestable, controversial, debatable, doubtful, dubious, dubitative, equivocal, forensic, justiciable, litigable, litigious, moot, problematic, uncertain (questionable), undecided, unsettled, unsound (fallacious)

disputant adversary, apologist, contender, contestant, foe, litigant, opponent, party (litigant), rival

disputare discuss, dispute (debate)

disputatio argument (contention), contention (argument)

disputation altercation, argument (contention), argument (pleading), belligerency, collision (dispute), contention *(argument)*, contention *(opposition)*, contest *(dispute)*, controversy *(argument)*, disaccord, disagreement, fight *(argument)*, impugnation, strife

disputatious argumentative, competitive *(antagonistic)*, contentious, debatable, disputable, dissenting, fractious, hostile, litigious, moot, petulant, polemic, pugnacious, querulous, remonstrative

disputative dissenting, forensic, litigious

dispute altercation, answer *(reply)*, argue, argument *(contention)*, bicker, brawl, challenge, collide *(clash)*, conflict, conflict, confront *(oppose)*, confrontation *(altercation)*, contention *(argument)*, contention *(opposition)*, contest *(dispute)*, contest, contradict, contradiction, contravene, controversy *(argument)*, controvert, cross *(disagree with)*, debate, deny *(contradict)*, differ *(disagree)*, disaccord, disaccord, disaffirm, disagree, disallow, disapprove *(reject)*, disbelieve, discord, dissension, dissent *(differ in opinion)*, doubt *(distrust)*, except *(object)*, exception *(objection)*, feud, fight *(argument)*, fight *(battle)*, fracas, fray, gainsay, haggle, impeach, impugn, impugnation, incompatibility *(difference)*, lawsuit, matter *(case)*, matter *(subject)*, negate, nonconformity, object, oppose, oppugn, proceeding, protest, rebut, reject, remonstrate, rift *(disagreement)*, strife, variance *(disagreement)*

dispute angrily brawl

disputed moot

disputed point conflict, contention *(argument)*, controversy *(argument)*, discrepancy

disputed point of law issue *(matter in dispute)*

disputed question controversy *(argument)*, issue *(matter in dispute)*

disputer malcontent

disputing dissenting, negative

disqualification disability *(physical inability)*, expulsion, inability, incapacity, invalidity, prohibition

disqualified disabled *(deprived of legal right)*, incompetent, ineligible, inept *(incompetent)*, powerless, unqualified *(not competent)*

disqualify ban, censor, condemn *(ban)*, disable, eliminate *(exclude)*, exclude, invalidate, prohibit, recall *(call back)*

disqualify as an attorney disbar

disqualifying prohibitive *(restrictive)*

disquiet affront, agitate *(perturb)*, annoy, badger, commotion, confusion *(turmoil)*, consternation, discommode, discompose, disconcert, disrupt, dissatisfaction, distress *(anguish)*, distress, disturb, disturbance, embarrass, embroilment, frighten, harass, harrow, ill will, incense, inflict, intimidate, menace, misgiving, molest *(annoy)*, outburst, perplex, perturb, pique, plague, press *(goad)*, provoke, qualm, remorse, stress *(strain)*, strife, trepidation, turmoil, upset

disquieting ominous, sinister, unsatisfactory

disquietude commotion, concern *(in-*

terest), confusion *(turmoil)*, consternation, distress *(anguish)*, disturbance, fear, fright, outburst, pandemonium, panic, stress *(strain)*, trepidation

disquisition charge *(statement to the jury)*, discourse, harangue, inquiry *(systematic investigation)*, narration, pandect *(treatise)*

disquisitional discursive *(analytical)*, narrative

disrank humiliate

disrate contemn, demote, derogate, humiliate, smear

disregard anarchy, breach, break *(violate)*, condonation, condone, contemn, contempt *(disdain)*, contravene, default, defiance, defy, dereliction, disaffirm, discount *(disbelieve)*, disdain, disdain, disfavor, dishonor *(nonpayment)*, dishonor *(refuse to pay)*, disinterest *(lack of interest)*, dismiss *(put out of consideration)*, disobey, disoblige, disown *(deny the validity)*, disparage, disrespect, disuse, eliminate *(exclude)*, except *(exclude)*, exclude, flout, ignore, inconsideration, indifference, jeer, laxity, misprize, muse, negate, neglect, neglect, negligence, nonfeasance, nonperformance, omission, overlook *(excuse)*, override, pretermit, rebuff, rebuff, reject, remit *(release from penalty)*, resist *(withstand)*, shun, spurn, trespass, violate

disregard of duty nonfeasance

disregard of orders contempt *(disobedience to the court)*, defiance, noncompliance *(nonobservance)*

disregard one's duty default

disregard one's obligations default

disregard prestige condescend *(deign)*

disregard the law offend *(violate the law)*

disregardant negligent, remiss

disregarded broken *(unfulfilled)*, inappreciable, null *(insignificant)*

disregardful broken *(unfulfilled)*, careless, contemptuous, derelict *(negligent)*, heedless, inadvertent, insolent, negligent, perfunctory, reckless, remiss, thoughtless

disregardfulness disregard *(lack of respect)*, disregard *(omission)*, disregard *(unconcern)*

disregarding disobedient, lax

disrelated alien *(unrelated)*, apart, separate

disrepair damage, deterioration, impairment *(damage)*

disreputability attaint, bad character, bad repute, discredit, disgrace, dishonor *(shame)*, disrepute, ignominy, ill repute, notoriety

disreputable arrant *(onerous)*, bad *(offensive)*, base *(bad)*, blameful, blameworthy, contemptible, delinquent *(guilty of a misdeed)*, depraved, disgraceful, dishonest, fraudulent, ignoble, immoral, iniquitous, lawless, notorious, profligate *(corrupt)*, reprehensible, reprobate, scandalous, sinister, unbecoming, unethical, unseemly

disreputable person degenerate

disreputableness bad repute, disrepute, ignominy, notoriety

disreputation ignominy, ill repute

disrepute attaint, bad character, bad faith, bad repute, contempt *(disdain)*, corruption, defamation, degradation, discredit, disgrace, dishonor *(shame)*, disparagement, ignominy, impeachability, infamy, notoriety, obloquy, odium, opprobrium, reproach, scandal, shame, stigma, turpitude

disreputed blameful

disrespect attaint, blasphemy, condescend *(patronize)*, contemn, contempt *(disobedience to the court)*, contumely, decry, disapprobation, disdain, disfavor, disgrace, disgrace, dishonor *(shame)*, disparage, disparagement, disregard *(lack of respect)*, disrepute, inconsideration, infamy, jeer, notoriety, obloquy, opprobrium, profanity, ridicule, shame, violate

disrespectability bad repute, ill repute

disrespectable blameworthy, disreputable, notorious, scandalous

disrespectful brazen, calumnious, contemptuous, disdainful, disobedient, harsh, impertinent *(insolent)*, insolent, offensive *(offending)*, outrageous, pejorative, presumptuous, profane, scurrilous, supercilious

disrespectfulness bad repute, contempt *(disobedience to the court)*, disparagement, disrespect, inconsideration

disrobe denude, divest

disroot remove *(eliminate)*

disrupt circumvent, counteract, damage, disconcert, discontinue *(break continuity)*, disorganize, foil, overthrow, subvert

disrupter insurgent

disruption abandonment *(discontinuance)*, alienation *(estrangement)*, check *(bar)*, debacle, disaccord, disassociation, discontinuance *(act of discontinuing)*, dissolution *(disintegration)*, estrangement, exception *(exclusion)*, furor, havoc, outbreak, outburst, pandemonium, shambles, split, subversion

disruptive offensive *(taking the initiative)*

dissatisfaction disapprobation, disapproval, dissent *(nonconcurrence)*, distress *(anguish)*, exception *(objection)*, ill will, objection, outcry, plaint, resentment, trouble, umbrage

dissatisfactory loathsome

dissatisfied disappointed, dissident, jealous, querulous

dissatisfiedness dissatisfaction

dissatisfy disaffect, disappoint

disscindere rend

dissect analyze, canvass, dichotomize, disjoint, examine *(study)*, investigate, partition, probe, rend, research, scrutinize, split, study, subdivide

dissectible divisible

dissection analysis, dichotomy, hornbook, indagation, split

disseise abridge *(divest)*, adeem, annex *(arrogate)*, attach *(seize)*, condemn *(seize)*, confiscate, dispossess, impress *(procure by force)*, impropriate, levy, seize *(confiscate)*

disseised attached *(seized)*

disseisin appropriation *(taking)*, distress *(seizure)*, expropriation *(divestiture)*

disseize deprive, dispossess, divest
disseizing confiscatory
dissemblance color *(deceptive appearance)*, difference, distortion, false pretense, story *(falsehood)*
dissemble assume *(simulate)*, camouflage, cheat, cloak, deceive, delude, disguise, distort, equivocate, evade *(deceive)*, fabricate *(make up)*, fake, falsify, feign, hide, misguide, mislead, misrepresent, misstate, palter, pretend, prevaricate, profess *(pretend)*
dissembling deceit, fraud, hypocrisy, lying, perfidious, recreant, tartuffish
disseminare disseminate
disseminate annunciate, apportion, cast *(throw)*, circulate, convey *(communicate)*, correspond *(communicate)*, diffuse, disburse *(distribute)*, disclose, dispel, dispense, dissipate *(spread out)*, distribute, herald, intersperse, issue *(publish)*, notify, proclaim, promulgate, propagate *(spread)*, publish, report *(disclose)*, reveal, signify *(inform)*, spread
disseminated pervade, public *(known)*
disseminating disbursement *(act of disbursing)*
dissemination circulation, common knowledge, communication *(statement)*, disbursement *(act of disbursing)*, disclosure *(act of disclosing)*, dispensation *(act of dispensing)*, distribution *(apportionment)*, division *(act of dividing)*, divulgation, notification, publication *(disclosure)*, publicity, report *(detailed account)*
dissensio conflict, disagreement, discord, dissent *(difference of opinion)*, variance *(disagreement)*
dissension argument *(contention)*, belligerency, breach, case *(lawsuit)*, conflict, contempt *(disobedience to the court)*, contention *(opposition)*, contest *(dispute)*, contradiction, controversy *(argument)*, difference, disaccord, disagreement, discord, dispute, dissent *(difference of opinion)*, dissent *(nonconcurrence)*, dissidence, distinction *(difference)*, division *(act of dividing)*, embroilment, faction, feud, fight *(argument)*, fracas, fray, incompatibility *(difference)*, opposition, revolt, schism, split, strife, struggle, variance *(disagreement)*
dissent argument *(contention)*, bicker, challenge, collide *(clash)*, conflict, conflict, contend *(dispute)*, contention *(opposition)*, contest *(dispute)*, contradict, contradiction, contravention, demonstrate *(protest)*, demur, denial, deny *(contradict)*, differ *(vary)*, disaccord, disaccord, disaffirm, disagree, disagreement, disallow, disapprobation, disapproval, disavow, discord, disown *(deny the validity)*, dispute *(debate)*, dissatisfaction, dissension, dissidence, except *(object)*, exception *(objection)*, faction, gainsay, impugnation, incompatibility *(difference)*, negation, nonconformity, object, objection, oppugn, outcry, protest, protest, refuse, reject, rejection, reluctance, renounce, repudiate, repudiation, resist *(oppose)*, schism, secede, strife, variance *(disagreement)*
dissent from dispute *(contest)*

dissenter disputant, heretic, malcontent
dissentience breach, disapproval, discord, dispute, dissension, dissent *(difference of opinion)*, embroilment
dissentient adversary, argumentative, contradictory, discordant, dissenting, dissident, divisive, heretic, hostile, malcontent, negative, nonconforming, nonconsenting, polemic, recusant
dissentient voice dissent *(nonconcurrence)*
dissenting contradictory, discordant, disinclined, dissident, hostile, nonconforming, nonconsenting, recusant, reluctant, renitent
dissentious contentious, dissenting, dissident, hostile, litigious, pugnacious, reluctant
dissentire conflict, differ *(vary)*, disagree, dissent *(differ in opinion)*
disserere discuss
dissertate converse, declaim, discourse, discuss
dissertation communication *(discourse)*, conversation, discourse, pandect *(treatise)*, recital
dissertation on the law hornbook
disserve damage, harm
disservice grievance, harm, injury, mischief, prejudice *(injure)*
disserviceable adverse *(negative)*, deleterious, disadvantageous, harmful, peccant *(unhealthy)*, pernicious, prejudicial
dissever detach, dichotomize, disband, discontinue *(abandon)*, discontinue *(break continuity)*, disengage, disjoint, dissociate, dissolve *(separate)*, divide *(separate)*, estrange, excise *(cut away)*, interrupt, isolate, luxate, part *(separate)*, rend, separate, sever, split, subdivide
disseverable divisible
disseverance division *(act of dividing)*, separation, split
disseverence disassociation
dissevering estrangement
dissidence argument *(contention)*, conflict, contention *(opposition)*, contravention, controversy *(argument)*, deviation, disaccord, disagreement, disapprobation, disapproval, discord, dispute, dissension, dissent *(difference of opinion)*, incompatibility *(difference)*, nonconformity, protest, sedition, strife, variance *(disagreement)*
dissident competitive *(antagonistic)*, deviant, discordant, dissenting, divisive, heretic, hostile, insubordinate, malcontent, negative, nonconforming, nonconsenting, recusant
dissidere differ *(vary)*, disagree, dissent *(differ in opinion)*
dissidium disagreement, discord
dissimilar atypical, different, discordant, disparate, distinct *(distinguished from others)*, divergent, diverse, heterogeneous, multifarious, nonconforming, peculiar *(distinctive)*, separate, unequal *(unequivalent)*, unique, unrelated
dissimilarity contradistinction, contraposition, deviation, difference, discord, discrepancy, distortion, diversity, identity *(individuality)*, incompatibility *(inconsistency)*, incongruity, in-

consistency, inequality, nonconformity, specialty *(distinctive mark)*
dissimilis dissimilar, heterogeneous
dissimilitude difference, disagreement, discrepancy, disparity, distortion, diversity, incompatibility *(inconsistency)*, incongruity, inconsistency, inequality
dissimilitudo disparity, inequality
dissimulare cloak, pretend
dissimulate assume *(simulate)*, cloak, deceive, disguise, equivocate, fabricate *(make up)*, fake, feign, lie *(falsify)*, misrepresent, palter, pretend, prevaricate, profess *(pretend)*
dissimulatio hypocrisy, irony
dissimulation color *(deceptive appearance)*, deceit, deception, disguise, duplicity, false pretense, falsehood, falsification, fraud, indirection *(deceitfulness)*, story *(falsehood)*
dissipare dispel, disperse *(scatter)*, dissipate *(spread out)*
dissipate carouse, debauch, deplete, diffuse, disappear, disorganize, dispel, disperse *(scatter)*, dissolve *(disperse)*, exhaust *(deplete)*, expend *(consume)*, impair, misemploy, obliterate, overdraw
dissipated depraved, dissolute, immoral, improvident, irredeemable, irretrievable, lascivious, lecherous, licentious, lost *(taken away)*, prodigal, profligate *(corrupt)*, prurient
dissipation consumption, debauchery, decentralization, decrease, decrement, dissolution *(disintegration)*, division *(act of dividing)*, expense *(sacrifice)*, privation, vice, waste
dissipative prodigal, profligate *(corrupt)*
dissociability ostracism
dissociate abstract *(separate)*, break *(separate)*, depart, detach, disband, disengage, disjoint, disrupt, dissolve *(separate)*, divide *(separate)*, divorce, estrange, isolate, luxate, part *(separate)*, remove *(dismiss from office)*, remove *(eliminate)*, seclude, separate, sever, withdraw
dissociate oneself disagree, disavow, disown *(refuse to acknowledge)*
dissociated alien *(unrelated)*, apart, discrete, foreign, independent, separate
dissociation disassociation, disclaimer, division *(act of dividing)*, estrangement, inconsequence, privacy, repudiation, segregation *(separation)*, separation
dissoluable severable
dissoluble defeasible
dissolute culpable, depraved, disorderly, disreputable, felonious, immoral, iniquitous, lascivious, lecherous, lewd, licentious, nefarious, profligate *(corrupt)*, promiscuous, prurient, reprobate, salacious, tainted *(corrupted)*, unrestrained *(not repressed)*, wanton
dissoluteness debauchery, delinquency *(misconduct)*, vice
dissolutio abolition, dissolution *(termination)*
dissolution abatement *(extinguishment)*, abolition, ademption, annulment, cancellation, cessation *(termination)*, debacle, decentralization, decline,

defeasance, denouement, destruction, disassociation, discharge *(annulment)*, end *(termination)*, erosion, expense *(sacrifice)*, expiration, extremity *(death)*, interruption, rescision, separation, spoilage, wear and tear

dissolution of marriage divorce, separation

dissolution of the marriage bond divorce

dissolutus dissolute, lax, licentious

dissolvable destructible

dissolve abate *(extinguish)*, abolish, abrogate *(annul)*, cancel, degenerate, destroy *(efface)*, disappear, discharge *(release from obligation)*, discontinue *(abandon)*, discontinue *(break continuity)*, disintegrate, disorganize, dispel, disperse *(scatter)*, dissipate *(spread out)*, eliminate *(eradicate)*, eradicate, erode, extirpate, interrupt, nullify, obliterate, part *(separate)*, quash, recess, renege, repudiate, rescind, revoke, separate, sever

dissolve by dismissal disband

dissolve of the bonds of matrimony divorce

dissolve the marriage of divorce

dissolved irretrievable

dissolvere disburse *(pay out)*, dissolve *(disperse)*, refund, solve

dissolving cancellation

dissonance conflict, contention *(opposition)*, contest *(dispute)*, controversy *(argument)*, deviation, difference, disaccord, disagreement, discord, discrepancy, disparity, dissension, dissent *(difference of opinion)*, dissidence, distinction *(difference)*, division *(act of dividing)*, estrangement, incompatibility *(inconsistency)*, incongruity, inconsistency, inequality, paradox

dissonant deranged, deviant, different, discordant, dissenting, divisive, inapposite, inappropriate, inapt, incongruous, inconsistent, inept *(inappropriate)*, peculiar *(distinctive)*, polemic, unsuitable

dissonus discordant

dissuade caution, check *(restrain)*, counsel, debar, deter, discourage, expostulate, forewarn, reason *(persuade)*, remonstrate

dissuade from entering picket

dissuadere dissuade

dissuasion admonition, deterrence, deterrent, disincentive, persuasion, remonstrance, restraint

dissuasive adverse *(hostile)*, remonstrative

distance extent, ostracism, perspective, range, space, surpass

distant controlled *(restrained)*, disdainful, distinct *(distinguished from others)*, foreign, inaccessible, insusceptible *(uncaring)*, obscure *(remote)*, phlegmatic, remote *(not proximate)*, remote *(secluded)*, unapproachable

distantly related consanguineous

distare apart

distaste dissatisfaction, odium, phobia, reluctance

distasteful bitter *(acrid tasting)*, deplorable, heinous, loathsome, objectionable, offensive *(offending)*, repugnant *(exciting aversion)*, repulsive, unaccept-

able, undesirable, unsavory, unseemly

distemper discompose, disease, disorder *(abnormal condition)*, disturb, pique

distend compound, enlarge, expand, extend *(enlarge)*, inflate, overextend

distended inflated *(enlarged)*

distension boom *(increase)*, inflation *(increase)*

distention extension *(expansion)*, growth *(increase)*, stress *(strain)*

distill extract

distillation corpus

distinct apparent *(perceptible)*, categorical, certain *(particular)*, certain *(positive)*, certain *(specific)*, clear *(apparent)*, cognizable, coherent *(clear)*, concrete, conspicuous, definite, different, discrete, disjunctive *(tending to disjoin)*, disparate, distinctive, diverse, evident, exclusive *(singular)*, explicit, express, individual, insular, lucid, manifest, naked *(perceptible)*, nonconforming, obvious, open *(in sight)*, overt, palpable, particular *(individual)*, particular *(specific)*, peculiar *(distinctive)*, perceivable, perceptible, personal *(individual)*, precise, prominent, remarkable, salient, separate, singular, trenchant, unambiguous, unmistakable, visible *(in full view)*

distinct indivisible entity individual

distinct intention deliberation

distinct purpose forethought, premeditation

distinct statement count

distincte fairly *(clearly)*

distinctio discrimination *(differentiation)*, distinction *(difference)*

distinction alternative *(option)*, character *(reputation)*, characteristic, color *(complexion)*, consequence *(significance)*, contradistinction, credit *(recognition)*, degree *(academic title)*, denomination, difference, differential, discretion *(power of choice)*, discretion *(quality of being discreet)*, discrimination *(differentiation)*, eminence, emphasis, feature *(characteristic)*, honor *(outward respect)*, identity *(individuality)*, importance, inequality, materiality *(consequence)*, merit, notoriety, nuance, personality, prestige, prize, property *(distinctive attribute)*, quality *(grade)*, regard *(esteem)*, reputation, restriction, severance, significance, speciality, specialty *(distinctive mark)*, specification, stress *(accent)*

distinctive different, discriminating *(distinguishing)*, distinct *(distinguished from others)*, individual, meritorious, noteworthy, novel, outstanding *(prominent)*, particular *(individual)*, particular *(specific)*, prominent, remarkable, representative, several *(separate)*, special, specific, uncommon, unusual

distinctive characteristic speciality

distinctive feature characteristic, differential, highlight, identity *(individuality)*, particularity, specialty *(distinctive mark)*, technicality

distinctive mark speciality

distinctive quality speciality

distinctive social attitude manner *(behavior)*

distinctive trait feature *(characteris-*

tic)

distinctively fairly *(clearly)*

distinctiveness caliber *(quality)*, identity *(individuality)*, personality, speciality, specialty *(distinctive mark)*

distinctly fairly *(clearly)*, particularly

distinctly expressed explicit

distinctly indicated express

distinctly stated explicit, express

distinctness contradistinction, deviation, difference, emphasis, identity *(individuality)*, nonconformity, specialty *(distinctive mark)*

distinctus distinct *(clear)*, distinct *(distinguished from others)*

distinguere discriminate *(distinguish)*, distinguish

distinguish call *(title)*, characterize, circumscribe *(define)*, classify, contrast, demarcate, detect, diagnose, differentiate, discern *(discriminate)*, elevate, honor, identify, notice *(observe)*, perceive, pierce *(discern)*, recognize *(perceive)*, secern, spy

distinguish between compare, contrast, select

distinguish by a mark label

distinguish by mark brand *(mark)*

distinguish by name denominate

distinguish by special selection elect *(choose)*

distinguishable appreciable, ascertainable, cognizable, conspicuous, determinable *(ascertainable)*, distinct *(clear)*, diverse, individual, naked *(perceptible)*, obvious, particular *(specific)*, peculiar *(distinctive)*, perceivable, perceptible, ponderable, several *(separate)*, unambiguous, unmistakable

distinguishably fairly *(clearly)*

distinguished best, certain *(specific)*, conspicuous, discrete, disparate, elegant, famous, illustrious, important *(significant)*, influential, major, meritorious, nonconforming, notable, noteworthy, outstanding *(prominent)*, paramount, particular *(individual)*, particular *(specific)*, peculiar *(distinctive)*, preferential, prominent, remarkable, renowned, reputable, salient, special, stellar, superior *(excellent)*, unusual

distinguished by nature distinct *(distinguished from others)*

distinguished by station distinct *(distinguished from others)*

distinguished quality trait

distinguishing discovery, discreet, distinctive, personal *(individual)*

distinguishing characteristic distinction *(difference)*, identity *(individuality)*

distinguishing feature differential

distinguishing mark designation *(symbol)*, earmark

distinguishing quality distinction *(difference)*, identity *(individuality)*, property *(distinctive attribute)*

distinguishing trait characteristic, property *(distinctive attribute)*

distinguishment discrimination *(differentiation)*, recognition, segregation *(separation)*, severance

distorquere contort, distort

distort bear false witness, camouflage, cloak, contort, corrupt, deface, denature, disguise, fabricate *(make up)*,

fake, falsify, invent *(falsify)*, misapprehend, misconstrue, misemploy, misguide, misinform, misinterpret, mislead, misread, misrepresent, misstate, misunderstand, mutilate, palter, prejudice *(influence)*, prevaricate, slant
distort intentionally misrepresent
distort the meaning misconceive
distort the truth feign
distorted defective, fallacious, false *(inaccurate)*, faulty, mendacious
distorted conception error
distorted idea misestimation
distorted impression misestimation
distortio distortion
distortion abuse *(corrupt practice)*, artifice, catachresis, color *(deceptive appearance)*, defacement, difference, error, evasion, exaggeration, fallacy, falsehood, falsification, irregularity, lie, misapplication, misrepresentation, misstatement, misusage, overstatement, parody, propaganda, sophistry, story *(falsehood)*, travesty
distortion of the truth perjury
distortion of truth falsehood
distract bait *(harass)*, confuse *(bewilder)*, disorganize, disorient, disrupt, disturb, divert, interrupt, perturb
distracted oblivious, thoughtless
distraction confusion *(ambiguity)*, confusion *(turmoil)*, preoccupation, turmoil
distrahere perplex
distrain annex *(arrogate)*, assume *(seize)*, attach *(seize)*, compel, condemn *(seize)*, confiscate, deprive, divest, garnish, impound, levy, mulct *(fine)*, seize *(confiscate)*, sequester *(seize property)*
distrained attached *(seized)*
distrainer attachment *(seizure)*
distraining confiscatory
distraint attachment *(seizure)*, condemnation *(seizure)*, disseisin, distress *(seizure)*, expropriation *(divestiture)*, foreclosure, garnishment, sequestration, taking
distrait thoughtless
distraught deranged, non compos mentis
distress adversity, affront, aggravation *(annoyance)*, annoy, attach *(seize)*, attachment *(seizure)*, badger, bait *(harass)*, condemnation *(seizure)*, discommode, disseisin, distraint, disturb, embarrass, expropriation *(divestiture)*, foreclosure, garnishment, harass, harry *(harass)*, hector, inflict, mistreat, obsess, offend *(insult)*, pain, persecute, perturb, plague, plaint, poverty, privation, prostration, provoke, quagmire, sequestration, toll *(effect)*, trouble, upset
distressed aggrieved *(harmed)*, destitute, disappointed, disconsolate, impecunious, poor *(underprivileged)*
distressful lamentable, painful
distressing bleak *(not favorable)*, cruel, deplorable, detrimental, disastrous, insufferable, irksome, lamentable, loathsome, oppressive, painful, pernicious, unsatisfactory
distribuere allot, apportion, dispense, distribute, divide *(distribute)*, parcel
distribute administer *(tender)*, allocate, allot, apportion, assign *(allot)*, be-

queath, bestow, cast *(throw)*, circulate, classify, deploy, detail *(assign)*, diffuse, dispense, disperse *(disseminate)*, dispose *(apportion)*, disseminate, dole, expend *(disburse)*, file *(arrange)*, fix *(arrange)*, give *(grant)*, intersperse, issue *(publish)*, marshal, mete, parcel, partition, post, prorate, publish, sort, split, spread, subdivide, supply
distribute again reapportion
distribute anew reapportion
distribute assets liquidate *(convert into cash)*
distribute proportionally prorate
distribute proportionately apportion
distributed pro rata
distributed by will testamentary
distributee legatee
distributer merchant
distributing center headquarters
distributing justice equitable
distribution administration, allotment, appointment *(act of designating)*, apportionment, appropriation *(allotment)*, assignment *(allotment)*, assignment *(transfer of ownership)*, budget, circulation, classification, consignment, decentralization, dispensation *(act of dispensing)*, disposition *(final arrangement)*, disposition *(transfer of property)*, division *(act of dividing)*, form *(arrangement)*, hierarchy *(arrangement in a series)*, order *(arrangement)*, proportion, ration
distribution by lot allotment
distribution of earnings dividend
distribution of profits dividend
distributional proportionate
distributor merchant
distributor of largess donor
district bailiwick, circuit, constituency, department, division *(administrative unit)*, local, locality, location, parcel, province, region, regional, territory
district attorney prosecutor
district officer caretaker *(one fulfilling the function of office)*
distrust apprehension *(fear)*, cloud *(suspicion)*, disbelieve, discount *(disbelieve)*, discredit, doubt *(suspicion)*, incredulity, misdoubt, misgiving, mistrust, qualm, rejection, suspicion *(mistrust)*
distrusted unbelievable
distrustful cynical, doubtful, inconvincible, incredulous, jealous, leery, pessimistic, resentful, skeptical
distrustfulness cloud *(suspicion)*, doubt *(suspicion)*, incredulity
distrusting skeptical
distrusting the motives of others cynical
disturb affront, aggravate *(annoy)*, agitate *(perturb)*, annoy, badger, bait *(harass)*, confuse *(create disorder)*, discommode, discompose, disconcert, discontinue *(break continuity)*, dislocate, dislodge, disorganize, disorient, displace *(remove)*, disrupt, distress, embarrass, evict, harass, harrow, harry *(harass)*, hector, impair, inconvenience, interfere, interrupt, irritate, menace, mistreat, molest *(annoy)*, muddle, obfuscate, offend *(insult)*, perplex, persecute, perturb, pique, plague, remove *(eliminate)*, upset

disturb keenly badger
disturb the composure of discompose
disturbance affray, altercation, belligerency, bluster *(commotion)*, brawl, cataclysm, commotion, confusion *(turmoil)*, consternation, detriment, disorder *(lack of order)*, dispute, embarrassment, embroilment, fracas, fray, furor, imbroglio, insurrection, molestation, nuisance, outbreak, outburst, outcry, pandemonium, panic, phobia, riot, trouble, turmoil, violation
disturbed disorderly, unsettled, unsound *(not strong)*
disturbing detrimental, formidable, ominous, painful, sinister, unsatisfactory, unsuitable, vexatious
disunion anarchy, argument *(contention)*, conflict, contravention, controversy *(argument)*, disaccord, disagreement, disassociation, discord, dissension, dissidence, division *(act of dividing)*, divorce, estrangement, hiatus, incompatibility *(difference)*, interruption, schism, segregation *(separation)*, separation, split
disunite abstract *(separate)*, alienate *(estrange)*, bicker, break *(separate)*, demarcate, detach, dichotomize, disaccord, disaffect, disband, discontinue *(abandon)*, discontinue *(break continuity)*, disengage, disintegrate, disjoint, dislocate, disperse *(scatter)*, dissociate, dissolve *(separate)*, divide *(separate)*, divorce, estrange, interrupt, isolate, luxate, part *(separate)*, rend, separate, sever, split
disunited apart, bipartite, disconnected, discrete, disjunctive *(tending to disjoin)*, dissenting, separate, unbound
disuniting division *(act of dividing)*
disunity argument *(contention)*, conflict, contravention, controversy *(argument)*, disaccord, disagreement, discord, disparity, dispute, dissension, dissent *(nonconcurrence)*, dissidence, division *(act of dividing)*, estrangement, incompatibility *(difference)*, variance *(disagreement)*
disusage abolition, desuetude, disuse, nonuse
disuse abandon *(relinquish)*, abolition, cancellation, desuetude, discontinuance *(act of discontinuing)*, dissolution *(termination)*, leave *(allow to remain)*, nonuse, set aside *(annul)*
disused barren, obsolete, otiose, outdated, outmoded, unemployed
disvaluation contempt *(disdain)*, criticism, ignominy
disvalue denounce *(condemn)*, deprecate, discommend, lessen
dithyrambic ecstatic
ditto copy, duplicate, reflect *(mirror)*, resemblance, tantamount
diurna record
diurnal daily
diuturnity period
divagate digress
divagation deviation, digression, indirection *(indirect action)*
divaricate bifurcate, bipartite, break *(separate)*, conflict, deviate, dichotomize, digress, disaccord, disagree, disjoint, spread

divaricate from differ *(vary)*

divaricating disparate, divergent

divarication dichotomy, digression, disassociation, split

divendere sell

diverge bifurcate, change, depart, deploy, detour, deviate, dichotomize, digress, disaccord, disagree, dissipate *(spread out)*, vary

diverge from conflict, differ *(vary)*

divergence antithesis, circulation, conflict, contention *(opposition)*, contradiction, contradistinction, controversy *(argument)*, deviation, difference, digression, disaccord, disassociation, discrepancy, disparity, dispute, dissension, dissent *(difference of opinion)*, dissidence, incompatibility *(difference)*, incompatibility *(inconsistency)*, inconsistency, inequality, innovation, irregularity, nonconformity, quirk *(idiosyncrasy)*, split, variance *(disagreement)*, variance *(exemption)*

divergent anomalous, deviant, different, disconnected, discordant, disordered, disparate, disproportionate, dissenting, dissident, dissimilar, distinct *(distinguished from others)*, diverse, eccentric, inapplicable, inappropriate, incongruous, inconsistent, irregular *(not usual)*, multiple, peculiar *(distinctive)*, separate, unorthodox, unsuitable

divergent opinion contradiction

divergent opinions conflict, controversy *(argument)*, disagreement, discord, dispute, dissension

diverging divergent, divisive

divers dissimilar, diverse, manifold

diverse atypical, different, discordant, disordered, dissimilar, distinct *(distinguished from others)*, divergent, heterogeneous, manifold, miscellaneous, multifarious, multiple, promiscuous, separate, several *(plural)*, unrelated

diverseness deviation, difference, distinction *(difference)*, diversity, nonconformity

diversification innovation

diversified composite, dissimilar, divergent, diverse, heterogeneous, manifold, miscellaneous, multifarious, multifold, multiple, nonconforming

diversiform different, diverse, heterogeneous, miscellaneous, multifold

diversify convert *(change use)*, differ *(vary)*, differentiate, vary

diversion decoy, detour, deviation, digression, enjoyment *(pleasure)*, misappropriation, misusage, treat

diversitas difference, diversity

diversity difference, discord, disparity, inconsistency, inequality, nonconformity, variance *(disagreement)*

diversity of opinion disaccord, disagreement, dissension, dissent *(difference of opinion)*

diversus apart, contradictory, different, diverse, heterogeneous, miscellaneous, repugnant *(exciting aversion)*

divert alleviate, avert, cloak, deter, detour, digress, discourage, entice, hold up *(rob)*, misemploy, peculate, pervert, repel *(drive back)*

divert by appeal dissuade, expostulate

divert by persuasion expostulate

divert from deter, dissuade

divert from its course detour, deviate

divert from original use estrange

divert from the original possessor estrange

divert funds defalcate

divert one's attention interest

divert to one's own use embezzle

diverting jocular

divest adeem, confiscate, demote, denude, depose *(remove)*, deprive, despoil, diminish, disinherit, disown *(refuse to acknowledge)*, dispossess, distrain, eject *(evict)*, excise *(cut away)*, expose, levy, plunder, remove *(dismiss from office)*, remove *(eliminate)*, unveil

divest of abridge *(divest)*

divest of legal office disbar

divest of office dislodge, oust

divest of property condemn *(seize)*

divest of right disqualify

divest of suspicion disarm *(set at ease)*

divest oneself forswear

divest oneself of abandon *(relinquish)*, disclaim, resign

divesting confiscatory

divestiture abridgment

divestiture *(disentitlement)*, garnishment

divestiture of property forfeiture *(act of forfeiting)*

divestment appropriation *(taking)*, attachment *(seizure)*, condemnation *(seizure)*, curtailment, denial, disseisin, distraint, distress *(seizure)*, eviction, expropriation *(divestiture)*, foreclosure, forfeiture *(act of forfeiting)*, privation, removal, sequestration, taking

dividable divisible

divide alienate *(estrange)*, allocate, allot, apportion, classify, codify, cross *(intersect)*, demarcate, detach, dichotomize, disaccord, disaffect, disagree, disburse *(distribute)*, discontinue *(break continuity)*, discriminate *(distinguish)*, disjoint, disperse *(disseminate)*, disperse *(scatter)*, dissociate, dissolve *(separate)*, distinguish, distribute, dole, estrange, fix *(arrange)*, hedge, interrupt, lancinate, mete, parcel, part *(separate)*, partition, pigeonhole, prorate, rend, separate, sever, sort, split, subdivide

divide according to rule apportion

divide and bestow in shares allocate

divide in portions assign *(allot)*, dispense

divide into distinct portions partition

divide into parcels subdivide

divide into portions partition

divide into shares apportion, parcel, partition

divide into two bifurcate

divide on differ *(disagree)*, dispute *(debate)*

divide proportionally prorate

divide proportionately apportion, partition

divide up apportion, partition, subdivide

divided bicameral, bipartite, broken *(fractured)*, broken *(interrupted)*, discrete, disjunctive *(tending to disjoin)*, dissident, hostile, partial *(part)*, partial *(relating to a part)*, polemic, separate

divided on dissenting

dividend bonus, commission *(fee)*, coupon, installment, interest *(profit)*, profit

dividends revenue

dividere distribute, divide *(distribute)*, divide *(separate)*, parcel, part *(separate)*, sever

dividing disbursement *(act of disbursing)*, divisive

dividing line edge *(border)*

dividing point crossroad *(turning point)*

dividual divisible, severable

dividuus severable

divinare guess

divination deduction *(conclusion)*, premonition, recognition

divinatory ominous, oracular, portentous *(ominous)*, prophetic

divine anticipate *(prognosticate)*, assume *(suppose)*, construe *(comprehend)*, deduce, deduct *(conclude by reasoning)*, detect, discover, expect *(consider probable)*, find *(discover)*, guess, portend, predict, presage, presume, presuppose, prognosticate, sacrosanct, surmise, suspect *(think)*

divinus prophetic

divisible divisive, partial *(part)*, partial *(relating to a part)*, separable, severable

divisio division *(act of dividing)*

division affiliate, alienation *(estrangement)*, apportionment, argument *(contention)*, article *(distinct section of a writing)*, assignment *(allotment)*, bureau, capacity *(sphere)*, chamber *(compartment)*, chapter *(branch)*, class, classification, component, conflict, constituency, constituent *(part)*, decentralization, denomination, department, detail, dichotomy, disaccord, disassociation, discord, discrimination *(differentiation)*, dispensation *(act of dispensing)*, dissension, distribution *(apportionment)*, equity *(share of ownership)*, estrangement, faction, incompatibility *(difference)*, installment, kind, manner *(kind)*, member *(constituent part)*, moiety, offshoot, organ, part *(place)*, part *(portion)*, plot *(land)*, province, ration, region, rubric *(title)*, schism, segment, segregation *(separation)*, separation, severance, split, subdivision, subheading, territory, unit *(department)*, variance *(disagreement)*

division by races segregation *(isolation by races)*

division in proportion apportionment

division line boundary, mete

division lines confines

divisional local, provincial, regional, specific

divisiveness argument *(contention)*, contravention, discord

divorce depart, detach, disassociation, disband, disengage, disjoint, disown *(refuse to acknowledge)*, dissociate, dissolve *(separate)*, divide *(separate)*, division *(act of dividing)*, estrangement, separation, sever, severance, split

divorce oneself from renounce

divorced disconnected, disjunctive

(tending to disjoin), distinct *(distinguished from others),* separate

divorcement disassociation, estrangement, separation

divortium divorce

divulgare circulate, circulation, publish, spread

divulgate bare, circulate, confide *(divulge),* convey *(communicate),* divulge, report *(disclose),* reveal

divulgation disclosure *(act of disclosing),* notification, publicity

divulge adduce, admit *(concede),* apprise, bare, bear *(adduce),* betray *(disclose),* circulate, communicate, confess, convey *(communicate),* declare, denounce *(inform against),* disabuse, disclose, display, enlighten, expose, find *(discover),* inform *(betray),* inform *(notify),* issue *(publish),* manifest, mention, notice *(give formal warning),* notify, proclaim, produce *(offer to view),* profess *(avow),* promulgate, publish, recite, recount, relate *(tell),* report *(disclose),* reveal, signify *(inform),* speak, spread, unveil, utter

divulged alleged, public *(known)*

divulgement communication *(statement),* confession, disclosure *(act of disclosing),* divulgation, publicity

divulgence admission *(disclosure),* confession, disclosure *(act of disclosing),* disclosure *(something disclosed),* discovery, divulgation, manifestation, publicity

divulger informant, informer *(a person who provides information)*

divulsion avulsion, split

dizen embellish

do conduct, discharge *(perform),* execute *(accomplish),* fulfill, generate, implement, operate, perform *(execute),* perpetrate, realize *(make real)*

do a favor for accommodate

do a job labor

do a service assist, help, serve *(assist)*

do a service for accommodate

do again reproduce

do all one can endeavor, strive

do an injustice to exploit *(take advantage of),* ill use, mistreat, persecute

do away with delete, destroy *(efface),* dispatch *(put to death),* dispel, dispense, eliminate *(eradicate),* eliminate *(exclude),* eradicate, expunge, extinguish, extirpate, override, rescind, vacate *(void)*

do away with completely eradicate

do battle with grapple

do business deal, handle *(trade),* trade, transact

do business with deal, patronize *(trade with)*

do disservice to damage

do duty exercise *(discharge a function),* officiate

do evil harm, ill use

do harm persecute

do harm to ill use

do honor dedicate

do honor to defer *(yield in judgment)*

do like copy

do likewise mock *(imitate)*

do mischief harm, persecute

do nothing procrastinate

do of one's own accord choose

do one's best attempt, endeavor, strive

do one's bidding serve *(assist)*

do one's utmost endeavor, strive

do over emend, repeat *(do again),* transform

do penance redeem *(satisfy debts),* repent

do repairs fix *(repair)*

do repeatedly practice *(train by repetition)*

do research study

do scant justice to underestimate

do service avail *(be of use),* pander

do subtraction diminish

do the deed dispatch *(dispose of)*

do the needful attempt

do the will of obey, observe *(obey)*

do thoroughly consummate

do violence harm, ill use, persecute

do violence to damage, mistreat, violate

do well pass *(satisfy requirements),* succeed *(attain)*

do without dispense, eschew, forbear, forgo, forswear, refrain, relinquish

do work labor

do work with ply

do wrong ill use, lapse *(fall into error),* mistreat

do wrong to persecute

doable potential, practicable, viable

docere edify, inform *(notify),* instruct *(teach)*

docile facile, malleable, obedient, obsequious, passive, patient, pliable, pliant, sequacious, suasible, tractable, yielding

docilis tractable

docility amenability, capitulation, resignation *(passive acceptance)*

dock diminish, lessen

docket agenda, book, calendar *(list of cases),* calendar *(record of yearly periods),* empanel, enroll, file, file *(place among official records),* label, label, note *(record),* pigeonhole, program, program, record, record, register, roll, schedule, set down, tabulate

docket incorrectly mislabel

doctor cure, denature, falsify, meliorate, palter, revise, slant

doctor up restore *(renew)*

doctrina instruction *(teaching),* knowledge *(learning),* theoretical, theory

doctrinaire bigot, dogmatic, theoretical

doctrinaire opinion dogma

doctrinal disciplinary *(educational),* dogmatic, informatory, orthodox

doctrinal statement belief *(something believed)*

doctrine belief *(something believed),* codification, concept, conviction *(persuasion),* discipline *(field of study),* dogma, idea, platform, policy *(plan of action),* precept, prescription *(directive),* principle *(axiom),* rule *(legal dictate),* theory, thesis

doctrines of lawmaking jurisprudence

doctus learned

document bear *(adduce),* blank *(form),* certify *(attest),* cite *(state),* confirm, corroborate, deed, dossier, estab-

lish *(show),* evidence, file *(place among official records),* index *(relate),* itemize, note *(record),* quote, record, roll, sustain *(confirm),* verify *(confirm),* will *(testamentary instrument)*

document granting permission permit

document produced as evidence exhibit

document which passes a present interest deed

documentable deductible *(provable)*

documental documentary

documentary convincing, informatory

documentary evidence certification *(attested copy)*

documentation certification *(attested copy),* certification *(certification of proficiency),* confirmation, corroboration, deposition, dossier, evidence, jurat, proof, record, reference *(citation),* support *(corroboration)*

documented authentic, convincing, documentary

documented event fact

documents credentials, data, evidence

documentum example, sample, specimen

dodge abscond, avoid *(evade),* avoidance *(evasion),* contrivance, deception, default, elude, equivocate, evade *(deceive),* evade *(elude),* evasion, hedge, ignore, imposture, machination, maneuver *(trick),* omit, palter, parry, pettifog, prevaricate, reject, ruse, shirk, shun, stratagem, subterfuge, tergiversate

dodgery artifice, pettifoggery

dodging disingenuous

doff denude

dogged diligent, faithful *(diligent),* inexorable, inflexible, intractable, obdurate, patient, persistent, pertinacious, purposeful, resolute, sedulous, serious *(devoted)*

doggedness diligence *(perseverance),* prowess *(bravery),* purpose, tenacity

dogma article *(precept),* belief *(something believed),* conviction *(persuasion),* doctrine

dogma dogma

dogma idea, precept, principle *(axiom),* rule *(legal dictate),* theory, thesis

dogmatic arbitrary and capricious, assertive, categorical, dictatorial, fanatical, illiberal, insistent, narrow, obdurate, parochial, provincial

dogmatic theorist bigot

dogmatical obdurate

dogmatist bigot, pedant

dogmatizer bigot

doing act *(undertaking),* action *(performance),* commission *(act)*

doing away with dispatch *(act of putting to death)*

doing good benevolent

doing nothing unemployed

doings dealings, overt act

dole allot, allotment, bestow, disperse *(disseminate),* distribute, distribution *(apportionment),* divide *(distribute),* fund, gratuity *(present),* largess *(gift),* loan, prorate, ration, share *(interest),* split

dole out administer *(tender),* allocate,

apportion, assign (allot), contribute (supply), disburse (distribute), dispense, disperse (disseminate), dispose (apportion), divide (distribute), mete, parcel, partition, present (make a gift), reapportion

dole out again redistribute
doleful deplorable, disconsolate, lamentable, lugubrious
dolefulness depression, pessimism
doling out apportionment
dollar currency cash
dolmen monument
dolor pain
dolorous deplorable, despondent, disconsolate, grave (solemn), lugubrious
dolosus fraudulent, insidious
doltish obtuse, opaque, uncouth
doltishness opacity
dolus deceit, machination, maneuver (trick), ruse, sham, stratagem
domain ambit, area (province), bailiwick, capacity (sphere), circuit, coverage (scope), demesne, department, district, dominion (absolute ownership), freehold, holding (property owned), jurisdiction, locality, possessions, property (land), province, real estate, realm, region, sphere, territory, title (right)
domare subdue
domestic internal, local, national, native (domestic), residential
domestic circle family (household), household
domestic domicile household
domestic establishment family (household), household
domesticate inure (accustom)
domestication cohabitation (married state)
domesticus household (domestic), internal
domicile abode, address, building (structure), dwell (reside), dwelling, habitation (dwelling place), house, inhabit, inhabitation (place of dwelling), lodge (house), lodge (reside), lodging, reside, residence
domiciled household (domestic)
domiciles premises (buildings)
domiciliary domestic (household), habitant, household (domestic), residential
domiciliate dwell (reside), reside
domiciliated household (domestic)
domiciliation residence
domicilium domicile, dwell (reside), dwelling, habitation (dwelling place), home (domicile), house, inhabitation (place of dwelling), residence, seat
dominance advantage, authority (power), control (supervision), dominion (supreme authority), duress, hegemony, influence, patronage (power to appoint jobs), power, predominance, preponderance, puissance
dominancy clout, dominance, dominion (supreme authority)
dominant cardinal (outstanding), causative, central (essential), compelling, considerable, forcible, influential, leading (ranking first), master, omnipotent, potent, powerful, predominant, prevailing (current), prevailing (having superior force), prevalent, primary,

prime (most valuable), principal, rampant, rife, salient, sovereign (absolute), stellar
dominant characteristic specialty (distinctive mark)
dominant quality character (personal quality)
dominant strength main force
dominant theme motif
dominate coerce, constrain (compel), control (regulate), direct (supervise), discipline (control), govern, handle (manage), hold (possess), manage, manipulate (control unfairly), monopolize, obsess, occupy (take possession), outbalance, outweigh, overcome (surmount), override, oversee, own, predominate (command), prevail (be in force), prevail (triumph), subdue, subject, subjugate, surmount
dominating leading (ranking first), omnipotent, powerful, predominant, prevailing (having superior force), salient
dominating action obsession
dominatio supremacy
domination authority (power), compulsion (coercion), control (supervision), dominance, dominion (supreme authority), force (strength), hegemony, influence, jurisdiction, monopoly, occupation (possession), oppression, patronage (power to appoint jobs), possession (ownership), power, predominance, preponderance, primacy, supremacy
domineer browbeat, dominate, impose (subject), prevail (be in force), repress, rule (govern)
domineering brutal, dictatorial, dogmatic, influential, peremptory (imperative), presumptuous, severe, supercilious, tyrannous
dominion agency (legal relationship), ambit, bailiwick, circuit, clout, control (supervision), coverage (scope), demesne, domain (sphere of influence), dominance, force (strength), government (administration), hegemony, influence, interest (ownership), jurisdiction, occupancy, occupation (possession), ownership, possession (ownership), power, predominance, primacy, province, realm, regime, supremacy, territory
dominions possessions, property (land)
dominium ownership
dominus proprietor
domus abode, building (structure), domicile, dwelling, habitation (dwelling place), home (domicile), house, household, premises (buildings), residence
don assume (simulate), pedagogue
donare impart, present (make a gift)
donate bequeath, bestow, cede, contribute (supply), convey (transfer), dedicate, dispense, endow, endue, fund, give (grant), leave (give), present (make a gift), proffer, provide (supply), spend
donate to subscribe (promise)
donated gratuitous (given without recompense)
donation benefit (conferment), bonus, cession, charity, endowment, gift (present), grant, largess (gift), perquisite, provision (act of supplying), reward, tip

(gratuity)
donative gift (present), gratuity (present), largess (gift), tip (gratuity)
donator contributor (giver), donor, grantor
done complete (ended), through
done again repeated
done at pleasure arbitrary
done by force forcible
done by one person ex parte
done by stealth surreptitious
done for effect flagrant
done on purpose deliberate
done over repeated
done quickly expeditious
done reciprocally mutual (reciprocal)
done with through
done with expedition expeditious
done with intent to commit crime felonious
done with skill artful
done with thoroughness elaborate
done without delay summary
done without reason random
donee assignee, beneficiary, devisee, feoffee, grantee, heir, legatee, licensee, payee, recipient, transferee
donee of a corporeal hereditament feoffee
donor benefactor, contributor (giver), feoffor, good samaritan, maker, transferor
donum donation, gift (present), grant
doom condemn (punish), convict, predetermine, sentence, tragedy
doomed unproductive
doomful portentous (ominous)
door entrance, outlet, portal, threshold (entrance)
doorway egress, portal
dope narcotic
doppelganger counterpart (complement)
dormancy abeyance, cessation (interlude), desuetude, inaction, inertia
dormant dead, inactive, insensible, lifeless (dull), otiose, passive, potential, stagnant, static, torpid
dormant energy potential
dormitory dwelling, home (domicile), lodging
dos dower
dose drug
dossier blank (form), file, record
dotage caducity, incapacity
dotation charity, donation, dower, largess (gift), legacy
doted on popular
double alter ego, copy, correlate, counterpart (parallel), duplicate, reflection (image), reproduce, resemblance, same, substitute
double back return (go back)
double dealing deceptive
double for displace (replace), impersonate, pose (impersonate)
double prosecution double jeopardy
double punishment double jeopardy
double talk jargon (unintelligible language)
double-cross betray (disclose), mislead
double-crossing machiavellian, perfidious
double-dealing bad faith, bunko, col-

lusion, deceit, deception, dishonest, duplicity, faithless, false (disloyal), fraud, fraudulent, hypocrisy, infidelity, knavery, lying, machiavellian, perfidious, recreant, sly, undependable, untrustworthy

double-edged bitter (penetrating)

double-tongued false (disloyal), machiavellian

doubling boom (increase)

doubt cloud (suspicion), confusion (ambiguity), disbelieve, discount (disbelieve), dispute (contest), hesitate, hesitation, improbability, incertitude, incredulity, indecision, misdoubt, misgiving, mistrust, qualm, quandary, reluctance, scruple, suspect (distrust), suspicion (mistrust)

doubt the truth of impugn

doubtable debatable, disputable, doubtful, dubitative, impalpable, implausible, ludicrous

doubtful ambiguous, controversial, cynical, debatable, disputable, dubious, dubitative, equivocal, hesitant, implausible, inconclusive, inconvincible, incredible, incredulous, indefinite, irresolute, leery, moot, precarious, problematic, speculative, suspicious (questionable), unbelievable, uncertain (questionable), undecided, unsettled, unsustainable, vague

doubtful event contingency

doubtful meaning ambiguity

doubtful narrative myth

doubtfulness ambiguity, confusion (ambiguity), doubt (suspicion), improbability, incertitude, incredulity, indecision, misgiving, qualm, quandary, scruple, suspicion (mistrust), suspicion (uncertainty)

doubting cynical, disputable, doubtful, hesitant, inconvincible, incredulous, irresolute, jealous, leery, skeptical, suspicious (distrustful), undecided

doubtless axiomatic, categorical, certain (positive), clear (certain), definite, demonstrable, indubious, uncontroverted, undisputed, unrefutable

doubtlessly a priori, admittedly, fairly (clearly)

douceur grant

doughtiness prowess (bravery)

doughty heroic, indomitable, spartan, undaunted

dour astringent, bleak (severely simple), rigid, severe

douse immerse (plunge into)

dovetail correspond (be equivalent)

down payment deposit, handsel, installment

down to until

downcast despondent, disconsolate, lugubrious, pessimistic

downcastness pessimism

downfall catastrophe, debacle, decline, defeat, disaster, failure (lack of success), fatality, miscarriage, prostration

downgrade debase, decline, deduct (reduce), demote, deteriorate, discredit, disgrace, disparage, humiliate, reduce

downhearted disconsolate, pessimistic

downheartedness damper (depres-

sant), pessimism

downhill decline

downright absolute (complete), clear (apparent), honest, ingenuous, outright, purely (positively), simple, stark, thorough, total, unaffected (sincere), unequivocal, unmitigated, unqualified (unlimited)

downrush descent (declination)

downthrow prostration

downtrend decline, decrease

downtrodden servile

downturn decline, decrease

downward inclination decline

downward incline decline

downward trend decline, decrease

dowry endowment

doxology laudation

doxy dogma

drab ordinary, pedestrian

drabble sully

draconian harsh, stringent

draft bill (proposed act), blueprint, check (instrument), coerce, compose, conceive (invent), contrive, delineate, design (construction plan), direction (course), enroll, formulate, frame (construct), frame (formulate), instrument (document), invent (produce for the first time), make, nominate, note (written promise to pay), originate, pattern, plan, program, program, proposal (suggestion), recruit, require (compel), select

draft holder bearer

drafter author (writer)

draftsman architect

drag impede

drag away carry away

drag on persist

drag out continue (prolong), prolong, protract (prolong)

dragged out protracted

dragonnade onset (assault)

dragoon bait (harass), coerce, persecute

drain consume, decrease, decrement, deplete, diminish, dissipate (expend foolishly), exhaust (deplete), expense (sacrifice), exude, outflow, outpour, remove (eliminate), spend, tax (overwork)

drain of resources deplete

drain on resources expense (cost), expense (sacrifice), maintenance (upkeep), overhead

drainage outflow

drained insufficient, nonsubstantial (not sufficient), poor (underprivileged), vacuous

dramatic histrionic, moving (evoking emotion), potent

dramatic art histrionics

dramatic representation histrionics

dramatize produce (offer to view), recite

dramaturgy histrionics

drape clothe

drastic extreme (exaggerated), forcible, harsh, outrageous, severe

draw bait (lure), bet, characterize, choose, copy, deadlock, delineate, depict, detail (particularize), educe, exhaust (deplete), extract, gain, inveigle, lottery, motivate, portray, reap, receive (acquire), trace (delineate)

draw a comparison contrast

draw a conclusion ascertain, deduce, deduct (conclude by reasoning), derive (deduce), determine, find (determine), infer, judge, read, rule (decide)

draw a distinction distinguish

draw a parallel compare, connect (relate), correspond (be equivalent), relate (establish a connection)

draw a picture delineate

draw an inference construe (comprehend), derive (deduce), gauge, infer, presuppose

draw apart estrange

draw as an implication construe (comprehend)

draw as by a lure entrap

draw aside divert

draw away divert

draw back retreat, shun

draw by artful inducements entrap

draw forth disinter, distill, educe, elicit, evoke, extract

draw from derive (receive), exact

draw gradually together converge

draw in converge, engage (involve), entrap, implicate, incriminate, involve (implicate)

draw inferences generalize, reason (conclude)

draw lots bet

draw near accost, approach, approximate, border (approach), gravitate, impend

draw off disengage

draw on exercise (use), lure

draw one's sword brandish

draw out compose, continue (prolong), disinter, distill, educe, elicit, evoke, exhaust (deplete), extend (enlarge), extract, prolong, withdraw

draw out by compulsion extort

draw out by force extort

draw out the essence distill

draw profit from profit

draw rein check (restrain)

draw the inference assume (suppose)

draw the line delimit, differentiate, discriminate (distinguish)

draw the veil camouflage

draw to a close cease, complete, dissolve (terminate), expire

draw together collect (gather), compile, consolidate (unite), constrict (compress), convene, glean, hoard

draw toward gravitate

draw up compile, compose, devise (invent), formulate, frame (construct), frame (formulate), make, produce (manufacture)

drawback burden, check (bar), defect, disadvantage, encumbrance, fault (weakness), handicap, hindrance, impediment, liability, obstacle, onus (burden), scruple

drawee debtor, obligor

drawer payee

drawing attractive, design (construction plan), lottery

drawing conclusions dialectic

drawing near forthcoming, immediate (imminent), imminent

drawing out evulsion

drawing to a close determinable (liable to be terminated)

drawn undecided

drawn battle deadlock

drawn game deadlock
drawn out chronic, protracted
drayage carriage
dread consternation, fear (noun), fear (verb), fright, mistrust, panic, phobia, portentous (ominous), stress (strain), trepidation
dreaded dire, undesirable
dreadful adverse (negative), bad (inferior), deplorable, detrimental, dire, disastrous, disreputable, formidable, gross (flagrant), heinous, hostile, insufferable, lamentable, loathsome, nefarious, portentous (ominous), regrettable, repulsive, serious (grave), sinister
dreadful event tragedy
dreadless undaunted
dream end (intent), objective, phantom, reflect (ponder)
dream up conceive (invent), conjure, invent (produce for the first time)
dreaminess preoccupation
dreaming pensive
dreamy delusive, oblivious, pensive, quixotic
drear bleak (severely simple)
drearisome jejune (dull), lifeless (dull), pedestrian, ponderous, prolix
dreary bleak (severely simple), deplorable, despondent, insipid, jejune (dull), lifeless (dull), lugubrious, pedestrian, ponderous, portentous (ominous)
drench imbue, immerse (plunge into), inundate, overload, permeate, pervade
dress clothe
dress as impersonate
dress down browbeat, denounce (condemn), disapprove (condemn), fault, reprehend, reprimand
dress to conceal disguise
dress up camouflage, cloak, disguise, embellish
dressing down diatribe, obloquy, reprimand, reproach
dried up otiose
drift conatus, connotation, content (meaning), contents, detour, deviate, digress, digression, direction (course), gist (substance), import, main point, meaning, prowl, signification, substance (essential nature), tenor
drifter derelict, itinerant
drifting discursive (digressive), moving (in motion), shifting
drill discipline (training), educate, enter (penetrate), practice (train by repetition)
drilling discipline (training)
drink carouse
drink to excess carouse
drinkable palatable
drip exude
drive activity, ardor, bind (obligate), browbeat, campaign, causeway, coerce, compel, compulsion (obsession), constrain (compel), enforce, foray, force (compulsion), impact, impetus, impose (enforce), impulse, incite, inducement, industry (activity), life (vitality), manipulate (utilize skillfully), obsess, operate, press (constrain), press (goad), pressure, pressure, project (impel forward), provoke, purpose, require (compel), send, stimulate, stimulus, urge
drive a bargain dicker, haggle, handle (trade), trade

drive a trade deal, sell
drive against collide (crash against)
drive apart estrange
drive at attempt, intend, strive
drive away deport (banish), dispel, parry, repel (drive back), repulse, spurn, stave, supplant
drive away by scattering dispel
drive back parry, rebuff, repel (drive back), repulse, spurn
drive firmly in impact
drive forward hasten, impel
drive from one's native land expatriate
drive in inject
drive into collide (crash against), pierce (lance)
drive off in various directions dispel
drive on expedite
drive onward impel
drive out deport (banish), depose (remove), divest, expel, oust, supplant, transport
driveway causeway
driving compelling, important (urgent), impulsive (impelling), insistent
driving force determinant, incentive, motive
driving out deportation, expulsion
droit birthright, capacity (authority), due, franchise (license), interest (ownership), prerogative, title (right)
droning ponderous
dronish lifeless (dull), obtuse
droop descent (declination), languish, succumb
drooping languid, powerless
droopy powerless
drop abandon (relinquish), cancel, cease, decline, decline (fall), decrease, decrease, delete, demote, depose (remove), depreciate, depress, descent (declination), discharge (dismiss), discontinue (abandon), distill, ebb, exude, forswear, iota, languish, leave (allow to remain), minimum, omit, precipitate (throw down violently), quit (discontinue), relinquish, renounce, set aside (annul), stop, subside, succumb, terminate
drop a hint imply, remind
drop by drop piecemeal
drop charges remit (release from penalty)
drop in strength decline (fall)
drop off diminish, ebb, lessen
drop out leave (depart), resign, retire (conclude a career)
drought paucity
drove assemblage, mass (body of persons)
drown immerse (plunge into), overcome (overwhelm), stifle
drown out extinguish
drowsiness languor
drowsy torpid
drub defeat, lash (strike), overcome (surmount)
drubbing failure (lack of success)
drudge labor, palliative (abating), strive
drudgery work (effort)
drug cannabis, narcotic
drugged insensible
drum repeat (state again)

drum out of the legal profession disbar
drunkenness dipsomania, inebriation
dry jejune (dull), languid, lifeless (dull), pedestrian, prosaic, unproductive
dry run experiment
dry up deplete
dual bilateral
dual chambered bicameral
duality duplicity
dub denominate, phrase
dubiety ambiguity, ambivalence, confusion (ambiguity), doubt (suspicion), hesitation, incertitude, incredulity, indecision, misgiving, qualm, quandary, rejection, scruple, suspicion (mistrust)
dubiosity incertitude, quandary
dubious aleatory (uncertain), ambiguous, controversial, cynical, debatable, disputable, doubtful, dubitative, equivocal, inconvincible, incredulous, indefinite, leery, moot, poor (inferior in quality), precarious, problematic, skeptical, speculative, suspicious (distrustful), suspicious (questionable), unbelievable, uncertain (questionable), undecided, unsettled, vague
dubiousness ambiguity, confusion (ambiguity), doubt (suspicion), incertitude, incredulity, indecision, qualm, quandary, rejection, scruple, suspicion (mistrust)
dubitable controversial, debatable, disputable, doubtful, dubitative, impalpable, implausible, ludicrous
dubitancy ambivalence, incertitude, indecision
dubitare hesitate
dubitate doubt (hesitate)
dubitatio doubt (indecision), hesitation, indecision, scruple
dubitation confusion (ambiguity), doubt (suspicion), hesitation, incertitude, indecision, quandary
dubitative debatable, disputable, dubious
dubito doubt (indecision)
dubius critical (crucial), doubtful, dubious, equivocal, indefinite, indeterminate, irresolute, precarious, problematic, undecided, vague
ducere regard (pay attention)
duck immerse (plunge into), shirk
ductile flexible, malleable, obedient, pliable, pliant, sequacious, tractable
ductilis malleable
ductility amenability
ductus generalship, guidance
dudgeon estrangement, odium, resentment, umbrage
due birthright, charge (cost), claim (right), condign, delinquent (overdue), droit, entitled, expense (cost), forthcoming, just, liability, opportune, outstanding (unpaid), overdue, payable, prerogative, price, receivable, reprisal, retribution, right (entitlement), right (righteousness), rightful, seasonable, suitable, unpaid, unsettled
due date maturity
due order array (order)
due punishment reprisal
due to contingent, dependent
due to be paid receivable
duel compete, fight (battle)
dueness droit, propriety (appropriate-

ness)

dues charge *(cost),* fee *(charge),* tax
dulce domum building *(structure)*
dulcet nectarious, palatable, sapid
dulcification mollification
dulcify alleviate, lull, mollify, pacify, placate, soothe
dulcis palatable
dull allay, alleviate, bleak *(severely simple),* diminish, drug, impair, inexpressive, insensible, insipid, languid, lessen, moderate *(temper),* mollify, nondescript, obfuscate, obnubilate, obscure, obtund, obtuse, opaque, pedestrian, phlegmatic, ponderous, prosaic, repress, soothe, stagnant, stale, stifle, subdue, sully, tarnish, thoughtless, torpid, trite, vacuous
dull comment platitude
dull-witted non compos mentis, obtuse, opaque
dull-wittedness opacity
dulling narcotic
dullness indistinctness, inertia, languor, opacity, sloth
duly as a matter of right, ex officio
dumb fatuous, mute, speechless, taciturn
dumb-struck speechless
dumbfound confound
dumbfounding prodigious *(amazing)*
dummy imitation, proxy
dump deposit *(place)*
dun charge *(assess),* claim *(demand),* exact, importune, request
duncelike opaque
duncical opaque
dunk immerse *(plunge into)*
dupable naive
dupe bait *(lure),* betray *(lead astray),* bilk, cheat, cloak, deceive, defraud, delude, ensnare, entrap, fake, hoodwink, illude, mislead, misrepresent, overreach, palter, pettifog, pretend, prevaricate
dupery bunko, deception, false pretense, falsification, fraud, hoax, knavery
duplexity duplicity
duplexity in meaning ambiguity
duplicate copy (noun), copy (verb), correlate, counterpart *(parallel),* expendable, facsimile, identical, mock *(imitate),* plagiarize, quote, reconstruct, recreate, reflection *(image),* reiterate, repeat *(do again),* replace, reproduce, same, superfluous, trace *(delineate)*
duplicated repeated
duplication boom *(increase),* copy, counterpart *(parallel),* identity *(similarity),* plagiarism, redundancy, resemblance, tautology
duplicative iterative, repetitious
duplicitous agreement conspiracy
duplicity artifice, bad faith, collusion, concealment, deceit, deception, dishonesty, false pretense, falsification, fraud, hoax, hypocrisy, imposture, improbity, indirection *(deceitfulness),* knavery, misstatement, pettifoggery, pretense *(pretext),* ruse, story *(falsehood),* subterfuge
durability indestructibility, longevity, strength, survival, tolerance
durable constant, firm, immutable, indelible, indestructible, infrangible,

noncancellable, permanent, persistent, resilient, solid *(sound),* stable, strong, unremitting
durableness indestructibility, longevity
durables goods
durance bondage, captivity, commitment *(confinement),* custody *(incarceration),* restraint, thrall
durance vile detention
durare continue *(prolong),* endure *(last),* last, remain *(stay)*
duration life *(period of existence),* longevity, period, phase *(period),* survival, tenure, time
duration of existence age
duration of life lifetime
duress captivity, coercion, compulsion *(coercion),* constraint *(restriction),* force *(compulsion),* intimidate, main force, pressure, stress *(strain),* subjection
during ad interim
during the interval ad interim
during the journey en route
during the last moments of life in extremis
during travel en route
duritia rigor
durus callous, rigid, severe, unbending
dusk obscure
dusky indistinct, nebulous
duteous conscientious, faithful *(loyal),* loyal, meritorious, moral, obedient, obeisant, passive, true *(loyal)*
duteously faithfully
duteousness allegiance, fealty
dutiable ad valorem
dutiful conscientious, faithful *(loyal),* law-abiding, loyal, meritorious, moral, obedient, obeisant, passive, patient, punctilious, serious *(devoted),* true *(loyal)*
dutiful adherence fidelity
dutifully faithfully, respectfully
dutifulness adhesion *(loyalty),* allegiance, compliance, conformity *(obedience),* discipline *(obedience),* fidelity
dutiless broken *(unfulfilled),* derelict *(negligent),* irresponsible, remiss
dutilessness dereliction, infidelity, misdeed, misdoing, nonperformance
duty ad valorem, agency *(legal relationship),* assignment *(task),* burden, business *(affair),* business *(occupation),* charge *(lien),* commitment *(responsibility),* compulsion *(coercion),* employment, excise, fealty, function, imposition *(tax),* job, labor *(work),* levy, liability, loyalty, mission, office, position *(business status),* province, responsibility *(accountability),* right *(righteousness),* tariff *(duties),* tax, trade *(occupation),* trust *(custody),* weight *(burden),* work *(employment)*
duty owed obligation *(duty)*
duty to pay liability
duty to pay money obligation *(liability)*
duty unfulfilled delict
dux chief, marshal
dwarf lessen, minimize
dwell lodge *(reside),* occupy *(take possession),* pause, remain *(occupy),* reside
dwell in inhabit, occupy *(take possession)*
dwell on repeat *(state again)*

dwell permanently inhabit
dwell together cohabit
dwell upon brood, recall *(remember),* reflect *(ponder)*
dweller citizen, denizen, domiciliary, habitant, inhabitant, inmate, lodger, occupant, resident, tenant
dwellers population
dwelling abode, address, building *(structure),* domicile, habitation *(act of inhabiting),* habitation *(dwelling place),* home *(domicile),* house, inhabitation *(act of dwelling in),* inhabitation *(place of dwelling),* lodging, residence
dwelling place abode, address, building *(structure),* home *(domicile),* house, inhabitation *(place of dwelling),* lodging
dwellings premises *(buildings)*
dwindle consume, decrease, deduct *(reduce),* depreciate, diminish, ebb, lessen, subside
dwindling attrition, decrease, deduction *(diminution)*
dye stain
dying death, expiration, in extremis
dynamic impulsive *(impelling),* intense, potent, powerful, progressive *(going forward),* trenchant
dynamic quality life *(vitality)*
dynamical impulsive *(impelling)*
dynamism industry *(activity),* life *(vitality)*
dynamite bomb
dynasty bloodline, descent *(lineage),* family *(common ancestry),* origin *(ancestry)*
dyspeptic bilious, bitter *(penetrating)*

E

each respectively
each and every collective, in solido
each in turn respectively
each to each per capita, pro rata
eadem sentire sympathize
eager earnest, fervent, hot-blooded, inclined, industrious, prompt, prone, ready *(willing),* sedulous, serious *(devoted),* solicitous, vehement, willing *(desirous),* zealous
eager for knowledge inquisitive
eager to please obeisant
eagerly readily
eagerness ardor, desire, emotion, greed, industry *(activity),* interest *(concern),* life *(vitality),* passion, penchant, purpose
eagerness to act quickly haste
earlier antecedent, back *(in arrears),* before mentioned, former, heretofore, last *(preceding),* precursory, preexisting, previous, prior, said, theretofore
earliest original *(initial),* primary, prime *(original)*
earliest stage embryo
early initial, instant, obsolete, old, preliminary, preparatory, previous, prime *(original),* prompt, punctual
early stage nonage
earmark allocate, allot, brand, brand *(mark),* designate, designation *(symbol),* device *(distinguishing mark),* distinction *(difference),* index *(catalog),* label, property *(distinctive attribute),* quality *(grade),* reserve, specialty *(dis-*

tinctive mark)

earmarked prospective

earn attain, bear *(yield)*, gain, obtain, pass *(satisfy requirements)*, procure, realize *(obtain as a profit)*, reap, receive *(acquire)*, succeed *(attain)*

earned condign, due *(owed)*, entitled

earned income earnings

earnest bail, binder, close *(rigorous)*, eager, fervent, honest, industrious, intense, painstaking, pertinacious, pledge *(security)*, purposeful, resolute, security *(pledge)*, serious *(devoted)*, solemn, true *(loyal)*, urgent, vehement, willing *(desirous)*, zealous

earnest averment surety *(certainty)*

earnest avowal surety *(certainty)*

earnest declaration assurance, surety *(certainty)*

earnest entreaty prayer

earnest money handsel

earnest payment pledge *(security)*

earnest pledge deposit

earnest request call *(appeal)*, entreaty, petition, prayer

earnest seeking market *(demand)*

earnestly faithfully

earnestness adhesion *(loyalty)*, compulsion *(obsession)*, diligence *(care)*, diligence *(perseverance)*, goodwill, industry *(activity)*, intention, resolution *(decision)*, spirit

earnings annuity, boom *(prosperity)*, commission *(fee)*, compensation, honorarium, income, interest *(profit)*, output, pay, payment *(remittance)*, possessions, proceeds, profit, recompense, revenue, wage

earshot range

earthly material *(physical)*, mundane, physical

earthly possessions estate *(property)*

earthquake cataclysm

earthshaking momentous

earthy inelegant

earwitness bystander

ease alleviate, ameliorate, assuage, commute, disencumber, disentangle, expedite, facilitate, facility *(easiness)*, favor, give *(yield)*, help, informality, lessen, lull, mitigate, moderate *(temper)*, modify *(moderate)*, mollify, obtund, pacify, palliate *(abate)*, prosperity, reassure, redress, relax, relieve *(give aid)*, remedy, remit *(relax)*, skill, solace, soothe

ease of movement latitude

ease the burden alleviate, disencumber, ease

easeful palliative *(abating)*, placid

easement advantage, droit, instigation, mollification, relief *(release)*, solace

easily readily

easily accessible convenient

easily affected perceptive, susceptible *(responsive)*

easily bent flexible, malleable, pliable, pliant

easily convinced credulous, suasible

easily deceived credulous, unsuspecting

easily done convenient, facile

easily duped credulous

easily excited sensitive *(easily affected)*

easily influenced facile, malleable, pliable, sequacious

easily lead tractable

easily led sequacious

easily managed flexible, resigned, tractable

easily managed job sinecure

easily observed scrutable

easily offended sensitive *(easily affected)*

easily perceived distinct *(clear)*, palpable

easily persuaded facile, malleable, pliable, pliant, prone, suasible

easily seen apparent *(perceptible)*, evident, gross *(flagrant)*, overt, palpable, scrutable

easily taken in credulous

easily taught sequacious, tractable

easily understood coherent *(clear)*, comprehensible, distinct *(clear)*, scrutable

easiness informality

easiness of belief credulity

easing mitigating, mitigation, mollification, remedial

easy convenient, elementary, facile, lenient, malleable, passable, promiscuous, yielding

easy chore sinecure

easy employment sinecure

easy job sinecure

easy labor sinecure

easy to be seen patent, perceptible

easy to believe presumptive

easy to grasp coherent *(clear)*

easy to perceive evident

easy to see evident, manifest, naked *(perceptible)*, perceivable

easy to understand coherent *(clear)*, comprehensible, elementary, explicit, pellucid

easy-mannered civil *(polite)*

easygoing facile, lenient, malleable, nonchalant, patient, peaceable, placid, pliable, sequacious, suasible, tractable, yielding

easygoingness informality

eat consume, prey

eat away diminish

eat excessively overindulge

eatable palatable

eavesdrop monitor, overhear, spy

ebb decline, decline *(fall)*, decrease (noun), decrease (verb), degenerate, depreciate, depress, deteriorate, diminish, languish, lessen, outflow, retreat, subside

ebb and flow beat *(pulsate)*

ebb of life death

eblandiri elicit

ebrietas inebriation

ebriosity dipsomania

ebrius drunk

ebullition bluster *(speech)*, commotion, emotion, outbreak, outburst

eccentric anomalous, deviant, divergent, irregular *(not usual)*, ludicrous, nonconforming, novel, original *(creative)*, particular *(specific)*, peculiar *(curious)*, singular, unaccustomed, uncommon, unorthodox, unpredictable

eccentricity irregularity, nonconformity, quirk *(idiosyncrasy)*, specialty *(distinctive mark)*

echelon class, degree *(station)*, posi-

tion *(business status)*

echo concur *(agree)*, copy, mock *(imitate)*, reflection *(image)*, reiterate, repeat *(state again)*, repercussion

echoed repeated

echoic repetitious

echoing iterative, repetitious, resounding

eclat notoriety

éclat prestige

eclat prestige

eclectic miscellaneous

eclipse blind *(obscure)*, cloak, conceal, ensconce, enshroud, obfuscate, obnubilate, obscure, outbalance, outweigh, overcome *(surmount)*, predominate *(outnumber)*, shroud, surpass, transcend

eclipsed allusive, hidden

economic commercial, fiscal, mercantile, pecuniary

economic decline depression

economic downfall failure *(bankruptcy)*

economic prosperity boom *(prosperity)*

economic resources capital, principal *(capital sum)*

economic science economy *(economic system)*

economic use management *(judicious use)*

economical economic, frugal, parsimonious, pecuniary, provident *(frugal)*, prudent

economical of space compact *(dense)*

economical of words laconic, sententious

economically imprudent profligate *(extravagant)*

economicalness austerity, economy *(frugality)*

economics finance

economize diminish, preserve, retrench, save *(hold back)*

economizing economical

economy austerity, conservation, moderation, prudence, regulation *(management)*

economy-minded frugal

ecphonesis expletive

ecstasy enjoyment *(pleasure)*, passion

ectype copy, duplicate

ecumenical general, nonsectarian

edacious gluttonous

edacity greed

eddying fluvial

edere issue *(publish)*

edge advantage, border, border *(bound)*, boundary, circumscribe *(surround by boundary)*, delimit, enclosure, encompass *(surround)*, end *(termination)*, envelop, extremity *(furthest point)*, frontier, hedge, margin *(outside limit)*, outline *(boundary)*, penumbra, periphery, threshold *(verge)*

edge close to approach

edges configuration *(confines)*, confines

edging border, contiguous, edge *(border)*, outline *(boundary)*, proximate

edible palatable

edicere enunciate, order

edico direction *(order)*

edict act *(enactment)*, adjudication, award, brevet, canon, constitution, dec-

laration, decree, dictate, direction
(*order*), directive, enactment, fiat, mandate, measure, mittimus, monition
(*legal summons*), order (*judicial directive*), ordinance, precept, prescription
(*directive*), proclamation, pronouncement, regulation (*rule*), requirement,
rule (*legal dictate*), ruling, sentence,
statute, warrant (*judicial writ*)
edictum declaration, decree, edict,
order (*judicial directive*), ordinance,
proclamation
edification education, guidance, instruction (*direction*), instruction (*teaching*)
edifice building (*structure*), dwelling,
inhabitation (*place of dwelling*)
edifices premises (*buildings*)
edify disabuse, educate, enlighten, instruct (*teach*), profit
edifying beneficial, didactic, informative, meritorious, profitable, salutary,
valuable
edit amend, digest (*summarize*),
redact, revise, treat (*process*)
edit out bowdlerize, delete, expunge,
redact
editing revision (*process of correcting*)
editio libri publication (*printed matter*)
edition publication (*printed matter*)
editorial review (*critical evaluation*)
editors press
educare develop, educate
educate convey (*communicate*), direct
(*supervise*), disabuse, discipline (*train*),
edify, enlighten, impart, inculcate, inform (*notify*), instill, instruct (*teach*),
nurture
educate oneself study
educated cognizant, familiar (*informed*), knowing, learned, literate,
sciential
educated guess estimate (*approximate cost*), estimation (*calculation*)
educating didactic
education direction (*guidance*), discipline (*field of study*), edification, experience (*background*), guidance, information (*knowledge*), instruction (*teaching*),
knowledge (*learning*), preparation
educational didactic, informative,
informatory
educational clarification edification
educational institution institute
educational knowledge edification
educative didactic, disciplinary (*educational*), informative
educator pedagogue
educe deduce, deduct (*conclude by
reasoning*), detect, disinter, elicit,
evoke, extract, solve
edulcorate purge (*purify*)
eel-shaped circuitous
eellike circuitous
eerie sinister
efface annul, deface, delete, dissolve
(*terminate*), eliminate (*eradicate*), eradicate, expunge, expurgate, extinguish,
extirpate, obliterate
effaced lost (*taken away*)
effacement annulment, defacement,
dissolution (*termination*)
effect accomplish, administer (*conduct*), amount (*result*), article (*commodity*), attain, avail (*bring about*),

carry (*succeed*), cast (*register*), cause,
chattel, chilling effect, commit (*perpetrate*), compose, conclusion (*outcome*),
conduce, consequence (*conclusion*), consequence (*significance*), constitute (*establish*), consummate, contrive, create,
culminate, development (*outgrowth*),
discharge (*perform*), dispatch (*dispose
of*), effectuate, elicit, enforce, engender,
evoke, execute (*accomplish*), fulfill,
generate, holding (*property owned*), implement, impose (*subject*), impression,
induce, influence, inspire, item, legislate, lobby, magnitude, make, occasion,
operate, originate, outcome, outgrowth,
perform (*execute*), perpetrate, possession (*property*), proceeds, procure, produce (*manufacture*), product, provoke,
reaction (*response*), realize (*make real*),
redound, result, semblance, signification (*effect*), value, weight (*importance*)
effect a change modify (*alter*)
effect a cure cure
effect a dissolution dissolve (*terminate*)
effect a sale handle (*trade*), sell
effect an agreement mediate
effect an entrance enter (*go in*)
effect by legislation constitute (*establish*)
effected complete (*ended*)
effected by choice voluntary
effecter author (*originator*)
effectible practicable
effecting commission (*act*)
effectio operation
effective active, capable, causal, cogent, competent, constructive (*creative*),
efficient, eloquent, expert, felicitous,
functional, incisive, influential, material (*important*), omnipotent, operative,
persuasive, politic, potent, powerful,
practical, predominant, prevailing (*having superior force*), proficient, sound,
strong, successful, valid, valuable, viable
effective before retroactive
effective help remedy (*legal means of
redress*)
effective rejoinder confutation
effectiveness competence (*ability*),
dint, efficiency, force (*strength*), influence, sinew
effectless null (*invalid*), null and void
effects assets, dower, estate (*property*), goods, merchandise, movable,
paraphernalia (*personal belongings*),
personalty, possessions, property (*possessions*), stock (*store*)
effectual active, adequate, capable,
causal, cogent, competent, constructive
(*creative*), decisive, effective (*efficient*),
effective (*operative*), efficient, functional, influential, ministerial, omnipotent, operative, potent, powerful, practical, prevailing (*having superior force*),
sound, valid, valuable, viable
effectuality capacity (*aptitude*), competence (*ability*), dint, force (*strength*),
influence
effectuate administer (*conduct*), attain, avail (*bring about*), bear (*yield*),
carry (*succeed*), cause, constitute (*establish*), consummate, discharge (*perform*), dispatch (*dispose of*), elicit, en-

force, engender, evoke, execute (*accomplish*), fulfill, function, generate, implement, induce, inspire, make, operate,
perfect, perform (*execute*), perpetrate,
produce (*manufacture*), realize (*make
real*)
effectuated complete (*ended*)
effectuation act (*undertaking*), action
(*performance*), building (*business of assembling*), commission (*act*), conclusion
(*outcome*), course, development (*progression*), discharge (*performance*), effect, enforcement, fait accompli, fruition, output, realization, transaction
effectus effect, realization
effervescence life (*vitality*)
effervescent volatile
effete decadent, ineffective, ineffectual, otiose, powerless, stale, unproductive
efficacious active, beneficial, cogent,
competent, effective (*efficient*), functional, influential, politic, potent, powerful, practical, predominant, prevailing (*having superior force*), proficient,
qualified (*competent*), sciential, sound,
successful, valuable, viable
efficacy caliber (*mental capacity*),
competence (*ability*), dint, efficiency,
force (*strength*), strength, utility (*usefulness*), weight (*importance*)
efficax effective (*efficient*), operative
efficere compose, constitute (*compose*),
execute (*accomplish*), exercise (*discharge a function*), fulfill, realize (*make
real*)
efficiency caliber (*mental capacity*),
qualification (*fitness*)
efficient active, competent, constructive (*creative*), deft, economical, expeditious, expert, functional, operative, potent, practical, practiced, productive,
proficient, prompt, resourceful
efficientia efficiency
effigies counterpart (*parallel*), embodiment, imitation, representation (*statement*)
effigy counterpart (*parallel*), resemblance
effingere depict
efflagitare insist
effluence issuance, outflow
effluency issuance
efflux outflow
effodere disinter
efform compose, forge (*produce*), formulate, make
efformation building (*business of assembling*), composition (*makeup*), form
(*arrangement*), formation
effort campaign, course, endeavor, enterprise (*undertaking*), industry (*activity*), labor (*exertion*), main force, performance (*workmanship*), pursuit (*effort to
secure*), struggle, test, undertaking (*attempt*), undertaking (*enterprise*)
effort to secure pursuit (*chase*)
effortful operose
effortless convenient, facile, practiced
effortless assignment sinecure
effortless employment sinecure
effortless undertaking sinecure
effortless work sinecure
effortlessly readily
effortlessness facility (*easiness*)
effractura burglary

effrenatus lawless, uncurbed, unrestricted, unruly

effrontery contumely, disrespect, temerity

effugere flee

effugium flight

effulgent lucid

effundi emanate

effuse diffuse, emanate, exude, outpour

effusio waste

effusion expulsion, harangue, issuance, outflow, prolixity

effusive demonstrative *(expressive of emotion)*, loquacious, unrestrained *(not repressed)*, voluble

effusiveness ardor

effusus profuse, uncurbed

egens poor *(underprivileged)*

egere require *(need)*

egestas indigence, necessity, privation

egg on provoke, stimulate

egocentric inflated *(vain)*, orgulous

egohood personality

egoism pride

egoistic inflated *(vain)*, orgulous, presumptuous, proud *(conceited)*

egoistical inflated *(vain)*, orgulous, proud *(conceited)*

egotism pride

egotistic inflated *(vain)*, orgulous, presumptuous, supercilious

egotistical inflated *(vain)*, orgulous, presumptuous

egredi issue *(send forth)*

egregious contemptible, gross *(flagrant)*, heinous, noteworthy, notorious, outrageous, remarkable

egregius singular, special

egress alight, avenue *(route)*, issuance, issue *(send forth)*, outlet, quit *(evacuate)*

egression egress, issuance, outflow

egressus egress, outlet

eicere eject *(expel)*, expel

eidetic distinct *(clear)*

eidolon phantom, specter

eiuratio abdication

ejaculate precipitate *(throw down violently)*, send

ejaculation outburst

eject cast *(throw)*, censor, deport *(banish)*, depose *(remove)*, discharge *(dismiss)*, dislocate, dislodge, dismiss *(discharge)*, dispel, displace *(remove)*, eliminate *(exclude)*, emanate, emit, eradicate, evict, exclude, expatriate, expel, jettison, launch *(project)*, luxate, oust, outpour, project *(impel forward)*, reject, remove *(dismiss from office)*, send, supplant

eject from possession dispossess

ejection banishment, deportation, discharge *(dismissal)*, dismissal *(discharge)*, disqualification *(rejection)*, eviction, evulsion, exclusion, expropriation *(divestiture)*, expulsion, layoff, ostracism, ouster, removal

ejectment deportation, eviction, expulsion, layoff

elabi escape

elaborare elaborate

elaborate amplify, compound, compound, develop, embellish, enhance, enlarge, expand, intricate, meliorate, painstaking

elaborated complex, detailed

elaboration accession *(enlargement)*, advance *(increase)*, advancement *(improvement)*, amendment *(correction)*, development *(progression)*, overstatement, revision *(process of correcting)*

elaboratus elaborate

élan ardor

elapse expire

elapsed back *(in arrears)*

elastic flexible, malleable, pliable, pliant, resilient, sequacious, tractable, volatile, yielding

elated ecstatic

elatio elevation

elbow jostle *(bump into)*

elbowroom margin *(spare amount)*

elder adult, predecessor, primogenitor

elderliness longevity

elderly old

elect adopt, choose, decide, entrust, intend, prefer, premium, select, vote

elected preferred *(favored)*, select

elected representative officer

electio election *(choice)*, selection *(choice)*

election adoption *(acceptance)*, alternative *(option)*, choice *(alternatives offered)*, choice *(decision)*, discretion *(power of choice)*, nomination, option *(choice)*, plebiscite, poll *(casting of votes)*, preference *(choice)*, primary, referendum, selection *(choice)*, volition, vote

election contest primary

electioneering politics

elective adoptive, discretionary, disjunctive *(alternative)*, spontaneous, voluntary

elective preference volition

elective privilege poll *(casting of votes)*

electorate constituency

electors constituency

electric incisive, provocative

electrify agitate *(activate)*, impress *(affect deeply)*

electrifying moving *(evoking emotion)*, provocative

electus select

eleemosynary benevolent, charitable *(benevolent)*, donative, nonprofit, philanthropic

eleemosynary corporation foundation *(organization)*

elegance propriety *(correctness)*

elegance of manners courtesy

elegans critical *(faultfinding)*, elegant, particular *(exacting)*, precise

elegant attractive

elegiac disconsolate, lugubrious

element aspect, atmosphere, component, constituent *(part)*, detail, determinant, factor *(ingredient)*, feature *(characteristic)*, ingredient, item, member *(constituent part)*, segment, unit *(item)*

elemental cardinal *(basic)*, central *(essential)*, elementary, essential *(inherent)*, fundamental, inchoate, incipient, integral, organic, original *(initial)*, primary, prime *(original)*, primordial, rudimentary, simple, substantive, ultimate, underlying

elementary cardinal *(basic)*, fundamental, inchoate, incipient, initial,

naked *(lacking embellishment)*, original *(initial)*, primary, prime *(original)*, primordial, rudimentary, simple, ultimate, underlying

elementary detail necessity

elementary unit component, factor *(ingredient)*

elementum constituent *(part)*, element

elephantine ponderous, prodigious *(enormous)*

elevare disparage

elevate ameliorate, build *(augment)*, build *(construct)*, cultivate, enhance, expand, honor, meliorate, parlay *(exploit successfully)*, prefer, promote *(advance)*, raise *(advance)*, uphold

elevated ecstatic, famous, magnanimous, meritorious, outstanding *(prominent)*, prominent, sacrosanct

elevated place elevation

elevated rank eminence

elevation advance *(progression)*, advancement *(improvement)*, building *(structure)*, eminence, inflation *(increase)*, precedence, promotion *(advancement)*, reform, remembrance *(commemoration)*, status

elevation in rank promotion *(advancement)*

élève disciple

eleventh hour crossroad *(turning point)*, dilatory

elicere elicit, evoke

elicit cause, compel, discover, disinter, educe, evoke, exact, extract, ferret, find *(discover)*, generate, inspire, originate, provoke

elicit by threat coerce, extort

elicitation evulsion

elide delete, eliminate *(exclude)*, relegate

eligere elect *(choose)*, select

eligibility admissibility, competence *(ability)*, droit, qualification *(fitness)*

eligible admissible, allowed, convenient, desirable *(qualified)*, entitled, fit, qualified *(competent)*, suitable

eliminate abate *(extinguish)*, abolish, abrogate *(annul)*, abrogate *(rescind)*, censor, close *(terminate)*, debar, delete, deplete, destroy *(efface)*, dislodge, eject *(expel)*, eradicate, except *(exclude)*, exclude, expel, expurgate, extirpate, exude, forgo, jettison, obliterate, palliate *(abate)*, purge *(purify)*, reject, relegate, relinquish, remove *(eliminate)*, renounce, repeal, screen *(select)*, select, terminate, vacate *(void)*

eliminate racial segregation desegregate

eliminate the alternatives choose, elect *(choose)*

eliminated ineligible, lost *(taken away)*

elimination abatement *(extinguishment)*, aberemurder, abolition, cancellation, censorship, curtailment, deduction *(diminution)*, deportation, discharge *(dismissal)*, dismissal *(discharge)*, disqualification *(rejection)*, dissolution *(termination)*, end *(termination)*, evulsion, expulsion, homicide, killing, layoff, murder, obviation, ostracism, ouster, prohibition, proscription, rejection, removal, renunciation

elimination of ambiguousness clarification

elimination of complexity clarification

elimination of complication clarification

elinguis speechless

elite preferential, select

elixir cure, main point

elliptical brief

elocutio delivery

elocution declamation, parlance, rhetoric *(skilled speech)*

elocutionary orotund

elongate extend *(enlarge)*, protract *(stall)*, sustain *(prolong)*

elongated protracted

eloquence parlance, rhetoric *(skilled speech)*

eloquens eloquent

eloquent descriptive, persuasive, voluble

else further

elsewhere known as alias

elucidate argue, bear *(adduce)*, characterize, clarify, comment, construe *(translate)*, convey *(communicate)*, define, demonstrate *(establish)*, describe, detail *(particularize)*, enlighten, exemplify, explain, explicate, exposit, expound, illustrate, instruct *(teach)*, notice *(observe)*, relate *(tell)*, render *(depict)*, resolve *(solve)*, simplify *(clarify)*, solve

elucidating declaratory

elucidation answer *(solution)*, clarification, comment, definition, discourse, education, explanation, illustration, instance, paraphrase, rationale

elucidative demonstrative *(illustrative)*, interpretive

elucidatory informatory

elude abscond, avoid *(evade)*, bilk, circumvent, default, equivocate, escape, eschew, ignore, parry, prevaricate, shirk, shun, spurn

eludere balk, elude, foil

eludication solution *(answer)*

eluding evasive

eluding clear perception elusive

elusion abstention, avoidance *(evasion)*, flight, subterfuge

elusive delusive, ephemeral, evasive, inaccessible, oblique *(evasive)*, recondite, stealthy, temporary, transient, unresponsive, volatile

elusiveness evasion

elusory elusive, evasive, oblique *(evasive)*

elutriate purge *(purify)*

emaciate decrease

emaciation deterioration

emanare emanate

emanate accrue *(arise)*, arise *(originate)*, develop, emerge, issue *(send forth)*, proceed *(go forward)*, result, spread, stem *(originate)*

emanate in rays radiate

emanation circulation, consequence *(conclusion)*, development *(outgrowth)*, discharge *(shot)*, face value *(first blush)*, issuance, outflow, output, product

emancipate discharge *(liberate)*, disencumber, disengage, disenthrall, enable, enfranchise, free, liberate, pardon, parole, quit *(free of)*, redeem *(repur-*

chase), release, relieve *(free from burden)*, rescue

emancipated free *(enjoying civil liberty)*, liberal *(broad minded)*

emancipation discharge *(liberation)*, discharge *(release from obligation)*, freedom, liberation, liberty, parole, release, suffrage

emasculate bowdlerize, debilitate, disable, inadequate

emasculated ineffective, ineffectual, powerless

emasculating operose

emasculation fault *(weakness)*, languor

embankment bulwark

embar bar *(hinder)*, obstruct, toll *(stop)*

embargo attachment *(seizure)*

embargo ban, bar *(obstruction)*, boycott, check *(bar)*, condemn *(ban)*, debar, enjoin, hindrance, interdict, obstacle, obstruction, prohibit, prohibition, proscribe *(prohibit)*, proscription, restraint, seclude, veto

embargoed goods contraband

embark launch *(initiate)*, leave *(depart)*

embark on commence

embark upon assume *(undertake)*, maintain *(commence)*, undertake

embarkation birth *(beginning)*, inception, onset *(commencement)*, outset, start

embarrass confuse *(bewilder)*, disgrace, humiliate, impede, offend *(insult)*, perplex, perturb, upset

embarrassed diffident, impecunious, poor *(underprivileged)*

embarrassed circumstances poverty

embarrassing position plight, predicament

embarrassing situation imbroglio, plight

embarrassment confusion *(ambiguity)*, disadvantage, disgrace, ignominy, indigence, obstruction, predicament

embassage embassy

embassy commission *(agency)*, delegation *(envoy)*, mission

embed fix *(make firm)*, inseminate, plant *(place firmly)*

embedded ingrained, situated

embellish camouflage, cloak, falsify, meliorate

embellished elaborate, inflated *(overestimated)*, pretentious *(ostentatious)*

embellishment bombast, exaggeration, expletive, motif

embezzle bilk, cheat, convert *(misappropriate)*, defalcate, defraud, impropriate, loot, mulct *(defraud)*, peculate, pilfer, purloin, steal

embezzlement conversion *(misappropriation)*, larceny, misappropriation, theft

embezzler hoodlum, thief

embitter affront, alienate *(estrange)*, antagonize, bait *(harass)*, discompose, incense

embittered bitter *(reproachful)*, dyseptic, hostile, malevolent, resentful

embittering operose

emblaze brand *(mark)*

emblazon embellish

emblem brand, designation *(symbol)*,

device *(distinguishing mark)*, earmark, indicant, indication, indicator, label, manifestation, symbol, token

emblematic representative

embodied bodily, compound, concrete, corporeal, physical, tangible

embodied terms contract

embodiment affiliation *(amalgamation)*, appearance *(look)*, body *(person)*, composition *(makeup)*, corpus, coverage *(scope)*, cross section, entity, epitome, essence, instance, materiality *(physical existence)*

embody attach *(join)*, commingle, comprehend *(include)*, comprise, concern *(involve)*, consist, constitute *(compose)*, contain *(comprise)*, depict, exemplify, form, include, incorporate *(include)*, personify, substantiate

embodying inclusive

embolden abet, assure *(give confidence to)*, encourage, promise *(raise expectations)*, reassure

embolium cessation *(interlude)*

emboss brand *(mark)*, embellish

embowel eviscerate

embox contain *(enclose)*, envelop

embrace accept *(embrace)*, adopt, affiliate, attach *(join)*, border *(bound)*, choose, circumscribe *(surround by boundary)*, collect *(gather)*, comprehend *(include)*, comprise, concern *(involve)*, constitute *(compose)*, contact *(touch)*, contain *(comprise)*, contain *(enclose)*, coverage *(scope)*, enclose, enclosure, encompass *(include)*, envelop, espouse, include, incorporate *(include)*, keep *(shelter)*, personify, prefer, receive *(permit to enter)*

embrace an offer assent

embrace an opinion deem

embraced select

embracement adoption *(acceptance)*, alternative *(option)*

embracing inclusive

embracing a large area extensive

embrangle confound, disorganize, muddle

embrangled inextricable

embranglement brawl, disaccord, dispute, embroilment, imbroglio

embroider camouflage, cloak, clothe, embellish, falsify, invent *(falsify)*, misrepresent, slant

embroidered histrionic, mendacious

embroidery distortion, exaggeration, overstatement, rodomontade

embroil bicker, collide *(clash)*, confound, confuse *(create disorder)*, disrupt, implicate, incense

embroilment affray, belligerency, bluster *(commotion)*, brawl, collision *(dispute)*, commotion, conflict, contest *(dispute)*, controversy *(argument)*, disaccord, dispute, disturbance, entanglement *(confusion)*, fight *(argument)*, imbroglio, involution, pandemonium

embryonic inchoate, incipient, initial, original *(initial)*, premature, prime *(original)*, rudimentary

emend amend, convert *(change use)*, edit, fix *(repair)*, meliorate, modify *(alter)*, rectify, reform

emendable ambulatory, corrigible

emendare amend, emend, rectify

emendate adjust *(resolve)*, amend,

edit, emend, modify *(alter)*, rectify

emendatio amendment *(correction)*, correction *(change)*, reform, revision *(corrected version)*

emendation advancement *(improvement)*, amendment *(correction)*, correction *(change)*, progress

emendatory ambulatory, curative, progressive *(advocating change)*

emerge appear *(materialize)*, arise *(appear)*, develop, emanate, evolve, germinate, issue *(send forth)*, occur *(come to mind)*, occur *(happen)*, result

emergence egress, expression *(manifestation)*, issuance, manifestation, nascency, origination, outflow, start

emergency casualty, catastrophe, debacle, disaster, peril, plight, predicament, quagmire

emergere emerge, recover

emersion egress, outflow

emigrant alien

emigrate abandon *(physically leave)*, abscond, depart, leave *(depart)*, move *(alter position)*, quit *(evacuate)*

emigration egress, outflow

eminence advantage, caliber *(quality)*, character *(reputation)*, clout, distinction *(reputation)*, dominance, elevation, emphasis, importance, influence, magnitude, materiality *(consequence)*, notoriety, power, prestige, primacy, regard *(esteem)*, reputation, significance, status, weight *(importance)*

eminency elevation

eminent consequential *(substantial)*, dominant, famous, illustrious, influential, master, meritorious, notable, noteworthy, outstanding *(prominent)*, prime *(most valuable)*, prominent, renowned, reputable, salient, singular, stellar

eminent domain dominion *(supreme authority)*

eminent person paragon

eminently particularly

emissaries deputation *(delegation)*

emissarium outlet

emissarius spy

emissary agent, conduit *(intermediary)*, deputy, intermediary, liaison, medium, plenipotentiary, procurator, proxy, representative *(proxy)*, spokesman, substitute

emissio discharge *(shot)*

emission issuance, outburst

emit bear *(yield)*, cast *(throw)*, discharge *(shoot)*, emanate, enunciate, expel, exude, outpour, project *(impel forward)*, promulgate, pronounce *(speak)*, publish, remark, send, utter

emit heat radiate

emit rays radiate

emittere emit, send

emmission discharge *(shot)*

emollient cure, medicinal, remedial

emolument advance *(allowance)*, alimony, bounty, brokerage, commission *(fee)*, compensation, consideration *(recompense)*, disbursement *(funds paid out)*, earnings, fee *(charge)*, honorarium, pay, payment *(remittance)*, pension, perquisite, profit, recompense, requital, restitution, revenue, reward, wage

emolumental profitable

emotion ardor, passion, reaction *(response)*, sensibility

emotional demonstrative *(expressive of emotion)*, ecstatic, impulsive *(rash)*, intense, subjective

emotional display for effect histrionics

emotional release catharsis

emotional tone outlook

emotionless insensible, unresponsive

emotive demonstrative *(expressive of emotion)*, sensitive *(easily affected)*

empathetic benevolent, charitable *(lenient)*

empathic vicarious *(delegated)*

empathize sympathize

empathy rapport, understanding *(tolerance)*

emper charge *(empower)*

empery dominion *(supreme authority)*

emphasis content *(meaning)*

emphasis emphasis

emphasis importance, inflection, strength, stress *(accent)*, weight *(importance)*

emphasize argue, assert, bear *(adduce)*, contend *(maintain)*, dwell *(linger over)*, enhance, insist, intensify, magnify, plead *(allege in a legal action)*, pronounce *(speak)*, reaffirm, repeat *(state again)*

emphatic categorical, clear *(apparent)*, compelling, dogmatic, express, forcible, insistent, resounding, vehement

emphatic assertion asseveration

emphatic inquiry demand

empierce enter *(penetrate)*, lancinate, penetrate, pierce *(lance)*

empire demesne, realm

empiric probative

empirical probative

empiricism casuistry, experience *(background)*

employ agency *(legal relationship)*, apply *(put in practice)*, appoint, capitalize *(seize the chance)*, commit *(entrust)*, delegate, employment, engage *(hire)*, exercise *(use)*, exert, expend *(consume)*, exploit *(make use of)*, exploitation, hire, impropriate, induct, labor *(work)*, manipulate *(utilize skillfully)*, ply, practice *(engage in)*, recruit, resort, spend, wield

employ capital invest *(fund)*

employ force compel, enforce

employ improperly misemploy

employ one's professional skill practice *(engage in)*

employ one's time strive

employ oneself attempt, commit *(perpetrate)*, perform *(execute)*, strive

employ oneself in practice *(engage in)*

employ stratagem compete

employability utility *(usefulness)*, utilization

employable disposable, eligible, functional, practical

employed operative

employee assistant

employees personnel, staff

employees' earnings payroll

employees' salaries payroll

employer chief, executive, principal *(director)*

employer of legal advice client

employer work stoppage lockout

employment agency *(legal relationship)*, appointment *(position)*, business *(occupation)*, calling, career, course, enjoyment *(use)*, function, industry *(activity)*, job, labor *(work)*, livelihood, management *(judicious use)*, means *(opportunity)*, occupation *(vocation)*, office, position *(business status)*, post, practice *(professional business)*, profession *(vocation)*, project, pursuit *(occupation)*, title *(position)*, trade *(occupation)*, usage, use

employment fee retainer

employment of capital investment

employment of force compulsion *(coercion)*

empoison infect

emporium market *(business)*, market place, store *(business)*

empower allow *(authorize)*, appoint, assign *(designate)*, authorize, bestow, certify *(approve)*, clothe, commit *(entrust)*, constitute *(establish)*, countenance, delegate, detail *(assign)*, employ *(engage services)*, enable, endue, enfranchise, entrust, grant *(concede)*, invest *(vest)*, let *(permit)*, permit, qualify *(meet standards)*, sanction, suffer *(permit)*, vest

empower to act for another delegate

empowered allowed, entitled, ex officio, influential, permissible, powerful, privileged

empowering consent, deputation *(selection of delegates)*

empowerment charter *(sanction)*, droit, force *(strength)*, freedom, license, sanction *(permission)*

emprise campaign, endeavor, undertaking *(enterprise)*

emptiness insufficiency

emptor consumer

emptor customer, patron *(regular customer)*

empty barren, baseless, consume, deficient, deplete, devoid, diminish, dissipate *(expend foolishly)*, evacuate, exhaust *(deplete)*, ill-founded, inexpressive, languid, lifeless *(dull)*, null *(insignificant)*, outpour, purge *(purify)*, spend, superficial, trivial, unavailing, unfounded, vacant, vacate *(leave)*, vacuous

empty of devoid

empty out deplete

empty show pretense *(ostentation)*

empty talk bombast, fustian, jargon *(unintelligible language)*, rodomontade

empty words pretense *(pretext)*

empty-handed poor *(underprivileged)*

empty-headed vacuous

emulate copy, mock *(imitate)*, pose *(impersonate)*, reflect *(mirror)*

emulation contest *(competition)*, fake

emulative competitive *(antagonistic)*

emulsion solution *(substance)*

en attendant ad interim

en bloc en banc, en masse

en masse en banc

en rapport concurrent *(united)*, conjoint

enable allow *(authorize)*, authorize, charge *(empower)*, clothe, delegate, empower, endue, facilitate, furnish, grant *(concede)*, invest *(vest)*, let *(permit)*,

permit, qualify *(meet standards)*, sanction, vest
enable to comprehend enlighten
enable to see enlighten
enablement ability, capacity *(authority)*, competence *(ability)*, faculty *(ability)*, force *(strength)*
enact accomplish, command, conduct, constitute *(establish)*, effectuate, execute *(accomplish)*, govern, impersonate, implement, impose *(enforce)*, instruct *(direct)*, legislate, make, pass *(approve)*, perform *(adhere to)*, perform *(execute)*, pursue *(carry on)*, recite, require *(compel)*, rule *(govern)*
enact beforehand preordain
enact by law legalize
enact laws legislate
enacted legitimate *(rightful)*, positive *(prescribed)*
enacting legislative
enacting laws legislation *(lawmaking)*
enacting punishment penal
enactment code, codification, commission *(act)*, constitution, dictate, direction *(order)*, edict, fiat, law, mandate, measure, ordinance, pandect *(code of laws)*, performance *(execution)*, prescription *(directive)*, regulation *(rule)*, rubric *(authoritative rule)*, rule *(legal dictate)*, statute, symbol, transaction
enactment of rules code
enarrare recount, relate *(tell)*
enarratio description
encage immure
encamp lodge *(reside)*
encapsulate comprise, contain *(enclose)*, envelop
encase border *(bound)*, clothe, contain *(enclose)*, enclose, encompass *(surround)*, ensconce, enshroud, envelop, shroud, shut
encasement enclosure
enchain confine, contain *(restrain)*, fetter, handcuff, repress, restrain, restrict, trammel
enchanted ecstatic
enchanting attractive, moving *(evoking emotion)*, provocative, sapid
enchantment affection, compulsion *(obsession)*, seduction
enchase border *(bound)*
enchorial native *(domestic)*
enchoric native *(domestic)*
encincture blockade *(enclosure)*, constraint *(imprisonment)*, contain *(enclose)*, embrace *(encircle)*, enclose, encompass *(surround)*
encircle border *(bound)*, circumscribe *(surround by boundary)*, comprehend *(include)*, contain *(enclose)*, delimit, detour, enclose, encompass *(surround)*, envelop, hedge, include, incorporate *(include)*, lock
encirclement blockade *(enclosure)*, enclosure
encircling comprehensive, inclusive
enclasp concern *(involve)*, contain *(enclose)*
enclave bailiwick, parcel
enclose affix, border *(bound)*, circumscribe *(surround by boundary)*, confine, constrain *(imprison)*, delimit, demarcate, embrace *(encircle)*, encompass *(surround)*, ensconce, enshroud, en-

velop, fetter, hedge, immure, imprison, keep *(restrain)*, limit, lock, restrain, shut
enclose on all sides encompass *(surround)*
enclose within bounds border *(bound)*
enclose within walls immure
enclosed internal, limited
enclosed cage cell
enclosed space enclosure
enclosing blockade *(enclosure)*, inclusive
enclosure barrier, boundary, chamber *(compartment)*, close *(enclosed area)*, constraint *(imprisonment)*, coverage *(scope)*, curtilage, parcel
enclosures confines
encloud obscure
encomiastic favorable *(expressing approval)*
encomium laudation
encompass border *(bound)*, circumscribe *(surround by boundary)*, comprehend *(include)*, comprise, consist, constitute *(compose)*, contain *(enclose)*, delimit, demarcate, embrace *(encircle)*, enclose, envelop, hedge, include, incorporate *(include)*
encompass with gloom obnubilate
encompassed with difficulties difficult
encompassing a wide area extensive
encompassment blockade *(enclosure)*, coverage *(scope)*, enclosure
encore de novo
encounter affray, affront, assail, assault, belligerency, collide *(clash)*, collision *(accident)*, collision *(dispute)*, commotion, compete, competition, conflict, confrontation *(act of setting face to face)*, contact *(touch)*, contend *(dispute)*, contest *(competition)*, contest *(dispute)*, discover, embroilment, endure *(suffer)*, engage *(involve)*, fight *(battle)*, find *(discover)*, grapple, meet, meeting *(conference)*, onset *(assault)*, oppose, rendezvous, rendezvous, strife, strike *(collide)*, struggle
encounter the risk bet
encounter with a shock collide *(crash against)*
encourage abet, assure *(give confidence to)*, coax, conduce, contribute *(assist)*, counsel, exhort, expedite, facilitate, favor, foment, foster, help, impel, incite, indorse, inspire, lobby, motivate, nurture, prevail upon, promise *(raise expectations)*, promote *(advance)*, promote *(organize)*, prompt, reassure, side, spirit, stimulate, uphold, urge
encourage repose lull
encouraged sanguine
encouragement advocacy, approval, auspices, catalyst, contribution *(participation)*, favor *(sanction)*, guidance, help, impetus, impulse, incentive, indorsement, inducement, influence, instigation, invitation, motive, patronage *(support)*, persuasion, recommendation, relief *(aid)*, sanction *(permission)*, solace, stimulus, support *(assistance)*
encourager abettor, accessory, accomplice, advocate *(espouser)*, catalyst, partisan, promoter

encouraging auspicious, favorable *(advantageous)*, favorable *(expressing approval)*, moving *(evoking emotion)*, propitious, viable
encroach accroach, border *(approach)*, impinge, impose *(intrude)*, interfere, intervene, intrude, invade, obtrude, overlap, overreach, overstep, trespass, usurp
encroach upon violate
encroached upon broken *(unfulfilled)*
encroaching culpable, obtrusive
encroachment assumption *(seizure)*, breach, contempt *(disobedience to the court)*, crime, imposition *(excessive burden)*, incursion, infraction, injustice, intrusion, invasion, offense, transgression, violation
encrust embellish
encumber bind *(obligate)*, bind *(restrain)*, block, check *(restrain)*, contain *(restrain)*, detain *(restrain)*, disadvantage, embarrass, estop, hamper, hinder, hold up *(delay)*, impede, impose *(enforce)*, inconvenience, interfere, obstruct, overcome *(overwhelm)*, overload, perplex, preclude, restrict, tax *(overwork)*, trammel, weigh
encumbered arrested *(checked)*, disconsolate, indebted
encumbrance barrier, burden, charge *(lien)*, constraint *(restriction)*, damper *(stopper)*, debt, disadvantage, fetter, handicap, hindrance, impediment, imposition *(excessive burden)*, liability, mortgage, onus *(burden)*, pressure, responsibility *(accountability)*, weight *(burden)*
encyclic public *(known)*
encyclical public *(known)*
encyclopedia hornbook
encyclopedic broad, collective, complete *(all-embracing)*, comprehensive, expert, omnibus, omniscient
encyclopedical omnibus
end annul, arrest *(stop)*, border, cancel, cap, cause *(reason)*, cease, cessation *(termination)*, close *(conclusion)*, close *(terminate)*, complete, conclude *(complete)*, conclusion *(outcome)*, consummate, culminate, decide, defeasance, denouement, design *(intent)*, desist, destination, discontinue *(abandon)*, dispatch *(put to death)*, dissolution *(termination)*, dissolve *(terminate)*, eliminate *(eradicate)*, expiration, expire, extinguish, extirpate, extremity *(death)*, extremity *(furthest point)*, final, finality, finish, goal, halt, halt, impasse, intent, lapse *(cease)*, last *(final)*, mete, moratorium, motive, object, objective, outcome, output, payoff *(result)*, perform *(adhere to)*, periphery, point *(purpose)*, project, purpose, pursuit *(goal)*, quash, reason *(basis)*, rescind, rest *(cease from action)*, result, result, settle, shut, stop, succumb, suppress, target, terminate, ultimate
end at abut
end by a decision arbitrate *(adjudge)*, conclude *(decide)*, determine
end in view design *(intent)*, intention
end intended intention
end life dispatch *(put to death)*, execute *(sentence to death)*

end of hostilities peace
end of life death, demise *(death)*, extremity *(death)*
end of the matter defeasance, time
end one's life decease, die
end product conclusion *(outcome)*, effect, outcome, output
end result amount *(result)*, conclusion *(outcome)*, destination, effect, outgrowth, proceeds, product
end the introduction of evidence rest *(end a legal case)*
end the presentation of evidence rest *(end a legal case)*
end to end contiguous
endamage disable, harm, persecute
endanger expose, jeopardize
endangered aleatory *(perilous)*, insecure
endangerment hazard, jeopardy, peril, risk
endearment affection
endeavor activity, attempt, business *(occupation)*, calling, campaign, conatus, course, creation, effort, enterprise *(undertaking)*, experiment, industry *(activity)*, intend, labor *(exertion)*, labor, profession *(vocation)*, project, pursuit *(effort to secure)*, pursuit *(occupation)*, strive, struggle, test, trial *(experiment)*, try *(attempt)*, undertake, undertaking *(enterprise)*, venture, work *(effort)*
endeavor to accomplish strive
endeavor to effect strive
endeavor to gain pursue *(strive to gain)*
endeavor to overtake chase
ended dead, defunct, lifeless *(dead)*, through
endemic domestic *(indigenous)*, native *(domestic)*, special, specific
endemical native *(domestic)*, specific
endenizen adopt
ending cessation *(termination)*, close *(conclusion)*, conclusion *(outcome)*, defeasance, denouement, destination, development *(outgrowth)*, dissolution *(termination)*, end *(termination)*, expiration, extreme *(last)*, final, finality, halt, last *(final)*, moratorium, outcome, ultimate
ending of a proceeding dismissal *(termination of a proceeding)*
ending of an action dismissal *(termination of a proceeding)*
endless chronic, constant, continual *(perpetual)*, continuous, durable, far reaching, incessant, indestructible, indeterminate, infinite, innumerable, myriad, permanent, perpetual, profuse, progressive *(going forward)*, relentless, rife, stable, unlimited, unrelenting
endless duration perpetuity
endless time perpetuity
endlessly ad infinitum
endlessness indestructibility, perpetuity
endmost extreme *(last)*, last *(final)*
endorse abet, accept *(assent)*, accredit, acknowledge *(declare)*, advocate, affirm *(uphold)*, allow *(authorize)*, approve, assent, assist, assure *(insure)*, attest, authorize, avouch *(guarantee)*, bear *(adduce)*, bond *(secure a debt)*, brand *(mark)*, certify *(approve)*, certify

(attest), close *(agree)*, coincide *(concur)*, concede, concur *(agree)*, confirm, consent, constitute *(establish)*, corroborate, cosign, countenance, countersign, embrace *(accept)*, encourage, ensure, espouse, favor, justify, let *(permit)*, pass *(approve)*, qualify *(meet standards)*, recommend, sanction, seal *(solemnize)*, side, sponsor, subscribe *(sign)*, support *(assist)*, sustain *(confirm)*, underwrite, uphold, validate, vouch, witness *(attest to)*
endorse over assign *(transfer ownership)*
endorsed agreed *(promised)*, allowed, consensual, official, preferred *(favored)*
endorsee holder, payee
endorsement acceptance, accommodation *(backing)*, acknowledgment *(acceptance)*, advocacy, affirmance *(authentication)*, affirmance *(judicial sanction)*, affirmation, aid *(help)*, approval, assent, attestation, avowal, certificate, certification *(attested copy)*, charter *(sanction)*, confirmation, consent, corroboration, favor *(sanction)*, guaranty, jurat, leave *(permission)*, license, ratification, recommendation, reference *(recommendation)*, rider, sanction *(permission)*, stamp, subscription, support *(corroboration)*, vow
endorser backer, comaker, patron *(influential supporter)*, proponent, surety *(guarantor)*, undersigned
endow authorize, bear *(yield)*, bestow, charge *(empower)*, clothe, confer *(give)*, contribute *(supply)*, convey *(transfer)*, dedicate, demise, descend, devise *(give)*, divide *(distribute)*, empower, enable, endue, fund, furnish, give *(grant)*, impart, instate, leave *(give)*, pass *(advance)*, present *(make a gift)*, provide *(supply)*, subsidize, supply, vest
endow the power charge *(empower)*
endow with bequeath
endow with authority invest *(vest)*
endow with political privilege enfranchise
endow with power authorize
endow with rights of citizenship naturalize *(make a citizen)*
endowed resourceful
endowed institution foundation *(organization)*
endowed with consciousness cognizant
endowed with life conscious *(awake)*, live *(conscious)*
endowed with reason cognizant, rational
endowing donative
endowment aid *(subsistence)*, appropriation *(donation)*, aptitude, behalf, benefit *(conferment)*, bequest, caliber *(mental capacity)*, charity, color *(complexion)*, competence *(ability)*, concession *(authorization)*, contribution *(donation)*, dedication, donation, dower, faculty *(ability)*, foundation *(organization)*, fund, gift *(flair)*, gift *(present)*, grant, inheritance, investment, largess *(gift)*, legacy, pension, performance *(workmanship)*, perquisite, potential, provision *(act of supplying)*, qualification *(fitness)*, quality *(attribute)*, quality *(grade)*, skill, specialty *(special aptitude)*, support *(assistance)*
ends confines
endue clothe, endow, fund, furnish, supply
endurance continuance, diligence *(perseverance)*, force *(strength)*, indestructibility, industry *(activity)*, lenience, life *(period of existence)*, longanimity, longevity, resignation *(passive acceptance)*, sinew, strength, survival, tenacity, tolerance
endure abide, adhere *(persist)*, bear *(tolerate)*, concede, exist, forbear, keep *(continue)*, last, persevere, persist, remain *(continue)*, resist *(withstand)*, stay *(continue)*, submit *(yield)*, subsist, suffer *(sustain loss)*, tolerate, withstand
endure the cost of disburse *(pay out)*
enduring chronic, constant, diligent, durable, indelible, indestructible, infallible, infinite, lasting, lenient, live *(existing)*, passive, patient, permanent, perpetual, persistent, pertinacious, resigned, solid *(sound)*, stable, standing, steadfast, strong, unrelenting, unremitting, unyielding
enduring only a very short time ephemeral
enemy adversary, foe, rival
energetic active, forcible, indomitable, industrious, intense, painstaking, potent, sedulous, strong, trenchant
energize agitate *(activate)*, empower, incite, reinforce, restore *(renew)*, stimulate
energizing impulsive *(impelling)*
energumen bigot
energy ardor, force *(strength)*, impetus, industry *(activity)*, labor *(exertion)*, life *(vitality)*, main force, puissance, sinew, spirit, strength
enervare disable
enervate debilitate, depreciate, disable, disarm *(divest of arms)*, eviscerate, exhaust *(deplete)*, extenuate, impair, tax *(overwork)*
enervate oneself carouse
enervated helpless *(powerless)*, nonsubstantial *(not sturdy)*
enervating operose
enervation frailty, languor, prostration
enfeeble debilitate, depreciate, disable, disarm *(divest of arms)*, eviscerate, exhaust *(deplete)*, extenuate, impair
enfeebled disabled *(made incapable)*, old
enfeeblement decline
enfeebling disabling
enfeoff alienate *(transfer title)*, bequeath, convey *(transfer)*
enfeoffment alienation *(transfer of title)*
enflame bait *(harass)*
enfold clothe, consist, contain *(comprise)*, embrace *(encircle)*, enclose, envelop
enfoldment enclosure
enforce administer *(conduct)*, compel, constrain *(compel)*, discharge *(perform)*, effectuate, exact, force *(coerce)*, implement, inflict, insist, make, operate, perform *(adhere to)*, press *(constrain)*, require *(compel)*
enforce censorship censor, expurgate

enforce obedience constrain (compel), force (coerce), rule (govern)
enforce payment excise (levy a tax)
enforceable choate lien, valid
enforceable claim cause of action
enforceable in a court of law legal
enforced compulsory, forcible, obligatory
enforced abstention prohibition
enforced withdrawal expulsion
enforcement action (performance), commission (act), compulsion (coercion), discharge (performance), duress, force (compulsion), requirement
enforcement of judgment collection (payment)
enforcement of mortgage foreclosure
enforcing compelling
enframe frame (construct)
enframement border
enfranchise allow (authorize), authorize, bestow, disenthrall, free, let (permit), liberate, release
enfranchised allowed, autonomous (self governing), free (enjoying civil liberty), rightful
enfranchisement charter (sanction), copyright, emancipation, franchise (right to vote), freedom, home rule, liberation, liberty, license, privilege, suffrage
engage agree (contract), appoint, assume (undertake), book, charge (empower), coax, commit (entrust), contend (dispute), contract, delegate, employ (engage services), fight (battle), hire, immerse (engross), implicate, induct, lease, monopolize, nominate, participate, promise (vow), provide (arrange for), pursue (carry on), register, rent, retain (employ), stipulate
engage in commence, endeavor, exercise (discharge a function), labor, operate, participate, ply, practice (engage in), undertake
engage in a contest compete
engage in a contest of speed race
engage in a conversation communicate, discuss, speak
engage in a dialogue speak
engage in an enterprise embark
engage in conflict with confront (oppose)
engage in conversation discuss
engage in hostilities attack
engage in oral controversy debate, discuss
engage in solemn manner promise (vow)
engage premises for a designated period lease
engage solemnly pledge (promise the performance of)
engage the attention interest, occupy (engage)
engage the mind interest, occupy (engage)
engage the thoughts interest, occupy (engage)
engage to give pledge (promise the performance of)
engage with grapple
engaged bound, indentured
engaged in business industrial
engaged in commerce commercial,

retail
engaged in traffic industrial
engagement agreement (contract), appointment (meeting), assurance, burden, charge (responsibility), commitment (responsibility), competition, conflict, confrontation (act of setting face to face), confrontation (altercation), contest (competition), contract, covenant, duty (obligation), embroilment, employment, enterprise (undertaking), fight (battle), meeting (encounter), mortgage, profession (vocation), project, promise, pursuit (occupation), rendezvous, responsibility (accountability), specialty (contract), stipulation, strife, struggle, testament, trade (occupation), undertaking (business), undertaking (enterprise), undertaking (pledge), work (employment)
engagements ties
engager of services principal (director)
engaging attractive, sapid
engaging fee retainer
engaging in bigamy polygamous
engaging in unlawful marriage polygamous
engender avail (bring about), bear (yield), cause, constitute (establish), create, foment, generate, make, originate, produce (manufacture), propagate (increase), reproduce
engenderment creation
engineer administer (conduct), arrange (plan), build (construct), cause, compose, connive, contractor, control (regulate), create, devise (invent), direct (supervise), manage, maneuver, manipulate (utilize skillfully), manufacture, materialman, militate, operate, originate, oversee, plan, plot, program, realize (make real), scheme
engineered tactical
engineering building (business of assembling), contrivance, strategy
engird circumscribe (surround by boundary), contain (enclose), embrace (encircle), encompass (surround), include
engorgement plethora
engraft embed, plant (place firmly)
engrafted ingrained, permanent
engrave brand (mark), delineate, inscribe
engraving inscription, stamp
engross engage (involve), interest, monopolize, occupy (engage)
engross the mind interest, occupy (engage)
engross the thoughts interest, occupy (engage)
engrossed pensive
engrossment compulsion (obsession), contemplation, notice (heed), obsession, preoccupation
engulf immerse (plunge into), inundate, overcome (overwhelm)
engulfing oppressive
engulfment osmosis
enhance ameliorate, amend, build (augment), compound, embellish, enlarge, expand, heighten (augment), intensify, inure (benefit), magnify, meliorate, progress, raise (advance), reform, renew (refurbish), supplement

enhance the degree of appreciate (increase)
enhancement accession (enlargement), additive, advance (increase), amendment (correction), augmentation, boom (increase), development (progression), hyperbole, progress, reform, renewal
enhancing cumulative (intensifying)
enhearten assure (give confidence to), promise (raise expectations), reassure
enigma confusion (ambiguity), mystery, paradox, problem, question (issue), secret
enigmatic complex, debatable, difficult, disputable, elusive, equivocal, esoteric, inapprehensible, incomprehensible, indefinable, indefinite, indistinct, inexplicable, inexpressive, inscrutable, mysterious, obscure (abstruse), opaque, oracular, problematic, recondite, suspicious (questionable), vague
enigmatical equivocal, esoteric, hidden, inapprehensible, incomprehensible, indefinable, indefinite, indistinct, inexplicable, inexpressive, mysterious, obscure (abstruse), problematic, uncertain (ambiguous)
enisle isolate
enisled insular, solitary
eniti endeavor, strive
enixus earnest
enjoin admonish (advise), arrest (stop), ban, bar (hinder), coerce, condemn (ban), debar, demand, detail (assign), dictate, direct (order), enact, exact, exhort, expostulate, forbid, force (coerce), forestall, impose (enforce), inhibit, insist, interdict, necessitate, prescribe, press (beseech), prohibit, proscribe (prohibit), request, require (compel), restrain
enjoin from contain (restrain)
enjoinder injunction
enjoined positive (prescribed)
enjoining bar (obstruction), obstacle, obstruction, prohibition, remonstrative
enjoinment directive, refusal, requirement
enjoy own, possess, realize (obtain as a profit), relish, remain (occupy)
enjoy the use of premises rent
enjoyable desirable (pleasing), palatable, preferable
enjoyed popular
enjoying liberty free (enjoying civil liberty), sovereign (independent)
enjoying political independence sovereign (independent)
enjoyment benefit (betterment), occupancy, satisfaction (fulfilment), use
enkindle burn, foment, incense, inspire, provoke, stimulate
enlace intertwine
enlarge accrue (increase), amplify, bear (yield), build (augment), compound, develop, enhance, expand, extricate, heighten (augment), increase, inflate, magnify, overestimate, raise (advance), recruit, supplement
enlarge in size accumulate (enlarge)
enlarge on expand
enlarge the mind disabuse, edify
enlarge the scope of extend (enlarge)
enlarge upon develop, elaborate,

outpour

enlarged extreme *(exaggerated)*, inflated *(overestimated)*, liberal *(not literal)*

enlarged by swelling inflated *(enlarged)*

enlargement accretion, addition, advance *(increase)*, advancement *(improvement)*, aggravation *(exacerbation)*, augmentation, bombast, boom *(increase)*, distortion, exaggeration, extension *(expansion)*, growth *(increase)*, hyperbole, increment, inflation *(increase)*, overstatement

enlarging augmentation, cumulative *(increasing)*

enlighten admit *(concede)*, advise, apprise, clarify, comment, communicate, construe *(translate)*, convey *(communicate)*, disabuse, discipline *(train)*, disclose, divulge, edify, educate, elucidate, explain, explicate, exposit, herald, illustrate, impart, inform *(notify)*, initiate, instruct *(teach)*, mention, notify, report *(disclose)*, reveal, signify *(inform)*

enlightened acquainted, cognizant, familiar *(informed)*, informed *(educated)*, informed *(having information)*, judicious, juridical, learned, literate, politic, rational, sensible

enlightener bystander, deponent, informant

enlightening advisory, demonstrative *(illustrative)*, didactic, informative, informatory, interpretive

enlightenment admission *(disclosure)*, civilization, clarification, cognition, comprehension, direction *(guidance)*, disclosure *(act of disclosing)*, dispatch *(message)*, edification, education, experience *(background)*, guidance, information *(knowledge)*, insight, intelligence *(news)*, knowledge *(awareness)*, knowledge *(learning)*, mention *(reference)*, monition *(warning)*, notice *(announcement)*, notification, publication *(disclosure)*, sense *(intelligence)*, tip *(clue)*

enlist appoint, bait *(lure)*, coax, convert *(persuade)*, convince, employ *(engage services)*, engage *(hire)*, enroll, hire, instate, join *(associate oneself with)*, levy, lobby, persuade, prevail *(persuade)*, prevail upon, procure, recruit, register, resort, retain *(employ)*

enlist employees in a labor union organize *(unionize)*

enlist in a labor union organize *(unionize)*

enlist in one's service engage *(hire)*

enlist jurors empanel

enlist with combine *(act in concert)*

enlisted man volunteer

enlisted person volunteer

enlistee member *(individual in a group)*, volunteer

enlistment persuasion, registration

enliven inspire, spirit, stimulate

enlivened born *(alive)*, conscious *(awake)*

enmesh bait *(lure)*, betray *(lead astray)*, engage *(involve)*, ensnare, entrap, implicate, incriminate, intertwine

enmeshed interrelated, related

enmeshment complex *(entanglement)*, entanglement *(confusion)*, implication

(incriminating involvement)

enmity alienation *(estrangement)*, belligerency, breach, conflict, contention *(opposition)*, cruelty, disaccord, discord, estrangement, feud, hatred, ill will, malice, odium, opposition, rancor, resentment, spite, umbrage, vengeance

ennoble honor, raise *(advance)*

enodare explicate, solve

enormity degree *(magnitude)*, magnitude, weight *(importance)*

enormous exorbitant, far reaching, flagrant, grandiose, gross *(flagrant)*, major, outrageous, ponderous

enough adequate, quorum, sufficiency

enounce declare, enunciate, proclaim, promulgate, pronounce *(speak)*

enquiry cross-examination

enrage aggravate *(annoy)*, alienate *(estrange)*, annoy, bait *(harass)*, discompose, disturb, exacerbate, harass, incense, irritate, offend *(insult)*, persecute, pique, provoke, upset

enraptured ecstatic

enregister note *(record)*

enrich amend, bestow, compound, contribute *(supply)*, cultivate, elaborate, embellish, endow, endue, enhance, impart, inure *(benefit)*, meliorate, nurture, progress, replenish, supplement

enriched literate

enriching didactic, informative

enrichment advance *(increase)*, development *(progression)*, endowment, progress, reform

enring encompass *(surround)*

enrobe clothe

enroll empanel, employ *(engage services)*, enter *(record)*, enumerate, file *(place among official records)*, inscribe, instate, join *(associate oneself with)*, record, recruit, register, subscribe *(promise)*, survey *(poll)*

enrolled person member *(individual in a group)*

enrolling registration

enrollment constituency, registration, subscription

ensample instance, sample, specimen

ensconce blind *(obscure)*, camouflage, cloak, enshroud, harbor, hide, instate, plant *(place firmly)*, preserve, shroud

ensconce oneself lurk

ensconced clandestine, safe, situated

enscroll inscribe

ensemble assemblage, corpus, en masse, entirety

enshield ensconce

enshrine dedicate

enshrined sacrosanct

enshrinement dedication, remembrance *(commemoration)*

enshrining honorary

enshroud blind *(obscure)*, camouflage, cloak, conceal, cover *(conceal)*, ensconce, envelop, obnubilate, obscure

enshrouded hidden

ensign device *(distinguishing mark)*, indicant, indicator, symbol

enslave force *(coerce)*, impose *(subject)*, subject, subjugate

enslaved indentured, obsequious, subservient

enslavement bondage, captivity, oppression, servitude, subjection, thrall

enslaving dictatorial

ensnare abduct, ambush, bait *(lure)*, betray *(lead astray)*, bilk, coax, deceive, dupe, entrap, hunt, illude, inveigle, kidnap, mislead, pettifog, trap

ensnarement bunko

ensnaring insidious

ensphere border *(bound)*, circumscribe *(surround by boundary)*, contain *(enclose)*, encompass *(surround)*, envelop, hedge

enstamp seal *(solemnize)*

ensual consequence *(conclusion)*, development *(outgrowth)*

ensue accrue *(arise)*, arise *(originate)*, proceed *(go forward)*, redound, result, stem *(originate)*, succeed *(follow)*, supervene, trace *(follow)*

ensue from emanate

ensuing ancillary *(subsidiary)*, consecutive, derivative, forthcoming, future, subsequent, successive

ensure avouch *(guarantee)*, bond *(secure a debt)*, certify *(attest)*, cover *(guard)*, guarantee, preserve, protect, sponsor

ensure a result frame *(prearrange)*, prearrange

ensured certain *(positive)*, definite

ensurer backer

entail bequest, concern *(involve)*, consist, require *(compel)*

entailed proprietary, requisite

entangle bait *(lure)*, bicker, bilk, collide *(clash)*, confound, confuse *(create disorder)*, disorganize, encumber *(hinder)*, engage *(involve)*, ensnare, entrap, implicate, incriminate, interest, intertwine, inveigle, involve *(implicate)*, muddle, perplex, perturb, trammel, trap

entangled complex, compound, disordered, inextricable, labyrinthine, sinuous

entangled by difficulties difficult

entanglement commotion, complication, confusion *(turmoil)*, embroilment, imbroglio, implication *(incriminating involvement)*, involution, pandemonium, predicament, quagmire, snarl

entente arrangement *(understanding)*, bargain, compact

entente compatibility

entente conciliation

entente contract

entente mutual understanding, pact, treaty

entente cordiale accordance *(compact)*, compact

enter book, compete, embark, enroll, file *(place among official records)*, impanel, inscribe, introduce, join *(associate oneself with)*, note *(record)*, penetrate, pervade, record, register, set down

enter a competition race

enter a demurrer demur, object

enter a plea address *(petition)*

enter a protest challenge, object

enter a suit for address *(petition)*

enter an appearance appear *(attend court proceedings)*

enter by stealth encroach

enter competition compete

enter hostilely invade

enter into contract, contribute *(assist)*, engage *(involve)*, espouse, incur, involve (*participate*), participate, undertake

enter into a contract sign

enter into a contractual obligation close (*agree*)

enter into a league organize (*unionize*)

enter into an account deposit (*submit to a bank*)

enter into collision collide (*crash against*)

enter into conflict with engage (*involve*)

enter into detail designate, develop, expand, itemize

enter into partnership with combine (*act in concert*), pool

enter into possession obtain, possess

enter on a list enroll

enter on a record enroll

enter on a register enroll

enter the mind occur (*come to mind*)

enter the picture emerge, occur (*come to mind*)

enter those names designated as jurors empanel

enter uninvited intrude

enter unlawfully impose (*intrude*), intrude, trespass

enter upon assume (*undertake*), commence, embark, initiate, undertake

enter upon the domain of another encroach

enter wrongfully encroach

enterprise act (*undertaking*), activity, calling, campaign, corporation, employment, endeavor, firm, industry (*activity*), industry (*business*), labor (*exertion*), livelihood, occupation (*vocation*), operation, project, pursuit (*occupation*), scheme, spirit, transaction, undertaking (*business*), venture, work (*effort*)

enterpriser architect, developer, promoter

enterprising active, competent, progressive (*advocating change*), resourceful

entertain engage (*involve*), interest, occupy (*engage*), receive (*permit to enter*), treat (*process*)

entertain doubts doubt (*distrust*), misdoubt, mistrust

entertain suspicions doubt (*distrust*), misdoubt, mistrust

entertaining sapid

entertaining suspicion leery

entertainment enjoyment (*pleasure*)

entêté contumacious

enthrall coerce, commit (*institutionalize*), confine, constrain (*imprison*), detain (*hold in custody*), force (*coerce*), immerse (*engross*), interest, lock, monopolize, obsess, occupy (*engage*), subdue, subject, subjugate

enthralling attractive, sapid

enthrallment constraint (*imprisonment*), constraint (*restriction*), custody (*incarceration*), preoccupation, servitude, subjection, thrall

enthuse incite

enthusiasm ardor, compulsion (*obsession*), emotion, industry (*activity*), interest (*concern*), life (*vitality*), penchant, spirit

enthusiast addict, partisan, proponent

enthusiastic eager, earnest, ecstatic,

fanatical, fervent, industrious, ready (*willing*), sanguine, vehement, willing (*desirous*), zealous

enthusiastically readily

entice bait (*lure*), betray (*lead astray*), cajole, coax, ensnare, entrap, interest, inveigle, lure, prevail upon

enticement bribery, cause (*reason*), decoy, draw (*attraction*), hush money, incentive, inducement, invitation, persuasion, seduction

enticing attractive, sapid

entire absolute (*complete*), collective, complete (*all-embracing*), full, gross (*total*), intact, outright, plenary, pure, radical (*extreme*), stark, thorough, total, whole (*undamaged*)

entire amount entirety

entire number aggregate

entire quantity aggregate

entirely en banc, in toto, purely (*positively*), solely (*singly*), wholly

entirely defensible blameless, clean, inculpable

entirely occupied full

entireness entirety, finality, totality

entirety aggregate, finality, sum (*total*), totality, whole

entitle allow (*authorize*), authorize, bestow, call (*title*), certify (*approve*), delegate, denominate, designate, label, let (*permit*), nominate, permit, phrase, qualify (*meet standards*), sanction

entitled desirable (*qualified*), meritorious, privileged, qualified (*competent*)

entitled to acceptance and belief authentic

entitlement birthright, certification (*certification of proficiency*), charter (*sanction*), consent, droit, due, freedom, license, privilege, qualification (*fitness*), title (*right*)

entitlement for a term of years copyright

entity body (*collection*), body (*person*), item, materiality (*physical existence*), totality

entomb conceal, constrain (*imprison*), immure, imprison

entombment bondage, captivity

entrammel arrest (*apprehend*), encumber (*hinder*), fetter, handcuff, interfere, restrict, trammel

entrance access (*right of way*), admission (*entry*), admittance (*acceptance*), admittance (*means of approach*), avenue (*route*), entry (*entrance*), incursion, inflow, ingress, nascency, occupy (*engage*), onset (*commencement*), outset, portal

entrance by stealth encroachment

entrance in a case appearance (*coming into court*)

entrance into a lawsuit intervention (*imposition into a lawsuit*)

entrance of a third party intervention (*imposition into a lawsuit*)

entrance upon domain of another infringement

entrance upon the domain of another encroachment

entrance way access (*right of way*), threshold (*entrance*)

entranced ecstatic

entrances approaches

entranceway portal

entranceways approaches

entrancing attractive, provocative, sapid

entrant amateur, applicant (*candidate*), candidate, contender, neophyte, novice, probationer (*one being tested*), rival

entrap ambush, bait (*lure*), betray (*lead astray*), deceive, dupe, ensnare, inveigle, mislead, trap

entrapment entanglement (*involvement*)

entreat bait (*lure*), call (*appeal to*), desire, exhort, invoke, petition, plead (*implore*), pray, press (*beseech*), pressure, prevail upon, request, solicit, sue, urge

entreat against except (*object*)

entreat earnestly petition

entreat persistently importune, pray

entreating precatory

entreaty bait (*lure*), call (*appeal*), dun, petition, prayer, request

entree admittance (*acceptance*)

entrench embed, fix (*make firm*), impose (*intrude*), overstep

entrench on impinge

entrenched chronic, constant, fixed (*settled*), indefeasible, ingrained, inveterate, irreversible, permanent, safe

entrepreneur merchant, speculator

entries ledger

entrust appoint, assign (*designate*), assign (*transfer ownership*), authorize, charge (*empower*), confide (*trust*), consign, delegate, deliver, deposit (*submit to a bank*), descend, detail (*assign*), empower, endue, give (*grant*), instate, invest (*vest*), leave (*give*), lend, let (*permit*), refer (*send for action*), relegate, rely, remand, vest

entrust to the care of another delegate

entrust with a task employ (*engage services*)

entrust with information notice (*give formal warning*)

entrust with management employ (*engage services*)

entrust with private information confide (*divulge*)

entrusted cause charge (*custody*)

entrusted object charge (*custody*)

entrusting delegation (*assignment*)

entrustment delegation (*assignment*), deputation (*selection of delegates*), escrow, loan

entry access (*right of way*), admittance (*acceptance*), admittance (*means of approach*), avenue (*route*), entrance, file, inflow, ingress, inscription, insertion, item, marginalia, nascency, notation, note (*brief comment*), portal, record, threshold (*entrance*)

entry book docket

entry of aliens immigration

entry under paramount title eviction

entryway admission (*entry*), admittance (*means of approach*), entrance

entryways approaches

entwine combine (*join together*), commingle, conjoin, connect (*join together*), intertwine, join (*bring together*), lock, merge, unite

entwined cognate, collateral (*accom-*

panying)

enucleate comment, elucidate, enlighten, exemplify, explain, explicate, exposit, expound, resolve *(solve)*, solve
enucleation comment, explanation, illustration, paraphrase
enumerare enumerate, recite, specify
enumerate book, calculate, define, detail *(particularize)*, express, impanel, index *(relate)*, itemize, mention, pinpoint, poll, recapitulate, recite, signify *(inform)*, specify, survey *(poll)*, tabulate
enumerated detailed
enumeratio recital, restatement
enumeration account *(evaluation)*, census, computation, disclosure *(act of disclosing)*, docket, index *(catalog)*, inventory, invoice *(itemized list)*, poll *(canvass)*, reference *(citation)*, roll, schedule, specification, statement
enumeration of causes arranged for trial calendar *(list of cases)*
enumeration of the essential qualities delineation
enunciate affirm *(claim)*, allege, annunciate, argue, assert, avow, cite *(state)*, communicate, construe *(translate)*, declare, depict, express, herald, issue *(publish)*, notify, pass *(determine)*, phrase, plead *(allege in a legal action)*, posit, pronounce *(speak)*, propagate *(spread)*, speak, utter
enunciated alleged, nuncupative, oral
enunciation assertion, declaratory judgment, disclosure *(something disclosed)*, notice *(announcement)*, notification, profession *(declaration)*, pronouncement, publicity, speech
enunciative declaratory
enunciatory declaratory
enuntiare pronounce *(speak)*
envelop blind *(obscure)*, border *(bound)*, camouflage, circumscribe *(surround by boundary)*, cloak, clothe, comprehend *(include)*, conceal, consist, contain *(comprise)*, contain *(enclose)*, embrace *(encircle)*, enclose, encompass *(surround)*, ensconce, enshroud, hide, include, shroud, shut
envelopment blockade *(enclosure)*, coverage *(scope)*, enclosure, panoply
envenom aggravate *(annoy)*, alienate *(estrange)*, antagonize, bait *(harass)*, disaffect, discompose, incense, infect, provoke, taint *(contaminate)*
envenomed bitter *(reproachful)*, caustic, deadly, deleterious, malevolent, malignant, peccant *(unhealthy)*, pernicious, scathing, sinister, spiteful, tainted *(contaminated)*, virulent
envenomed tongue aspersion
enviable meritorious
envious jealous, resentful
environ border *(bound)*, enclose, envelop
environing influence atmosphere
environment atmosphere, climate, locality, location, situation
environmental conditions climate
environmental science ecology
environmental studies ecology
environs confines, environment, locality, region, section *(vicinity)*, site, territory, vicinity
envisage compose, conceive *(comprehend)*, conjure, invent *(produce for the*

first time)
envisagement contemplation
envision conceive *(comprehend)*, expect *(consider probable)*, predict, presage
envisioning original *(creative)*
envisionment contemplation
envoy agent, conduit *(intermediary)*, deputy, factor *(commission merchant)*, informant, informer *(a person who provides information)*, liaison, medium, plenipotentiary, procurator, proxy, replacement, representative *(proxy)*, spokesman, substitute
envoys deputation *(delegation)*
envy resentment
enwrap clothe, contain *(enclose)*, encompass *(surround)*, ensconce, enshroud, envelop, shroud, shut
eodem tempore simultaneous
eon age, cycle, period
epagogic discursive *(analytical)*
epexegesis clarification
ephemeral brief, insubstantial, nonsubstantial *(not sturdy)*, temporary, transient, transitory, volatile
ephemeris journal
ephemeris register
ephemerous ephemeral, transient
epic narrative, story *(narrative)*
epicenter center *(central position)*
epicurean palatable, particular *(exacting)*
epidemic contagious, disease, far reaching, general, pestilent, predominant, prevailing *(current)*, prevalent, rife
epigrammatic brief, compact *(pithy)*, concise, laconic, pithy, proverbial, sententious, succinct
epigrammatical sententious
epilogue codicil, denouement
epilogus peroration
episode event, experience *(encounter)*, happening, incident, occasion, occurrence, scene
epistle dispatch *(message)*
epistolize correspond *(communicate)*
epistula dispatch *(message)*, note *(brief comment)*
epistulae correspondence *(communication by letters)*
epithet blasphemy, call *(title)*, term *(expression)*
epitoma abstract, compendium, summary
epitome abridgment *(condensation)*, abstract, capsule, compendium, cross section, digest, outline *(synopsis)*, restatement, summary
epitome synopsis
epitomization abridgment *(condensation)*
epitomize abridge *(shorten)*, abstract *(summarize)*, condense, extract, review
epitomized brief, compact *(pithy)*, concise
epoch age, cycle, duration, lifetime, period, phase *(period)*
eponym call *(title)*
equability composure, parity, uniformity
equable agreed *(harmonized)*, coextensive, comparable *(equivalent)*, consistent, consonant, equal, harmonious, just, peaceable, placid, uniform

equably fairly *(impartially)*
equal agreed *(harmonized)*, coequal, coextensive, cognate, commensurable, competitive *(open)*, congruous, consistent, consonant, correlate, correspond *(be equivalent)*, counterpart *(parallel)*, equitable, equivalent, evenhanded, fair *(just)*, identical, peer, reach, same, same, tantamount, uniform
equal distribution of weight equipoise
equal footing par *(equality)*
equal in effect equivalent
equal in extent commensurate
equal in force equivalent
equal in measure commensurate
equal in power equivalent
equal in scope coextensive
equal in significance equivalent
equal in space coextensive
equal in time coextensive
equal in value comparable *(equivalent)*, equivalent
equal part moiety
equal share moiety
equal to capable, commensurate, effective *(efficient)*, proficient, qualified *(competent)*
equal to the need adequate
equal value par *(equality)*
equal worth par *(equality)*
equality fairness, identity *(similarity)*, par *(equality)*, parity, resemblance
equality of force equipoise
equality of weight equipoise
equalization balance *(equality)*, offset
equalize compensate *(counterbalance)*, conform, coordinate, counteract, neutralize, outbalance
equalized agreed *(harmonized)*, coextensive, equal, equivalent
equally fairly *(impartially)*
equally divided equal
equalness par *(equality)*
equanimity compatibility, composure, moderation
equate compare, compensate *(counterbalance)*
equation balance *(equality)*, comparison, parity
equibalanced coequal
equidistance center *(central position)*
equidistant central *(situated near center)*, coextensive, equal, intermediate
equilateral coextensive, equal
equilibrate compensate *(counterbalance)*
equilibration balance *(equality)*, equipoise
equilibrium balance *(equality)*, composure, equipoise, parity, status quo
equip bear *(yield)*, bestow, clothe, contribute *(supply)*, fund, furnish, give *(grant)*, provide *(supply)*, supply
equipage paraphernalia *(apparatus)*
equipment appliance, chattel, competence *(ability)*, device *(mechanism)*, expedient, faculty *(ability)*, instrument *(tool)*, instrumentality, paraphernalia *(apparatus)*, preparation, stock in trade
equipoise balance *(equality)*, parity, quid pro quo
equipollence balance *(equality)*, identity *(similarity)*, par *(equality)*
equipollency identity *(similarity)*

equipollent analogous, coequal, coextensive, comparable *(equivalent)*, equal, equivalent

equiponderance balance *(equality)*, equipoise

equiponderant coequal, coextensive

equiponderate counteract, countervail, outbalance

equipondious coextensive

equipped practiced, provident *(showing foresight)*, qualified *(competent)*, ready *(prepared)*

equipped with arms armed

equitable equal, evenhanded, fair *(just)*, honest, impartial, judicial, juridical, just, neutral, nonpartisan, objective, open-minded, reasonable *(fair)*, right *(correct)*, rightful, scrupulous, unbiased, unprejudiced

equitable interest claim *(right)*

equitable treatment fairness

equitableness candor *(impartiality)*, disinterest *(lack of prejudice)*, fairness, justice, objectivity, probity, right *(righteousness)*

equitably fairly *(impartially)*

equity candor *(impartiality)*, disinterest *(lack of prejudice)*, estate *(property)*, fairness, justice, objectivity, possessions, probity, propriety *(appropriateness)*, rectitude, right *(righteousness)*, stake *(interest)*, title *(right)*

equivalence analogy, balance *(equality)*, correspondence *(similarity)*, identity *(similarity)*, par *(equality)*, parity, propinquity *(similarity)*

equivalency parity

equivalent agreed *(harmonized)*, analogous, coequal, coextensive, cognate, commensurable, commensurate, compensatory, congruous, correlate, correlative, counterpart *(parallel)*, disjunctive *(alternative)*, faithful *(true to fact)*, identical, mutual *(reciprocal)*, offset, peer, pendent, proportionate, replacement, same, same, similar, tantamount, value, vicarious *(substitutional)*, virtual

equivalent claim setoff

equivalent given for injury compensation

equivalent given for loss sustained compensation

equivalent item cover *(substitute)*

equivalent meaning definition, paraphrase

equivalently pro rata

equivocal aleatory *(uncertain)*, ambiguous, conditional, disputable, doubtful, dubious, elusive, hesitant, impalpable, indefinite, indeterminate, oblique *(evasive)*, precarious, problematic, provisional, suspicious *(questionable)*, uncertain *(questionable)*, unclear, vague

equivocalness ambiguity, ambivalence, color *(deceptive appearance)*, indecision, qualm

equivocate bicker, doubt *(hesitate)*, evade *(deceive)*, lie *(falsify)*, misrepresent, palter, prevaricate, tergiversate, vacillate

equivocating equivocal, evasive, lying, oblique *(evasive)*

equivocation ambiguity, color *(deceptive appearance)*, deceit, deception, duplicity, evasion, falsehood, hesitation,

pettifoggery, sophistry

equivocatory equivocal

era age, cycle, duration, lifetime, period, phase *(period)*, term *(duration)*, time

eradere eradicate

eradicable destructible

eradicare extirpate

eradicate abolish, cancel, censor, consume, delete, destroy *(efface)*, excise *(cut away)*, exclude, expunge, extinguish, extirpate, overthrow, purge *(purify)*, quash, reject, relegate, remove *(eliminate)*, supplant

eradicated lost *(taken away)*

eradication abolition, cancellation, catastrophe, destruction, dissolution *(termination)*, evulsion, prohibition, rejection, removal, rescision

eradicative dire, disastrous, fatal

erase censor, deface, delete, destroy *(efface)*, dissolve *(terminate)*, edit, eliminate *(eradicate)*, eradicate, expunge, expurgate, extinguish, extirpate, invalidate, obliterate, redact, rescind

erasure cancellation, defacement, dissolution *(termination)*, rejection, removal

erasure of ambiguity clarification

eratic disjunctive *(tending to disjoin)*

erect build *(construct)*, create, devise *(invent)*, elevate, fabricate *(construct)*, frame *(construct)*, honest, make, produce *(manufacture)*, upright

erect a barrier bar *(hinder)*, impede

erection building *(structure)*, development *(building)*, elevation, structure *(edifice)*

erectus intent

eremetical solitary

eremitic solitary

eremitish solitary

ergo a fortiori, a priori, consequently

eripere disabuse, hold up *(rob)*

eristic argumentative, controversial, debatable, disputable, litigious, polemic

eristical argumentative, litigious, polemic

ernest decisive

erode degenerate, depreciate, diminish, impair, lessen

erogare expend *(disburse)*

erosion attrition, decline, decrement, deterioration, detriment, dissolution *(disintegration)*, expense *(sacrifice)*, spoilage, wear and tear

erosive caustic

erotic lascivious, lecherous, prurient, salacious, suggestive *(risqué)*

erotica pornography

erotical lecherous

err deviate, fail *(lose)*, lapse *(fall into error)*, misapprehend, miscalculate, misconceive, misinterpret, misjudge, misread, mistake, misunderstand, offend *(violate the law)*

err in judgment misjudge

errable fallible

errancy misapplication

errand burden, mission

errant astray, blameful, blameworthy, deviant, devious, discursive *(digressive)*, fallible, faulty, truant

errare err, lapse *(fall into error)*, miscalculate

erratic anomalous, astray, broken *(in-*

terrupted), capricious, desultory, disjointed, eccentric, inconsistent, infrequent, irregular *(not usual)*, irresolute, periodic, sporadic, undependable, unpredictable, variable, volatile

erratum error

erratum fault *(mistake)*, miscue, misstatement

erratum oversight *(carelessness)*

erring at fault, blameworthy, delinquent *(guilty of a misdeed)*, errant, erroneous, fallible, guilty, inaccurate, incorrect, peccable

erroneous baseless, errant, fallacious, false *(inaccurate)*, faulty, fictitious, ill-founded, improper, inaccurate, incorrect, inexact, peccant *(culpable)*, sophistic, specious, unfounded, unsound *(fallacious)*, unsustainable, untenable, untrue

erroneous in date untimely

erroneous reasoning fallacy

erroneous statement error

erroneous trial mistrial

erroneous use abuse *(corrupt practice)*, misuse

erroneousness fallacy, invalidity, misestimation

error delinquency *(failure of duty)*

error error

error failure *(lack of success)*, fallacy, fault *(mistake)*, flaw, indiscretion

error lapse *(expiration)*

error lapse *(expiration)*, misapplication, misconduct, miscue, misdoing, misestimation, misjudgment, misstatement, onus *(blame)*, oversight *(carelessness)*, tort, transgression

error in naming misnomer

error of judgment fault *(mistake)*

error of the court injustice

errori obnoxius fallible

errorless accurate, factual, infallible

ersatz artificial, counterfeit, imitation, spurious, succedaneum, synthetic, vicarious *(substitutional)*

erstwhile former, late *(defunct)*, previous

eruct eject *(expel)*, outpour

eructate eject *(expel)*, emit, outpour

erudire educate, instruct *(teach)*

erudite cognizant, didactic, familiar *(informed)*, informed *(educated)*, learned, literate, profound *(esoteric)*

eruditio instruction *(teaching)*, research

erudition comprehension, education, information *(knowledge)*, knowledge *(learning)*

eruditus learned

eruere disinter

erumpere issue *(send forth)*

erupt emit, penetrate

eruption bluster *(commotion)*, cataclysm, commotion, disturbance, expulsion, furor, outbreak, outburst, outflow, passion, recrudescence, strife, violence

escalate accrue *(increase)*, enhance, enlarge, expand, increase, inflate, intensify, parlay *(exploit successfully)*

escalating cumulative *(intensifying)*

escalation boom *(increase)*, boom *(prosperity)*, growth *(increase)*, inflation *(increase)*

escapade experience *(encounter)*

escape abscond, avoid *(evade)*, circumvent, disappear, egress, elude, evacuate, evade *(elude)*, exude, flee, impunity, issuance, leave *(depart)*, outflow, parry, part *(leave)*, quit *(evacuate)*, retreat, shun

escape by artifice elude
escape by cleverness evasion
escape by trickery evasion
escape clause loophole, salvo
escape detection elude, lurk
escape from shirk
escape hatch loophole
escape notice elude, evade *(elude)*, lurk
escape observation lurk
escape recognition lurk
escape valve loophole
escape-clause dispensation *(exception)*
escaped prisoner fugitive
escapee convict, fugitive
escaper fugitive
escaping elusive, flight
escheat forfeit, relapse
eschew abscond, avoid *(evade)*, decline *(reject)*, forgo, forswear, refrain, repulse, shun
eschewal abstention, continence
eschewment avoidance *(evasion)*
escort consort, guardian, protect
escrow binder
esculent palatable
esoteric certain *(specific)*, enigmatic, exclusive *(limited)*, hidden, incomprehensible, inexplicable, mysterious, obscure *(abstruse)*, private *(confidential)*, profound *(esoteric)*, recondite, secret, special, specific, undefinable
esoterical esoteric, private *(confidential)*
especial certain *(particular)*, certain *(specific)*, exclusive *(singular)*, extraordinary, noteworthy, outstanding *(prominent)*, particular *(individual)*, particular *(specific)*, singular, special, specific
especially a fortiori, particularly
especially liked preferred *(favored)*
especially prepared express
espial discovery, espionage, observation, perception, recognition
espieglerie artifice
espier detective
espionage observation
espousal adoption *(acceptance)*, aid *(help)*, alternative *(option)*, defense, favor *(sanction)*, marriage *(wedlock)*, matrimony
espouse adhere *(maintain loyalty)*, adopt, advocate, assert, assure *(insure)*, defend, embrace *(accept)*, justify, lobby, prefer, spouse, uphold
espouse the cause of justify, maintain *(sustain)*
espoused conjugal, nuptial
espousement marriage *(wedlock)*, matrimony
espouser proponent
espy detect, discern *(detect with the senses)*, identify, observe *(watch)*, perceive, recognize *(perceive)*, spy
essay attempt, effort, endeavor, endeavor, experiment, pandect *(treatise)*, project, question *(inquiry)*, review *(critical evaluation)*, struggle, undertaking *(enterprise)*, venture, work *(effort)*
essayist author *(writer)*

esse exist, subsist
esse participem participate
essence basis, capsule, character *(personal quality)*, characteristic, compendium, connotation, consequence *(significance)*, content *(meaning)*, contents, cornerstone, corpus, digest, epitome, gist *(substance)*, gravamen, import, interior, main point, necessary, outline *(synopsis)*, point *(purpose)*, scenario, signification, spirit, structure *(composition)*, substance *(essential nature)*, sum *(tally)*
essence of a grievance gravamen
essential actual, cardinal *(basic)*, critical *(crucial)*, crucial, exigent, fundamental, grave *(important)*, imperative, important *(urgent)*, indispensable, ingrained, inherent, innate, integral, major, mandatory, material *(important)*, native *(inborn)*, necessary *(required)*, necessary, necessity, obligatory, peremptory *(imperative)*, primary, principal, requirement, requisite, resource, rudimentary, substantive, ultimate, underlying, urgent, virtual, vital
essential clause sine qua non
essential condition sine qua non
essential desideratum prerequisite, requirement
essential element necessity, need *(requirement)*
essential ground gist *(ground for a suit)*
essential matter content *(meaning)*, cornerstone, gist *(ground for a suit)*, main point, sine qua non
essential meaning connotation, content *(meaning)*, gist *(substance)*
essential nature materiality *(physical existence)*
essential object of desire desideratum
essential part body *(main part)*, center *(essence)*, character *(personal quality)*, characteristic, content *(meaning)*, element, essence, gist *(ground for a suit)*, gist *(substance)*, gravamen, ingredient, main point, sine qua non, spirit, substance *(essential nature)*
essential point gravamen, main point
essential provision condition *(contingent provision)*
essential qualification sine qua non
essential quality consequence *(significance)*
essential quality of one's nature character *(personal quality)*
essential status priority
essential to completeness integral
essentiality importance, magnitude, market *(demand)*, necessary, need *(requirement)*, significance
essentially ipso facto, purely *(positively)*, purely *(simply)*
essentially different disparate
essentialness character *(personal quality)*, main point, need *(requirement)*
essentials basic facts
establish affirm *(claim)*, affirm *(uphold)*, appoint, argue, ascertain, authorize, award, bear *(adduce)*, build *(construct)*, cast *(register)*, certify *(approve)*, circumscribe *(define)*, cite *(state)*, confirm, create, decide, decree,

define, document, enact, evidence, fabricate *(construct)*, fix *(arrange)*, fix *(make firm)*, fix *(settle)*, form, instate, launch *(initiate)*, legislate, locate, make, organize *(unionize)*, originate, pass *(approve)*, plant *(place firmly)*, prove, quote, reason *(persuade)*, repose *(place)*, rule *(decide)*, stabilize, support *(corroborate)*, sustain *(confirm)*, testify, verify *(confirm)*, vest
establish a corporation incorporate *(form a corporation)*
establish as facts find *(determine)*
establish as truth prove
establish beforehand preordain
establish boundaries demarcate
establish by agreement close *(agree)*
establish by law enact, legislate, pass *(approve)*
establish by proof substantiate
establish connection contact *(communicate)*, contact *(touch)*
establish equilibrium adjust *(regulate)*
establish guide lines organize *(arrange)*
establish guidelines for plan
establish in an office instate
establish oneself lodge *(reside)*, reside
establish parameters organize *(arrange)*
establish the authenticity of a will probate
establish the genuineness of prove
establish the genuineness of a will probate
establish the truth of verify *(confirm)*
establish the validity of prove
establish the validity of a will probate
establish with certainty ascertain
establishable convincing, provable
established accustomed *(customary)*, certain *(positive)*, chronic, common *(customary)*, conventional, convincing, customary, daily, definite, demonstrable, durable, familiar *(customary)*, firm, fixed *(settled)*, habitual, inappealable, incontrovertible, indefeasible, ingrained, inveterate, lawful, normal *(regular)*, official, ordinary, orthodox, permanent, positive *(prescribed)*, prescriptive, prevailing *(current)*, prevalent, professional *(trained)*, prosperous, regular *(orderly)*, routine, situated, solid *(sound)*, stable, standing, stated, statutory, steadfast, substantial, traditional, undeniable, usual
established by custom customary
established by general consent conventional
established by law legal
established by the federal government national
established custom usage
established division of time calendar *(record of yearly periods)*
established law code
established matter fact
established method procedure
established mode formality
established order code, method, policy *(plan of action)*, practice *(custom)*, practice *(procedure)*

established patronage goodwill
established phenomenon fact
established popularity goodwill
established practice conduct, form *(arrangement)*, usage
established principle canon, maxim
established reputation goodwill
established rule law, principle *(axiom)*
established way of doing things custom
establisher developer, pioneer
establishing guilt incriminatory, inculpatory
establishment affirmance *(authentication)*, affirmation, birth *(beginning)*, building *(business of assembling)*, building *(structure)*, business *(commercial enterprise)*, company *(enterprise)*, composition *(makeup)*, concern *(business establishment)*, corporation, corroboration, creation, enactment, facility *(institution)*, firm, formation, foundation *(organization)*, household, industry *(business)*, inhabitation *(place of dwelling)*, installation, institute, market *(business)*, onset *(commencement)*, organization *(association)*, preparation, proof, store *(business)*, structure *(edifice)*
establishment of a firm incorporation *(formation of a business entity)*
establishment of an ambassador embassy
establishment of foreign residence immigration
establishment of proof corroboration
estate assets, demesne, domain *(land owned)*, dower, effects, freehold, holding *(property owned)*, homestead, paraphernalia *(personal belongings)*, parcel, possessions, property *(land)*, property *(possessions)*, rating, real estate, realty, remainder *(estate in property)*, resource, substance *(material possessions)*
estate for a fixed term leasehold
estate for a fixed term of years leasehold
estate for life freehold
estate in fee freehold
estate in realty leasehold
estate owner landholder, landowner
esteem appreciate *(value)*, character *(reputation)*, consideration *(sympathetic regard)*, credit *(recognition)*, deem, defer *(yield in judgment)*, deference, eminence, homage, honor *(outward respect)*, honor, indorsement, interest *(concern)*, mention *(tribute)*, opine, prestige, rate, recommend, recommendation, regard *(hold in esteem)*, reputation, respect, status, surmise, value, worth
esteem of no account disdain
esteem of small account disdain
esteem slightly flout
esteemed famous, important *(significant)*, influential, outstanding *(prominent)*, popular, reputable, valuable
estimable appreciable, considerable, determinable *(ascertainable)*, high-minded, honest, laudable, meritorious, moral, popular, premium, reputable, upright, valuable
estimableness honesty, integrity
estimate appraisal, assess *(appraise)*,

assessment *(estimation)*, bid, calculate, charge *(assess)*, computation, concept, determine, diagnose, estimation *(calculation)*, evaluate, gauge, generalization, guess, idea, judge, judgment *(discernment)*, measure, measurement, opine, opinion *(belief)*, perception, presume, presuppose, price, prognosis, rate, survey *(poll)*, value, weigh
estimate incorrectly miscalculate, misconceive, misjudge
estimate relatively compare
estimate too highly overestimate
estimated approximate, inexact
estimated by comparison comparative
estimated expenditures budget
estimated value appraisal
estimation appraisal, appreciation *(perception)*, character *(reputation)*, computation, conclusion *(determination)*, consideration *(sympathetic regard)*, diagnosis, discrimination *(differentiation)*, estimate *(approximate cost)*, generalization, homage, honor *(outward respect)*, idea, judgment *(discernment)*, measurement, notion, observation, opinion *(belief)*, prestige, price, rating, regard *(esteem)*, reputation, respect, value, worth
estimator juror
estop balk, ban, bar *(hinder)*, block, check *(restrain)*, constrict *(inhibit)*, debar, forestall, halt, hamper, impede, inhibit, obstruct, preclude, prevent, toll *(stop)*
estoppage end *(termination)*, halt
estoppel bar *(obstruction)*, check *(bar)*, halt, impediment, obstacle, prohibition
estrange antagonize, disaffect
estranged hostile, inimical, irreconcilable, solitary
estrangement feud, fight *(argument)*, rift *(disagreement)*, separation, umbrage
etch delineate
eternal constant, continual *(perpetual)*, durable, immutable, incessant, infinite, permanent, perpetual
eternally ad infinitum
eternalness indestructibility, perpetuity
eternity perpetuity
eternization preservation
eternize perpetuate
ethereal immaterial, incorporeal, intangible
ethical high-minded, honest, incorruptible, just, law-abiding, meritorious, moral, proper, reputable, right *(correct)*, scrupulous, upright
ethical judgment conscience, responsibility *(conscience)*
ethical philosophy casuistry, conscience
ethical self conscience
ethicality propriety *(correctness)*
ethics conduct, conscience, principle *(virtue)*
ethnic group blood, family *(common ancestry)*, race
ethnic stock race
ethnicity family *(common ancestry)*
ethology casuistry
ethos character *(personal quality)*,

temperament
etiquette conduct, courtesy, custom, decorum, formality, manner *(behavior)*, propriety *(correctness)*, respect
étranger alien
etymology origination
eulogistic favorable *(expressing approval)*
eulogistic speech mention *(tribute)*
eulogistical favorable *(expressing approval)*
eulogize belaud, honor
eulogy laudation, mention *(tribute)*
euphemism bombast
euphuism fustian, rhetoric *(insincere language)*
euphuistic turgid
eurhythmy proportion
evacuate abandon *(physically leave)*, alight, depart, deplete, dislocate, dislodge, eliminate *(eradicate)*, eliminate *(exclude)*, flee, leave *(depart)*, outpour, part *(leave)*, purge *(purify)*, retreat, secede, vacate *(leave)*, vacate *(void)*, withdraw
evacuation abandonment *(desertion)*, egress, flight, outflow, removal, resignation *(relinquishment)*
évacué discard
evade abscond, bilk, circumvent, default, dishonor *(refuse to pay)*, elude, equivocate, escape, eschew, fail *(neglect)*, flee, hedge, ignore, palter, parry, pettifog, prevaricate, refrain, shirk, shun, spurn, tergiversate
evade the truth palter, prevaricate
evader fugitive
evadere escape
evagari maneuver
evagation vagrancy
evaluate assess *(appraise)*, calculate, consider, estimate, gauge, measure, ponder, rate, screen *(select)*, survey *(examine)*, weigh
evaluated ad valorem
evaluation appraisal, census, computation, concept, conclusion *(determination)*, determination, discretion *(power of choice)*, discrimination *(differentiation)*, estimate *(approximate cost)*, estimation *(calculation)*, idea, inspection, judgment *(discernment)*, judgment *(formal court decree)*, opinion *(belief)*, par *(face amount)*, perception, poll *(canvass)*, rating, trial *(experiment)*
evaluator juror
evanesce disappear, dissipate *(spread out)*, dissolve *(disperse)*, perish
evanescence mortality
evanescent elusive, ephemeral, indiscernible, temporary, transient, transitory, volatile
evanescere disappear
evaporable volatile
evaporate consume, disappear, lessen, perish
evasion abstention, artifice, avoidance *(evasion)*, color *(deceptive appearance)*, concealment, dereliction, duplicity, falsehood, flight, loophole, nonpayment, nonperformance, pettifoggery, pretext, privacy, ruse, salvo, sophistry, story *(falsehood)*, stratagem, subterfuge
evasion of duty default, infidelity, infraction, maladministration, nonperformance

evasion of truth false pretense

evasive allusive, clandestine, disingenuous, elusive, furtive, indefinite, machiavellian, noncommittal, reluctant, sly, stealthy, surreptitious, unresponsive, vague

evasive action avoidance (evasion)

evasive reasoning sophistry

evasiveness privacy

evellere eradicate, extract

even adjust (regulate), coequal, coextensive, commensurable, comparable (equivalent), compensate (counterbalance), equal, equivalent, impartial, notwithstanding, placid, precise, proportionate, regular (orderly), uniform

even balance equipoise

even more a fortiori

even tenor regularity

even the score settle

even though regardless

even-handed dispassionate, unprejudiced

even-handedness candor (impartiality)

even-sided coextensive

even-tempered dispassionate

evenhanded equal, equitable, fair (just), honest, impartial, just, law-abiding, nonpartisan, open-minded

evenhanded justice fairness, right (righteousness)

evenhandedly fairly (impartially)

evenhandedness disinterest (lack of prejudice), equity (justice), fairness

evenire result

evenly fairly (impartially)

evenly balanced impartial

evenness candor (impartiality), composure, equipoise, par (equality), regularity, uniformity

event chance (fortuity), development (outgrowth), experience (encounter), fact, happening, incident, landmark (significant change), occasion, occurrence, particular

eventful cardinal (outstanding), critical (crucial), stellar

events circumstances

eventual forthcoming, future, pending (imminent), prospective, subsequent, ultimate

eventuality conclusion (outcome), consequence (conclusion), development (outgrowth), occurrence, outcome, outgrowth, result

eventually in due course

eventuate accrue (arise), arise (occur), arise (originate), crystallize, ensue, result, supervene

eventuation denouement, development (outgrowth), effect, outcome, outgrowth

eventus effect, event

ever-abiding perpetual

ever-present chronic, ubiquitous

ever-victorious invincible

ever-widening cumulative (increasing)

everchanging capricious, protean

everlasting chronic, continual (perpetual), durable, incessant, indestructible, infallible, infinite, infrangible, permanent, perpetual, perpetuity, persistent, stable

everlastingness indestructibility

evermore now and forever

eversio subversion

evertere overturn, subvert, upset

every collective

every bit throughout (all over)

everyday common (customary), conventional, customary, familiar (customary), household (familiar), mediocre, mundane, nondescript, normal (regular), prevailing (current), prevalent, prosaic, regular (conventional), repeated, routine, typical, usual

everything entirety, sum (total), totality, whole

everywhere rampant

evict deport (banish), depose (remove), dislocate, dislodge, displace (remove), dispossess, divest, eliminate (exclude), expel

evictio eviction, recovery (repossession)

eviction banishment, deportation, discharge (dismissal), disqualification (rejection), expropriation (divestiture), expulsion, foreclosure, forfeiture (act of forfeiting), ostracism, ouster, proscription, rejection

evidence adduce, bear (adduce), certification (attested copy), certify (attest), cite (state), clue, connote, corroboration, data, disclose, display, document, documentation, evince, exemplify, exhibit, exhibit, expression (manifestation), ground, indicate, indication, indicia, manifest, manifestation, notarize, produce (offer to view), proof, record, signify (denote), substantiate, sustain (confirm), symptom, testimony, token, verify (swear)

evidence against confutation

evidence by a competent witness testimony

evidence from impersonal knowledge hearsay

evidence in support of testimony

evidence of a debt bond

evidence on oath affidavit, affirmance (legal affirmation)

evidence on the other side confutation

evidence-seeking cross-examination

evidenced solely by speech parol

evidences of debts securities

evidences of obligations securities

evidens evident, manifest, palpable, undeniable

evident apparent (perceptible), appreciable, certain (positive)

évident clear (apparent)

evident clear (apparent), coherent (clear), comprehensible, conclusive (determinative), conspicuous, convincing, definite, demonstrable, discernible, distinct (clear), explicit, gross (flagrant), lucid, manifest, naked (perceptible), obvious, open (in sight), ostensible, overt, palpable, patent, perceivable, perceptible, positive (incontestable), prominent, public (known), salient, scrutable, tangible, unambiguous, undeniable, unequivocal, unmistakable

evident demonstration proof

evidential apparent (presumptive), categorical, certain (positive), cogent, conclusive (settled), deductive, definite, documentary, presumptive, probative, reliable

evidential record documentation

evidential writing instrument (document)

evidentiary probative

evidentiary record document, documentation

evidently fairly (clearly)

evil arrant (onerous), bad (offensive), contemptible, delinquency (misconduct), delinquent (guilty of a misdeed), depraved, detriment, diabolic, harm, harmful, heinous, immoral, inexpiable, iniquitous, lethal, malevolent, malicious, malignant, mischief, nefarious, objectionable, odious, peccant (culpable), pernicious, perverse, pestilent, profane, profligate (corrupt), reprehensible, sinister, tainted (corrupted), vice, vicious, wrong

evil adumbration premonition

evil behavior delinquency (misconduct), offense, perversion

evil conduct mischief

evil deed misdeed, offense

evil disposition malice

evil fame infamy

evil fortune calamity, misfortune

evil intent malice

evil lot calamity

evil luck calamity

evil-doing delinquent (guilty of a misdeed), diabolic

evil-minded cruel, delinquent (guilty of a misdeed), diabolic, dissolute, malevolent, malicious, malignant, perverse, profligate (corrupt), reprobate, spiteful, vicious

evil-speaking calumnious, malediction

evildoer convict, criminal, delinquent, embezzler, felon, hoodlum, malefactor, offender, outlaw, vandal, wrongdoer

evildoing felonious, misdoing

evince adduce, allude, attest, bare, bear (adduce), certify (attest), cite (state), convey (communicate), demonstrate (establish), depict, disclose, disinter, display, divulge, evidence, exemplify, exhibit, expose, indicate, manifest, produce (offer to view), prove, reveal, signify (denote)

evincement appearance (emergence), expression (manifestation), indication, manifestation, symptom

evincible ascertainable, convincing

evincive explicit

eviscerate bowdlerize, debilitate, extract

evitare elude

evocare elicit, evoke

evocative moving (evoking emotion)

evoke bait (lure), cause, coax, depict, disinter, educe, elicit, extract, generate, inspire, originate, provoke, recall (remember), represent (portray), urge

evolution civilization, course, development (progression), maturity, nascency, preparation, start

evolve arise (originate), avail (bring about), bear (yield), build (construct), change, convert (change use), develop, devise (invent), educe, forge (produce), germinate, make, manufacture, mature

evolved derivative

evolved from dependent

evolvement development *(progression)*, growth *(evolution)*, nascency
evolvere evolve
evulgare reveal
evulgate bare, propagate *(spread)*, reveal
evulgation divulgation, notification, publicity
evulse disinter
evulsion avulsion, removal
ex concesso a priori
ex officio clerical
ex parte determinative
exacerbare exacerbate
exacerbate compound, distress, expand, harm, heighten *(augment)*, incense, intensify, irritate, prejudice *(injure)*, provoke
exacerbation damage
exact absolute *(conclusive)*, accurate, acquire *(secure)*, actual, appropriate, attach *(seize)*, bind *(obligate)*, brief, call *(demand)*, certain *(particular)*, certain *(specific)*, charge *(assess)*, clear *(apparent)*, close *(rigorous)*, coerce, coherent *(clear)*, command, compel, constrain *(compel)*, decree, definite, definitive, demand, detailed, diligent, dun, enforce, enjoin, excise *(levy a tax)*, explicit, express, extort, factual, faithful *(true to fact)*, genuine, honest, identical, impose *(enforce)*, insist, instruct *(direct)*, laconic, levy, literal, meticulous, narrow, necessitate, need, precise, prescribe, press *(constrain)*, punctilious, punctual, realistic, reliable, request, require *(compel)*, right *(direct)*, rigid, said, specific, strict, stringent, subtle *(refined)*, systematic, tax *(levy)*, tax *(overwork)*, true *(authentic)*, unambiguous, undistorted, verbatim
exact a charge assess *(tax)*
exact a fine mulct *(fine)*
exact a penalty condemn *(punish)*, discipline *(punish)*, fine, penalize
exact a toll assess *(tax)*
exact amount face amount
exact as due claim *(demand)*
exact by force extort
exact copy facsimile
exact data information *(facts)*
exact meaning definition
exact moment point *(period of time)*
exact payment collect *(recover money)*
exact retribution condemn *(punish)*, discipline *(punish)*, fine, penalize, punish
exact statement definition
exact tribute toll *(exact payment)*
exacted positive *(prescribed)*
exacter extortionist
exacting circumspect, confiscatory, conscientious, critical *(faultfinding)*, dictatorial, draconian, faithful *(diligent)*, ironclad, mercenary, meticulous, onerous, operose, oppressive, painstaking, punctilious, punctual, rigid, severe, strict, stringent, uncompromising
exactingness particularity
exactio expulsion
exaction assessment *(levy)*, assumption *(seizure)*, blackmail, charge *(cost)*, claim *(legal demand)*, coercion, dun, duress, duty *(tax)*, enforcement, excise, expense *(cost)*, extortion, force *(compul-

sion)*, forfeiture *(act of forfeiting)*, levy, price, request, requirement, requisition, tax, toll *(effect)*, toll *(tax)*, ultimatum
exaction by oppression extortion
exaction of penalty condemnation *(punishment)*, conviction *(finding of guilt)*
exactitude caution *(vigilance)*, diligence *(care)*, honesty, particularity, rigor, veracity
exactly faithfully
exactly alike identical
exactly like same
exactly the same identical
exactment assessment *(levy)*, charge *(cost)*, duty *(tax)*, excise, expense *(cost)*, fee *(charge)*, levy, tax
exactness caution *(vigilance)*, diligence *(care)*, particularity, regularity, rigor, truth, veracity
exactus exact
exaggerare accumulate *(enlarge)*, heighten *(augment)*, magnify
exaggerate cloak, compound, distort, enhance, enlarge, expand, falsify, inflate, intensify, invent *(falsify)*, magnify, misinform, misrepresent, overestimate, slant
exaggerated excessive, histrionic, inflated *(overestimated)*, inordinate, lurid, outrageous, unreasonable
exaggerated likeness caricature
exaggerated statement overstatement
exaggerating cumulative *(intensifying)*
exaggeration bombast, caricature, catachresis, color *(deceptive appearance)*, distortion, falsification, histrionics, hyperbole, inflation *(increase)*, misrepresentation, overstatement, parody, rodomontade, travesty
exaggerative inflated *(overestimated)*
exagitare harass, plague
exalt belaud, compound, elevate, honor, magnify, overestimate, parlay *(exploit successfully)*, promote *(advance)*, raise *(advance)*, recognize *(acknowledge)*, recommend, regard *(hold in esteem)*
exaltation distinction *(reputation)*, elevation, eminence, homage, honor *(outward respect)*, laudation, mention *(tribute)*, precedence, prestige, promotion *(advancement)*, remembrance *(commemoration)*
exalted famous, irreprehensible, magnanimous, outstanding *(prominent)*, prominent, renowned, salient
examinant detective
examination analysis, appraisal, collation, consideration *(contemplation)*, contemplation, cross-examination, deliberation, discretion *(power of choice)*, discrimination *(differentiation)*, experiment, habeas corpus, hearing, indagation, inquest, inquiry *(request for information)*, inquiry *(systematic investigation)*, inspection, interrogation, investigation, judgment *(discernment)*, observation, probe, proposal *(report)*, question *(inquiry)*, regard *(attention)*, research, scrutiny, surveillance, test, treatment, trial *(experiment)*, trial *(legal proceeding)*
examination for qualification for

jury service voir dire
examination for the purpose of ascertaining facts discovery
examination into facts or principles inquiry *(request for information)*
examine analyze, audit, canvass, check *(inspect)*, consider, criticize *(evaluate)*, cross-examine, deliberate, delve, discern *(detect with the senses)*, frisk, inquire, investigate, judge, monitor, muse, observe *(watch)*, overlook *(superintend)*, oversee, peruse, ponder, probe, reason *(conclude)*, research, review, revise, scrutinize, search, study, treat *(process)*, try *(conduct a trial)*, weigh
examine a question debate
examine a source consult *(seek information from)*
examine by argument debate
examine by inspection search
examine carefully deliberate
examine closely concentrate *(pay attention)*, focus, frisk, notice *(observe)*
examine critically analyze, diagnose
examine financial accounts audit
examine in detail investigate
examine intently concern *(care)*, frisk, notice *(observe)*
examine judicially hear *(give a legal hearing)*, try *(conduct a trial)*
examine searchingly canvass
examine secretely spy
examine the accounts officially audit
examine the particulars investigate
examine the witnesses hear *(give a legal hearing)*
examine with care and accuracy investigate
examinee contender
examiner detective, juror
examiner of business accounts comptroller
example comment, criterion, cross section, exemplar, illustration, indicant, instance, model, paradigm, paragon, pattern, precedent, prototype, sample, semblance, specimen, standard
examples selection *(collection)*
exanimate dead, deceased, defunct, insensible, languid, lifeless *(dead)*
exanimis dead
exanimus dead, lifeless *(dead)*
exasperate aggravate *(annoy)*, annoy, badger, bait *(harass)*, discommode, discompose, disturb, incense, irritate, perturb, pique, plague, provoke
exasperating provocative, vexatious
exasperation provocation
exauctorare disband
exaudire overhear
excavate disinter, extract
excavation evulsion
excedere leave *(depart)*
exceed carouse, outbalance, outweigh, overestimate, overlap, overreach, overstep, predominate *(outnumber)*, prevail *(triumph)*, surmount, surpass, transcend, trespass
exceed in importance outweigh
exceed in value outweigh
exceeding drastic, excessive, extreme *(exaggerated)*, inordinate, intemperate
exceeding propriety undue *(excessive)*
exceeding the bounds of modera-

tion extreme *(exaggerated)*
exceeding the law illegal, illicit
exceeding the usual extraordinary
exceeding what is usual excessive
exceedingly ardent perfervid
excel beat *(defeat)*, outweigh, prevail *(triumph)*, surmount, surpass, transcend
excellence caliber *(quality)*, efficiency, merit, prowess *(ability)*, right *(righteousness)*, significance, skill, value, worth
excellence of behavior courtesy
excellency primacy
excellent cardinal *(outstanding)*, competent, exemplary, felicitous, illustrious, laudable, meritorious, noteworthy, outstanding *(prominent)*, preferable, premium, professional *(stellar)*, proficient, rare, select, sterling, superlative, unimpeachable, valuable
excellent judgment sagacity
excellent prospect likelihood
exceller paragon
excellere surpass, transcend
excelling absolute *(ideal)*, outstanding *(prominent)*, preferable, prime *(most valuable)*
except bar *(exclude)*, eliminate *(exclude)*, exclude, object, remove *(eliminate)*, reserve, save, unless
excepted barred, inadmissible, privileged
excepting palliative *(excusing)*, save, unless
excepting that only
exceptio exception *(exclusion)*, plea, qualification *(condition)*, reservation *(condition)*
exception clause, condition *(contingent provision)*, criticism, demurrer, disagreement, disapproval, discharge *(release from obligation)*, disparagement, dispensation *(exception)*, exemption, extenuating circumstances, immunity, irregularity, license, loophole, modification, nonconformity, objection, phenomenon *(unusual occurrence)*, qualification *(condition)*, quirk *(idiosyncrasy)*, remonstrance, removal, reprimand, reservation *(condition)*, salvo, stricture, variance *(exemption)*
exception in favor of dispensation *(exception)*
exception to a pleading demurrer
exceptionable blameful, objectionable, peccable, reprehensible, sinister, unacceptable, undesirable
exceptional atypical, best, extraordinary, individual, infrequent, irregular *(not usual)*, notable, noteworthy, novel, original *(creative)*, outstanding *(prominent)*, particular *(specific)*, peculiar *(distinctive)*, portentous *(eliciting amazement)*, preferential, prime *(most valuable)*, prodigious *(amazing)*, rare, remarkable, select, singular, special, specific, sterling, superior *(excellent)*, unaccustomed, uncanny, uncommon, unique, unprecedented, unusual
exceptionality nonconformity
exceptionem facere demur
exceptious fractious, litigious, querulous, restive
excerpere extract
excerpt choose, digest *(summarize)*,

extract, part *(portion)*, quote, select
excerption excerpt
excess balance *(amount in excess)*, boom *(prosperity)*, debauchery, exaggeration, expendable, greed, needless, nonessential, overage, plethora, redundancy, remainder *(estate in property)*, remainder *(remaining part)*, residual, residuary, superfluous, surfeit, surplus, unnecessary, vice
excessive brutal, disproportionate, drastic, egregious, excess, exorbitant, expendable, extreme *(exaggerated)*, fanatical, gluttonous, gratuitous *(unwarranted)*, harsh, hot-blooded, inflated *(overestimated)*, inordinate, intemperate, needless, onerous, outrageous, prodigal, profuse, rampant, redundant, residuary, superlative, unconscionable, undue *(excessive)*, unendurable, unnecessary, unreasonable, unrestrained *(not repressed)*, unwarranted, usurious
excessive amount surfeit
excessive burden surcharge
excessive charge premium *(excess value)*, surcharge
excessive demand imposition *(excessive burden)*
excessive drinking dipsomania
excessive interest usury
excessive rate usury
excessive use abuse *(corrupt practice)*, waste
excessively unduly
excessively bold presumptuous
excessively confident presumptuous
excessively critical particular *(exacting)*
excessively frugal parsimonious
excessiveness debauchery, dipsomania, exaggeration, redundancy
exchange barter, business *(commerce)*, change, commerce, communication *(discourse)*, commute, conference, contact *(association)*, conversation, convert *(change use)*, cover *(substitute)*, deal, deal, dealings, displace *(replace)*, finance, handle *(trade)*, interchange, market *(business)*, market place, mercantile, mutuality, novation, quid pro quo, reciprocate, reciprocity, replace, replacement, return *(respond)*, revise, sale, sell, store *(business)*, subrogation, succedaneum, trade *(commerce)*, trade, vary
exchange blows fight *(battle)*, retaliate
exchange fisticuffs fight *(battle)*
exchange for money liquidate *(convert into cash)*
exchange ideas converse
exchange in commerce handle *(trade)*
exchange letters correspond *(communicate)*
exchange observations confer *(consult)*, consult *(ask advice of)*, counsel, discourse, discuss
exchange of blows fight *(battle)*
exchange of commodities trade *(commerce)*
exchange of letters correspondence *(communication by letters)*
exchange of obligations innovation
exchange of views conversation, discourse, interview, meeting *(conference)*,

negotiation, panel *(discussion group)*, parley
exchange opinions discuss, respond, speak
exchange penalties commute
exchange value price
exchange views converse
exchangeable assignable, convertible, correlative, heritable, marketable, negotiable
exchequer treasury
excidere eradicate, extirpate
excipere disqualify, except *(exclude)*, overhear, succeed *(follow)*
excisable ad valorem
excise assess *(tax)*, bowdlerize, cancel, delete, diminish, duty *(tax)*, expunge, imposition *(tax)*, levy, redact, reject, tariff *(duties)*, tax, toll *(tax)*
exciseman assessor
excision cancellation, expulsion, rejection, removal
excitability passion
excitable demonstrative *(expressive of emotion)*, fractious, hot-blooded, restive, volatile
excitant catalyst, stimulus
excitare evoke, inspire, spirit, stimulate
excitation aggravation *(exacerbation)*, dispatch *(promptness)*, instigation, provocation
excitation of feeling affection
excitation of feelings ardor
excite aggravate *(annoy)*, agitate *(activate)*, bait *(harass)*, bait *(lure)*, discompose, engender, evoke, exacerbate, foment, harass, incense, incite, interest, perturb, prompt, provoke, spirit, stimulate
excite anger irritate
excite disapprobation brand *(stigmatize)*, denounce *(condemn)*
excite dislike repel *(disgust)*
excite expectation promise *(raise expectations)*
excite hate antagonize
excite hatred incense
excite impatience irritate
excite indignation bait *(harass)*, incense
excite the attention occupy *(engage)*
excited eager, ecstatic, fervent, frenetic, restive, vehement
excitement ardor, commotion, furor, interest *(concern)*, passion, provocation, turmoil
exciter catalyst, demagogue
exciting moving *(evoking emotion)*, offensive *(taking the initiative)*, provocative, sapid
exciting fear formidable
excitive moving *(evoking emotion)*
exclaim interject, observe *(remark)*, proclaim
exclaim against censure, denounce *(condemn)*, disapprove *(condemn)*, expostulate, inveigh, protest
exclamation confession, proclamation, remark, statement
exclude abrogate *(rescind)*, ban, block, censor, clog, condemn *(ban)*, debar, deport *(banish)*, discharge *(dismiss)*, dislodge, displace *(remove)*, disqualify, eject *(expel)*, eliminate *(exclude)*, estrange, expatriate, expel, for-

bid, isolate, omit, outlaw, preclude, preempt, prohibit, proscribe *(prohibit)*, refuse, reject, relegate, remove *(eliminate)*, renounce, repudiate, restrict, screen *(select)*, seclude, select, separate, sequester *(seclude)*

exclude from inheritance disinherit
exclude from the profession of law disbar
excluded barred, derelict *(abandoned)*, exempt, inadmissible, ineligible, privileged
excludere debar, exclude
excluding omission
exclusio exclusion
exclusion bar *(obstruction)*, blockade *(limitation)*, boycott, control *(restriction)*, deportation, disapprobation, dismissal *(discharge)*, dispensation *(exception)*, disqualification *(rejection)*, disregard *(unconcern)*, expulsion, omission, ostracism, ouster, preemption, prohibition, proscription, refusal, rejection, removal, renunciation, repudiation
exclusion from commerce embargo
exclusion from favor disgrace
exclusion of entitled owner disseisin
exclusion of workers lockout
exclusionary exclusive *(limited)*
exclusive certain *(particular)*, certain *(specific)*, distinctive, only *(sole)*, particular *(individual)*, preferential, private *(not public)*, privy, prohibitive *(restrictive)*, proprietary, restrictive, select, several *(separate)*, singular, specific
exclusive application diligence *(care)*
exclusive area circuit
exclusive attention diligence *(care)*, obsession
exclusive competition primary
exclusive contest primary
exclusive control monopoly
exclusive election primary
exclusive license patent
exclusive of save
exclusive political competition primary
exclusive political contest primary
exclusive possession holding *(property owned)*, monopoly
exclusive privilege patent, prerogative
exclusive privilege of publication copyright
exclusive privilege of publication and sale copyright
exclusive privilege to carry on a traffic monopoly
exclusive right monopoly, patent, possession *(ownership)*, prerogative
exclusive right of production copyright
exclusive study diligence *(care)*
exclusive thought diligence *(care)*
exclusive title patent
exclusively only, solely *(singly)*
exclusory exclusive *(limited)*, prohibitive *(restrictive)*
excogitare conjure, contrive, devise *(invent)*, invent *(produce for the first time)*, program
excogitate conceive *(invent)*, conjure, deliberate, frame *(formulate)*, invent *(produce for the first time)*, ponder, ra-

tionalize, reason *(conclude)*, reflect *(ponder)*, scheme, study
excogitatio contrivance
excogitation contemplation, deliberation, idea, reflection *(thought)*
excogitative deliberate
excolere develop
excommunicate condemn *(ban)*, debar, eliminate *(exclude)*, exclude, expel, isolate, relegate, seclude
excommunication banishment, expulsion, ostracism, rejection
excorciating caustic
excoriate castigate, censure, denounce *(condemn)*, deprecate, disapprove *(condemn)*, lash *(attack verbally)*, reproach
excoriating scathing
excoriation bad repute, blame *(culpability)*, denunciation, disapprobation
excrescence outgrowth
excrescent superfluous
excrete exude, purge *(purify)*
excruciare harrow
excruciate badger, harass
excruciating caustic, insufferable, painful, severe
exculpable blameless, inculpable, not guilty, palliative *(excusing)*
exculpate absolve, acquit, clear, discharge *(liberate)*, excuse, exonerate, extenuate, forgive, free, justify, liberate, palliate *(excuse)*, purge *(wipe out by atonement)*, release, remit *(release from penalty)*, vindicate
exculpated acquitted, blameless, clear *(free from criminal charges)*
exculpating palliative *(excusing)*
exculpation absolution, acquittal, amnesty, compurgation, discharge *(liberation)*, discharge *(release from obligation)*, dispensation *(exception)*, excuse, exoneration, immunity, innocence, justification, liberation, release, remission
exculpatory defensible, mitigating
exculpatory excuse alibi
excurse detour
excursion detour
excursive circuitous, devious, indirect, labyrinthine, tangential
excursus appendix *(supplement)*, digression, discourse, hornbook, pandect *(treatise)*
excusabilis pardonable
excusable allowable, defensible, justifiable, pardonable
excusal condonation, release, waiver
excusare exculpate, excuse, justify
excusatio excuse, justification, plea
excusatory palliative *(excusing)*
excuse absolve, acquit, alibi, clear, clemency, compurgation, condone, cover *(pretext)*, discharge *(release from obligation)*, discharge *(liberate)*, discharge *(release from obligation)*, dispensation *(exception)*, exclude, exculpate, exonerate, exoneration, extenuate, forgive, free, grace, justification, justify, loophole, overlook *(excuse)*, pardon, pretense *(pretext)*, pretext, purge *(wipe out by atonement)*, rationalize, reason *(basis)*, release, release, remit *(release from penalty)*, stratagem, subterfuge, vindicate
excuse oneself decline *(reject)*
excused clear *(free from criminal*

charges)*, exempt, free *(relieved from a burden)*, immune, privileged
excuser apologist
excusing mitigating
execrable arrant *(onerous)*, bad *(offensive)*, blameful, blameworthy, contemptible, contemptuous, depraved, diabolic, heinous, loathsome, malignant, nefarious, objectionable, obnoxious, odious, offensive *(offending)*, outrageous, peccant *(culpable)*, repulsive, scandalous
execrableness disrepute
execrate blame, castigate, censure, condemn *(blame)*, contemn, denounce *(condemn)*, proscribe *(denounce)*, reprimand
execration alienation *(estrangement)*, aspersion, blasphemy, condemnation *(blame)*, condemnation *(punishment)*, denunciation, disapprobation, expletive, imprecation, malediction, obloquy, odium, outcry, phillipic, profanity, revilement, slander
execrative profane
execute abide, accomplish, apply *(put in practice)*, certify *(attest)*, close *(agree)*, collect *(recover money)*, commit *(perpetrate)*, compose, conclude *(complete)*, conduct, consummate, countersign, culminate, discharge *(perform)*, dispatch *(dispose of)*, dispatch *(put to death)*, effectuate, enforce, engender, exercise *(discharge a function)*, fabricate *(construct)*, fulfill, function, garnish, generate, handle *(manage)*, implement, impose *(enforce)*, kill *(murder)*, levy, make, manage, obey, observe *(obey)*, officiate, operate, oversee, perfect, perform *(adhere to)*, perpetrate, produce *(manufacture)*, pursue *(carry on)*, render *(administer)*, render *(deliver)*, sign, slay, transact, undertake
execute a sentence condemn *(punish)*, discipline *(punish)*, penalize
execute judgment discipline *(punish)*, penalize
execute justice condemn *(punish)*, discipline *(punish)*
executed complete *(ended)*, fully executed *(signed)*
executed and delivered writing instrument *(document)*
executed with care accurate
executed with exactness elaborate
executed with proper formalities valid
execution act *(undertaking)*, action *(performance)*, administration, assassination, attachment *(seizure)*, capital punishment, commission *(act)*, consequence *(conclusion)*, course, discharge *(performance)*, dispatch *(act of putting to death)*, distraint, enforcement, fait accompli, finality, fruition, garnishment, infliction, killing, manufacture, operation, realization, sequestration, transaction, treatment
execution of sentence conviction *(finding of guilt)*
executions dealings
executive administrator, director, employer, official, principal *(director)*
executive arm management *(supervision)*
executive charge administration

executive committee commission *(agency)*, management *(directorate)*
executive office management *(directorate)*
executive officer official, principal *(director)*
executives authorities, management *(directorate)*, management *(supervision)*
executor director, fiduciary, procurator
exegesis comment, construction, content *(meaning)*, explanation, note *(brief comment)*
exegetic demonstrative *(illustrative)*, narrative
exegetical demonstrative *(illustrative)*, narrative, solvable
exemplar criterion, cross section
exemplar duplicate
exemplar example, illustration, instance
exemplar model
exemplar paradigm, paragon
exemplar pattern, prototype
exemplar representative *(example)*, sample, standard
exemplar transcript
exemplary absolute *(ideal)*, best, laudable, meritorious, moral, prime *(most valuable)*, professional *(stellar)*, representative, sterling
exempli gratia cross section
exemplification case *(example)*, clarification, comment, construction, corroboration, cross section, epitome, example, explanation, illustration, instance, sample
exemplify bear *(adduce)*, characterize, cite *(state)*, clarify, comment, define, demonstrate *(establish)*, depict, elucidate, evidence, explain, illustrate, personify, represent *(portray)*, signify *(denote)*
exemplifying a class typical
exemplum cross section, duplicate, example, exemplar, illustration, instance, model, pattern, precedent, prototype, sample, specimen, tenor, transcript
exempt acquit, clear *(unencumbered)*, clear, condone, discharge *(release from obligation)*, eliminate *(exclude)*, except *(exclude)*, exclude, excuse, forgive, free, immune, palliate *(excuse)*, privileged, purge *(wipe out by atonement)*, release, relieve *(free from burden)*, remit *(release from penalty)*, unbound
exempt from external authority free *(enjoying civil liberty)*, sovereign *(independent)*
exempted clear *(free from criminal charges)*, exempt, free *(relieved from a burden)*, privileged
exemptible justifiable
exempting palliative *(excusing)*
exemption clause, clemency, condonation, discharge *(liberation)*, discharge *(release from obligation)*, dispensation *(exception)*, exception *(exclusion)*, exclusion, excuse, franchise *(license)*, freedom, grace period, immunity, impunity, leave *(permission)*, privilege, probation, qualification *(condition)*, release, remission, reservation *(condition)*, respite *(reprieve)*, salvo
exemption from control latitude, liberty, suffrage

exemption from external control freedom, liberty
exemption from judgment impunity
exemption from law dispensation *(exception)*
exemption from penalty impunity
exemption from punishment immunity, impunity, pardon
exemption from restraint freedom, liberty, suffrage
exenterate eviscerate
exercere discipline *(control)*, exercise *(discharge a function)*, plague, ply, practice *(engage in)*
exercise apply *(put in practice)*, campaign, commission *(act)*, discipline *(training)*, employ *(make use of)*, endeavor, exert, exploit *(make use of)*, labor, officiate, operate, ply, practice *(train by repetition)*, problem, resort, transaction, undertaking *(enterprise)*, wield, work *(effort)*
exercise an option elect *(choose)*
exercise authority command, dictate, direct *(supervise)*, govern, handle *(manage)*, manage, police, prescribe, rule *(govern)*
exercise charge over superintend
exercise critical judgment compare
exercise direction over discipline *(control)*, handle *(manage)*, hold *(possess)*
exercise discretion discern *(discriminate)*, distinguish, elect *(choose)*
exercise discrimination differentiate, distinguish
exercise exclusive rights monopolize
exercise federal authority over federalize *(place under federal control)*
exercise influence lobby, persuade
exercise influence over induce, prejudice *(influence)*, prevail upon
exercise influence upon prejudice *(influence)*, prevail upon
exercise influence with prevail upon
exercise judgment adjudge, gauge, rule *(decide)*
exercise judicial authority adjudicate
exercise of the intellect reflection *(thought)*
exercise of will volition
exercise one's choice cast *(register)*, choose
exercise one's discretion choose
exercise one's option adopt, choose
exercise one's options cast *(register)*
exercise one's preference choose
exercise power over force *(coerce)*, govern, handle *(manage)*, operate
exercise self-control refrain
exercise supervision direct *(supervise)*, preside
exercise supervision over superintend
exercise the function of legislation legislate
exercise the judgment determine
exercise the right of suffrage vote
exercise the will choose
exercising commission *(act)*
exercising reason rational
exercitatio practice *(procedure)*
exercitation course, use
exert apply *(put in practice)*, expend *(consume)*, operate, wield

exert authority federalize *(place under federal control)*, govern, handle *(manage)*, police, rule *(govern)*
exert effort endeavor
exert energy labor
exert federal control federalize *(place under federal control)*
exert influence affect, constrain *(compel)*, convince, incite, inspire, lobby, motivate, persuade, prejudice *(influence)*
exert one's energies strive
exert oneself attempt, endeavor, labor, persevere, strive, try *(attempt)*
exert oneself for pursue *(strive to gain)*
exert pressure bait *(lure)*, coax, incite, insist, lobby
exert pressure on browbeat
exertion campaign, effort, endeavor, industry *(activity)*, pressure, pursuit *(effort to secure)*, stress *(strain)*, struggle, work *(effort)*
exhale emit
exhaurire exhaust *(try all possibilities)*
exhaust conclude *(complete)*, consume, debilitate, deplete, disable, dissipate *(expend foolishly)*, emit, expend *(consume)*, outlet, outpour, overdraw, spend
exhausted inadequate, languid, lost *(taken away)*, otiose, powerless, unproductive, unsound *(not strong)*, vacant, vacuous
exhaustible destructible
exhausting operose, oppressive
exhaustion consumption, decrement, impuissance, insufficiency, privation, prostration, waste, wear and tear
exhaustive absolute *(complete)*, complete *(all-embracing)*, comprehensive, definitive, detailed, full, gross *(total)*, inclusive, intensive, omnibus, outright, plenary, radical *(extreme)*, thorough, unmitigated
exhaustive inquiry analysis, examination *(study)*, hearing, indagation, judgment *(discernment)*
exhaustive study indagation, investigation, probe
exhaustive tract pandect *(treatise)*
exhaustiveness entirety
exhaustless infallible, infinite, innumerable
exheredare disinherit
exhibere exhibit
exhibit bare, bear *(adduce)*, brandish, cite *(state)*, demonstrate *(establish)*, denude, depict, disclose, disinter, display, document, documentation, evidence, evince, exemplify, expose, expression *(manifestation)*, flaunt, illustrate, manifest, manifestation, present *(introduce)*, produce *(offer to view)*, propound, unveil
exhibit boastfully flaunt
exhibit hostile intentions menace
exhibit in visible form embody
exhibit the differences between contrast
exhibited palpable
exhibiting equity equitable
exhibiting lust lewd
exhibiting pros and cons controversial
exhibiting purpose pertinacious
exhibition exhibit, expression *(mani-*

festation), manifestation, performance *(workmanship)*

exhibitionistic histrionic

exhibits evidence

exhibits submitted to jury evidence

exhilarate spirit

exhilaration ardor, enjoyment *(pleasure)*

exhort admonish *(advise),* admonish *(warn),* advocate, agitate *(activate),* bait *(harass),* bait *(lure),* caution, charge *(instruct on the law),* coax, coerce, confer *(consult),* enjoin, forewarn, incite, insist, motivate, notify, persuade, press *(beseech),* pressure, prevail upon, prompt, recommend, remonstrate, spirit, urge

exhort against dissuade, expostulate, protest

exhort to take heed caution

exhortation admonition, caution *(warning),* charge *(statement to the jury),* direction *(guidance),* discourse, guidance, harangue, inducement, instigation, monition *(warning),* persuasion, pressure, proposal *(suggestion),* recommendation, remonstrance, rhetoric *(skilled speech),* suggestion

exhortative hortative

exhortatory hortative

exhume disinter, remove *(eliminate)*

exigence exigency

exigency coercion, cornerstone, demand, desideratum, emergency, necessity, need *(deprivation),* paucity, poverty, predicament, prerequisite, pressure, priority, quagmire, requirement, situation, stress *(strain)*

exigent astringent, compulsory, critical *(crucial),* crucial, essential *(required),* grave *(important),* imperative, important *(urgent),* indispensable, insistent, mandatory, necessary *(required),* obligatory, particular *(exacting),* peremptory *(imperative),* requisite, severe, stringent, uncompromising, urgent

exigere expel, require *(compel)*

exiguitas insignificance

exiguity dearth, insufficiency, paucity

exiguous minimal, slight

exiguousness dearth, insufficiency

exiguus inconsiderable, slight

exile asylum *(hiding place),* banishment, bar *(exclude),* deport *(banish),* deportation, depose *(remove),* derelict, dislodge, displace *(remove),* eliminate *(exclude),* exclude, exclusion, expatriate, expel, expulsion, isolate, ostracism, pariah, rejection, relegate, removal, seclude, transport

exilement banishment, deportation, ostracism, rejection

eximere except *(exclude),* exclude, free

eximious illustrious, outstanding *(prominent)*

eximius special, superlative

exire issue *(send forth)*

exist continue *(persevere),* endure *(last),* last, lie *(be sustainable),* remain *(continue),* subsist

exist together coincide *(correspond),* concur *(coexist)*

exist uninterruptedly endure *(last)*

exist widely prevail *(be in force)*

exist without break endure *(last)*

existence entity, life *(period of existence),* materiality *(physical existence),* reality, survival

existenceless nonentity

existent actual, bodily, concrete, conscious *(awake),* corporeal, current, de facto, extant, instant, live *(conscious),* live *(existing),* present *(current),* substantial, substantive

existent thing fact

existimatio character *(reputation),* honor *(good reputation)*

existing actual, bodily, certain *(positive),* concrete, conscious *(awake),* current, de facto, definite, extant, live *(conscious),* present *(current),* substantial, substantive

existing as an independent entity autonomous *(independent)*

existing conditions status quo

existing for a short time ephemeral

existing from birth innate

existing in equity equitable

existing in fact de facto

existing state case *(set of circumstances),* posture *(situation),* status quo

exit alight, depart, disappear, egress, emerge, evacuate, issuance, issue *(send forth),* leave *(depart),* move *(alter position),* outlet, quit *(evacuate),* vacate *(leave)*

exitialis deadly, fatal, lethal

exitiosus pernicious

exitus egress, end *(termination),* event, outlet, result

exodus egress, flight, outflow

exomologesis confession

exonerate absolve, acquit, clear, condone, discharge *(liberate),* discharge *(release from obligation),* disencumber, exculpate, excuse, extenuate, extricate, forgive, free, justify, liberate, palliate *(excuse),* pardon, quit *(free of),* release, remit *(release from penalty),* vindicate

exonerated acquitted, blameless, clear *(free from criminal charges),* free *(relieved from a burden)*

exonerating circumstance justification

exonerating fact justification

exoneration absolution, acquittal, amnesty, compurgation, condonation, discharge *(liberation),* discharge *(release from obligation),* dispensation *(exception),* excuse, innocence, justification, liberation, pardon, release, remission

exorabilis placable

exorable charitable *(lenient),* lenient, placable

exorare prevail upon

exorbitance boom *(prosperity),* exaggeration, plethora

exorbitancy boom *(prosperity),* exaggeration, plethora

exorbitant excess, excessive, extreme *(exaggerated),* grandiose, inordinate, intemperate, needless, outrageous, profuse, prohibitive *(costly),* unconscionable, undue *(excessive),* unreasonable, usurious

exorbitant interest usury

exorbitantly unduly

exordial preliminary

exordium birth *(beginning)*

exordium genesis, inception, onset

(commencement), origination, outset, overture

exordium preamble

exordium preface, prelude, start

exornare embellish, garnish

exoteric coherent *(clear),* comprehensible, obvious, pellucid, perceivable, public *(known)*

exoterical coherent *(clear),* obvious

exotic nonconforming, unaccustomed, uncommon

expand accrue *(increase),* accumulate *(enlarge),* amplify, build *(augment),* compound, declaim, deploy, develop, elaborate, enhance, extend *(enlarge),* heighten *(augment),* increase, inflate, magnify, overestimate, parlay *(exploit successfully),* progress, spread, supplement

expand on comment

expand upon develop

expanded capacious, extensive, inflated *(enlarged)*

expanding cumulative *(increasing)*

expange deface

expanse area *(province),* area *(surface),* caliber *(measurement),* coverage *(scope),* degree *(magnitude),* extent, latitude, scope, space, territory

expansion accession *(enlargement),* advance *(increase),* advancement *(improvement),* area *(surface),* augmentation, bombast, boom *(increase),* boom *(prosperity),* development *(progression),* distortion, exaggeration, growth *(evolution),* growth *(increase),* increment, inflation *(increase),* latitude, overstatement, prosperity

expansive ample, broad, capacious, complete *(all-embracing),* comprehensive, extensive, omnibus, open-ended, voluble

exparte one-sided

expatiate declaim, digress, discourse, enlarge

expatiate on expand

expatiation harangue

expatriate alien, deport *(banish),* dislodge, displace *(remove),* eliminate *(exclude),* exclude, expel, pariah, relegate, seclude

expatriate oneself abscond, depart

expatriation banishment, deportation, exclusion, expulsion, immigration, ostracism, rejection

expect intend, plan, presume, presuppose, trust

expectable deductible *(provable)*

expectance contemplation, expectation, likelihood, possibility, prospect *(outlook)*

expectancy claim *(right),* expectation, likelihood, possibility, prospect *(outlook),* remainder *(estate in property)*

expectant pending *(imminent),* preparatory, prospective, ready *(prepared),* sanguine

expectare expect *(anticipate)*

expectation belief *(something believed),* belief *(state of mind),* contemplation, design *(intent),* end *(intent),* likelihood, objective, possibility, probability, prospect *(outlook),* purpose, reliance

expectations heritage

expected apparent *(presumptive),* customary, foreseeable, forseen, forthcoming, future, habitual, immediate *(imminent)*, imminent, necessary *(inescapable)*, ordinary, potential, prospective, proximate, regular *(conventional)*, routine, usual

expedience advantage, behalf, feasibility, pragmatism, propriety *(appropriateness)*, qualification *(fitness)*

expediency artifice, benefit *(betterment)*, boom *(prosperity)*, expedience, feasibility, pragmatism, propriety *(appropriateness)*

expedient appropriate, convenient, due *(regular)*, effective *(efficient)*, efficient, favorable *(advantageous)*, fitting, functional, help, instrumentality, loophole, medium, necessary *(required)*, opportune, plan, politic, practical, pragmatic, profitable, propitious, requisite, resource, seasonable, step, stopgap, stratagem, suitable, viable

expediential practical

expediousness dispatch *(promptness)*

expedire disengage, disentangle, expedite, explain, extricate, facilitate, solve

expedite conduce, dispatch *(send off)*, ease, facilitate, hasten, help, precipitate *(hasten)*

expedited determination accelerated judgment

expedited judgment accelerated judgment

expedition acceleration, advance *(progression)*, campaign

expédition dispatch *(promptness)*

expedition haste, quest

expeditious alert *(agile)*, efficient, instantaneous, prompt, punctual, rapid, ready *(willing)*, summary

expeditious performance acceleration, dispatch *(promptness)*

expeditiously as soon as feasible, instantly

expeditiousness haste

expel condemn *(ban)*, delete, deport *(banish)*, depose *(remove)*, discharge *(dismiss)*, discharge *(shoot)*, dislocate, dislodge, dismiss *(discharge)*, displace *(remove)*, dispossess, distill, divest, eject *(evict)*, eliminate *(exclude)*, emit, evict, exclude, expatriate, jettison, luxate, oust, outlaw, outpour, precipitate *(throw down violently)*, project *(impel forward)*, purge *(purify)*, reject, relegate, remove *(dismiss from office)*, supplant, transport

expel from the bar disbar

expel from the legal profession disbar

expelled ineligible

expellere dislodge, eject *(expel)*, expel

expelling expulsion

expend bear the expense, consume, defray, deplete, disburse *(pay out)*, dissipate *(expend foolishly)*, emit, exert, exhaust *(deplete)*, pay, spend

expend gradually conserve

expend slowly conserve

expendable disposable, minor, needless, negligible, nonessential, null *(insignificant)*, otiose, petty, superfluous, unnecessary

expended irredeemable

expendere consider, expend *(disburse)*

expenditure advance *(allowance)*, charge *(cost)*, collection *(payment)*, consumption, cost *(expenses)*, decrement, disbursement *(funds paid out)*, expense *(cost)*, fee *(charge)*, finance, maintenance *(upkeep)*, outflow, outlay, payment *(act of paying)*, payment *(remittance)*, price, remittance, waste

expenditure of energy effort

expenditures bill *(invoice)*, overhead

expense charge *(cost)*, disbursement *(funds paid out)*, expenditure, fare, fee *(charge)*, maintenance *(upkeep)*, outflow, outlay, overhead, payment *(remittance)*, price, rate, value, worth

expense of transportation fare

expense outlay binder

expenseless free *(at no charge)*, gratis, gratuitous *(given without recompense)*

expenses bill *(invoice)*, damages, expenditure, out of pocket

expensive exorbitant, invaluable, priceless, prohibitive *(costly)*, valuable

expensiveness cost *(price)*

expensum debit

experience bear *(tolerate)*, common knowledge, common sense, competence *(ability)*, discern *(detect with the senses)*, endure *(suffer)*, event, fact, happening, incident, information *(knowledge)*, occasion, occurrence, partake, particular, perceive, phenomenon *(unusual occurrence)*, skill, test

experience a loss lose *(be deprived of)*

experience loss suffer *(sustain loss)*

experience unpleasantly endure *(suffer)*

experienced artful, competent, expert, familiar *(informed)*, learned, practiced, professional *(trained)*, proficient, qualified *(competent)*, resourceful, veteran

experienced hand expert

experienced person expert, professional, specialist

experienced personnel expert

experienced view common sense

experientia experience *(background)*

experiment check *(inspect)*, endeavor, research, test, venture

experimental probative, speculative, tentative

experimental method trial *(experiment)*

experimentation research

experimentee subject *(object)*

experimenter speculator

experimentum experiment, trial *(experiment)*

expers corporis immaterial

expert capable, cognizant, competent, deft, efficient, familiar *(informed)*, informed *(educated)*, learned, mastermind, practiced, professional *(trained)*, professional, proficient, qualified *(competent)*, specialist, subtle *(refined)*, veteran, veteran

expertise comprehension, experience *(background)*, facility *(easiness)*, faculty *(ability)*, gift *(flair)*, knowledge *(learning)*, prowess *(ability)*, specialty *(special aptitude)*

expertness discretion *(quality of being discreet)*, efficiency, experience *(background)*, facility *(easiness)*, faculty

(ability), gift *(flair)*, performance *(workmanship)*, prowess *(ability)*, science *(technique)*, skill, specialty *(special aptitude)*

expetere desire

expiable justifiable, pardonable

expiate redeem *(satisfy debts)*, redress, repent

expiating compensatory, palliative *(excusing)*

expiatio expiation

expiation condonation, damages, reparation *(indemnification)*, restitution

expiatory compensatory, penitent

expilare hold up *(rob)*, plunder

expilatio pillage, spoliation

expiration cessation *(termination)*, close *(conclusion)*, death, defeasance, demise *(death)*, dissolution *(termination)*, end *(termination)*, extremity *(death)*, finality

expire cease, close *(terminate)*, decease, die, discontinue *(abandon)*, dissolve *(terminate)*, lapse *(cease)*, perish, stop, succumb, terminate

expired back *(in arrears)*, dead, defunct, lifeless *(dead)*, obsolete, outdated, outmoded

expiring in extremis

expiry end *(termination)*, expiration, finality, lapse *(expiration)*

explain annunciate, argue, clarify, comment, construe *(comprehend)*, construe *(translate)*, convey *(communicate)*, define, depict, describe, detail *(particularize)*, discourse, discuss, educate, elucidate, enlighten, enunciate, explicate, exposit, expound, illustrate, inform *(notify)*, instruct *(teach)*, interject, interpret, justify, manifest, rationalize, reason *(persuade)*, respond, reveal, review, simplify *(clarify)*, solve, speak, specify, support *(justify)*, trace *(delineate)*

explain away negate, rationalize

explain incorrectly misinterpret

explain the meaning interpret

explain the nature of define

explain wrongly misrepresent

explainable ascertainable, determinable *(ascertainable)*, solvable

explained coherent *(clear)*

explanare elucidate, explain, interpret

explanatio explanation

explanation alibi, answer *(solution)*, clarification, comment, construction, content *(meaning)*, definition, description, disclosure *(something disclosed)*, education, illustration, instruction *(teaching)*, justification, meaning, pandect *(treatise)*, paraphrase, rationale, reason *(basis)*, recital, rendition *(explication)*, representation *(statement)*, response, restatement, signification, solution *(answer)*, statement

explanation for some delinquency excuse

explanatory coherent *(clear)*, declaratory, demonstrative *(illustrative)*, descriptive, explicit, informative, informatory, interpretive, narrative

explanatory comment note *(brief comment)*

explanatory note comment

explanatory remark note *(brief comment)*

explere fulfill

expletio satisfaction *(fulfilment)*

expletive blasphemy, expendable, imprecation, needless, surplus, unnecessary

explicability construction

explicable accountable *(explainable)*, cognizable, coherent *(clear)*, comprehensible, determinable *(ascertainable)*, scrutable

explicare clear, deploy, describe, disentangle, evolve, explicate, spread

explicate clarify, comment, construe *(translate)*, depict, elucidate, enlighten, exemplify, explain, exposit, expound, interpret

explicatio analysis, development *(progression)*, explanation, solution *(answer)*

explication clarification, comment, construction, content *(meaning)*, definition, explanation, illustration, paraphrase, rationale, solution *(answer)*

explicative demonstrative *(illustrative)*, informative, informatory, interpretive, narrative, solvable

explicators of the law judiciary

explicatory coherent *(clear)*, demonstrative *(illustrative)*, descriptive, informative, informatory, narrative, solvable

explicit absolute *(conclusive)*, accurate, apparent *(perceptible)*, candid, certain *(specific)*, clear *(apparent)*, cognizable, coherent *(clear)*, comprehensible, concrete, demonstrative *(illustrative)*, detailed, direct *(forthright)*, distinct *(clear)*, evident, exact, express, informative, lucid, manifest, naked *(perceptible)*, obvious, ostensible, overt, palpable, pellucid, perceivable, perceptible, positive *(incontestable)*, precise, resounding, salient, scrutable, specific, trenchant, unambiguous, unequivocal, unmistakable

explicit utterance declaration

explicitly fairly *(clearly)*

explode discharge *(shoot)*, rebut, refute

exploit bilk, capitalize *(seize the chance)*, employ *(make use of)*, endeavor, manipulate *(control unfairly)*, operation, ply, transaction

exploitable disposable, naive

exploitation abuse *(corrupt practice)*, function, graft, misusage, use, usury

exploitative immoral, mercenary

explorare ascertain, spy

exploration analysis, cross-examination, cross-questioning, discovery, examination *(study)*, indagation, inquiry *(request for information)*, inquiry *(systematic investigation)*, inspection, interrogation, investigation, probe, quest, question *(inquiry)*, research, scrutiny, test, trial *(experiment)*

explorator spy

exploratory interrogative, precursory, probative, tentative

exploratory examination indagation, probe

explore analyze, canvass, check *(inspect)*, delve, examine *(study)*, find *(discover)*, frisk, hunt, inquire, investigate, peruse, probe, research, scrutinize, search, study

explorer pioneer

explosion discharge *(shot)*, outbreak, outburst, outcry, passion, repercussion, salvo, violence

explosions barrage

explosive ammunition, bomb, dangerous, disorderly, vehement, volatile

explosive device bomb

exponent abettor, advocate *(espouser)*, amicus curiae, apologist, backer, example, exemplar, illustration, indicant, indication, proponent, specimen, symbol

exponere elucidate, exhibit, explain, expose, recite

export displace *(remove)*, outflow, remove *(eliminate)*, send

export and import deal

exportation outflow

exporter dealer

exposcere dun, insist

expose accuse, admit *(concede)*, bare, bear *(adduce)*, betray *(disclose)*, clarify

exposé common knowledge

expose confess, contemn, convey *(communicate)*, debunk, denigrate, denude

exposé denunciation

expose detect, disabuse, disclose

exposé disclosure *(something disclosed)*

expose discover, dishonor *(deprive of honor)*, disinter, divulge, emerge, endanger, evidence, exhibit, find *(discover)*, impeach, implicate, incriminate, inform *(betray)*, issue *(publish)*, locate, manifest, manifestation, pillory, produce *(offer to view)*, publish, report *(disclose)*, reveal, subject, unveil

expose onself to incur

expose to danger compromise *(endanger)*, endanger, jeopardize

expose to infamy humiliate, pillory, smear

expose to injury endanger

expose to loss endanger

expose to public contempt libel

expose to view bare, disinter, manifest, present *(introduce)*

exposed aleatory *(perilous)*, apparent *(perceptible)*, blatant *(conspicuous)*, bleak *(exposed and barren)*, conspicuous, evident, helpless *(defenseless)*, indefensible, insecure, manifest, naked *(perceptible)*, obvious, open *(in sight)*, overt, patent, perceivable, perceptible, precarious, susceptible *(unresistent)*, untenable, vulnerable

exposed to liable

exposed to penalty liable

exposed to risk aleatory *(perilous)*, dangerous, insecure

exposed to view conspicuous, distinct *(clear)*, open *(in sight)*, patent, perceivable, perceptible

exposit clarify, construe *(translate)*, elucidate, expound

exposit on comment

expositer apologist

expositio description, narration, publication *(disclosure)*

exposition body *(main part)*, clarification, comment, construction, content *(meaning)*, declaration, disclosure *(act of disclosing)*, disclosure *(something disclosed)*, discourse, discovery, exhibit,

explanation, expression *(manifestation)*, hornbook, illustration, instruction *(teaching)*, justification, manifestation, market place, narration, pandect *(treatise)*, rationale, recital, report *(detailed account)*, review *(critical evaluation)*, solution *(answer)*, statement

expositive descriptive, informative, informatory, narrative

expository declaratory, demonstrative *(illustrative)*, descriptive, didactic, informative, informatory, narrative, solvable

expostulate admonish *(warn)*, argue, blame, castigate, censure, charge *(accuse)*, counsel, demonstrate *(protest)*, discourage, forewarn, reason *(persuade)*, remonstrate, reprehend, urge

expostulation admonition, blame *(culpability)*, complaint, condemnation *(blame)*, criticism, disapprobation, dissent *(difference of opinion)*, guidance, objection, objurgation, remonstrance

expostulative hortative

expostulatory hortative, remonstrative

exposure admission *(disclosure)*, bad repute, detection, disclosure *(act of disclosing)*, discovery, expression *(manifestation)*, impeachment, manifestation, publicity, risk

exposure to danger peril, pitfall

exposure to destruction peril

exposure to harm danger, peril, pitfall, risk

exposure to injury peril

exposure to loss peril

expound clarify, comment, construe *(translate)*, declaim, define, describe, discourse, elucidate, enlighten, explain, explicate, exposit, illustrate, instruct *(teach)*, interpret, reason *(persuade)*, remark, report *(disclose)*, speak

expounder advocate *(espouser)*, apologist, pedagogue

expounding comment, construction, explanation

express absolute *(conclusive)*, acknowledge *(declare)*, advise, affirm *(claim)*, allege, annunciate, apparent *(perceptible)*, argue, assert, avow, bear *(adduce)*, bespeak, candid, causeway, certain *(specific)*, cite *(state)*, clear *(apparent)*, coherent *(clear)*, comment, communicate, compose, comprehensible, connote, construe *(translate)*, contend *(maintain)*, convey *(communicate)*, declaratory, definite, denote, depict, designate, display, distinct *(clear)*, enunciate, evident, exact, exemplify, exhibit, expeditious, explicit, frame *(formulate)*, interject, lucid, manifest, manifest, mention, naked *(perceptible)*, observe *(remark)*, ostensible, overt, particular *(specific)*, pellucid, perceivable, perceptible, peremptory *(absolute)*, phrase, portray, posit, precise, pronounce *(speak)*, publish, purport, rapid, recite, relate *(tell)*, remark, report *(disclose)*, signify *(inform)*, speak, specific, specify, testify, unambiguous, unmistakable, utter

express a wish to obtain desire

express agreement quid pro quo

express an objection object

express an opinion evaluate, opine

express annoyance resent
express briefly indicate
express concurrence assent, grant *(concede)*
express deep grief for deplore
express disagreement demonstrate *(protest)*
express disapproval demonstrate *(protest)*, except *(object)*, object, remonstrate
express displeasure reproach
express dissatisfaction criticize *(find fault with)*, demonstrate *(protest)*
express generally indicate
express highway causeway
express ill will resent
express in a formula formulate
express in a systematic way formulate
express in concrete form embody
express in fuller form expand
express in precise form formulate
express opposition protest
express permission charter *(license)*
express precisely characterize
express shipper carrier
express sympathy sympathize
expressage consignment
expressed certain *(specific)*, oral, parol, stated, verbal
expressed command law
expressed concisely compact *(pithy)*
expressed desire request
expressed in few words succinct
expressed in words nuncupative, oral
expressed in writing in writing
expressed indirectly implied
expressed meaning definition
expressed opinion expression *(comment)*
expressed outright explicit
expressed solely by speech parol
expressing disdain contemptuous
expressing entreaty precatory
expression admission *(disclosure)*, assertion, call *(title)*, comment, connotation, creation, declaration, demeanor, disclosure *(something disclosed)*, inflection, language, manifestation, maxim, mention *(reference)*, parlance, phraseology, pronouncement, remark, rhetoric *(skilled speech)*, speech, style, testimony, token
expression of choice referendum
expression of contrary opinions fight *(argument)*
expression of conviction testament
expression of disapproval reaction *(opposition)*
expression of discontent plaint
expression of grief plaint
expression of ideas phraseology
expression of merit mention *(tribute)*
expression of opinion observation
expression of opinion for or against argument *(pleading)*
expression of pain plaint
expression of satisfaction approval
expression of views discourse
expression of will poll *(casting of votes)*
expressionless inexpressive, inscrutable, vacuous
expressions indicia
expressive clear *(apparent)*, coherent

(clear), declaratory, demonstrative *(expressive of emotion)*, demonstrative *(illustrative)*, eloquent, informative, moving *(evoking emotion)*, sententious, suggestive *(evocative)*
expressive of opinion advisory
expressly faithfully, particularly, purposely
expressway causeway
exprimere express, extort, force *(coerce)*, represent *(portray)*
exprobate contemn, deprecate, remonstrate, reprehend
exprobation blame *(culpability)*
exprobrate lash *(attack verbally)*, rebuke, reprimand, reproach
exprobratio reproach
exprobration obloquy, remonstrance, reprimand, reproach, revilement
exprobrative remonstrative
exprobratory remonstrative
expropriate abridge *(divest)*, annex *(arrogate)*, assume *(seize)*, attach *(seize)*, carry away, condemn *(seize)*, confiscate, convert *(misappropriate)*, deprive, dislodge, displace *(remove)*, dispossess, divest, hijack, impress *(procure by force)*, occupy *(take possession)*, plagiarize, seize *(confiscate)*
expropriated attached *(seized)*
expropriation appropriation *(taking)*, assumption *(seizure)*, attachment *(seizure)*, condemnation *(seizure)*, disseisin, distraint, distress *(seizure)*, foreclosure, forfeiture *(act of forfeiting)*, garnishment, taking
expropriatory confiscatory
expugnable helpless *(defenseless)*
expulsio expulsion
expulsion banishment, deportation, discharge *(dismissal)*, dismissal *(discharge)*, disqualification *(rejection)*, eviction, exception *(exclusion)*, exclusion, expropriation *(divestiture)*, foreclosure, layoff, ostracism, outburst, outflow, rejection, removal
expulsion of a fetus abortion *(feticide)*
expunction cancellation, dissolution *(termination)*
expunge annul, bowdlerize, cancel, censor, delete, destroy *(efface)*, edit, eliminate *(eradicate)*, eradicate, excise *(cut away)*, expurgate, extinguish, obliterate, redact, remove *(eliminate)*, revoke
expunge the record of pardon
expurgare excuse, expurgate
expurgate bowdlerize, censor, censure, diminish, eliminate *(eradicate)*, eradicate, excise *(cut away)*, purge *(purify)*
expurgated pure
expurgation censorship
exquisite attractive, elegant, prime *(most valuable)*, rare
exquisitus recondite, select
exsanguis lifeless *(dull)*
exsecratio imprecation, malediction
exsect eviscerate
exsection evulsion
exsequi enforce
exsistere appear *(materialize)*, exist
exsolvere disburse *(pay out)*, disentangle, extricate, pay, release, rescue
exspectatio expectation

exspirare expire
exspiratio expiration
exspoliare rob
exstare exist, extant
exstinguere abolish, suppress
exstirpare eradicate, extirpate
exsuperare surmount, transcend
extant conscious *(awake)*, live *(existing)*, present *(current)*
extemperaneous unexpected
extemplo instantly
extemporal spontaneous
extemporaneous ad hoc, impulsive *(rash)*, informal, spontaneous, unpremeditated
extemporaneousness informality
extemporary impulsive *(rash)*, spontaneous
extempore informal, spontaneous, unexpected, unpremeditated
extend accrue *(increase)*, accumulate *(enlarge)*, administer *(tender)*, amplify, append, bestow, build *(augment)*, compound, continue *(prolong)*, defer *(put off)*, deploy, develop, dwell *(linger over)*, endure *(last)*, enhance, enlarge, expand, increase, inflate, keep *(continue)*, lie *(be sustainable)*, magnify, offer *(tender)*, postpone, present *(make a gift)*, proceed *(go forward)*, proffer, prolong, protract *(stall)*, remain *(continue)*, spread, stay *(continue)*, submit *(give)*, sustain *(prolong)*, tender
extend beyond overlap, overreach
extend citizenship to an alien naturalize *(make a citizen)*
extend credit capitalize *(provide capital)*, lend, loan
extend in duration continue *(prolong)*
extend over overreach
extend through pervade
extend to abut, border *(bound)*, reach
extended broad, capacious, chronic, comprehensive, continuous, extensive, far reaching, inflated *(enlarged)*, liberal *(not literal)*, prolix, prominent, protracted
extended meaning context
extendere expand, extend *(enlarge)*, prolong
extending broad, cumulative *(intensifying)*, extensive
extension accession *(enlargement)*, accretion, addition, additive, adjournment, adjunct, advance *(increase)*, appendix *(accession)*, appurtenance, augmentation, boom *(increase)*, continuance, continuation *(prolongation)*, deferment, development *(progression)*, growth *(increase)*, increment, inflation *(increase)*, insertion, latitude, magnitude, offshoot, organ, rider, stress *(strain)*, survival
extension in time duration
extension of credit loan
extension of time deferment
extensive ample, broad, capacious, complete *(all-embracing)*, comprehensive, far reaching, general, inclusive, major, material *(important)*, omnibus, predominant, prevailing *(current)*, prevalent, rife, thorough
extensive flood cataclysm
extensively generally, throughout *(all over)*

extent amount *(quantity)*, caliber *(measurement)*, capacity *(maximum)*, capacity *(sphere)*, circuit, configuration *(confines)*, degree *(magnitude)*, duration, gamut, magnitude, mass *(weight)*, measurement, purview, quota, range, scope, space, time

extent of authority jurisdiction

extent of surface area *(surface)*

extent of the court's authority judicature

extent of view coverage *(scope)*

extents confines

extenuare attenuate, decrease, disparage, qualify *(condition)*

extenuate alleviate, attenuate, dilute, diminish, ease, excuse, lessen, modify *(moderate)*, palliate *(excuse)*

extenuating mitigating, palliative *(excusing)*

extenuation clemency, condonation, excuse, extenuating circumstances, justification, reason *(basis)*

extenuative palliative *(excusing)*

exterior extrinsic, peripheral, periphery, semblance, specious, superficial

exterminate abate *(extinguish)*, abolish, annul, cancel, destroy *(efface)*, dispatch *(put to death)*, eliminate *(eradicate)*, eradicate, extinguish, extirpate, kill *(murder)*, obliterate, overthrow, remove *(eliminate)*, slay

exterminated lost *(taken away)*

extermination abatement *(extinguishment)*, aberemurder, abolition, dispatch *(act of putting to death)*, homicide, killing, removal

exterminative dire, disastrous, fatal

exterminatory disastrous

external alien *(foreign)*, extrinsic, peripheral, physical, specious, superficial

external appearance color *(deceptive appearance)*, complexion, feature *(appearance)*

external aspect appearance *(look)*

external form configuration *(form)*, outline *(boundary)*

externalize perceive

externus foreign

exterrere frighten

extinct dead, defunct, lifeless *(dead)*, null *(invalid)*, null and void, obsolete, outdated, outmoded

extinction aberemurder, abolition, ademption, cancellation, catastrophe, death, demise *(death)*, destruction, dissolution *(termination)*, end *(termination)*, extremity *(death)*, mortality, prostration, subversion

extinction of a debt amortization

extinguere extinguish

extinguish abolish, annul, cancel, cease, destroy *(efface)*, destroy *(void)*, disappear, eradicate, expunge, extirpate, inhibit, kill *(defeat)*, obliterate, quash, stifle, strangle, subvert, suppress

extinguish indebtedness liquidate *(determine liability)*

extinguish visual discernment blind *(deprive of sight)*

extinguishable destructible

extinguished dead, lost *(taken away)*, null *(invalid)*, null and void

extinguishment abolition, death, demise *(death)*, deterrence, dissolution *(termination)*, end *(termination)*, extremity *(death)*

extinguishment of claim amortization

extirpate abolish, bowdlerize, delete, destroy *(efface)*, eliminate *(eradicate)*, eradicate, expunge, extinguish, obliterate, overthrow, quash, redact, reject, remove *(eliminate)*, subvert, supplant

extirpated lost *(taken away)*

extirpation abolition, destruction, dissolution *(termination)*, evulsion, rejection, removal, subversion

extirpative detrimental, dire, disastrous, fatal, pernicious

extirpatory dire

extol belaud, honor, overestimate, recommend, regard *(hold in esteem)*

extorquere extort, force *(coerce)*

extort acquire *(secure)*, coerce, deprive, exact, force *(coerce)*, impose *(enforce)*, press *(constrain)*, prey, toll *(exact payment)*

extort belief convince

extorter racketeer

extortion blackmail, coercion

extortionary confiscatory

extortionate exorbitant, inordinate, prohibitive *(costly)*, usurious, venal

extortionist criminal

extra additional, also, ancillary *(auxiliary)*, balance *(amount in excess)*, bonus, excess, excessive, expendable, extraneous, extrinsic, further, gratuity *(present)*, needless, nonessential, overage, premium *(excess value)*, superfluous, supplementary, unnecessary

extra amount for contingencies margin *(spare amount)*

extra amount for emergencies margin *(spare amount)*

extra charge surcharge

extra compensation commission *(fee)*

extra fee surcharge

extra time extension *(postponement)*

extract abridgment *(condensation)*, abstract, acquire *(secure)*, brief, compendium, deduce, deduct *(conclude by reasoning)*, derive *(deduce)*, derive *(receive)*, detect, digest, disencumber, disinter, dislodge, distill, educe, elicit, eradicate, eviscerate, evoke, except *(exclude)*, excerpt, excise *(cut away)*, gain, glean, infer, liberate, quote, reject, remove *(eliminate)*, select, unveil, withdraw

extract from other works compile

extracted individual

extraction birth *(lineage)*, blood, bloodline, degree *(kinship)*, derivation, descent *(lineage)*, evulsion, family *(common ancestry)*, lineage, origin *(ancestry)*, parentage, race, relationship *(family tie)*, removal, selection *(choice)*

extradite deport *(banish)*, transport

extradition banishment, deportation, expulsion

extrahere extract

extrajudicial opinion dictum

extralegal felonious

extramarital promiscuity adultery

extramarital relations adultery

extraneous circumstantial, collateral *(immaterial)*, expendable, extrinsic, foreign, gratuitous *(unwarranted)*, immaterial, impertinent *(irrelevant)*, inapposite, irrelevant, needless, nonessential, peripheral, tangential, unessential, unnecessary, unrelated

extraneus extraneous

extraordinally particularly

extraordinarily burdensome requirement imposition *(excessive burden)*

extraordinarius extraordinary

extraordinary best, eccentric, individual, infrequent, inordinate, irregular *(not usual)*, major, meritorious, notable, noteworthy, novel, outstanding *(prominent)*, paramount, particular *(specific)*, peculiar *(distinctive)*, portentous *(eliciting amazement)*, preferential, priceless, prodigious *(amazing)*, rare, remarkable, renowned, salient, singular, special, stellar, sterling, unaccustomed, uncommon, unique, unprecedented, unusual

extraordinary remedy habeas corpus

extraordinary writ habeas corpus

extravagance exaggeration, hyperbole, misapplication, overstatement, rodomontade, waste

extravagancy overstatement

extravagant copious, egregious, excess, excessive, exorbitant, improvident, inordinate, intemperate, pretentious *(pompous)*, prodigal, profuse, prohibitive *(costly)*, rampant, superfluous, undue *(excessive)*, unreasonable, unrestrained *(not repressed)*

extravagant statement exaggeration

extravasate outpour

extravasation outflow

extrema condicio ultimatum

extrema lineamenta outline *(boundary)*

extreme brutal, ceiling, conclusive *(settled)*, contra, dire, draconian, drastic, end *(termination)*, excess, excessive, exorbitant, fanatical, final, gross *(flagrant)*, harsh, hot-blooded, inordinate, insufferable, intemperate, intense, last *(final)*, lurid, noteworthy, outrageous, strict, superlative, ultimate, unconscionable, undue *(excessive)*, unendurable, unreasonable, unusual, utmost

extreme boundary limit

extreme edge periphery

extreme fear fright

extreme limit extremity *(furthest point)*, utmost

extreme penalty capital punishment

extreme point end *(termination)*

extremely unduly

extremely important vital

extremes exaggeration

extremist bigot, malcontent

extremitas extremity *(furthest point)*

extremities confines

extremity border, boundary, ceiling, disaster, edge *(border)*, emergency, end *(termination)*, finality, need *(deprivation)*, outline *(boundary)*, pinnacle, prostration, requirement, utmost

extremus extreme *(last)*, final, ultimate

extricable corrigible

extricate clear, discharge *(liberate)*, disencumber, disengage, disentangle, disenthrall, disinter, educe, free, quit *(free of)*, release, relieve *(free from burden)*, remove *(eliminate)*, rescue

extrication condonation, discharge

(liberation), discharge *(release from obligation),* emancipation, evulsion, freedom, ransom, release, removal, salvage
extrinsic alien *(foreign),* extraneous, foreign, incidental, nonessential, unessential, unnecessary
extrinsical extraneous, extrinsic, nonessential
extrude expel
extrudere eject *(expel)*
extrusion deportation, eviction, expulsion, ostracism, outflow
exuberance life *(vitality)*
exuberant copious, loquacious, profuse, rampant
exudation outflow
exude emanate, emit, issue *(send forth),* radiate
exultant ecstatic
eye center *(central position),* observe *(watch),* scrutinize, study
eye opener bombshell
eye-catching manifest, open *(in sight),* remarkable
eyeless blind *(sightless)*
eyereach perspective, scene
eyeshot scene
eyewitness bystander

F

faber artisan
fable fiction, lie *(falsify),* myth
fabled famous, fictitious
fabric building *(structure),* frame *(structure),* structure *(composition)*
fabrica manufacture
fabricari fabricate *(construct),* form, make, manufacture
fabricate build *(construct),* conceive *(invent),* conjure, contrive, create, devise *(invent),* fake, falsify, feign, forge *(produce),* form, formulate, frame *(construct),* generate, invent *(falsify),* invent *(produce for the first time),* lie *(falsify),* make, manufacture, misrepresent, originate, palter, plagiarize, prevaricate, produce *(manufacture),* profess *(pretend),* scheme, simulate
fabricate evidence frame *(charge falsely)*
fabricated assumed *(feigned),* fictitious, illusory, mendacious, spurious, unfounded
fabricating lying
fabrication artifice, building *(business of assembling),* canard, composition *(makeup),* counterfeit, creation, deceit, deception, evasion, fake, false pretense, falsehood, falsification, fiction, figment, formation, fraud, hoax, invention, lie, manufacture, misrepresentation, myth, origination, pretense *(pretext),* pretext, sham, story *(falsehood),* subreption, subterfuge
fabricative constructive *(creative)*
fabricator author *(originator)*
fabula fiction, myth, story *(narrative)*
fabulous exorbitant, remarkable, special
facade disguise, false pretense
face appearance *(look),* confront *(encounter),* endure *(suffer),* withstand
face danger fight *(battle),* withstand
face to face direct *(forthright)*
face up to withstand

face value cost *(price),* par *(face amount)*
facere appoint, exercise *(discharge a function),* glean, make, practice *(engage in),* realize *(make real)*
facet aspect, complexion, phase *(aspect),* side
facetious jocular
facies form *(arrangement)*
facile artful, capable, deft, expert, pliable, practiced, proficient, resourceful, sequacious, suasible, tractable, veteran, yielding
facillity instrument *(tool)*
facilis facile, flexible, tractable, yielding
facilitas facility *(easiness)*
facilitate abet, aid, bestow, ease, enable, expedite, favor, further, hasten, help, permit, promote *(organize),* support *(assist)*
facilitated decision accelerated judgment
facilitation advance *(progression),* aid *(help),* help
facility appliance, competence *(ability),* device *(mechanism),* discretion *(quality of being discreet),* gift *(flair),* power, prison, proclivity, propensity, prowess *(ability),* science *(technique),* skill, tendency
facing opposite
facinorous heinous, inexpiable, iniquitous, reprobate, scandalous, sinister
facinus crime, venture
facsimile copy, delineation, duplicate, fake, model
fact fait accompli, ground, particular, technicality, truth
fact of comprehending coverage *(scope)*
fact put in controversy by the pleadings issue *(matter in dispute)*
fact-finding interrogative
factfinding research
factio cabal, faction
faction cabal, conflict, constituency, contention *(opposition),* denomination, disaccord, disagreement, discord, dissidence, disturbance, division *(act of dividing),* feud, incompatibility *(difference),* organization *(association),* party *(political organization),* schism, side, society, sodality, split, strife
factional divergent, partial *(part),* partisan
factional part proportion
factionalism strife
factionary demagogue, partisan
factioneer demagogue
factious argumentative, contentious, controversial, contumacious, dissenting, dissident, divergent, divisive, hostile, negative, polemic, pugnacious
factious leader demagogue
factiousness contention *(opposition)*
factitare practice *(engage in)*
factitious assumed *(feigned),* colorable *(specious),* false *(not genuine),* imitation, synthetic
factor aspect, broker, cause *(reason),* component, constituent *(part),* dealer, deputy, determinant, element, feature *(characteristic),* ingredient, member *(constituent part),* part *(portion),* plenipotentiary, procurator, represent *(sub-*

stitute), substitute
factorage brokerage
factors case *(set of circumstances),* circumstances, deputation *(delegation)*
factory-made industrial
factotum employee
factotums personnel
facts circumstances, data, dossier, evidence, proof, science *(study)*
facts admitted at trial evidence
facts judicially noted evidence
facts which bear on the point in question evidence
facts which establish the point in issue evidence
factual accurate, actual, authentic, certain *(positive),* de facto, documentary, genuine, honest, incontrovertible, indubious, literal, objective, real, sound, true *(authentic),* unrefutable, valid
factual basis documentation
factual matter evidence
factual statement affirmation
factualness honesty, reality, veracity
factum action *(performance),* event, fact
facultas ability, facility *(instrumentality),* permission, possibility
facultate bestow
facultatem facere enable
facultates resource
facultative voluntary
faculty ability, aptitude, caliber *(mental capacity),* capacity *(aptitude),* color *(complexion),* competence *(ability),* droit, gift *(flair),* performance *(workmanship),* specialty *(special aptitude),* staff
faculty member pedagogue
faculty of speech language
fad mode
fade decay, depart, disappear, dissipate *(spread out),* languish, perish, tarnish
fade away diminish, disappear, dissipate *(spread out),* ebb, expire, perish
fade out perish
faded blemished, indistinct, stale
faded reputation ignominy
fadeless indelible, indestructible
fading attrition, brief, transient
faeneratio usury
faenus interest *(profit)*
fagging operose
fail decay, default, disappoint, ebb, languish, lapse *(fall into error),* lose *(undergo defeat),* mismanage, neglect, perish, succumb
fail in duty default
fail in health languish
fail to accommodate disoblige
fail to act default
fail to answer default
fail to appear default
fail to appreciate decry, overlook *(disregard)*
fail to comply disobey
fail to comply with disoblige
fail to do omit
fail to exact a penalty pardon
fail to find lose *(be deprived of)*
fail to include omit
fail to insert omit
fail to keep forfeit, lose *(be deprived of),* violate

fail to meet financial engagements default
fail to mention omit
fail to notice disregard
fail to observe disregard, overlook *(disregard),* violate
fail to pay default
fail to perform default
fail to recognize misjudge
fail to retain forfeit
fail to see overlook *(disregard)*
fail to understand misapprehend, misconceive, misconstrue, misinterpret, misunderstand
fail to win lose *(undergo defeat)*
failed bankrupt, insolvent
failing decadent, decline, defect, deficiency, disadvantage, fault *(mistake),* fault *(weakness),* flaw, foible, frailty, imperfect, insufficient, misconduct, perfunctory, vice
failing in duty delinquent *(overdue),* derelict *(negligent)*
failure abortion *(fiasco),* bankruptcy, breach, debacle, defeat, delinquency *(failure of duty),* disaster, dishonor *(nonpayment),* disqualification *(factor that disqualifies),* flaw, foible, frailty, frustration, impossibility, impotence, impuissance, inability, incapacity, inefficacy, infraction, lapse *(expiration),* loss, miscarriage, misconduct, mistrial, neglect, negligence, nonfeasance, nonpayment, offense, omission, oversight *(carelessness),* vice
failure in duty culpability, dereliction
failure of credit default
failure of duty default, infraction, laches, maladministration
failure of obligation delinquency *(failure of duty)*
failure of strength frailty
failure of vital functions death
failure to act delinquency *(failure of duty),* inaction
failure to agree conflict, contest *(dispute),* controversy *(argument),* difference, disaccord, disagreement, discord, disparity, dispute, dissent *(difference of opinion)*
failure to answer default
failure to appear default, nonappearance
failure to carry out disregard *(omission)*
failure to comply deficiency
failure to correspond discrepancy
failure to establish a cause of action nonsuit
failure to litigate within reasonable period laches
failure to maintain solvency failure *(bankruptcy)*
failure to make a case nonsuit
failure to meet one's obligations default
failure to meet the burden of proof nonsuit
failure to notice oversight *(carelessness)*
failure to pay default, nonpayment
failure to perform nonperformance, omission
failure to present sufficient evidence nonsuit

failure to use desuetude, disuse
fain willing *(not averse)*
fainaigue deceive
faineance sloth
faineant otiose
faint inconspicuous, indefinite, indistinct, insufficient, languid, nebulous, powerless, prostration, remote *(small),* unclear, vague
faint hope pessimism
faint outline hint
faint suggestion hint
faint-hearted caitiff
fainthearted diffident, recreant
faintheartedness fear
faintish powerless
faintness indistinctness, obscuration
fair adequate, attractive, average *(standard),* clean, dispassionate, equal, equitable, evenhanded, high-minded, honest, impartial, imperfect, judicial, juridical, just, marginal, market *(business),* mediocre, neutral, nonpartisan, objective, open-minded, passable, right *(correct),* rightful, scrupulous, unbiased, unprejudiced, upright
fair chance likelihood, opportunity, probability, prospect *(outlook)*
fair claim right *(entitlement)*
fair expectation probability
fair notice adequate notice
fair play disinterest *(lack of prejudice),* fairness, justice, objectivity, probity
fair prospect likelihood
fair sample cross section
fair sharing dispensation *(act of dispensing)*
fair treatment candor *(impartiality),* disinterest *(lack of prejudice),* equity *(justice),* fairness, justice, right *(righteousness)*
fair value expense *(cost)*
fair-dealing honest
fair-haired popular
fair-minded equal, equitable, evenhanded, fair *(just),* impartial, just, liberal *(broad minded),* neutral, nonpartisan, objective, open-minded, unbiased
fair-mindedness equity *(justice),* fairness, justice, objectivity
fairish mediocre
fairly duly, in good faith
fairminded unprejudiced
fairness candor *(impartiality),* disinterest *(lack of prejudice),* equity *(justice),* honesty, integrity, justice, mediocrity, moderation, objectivity, probity, rectitude, right *(righteousness)*
fait accompli denouement
faith allegiance, conviction *(persuasion),* credence, fealty, fidelity, probity, prospect *(outlook),* reliance, security *(safety),* trust *(confidence),* weight *(credibility)*
faithful accurate, actual, authentic, bona fide, close *(intimate),* conscientious, constant, credible, dependable, diligent, exact, factual, identical, infallible, intimate, literal, loyal, meticulous, obedient, persistent, pertinacious, precise, punctilious, realistic, reliable, representative, reputable, resolute, serious *(devoted),* stable, staunch, steadfast, strict, true *(loyal),* undistorted, unyielding

faithful companion cohort
faithfully in good faith, invariably
faithfulness adherence *(devotion),* adhesion *(loyalty),* allegiance, commitment *(responsibility),* conformity *(obedience),* credibility, discipline *(obedience),* fealty, fidelity, homage, integrity, loyalty, rectitude, responsibility *(conscience),* trustworthiness, veracity
faithless derelict *(negligent),* dishonest, false *(disloyal),* lying, machiavellian, malevolent, perfidious, profane, recreant, skeptical, unreliable, unscrupulous, untrue, untrustworthy, variable
faithlessness dereliction, dishonesty, disloyalty, doubt *(suspicion),* incredulity, infidelity, revolt, story *(falsehood)*
faithworthy credible, solid *(sound)*
fake assumed *(feigned),* camouflage, cloak, copy, counterfeit, deceive, deception, disguise, dishonest, fabricate *(make up),* false *(not genuine),* false pretense, falsification, falsify, fictitious, forge *(counterfeit),* forgery, frame *(prearrange),* fraudulent, hoax, imposture, invent *(falsify),* meretricious, misrepresent, mock *(imitate),* palter, pretend, sham, specious, spurious, untrue
fake charges against frame *(charge falsely)*
fake the evidence frame *(prearrange)*
faked artificial, dishonest, fictitious, fraudulent, imitation, lying, spurious, surreptitious
faked charge frame up
fakery false pretense
faking disguise
fall debacle, decline, decline *(fall),* decrease, decrease, depreciate, ebb, failure *(lack of success),* prostration, relapse, relapse, subside, succumb
fall again into regress
fall against impinge
fall apart decay, degenerate
fall away degenerate, diminish, ebb, subside
fall back regress, relapse, retire *(retreat),* retreat
fall back on exploit *(make use of)*
fall back upon resort
fall behind decrease, regress
fall below decrease
fall by inheritance devolve
fall by succession devolve
fall due accrue *(arise),* mature
fall exactly together coincide *(correspond)*
fall foul of bicker
fall from grace lapse *(fall35into error)*
fall from repute degradation
fall heir to inherit
fall ill languish
fall in conform
fall in with comply, comport *(agree with),* defer *(yield in judgment),* obey, unite
fall into incur
fall into decay degenerate
fall into error deviate, err, miscalculate, misconceive, misread, mistake, misunderstand
fall into line conform, crystallize
fall off decrease, degenerate, ebb, subside
fall out alienate *(estrange),* bicker, disaccord, emanate, estrange

fall short fail *(lose),* lack, require *(need)*
fall sick languish
fall to pieces decay, degenerate, disintegrate
fall to the rear retreat
fall upon accost, assail, attack, oppugn, strike *(assault)*
fallabity frailty
fallacia deceit, fraud, imposture, sham
fallacious deceptive, delusive, dishonest, errant, erroneous, false *(inaccurate),* faulty, fraudulent, ill-founded, illogical, illusory, inaccurate, incorrect, invalid, ludicrous, nonsubstantial *(not sturdy),* sophistic, specious, unfounded, untenable, untrue
fallacious argument fallacy, non sequitur
fallacious reasoning non sequitur, sophistry
fallaciousness bad faith, deceit, fraud, invalidity, misestimation
fallacy invalidity, misjudgment, non sequitur
fallax delusive, fallacious, insidious
fallen peccable, profligate *(corrupt)*
fallen into desuetude obsolete, outdated, outmoded
fallen into disuse obsolete, outdated, outmoded
fallen into ruin dilapidated
fallere hoodwink, mislead
falli err, miscalculate
fallible disputable, dubious, peccable, unreliable, untrustworthy, vulnerable
falling decadent, descent *(declination)*
falling away decline
falling due maturity
falling into ruin decadent
falling off attrition
falling out disaccord, schism
falling short defective, deficiency, deficient, insufficiency
falling-off decline, decrease
fallow barren, idle, otiose, unproductive
falsa docere misinform
false artificial, assumed *(feigned),* baseless, bogus, colorable *(specious),* deceptive, delusive, dishonest, disingenuous, erroneous, faithless, fallacious, faulty, fictitious, fraudulent, ill-founded, illusory, imitation, immoral, improper, inaccurate, incorrect, insidious, lying, mendacious, meretricious, perfidious, recreant, sophistic, specious, spurious, tartuffish, unfounded, unreliable, unscrupulous, unsound *(fallacious),* unsustainable, untenable, untrue, untrustworthy
false accusation defamation, libel
false alarm hoax
false and injurious libelous
false appearance color *(deceptive appearance),* deception, disguise, fallacy, pretense *(ostentation),* pretense *(pretext),* pretext
false assertion falsehood
false charge frame up
false claim artifice
false coloring catachresis, distortion
false colors disguise
false conception error
false conduct duplicity, fraud, imposture

false construction catachresis, distortion, misapplication
false copy counterfeit, disguise, distortion
false duplication counterfeit
false evidence frame up
false fabrication forgery
false front deception, disguise
false ground pretext
false hearted disingenuous, false *(disloyal)*
false idea misestimation
false impression error, misestimation
false information frame up
false logic sophistry
false motive pretext
false plea pretense *(pretext)*
false pretense pretext
false pretenses bad faith
false pretension bad faith
false pretensions artifice
false profession hypocrisy
false publication defamation, libel
false reading catachresis, distortion
false reason pretext
false reasoning non sequitur
false report canard, defamation, hoax, slander
false representation counterfeit, fake, fraud, misrepresentation
false representation of fact false pretense
false reproduction counterfeit
false rumor canard
false show histrionics, pretense *(ostentation),* pretense *(pretext),* pretext, role, sham
false statement canard, falsehood, fiction, libel, lie, misrepresentation, misstatement, perjury, story *(falsehood)*
false step fault *(mistake)*
false story myth
false swearing bad faith, dishonesty, perjury, subreption
false teaching propaganda
false-hearted dishonest
falsehearted faithless, insidious, machiavellian, perfidious, recreant
falseheartedness bad faith, deceit, dishonesty, duplicity, infidelity
falsehood canard, counterfeit, deceit, deception, dishonesty, fake, false pretense, fiction, figment, improbity, indirection *(deceitfulness),* libel, lie, misrepresentation, misstatement, myth, perjury, pretense *(pretext),* subreption, subterfuge
falsely call to account frame *(charge falsely)*
falsely characterize mislabel
falsely testify bear false witness
falseness bad faith, color *(deceptive appearance),* counterfeit, deceit, deception, dishonesty, disloyalty, duplicity, fallacy, false pretense, fraud, improbity, indirection *(deceitfulness),* invalidity, libel, perjury, pretense *(pretext)*
falsification artifice, canard, color *(deceptive appearance),* counterfeit, deceit, deception, dishonesty, distortion, fake, false pretense, falsehood, fiction, figment, forgery, fraud, hoax, hypocrisy, libel, lie, misrepresentation, misstatement, overstatement, perjury, pretense *(pretext),* pretext, story *(false-*

hood), subreption
falsified dishonest, fraudulent, mendacious
falsify bear false witness, cloak, copy, deceive, defame, delude, disguise, distort, evade *(deceive),* fabricate *(make up),* fake, feign, forge *(counterfeit),* invent *(falsify),* lie *(falsify),* malign, misguide, misinform, mislead, misrepresent, misstate, negate, palter, perjure, pervert, plagiarize, pretend, prevaricate, refute, slant
falsify accounts defalcate
falsify testimony perjure
falsity counterfeit, deceit, dishonesty, disloyalty, fallacy, false pretense, falsehood, fraud, improbity, infidelity, invalidity, lie, misrepresentation, story *(falsehood)*
falsum falsehood, lie
falsus counterfeit, delusive, erroneous, false pretense, illusory, inaccurate, incorrect, putative, untrue
falter beat *(pulsate),* doubt *(hesitate),* hesitate, oscillate, vacillate
faltering diffident, disinclined, doubt *(indecision),* hesitant, hesitation, irresolute, noncommittal
fama character *(reputation),* honor *(good reputation),* notoriety, prestige, report *(rumor),* reputation
fame character *(reputation),* credit *(recognition),* distinction *(reputation),* eminence, importance, notoriety, prestige, publicity, regard *(esteem),* reputation
famed famous, illustrious, notable, notorious, outstanding *(prominent),* renowned, reputable
familia family *(household),* household
familiar accustomed *(familiarized),* brazen, close *(intimate),* cognizable, cognizant, common *(customary),* conventional, customary, frequent, habitual, informal, informed *(having information),* intimate, learned, mundane, nondescript, ordinary, presumptuous, prevailing *(current),* prevalent, proverbial, public *(known),* regular *(conventional),* routine, trite, typical, usual
familiar discourse conversation
familiar object landmark *(conspicuous object)*
familiar through use accustomed *(familiarized)*
familiar way custom
familiaris familiar *(customary),* intimate
familiarity cognition, common knowledge, comprehension, consortium *(marriage companionship),* experience *(background),* informality, information *(knowledge),* knowledge *(awareness),* knowledge *(learning),* scienter
familiarization habituation, knowledge *(learning)*
familiarize advise, apprise, communicate, educate, inform *(notify),* initiate, instruct *(teach),* inure *(accustom),* naturalize *(acclimate)*
familiarize oneself perceive
familiarize with instill, practice *(train by repetition)*
familiarized informed *(having information)*
family affiliation *(bloodline),* affinity

(family ties), ancestry, bloodline, derivation, descendant, domestic *(household)*, house, household *(domestic)*, household, issue *(progeny)*, kindred, kinship, lineage, next of kin, offspring, origin *(ancestry)*, parentage, paternal, posterity, progeny, race, relative, succession

family abode household

family circle household

family connection affiliation *(bloodline)*, affinity *(family ties)*, ancestry, blood, degree *(kinship)*, filiation, kinship, next of kin, parentage, propinquity *(kinship)*, relation *(kinship)*, relationship *(family tie)*

family dwelling place household

family patronage nepotism

family related consanguineous

family relationship blood, degree *(kinship)*

family tie affiliation *(bloodline)*, blood, degree *(kinship)*, next of kin, relation *(kinship)*

family tree ancestry, blood, bloodline, descent *(lineage)*, parentage

family unit family *(household)*

famine paucity, poverty, privation

famous blatant *(conspicuous)*, household *(familiar)*, illustrious, important *(significant)*, notable, noteworthy, notorious, outstanding *(prominent)*, popular, prominent, renowned, stellar

famousness notoriety, prestige, publicity, regard *(esteem)*, reputation

fan addict, spread, stimulate

fan out deploy, expand

fanatic addict, addicted, bigot, demagogue, dictatorial, drastic, eager, fanatical, malcontent, outrageous, partisan, uncompromising

fanatical demonstrative *(expressive of emotion)*, dogmatic, draconian, drastic, eager, excessive, extreme *(exaggerated)*, illiberal, inordinate, narrow, outrageous, parochial, provincial, radical *(favoring drastic change)*, uncompromising, vehement, zealous

fanaticism ardor, compulsion *(obsession)*, obsession, passion

fanaticus fanatical

fancied delusive, fictitious, illusory, nonexistent, preferred *(favored)*

fancier addict

fanciful arbitrary, arbitrary and capricious, capricious, delusive, fictitious, ill-founded, illusory, insubstantial, original *(creative)*, quixotic, unpredictable, variable

fanciful name sobriquet

fancy affection, compulsion *(obsession)*, conatus, concept, conjure, desire, elaborate, expect *(consider probable)*, favor, fiction, figment, idea, notion, obsession, opine, opinion *(belief)*, penchant, predilection, predisposition, prefer, preference *(choice)*, propensity, quirk *(idiosyncrasy)*, relish, surmise, suspect *(think)*

fanfare noise

fanfaronade histrionics, jactation, pretense *(ostentation)*, rodomontade

fanfaronading orgulous

fantasied capricious

fantastic delusive, ludicrous, nonexistent, noteworthy, prodigious *(amaz-*

ing), special, unusual

fantastical capricious, delusive, ludicrous, nonexistent

fantasy fiction, figment, myth, story *(falsehood)*, vision *(dream)*

far inaccessible, obscure *(remote)*, remote *(not proximate)*, remote *(secluded)*

far away inaccessible

far from the point irrelevant

far off inaccessible

far removed remote *(not proximate)*

far-famed outstanding *(prominent)*, renowned

far-fetched inapposite

far-flung broad, extensive, far reaching

far-gone dilapidated

far-off remote *(not proximate)*, remote *(secluded)*, unapproachable

far-ranging extensive, far reaching

far-reaching broad, comprehensive, critical *(crucial)*, extensive, important *(significant)*, major, material *(important)*, momentous, rife

far-spread broad

faraway oblivious, remote *(secluded)*, unapproachable

farce caricature, parody, travesty

farcical ludicrous

fare fee *(charge)*, price, rate, toll *(tax)*

fare well succeed *(attain)*

farfetched suspicious *(questionable)*, unbelievable

farm cultivate, homestead

farm land homestead

farmplace homestead

farmstead homestead

farrago confusion *(turmoil)*, melange

farseeing omniscient, perspicacious, prophetic, provident *(showing foresight)*

farsighted perspicacious, politic, prophetic, prudent, sapient, sensible

farsightedness sagacity

farthest extreme *(last)*, last *(final)*, peripheral, ultimate

farthest end extremity *(furthest point)*

farthest point ceiling, extremity *(furthest point)*

farthest reach extremity *(furthest point)*, utmost

farthest removed extreme *(last)*

fascicle serial

fascimile recreate, resemblance, transcript

fascinate immerse *(engross)*, interest, occupy *(engage)*

fascinating attractive, sapid

fascination compulsion *(obsession)*, obsession, preoccupation, seduction

fascist dictatorial

fashion adapt, build *(construct)*, complexion, compose, conduct, contrive, create, crystallize, custom, devise *(invent)*, fabricate *(construct)*, forge *(produce)*, form *(arrangement)*, form, formulate, frame *(construct)*, frame *(formulate)*, habit, invent *(produce for the first time)*, make, manner *(behavior)*, manner *(kind)*, manufacture, means *(opportunity)*, mode, parlance, prescription *(custom)*, produce *(manufacture)*, scheme, style, usage, way *(manner)*

fashionable customary, elegant, popular

fashionable society elite

fashionableness custom

fashioning building *(business of assembling)*, creation, manufacture, onset *(commencement)*

fast close *(intimate)*, expeditious, firm, fixed *(securely placed)*, indelible, inextricable, inseparable, instantly, loyal, permanent, rapid, secure *(sound)*, solid *(sound)*, stable, staunch, steadfast

fast and loose variable

fast rate dispatch *(promptness)*

fasten affix, annex *(add)*, append, attach *(join)*, bar *(hinder)*, cement, cohere *(adhere)*, combine *(join together)*, commingle, handcuff, lock, occlude, restrain, shut, trammel

fasten in position securely fix *(make firm)*

fasten oneself upon hunt

fasten securely fix *(make firm)*

fasten together attach *(join)*, connect *(join together)*

fasten upon grapple

fastened attached *(annexed)*, firm, fixed *(securely placed)*, secure *(sound)*, stable

fastened together conjoint

fastener connection *(fastening)*, handcuff

fastening accession *(annexation)*, attachment *(act of affixing)*

fastidiosus disdainful, supercilious

fastidious conscientious, diligent, discriminating *(judicious)*, meticulous, particular *(exacting)*, precise, punctilious, sensitive *(discerning)*, strict

fastidiousness decorum, diligence *(care)*, particularity

fastidire disdain, spurn

fastidium contempt *(disdain)*, disdain

fastigium eminence

fastness dispatch *(promptness)*

fatal deadly, deleterious, dire, lethal, malignant, noxious, pernicious, pestilent, serious *(grave)*, toxic

fatal accident fatality

fatal affair tragedy

fatal casualty dead, fatality

fatal mishap fatality

fatalism resignation *(passive acceptance)*

fatality dead, death, mortality

fate end *(termination)*, happenstance, predetermination, predetermine, prospect *(outlook)*, quirk *(accident)*

fated forthcoming, future, inevitable, necessary *(inescapable)*, unalterable, unavoidable *(inevitable)*

fateful critical *(crucial)*, fatal, key, major, momentous, necessary *(inescapable)*, portentous *(ominous)*, prophetic

fateri admit *(concede)*, avow, confess

father generate, originate, parents, primogenitor, propagate *(increase)*, reproduce

fatherhood filiation, paternity

fatherland home *(place of origin)*, nationality

fatherlike paternal

fatherly paternal

fathership filiation, paternity

fathom apprehend *(perceive)*, ascertain, comprehend *(understand)*, conceive *(comprehend)*, construe *(comprehend)*, delve, digest *(comprehend)*, discern *(detect with the senses)*, find *(dis-*

cover), gauge, measure, pierce *(discern),* realize *(understand),* solve, understand

fathomable appreciable, cognizable, coherent *(clear),* comprehensible, determinable *(ascertainable),* scrutable, solvable

fathomless incomprehensible, profound *(intense)*

fatidic ominous, oracular, prophetic

fatidical ominous, oracular, prophetic

fatidicus prophetic

fatigare importune

fatigue exhaust *(deplete),* languor, prostration, tax *(overwork)*

fatigued languid

fatiguing difficult, onerous, operose, oppressive

fatiloquent portentous *(ominous),* prophetic

fatten enlarge, expand, inflate

fatten upon prey

fatuitous fatuous, illusory, opaque

fatuity opacity

fatuous ludicrous, misadvised, nugatory, opaque, puerile, vacuous

fatuus fatuous

faubourg frontier

fault blame *(culpability),* blame, culpability, decry, defacement, defect, deficiency, delinquency *(misconduct),* deprecate, depreciate, disadvantage, discommend, drawback, error, flaw, foible, frailty, guilt, impeach, mischief, misconduct, misdeed, misdoing, onus *(blame),* rift *(gap),* tort, transgression, vice

fault finding cynical

fault of the court injustice

fault-finding criticism, dissatisfaction

faultfind cavil, complain *(criticize)*

faultfinder malcontent

faultfinding denunciation, derogatory, diatribe, disapproval, disparagement, fractious, impugnation, inculpation, nonconsenting, obloquy, particular *(exacting),* pejorative, querulous, severe, stricture

faultful defective, errant, fallacious, peccant *(culpable)*

faultiness defect, deficiency, fallacy, handicap

faultless absolute *(ideal),* accurate, best, blameless, clean, faithful *(true to fact),* incorruptible, inculpable, infallible, innocent, intact, irreprehensible, literal, not guilty, pardonable, precise, pure, unblemished, unimpeachable

faultlessness rectitude

faulty bad *(inferior),* blameful, blemished, defective, deficient, derelict *(negligent),* errant, erroneous, fallacious, fallible, false *(inaccurate),* illogical, imperfect, inaccurate, incorrect, inexact, inferior *(lower in quality),* invalid, marred, obnoxious, peccable, poor *(inferior in quality),* unsatisfactory, unsound *(fallacious),* unsound *(not strong),* untenable

faulty in logic fallacious, sophistic

faulty reasoning fallacy

faulty work noncompliance *(improper completion)*

fautor backer

fautor partisan, promoter

favere favor, patronize *(trade with)*

favor accommodate, advantage, advocate, approval, approve, assent, auspices, behalf, benefit *(conferment),* benevolence *(act of kindness),* bounty, capitalize *(provide capital),* complexion, concur *(agree),* conduce, countenance, deign, discriminate *(treat differently),* embrace *(accept),* espouse, estimation *(esteem),* foster, franchise *(license),* further, gift *(present),* goodwill, grace, grant, grant *(concede),* gratuity *(present),* help, honor *(outward respect),* indorsement, indulgence, inequity, largess *(gift),* leave *(permission),* lenience, let *(permit),* nepotism, option *(contractual provision),* partiality, pass *(approve)*

favor patronage *(power to appoint jobs)*

favor patronage *(support),* patronize *(condescend toward),* predilection, predisposition, prefer, preserve, prestige, privilege, promote *(advance),* propensity, recommend, regard *(esteem),* respect, sanction *(permission),* service *(assistance),* side, sponsor, token, uphold

favor excessively overindulge

favor owed due

favor with bestow, impart, vouchsafe

favor with one's patronage patronize *(trade with)*

favorable auspicious, beneficial, constructive *(creative),* fitting, inclined, profitable, prone, propitious, receptive, salutary, seasonable, suitable, valuable, viable, willing *(not averse)*

favorable chance likelihood, opportunity, probability

favorable disposition goodwill

favorable opinion credit *(recognition),* estimation *(esteem)*

favorable opportunity advantage, possibility

favorable position edge *(advantage)*

favorable prospect chance *(possibility),* high probability, likelihood, possibility

favorable reception adoption *(acceptance)*

favorable recognition estimation *(esteem)*

favorable regard goodwill

favorable repute estimation *(esteem)*

favorable time chance *(fortuity),* opportunity

favorable to health salubrious

favorable trade balance boom *(prosperity)*

favorable verdict acquittal

favorable verdict to the defendant compurgation

favorableness expedience

favorably disposed partial *(biased)*

favorably inclined consenting, propitious, willing *(not averse)*

favorably minded ready *(willing)*

favorably prejudiced favorable *(expressing approval)*

favored exempt, popular, preferential, privileged

favored by fortune auspicious

favored treatment preference *(priority)*

favorer abettor, advocate *(espouser),* apologist, benefactor, disciple, partisan,

patron *(influential supporter),* sponsor

favoring auspicious, favorable *(expressing approval),* inequitable, lenient

favoring circumstance advantage

favoring influence auspices

favorite best, popular, preferable, preference *(choice),* preferred *(favored)*

favoritism bias, discrimination *(bigotry),* favor *(partiality),* inequity, injustice, nepotism, partiality, predisposition, prejudice *(preconception)*

fawn truckle

fawning obsequious, servile, subservient

fealty adherence *(devotion),* adhesion *(loyalty),* allegiance, fidelity, loyalty

fear cloud *(suspicion),* consternation, fright, misgiving, mistrust, panic, phobia, scruple, stress *(strain),* suspicion *(mistrust),* trepidation

fear of danger fright

fear-inspiring formidable, ominous, sinister

fear-stricken caitiff

fearful dire, formidable, ineffable, ominous, pending *(imminent),* portentous *(ominous),* recreant, repulsive, suspicious *(distrustful)*

fearfulness consternation, fear, misgiving, panic, scruple, stress *(strain),* suspicion *(mistrust)*

fearless heroic, indomitable, spartan, undaunted

fearlessness confidence *(faith),* prowess *(bravery)*

fearsome dangerous, sinister

feasibility expedience, possibility, potential

feasible colorable *(plausible),* plausible, possible, potential, practicable, pragmatic, presumptive, probable, suitable, viable

feasibleness feasibility

feast carouse

feast upon prey

feat act *(undertaking),* endeavor

featherbrained opaque

feature aspect, characteristic, complexion, component, constituent *(part),* contour *(shape),* detail, differential, element, exhibit, expose, factor *(ingredient),* ingredient, item, member *(constituent part),* particular, particularity, phase *(aspect),* phenomenon *(manifestation),* point *(item),* property *(distinctive attribute),* quality *(attribute),* quality *(grade),* speciality, specialty *(distinctive mark),* symptom, technicality, trait

featured attraction feature *(special attraction)*

featureless indeterminate

features character *(personal quality),* circumstances, color *(complexion),* configuration *(form),* indicia

febrifugal medicinal

febrile hot-blooded

feckless futile, inadept, inadequate, ineffective, ineffectual, lax, otiose, unable

feculent repulsive

fecund fertile, original *(creative),* productive, prolific

fecundate proliferate, propagate *(increase),* reproduce

fecundify proliferate

fecundus fertile

federal mutual (collective), national, public (affecting people)
federal officer marshal
federal union federation
federalization integration (amalgamation)
federalize affiliate, join (bring together)
federate affiliate, allied, associated, combine (act in concert), consolidate (unite), cooperate, federal, federalize (associate), intimate, join (bring together), mutual (collective), organize (unionize), pool
federated affiliated, associated, conjoint, mutual (collective)
federation affiliation (amalgamation), association (alliance), cartel, chamber (body), coaction, coalescence, coalition, committee, company (enterprise), confederacy (compact), consolidation, contact (association), contribution (participation), cooperative, corporation, integration (assimilation), league, merger, organization (association), partnership, pool, society, sodality, syndicate, union (labor organization)
federative collective, conjoint, corporate (associate), federal, mutual (collective)
fee advance (allowance), brokerage, charge (cost), compensation, due, excise, expense (cost), fare, honorarium, pay, payment (remittance), pension, perquisite, price, rate, real estate, recompense, rent, reward, toll (tax), wage
fee contingent on future legal services retainer
fee paid to secure legal services retainer
fee simple freehold
feeble decadent, helpless (powerless), imperfect, inadept, inadequate, incapable, inconspicuous, ineffective, ineffectual, insipid, insubstantial, insufficient, languid, lifeless (dull), nonsubstantial (not sturdy), passive, powerless, unsatisfactory, unsound (not strong)
feeble-eyed blind (sightless)
feeble-minded non compos mentis
feebleness caducity, disability (physical inability), fault (weakness), frailty, impotence, impuissance, incapacity, inefficacy, languor, prostration
feed maintain (sustain), nurture, provide (supply), supply, support (assist)
feed upon prey
feel deem, detect, endure (suffer), opine, perceive, surmise
feel a dearth lack
feel annoyance resent
feel compassion relent
feel conscience stricken regret
feel contempt for contemn, disdain, flout, misprize
feel contrition repent
feel disapproval except (object)
feel displeasure resent
feel distrust doubt (distrust), suspect (distrust)
feel for relent, sympathize
feel gratification relish
feel hurt resent
feel ill will resent
feel joy relish
feel no concern disregard

feel out peruse
feel pain suffer (sustain loss)
feel pleasure relish
feel regret repent
feel remorse repent
feel resentment resent
feel sure rely, trust
feel sure of confide (trust)
feel terror fear
feel the necessity for need, require (need)
feel the want of need
feel uncertain vacillate
feel uneasy about regret
feel unsure doubt (hesitate)
feel utter contempt for decry, disdain
feeling affection, climate, concept, fervent, humanity (humaneness), impression, notion, opinion (belief), passion, perceptive, perspective, pity, position (point of view), posture (attitude), premonition, reaction (response), sensibility, sensitive (easily affected), tenor
feeling of dejection damper (depressant)
feeling of depression damper (depressant)
feeling of obligation responsibility (conscience)
feeling of uncertainty doubt (indecision), qualm
feelingless cold-blooded
feelings of guilt remorse
fees consideration (recompense), disbursement (funds paid out)
feign assume (simulate), cloak, disguise, fabricate (make up), fake, falsify, forge (counterfeit), invent (falsify), misrepresent, mock (imitate), palter, perjure, pretend, prevaricate, profess (pretend), simulate
feigned artificial, colorable (specious), deceptive, delusive, dishonest, disingenuous, evasive, false (not genuine), fictitious, fraudulent, illusory, imitation, lying, mendacious, spurious, tartuffish
feigned copy fake
feigned story fiction, figment
feint artifice, color (deceptive appearance), deception, false pretense, maneuver (trick), pretense (pretext), pretext, ruse, sham, stratagem
felicitous auspicious, ecstatic, favorable (advantageous), propitious, relevant, resourceful, successful, suitable
felicitousness expedience, timeliness
felicity gift (flair), propensity, propriety (appropriateness), prosperity, skill
feline furtive, machiavellian, politic, sly, stealthy, subtle (insidious)
felix auspicious, successful
fell brutal, dire, disastrous, fatal, harmful, lethal, malignant, overthrow, pernicious, precipitate (throw down violently), ruthless
fell stroke disaster
fellow cohort, colleague, confederate, consort, contributor (contributor), copartner (business associate), correlate, correlative, member (individual in a group), participant, peer, person, resemblance
fellow companion colleague, consociate, consort
fellow conspirator accessory, accom-

plice, coactor, coconspirator, cohort, colleague, consociate, conspirer
fellow feeling comity, philanthropy, pity, rapprochement
fellow machinator coconspirator
fellow plotter coconspirator
fellow schemer coconspirator
fellow strategist coconspirator
fellow suffering pity
fellow traiter coconspirator
fellow worker associate, coadjutant, colleague, consociate, copartner (business associate), participant, partisan, partner
fellow workers personnel
fellowless solitary
fellowship coaction, coalition, committee, confederacy (compact), contact (association), contribution (participation), informality, integration (assimilation), league, merger, partnership, peace, rapprochement, society, sodality, union (labor organization)
fellowship in sorrow pity
felon assailant, captive, convict, criminal, hoodlum, lawbreaker, malefactor, offender, outlaw, prisoner
felonious culpable, illegal, illicit, impermissible, iniquitous, larcenous, lawless, nefarious, reprobate, wrongful
felonious abreption asportation
felonious act tortious act
felonious conduct criminality, guilt
felonious removal asportation
felonious stealing larceny
felonious taking robbery, theft
felonious taking of the property of another robbery
felonious transference asportation
felonious translocation asportation
feloniously illegally
feloniousness corruption, criminality
felony burglary, crime, delict, homicide, housebreaking, misdeed, offense
felony murder homicide
fence bar (hinder), barrier, bicker, enclosure, equivocate, hedge, obstacle, obstruction, palter, parry, pettifog, prevaricate, receiver, screen (guard)
fence in circumscribe (surround by boundary), confine, contain (enclose), enclose, encompass (surround), envelop, shut
fence off demarcate
fenced curtilage, guarded
fenced in area enclosure
fend counter, deter
fend off avert, block, deter, estop, parry, prevent, repel (drive back), repulse, resist (withstand), save (rescue), stave
fender panoply
feod fee (estate)
feoffee legatee
feracious fertile, prolific
feral deadly, destructive, fatal, harsh, lethal, malicious, malignant, pestilent, ruthless
ferax fertile, productive
fergiversate prevaricate
feriae holiday
ferine harsh, ruthless
ferire beat (strike)
ferity atrocity, cruelty, severity
ferment agitate (activate), catalyst, commotion, confusion (turmoil), discom-

pose, disturb, disturbance, embroil-
ment, emotion, entanglement *(confusion)*, foment, furor, pandemonium,
passion, perturb, riot, stress *(strain)*,
turmoil
fermentation commotion
ferocious brutal, cruel, harsh, malevolent, malicious, malignant, outrageous, ruthless, vicious
ferociousness bestiality, cruelty, severity
ferocity atrocity, bestiality, cruelty,
furor, outbreak, severity, violence
ferox rampant, unruly
ferre bear *(support)*, legalize
ferret hunt, search
ferret out ascertain, cross-examine,
delve, detect, discover, disinter, educe,
find *(discover)*, locate, pursue *(chase)*,
solve, trace *(follow)*
ferrier carrier
fertile beneficial, gainful, lucrative,
original *(creative)*, productive, prolific,
resourceful
fertilis fertile
fertility maternity
ferule cudgel
ferus brutal
fervency affection, ardor, compulsion
(obsession), furor, passion
fervens fervent, vehement
fervent demonstrative *(expressive of
emotion)*, eager, earnest, fanatical,
hot-blooded, intense, intensive, ready
(willing), serious *(devoted)*, true *(loyal)*,
vehement, zealous
fervid fervent, hot-blooded, vehement,
zealous
fervidness ardor
fervidus eager, fervent
fervor affection
fervor ardor
fervor emotion, passion, strength
Fescennine salacious
fester annoy
festering toxic
festinatio dispatch *(promptness)*, haste
festival holiday, treat
festive occasion ceremony
festivity ceremony
festooned elaborate
fetch procure, ruse, transport, yield
(produce a return)
fetching attractive
fete holiday
fetid stale
fetish compulsion *(obsession)*, obsession
fetter apprehend *(arrest)*, bind *(restrain)*, constraint *(imprisonment)*, constraint *(restriction)*, constrict *(inhibit)*,
contain *(restrain)*, custody *(incarceration)*, detain *(restrain)*, detention, deter,
hamper, handcuff, handcuff, hinder,
impede, impediment, interfere, restrain, restrict, trammel
fetters bondage, servitude
fettle color *(complexion)*
fetus embryo
feud altercation, argument *(contention)*, belligerency, brawl, collide
(clash), contention *(opposition)*, contest
(dispute), controversy *(argument)*, disaccord, disagreement, dispute, fee *(estate)*, freehold, revenge, struggle
feuder contender

feuding malevolent
fever furor
feverish demonstrative *(expressive of
emotion)*, frenetic, hot-blooded, rapid
feverish haste dispatch *(promptness)*
feverishness ardor
few deficient, infrequent, scarce, several *(plural)*
fewness insufficiency, paucity
fiasco debacle, disaster, failure *(lack
of success)*, miscarriage
fiat brevet, canon, declaration, decree,
dictate, direction *(order)*, directive,
edict, enactment, law, license, mandate, monition *(legal summons)*, order
(judicial directive), ordinance, permit,
precept, proclamation, pronouncement,
requirement, writ
fib invent *(falsify)*, lie *(falsify)*, mislead, prevaricate, story *(falsehood)*,
subterfuge
fibbing falsification
fiber character *(personal quality)*,
frame *(mood)*, prowess *(bravery)*
fickle capricious, faithless, false *(disloyal)*, inconsistent, irresolute, mutable,
undependable, unpredictable, unreliable, unsettled, untrustworthy, variable,
volatile
fickleness disloyalty, indecision, infidelity
fictile pliable, sequacious
fiction canard, falsehood, figment, lie,
misstatement, myth, phantom, story
(falsehood), subterfuge
fiction of the mind figment
fictional fictitious
fictionalize fabricate *(make up)*, invent *(falsify)*
fictitious artificial, assumed *(feigned)*,
erroneous, evasive, false *(inaccurate)*,
illusory, lying, mendacious, sobriquet,
spurious, unfounded, untrue
fictitious story myth
fictive evasive, fictitious, original
(creative)
fictive creation phantom
fictus apparent *(perceptible)*, false *(not
genuine)*, false pretense, fictitious, ostensible, unfounded
fidelis faithful *(diligent)*, loyal, true
(authentic)
fidelitas fidelity, loyalty
fideliter faithfully
fidelity adherence *(devotion)*, adhesion *(loyalty)*, allegiance, conformity
(obedience), discipline *(obedience)*, faith,
fealty, homage, honesty, integrity, loyalty, rectitude
fides allegiance, confidence *(faith)*,
credibility, duty *(obligation)*, faith, fidelity, guarantee, honesty, loyalty,
promise, reliance, trust *(confidence)*,
vow
fidgety restive
fiducia assurance, confidence *(faith)*,
reliance, trust *(confidence)*
fiducial fiduciary, pecuniary
fiduciary executor, pecuniary, trustee
fiduciary currency check *(instrument)*
fidus confidential, faithful *(diligent)*,
loyal, safe, staunch, true *(authentic)*
fief fee *(estate)*, freehold
field area *(province)*, bailiwick, calling, capacity *(sphere)*, career, circuit,

coverage *(scope)*, department, employment, latitude, occupation *(vocation)*,
parcel, plot *(land)*, post, profession *(vocation)*, province, pursuit *(occupation)*,
range, realm, region, scene, scope, section *(vicinity)*, space, sphere, territory
field of activity department, sphere
field of inquiry issue *(matter in dispute)*, matter *(subject)*
field of interest discipline *(field of
study)*
field of learning discipline *(field of
study)*
field of operation sphere
field of view outlook, perspective, vision *(sight)*
field of vision perception, perspective
field questions return *(respond)*
fiendish cold-blooded, cruel, diabolic,
harmful, malevolent, malignant, peccant *(culpable)*, pernicious, ruthless,
sinister
fiendishness atrocity, bestiality
fiendlike diabolic, malignant
fierce brutal, cruel, demonstrative
(expressive of emotion), fervent, formidable, intense, severe, spartan, vehement, vicious
fierceness bestiality, cruelty, passion,
severity
fieri occur *(happen)*, result
fieriness life *(vitality)*
fiery demonstrative *(expressive of
emotion)*, fervent, hot-blooded, intense,
vehement, zealous
fifty percent moiety
fifty-two weeks annum
fight affray, altercation, beat *(strike)*,
bicker, brawl, brawl, collision *(dispute)*,
commotion, conflict, confrontation *(altercation)*, contend *(dispute)*, contention
(opposition), contest *(dispute)*, contest,
disagree, fracas, fray, grapple, incompatibility *(difference)*, oppose, oppugn,
resist *(oppose)*, resistance, rift *(disagreement)*, strife, strive, struggle,
withstand
fight against counter, counteract
fight for protect
fight off counter, parry, repel *(drive
back)*
fight offensively attack
fight with engage *(involve)*
fighter aggressor, contender, foe, malcontent
fighting belligerency, conflict, litigious, offensive *(taking the initiative)*,
pugnacious, strife
figment fiction, myth, phantom, story
(falsehood)
figment of the imagination phantom
figmental fictitious
figura contour *(shape)*, form *(arrangement)*
figurare form
figuration configuration *(form)*, contour *(outline)*, contour *(shape)*, formation, motif, organization *(structure)*
figurative representative
figure bill *(invoice)*, body *(main part)*,
build *(construct)*, calculate, character
(an individual), color *(complexion)*,
complexion, configuration *(form)*, contour *(outline)*, contour *(shape)*, delineate, estimate, indicant, motif, organization *(structure)*, phenomenon *(manifes-*

tation), plan, price, rate, sum _(tally)_
figure costs estimate, evaluate
figure of speech phrase
figure out ascertain, calculate, conceive _(comprehend)_, construe _(comprehend)_, find _(discover)_, interpret, reason _(conclude)_, resolve _(solve)_, solve
figure up sum
figure work computation
figure-work census
figurehead ineffective, ineffectual, nonentity, powerless, token
figures census, information _(facts)_
figuring census, computation
filch embezzle, pilfer, poach, purloin, steal
filcher burglar, criminal
filchery theft
filching burglary, housebreaking
file book, classify, defer _(put off)_, distribute, dossier, enroll, enter _(record)_, entry _(record)_, erode, fix _(arrange)_, index _(docket)_, ledger, lineup, organize _(arrange)_, pigeonhole, record, record, register, register, sort, tabulate
file a charge complain _(charge)_, prosecute _(charge)_
file a claim charge _(accuse)_, complain _(charge)_, impeach, lodge _(bring a complaint)_, prosecute _(charge)_
file a legal claim sue
file a suit complain _(charge)_, lodge _(bring a complaint)_
file for petition
file suit sue
filed charges accused _(charged)_
filed notice lis pendens
filia child
filial loyal
filiality affiliation _(bloodline)_
filiate ascribe, relate _(establish a connection)_
filiation affiliation _(bloodline)_, affinity _(family ties)_, ancestry, blood, degree _(kinship)_, descent _(lineage)_, family _(common ancestry)_, origin _(ancestry)_, parentage, propinquity _(kinship)_, relationship _(family tie)_
filibuster detain _(restrain)_, forestall, hold up _(delay)_, procrastinate, protract _(prolong)_, stall
filing registration
filing of charges accusation
filius child
filius familias minor
fill fulfill, imbue, impact, load, penetrate, permeate, pervade, replenish, satisfy _(fulfill)_, sufficiency
fill a position employ _(engage services)_, engage _(hire)_, hire
fill a post hold _(possess)_
fill a vacancy employ _(engage services)_, hire
fill an office officiate, serve _(assist)_
fill an opening employ _(engage services)_
fill another's position displace _(replace)_
fill identical times coincide _(correspond)_
fill in compound, develop, replacement, replenish
fill in for displace _(replace)_, replace
fill one's time engage _(involve)_
fill out compound, develop, enlarge, expand, inflate, spread

fill to capacity impact
fill to superfluity inundate
fill up load, replenish, supply
fill with air inflate
fill with doubt perplex
fill with enthusiasm inspire
fill with information disabuse, instruct _(teach)_
fill with loathing repel _(disgust)_
fill with longing motivate
fill with shame humiliate
filled copious, full, inflated _(enlarged)_, replete
filled out ripe
filled to repletion replete
filled to utmost capacity full
filled with pride disdainful
fillip inducement, stimulate, stimulus
filminess indistinctness
filmy indistinct
filter distill, purge _(purify)_, screen _(select)_
filter in penetrate
filter through pervade
filth pornography
filthify pollute
filthiness defilement
filthy objectionable, repulsive, salacious
filtrate distill
fimbriae edge _(border)_
finagling fraudulent
final absolute _(complete)_, absolute _(conclusive)_, binding, categorical, certain _(positive)_, complete _(ended)_, conclusive _(determinative)_, conclusive _(settled)_, crucial, decisive, definitive, determinative, extreme _(last)_, inappealable, irrevocable, last _(final)_, peremptory _(absolute)_, positive _(incontestable)_, ultimate
final assessment determination
final authority arbiter
final cause object, purpose
final condemnation conviction _(finding of guilt)_
final condition ultimatum
final demand dun
final determination adjudication
final event end _(termination)_
final happening denouement
final judgment adjudication, conclusion _(determination)_, decree, holding _(ruling of a court)_, opinion _(judicial decision)_
final notice dun
final offer ultimatum
final outcome product
final point extremity _(furthest point)_, limit, objective
final proposal ultimatum
final proposition ultimatum
final result conclusion _(outcome)_, consequence _(conclusion)_, effect, issuance
final settlement of a matter disposition _(determination)_
final state end _(termination)_
final statement denouement
final terms condition _(contingent provision)_, settlement
final touch denouement
finale cessation _(termination)_, close _(conclusion)_, conclusion _(outcome)_, consequence _(conclusion)_
finale denouement
finale end _(termination)_, payoff _(re-

sult)
finality divorce, end _(termination)_
finalization denouement
finalize close _(agree)_, complete, conclude _(complete)_, consummate, decide, finish
finalize an agreement close _(agree)_
finally consequently
finally settled inappealable
finalty conclusion _(outcome)_
finance bear _(support)_, bestow, capitalize _(provide capital)_, fund, invest _(fund)_, lend, maintain _(sustain)_, pay, sponsor, subsidize, support _(assist)_, underwrite
finance again refinance
financer patron _(influential supporter)_, surety _(guarantor)_
finances capital, cash, means _(funds)_, money
financial commercial, fiscal, mercantile, monetary, pecuniary
financial affairs finance
financial assistance consideration _(recompense)_
financial backer promoter
financial backing investment, maintenance _(support of spouse)_
financial center market _(business)_, market place
financial disaster bankruptcy, default, failure _(bankruptcy)_
financial failure bankruptcy
financial loss failure _(bankruptcy)_
financial officer comptroller
financial provision capital
financial remuneration compensation, honorarium, income, pension, perquisite, recovery _(award)_, reparation _(indemnification)_
financial resources capital, finance, income, property _(possessions)_
financial reward perquisite, profit
financial ruin bankruptcy, failure _(bankruptcy)_
financial shortage deficit
financial statement account _(evaluation)_
financial straits privation
financially prudent economical
financially sound solvent
financier obligee, promoter, sponsor, trustee
financing investment, loan, maintenance _(support of spouse)_
find acquisition, adjudge, adjudicate, ascertain, award, conclude _(decide)_, decide, decree, detect, determine, disinter, ferret, hold _(decide)_, invent _(produce for the first time)_, judge, locate, prize, procure, pronounce _(pass judgment)_, rule _(decide)_, sentence
find a clue elucidate
find a middle ground compromise _(settle by mutual agreement)_
find a place for lodge _(house)_
find a remedy counteract
find a solution resolve _(solve)_
find a way devise _(invent)_
find against convict
find an indictment against impeach
find cause to blame criticize _(find fault with)_
find fault blame, complain _(criticize)_, decry, deprecate, discommend, except _(object)_, object, remonstrate, reprimand

find fault with cavil, censure, complain *(criticize)*, denounce *(condemn)*, depreciate, disapprove *(condemn)*, disparage, expostulate, impugn, incriminate, rebuke, reprehend, reproach
find flaws remonstrate
find freedom escape
find guilty condemn *(blame)*, convict, sentence
find hard to believe doubt *(distrust)*
find help employ *(engage services)*
find indispensable need
find intolerable resent
find liable convict
find manpower recruit
find necessary need
find not guilty absolve, acquit, clear
find nothing to praise decry
find one's advantage in capitalize *(seize the chance)*
find out ascertain, detect, discover, disinter, overhear, solve
find out exactly ascertain
find out the meaning of construe *(comprehend)*
find outlet exude
find passage exude
find probable assume *(suppose)*
find room for lodge *(house)*
find the answer ascertain, resolve *(solve)*
find the cause solve
find the key solve
find the solution ascertain, solve
find the value of evaluate
find the weight of weigh
find unfounded disprove
find useful exploit *(make use of)*
find vent exude
find words for express
find words to express communicate, phrase
finding adjudication, answer *(solution)*, arbitration, award, choice *(decision)*, clue, cognovit, comment, conclusion *(determination)*, consequence *(conclusion)*, conviction *(finding of guilt)*, decree, detection, determination, dictum, disposition *(determination)*, holding *(ruling of a court)*, invention, judgment *(formal court decree)*, observation, opinion *(judicial decision)*, outcome, perception, recognition, result, ruling, solution *(answer)*, verdict
finding a middle course mediation
finding another mate digamy
finding another spouse digamy
finding of guilty condemnation *(punishment)*
finding out discovery
findings of fact and conclusions of law ruling
fine acute, amercement, appropriate, cost *(penalty)*, damages, forfeiture *(thing forfeited)*, impalpable, meritorious, narrow, penalize, penalty, premium, rare, sapid, tenuous, trover, valuable
fine-mannered civil *(polite)*
fine point technicality
fineness quality *(excellence)*, sensibility
finer superior *(excellent)*
finesse artifice, discretion *(quality of being discreet)*, management *(judicious use)*, performance *(workmanship)*,

prowess *(ability)*, ruse, science *(technique)*, skill, stratagem, subterfuge
finest cardinal *(outstanding)*, leading *(ranking first)*, premium, prime *(most valuable)*
fingere conjure, create, feign, pretend
finical meticulous, particular *(exacting)*, precise, punctilious
finicality particularity
finicalness particularity
finicking meticulous, punctilious
finicky meticulous, particular *(exacting)*, precise, punctilious
finire conclude *(complete)*, limit
finis boundary, cessation *(termination)*, close *(conclusion)*, conclusion *(outcome)*
finis denouement, dissolution *(termination)*
finis end *(termination)*, frontier, limit, object, restriction
finish accomplish, attain, cap, cease, cessation *(termination)*, close *(conclusion)*, close *(terminate)*, commit *(perpetrate)*, complete, conclude *(complete)*, conclusion *(outcome)*, consequence *(conclusion)*, consummate, culminate, defeasance, denouement, deplete, desist, destination, discontinue *(abandon)*, dispatch *(dispose of)*, dissolution *(termination)*, dissolve *(terminate)*, end *(termination)*, exhaust *(try all possibilities)*, expend *(consume)*, expiration, expire, extremity *(death)*, finality, fulfill, liquidate *(convert into cash)*, mature, outcome, pass *(satisfy requirements)*, payoff *(result)*, perfect, perform *(adhere to)*, quit *(discontinue)*, shut, stop, terminate
finish litigation rest *(end a legal case)*
finish off cap, extinguish
finish up close *(terminate)*
finished absolute *(complete)*, choate lien, complete *(ended)*, conclusive *(settled)*, defunct, expert, irredeemable, ripe, through, veteran
finished product fait accompli, performance *(execution)*
finishing conclusive *(settled)*, extreme *(last)*, final, last *(final)*
finishing stroke denouement
finite terminable
finite quantity paucity
finitimus adjacent
fire ardor, barrage, burn, conflagration, deflagrate, depose *(remove)*, discharge *(dismiss)*, discharge *(shoot)*, dismiss *(discharge)*, foment, life *(vitality)*, passion, provoke, remove *(dismiss from office)*, spirit, stimulate, supplant
fire at discharge *(shoot)*
fire from employment terminate
fire up motivate
fire-raising arson
firearm gun
firearms ammunition
fireball bomb
firebrand demagogue, hoodlum
fireside home *(domicile)*
firing arson, discharge *(dismissal)*, discharge *(shot)*, dismissal *(discharge)*, layoff, rejection
firing a charge discharge *(shot)*
firm business *(commercial enterprise)*, certain *(fixed)*, cohesive *(compact)*, com-

pact *(dense)*, company *(enterprise)*, concern *(business establishment)*, concrete, constant, corporation, corporeal, definite, durable, earnest, enterprise *(economic organization)*, faithful *(loyal)*, fixed *(securely placed)*, house, immutable, indomitable, inexorable, inflexible, infrangible, inseparable, institute, intractable, ironclad, irreconcilable, irrevocable, loyal, obdurate, ossified, partnership, patient, peremptory *(imperative)*, pertinacious, purposeful, renitent, resolute, rigid, secure *(sound)*, sedulous, serious *(devoted)*, severe, solid *(compact)*, solid *(sound)*, spartan, stable, staunch, steadfast, strong, unalterable, unbending, uncompromising, undaunted, undeniable, unyielding, well-grounded
firm advice instruction *(direction)*
firm attachment affection
firm belief confidence *(faith)*, conviction *(persuasion)*, credence, faith
firm hold coherence
firm in adherence true *(loyal)*
firm in allegiance true *(loyal)*
firm in principle high-minded
firm opposition conflict
firm principle code, law
firm up stabilize
firmly faithfully
firmly established fixed *(securely placed)*, ingrained, inveterate, steadfast
firmly fixed ingrained
firmly implanted fixed *(securely placed)*
firmly seated fixed *(securely placed)*
firmly set fixed *(securely placed)*, rigid
firmly united compact *(dense)*
firmness adherence *(adhesion)*, adhesion *(loyalty)*, certainty, constant, force *(strength)*, inertia, prowess *(bravery)*, purpose, resolution *(decision)*, rigor, spirit, strength, surety *(certainty)*, tenacity
firmness of belief certainty
firmness of purpose diligence *(perseverance)*
firmus constant (adjective), constant (noun), durable, firm, irrefutable, resolute, solid *(sound)*, stable, staunch, steadfast, substantial, valid
first ab initio, cardinal *(basic)*, central *(essential)*, dominant, important *(significant)*, initial, leading *(ranking first)*, original *(initial)*, paramount, precursory, preferred *(given priority)*, previous, primary, prime *(original)*, primordial, principal, prior, prototype, stellar, unprecedented
first and foremost ab initio
first and last only *(sole)*
first appearance nascency, onset *(commencement)*
first attempt experiment
first cause derivation
first charge first offense
first competition primary
first contest primary
first crime first offense
first criminal violation first offense
first election primary
first in quality prime *(most valuable)*
first installment handsel
first move onset *(commencement)*,

outset
first occasion derivation
first of all ab initio
first offender convict
first payment handsel
first place primacy, priority, prize
first pleading complaint
first political competition primary
first political contest primary
first receipts handsel
first sight discovery
first stage embryo, nascency
first step nascency, onset *(commencement)*, outset, start
first violation first offense
first-class best, premium, prime *(most valuable)*
first-rate best, meritorious, preferential, premium, prime *(most valuable)*, select, superior *(excellent)*, superlative
firstly ab initio
fiscal commercial, financial, mercantile, monetary, pecuniary
fiscal exchange commerce
fiscalis fiscal
fiscus finance, treasury
fish out ferret
fissile divisible, severable
fission severance
fissionable divisible, severable
fissura split
fissure break *(fracture)*, force *(break)*, part *(separate)*, rift *(gap)*, sever, split *(noun)*, split *(verb)*
fisticuffs affray, brawl
fit accommodate, adapt, adequate, agree *(comply)*, applicable, apposite, appropriate, available, capable, competent, comply, comport *(agree with)*, condign, conform, congruous, consonant, due *(regular)*, effective *(efficient)*, eligible, entitled, familiar *(informed)*, favorable *(advantageous)*, felicitous, just, normal *(sane)*, opportune, outbreak, outburst, pertinent, qualified *(competent)*, ready *(prepared)*, reasonable *(fair)*, reasonable *(rational)*, relative *(relevant)*, relevant, right *(suitable)*, ripe, satisfy *(fulfill)*, seasonable, suitable
fit exactly coincide *(correspond)*
fit for a purpose attune
fit for appointment eligible
fit for dwelling habitable
fit for election eligible
fit for habitation habitable, residential
fit for sale marketable
fit for selection eligible
fit for travel open *(accessible)*, passable
fit for use disposable, effective *(operative)*, functional
fit in comport *(agree with)*, conform
fit out clothe, furnish, supply
fit the pattern naturalize *(acclimate)*
fit time opportunity
fit to be chosen eligible
fit to be occupied habitable
fit to live in habitable
fit together comport *(agree with)*, frame *(construct)*, join *(bring together)*
fitful broken *(interrupted)*, disjunctive *(tending to disjoin)*, disorderly, haphazard, inconsistent, intermittent, sporadic, unpredictable, variable

fitfulness inconsistency, irregularity
fitness ability, admissibility, aptitude, competence *(ability)*, expedience, faculty *(ability)*, health, instinct, propriety *(appropriateness)*, timeliness
fitted capable, commensurate, convenient, familiar *(informed)*, fit, sciential
fitted for legal argumentation forensic
fitted for public argumentation forensic
fitted to teach didactic
fittedness ability
fitting applicable, apposite, appropriate, as a matter of right, condign, congruous, consonant, convenient, conventional, correlative, eligible, fair *(just)*, favorable *(advantageous)*, felicitous, fit, germane, just, opportune, permissible, pertinent, practical, proper, reasonable *(fair)*, relative *(relevant)*, relevant, right *(suitable)*, rightful, suitable, tenable
fitting occasion opportunity
fitting time opportunity
fittingness decorum, expedience, qualification *(fitness)*
fix adjust *(resolve)*, affix, allocate, annex *(add)*, arrange *(methodize)*, award, bind *(restrain)*, bond *(hold together)*, cement, decide, define, delimit, designate, dispose *(apportion)*, embed, emend, entanglement *(involvement)*, help, hold *(decide)*, marshal, plant *(place firmly)*, predicament, redress, reform, rehabilitate, remedy, renew *(refurbish)*, renovate, repair, repose *(place)*, restore *(renew)*
fix a charge charge *(assess)*
fix a valuation assess *(tax)*
fix attention on note *(notice)*
fix beforehand preordain
fix blame accuse
fix bounds circumscribe *(surround by boundary)*
fix by agreement close *(agree)*
fix conclusively arbitrate *(adjudge)*, rule *(decide)*
fix deeply establish *(entrench)*
fix firmly embed
fix in pinpoint
fix in purpose resolve *(decide)*
fix in the mind recall *(remember)*, remember
fix limits circumscribe *(surround by boundary)*, demarcate
fix on focus
fix one's attention concentrate *(pay attention)*
fix permanently establish *(entrench)*
fix the blame for lodge *(bring a complaint)*
fix the burden of impute
fix the date date
fix the meaning define
fix the mind upon intend
fix the order arrange *(methodize)*, file *(arrange)*
fix the position locate
fix the price at charge *(assess)*
fix the price of rate
fix the responsibility present *(prefer charges)*
fix the responsibility for impute
fix the thoughts upon focus
fix the time date

fix the value assess *(appraise)*
fix together cement
fix up embellish
fix upon determine, impute, prefer, select
fix with precision define
fixable ascertainable, corrigible, determinable *(ascertainable)*
fixation compulsion *(obsession)*, constant, location, obsession, preoccupation
fixed absolute *(conclusive)*, accustomed *(customary)*, attached *(annexed)*, certain *(specific)*, constant, conventional, customary, definite, definitive, deliberate, durable, express, firm, formal, habitual, immutable, inappealable, indelible, inevitable, inextricable, inflexible, ingrained, inherent, inveterate, irrevocable, limited, necessary *(inescapable)*, ordinary, permanent, perpetual, positive *(prescribed)*, prescriptive, regular *(orderly)*, resolute, rigid, routine, secure *(sound)*, serious *(devoted)*, several *(separate)*, situated, stable, standing, stated, static, statutory, steadfast, traditional, unalienable, unalterable, unavoidable *(inevitable)*, unavoidable *(not voidable)*, unbending, unyielding
fixed amount of damages ad damnum clause
fixed assets immovable
fixed belief credence
fixed capital principal *(capital sum)*
fixed charge fee *(charge)*
fixed chattel immovable
fixed conviction compulsion *(obsession)*
fixed direction intention
fixed future predetermination
fixed idea compulsion *(obsession)*, obsession, preconception, preoccupation
fixed intention project
fixed opinion conviction *(persuasion)*
fixed order array *(order)*, method
fixed procedure usage
fixed property immovable
fixed purpose animus, design *(intent)*, forethought, goal, intention, objective
fixed residence abode, home *(domicile)*
fixed ways practice *(custom)*
fixedly invariably
fixedness adherence *(adhesion)*
fixing attachment *(act of affixing)*, designation *(naming)*, renewal, repair
fixing a price appraisal
fixity of purpose diligence *(perseverance)*
fixture attachment *(thing affixed)*, device *(mechanism)*, immovable
flaccid powerless
flag indicant, indicator, languish, succumb
flag bearer nominee *(candidate)*
flagellare lash *(strike)*
flagellate beat *(strike)*, ill use, lash *(strike)*
flagging languid
flagitare call *(demand)*, dun, solicit
flagitiosus disgraceful
flagitious bad *(offensive)*, blameworthy, depraved, disgraceful, flagrant, heinous, immoral, inexcusable, inexpiable, iniquitous, nefarious, outra-

geous, profligate *(corrupt)*, reprehensible, reprobate, scandalous, sinister
flagitious villainy atrocity
flagitiousness atrocity, bad repute, crime
flagitous blameful
flagrancy atrocity, bad repute, notoriety, pretense *(ostentation)*
flagrant arrant *(onerous)*, bad *(offensive)*, blameworthy, brazen, conspicuous, delinquent *(guilty of a misdeed)*, disgraceful, egregious, extreme *(exaggerated)*, heinous, manifest, nefarious, notorious, outrageous, outright, prominent, remarkable, reprehensible, reprobate, salient, scandalous
flagrant abuse of the law lynch law
flagrante delicto blameworthy, delinquency *(misconduct)*
flagrantly bad arrant *(onerous)*
flail beat *(strike)*
flair aptitude, competence *(ability)*, faculty *(ability)*
flam falsehood
flamboyant elaborate, grandiose, pretentious *(ostentatious)*
flame deflagrate
flame up burn, deflagrate
flaming hot-blooded, intense
flaming into notice flagrant
flange border
flank border *(bound)*, hedge, protect
flap brandish, oscillate
flare burn, deflagrate, discharge *(shot)*
flare up deflagrate, outburst
flare-up bluster *(commotion)*, furor, outbreak
flaring blatant *(obtrusive)*
flash deflagrate, discharge *(shot)*, flaunt, immediate *(at once)*
flashiness pretense *(ostentation)*
flashy elaborate, flagrant, grandiose, pretentious *(ostentatious)*, tawdry
flat impecunious, insipid, jejune *(dull)*, lifeless *(dull)*, pedestrian, prosaic, stale
flat broke impecunious
flat refusal rebuff
flat saying platitude
flatten depress
flatter overestimate
flattering obsequious
flattery mention *(tribute)*
flatulence bombast
flatulent fustian, inflated *(bombastic)*, loquacious, orotund
flaunt brandish, display
flaunting blatant *(obtrusive)*, brazen, flagrant, grandiose, orgulous, proud *(conceited)*
flavor color *(complexion)*, savory
flavored savory
flavorful palatable, sapid
flavorless insipid, jejune *(dull)*, stale
flavorous palatable, sapid, savory
flavorsome palatable, sapid, savory
flavory sapid
flaw deface, defacement, defect, deficiency, drawback, error, fault *(mistake)*, fault *(weakness)*, foible, frailty, miscue, onus *(blame)*, stigma, vice
flaw in reasoning fallacy
flaw in the argument non sequitur
flawed blemished, defective, deficient, fallible, faulty, imperfect, incorrect, in-

exact, marred, peccable, sinister, vicious
flawless absolute *(ideal)*, best, infallible, intact, precise, pure, unblemished
flay denude, lash *(attack verbally)*, lash *(strike)*, plunder, reprimand, reproach
flebilis deplorable, lamentable, lugubrious
fledging amateur
fledgling juvenile, neophyte, novice
flee abscond, depart, disappear, elude, escape, evacuate, evade *(elude)*, leave *(depart)*, move *(alter position)*, quit *(evacuate)*, retreat
flee from avoid *(evade)*, eschew
fleece betray *(lead astray)*, defraud, deprive, dupe, prey, steal
fleeced aggrieved *(victimized)*
fleeing flight
fleer flout, fugitive, mock *(deride)*
fleet expeditious, rapid
fleeting brief, elusive, ephemeral, temporary, transient, transitory, volatile
flesh and blood physical
fleshly corporeal, lascivious, lecherous, mundane, physical, prurient
fleshy corporal
flexibilis flexible, pliable
flexibility amenability, facility *(easiness)*, informality, lenience
flexible amenable, deft, facile, liberal *(broad minded)*, malleable, open *(persuasible)*, passive, pliable, pliant, receptive, resilient, sequacious, suasible, susceptible *(responsive)*, tractable, yielding
flexibleness amenability
flexile flexible, malleable, pliable, resilient, sequacious, tractable
flexuous circuitous, complex, labyrinthine, sinuous
flicker beat *(pulsate)*
flickering intermittent
flier notice *(announcement)*
flight abandonment *(desertion)*, desertion, evasion
flight of fancy figment
flightiness inconsistency
flighty capricious, frivolous, inconsistent, irresponsible, thoughtless, volatile
flimflam bunko, falsification, ruse
flimsiness frailty, impalpability
flimsy frivolous, inconclusive, inconsequential, inferior *(lower in quality)*, insubstantial, nonsubstantial *(not sturdy)*, poor *(inferior in quality)*, tenuous
fling cast *(throw)*, dispatch *(send off)*, impel, launch *(project)*, precipitate *(throw down violently)*, project *(impel forward)*, send
fling dishonor upon disgrace
fling downward precipitate *(throw down violently)*
fling off dispel
flint-hearted brutal, malignant
flinty rigid
flip a coin bet
flippancy disrespect
flippant brazen, frivolous, impertinent *(insolent)*, insolent, presumptuous
flitter beat *(pulsate)*
flitting transitory
float finance

flock assemblage, mass *(body of persons)*, meet
flog beat *(strike)*, lash *(strike)*, punish
flood assemblage, cataclysm, immerse *(plunge into)*, inundate, load, outflow, overcome *(overwhelm)*, overload, plethora, spate
floodgate crossroad *(turning point)*, outlet
floor recognition
florens prosperous
floridness bombast
flounder mismanage
floundering incompetent
flourish brandish, display, flaunt, gain, germinate, increase, pretense *(ostentation)*, proliferate, pullulate, succeed *(attain)*
flourishing cumulative *(increasing)*, opulent, prosperous, rampant, successful
flourishing condition boom *(prosperity)*
flout contemn, defy, disdain, disrespect, jape, mock *(deride)*, override, spurn
flouting contemptuous, disdainful
flow accrue *(arise)*, arise *(originate)*, circulate, circulation, cycle, ensue, issue *(send forth)*, pass *(advance)*, proceed *(go forward)*, progress, result, sequence, spread, stem *(originate)*
flow forth emanate
flow from redound
flow in penetrate
flow into pervade
flow of language parlance
flow of words parlance
flow out exude, issue *(send forth)*
flow over inundate
flower proliferate, pullulate
flowering fertile, fruition, growth *(evolution)*
flowery turgid
flowery language rhetoric *(skilled speech)*
flowing circulation, copious, eloquent, facile, fluvial, full
flown truant
fluctuant indeterminate
fluctuare fluctuate
fluctuate beat *(pulsate)*, change, doubt *(hesitate)*, oscillate, vacillate, vary
fluctuating capricious, disorderly, faithless, hesitant, intermittent, irresolute, irresponsible, mutable, periodic, shifting, sporadic, undependable, variable
fluctuation hesitation, indecision
fluctuations vicissitudes
fluency facility *(easiness)*, parlance, skill
fluent eloquent, facile, fluvial, loquacious, voluble
fluere emanate
fluid fluvial, indeterminate, protean
fluidic fluvial
flunk fail *(lose)*
flurry confuse *(bewilder)*, dispatch *(promptness)*, haste, outburst, perturb
flush full, opulent, profuse, prosperous, replete, substantial
fluster agitate *(perturb)*, confuse *(bewilder)*, confusion *(ambiguity)*, discompose, disconcert, disorient, disrupt, dis-

turb, embarrass, embarrassment, harry *(harass)*, muddle, obfuscate, perturb, stress *(strain)*, upset

flutter beat *(pulsate)*, oscillate, panic, trepidation

fluviatic fluvial

fluviatile fluvial

fluvicoline fluvial

flux circulation, outflow, transition

fluxus transient

fly flee, leave *(depart)*, race

fly at attack

fly in the face of override

fly off at a tangent deviate, digress

fly-by-night untrustworthy

fob off on foist

focal central *(situated near center)*

focal point center *(central position)*, focus, gravamen, highlight

focal point of the complaint gist *(ground for a suit)*

focalization centralization

focalize concentrate *(consolidate)*, converge

focus center *(central position)*, concentrate *(consolidate)*, concentrate *(pay attention)*, converge, devote, gravamen, pinpoint

focus attention on concentrate *(pay attention)*, specialize

focus of attention center *(central position)*

fodere delve

fodicare jostle *(bump into)*

foe adversary, aggressor, contender, contestant, rival

foedare deface

foederatus federal

foedere sociatus federal

foedus confederacy *(compact)*, league, loathsome, pact, repulsive

foeman foe

fog confuse *(bewilder)*, discompose, ignorance, incertitude, indistinctness, muddle, obfuscate, obnubilate, obscure, perplex

fogginess indistinctness, obscuration

foggy indistinct, nebulous, opaque, unclear

foible defect, deficiency, fault *(weakness)*, flaw, frailty, vice

foil arrest *(stop)*, balk, check *(bar)*, circumvent, constrict *(inhibit)*, contravene, counter, counteract, defeat, deter, disadvantage, discontinue *(break continuity)*, enjoin, fight *(counteract)*, frustrate, frustration, halt, hamper, interfere, interrupt, keep *(restrain)*, oppugn, overturn, parry, preclude, prevent, repel *(drive back)*, stem *(check)*, stop, subdue, thwart, withstand

foiled disappointed

foist coerce

foist off fake

foist oneself intrude

foist upon bilk

fold fail *(lose)*, society

folder file

folio publication *(printed matter)*

folk family *(common ancestry)*, kindred, lineage, populace, population, public, race, society

folk speech language

folklore myth

folks populace

folktale myth

follow abide, accrue *(arise)*, adhere *(maintain loyalty)*, adopt, arise *(originate)*, chase, conform, copy, ensue, evolve, fulfill, heed, hunt, keep *(fulfill)*, mock *(imitate)*, obey, observe *(obey)*, observe *(watch)*, proceed *(go forward)*, pursue *(carry on)*, pursue *(chase)*, redound, result, resume, spy, stem *(originate)*, supervene

follow a calling practice *(engage in)*

follow a course proceed *(go forward)*

follow a profession practice *(engage in)*

follow a trail pursue *(chase)*

follow after succeed *(follow)*

follow as a consequence ensue

follow as a model plagiarize

follow as an occupation practice *(engage in)*

follow close upon hunt

follow from emanate

follow in a train of events ensue

follow in order accede *(succeed)*, succeed *(follow)*

follow one another interchangeably alternate *(take turns)*

follow one another reciprocally alternate *(take turns)*

follow one's vocation labor

follow orders obey

follow precedent conform

follow routine conform

follow successively reciprocate

follow suit copy, mock *(imitate)*

follow the example of copy, mock *(imitate)*

follow the trail delve, hunt

follow the trail of search

follow through complete, consummate, exhaust *(try all possibilities)*, follow-up, perpetrate

follow to a conclusion perfect

follow up maintain *(carry on)*, persevere, probe, prosecute *(carry forward)*

follow up an inquiry canvass

follower addict, coadjutant, cohort, consociate, disciple, member *(individual in a group)*, parasite, partisan, protégé, successor

following ancillary *(subsidiary)*, business *(occupation)*, consequential *(deducible)*, continuous, deductible *(provable)*, deductive, derivative, ensuing, forthcoming, future, immediate *(imminent)*, imminent, inevitable, malleable, proximate, secondary, subsequent, successive

following death posthumous

following established custom formal

following established form formal

following established rules formal

following in a series consecutive

following in time ex post facto

following the letter verbatim

following upon incident

folly abortion *(fiasco)*, inexpedience, lunacy

foment abet, agitate *(activate)*, cause, conduce, incite, outbreak, outburst, stimulate

fomentation aggravation *(exacerbation)*, commotion, disturbance, instigation, origination, outbreak, outburst, provocation

fomenter demagogue

fomentor abettor, determinant

fond of home household *(domestic)*

fond of investigation inquisitive

fondness affection, affinity *(regard)*, desire, estimation *(esteem)*, favor *(partiality)*, favoritism, inclination, partiality, penchant, predilection, predisposition, propensity, regard *(esteem)*

fons origin *(source)*, source

font origin *(source)*, origination, source

food sustenance

fool bilk, deceive, defraud, delude, dupe, ensnare, entrap, evade *(deceive)*, illude, inveigle, jape, lie *(falsify)*, misguide, mislead, misrepresent, overreach, palter, pretend

foolable naive

foolhardiness inconsideration, temerity

foolhardy hot-blooded, imprudent, impulsive *(rash)*, precipitate, presumptuous, reckless, thoughtless

foolish fatuous, ill-advised, impolitic, imprudent, inept *(incompetent)*, irrational, ludicrous, lunatic, puerile, reckless, trivial, unfit, unpolitic, unreasonable, vacuous

foolishness credulity, ignorance, inexpedience, jargon *(unintelligible language)*, lunacy, temerity

foolproof indubious, infallible, safe

foot pay

foot passenger pedestrian

foot the bill defray

foot traveler pedestrian

footage space

footing ground, plight, position *(situation)*, posture *(situation)*, status

footnote comment, marginalia, notation, note *(brief comment)*

footpace space

footstep step

foppishness pride

for in furtherance, in lieu of

for a beginning ab initio

for a certainty a fortiori

for a select few esoteric

for a still stronger reason a fortiori

for a time ad interim, pro tempore, provisional

for all history always *(forever)*

for all to see distinct *(clear)*

for each and every day per diem

for each day per diem

for ever and ever now and forever

for every day per diem

for just reason for cause

for legitimate reason for cause

for mere discussion only arguendo

for nothing free *(at no charge)*, gratis, gratuitous *(given without recompense)*

for one party ex parte

for one's good beneficial

for one's interest beneficial

for reasons given consequently

for that cause consequently

for that reason a priori, consequently

for the duration throughout *(during)*

for the moment pro tempore

for the most part as a rule, generally

for the period of throughout *(during)*

for the present occasion pro tempore

for the sake of ad hoc, in further-ance
for the sake of appearances pro forma
for the sake of argument arguendo
for the sake of form pro forma
for the time being ad interim, pro tempore
for the use of all common *(shared)*
for this case alone ad hoc
for this reason a priori, consequently
for which reason a priori, conse-quently
forage despoil, harry *(plunder)*, hunt, loot, prey, spoil *(pillage)*
foramen loophole
foraminated penetrable
foraminous penetrable
foray depredation, despoil, harry *(plunder)*, impinge, incursion, invasion, onset *(assault)*, pillage, plunder, prey, spoil *(pillage)*, spoliation
forbear abandon *(relinquish)*, allow *(endure)*, avoid *(evade)*, bear *(tolerate)*, cease, condone, defer *(put off)*, desist, endure *(suffer)*, eschew, forgo, leave *(allow to remain)*, palliate *(excuse)*, pause, refrain, renounce, stop, tolerate, withhold
forbearance abstention, benevolence *(disposition to do good)*, clemency, com-posure, continence, grace, lenience, longanimity, moderation, remission, resignation *(passive acceptance)*, re-straint, sufferance, temperance
forbearant passive, placable, resigned
forbearing charitable *(lenient)*, leni-ent, patient, placable, resigned
forbid ban, bar *(exclude)*, bar *(hin-der)*, block, censor, clog, condemn *(ban)*, constrain *(restrain)*, debar, deny *(refuse to grant)*, deter, enjoin, estop, forestall, forewarn, gainsay, halt, in-hibit, interdict, interfere, obstruct, pre-clude, prevent, prohibit, proscribe *(pro-hibit)*, reject, renounce, repel *(drive back)*, restrain, restrict, stay *(halt)*, stop, withhold
forbid by law enjoin, outlaw
forbiddance bar *(obstruction)*, con-straint *(restriction)*, embargo, estoppel, obstacle, obstruction, prohibition, pro-scription, restraint, veto
forbidden illegal, illegitimate *(ille-gal)*, illicit, impermissible, improper, unauthorized, unlawful
forbidden by law illicit
forbidding bleak *(not favorable)*, cen-sorship, loathsome, lugubrious, odious, ominous, portentous *(ominous)*, repug-nant *(exciting aversion)*, repulsive, se-vere, unapproachable
forbodement misgiving
forboding ominous
force ardor, attack, authority *(power)*, band, bind *(obligate)*, cast *(throw)*, cat-alyst, clout, coerce, coercion, command, compel, compulsion *(coercion)*, connota-tion, consequence *(significance)*, con-strain *(compel)*, constraint *(restriction)*, content *(meaning)*, context, dint, domi-nance, draw *(attraction)*, duress, em-phasis, enforce, enforcement, entail, exact, extort, foist, hijack, impact, im-petus, impose *(subject)*, inflict, inflic-tion, infringement, leverage, levy, main

point, make, mistreat, misusage, neces-sitate, obtrude, oppression, overload, potential, power, press *(constrain)*, pressure, pressure, prestige, puissance, purpose, repercussion, require *(compel)*, rigor, severity, significance, significa-tion, sinew, spirit, staff, strength, stress *(accent)*, stress *(strain)*, struggle, subjection, substance *(essential nature)*, validity, value, violence, weight *(im-portance)*
force a passage penetrate, pervade
force an entrance impose *(intrude)*
force apart break *(separate)*
force armed with legal authority posse
force away expel
force back parry, repel *(drive back)*
force from acquire *(secure)*, preempt, procure
force in inject, interject, interpose
force of argument dialectic
force of circumstances predetermi-nation
force of expression emphasis
force of voice emphasis
force oneself intrude
force oneself in impinge, impose *(in-trude)*
force open break *(separate)*
force out deport *(banish)*, dislodge, eject *(expel)*, exclude, expel, oust, sup-plant
force payment exact, excise *(levy a tax)*
force together impact
force upon foist, impose *(enforce)*, in-flict, insist
forced bound, compulsory, inappropri-ate, involuntary, obligatory, ponderous
forced confinement bondage, dur-ance
forced departure deportation
forced entrance intrusion, onset *(as-sault)*
forced entry incursion
forced into smaller space compact *(dense)*
forced labor bondage
forced leave taking deportation
forced sale condemnation *(seizure)*
forceful categorical, cogent, convinc-ing, decisive, dogmatic, drastic, elo-quent, forcible, indomitable, insistent, intensive, irresistible, orotund, persua-sive, potent, powerful, predominant, prevailing *(having superior force)*, re-sounding, sound, stringent, strong, trenchant, vehement
forceful persuasion advocacy
forcefulness ardor, dint, force *(strength)*, influence, main force, sinew, validity
forceless null *(invalid)*, null and void, powerless, unable
forcelessness impotence, inefficacy
forces of law and order police
forces of nature climate
forcible cogent, compelling, compul-sory, indomitable, irresistible, obliga-tory, potent, powerful, strong, valid, ve-hement
forcible demand dun, requisition
forcible detention durance
forcible entry burglary, housebreaking

forcible expulsion from property eviction
forcible extraction avulsion
forcible inducement compulsion *(co-ercion)*
forcible restraint of liberty bondage
forcible seizure condemnation *(sei-zure)*, disseisin, distraint, expropriation *(divestiture)*, forfeiture *(act of forfeiting)*
forcible urging compulsion *(coer-cion)*, enforcement
forcible violation rape
forcing coercion, compulsion *(coer-cion)*
ford traverse
fordable passable
fore antecedent, back *(in arrears)*, last *(preceding)*, previous
forearm anticipate *(expect)*, caution, prearrange
forearmed prudent
forearming precaution
forebear ancestor, ascendant, fore-runner, parents, primogenitor, progeni-tor
forebearance nonuse
forebearer precursor, predecessor
forebears ancestry, lineage, parent-age
forebode admonish *(warn)*, anticipate *(prognosticate)*, forewarn, portend, pre-dict, presage, prognosticate, promise *(raise expectations)*, threaten
foreboding admonition, apprehension *(fear)*, caution *(warning)*, expectation, fear, misgiving, pessimistic, portentous *(ominous)*, precognition, premonition, presageful, prognosis, prophetic, qualm, threat, warning
forecast anticipate *(prognosticate)*, contrive, expect *(consider probable)*, forseen, forewarn, herald, portend, pre-determine, predict, presage, prognosis, prognosticate, promise *(raise expecta-tions)*, prospect *(outlook)*
forecasted foreseeable, imminent
forecasting prophetic, provident *(showing foresight)*
foreclose arrest *(stop)*, ban, bar *(hin-der)*, block, clog, condemn *(seize)*, con-fiscate, deprive, deter, dispossess, im-pede, preclude, prevent, prohibit, repos-sess, stay *(halt)*
foreclosed attached *(seized)*
foreclosing confiscatory
foreclosure attachment *(seizure)*, bar *(obstruction)*, condemnation *(seizure)*, disseisin, expropriation *(divestiture)*, forfeiture *(act of forfeiting)*, taking
foredate antedate
foredoom predetermination, preor-dain
forefather ancestor, ascendant, pre-cursor, predecessor, primogenitor, pro-genitor
forefathers ancestry, lineage, parent-age
forefeeling expectation, premonition
forefeiture penalty
forefend balk
foregathering caucus
forego abandon *(relinquish)*, disclaim, forswear, resign, surrender *(give back)*
foregoer ancestor, precursor, prede-cessor, progenitor
foregoing aforesaid, antecedent, be-

fore mentioned, former, last *(preceding)*, precursory, preliminary, previous, prior, said

foregone previous

foregone conclusion bias, inequity, preconception, predetermination, predisposition

forehanded economical, provident *(showing foresight)*

forehandedness economy *(frugality)*

foreign apart, different, extraneous, extrinsic, inapplicable, inapposite, irrelevant, novel, obscure *(remote)*, peculiar *(curious)*, unaccustomed, unrelated

foreign influx immigration

foreign person stranger

foreign-born alien *(foreign)*

foreigner alien, stranger

forejudge guess, preconceive, predetermine, prejudge, preordain, presume, presuppose

forejudgment foregone conclusion, preconception, predetermination, prejudice *(preconception)*

foreknow anticipate *(prognosticate)*, predict, presage

foreknowable foreseeable

foreknowing oracular, prophetic

foreknowledge expectation, precognition, prognosis

forelay bait *(lure)*

foreman chief, director, superintendent

forementioned before mentioned, previous, said

foremost best, cardinal *(basic)*, cardinal *(outstanding)*, central *(essential)*, critical *(crucial)*, dominant, famous, important *(significant)*, influential, leading *(ranking first)*, master, notable, noteworthy, outstanding *(prominent)*, paramount, predominant, prime *(most valuable)*, principal, professional *(stellar)*, prominent, renowned, salient, stellar, superior *(excellent)*, superlative

forenamed aforesaid, before mentioned

forensic juridical

forensic oratory rhetoric *(skilled speech)*

forensis forensic, judicial

foreordain prearrange, predetermine

foreordained inevitable, necessary *(inescapable)*, premeditated

foreordainment predetermination

foreordinate predetermine

foreordination foregone conclusion

foreparent predecessor

foreparents parentage

foreperson chief, principal *(director)*

forerun antecede, herald, precede

forerunner ancestor, ascendant, harbinger, pioneer, precursor, predecessor, primogenitor, progenitor

forerunning antecedent, precursory, previous

foresee expect *(consider probable)*, preconceive, predict, presage, prognosticate

foresee the future prognosticate

foreseeable forthcoming, future, probable

foreseeing acute, omniscient, prophetic, provident *(showing foresight)*, prudent

foreseen foreseeable, immediate *(im-*

minent)*, pending *(imminent)*, prospective

foreshadow forewarn, portend, predict, preordain, presage, prognosticate, promise *(raise expectations)*, threaten, warning

foreshadowing hint, indicator, pending *(imminent)*, precursory, premonition

foreshorten abridge *(shorten)*, condense

foreshow anticipate *(prognosticate)*, caution, forewarn, herald, portend, predict, presage, prognosticate, promise *(raise expectations)*

foresight diligence *(care)*, expectation, precaution, precognition, preparation, prognosis, prudence, sagacity, sense *(intelligence)*

foresighted careful, perspicacious, prophetic, prudent

forespeak anticipate *(prognosticate)*, predict

forestall arrest *(stop)*, avert, balk, clog, condemn *(ban)*, debar, defer *(put off)*, detain *(restrain)*, deter, discourage, enjoin, estop, frustrate, prevent, refrain, repel *(drive back)*, stay *(halt)*, stop, thwart

forestalling bar *(obstruction)*, deterrence, deterrent, obviation, preventive

foretell herald, portend, predict, presage, prognosticate, promise *(raise expectations)*

foretellable foreseeable

foretelling caution *(warning)*, oracular, portentous *(ominous)*, prognosis, prophetic

forethought caution *(vigilance)*, consideration *(contemplation)*, contemplation, deliberation, design *(intent)*, plan, precaution, precognition, predetermination, premeditation, preparation, prudence, strategy

forethoughtful discreet, perspicacious

foretoken caveat, harbinger, herald, indicant, indicate, indication, portend, predict, premonition, presage, prognosticate

foretold forseen

forever chronic, now and forever, perpetuity

forevermore now and forever

forewarn admonish *(warn)*, advise, caution, counsel, notice *(give formal warning)*, notify, portend, predict, presage, promise *(raise expectations)*, threaten

forewarned informed *(having information)*

forewarning admonition, caution *(warning)*, caveat, harbinger, monition *(warning)*, notice *(warning)*, portentous *(ominous)*, precursory, premonition, prophetic, symptom, tip *(clue)*

foreword overture, preamble, preface, prelude, threshold *(commencement)*

forfeit amercement, confiscate, deposit, detriment, discontinue *(abandon)*, disfranchise, disinherit, divest, expense *(sacrifice)*, fine, lose *(be deprived of)*, lose *(undergo defeat)*, loss, penalize, penalty, surrender *(give back)*, toll *(effect)*

forfeited attached *(seized)*, irretrievable, lost *(taken away)*

forfeiting confiscatory

forfeiture amercement, cost *(penalty)*, detriment, disqualification *(rejection)*, escheatment, expense *(sacrifice)*, fine, foreclosure, loss, punishment, trover

forfend ban, contain *(restrain)*, deter, forbid, forestall, prevent, prohibit

forgather meet, rendezvous

forgathering collection *(assembly)*, conglomeration, congregation, session

forge copy, create, fake, form, formulate, frame *(construct)*, frame *(formulate)*, invent *(produce for the first time)*, make, manufacture, originate, plagiarize

forge ahead continue *(persevere)*, endure *(last)*, keep *(continue)*, progress, resume

forged artificial, false *(not genuine)*, fictitious, spurious, untrue

forged check bad check

forged copy counterfeit

forged duplicate fake

forgery artifice, copy, counterfeit, deceit, deception, fake, false pretense, falsification, imposture, plagiarism, pretense *(pretext)*, sham, subterfuge

forget condone, forgive, leave *(allow to remain)*, lose *(be deprived of)*, neglect, overlook *(disregard)*, pretermit

forgetful careless, lax, oblivious, remiss

forgetfulness inconsideration

forging manufacture, onset *(commencement)*

forgivable justifiable, pardonable

forgive absolve, clear, condone, discharge *(liberate)*, discharge *(release from obligation)*, excuse, exonerate, extenuate, free, justify, overlook *(excuse)*, palliate *(excuse)*, pardon, purge *(wipe out by atonement)*, release, relent, remit *(release from penalty)*

forgiven clear *(free from criminal charges)*

forgiveness absolution, amnesty, clemency, condonation, dispensation *(exception)*, exoneration, grace, indulgence, lenience, longanimity, pardon, reconciliation, release, remission

forgiveness of sins absolution

forgiving charitable *(lenient)*, lenient, magnanimous, nonmilitant, palliative *(excusing)*, patient, peaceable, placable

forgivingness clemency, lenience, longanimity

forgo forbear, forfeit, quit *(discontinue)*, refrain, relinquish, renounce, vacate *(leave)*, waive, yield *(submit)*

forgoing waiver

forgotten back *(in arrears)*, derelict *(abandoned)*, outdated, outmoded, unclaimed

fork bifurcate, split, spread

forking divergent

forlorn derelict *(abandoned)*, disappointed, disconsolate, lugubrious, pessimistic

forlorn hope pessimism

form appearance *(look)*, body *(main part)*, build *(construct)*, color *(complexion)*, complexion, compose, consist, constant, constitute *(compose)*, construction, content *(structure)*, contour *(outline)*, contour *(shape)*, contrive, create, criterion, crystallize, decorum, delineation, devise *(invent)*, discipline *(train)*, embodiment, embody, establish *(launch)*, fabricate *(construct)*, feature *(appearance)*, fix *(arrange)*, forge *(produce)*, formalize, formulate, frame *(construct)*, frame *(formulate)*, generate, influence, invent *(produce for the first time)*, kind, make, manner *(kind)*, manufacture, means *(opportunity)*, mode, motif, order *(arrangement)*, organization *(structure)*, organize *(unionize)*, originate, pattern, phenomenon *(manifestation)*, practice *(procedure)*, principle *(axiom)*, produce *(manufacture)*, pronounce *(speak)*, protocol *(etiquette)*, specter, stamp, structure *(composition)*, style, tenor, usage, vision *(dream)*

form a cartel federalize *(associate)*
form a circle round circumscribe *(surround by boundary)*, encompass *(surround)*
form a coalition conspire
form a company incorporate *(form a corporation)*
form a conception conceive *(comprehend)*
form a connection affiliate
form a core crystallize
form a fork bifurcate
form a judgment conclude *(decide)*, deem, determine
form a labor union organize *(unionize)*
form a league unite
form a network intertwine
form a plan plot, program
form a plot maneuver
form a resolution conclude *(decide)*, decide, determine
form a single unit unite
form a union combine *(act in concert)*, combine *(join together)*, federalize *(associate)*
form an alliance unite
form an estimate calculate, gauge, measure
form an estimation guess
form an image conjure
form an opinion conclude *(decide)*, construe *(comprehend)*, decide, deem, estimate, evaluate, gauge, measure, presume
form anew reform
form into a body organize *(unionize)*
form into classes classify, organize *(arrange)*, partition, pigeonhole
form into ranks marshal
form of expression language
form of government polity
form plots conspire
forma aspect, contour *(shape)*, design *(construction plan)*, form *(arrangement)*, formation, kind
formable flexible, malleable, pliable, pliant, tractable
formal official, orthodox, perfunctory, proper, punctilious, rigid, solemn, strict
formal accusal arraignment
formal accusation indictment, information *(charge)*
formal allegation complaint
formal assertion declaration, pleading
formal averment allegation, information *(charge)*, pleading
formal charge accusation, informa-

tion *(charge)*
formal complaint charge *(accusation)*
formal consent permission
formal contract treaty
formal criminal charge information *(charge)*
formal criminal complaint information *(charge)*
formal criticism protest
formal declaration acknowledgment *(avowal)*, affirmation, protest, testament
formal declaration of dissent protest
formal discourse pandect *(treatise)*
formal discussion discourse
formal essay pandect *(treatise)*
formal examination by a court of law trial *(legal proceeding)*
formal examination of facts by a court trial *(legal proceeding)*
formal expression resolution *(formal statement)*
formal expression of choice poll *(casting of votes)*, vote
formal guaranty vow
formal notice declaration
formal occasion ceremony
formal permission license
formal petition bill *(formal declaration)*
formal presentation introduction
formal proceeding hearing
formal prosecution action *(proceeding)*
formal questioning hearing, interrogation
formal request requisition
formal scrutiny investigation
formal speech peroration
formal statement opinion *(judicial decision)*, pronouncement
formal writing instrument *(document)*
formal writing embodying a request petition
formal written plea petition
formal written request petition
formalis formal
formalistic draconian, formal
formalities decorum, protocol *(etiquette)*
formality ceremony, custom, decorum, form *(arrangement)*
formalization of laws codification
formalize authorize, characterize, codify, define, frame *(formulate)*, record
formally pro forma
formally accuse arraign
formally advise notice *(give formal warning)*
formally charge arraign, indict
formally charge with a crime indict
formally criminate arraign
formally incriminate arraign
formally pronounced judgment sentence
formally sanction authorize
formally urge petition
formally withdraw repeal
formalness formality
format configuration *(form)*, content *(structure)*, form *(arrangement)*, formation, motif
formation arrangement *(ordering)*, building *(business of assembling)*, com-

position *(makeup)*, configuration *(form)*, content *(structure)*, contour *(shape)*, coverage *(scope)*, creation, distribution *(arrangement)*, embodiment, form *(arrangement)*, genesis, invention, lineup, manufacture, nascency, order *(arrangement)*, organization *(structure)*, performance *(workmanship)*, structure *(composition)*, unit *(item)*
formation of a company incorporation *(formation of a business entity)*
formation of a corporation incorporation *(formation of a business entity)*
formation of an organization incorporation *(formation of a business entity)*
formative causal, causative, constructive *(creative)*, original *(initial)*, pliable, primary, prime *(original)*, productive, rudimentary
formative notion concept
former aforesaid, antecedent, back *(in arrears)*, before mentioned, deceased, last *(preceding)*, late *(defunct)*, outdated, outmoded, preliminary, previous, prior
former generations ancestry, parentage
former incumbent predecessor
former officeholder predecessor
formerly heretofore, theretofore
formidable important *(significant)*, indomitable, inexpugnable, insuperable, insurmountable, irresistible, onerous, operose, oppressive, potent, spartan, strong, unapproachable
formidolosus formidable
forming creation, manufacture, onset *(commencement)*
formless indefinite, indeterminate
formula avenue *(means of attainment)*, criterion, expedient, expression *(comment)*, form *(arrangement)*, method, mode, phrase, prescription *(directive)*, principle *(axiom)*, rule *(guide)*, rule *(legal dictate)*
formula system
formula usage
formularize formulate
formulary boiler plate, code, form *(arrangement)*, prescription *(directive)*, rule *(legal dictate)*
formulate arrange *(plan)*, avow, bear *(adduce)*, codify, compose, conceive *(invent)*, conjure, constitute *(establish)*, create, crystallize, define, designate, devise *(invent)*, express, forge *(produce)*, form, frame *(construct)*, generate, legislate, make, manufacture, organize *(unionize)*, originate, phrase, produce *(manufacture)*
formulate by law constitute *(establish)*
formulated belief doctrine, principle *(axiom)*
formulated intention objective, proposition
formulating questions cross-examination
formulating rules for the future legislation *(lawmaking)*
formulation averment, avouchment, building *(business of assembling)*, code, composition *(makeup)*, construction, creation, definition, description, expression *(comment)*, language, parlance, phraseology, rule *(legal dictate)*

formulation of a mental image creation

formulation of a principle creation

formulation of an idea creation

formulation of laws codification

formulator of laws lawmaker

formulize formulate

fors hazard

forsake abandon *(physically leave)*, abandon *(relinquish)*, abandon *(withdraw)*, avoid *(evade)*, default, defect, depart, disclaim, discontinue *(abandon)*, disinherit, disown *(refuse to acknowledge)*, fail *(neglect)*, forgo, forswear, leave *(depart)*, quit *(discontinue)*, quit *(evacuate)*, refrain, relinquish, renounce, resign, surrender *(give back)*

forsaken derelict *(abandoned)*, helpless *(defenseless)*, solitary, void *(empty)*

forsaking desertion, resignation *(relinquishment)*

forswear abandon *(relinquish)*, answer *(reply)*, bear false witness, betray *(lead astray)*, cloak, deceive, deny *(contradict)*, disaffirm, disavow, disclaim, disown *(deny the validity)*, eschew, exclude, fabricate *(make up)*, forfeit, forgo, lie *(falsify)*, palter, perjure, prevaricate, quit *(discontinue)*, refuse, reject, relinquish, renounce, repudiate, surrender *(give back)*

forswearing abjuration, bad faith, desertion, falsification, negation, renunciation, repudiation

forsworn fraudulent, lying

fort bulwark

forte competence *(ability)*, gift *(flair)*, performance *(workmanship)*, propensity, specialty *(special aptitude)*

forte oblatus fortuitous, incidental

forthcoming close *(near)*, future, immediate *(imminent)*, imminent, inevitable, instant, pending *(imminent)*, portentous *(ominous)*, prospective, proximate

forthright bona fide, candid, coherent *(clear)*, direct *(forthright)*, explicit, genuine, honest, ingenuous, scrupulous, straightforward, unaffected *(sincere)*, unequivocal, upright

forthrightness candor *(straightforwardness)*

forthwith as soon as feasible, instant, instantly

fortification barrier, bulwark, corroboration, panoply, protection, safeguard, support *(corroboration)*

fortified armed, insusceptible *(resistant)*, protective

fortify bear *(support)*, certify *(attest)*, compound, confirm, consolidate *(strengthen)*, corroborate, document, endue, help, nurture, protect, reaffirm, reinforce, supplement, sustain *(prolong)*

fortis heroic, resolute, spartan, strong

fortis et invictus heroic

fortitude composure, longanimity, resignation *(passive acceptance)*, spirit, sufferance, tolerance

fortress bear *(support)*, bulwark

fortuitous casual, coincidental, random, unexpected, unintentional, unwitting

fortuitous event accident *(chance occurrence)*, quirk *(accident)*

fortuitously unknowingly

fortuitousness act of god, chance *(fortuity)*, happenstance

fortuitus coincidental, fortuitous

fortuity accident *(chance occurrence)*, act of god, happenstance, occurrence, opportunity, quirk *(accident)*, speculation *(risk)*

fortuna adversa misfortune

fortunate auspicious, favorable *(advantageous)*, felicitous, propitious, prosperous, successful

fortunate condition prosperity

fortunatus successful

fortune chattel, contingency, money, possessions, predetermination, prospect *(outlook)*, speculation *(risk)*, substance *(material possessions)*, welfare

fortuneless poor *(underprivileged)*

forum bar *(court)*

forum bench, chamber *(body)*, conference, council *(assembly)*

forum forum *(court)*

forum judicatory, judicature

forum market place

forum meeting *(conference)*, panel *(discussion group)*, session, tribunal

forum for adjusting disputes court

forum of justice bench, court, judiciary

forward along, ameliorate, brazen, bumptious, contemptuous, countenance, cultivate, deliver, dispatch *(send off)*, eager, expedite, facilitate, foster, further, hasten, help, impertinent *(insolent)*, inure *(benefit)*, meliorate, nurture, obtrusive, precipitate *(hasten)*, presumptuous, progressive *(going forward)*, promote *(advance)*, redirect, remit *(submit for consideration)*, remove *(transfer)*, send, serve *(assist)*, serve *(deliver a legal instrument)*, transfer, transmit, unabashed, vanward

forward looking progressive *(advocating change)*, sophisticated

forward motion advance *(progression)*, headway

forward movement advance *(progression)*

forward moving progressive *(going forward)*

forward payment remit *(send payment)*

forwarding advance *(progression)*, promotion *(advancement)*, transmittal

fossil prime *(original)*

fossilized ossified

foster abet, adopt, assist, bear *(support)*, bestow, care *(regard)*, concern *(care)*, conduce, cultivate, discipline *(train)*, expedite, facilitate, foment, further, keep *(shelter)*, nurture, preserve, promote *(organize)*, protect, sanction, subsidize, surrogate

foster child child

foster hope promise *(raise expectations)*

fosterage adoption *(affiliation)*, auspices, favor *(sanction)*, guidance, help

fostering conservation, promotion *(encouragement)*

foul arrant *(onerous)*, bad *(inferior)*, contemptible, debase, deface, deleterious, depraved, disgraceful, disreputable, harmful, heinous, infect, iniquitous, irregular *(improper)*, loathsome,

malignant, nefarious, objectionable, obnoxious, obscene, odious, offensive *(offending)*, outrageous, peccant *(culpable)*, pestilent, pollute, profligate *(corrupt)*, prurient, reprehensible, repulsive, salacious, scurrilous, sordid, sully, taint *(contaminate)*, tainted *(contaminated)*, tarnish, unfavorable, vicious

foul invective expletive

foul language expletive, imprecation, malediction, profanity

foul play collusion, frame up, grievance, inequity, knavery, machination, mischief, misdoing, pettifoggery

foul talk profanity

foul-spoken profane

fouled marred, sordid

foulmouthed profane

foulness defilement, delinquency *(misconduct)*, perversion

found build *(construct)*, create, establish *(launch)*, generate, initiate, instate, launch *(initiate)*, originate, situated

found guilty blameful, blameworthy

found wanting blameful, devoid, faulty

foundation assumption *(supposition)*, basis, building *(business of assembling)*, cause *(reason)*, cornerstone, corporation, creation, criterion, derivation, facility *(institution)*, formation, fund, genesis, ground, institute, mainstay, nascency, onset *(commencement)*, organization *(association)*, origin *(source)*, origination, outset, postulate, preamble, precedent, preparation, principle *(axiom)*, reason *(basis)*, source, stare decisis, start

foundation of a suit gist *(ground for a suit)*

foundational central *(essential)*, elementary, incipient, original *(initial)*, precursory, preparatory

foundationless baseless

foundations premises *(hypotheses)*

founded in confidence fiduciary

founded in law jural

founded on based on

founded on circumstances circumstantial

founded on fact authentic, documentary, true *(authentic)*

founded on fiction fictitious

founder architect, author *(originator)*, pioneer, predecessor, promoter

founder of the family parents, primogenitor

founding nascency

founding father pioneer

foundling discard, orphan

fount derivation, fund, source

fountain origination, source

fountainhead derivation, origin *(source)*, origination, source

four corners crossroad *(intersection)*

fovea pitfall

fovere foment

foxy devious, insidious, machiavellian, politic, sly

foyer entrance

fracas affray, altercation, belligerency, bluster *(commotion)*, brawl, collision *(dispute)*, commotion, confrontation *(altercation)*, contest *(dispute)*, disaccord, disorder *(lack of order)*, disturbance, embroilment, fight *(battle)*, fray, furor, imbroglio, noise, outbreak, outcry, pandemonium, riot, struggle, turmoil, violence

fraction constituent *(part)*, element, installment, member *(constituent part)*, modicum, moiety, part *(portion)*, paucity, proportion, section *(division)*, segment, subdivision

fractional broken *(fractured)*, partial *(relating to a part)*, semi, severable

fractional part detail, segment

fractionalize lancinate

fractionize divide *(separate)*, separate

fractious adverse *(hostile)*, contumacious, disobedient, froward, insubordinate, negative, perverse, petulant, pugnacious, querulous, recalcitrant, restive, uncontrollable, unruly

fractiousness contempt *(disobedience to the court)*

fracture hiatus, rend, rift *(gap)*, split, split

fradulent copy counterfeit

fragile insecure, insubstantial, nonsubstantial *(not sturdy)*, powerless

fragilitas frailty

fragility frailty

fragment break *(fracture)*, chapter *(division)*, component, constituent *(part)*, detail, dichotomize, disintegrate, divide *(separate)*, element, ingredient, iota, lancinate, minimum, modicum, moiety, part *(portion)*, section *(division)*, segment, subdivision

fragmentable divisive

fragmentary broken *(fractured)*, imperfect, inchoate, minimal, partial *(part)*, partial *(relating to a part)*, semi

fragmentation decentralization

fragmentum segment

frail imperfect, insecure, insubstantial, nonsubstantial *(not sturdy)*, powerless

fraility vice

frailty defect, disability *(physical inability)*, disadvantage, fault *(weakness)*, flaw, foible, impuissance

frailty of character foible

frame arrange *(plan)*, border, border *(bound)*, build *(construct)*, building *(structure)*, circumscribe *(surround by boundary)*, compose, conceive *(invent)*, configuration *(form)*, conjure, conspire, construction, contain *(enclose)*, contour *(outline)*, contour *(shape)*, contrive, create, delineate, devise *(invent)*, edge *(border)*, envelop, forge *(produce)*, form, formulate, foundation *(basis)*, frame up, generate, make, maneuver, margin *(outside limit)*, originate, outline *(boundary)*, plan, plot, program, pronounce *(speak)*, scheme

frame of mind character *(personal quality)*, disposition *(inclination)*, outlook, position *(point of view)*, spirit

frame of reference cornerstone, criterion, exemplar, instance, outlook, precedent, standard

framer architect

framework building *(structure)*, configuration *(confines)*, configuration *(form)*, construction, content *(structure)*, contour *(outline)*, delineation, foundation *(basis)*, frame *(structure)*, organization *(structure)*, perspective

framing blockade *(enclosure)*, building *(business of assembling)*, creation

franchise charter *(sanction)*, droit, empower, enfranchise, free, freedom, home rule, immunity, let *(permit)*, liberate, liberty, license, prerogative, privilege, suffrage, tolerance

franchised free *(enjoying civil liberty)*, permissible, privileged

franchisement freedom, liberation

frangere impair, infringe

frangible nonsubstantial *(not sturdy)*

frank candid, clear *(apparent)*, credible, direct *(forthright)*, genuine, honest, ingenuous, simple, straightforward, unaffected *(sincere)*

frankhearted candid

frankness candor *(straightforwardness)*, honesty, probity, veracity

frantic frenetic, hot-blooded

fraternal akin *(related by blood)*, close *(intimate)*, consanguineous, harmonious, humane, interrelated, intimate

fraternal order society

fraternalism peace

fraternity coaction, concordance, society, sodality, union *(labor organization)*

fraternization rapprochement, society, sodality

fraternize cooperate, join *(associate oneself with)*

fraud bad faith, bad repute, betray *(lead astray)*, bilk, canard, collusion, conversion *(misappropriation)*, deceit, deception, duplicity, embezzlement, fake, false pretense, falsehood, falsification, forgery, hoax, hypocrisy, imposture, improbity, indirection *(deceitfulness)*, knavery, lie, maneuver *(trick)*, misappropriation, misrepresentation, pettifoggery, pretense *(pretext)*, pretext, racket, ruse, sham

fraudare cheat

fraudulence artifice, bad repute, collusion, corruption, criminality, deceit, deception, dishonesty, false pretense, falsehood, forgery, fraud, hoax, hypocrisy, imposture, improbity, knavery, pettifoggery, pretense *(pretext)*, racket

fraudulency abuse *(corrupt practice)*, bad faith, corruption, deception, dishonesty, false pretense, hoax, improbity, indirection *(deceitfulness)*, pettifoggery

fraudulent assumed *(feigned)*, collusive, colorable *(specious)*, deceptive, delusive, dishonest, disingenuous, fallacious, false *(not genuine)*, felonious, insidious, larcenous, lying, machiavellian, mendacious, meretricious, perfidious, spurious, tortuous *(corrupt)*, unfair, unfounded, unscrupulous, untrue, untrustworthy

fraudulent application misapplication

fraudulent appropriation embezzlement

fraudulent appropriation of money embezzlement

fraudulent check bad check

fraudulent conversion embezzlement, misappropriation

fraudulent document forgery

fraudulent expedient maneuver *(trick)*

fraudulent imitation counterfeit

fraudulent income graft

fraudulent practice pettifoggery

fraudulent replica fake

fraudulent taking larceny, theft

fraudulently induce suborn

fraudulently introduced surreptitious

fraudulentus dishonest, fraudulent

fraught full, replete

fraught with danger aleatory *(perilous)*, dangerous, insalubrious, insecure, noxious, precarious

fraught with evil pernicious

fraught with harm disastrous, pernicious

fraught with peril dangerous

fraus deceit, dishonesty, fraud, hypocrisy, imposture, knavery, sham

fray affray, brawl, collision *(dispute)*, commotion, confrontation *(altercation)*, contest *(dispute)*, embroilment, fight *(battle)*, fracas, furor, outbreak, outburst, riot, strife

frayed dilapidated

freak quirk *(accident)*

freak occurrence phenomenon *(unusual occurrence)*

freakish irregular *(not usual)*, prodigious *(amazing)*, unaccustomed

free absolve, alleviate, autonomous *(independent)*, autonomous *(self governing)*, clear *(unencumbered)*, clear, competitive *(open)*, condone, discharge *(liberate)*, disencumber, disengage, disentangle, disenthrall, dissociate, enfranchise, exculpate, excuse, exempt, extricate, gratis, gratuitous *(given without recompense)*, immune, independent, liberal *(generous)*, liberate, licentious, parole, passable, philanthropic, promiscuous, release, relieve *(free from burden)*, remit *(release from penalty)*, rescue, salacious, sovereign *(independent)*, spontaneous, unbound, unlimited, unpaid, unrestrained *(not in custody)*, unrestricted, unsolicited, vacant, void *(empty)*, voluntary

free agency volition

free course latitude

free decision discretion *(power of choice)*, latitude, option *(choice)*

free fight affray

free for use disposable

free from a mistaken belief disabuse

free from accusation exonerate

free from affectation natural, unaffected *(sincere)*

free from ambiguity clarify

free from anxiety ease, soothe

free from bias impartial

free from blame exculpate, exonerate

free from bondage disenthrall

free from burden clear *(unencumbered)*

free from confinement rescue

free from confusion clarify

free from danger rescue, safe

free from desecration inviolate

free from difficulty facilitate

free from doubt assure *(give confidence to)*, clear *(certain)*

free from encumbrance clear *(unencumbered)*, disencumber

free from engagement disengage

free from error disabuse

free from extraneous matter distill
free from fault inculpable, irreprehensible
free from fraud honest
free from guilt blameless, clean, inculpable, innocent, not guilty
free from harm safe
free from hindrance clear *(unencumbered)*, facilitate
free from hurt safe
free from ignorance enlighten
free from impairment inviolate
free from impediment clear *(unencumbered)*, facilitate
free from imperfection infallible, intact, unblemished
free from impurities clean
free from impurity purge *(purify)*
free from injury safe
free from limitation clear *(unencumbered)*
free from mistake infallible
free from narrowness liberal *(not literal)*
free from objectionable content expurgate
free from obstruction clear *(unencumbered)*, facilitate
free from pain soothe
free from pledge disengage
free from political disabilities enfranchise
free from prejudice enlighten, fairly *(impartially)*
free from reserve ingenuous
free from risk safe
free from sin clean
free from superstition enlighten
free from thralldom disenthrall
free from uncertainty assure *(give confidence to)*
free from vindictiveness charitable *(lenient)*, lenient
free from vow disengage
free from war peaceable
free from waste economical
free from wrong blameless
free giver benefactor, donor
free giving largess *(generosity)*, philanthropy
free hand latitude
free in expression demonstrative *(expressive of emotion)*
free of privileged
free of access open *(accessible)*
free of binding obligation exempt
free of charge gratis
free of cost gratis, gratuitous *(given without recompense)*
free of duplicity simple
free of error accurate, proper
free of expense gratis, gratuitous *(given without recompense)*
free of guilt irreprehensible
free of pettiness magnanimous
free play latitude
free selection alternative *(option)*, option *(choice)*
free thought latitude
free to all competitive *(open)*, open *(accessible)*, patent, public *(open)*
free to choose autonomous *(independent)*, impartial
free translation paraphrase
free will discretion *(power of choice)*, latitude, liberty, option *(choice)*, voli-

tion
free wording paraphrase
free-handedness philanthropy
free-living dissolute
free-willed spontaneous
freed clear *(free from criminal charges)*, free *(enjoying civil liberty)*
freed from exempt
freed of wrongdoing acquitted
freedom dispensation *(exception)*, emancipation, exemption, exoneration, immunity, impunity, informality, latitude, liberation, liberty, license, option *(choice)*, parole, prerogative, privilege, probation, suffrage, tolerance
freedom from accusation exoneration
freedom from affectation informality
freedom from ailment health
freedom from bias disinterest *(lack of prejudice)*, justice
freedom from bigotry tolerance
freedom from blame innocence
freedom from captivity liberty
freedom from danger asylum *(protection)*, preservation, protection, security *(safety)*
freedom from deviation rigor
freedom from difficulty facility *(easiness)*
freedom from disease health
freedom from domination home rule
freedom from doubt faith
freedom from duty exemption, leave *(absence)*
freedom from error certification *(certainness)*, certitude
freedom from exemption immunity
freedom from extravagance economy *(frugality)*
freedom from guilt exoneration, innocence
freedom from harm security *(safety)*
freedom from illegality innocence
freedom from interference home rule
freedom from judgment impunity
freedom from liability exemption
freedom from obligation exemption, immunity
freedom from penalty impunity
freedom from prejudice disinterest *(lack of prejudice)*, tolerance
freedom from prosecution immunity
freedom from punishment impunity
freedom from requirements exemption
freedom from self-interest disinterest *(lack of prejudice)*
freedom from service exemption
freedom from vindictiveness lenience
freedom from war peace
freedom of action home rule, latitude, liberty
freedom of choice call *(option)*, discretion *(power of choice)*, franchise *(right to vote)*, home rule, liberty, option *(choice)*, suffrage
freehanded benevolent, charitable *(benevolent)*, donative, philanthropic
freehandedness largess *(generosity)*
freehold demesne, domain *(land*

owned*)*, dominion *(absolute ownership)*, estate *(property)*, fee *(estate)*, leasehold, property *(land)*, real estate
freeholder landholder, landowner, occupant
freeing liberation, release
freeing from blame exoneration
freeing from prison parole
freelance independent
freely readily
freely giving liberal *(generous)*
freeness largess *(generosity)*
freethinking liberal *(broad minded)*, licentious, radical *(favoring drastic change)*, skeptical
freeway causeway
freewill worker volunteer
freeze check *(restrain)*, desist, embargo, stop
freight cargo, load, merchandise, send
freightage cargo, freight
frenetic deranged, lunatic
frenzied deranged, frenetic, lunatic, uncontrollable, vehement
frenzy bluster *(commotion)*, confusion *(turmoil)*, furor, haste, insanity, lunacy, outburst, pandemonium, panic, passion
frequence draw *(attendance)*, frequency
frequens frequent, populous
frequent attend *(be present at)*, chronic, common *(customary)*, customary, familiar *(customary)*, habitual, incessant, innumerable, inveterate, mundane, ordinary, patronize *(trade with)*, periodic, prevailing *(current)*, prevalent, repeated, routine, usual
frequent as a customer patronize *(trade with)*
frequent repetition practice *(custom)*
frequenter addict, patron *(regular customer)*
frequentia frequency
frequently invariably
frequently met prevalent
frequently repeated act habit
fresh impertinent *(insolent)*, insolent, novel, original *(creative)*, recent, unusual
fresh outbreak recrudescence
fresh spurt resurgence
fresh start continuation *(resumption)*
fresh supply reinforcement
freshen fix *(repair)*, renew *(refurbish)*
freshen up fix *(repair)*
freshening revival
freshest last *(preceding)*
freshly de novo
freshman amateur, neophyte, novice
fret agitate *(perturb)*, annoy, badger, brood, discompose, fear, harrow, harry *(harass)*, hector, irritate, languish, oscillate, perturb, pique, plague, provoke, regret, trepidation
fret over deplore
fretful fractious, petulant, querulous, restive
fretter malcontent
friable dilapidated
fribble petty
friction collision *(dispute)*, conflict, contention *(opposition)*, contravention, controversy *(argument)*, disaccord, discord, dissension, dissent *(difference of opinion)*, strife
frictional hostile

frictionless harmonious

friend associate, benefactor, cohort, confederate, partisan, patron (influential supporter), proponent, samaritan

friend at court advocate (counselor)

friend in court advocate (counselor), amicus curiae

friendless derelict (abandoned), helpless (defenseless), solitary

friendliness affinity (regard), benevolence (disposition to do good), comity, consideration (sympathetic regard), courtesy, informality, peace, rapprochement, sodality

friendly amicable, benevolent, close (intimate), harmonious, intimate, peaceable, propitious, receptive

friendly agreement accommodation (adjustment)

friendly association affiliation (connectedness)

friendly disposition goodwill

friendly interest patronage (support)

friendly relations sodality

friendly turn favor (act of kindness)

friendship affinity (regard), benevolence (disposition to do good), concordance, consortium (marriage companionship), patronage (support), peace, rapprochement, sodality

fright consternation, fear, frighten, panic, phobia, stress (strain), trepidation

frighten browbeat, intimidate, menace, repel (disgust), threaten

frighten away discourage, dissuade

frightened leery, recreant

frightening dire, formidable, odious, portentous (ominous), sinister

frightful deplorable, disastrous, formidable, insufferable, loathsome, ominous, portentous (ominous), repulsive, vicious

frigid cold-blooded, insensible, insusceptible (uncaring), phlegmatic, unaffected (uninfluenced)

frigidus insipid, lifeless (dull), prosaic

frill embellish

fringe border, edge (border), extremity (furthest point), frontier, limit, margin (outside limit), penumbra, peripheral, periphery

fringement crime

fringes confines, outline (boundary)

fringing contiguous, proximate

frisky jocular

frivolous capricious, inconsequential, irresolute, irresponsible, jocular, nonessential, nugatory, petty, superficial, trivial, undependable, untrustworthy

frock clothe

frolic carouse

frolicsome jocular

frolicsomeness mischief

from a general law to a particular instance a priori

from abroad alien (foreign)

from beginning to end throughout (all over)

from cause to effect a priori

from competent sources authentic

from first to last throughout (all over)

from here on hereafter (henceforth)

from its birth ab initio

from now on hereafter (henceforth)

from nowhere alien (unrelated)

from that cause a priori, consequently

from that time thereafter

from the beginning ab initio, de novo

from the ground up throughout (all over)

from the original data authentic

from the river fluvial

from the start heretofore

from the word go throughout (all over)

from this cause a priori

from this time on hereafter (henceforth)

fronder censure

front defy, hypocrisy, prime (most valuable)

front office management (directorate)

front position preference (priority)

frontier border, edge (border), extremity (furthest point), limit, outline (boundary), periphery

frontiers configuration (confines)

frontiersman pioneer

frontward vanward

frothy nugatory

froward disobedient, disorderly, insolent, insubordinate, intractable, perverse, petulant, spiteful, unruly, wanton

frown on disfavor

frown upon denounce (condemn), disparage, remonstrate, reproach, spurn

frowning grave (solemn)

fructiferous fertile, productive

fructify ameliorate, bear (yield), reproduce

fructuosus profitable

fructuous fertile, productive

fructus enjoyment (pleasure), fruition, profit, result

frugal economical, parsimonious, penurious, prudent

frugality austerity, management (judicious use), moderation, prudence, temperance

frugalness austerity, economy (frugality)

frugi economical, frugal

frugifer profitable

fruit effect, issuance, outcome, outgrowth, output, product, progeny, result

fruit of labor earnings

fruitbearing prolific

fruitful fertile, gainful, lucrative, operative, productive, profitable, prolific, successful

fruitfulness utility (usefulness)

fruition commission (act), consequence (conclusion), creation, denouement, discharge (performance), effect, fait accompli, growth (evolution), outcome, realization, result, satisfaction (fulfilment)

fruitless barren, futile, idle, ineffective, ineffectual, needless, otiose, unavailing, unproductive

fruitless effort failure (lack of success)

fruitless trial mistrial

fruits profit

frustrari balk, disappoint

frustrari frustrate

frustrate arrest (stop), balk, bar (hinder), block, check (restrain), clog, condemn (ban), constrict (inhibit), contravene, counteract, defeat, deter, disadvantage, discontinue (break continuity), encumber (hinder), enjoin, fight (counteract), foil, forestall, halt, hamper, impede, inhibit, interrupt, keep (restrain), obstruct, perturb, preclude, prevent, repel (drive back), repulse, restrict, stay (halt), stem (check), stifle, thwart, toll (stop), trammel

frustrate by contrary action counter, counteract

frustrated disappointed

frustration abortion (fiasco), aggravation (annoyance), check (bar), deadlock, deterrence, failure (lack of success), impediment, miscarriage

fuddle confusion (ambiguity), muddle

fudge mulct (defraud)

fuga flight, lapse (break)

fugacious ephemeral, temporary, transient, transitory

fugaciousness mortality

fugacity mortality

fugam petere flee

fugare repel (drive back), stave

fugax transient

fugere escape, retreat

fugitive convict, criminal, derelict, elusive, ephemeral, moving (in motion), outlaw, pariah, temporary, transient, truant

fugitive from the law outlaw

fugitivus fugitive

fulcrum basis, center (central position)

fulfill accomplish, close (terminate), commit (perpetrate), complete, comply, conclude (complete), consummate, discharge (perform), dispatch (dispose of), effectuate, execute (accomplish), implement, obey, observe (obey), operate, pass (satisfy requirements), perform (adhere to), perpetrate, succeed (attain), transact

fulfill an engagement report (present oneself)

fulfill an obligation satisfy (discharge)

fulfill the commands of obey

fulfilled complacent, fully executed (consummated)

fulfillment cessation (termination), conclusion (outcome), discharge (performance), end (termination), fait accompli, finality, fruition, maturity, outcome

fulfilment collection (payment), commission (act), performance (execution), realization

fulgent pretentious (ostentatious)

fulgere radiate

fulgid lucid, pretentious (ostentatious)

fulguration discharge (shot)

full absolute (complete), broad, complete (all-embracing), comprehensive, copious, gross (total), inclusive, intact, orotund, outright, plenary, populous, profuse, replete, ripe, thorough, total, unmitigated, unqualified (unlimited)

full age majority (adulthood), maturity

full appraisal appreciation (perception)

full array panoply

full assurance credence
full authority permission
full belief credence
full chance day in court
full complement capacity *(maximum)*
full development maturity
full effect amount *(result)*
full extent capacity *(maximum)*
full force main force
full growth maturity
full legal age majority *(adulthood)*
full measure plethora, quorum, sufficiency
full observance conformity *(obedience)*
full of affectation pretentious *(pompous)*
full of contempt disdainful
full of curves labyrinthine
full of details detailed
full of enterprise eager
full of enthusiasm eager
full of exhortation hortative
full of faults faulty
full of feeling ecstatic, eloquent
full of fun jocular
full of good will benevolent
full of hate hostile, malevolent
full of hope sanguine
full of initiative eager
full of life live *(conscious)*
full of malice hostile, malevolent
full of meaning eloquent, pithy, sententious
full of mischief peccant *(culpable)*
full of power forcible
full of promise favorable *(advantageous)*, probable, propitious
full of regret remorseful
full of regrets contrite, penitent, repentant
full of remorse contrite
full of revenge malevolent
full of risk aleatory *(perilous)*, dangerous, precarious
full of sin diabolic
full of spirit volatile
full of spite malevolent
full of strength forcible
full of substance eloquent
full of thought deliberate, pensive
full of turns labyrinthine
full of urgency hortative
full of verbiage prolix
full pardon condonation
full particulars circumstances
full play latitude
full purse prosperity
full report accounting
full round of the seasons annum
full satisfaction collection *(payment)*, discharge *(payment)*, expiation, indemnity
full size caliber *(measurement)*
full stop check *(bar)*
full volume capacity *(maximum)*
full-blown plenary, ripe
full-bodied sapid, savory
full-charged plenary
full-flavored sapid, savory
full-fledged outright
full-grown ripe
fullness capacity *(maximum)*, corpus, entirety, finality, mass *(weight)*, maximum *(amplitude)*, plethora, quantity, sufficiency, surfeit

fullness of heart affection
fully fairly *(clearly)*, in toto, wholly
fully constituted plenary
fully convinced certain *(positive)*, definite, positive *(confident)*
fully detailed analysis accounting
fully developed ripe
fully developed person adult
fully executed thorough
fully furnished plenary
fully grown ripe
fully grown person adult
fully realized comprehensive
fully sufficient adequate
fully supplied replete
fulminate defame, discharge *(shoot)*, inveigh, threaten
fulminate against censure, condemn *(blame)*, denounce *(condemn)*, disapprove *(condemn)*, lash *(attack verbally)*, malign, reprimand
fulmination denunciation, discharge *(shot)*, imprecation, malediction, threat
fulsome arrant *(onerous)*, bad *(inferior)*, bad *(offensive)*, contemptible, detrimental, excessive, gross *(flagrant)*, heinous, loathsome, lurid, objectionable, obnoxious, odious, outrageous, repugnant *(exciting aversion)*, scandalous, sordid, unwarranted
fumble miscue, mismanage
fumigate decontaminate
function activity, agency *(legal relationship)*, appointment *(position)*, assignment *(task)*, business *(occupation)*, calling, capacity *(job)*, charge *(responsibility)*, demean *(deport oneself)*, duty *(obligation)*, employment, job, office, officiate, operate, operation, part *(role)*, perform *(execute)*, position *(business status)*, post, province, purpose, pursuit *(occupation)*, role, specialty *(special aptitude)*, sphere, trade *(occupation)*, use, utility *(usefulness)*, work *(employment)*
functional beneficial, corrigible, effective *(efficient)*, efficient, ministerial, operative, practical, procedural, viable
functionary agent, conduit *(intermediary)*, incumbent, notary public, officer, official, proctor, trustee
functioning acting, active, in full force, operative
functionless barren, expendable
functus officio defeasible
fund bear *(yield)*, bestow, capitalize *(provide capital)*, endow, endowment, finance, garner, hoard, principal *(capital sum)*, provide *(supply)*, provision *(something provided)*, reserve, resource, stock *(shares)*, store *(depository)*, sufficiency, treasury, underwrite
fund again refinance
fund invested for a charitable purpose foundation *(organization)*
fundamenta foundation *(basis)*
fundamental born *(innate)*, cardinal *(basic)*, central *(essential)*, cornerstone, elementary, essential *(inherent)*, essential *(required)*, gravamen, inchoate, incipient, indispensable, initial, innate, integral, material *(important)*, naked *(lacking embellishment)*, native *(inborn)*, natural, necessary *(required)*, necessity, need *(requirement)*, organic, original *(initial)*, prerequisite, primary, prime *(original)*, primordial, rudimen-

tary, simple, substantive, ultimate, underlying, virtual, vital
fundamental doctrine principle *(axiom)*
fundamental feature main point
fundamental law constitution, principle *(axiom)*
fundamental part component, essence, ingredient, main point
fundamental point main point
fundamental principle canon, foundation *(basis)*, necessity
fundamental principles policy *(plan of action)*
fundamental principles of government polity
fundamental reason rationale
fundamental research inquiry *(systematic investigation)*
fundamental rule principle *(axiom)*
fundamental unit necessity
fundamentally purely *(positively)*
fundamentals basis, gist *(substance)*
fundemental part element
funding appropriation *(donation)*, endowment, loan
funds assets, capital, cash, finance, money, personalty, possessions, principal *(capital sum)*, property *(possessions)*, security *(stock)*
funds for investment capital
funds in hand capital
funds paid out expenditure
fundus basis
funereal disconsolate, lugubrious, solemn
funestus disastrous, fatal, lethal
funk shirk, trepidation
funny jocular, ludicrous
furari pilfer, purloin, steal
furbish rehabilitate
furcate bifurcate, bipartite, dichotomize, divergent
furcated divergent
furcular bipartite
furens frenetic
furibund frenetic
furious demonstrative *(expressive of emotion)*, resentful, severe, vehement
furiousness violence
furlough holiday, leave *(absence)*
furnish accommodate, adduce, bear *(yield)*, bequeath, bestow, clothe, contribute *(supply)*, dole, endow, endue, engender, fund, give *(grant)*, lend, pander, present *(make a gift)*, produce *(manufacture)*, provide *(supply)*, render *(administer)*, replenish, sell, supply, tender, vest, yield *(produce a return)*
furnish aid abet, assist, capitalize *(provide capital)*, contribute *(assist)*, inure *(benefit)*, serve *(assist)*, subsidize
furnish an equivalent compensate *(counterbalance)*
furnish an estimate calculate
furnish an example illustrate
furnish assistance bear *(support)*, help, serve *(assist)*
furnish credit lend
furnish evidence bear *(adduce)*, evince
furnish foundations capitalize *(provide capital)*
furnish funds loan, support *(assist)*
furnish occupation for employ *(engage services)*, hire

furnish room for lodge *(house)*
furnish support bear *(support)*, capitalize *(provide capital)*, subsidize
furnish sustenance bear *(support)*
furnish with a date date
furnish with quarters lodge *(house)*
furnish with rank invest *(vest)*
furnished with weapons armed
furnisher supplier
furnishing donative, provision *(act of supplying)*
furnishings cargo
furor ardor, commotion, emotion, outburst, outcry, passion, riot
furrow split
further accrue *(increase)*, additional, aggravate *(exacerbate)*, aid, assist, compound, countenance, cultivate, develop, expand, expedite, facilitate, favor, foster, help, inure *(benefit)*, nurture, parlay *(exploit successfully)*, precipitate *(hasten)*, prefer, promote *(advance)*, promote *(organize)*, raise *(advance)*, side, subsidize, support *(assist)*
further time extension *(postponement)*
furtherance advancement *(improvement)*, advocacy, aid *(help)*, assistance, behalf, course, development *(progression)*, favor *(sanction)*, headway, help, longevity, progress, promotion *(encouragement)*, reinforcement
furthermore also, further
furthermost ultimate
furthermost part end *(termination)*
furthest extreme *(last)*, last *(final)*, ultimate, utmost
furthest extent ambit
furthest point ambit, limit, utmost
furtim feras intercipere poach
furtive clandestine, collusive, covert, evasive, fraudulent, insidious, mysterious, oblique *(evasive)*, privy, secret, sly, stealthy, surreptitious
furtive removal asportation
furtiveness bad faith, concealment, deceit, dishonesty, fraud, improbity
furtivus clandestine, furtive, stealthy, surreptitious
furtum burglary, larceny, theft
fury furor, outbreak, outburst, passion, resentment, severity, violence
fuscus dun
fuse adhere *(fasten)*, amalgamate, bond *(hold together)*, cement, combine *(join together)*, commingle, conjoin, connect *(join together)*, consolidate *(strengthen)*, consolidate *(unite)*, desegregate, incorporate *(include)*, join *(bring together)*, lock, merge, unite
fused coadunate, coherent *(joined)*, composite, compound, concerted, concurrent *(united)*, conjoint, inseparable, promiscuous
fusillade discharge *(shot)*, onset *(assault)*, salvo
fusing coalescence, coalition, concordant
fusion accession *(annexation)*, adhesion *(affixing)*, affiliation *(amalgamation)*, cartel, centralization, coaction, coalescence, coalition, coherence, combination, concrescence, confederacy *(compact)*, consolidation, incorporation *(blend)*, integration *(amalgamation)*, league, meeting *(encounter)*, merger,

union *(unity)*
fusion of interests coalition, concert
fuss disturbance, fracas, furor, outburst, pretense *(ostentation)*, trouble, turmoil
fussiness particularity
fussy meticulous, particular *(exacting)*, precise, punctilious, punctual
fustian bombast, flatulent, grandiose, inflated *(bombastic)*, orotund, turgid
fustigate beat *(strike)*, lash *(strike)*
fustis cudgel
fusty sordid, stale
futile expendable, idle, ineffective, ineffectual, invalid, minor, needless, nugatory, otiose, powerless, unavailing, unproductive
futile effort frustration, miscarriage
futilis futile, unavailing
futility impossibility
future forthcoming, imminent, potential, prospective, subsequent
future generation descendant
future interest reversion *(remainder of an estate)*
future payment credit *(delayed payment)*
future possession heritage, reversion *(remainder of an estate)*
future relatives posterity
futures portfolio
futurity prospect *(outlook)*
futurus future, prospective
fuzziness indistinctness, obscuration
fuzzy unclear

G

gab prattle
gabble prattle
gabby loquacious
gad prowl
gadget device *(mechanism)*, item
gag inhibit, repress, stifle, suppress
gage bail, binder, defiance, deposit, guaranty, security *(pledge)*
gagged speechless
gaiety enjoyment *(pleasure)*
gain accession *(enlargement)*, accretion, accrue *(increase)*, accumulate *(enlarge)*, acquire *(receive)*, acquire *(secure)*, acquisition, advancement *(improvement)*, advantage, appreciation *(increased value)*, attain, augmentation, bear *(yield)*, benefit *(betterment)*, boom *(increase)*, boom *(prosperity)*, carry *(succeed)*, collect *(gather)*, collect *(recover money)*, development *(progression)*, dividend, earn, edification, expand, headway, increase, increment, inherit, interest *(profit)*, inure *(benefit)*, obtain, output, perquisite, possess, prize, proceeds, procure, profit, profit, progress, progress, purchase, reach, realize *(obtain as a profit)*, reap, receipt *(act of receiving)*, receive *(acquire)*, recruit, revenue, shelter *(tax benefit)*, succeed *(attain)*
gain a victory prevail *(triumph)*, succeed *(attain)*
gain admittance enter *(go in)*
gain advantage profit
gain anew recoup *(regain)*, recover
gain by labor earn
gain by service earn
gain by wrongful methods extort

gain control over defeat
gain derived from capital income
gain derived from labor income
gain entry enter *(go in)*
gain for oneself possess
gain ground compound, increase, proceed *(go forward)*, progress
gain in worth appreciate *(increase)*, appreciation *(increased value)*
gain indemnity against loss insure
gain insight comprehend *(understand)*
gain insight into perceive
gain knowledge detect
gain liberty escape
gain more time postpone
gain one's end attain
gain over disarm *(set at ease)*, prejudice *(influence)*
gain possession obtain, preempt, recover
gain strength compound, expand
gain the advantage prevail *(triumph)*
gain the ascendancy outbalance
gain the confidence of convince, disarm *(set at ease)*, persuade, prevail *(persuade)*
gain the favor of propitiate
gain the upper hand predominate *(command)*, prevail *(triumph)*
gain time defer *(put off)*, hold up *(delay)*, procrastinate, protract *(prolong)*
gain wrongfully extort
gainful beneficial, functional, lucrative, productive, profitable, successful, valuable
gaingiving misgiving
gainless disadvantageous, futile, ineffective, ineffectual
gains earnings, income, spoils
gainsay contend *(dispute)*, contest, contravene, cross *(disagree with)*, debar, deny *(contradict)*, disaccord, disaffirm, disagree, disapprove *(reject)*, dispute *(contest)*, except *(object)*, expostulate, negation, oppugn, prohibit, refute, reject, repulse
gainsaying contravention, counterargument, denial, diatribe, disagreement, disapprobation, negation, negative, rejection, remonstrance, retraction
gait step
gala holiday, special
galbe configuration *(form)*
gall affront, annoy, irritate, offend *(insult)*, perturb, pique, plague, provoke, resentment, spite, temerity
gallant heroic, magnanimous, undaunted
gallant acts prowess *(bravery)*
gallantness prowess *(bravery)*
gallantry consideration *(sympathetic regard)*, courtesy, prowess *(bravery)*
galled resentful
gallimaufry melange
galling malevolent, oppressive, outrageous, provocative, vexatious
gallop race
galloping rapid
galore rife
galvanic incisive, provocative
galvanical provocative
galvanize foment, impress *(affect deeply)*

gambit first appearance

gamble bet, hazard, invest *(fund)*, lottery, parlay *(bet)*, possibility, risk, speculate *(chance)*, speculation *(risk)*, venture

gambler bettor, speculator

gambling speculation *(risk)*

game bet, contest *(competition)*, ridicule

game of chance lottery

gamesome jocular

gamester bettor

gaming risk, speculation *(risk)*

gammon bait *(lure)*, betray *(lead astray)*, palter

gamut range

gang assemblage, band, cabal, league

gangleader racketeer

gangster burglar, criminal, malefactor, racketeer

gangway entrance

gannitus snarl

gap flaw, hiatus, interruption, interval, pause, space, split

gaping open *(unclosed)*, penetrable

garb clothe

garble cloak, falsify, misconstrue, misinterpret, misread

garbled imperfect, inaccurate, marred

garbling catachresis

garden cultivate, curtilage

gargantuan prodigious *(enormous)*

garish meretricious, pretentious *(ostentatious)*, tawdry

garishness pretense *(ostentation)*

garner accumulate *(amass)*, collect *(gather)*, compile, fund, glean, hoard, repository, reserve, store

garner up hoard

garnering arsenal

garnish attach *(seize)*, distrain, embellish, impress *(procure by force)*, levy

garnished elaborate

garnisheed attached *(seized)*

garnishing bombast, confiscatory

garnishment attachment *(seizure)*, distraint, motif, sequestration

garrison bear *(support)*, lodge *(house)*, protect

garrulous flatulent, loquacious, profuse, voluble

garrulus loquacious

gasconade exaggeration, jactation, rodomontade

gasconading orgulous

gash lancinate, mutilate, rift *(gap)*, split

gate egress, entrance, immure, outlet, portal

gatekeeper guardian, warden

gates approaches

gateway easement, egress, entrance, outlet, portal, threshold *(entrance)*

gather accrue *(increase)*, accumulate *(amass)*, aggregate, assume *(suppose)*, call *(summon)*, compile, concentrate *(consolidate)*, congregate, conjoin, connect *(join together)*, construe *(comprehend)*, convene, converge, cull, deduce, deduct *(conclude by reasoning)*, expect *(consider probable)*, extract, gain, garner, glean, guess, hold *(possess)*, infer, join *(bring together)*, levy, obtain, presume, presuppose, procure, read, reap, reason *(conclude)*, receive *(acquire)*, recruit, rendezvous, store, surmise, sus-

pect *(think)*, understand

gather for oneself hoard

gather in hoard

gather into a mass accumulate *(amass)*

gather knowledge find *(discover)*

gather together accumulate *(amass)*, aggregate, collect *(gather)*, compile, consolidate *(unite)*, convene, meet, raise *(collect)*, unite

gather up accumulate *(amass)*, hoard

gathered collective, composite

gathered into a round mass conglomerate

gathered into a whole composite

gathering assemblage, assembly, body *(collection)*, caucus, chamber *(body)*, collection *(assembly)*, company *(assemblage)*, compilation, conference, congregation, levy, mass *(body of persons)*, meeting *(conference)*, rendezvous, selection *(collection)*, session

gathering place focus, rendezvous

gathering together centralization

gauche incompetent, provincial

gaudiness pretense *(ostentation)*

gaudium enjoyment *(pleasure)*

gaudy blatant *(obtrusive)*, meretricious, pretentious *(ostentatious)*, tawdry

gauge assess *(appraise)*, calculate, consider, criterion, criticize *(evaluate)*, estimate *(approximate cost)*, estimate, estimation *(calculation)*, evaluate, extent, magnitude, mass *(weight)*, measure, measurement, model, rate, standard, weigh

gaugeable appreciable, determinable *(ascertainable)*

gausape fustian (adjective), fustian (noun)

gawky incompetent, provincial, uncouth

gay jocular

gaze regard *(pay attention)*

gaze at observe *(watch)*

gazette herald, journal, proclaim

gear clothe, device *(mechanism)*, furnish, paraphernalia *(apparatus)*

gear with engage *(involve)*

geared to fitting

gelatinization congealment

gelling congealment

gemination duplicate

gemmate germinate

genealogical hereditary

genealogical tree blood, origin *(ancestry)*, parentage

genealogy ancestry, blood, bloodline, descent *(lineage)*, family *(common ancestry)*, lineage, origin *(ancestry)*, parentage, race

genera class

general broad, chief, collective, competitive *(open)*, conventional, customary, familiar *(customary)*, generic, habitual, inaccurate, inclusive, inexact, liberal *(not literal)*, mutual *(collective)*, national, nonsectarian, omnibus, ordinary, predominant, prevailing *(current)*, prevalent, proverbial, public *(affecting people)*, regular *(conventional)*, rife, routine, unspecified, usual, vague

general agreement consensus

general course practice *(custom)*

general denial demurrer

general discharge salvo

general expenses overhead

general fire conflagration

general guidelines policy *(plan of action)*, practice *(procedure)*

general information common knowledge, education

general law generality *(vague statement)*

general meaning connotation, content *(meaning)*, gist *(substance)*

general notion impression

general pardon amnesty

general performance norm

general principle generality *(vague statement)*

general principles policy *(plan of action)*

general public populace, population, public

general reciprocity comity

general rule canon, generality *(vague statement)*

general run matter of course

general statement generality *(vague statement)*, generalization

general store market *(business)*

general uprising revolution

generalis general

generality generalization, majority *(greater part)*, norm

generalization generality *(vague statement)*

generalized broad, inaccurate

generally as a rule, invariably

generally accepted prevailing *(current)*, prevalent

generally known common *(customary)*, notorious

generally practiced ordinary

generally seen familiar *(customary)*

generally speaking as a rule

generals management *(directorate)*

generalship management *(supervision)*

generare engender, generate

generate avail *(bring about)*, bear *(yield)*, cause, compose, conceive *(invent)*, create, elicit, engender, evoke, fabricate *(construct)*, germinate, induce, inspire, launch *(initiate)*, make, manufacture, occasion, originate, produce *(manufacture)*, propagate *(increase)*, provoke, pullulate, reproduce, yield *(produce a return)*

generatim generalize

generating causal

generation formation, lifetime

generations of man humanity *(mankind)*

generative causal, causative, constructive *(creative)*, potent, prime *(original)*, prolific

generator architect, author *(originator)*, cause *(reason)*, derivation, determinant, source

generic broad, omnibus, unspecified

generic class kind

generical omnibus

generis kind

generosity benevolence *(disposition to do good)*, charity, clemency, consideration *(sympathetic regard)*, contribution *(donation)*, indulgence, largess *(generosity)*, philanthropy

generous ample, benevolent, capacious, charitable *(benevolent)*, copious,

donative, favorable *(expressing approval)*, humane, lenient, liberal *(generous)*, magnanimous, meritorious, multiple, philanthropic, placable, profuse, propitious
generous giver donor
generous giving charity
generousness clemency, indulgence, largess *(generosity)*, lenience
genesis ancestry, birth *(beginning)*, cause *(reason)*, derivation, determinant, embryo, formation, inception, nascency, onset *(commencement)*, origin *(source)*, origination, outset, parentage, reason *(basis)*, source, start
genetic born *(innate)*, hereditary, native *(inborn)*
genial amicable, benevolent, civil *(polite)*, willing *(not averse)*
genialis nuptial
geniality consideration *(sympathetic regard)*, courtesy, goodwill
genitor ancestor, ascendant, parents, progenitor
genius caliber *(mental capacity)*, expert *(flair)*, intellect, intelligence *(intellect)*, mastermind, propensity, sagacity, science *(technique)*, sense *(intelligence)*, specialty *(special aptitude)*
genocide murder
genre class, denomination, kind, style
gens lineage
gens humana humanity *(mankind)*
genteel civil *(polite)*
gentility blood, comity, courtesy, decorum, presence *(poise)*, society
gentle harmless, lenient, nonmilitant, peaceable, placid
gentleman of fortune bettor
gentlemanlike civil *(polite)*
gentlemanliness decorum
gentlemanly civil *(polite)*
gentleness clemency, consideration *(sympathetic regard)*, humanity *(humaneness)*, lenience, moderation
gentry elite
genuflection prostration
genuine accurate, actual, authentic, bona fide, convincing, de facto, direct *(forthright)*, documentary, factual, faithful *(true to fact)*, honest, ingenuous, legitimate *(rightful)*, natural, prime *(original)*, real, realistic, reliable, rightful, sterling, substantial, true *(authentic)*, unadulterated, undistorted, veridical
genuine in origin authentic
genuinely admittedly
genuineness candor *(straightforwardness)*, honesty, legitimacy, reality, truth, validity
genuiness veracity
genus ancestry, blood, class
genus kind
genus lineage, parentage
genus race
genus range
genus rubric *(title)*
genus style
geographical regional
gerere conduct, transact
germ consequence *(significance)*, embryo, source
germane applicable, apposite, appropriate, cognate, congruous, correlative, felicitous, interrelated, pertinent, re-

lated, relative *(relevant)*, relevant, suitable, tangential
germanus genuine, real
germicidal preventive
germinal original *(initial)*, prime *(original)*, rudimentary
germinare germinate
germinate develop, pullulate, stem *(originate)*
germinate from redound
germination development *(progression)*, growth *(evolution)*
germinative rudimentary
gerrymander illude
gestare bear *(support)*
gesture brandish, symbol
get acquire *(secure)*, attain, derive *(receive)*, gain, incur, obtain, possess, procure, raise *(collect)*, reach, realize *(obtain as a profit)*, reap, receive *(acquire)*
get a fresh start resume
get a glimpse of discover
get a profit earn
get abroad circulate
get across annunciate, convey *(communicate)*
get ahead compound, proceed *(go forward)*, progress, surpass
get ahead of outbalance, outweigh
get as one's own possess
get at reach
get away elude
get away from evade *(elude)*, part *(leave)*
get back collect *(recover money)*, reclaim, recoup *(regain)*, recover, redeem *(repurchase)*, retaliate
get back to work proceed *(continue)*
get by pass *(satisfy requirements)*
get by effort attain, earn
get by judgment recover
get control hold *(possess)*
get done attain, cap
get down alight
get even repay, retaliate
get even with discipline *(punish)*, recriminate
get free break *(separate)*
get going originate
get hold of grapple, obtain
get in exchange buy
get in formation organize *(arrange)*
get in the act participate
get in the way disrupt, hinder, interrupt
get in the way of foil
get in touch convey *(communicate)*
get in touch with reach
get loose break *(separate)*
get money collect *(recover money)*
get near approach
get off alight
get off the subject deviate
get on proceed *(continue)*, proceed *(go forward)*
get on credit borrow
get on the nerves of annoy
get out quit *(evacuate)*
get possession of attain, collect *(recover money)*, gain, hold *(possess)*, obtain
get ready provide *(arrange for)*
get rid of delete, discharge *(dismiss)*, disown *(refuse to acknowledge)*, dispel, eject *(evict)*, eliminate *(eradicate)*, expel, extirpate, jettison, purge *(pu-*

rify), reject, remove *(dismiss from office)*
get temporary use of borrow
get the best of beat *(defeat)*
get the better of beat *(defeat)*, overcome *(surmount)*, overreach, subdue, subject, surmount
get the start on anticipate *(expect)*
get the upper hand overcome *(overwhelm)*, overcome *(surmount)*, prevail *(triumph)*
get through annunciate, cease, pass *(satisfy requirements)*
get through to contact *(communicate)*, reach
get through with cap
get to contact *(communicate)*
get to safety escape
get to the bottom of find *(discover)*
get together congregate, hoard, meet
get under way arise *(occur)*, dispatch *(send off)*, embark
get up originate
get used to inure *(accustom)*, naturalize *(acclimate)*
get worse degenerate, depreciate
get wrong misconstrue, mistake
get-together rendezvous
getting even reprisal
getting less decrease
getting together congregation
ghastly deplorable, heinous, loathsome, lurid, repulsive
ghost phantom
ghostly nonsubstantial *(not sturdy)*
ghostly form phantom
ghoulish sinister
giant prodigious *(enormous)*
gibberish jargon *(unintelligible language)*
gibbet defame, denigrate, denounce *(condemn)*, pillory, sully
gibe disdain, disparage, flout, hector, jeer, mock *(deride)*, plague, ridicule
gibe at jape
giddy capricious, frivolous, thoughtless, volatile
gift appropriation *(donation)*, aptitude, behalf, benefit *(conferment)*, bequest, bonus, bounty, caliber *(mental capacity)*, cession, charity, competence *(ability)*, contribution *(donation)*, donation, endowment, faculty *(ability)*, grant, gratuity *(present)*, inheritance, perquisite, proclivity, propensity, reward, skill, subsidy, tendency, tip *(gratuity)*
gift by succession estate *(hereditament)*
gift by will legacy
gift of a freehold interest feoffment
gift of property by will legacy
gifted artful, capable, deft, original *(creative)*, practiced, resourceful, sciential
giftedness capacity *(aptitude)*
gigantic capacious, copious, gross *(flagrant)*, prodigious *(enormous)*
gignere engender, generate, propagate *(increase)*
gild camouflage, embellish
gimcrack poor *(inferior in quality)*
gimmick device *(contrivance)*, stratagem
gingerly meticulous
gird border *(bound)*, circumscribe

(surround by boundary), embrace *(encircle)*, enclose, encompass *(surround)*
girdle circumscribe *(surround by boundary)*, embrace *(encircle)*, enclose, enclose, encompass *(surround)*, hedge, include
girdling blockade *(enclosure)*
girl child
girlishness puerility
girth caliber *(measurement)*, measurement
gist center *(essence)*, connotation, content *(meaning)*, contents, context, essence, gravamen, import, main point, significance, signification, spirit, subject *(topic)*, substance *(essential nature)*, sum *(tally)*, tenor
gist of a charge gravamen
gite abode
givable heritable
give adduce, administer *(tender)*, allow *(authorize)*, ascribe, attorn, bear *(yield)*, bequeath, bestow, cede, confer *(give)*, contribute *(supply)*, convey *(transfer)*, dedicate, delegate, descend, devise *(give)*, devolve, disburse *(distribute)*, dole, endow, endue, extend *(offer)*, fund, furnish, grant *(concede)*, grant *(transfer formally)*, lend, loan, mete, pander, present *(make a gift)*, proffer, provide *(supply)*, relax, relent, render *(administer)*, render *(deliver)*, replenish, send, spend, subsidize, supply, tender, transmit, yield *(produce a return)*
give a bad name defame, denigrate, pillory
give a beating lash *(strike)*
give a blow beat *(strike)*
give a color to camouflage
give a detailed explanation explicate
give a directive direct *(order)*, instruct *(direct)*, prescribe
give a false appearance camouflage, pretend
give a false coloring camouflage, cloak, disguise, misrepresent
give a false idea delude, distort, mislead
give a false impression delude, distort, misdirect, misinform, mislead, misstate, profess *(pretend)*
give a false representation misrepresent
give a favorable verdict acquit
give a final notice charge *(assess)*
give a formal hearing to hear *(give a legal hearing)*
give a formal speech declaim
give a grant to subsidize
give a guarantee certify *(attest)*, pledge *(promise the performance of)*
give a guilty verdict convict
give a hand assist
give a hint imply, mention
give a job retain *(employ)*
give a job to employ *(engage services)*, engage *(hire)*, hire
give a judicial hearing to hear *(give a legal hearing)*
give a lesson exposit
give a mandate appoint, delegate, entrust, instruct *(direct)*, invest *(vest)*, prescribe
give a name call *(title)*

give a name to denominate, identify
give a new form to modify *(alter)*
give a performance produce *(offer to view)*
give a permit qualify *(meet standards)*
give a position to employ *(engage services)*
give a post to employ *(engage services)*
give a present bestow
give a prize dedicate
give a promise swear
give a recommendation counsel
give a report inform *(notify)*, relate *(tell)*
give a reprieve clear, condone, free
give a responsibility to delegate, entrust
give a right authorize
give a ruling conclude *(decide)*, determine, pronounce *(pass judgment)*
give a sense to comment
give a signal indicate
give a situation to engage *(hire)*
give a solemn declaration depose *(testify)*
give a speech address *(talk to)*, discourse
give a start expedite
give a strained meaning distort
give a summary of recapitulate
give a talk discourse, speak
give a thrashing beat *(strike)*, lash *(strike)*
give a turn distort
give a verbal account recite
give a vote cast *(register)*
give a warrant qualify *(meet standards)*
give a wide berth eschew
give a wide berth to shun
give a wrong idea misstate
give ability empower, enable
give absolution clear, condone, exonerate, forgive, free, pardon
give absolution to exculpate, excuse
give additional information elaborate
give admittance to instate
give advice admonish *(advise)*, advise, advocate, caution, charge *(instruct on the law)*, confer *(consult)*, counsel, incite
give advice against expostulate
give aid aid, assist, capitalize *(provide capital)*, contribute *(assist)*, nurture, subsidize
give allegiance to obey
give amnesty condone, palliate *(excuse)*, remit *(release from penalty)*
give an account communicate, convey *(communicate)*, depict, describe, detail *(particularize)*, inform *(notify)*, recount, relate *(tell)*
give an account of characterize, depose *(testify)*, report *(disclose)*
give an address discourse
give an answer respond, return *(respond)*
give an appellation to identify
give an approximate value estimate
give an encore copy, repeat *(do again)*
give an estimate evaluate
give an example exemplify

give an explanation elucidate
give an impetus impel, inspire
give an inclination prejudice *(influence)*
give an inkling hint
give an instance exemplify, illustrate
give an interpretation elucidate
give an introduction present *(introduce)*
give an official hearing to hear *(give a legal hearing)*
give an opinion adjudge, advise, conclude *(decide)*, determine, evaluate, find *(determine)*, pass *(determine)*, pronounce *(pass judgment)*, rule *(decide)*
give an order direct *(order)*, instruct *(direct)*, prescribe
give and bequeath devise *(give)*
give and take barter, interchange, quid pro quo, reciprocal, reciprocate, reciprocity
give approval bestow, consent, pass *(approve)*, sanction
give as a gift present *(make a gift)*
give as a guarantee pledge *(deposit)*
give as an excuse justify
give as example cite *(state)*
give as security pawn
give as security for a debt pledge *(deposit)*
give as security for an obligation pledge *(deposit)*
give as surety pledge *(deposit)*
give assent accede *(concede)*, agree *(comply)*, bestow, certify *(approve)*, coincide *(concur)*, defer *(yield in judgment)*
give assurance agree *(contract)*, avouch *(guarantee)*, close *(agree)*, cosign, guarantee, pledge *(promise the performance of)*, promise *(vow)*, vouch
give attention concern *(care)*, devote, focus
give attention to concentrate *(pay attention)*, note *(notice)*, observe *(watch)*, perceive, specialize
give audience hear *(give attention to)*
give authoritative instructions to instruct *(direct)*
give authority allow *(authorize)*, authorize, empower, enable, grant *(concede)*, invest *(vest)*, vest
give authority to charge *(empower)*, delegate
give away abandon *(relinquish)*, bestow, betray *(disclose)*, cede, contribute *(supply)*, devise *(give)*, disburse *(distribute)*, disperse *(disseminate)*, dole, expose, forfeit, grant *(transfer formally)*, parcel, post, renounce
give away at death bequeath
give back bestow, contribute *(indemnify)*, indemnify, rebate, recommit, recoup *(reimburse)*, reflect *(mirror)*, refund, remise, render *(deliver)*, repay, restore *(return)*, return *(refund)*
give base bear *(support)*
give being to develop
give birth propagate *(increase)*
give birth to conceive *(invent)*, create, make, originate, produce *(manufacture)*, reproduce
give by way of information instruct *(teach)*
give by will bequeath, demise, descend, devise *(give)*, leave *(give)*

give cause for occasion

give cause for alarm disconcert, frighten, perturb

give chase hunt

give clearance bestow, certify *(approve)*, facilitate, grant *(concede)*, permit, release

give close attention scrutinize

give color to disguise

give compensation for defray

give compensation for in advance prepay

give concrete form to embody, exemplify

give confidence reassure

give consent agree *(comply)*, assent, bestow, certify *(approve)*, consent, defer *(yield in judgment)*, grant *(concede)*, permit, suffer *(permit)*

give consent to comply

give control vest

give counsel admonish *(advise)*, advise

give credence to trust

give credit concur *(agree)*, lend, recommend

give credit to trust

give currency promulgate

give currency to circulate

give definite form to embody

give denial to contradict, controvert, dispute *(contest)*

give details detail *(particularize)*

give directions command, direct *(order)*, discipline *(train)*, prescribe

give dispensation bestow, excuse, palliate *(excuse)*

give earnestly dedicate

give employment delegate, employ *(engage services)*

give employment to engage *(hire)*, hire

give entrance receive *(permit to enter)*

give entrance to induct, initiate, instate, penetrate

give equal value compensate *(remunerate)*

give evidence bear *(adduce)*, confess, depose *(testify)*, swear, testify, verify *(confirm)*, vouch, witness *(attest to)*

give expectation promise *(raise expectations)*

give explanation to construe *(translate)*

give expression communicate, enunciate, recite, speak

give expression to depict, express, observe *(remark)*, phrase, utter

give fair warning caution, forewarn, notice *(give formal warning)*

give final notice dun

give force to implement

give form to formalize, formulate

give formal approval to formalize

give formal status to formalize

give forth circulate, develop, emit, post, reflect *(mirror)*, send, utter

give foundation bear *(support)*

give freedom liberate

give freely bestow

give full particulars specify

give good reasons for vindicate

give ground bear *(support)*

give grounds for support *(justify)*

give heed concentrate *(pay attention)*

give heed to attend *(heed)*, care *(be cautious)*, notice *(observe)*, observe *(watch)*, regard *(pay attention)*

give help relieve *(give aid)*, serve *(assist)*

give honor dedicate

give hope assure *(give confidence to)*, promise *(raise expectations)*, reassure

give impetus incite

give impulse to originate

give in accede *(concede)*, concede, defer *(yield in judgment)*, relent, submit *(yield)*, succumb, surrender *(yield)*, vouchsafe, yield *(submit)*

give in charge delegate

give in custody arrest *(apprehend)*

give in earnest pawn

give in exchange barter, change, repay

give in kind recriminate

give in return reciprocate

give in trust confide *(trust)*, consign, delegate

give increase bear *(yield)*

give indication of evidence, speak

give indirect information connote, imply

give information advise, apprise, bear *(adduce)*, notice *(give formal warning)*

give inside information reveal

give instructions direct *(order)*, discipline *(train)*

give intimation of impending evil caution, forewarn

give into another's keeping deliver

give judgment adjudicate, arbitrate *(adjudge)*, conclude *(decide)*, decree, determine, find *(determine)*, pronounce *(pass judgment)*, rule *(decide)*

give leave allow *(authorize)*, authorize, bestow, grant *(concede)*, let *(permit)*, permit, suffer *(permit)*

give legal force validate

give legal form to constitute *(establish)*

give legislative sanction enact

give legislative sanction to pass *(approve)*

give lessons educate

give lessons in discipline *(train)*, instruct *(teach)*

give liberty to disenthrall, enfranchise, liberate

give life to generate

give means enable

give measure for measure retaliate

give money bear the expense, disburse *(pay out)*, expend *(disburse)*, fund

give money over lend

give new life to renew *(refurbish)*

give no credence to disbelieve, doubt *(distrust)*, misdoubt

give no credit to disbelieve, misdoubt, mistrust

give no heed disregard

give notice admonish *(advise)*, advise, alert, annunciate, apprise, caution, communicate, convey *(communicate)*, demand, discharge *(dismiss)*, forewarn, inform *(notify)*, mention, notify, predict, remind, resign, retire *(conclude a career)*, signify *(inform)*

give notice of proclaim, promulgate

give notice to serve *(deliver a legal instrument)*

give notification communicate

give occasion for cause

give occupation rent

give off emit, exude

give offense irritate, pique, provoke, repel *(disgust)*

give offense to affront, bait *(harass)*, disoblige, humiliate

give one a talking to browbeat

give one an idea of interpret

give one an impression of interpret

give one his deserts discipline *(punish)*

give one pause discourage

give one to understand advise, communicate

give one's attention concern *(care)*

give one's blessing countenance

give one's hand to bestow

give one's honor promise *(vow)*

give one's signature cosign, pledge *(deposit)*

give one's word bear *(adduce)*, certify *(attest)*, guarantee, pledge *(promise the performance of)*, promise *(vow)*, swear, testify, vouch

give one's word for confirm

give one's word of honor promise *(vow)*

give opportunity for permit

give oral evidence affirm *(declare solemnly)*

give orders command, decree, dictate, direct *(order)*, enjoin, govern, rule *(govern)*, summon

give origin provoke

give origin to avail *(bring about)*, cause, create, make, originate

give out allocate, assign *(allot)*, bestow, circulate, deliver, disburse *(distribute)*, dispense, distribute, divide *(distribute)*, dole, emit, issue *(publish)*, mete, parcel, post, proclaim, publish, reveal

give out again redistribute

give out among a number disperse *(disseminate)*

give out in payment disburse *(pay out)*

give out in shares bestow

give out information inform *(notify)*

give over abandon *(relinquish)*, cease, present *(make a gift)*, relinquish

give over to grant *(transfer formally)*

give over to the foe betray *(lead astray)*, inform *(betray)*

give pain aggravate *(annoy)*, harrow, inflict, mistreat

give payment pay, remunerate

give permission allow *(authorize)*, authorize, bestow, certify *(approve)*, consent, empower, enable, grant *(concede)*, let *(permit)*, permit, sanction, suffer *(permit)*

give place to succeed *(follow)*

give play to the imagination conjure

give political privileges to enfranchise

give power authorize, bestow, delegate, empower, enable, invest *(vest)*, permit

give power of attorney delegate

give power to charge *(empower)*

give precise meaning to characterize

give previous notice to forewarn

give previous warning to forewarn

give proof depose *(testify)*

give proof by a witness depose *(testify)*

give public notice of issue *(publish)*, post, publish

give publicity to promulgate

give quarter relent

give reason for enlighten, explain, exposit

give references document

give refuge harbor

give relief mitigate, mollify, relieve *(give aid)*, soothe

give repose ease

give rest ease

give right empower

give right of entry to admit *(give access)*

give rise provoke

give rise to avail *(bring about)*, cause, compose, create, develop, engender, establish *(launch)*, evoke, generate, make, originate, produce *(manufacture)*

give salvation save *(rescue)*

give satisfaction indemnify, redeem *(satisfy debts)*

give satisfaction for damage compensate *(remunerate)*

give satisfaction for injury compensate *(remunerate)*

give security assure *(insure)*, bond *(secure a debt)*, confirm, ensure, pledge *(deposit)*, promise *(vow)*

give sense to construe *(translate)*

give shape to form

give sign signify *(inform)*

give strength to compound

give suggestions advise

give suggestions to charge *(instruct on the law)*, counsel

give support adhere *(maintain loyalty)*, aid, assist, bear *(support)*, capitalize *(provide capital)*, preserve

give support to subsidize

give surety ensure

give sworn evidence affirm *(declare solemnly)*

give sworn testimony depose *(testify)*

give tangible form to embody

give terms dicker

give testimony witness *(attest to)*

give the cold shoulder ignore

give the death blow dispatch *(put to death)*

give the details of characterize, delineate

give the effect appear *(seem to be)*

give the facts communicate, inform *(notify)*, notify, recount, report *(disclose)*

give the floor to recognize *(acknowledge)*

give the impression appear *(seem to be)*

give the meaning define

give the mind to focus

give the nod to recognize *(acknowledge)*

give the particulars recount

give the right to vote enfranchise

give the signal instruct *(direct)*

give the sum and substance abridge *(shorten)*

give the word instruct *(direct)*

give the word of command instruct

give thought to ponder, reflect *(ponder)*

give tidings herald, inform *(notify)*

give title to denominate, sell

give to delegate

give to the world circulate

give to understand disabuse, instruct *(teach)*, notify

give token portend

give tongue communicate

give tongue to observe *(remark)*, phrase

give trouble balk, inconvenience

give twist distort

give umbrage pique

give umbrage to bait *(harass)*

give up abandon *(relinquish)*, bestow, cede, demit, disclaim, discontinue *(abandon)*, disown *(refuse to acknowledge)*, forfeit, forgo, forswear, leave *(allow to remain)*, quit *(discontinue)*, release, relinquish, remise, remit *(relax)*, renounce, resign, submit *(yield)*, waive, yield *(submit)*

give up claim to abandon *(relinquish)*, cede, forfeit, forgo, relinquish, renounce, waive

give up office retire *(conclude a career)*

give up the argument forfeit

give up the point forfeit

give up the right to forgo

give up treacherously betray *(lead astray)*

give up work retire *(conclude a career)*

give utterance communicate, enunciate, mention, phrase, remark

give utterance to betray *(disclose)*, disclose, observe *(remark)*

give validity to implement

give variety vary

give vent to express

give verbal evidence affirm *(declare solemnly)*

give voice communicate, speak

give voice to express, observe *(remark)*, phrase

give warning admonish *(warn)*, advise, caution, notice *(give formal warning)*, notify

give warning of possible harm caution, forewarn

give way defer *(yield in judgment)*, hear *(give attention to)*, obey, relent, retreat, split, succumb, yield *(submit)*

give way to submit *(yield)*

give witness bear *(adduce)*

give word for word quote

give words to phrase, portray, speak

give work to employ *(engage services)*, hire

given assumed *(inferred)*, free *(at no charge)*, gratuitous *(given without recompense)*, prone, ready *(willing)*, unpaid

given away donative, free *(at no charge)*, gratuitous *(given without recompense)*

given by testament testamentary

given due consideration deliberate

given name call *(title)*

given over addicted

given preference preferred *(given priority)*

given to accustomed *(familiarized)*

given to controversy argumentative

given to deceit false *(not genuine)*

given to disputation litigious

given to fighting pugnacious

given to joking jocular

given to lying mendacious

given to research inquisitive

given to suspicion inconvincible

given to thought pensive

given to vice vicious

given up derelict *(abandoned)*, irretrievable

giver benefactor, donor, feoffor, good samaritan, grantor, supplier

giver of evidence eyewitness

giving charitable *(benevolent)*, concession *(authorization)*, dedication, disposition *(transfer of property)*, donative, philanthropic, sequacious

giving back reimbursement, restitution

giving beforehand advance *(allowance)*

giving each his due equitable

giving in concession *(compromise)*

giving over delegation *(assignment)*

giving up bailment, cession, renunciation, resignation *(relinquishment)*, waiver

giving up claim to cession

giving way capitulation

glad ecstatic, inclined, ready *(willing)*

gladly readily

glamor prestige

glamorize embellish

glamorous attractive

glance vision *(dream)*

glance at notice *(observe)*

glance off deviate

glance over peruse

glare pretense *(ostentation)*

glaring blatant *(obtrusive)*, clear *(apparent)*, distinct *(clear)*, egregious, evident, flagrant, gross *(flagrant)*, manifest, notorious, obvious, open *(in sight)*, outrageous, overt, palpable, patent, perceivable, perceptible, prominent, salient, stark, tawdry, unmistakable

glaringly bad arrant *(onerous)*

glaringly vivid lurid

glean acquire *(receive)*, compile, construe *(comprehend)*, cull, derive *(receive)*, extract, gain, infer, procure, read, reap, select, understand

glean information peruse

glean knowledge of overhear

gleaning acquisition

gleeful jocular

gleesome jocular

glib loquacious, voluble

glimmer suggestion

glimpse find *(discover)*, pierce *(discern)*, spy, vision *(dream)*

gliscere increase

glitter pretense *(ostentation)*

glittering tawdry

gloat over relish

global complete *(all-embracing)*, nonsectarian, prevailing *(current)*, prevalent, total

globe sphere

globoid sphere

globular mass sphere

glomerate composite, conglomerate

glomeration agglomeration, conglomeration, cumulation

gloom damper *(depressant)*, depression, indistinctness, obscuration, pessimism

gloominess obscuration, pessimism

gloomy bleak *(not favorable)*, bleak *(severely simple)*, despondent, disconsolate, lugubrious, ominous, pessimistic, portentous *(ominous)*, solemn

gloomy outlook pessimism

gloria prestige

glorification doxology, homage, honor *(outward respect)*, laudation, mention *(tribute)*, remembrance *(commemoration)*

glorified famous

glorify belaud, compound, elevate, honor, magnify, overestimate, raise *(advance)*, recommend, regard *(hold in esteem)*

gloriosus pretentious *(pompous)*

glorious famous, illustrious, meritorious

glory eminence, honor *(outward respect)*, prestige, reputation

gloss color *(deceptive appearance)*, comment, comment, distortion, note *(brief comment)*

gloss over cloak, discount *(disbelieve)*, neglect, pretermit, prevaricate

glow passion

glowing moving *(evoking emotion)*, vehement

glue adhere *(fasten)*, bond *(hold together)*, cement, combine *(join together)*, join *(bring together)*, lock

glued inseparable

glum disconsolate, lugubrious, pessimistic

glumness damper *(depressant)*, pessimism

glut inundate, overage, overcome *(overwhelm)*, overload, plethora, sufficiency, surfeit, surplus

glutinosity adhesion *(affixing)*

glutinous cohesive *(sticking)*

glutted full

gluttonous inordinate, insatiable, lecherous

gluttonous appetite greed

gluttony greed

gnarus familiar *(informed)*

gnaw obsess, pique

gnomic compact *(pithy)*, pithy, sententious

gnomic saying maxim

gnomical compact *(pithy)*

gnostic profound *(esoteric)*

go expire, leave *(depart)*, move *(alter position)*, part *(leave)*, pass *(advance)*, perish, proceed *(go forward)*, quit *(evacuate)*

go about discharge *(perform)*, occupy *(engage)*

go about stealthily prowl

go across cross *(intersect)*, traverse

go adrift deviate

go after attempt, chase, hunt, prosecute *(carry forward)*, pursue *(chase)*, strive, succeed *(follow)*

go against antagonize, confront *(oppose)*, contradict, contravene, counter, counteract, disapprove *(reject)*, oppose, oppugn

go ahead proceed *(go forward)*, progress

go ahead of precede

go all out for attempt

go along with attend *(accompany)*, authorize, coincide *(concur)*, comply, concur *(agree)*, conform, cooperate, countenance, defer *(yield in judgment)*, participate, sanction

go amiss deviate, err, miscalculate, mistake

go apart disband

go around detour, envelop, perambulate

go astray deviate, digress, err, lapse *(fall into error)*, miscalculate, mistake, trespass

go away leave *(depart)*, move *(alter position)*, part *(leave)*, quit *(evacuate)*, retreat, vacate *(leave)*

go awry deviate, lapse *(fall into error)*, miscalculate

go back escheat, recollect, regress, retire *(retreat)*, retreat

go back on abandon *(relinquish)*

go back on a commitment renege

go back on a promise renege

go back on one's word bear false witness

go back over reexamine

go back to continue *(resume)*

go bad degenerate, spoil *(impair)*

go before antecede, precede

go beyond outweigh, overlap, overstep, predominate *(outnumber)*, surmount, surpass, transcend

go by pass *(advance)*

go contrary to collide *(clash)*, conflict, contradict, counter, except *(object)*, oppose, protest

go counter to contradict, countervail, disobey

go deep into delve

go different ways disband, disperse *(scatter)*

go down succumb

go down in defeat lose *(undergo defeat)*

go downhill decrease

go for a walk perambulate

go forth circulate, leave *(depart)*, move *(alter position)*, part *(leave)*, proceed *(go forward)*, quit *(evacuate)*

go forward persevere, persist, progress

go from home move *(alter position)*

go in advance precede

go in different directions diffuse, disperse *(scatter)*

go in for pursue *(carry on)*, undertake

go in front of precede

go in many directions diffuse

go in opposition to collide *(clash)*, conflict, contradict, counter, counteract

go in pursuit of chase, delve, hunt, pursue *(chase)*

go in quest of chase, research

go in search of delve, hunt

go into deliberate, embark, enter *(go in)*, investigate

go into a decline languish

go into detail develop, elaborate, expand, quote, specify

go into litigation litigate

go into partnership cooperate, federalize *(associate)*

go into retirement demit, quit *(dis-*

continue)

go into the particulars detail *(particularize)*

go near approach

go next succeed *(follow)*

go off on a tangent deviate

go on continue *(persevere)*, endure *(last)*, exist, keep *(continue)*, maintain *(carry on)*, move *(alter position)*, pass *(advance)*, persevere, persist, progress, remain *(continue)*, resume, subsist

go on a spree carouse

go on an outing perambulate

go on foot perambulate

go one better surpass

go one's way move *(alter position)*

go out quit *(evacuate)*

go out of emanate

go out of business fail *(lose)*, quit *(discontinue)*

go out of one's way detour, deviate

go out of the path detour

go out of the way detour

go over check *(inspect)*, examine *(study)*, overstep, peruse, reaffirm, recapitulate, reconsider, reiterate, review, trace *(delineate)*

go past pass *(advance)*

go round about detour, deviate

go separate ways disband, disperse *(scatter)*

go the rounds patrol

go through bear *(tolerate)*, delve, endure *(suffer)*, penetrate, permeate, pervade, search, spend

go through phases change

go through the books audit

go through the motions fake

go through with commit *(perpetrate)*, discharge *(perform)*, follow-up

go to attend *(be present at)*

go to any lengths adhere *(persist)*

go to contract close *(agree)*

go to pieces degenerate

go to press publish

go to the limit adhere *(persist)*

go to the polls cast *(register)*

go to war fight *(battle)*

go too far overextend, overstep

go under fail *(lose)*, succumb

go undercover cloak

go with coincide *(correspond)*

go without relinquish, renounce

go wrong deviate, err, mistake

go-between agent, broker, conduit *(intermediary)*, interagent, intermediary, liaison, medium, procurator, representative *(proxy)*, spokesman, umpire

goad abet, agitate *(activate)*, badger, bait *(harass)*, bait *(lure)*, browbeat, catalyst, constrain *(compel)*, discompose, exhort, foment, harass, hector, impetus, incentive, incite, inducement, motivate, pique, pressure, prompt, provocation, stimulate, stimulus, urge

goading instigation

goal cause *(reason)*, contemplation, desideratum, design *(intent)*, destination, end *(intent)*, focus, intention, mission, motive, object, objective, point *(purpose)*, predetermination, project, purpose, reason *(basis)*, target

goatish lascivious, lecherous, salacious

god-forsaken diabolic

godless profane

godlike omnipotent, omniscient
godly sacrosanct
going before in time antecedent
going contrary to dissenting
going down descent (declination)
going on open-ended, present (current)
going over restatement
going to the utmost lengths extreme (exaggerated)
going too far extreme (exaggerated)
golden propitious
gone defunct, irredeemable, irretrievable, lifeless (dead), lost (taken away), null (invalid)
gone by outdated
gone out outdated, outmoded
gone out of existence defunct
gone to waste irredeemable, lost (taken away)
good advantage, appropriate, auspicious, behalf, benefit (betterment), clean, competent, ethical, favorable (advantageous), item, meritorious, moral, palatable, preferable, proficient, salutary, sapid, savory, select, sterling, upright, valid, valuable, welfare
good actions merit, right (righteousness)
good and effectual in law legal
good at deft
good behavior courtesy, merit, propriety (correctness), protocol (etiquette), right (righteousness)
good breeding courtesy, propriety (correctness)
good chance likelihood, opportunity, prospect (outlook)
good conduct ethics
good deed benevolence (act of kindness), favor (act of kindness)
good disposition benevolence (disposition to do good)
good enough fair (satisfactory), mediocre
good example exemplar, paragon
good excuse justification
good faith fidelity, integrity, loyalty, probity
good for nothing ineffective, ineffectual
good for one's advantage beneficial
good form decorum, protocol (etiquette)
good fortune boom (prosperity), chance (fortuity), opportunity, prosperity
good intention benevolence (disposition to do good)
good judgment caliber (mental capacity), common sense, sagacity, sense (intelligence)
good luck prosperity
good management austerity, economy (frugality)
good manners consideration (sympathetic regard), courtesy, decorum, propriety (correctness), protocol (etiquette), respect
good men and true array (jury)
good name credit (recognition), goodwill, honor (good reputation), regard (esteem), reputation
good nature benevolence (disposition to do good), goodwill, philanthropy
good neighbor samaritan

good notice adequate notice
good offices patronage (power to appoint jobs)
good opinion estimation (esteem), favor (sanction), honor (good reputation), recommendation
good order array (order)
good prospect likelihood
good reputation estimation (esteem), goodwill
good repute prestige
Good Samaritan benefactor, donor
good sense common sense, discretion (quality of being discreet), discrimination (good judgment), reason (sound judgment)
good service favor (act of kindness)
good standing estimation (esteem)
good taste decorum
good times prosperity
good to eat palatable
good treatment benevolence (act of kindness)
good turn benefit (conferment), benevolence (act of kindness), favor (act of kindness), help
good understanding agreement (concurrence)
good will affinity (regard), benevolence (disposition to do good), charity, clemency, comity, humanity (humaneness), peace, philanthropy, respect, tolerance, understanding (tolerance)
good works philanthropy
good-fellowship comity
good-hearted philanthropic
good-heartedness philanthropy
good-humored benevolent, obeisant
good-natured benevolent, obeisant, philanthropic
good-quality meritorious
good-tasting palatable, sapid, savory
good-tempered peaceable
goodly major
goodness benevolence (disposition to do good), decorum, ethics, good faith, honor (good reputation), integrity, merit, principle (virtue), probity, quality (excellence), rectitude, right (righteousness)
goodness and mercy benevolence (disposition to do good)
goods assets, cargo, commodities, effects, estate (property), freight, merchandise, movable, paraphernalia (personal belongings), possession (property), possessions, property (possessions), stock in trade
goods exported illegally contraband
goods for sale merchandise
goods imported illegally contraband
goods shipped consignment
goods subject to confiscation contraband
goods subject to seizure contraband
gore enter (penetrate), lancinate, penetrate, pierce (lance)
gorge overload
gorged full, replete
gorgeous elegant
gospel doctrine, principle (axiom)
gossip hearsay, report (rumor)
gossipy informatory
govern administer (conduct), command, control (regulate), curb, direct (order), direct (supervise), discipline

(control), dominate, handle (manage), inhibit, manage, manipulate (utilize skillfully), moderate (preside over), officiate, operate, overlook (superintend), oversee, predominate (command), preside, prevail (be in force), qualify (condition), regulate (manage), restrain, subject, subjugate, superintend, wield
govern badly misgovern
govern strictly discipline (control)
governable corrigible, malleable, obedient, pliable, sequacious, tractable
governance agency (legal relationship), authority (power), bureaucracy, dominance, government (administration), hegemony, influence, management (supervision), politics, regime, supremacy
governed arrested (checked)
governed by inferior (lower in position)
governed by law legal
governing dominant, influential, master, predominant, prevailing (having superior force), sovereign (absolute)
governing body board, management (directorate)
governing course of action policy (plan of action), practice (procedure)
governing factors circumstances
governing plan policy (plan of action), practice (procedure)
governing principle policy (plan of action)
government authorities, bureaucracy, civic, control (supervision), dominion (supreme authority), hierarchy (persons in authority), management (directorate), national, politics, public (affecting people), regime, regulation (management), supervision
government appropriation of private land expropriation (right of eminent domain)
government attorney prosecutor
government by bureaus bureaucracy
government notes currency
government office bureaucracy
government officers police
government paper bond
government servant caretaker (one fulfilling the function of office)
government-owned national
governmental civic, civil (public), federal, national, political, public (affecting people)
governmental body congress
governmental control censorship
governmental grant patent
governmental leader politician
governmental order of prohibition embargo
governmental procedure bureaucracy
governmental system for decision-making bureaucracy
governmental unit state (political unit)
governor caretaker (one caring for property), director, pedagogue, principal (director), superintendent
governorship direction (guidance)
grab obtain, prey, spoils
grace absolution, amenity, amnesty, charity, clemency, condonation, con-

sent, decorum, dispensation *(exception)*, embellish, facility *(easiness)*, favor *(act of kindness)*, franchise *(license)*, leave *(permission)*, lenience, permission, proportion, propriety *(correctness)*, remission, respite *(reprieve)*

graceful diplomatic, elegant, eloquent

gracefulness facility *(easiness)*

graceless dissolute, immoral, inelegant, pedestrian, unbecoming, uncouth

gracious benevolent, charitable *(benevolent)*, charitable *(lenient)*, civil *(polite)*, favorable *(expressing approval)*, meritorious, obeisant, philanthropic, placable, propitious, receptive

graciously readily

graciousness benevolence *(disposition to do good)*, comity, consideration *(sympathetic regard)*, courtesy, largess *(generosity)*, philanthropy

gradation array *(order)*, chain *(series)*, class, classification, degree *(station)*, differential, distribution *(arrangement)*, hierarchy *(arrangement in a series)*, order *(arrangement)*, sequence, step

grade caliber *(measurement)*, caliber *(quality)*, class, classify, condition *(state)*, degree *(station)*, differential, file *(arrange)*, fix *(arrange)*, measure, organize *(arrange)*, pigeonhole, quality *(excellence)*, rate, rating, screen *(select)*, sort, state *(condition)*, status, step, tabulate

grade A premium

grade of excellence standard

grading rating

gradual deliberate

gradual crumbling decline

gradual decline deterioration

gradual eating away erosion

gradual evolution development *(progression)*

gradual impairment decline, deterioration

gradual wearing away erosion

gradually piecemeal

gradually eat away erode

graduate file *(arrange)*, fix *(arrange)*, measure, prefer, promote *(advance)*, sort, subdivide, tabulate

graduation differential, distribution *(arrangement)*, promotion *(advancement)*, transition

graduation certificate degree *(academic title)*

gradus degree *(station)*

gradus amplior advancement *(improvement)*

graft bribe, connect *(join together)*, corruption, crime, gratuity *(bribe)*, hush money, improbity, spoils

grafter criminal

grain character *(personal quality)*, disposition *(inclination)*, frame *(mood)*, iota, modicum, scintilla

grand elegant, illustrious, important *(significant)*, momentous, orgulous, paramount, prodigious *(enormous)*, proud *(self-respecting)*, stellar

grand jury's accusation indictment

grand total corpus

grand vizier caretaker *(one fulfilling the function of office)*

grandchild child

grandeur character *(reputation)*, dis-

---

tinction *(reputation)*, eminence, importance, prestige

grandiloquence bombast, declamation, peroration, rhetoric *(insincere language)*

grandiloquent flatulent, fustian, grandiose, inflated *(bombastic)*, orotund, pretentious *(pompous)*, sesquipedalian, turgid

grandiose elaborate, fustian, inflated *(vain)*, orgulous, orotund, pretentious *(pompous)*

grandiosity bombast, pretense *(ostentation)*, rhetoric *(insincere language)*

grandsire ancestor, primogenitor

grant abalienate, accede *(concede)*, acquiescence, admit *(concede)*, alimony, allocate, allow *(authorize)*, appropriation *(donation)*, assign *(transfer ownership)*, assignment *(transfer of ownership)*, attorn, authorize, award, bear *(yield)*, bequeath, bestow, bounty, brevet, cede, cession, charge *(empower)*, charity, charter *(license)*, charter *(sanction)*, concede, concession *(authorization)*, concession *(compromise)*, condescend *(deign)*, confer *(give)*, consent, consent, contribute *(supply)*, contribution *(donation)*, convey *(transfer)*, copyright, deign, descend, devise *(give)*, devolve, dispensation *(exception)*, dispense, dole, donation, empower, enable, endow, endowment, endue, enfranchise, franchise *(license)*, fund, furnish, gift *(present)*, gratuity *(present)*, indulgence, largess *(gift)*, lease, leave *(permission)*, leave *(give)*, legacy, lend, let *(lease)*, let *(permit)*, liberty, license, loan, option *(contractual provision)*, parcel, patent, patronize *(condescend toward)*, pay, pension, permit, prerogative, present *(make a gift)*, privilege, provide *(supply)*, recognize *(acknowledge)*, remise, reveal, reward, sanction *(permission)*, sanction, subsidy, suffer *(permit)*, supply, tender, transfer, vouchsafe, yield *(submit)*

grant a boon bestow

grant a demise sublease

grant a lease rent, sublease

grant a reprieve clear, exonerate, free

grant a request bestow

grant absolution palliate *(excuse)*, purge *(wipe out by atonement)*

grant again recover

grant amnesty clear, condone, exonerate, forgive, free, palliate *(excuse)*, pardon

grant amnesty to excuse, quit *(free of)*

grant asylum harbor, receive *(permit to enter)*

grant authority empower, invest *(vest)*

grant authority to commit *(entrust)*

grant by favor vouchsafe

grant by will demise

grant claims authorize

grant clemency pardon

grant exclusive possession for a designated period lease

grant exemption palliate *(excuse)*

grant favors to favor, prefer

grant for support pension

grant forgiveness pardon

---

grant immunity condone, palliate *(excuse)*

grant in aid pension

grant monetary compensation indemnify

grant of a share contribution *(donation)*

grant of authority patent

grant of realty lease

grant of use and possession lease

grant pardon forgive, free

grant permission allow *(authorize)*, authorize, bestow, permit, suffer *(permit)*

grant power empower, invest *(vest)*

grant remission acquit, clear, pardon

grant the occupancy of let *(lease)*

grant use and possession lease

grant-in-aid subsidy

grantable assignable, plausible, possible

granted allowable, allowed, assumed *(inferred)*, consensual, definite, permissible

granted amnesty immune

granted on certain terms conditional, dependent

grantee assignee, bearer, beneficiary, devisee, donee, feoffee, legatee, payee, receiver, recipient, successor, transferee

granter contributor *(giver)*

granting concession *(compromise)*, donative, permissive

granting freedom parole

grantor contributor *(giver)*, donor, feoffor, obligee, transferor

grapevine report *(rumor)*

graph delineation, design *(construction plan)*, measure

graphic clear *(apparent)*, coherent *(clear)*, comprehensible, demonstrative *(illustrative)*, descriptive, detailed, distinct *(clear)*, holographic, lurid, narrative, realistic, representative, suggestive *(evocative)*

graphic account recital

graphic treatment caricature

graphical comprehensible, representative, suggestive *(evocative)*

grapple lock

grapple with contest, fight *(battle)*, repulse

grasp apprehension *(perception)*, cognition, cohere *(adhere)*, competence *(ability)*, comprehend *(understand)*, comprehension, conceive *(comprehend)*, coverage *(scope)*, digest *(comprehend)*, gain, grapple, hold *(possess)*, information *(knowledge)*, judgment *(discernment)*, jurisdiction, knowledge *(awareness)*, perception, pierce *(discern)*, read, realize *(understand)*, retain *(keep in possession)*, retention, seize *(confiscate)*, sense *(intelligence)*, understand, understanding *(comprehension)*

grasp mentally construe *(comprehend)*

grasping illiberal, insatiable, mercenary, parsimonious, rapacious, venal

grass cannabis

grate annoy, badger, bait *(harass)*, irritate, plague, provoke, repel *(disgust)*

gratia patronage *(power to appoint jobs)*

gratification benefit *(betterment)*, bounty, enjoyment *(pleasure)*, fruition,

indulgence, satisfaction *(fulfilment)*
gratification of desire indulgence
gratified complacent, proud *(self-respecting)*
gratify accommodate, bestow, consent, favor, grant *(concede)*, pander, sanction, satisfy *(fulfill)*, vouchsafe
gratify to excess overindulge
gratifying desirable *(pleasing)*, palatable, sapid
gratiis gratis
grating harsh, provocative
gratis free *(at no charge)*, gratuitous *(given without recompense)*, unpaid
gratitude recognition
gratuito gratis
gratuitous baseless, donative, elective *(voluntary)*, expendable, free *(at no charge)*, impertinent *(irrelevant)*, inappropriate, irrelevant, needless, nonessential, unnecessary, unpaid, unsolicited, willing *(uncompelled)*
gratuitous remark dictum
gratuitous worker volunteer
gratuitus free *(at no charge)*, gratuitous *(unwarranted)*
gratuity benefit *(conferment)*, bonus, bounty, consideration *(recompense)*, contribution *(donation)*, dedication, donation, gift *(present)*, grant, honorarium, hush money, largess *(gift)*, payment *(remittance)*, perquisite, recompense, reward
gravamen center *(essence)*, content *(meaning)*, cornerstone, gist *(ground for a suit)*, impugnation, main point
gravamen of a charge complaint, gist *(ground for a suit)*
gravamen of the complaint gist *(ground for a suit)*
grave bleak *(not favorable)*, critical *(crucial)*, crucial, deadly, dire, earnest, exigent, gross *(flagrant)*, important *(significant)*, lamentable, major, momentous, solemn, urgent
grave culpability impeachability
grave injustice ground, misjudgment
graveness solemnity
gravis compelling, considerable, earnest, grave *(important)*, important *(significant)*, influential, insalubrious, irksome, offensive *(offending)*, onerous, peccant *(unhealthy)*, ponderous, serious *(grave)*, solemn, substantial, urgent, valid, virulent
gravitas severity, solemnity, validity
gravitate toward border *(approach)*
gravitation penchant, proclivity, tendency
gravity draw *(attraction)*, import, importance, interest *(concern)*, magnitude, materiality *(consequence)*, severity, significance, solemnity
grayness indistinctness
graze contact *(touch)*
graze against jostle *(bump into)*
great capacious, compelling, consequential *(substantial)*, considerable, copious, extensive, far reaching, gross *(flagrant)*, illustrious, ineffable, inordinate, magnanimous, major, master, meritorious, momentous, outstanding *(prominent)*, paramount, portentous *(eliciting amazement)*, powerful, prodigious *(enormous)*, profound *(intense)*, remarkable, renowned, serious *(grave)*,

substantial
great fear panic
great feeling emotion
great misfortune catastrophe, disaster
great mishap disaster
great number plurality
great person paragon
great point gist *(ground for a suit)*
great quantity boom *(prosperity)*, plethora, store *(depository)*
great span of life longevity
great station eminence
greaten accrue *(increase)*, accumulate *(enlarge)*, compound, expand, heighten *(augment)*, increase
greater best, superior *(excellent)*, superior *(higher)*
greater number majority *(greater part)*
greater part body *(main part)*, generality *(bulk)*
greatest cardinal *(outstanding)*, leading *(ranking first)*, maximum *(amplitude)*, paramount, primary, prime *(most valuable)*, superlative, utmost
greatest amount cap, capacity *(maximum)*, utmost
greatest degree utmost
greatest extent capacity *(maximum)*
greatest number generality *(bulk)*
greatest part bulk
greatest possible cardinal *(outstanding)*, ultimate
greatest size capacity *(maximum)*
greathearted charitable *(benevolent)*, meritorious
greatness degree *(magnitude)*, dint, distinction *(reputation)*, eminence, importance, mass *(weight)*, materiality *(consequence)*, measurement, merit, prestige, primacy, significance
greediness greed
greedy exorbitant, gluttonous, illiberal, insatiable, jealous, mercenary, penurious, predatory, rapacious, venal
green credulous, inexperienced, naive, premature, puerile, unaccustomed
greenback money
greenness ignorance, nescience
greet recognize *(acknowledge)*
greet with skepticism doubt *(distrust)*
grenade bomb
grew accrued
grex band, company *(enterprise)*
grief pain, plaint, remorse
grief-stricken disconsolate
grievance aggravation *(annoyance)*, complaint, criticism, damage, dissatisfaction, exception *(objection)*, gravamen, impugnation, nuisance, objection, outcry, provocation, trouble, wrong
grieve affront, annoy, brood, discommode, distress, harass, languish, perturb, repent
grieve at regret
grieve for deplore
grieve with sympathize
grieved aggrieved *(harmed)*, disconsolate, pessimistic
grieving disconsolate, lugubrious, plaint
grievous arrant *(onerous)*, deplorable, detrimental, dire, disastrous, gross *(flagrant)*, lamentable, oppressive, painful,

regrettable, severe
grievous harm calamity
grievous price toll *(effect)*
grievous trouble pain
grill cross-examine
grilling cross-examination, interrogation
grim bleak *(not favorable)*, bleak *(severely simple)*, brutal, dire, disastrous, grave *(solemn)*, harsh, malevolent, ominous, portentous *(ominous)*, repulsive, ruthless, serious *(grave)*, severe, solemn
grime pollute, stain
grimness severity
grimy sordid
grind erode, ill use, struggle, work *(effort)*
grinding erosion, onerous, operose, oppressive, tyrannous
grip dominion *(supreme authority)*, grapple, immerse *(engross)*, interest, monopolize, tenacity
gripe discompose
griper malcontent
gripping moving *(evoking emotion)*
grisly repulsive
grit prowess *(bravery)*, sinew, tenacity, will *(desire)*
gritty steadfast, undaunted
groan deplore, plaint
groom discipline *(train)*
groomed ready *(prepared)*
grooming discipline *(training)*
grope for hunt
groping blind *(sightless)*, hesitant, tentative
gross aggregate, blatant *(obtrusive)*, brutal, depraved, entirety, excessive, exorbitant, extreme *(exaggerated)*, flagrant, heinous, improper, inelegant, iniquitous, lurid, manifest, nefarious, objectionable, obnoxious, outrageous, repulsive, salacious, scurrilous, stark, total, totality, uncouth, unseemly, whole *(undamaged)*
gross amount aggregate, corpus, entirety, principal *(capital sum)*, sum *(total)*, whole
gross injustice misjudgment
gross offense atrocity, felony
gross offense against law crime
gross profit proceeds
gross return income
gross wrong ground
grossly inadequate representation understatement
grossly offensive outrageous
grossness bestiality, brutality, debauchery
grotesque odious, prodigious *(amazing)*
grotesque portrayal caricature
grotesque rendition caricature
grouchy fractious, petulant, querulous, resentful
ground assumption *(supposition)*, basis, cause *(reason)*, cause of action, contention *(argument)*, derivation, fix *(make firm)*, gist *(ground for a suit)*, instill, parcel, plant *(place firmly)*, plot *(land)*, point *(item)*, position *(situation)*, property *(land)*, rationale, real estate, reason *(basis)*
ground for believing presumption
ground for excusing justification
ground gained headway

ground of argument discrepancy
ground of proof evidence
ground oneself alight
ground plan arrangement *(plan)*, blueprint
ground rules criterion
grounded stable
grounded on based on
groundless arbitrary and capricious, baseless, erroneous, fallacious, false *(inaccurate)*, gratuitous *(unwarranted)*, ill-founded, illogical, immaterial, inaccurate, insubstantial, needless, sophistic, unfounded, unjustifiable, unreasonable, unsound *(fallacious)*, unsupported, unsustainable, untenable, untrue, unwarranted, wanton
groundless rumor hearsay
groundless story canard
grounds case *(set of circumstances)*, circumstances, close *(enclosed area)*, data, documentation, estate *(property)*, homestead, premises *(buildings)*, premises *(hypotheses)*, property *(land)*, realty
grounds for belief documentation, evidence
grounds for complaint grievance
groundwork basis, cornerstone, foundation *(basis)*, frame *(structure)*, preparation, prerequisite
group aggregate, allocate, arrange *(methodize)*, assemblage, assembly, band, call *(summon)*, cartel, chamber *(body)*, class, classification, classify, coalition, codify, collect *(gather)*, collection *(accumulation)*, collection *(assembly)*, combine *(join together)*, community, company *(assemblage)*, compile, complex *(development)*, conglomeration, congregate, connect *(relate)*, constituency, convene, denomination, division *(administrative unit)*, file *(arrange)*, fix *(arrange)*, garner, hoard, index *(relate)*, join *(bring together)*, kind, league, marshal, meet, organization *(association)*, organize *(arrange)*, partition, party *(political organization)*, pigeonhole, race, relate *(establish a connection)*, screen *(select)*, section *(division)*, selection *(collection)*, sequence, society, sodality, sort, subdivide, subdivision, tabulate, unit *(department)*, unite
group feeling loyalty
group of delegates committee
group of deputies posse
group of jurors panel *(jurors)*
group of persons organized with legal authorization posse
group refusal to work strike
group together compile
grouped collective
grouping building *(business of assembling)*, centralization, class, classification, corpus, denomination, disposition *(final arrangement)*, distribution *(arrangement)*, division *(administrative unit)*, form *(arrangement)*, hierarchy *(arrangement in a series)*, lineup, manner *(kind)*, order *(arrangement)*, organization *(structure)*, rating, rubric *(title)*, section *(division)*, segregation *(separation)*, subdivision
grovel truckle
groveling obsequious, servile
grow accrue *(increase)*, accumulate

(enlarge), build *(augment)*, develop, enlarge, expand, germinate, increase, inflate, progress, proliferate, stem *(originate)*
grow aware comprehend *(understand)*, construe *(comprehend)*
grow better develop, progress
grow from develop, emanate, evolve
grow in number proliferate
grow in value appreciate *(increase)*
grow larger accumulate *(enlarge)*, compound, expand
grow lenient relent
grow less decrease, depreciate, diminish, subside
grow less severe relent
grow out of arise *(originate)*, emanate, ensue
grow together cohere *(adhere)*, unite
grow too fast overextend
grow too much overextend
grow up mature, progress
grow weak degenerate, languish
grow worse decay, degenerate, depreciate
growing cumulative *(increasing)*, live *(conscious)*, progressive *(going forward)*, rampant
growing by successive additions cumulative *(increasing)*
growling petulant
grown ripe
grown old outdated, outmoded
grown-up person adult
growth accession *(enlargement)*, accretion, advancement *(improvement)*, appreciation *(increased value)*, augmentation, boom *(increase)*, boom *(prosperity)*, development *(progression)*, extension *(expansion)*, headway, increment, inflation *(increase)*, profit, progress, transition
growth by addition collection *(accumulation)*, cumulation
growth in value appreciation *(increased value)*
grudge dissatisfaction, feud, rancor, refuse, resentment, spite, umbrage
grudgeful malevolent, vindictive
grudging disinclined, illiberal, jealous, malevolent, parsimonious, penurious, reluctant, resentful
grueling difficult, harsh, onerous, operose, painful
gruesome lurid, sordid
gruff brutal, harsh, severe
grumbler malcontent
grumbling criticism, petulant, querulous
grumbly petulant
grumose solid *(compact)*
grumpy petulant, resentful, restive
guage caliber *(measurement)*
guarantee accommodation *(backing)*, assure *(insure)*, bear *(adduce)*, bond, bond *(secure a debt)*, certificate, certify *(attest)*, charge *(lien)*, close *(agree)*, confirm, consent, contract, corroborate, cosign, covenant, coverage *(insurance)*, deposit, ensure, hostage, hypothecation, indemnify, indorse, insurer, oath, pact, pawn, pledge *(binding promise)*, pledge *(security)*, pledge *(deposit)*, pledge *(promise the performance of)*, precaution, promise, promise *(vow)*, protection, reassure, recommend, security

(pledge), sponsor, stipulate, subscribe *(promise)*, swear, undertake, undertaking *(pledge)*, underwrite, verify *(swear)*, vouch, warranty
guarantee against loss insurance, insure
guaranteed agreed *(promised)*, certain *(fixed)*, certain *(positive)*, conclusive *(determinative)*, definite, dependable, fully secured, indubious, inevitable, official, promissory, reliable, safe, secure *(free from danger)*, solid *(sound)*
guarantor backer, insurer, sponsor
guaranty assurance, bail, binder, bond, certify *(attest)*, charge *(lien)*, coverage *(insurance)*, letter of credit, option *(contractual provision)*, recognizance, specialty *(contract)*, surety *(certainty)*, underwrite, warranty
guard attend *(take care of)*, bulwark, care *(be cautious)*, caretaker *(one caring for property)*, conserve, control *(restrain)*, cover *(protection)*, defend, detain *(hold in custody)*, diligence *(care)*, ensconce, enshroud, guarantee, guaranty, guardian, harbor, hedge, keep *(shelter)*, maintain *(sustain)*, monitor, notice *(heed)*, panoply, patrol, peace officer, preserve, protect, protection, safekeeping, security *(safety)*, shield, surveillance, sustain *(prolong)*, uphold, ward, warden
guard against anticipate *(expect)*
guarded alert *(vigilant)*, careful, circumspect, controlled *(restrained)*, discreet, inarticulate, intimate, leery, noncommittal, politic, preventive, prudent, safe, secure *(free from danger)*, taciturn, vigilant
guardedness caution *(vigilance)*, discretion *(quality of being discreet)*, precaution
guardian administrator, caretaker *(one caring for property)*, custodian *(protector)*, fiduciary, patron *(influential supporter)*, protective, sponsor, superintendent, trustee, warden
guardian of the peace peace officer
guardianship administration, adoption *(affiliation)*, auspices, bondage, charge *(custody)*, control *(supervision)*, custody *(supervision)*, detention, patronage *(support)*, preservation, protection, restraint, safekeeping, trust *(custody)*, ward
guarding bondage, conservation, preservation, preventive
guardless helpless *(defenseless)*, precarious, vulnerable
gubernare overrule
gubernatio direction *(guidance)*, government *(administration)*
gubernation supervision
guerdon appropriation *(donation)*, bounty, collection *(payment)*, compensation, consideration *(recompense)*, contribution *(indemnification)*, expiation, honorarium, payment *(remittance)*, prize, recompense, requital, reward, satisfaction *(discharge of debt)*, tip *(gratuity)*
guess concept, conjecture, deduce, deduct *(conclude by reasoning)*, estimate *(idea)*, estimate, estimation *(calculation)*, expect *(consider probable)*, hypothesis, idea, infer, inference, opine,

opinion *(belief)*, postulate, presume, presuppose, prognosis, read, speculate *(conjecture)*, supposition, surmise, suspect *(think)*, suspicion *(uncertainty)*
guess correctly solve
guess right solve
guess wrong misconceive
guessed inexact
guesswork conjecture, estimate *(idea)*, estimation *(calculation)*, inference, speculation *(conjecture)*, theory
guidable tractable
guidance administration, advice, advocacy, aid *(help)*, auspices, charge *(custody)*, charge *(statement to the jury)*, control *(supervision)*, custody *(supervision)*, discipline *(training)*, edification, education, generalship, government *(administration)*, help, instruction *(direction)*, instruction *(teaching)*, management *(supervision)*, patronage *(support)*, recommendation, regulation *(management)*, service *(assistance)*, supervision, tip *(clue)*
guide administer *(conduct)*, advise, charge *(instruct on the law)*, clue, code, conduct, control *(regulate)*, counsel, criterion, direct *(show)*, direct *(supervise)*, director, discipline *(train)*, edify, educate, example, exemplar, generalization, govern, guideline, handle *(manage)*, inculcate, index *(gauge)*, indicate, indication, influence, instill, instruct *(direct)*, instruct *(teach)*, manage, manipulate *(utilize skillfully)*, marshal, model, motivate, officiate, overlook *(superintend)*, oversee, paradigm, pattern, pedagogue, precedent, precept, precursor, predominate *(command)*, prescribe, preside, prevail *(be in force)*, prevail *(persuade)*, prototype, recommend, regulate *(manage)*, rule *(govern)*, sample, specimen, standard, superintend, symptom
guide astray mislead
guide into error mislead
guide the studies of instruct *(teach)*
guide wrongly mislead
guidebook directory
guided direct *(straight)*
guided by experiment empirical
guideline code
guidepost landmark *(conspicuous object)*
guiding administrative, advisory
guiding conception impression
guiding principle end *(intent)*, purpose
guild association *(alliance)*, company *(enterprise)*, confederacy *(compact)*, cooperative, institute, league, partnership, society, sodality, syndicate, union *(labor organization)*
guildsman member *(individual in a group)*
guile artifice, bad faith, collusion, color *(deceptive appearance)*, deception, duplicity, evasion, fraud, hoax, hypocrisy, imposture, improbity, indirection *(deceitfulness)*, knavery, pettifoggery, ruse, subreption
guileful collusive, delusive, dishonest, evasive, fallacious, fraudulent, insidious, machiavellian, perfidious, recreant, sly, subtle *(insidious)*, surreptitious

guileless clean, direct *(forthright)*, genuine, honest, ingenuous, pure, simple, straightforward, unaffected *(sincere)*, upright
guilelessness candor *(straightforwardness)*, honesty, probity, veracity
guilt blame *(culpability)*, criminality, culpability
guilt-free blameless, not guilty
guiltiness blame *(culpability)*, culpability, impeachability, onus *(blame)*
guiltless blameless, clean, clear *(free from criminal charges)*, incorruptible, inculpable, innocent, irreprehensible, meritorious, not guilty, pardonable, pure, unblemished, unimpeachable
guiltlessness innocence
guilty arrant *(onerous)*, at fault, blameful, blameworthy, contrite, culpable, delinquent *(guilty of a misdeed)*, diabolic, illicit, peccable, peccant *(culpable)*, reprehensible, vicious
guilty act crime, misconduct, misdeed, misdemeanor, misdoing, transgression
guilty man convict, delinquent
guilty of transgression peccant *(culpable)*
guilty person convict, criminal, felon, lawbreaker, recidivist
guilty verdict condemnation *(punishment)*
guise appearance *(look)*, color *(deceptive appearance)*, complexion, conduct, cover *(pretext)*, demeanor, deportment, disguise, false pretense, manner *(behavior)*, means *(opportunity)*, mode, presence *(poise)*, pretense *(pretext)*, pretext, role, semblance, sham, style, subterfuge, veil
gulf hiatus, split
gull deceive, delude, dupe, ensnare, foist, illude, inveigle
gullibility credulity
gullible credulous, naive, unsuspecting
gullibleness credulity
gulosity greed
gumminess adhesion *(affixing)*
gummosity adhesion *(affixing)*
gumshoe prowl
gun for hunt
gunfire barrage
gunman criminal, hoodlum
gunnery ammunition
gunpowder ammunition, bomb
gunrunner bootlegger
gush emit, exude, issuance, outburst, outflow
gushy loquacious
gustable sapid, savory
gustative savory
gustful sapid
gusto enjoyment *(pleasure)*, passion
gut burn, destroy *(efface)*, devastate, eviscerate, extirpate, obliterate, prey
gyp bunko
gypsy migrant
gyve detain *(restrain)*, fetter (noun), fetter (verb), handcuff

H

habere dwell *(reside)*, hold *(possess)*, own, possess
habile resourceful

habilis convenient, efficient
habilitated proficient
habit custom, manner *(behavior)*, method, mode, norm, practice *(custom)*, prescription *(custom)*, procedure, quirk *(idiosyncrasy)*, rule *(guide)*, style, trait, usage, way *(manner)*
habit of a majority custom
habitabilis habitable
habitance domicile
habitancy abode, domicile, habitation *(act of inhabiting)*, inhabitation *(act of dwelling in)*, nationality, population, residence
habitant citizen, denizen, domiciliary, inhabitant, inmate, lodger, occupant, resident
habitants populace, population
habitare dwell *(reside)*, inhabit, reside
habitat abode, building *(structure)*, domicile, habitation *(dwelling place)*, home *(domicile)*, locality, lodging, residence, site
habitation abode, address, building *(structure)*, domicile, dwelling, enjoyment *(use)*, home *(domicile)*, house, household, inhabitation *(act of dwelling in)*, lodging, occupancy, residence, shelter *(protection)*
habitator habitant, inhabitant, resident
habits behavior, conduct
habitual accustomed *(customary)*, boiler plate, chronic, constant, conventional, customary, daily, familiar *(customary)*, frequent, general, household *(familiar)*, ingrained, inveterate, mundane, normal *(regular)*, ordinary, orthodox, periodic, prevailing *(current)*, prevalent, regular *(conventional)*, repeated, routine, systematic, traditional, typical, usual
habitual activity custom
habitual course practice *(custom)*
habitual criminal outlaw, recidivist
habitual devotion diligence *(perseverance)*
habitual offender outlaw
habitual practice custom, manner *(behavior)*
habitual relapse into crime recidivism
habitual use usage
habitually generally, invariably
habitually silent taciturn
habituate discipline *(train)*, inure *(accustom)*, naturalize *(acclimate)*
habituated accustomed *(familiarized)*, addicted, inveterate, practiced
habituation behavior, custom, practice *(custom)*
habitude behavior, condition *(state)*, custom, practice *(custom)*, usage
habitus deportment, habit
hack split
hackneyed familiar *(customary)*, mundane, nondescript, ordinary, pedestrian, prosaic, stale, trite
hackneyed expression platitude
hackneyed idea platitude
hackneyed phrase platitude
hackneyed saying platitude
hactenus extent
haerere hesitate
haereticus heretic
haesitatio hesitation, indecision, scru-

ple

haggle barter, cavil, dicker, negotiate

haggling negotiation

hail honor

hairsplitting particular *(exacting)*

halcyon harmonious, nonmilitant, peaceable, placid

halcyonian peaceable, placid

haleness health, welfare

half moiety, semi

half believe doubt *(distrust)*

half distance center *(central position)*

half finished semi

half-begun inchoate

half-done inchoate

half-seen indistinct

halfhearted hesitant, insipid, lax, perfunctory, phlegmatic

halfway center *(central position)*, central *(situated near center)*, intermediate

hall chamber *(compartment)*

hallmark brand, designation *(symbol)*, device *(distinguishing mark)*, label, stamp, trademark

hallow dedicate

hallowed infrangible, inviolate, laudable, sacrosanct, solemn

hallowing honorary

hallucination figment, insanity, phantom

hallucinative delusive

hallucinatory delusive, insubstantial, nonexistent

halt abeyance, balk, block, cease, cessation *(interlude)*, check *(bar)*, check *(restrain)*, close *(terminate)*, cloture, conclude *(complete)*, condemn *(ban)*, constrict *(inhibit)*, curtail, debar, defeat, desist, desuetude, detain *(restrain)*, deterrence, discontinue *(abandon)*, dissolve *(terminate)*, embargo, end *(termination)*, estop, finality, finish, forestall, hiatus, hinder, hold up *(delay)*, impasse, interdict, interruption, interval, keep *(restrain)*, layoff, lull, moratorium, obstruct, pause, pause, pendency, prevent, prohibit, proscribe *(prohibit)*, quit *(discontinue)*, recess, recess, refrain, remission, remit *(relax)*, respite *(interval of rest)*, rest *(cease from action)*, shut, stall, stay, stay *(rest)*, stem *(check)*, stop, suspend, terminate, toll *(stop)*

halt work strike *(refuse to work)*

halting broken *(interrupted)*

halve bifurcate, cross *(intersect)*, dichotomize, divide *(separate)*, part *(separate)*, split

halved bipartite

halving dichotomy

hammer in impact

hammer out forge *(produce)*, formulate, make

hammer together frame *(construct)*

hamper balk, bar *(hinder)*, bind *(restrain)*, block, clog, condemn *(ban)*, constrain *(restrain)*, constrict *(inhibit)*, control *(restrain)*, damper *(stopper)*, debar, delay, detain *(restrain)*, deter, disadvantage, disadvantage, encumber *(hinder)*, enjoin, estop, fetter, fetter, foil, halt, handcuff, hinder, hindrance, hold up *(delay)*, impede, impediment, inconvenience, interfere, keep *(restrain)*, limit, lock, obstacle, obstruct, obstruction, occlude, overcome *(over-*

whelm), prevent, prohibit, restrain, restraint, restrict, stall, stave, stay *(halt)*, stem *(check)*, stop, thwart, trammel, withstand

hampered arrested *(checked)*, limited

hampering binding, deterrent, encumbrance, limiting

hamstring deter, hinder, obstruct

hamstrung marred

hand deliver, employee, handwriting, help, present *(make a gift)*

hand back restore *(return)*

hand down abalienate, bequeath, confer *(give)*, convey *(transfer)*, deliver, demise, descend, endow, leave *(give)*, render *(deliver)*

hand grenade bomb

hand in one's resignation demit

hand on bequeath, descend, transfer, transmit

hand out allocate, bestow, convey *(transfer)*, disburse *(distribute)*, dispense, dole, endow, endue, fund, mete

hand out again redistribute

hand over abalienate, bestow, consign, contribute *(supply)*, delegate, discharge *(pay a debt)*, dole, endow, pay, present *(make a gift)*, relinquish, render *(deliver)*, serve *(deliver a legal instrument)*, surrender *(give back)*, transmit

hand over to bequeath

hand-to-hand fight affray

handbook directory, pandect *(treatise)*

handcuff fetter, restrain, restrict

handed down traditional

handicap burden, clog, constrict *(inhibit)*, detriment, disability *(physical inability)*, disadvantage, disadvantage, disease, disorder *(abnormal condition)*, disqualification *(factor that disqualifies)*, estop, fetter, fetter, hamper, hinder, hindrance, impede, impediment, incumbrance *(burden)*, interfere, liability, nuisance, obstacle, obstruct, onus *(burden)*, penalty, preclude, prevent, restrain, restrict, trammel

handicapped disabled *(made incapable)*, disadvantaged

handicraft business *(occupation)*, performance *(workmanship)*, specialty *(special aptitude)*, trade *(occupation)*

handicraftsman artisan

handiness efficiency, faculty *(ability)*, gift *(flair)*, means *(opportunity)*, performance *(workmanship)*, skill

handing out disbursement *(act of disbursing)*, distribution *(apportionment)*

handing over cession

handing over into custody commitment *(confinement)*

handing over legal papers service *(delivery of legal process)*

handiwork building *(business of assembling)*, invention, performance *(workmanship)*, product

handle administer *(conduct)*, conduct, control *(regulate)*, deal, manage, manipulate *(utilize skillfully)*, militate, operate, oversee, ply, regulate *(manage)*, sell, superintend, treat *(process)*, wield

handle badly mishandle *(maltreat)*, mishandle *(mismanage)*

handler merchant

handling administration, agency

(legal relationship), course, management *(judicious use)*, operation, process *(course)*, regulation *(management)*, treatment

handout donation, gratuity *(present)*, largess *(gift)*

handpicked preferred *(favored)*, select

hands-off policy laissez faire

handsel binder, bounty, grant, largess *(gift)*, launch *(initiate)*, originate

handsome elegant, liberal *(generous)*, magnanimous

handwriting script

handwritten holographic

handy available, close *(near)*, deft, effective *(efficient)*, expert, functional, immediate *(not distant)*, practical, practiced, present *(attendant)*, proficient, resourceful

hang around loiter

hang back pause, procrastinate

hang on cohere *(adhere)*, endure *(last)*, grapple, last, persevere, remain *(continue)*

hang on to hoard

hang over project *(extend beyond)*

hang together cohere *(be logically consistent)*

hangdog furtive

hanger on partisan

hanger-on disciple

hankering desire, will *(desire)*

hap contingency, event, opportunity, quirk *(accident)*

haphazard casual, fortuitous, indiscriminate, random, slipshod

hapless ominous

happen arise *(occur)*, supervene

happen again recur

happen at the same time concur *(coexist)*

happen simultaneously concur *(coexist)*

happen together coincide *(correspond)*, concur *(coexist)*

happen upon find *(discover)*

happening accident *(chance occurrence)*, chance *(fortuity)*, contingency, event, experience *(encounter)*, incident, occasion, occurrence, situation

happening by chance fortuitous

happenings circumstances

happenstance occurrence

happiness welfare

happy ecstatic, felicitous, inclined, propitious, prosperous, proud *(self-respecting)*, ready *(willing)*

happy medium compromise

happy-go-lucky improvident

harangue address *(talk to)*, bombast, declaim, declamation, diatribe, outpour, phillipic

haranguer demagogue

harass annoy, badger, browbeat, discompose, distress, harrow, hector, importune, incense, inflict, intimidate, irritate, mistreat, molest *(annoy)*, persecute, perturb, pique, prey, provoke

harassing vexatious

harassment aggravation *(annoyance)*, infliction, nuisance, oppression

harbinger anticipate *(prognosticate)*, forerunner, herald, indicator, informant, informer *(a person who provides information)*, precede, precursor

harbor conceal, cover *(guard)*, foster, haven, hide, lodge *(house)*, lodging, nurture, preserve, protect, refuge, screen *(guard)*, shelter *(protection)*
harbor a design intend, plan
harbor a grudge harass, resent
harbor doubts disbelieve, doubt *(distrust)*, mistrust
harbor suspicions disbelieve, discount *(disbelieve)*, doubt *(distrust)*, misdoubt, mistrust
harbor suspicious suspect *(distrust)*
harboring conservation
harborless insecure
hard callous, close *(rigorous)*, cohesive *(compact)*, cold-blooded, compact *(dense)*, cruel, difficult, durable, impervious, inflexible, insusceptible *(uncaring)*, obdurate, onerous, operose, oppressive, ossified, powerful, relentless, rigid, ruthless, severe, solid *(compact)*, strict, stringent, strong, tyrannous, unbending, uncompromising, unrelenting, unyielding
hard bargaining counteroffer
hard blow disaster
hard cash currency, money
hard feelings argument *(contention)*, ill will, malice
hard money cash
hard of heart callous, malignant, relentless
hard task campaign
hard to believe debatable, disputable, implausible, incredible, ludicrous, suspicious *(questionable)*, unbelievable
hard to comprehend opaque
hard to control unruly
hard to convince impervious, inconvincible, incredulous, suspicious *(distrustful)*
hard to cope with operose
hard to deal with difficult, impracticable, perverse
hard to define elusive
hard to endure painful, severe
hard to explain indefinable
hard to express elusive
hard to get rid of pertinacious
hard to grasp elusive
hard to lift ponderous
hard to maintain elusive
hard to manage difficult, perverse
hard to overcome formidable
hard to please particular *(exacting)*, querulous
hard to see obscure *(faint)*
hard to translate indefinable
hard to understand difficult, elusive, enigmatic, equivocal, incomprehensible, indefinable, inexplicable, opaque
hard up impecunious, poor *(underprivileged)*
hard upon critical *(faultfinding)*
hard work effort, industry *(activity)*
hard working industrious, patient
hard-bitten obdurate
harden cement, cohere *(adhere)*, consolidate *(strengthen)*, fix *(make firm)*, inure *(accustom)*
harden the heart alienate *(estrange)*
hardened callous, cold-blooded, impervious, incorrigible, inexpressive, inflexible, insusceptible *(uncaring)*, inveterate, obdurate, ossified, recalcitrant, remorseless, reprobate, solid *(compact)*,

unabashed
hardened criminal malefactor, outlaw
hardened offender criminal, recidivist
hardheaded perspicacious
hardhearted brutal, callous, cold-blooded, cruel, malevolent, obdurate, relentless, ruthless, unaffected *(uninfluenced)*
hardheartedness malice
hardhitting critical *(faultfinding)*
hardihood audacity, prowess *(bravery)*, surety *(certainty)*
hardiness force *(strength)*, health, prowess *(bravery)*, strength
hardly begun inchoate
hardly credible incredible
hardly possible implausible, insurmountable
hardly worth mention nominal
hardness brutality, congealment
hardness of heart brutality
hardship adversity, burden, calamity, casualty, catastrophe, damage, detriment, grievance, misfortune, nuisance, plight, pressure, privation, tragedy, trouble
hardworking diligent, painstaking, sedulous
hardy durable, indestructible, indomitable, inexpugnable, spartan, strong
harebrained impolitic, precipitate, thoughtless, unpolitic
hark heed
harm abuse *(violate)*, annoy, assault, cost *(penalty)*, damage, damage, detriment, disable, disadvantage, disadvantage, disaster, disservice, drawback, endanger, eviscerate, expense *(sacrifice)*, harrow, ill use, impair, impairment *(damage)*, infect, inflict, injury, mischief, mistreat, molest *(annoy)*, penalize, prejudice *(injury)*, prejudice *(injure)*, spoil *(impair)*, strike *(assault)*, wrong
harmed imperfect, marred
harmful adverse *(negative)*, dangerous, deleterious, destructive, detrimental, disadvantageous, disastrous, fatal, hostile, inadvisable, incendiary, inimical, insalubrious, invidious, lethal, malevolent, malicious, malignant, noxious, oppressive, outrageous, painful, peccant *(unhealthy)*, pernicious, pestilent, prejudicial, scathing, sinister, toxic, virulent
harmful act injury
harmful action mischief
harmful desire malice
harmful physical contact battery
harming disabling, incriminatory
harmless innocuous, nontoxic, powerless, safe, salutary, unobjectionable
harmonious amicable, appropriate, concerted, concordant, congruous, consensual, consistent, consonant, felicitous, fit, joint, proportionate, suitable, uniform
harmonious relation rapport
harmoniousness peace
harmonization accommodation *(adjustment)*, accordance *(understanding)*, arrangement *(understanding)*
harmonize accommodate, arbitrate *(conciliate)*, attune, cohere *(be logically consistent)*, coincide *(concur)*, combine

(act in concert), commingle, comport *(agree with)*, compromise *(settle by mutual agreement)*, concur *(agree)*, coordinate, correspond *(be equivalent)*, merge, naturalize *(acclimate)*, orchestrate, reconcile, settle, unite
harmonize with comply
harmonized concerted, congruous, consensual
harmonizing concurrent *(united)*
harmony accordance *(understanding)*, adjustment, agreement *(concurrence)*, coherence, comity, compatibility, compliance, composure, concert, conciliation, concordance, conformity *(agreement)*, conjunction, consensus, consent, contribution *(participation)*, correspondence *(similarity)*, peace, propinquity *(similarity)*, proportion, propriety *(appropriateness)*, rapport, rapprochement, reconciliation, regularity, synchronism, understanding *(agreement)*, union *(unity)*
harness confine, constrain *(imprison)*, constrain *(restrain)*, curb, discipline *(control)*, handcuff, inhibit, join *(bring together)*, restrain, subdue
harness together connect *(join together)*
harnessed servile
harp on repeat *(state again)*
harp upon dwell *(linger over)*, reiterate
harping insistent, iterative, repetitious
harrassed aggrieved *(victimized)*
harried aggrieved *(victimized)*
harrow badger, distress, harass, hector, mistreat, prey
harrowing disastrous, insufferable, onerous, painful
harry annoy, badger, bait *(harass)*, discommode, discompose, distress, harass, harrow, hector, loot, mistreat, molest *(annoy)*, perturb, pique, plague, press *(goad)*
harsh astringent, bitter *(penetrating)*, blatant *(obtrusive)*, brutal, caustic, close *(rigorous)*, contemptuous, cruel, draconian, drastic, hostile, incisive, insufferable, lurid, malevolent, mordacious, obdurate, offensive *(offending)*, onerous, oppressive, pejorative, relentless, rigid, ruthless, scathing, severe, spiteful, strict, stringent, strong, tyrannous
harsh feeling spite
harsh sound noise
harshness brutality, cruelty, oppression, rancor, severity
haruspical prophetic
harvest gain, glean, output, product, profit, profit, reap, result
has as a component consist
hash cannabis, melange
hashish cannabis
haste dispatch *(promptness)*
hasten dispatch *(send off)*, evoke, expedite, facilitate, induce, race
hasten away flee
hasten on dispatch *(send off)*
hasten one's end dispatch *(put to death)*
hastening acceleration
hastily instantly
hastiness dispatch *(promptness)*, in-

consideration, temerity

hasty brief, careless, cursory, expeditious, heedless, hot-blooded, ill-advised, ill-judged, impolitic, improvident, imprudent, impulsive *(rash),* injudicious, instantaneous, perfunctory, precipitate, premature, rapid, reckless, summary, superficial, transient, unpolitic, unpremeditated

hasty departure abandonment *(desertion),* flight

hatch conceive *(invent),* engender, frame *(formulate),* make, outlet, produce *(manufacture),* scheme

hatch a plot conspire

hatch a plot against frame *(charge falsely)*

hatched illusory

hate malice, odium, rancor, resent, spite

hateful antipathetic *(distasteful),* contemptible, contemptuous, disreputable, heinous, invidious, loathsome, malevolent, malicious, malignant, nefarious, objectionable, obnoxious, odious, offensive *(offending),* outrageous, reprehensible, repugnant *(exciting aversion),* repulsive, spiteful, vicious, virulent

hatred conflict, incompatibility *(difference),* intolerance, malice, odium, rancor, rejection, resentment, spite, umbrage

haud accuratus inexact

haud dubius infallible, undeniable, undisputed

haud sufficiens insufficient

haughtiness contumely, disdain, pride

haughty cynical, disdainful, impertinent *(insolent),* inflated *(vain),* insolent, orgulous, presumptuous, pretentious *(pompous),* proud *(conceited),* supercilious

haughty contempt disdain

haughty indifference disdain

haul cargo, carry *(transport),* deliver, plunder, spoils, struggle

haunt bailiwick, harass, obsess, plague, recur, remind

haunting ominous, portentous *(ominous)*

hauteur disdain

have accommodate, hold *(possess),* keep *(shelter),* own, possess, remain *(occupy),* retain *(keep in possession)*

have a bad conscience regret

have a bearing on concern *(involve),* relate *(establish a connection)*

have a bias forejudge, preconceive, presuppose, select

have a care beware

have a certain semblance appear *(seem to be)*

have a common origin evolve

have a comparison correspond *(be equivalent)*

have a conference on discuss

have a connection concern *(involve),* correspond *(be equivalent)*

have a connection to apply *(pertain)*

have a deed for own, possess

have a dialogue speak

have a dissimilar opinion differ *(vary)*

have a fancy for prefer

have a feud with dispute *(contest)*

have a firm grip on hold *(possess)*

have a good influence meliorate

have a guilty conscience repent

have a habitation dwell *(reside)*

have a hand in involve *(participate),* partake, participate

have a hunch expect *(consider probable),* guess, opine

have a impulse desire

have a liking for regard *(hold in esteem)*

have a loan owe

have a part in participate

have a part of participate

have a policy plan

have a portion of partake

have a prejudice forejudge

have a prepossession forejudge

have a presentiment anticipate *(prognosticate),* expect *(consider probable),* presage

have a proclivity desire

have a proclivity for gravitate

have a propensity for gravitate

have a reference concern *(involve)*

have a relation concern *(involve),* correspond *(be equivalent)*

have a right claim *(demand)*

have a right to earn

have a row brawl

have a share of partake, participate

have a strong effect impress *(affect deeply)*

have a theory speculate *(conjecture)*

have a title to hold *(possess),* own, possess

have a verbal controversy over dispute *(debate)*

have a vision conjure

have a wrong impression misjudge

have a yearning desire

have absolute disposal of hold *(possess),* possess

have all to oneself monopolize

have an address reside

have an affection for discriminate *(treat differently)*

have an altercation bicker, contend *(dispute),* dispute *(contest)*

have an appetite desire

have an effect upon affect

have an exchange contact *(communicate)*

have an idea conceive *(comprehend),* devise *(invent),* opine, surmise

have an idea that assume *(suppose)*

have an impression apprehend *(perceive)*

have an incorrect impression misconstrue

have an insufficiency require *(need)*

have an obligation owe

have an opinion deem, opine

have an understanding of apprehend *(perceive)*

have an urge for need

have anxiety mistrust

have as its foundation consist

have as property hold *(possess),* possess

have at one's command possess

have at one's disposal possess

have authority govern, handle *(manage),* police, rule *(govern)*

have authority over oversee, preside, prevail *(be in force),* regulate *(manage)*

have bearing on apply *(pertain)*

have being exist

have business relations deal

have by inheritance hold *(possess)*

have by tenure hold *(possess)*

have capacity for accommodate

have charge of control *(regulate),* handle *(manage),* moderate *(preside over),* operate, overlook *(superintend),* oversee, police, prevail *(be in force),* regulate *(manage),* superintend

have charges against accused *(charged)*

have claim upon hold *(possess),* own

have cognizance of apprehend *(perceive),* perceive

have commerce deal, handle *(trade)*

have confidence in confide *(trust),* rely

have control command, conduct, manage, preside, rule *(govern)*

have conveyed consign, dispatch *(send off)*

have currency circulate

have dealings dicker

have dealings with contact *(communicate),* deal, patronize *(trade with)*

have designs plot, scheme

have designs on desire

have dialogue converse

have differences conflict, disaccord, dispute *(contest)*

have dissension disagree

have dominion over prevail *(be in force)*

have done with discontinue *(abandon),* quit *(discontinue)*

have doubts disbelieve, doubt *(distrust),* mistrust

have doubts about misdoubt

have duration endure *(last)*

have effect function, prevail *(persuade)*

have effect on militate

have efficacy avail *(be of use)*

have every indication appear *(seem to be)*

have evidence bear *(adduce)*

have executed enforce

have executive charge of administer *(conduct),* govern

have existence exist

have faith opine

have faith in confide *(trust),* rely, trust

have fears doubt *(distrust),* misdoubt, mistrust

have for one's own possess

have for sale handle *(trade)*

have force avail *(bring about),* prevail *(be in force)*

have foreknowledge preconceive

have hold of own

have ill feelings toward discriminate *(treat differently)*

have implications for pertain

have in hand hold *(possess),* own, possess

have in mind intend

have in one's charge control *(regulate)*

have in one's possession hold *(possess)*

have in production make

have in prospect anticipate *(expect),* expect *(anticipate)*

have in sight discern *(detect with the senses)*, observe *(watch)*, pierce *(discern)*
have in store hoard
have in view intend
have influence affect, constrain *(compel)*, predominate *(command)*
have influence on militate
have influence over prejudice *(influence)*, prevail upon
have influence upon prejudice *(influence)*, prevail upon
have influence with prevail upon
have inherited hold *(possess)*
have insight diagnose, discern *(discriminate)*
have intercourse communicate
have interrelationship with concern *(involve)*, pertain
have it out bicker
have jurisdiction over govern, rule *(govern)*
have knowledge of apprehend *(perceive)*, perceive, pierce *(discern)*
have life exist
have mastery prevail *(triumph)*
have memories of recall *(remember)*
have mercy relent
have misgivings doubt *(distrust)*, mistrust
have need for need
have no concern with dissociate
have no confidence in misdoubt, suspect *(distrust)*
have no doubt opine, trust
have no end endure *(last)*
have no faith in misdoubt, mistrust
have no objection authorize, consent, grant *(concede)*, let *(permit)*, permit
have no part of shun
have no regard for decry, disfavor, jeer
have no reservations trust
have no respect for decry, disfavor, disgrace
have no trust in mistrust
have no use for decry, disdain, disfavor
have nothing to do with avoid *(evade)*, disown *(refuse to acknowledge)*, eschew, exclude, refrain, shun, spurn
have occasion for need
have offspring proliferate
have one's address at dwell *(reside)*
have one's heart set on desire
have one's plans backfire overreach
have origin arise *(originate)*
have pity sympathize
have possession remain *(occupy)*
have possession of occupy *(take possession)*
have power dominate
have precedence antecede
have predominating influence rule *(govern)*
have printed publish
have progeny proliferate
have qualms disbelieve, doubt *(hesitate)*, fear, mistrust, repent
have qualms about regret
have quarters inhabit
have questions doubt *(distrust)*, misdoubt
have recourse resort
have recourse to employ *(make use*

of)*
have reference appertain, apply *(pertain)*
have reference to pertain
have regard care *(be cautious)*
have regard for regard *(hold in esteem)*
have relation appertain, apply *(pertain)*
have relation to pertain
have relevance pertain
have reservations disbelieve, doubt *(hesitate)*, hesitate, misdoubt, mistrust
have responsibility rule *(govern)*
have revenge recriminate
have rights to hold *(possess)*, occupy *(take possession)*, own, possess
have run its course close *(terminate)*
have second thoughts reconsider
have significance for pertain
have succession as an heir inherit
have superiority prevail *(triumph)*
have superiority over prevail *(be in force)*
have suspicions doubt *(distrust)*, misdoubt, mistrust
have sway predominate *(command)*
have sympathy relent
have tenacity adhere *(persist)*
have the advantage beat *(defeat)*, outbalance
have the care of handle *(manage)*, hold *(possess)*
have the charge of hold *(possess)*
have the direction of control *(regulate)*, handle *(manage)*, hold *(possess)*, oversee
have the edge on outbalance
have the idea suspect *(think)*
have the impression deem
have the mien demean *(deport oneself)*
have the qualifications qualify *(meet standards)*
have the requisites qualify *(meet standards)*
have the upper hand predominate *(command)*, surpass
have the wrong impression misapprehend, miscalculate
have title to hold *(possess)*, occupy *(take possession)*
have to do with deal
have to one's name own
have under command manage
have under control control *(regulate)*, handle *(manage)*, hold *(possess)*
have underwritten insure
have use of need
have verbal intercourse converse
have volition choose
have words bicker
have words with brawl, contend *(dispute)*, disaccord, dispute *(contest)*, fight *(battle)*
haven asylum *(hiding place)*, bulwark, harbor, home *(domicile)*, preserve, protect, protection, refuge, screen *(guard)*, shelter *(protection)*
having a bad reputation disreputable
having a common measure commensurate
having a double meaning ambiguous
having a natural contrariety anti-

pathetic *(oppositional)*
having a significant impact far reaching
having a strong effect forcible
having direct bearing pertinent
having fixed limits definite
having force forcible
having formal education literate
having great strength forcible
having home interests household *(domestic)*
having immunity insusceptible *(resistant)*
having independent qualities apart
having integrity incorruptible
having investments in interested
having left a will testate
having legal force effective *(operative)*, valid
having legal strength valid
having multiple husbands polygamous
having multiple wives polygamous
having no acknowledged name anonymous
having no alternative bound
having no force invalid
having no foundation baseless
having no limit comprehensive, perpetual
having plurality of wives or husbands polygamous
having prior application retroactive
having prior effect retroactive
having priority preferred *(given priority)*
having resistance insusceptible *(resistant)*
having seniority preferred *(given priority)*
having substance corporeal
having suffered invasion of legal rights aggrieved *(harmed)*
having the possibility of termination determinable *(liable to be terminated)*
having the privilege to choose disjunctive *(alternative)*
having the right entitled
having to do with pertinent
having unique features apart
having unique qualities apart
having violated the law culpable
having written a testament testate
havoc catastrophe, confusion *(turmoil)*, debacle, depredation, disturb, pillage, shambles, turmoil
hawk handle *(trade)*, hunt, sell
hawk about proclaim, promulgate, propagate *(spread)*
hawker dealer, merchant, vendor
hayseed provincial
hazard accident *(chance occurrence)*, bet, compromise *(endanger)*, danger, endanger, expose, jeopardy, menace, parlay *(bet)*, peril, pitfall, risk, speculate *(chance)*, speculation *(risk)*, threat, venture
hazard a guess presume, surmise
hazard a supposition postulate
hazard an opinion deem
hazarder bettor, speculator
hazardous aleatory *(perilous)*, dangerous, imprudent, insalubrious, insecure, noxious, precarious, speculative
haze bait *(harass)*, harry *(harass)*, ig-

norance, incertitude, obnubilate, obscure

haziness confusion *(ambiguity)*, indistinctness

hazy dubious, equivocal, indeterminate, indistinct, inexact, nebulous, opaque, unclear

he who has passed away decedent

head call *(title)*, caption, chairman, chapter *(division)*, chief, culmination, derivation, direct *(supervise)*, employer, govern, heading, manage, master, moderate *(preside over)*, officiate, oversee, paramount, pinnacle, preface, preside, prime *(most valuable)*, principal *(director)*, regulate *(manage)*, rubric *(title)*, superintend, tip *(clue)*

head of affairs administrator

head of government official

head of the household parents

head off avert, check *(restrain)*

head start advantage, edge *(advantage)*

head toward gravitate

heading caption, chapter *(division)*, denomination, direction *(course)*, prevailing *(having superior force)*, rubric *(title)*, subheading, term *(expression)*, title *(designation)*

headline caption, heading, rubric *(title)*

headlong blind *(not discerning)*, impolitic, improvident, precipitate, thoughtless

headman chairman, chief

headmaster pedagogue

headmen management *(directorate)*

headnote caption

headperson chief, principal *(director)*

headquarters address, base *(place)*, building *(structure)*, habitation *(dwelling place)*, management *(directorate)*, seat

heads authorities, hierarchy *(persons in authority)*

headship direction *(guidance)*, generalship, hegemony, primacy, supremacy

headspring source

headstrong contumacious, disobedient, froward, hot-blooded, ill-judged, inexorable, inflexible, intractable, obdurate, pertinacious, perverse, precipitate, recalcitrant, restive, uncontrollable, unruly, unyielding, vehement

headward vanward

headway advance *(progression)*, margin *(spare amount)*, progress, promotion *(advancement)*

heady precipitate

heal cure, drug, fix *(repair)*, help, recreate, redress, relieve *(give aid)*, remedy, restore *(renew)*, treat *(process)*

heal the breach placate, reconcile

healing curative, medicinal, remedial, salubrious, salutary

healing agent cure, panacea

health strength, welfare

health of mind sanity

health-giving medicinal, remedial, salutary

health-preserving salutary

health-promoting salubrious

healthful remedial, salubrious, salutary

healthy salubrious, salutary, strong

healthy mind sanity

healthy mindedness competence *(sanity)*

heap assemblage, bulk, collection *(accumulation)*, hoard, hoard, plethora, quantity

heap upon bestow

hear adjudicate, heed, notice *(observe)*, overhear

hear a case try *(conduct a trial)*

hear a cause try *(conduct a trial)*

hear the case adjudicate

hearer juror

hearing action *(proceeding)*, day in court, inquest, inquiry *(request for information)*, inquiry *(systematic investigation)*, interview, parley, proceeding, range, session, trial *(legal proceeding)*

hearing before the court voir dire

hearing of evidence inquiry *(systematic investigation)*

hearing on the merits action *(proceeding)*

hearing without jury's presence voir dire

hearken concentrate *(pay attention)*, defer *(yield in judgment)*, eavesdrop

hearken to heed, note *(notice)*

hearsay report *(rumor)*

heart center *(essence)*, confidence *(faith)*, consequence *(significance)*, cornerstone, essence, focus, frame *(mood)*, main point, substance *(essential nature)*

heart of stone brutality

heart-stirring profound *(intense)*

heartbreaking disastrous

heartbroken disconsolate

hearten assure *(give confidence to)*, encourage, reassure

heartening propitious

heartfelt ecstatic, profound *(intense)*

heartily readily

heartiness health

heartless callous, cold-blooded, cruel, dispassionate, insusceptible *(uncaring)*, obdurate, remorseless, ruthless, sinister, unaffected *(uninfluenced)*

heartlessness brutality, cruelty

heartsick disconsolate

hearty fervent, powerful, zealous

heat passion

heated hot-blooded, vehement

heated debate altercation

heave impel, launch *(project)*, precipitate *(throw down violently)*

heave up elevate

heaven sent propitious

heavenly sacrosanct, stellar

heaviness damper *(depressant)*, languor, pressure

heaviness of heart pessimism

heaviness of spirit damper *(depressant)*, pessimism

heavy grave *(solemn)*, onerous, oppressive, pedestrian, ponderous, profound *(intense)*, torpid

heavy demand market *(demand)*

heavy-handed uncouth

heavy-hearted lugubrious

heavy-laden disconsolate

heavyhearted pessimistic

hebes obtuse

hebetude languor, opacity

hebetudinous languid, lifeless *(dull)*, phlegmatic, stagnant

heckle annoy, badger, bait *(harass)*, discompose, harass, harry *(harass)*, hec-

tor, mistreat, mock *(deride)*, pique, plague, press *(goad)*, provoke

hector annoy, badger, bait *(harass)*, intimidate, irritate, plague, press *(goad)*, provoke, threaten

hectoring insolent

hedge equivocate, evade *(deceive)*, offset, outbalance, parry, prevaricate, protection, shelter *(tax benefit)*, tergiversate

hedge in circumscribe *(surround by boundary)*, envelop, occlude, restrict

hedging evasive, noncommittal

heed abide, care *(be cautious)*, caution *(vigilance)*, consider, consideration *(contemplation)*, deliberation, devote, diligence *(care)*, discretion *(quality of being discreet)*, fulfill, hear *(give attention to)*, interest *(concern)*, keep *(fulfill)*, note *(notice)*, notice *(observe)*, obey, observation, observe *(obey)*, observe *(watch)*, precaution, prudence, regard *(attention)*, regard *(pay attention)*, submit *(yield)*, surveillance

heedful careful, circumspect, conscientious, conscious *(aware)*, diligent, guarded, judicious, knowing, leery, meticulous, noncommittal, painstaking, particular *(exacting)*, politic, protective, provident *(showing foresight)*, prudent, sensitive *(discerning)*, vigilant

heedfulness caution *(vigilance)*, deliberation, diligence *(care)*, discretion *(quality of being discreet)*, interest *(concern)*, notice *(heed)*, observation, precaution, prudence, regard *(attention)*

heedless blind *(not discerning)*, careless, cursory, derelict *(negligent)*, hot-blooded, ill-judged, impolitic, improvident, imprudent, impulsive *(rash)*, inadvertent, incognizant, injudicious, insensible, intractable, irrational, lawless, lax, negligent, oblivious, passive, perfunctory, prodigal, reckless, relentless, remiss, slipshod, thoughtless, unaware, unpolitic, wanton

heedlessness dereliction, disinterest *(lack of interest)*, disregard *(lack of respect)*, disregard *(unconcern)*, inconsideration, ingratitude, laxity, neglect, negligence, oversight *(carelessness)*, temerity

heft elevate

hegemonic influential, master, paramount, powerful, prevailing *(having superior force)*, principal, sovereign *(absolute)*

hegemonical dominant, influential, master, paramount, powerful, prevailing *(having superior force)*, principal, sovereign *(absolute)*

hegemony clout, dominion *(supreme authority)*, influence, primacy

hegira flight

height ceiling, culmination, elevation, eminence, pinnacle, primacy

height of one's ambition objective

height of perfection paragon

heighten accrue *(increase)*, aggravate *(exacerbate)*, build *(augment)*, compound, elevate, enhance, exacerbate, expand, intensify, magnify, raise *(advance)*

heightened inflated *(overestimated)*, intense

heightening aggravation *(exacerba-*

tion), boom *(increase),* cumulative *(intensifying),* growth *(increase)*

heinous arrant *(onerous),* bad *(offensive),* base *(bad),* blameful, contemptible, depraved, diabolic, disgraceful, disorderly, disreputable, gross *(flagrant),* immoral, inexcusable, inexpiable, iniquitous, loathsome, malevolent, malignant, nefarious, objectionable, obnoxious, odious, offensive *(offending),* outrageous, peccant *(culpable),* profligate *(corrupt),* reprehensible, reprobate, scandalous, sinister, unjust, vicious

heinous conduct criminality

heinous crime felony

heinous misconduct felony

heinousness atrocity, delinquency *(misconduct),* disrepute

heir beneficiary, descendant, devisee, offspring, recipient, transferee

heir apparent legatee

heir at law legatee

heirdom bequest

heiress beneficiary, legatee

heirloom bequest, hereditament

heirs children, issue *(progeny),* posterity, progeny

held arrested *(apprehended),* in custody

held back arrested *(checked)*

held in contempt blameful, disreputable, notorious

held in custody arrested *(apprehended)*

held in esteem reputable

held in good repute reputable

held in high esteem famous

held in pledge bailment, in trust

held in trust in trust

held responsible accused *(charged)*

held up late *(tardy)*

helical circuitous

helicoid circuitous

helicoidal circuitous

hellbent precipitate

hellish cruel, diabolic, heinous, loathsome, malevolent, malignant, obnoxious

helot captive

helotism servitude

helotry bondage, servitude, subjection, thrall

help abet, accommodate, advantage, advocacy, aid *(help),* aid, ameliorate, assist, assistance, avail *(be of use),* behalf, benefactor, capitalize *(provide capital),* charity, coadjutant, consortium *(marriage companionship),* contribute *(assist),* contribution *(participation),* countenance, emend, employee, enable, endow, espouse, expedite, facilitate, favor *(sanction),* favor, foster, guidance, inure *(benefit),* largess *(generosity),* largess *(gift),* mainstay, nurture, pander, patronage *(support),* personnel, profit, promote *(advance),* promote *(organize),* promotion *(encouragement),* reassure, redress, reinforcement, relief *(aid),* relieve *(give aid),* remedy *(legal means of redress),* remedy *(that which corrects),* remedy, samaritan, save *(rescue),* serve *(assist),* service *(assistance),* side, solace, staff, subsidize, support *(assistance),* support *(assist),* uphold

help a judge clerk

help along assist, ease, hasten

help oneself to assume *(seize),* hijack, impropriate, occupy *(take possession),* pirate *(reproduce without authorization),* procure, usurp

help to bestow

help with money subsidize

helper abettor, accessory, accomplice, assistant, backer, benefactor, coactor, coadjutant, cohort, colleague, confederate, consociate, conspirer, contributor *(contributor),* copartner *(business associate),* copartner *(coconspirator),* donor, employee, good samaritan, participant, partner, patron *(influential supporter),* samaritan

helpful ancillary *(auxiliary),* beneficial, benevolent, charitable *(lenient),* constructive *(creative),* contributory, convenient, disposable, effective *(efficient),* favorable *(advantageous),* favorable *(expressing approval),* functional, humane, instrumental, medicinal, ministerial, obeisant, operative, palliative *(abating),* philanthropic, practical, profitable, propitious, purposeful, salutary, subservient, valuable

helpfulness aid *(help),* assistance, benevolence *(act of kindness),* benevolence *(disposition to do good),* consideration *(sympathetic regard),* efficiency, goodwill, help, instigation, largess *(generosity),* philanthropy, utility *(usefulness)*

helping beneficial, clerical, contributory, ministerial, part *(portion),* propitious, ration, subsidiary

helping hand good samaritan, reinforcement, samaritan, service *(assistance),* support *(assistance)*

helpless dependent, derelict *(abandoned),* disabled *(deprived of legal right),* disabled *(made incapable),* inadequate, indefensible, insecure, powerless, susceptible *(unresistent),* unable

helpless person dependent

helplessness danger, disability *(physical inability),* impotence, impuissance, inability, incapacity, inefficacy, languor, peril, prostration

helpmate accessory, accomplice, assistant, confederate, consociate, consort, conspirer, contributor *(contributor),* copartner *(coconspirator),* spouse

helpmeet spouse

hem border, margin *(outside limit)*

hem in border *(bound),* circumscribe *(surround by boundary),* enclose, encompass *(surround),* envelop, limit, occlude, restrict, shut

hemisphere circuit, zone

hemp cannabis

hence a savoir, consequently

henchman abettor, coactor, coadjutant

her honor judge

herald anticipate *(prognosticate),* declare, forerunner, harbinger, indicator, inform *(notify),* informant, informer *(a person who provides information),* notify, portend, precede, precursor, predict, preface, proclaim, prognosticate, promulgate, propagate *(spread),* publish, report *(disclose)*

heralding portentous *(ominous)*

Herculean omnipotent, onerous, operose, powerful, prodigious *(enor-*

mous), strong

herd together congregate

here present *(current)*

hereditable hereditary, heritable

hereditament bequest, demesne, domain *(land owned),* estate *(property),* fee *(estate),* freehold, heritage, real estate

hereditaments property *(possessions)*

hereditarius hereditary

hereditary born *(innate),* consanguineous, derivative, genetic, heritable, native *(inborn),* testamentary

hereditary enmity feud

hereditas heritage, inheritance, reversion *(remainder of an estate)*

hereditas caduca escheat

heredity affiliation *(bloodline),* ancestry, birth *(lineage),* blood, bloodline, descent *(lineage)*

heredium heritage

herein wherein

heresy blasphemy, nonconformity

heretic malcontent, pariah, recusant

heretical deviant, nonconforming, skeptical, unorthodox

heretofore theretofore

hereunder a savoir

hereupon a savoir

heriditary innate

heritable bequest, hereditament, hereditary

heritage affinity *(family ties),* bequest, birth *(lineage),* birthright, blood, claim *(right),* descent *(lineage),* estate *(hereditament),* hereditament, inheritance, origin *(ancestry),* right *(entitlement)*

heritance birthright, estate *(hereditament),* hereditament, heritage, legacy

hermetic impervious

hermitic solitary

hermitical solitary

hero paragon, protagonist

hero worship doxology

hero-like spartan

heroic illustrious, meritorious, spartan, undaunted

heroic achievement prowess *(bravery)*

heroism prowess *(bravery)*

herolike heroic

hesitance pause, qualm, reluctance

hesitancy doubt *(indecision),* hesitation, incertitude, indecision, pause, qualm, reluctance, scruple

hesitant disinclined, irresolute, leery, noncommittal, recreant, reluctant, suspicious *(distrustful),* undecided

hesitate defer *(put off),* discontinue *(break continuity),* misdoubt, mistrust, oscillate, pause, procrastinate, recess, refuse, vacillate

hesitating diffident, disinclined, hesitant, irresolute, leery, noncommittal, reluctant

hesitation ambivalence, cloud *(suspicion),* doubt *(suspicion),* halt, incertitude, indecision, misgiving, pause, qualm, reluctance, scruple

hesitative hesitant, reluctant

hest directive, fiat

heteroclite irregular *(not usual)*

heterodox recusant, skeptical, unorthodox

heterodoxy disaccord, nonconformity

heterogeneity difference, diversification, diversity, nonconformity

heterogeneous composite, different, disordered, dissimilar, diverse, miscellaneous, multifarious, promiscuous, unrelated

hew break *(fracture)*, split

heyday prosperity

hiatus absence *(omission)*, blank *(emptiness)*, cessation *(interlude)*

hiatus hiatus

hiatus interruption, interval, lapse *(break)*, pendency, recess, rift *(gap)*, split

hibernating dormant

hic current

hidden blind *(concealed)*, clandestine, confidential, covert, enigmatic, esoteric, furtive, impalpable, inapprehensible, incomprehensible, inconspicuous, indirect, indiscernible, inexplicable, inscrutable, lost *(taken away)*, mysterious, obscure *(abstruse)*, obscure *(faint)*, personal *(private)*, private *(confidential)*, private *(secluded)*, privy, recondite, remote *(secluded)*, secret, sly, stealthy, surreptitious, ulterior, undisclosed

hidden from view latent

hidden knowledge secret

hidden meaning implication *(inference)*, mystery, nuance

hide abscond, blind *(obscure)*, camouflage, cloak, conceal, cover *(conceal)*, disguise, elude, ensconce, enshroud, envelop, flee, harbor, hedge, hoard, lurk, obfuscate, obnubilate, obscure, reserve, screen *(guard)*, seclude, shroud, withhold

hide away blind *(obscure)*, camouflage, cloak, ensconce, hoard, plant *(covertly place)*

hide from evade *(elude)*, shun

hide from view ensconce

hide one's identity camouflage, disguise

hide securely ensconce

hide the identity of blind *(obscure)*

hide the truth perjure

hide under a mask pretend

hide underground blind *(obscure)*

hideaway cache *(hiding place)*

hidebound illiberal, parochial, rigid

hideous loathsome, odious, offensive *(offending)*, repulsive

hideout haven

hiding concealment, disguise, nonappearance

hiding place refuge

hie race

hierarchy class

hieroglyphic hidden

higgle haggle

high disdainful, priceless

high character honesty, integrity

high coloring bombast

high explosive bomb

high honor prestige

high ideals conscience

high interest usury

high land elevation

high level executive

high official caretaker *(one fulfilling the function of office)*

high opinion estimation *(esteem)*, mention *(tribute)*

high point landmark *(significant change)*

high position eminence, primacy

high powered in full force

high pressure duress

high pressure methods compulsion *(coercion)*

high prices inflation *(decrease in value of currency)*

high principles honesty, probity

high priority exigent

high rank eminence

high regard credit *(recognition)*, estimation *(esteem)*, homage, honor *(good reputation)*, honor *(outward respect)*

high repute prestige

high reward character *(reputation)*

high society elite

high spot highlight

high standards conscience

high station eminence

high structure edifice

high worth cost *(price)*

high-class superior *(excellent)*

high-flown flatulent, fustian, inflated *(bombastic)*, orotund, turgid

high-grade preferential, premium, sterling, superior *(excellent)*

high-handed tyrannous

high-level important *(significant)*, major

high-minded clean, law-abiding, magnanimous, meritorious, moral

high-mindedness honesty, integrity

high-paying lucrative

high-potency powerful

high-pressure intense

high-priced exorbitant, priceless, prohibitive *(costly)*

high-principled clean, high-minded, incorruptible, law-abiding, meritorious, moral, reputable, strict

high-priority important *(urgent)*, indispensable

high-quality premium, sterling, superior *(excellent)*

high-sounding fustian, grandiose, inflated *(bombastic)*

high-sounding words bombast, fustian

high-spirited hot-blooded

high-strung hot-blooded, sensitive *(easily affected)*

higher class society

higher court appellate court

highest absolute *(ideal)*, best, cardinal *(outstanding)*, paramount, primary, prime *(most valuable)*, principal, superlative, utmost, utmost

highest degree ceiling, pinnacle

highest point ceiling, culmination, pinnacle

highest position supremacy

highest quality professional *(stellar)*

highest ranking person chief

highhanded dictatorial

highlight cornerstone, emphasis, feature *(special attraction)*, indicate

highly developed skill science *(technique)*

highly disciplined spartan

highly important central *(essential)*

highly important detail necessity, need *(requirement)*

highly principled upright

highly reputed famous

highly serious serious *(grave)*

highly specialized technical

highly specific technical

highly thought of popular

highly wrought elaborate

highness elevation

highroad causeway

highway causeway

highways approaches

hike boom *(increase)*, perambulate

hike in prices inflation *(decrease in value of currency)*

hilarious jocular

hinder arrest *(stop)*, balk, bind *(restrain)*, block, check *(restrain)*, clog, conflict, constrain *(restrain)*, constrict *(inhibit)*, contain *(restrain)*, control *(restrain)*, counter, counteract, countervail, curb, debar, defer *(put off)*, delay, detain *(restrain)*, deter, disable, disadvantage, disappoint, discommode, discontinue *(break continuity)*, discourage, disrupt, enjoin, estop, fetter, fight *(counteract)*, foil, forbid, forestall, frustrate, halt, hamper, hold up *(delay)*, impair, impede, inconvenience, inhibit, interdict, interfere, interpose, interrupt, keep *(restrain)*, limit, lock, obstruct, obturate, occlude, oppugn, preclude, prevent, prohibit, repress, repulse, resist *(oppose)*, restrain, stall, stave, stay *(halt)*, stem *(check)*, stop, suspend, tamper, thwart, toll *(stop)*, trammel, withhold, withstand

hinder movement encumber *(hinder)*

hindered arrested *(checked)*, broken *(interrupted)*

hinderer deterrent

hindering binding, detrimental, disadvantageous, encumbrance, intrusive, limiting, preventive, prohibitive *(restrictive)*, restrictive

hindermost back *(in reverse)*, extreme *(last)*, last *(final)*

hindmost back *(in reverse)*, extreme *(last)*, last *(final)*

hindrance admonition, bar *(obstruction)*, barrier, burden, censorship, check *(bar)*, complication, constraint *(restriction)*, damper *(stopper)*, deterrence, deterrent, disadvantage, disincentive, disturbance, encumbrance, estoppel, fetter, filibuster, frustration, handicap, impediment, imposition *(excessive burden)*, interruption, liability, nuisance, obstacle, obstruction, onus *(burden)*, pressure, prohibition, resistance, restraint, stay, trouble

hindsight retrospect

hindward back *(in reverse)*

hinge crossroad *(turning point)*

hint allude, clue, connotation, connote, guidance, implication *(inference)*, indicant, indicate, indication, indicator, infer, inference, innuendo, insinuation, intimation, mention *(reference)*, monition *(warning)*, prompt, reference *(allusion)*, remind, reminder, report *(rumor)*, signify *(denote)*, suggestion, suspicion *(uncertainty)*, tip *(clue)*

hint at imply, mention, refer *(direct attention)*

hints indicia

hire delegate, employ *(engage services)*, fare, let *(lease)*, pay, procure, rate, retain *(employ)*, revenue, sublease, wage

hire out let *(lease)*, rent
hired mercenary
hired hand employee
hireling employee, mercenary
hirer client
his honor judge
historic traditional
historical honest, traditional
historical record journal
historically speaking heretofore
historiette story *(narrative)*
historify record
historize record
history account *(report)*, ancestry, bloodline, calendar *(record of yearly periods)*, common knowledge, record, report *(detailed account)*, story *(narrative)*
histrionic demonstrative *(expressive of emotion)*, orotund
histrionics exaggeration, pretense *(ostentation)*
hit attack, beat *(strike)*, collide *(crash against)*, contact *(touch)*, impinge, impress *(affect deeply)*, lash *(strike)*, strike *(assault)*, strike *(collide)*
hit against jostle *(bump into)*, strike *(collide)*
hit back recriminate
hit upon find *(discover)*
hit upon a solution resolve *(solve)*
hitch connection *(fastening)*, damper *(stopper)*, encumbrance, obstruction, period
hive hoard
hoard accumulate *(amass)*, collection *(accumulation)*, fund, fund, garner, preserve, provision *(something provided)*, reserve, save *(hold back)*, selection *(collection)*, stock *(store)*, store *(depository)*, store, sufficiency
hoary elderly, old
hoax artifice, betray *(lead astray)*, bilk, bunko, canard, circumvent, collusion, deceive, deception, defraud, delude, dupe, ensnare, evade *(deceive)*, fake, fake, false pretense, falsification, frame up, hoodwink, illude, imposture, knavery, maneuver *(trick)*, misrepresent, palter, pretense *(pretext)*, ruse
hobble block, maim, repress, restrict, trammel
hoboism vagrancy
hodgepodge melange
hoggish insatiable
hoist elevate
hold accommodate, adjudge, advantage, apprehend *(arrest)*, arrest *(apprehend)*, arrest *(stop)*, chamber *(compartment)*, claim *(maintain)*, comprise, conclude *(decide)*, confine, consist, constrain *(imprison)*, contain *(comprise)*, contend *(maintain)*, decide, deem, delay, depository, desist, detain *(hold in custody)*, determine, dominance, dominion *(supreme authority)*, embrace *(encircle)*, encompass *(include)*, find *(determine)*, grapple, halt, handcuff, immerse *(engross)*, immure, include, influence, judge, keep *(restrain)*, keep *(shelter)*, lock, moratorium, obtain, occupy *(take possession)*, opine, own, possess, power, primacy, remain *(occupy)*, remain *(stay)*, reserve, restrain, retain *(keep in possession)*, retention, rule *(decide)*, save *(conserve)*, seisin, sentence, stay *(halt)*, stop, store, suspect *(think)*,

withhold
hold a brief for bear *(support)*
hold a conference confer *(consult)*, discourse
hold a consultation confer *(consult)*, deliberate
hold a conversation speak
hold a convocation meet
hold a discussion speak
hold a high opinion of regard *(hold in esteem)*
hold a meeting convene, meet
hold a position of authority preside
hold a session convene, meet
hold accountable denounce *(inform against)*, incriminate
hold aloft elevate
hold an argument dispute *(debate)*
hold an inquiry analyze, audit, canvass, delve, investigate
hold an office officiate
hold an opinion deem
hold apart separate
hold as a hostage confine
hold as hostage constrain *(imprison)*
hold at bay counter, parry
hold at fault impeach
hold authority govern, handle *(manage)*, preside, rule *(govern)*
hold back arrest *(stop)*, avoid *(evade)*, balk, clog, confine, constrain *(restrain)*, constrict *(inhibit)*, contain *(restrain)*, control *(restrain)*, curb, debar, decline *(reject)*, defer *(put off)*, delay, detain *(restrain)*, deter, disadvantage, forbear, forestall, hamper, hesitate, hinder, hoard, impede, inhibit, keep *(restrain)*, limit, mistrust, parry, pause, prevent, procrastinate, refrain, refuse, repress, reserve, restrain, restrict, stem *(check)*, stop, toll *(stop)*, trammel, withhold
hold back action encumber *(hinder)*
hold back by force constrain *(imprison)*, constrain *(restrain)*
hold by force usurp
hold captive capture, confine, constrain *(imprison)*, detain *(hold in custody)*, immure, imprison, jail, obsess, subjugate
hold cheap decry, disdain, disfavor, misprize
hold conclave deliberate, discuss
hold conference converse, discuss
hold conversations discuss
hold court adjudicate, hear *(give a legal hearing)*
hold dear foster, regard *(hold in esteem)*
hold different views differ *(disagree)*
hold dominion predominate *(command)*, rule *(govern)*
hold down constrain *(restrain)*, dominate, extinguish, subject
hold fast adhere *(fasten)*, cohere *(adhere)*, grapple, hold *(possess)*, hold out *(resist)*, persevere, persist, retain *(keep in possession)*
hold firmly adhere *(fasten)*
hold for ransom kidnap
hold forth declaim, exposit, offer *(propose)*, recite, recount
hold in constrain *(restrain)*, inhibit, keep *(restrain)*, repress, withhold
hold in abeyance adjourn, defer *(put off)*, delay, discontinue *(break continuity)*, forbear, hold up *(delay)*, suspend

hold in affection regard *(hold in esteem)*
hold in belief deem
hold in bondage subject, subjugate
hold in captivity capture, confine, immure, imprison, jail
hold in check balk, check *(restrain)*, clog, confine, constrain *(restrain)*, contain *(restrain)*, control *(restrain)*, curb, detain *(hold in custody)*, disadvantage, enjoin, immure, impede, moderate *(preside over)*, restrain
hold in constraint commit *(institutionalize)*
hold in contempt condescend *(patronize)*, contemn, decry, disdain, flout, ignore, misprize, reject, spurn
hold in custody contain *(restrain)*, jail, restrain
hold in derision flout, humiliate, jeer, mock *(deride)*
hold in despite contemn
hold in disrespect condescend *(patronize)*, flout, humiliate
hold in esteem defer *(yield in judgment)*, honor
hold in leash discipline *(control)*
hold in legal custody impound
hold in line discipline *(control)*
hold in one's grasp hold *(possess)*
hold in possession retain *(keep in possession)*
hold in preventive custody detain *(hold in custody)*
hold in regard regard *(hold in esteem)*
hold in restraint commit *(institutionalize)*, constrain *(imprison)*, imprison
hold in subjection subject
hold in thrall confine, detain *(hold in custody)*
hold in view anticipate *(expect)*, observe *(watch)*
hold intercourse discuss
hold liable convict, encumber *(financially obligate)*
hold no brief for blame, disown *(deny the validity)*
hold not to be true disbelieve
hold off cease, counter, defer *(put off)*, doubt *(hesitate)*, forbear, parry, pause, postpone, resist *(withstand)*, stave
hold office govern, predominate *(command)*, rule *(govern)*
hold on adhere *(persist)*, cohere *(adhere)*, last, persevere, persist, subsist
hold on property charge *(lien)*, cloud *(incumbrance)*, lien, mechanics lien
hold one's ground endure *(last)*
hold ones own hold out *(resist)*
hold opposite views collide *(clash)*, conflict, disaccord, disagree
hold out endure *(last)*, extend *(offer)*, last, offer *(propose)*, persevere, persist, profess *(avow)*, proffer, remain *(continue)*, resist *(withstand)*, submit *(give)*, tender, withhold, withstand
hold out against counter, oppugn
hold out allurement bait *(lure)*, entrap, lure
hold out hope reassure
hold out temptation entrap, lure
hold over adjourn, continue *(adjourn)*, delay, prolong
hold possession remain *(occupy)*

hold prisoner confine

hold questionable misdoubt

hold responsible blame, charge (accuse), convict, delegate, denounce (inform against), implicate

hold responsible for confide (trust)

hold spellbound immerse (engross), monopolize

hold sway govern, preside

hold sway over moderate (preside over), subjugate

hold the advantage beat (defeat)

hold the attention interest

hold the chair moderate (preside over), preside

hold the interest of engage (involve), monopolize

hold the opinion assume (suppose), contend (maintain)

hold the reins overlook (superintend)

hold tight adhere (persist)

hold to blame fault

hold together annex (add), cement, cohere (adhere), cohere (be logically consistent), conjoin, conspire

hold under duress detain (hold in custody)

hold up bear (support), clog, cohere (adhere), curb, defer (put off), delay, detain (restrain), deter, elevate, encumber (hinder), heighten (elevate), impede, keep (restrain), last, maintain (sustain), manifest, procrastinate, promote (organize), protract (prolong), remit (relax), resist (withstand), rob, stall, steal, uphold

hold up one's hand cast (register)

hold up to execration censure, disapprove (condemn)

hold up to public ridicule expose

hold up to reprobation blame, censure, disapprove (condemn)

hold up to ridicule mock (deride), pillory

hold up to scorn flout

hold up to shame brand (stigmatize), discredit, disgrace, pillory, smear

hold up to view manifest, produce (offer to view)

hold upon the property of another lien

hold with concur (agree), countenance

hold within bounds immure

hold-over adjournment

holdback disadvantage, hindrance, impediment, restraint

holder bearer, catchall, coffer, depository, receiver, recipient, tenant

holder of an estate by virtue of a lease lessee

holder of an office incumbent

holder of legal title landholder, landowner

holder of the legal estate trustee

holdfast connection (fastening)

holding chattel, custody (incarceration), demesne, domain (land owned), dominion (absolute ownership), fee (estate), interest (ownership), occupancy, ownership, possession (property), property (land), ruling, share (stock), stake (interest), tenancy, tenure, trust (custody)

holding a low opinion of mankind cynical

holding ability capacity (maximum)

holding action retention

holding back hesitation

holding by title tenancy

holding company corporation, firm

holding in constraint commitment (confinement)

holding in custody apprehension (act of arresting)

holding in restraint commitment (confinement)

holding legal rights conferred by another acting

holding off abstention

holding power retention

holding property proprietary

holding public interest famous

holding to a purpose pertinacious

holding together adherence (adhesion), coherence, coherent (joined), cohesive (sticking)

holding up well durable

holdings assets, capital, commodities, effects, estate (property), paraphernalia (personal belongings), personalty, portfolio, possessions, principal (capital sum), property (possessions), realty, securities, stock (shares)

holdup robbery

holdup man burglar, hoodlum

hole outlet, predicament

holiday furlough, leave (absence), remembrance (commemoration)

holistic whole (unified)

hollow chamber (compartment), deficient, jejune (dull), perfunctory, untenable, vacant, vacuous, void (empty)

hollow place chamber (compartment)

hollow pretense hypocrisy, imposture

hollowness blank (emptiness)

holocaust atrocity, cataclysm, catastrophe, disaster, havoc, shambles

holy infrangible, sacrosanct, solemn

homage adherence (devotion), adhesion (loyalty), allegiance, estimation (esteem), fealty, fidelity, honor (outward respect), mention (tribute), remembrance (commemoration), respect

home abode, address, apartment, building (structure), domestic (household), domestic (indigenous), domicile, habitation (dwelling place), house, household (domestic), household, inhabitation (place of dwelling), lodging, residence, residential, seat, shelter (protection)

home base headquarters

home circle family (household)

home office headquarters

home-grown native (domestic)

home-loving household (domestic)

home-owning household (domestic)

homeland home (domicile), home (place of origin), nationality

homeless derelict (abandoned), solitary

homeless child orphan

homely familiar (customary), inelegant, nondescript, ordinary

homemade domestic (indigenous)

homemaking domestic (household), household (domestic)

homeostasis balance (equality)

homes premises (buildings)

homespun inelegant, mundane, ordinary, simple

homestead abode, building (struc-

ture), dwelling, habitation (dwelling place), home (domicile), house, household, property (land)

homicidal deadly

homicide aberemurder, assassination, dispatch (act of putting to death), killing, manslaughter, murder

homicidium manslaughter

homiletic informative

homiletical informative

homily peroration

hominem endow

hominem adire apply (request)

hominem adloqui address (talk to)

hominem armis exuere disarm (divest of arms)

hominem deserere abandon (physically leave)

hominem imitari impersonate

hominem iubere facere command

hominem permulcere coax

homines public, society

homini blandiri coax

homini civitatem dare naturalize (make a citizen)

homini gratiam debere obligation (duty)

homini imperare command

homini obsistere cross (disagree with)

homini placere appeal

homini praecipere ut faciat command

homini rei empower, enable

homini suadere advise

homini viam monstrare direct (show)

hominis welfare

hominis bona vendere distrain

hominis caedes manslaughter

hominis nomen deferre inform (betray)

hominum generis humanity (mankind)

homo inhabitant, person

homo maleficus delinquent (guilty of a misdeed), delinquent, malefactor, wrongdoer

homo peritus specialist

homo rerum novarum cupidus malcontent

homo sapiens humanity (mankind)

homo sceleratus malefactor

homo studiosus partisan

homo trium literarum burglar

homogeneity identity (similarity), propinquity (similarity), regularity, resemblance, uniformity, union (unity)

homogeneous boiler plate, cognate, comparable (capable of comparison), identical, pure, similar, simple, uniform

homologate agree (comply), assent, authorize, concur (agree), confirm, correspond (be equivalent), countenance, sanction

homologation sanction (permission)

homological correlative

homologize coordinate, correspond (be equivalent)

homologous analogous, coequal, coextensive, cognate, comparable (capable of comparison), equal

homologue counterpart (complement)

homology analogy, relation (connection)

honest actual, authentic, bona fide, candid, clean, conscientious, credible, direct (forthright), equitable, ethical, factual, fair (just), faithful (true to *fact),* genuine, high-minded, impartial, incorruptible, ingenuous, irreprehensible, just, law-abiding, meritorious, moral, proper, reliable, reputable, right *(correct),* rightful, scrupulous, sterling, straightforward, true *(authentic),* unaffected *(sincere),* upright, veridical

honest effort good faith

honestly fairly *(impartially),* faithfully, in good faith

honestus moral, reputable, upright

honesty candor *(straightforwardness),* conscience, equity *(justice),* ethics, fairness, integrity, principle *(virtue),* probity, rectitude, trustworthiness, truth, veracity

honeyed nectarious

honor accept *(recognize),* character *(reputation),* compensate *(remunerate),* conscience, credit *(recognition),* dedicate, defer *(yield in judgment),* deference, discharge *(pay a debt),* distinction *(reputation),* elevate, eminence, estimation *(esteem),* ethics, homage, integrity, keep *(fulfill),* laudation, mention *(tribute),* merit, observe *(obey),* pay, prestige, principle *(virtue),* privilege, prize, probity, raise *(advance),* recognize *(acknowledge),* rectitude, regard *(esteem),* regard *(hold in esteem),* respect, right *(righteousness)*

honor a bill defray

honor a claim refund

honor with bestow

honorable bona fide, clean, conscientious, equitable, ethical, exemplary, fair *(just),* high-minded, honest, impartial, incorruptible, ingenuous, just, law-abiding, loyal, magnanimous, meritorious, moral, obeisant, outstanding *(prominent),* pure, reliable, reputable, right *(correct),* scrupulous, sterling, straightforward, upright

honorable justice judge

honorableness honesty, integrity, principle *(virtue),* probity, rectitude

honorably fairly *(impartially),* faithfully

honorarium bonus, bounty, contribution *(donation),* payment *(remittance),* reward

honorary nominal

honored famous, illustrious, influential, outstanding *(prominent),* prominent, proud *(self-respecting),* renowned, reputable

honorific honorary

honorifical honorary

honoring dedication, obedient, remembrance *(commemoration)*

hood enshroud

hoodlum lawbreaker, malefactor

hoodwink betray *(lead astray),* bilk, deceive, delude, ensnare, fake, pretend, prevaricate

hook connect *(join together),* ensnare, trap

hooligan malefactor

hoot mock *(deride)*

hope chance *(possibility),* design *(intent),* end *(intent),* expectation, faith, goal, objective, plan, possibility, prospect *(outlook),* purpose, target, trust, will *(desire)*

hope for desire

hoped for prospective

hopeful apparent *(presumptive),* auspicious, candidate, novice, propitious, sanguine, solicitous

hopeless despondent, diabolic, disconsolate, futile, impossible, impracticable, incorrigible, inoperable *(incurable),* irredeemable, irremediable, irreversible, ominous, pessimistic, unfavorable, unpropitious

hopeless failure miscarriage

hopelessly lost irretrievable

hopelessness impasse, impossibility, peril, pessimism

horde assemblage, band, congregation

horizontality prostration

horn in intrude

horrendous contemptible, depraved, disastrous, disreputable, heinous, reprehensible

horrible contemptible, deplorable, diabolic, dire, disastrous, disgraceful, formidable, gross *(flagrant),* heinous, lamentable, loathsome, lurid, nefarious, obnoxious, odious, offensive *(offending),* repulsive, sinister

horrid deplorable, dire, disastrous, disreputable, heinous, lamentable, loathsome, objectionable, obnoxious, odious, offensive *(offending),* repulsive, sinister, vicious

horrific deplorable

horrify frighten, offend *(insult),* repel *(disgust)*

horrifying deplorable, dire, formidable, lurid, outrageous, repulsive, scandalous

horror consternation, fear, fright, odium, panic, phobia, trepidation

hors de combat disabled *(made incapable)*

hortans hortative

hortation instigation

hortative informative, informatory, persuasive

hortatory hortative, informative, informatory, persuasive

hospes stranger

hospitable benevolent, humane, liberal *(generous),* philanthropic, receptive

hospitableness largess *(generosity),* philanthropy

hospital case patient

hospitality charity, largess *(generosity),* philanthropy

hospitalized person patient

hospitio excipere lodge *(house)*

host body *(collection),* mass *(body of persons),* plurality, quantity

hostage captive, prisoner

hostel lodge *(house)*

hostia victim

hostile averse, bitter *(reproachful),* discordant, disobedient, impertinent *(insolent),* inimical, irreconcilable, litigious, malevolent, malicious, malignant, negative, nonconsenting, offensive *(taking the initiative),* opposite, prejudicial, pugnacious, recusant, repugnant *(incompatible),* spiteful, unfavorable, virulent

hostile attack diatribe, impugnation

hostile contest confrontation *(altercation)*

hostile criticism diatribe, disparagement, impeachment

hostile demonstration protest

hostile eloquence diatribe

hostile encounter confrontation *(altercation),* fight *(battle)*

hostile entrance incursion

hostile entry invasion

hostile invasion foray

hostile person foe

hostile verdict conviction *(finding of guilt),* nonsuit

hostilities conflict

hostility alienation *(estrangement),* argument *(contention),* belligerency, collision *(dispute),* conflict, contention *(opposition),* discord, estrangement, feud, hatred, ill will, impugnation, incompatibility *(difference),* malice, odium, ostracism, rancor, spite, umbrage

hostis foe

hot vehement

hot-headed hot-blooded, imprudent, outrageous, petulant, precipitate

hot-tempered fractious, hot-blooded, petulant

hotheaded impulsive *(rash)*

hound badger, bait *(harass),* harry *(harass),* hector, hunt, importune, molest *(annoy),* obsess, press *(goad),* prompt, provoke, trace *(follow)*

hour point *(period of time)*

hour of decision crossroad *(turning point)*

house abode, building *(structure),* concern *(business establishment),* domicile, dwelling, enterprise *(economic organization),* family *(common ancestry),* firm, habitation *(dwelling place),* home *(domicile),* homestead, inhabitation *(place of dwelling),* institute, locate, market *(business),* parentage, preserve, protect, shelter *(protection)*

house of correction jail, penitentiary, prison, reformatory

house of detention jail, penitentiary, prison, reformatory

house of reform prison

house of representatives legislature

house with the grounds belonging to it premises *(buildings)*

house-building program development *(building)*

housebreaker burglar

housebreaking burglary

housed situated

household domestic *(household),* familiar *(customary),* home *(domicile),* homestead, house, ordinary, prevalent, property *(land),* residential

householder inhabitant, occupant, proprietor, tenant

housekeeping domestic *(household),* household *(domestic)*

housing development *(building),* habitation *(dwelling place),* lodging, residence

hover prowl, vacillate

however notwithstanding, regardless, unless

howl outcry

hub body *(main part),* focus

hubbub bluster *(commotion),* brawl, noise, riot

hubris pride

huckster dealer, merchant, sell, trade, vendor

huddle meet, turmoil
hue color *(complexion)*
huff resentment
huffy petulant, resentful
huge capacious, exorbitant, far reaching, formidable, grandiose, gross *(flagrant)*, prodigious *(enormous)*
hulking ponderous
hullabaloo noise, outcry
human bodily, character *(an individual)*, person, physical
human being body *(person)*, character *(an individual)*, individual, person
human beings humanity *(mankind)*
human creature person
human environment ecology
human race mortality
human weakness foible, frailty
humane benevolent, charitable *(lenient)*, lenient, liberal *(generous)*, philanthropic
humaneness benevolence *(disposition to do good)*, charity, clemency, philanthropy
humanism benevolence *(disposition to do good)*
humanitarian benefactor, benevolent, charitable *(lenient)*, donor, good samaritan, humane, liberal *(generous)*, nonprofit, philanthropic
humanitarianism aid *(subsistence)*, charity, help, philanthropy
humanitas civilization, humanity *(humaneness)*, philanthropy
humanity benevolence *(disposition to do good)*, charity, clemency, consideration *(sympathetic regard)*, goodwill, lenience, mortality, populace, population, tolerance, understanding *(tolerance)*
humanize personify
humankind humanity *(mankind)*
humanness mortality
humanum genus humanity *(mankind)*
humanus humane, philanthropic
humble browbeat, contrite, debase, demean *(make lower)*, demote, derogate, diffident, familiar *(customary)*, humiliate, ignoble, marginal, obeisant, obsequious, paltry, penitent, reduce, repentant, servile, subaltern, subdue, subject, subjugate, subordinate, unobtrusive, unpretentious
humble entreaty prayer
humble oneself condescend *(deign)*, repent
humble oneself to obey
humble service fealty
humbled contrite, diffident
humbled pride disgrace
humbleness poverty, respect
humbling disgrace
humbly respectfully
humbug bilk, deceive, invent *(falsify)*, pettifoggery, ruse
humbuggery deception, knavery
humdrum ordinary, prosaic, stale, usual
humiliate browbeat, debase, demean *(make lower)*, denigrate, disgrace, disparage, smear
humiliating disgraceful, libelous
humiliating rudeness contumely
humiliation attaint, contumely, degradation, disgrace, dishonor *(shame)*, embarrassment, ignominy, infamy, ob-

loquy, odium, opprobrium, scandal, shame
humiliative disgraceful
humilis ignoble, servile
humility homage, respect
humor characteristic, disposition *(inclination)*, notion, pander, placate, propitiate, soothe, spirit, vouchsafe
humor excessively overindulge
humoring indulgence, lenient
humorless grave *(solemn)*, pedestrian
humorous jocular, ludicrous
humorsome restive, volatile
hunch premonition
hunger desire, passion
hunger for lack, need
hunt chase, ferret, frisk, prey, pursue *(chase)*, pursuit *(chase)*, pursuit *(effort to secure)*, quest, research, search
hunt down expose
hunt for delve
hunt out trace *(follow)*
hunt through delve, frisk
hunted person fugitive
hurdle bar *(obstruction)*, barrier, deterrence, deterrent, encumbrance, handicap, negotiate, obstacle, obstruction
hurl cast *(throw)*, emit, impel, launch *(project)*, project *(impel forward)*, send
hurl defiance at challenge
hurl headlong precipitate *(throw down violently)*
hurried brief, careless, cursory, ephemeral, impulsive *(rash)*, instantaneous, perfunctory, precipitate, rapid, summary, superficial
hurriedly instantly
hurriedness haste
hurry dispatch *(promptness)*, dispatch *(send off)*, expedite, haste, hasten, precipitate *(hasten)*, race, urge
hurry along dispatch *(send off)*, hasten
hurry away quit *(evacuate)*
hurry off with distrain
hurry on dispatch *(send off)*
hurrying acceleration
hurt abuse *(physical misuse)*, aggravate *(annoy)*, aggrieved *(harmed)*, brutalize, damage, damage, deface, detriment, disable, disconsolate, distress, drawback, endanger, expense *(sacrifice)*, harm, harm, harrow, ill use, impair, impairment *(damage)*, imperfect, inflict, injury, maim, marred, mischief, mistreat, molest *(annoy)*, offend *(insult)*, pain, penalize, pique, prejudice *(injury)*, prejudice *(injure)*, resentful, spoil *(impair)*, strike *(assault)*, suffer *(sustain loss)*
hurt the feelings affront, discompose
hurtful adverse *(negative)*, bitter *(reproachful)*, caustic, dangerous, detrimental, disadvantageous, disastrous, fatal, harmful, inadvisable, inimical, insalubrious, insufferable, invidious, lethal, malevolent, malignant, noxious, oppressive, painful, pernicious, pestilent, prejudicial, scathing, sinister, virulent
hurtfulness harm
hurting disabling, painful
hurtle against collide *(crash against)*
hurtless harmless, innocuous, nontoxic, salutary

husband consort, hoard, keep *(shelter)*, preserve, spouse, store
husband one's resources hoard
husbanding of resources economy *(frugality)*
husbandry austerity, prudence
hush allay, lull, lull, moderate *(temper)*, mollify, peace, placate, repress, silence, soothe, stifle, strangle
hush money blackmail, bribe, graft, gratuity *(bribe)*
hush up hide, suppress, withhold
hushed mute
husky strong
hustle haste, hasten, jostle *(bump into)*, race
hyaline pellucid
hybridize commingle
hybridized compound
hygienic preventive, salutary
hygienize decontaminate
hyperbole bombast, caricature, distortion, exaggeration, overstatement, rodomontade
hyperbolic extreme *(exaggerated)*, inflated *(overestimated)*
hyperbolical outrageous
hyperbolism overstatement
hypercritical critical *(faultfinding)*, particular *(exacting)*, querulous, sensitive *(easily affected)*, severe
hypercriticism diatribe, disparagement
hypersensitive querulous
hyphenate connect *(join together)*
hypnotic narcotic, narcotic
hypocrisy bad faith, duplicity, indirection *(deceitfulness)*, pretense *(pretext)*
hypocritical dishonest, disingenuous, evasive, faithless, false *(disloyal)*, insidious, machiavellian, perfidious, specious, tartuffish, untrue
hypostasis center *(essence)*, essence, spirit, substance *(essential nature)*
hypothecate bond *(secure a debt)*, guarantee, pawn, pledge *(deposit)*, promise *(vow)*
hypothecated fully secured
hypothecation charge *(lien)*, cloud *(incumbrance)*, guaranty, specialty *(contract)*
hypothesis assumption *(supposition)*, basis, conjecture, deduction *(conclusion)*, generalization, idea, inference, opinion *(belief)*, postulate, presumption, prolepsis, proposition, speculation *(conjecture)*, supposition, theory, thesis
hypothesization assumption *(supposition)*
hypothesize generalize, guess, opine, posit, postulate, presume, presuppose, propound, reason *(conclude)*, speculate *(conjecture)*, surmise, suspect *(think)*
hypothesized assumed *(inferred)*, presumptive
hypothetic hypothetical
hypothetical conditional, debatable, disputable, moot, nonexistent, speculative, theoretical
hypothetically arguendo
hysteria furor, outburst, panic
hysterical frenetic, uncontrollable
hysterical state outburst
hystericalness panic
hysterics outburst

I

iacere dormant

iactans pretentious *(ostentatious)*, pretentious *(pompous)*

iactare cast *(throw)*, flaunt

iactura loss

iconoclasm blasphemy

iconoclast heretic

iconoclastic radical *(favoring drastic change)*, recusant, skeptical

icy disdainful, unaffected *(uninfluenced)*

icy aloofness disdain

idea apprehension *(perception)*, clue, concept, connotation, end *(intent)*, hint, import, intimation, meaning, notion, objective, opinion *(belief)*, perception, project, proposal *(suggestion)*, proposition, purpose, sense *(feeling)*, substance *(essential nature)*, suggestion, tenor

idea conveyed gist *(substance)*, sum *(tally)*

ideal criterion, example, exemplar, exemplary, felicitous, model, nonexistent, paradigm, paragon, pattern, prototype, ripe, standard, unimpeachable

ideal justice equity *(justice)*

idealism casuistry

idealistic ethical, meritorious, moral, quixotic

idealize magnify

ideals conscience, ethics

ideate conceive *(comprehend)*, create

ideational theoretical

ideative cogitative, theoretical

idée fixe preoccupation

idem identical

idem same

identical comparable *(equivalent)*, equivalent, same, same, similar, tantamount, uniform

identical in amount equal

identical in quantity equal

identical in size commensurable, equal, equivalent

identical in value coequal, equal, equivalent

identical value parity

identicalness identity *(similarity)*, par *(equality)*, parity, resemblance

identifiable apparent *(perceptible)*, arrant *(definite)*, clear *(apparent)*, manifest, palpable, unmistakable

identification classification, connection *(relation)*, credentials, definition, denomination, designation *(naming)*, discovery, earmark, fingerprints, label, recognition, speciality, stamp, trademark

identification mark brand, designation *(symbol)*, device *(distinguishing mark)*

identification records fingerprints

identification tag brand, label

identified with congruous

identifier eyewitness

identify brand *(mark)*, call *(title)*, characterize, classify, define, describe, detect, diagnose, discover, find *(discover)*, label, recognize *(perceive)*, relate *(establish a connection)*

identify by name call *(title)*

identify incorrectly mislabel, mistake

identify with compare, sympathize

identifying descriptive

identity par *(equality)*, personality, resemblance, semblance

identity classification identification

identity comparison identification

identity verification identification

ideological theoretical

ideology theory

idiocrasy characteristic, quality *(attribute)*, quirk *(idiosyncrasy)*

idiom expression *(comment)*, language, parlance, phrase, phraseology, speech, term *(expression)*

idiomatic distinctive, specific

idiosyncrasy characteristic, disposition *(inclination)*, feature *(characteristic)*, identity *(individuality)*, irregularity, nonconformity, quality *(attribute)*, specialty *(distinctive mark)*, tendency, trait

idiosyncratic different, distinct *(distinguished from others)*, distinctive, eccentric, noteworthy, particular *(specific)*, peculiar *(distinctive)*, personal *(individual)*, specific

idiosyncratical specific

idiotic fatuous, ludicrous, non compos mentis, obtuse

idle barren, baseless, inactive, indolent, ineffectual, lax, loiter, otiose, procrastinate, remiss, rest *(cease from action)*, stagnant, torpid, trivial, truant, unavailing, unemployed, unfounded, vacant, vacuous

idle expenditure misapplication

idle fancy figment

idle speech fustian

idle speeches bombast

idleness desuetude, inaction, languor, lull, neglect, nonperformance, sloth

idling layoff

idolatory doxology

idolatry laudation

idolization respect

idolize honor, regard *(hold in esteem)*

idoneous suitable

idoneus adequate, capable, convenient, eligible, fit, opportune, proper, qualified *(conditioned)*, suitable

ieiunus prosaic

if it were not that only

igitur consequently

ignarus inexperienced, unacquainted, unaware

ignavia sloth

ignavus idle, inactive, indolent

ignis conflagration

ignite burn, deflagrate, discharge *(shoot)*

igniting discharge *(shot)*

ignobility bad character, bad repute, dishonor *(shame)*, disrepute, ignominy, infamy, odium, opprobrium

ignoble bad *(offensive)*, caitiff, calumnious, disgraceful, disreputable, immoral, machiavellian, nefarious, notorious, odious, offensive *(offending)*, outrageous, reprehensible, scandalous, sinister, unethical, unseemly

ignominia degradation, discredit, disgrace, dishonor *(shame)*, ignominy, infamy, shame

ignominious blameful, blameworthy, caitiff, calumnious, contemptible, contemptuous, disgraceful, disreputable, ignoble, libelous, notorious, odious, scandalous

ignominiousness bad repute, disrepute, infamy, opprobrium

ignominy attaint, bad character, bad faith, bad repute, degradation, discredit, disgrace, dishonor *(shame)*, disrepute, infamy, notoriety, obloquy, odium, opprobrium, scandal, shame

ignomy ignominy, notoriety

ignorance nescience

ignorant incognizant, incompetent, inept *(incompetent)*, inexperienced, insensible, obtuse, opaque, unacquainted, unaware, unversed, unwitting

ignorantly unknowingly

ignorare mistake

ignoration nescience

ignore discount *(disbelieve)*, disdain, dismiss *(put out of consideration)*, disobey, disoblige, disregard, exclude, fail *(neglect)*, neglect, overlook *(superintend)*, override, pretermit, rebuff, reject, shirk, shun, spurn

ignore distinctions generalize, muddle

ignore ethics cheat

ignore limits trespass

ignore one's obligations default

ignored derelict *(abandoned)*

ignorement disuse

ignoscere amnesty, forgive, overlook *(superintend)*

ii qui reipublicae praesunt government *(political administration)*

ilk class, kind, manner *(kind)*

ill pain, trouble, unsound *(not strong)*

ill at ease restive

ill conduct guilt, malfeasance

ill consequence mischief

ill disposition ill will

ill fame attaint, opprobrium

ill favor attaint, bad character, ignominy, obloquy

ill feeling argument *(contention)*, discord, hatred, malice, rancor, spite

ill fortune calamity, casualty, expense *(sacrifice)*, loss, misfortune

ill hap casualty

ill health disease

ill humor umbrage

ill individual patient

ill judgment indiscretion

ill luck loss, misfortune

ill management misconduct

ill nature spite

ill repute attaint, bad character, bad repute, ignominy, infamy, notoriety, obloquy, opprobrium, scandal, shame, turpitude

ill treat misemploy, mishandle *(maltreat)*, mistreat, persecute

ill treatment abuse *(physical misuse)*, injury, misusage, misuse, molestation, oppression

ill turn disservice

ill usage abuse *(corrupt practice)*, abuse *(physical misuse)*, misusage, misuse, molestation

ill use abuse *(corrupt practice)*, abuse *(physical misuse)*, misemploy, mishandle *(maltreat)*, mistreat, misuse, persecute

ill will argument *(contention)*, discord, estrangement, feud, hatred, malice, odium, rancor, resentment, spite, umbrage

ill wishes imprecation, malediction
ill-adapted disproportionate, improper, inapplicable, inapposite, inapt, inept *(inappropriate)*, unfit, unsuitable
ill-advised detrimental, fatuous, ill-judged, impolitic, imprudent, inadvisable, inept *(inappropriate)*, injudicious, irrational, misadvised, regressive, thoughtless, undue *(excessive)*, unfit, unpolitic, unreasonable, untimely
ill-behaved blatant *(obtrusive)*, disobedient, perverse
ill-boding dire, ominous, portentous *(ominous)*, regrettable, unfavorable
ill-bred blatant *(obtrusive)*, inelegant, offensive *(offending)*, presumptuous, uncouth
ill-chosen ill-judged, inopportune
ill-consequence harm
ill-considered ill-advised, ill-judged, impolitic, imprudent, impulsive *(rash)*, inadvisable, irrational, misadvised, negligent, premature, untimely
ill-contrived detrimental, ill-judged
ill-defined inconspicuous, indefinite, indeterminate, indistinct, nebulous, opaque, unclear, vague
ill-disciplined lawless
ill-disposed hostile, malevolent, malicious, resentful, sinister, spiteful, unfavorable, unpropitious, vicious
ill-done perfunctory
ill-fame dishonor *(shame)*, disrepute
ill-fated ominous, portentous *(ominous)*, regrettable
ill-favor disgrace, dishonor *(shame)*, disrepute
ill-feeling ill will
ill-founded baseless, improper, unsound *(fallacious)*
ill-furnished devoid
ill-gotten gains spoils
ill-gotten goods plunder
ill-humored petulant
ill-intent ill will
ill-intentioned cruel, harmful, malevolent, malignant, spiteful
ill-judged ill-advised, impolitic, imprudent, inadvisable, injudicious, irrational, misadvised, unpolitic, unreasonable
ill-manage mismanage
ill-mannered blatant *(obtrusive)*, disorderly, impertinent *(insolent)*, inelegant, presumptuous, provincial, uncouth
ill-matched disparate, disproportionate, incongruous
ill-nature cruelty
ill-natured cruel, harsh, malevolent, malicious, perverse, severe, spiteful, vicious
ill-omened dire, disastrous, ominous, regrettable, unfavorable, unpropitious
ill-proportioned disproportionate
ill-provided devoid
ill-provided for poor *(underprivileged)*
ill-qualified inept *(incompetent)*, inexperienced, unqualified *(not competent)*
ill-reasoned sophistic
ill-repute disgrace, dishonor *(shame)*, disrepute
ill-seasoned inopportune
ill-sorted disproportionate
ill-starred ominous, portentous *(omi-*

nous)
ill-stored devoid
ill-suited disproportionate, inapt, inept *(inappropriate)*
ill-tempered fractious, perverse, petulant, severe
ill-timed improper, inapposite, inapt, inauspicious, inept *(inappropriate)*, inopportune, premature, unpropitious, untimely
ill-treat affront, exploit *(take advantage of)*, harass, harm, harrow, ill use, maltreat
ill-treated aggrieved *(harmed)*
ill-treatment harm
ill-usage cruelty, waste
ill-use abuse *(misuse)*, abuse *(violate)*, exploit *(take advantage of)*, harass, harm, harrow, maltreat
ill-used aggrieved *(victimized)*
ill-will cruelty
ill-willed cruel, hostile, libelous, negative
ill-wishing malevolent
illapse entrance
illaqueate inveigle
illation consequence *(conclusion)*, deduction *(conclusion)*, generalization, inference
illative deductible *(provable)*
illaudable blameful, blameworthy, immoral, objectionable, peccable, reprehensible, scandalous, sinister
illegal felonious, illicit, immoral, impermissible, irregular *(improper)*, lawless, peccant *(culpable)*, unauthorized, unlawful, usurious, wrongful
illegal act offense
illegal action malfeasance, transgression
illegal agreement confederacy *(conspiracy)*
illegal amotion asportation
illegal application misapplication
illegal carriage asportation
illegal compact confederacy *(conspiracy)*
illegal compulsion blackmail, coercion, extortion
illegal conduct offense
illegal custody detainer
illegal detention detainer
illegal donation bribe
illegal evasion breach
illegal exacter extortionist
illegal gain gratuity *(bribe)*
illegal incentive bribe
illegal incitation bribe, bribery
illegal inducement bribe, bribery
illegal infliction of punishment lynch law
illegal interest usury
illegal intrusion encroachment
illegal lure bribe
illegal offer bribe
illegal offering bribe
illegal pact collusion
illegal present bribe
illegal profit graft
illegal property contraband
illegal restraint detainer
illegal reward bribe
illegal subduction asportation
illegal taker extortionist
illegal traffic contraband
illegal transmittance asportation

illegal transplantation asportation
illegal transshipment asportation
illegal use of property misappropriation
illegal withholding detainer
illegality burglary, corruption, crime, criminality, felony, infringement, injustice, irregularity, misconduct, misdeed, misdemeanor, misdoing, offense, prohibition, transgression, violation, wrong
illegalize disfranchise
illegally exported goods contraband
illegally imported goods contraband
illegibility incoherence
illegible indistinct, unclear
illegitimacy bar sinister, illegality, incompetence, prohibition
illegitimate felonious, illegal, illicit, impermissible, irregular *(improper)*, spurious, synthetic, ultra vires, unauthorized, unlawful, wrongful
illegitimate act tortious act
illegitimate child bastard
illegitimate undertaking racket
illegitimately illegally
illegitimateness bar sinister
illegitimation bar sinister
illiberal bigot, exclusive *(limited)*, narrow, parochial, parsimonious, penurious, provincial
illiberality discrimination *(bigotry)*, intolerance
illicit illegal, illegitimate *(illegal)*, immoral, impermissible, improper, irregular *(improper)*, unlawful, wrongful
illicit business racket
illicit dealer bootlegger, racketeer
illicit gains contraband, plunder
illicit intercourse adultery
illicit love adultery
illicit procreation bar sinister
illicit profit graft
illicit revenue graft
illicit scheme racket
illicit sexual intercourse adultery
illicitly illegally
illicitly covert collusive
illicitness breach, criminality
illimitable infinite, myriad, omnipotent, open-ended, profuse, unqualified *(unlimited)*
illimitably ad infinitum
illimited open-ended
illiteracy ignorance
illiterate unversed
illiterateness ignorance
illness disability *(physical inability)*, disease, disorder *(abnormal condition)*, prostration
illogical arbitrary, baseless, disordered, disproportionate, erroneous, fatuous, ill-judged, improper, inapposite, incongruous, inconsistent, inept *(inappropriate)*, irrational, misadvised, nonsubstantial *(not sturdy)*, sophistic, unfounded, unreasonable, unsound *(fallacious)*, untenable
illogical conclusion non sequitur
illogical deduction non sequitur
illogical result non sequitur
illude delude
illuminate clarify, comment, construe *(translate)*, delineate, demonstrate *(establish)*, depict, describe, detail *(particularize)*, elucidate, embellish, enlighten, exemplify, explain, explicate,

exposit, illustrate, interpret, manifest, resolve (solve)

illuminated coherent (clear), lucid

illuminating demonstrative (illustrative), descriptive, informative, informatory, interpretive, narrative

illumination civilization, clarification, cognition, comment, construction, definition, explanation, illustration, motif, realization, solution (answer)

illuminative demonstrative (illustrative), descriptive, narrative

illumine disabuse, enlighten, instruct (teach)

illumined lucid

illusion artifice, deception, distortion, fallacy, figment, phantom, prestidigitation, semblance, specter, vision (dream)

illusional ostensible, specious

illusionary delusive, ostensible

illusive deceptive, delusive, fallacious, fictitious, illusory, insubstantial, ostensible, specious, subtle (insidious), untrustworthy

illusory artificial, deceptive, delusive, fallacious, fictitious, insubstantial, nonexistent, ostensible, quixotic, specious, tenuous

illustrate bear (adduce), characterize, cite (state), clarify, comment, construe (translate), define, delineate, demonstrate (establish), depict, describe, detail (particularize), display, elucidate, embellish, enlighten, evidence, evince, exemplify, exhibit, explain, explicate, expound, interpret, manifest, portray, render (depict), represent (portray), signify (denote)

illustration case (example), clarification, comment, example, explanation, expression (manifestation), instance, representation (statement), sample, specimen

illustrational representative

illustrative descriptive, exemplary, general, narrative, representative, typical

illustrative statement dictum

illustrious famous, important (significant), influential, magnanimous, notable, noteworthy, outstanding (prominent), professional (stellar), prominent, renowned, reputable, salient, superior (excellent)

illustriousness distinction (reputation), prestige, reputation

image apprehension (perception), color (complexion), complexion, conceive (comprehend), concept, copy, counterpart (parallel), impression, model, perception, phantom, phenomenon (manifestation), presence (poise), represent (portray), resemblance, semblance, symbol, vision (dream)

image in the mind impression

imaginability chance (possibility)

imaginable plausible, possible, potential, prospective, viable

imaginal original (creative)

imaginary artificial, delusive, fictitious, hypothetical, illusory, insubstantial, nonexistent, speculative

imagination comprehension, creation

imaginative artful, fertile, original (creative), productive, resourceful

imagine compose, conceive (comprehend), conjure, contrive, deem, devise (invent), expect (consider probable), feign, gauge, guess, invent (produce for the first time), opine, presuppose, pretend, profess (pretend), surmise, suspect (think)

imagined artificial, delusive, fictitious, illusory, insubstantial, nonexistent, presumptive

imagined thought figment

imago phantom, reflection (image), representation (statement), semblance

imbalance difference, disparity, distortion, inequality

imbecilic fatuous, obtuse, opaque

imbecillitas impotence

imbed inject

imbibe carouse

imbricate overlap

imbroglio brawl, commotion, complex (entanglement), complication, confusion (turmoil), dilemma, disaccord, dispute, embroilment, entanglement (confusion), fight (argument), involution, pandemonium, plight, predicament, quagmire, snarl, strife, turmoil

imbrue infuse, penetrate, pervade

imbruement infusion

imbue inculcate, infuse, inject, inspire, permeate, pervade

imbued full

imbued with addicted

imbued with life conscious (awake), live (conscious)

imbuement infusion

imbuere imbue, initiate, taint (contaminate)

imitari copy

imitate adopt, copy, fake, forge (counterfeit), impersonate, plagiarize, pose (impersonate), pretend, reflect (mirror), repeat (do again), reproduce, simulate

imitate deceptively feign

imitate falsely forge (counterfeit)

imitate fraudulently forge (counterfeit)

imitate insultingly disparage, jape

imitated imitation, repeated

imitation artificial, caricature, copy, counterfeit, decoy, disguise, duplicate, fake, false (not genuine), forgery, imposture, meretricious, model, parody, plagiarism, pretense (pretext), quasi, resemblance, sham, spurious, surrogate, travesty

imitation of an original plagiarism

imitative artificial, derivative, imitation

imitator disciple

immaculate absolute (ideal), blameless, clean, pure, unblemished

immanence characteristic

immanent born (innate), essential (inherent), inherent, innate

immanis brutal, outrageous, prodigious (enormous)

immanitas brutality

immaterial frivolous, impertinent (irrelevant), imponderable, inapposite, inconsequential, inconsiderable, incorporeal, insubstantial, intangible, irrelevant, minor, negligible, nugatory, null (insignificant), slight, trivial, unessential

immaterial substance spirit

immateriality impalpability, inconsequence, insignificance

immaterialness impalpability

immateriate impalpable, imponderable, incorporeal

immature inchoate, incipient, inexperienced, jejune (lacking maturity), juvenile, naive, puerile, rudimentary

immature person juvenile

immature stage embryo

immaturity adolescence, minority (infancy), nonage

immaturus premature, untimely

immeasurable far reaching, indeterminate, inestimable, infinite, innumerable, profuse, unlimited

immeasurably ad infinitum

immediate current, direct (straight), expeditious, instantaneous, pending (imminent), precipitate, present (current), prompt, prospective, proximate, right (direct), summary

immediate forebear parents

immediately forthwith, instantly

immediateness dispatch (promptness)

immedicable chronic, inoperable (incurable), irremediable

immemor oblivious

immense broad, capacious, exorbitant, far reaching, grandiose, gross (flagrant), innumerable, myriad, outrageous, prodigious (enormous)

immensity magnitude, mass (weight)

immensurable inestimable

immensus unlimited

immeritorious arrant (onerous), blameful, depraved, sinister

immerse concern (involve), inundate, occupy (engage), overcome (overwhelm), overwhelm

immersion obsession, preoccupation

immethodical cursory, disordered, disorderly, haphazard, indiscriminate, random, sporadic

immigrant alien (foreign), alien

immigration entry (entrance), inflow

imminence threat

imminent close (near), forthcoming, future, inevitable, instant, necessary (inescapable), prospective, proximate

imminent danger menace, pitfall

imminere command, imminent, impend, overlap

imminuere decrease, impair, lessen, reduce

imminui abate (lessen)

imminutio decrease

immiscere intersperse

immisericors relentless, remorseless, ruthless

immitigable irredeemable, irremediable, irrevocable

immitis unrelenting

immittere launch (project)

immix combine (join together), commingle

immixture coalescence

immobile firm, inflexible, stagnant, static, unbending, unyielding

immobilis immovable, static

immobility abeyance, inaction, inertia, insentience, languor

immobilization inertia

immobilize bind (restrain), fetter, lock

immoderacy exaggeration

immoderate disorderly, dissolute,

drastic, egregious, excess, excessive, exorbitant, extreme *(exaggerated),* fanatical, gluttonous, hot-blooded, incendiary, inordinate, intemperate, outrageous, prodigal, profligate *(extravagant),* profuse, prohibitive *(costly),* superlative, unconscionable, undue *(excessive),* unqualified *(unlimited),* unreasonable, unrestrained *(not repressed),* unrestricted, unwarranted, usurious
immoderately unduly
immoderateness exaggeration
immoderation debauchery, exaggeration, redundancy
immoderatus excessive, inordinate, outrageous
immodest brazen, flagrant, improper, inflated *(vain),* lascivious, lewd, obscene, orgulous, pretentious *(pompous),* promiscuous, prurient, scandalous, unabashed
immodesty obscenity, pride
immodicus excessive, exorbitant, inordinate, undue *(excessive)*
immoral bad *(offensive),* base *(bad),* brazen, decadent, delinquent *(guilty of a misdeed),* depraved, diabolic, dishonest, disreputable, dissolute, felonious, illicit, improper, inexcusable, iniquitous, irregular *(improper),* lascivious, lawless, lecherous, lewd, licentious, machiavellian, nefarious, obscene, peccant *(culpable),* profligate *(corrupt),* promiscuous, reprehensible, reprobate, salacious, scandalous, sinister, tainted *(corrupted),* tortuous *(corrupt),* unethical, unjust, unscrupulous, vicious, wanton
immoral habit vice
immoral person degenerate
immorality bad repute, delinquency *(misconduct),* guilt, misdoing, obscenity, perversion, turpitude, vice, wrong
immortal constant, durable, permanent, perpetual
immortal part spirit
immortality distinction *(reputation),* indestructibility
immortalization dedication, preservation, remembrance *(commemoration)*
immortalize dedicate, perpetuate
immotile firm
immotus immovable, static, unaffected *(uninfluenced)*
immovability inertia, objectivity, security *(safety),* tenacity
immovable dispassionate, durable, firm, fixed *(securely placed),* immutable, implacable, indelible, inexorable, inextricable, inflexible, irreconcilable, irrevocable, obdurate, pertinacious, recalcitrant, secure *(sound),* severe, stable, unbending, uncompromising, unyielding
immovables property *(possessions)*
immune clear *(free from criminal charges),* exempt
immune freehold
immune inexpugnable, insusceptible *(resistant),* privileged, tenable
immune from restriction free *(not restricted)*
immunis exempt, free *(relieved from a burden),* immune, privileged
immunitas exemption, immunity, privilege

immunitio infraction, infringement
immunity dispensation *(exception),* exclusion, exemption, franchise *(license),* impunity, privilege, protection, release, resistance, respite *(reprieve),* sanction *(permission),* security *(safety),* tolerance
immunity from assault inviolability
immunization tolerance
immunize protect
immunized immune, insusceptible *(resistant),* privileged
immuration bondage, captivity, constraint *(imprisonment),* custody *(incarceration),* detention
immure arrest *(apprehend),* capture, commit *(institutionalize),* confine, constrain *(imprison),* contain *(enclose),* detain *(hold in custody),* enclose, encompass *(surround),* imprison, jail, lock, restrain, restrict, sentence
immurement bondage, captivity, constraint *(imprisonment),* custody *(incarceration),* detention, durance, enclosure, incarceration
immuring commitment *(confinement)*
immurred arrested *(apprehended)*
immutabilis immutable, unalterable
immutability constant, indestructibility
immutable conclusive *(determinative),* constant, definite, durable, indefeasible, indelible, inexorable, inflexible, ironclad, irreconcilable, irreversible, irrevocable, obdurate, permanent, pertinacious, resolute, stable, unalterable
immutably invariably
immutare alter, change
impact collision *(accident),* connotation, contact *(touching),* content *(meaning),* effect, force *(strength),* impression, reaction *(response),* repercussion, signification, value
impacted inextricable
impair abrogate *(annul),* adulterate, aggravate *(exacerbate),* check *(restrain),* contaminate, damage, debase, debilitate, deface, denature, disable, disadvantage, disorient, endanger, eviscerate, harm, hinder, impede, infect, maim, mistreat, mutilate, pollute, prejudice *(injure),* spoil *(impair),* stain, subvert, vitiate
impair in worth debase
impair one's reputation libel
impair the force of obtund
impair the legibility of deface
impair the looks of deface
impair the reputation of discredit
impaired defective, deficient, dilapidated, disabled *(made incapable),* faulty, imperfect, inadequate, marred, tainted *(contaminated),* unsound *(not strong)*
impaired condition disrepair
impaired reputation bad repute, discredit
impairing disabling, noxious
impairment abuse *(physical misuse),* cost *(penalty),* damage, defacement, defect, deficiency, defilement, deterioration, detriment, disability *(legal disqualification),* disability *(physical inability),* disrepair, expense *(sacrifice),* fault *(weakness),* handicap, harm, injury, prejudice *(injury),* wear and tear

impairment of mental faculties lunacy
impairment of reputation libel
impalatable objectionable, obnoxious, unendurable
impale enter *(penetrate),* lancinate, penetrate, pierce *(lance)*
impalpable elusive, imponderable, inappreciable, incorporeal, indiscernible, insubstantial, intangible, minimal, obscure *(abstruse),* obscure *(faint),* vague
impar disproportionate, inadequate, insufficient, one-sided, unequal *(unequivalent)*
imparity difference, inequality
impart administer *(tender),* advise, annunciate, attorn, bear *(yield),* bestow, betray *(disclose),* cast *(throw),* communicate, concede, confer *(give),* contribute *(supply),* convey *(communicate),* convey *(transfer),* deliver, disabuse, disclose, disseminate, divulge, enlighten, express, give *(grant),* grant *(transfer formally),* inform *(betray),* inform *(notify),* instill, instruct *(teach),* leave *(give),* manifest, mention, notify, observe *(remark),* pass *(determine),* phrase, post, present *(make a gift),* produce *(offer to view),* provide *(supply),* publish, recount, relate *(tell),* render *(deliver),* report *(disclose),* reveal, signify *(inform),* transmit, utter
impart gradually instill
impart knowledge apprise
impart knowledge of notice *(give formal warning)*
impart momentum impel, incite
impart motion dispatch *(send off),* impel
impart motion to agitate *(shake up)*
impart power to empower
impart thoughts converse
impart to notice *(give formal warning)*
impartation dispensation *(act of dispensing),* donation, transmittal
imparted alleged
imparted in secret confidential
impartial discriminating *(judicious),* dispassionate, equal, equitable, even-handed, fair *(just),* honest, judicial, juridical, just, liberal *(broad minded),* neutral, nonpartisan, objective, open-minded, receptive, unbiased, unprejudiced
impartial justice equity *(justice)*
impartiality disinterest *(lack of prejudice),* fairness, honesty, justice, neutrality, objectivity, probity, rectitude
impartialness disinterest *(lack of prejudice)*
impartible contagious, indivisible, inseparable
imparting donative
imparting of skill education
imparting of thoughts conversation
impartment concession *(authorization),* delivery, dispensation *(act of dispensing),* donation, legacy
impassable difficult, impervious, impossible, impracticable, insurmountable
impasse deadlock, dilemma, draw *(tie),* halt, imbroglio, predicament, quagmire
impassible insuperable
impassion foment, incite, inspire,

spirit

impassionable sensitive *(easily affected)*

impassioned eager, earnest, eloquent, fanatical, fervent, fervid, intense, perfervid, vehement, zealous

impassionedness ardor, life *(vitality)*

impassive callous, controlled *(restrained)*, dispassionate, impervious, inexpressive, inscrutable, insusceptible *(uncaring)*, nonchalant, phlegmatic, stoical, unaffected *(uninfluenced)*, unresponsive

impassiveness indifference

impatient eager, fractious, hot-blooded, ill-judged, petulant, restive

impavidus undaunted

impeach accuse, blame, cite *(accuse)*, condemn *(blame)*, defame, denounce *(inform against)*, depose *(remove)*, disapprove *(condemn)*, discharge *(dismiss)*, except *(object)*, fault, impugn, inform *(betray)*, remove *(dismiss from office)*, reprehend, reprimand, sully

impeach falsely frame *(charge falsely)*

impeach unfairly frame *(charge falsely)*

impeach unjustly frame *(charge falsely)*

impeachability guilt

impeachable blameful, blameworthy, reprehensible, unjustifiable

impeached accused *(charged)*

impeacher accuser, complainant, informer *(one providing criminal information)*

impeachment charge *(accusation)*, condemnation *(blame)*, disparagement, incrimination, reproach

impeachment of virtue libel

impeccability rectitude

impeccable absolute *(ideal)*, best, blameless, clean, honest, incorruptible, inculpable, irreprehensible, meritorious, not guilty, unblemished, unimpeachable

impecuniosity bankruptcy, indigence, poverty, privation

impecunious bankrupt, destitute, insolvent, poor *(underprivileged)*

impecuniousness poverty, privation

impedance deterrent, offset

impede arrest *(stop)*, balk, bar *(hinder)*, bind *(restrain)*, block, check *(restrain)*, clog, condemn *(ban)*, constrain *(restrain)*, constrict *(inhibit)*, contain *(restrain)*, control *(restrain)*, counter, curb, debar, defer *(put off)*, delay, detain *(restrain)*, deter, disadvantage, discommode, disrupt, encumber *(hinder)*, enjoin, estop, fetter, fight *(counteract)*, foil, forbid, forestall, halt, hamper, hinder, hold up *(delay)*, inconvenience, inhibit, interdict, interfere, interpose, keep *(restrain)*, limit, lock, obstruct, occlude, preclude, prevent, prohibit, repulse, stall, stave, stay *(halt)*, stem *(check)*, stop, thwart, toll *(stop)*, trammel, withstand

impede the progress of delay, hold up *(delay)*

impeded arrested *(checked)*, disadvantaged, limited

impeder deterrent

impediment bar *(obstruction)*, bar-

rier, blockade *(barrier)*, burden, censorship, check *(bar)*, complication, constraint *(restriction)*, damper *(stopper)*, delay, deterrence, disadvantage, drawback, encumbrance, estoppel, fetter, filibuster, frustration, halt, handicap, hindrance, impasse, imposition *(excessive burden)*, incumbrance *(burden)*, interruption, obstacle, obstruction, onus *(burden)*, predicament, prohibition, restraint, restriction

impedimenta cargo, paraphernalia *(apparatus)*

impedimental preventive, unfavorable

impedimentary unfavorable

impedimentive unfavorable

impedimentum check *(bar)*, encumbrance, handicap, hindrance, impediment, obstacle, obstruction, restraint

impeding limiting, preventive, prohibitive *(restrictive)*

impedire clog, embarrass, encumber *(financially obligate)*, fetter, hamper, hinder, impede, incriminate, prevent

impedite balk, check *(restrain)*, clog, disadvantage, hamper, obstruct

impedition bar *(obstruction)*, check *(bar)*, damper *(stopper)*, deterrence, obstruction

impeditive preventive, restrictive

impeditus difficult, impervious, labyrinthine

impel agitate *(activate)*, bait *(harass)*, bait *(lure)*, cast *(throw)*, coax, coerce, compel, constrain *(compel)*, convince, dispatch *(send off)*, enforce, entail, exact, exhort, further, impose *(enforce)*, influence, inspire, motivate, necessitate, operate, persuade, press *(constrain)*, prevail *(persuade)*, prevail upon, prompt, provoke, send, spirit, stimulate, urge

impel forward launch *(project)*

impelled bound

impellent impetus, impulsive *(impelling)*

impeller abettor, catalyst

impellere induce, influence, urge

impelling causative, coercion, compelling, decisive, force *(compulsion)*, forcible, important *(urgent)*, insistent, moving *(evoking emotion)*, persuasive, potent, powerful, urgent

impelling force impetus, impulse

impelling power motive

impend menace, presage

impendence threat

impendency threat

impendent immediate *(imminent)*, imminent, proximate

impendere expend *(disburse)*, imminent, impend, overlap

impending close *(near)*, forthcoming, future, immediate *(imminent)*, imminent, inevitable, instant, necessary *(inescapable)*, pending *(imminent)*, prospective, proximate, unavoidable *(inevitable)*

impendium expense *(cost)*

impenetrabilis impervious

impenetrability congealment, inviolability, opacity

impenetrable callous, cohesive *(compact)*, complex, difficult, impervious, inapprehensible, incomprehensible, inde-

finable, inexplicable, inexpressive, inexpugnable, inscrutable, insurmountable, mysterious, opaque, recondite, solid *(compact)*

impenitent callous, incorrigible, recusant, relentless, remorseless

impensa cost *(price)*, expense *(cost)*, outlay

imperare order

imperative binding, canon, charge *(command)*, compelling, compulsory, critical *(crucial)*, crucial, decisive, decree, dictate, dictatorial, direction *(order)*, directive, exigent, grave *(important)*, important *(urgent)*, indispensable, injunction, insistent, mandate, mandatory, necessary *(required)*, necessity, obligatory, order *(judicial directive)*, ordinance, positive *(prescribed)*, pronouncement, requirement, requisite, subpoena, unavoidable *(inevitable)*, urgent

imperative duty allegiance, charge *(responsibility)*, responsibility *(accountability)*

imperative request demand

imperativeness exigency, pressure

imperceptibility impalpability, indistinctness, nonappearance, opacity

imperceptible blind *(concealed)*, impalpable, inappreciable, inconspicuous, indiscernible, indistinct, intangible, latent, negligible, obscure *(faint)*

imperceptive insensible, obtuse, opaque

impercipient insensible, lifeless *(dead)*, obtuse

imperdible inexpugnable, tenable

imperfect bad *(inferior)*, blemished, defective, deficient, dilapidated, errant, fallible, faulty, inchoate, incorrect, inexact, inferior *(lower in quality)*, insufficient, marred, partial *(relating to a part)*, peccable, perfunctory, poor *(inferior in quality)*, unsatisfactory, unsound *(not strong)*, vicious

imperfection defect, deficiency, disadvantage, fault *(weakness)*, flaw, foible, frailty, handicap, irregularity, vice

imperfectness disadvantage, flaw, frailty

imperfectus defective, executory, imperfect

imperforate impervious

imperial sovereign *(absolute)*

imperil compromise *(endanger)*, endanger, expose, jeopardize

imperiled aleatory *(perilous)*

imperilment danger, hazard, jeopardy, menace, peril, risk

imperiosus dictatorial, impervious

imperious dictatorial, disdainful, dogmatic, influential, insolent, oppressive, orgulous, peremptory *(absolute)*, peremptory *(imperative)*, powerful, presumptuous, proud *(conceited)*, relentless, strict, supercilious, tyrannous

imperious commandant dictator

imperious direction dictate

imperishability indestructibility

imperishable constant, durable, indefeasible, indelible, indestructible, infallible, infinite, permanent, perpetual

imperitus inexperienced, unversed

imperium direction *(order)*, dominion

(supreme authority), fiat, injunction
imperium predominance
impermanence mortality
impermanent acting, ephemeral, interim, precarious, temporary, transient, transitory
impermanent fixture stopgap
impermeability congealment
impermeable cohesive *(compact),* impervious, solid *(compact)*
impermissible illegal, illegitimate *(illegal),* illicit
impermissibly illegally
impero imperative
impersonal clinical, dispassionate, impartial, neutral, objective, unbiased
impersonality disinterest *(lack of prejudice),* objectivity
impersonally fairly *(impartially)*
impersonate assume *(simulate),* copy, feign, mock *(imitate),* pretend
impersonation artifice, part *(role),* role, sham
imperspicuity incoherence
imperspicuous allusive, equivocal, indefinite, nebulous, opaque, problematic, recondite, unclear
impersuadable impervious
impersuadible inflexible
impersuasible impervious, inflexible
impertinence contempt *(disobedience to the court),* disrespect, inconsequence
impertinency inconsequence
impertinent brazen, collateral *(immaterial),* contemptuous, extraneous, immaterial, inapplicable, inapposite, inappropriate, inconsequential, insolent, irrelative, irrelevant, obtrusive, offensive *(offending),* peripheral, presumptuous, unfit, unsuitable
impertire bestow, impart
imperturable placid
imperturbability composure, indifference
imperturbable callous, clinical, cold-blooded, controlled *(restrained),* dispassionate, impervious, inexpressive, nonchalant, patient, peaceable, phlegmatic, stoical
imperturbation composure, longanimity, sufferance
imperviable impervious
impervious callous, cold-blooded
impervious impervious
impervious inexpressive, insuperable, insusceptible *(uncaring),* obdurate, opaque, safe, torpid, unaffected *(uninfluenced)*
impervious to change durable
imperviousness resistance
impetrate call *(appeal to),* importune, pray, press *(beseech),* request
impetration call *(appeal),* dun, entreaty, request
impetuosity dispatch *(promptness),* inconsideration, outburst, passion, temerity
impetuous arbitrary and capricious, careless, disordered, impulsive *(rash),* precipitate, reckless, spontaneous, uncontrollable, unexpected, vehement, zealous
impetus assault
impetus boom *(prosperity),* catalyst, determinant
impetus force *(strength),* impulse

impetus incentive, instigation, reason *(basis),* stimulus
impietas profanity
impiety blasphemy, violation
impiger active
impignorate guarantee, pawn, pledge *(deposit)*
impinge border *(bound),* collide *(crash against),* contact *(touch),* encroach, infringe, invade, overlap, overstep
impingement collision *(accident),* encroachment
impingi impinge
impious diabolic, nefarious, offensive *(offending),* peccant *(culpable),* profane, sinister
impious utterance blasphemy
impiousness blasphemy
impishness mischief
impius profane
implacabilis implacable, irreconcilable
implacability alienation *(estrangement),* revenge, vengeance
implacable callous, cruel, immutable, inexorable, irreconcilable, malevolent, pertinacious, relentless, remorseless, resentful, ruthless, severe, unaffected *(uninfluenced),* unbending, uncompromising, unrelenting, vindictive
implacably opposed irreconcilable
implant educate, embed, enter *(insert),* fix *(make firm),* imbue, inculcate, infuse, initiate, inject, inseminate, instill, instruct *(teach),* interject, pervade, plant *(place firmly)*
implant firmly establish *(entrench)*
implantation infusion, propaganda
implanted ingrained, internal, organic, situated
implausibility improbability
implausible doubtful, incredible, ludicrous, unbelievable, untenable
implement appliance, consummate, device *(mechanism),* discharge *(perform),* dispatch *(dispose of),* empower, enable, enforce, expedient, exploit *(make use of),* facility *(instrumentality),* instrument *(tool),* instrumentality, operate, perpetrate, realize *(make real),* tool
implemental effective *(efficient),* ministerial, practical
implementation act *(undertaking),* action *(performance),* building *(business of assembling),* campaign, commission *(act),* course, discharge *(performance),* enforcement, fait accompli, finality, fruition, performance *(execution),* realization
implements paraphernalia *(apparatus)*
implere fulfill
impletion plethora
impliant unyielding
implicare hamper, implicate, incriminate
implicate accuse, arraign, blame, cite *(accuse),* complain *(charge),* condemn *(blame),* denigrate, denounce *(inform against),* impeach, incriminate, indict, inform *(betray),* present *(prefer charges)*
implicate falsely frame *(charge falsely)*
implicate oneself acknowledge *(declare)*
implicate unfairly frame *(charge*

falsely)
implicate unjustly frame *(charge falsely)*
implicated complex, incident, related
implicating incriminatory, inculpatory
implicatio complication, embarrassment, entanglement *(involvement),* involution
implication affiliation *(connectedness),* attribution, blame *(responsibility),* caveat, condemnation *(blame),* connotation, content *(meaning),* context, deduction *(conclusion),* entanglement *(involvement),* gist *(substance),* hint, incrimination, inculpation, indicant, indication, inference, innuendo, insinuation, intimation, main point, mention *(reference),* nuance, reference *(allusion),* referral, signification, suggestion
implicational allusive, circumstantial, leading *(guiding)*
implicative allusive, circumstantial, constructive *(inferential),* incriminatory, inculpatory, leading *(guiding),* suggestive *(evocative)*
implicatory circumstantial, constructive *(inferential),* incriminatory, inculpatory, leading *(guiding)*
implicit assumed *(inferred),* constructive *(inferential),* essential *(inherent),* implied, indirect, inherent, intrinsic *(belonging),* peremptory *(absolute),* tacit, virtual
implicit belief credence, faith
implicit confidence faith
implied constructive *(inferential),* implicit, subtle *(insidious),* tacit
implied assent connivance
implied consent acquiescence
implied in law constructive *(inferential)*
implied indication innuendo, reference *(allusion)*
implied rather than expressly stated implicit
implorare invoke, petition, request
imploratio prayer
imploration call *(appeal),* entreaty, prayer, request
imploratory precatory
implore call *(appeal to),* exhort, importune, invoke, petition, pray, press *(beseech),* pressure, request, solicit, sue, urge
imploring precatory
imply allude, bear *(adduce),* bespeak, connote, denote, evidence, hint, indicate, infer, purport, signify *(denote)*
impolicy misrule
impolite disorderly, impertinent *(insolent),* insolent, perverse, presumptuous, uncouth
impoliteness disregard *(lack of respect),* disrespect
impolitic detrimental, disadvantageous, ill-advised, imprudent, inadvisable, inappropriate, inapt, inept *(inappropriate),* injudicious, misadvised, unpolitic
impolitical injudicious
impoliticness indiscretion
imponderable intangible
imponderous imponderable
imponere impose *(enforce),* inflict
imporous impervious

import allude, amount *(result)*, bespeak, connotation, consequence *(significance)*, content *(meaning)*, context, corpus, degree *(magnitude)*, gist *(substance)*, implication *(inference)*, importance, interest *(concern)*, magnitude, main point, materiality *(consequence)*, meaning, point *(purpose)*, prestige, significance, signification, stress *(accent)*, substance *(essential nature)*, tenor, weight *(importance)*

importance authority *(power)*, caliber *(quality)*, clout, concern *(interest)*, consequence *(significance)*, corpus, degree *(magnitude)*, distinction *(reputation)*, dominance, eminence, emphasis, force *(strength)*, hegemony, import, influence, interest *(concern)*, magnitude, materiality *(consequence)*, power, precedence, prestige, primacy, priority, relevance, reputation, significance, signification, status, stress *(accent)*, supremacy, value, worth

important consequential *(substantial)*, considerable, constructive *(creative)*, critical *(crucial)*, crucial, decisive, determinative, essential *(required)*, exigent, famous, germane, illustrious, indispensable, influential, key, major, momentous, necessary *(required)*, notable, noteworthy, outstanding *(prominent)*, peremptory *(imperative)*, potent, powerful, predominant, primary, prime *(most valuable)*, prominent, relevant, remarkable, renowned, requisite, salient, serious *(grave)*, special, strategic, substantial, substantive, unusual, urgent, valuable, vital

important event highlight
important feature main point
important part center *(essence)*, main point
important point gist *(ground for a suit)*, main point
important station eminence
importation inflow
imported alien *(foreign)*
importunate important *(urgent)*, insistent, obligatory, precatory, urgent
importunateness pressure
importune annoy, badger, bait *(harass)*, bait *(lure)*, cajole, call *(appeal to)*, dun, exhort, harry *(harass)*, insist, inveigle, persuade, plead *(implore)*, pray, press *(beseech)*, prevail upon, request, solicit, urge
importunitas intrusion
importunity call *(appeal)*, dun, entreaty, prayer, request
impose bind *(obligate)*, charge *(assess)*, coerce, command, compel, constrain *(compel)*, decree, demand, detail *(assign)*, encumber *(hinder)*, enforce, enjoin, exact, foist, force *(coerce)*, impinge, impose *(intrude)*, inflict, infringe, insist, intrude, levy, necessitate, obtrude, order, perpetrate, prescribe, press *(constrain)*, require *(compel)*
impose a ban censor, enjoin, exclude
impose a charge assess *(tax)*, encumber *(financially obligate)*
impose a duty compel, constrain *(compel)*, delegate, enjoin, exact, instruct *(direct)*, order
impose a duty on excise *(levy a tax)*
impose a fine mulct *(fine)*

impose a forfeiture fine
impose a levy assess *(tax)*
impose a lien encumber *(financially obligate)*
impose a mulct fine
impose a penalty condemn *(punish)*, demote, discipline *(punish)*, fine, penalize
impose a penalty on convict
impose a task enjoin, instruct *(direct)*, order
impose a tax exact
impose an order dictate
impose by fraud foist
impose difficulties discourage
impose hardship inconvenience
impose payment for misconduct fine
impose pecuniary punishment fine
impose penalty condemn *(punish)*, sentence
impose punishment inflict
impose restraint fetter
impose restrictions coerce, constrain *(restrain)*
impose upon accroach, discommode, mishandle *(maltreat)*
impose with authority enjoin
imposed indispensable, necessary *(required)*, obligatory, positive *(prescribed)*
imposed upon aggrieved *(victimized)*
imposing critical *(crucial)*, important *(significant)*, major, moving *(evoking emotion)*, outstanding *(prominent)*, prominent, proud *(self-respecting)*, remarkable, salient, solemn, special
imposing a condition conditional, dependent
imposing building edifice
imposition ad valorem, assessment *(levy)*, burden, canon, charge *(command)*, compulsion *(coercion)*, conviction *(finding of guilt)*, deception, demand, disadvantage, duty *(tax)*, encroachment, encumbrance, enforcement, excise, fiat, force *(compulsion)*, forgery, hoax, incumbrance *(lien)*, infliction, injustice, intrusion, misjudgment, nuisance, requirement, sanction *(punishment)*, tax
imposition of veil of secrecy censorship
impossibility impasse, improbability
impossible impracticable, incredible, infeasible, insufferable, insuperable, insurmountable, intolerable, ludicrous, prohibitive *(restrictive)*, unacceptable, unattainable, unendurable
impossible task impasse
impossible to alter ironclad
impossible to better irremediable
impossible to break ironclad
impossible to calculate imponderable
impossible to change ironclad, irreversible, irrevocable
impossible to defeat invincible
impossible to describe ineffable
impossible to explain indefinable
impossible to express ineffable
impossible to influence obdurate
impossible to measure imponderable
impossible to overcome irresistible
impossible to reach inaccessible
impossible to resist irresistible
impossible to reverse irreversible

impossible to stop perpetual
impossible to translate indefinable
impossible to understand inapprehensible, incomprehensible, indefinable, inscrutable
impossible to vanquish invincible
impossible to weigh imponderable
impossible to withstand irresistible
impossibleness impossibility
impost assessment *(levy)*, duty *(tax)*, excise, excise *(levy a tax)*, levy, tariff *(duties)*, tax, toll *(tax)*
imposter fake
impostor sham
impostrous deceptive
imposture artifice, deception, false pretense, falsification, forgery, hoax, hypocrisy, ruse, sham, subterfuge
impotence desuetude, detriment, disability *(physical inability)*, fault *(weakness)*, frailty, impuissance, inability, inaction, incapacity, inefficacy, languor, prostration
impotency defect, disability *(physical inability)*, impotence
impotens powerless, uncontrollable
impotent barren, devoid, disabled *(deprived of legal right)*, disabled *(made incapable)*, expendable, harmless, helpless *(powerless)*, inadept, inadequate, ineffective, ineffectual, inept *(incompetent)*, insipid, languid, null *(invalid)*, null and void, otiose, powerless, unable, unavailing, unproductive
impound annex *(arrogate)*, attach *(seize)*, commit *(institutionalize)*, condemn *(seize)*, confine, confiscate, constrain *(imprison)*, contain *(restrain)*, deprive, detain *(hold in custody)*, distrain, enclose, garnish, immure, impress *(procure by force)*, jail, lock, restrain, seize *(confiscate)*, sequester *(seize property)*
impoundage attachment *(seizure)*, distraint, distress *(seizure)*, sequestration, taking
impounded attached *(seized)*
impounding condemnation *(seizure)*, confiscatory
impoundment appropriation *(taking)*, attachment *(seizure)*, bondage, captivity, commitment *(confinement)*, constraint *(imprisonment)*, custody *(incarceration)*, detention, distraint, distress *(seizure)*, enclosure, garnishment, incarceration, sequestration, taking
impoverish deplete, depreciate, deprive, despoil, plunder, spend
impoverished bankrupt, deficient, destitute, impecunious, insolvent, penurious, poor *(underprivileged)*
impoverishment dearth, indigence, poverty
impower delegate
impracticability impossibility
impracticable impossible, infeasible, insuperable, insurmountable, otiose, quixotic, unattainable
impractical hot-blooded, impracticable, otiose, quixotic, speculative, theoretical, unattainable
impracticality impossibility
imprecation contempt *(disdain)*, expletive, malediction, slander
imprecation of evil blasphemy
imprecative calumnious, profane
imprecatory calumnious, profane

imprecise approximate, equivocal, faulty, inaccurate, incorrect, indefinite, inexact, lax, liberal *(not literal)*, slipshod, vague

imprecise statement generalization

imprecision generality *(vague statement)*, laxity, misstatement

impregnability incontestability, inviolability, security *(safety)*, strength

impregnable defensible, immune, inappealable, incontestable, indomitable, inexpugnable, insuperable, insurmountable, powerful, safe, secure *(free from danger)*, tenable, unapproachable

impregnate infuse, inject, inseminate, penetrate, permeate, pervade, plant *(place firmly)*

impregnation infusion

imprescriptible indefeasible, unalienable

impress abduct, affect, attach *(seize)*, brand, brand *(mark)*, capture, coerce, confiscate, convince, copy, distrain, distress *(seizure)*, dwell *(linger over)*, embed, hijack, hold up *(rob)*, inculcate, induct, influence, kidnap, overwhelm, persuade, reach, seize *(confiscate)*, sequester *(seize property)*, specialty *(distinctive mark)*, stamp

impress by repeated statement inculcate

impress on insist

impress upon the memory instruct *(teach)*, retain *(keep in possession)*

impress upon the mind discipline *(train)*, imbue, inculcate, instill, instruct *(teach)*

impress with mark seal *(solemnize)*

impressed with oneself inflated *(vain)*

impressibility credulity, sensibility

impressible open *(persuasible)*, perceptive, pliant, receptive, sensitive *(easily affected)*, sequacious, susceptible *(responsive)*, yielding

impression apprehension *(perception)*, assumption *(supposition)*, color *(deceptive appearance)*, complexion, concept, conviction *(persuasion)*, copy, estimate *(idea)*, fingerprints, idea, inference, notion, opinion *(belief)*, pattern, perception, perspective, reaction *(response)*, reflection *(image)*, sense *(feeling)*, stamp, suspicion *(uncertainty)*

impression of fingers fingerprints

impressionable amenable, facile, malleable, open *(persuasible)*, perceptive, pliable, pliant, receptive, sensitive *(easily affected)*, sequacious, susceptible *(responsive)*, tractable, yielding

impressive considerable, eloquent, forcible, important *(significant)*, influential, major, momentous, moving *(evoking emotion)*, notable, noteworthy, outstanding *(prominent)*, persuasive, potent, prodigious *(amazing)*, profound *(intense)*, proud *(self-respecting)*, remarkable, sapid, solemn, stellar

impressive effect pretense *(ostentation)*

impressiveness emphasis, solemnity, weight *(credibility)*, weight *(importance)*

impressment abduction, attachment *(seizure)*, compulsion *(coercion)*, distress *(seizure)*, duress, force *(compulsion)*, levy, sequestration

imprest loan

imprimatur charter *(license)*, leave *(permission)*, license

imprint brand, brand *(mark)*, caption, copy, embed, fingerprints, impression, inculcate, inscribe, label, seal *(solemnize)*, stamp, trademark

imprison arrest *(apprehend)*, capture, commit *(institutionalize)*, confine, contain *(restrain)*, detain *(hold in custody)*, enclose, immure, jail, lock, restrain, seclude, seize *(apprehend)*, sentence, transport

imprison again remand

imprisoned arrested *(apprehended)*, in custody

imprisoned person captive

imprisonment apprehension *(act of arresting)*, arrest, bondage, captivity, commitment *(confinement)*, custody *(incarceration)*, detention, enclosure, fetter, incarceration, restraint

improbability doubt *(indecision)*, doubt *(suspicion)*

improbable disputable, doubtful, implausible, impossible, incredible, unbelievable, unforeseeable, unsound *(fallacious)*

improbare impugn

improbatio disapproval

improbation bad repute, exception *(objection)*, reprimand

improbitas dishonesty

improbity attaint, bad faith, bad repute, bribery, contempt *(disobedience to the court)*, corruption, culpability, delinquency *(misconduct)*, dishonesty, dishonor *(nonpayment)*, dishonor *(shame)*, disloyalty, fraud, guilt, hypocrisy, indirection *(deceitfulness)*, injustice, misdemeanor, misdoing, racket, wrong

improbus bad *(offensive)*, dishonest, incorrect, iniquitous

improficient incompetent, libelous

impromptu impulsive *(rash)*, spontaneous, unexpected, unpremeditated

improper bad *(offensive)*, blatant *(obtrusive)*, culpable, delinquent *(guilty of a misdeed)*, disgraceful, disorderly, disreputable, drastic, false *(inaccurate)*, faulty, illegal, illegitimate *(illegal)*, illicit, immoral, impertinent *(insolent)*, inaccurate, inadmissible, inapplicable, inapposite, inappropriate, inapt, incongruous, incorrect, inelegant, ineligible, inept *(inappropriate)*, iniquitous, lascivious, nefarious, objectionable, perverse, profane, slipshod, suggestive *(risqué)*, unauthorized, unbecoming, undesirable, undue *(excessive)*, unfit, unjust, unprofessional, unseemly, unsuitable, untimely, unwarranted, vicious, wrongful

improper act tortious act

improper action impropriety, misfeasance

improper behavior impropriety, misdeed

improper conduct guilt, misconduct

improper jurisdiction want of jurisdiction

improper performance misfeasance

improper professional action malpractice

improper professional conduct malpractice

improper rate of interest usurious

improper usage abuse *(corrupt practice)*, misusage, misuse

improper use abuse *(corrupt practice)*, misapplication, misusage, misuse

improperly illegally

improperly proportioned disproportionate

improperness ill repute, irregularity

impropriate condemn *(seize)*, hold *(possess)*, impress *(procure by force)*, preempt

impropriation appropriation *(taking)*, arrogation, assignment *(transfer of ownership)*, assumption *(seizure)*, condemnation *(seizure)*, disseisin, distress *(seizure)*

impropriety bad repute, breach, delinquency *(misconduct)*, fault *(mistake)*, ill repute, illegality, incongruity, indecency, misapplication, misconduct, miscue, misdeed, misdemeanor, misdoing, misusage, obscenity, offense

improvable corrigible

improve accrue *(increase)*, ameliorate, amend, appreciate *(increase)*, cultivate, cure, develop, edify, edit, elevate, embellish, emend, enhance, fix *(repair)*, gain, heighten *(augment)*, help, inure *(benefit)*, meliorate, modify *(alter)*, mollify, nurture, profit, progress, rectify, redress, reform, rehabilitate, relieve *(give aid)*, remedy, renew *(refurbish)*, renovate, repair, restore *(renew)*, revise, supplement, treat *(remedy)*

improve upon elaborate, fix *(repair)*, modify *(alter)*, surpass

improved relations rapprochement, reconciliation

improved version correction *(change)*, revision *(corrected version)*

improvement advance *(increase)*, advantage, amendment *(correction)*, augmentation, behalf, benefit *(betterment)*, boom *(increase)*, boom *(prosperity)*, correction *(change)*, development *(progression)*, edification, growth *(evolution)*, headway, panacea, profit, progress, promotion *(advancement)*, reform, rehabilitation, renewal, reorganization, repair, revision *(corrected version)*, revival

improvement of the mind education

improvement-minded progressive *(advocating change)*

improvidence disregard *(unconcern)*, inconsideration, laches, laxity, neglect, negligence, temerity, waste

improvident careless, derelict *(negligent)*, heedless, imprudent, injudicious, lax, negligent, prodigal, profligate *(extravagant)*, profuse, reckless, remiss, thoughtless, unpolitic

improvidus improvident

improving beneficial, constructive *(creative)*

improvisate unpremeditated

improvisation invention

improvisatorial spontaneous

improvise compose, conjure, contrive, create, devise *(invent)*, invent *(produce for the first time)*, make, originate, scheme

improvised ad hoc, impulsive *(rash)*, spontaneous, unpremeditated

improvisus unanticipated

imprudence disregard *(unconcern)*,

impropriety, inconsideration, indiscretion, inexpedience, neglect, negligence, res ipsa loquitur, temerity

imprudens impolitic, improvident, inadvertent, thoughtless

imprudent careless, heedless, hot-blooded, ill-advised, ill-judged, impolitic, improvident, impulsive *(rash)*, inadvisable, inept *(inappropriate)*, injudicious, irrational, lax, misadvised, negligent, precipitate, prodigal, reckless, remiss, thoughtless, unpolitic, unprofessional, unsuitable, untimely

imprudentia ignorance

impudence contempt *(disobedience to the court)*, defiance, disregard *(lack of respect)*, disrespect, temerity

impudency defiance

impudens brazen, flagrant, insolent, unabashed

impudent brazen, contemptuous, impertinent *(insolent)*, insolent, offensive *(offending)*, perverse, presumptuous

impudentia indiscretion

impudicity debauchery

impudicus lewd, licentious, wanton

impugn answer *(reply)*, attack, bear false witness, blame, brand *(stigmatize)*, censure, condemn *(blame)*, contend *(dispute)*, contest, contradict, contravene, criticize *(find fault with)*, demonstrate *(protest)*, denounce *(condemn)*, deprecate, disaccord, disaffirm, disallow, disapprove *(condemn)*, disown *(deny the validity)*, dispute *(contest)*, doubt *(distrust)*, except *(object)*, fault, gainsay, impeach, inveigh, lash *(attack verbally)*, malign, negate, protest, refute, reject, reprehend, reprimand, resist *(oppose)*, sully

impugnare impugn

impugnation bad repute, belligerency, contest *(dispute)*, controversy *(argument)*, disparagement, dispute, exception *(objection)*, opposition

impugning negative

impugnment belligerency, contest *(dispute)*, impugnation, opposition, vilification

impuissance fault *(weakness)*, impotence, inability, incapacity

impuissant incapable, null *(insignificant)*, powerless

impulse catalyst, cause *(reason)*, desire, impetus, incentive, motive, passion, stimulus

impulsio impulse

impulsion impetus, impulse, incentive, instigation, provocation

impulsive careless, heedless, improvident, imprudent, precipitate, reckless, spontaneous, thoughtless, unexpected, unpremeditated, vehement

impulsiveness inconsideration

impulsus impulse

impunitas impunity

impunity condonation, tolerance

impure bad *(inferior)*, blemished, disreputable, dissolute, immoral, lewd, licentious, marred, obscene, profane, prurient, salacious, tainted *(contaminated)*, vicious

impure air air pollution

impurity vice

impurus lascivious, lewd

imputable blameful, guilty

imputation accusation, allegation, aspersion, assignation, attaint, attribution, blame *(responsibility)*, charge *(accusation)*, condemnation *(blame)*, conjecture, count, criticism, defamation, disapprobation, discredit, disgrace, dishonor *(shame)*, disparagement, ignominy, incrimination, inculpation, innuendo, notoriety, onus *(stigma)*, opprobrium, presentment, reference *(allusion)*, scandal, stigma

imputation from criminal proceeding arraignment

imputation of blame accusation

imputation of dereliction impeachment

imputation of fault impeachment

imputation of wrongdoing incrimination

imputative calumnious, incriminatory, inculpatory

impute ascribe, attribute, charge *(accuse)*, cite *(accuse)*, complain *(charge)*, denounce *(inform against)*, fault, implicate, present *(prefer charges)*

impute fault to impeach

impute guilt to incriminate

impute shame to discredit, disgrace, pillory

impute to blame

imputed accused *(attacked)*, alleged

imputing blame incriminatory, inculpatory

in herein

in a body en banc

in a certain sense quasi

in a different class peculiar *(distinctive)*

in a dilemma doubtful

in a fair manner fairly *(impartially)*

in a huff resentful

in a line consecutive

in a manner quasi

in a mass en banc

in a quandary doubtful

in a row consecutive

in a state of action active

in a state of uncertainty contingent, indeterminate, pending *(unresolved)*, provisional

in abeyance back *(in arrears)*, dormant, pending *(unresolved)*

in accord commensurate, concerted, concordant, concurrent *(united)*, congruous, consenting, consonant, contractual

in accord with pursuant to

in accord with ethics ethical

in accordance therefore consequently

in accordance with apposite, concerted, congruous, contractual, in strict conformity, pursuant to

in accordance with conventional requirements formal

in accordance with duty right *(correct)*

in accordance with justice right *(correct)*

in accordance with law de jure, legitimate *(rightful)*

in accordance with legal provisions legitimate *(rightful)*

in accordance with morality right *(correct)*

in accordance with the contract as

agreed upon

in accordance with the law juridical, lawful, licit

in accordance with the ordinance de jure

in accordance with the rules for right conduct ethical

in accordance with the standards of a profession ethical

in accordance with the statute de jure

in accordance with truth right *(correct)*

in action effective *(operative)*, functional, operative

in actual process active

in addition also, ancillary *(auxiliary)*, further

in advance vanward

in agreement commensurate, concerted, concordant, concurrent *(united)*, consensual, consenting, consonant, synergetic

in album register

in alienum fundum ingredi trespass

in all in toto

in all cases invariably

in all likelihood high probability

in all respects in toto, purely *(positively)*, wholly

in alliance concerted, conjoint, consensual

in any case notwithstanding, regardless

in any event notwithstanding, regardless

in arms armed

in arrears deficient, delinquent *(overdue)*, due *(owed)*, indebted, insolvent, outstanding *(unpaid)*, overdue, past due, receivable, unpaid

in assembly en masse

in attendance present *(attendant)*

in authority ex officio

in bad taste inappropriate, inelegant, unbecoming, unseemly, unsuitable

in behalf of one party ex parte

in being extant

in black and white holographic, in writing

in bold relief clear *(apparent)*, conspicuous, manifest, perceptible

in carcerem imprison, jail

in chaos disordered

in character typical

in charge ex officio

in check controlled *(restrained)*

in chief a fortiori

in close proximity close *(near)*, contiguous, proximate

in clover prosperous

in cogitatione defixus pensive

in common conjoint, mutual *(collective)*

in common boundaries with contiguous

in common with cognate

in company with along

in compensation compensatory

in competition competitive *(antagonistic)*

in concert concordant, simultaneous

in conclusion consequently

in concord consonant, synergetic

in conflict dissenting

in conflict with contra (adverb), con-

tra (preposition)
in conformity contractual
in conformity to the law juridical, lawful
in conformity with law legal
in conjunction concordant, conjoint
in conjunction with along, apposite
in connection with comparative, incident
in consequence a priori
in consequence of thereby
in consideration of ad hoc
in consonance pari materia
in contact contiguous
in contemplation at issue
in contrast to contra
in control ex officio
in correspondence with the contract as agreed upon
in current use extant
in custodiam imprison, jail
in custodiam dare arrest *(apprehend)*
in custody guarded
in danger helpless *(defenseless)*, liable, susceptible *(unresistent)*
in darkness blind *(sightless)*
in debt indebted, past due
in decadence decadent
in decline decadent
in default insufficient, past due
in default of devoid
in defiance of the law lawless
in demand important *(urgent)*, popular, requisite, valuable
in despair despondent, disconsolate
in disagreement different, discordant, dissenting
in disarray disjointed, disordered
in discrimen endanger
in disgrace disreputable
in disguise evasive
in disorder anomalous, deranged, disjointed
in dispute arguable, at issue, controversial, debatable, disputable, doubtful, dubious, litigable, moot
in distress penurious, poor *(underprivileged)*
in doubt disputable, doubtful, dubious, dubitative, indefinite, indeterminate, leery
in dubio esse abeyance
in due form pro forma
in easy circumstances prosperous
in effect constructive *(inferential)*, effective *(operative)*, operative
in embarrassed circumstances poor *(underprivileged)*
in equal shares pro rata
in equilibrium coextensive
in error at fault, culpable, delinquent *(guilty of a misdeed)*, fallacious, false *(inaccurate)*, guilty, misadvised
in errorem inducere mislead
in errorum inducere misguide
in escrow bailment, in trust
in essence constructive *(inferential)*
in essence is consist
in established usage conventional, customary
in every instance invariably
in every respect faithfully
in evidence clear *(apparent)*, coherent *(clear)*, conspicuous, evident, manifest, obvious, palpable, perceivable, perceptible

in exact agreement commensurate
in existence conscious *(awake)*, corporeal, de facto, extant
in fact actual, de facto
in fashion current
in fault blameworthy, delinquent *(guilty of a misdeed)*
in favor popular
in favor of in furtherance
in focus manifest, visible *(in full view)*
in force effective *(operative)*, operative
in front vanward
in full in toto
in full effect in full force
in full force undiminished
in full view distinct *(clear)*, evident, manifest, open *(in sight)*, overt, patent, perceivable, perceptible, visible *(in full view)*
in genera describere classify
in general as a rule, generally
in good faith bona fide, faithfully
in good financial condition solvent
in good order intact
in good spirits sanguine
in good taste elegant
in good time in due course
in harmony concordant, consonant, pari materia
in harmony with congruous, consenting, pursuant to
in harness operative, ready *(prepared)*
in heavy spirits disconsolate
in high dudgeon resentful
in high esteem popular
in high favor popular
in hysterics disordered
in installments in part, piecemeal
in issue debatable, disputable, moot
in its entirety in toto
in its infancy ab initio, inchoate
in its present condition as is
in its present form as is
in its present state as is
in iudicium venire appear *(attend court proceedings)*
in ius vocare implead
in keeping fit
in keeping with in strict conformity
in league conjoint
in line with in strict conformity
in loco apposite
in longhand holographic
in margine positus marginal
in margine scriptus marginal
in mass en masse
in memory of honorary
in most cases as a rule, generally
in most instances high probability
in name only nominal, purported, quasi
in narrow circumstances poor *(underprivileged)*
in nature is consist
in need impecunious, penurious, poor *(underprivileged)*
in obedience to the agreement as agreed upon
in obedience with in strict conformity
in office ex officio
in one piece intact
in one's last moments in extremis

in one's own person in person
in operation active, effective *(operative)*, functional, operative
in opposition hostile
in opposition to contra, contra, contrary
in order consecutive, functional, ready *(prepared)*, systematic
in partnership common *(shared)*
in passage en route
in penury poor *(underprivileged)*
in perfect condition intact
in periculum endanger, jeopardize
in perpetuum ratus indefeasible
in pinched circumstances poor *(underprivileged)*
in place felicitous, fit
in place of in lieu of
in place of a parent loco parentis
in plain sight conspicuous, overt, perceivable, perceptible, visible *(in full view)*
in plain view naked *(perceptible)*
in play operative
in point congruous, exemplary
in point of fact de facto
in position ready *(prepared)*
in posse colorable *(plausible)*
in practice active, constructive *(inferential)*
in print holographic
in prison in custody
in process instant
in profusion copious
in progress en route
in proportion pro rata
in proportion to comparative
in prospect prospective
in question aleatory *(uncertain)*, arguable, at issue, controversial, debatable, disputable, doubtful, dubious, moot, pending *(unresolved)*
in rapport concordant, congruous, consonant
in re commorari dwell *(linger over)*
in re connivere connive
in re stare adhere *(persist)*
in re versari occupy *(engage)*
in readiness ready *(prepared)*
in reality de facto
in receivership bankrupt
in reduced circumstances poor *(underprivileged)*
in regard to which wherein
in regular order consecutive
in relation to comparative, incident
in relation with apposite, comparative
in residence household *(domestic)*
in respect to comparative
in safety secure *(free from danger)*
in se recipere undertake
in sequence consecutive
in set form pro forma
in sight apparent *(perceptible)*, discernible, evident, manifest, perceivable, perceptible, visible *(in full view)*
in small amount remote *(small)*
in small doses piecemeal
in small quantities piecemeal
in solitude alone *(solitary)*
in some measure in part
in spite of irrespective, notwithstanding, regardless
in store forthcoming, imminent, inevitable, prospective

in straitened circumstances impecunious, poor *(underprivileged)*
in strict compliance with in strict conformity
in strong relief clear *(apparent)*
in style current
in substance is consist
in sum en banc
in suspense dormant, doubtful, outstanding *(unresolved)*
in tabulas referre record
in tempus provisional
in that case consequently
in that event consequently
in the absence of devoid
in the aggregate en masse, in toto, wholly
in the area close *(near)*
in the background clandestine
in the beginning ab initio
in the blood born *(innate)*
in the clear clean
in the company of present *(attendant)*
in the course of ad interim, throughout *(during)*
in the eyes of the law de jure
in the fad current
in the field of public debate forensic
in the final moments of life in extremis
in the first place ab initio
in the foreground conspicuous, manifest
in the general time frame on or about
in the habit addicted
in the habit of accustomed *(familiarized)*
in the hands of receivers bankrupt
in the immediate vicinity of on or about
in the interest of one party ex parte
in the interim ad interim
in the intervening time ad interim
in the jaws of death in extremis
in the lead vanward
in the limelight famous
in the long run in due course
in the main a fortiori, as a rule, generally, wholly
in the market commercial
in the mass wholly
in the meantime ad interim
in the meanwhile ad interim
in the middle of among
in the name of in furtherance
in the neighborhood close *(near)*
in the neighborhood of on or about
in the offing immediate *(imminent)*, imminent, inevitable
in the opposite scale contradictory
in the past heretofore
in the power of inferior *(lower in position)*
in the presence of present *(attendant)*
in the public eye famous
in the red impecunious
in the same category cognate, comparative
in the same way as is
in the same words verbatim
in the service of in furtherance
in the spotlight famous

in the usual course of things as a rule, generally
in the vicinity close *(near)*, present *(attendant)*
in the vicinity of approximate
in the whole in toto
in the wind imminent
in the wrong blameful, blameworthy, culpable, delinquent *(guilty of a misdeed)*, guilty
in the wrong place anomalous
in time in due course
in toto en banc
in toto wholly
in transit en route
in tribute honorary
in truth purely *(positively)*
in turn consecutive, respectively
in two bipartite
in unbroken sequence consecutive
in uninterrupted succession consecutive
in unison concerted, concordant, concurrent *(united)*, consonant
in unison with congruous
in unum vergere converge
in view apparent *(perceptible)*, conspicuous, evident, immediate *(imminent)*, imminent, manifest, obvious, patent, perceivable, perceptible, present *(attendant)*, present *(current)*, prospective, visible *(in full view)*
in violation of deviant
in violation of law felonious, illegally
in vogue current, popular, prevailing *(current)*
in want impecunious, penurious, poor *(underprivileged)*
in want of devoid
in which case consequently
in whole in solido
in working order ready *(prepared)*
in writing documentary, holographic
in-depth analysis proposal *(report)*, trial *(experiment)*
inability abortion *(fiasco)*, disability *(physical inability)*, disqualification *(factor that disqualifies)*, failure *(falling short)*, impairment *(drawback)*, impotence, impuissance, incapacity, inefficacy
inability of performance frustration
inability to accept incredulity
inability to act inertia, insentience
inability to be completed frustration
inability to believe incredulity
inability to decide doubt *(indecision)*, indecision
inability to doubt certainty
inability to maintain solvency failure *(bankruptcy)*
inability to meet financial obligations failure *(bankruptcy)*
inability to pay bankruptcy, delinquency *(shortage)*, dishonor *(nonpayment)*
inability to perceive insentience
inability to wait dispatch *(promptness)*, haste
inability to work disability *(physical inability)*
inabstinence indulgence
inabstinent gluttonous, inordinate, intemperate
inaccessibility impossibility, unavail-

ability
inaccessible immune, impervious, impossible, infeasible, insuperable, insurmountable, private *(secluded)*, remote *(secluded)*, unapproachable, unattainable
inaccessus inaccessible
inaccordance controversy *(argument)*, difference, discrepancy
inaccordant discordant, dissident, inapposite, inapt, incommensurate, incongruous, inept *(inappropriate)*, repugnant *(incompatible)*
inaccuracy error, exaggeration, fallacy, falsehood, fault *(mistake)*, figment, laxity, misestimation, misjudgment, misrepresentation, misstatement, story *(falsehood)*
inaccurate erroneous, fallacious, faulty, ill-founded, improper, incorrect, inexact, lax, slipshod, untrue
inaccurateness misestimation, misjudgment
inacquiescent dissident, hostile, nonconsenting, reluctant
inaction abeyance, abstention, cessation *(interlude)*, desuetude, inertia, insentience, languor, neglect, sloth
inactivate disable
inactive barren, dead, defunct, dormant, idle, indolent, insipid, languid, lifeless *(dull)*, otiose, powerless, stagnant, static, torpid, unemployed
inactivity abeyance, cessation *(interlude)*, desuetude, halt, inertia, insentience, languor, leave *(absence)*, lull, nonperformance, sloth
inadept inept *(incompetent)*
inadequacy absence *(omission)*, dearth, defect, deficiency, deficit, delinquency *(shortage)*, detriment, disability *(physical inability)*, disadvantage, disqualification *(factor that disqualifies)*, fault *(weakness)*, frailty, impotence, inability, incapacity, incompetence, inefficacy, insufficiency, invalidity, need *(deprivation)*, paucity, vice
inadequate defective, deficient, faulty, imperfect, incapable, incompetent, ineffective, ineffectual, inept *(incompetent)*, inferior *(lower in quality)*, insubstantial, insufficient, invalid, nonsubstantial *(not sturdy)*, nonsubstantial *(not sufficient)*, nugatory, paltry, peccable, perfunctory, poor *(inferior in quality)*, powerless, puerile, scarce, unable, unavailing, unfit, unqualified *(not competent)*, unsatisfactory, unsuitable, vacuous
inadequate final work noncompliance *(improper completion)*
inadequateness dearth, deficiency, insufficiency
inadfectatus unpretentious
inadmissable unacceptable
inadmissibility disqualification *(rejection)*
inadmissible impertinent *(irrelevant)*, improper, inapplicable, inapposite, inappropriate, inapt, ineligible, inept *(inappropriate)*, unsuitable
inadvertence contingency, inconsideration, laxity, miscue, neglect, negligence, omission, quirk *(accident)*
inadvertency inconsideration, laxity, miscue, negligence, oversight *(careless-*

ness)

inadvertent blind *(not discerning)*, careless, lax, negligent, thoughtless, unintentional, unwitting

inadvertently unknowingly

inadvisability detriment, inexpedience

inadvisable disadvantageous, ill-advised, impolitic, imprudent, inapt, inauspicious, inept *(inappropriate)*, inopportune, misadvised, objectionable, undesirable, unfavorable, unfit, unsuitable

inaequabilis irregular *(not usual)*

inaequalis disproportionate, one-sided, unequal *(unequivalent)*

inaequalitas inequality

inaestimabilis inestimable, invaluable, priceless

inaffable offensive *(offending)*, perverse, unapproachable

inalienable absolute *(conclusive)*, indefeasible, rightful, unalienable

inalienable interest right *(entitlement)*

inalienable right prerogative, prescription *(claim of title)*

inalterable certain *(positive)*, constant, unalterable

inane barren, fatuous, ludicrous, nugatory, puerile, superficial, thoughtless, trivial, vacuous

inanimate inactive, insensible, lifeless *(dead)*, torpid

inanimateness insentience

inanimation desuetude, insentience

inanis frivolous, futile, void *(empty)*

inanitas nullity

inanity bombast, jargon *(unintelligible language)*, platitude

inappealable certain *(positive)*, definite, incontestable, incontrovertible, irrefutable, positive *(incontestable)*, undeniable, unequivocal, unrefutable

inappetance disinterest *(lack of interest)*

inappetancy disinterest *(lack of interest)*

inapplicability incongruity, inconsequence, inconsistency

inapplicable collateral *(immaterial)*, disproportionate, expendable, extraneous, immaterial, impertinent *(irrelevant)*, impracticable, improper, inadmissible, inapposite, inappropriate, inapt, incongruous, inconsequential, inept *(inappropriate)*, irrelative, irrelevant, unfit, unsuitable

inapposite disproportionate, extraneous, gratuitous *(unwarranted)*, impertinent *(irrelevant)*, improper, inadmissible, inapplicable, inappropriate, inapt, incongruous, inept *(inappropriate)*, irrelative, irrelevant, unbecoming, unessential, unfit, unsuitable, untimely

inappositeness inconsequence

inappreciability impalpability

inappreciable immaterial, impalpable, inconsequential, inconsiderable, intangible, marginal, minimal, minor, negligible, null *(insignificant)*, petty, remote *(small)*, slight, trivial

inappreciation disregard *(lack of respect)*, ingratitude

inapprehensibility incoherence, opacity

inapprehensible impalpable, incomprehensible, inexplicable, inscrutable

inapproachable inaccessible

inappropos irrelevant

inappropriate alien *(unrelated)*, collateral *(immaterial)*, detrimental, disproportionate, gratuitous *(unwarranted)*, ill-advised, immaterial, impertinent *(irrelevant)*, improper, inadmissible, inadvisable, inapplicable, inapposite, inapt, incongruous, inconsequential, incorrect, ineligible, injudicious, inopportune, irrelevant, objectionable, unacceptable, unauthorized, unbecoming, undesirable, undue *(excessive)*, unfavorable, unfit, unprofessional, unsatisfactory, unseemly, unsuitable, untimely

inappropriate behavior impropriety

inappropriately timed untimely

inappropriateness impropriety, incongruity, inconsistency, inexpedience

inapropos impertinent *(irrelevant)*

inapt improper, inapplicable, inapposite, inappropriate, ineligible, inept *(inappropriate)*, inept *(incompetent)*, inexperienced, irrelevant, nugatory, powerless, unfit, unsatisfactory, unsuitable

inaptitude disadvantage, disqualification *(factor that disqualifies)*, impuissance, incapacity

inarticulate mute, speechless, taciturn

inarticulated indeterminate

inartificial authentic, genuine, honest, ingenuous, real, simple, unaffected *(sincere)*, veridical

inartificiality honesty

inartistic poor *(inferior in quality)*

inattention dishonor *(nonpayment)*, disinterest *(lack of interest)*, disregard *(unconcern)*, disuse, inconsideration, indifference, laches, laxity, neglect, negligence, nonfeasance, oversight *(carelessness)*

inattention to consequences inconsideration

inattentive blind *(not discerning)*, careless, casual, cursory, derelict *(negligent)*, heedless, hot-blooded, inadvertent, lax, negligent, oblivious, perfunctory, reckless, remiss, thoughtless, truant, unaware, unresponsive

inattentiveness disinterest *(lack of interest)*, disregard *(lack of respect)*, disregard *(unconcern)*, laxity, neglect, negligence

inaudibility indistinctness

inaudible inarticulate, indistinct

inauditus unprecedented

inaugural initial, original *(initial)*, precursory, preliminary, preparatory, primary, prime *(original)*, prior

inaugural competition primary

inaugural contest primary

inaugural election primary

inaugural political competition primary

inaugural political contest primary

inaugurare induct, instate

inaugurate admit *(give access)*, cause, commence, constitute *(establish)*, create, embark, establish *(launch)*, generate, induct, initiate, instate, invest *(vest)*, launch *(initiate)*, originate, preface

inauguration birth *(beginning)*, first appearance, inception, installation, nascency, onset *(commencement)*, origination, outset, prelude, start

inaugurator author *(originator)*

inauguratory original *(initial)*, precursory

inauspicious adverse *(hostile)*, bleak *(not favorable)*, dire, inopportune, ominous, portentous *(ominous)*, regrettable, sinister, unfavorable, unpropitious, untimely

inavertible unavoidable *(inevitable)*

inborn born *(innate)*, hereditary, ingrained, inherent, innate, natural, organic

inborn ability penchant

inborn aptitude gift *(flair)*, specialty *(special aptitude)*

inborn proclivity instinct

inbred born *(innate)*, hereditary, ingrained, inherent, innate, native *(inborn)*, natural, organic

incalculable aleatory *(uncertain)*, imponderable, incomprehensible, indeterminate, inestimable, infinite, innumerable, invaluable, myriad, priceless, profuse, unlimited, unpredictable

incalculably ad infinitum

incandesce burn, deflagrate

incapabable of being done impossible

incapability disability *(physical inability)*, disqualification *(factor that disqualifies)*, impotence, impuissance, inability, incapacity, incompetence, inefficacy

incapable helpless *(powerless)*, inadept, inadequate, incompetent, inept *(incompetent)*, insufficient, powerless, unable, unfit, unqualified *(not competent)*

incapable of being accomplished impracticable

incapable of being affected impervious

incapable of being appraised invaluable

incapable of being bought back irredeemable

incapable of being conveyed inalienable

incapable of being counted innumerable

incapable of being defeated indefeasible

incapable of being defended untenable

incapable of being deleted indelible

incapable of being divided indivisible

incapable of being done insurmountable

incapable of being evaluated imponderable

incapable of being explained inexplicable

incapable of being held untenable

incapable of being impaired impervious

incapable of being influenced impervious

incapable of being injured impervious

incapable of being justified inexcusable

incapable of being maintained untenable

incapable of being overcome insuperable, insurmountable, invincible

incapable of being parted inseparable

incapable of being perceived impalpable

incapable of being reviewed inappealable

incapable of being revoked indefeasible

incapable of being satisfied insatiable

incapable of being separated indivisible

incapable of being sold inalienable

incapable of being subdued indomitable

incapable of being surmounted insuperable

incapable of being surrendered unalienable

incapable of being transferred inalienable

incapable of caring insusceptible *(uncaring)*

incapable of correction incorrigible

incapable of deceit honest

incapable of discharging liabilities bankrupt

incapable of error infallible

incapable of existing impossible

incapable of feeling insensible

incapable of happening impossible

incapable of managing one's own affairs fatuous

incapable of perceiving insensible

incapable of revocation irrevocable

incapable of speech mute

incapable of success insurmountable

incapable of utterance speechless

incapacious narrow

incapacitate damage, debilitate, disable, disarm *(divest of arms)*, disqualify, harm, maim, mutilate, neutralize, stall

incapacitated disabled *(deprived of legal right)*, disabled *(made incapable)*, incompetent, powerless

incapacitating disabling

incapacitation disability *(physical inability)*, disqualification *(factor that disqualifies)*, impotence, inability, incapacity, inefficacy

incapacity abortion *(fiasco)*, disability *(physical inability)*, disqualification *(factor that disqualifies)*, fault *(weakness)*, frustration, ignorance, impotence, impuissance, inability, incompetence, inefficacy

incapacity to endure intolerance

incarcerate arrest *(apprehend)*, capture, commit *(institutionalize)*, confine, constrain *(imprison)*, contain *(restrain)*, detain *(hold in custody)*, enclose, immure, imprison, jail, lock, restrain, seize *(apprehend)*

incarcerated arrested *(apprehended)*, in custody

incarcerated person captive, prisoner

incarcerating commitment *(confinement)*

incarceration apprehension *(act of arresting)*, arrest, bondage, captivity,

cell, commitment *(confinement)*, constraint *(imprisonment)*, detention, durance, enclosure, fetter, restraint

incarceration facility prison

incarnate bodily, born *(innate)*, corporal, corporeal, embody, genetic, live *(conscious)*, personify, physical

incarnation embodiment

incase contain *(enclose)*

incaution disregard *(unconcern)*, inconsideration, indiscretion

incautious careless, cursory, heedless, hot-blooded, impolitic, improvident, imprudent, impulsive *(rash)*, injudicious, lax, misadvised, negligent, perfunctory, reckless, unpolitic

incautiousness inconsideration, indiscretion, negligence, temerity

incautus heedless, improvident, reckless, unsuspecting

incendere incense, inspire

incendiarism arson, conflagration, subversion

incendiarize burn

incendiary disorderly

incendium conflagration

incense aggravate *(annoy)*, alienate *(estrange)*, bait *(harass)*, disaffect, discompose, exacerbate, harass, irritate, molest *(annoy)*, offend *(insult)*, pique, provoke, repel *(disgust)*

incensurable blameless

incentive bonus, catalyst, consideration *(recompense)*, impetus, impulse, instigation, motive, premium *(excess value)*, profit, provocation, reason *(basis)*, reward, stimulus

incentor demagogue

incept commence

inception birth *(beginning)*, causal, derivation, genesis, nascency, onset *(commencement)*, origin *(source)*, origination, outset, prelude, start, threshold *(commencement)*

inceptive causative, elementary, inchoate, incipient, initial, preparatory, prime *(original)*, rudimentary

inceptum enterprise *(undertaking)*, inception, project, undertaking *(enterprise)*

incertitude ambiguity, ambivalence, confusion *(ambiguity)*, doubt *(indecision)*, hesitation, indecision, qualm, quandary, suspicion *(uncertainty)*

incertus dubious, indefinite, indeterminate, insecure, irresolute, precarious, problematic, undecided, unsettled, vague

incessancy continuity, perpetuity

incessant chronic, constant, continual *(perpetual)*, continuous, durable, insistent, perpetual, repeated, repetitious, unrelenting, unremitting

incessere inveigh

incestus lewd

inch by inch piecemeal

inchoate conceive *(invent)*, establish *(launch)*, incipient, initial, initiate, original *(initial)*, premature, rudimentary

inchoation embryo, genesis, inception, nascency, onset *(commencement)*, origination, outset, start

inchoative fundamental, incipient, original *(initial)*

incidence situation

incident accident *(chance occurrence)*, appurtenant, casualty, contingency, event, experience *(encounter)*, happening, occasion, occurrence, particular

incident to contingent, dependent, subject *(conditional)*

incidental appurtenance, casual, circumstantial, collateral *(immaterial)*, extraneous, extrinsic, impertinent *(irrelevant)*, inapposite, nonessential, particular, random, subject *(conditional)*, supplementary, tangential, unessential

incidental mention reference *(allusion)*

incidental opinion dictum

incidental profits perquisite

incidentals circumstances

incidere impinge, occur *(happen)*

incinerate burn, deflagrate, destroy *(efface)*

incipere commence, engage *(involve)*, initiate

incipience birth *(beginning)*, embryo, genesis, inception, nascency, onset *(commencement)*, origination, outset, start

incipiency birth *(beginning)*, genesis, inception, nascency, origination, outset, start

incipient inchoate, initial, original *(initial)*, preliminary, preparatory, prime *(original)*

incipient organism embryo

incircumspection inconsideration, indiscretion, negligence

incise break *(separate)*, lancinate, split

incision split

incisive bitter *(penetrating)*, compelling, eloquent, harsh, mordacious, pithy, trenchant

incisiveness judgment *(discernment)*, sagacity

incitamentum incentive, inducement, stimulus

incitare impel, incite, inspire, spirit, stimulate, urge

incitation catalyst, inducement, influence, instigation, persuasion, reason *(basis)*

incitatus vehement

incite abet, agitate *(activate)*, bait *(harass)*, bait *(lure)*, cause, coax, engender, evoke, exacerbate, exhort, foment, hasten, impel, induce, influence, inspire, motivate, pique, press *(goad)*, prevail *(persuade)*, prompt, provoke, spirit, stimulate, urge

incite to action impel

incitement catalyst, cause *(reason)*, incentive, inducement, influence, instigation, invitation, persuasion, provocation, stimulus

inciter demagogue

inciting incendiary, moving *(evoking emotion)*, offensive *(taking the initiative)*, provocative

incitive incendiary

incivility contempt *(disdain)*, disregard *(lack of respect)*, disrespect

inclemency severity, violence

inclement callous, harsh, relentless, ruthless, severe, unfavorable, unrelenting

inclinatio bias, inclination, penchant, predisposition, tendency

inclination affection, affinity *(regard)*, amenability, animus, aptitude, bias, character *(personal quality)*, characteristic, color *(complexion)*, conatus, conviction *(persuasion)*, design *(intent)*, desire, direction *(course)*, disposition *(inclination)*, favor *(partiality)*, habit, instinct, notion, partiality, penchant, perspective, position *(point of view)*, posture *(attitude)*, preconception, predilection, predisposition, preference *(choice)*, prejudice *(preconception)*, proclivity, propensity, stand *(position)*, standpoint, tendency, will *(desire)*
inclination downward descent *(declination)*
inclination to ask questions interest *(concern)*
incline convince, desire, dispose *(incline)*, gravitate, lobby, motivate, preconceive, prompt, slant
incline to conduce
incline toward discriminate *(treat differently)*
incline toward each other converge
inclined eager, oblique *(slanted)*, partial *(biased)*, pliable, prone, ready *(willing)*, receptive, solicitous
inclined to anger fractious
inclined to assent consenting
inclined to delay dilatory
inclined to judge with severity critical *(faultfinding)*
inclined to lewdness lecherous
inclined to suspect inconvincible
inclined to vengeance vindictive
inclining oblique *(slanted)*
inclose contain *(enclose)*
inclosure jail
include append, circumscribe *(surround by boundary)*, comprise, consist, constitute *(compose)*, contain *(comprise)*, embrace *(encircle)*, implicate, interject, receive *(permit to enter)*
include as a necessary consequence entail
include by implication imply
include in an agreement stipulate
included additional, constituent *(part)*
includere confine, embody, enclose, immure, imprison, shut
including also
inclusion accession *(annexation)*, addendum, admittance *(acceptance)*, affiliation *(connectedness)*, appendix *(accession)*, composition *(makeup)*, coverage *(scope)*, insertion
inclusive broad, complete *(all-embracing)*, comprehensive, detailed, extensive, general, gross *(total)*, omnibus, thorough, total
inclusiveness corpus, coverage *(scope)*, entirety
inclusivity coverage *(scope)*
inclusory inclusive, omnibus
incogitant thoughtless
incogitative vacuous
incognito anonymous, concealment
incognizable inapprehensible, inscrutable
incognizance ignorance, insentience, nescience
incognizant blind *(not discerning)*, unaware
incognoscible incomprehensible

incohatus inchoate, rudimentary
incoherence jargon *(unintelligible language)*
incoherent disconnected, disjointed, disordered, incomprehensible
incoherent discourse jargon *(unintelligible language)*
incola denizen, habitant, inhabitant, tenant
incolarum numerus population
incolere inhabit, reside
incolumitas security *(safety)*
income alimony, annuity, capital, earnings, finance, honorarium, money, pay, proceeds, profit, receipt *(act of receiving)*, recompense, rent, resource, retainer, revenue, substance *(material possessions)*, wage
income from real estate rent
incoming inflow, ingress
incoming population immigration
incommensurability difference, disparity
incommensurable different, disparate, disproportionate, inapplicable, incommensurate
incommensurate disproportionate, insufficient
incommode annoy, badger, bait *(harass)*, deter, disadvantage, discommode, disoblige, disturb, embarrass, encumber *(hinder)*, harass, hinder, hold up *(delay)*, impede, inconvenience, molest *(annoy)*, pique, plague, trammel
incommoded aggrieved *(harmed)*
incommodious undesirable, unsuitable
incommodum detriment, disadvantage, disadvantage, disservice, infliction, injury, mischief, misfortune
incommodus disadvantageous, unfit, unsuitable
incommunicable ineffable
incommunicative inarticulate, mute, noncommittal
incommutable certain *(positive)*, conclusive *(determinative)*, definite, irreversible, irrevocable, permanent, unalterable
incomparable absolute *(ideal)*, best, cardinal *(outstanding)*, different, diverse, master, outstanding *(prominent)*, paramount, premium, priceless, professional *(stellar)*, rare, superior *(excellent)*, superlative, unapproachable, unique, unprecedented, unrelated, unusual
incompatability feud
incompatibility antithesis, conflict, contraposition, contrary, disaccord, disagreement, discord, discrepancy, disparity, estrangement, ill will, incongruity, inconsistency, inequality, paradox, strife, variance *(disagreement)*
incompatible different, discordant, disproportionate, dissident, divergent, hostile, inapplicable, inapposite, inappropriate, inapt, incongruous, inconsistent, inept *(inappropriate)*, negative, opposite, unrelated, unsuitable
incompetence abortion *(fiasco)*, disability *(physical inability)*, disqualification *(factor that disqualifies)*, impotence, impuissance, inability, incapacity, inefficacy, insufficiency, invalidity
incompetency abortion *(fiasco)*, dis-

ability *(physical inability)*, disqualification *(factor that disqualifies)*, impotence, inability, incapacity, inefficacy, maladministration
incompetent deficient, deranged, disabled *(made incapable)*, helpless *(powerless)*, inadept, inadequate, inadmissible, incapable, ineffective, ineffectual, inept *(incompetent)*, insufficient, nugatory, powerless, unable, unavailing, unfit, unqualified *(not competent)*
incomplete broken *(interrupted)*, defective, deficient, devoid, imperfect, inadequate, inchoate, insufficient, nonsubstantial *(not sufficient)*, outstanding *(unresolved)*, paltry, partial *(part)*, partial *(relating to a part)*, perfunctory, rudimentary, scarce
incompletely in part
incompleteness dearth, defect, deficiency, deficit, hiatus, insufficiency, need *(deprivation)*
incompletion defect, deficiency, delinquency *(failure of duty)*
incomplex simple
incompliance refusal
incompositus disjointed
incomprehensibility complication, incoherence, opacity
incomprehensible difficult, inapprehensible, inarticulate, indefinable, indistinct, inexplicable, inexpressive, innumerable, inscrutable, mysterious, obscure *(abstruse)*, opaque, unclear, vague
incomprehensibly ad infinitum
incomprehension ignorance, incapacity, insentience
incompressibility congealment
incompressible solid *(compact)*
incomputable imponderable, innumerable
inconceivability impossibility
inconceivable debatable, doubtful, implausible, impossible, impracticable, incomprehensible, incredible, ineffable, infeasible, portentous *(eliciting amazement)*, prodigious *(amazing)*, rare, unbelievable, uncanny, unusual
inconclusive circumstantial, indeterminate, uncertain *(ambiguous)*, unconfirmed
inconclusiveness suspicion *(uncertainty)*
incondite defective
inconditus simple
inconformable disproportionate, incongruous, peculiar *(distinctive)*
inconformity diversity
incongruence conflict, controversy *(argument)*, difference, disaccord, discord, discrepancy, disparity, dissidence
incongruency discrepancy
incongruens incongruous
incongruent discordant, disjointed, disparate, disproportionate, dissimilar, distinct *(distinguished from others)*, inapplicable, inapposite, inappropriate, inapt, incongruous, inept *(inappropriate)*, peculiar *(distinctive)*
incongruity conflict, contradiction, deviation, difference, disaccord, discord, discrepancy, disparity, dissidence, incompatibility *(inconsistency)*, inconsistency, inequality, misjoinder, noncon-

formity, paradox

incongruous different, discordant, disjointed, disparate, disproportionate, dissenting, distinct *(distinguished from others)*, heterogeneous, impertinent *(irrelevant)*, improper, inapplicable, inapposite, inappropriate, inapt, inconsistent, inept *(inappropriate)*, irrelevant, ludicrous, nonconforming, peculiar *(distinctive)*, repugnant *(incompatible)*, unbecoming, unfit, unrelated, unseemly, unsound *(fallacious)*, unsuitable

incongruousness difference, impropriety, incongruity, inconsistency, inequality

inconsequence immateriality, insignificance, non sequitur

inconsequent disproportionate, extraneous, impertinent *(irrelevant)*, inapposite, incongruous, inconsequential, irrelevant, sophistic

inconsequential collateral *(immaterial)*, de minimus, expendable, extraneous, immaterial, inapposite, inappreciable, inconsiderable, insubstantial, irrelevant, mediocre, minor, negligible, nonessential, nugatory, null *(insignificant)*, paltry, peripheral, petty, remote *(small)*, slight, tenuous, trivial, unessential

inconsequentiality inconsequence, insignificance

inconsiderable inappreciable, inconsequential, insubstantial, insufficient, minimal, minor, negligible, nominal, null *(insignificant)*, paltry, petty, remote *(small)*, scarce, slight, trivial, unessential

inconsiderableness inconsequence, mediocrity

inconsiderate blind *(not discerning)*, careless, derelict *(negligent)*, ill-advised, ill-judged, impolitic, imprudent, injudicious, oblivious, reckless, remiss, thoughtless, unpolitic

inconsiderateness disregard *(lack of respect)*, inconsideration, ingratitude, temerity

inconsideration disinterest *(lack of interest)*, disregard *(lack of respect)*, disregard *(unconcern)*, indifference, ingratitude, negligence

inconsideratus injudicious, reckless

inconsistence inconsequence

inconsistency antipode, conflict, contradiction, contrary, controversy *(argument)*, deviation, difference, disaccord, discrepancy, exception *(exclusion)*, incongruity, inconsequence, inequality, irregularity, nonconformity, paradox, specialty *(distinctive mark)*

inconsistent anomalous, contradictory, deranged, desultory, disconnected, discordant, discriminating *(distinguishing)*, disjunctive *(tending to disjoin)*, disordered, disparate, disproportionate, dissenting, divergent, illogical, inapplicable, inapposite, inappropriate, inapt, incommensurate, incongruous, inept *(inappropriate)*, ludicrous, miscellaneous, opposite, repugnant *(incompatible)*, sophistic, unusual

inconsistent with dissident, hostile

inconsolable despondent, disconsolate

inconsonance deviation, difference, disaccord, disagreement, incompatibil-

ity *(inconsistency)*, incongruity, inconsistency, inequality, paradox

inconsonant discordant, disparate, disproportionate, incongruous, inconsistent

inconspicuous blind *(concealed)*, impalpable, indiscernible, intangible, obscure *(faint)*, unclear, usual

inconspicuousness concealment

inconstancy disloyalty, inconsistency, infidelity, lapse *(expiration)*, revolt

inconstans capricious, desultory, inconsistent, mutable, unsettled

inconstant broken *(interrupted)*, capricious, desultory, faithless, false *(disloyal)*, inconsistent, infrequent, insidious, irresponsible, mutable, noncommittal, perfidious, shifting, sporadic, transient, undependable, unpredictable, unreliable, unsettled, untrue, untrustworthy, variable, volatile

inconstantia inconsistency, indecision

inconsultus ill-advised, impolitic, imprudent, injudicious, precipitate, thoughtless

incontestability certainty, certification *(certainness)*, certitude

incontestable axiomatic, believable, categorical, certain *(fixed)*, certain *(positive)*, clear *(certain)*, cogent, conclusive *(determinative)*, decisive, definite, definitive, demonstrable, factual, inappealable, incontrovertible, indefeasible, indubious, infallible, irrebuttable, irrefutable, positive *(incontestable)*, provable, real, reliable, resounding, solid *(sound)*, uncontested, undeniable, undisputed, unequivocal, unimpeachable, unrefutable

incontestably admittedly

incontinence debauchery, greed, vice

incontinent dissolute, gluttonous, promiscuous, salacious, uncurbed, unrestrained *(not repressed)*

incontrollable disordered

incontrovertibility certainty, certification *(certainness)*, certitude, incontestability

incontrovertible axiomatic, believable, categorical, certain *(fixed)*, certain *(positive)*, clear *(certain)*, cogent, conclusive *(determinative)*, definitive, factual, immutable, inappealable, incontestable, indefeasible, infallible, irrefutable, peremptory *(absolute)*, positive *(incontestable)*, reliable, resounding, solid *(sound)*, sound, uncontested, undeniable, undisputed, unequivocal, unimpeachable, unrefutable

incontrovertible incident fact

incontrovertibly admittedly

inconvenience aggravation *(annoyance)*, annoy, bait *(harass)*, detriment, disadvantage, disadvantage, discommode, drawback, encumber *(hinder)*, encumbrance, handicap, hinder, hindrance, hold up *(delay)*, impede, impediment, molest *(annoy)*, molestation, nuisance, obstacle, trammel, trouble

inconvenient ill-advised, inopportune, undesirable, unfavorable, unfit, unsuitable, untimely

inconversable inarticulate

inconvertible certain *(positive)*, constant, irredeemable

inconvertible bill bad debt

inconvincability incredulity

inconvincible cynical, doubtful, suspicious *(distrustful)*

incorporal incorporeal, intangible

incorporality impalpability

incorporate affix, annex *(add)*, attach *(join)*, cement, collect *(gather)*, commingle, comprehend *(include)*, comprise, conjoin, consist, consolidate *(unite)*, constitute *(compose)*, contain *(comprise)*, corporate *(associate)*, desegregate, digest *(comprehend)*, embody, embrace *(encircle)*, encompass *(include)*, federalize *(associate)*, include, intangible, interject, join *(bring together)*, merge, organize *(unionize)*, unite

incorporated affiliated, associated, coadunate, coherent *(joined)*, composite, compound, conjoint

incorporation accession *(annexation)*, building *(business of assembling)*, centralization, coalescence, combination, compilation, consolidation, coverage *(scope)*, integration *(amalgamation)*, merger

incorporeal immaterial, impalpable, insubstantial, intangible

incorporeal being phantom

incorporeal entity intangible

incorporeal hereditament heritage

incorporealism impalpability

incorporeality immateriality, impalpability

incorporeity impalpability

incorrect defective, errant, erroneous, fallacious, false *(inaccurate)*, faulty, ill-founded, improper, inaccurate, inexact, mendacious, sophistic, unauthorized, unbecoming, unseemly, unsound *(fallacious)*, unsustainable, untenable, untrue, wrongful

incorrect act tortious act

incorrect application misapplication

incorrect appraisal misestimation

incorrect assertion misrepresentation

incorrect belief error

incorrect evaluation misestimation

incorrect statement misstatement

incorrect usage catachresis, misapplication, misuse

incorrect use misapplication, misuse

incorrect valuation misestimation

incorrectness impropriety, misdoing, story *(falsehood)*

incorrigible delinquent *(guilty of a misdeed)*, disobedient, disorderly, dissolute, inexcusable, iniquitous, intractable, irrecoverable, irredeemable, lawless, obdurate, peccant *(culpable)*, perverse, reprehensible, reprobate, restive, uncontrollable, unruly, vicious

incorrupt blameless, clean, dependable, equitable, high-minded, honest, impartial, law-abiding, loyal, meritorious, moral, not guilty, pure

incorruptibility adhesion *(loyalty)*, honesty, honor *(good reputation)*, integrity, inviolability, loyalty, principle *(virtue)*, probity, responsibility *(conscience)*

incorruptible clean, conscientious, credible, equitable, faithful *(loyal)*, high-minded, honest, irreprehensible, just, law-abiding, loyal, meritorious, moral, reputable, true *(loyal)*, uncom-

promising, upright
incorruptibly faithfully
incorruption innocence
incorruptus impartial, incorruptible
incrassate ossified
incrassated ossified
increase accession *(enlargement)*, accumulate *(enlarge)*, addition, advance *(increase)*, advancement *(improvement)*, aggravate *(exacerbate)*, aggravation *(exacerbation)*, amplify, appreciation *(increased value)*, augmentation, build *(augment)*, compound, enlarge, exacerbate, expand, extend *(enlarge)*, extension *(expansion)*, heighten *(augment)*, increment, inflate, inflation *(increase)*, intensify, magnify, profit, progress, progress, prolong, promotion *(advancement)*, pullulate, raise *(advance)*, recruit, reinforcement, supplement
increase clarity explain
increase dimensions inflate
increase in amount of wealth income
increase in bulk expand
increase in extent expand
increase in size development *(progression)*
increase of clarity clarification
increase of clearness clarification
increase of damages additur
increase of intelligibility clarification
increase of jury award additur
increase of size extension *(expansion)*
increase of speed acceleration
increase the capacity of expand
increase the chances conduce
increase the length of extend *(enlarge)*
increase the market price of appreciate *(increase)*
increase the number of proliferate
increase the numbers compound
increase the size of magnify
increase the strength of develop
increase the value of enhance
increased accrued
increased price appreciation *(increased value)*
increased value premium *(excess value)*
increasement boom *(increase)*
increasing augmentation, boom *(increase)*
incredibilis gross *(total)*, incredible, ineffable
incredibility doubt *(suspicion)*
incredible debatable, disputable, doubtful, implausible, impossible, ludicrous, noteworthy, portentous *(eliciting amazement)*, prodigious *(amazing)*, remarkable, special, unbelievable, uncanny, unusual
incredulity cloud *(suspicion)*, discredit, doubt *(suspicion)*, suspicion *(mistrust)*
incredulous inconvincible, skeptical
incredulousness cloud *(suspicion)*, doubt *(suspicion)*, incredulity
incredulus incredulous
increment accretion, addition, additive, advance *(increase)*, appreciation *(increased value)*, augmentation, behalf, boom *(increase)*, boom *(prosperity)*, com-

mission *(fee)*, dividend, extension *(expansion)*, growth *(increase)*, interest *(profit)*, profit, progress
incremental cumulative *(increasing)*
incrementum growth *(increase)*, increment
increpare inveigh
increpate lash *(attack verbally)*, reprehend, reproach
increpation admonition, bad repute, reprimand, reproach, revilement
increpitare reproach
incriminate accuse, arraign, blame, charge *(accuse)*, cite *(accuse)*, complain *(charge)*, condemn *(blame)*, denigrate, denounce *(inform against)*, implicate, indict, inform *(betray)*, involve *(implicate)*, libel, lodge *(bring a complaint)*, present *(prefer charges)*, proscribe *(denounce)*, reproach
incriminate unjustly frame *(charge falsely)*, frame *(prearrange)*
incriminated guilty
incriminating inculpatory
incriminating statement confession
incrimination accusation, arraignment, attribution, blame *(culpability)*, charge *(accusation)*, complaint, condemnation *(blame)*, denunciation, entanglement *(involvement)*, inculpation, innuendo, reproach
incriminator accuser, complainant
incriminatory inculpatory
incubare brood
incubus weight *(burden)*
inculcare inculcate, obtrude
inculcate discipline *(train)*, educate, imbue, infuse, instill, instruct *(teach)*
inculcation discipline *(training)*, education, guidance, infusion, instruction *(teaching)*, propaganda
inculcator pedagogue
inculculate initiate
inculpable blameless, incorruptible, irreprehensible, justifiable, not guilty, unimpeachable
inculpate accuse, arraign, blame, charge *(accuse)*, complain *(charge)*, confess, denigrate, denounce *(condemn)*, denounce *(inform against)*, deprecate, impeach, implicate, incriminate, indict, inform *(betray)*, involve *(implicate)*, lodge *(bring a complaint)*, reproach
inculpate falsely frame *(charge falsely)*
inculpate unfairly frame *(charge falsely)*
inculpate unjustly frame *(charge falsely)*
inculpating inculpatory
inculpation accusation, allegation, bad repute, blame *(culpability)*, charge *(accusation)*, condemnation *(blame)*, count, denunciation, diatribe, entanglement *(involvement)*, implication *(incriminating involvement)*, incrimination, reproach
inculpation by prosecution arraignment
inculpatory incriminatory
inculpatory statement confession
incultus uncouth
incumbency appointment *(position)*, commitment *(responsibility)*, employment, office, position *(business status)*, post, regime, term *(duration)*, work

(employment)
incumbent binding, forcible, necessary *(required)*
incumbent on mandatory, obligatory, requisite
incumbent upon compulsory, essential *(required)*
incumbere study
incumbrance lien
incunabula birth *(beginning)*, genesis, nascency, onset *(commencement)*, origination, source
incunabular incipient, original *(initial)*
incur a debt charge *(assess)*, overdraw, owe
incur a duty assume *(undertake)*, promise *(vow)*, undertake
incur a loss forfeit, lose *(be deprived of)*
incur an expense expend *(disburse)*
incur blame denounce *(inform against)*, humiliate, impeach
incur costs bear the expense, disburse *(pay out)*, expend *(disburse)*
incur disapproval disoblige
incur disgrace derogate
incur expense spend
incur expenses bear the expense, disburse *(pay out)*
incur loss suffer *(sustain loss)*
incur the hostility of antagonize
incur the risk bet
incurable deadly, incorrigible, irredeemable, irremediable, irreparable, irreversible
incuria neglect, negligence, oversight *(carelessness)*
incuriosity disinterest *(lack of interest)*
incuriosus regardless
incuriousness disinterest *(lack of interest)*
incurrere incur, invade
incursio incursion, invasion
incursion assault, encroachment, foray, inflow, infringement, ingress, intrusion, invasion, onset *(assault)*
incursionem invade
incursive offensive *(taking the initiative)*
incursus assault
incusare reproach
incutere infuse, intimidate
indagate probe, research, search
indagatio investigation
indagation probe, research, scrutiny
indagator detective
indebted insolvent, loyal
indebtedness arrears, charge *(lien)*, cloud *(incumbrance)*, debit, debt, due, duty *(obligation)*, liability, lien, mortgage, obligation *(liability)*
indebtment arrears, cloud *(incumbrance)*, delinquency *(shortage)*, lien
indecency impropriety, obscenity, pornography, sodomy, vice
indecent bad *(offensive)*, brazen, depraved, disgraceful, disreputable, dissolute, ignoble, immoral, improper, lascivious, lewd, licentious, nefarious, obscene, offensive *(offending)*, profligate *(corrupt)*, prurient, salacious, scandalous, scurrilous, suggestive *(risqué)*, unbecoming, unseemly

indecent assault abuse *(physical misuse)*

indeciduous constant, durable

indecision ambivalence, dilemma, hesitation, incertitude, inertia, quandary

indecisive circumstantial, debatable, doubtful, equivocal, hesitant, inconclusive, indefinite, ineffective, ineffectual, irresolute, noncommittal, open-ended, pliant, unconfirmed, undecided, vague

indecisiveness ambivalence, confusion *(ambiguity)*

indecorous blatant *(obtrusive)*, brazen, disorderly, disreputable, improper, inappropriate, inelegant, inept *(inappropriate)*, unbecoming, undue *(excessive)*, unseemly, unsuitable

indecorousness impropriety, indecency

indecorum bad repute, disrespect, impropriety, obscenity

indecorus improper, unbecoming, unseemly

indefatigability diligence *(perseverance)*, industry *(activity)*, resolution *(decision)*, tenacity

indefatigable diligent, faithful *(diligent)*, incessant, indomitable, industrious, infallible, patient, permanent, persistent, pertinacious, potent, relentless, resolute, sedulous, undaunted, unrelenting, unremitting

indefeasable unimpeachable

indefeasibility incontestability, indestructibility

indefeasible certain *(positive)*, clear *(certain)*, compulsory, conclusive *(determinative)*, definite, incontestable, indelible, indestructible, irreversible, irrevocable, permanent, unalienable, unavoidable *(not voidable)*

indefeasible right birthright

indefectible infallible

indefective infallible

indefensible blameful, blameworthy, illogical, inadequate, inexcusable, inexpiable, powerless, reprehensible, unjustifiable, unreasonable, untenable, unwarranted, vulnerable

indefinable ineffable, inexplicable, undefinable, unspecified

indefinite aleatory *(uncertain)*, ambiguous, broad, conditional, debatable, disputable, equivocal, impalpable, incomprehensible, inconspicuous, indeterminate, intangible, obscure *(faint)*, open-ended, outstanding *(unresolved)*, pending *(unresolved)*, provisional, speculative, sporadic, undecided, unlimited, unspecified, vague

indefinite meaning ambiguity

indefinite portion moiety

indefinite share moiety

indefinitely ad infinitum

indefiniteness ambiguity, confusion *(ambiguity)*, doubt *(indecision)*, indistinctness, perpetuity

indelibatus undiminished

indeliberate impulsive *(rash)*, spontaneous, unpremeditated

indelibilis indelible

indelibility indestructibility

indelible constant, durable, indestructible, ingrained, irrevocable, noncancellable, permanent, perpetual, profound *(intense)*

indelicacy impropriety, indecency, obscenity

indelicate blatant *(obtrusive)*, disreputable, gross *(flagrant)*, improper, inelegant, lewd, licentious, lurid, obscene, profane, scurrilous, suggestive *(risqué)*, thoughtless, unbecoming, uncouth, unseemly

indemnification collection *(payment)*, compensation, consideration *(recompense)*, damages, expiation, indemnity, insurance, payment *(remittance)*, recompense, recovery *(award)*, redemption, refund, reimbursement, relief *(legal redress)*, remuneration, rendition *(restoration)*, requital, restitution, retribution, reward, satisfaction *(discharge of debt)*, trover

indemnificatory compensatory

indemnifier insurer

indemnify bear the expense, compensate *(remunerate)*, defray, outbalance, pay, quit *(repay)*, recoup *(reimburse)*, refund, reimburse, remedy, remunerate, repay, restore *(return)*, return *(refund)*

indemnify against loss ensure

indemnitor insurer, surety *(guarantor)*

indemnity bail, binder, clemency, collection *(payment)*, compensation, condonation, consideration *(recompense)*, contribute *(indemnify)*, contribution *(indemnification)*, coverage *(insurance)*, damages, expiation, guaranty, honorarium, indemnification, pay, payment *(remittance)*, recompense, recovery *(award)*, reimbursement, remuneration, reparation *(indemnification)*, requital, reward, satisfaction *(discharge of debt)*, security *(pledge)*, trover

indemnity against loss insurance

indent bind *(obligate)*, depress, requisition, undertake

identification relation *(connection)*

indenture bind *(obligate)*, bond, bond *(secure a debt)*, compact, obligation *(liability)*, pact, security *(stock)*, servitude, specialty *(contract)*, undertake

independence freedom, home rule, latitude, liberty, nonconformity

independent alien *(unrelated)*, apart, disparate, eccentric, foreign, free *(enjoying civil liberty)*, free *(not restricted)*, impartial, impertinent *(irrelevant)*, individual, irrelative, neutral, nonconforming, nonpartisan, open-minded, peremptory *(absolute)*, separate, several *(separate)*, spontaneous, substantive, unbiased, unilateral, unprejudiced, unrelated, unrestrained *(not in custody)*, unrestricted

independent of law arbitrary

independent of rule arbitrary

independent of volition involuntary

independently alone *(solitary)*, respectively

indescribable indefinable, ineffable, nondescript, portentous *(eliciting amazement)*, prodigious *(amazing)*, undefinable, unusual

indestructibility inviolability

indestructible certain *(positive)*, constant, immutable, indefeasible, indelible, infinite, infrangible, invincible, irrevocable, permanent, perpetual

indeterminable conditional, open-ended

indeterminableness confusion *(ambiguity)*

indeterminacy ambiguity, ambivalence, chance *(possibility)*

indeterminate broad, casual, conditional, debatable, disputable, equivocal, generic, indefinite, nebulous, oblique *(evasive)*, pending *(unresolved)*, provisional, uncertain *(ambiguous)*, undefinable, unspecified, vague

indeterminately ad infinitum

indeterminateness chance *(possibility)*, confusion *(ambiguity)*, doubt *(indecision)*

indetermination ambivalence, doubt *(indecision)*, incertitude, indecision, quandary

index book, classify, clue, codify, directory, enumerate, fix *(arrange)*

index gist *(substance)*

index indicant, indicate, indication, indicator

index inscription, inventory

index itemize, ledger, marshal, pigeonhole, record, register, roll, schedule, symbol, symptom, tabulate

indicant device *(distinguishing mark)*, index *(catalog)*, indication, suggestive *(evocative)*, symptom, token

indicare denote, disclose, enunciate, imply, indicate, purport

indicate adduce, allot, allude, bear *(adduce)*, bespeak, cite *(state)*, connote, construe *(translate)*, convey *(communicate)*, demonstrate *(establish)*, denote, depict, designate, direct *(show)*, disabuse, disclose, display, evidence, evince, exemplify, exhibit, express, hint, imply, infer, label, manifest, mention, notify, portend, predict, purport, refer *(direct attention)*, represent *(portray)*, reveal, signify *(denote)*, speak, specify, testify

indicate beforehand portend, predict, presage, prognosticate

indicate in advance presage, prognosticate

indicate willingness consent

indicated assumed *(inferred)*, constructive *(inferential)*, implied, tacit

indicating reference *(citation)*

indicating difference distinctive

indication admonition, attribution, call *(title)*, caveat, clue, designation *(naming)*, earmark, expression *(comment)*, expression *(manifestation)*, guideline, hint, implication *(inference)*, indicant, innuendo, manifestation, mention *(reference)*, monition *(warning)*, reference *(allusion)*, representation *(statement)*, selection *(choice)*, signification, suggestion, symbol, symptom, tip *(clue)*

indication of contents caption

indications indicia

indicative allusive, circumstantial, distinctive, portentous *(ominous)*, prophetic, representative, suggestive *(evocative)*, typical

indicator bystander, clue, deponent, designation *(symbol)*, index *(catalog)*, indicant, indication, symptom, token

indicatory circumstantial, represent-

ative, suggestive *(evocative)*, typical
indice symptom
indicium designation *(symbol)*
indicium disclosure *(something disclosed)*, evidence, evidence, indication, manifestation, proof, symptom
indict accuse, blame, charge *(accuse)*, condemn *(blame)*, defame, denounce *(inform against)*, impeach, incriminate
indict for maladministration impeach
indictable blameful, blameworthy, culpable, guilty
indictable offense crime, felony
indicted accused *(charged)*
indicter complainant, informer *(one providing criminal information)*
indictment accusation, bill *(formal declaration)*, charge *(accusation)*, complaint, count, criticism, denunciation, diatribe, disapprobation, impeachment, incrimination, presentment
indictor accuser, complainant
indifference dereliction, disinterest *(lack of interest)*, disregard *(lack of respect)*, disregard *(unconcern)*, insentience, languor, laxity, neglect, negligence, neutrality, nonfeasance, sloth
indifference to act delinquency *(failure of duty)*
indifferent blind *(not discerning)*, callous, careless, casual, cold-blooded, collateral *(immaterial)*, cursory, derelict *(negligent)*, disdainful, dispassionate, evenhanded, faithless, impartial, imperfect, impervious, inactive, indolent, inferior *(lower in quality)*, insusceptible *(uncaring)*, jejune *(dull)*, languid, lax, marginal, mediocre, negligent, neutral, nonchalant, obdurate, oblivious, openminded, passive, perfunctory, phlegmatic, poor *(inferior in quality)*, reckless, remiss, slipshod, stoical, thoughtless, torpid, trivial, truant, unaffected *(uninfluenced)*, unbiased, unresponsive, usual
indifferent to suffering cruel
indigen citizen
indigence bankruptcy, dearth, need *(deprivation)*, poverty, privation
indigene citizen
indigenous born *(innate)*, hereditary, innate, native *(domestic)*, native *(inborn)*, natural, organic, specific
indigent bankrupt, destitute, impecunious, penurious, poor *(underprivileged)*
indignant bitter *(reproachful)*, contemptuous, disdainful, resentful
indignant aversion contempt *(disdain)*, disdain
indignation disparagement, resentment, umbrage
indignity contumely, defilement, disgrace, dishonor *(shame)*, notoriety, opprobrium, reproach
indignus improper, unbecoming, unfit
indiligence neglect
indiligens inaccurate, negligent
indiligentia neglect, negligence
indirect allusive, astray, circuitous, circumstantial, collusive, constructive *(inferential)*, deceptive, devious, discursive *(digressive)*, furtive, insidious, labyrinthine, oblique *(evasive)*, remote *(not proximate)*, secondary, sinuous, surrep-

titious, tortuous *(bending)*, virtual
indirect allusion innuendo, insinuation
indirect comment insinuation
indirect evidence hearsay
indirect hint mention *(reference)*
indirect implication insinuation, reference *(allusion)*
indirect influence impression
indirect path detour
indirect quotation paraphrase
indirect suggestion hint
indirection corruption, deceit, deception, falsification, improbity, pettifoggery
indirectly meant constructive *(inferential)*
indirectly state imply
indirectness deception
indiscernable hidden
indiscernibility nonappearance, opacity
indiscernible blind *(concealed)*, inconspicuous, inscrutable, intangible, latent, obscure *(faint)*
indiscerptibility entirety
indiscerptible indivisible, infrangible, inseparable, solid *(compact)*
indiscerptibleness entirety
indiscipline anarchy, contempt *(disobedience to the court)*, latitude, rebellion
indiscreet careless, culpable, impolitic, improvident, imprudent, misadvised, precipitate, reckless, thoughtless, unpolitic, unprofessional
indiscrete injudicious
indiscretion bad faith, delinquency *(misconduct)*, impropriety, inconsideration, misconduct, misdemeanor, misdoing, temerity
indiscriminate blind *(not discerning)*, broad, casual, conglomerate, disjointed, haphazard, miscellaneous, omnibus, promiscuous, random
indiscriminating blind *(not discerning)*
indiscrimination disinterest *(lack of prejudice)*
indiscriminative promiscuous
indispensability market *(demand)*, need *(requirement)*
indispensable cardinal *(basic)*, central *(essential)*, compulsory, essential *(required)*, exigent, fundamental, grave *(important)*, imperative, important *(urgent)*, instrumental, integral, mandatory, material *(important)*, necessary *(required)*, necessity, obligatory, requisite, urgent, vital
indispensable condition sine qua non
indispensable item prerequisite, requirement, sine qua non
indispensable person key man
indispensable provision necessity, need *(requirement)*
indispensable thing necessary
indispose deter, disable, discourage
indisposed adverse *(hostile)*, averse, disabled *(made incapable)*, disinclined, disobedient, reluctant, renitent, unfavorable
indisposed to action indolent
indisposed to believe cynical, inconvincible, incredulous

indisposed to mercy callous
indisposed to talk mute
indisposed to words speechless
indisposedly unwillingly
indisposedness reluctance
indisposition disability *(physical inability)*, disease, disincentive, disorder *(abnormal condition)*, reluctance
indisposition to admit incredulity
indisposition to believe incredulity
indisposition to move inertia
indisputability certainty, certification *(certainness)*, certitude, incontestability
indisputable absolute *(conclusive)*, believable, categorical, certain *(fixed)*, certain *(positive)*, clear *(certain)*, conclusive *(determinative)*, credible, definite, definitive, demonstrable, evident, explicit, inappealable, incontestable, incontrovertible, irrebuttable, irrefutable, lucid, manifest, obvious, official, palpable, positive *(incontestable)*, provable, real, reliable, undeniable, undisputed, unequivocal, unrefutable
indisputable event fact
indisputably admittedly
indissolubility indestructibility
indissoluble constant, firm, indefeasible, indestructible, inextricable, infrangible, inseparable, irreversible, irrevocable, stable, steadfast
indissoluble entity aggregate
indissolvable infrangible, irreversible, irrevocable
indistinct ambiguous, impalpable, inapprehensible, inarticulate, inconspicuous, indefinite, indeterminate, nebulous, obscure *(faint)*, opaque, speculative, subtle *(insidious)*, uncertain *(ambiguous)*, unclear, undefinable, unspecified, vague
indistinct in character or meaning doubtful
indistinctness confusion *(ambiguity)*, obscuration, opacity
indistinguishability indistinctness, opacity
indistinguishable identical, inarticulate, indefinite, indiscernible, indistinct, promiscuous, similar, unclear, vague
indisturbance composure
indite formulate
individual certain *(particular)*, certain *(specific)*, corpse, different, discrete, disjunctive *(tending to disjoin)*, distinct *(distinguished from others)*, eccentric, entity, noteworthy, only *(sole)*, original *(creative)*, particular *(specific)*, patent, peculiar *(distinctive)*, person, private *(not public)*, separate, singular, sole, specific, subjective, unique, unusual
individual admitted to the bar counselor
individual characteristic speciality
individual held in custody prisoner
individual in possession holder
individual jailed prisoner
individual method style
individual part detail
individual selected for jury service juror
individual trait speciality
individual under age minor
individual under guardianship de-

pendent
individual under suspicion suspect
individual under the age of majority
minor
individual who brings a lawsuit
plaintiff
individual who stays on holdover
individual's nearest relative next of
kin
individualism character *(personal
quality),* disposition *(inclination),* home
rule, identity *(individuality),* personality, quality *(attribute),* specialty *(distinctive mark),* trait
individualistic distinctive, noteworthy, special, specific
individuality character *(personal
quality),* characteristic, difference, distinction *(difference),* feature *(characteristic),* individual, nonconformity, particularity, personality, property *(distinctive attribute),* quirk *(idiosyncrasy),* speciality
individualization discrimination *(differentiation)*
individualize call *(title),* characterize,
define, detail *(particularize),* discriminate *(distinguish),* distinguish
individualized individual, private
(not public), subjective
individualizing discriminating *(distinguishing),* distinctive
individually in person, particularly,
respectively
individuals populace
individuate characterize, define
individuus indivisible
indivisibility congealment, whole
indivisible coherent *(joined),* cohesive
(compact), conjoint, inextricable, infrangible, inseparable, solid *(compact),*
whole *(unified)*
indivisible entity aggregate
indocile contumacious, fractious, froward, indomitable, inflexible, insubordinate, intractable, petulant, renitent,
uncontrollable, unruly
indocilis intractable
indocility contempt *(disobedience to
the court),* reluctance
indoctrinate convince, discipline
(train), educate, imbue, inculcate, initiate, instill, instruct *(teach),* persuade,
prevail *(persuade)*
indoctrination discipline *(training),*
education, guidance, instruction *(teaching),* propaganda
indolen truant
indolence inaction, inertia, languor,
laxity, sloth, vagrancy
indolent dilatory, idle, inactive, lax,
lifeless *(dull),* otiose, passive, remiss,
stagnant, torpid
indoles disposition *(inclination)*
indomitable contumacious, formidable, inexorable, inexpugnable, infallible, inflexible, insuperable, insurmountable, intractable, invincible, irresistible, pertinacious, potent, powerful,
resolute, spartan, stable, steadfast, uncontrollable, undaunted, unyielding
indomitus indomitable
indorse certify *(approve),* cosign,
pledge *(deposit),* sign
indorsement certification *(certification of proficiency),* leave *(permission)*

indorser notary public
indubious axiomatic, decisive, definite, incontestable, incontrovertible, irrefutable, uncontroverted
indubitability certainty, certification
(certainness), certitude
indubitable absolute *(conclusive),* apparent *(perceptible),* axiomatic, believable, categorical, certain *(fixed),* certain
(positive), clear *(certain),* cogent, conclusive *(determinative),* credible, definite, definitive, demonstrable, distinct
(clear), evident, incontestable, incontrovertible, indefeasible, irrebuttable, irrefutable, manifest, ostensible, palpable, perceptible, positive *(incontestable),*
probable, reliable, salient, uncontested,
undeniable, undisputed, unequivocal,
unmistakable, unrefutable
indubitable fact certification
(certainness), certitude
indubitableness certainty, certitude,
incontestability
indubitably admittedly, fairly
(clearly)
induce affect, agitate *(activate),* bait
(lure), cause, coax, coerce, constrain
(compel), contrive, convert *(persuade),*
convince, create, dispose *(incline),* engender, entice, evoke, exhort, generate,
impel, incite, influence, inspire, inveigle, launch *(initiate),* lobby, lure, motivate, occasion, originate, persuade,
pressure, prevail *(persuade),* prevail
upon, prompt, provoke, solicit, suborn
induce another to commit perjury
suborn
induce by illegal gratuity suborn
induce forgetfulness lull
induce pain mistreat
induced causative
inducement bribery, catalyst, cause
(reason), coercion, consideration *(recompense),* decoy, determinant, force *(compulsion),* hush money, incentive, instigation, invitation, motive, persuasion,
prize, provocation, reason *(basis),* seduction, stimulus
inducer abettor
inducere cancel, expunge, induce, introduce
inducible open *(persuasible),* suasible
inducing causal, causative
inducive advisory, cogent, compelling
induct admit *(give access),* enroll,
hire, initiate, instate, introduce, invest
(vest), receive *(permit to enter),* recruit
inductile unyielding
inductio introduction
induction admittance *(acceptance),*
consequence *(conclusion),* dialectic, inflow, installation, introduction,
nascency, outset, prelude
inductional logical
inductive causative, discursive *(analytical),* logical, persuasive
induere sibi vestem clothe
indulge bestow, enable, foster, furnish, give *(grant),* grant *(concede),* let
(permit), pander, patronize *(condescend
toward),* sanction, suffer *(permit),* tolerate, vouchsafe
indulge in argument discuss, dispute
(debate)
indulge in dissipation carouse
indulge in extravagance dissipate

(expend foolishly)
indulge one's fancy prefer
indulge oneself carouse, dissipate
(expend foolishly)
indulgence benevolence *(disposition
to do good),* clemency, condonation,
consent, dispensation *(exception),* favor
(act of kindness), franchise *(license),*
grace, grant, greed, largess *(generosity),*
leave *(permission),* lenience,
longanimity, philanthropy, privilege,
remission, sanction *(permission),*
sufferance, temperance, tolerance, understanding *(tolerance),* vice
indulgent addicted, benevolent, dissolute, gluttonous, intemperate, lenient,
patient, permissive, philanthropic, placable, pliant, propitious
indulgentia connivance, indulgence,
patronage *(power to appoint jobs),* tolerance
indulging lenient
indurate callous, cold-blooded, impervious, insusceptible *(uncaring),* obdurate, remorseless, rigid, tempered
indurated callous, cold-blooded, impervious, insusceptible *(uncaring),* obdurate, ossified, remorseless, rigid,
tempered
indurative rigid
industria diligence *(care),* industry
(activity)
industrial commercial, mercantile,
productive, technical
industrial area development *(building)*
industrial building development
(building)
industrialist executive
industrialized industrial
industrious active, diligent, eager,
faithful *(diligent),* meticulous, painstaking, pertinacious, resolute, sedulous,
stable, steadfast, zealous
industriousness diligence *(perseverance)*
industrius active, diligent, industrious
industry building *(business of assembling),* business *(commerce),* business
(commercial enterprise), calling, commerce, corporation, effort, employment,
enterprise *(economic organization),*
firm, labor *(exertion),* occupation *(vocation),* work *(effort),* work *(employment)*
industry and trade commerce
indwell dwell *(reside),* occupy *(take
possession),* reside
indweller citizen, denizen, domiciliary, habitant, inhabitant, lodger, resident
indwelling ingrained
inebriant alcohol
inebriated drunk
inebriation dipsomania
inebriety dipsomania, inebriation
inedible repugnant *(exciting aversion)*
ineducation illiteracy
ineffable mysterious, sacrosanct, undefinable
ineffaceable indelible, indestructible,
ingrained, inherent, noncancellable
ineffective disabled *(made incapable),*
futile, inadept, inadequate, incapable,
incompetent, inconclusive, ineffectual,
inept *(incompetent),* insipid, invalid,
languid, nugatory, null *(invalid),* null

and void, otiose, powerless, unable, unavailing, unqualified *(not competent)*, void *(invalid)*

ineffective trial mistrial

ineffectiveness disability *(physical inability)*, impotence, inefficacy, invalidity, miscarriage

ineffectual disabled *(deprived of legal right)*, expendable, futile, inadept, inadequate, incapable, incompetent, ineffective, inept *(incompetent)*, invalid, minor, nugatory, null *(invalid)*, null and void, otiose, powerless, unavailing, unproductive, void *(invalid)*

ineffectual attempt miscarriage

ineffectuality abortion *(fiasco)*, disability *(physical inability)*, impotence, inefficacy

ineffectualness detriment, disability *(physical inability)*, failure *(lack of success)*, impotence, inability, inefficacy

inefficacious defunct, disabled *(made incapable)*, futile, inadept, inadequate, ineffective, ineffectual, inept *(incompetent)*, invalid, nugatory, null *(invalid)*, null and void, otiose, powerless, unavailing, unproductive

inefficaciousness impotence, inefficacy

inefficacy abortion *(fiasco)*, disability *(physical inability)*, impotence, impuissance, inability, incapacity, nullity

inefficiency detriment, disability *(physical inability)*, impotence, impuissance, inability, incapacity, incompetence, inefficacy, maladministration

inefficient inadept, incompetent, inept *(incompetent)*, otiose, unable, unavailing, unproductive, unqualified *(not competent)*

inefficient management maladministration

inelastic inflexible, rigid

inelegance impropriety

inelegans inelegant

inelegant disreputable, imperfect, inferior *(lower in quality)*, pedestrian, tawdry, uncouth, unseemly

ineligibility disqualification *(rejection)*

ineligible inadmissible, inappropriate, undesirable, unfit, unqualified *(not competent)*

ineluctable inevitable, irrevocable, necessary *(inescapable)*, requisite, unavoidable *(inevitable)*

ineludible inevitable, necessary *(inescapable)*, unavoidable *(inevitable)*

inept amateur, disabled *(made incapable)*, fatuous, ill-judged, improper, inadept, inadequate, inapposite, incapable, incompetent, ineffective, ineffectual, inexperienced, nugatory, powerless, unable, unfit, unqualified *(not competent)*, unsatisfactory

ineptitude abortion *(fiasco)*, disqualification *(factor that disqualifies)*, ignorance, impotence, impuissance, inability, incapacity

ineptness inability

ineptus fatuous, inept *(incompetent)*, insipid

inequality difference, discrepancy, disparity, favoritism, incompatibility

(inconsistency), inconsistency, injustice

inequitable iniquitous, unequal *(unjust)*, unfair, unjust, unscrupulous

inequitable action injustice

inequitableness inequity, misjudgment, nepotism

inequity favoritism, ground, injustice, misjudgment, nepotism

ineradicable durable, indefeasible, indelible, invincible, irreversible, irrevocable, permanent, perpetual

ineradicableness indestructibility

inerasable durable, indelible, indestructible

inerasableness indestructibility

inermis helpless *(defenseless)*

inerrability certainty, certitude

inerrable infallible, reliable

inerrancy certainty, certification *(certainness)*, certitude

inerrant accurate, certain *(positive)*, infallible, reliable

iners inactive, indolent, torpid

inert dead, dormant, idle, inactive, languid, lifeless *(dull)*, otiose, phlegmatic, stable, stagnant, static, torpid

inertia desuetude

inertia insentience

inertia sloth

inertion abeyance

inertness abeyance, inaction, inertia, insentience, languor, sloth

inerudition ignorance, illiteracy

inescapable certain *(fixed)*, certain *(positive)*, compulsory, definite, exigent, forthcoming, important *(urgent)*, inevitable, irrevocable, obligatory, positive *(incontestable)*, stringent, unavoidable *(inevitable)*, undeniable

inescapable duty allegiance, charge *(responsibility)*, onus *(burden)*

inessential circumstantial, expendable, gratuitous *(unwarranted)*, immaterial, inapposite, inappropriate, inconsequential, irrelevant, minor, nonessential, null *(insignificant)*, peripheral, superfluous, unnecessary

inessentiality immateriality, insignificance, technicality

inestimable imponderable, invaluable, priceless, valuable

inevasible definite, inevitable, irrevocable, requisite, unavoidable *(inevitable)*

inevitabilis inevitable, unavoidable *(inevitable)*

inevitability predetermination

inevitable categorical, certain *(fixed)*, certain *(positive)*, definite, forthcoming, future, irremediable, irrevocable, necessary *(inescapable)*, necessity, unalterable

inevitable occurrence accident *(chance occurrence)*

inevitable result foregone conclusion

inevitableness certification *(certainness)*, certitude, predetermination

inexact ambiguous, approximate, erroneous, generic, ill-judged, imperfect, improper, inaccurate, incorrect, indefinite, lax, liberal *(not literal)*, oblique *(evasive)*, open-ended, partial *(relating to a part)*, perfunctory, slipshod

inexact statement generalization

inexactitude exaggeration, generality

(vague statement), informality, laxity, misestimation, misjudgment, misstatement

inexactness confusion *(ambiguity)*, error, exaggeration, generality *(vague statement)*, informality, laxity, misestimation, misjudgment, misstatement

inexcitability composure, inertia, languor, longanimity

inexcitable callous, dispassionate, insensible, lifeless *(dull)*, torpid

inexcusability misdoing

inexcusable blameful, indefensible, inexpiable, peccant *(culpable)*, reprehensible, unjustifiable, unwarranted

inexcusable delay laches

inexcusable delay in assertion of rights laches

inexecution neglect, nonperformance

inexertion neglect, sloth

inexhaustible copious, durable, infallible, infinite, innumerable, myriad, perpetual, profuse, unlimited

inexistence blank *(emptiness)*, nonappearance, nonentity, nullity

inexistent nonexistent

inexorabilis implacable, inexorable, irreconcilable, relentless, ruthless, unrelenting

inexorability certainty, certitude, severity

inexorable brutal, callous, certain *(positive)*, definite, dictatorial, immutable, implacable, inflexible, ironclad, irreconcilable, necessary *(inescapable)*, obdurate, peremptory *(imperative)*, pertinacious, purposeful, relentless, resolute, rigid, ruthless, severe, stable, steadfast, strict, unavoidable *(inevitable)*, uncompromising, unrelenting, unyielding

inexorable fate predetermination

inexpectant unaware

inexpectation bombshell, happenstance, improbability

inexpectatus unexpected

inexpedience detriment, disadvantage, hindrance, impropriety

inexpediency detriment, impropriety, inexpedience

inexpedient harmful, ill-advised, illjudged, impolitic, imprudent, inadvisable, inappropriate, inapt, inauspicious, inept *(inappropriate)*, injudicious, inopportune, misadvised, objectionable, undesirable, unfavorable, unfit, unpolitic, unsatisfactory, unsuitable

inexpensive economical, nominal

inexperience ignorance, minority *(infancy)*, nescience

inexperienced incompetent, jejune *(lacking maturity)*, juvenile, unaccustomed, unacquainted, unqualified *(not competent)*, unversed

inexperienced person amateur, juvenile, novice

inexpert inadept, incompetent, inept *(incompetent)*, inexperienced, unfit, unqualified *(not competent)*, unversed

inexpertness abortion *(fiasco)*, disqualification *(factor that disqualifies)*, incompetence

inexpiable implacable, indefensible, inexcusable, irreconcilable, irremediable, peccant *(culpable)*, reprehensible

inexplebilis insatiable

inexplicabilis inexpiable, inexplicable, inextricable

inexplicable enigmatic, inapprehensible, incomprehensible, indefinable, inexpressive, inscrutable, mysterious, peculiar *(curious)*, undefinable

inexplicable statement enigma

inexplicableness mystery

inexplicit indefinite, vague

inexpressible inapprehensible, indefinable, ineffable, undefinable

inexpugnabilis inexpugnable

inexpugnability inviolability

inexpugnable immune, insurmountable, invincible

inexpungeable durable

inexspectatus unanticipated

inexsuperabilis invincible

inextinguishable certain *(positive)*, constant, indefeasible, indelible, indestructible, indomitable, inexpugnable, invincible, irreversible, irrevocable, permanent

inextinguished chronic

inextricabilis inextricable, labyrinthine

inextricability complication, constant, impasse

inextricable complex, inseparable

infallibilism certitude

infallibility certainty, certification *(certainness)*, certitude

infallible certain *(fixed)*, certain *(positive)*, conclusive *(determinative)*, factual, positive *(incontestable)*, reliable, secure *(sound)*, undeniable

infallibleness certitude

infamia discredit, disgrace, dishonor *(shame)*, disrepute, ignominy, infamy, notoriety, shame

infamis disputable, disreputable

infamous arrant *(onerous)*, bad *(offensive)*, contemptible, contemptuous, disgraceful, disreputable, flagrant, heinous, ignoble, illicit, inexpiable, iniquitous, machiavellian, malevolent, nefarious, notorious, odious, outrageous, peccant *(culpable)*, profligate *(corrupt)*, reprehensible, reprobate, scandalous, sinister

infamous conduct criminality, misconduct, misdeed, misdemeanor, misdoing

infamous misbehavior criminality

infamousness bad repute, disrepute, infamy, notoriety, opprobrium, stigma

infamy atrocity, attaint, bad character, bad repute, contempt *(disdain)*, defamation, discredit, disgrace, dishonor *(shame)*, disrepute, ignominy, ill repute, notoriety, obloquy, odium, onus *(stigma)*, opprobrium, scandal, shame, stigma, turpitude, vice

infancy birth *(beginning)*, nascency, nonage, onset *(commencement)*, origination, outset, start

infandus ineffable

infans child, infant

infant child, inchoate, incipient, minor, original *(initial)*

infant status minority *(infancy)*

infantile jejune *(lacking maturity)*, puerile

infantilism puerility

infantine jejune *(lacking maturity)*, juvenile, puerile

infants children

infarction bar *(obstruction)*

infatuate bigot, obsess

infatuated zealous

infatuation affection, compulsion *(obsession)*, obsession, passion, predilection

infeasibility impossibility

infeasible impossible, unattainable

infect adulterate, contaminate, foment, harm, motivate, pervert, pollute, taint *(contaminate)*

infected marred, tainted *(contaminated)*

infection contaminate, disease

infectious contagious, harmful, pestilent

infective contagious

infectus executory

infecund barren, unproductive

infecundus unproductive

infelicitous disconsolate, disproportionate, ill-advised, improper, inadvisable, inapplicable, inapposite, inappropriate, inapt, inept *(inappropriate)*, misadvised, unbecoming, unfavorable, unsuitable, untimely

infelicity distress *(anguish)*, inexpedience, misfortune

infelix inauspicious

infensus adverse *(hostile)*, hostile

infer allude, assume *(suppose)*, conclude *(decide)*, connote, construe *(comprehend)*, deduce, deduct *(conclude by reasoning)*, derive *(deduce)*, determine, educe, evidence, expect *(consider probable)*, guess, hint, implicate, imply, judge, opine, postulate, presume, presuppose, purport, read, reason *(conclude)*, surmise, suspect *(think)*, understand

inferable constructive *(inferential)*, deductible *(provable)*, deductive, presumptive, provable

inference conclusion *(determination)*, conjecture, connotation, construction, generalization, hint, hypothesis, idea, innuendo, insinuation, intimation, mention *(reference)*, presumption, reference *(allusion)*, referral, signification, speculation *(conjecture)*, suggestion, suspicion *(uncertainty)*

inferential accountable *(explainable)*, allusive, circumstantial, consequential *(deducible)*, deductible *(provable)*, deductive, discursive *(analytical)*, implied, leading *(guiding)*, suggestive *(evocative)*, tacit

inferentially a priori

inferior deficient, faulty, ignoble, imperfect, inadequate, mediocre, minor, null *(insignificant)*, pedestrian, poor *(inferior in quality)*, secondary, slight, subaltern, subordinate, subservient, trivial, unsatisfactory, unworthy

inferior rank subjection

inferiority disadvantage, flaw, handicap, mediocrity

inferiorness mediocrity

infernal blameworthy, diabolic, heinous, malevolent, malignant, nefarious, odious

infernal machine bomb

inferre entail, inflict

inferred allusive, constructive *(inferential)*, implied, presumptive, subtle *(insidious)*, tacit

inferred in law constructive *(inferential)*

inferring dialectic

infertile barren, otiose, unproductive

infest annoy, harass

infestus hostile

inficere imbue

infidel heretic

infidelis faithless

infidelitas disloyalty, infidelity

infidelity adultery, bad faith, bad repute, breach, dishonesty, disloyalty, sedition, treason

infiltrate encroach, enter *(penetrate)*, interject, interpose, penetrate, permeate, pervade

infiltration encroachment, entrance, incursion, inflow, infusion, intrusion, invasion, osmosis

infinite continual *(perpetual)*, far reaching, incessant, indeterminate, inestimable, innumerable, myriad, open-ended, permanent, perpetual, profuse, unlimited

infinite duration perpetuity

infinitely powerful omnipotent

infinitely wise omniscient

infiniteness perpetuity

infinitesimal impalpable, inappreciable, intangible, minimal, tenuous

infinitus arbitrary, infinite, unlimited

infinity perpetuity

infirm defective, imperfect, insecure, insubstantial, nonsubstantial *(not sturdy)*, powerless, precarious, unsound *(not strong)*

infirm of purpose irresolute, irresponsible, noncommittal

infirmare quash

infirmitas frailty, impotence, inability

infirmity defect, deficiency, disability *(physical inability)*, disadvantage, disease, disorder *(abnormal condition)*, fault *(weakness)*, flaw, frailty, impuissance, inability, incapacity, vice

infirmity of old age caducity

infirmity of purpose doubt *(indecision)*, indecision

infirmus invalid, powerless

infitiari disavow, disown *(deny the validity)*, disown *(refuse to acknowledge)*

infitias ire deny *(contradict)*, disavow

infitiatio negation

infix embed, fix *(make firm)*, inculcate, inject, instill, plant *(place firmly)*

infixed ingrained, innate, internal

inflame aggravate *(annoy)*, agitate *(activate)*, bait *(harass)*, burn, deflagrate, discompose, exacerbate, foment, incense, intensify, irritate, molest *(annoy)*, motivate, offend *(insult)*, perturb, pique, provoke, stimulate

inflame with wrath incense

inflamed hot-blooded, painful, vehement

inflamer demagogue

inflaming moving *(evoking emotion)*, provocative

inflammable fractious

inflammation aggravation *(exacerbation)*, provocation

inflammatory disorderly, hot-blooded, incendiary, offensive *(taking the initiative)*, provocative

inflare inflate

inflate compound, distort, enlarge, expand, extend *(enlarge)*, increase, magnify, overestimate, spread

inflated flatulent, fustian, grandiose, orgulous, orotund, pretentious *(pompous)*, superlative, turgid

inflated language fustian, rhetoric *(insincere language)*

inflated speech fustian

inflated statement overstatement

inflated style fustian

inflatio inflation *(increase)*

inflation bombast, boom *(prosperity)*, exaggeration, growth *(increase)*, overstatement, pretense *(ostentation)*, rodomontade

inflatus inflated *(bombastic)*, inflated *(enlarged)*, pretentious *(pompous)*

inflection intonation, stress *(accent)*

inflexibility severity

inflexible callous, certain *(positive)*, constant, decisive, definite, draconian, firm, formal, immutable, implacable, inexorable, insusceptible *(uncaring)*, intractable, ironclad, irreconcilable, irrevocable, obdurate, orthodox, particular *(exacting)*, peremptory *(imperative)*, pertinacious, precise, provincial, recusant, relentless, resolute, restive, restrictive, rigid, ruthless, severe, solid *(compact)*, staunch, steadfast, strict, stringent, strong, unaffected *(uninfluenced)*, unalterable, unbending, uncompromising, unrelenting, unyielding, willful

inflexible routine bureaucracy

inflict bait *(harass)*, beat *(strike)*, commit *(perpetrate)*, compel, encumber *(hinder)*, foist, levy, perpetrate

inflict a penalty penalize

inflict a penalty on convict

inflict a penalty upon fine

inflict capital punishment execute *(sentence to death)*

inflict evil mistreat, persecute

inflict harm strike *(assault)*

inflict injury harm, prejudice *(injure)*, strike *(assault)*

inflict pain harrow, mistreat

inflict pain on plague

inflict penalty condemn *(punish)*, discipline *(punish)*, punish, sentence

inflict penance upon discipline *(punish)*

inflict punishment condemn *(punish)*, convict, penalize

inflicting commission *(act)*

infliction casualty, catastrophe, commission *(act)*, condemnation *(punishment)*, correction *(punishment)*, damage, discipline *(punishment)*, encumbrance, ground, imposition *(excessive burden)*, mischief, nuisance, pain, penalty, punishment, sanction *(punishment)*

infliction of pain cruelty

inflictive disciplinary *(punitory)*, penal

infligere inflict

inflow penetrate

influence advantage, affect, agitate *(activate)*, authority *(power)*, bait *(lure)*, cause *(reason)*, cause, clout, coax, concern *(involve)*, conduce, consequence *(significance)*, convert *(persuade)*, convince, dint, dispose *(incline)*, dominance, dominate, draw *(attraction)*, em-

inence, exhort, force *(strength)*, hegemony, imbue, impetus, importance, impress *(affect deeply)*, impression, incentive, incite, induce, inducement, inspire, instigation, inveigle, leverage, lobby, manipulate *(control unfairly)*, militate, motivate, motive, occupation *(possession)*, patronage *(power to appoint jobs)*, patronage *(support)*, persuade, persuasion, power, predominance, predominate *(command)*, pressure, pressure, prestige, prevail *(persuade)*, prevail upon, primacy, prompt, reach, redound, sphere, stimulus, supremacy, weight *(importance)*

influence against prejudice *(influence)*

influence by a gift gratuity *(bribe)*

influence of liquor inebriation

influenceability amenability

influenceable amenable, open *(persuasible)*, pliant, receptive, suasible, susceptible *(responsive)*

influenced interested, one-sided, partial *(biased)*, partisan, passive, unequal *(unjust)*, unjust

influencer special interest

influencers ,lobby

influences climate

influencing moving *(evoking emotion)*

influential assertive, causal, causative, cogent, compelling, consequential *(substantial)*, considerable, contributory, convincing, crucial, decisive, dominant, forcible, important *(significant)*, key, master, material *(important)*, outstanding *(prominent)*, persuasive, potent, powerful, predominant, prevailing *(having superior force)*, prominent, provocative, sovereign *(absolute)*

influential persons lobby

influential sponsor patron *(influential supporter)*

influentiality clout, force *(strength)*, patronage *(power to appoint jobs)*, pressure, prestige

influx entrance, incursion, inflow

infold contain *(enclose)*

inform admonish *(advise)*, advise, annunciate, apprise, bear *(adduce)*, betray *(disclose)*, caution, charge *(instruct on the law)*, communicate, construe *(translate)*, contact *(communicate)*, converse, convey *(communicate)*, declare, denounce *(inform against)*, disabuse, disclose, disseminate, divulge, edify, educate, enlighten, enunciate, forewarn, herald, impart, initiate, instill, instruct *(teach)*, issue *(publish)*, mention, notice *(give formal warning)*, notify, posit, proclaim, publish, relate *(tell)*, report *(disclose)*, reveal, speak

inform against betray *(disclose)*, cite *(accuse)*, complain *(charge)*, implicate, incriminate

inform on betray *(disclose)*, denounce *(inform against)*, expose

informal casual, unofficial, unpretentious

informalness informality

informant bystander, deponent, eyewitness, indicator, informer *(one providing criminal information)*, source, spy, witness

information accusation, advice, charge *(accusation)*, clue, communica-

tion *(statement)*, complaint, comprehension, connotation, data, direction *(guidance)*, disclosure *(something disclosed)*, dispatch *(message)*, edification, file, guidance, intelligence *(news)*, knowledge *(awareness)*, knowledge *(learning)*, monition *(warning)*, notice *(announcement)*, notification, presentment, publicity, report *(detailed account)*, science *(study)*

information against complaint

information blank form *(document)*

information giver informant

information preserved in writing entry *(record)*

information supplier informer *(one providing criminal information)*

informational didactic, disciplinary *(educational)*, informatory, narrative

informative demonstrative *(illustrative)*, didactic, disciplinary *(educational)*, eloquent, informatory, loquacious, narrative

informed acquainted, cognizant, conscious *(aware)*, knowing, learned, literate, omniscient, perspicacious, practiced, sensible

informer accuser, bystander, deponent, eyewitness, harbinger, indicator, informant, spy, witness

informing demonstrative *(illustrative)*, disclosure *(act of disclosing)*

informing against denunciation

infract infringe

infraction bad faith, breach, delinquency *(misconduct)*, disregard *(omission)*, encroachment, illegality, infringement, invasion, misdeed, offense, perversion, sedition, transgression, violation, wrong

infraction of rule exception *(exclusion)*

infraction of the law delinquency *(misconduct)*

infrangible callous, inseparable

infrenatus uncurbed

infrequency improbability, paucity

infrequent extraordinary, intermittent, noteworthy, rare, special, sporadic, uncommon, unusual

infringe accroach, break *(violate)*, contravene, disobey, disrupt, encroach, impinge, impose *(intrude)*, interfere, interpose, intervene, intrude, invade, obtrude, offend *(violate the law)*, overlap, overstep, plagiarize, trespass, violate

infringe a law deviate, offend *(violate the law)*

infringe copyright copy

infringe custom deviate

infringed broken *(unfulfilled)*

infringement assumption *(seizure)*, breach, conflict, contempt *(disobedience to the court)*, contravention, crime, delinquency *(misconduct)*, disregard *(omission)*, encroachment, illegality, imposition *(excessive burden)*, incursion, infraction, injustice, intrusion, invasion, irregularity, malfeasance, misdeed, misfeasance, nuisance, offense, plagiarism, transgression, violation

infringement of custom quirk *(idiosyncrasy)*

infringing broken *(unfulfilled)*, intrusive

infundere infuse, inject

infuriate aggravate *(annoy)*, bait *(harass)*, discompose, exacerbate, harass, incense, irritate, offend *(insult)*, perturb, pique, provoke

infuriated resentful

infuriating outrageous

infuse denature, develop, discipline *(train)*, enter *(insert)*, imbue, inculcate, inject, instill, permeate, pervade

infuse courage reassure

infuse funds invest *(fund)*

infuse life into foment

infused compound

infusio infusion

infusion incorporation *(blend)*

ingather congregate

ingathering assemblage, caucus, chamber *(body)*, collection *(assembly)*, company *(assemblage)*, conglomeration, congregation, rendezvous

ingeminate recapitulate, reiterate, repeat *(do again)*

ingenerate hereditary, native *(inborn)*, natural

ingeniosus resourceful

ingenious artful, competent, deft, expert, fertile, original *(creative)*, politic, proficient, resourceful

ingeniousness gift *(flair)*, skill

ingenit native *(inborn)*

ingenium ability, character *(personal quality)*, disposition *(inclination)*, personality, spirit, understanding *(comprehension)*

ingens prodigious *(enormous)*

ingenue child

ingenuity artifice, gift *(flair)*, performance *(workmanship)*, skill, specialty *(special aptitude)*

ingenuous bona fide, candid, credible, direct *(forthright)*, honest, simple, straightforward, unaffected *(sincere)*

ingenuousness candor *(straightforwardness)*, honesty, informality, probity, veracity

ingerere obtrude

inglorious blameworthy, contemptible, disgraceful, disreputable, ignoble, mediocre, notorious, recreant, scandalous, unethical

ingloriousness attaint, degradation, discredit, disgrace, dishonor *(shame)*, disrepute, ignominy, infamy, notoriety, obloquy, opprobrium, scandal

ingoing inflow, ingress

ingraft fix *(make firm)*

ingrain embed, establish *(entrench)*, fix *(make firm)*, infuse

ingrained born *(innate)*, genetic, habitual, indelible, inherent, innate, internal, inveterate, native *(inborn)*, natural, organic, permanent, routine, traditional

ingrained with accustomed *(familiarized)*

ingratiate propitiate

ingratiate oneself pander

ingratiating obsequious, servile, subservient

ingratus unacceptable

ingredient component, constituent *(part)*, detail, element, feature *(characteristic)*, inherent, item, member *(constituent part)*, part *(portion)*, segment

ingress access *(right of way)*, admission *(entry)*, admittance *(means of approach)*, avenue *(route)*, entrance, entry *(entrance)*, immigration, incursion, inflow, osmosis, portal

ingress wrongfully encroach

ingresses approaches

ingression entry *(entrance)*, incursion, inflow, ingress

ingressus ingress

ingrown ingrained, provincial

inhabilis incapable, incompetent

inhabit dwell *(reside)*, lodge *(reside)*, occupy *(take possession)*, remain *(occupy)*, reside

inhabitable habitable

inhabitance domicile, habitation *(act of inhabiting)*, lodging

inhabitancy abode, address, domicile, habitation *(act of inhabiting)*, inhabitation *(act of dwelling in)*, lodging, nationality, occupancy, residence

inhabitant citizen, denizen, domiciliary, habitant, inmate, lodger, occupant, resident, tenant

inhabitants community, populace, population

inhabitare reside

inhabitation abode, habitation *(act of inhabiting)*, nationality, occupation *(possession)*, residence

inhabited populous, residential

inhabiter citizen, domiciliary, habitant, inhabitant, lodger, resident

inhabitual infrequent

inhaerere adhere *(fasten)*

inharmonious different, discordant, disproportionate, dissenting, divisive, harsh, improper, inapposite, inapt, incongruous, inept *(inappropriate)*, offensive *(offending)*, opposite, polemic, repugnant *(incompatible)*, unsuitable

inharmoniousness conflict, controversy *(argument)*, deviation, difference, disaccord, disagreement, disparity, dissidence, incompatibility *(inconsistency)*, incongruity

inharmony contest *(dispute)*, controversy *(argument)*, difference, disaccord, incompatibility *(inconsistency)*, inconsistency

inhere appertain, exist

inhere in constitute *(compose)*

inherence characteristic

inherent implicit, ingrained, innate, interior, intrinsic *(belonging)*, native *(inborn)*, organic, virtual

inherent ability proclivity

inherent in incident

inherit accede *(succeed)*, hold *(possess)*, receive *(acquire)*

inheritable heritable

inheritable property hereditament

inheritance bequest, birth *(lineage)*, birthright, dower, estate *(hereditament)*, hereditament, heritage, legacy

inherited born *(innate)*, genetic, hereditary, innate, native *(inborn)*, traditional

inherited characteristics character *(personal quality)*

inherited lot heritage

inherited portion heritage

inherited property inheritance

inherited rights birthright

inheritor beneficiary, devisee, heir, legatee, recipient, transferee

inheritrix heir

inhersion characteristic

inhibere stop

inhibit arrest *(stop)*, bar *(hinder)*, bind *(restrain)*, censor, check *(restrain)*, constrain *(restrain)*, contain *(restrain)*, control *(restrain)*, counter, counteract, countervail, curb, debar, detain *(restrain)*, deter, disadvantage, disqualify, encumber *(hinder)*, enjoin, estop, fight *(counteract)*, forbid, forestall, halt, hamper, hinder, hold up *(delay)*, impede, interdict, interfere, interrupt, keep *(restrain)*, lock, obstruct, occlude, prevent, prohibit, repress, restrain, restrict, stall, stave, stifle, strangle, subdue, suppress, thwart, toll *(stop)*, withhold, withstand

inhibit motion fetter

inhibit movement fetter

inhibited arrested *(checked)*, controlled *(restrained)*

inhibiting binding

inhibition censorship, constraint *(restriction)*, control *(restriction)*, damper *(stopper)*, deterrence, deterrent, disadvantage, estoppel, fetter, hindrance, impediment, obstacle, prohibition, proscription, quota, restraint, veto

inhibitive preventive, prohibitive *(restrictive)*, unfavorable

inhibitor deterrent

inhibitory preventive, prohibitive *(restrictive)*

inhonestus disgraceful, ignoble

inhospitable illiberal

inhospitality ostracism

inhuman brutal, cruel, diabolic, harsh, malignant, oppressive, ruthless, vicious

inhumane cold-blooded, cruel, harsh, ruthless

inhumanity atrocity, bestiality, brutality, cruelty, oppression, severity

inhumanus brutal, ruthless

inicere infuse, intimidate

inimical adverse *(hostile)*, antipathetic *(oppositional)*, averse, contentious, detrimental, discordant, hostile, irreconcilable, litigious, negative, opposite, pernicious, perverse, prejudicial, pugnacious, recusant, repugnant *(incompatible)*, spiteful, unfavorable, vicious

inimical descent foray

inimicality belligerency, conflict, contention *(opposition)*, feud, ill will, incompatibility *(difference)*, spite

inimicalness odium

inimicitia feud

inimicus foe, hostile, inimical

inimitable best, cardinal *(outstanding)*, inestimable, original *(creative)*, paramount, premium, superlative, unapproachable

iniquitas disadvantage, partiality

iniquitous bad *(offensive)*, blameful, blameworthy, delinquent *(guilty of a misdeed)*, depraved, diabolic, disgraceful, dishonest, disreputable, dissolute, fraudulent, heinous, illicit, immoral, impermissible, malevolent, malignant, nefarious, outrageous, peccable, peccant *(culpable)*, profligate *(corrupt)*, reprehensible, reprobate, scandalous, unfair, unjust, unscrupulous, vicious, wrongful

iniquity atrocity, delinquency *(misconduct)*, grievance, ground, guilt, injustice, misdeed, transgression, vice, wrong

iniquus detrimental, iniquitous, one-sided, oppressive, partial *(biased)*, unfavorable, unjust, unjustifiable, unreasonable

inire enter *(go in)*

initial designation *(symbol)*, first appearance, inchoate, incipient, indorse, original *(initial)*, preliminary, preparatory, previous, primary, prime *(original)*, rudimentary, sign, unprecedented

initially ab initio

initiare initiate, instate

initiate admit *(give access)*, amateur, arise *(originate)*, cause, commence, conceive *(invent)*, create, educate, elicit, embark, enroll, establish *(launch)*, evoke, form, generate, incite, induct, instate, invent *(produce for the first time)*, maintain *(commence)*, make, novice, originate, preface, probationer *(one being tested)*, prompt, protégé, receive *(permit to enter)*, stimulate, undertake

initiate a civil action sue

initiate a corporation incorporate *(form a corporation)*

initiated practiced

initiation admittance *(acceptance)*, discipline *(training)*, genesis, inception, inflow, installation, instigation, nascency, onset *(commencement)*, origin *(source)*, origination, outset, prelude, preparation, propaganda, start

initiative initial, original *(initial)*, overture, preparatory, rudimentary

initiative seizer aggressor

initiator author *(originator)*, maker

initiatory elementary, incipient, initial, original *(initial)*, precursory, preliminary, preparatory, previous, rudimentary

initium creation, inception, outset, start

iniucundus unacceptable

iniungere impose *(enforce)*

iniuria encroachment, grievance, injustice, oppression, wrong

iniuriosus wrongful

iniurius unjust, unjustifiable

iniustitia injustice

iniustus iniquitous, unjust, unjustifiable, wrongful

inject drug, enter *(insert)*, imbue, impact, infuse, inseminate, instill, interject, interpose, introduce, penetrate, permeate, pervade, plant *(place firmly)*

injection expletive, infusion

injudicial illicit

injudicious arbitrary, careless, ill-advised, ill-judged, impolitic, improvident, imprudent, impulsive *(rash)*, inadvisable, inept *(inappropriate)*, irrational, misadvised, negligent, precipitate, puerile, reckless, remiss, unfit, unpolitic, unprofessional, unreasonable

injudicious treatment malpractice

injudiciousness inconsideration, indiscretion, inexpedience, temerity

injunction bar *(obstruction)*, charge *(command)*, check *(bar)*, dictate, direction *(guidance)*, direction *(order)*, fiat, obstacle, obstruction, precept, prescription *(directive)*, prohibition, proscription, recommendation, regulation *(rule)*, requirement, requisition, restraint, veto

injunctive prohibitive *(restrictive)*

injure abuse *(misuse)*, abuse *(victimize)*, aggravate *(annoy)*, brutalize, damage, debase, debilitate, deface, disable, disadvantage, endanger, eviscerate, harm, harrow, ill use, impair, inflict, maim, mishandle *(maltreat)*, mistreat, molest *(annoy)*, mutilate, offend *(insult)*, persecute, spoil *(impair)*, subvert, sully, violate, vitiate

injure another's reputation libel

injure by a published writing libel

injure fatally kill *(murder)*

injure one's reputation libel

injure persistently harass

injure the credit of discredit

injure the good name of defame

injure the good reputation of defame

injured aggrieved *(harmed)*, aggrieved *(victimized)*, blemished, broken *(fractured)*, defective, faulty, imperfect, marred, victim

injuring contemptuous, disabling, inculpatory

injurious adverse *(negative)*, bad *(inferior)*, bad *(offensive)*, blameworthy, calumnious, contemptuous, dangerous, derogatory, destructive, detrimental, disadvantageous, disastrous, fatal, harmful, inadvisable, insalubrious, invidious, lethal, libelous, malevolent, malignant, noxious, outrageous, peccant *(unhealthy)*, pejorative, pernicious, pestilent, prejudicial, sinister, toxic, virulent

injurious act delict

injurious action malfeasance

injurious conduct mischief

injurious exercise of authority misfeasance

injurious exercise of lawful authority misfeasance

injurious force battery

injurious interference nuisance

injurious occurrence accident *(misfortune)*

injurious to health deleterious

injurious treatment by a professional malpractice

injuriousness adversity, detriment, mischief

injury abuse *(physical misuse)*, adversity, assault, casualty, cost *(penalty)*, damage, damages, defacement, delict, detriment, disadvantage, disservice, drawback, expense *(sacrifice)*, flaw, grievance, ground, harm, impairment *(damage)*, infliction, mischief, misdeed, offense, pain, wrong

injury to character libel

injury to one's reputation libel

injury to outward appearance defacement

injustice corruption, disservice, error, grievance, ground, inequality, inequity, infringement, mischief, misdeed, misdoing, misjudgment, nepotism, oppression, partiality, prejudice *(injury)*, wrong

inkling clue, hint, inference, intimation, notion, perception, reference *(allusion)*, suggestion, suspicion *(uncertainty)*

inland interior

inlay plant *(place firmly)*

inlecebra inducement

inlet access *(right of way)*, admission *(entry)*, admittance *(means of approach)*, entrance, ingress, portal

inlets approaches

inlex decoy

inlibatus undiminished

inliberalis ignoble, illiberal, sordid

inlicere ensnare, entrap, lure

inlicitus felonious, illegal, illicit, inadmissible, unlawful

inligare implicate

inlinere smear

inludere hoodwink

inluminare enlighten

inlustrare enlighten, illustrate

inlustris famous, illustrious, renowned

inmate captive, citizen, convict, denizen, habitant, inhabitant, lodger, occupant, patient, prisoner, resident

inmost central *(situated near center)*, internal, intimate, privy

inmost nature center *(essence)*, essence

inmost recesses cache *(hiding place)*

inmost substance center *(essence)*

innate genetic, hereditary, implicit, ingrained, inherent, interior, internal, native *(inborn)*, natural, organic

innate ability aptitude, gift *(flair)*, penchant, specialty *(special aptitude)*

innate disposition proclivity

innate inclination instinct

innate proclivity instinct

innate quality gift *(flair)*

innate sense proclivity

innatus inherent, innate, natural

innavigable impossible, insuperable

innectere intertwine

inner central *(situated near center)*, interior, internal, intrinsic *(deep down)*

inner being essence

inner drive motive

inner nature character *(personal quality)*

inner part interior

inner reality center *(essence)*

inner voice conscience

innermost interior, internal, intimate

innermost thoughts introspection

innocence compurgation, credulity, ignorance

innocency innocence

innocens harmless, inculpable, innocent, irreprehensible

innocent blameless, clean, harmless, honest, inculpable, inexperienced, infant, ingenuous, innocuous, irreprehensible, moral, naive, nontoxic, not guilty, pardonable, pure, unaffected *(sincere)*, unblemished, unimpeachable, unsuspecting

innocentia innocence, integrity

innocently unknowingly

innocents children

innocuous blameless, harmless, nontoxic, salutary

innocuousness moderation

innocuus harmless, innocuous

innominate anonymous

innovate alter, change, conceive *(invent)*, vary

innovater author *(originator)*
innovation invention, reform
innovative novel, sophisticated
innovator pioneer
innoxious harmless, innocuous, irreprehensible, nontoxic, salutary
innoxius harmless
innuendo connotation, implication *(inference)*, indication, insinuation, intimation, reference *(allusion)*, referral, suggestion
innumerabilis innumerable
innumerable copious, infinite, manifold, multiple, myriad, profuse
innumerably ad infinitum
innumerous myriad
innumerus innumerable
inobservance breach, contempt *(disobedience to the court)*, delinquency *(failure of duty)*, dishonor *(nonpayment)*, disregard *(unconcern)*, informality, infraction, laches, laxity, negligence, offense
inobservant broken *(unfulfilled)*, negligent
inoccupation inaction
inoculate inject, protect
inoculation propaganda
inoffensive blameless, harmless, innocuous, irreprehensible, nontoxic, pardonable, peaceable, unobjectionable
inoperability impossibility
inoperable impracticable
inoperative defective, defunct, disabled *(deprived of legal right)*, dormant, expendable, inactive, inadequate, ineffective, ineffectual, invalid, nugatory, null *(invalid)*, null and void, otiose, powerless, unable, unavailing, unproductive, void *(invalid)*
inopia dearth, inability, indigence, insufficiency, privation
inopportune detrimental, disadvantageous, ill-advised, improper, imprudent, inadvisable, inapposite, inappropriate, inapt, inauspicious, inept *(inappropriate)*, injudicious, premature, regrettable, unfavorable, unfit, unsuitable, untimely
inopportuneness impropriety, inexpedience
inopportunus ineligible, inopportune
inops deficient, destitute, helpless *(defenseless)*, poor *(underprivileged)*
inordinacy exaggeration, redundancy
inordinate disproportionate, drastic, egregious, excess, excessive, exorbitant, extreme *(exaggerated)*, fanatical, gluttonous, intemperate, needless, outrageous, profuse, prohibitive *(costly)*, redundant, superfluous, unconscionable, undue *(excessive)*, unreasonable, unwarranted, usurious
inordinate amount redundancy
inordinate desire greed
inordinate desire to gain greed
inordinately particularly, unduly
inordinateness exaggeration
inornate simple
inosculate amalgamate, combine *(join together)*, contact *(touch)*, intertwine, join *(bring together)*
inosculated associated
inpermeable invincible
inpour inflow
inpouring inflow

inquest cross-examination, examination *(study)*, hearing, indagation, inquiry *(systematic investigation)*, inspection, interrogation, pursuit *(chase)*, research, scrutiny, test, trial *(legal proceeding)*
inquietude commotion, consternation, dissatisfaction, distress *(anguish)*, disturbance, misgiving, pandemonium, panic
inquilinus lodger, tenant
inquinare stain, sully, tarnish
inquinatus obscene
inquire canvass, examine *(interrogate)*, research, trace *(follow)*
inquire for delve, hunt
inquire into analyze, canvass, check *(inspect)*, delve, examine *(study)*, hear *(give a legal hearing)*, investigate, monitor, peruse, probe, scrutinize, search, study
inquire into systematically investigate
inquire of consult *(seek information from)*, cross-examine
inquire to ascertain facts investigation
inquirer applicant *(candidate)*, detective
inquirere examine *(interrogate)*
inquiries interrogatories
inquiring inquisitive
inquiry analysis, conversation, cross-examination, cross-questioning, deliberation, discovery, hearing, indagation, inquest, inspection, interrogation, investigation, judgment *(discernment)*, market *(demand)*, matter *(case)*, poll *(canvass)*, probe, pursuit *(chase)*, quest, research, scrutiny, test, trial *(experiment)*, trial *(legal proceeding)*, voir dire
inquiry agent detective
inquisitio examination *(study)*, inquiry *(systematic investigation)*, investigation
inquisition cross-examination, examination *(study)*, hearing, indagation, inquiry *(request for information)*, inquiry *(systematic investigation)*, interrogation, pursuit *(chase)*, question *(inquiry)*, research, scrutiny, test, trial *(legal proceeding)*
inquisitional interrogative
inquisitive interrogative
inquisitive attention diligence *(care)*
inquisitor detective, dictator
inquisitorial dictatorial, interrogative
inquitous sinister
inreparabilis irretrievable
inretire ensnare, entrap
inrevocabilis irrevocable, unavoidable *(not voidable)*
inridere jeer, mock *(deride)*
inritamentum incentive, stimulus
inritare irritate, stimulate
inritum facere invalidate, quash
inritus invalid, null *(invalid)*, unavailing, void *(invalid)*
inroad encroachment, entrance, foray, incursion, inflow, ingress, invasion
inrumpere force *(break)*
inruptio invasion
inrush inflow
insagacious inept *(inappropriate)*
insalubrious adverse *(negative)*, blameful, blameworthy, deleterious, detrimental, disadvantageous, harmful,

inadvisable, malignant, noxious, peccant *(unhealthy)*, pernicious, pestilent, toxic
insalubriousness disadvantage
insalubris insalubrious, peccant *(unhealthy)*
insalubrity disease
insane deranged, lunatic, non compos mentis
insanely deluded non compos mentis
insaneness lunacy
insania insanity
insanity lunacy, paranoia
insanus deranged, frenetic
insatiabilis insatiable
insatiability greed
insatiable gluttonous, rapacious
insatiableness greed
insatiate rapacious
insciens unintentional, unwitting
inscientia ignorance
inscitia ignorance, incapacity
inscitus incompetent
inscius unacquainted, unaware, unwitting
inscribe book, brand *(mark)*, dedicate, enroll, enter *(record)*, file *(place among official records)*, record, register, seal *(solemnize)*, subscribe *(sign)*
inscribe one's name sign
inscribe one's signature indorse, sign
inscribed holographic
inscribere inscribe
inscribing registration
inscriptio address, device *(distinguishing mark)*, inscription
inscription caption, dedication, entry *(record)*, marginalia, notation, phrase, title *(designation)*
inscriptional holographic
inscroll enter *(record)*
inscrutability complication, mystery, opacity
inscrutable complex, dispassionate, inapprehensible, incomprehensible, indefinable, inexplicable, inexpressive, mysterious, opaque
inscrutable person enigma
inscrutableness mystery
insecable solid *(compact)*
insectari inveigh
insecure dubious, open *(accessible)*, precarious, speculative, uncertain *(questionable)*, unreliable, unsound *(not strong)*, untrustworthy, vulnerable
insecurity doubt *(indecision)*, hazard, incertitude, jeopardy, peril, risk, suspicion *(uncertainty)*, threat
insensate callous, deranged, impervious, insensible, insusceptible *(uncaring)*, irrational, lifeless *(dead)*, lunatic, thoughtless, torpid
insensateness insentience
insensibility ignorance, ingratitude, insentience
insensible blind *(not discerning)*, callous, incognizant, insusceptible *(uncaring)*, intangible, lifeless *(dull)*, oblivious, phlegmatic, reckless, torpid, unaware
insensibleness insentience
insensibly unknowingly
insensient lifeless *(dead)*
insensitive blind *(not discerning)*, callous, cold-blooded, cruel, draconian, im-

pervious, insensible, insusceptible (uncaring), obdurate, obtuse, relentless, remorseless, ruthless, unaffected (uninfluenced), unresponsive

insensitivity disinterest (lack of interest), disregard (lack of respect), insentience

insentient callous, inactive, insensible, unaffected (uninfluenced)

inseparability adhesion (affixing)

inseparable close (intimate), coherent (joined), cohesive (compact), compound, conglomerate, conjoint, indivisible, inextricable, infrangible, joint, solid (compact)

inseparable intermixture confusion (turmoil)

inseparableness adhesion (affixing)

insequens subsequent

inserere graft, incorporate (form a corporation)

insert affix, append, attach (join), book, embed, immerse (plunge into), impact, infuse, inject, inscribe, inseminate, interject, interpose, introduce, penetrate, pierce (lance), plant (place firmly), record

insert in a wrapper enclose

insert in an envelope enclose

insert names on a register empanel

insert surreptitiously foist

inserted intermediate

insertion addendum, appendix (accession), attachment (act of affixing), codicil, enclosure, entrance, expletive, inflow, infusion, intervention (imposition into a lawsuit), rider

inset insertion, plant (place firmly)

inseverable indivisible, inextricable, inseparable

inside herein, interior, internal

inside and out throughout (all over)

inside information disclosure (something disclosed), secret, tip (clue)

insider bystander, member (individual in a group)

insidiosus insidious

insidious bad (offensive), collusive, contemptible, covert, deceptive, detrimental, devious, dishonest, disingenuous, fraudulent, furtive, harmful, illusory, lawless, machiavellian, perfidious, pernicious, recreant, sinister, sly, surreptitious, untrue, untrustworthy

insidiousness artifice, bad faith, deceit, fraud, improbity

insight cognition, comprehension, discretion (quality of being discreet), discrimination (good judgment), intelligence (intellect), judgment (discernment), perception, reason (sound judgment), recognition, sagacity, sense (intelligence), understanding (comprehension)

insignia brand, designation (symbol), device (distinguishing mark), label

insignificance immateriality, inconsequence, mediocrity, nonentity, nullity

insignificancy nonentity

insignificant collateral (immaterial), de minimus, expendable, frivolous, futile, ignoble, immaterial, inapposite, inappreciable, inconsequential, inconsiderable, inferior (lower in position), insubstantial, irrelevant, mediocre, minor, negligible, nominal, nonessen-

tial, nonsubstantial (not sufficient), nugatory, paltry, petty, remote (small), slight, tenuous, trivial, unessential, usual

insignificant amount modicum, scintilla

insignificant number minority (outnumbered group)

insincere deceptive, dishonest, disingenuous, disreputable, faithless, false (disloyal), histrionic, machiavellian, mendacious, tartuffish, untrue

insincerity bad faith, deceit, deception, dishonesty, disloyalty, duplicity, falsification, hypocrisy, improbity, indirection (deceitfulness), knavery, misstatement, pretense (ostentation), pretext, story (falsehood)

insinuate allude, connote, hint, imply, impose (intrude), incriminate, indicate, infer, mention, purport

insinuated assumed (inferred), constructive (inferential), implied, subtle (insidious)

insinuates signify (denote)

insinuating calumnious, contemptuous, leading (guiding)

insinuation attribution, charge (accusation), clue, connotation, criticism, defamation, disparagement, hint, implication (inference), indication, innuendo, intimation, mention (reference), reference (allusion), referral, slander, suggestion, tip (clue)

insinuative leading (guiding), suggestive (evocative)

insinuatory circumstantial, suggestive (evocative)

insipid inferior (lower in quality), jejune (dull), lifeless (dull), nondescript, ordinary, pedestrian, stale

insipid remark platitude

insist certify (attest), claim (maintain), coax, coerce, compel, constrain (compel), contend (maintain), demand, dun, dwell (linger over), force (coerce), importune, persist, posit, press (constrain), pressure, reaffirm, urge

insist on call (demand), constrain (compel), enforce, enjoin, order, require (compel)

insist upon assert, claim (demand), enforce, exact, impose (enforce), necessitate, repeat (state again)

insistance instigation

insisted alleged

insistence assertion, coercion, diligence (perseverance), dun, enforcement, force (compulsion), instigation, persuasion, pressure, request, stress (accent)

insistence on a claim assertion

insistence on a right assertion

insistence upon enforcement

insistent dogmatic, exigent, persistent, pertinacious, positive (confident), relentless, urgent, vehement

insistent demand call (appeal), dun

insisting on notice insistent

insite recognition

insitus ingrained, inherent, innate

insobriety dipsomania, inebriation

insolence bad repute, contempt (disdain), contempt (disobedience to the court), contumely, defiance, disdain, disregard (lack of respect), disrespect

insolens impertinent (insolent), inso-

lent

insolent brazen, calumnious, contemptuous, contumacious, disdainful, disorderly, lawless, obtrusive, offensive (offending), orgulous, outrageous, presumptuous, proud (conceited), supercilious

insolentia disrespect

insolently disobedient contumacious

insolicitous insusceptible (uncaring)

insolitus unaccustomed, uncommon

insoluble difficult, incomprehensible, inexplicable, inextricable, infrangible, inscrutable, inseparable, insurmountable, problematic

insoluble difference deadlock, impasse

insolvable incomprehensible, inexplicable

insolvency bankruptcy, default, dishonor (nonpayment), failure (bankruptcy), indigence, poverty

insolvent bankrupt, destitute, impecunious, poor (underprivileged), unsound (not strong)

insolvent debtor delinquent

insons innocent

insouciance disinterest (lack of interest), disregard (unconcern), indifference

insouciant careless, casual, heedless, insusceptible (uncaring), nonchalant

inspect audit, canvass, consider, discern (detect with the senses), examine (study), frisk, investigate, monitor, notice (observe), observe (watch), overlook (superintend), patrol, peruse, probe, research, review, scrutinize, search, study, survey (examine)

inspect accounts officially audit

inspect secretely spy

inspection contemplation, cross-questioning, deliberation, diligence (care), discovery, examination (study), indagation, interrogation, judgment (discernment), observation, probe, research, scrutiny, supervision, surveillance, test, trial (experiment)

inspector detective, director

inspector of accounts comptroller

insperatus unanticipated, unexpected

inspicere examine (interrogate), review, scrutinize

inspiration catalyst, incentive, inducement, influence, instigation, motive, provocation, reason (basis), source

inspirational provocative

inspire agitate (activate), assure (give confidence to), cause, coax, convince, encourage, evoke, exhort, imbue, impress (affect deeply), incite, inculcate, influence, infuse, interest, motivate, originate, prevail (persuade), prompt, reassure, spirit, stimulate

inspire fear discourage, menace

inspire hope assure (give confidence to)

inspired causative, felicitous, original (creative)

inspirer abettor, catalyst

inspiring persuasive, potent, sapid

inspirit agitate (activate), exhort, foment, incite, infuse, lobby, motivate, promise (raise expectations), reassure, spirit, stimulate

inspirited conscious (awake), sanguine

inspiriting auspicious, moving *(evoking emotion)*, potent, propitious
instabilis insecure
instability doubt *(indecision)*, fault *(weakness)*, frailty, inconsistency, indecision, jeopardy, risk
instability of mental powers lunacy
instable volatile
install admit *(give access)*, bestow, commence, constitute *(establish)*, deposit *(place)*, hire, induct, initiate, instate, invest *(vest)*, locate, lodge *(house)*, nominate, plant *(place firmly)*, receive *(permit to enter)*
installation appointment *(act of designating)*, building *(business of assembling)*, deputation *(selection of delegates)*, designation *(naming)*
installed situated
installing registration
installment advance *(allowance)*, binder, collection *(payment)*, component, constituent *(part)*, deposit, downpayment, handsel, honorarium, installation, pledge *(security)*, segment
installment buying credit *(delayed payment)*
instance call *(appeal)*, case *(example)*, detail, evidence, example, exemplify, expression *(manifestation)*, illustrate, illustration, occasion, occurrence, particular, quote, sample, situation, specify, specimen
instances circumstances
instant crucial, current, expeditious, immediate *(at once)*, imminent, important *(urgent)*, insistent, instantaneous, pending *(imminent)*, point *(period of time)*, present *(current)*, prompt, rapid, requisite, urgent
instantaneity dispatch *(promptness)*
instantaneous immediate *(at once)*, prompt, summary, unexpected
instantaneously forthwith, instantly
instantly forthwith
instar omnium pendent
instare insist
instate delegate, induct, invest *(vest)*
instatement installation
instauration rehabilitation, renewal, reparation *(keeping in repair)*
instead of in lieu of
instead of a parent loco parentis
instigare incite, press *(goad)*
instigate abet, agitate *(activate)*, bait *(harass)*, evoke, exhort, foment, impel, incite, induce, inspire, lobby, motivate, pique, press *(goad)*, prompt, provoke, spirit, stimulate, suborn, urge
instigating moving *(evoking emotion)*, offensive *(taking the initiative)*
instigation cause *(reason)*, determinant, impetus, incentive, inducement, influence, origination, provocation, reason *(basis)*
instigative incendiary, offensive *(taking the initiative)*
instigator abettor, catalyst, demagogue, malcontent, special interest
instill communicate, discipline *(train)*, imbue, inculcate, infuse, initiate, inject, instruct *(teach)*, pervade, plant *(place firmly)*
instillare instill
instillation infusion
instinct caliber *(mental capacity)*, gift

(flair), proclivity, sense *(feeling)*, tendency
instinctive born *(innate)*, hereditary, inherent, innate, native *(inborn)*, natural, organic
instinctive belief credence
instinctual born *(innate)*, hereditary, native *(inborn)*, natural
instituere discipline *(train)*, educate, establish *(launch)*, instate, instruct *(teach)*
institute admit *(give access)*, building *(structure)*, cause, chamber *(body)*, commence, company *(enterprise)*, constitute *(establish)*, corporation, create, embark, establish *(launch)*, facility *(institution)*, foundation *(organization)*, generate, initiate, invest *(vest)*, launch *(initiate)*, legislate, maintain *(commence)*, make, organization *(association)*, organize *(unionize)*, originate, pass *(approve)*, preface, produce *(manufacture)*, society
institute a comparison contrast
institute a lawsuit complain *(charge)*
institute a legal proceeding sue
institute an action against a third party implead
institute an inquiry analyze, canvass, delve, probe
institute by law enact, pass *(approve)*
institute commingling of races desegregate
institute legal proceedings litigate
institute process sue
instituted positive *(prescribed)*
institutio instruction *(teaching)*
institution building *(business of assembling)*, concern *(business establishment)*, corporation, custom, firm, formation, foundation *(organization)*, installation, institute, organization *(association)*, prescription *(custom)*, rubric *(authoritative rule)*
institution of commercial sites development *(building)*
institution of learning institute
institution of proceedings service *(delivery of legal process)*
institution where justice is rendered judicatory
institutionalize confine, constrain *(imprison)*, jail
institutive causal, causative, prime *(original)*
institutor author *(originator)*
institutum determination, intention, matter *(subject)*, principle *(axiom)*, purpose
instruct admonish *(advise)*, apprise, charge *(instruct on the law)*, command, communicate, control *(regulate)*, convey *(communicate)*, counsel, decree, demonstrate *(establish)*, dictate, direct *(order)*, direct *(show)*, disabuse, discipline *(train)*, edify, educate, enjoin, enlighten, exhort, impart, inculcate, inform *(notify)*, initiate, instill, notice *(give formal warning)*, notify, nurture, order, oversee, prescribe, recommend, signify *(inform)*, superintend
instruct badly misdirect
instructed acquainted, familiar *(informed)*, informed *(educated)*, knowing, learned
instructing advisory
instruction admonition, advice,

canon, caveat, charge *(command)*, dictate, direction *(guidance)*, directive, discipline *(training)*, dispatch *(message)*, edification, education, experience *(background)*, fiat, guidance, law, mandate, order *(judicial directive)*, precept, preparation, prescription *(directive)*, principle *(axiom)*, recommendation, regulation *(rule)*, subpoena, tip *(clue)*
instruction to appear process *(summons)*
instructional didactic, disciplinary *(educational)*, informative, leading *(guiding)*
instructional corps faculty *(teaching staff)*
instructional personnel faculty *(teaching staff)*
instructions charge *(statement to the jury)*, direction *(order)*
instructive decretal, didactic, disciplinary *(educational)*, informative, informatory, leading *(guiding)*
instructor counselor, pedagogue
instructors faculty *(teaching staff)*
instruere endow, furnish, garnish, marshal
instrument appliance, blank *(form)*, certificate, charter *(license)*, conduit *(channel)*, deed, device *(mechanism)*, document, expedient, facility *(instrumentality)*, form *(document)*, forum *(medium)*, indenture, instrumentality, interagent, lease, medium, organ, proctor, resource, tool, will *(testamentary instrument)*
instrument evidencing an agreement contract
instrument for use in combat cudgel
instrument granting possession of premises lease
instrument held until the performance of a condition escrow
instrument in proof affidavit, averment
instrument of proof certification *(attested copy)*, evidence
instrument of war cudgel
instrument of warfare bomb
instrument which transfers title to realty deed
instrumental causal, clerical, constructive *(creative)*, contributory, effective *(efficient)*, functional, intermediate, ministerial, operative, practical
instrumentality agency *(legal relationship)*, intercession, medium, organ
instruments paraphernalia *(apparatus)*
instruments of combat weapons
instrumentum appliance, document, instrument *(tool)*
insubmission contempt *(disobedience to the court)*, defiance
insubmissive froward, insubordinate
insubordinate broken *(unfulfilled)*, contumacious, disobedient, froward, impertinent *(insolent)*, insurgent, intractable, lawless, malcontent, nonconsenting, perverse, recalcitrant, recusant, restive, unruly
insubordination anarchy, contempt *(disobedience to the court)*, defiance, disloyalty, disrespect, insurrection, mutiny, rebellion, resistance, revolt, sedi-

tion

insubstantial circumstantial, collateral *(immaterial)*, deficient, delusive, ill-founded, illusory, immaterial, inadequate, inappreciable, inconsiderable, insipid, intangible, minor, negligible, nonsubstantial *(not sufficient)*, nugatory, null *(insignificant)*, perfunctory, remote *(small)*, superficial, unfounded, unsound *(fallacious)*, void *(invalid)*

insubstantiality artifice, blank *(emptiness)*, immateriality, impalpability, insignificance, nonentity

insuetus unaccustomed

insufferable contemptible, deplorable, intolerable, loathsome, objectionable, obnoxious, odious, painful, repugnant *(exciting aversion)*, repulsive, severe, undesirable, unendurable

insufficiency abortion *(fiasco)*, dearth, defect, deficiency, deficit, delinquency *(shortage)*, detriment, disability *(physical inability)*, disadvantage, disqualification *(factor that disqualifies)*, failure *(falling short)*, fault *(weakness)*, handicap, immateriality, impotence, inability, incompetence, indigence, inefficacy, market *(demand)*, need *(deprivation)*, paucity, privation

insufficiency as a matter of law nonsuit

insufficiency of funds failure *(bankruptcy)*

insufficiency of service emergency

insufficient barren, defective, deficient, devoid, imperfect, inadept, inadequate, incapable, incompetent, ineffective, ineffectual, inferior *(lower in quality)*, minimal, null *(insignificant)*, partial *(relating to a part)*, scarce, unable, unsatisfactory, vacuous

insufficient evidence nonsuit

insufficient funds default

insufficient income indigence

insufficiently considered injudicious

insular alien *(unrelated)*, alone *(solitary)*, disjunctive *(tending to disjoin)*, limited, parochial, private *(secluded)*, provincial, regional, remote *(secluded)*, separate, sole, solitary

insulate isolate, protect, seclude

insulation buffer zone, bulwark

insulator bulwark

insulse lifeless *(dull)*

insulsus insipid

insult affront, aspersion, bait *(harass)*, contumely, defamation, defilement, denigrate, diatribe, disoblige, disparage, disregard *(lack of respect)*, disrespect, flout, hector, humiliate, jeer, mock *(deride)*, pique, provocation, provoke, rebuff, rebuff, revilement

insulting abusive, calumnious, caustic, contemptuous, disdainful, impertinent *(insolent)*, insolent, libelous, offensive *(offending)*, outrageous, pejorative, perverse, presumptuous, scathing, scurrilous

insumere spend

insuperabilis irresistible

insuperability impasse, impossibility

insuperable impossible, impracticable, indomitable, inexpugnable, insurmountable, invincible, unattainable

insuperable obstacle deterrent, impasse

insuperableness impossibility

insupportable indefensible, insufferable, intolerable, unsustainable, untenable

insuppressible hot-blooded, intractable, manifest, uncontrollable

insurance guaranty, safeguard, security *(pledge)*, undertaking *(pledge)*

insurance adviser actuary

insurance company insurer

insurance contract policy *(contract)*

insure avouch *(guarantee)*, bond *(secure a debt)*, certify *(attest)*, cosign, cover *(guard)*, cover *(provide for)*, ensure, guarantee, harbor, indemnify, pledge *(deposit)*, preserve, promise *(vow)*, sponsor, underwrite

insured agreed *(promised)*, definite, fully secured, official, safe, secure *(free from danger)*

insurer sponsor, surety *(guarantor)*

insurgence anarchy, commotion, defiance, insurrection, mutiny, outbreak, outburst, rebellion, resistance, riot, sedition, treason

insurgency defiance, disloyalty, insurrection, mutiny, rebellion, revolt

insurgent disobedient, insubordinate, malcontent, radical *(favoring drastic change)*, restive, uncontrollable

insurmountability impossibility

insurmountable cardinal *(outstanding)*, difficult, impossible, impracticable, indomitable, inexpugnable, insuperable, invincible, unattainable

insurrect disobey, rebel, secede

insurrection anarchy, commotion, defiance, disloyalty, mutiny, outbreak, outburst, rebellion, resistance, revolt, revolution, riot, sedition, treason

insurrectional disobedient, renitent

insurrectionary disorderly, insubordinate, insurgent, radical *(favoring drastic change)*

insurrectionist insurgent, malcontent

insusceptibility to change indestructibility

insusceptible indestructible

insusceptible of change indefeasible

insusceptible to change permanent

insusceptire insusceptible *(uncaring)*

intact gross *(total)*, inviolate, live *(existing)*, safe, stable, unblemished, undiminished, whole *(undamaged)*

intactilis intangible (adjective), intangible (noun)

intactness entirety, whole

intactus intact, inviolate

intaglio stamp

intake receipt *(act of receiving)*, revenue

intakes approaches

intaking acquisition

intangibility immateriality, impalpability

intangible elusive, immaterial, impalpable, imponderable, inappreciable, incorporeal, nonsubstantial *(not sturdy)*, vague

intangible assets estate *(property)*

integer full, impartial, incorruptible, inculpable

integer individual

integer intact, inviolate, pure, unadulterated, unblemished, undiminished,

unprejudiced, upright

integer whole

integral essential *(inherent)*, indispensable, inherent, necessary *(required)*, total, unit *(item)*

integral part component, constituent *(part)*, detail, element, factor *(ingredient)*, ingredient, member *(constituent part)*, necessity, need *(requirement)*

integrality corpus

integrant constituent *(part)*, detail, integral

integrant part constituent *(part)*

integrate aggregate, connect *(relate)*, coordinate, desegregate, embody, embrace *(encircle)*, relate *(establish a connection)*

integrated coadunate, collective, composite, compound, conjoint, inseparable

integration affiliation *(amalgamation)*, coalition, consolidation, corpus, federation, merger, totality

integrative collective

integritas innocence, integrity, principle *(virtue)*, rectitude

integrity adhesion *(loyalty)*, conscience, credibility, ethics, fairness, honesty, honor *(good reputation)*, principle *(virtue)*, probity, rectitude, right *(righteousness)*, trustworthiness, truth, veracity, whole

integument cover *(protection)*

integumentum veil

intellect caliber *(mental capacity)*, character *(personal quality)*, comprehension, mastermind, reason *(sound judgment)*, sense *(intelligence)*

intellection apprehension *(perception)*, cognition, deliberation, knowledge *(awareness)*, ratiocination, reflection *(thought)*

intellectual faculty intelligence *(intellect)*

intellectual literate, mastermind, profound *(esoteric)*, sapient

intellectual ability sense *(intelligence)*

intellectual faculties judgment *(discernment)*

intellectual power caliber *(mental capacity)*, comprehension, intelligence *(intellect)*

intellectual powers intellect, judgment *(discernment)*

intellectual prodigy mastermind

intellectualism comprehension

intellectuality comprehension, education, intellect, intelligence *(intellect)*, sense *(intelligence)*

intellectualization concept, contemplation, ratiocination

intellectualize muse, ponder, reason *(conclude)*, study

intellectually deep profound *(esoteric)*

intellegentia comprehension, discrimination *(good judgment)*, insight, intellect, intelligence *(intellect)*

intellegere realize *(understand)*, understand

intellegi non potest incomprehensible

intelligence aptitude, caliber *(mental capacity)*, common sense, competence *(ability)*, discrimination *(good judgment)*, espionage, information *(knowledge)*, intellect, knowledge *(awareness)*, notification, reason *(sound judgment)*, report *(detailed account)*, sagacity, understanding *(comprehension)*

intelligence agent spy

intelligencer harbinger, informant, informer *(a person who provides information)*, spy

intelligent discreet, perspicacious, rational, reasonable *(rational)*, sapient, sciential, sensible

intelligent grip information *(knowledge)*

intelligibility coherence

intelligible clear *(apparent)*, cognizable, coherent *(clear)*, comprehensible, distinct *(clear)*, explicit, lucid, obvious, pellucid, scrutable, simple, solvable, unambiguous, unmistakable

intelligibly fairly *(clearly)*

intemperance debauchery, dipsomania, exaggeration, greed, inebriation, waste

intemperate disorderly, dissolute, drastic, drunk, egregious, excessive, exorbitant, extreme *(exaggerated)*, gluttonous, hot-blooded, incendiary, inordinate, insatiable, lawless, prodigal, profligate *(extravagant)*, profuse, promiscuous, unconscionable, unreasonable, unrestrained *(not repressed)*, wanton

intemperately unduly

intemperateness exaggeration

intempestivus untimely

intend allocate, attempt, plan, predetermine, purport, pursue *(strive to gain)*

intendance generalship

intendancy generalship

intendant administrator, director, procurator, superintendent

intended aforethought, apparent *(presumptive)*, bona fide, deliberate, express, intentional, knowing, premeditated, prospective, purposeful, tactical, voluntary, willful

intended for a specific purpose express

intended for instruction didactic

intended for teaching didactic

intended for youth juvenile

intended result end *(intent)*, purpose

intended to bring about delay dilatory

intended to defer decision dilatory

intended to gain time dilatory

intendere exert, intend

intendment animus, end *(intent)*, plan

intense acute, close *(rigorous)*, drastic, eager, fervent, forcible, harsh, hot-blooded, intensive, major, potent, powerful, profound *(intense)*, purposeful, serious *(grave)*, severe, strong, trenchant, vehement

intense application diligence *(care)*

intense desire ardor, greed

intense study diligence *(care)*

intense thought diligence *(care)*

intensification advance *(increase)*, aggravation *(exacerbation)*, augmentation, boom *(increase)*, exaggeration, growth *(increase)*

intensified intense

intensify accrue *(increase)*, aggravate *(exacerbate)*, compound, consolidate *(strengthen)*, develop, dwell *(linger over)*, enhance, enlarge, exacerbate, ex-

pand, heighten *(augment)*, magnify, reinforce

intensity degree *(magnitude)*, force *(strength)*, life *(vitality)*, main force, passion, pressure, rigor, severity, strength

intensity of expression emphasis

intensive comprehensive, cumulative *(intensifying)*, radical *(extreme)*, resounding, thorough, unmitigated

intent animus, cause *(reason)*, circumspect, connotation, contemplation, content *(meaning)*, destination, earnest, forethought, goal, hot-blooded, idea, industrious, intense, objective, pertinacious, plan, point *(purpose)*, project, purpose, purposeful, reason *(basis)*, scienter, serious *(devoted)*, signification, spirit, volition, will *(desire)*

intent on solicitous

intent upon decisive, insistent, resolute

intention animus, cause *(reason)*, conatus, connotation, contemplation, content *(meaning)*, design *(intent)*, destination, end *(intent)*, expectation, forethought, goal, idea, objective, plan, point *(purpose)*, predetermination, project, prospect *(outlook)*, purpose, reason *(basis)*, resolution *(decision)*, scienter, signification, target

intentional deliberate, express, knowing, premeditated, purposeful, voluntary, willful

intentional act overt act

intentional deception fraud

intentional distortion lie

intentional exaggeration lie

intentional exclusion of lessee eviction

intentional killing murder

intentional misstatement falsehood, lie, misrepresentation, perjury, story *(falsehood)*

intentional relinquishment waiver

intentional untruth lie, story *(falsehood)*

intentional wrongdoing malice

intentionality animus, design *(intent)*

intentionally knowingly, purposely

intentionally disregard ignore

intentionally untrue false *(not genuine)*

intentiveness interest *(concern)*

intentivus intensive

intentness compulsion *(obsession)*, diligence *(care)*, diligence *(perseverance)*, industry *(activity)*, interest *(concern)*, observation, preoccupation, regard *(attention)*

intentus earnest, intense, intent, vigilant

inter se congredi meet

inter se dare reciprocate

inter se repugnare contradict

interacting correlative, interlocking

interaction course

interactive concerted, mutual *(reciprocal)*

interaffiliated interrelated

interaffiliation mutuality

interagency medium

interagent adjuster, advocate *(counselor)*, arbiter, arbitrator, factor *(commission merchant)*, go-between, instrumentality, liaison, medium, umpire

interallied associated, concurrent *(united)*, interrelated

interassociated interrelated

interassociation mutuality

interblend combine *(join together)*, consolidate *(unite)*, desegregate, embody, incorporate *(include)*

interbreed commingle

intercalate enter *(insert)*, interject, interpose

intercalation insertion, intervention *(interference)*

intercapedo interruption, pause

intercede arbitrate *(conciliate)*, impose *(intrude)*, interfere, interpose, intervene, mediate, negotiate, reconcile

intercede for assist, contribute *(assist)*, help

interceder adjuster, advocate *(counselor)*, arbiter, arbitrator, go-between, intermediary, referee

intercedere intervene, protest

intercept avert, block, check *(restrain)*, clog, discontinue *(break continuity)*, disrupt, eavesdrop, foil, forestall, hamper, hijack, hinder, inhibit, interfere, interpose, interrupt, occlude, overhear, parry, prevent, stave, stay *(halt)*, stem *(check)*, stop, thwart

interception interruption, intervention *(interference)*, restraint

interceptor embezzler

intercessio veto

intercession advocacy, arbitration, assistance, collective bargaining, intervention *(interference)*, mediation

intercessor adjuster, advocate *(counselor)*, amicus curiae, arbiter, arbitrator, counselor, intermediary, judge, jurist, liaison, referee, umpire

interchange alternate *(take turns)*, barter, bequeath, change, commerce, communication *(discourse)*, consignment, contact *(association)*, contact *(communicate)*, conversation, conversion *(change)*, convert *(change use)*, crossroad *(intersection)*, devolution, devolve, displace *(replace)*, exchange, handle *(trade)*, mutuality, quid pro quo, reciprocate, reciprocity, replace, replacement, return *(respond)*, subrogation, trade *(commerce)*, trade, vary

interchange ideas converse

interchange information converse

interchange of commodities commerce

interchange of goods commerce

interchange of information conversation

interchange of opinions conference, conversation

interchange of speech conversation

interchange of thoughts conversation

interchange of views discourse, meeting *(conference)*

interchange opinions converse

interchange regularly alternate *(take turns)*

interchange successively alternate *(take turns)*

interchange thoughts communicate, converse

interchange views confer *(consult)*, consult *(ask advice of)*, discuss

interchangeability identity *(similar-*

ity), mutuality

interchangeable akin *(germane),* co-equal, cognate, comparable *(equivalent),* convertible, disjunctive *(alternative),* equivalent, identical, negotiable, reciprocal

interchangeable commitment mutual understanding

interchangeableness par *(equality)*

interchanged mutual *(reciprocal)*

interchanges vicissitudes

intercipere embezzle

interclasped conjoint

interclude deter, occlude

intercommunicate communicate, contact *(communicate)*

intercommunication communication *(discourse),* contact *(association),* conversation, notification, parley

intercommunion consortium *(marriage companionship),* contact *(association)*

interconnect connect *(relate),* contact *(touch),* involve *(implicate),* juxtapose, relate *(establish a connection)*

interconnected interrelated, reciprocal, related, relative *(relevant)*

interconnection chain *(nexus),* coalescence, connection *(fastening),* intersection, mutuality, nexus, privity, relation *(connection),* relationship *(connection)*

interconnections ties

intercourse business *(commerce),* commerce, communication *(discourse),* contact *(association),* dealings, exchange, interchange, sodality

intercross cross *(intersect)*

intercrossing crossroad *(intersection),* intersection

intercurrent intermediate

interdenominational nonsectarian

interdependence mutuality, relationship *(connection)*

interdependent cognate, conjoint, correlative, inseparable, mutual *(collective),* reciprocal, related

interdicere forbid, inhibit, interdict

interdict ban, bar *(obstruction),* bar *(exclude),* block, coerce, condemn *(ban),* constraint *(restriction),* debar, enjoin, forbid, inhibit, prohibit, prohibition, proscription, renounce, restrain, restrict, veto

interdicted illegitimate *(illegal),* illicit

interdictio aquae et ignis banishment

interdiction canon, constraint *(restriction),* decree, injunction, obviation, prohibition, proscription, refusal, restriction, veto

interdictive prohibitive *(restrictive),* restrictive

interdictory prohibitive *(restrictive),* restrictive

interdictum prohibition

interest activity, advocacy, appertain, behalf, benefit *(betterment),* birthright, boom *(increase),* business *(affair),* claim *(right),* commission *(fee),* concern *(involve),* contribution *(participation),* dividend, dominion *(absolute ownership),* engage *(involve),* equity *(share of ownership),* fee *(estate),* holding *(property owned),* immerse *(engross),* market *(demand),* motivate, nepotism, occupy *(en-*

gage), part *(portion),* patronage *(support),* prescription *(claim of title),* profit, regard *(attention),* regard *(esteem),* remainder *(estate in property),* revenue, significance, title *(right),* weight *(importance),* welfare

interest certificate coupon

interest group constituency

interest in land easement, estate *(property)*

interest in real estate leasehold

interest in real property freehold

interest of a lessee leasehold

interested eager, inquisitive, interrogative, one-sided, partial *(biased),* receptive, unjust

interested party privy, prospect *(prospective patron)*

interesting attractive, moving *(evoking emotion),* provocative, sapid

interests affairs, dealings

interfere arrest *(stop),* censor, clog, constrict *(inhibit),* counter, countervail, debar, defer *(put off),* delay, disqualify, disrupt, disturb, encroach, encumber *(hinder),* estop, fight *(counteract),* forestall, hamper, hinder, hold up *(delay),* impede, impose *(intrude),* infringe, intercede, interpose, interrupt, intervene, intrude, mediate, militate, obtrude, obturate, overstep, parry, prevent, prohibit, tamper, thwart

interfere with bar *(hinder),* block, collide *(clash),* conflict, counteract, deter, disadvantage, discontinue *(break continuity),* molest *(annoy),* obstruct, oppugn, preclude, suspend

interference bar *(obstruction),* barrier, check *(bar),* collision *(dispute),* conflict, damper *(stopper),* deterrence, deterrent, disadvantage, embargo, encroachment, encumbrance, fetter, filibuster, frustration, handicap, hiatus, hindrance, impediment, imposition *(excessive burden),* infringement, intercession, interruption, intervention *(imposition into a lawsuit),* intrusion, invasion, mediation, molestation, nuisance, obstruction, onus *(burden),* opposition, prohibition, resistance, restraint, veto

interfering intrusive, mesne, obtrusive, preventive, prohibitive *(restrictive)*

interficere dispatch *(put to death),* kill *(defeat),* kill *(murder),* slay

interfuse combine *(join together),* consolidate *(unite),* converge, desegregate, embody, incorporate *(include),* intersperse, penetrate, pervade, unite

interfused conjoint

interfusion coalescence, incorporation *(blend)*

intericere interject, interpose

interim abeyance, cessation *(interlude),* hiatus, interlocutory, interruption, interval, moratorium, pause, pendency, provisional, recess, respite *(interval of rest),* shifting, temporary, tentative, time, transient

interim agreement modus vivendi

interim dividend coupon

interimere dispatch *(put to death),* slay

interior internal

interire perish

interjacence arbitration, intervention *(interference)*

interjacent intermediate, mesne

interjaculate inject, interject

interject comment, discontinue *(break continuity),* enter *(insert),* inject, interfere, interpose

interjection expletive, insertion, intercession, intervention *(imposition into a lawsuit),* intervention *(interference),* remark

interjection into a lawsuit intervention *(imposition into a lawsuit)*

interknit intertwine

interlace commingle, conjoin, desegregate, implicate, incorporate *(include),* intertwine

interlaced complex, compound

interlacement incorporation *(blend)*

interlard commingle, desegregate, intersperse

interlarded promiscuous

interlink annex *(add),* combine *(join together),* connect *(join together),* intertwine, join *(bring together)*

interlinked coadunate, coherent *(joined),* correlative, interrelated

interlinking interlocking

interlock bond *(hold together),* conjoin, connect *(join together),* engage *(involve),* join *(bring together)*

interlocked coadunate, coherent *(joined)*

interlocking coalition

interlocution communication *(discourse),* conference, conversation, discourse, parlance, parley, speech

interlocutor adjuster, advocate *(counselor),* spokesman

interlope accroach, balk, encroach, impinge, impose *(intrude),* infringe, intrude, obtrude

interloper alien

interloping encroachment, intervention *(interference),* intrusion, intrusive, invasion

interlude abeyance, hiatus, interruption, interval, lapse *(break),* leave *(absence),* lull, pause, pendency, recess, respite *(interval of rest),* time

intermeddle intercede, interfere, interpose, intervene, obtrude, tamper

intermeddling intercession, intervention *(interference)*

intermedial interlocutory, ministerial

intermediary adjuster, advocate *(counselor),* agent, arbiter, arbitrator, broker, clerical, deputy, factor *(commission merchant),* forum *(medium),* go-between, instrumentality, interagent, interlocutory, intermediate, liaison, medium, mesne, ministerial, procurator, referee, umpire, vicarious *(delegated)*

intermediate adjuster, advocate *(counselor),* agent, arbiter, arbitrator, average *(midmost),* go-between, instrumentality, interagent, intercede, interim, interpose, medium, mesne, ministerial, negotiate, procurator, referee

intermediate agent advocate *(counselor),* go-between, interagent, medium

intermediate time cessation *(interlude),* pendency, respite *(interval of rest)*

intermediation agency *(legal relationship),* arbitration, collective bargaining, intercession, intervention *(interference)*

intermediator adjuster, advocate *(counselor)*, arbiter, go-between, interagent, referee, umpire
intermedium adjuster, advocate *(counselor)*, agent, broker, chain *(nexus)*, conduit *(intermediary)*, instrumentality, liaison, nexus, procurator, umpire
interminability indestructibility, perpetuity
interminable continual *(perpetual)*, durable, incessant, indeterminate, infinite, innumerable, open-ended, permanent, perpetual, profuse, unlimited
interminably ad infinitum
interminate incessant
intermingle commingle, confuse *(create disorder)*, desegregate, interject, intersperse, merge
intermingled compound
intermissio cessation *(interlude)*, cessation *(termination)*, halt, interruption, pause
intermission abeyance, adjournment, cessation *(interlude)*, delay, extension *(postponement)*, halt, hiatus, interruption, interval, leave *(absence)*, lull, pause, pendency, recess, remission, respite *(interval of rest)*
intermit adjourn, cease, delay, desist, discontinue *(break continuity)*, disrupt, fluctuate, interfere, interrupt, pause, quit *(discontinue)*, recess, recur, suspend
intermittence irregularity
intermittent broken *(interrupted)*, disjunctive *(tending to disjoin)*, infrequent, periodic, sporadic
intermittere interrupt, neglect, pause, suspend
intermitti abeyance
intermitting disjunctive *(tending to disjoin)*, intermittent, sporadic
intermix combine *(join together)*, commingle, denature, desegregate, diffuse, embody, incorporate *(include)*, intertwine, merge
intermixed composite, conjoint, miscellaneous, promiscuous
intermixture incorporation *(blend)*, integration *(amalgamation)*, melange, solution *(substance)*
intermutation mutuality
intern arrest *(apprehend)*, commit *(institutionalize)*, confine, constrain *(imprison)*, detain *(hold in custody)*, imprison, lock, shut
internal domestic *(household)*, inherent, interior, intrinsic *(deep down)*, subjective
internalize accept *(embrace)*, understand
international compact treaty
internecine deadly, destructive, detrimental, harmful, lethal, noxious
internecive lethal
interned arrested *(apprehended)*
internee captive, convict, hostage, prisoner
interning commitment *(confinement)*
internment apprehension *(act of arresting)*, arrest, bondage, captivity, commitment *(confinement)*, constraint *(imprisonment)*, detention, durance, incarceration
internoscere discriminate *(distin-*

guish), distinguish
internuncio advocate *(counselor)*, broker, plenipotentiary, referee
interpellare interfere, interrupt
interpellate cross-examine, examine *(interrogate)*
interpellation citation *(charge)*, cross-examination, question *(inquiry)*
interpenetrate break *(fracture)*, enter *(penetrate)*, intersperse, permeate, pervade
interpenetration osmosis
interplay mutuality, reciprocity
interpolare falsification, falsify
interpolate inject, interject, intersperse
interpolation expletive, insertion, intervention *(interference)*
interponere interject, interpose
interpose comment, discontinue *(break continuity)*, enter *(insert)*, impose *(intrude)*, inject, intercede, interfere, interject, interrupt, intersperse, intervene, introduce, obtrude
interpose no obstacles authorize
interposed intermediate
interpositio insertion
interposition arbitration, collective bargaining, deterrent, hindrance, intercession, intervention *(imposition into a lawsuit)*, intervention *(interference)*, introduction
interpres broker, go-between
interpret characterize, clarify, comment, construe *(comprehend)*, construe *(translate)*, define, determine, educate, elucidate, enlighten, explain, explicate, expound, illustrate, judge, read, recite, render *(depict)*, resolve *(solve)*, review, solve
interpret falsely slant
interpret incorrectly misconceive, misread
interpretability construction
interpretable accountable *(explainable)*, determinable *(ascertainable)*
interpretari construe *(translate)*, elucidate, explicate, interpret
interpretatio construction, explanation, paraphrase
interpretation clarification, comment, connotation, construction, content *(meaning)*, definition, diagnosis, explanation, meaning, paraphrase, rendition *(explication)*, signification, solution *(answer)*
interpretational interpretive
interpretative demonstrative *(illustrative)*, discursive *(analytical)*
interpreted coherent *(clear)*
interpreter judge
interpreters of the law judiciary
interpretive demonstrative *(illustrative)*, descriptive
interregnum abeyance, anarchy, cessation *(interlude)*, duration, hiatus, interval, lull, pendency
interrelate connect *(relate)*, involve *(implicate)*, relate *(establish a connection)*
interrelated coadunate, cognate, coherent *(joined)*, collateral *(accompanying)*, correlative, mutual *(reciprocal)*, reciprocal, related, tangential
interrelation building *(business of assembling)*, chain *(nexus)*, coherence,

connection *(relation)*, contact *(association)*, content *(structure)*, mutuality, nexus, proportion, relationship *(connection)*
interrelation of parts organization *(structure)*
interrelationship relation *(connection)*, relationship *(connection)*
interritus undaunted
interrogate cross-examine, inquire, investigate, pose *(propound)*, probe
interrogatio inquiry *(request for information)*, interrogation
interrogation cross-examination, cross-questioning, examination *(test)*, hearing, indagation, inquest, inquiry *(request for information)*, inquiry *(systematic investigation)*, investigation, question *(inquiry)*, test
interrogational interrogative
interrogative inquisitive
interrogativus interrogative
interrogatory question *(inquiry)*
interrumpere break *(fracture)*
interrupt arrest *(stop)*, balk, cease, check *(restrain)*, close *(terminate)*, condemn *(ban)*, continue *(adjourn)*, cross *(intersect)*, defer *(put off)*, desist, discontinue *(break continuity)*, disorganize, disrupt, disturb, encumber *(hinder)*, estop, halt, hamper, hinder, hold up *(delay)*, impede, inhibit, interfere, interject, interpose, intervene, intrude, molest *(annoy)*, obstruct, obtrude, occlude, pause, preclude, prevent, recess, stall, stay *(halt)*, stem *(check)*, stop, suspend, thwart, toll *(stop)*, withstand
interrupt work strike *(refuse to work)*
interrupted arrested *(checked)*, desultory, disconnected, disjointed, disjunctive *(tending to disjoin)*, intermittent
interrupting obtrusive
interruption abeyance, adjournment, cessation *(interlude)*, check *(bar)*, cloture, damper *(stopper)*, deferment, delay, disassociation, discontinuance *(act of discontinuing)*, disturbance, frustration, halt, hiatus, hindrance, impediment, interval, intervention *(interference)*, intrusion, lapse *(break)*, layoff, lull, molestation, obstruction, pause, pendency, recess, remission, respite *(interval of rest)*, split, stay, violation
interruptive intrusive, obtrusive
intersect cross *(intersect)*, separate, split, traverse
intersecting road crossroad *(intersection)*
intersection crossroad *(intersection)*, meeting *(encounter)*
intersperse diffuse, dissolve *(disperse)*
interstate commerce commerce
interstice hiatus, interruption, interval, rift *(gap)*, space
interthread intertwine
intertwine combine *(join together)*, connect *(join together)*, consolidate *(unite)*, implicate, join *(bring together)*, merge
intertwined inseparable, related
intertwist annex *(add)*, combine *(join together)*, conjoin, intertwine, join *(bring together)*
interval abeyance, cessation *(interlude)*, discontinuance *(act of discontinu-*

ing), duration, hiatus, moratorium, pause, pendency, period, point *(period of time),* recess, remission, space, term *(duration),* time
interval of ease reprieve
interval of rest leave *(absence)*
interval of years age
intervallum interruption, interval, pause
intervene arbitrate *(conciliate),* check *(restrain),* defer *(put off),* discontinue *(break continuity),* disrupt, estop, forestall, hold up *(delay),* impose *(intrude),* intercede, interfere, interject, interpose, mediate, obstruct, obtrude, parry, tamper
intervener actor, adjuster, advocate *(counselor),* arbiter, interagent, medium, party *(litigant),* referee
intervenient intermediate, mesne
intervening interlocutory, intermediate, mesne, ministerial
intervening agent interagent
intervening episode cessation *(interlude)*
intervening party amicus curiae
intervening period cessation *(interlude),* hiatus, pause, pendency, recess
intervening space cessation *(interlude)*
intervening time cessation *(interlude),* interval
intervenire interfere, intervene
intervenor amicus curiae, arbitrator, litigant, umpire
intervention agency *(legal relationship),* arbitration, collective bargaining, intercession, invasion, mediation
intervention to facilitate a compromise mediation
interventional interlocutory
interventionist advocate *(counselor),* arbitrator
interventor advocate *(counselor)*
interventus intervention *(interference)*
intervertere embezzle
interview appointment *(meeting),* confrontation *(act of setting face to face),* conversation, converse, examination *(test),* examine *(interrogate),* parley
interviewers press
interweave combine *(join together),* conjoin, connect *(join together),* interject, intersperse, intertwine, join *(bring together)*
interwoven complex, compound, interrelated, promiscuous, related
intestate individual decedent
intestinus internal
intimacy confidence *(relation of trust),* consortium *(marriage companionship),* contact *(association),* marriage *(intimate relationship),* privacy, rapport, secret
intimate advise, connote, consociate, familiar *(informed),* hint, imply, indicate, infer, inseparable, mention, personal *(private),* private *(confidential),* purport, signify *(denote)*
intimate connection affiliation *(connectedness)*
intimated assumed *(inferred)*
intimately allied affiliated, cognate
intimately related affiliated, cognate, consanguineous
intimation cloud *(suspicion),* clue,

hint, implication *(inference),* indication, insinuation, mention *(reference),* premonition, reference *(allusion),* report *(rumor),* suggestion, suspicion *(uncertainty),* symptom, tip *(clue)*
intimidate bait *(harass),* browbeat, coerce, deter, discourage, frighten, harass, hector, menace, pressure, threaten
intimidating chilling effect, dictatorial, portentous *(ominous),* sinister
intimidating force menace
intimidation admonition, coercion, deterrence, deterrent, fear, fright, menace, pressure, threat
intimus intimate
intitle delegate
intolerabilis insufferable
intolerable deplorable, insufferable, loathsome, objectionable, obnoxious, odious, offensive *(offending),* onerous, oppressive, outrageous, painful, peccant *(culpable),* unacceptable, undesirable, unendurable, unsatisfactory, unsavory, unsuitable
intolerance bias, cruelty, discrimination *(bigotry),* exclusion, feud, hatred, ill will, incompatibility *(difference),* inequity, ostracism, partiality, prejudice *(preconception),* proscription, rejection, spite
intolerandus insufferable
intolerant adverse *(hostile),* bigot, callous, disdainful, dogmatic, draconian, illiberal, insolent, narrow, orgulous, parochial, provincial, relentless, remorseless, supercilious
intoleration rejection
intonate enunciate
intonation inflection, stress *(accent)*
intone enunciate
intorted circuitous
intoxicant alcohol
intoxicated drunk
intoxicating provocative
intoxicating liquor alcohol
intoxication dipsomania, inebriation, passion
intractable contumacious, difficult, disobedient, froward, immutable, incorrigible, indomitable, inexorable, inflexible, insubordinate, lawless, nonconsenting, obdurate, pertinacious, perverse, recalcitrant, renitent, restive, rigid, severe, unbending, uncontrollable, unruly, unyielding, willful
intractableness contempt *(disobedience to the court)*
intransient permanent, perpetual
intransigence incompatibility *(difference),* tenacity
intransigency incompatibility *(difference)*
intransigent implacable, incorrigible, inflexible, irreconcilable, obdurate, purposeful, relentless, renitent, resolute, restive, steadfast, unbending, uncompromising, unyielding, willful
intransmutable definite, durable, indefeasible, irrevocable, permanent
intransparency density
intrare enter *(go in)*
intrepid heroic, spartan, undaunted
intrepidity audacity, confidence *(faith),* diligence *(perseverance),* prowess *(bravery)*
intrepidus undaunted

intricacy complex *(entanglement),* complication, entanglement *(confusion),* involution, predicament
intricate complex, compound, elaborate, incomprehensible, inextricable, labyrinthine, obscure *(abstruse),* recondite, sinuous
intricate involvement imbroglio
intricate plot imbroglio
intricately wrought elaborate
intrigant confederate, conspirator, conspirer
intrigant copartner *(coconspirator)*
intrigue artifice, cabal, coax, collusion, complication, confederacy *(conspiracy),* connivance, connive, conspiracy, conspire, contrivance, contrive, deceive, deception, frame up, fraud, impress *(affect deeply),* indirection *(deceitfulness),* machination, maneuver, pettifoggery, plan, plot *(secret plan),* plot, scheme, secret, stratagem, strategy
intriguer conspirator, conspirer, copartner *(coconspirator)*
intriguery collusion, conspiracy, strategy
intriguing artful, attractive, collusive, insidious, machiavellian, perfidious, provocative, sapid, sly, subtle *(insidious),* suggestive *(evocative),* tactical, unconscionable
intrinsic born *(innate),* central *(essential),* essential *(inherent),* implicit, ingrained, inherent, innate, native *(inborn),* organic, virtual
intrinsic nature gist *(substance)*
intrinsical central *(essential),* essential *(inherent),* organic
intrinsicality character *(personal quality)*
intrinsicalness character *(personal quality)*
introduce adduce, bear *(adduce),* commence, enter *(insert),* establish *(launch),* extend *(offer),* herald, induct, infuse, initiate, inject, inseminate, instate, interject, interpose, invent *(produce for the first time),* launch *(initiate),* maintain *(commence),* move *(judicially request),* originate, pose *(propound),* precede, preface, propose, propound, submit *(give)*
introduce a change affect
introduce a system classify, organize *(arrange)*
introduce as an example cite *(state)*
introduce changes denature, modify *(alter),* qualify *(condition)*
introduce into office induct, instate
introduce new conditions qualify *(condition)*
introduce order codify, marshal, organize *(arrange)*
introduce order into fix *(arrange)*
introduced alleged
introduced to acquainted
introducer architect, author *(originator)*
introducere introduce, present *(introduce)*
introductio introduction
introduction appearance *(emergence),* birth *(beginning),* genesis, inflow, infusion, insertion, installation, nascency, onset *(commencement),* origination, out-

set, overture, preamble, preface, prelude

introductory aforesaid, antecedent, elementary, inchoate, incipient, initial, last *(preceding)*, original *(initial)*, precursory, preliminary, preparatory, previous, prime *(original)*, prior

introductory part preamble, preface

introductory statement preamble

introgression entrance, incursion, inflow, osmosis

introire enter *(go in)*

introitus entrance

intromit enter *(insert)*, inject, interject

introspect muse, ponder

introspection contemplation

introspective circumspect, cogitative, pensive, subjective

introversion introspection

intrude accroach, discontinue *(break continuity)*, disrupt, disturb, encroach, impinge, infringe, interfere, interpose, interrupt, intervene, invade, obtrude, overstep, pervade, trespass

intrude illegally encroach

intrude upon harass

intruder alien

intruding obtrusive

intrusion assault, disturbance, encroachment, incursion, infringement, interruption, intervention *(imposition into a lawsuit)*, intervention *(interference)*, invasion, molestation, nuisance, onset *(assault)*

intrusive impertinent *(insolent)*, obtrusive, presumptuous

intrust delegate

intuit anticipate *(expect)*, preconceive, presuppose

intuition belief *(state of mind)*, common sense, comprehension, discretion *(quality of being discreet)*, discrimination *(good judgment)*, insight, instinct, judgment *(discernment)*, sagacity

intuitional uncanny

intuitive acute, innate

intuitive truth principle *(axiom)*

intuitiveness insight

intwine combine *(join together)*

inundate immerse *(plunge into)*, load, outpour, overcome *(overwhelm)*, overload, overwhelm

inundation cataclysm, inflow, overage, plethora, surfeit

inurbane provincial

inurbanity disrespect

inurbanus inelegant

inure accrue *(arise)*, naturalize *(acclimate)*

inured impervious, inveterate, nonchalant, unaffected *(uninfluenced)*

inurement habituation

inusitate novel, unaccustomed, uncommon, unusual

inusitation desuetude, disuse

inusitatus eccentric, extraordinary, irregular *(not usual)*, rare, sporadic, uncommon

inutile expendable, futile, ineffective, ineffectual, nugatory, unavailing, unfit

inutile check bad check

inutilis incompetent, ineffective, ineffectual, unfit

inutilitas inexpedience

inutility desuetude

invade accroach, assail, attack, break *(violate)*, despoil, encroach, enter *(penetrate)*, force *(break)*, harry *(plunder)*, impinge, impose *(intrude)*, infringe, interfere, intrude, obtrude, occupy *(take possession)*, overlap, overstep, pervade, preempt, trespass, violate

invade unlawfully encroach

invader aggressor, assailant

invadere encroach, invade

invading intrusive, offensive *(taking the initiative)*

invalid disabled *(deprived of legal right)*, disabled *(made incapable)*, fallacious, false *(inaccurate)*, faulty, helpless *(powerless)*, illegal, inactive, inconsequential, ineffective, ineffectual, nugatory, null and void, otiose, patient, sophistic, unavailing, unsound *(fallacious)*, untenable

invalid check bad check

invalid trial mistrial

invalidate abate *(extinguish)*, abolish, abrogate *(annul)*, abrogate *(rescind)*, annul *(cancel)*, avoid *(cancel)*, cancel, denature, destroy *(void)*, disable, disarm *(divest of arms)*, disavow, discharge *(release from obligation)*, discontinue *(abandon)*, disown *(deny the validity)*, disprove, disqualify, frustrate, kill *(defeat)*, negate, neutralize, nullify, obliterate, override, overrule, quash, recall *(call back)*, refute, renege, repeal, rescind, revoke, vacate *(void)*, vitiate, withdraw

invalidate an attorney's license disbar

invalidated disabled *(deprived of legal right)*

invalidating cancellation

invalidation abatement *(extinguishment)*, abolition, ademption, annulment, avoidance *(cancellation)*, cancellation, counterargument, countermand, defeasance, defeat, disability *(legal disqualification)*, discharge *(annulment)*, discharge *(release from obligation)*, discontinuance *(act of discontinuing)*, dismissal *(termination of a proceeding)*, disqualification *(factor that disqualifies)*, disqualification *(rejection)*, dissolution *(termination)*, negation, rescision, reversal, revocation

invalidism disease

invalidity disability *(legal disqualification)*, disqualification *(factor that disqualifies)*, impuissance, nullity

invalidus ineffective, ineffectual, powerless

invaluable beneficial, constructive *(creative)*, functional, inestimable, lucrative, practical, priceless, profitable, valuable

invariability constant, regularity

invariable certain *(positive)*, chronic, constant, constant, definite, durable, immutable, indefeasible, inflexible, obdurate, regular *(orderly)*, repetitious, stable, unalterable, uniform, unyielding

invariably always *(without exception)*

invariant constant, constant

invasion encroachment, entrance, foray, incursion, inflow, infringement, intrusion, onset *(assault)*, outbreak, violation

invasion of a legal right injury, tort

invasion of a right infringement

invasive intrusive, obtrusive, offensive *(taking the initiative)*

invectio introduction

invective aspersion, condemnation *(blame)*, contumely, correction *(punishment)*, defamation, denunciation, diatribe, disparagement, harangue, libel, malediction, obloquy, outcry, phillipic, profanity, revilement, slander, vilification

invehere introduce

invehi in attack

inveigh demonstrate *(protest)*, denounce *(condemn)*, entice, lash *(attack verbally)*, protest

inveigh against censure, condemn *(blame)*, contemn, decry, defame, impugn, reprimand, reproach

inveigle bait *(lure)*, betray *(lead astray)*, bilk, cheat, coax, convince, deceive, defraud, delude, dupe, entrap, hoodwink, illude, importune, influence, lure, palter, persuade, prevail *(persuade)*, trap

inveiglement bribery, decoy, persuasion, seduction

invenire contrive, devise *(invent)*, discover, find *(discover)*, invent *(produce for the first time)*

invent compose, conjure, contrive, create, fabricate *(make up)*, find *(discover)*, forge *(produce)*, frame *(formulate)*, generate, initiate, lie *(falsify)*, make, manufacture, originate, palter, prevaricate, produce *(manufacture)*, scheme

invented assumed *(feigned)*, fictitious, illusory, mendacious, unfounded, untrue

inventio contrivance

invention contrivance, creation, device *(mechanism)*, expedient, false pretense, falsehood, falsification, fiction, figment, formation, innovation, lie, myth, nascency, origination, pretense *(pretext)*, pretext, product, story *(falsehood)*, strategy, subreption

invention of lies perjury

inventive fertile, original *(creative)*, productive, resourceful

inventiveness contrivance

inventor architect, author *(originator)*, pioneer

inventories assets

inventory check *(inspect)*, enumerate, index *(relate)*, inspection, invoice *(itemized list)*, itemize, roll, schedule, stock *(store)*, store *(depository)*, tabulate

inventory expert comptroller

inventum invention

invenustus inelegant

inveracity bad faith, dishonesty, falsehood, improbity, story *(falsehood)*

inverse adverse *(opposite)*, antipode, antithesis, contra, contradictory, contrary, discordant, negative, opposite

inversely contra

inversion antipode, reversal, subversion

inversus inverse

invert alter, disorganize, disorient, overthrow, overturn, upset

inverted disordered, inverse, opposite

invest admit *(give access)*, allow *(authorize)*, assign *(designate)*, bequeath, bestow, capitalize *(provide capital)*, clothe, commit *(entrust)*, confer *(give)*,

constitute *(establish)*, contribute *(supply)*, delegate, deposit *(submit to a bank)*, embrace *(encircle)*, empower, enable, endue, enshroud, finance, induct, instate, lend, repose *(place)*, speculate *(chance)*, spend, supply, vest
invest empower entrust
invest in purchase
invest in again refinance
invest money fund
invest the power charge *(empower)*
invest with devolve
invest with a body embody
invest with authoritative power charge *(empower)*, delegate
invest with matter embody
invest with power authorize, clothe, commit *(entrust)*
invested capital investment
invested money investment
invested property investment, securities, security *(stock)*, share *(stock)*, stock *(shares)*
invested sum principal *(capital sum)*
investigare examine *(interrogate)*, scrutinize, trace *(follow)*
investigate analyze, audit, canvass, check *(inspect)*, consider, deliberate, delve, discover, examine *(study)*, frisk, inquire, monitor, notice *(observe)*, peruse, probe, research, review, scrutinize, search, study, trace *(follow)*, treat *(process)*
investigate judicially hear *(give a legal hearing)*
investigating committee commission *(agency)*
investigatio examination *(study)*, investigation
investigation analysis, cross-examination, cross-questioning, discovery, examination *(study)*, experiment, hearing, indagation, inquest, inquiry *(request for information)*, inquiry *(systematic investigation)*, interrogation, observation, probe, pursuit *(chase)*, pursuit *(effort to secure)*, question *(inquiry)*, research, review *(official reexamination)*, scrutiny, test, treatment
investigation to uncover facts discovery
investigative inquisitive, interrogative
investigator detective, spy
investing with authority delegation *(assignment)*
investiture delegation *(assignment)*, deputation *(selection of delegates)*, installation
investiture of title feoffment
investment advance *(allowance)*, advancement *(loan)*, binder, deputation *(selection of delegates)*, equity *(share of ownership)*, expenditure, fund, securities, security *(stock)*, share *(stock)*, stock *(shares)*, venture
investment portfolio capital
investments capital, finance, personalty, portfolio, property *(possessions)*
investor backer, contributor *(giver)*, creditor, customer, grantor, patron *(influential supporter)*, shareholder
inveteracy behavior, constant, habituation
inveterate constant, durable, familiar *(customary)*, habitual, incorrigible, in-

grained, pertinacious, stable, traditional
inveterate habit habituation, practice *(custom)*
inveterate hatred feud
inveterate practice habit
inveterate strife feud
inveterateness habituation
inveteratus habitual, ingrained, inveterate, old
invictus indomitable, insuperable, invincible, irresistible
invidia disfavor, malice, rancor
invidiosus invidious, odious
invidious caustic, heinous, loathsome, malevolent, malicious, malignant, objectionable, obnoxious, odious, offensive *(offending)*, provocative, spiteful
invidiousness malice
invidus jealous, malicious
invigilate police
invigorate develop, endue, fix *(repair)*, meliorate, nurture, recreate, renew *(refurbish)*, stimulate
invigorating medicinal, remedial, salubrious, salutary
invigoration instigation, revival
invincible defensible, forcible, indomitable, inexpugnable, insuperable, insurmountable, irresistible, potent, powerful
inviolability responsibility *(conscience)*
inviolable clean, immune, indefeasible, inexpugnable, infrangible, invincible, lawful, private *(confidential)*, sacrosanct, secure *(free from danger)*, tenable, unalienable
inviolable refuge asylum *(hiding place)*
inviolableness inviolability
inviolate certain *(positive)*, clean, definite, durable, gross *(total)*, honest, intact, law-abiding, sacrosanct
inviolatus inviolate
invious impervious
invisibility concealment, nonappearance
invisible covert, hidden, impalpable, inconspicuous, indiscernible, intangible, obscure *(faint)*, undisclosed
invisibleness nonappearance
invisus obnoxious, odious
invitatio invitation
invitation instigation, monition *(legal summons)*, overture, provocation, request, seduction
invitation to combat defiance
invite call *(appeal to)*, call *(summon)*, motivate, offer *(propose)*, proffer, request, urge
invite competition challenge
invite the attention occupy *(engage)*
invite to contest challenge
inviting attractive, palatable, persuasive, provocative, sapid
invitingness amenity
invitus involuntary, reluctance
invocare invoke
invocate invoke
invocation call *(appeal)*, entreaty, laudation, petition, prayer, request, subpoena, summons
invocation of evil imprecation
invocatory plea call *(appeal)*
invocatory prayer call *(appeal)*

invoice charge *(assess)*, register
invoke bear *(adduce)*, call *(appeal to)*, call *(summon)*
involucrum veil
involuntarily unwillingly
involuntariness happenstance, instinct
involuntary compelling, fortuitous, innate, mandatory, obligatory, reluctant, unavoidable *(inevitable)*, unintentional, unwitting
involuntary exile banishment
involuntary liquidation bankruptcy
involuntary loss of right forfeiture *(act of forfeiting)*
involuntary servitude bondage, subjection
involute elaborate, inextricable, labyrinthine, sinuous, snarl
involuted complex, inextricable, labyrinthine, sinuous
involution complex *(entanglement)*, complication
involutional complex, sinuous
involutionary sinuous
involve appertain, apply *(pertain)*, bear *(adduce)*, comprehend *(include)*, comprise, confound, connote, consist, constitute *(compose)*, denounce *(inform against)*, embrace *(encircle)*, entail, immerse *(engross)*, implicate, imply, include, incorporate *(include)*, incriminate, interest, monopolize, occupy *(engage)*, perplex
involve in criminal proceeding incriminate
involve in error misdirect
involve in guilt incriminate
involve in shame brand *(stigmatize)*, discredit, disgrace
involve in suspicion impugn
involve together commingle, pool
involved at risk, complex, compound, constructive *(inferential)*, difficult, disordered, elaborate, esoteric, inextricable, interested, intricate, labyrinthine, obscure *(abstruse)*, problematic, recondite, sinuous, tortuous *(bending)*
involved situation imbroglio
involved state complication
involvement affiliation *(connectedness)*, association *(connection)*, complex *(entanglement)*, complication, embroilment, involution, preoccupation, quagmire, relationship *(connection)*
involvere envelop
involving death fatal
involving in guilt incriminatory, inculpatory
involving risk dangerous
involving ruin fatal
invulnerability inviolability, protection, security *(safety)*
invulnerable certain *(positive)*, defensible, immune, indestructible, inexpugnable, infrangible, insuperable, invincible, permanent, safe, secure *(free from danger)*, tenable
inward interior, intrinsic *(deep down)*
inward monitor conscience, responsibility *(conscience)*
inward perception impression
inwardly herein, wherein
inweave intertwine
inwrought born *(innate)*, ingrained
iocosus jocular

iocularis jocular

iota minimum, modicum, scintilla

ipse actual

ipse dixit allegation, assertion, bigot, declaration

ipsum se inspicere introspection

ira resentment

iracund petulant

iracundus resentful

iram remittere relent

irascibility outburst

irascible contentious, disobedient, fractious, froward, perverse, petulant

irascibleness outburst

ire passion, resentment

irenic nonmilitant, placid

irenical nonmilitant, placid

irk aggravate *(annoy)*, annoy, badger, bait *(harass)*, discommode, discompose, distress, disturb, irritate, molest *(annoy)*, offend *(insult)*, perturb, pique, plague, provoke

irksome invidious, operose, oppressive, painful, provocative, vexatious

iron fetter, relentless, staunch

iron grip adhesion *(affixing)*

iron rule oppression

iron will tenacity

iron-handed peremptory *(imperative)*

iron-hearted obdurate, spartan

ironbound ironclad

ironclad severe

ironclad agreement contract

ironhanded dictatorial, severe, stringent

ironia irony

ironical ironic

irradiate radiate, spread

irrational arbitrary, disconnected, disproportionate, fatuous, ill-judged, illogical, injudicious, ludicrous, lunatic, misadvised, reckless, sophistic, thoughtless, unreasonable, unsound *(fallacious)*, untenable

irrational conclusion non sequitur

irrational terror panic

irrebuttable unavoidable *(not voidable)*

irreclaimable incorrigible, iniquitous, irredeemable, irretrievable, irreversible, irrevocable, lost *(taken away)*, obdurate, reprobate

irreconcilability antithesis, conflict, contention *(opposition)*, difference, discrepancy, disparity, incompatibility *(difference)*, paradox

irreconcilable adverse *(opposite)*, contradictory, discordant, disparate, disproportionate, dissenting, dissident, hostile, implacable, inapposite, inapt, incongruous, inconsistent, inept *(inappropriate)*, inimical, litigious, reluctant, repugnant *(incompatible)*, restive, uncompromising

irreconcilable difference incompatibility *(difference)*

irreconcilableness incompatibility *(difference)*

irrecoverable incorrigible, irredeemable, irremediable, irreparable, irretrievable, irreversible, lifeless *(dead)*, lost *(taken away)*

irredeemable delinquent *(guilty of a misdeed)*, diabolic, incorrigible, irrecoverable, irremediable, irreparable, irretrievable, irreversible, irrevocable, lost *(taken away)*, reprobate

irredeemable bill bad debt

irreducible certain *(positive)*, complex, inextricable, net, simple, succinct

irreformable incorrigible, irredeemable, irreversible

irrefragability certainty, certification *(certainness)*, certitude

irrefragable believable, categorical, certain *(fixed)*, certain *(positive)*, clear *(certain)*, cogent, conclusive *(determinative)*, convincing, definite, incontestable, incontrovertible, indefeasible, infallible, irrefutable, positive *(incontestable)*, uncontested, undeniable, undisputed, unequivocal, unimpeachable, unrefutable

irrefragably admittedly, fairly *(clearly)*

irrefragibility incontestability

irrefutability certainty, certification *(certainness)*, certitude, incontestability

irrefutable axiomatic, believable, categorical, certain *(fixed)*, certain *(positive)*, clear *(certain)*, cogent, conclusive *(determinative)*, convincing, credible, definite, definitive, factual, inappealable, incontestable, incontrovertible, indubious, irrebuttable, positive *(incontestable)*, provable, real, reliable, solid *(sound)*, sound, unavoidable *(not voidable)*, uncontested, undeniable, undisputed, unequivocal, unimpeachable, unrefutable

irrefutably admittedly, fairly *(clearly)*

irregular anomalous, broken *(interrupted)*, casual, deviant, disjunctive *(tending to disjoin)*, disorderly, disparate, dissimilar, eccentric, extraordinary, haphazard, impermissible, incongruous, infrequent, intermittent, multifarious, nonconforming, novel, peculiar *(curious)*, random, sporadic, suspicious *(questionable)*, tortuous *(bending)*, unaccustomed, unequal *(unequivalent)*, unorthodox, unpredictable, unusual, variable

irregularity deviation, disorder *(lack of order)*, diversity, entanglement *(confusion)*, exception *(exclusion)*, inequality, informality, misapplication, miscue, misdoing, nonconformity, quirk *(idiosyncrasy)*

irrelated alien *(unrelated)*

irrelation difference, disparity, distinction *(difference)*, distortion

irrelative apart, disconnected, dissimilar, extraneous, gratuitous *(unwarranted)*, heterogeneous, impertinent *(irrelevant)*, inapposite, independent, irrelevant, unrelated

irrelevance immateriality, inconsequence, insignificance

irrelevancy immateriality, inconsequence, insignificance, non sequitur

irrelevant collateral *(immaterial)*, expendable, extraneous, extrinsic, gratuitous *(unwarranted)*, immaterial, improper, inadmissible, inapplicable, inapposite, inappreciable, inappropriate, inconsequential, inconsiderable, irrelative, minor, needless, negligible, nugatory, null *(insignificant)*, paltry, peripheral, unessential, unfit, unnecessary, unrelated, unsuitable

irreligious diabolic, mundane, profane

irremediable blameworthy, incorrigible, irrevocable

irremedial irreversible

irremissible inexcusable, unjustifiable

irremovable durable, firm, fixed *(securely placed)*, immutable, indefeasible, indelible, inextricable, irreversible, irrevocable, permanent, stable

irrepair deterioration

irreparable incorrigible, irrecoverable, irredeemable, irremediable, irretrievable, irreversible, irrevocable

irrepealable conclusive *(determinative)*, irreversible, irrevocable, noncancellable

irreplaceability importance, need *(requirement)*

irreplaceable indispensable, inestimable, integral, priceless, vital

irreplaceable feature necessity, need *(requirement)*

irrepoachable honest

irreppproachable law-abiding

irreprehensible blameless, clean, inculpable, unimpeachable, unobjectionable

irrepressible hot-blooded, indomitable, intractable, rampant, uncontrollable, unruly

irreproachable blameless, clean, incorruptible, inculpable, infallible, irreprehensible, meritorious, unimpeachable, unobjectionable

irreprovable blameless, clean, irreprehensible, unobjectionable

irresistable uncontrollable

irresistible certain *(positive)*, cogent, compelling, compulsory, definite, indomitable, inexpugnable, invincible, necessary *(inescapable)*, omnipotent, powerful, provocative, unavoidable *(inevitable)*

irresistible compulsion necessity

irresistible impulse compulsion *(obsession)*, obsession

irresistible urge passion

irresoluble certain *(positive)*

irresolute capricious, doubtful, hesitant, insipid, mutable, noncommittal, passive, pliant, speculative, undecided, volatile

irresoluteness ambivalence, indecision

irresolution ambivalence, doubt *(indecision)*, hesitation, incertitude, indecision, inertia, quandary

irresolved noncommittal, outstanding *(unresolved)*

irrespective of regardless

irresponsibility anarchy, inconsideration, negligence, res ipsa loquitur

irresponsible capricious, careless, disobedient, heedless, ill-advised, lawless, misadvised, negligent, reckless, thoughtless, uncurbed, undependable, unreliable, untrustworthy, variable

irresponsive unresponsive

irretrievable irrecoverable, irredeemable, irremediable, irreversible, irrevocable, lost *(taken away)*

irretrievable debt bad debt

irrevealable clandestine, confidential

irreverant profane

irreverence bad repute, blasphemy,

contempt *(disobedience to the court),* disparagement, disrespect, expletive, ignominy, violation

irreverent contemptuous, impertinent *(insolent),* pejorative, presumptuous, reprobate, supercilious

irreverent behavior blasphemy

irreversible certain *(positive),* decisive, definite, indefeasible, indelible, ironclad, irrecoverable, irredeemable, irremediable, irreparable, irrevocable, noncancellable, permanent, stable, unalterable

irreversible damage prejudice *(injury)*

irrevocability certitude

irrevocable certain *(positive),* compulsory, conclusive *(determinative),* decisive, definite, final, immutable, inappealable, indefeasible, indelible, indestructible, ironclad, irredeemable, irremediable, irreversible, lost *(taken away),* necessary *(inescapable),* permanent, stable, unavoidable *(inevitable),* unavoidable *(not voidable)*

irrevocable decision adjudication

irritable fractious, froward, petulant, querulous, sensitive *(easily affected)*

irritant aggravation *(annoyance)*

irritate affront, aggravate *(annoy),* agitate *(activate),* annoy, antagonize, badger, bait *(harass),* disaffect, discommode, discompose, distress, exacerbate, harass, harrow, harry *(harass),* hector, incense, inconvenience, molest *(annoy),* offend *(insult),* perturb, pique, plague, press *(goad),* provoke, repel *(disgust)*

irritating caustic, irksome, loathsome, offensive *(offending),* painful, provocative, vexatious

irritation aggravation *(annoyance),* dissatisfaction, instigation, molestation, nuisance, provocation, umbrage

irrupt encroach, intrude

irruption assault, encroachment, incursion, inflow, intrusion, outbreak, outburst

is composed of consist

is essentially consist

island isolate

isolate abstract *(separate),* constrain *(imprison),* detain *(hold in custody),* dissociate, estrange, exclude, immure, insulate, jail, part *(separate),* relegate, remove *(eliminate),* seclude, select, sequester *(seclude),* sever, split

isolated alone *(solitary),* apart, derelict *(abandoned),* disconnected, discrete, disjunctive *(tending to disjoin),* exclusive *(singular),* inapposite, individual, insular, obscure *(remote),* private *(secluded),* remote *(secluded),* separate, singular, sole, solitary, sporadic

isolation exclusion, expulsion, ostracism, privacy, removal, segregation *(separation),* severance

isolationist neutral

issuance apportionment, circulation, dispensation *(act of dispensing),* distribution *(apportionment),* output, publication *(disclosure),* publicity

issue accrue *(arise),* administer *(tender),* bestow, blood, cause of action, cessation *(termination),* child, children, circulate, confer *(give),* contention *(argument),* denouement, derivation, descendant, dispense, disperse *(disseminate),* disseminate, divide *(distribute),* dole, effect, emanate, emerge, emit, ensue, evolve, exude, family *(household),* impart, issuance, matter *(subject),* mete, offshoot, offspring, outcome, outflow, outgrowth, output, point *(item),* post, posterity, proceed *(go forward),* product, progeny, promulgate, propagate *(spread),* publication *(printed matter),* publish, result, send, serial, serve *(deliver a legal instrument),* signify *(inform),* stem *(originate),* subject *(topic),* succession, supervene, tender, thesis, transmit, utter

issue a command command, constrain *(compel),* dictate, direct *(order),* enact, instruct *(direct),* require *(compel),* subpoena, summon

issue a court directive subpoena, summon

issue a decree command, direct *(order),* instruct *(direct),* order

issue a fiat decree

issue a proclamation decree, notify

issue a pronouncement notify

issue a statement certify *(attest),* posit, post, publish, speak

issue a ukase decree

issue a writ charge *(accuse),* subpoena

issue an edict decree

issue an invitation call *(summon)*

issue an order command, dictate, direct *(order),* enjoin, instruct *(direct),* prescribe

issue counterfeit money forge *(counterfeit)*

issue for distribution publish

issue for public sale publish

issue forth arise *(originate),* depart

issue one's fiat order

issue process subpoena, summon

issue rays radiate

issue threats coerce

issued positive *(prescribed)*

issued weapons armed

issueless barren, otiose, unproductive

it follows that consequently

itaque consequently

itch passion

item article *(commodity),* article *(distinct section of a writing),* component, count, detail, element, entity, entry *(record),* member *(constituent part),* object, particular, particularity, possession *(property),* product, specification, technicality, term *(provision),* title *(division),* trait

item in the indictment count

item of evidence exhibit

item of information particular

item of personalty possession *(property)*

item on the agenda issue *(matter in dispute),* matter *(subject)*

itemization inventory, specification

itemize delineate, describe, designate, detail *(particularize),* enumerate, impanel, index *(relate),* specify, tabulate

itemized detailed

itemized account bill *(invoice),* invoice *(itemized list),* tariff *(bill)*

itemized list inventory

itemized specification bill *(formal declaration)*

items circumstances, commodities, contents, goods

items for sale merchandise

items of business agenda

items of personalty possessions

iter course

iterare reiterate, renew *(begin again),* repeat *(do again)*

iterate copy, reaffirm, recount, reiterate, repeat *(state again)*

iteration narration, recital, restatement

iterative incessant, insistent

iterum reopen

itinerancy vagrancy

itinerant moving *(in motion)*

itinerary plan

iubeo direction *(order)*

iubere order, pass *(approve)*

iucundus palatable

iudex judge, juror

iudicare criticize *(evaluate),* judge, try *(conduct a trial)*

iudices jury

iudicialis forensic, judicial

iudicium court, criticism, determination, discretion *(quality of being discreet),* discrimination *(good judgment),* estimate *(idea),* holding *(ruling of a court),* insight, judgment *(discernment),* judgment *(formal court decree),* opinion *(belief),* perception, sense *(intelligence),* sentence, trial *(legal proceeding),* tribunal, verdict

iudicium exercere judge

iungere connect *(join together)*

iurare swear

iureiurando adfirmare swear

iurgium altercation

iuridicialis forensic, juridical

iuris consultus jurist

iuris peritus jurist

iuris prudentia jurisprudence

iurisconsultus lawyer

iurisdictio judicature, jurisdiction

iurisperitus lawyer

ius law, right *(entitlement),* statute

iusiurandum oath

iussum fiat, injunction, order *(judicial directive),* regulation *(rule)*

iusta right *(entitlement)*

iuste fairly *(impartially)*

iustitia equity *(justice),* fairness, justice

iustus equitable, just, justifiable, regular *(conventional),* rightful, valid

iuvenilis juvenile (adjective), juvenile (noun)

J

jab jostle *(bump into)*

jabber jargon *(unintelligible language),* prattle

jabbering loquacious

jack up elevate

jackpot prize

jactitation jactation, rodomontade

jaculate impel, launch *(project),* precipitate *(throw down violently),* send

jaggedness irregularity

jail arrest *(apprehend),* captivity, capture, cell, commit *(institutionalize),* confine, constrain *(imprison),* contain *(restrain),* detain *(hold in custody),* im-

prison, lock, penitentiary, prison, reformatory, restrain, seize *(apprehend)*
jail inmate convict
jailed arrested *(apprehended),* in custody
jailed person prisoner
jailer custodian *(warden),* warden
jailhouse cell, penitentiary
jailing commitment *(confinement)*
jam block, imbroglio, impact
jam-packed replete
jammed inextricable, replete
jangle altercation, brawl, brawl, controversy *(argument),* fracas, fray, noise
jangling altercation
jar agitate *(perturb),* bicker, collision *(accident),* discompose, fracas, irritate, jostle *(bump into),* perturb, strike *(collide)*
jargon language, phraseology
jarring inapplicable, inapposite, inapt, incongruous, inconsistent, inept *(inappropriate),* repugnant *(incompatible)*
jaundice bias, intolerance, predetermination, prejudice *(influence)*
jaundiced bilious, dyseptic, one-sided, parochial, partial *(biased),* unequal *(unjust),* unfair, unjust
jaunt perambulate
jaunty resilient
jealous resentful, suspicious *(distrustful)*
jealousy resentment
jeer disdain, disparage, flout, hector, jape, mock *(deride),* reject, ridicule
jeering disdainful
jejune deficient, irksome, nugatory, otiose, pedestrian, prosaic, puerile, stale, unproductive
jellification congealment
jeopardize compromise *(endanger),* endanger, expose
jeopardous noxious, precarious
jeopardy danger, hazard, peril, predicament, risk, threat, venture
jest jape
jesting jocular
jet emit, outburst, outflow
jettison abandon *(relinquish),* disown *(refuse to acknowledge),* eject *(expel),* evict, reject, relinquish
jettisoned derelict *(abandoned)*
jibe comport *(agree with),* concur *(agree)*
jilt rebuff, reject, spurn
jingoism intolerance
jitteriness trepidation
job appointment *(position),* burden, business *(occupation),* calling, career, employment, enterprise *(undertaking),* labor *(work),* livelihood, mission, occupation *(vocation),* office, part *(role),* position *(business status),* post, profession *(vocation),* project, province, pursuit *(occupation),* role, trade *(occupation),* undertaking *(enterprise),* work *(employment)*
job action strike
job holder incumbent
job seeker candidate
jobation reprimand, reproach
jobber dealer
jobbery abuse *(corrupt practice),* artifice, bribery, corruption, crime, gratuity *(bribe),* improbity, pettifoggery

jobbing commercial
jobholder employee
jobless idle, otiose, unemployed
jockey maneuver
jocose jocular
jocularity life *(vitality)*
jocund jocular
jocundity life *(vitality)*
jog impetus, reminder, stimulate
jog the memory remind
join abut, accompany, adhere *(fasten),* affiliate, affix, aggregate, amalgamate, annex *(add),* append, bond *(hold together),* border *(approach),* border *(bound),* cement, collect *(gather),* commingle, congregate, connect *(join together),* consolidate *(unite),* conspire, contact *(touch),* correspond *(be equivalent),* enroll, espouse, federalize *(associate),* federate, incorporate *(include),* juxtapose, lock, meet, merge, organize *(unionize),* participate, register, unite
join as a third party implead
join battle with engage *(involve)*
join forces affiliate, combine *(act in concert),* concur *(agree),* connive, consolidate *(unite),* conspire, cooperate, federalize *(associate),* federate, involve *(participate),* merge, participate, unite
join forces with consolidate *(unite)*
join in concur *(agree),* contribute *(assist),* cooperate, involve *(participate),* participate
join in a compact confirm
join in a conversation discuss, speak
join in partnership with participate
join issue bicker, collide *(clash),* disaccord, oppose, reason *(persuade),* rebut, respond
join the majority conform
join together affiliate, concur *(agree),* conjoin, converge, desegregate, organize *(unionize)*
join with combine *(act in concert),* concur *(agree),* connive, cooperate
joinder attachment *(act of affixing),* merger
joined additional, associated, attached *(annexed),* coadunate, collective, composite, concerted, concurrent *(united),* conjoint, contiguous, correlative, inextricable, inseparable, interrelated, joint, promiscuous
joined in a union federal
joined together conjoint
joined with affiliated
joiner connection *(fastening)*
joining accession *(annexation),* addition, attachment *(act of affixing),* coalescence, combination, contact *(touching),* joinder, marriage *(intimate relationship),* matrimony, meeting *(encounter),* union *(unity)*
joining place intersection
joining road crossroad *(intersection)*
joint common *(shared),* concerted, concomitant, concordant, concurrent *(united),* conjoint, connection *(fastening),* consensual, federal, harmonious, intersection, mutual *(collective)*
joint action concert, cooperative
joint agreement mutual understanding
joint and several in solido
joint concern cartel, coalition, company *(enterprise),* corporation, firm,

merger, organization *(association),* pool
joint discussion panel *(discussion group)*
joint effect synergy
joint effort coaction, collusion, conformity *(agreement),* conjunction, connivance, conspiracy
joint endeavor coalition
joint enterprise affiliation *(connectedness),* association *(connection)*
joint interest partnership
joint operation concert, cooperative
joint ownership pool
joint pact mutual understanding
joint participation coaction
joint planning collusion, conformity *(agreement),* connivance, conspiracy
joint possession cooperative, pool
joint-operator coactor
jointure dower
joke jape
joke about mock *(deride)*
joking jocular
jolly jocular
jolt bombshell, collision *(accident),* discompose, impetus, jostle *(bump into),* perturb, strike *(collide)*
joshing jocular
jot iota, minimum
jot down enter *(record),* note *(record),* record, set down
jottings script
journal calendar *(record of yearly periods),* dossier, record, register
journalistic writers press
journalists press
journalize record
journey move *(alter position),* perambulate, quest
journey's end destination
journeying itinerant, moving *(in motion)*
journeyman artisan, practitioner
joust compete, fight *(battle)*
jovial jocular
joviality life *(vitality)*
joyful ecstatic, felicitous, jocular
joyless bleak *(not favorable),* bleak *(severely simple),* despondent, disconsolate, grave *(solemn),* lamentable, lugubrious, pessimistic
joylessness damper *(depressant),* pessimism
joyous ecstatic, felicitous, jocular
jubilant ecstatic
jubilee holiday
judge adjudge, adjudicate, arbitrate *(adjudge),* assess *(appraise),* bench, censor, conclude *(decide),* construe *(comprehend),* criticize *(evaluate),* decide, decree, deduce, deduct *(conclude by reasoning),* deem, deliberate, determine, diagnose, discern *(discriminate),* distinguish, estimate, evaluate, expect *(consider probable),* find *(determine),* gauge, guess, hear *(give a legal hearing),* hold *(decide),* intercede, jurist, magistrate, measure, opine, presume, presuppose, pronounce *(pass judgment),* rate, reason *(conclude),* rebuke, referee, speculate *(conjecture),* surmise, suspect *(think),* try *(conduct a trial),* umpire, vote
judge at random guess
judge before hearing prejudge
judge beforehand forejudge,

preconceive, prejudge
judge erroneously misjudge
judge from premises infer
judge in advance forejudge, prejudge, presuppose
judge inaccurately misjudge
judge innocent palliate *(excuse)*
judge the future presage
judge with indulgence excuse
judge with uncertainty guess
judge wrongly misjudge
judged deliberate
judged by comparison comparative
judgelike judicial, juridical
judges tribunal
judges of the facts jury
judgmatic determinative, discriminating *(judicious)*, judicial, judicious, juridical
judgment adjudication, alternative *(option)*, apprehension *(perception)*, arbitration, authority *(documentation)*, belief *(state of mind)*, caliber *(mental capacity)*, choice *(decision)*, common sense, concept, conclusion *(determination)*, condemnation *(punishment)*, consideration *(contemplation)*, conviction *(finding of guilt)*, conviction *(persuasion)*, decision *(election)*, decree, deliberation, determination, diagnosis, dialectic, dictate, direction *(order)*, discipline *(punishment)*, edict, estimate *(idea)*, estimation *(calculation)*, experience *(background)*, fiat, finding, holding *(ruling of a court)*, idea, inference, notion, opinion *(belief)*, opinion *(judicial decision)*, outcome, perception, position *(point of view)*, pronouncement, prudence, recommendation, regard *(esteem)*, relief *(legal redress)*, res judicata, result, ruling, sagacity, sense *(intelligence)*, sensibility, standpoint, verdict, vote
judgment dissolving a marriage divorce
judgment for the defendant as a matter of law nonsuit
judgment of the court declaratory judgment
judgment on facts adjudication, determination, holding *(ruling of a court)*, opinion *(judicial decision)*
judgment seat bench, court, tribunal
judicable determinable *(ascertainable)*
judicate adjudge, arbitrate *(adjudge)*
judication award
judicative judicial, juridical
judicator arbitrator, referee
judicatorial juridical
judicatory bench, board, chamber *(body)*, forensic, forum *(court)*, judicature, judiciary, jural, juridical, licit
judicature bar *(court)*, bench, council *(assembly)*, forum *(court)*, judgment *(formal court decree)*, judicatory, judiciary
judicial forensic, jural, juridical, licit, objective, open-minded, politic, unprejudiced
judicial administrator clerk
judicial antecedent precedent
judicial assembly bench, court
judicial assertion dictum, judgment *(formal court decree)*
judicial assistant clerk

judicial authorization warrant *(judicial writ)*
judicial branch chamber *(body)*, judiciary
judicial branch of government judiciary
judicial charge arraignment
judicial command mandate, order *(judicial directive)*
judicial comment dictum
judicial conclusion finding
judicial contest action *(proceeding)*, case *(lawsuit)*, controversy *(lawsuit)*, lawsuit, suit, trial *(legal proceeding)*
judicial decision adjudication, award, decree, holding *(ruling of a court)*
judicial decision establishing a rule authority *(documentation)*
judicial decree mandate
judicial department chamber *(body)*, judiciary
judicial determination ruling
judicial examination hearing, voir dire
judicial forum bench, court, judiciary
judicial imperative subpoena
judicial inquiry inquest
judicial instruction order *(judicial directive)*
judicial investigation hearing
judicial murder capital punishment
judicial order mandate, warrant *(judicial writ)*
judicial order to refrain from an act injunction
judicial order to search search warrant
judicial outcome finding
judicial precedent authority *(documentation)*
judicial proceeding action *(proceeding)*
judicial process search warrant
judicial proclamation ruling
judicial pronouncement ruling
judicial reconsideration review *(official reexamination)*
judicial recorder clerk
judicial reexamination habeas corpus
judicial remark dictum
judicial reprimand admonition
judicial secretary clerk
judicial sentence award
judicial separation of a husband and wife divorce
judicial tribunal bench, court, forum *(court)*
judicial validation of a will probate
judicial verdict finding
judicially determine adjudge
judiciary bar *(court)*, bench, judicatory, jural, juridical, tribunal
judicious careful, circumspect, determinative, discreet, impartial, judicial, juridical, nonpartisan, perspicacious, politic, preventive, provident *(showing foresight)*, prudent, rational, reasonable *(fair)*, reasonable *(rational)*, sane, sapient, sensible, solid *(sound)*, vigilant
judiciousness discretion *(quality of being discreet)*, discrimination *(good judgment)*, judgment *(discernment)*, prudence, reason *(sound judgment)*, sense *(intelligence)*
judicium bench

jugglery deceit, machination, pettifoggery, ruse, subterfuge
juggling pettifoggery, prestidigitation
juicy pithy
jumble complex *(entanglement)*, confuse *(bewilder)*, confuse *(create disorder)*, discompose, entanglement *(confusion)*, jargon *(unintelligible language)*, melange, misinterpret, misunderstand, muddle, pandemonium, shambles, turmoil
jumbled complex, disconnected, disjointed, disordered, labyrinthine, miscellaneous, promiscuous
jump edge *(advantage)*, transition
jump in prices inflation *(decrease in value of currency)*
jump to a conclusion forejudge, preconceive, predetermine, prejudge, presuppose
jump to conclusions presume
jumpiness trepidation
junction adhesion *(affixing)*, attachment *(act of affixing)*, chain *(nexus)*, coalescence, coalition, collusion, combination, conjunction, connection *(abutment)*, connection *(fastening)*, connivance, consolidation, contact *(touching)*, crossroad *(intersection)*, intersection, joinder, meeting *(encounter)*, union *(unity)*
junction of bodies contact *(touching)*
juncture case *(set of circumstances)*, connection *(fastening)*, contact *(touching)*, crossroad *(turning point)*, intersection, meeting *(encounter)*, occasion, period, point *(period of time)*, posture *(situation)*, situation
jungle imbroglio
junior adolescent, inferior *(lower in position)*, juvenile, minor, minor, secondary, subaltern, subordinate, subservient
juniority adolescence
junta cabal
jural forensic, juridical
jurat juror
jurgium brawl
juridic forensic, juridical, lawful, licit
juridical civic, forensic, judicial, jural
jurisconsult advocate *(counselor)*, attorney, barrister, counsel, counselor, esquire, jurist, lawyer
jurisdiction agency *(legal relationship)*, ambit, area *(province)*, authority *(right)*, bailiwick, capacity *(authority)*, capacity *(sphere)*, charge *(custody)*, circuit, control *(supervision)*, custody *(supervision)*, department, direction *(guidance)*, domain *(sphere of influence)*, dominion *(supreme authority)*, generalship, government *(administration)*, judicature, occupation *(possession)*, power, predominance, primacy, province, realm, supervision, venue
jurisdiction of the court judicature
jurisdictional forensic, justiciable
jurisdictionally sound cognizable
jurisprudence law
jurisprudent attorney, barrister, esquire, jurist, lawyer, licit
jurisprudential forensic, juridical, licit
jurist advocate *(counselor)*, attorney, barrister, counsel, counselor, esquire, judge, lawyer, magistrate

juristic forensic, judicial, jural, juridical, legitimate *(rightful)*
juristical judicial
jurists bar *(body of lawyers)*
jurors array *(jury)*
jury panel *(jurors)*
jury charge instruction *(direction)*
juryman juror
jurymen array *(jury)*, jury
jussive decretal
just bona fide, condign, conscientious, equal, equitable, ethical, evenhanded, honest, impartial, incorruptible, judicial, juridical, licit, mere, meritorious, moral, objective, open-minded, reasonable *(fair)*, rightful, solid *(sound)*, suitable, unbiased, allowable, unprejudiced, upright
just as quasi
just begun inchoate
just cause compurgation
just claim cause of action, droit, right *(entitlement)*
just compensation damages, out of pocket
just dealing fairness
just deserts discipline *(punishment)*
just division apportionment
just estimation appreciation *(perception)*
just the same as is
justice bench, condemnation *(punishment)*, court, disinterest *(lack of prejudice)*, equity *(justice)*, ethics, fairness, judge, jurist, magistrate, moderation, objectivity, principle *(virtue)*, probity, rectitude, retribution, right *(righteousness)*
justice as distinguished from conformity to enactments or statutes equity *(justice)*
justice ascertained by natural reason equity *(justice)*
justice seat bench, court
justice under the law equity *(justice)*
justicer judge
justices judiciary
justiciable actionable, blameworthy, litigable, triable
justifiability admissibility, legitimacy
justifiable admissible, allowable, defensible, juridical, just, pardonable, plausible, rational, reasonable *(rational)*, rightful, sensible, tenable
justifiable excuse alibi
justification alibi, basis, capacity *(authority)*, compurgation, defense, determinant, excuse, explanation, ground, precedent, pretext, right *(entitlement)*, support *(corroboration)*
justificatory palliative *(excusing)*
justificatory excuse alibi
justified allowed, clear *(free from criminal charges)*, condign, defensible, entitled, juridical, justifiable, pardonable, sound
justifier advocate *(counselor)*, apologist, proponent
justify bear *(support)*, corroborate, defend, document, exculpate, excuse, extenuate, maintain *(sustain)*, palliate *(excuse)*, rationalize, reason *(persuade)*, sustain *(confirm)*, uphold, vindicate
justifying palliative *(excusing)*
justly fairly *(impartially)*
justly claimable payable
justly complaining aggrieved *(victimized)*

justly responsible liable
justness candor *(impartiality)*, disinterest *(lack of prejudice)*, equity *(justice)*, fairness, integrity, justice, objectivity, propriety *(appropriateness)*, rectitude, right *(righteousness)*
jut project *(extend beyond)*
jut out project *(extend beyond)*
jutting prominent
juvenal juvenile
juvenile adolescent, child, infant, jejune *(lacking maturity)*, minor, puerile
juvenile charge dependent
juvenile delinquent criminal
juvenility adolescence
juxtapose adjoin, border *(approach)*, border *(bound)*, compare
juxtaposed adjacent, proximate
juxtaposit adjoin, border *(approach)*, border *(bound)*
juxtaposition collation, connection *(abutment)*, contact *(touching)*, propinquity *(proximity)*
juxtapositional immediate *(not distant)*

K

kaleidoscopic complex, protean
keen acute, bitter *(penetrating)*, close *(rigorous)*, cognizant, discriminating *(judicious)*, eager, fervent, incisive, intense, perceptive, perspicacious, ready *(willing)*, receptive, responsive, sapient, sedulous, sensitive *(discerning)*, sly, solicitous, subtle *(refined)*, trenchant, zealous
keen sight perception
keen-eyed perspicacious
keen-sighted perspicacious
keen-witted perspicacious
keeness comprehension, perception
keenly aware vigilant
keenly sensitive acute
keenness insight, intelligence *(intellect)*, judgment *(discernment)*, predisposition, rigor, sagacity, sensibility
keensightedness sagacity
keep accompany, concern *(care)*, conserve, constrict *(inhibit)*, continue *(persevere)*, detain *(restrain)*, endure *(last)*, fulfill, fund, harbor, hoard, hold *(possess)*, jail, livelihood, obey, observe *(obey)*, occupy *(take possession)*, own, perform *(adhere to)*, possess, preserve, prolong, protect, remain *(continue)*, reserve, restrain, retain *(employ)*, retain *(keep in possession)*, save *(hold back)*, store, subsidize, sustenance, uphold, withhold
keep a date rendezvous
keep a secret cloak
keep accounts note *(record)*, record
keep alive keep *(shelter)*, maintain *(carry on)*, perpetuate, preserve
keep aloof elude, estrange
keep aloof from forgo
keep an account deposit *(submit to a bank)*
keep an appointment rendezvous
keep an eye on observe *(watch)*, patrol
keep an eye upon survey *(examine)*
keep apart dichotomize, dissociate,

estrange, insulate, isolate, part *(separate)*, seclude, separate, sever, withdraw
keep as captive constrain *(imprison)*, imprison
keep as one's own hold *(possess)*
keep at persist
keep at a distance eschew, estrange, rebuff
keep at a distance from avoid *(evade)*
keep at bay parry, repel *(drive back)*, repulse, stave, stem *(check)*
keep away eschew, parry
keep away from avoid *(evade)*, forgo, shirk, shun
keep back arrest *(stop)*, check *(restrain)*, constrain *(restrain)*, constrict *(inhibit)*, delay, detain *(restrain)*, deter, discourage, encumber *(hinder)*, forbear, hinder, hoard, impede, reserve, stall, strangle, suppress, withhold
keep behind bars enclose, imprison
keep busy occupy *(engage)*
keep clandestine blind *(obscure)*, conceal, enshroud, plant *(covertly place)*
keep clear of avoid *(evade)*, eschew, evade *(elude)*, parry, shun
keep company with accompany
keep count enumerate
keep count of poll
keep down extinguish, repress, strangle, subject, suppress
keep driving persevere
keep entirely to oneself monopolize
keep faith adhere *(maintain loyalty)*
keep for hold *(possess)*
keep for future action postpone
keep from conceal, deny *(refuse to grant)*, deter, discourage, forbear, forgo, prevent, refrain
keep from being successful foil
keep from contact with others isolate
keep from danger ensconce
keep from entering exclude
keep from happening enjoin, prevent
keep from harm ensure, preserve
keep from loss conserve
keep from notice enshroud
keep from proceeding delay
keep from public view seal *(close)*
keep from sight camouflage
keep from view camouflage, enshroud
keep going adhere *(persist)*, keep *(continue)*, maintain *(carry on)*, persevere, proceed *(go forward)*, progress, remain *(continue)*, sustain *(prolong)*
keep guard patrol, police
keep guarded ensconce
keep hidden cloak, ensconce, enshroud, plant *(covertly place)*
keep hold of occupy *(take possession)*, retain *(keep in possession)*
keep house inhabit, occupy *(take possession)*
keep in circumscribe *(surround by boundary)*, contain *(enclose)*, enclose, encompass *(surround)*, immure, inhibit, repress, stem *(check)*, withhold
keep in bounds condemn *(ban)*, enjoin
keep in captivity contain *(restrain)*, immure, imprison

keep in check balk, constrain *(restrain)*, contain *(restrain)*, control *(restrain)*, fetter, immure, impede, repress
keep in confidence seal *(close)*
keep in countenance coax
keep in custody confine, constrain *(imprison)*, detain *(hold in custody)*, enclose, immure, imprison
keep in detention constrain *(imprison)*, detain *(hold in custody)*, immure, imprison, seclude
keep in existence conserve, perpetuate
keep in hand hold *(possess)*
keep in ignorance cloak
keep in mind recall *(remember)*, remember, retain *(keep in possession)*
keep in order handle *(manage)*, manage, police, rule *(govern)*, superintend
keep in pay retain *(employ)*
keep in perspective discern *(discriminate)*
keep in private seclude
keep in readiness hold *(possess)*
keep in reserve fund, garner, hoard, hold *(possess)*, reserve, set aside *(reserve)*
keep in safety cover *(guard)*
keep in secrecy seal *(close)*
keep in service employ *(engage services)*
keep in sight monitor, observe *(watch)*, regard *(pay attention)*
keep in solitude isolate
keep in the dark camouflage, obscure
keep in the shade camouflage
keep in view monitor, observe *(watch)*, patrol, police
keep intact preserve
keep moving proceed *(go forward)*, progress
keep off deter, parry, stave
keep on adhere *(persist)*, bear *(tolerate)*, hold *(possess)*, maintain *(carry on)*, persevere, persist, pursue *(carry on)*, recur, remain *(continue)*, stay *(continue)*
keep on hand reserve
keep one guessing obfuscate
keep one waiting delay, hold up *(delay)*, procrastinate
keep one's countenance bear *(tolerate)*
keep one's distance shun
keep one's word perform *(adhere to)*
keep order handle *(manage)*, police, preside
keep orderly police
keep out bar *(exclude)*, clog, condemn *(ban)*, eliminate *(exclude)*, exclude, reject, screen *(select)*, seclude
keep out of harm's way beware
keep out of sight blind *(obscure)*, conceal, cover *(conceal)*, elude, enshroud, harbor, hide, lurk, suppress
keep out of the way eschew
keep out of view camouflage, hide
keep pace with concur *(coexist)*, reach
keep pending adjourn, continue *(adjourn)*, defer *(put off)*, delay, hold up *(delay)*
keep posted annunciate, convey *(communicate)*, inform *(notify)*
keep prepared hold *(possess)*

keep prisoner constrain *(imprison)*, contain *(restrain)*, immure
keep quiet rest *(cease from action)*
keep safe conserve, ensconce, ensure, harbor, keep *(shelter)*, preserve, save *(conserve)*
keep safe from harm cover *(guard)*
keep score poll
keep secret camouflage, cloak, conceal, ensconce, harbor, hide, plant *(covertly place)*, suppress, withhold
keep sound preserve
keep subjugated dominate
keep to conform
keep to oneself conceal, hide
keep under arrest contain *(restrain)*, detain *(hold in custody)*, immure, imprison
keep under close watch cover *(guard)*
keep under control check *(restrain)*, confine, contain *(restrain)*, control *(restrain)*, detain *(hold in custody)*, detain *(restrain)*, handle *(manage)*, police, repress, restrain
keep under cover ensconce, enshroud, hide, preserve
keep under surveillance examine *(study)*, scrutinize
keep undercover cloak
keep underground conceal
keep unimpaired conserve
keep up last, maintain *(carry on)*, persevere, preserve, pursue *(carry on)*, sustain *(prolong)*
keep vigil patrol, police
keep watch check *(inspect)*, patrol, police, survey *(examine)*
keep watch over preserve
keep within bounds censor, condemn *(ban)*, confine, detain *(hold in custody)*, detain *(restrain)*, immure, moderate *(temper)*, restrain, trammel
keep within limits curb, qualify *(condition)*, restrict
keeper caretaker *(one caring for property)*, custodian *(protector)*, guardian, holder
keeping administration, charge *(custody)*, compliance, conservation, constraint *(imprisonment)*, control *(supervision)*, custody *(supervision)*, detention, retention, safekeeping, trust *(custody)*, ward
keeping back detention
keeping in detention
keeping in custody detention
keepsake remembrance *(commemoration)*, reminder, token
ken apprehend *(perceive)*, cognition, comprehend *(understand)*, construe *(comprehend)*, digest *(comprehend)*, experience *(background)*, find *(discover)*, insight, knowledge *(awareness)*, knowledge *(learning)*, perceive, realization
kept in custody arrested *(apprehended)*
kept in prison in custody
kept in remembrance honorary
kept out ineligible
kernel main point
key cardinal *(basic)*, cardinal *(outstanding)*, catchword, central *(essential)*, clue, cornerstone, critical *(crucial)*, explanation, fundamental, gravamen, indispensable, main point, major,

material *(important)*, necessary *(required)*, primary, solution *(answer)*, strategic, tip *(clue)*
key man chairman, executive
key person caretaker *(one fulfilling the function of office)*, executive
key point landmark *(significant change)*
key woman executive
keynote cornerstone, corpus, highlight, main point
keystone cornerstone, foundation *(basis)*, gist *(ground for a suit)*, gravamen, main point, mainstay
kick beat *(strike)*, impetus, spurn
kick out evict, expel
kickback graft, gratuity *(bribe)*
kicker malcontent
kiddish puerile
kidnap abduct, carry away
kidnapper criminal
kidnapping abduction
kill destroy *(efface)*, dispatch *(put to death)*, eliminate *(eradicate)*, execute *(sentence to death)*, extinguish, prey, remove *(eliminate)*, repress, slay, stifle
kill by suffocation extinguish
kill time procrastinate
killer criminal
killing aberemurder, assassination, capital punishment, deadly, dispatch *(act of putting to death)*, fatal, homicide, lethal, manslaughter, murder, pernicious, pestilent
killing with malice aforethought aberemurder
kin descendant, descent *(lineage)*, family *(common ancestry)*, house, kindred, next of kin, relation *(kinship)*, relative
kind benevolent, blood, character *(personal quality)*, charitable *(lenient)*, class, color *(complexion)*, denomination, favorable *(expressing approval)*, form *(arrangement)*, humane, lenient, magnanimous, manner *(kind)*, philanthropic, propitious, race, style
kind act favor *(act of kindness)*
kind office benevolence *(act of kindness)*
kind person benefactor, good samaritan, samaritan
kind regard favor *(partiality)*
kind treatment benevolence *(act of kindness)*
kindhearted benevolent, charitable *(lenient)*, humane, lenient, philanthropic, propitious
kindheartedness benevolence *(disposition to do good)*, consideration *(sympathetic regard)*, humanity *(humaneness)*
kindle agitate *(activate)*, burn, create, foment, generate, incite, induce, inspire, make, originate, provoke, spirit, stimulate
kindle one's wrath incense
kindle wrath pique
kindliness benevolence *(disposition to do good)*, consideration *(sympathetic regard)*, largess *(generosity)*, philanthropy, pity, solace, understanding *(tolerance)*
kindly benevolent, humane, paternal, peaceable, philanthropic, propitious
kindly disposed benevolent

kindness affection, benefit *(conferment)*, benevolence *(disposition to do good)*, charity, clemency, consideration *(sympathetic regard)*, goodwill, help, humanity *(humaneness)*, largess *(generosity)*, lenience, philanthropy

kindred affiliation *(bloodline)*, affinity *(family ties)*, akin *(related by blood)*, allied, analogous, blood, comparable *(capable of comparison)*, consanguineous, family *(common ancestry)*, house, interrelated, next of kin, propinquity *(kinship)*, related, relation *(kinship)*, relative *(relevant)*, relative, similar

kindredship kinship, relationship *(family tie)*

kinetic impulsive *(impelling)*, moving *(in motion)*

kinfolk affiliation *(bloodline)*

kingdom domain *(sphere of influence)*, realm

kink quirk *(idiosyncrasy)*, snarl

kinsfolk blood, kindred

kinship affiliation *(bloodline)*, affinity *(family ties)*, ancestry, blood, chain *(nexus)*, community, connection *(relation)*, contact *(association)*, family *(common ancestry)*, filiation, nexus, relationship *(family tie)*, resemblance

kinsman blood, next of kin, relation *(kinship)*, relative

kinsmen affiliation *(bloodline)*, blood, family *(common ancestry)*, kindred

kinspeople kindred, next of kin

kinswoman blood

kismet predetermination

kith relative

kith and kin origin *(ancestry)*

kithless solitary

knack faculty *(ability)*, gift *(flair)*, propensity, skill

knave criminal, hoodlum

knavery artifice, collusion, corruption, deception, dishonesty, evasion, hoax, imposture, improbity, mischief, misdoing, pettifoggery

knavish artful, deceptive, disreputable, false *(disloyal)*, immoral, iniquitous, lawless, machiavellian, perfidious, recreant, reprobate, tortuous *(corrupt)*, unconscionable

knavishness dishonesty, knavery

kneel to obey

kneeling prostration

knife lancinate, pierce *(lance)*

knifelike mordacious

knit connect *(join together)*, join *(bring together)*, related

knock impinge, jostle *(bump into)*, sully

knock about ill use

knock against collide *(crash against)*, impinge, jostle *(bump into)*

knock down beat *(strike)*

knock into collide *(crash against)*, strike *(collide)*

knock out of shape mutilate

knot connection *(fastening)*, contort, intertwine, involution, snarl

knots ties

knotted complex, inextricable

knotty problematic, recondite

knotty point enigma

know appreciate *(comprehend)*, comprehend *(understand)*, conceive *(comprehend)*, digest *(comprehend)*, discern *(detect with the senses)*, find *(discover)*, identify, perceive, pierce *(discern)*, read, realize *(understand)*, recognize *(perceive)*, understand

know again recall *(remember)*, recollect, remember

know by heart recall *(remember)*, remember

know entirely apprehend *(perceive)*

know of apprehend *(perceive)*

know well apprehend *(perceive)*

know-all bigot

know-how experience *(background)*, faculty *(ability)*, knowledge *(awareness)*, knowledge *(learning)*, prowess *(ability)*, science *(technique)*

know-it-all bigot

knowable appreciable, ascertainable, cognizable, coherent *(clear)*, comprehensible, determinable *(ascertainable)*, discernible, perceivable, perceptible, ponderable, scrutable

knowing certain *(positive)*, cognizant, conscious *(aware)*, discriminating *(judicious)*, expert, familiar *(informed)*, intentional, judicial, learned, literate, omniscient, oracular, perceptive, perspicacious, politic, practiced, proficient, profound *(esoteric)*, qualified *(competent)*, rational, sapient, sciential, sensible, tactical, veteran

knowing person expert, specialist, veteran

knowingly purposely

knowledge apprehension *(perception)*, caliber *(mental capacity)*, certainty, certification *(certainness)*, cognition, comprehension, concept, disclosure *(something disclosed)*, discrimination *(good judgment)*, edification, education, experience *(background)*, information *(knowledge)*, intelligence *(news)*, notification, realization, reason *(sound judgment)*, recognition, science *(study)*, scienter, skill, specialty *(special aptitude)*, understanding *(comprehension)*

knowledge of facts information *(knowledge)*

knowledge of law jurisprudence

knowledgeable acquainted, acute, cognizant, expert, familiar *(informed)*, informed *(educated)*, knowing, learned, literate, omniscient, sciential, sensible, sophisticated

known apparent *(perceptible)*, cognizable, famous, illustrious, ordinary, outstanding *(prominent)*, prominent, proverbial, renowned, reputable, trite, unmistakable, usual

known elsewhere as alias

known elsewhere by alias

known elsewhere under the name alias

known facts information *(knowledge)*, intelligence *(news)*

known in advance foreseeable

known name goodwill

known otherwise as alias

known previously as alias

known variously as alias

knuckle under succumb

L

"lettre de change" draft

labefactare invalidate

label brand, brand *(mark)*, call *(title)*, classify, define, denominate, denomination, denote, designation *(naming)*, designation *(symbol)*, device *(distinguishing mark)*, discriminate *(distinguish)*, earmark, heading, identification, identify, nominate, pigeonhole, rubric *(title)*, title *(designation)*, trademark

label incorrectly mislabel

labeled entitled

labor employment, endeavor (noun), endeavor (verb), industry *(activity)*, job, persevere, struggle, work *(effort)*

labor at one's vocation practice *(engage in)*

labor dispute strike

labor expense payroll

labor for attempt, pursue *(strive to gain)*, strive

labor in vain failure *(lack of success)*

labor saving economic

labor supply personnel

labor under bear *(tolerate)*

labor under a misapprehension err, miscalculate, misconceive, mistake, misunderstand

labor under an error miscalculate

labor-saving economical

labor-saving device appliance

laborare labor

labored difficult, elaborate, painstaking, ponderous

laborer artisan, employee

laborers personnel

laboring force personnel

laborious difficult, faithful *(diligent)*, industrious, onerous, operose, oppressive, painful, painstaking, sedulous

laborious application pursuit *(effort to secure)*

laboriousness effort, industry *(activity)*

labyrinth complex *(entanglement)*, complication, confusion *(ambiguity)*, imbroglio, involution, snarl

labyrinthian labyrinthine, sinuous

labyrinthic labyrinthine

labyrinthine circuitous, complex, devious, difficult, indirect, inextricable, sinuous, tortuous *(bending)*

lace connect *(join together)*, intertwine

lacerate damage, harrow, lancinate, mutilate, rend, sever

lacerated broken *(fractured)*

laches neglect

lachrymose disconsolate

lack absence *(omission)*, dearth, defect, deficiency, deficit, delinquency *(shortage)*, disadvantage, failure *(falling short)*, foible, insufficiency, market *(demand)*, need *(deprivation)*, paucity, poverty, privation, require *(need)*, vice

lack belief in mistrust

lack candor feign, palter

lack confidence misdoubt

lack confidence in doubt *(distrust)*, mistrust, suspect *(distrust)*

lack conviction misdoubt

lack faith disbelieve, misdoubt

lack faith in mistrust

lack harmony disaccord, disagree

lack honesty cheat

lack information misunderstand

lack of ability inability

lack of accord discrepancy, inconsis-

tency
lack of activity inertia
lack of agreement discrepancy, exception *(objection)*, incompatibility *(difference)*, incompatibility *(inconsistency)*, nonconformity, paradox
lack of allurement disincentive
lack of appreciation ingratitude
lack of attention disinterest *(lack of interest)*, negligence, res ipsa loquitur
lack of awareness insentience, nescience
lack of belief incredulity
lack of bias objectivity, tolerance
lack of candidness indirection *(deceitfulness)*
lack of capacity incapacity
lack of care disregard *(unconcern)*, inconsideration
lack of caution inconsideration
lack of certainty cloud *(suspicion)*, indecision, misgiving, qualm
lack of certitude doubt *(indecision)*
lack of charm disincentive
lack of circumspection indiscretion
lack of clarity incoherence
lack of clearness confusion *(ambiguity)*
lack of competence inability
lack of complaint resignation *(passive acceptance)*
lack of comprehension insentience
lack of concern disinterest *(lack of interest)*
lack of concert discrepancy
lack of concord argument *(contention)*, contravention, controversy *(argument)*, discord
lack of confidence cloud *(suspicion)*, discredit, doubt *(indecision)*, doubt *(suspicion)*, misgiving, qualm
lack of conformity discrepancy, exception *(objection)*
lack of congruence discrepancy
lack of congruity discrepancy
lack of connection difference
lack of conscience bad faith, corruption, dishonesty, dishonor *(shame)*, improbity, indirection *(deceitfulness)*
lack of consideration disregard *(unconcern)*, disrespect, inconsideration, indiscretion, ingratitude
lack of consonance discrepancy, incongruity
lack of control laxity
lack of conviction doubt *(indecision)*, qualm
lack of corruption fairness
lack of courteousness disrespect
lack of courtesy disrespect
lack of decision indecision
lack of depth immateriality
lack of desire disincentive
lack of dexterity disqualification *(factor that disqualifies)*
lack of diligence laches, negligence
lack of discipline rebellion
lack of doubt credulity
lack of dubiety credulity
lack of dubiousness credulity
lack of due process lynch law
lack of education ignorance
lack of enthusiasm pessimism
lack of enticement disincentive
lack of equality inequality
lack of esteem discredit

lack of excess moderation
lack of expectation pessimism
lack of faith cloud *(suspicion)*, doubt *(indecision)*, doubt *(suspicion)*, incredulity, infidelity, suspicion *(mistrust)*
lack of feeling brutality
lack of fidelity bad faith, disloyalty
lack of fitness incapacity
lack of force impuissance
lack of funds failure *(bankruptcy)*
lack of good taste impropriety
lack of gratitude ingratitude
lack of harmony dissension, dissent *(difference of opinion)*, impugnation, incompatibility *(inconsistency)*, incongruity, paradox
lack of honesty dishonesty
lack of honor dishonor *(shame)*
lack of impetus disincentive
lack of incentive disincentive
lack of inducement disincentive
lack of integrity bad repute, dishonesty, improbity
lack of interest disregard *(unconcern)*, laxity
lack of jaundice objectivity
lack of judgment indiscretion
lack of justice lynch law
lack of knowledge ignorance, insentience, nescience
lack of learning ignorance, nescience
lack of legal sanction lynch law
lack of loyalty disloyalty, infidelity
lack of luxury austerity
lack of maintenance disrepair
lack of might impuissance
lack of motion inertia
lack of motivation disincentive
lack of movement inertia
lack of observation disregard *(unconcern)*
lack of order irregularity, pandemonium
lack of perception insentience
lack of piety blasphemy
lack of politeness disrespect
lack of possibility impossibility
lack of potentiality impossibility
lack of power impotence, impuissance, inability, incapacity, inefficacy
lack of prejudice fairness, objectivity, understanding *(tolerance)*
lack of principle bad faith, corruption, dishonesty, dishonor *(shame)*, improbity, knavery
lack of probity bad faith, corruption, dishonesty, dishonor *(shame)*, fraud, indirection *(deceitfulness)*, knavery
lack of proficiency disqualification *(factor that disqualifies)*
lack of propriety irregularity
lack of protection danger
lack of qualification disqualification *(factor that disqualifies)*
lack of regular order disorder *(lack of order)*
lack of relation disparity
lack of resemblance difference, discrepancy
lack of resistance resignation *(passive acceptance)*
lack of respect disrespect, ignominy, inconsideration
lack of reverence blasphemy, inconsideration

lack of safety danger
lack of skepticism credulity
lack of sophistication credulity
lack of sound silence
lack of spirit damper *(depressant)*
lack of stimulus disincentive
lack of strength fault *(weakness)*, impotence, impuissance, inefficacy, languor
lack of strictness lenience
lack of substance immateriality, impalpability
lack of suspicion credulity
lack of symmetry disparity, inequality, irregularity
lack of temptation disincentive
lack of thoroughness laxity
lack of toleration intolerance
lack of trust doubt *(suspicion)*, suspicion *(mistrust)*
lack of understanding opacity
lack of vigor impuissance
lack of warmth damper *(depressant)*
lack of warning surprise
lack resemblance differ *(vary)*
lack self-control carouse, overindulge
lack trust in mistrust
lackadaisical careless, dilatory, indolent, languid, lax, lifeless *(dull)*, otiose, phlegmatic, remiss, slipshod
lacking defective, deficient, delinquent *(overdue)*, devoid, essential *(required)*, faulty, imperfect, inadept, inadequate, insufficient, nonsubstantial *(not sufficient)*, paltry, peccable, perfunctory, save, void *(empty)*
lacking accord inconsistent
lacking activity stagnant
lacking agreement incongruous
lacking authority invalid
lacking caution imprudent
lacking clarity indistinct, nebulous, oblique *(evasive)*, opaque
lacking clearness ambiguous
lacking confidence hesitant
lacking content vacuous
lacking continuity desultory
lacking decency profligate *(corrupt)*
lacking dexterity inept *(incompetent)*
lacking dexterousness inept *(incompetent)*
lacking discretion ill-judged, injudicious
lacking elegance inelegant
lacking enthusiasm nonchalant
lacking experience inexperienced
lacking feeling insusceptible *(uncaring)*
lacking firmness insubstantial
lacking force invalid
lacking foresight improvident
lacking frankness disingenuous
lacking funds destitute, insolvent
lacking good taste inelegant
lacking grace inelegant
lacking harmony incongruous, inconsistent
lacking importance inapposite
lacking in quality poor *(inferior in quality)*
lacking individuality sequacious
lacking interest nonchalant
lacking judgment imprudent
lacking morals immoral
lacking nothing gross *(total)*
lacking order disjointed

lacking precision indistinct
lacking prejudice impartial
lacking principle profligate (corrupt)
lacking proficiency inexperienced
lacking proportion disproportionate
lacking prudence imprudent
lacking qualification incompetent
lacking refinement inelegant
lacking relevance inapposite
lacking remorse remorseless
lacking respect presumptuous
lacking self-confidence diffident
lacking shame profligate (corrupt)
lacking skill inept (incompetent), in-experienced
lacking stability insecure
lacking strength invalid
lacking substance insubstantial
lacking truth mendacious
lacking vigor indolent
lacking warmth nonchalant
lacking worth unworthy
lackluster inexpressive, lifeless (dull)
laconic brief, compact (pithy), concise, inarticulate, noncommittal, pithy, sententious, succinct, taciturn, unresponsive
lactare dupe
lacuna hiatus, split
lade encumber (hinder), load
laden full, replete
lading cargo, freight
lading of a ship cargo
laedere harm, offend (insult)
lag delay, pause, procrastinate, stall
laggard disinclined, indolent, lifeless (dull), otiose, truant
laggardness laches
lagging late (tardy), otiose
lagniappe contribution (donation), grant
laic civil (public), layman, profane
laical civil (public), profane
laid situated
laid bare naked (lacking embellishment)
laid down positive (prescribed)
lakeside littoral
lambaste beat (strike)
lamblike passive, patient, peaceable, pliable
lame defective, disable, imperfect, inadept, ineffective, ineffectual, insubstantial, maim, nonsubstantial (not sturdy), otiose, unable, unsatisfactory
lamed marred
lament deplore, languish, outcry, plaint, regret, repent
lament with sympathize
lamenta plaint
lamentabilis lamentable
lamentable deplorable, gross (flagrant), regrettable
lamentation disapprobation, plaint
lamentative querulous
lamenting disconsolate, querulous, remorseful, repentant
laming detriment
lampoon caricature, disparage, jape, mock (deride), parody, pillory, travesty
lampoonery ridicule
lance enter (penetrate), lancinate, launch (project), penetrate, split
lancinate harrow, rend
land alight, circuit, curtilage, demesne, domain (land owned), fee (es-

tate), freehold, holding (property owned), immovable, parcel, premises (buildings), property (land), real estate, realm, realty, region, territory
land a blow beat (strike)
land and buildings estate (property)
land developer developer
land held by lease leasehold
land leased leasehold
land owned realty
land revenue rent
landed proprietary
landed estate demesne, fee (estate), freehold, holding (property owned), real estate
landed interests property (land)
landed property demesne, fee (estate), freehold, property (land)
landed proprietor landowner
landholder landowner, tenant
landing haven
landlord landholder, landowner, lessor, proprietor
landmark cornerstone, crossroad (turning point), indicant, indicator
landowner landholder, proprietor, tenant
lands estate (property), fee (estate)
landscape scene
lane causeway, way (channel)
langour disinterest (lack of interest)
language discourse, phraseology, rhetoric (skilled speech), speech
language of a particular profession jargon (technical language)
languens languid
languere languish
languescere languish
languid inactive, indolent, insipid, lifeless (dull), phlegmatic, powerless, torpid
languidness disinterest (lack of interest), sloth
languish decay, degenerate, suffer (sustain loss)
languishing disconsolate, powerless
languor inaction, inertia
languour languor
languorous languid, otiose, passive, phlegmatic, torpid
languourness lifeless (dull)
laniena shambles
lap embrace (encircle)
lap over overlap
lapidified ossified
lapis landmark (conspicuous object)
lapse abeyance, cease, cessation (interlude), cloture, decline (fall), default, degenerate, descent (declination), deteriorate, error, expire, halt, hiatus, interval, misdeed, nonpayment, oversight (carelessness), pendency, recrudescence, relapse, remission, respite (interval of rest), revert, stop, subside
lapse in conduct delinquency (failure of duty)
lapsing regressive
lapsus lapse (expiration)
larcener burglar, hoodlum
larcenist hoodlum
larceny burglary, conversion (misappropriation), embezzlement, housebreaking, misappropriation, theft
larceny by force robbery
lard meliorate
lares household (domestic)

large broad, capacious, considerable, copious, extensive, gross (flagrant), major, ponderous, prodigious (enormous), substantial
large amount plurality, sufficiency
large asset transfer bulk transfer
large enough ample
large number plurality, quantity
large quantity plurality
large scale far reaching
large undertaking campaign
large-scale broad, extensive
largehearted magnanimous
largeness capacity (maximum), degree (magnitude), latitude, mass (weight), measurement
larger number majority (greater part)
larger part majority (greater part)
largess benefit (conferment), bounty, consideration (recompense), donation, grant, philanthropy
largesse contribution (donation), grant
largest part generality (bulk)
largiri bestow
largitas bounty
largitio largess (generosity)
larrup lash (strike)
lascivious dissolute, lecherous, lewd, licentious, obscene, prurient, salacious, scurrilous, suggestive (risqué)
lasciviousness debauchery
lascivire frisk
lascivus lascivious, wanton
lash beat (strike), denounce (condemn), handcuff, inveigh, punish, reprehend, reprimand
lash back recriminate
lashing caustic, obloquy
lassitude inertia, languor, prostration
lassus languid
last continue (persevere), definitive, exist, extreme (last), final, keep (continue), persevere, persist, remain (continue), remain (stay), resist (withstand), stay (continue), subsist, ultimate, withstand
last act denouement
last minute dilatory
last minute need emergency
last of a series end (termination)
last offer ultimatum
last part close (conclusion), end (termination)
last stage close (conclusion), conclusion (outcome)
last stop destination
lasting chronic, constant, continuance, durable, indelible, indestructible, infallible, infinite, infrangible, irreversible, irrevocable, live (existing), noncancellable, permanent, perpetual, persistent, solid (sound), stable, standing, steadfast, strong
lasting a very short time ephemeral
lasting period duration
lasting reminder monument
lastingness indestructibility, life (period of existence), longevity
latch adhere (fasten), shut
late back (in arrears), deceased, dilatory, former, lifeless (dead), overdue, prior, remiss
late patens comprehensive
late payment delinquency (shortage)

latebra evasion, subterfuge

lately recent

latency cessation *(interlude)*, inaction

lateness delay

latent blind *(concealed)*, covert, dormant, hidden, inactive, potential, secret, underlying, undisclosed

latent power potential

later ensuing, ex post facto, future, hereafter *(eventually)*, subsequent, successive, thereafter

later generations posterity

later in time ex post facto

later meditation hindsight

later thought hindsight

laterality contour *(outline)*

latere abscond, lurk

latest contemporary, current, present *(current)*, prevailing *(current)*

latitare lurk

latitude coverage *(scope)*, freedom, informality, liberty, margin *(spare amount)*, purview, region, scope, space, territory, zone

latitudinarian nonpartisan, open-minded

latitudinous broad

latitudo purview

latrocinium robbery

latter before mentioned, subsequent

latter day current

latus broad, extensive

laud belaud, honor *(outward respect)*, honor, mention *(tribute)*, recommend

laudabilis laudable, meritorious

laudable exemplary, honest, meritorious, moral, professional *(stellar)*, scrupulous, unimpeachable, upright

laudatio recommendation

laudation doxology, honor *(outward respect)*, mention *(tribute)*, recommendation, reference *(recommendation)*, respect

laudatory favorable *(expressing approval)*, meritorious

laudatus laudable

laude dignus laudable, meritorious

laugh at disdain, disparage, flout, humiliate, jape, jeer, mock *(deride)*, pillory, spurn

laugh-provoking ludicrous

laughable ludicrous

laughing jocular

launch cast *(throw)*, cause, commence, create, discharge *(shoot)*, embark, generate, impel, incite, initiate, inspire, instate, maintain *(commence)*, originate, precipitate *(throw down violently)*, preface, project *(impel forward)*, send, undertake

launch again renew *(begin again)*

launching genesis, installation, nascency, onset *(commencement)*, outset

lavish bestow, copious, excess, furnish, inordinate, liberal *(generous)*, philanthropic, prodigal, profuse, replete, superfluous, supply

lavishment largess *(generosity)*

lavishness largess *(generosity)*, philanthropy, waste

law act *(enactment)*, brevet, canon, constitution, criterion, dictate, edict, enactment, holding *(ruling of a court)*, measure, ordinance, precept, prescription *(directive)*, principle *(axiom)*, regulation *(rule)*, rubric *(authoritative rule)*,

rule *(legal dictate)*, statute

law and order peace

law court bench, judicatory, tribunal

law courts judiciary

law enforcement agency police

law enforcement agent district attorney, marshal, peace officer

law enforcement agents police

law enforcement body police, posse

law of conduct principle *(axiom)*

law of the case holding *(ruling of a court)*

law officer peace officer

law-abiding clean, ethical, honest, lawful, legitimate *(rightful)*, licit, moral, obedient

law-breaker delinquent

law-breaking guilt

law-giving decretal

law-making body chamber *(body)*, legislature

law-making branch of government legislature

law-revering law-abiding

lawbreaker convict, criminal, embezzler, felon, hoodlum, inmate, malefactor, offender, outlaw, recidivist, thief, vandal, wrongdoer

lawbreaker under suspension of sentence probationer *(released offender)*

lawbreaking bribery, culpable, delinquency *(misconduct)*, delinquent *(guilty of a misdeed)*, disobedient, disorderly, felonious, illegitimate *(illegal)*, larcenous, lawless, offense, racket, violation

lawcourt court, courtroom

lawful allowable, allowed, choate lien, civic, clean, de jure, due *(regular)*, forensic, juridical, just, justifiable, legal, legitimate *(rightful)*, licit, permissible, rightful, statutory, unalienable, valid

lawful authority hegemony

lawful cause cause of action

lawful claim due

lawful possession dominion *(absolute ownership)*, interest *(ownership)*

lawful power force *(legal efficacy)*

lawful vigor force *(legal efficacy)*

lawfully de jure, fairly *(impartially)*

lawfully sufficient prima facie *(legally sufficient)*

lawfulness legality, legitimacy, validity

lawgiver lawmaker, legislator, politician

lawgivers government *(political administration)*, legislature

lawgiving legislative

lawless broken *(unfulfilled)*, culpable, disobedient, disordered, disorderly, felonious, illegal, illicit, iniquitous, insubordinate, irresponsible, nonconforming, profligate *(corrupt)*, restive, sinister, uncontrollable, uncurbed, unlawful, unorthodox, unrestrained *(not repressed)*, unruly, unscrupulous, wrongful

lawless individual malefactor, outlaw

lawlessness anarchy, burglary, criminality, delinquency *(misconduct)*, disorder *(lack of order)*, illegality, irregularity, lynch law, misdeed, misdoing, misrule, offense, racket, revolution, riot, wrong

lawlike licit

lawmaker legislator, politician

lawmakers chamber *(body)*, government *(political administration)*, legislature

lawmaking codification, legislative, regulation *(management)*

laws code, legislation *(enactments)*

laws of a profession ethics

lawsuit action *(proceeding)*, matter *(case)*, proceeding, suit, trial *(legal proceeding)*

lawyer advocate *(counselor)*, attorney, barrister, counsel, counselor, esquire, jurist, practitioner, proctor, representative *(proxy)*

lawyers bar *(body of lawyers)*

lax careless, cursory, derelict *(negligent)*, improvident, indolent, negligent, peccable, perfunctory, promiscuous, remiss, slipshod, superficial, uncurbed

laxare release

laxity bad repute, dereliction, disinterest *(lack of interest)*, indifference, informality, laches, neglect, negligence, nonfeasance, nonperformance, omission, oversight *(carelessness)*

laxness dereliction, laches, neglect, negligence, omission, oversight *(carelessness)*, sloth

lay deposit *(place)*, profane, rest *(be supported by)*

lay a duty tax *(levy)*

lay a duty on exact, excise *(levy a tax)*

lay a duty upon charge *(assess)*

lay a plan program, scheme

lay a plot frame *(charge falsely)*

lay a snare for entrap

lay a trap inveigle

lay a trap for ambush, ensnare, entrap

lay a wager bet, gamble, parlay *(bet)*

lay an embargo on condemn *(ban)*, stop

lay an impost assess *(tax)*

lay an information complain *(charge)*

lay aside abandon *(relinquish)*, continue *(adjourn)*, defer *(put off)*, dismiss *(put out of consideration)*, exclude, forgo, forswear, hold *(possess)*, hold up *(delay)*, keep *(shelter)*, neglect, postpone, pretermit, quit *(discontinue)*, reject, relinquish, renounce, select, set aside *(reserve)*, suspend

lay away hold *(possess)*, keep *(shelter)*, reserve, store

lay bare bare, betray *(disclose)*, denude, disclose, divest, divulge, evidence, exhibit, expose, inform *(betray)*, manifest, produce *(offer to view)*, profess *(avow)*

lay before communicate, offer *(propose)*, pose *(propound)*, proffer, propose, propound, tender

lay before the public circulate, issue *(publish)*, publish

lay blame upon complain *(charge)*, denounce *(inform against)*, incriminate, reprehend

lay by deposit *(submit to a bank)*, hoard

lay charges against denounce *(inform against)*

lay claim to call *(demand)*, exact, excise *(levy a tax)*

lay down pose *(propound)*, posit, stipulate

lay down a plan devise *(invent)*, prearrange

lay down guide lines organize *(arrange)*

lay down limits demarcate

lay down one's office demit

lay down the law instruct *(direct)*

lay even money bet

lay eyes on discern *(detect with the senses)*, observe *(watch)*, pierce *(discern)*

lay hands on attack, procure

lay hands upon obtain

lay hold of distrain, hijack, impropriate, pirate *(take by violence)*, usurp

lay in ashes pillage

lay in ruins pillage, plunder

lay in store fund, glean, hoard

lay into attack

lay money down bet

lay money on gamble, parlay *(bet)*, speculate *(chance)*

lay odds bet

lay off dislodge, dismiss *(discharge)*, recess, suspend

lay on levy

lay oneself open to incur

lay open bare, clarify, confess, denude, disabuse, disinter, divest, divulge, educe, elucidate, exhibit, expose, inform *(betray)*, manifest, profess *(avow)*, unveil

lay open to harm expose

lay open to view expose

lay out demonstrate *(establish)*, devise *(invent)*, disburse *(pay out)*, invest *(fund)*, manifest, orchestrate, plan, prescribe, produce *(offer to view)*, program

lay out a boundary delimit

lay out money spend

lay over continue *(adjourn)*, delay

lay plans contrive, frame *(formulate)*, maneuver

lay responsibility on complain *(charge)*

lay responsibility upon charge *(accuse)*

lay stress on insist

lay the blame on complain *(charge)*, involve *(implicate)*

lay the foundation build *(construct)*, initiate, plan, plant *(place firmly)*

lay the foundation for originate

lay the foundation of generate

lay the foundations cause, commence, create, establish *(launch)*, instate, launch *(initiate)*

lay under embargo enjoin

lay under restraint arrest *(apprehend)*, check *(restrain)*, constrain *(restrain)*, detain *(restrain)*, hold up *(delay)*, immure

lay up fund, hoard

lay upon impose *(enforce)*

lay waste beat *(defeat)*, damage, denude, despoil, destroy *(efface)*, eliminate *(eradicate)*, eradicate, extirpate, harry *(plunder)*, loot, mistreat, pillage, plunder, spoil *(impair)*, subvert

lay waste to extinguish

layer of society class

laying aside release

laying out disbursement *(act of dis-*

bursing)

layman amateur

laymen public

layoff dismissal *(discharge)*, removal

layout arrangement *(plan)*, array *(order)*, configuration *(form)*, design *(construction plan)*, formation, method, order *(arrangement)*, pattern, structure *(composition)*

lazare expand

lazaretto asylum *(hospital)*

laziness inertia, laches, languor, laxity, sloth

lazy idle, inactive, indolent, lax, lifeless *(dull)*, otiose, phlegmatic, remiss, stagnant, torpid, truant

lead advantage, clue, coax, command, conduct, control *(regulate)*, direct *(show)*, direct *(supervise)*, dominate, edge *(advantage)*, generalship, govern, guidance, influence, initiate, manage, manipulate *(utilize skillfully)*, marshal, moderate *(preside over)*, motivate, officiate, operate, originate, oversee, persuade, pioneer, plurality, preamble, precede, predominance, predominate *(command)*, prescribe, preside, prevail *(triumph)*, prevail upon, primacy, prior, prompt, protagonist, redound, regulate *(manage)*, suggestion, superintend, tip *(clue)*

lead astray bait *(lure)*, brutalize, corrupt, debauch, delude, ensnare, entrap, illude, inveigle, misdirect, misguide, mislabel, mislead, misstate, palter, pervert

lead by inducement entrap

lead in preface

lead into captivity immure

lead into danger by artifice entrap

lead into error delude, illude, misdirect, misguide, mislabel, mislead, misstate

lead into temptation bait *(lure)*, entrap

lead into trouble mistreat

lead item feature *(special attraction)*

lead on entrap, inveigle

lead on by artifice ensnare

lead one to induce

lead one to expect promise *(raise expectations)*

lead the way initiate, instate, precede, preface

lead to cause, conduce, engender

lead to a decision arbitrate *(adjudge)*

lead to believe assure *(give confidence to)*, convert *(persuade)*, convince, persuade

leadable tractable

leaden indolent, languid, lifeless *(dull)*, otiose, ponderous, torpid

leadenness sloth

leader administrator, chairman, chief, demagogue, director, employer, forerunner, mastermind, official, patron *(influential supporter)*, pioneer, protagonist, superintendent

leader of affairs official

leaders management *(directorate)*

leadership direction *(guidance)*, generalship, guidance, hegemony, influence, management *(directorate)*, management *(supervision)*, predominance, primacy, supremacy

leadership power hierarchy *(persons in authority)*

leading cardinal *(outstanding)*, dominant, famous, important *(significant)*, influential, initial, major, master, material *(important)*, notable, noteworthy, paramount, precursory, prevailing *(having superior force)*, primary, prime *(most valuable)*, principal, prior, prominent, renowned, salient, sovereign *(absolute)*, stellar

leading character protagonist

leading inquiry cross-examination

leading nowhere blind *(impassable)*

leaf through read

league affiliation *(amalgamation)*, association *(alliance)*, band, cabal, cartel, chamber *(body)*, coaction, coalescence, coalition, collusion, commingle, committee, company *(assemblage)*, conciliation, confederacy *(compact)*, conformity *(agreement)*, connect *(join together)*, connection *(relation)*, connivance, consolidate *(unite)*, consolidation, consortium *(business cartel)*, consortium *(marriage companionship)*, contribution *(participation)*, cooperate, federalize *(associate)*, federate, federation, organization *(association)*, pact, partnership, party *(political organization)*, pool, pool, society, sodality, syndicate, union *(labor organization)*, unite

league together concur *(agree)*, conspire, join *(associate oneself with)*

league with combine *(act in concert)*, conspire

leagued affiliated, allied, associated, coadunate, collective, concurrent *(united)*, conjoint, corporate *(associate)*, federal, harmonious, joint, mutual *(collective)*, partisan

leak decrement, divulge, exude

leak into penetrate

leakage decrement, outflow

lean gravitate, insufficient, minimal, rest *(be supported by)*, select

lean against abut, border *(bound)*

lean on rely, trust

lean toward discriminate *(treat differently)*, prefer

leaning character *(personal quality)*, characteristic, conatus, conviction *(persuasion)*, disposition *(inclination)*, favor *(partiality)*, favoritism, habit, inclination, inclined, inequity, nepotism, oblique *(slanted)*, partiality, penchant, perspective, position *(point of view)*, posture *(attitude)*, preconception, predilection, predisposition, preference *(choice)*, prejudice *(preconception)*, proclivity, propensity, stand *(position)*, standpoint, tendency

leanness dearth, poverty

leap transition

learn apprehend *(perceive)*, detect, discover, find *(discover)*, gain, perceive, realize *(understand)*, study, understand

learn a habit naturalize *(acclimate)*, practice *(train by repetition)*

learn a lesson from profit

learn about ascertain

learn for a certainty discover

learn of discover

learn the answer solve

learnable ascertainable

learned cognizant, competent, didactic, expert, familiar *(informed)*, informed *(educated)*, literate, practiced, professional *(trained)*, profound *(esoteric)*, sapient, sciential

learned counsel advocate *(counselor)*, attorney, barrister, jurist

learned in the law forensic

learned man pedagogue

learned person mastermind, specialist

learned profession calling, profession *(vocation)*

learnedly knowingly

learner apprentice, disciple, neophyte, novice, probationer *(one being tested)*, protégé

learning aptitude, common knowledge, comprehension, detection, discipline *(field of study)*, edification, education, experience *(background)*, information *(knowledge)*, science *(study)*

lease convey *(transfer)*, engage *(hire)*, rent, sublet

leased mercenary

leasehold property *(land)*

leaseholder landholder, lessee, lodger, occupant, tenant

leaser consumer, customer

leash handcuff, inhibit, limit, repress

leasing tenancy

least minimal

least amount minimum

least part minimum

least quantity minimum

leave abscond, alight, bequeath, capacity *(authority)*, charter *(sanction)*, concession *(authorization)*, consent, defect, demise, demit, depart, devise *(give)*, disappear, discontinue *(abandon)*, dispensation *(exception)*, evacuate, fail *(neglect)*, favor *(sanction)*, forgo, forswear, franchise *(license)*, freedom, furlough, give *(grant)*, holiday, indulgence, liberty, license, move *(alter position)*, option *(choice)*, permission, permit, pretermit, quit *(evacuate)*, relinquish, renounce, resign, retire *(conclude a career)*, retire *(retreat)*, retreat, secede, shun, sufferance, variance *(exemption)*, withdraw, yield *(submit)*

leave a legacy bequeath, demise, descend

leave a place move *(alter position)*

leave alone neglect

leave an inference allude, imply

leave behind abandon *(physically leave)*, surpass

leave by will bequeath, demise, devise *(give)*

leave defenseless endanger

leave destitute deprive, despoil

leave empty evacuate

leave in the lurch abandon *(physically leave)*

leave no choice necessitate

leave no option compel, constrain *(compel)*, impose *(enforce)*, necessitate

leave no trace disappear, expunge, perish

leave no trace of eradicate

leave no vestige of eradicate

leave nothing to be desired consummate

leave of absence furlough

leave off cease, desist, discontinue *(abandon)*, discontinue *(break continu-*

ity*)*, forbear, interrupt, quit *(discontinue)*, refrain, stop, suspend

leave one's country expatriate

leave out bar *(exclude)*, block, censor, delete, disregard, eliminate *(exclude)*, estrange, except *(exclude)*, exclude, omit, overlook *(disregard)*, pretermit, reject

leave out of consideration disregard

leave the impression demean *(deport oneself)*

leave the job strike *(refuse to work)*

leave to bequeath, devolve

leave to chance bet

leave undone omit, overlook *(disregard)*, pretermit, shirk

leave unfinished quit *(discontinue)*

leave unlawfully defect

leave unprotected endanger, jeopardize

leave unregarded exclude

leaven determinant, imbue, penetrate, permeate

leavetaking egress

leaving abdication, desertion, discard, flight, resignation *(relinquishment)*

leaving no choice obligatory

leaving off moratorium

leaving out disregard *(unconcern)*, omission, save

leavings surplus

lecherous depraved, immoral, lascivious, lewd, obscene, prurient, salacious, suggestive *(risqué)*

lechery debauchery, obscenity

lecture address *(talk to)*, charge *(statement to the jury)*, criticism, declaim, declamation, discourse, discourse, harangue, inculcate, instruct *(teach)*, instruction *(teaching)*, objurgation, peroration, rebuke, recital, recite, reprehend, reprimand, reprimand, reproach, speech

lecturer pedagogue

lecturers faculty *(teaching staff)*

led astray blind *(not discerning)*

ledge border, margin *(outside limit)*

ledger account *(evaluation)*, journal, register, roll

lee refuge, safekeeping

leech parasite

leery suspicious *(distrustful)*

leeway freedom, margin *(spare amount)*

left derelict *(abandoned)*

left in penury bankrupt

left over residuary

left to discretion discretionary

left to individual judgment discretionary

leftover balance *(amount in excess)*, expendable, net, overage, remainder *(remaining part)*, residual

legacy benefit *(conferment)*, bequest, claim *(right)*, dower, estate *(hereditament)*, gift *(present)*, grant, heritage, inheritance, will *(testamentary instrument)*

legal admissible, allowable, allowed, choate lien, civic, de jure, due *(regular)*, forensic, honest, jural, juridical, just, justifiable, lawful, legitimate *(rightful)*, licit, permissible, rightful, statutory, valid

legal abstract brief

legal action action *(proceeding)*,

cause *(lawsuit)*, controversy *(lawsuit)*, day in court, lawsuit, matter *(case)*, proceeding, prosecution *(criminal trial)*, suit

legal administration bench

legal adversary litigant

legal adviser advocate *(counselor)*, attorney, barrister, counsel, counselor, esquire, jurist

legal advisor lawyer

legal advocate lawyer

legal age majority *(adulthood)*

legal agreement lease, specialty *(contract)*

legal appointee attorney in fact

legal approval affirmance *(judicial sanction)*

legal argument answer *(judicial response)*, case *(lawsuit)*, controversy *(lawsuit)*, lawsuit, plea

legal arrangement before marriage antenuptial agreement

legal assertion cause of action

legal assistance maintenance *(support of spouse)*

legal authority judicature, jurisdiction

legal authorization affirmance *(judicial sanction)*

legal battle dispute

legal body corporation, corpus

legal call process *(summons)*

legal capacity capacity *(authority)*

legal cession grant

legal chicanery bunko

legal claim demand, right *(entitlement)*

legal code code, constitution, jurisprudence, law, pandect *(code of laws)*

legal command ordinance

legal competence competence *(ability)*, majority *(adulthood)*

legal confinement commitment *(confinement)*

legal constraint commitment *(confinement)*

legal consultant lawyer

legal contest action *(proceeding)*, day in court, lawsuit

legal controversy lawsuit

legal costs damages

legal counsel advice

legal course to adhere to adjective law

legal decision cognovit, judgment *(formal court decree)*

legal defender counselor

legal defense compurgation, justification, plea

legal dispute case *(lawsuit)*, contention *(argument)*, lawsuit, trial *(legal proceeding)*

legal dissolution of marriage divorce, separation

legal document agreement *(contract)*, blank *(form)*, brief, contract, policy *(contract)*

legal document to search search warrant

legal enforcement of a lien foreclosure

legal entity corporation, corpus, partnership

legal epitome brief

legal estate effects, fee *(estate)*, holding *(property owned)*

legal evidence admissible evidence, affirmance *(legal affirmation)*, affirmation, corroboration
legal expense cost *(expenses)*
legal expert jurist
legal fitness competence *(ability)*
legal force validity
legal forum judiciary
legal heir legatee
legal immaturity minority *(infancy)*, nonage
legal incapacity disability *(legal disqualification)*, minority *(infancy)*
legal incompetence minority *(infancy)*
legal inquiry investigation
legal instructions charge *(statement to the jury)*
legal investigation inquest
legal issue case *(lawsuit)*, contention *(argument)*
legal learning jurisprudence
legal liability damages, fine
legal mandate subpoena
legal maturity majority *(adulthood)*
legal memorandum brief
legal methods adjective law
legal minimum quorum
legal minority nonage
legal notice monition *(legal summons)*, notification
legal nullification of marriage divorce
legal obligation liability
legal opponent litigant
legal order mittimus, precept, search warrant
legal philosophy jurisprudence
legal pledge adjuration, affirmance *(legal affirmation)*, affirmation, asseveration, avowal, certification *(attested copy)*, confirmation
legal power authority *(right)*, droit, judicature, jurisdiction, prerogative, right *(entitlement)*
legal power to decide a case jurisdiction
legal practice jurisprudence
legal practitioner advocate *(counselor)*, attorney, barrister, counsel, counselor, esquire, jurist, lawyer
legal precedent jurisprudence
legal procedure certiorari, proceeding
legal proceeding action *(proceeding)*, controversy *(lawsuit)*, suit
legal proceedings case *(lawsuit)*, cause *(lawsuit)*, hearing, lawsuit, matter *(case)*
legal process certiorari, citation *(charge)*, controversy *(lawsuit)*, prosecution *(criminal trial)*, search warrant, subpoena, summons, warrant *(judicial writ)*
legal profession bar *(body of lawyers)*
legal program agenda
legal ratification affirmance *(judicial sanction)*
legal redress recourse
legal relation of spouses to each other cohabitation *(married state)*
legal relationship privity
legal release from confinement discharge *(liberation)*
legal remedy suit

legal representative administrator, advocate *(counselor)*, attorney in fact, counselor, executor, jurist
legal residence address
legal responsibility liability, obligation *(duty)*
legal restraint constraint *(imprisonment)*, detention, deterrence, deterrent, durance, embargo, estoppel, incarceration
legal right birthright, droit, freedom, jurisdiction, patent
legal science jurisprudence
legal status of a married woman coverture
legal support maintenance *(support of spouse)*
legal tender cash, currency, money
legal termination of marriage divorce
legal title droit, right *(entitlement)*, title *(right)*
legal trial day in court, hearing, inquiry *(systematic investigation)*, prosecution *(criminal trial)*
legal union of a man and a woman cohabitation *(married state)*
legal vitality force *(legal efficacy)*
legal will testament
legal wrong tort
legalese jargon *(technical language)*
legalism legality
legalist jurist
legalistic forensic, juridical
legality admissibility, legitimacy, sanction *(permission)*, validity
legalization consent, leave *(permission)*, permit
legalize allow *(authorize)*, authorize, certify *(approve)*, confirm, constitute *(establish)*, formalize, legitimate, notarize, pass *(approve)*, seal *(solemnize)*, validate
legalized allowable, allowed, choate lien, entitled, juridical, justifiable, lawful, legal, legitimate *(rightful)*, licit, prescriptive, rightful, statutory, valid
legally de jure, fairly *(impartially)*
legally adequate prima facie *(legally sufficient)*
legally binding valid
legally bound liable
legally determine try *(conduct a trial)*
legally discard a spouse divorce
legally enforceable triable
legally incapable disabled *(deprived of legal right)*
legally obliged to repay indebted
legally pursue sue
legally qualified eligible
legally responsible liable
legally restrain apprehend *(arrest)*, arrest *(apprehend)*
legally restrain again rearrest
legally restrained arrested *(apprehended)*
legally sound permissible
legare leave *(give)*
legatary legatee
legate advocate *(counselor)*, plenipotentiary
legatee beneficiary, devisee, donee, feoffee, heir, recipient, transferee
legateship embassy
legati deputation *(delegation)*

legatio deputation *(delegation)*, embassy, staff
legation delegation *(envoy)*, deputation *(delegation)*, embassy, mission
legatum bequest, legacy
legatus deputy, procurator
legend caption, fiction, inscription, myth, story *(narrative)*
legendary famous, fictitious, nonexistent, proverbial
legendary story myth
legerdemain deception, knavery, maneuver *(trick)*, prestidigitation
legere cull, select
leges facere legislate
legible coherent *(clear)*, comprehensible
legibly fairly *(clearly)*
legion assemblage, band, quantity
legionary innumerable
legis violator lawbreaker
legislate authorize, constitute *(establish)*, enact, govern, legalize, mandamus, pass *(approve)*
legislated due *(regular)*, legitimate *(rightful)*, licit, positive *(prescribed)*
legislating legislative
legislation act *(enactment)*, amendment *(legislation)*, bill *(proposed act)*, canon, code, codification, edict, enactment, measure, ordinance, regulation *(rule)*, rubric *(authoritative rule)*, rule *(legal dictate)*, statute
legislative executive, statutory
legislative act amendment *(legislation)*
legislative bill amendment *(legislation)*
legislative body chamber *(body)*, congress, legislature
legislative cure remedial statute
legislative declaration bill *(formal declaration)*
legislative decree act *(enactment)*, ordinance
legislative draftsman lawmaker
legislative edict ordinance
legislative enactment measure, statute
legislative mandate measure
legislative precedent authority *(documentation)*
legislative process legislation *(lawmaking)*
legislative proclamation measure
legislative redress remedial statute
legislative sanction legalization
legislator lawmaker, politician
legislatorial statutory
legislators government *(political administration)*
legislature chamber *(body)*, congress
legist advocate *(counselor)*, attorney, barrister, counsel, counselor, esquire, jurist, lawyer, magistrate
legists bar *(body of lawyers)*
legitimacy admissibility, authority *(right)*, honesty, legality, reality, validity
legitimate admissible, allowable, allowed, authentic, authorize, bona fide, choate lien, constitute *(establish)*, de jure, due *(regular)*, ethical, fit, formalize, genuine, honest, justifiable, justify, lawful, legal, legalize, licit, official, permissible, plausible, proper, rational,

real, reliable, right *(correct)*, rightful, sanction, sane, scrupulous, sound, straightforward, tenable, true *(authentic)*, upright, valid, veridical, viable, well-grounded

legitimate puissance force *(legal efficacy)*

legitimately de jure, duly, in good faith

legitimateness legality, legitimacy, validity

legitimation legitimacy

legitimatization legalization

legitimatize allow *(authorize)*, authorize, constitute *(establish)*, formalize, legalize, legitimate, sanction, validate

legitimization legitimacy

legitimize authorize, constitute *(establish)*, pass *(approve)*, sanction, validate

legitimized choate lien, fully executed *(signed)*

legitimus justifiable, lawful, legal, licit

leisure furlough, holiday, leave *(absence)*

leisured unemployed

leisurely deliberate

lend bestow, capitalize *(provide capital)*, finance, invest *(fund)*, let *(lease)*, loan, rent

lend a hand facilitate, help, promote *(organize)*

lend aid help, serve *(assist)*

lend approval recommend

lend assistance contribute *(assist)*

lend force to compound

lend money to support *(assist)*

lend on security invest *(fund)*, lease

lend one's aid capitalize *(provide capital)*, subsidize

lend one's name to indorse

lend one's support to cooperate

lend oneself to cooperate, espouse, involve *(participate)*, partake

lend support bear *(support)*, capitalize *(provide capital)*, help, preserve, recommend, subsidize

lend to again refinance

lender backer, creditor, obligee

lending assistance contributory

length extent, gamut

length of life longevity

length of time duration, period

lengthen compound, continue *(prolong)*, enlarge, expand, extend *(enlarge)*, increase, keep *(continue)*, project *(extend beyond)*, prolong, spread, supplement, sustain *(prolong)*

lengthen out protract *(stall)*

lengthened protracted

lengthening continuance, continuation *(prolongation)*, cumulative *(increasing)*, development *(progression)*

lengthwise along

lengthy prolix, protracted, sesquipedalian

lenience clemency, condonation, humanity *(humaneness)*, indulgence, longanimity, moderation, pity

leniency clemency, grace period, humanity *(humaneness)*, indulgence, lenience, longanimity, moderation, pardon, pity

lenient palliative *(abating)*, perfunctory, permissive, placable

lenify palliate *(abate)*, relax, remit

(relax), soothe

lenire allay, mitigate, mollify, pacify, soothe

lenis lenient

lenitive medicinal, narcotic, remedial

lenity clemency, humanity *(humaneness)*, indulgence, lenience, moderation, pity

lentus flexible, intentional, malleable, phlegmatic, pliable, pliant, stagnant, torpid

leonine powerful

lese majesty rebellion

less save, subaltern

less important minor, secondary, subordinate

less powerful inferior *(lower in position)*

less significant subordinate

less than necessary deficient

less than perfect faulty, peccable

less valuable inferior *(lower in quality)*

lessee consumer, customer, lodger, occupant, tenant

lessen abridge *(shorten)*, adulterate, allay, alleviate, assuage, attenuate, commute, curtail, debilitate, decrease, deduct *(reduce)*, deplete, depreciate, depress, derogate, diminish, discount *(minimize)*, ease, erode, expend *(consume)*, extenuate, minimize, mitigate, moderate *(temper)*, modify *(moderate)*, mollify, palliate *(abate)*, rebate, reduce, relax, remit *(relax)*, retrench, soothe, subdue, subside

lessen importance of demote

lessen in force mitigate

lessen in power impair

lessen in value impair

lessen in worth degenerate

lessen one's reputation defame

lessen the labor facilitate

lessen the price of depreciate

lessen the reputation of derogate

lessen the self-confidence of discourage

lessen the strength of dilute

lessening abatement *(reduction)*, attrition, curtailment, decline, decrease, decrement, deduction *(diminution)*, derogatory, diminution, erosion, mitigating, mitigation, mollification, remission

lessening of price rebate

lesser ancillary *(subsidiary)*, inferior *(lower in position)*, inferior *(lower in quality)*, mediocre, minimal, minor, secondary, subaltern, subordinate, subservient

lesser group minority *(outnumbered group)*

lesser part minority *(outnumbered group)*

lesson caveat, correction *(punishment)*, guidance

lessor landlord, obligee, transferor

let attorn, bestow, enable, engage *(hire)*, grant *(concede)*, lease, permit, rent, suffer *(permit)*, vouchsafe

let alone forswear, shun

let be leave *(allow to remain)*

let continue leave *(allow to remain)*

let down betray *(lead astray)*, disappoint, disappointed, frustrate

let drop divulge

let escape free, rescue

let fall outpour, precipitate *(throw down violently)*, remark

let fly precipitate *(throw down violently)*, project *(impel forward)*

let go acquitted, clear, disband, discharge *(dismiss)*, discharge *(liberate)*, disenthrall, disown *(refuse to acknowledge)*, forfeit, free, leave *(allow to remain)*, liberate, omit, palliate *(excuse)*, release, relinquish, remit *(release from penalty)*, renounce, surrender *(give back)*, terminate, yield *(submit)*

let go free parole

let have present *(make a gift)*

let in receive *(permit to enter)*

let know apprise, communicate, confide *(divulge)*, disabuse, inform *(notify)*, mention, notify

let lapse discontinue *(abandon)*

let loose discharge *(dismiss)*, discharge *(liberate)*, disenthrall, extricate, free, liberate, pardon

let off absolve, acquit, acquitted, cast *(throw)*, clear, excuse, palliate *(excuse)*

let one down fail *(neglect)*

let out communicate, disband, discharge *(liberate)*, disengage, disenthrall, emit, free *(not restricted)*, free, liberate, release, remit *(release from penalty)*, rent, rescue, sublease, sublet

let out of jail parole

let out of prison discharge *(liberate)*, disenthrall, free, parole

let pass condone, forgo, omit, pretermit

let premises for a designated period lease

let ride overlook *(disregard)*

let slacken remit *(relax)*

let slide ignore, procrastinate

let slip betray *(disclose)*, divulge, forfeit, ignore, omit, procrastinate

let stand leave *(allow to remain)*

let the matter stand procrastinate

let through receive *(permit to enter)*

let up diminution, ease, lessen, remit *(relax)*, subside

letdown damper *(depressant)*

lethal deadly, deleterious, dire, fatal, insalubrious, malevolent, malignant, noxious, peccant *(unhealthy)*, pernicious, pestilent, ruthless, toxic, virulent

lethal instrument cudgel, gun

lethal instruments weapons

lethal weapon cudgel

lethal weapons weapons

lethality fatality

lethargic inactive, indolent, languid, lifeless *(dull)*, otiose, phlegmatic, stagnant, torpid

lethargical inactive, languid, lifeless *(dull)*, otiose, phlegmatic

lethargy inertia, languor, sloth

lethiferous deadly, fatal, insalubrious, lethal, pestilent

letter dispatch *(message)*, inscribe, transmittal

letter in support reference *(recommendation)*

letter of credit draft

letter of introduction reference *(recommendation)*

letter of recognition certification *(certification of proficiency)*

letter of recommendation reference *(recommendation)*

letter writing correspondence *(communication by letters)*
lettered cognizant, familiar *(informed)*, informed *(educated)*, learned, literate
letters correspondence *(communication by letters)*, education
letting go layoff
letting off acquittal
lettre de cachet durance
letup cloture, pause, remission, respite *(interval of rest)*
levamentum mitigation
levant abscond, bilk, defraud, escape
levanter fugitive
levare assuage, elevate, extenuate
levatio mitigation
level balance *(equality)*, coequal, commensurable, destroy *(efface)*, extirpate, obliterate, pillage, regulate *(adjust)*, subvert
level of attendance draw *(attendance)*
level of development degree *(station)*
level of education civilization
level of excellence standard
level off compensate *(counterbalance)*, decrease
level with inform *(notify)*
level-headedness common sense, deliberation
levelheaded patient, prudent, rational, sane, sensible
levelheadedness sagacity, sanity
levelness regularity, uniformity
lever devastate
leverage advantage, clout, influence, latitude
leviable ad valorem
leviathan prodigious *(enormous)*
levied attached *(seized)*
levis capricious, frivolous, inconsiderable, negligible, slight, superficial, trivial, volatile
levy ad valorem, assess *(tax)*, attach *(seize)*, charge *(assess)*, collect *(recover money)*, confiscate, distrain, distraint, distress *(seizure)*, dun, duty *(tax)*, exact, excise, excise *(levy a tax)*, garnishment, imposition *(tax)*, impress *(procure by force)*, raise *(collect)*, require *(compel)*, requisition, sequester *(seize property)*, sequestration, tariff *(duties)*, tax, toll *(tax)*, toll *(exact payment)*
levy a distress distrain
levy an excise on excise *(levy a tax)*
levy upon garnish
lewd depraved, immoral, lascivious, lecherous, licentious, obscene, promiscuous, prurient, salacious, scandalous, scurrilous, suggestive *(risqué)*, unrestrained *(not repressed)*, wanton
lewdness debauchery, obscenity, perversion, pornography, vice
lex act *(enactment)*, canon, code, enactment, law, statute, term *(provision)*
lex oblivionis indemnity
liabilities overhead
liability arrears, attornment, blame *(responsibility)*, burden, chance *(possibility)*, characteristic, charge *(lien)*, cloud *(incumbrance)*, debit, debt, delinquency *(shortage)*, detriment, disadvantage, drawback, due, duty *(obligation)*, encumbrance, excise, fault *(responsibility)*, fine, impairment *(drawback)*,

impeachability, incumbrance *(lien)*, lien, penalty, probability, responsibility *(accountability)*, weight *(burden)*
liability to disaster fatality
liability to err frailty
liability to injury danger, hazard, peril
liable accountable *(responsible)*, at fault, blameful, blameworthy, bound, inclined, possible, probable, prone, subject *(exposed)*, susceptible *(unresistent)*
liable to conditional
liable to attack vulnerable
liable to be annulled voidable
liable to be completed determinable *(liable to be terminated)*
liable to be discontinued determinable *(liable to be terminated)*
liable to be dropped determinable *(liable to be terminated)*
liable to be ended determinable *(liable to be terminated)*
liable to be erroneous fallible
liable to come to an end determinable *(liable to be terminated)*
liable to disappear elusive
liable to err peccable
liable to expire determinable *(liable to be terminated)*
liable to mistake fallible
liable to prosecution actionable, blameful, blameworthy, justiciable
liable to question uncertain *(questionable)*
liable to sin peccable
liableness probability
liaison chain *(nexus)*, collusion, connection *(fastening)*, connection *(relation)*, connivance, contact *(association)*, nexus, relation *(connection)*
liaisons ties
libation grant
libel aspersion, defamation, defame, denigrate, malign, slander, smear
libelant accuser, claimant, complainant, contender, contestant, party *(litigant)*
libellus indictment, invoice *(itemized list)*, petition, schedule
libellus famosus libel
libelous calumnious, contemptuous, derogatory
liber candid, exempt, free *(not restricted)*, independent, ingenuous, liberty, register
liberal ample, benevolent, broad, charitable *(benevolent)*, charitable *(lenient)*, copious, extensive, lenient, magnanimous, open-minded, permissive, philanthropic, prodigal, profuse, progressive *(advocating change)*, unbiased
liberalis charitable *(lenient)*, liberal *(broad minded)*
liberalism latitude
liberalistic broad
liberalitas bounty, charity
liberality benefit *(conferment)*, benevolence *(disposition to do good)*, candor *(impartiality)*, clemency, disinterest *(lack of prejudice)*, largess *(generosity)*, lenience, philanthropy, tolerance
liberalness charity, largess *(generosity)*
liberare absolve, acquit, disengage, exonerate, extricate, free, liberate, release, rescue

liberate absolve, acquit, clear, disencumber, disengage, disentangle, disenthrall, dissociate, enable, enfranchise, exclude, exculpate, excuse, exonerate, extricate, free, let *(permit)*, palliate *(excuse)*, pardon, parole, quit *(free of)*, redeem *(repurchase)*, release, relieve *(free from burden)*, remit *(release from penalty)*, rescue, save *(rescue)*
liberate from connection disengage
liberate from oppression disenthrall
liberated exempt, free *(enjoying civil liberty)*, free *(not restricted)*, free *(relieved from a burden)*, liberal *(broad minded)*, sovereign *(independent)*, unbound
liberatio acquittal, emancipation, liberation, release
liberation absolution, acquittal, compurgation, emancipation, exemption, exoneration, freedom, immunity, impunity, parole, probation, release, relief *(release)*, remission, suffrage
liberation from foreign restraint liberty
liberi issue *(progeny)*
libertas freedom, latitude, liberty
liberticide oppression
libertinage debauchery
libertine dissolute, lascivious, lecherous, lewd, licentious, salacious, unrestrained *(not repressed)*
libertinism debauchery, vice
liberty capacity *(authority)*, charter *(sanction)*, dispensation *(exception)*, emancipation, exemption, freedom, furlough, immunity, informality, latitude, leave *(absence)*, leave *(permission)*, license, opportunity, option *(choice)*, parole, prerogative, privilege, suffrage
liberty of action call *(option)*
liberty of approach admittance *(means of approach)*
liberty of choice franchise *(right to vote)*
liberty of choosing discretion *(power of choice)*
liberty of judgment discretion *(power of choice)*
liberty of use easement
liberty to enter ingress
liberty to vote franchise *(right to vote)*
libidinosus arbitrary, lascivious, licentious, prurient
libidinous dissolute, immoral, lascivious, lecherous, lewd, obscene, prurient, salacious, scurrilous, suggestive *(risqué)*, wanton
librate oscillate, vacillate
libretto script
libro balance *(equality)*
librum edere edit
license allow *(authorize)*, appoint, approval, authorize, bestow, brevet, capacity *(authority)*, certificate, certification *(certification of proficiency)*, certify *(approve)*, charter *(sanction)*, concession *(authorization)*, confirm, consent, consent, constitute *(establish)*, copyright, countenance, delegate, delegation *(assignment)*, discretion *(power of choice)*, dispensation *(exception)*, droit, empower, enable, enfranchise, entrust, exemption, freedom, grant *(concede)*, immunity, impunity, induct, indulgence,

informality, invest *(vest)*, latitude, leave *(permission)*, let *(permit)*, liberty, option *(contractual provision)*, palliate *(excuse)*, patent, permission, permit, permit, prerogative, prescription *(claim of title)*, privilege, qualify *(meet standards)*, sanction *(permission)*, sanction, seal *(solemnize)*, sign, suffer *(permit)*, sufferance, suffrage, tolerance, warrant *(authorization)*

licensed admissible, allowed, entitled, lawless, legitimate *(rightful)*, licit, official, permissible, privileged, qualified *(competent)*

licensee nominee *(delegate)*, transferee

licensor transferor

licentia anarchy, freedom, latitude, leave *(permission)*, liberty

licentious depraved, disobedient, disorderly, disreputable, dissolute, immoral, lecherous, lewd, obscene, promiscuous, prurient, salacious, scandalous, scurrilous, uncurbed, unrestrained *(not repressed)*, wanton

licentiousness debauchery, vice

licet permissible

licit allowable, allowed, de jure, due *(regular)*, honest, just, justifiable, law-abiding, lawful, legal, legitimate *(rightful)*, permissible, rightful, statutory, valid

licitatio bid

licitly de jure

licitness droit, legitimacy

licitus permissible

lickerish lascivious, lecherous, prurient, salacious, suggestive *(risqué)*

lickerous salacious

lid cap

lidless open *(unclosed)*

lie bear false witness, canard, deceive, deception, equivocate, evade *(deceive)*, fabricate *(make up)*, fake, false pretense, falsehood, falsify, fiction, figment, hoax, invent *(falsify)*, misguide, mislead, misrepresent, misrepresentation, misstate, misstatement, palter, perjure, posture *(attitude)*, pretend, pretense *(pretext)*, pretext, prevaricate, rest *(be supported by)*, story *(falsehood)*, subterfuge

lie about feign

lie across cross *(intersect)*

lie adjacent to contact *(touch)*

lie against frame *(charge falsely)*, frame *(prearrange)*

lie beside adjoin

lie concealed lurk

lie contiguous to border *(bound)*

lie down repose *(rest)*

lie hidden lurk

lie in ambush lurk, prowl

lie in wait lurk, prowl

lie in wait for ambush

lie low lurk

lie near border *(approach)*

lie near to adjoin

lie next to border *(bound)*

lie over overlap

lief readily

liegeman subject *(object)*

lien encumbrance, hypothecation, security *(pledge)*

lien on an estate encumbrance

lieutenant coadjutant, deputy, liaison,

plenipotentiary, proctor, procurator, proxy, substitute

life entity, lifetime, practice *(professional business)*, spirit, survival

life estate freehold

life span lifetime

life's duration lifetime

life's work practice *(professional business)*

life-giving productive, salubrious

life-supporting vital

lifeblood main point

lifeless dead, deceased, defunct, languid, mediocre, otiose, pedestrian, phlegmatic, ponderous, stagnant, torpid

lifeless body corpse

lifeless object article *(commodity)*

lifelessness inertia, insentience, languor

lifelike descriptive, natural, realistic, suggestive *(evocative)*

lifelong durable

lifetime life *(period of existence)*, term *(duration)*

lifework calling, career, employment, profession *(vocation)*, pursuit *(occupation)*

lift bolster, build *(augment)*, elevate, elevation, enhance, jostle *(pickpocket)*, promotion *(advancement)*, raise *(advance)*, steal, support *(assistance)*

lift a ban facilitate

lift controls disengage, quit *(free of)*

lift up heighten *(elevate)*

lifter thief

ligament chain *(nexus)*

ligation attachment *(act of affixing)*

ligature chain *(nexus)*, connection *(fastening)*

light deft, frivolous, jocular, minimal, negligible, slight, subtle *(refined)*, trivial

light labor sinecure

light up burn

light upon find *(discover)*

light work sinecure

light-footed rapid

light-minded frivolous

lighten abate *(lessen)*, allay, alleviate, attenuate, commute, diminish, ease, extenuate, facilitate, lessen, mitigate, moderate *(temper)*, modify *(moderate)*, relieve *(free from burden)*

lighten the labor disencumber

lightening abatement *(reduction)*, mitigation, mollification

lightness immateriality, informality

lightweight immaterial

likable palatable, preferable, sapid, savory

like akin *(germane)*, analogous, approximate, cognate, comparable *(capable of comparison)*, congruous, correlate, equal, equivalent, faithful *(true to fact)*, identical, related, relish, similar

like better prefer

like in degree coequal, equal

like in quantity coequal, equal

like quality analogy

like to desire

like-minded consensual

likeable attractive

liked popular, preferred *(favored)*

likelihood chance *(possibility)*, feasibility, possibility, presumption, probability, prospect *(outlook)*, supposition,

weight *(credibility)*

likeliness likelihood, probability, prospect *(outlook)*, supposition

likely apparent *(presumptive)*, appropriate, believable, circumstantial, convincing, deductible *(provable)*, fitting, future, ostensible, possible, potential, presumptive, probable, prone, prospective, suitable, viable

likely client prospect *(prospective patron)*

likely customer prospect *(prospective patron)*

likely patron prospect *(prospective patron)*

likely person prospect *(prospective patron)*

likely to decrease taxes deductible *(capable of being deducted from taxes)*

likely to excite ill will invidious

likely to happen imminent

likely to harm dangerous

likeminded consenting

likemindedness concordance, understanding *(agreement)*

liken compare, conform, correspond *(be equivalent)*, measure

likeness analogy, appearance *(look)*, color *(complexion)*, conformity *(agreement)*, cocopy, correspondence *(similarity)*, counterpart *(parallel)*, duplicate, identity *(similarity)*, par *(equality)*, parity, peer, propinquity *(similarity)*, reflection *(image)*, relation *(connection)*, relationship *(connection)*, resemblance, semblance

likewise also

liking affinity *(regard)*, desire, disposition *(inclination)*, favor *(partiality)*, inclination, indorsement, partiality, penchant, predilection, predisposition, preference *(choice)*, proclivity, propensity, regard *(esteem)*

Lilliputian minimal

lilylivered recreant

limare file *(arrange)*

limber flexible, malleable, pliable, pliant

limelight publicity

limit abate *(lessen)*, abridge *(divest)*, ambit, bar *(obstruction)*, bar *(exclude)*, barrier, bind *(restrain)*, block, border, border *(bound)*, boundary, cap, capacity *(maximum)*, ceiling, censor, check *(restrain)*, commute, compel, condemn *(ban)*, confine, constrain *(imprison)*, constrain *(restrain)*, constrict *(inhibit)*, control *(restrain)*, curb, debar, defeasance, define, demarcate, detain *(restrain)*, deter, determine, diminish, disadvantage, discipline *(control)*, disfranchise, duration, edge *(border)*, enclose, enclosure, encumber *(hinder)*, end *(termination)*, enjoin, expiration, extent, extremity *(furthest point)*, frontier, gamut, guideline, hamper, hedge, impede, margin *(outside limit)*, maximum *(pinnacle)*, measurement, mete, moderate *(temper)*, modify *(moderate)*, obstruct, palliate *(abate)*, periphery, prevent, prohibit, prohibition, purview, qualify *(condition)*, quota, range, repress, restrain, restrict, retrench, scope, specialize, toll *(stop)*

limit of endurance capacity *(maximum)*

limitable terminable

limitary qualified *(conditioned)*, restrictive

limitation abatement *(reduction)*, abridgment *(disentitlement)*, alienation *(transfer of title)*, bar *(obstruction)*, boundary, capacity *(maximum)*, censorship, check *(bar)*, clause, compulsion *(coercion)*, condition *(contingent provision)*, constraint *(restriction)*, control *(restriction)*, custody *(incarceration)*, damper *(stopper)*, detention, deterrence, deterrent, disadvantage, discipline *(obedience)*, enclosure, end *(termination)*, extent, fetter, flaw, foible, guideline, handicap, impairment *(drawback)*, impediment, mete, moderation, modification, obstacle, obstruction, periphery, prohibition, provision *(clause)*, purview, qualification *(condition)*, quota, reservation *(condition)*, restraint, restriction, term *(provision)*

limitations configuration *(confines)*, confines, frontier, outline *(boundary)*

limitative conditional, prohibitive *(restrictive)*, restrictive

limited arrested *(checked)*, brief, certain *(specific)*, conditional, dependent, imperfect, infrequent, local, minimal, narrow, parochial, partial *(part)*, partial *(relating to a part)*, petty, private *(not public)*, privy, provisional, qualified *(conditioned)*, scarce, slight, specific, strict, temporary

limited amount paucity

limited area region

limited choice dilemma

limited time period

limiting binding, determinative, mitigating, prohibitive *(restrictive)*, restrictive

limitive determinative

limitless far reaching, indeterminate, infinite, innumerable, myriad, omnibus, open-ended, plenary, profuse, unbound, unlimited, unqualified *(unlimited)*, unrestricted

limitlessly ad infinitum

limits area *(province)*, boundary, capacity *(sphere)*, configuration *(confines)*, confines, outline *(boundary)*, premises *(buildings)*, purview

limn delineate, depict, portray

limp insipid, languid, nonsubstantial *(not sturdy)*

limpid clear *(apparent)*, lucid, pellucid

line ancestry, birth *(lineage)*, blood, bloodline, business *(occupation)*, calling, career, chain *(series)*, derivation, descent *(lineage)*, direction *(course)*, employment, family *(common ancestry)*, lineage, merchandise, occupation *(vocation)*, origin *(ancestry)*, parentage, policy *(plan of action)*, polity, post, posterity, progeny, pursuit *(occupation)*, race, range, stock in trade, trade *(occupation)*, work *(employment)*

line drawn round delineation

line of achievement calling

line of action action *(performance)*, campaign, course, maneuver *(tactic)*, manner *(behavior)*, policy *(plan of action)*, practice *(custom)*, practice *(procedure)*, procedure, process *(course)*

line of ancestors bloodline, descent *(lineage)*, family *(common ancestry)*, or-

igin *(ancestry)*, parentage

line of business calling, labor *(work)*, position *(business status)*, practice *(professional business)*

line of circumvallation boundary, mete

line of conduct behavior, campaign, course, manner *(behavior)*, modus operandi, platform, policy *(plan of action)*, practice *(procedure)*

line of credit capital

line of demarcation border, boundary, configuration *(confines)*, crossroad *(turning point)*, frontier, limit, mete, outline *(boundary)*, periphery

line of descent affiliation *(bloodline)*, birth *(lineage)*, degree *(kinship)*, family *(common ancestry)*, lineage, origin *(ancestry)*

line of duty burden

line of goods merchandise

line of proceeding campaign, practice *(custom)*

line of sight perspective

line of work calling, labor *(work)*, livelihood, position *(business status)*, practice *(professional business)*, profession *(vocation)*, trade *(occupation)*

line up allocate, file *(arrange)*, fix *(arrange)*, juxtapose, marshal, set down

lineage affiliation *(bloodline)*, affinity *(family ties)*, ancestry, blood, bloodline, children, derivation, descendant, family *(common ancestry)*, filiation, heritage, house, issue *(progeny)*, kindred, offspring, origin *(ancestry)*, parentage, paternity, posterity, progeny, relationship *(family tie)*, source, succession

lineal hereditary

lineal descendant child

lineal descendants issue *(progeny)*

lineament color *(complexion)*, feature *(appearance)*, particularity, trait

lineamenta contour *(outline)*, design *(construction plan)*

lineaments boundary, outline *(boundary)*

lineamentum feature *(appearance)*

linear direct *(straight)*

lined up coextensive

lines ambit, boundary, configuration *(form)*, contour *(outline)*, contour *(shape)*, feature *(appearance)*, script

lines of demarcation confines

lineup order *(arrangement)*

linger continue *(persevere)*, defer *(put off)*, delay, last, loiter, pause, persist, procrastinate, prolong, remain *(continue)*, remain *(stay)*, stall

linger on endure *(last)*

lingering chronic, lasting, protracted

lingo phraseology, speech

lingua language

lingual parol

linguistics language

link affiliation *(connectedness)*, affix, appertain, association *(connection)*, attach *(join)*, broker, chain *(nexus)*, combine *(join together)*, commingle, connection *(fastening)*, connection *(relation)*, consolidate *(unite)*, contact *(association)*, contact *(touch)*, engage *(involve)*, go-between, implicate, implication *(incriminating involvement)*, intermediary, join *(bring together)*, kinship, liaison, lock, medium, member *(constituent*

part), nexus, privity, propinquity *(kinship)*, relate *(establish a connection)*, relation *(connection)*, relationship *(connection)*, unite

link together connect *(join together)*, connect *(relate)*, involve *(implicate)*

linkage affiliation *(connectedness)*, affinity *(family ties)*, association *(connection)*, chain *(nexus)*, coalescence, connection *(fastening)*, connection *(relation)*, contact *(association)*, joinder, liaison, marriage *(intimate relationship)*, relationship *(connection)*

linked affiliated, akin *(germane)*, associated, coadunate, cognate, concurrent *(united)*, conjoint, correlative, interrelated, intimate, related

linking joinder, marriage *(intimate relationship)*

links chain *(series)*, ties

lion's share majority *(greater part)*

lionhearted heroic, spartan

lionize honor

lip edge *(border)*, margin *(outside limit)*

liquefacere dissolve *(disperse)*

liquid assets capital, estate *(property)*

liquidate defray, destroy *(efface)*, discharge *(pay a debt)*, disorganize, dispatch *(put to death)*, eliminate *(eradicate)*, eradicate, extinguish, extirpate, kill *(murder)*, obliterate, pay, remove *(eliminate)*, slay

liquidation aberemurder, assassination, cancellation, composition *(agreement in bankruptcy)*, discharge *(payment)*, dispatch *(act of putting to death)*, dissolution *(termination)*, homicide, killing, murder, payment *(act of paying)*

liquidation of a debt amortization

liquidator recipient

liquor alcohol

lis action *(proceeding)*, lawsuit, process *(summons)*, suit

lissome flexible, malleable, pliable

list bill *(invoice)*, book, census, classify, codify, docket, enroll, enter *(record)*, enumerate, file, file *(place among official records)*, fix *(arrange)*, impanel, index *(catalog)*, index *(relate)*, inscribe, inventory, itemize, organize *(arrange)*, pigeonhole, poll, program, program, recite, record, record, register, roll, schedule, sequence, set down, specify, survey *(poll)*, tabulate, tariff *(bill)*

list for jury duty empanel

list jurors empanel

list of appointments calendar *(record of yearly periods)*

list of cases docket

list of cases set down for hearing calendar *(list of cases)*

list of causes arranged for trial calendar *(list of cases)*

list of causes instituted in court calendar *(list of cases)*

list of causes ready for trial calendar *(list of cases)*

list of events calendar *(record of yearly periods)*

list of goods invoice *(itemized list)*

list of items invoice *(itemized list)*, tariff *(bill)*

list of items shipped invoice *(itemized list)*

list of jurors panel *(jurors)*
list of mercantile goods invoice *(itemized list)*
list of paid employees payroll
list of properties inventory
list of receipts and payments account *(evaluation)*
list of salaried employees payroll
list of wages to be paid out payroll
listen attend *(heed)*, concentrate *(pay attention)*, eavesdrop, hear *(give attention to)*, monitor, obey
listen in on overhear
listen stealthily eavesdrop, overhear
listen to heed, submit *(yield)*
listener bystander
listing census, docket, index *(catalog)*, registration
listing of contents index *(catalog)*
listless despondent, idle, inactive, indolent, inexpressive, languid, lifeless *(dull)*, otiose, phlegmatic, powerless, stagnant, torpid
listlessness disinterest *(lack of interest)*, languor, sloth
literacy education
literal accurate, actual, authentic, exact, factual, faithful *(true to fact)*, honest, narrow, orthodox, parochial, precise, strict, true *(authentic)*, verbatim
literal interpretation connotation, content *(meaning)*
literal meaning connotation, content *(meaning)*
literal sense connotation, content *(meaning)*
literality connotation, content *(meaning)*
literalize construe *(translate)*
literally faithfully, verbatim
literary literate
literary artistry phraseology
literary forgery plagiarism
literary magazine publication *(printed matter)*
literary person author *(writer)*
literary piracy plagiarism
literary publications press
literary style phraseology
literary theft plagiarism
literate familiar *(informed)*, informed *(educated)*, learned
literati faculty *(teaching staff)*
literatim verbatim
literature publication *(printed matter)*
lithe flexible, malleable, pliable, pliant
lithesome malleable, pliable
litigable actionable, justiciable
litigant accuser, actionable, actor, adversary, appellant, claimant, complainant, contender, contestant, disputant, petitioner, plaintiff, rival, suitor
litigare litigate
litigate contend *(dispute)*
litigate against sue
litigate completely exhaust *(try all possibilities)*
litigation action *(proceeding)*, case *(lawsuit)*, cause *(lawsuit)*, complaint, contest *(dispute)*, controversy *(lawsuit)*, day in court, dispute, hearing, lawsuit, matter *(case)*, proceeding, prosecution *(criminal trial)*, suit, trial *(legal proceeding)*

litigation of the charges action *(proceeding)*
litigationist litigant
litigator contender, litigant, suitor
litigatory litigious
litigiosus litigious
litigious actionable, argumentative, contentious, forensic
litterae correspondence *(communication by letters)*, dispatch *(message)*, document
litteratus learned
little impalpable, inappreciable, minimal, minor, negligible, nominal, paltry, petty, remote *(small)*, scarce, slight, tenuous, trivial
little by little piecemeal
little chance improbability
little one infant
little-known peculiar *(curious)*, recondite, unusual
littleness dearth
livable habitable
live born *(alive)*, conscious *(awake)*, dwell *(reside)*, exist, inhabit, lodge *(reside)*, occupy *(take possession)*, reside, subsist
live at reside
live by obey
live dissolutely carouse
live idly dissipate *(expend foolishly)*
live in occupy *(take possession)*, remain *(occupy)*
live in sexual intimacy cohabit
live in terror fear
live on endure *(last)*, exist, keep *(continue)*, last, persist
live through bear *(tolerate)*
live together cohabit
live under unfavorable conditions languish
live up to fulfill, keep *(fulfill)*
live with cohabit
livelihood business *(occupation)*, calling, career, employment, occupation *(vocation)*, revenue, support *(assistance)*, trade *(occupation)*
liveliness ardor, dispatch *(promptness)*, life *(vitality)*, spirit
lively rapid, volatile
lively pace dispatch *(promptness)*
liverish petulant
livery of seisin feoffment
lividus jealous, spiteful
living appointment *(position)*, bodily, born *(alive)*, business *(occupation)*, calling, conscious *(awake)*, durable, employment, extant, inhabitation *(act of dwelling in)*, live *(conscious)*, livelihood, present *(current)*, pursuit *(occupation)*, residential, sustenance, trade *(occupation)*, viable
living as man and wife coverture
living being person
living by prey predatory
living expenses overhead
living image alter ego
living on prey rapacious
living place abode, house, lodging, residence
living quarters building *(structure)*, domicile, dwelling, habitation *(dwelling place)*, home *(domicile)*, house, inhabitation *(place of dwelling)*, residence
living soul person

living space inhabitation *(place of dwelling)*
living thing entity
living together in sexual intimacy cohabitation *(living together)*
livor spite
load burden, cargo, encumbrance, freight, impact, impede, incumbrance *(burden)*, onus *(burden)*, plethora, pressure, stress *(strain)*, tax *(overwork)*, weight *(burden)*
load down weigh
load to excess overload
load up hoard
loaded full, ready *(prepared)*, replete
loaf procrastinate
loafer parasite
loafing indolent, remiss
loan capitalize *(provide capital)*, credit *(delayed payment)*, finance, invest *(fund)*, investment, lend, let *(lease)*
loan applicant obligor
loan at interest investment
loan to again refinance
loan transaction mortgage
loanee debtor, obligor
loath averse, disinclined, disobedient, dissident, hesitant, renitent, restive
loathe contemn, disdain
loathe to contra
loathed undesirable
loathful loathsome, obnoxious
loathing alienation *(estrangement)*, hatred, malice, odium, phobia
loathsome antipathetic *(distasteful)*, bad *(offensive)*, contemptible, disreputable, heinous, invidious, objectionable, obnoxious, odious, offensive *(offending)*, repugnant *(exciting aversion)*, repulsive, undesirable, unsavory
loathsomeness disrepute
lobby bait *(lure)*, constituency, entrance, party *(political organization)*, special interest
lobbyist special interest
local chapter *(branch)*, domestic *(indigenous)*, native *(domestic)*, organ, provincial, regional
local law ordinance
local legislation ordinance
local office chapter *(branch)*
local representative dealer
local rule ordinance
locale district, locality, location, part *(place)*, region, scene, seat, section *(vicinity)*, site, situs, territory, venue
locality community, district, environment, home *(domicile)*, location, region, scene, seat, section *(vicinity)*, site, situs, venue
localize restrict, site
localized local, regional
locally born native *(domestic)*
locare contract, lease, rent
locate allocate, deposit *(place)*, detect, discover, find *(discover)*, lodge *(house)*, pinpoint, plant *(place firmly)*, site
locate oneself lodge *(reside)*
located situated
location area *(province)*, locality, part *(place)*, region, scene, seat, section *(vicinity)*, site, situs, standpoint, structure *(edifice)*, venue
lock connect *(join together)*, fetter, fix *(make firm)*, occlude, seal *(close)*, shut
lock in immure, imprison, jail

lock out bar *(exclude)*, eliminate *(exclude)*

lock up capture, commit *(institutionalize)*, confine, contain *(restrain)*, detain *(hold in custody)*, fetter, immure, imprison, jail, lock, restrain

locked conjoint, impervious, inseparable

locker coffer

locking up commitment *(confinement)*

lockout ostracism

lockup penitentiary

loco movere depose *(remove)*

loco suo movere displace *(remove)*

locomotive moving *(in motion)*

locum vacuefacere evacuate

locuples unimpeachable

locus address, circuit, locality

locus location

locus position *(situation)*, post, purview, region, scene, scope, section *(vicinity)*

locus situs

locus space

locus classicus cross section

locus qui petitur objective

locus standi character *(reputation)*

locutio phraseology

locution expression *(comment)*, parlance, phraseology, speech, term *(expression)*

lodge chapter *(branch)*, deposit *(place)*, dwell *(reside)*, embed, fix *(make firm)*, harbor, inhabit, locate, occupy *(take possession)*, organ, remain *(occupy)*, remain *(stay)*, repose *(place)*, reside, stay *(rest)*

lodge a complaint accuse, blame, charge *(accuse)*, cite *(accuse)*, complain *(charge)*, denounce *(inform against)*, implicate, incriminate, indict, involve *(implicate)*, present *(prefer charges)*

lodge together cohabit

lodged situated

lodger habitant, inhabitant, lessee, occupant, resident, tenant

lodging address, building *(structure)*, chamber *(compartment)*, domicile, dwelling, habitation *(dwelling place)*, home *(domicile)*, house, household, inhabitation *(act of dwelling in)*, inhabitation *(place of dwelling)*, shelter *(protection)*

lodging house building *(structure)*

lodging place address, building *(structure)*, dwelling, home *(domicile)*, inhabitation *(place of dwelling)*, lodging

lodging together cohabitation *(living together)*

lodging together as husband and wife cohabitation *(living together)*

lodgings building *(structure)*, premises *(buildings)*, residence

lodgment address, building *(structure)*, domicile, dwelling, habitation *(act of inhabiting)*, habitation *(dwelling place)*, inhabitation *(act of dwelling in)*, inhabitation *(place of dwelling)*, lodging, residence

loftiness bombast, distinction *(reputation)*, elevation, eminence, pretense *(ostentation)*, rhetoric *(insincere language)*

lofty grandiose, magnanimous, meritorious, orgulous, presumptuous, prominent, proud *(self-respecting)*, remarka-

ble, supercilious

log book, calendar *(record of yearly periods)*, enter *(record)*, journal, ledger, note *(record)*, record, record, register

log book register

logbook calendar *(record of yearly periods)*, journal, ledger

logic common sense, data, dialectic, ratiocination, reason *(sound judgment)*

logic of discursive argument dialectic

logical apparent *(presumptive)*, cogent, coherent *(clear)*, colorable *(plausible)*, consistent, convincing, deductive, discursive *(analytical)*, normal *(sane)*, persuasive, plausible, probable, rational, reasonable *(rational)*, sane, sensible, solid *(sound)*, tenable, valid, viable

logical argumentation dialectic

logical discussion deliberation, dialectic

logical order array *(order)*, method, sequence

logical process deduction *(conclusion)*, dialectic, system

logical reasoning rationale

logical relation analogy

logical result consequence *(conclusion)*

logical sequence corollary, deduction *(conclusion)*, dialectic

logically appealing coherent *(clear)*

logically consistent coherent *(clear)*, consonant

logically then consequently

logically unsound illogical

logicalness reason *(sound judgment)*

logomachic argumentative

logomachical argumentative

logomachy fight *(argument)*

loiter delay, pause, procrastinate, prowl

loitering truant

lone exclusive *(singular)*, only *(sole)*, separate, singular, sole, solitary, unilateral

lonely derelict *(abandoned)*, solitary

lonesome derelict *(abandoned)*, solitary

long prolix, protracted, sesquipedalian

long for desire, lack, need

long gone dead

long life longevity

long odds improbability

long vehement speech diatribe

long windedness prolixity

long-continued protracted

long-continuing chronic, durable

long-delayed back *(in arrears)*, overdue

long-drawn protracted

long-enduring durable

long-established conventional, customary, prescriptive, traditional

long-lasting durable, incessant, permanent, stable, steadfast

long-lived chronic, durable, stable

long-spun prolix

long-standing chronic, durable, inveterate, stable, traditional

long-suffering lenient, patient, resigned, stoical

long-winded flatulent, loquacious, profuse, prolix, turgid, voluble

longanimity lenience, resignation

(passive acceptance), sufferance

longanimous lenient, patient, placable

longevity age

longevous durable

longhand handwriting, holographic, script

longiloquent loquacious

longing desire, eager, jealous, predisposition, will *(desire)*

longlivedness longevity

longsighted perspicacious

longstanding chronic, prescriptive

longus prolix

look appear *(seem to be)*, aspect, complexion, condition *(state)*, configuration *(form)*, demean *(deport oneself)*, demeanor, deportment, feature *(appearance)*, manner *(behavior)*, notice *(observe)*, observation, observe *(watch)*, presence *(poise)*, regard *(pay attention)*, semblance, vision *(dream)*

look about for canvass

look about one beware

look after concern *(care)*, conduct, control *(regulate)*, direct *(supervise)*, foster, handle *(manage)*, harbor, keep *(shelter)*, maintain *(sustain)*, manage, operate, overlook *(superintend)*, oversee, preserve, protect, provide *(arrange for)*, superintend

look ahead plan

look ahead to prognosticate

look around for delve

look as if appear *(seem to be)*

look askance at disfavor

look at discern *(detect with the senses)*, note *(notice)*, notice *(observe)*, observe *(watch)*, regard *(pay attention)*, spy, survey *(examine)*

look at closely scrutinize

look back remember

look back upon recall *(remember)*, recollect

look behind the scenes delve

look down on condescend *(patronize)*, disdain, disfavor, disparage, patronize *(condescend toward)*

look down upon discriminate *(treat differently)*, misprize, spurn

look for delve, expect *(anticipate)*, ferret, hunt, spy

look for flaws check *(inspect)*, examine *(study)*

look forward to anticipate *(prognosticate)*, expect *(anticipate)*, forestall, prognosticate

look into canvass, check *(inspect)*, delve, examine *(study)*, frisk, inquire, investigate, probe, research, scrutinize, search

look on discern *(detect with the senses)*

look out beware, overlook *(superintend)*, patrol

look out for care *(be cautious)*

look over check *(inspect)*, examine *(study)*, frisk, overlook *(superintend)*, peruse, review, scrutinize, search

look through delve, examine *(study)*, frisk, search

look to focus, heed, rely, resort

look up information in consult *(seek information from)*

look up to honor, regard *(hold in esteem)*

look upon deem, discern *(detect with the senses),* opine, regard *(pay attention)*

look with scorn on disdain

look with scorn upon condescend *(patronize)*

looked after safe

looked for foreseeable, forseen, immediate *(imminent),* prospective

looked toward future

looker bystander, witness

looker-on bystander, eyewitness, witness

looking back hindsight, retrospect

looking within introspection

lookout caretaker *(one caring for property),* spy, surveillance

loom emerge, impend

looming forthcoming, future, imminent, inevitable, instant, pending *(imminent),* prospective

loop detour

loophole flaw, subterfuge

loose careless, discharge *(liberate),* disconnected, disencumber, disengage, disjunctive *(tending to disjoin),* dispel, free *(not restricted),* inaccurate, inexact, lax, lecherous, liberal *(not literal),* liberate, licentious, open-ended, promiscuous, salacious, separate, suggestive *(risqué),* unrestrained *(not repressed)*

loose rendering paraphrase

loose statement generality *(vague statement)*

loose thinking non sequitur

loose translation paraphrase

loosen disencumber, disentangle, disenthrall, dissociate, ease, extricate, give *(yield),* remit *(relax)*

looseness informality, laxity, vice

looseness of morals perversion

loosing discharge *(liberation),* discharge *(release from obligation)*

loot despoil, jostle *(pickpocket),* pilfer, pillage, pirate *(take by violence),* plunder, plunder, prey, prize, rob, spoil *(pillage),* spoils

looting burglary, foray, housebreaking, spoliation, theft

lop break *(separate),* curtail, retrench

lop off sever

loquacious profuse, voluble

loquacity prolixity, tautology

loquax loquacious

loqui generalize

lordliness pride

lordly dictatorial, disdainful, inflated *(vain),* orgulous, presumptuous, proud *(conceited),* supercilious, tyrannous

lordship dominion *(supreme authority),* hegemony, possession *(ownership),* supremacy

lore discipline *(field of study),* information *(knowledge)*

lose deplete, erode, fail *(lose),* forfeit, succumb, suffer *(sustain loss)*

lose an opportunity forfeit

lose by breach of condition forfeit

lose by default forfeit

lose by failure to appear default, forfeit

lose control carouse

lose courage fear

lose ground retreat

lose heart languish

lose identity merge

lose individuality merge

lose life decease, perish

lose luster tarnish

lose morale degenerate

lose no time hasten

lose one's life die

lose sight of neglect

lose spirit languish

lose strength languish

lose value depreciate

losel improvident

loss abridgment *(disentitlement),* bad debt, bankruptcy, calamity, consumption, cost *(penalty),* damage, damages, decline, decrease, decrement, defeat, deficiency, deficit, detriment, disadvantage, erosion, expense *(sacrifice),* failure *(lack of success),* forfeiture *(thing forfeited),* impairment *(damage),* injury, miscarriage, penalty, prejudice *(injury),* privation, toll *(effect)*

loss consequent to a default forfeiture *(thing forfeited)*

loss of affection estrangement

loss of belief discredit

loss of credence discredit

loss of credit discredit

loss of fortune bankruptcy, poverty, privation

loss of freedom bondage, subjection

loss of health disease

loss of honor bad repute, disgrace, disrepute, ignominy, notoriety, opprobrium, scandal, shame

loss of identity merger

loss of life death, demise *(death)*

loss of power prostration

loss of reason insanity

loss of reputation attaint, bad repute, disgrace, dishonor *(shame),* disrepute, ignominy, infamy, notoriety, opprobrium, scandal, shame

loss of repute discredit

loss of respect ignominy

loss of right disqualification *(rejection),* forfeiture *(act of forfeiting),* waiver

loss of standing opprobrium

loss of strength failure *(falling short),* fault *(weakness),* frailty

loss of value decline, decrease

lost astray, disconsolate, incorrigible, irredeemable, irretrievable, reprobate

lost connection anacoluthon, non sequitur

lost labor miscarriage

lost to principle profligate *(corrupt)*

lost to virtue profligate *(corrupt)*

lot assemblage, bulk, conglomeration, entirety, lottery, parcel, plight, plot *(land),* posture *(situation),* predetermination, property *(land),* quantity, real estate, situation

loud blatant *(obtrusive),* disorderly, flagrant, powerful, resounding, tawdry

loud noise outcry

loud protest outcry

loudness noise

lounge rest *(be supported by),* rest *(cease from action)*

loutish opaque, provincial, uncouth

love affection, affinity *(regard),* predilection

love of mankind philanthropy

loved popular

lovely elegant, sapid

loving zealous

low caitiff, depraved, heinous, ignoble, inelegant, lamentable, minimal, nominal, nonsubstantial *(not sufficient),* odious, offensive *(offending),* outrageous, poor *(inferior in quality),* scandalous, scarce, scurrilous, servile, subaltern, tainted *(corrupted)*

low comedy travesty

low estimation dishonor *(shame),* disparagement, disregard *(lack of respect)*

low grade mediocrity

low opinion disapproval, disparagement

low quality mediocrity

low regard bad repute

low spirited disconsolate

low spirits damper *(depressant),* pessimism

low standard bad repute

low standing ignominy

low valuation disparagement

low-class mediocre

low-grade inferior *(lower in quality),* mediocre, poor *(inferior in quality)*

low-level minor, subordinate

low-minded depraved, dissolute

low-priced nominal

low-quality marginal, mediocre

low-spirited lugubrious, pessimistic

low-spiritedness pessimism

lowborn caitiff, ignoble

lower debase, decrease, deduct *(reduce),* defame, demean *(make lower),* demote, denigrate, depreciate, depress, derogate, deteriorate, diminish, discount *(reduce),* disgrace, humiliate, inferior *(lower in position),* lessen, minimize, minor, modify *(moderate),* pervert, pillory, reduce, subaltern, subdue, subordinate, subservient

lower in authority inferior *(lower in position)*

lower in price depreciate

lower in rank demote, inferior *(lower in position),* subaltern, subordinate

lower in reputation depreciate

lower in the scale inferior *(lower in position)*

lower in value debase, depreciate

lower morally taint *(corrupt)*

lower oneself condescend *(deign),* patronize *(condescend toward)*

lower price discount

lower the courage of discourage

lower the estimation of disparage

lower the sale price discount *(reduce)*

lower the standard adulterate

lower the value of depreciate

lowering decline, decrease, deduction *(diminution),* depression, diminution

lowest quantity minimum

lowliness prostration

lowly base *(inferior),* ignoble, inferior *(lower in position),* subaltern, subordinate

lowness bad character, depression

loyal constant, dependable, obedient, reliable, serious *(devoted),* staunch, steadfast

loyalist disciple

loyally faithfully

loyalty adherence *(devotion),* allegiance, discipline *(obedience),* faith, fealty, fidelity, homage, rectitude, regard *(esteem)*, trustworthiness

lubric lascivious, lecherous

lubricious prurient

lubricity obscenity, pornography

lubricous lascivious, lecherous, lewd, licentious, obscene

lucent lucid

lucid cognizable, coherent *(clear)*, comprehensible, distinct *(clear)*, evident, explicit, manifest, normal *(sane)*, obvious, palpable, pellucid, rational, reasonable *(rational)*, sane, unambiguous, unmistakable

lucidity competence *(sanity)*, reason *(sound judgment)*, sanity

lucidly fairly *(clearly)*

lucidus lucid

luck contingency, opportunity, prosperity, quirk *(accident)*, welfare

luckless ominous

lucky auspicious, fortuitous, propitious, prosperous

lucrari gain

lucrative gainful, profitable

lucre boom *(prosperity)*

lucrosus gainful, lucrative

lucrum earnings, profit

luctatio struggle

lucubration pandect *(treatise)*

luculent comprehensible, lucid

ludibrio mock *(deride)*

ludicrous fatuous, inept *(inappropriate)*, irrational, unreasonable

ludicrous imitation parody

ludicrous presentation travesty

ludicrous representation ridicule

ludicrousness incongruity, inexpedience

ludificari flout, hoodwink

ludificatio hoax

luggage cargo

lugubrious despondent, lamentable

lugubris lugubrious

lukewarm irresolute, languid, nonchalant, noncommittal, perfunctory

lukewarmness indifference

lull allay, alleviate, cessation *(interlude)*, cloture, halt, hiatus, holiday, interruption, interval, lapse *(break)*, mollification, mollify, moratorium, pause, peace, pendency, recess, remission, respite *(interval of rest)*, soothe, subside

lumbering ponderous

luminary mastermind

luminous cognizable, coherent *(clear)*, notable, outstanding *(prominent)*

lump assemblage, entirety, part *(portion)*, totality

lump together commingle, compile, consolidate *(unite)*, hoard

lumpiness irregularity

lumpish lifeless *(dull)*, obtuse, opaque, ponderous, stagnant

lumpishness opacity, sloth

lunacy insanity, paranoia

lunatic non compos mentis

lunge at beat *(strike)*, strike *(assault)*

lupine predatory, rapacious

lurch oscillate

lure amenity, betray *(lead astray)*, cajole, coax, ensnare, entice, entrap, incentive, inveigle, persuade, prevail *(persuade)*, seduction, trap

lure into a compromising act entrap

lurid licentious, obscene, salacious, suggestive *(risqué)*

luridus lurid

luring attractive, bribery

lurk prowl

lurking hidden, surreptitious

luscious nectarious, palatable, sapid, savory

lush fertile

lust debauchery, desire, passion

lust for need

lust for money greed

luster prestige, reputation

lusterless lifeless *(dull)*, ponderous

lustful dissolute, hot-blooded, lascivious, lecherous, lewd, obscene, prurient, salacious, suggestive *(risqué)*, wanton

lustiness life *(vitality)*, prowess *(bravery)*, puissance, sinew

lustless languid, powerless

lustrate decontaminate

lustrous outstanding *(prominent)*

lusty powerful, strong, vehement

luxate disjoint, dislocate

luxuriant copious, fertile, productive, profuse, superfluous, wanton

luxuriate pullulate

luxuriate in relish

luxuriosus dissolute

luxurious replete, superfluous

luxury prosperity

lyceum institute

lying deceit, deceptive, dishonest, dishonesty, disingenuous, falsification, improbity, insidious, mendacious, perfidious, subreption, untrue

lymphatic languid, otiose, phlegmatic, ponderous

M

macellum market *(business)*

macerate bait *(harass)*, plague

Machiavellian artful

Machiavellism artifice

machina device *(contrivance)*, expedient, machination

machinari conjure, contrive

machinate connive, conspire, contrive, maneuver, plan, plot, scheme

machination artifice, cabal, connivance, contrivance, deception, device *(contrivance)*, expedient, frame up, hoax, maneuver *(trick)*, premeditation, ruse, scheme, stratagem, strategy, subterfuge

machinator conspirator, copartner *(coconspirator)*

machine appliance, expedient, instrument *(tool)*, make, syndicate, tool

machine like controlled *(automatic)*

machine-made industrial

machiner artisan

machinery conduit *(channel)*, facility *(instrumentality)*, instrument *(tool)*, instrumentality, medium

macroscopic perceivable, perceptible

macula defilement

maculare stain, sully

maculate pollute, stain, tarnish

maculation bad repute, flaw

mad deranged, lunatic, non compos mentis, outrageous, quixotic

madcap hot-blooded, outrageous, precipitate

madden aggravate *(annoy)*, incense,

irritate, obsess, offend *(insult)*, perturb, pique, provoke

maddened deranged, non compos mentis

maddening vexatious

made captive arrested *(apprehended)*

made fast fixed *(securely placed)*

made poorly insubstantial

made prisoner arrested *(apprehended)*

made public naked *(perceptible)*

made up mendacious

madhouse shambles

madness furor, insanity, lunacy, paranoia

maelstrom bluster *(commotion)*, commotion, disturbance, furor, shambles

maeror depression

maestus disconsolate

magazine depository, journal, publication *(printed matter)*

magic prestidigitation

magical mysterious, uncanny

magister pedagogue, principal *(director)*

magisterial dogmatic, insolent, juridical, official, powerful, presumptuous, supercilious

magistracy bench, judiciary

magistrate bench, caretaker *(one fulfilling the function of office)*, judge, jurist

magistrates court

magistrature bench

magistratus authorities, magistrate

magnanimity charity, clemency, condonation, indulgence, largess *(generosity)*, longanimity, philanthropy

magnanimous benevolent, charitable *(benevolent)*, lenient, liberal *(generous)*, meritorious, philanthropic, placable

magnanimousness clemency, largess *(generosity)*

magnanimus magnanimous

magnetic attractive

magnetism draw *(attraction)*

magni momenti momentous

magnification aggravation *(exacerbation)*, augmentation, bombast, boom *(increase)*, distortion, exaggeration, extension *(expansion)*, hyperbole, laudation, overstatement

magnificent elegant, meritorious, proud *(self-respecting)*

magnified extreme *(exaggerated)*, inflated *(overestimated)*

magnify aggravate *(exacerbate)*, build *(augment)*, compound, develop, elaborate, enhance, enlarge, expand, extend *(enlarge)*, heighten *(augment)*, inflate, intensify, overestimate, promote *(advance)*, supplement

magnifying cumulative *(intensifying)*

magniloquence ardor, bombast, fustian, overstatement, peroration, rhetoric *(insincere language)*

magniloquent grandiose, inflated *(bombastic)*, orotund, sesquipedalian, turgid

magnitude amount *(quantity)*, bulk, caliber *(measurement)*, consequence *(significance)*, extent, importance, mass *(weight)*, materiality *(consequence)*, measurement, purview, weight *(importance)*

magnitudo bulk, magnitude

magno rate

magnus considerable, extensive, gross *(total)*, important *(significant)*

maiden incipient, initial, original *(initial)*

maiestas treason

mail correspondence *(communication by letters)*, dispatch *(message)*, send

mail again redirect

maim damage, disable, harm, mutilate, prejudice *(injure)*

maimed disabled *(made incapable)*, marred

maiming disabling

main cardinal *(basic)*, central *(essential)*, dominant, essential *(inherent)*, important *(significant)*, indispensable, leading *(ranking first)*, master, material *(important)*, noteworthy, paramount, primary, principal, prominent, salient, stellar, strength, substantive, vital

main asset transfer bulk transfer

main attraction feature *(special attraction)*

main body cornerstone, corpus, generality *(bulk)*, majority *(greater part)*, principal *(capital sum)*

main business agenda

main character protagonist

main charge complaint, count, gist *(ground for a suit)*, indictment

main element cornerstone

main feature motif

main features contour *(outline)*

main idea main point

main ingredient necessity

main interest specialty *(special aptitude)*

main item feature *(special attraction)*

main meaning context

main office headquarters

main part body *(main part)*, bulk, center *(essence)*, corpus, generality *(bulk)*, majority *(greater part)*, plurality

main point center *(essence)*, content *(meaning)*, cornerstone, gist *(ground for a suit)*, gravamen

main thing cornerstone, main point

mainly a fortiori, ab initio, as a rule, generally, particularly

mainspring cause *(reason)*, derivation, reason *(basis)*

mainstay abettor, backer, cornerstone, partisan, strength, support *(assistance)*

maintain adhere *(persist)*, allege, argue, assert, authorize, avouch *(avow)*, avow, bear *(adduce)*, bear *(support)*, bestow, cite *(state)*, conserve, continue *(persevere)*, continue *(prolong)*, control *(regulate)*, corroborate, declare, defend, endure *(last)*, fund, harbor, justify, keep *(continue)*, keep *(shelter)*, nurture, own, perpetuate, persevere, persist, plead *(allege in a legal action)*, posit, possess, preserve, profess *(avow)*, prolong, promote *(organize)*, propound, prosecute *(carry forward)*, protect, provide *(supply)*, pursue *(carry on)*, remain *(continue)*, remain *(occupy)*, reserve, resist *(withstand)*, retain *(employ)*, retain *(keep in possession)*, store, subsidize, subsist, supply, support *(assist)*, sustain *(prolong)*, uphold

maintain a course persevere

maintain a middle position compromise *(settle by mutual agreement)*

maintain as conformable to duty justify

maintain as conformable to justice justify

maintain by affirmation vouch

maintain by arguments plead *(argue a case)*

maintain continuity continue *(prolong)*

maintain under oath swear

maintainable defensible, justifiable, tenable

maintained alleged, chronic, durable, lasting, plausible, safe

maintained in prison in custody

maintainer abettor, advocate *(counselor)*, advocate *(espouser)*, backer, benefactor, mainstay, partisan

maintaining conservation, convincing

maintenance aid *(help)*, aid *(subsistence)*, alimony, conservation, continuation *(prolongation)*, ecology, livelihood, longevity, preservation, promotion *(encouragement)*, provision *(something provided)*, security *(safety)*, support *(assistance)*, survival, sustenance

maintenance allowance alimony

maintenance of regularity status quo

maior numerus majority *(greater part)*

maior pars majority *(greater part)*

majestic important *(significant)*, outstanding *(prominent)*, proud *(self-respecting)*, solemn

majesty eminence, prestige

major cardinal *(outstanding)*, central *(essential)*, critical *(crucial)*, important *(significant)*, indispensable, key, material *(important)*, momentous

major business asset transfer bulk transfer

major event cornerstone

major misfortune calamity

major part body *(main part)*, bulk, cornerstone, corpus, main point, majority *(greater part)*

majority bulk, generality *(bulk)*, maturity, plurality, preponderance

make build *(construct)*, cause, color *(complexion)*, create, fabricate *(construct)*, forge *(produce)*, form, frame *(construct)*, gain, generate, impose *(enforce)*, manner *(kind)*, manufacture, occasion, originate, press *(constrain)*, produce *(manufacture)*, realize *(obtain as a profit)*, receive *(acquire)*, require *(compel)*, style

make a bargain agree *(contract)*, close *(agree)*, contract, handle *(trade)*

make a beginning embark

make a benefaction bestow

make a bequest bequeath, demise, descend, devise *(give)*, leave *(give)*

make a bet parlay *(bet)*

make a bid attempt, endeavor, offer *(propose)*, proffer, strive

make a butt of mock *(deride)*

make a change affect, vary

make a choice cast *(register)*, decide, discriminate *(distinguish)*, elect *(choose)*, resolve *(decide)*, select

make a circuit detour

make a clean breast betray *(disclose)*

make a common cause with federalize *(associate)*

make a commotion brawl

make a compact settle

make a comparison contrast, measure

make a complaint cite *(accuse)*

make a compromise compromise *(settle by mutual agreement)*

make a computation calculate

make a condition stipulate

make a confession confess

make a deal compromise *(settle by mutual agreement)*

make a decision adjudge, adjudicate, arbitrate *(adjudge)*, cast *(register)*, choose, conclude *(decide)*, decide, determine, find *(determine)*, fix *(settle)*, hold *(decide)*, resolve *(decide)*, rule *(decide)*

make a declaration declare

make a decree instruct *(direct)*

make a deduction derive *(deduce)*

make a demand call *(demand)*, move *(judicially request)*

make a departure evacuate, quit *(evacuate)*

make a detour deviate

make a distinction differentiate, discriminate *(distinguish)*, discriminate *(treat differently)*, select

make a duplicate of copy

make a false show of feign

make a fool of delude, dupe, hoodwink, humiliate, illude, mock *(deride)*

make a formal proclamation notice *(give formal warning)*

make a gaudy display flaunt

make a generalization generalize

make a getaway escape

make a gift give *(grant)*

make a good return pay

make a hit succeed *(attain)*

make a judgment diagnose

make a legacy demise, descend

make a likeness delineate

make a list enumerate

make a loan bestow

make a member enroll

make a memorandum note *(record)*, record

make a mess of muddle

make a mistake err, miscalculate, misconceive, misconstrue, misinterpret, misjudge, misread, misunderstand

make a mixture combine *(join together)*

make a motion move *(judicially request)*, pose *(propound)*, proffer, propose, propound, submit *(give)*

make a new beginning continue *(resume)*

make a note record

make a party to implicate, incriminate, involve *(implicate)*

make a passage penetrate

make a path for facilitate

make a petition call *(appeal to)*, move *(judicially request)*

make a place for locate, lodge *(house)*, plant *(place firmly)*

make a plan devise *(invent)*, maneuver, plot

make a positive statement affirm *(claim)*

make a prediction predict, presage, prognosticate, promise *(raise expecta-*

tions)

make a present grant *(transfer formally)*

make a present of bequeath, bestow

make a presentation give *(grant)*

make a pretext of pretend

make a proclamation proclaim

make a profit gain

make a prognosis predict

make a promise assure *(insure)*, pledge *(promise the performance of)*

make a proposition offer *(propose)*

make a public announcement issue *(publish)*

make a purchase buy, procure

make a racket brawl

make a reality implement

make a rebuttal converse, retort, return *(respond)*

make a reconnaissance check *(inspect)*, spy

make a record enroll

make a rejoinder answer *(reply)*, controvert, dispute *(debate)*, respond, return *(respond)*

make a remark observe *(remark)*

make a replica copy

make a request call *(appeal to)*, move *(judicially request)*, plead *(implore)*, pray, solicit

make a request for desire

make a requisition call *(appeal to)*, move *(judicially request)*, order, petition

make a resolute stand hold out *(resist)*

make a resolution conclude *(decide)*, determine, rule *(decide)*

make a sale handle *(trade)*, sell, vend

make a selection cast *(register)*, cull, decide, discriminate *(distinguish)*, elect *(choose)*, extract, select

make a shambles pillage

make a shift with displace *(replace)*

make a show pretend

make a show of fake, flaunt, profess *(pretend)*

make a showy appearance flaunt

make a solemn declaration affirm *(declare solemnly)*

make a solemn resolution promise *(vow)*

make a spectacle flaunt

make a speech converse, declaim, discourse, recite, speak

make a spurious copy of forge *(counterfeit)*

make a stand repulse

make a stand against counter, counteract, cross *(disagree with)*, fight *(counteract)*, repel *(drive back)*, resist *(oppose)*

make a start preface

make a statement avow, bear *(adduce)*, claim *(maintain)*, contend *(maintain)*, converse, declare, express, profess *(avow)*, speak

make a suggestion propose, submit *(give)*

make a summary of digest *(summarize)*

make a survey canvass, poll

make a testamentary disposition leave *(give)*

make a transcript of copy

make a transition change

make a trial run check *(inspect)*

make a try attempt

make able charge *(empower)*, empower, enable

make absolute certify *(attest)*, support *(corroborate)*

make acceptable rationalize

make accordant attune

make accountable for encumber *(financially obligate)*

make acknowledgment return *(respond)*

make acquainted convey *(communicate)*, present *(introduce)*

make acquainted with forewarn, notice *(give formal warning)*

make active implement, launch *(initiate)*

make adjustments attune, modify *(alter)*

make again reproduce

make agree attune

make allowance condone, rebate

make allowance for discount *(reduce)*, extenuate, palliate *(excuse)*, provide *(arrange for)*

make allowances rationalize

make allowances for countenance, excuse

make allusion to mention

make amends propitiate, recoup *(reimburse)*, redeem *(satisfy debts)*, redress, refund, remedy, repay, repent, replace, restore *(return)*

make an accusation complain *(charge)*

make an adjustment compromise *(settle by mutual agreement)*

make an affidavit depose *(testify)*, plead *(allege in a legal action)*

make an agenda program

make an agreement agree *(contract)*, close *(agree)*

make an agreement with connive, conspire, cooperate, join *(associate oneself with)*

make an allusion hint

make an allusion to imply, remind

make an analysis analyze, examine *(study)*

make an announcement enunciate, notice *(give formal warning)*, notify, report *(disclose)*

make an antagonist of antagonize

make an appearance appear *(attend court proceedings)*, arise *(appear)*, emerge

make an arrest capture

make an assertion affirm *(claim)*, allege, argue, avouch *(avow)*, avow, bear *(adduce)*, claim *(maintain)*, contend *(maintain)*, express, plead *(allege in a legal action)*, profess *(avow)*

make an asseveration affirm *(declare solemnly)*

make an attempt endeavor, strive

make an attestation affirm *(declare solemnly)*

make an authoritative request call *(demand)*, exact

make an averment affirm *(declare solemnly)*

make an avowal promise *(vow)*

make an effort endeavor, strive, try *(attempt)*, undertake

make an effort at attempt

make an end of cease, close *(terminate)*, conclude *(complete)*, dispatch *(dispose of)*, quit *(discontinue)*

make an engagement promise *(vow)*

make an entrance enter *(go in)*, pervade

make an entry book, cast *(register)*, enter *(record)*, inscribe, note *(record)*, record

make an error misinterpret, misjudge

make an escape elude, flee

make an estimate calculate, measure

make an estimation gauge

make an examination probe

make an example of discipline *(punish)*

make an exception except *(exclude)*, exclude

make an exit depart, quit *(evacuate)*

make an expenditure expend *(disburse)*

make an impact upon impress *(affect deeply)*

make an impression on impress *(affect deeply)*

make an incision lancinate

make an incursion encroach

make an inquiry analyze

make an introduction present *(introduce)*

make an investment invest *(fund)*

make an issue contend *(dispute)*

make an oath promise *(vow)*

make an offer proffer

make an onset against attack

make an opening capitalize *(seize the chance)*

make an order instruct *(direct)*

make an overture offer *(propose)*, proffer

make an uproar brawl

make angry affront, offend *(insult)*

make apparent bare, characterize, delineate, elucidate

make appeal call *(appeal to)*

make appeal to sue

make application call *(appeal to)*, demand, move *(judicially request)*, petition, request

make application for desire

make arrangements arrange *(plan)*, deal, devise *(invent)*, frame *(formulate)*, maneuver, plan, plot, program, scheme

make aseptic decontaminate

make ashamed demean *(make lower)*, derogate

make available disburse *(distribute)*, let *(lease)*, rent

make available for rent sublease

make averse alienate *(estrange)*

make aware apprise, caution, convey *(communicate)*, enlighten, forewarn

make away with dispatch *(put to death)*, distrain

make beautiful embellish

make believe assume *(simulate)*, fake, false *(not genuine)*, feign, invent *(falsify)*, pretend, prevaricate, profess *(pretend)*, simulate

make better ameliorate, cultivate, emend, enhance, expurgate, meliorate, mollify, reform, remedy, renovate, repair, restore *(renew)*

make binding validate

make blunt obtund

make bold to ask call *(appeal to)*, importune

make book parlay *(bet)*

make brief condense, constrict *(compress)*, decrease, digest *(summarize)*, minimize

make by mechanical industry manufacture

make calm lull

make capable empower, enable, qualify *(meet standards)*

make capital gain

make capital out of profit

make captive arrest *(apprehend)*, fetter, immure

make captive again rearrest

make certain ascertain, assure *(give confidence to)*, assure *(insure)*, certify *(attest)*, document, ensure, find *(discover)*, reconfirm, verify *(confirm)*

make charges against denounce *(inform against)*

make claims upon call *(demand)*, charge *(assess)*, dun

make clear characterize, clarify, comment, define, delineate, demonstrate *(establish)*, describe, detail *(particularize)*, elucidate, enlighten, evince, exhibit, explain, explicate, exposit, expound, interpret, manifest, profess *(avow)*, resolve *(solve)*, simplify *(clarify)*, stipulate

make clear by examples exemplify

make cognizant apprise

make comfortable ease

make common cause affiliate

make common cause with combine *(act in concert)*, cooperate, involve *(participate)*

make compatible arbitrate *(conciliate)*, reconcile

make compensation bear the expense, contribute *(indemnify)*, cover *(provide for)*, outbalance, pay, quit *(repay)*, refund, return *(refund)*, satisfy *(discharge)*

make competent qualify *(meet standards)*

make complete conclude *(complete)*, replenish

make comprehensible clarify

make compulsory enforce

make concessions compromise *(settle by mutual agreement)*

make concise condense, digest *(summarize)*

make confident assure *(give confidence to)*, convince

make conformable adapt

make connection contact *(communicate)*

make consistent reconcile

make conspicuous manifest

make contact collide *(crash against)*, overlap

make contented pander, reconcile

make contiguous juxtapose

make conveyance of grant *(transfer formally)*

make corporeal embody

make corrections edit, emend, fix *(repair)*, modify *(alter)*, rectify, review

make corrupt pervert

make deductions construe *(comprehend)*, reason *(conclude)*

make defense for justify, support

(justify)

make definite stipulate

make deletions redact

make delivery of legal process serve *(deliver a legal instrument)*

make demands exact, petition

make demands on claim *(demand)*, dun, order

make dense constrict *(compress)*

make denser condense

make deposition depose *(testify)*

make desirable recommend

make despondent depress

make different change, vary

make difficult perplex

make dim obscure

make discontented disaffect

make disease-free decontaminate

make disloyal disaffect

make dissatisfied disappoint

make distasteful discredit

make distinctions discern *(discriminate)*, distinguish

make distinctive differentiate

make distribution of disburse *(distribute)*

make docile subdue

make durable establish *(entrench)*

make earnest entreaty call *(appeal to)*

make earnest petition for pray

make easier favor

make easy ease, facilitate, help, naturalize *(acclimate)*

make effective enforce

make elaborate embellish

make equal compensate *(counterbalance)*

make essential entail

make eternal perpetuate

make even juxtapose

make everlasting perpetuate

make evident bare, bear *(adduce)*, cite *(state)*, demonstrate *(establish)*, document, evince, exemplify, explain, illustrate, manifest, profess *(avow)*

make excessive demands tax *(overwork)*

make excessive use of abuse *(misuse)*

make exchanges barter

make excuses rationalize

make excuses for extenuate, justify

make expenditure bear the expense, disburse *(pay out)*, spend

make explanation of justify

make explicit clarify, explain, explicate, express

make extinct superannuate

make eyeless blind *(deprive of sight)*

make false pretenses palter

make false statements falsify, frame *(charge falsely)*, palter

make fast fix *(make firm)*, handcuff, lock

make faulty vitiate

make favorably inclined propitiate

make feeble debilitate

make final disposition of dispatch *(dispose of)*

make firm affirm *(uphold)*, cement, concentrate *(consolidate)*, confirm, consolidate *(strengthen)*, establish *(entrench)*, sustain *(confirm)*

make forbidden forbid

make formal formalize

make formal accusation against denounce *(inform against)*, indict

make formal application move *(judicially request)*

make formal request apply *(request)*

make foul pollute

make free acquit, disengage, disenthrall, extricate, parole

make free with assume *(seize)*

make friendly disarm *(set at ease)*

make full replenish

make fun of disparage, jape, jeer, mock *(deride)*, pillory

make germ-free decontaminate

make good fulfill, indemnify, keep *(fulfill)*, pay, recoup *(reimburse)*, redress, refund, reimburse, repair, restore *(return)*, return *(refund)*, satisfy *(discharge)*, substantiate, support *(corroborate)*

make good against anticipated loss indemnify

make good use of profit

make great magnify

make greater accumulate *(enlarge)*, compound, enlarge, expand, increase, inflate

make haste hasten, precipitate *(hasten)*

make havoc confound, disorganize, disorient, muddle, perturb, pillage

make headway develop, persist, proceed *(go forward)*, progress

make healthful decontaminate

make heavy load, overload

make higher build *(augment)*, elevate, heighten *(augment)*, heighten *(elevate)*

make hostile disaffect

make hygienic decontaminate

make ill infect

make illegal annul, prohibit

make illegible deface

make illegitimate disfranchise

make impact collide *(crash against)*, impinge

make imperfect vitiate

make important honor

make impossible condemn *(ban)*, disqualify, preclude

make improper use of abuse *(misuse)*

make improvement profit

make improvements edit, embellish, emend, enhance, meliorate, modify *(alter)*, repair, review

make impure adulterate, denature, infect, vitiate

make inactive close *(terminate)*, delay, desist, disable, disarm *(divest of arms)*, halt

make incapable disable

make inconspicuous blind *(obscure)*, conceal

make incumbent entail

make indifferent alienate *(estrange)*

make indirect reference allude

make indirect suggestion connote

make indiscernible blind *(obscure)*, conceal

make indispensable necessitate

make indistinct obnubilate, obscure

make ineffective neutralize, vitiate

make ineffectual override

make inescapable entail

make inevitable necessitate

make inferior in value degenerate
make inimical alienate (*estrange*), disaffect
make innovations alter
make innoxious decontaminate
make inoperative avoid (*cancel*)
make inquiries probe
make inquiry delve
make inroads encroach, impinge
make inroads on impair
make insecure endanger
make insensitive brutalize
make inseperable lock
make intelligible clarify, construe (*translate*), elucidate
make into convert (*change use*)
make into a statute enact
make into law legislate, pass (*approve*)
make intricate perplex
make its appearance issue (*send forth*)
make known advise, annunciate, apprise, bare, betray (*disclose*), circulate, communicate, confide (*divulge*), convey (*communicate*), declare, disabuse, disclose, disinter, divulge, enlighten, exhibit, express, herald, impart, inform (*betray*), inform (*notify*), instruct (*teach*), issue (*publish*), manifest, mention, notice (*give formal warning*), notify, phrase, post, present (*introduce*), proclaim, produce (*offer to view*), profess (*avow*), promulgate, propagate (*spread*), publish, relate (*tell*), report (*disclose*), reveal, signify (*inform*), spread, unveil, utter
make known publicly annunciate
make languid debilitate
make larger build (*augment*), compound, enlarge, expand, extend (*enlarge*), heighten (*augment*), increase, inflate, magnify
make last perpetuate
make lasting establish (*entrench*)
make lawful legalize, legitimate
make laws enact, legislate
make leeway outbalance
make legacies bequeath
make legal authorize, constitute (*establish*), legalize, legislate, legitimate, pass (*approve*), validate
make legitimate justify, legitimate, support (*justify*)
make less decrease, deduct (*reduce*), diminish, minimize, moderate (*temper*), reduce
make less concentrated dilute
make less confusing elucidate
make less extreme commute, modify (*moderate*)
make less friendly disaffect
make less harsh commute
make less important demote
make less intense commute, modify (*moderate*)
make less rigorous commute
make less rough commute
make less serious extenuate
make less severe commute, mitigate, modify (*moderate*), palliate (*abate*)
make less violent obtund, remit (*relax*)
make level compensate (*counterbalance*)
make liable expose, subject

make liable to danger compromise (*endanger*), endanger
make liable to injury endanger
make light of discount (*disbelieve*), disparage, underestimate
make lighter commute
make little of decry, depreciate, derogate, minimize, misprize
make longer prolong
make lower in character degenerate
make lower in quality adulterate, denature
make lowly demean (*make lower*), derogate, humiliate
make lucid clarify, elucidate, exposit
make manifest bare, elicit, evince, exemplify, explain
make manifold proliferate
make mention remark, speak
make mention of notice (*give formal warning*), observe (*remark*)
make mild palliate (*abate*)
make milder commute
make mischief mistreat
make miserable distress
make money gain
make money by profit
make more attractive enhance
make more certain support (*corroborate*)
make more comprehensive expand, extend (*enlarge*)
make more fluid dilute
make more important magnify
make more liquid dilute
make more offensive aggravate (*exacerbate*)
make more serious aggravate (*exacerbate*)
make more severe aggravate (*exacerbate*), exacerbate
make more valuable enhance
make much of belaud
make naked denude
make national nationalize
make national in character nationalize
make natural naturalize (*acclimate*)
make necessary constrain (*compel*), entail, indicate, necessitate, press (*constrain*)
make needed indicate
make nervous browbeat
make new renovate
make no racial distinctions desegregate
make note of remark
make notes comment
make nothing of misprize
make noxious taint (*contaminate*)
make null destroy (*void*), overrule
make null and void override
make objection except (*object*)
make objections remonstrate
make obligatory exact, force (*coerce*), impose (*enforce*)
make observations comment
make obsolete superannuate, supersede
make obvious educe, evidence, exemplify, exhibit, manifest, signify (*inform*)
make of greater value appreciate (*increase*)
make of no effect avoid (*cancel*)
make off abscond, avoid (*evade*), flee
make off with carry away, despoil,

hijack, hold up (*rob*), loot, pilfer, poach
make official formalize
make one attach (*join*), conjoin, consolidate (*unite*)
make one a third party implead
make one feel small browbeat
make one lose one's temper incense
make one shudder repel (*disgust*)
make one sick repel (*disgust*)
make one's choice cast (*register*), choose, determine
make one's debut commence
make one's exit abandon (*physically leave*)
make one's home dwell (*reside*)
make one's home at lodge (*reside*), occupy (*take possession*)
make one's mark pass (*satisfy requirements*)
make one's oath certify (*attest*)
make one's own acquire (*secure*), adopt, buy, embrace (*accept*), impropriate
make one's point persuade
make one's selection cast (*register*), choose
make one's submission move (*judicially request*)
make oneself acquainted with ascertain
make oneself answerable promise (*vow*)
make oneself answerable for guarantee
make oneself felt persuade
make oneself scarce retreat
make oneself useful pander
make open affirmation avouch (*avow*)
make oral communication speak
make oral mention speak
make orderly file (*arrange*)
make out detect, discern (*detect with the senses*), hear (*perceive by ear*), note (*notice*), perceive, pierce (*discern*), read, realize (*understand*), recognize (*perceive*), solve, spy
make outdated superannuate
make over change, convert (*change use*), deliver, devolve, fix (*repair*), grant (*transfer formally*), present (*make a gift*), reconstitute, reconstruct, recreate, reform, rehabilitate, renew (*refurbish*), renovate, transform
make over to another assign (*transfer ownership*)
make overtures hold out (*deliberate on an offer*)
make participator involve (*implicate*)
make pay exact
make payment bear (*yield*), bear the expense, compensate (*remunerate*), defray, disburse (*pay out*), expend (*disburse*), pay, quit (*repay*), remit (*send payment*), remunerate, repay, satisfy (*discharge*)
make payment for purchase
make payment in advance prepay
make peace negotiate, pacify, placate, propitiate, reconcile
make peace between arbitrate (*conciliate*), intercede
make pecuniary provision endow
make perfect renew (*refurbish*)
make permanent establish (*en-

trench), perpetuate
make perpetual perpetuate
make plain demonstrate *(establish)*, describe, elucidate, evidence, evince, exemplify, exhibit, explain, explicate, exposit, expound, express, illustrate, interpret, manifest, resolve *(solve)*, signify *(inform)*, simplify *(clarify)*, simplify *(make easier)*, solve, unveil
make possible enable, facilitate, let *(permit)*, permit, proffer
make possible the avoidance of avert
make potent empower
make practicable enable
make preferable recommend
make preparations anticipate *(expect)*, arrange *(plan)*, plan, plot, provide *(arrange for)*
make prisoner arrest *(apprehend)*, capture, fetter, hijack
make probable conduce
make proclamation annunciate
make progress ameliorate, develop, proceed *(go forward)*, progress
make provision bear *(yield)*, maintain *(sustain)*, provide *(arrange for)*
make provision for bestow, cover *(provide for)*, endue
make provisions forestall
make provisions for nurture
make public bare, betray *(disclose)*, circulate, convey *(communicate)*, denude, disclose, disseminate, divulge, notice *(give formal warning)*, notify, post, proclaim, propagate *(spread)*, publish, reveal, signify *(inform)*, spread
make publicly known reveal
make pure decontaminate
make putrid taint *(contaminate)*
make rapid strides proceed *(go forward)*
make ready plan, provide *(arrange for)*
make ready for publication edit
make realize convince
make reference quote
make reference to bear *(adduce)*, cite *(state)*
make rejoinder reply
make relevant connect *(relate)*
make remarks comment
make repairs emend
make reparation contribute *(indemnify)*, discharge *(pay a debt)*, indemnify, quit *(repay)*, redress, reimburse, repay, restore *(return)*, return *(refund)*
make reparations recoup *(reimburse)*
make repayment defray
make requisite entail‧
make requisition call *(demand)*, exact
make requital repay
make resplendent embellish
make responsible for commit *(entrust)*, encumber *(financially obligate)*
make restitution bear the expense, compensate *(remunerate)*, contribute *(indemnify)*, defray, discharge *(pay a debt)*, indemnify, liquidate *(determine liability)*, pay, quit *(repay)*, recoup *(reimburse)*, refund, reimburse, repay, restore *(return)*, return *(refund)*
make restoration fix *(repair)*
make right rectify, regulate *(adjust)*
make rigid fix *(make firm)*

make rounds perambulate
make routine inure *(accustom)*
make sad depress
make safe cover *(guard)*, maintain *(sustain)*
make salubrious decontaminate
make scandal smear
make secret arrangements conspire
make secret observations spy
make self-conscious embarrass
make sense cohere *(be logically consistent)*
make sense of elucidate, interpret
make sensible pierce *(discern)*
make sightless blind *(deprive of sight)*
make simple elucidate, exposit
make smaller constrict *(compress)*, curtail, decrease, deduct *(reduce)*, derogate, diminish, minimize, reduce
make solemn bear *(adduce)*
make solemn affirmation avouch *(avow)*, confess, speak
make solemn declaration speak, testify
make solid concentrate *(consolidate)*, consolidate *(strengthen)*
make someone a trustee of delegate
make someone guardian of delegate, entrust
make sorrowful distress
make sound fix *(repair)*, remedy, renew *(refurbish)*, renovate
make sport of disparage
make stable establish *(entrench)*
make steadfast establish *(entrench)*
make steady compensate *(counterbalance)*
make strong nurture
make submissive impose *(subject)*, subdue, subject
make subordinate subject
make subservient subject
make suitable adapt, qualify *(meet standards)*
make supplication pray
make sure ascertain, assure *(insure)*, certify *(attest)*, ensure, verify *(confirm)*
make sure again reconfirm
make swollen inflate
make terms agree *(contract)*, conclude *(decide)*, contract, determine, dicker, haggle, negotiate, transact
make terse condense
make testamentary disposition demise
make testamentary dispositions devise *(give)*
make the best of endure *(suffer)*, submit *(yield)*, tolerate
make the effort attempt
make the most of capitalize *(seize the chance)*, exploit *(make use of)*
make the round of circulate
make thin attenuate, dilute, diminish, erode, minimize
make toe the line discipline *(control)*
make too much of overestimate
make tractable subdue
make tumid inflate
make ugly deface
make unable to see blind *(deprive of sight)*
make unapparent blind *(obscure)*, conceal
make unavoidable entail, necessitate

make unclean disgrace, sully
make uncomfortable embarrass
make understandable elucidate, exposit
make understood clarify
make uneasy discommode, discompose, disturb, perturb
make unfaithful disaffect
make unfit disable
make unfriendly alienate *(estrange)*, antagonize
make unhappy distress
make uniform conform, juxtapose, regulate *(adjust)*
make unlawful enjoin, outlaw
make unlike distort
make unperceptible blind *(obscure)*, conceal
make unrecognizable camouflage, disguise
make unsafe endanger
make unsightly deface
make unsound damage
make unwelcome eschew, ignore, repel *(disgust)*
make up compile, conceive *(invent)*, conjure, consist, constitute *(compose)*, contrive, create, devise *(invent)*, feign, indemnify, invent *(falsify)*, manufacture, originate, produce *(manufacture)*, reconcile, replenish, structure *(composition)*
make up a lack replenish
make up for compensate *(counterbalance)*, outbalance, recoup *(reimburse)*, redeem *(satisfy debts)*, redress, remunerate, repent
make up one's mind conclude *(decide)*, decide, determine, resolve *(decide)*
make use of capitalize *(seize the chance)*, exercise *(use)*, exert, impropriate, manipulate *(utilize skillfully)*, ply, profit, resort, wield
make use of without permission pirate *(reproduce without authorization)*
make useless disable, disarm *(divest of arms)*, disqualify, maim, nullify
make valid approve, authorize, certify *(approve)*, confirm, countenance, formalize, implement, indorse, notarize, validate
make valueless nullify
make visible embody, expose, manifest, produce *(offer to view)*, unveil
make vivid characterize, delineate, describe, detail *(particularize)*, illustrate
make void abrogate *(annul)*, adeem, annul, avoid *(cancel)*, cancel, discharge *(release from obligation)*, invalidate, nullify, override, overrule, quash, repeal, revoke, supersede, vacate *(void)*, vitiate
make vulnerable compromise *(endanger)*, endanger
make war fight *(battle)*
make way yield *(submit)*
make way for demit, displace *(replace)*
make weak dilute
make well cure, renew *(refurbish)*
make whole cure, fix *(repair)*, renew *(refurbish)*, renovate, replenish, restore *(renew)*
make wholesome decontaminate

make wholly without effect avoid (cancel)

make wicked brutalize

make worse aggravate (exacerbate), degenerate, exacerbate, impair

make wrathful bait (harass), pique

make written application petition

make-believe delusive, fictitious, hypothetical, illusory, imitation, mendacious, pretext

maker architect, author (originator), contractor

makeshift expedient, interim, provisional, replacement, stopgap, surrogate, temporary, vicarious (substitutional)

makeup character (personal quality), characteristic, configuration (form), content (structure), disposition (inclination), frame (mood), organization (structure), personality, temperament

making building (business of assembling), commission (act), manufacture, onset (commencement)

making amends collection (payment), penitent

making apparent clarification

making aware disclosure (act of disclosing)

making distinct clarification

making evident clarification

making intelligible definition

making less decrease, deduction (diminution)

making lucid clarification

making one concrescence

making over renewal

making perspicuous clarification

making precise clarification

making public disclosure (act of disclosing), divulgation

making ready preparation

making reference referral

making sense coherent (clear)

making specific clarification

making trenchant clarification

making useless avoidance (cancellation)

mala fides bad faith

maladjusted inappropriate, unfit

maladjustment disaccord

maladminister misgovern, misguide, mishandle (mismanage), mismanage

maladministration misconduct, misdoing, misrule, misusage, misuse

maladroit incompetent, inept (incompetent)

malady disability (physical inability), disease, disorder (abnormal condition), pain

malaise pain

malapert brazen, impertinent (insolent), insolent, obtrusive, presumptuous

malapropism error, misapplication, misusage

malapropos impertinent (irrelevant), inapplicable, inapposite, inappropriate, inapt, inept (inappropriate), inopportune, irrelevant, unfavorable, unsuitable, untimely

malapropros unfit

malcontent actor, dissident

male administrare misgovern

male computare miscalculate

male interpretari misinterpret

male iudicare misjudge

male moratus immoral

male parentage paternity

male regere misgovern

maledicent contemptuous, querulous

maledictio revilement, slander

malediction aspersion, blasphemy, contempt (disdain), denunciation, expletive, imprecation, phillipic, profanity, revilement, vilification

maledictive profane

maledictory abusive, calumnious, profane

maledictum obloquy

malefaction delict, delinquency (misconduct), disregard (omission), fault (responsibility), guilt, illegality, misdeed, misdoing, misprision, offense, perversion

malefactor convict, criminal, delinquent, embezzler, felon, hoodlum, lawbreaker, offender, outlaw, racketeer, recidivist

malefactor wrongdoer

malefactor under suspension of sentence probationer (released offender)

malefic adverse (negative), deleterious, detrimental, disadvantageous, disastrous, harmful, heinous, insalubrious, lethal, malevolent, malicious, malignant, noxious, peccant (unhealthy), pernicious, pestilent, sinister

maleficence vice

maleficent bad (offensive), dangerous, deleterious, delinquent (guilty of a misdeed), diabolic, disadvantageous, harmful, insalubrious, lethal, malevolent, malicious, malignant, peccant (culpable), peccant (unhealthy), pernicious, pestilent, ruthless, scathing, sinister

maleficial lethal, malicious, peccant (culpable), pernicious, sinister

maleficient adverse (negative)

maleficium crime, mischief, misdeed

malevolence alienation (estrangement), atrocity, bad repute, belligerency, feud, hatred, ill will, malediction, malice, odium, rancor, spite, vengeance

malevolent bad (offensive), calumnious, caustic, cold-blooded, contemptuous, convict, cruel, delinquent (guilty of a misdeed), diabolic, hoodlum, hostile, inimical, iniquitous, libelous, malicious, malignant, outrageous, pernicious, resentful, ruthless, scathing, sinister, spiteful, vicious, vindictive, virulent

malevolentia ill will, malice, spite

malevolus malevolent, malicious, spiteful

malfeasance abuse (corrupt practice), blame (culpability), conversion (misappropriation), crime, delict, delinquency (misconduct), disloyalty, disservice, guilt, knavery, maladministration, misconduct, misdeed, misdemeanor, misprision, misrule, offense, tort, wrong

malfeasant convict, criminal, delinquent (guilty of a misdeed), felonious, hoodlum, illegitimate (illegal), offender, recidivist, wrongdoer

malfeasor convict, delinquent, hoodlum, lawbreaker, recidivist

malformation irregularity

malformed blemished, faulty, inferior (lower in quality)

malfunction disorder (abnormal condition), irregularity

malice alienation (estrangement), cruelty, ill will, odium, rancor, resentment, spite

malice aforethought cruelty

malice prepense cruelty

malicious caustic, cold-blooded, contemptuous, cruel, felonious, harmful, invidious, libelous, malevolent, malignant, mordacious, noxious, outrageous, resentful, scathing, sinister, spiteful, vicious, vindictive, virulent, wrongful

malicious action mischief

malicious burning of property arson

malicious defamation libel

malicious falsehood libel

malicious gossip scandal

malicious publication libel

malicious report slander

maliciously defame libel

maliciousness cruelty, ill will, malice, odium, spite

malific bad (offensive)

malign bait (harass), brand (stigmatize), cold-blooded, complain (criticize), contemn, cruel, damage, decry, defame, denigrate, denounce (condemn), depreciate, derogate, destructive, disapprove (condemn), disastrous, discommend, discredit, dishonor (deprive of honor), disoblige, disparage, harass, harmful, humiliate, ill use, lessen, lethal, libel, malevolent, malignant, misrepresent, mistreat, outrageous, pernicious, pestilent, pillory, reproach, ruthless, sinister, smear, spiteful, stain, sully, toxic, unfavorable, vicious, virulent

malignance cruelty, fatality, harm, ill will, spite, vice

malignancy corruption, cruelty, fatality, harm, ill will, spite

malignant bad (inferior), caustic, contemptuous, cruel, dangerous, deadly, deleterious, detrimental, diabolic, disadvantageous, fatal, lethal, libelous, malevolent, malicious, nefarious, noxious, offensive (offending), outrageous, peccant (unhealthy), pernicious, pestilent, resentful, ruthless, scathing, sinister, spiteful, vicious, vindictive, virulent

maligned accused (attacked)

maligning contemptuous

malignitas malice, spite

malignity bad repute, cruelty, fatality, harm, malice, mischief, rancor, resentment, spite

malignus spiteful

malinger fake, pretend, shirk, shun

malison imprecation, malediction

malitia knavery

malleability amenability, discipline (obedience)

malleable facile, flexible, open (persuasible), passive, pliable, pliant, resilient, sequacious, tractable, yielding

mallet cudgel

malpractice delinquency (failure of duty), disregard (omission), guilt, misapplication, misconduct, misdeed, misdoing, misprision, misusage, misuse, offense, wrong

maltreat abuse (misuse), abuse (victimize), bait (harass), brutalize, damage, disoblige, endanger, exploit (take advantage of), harass, harm, harrow, ill use, inflict, misemploy, mistreat, persecute

maltreatment abuse *(physical misuse)*, atrocity, infliction, injustice, mischief, misuse, molestation, oppression

malum delinquency *(misconduct)*

malus bad *(inferior)*, bad *(offensive)*, dishonest

malversation abuse *(corrupt practice)*, bad faith, bad repute, crime, criminality, delict, delinquency *(misconduct)*, embezzlement, guilt, maladministration, misappropriation, misconduct, misdeed, misdemeanor, misdoing, misprision, misusage, offense

mammoth prodigious *(enormous)*

man character *(an individual)*, humanity *(mankind)*, mortality

man of business dealer

man of erudition expert

man of law advocate *(counselor)*

man of learning expert

man of letters author *(writer)*, pedagogue

man of mark key man, paragon

man with a grievance actor

man-made artificial, synthetic

manacle constrain *(imprison)*, contain *(restrain)*, detain *(restrain)*, fetter, fetter, hamper, handcuff, handcuff, restrain, restrict, trammel

manacles bondage

manage administer *(conduct)*, arrange *(methodize)*, assume *(undertake)*, comport *(behave)*, conduct, control *(regulate)*, demean *(deport oneself)*, direct *(supervise)*, discipline *(control)*, dominate, effectuate, execute *(accomplish)*, function, govern, maneuver, manipulate *(control unfairly)*, marshal, militate, moderate *(preside over)*, officiate, operate, oversee, predominate *(command)*, preside, program, provide *(arrange for)*, rule *(govern)*, succeed *(attain)*, superintend, transact, wield

manage badly misgovern, mishandle *(mismanage)*

manage poorly mismanage

manage unskillfully mismanage

manageability amenability

manageable corrigible, facile, flexible, malleable, obedient, pliable, pliant, resigned, sequacious, tractable, yielding

management administration, agency *(legal relationship)*, auspices, authorities, board, bureaucracy, conduct, control *(supervision)*, course, custody *(supervision)*, direction *(guidance)*, disposition *(final arrangement)*, distribution *(arrangement)*, dominion *(supreme authority)*, economy *(economic system)*, economy *(frugality)*, employer, generalship, government *(administration)*, guidance, hierarchy *(persons in authority)*, maneuver *(tactic)*, operation, oversight *(control)*, policy *(plan of action)*, regime, staff, strategy, supervision, supremacy, transaction, treatment, trust *(custody)*, usage

management of money finance

management of natural resources ecology

management of resources economy *(economic system)*

manager administrator, caretaker *(one fulfilling the function of office)*,

chief, comptroller, custodian *(protector)*, director, employer, executive, factor *(commission merchant)*, principal *(director)*, proctor, procurator, proprietor, superintendent

manager's office headquarters

managerial administrative

managers hierarchy *(persons in authority)*, management *(supervision)*

managership control *(supervision)*, direction *(guidance)*, generalship, management *(supervision)*

managing administrative, executive, ministerial

manare exude

mancus deficient

mandamus fiat

mandare delegate, devolve, entrust, instruct *(direct)*, invest *(vest)*, trust

mandate act *(enactment)*, agency *(legal relationship)*, article *(precept)*, assignment *(designation)*, brevet, burden, canon, charge *(command)*, citation *(charge)*, command, decree, delegation *(assignment)*, dictate, direction *(order)*, directive, edict, instruction *(direction)*, law, measure, mission, mittimus, monition *(legal summons)*, order *(judicial directive)*, ordinance, plebiscite, precept, prescribe, proclamation, referendum, regulation *(rule)*, requirement, requisition, statute, subpoena, summons, writ

mandate of a court warrant *(judicial writ)*

mandated legitimate *(rightful)*, licit

mandated territory state *(political unit)*

mandatorily will shall

mandatory binding, compulsory, conclusive *(determinative)*, decretal, essential *(required)*, exigent, imperative, indispensable, involuntary, necessary *(required)*, obligatory, peremptory *(imperative)*, positive *(prescribed)*, requisite, unavoidable *(inevitable)*, unavoidable *(not voidable)*

mandatory factor necessity, need *(requirement)*

mandatum charge *(command)*, commission *(act)*, fiat, injunction, instruction *(direction)*, mandate, order *(judicial directive)*, warrant *(authorization)*

manere adhere *(persist)*

maneuver act *(undertaking)*, connive, conspire, contrivance, contrive, device *(contrivance)*, devise *(invent)*, evasion, expedient, inveigle, machination, manage, manipulate *(utilize skillfully)*, militate, operate, overt act, perpetrate, plot, ploy, ruse, scheme, scheme, step, stratagem, subterfuge, trap

maneuverability latitude

maneuverable negotiable

maneuverer catalyst

maneuvering artifice, campaign, conspiracy, strategy, tactical

maneuvers campaign, strategy

manger liaison

mangle damage, deface, disable, mutilate, spoil *(impair)*

mangled broken *(fractured)*, marred

manhandle abuse *(misuse)*, abuse *(victimize)*, ill use, mishandle *(maltreat)*, mistreat, persecute

manhood majority *(adulthood)*

mania compulsion *(obsession)*, furor, lunacy, market *(demand)*, obsession, paranoia, passion

maniacal deranged, frenetic, lunatic, non compos mentis, outrageous

manic lunatic, non compos mentis

manicae handcuff

manifest adduce, apparent *(perceptible)*, apparent *(presumptive)*, appreciable, axiomatic, bare, bear *(adduce)*, bear *(yield)*, bill *(invoice)*, blatant *(conspicuous)*, bodily, cite *(state)*, clear *(apparent)*, coherent *(clear)*, comprehensible, conspicuous, convey *(communicate)*, corroborate, demonstrate *(establish)*, denude, depict, disabuse, discernible, discover, disinter, distinct *(clear)*, divulge, document, elucidate, embody, emerge, establish *(show)*, evidence, evident, evince, exemplify, exhibit, explain, explicit, expose, flagrant, gross *(flagrant)*, illustrate, inventory, lucid, naked *(perceptible)*, obvious, open *(in sight)*, ostensible, overt, palpable, patent, pellucid, perceivable, perceptible, personify, produce *(offer to view)*, prominent, prove, public *(known)*, reveal, scrutable, signify *(denote)*, tangible, unmistakable, unveil, visible *(in full view)*

manifest act overt act

manifest directly express

manifest itself appear *(materialize)*, arise *(appear)*, issue *(send forth)*, occur *(come to mind)*

manifestation appearance *(emergence)*, common knowledge, complexion, disclosure *(something disclosed)*, embodiment, face value *(first blush)*, illustration, indicant, proof, symbol, symptom, token

manifestations indicia

manifesting contempt contemptuous

manifestly fairly *(clearly)*

manifesto brevet, canon, issuance, proclamation, pronouncement, report *(detailed account)*, statement

manifestus apparent *(perceptible)*, conspicuous, evident, flagrant, obvious, open *(in sight)*, overt, palpable, patent, perceptible

manifold compound, diverse, miscellaneous, multifarious, multifold, myriad, reproduce, rife

manifoldness diversity

manipulable pliable

manipulate capitalize *(seize the chance)*, coax, control *(regulate)*, employ *(make use of)*, exercise *(use)*, exert, exploit *(make use of)*, exploit *(take advantage of)*, handle *(manage)*, ill use, manage, militate, operate, perpetrate, ply, rule *(govern)*, scheme, tamper, wield

manipulate improperly misemploy

manipulation act *(undertaking)*, connivance, contrivance, machination, management *(judicious use)*, maneuver *(tactic)*, performance *(workmanship)*, plot *(secret plan)*, stratagem, strategy

mankind mortality

manliness prowess *(bravery)*

manly potent, spartan, strong

manner appearance *(look)*, avenue *(means of attainment)*, behavior, character *(personal quality)*, color *(complex-*

ion), complexion, conduct, conduit *(channel),* course, custom, degree *(station),* demeanor, deportment, facility *(instrumentality),* form *(arrangement),* instrumentality, means *(opportunity),* method, mode, modus operandi, parlance, posture *(attitude),* practice *(custom),* presence *(poise),* process *(course),* style, system, tenor, trait, usage

manner of conduct dealings

manner of construction organization *(structure)*

manner of disposal disposition *(transfer of property)*

manner of expression phraseology

manner of life behavior

manner of living modus vivendi

manner of operating modus operandi

manner of presentation style

manner of proceeding policy *(plan of action),* practice *(procedure),* procedure

manner of speaking parlance

manner of working avenue *(means of attainment),* procedure

mannered formal, histrionic

mannerism characteristic, habit, identity *(individuality),* quirk *(idiosyncrasy),* specialty *(distinctive mark),* trait

mannerless disorderly

manneriliness decorum

mannerly civil *(polite)*

manners behavior, conduct, courtesy, decorum, propriety *(correctness),* protocol *(etiquette)*

manor demesne, domain *(land owned),* dominion *(absolute ownership),* homestead

manpower personnel

mansio stay

manslaughter homicide

manslayer criminal

mansuetuda clemency

mansuetude amenability, comity

mantic portentous *(ominous),* prophetic

mantle enshroud, plant *(covertly place),* spread, veil

manual directory, hornbook, pandect *(treatise)*

manual of instruction hornbook

manufactural industrial

manufacture build *(construct),* building *(business of assembling),* business *(commercial enterprise),* composition *(makeup),* creation, devise *(invent),* engender, fabricate *(construct),* forge *(produce),* form, formation, frame *(construct),* generate, industry *(business),* invent *(produce for the first time),* make, originate, palter, performance *(workmanship)*

manufactured assumed *(feigned),* industrial, synthetic

manufactured for sale commercial, industrial

manufactured goods merchandise

manufactured product output

manufacturer author *(originator)*

manufacturing productive

manumissio emancipation, liberation

manumission emancipation, liberation, release, suffrage

manumit disengage, disenthrall, en-

franchise, free, liberate, quit *(free of),* release, relieve *(free from burden),* rescue

manumitted clear *(free from criminal charges),* free *(enjoying civil liberty),* unbound

manumittere liberate

manus force *(strength),* handwriting, profession *(vocation),* violence

manuscript holographic, script

many ample, innumerable, manifold, miscellaneous, multifarious, multifold, multiple, myriad, rife

many sidedness multiplicity

map blueprint, delineate, delineation, design *(construction plan),* direction *(course),* scheme

map out devise *(invent),* frame *(construct),* frame *(formulate),* locate, plan, prearrange, predetermine, program, scheme

mar adulterate, contaminate, damage, deface, eviscerate, frustrate, harm, impair, impede, mutilate, prejudice *(injure),* smear, spoil *(impair),* stain, sully, vice, vitiate

mar the appearance of deface

maraud despoil, foray, harry *(plunder),* hold up *(rob),* loot, onset *(assault),* pillage, pillage, plunder, plunder, prey, spoil *(pillage)*

marauder burglar, criminal, thief

marauding burglary, depredation, rapacious, spoliation

marble-hearted malignant, ruthless

marcescence decline

march demonstrate *(protest),* frontier, patrol, perambulate, periphery, progress, traverse

march off depart, part *(leave)*

march out evacuate

marcher pedestrian

marge border

margin balance *(amount in excess),* border, edge *(border),* extremity *(furthest point),* latitude, mete, outline *(boundary),* penumbra, periphery, plethora, scope, space, surplus

marginal inappreciable, petty

marginal annotation comment, note *(brief comment)*

marginalia notation

margo edge *(border)*

marijuana cannabis

marital conjugal, nuptial

marital infidelity adultery

marital partner consort, spouse

maritus consort

mark attaint, attend *(heed),* brand, characterize, clue, color *(complexion),* consider, deface, degree *(station),* demarcate, denote, designate, designation *(symbol),* discriminate *(distinguish),* earmark, eminence, expression *(manifestation),* feature *(characteristic),* goal, heed, importance, impression, index *(catalog),* indicant, indication, indicator, inscribe, inscription, intention, interest *(concern),* label, label, magnitude, manifest, manifestation, monument, note *(notice),* note *(record),* notice *(observe),* objective, observe *(watch),* particularity, perceive, prestige, property *(distinctive attribute),* recognize *(perceive),* record, regard *(pay attention),* reputation, select, significance,

signify *(denote),* smear, speciality, specialty *(distinctive mark),* stain, stamp, subscribe *(sign),* symbol, symptom, target, trademark, trait, witness *(have direct knowledge of)*

mark against confront *(oppose)*

mark down book, cast *(register),* decrease, deduct *(reduce),* discount *(reduce),* enter *(record),* note *(record),* rebate

mark incorrectly mislabel

mark limits delimit, demarcate

mark of Cain onus *(stigma)*

mark of disgrace stigma

mark of honor mention *(tribute)*

mark of identification caption, earmark, label

mark of identity earmark

mark of shame stigma

mark off border *(bound),* characterize, circumscribe *(surround by boundary),* delimit, hedge, measure

mark off by differences differentiate

mark out circumscribe *(surround by boundary),* delimit, demarcate, designate, differentiate, distinguish, indicate, prescribe, specify, trace *(delineate)*

mark out a course arrange *(plan),* plan

mark out for choose

mark that designates device *(distinguishing mark)*

mark the difference between discriminate *(distinguish)*

mark the limits define

mark the time of date

mark time pause

mark up cost *(price)*

markdown discount, rebate

marked certain *(particular),* certain *(specific),* considerable, conspicuous, distinct *(distinguished from others),* distinctive, important *(significant),* manifest, marred, momentous, notable, noteworthy, open *(in sight),* outstanding *(prominent),* palpable, particular *(specific),* peculiar *(distinctive),* perceptible, preferential, prominent, remarkable, resounding, salient, several *(separate),* special, specific, stellar, uncommon, unusual

marked by consent consenting

marked by excessive effort elaborate

marked feature characteristic, property *(distinctive attribute)*

marked occurrence event

marked price cost *(price)*

marked quality characteristic, property *(distinctive attribute)*

marked superiority distinction *(reputation)*

marked time date

marked traits character *(personal quality)*

markedly fairly *(clearly),* particularly

marker indication, label, landmark *(conspicuous object)*

market barter, deal, exchange, handle *(trade),* mercantile, outlet, sell, store *(business),* vend

market place store *(business)*

market price estimate *(approximate cost),* expense *(cost),* par *(face amount)*

marketable negotiable, valuable

marketing commerce, retail, trade

(commerce)

marks fingerprints, indicia

marks left by a person's finger fingerprints

maroon isolate, seclude

marred blemished, defective, deficient, dilapidated, imperfect, poor *(inferior in quality)*

marriage cohabitation *(married state)*, matrimony

marriage accord consortium *(marriage companionship)*

marriage compatibility consortium *(marriage companionship)*

marriage concord consortium *(marriage companionship)*

marriage lines coverture

marriage partner consort, spouse

marriage tie marriage *(wedlock)*, matrimony

marriage to a second partner digamy

married conjugal, nuptial

married life marriage *(wedlock)*, matrimony

married state coverture, marriage *(wedlock)*, matrimony

married status cohabitation *(married state)*, marriage *(wedlock)*, matrimony

married tie coverture

marring defacement

marring feature flaw

marrow consequence *(significance)*, gist *(substance)*, main point, substance *(essential nature)*

marrowless powerless

marry combine *(act in concert)*, connect *(join together)*, join *(bring together)*, unite

marshal allocate, arrange *(methodize)*, classify, file *(arrange)*, fix *(arrange)*, organize *(arrange)*, tabulate

marshaling array *(order)*, disposition *(final arrangement)*, distribution *(arrangement)*

mart exchange, market *(business)*, store *(business)*

martial spartan

martial law force *(compulsion)*

martiality belligerency

martinet dictator

marvel phenomenon *(unusual occurrence)*

marvelous ineffable, meritorious, portentous *(eliciting amazement)*, prodigious *(amazing)*, remarkable, special, unusual

mask camouflage, cloak, conceal, cover *(pretext)*, cover *(conceal)*, denature, disguise, disguise, ensconce, enshroud, envelop, false pretense, hide, obliterate, obnubilate, obscure, plant *(covertly place)*, pretend, pretense *(pretext)*, pretext, ruse, screen *(guard)*, shroud, stifle, strangle, subterfuge, suppress, veil

masked blind *(concealed)*, clandestine, furtive, hidden, mysterious, stealthy

masquerade camouflage, deception, disguise, disguise, evasion, false pretense, hoax, palter, pretend, ruse, sham

masquerade as impersonate, pose *(impersonate)*

mass accumulate *(amass)*, agglomeration, aggregate, aggregate, amount

(quantity), assemblage, assembly, body *(collection)*, bulk, caliber *(measurement)*, chamber *(body)*, cohere *(adhere)*, collect *(gather)*, collection *(accumulation)*, compile, concentrate *(consolidate)*, conglomerate, conglomeration, congregate, congregation, conjoin, consolidate *(strengthen)*, corpus, cumulation, desegregate, entirety, generality *(bulk)*, hoard, join *(bring together)*, load, majority *(greater part)*, materiality *(physical existence)*, measurement, meet, quantity, selection *(collection)*, store, totality, unite, weight *(burden)*

mass meeting assemblage, caucus, congregation

mass produce manufacture

mass produced industrial

massacre aberemurder, dispatch *(act of putting to death)*, dispatch *(put to death)*, homicide, kill *(murder)*, killing, murder, slay

massed collective, compact *(dense)*, populous, solid *(compact)*

masses populace, population

massing centralization

massive capacious, compact *(dense)*, copious, gross *(flagrant)*, major, ponderous, prodigious *(enormous)*, solid *(compact)*

master apprehend *(perceive)*, comprehend *(understand)*, construe *(comprehend)*, defeat, dominant, dominate, employer, expert, gain, impose *(subject)*, manage, mastermind, moderate *(preside over)*, overcome *(surmount)*, oversee, overthrow, overwhelm, paramount, pass *(satisfy requirements)*, pedagogue, predominate *(command)*, prevail *(triumph)*, principal *(director)*, professional, proprietor, remember, repress, rule *(govern)*, sovereign *(absolute)*, specialist, subdue, subject, subjugate, succeed *(attain)*, superintendent, surmount, understand

master craftsman artisan

master hand expert

master of ceremonies chairman

master of jurisprudence jurist

master plan arrangement *(plan)*, blueprint, direction *(course)*, method

master worker practitioner

master workman artisan

masterdom supremacy

masterful competent, deft, dictatorial, expert, indomitable, potent, practiced, proficient, tyrannous

masterfulness influence, puissance

masterless independent

masterly artful, capable, competent, deft, expert, practiced, subtle *(refined)*

mastermind administer *(conduct)*, direct *(supervise)*, expert, manage, operate, oversee, predominate *(command)*

masters hierarchy *(persons in authority)*

mastership ability, clout, generalship, performance *(workmanship)*, power, prowess *(ability)*, specialty *(special aptitude)*, supremacy

mastery ability, advantage, apprehension *(perception)*, cognition, competence *(ability)*, control *(supervision)*, dominance, dominion *(supreme authority)*, efficiency, experience *(background)*, force *(strength)*, gift *(flair)*, hegemony,

influence, knowledge *(learning)*, occupation *(possession)*, ownership, performance *(workmanship)*, power, predominance, prowess *(ability)*, science *(technique)*, seisin, skill, specialty *(special aptitude)*, supremacy

mastery of thought comprehension

mat snarl

match alter ego, coincide *(correspond)*, compare, comport *(agree with)*, conform, connect *(join together)*, connect *(relate)*, connection *(relation)*, contest *(competition)*, correlate, correspond *(be equivalent)*, counterpart *(parallel)*, countervail, duplicate, equipoise, identity *(similarity)*, join *(bring together)*, matrimony, measure, peer, recriminate, resemblance, retaliate, same, strife

match against confront *(oppose)*, counteract

match strength with compete

match wits with compete

matched coextensive, comparable *(equivalent)*, conjugal, correlative, equal, fit, uniform

matching agreed *(harmonized)*, analogous, coequal, commensurable, commensurate, comparable *(equivalent)*, comparative, congruous, harmonious, identical, pendent, similar

matchless absolute *(ideal)*, best, inestimable, invaluable, laudable, major, paramount, premium, priceless, prime *(most valuable)*, rare, renowned, select, singular, sterling, superior *(excellent)*, superlative, unapproachable, unique, unusual

matchless effort main force

matchmaker broker

mate coadjutant, colleague, consociate, consort, contributor *(contributor)*, copartner *(business associate)*, correlate, counterpart *(complement)*, participant, peer, resemblance, same, spouse

mated conjugal, nuptial

material appreciable, article *(commodity)*, bodily, cardinal *(basic)*, concrete, considerable, corporal, corporeal, critical *(crucial)*, crucial, equipment, essential *(required)*, expedient, important *(significant)*, major, momentous, mundane, noteworthy, objective, paraphernalia *(apparatus)*, pertinent, physical, relative *(relevant)*, relevant, resource, subject *(topic)*, substance *(essential nature)*, substantive, tangible, virtual

material assets estate *(property)*, merchandise, principal *(capital sum)*, property *(possessions)*

material existence body *(person)*, materiality *(physical existence)*

material figuration embodiment

material object article *(commodity)*

material part component, gravamen

material point cornerstone, issue *(matter in dispute)*, landmark *(significant change)*, main point

material point deduced by the pleadings issue *(matter in dispute)*

material product object

material representation embodiment

material substance object

material things which are owned estate *(property)*

material wealth possessions
materialistic mercenary
materiality corpus, importance, magnitude, relevance, significance
materialization corpus, embodiment, manifestation, phenomenon *(manifestation)*, realization
materialize embody, emerge, form, occur *(happen)*, realize *(make real)*, substantiate
materialness consequence *(significance)*, importance, magnitude, materiality *(consequence)*, materiality *(physical existence)*, significance
materials goods, merchandise
materials of combat ammunition
materiate bodily, physical
maternal consanguineous
mating matrimony
matriarch parents
matriculate register
matriculation registration
matrilinear consanguineous
matrimonial conjugal, nuptial
matrimonium marriage *(wedlock)*, matrimony
matrimony cohabitation *(married state)*, coverture, marriage *(wedlock)*
matrix pattern
matronage coverture
matronhood coverture
matronship coverture
matronymic call *(title)*
matted inextricable
matter article *(commodity)*, business *(affair)*, case *(lawsuit)*, content *(meaning)*, corpus, entity, gist *(substance)*, happening, import, issue *(matter in dispute)*, materiality *(consequence)*, materiality *(physical existence)*, object, particular, point *(item)*, proceeding, significance, subject *(topic)*
matter for judgment case *(lawsuit)*, controversy *(lawsuit)*, lawsuit
matter in dispute problem
matter in hand issue *(matter in dispute)*
matter in question issue *(matter in dispute)*
matter legally submitted to the jury evidence
matter of cognition content *(meaning)*
matter of concern cornerstone
matter of contention issue *(matter in dispute)*
matter of course behavior, custom, practice *(custom)*, procedure, rule *(guide)*
matter of disputation discrepancy
matter of dubitation doubt *(indecision)*, doubt *(suspicion)*
matter of duty allegiance
matter of fact certification *(certainness)*, fait accompli, prosaic, unpretentious
matter of factness pragmatism
matter of importance cornerstone
matter of necessity requirement
matter of no consequence nonentity
matter of no importance nonentity
matter of record certificate
matter-of-fact pragmatic
mattering much important *(significant)*
matters affairs, dealings

matters of fact evidence
matters of state politics
matters to be attended to agenda
maturare expedite, hasten, mature, precipitate *(hasten)*
maturate conclude *(complete)*, mature, progress
maturation finality, growth *(evolution)*
mature accrue *(arise)*, develop, full, payable, progress, ready *(prepared)*, receivable, ripe
mature consideration deliberation
mature person adult
mature reflection deliberation
mature responsibility discretion *(quality of being discreet)*
matured choate lien, elderly, old
maturely considered deliberate, premeditated
matureness majority *(adulthood)*, maturity, timeliness
maturing payable
maturitas maturity
maturity age, discretion *(quality of being discreet)*, experience *(background)*, finality, majority *(adulthood)*
maturus expeditious, ripe
maudlin demonstrative *(expressive of emotion)*
maul beat *(strike)*, lash *(strike)*, mishandle *(maltreat)*, mistreat
maundering prolix
mawkish unsavory
maxim article *(precept)*, belief *(something believed)*, catchword, code, constant, constitution, doctrine, dogma, expression *(comment)*, holding *(ruling of a court)*, law, ordinance, precedent, prescription *(directive)*, principle *(axiom)*, rule *(legal dictate)*
maxim effort main force
maximal cardinal *(outstanding)*, radical *(extreme)*, utmost
maxime particularly
maximize enhance, expand, increase, magnify, overestimate, parlay *(exploit successfully)*
maximizing cumulative *(intensifying)*
maximum best, ceiling, full, ultimate, utmost, utmost
maximum amount cap
mayhem commotion, outbreak, outburst, shambles
maze complex *(entanglement)*, entanglement *(confusion)*, ignorance, imbroglio, involution, snarl
mazy circuitous, inextricable, labyrinthine, sinuous, tortuous *(bending)*
meager de minimus, deficient, inappreciable, inconsiderable, insufficient, marginal, mediocre, minimal, negligible, nominal, nonsubstantial *(not sufficient)*, paltry, petty, poor *(inferior in quality)*, scarce, slight, trivial, unworthy
meagerness austerity, dearth, deficiency, deficit, immateriality, insufficiency, poverty
mean average *(midmost)*, base *(inferior)*, bespeak, brutal, connote, denote, heinous, ignoble, illiberal, inappreciable, inconsiderable, inimical, intend, intermediate, loathsome, machiavellian, malevolent, mediocre, mediocrity, mesne, moderation, odious, paltry, par-

simonious, penurious, perverse, petty, petulant, poor *(inferior in quality)*, purport, represent *(portray)*, scandalous, scurrilous, servile, signify *(denote)*, slight, spiteful, vicious
mean proportioned average *(midmost)*
mean-spirited caitiff
mean-tempered petulant
meander detour, deviate, digress, perambulate, prowl
meandering circuitous, discursive *(digressive)*, indirect, labyrinthine, moving *(in motion)*, protracted, sinuous, tortuous *(bending)*
meandrous circuitous, sinuous
meaning connotation, consequence *(significance)*, construction, contents, context, definition, design *(intent)*, essence, explanation, gist *(substance)*, import, intent, main point, paraphrase, purview, significance, signification, spirit, substance *(essential nature)*, sum *(tally)*, tenor
meaningful cognizable, coherent *(clear)*, eloquent, pithy, sententious, suggestive *(evocative)*
meaningfulness content *(meaning)*, import
meaningless collateral *(immaterial)*, frivolous, immaterial, incomprehensible, inexpressive, minor, nominal, null *(insignificant)*, pedestrian, trivial, unessential, void *(invalid)*
meaningless saying platitude
meaninglessness incoherence
meanness inconsideration, mediocrity, mischief
means access *(opening)*, appliance, conduit *(channel)*, determinant, effects, expedient, facility *(instrumentality)*, forum *(medium)*, instrument *(tool)*, instrumentality, livelihood, medium, method, mode, modus operandi, money, organ, process *(course)*, recourse, reserve, resource, stopgap, substance *(material possessions)*, system, tool, use, way *(manner)*
means of access access *(right of way)*, approaches, avenue *(means of attainment)*, entrance, ingress, portal
means of approach access *(right of way)*
means of attack ammunition
means of communication language
means of earning a living calling
means of entering entrance
means of entry ingress
means of escape loophole, outlet
means of exit egress
means of expression forum *(medium)*
means of identification fingerprints
means of livelihood employment, position *(business status)*, post, pursuit *(occupation)*
means of offense cudgel
means of proof evidence
means of protection panoply
means of proving a fact evidence
means of recognition indicia, symptom
means of restraint deterrence, deterrent, fetter
means of subsistence maintenance *(support of spouse)*

means of support business *(occupation)*, employment
means of sustaining life sustenance
means to an end contrivance, device *(contrivance)*, expedient
meant bona fide, express, implied, knowing, purposeful
meantime ad interim
meanwhile ad interim
measly paltry
measurable appreciable, determinable *(ascertainable)*
measure act *(undertaking)*, allot, amendment *(legislation)*, amount *(quantity)*, assess *(appraise)*, assessment *(estimation)*, bill *(proposed act)*, calculate, caliber *(measurement)*, capacity *(maximum)*, compare, coverage *(scope)*, criterion, criticize *(evaluate)*, degree *(magnitude)*, delimit, dimension, enactment, evaluate, expedient, extent, gauge, index *(gauge)*, magnitude, mass *(weight)*, measurement, mete, mete, moiety, parcel, part *(portion)*, prescription *(directive)*, procedure, proportion, proposal *(suggestion)*, quantity, quota, rate, ration, regulation *(rule)*, rubric *(authoritative rule)*, segment, share *(interest)*, standard, statute, stopgap, transaction, unit *(item)*
measure according to weight weigh
measure for measure quid pro quo, reprisal, retribution
measure of value money
measure out administer *(tender)*, apportion, dole, mete
measure up qualify *(meet standards)*
measure up to conform
measured deliberate, periodic, regular *(orderly)*
measured size area *(surface)*, caliber *(measurement)*
measured time phase *(period)*
measureless indeterminate, inestimable, infinite, myriad, open-ended, profuse, unlimited, unqualified *(unlimited)*
measurelessly ad infinitum
measurement amount *(quantity)*, appraisal, appreciation *(perception)*, census, comparison, computation, degree *(magnitude)*, estimate *(approximate cost)*, estimation *(calculation)*, magnitude, mass *(weight)*, quantity, rating
measurement across caliber *(measurement)*
measurements area *(surface)*
measures campaign, course, legislation *(enactments)*, means *(opportunity)*
measuring out apportionment
meat signification
meaty compact *(pithy)*, pithy, sententious
mechanic artisan
mechanical controlled *(automatic)*, industrial, perfunctory, routine, technical
mechanical aid device *(mechanism)*
mechanical construction instrument *(tool)*
mechanical drawing blueprint
mechanician artisan
mechanism appliance, contrivance, expedient, facility *(instrumentality)*, forum *(medium)*, instrument *(tool)*, medium, ploy, tool
mechanism for evasion loophole

mechanistic controlled *(automatic)*
mechanized industrial
medal prize
meddle disrupt, disturb, infringe, intercede, interfere, interrupt, intervene, militate, obtrude, overstep, tamper
meddlesome obtrusive
meddling interest *(concern)*, intrusion, molestation, obtrusive
mederi cure
media press
media pars center *(central position)*
medial average *(midmost)*, central *(situated near center)*, intermediate
median average *(midmost)*, central *(situated near center)*, intermediate, mesne, norm
mediary agent, conduit *(intermediary)*, go-between, intermediary, spokesman
mediate adjudicate, average *(midmost)*, compromise *(settle by mutual agreement)*, intercede, interpose, mollify, negotiate, pacify, reconcile
mediated agreed *(harmonized)*
mediating agency interagent, liaison, medium
mediation collective bargaining, conciliation, intercession, mollification, negotiation, reconciliation
mediator adjuster, advocate *(counselor)*, arbiter, broker, conduit *(intermediary)*, go-between, interagent, intermediary, liaison, medium, referee, spokesman, umpire
mediatorial intermediate
mediatorship collective bargaining
mediatory intermediate
medical medicinal, remedial
medical case patient
medical preparation drug
medical segregation quarantine
medical treatment cure
medicament cure, drug, panacea
medicamentum drug, remedy
medicare drug
medicate cure, drug, relieve *(give aid)*, remedy
medication drug, narcotic
medicative medicinal, remedial
medicina remedy *(that which corrects)*, remedy
medicinal remedial, salubrious, salutary
medicinal component drug
medicinal ingredient drug
medicine cure, narcotic, panacea
mediocre average *(standard)*, fair *(satisfactory)*, imperfect, inferior *(lower in quality)*, marginal, nondescript, nonsubstantial *(not sturdy)*, ordinary, paltry, passable, pedestrian, poor *(inferior in quality)*, prosaic, trivial, usual
mediocris mediocre, poor *(inferior in quality)*
mediocritas mediocrity
mediocriter fairly *(moderately)*
meditari practice *(train by repetition)*
meditate concentrate *(pay attention)*, deliberate, muse, ponder, reflect *(ponder)*, study
meditate on brood, consider
meditate upon devote, focus, weigh
meditated deliberate, intentional
meditation consideration *(contemplation)*, deliberation, hindsight, introspec-

tion, reflection *(thought)*
meditative circumspect, cogitative, deliberate, pensive, solemn, speculative
medium advocate *(counselor)*, agent, atmosphere, average *(midmost)*, broker, buffer zone, conduit *(channel)*, conduit *(intermediary)*, determinant, expedient, facility *(instrumentality)*, factor *(commission merchant)*, fair *(satisfactory)*, instrument *(tool)*, instrumentality, interagent, intermediary, intermediate, mediocre, tool
medium of exchange cash, currency, money
medium of proof documentation, evidence
medius center *(central position)*, intermediate, neutral
medley assemblage, composite, diversity, integration *(amalgamation)*, melange, miscellaneous
medullosus pithy
meed appropriation *(donation)*, compensation, honorarium, pay, prize, profit, recompense, requital, reward, tip *(gratuity)*, wage
meek malleable, nonmilitant, obedient, obeisant, patient, placid, pliable, pliant, resigned, sequacious, servile, unobtrusive, unpretentious
meekness resignation *(passive acceptance)*
meet abut, adjoin, appropriate, border *(approach)*, caucus, coincide *(concur)*, collection *(assembly)*, collide *(crash against)*, concur *(agree)*, confront *(encounter)*, congregate, connect *(join together)*, consolidate *(unite)*, contact *(touch)*, convene, converge, discharge *(pay a debt)*, endure *(suffer)*, engage *(involve)*, felicitous, fulfill, keep *(fulfill)*, pay, reach, rendezvous, report *(present oneself)*, rightful, strike *(collide)*, suitable, unite
meet an obligation satisfy *(discharge)*
meet charges disburse *(pay out)*
meet death decease, perish
meet end to end border *(bound)*
meet halfway compromise *(settle by mutual agreement)*, negotiate
meet in a body congregate
meet in conflict confront *(oppose)*
meet one's death die
meet payments liquidate *(determine liability)*
meet requirements pass *(satisfy requirements)*, satisfy *(fulfill)*
meet the bill bear the expense, defray, disburse *(pay out)*
meet the bill ahead of time prepay
meet the demand avail *(bring about)*
meet the demands qualify *(meet standards)*
meet the expense of disburse *(pay out)*, expend *(disburse)*
meet the specifications qualify *(meet standards)*
meet the wants of accommodate
meet with bear *(tolerate)*, border *(bound)*, contact *(communicate)*, find *(discover)*, incur
meet with a loss forfeit, lose *(be deprived of)*
meet with success prevail *(triumph)*, succeed *(attain)*

meeting adjacent, assemblage, assembly, caucus, chamber *(body)*, coalition, collection *(assembly)*, collision *(accident)*, company *(assemblage)*, concurrent *(united)*, conference, confrontation *(act of setting face to face)*, congregation, contact *(touching)*, contiguous, interview, parley, rendezvous, session
meeting hall chamber *(compartment)*
meeting of events crossroad *(turning point)*
meeting of minds accordance *(understanding)*, mutual understanding, understanding *(agreement)*
meeting of political leaders caucus
meeting of the minds agreement *(concurrence)*
meeting place intersection, rendezvous
meeting point intersection
meeting standards palatable
meetness expedience
megalopolis city
melancholia pessimism
melancholic despondent, disconsolate, pessimistic
melancholy despondent, disconsolate, lamentable, lugubrious, pessimism, pessimistic
meld amalgamate, combine *(join together)*, desegregate, incorporate *(include)*, join *(bring together)*, unite
melee affray
melee altercation, belligerency, bluster *(commotion)*
mêlée brawl
mêlée collision *(dispute)*, commotion, confrontation *(altercation)*
melee fracas, fray, imbroglio, pandemonium, riot, turmoil
melior preferable, superior *(excellent)*
meliorate ameliorate, commute, cure, develop, embellish, emend, fix *(repair)*, mitigate, modify *(alter)*, mollify, progress, rectify, reform, rehabilitate, relieve *(give aid)*, remedy, renew *(refurbish)*, renovate, repair, restore *(renew)*
melioration amendment *(correction)*, correction *(change)*, development *(progression)*, improvement, mollification, progress, reform, rehabilitation, renewal, reorganization, repair, solace
meliorative mitigating
melliferous nectarious
mellifluous eloquent
mellow mollify, orotund, pacify, ripe
melodramatic histrionic
melodramatics histrionics
melt burn
melt away decrease, disappear, dissolve *(disperse)*, lessen, perish, subside
melt into one consolidate *(unite)*, merge
member chapter *(branch)*, element, ingredient, offshoot, organ, party *(participant)*
member of a governmental body legislator
member of a jury juror
member of a legislative body legislator
member of a legislature lawmaker
member of a partnership partner
member of Congress lawmaker
member of organized crime racketeer

member of parliament legislator
member of the Assembly lawmaker
member of the bar attorney, barrister, counsel, counselor, esquire, jurist
member of the family relative
member of the House lawmaker
member of the human race person
member of the legal profession advocate *(counselor)*, counsel, counselor, esquire, jurist, lawyer
member of the police force peace officer
member of the Senate lawmaker
members constituency, personnel
members of the bar chamber *(body)*
members of the media press
members of the press press
membership affiliation *(connectedness)*, constituency, roll
membrum clause, ingredient
memento remembrance *(commemoration)*, reminder, token
memo entry *(record)*, reminder
memoir account *(report)*, memorandum, recollection, story *(narrative)*
memorability importance, materiality *(consequence)*
memorable famous, illustrious, important *(significant)*, major, material *(important)*, momentous, notable, noteworthy, outstanding *(prominent)*, paramount, portentous *(eliciting amazement)*, prominent, remarkable, salient, special, stellar, unusual
memorable part highlight
memorableness importance
memoranda calendar *(record of yearly periods)*
memorandum brief, entry *(record)*, marginalia, notation, note *(brief comment)*, notice *(announcement)*, record, register, reminder
memorandum of law brief
memoria account *(report)*, recollection, remembrance *(recollection)*
memorial honorary, monument, remembrance *(commemoration)*, reminder
memorialization ceremony, remembrance *(commemoration)*
memorialize honor, recall *(remember)*, remember
memorize recall *(remember)*, remember
memory hindsight, recognition, recollection, remembrance *(recollection)*, retention, retrospect
menace bait *(harass)*, challenge, danger, endanger, frighten, hazard, hector, impend, intimidate, jeopardize, jeopardy, portend, threat, threaten
menacing abusive, dangerous, formidable, imminent, insalubrious, noxious, ominous, pernicious, portentous *(ominous)*, precarious, prophetic, sinister
mend ameliorate, amend, cure, develop, emend, fix *(repair)*, meliorate, progress, reconcile, recreate, rectify, redress, reform, rehabilitate, remedy, renew *(refurbish)*, renovate, repair, restore *(renew)*, settle
mendable corrigible
mendacious deceptive, disingenuous, false *(inaccurate)*, fictitious, lying, untrue
mendaciousness bad faith, dishonesty, improbity, indirection *(deceitful-*

ness)
mendacity artifice, bad faith, deceit, deception, dishonesty, false pretense, falsification, fraud, improbity, indirection *(deceitfulness)*, lie, misstatement, pretense *(pretext)*, subreption
mendacium falsehood, lie, misstatement, story *(falsehood)*
mendax mendacious
mendicancy poverty, privation
mendicant parasite
mendicate request
mendicitas indigence
mendicity poverty, privation
mendicus poor *(underprivileged)*
mending correction *(change)*, renewal, repair
mendosus faulty
mendum defect, flaw
menial base *(inferior)*, ignoble, inferior *(lower in position)*, servile, subservient
menology calendar *(record of yearly periods)*
mens intellect, intelligence *(intellect)*, purpose, reason *(sound judgment)*, understanding *(comprehension)*
mensio measurement
mensura measurement
mensurable appreciable, determinable *(ascertainable)*
mensural appreciable
mensurate assess *(appraise)*
mensuration assessment *(estimation)*, estimation *(calculation)*, measurement
mental non compos mentis, vicarious *(delegated)*
mental aberration lunacy, paranoia
mental ability intellect, intelligence *(intellect)*, understanding *(comprehension)*
mental abnormality insanity, lunacy
mental acuteness intellect, intelligence *(intellect)*
mental agony distress *(anguish)*
mental alienation insanity
mental and spiritual makeup character *(personal quality)*
mental attitude impression
mental balance competence *(sanity)*, sanity
mental capacity apprehension *(perception)*, competence *(sanity)*, comprehension, intellect, intelligence *(intellect)*, reason *(sound judgment)*
mental constitution disposition *(inclination)*, frame *(mood)*
mental cultivation edification
mental decay insanity
mental deficiency insanity
mental derangement insanity
mental disease insanity, paranoia
mental dissociation lunacy
mental equilibrium competence *(sanity)*, sanity
mental faculty intellect, intelligence *(intellect)*, judgment *(discernment)*
mental giant mastermind
mental grasp comprehension, information *(knowledge)*
mental health competence *(sanity)*, sanity
mental hospital asylum *(hospital)*
mental illness lunacy
mental image concept, impression, notion, perception, phantom, recollec-

tion, remembrance *(recollection)*, sense *(feeling)*
mental imbalance lunacy
mental impression concept, perception
mental incapacity insanity
mental infirmities insanity
mental instability insanity
mental institution asylum *(hospital)*
mental outlook position *(point of view)*
mental picture recollection
mental poise common sense
mental representation concept
mental reservation ambivalence
mental sickness insanity, lunacy
mental toil labor *(exertion)*
mental unsoundness insanity
mental view impression, perspective
mentality caliber *(mental capacity)*, comprehension, intellect, intelligence *(intellect)*, sagacity, sense *(intelligence)*, temperament
mentally aberrant lunatic
mentally appreciate discern *(detect with the senses)*
mentally capable competent
mentally deficient non compos mentis
mentally diseased non compos mentis
mentally ill lunatic, non compos mentis
mentally sick non compos mentis
mentally sound normal *(sane)*, sane
mentally unbalanced lunatic
mentally unsound non compos mentis
mentation reflection *(thought)*
mentio mention *(reference)*
mention adduce, advise, allude, attribution, citation *(attribution)*, cite *(state)*, comment, comment, communicate, convey *(communicate)*, designate, disclose, disclosure *(act of disclosing)*, enumerate, expression *(comment)*, impart, indication, inform *(notify)*, innuendo, intimation, itemize, notice *(announcement)*, notice *(observe)*, notification, notify, observation, observe *(remark)*, refer *(direct attention)*, reference *(allusion)*, reference *(citation)*, referral, relate *(tell)*, remark, remark, report *(disclose)*, reveal, signify *(inform)*, specify, tip *(clue)*
mention in detail itemize
mention one by one enumerate
mention specifically enumerate
mentioned aforesaid
mentioned previously aforesaid
mentioning reference *(citation)*
mentiri lie *(falsify)*
mentis acies perception
mentis compos sane
mentor mastermind
mentors faculty *(teaching staff)*
Mephistophelian diabolic
mephitic deadly, harmful, insalubrious, malignant, pernicious, pestilent
mercantile commercial, industrial, retail
mercantile business commerce, industry *(business)*, trade *(commerce)*
mercantile relations commerce, trade *(commerce)*

mercantilism commerce
mercari buy
mercator dealer, merchant
mercatura commerce
mercaturam trade
mercatus market *(business)*, trade *(commerce)*
mercenarius mercenary
mercenary employee, illiberal, parsimonious, penurious, venal
merces fee *(charge)*, pay, recompense, rent, wage
merces mutare barter
merces vetitae contraband
merchandise barter, cargo, commodities, deal, freight, handle *(trade)*, item, output, paraphernalia *(personal belongings)*, product, sell, stock in trade, trade
merchandise list inventory
merchandise sent consignment
merchandise specification invoice *(itemized list)*
merchandiser dealer, merchant
merchandising business *(commerce)*, commerce, commercial, mercantile, trade *(commerce)*
merchant dealer, supplier, vendor
merchantable marketable
merchantry business *(commerce)*, commerce, deal, exchange, trade *(commerce)*
merciful benevolent, charitable *(lenient)*, humane, lenient, placable, propitious, sensitive *(easily affected)*
mercifulness clemency, humanity *(humaneness)*, lenience, pity
merciless brutal, cruel, diabolic, harmful, harsh, inexorable, malevolent, malicious, obdurate, relentless, remorseless, ruthless, unrelenting, vicious
mercilessness atrocity, brutality, cruelty
mercurial capricious, inconsistent, irresolute, moving *(in motion)*, undependable, unpredictable, untrustworthy, variable, volatile
mercurialness inconsistency
mercy benevolence *(disposition to do good)*, clemency, condonation, consideration *(sympathetic regard)*, humanity *(humaneness)*, lenience, pity, understanding *(tolerance)*
mere marginal, minor, naked *(lacking embellishment)*, only *(no more than)*, simple
merely only, purely *(simply)*, solely *(purely)*
merere earn
meretricious dishonest, disreputable, fraudulent, pretentious *(ostentatious)*, tawdry
meretriciousness bad faith
merge amalgamate, annex *(add)*, attach *(join)*, bond *(hold together)*, cement, coincide *(concur)*, combine *(join together)*, commingle, conjoin, connect *(join together)*, consolidate *(unite)*, converge, desegregate, federalize *(associate)*, federate, include, incorporate *(include)*, join *(bring together)*, organize *(unionize)*, pool, unite
merge in desegregate
merged compound, concordant, concurrent *(united)*, conjoint, federal, joint,

miscellaneous
merger accession *(annexation)*, affiliation *(amalgamation)*, cartel, coalescence, coalition, combination, concert, consolidation, consortium *(business cartel)*, federation, integration *(amalgamation)*, integration *(assimilation)*, meeting *(encounter)*, syndicate, trust *(combination of businesses)*
merging centralization, coalescence, coalition, concerted, concordant
meridian pinnacle
merit caliber *(quality)*, consequence *(significance)*, credit *(recognition)*, earn, importance, probity, quality *(excellence)*, quality *(grade)*, rate, rectitude, right *(righteousness)*, significance, value, weight *(importance)*, worth
merit as compensation earn
merited condign, due *(owed)*, entitled, equitable, fair *(just)*, just, justifiable, rightful, suitable
meriting blame peccant *(culpable)*
meriting censure culpable
meriting condemnation culpable
meritless unworthy
meritoria lodging
meritorious cogent, conscientious, exemplary, high-minded, incorruptible, justifiable, laudable, major, moral, reputable, sterling, unimpeachable
meritoriousness merit, validity
meritum merit
meritus condign, equitable, just
merriment enjoyment *(pleasure)*
merry jocular
merrymaking jocular
merus genuine, unadulterated
merx commodities, merchandise
mesh intertwine
mesh together engage *(involve)*
mesh with comport *(agree with)*
meshing interlocking
mesial central *(situated near center)*, intermediate
mesne intermediate
mess confuse *(create disorder)*, imbroglio, pollute, predicament, quagmire, quantity, shambles, snarl
mess up confuse *(create disorder)*, disrupt, spoil *(impair)*
message communication *(statement)*, disclosure *(something disclosed)*, intelligence *(news)*, issuance, note *(brief comment)*, notice *(announcement)*, notification, proclamation, report *(detailed account)*
messenger forerunner, harbinger, informer *(a person who provides information)*, liaison, plenipotentiary, proxy, representative *(proxy)*, spokesman
messuage homestead
messy disordered
metabolize convert *(change use)*
metage measurement
metamorphic protean
metamorphose alter, change, convert *(change use)*, modify *(alter)*, transform
metamorphosis conversion *(change)*
metaphor example
metaphorical comparative
metaphysical incomprehensible
metari measure
metastasis transition
mete allocate, allot, apportion, assess *(appraise)*, bestow, calculate, disburse

(distribute), dispense, distribute, divide
(distribute), dole, measure, parcel, partition, periphery, split
mete out administer (tender), allot, apportion, arbitrate (adjudge), assign (allot), contribute (supply), disperse (disseminate), dispose (apportion), divide (distribute), dole, inflict, partition, present (make a gift), prorate, render (administer)
meteoric brief, ephemeral, transient
meteorical ephemeral
meter measure
meterable appreciable
meterage measurement
metes confines, outline (boundary)
method act (undertaking), arrangement (ordering), arrangement (plan), array (order), avenue (means of attainment), campaign, conduct, conduit (channel), contrivance, course, device (contrivance), direction (course), disposition (final arrangement), expedient, facility (instrumentality), form (arrangement), instrumentality, key (solution), manner (behavior), means (opportunity), mode, modus operandi, policy (plan of action), practice (custom), practice (procedure), procedure, process (course), regularity, rule (guide), scheme, science (technique), strategy, style, system, technicality, usage
method of action manner (behavior)
method of attack avenue (means of attainment)
method of business dealings
method of communication forum (medium)
method of expression forum (medium)
method of living modus vivendi
method of treatment cure
methodical precise, procedural, punctilious, regular (orderly), systematic
methodicalness array (order), regularity
methodization classification
methodize adjust (regulate), classify, codify, coordinate, disentangle, fix (arrange), orchestrate, organize (arrange), pigeonhole, regulate (adjust), sort, tabulate
methodology array (order), modus operandi, order (arrangement), procedure, process (course)
meticulosity diligence (perseverance), interest (concern)
meticulous accurate, careful, circumspect, close (rigorous), conscientious, detailed, discriminating (judicious), exact, faithful (diligent), literal, painstaking, particular (exacting), precise, punctilious, punctual, strict, subtle (refined), thorough
meticulously faithfully
meticulousness caution (vigilance), diligence (care), particularity, rigor
metier calling, career, industry (business), pursuit (occupation), trade (occupation), work (employment)
meting out apportionment
metiri gauge
metropolis city
metropolitan civic, civil (public)
metropolitan area city
mettle character (personal quality),

frame (mood), prowess (bravery), spirit
mettlesome undaunted
metuere fear
metus fear
metus timor misgiving
mew imprison
miasmal deleterious, destructive, harmful, insalubrious, malignant, peccant (unhealthy)
miasmatic destructive, insalubrious, malignant
miasmatical insalubrious, malignant
miasmic deadly, destructive, insalubrious
microscopic impalpable
mid average (midmost), intermediate
middle average (midmost), center (central position), central (situated near center), interior, intermediate, mediocre, mesne
middle class average (midmost)
middle distance center (central position)
middle grade average (midmost)
middle ground compromise
middle man representative (proxy)
middle point center (central position)
middle position center (central position)
middle state mediocrity
middleman agent, broker, conduit (intermediary), dealer, factor (commission merchant), go-between, interagent, intermediary, medium, merchant, procurator
middlemost average (midmost), central (situated near center)
middling average (midmost), fair (satisfactory), imperfect, marginal, mediocre, nondescript, ordinary, passable, usual
midmost central (situated near center), intermediate
midmost point center (central position)
midpoint center (central position), norm
midst center (central position)
midway en route
mien appearance (look), aspect, behavior, complexion, conduct, demeanor, deportment, manner (behavior), presence (poise), semblance, state (condition)
miff aggravate (annoy)
miffed resentful
might degree (magnitude), dint, force (strength), influence, main force, potential, prowess (bravery), puissance, quality (excellence), severity, sinew, strength
mightiness dint, dominance, eminence, force (strength), influence, potential, predominance, puissance, strength
mightless powerless
mighty efficient, grandiose, important (significant), in full force, inexpugnable, influential, irresistible, omnipotent, potent, powerful, predominant, prevailing (having superior force), prodigious (enormous), spartan, strong, vehement
migrate leave (depart), move (alter position), part (leave)
migration immigration

migratory moving (in motion), transient, unsettled
mild civil (polite), innocuous, lenient, patient, peaceable, permissive, placable, placid
mild-tempered patient
milden mollify, relax
mildewed stale
mildly fairly (moderately)
mildness amenity, humanity (humaneness), lenience, moderation
mileage space
milestone cornerstone, crossroad (turning point), event, landmark (significant change), step
milieu atmosphere, case (set of circumstances), environment, section (vicinity)
militancy belligerency
militant aggressor, contentious, litigious, offensive (taking the initiative), pugnacious, radical (favoring drastic change), spartan
militaristic offensive (taking the initiative), pugnacious
military evolutions strategy
military science strategy
militate influence, operate
militate against counter, counteract, countervail, oppugn
milk exploit (take advantage of)
millstone incumbrance (burden)
mime impersonate, mock (imitate), parody
mimesis part (role)
mimic impersonate, jape, mock (imitate), pose (impersonate), pretend
mimicking caricature
mimicry caricature, parody, ridicule, travesty
minacious ominous, pending (imminent), portentous (ominous), prophetic
minacious force menace
minacity menace
minae threat
minatorial imminent, portentous (ominous), prophetic
minatory aleatory (perilous), dangerous, imminent, ominous, portentous (ominous), prophetic, sinister, unpropitious
mince the truth prevaricate
mind animus, attend (heed), beware, care (be cautious), care (regard), comprehension, conatus, concern (care), conscience, conviction (persuasion), frame (mood), hear (give attention to), heed, intellect, intelligence (intellect), intent, memory (retention), note (notice), obey, observe (watch), preserve, propensity, reason (sound judgment), regard (pay attention), submit (yield), will (desire)
mind set position (point of view)
minded prone
mindful careful, circumspect, cognizant, conscious (aware), discreet, faithful (diligent), familiar (informed), judicious, knowing, meticulous, particular (exacting), perceptive, politic, prudent, sensitive (discerning)
mindfulness caution (vigilance), comprehension, diligence (care), discretion (quality of being discreet), interest (concern), knowledge (awareness), notice (heed), observation, perception, realiza-

tion, recollection, regard *(attention)*, sense *(feeling)*, sensibility

mindless blind *(not discerning)*, heedless, irrational, lax, negligent, non compos mentis, oblivious, opaque, perfunctory, reckless, unaware

mindlessness disinterest *(lack of interest)*, disregard *(unconcern)*

mine bomb, contrive, extract, fund

mingle combine *(join together)*, confuse *(create disorder)*, desegregate, join *(associate oneself with)*, unite

mingle confusedly confound

mingled complex, compound, conglomerate, promiscuous

minglement incorporation *(blend)*, melange

mingling concrescence, integration *(amalgamation)*, integration *(assimilation)*

miniature model, tenuous

minify diminish, lessen

minim minimum, scintilla

minimal minor, remote *(small)*

minimalize discount *(minimize)*

minime suspicax unsuspecting

minimization curtailment, deduction *(diminution)*, understatement

minimize allay, commute, decrease, depreciate, dilute, diminish, disparage, lessen, misprize, palliate *(abate)*, reduce, remit *(relax)*, underestimate

minimum minimal, minor, modicum, nominal, paucity

minimus inappreciable

minister administer *(conduct)*, caretaker *(one fulfilling the function of office)*, contribute *(assist)*, deputy, incumbent, officiate, operate, pander, proctor, supply

minister to accommodate, aid, assist, attend *(take care of)*, bear *(yield)*, bestow, care *(regard)*, concern *(care)*, cure, foster, preserve, relieve *(give aid)*, remedy, serve *(assist)*, support *(assist)*

ministerial administrative, executive

ministering angel samaritan

ministerium service *(assistance)*

ministers government *(political administration)*

ministrant ancillary *(auxiliary)*, benefactor, samaritan, subservient

ministrare supply

ministration administration, aid *(help)*, aid *(subsistence)*, attendance, behalf, bureaucracy, direction *(guidance)*, help, relief *(aid)*, service *(assistance)*

ministry aid *(help)*, aid *(subsistence)*, bureau, control *(supervision)*, department, relief *(aid)*

minor adolescent, child, collateral *(immaterial)*, dependent, dependent, frivolous, immaterial, inappreciable, incidental, inconsequential, inconsiderable, infant, inferior *(lower in position)*, juvenile, juvenile, minimal, negligible, nonessential, null *(insignificant)*, petty, secondary, slight, subaltern, subordinate, unessential

minor amount modicum

minor officer of the law marshal

minor part detail

minor point technicality

minor under guardianship dependent

minor under protectorship dependent

minoris aestimare underestimate

minoris facere underestimate

minority adolescence, nonage, paucity

minors children

mintage money

minted monetary

minuere curtail, diminish, extenuate

minui suffer *(sustain loss)*

minus save

minute accurate, capsule, conscientious, detailed, entry *(record)*, exact, impalpable, inconsiderable, meticulous, minimal, minor, negligible, nominal, notation, note *(brief comment)*, outline *(synopsis)*, paltry, paraphrase, petty, record, remote *(small)*, report *(detailed account)*, scarce, slight, summary, synopsis, tenuous, trivial

minute account specification

minute application diligence *(care)*

minute attention diligence *(care)*, interest *(concern)*, scrutiny

minute circumstance particularity

minute examination cross-examination

minute investigation indagation

minute part detail

minute quantity iota

minute study diligence *(care)*

minute thought diligence *(care)*

minutely careful meticulous

minutely correct punctilious, punctual

minuteness diligence *(care)*, interest *(concern)*, particularity

minutes register, transcript

minutia particular

minutiae circumstances, technicality

minutus paltry, petty

miracle phenomenon *(unusual occurrence)*

miraculous incomprehensible, ineffable, portentous *(eliciting amazement)*, prodigious *(amazing)*, remarkable, special, unprecedented

mirage deception, figment, phantom

miratio surprise

mire pollute

mirror copy, impersonate, mock *(imitate)*, reproduce

mirth-loving jocular

mirthful jocular

mirthless solemn

mirus eccentric

misaddress misdirect

misadminister misgovern, mismanage

misadministration maladministration, misconduct

misadventure accident *(misfortune)*, adversity, casualty, catastrophe, debacle, disaster, miscarriage, misfortune, quirk *(accident)*, tragedy

misadvise misdirect, misguide, misinform, mislead

misadvised ill-advised, ill-judged, inadvisable

misalliance disaccord, incongruity, misjoinder

misanthropic cynical

misapplication abuse *(corrupt practice)*, catachresis, conversion *(misappropriation)*, distortion, exploitation, maladministration, misappropriation, misdoing, misrepresentation, misusage,

misuse, waste

misapplied inapplicable, inappropriate

misapplied name misnomer

misapply abuse *(misuse)*, bilk, convert *(misappropriate)*, embezzle, exploit *(take advantage of)*, misemploy, mismanage, pervert, purloin, slant

misapply funds defalcate

misapprehend err, misconceive, misconstrue, misinterpret, misjudge, misread, mistake, misunderstand

misapprehension catachresis, fallacy, misestimation, misjudgment

misappropriate abuse *(misuse)*, bilk, divert, embezzle, exploit *(take advantage of)*, hold up *(rob)*, impropriate, jostle *(pickpocket)*, misemploy, mismanage, peculate, pilfer, plagiarize, poach, purloin, rob

misappropriate funds embezzle

misappropriate intrusted funds embezzle

misappropriate money defalcate

misappropriation abuse *(corrupt practice)*, embezzlement, larceny, misapplication, misusage, misuse, plagiarism, theft

misappropriation of funds conversion *(misappropriation)*

misarrange disorganize

misarrangement disturbance

misbecoming inappropriate

misbegetting bar sinister

misbegot illegitimate *(born out of wedlock)*

misbegotten illegitimate *(born out of wedlock)*

misbehave disobey, lapse *(fall into error)*

misbehaved disorderly

misbehaving delinquent *(guilty of a misdeed)*, disobedient, disorderly

misbehavior bad repute, culpability, delinquency *(misconduct)*, disregard *(omission)*, fault *(responsibility)*, guilt, impropriety, malfeasance, miscarriage, mischief, misconduct, misdeed, misdoing, transgression, violation

misbelief error, fallacy

misbelieve doubt *(distrust)*, misdoubt

misbeliever heretic

misbelieving doubtful

misbrand mislabel

miscalculate err, misapprehend, misconceive, misinterpret, misjudge, mistake, misunderstand

miscalculated fallacious, ill-judged, incorrect, inexact, inflated *(overestimated)*

miscalculation confusion *(ambiguity)*, error, fallacy, fault *(mistake)*, miscue, misestimation, misjudgment

miscalling misnomer

miscarriage accident *(misfortune)*, disaster, failure *(lack of success)*

miscarriage of justice error, inequity, injustice, misjudgment

miscarry fail *(lose)*

miscellaneous composite, conglomerate, diverse, heterogeneous, manifold, multifarious, multiple, omnibus, promiscuous

miscellaneous collection melange

miscellany assemblage, compilation, conglomeration, diversity, melange *miscere* combine *(join together),* disorganize, unite

mischance accident *(misfortune),* adversity, calamity, casualty, catastrophe, debacle, fatality, miscarriage, misfortune, quirk *(accident)*

mischaracterize mislabel

mischief disservice, harm, misdoing

mischief-maker delinquent, malefactor

mischievous harmful, malevolent, malicious, noxious, peccant *(culpable),* pernicious, sinister, vicious, wrongful

miscitation catachresis

miscite bear false witness, distort, falsify, misrepresent

misclassify mislabel

miscolor camouflage, cloak, distort, falsify, misinform, misrepresent, slant

miscomprehend misapprehend

miscomputation error, misestimation, misjudgment

miscompute err, miscalculate, misjudge

misconceive misapprehend, miscalculate, misconstrue, misinterpret, misjudge, mistake, misunderstand

misconception catachresis, confusion *(ambiguity),* error, fallacy, misapplication, misestimation, misjudgment

misconduct blame *(culpability),* crime, culpability, disregard *(omission),* fault *(responsibility),* guilt, indiscretion, maladministration, malpractice, miscarriage, mischief, misdeed, misdoing, misemploy, misfeasance, misguide, mishandle *(mismanage),* mismanage, misprision, misrule, offense, transgression, vice

misconduct oneself offend *(violate the law)*

misconducted misadvised

misconjecture error, miscalculate, misconceive, misestimation, misinterpret

misconstructed fallacious

misconstruction catachresis, distortion, fallacy, falsification, misapplication, misjudgment, misrepresentation

misconstrue distort, err, misapprehend, miscalculate, misconceive, misinterpret, misjudge, misread, mistake, misunderstand, slant

misconstrued incorrect

miscounseled ill-advised

miscount error, miscalculate

miscreancy wrong

miscreant bad *(offensive),* convict, delinquent, hoodlum, immoral, iniquitous, malefactor, nefarious, outlaw, profane, racketeer, sinister, wrongdoer

misdealing bribery, crime, disingenuous, disreputable, machiavellian, racket

misdeed crime, delinquency *(misconduct),* disservice, fault *(responsibility),* guilt, illegality, lapse *(expiration),* malfeasance, misconduct, misdemeanor, misdoing, misfeasance, misprision, offense, onus *(blame),* tort, transgression, vice, wrong

misdeed punishable by imprisonment felony

misdeem misapprehend, miscalculate, misconceive, misinterpret, misjudge, misread, misunderstand

misdemeanant convict, criminal, cul-

pable, delinquent, lawbreaker, malefactor, wrongdoer

misdemeanor crime, delict, guilt, misconduct, misdeed, misdoing, offense

misdenominate mislabel

misdescribe distort, mislabel, mislead, misrepresent

misdesignate mislabel

misdirect convert *(misappropriate),* corrupt, deceive, delude, disorient, distort, divert, dupe, ensnare, exploit *(take advantage of),* illude, misemploy, misgovern, misguide, mishandle *(mismanage),* misinform, mislabel, mislead, mismanage, palter, slant

misdirected errant, inappropriate, misadvised

misdirection abuse *(corrupt practice),* digression, distortion, maladministration, misrule

misdo misemploy, mismanage

misdoer delinquent, wrongdoer

misdoing crime, criminality, culpability, delinquency *(misconduct),* disservice, guilt, infringement, malfeasance, mischief, misconduct, misdeed, misdemeanor, misfeasance, offense, tort, transgression, wrong

misdoubt apprehension *(fear),* cloud *(suspicion),* doubt *(suspicion),* doubt *(distrust),* mistrust, suspect *(distrust),* suspicion *(mistrust)*

miseducate distort, misdirect, misguide, misinform, mislead

misemploy abuse *(misuse),* convert *(misappropriate),* exploit *(take advantage of),* mishandle *(maltreat),* mismanage, mistreat, persecute

misemploy funds defalcate

misemployment abuse *(corrupt practice),* conversion *(misappropriation),* misapplication, misappropriation, misusage, misuse, waste

miserabilis deplorable, moving *(evoking emotion)*

miserable deplorable, disconsolate, lamentable, lugubrious, paltry, pessimistic, poor *(inferior in quality)*

misereri sympathize

miseria adversity

misericordia humanity *(humaneness),* pity

misericors humane

miserly illiberal, parsimonious, penurious

misery calamity, disaster, distress *(anguish),* pain, pessimism, prostration

misesteem misjudge

misestimate distort, miscalculate, misconceive, misjudge, overestimate

misestimation misjudgment

misexplain distort, misrepresent

misexplanation catachresis, distortion, misapplication

misexplication catachresis, misapplication

misexposition catachresis

misexpress distort

misfeasance bad faith, crime, delict, fault *(responsibility),* guilt, infringement, maladministration, misconduct, misdeed, misdemeanor, misdoing, misprision, offense, tort, transgression

misfeasor convict, delinquent, lawbreaker

misfigured fallacious, incorrect, inex-

act

misfire miscarriage

misfit misjoinder

misfortunate unfavorable

misfortune adversity, calamity, casualty, catastrophe, debacle, detriment, disaster, failure *(lack of success),* fatality, hardship, harm, infliction, loss, plight, predicament, quagmire, tragedy, trouble

misgive doubt *(distrust),* misdoubt, mistrust, suspect *(distrust)*

misgiving apprehension *(fear),* cloud *(suspicion),* disturbance, doubt *(indecision),* doubt *(suspicion),* expectation, fear, fright, incertitude, premonition, qualm, reluctance, scruple, stress *(strain),* suspicion *(mistrust)*

misgovern exploit *(take advantage of),* mismanage, mistreat

misgovernment anarchy, lynch law, maladministration, malfeasance, misconduct, misrule

misguidance error, maladministration, misconduct, misrepresentation, misrule

misguide deceive, delude, dupe, ensnare, equivocate, fabricate *(make up),* illude, lie *(falsify),* misdirect, misgovern, misinform, mislabel, mislead, mismanage, misrepresent, misstate, palter, prevaricate

misguided astray, ill-advised, inadvisable, injudicious, misadvised

mishandle abuse *(misuse),* exploit *(take advantage of),* ill use, maltreat, misemploy, misguide, mismanage, mistreat, persecute

mishandling abuse *(corrupt practice),* abuse *(physical misuse),* maladministration, misapplication, misuse

mishap accident *(misfortune),* adversity, casualty, catastrophe, debacle, misfortune, quirk *(accident),* situation, tragedy

misidentify mislabel, misread, mistake

misinform betray *(lead astray),* bilk, cloak, deceive, delude, distort, equivocate, fabricate *(make up),* hoodwink, illude, lie *(falsify),* misdirect, misguide, mislabel, mislead, misstate, palter, prevaricate

misinformation distortion, false pretense, misstatement

misinformed misadvised

misinstruct distort, misdirect, misguide, misinform, mislead

misinstructed misadvised

misinstruction distortion, propaganda

misinterpret distort, err, misapprehend, misconceive, misconstrue, misjudge, misread, mistake, misunderstand, slant

misinterpretation catachresis, distortion, error, fallacy, misapplication, misestimation, misjudgment

misinterpreted inexact

misjoined incongruous

misjudge err, misapprehend, miscalculate, misconceive, misconstrue, misinterpret, misprize, mistake, misunderstand, overestimate, underestimate

misjudged incorrect, inopportune, untimely

misjudging credulous

misjudgment catachresis, error, fallacy, fault *(mistake)*, indiscretion, misapplication, miscue, misestimation, overstatement

mislaid lost *(taken away)*

mislay dislocate, disorient, lose *(be deprived of)*

mislead betray *(lead astray)*, brutalize, circumvent, cloak, confound, confuse *(bewilder)*, corrupt, deceive, defraud, delude, disorient, distort, divert, dupe, ensnare, equivocate, evade *(deceive)*, fabricate *(make up)*, fake, feign, hoodwink, illude, inveigle, lie *(falsify)*, misdirect, misguide, misinform, mislabel, misrepresent, misstate, obscure, overreach, palter, pervert, pettifog, pretend, prevaricate

misleader decoy

misleading assumed *(feigned)*, deceptive, delusive, dishonest, disingenuous, equivocal, evasive, fallacious, false *(inaccurate)*, fictitious, fraudulent, illusory, incorrect, lying, meretricious, ostensible, propaganda, sophistic, specious, untrue

misleading enlargement exaggeration

misleading notion fallacy

misled astray, misadvised

misled by deception blind *(not discerning)*

mislike disaffect

mismanage convert *(misappropriate)*, exploit *(take advantage of)*, fail *(neglect)*, misemploy, misgovern, misguide, mistreat, muddle

mismanagement abuse *(corrupt practice)*, incompetence, maladministration, malfeasance, misapplication, misconduct, misdoing, misrule, misusage, misuse

mismark mislabel

mismatch conflict, incongruity, misjoinder

mismatched different, disproportionate, dissimilar, inapplicable, inapt, incommensurate, incongruous, inept *(inappropriate)*, unrelated, unsuitable

mismated different, incongruous, opposite

misname mislabel

misnaming misnomer

misperceive misunderstand

misplace dislocate, disorganize, disorient, lose *(be deprived of)*

misplaced anomalous, inapplicable, inappropriate, inapt, inept *(inappropriate)*, lost *(taken away)*

misprint error

misprision contempt *(disdain)*, crime, delict, delinquency *(failure of duty)*, dereliction, guilt, misconduct, misdoing, neglect, nonfeasance, offense

misprize contemn, depreciate, derogate, discount *(disbelieve)*, disdain, disfavor, disparage, humiliate, minimize, underestimate

mispronunciation misusage

misquotation catachresis, distortion, falsification, misrepresentation

misquote distort, falsify, misrepresent, slant

misread distort, misconstrue, misinterpret, misjudge, mistake, misunderstand

misreading catachresis

misreckon distort, err, misapprehend, miscalculate, misconceive, misinterpret, misjudge, misunderstand

misreckoning error, misestimation

misrender palter, slant

misrendering catachresis, distortion

misreport bear false witness, distort, falsify, feign, misrepresent, misrepresentation, misstate, palter

misreported inaccurate, inexact

misrepresent cloak, deceive, delude, disguise, distort, equivocate, evade *(deceive)*, fabricate *(make up)*, fake, falsify, feign, invent *(falsify)*, lie *(falsify)*, misguide, misinform, misinterpret, mislabel, mislead, misrepresent, misstate, overestimate, palter, perjure, pervert, pretend, prevaricate, slant

misrepresentation abuse *(corrupt practice)*, artifice, bad faith, catachresis, color *(deceptive appearance)*, deceit, deception, distortion, evasion, false pretense, falsehood, falsification, forgery, fraud, hoax, lie, misstatement, overstatement, perjury, pretense *(pretext)*, pretext, sham, sophistry, story *(falsehood)*, subreption, understatement

misrepresentative evasive, fallacious, false *(not genuine)*, fictitious, lying, mendacious

misrepresented assumed *(feigned)*, mendacious, spurious

misrule anarchy, lynch law, maladministration, misemploy, misgovern, mismanage, mistreat, oppression

miss fail *(neglect)*, ignore, lack, lose *(be deprived of)*, miscue, need, omit, overlook *(disregard)*, pretermit, require *(need)*

miss an opportunity fail *(neglect)*

miss the mark fail *(lose)*

missend mismanage

misserved aggrieved *(victimized)*

misshape contort, deface, distort

misshapen blemished, repulsive

missile bomb

missing deficient, delinquent *(overdue)*, devoid, insufficient, lost *(taken away)*, truant, vacuous

missio release

mission agency *(legal relationship)*, assignment *(task)*, business *(affair)*, business *(occupation)*, calling, charge *(responsibility)*, charge *(empower)*, commitment *(responsibility)*, delegation *(envoy)*, deputation *(delegation)*, design *(intent)*, embassy, end *(intent)*, function, goal, job, objective, occupation *(vocation)*, purpose, role

mission of the ambassador embassy

missive dispatch *(message)*, note *(brief comment)*

missives correspondence *(communication by letters)*

misspend dissipate *(expend foolishly)*, misemploy

misstate delude, equivocate, fabricate *(make up)*, falsify, feign, invent *(falsify)*, lie *(falsify)*, misguide, misinform, mislabel, mislead, misrepresent, palter, prevaricate, slant

misstated inaccurate, inexact, mendacious

misstatement abuse *(corrupt practice)*, color *(deceptive appearance)*, error, false pretense, falsehood, falsification, lie, miscue, misestimation, misrepresentation, overstatement, perjury, pretext, story *(falsehood)*

misstatement of fact misrepresentation

misstep delinquency *(misconduct)*, fault *(mistake)*, indiscretion, lapse *(expiration)*, lapse *(fall into error)*, miscue

missum facere discharge *(dismiss)*

mist obfuscate

mistakable uncertain *(ambiguous)*

mistake catachresis, defect, err, error, failure *(lack of success)*, fallacy, indiscretion, lapse *(expiration)*, misapplication, misapprehend, miscalculate, miscarriage, misconstrue, miscue, misdeed, misestimation, misinterpret, misjudge, misjudgment, misread, misstatement, misunderstand, oversight *(carelessness)*, wrong

mistake of the court injustice

mistaken errant, erroneous, fallacious, false *(inaccurate)*, faulty, illogical, improper, inaccurate, incorrect, misadvised, unsound *(fallacious)*

mistaken belief error

mistaken idea fallacy

mistaken judgment error

misteach distort, misdirect, misguide, misinform, mislead, misrepresent

misterm misnomer

misthink misjudge

misticket mislabel

mistimed inauspicious, inopportune, premature, untimely

mistiness indistinctness

mistitle mislabel

mistranslate distort, misinterpret, misread

mistranslated inexact

mistranslation catachresis, distortion, error, misapplication

mistreat abuse *(misuse)*, abuse *(victimize)*, exploit *(take advantage of)*, ill use, maltreat, misemploy, persecute

mistreatment abuse *(physical misuse)*, disservice, misuse, molestation, oppression, violation, wrong

mistrust apprehension *(fear)*, cloud *(suspicion)*, disbelieve, discount *(disbelieve)*, discredit, doubt *(suspicion)*, doubt *(distrust)*, incredulity, misdoubt, misgiving, qualm, rejection, suspect *(distrust)*

mistrustful cynical, doubtful, incredulous, leery, resentful, suspicious *(distrustful)*

mistrustfulness cloud *(suspicion)*, doubt *(suspicion)*, incredulity, misgiving

mistrusting doubtful

misty inconspicuous, indistinct, opaque, unclear

misunderstand err, misapprehend, misconceive, misconstrue, misinterpret, misjudge, misread, mistake

misunderstanding argument *(contention)*, catachresis, conflict, difference, error, fault *(mistake)*, incompatibility *(difference)*, misapplication, miscue, misestimation, misjudgment, rift *(disagreement)*

misunderstood vague

misusage abuse *(corrupt practice)*, abuse *(physical misuse)*, catachresis,

distortion, misapplication, misappropriation, mischief, misuse, waste
misuse abuse *(corrupt practice)*, conversion *(misappropriation)*, convert
(misappropriate), dissipate *(expend foolishly)*, embezzle, endanger, exploit *(take
advantage of)*, exploitation, harass,
harm, harrow, ill use, manipulate *(control unfairly)*, misapplication, misappropriation, misemploy, mishandle *(maltreat)*, mishandle *(mismanage)*, mismanage, mistreat, misusage, molest
(annoy), persecute, perversion, pervert,
purloin, taint *(corrupt)*, violation, waste
misuse entrusted monies defalcate
misuse of funds misapplication
misuse of power oppression
misuse of words distortion, error,
misapplication
misused aggrieved *(harmed)*
misventure disaster
mitite modicum
mitigare allay, assuage, extenuate,
mitigate, mollify
mitigate abate *(lessen)*, adjust *(resolve)*, allay, alleviate, ameliorate, assuage, commute, curb, decrease, dilute,
diminish, ease, extenuate, justify,
lessen, lull, meliorate, moderate *(temper)*, modify *(moderate)*, mollify, obtund, palliate *(abate)*, relax, relieve
(free from burden), remedy, remit
(relax), soothe, subside
mitigating narcotic, palliative *(abating)*
mitigating circumstance justification
mitigating circumstances extenuating circumstances
mitigatio mitigation
mitigation abatement *(reduction)*, decrease, diminution, excuse, extenuating
circumstances, justification, moderation, mollification, relief *(release)*, remission, solace
mitigative narcotic, palliative *(abating)*
mitiorem facere mitigate
mitis lenient
mittere cast *(throw)*, discharge *(shoot)*,
dispatch *(send off)*, remit *(send payment)*, send
mittimus citation *(charge)*, commitment *(confinement)*
mix agitate *(shake up)*, amalgamate,
combine *(join together)*, commingle,
conjoin, consolidate *(strengthen)*, consolidate *(unite)*, denature, desegregate,
diffuse, incorporate *(include)*, integration *(amalgamation)*, intersperse, join
(bring together), merge, pool, solution
(substance), unite
mix together commingle
mix up agitate *(shake up)*, confuse
(bewilder), confuse *(create disorder)*,
discompose, disrupt, muddle, obfuscate,
perplex
mix-up embroilment, entanglement
(confusion)
mixed composite, compound, conglomerate, conjoint, dissimilar, diverse, heterogeneous, inextricable, joint, miscellaneous, multifarious, multiple, nonsectarian, promiscuous
mixed up labyrinthine
mixing concrescence
mixture coalescence, coalition, consol-

idation, diversity, incorporation *(blend)*,
melange, merger, solution *(substance)*
mixup pandemonium
mnemonic reminder
mnemonic device reminder
moan deplore, plaint
mob assemblage, mass *(body of persons)*
mob law anarchy
mob rule anarchy, lynch law
mob swayer demagogue
mobile moving *(in motion)*, protean
mobilis movable, volatile
mobilization campaign
mobilize call *(summon)*, consolidate
(unite), convene, dispatch *(send off)*,
employ *(make use of)*, impel
mobilized ready *(prepared)*
mobocracy lynch law
mobster hoodlum, racketeer
mock copy, deceptive, delusive, disdain, disgrace, disparage, false *(not
genuine)*, flout, harass, humiliate,
illude, imitation, jape, jeer, meretricious, misrepresent, pillory, pose *(impersonate)*, quasi, sham, simulate, spurious, synthetic, untrue
mockery caricature, dishonor
(shame), disparagement, disrespect, falsification, irony, parody, pretense *(ostentation)*, ridicule, travesty
mocking caustic, cynical, disdainful
mode avenue *(means of attainment)*,
conduit *(channel)*, course, form *(arrangement)*, habit, instrumentality,
manner *(behavior)*, means *(opportunity)*, method, modus operandi, parlance, practice *(custom)*, practice *(procedure)*, procedure, style, tenor, usage,
way *(channel)*
mode of action behavior, conduct
mode of behavior conduct
mode of communication forum *(medium)*
mode of expression context, phraseology
mode of living modus vivendi
mode of management course, policy
(plan of action), practice *(procedure)*,
system
mode of operation avenue *(means of
attainment)*, modus operandi, procedure, process *(course)*, strategy
mode of procedure course, expedient, maneuver *(tactic)*, modus operandi,
practice *(custom)*
mode of proceeding manner *(behavior)*
mode of reasoning dialectic
mode of speech phraseology
mode of use procedure
model absolute *(ideal)*, build *(construct)*, case *(example)*, code, copy, criterion, design *(construction plan)*, epitome, example, exemplar, exemplary,
forge *(produce)*, form *(arrangement)*, illustration, instance, laudable, make,
norm, paradigm, paragon, paramount,
pattern, precedent, principle *(axiom)*,
professional *(stellar)*, prototype, representative *(example)*, rule *(guide)*, sample, specimen, standard, style, symbol,
typical
model after mock *(imitate)*
model instance precedent
model of virtue paragon

model oneself after pose *(impersonate)*
moderari control *(regulate)*, modify
(moderate)
moderate adjust *(regulate)*, allay, alleviate, alter, arbitrate *(conciliate)*, assuage, average *(standard)*, controlled
(restrained), curb, de minimus, ease,
extenuate, fair *(satisfactory)*, imperfect,
intercede, intermediate, judge, judicious, lenient, lessen, marginal, mediate, mediocre, minimal, mitigate, mollify, negligible, nominal, nonpartisan,
obtund, officiate, palliate *(abate)*, passable, peaceable, regulate *(adjust)*,
relax, relieve *(free from burden)*, remit
(relax), restrain, soothe, subdue, subside, usual
moderate in severity mitigate
moderated qualified *(conditioned)*,
tempered
moderately good fair *(satisfactory)*
moderately large major
moderateness continence, moderation, neutrality, temperance
moderatio control *(supervision)*, restraint, temperance
moderation composure, continence,
control *(restriction)*, lenience, mitigation, regulation *(management)*, remission, restraint, temperance
moderatism moderation
moderator arbiter, arbitrator, chairman, go-between, intermediary, judge,
magistrate
moderator procurator
moderator referee, umpire
modern contemporary, novel, present
(current), progressive *(advocating
change)*, sophisticated, unprecedented,
unusual
modernist pioneer
modernization development *(progression)*, innovation, renewal
modernize meliorate, modify *(alter)*,
reconstruct, renew *(refurbish)*, renovate
modest de minimus, diffident, inconsiderable, inconspicuous, insubstantial,
marginal, mediocre, minimal, minor,
negligible, nominal, paltry, slight, unaffected *(sincere)*, unobtrusive, unpretentious
modestly fairly *(moderately)*
modesty decorum, propriety *(correctness)*
modicum minimum, paucity, scintilla
modicus reasonable *(fair)*, unpretentious
modifiable ambulatory, open-ended,
pliable, protean, provisional, variable
modification abatement *(reduction)*,
amendment *(correction)*, correction
(change), curtailment, innovation, qualification *(condition)*, transition, treatment
modification of the law amendment
(legislation)
modifications vicissitudes
modificatory restrictive
modified qualified *(conditioned)*, tempered
modified by conditions conditional,
dependent
modify abate *(lessen)*, adapt, alter,
amend, change, convert *(change use)*,
influence, moderate *(temper)*, qualify

(condition), reform, relax, restrict, revise, transform, treat *(process),* vary
modify by excisions delete, edit
modify sentence commute
modifying mitigating, palliative *(abating),* restrictive
modifying cause catalyst
modulate adapt, alleviate, alter, change, lessen, limit, obtund, palliate *(abate),* regulate *(adjust),* relax
modulation inflection, remission
modulatory palliative *(abating)*
module entity
modus kind, method, mode, moderation, restriction, style
modus operandi course
modus operandi procedure
moiety segment
moil commotion
mold character *(personal quality),* delineate, disposition *(inclination),* fabricate *(construct),* facsimile, forge *(produce),* form, frame *(construct),* influence, make, manufacture, militate, model, norm, nurture, organize *(unionize),* pattern, prototype, resemblance
moldable facile, flexible, malleable, pliable, pliant, sequacious
molded together inseparable
molder decay
moldering decadent
molding creation, edge *(border),* facsimile, manufacture
moldy stale
moles bulk
molest abuse *(victimize),* brutalize, debauch, distress, disturb, endanger, harrow, hector, irritate, misemploy, mishandle *(maltreat),* mistreat, pique, plague, press *(goad)*
molestation abuse *(physical misuse),* disturbance, mischief, nuisance
moleste ferre resent
molestia dissatisfaction
molestus irksome, oppressive
mollification reconciliation
mollify allay, assuage, disarm *(set at ease),* mitigate, moderate *(temper),* modify *(moderate),* pacify, placate, propitiate, reconcile, remedy, soothe, subdue
mollifying palliative *(abating)*
mollire mollify
molliri relent
mollis malleable, pliant, resilient, sensitive *(easily affected),* susceptible *(responsive)*
Molotov cocktail bomb
moment date, degree *(magnitude),* emphasis, import, importance, interest *(concern),* occasion, phase *(period),* point *(period of time),* significance, weight *(importance)*
moment of change landmark *(significant change)*
momentarily pro tempore
momentariness insignificance
momentary brief, ephemeral, immediate *(imminent),* pending *(imminent),* temporary, transient, transitory, volatile
momentous cardinal *(outstanding),* consequential *(substantial),* considerable, critical *(crucial),* crucial, decisive, important *(significant),* key, major, material *(important),* notable, noteworthy,

remarkable, serious *(grave),* stellar, strategic
momentousness importance, magnitude, materiality *(consequence),* significance
momentum headway, impetus
momentum importance, stress *(strain)*
momumental notable
monad individual, unit *(item)*
monarchy realm
monas individual
monens hortative
monere admonish *(warn),* caution
moneta currency
monetary commercial, financial, fiscal, mercantile, pecuniary
monetary benefit interest *(profit)*
monetary clause ad damnum clause
monetary exchange commerce
monetary gain interest *(profit)*
monetary help maintenance *(support of spouse)*
monetary remuneration compensation, indemnification
monetary reservoir bank
monetary return pay
monetary theory finance
monetary unit cash
monetary value expense *(cost)*
money assets, capital, cash, currency, finance, payment *(remittance),* possession *(property),* principal *(capital sum),* remuneration, substance *(material possessions)*
money back refund
money box bank
money chest coffer
money coming in income, proceeds
money conscious mercenary, provident *(frugal)*
money dealings finance
money due debt, setoff
money earned earnings
money expended cost *(expenses),* expenditure, expense *(cost),* overhead
money going out disbursement *(funds paid out)*
money hungry mercenary
money illegally acquired graft
money in actual use currency
money in bank deposit
money invested security *(stock)*
money matters finance
money order check *(instrument),* draft, note *(written promise to pay)*
money owed debt
money paid collection *(payment)*
money paid for passage fare
money saving economic
money sent remittance
money's worth tariff *(bill)*
money-conscious economical
money-making finance, gainful, profitable
money-saving economical
moneyed opulent, prosperous, solvent
moneyless bankrupt, destitute, insolvent, poor *(underprivileged)*
moneylessness poverty
moneymaking lucrative
moneys cash
moneys borrowed loan
moneys expended disbursement *(funds paid out)*
moneys paid out disbursement *(funds paid out)*

monger broker, dealer, merchant, vendor
monitio premonition
monition admonition, caution *(warning),* caveat, citation *(charge),* deterrence, deterrent, dispatch *(message),* guidance, indication, intelligence *(news),* notice *(warning),* notification, symptom, warning
monitor audit, bystander, chairman, check *(inspect),* examine *(study),* overhear, patrol, proctor, procurator, superintendent, symptom
monitorial hortative, prophetic
monitory informatory, ominous, portentous *(ominous),* presageful, prophetic
monitum premonition
monitus warning
monocratic dictatorial
monohemerous temporary
monolithical solid *(compact)*
monologue peroration
monomachy contest *(dispute)*
monomania obsession
monomaniac bigot
monopolistic organization trust *(combination of businesses)*
monopolium monopoly
monopolize immerse *(engross),* occupy *(engage),* possess
monopolize the thoughts occupy *(engage)*
monopoly consortium *(business cartel),* exclusion, franchise *(license),* trust *(combination of businesses)*
monosyllabic inarticulate
monotone prosaic
monotonous insistent, jejune *(dull),* lifeless *(dull),* pedestrian, ponderous, prolix, prosaic, repeated, repetitious, stale, usual
monster prodigious *(enormous)*
monstrosity atrocity
monstrous arrant *(onerous),* bad *(offensive),* delinquent *(guilty of a misdeed),* diabolic, flagrant, gross *(flagrant),* heinous, inexcusable, inordinate, malignant, nefarious, odious, offensive *(offending),* outrageous, prodigious *(enormous),* reprehensible, repulsive, unconscionable
monstrousness bestiality, disrepute
monument landmark *(conspicuous object),* remembrance *(commemoration)*
monumental noteworthy, prodigious *(enormous),* remarkable
monumentum monument
mood atmosphere, climate, disposition *(inclination),* emotion, spirit, state *(condition),* tenor
moodish fractious
moody despondent, disconsolate, fractious, froward, inconsistent, petulant, resentful, restive
moonshiner bootlegger
moored firm, stable
moot debate, dubious, equivocal, pose *(propound),* posit, problematic, propound, undecided
moot point problem, thesis
mope brood
mora check *(bar),* delay
moral blameless, clean, conscientious, ethical, high-minded, honest, incorruptible, just, law-abiding, meritorious,

proper, reputable, scrupulous, signification, upright
moral behavior ethics
moral certainty certitude
moral compulsion coercion
moral conduct ethics
moral consciousness conscience, responsibility *(conscience)*
moral degeneracy bad repute
moral excellence principle *(virtue)*, probity
moral faculty conscience, responsibility *(conscience)*
moral insensibility brutality
moral judgment ethics
moral necessity duty *(obligation)*
moral obligation allegiance, conscience, duty *(obligation)*, ethics, responsibility *(conscience)*
moral philosophy ethics
moral practice ethics
moral principles conscience, ethics
moral qualities character *(personal quality)*
moral rectitude ethics, honor *(good reputation)*, principle *(virtue)*
moral responsibility obligation *(duty)*
moral science casuistry
moral sense conscience, responsibility *(conscience)*
moral soundness integrity
moral strength ethics, integrity
moral tone ethics
moral turpitude bad repute
moral weakness foible
morale confidence *(faith)*
moralis ethical
moralism maxim
morality ethics, integrity, principle *(virtue)*, probity, propriety *(correctness)*, rectitude, responsibility *(conscience)*, right *(righteousness)*
morally fairly *(impartially)*
morally abandoned reprobate
morally evil profligate *(corrupt)*
morally impure lewd
morally unrestrained lewd
morals conduct, ethics, probity, right *(righteousness)*
morari pause
moratorium adjournment, cancellation, cessation *(interlude)*, deferment, delay, discontinuance *(interruption of a legal action)*, extension *(postponement)*, hiatus, pause, pendency, reprieve
moratory late *(tardy)*
morbid malignant, ominous, peccant *(unhealthy)*, pessimistic, pestilent
morbidly meditate brood
morbiferous deleterious, malignant, pernicious, pestilent
morbific deleterious, harmful, insalubrious, malignant, peccant *(unhealthy)*, pernicious, pestilent
morbifical insalubrious, malignant, pestilent
morbus disease
mordacious caustic, harsh, incisive, malignant, scathing, virulent
mordant astringent, bitter *(penetrating)*, harsh, incisive, mordacious, severe, trenchant
mordax caustic, cynical, incisive, scathing
mordent caustic

more additional, ancillary *(auxiliary)*
more advantageous preferable
more desirable preferable
more elevated superior *(higher)*
more in demand preferable
more or less inexact, on or about
more pleasing preferable
more popular preferable
more select preferable
more than due overdue
more than enough copious, excess, superfluous
more than half majority *(greater part)*
more than one multiple, several *(plural)*
more than one can tell innumerable
more than sufficient superfluous
more time extension *(postponement)*
morem gerere comply
moreover also
mores behavior, character *(personal quality)*
mores decorum
mori die
moribund decadent, in extremis
moronic fatuous, non compos mentis, obtuse, opaque
morose disconsolate, lugubrious, pessimistic
morosis incapacity
morosus fractious
morsel iota, minimum
mortal character *(an individual)*, conscious *(awake)*, deadly, ephemeral, lethal, live *(conscious)*, pernicious, person, pestilent
mortal body person
mortal remains corpse
mortalis person
mortalitas mortality
mortality death, demise *(death)*, fatality
mortalness mortality
mortals humanity *(mankind)*
mortar cement
mortem obire die
mortgage cloud *(incumbrance)*, encumber *(financially obligate)*, encumbrance, hypothecation, pawn
mortgage holder obligee
mortgaged fully secured
mortgagee creditor, obligee
mortgagor debtor, obligor
mortgatee backer
mortifer deadly, lethal
mortiferous deadly, fatal, insalubrious, lethal
mortification disgrace, embarrassment, ignominy
mortify badger, demean *(make lower)*, discompose, disgrace, embarrass, humiliate, offend *(insult)*, plague
mortuus dead, defunct
mos habit, practice *(procedure)*, usage
mosaic composite, compound, miscellaneous
most majority *(greater part)*, maximum *(pinnacle)*, utmost
most carefully selected group elite
most complete definitive
most considerable principal
most desirable best
most distant extreme *(last)*, ultimate
most eminent superlative
most excellent best

most frequently as a rule, generally
most important cardinal *(outstanding)*, master, principal
most important character protagonist
most important point emphasis
most influential leading *(ranking first)*
most often as a rule, generally
most powerful principal, sovereign *(absolute)*
most precise definitive
most recent last *(preceding)*
most remote extreme *(last)*, ultimate
mostly as a rule, purely *(simply)*, quasi
mot catchword
mote minimum
mother parents
mother country home *(place of origin)*
motherhood maternity
motherland home *(place of origin)*
motherliness maternity
motif content *(meaning)*, subject *(topic)*
motile moving *(in motion)*
motion application, call *(appeal)*, campaign, circulation, course, overture, petition, prayer, procedure, proposal *(suggestion)*, recommendation, request, suggestion, transition
motion docket calendar *(list of cases)*
motionless firm, idle, inactive, indolent, otiose, placid, rigid, stable, stagnant, static, torpid
motionlessness inaction, inertia
motivate cause, coax, evoke, further, impel, induce, influence, inspire, lobby, originate, persuade, prevail *(persuade)*, prevail upon, prompt, provoke, spirit, stimulate, urge
motivated by a desire for money mercenary
motivated by greed mercenary
motivating provocative
motivating force catalyst, stimulus
motivating idea end *(intent)*, purpose
motivation catalyst, cause *(reason)*, determinant, end *(intent)*, impulse, incentive, instigation, origination, persuasion, provocation, rationale, reason *(basis)*
motivator abettor
motive animus, basis, cause *(reason)*, design *(intent)*, desire, determinant, end *(intent)*, ground, impetus, impulse, incentive, intent, moving *(in motion)*, origination, point *(purpose)*, provocation, purpose, rationale, reason *(basis)*, source, stimulus, target
motiveless arbitrary and capricious
motley composite, compound, diverse, heterogeneous, miscellaneous, multifarious
motor road causeway
motorway causeway
motto expression *(comment)*, phrase
motus commotion, disturbance, insurrection, mutiny, rebellion, revolt, sedition
moulder degenerate
mouldering dilapidated
mount accrue *(increase)*, increase, originate, progress
mount guard protect

mounted accrued

mourn deplore, repent

mourn for regret

mourn with sympathize

mournful despondent, disconsolate, lamentable, lugubrious, querulous, solemn

mourning disconsolate

mouth entrance, enunciate, express, phrase, recite, utter

mouthpiece medium, protagonist, spokesman

mouthy flatulent, fustian, inflated *(bombastic)*

movable ambulatory, amenable, disposable, open *(persuasible)*, pliant, possession *(property)*, protean, receptive, suasible, susceptible *(responsive)*

movable article of property chattel

movable property effects

movables chattel, commodities, merchandise, paraphernalia *(personal belongings)*, possessions, property *(possessions)*

movant petitioner

move act *(undertaking)*, carry *(transport)*, constrain *(compel)*, dislocate, displace *(remove)*, further, impress *(affect deeply)*, incite, influence, inspire, interest, maneuver *(tactic)*, maneuver, motivate, operate, operation, persuade, pose *(propound)*, prevail *(persuade)*, prevail upon, proffer, prompt, propose, propound, provoke, reach, reason *(persuade)*, recommend, remove *(transfer)*, spirit, step, stimulate, transport, undertaking *(enterprise)*, urge, vacate *(leave)*, venture

move across cross *(intersect)*

move ahead continue *(persevere)*, endure *(last)*, keep *(continue)*, proceed *(go forward)*, progress, resume

move aimlessly loiter

move at an accelerated rate of speed race

move away part *(leave)*, quit *(evacuate)*

move back ebb, retreat

move backward regress

move by persuasion prevail upon

move fast hasten

move forward gain, impel, proceed *(go forward)*

move furtively lurk

move in waves fluctuate, oscillate

move into occupy *(take possession)*

move near approach

move off abandon *(physically leave)*

move on dispatch *(send off)*, leave *(depart)*, progress

move onward progress

move out evacuate, move *(alter position)*, part *(leave)*, vacate *(leave)*

move quickly hasten

move secretly prowl

move speedily hasten

move strongly impress *(affect deeply)*

move to locate

move to action constrain *(compel)*, motivate, stimulate

move to and fro oscillate, vacillate

move to anger provoke

move toward approach, border *(approach)*, gravitate

move under cover prowl

move up expedite, prefer, promote

(advance), raise *(advance)*

move up and down beat *(pulsate)*

moveant applicant *(petitioner)*

moved inclined

movement activity, band, campaign, circulation, course, denomination, dispatch *(promptness)*, operation, outflow, progress, transition, transmittal

movement forward progress

movement of population immigration

movement toward adulthood growth *(evolution)*

movement toward maturity growth *(evolution)*

mover advocate *(counselor)*, catalyst, special interest

movere impress *(affect deeply)*, influence

moving convincing, eloquent, impulsive *(impelling)*, incisive, itinerant, persuasive, potent, prevailing *(having superior force)*, profound *(intense)*, progressive *(going forward)*, sensitive *(easily affected)*

moving cause motive

moving force impetus

moving power motive

moving spirit catalyst, motive

movingly expressive eloquent

mow down obliterate

much innumerable

much the same approximate, comparable *(capable of comparison)*, pendent

much touted renowned

much used trite

muchness quantity

muck pollute

muckrake disapprove *(condemn)*, expose

muckraking disparagement

mucky sordid

muddle blind *(obscure)*, complex *(entanglement)*, confound, confuse *(bewilder)*, confuse *(create disorder)*, confusion *(turmoil)*, discompose, disorder *(lack of order)*, disorganize, disorient, embroilment, imbroglio, obfuscate, perplex, plight, quagmire, turmoil

muddled complex, labyrinthine

muddleheaded opaque

muddy opaque, pollute, unclear

muffle cloak, disguise, repress, shroud, stifle, subdue, suppress

muffled covert, indistinct

muffler damper *(stopper)*

mug assail

mulcere soothe

mulct bilk, deceive, defraud, deprive, dupe, exact, fine, fine, forfeiture *(thing forfeited)*, peculate, penalize, punishment, seize *(confiscate)*, steal, trover

mulctuary penal, punitive

mulish inflexible, intractable, obdurate, pertinacious, recalcitrant, restive, uncontrollable

mull muse

mull over brood, consider, deliberate, ponder, reflect *(ponder)*, review, study, weigh

multa fine, penalty

multare fine, sentence

multifarious composite, compound, diverse, manifold, miscellaneous, multifold, multiple

multifariousness difference, diversifi-

cation, diversity

multifold manifold, multiple

multiform compound, dissimilar, diverse, heterogeneous, manifold, miscellaneous, multifarious, multifold, protean

multiformity diversification, diversity

multigenerous multifarious, multifold

multilateral trade commerce

multiloquent voluble

multipartite bicameral

multiphase protean

multiple composite, compound, manifold, multifold, repeated

multiplex complex, complex *(entanglement)*, composite, compound, manifold

multiplex miscellaneous, multifarious, multifold, multiple

multiplicare proliferate

multiplicate manifold, multifold

multiplication accession *(enlargement)*, growth *(increase)*

multiplicity diversity, quantity

multiplied accrued

multiply accrue *(increase)*, accumulate *(enlarge)*, bear *(yield)*, compound, enlarge, expand, heighten *(augment)*, increase, proliferate, propagate *(increase)*, pullulate, reproduce

multiplying cumulative *(increasing)*, cumulative *(intensifying)*

multipotent influential, powerful

multisyllabic sesquipedalian

multitude assemblage, assembly, body *(collection)*, collection *(assembly)*, conglomeration, congregation, mass *(body of persons)*, plurality, populace, quantity

multitudinary profuse

multitudinous innumerable, manifold, multifold, multiple, multiplicity, myriad, populous, profuse, rife

multitudinousness quantity

multitudo mass *(body of persons)*, plurality

mum laconic, speechless, taciturn, unresponsive

mummery parody

mundane civil *(public)*, material *(physical)*, physical, profane, prosaic

mundivagant moving *(in motion)*

mundus clean

munerari present *(make a gift)*

municipal civic, civil *(public)*, local, public *(affecting people)*

municipal code ordinance

municipal regulation bylaw, ordinance

municipality city, community

municipalization condemnation *(seizure)*

municipalize condemn *(seize)*

munificence benevolence *(disposition to do good)*, charity, donation, goodwill, largess *(generosity)*, philanthropy

munificent benevolent, charitable *(benevolent)*, liberal *(generous)*, nonprofit, philanthropic, profuse

munificus liberal *(generous)*

muniment ammunition, certificate, charter *(license)*, form *(document)*

muniments deed

munimentum safeguard

munition ammunition, gun

munitions bomb, weapons

munus calling, department, duty *(obligation)*, function, gift *(present)*, office, post

munus obire discharge *(perform)*

murder assassination, destroy *(efface)*, dispatch *(act of putting to death)*, dispatch *(put to death)*, extinguish, homicide, killing, manslaughter, slay

murder by stealth assassination

murder victim corpse

murderer criminal, lawbreaker

murderous deadly, diabolic, fatal, lethal, malignant, pernicious, pestilent, ruthless, sinister

murderous assault killing

mure detain *(hold in custody)*

murkiness indistinctness

murky obscure *(faint)*, privy, unclear

murmur speak

muscle sinew, strength

muscular powerful

muse brood, concentrate *(pay attention)*, consider, digest *(comprehend)*, observe *(remark)*, ponder, reflect *(ponder)*, speculate *(conjecture)*, study

museful cogitative, pensive

mushroom proliferate

musing contemplation, hindsight, introspection, pensive, preoccupation, reflection *(thought)*

must requirement, requisite

muster call *(summon)*, collect *(gather)*, collection *(assembly)*, convene, garner, levy, marshal, meet, raise *(collect)*, recruit, rendezvous, rendezvous, roll

muster up call *(summon)*

mustering company *(assemblage)*

musty stale

mutabilis mutable

mutabilitas inconsistency

mutability irregularity

mutable aleatory *(uncertain)*, ambulatory, convertible, faithless, inconsistent, irresolute, noncommittal, pliable, protean, unpredictable, unsettled

mutare alter, innovation, modify *(alter)*, vary

mutate convert *(change use)*, transform, vary

mute inarticulate, moderate *(temper)*, repress, speechless, stifle, subdue, taciturn, unresponsive

mutilare mutilate

mutilate damage, deface, destroy *(efface)*, disable, harm, maim, spoil *(impair)*

mutilated broken *(fractured)*, defective, imperfect, marred

mutilation defacement, defect, detriment, harm

mutineer insurgent, malcontent

mutineering disloyalty, insurrection

mutinous contumacious, disobedient, disorderly, insubordinate, irresponsible, lawless, radical *(favoring drastic change)*, recalcitrant, renitent, restive, unruly

mutinousness disloyalty, outbreak

mutiny defect, defiance, defy, desertion, disloyalty, disobey, infidelity, insurrection, outbreak, rebel, rebellion, resistance, revolt, secede, sedition, treason

mutter speak

mutual cognate, collective, common

(shared), concordant, correlative, joint, reciprocal, related

mutual accord conciliation

mutual agreement arrangement *(understanding)*, bargain, composition *(agreement in bankruptcy)*, conciliation, consensus, contract, indenture, pact, policy *(contract)*, quid pro quo

mutual appreciation rapport

mutual assent agreement *(concurrence)*, arrangement *(understanding)*

mutual assistance coaction, concert

mutual attraction affection

mutual aversion feud

mutual company partnership

mutual concern coalition

mutual concession adjustment, composition *(agreement in bankruptcy)*, compromise, conciliation

mutual consideration comity, quid pro quo

mutual dependence mutuality

mutual exchange interview

mutual exclusiveness antithesis, difference

mutual forgiveness reconciliation

mutual friendliness rapprochement

mutual intercourse contact *(association)*

mutual ownership pool

mutual pledge agreement *(contract)*, bargain, compact, contract, pact, understanding *(agreement)*

mutual profit boom *(prosperity)*

mutual promise agreement *(concurrence)*, arrangement *(understanding)*, compact, contract, mutual understanding, pact

mutual relation mutuality

mutual relationship privity

mutual respect comity

mutual sympathy consensus

mutual transfer assignment *(transfer of ownership)*, delivery

mutual understanding accommodation *(adjustment)*, accord, adjustment, agreement *(concurrence)*, bargain, cartel, compatibility, conciliation, consensus, covenant, quid pro quo

mutual undertaking arrangement *(understanding)*, bargain, contract, indenture, league, policy *(contract)*

mutuality coaction, rapport, rapprochement, reciprocity, relation *(connection)*, relationship *(connection)*

mutuality of interest privity

mutually agreeable consensual

mutually agreed concerted

mutually assent agree *(contract)*

mutually opposed opposite

mutually related correlative

mutually understood consensual

mutuari borrow

mutus mute, speechless

mutuum loan

mutuus mutual *(reciprocal)*, reciprocal

muzzle constraint *(restriction)*, curb, disadvantage, disarm *(divest of arms)*, discipline *(control)*, hamper, inhibit, prevent, repress, restrict, stifle, strangle, withhold

myriad innumerable, manifold, multiple, profuse

myriads quantity

mysterious covert, elusive, enigmatic, esoteric, evasive, furtive, hidden, inap-

prehensible, incomprehensible, indefinable, indefinite, indistinct, ineffable, inexplicable, inscrutable, obscure *(abstruse)*, oracular, peculiar *(curious)*, private *(confidential)*, privy, problematic, recondite, secret, surreptitious, uncanny, uncertain *(ambiguous)*, undisclosed, vague

mysteriousness indistinctness

mystery enigma, problem, question *(issue)*, secret

mystic covert, esoteric, hidden, inapprehensible, incomprehensible, inexplicable, mysterious, recondite

mystical covert, esoteric, hidden, inapprehensible, incomprehensible, inexplicable, mysterious, oracular, recondite, sacrosanct

mysticism mystery

mystification confusion *(ambiguity)*

mystified incognizant, lost *(disoriented)*

mystify confound, confuse *(bewilder)*, delude, disorient, elude, equivocate, hoodwink, obfuscate, perplex

mystifying enigmatic, labyrinthine, mysterious, peculiar *(curious)*, uncanny, uncertain *(ambiguous)*

myth fiction, figment, story *(falsehood)*

mythic fictitious, illusory

mythical fictitious

mythological fictitious, illusory

N

nafarius heinous

nag annoy, bicker, browbeat, hector, importune, irritate, obsess, plague, request

nagging critical *(faultfinding)*, petulant, querulous

naive credulous, inexperienced, ingenuous, puerile, unaccustomed, unaffected *(sincere)*, unsuspecting

naiveness credulity

naivete credulity, nescience

naked manifest, perceivable, perceptible

name appoint, assign *(designate)*, bear *(adduce)*, call *(title)*, call *(title)*, character *(reputation)*, cite *(state)*, classify, cognomen, define, delegate, denominate, denomination, denounce *(inform against)*, designate, designation *(symbol)*, distinction *(reputation)*, elect *(choose)*, identify, induct, instate, invest *(vest)*, label, mention, nominate, notoriety, phrase, pigeonhole, prestige, reputation, select, specify, stipulate, term *(expression)*, title *(designation)*

name expressly enumerate

name for office nominate

name inaccurately mistake

name incorrectly mislabel

name one by one enumerate

name to fill an appointment delegate

named aforesaid, before mentioned, said, select

named representative nominee *(candidate)*, officer

nameless anonymous, ineffable

namely a savoir

namesake call *(title)*

naming appointment *(act of designat-*

ing), call *(title)*, nomination, selection *(choice)*
nancisci obtain
narcissism pride
narcissistic orgulous
narcotic cannabis
narcotic preparation drug
narcotic substance drug
narcotical narcotic
narcotize drug
narrare narrative
narrate communicate, convey *(communicate)*, detail *(particularize)*, inform *(notify)*, recite, recount, relate *(tell)*
narratio account *(report)*, narration, recital, story *(narrative)*
narration account *(report)*, recital, report *(detailed account)*, representation *(statement)*, story *(narrative)*
narrative description, descriptive, journal, narration, recital, representation *(statement)*, scenario, statement
narrator informant
narrow attenuate, constrict *(compress)*, decrease, illiberal, limit, limited, minimal, moderate *(temper)*, one-sided, parochial, partial *(part)*, precise, provincial, qualify *(condition)*, reduce, restrict, restrictive, specialize, specific, tenuous, uncompromising
narrow means indigence, poverty, privation
narrow search indagation, inquiry *(systematic investigation)*
narrow-minded dogmatic, illiberal, narrow, one-sided, parochial, partial *(biased)*, provincial, unbending
narrow-minded person pedant
narrow-mindedness intolerance, prejudice *(preconception)*
narrowing centralization, decrease
narrowness intolerance
nascence nascency
nascency birth *(beginning)*, origin *(source)*, origination
nascent inchoate, incipient, initial, original *(initial)*, primary
nastiness mischief
nasty bad *(offensive)*, bitter *(penetrating)*, harmful, heinous, loathsome, malignant, objectionable, obnoxious, odious, offensive *(offending)*, perverse, repulsive, severe, unsavory, vicious
nasty blow disaster
natal native *(inborn)*, original *(initial)*
nation nationality, polity, populace, population, public, state *(political unit)*
national domestic *(indigenous)*, federal, public *(affecting people)*
national culture civilization
national group nationality
national status nationality
nationality blood, polity
nationalization condemnation *(seizure)*
nationalize condemn *(seize)*, naturalize *(make a citizen)*
nationwide public *(affecting people)*
native born *(innate)*, citizen, domestic *(indigenous)*, domiciliary, hereditary, inhabitant, inherent, innate, intrinsic *(belonging)*, local, natural, organic, original *(initial)*, prime *(original)*, regional, resident
native character disposition *(inclination)*

native environment home *(domicile)*
native ground home *(place of origin)*
native grown domestic *(indigenous)*
native hearth home *(place of origin)*
native land home *(place of origin)*, nationality
native reason common sense
native soil home *(place of origin)*
native tendency instinct
natives population
nativity birth *(emergence of young)*, genesis, nascency, nationality, origin *(source)*, origination
nativus natural
natura character *(personal quality)*, disposition *(inclination)*, essence
natura et ingenium gift *(flair)*
natural bodily, born *(innate)*, common *(customary)*, conventional, familiar *(customary)*, genuine, habitual, informal, ingenuous, inherent, innate, legitimate *(lawfully conceived)*, naive, native *(inborn)*, normal *(regular)*, organic, physical, prevailing *(current)*, real, realistic, regular *(conventional)*, simple, spontaneous, unaffected *(sincere)*, undistorted, unobtrusive, unpretentious, usual, veridical
natural ability gift *(flair)*, specialty *(special aptitude)*
natural course practice *(custom)*
natural courtesy decorum
natural disposition tendency
natural fitness disposition *(inclination)*
natural impulse conatus
natural liking affinity *(regard)*
natural meaning connotation
natural quality gift *(flair)*
natural right equity *(justice)*
natural sagacity common sense
natural science ecology
natural sense instinct, proclivity
natural state matter of course
natural tendency conatus, disposition *(inclination)*, instinct, predisposition
natural turn of mind character *(personal quality)*
naturalistic realistic
naturalize adopt, inure *(accustom)*
naturally consequently, generally
naturalness informality
nature animus, center *(essence)*, character *(personal quality)*, characteristic, color *(complexion)*, complexion, composition *(makeup)*, consequence *(significance)*, content *(meaning)*, content *(structure)*, disposition *(inclination)*, essence, frame *(mood)*, kind, personality, posture *(attitude)*, predisposition, quality *(attribute)*, quality *(grade)*, spirit, temperament, tendency, tenor, trait
nature study ecology
naught nullity
naughtiness mischief
naughty improper, iniquitous, peccant *(culpable)*, perverse, reprehensible, reprobate
naulum fare
nauseate repel *(disgust)*
nauseating loathsome, obnoxious, offensive *(offending)*, repugnant *(exciting aversion)*, repulsive, unsavory
nauseous loathsome, repulsive, unsavory

navigable open *(accessible)*, passable
navigate direct *(show)*, oversee
navus active
ne plus ultra absolute *(ideal)*
ne plus ultra maximum *(pinnacle)*
ne'er-do-well derelict
near border *(approach)*, cognate, congruous, contiguous, forthcoming, future, immediate *(not distant)*, imminent, inevitable, instant, local, pending *(imminent)*, present *(current)*, proximate, quasi
near at hand close *(near)*, future, immediate *(imminent)*, imminent, instant, present *(attendant)*
near by immediate *(not distant)*
near death in extremis
near in time present *(current)*
near one's end in extremis
near relation next of kin
nearby close *(near)*, local, present *(attendant)*
nearest proximate
nearest blood relation next of kin
nearest relative by blood next of kin
nearing forthcoming, immediate *(imminent)*, imminent
nearing completion determinable *(liable to be terminated)*
nearly almost
nearly accurate approximate, inexact
nearly allied consanguineous
nearly correct approximate, inexact
nearly equal approximate, approximate
nearly perfect approximate
nearly related consanguineous
nearly resembling approximate
nearly rival approximate
nearness comparison, connection *(abutment)*, presence *(attendance)*, propinquity *(proximity)*, relation *(connection)*, relationship *(connection)*
nearness of blood propinquity *(kinship)*
nearness of relation propinquity *(kinship)*
neat meticulous, unadulterated
nebulose nebulous
nebulosity indistinctness, opacity
nebulosus nebulous
nebulous debatable, elusive, enigmatic, equivocal, inconspicuous, indistinct, inexpressive, obscure *(faint)*, opaque, recondite, uncertain *(ambiguous)*, vague
nebulousness incomprehensible
necessaries maintenance *(support of spouse)*
necessarii kindred
necessarily a priori, consequently
necessarily connected appurtenant
necessarius indispensable, inevitable, integral, requisite, unavoidable *(inevitable)*, urgent
necessary binding, cardinal *(basic)*, central *(essential)*, compelling, compulsory, desideratum, essential *(required)*, exigent, fundamental, imperative, important *(urgent)*, indispensable, integral, mandatory, material *(important)*, need *(requirement)*, obligatory, peremptory *(imperative)*, primary, requisite, unavoidable *(inevitable)*, urgent
necessary attribute necessity, need

(requirement)

necessary component necessity, need *(requirement)*

necessary condition prerequisite

necessary item prerequisite

necessary to life vital

necessitas compulsion *(coercion)*, necessary, necessity

necessitate call *(demand)*, coerce, compel, constrain *(compel)*, enforce, entail, exact, force *(coerce)*, impose *(enforce)*, press *(constrain)*, require *(compel)*, require *(need)*

necessitated bound, indispensable, mandatory, necessary *(required)*, obligatory, requisite

necessitation duress, enforcement, force *(compulsion)*, requirement, requisition

necessities necessary, sustenance

necessities of life maintenance *(support of spouse)*

necessitous destitute, exigent, impecunious, important *(urgent)*, mandatory, necessary *(required)*, poor *(underprivileged)*, urgent

necessitousness emergency, indigence, necessary, need *(deprivation)*, poverty

necessitude force *(compulsion)*, necessary, need *(deprivation)*, privation

necessitudo affinity *(family ties)*

necessity burden, coercion, compulsion *(coercion)*, desideratum, enforcement, exigency, force *(compulsion)*, market *(demand)*, necessary, need *(deprivation)*, need *(requirement)*, obligation *(duty)*, poverty, prerequisite, pressure, priority, privation, requirement, requisition, sine qua non

necrosis demise *(death)*

nectarean savory

nectareous palatable, sapid, savory

need absence *(omission)*, compulsion *(obsession)*, contribution *(indemnification)*, dearth, deficiency, desideratum, emergency, entail, exigency, foible, force *(compulsion)*, indigence, insufficiency, lack, market *(demand)*, necessary, necessity, paucity, poverty, prerequisite, pressure, privation, requirement, requisition, stress *(strain)*

need for action emergency

needed essential *(required)*, exigent, fundamental, important *(urgent)*, indispensable, integral, necessary *(required)*, requisite, vital

needed item prerequisite

needful destitute, essential *(required)*, exigent, imperative, integral, poor *(underprivileged)*, requisite

needfulness emergency, priority

neediness indigence, poverty, privation

needing perfunctory

needing outside support dependent

needle annoy, harrow, harry *(harass)*, irritate, pique, plague, stimulus

needless excess, excessive, expendable, extraneous, gratuitous *(unwarranted)*, injudicious, inordinate, nonessential, redundant, superfluous, undue *(excessive)*, unessential, unnecessary, unwarranted

needlessness redundancy

needy destitute, impecunious, penuri-

ous, poor *(underprivileged)*

needy circumstances indigence, poverty

nefandus heinous

nefarious bad *(offensive)*, blameful, blameworthy, contemptible, contemptuous, delinquent *(guilty of a misdeed)*, diabolic, dishonest, disreputable, felonious, flagrant, heinous, immoral, inexpiable, iniquitous, irregular *(improper)*, malignant, objectionable, obnoxious, outrageous, peccant *(culpable)*, profligate *(corrupt)*, reprehensible, reprobate, scandalous, sinister

nefarious act tortious act

nefariousness atrocity, delinquency *(misconduct)*, disrepute

nefarius felon, nefarious

nefas atrocity

nefastus inauspicious

negans negative

negare deny *(contradict)*, deny *(refuse to grant)*

negate abolish, abrogate *(annul)*, adeem, annul, cancel, challenge, contradict, contravene, controvert, counter, counteract, countercharge, countervail, demonstrate *(protest)*, deny *(contradict)*, disaccord, disaffirm, disallow, disapprove *(reject)*, disavow, disobey, disown *(deny the validity)*, disprove, dissent *(withhold assent)*, fight *(counteract)*, gainsay, impugn, neutralize, nullify, oppose, prohibit, protest, rebut, recant, refute, repeal, repudiate, rescind, revoke, vacate *(void)*, vitiate

negated null *(invalid)*, null and void

negating contradictory

negatio denial, negation

negation absence *(omission)*, ademption, annulment, answer *(judicial response)*, answer *(reply)*, antipode, cancellation, confutation, contradiction, contravention, counterargument, declination, defeasance, denial, disagreement, disapprobation, disapproval, discharge *(annulment)*, disclaimer, prohibition, refusal, rejection, renunciation, repudiation, rescision, retraction, revocation

negation of allegations demurrer

negative challenge, contradict, contrary, disadvantageous, disapprove *(reject)*, disavow, disown *(deny the validity)*, dispute *(contest)*, dissent *(withhold assent)*, negate, opposite, perverse, prohibit, rebut, recusant, refuse, veto, vitiate

negative answer denial, refusal

negative compulsion coercion

negative evidence answer *(judicial response)*, contradiction

negative result miscarriage

negativistic perverse

negatory antipathetic *(oppositional)*, contradictory, contrary, negative

neglect blame *(culpability)*, break *(violate)*, default, delinquency *(failure of duty)*, dereliction, desuetude, disinterest *(lack of interest)*, disobey, disregard *(omission)*, disregard *(unconcern)*, disregard, disrepair, disuse, eschew, exclude, ignore, inconsideration, indifference, laches, laxity, leave *(allow to remain)*, maladministration, mismanage, misprision, nonpayment, nonperfor-

mance, nonuse, omission, omit, overlook *(disregard)*, override, oversight *(cacarelessness)*, pretermit, procrastinate, rebuff, reject, rejection, repudiate, shirk, shun, spurn

neglect of duty delict, nonfeasance

neglect of obligation delinquency *(failure of duty)*

neglect one's duty default

neglect to obey disoblige

neglect to perform omission

neglected derelict *(abandoned)*, outmoded

neglectful blameful, careless, derelict *(negligent)*, disobedient, heedless, improvident, imprudent, inadvertent, lax, negligent, oblivious, otiose, perfunctory, reckless, remiss, thoughtless, truant

neglectful of obligation delinquent *(overdue)*

neglectfulness dereliction, disinterest *(lack of interest)*, disregard *(omission)*, disregard *(unconcern)*, laches, laxity, negligence, sloth

neglecting derelict *(negligent)*

neglection breach

neglector of duty delinquent

neglegens careless, heedless, lax, negligent, reckless, regardless, remiss, thoughtless

neglegentia laxity, neglect, negligence

neglegere disregard, ignore, neglect

negligence delinquency *(failure of duty)*, dereliction, disinterest *(lack of interest)*, disregard *(unconcern)*, fault *(responsibility)*, incompetence, inconsideration, indifference, inertia, laches, lapse *(expiration)*, laxity, maladministration, misconduct, misprision, neglect, nonfeasance, nonperformance, omission, oversight *(carelessness)*

negligent blameful, blameworthy, careless, delinquent *(guilty of a misdeed)*, disobedient, heedless, improvident, inadvertent, indolent, injudicious, lax, oblivious, perfunctory, reckless, remiss, slipshod, thoughtless

negligent act tort

negligent act of injury delict

negligent offense delict

negligent wrongdoing delict

negligibility inconsequence

negligible collateral *(immaterial)*, de minimus, expendable, inapposite, inappreciable, inconsiderable, insufficient, minor, nominal, nonessential, null *(insignificant)*, paltry, petty, slight, trivial, unessential

negotia commerce

negotiable assignable, conditional, heritable

negotiable instrument coupon, debenture, draft, letter of credit, note *(written promise to pay)*, security *(stock)*

negotiable paper check *(instrument)*, draft, note *(written promise to pay)*, security *(stock)*

negotiables portfolio, securities, stock *(shares)*

negotiant adjuster, advocate *(counselor)*, agent, arbiter, arbitrator, broker, intermediary, liaison, medium

negotiate arbitrate *(conciliate)*, assign *(transfer ownership)*, close *(agree)*, compromise *(settle by mutual agreement)*, confer *(consult)*, deal, debate, deliberate, dicker, discuss, haggle, intercede, judge, lobby, mediate, reconcile, settle, trade, transact, treat *(process)*

negotiated agreed *(harmonized)*, contractual, res judicata

negotiated agreement contract

negotiation adjustment, collective bargaining, commerce, compromise, conciliation, conference, counteroffer, deal, intercession, mediation, meeting *(conference)*, parley, settlement, trade *(commerce)*, transaction, treaty

negotiation process mediation

negotiations conference

negotiator adjuster, advocate *(counselor)*, agent, arbiter, arbitrator, broker, conduit *(intermediary)*

negotiator dealer

negotiator go-between, interagent, intermediary, judge, liaison, medium, spokesman

negotium employment, occupation *(vocation)*, pursuit *(occupation)*, transaction

neighbor adjoin, border *(approach)*, juxtapose

neighborhood civic, community, district, local, locality, location, region, regional, section *(vicinity)*, site, venue, vicinity

neighboring adjacent, close *(near)*, contiguous, immediate *(not distant)*, proximate

neighborliness comity, concordance, consideration *(sympathetic regard)*, rapprochement

neighborly benevolent

neither more nor less coequal

nemesis punishment, reprisal, retribution, revenge, vengeance

neologism jargon *(technical language)*

neology jargon *(technical language)*

neophyte amateur, novice, probationer *(one being tested)*

neophytism preparation

neoteric novel

neoterical novel

neoterism innovation

nepenthe drug

nequam bad *(offensive)*

nequitia knavery

nerve audacity, confidence *(faith)*, prowess *(bravery)*, reassure, temerity

nerveless powerless

nervous suspicious *(distrustful)*, unsettled

nervousness hesitation, misgiving, panic, qualm, stress *(strain)*, trepidation

nervus sinew

nervy insolent

nescience ignorance

nescient blind *(not discerning)*, incognizant, opaque, unaware

nescius unaware

nest habitation *(dwelling place)*

nest egg fund, store *(depository)*

net capture, earn, ensnare, gain, realize *(obtain as a profit)*, trap

net profit dividend, proceeds

net quantity amount *(quantity)*, amount *(result)*

net return income

nettle aggravate *(annoy)*, badger, discompose, disturb, hector, incense, irri-

tate, offend *(insult)*, pique, plague, provoke

network complex *(development)*, conjunction, league

neutral dispassionate, equitable, evenhanded, impartial, independent, intermediate, liberal *(broad minded)*, noncommittal, nonmilitant, nonpartisan, objective, open-minded, peaceable, unbiased, unprejudiced

neutralism neutrality

neutrality candor *(impartiality)*, disinterest *(lack of prejudice)*, objectivity, peace

neutralization of forces balance *(equality)*

neutralize compensate *(counterbalance)*, counteract, countervail, cross *(disagree with)*, disable, disarm *(divest of arms)*, disqualify, dissolve *(terminate)*, frustrate, negate, nullify, outbalance, prevent, remedy, vitiate

neutralized ineffective, ineffectual

neutralizer offset

neutralizing preventive

neutrius partis neutral

never sine die

never again sine die

never cease keep *(continue)*, persist

never changing immutable

never ending continuous

never idle diligent, industrious

never late punctual

never the same atypical

never tiring diligent

never to be forgotten critical *(crucial)*

never varying immutable

never-ceasing chronic, permanent, perpetual

never-dying perpetual

never-ending continual *(perpetual)*, durable, incessant, permanent, protracted

never-endingness perpetuity

never-fading perpetual

never-failing infallible, perpetual

never-stopping chronic, permanent, perpetual

never-tiring painstaking, pertinacious

never-wearying pertinacious

nevertheless notwithstanding, regardless

new contemporary, current, de novo, inexperienced, novel, recent, sophisticated, unaccustomed, unacquainted, unprecedented, unsettled, unusual

new arrival novice

new beginning continuation *(resumption)*

new departure creation

new device innovation

new edition revision *(corrected version)*

new energy resurgence

new hearing rehearing

new idea innovation

new method innovation

new offer counteroffer

new outbreak recrudescence

new phase innovation

new start continuation *(resumption)*, renewal

new version revival

newborn child

newcomer neophyte, novice, proba-

tioner *(one being tested)*, stranger, successor

newest last *(preceding)*

newfangled unprecedented, unusual

newly anew, de novo

newly arrived recent

newly come novel

news communication *(statement)*, disclosure *(something disclosed)*, dispatch *(message)*, information *(facts)*, notice *(announcement)*, notification, publicity, report *(detailed account)*, story *(narrative)*

news article story *(narrative)*

news blackout censorship

news business press

news gatherers press

news item story *(narrative)*

news story report *(detailed account)*

newsmen press

newspaper organ

newspaper report story *(narrative)*

newspaper world press

newspaperman press

newspapers press

newsworthy notable, noteworthy

newswriters press

newsy informative, informatory

next a savoir, ensuing, future, immediate *(imminent)*, imminent, inevitable, proximate, subsequent, thereafter

next generation offspring

next in line successor

next of kin affiliation *(bloodline)*, blood, kindred

next to adjacent, contiguous, immediate *(not distant)*

nexus attachment *(act of affixing)*, connection *(fastening)*, contact *(touching)*, liaison, privity, relation *(connection)*, sequence

nice palatable

nice appreciation decorum

niceness amenity

nicety decorum, discretion *(quality of being discreet)*, nuance, specification

nickname cognomen, sobriquet

niggard penurious

niggardly economical, illiberal, nonsubstantial *(not sufficient)*, paltry, parsimonious, penurious, slight

niggling inconsequential

nigh approximate, close *(near)*, forthcoming, future, immediate *(imminent)*, present *(attendant)*, present *(current)*, proximate

night stick cudgel

nihil nonentity

nihil ad rem pertinet irrelevant

nihilism anarchy, lynch law

nihilist insurgent, malcontent

nihilistic disorderly, incendiary

nihility nullity

nil blank *(emptiness)*

nim steal

nimble alert *(agile)*, deft, rapid

nimble-fingered deft

nimble-witted perspicacious

nimbleness dispatch *(promptness)*

nimiety plethora, redundancy, surfeit, surplus

nimious inordinate

nimium excess

nimius excessive, gross *(total)*, undue *(excessive)*

nip foil, thwart

nip in the bud deter

nisus conatus

nisus endeavor

nitid lucid

no decision deadlock

no longer conventional outmoded

no longer customary outdated, outmoded

no longer fashionable outdated

no longer in perfect condition marred

no longer in style outdated

no longer in use obsolete

no longer law null *(invalid),* null and void

no longer living dead, deceased, defunct

no longer prevailing outdated, outmoded

no longer prevalent outdated

no longer stylish outdated

no longer young old

no matter when whenever

no matter who whoever

no more defunct

no one nonentity

no relation alien *(unrelated),* apart

no reputation disrepute

no repute dishonor *(shame),* disrepute

no standing dishonor *(shame)*

nobilis notorious

nobility character *(reputation),* distinction *(reputation),* elite, eminence, prestige

noble heroic, high-minded, illustrious, laudable, law-abiding, magnanimous, meritorious, moral, prominent, proud *(self-respecting),* reputable, scrupulous, sterling, superior *(excellent)*

noble-minded magnanimous

nobleness integrity, principle *(virtue),* right *(righteousness)*

nobody nonentity

nocens harmful, prejudicial

nocent harmful, lethal, noxious, pernicious, pestilent

nocere harm

nocuous bad *(offensive),* deleterious, harmful, inadvisable, lethal, malignant, peccant *(unhealthy),* pestilent, sinister

nod recognition

nod assent to coincide *(concur)*

nod of approbation approval

noesis insight, perception

noise outcry, pandemonium

noise abroad circulate, divulge, proclaim, propagate *(spread)*

noiseless mute, speechless

noiselessness silence

noisiness brawl

noisome deleterious, detrimental, fatal, harmful, harsh, heinous, insalubrious, malignant, noxious, objectionable, obnoxious, peccant *(unhealthy),* pernicious, pestilent, repugnant *(exciting aversion),* repulsive, sinister

noisy blatant *(obtrusive),* loquacious

noisy quarrel altercation, fracas

noisy strife commotion

nol-pros quit *(discontinue)*

nolition reluctance

nom de plume sobriquet

nomad migrant

nomadic moving *(in motion)*

nomen entry *(record),* prestige

nomen alienum alias

nomen deferre indict

nomenclature call *(title),* classification, denomination

nominal immaterial, inconsiderable, negligible, null *(insignificant),* trivial

nominalness insignificance

nominare call *(title),* designate, nominate

nominate charge *(empower),* delegate, designate, induct, instate, invest *(vest),* propose, select

nominatio nomination

nomination appointment *(act of designating),* assignment *(designation),* deputation *(selection of delegates),* selection *(choice)*

nomination contest primary

nominative competition primary

nominative contest primary

nominative election primary

nominator licensor

nomine nominal

nominee candidate, contender, licensee

nomography jurisprudence

nomology jurisprudence

nomothetic decretal, due *(regular),* lawful

nomothetical de jure

non aptus incongruous

non credere disbelieve

non idoneus inapposite, inappropriate, unsatisfactory

non legitimus felonious, illegitimate *(illegal),* unlawful

non necessarius needless, unnecessary

non obsequi disobedient

non occurrence noncompliance *(nonobservance)*

non rectus indirect

non salable unmarketable

non sequitur anacoluthon

non specific unspecified

non valere inapplicable

non verisimilis improbability

non voluntarius involuntary

non-esse blank *(emptiness)*

non-executional judgment declaratory judgment

non-uniform atypical

nonabolishable noncancellable

nonabstract actual

nonacceptance declination, denial, disapproval, disdain, dishonor *(nonpayment),* exclusion, impugnation, negation, refusal, rejection

nonactual baseless

nonadherence breach, contempt *(disobedience to the court),* dishonor *(nonpayment)*

nonadhering broken *(unfulfilled),* nonconforming

nonadmission bar *(obstruction),* disqualification *(rejection),* exclusion, ostracism, prohibition

nonadmission of employees lockout

nonage adolescence, minority *(infancy)*

nonaggresive nonmilitant

nonaggressive lax

nonagreement disaccord, discord, discrepancy, disparity, dispute, dissension, dissent *(difference of opinion),* dissent

(nonconcurrence), exception *(objection),* impugnation, incompatibility *(difference),* negation, nonconformity, variance *(disagreement)*

nonaligned neutral, nonpartisan

nonannullable noncancellable

nonapparent covert

nonappearance absence *(nonattendance),* concealment, leave *(absence)*

nonapproval disapprobation, disapproval, disparagement, dissatisfaction, exception *(objection),* reversal

nonassent dissension, dissent *(nonconcurrence)*

nonattendance leave *(absence),* nonappearance

nonattendant truant

nonavailability desuetude

nonbeing absence *(omission),* nonentity, nullity

nonbelligerence neutrality

nonbelligerent neutral

nonchalance disinterest *(lack of interest),* indifference

nonchalant careless, casual, dispassionate, informal

nonchallengeable noncontestable

noncitizen alien

noncohesive disconnected

noncombatance neutrality

noncombatant neutral, nonmilitant

noncombative nonmilitant, peaceable

noncomformity contest *(dispute)*

noncommittal guarded, neutral

noncompletion breach, deficiency, delinquency *(failure of duty),* dishonor *(nonpayment),* failure *(falling short),* frustration, laxity, miscarriage, neglect, nonperformance

noncompletion of a task delinquency *(failure of duty)*

noncompliance contempt *(disobedience to the court),* declination, defiance, dishonor *(nonpayment),* disregard *(omission),* dissent *(difference of opinion),* dissidence, impugnation, informality, infraction, insurrection, negation, neglect, nonperformance, offense, refusal, resistance, revolt, sedition, transgression

noncompliance with law crime

noncompliant disobedient, dissident, insubordinate, nonconforming, perverse

noncompulsory disjunctive *(alternative),* extraneous, needless, unnecessary

nonconcurrence dissension, dissidence, nonconformity

nonconformance resistance

nonconformant nonconsenting

nonconforming dissident, eccentric, individual, licentious

nonconformism deviation

nonconformist deviant, dissident, eccentric, heretic, lawless, malcontent, novel, original *(creative),* recusant

nonconformity breach, deviation, difference, disaccord, discrepancy, disparity, dissent *(nonconcurrence),* dissidence, exception *(exclusion),* incompatibility *(inconsistency),* incongruity, inconsistency, inequality, informality, irregularity, noncompliance *(nonobservance),* quirk *(idiosyncrasy),* schism

nonconformity to fact falsehood

nonconsent declination, denial, disagreement, disapproval, dissent *(nonconcurrence),* dissent *(withhold assent),* impugnation, negation, refusal

nonconsideration exclusion

nonconstitutional illicit

noncontent nonconsenting

noncontinuance cloture

noncontinuous discrete, disjunctive *(tending to disjoin)*

noncontroversial incontestable, incontrovertible, unimpeachable

noncontrovertible noncontestable

noncooperating contentious, disinclined, hostile

noncooperation contempt *(disobedience to the court),* defiance, dereliction, disaccord, division *(act of dividing),* impugnation, nonperformance

noncooperative recalcitrant

noncooperator malcontent

noncorroboration negation

noncriminal civil *(public)*

nondebatable noncontestable

nondescript indefinite, usual

nondisputable noncontestable

nondivisible indivisible, inseparable

nondomicile nonresidence

nondurable ephemeral, temporary

none the less notwithstanding

nonecliastical civil *(public)*

nonelastic immutable, inflexible

nonemployment disuse, nonuse

nonentity blank *(emptiness),* nullity

nonerasable noncancellable

nonessential circumstantial, collateral *(immaterial),* excessive, expendable, extraneous, extrinsic, immaterial, inconsequential, inconsiderable, minor, needless, petty, slight, supplementary, tangential, trivial, unessential

nonessentiality immateriality

nonesuch exemplar, paragon, phenomenon *(unusual occurrence)*

nonetheless regardless

nonexclusive competitive *(open),* generic

nonexistence absence *(omission),* blank *(emptiness),* nonentity, nullity

nonexistent fictitious, insubstantial

nonexpectation bombshell, improbability

nonexpert unprofessional

nonfatal nontoxic

nonfeasance crime, delict, dereliction, dishonor *(nonpayment),* laches, laxity, misconduct, neglect, nonperformance, omission

nonfertile barren

nonfinal interlocutory

nonfulfillment default, defeat, deficiency, delinquency *(failure of duty),* delinquency *(shortage),* dishonor *(nonpayment),* failure *(falling short),* frustration, laxity, miscarriage, mistrial, neglect, nonfeasance, nonperformance

nonfulfillment of one's hopes dissatisfaction

nonfulfilment abortion *(fiasco),* breach

nonfunctional expendable, otiose

nonfunctioning otiose

nongregarious unapproachable

nonhabitancy nonresidence

nonhabitation nonresidence

nonhampering laissez faire

nonidentical different, dissimilar

nonimitation deviation, difference

nonimitative original *(initial)*

nonimmunity danger

noninclusion bar *(obstruction),* dispensation *(exception),* disqualification *(rejection),* exception *(exclusion),* exclusion, omission, ostracism, prohibition, rejection, removal

noninfringement laissez faire

noninhabitance nonresidence

noninhabitancy nonresidence

nonintentional occurrence quirk *(accident)*

noninterference freedom, home rule, laissez faire, latitude, liberty, neutrality

noninterfering neutral

nonintermeddling laissez faire

noninterruption laissez faire

nonintervention home rule, laissez faire, latitude, neutrality

noninterventionist neutral

nonintrusion laissez faire

noninvolvement disinterest *(lack of interest),* disinterest *(lack of prejudice),* objectivity

nonirritating innocuous, nontoxic

nonjuring recusant

nonlegal felonious, illicit, impermissible, lawless

nonlethal nontoxic

nonliability condonation, dispensation *(exception),* immunity, impunity

nonliable clear *(free from criminal charges)*

nonliteral translation paraphrase

nonmalignant harmless, innocuous, nontoxic

nonmaterial impalpable

nonmilitary civil *(public)*

nonobjective subjective

nonobligatory disjunctive *(alternative)*

nonobservance breach, contempt *(disobedience to the court),* default, delinquency *(failure of duty),* desuetude, deviation, dishonor *(nonpayment),* disregard *(omission),* disregard *(unconcern),* dissent *(nonconcurrence),* failure *(falling short),* indifference, informality, infraction, infringement, neglect, offense, oversight *(carelessness),* repudiation, transgression, violation

nonobservance of law crime

nonobservance of rules infraction

nonobservant broken *(unfulfilled),* disorderly, dissident, heedless, lawless, nonconforming, recusant

nonobservence dereliction

nonoccupance nonresidence

nonoccupancy nonresidence

nonoccupation nonresidence

nonofficial private *(not public)*

nonpacific contentious

nonpareil exemplar, outstanding *(prominent),* paragon, phenomenon *(unusual occurrence),* primary, prime *(most valuable),* singular, superior *(excellent),* superlative, unique, unusual

nonparticipance neutrality

nonparticipant neutral

nonparticipating neutral, otiose

nonparticipation abstention, neutrality

nonpartisan impartial, independent, liberal *(broad minded),* neutral, objective, unbiased, unprejudiced

nonpartisanship candor *(impartiality),* disinterest *(lack of prejudice),* neutrality, objectivity

nonpayer delinquent

nonpaying penurious

nonpayment debt, delinquency *(shortage)*

nonpayment at maturity dishonor *(nonpayment)*

nonperformance breach, default, deficiency, delinquency *(failure of duty),* dereliction, failure *(falling short),* frustration, laches, laxity, miscarriage, neglect, nonfeasance

nonperishable indelible, indestructible

nonpermanent interlocutory, provisional

nonpermanent agreement modus vivendi

nonpermanent arrangement modus vivendi

nonpertinent extraneous, gratuitous *(unwarranted)*

nonphysical immaterial, incorporeal, intangible

nonplus confound, confuse *(bewilder),* confusion *(ambiguity),* discompose, disorient, disturb, embarrass, obfuscate, perplex, perturb, quagmire, quandary

nonpoisonous harmless, nontoxic

nonporous solid *(compact)*

nonpractice nonperformance

nonpresence absence *(nonattendance),* nonappearance, nonresidence

nonproblematical noncontestable

nonproducing barren

nonproductive barren

nonprofessional layman, volunteer

nonprohibitive permissive

nonprosecution compurgation, impunity

nonpublic private *(not public),* privy

nonquestionable noncontestable

nonrational arbitrary

nonrecognition disdain, insentience

nonrecurrent desultory

nonrefutable noncontestable

nonrescindable noncancellable

nonresident foreign

nonresistance acquiescence, capitulation, compliance, deference, discipline *(obedience),* resignation *(passive acceptance)*

nonresistant passive, resigned, susceptible *(unresistent)*

nonresisting obeisant, passive, patient, pliable, pliant

nonresponsibility dispensation *(exception)*

nonresumption impasse

nonretention alienation *(transfer of title),* assignment *(transfer of ownership),* cession, desuetude, devolution

nonretractable noncancellable

nonreversible indefeasible, irreversible, irrevocable, noncancellable, permanent

nonsacred mundane

nonscientific illogical

nonsense jargon *(unintelligible language),* platitude

nonsensical fatuous, incredible, inexpressive, irrational, ludicrous, lunatic, puerile, unreasonable

nonsensical language jargon *(unin-*

telligible language)
nonsensical talk jargon (unintelligible language), prattle
nonsensicality non sequitur
nonsensicalness jargon (unintelligible language), non sequitur
nonspecialist layman
nonspecific broad, generic, indefinite, indeterminate
nonspiritual material (physical), mundane, physical
nonstandard anomalous
nonstop consecutive, continual (connected), incessant
nonsubjective objective
nonsubjectivity objectivity
nonsubsistence blank (emptiness)
nonsubstantial intangible
nonsuccess miscarriage, mistrial
nonsuit dismissal (termination of a proceeding)
nonsystematic haphazard
nontampering laissez faire
nontenancy nonresidence
nontoxic harmless, innocuous
nontransferable inalienable
nontranslucent opaque
nonuniform anomalous, desultory, deviant, disjointed, disordered, disparate, dissimilar, distinct (distinguished from others), divergent, heterogeneous, individual, intermittent, miscellaneous, multifarious, nonconforming, protean, sporadic, unique
nonuniformity deviation, difference, discrepancy, disparity, distinction (difference), diversity, exception (exclusion), incompatibility (inconsistency), inequality, nonconformity
nonuse abatement (extinguishment), abolition, cancellation, desuetude, discontinuance (act of discontinuing), disuse
nonutilization nonuse
nonvenomous harmless, nontoxic
nonviolence moderation
nonviolent harmless, nonmilitant
nonvirulent harmless, nontoxic
nonworker parasite
norm code, criterion, cross section, example, law, paradigm, pattern, rule (guide), standard
norma canon, rule (guide), standard
normal accustomed (customary), average (standard), common (customary), conventional, customary, exemplary, familiar (customary), habitual, mediocre, natural, ordinary, prevailing (current), prevalent, regular (conventional), routine, sane, typical, usual
normalcy competence (sanity), sanity
normality competence (sanity), sanity
normalize adjust (regulate), naturalize (acclimate), regulate (adjust)
normally as a rule, generally, invariably
normalness competence (sanity)
normative average (standard), exemplary
noscere recognize (acknowledge)
noscitare recognize (perceive)
not abide conflict, disapprove (reject)
not abiding dissenting
not able unable
not able to be conveyed inalienable
not absolute conditional, qualified

(conditioned)
not abundant scarce
not accept abrogate (rescind), conflict, disagree, disallow, disapprove (reject), disavow, disbelieve, disclaim, disdain, disoblige, disown (deny the validity), dissent (withhold assent)
not accepting dissenting
not accidental express
not according to law illegal, illegitimate (illegal), illicit
not accountable immune, privileged
not admit disapprove (reject), disavow, disclaim, disown (deny the validity), doubt (distrust)
not admitted inadmissible
not agree differ (vary), dispute (contest), dispute (debate), dissent (differ in opinion)
not agreeing dissenting
not alien native (domestic)
not allow estop, forbid
not allowed illegal, illicit, inadmissible
not allowed by law unlawful
not answerable clear (unencumbered), exempt, immune
not apocryphal authentic
not applicable irrelevant
not approve disapprove (reject), disavow, dissent (withhold assent)
not approved illegal, illicit
not argued over uncontested
not ascertained indeterminate
not ashamed unabashed
not authenticated unsupported
not authorized by law illegal
not averruncated chronic
not axiomatic controversial, disputable
not badly fairly (moderately)
not baneful nontoxic
not believe disbelieve, doubt (distrust)
not belonging disordered
not biased impartial
not binding invalid, void (invalid)
not blamable inculpable
not bother with disregard
not budge hold out (resist)
not by chance express
not capable of annulment irreversible
not capable of being introduced as evidence inadmissible
not care for disfavor, neglect, pretermit
not certain conditional, uncertain (ambiguous)
not challenged uncontested
not charged gratuitous (given without recompense)
not charged for free (at no charge), gratuitous (given without recompense)
not choosy indiscriminate
not clear ambiguous, nebulous, uncertain (ambiguous)
not clear to the mind intangible
not close remote (secluded)
not cohesive disjunctive (tending to disjoin)
not commercial residential
not committed to writing parol
not comparable alien (unrelated), disparate, dissimilar
not compare with differ (vary)

not complete partial (part)
not completed partial (part)
not completely formed inchoate
not compliant contumacious
not comply disallow, disobey
not comply with disoblige
not compromise hold out (resist)
not compulsory disjunctive (alternative)
not concealed manifest
not confirm demur, disallow, disavow, disown (deny the validity)
not conform conflict, deviate, differ (vary)
not conforming dissenting
not conforming to the usual anomalous
not connected with immaterial
not consenting dissident
not consider disapprove (reject), disdain, disregard, dissent (withhold assent)
not considered ineligible
not contradictory consistent
not cooperate disobey
not countenance disapprove (reject), enjoin
not covered by law illegal, illicit
not current outdated
not dangerous nontoxic
not deadly nontoxic
not declared openly implicit
not decreased undiminished
not defend dissent (withhold assent)
not definite intangible
not deleterious nontoxic
not designated indeterminate
not discharged delinquent (overdue)
not disconcerted unabashed
not dispose of hold (possess)
not disposed reluctant
not disputed uncontested
not do justice to derogate
not domestic alien (foreign)
not easily governed intractable
not easily worn out durable
not eligible ineligible
not elusive tangible
not employed unemployed
not endowed with life defunct
not enough deficient, inadequate, insufficiency, insufficient
not enslaved free (enjoying civil liberty)
not entirely quasi
not equal to incapable
not equate differ (vary)
not equitable unfair
not established unsupported
not evident underlying
not excessive reasonable (fair)
not existing defunct
not expressed implicit
not expressed by writing parol
not extinct extant
not extraordinary nondescript
not extreme reasonable (fair)
not false authentic, true (authentic)
not faulty true (authentic)
not fictitious actual, authentic, documentary, true (authentic)
not final inconclusive, interlocutory
not find tenable disbelieve
not fit unworthy
not fitting gratuitous (unwarranted), unacceptable

not fixed aleatory *(uncertain)*, ambulatory, indeterminate
not fixed in extent indeterminate
not fluctuating fixed *(settled)*
not following disproportionate, gratuitous *(unwarranted)*
not for publication confidential
not foreign domestic *(indigenous)*, native *(domestic)*
not forfeitable indefeasible
not forget remember
not fully executed inchoate
not genuine synthetic
not give up hold out *(resist)*
not guilty acquitted, blameless, clean, clear *(free from criminal charges)*, inculpable, irreprehensible
not have any part of conflict, disapprove *(reject)*
not hear disregard
not hear of dismiss *(put out of consideration)*
not heed disobey, disregard
not hold with dissent *(withhold assent)*
not honest dishonest, fraudulent
not honorable blameworthy
not ideal faulty
not identical distinct *(distinguished from others)*
not imaginary actual
not immediate remote *(not proximate)*
not important immaterial
not imported domestic *(indigenous)*
not impossible allowable
not improbable credible
not improper allowable
not in action defunct
not in bondage free *(enjoying civil liberty)*
not in force defunct, void *(invalid)*
not in keeping disproportionate
not in use vacant
not in vogue outdated, outmoded
not inclined reluctant
not include censor, disregard
not included inadmissible
not including save
not indigenous alien *(foreign)*
not indiginous foreign
not integrated disjunctive *(tending to disjoin)*
not intended unpremeditated
not lasting ephemeral
not legitimate want of jurisdiction
not lessened undiminished
not liable blameless, exempt, immune
not like disfavor
not limited by conditions unconditional
not listen disobey, disregard
not long past recent
not lost extant
not lying candid
not made certain indeterminate
not maintain disavow, disown *(deny the validity)*, disown *(refuse to acknowledge)*
not manifest impalpable, ulterior
not mature undue *(not owing)*
not merely supposed actual
not met delinquent *(overdue)*
not mind disobey
not modern old, outdated
not modified unqualified *(unlimited)*

not narrow-minded liberal *(broad minded)*
not native alien *(foreign)*, foreign
not natural artificial, synthetic
not naturalized alien *(foreign)*
not near remote *(secluded)*
not nearby remote *(secluded)*
not necessitated gratuitous *(unwarranted)*
not nervous secure *(confident)*
not obey disobey, disoblige
not objectionable allowable
not obscure manifest, naked *(perceptible)*
not observant of the law lawless
not observe dishonor *(refuse to pay)*, overstep
not occupied vacant
not odd nondescript
not of high standards unprofessional
not of material nature incorporeal
not on point irrelevant
not on time overdue
not open private *(not public)*
not openly expressed tacit
not owing solvent
not paid on time delinquent *(overdue)*
not part with hold *(possess)*
not partial competitive *(open)*, general, impartial
not particular generic, open-ended
not particularly designated indeterminate
not pass disavow
not pay default, dishonor *(refuse to pay)*
not perfect fallible
not perfectly accurate approximate
not permanent transitory
not permit enjoin
not permitted illegal, illegitimate *(illegal)*, illicit
not permitting passage impervious
not permitting penetration impervious
not pernicious nontoxic
not pertaining to immaterial, irrelevant
not pertinent gratuitous *(unwarranted)*, immaterial, improper, irrelevant
not plain ambiguous, uncertain *(ambiguous)*
not plainly apparent implicit
not plentiful scarce
not pliable intractable
not positive indefinite
not possessing life dead
not precise indeterminate
not private public *(open)*
not privileged competitive *(open)*
not proceed with cancel, forbear
not protracted brief
not public residential, secret
not readily discerned impalpable
not readily salable unmarketable
not receivable as evidence inadmissible
not receivable in evidence inadmissible
not reciprocal unilateral
not reputable disreputable
not required elective *(voluntary)*
not resist comply
not respect contemn, decry, disdain,

disfavor
not respectable blameworthy, disreputable
not responsible clean, clear *(unencumbered)*, exempt, immune, not guilty
not restorable chronic
not restricted exempt
not retain displace *(remove)*, waive
not reveal conceal
not right errant, improper
not satisfying deficient
not scared secure *(confident)*
not select general
not selective indiscriminate
not sensitive to insusceptible *(resistant)*
not settled indeterminate
not sharp indefinite
not significant irrelevant
not similar dissimilar
not singular nondescript
not speak well of censure, decry
not special generic, nondescript
not specific open-ended
not spiritual corporal
not spurious authentic
not straightforward mendacious
not subject immune, privileged
not subject to exempt
not subject to a payment gratuitous *(given without recompense)*
not subject to regulation free *(enjoying civil liberty)*
not submit hold out *(resist)*, oppose
not subordinate substantive
not substantiated unsupported
not succeed fail *(lose)*
not sufficient insufficient
not suitable improper
not support counter, disapprove *(reject)*
not sure conditional, uncertain *(questionable)*
not tainted blameless
not take kindly to disapprove *(condemn)*
not tampered with authentic
not the same different, disparate, distinct *(distinguished from others)*
not think about disregard
not think of disregard
not thought much of disreputable
not to be abrogated indefeasible
not to be admitted inadmissible
not to be allowed inadmissible
not to be annulled indefeasible
not to be avoided obligatory
not to be believed disputable
not to be changed immutable
not to be communicated confidential
not to be delayed exigent
not to be disclosed confidential
not to be disputed demonstrable, inappealable
not to be evaded obligatory
not to be made void indefeasible
not to be moved immutable
not to be overlooked considerable, exigent
not to be quoted confidential, unofficial
not to be recommended blameworthy
not to be spoken of confidential
not to the point irrelevant

not to the purpose irrelevant
not too difficult practicable
not toxiferous nontoxic
not trouble oneself disregard
not true dishonest, fraudulent, illusory
not unique nondescript
not up to expectation inadequate
not up to normal deficient
not up to par deficient, unsatisfactory
not use neglect, waive
not vague tangible, unambiguous
not valid illegal, null *(invalid)*, null and void
not varying fixed *(settled)*
not vital incidental, inconsequential, irrelevant, minor
not wanted inadmissible
not weaken hold out *(resist)*
not well off impecunious
not well-founded baseless
not whole semi
not wholly in part
not working unemployed
not worth considering inconsiderable
not worth mentioning minor
not worthy of notice inconsiderable
not written nuncupative, parol
not yet carried into operation executory
not yet due undue *(not owing)*
not yet payable undue *(not owing)*
not yield hold out *(resist)*, oppose
nota brand, stamp, stigma, symptom, trait
notabilis notable
notability character *(reputation)*, clout, distinction *(reputation)*, eminence, emphasis, feature *(characteristic)*, importance, materiality *(consequence)*, notoriety, prestige, reputation, significance, status
notable appreciable, cardinal *(outstanding)*, considerable, conspicuous, critical *(crucial)*, extraordinary, famous, illustrious, important *(significant)*, influential, major, manifest, momentous, noteworthy, obvious, outstanding *(prominent)*, palpable, paramount, perceivable, perceptible, portentous *(eliciting amazement)*, prominent, remarkable, renowned, reputable, salient, special, unusual
notable disaster catastrophe
notable feature consequence *(significance)*
notableness materiality *(consequence)*
notably particularly
notam homini inurere brand *(mark)*
notare brand *(mark)*, characterize, designate
notary notary public
notatio notice *(heed)*, notice *(observe)*, observation
notation comment, marginalia, memorandum, reminder, symbol
note attend *(heed)*, book, capsule, check *(instrument)*, comment, comment, coupon, denote, designate, discern *(detect with the senses)*, dispatch *(message)*, distinction *(reputation)*, draft, eminence, emphasis, enter *(record)*, entry *(record)*, hear *(give attention to)*, heed, importance, indicant, indication,

indicator, interest *(concern)*, invoice *(bill)*, itemize, marginalia, memorandum, mention *(reference)*, mention, muse, notation, notice *(announcement)*, notice *(observe)*, observation, observe *(watch)*, outline *(synopsis)*, perceive, perception, pierce *(discern)*, prestige, record, record, regard *(esteem)*, regard *(pay attention)*, remark, remark, remind, reminder, report *(detailed account)*, reputation, respect, set down, significance, study, summary, symbol, transmittal, witness *(have direct knowledge of)*
note differences discriminate *(distinguish)*, distinguish
note down register
note of explanation comment
note the distinctions discern *(discriminate)*, secern
note the similarities and differences compare
note the time of date
notebook file
noted famous, illustrious, notable, notorious, outstanding *(prominent)*, popular, renowned
notedness notoriety
notes caption, currency, register
noteworthiness distinction *(reputation)*, eminence, importance, prestige
noteworthy certain *(specific)*, considerable, distinctive, extraordinary, famous, important *(significant)*, influential, major, momentous, notable, outstanding *(prominent)*, particular *(specific)*, peculiar *(distinctive)*, portentous *(eliciting amazement)*, prodigious *(amazing)*, rare, remarkable, renowned, special, stellar, uncanny, uncommon, unusual
nothing blank *(emptiness)*, nonentity, nullity
nothing but mere
nothingness blank *(emptiness)*, nonentity, nullity
nothus bastard, illegitimate *(born out of wedlock)*
notice admonition, advice, appreciate *(comprehend)*, attend *(heed)*, caution *(warning)*, caveat, character *(reputation)*, citation *(charge)*, comment, consider, declaration, detect, discern *(detect with the senses)*, disclosure *(something disclosed)*, dispatch *(message)*, dun, find *(discover)*, hear *(perceive by ear)*, heed, information *(facts)*, intelligence *(news)*, issuance, monition *(warning)*, notification, observation, observe *(watch)*, perceive, perception, pierce *(discern)*, pronouncement, publication *(disclosure)*, publicity, recognition, recognize *(perceive)*, regard *(attention)*, regard *(pay attention)*, report *(detailed account)*, symptom, ultimatum, witness *(have direct knowledge of)*
notice critically review
notice of an action lis pendens
notice of claim demand
notice of danger warning
notice of pending suit lis pendens
notice of right lis pendens
notice on file lis pendens
notice to appear citation *(charge)*, monition *(legal summons)*
noticeable apparent *(perceptible)*, ap-

preciable, blatant *(conspicuous)*, conspicuous, determinable *(ascertainable)*, distinct *(clear)*, distinctive, evident, flagrant, manifest, naked *(perceptible)*, noteworthy, obvious, open *(in sight)*, ostensible, overt, palpable, patent, perceivable, perceptible, prominent, salient, scrutable
noticeably fairly *(clearly)*
notification admonition, advice, caveat, citation *(charge)*, communication *(statement)*, declaration, directive, disclosure *(act of disclosing)*, disclosure *(something disclosed)*, dispatch *(message)*, information *(facts)*, issuance, monition *(legal summons)*, monition *(warning)*, notice *(announcement)*, proclamation, profession *(declaration)*, pronouncement, publication *(disclosure)*, publicity, report *(detailed account)*, subpoena
notification of legal action service *(delivery of legal process)*
notification to appear summons, venire
notificatory declaratory
notified acquainted, informed *(having information)*
notifier informant, informer *(a person who provides information)*
notify admonish *(advise)*, advise, alert, annunciate, apprise, communicate, contact *(communicate)*, convey *(communicate)*, correspond *(communicate)*, disabuse, disclose, disseminate, enlighten, enunciate, forewarn, herald, inform *(notify)*, issue *(publish)*, mention, notice *(give formal warning)*, portend, predict, promulgate, propagate *(spread)*, relate *(tell)*, report *(disclose)*, reveal, signify *(inform)*
notify of danger caution
notify publicly issue *(publish)*
notify to appear subpoena, summon
notifying informatory
noting down registration
notio idea, notion
notion apprehension *(perception)*, assumption *(supposition)*, concept, idea, impression, opinion *(belief)*, perception, sense *(feeling)*, suspicion *(uncertainty)*
notional allusive, delusive, fictitious, illusory, inconsistent, insubstantial, nonexistent, quixotic
notoriety bad repute, character *(reputation)*, common knowledge, disgrace, dishonor *(shame)*, ill repute, infamy, opprobrium, prestige, publicity, reputation, scandal, stigma
notorious apparent *(perceptible)*, blatant *(conspicuous)*, conspicuous, disreputable, famous, flagrant, outrageous, overt, prominent, proverbial, public *(known)*, renowned, scandalous, unmistakable
notorious criminal outlaw
notoriousness character *(reputation)*, stigma
notus acquainted, familiar *(customary)*, notorious
notwithstanding regardless
nought nonentity
nourish abet, bear *(support)*, cultivate, foster, maintain *(sustain)*, nurture, preserve, promote *(organize)*, support *(assist)*, sustain *(prolong)*

nourishing conservation, salubrious, salutary

nourishment preservation, sustenance

nouveau riche philistine

novare innovation

novel different, noteworthy, original *(creative)*, portentous *(eliciting amazement)*, recent, unaccustomed, uncommon, unique, unprecedented, unusual

novelty innovation

novice amateur, apprentice, neophyte, probationer *(one being tested)*, protégé

novitiate apprentice, preparation, probationer *(one being tested)*

novus eccentric, extraordinary, novel, unprecedented

now instantly

now and then sporadic

now to be accounted for a savoir

now to be announced a savoir

now to be described a savoir

now to be enunciated a savoir

now to be itemized a savoir

now to be listed a savoir

now to be mentioned a savoir

now to be narrated a savoir

now to be presented a savoir

now to be read a savoir

now to be recited a savoir

now to be recounted a savoir

now to be reported a savoir

now to be set forth a savoir

now to be stated a savoir

now to follow a savoir

nowhere to be found lost *(taken away)*

noxia guilt

noxious bad *(inferior)*, contemptible, deadly, deleterious, detrimental, fatal, harmful, harsh, inimical, insalubrious, lethal, malignant, objectionable, obnoxious, offensive *(offending)*, peccant *(unhealthy)*, pernicious, pestilent, repulsive, sinister, tainted *(contaminated)*, toxic, unfavorable, virulent

noxiousness harm

noxius deleterious, harmful, obnoxious, pernicious, prejudicial

nuance difference, differential, technicality

nubilous indistinct

nucleation centralization

nucleus center *(essence)*, consequence *(significance)*, cornerstone, gravamen, main point, mainstay

nudge jostle *(bump into)*

nugatorius invalid, nugatory

nugatory collateral *(immaterial)*, expendable, futile, inactive, inadequate, inconsequential, inconsiderable, ineffective, ineffectual, invalid, minor, negligible, null *(insignificant)*, null *(invalid)*, null and void, otiose, paltry, petty, powerless, slight, trivial, unavailing, unproductive, void *(invalid)*

nugatory check bad check

nugatory trial mistrial

nugax frivolous

nuisance aggravation *(annoyance)*, disadvantage, mischief, molestation

null inactive, ineffective, ineffectual, invalid, lifeless *(dead)*, nugatory, vacuous, void *(invalid)*

null and void nugatory, otiose, powerless, void *(invalid)*

nullifiable defeasible, voidable

nullification abatement *(extinguishment)*, abolition, ademption, annulment, cancellation, countermand, defeasance, destruction, discharge *(annulment)*, discharge *(release from obligation)*, disclaimer, discontinuance *(act of discontinuing)*, dissolution *(termination)*, mistrial, negation, repudiation, rescision, retraction, reversal, revocation

nullified null *(invalid)*, null and void

nullifier offset

nullify abate *(extinguish)*, abolish, abrogate *(annul)*, abrogate *(rescind)*, adeem, alleviate, annul, balk, cancel, contravene, counteract, destroy *(void)*, disable, disavow, discharge *(release from obligation)*, disinherit, disown *(deny the validity)*, disprove, dissolve *(terminate)*, eliminate *(eradicate)*, expunge, extinguish, extirpate, frustrate, invalidate, kill *(defeat)*, negate, neutralize, obliterate, override, overrule, overthrow, quash, recall *(call back)*, recant, renege, repeal, repudiate, rescind, revoke, supersede, vacate *(void)*, vitiate, withdraw

nullify a marriage divorce

nullify one's gains overreach

nullifying avoidance *(cancellation)*, cancellation

nullity blank *(emptiness)*, invalidity, mistrial, nonentity

nullius filius bastard

nullius momenti immaterial

nullo modo fieri potest impossible

numb drug, insusceptible *(uncaring)*, obtund, torpid

number amount *(quantity)*, calculate, contain *(comprise)*, enumerate, itemize, quantity, quota

number of people population

numbering census, poll *(canvass)*

numberless frequent, infinite, innumerable, myriad, profuse

numerare pay

numerate enumerate

numeration amount *(quantity)*, census, computation, poll *(canvass)*

numerous copious, frequent, manifold, multifarious, multifold, multiple, myriad, populous, profuse, rife

numerousness multiplicity

numerus quantity

numismatical monetary, pecuniary

nummarius venal

nummary financial, pecuniary

nummi principal *(capital sum)*

nummulary monetary

nummus money

nuncupative parol, verbal

nundinae market *(business)*

nundination trade *(commerce)*

nuntiare inform *(notify)*

nuntius innuendo, intelligence *(news)*, intimation

nuptiae marriage *(wedlock)*

nuptial conjugal

nuptial bond cohabitation *(married state)*, coverture, marriage *(wedlock)*, matrimony

nuptial state matrimony

nuptial tie cohabitation *(married state)*, marriage *(wedlock)*, matrimony

nuptialis nuptial

nurse cure, foster, maintain *(sustain)*, nurture, promote *(organize)*, protect

nursing conservation

nursing home asylum *(hospital)*

nursling infant

nurture abet, aid, assist, care *(regard)*, conjure, cultivate, discipline *(train)*, educate, foster, keep *(shelter)*, maintain *(sustain)*, mature, preservation, promote *(organize)*

nurture a belief opine

nutriment sustenance

nutrire foster, nurture

nutrition sustenance

nutritious salubrious, salutary

nutritive salubrious, salutary

O

oafish obtuse, opaque, provincial

oafishness opacity

oath adjuration, affirmation, asseveration, assurance, attestation, avouchment, confirmation, covenant, obligation *(duty)*, pledge *(binding promise)*, profession *(declaration)*, promise, undertaking *(pledge)*, vow

oath-giving affirmation

oath-taking affirmation

obaeratus indebted

obducere envelop

obduracy resolution *(decision)*, tenacity

obdurate callous, cold-blooded, disobedient, implacable, incorrigible, inexorable, inflexible, insusceptible *(uncaring)*, intractable, pertinacious, recusant, relentless, remorseless, reprobate, resolute, restive, rigid, ruthless, severe, strict, unaffected *(uninfluenced)*, unalterable, unbending, uncompromising, uncontrollable, unrelenting, unyielding, willful

obdurescere insensible

obedience adherence *(devotion)*, adhesion *(loyalty)*, allegiance, capitulation, compliance, deference, duty *(obligation)*, fealty, homage, loyalty, resignation *(passive acceptance)*, servitude

obedient amenable, controlled *(restrained)*, faithful *(loyal)*, law-abiding, lawful, licit, loyal, obeisant, obsequious, passive, pliable, pliant, sequacious, servile, subservient, tractable, true *(loyal)*, yielding

obediently faithfully, respectfully

obeisance conformity *(obedience)*, homage, honor *(outward respect)*, prostration, respect

obeisant obedient, passive, pliant, sequacious, servile, subservient

obey abide, accede *(concede)*, adhere *(maintain loyalty)*, bear *(tolerate)*, comply, conform, fulfill, hear *(give attention to)*, heed, observe *(obey)*, pander, submit *(yield)*, surrender *(yield)*, yield *(submit)*

obey orders conform

obey regulations conform

obey rules conform

obeyed powerful

obfuscate blind *(obscure)*, camouflage, confound, confuse *(bewilder)*, disorganize, disorient, muddle, obnubilate, obscure

obfuscated lost *(disoriented)*, nebulous, opaque

obfuscation concealment, evasion, obscuration, opacity, pretext

object article *(commodity)*, cause *(reason)*, collide *(clash)*, complain *(criticize)*, condemn *(ban)*, conflict, confront *(oppose)*, connotation, content *(meaning)*, contest, counter, demonstrate *(protest)*, demur, deprecate, design *(intent)*, destination, determinant, differ *(disagree)*, disaccord, disaffirm, disagree, disallow, disapprove *(reject)*, disown *(deny the validity)*, dissent *(withhold assent)*, doubt *(distrust)*, end *(intent)*, entity, expostulate, fight *(counteract)*, goal, idea, intent, intention, item, motive, negate, oppose, oppugn, point *(purpose)*, predetermination, project, purpose, pursuit *(goal)*, reason *(basis)*, recipient, reject, remonstrate, reprehend, signification, target

object frivolously cavil

object lesson admonition

object of responsibility charge *(custody)*

object of study specialty *(special aptitude)*

object of the action gist *(ground for a suit)*

object produced as evidence exhibit

object submitted in proof of facts exhibit

object to challenge, complain *(criticize)*, criticize *(find fault with)*, disapprove *(condemn)*, discriminate *(treat differently)*, disfavor, dispute *(contest)*, except *(object)*, refuse

objectify substantiate

objecting critical *(faultfinding)*, disobedient, dissenting, dissident, nonconsenting, remonstrative

objection admonition, complaint, condemnation *(blame)*, criticism, demurrer, denial, disadvantage, disagreement, disapprobation, disapproval, disparagement, dissent *(difference of opinion)*, dissent *(nonconcurrence)*, drawback, grievance, ground, misgiving, negation, nonconformity, opposition, outcry, reaction *(opposition)*, rejection, reluctance, remonstrance, reprimand, reproach, scruple, stricture

objection to a pleading demurrer

objectionable bad *(inferior)*, bad *(offensive)*, blameful, blameworthy, contemptuous, disreputable, heinous, immoral, impermissible, improper, inadmissible, inadvisable, inappropriate, inapt, ineligible, inept *(inappropriate)*, inexcusable, iniquitous, injudicious, invidious, loathsome, obnoxious, odious, offensive *(offending)*, peccable, reprehensible, repugnant *(exciting aversion)*, repulsive, unacceptable, undesirable, undue *(excessive)*, unendurable, unfit, unjustifiable, unsatisfactory, unsavory, unsuitable, unwarranted

objective actual, candid, cause *(reason)*, desideratum, design *(intent)*, destination, dispassionate, end *(intent)*, equitable, evenhanded, factual, fair *(just)*, focus, goal, impartial, intent, intention, just, liberal *(broad minded)*, mission, motive, neutral, nonpartisan, openminded, point *(purpose)*, predetermination, project, purpose, pursuit *(goal)*, rational, substantive, target, unbiased, unprejudiced

objective certainty certification *(certainness)*, certitude

objective certitude certainty

objective necessity compulsion *(coercion)*

objectivity candor *(impartiality)*, disinterest *(lack of prejudice)*, fairness, justice

objector appellant, disputant, malcontent

objects commodities

objuration disparagement, imprecation

objurgate admonish *(warn)*, blame, castigate, censure, contemn, criticize *(find fault with)*, defame, deprecate, disapprove *(condemn)*, expostulate, lash *(attack verbally)*, rebuke, remonstrate, reprehend, reprimand, reproach

objurgation aspersion, bad repute, blame *(culpability)*, charge *(accusation)*, condemnation *(blame)*, contempt *(disdain)*, contumely, denunciation, diatribe, disapprobation, obloquy, remonstrance, reprimand, reproach, revilement, stricture

objurgatory blameful, contemptible, critical *(faultfinding)*, derogatory, remonstrative, scandalous

oblation benefit *(conferment)*, grant

obliga agreement *(contract)*

obligare bind *(obligate)*, pledge *(promise the performance of)*

obligate compel, constrain *(compel)*, detail *(assign)*, encumber *(financially obligate)*, entail, exact, force *(coerce)*, guarantee, necessitate, press *(constrain)*, require *(compel)*

obligate oneself contract, promise *(vow)*, undertake

obligated accountable *(responsible)*, bound, contractual, indebted, indentured, liable

obligation agreement *(contract)*, allegiance, arrears, assurance, bond, burden, charge *(cost)*, charge *(lien)*, charge *(responsibility)*, cloud *(incumbrance)*, commitment *(responsibility)*, compact, compulsion *(coercion)*, condition *(contingent provision)*, contract, coverage *(insurance)*, debit, debt, delinquency *(shortage)*, duress, enforcement, excise, expense *(cost)*, incumbrance *(lien)*, job, liability, lien, mortgage, need *(requirement)*, pledge *(binding promise)*, policy *(contract)*, pressure, promise, provision *(clause)*, rate, recognizance, requirement, responsibility *(accountability)*, restriction, security *(stock)*, specialty *(contract)*, trust *(custody)*, undertaking *(commitment)*, undertaking *(pledge)*, weight *(burden)*

obligation accrued due

obligation incurred cost *(expenses)*

obligation repudiated delict

obligatorily will shall

obligatoriness responsibility *(accountability)*

obligatory binding, choate lien, compelling, compulsory, conclusive *(determinative)*, contractual, essential *(required)*, imperative, indispensable, involuntary, mandatory, necessary *(required)*, peremptory *(imperative)*, positive *(prescribed)*, prescriptive, requisite, strict, unavoidable *(inevitable)*

obligatus indebted

oblige accommodate, aid, assist, bear *(support)*, bestow, bind *(obligate)*, call *(demand)*, coerce, compel, constrain *(compel)*, delegate, detail *(assign)*, dictate, enjoin, exact, excise *(levy a tax)*, force *(coerce)*, help, impose *(enforce)*, impose *(subject)*, let *(permit)*, necessitate, order, pander, patronize *(condescend toward)*, press *(constrain)*, require *(compel)*, suffer *(permit)*, supply, tolerate

obliged accountable *(responsible)*, bound, indebted, indentured, liable

obliged in law liable

obligement enforcement, obligation *(duty)*

obliging accommodation *(adjustment)*, beneficial, benevolent, binding, charitable *(lenient)*, civil *(polite)*, favorable *(expressing approval)*, malleable, obedient, obeisant, philanthropic, pliable, propitious, sequacious, yielding

obligingness amenability, benevolence *(disposition to do good)*, clemency, comity, consideration *(sympathetic regard)*, indulgence

obligor debtor

oblinere smear

obliquation indirection *(indirect action)*

oblique circuitous, deceptive, deviant, indirect, labyrinthine, sinuous

oblique allusion innuendo

oblique hint insinuation

obliqueness indirection *(deceitfulness)*, indirection *(indirect action)*

obliquitous deceptive, sinister

obliquity bad faith, bad repute, corruption, crime, deception, delinquency *(misconduct)*, improbity, indirection *(deceitfulness)*, indirection *(indirect action)*, vice, wrong

obliquus indirect, oblique *(slanted)*

obliterate abate *(extinguish)*, abolish, adeem, annul, cancel, deface, delete, destroy *(efface)*, dissolve *(terminate)*, eliminate *(eradicate)*, eradicate, expunge, extinguish, extirpate, negate, nullify, overthrow, overturn, quash, remove *(eliminate)*, repeal, rescind

obliterated lost *(taken away)*, null *(invalid)*, null and void

obliteration abatement *(extinguishment)*, abolition, annulment, catastrophe, censorship, defacement, destruction, dissolution *(termination)*, obscuration, removal

obliteration of grievances pardon

oblitterare expunge

oblivion disregard *(unconcern)*, nullity

obliviosus oblivious

oblivious careless, heedless, inadvertent, incognizant, lax, negligent, unaware

obliviousness disinterest *(lack of interest)*, disregard *(unconcern)*, negligence

obloquial calumnious

obloquious calumnious

obloquy aspersion, attaint, bad repute, blame *(culpability)*, contempt *(disdain),* contumely, criticism, defamation, degradation, denunciation, diatribe, disgrace, dishonor *(shame),* disparagement, disrepute, ignominy, infamy, malediction, notoriety, odium, opprobrium, ostracism, phillipic, profanity, reproach, revilement, scandal, shame, slander, stricture

obnoxious bad *(offensive),* blameworthy, contemptuous, disreputable, heinous, invidious, loathsome, nefarious, objectionable, odious, offensive *(offending),* reprehensible, repugnant *(exciting aversion),* repulsive, undesirable, unendurable, unsavory

obnoxiousness bad repute, disrepute, indecency

obnoxium reddere subject
obnoxius dependent, liable
oboediens obedient
oboedire obey
obreptitious collusive, sly, stealthy, surreptitious
obruere overwhelm
obrussa criterion
obscene depraved, lascivious, lewd, licentious, objectionable, prurient, repulsive, salacious, scurrilous, suggestive *(risqué)*
obscene art pornography
obscene literature pornography
obscenitas obscenity
obscenity debauchery, pornography, turpitude
obscenus obscene
obscuration indistinctness, opacity
obscure allusive, ambiguous, blind *(concealed),* camouflage, clandestine, cloak, complex, conceal, confound, cover *(conceal),* de minimus, debatable, difficult, disguise, disorganize, disorient, elusive, enigmatic, ensconce, enshroud, envelop, equivocal, esoteric, hidden, hide, impalpable, inapprehensible, incomprehensible, inconspicuous, indefinable, indefinite, indeterminate, inexplicable, inscrutable, minor, mysterious, nebulous, obfuscate, obliterate, obnubilate, opaque, oracular, plant *(covertly place),* privy, recondite, secret, shroud, stealthy, ulterior, uncertain *(ambiguous),* unclear, underlying, unspecified, vague
obscure information secret
obscure meaning ambiguity
obscure question enigma
obscure statement enigma
obscured hidden, lost *(taken away)*
obscurity ambiguity, complication, concealment, indistinctness, mystery, nonappearance, obscuration, opacity, privacy
obscurus inconspicuous, indistinct, inscrutable, lurid
obsecrare appeal, plead *(implore),* request
obsecrate importune, solicit
obsecratio entreaty
obsecration call *(appeal),* claim *(legal demand),* dun, entreaty, imprecation, request
obsequens subservient, yielding
obsequi defer *(put off),* defer *(yield in judgment),* obey
obsequious law-abiding, passive, sequacious, servile, subservient, yield-

ing
obsequiousness allegiance, discipline *(obedience)*
obsequium compliance
obserere lock
observable appreciable, blatant *(conspicuous),* clear *(apparent),* conspicuous, determinable *(ascertainable),* discernible, manifest, naked *(perceptible),* obvious, open *(in sight),* ostensible, palpable, patent, perceivable, perceptible, scrutable, visible *(noticeable)*
observably particularly
observably different distinct *(distinguished from others)*
observance acquiescence, adherence *(devotion),* allegiance, ceremony, compliance, conformity *(obedience),* contemplation, custom, discharge *(performance),* discipline *(obedience),* habit, manner *(behavior),* notice *(heed),* practice *(procedure),* prescription *(custom),* remembrance *(commemoration),* scrutiny
observance of form formality
observance of obligation allegiance
observant alert *(vigilant),* circumspect, conscientious, conscious *(aware),* law-abiding, obedient, perspicacious, punctilious, receptive, sensible, sensitive *(discerning),* vigilant
observant of decorum punctilious
observant of form formal
observantia homage, respect
observantly faithfully
observare heed, keep *(fulfill),* observe *(obey),* observe *(watch),* regard *(pay attention)*
observatio observation
observation apprehension *(perception),* comment, comprehension, concept, conclusion *(determination),* dictum, diligence *(care),* discovery, estimate *(idea),* examination *(study),* generalization, indagation, inference, inspection, judgment *(discernment),* notice *(heed),* outlook, perception, pronouncement, regard *(attention),* remark, research, scrutiny, sense *(intelligence),* statement, surveillance, test
observation post standpoint
observe abide, bear *(tolerate),* check *(inspect),* comment, comply, conform, consider, detect, discern *(detect with the senses),* discover, examine *(study),* express, find *(discover),* fulfill, heed, keep *(fulfill),* mention, monitor, note *(notice),* notice *(observe),* obey, patrol, perceive, perform *(adhere to),* peruse, phrase, pierce *(discern),* police, probe, regard *(pay attention),* relate *(tell),* remark, scrutinize, spy, study, survey *(examine),* witness *(have direct knowledge of)*
observe discipline conform
observer bystander, eyewitness, spy, witness
observing circumspect
obses hostage
obsess harass, occupy *(engage)*
obsessed fanatical, lunatic, pensive
obsessed with addicted
obsessing compelling
obsessio blockade *(barrier)*
obsession dipsomania, phobia, preoccupation, requirement

obsessional compelling
obsessive compelling, fanatical
obsidio blockade *(barrier)*
obsistere withstand
obsolescence desuetude, disuse
obsolescent obsolete, outdated, outmoded
obsolete defunct, inactive, old, outdated, outmoded
obsoleteness desuetude
obsoletus dilapidated, obsolete, stale
obstacle bar *(obstruction),* barrier, blockade *(barrier),* check *(bar),* complication, damper *(stopper),* deterrence, deterrent, detriment, disadvantage, drawback, encumbrance, fetter, handicap, hindrance, impasse, impediment, interruption, nuisance, obstruction, pitfall, predicament, problem, prohibition, restraint, stay
obstare prevent, withstand
obstinacy contempt *(disobedience to the court),* contest *(dispute),* reluctance, resistance, resolution *(decision),* tenacity
obstinate contentious, contumacious, difficult, disobedient, froward, immutable, impervious, implacable, incorrigible, inexorable, inflexible, insusceptible *(uncaring),* intractable, obdurate, persistent, pertinacious, perverse, proud *(conceited),* purposeful, recalcitrant, recusant, relentless, resolute, restive, rigid, steadfast, unbending, uncompromising, uncontrollable, unruly, unyielding, willful
obstinatus inflexible, pertinacious, willful
obstreperous blatant *(obtrusive),* disobedient, disorderly, intractable, perverse, recalcitrant, uncontrollable, unruly
obstruct abrogate *(annul),* arrest *(stop),* balk, ban, bar *(hinder),* block, check *(restrain),* clog, condemn *(ban),* constrain *(restrain),* constrict *(inhibit),* contain *(restrain),* control *(restrain),* counter, curb, debar, defer *(put off),* delay, detain *(restrain),* deter, disadvantage, discontinue *(break continuity),* disrupt, estop, fight *(counteract),* foil, forbid, forestall, frustrate, halt, hamper, hinder, hold up *(delay),* impede, inconvenience, inhibit, interdict, interfere, interpose, interrupt, keep *(restrain),* lock, obturate, occlude, oppose, oppugn, preclude, prevent, prohibit, repulse, resist *(oppose),* restrain, restrict, shut, stall, stave, stay *(halt),* stem *(check),* stifle, stop, suppress, thwart, toll *(stop),* trammel, withstand
obstruct action encumber *(hinder)*
obstruct by opposition discourage
obstruct one's vision blind *(deprive of sight)*
obstruct the course of descent escheat
obstruct the view of cloak, enshroud
obstruct work strike *(refuse to work)*
obstructed arrested *(checked),* blind *(impassable),* broken *(interrupted),* impervious
obstructer deterrent
obstructio obstruction
obstruction barrier, blockade *(barrier),* check *(bar),* cloud *(incumbrance),*

complication, constraint *(restriction),* damper *(stopper),* deadlock, deterrence, deterrent, disadvantage, encumbrance, estoppel, fetter, filibuster, frustration, halt, handicap, hindrance, impasse, impediment, impugnation, interruption, obstacle, onus *(burden),* predicament, prohibition, resistance, restraint, stay, trouble

obstruction of justice misprision

obstruction to congressional action filibuster

obstructionism constraint *(restriction),* contempt *(disobedience to the court)*

obstructionist assailant, disputant, malcontent

obstructive deterrent, preventive, prohibitive *(restrictive)*

obstruent obstruction

obstupefacere confound

obsuration concealment

obtain accept *(take),* acquire *(receive),* attain, buy, derive *(receive),* educe, engage *(hire),* evoke, extract, gain, glean, induce, inherit, occupy *(take possession),* perform *(adhere to),* possess, preempt, procure, purchase, raise *(collect),* reach, realize *(obtain as a profit),* reap, receive *(acquire),* recover, recruit, redeem *(repurchase),* succeed *(attain)*

obtain a mortgage borrow

obtain a return profit, realize *(obtain as a profit)*

obtain a victory beat *(defeat),* earn

obtain again repossess

obtain by any means acquire *(secure)*

obtain by compulsion enforce, extort

obtain by course of law recover

obtain by force enforce, impose *(enforce)*

obtain by reasoning derive *(deduce)*

obtain by search find *(discover)*

obtain exclusive possession monopolize

obtain in an unlawful manner extort

obtain insurance insure

obtain knowledge of overhear

obtain money by false pretenses cheat

obtain money on false pretenses defraud, peculate

obtain money under false pretenses defalcate

obtain payment collect *(recover money)*

obtain the use of borrow

obtain under false pretenses peculate

obtain unlawfully extort

obtainable available, open *(accessible),* possible, potential, practicable, vulnerable

obtainer consumer

obtaining by force extortion

obtaining by threat extortion

obtaining national defense secrets espionage

obtaining of classified information espionage

obtainment adverse possession, collection *(accumulation),* distraint, receipt *(act of receiving),* recovery *(repossession),* takeover

obtainment of property acquisition

obtegere cover *(pretext)*

obtemperans obedient

obtemperare conform

obtest importune, petition, pray, request, solicit

obtestatio appeal, entreaty

obtestation call *(appeal),* dun

obtrectare decry, defame, depreciate

obtrectatio disparagement

obtrectation bad repute

obtrude accroach, encroach, impinge, impose *(intrude),* interpose, intervene, intrude, invade, overstep

obtrude on compel

obtrusion deterrent, encroachment, intrusion

obtrusive brazen, bumptious, contemptuous, flagrant, intrusive, prominent

obtrusiveness pretense *(ostentation)*

obtund assuage, impair, palliate *(abate),* soothe, subdue

obturate balk, deter, occlude

obturation blockade *(limitation),* obstruction

obtuse blind *(not discerning),* fatuous, impervious, inexpressive, opaque, unaffected *(uninfluenced)*

obtuseness ignorance, opacity

obtusus obtuse

obumbrate obfuscate

obverse adverse *(opposite),* antipode, contra, contradictory, contraposition, contrary, counterpart *(complement)*

obviate balk, bar *(hinder),* deter, estop, forestall, overrule, overthrow, prevent, remove *(eliminate),* stay *(halt),* supersede

obvious absolute *(conclusive),* apparent *(perceptible),* arrant *(definite),* blatant *(conspicuous),* coherent *(clear),* comprehensible, conspicuous, distinct *(clear),* elementary, evident, explicit, flagrant, gross *(flagrant),* lucid, manifest, naked *(perceptible),* open *(in sight),* ostensible, outright, overt, palpable, patent, pellucid, perceivable, perceptible, prominent, public *(known),* salient, scrutable, stark, tangible, unambiguous, undeniable, unmistakable

obvious interpretation connotation, content *(meaning)*

obvious meaning connotation, content *(meaning)*

obvious sense connotation, content *(meaning)*

obviously fairly *(clearly)*

occasio occasion, opportunity

occasion access *(opening),* avail *(bring about),* cause, chance *(fortuity),* create, day in court, engender, entail, event, evoke, experience *(encounter),* generate, happening, incident, inspire, occurrence, opportunity, particular, point *(period of time),* prompt, provoke, qualification *(fitness)*

occasional casual, infrequent, intermittent, periodic, sporadic, uncommon, unusual

occasioner author *(originator)*

occasions circumstances

occidere kill *(murder),* perish, slay

occisio murder

occlude balk, bar *(exclude),* bar *(hinder),* block, clog, constrict *(inhibit),*

debar, hinder, lock, obstruct, seal *(close),* shut, stop

occlusion blockade *(limitation),* damper *(stopper),* deterrent, obstruction

occulere conceal

occult blind *(obscure),* cloak, covert, elusive, esoteric, hidden, incomprehensible, inexplicable, inscrutable, mysterious, obfuscate, obnubilate, obscure, recondite, secret, uncertain *(ambiguous),* undisclosed

occultare disguise

occultari abscond

occultate camouflage

occultation obscuration

occultism mystery

occultness mystery

occultus hidden, inscrutable, latent, mysterious, secret, stealthy

occupancy enjoyment *(use),* habitation *(act of inhabiting),* inhabitation *(act of dwelling in),* occupation *(possession),* ownership, possession *(ownership),* seisin, tenancy, tenure

occupant citizen, denizen, domiciliary, habitant, inhabitant, inmate, lessee, lodger, resident, tenant

occupant of an office incumbent

occupare assume *(seize),* encroach, invest *(fund),* occupy *(engage),* occupy *(take possession)*

occupatio occupation *(possession),* pursuit *(occupation),* taking

occupation appointment *(position),* calling, capacity *(job),* career, employment, enjoyment *(use),* enterprise *(undertaking),* function, habitation *(act of inhabiting),* industry *(activity),* inhabitation *(act of dwelling in),* job, labor *(work),* livelihood, occupancy, office, position *(business status),* post, practice *(professional business),* profession *(vocation),* project, province, seisin, specialty *(special aptitude),* tenancy, tenure, undertaking *(enterprise),* work *(employment)*

occupational technical

occupatum employ *(engage services)*

occupiable habitable

occupied full, pensive, populous, residential

occupier citizen, denizen, domiciliary, habitant, inhabitant, inmate, lessee, lodger, occupant, resident, tenant

occupy consist, dwell *(reside),* engage *(involve),* hold *(possess),* immerse *(engross),* inhabit, interest, monopolize, own, possess, preempt, reside

occupy oneself with address *(direct attention to),* commit *(perpetrate),* devote, notice *(observe),* ply

occupy the attention interest

occupy the chair manage, officiate, preside

occupy the mind with concentrate *(pay attention)*

occupy the thoughts with concentrate *(pay attention),* focus, ponder

occupying situated

occupying the same domicile cohabitation *(living together)*

occur accrue *(arise),* appear *(materialize),* ensue, supervene

occur again recur

occur at the same time concur *(coexist)*

occur concurrently concur *(coexist)*
occurrence appearance *(emergence)*, case *(example)*, case *(set of circumstances)*, contingency, development *(outgrowth)*, event, experience *(encounter)*, happening, incident, occasion, particular, predicament, situation
occurrences circumstances
occurring current
occurring after death posthumous
occurring again periodic
occurring at the same time concurrent *(at the same time)*
occurring by chance fortuitous
occurring in an instant instantaneous
occurring simultaneously coincidental
occurring together coincidental
ochlocracy lynch law
oculis captus blind *(not discerning)*
odd dissimilar, eccentric, inappropriate, irregular *(not usual)*, ludicrous, noteworthy, novel, original *(creative)*, particular *(specific)*, peculiar *(curious)*, singular, unaccustomed, uncanny, uncommon, unique, unusual
oddity exception *(exclusion)*, irregularity, quirk *(idiosyncrasy)*, speciality, specialty *(distinctive mark)*, trait
oddment discard
oddments balance *(amount in excess)*
oddness irregularity
odds advantage, contraposition, disaccord, disagreement, edge *(advantage)*, embroilment, feud, probability, variance *(disagreement)*
odiosus irksome, odious, repulsive
odiosus molestus offensive *(offending)*
odious antipathetic *(distasteful)*, bad *(offensive)*, base *(bad)*, blameworthy, contemptible, disgraceful, disreputable, gross *(flagrant)*, heinous, invidious, libelous, loathsome, nefarious, notorious, objectionable, obnoxious, offensive *(offending)*, outrageous, reprehensible, repugnant *(exciting aversion)*, repulsive, scandalous, sordid
odiousness bad repute, disrepute, odium
odium alienation *(estrangement)*, attaint, bad repute, contempt *(disdain)*, criticism, degradation, discredit, disgrace, disrepute, hatred, ignominy, ill will, infamy, malice, notoriety, obloquy, opprobrium, scandal, shame
odium rancor
odorari trace *(follow)*
of construe *(translate)*
of a different kind dissimilar
of a previous fashion outdated, outmoded
of a previous style outdated, outmoded
of all sorts dissimilar
of an equal size commensurable
of any description whatever
of any kind or sort whatever
of bad character disreputable
of consequence cogent
of course consequently
of decisive importance critical *(crucial)*
of doubtful certainty disputable
of doubtful meaning equivocal
of equal dignity coequal

of equal duration commensurate
of equal extent commensurate
of equal force equivalent
of equal length or volume commensurable
of equal power coequal
of equal rank commensurate
of equal value equivalent
of equal weight equivalent
of every description miscellaneous
of everyday occurrence typical
of external origin alien *(unrelated)*
of foreign origin alien *(foreign)*
of frequent occurrence typical
of general utility beneficial, practical
of good omen auspicious
of great age outdated
of great consequence critical *(crucial)*, decisive, important *(significant)*
of great extent copious, far reaching
of great magnitude important *(significant)*
of great scope complete *(all-embracing)*, far reaching, omnibus
of great weight important *(significant)*
of greater influence superior *(higher)*
of hidden meaning enigmatic
of high standing important *(significant)*
of high station important *(significant)*
of higher rank superior *(higher)*
of highest excellence prime *(most valuable)*
of humble birth ignoble
of ill fame disreputable, notorious
of ill repute notorious
of illicit union illegitimate *(born out of wedlock)*
of importance considerable, critical *(crucial)*, important *(significant)*, indispensable
of inestimable value invaluable
of law jural
of lawful parentage legitimate *(lawfully conceived)*
of less importance inferior *(lower in position)*
of like rank coequal
of little account immaterial, inappreciable, negligible
of little consequence negligible, nonessential, paltry, trivial
of little importance inapposite, inappreciable, negligible, nonessential
of little moment collateral *(immaterial)*
of little value paltry
of little weight frivolous
of long duration chronic, durable
of long standing conventional, customary, durable
of loose morals brazen
of low character ignoble
of low extraction caitiff, ignoble
of low origin caitiff
of low station ignoble
of lower rank subaltern
of many kinds dissimilar
of mean extraction caitiff
of mean origin caitiff
of minor importance de minimus, inconsequential
of mixed character miscellaneous

of moment crucial
of necessity compelling, consequently
of no account de minimus, expendable, frivolous, inconsequential, minor, nonessential, null *(insignificant)*, paltry, unessential
of no avail unavailing
of no binding force null *(invalid)*, null and void
of no concern nonessential
of no consequence immaterial, inconsequential, inconsiderable, insubstantial, nonessential, unessential
of no effect null *(insignificant)*, null *(invalid)*, null and void
of no essential consequence immaterial
of no importance immaterial, nonessential
of no legal weight null and void
of no moment immaterial, inconsiderable, negligible, null *(insignificant)*
of no repute blameworthy
of no significance immaterial, negligible, nonessential
of no validity null *(invalid)*, null and void
of no value null *(insignificant)*
of no weight null *(invalid)*
of note considerable, crucial
of old outdated
of one accord concurrent *(united)*, consensual, consenting
of one mind consensual
of promise auspicious
of recent occurrence recent
of regular recurrence continual *(connected)*
of repute credible
of right de jure
of second rank minor
of service beneficial, disposable, effective *(efficient)*
of short duration provisional
of small account petty, slight
of small importance nonessential, slight
of small moment petty
of small value paltry
of sound judgment normal *(sane)*
of supreme importance crucial
of that kind cognate
of that sort cognate
of the best quality prime *(most valuable)*
of the blood consanguineous
of the moment current
of the old order outdated
of the old school outdated, outmoded
of the origin reputed authentic
of the present current
of the quality of a felon felonious
of the same degree equal
of the same family consanguineous, interrelated
of the same kind consanguineous
of the same mind collective, concordant, consensual
of the same rank coequal, equal
of the same stock akin *(related by blood)*
of this date current
of todays date current
of uncertain issue doubtful
of uncertain significance equivocal
of unknown authorship anonymous

of unsound mind deranged, lunatic, non compos mentis
of use disposable, effective *(efficient)*
of value beneficial
of various kinds miscellaneous
of vital importance critical *(crucial)*, essential *(required)*
of which wherein
off stale
off guard heedless, negligent, unaware, unsuspecting
off the mark improper
off the point immaterial
off the record confidential, unofficial
off the subject impertinent *(irrelevant)*, irrelevant
off the topic immaterial, irrelevant
off-center astray
off-color improper, suggestive *(risqué)*
off-the-record private *(confidential)*
offbeat unusual
offence crime
offend affront, aggravate *(annoy)*, annoy, antagonize, bait *(harass)*, disoblige, distress, estrange, harry *(harass)*, hector, humiliate, irritate, mistreat, persecute, pique, plague, provoke, repel *(disgust)*, trespass
offend against the law violate
offended aggrieved *(victimized)*, resentful
offender convict, criminal, delinquent, felon, lawbreaker, malefactor, outlaw, pariah, racketeer, recidivist, wrongdoer
offender against society outlaw
offender against the law malefactor
offender under suspension of sentence probationer *(released offender)*
offendere disoblige, offend *(insult)*
offending delinquent *(guilty of a misdeed)*, felonious, offensive *(offending)*, repugnant *(exciting aversion)*
offensa disfavor, dissatisfaction
offense assault, crime, delict, delinquency *(misconduct)*, disrespect, exception *(objection)*, felony, foray, guilt, indiscretion, infraction, injury, injustice, misconduct, misdeed, misdemeanor, misdoing, misfeasance, misprision, onset *(assault)*, provocation, resentment, transgression, umbrage, violation, wrong
offense against the law crime, guilt, misdemeanor, misfeasance
offense against the state crime
offense punishable by imprisonment felony
offenseless blameless
offensio dissatisfaction, offense
offensive antipathetic *(distasteful)*, bad *(offensive)*, blatant *(obtrusive)*, calumnious, contemptible, contemptuous, foray, gross *(flagrant)*, heinous, impertinent *(insolent)*, inelegant, insolent, invidious, lewd, litigious, loathsome, lurid, noxious, objectionable, obnoxious, obscene, odious, onset *(assault)*, outrageous, peccant *(culpable)*, presumptuous, profligate *(corrupt)*, pugnacious, reprehensible, repugnant *(exciting aversion)*, repulsive, salacious, scandalous, scurrilous, unacceptable, unbecoming, unendurable, unsatisfactory, unsavory, unseemly, vicious

offensive action battery
offensive to decency obscene
offensive to modesty obscene
offensively assertive blatant *(obtrusive)*
offensively obtrusive blatant *(obtrusive)*
offensiveness guilt, obscenity
offer adduce, administer *(tender)*, bear *(yield)*, bid, hold out *(deliberate on an offer)*, introduce, invitation, overture, pose *(propound)*, present *(introduce)*, present *(make a gift)*, proffer, proposal *(suggestion)*, propose, proposition, propound, remit *(submit for consideration)*, tender
offer a discount rebate
offer a job to delegate
offer a post delegate
offer a word of caution forewarn, notice *(give formal warning)*
offer advice exhort
offer an explanation explain
offer an explanation of interpret
offer an inducement coax, suborn
offer an opinion advise
offer an opinion to counsel
offer as an exhibit introduce
offer assurances to assure *(give confidence to)*
offer collateral ensure, pawn, pledge *(deposit)*
offer compensation indemnify
offer counsel admonish *(advise)*, advise, charge *(instruct on the law)*
offer evidence present *(introduce)*
offer for consideration move *(judicially request)*
offer for inspection exhibit
offer for sale handle *(trade)*, sell, vend
offer in defense justify
offer in exchange displace *(replace)*
offer performance offer *(tender)*
offer reparation indemnify
offer resistance confront *(oppose)*, hold out *(resist)*, oppose, parry, resist *(oppose)*, withstand
offer sacrifice propitiate
offer satisfaction indemnify
offer to give dedicate
offer to the public issue *(publish)*, post
offered unsolicited, voluntary
offered price bid
offerer client
offering benefit *(conferment)*, bribe, contribution *(donation)*, dedication, donation, gratuity *(present)*, introduction, largess *(gift)*, tip *(gratuity)*
offering a problem difficult
offering as an exhibit introduction
offering evidence probative
offerre offer *(propose)*
offertory benefit *(conferment)*
offhand cursory, impulsive *(rash)*, informal, nonchalant, perfunctory, slipshod, unpremeditated
offhandedness informality
office agency *(commission)*, appointment *(position)*, bureau, business *(occupation)*, calling, career, chamber *(compartment)*, chapter *(branch)*, duty *(obligation)*, employment, firm, function, mission, occupation *(vocation)*, organ, position *(business status)*, post, profes-

sion *(vocation)*, province, pursuit *(occupation)*, sphere, title *(position)*, trade *(occupation)*, work *(employment)*
office bearer official
office force personnel
office holder clerk, functionary
office hunter candidate
office seeker candidate, politician
office worker clerk
office-seeker contender
officebearer incumbent
officeholder caretaker *(one fulfilling the function of office)*, incumbent, officer, official, politician
officeholders authorities
officer caretaker *(one fulfilling the function of office)*, functionary, incumbent, key man, magistrate, marshal, official, peace officer, proctor
officer in charge caretaker *(one fulfilling the function of office)*
officer of court counsel, counselor
officer of state caretaker *(one fulfilling the function of office)*, legislator, politician
officer of the court administrator, attorney, esquire
officer of the law marshal, peace officer
officer who carries out orders of the court marshal
officers management *(directorate)*, police
officers of instruction faculty *(teaching staff)*
officers of the law police
official actual, certain *(fixed)*, choate lien, civic, clerk, ex officio, factual, formal, functionary, genuine, incumbent, indubious, legitimate *(rightful)*, magistrate, notary public, officer, politician, valid
official announcement charter *(declaration of rights)*
official bulletin declaration
official call monition *(legal summons)*, process *(summons)*, summons
official correspondence dispatch *(message)*
official count census
official court order summons
official criminal charge information *(charge)*
official document charter *(license)*
official enumeration of inhabitants census
official enumeration of the population census
official headquarters of an ambassador embassy
official inquiry investigation
official misconduct crime, criminality, delict, guilt, misfeasance, offense
official mission embassy
official notice citation *(charge)*, monition *(legal summons)*, process *(summons)*, summons
official order mittimus, summons
official procedure bureaucracy
official publication document, proclamation
official receiver assessor
official reception ceremony
official reckoning census
official recognition mention *(tribute)*
official record instrument *(docu-*

ment)
official registration census
official reply answer *(judicial response)*
official representative legislator, plenipotentiary
official writing certificate, instrument *(document)*
officialdom bureaucracy
officially utter pronounce *(pass judgment)*
officially withdraw repeal
officials authorities, hierarchy *(persons in authority)*, management *(directorate)*
officiary official
officiate administer *(conduct)*, exercise *(discharge a function)*, govern, handle *(manage)*, manage, moderate *(preside over)*, operate, oversee, preside, rule *(govern)*
officiate at conduct
officiating executive, ministerial
officiation bureaucracy, direction *(guidance)*
officio fungi officiate
officious dictatorial, obtrusive
officium courtesy, duty *(obligation)*, function, obligation *(duty)*, office, subjection
offprint copy
offset adeem, compensate *(counterbalance)*, contra, counteract, countervail, cover *(provide for)*, equipoise, negate, neutralize, nullify, outbalance, overreach, reaction *(opposition)*, setoff
offset bad debts redeem *(satisfy debts)*
offsetting contribution *(indemnification)*
offsetting claim setoff
offshoot affiliate, consequence *(conclusion)*, corollary, descendant, development *(outgrowth)*, organ, outgrowth
offshoots offspring
offspring affinity *(family ties)*, blood, child, children, descendant, family *(household)*, issue *(progeny)*, offshoot, outcome, outgrowth, posterity, product, progeny, succession
oft repeated proverbial, trite
oft-repeated customary, frequent, ordinary, periodic, typical
often chronic
often done frequent
often met with common *(customary)*
oftentime periodic
old antique, elderly, obsolete, outdated, outmoded, prior, stale, traditional, trite
old age longevity
old campaigner veteran
old fashioned antique
old soldier veteran
old-fashioned defunct, obsolete, outdated, outmoded
old-time outdated
old-world outdated, outmoded
olden old, outdated
older antique
oldest prime *(original)*
oldness longevity
oligopoly monopoly
olio melange
omega close *(conclusion)*, end *(termination)*

omen anticipate *(prognosticate)*, caution *(warning)*, forerunner, harbinger, herald, indicant, indication, portend, precursor, predict, premonition, presage, threat, token, warning
ominate forewarn, portend, predict, presage, prognosticate
ominous aleatory *(perilous)*, bleak *(not favorable)*, dangerous, dire, imminent, inauspicious, insalubrious, oracular, pending *(imminent)*, portentous *(ominous)*, presageful, prophetic, suggestive *(evocative)*, unfavorable, unpropitious
omission breach, default, deficiency, deficit, delinquency *(failure of duty)*, dereliction, desuetude, dishonor *(nonpayment)*, dispensation *(exception)*, exception *(exclusion)*, exclusion, failure *(falling short)*, fault *(mistake)*, flaw, infraction, laches, miscue, neglect, negligence, nonfeasance, nonperformance, offense, ostracism, rejection, removal, renunciation
omission of a court injustice
omission of duty delinquency *(failure of duty)*
omission of obligation delinquency *(failure of duty)*
omission prohibited by law crime
omissive remiss
omit abrogate *(rescind)*, bar *(exclude)*, censor, delete, eliminate *(exclude)*, except *(exclude)*, exclude, fail *(neglect)*, forgo, forswear, ignore, neglect, obliterate, overlook *(disregard)*, pretermit, prohibit, relegate, remove *(eliminate)*, set aside *(annul)*
omit using conserve
omit what is due default
omitted null *(invalid)*, null and void
omittere abandon *(withdraw)*, disregard, omit
omitting perfunctory, save
omniform protean
omnino in toto
omnipotence force *(strength)*, influence, predominance, supremacy
omnipotens omnipotent
omnipotent compelling, in full force, indomitable, influential, irresistible, powerful, predominant, strong
omnipresent ubiquitous
omnis total
omniscient expert, learned
omnivorous gluttonous
omnivorousness greed
on a footing with coequal
on a level with coequal
on a par coequal, commensurate, equal
on a par with coequal, equivalent
on a proper scale commensurate
on a suitable scale commensurate
on account of ad hoc, in furtherance
on account of this a priori, consequently
on all counts in toto
on approval elective *(selective)*
on bad terms inimical
on behalf of in furtherance, in lieu of
on call available, disposable, ready *(prepared)*
on condition that provided
on duty operative
on edge restive

on even terms commensurate, equal, pro rata
on familiar terms intimate
on fire perfervid
on guard alert *(vigilant)*, circumspect, noncommittal, provident *(showing foresight)*, safe, vigilant
on hand present *(attendant)*
on intimate terms familiar *(informed)*
on no occasion sine die
on oath promissory
on one side only ex parte
on one's deathbed in extremis
on one's guard careful
on one's word promissory
on one's word of honor promissory
on paper holographic, in writing
on par comparable *(equivalent)*
on presentation prima facie *(self-evident)*
on purpose purposely
on record documentary
on schedule punctual
on that account a priori, consequently
on that ground a priori
on the agenda at issue, forthcoming
on the alert careful
on the anniversary per annum
on the application of one party ex parte
on the basis of a year per annum
on the brink of almost
on the confines of contiguous
on the contrary contra
on the decline regressive
on the docket forthcoming
on the edge peripheral
on the edge of contiguous
on the face of the matter prima facie *(self-evident)*
on the first view prima facie *(self-evident)*
on the fringe of society derelict *(abandoned)*
on the horizon forthcoming, pending *(imminent)*, prospective
on the increase cumulative *(increasing)*
on the journey en route
on the market available
on the other hand contra
on the road en route
on the same footing coequal
on the same level equal
on the same matter pari materia
on the spot present *(attendant)*, present *(current)*
on the verge of almost
on the wane decadent, dilapidated
on the way en route, imminent
on the whole as a rule, generally
on this account consequently
on time prompt, punctual
once late *(defunct)*, whenever
once more anew, de novo
oncoming forthcoming, imminent, onset *(commencement)*, pending *(imminent)*
one exclusive *(singular)*, individual, indivisible, sole, unit *(item)*, whole *(unified)*
one after another consecutive
one after the other consecutive
one and all en banc, in solido

one and the same same
one at a time respectively
one authorized to deliver a verdict
juror
one by one respectively
one called to the bar advocate
(*counselor*), counselor, jurist
one engaged in a manual enterprise
artisan
one engaged in buying and selling
dealer
one excluded from some privilege
alien
one held in captivity captive
one held in confinement captive
one held in subjegation captive
one holding land of another tenant
one implicated in the commission of
a crime offender
one instigating an action complainant
one not legally competent minor
one occupying another's land tenant
one occupying real property tenant
one of constituent (*part*)
one of an adjudgment body juror
one of several parts installment
one of several payments installment
one of successive parts installment
one of the clientele customer
one of the contents component
one of the purchasing public customer
one seeking cure patient
one seeking relief patient
one sided ex parte, inequitable
one skilled in an industrial art artisan
one suspected of a crime suspect
one sworn to deliver a verdict juror
one thing in return for another
quid pro quo
one to whom a fee is conveyed
feoffee
one to whom seisin passes feoffee
one to whom something is entrusted
trustee
one to whom title is passed feoffee
one trained in a mechanic trade artisan
one undergoing therapy patient
one undergoing treatment patient
one using real property tenant
one who affirms declarant
one who applies for relief petitioner
one who asserts declarant
one who asserts a demand claimant
one who attests deponent
one who bears witness bystander,
deponent
one who breaks the law offender
one who brings an action plaintiff
one who claims a right claimant
one who commits a crime offender
one who commits larceny embezzler
one who dispenses justice judge
one who enfeoffs another feoffor
one who exacts assessor
one who files an application for relief petitioner
one who flees fugitive
one who formulates laws legislator
one who gives a corporeal hereditament feoffor
one who gives assistance good sa-

maritan
one who gives evidence deponent
one who gives or makes laws legislator
one who gives testimony witness
one who handles property for another fiduciary
one who has attained legal majority
adult
one who has land landholder
one who has no specialized training
layman
one who has not come of age infant
one who has not reached his majority infant
one who helps another good samaritan
one who helps to pass laws legislator
one who imposes a charge assessor
one who inherits heir, legatee
one who is enfeoffed feoffee
one who is unfriendly foe
one who levies assessor
one who makes an affidavit deponent
one who obtains evidence first hand
eyewitness
one who opposes foe, opponent
one who personally observes an occurrence eyewitness
one who proclaims declarant
one who receives beneficiary
one who remains holdover
one who renders aid good samaritan
one who requests relief petitioner
one who sells for factorage factor
(*commission merchant*)
one who stays on holdover
one who supplies criminal information to the police informer (*one providing criminal information*)
one who testifies to what he has
seen eyewitness
one who testifies under oath
affirmant, deponent
one who transacts business for another fiduciary
one who transfers property by deed
feoffor
one who transfers real property to
another feoffor
one's due birthright
one's duty charge (*responsibility*)
one's own land demesne
one's people blood
one-sided ex parte, illiberal, interested, parochial, partial (*biased*), unequal (*unjust*), unfair, unilateral
one-sided conception distortion
one-sided view distortion
one-sidedness favoritism, inequity,
intolerance, partiality, predetermination, prejudice (*preconception*)
one-time late (*defunct*), previous
one-track mind compulsion (*obsession*)
oneness agreement (*concurrence*),
concordance, conformity (*agreement*),
entity, facsimile, identity (*individuality*), identity (*similarity*), peace, personality, union (*unity*)
onerare encumber (*financially obligate*), load
onerous bad (*offensive*), operose, oppressive, ponderous

onesidedness foregone conclusion
ongoing chronic, live (*existing*),
open-ended, progressive (*going forward*), protracted
onlooker bystander, eyewitness, witness
only exclusive (*singular*), mere, sole,
solely (*singly*)
onrush onset (*assault*)
onset assault, birth (*beginning*), genesis, inception, nascency, origin (*source*),
origination, outset, start, threshold
(*commencement*)
onset with force assault
onslaught assault, battery, incursion,
onset (*assault*), outbreak, violence
onus allegiance, burden, commitment
(*responsibility*), duty (*tax*), handicap,
imposition (*excessive burden*), incumbrance (*burden*), liability, penalty, requirement, weight (*burden*)
onus cargo, encumbrance, freight
onus imponere load
onus probandi cloud (*suspicion*)
onward vanward
onward motion progress
ooze exude, outflow
opacity density, indistinctness, obscuration
opaque impervious, inapprehensible,
indefinable, indefinite, obtuse
opaqueness density, obscuration,
opacity
open aleatory (*uncertain*), apparent
(*perceptible*), available, bare, bona fide,
break (*separate*), candid, commence,
conspicuous, denude, direct (*forthright*),
equivocal, establish (*launch*), evident,
explicit, flagrant, generate, honest, impartial, indeterminate, ingenuous, initiate, launch (*initiate*), liberal (*broad
minded*), liberal (*not literal*), manifest,
manifest, naive, naked (*perceptible*), obvious, open-minded, originate, outstanding (*unresolved*), overt, passable,
patent, penetrable, perceivable, perceptible, preface, pullulate, receptive, reveal, scrutable, simple, split, spread,
straightforward, suasible, subject (*exposed*), susceptible (*unresistent*), unaffected (*sincere*), unbiased, undecided,
unmistakable, unprejudiced, unrestricted, unsettled, vacant, vulnerable
open a passage admit (*give access*)
open a path admit (*give access*)
open a road admit (*give access*)
open a route admit (*give access*)
open a trade deal
open act overt act
open again reopen
open an account with deal
open an entryway admit (*give access*)
open an inlet admit (*give access*)
open breach feud
open contest competition
open court bench
open declaration avowal, oath
open discussion meeting (*conference*), panel (*discussion group*)
open enemy foe
open fire discharge (*shoot*)
open fire upon attack
open forum panel (*discussion group*)
open market market place, trade
(*commerce*)

open mart market *(business)*
open out compound
open position access *(opening)*
open quarrel feud
open statement of affirmation avouchment
open the mind disabuse
open the way for facilitate
open to disposable
open to all general
open to attack helpless *(defenseless)*
open to choice disjunctive *(alternative)*, elective *(selective)*
open to criticism blameful, blameworthy, reprehensible
open to debate debatable, disputable, litigious, polemic
open to discussion controversial, debatable, disputable, forensic, moot, pending *(unresolved)*, polemic, uncertain *(questionable)*
open to dispute debatable
open to doubt controversial, debatable, disputable, doubtful, implausible, incredible, ludicrous, problematic, suspicious *(questionable)*, unbelievable
open to error undependable
open to objection irregular *(improper)*
open to proof theoretical
open to question controversial, debatable, disputable, doubtful, dubitative, equivocal, indefinite, indeterminate, litigious, moot, pending *(unresolved)*, polemic, suspicious *(questionable)*, uncertain *(questionable)*
open to suggestion receptive
open to suggestions amenable
open to suspicion debatable, disputable, doubtful, implausible, incredible, unbelievable
open to the public competitive *(open)*
open to the vision evident
open to various interpretations ambiguous, uncertain *(ambiguous)*
open to view apparent *(perceptible)*, evident, expose, perceivable, perceptible, present *(introduce)*
open up bare, exhibit, liberate, manifest, unveil
open-handed philanthropic
open-handedness philanthropy
open-minded dispassionate, impartial, liberal *(broad minded)*, objective, open *(persuasible)*, progressive *(advocating change)*, receptive, suasible, unbiased
open-mindedness disinterest *(lack of prejudice)*, objectivity
open-mouthed speechless
opened penetrable
openhanded benevolent, charitable *(benevolent)*, donative, liberal *(generous)*
openhandedness largess *(generosity)*
openhearted liberal *(generous)*
opening access *(right of way)*, admission *(entry)*, admittance *(means of approach)*, chance *(fortuity)*, egress, entrance, first appearance, hiatus, inception, initial, loophole, margin *(spare amount)*, occasion, onset *(commencement)*, opportunity, original *(initial)*, origination, outlet, outset, portal, preamble, preface, preliminary, prelude,

preparatory, rift *(gap)*, start
opening argument opening statement
opening of negotiations overture
openly fairly *(clearly)*
openminded unprejudiced
openmindedness fairness
openness candor *(straightforwardness)*, honesty, latitude
opera effort, service *(assistance)*
operable functional, practicable
operant active, functional
operate administer *(conduct)*, commit *(perpetrate)*, conduct, control *(regulate)*, employ *(make use of)*, exercise *(use)*, exert, exploit *(make use of)*, function, handle *(manage)*, manage, manipulate *(utilize skillfully)*, militate, ply, transact, wield
operate jointly concur *(agree)*
operating active, in full force
operating company corporation
operating expenses overhead
operation act *(undertaking)*, activity, calling, campaign, commission *(act)*, conduct, course, deal, enterprise *(undertaking)*, instrumentality, management *(judicious use)*, maneuver *(tactic)*, manner *(behavior)*, method, modus operandi, performance *(execution)*, performance *(workmanship)*, practice *(procedure)*, process *(course)*, scheme, system, transaction, undertaking *(enterprise)*, usage
operational effective *(operative)*, functional, operative, practical
operational before retroactive
operative constructive *(creative)*, functional, ministerial, potent, practical, prevailing *(having superior force)*, procedural, valuable, viable
operative with respect to the past nunc pro tunc
operator actor, artisan, dealer
operire close *(terminate)*, cover *(pretext)*
operose difficult, diligent, industrious, oppressive, painstaking
operosus painstaking
opes strength
opiate cannabis, drug, narcotic, narcotic
opifex artisan
opinabilis hypothetical
opinari guess, opine
opine advise, comment, construe *(comprehend)*, counsel, deem, determine, gauge, guess, presume, presuppose, surmise, suspect *(think)*
opinio belief *(state of mind)*, character *(reputation)*, conviction *(persuasion)*, expectation, faith, impression, presumption, reputation, supposition
opinio praeiudicata prejudice *(preconception)*
opinion adjudication, advice, apprehension *(perception)*, assumption *(supposition)*, award, belief *(state of mind)*, concept, conclusion *(determination)*, conjecture, conviction *(persuasion)*, decree, deduction *(conclusion)*, determination, dictum, estimate *(idea)*, estimation *(calculation)*, finding, guidance, holding *(ruling of a court)*, idea, impression, judgment *(discernment)*, judgment *(formal court decree)*, notion, ob-

servation, position *(point of view)*, posture *(attitude)*, presumption, prognosis, pronouncement, recommendation, regard *(esteem)*, sense *(feeling)*, stand *(position)*, standpoint, supposition, theory
opinion of the court finding, ruling
opinion of the jury verdict
opinionated dogmatic, illiberal, inexorable, inflexible, narrow, obdurate, parochial, prejudicial, pretentious *(pompous)*, uncontrollable, unyielding
opinionated person bigot, pedant
opinionative dogmatic, inexorable, inflexible, obdurate, parochial
opinionativeness discrimination *(bigotry)*
opinionist bigot
opitulari assist
oppidan civil *(public)*, denizen, resident
oppignerare pawn
oppignerare pledge *(promise the performance of)*
oppilate obstruct, occlude
oppilation damper *(stopper)*
opponent adversary, contender, contestant, contradictory, disputant, foe, litigant, plaintiff, rival
opponent in a lawsuit litigant
opportune appropriate, auspicious, convenient, favorable *(advantageous)*, felicitous, fit, fitting, proper, propitious, seasonable, suitable
opportune moment opportunity
opportune time opportunity
opportuneness expedience, feasibility, timeliness
opportunism bribery
opportunist machiavellian
opportunistic mercenary
opportunities choice *(alternatives offered)*
opportunity access *(opening)*, behalf, call *(option)*, day in court, latitude, occasion, option *(choice)*, possibility, privilege
opportunity to obtain goods on time credit *(delayed payment)*
opportunus eligible, opportune, seasonable
oppose answer *(reply)*, antagonize, argue, block, challenge, collide *(clash)*, compensate *(counterbalance)*, compete, complain *(criticize)*, condemn *(ban)*, conflict, contend *(dispute)*, contest, contradict, contrast, contravene, controvert, counter, counteract, countervail, cross *(disagree with)*, defy, demonstrate *(protest)*, demur, deprecate, differ *(disagree)*, disaccord, disaffirm, disagree, disallow, disapprove *(reject)*, discourage, disobey, disown *(deny the validity)*, dissent *(differ in opinion)*, dissent *(withhold assent)*, engage *(involve)*, except *(object)*, expostulate, fight *(battle)*, fight *(counteract)*, forbid, frustrate, gainsay, grapple, hamper, impugn, negate, object, oppugn, parry, polarize, preclude, prevent, prohibit, proscribe *(prohibit)*, protest, rebel, rebut, refuse, refute, reject, remonstrate, renounce, repel *(drive back)*, repulse, restrain, stem *(check)*, thwart, trammel, withstand
oppose as false impugn
oppose by argument dispute *(con-*

test)

oppose by contrary proof counter-charge

opposed adverse *(hostile)*, antipathetic *(oppositional)*, averse, contradictory, contrary, different, discordant, disinclined, disobedient, hostile, inimical, negative, opposite, reluctant, renitent, repugnant *(incompatible)*, unfavorable

opposed to contra, contra

opposer adversary, contender, contestant, disputant, foe, opponent

opposing antipathetic *(oppositional)*, competitive *(antagonistic)*, contradictory, contrary, contravention, discordant, disobedient, dissenting, dissident, hostile, inimical, litigious, negative, opposite, preventive, recalcitrant, renitent, repugnant *(incompatible)*

opposing causes conflict

opposing litigant opponent

opposing party adversary, complainant, contestant, foe, opponent, party *(litigant)*

opposing suit counterclaim

opposite antipathetic *(oppositional)*, antipode, antithesis, contra, contra, contradictory, contraposition, contrary, contrary, discordant, hostile, inverse, negative, offset, opponent, pertinent

opposite camp foe

opposite evidence answer *(judicial response)*

opposite extreme antipode, contradiction

opposite in character contrary

opposite in nature contrary

opposite number peer

opposite pole antipode, antithesis

opposite side antipode, contraposition, foe, opponent

opposite to contra

oppositely contra

oppositeness antipode, contradiction, contradistinction, difference, dissent *(difference of opinion)*

opposites contradiction

opposition antipode, antithesis, argument *(contention)*, belligerency, check *(bar)*, collision *(dispute)*, competition, condemnation *(blame)*, conflict, confrontation *(altercation)*, contender, contest *(competition)*, contest *(dispute)*, contestant, contradiction, contradistinction, contraposition, contrary, contravention, controversy *(argument)*, counterargument, criticism, defiance, deterrence, deterrent, difference, disaccord, disagreement, disapprobation, disapproval, discord, dispute, dissatisfaction, dissent *(difference of opinion)*, dissent *(nonconcurrence)*, dissidence, division *(act of dividing)*, exception *(objection)*, feud, ill will, impediment, impugnation, incompatibility *(difference)*, mutiny, negation, objection, offset, opponent, outcry, protest, rebellion, rebuff, rejection, remonstrance, restraint, revolt, rival, strife, struggle, variance *(disagreement)*

opposition to allegations demurrer

oppositional contradictory, contrary, discordant, hostile

oppositionist adversary, contender, contestant, disputant

oppositive antipathetic *(oppositional)*, contradictory

opposure confrontation *(altercation)*, contempt *(disdain)*

oppress abuse *(victimize)*, badger, bait *(harass)*, brutalize, coerce, constrain *(restrain)*, contemn, discommode, dominate, exploit *(take advantage of)*, harass, harry *(harass)*, ill use, maltreat, mistreat, overload, persecute, plague, pressure, prey, subdue, subject, tax *(overwork)*

oppressed aggrieved *(victimized)*

oppression adversity, burden, coercion, compulsion *(coercion)*, cruelty, encumbrance, extortion, force *(compulsion)*, grievance, ground, incumbrance *(burden)*, infliction, injustice, molestation, pressure, servitude, thrall, weight *(burden)*

oppressive bad *(offensive)*, brutal, cruel, detrimental, dictatorial, disastrous, forcible, harsh, malignant, onerous, ponderous, severe, tyrannous

oppressive act ground

oppressive exaction blackmail, coercion, extortion

oppressive taskmaster dictator

oppressor dictator, hoodlum

opprimere overwhelm, repress, stifle

opprobrious bad *(offensive)*, blameful, blameworthy, calumnious, contemptible, contemptuous, disgraceful, disreputable, heinous, insolent, loathsome, notorious, objectionable, obnoxious, offensive *(offending)*, outrageous, reprehensible, scandalous, scurrilous

opprobrium aspersion

opprobrium attaint, bad repute, blame *(culpability)*, contempt *(disdain)*, contumely, criticism, degradation, denunciation, disapprobation, discredit, disdain, disgrace, dishonor *(shame)*, disrepute, ignominy, infamy, notoriety, obloquy, odium, reproach, revilement, scandal, shame, slander, vilification

oppugn answer *(reply)*, assail, assault, attack, collide *(clash)*, confront *(oppose)*, contest, contradict, counteract, disaffirm, disagree, disprove, gainsay, hold out *(resist)*, oppose, refute, repulse, resist *(oppose)*

oppugnance resistance

oppugnancy belligerency, conflict, contest *(dispute)*, contravention, disagreement, impugnation, mutiny, opposition

oppugnant adversary, antipathetic *(oppositional)*, competitive *(antagonistic)*, contrary, discordant, hostile, malevolent, opposite, recalcitrant, recusant

oppugnare assail, attack, impugn

oppugnatio assault

oppugnation belligerency, defiance, opposition, resistance

opt decide, espouse

opt for choose, elect *(choose)*

optative solicitous

optimal best

optimas prime *(most valuable)*

optimates elite

optimism confidence *(faith)*, faith, longanimity

optimistic sanguine

optimum ceiling, utmost

optimus best, superlative

option choice *(alternatives offered)*, conatus, discretion *(power of choice)*, election *(choice)*, franchise *(right to vote)*, latitude, preference *(choice)*, suffrage, volition, vote

optional discretionary, disjunctive *(alternative)*, elective *(voluntary)*, extraneous, needless, nonessential, spontaneous, unnecessary, voluntary

optionality discretion *(power of choice)*

opulence boom *(prosperity)*, prosperity

opulency boom *(prosperity)*

opulent copious

opulentus opulent

opus enterprise *(undertaking)*, performance *(workmanship)*, product, work *(effort)*

ora edge *(border)*

oracular indefinite, mysterious, omniscient, portentous *(ominous)*, profound *(esoteric)*, prophetic

oral language, nuncupative, parol, verbal

oral communication conversation, discourse, parlance, parley, speech

oral contention argument *(contention)*, fight *(argument)*

oral declaration nuncupative

oral evidence affirmance *(legal affirmation)*, deposition

oral examination interview

oral expression speech

oral statement under oath deposition

oral testimony nuncupative

orare plead *(implore)*, pray, sue

orate address *(talk to)*, declaim, discourse, recite

oratio language, speech

oration bombast, declamation, diatribe, discourse, peroration, recital, speech

orationem attribuere personify

orationem facere discourse

orationem habere discourse

oratorical flatulent, inflated *(bombastic)*, nuncupative, orotund

oratorical display declamation, peroration

oratory declamation, parlance, phraseology, rhetoric *(skilled speech)*, speech

orb sphere, zone

orbis circuit

orbit ambit, area *(province)*, bailiwick, capacity *(sphere)*, circuit, province, purview, realm, scope, sphere

orbus orphan

orchestrate compose

ordain award, bestow, command, constitute *(establish)*, decide, dictate, direct *(order)*, impose *(enforce)*, induct, invest *(vest)*, necessitate, nominate, order, pass *(approve)*, pass *(determine)*, predetermine, prescribe, require *(compel)*

ordain by law enact, pass *(approve)*

ordained entitled, inevitable, mandatory, necessary *(inescapable)*, positive *(prescribed)*, rightful

ordained by custom prescriptive

ordained by legislation legislative

ordaining legislative

ordainment designation (naming), nomination, ordinance, selection (choice)

ordeal aggravation (annoyance), burden, infliction, nuisance, pain, trouble

order adjudge, adjudicate, adjudication, agenda, appointment (act of designating), arbitrate (adjudge), arrange (methodize), authority (documentation), award, award, book, buy, call (demand), canon, caveat, chain (series), charge (command), choice (decision), class, classification, coerce, command, compel, constrain (compel), control (regulate), course, decree, decree, delegate, demand, demand, denomination, detail (assign), determination, dictate, dictate, directive, disposition (determination), disposition (final arrangement), draft, edict, enact, enjoin, exact, fiat, finding, force (coerce), form (arrangement), formation, govern, hierarchy (arrangement in a series), holding (ruling of a court), impose (enforce), injunction, insist, instruct (direct), instruction (direction), judgment (formal court decree), law, legislate, lineup, manage, mandamus, mandate, manner (kind), method, mittimus, modus operandi, monition (legal summons), opinion (judicial decision), orchestrate, ordinance, organization (structure), organize (arrange), peace, pigeonhole, precept, prescribe, prescription (directive), press (constrain), procedure, program, purchase, register, regularity, regulate (adjust), regulate (manage), regulation (rule), request, request, require (compel), requirement, requisition, rule (guide), rule (legal dictate), rule (govern), ruling, scheme, sentence, sequence, society, sodality, sort, statute, subpoena, subpoena, succession, summon, system, uniformity, warrant (judicial writ), writ

order authorizing a search search warrant

order back recommit, remand

order by law legalize

order for payment draft

order not to do forbid

order of business calendar (record of yearly periods)

order of cases calendar (list of cases)

order of penalty sentence

order of succession hierarchy (arrangement in a series)

order of the court adjudication, award, decree, holding (ruling of a court), ruling, sentence

order of the day agenda, docket, practice (custom), practice (procedure)

order on a bank check (instrument)

order to appear subpoena, subpoena, summon, summons

order to appear in court subpoena

order with authority command

ordered decretal, systematic

ordering allotment, array (order), classification, array (final arrangement), distribution (arrangement)

orderless casual, disjointed, disordered, disorderly, haphazard, indiscriminate, random, slipshod

orderliness decorum, diligence (care), method, peace, regularity, system

orderly meticulous, normal (regular), peaceable, right (suitable), systematic, uniform

orderly arrangement classification, method

orderly arrangement of papers file

orderly combination system

orderly disposition method

ordinance act (enactment), brevet, bylaw, canon, code, codification, dictate, direction (order), directive, edict, enactment, law, precept, prescription (directive), regulation (rule), rubric (authoritative rule), rule (legal dictate), statute, writ

ordinances legislation (enactments)

ordinare arrange (methodize), fix (arrange), organize (arrange)

ordinarily as a rule, generally, invariably

ordinariness mediocrity

ordinarius regular (conventional)

ordinary accustomed (customary), average (standard), common (customary), conventional, customary, daily, familiar (customary), general, habitual, household (familiar), imperfect, informal, jejune (dull), mediocre, mundane, nondescript, normal (regular), orthodox, passable, pedestrian, poor (inferior in quality), prevalent, prosaic, regular (conventional), trite, typical, usual

ordinary course practice (custom)

ordinary judgment common sense

ordinary manner custom

ordinary run norm

ordinary run of things matter of course

ordinary sense common sense

ordinary state matter of course

ordinate nominate

ordinatio disposition (final arrangement)

ordination appointment (act of designating), brevet, citation (charge), classification, dedication, delegation (assignment), designation (naming), dictate, installation, nomination, ordinance, selection (choice)

ordo class, degree (station), order (arrangement), regularity, sequence

organ chapter (branch), publication (printed matter)

organic bodily, born (innate), fundamental, native (inborn), natural, physical

organic law constitution

organic remains corpse

organism entity, individual

organization array (order), association (connection), building (business of assembling), bureaucracy, business (commercial enterprise), campaign, cartel, centralization, chamber (body), citation (attribution), classification, committee, company (enterprise), complex (development), composition (makeup), concern (business establishment), content (structure), corporation, denomination, disposition (final arrangement), distribution (arrangement), facility (institution), firm, form (arrangement), formation, institute, league, method, order (arrangement), practice (procedure), regulation (management), scheme, society, sodality, structure (composition), syndicate, system, union (labor organization)

organization of a commercial concern incorporation (formation of a business entity)

organization of a company incorporation (formation of a business entity)

organization to aid the needy foundation (organization)

organize arrange (methodize), classify, codify, compose, constitute (establish), contrive, coordinate, create, disentangle, establish (launch), fabricate (construct), federalize (associate), federate, file (arrange), fix (arrange), form, frame (construct), frame (formulate), make, marshal, orchestrate, pigeonhole, plan, plot, program, provide (arrange for), regulate (adjust), scheme, sort, tabulate

organize a corporation incorporate (form a corporation)

organized systematic, tactical

organized body federation

organized body for charity foundation (organization)

organized group committee, party (political organization), society

organized illegal activity racket

organized knowledge science (study)

organized labor union (labor organization)

organized observation experiment

organized refusal to work strike

organized society facility (institution)

organizer architect, author (originator), chief, developer, promoter

organizer of business enterprises promoter

organizer of commercial enterprises promoter

organizing conception impression

orgiastic gluttonous

orgulous proud (conceited)

orgy debauchery

orient apprise, inform (notify)

orientation guidance, perspective, standpoint

origin affiliation (bloodline), ancestry, basis, birth (beginning), bloodline, cause (reason), derivation, descent (lineage), determinant, embryo, family (common ancestry), foundation (basis), genesis, ground, inception, lineage, nascency, nationality, onset (commencement), outset, parentage, paternity, progenitor, reason (basis), source, start

original authentic, causative, fertile, genuine, incipient, initial, native (domestic), native (inborn), natural, nonconforming, novel, old, organic, paradigm, particular (individual), pattern, peculiar (distinctive), preliminary, primary, primordial, productive, prototype, resourceful, rudimentary, sample, source, true (authentic), underlying, undistorted, unique, unprecedented, unusual

original meaning connotation

original sum principal (capital sum)

original work creation

originality identity (individuality), legitimacy, nonconformity, personality

originally ab initio

originate accrue (arise), build (con-

struct), cause, commence, compose, conceive *(invent)*, conjure, constitute *(establish)*, create, embark, engender, establish *(launch)*, forge *(produce)*, frame *(construct)*, frame *(formulate)*, generate, induce, initiate, inspire, invent *(produce for the first time)*, launch *(initiate)*, legislate, maintain *(commence)*, make, manufacture, produce *(manufacture)*, propagate *(increase)*, provoke, result, stem *(originate)*, unveil

originate from evolve

originate in emanate

originating causal

origination ancestry, birth *(beginning)*, building *(business of assembling)*, creation, derivation, embryo, formation, genesis, inception, invention, manufacture, nascency, onset *(commencement)*, outset, source, start

originative causal, causative, constructive *(creative)*, fertile, original *(creative)*, prime *(original)*, productive, rudimentary

originator architect, developer, predecessor

origo ancestry, lineage, origin *(ancestry)*, origin *(source)*, primogenitor, source

ornament embellish, motif

ornamental aesthetic

ornamentation bombast, motif

ornamented elaborate, pretentious *(ostentatious)*

ornare provide *(supply)*

ornate elaborate, grandiose, meretricious, pretentious *(ostentatious)*

ornatus pretentious *(ostentatious)*

ornery malicious

orotund flatulent, fustian, grandiose, histrionic, turgid

orotundity bombast, declamation, fustian, histrionics, peroration

orphaned solitary

orphaned child orphan

orphaned infant orphan

orphic recondite

orthodox conventional, dogmatic, parochial, popular, proper, rigid, strict, traditional, typical, uncompromising, uniform, usual

orthodoxus orthodox

orthodoxy doctrine, dogma

ortus birth *(beginning)*

os impudens indiscretion

oscillate alternate *(fluctuate)*, beat *(pulsate)*, hesitate, vacillate

oscillating irresolute, variable

oscillation hesitation, indecision, trepidation

oscitancy inertia, languor

oscitant lifeless *(dull)*, otiose, phlegmatic

osculate contact *(touch)*, juxtapose

osmose penetrate, permeate

ossified solid *(compact)*

ostendere evince, prove, reflect *(mirror)*

ostensibility probability

ostensible apparent *(presumptive)*, circumstantial, colorable *(plausible)*, evident, manifest, naked *(perceptible)*, overt, patent, plausible, probable, purported, putative, specious

ostensible motive pretext

ostensible purpose pretense *(pre-*

text), pretext

ostensible reason excuse, pretense *(pretext)*, pretext

ostensibly prima facie *(self-evident)*

ostent presence *(poise)*

ostentare flaunt

ostentatio pretense *(ostentation)*

ostentation bombast, histrionics, jactation, rodomontade

ostentatious elaborate, grandiose, histrionic, inflated *(bombastic)*, tawdry

ostentatiousness pretense *(ostentation)*

ostentum phenomenon *(unusual occurrence)*

ostium entrance

ostracism banishment, boycott, exclusion, expulsion, ignominy, prohibition, rejection, segregation *(isolation by races)*

ostracization banishment

ostracize bar *(exclude)*, condemn *(ban)*, defame, denounce *(condemn)*, eliminate *(exclude)*, exclude, expel, ignore, isolate, proscribe *(denounce)*, reject, relegate, renounce, seclude, spurn, transport

other additional, alter ego, ancillary *(auxiliary)*

other choice alternative *(substitute)*

other extreme antipode, antithesis, contradiction, contrary

other half alter ego

other person alter ego

other self alter ego

other side foe, opponent

other than different

other wordly immaterial

otherness contraposition, nonconformity

otherwise contra

otherwise called alias

otherwise known as alias

otherwise known by alias

otherwise named alias

otherwordly demote

otherworldliness immateriality

otiose futile, inactive, indolent, nugatory, passive, redundant, stagnant, torpid, unproductive

otiosity sloth

otiosus idle, unemployed

otium ease, inaction, peace

oust deport *(banish)*, depose *(remove)*, disinherit, dislocate, dislodge, dismiss *(discharge)*, disown *(refuse to acknowledge)*, displace *(remove)*, dispossess, divest, eject *(evict)*, eject *(expel)*, eliminate *(exclude)*, evict, exclude, expel, reject, relegate, remove *(dismiss from office)*, supersede, supplant

oust from office depose *(remove)*

ouster deportation, discharge *(dismissal)*, dismissal *(discharge)*, disqualification *(rejection)*, disseisin, eviction, expulsion, layoff, rejection

ouster by paramount title eviction

ousting banishment, defeasance, discharge *(dismissal)*, removal

out of devoid

out of accord discordant

out of bounds excessive, extreme *(exaggerated)*, illicit, impermissible, inordinate, undue *(excessive)*

out of cash poor *(underprivileged)*

out of character inappropriate,

inapt, incongruous, inept *(inappropriate)*, undesirable, unseemly, unsuitable

out of circulation rare

out of control uncontrollable, uncurbed, unruly

out of danger safe

out of debt solvent

out of employment unemployed

out of fashion defunct, outmoded

out of favor blameful, repugnant *(exciting aversion)*

out of focus indistinct, nebulous, unclear

out of funds bankrupt, insolvent

out of hand uncurbed

out of humor petulant

out of joint disproportionate

out of keeping anomalous, disproportionate, inapplicable, inappropriate, inapt, incommensurate, incongruous, inept *(inappropriate)*, unbecoming, undesirable, unfit, unsuitable, untimely

out of limits inordinate

out of line nonconforming

out of money bankrupt, destitute, impecunious, insolvent, poor *(underprivileged)*

out of one's bearings astray

out of one's mind lunatic, non compos mentis

out of one's reckoning astray

out of one's senses lunatic, non compos mentis

out of one's wits non compos mentis

out of order anomalous, defective, deviant, disjointed, disordered, disorderly, faulty, imperfect, irregular *(not usual)*, irrelevant

out of place disordered, disproportionate, immaterial, impertinent *(irrelevant)*, improper, inapplicable, inappropriate, inapt, incongruous, inept *(inappropriate)*, irregular *(improper)*, irregular *(not usual)*, irrelevant, peculiar *(curious)*, unbecoming, unfit, unseemly, unsuitable, untimely

out of proportion disparate, disproportionate, extreme *(exaggerated)*, inapt, incommensurate, inept *(inappropriate)*

out of reach difficult, inaccessible, infeasible, insuperable, insurmountable, unapproachable, unattainable

out of sight covert, hidden, inconspicuous, lost *(taken away)*

out of sorts petulant

out of step deviant, nonconforming, unorthodox

out of the common run eccentric, prodigious *(amazing)*

out of the ordinary anomalous, different, distinct *(distinguished from others)*, eccentric, extraordinary, irregular *(not usual)*, noteworthy, original *(creative)*, peculiar *(curious)*, peculiar *(distinctive)*, portentous *(eliciting amazement)*, prodigious *(amazing)*, rare, singular, specific, unaccustomed, unusual

out of the question impossible, impracticable, ineligible, infeasible, insuperable, insurmountable, unattainable

out of the regular order extraordinary

out of the way circuitous, indirect, irrelevant, peculiar *(curious)*, remote *(secluded)*, scarce, uncommon

out of touch inaccessible

out of use obsolete, outmoded

out of view blind (concealed), hidden

out of work unemployed

out-and-out outright

out-of-date obsolete, outdated, outmoded

out-of-fashion outdated

out-of-sorts restive

out-of-the-way immaterial, private (secluded), unapproachable

out-of-use outdated

outbalance countervail, outweigh

outbreak bluster (commotion), brawl, embroilment, fracas, furor, inception, insurrection, mutiny, onset (commencement), outburst, outset, rebellion, revolt, revolution, riot, start, strife, threshold (commencement)

outburst bluster (commotion), furor, outbreak, outflow, riot, spate, strife, violence

outcast derelict (abandoned), derelict, ineligible, notorious, pariah, undesirable

outclass beat (defeat), surpass

outcome amount (result), answer (solution), cessation (termination), choice (decision), conclusion (outcome), consequence (conclusion), corollary, denouement, development (outgrowth), effect, end (termination), finding, holding (ruling of a court), issuance, output, product, result

outcry disparagement, exception (objection), expletive, noise, pandemonium, panic, plaint, protest

outdated obsolete, outmoded

outdistance transcend

outdo beat (defeat), outbalance, outweigh, overcome (surmount), surmount, surpass, transcend

outer peripheral

outer boundary periphery

outer district frontier

outer edge edge (border), extremity (furthest point), frontier, limit

outer edges confines

outer limit ambit

outer line limit

outer part frontier, periphery

outer point limit

outermost extreme (last), last (final), peripheral

outface defy, oppugn, parry

outfit assemblage, band, clothe, furnish, supply

outfitter materialman

outflank beat (defeat)

outflow issuance

outgo cost (expenses), disbursement (act of disbursing), disbursement (funds paid out), expenditure, expense (cost), issuance, outlay

outgrowth amount (result), boom (prosperity), conclusion (outcome), consequence (conclusion), corollary, denouement, effect, offshoot, outcome, result

outgush outflow

outland peripheral

outlander alien

outlandish eccentric, ludicrous, peculiar (curious), prodigious (amazing), unaccustomed, unusual

outlandishness quirk (idiosyncrasy)

outlast endure (last), persevere, persist, remain (continue), subsist

outlaw ban, bar (exclude), condemn (ban), convict, criminal, debar, deport (banish), disfranchise, eliminate (exclude), exclude, expatriate, expel, felon, foe, forbid, hoodlum, isolate, lawless, malefactor, pariah, proscribe (denounce), proscribe (prohibit), recidivist, relegate, seclude, thief, wrongdoer

outlawed felonious, illegal, illegitimate (illegal), illicit, impermissible, unlawful

outlawing expulsion

outlawry banishment, criminality, lynch law, prohibition

outlay bear the expense, charge (cost), cost (expenses), disburse (pay out), disbursement (act of disbursing), disbursement (funds paid out), expenditure, expense (cost), invest (fund), investment, maintenance (upkeep), overhead, payment (act of paying), price, spend

outlet catharsis, egress, issuance, loophole, market (demand), store (business)

outline ambit, arrangement (plan), blueprint, border, border (bound), boundary, brief, capsule, characterize, circumscribe (define), circumscribe (surround by boundary), compendium, complexion, condense, configuration (confines), configuration (form), construe (translate), delineate, delineation, demarcate, depict, describe, description, design (construction plan), digest, digest (summarize), dimension, direction (course), edge (border), form (arrangement), hedge, inform (notify), mete, mode, pandect (treatise), pattern, periphery, plan, plot, portray, practice (procedure), program, program, project, prospectus, render (depict), report (disclose), represent (portray), scenario, schedule, scheme, suggestion, summary, synopsis

outline on the law brief

outlined compact (pithy)

outlined before hand intentional

outlined beforehand deliberate, express, premeditated

outlines confines, frontier

outlive endure (last), last, remain (continue), subsist

outlook conviction (persuasion), opinion (belief), perspective, platform, position (point of view), posture (attitude), side, stand (position), standpoint

outlying peripheral, provincial

outlying area frontier

outlying borders frontier

outlying districts frontier

outmaneuver beat (defeat), circumvent, dupe, elude, ensnare, illude, pettifog, surmount, surpass, thwart

outmatch surpass

outmode succeed (follow)

outmoded obsolete, outdated

outmost peripheral

outnumber surpass

outplay beat (defeat), surpass

outpoint beat (defeat), outbalance

outpost border, frontier, periphery

outpour issuance, outburst, outflow

outpouring boom (prosperity)

output product, profit, result

outrage abuse (physical misuse), bait (harass), cruelty, defilement, delinquency (misconduct), dishonor (shame), disregard (lack of respect), disservice, disturb, flout, ground, harass, harrow, mischief, misdoing, offend (insult), offense, persecute, perturb, vice, wrong

outraged resentful

outrageous arrant (onerous), deplorable, diabolic, disgraceful, disorderly, drastic, egregious, excessive, exorbitant, extreme (exaggerated), flagrant, gross (flagrant), heinous, inept (inappropriate), inexcusable, inordinate, insolent, irrational, nefarious, notorious, offensive (offending), presumptuous, scandalous, unconscionable, undue (excessive), unwarranted

outrageous act misdeed

outrageousness exaggeration

outrange beat (defeat)

outrank outweigh, predominate (outnumber), surpass, transcend

outre egregious

outreach circumvent

outright candid, stark, total, unequivocal, unqualified (unlimited), wholly

outrival beat (defeat), outbalance, outweigh, overcome (surmount), predominate (outnumber), surmount, surpass, transcend

outrivalry competition

outrun surpass

outset genesis, inception, nascency, onset (commencement), origination, prelude, start

outshine overcome (surmount), surpass, transcend

outside alien (foreign), alien (unrelated), border, contour (outline), exempt, extremity (furthest point), extrinsic, foreign, peripheral, periphery

outside surface periphery

outside the law felonious, illegal, illegitimate (illegal), illicit, impermissible

outside the question immaterial

outsider alien, pariah, stranger

outskirt margin (outside limit), penumbra

outskirts border, edge (border), frontier, periphery, vicinity

outsmart dupe, overreach

outspoken brazen, candid, clear (apparent), direct (forthright), explicit, express, honest, ingenuous, parol, straightforward, unaffected (sincere)

outspokenness candor (straightforwardness)

outspread broad, deploy, expand, spread

outstanding best, blatant (conspicuous), critical (crucial), delinquent (overdue), due (owed), extraordinary, famous, flagrant, important (significant), infrequent, leading (ranking first), major, master, momentous, notable, noteworthy, open (in sight), overdue, particular (specific), past due, payable, portentous (eliciting amazement), preferential, principal, prominent, receivable, remarkable, renowned, residuary, salient, special, stellar, uncommon, unpaid, unsettled, unusual

outstanding debt arrears, bad debt,

cloud (*incumbrance*), delinquency (*shortage*), due, nonpayment, obligation (*liability*)

outstanding feature emphasis, gist (*ground for a suit*), highlight, main point

outstanding item feature (*special attraction*)

outstanding property feature (*characteristic*)

outstanding quality importance

outstream outflow

outstretch expand

outstretched broad

outstrip outbalance, overcome (*surmount*), predominate (*outnumber*), surpass, transcend

outvie outbalance, surpass, transcend

outward ostensible, specious, superficial

outward act overt act

outward appearance color (*deceptive appearance*), complexion, feature (*appearance*)

outward flow outflow

outward form configuration (*form*), formality, semblance

outward look appearance (*look*)

outward perception impression

outward show appearance (*look*), presence (*poise*), pretense (*ostentation*)

outward sweep outflow

outwardly seem assume (*simulate*)

outweigh convince, nullify, outbalance, override, predominate (*outnumber*), surpass, transcend

outweighing preponderance

outwit betray (*lead astray*), circumvent, defeat, dupe, elude, ensnare, evade (*deceive*), frustrate, hoodwink, illude, overreach

outwitting fraud

outworn obsolete, outdated, outmoded

ovation respect

over complete (*ended*), de novo

over again anew, de novo

over against contra

over all throughout (*all over*)

over and above a fortiori, also

over pass traverse

over-all complete (*all-embracing*)

over-coloring distortion

over-harsh brutal

overabound overload

overabounding profuse

overabundance overage, plethora, surfeit, surplus

overabundant excess, needless, rampant

overact overreach

overacted histrionic

overacting histrionics

overage surplus

overall comprehensive, omnibus

overall theme motif

overanxiety apprehension (*fear*)

overanxious diffident

overapprehensive diffident

overassess overestimate

overassessment exaggeration, surcharge

overawe browbeat, deter, intimidate

overbalance outbalance, outweigh

overbear beat (*defeat*), browbeat, repress, subdue, subjugate

overbearing brutal, dictatorial, dis-

dainful, dogmatic, inflated (*vain*), insolent, onerous, oppressive, orgulous, peremptory (*absolute*), presumptuous, proud (*conceited*), severe, supercilious, tyrannous

overbid beat (*defeat*)

overblown inflated (*bombastic*)

overboard extreme (*exaggerated*)

overboldness audacity

overburden disadvantage, exploit (*take advantage of*), harass, impact, mishandle (*maltreat*), mistreat, overload, persecute, surcharge

overcalculate overestimate

overcareful meticulous

overcast obnubilate, obscure

overcaution hesitation

overcautious careful

overcharge exploitation, overdraw, premium (*excess value*), surcharge, usury

overcharged disproportionate, inordinate

overcloud blind (*obscure*), obnubilate, obscure

overcoloring caricature

overcome attach (*seize*), beat (*defeat*), carry away, defeat, disconsolate, drunk, hijack, impose (*subject*), outbalance, override, overturn, overwhelm, prevail (*triumph*), repress, subdue, subject, subjugate, suppress, surmount

overcome another's resistence prevail upon

overcome by argument convince, impugn

overcome by liquor drunk

overcoming prevailing (*having superior force*)

overcommit overextend

overconfidence temerity

overconfident precipitate, presumptuous, reckless

overconscientious particular (*exacting*)

overcount overestimate

overcritical critical (*faultfinding*), nonconsenting, particular (*exacting*), querulous

overcriticalness disparagement

overcrowd impact

overdaring audacity

overdevelop overextend

overdo distort, overestimate, overindulge, overload, overreach

overdone extreme (*exaggerated*), outrageous

overdose overload, surfeit

overdraft deficit

overdramatize distort

overdramatized pretentious (*pompous*)

overdraw dissipate (*expend foolishly*)

overdrawing caricature

overdrawn inflated (*overestimated*), past due

overdrive harass, ill use

overdue back (*in arrears*), dilatory, late (*tardy*), outstanding (*unpaid*), past due

overdue bill arrears

overdue payment arrears, due

overeat overindulge

overemotional fanatical, sensitive (*easily affected*)

overemphasis exaggeration, histrion-

ics, hyperbole

overenlargement hyperbole

overenthusiasm exaggeration

overenthusiastic fanatical

overestimate magnify

overestimation caricature, overstatement

overexercise tax (*overwork*)

overexert overload, tax (*overwork*)

overexertion stress (*strain*)

overexpand overextend

overextend overdraw, overreach

overfamiliar presumptuous

overfastidious particular (*exacting*)

overfatigue tax (*overwork*)

overfeed overload

overfill overload

overflood inundate

overflow balance (*amount in excess*), cataclysm, inundate, outflow, overage, plethora, surfeit, surplus

overflowing cataclysm, copious, demonstrative (*expressive of emotion*), excess, excessive, full, inordinate, profuse, replete, superfluous

overfullness surfeit

overgenerous profuse

overgorge overindulge

overgratify overindulge

overgrow overlap

overhang overlap, project (*extend beyond*)

overhanging imminent, pending (*imminent*)

overhasty careless, imprudent, premature, reckless

overhaul check (*inspect*), fix (*repair*), modify (*alter*), remedy, renew (*refurbish*), repair, repair, reparation (*keeping in repair*), revise, scrutinize

overhauled renascent

overhauling reorganization, revision (*process of correcting*)

overhead cost (*expenses*), expense (*cost*), maintenance (*upkeep*)

overhear eavesdrop

overheat burn

overindulge carouse

overindulgence greed

overjoyed ecstatic

overjudge overestimate

overlap contact (*touch*), encroachment

overlaud overestimate

overlay overcome (*overwhelm*), overlap

overlie overlap

overload disadvantage, impact, overcome (*overwhelm*), plethora, surcharge, surfeit, tax (*overwork*)

overlook administer (*conduct*), check (*inspect*), condone, contemn, control (*regulate*), disregard, exclude, excuse, forgive, ignore, misprize, monitor, neglect, palliate (*excuse*), pardon, patrol, peruse, police, preside, pretermit, remit (*release from penalty*), review, superintend, survey (*examine*)

overlook an offense condone

overlooker chief, custodian (*protector*), principal (*director*)

overlooking condonation, disregard (*unconcern*), oblivious, oversight (*control*)

overly unduly

overly bold presumptuous

overly confident presumptuous

overly decorated pretentious *(ostentatious)*

overly hasty precipitate

overly liberal profligate *(extravagant)*

overly passionate perfervid

overly trustful credulous

overmaster beat *(defeat)*, defeat, overthrow, repress, subject

overmastering abduction

overmatch beat *(defeat)*, outbalance, overcome *(surmount)*

overmeasure balance *(amount in excess)*, overage, overestimate, surplus

overmeticulous particular *(exacting)*

overmuch disproportionate, excess, excessive, exorbitant, inordinate, needless, redundant, superfluous, undue *(excessive)*, unnecessary, unwarranted

overpass overstep, surmount, transcend

overplentiful needless

overplus balance *(amount in excess)*, expendable, overage, plethora, redundancy, remainder *(remaining part)*, surplus

overpoise outweigh

overpower beat *(defeat)*, carry away, check *(restrain)*, defeat, force *(coerce)*, hijack, obsess, outweigh, overcome *(overwhelm)*, overcome *(surmount)*, override, overthrow, overturn, overwhelm, repress, subdue, subjugate, supplant, suppress, surmount, upset

overpowered with emotion ecstatic

overpowering compelling, formidable, in full force, indomitable, invincible, irresistible, moving *(evoking emotion)*, onerous, oppressive, powerful, predominant, severe, strong

overpowering fright panic

overpraise doxology, exaggeration, overestimate

overpraised inflated *(overestimated)*

overpriced inflated *(overestimated)*

overprize magnify, overestimate

overprized inflated *(overestimated)*

overproud inflated *(vain)*, orgulous

overrate magnify, overestimate

overrated inflated *(overestimated)*

overreach betray *(lead astray)*, impose *(intrude)*

override abolish, abrogate *(rescind)*, beat *(defeat)*, browbeat, cancel, foil, frustrate, insist, invalidate, negate, nullify, overlap, overrule, preclude, predominate *(command)*, prevent, repeal, repudiate, rescind, revoke, supersede, thwart

overriding compelling, primary, reversal

overrule abolish, abrogate *(rescind)*, annul, cancel, disaffirm, disown *(deny the validity)*, dominate, invalidate, negate, nullify, override, predominate *(command)*, prevent, quash, reject, repeal, repudiate, rescind, subjugate, supersede, vacate *(void)*, withdraw

overruled null *(invalid)*, null and void

overruling cancellation, cardinal *(basic)*, compelling, considerable, critical *(crucial)*, predominant, prevailing *(having superior force)*, primary, rejection, rescision, reversal

overrun balance *(amount in excess)*, despoil, harass, impinge, incursion, invade, overlap, overstep, overthrow, overwhelm, permeate, spread, surplus, trespass

overrunning cataclysm, intrusion

oversee administer *(conduct)*, censor, check *(inspect)*, conduct, control *(regulate)*, direct *(supervise)*, discipline *(control)*, govern, maintain *(sustain)*, manage, moderate *(preside over)*, monitor, officiate, operate, overlook *(superintend)*, police, predominate *(command)*, preside, regulate *(manage)*, rule *(govern)*, superintend, survey *(examine)*

overseer administrator, caretaker *(one caring for property)*, caretaker *(one fulfilling the function of office)*, chairman, chief, custodian *(protector)*, director, employer, guardian, official, principal *(director)*, procurator, superintendent, warden

oversensitive hot-blooded

overset overthrow, overturn, prostration, subversion, subvert

overshadow minimize, obfuscate, obnubilate, obscure, outweigh, overcome *(surmount)*, predominate *(command)*, shroud, surpass, transcend

overshadowing critical *(crucial)*, dominant, important *(significant)*, obscuration

overshoot overreach

overshy diffident

oversight administration, auspices, control *(supervision)*, delinquency *(failure of duty)*, direction *(guidance)*, disregard *(unconcern)*, error, failure *(falling short)*, fault *(mistake)*, inconsideration, laxity, management *(supervision)*, miscue, neglect, negligence, nonpayment, omission, protection, supervision, surveillance

overspend dissipate *(expend foolishly)*, overdraw

overspread diffuse, dissipate *(spread out)*, inundate, overlap, penetrate, permeate, pervade, radiate, spread

overstate distort, magnify, misrepresent, overestimate, slant

overstated extreme *(exaggerated)*, inflated *(overestimated)*

overstatement bombast, distortion, exaggeration, hyperbole, misrepresentation

overstep accroach, encroach, impinge, impose *(intrude)*, infringe, transcend, trespass

overstep boundaries impinge

overstepping encroachment, incursion, infraction, invasion, malfeasance

overstrain dissipate *(expend foolishly)*, harass, overdraw, overload, tax *(overwork)*

overstress magnify

overstressed inflated *(overestimated)*

overstretch overdraw

overstuff overload

oversufficient needless

oversupply balance *(amount in excess)*, overage, plethora, redundancy, surfeit, surplus

oversweet nectarious

overt apparent *(perceptible)*, blatant *(conspicuous)*, candid, clear *(apparent)*, comprehensible, conspicuous, evident, lucid, manifest, naked *(perceptible)*, obvious, open *(in sight)*, ostensible, palpable, patent, pellucid, perceivable, perceptible, public *(known)*, salient, scrutable, unmistakable

overtake beat *(defeat)*, invade, reach

overtask exploit *(take advantage of)*, mistreat, overload

overtax exploit *(take advantage of)*, harass, misemploy, mistreat, overcome *(overwhelm)*, overload, persecute

overtaxing onerous

overthrow beat *(defeat)*, commotion, debacle, defeat, defeat, destroy *(efface)*, dislodge, dissolution *(termination)*, eliminate *(eradicate)*, insurrection, invalidate, kill *(defeat)*, miscarriage, negate, overcome *(surmount)*, overturn, overwhelm, plunder, prostration, quash, rebel, rebellion, refute, repulse, rescision, revolt, revolution, sedition, subject, subjugate, subversion, subvert, supplant, suppress, surmount, upset

overthrow of authority outbreak, revolution

overthrowing reversal

overtire exhaust *(deplete)*, tax *(overwork)*

overtone implication *(inference)*, innuendo, intimation, suggestion

overtop outbalance, outweigh, predominate *(outnumber)*, transcend

overtrump beat *(defeat)*

overtrustfulness credulity

overture bid, invitation, preface, prelude, proposal *(suggestion)*, proposition, threshold *(commencement)*

overturn abolish, debacle, destroy *(efface)*, disaffirm, disorient, disrupt, disturb, extirpate, kill *(defeat)*, nullify, override, overrule, overthrow, prostration, quash, rebellion, revolt, subversion, subvert, surmount, upset, vitiate

overturn of authority revolution

overturn of government revolution

overturning havoc

overuse exploit *(take advantage of)*, overload, tax *(overwork)*

overused trite

overvaluation exaggeration

overvalue magnify, overestimate

overvalued inflated *(overestimated)*

overview inquiry *(systematic investigation)*

overweening disdainful, inflated *(vain)*, orgulous, presumptuous, proud *(conceited)*, supercilious

overweigh convince, outbalance, outweigh, overload

overweight ponderous

overwelm quash

overwhelm beat *(defeat)*, controvert, defeat, devastate, force *(coerce)*, hijack, immerse *(engross)*, inundate, overload, overthrow, overturn, subdue, subjugate, suppress, upset

overwhelming compelling, formidable, indomitable, ineffable, invincible, irresistible, lurid, moving *(evoking emotion)*, omnipotent, oppressive, powerful, prodigious *(amazing)*, remarkable, resounding, strong

overwhelming part bulk

overwork exploit *(take advantage of)*, harass, misemploy, mistreat, overload, persecute

overwrought demonstrative *(expressive of emotion)*, frenetic

overzealous extreme *(exaggerated)*, fanatical
owe overdraw
owe money overdraw
owed delinquent *(overdue)*, receivable
owing accountable *(responsible)*, delinquent *(overdue)*, due *(owed)*, indebted, outstanding *(unpaid)*, payable, receivable, unpaid, unsettled
owing nothing solvent
own hold *(possess)*, occupy *(take possession)*, particular *(individual)*, personal *(individual)*, possess, profess *(avow)*, recognize *(acknowledge)*, remain *(occupy)*
own exclusively monopolize
own up betray *(disclose)*, confess
owned jointly common *(shared)*
owner employer, holder, lessor, principal *(director)*, proprietor, shareholder, tenant
owner of an estate in land landholder, landlord, landowner
owner of land landowner
owner of lands landlord
owner of real estate landowner
owner of real property landowner
owner of tenements landlord
owner of the fee landholder, landowner
owner of the fee simple absolute landholder
owner's mark brand
owner's sign brand
ownership adverse possession, claim *(right)*, dominion *(absolute ownership)*, enjoyment *(use)*, occupancy, occupation *(possession)*, property *(possessions)*, right *(entitlement)*, seisin, stake *(interest)*, substance *(material possessions)*, tenancy, title *(right)*

P

pace patrol, perambulate, rate, step
pace off measure
pacem conciliare mediate
pacesetter pioneer
pachydermatous impervious, insusceptible *(uncaring)*
pacifiable placable
pacific harmonious, neutral, patient, peaceable, placid
pacificate mollify, pacify, placate, propitiate, soothe
pacification conciliation, expiation, mollification, peace, reconciliation
pacificatory nonmilitant, peaceable
pacifier go-between
pacifistic neutral, nonmilitant, peaceable
pacify allay, alleviate, assuage, disarm *(set at ease)*, ease, lull, moderate *(temper)*, mollify, palliate *(abate)*, placate, propitiate, reconcile, redress, soothe
pacifying palliative *(abating)*
pacisci agree *(contract)*, close *(agree)*, covenant
pack assemblage, band, cargo, impact, load, overload, quantity
pack away hoard
pack close impact
pack in impact
pack tightly constrict *(compress)*
pack together impact

package bargaining collective bargaining
packages cargo, freight
packed compact *(dense)*, full, pithy, populous, replete, solid *(compact)*
packed together solid *(compact)*
packed with meaning sententious
packet assemblage
packman dealer
packwoman dealer
pact accordance *(compact)*, adjustment, agree *(contract)*, agreement *(contract)*, arrangement *(understanding)*, assurance, bargain, cartel, compact, condition *(contingent provision)*, contract, covenant, deal, guaranty, indenture, league, mutual understanding, obligation *(duty)*, peace, policy *(contract)*, promise, protocol *(agreement)*, settlement, specialty *(contract)*, stipulation, treaty, understanding *(agreement)*
pact before marriage antenuptial agreement
pactio bargain, compact, covenant, pact, treaty
paction assurance, contract, pact, promise
pactum compact, confederacy *(compact)*, contract, covenant, indenture, league, pact, settlement, stipulation
pad inflate
padded profuse, prolix
padlock handcuff, lock
paean doxology
paedeutic disciplinary *(educational)*
paenitendus regrettable
paenitens repentant
paenitet contrite
page call *(summon)*
paid mercenary
pain aggravate *(annoy)*, annoy, distress *(anguish)*, distress, irritate, nuisance, offend *(insult)*, perturb, pique, plague
pain reliever narcotic
pain-killing narcotic
pained aggrieved *(harmed)*, disconsolate, resentful
painful cruel, insufferable, lamentable, loathsome, oppressive, pernicious, repugnant *(exciting aversion)*, severe
painkiller drug, narcotic
painless innocuous
pains burden, effort, endeavor, labor *(exertion)*, struggle
painstaking careful, circumspect, conscientious, difficult, diligence *(care)*, diligent, elaborate, faithful *(diligent)*, industrious, meticulous, operose, particular *(exacting)*, pertinacious, precise, sedulous, thorough
paint delineate, describe, portray
paint a picture delineate
pair connect *(join together)*, join *(bring together)*
pair with combine *(act in concert)*, commingle
paired attached *(annexed)*, concurrent *(united)*, conjoint, conjugal, correlative
palatable popular, sapid, savory
palatial elaborate
palaver confer *(consult)*, conference, council *(assembly)*, speak, speech
pale ambit, border, capacity *(sphere)*, circuit, district, locality, nebulous, obscure *(faint)*, outline *(boundary)*, pe-

riphery, sphere
paleness indistinctness
palingenesis reconversion, revival
palinode retraction
pall veil
Palladian omniscient
palladium bulwark, protection, safeguard, security *(safety)*
palliate abate *(lessen)*, allay, alleviate, ameliorate, assuage, commute, condone, cure, drug, extenuate, forgive, justify, lessen, lull, meliorate, mitigate, moderate *(temper)*, mollify, obtund, redress, relieve *(give aid)*, remedy, remit *(relax)*, soothe
palliation abatement *(reduction)*, extenuating circumstances, justification, mitigation, moderation, mollification, relief *(release)*, solace
palliative cure, drug, medicinal, mitigating, narcotic, narcotic, panacea, remedial, remedy *(that which corrects)*, salutary
palliative circumstances extenuating circumstances
palm off foist
palm off fraudulently foist
palming prestidigitation
palmy prosperous
palmy days prosperity
palpability density, materiality *(physical existence)*
palpable actual, apparent *(perceptible)*, appreciable, arrant *(definite)*, bodily, coherent *(clear)*, comprehensible, concrete, corporal, corporeal, distinct *(clear)*, evident, lucid, manifest, material *(physical)*, obvious, overt, pellucid, perceivable, perceptible, physical, ponderable, sensible, substantive, tangible, unmistakable
palpable episode fact
palpably fairly *(clearly)*
palpably false unbelievable
palpitate beat *(pulsate)*
palsied powerless
palter equivocate, evade *(deceive)*, fabricate *(make up)*, feign, haggle, lie *(falsify)*, misrepresent, perjure, pettifog, prevaricate
palter with the truth distort
paltriness immateriality, inconsequence, insignificance
paltry de minimus, deficient, frivolous, inappreciable, inconsequential, inconsiderable, inferior *(lower in quality)*, insubstantial, insufficient, minimal, minor, negligible, nonsubstantial *(not sufficient)*, nugatory, null *(insignificant)*, petty, poor *(inferior in quality)*, scarce, slight, tenuous
paltry few minority *(outnumbered group)*
pamper pander
pamper excessively overindulge
pampering indulgence, lenience, lenient
panacea cure
panache pretense *(ostentation)*
pandect abstract, capsule, compendium, constitution, digest, hornbook, outline *(synopsis)*, summary
pandemic general, omnibus, predominant, prevailing *(current)*, prevalent, rife
pandemonium bluster *(commotion)*,

brawl, commotion, confusion *(turmoil)*, disorder *(lack of order)*, embroilment, furor, noise, outcry, panic, riot, shambles, turmoil

panegyric mention *(tribute)*

panegyrical favorable *(expressing approval)*

panel array *(jury)*, band, chamber *(body)*, jury, meeting *(conference)*

panel of judges bench, chamber *(body)*, forum *(court)*, tribunal

pang pain

pangs of conscience remorse

panhandler parasite

panic fear, fright, frighten, pandemonium, phobia, trepidation

panoplied armed, safe

panoply ammunition, protection

panorama scene

panoramic comprehensive

pansophic learned, omniscient

pansophical omniscient

pantomine mock *(imitate)*

panurgic practiced

paper blank *(form)*, certificate, document, instrument *(document)*, pandect *(treatise)*

paper credit letter of credit

paper money check *(instrument)*, currency, debenture

papers credentials, data, dossier

Paphian lascivious, salacious

par peer, similar

par worth

paraclete advocate *(counselor)*

parade demonstrate *(protest)*, display, flaunt, histrionics, lineup, pretense *(ostentation)*, produce *(offer to view)*

parade conspicuously flaunt

paradigm case *(example)*, example, exemplar, instance, model, pattern, prototype, sample, specimen, standard

paradigma paradigm

paradigmatic exemplary

paradisiacal placid

paradox enigma

paradoxical debatable, disputable, impossible, inconsistent, inexplicable, ironic, problematic

paragon exemplar, expert, model, pattern, prototype, representative *(example)*, standard

paragraph chapter *(division)*, clause, subheading, title *(division)*

parallel agreed *(harmonized)*, akin *(germane)*, analogous, coequal, coextensive, cognate, collateral *(accompanying)*, commensurable, comparable *(capable of comparison)*, compare, comparison, concerted, concomitant, concurrent *(at the same time)*, congruous, connection *(relation)*, consensual, consonant, constructive *(inferential)*, correlate, correlative, correspond *(be equivalent)*, equivalent, mutual *(reciprocal)*, peer, reciprocal, relate *(establish a connection)*, reproduce, resemblance, same, similar, tantamount

parallel relation analogy

paralleling commensurate

parallelism analogy, identity *(similarity)*, parity, propinquity *(similarity)*

parallelize compare

paralogical sophistic

paralogism fallacy, non sequitur

paralogistic fallacious, illogical

paralogize distort

paralysis deadlock, inaction, inertia

paralysis of authority lynch law

paralytic disabled *(made incapable)*, powerless

paralyze debar, disable, disarm *(divest of arms)*, fetter, impair, impede, inhibit, prevent, stall

paralyzed disabled *(made incapable)*, helpless *(powerless)*, powerless

paralyzing chilling effect, disabling

parameter guideline

paramount absolute *(ideal)*, best, cardinal *(outstanding)*, central *(essential)*, critical *(crucial)*, dominant, important *(significant)*, influential, leading *(ranking first)*, major, master, material *(important)*, necessary *(required)*, noteworthy, outstanding *(prominent)*, peremptory *(imperative)*, predominant, preferential, prevailing *(having superior force)*, primary, prime *(most valuable)*, principal, professional *(stellar)*, salient, sovereign *(absolute)*, stellar, superior *(higher)*, superlative, vital

paramount law constitution

paramountcy hegemony, importance, influence, predominance, preponderance, prestige, primacy, significance, stress *(accent)*, supremacy

paramountly a fortiori

paranoia insanity

parapet bulwark

paraph sign

paraphernalia effects, goods

paraphrase construe *(translate)*, elucidate, explain, plagiarize, quote, recapitulate, repeat *(state again)*, restatement

paraphrased repeated

paraphrasis paraphrase

parasitize prey

paratus ready *(prepared)*

parcel installment, lot, moiety, part *(separate)*, property *(land)*, ration, real estate, reapportion, subdivide

parcel of land plot *(land)*, section *(vicinity)*

parcel out allocate, allot, apportion, disburse *(distribute)*, dispense, disperse *(disseminate)*, dispose *(apportion)*, distribute, divide *(distribute)*, dole, marshal, mete, partition, prorate, sort, split

parcel out again redistribute

parcel out to delegate

parceling out disbursement *(act of disbursing)*, distribution *(apportionment)*

parcelling division *(act of dividing)*

parcels paraphernalia *(personal belongings)*

parcener heir

parcere forbear

parch burn

parcus close *(rigorous)*, frugal, parsimonious

pardon absolution, absolve, acquit, acquittal, amnesty, clear, clemency, compurgation, condonation, condone, discharge *(release from obligation)*, discharge *(exception)*, dispensation *(exception)*, emancipation, exculpate, excuse, exonerate, exoneration, extenuate, forgive, free, grace, grace period, impunity, indulgence, liberate, liberation, longanimity, overlook *(excuse)*, palliate

(excuse), purge *(wipe out by atonement)*, quit *(free of)*, release, remission, remit *(release from penalty)*, respite *(reprieve)*, vindicate

pardonable allowable, defensible, justifiable

pardoned clear *(free from criminal charges)*, free *(relieved from a burden)*

pardoning clemency, lenient, palliative *(excusing)*

pardonment release

pare curtail, decrease, denude, diminish, discount *(minimize)*, excise *(cut away)*, lessen, minimize, rebate, retrench

pare down curtail

paregoric narcotic

parens parents, progenitor

parent ancestor, author *(originator)*, derivation, precursor, primogenitor, progenitor, source

parentage adoption *(affiliation)*, affiliation *(bloodline)*, affinity *(family ties)*, ancestry, birth *(lineage)*, blood, bloodline, citation *(attribution)*, derivation, descent *(lineage)*, family *(common ancestry)*, filiation, lineage, origin *(ancestry)*, origination, paternity, race, source

parental paternal

parenthesis insertion

parenthesize interpose

parenthetic incidental, nonessential

parenthetical nonessential

parenthetically among

parenthood maternity, origin *(ancestry)*

parentless child orphan

parents ancestry

parents and children household

parere bear *(yield)*, comply, generate, heed, obey

pariah derelict

paring economy *(frugality)*

parity analogy, balance *(equality)*, correspondence *(similarity)*, equipoise, identity *(similarity)*, resemblance

park locate, lodge *(house)*, stay *(rest)*

parkway causeway

parlance conference, language, phraseology, rhetoric *(skilled speech)*, speech

parlay bet, build *(augment)*, compound

parley communicate, confer *(consult)*, conference, confrontation *(act of setting face to face)*, consult *(ask advice of)*, conversation, converse, council *(assembly)*, deliberate, discourse, discuss, mediate, mediation, meet, meeting *(conference)*, negotiate, negotiation, session, speak, treat *(process)*

parliament chamber *(body)*, council *(assembly)*, legislature

parliamentarian legislator

parlor chamber *(compartment)*

parlous aleatory *(perilous)*

parlous state peril

parochial illiberal, narrow, provincial, regional

parochialis parochial

parody caricature, distort, jape, mock *(imitate)*, pose *(impersonate)*, travesty

parol nuncupative

parole discharge *(liberate)*, free, liberate, liberation, probation, undertaking *(pledge)*, verbal

paroled free *(relieved from a burden)*, unbound
parolee convict, probationer *(released offender)*
paroxysm outbreak, outburst
parrot copy, impersonate, mock *(imitate)*, recite, repeat *(state again)*
parry avert, bicker, block, defense, dispute *(debate)*, divert, elude, equivocate, prevaricate, prevent, rebut, refute, repel *(drive back)*, reply, resist *(oppose)*, respond, retort
parrying avoidance *(evasion)*
pars clause, constituent *(part)*, department, faction, ingredient, installment, item, proportion, segment, share *(interest)*, side, subdivision
pars interior chamber *(compartment)*
pars minima minimum
parsimonia economy *(frugality)*
parsimonious economical, frugal, illiberal, penurious, provident *(frugal)*
part alienate *(estrange)*, alight, aspect, assignment *(task)*, bifurcate, break *(separate)*, chapter *(division)*, circuit, component, constituent *(part)*, courtroom, depart, department, detach, detail, dichotomize, disband, discontinue *(break continuity)*, disengage, disjoint, disperse *(scatter)*, dissociate, dissolve *(separate)*, divide *(separate)*, divorce, element, equity *(share of ownership)*, estrange, excerpt, factor *(ingredient)*, feature *(characteristic)*, ingredient, interest *(ownership)*, isolate, item, leave *(depart)*, lot, luxate, member *(constituent part)*, moiety, organ, phase *(aspect)*, proportion, province, quit *(evacuate)*, ration, region, remove *(eliminate)*, retire *(retreat)*, role, section *(division)*, section *(vicinity)*, segment, separate, sever, share *(interest)*, split, subdivision, title *(division)*, unit *(item)*
part and parcel constituent *(part)*
part company avoid *(evade)*, disband, estrange, move *(alter position)*, separate, split
part exemplifying a mass cross section
part exemplifying a number cross section
part of the bargain counteroffer
part payment deposit, installment
part payment of a debt installment
part ways separate
part with abandon *(relinquish)*, alienate *(transfer title)*, attorn, bestow, cede, disown *(refuse to acknowledge)*, forfeit, forgo, forswear, jettison, lose *(be deprived of)*, parcel, relinquish, renounce, spend, surrender *(give back)*
part with life die
partage split
partake contribute *(assist)*, engage *(involve)*, involve *(participate)*, participate
partake in cooperate
partake in a symposium discuss
partake of contribute *(assist)*
partaken privy
partaker accessory, accomplice, participant, partner, party *(participant)*
parted discrete, disjunctive *(tending to disjoin)*, separate
partes office, part *(role)*, role
partes hominis agere impersonate

partial deficient, ex parte, illiberal, imperfect, inchoate, inequitable, interested, one-sided, parochial, partisan, preferential, prone, semi, unequal *(unjust)*, unjust
partial change modification
partial excuse extenuating circumstances
partial payment installment
partial similarity analogy
partial to inclined, willing *(desirous)*
partial truth evasion
partialism favoritism
partiality affection, affinity *(regard)*, bias, favoritism, foregone conclusion, inclination, inequality, inequity, injustice, intolerance, nepotism, penchant, preconception, predetermination, predilection, predisposition, preference *(choice)*, prejudice *(preconception)*, proclivity, propensity, tendency
partially in part, piecemeal
partible divisible, divisive, separable, severable
particeps participant, partner
particeps criminis abettor, accessory, accomplice, cohort, colleague, copartner *(coconspirator)*
participant accessory, accomplice, actor, contestant, contributor *(contributor)*, partisan, partner, privy
participate assist, connive, contribute *(assist)*, cooperate, engage *(involve)*, espouse, federalize *(associate)*, federate, join *(associate oneself with)*, partake
participate in commit *(perpetrate)*, compete
participate in an unlawful scheme conspire
participate surreptitiously connive
participate with combine *(act in concert)*
participating common *(shared)*, concurrent *(united)*
participation affiliation *(connectedness)*, assistance, association *(connection)*, collusion, connivance, contact *(association)*, coverage *(scope)*, integration *(assimilation)*, interest *(ownership)*, league, partnership
participation in fraud collusion
participator accessory, accomplice, colleague, confederate, consociate, contributor *(contributor)*, member *(individual in a group)*, participant, partner, party *(participant)*
participatory common *(shared)*, mutual *(collective)*
particle constituent *(part)*, element, iota, minimum, modicum, part *(portion)*, scintilla
particular accurate, certain *(specific)*, circumspect, concrete, conscientious, detail, detailed, distinct *(clear)*, distinct *(distinguished from others)*, distinctive, exact, express, faithful *(diligent)*, feature *(characteristic)*, individual, item, meticulous, painstaking, peculiar *(distinctive)*, personal *(individual)*, point *(item)*, precise, proper, punctilious, singular, special, specific, specification, strict, technicality, term *(provision)*, unusual
particular aptitude penchant
particular characteristic specialty *(distinctive mark)*

particular charge complaint, count
particular course of action procedure
particular item specialty *(distinctive mark)*
particular manner of proceeding course
particular matter specialty *(distinctive mark)*
particular object article *(commodity)*
particular object of pursuit specialty *(special aptitude)*
particular one individual
particular part component
particular point specialty *(distinctive mark)*
particular point of time date
particularity characteristic, color *(complexion)*, detail, differential, diligence *(care)*, habit, identity *(individuality)*, particular, personality, property *(distinctive attribute)*, quality *(attribute)*, quality *(grade)*, quirk *(idiosyncrasy)*, speciality, specialty *(distinctive mark)*, technicality, trait
particularization designation *(naming)*, specification
particularize delineate, depict, describe, designate, detail *(particularize)*, differentiate, distinguish, itemize, portray, recount, relate *(tell)*, specify
particularized descriptive, detailed
particularly a fortiori
particularness discretion *(quality of being discreet)*, particularity
particulars circumstances, description, story *(narrative)*
partim partial *(part)*, partial *(relating to a part)*
parting divergent, division *(act of dividing)*, egress, estrangement, leave *(absence)*, rift *(disagreement)*, rift *(gap)*, separation
parting with cession
partiri parcel, part *(separate)*
partisan addict, advocate *(espouser)*, backer, ex parte, inequitable, interested, one-sided, parochial, partial *(biased)*, party *(participant)*, political, politician, preferential, prejudicial, proponent
partisan competition primary
partisan conflict faction
partisan contest primary
partisan election primary
partisan outlook posture *(attitude)*
partisanism bias, inequity, nepotism, politics
partisanship bias, constituency, faction, favor *(partiality)*, favoritism, indorsement, inequity, injustice, nepotism, partiality, predilection, prejudice *(preconception)*
partitio division *(act of dividing)*
partition allot, allotment, apportion, apportionment, assign *(allot)*, assignment *(allotment)*, barrier, bifurcate, chapter *(division)*, classify, decentralization, demarcate, dichotomize, disassociation, dispensation *(act of dispensing)*, disperse *(disseminate)*, disperse *(scatter)*, distribution *(apportionment)*, divide *(separate)*, division *(act of dividing)*, parcel, part *(separate)*, schism, segregation *(separation)*, sever, split, split, subdivide, subdivision

partitioned bipartite, disconnected, disjunctive (*tending to disjoin*)
partitioned space chamber (*compartment*)
partitionment apportionment
partly in part
partner accessory, accomplice, assistant, associate, coactor, coadjutant, coconspirator, cohort, colleague, confederate, connect (*join together*), consociate, consort, conspirer, contributor (*contributor*), copartner (*business associate*), member (*individual in a group*), participant, partisan, party (*participant*)
partner in crime accessory, accomplice, coactor, coconspirator, conspirer, copartner (*coconspirator*)
partner in wrongdoing accomplice, coconspirator
partnered conjoint, conjugal, corporate (*associate*)
partnership affiliation (*connectedness*), association (*connection*), coaction, coalition, community, company (*enterprise*), consortium (*business cartel*), consortium (*marriage companionship*), contribution (*participation*), cooperative, firm, integration (*assimilation*), league, matrimony, merger, pool, sodality, syndicate
parts contents
parturient fertile
parturition birth (*emergence of young*)
partus embryo
party actor, amicus curiae, appellant, applicant (*petitioner*), assemblage, character (*an individual*), complainant, constituency, contender, contributor (*contributor*), denomination, individual, litigant, participant, person, petitioner, privy, side
party against whom a complaint is lodged defendant
party against whom charges are pending defendant
party answering a summons or bill respondent
party competition primary
party contest primary
party election primary
party in power management (*directorate*)
party leadership politics
party line platform, policy (*plan of action*)
party machine party (*political organization*)
party making an affidavit deponent
party member partisan, politician
party planks platform
party politics politics
party system politics
party to a suit accuser, appellant, claimant, complainant, contender, contestant, litigant, suitor
party to an instrument comaker
party to the suit plaintiff
party who is sued defendant
party who sues plaintiff
party-liner partisan
parum candidus disingenuous
parum clarus indistinct
parum distinctus inarticulate
parum insignis inconspicuous

parum procedere miscarriage
parvi facere disregard
parvo emere rate
parvus limited
pasquinade parody, ridicule
pass alienate (*transfer title*), circulate, confirm, constitute (*establish*), convey (*transfer*), decide, enact, experience (*encounter*), expire, exude, forgo, franchise (*license*), give (*grant*), grant (*transfer formally*), incident, key (*passport*), legislate, outbalance, penetrate, perambulate, perish, permit, plight, posture (*situation*), predicament, pretermit, promote (*advance*), surmount, surpass, transcend, transfer, transmit, traverse
pass an opinion determine, find (*determine*)
pass and repass beat (*pulsate*)
pass away decease, die, expire, perish
pass back regress
pass by disdain, disregard, ignore, neglect, omit, reject
pass by devise descend
pass by inheritance descend
pass by operation of law descend
pass by succession descend
pass by will demise
pass censure on condemn (*blame*), convict, denounce (*condemn*)
pass censure upon disapprove (*condemn*)
pass current circulate
pass down attorn, confer (*give*), contribute (*supply*), convey (*transfer*), demise, endow, render (*deliver*)
pass down from generation to generation descend
pass for assume (*simulate*), displace (*replace*), impersonate, pose (*impersonate*), profess (*pretend*)
pass from one to another circulate
pass from point to point traverse
pass in the mind occur (*come to mind*)
pass into enter (*go in*)
pass judgment adjudge, adjudicate, arbitrate (*adjudge*), award, conclude (*decide*), decide, decree, determine, find (*determine*), hold (*decide*), rule (*decide*)
pass judgment upon sentence
pass laws legislate
pass off fake, pretend
pass off another's ideas as one's own plagiarize
pass off another's writings as one's own plagiarize
pass off as genuine foist
pass off for disguise, misrepresent
pass on abalienate, annunciate, comment, convey (*communicate*), decease, deliver, descend, die, perish, proceed (*go forward*), transfer, transmit
pass on again recover
pass on information annunciate, notice (*give formal warning*)
pass on to bequeath
pass orders instruct (*direct*)
pass out disburse (*distribute*), disperse (*disseminate*), divide (*distribute*), parcel
pass out of sight disappear
pass over alienate (*transfer title*), condone, discount (*disbelieve*), disdain, dismiss (*put out of consideration*), exclude, excuse, grant (*transfer formally*),

ignore, neglect, omit, overlook (*disregard*), override, pretermit, reject, remit (*release from penalty*)
pass over to bequeath
pass round circulate
pass sentence adjudicate, award, decide, determine, rule (*decide*)
pass sentence on condemn (*punish*), convict
pass sentence upon judge, pronounce (*pass judgment*)
pass through endure (*suffer*), perambulate, permeate, pervade, traverse
pass time in idleness loiter
pass title convey (*transfer*)
pass to devolve
pass to another lapse (*cease*)
pass under review censor, judge, notice (*observe*), peruse
pass unfavorable judgment upon disapprove (*condemn*)
pass up disapprove (*reject*), disavow, refuse
pass upon award, rule (*decide*)
pass without notice ignore
passable admissible, allowable, average (*standard*), fair (*satisfactory*), imperfect, marginal, mediocre, pardonable, penetrable, unobjectionable
passableness mediocrity
passably fairly (*moderately*)
passage access (*right of way*), admission (*entry*), admittance (*means of approach*), avenue (*route*), chapter (*division*), circulation, clause, conversion (*change*), entrance, entry (*entrance*), excerpt, fare, ingress, osmosis, progress, reconversion, transition, transmittal
passage at arms affray
passage money fare
passage out egress, outlet
passage taken from a book excerpt
passages approaches
passageway access (*right of way*), admission (*entry*), admittance (*means of approach*), avenue (*route*), entrance, portal
passbook ledger
passe outdated, outmoded
passed allowed
passed away dead, deceased, defunct, lifeless (*dead*)
passed down hereditary
passed on deceased, late (*defunct*), lifeless (*dead*)
passer-by bystander
passing brief, circulation, cursory, ephemeral, extremity (*death*), itinerant, moving (*in motion*), promotion (*advancement*), provisional, temporary, transient, transition, volatile
passing away death, demise (*death*), in extremis, transitory
passing into law legalization
passing judgment conviction (*finding of guilt*)
passing of seisin feoffment
passing over omission
passing word mention (*reference*)
passion affection, ardor, emotion, furor, obsession, penchant, propensity, spirit
passionate demonstrative (*expressive of emotion*), eager, ecstatic, fanatical, fervent, hot-blooded, impulsive (*rash*), intense, serious (*devoted*), vehement,

zealous

passionateness ardor

passionless cold-blooded, controlled *(restrained)*, dispassionate, languid, lifeless *(dull)*, nonchalant, perfunctory, phlegmatic, stoical

passive dormant, indolent, insensible, languid, lifeless *(dull)*, obedient, otiose, patient, phlegmatic, pliant, resigned, sequacious, servile, stagnant, static, stoical, torpid, unobtrusive, yielding

passive agreement acquiescence

passive consent acquiescence

passiveness capitulation, inaction, inertia, resignation *(passive acceptance)*

passivity capitulation, inaction, inertia, languor, resignation *(passive acceptance)*, sloth

passport credentials, permit

password catchword

past back *(in arrears)*, defunct, former, last *(preceding)*, obsolete, old, outdated, outmoded, previous, prior

past bearing insufferable, unendurable

past comprehension inapprehensible, inscrutable

past cure incorrigible, irredeemable, irremediable

past dispute categorical, certain *(positive)*, cogent, inappealable, incontestable, incontrovertible, indubious, irrefutable, positive *(incontestable)*, uncontroverted, undeniable, undisputed

past due delinquent *(overdue)*, late *(tardy)*, outstanding *(unpaid)*, overdue

past enduring insufferable, unendurable

past help irremediable

past hope incorrigible, irrecoverable, irredeemable

past mending irredeemable, irremediable

past recall irredeemable, irretrievable

past the time for payment overdue

paste combine *(join together)*

pastiche melange

pastoral placid

pat suitable, usual

patch fix *(repair)*, flaw, parcel, plot *(land)*, repair, restore *(renew)*

patch up fix *(repair)*, renew *(refurbish)*, restore *(renew)*

patch up a quarrel placate

patching repair

patchwork melange

patefacere detect, manifest, reveal

patefactio common knowledge, disclosure *(act of disclosing)*

patens open *(unclosed)*

patent apparent *(perceptible)*, appreciable, blatant *(conspicuous)*, charter *(license)*, clear *(apparent)*, comprehensible, conspicuous, evident, explicit, lucid, manifest, naked *(perceptible)*, obvious, open *(in sight)*, ostensible, overt, palpable, pellucid, perceivable, perceptible, permit, unmistakable

patently bad arrant *(onerous)*

patently offensive obscene

patere open *(accessible)*

paternal consanguineous

paternal parentage paternity

paternity descent *(lineage)*, filiation, parentage

paternus hereditary, paternal

path access *(right of way)*, admission *(entry)*, admittance *(means of approach)*, avenue *(route)*, conduit *(channel)*, outlet, way *(channel)*

pathetic deplorable, disconsolate, lamentable, paltry

pathfinder pioneer, precursor

pathless impervious

pathogenic contagious, insalubrious

pathway way *(channel)*

pati bear *(tolerate)*, let *(permit)*, suffer *(permit)*

patience composure, diligence *(perseverance)*, indulgence, lenience, longanimity, moderation, resignation *(passive acceptance)*, sufferance, temperament, temperance, tolerance, understanding *(tolerance)*

patiens patient, phlegmatic

patient charitable *(lenient)*, lenient, peaceable, persistent, pertinacious, placid, resigned, sedulous, steadfast, stoical

patient endurance longanimity, sufferance

patientia sufferance

patois phraseology

patriarch ancestor, parents, precursor, predecessor, primogenitor

patriarchal consanguineous, paternal

patriarchs ancestry

patriciate society

patrilinear consanguineous

patrimonial paternal, testamentary

patrimonium birthright, heritage

patrimony bequest, birthright, estate *(hereditament)*, hereditament, heritage

patriotic faithful *(loyal)*, loyal

patrius paternal

patrocinium patronage *(power to appoint jobs)*

patrol perambulate, police, protect, traverse

patrolman peace officer, warden

patron abettor, advocate *(counselor)*, advocate *(espouser)*, backer, benefactor, client, consumer, contributor *(giver)*, customer, donor, employer, good samaritan, guardian, member *(individual in a group)*, partisan, promoter, proponent, samaritan, sponsor

patron of professional servies client

patronage advantage, advocacy, aid *(help)*, aid *(subsistence)*, auspices, charge *(custody)*, charity, control *(supervision)*, favor *(sanction)*, goodwill, guidance, help, nepotism, protection, safekeeping, support *(assistance)*, trade *(commerce)*

patroness donor

patronize deign, finance, foster, help, nurture, prefer, preserve, promote *(organize)*, protect, sponsor, subscribe *(promise)*, subsidize, support *(assist)*

patronizer client, patron *(regular customer)*

patronizing inflated *(vain)*, orgulous, proud *(conceited)*, supercilious

patronus advocate *(counselor)*, patron *(influential supporter)*, spokesman

patronymic call *(title)*

pattern array *(order)*, compose, configuration *(form)*, constant, content *(structure)*, contrive, create, criterion,

delineation, example, exemplar, form *(arrangement)*, habit, make, manner *(behavior)*, model, modus operandi, motif, norm, order *(arrangement)*, paradigm, practice *(custom)*, prototype, rule *(guide)*, specimen, stamp, standard, structure *(composition)*, style, system

pattern after copy, mock *(imitate)*

pattern bargaining collective bargaining

pattern of words phraseology

patterned boiler plate, periodic, regular *(orderly)*

patterning creation

patternless disordered

patulous open *(unclosed)*

patulus open *(unclosed)*

pauciloquent brief, laconic, mute, succinct, taciturn

paucitas paucity

paucity dearth, deficiency, deficit, delinquency *(shortage)*, insignificance, insufficiency, need *(deprivation)*, poverty

paululum modicum

paulum modicum

pauperism bankruptcy, indigence, poverty, privation

pauperize deplete, deprive

pauperized bankrupt, impecunious, poor *(underprivileged)*

paupertas poverty

pause cease, cessation *(interlude)*, defer *(put off)*, delay, discontinuance *(act of discontinuing)*, doubt *(hesitate)*, extension *(postponement)*, halt, halt, hesitate, hiatus, interruption, interval, lapse *(break)*, leave *(absence)*, lull, misdoubt, moratorium, pendency, procrastinate, qualm, recess, recess, remain *(stay)*, remission, reprieve, respite *(interval of rest)*, rest *(cease from action)*, stay *(rest)*, stop

pausing dilatory, hesitant

pave the way expedite, facilitate, precede, provide *(arrange for)*

paved road causeway

paved way causeway

pavor consternation, fear, fright, panic

pawn captive, deposit, security *(pledge)*

pax peace

pay advance *(allowance)*, commission *(fee)*, compensation, contribute *(supply)*, cover *(provide for)*, defray, disburse *(pay out)*, disbursement *(funds paid out)*, earnings, expend *(disburse)*, fund, income, indemnify, inure *(benefit)*, liquidate *(determine liability)*, offer *(tender)*, payment *(remittance)*, post, profit, recoup *(reimburse)*, remit *(send payment)*, remunerate, remuneration, requital, revenue, reward, satisfy *(discharge)*, spend, subsidize, tender, wage

pay a debt quit *(repay)*

pay a price for buy

pay allegiance adhere *(maintain loyalty)*

pay an indemnity bear the expense, defray, quit *(repay)*

pay and settle liquidate *(determine liability)*

pay attention devote, hear *(give attention to)*, heed, notice *(observe)*, observe *(watch)*

pay attention to care *(be cautious)*, care *(regard)*, concern *(care)*, consider, note *(notice)*, observe *(obey)*, oversee

pay back bear *(yield)*, contribute *(indemnify)*, indemnify, quit *(repay)*, rebate, reciprocate, recoup *(reimburse)*, recriminate, refund, reimburse, repay, replace, retaliate, return *(refund)*

pay cash for buy

pay compensation bear the expense, defray, indemnify

pay damages bear the expense, compensate *(remunerate)*, contribute *(indemnify)*

pay debts liquidate *(determine liability)*

pay deference honor

pay dividends disperse *(disseminate)*

pay for bear the expense, buy, compensate *(remunerate)*, defray, finance, fund, purchase, sponsor, subsidize

pay heed devote, observe *(watch)*

pay heed to note *(notice)*

pay homage honor

pay homage to regard *(hold in esteem)*, yield *(submit)*

pay honor dedicate

pay in advance prepay

pay in full bear the expense, compensate *(remunerate)*, discharge *(pay a debt)*, quit *(repay)*, satisfy *(discharge)*

pay in kind repay

pay little attention to minimize

pay little heed to minimize

pay load freight

pay no attention discount *(disbelieve)*, disregard, neglect

pay no attention to disobey, ignore, pretermit

pay no heed discount *(disbelieve)*

pay no heed to ignore, neglect

pay no mind discount *(disbelieve)*

pay no regard to dismiss *(put out of consideration)*, disregard, neglect, pretermit

pay off disburse *(pay out)*, discharge *(pay a debt)*, quit *(repay)*, satisfy *(discharge)*

pay old debts quit *(repay)*

pay on demand bear the expense

pay one's way defray

pay out disperse *(disseminate)*, divide *(distribute)*, dole, expend *(disburse)*, mete

pay reparations defray, indemnify

pay respect to defer *(yield in judgment)*

pay respects honor

pay the bill bear the expense

pay the costs bear the expense, defray

pay the equivalent compensate *(remunerate)*

pay the penalty repent

pay the value compensate *(remunerate)*

pay towards subsidize

pay tribute belaud, bestow, honor, regard *(hold in esteem)*

pay up discharge *(pay a debt)*, satisfy *(discharge)*

pay wages bear the expense, compensate *(remunerate)*

pay-off commission *(fee)*

pay-out payoff *(payment in full)*

payable delinquent *(overdue)*, outstanding *(unpaid)*, receivable, unpaid

payee beneficiary, heir, holder, recipi-

ent, transferee

paying beneficial, compensatory, gainful, lucrative, productive, profitable

paying back contribution *(indemnification)*, expiation, reimbursement, restitution

paying for collection *(payment)*

paying guest tenant

paying off discharge *(payment)*

payload cargo

payment amortization, binder, charge *(cost)*, collection *(payment)*, commission *(fee)*, compensation, consideration *(recompense)*, contribution *(indemnification)*, correction *(punishment)*, cost *(expenses)*, deposit, disbursement *(funds paid out)*, downpayment, earnings, expenditure, expense *(cost)*, expiation, fee *(charge)*, handsel, honorarium, income, indemnification, indemnity, out of pocket, outlay, pay, payroll, pension, perquisite, price, prize, profit, rate, receipt *(voucher)*, recompense, reimbursement, relief *(legal redress)*, remittance, remuneration, rent, reparation *(indemnification)*, requital, restitution, retainer, retribution, revenue, reward, satisfaction *(discharge of debt)*, settlement, tip *(gratuity)*, toll *(effect)*, toll *(tax)*, trover, wage

payment beforehand advance *(allowance)*

payment for delay demurrage

payment for expenses refund

payment for misconduct fine

payment for services payroll

payment for the right of carriage fare

payment in lieu composition *(agreement in bankruptcy)*

payment of damages compensation

payments overhead

payments past due arrears

payoff effect

payor transferor

peace composure, concordance, lull, reconciliation

peace of mind composure

peace offering reparation *(indemnification)*

peace officer marshal

peace officers police

peace-loving nonmilitant, peaceable

peaceable neutral, nonmilitant, patient, placid

peaceful dispassionate, harmonious, neutral, nonmilitant, peaceable, placid

peaceful of mind complacent

peacefulness composure

peacelike peaceable

peacemaker go-between, intermediary, referee, umpire

peacemaking compromise, conciliation, intercession, reconciliation

peak ceiling, culmination, maximum *(amplitude)*, pinnacle

pealing resounding

peasant ignoble

pecability offense

peccability bad repute, blame *(culpability)*, culpability, delinquency *(misconduct)*, frailty, impeachability

peccable blameful, blameworthy, imperfect, profane, reprehensible, sinister

peccadillo guilt, impropriety, malfeasance, misconduct, misdeed, misde-

meanor, misdoing, misfeasance

peccancy culpability, delinquency *(misconduct)*, guilt, malfeasance, misdeed

peccans offender, peccant *(culpable)*

peccant bad *(offensive)*, blameful, blameworthy, culpable, delinquent *(guilty of a misdeed)*, disgraceful, errant, guilty, iniquitous, malignant, nefarious, objectionable, offensive *(offending)*, profane, profligate *(corrupt)*, reprehensible, reprobate, sinister

peccare lapse *(fall into error)*, offend *(violate the law)*

peccatum error, fault *(responsibility)*, lapse *(expiration)*, misconduct, misdeed, offense, transgression

peculate bilk, cheat, convert *(misappropriate)*, defalcate, defraud, impropriate, loot, mulct *(defraud)*, poach, purloin, rob, steal

peculation bad faith, bad repute, conversion *(misappropriation)*, embezzlement, larceny, misappropriation, misusage, theft

peculator embezzler, hoodlum, thief

peculiar anomalous, certain *(particular)*, certain *(specific)*, different, distinct *(distinguished from others)*, distinctive, eccentric, express, extraordinary, irregular *(not usual)*, ludicrous, nonconforming, noteworthy, novel, particular *(individual)*, particular *(specific)*, personal *(individual)*, prodigious *(amazing)*, remarkable, several *(separate)*, singular, specific, suspicious *(questionable)*, unaccustomed, uncanny, uncommon, unique, unusual

peculiar expression phrase

peculiar feature aspect

peculiar idiom characteristic, specialty *(distinctive mark)*

peculiar temperament specialty *(distinctive mark)*

peculiaris specific

peculiarities color *(complexion)*, personality

peculiarity character *(personal quality)*, characteristic, differential, distinction *(difference)*, feature *(characteristic)*, habit, identity *(individuality)*, irregularity, nonconformity, property *(distinctive attribute)*, quality *(attribute)*, quirk *(idiosyncrasy)*, speciality, specialty *(distinctive mark)*, technicality, trait

peculiarity of phrasing phraseology

peculiarly particularly

pecunia fund, income, money, remittance

pecunia praesens cash

pecuniae aversor embezzler

pecuniae residuae arrears

pecuniam mutuam dare capitalize *(provide capital)*

pecuniam redigere realize *(obtain as a profit)*

pecuniaria finance

pecuniarius pecuniary

pecuniary commercial, financial, fiscal, monetary

pecuniary aid alimony, consideration *(recompense)*, pension

pecuniary assistance alimony

pecuniary burden charge *(cost)*, charge *(lien)*

pecuniary due debit
pecuniary management finance
pecuniary penalty amercement, fine, forfeiture *(thing forfeited)*
pecuniary punishment fine
pecuniary resource bank
pecuniary resources assets, capital, cash, possessions, property *(possessions)*
pecunious opulent, prosperous, solvent
pedagogic didactic, disciplinary *(educational)*
pedagogical disciplinary *(educational)*
pedagogy education, guidance, instruction *(teaching)*
pedantic dogmatic, inflated *(bombastic)*, learned, sesquipedalian
pedantical learned
pedantry diligence *(care)*
peddle barter, handle *(trade)*, sell, vend
peddler dealer, merchant, vendor
pedem referre retreat
pederasty sodomy
pedestal cornerstone
pedestrian inferior *(lower in quality)*, mundane, nondescript, ordinary, prevalent, prosaic, stale, usual
pedestrianize perambulate
pedigree ancestry, blood, bloodline, descent *(lineage)*, origin *(ancestry)*, parentage
pedogogic informative
peel denude
peep spy
peer contributor *(contributor)*, copartner *(business associate)*, delve, spy
peer at examine *(study)*, observe *(watch)*
peer into frisk, investigate, peruse, scrutinize
peerage society
peerless absolute *(ideal)*, best, inestimable, invaluable, laudable, noteworthy, outstanding *(prominent)*, paramount, premium, priceless, prime *(most valuable)*, rare, singular, sterling, superior *(excellent)*, superlative, unapproachable, unique, unusual
peeve bait *(harass)*, irritate
peevish fractious, froward, perverse, petulant, querulous, resentful, restive, sensitive *(easily affected)*
pejoration decline
pejorative calumnious, derogatory, libelous
pelf spoils
pellicere lure
pellucid clear *(apparent)*, cognizable, coherent *(clear)*, comprehensible, distinct *(clear)*, lucid
pellucidus lucid, pellucid
pelt beat *(strike)*, lash *(strike)*
pen close *(enclosed area)*, detain *(hold in custody)*, enclose, lock, note *(record)*, restrict
pen in confine, encompass *(surround)*
pen up repress
penal disciplinary *(punitory)*, punitive
penal colony penitentiary, prison
penal institution jail, penitentiary, prison, reformatory
penal restraint bondage
penal retribution correction *(punishment)*, cost *(penalty)*, discipline *(pun-*

ishment), forfeiture *(thing forfeited)*, penalty, punishment, sanction *(punishment)*
penal servitude bondage, correction *(punishment)*
penal settlement penitentiary
penalization condemnation *(punishment)*, conviction *(finding of guilt)*, correction *(punishment)*, cost *(penalty)*, forfeiture *(thing forfeited)*, punishment
penalize condemn *(punish)*, convict, demote, discipline *(punish)*, fine, mulct *(fine)*, punish
penalizing punitive
penalty amercement, condemnation *(punishment)*, conviction *(finding of guilt)*, correction *(punishment)*, damages, disadvantage, discipline *(punishment)*, expense *(sacrifice)*, fine, forfeiture *(thing forfeited)*, imposition *(tax)*, infliction, punishment, reparation *(indemnification)*, reprisal, retribution, sanction *(punishment)*, sentence, surcharge, trover
penalty for delay demurrage
penalty imposed on an offender punishment
penance cost *(penalty)*, discipline *(punishment)*, penalty, punishment
penance doer penitent
penates household *(domestic)*
penchant affection, animus, bias, characteristic, conatus, disposition *(inclination)*, favor *(partiality)*, favoritism, inclination, partiality, predilection, predisposition, proclivity, propensity, tendency
pencraft handwriting
pendant addition, appendix *(accession)*, appurtenance, complement, correlate, counterpart *(complement)*
pendency cessation *(interlude)*
pendent dependent
pendere pay
pending ad interim, conditional, forthcoming, future, outstanding *(unresolved)*, undecided, unsettled, until
pendulate alternate *(fluctuate)*, beat *(pulsate)*, fluctuate, oscillate
penes quos est reipublica government *(political administration)*
penetrabilis penetrable
penetrability danger
penetrable cognizable, coherent *(clear)*, comprehensible, passable, scrutable, vulnerable
penetralia privacy
penetrare penetrate
penetrate break *(fracture)*, delve, encroach, impress *(affect deeply)*, interpose, invade, lancinate, permeate, pervade, pierce *(lance)*, solve, spread
penetrating acute, incisive, interrogative, mordacious, perspicacious, potent, profound *(esoteric)*, profound *(intense)*, sensitive *(discerning)*, trenchant
penetration comprehension, encroachment, entrance, incursion, inflow, infusion, insertion, insight, judgment *(discernment)*, osmosis, perception, sagacity
penetrative trenchant
penitence remorse
penitent contrite, remorseful, repentant
penitential contrite, penitent, re-

morseful, repentant
penitentiary cell, jail, prison, reformatory
penitus defixus inveterate
penitus insitus inveterate
penmanship handwriting, script
penned holographic
penniless bankrupt, destitute, impecunious, insolvent, penurious, poor *(underprivileged)*
pennilessness indigence, poverty
penny-conscious frugal
penny-pinching parsimonious
penological disciplinary *(punitory)*
penology discipline *(punishment)*
penscript script
pensio installment
pension annuity, capitalize *(provide capital)*
pensioner dependent, protégé
pensive cogitative, grave *(solemn)*, serious *(grave)*, solemn
pensiveness contemplation, introspection, preoccupation
penuria dearth, insufficiency
penurious illiberal, impecunious, parsimonious, poor *(underprivileged)*, provident *(frugal)*
penury bankruptcy, dearth, deficiency, indigence, need *(deprivation)*, poverty, privation
people community, family *(common ancestry)*, humanity *(mankind)*, nationality, populace, population, race
people delegated delegation *(envoy)*
peopled populous
peoples of the earth humanity *(mankind)*
pepper intersperse
per thereby
per contra contra
per day per diem
per head per capita
per miscere confound
per vim factus forcible
peragrare perambulate, prowl
perceivable apparent *(perceptible)*, appreciable, blatant *(conspicuous)*, clear *(apparent)*, coherent *(clear)*, comprehensible, conspicuous, determinable *(ascertainable)*, discernible, distinct *(clear)*, evident, manifest, naked *(perceptible)*, obvious, open *(in sight)*, ostensible, palpable, patent, perceptible, tangible, visible *(noticeable)*
perceivable dissimilarity distinction *(difference)*, identity *(individuality)*
perceive appreciate *(comprehend)*, comprehend *(understand)*, conceive *(comprehend)*, conjure, construe *(comprehend)*, deem, detect, discern *(detect with the senses)*, discover, find *(discover)*, identify, judge, note *(notice)*, notice *(observe)*, observe *(watch)*, pierce *(discern)*, read, realize *(understand)*, regard *(pay attention)*, spy, understand
perceive as true presume
perceive clearly differentiate, distinguish
perceive differences secern
perceive something audible hear *(perceive by ear)*
perceive the worth of appreciate *(value)*
perceived cognizable, foreseeable
perceived from accompanying

words noscitur a sociis

perceived happening fact

perceiving reasonable *(rational)*

percellere disconcert

percent proportion, share *(interest)*

percentage commission *(fee)*, moiety, part *(portion)*, per capita, proportion, quota, ration, share *(interest)*

percentage compensation commission *(fee)*

percentage of ownership interest *(ownership)*

percept concept, idea

perceptible appreciable, ascertainable, bodily, clear *(apparent)*, cognizable, coherent *(clear)*, comprehensible, concrete, conspicuous, determinable *(ascertainable)*, discernible, distinct *(clear)*, evident, manifest, obvious, open *(in sight)*, ostensible, overt, palpable, patent, perceivable, ponderable, scrutable, tangible, visible *(in full view)*

perceptibly fairly *(clearly)*

perception cognition, comprehension, concept, detection, discovery, discretion *(quality of being discreet)*, discrimination *(good judgment)*, estimate *(idea)*, idea, impression, insight, judgment *(discernment)*, knowledge *(awareness)*, precognition, reaction *(response)*, realization, reason *(sound judgment)*, recognition, sagacity, scienter, sense *(feeling)*, sense *(intelligence)*, sensibility, understanding *(comprehension)*, vision *(dream)*

perception of difference diagnosis

perceptive acute, cognizant, conscious *(aware)*, discreet, discriminating *(judicious)*, judicious, juridical, knowing, lucid, omniscient, perspicacious, politic, profound *(esoteric)*, receptive, responsive, sapient, sensible, sensitive *(discerning)*, sensitive *(easily affected)*, subtle *(refined)*, vicarious *(delegated)*

perceptiveness judgment *(discernment)*, knowledge *(awareness)*

perceptivity sensibility

perch rest *(be supported by)*, seat

percipere hear *(perceive by ear)*, perceive

percipience cognition, insight, judgment *(discernment)*, knowledge *(awareness)*, perception, sagacity

percipiency insight, reason *(sound judgment)*

percipient circumspect, cognizant, conscious *(aware)*, judicious, juridical, knowing, omniscient, perceptive, perspicacious, reasonable *(rational)*, sensitive *(discerning)*

percolate permeate

percontatio inquiry *(request for information)*, interrogation

percussion collision *(accident)*

percutere beat *(strike)*

perdere destroy *(efface)*, lose *(be deprived of)*, spoil *(impair)*

perdition adversity, destruction, miscarriage, subversion

perditus immoral, incorrigible, profligate *(corrupt)*, reprobate

perdu hidden, recondite

perducere conduct

perdurable chronic, constant, durable, infinite, infrangible, permanent,

perpetual, persistent, stable

perdure endure *(last)*, last, persist, remain *(continue)*, subsist

perduring live *(existing)*, permanent

peregrinate perambulate, prowl

peregrine foreign

peregrinus alien, foreign

peremptory compelling, compulsory, decisive, dictatorial, dogmatic, inappealable, insistent, mandatory, severe, supercilious, tyrannous, unequivocal

peremptory claim demand

peremptory demand dun

peremptory refusal rebuff

perennial chronic, consecutive, constant, continual *(connected)*, continuous, immutable, incessant, indestructible, permanent, unremitting

perenniality perpetuity

perennis permanent, perpetual

pererration vagrancy

perfect absolute *(ideal)*, accurate, amend, attain, best, blameless, cap, complete, consummate, definitive, develop, elaborate, enhance, faithful *(true to fact)*, felicitous, finish, fulfill, infallible, intact, mature, meritorious, peremptory *(absolute)*, pure, rectify, renew *(refurbish)*, renovate, right *(suitable)*, ripe, thorough, unblemished, unimpeachable

perfect a routine practice *(train by repetition)*

perfect substitute alter ego

perfected choate lien, elaborate

perfected condition maturity

perfectible corrigible

perfection amendment *(correction)*, maturity, progress

perfectionism casuistry, particularity

perfectly purely *(positively)*

perfectly sure positive *(confident)*

perferre enact, endure *(suffer)*

perfervid eager, fervent, intense, vehement, zealous

perfervor ardor

perficere consummate, dispatch *(dispose of)*, perfect, perform *(execute)*

perfidia infidelity, treason

perfidiosus faithless, perfidious

perfidious bad *(offensive)*, collusive, contemptible, dishonest, disingenuous, disobedient, evasive, faithless, false *(disloyal)*, felonious, fraudulent, insidious, irresponsible, lying, machiavellian, malevolent, mendacious, outrageous, recreant, tortuous *(corrupt)*, undependable, unreliable, unscrupulous, untrue, untrustworthy

perfidiousness bad faith, bad repute, corruption, dishonesty, disloyalty, indirection *(deceitfulness)*, infidelity

perfidus faithless, false *(disloyal)*, perfidious

perfidy artifice, bad faith, bad repute, breach, bribery, collusion, corruption, deceit, dishonesty, disloyalty, duplicity, false pretense, fraud, indirection *(deceitfulness)*, infidelity, treason, turpitude

perforable penetrable

perforare pierce *(lance)*

perforate enter *(penetrate)*, lancinate, penetrate, pervade, pierce *(lance)*

perforated penetrable

perforation split

perform abide, commit *(perpetrate)*, comply, comport *(behave)*, demonstrate *(establish)*, dispatch *(dispose of)*, effectuate, execute *(accomplish)*, exercise *(discharge a function)*, fulfill, function, implement, inflict, keep *(fulfill)*, make, obey, observe *(obey)*, officiate, operate, perpetrate, pretend, pursue *(carry on)*, realize *(make real)*, recite, render *(administer)*, transact

perform a circuit detour, deviate

perform a function avail *(be of use)*

perform by turns alternate *(take turns)*, reciprocate

perform on militate

perform reciprocally alternate *(take turns)*

perform repeatedly practice *(train by repetition)*

perform responsively alternate *(take turns)*, reciprocate

perform sentry duty patrol

perform the duties of practice *(engage in)*

perform the functions of practice *(engage in)*

performability feasibility

performable facile, possible, potential, practicable, viable

performance act *(undertaking)*, conduct, course, finality, fruition, function, histrionics, infliction, operation, part *(role)*, proceeding, process *(course)*, realization, role, transaction

performance of executive duties administration

performance owed obligation *(duty)*

performed complete *(ended)*

performer actor

performing active, operative

perfringere breach

perfugium refuge

perfunctoriness disinterest *(lack of interest)*, laxity

perfunctory careless, casual, cursory, inadequate, informal, lax, superficial

pergere continue *(persevere)*

periculum danger, experiment, hazard, risk, venture

peril danger, endanger, hazard, jeopardize, jeopardy, menace, pitfall, risk, threat, venture

perilous dangerous, disastrous, insalubrious, insecure, noxious, ominous, peccant *(unhealthy)*, portentous *(ominous)*, precarious

perilousness danger, jeopardy

perimeter ambit, border, boundary, configuration *(confines)*, confines, contour *(outline)*, enclosure, frontier, guideline, limit, margin *(outside limit)*, mete, outline *(boundary)*, periphery, purview, range, zone

perimeters realm

perimetric peripheral

perimetrical peripheral

perimetros periphery

period age, annum, cycle, date, duration, expiration, life *(period of existence)*, moratorium, tenure, term *(duration)*, time

period of allowance grace period

period of being under legal age minority *(infancy)*

period of being under statutory age

minority *(infancy)*

period of decrease decline
period of detention quarantine
period of existence lifetime
period of indulgence grace period
period of isolation quarantine
period of legal immaturity nonage
period of legal minority nonage
period of life lifetime
period of obligatory delay moratorium
period of rest lull
period of survival life *(period of existence)*, lifetime
period of testing probation
period of time date, duration, phase *(period)*
period of tolerance grace period
period of trial probation
periodic disjunctive *(tending to disjoin)*, habitual, infrequent, intermittent, regular *(orderly)*, repeated, sporadic
periodic payment installment, premium *(insurance payment)*
periodic returns from property or labor income
periodical habitual, journal, organ, publication *(printed matter)*, regular *(orderly)*, serial, sporadic
periodicity frequency, regularity
peripatetic itinerant, itinerant, moving *(in motion)*, pedestrian
peripheral collateral *(immaterial)*, expendable, extraneous, extrinsic, minor, nonessential, null *(insignificant)*
peripheral group minority *(outnumbered group)*
periphery ambit, border, boundary, contour *(outline)*, edge *(border)*, frontier, margin *(outside limit)*, mete, outline *(boundary)*, zone
periphrasis digression, indirection *(indirect action)*
periphrastic indirect, redundant, turgid
periphrastical indirect
perire perish
perish decease, die, expire, succumb
perishable ephemeral, nonsubstantial *(not sturdy)*, temporary, transient
perished deceased, defunct, late *(defunct)*, lifeless *(dead)*, lost *(taken away)*
peritia experience *(background)*, skill
peritus acquainted, familiar *(informed)*, proficient
periurare perjure
periurium perjury
periurium facere perjure
perjure palter, prevaricate
perjure oneself bear false witness, fabricate *(make up)*, frame *(charge falsely)*, lie *(falsify)*, misrepresent
perjured dishonest, fraudulent, lying, mendacious, perfidious
perjured testimony frame up
perjury deceit, dishonesty, falsification, fiction, hypocrisy, misstatement, subreption
perlegere peruse
perlustrare perambulate
permanence constant, continuity, indestructibility, perpetuity, survival
permanent chronic, constant, continual *(perpetual)*, conventional, durable, fixed *(securely placed)*, fixed *(settled)*,

immutable, indefeasible, indelible, indestructible, infinite, ingrained, irreversible, irrevocable, last *(final)*, noncancellable, perpetual, stable, standing, static, unalterable
permanent attachment to real property fixture
permanent exclusion expulsion, ouster
permanent legal address home *(domicile)*
permanent resident inhabitant
permanent structure monument
permanere endure *(last)*, last, pursue *(carry on)*
permeable penetrable
permeare diffuse
permeate diffuse, imbue, penetrate, pervade, spread
permeation infusion, osmosis
permeative ubiquitous
permetiri measure
permiscere confuse *(bewilder)*, muddle
permissibility admissibility, legitimacy
permissible admissible, allowable, allowed, lawful, legal, licit, potential
permissible evidence admissible evidence
permissibleness legality
permissio leave *(permission)*
permission acquiescence, admittance *(acceptance)*, assent, capacity *(authority)*, charter *(sanction)*, concession *(authorization)*, consent, discretion *(power of choice)*, dispensation *(exception)*, favor *(sanction)*, franchise *(license)*, indorsement, indulgence, liberty, license, permit, privilege, sanction *(permission)*, sufferance, title *(right)*, warrant *(authorization)*
permission to defer payment credit *(delayed payment)*
permission to rent lease
permissioned allowed
permit abide, accede *(concede)*, allow *(authorize)*, allow *(endure)*, approval, assent, authorize, bear *(tolerate)*, bestow, capacity *(authority)*, certify *(approve)*, charge *(empower)*, charter *(license)*, charter *(sanction)*, concede, concession *(authorization)*, condone, confirm, consent, consent, copyright, dispensation *(exception)*, empower, enable, enfranchise, exemption, franchise *(license)*, freedom, grant *(concede)*, invest *(vest)*, key *(passport)*, leave *(allow to remain)*, license, palliate *(excuse)*, patent, qualify *(meet standards)*, receive *(permit to enter)*, recognize *(acknowledge)*, sanction *(permission)*, sanction, tolerate, vouchsafe, warrant *(authorization)*, yield *(submit)*
permit by law legalize
permit to borrow lend, loan
permit to vote enfranchise
permittance acquiescence, leave *(permission)*
permitted admissible, allowed, due *(regular)*, entitled, justifiable, lawful, licit, open *(accessible)*, pardonable, permissible, potential, privileged, public *(open)*, rightful, unrestricted
permitted by law legal
permittere concede, countenance, devolve, grant *(concede)*, grant *(transfer*

formally), suffer *(permit)*
permitting charitable *(lenient)*, consenting
permutable aleatory *(uncertain)*, ambulatory, convertible, protean
permutatio exchange, interchange
permutation exchange, mutuality
permute alternate *(take turns)*, change, convert *(change use)*
perniciosus deadly, detrimental, disastrous, fatal, pernicious
pernicious bad *(offensive)*, deadly, deleterious, destructive, detrimental, disadvantageous, disastrous, fatal, harmful, heinous, immoral, inadvisable, incendiary, inimical, iniquitous, insalubrious, lethal, malevolent, malicious, malignant, nefarious, noxious, objectionable, obnoxious, oppressive, pestilent, prejudicial, sinister, toxic, vicious, virulent
perniciousness fatality, harm
perorate converse, declaim, discourse
peroratio peroration
peroration close *(conclusion)*
perperam misunderstand
perperam accipere misconceive
perpetrate execute *(accomplish)*, operate, perform *(execute)*
perpetration act *(undertaking)*, commission *(act)*, course, discharge *(performance)*, infliction, performance *(execution)*
perpetual chronic, constant, continuous, durable, habitual, immutable, incessant, indestructible, infinite, periodic, permanent, stable, standing, unlimited, unremitting
perpetually invariably
perpetualness perpetuity
perpetuate continue *(prolong)*, establish *(entrench)*, keep *(continue)*, maintain *(carry on)*, persevere, preserve, prolong, remain *(continue)*, sustain *(prolong)*, uphold
perpetuated lasting, permanent, perpetual, standing
perpetuating honorary
perpetuation continuance, continuation *(prolongation)*, longevity, perpetuity, preservation, remembrance *(commemoration)*
perpetuitas continuance, continuation *(prolongation)*, continuity, perpetuity
perpetuity continuity, indestructibility
perpetuo comitari inseparable
perpetuus continual *(perpetual)*, incessant, indestructible
perplex agitate *(perturb)*, badger, bait *(harass)*, confound, confuse *(bewilder)*, discommode, discompose, disconcert, disorganize, disturb, obfuscate, perturb
perplexed lost *(disoriented)*
perplexing complex, debatable, difficult, disputable, dubious, enigmatic, equivocal, indefinable, labyrinthine, mysterious, peculiar *(curious)*, problematic, recondite, uncertain *(ambiguous)*, vague
perplexing state of affairs imbroglio
perplexity cloud *(suspicion)*, complication, confusion *(ambiguity)*, dilemma, doubt *(indecision)*, enigma, ignorance, impasse, incertitude, paradox, predicament, quagmire, quandary

perplexus indistinct, labyrinthine
perquisite bounty, gratuity *(present)*, pay, prerogative, privilege, reward, tip *(gratuity)*
perquisites bonus, paraphernalia *(personal belongings)*, revenue
perquisition examination *(study)*, indagation, probe, quest
perscribere record, register
perscrutari investigate, scrutinize
perscrutatio scrutiny
perscrutation indagation, probe
persecute abuse *(violate)*, badger, bait *(harass)*, brutalize, endanger, exploit *(take advantage of)*, harrow, harry *(harass)*, hector, ill use, irritate, maltreat, mishandle *(maltreat)*, mistreat, pique, plague, press *(goad)*, provoke
persecuted aggrieved *(victimized)*
persecuting brutal, callous, illiberal, malignant
persecution abuse *(physical misuse)*, cruelty, infliction, injustice, intolerance, molestation, oppression
persecutor bigot
persequi prosecute *(carry forward)*
perseverance continuance, continuation *(prolongation)*, industry *(activity)*, longanimity, purpose, resolution *(decision)*, tenacity, tolerance
perseverant diligent, insistent, lasting, patient, persistent, relentless, sedulous, steadfast, strong, undaunted, unrelenting, unremitting, unyielding, zealous
perseverare continue *(persevere)*, keep *(continue)*
persevere adhere *(persist)*, bear *(tolerate)*, continue *(persevere)*, endeavor, endure *(last)*, hold out *(resist)*, insist, keep *(continue)*, last, maintain *(carry on)*, persist, prolong, pursue *(carry on)*, recur, remain *(continue)*, resist *(withstand)*, stay *(continue)*
persevere at ply
persevere in prosecute *(carry forward)*
perseverence prowess *(bravery)*
persevering chronic, diligent, durable, faithful *(diligent)*, indelible, indestructible, indomitable, industrious, inexorable, inflexible, insistent, live *(existing)*, painstaking, patient, permanent, persistent, pertinacious, purposeful, relentless, resolute, sedulous, steadfast, strong, undaunted, unrelenting, unremitting, unyielding
persist continue *(persevere)*, endure *(last)*, exist, hold out *(resist)*, insist, keep *(continue)*, last, maintain *(carry on)*, persevere, prosecute *(carry forward)*, pursue *(carry on)*, recur, remain *(continue)*, repeat *(do again)*, resist *(withstand)*, stay *(continue)*, subsist
persist in adhere *(persist)*, bear *(tolerate)*
persistence continuance, continuation *(prolongation)*, diligence *(perseverance)*, industry *(activity)*, longevity, purpose, resolution *(decision)*, tenacity, tolerance, uniformity
persistency diligence *(perseverance)*, tenacity
persistent chronic, continual *(connected)*, diligent, durable, faithful *(diligent)*, frequent, immutable, incessant, indelible, industrious, inexorable, infinite, insistent, lasting, patient, permanent, perpetual, pertinacious, purposeful, relentless, repeated, resolute, sedulous, stable, steadfast, strong, undaunted, unrelenting, unremitting, unyielding, zealous

persistent exertion diligence *(perseverance)*
persistere continue *(persevere)*, persevere, persist, pursue *(carry on)*
persisting chronic, durable, indelible, indestructible, inexorable, insistent, irrevocable, lasting, live *(existing)*, patient, permanent, pertinacious, undaunted
persisting in error perverse
persisting in fault perverse
persnickety particular *(exacting)*
person actor, character *(an individual)*, individual
person accused of crime suspect
person affording evidence witness
person appointed to administer affairs trustee
person coming from a foreign country alien
person employing advice client
person entrusted with property of another fiduciary
person from foreign parts alien
person full of character individual
person in authority chairman, chief, incumbent, official, principal *(director)*
person in charge caretaker *(one fulfilling the function of office)*, chief, executor, principal *(director)*
person in possession holder, lessee
person in responsibility executor
person making a feoffment feoffor
person named to carry out the provisions of a will executor
person of age adult
person of experience veteran
person of importance key man
person of intellect mastermind
person of repute key man, paragon
person of voting age adult
person represented client
person represented by counsel client
person responsible official
person under 18 years of age minor
person under 18 years old infant
person under arrest captive, prisoner
person under guardianship dependent
person under legal age juvenile, minor
person under the age of majority infant
person who conveys a fee feoffor
person who flees justice fugitive
person who is not of full age infant, minor
person who makes a claim claimant
person who makes allegations declarant
person who writes author *(writer)*
person with a grievance claimant
personage body *(person)*, character *(an individual)*, individual, person
personal intimate, particular *(individual)*, private *(confidential)*, privy, several *(separate)*, subjective, unofficial

personal allowance alimony
personal bearing behavior, conduct, deportment, manner *(behavior)*
personal bias prejudice *(preconception)*
personal characteristic identity *(individuality)*, specialty *(distinctive mark)*
personal chattels which are not in possession intangible
personal effect chattel
personal effects assets, movable, paraphernalia *(personal belongings)*, property *(possessions)*
personal equation characteristic
personal estate goods, paraphernalia *(personal belongings)*
personal gain earnings
personal hatred malice
personal identity personality
personal judgment assumption *(supposition)*, conviction *(persuasion)*, estimate *(idea)*
personal mark personality
personal matter confidence *(relation of trust)*, secret
personal presence appearance *(look)*
personal property effects, movable, paraphernalia *(personal belongings)*, personalty, possessions
personal property capable of being inherited hereditament
personal reasons motive
personal representative administrator, executor
personal resources assets, personalty, property *(possessions)*
personal right not reduced to possession intangible
personal security pledge *(security)*
personal style manner *(behavior)*
personal traits character *(personal quality)*
personal wrong tort
personality character *(an individual)*, character *(personal quality)*, disposition *(inclination)*, identity *(individuality)*, individual, presence *(poise)*, property *(distinctive attribute)*, temperament
personalize call *(title)*
personalized private *(not public)*, subjective
personally in person
personally solicit lobby
personalty chattel, effects, estate *(property)*, movable, paraphernalia *(personal belongings)*, possessions
personate assume *(simulate)*, copy, feign, impersonate, mock *(imitate)*, pose *(impersonate)*
personation caricature, copy
personification embodiment
personify characterize, depict, embody, impersonate
personifying exemplary
personnel copartner *(business associate)*
personnel employee, staff
persons humanity *(mankind)*, populace, population, public
persons in office authorities
persons in power hierarchy *(persons in authority)*
persons of commanding influence authorities
persons summoned to attend the court as jurymen panel *(jurors)*

personship identity (individuality)
perspective aspect, opinion (belief), outlook, standpoint, vision (dream)
perspicacious acute, circumspect, cognizant, discriminating (judicious), judicious, juridical, lucid, perceptive, sapient, sensitive (discerning)
perspicaciousness comprehension, experience (background), perception, sagacity
perspicacitas sagacity
perspicacity caliber (mental capacity), discretion (quality of being discreet), discrimination (good judgment), insight, judgment (discernment), perception, sagacity, sense (intelligence)
perspicax acute, perspicacious
perspicuity discrimination (good judgment)
perspicuous appreciable, clear (apparent), cognizable, coherent (clear), comprehensible, evident, explicit, lucid, manifest, obvious, open (in sight), ostensible, overt, palpable, patent, perceivable, perceptible, unambiguous, unmistakable
perspicuousness judgment (discernment)
perspicuus comprehensible, distinct (clear), lucid, manifest, obvious
perstare persevere, persist
perstringere refer (direct attention)
persuable reasonable (rational)
persuadable amenable, open (persuasible), open-minded, pliable, receptive, suasible, susceptible (responsive)
persuade agitate (activate), assure (give confidence to), bait (lure), coax, convince, counsel, exhort, incite, induce, influence, inspire, inveigle, lobby, motivate, prejudice (influence), pressure, prevail upon, prompt, reason (persuade), recommend, urge
persuade against caution, deter, discourage
persuade by argument convince
persuade not to work picket
persuade oneself presuppose
persuade to believe error delude
persuaded affirmative, certain (positive), definite, positive (confident)
persuadere convince, prevail (persuade), prevail upon
persuaders lobby
persuading hortative, moving (evoking emotion)
persuasibility amenability, credulity
persuasible amenable, credulous, open-minded, pliable, suasible
persuasio belief (state of mind), faith
persuasion belief (something believed), concept, conclusion (determination), credence, denomination, dogma, force (compulsion), guidance, idea, incentive, inducement, instigation, motive, opinion (belief), patronage (power to appoint jobs), pressure, propaganda, seduction, standpoint, surety (certainty)
persuasive believable, cogent, colorable (plausible), convincing, determinative, eloquent, hortative, prevailing (having superior force), provocative, sound, specious, strong
persuasive facts evidence
persuasiveness inducement
persuasory persuasive

pert brazen, impertinent (insolent), insolent, presumptuous
pertain appertain, correspond (be equivalent), refer (direct attention), relate (establish a connection)
pertain to affiliate, concern (involve), connect (relate)
pertaining correlative, pertinent, relative (relevant)
pertaining to comparative, germane, incident, relevant
pertaining to business commercial
pertaining to financial matters fiscal
pertaining to government finances fiscal
pertaining to home household (domestic)
pertaining to law jural
pertaining to litigation actionable
pertaining to merchants commercial
pertaining to monetary receipts and expenditures fiscal
pertaining to one's household domestic (household)
pertaining to ownership proprietary
pertaining to property proprietary
pertaining to the courts forensic
pertaining to the family domestic (household), household (domestic)
pertaining to the home domestic (household)
pertaining to the law forensic
pertaining to the public revenues fiscal
pertaining to the public treasury fiscal
pertaining to the whole community common (shared)
pertaining to trade commercial
pertinacia tenacity
pertinacious diligent, faithful (diligent), inexorable, inflexible, insistent, intractable, obdurate, patient, persistent, purposeful, relentless, resolute, sedulous, steadfast, unrelenting, unremitting, unyielding
pertinaciousness tenacity
pertinacity diligence (perseverance), tenacity
pertinax contumacious, froward, inflexible, pertinacious, willful
pertinence connection (relation), interest (concern), propriety (appropriateness), qualification (fitness), relation (connection), relationship (connection), relevance
pertinent akin (germane), applicable, apposite, appropriate, felicitous, fit, germane, interrelated, intrinsic (belonging), material (important), noteworthy, related, relative (relevant), relevant, suitable, tangential
pertinent to comparative
pertinere concern (involve), relate (establish a connection)
pertinere ad apply (pertain)
pertness disrespect
perturb badger, bait (harass), discommode, discompose, disconcert, disorganize, disorient, disrupt, distress, disturb, embarrass, harrow, molest (annoy), obfuscate, perplex, pique, provoke, upset
perturbance panic
perturbare confuse (bewilder), discon-

cert, disorganize, disturb
perturbate agitate (perturb), perturb
perturbatio confusion (turmoil)
perturbation apprehension (fear), commotion, confusion (ambiguity), consternation, distress (anguish), disturbance, embarrassment, instigation, misgiving, panic, quandary, trepidation, turmoil
perturbed frenetic, unsettled
perturbing enigmatic
perturbo perturb
perusal analysis, discovery, examination (study), indagation, inquiry (systematic investigation), inspection, scrutiny
peruse check (inspect), examine (study), observe (watch), probe, read, regard (pay attention), scrutinize, study, survey (examine)
peruse carefully concentrate (pay attention)
pervade diffuse, enter (penetrate), imbue, obsess, penetrate, permeate, spread
pervadere penetrate
pervading ubiquitous
pervagari perambulate
pervasive broad, ubiquitous
perverse arbitrary, contentious, contumacious, difficult, disobedient, fractious, froward, intractable, opposite, petulant, restive, sinister, unruly, unyielding, vicious
perverseness contempt (disobedience to the court)
perversion abuse (corrupt practice), debauchment, distortion, lie, misapplication, misstatement, misusage, misuse, sodomy, travesty, vice
perversion of integrity corruption
perversion of the truth evasion
perversion of truth false pretense, falsehood, indirection (deceitfulness), perjury, story (falsehood)
perversity bad repute
perversus incorrect, perverse
pervert abuse (misuse), adulterate, bear false witness, brutalize, camouflage, contort, corrupt, damage, debase, debauch, degenerate, denature, deteriorate, distort, falsify, harm, infect, invent (falsify), lie (falsify), misconceive, misconstrue, misemploy, misguide, mislead, mismanage, misread, misrepresent, misstate, mistreat, misunderstand, palter, pollute, prevaricate, slant, subvert, taint (corrupt), vitiate
perverted depraved, dissolute, immoral, mendacious, perverse, tainted (corrupted)
pervicacious intractable, obdurate, pertinacious, recalcitrant, restive, unreasonable, unyielding
pervicax pertinacious
pervious amenable, disposable, open (persuasible), passable, penetrable, pliable, suasible
pervius penetrable
pervulgatus prevalent, trite
pessimism damper (depressant)
pessimistic cynical, despondent, disconsolate, ominous
pest nuisance
pester annoy, badger, discompose, harass, harry (harass), hector, impor-

tune, irritate, molest *(annoy)*, perturb, pique, plague, press *(goad)*
pestering vexatious
pestiferous contagious, dangerous, deadly, harmful, insalubrious, lethal, malignant, noxious, pernicious
pestilence nuisance
pestilens insalubrious, pestilent
pestilent insalubrious, lethal, noxious, peccant *(unhealthy)*, toxic
pestilential deleterious, detrimental, harmful, insalubrious, lethal, malignant, pernicious, pestilent
pet animal, popular
petard bomb
peter out perish, subside
petere petition, solicit
petit petty
petitio application, plea
petition appeal, application, apply *(request)*, bill *(formal declaration)*, call *(appeal)*, call *(appeal to)*, canvass, claim *(demand)*, complaint, cross-examine, entreaty, importune, invitation, motion, move *(judicially request)*, plead *(implore)*, pray, prayer, press *(beseech)*, request, requisition, solicit, sue, suit
petition for intercede, request
petition for release habeas corpus
petitionary solicitous
petitioner accuser, actor, appellant, applicant *(petitioner)*, candidate, claimant, complainant, contender, litigant, malcontent, party *(litigant)*, plaintiff, special interest, suitor, undersigned
petitioner for legal redress complainant
petitioners lobby
petitor contestant, plaintiff
petrification congealment
petrified ossified
petrify browbeat, frighten, intimidate
pettifog cheat, circumvent
pettifoggery artifice, bad faith, bribery, false pretense, knavery
pettifogging bunko, hoax, immoral
pettiness immateriality
pettish fractious, petulant, querulous
petty de minimus, frivolous, illiberal, inappreciable, inconsequential, inconsiderable, insubstantial, minor, nominal, nugatory, null *(insignificant)*, paltry, parsimonious, penurious, provincial, puerile, slight, tenuous, trivial
petty detail technicality
petty dishonesty pettifoggery
petulans petulant
petulant argumentative, brazen, fractious, froward, perverse, querulous
phalanx band, mass *(body of persons)*
phantasm phantom
phantasmal delusive, illusory
pharisaism hypocrisy
phase aspect, duration, transition
phenomenal extraordinary, infrequent, noteworthy, portentous *(eliciting amazement)*, prodigious *(amazing)*, unusual
phenomenon experience *(encounter)*, happening, occurrence, vision *(dream)*
philanthropic benevolent, charitable *(benevolent)*, donative, humane, liberal *(generous)*, magnanimous, meritorious, nonprofit
philanthropic gift charity

philanthropic institution foundation *(organization)*
philanthropist benefactor, contributor *(giver)*, donor, good samaritan, patron *(influential supporter)*, samaritan
philanthropize bestow, dedicate
philanthropy benefit *(conferment)*, benevolence *(act of kindness)*, benevolence *(disposition to do good)*, charity, dedication, donation, favor *(act of kindness)*, goodwill, help, largess *(generosity)*
Philippic denunciation
philippic outcry, revilement, stricture
philistine ordinary
philoprogenitive fertile, prolific
philosophaster pedant
philosophia moralis ethics
philosophic patient, stoical
philosophical cogitative, logical, profound *(esoteric)*, theoretical
philosophize reason *(conclude)*, speculate *(conjecture)*
philosophy doctrine, posture *(attitude)*, principle *(axiom)*, theory
philosophy of law jurisprudence
phlegm disinterest *(lack of interest)*, languor, sloth
phlegmatic dispassionate, indolent, languid, lifeless *(dull)*, obtuse, otiose, passive, stagnant, torpid
phlegmatical languid, phlegmatic, stagnant
phobia apprehension *(fear)*, fear, fright, panic, paranoia
phoenix revival
phonate enunciate
phonation intonation, speech
phonic nuncupative, oral
phoniness falsification
phony bogus, fictitious, fraudulent, imitation, specious
photographic descriptive
photostat duplicate
phrase chapter *(division)*, clause, denominate, express, observe *(remark)*, relate *(tell)*, speak, term *(expression)*
phraseology language, parlance, rhetoric *(skilled speech)*, speech
phrasing language, phraseology, rhetoric *(skilled speech)*
phrenetic fanatical
phrenetical fanatical
phylactery reminder
phylum race
physic drug, drug
physical bodily, concrete, corporal, corporeal, mundane, tangible
physical appearance demeanor
physical being body *(person)*, materiality *(physical existence)*
physical condition health
physical derangement disease
physical element component
physical force compulsion *(coercion)*
physical hurt injury
physical limit capacity *(maximum)*
physical nature materiality *(physical existence)*
physical power force *(strength)*
physically strong powerful
physicalness materiality *(physical existence)*
physiognomy appearance *(look)*, feature *(appearance)*
physique body *(person)*, configuration

(form)
piacular penitent
piaculum expiation
picayune inconsequential, insubstantial, minor, negligible, petty, trivial
pick alternative *(option)*, appoint, choice *(alternatives offered)*, choose, cull, decide, decision *(election)*, discretion *(power of choice)*, elect *(choose)*, election *(choice)*, extract, option *(choice)*, prefer, reap, screen *(select)*, select, volition, vote
pick a quarrel bicker
pick one's pockets jostle *(pickpocket)*
pick out appoint, choose, cull, eviscerate, except *(exclude)*, extract, prefer
pick up elevate, gain, glean, heighten *(elevate)*, obtain, overhear, procure, purchase, reap, receive *(acquire)*
picked preferable, select
picked out preferred *(favored)*
pickeer hold up *(rob)*
picket demonstrate *(protest)*
pickings spoils
pickle imbroglio
pickpocket hoodlum
pickpocketing larceny
picky particular *(exacting)*
pictorial descriptive, suggestive *(evocative)*
picture characterize, conceive *(comprehend)*, concept, contour *(outline)*, delineate, depict, describe, design *(construction plan)*, detail *(particularize)*, draw *(depict)*, exemplify, portray, recount, render *(depict)*, represent *(portray)*, symbol, vision *(dream)*
picturize delineate
piddling inconsiderable, paltry, petty, puerile
piece commingle, component, constituent *(part)*, detail, element, gun, item, lot, member *(constituent part)*, minimum, moiety, parcel, part *(portion)*, ration, repair, segment, story *(narrative)*, unit *(item)*
piece of apparatus appliance
piece of architecture building *(structure)*, edifice
piece of ground lot
piece of information item, particular
piece of land parcel, plot *(land)*, premises *(buildings)*
piece of landed property estate *(property)*
piece of legislation measure
piece of news item
piece together combine *(join together)*, consolidate *(unite)*, devise *(invent)*, fabricate *(construct)*, frame *(construct)*, join *(bring together)*, make, merge, solve
pieced together conjoint
pierce break *(fracture)*, enter *(penetrate)*, impress *(affect deeply)*, inject, lancinate, penetrate, pervade
piercing acute, bitter *(penetrating)*, caustic, harsh, incisive, interrogative, mordacious, perspicacious, profound *(intense)*, trenchant
pietas affection
pig-headed obdurate
pigeonhearted recreant
pigeonhole classify, defer *(put off)*, file *(arrange)*, hold up *(delay)*, parti-

tion, postpone, procrastinate, set aside *(reserve)*

piger stagnant

piggish insatiable

pigheaded pertinacious

pignerare pawn

pignoration security *(pledge)*

pignus bail, mortgage, pledge *(security)*, security *(stock)*

pignus judiciale charge *(lien)*, cloud *(incumbrance)*

pignus legale cloud *(incumbrance)*

piker bettor

pile agglomeration, assemblage, collect *(gather)*, collection *(accumulation)*, cumulation, hoard, load, selection *(collection)*

pile up accumulate *(amass)*, compound, hoard, keep *(shelter)*, set aside *(reserve)*, store

pileup collision *(accident)*

pilfer despoil, embezzle, hold up *(rob)*, jostle *(pickpocket)*, loot, peculate, poach, purloin, rob, steal

pilferage larceny, misappropriation, theft

pilferer burglar, criminal, embezzler, thief

pilfering burglary, embezzlement, housebreaking, plagiarism, spoliation, theft

piling up cumulative *(increasing)*

pillage despoil, devastate, harry *(plunder)*, havoc, hold up *(rob)*, loot, pilfer, pirate *(take by violence)*, plunder, plunder, prey, prize, rape, rob, seize *(confiscate)*, spoils, spoliation, steal

pillager burglar, criminal, thief, vandal

pillaging burglary, foray, predatory, rapacious, spoliation

pillar mainstay

pillory brand *(stigmatize)*, defame, denigrate, denounce *(condemn)*, disgrace, dishonor *(deprive of honor)*, smear

pilot administer *(conduct)*, conduct, control *(regulate)*, govern, manage, manipulate *(utilize skillfully)*, moderate *(preside over)*, officiate, operate, overlook *(superintend)*, oversee, prescribe, preside, superintend

pilotage direction *(guidance)*, management *(supervision)*

pilpulistic argumentative

pin fix *(make firm)*

pin down restrict

pinch constrict *(compress)*, dearth, plight, predicament, privation, quagmire, retrench, stress *(strain)*

pinch hitter substitute

pinchbeck spurious

pinched impecunious, narrow

pine languish

pine away languish

pinion contain *(restrain)*, handcuff, handcuff, restrict, trammel

pinnacle ceiling, culmination

pinpoint designate, discover, locate

pioneer commence, forerunner, initiate, originate, precede, precursor

pious tartuffish, zealous

piquancy instigation

piquant hot-blooded, incisive, moving *(evoking emotion)*, palatable, provocative, sapid, savory

pique affront, aggravate *(annoy)*, annoy, badger, bait *(harass)*, discommode, discompose, dissatisfaction, disturb, harrow, harry *(harass)*, incense, interest, irritate, malice, molest *(annoy)*, offend *(insult)*, perturb, plague, provoke, resentment, stimulate, umbrage

piqued bitter *(reproachful)*, petulant, resentful

piracy pillage, robbery, spoliation

pirate abduct, copy, criminal, hijack, hold up *(rob)*, impropriate, loot, pillage, plagiarize, plunder, poach, prey, seize *(confiscate)*, spoil *(pillage)*, steal, thief

piratic larcenous

piratical larcenous, rapacious

piste brand

pistol gun

pit against alienate *(estrange)*, counter, counteract

pit against one another polarize

pitch elevate, inflection, intonation, launch *(project)*, precipitate *(throw down violently)*

pitch into attack

piteous deplorable, lamentable, lugubrious

pitfall hazard, trap, trouble

pith center *(essence)*, contents, corpus, essence, gist *(substance)*, import, main point, significance, signification, subject *(topic)*, substance *(essential nature)*

pith of a matter gist *(ground for a suit)*

pithless languid, powerless

pithy brief, concise, eloquent, laconic, sententious, succinct

pithy saying catchword, maxim

pitiable deplorable, lamentable

pitiful deplorable, lamentable, paltry, poor *(inferior in quality)*

pitiless brutal, callous, cold-blooded, cruel, diabolic, harmful, harsh, implacable, inexorable, malevolent, relentless, remorseless, ruthless, severe, unaffected *(uninfluenced)*, unrelenting, unresponsive

pitilessness brutality, malice

pittance paucity, ration

pitted blemished, marred

pitting of strength competition

pitting of strengths contest *(competition)*

pitting of wits competition

pity lenience, relent, sympathize

pitying lenient

pivot cornerstone, crossroad *(turning point)*

pivotal cardinal *(basic)*, causative, central *(essential)*, critical *(crucial)*, crucial, decisive, indispensable, material *(important)*

pivotal argument base *(foundation)*

pivotal point gravamen, main point

placabilis peaceable, placable

placability amenability, benevolence *(disposition to do good)*, lenience, longanimity

placable lenient, nonmilitant

placableness lenience

placare pacify, placate, propitiate, soothe

placate disarm *(set at ease)*, lull, mollify, pacify, propitiate, reconcile, soothe

placation conciliation, mollification

placative nonmilitant

placatus dispassionate

place allocate, area *(province)*, base *(place)*, building *(structure)*, case *(set of circumstances)*, character *(reputation)*, circuit, class, deploy, dispose *(apportion)*, employ *(engage services)*, fix *(arrange)*, habitation *(dwelling place)*, identify, inhabitation *(place of dwelling)*, instate, levy, locality, locate, location, lodge *(house)*, lodge *(reside)*, marshal, organize *(arrange)*, pigeonhole, pinpoint, plant *(place firmly)*, position *(situation)*, post, premises *(buildings)*, prestige, recall *(remember)*, recognize *(perceive)*, recollect, region, remember, residence, role, scene, seat, set down, site, site, situs, source, stand *(witness' place in court)*, status, territory

place a cloud on encumber *(financially obligate)*

place a false construction on misinterpret

place a value on calculate, estimate, evaluate

place a wrong construction on misinterpret

place against contrast

place an erroneous construction on misinterpret

place an instrument in a place of deposit file *(place among official records)*

place at one's disposal extend *(offer)*, present *(make a gift)*

place at ones disposal hold out *(deliberate on an offer)*

place authority vest

place before introduce, preface

place between interpose

place by itself isolate

place close together juxtapose

place control vest

place for safe keeping depository

place in a category classify, partition, pigeonhole

place in a dubious position compromise *(endanger)*

place in a former state reinstate

place in a receptacle deposit *(place)*

place in an office delegate

place in authority nominate

place in charge of delegate

place in command nominate

place in confinement arrest *(apprehend)*, commit *(institutionalize)*, imprison, jail

place in custody again rearrest

place in danger jeopardize

place in durance confine, contain *(restrain)*, detain *(hold in custody)*

place in juxtaposition border *(approach)*, compare, contrast

place in office elect *(select by a vote)*, hire, induct, instate, nominate

place in official custody of the clerk file *(place among official records)*

place in order apportion, arrange *(methodize)*, classify, file *(arrange)*, fix *(arrange)*, marshal, organize *(arrange)*, sort

place in the condition of natural born subjects naturalize *(make a citizen)*

place in the foreground adduce

place in the possession of deliver

place in the protection of entrust
place in the record enter *(record)*
place into enter *(insert)*, inject, interject
place limitations border *(bound)*, clog
place near border *(approach)*, juxtapose
place next to juxtapose
place of abode habitation *(dwelling place)*, home *(domicile)*, household, inhabitation *(place of dwelling)*
place of assignation rendezvous
place of birth home *(place of origin)*
place of business address, market *(business)*, market place, office
place of business traffic market place
place of buying and selling market *(business)*, market place
place of commerce market *(business)*, market place
place of concealment cache *(hiding place)*
place of confinement jail, penitentiary
place of deposit cache *(storage place)*, depository, treasury
place of detention penitentiary
place of dwelling abode, home *(domicile)*
place of education institute
place of employment office
place of entry entrance
place of existence home *(domicile)*
place of exit egress
place of habitation building *(structure)*, house
place of immunity asylum *(hiding place)*
place of imprisonment penitentiary
place of jurisdiction venue
place of meeting rendezvous
place of occupancy domicile
place of one's domestic affections home *(domicile)*
place of protection refuge
place of refuge asylum *(hiding place)*, home *(domicile)*, shelter *(protection)*
place of residence apartment, domicile, dwelling, habitation *(dwelling place)*, home *(domicile)*, inhabitation *(place of dwelling)*, lodging, residence
place of rest home *(domicile)*, lodging
place of safety cache *(storage place)*, haven, refuge
place of settlement homestead
place of trade market *(business)*, market place
place on record cast *(register)*, file *(place among official records)*
place out of bounds exclude
place outside the protection of the law outlaw
place parallel border *(approach)*
place permanently fix *(make firm)*
place reliance in trust
place reliance on confide *(trust)*
place side by side adjoin, juxtapose
place the blame for lodge *(bring a complaint)*
place the blame on impute, incriminate
place the responsibility for impute

place to live in home *(domicile)*
place trust in delegate, rely
place under a liquid immerse *(plunge into)*
place under arrest apprehend *(arrest)*
place under federal administration federalize *(place under federal control)*
place under federal rule federalize *(place under federal control)*
place under government control nationalize
place under interdiction enjoin
place under protective custody confine
place under the ban enjoin
place upon a list empanel
place where justice is administered court, judicatory
place where one lives home *(domicile)*
placed situated
placed in advance preferred *(given priority)*
placement arrogation, assignation, classification, disposition *(final arrangement)*, distribution *(apportionment)*, distribution *(arrangement)*, installation, location, order *(arrangement)*, organization *(structure)*, rating, situs
placement against contraposition
placement opposite contraposition
placere interest
placet brevet
placid complacent, patient, peaceable, stoical
placidity composure, longanimity
placidness composure
placidus dispassionate, peaceable, placid
placing array *(order)*, introduction
placing in confinement commitment *(confinement)*
placing in office appointment *(act of designating)*, assignment *(designation)*, designation *(naming)*
placitum decision *(judgment)*
placitum decree, dogma
plagiarism counterfeit
plagiarize copy, fake, pirate *(reproduce without authorization)*, steal
plagiary counterfeit
plague annoy, badger, bait *(harass)*, discommode, discompose, disease, disturb, dun, embarrass, harass, harm, harrow, harry *(harass)*, hector, ill use, importune, infliction, irritate, mistreat, molest *(annoy)*, nuisance, obsess, persecute, perturb, pique, press *(goad)*, prey, provoke, trouble
plagued by conscience penitent
plagueful pestilent
plaguesome invidious
plain apparent *(perceptible)*, arrant *(definite)*, blatant *(conspicuous)*, clear *(apparent)*, coherent *(clear)*, comprehensible, conspicuous, direct *(forthright)*, elementary, evident, exact, explicit, express, flagrant, genuine, household *(familiar)*, ingenuous, jejune *(dull)*, lucid, manifest, mere, mundane, naive, naked *(lacking embellishment)*, naked *(perceptible)*, nondescript, obvious, only *(no more than)*, open *(in sight)*, ostensible, overt, palpable, patent, pedestrian,

pellucid, perceivable, perceptible, prosaic, salient, scrutable, simple, stark, tangible, unaffected *(sincere)*, unambiguous, unequivocal, unmistakable, unpretentious, usual, visible *(in full view)*
plain English plain language
plain interpretation explanation
plain meaning connotation, content *(meaning)*
plain sense common sense
plain speaking plain language
plain speech plain language
plain to be seen patent, perceivable
plain words plain language
plain-speaking bona fide, honest
plain-spoken straightforward
plainly fairly *(clearly)*, only, purely *(simply)*, solely *(purely)*
plainness honesty, informality
plainspeaking honesty
plainspoken unaffected *(sincere)*
plaint charge *(accusation)*, complaint, denunciation, outcry
plaintful querulous
plaintiff actor, claimant, complainant, litigant, party *(litigant)*, suitor
plaintiff's allegations pleading
plaintiff's initiatory pleading complaint
plaintive disconsolate, lugubrious, querulous
plait intertwine
plan agenda, blueprint, building *(business of assembling)*, calculate, campaign, conceive *(invent)*, conspiracy, conspire, contemplation, content *(structure)*, contour *(outline)*, contrivance, contrive, course, delineation, design *(construction plan)*, design *(intent)*, device *(contrivance)*, devise *(invent)*, direction *(course)*, enterprise *(undertaking)*, expedient, forethought, form *(arrangement)*, frame *(construct)*, frame *(formulate)*, frame *(prearrange)*, goal, idea, intend, intent, intention, maneuver, method, model, motif, motive, order *(arrangement)*, organization *(structure)*, originate, pattern, platform, ploy, policy *(plan of action)*, prearrange, predetermine, preparation, procedure, process *(course)*, program, project, proposal *(report)*, proposal *(suggestion)*, propose, proposition, prospect *(outlook)*, prospectus, provide *(arrange for)*, purpose, purview, resolution *(formal statement)*, resolve *(decide)*, schedule, scheme, scheme, set down, stratagem, strategy, structure *(composition)*, subterfuge, system, target, undertaking *(attempt)*, undertaking *(enterprise)*, way *(channel)*
plan a crime conspire
plan an unlawful act conspire
plan mischief plot
plan of action platform, polity, practice *(procedure)*, procedure, strategy
plan of attack design *(intent)*, maneuver *(tactic)*, strategy
plan of campaign policy *(plan of action)*
plan of offensive campaign
plan on anticipate *(expect)*, expect *(anticipate)*
plan out devise *(invent)*
plan secretly conspire, plot
plan strategy maneuver

plan to commit a crime conspire
plane degree *(station)*
plane in toto
plane surface area *(surface)*
planless haphazard
planned aforethought, deliberate, express, foreseeable, forthcoming, future, intentional, knowing, premeditated, prospective, purposeful, strategic, tactical, willful
planned beforehand aforethought, premeditated
planned campaign maneuver *(tactic)*, strategy
planned course of action forethought
planned disbursement budget
planned for future
planned in advance deliberate, express, premeditated
planned place of arrival destination
planner accessory, accomplice, architect, catalyst, coactor, conspirer, contractor, developer, promoter
planning agenda
planning ahead forethought
planning board commission *(agency)*
plans calendar *(record of yearly periods)*
plant deposit *(place)*, embed, engender, establish *(entrench)*, fix *(make firm)*, frame up, inculcate, initiate, inseminate, insertion, instate, repose *(place)*
plant the evidence frame *(prearrange)*
planted situated
plastic flexible, pliable, pliant, sequacious, tractable
plasticity amenability
plat intertwine, plot *(land)*
platform policy *(plan of action)*, polity, prospectus, stand *(witness' place in court)*, strategy
platitudinous ordinary, pedestrian, prosaic, trite
plaudit mention *(tribute)*
plausibility common sense, credibility, likelihood, possibility, probability
plausible apparent *(presumptive)*, believable, convincing, defensible, justifiable, ostensible, persuasive, possible, presumptive, probable, rational, reasonable *(rational)*, specious, tenable, viable
plausible excuse alibi
play bet, latitude, parlay *(bet)*, performance *(workmanship)*, pretend
play a direct part affect
play a leading part predominate *(command)*
play a long shot bet
play a part involve *(participate)*, mock *(imitate)*, pose *(impersonate)*
play a part in participate
play a trick dupe
play a trick on delude
play act pretend
play against counter, counteract
play at cross purposes conflict, counteract
play down disparage
play false betray *(lead astray)*, cheat, illude, pretend
play favorites prefer
play for bet
play for money gamble

play for stakes gamble
play for time procrastinate
play havoc with disorganize, prejudice *(injure)*
play one false ensnare
play out discontinue *(abandon)*
play safe hedge
play the market invest *(fund)*, speculate *(chance)*
play the part assume *(simulate)*
play tricks upon jape
play truant flee
play up magnify
play upon dupe
play upon words distort
play-act simulate
playact palter
playbook script
player bettor
player for stakes bettor
playful jocular
playfulness mischief
plaza market place
plea advocacy, allegation, answer *(judicial response)*, argument *(pleading)*, call *(appeal)*, claim *(legal demand)*, contention *(argument)*, counterargument, entreaty, invitation, nollo contendere, petition, pleading, prayer, pretense *(pretext)*, request, response
plea in being elsewhere alibi
plea in rebuttal answer *(judicial response)*, confutation, counterargument, rejoinder
plead address *(petition)*, adduce, allege, answer *(reply)*, answer *(respond legally)*, bear *(adduce)*, depose *(testify)*, exhort, importune, intercede, petition, pray, press *(beseech)*, pressure, reason *(persuade)*, respond, solicit, sue
plead a cause against a third party implead
plead for advocate, bear *(support)*, call *(appeal to)*, defend, justify, request, side
plead guilty repent
plead in favor of advocate
plead one's case advocate, assert
plead one's cause advocate, assert, defend, justify
plead with call *(appeal to)*
pleader advocate *(counselor)*, apologist, attorney, claimant, counsel, intermediary, jurist, petitioner, proponent, suitor
pleading argument *(pleading)*, persuasion, plea, precatory
pleading in a civil action complaint
pleadings matter *(case)*, plea
pleasant attractive, desirable *(pleasing)*, harmonious, jocular, palatable, sapid, savory
pleasantness amenity
please obey, pacify, pander, placate, propitiate, satisfy *(fulfill)*
pleased complacent, inclined, proud *(self-respecting)*
pleased with oneself inflated *(vain)*
pleasing attractive, harmonious, palatable, popular, sapid, savory
pleasingness amenity
pleasurable desirable *(pleasing)*, palatable, sapid
pleasure benefit *(betterment)*, satisfaction *(fulfilment)*, treat, will *(desire)*
pleasureful desirable *(pleasing)*

plebeian ordinary, uncouth
plebian ignoble
plebicola demagogue
plebis dux demagogue
plebiscite election *(selection by vote)*, poll *(casting of votes)*, referendum
plebiscitum enactment
plebs populace
pledge adjuration, agree *(contract)*, agreement *(contract)*, allegiance, assurance, assure *(insure)*, avouch *(guarantee)*, bail, bear *(adduce)*, bind *(obligate)*, binder, bond *(secure a debt)*, charge *(lien)*, cloud *(incumbrance)*, commitment *(responsibility)*, compact, contract, contract, covenant, coverage *(insurance)*, deal, debenture, deposit, due, duty *(obligation)*, guarantee, guaranty, hostage, hypothecation, insurance, lien, loan, mortgage, oath, pact, pawn, profess *(avow)*, profession *(declaration)*, promise, promise *(vow)*, responsibility *(accountability)*, specialty *(contract)*, stipulate, subscribe *(promise)*, undertake, undertaking *(bond)*, undertaking *(commitment)*, underwrite, vouch, vow, warrant *(guaranty)*, warranty
pledge for the payment of a debt mortgage
pledge of security mortgage
pledge one's credit promise *(vow)*
pledge one's honor promise *(vow)*
pledge one's word avouch *(guarantee)*, promise *(vow)*, undertake
pledge oneself promise *(vow)*
pledged agreed *(promised)*, bound, contractual, fully secured, loyal
pledged word contract, specialty *(contract)*, undertaking *(pledge)*
pledgee creditor
pledges ties
pledgor debtor, obligor
plenary complete *(all-embracing)*, detailed, full, gross *(total)*, radical *(extreme)*, thorough, unmitigated, unqualified *(unlimited)*
plenipotent omnipotent, powerful
plenipotentiaries deputation *(delegation)*
plenipotentiary deputy, omnipotent, spokesman, substitute
plenitude capacity *(maximum)*, sufficiency
plenitudinous replete
plenteous ample, copious, multiple, replete, rife
plentiful considerable, copious, liberal *(generous)*, ordinary, profuse, replete, rife, substantial, usual
plentifulness boom *(prosperity)*, plethora, quorum
plentitude boom *(prosperity)*, maximum *(amplitude)*
plenty overage, plethora, prosperity, quantity, quorum, store *(depository)*, sufficiency, surfeit
plenum body *(collection)*, chamber *(body)*, corpus, meeting *(conference)*, quorum, session
plenus full
pleonasm redundancy, tautology
pleonastic extraneous, needless, prolix, redundant, repetitious, turgid
pleonastical prolix, repetitious
plethora sufficiency
plethoric excessive, full, replete,

turgid
plexiform sinuous
pliability amenability, credulity
pliable amenable, facile, flexible, malleable, passive, pliant, resilient, sequacious, suasible, tractable, yielding
pliancy amenability, compliance, credulity, discipline *(obedience)*
pliant amenable, facile, flexible, malleable, obedient, obeisant, passive, patient, pliable, resilient, sequacious, suasible, susceptible *(responsive)*, tractable, yielding
plight case *(set of circumstances)*, condition *(state)*, emergency, imbroglio, position *(situation)*, posture *(situation)*, predicament, problem, promise *(vow)*, quagmire, quandary, situation, state *(condition)*
plight one's honor promise *(vow)*
plight one's word promise *(vow)*
plod bear *(tolerate)*, labor, persevere, persist
plodding operose, painstaking, patient, pedestrian, pertinacious, stable, steadfast
plot cabal, campaign, confederacy *(conspiracy)*, connivance, connive, conspiracy, conspire, contrivance, contrive, delineate, delineation, forethought, location, lot, machination, maneuver *(trick)*, maneuver, parcel, plan, plan, prearrange, program, property *(land)*, real estate, ruse, scenario, scheme, scheme, section *(vicinity)*, stratagem
plot an action in advance conspire
plot craftily conspire
plot of ground parcel, section *(vicinity)*
plot of land parcel, section *(vicinity)*
plot together conspire
plotted deliberate, premeditated, tactical
plotter coactor, conspirator, conspirer
plotting artful, collusion, collusive, insidious, machiavellian, malevolent, perfidious, sly
ploy artifice, machination, plot *(secret plan)*, stratagem
pluck cull, eviscerate, prowess *(bravery)*
pluck out excise *(cut away)*, extirpate
plucking out avulsion, evulsion
pluckless languid, phlegmatic
plucky indomitable, spartan
plug clog, damper *(stopper)*, obstruction, occlude, shut, stem *(check)*, stop
plug away labor, persevere, persist
plug up block, clog
plum prize
plumb probe
plunder despoil, devastate, hijack, hold up *(rob)*, loot, pillage, pillage, pirate *(take by violence)*, prey, prize, rape, rob, spoil *(pillage)*, spoils, spoliation, steal
plunder by stealth poach
plunderage burglary, pillage, rape, spoils, spoliation
plunderer burglar, criminal, vandal
plundering burglary, foray, havoc, housebreaking, larcenous, predatory, rapacious, robbery, spoliation
plunderous larcenous
plunge decline, depress, risk, speculate *(chance)*, venture

plunge ahead race
plunge in pierce *(lance)*
plunge into embark, occupy *(engage)*
plunge into a liquid immerse *(plunge into)*
plunger bettor
plural multiple
plurality majority *(greater part)*, mass *(body of persons)*, multiplicity, preponderance
plures esse predominate *(outnumber)*
plus advantage, also, balance *(amount in excess)*, further
ply cajole, employ *(make use of)*, importune, labor, manipulate *(utilize skillfully)*, occupy *(engage)*, propensity, wield
ply one's task attempt
ply one's trade labor
plying bribery
poach hold up *(rob)*, impose *(intrude)*, pilfer, purloin, steal
poached trade contraband
poached traffic contraband
pock-marked blemished
pocket obtain, receive *(acquire)*, steal
pococurante careless, casual, cold-blooded, inactive, insusceptible *(uncaring)*, lax, lifeless *(dull)*, nonchalant
pococurantism disinterest *(lack of interest)*
poena expiation, penalty, punishment, retribution
poenalis penal
poetic original *(creative)*
poignant bitter *(penetrating)*, moving *(evoking emotion)*
point case *(set of circumstances)*, consequence *(significance)*, content *(meaning)*, contention *(argument)*, degree *(station)*, detail, direct *(show)*, edge *(border)*, end *(termination)*, feature *(characteristic)*, gist *(ground for a suit)*, import, intent, issue *(matter in dispute)*, item, location, matter *(subject)*, motive, object, objective, occasion, particular, period, phase *(aspect)*, phase *(period)*, pinnacle, posture *(situation)*, property *(distinctive attribute)*, purpose, refer *(direct attention)*, remark, signification, situs, standpoint, subject *(topic)*, target, technicality, term *(provision)*, tip *(clue)*
point at denounce *(inform against)*, strive
point at issue matter *(subject)*, subject *(topic)*
point in common analogy
point in dispute problem, question *(issue)*
point in question issue *(matter in dispute)*, matter *(subject)*
point of connotation
point of cessation destination
point of comparison criterion, example, norm, precedent
point of concentration focus
point of convergence center *(central position)*, focus
point of difference characteristic, distinction *(difference)*, specialty *(distinctive mark)*
point of disembarkation destination
point of etiquette decorum
point of no return crossroad *(turning point)*

point of observation outlook, perspective
point of resemblance analogy
point of time date, phase *(period)*
point of view concept, conviction *(persuasion)*, idea, opinion *(belief)*, outlook, perception, perspective, platform, posture *(attitude)*, side, stand *(position)*, standpoint
point out apprise, bear *(adduce)*, charge *(instruct on the law)*, comment, convey *(communicate)*, demonstrate *(establish)*, denote, designate, direct *(show)*, disabuse, discriminate *(distinguish)*, enumerate, exhibit, explain, impart, indicate, inform *(notify)*, instruct *(teach)*, itemize, manifest, mention, quote, reason *(persuade)*, remind, select, signify *(denote)*, specify
point out an essential difference distinguish
point to allude, ascribe, attribute, bear *(adduce)*, cite *(state)*, connote, evince, exemplify, implicate, imply, indicate, mention, predict, presage
point to be settled problem
point up dwell *(linger over)*
point-blank direct *(forthright)*
pointed acute, compact *(pithy)*, conspicuous, direct *(forthright)*, eloquent, explicit, incisive, laconic, mordacious, persuasive, pithy, sententious, trenchant
pointedly fairly *(clearly)*, knowingly, purposely
pointer indicant, indication, indicator, suggestion, tip *(clue)*
pointing out designation *(naming)*, reference *(citation)*
pointless immaterial, inapposite, insipid, null *(insignificant)*, pedestrian, unavailing, unreasonable
pointlessness immateriality
points of comparison analogy
poise composure, confidence *(faith)*, decorum, demeanor, deportment
poison contaminate, degenerate, infect, pervert, pollute, taint *(contaminate)*, virulent, vitiate
poisoned deadly, peccant *(unhealthy)*, tainted *(contaminated)*
poisoning contaminate, detriment
poisonous deadly, deleterious, fatal, harmful, incendiary, insalubrious, lethal, malevolent, malignant, noxious, obnoxious, peccant *(unhealthy)*, pernicious, pestilent, ruthless, toxic, virulent
poke delve, jostle *(bump into)*, loiter
poke fun at jape, mock *(deride)*
poke into frisk, probe
poker-faced inexpressive, inscrutable
polarity antipode, antithesis, conflict, penchant, reaction *(opposition)*
polarized hostile
pole cudgel, end *(termination)*, extremity *(furthest point)*
polemic argumentative, contention *(argument)*, disputable, dispute, litigious
polemical argumentative, contentious, controversial, dissenting, forensic, litigious, polemic
polemicist disputant
polemics argument *(contention)*, contest *(dispute)*, controversy *(argument)*, disaccord, disagreement, fight *(argu-*

ment), strife
polemist contender
poles apart distinct *(distinguished from others)*
police censor, moderate *(preside over),* patrol, peace officer, regulate *(manage),* rule *(govern)*
police constable peace officer
police force police
police officer peace officer
police officers police
police tipper informer *(one providing criminal information)*
policeman peace officer
policewoman peace officer
policy course, direction *(course),* platform, polity, practice *(procedure),* principle *(axiom),* procedure, process *(course),* program, rule *(guide),* scheme, strategy, system
policy-fixing meeting caucus
polis city
polish amend, complete, cultivate, decorum, discretion *(quality of being discreet),* edit, embellish, enhance, meliorate, revise
polished civil *(polite),* literate
polished manners courtesy, decorum
polite diplomatic, discreet, formal, obeisant
polite act courtesy
polite regard respect
politely respectfully
politeness comity, consideration *(sympathetic regard),* courtesy, decorum, deference, propriety *(correctness),* protocol *(etiquette),* respect
politic diplomatic, discreet, favorable *(advantageous),* judicial, judicious, juridical, provident *(showing foresight),* prudent, sensible, solid *(sound),* strategic, subtle *(refined),* tactical
political civic, civil *(public)*
political affairs politics
political agitator malcontent
political aspirant candidate
political body congress
political community government *(political administration)*
political competition primary
political confluence caucus
political contention primary
political contestant candidate
political corruption graft
political disorder anarchy
political division state *(political unit)*
political election primary
political independence freedom, home rule, liberty
political influence politics
political involvement politics
political leaders government *(political administration)*
political machine party *(political organization)*
political maneuvers politics
political methods politics
political partisanship politics
political prisoner hostage
political process politics
political regime government *(political administration)*
political representative nominee *(candidate)*
political rivalry primary
political strategy politics

political subdivision venue
political system regime
political upheaval insurrection, revolt, revolution
politically independent autonomous *(self governing),* sovereign *(independent)*
politician demagogue, lawmaker, legislator
politicians government *(political administration)*
politico lawmaker, politician
politicos government *(political administration)*
polity body *(collection),* community, constituency, government *(political administration),* nationality, policy *(plan of action),* public, society, state *(political unit)*
poll canvass, cast *(register),* census, election *(selection by vote),* inquiry *(request for information),* plebiscite, primary, referendum, vote, vote
pollage tax
polliceri promise *(vow)*
pollinate inseminate
pollinize inseminate
polluere stain
pollute abuse *(violate),* adulterate, contaminate, corrupt, damage, debase, degenerate, denature, deteriorate, disgrace, harm, impair, infect, misemploy, mistreat, pervert, smear, stain, sully, taint *(contaminate),* tarnish, vitiate
polluted dissolute, harmful, profane, salacious, tainted *(contaminated)*
pollution contaminate, detriment, misusage, perversion
pollution control ecology
poltergeist phantom
poltroon recreant
poltroonish caitiff
polymorphic protean
polymorphous protean
polysyllabic profundity bombast
pommel impinge
pomp pretense *(ostentation),* solemnity
pomposity bombast, fustian, pretense *(ostentation),* pride, rhetoric *(insincere language)*
pompous dictatorial, flatulent, formal, fustian, grandiose, inflated *(bombastic),* inflated *(vain),* orgulous, orotund, presumptuous, proud *(conceited),* supercilious, turgid
pompous prolixity bombast
pompous speech rhetoric *(insincere language)*
pompousness pretense *(ostentation),* rhetoric *(insincere language)*
ponder brood, concentrate *(pay attention),* consider, debate, deliberate, doubt *(hesitate),* muse, reason *(conclude),* speculate *(conjecture),* study, weigh
ponder over deliberate
ponder reasons for and against deliberate
ponderable appreciable
ponderare ponder
pondered deliberate, intentional
pondering cogitative, consideration *(contemplation),* contemplation, deliberation, reflection *(thought)*
ponderosus ponderous

ponderous jejune *(dull),* major, oppressive, pedestrian
ponderousness weight *(burden)*
pondus importance, influence, pressure, stress *(strain),* validity
ponere invest *(fund),* propose
poniard pierce *(lance)*
pool combination, combine *(act in concert),* concert, consolidation, consortium *(business cartel),* contribution *(participation),* cooperate, federalize *(associate),* federation, fund, join *(associate oneself with),* join *(bring together),* league, partnership, syndicate, trust *(combination of businesses),* unite
pool one's interests federate
pooled common *(shared),* conjoint
poor base *(inferior),* deficient, deplorable, destitute, devoid, impecunious, imperfect, inadept, inadequate, inferior *(lower in quality),* insubstantial, insufficient, lamentable, marginal, mediocre, negligible, paltry, perfunctory, slipshod, unfavorable, unsatisfactory
poor administration maladministration
poor chance improbability
poor circumstances indigence, poverty
poor judgment error, indiscretion, misestimation, misjudgment
poor opinion disparagement
poor prospect improbability
poor quality work noncompliance *(improper completion)*
poor reputation ignominy
poor usage misapplication
poor visiblity indistinctness
poorly adapted disproportionate, unsuitable
poorly advised misadvised
poorly defined inconspicuous, unclear, vague
poorly done perfunctory
poorly off impecunious
poorly qualified inexperienced
poorly seen inconspicuous, unclear
poorly timed untimely
poorness dearth, indigence, mediocrity, poverty
populace community, nationality, population, public
populacy population
popular common *(customary),* common *(shared),* competitive *(open),* current, customary, familiar *(customary),* famous, general, household *(familiar),* illustrious, meritorious, ordinary, prescriptive, prevailing *(current),* prevalent, proverbial, public *(known),* regular *(conventional),* renowned, rife, routine, sapid, select, typical, usual
popular agitator demagogue
popular choice referendum
popular decision poll *(casting of votes),* referendum, suffrage
popular favor character *(reputation),* distinction *(reputation),* reputation
popular regard affection
popular report hearsay
popular repute notoriety
popular ringleader catalyst
popular vote referendum
popularity character *(reputation),* notoriety
popularize elucidate, explain

popularly believed consensual
populate dwell *(reside)*
populated populous
population community, populace, public, society
populous compact *(dense)*, copious, manifold, rife
populus public
pore over consider, notice *(observe)*, peruse, read, reflect *(ponder)*, study
pornographic lascivious, lewd, obscene, prurient, salacious, suggestive *(risqué)*
pornography obscenity
porous penetrable
port complexion, conduct, deportment, destination, haven, manner *(behavior)*
portage carriage
portage fee fare
portal admittance *(means of approach)*, entrance, margin *(outside limit)*, outlet
portare bear *(support)*
portend anticipate *(prognosticate)*, forewarn, indicate, predict, presage, prognosticate, promise *(raise expectations)*, threaten
portendance caveat
portendere portend, presage
portending evil ominous, portentous *(ominous)*, sinister
portending happiness auspicious
portendment caveat
portent caution *(warning)*, forerunner, harbinger, indicant, indication, phenomenon *(unusual occurrence)*, precursor, premonition, significance, threat, token, warning
portention caveat
portentous dire, imminent, important *(significant)*, ominous, oracular, presageful, prophetic, unusual
porter caretaker *(one caring for property)*
porterage carriage
portfolio dossier
portio installment, share *(interest)*
portion allotment, article *(distinct section of a writing)*, assignment *(allotment)*, chapter *(division)*, commission *(fee)*, component, detail, dole, element, equity *(share of ownership)*, excerpt, factor *(ingredient)*, heritage, installment, interest *(ownership)*, lot, member *(constituent part)*, moiety, parcel, part *(separate)*, partition, phase *(aspect)*, proportion, prorate, quantity, quota, ration, region, segment, share *(interest)*, subdivide, title *(division)*
portion off allocate
portion out allocate, allot, apportion, assign *(allot)*, dispense, disperse *(disseminate)*, distribute, divide *(distribute)*, measure, parcel, partition, reapportion
portion out again reassign
portion out equitably apportion
portioning division *(act of dividing)*
portorium tax, toll *(tax)*
portraiture representation *(statement)*
portray characterize, copy, delineate, denote, depict, describe, detail *(particularize)*, draw *(depict)*, exemplify, impersonate, mock *(imitate)*, pose *(impersonate)*, pretend, recite, recount, relate *(tell)*, render *(depict)*, reproduce,

signify *(denote)*
portray by example exemplify
portray falsely fake
portray in words delineate, describe
portrayal caricature, delineation, description, narration, part *(role)*, representation *(statement)*, story *(narrative)*, symbol
portus haven
poscere require *(compel)*
pose disguise, offer *(propose)*, palter, perplex, posit, position *(point of view)*, posture *(attitude)*, pretense *(ostentation)*, propose, propound, role
pose as assume *(simulate)*, fake, impersonate, purport
posed specious
poser enigma
posit comment, infer, pose *(propound)*, postulate, presume, presuppose, propound, surmise, suspect *(think)*
posited assumed *(inferred)*, situated
position advantage, aspect, calling, capacity *(job)*, career, case *(set of circumstances)*, character *(reputation)*, claim *(assertion)*, class, condition *(state)*, conviction *(persuasion)*, degree *(station)*, employment, file *(arrange)*, job, livelihood, locality, locate, location, marshal, occupation *(vocation)*, office, opinion *(belief)*, opinion *(judicial decision)*, outlook, perspective, platform, plight, post, posture *(attitude)*, posture *(situation)*, predicament, prestige, principle *(axiom)*, profession *(vocation)*, proposition, pursuit *(occupation)*, reputation, role, seat, side, site, site, situation, situs, stand *(position)*, stand *(witness' place in court)*, standpoint, state *(condition)*, status, supposition, thesis, trade *(occupation)*, venue, work *(employment)*
position in society character *(reputation)*, reputation
position of influence authority *(power)*, patronage *(power to appoint jobs)*
position of power authority *(power)*
position paper pandect *(treatise)*
position together juxtapose
positioned situated
positions premises *(hypotheses)*
positive absolute *(conclusive)*, actual, affirmative, authentic, axiomatic, categorical, certain *(fixed)*, clear *(certain)*, conclusive *(determinative)*, convincing, decisive, definite, demonstrable, distinct *(clear)*, dogmatic, explicit, express, incontrovertible, indubious, inexorable, irrefutable, obdurate, peremptory *(absolute)*, pure, resounding, secure *(confident)*, stark, strict, substantive, tangible, undisputed, unequivocal, unmistakable, unrefutable, well-grounded
positive action course
positive assertion allegation, avouchment
positive declaration affirmance *(legal affirmation)*, allegation, assertion, asseveration, averment
positive fact certification *(certainness)*
positive statement affirmance *(legal affirmation)*, affirmation, allegation, assertion, asseveration, averment, avouchment, avowal, declaration

positively de facto, fairly *(clearly)*, ipso facto
positively declared alleged
positively direct enjoin
positiveness belief *(state of mind)*, certainty, certification *(certainness)*, certitude, confidence *(faith)*, conviction *(persuasion)*, surety *(certainty)*, weight *(credibility)*
positivistic dogmatic
positus situated
posse possibility
possess appropriate, comprehend *(include)*, impropriate, keep *(shelter)*, obsess, obtain, occupy *(take possession)*, own, remain *(occupy)*, retain *(keep in possession)*
possess authority handle *(manage)*, rule *(govern)*
possess oneself of assume *(seize)*, distrain
possessed diabolic, fanatical, frenetic, lunatic
possessed of immunity exempt, immune
possessed of knowledge cognizant
possessing double meaning equivocal
possessing merit meritorious
possessing unlimited power omnipotent
possessio domain *(land owned)*, estate *(property)*, holding *(property owned)*, occupancy, possession *(ownership)*, possession *(property)*, possessions, retention, tenure
possession acquisition, chattel, compulsion *(obsession)*, dominion *(absolute ownership)*, enjoyment *(use)*, habitation *(act of inhabiting)*, holding *(property owned)*, interest *(ownership)*, item, occupancy, receipt *(act of receiving)*, seisin, tenancy, title *(right)*
possession and control trust *(custody)*
possession of full rights emancipation
possessione depellere dispossess
possessions assets, commodities, effects, estate *(property)*, goods, merchandise, movable, paraphernalia *(personal belongings)*, personalty, property *(possessions)*
possessive jealous, mercenary
possessiveness greed
possessor bearer, lessee, lodger, occupant, proprietor, tenant
possessor holder
possessor of descent heir
possessorship dominion *(absolute ownership)*, ownership, seisin, tenancy
possibility access *(opening)*, contingency, feasibility, likelihood, opportunity, potential, probability, proposal *(suggestion)*, prospect *(outlook)*, prospect *(prospective patron)*, risk, suggestion
possibility of injury risk
possibility of loss risk
possible conditional, contingent, convincing, debatable, future, plausible, potential, practicable, presumptive, probable, prospective, viable
possible client prospect *(prospective patron)*
possible customer prospect *(prospec-*

tive patron)

possible patron prospect *(prospective patron)*

possibleness chance *(possibility),* likelihood, potential

possidere hold *(possess),* own, tenure

post annunciate, appointment *(position),* bond *(secure a debt),* book, calling, career, convey *(communicate),* dispatch *(send off),* employment, enter *(record),* induct, inform *(notify),* inscribe, issue *(publish),* itemize, location, notify, office, organ, pawn, pledge *(deposit),* position *(business status),* pursuit *(occupation),* record, register, role, seat, send, set down, situation, stand *(witness' place in court),* standpoint, title *(position),* trade *(occupation),* work *(employment)*

post mortem posthumous

post on redirect

post road causeway

postal communication dispatch *(message)*

postdate succeed *(follow)*

posted acquainted, cognizant, informed *(having information),* knowing, situated

posterior back *(in reverse),* ensuing

posterior subsequent

posteritas posterity

posterity descendant, heir, offspring, progeny, succession

postern portal

posterus future

postfix attachment *(thing affixed)*

posthaste rapid

postnote memorandum

postpone adjourn, continue *(adjourn),* defer *(put off),* delay, discontinue *(break continuity),* hold up *(delay),* impede, procrastinate, recess, stall, suspend

postponed arrested *(checked),* late *(tardy)*

postponed payment bill *(invoice)*

postponement adjournment, cessation *(interlude),* continuance, deferment, delay, discontinuance *(act of discontinuing),* moratorium, pendency, reprieve

postponement of penalty reprieve

postscript addendum, allonge, codicil, insertion, rider

postulant claimant

postulare arraign

postulate assumption *(supposition),* avow, claim *(legal demand),* comment, comment, concept, condition *(contingent provision),* conjecture, deduction *(conclusion),* generalization, guess, hypothesis, infer, inference, maxim, opine, pose *(propound),* posit, presume, presumption, presuppose, principle *(axiom),* propose, proposition, propound, require *(compel),* supposition, suspicion *(uncertainty),* theory, thesis

postulate of reason principle *(axiom)*

postulated assumed *(inferred),* presumptive, requisite, theoretical

postulates premises *(hypotheses)*

postulatio claim *(legal demand),* pretense *(pretext),* request, requisition

postulation condition *(contingent provision),* conjecture, conviction *(persuasion),* deduction *(conclusion),* generalization, hypothesis, inference, prolepsis,

request, suspicion *(uncertainty),* thesis

postulational presumptive

postulatory theoretical

postulatum inference

posture appearance *(look),* aspect, case *(set of circumstances),* color *(complexion),* complexion, condition *(state),* conduct, conviction *(persuasion),* demeanor, deportment, disguise, manner *(behavior),* opinion *(belief),* outlook, position *(point of view),* position *(situation),* predicament, presence *(poise),* profess *(pretend),* role, situation, state *(condition),* status

pot cannabis, stake *(award)*

potable palatable

potare carouse

potation alcohol, dipsomania, inebriation

potence dint, force *(strength),* main force, puissance, sinew

potency caliber *(quality),* clout, competence *(ability),* dint, efficiency, faculty *(ability),* force *(strength),* influence, leverage, main force, potential, power, prestige, puissance, quality *(excellence),* sinew, strength, validity, weight *(importance)*

potens influential, predominant

potent assertive, capable, cogent, compelling, considerable, convincing, efficient, in full force, indomitable, inexpugnable, influential, irresistible, omnipotent, operative, persuasive, powerful, predominant, prevailing *(having superior force),* productive, sound, sovereign *(absolute),* strong, valid, virtual

potentia influence, predominance

potential chance *(possibility),* constructive *(inferential),* likelihood, possibility, possible, prospective, viable, virtual

potentialis potential (adjective), potential (noun)

potentiality ability, capacity *(aptitude),* chance *(possibility),* feasibility, likelihood, possibility, quality *(excellence)*

potentially liable at risk

potentiate empower

potestas ability, dominion *(supreme authority),* license, opportunity, permission, possibility, power, warrant *(authorization)*

potestatem facere authorize, empower

potestates authorities

pother furor, hector, perplex, perturb, pique, plague, turmoil

potior preferable

potiorem outweigh

potpourri melange

poultice drug

pounce upon attack, oppugn, seize *(confiscate)*

pound beat *(pulsate),* beat *(strike),* cell, enclosure, lash *(strike),* strike *(assault)*

pour forth emit, issue *(send forth),* outpour, speak

pour in imbue, penetrate

pour out emit, issue *(send forth),* outpour

pour out of emanate

pour over inundate

pourboire bonus, bounty

pourparler caucus

poverty dearth, deficiency, indigence, paucity, privation

poverty-stricken bankrupt, destitute, impecunious, penurious, poor *(underprivileged)*

power advantage, capacity *(aptitude),* capacity *(authority),* catalyst, clout, control *(supervision),* credit *(recognition),* dint, dominance, dominion *(supreme authority),* droit, faculty *(ability),* force *(strength),* government *(administration),* hegemony, influence, jurisdiction, license, main force, management *(directorate),* occupation *(possession),* option *(contractual provision),* patronage *(power to appoint jobs),* potential, predominance, prerogative, pressure, prestige, primacy, puissance, quality *(excellence),* range, realm, regime, right *(entitlement),* sinew, strength, supremacy, title *(right),* validity, warrant *(authorization),* weight *(importance)*

power of choice latitude, liberty, volition

power of choosing discretion *(power of choice),* will *(desire)*

power of determination will *(desire)*

power of directing pressure

power of disposal dominion *(absolute ownership)*

power of entrance ingress

power of impelling clout, pressure

power over trust *(custody)*

power to choose latitude, liberty, option *(choice)*

power to grasp ideas comprehension

power to reason intellect, intelligence *(intellect)*

power to understand comprehension, understanding *(comprehension)*

power-crazed dictatorial

power-hungry dictatorial

power-mad dictatorial

powerful assertive, cogent, consequential *(substantial),* considerable, convincing, decisive, drastic, efficient, eloquent, forcible, important *(significant),* incisive, indomitable, inexpugnable, influential, intense, intensive, irresistible, omnipotent, persuasive, potent, predominant, prevailing *(having superior force),* prominent, sound, sovereign *(absolute),* strong, trenchant, valid, vehement, virtual

powerfully expressive eloquent

powerfulness dint, force *(strength),* influence, main force, potential, sinew

powerless harmless, inactive, inadequate, ineffective, ineffectual, inept *(incompetent),* insipid, insubstantial, languid, nonsubstantial *(not sturdy),* null *(insignificant),* null *(invalid),* otiose, unable, untenable

powerless group minority *(outnumbered group)*

powerlessness disability *(physical inability),* fault *(weakness),* impotence, impuissance, inability, inefficacy, insentience

powerpacked powerful

powers hierarchy *(persons in authority)*

powers that be authorities, authority *(power),* bureaucracy

practicability feasibility, potential

practicable appropriate, beneficial,

effective *(efficient)*, functional, justifiable, potential, practical, probable, suitable, viable

practicableness feasibility

practical beneficial, constructive *(creative)*, effective *(efficient)*, efficient, functional, ministerial, politic, practicable, pragmatic, purposeful, realistic, viable, virtual

practical attitude pragmatism

practical demonstration illustration

practical discernment common sense

practical joke hoax

practical knowledge common sense, experience *(background)*

practical management administration

practical wisdom experience *(background)*

practicality common sense, expedience, feasibility, pragmatism, utility *(usefulness)*, utilization

practicalness pragmatism

practice business *(occupation)*, calling, conduct, course, custom, dealings, deportment, discipline *(training)*, employ *(make use of)*, employment, exercise *(discharge a function)*, exercise *(use)*, expedient, experience *(background)*, habit, manner *(behavior)*, method, mode, operate, operation, perform *(adhere to)*, ply, position *(business status)*, prescription *(custom)*, procedure, profession *(vocation)*, protocol *(etiquette)*, pursue *(carry on)*, pursuit *(occupation)*, qualify *(meet standards)*, resort, rule *(guide)*, system, trade *(occupation)*, usage, use

practice chicanery cheat, circumvent, deceive, defraud, delude, dupe, illude, profess *(pretend)*

practice deception deceive, mislead

practice economy retrench

practice exclusively specialize

practice extravagance dissipate *(expend foolishly)*

practice fraud cheat, mulct *(defraud)*

practice fraud upon defraud, delude

practice gaming gamble

practice of spying on others espionage

practice upon one's credulity delude

practiced cognizant, competent, convincing, deft, expert, facile, familiar *(informed)*, literate, proficient, qualified *(competent)*, resourceful, veteran

practiced hand expert, specialist, veteran

practiced individual professional

practicing lawyer jurist

practicing plural marriage polygamous

practitioner addict, attorney, esquire, expert, professional, specialist

practitioner of the law jurist

praebere furnish, provide *(supply)*

praeceps precipitate

praeceptum maxim, precept, regulation *(rule)*, rule *(legal dictate)*

praecidere abridge *(shorten)*

praecipere forestall, instruct *(direct)*

praecipitare precipitate *(hasten)*, precipitate *(throw down violently)*

praecipue particularly

praecipuus cardinal *(basic)*, cardinal

(outstanding), salient, special

praecurrentia precursory

praecursor precursor

praeda plunder

praedabundus predatory

praedari plunder, prey

praedatorius predatory

praedial proprietary

praedicare declare, proclaim, publish

praedicatio declaration, publication *(disclosure)*

praedicere predict

praedium liberum freehold

praeesse superintend

praefari preface

praefatio preface

praefectus official, superintendent

praefinire predetermine

praegravare encumber *(financially obligate)*

praeiudicare preconceive, prejudge

praeiudicata opinio preconception

praematurus premature

praemeditatio premeditation

praemium prize, recompense, remuneration

praemium proponere reward

praemonere forewarn

praenomen call *(title)*

praenuntius forerunner, harbinger, precursor

praeoccupatio preoccupation

praeoptare prefer

praepollens predominant

praepollere predominate *(command)*

praeponere prefer

praepositio preference *(priority)*

praesagire presage

praesagium misgiving

praesciens foreseeable

praescribere instruct *(direct)*, prescribe

praescriptum instruction *(direction)*, precept, rule *(legal dictate)*

praesens immediate *(at once)*, imminent, instantaneous, present *(attendant)*, present *(current)*

praesentia presence *(attendance)*

praesertim particularly

praeses guardian

praesidere preside

praesidium patronage *(power to appoint jobs)*, protection

praestantia eminence

praestantior superior *(excellent)*

praestare ascendant, evince, indorse

praestituere predetermine

praeterire ignore, overlook *(superintend)*

praetermissio omission

praetermittere omit

praetervehi pass *(advance)*

praetextum pretext

praetextus color *(deceptive appearance)*

praetor judge

praetorium headquarters

praevaricatio collusion

praevenire forestall

praevertere anticipate *(prognosticate)*

pragmatic constructive *(inferential)*, effective *(efficient)*, functional, realistic

pragmatic sanction charter *(sanction)*

pragmatism expedience

pragmatize justify

praise advocacy, belaud, doxology, es-

timation *(esteem)*, honor *(outward respect)*, honor, laudation, mention *(tribute)*, recommend, recommendation, regard *(hold in esteem)*, remembrance *(commemoration)*, respect

praised popular

praiseworthy exemplary, laudable, meritorious, moral, professional *(stellar)*

praiseworthy quality merit

praising favorable *(expressing approval)*

prankishness mischief

prate bombast, prattle

prattle jargon *(unintelligible language)*, prattle, speech

prattling loquacious

prava rerum administratio maladministration

pravitas distortion

pravus immoral, sinister

praxis course, manner *(behavior)*

pray apply *(request)*, importune, request

pray for petition

prayer call *(appeal)*, entreaty, petition, request

pre-trial inquiries interrogatories

preach address *(talk to)*, declaim, educate, inculcate, recite

preaching instruction *(teaching)*, propaganda

preamble overture, preface, preface, prelude, threshold *(commencement)*

preannounce anticipate *(prognosticate)*, predict, prognosticate

preannouncement prognosis

preapprehend preconceive

preapprehension bias, inequity, preconception, predetermination, predisposition

prearrange devise *(invent)*, frame *(prearrange)*, maneuver, plan, plot, predetermine

prearrange fraudulently frame *(charge falsely)*, frame *(prearrange)*

prearranged aforethought, deliberate, express, intentional, premeditated, stated

prearrangement premeditation

precari pray

precarious aleatory *(perilous)*, debatable, insecure, noxious, uncertain *(questionable)*, unreliable, unsound *(not strong)*, untrustworthy, volatile, vulnerable

precariousness danger, doubt *(indecision)*, hazard, jeopardy, peril, predicament, risk

precatio prayer

precaution caution, discretion *(quality of being discreet)*, panoply, preparation, prudence, safeguard

precautional solid *(sound)*

precautionary circumspect, noncommittal, preparatory, preventive, provident *(showing foresight)*, prudent, solid *(sound)*

precautious careful, circumspect, discreet, noncommittal, provident *(showing foresight)*, prudent, solid *(sound)*, vigilant

precede antecede, preface

precedence advantage, importance, magnitude, preference *(priority)*, prestige, priority, reputation, significance, supremacy

precedent aforesaid, antecedent, authority *(documentation)*, before mentioned, code, criterion, finding, forerunner, holding *(ruling of a court)*, judgment *(formal court decree)*, last *(preceding)*, law, mode, model, pattern, precursor, precursory, preparatory, prescription *(custom)*, previous, prior, prototype, standard, stare decisis

precedential exemplary

preceding aforesaid, antecedent, before mentioned, former, old, precursory, preferred *(given priority)*, preliminary, preparatory, previous, prior, said

preceding instance precedent

precept act *(enactment)*, authority *(documentation)*, belief *(something believed)*, brevet, canon, charge *(command)*, citation *(charge)*, code, codification, constitution, dictate, direction *(order)*, directive, doctrine, dogma, edict, guidance, holding *(ruling of a court)*, injunction, instruction *(direction)*, law, mandate, maxim, order *(judicial directive)*, precedent, prescription *(directive)*, principle *(axiom)*, recommendation, regulation *(rule)*, rubric *(authoritative rule)*, rule *(legal dictate)*, technicality, writ

preceptive decretal, disciplinary *(educational)*, informative, prescriptive

preceptor pedagogue

preceptoral disciplinary *(educational)*

precepts code, platform

precepts on securities blue sky law

preces entreaty, imprecation, request

precinct bailiwick, circuit, close *(enclosed area)*, department, district, province, region, territory

precincts confines, vicinity

preciosity bombast

precious inestimable, invaluable, premium, priceless, rare, sterling, valuable

preciousness bombast

precipitance dispatch *(promptness)*, haste, inconsideration

precipitancy dispatch *(promptness)*, haste, inconsideration

precipitant careless, impulsive *(rash)*, precipitate

precipitate careless, cause, evoke, expedite, hasten, heedless, impel, imprudent, impulsive *(rash)*, induce, injudicious, inspire, launch *(project)*, originate, premature, reckless, thoughtless, unexpected

precipitation congealment, dispatch *(promptness)*, haste

precipitous impulsive *(rash)*, precipitate

precipitousness dispatch *(promptness)*, haste

précis abridgment *(condensation)*

precis abstract, capsule, compendium, condense

precise absolute *(conclusive)*, accurate, actual, appropriate, brief, certain *(particular)*, certain *(specific)*, circumspect, close *(rigorous)*, coherent *(clear)*, conscientious, detailed, distinct *(clear)*, draconian, exact, explicit, express, factual, faithful *(true to fact)*, laconic, literal, meticulous, narrow, painstaking, particular *(exacting)*, positive *(incon-*

testable), prompt, proper, punctilious, punctual, rigid, sententious, specific, strict, stringent, subtle *(refined)*, systematic, true *(authentic)*, unambiguous, verbatim

precise amount face amount

precise moment point *(period of time)*

precisely faithfully

precisely bounded definite

precisely formulated specific

preciseness particularity, rigor

precisian precise

precision particularity, regularity, rigor, truth, veracity

precision tool appliance

preclude bar *(exclude)*, bar *(hinder)*, block, censor, clog, condemn *(ban)*, constrain *(restrain)*, debar, disable, disqualify, eliminate *(exclude)*, enjoin, estop, exclude, fight *(counteract)*, forbid, forestall, halt, hamper, impede, interdict, interfere, obstruct, occlude, preempt, prevent, prohibit, reject, restrict, stay *(halt)*, stop, supersede, thwart, withstand

precluded barred

precluding unless

preclusion bar *(obstruction)*, blockade *(limitation)*, check *(bar)*, constraint *(restriction)*, damper *(stopper)*, deterrence, deterrent, disqualification *(rejection)*, embargo, estoppel, exception *(exclusion)*, exclusion, hindrance, impasse, obstacle, obstruction, ostracism, preemption, prohibition

preclusion by act estoppel

preclusion by conduct estoppel

preclusion of work lockout

preclusive exclusive *(limited)*, preventive, prohibitive *(restrictive)*, restrictive

precognitive prophetic

precognize anticipate *(prognosticate)*, preconceive

preconceive anticipate *(expect)*, forejudge, opine, predetermine, prejudge, preordain, presume, presuppose

preconceived aforethought, prejudicial

preconceived idea bias, foregone conclusion, inequity, preconception, prejudice *(preconception)*

preconceived liking preference *(choice)*

preconceived notion inequity, prejudice *(preconception)*

preconception bias, expectation, inequity, intolerance, opinion *(belief)*, partiality, predetermination, predisposition, prejudice *(preconception)*

preconceptual prejudicial

preconcert orchestrate, plan, plot, prearrange, program

preconclude forejudge, preconceive, predetermine, prejudge, preordain, presuppose

preconclusion foregone conclusion, preconception, predetermination, predisposition

precondemn prejudge

precondition necessity, need *(requirement)*, prerequisite, requirement, sine qua non

preconsider predetermine, prejudge, preordain

preconsideration forethought, predisposition, premeditation

preconsidered aforethought, deliberate, intentional, premeditated

precontrive plan, prearrange

precontrived premeditated

precurse portend

precursive aforesaid, antecedent, before mentioned, ominous, oracular, precursory, preliminary, previous, prophetic

precursor ancestor, ascendant, caution *(warning)*, forerunner, harbinger, indicator, parents, pioneer, precedent, predecessor, primogenitor, progenitor

precursory aforesaid, antecedent, before mentioned, elementary, incipient, last *(preceding)*, ominous, oracular, original *(initial)*, preliminary, preparatory, previous, prior

predaceous larcenous

predacious predatory, rapacious

predate antecede, antedate

predative predatory

predatory larcenous, rapacious

predatory incursion foray

predecessor ancestor, ascendant, forerunner, parents, pioneer, precedent, precursor, primogenitor, progenitor

predecessors ancestry

predecide forejudge, preconceive, predetermine, prejudge, preordain, presuppose

predecision foregone conclusion, predetermination, predisposition

predecisive prejudicial

predeliberate preordain

predeliberated aforethought, deliberate, premeditated

predeliberation forethought, goal, plan, predetermination, premeditation

predesign contrive, frame *(prearrange)*, plan, prearrange, scheme

predesigned deliberate, intentional, premeditated

predesigned conclusion foregone conclusion

predestinate prearrange, predetermine

predestination predetermination

predestine prearrange, predetermine, preordain

predestined forthcoming, future, inevitable

predeterminated premeditated

predetermination animus, bias, design *(intent)*, foregone conclusion, forethought, goal, intent, preconception, predisposition, prejudice *(preconception)*, premeditation

predetermine anticipate *(prognosticate)*, devise *(invent)*, forejudge, frame *(prearrange)*, necessitate, orchestrate, plan, prearrange, preconceive, prejudge, prejudice *(influence)*, preordain, presuppose, program, scheme

predetermined aforethought, deliberate, express, fixed *(settled)*, intentional, premeditated, stated

predetermined conclusion foregone conclusion

predetermined course of events predetermination

predevised premeditated

predicament case *(set of circumstances)*, complication, condition *(state)*, confusion *(ambiguity)*, deadlock, dilemma, emergency, entanglement *(involvement)*, imbroglio, impasse, occurrence, peril, pitfall, plight, position *(situation)*, posture *(situation)*, problem, quagmire, quandary, situation, state *(condition)*

predicate ascribe, assume *(suppose)*, attribute, avow, cite *(state)*, claim *(maintain)*, contend *(maintain)*, declare, express, pose *(propound)*, posit, postulate, propound, surmise

predication affirmance *(authentication)*, affirmation, assertion, claim *(assertion)*, pronouncement

predict anticipate *(prognosticate)*, calculate, caution, expect *(consider probable)*, forewarn, portend, preconceive, presage, prognosticate, promise *(raise expectations)*

predictable foreseeable, regular *(conventional)*

predicted foreseeable, forseen, forthcoming, future, imminent

predicting omniscient, oracular

prediction premonition, prognosis, prospect *(outlook)*

prediction of danger monition *(warning)*

prediction of misfortune misgiving

predictive oracular, prophetic, provident *(showing foresight)*

predictory prophetic

predilection affinity *(regard)*, animus, bias, character *(personal quality)*, characteristic, choice *(decision)*, compulsion *(obsession)*, conatus, conviction *(persuasion)*, desire, disposition *(inclination)*, favor *(partiality)*, foregone conclusion, inclination, inequity, partiality, penchant, position *(point of view)*, predisposition, preference *(choice)*, prejudice *(preconception)*, presumption, proclivity, propensity, standpoint, vote

predispose anticipate *(expect)*, bait *(lure)*, convince, preconceive, predetermine, prejudice *(influence)*, prevail upon, slant

predispose to conduce

predisposed inclined, parochial, partial *(biased)*, partisan, prone, ready *(willing)*, susceptible *(unresistent)*

predisposition affection, animus, bias, conatus, conviction *(persuasion)*, disposition *(inclination)*, foregone conclusion, habit, inclination, instinct, partiality, penchant, personality, position *(point of view)*, predilection, prejudice *(preconception)*, presumption, proclivity, propensity, tendency

predispositional prejudicial

predominance advantage, dominance, force *(strength)*, hegemony, influence, majority *(greater part)*, occupation *(possession)*, patronage *(power to appoint jobs)*, power, precedence, preponderance, prestige, puissance, supremacy

predominancy clout, dominance, influence, occupation *(possession)*, predominance, primacy, supremacy

predominant cardinal *(outstanding)*, causative, compelling, considerable, customary, dominant, forcible, influential, leading *(ranking first)*, omnipotent, potent, prevailing *(current)*, pre-

vailing *(having superior force)*, prevalent, primary, prime *(most valuable)*, principal, rife, salient, sovereign *(absolute)*, stellar

predominant part bulk, generality *(bulk)*, majority *(greater part)*

predominantly the same in strict conformity

predominate beat *(defeat)*, dominate, outbalance, outweigh, prevail *(be in force)*, prevail *(triumph)*, rule *(govern)*, surpass, transcend

predominating dominant, master, prevailing *(having superior force)*

predominating influence hegemony

predomination predominance, preponderance, prestige, primacy, supremacy

predominent prominent, remarkable

preeminence advantage, character *(reputation)*, eminence, precedence, preference *(priority)*, preponderance, prestige, primacy, priority, reputation, significance, supremacy

preeminent absolute *(ideal)*, best, cardinal *(outstanding)*, compelling, conspicuous, dominant, famous, important *(significant)*, influential, leading *(ranking first)*, master, meritorious, notable, noteworthy, outstanding *(prominent)*, paramount, primary, prime *(most valuable)*, principal, professional *(stellar)*, prominent, renowned

preeminently particularly

preeminently bad arrant *(onerous)*

preempt attach *(seize)*, distrain, preclude, sequester *(seize property)*

preemption taking

preengagement reservation *(engagement)*

preestablish contrive, prearrange, predetermine, preordain, program

preestimate preconception, prejudge, presuppose

preexamine canvass

preexist precede

preexistent aforesaid, antecedent, before mentioned, former, preexisting, previous, prior

preexisting old, preliminary

prefabrication building *(business of assembling)*

preface caption, forerunner, overture, preamble, prelude

prefatorial previous

prefatory antecedent, before mentioned, elementary, inchoate, incipient, initial, last *(preceding)*, precursory, preliminary, preparatory, previous, prior

prefatory note preamble, preface

prefer choose, discriminate *(treat differently)*, favor, proffer, promote *(advance)*, relish, screen *(select)*, select

prefer a claim impeach, litigate, prosecute *(charge)*, sue

prefer a petition call *(appeal to)*, pray

prefer a request call *(appeal to)*, plead *(implore)*, pray

prefer a request to petition

prefer an appeal call *(appeal to)*

prefer charges accuse, arraign, book, complain *(charge)*, impeach, incriminate, indict, involve *(implicate)*, lodge *(bring a complaint)*, present *(prefer*

charges)*, prosecute *(charge)*

preferability choice *(decision)*

preferable preferred *(favored)*, select, superior *(excellent)*

preference advantage, bias, choice *(decision)*, conatus, discrimination *(bigotry)*, disposition *(inclination)*, election *(choice)*, favor *(partiality)*, favoritism, inclination, inequity, option *(choice)*, partiality, patronage *(power to appoint jobs)*, penchant, poll *(casting of votes)*, position *(point of view)*, precedence, predilection, predisposition, prejudice *(preconception)*, prerogative, primary, priority, propensity, referendum, selection *(choice)*, volition, vote, will *(desire)*

preferential adoptive, preferred *(favored)*

preferential treatment favor *(partiality)*, inequity, nepotism, partiality

preferment behalf, preference *(priority)*, progress, promotion *(advancement)*

preferment of charges complaint

preferred popular, preferable, preferential, select, superior *(excellent)*

preferred standing preference *(priority)*

preferring of charges accusation

preferror of charges complainant

prefigurate portend, presage, presuppose

prefiguration caution *(warning)*, caveat, prognosis

prefigurative prophetic

prefigure forewarn, portend, presage, presuppose

prefigurement forerunner, prognosis

pregnability danger

pregnable disabled *(made incapable)*, helpless *(defenseless)*, indefensible, open *(accessible)*, penetrable, powerless, untenable, vulnerable

pregnant eloquent, productive, replete, strategic

prehension adhesion *(affixing)*, arrest, condemnation *(seizure)*, disseisin, understanding *(comprehension)*

preindicate portend, predict, presage

preindication symptom

preindicative prophetic

preinstruct initiate

prejudge forejudge, opine, preconceive, predetermine, prejudice *(influence)*, preordain, presume, presuppose

prejudged conclusion foregone conclusion

prejudgment bias, foregone conclusion, inequity, intolerance, partiality, preconception, predetermination, predilection, prejudice *(preconception)*

prejudicate forejudge, prejudge

prejudication bias, preconception

prejudice bias, damage, detriment, disadvantage, disadvantage, discrimination *(bigotry)*, drawback, exclusion, favor *(partiality)*, favoritism, foregone conclusion, hatred, inclination, inequality, inequity, influence, injury, injustice, intolerance, ostracism, partiality, penchant, preconception, predetermination, predilection, predisposition, preference *(choice)*, proclivity, segregation *(isolation by races)*, slant, tendency

prejudiced disadvantaged, ex parte, exclusive *(limited)*, illiberal, inequitable, interested, one-sided, parochial, partial *(biased)*, subjective, unequal *(unjust)*, unfair, unjust

prejudiced view foregone conclusion, preconception

prejudicial adverse *(negative)*, detrimental, disadvantageous, unfavorable

prejudicial delay laches

prelect declaim, discourse, inculcate, recite

prelection discourse, harangue, peroration

preliminaries preparation

preliminary antecedent, before mentioned, inchoate, last *(preceding)*, original *(initial)*, overture, precursory, preparatory, previous, prior

preliminary comment preface

preliminary condition need *(requirement)*, prerequisite

preliminary drawing design *(construction plan)*

preliminary negotiation overture

preliminary part prelude

preliminary statement preface

preliminary step preparation

prelude overture, preamble, preface, preface, threshold *(commencement)*

preludial last *(preceding)*, precursory, preliminary, preparatory, prior

preluding aforesaid

preludious last *(preceding)*, precursory

prelusion preamble, preface, prelude

prelusive antecedent, last *(preceding)*, original *(initial)*, precursory, preliminary, preparatory, previous, prior

prelusory aforesaid, antecedent, last *(preceding)*, original *(initial)*, precursory, preliminary, preparatory, previous

premature undue *(not owing)*

premeditate intend, plan, plot, ponder, prearrange, predetermine, scheme

premeditated aforethought, deliberate, express, intentional, willful

premeditation conference, consideration *(contemplation)*, deliberation, forethought, goal, predetermination

premeditative circumspect

premier initial

premise assume *(suppose)*, assumption *(supposition)*, basis, foundation *(basis)*, generalization, ground, inference, postulate, postulate, presumption, proposition, supposition, thesis

premised apparent *(presumptive)*

premises apartment, area *(province)*, building *(structure)*, part *(place)*, property *(land)*, structure *(edifice)*

premium bonus, bounty, gratuity *(present)*, payment *(remittance)*, perquisite, price, prize, profit, reward

premium bond coupon

premium certificate coupon

premium for the use of money interest *(profit)*

premonish admonish *(warn)*, anticipate *(prognosticate)*, expostulate, forewarn, portend, predict, prognosticate

premonishment notice *(warning)*, premonition

premonition caveat, misgiving, prognosis

premonitive portentous *(ominous)*

premonitor indication, symptom

premonitory ominous, portentous *(ominous)*, prophetic

premonitory sign harbinger, indication, symptom

premonstrate portend, predict, presage, prognosticate

premunition precaution, preparation

prenomen call *(title)*

prenotice prognosis

prenotification notice *(warning)*, premonition, tip *(clue)*

prenotify caution

prenotion bias, foregone conclusion, inequity, precognition, preconception, predetermination

prentice neophyte

preoccupation compulsion *(obsession)*, contemplation, interest *(concern)*, obsession

preoccupied oblivious

preoccupy immerse *(engross)*, obsess, occupy *(engage)*, preempt

preordain predetermine

preordained inevitable

preorder prearrange

preordination foregone conclusion

preparation building *(business of assembling)*, composition *(makeup)*, creation, direction *(guidance)*, discipline *(training)*, edification, education, experience *(background)*, instruction *(teaching)*, manufacture, performance *(workmanship)*, plan, precursor, prelude, provision *(act of supplying)*, qualification *(fitness)*

preparation of laws legislation *(lawmaking)*

preparative preliminary, preparatory

preparatory precursory, preliminary, previous, prior

prepare arrange *(plan)*, charge *(instruct on the law)*, compile, conceive *(invent)*, contrive, devise *(invent)*, discipline *(train)*, educate, establish *(launch)*, fix *(arrange)*, forewarn, frame *(construct)*, induct, initiate, instill, instruct *(teach)*, make, nurture, originate, plan, plot, practice *(train by repetition)*, prearrange, produce *(manufacture)*, provide *(arrange for)*, qualify *(meet standards)*, scheme

prepare a complaint address *(petition)*

prepare a formal request address *(petition)*

prepare a petition address *(petition)*

prepare an estimate evaluate

prepare for anticipate *(expect)*, expect *(anticipate)*, forestall

prepare for crops cultivate

prepare for publication edit

prepare for the worst caution

prepare something specious fake

prepare the ground precede

prepared aforethought, alert *(vigilant)*, circumspect, competent, defensible, discreet, expert, familiar *(informed)*, fit, inclined, informed *(educated)*, practiced, provident *(showing foresight)*, prudent, resourceful, ripe, tactical

prepared announcement statement

prepared for sale commercial

prepared speech peroration

prepared text statement

preparedness diligence *(care)*, maturity, prudence, qualification *(fitness)*

preparer precursor

preparing prospective

prepense aforethought, deliberate

prepollence dominance, hegemony, influence, power, predominance, preponderance

prepollency dominance, influence, power, predominance, preponderance

prepollent influential, paramount, sovereign *(absolute)*

preponderance dominance, generality *(bulk)*, majority *(greater part)*, plurality

preponderancy generality *(bulk)*, plurality, preponderance

preponderant cardinal *(basic)*, cardinal *(outstanding)*, compelling, dominant, influential, predominant, prevailing *(having superior force)*, prevalent, prime *(most valuable)*

preponderate beat *(defeat)*, dominate, outbalance, outweigh, predominate *(outnumber)*, prevail *(be in force)*, prevail *(triumph)*

preponderating prevailing *(having superior force)*

preponderation generality *(bulk)*, majority *(greater part)*, preponderance

prepositional preparatory

prepositive before mentioned

prepossess forejudge, preconceive, slant

prepossess unfavorably prejudice *(influence)*

prepossessed interested, one-sided, parochial, partial *(biased)*, prejudicial, unequal *(unjust)*, unjust

prepossessing attractive, palatable, sapid

prepossession compulsion *(obsession)*, foregone conclusion, inequity, partiality, preconception, predetermination, predilection, predisposition, prejudice *(preconception)*, preoccupation

preposterous excessive, exorbitant, impossible, incredible, inept *(inappropriate)*, inordinate, irrational, ludicrous, outrageous, prohibitive *(costly)*, unconscionable, unreasonable, unseemly

prepotency dint, dominance, influence, predominance

prepotent dominant, forcible, influential, master, omnipotent, paramount, potent, sovereign *(absolute)*

prequisiteness need *(requirement)*

prerequirement condition *(contingent provision)*, necessary, necessity, need *(requirement)*

prerequisite attornment, compulsory, condition *(contingent provision)*, important *(urgent)*, integral, mandatory, necessary *(required)*, necessary, necessity, obligatory, qualified *(conditioned)*, requirement, requisite, sine qua non

preresolution predetermination, premeditation

preresolve prearrange, predetermine, preordain

preresolved aforethought, premeditated

prerogative authority *(right)*, birthright, capacity *(authority)*, droit, enjoyment *(use)*, franchise *(license)*, franchise *(right to vote)*, freedom, impunity, liberty, license, option *(contractual provision)*, prescription *(claim of title)*, privilege, right *(entitlement)*, suffrage, title *(right)*

presage anticipate *(prognosticate)*, caution *(warning)*, forerunner, forewarn, harbinger, herald, indicant, indicate, indication, misgiving, portend, precognition, precursor, predict, premonition, prognosis, prognosticate, promise *(raise expectations)*, threat, threaten, warning

presaged forseen

presageful inauspicious, ominous, portentous *(ominous)*, prophetic, sinister

presagement prognosis

presaging ominous, oracular, portentous *(ominous)*, prophetic

presaging good fortune auspicious

prescience precognition

prescient omniscient, prophetic, vigilant

prescribe administer *(conduct)*, admonish *(advise)*, advise, advocate, allocate, assign *(designate)*, authorize, call *(demand)*, caution, command, constitute *(establish)*, counsel, decree, define, detail *(assign)*, dictate, direct *(order)*, drug, enact, govern, impose *(enforce)*, instruct *(direct)*, order, pass *(approve)*, recommend, require *(compel)*, rule *(govern)*, urge

prescribe a task instruct *(direct)*

prescribe by law constitute *(establish)*

prescribe laws legislate

prescribe punishment condemn *(punish)*, convict, determine, pronounce *(pass judgment)*, sentence

prescribe the law charge *(instruct on the law)*

prescribed arrested *(checked)*, boiler plate, certain *(specific)*, fixed *(settled)*, juridical, legal, licit, limited, mandatory, necessary *(required)*, prescriptive, qualified *(conditioned)*, stated, traditional

prescribed by law lawful, legal

prescribed code of conduct decorum

prescribed form constant, criterion, custom, formality, law, matter of course, policy *(plan of action)*, practice *(procedure)*

prescribed method of action proceeding

prescribed mode of action proceeding

prescribed procedure ceremony

prescribed punishment conviction *(finding of guilt)*, fine, penalty, sentence

prescribed system course

prescribed usage practice *(procedure)*

prescriber arbiter

prescript act *(enactment)*, bylaw, canon, citation *(charge)*, code, dictate, direction *(order)*, directive, fiat, injunction, mandate, measure, order *(judicial directive)*, ordinance, precept, prescription *(directive)*, regulation *(rule)*, requirement

prescription assignment *(designa-*

tion), brevet, bylaw, canon, citation *(charge)*, cloud *(incumbrance)*, code, codification, condition *(contingent provision)*, constitution, dictate, direction *(order)*, directive, drug, fiat, guidance, law, mandate, measure, order *(judicial directive)*, practice *(custom)*, recommendation, regulation *(rule)*, requirement, rubric *(authoritative rule)*, rule *(legal dictate)*, title *(right)*, usage

prescriptive compulsory, decretal, formal, legislative, orthodox, rightful, traditional, unalienable

prescriptive right droit

prescripts legislation *(enactments)*

preselect reserve

presence attendance, behavior, complexion, conduct, demeanor, deportment, manner *(behavior)*, phenomenon *(manifestation)*, posture *(attitude)*, specter, vision *(dream)*

presence in court appearance *(coming into court)*

presence of mind common sense, composure, discretion *(quality of being discreet)*, prudence

present actual, adduce, allege, bear *(adduce)*, benefit *(conferment)*, bestow, confer *(give)*, contribute *(supply)*, contribution *(donation)*, convey *(transfer)*, current, de facto, dedicate, disclose, display, dole, donation, endow, endowment, endue, exhibit, expose, exposit, express, extant, extend *(offer)*, fund, furnish, gift *(present)*, give *(grant)*, grant, grant *(transfer formally)*, hold out *(deliberate on an offer)*, impart, initiate, instruct *(teach)*, introduce, largess *(gift)*, leave *(give)*, manifest, mete, offer *(tender)*, pass *(determine)*, pay, perquisite, phrase, plead *(allege in a legal action)*, portray, pose *(propound)*, post, produce *(offer to view)*, proffer, pronounce *(speak)*, propose, propound, provide *(supply)*, recite, remark, remit *(submit for consideration)*, render *(deliver)*, replenish, serve *(deliver a legal instrument)*, submit *(give)*, supply, tender, unveil

present a case show cause

present an answer appear *(attend court proceedings)*

present an opportunity extend *(offer)*

present an ultimatum call *(demand)*, charge *(assess)*

present argument show cause

present as proof cite *(state)*

present as worthy recommend

present cause show cause

present day contemporary, current

present facts communicate

present falsely pretend

present for acceptance offer *(tender)*

present for acceptance or rejection extend *(offer)*

present for consideration exhibit

present for payment tender

present formally introduce

present information inform *(notify)*

present itself arise *(appear)*, occur *(come to mind)*

present itself to the mind occur *(come to mind)*

present money fund

present money for safekeeping de-

posit *(submit to a bank)*

present one's claim call *(demand)*, charge *(assess)*, demand

present oneself appear *(attend court proceedings)*, comport *(behave)*, demean *(deport oneself)*, report *(present oneself)*

present reason show cause

present reasons against argue

present reasons for argue

present reasons for and against debate

present the appearance appear *(seem to be)*, demean *(deport oneself)*

present the meaning of expound

present to the court for acceptance introduce

present to the view appear *(materialize)*

present to view denude, disinter, exhibit

present varied opinions debate, discuss

present with bias prejudice *(influence)*

present-day present *(current)*

present-time present *(current)*

presentability admissibility

presentable admissible, passable

presentably fairly *(moderately)*

presentation account *(report)*, application, benefit *(conferment)*, bid, cession, claim *(assertion)*, clarification, concession *(authorization)*, contribution *(donation)*, declaration, dedication, disclosure *(something disclosed)*, dispensation *(act of dispensing)*, donation, endowment, exhibit, experience *(encounter)*, expression *(manifestation)*, gift *(present)*, gratuity *(present)*, inheritance, installation, introduction, largess *(gift)*, notice *(announcement)*, overture, presence *(poise)*, profession *(declaration)*, program, proposal *(suggestion)*, proposition, publicity, representation *(statement)*, resolution *(formal statement)*, reward, role, style

presentation of arguments and evidence hearing

presentation of basics opening statement

presentation of data opening statement

presentation of essentials opening statement

presentation of evidence corroboration

presentation of testimony hearing

presentation of the documentation opening statement

presentation of the evidence opening statement

presentation of the facts opening statement

presentation to the public publication *(disclosure)*

presentation to view disclosure *(act of disclosing)*

presented alleged

presenter contributor *(giver)*, donor, grantor

presentient ominous, portentous *(ominous)*, prophetic

presentiment apprehension *(fear)*, expectation, fear, foregone conclusion, inequity, misgiving, precognition, preconception, premonition

presenting donative
presenting favorable conditions propitious
presenting few difficulties convenient
presenting information informatory
presently in due course, instantly
presentment charge (accusation), claim (legal demand), dedication, dispensation (act of dispensing), endowment, expression (manifestation), indictment, largess (gift)
preservation bulwark, conservation, continuation (prolongation), custody (supervision), defense, ecology, maintenance (support of spouse), panoply, protection, safekeeping, security (safety), shelter (protection), support (assistance), ward
preservation from harm custody (supervision)
preservation from injury custody (supervision)
preservation of the same conditions status quo
preservative preventive, prophylactic, protective
preserve adhere (maintain loyalty), conserve, continue (prolong), ensconce, fund, harbor, hoard, hold (possess), keep (shelter), maintain (sustain), perpetuate, prolong, protect, protection, record, rescue, reserve, retain (keep in possession), save (conserve), sustain (prolong), uphold
preserve a memory remember
preserve permanently as a public record file (place among official records)
preserve public order police
preserve public tranquility police
preserved intact, lasting, permanent, safe
preserver guardian
preserving conservation
presettle prepay
preshow forewarn, portend, presage
preside direct (supervise), manage, officiate, overlook (superintend)
preside over administer (conduct), conduct, control (regulate), direct (supervise), dominate, govern, handle (manage), hear (give a legal hearing), manage, operate, regulate (manage), render (administer), rule (govern)
presidency management (directorate)
president chief, key man
presider chairman
presiding executive
presiding officer chairman, director
presidium board, management (directorate)
presignify caution, portend, predict, presage, prognosticate
press attach (seize), bait (lure), call (appeal to), call (demand), claim (demand), coax, coerce, compel, constrict (compress), demand, desire, duress, enforce, exact, exhort, exigency, force (coerce), hasten, impact, impede, importune, impose (enforce), incite, inculcate, insist, jostle (bump into), lobby, motivate, plead (implore), pray, pressure, pressure, prompt, solicit, spirit, urge, weigh
press a claim dun, sue

press advice on charge (instruct on the law)
press agentry publicity
press back repress
press by entreaty importune
press down depress
press earnestly insist
press in embed, inject
press in court litigate
press into service resort
press notice publicity, story (narrative)
press on impel, proceed (go forward), progress
press onward continue (persevere), endure (last), keep (continue), progress
press out distill
press together constrict (compress), impact
pressed by duty bound
pressed into smaller compass compact (dense)
pressed together cohesive (compact), compact (dense), solid (compact)
pressing compelling, compulsory, critical (crucial), crucial, essential (required), exigent, grave (important), imperative, important (urgent), indispensable, insistent, major, mandatory, obligatory, onerous, operose, peremptory (imperative), relentless, requisite, serious (grave), urgent, vital
pressing concern requirement
pressing necessity emergency, exigency
pressing need emergency, prerequisite
pressing requirement market (demand)
pressure aggravation (annoyance), bribery, cajole, coerce, coercion, compel, compulsion (coercion), constrain (compel), constraint (restriction), dint, duress, encumbrance, enforcement, exigency, force (compulsion), force (strength), hasten, impetus, impulse, inducement, influence, instigation, leverage, lobby, main force, persuasion, power, predicament, provocation, requirement, stress (strain), weight (burden)
pressure group faction, lobby, special interest
prestige advantage, character (reputation), clout, credit (recognition), distinction (reputation), eminence, importance, influence, power, precedence, primacy, reputation, respect, status
prestigious outstanding (prominent)
presumable apparent (presumptive), believable, circumstantial, colorable (plausible), constructive (inferential), ostensible, plausible, presumptive, probable
presumably prima facie (self-evident), reputedly
presume assume (suppose), deem, expect (consider probable), forejudge, guess, infer, intend, opine, postulate, preconceive, predetermine, prejudge, presuppose, prognosticate, read, surmise, suspect (think), trust
presume on accroach
presumed assumed (inferred), constructive (inferential), deductible (provable), forseen, presumptive, putative,

theoretical
presumed wrongdoer suspect
presuming obtrusive, presumptuous
presumption assumption (supposition), concept, condition (contingent provision), conjecture, disrespect, expectation, generalization, inequity, opinion (belief), position (point of view), preconception, predetermination, probability, prognosis, prospect (outlook), rationale, speculation (conjecture), supposition
presumptive circumstantial, colorable (plausible), deductible (provable), probable, putative, speculative, theoretical
presumptuous brazen, impertinent (insolent), insolent, obtrusive, orgulous, orotund, proud (conceited), supercilious
presumptuousness contumely, disrespect, temerity
presupposal foregone conclusion, inference, preconception, predetermination
presuppose assume (suppose), forejudge, guess, opine, postulate, preconceive, predetermine, prejudge, presume, surmise, suspect (think)
presupposed assumed (inferred), presumptive
presupposition assumption (supposition), condition (contingent provision), conjecture, conviction (persuasion), foregone conclusion, generalization, idea, inference, opinion (belief), preconception, predetermination, presumption, prolepsis, theory
presurmise conjecture, expectation, foregone conclusion, forejudge, preconceive, preconception, predetermination, predetermine, prejudge, premonition, presume, presuppose
pretend claim (demand), cloak, copy, evade (deceive), fabricate (make up), fake, false (not genuine), feign, invent (falsify), lie (falsify), misrepresent, mock (imitate), palter, prevaricate, purport, simulate, specious, spurious
pretend not to see ignore
pretend to be assume (simulate), impersonate, pose (impersonate)
pretended artificial, assumed (feigned), deceptive, delusive, evasive, fictitious, hypothetical, illusory, imitation, mendacious, ostensible, purported, specious, synthetic, tartuffish
pretender fake, pedant
pretense appearance (look), artifice, bad faith, color (deceptive appearance), counterfeit, cover (pretext), deceit, disguise, excuse, false pretense, falsehood, falsification, fraud, histrionics, hoax, hypocrisy, imposture, indirection (deceitfulness), misstatement, pretext, rodomontade, role, sham, story (falsehood), subterfuge
pretense of virtue hypocrisy
pretension artifice, disguise, droit, hypocrisy, jactation, pretense (ostentation), pretext, rhetoric (insincere language), rodomontade
pretentious flatulent, fustian, grandiose, histrionic, inflated (bombastic), inflated (vain), orotund, tawdry
pretentious speech fustian
pretentious talk rodomontade
pretentiousness bombast, pretense

(ostentation), rhetoric *(insincere language)*

preterition disregard *(omission)*

pretermission default, disregard *(omission)*, failure *(falling short)*, omission

pretermit defer *(put off)*, disregard, neglect

preternatural mysterious, peculiar *(curious)*, uncanny

pretexed purported

pretext artifice, bad faith, color *(deceptive appearance)*, deception, disguise, evasion, excuse, false pretense, falsehood, ruse, stratagem, subterfuge

pretexted assumed *(feigned)*

pretiosissimus invaluable, priceless

pretiosus valuable

pretium bribe, charge *(cost)*, price, ransom, worth

pretrial examination proceedings discovery

pretty attractive

pretty good passable

pretty well fairly *(moderately)*

prevail carry *(succeed)*, coax, continue *(persevere)*, convert *(persuade)*, dominate, endure *(last)*, last, outbalance, outweigh, pass *(satisfy requirements)*, persevere, persist, predominate *(command)*, remain *(continue)*, subsist, succeed *(attain)*, surpass, transcend

prevail against resist *(withstand)*, withstand

prevail on govern

prevail over beat *(defeat)*, defeat, kill *(defeat)*, operate, overcome *(surmount)*, override, prejudice *(influence)*, prescribe, surmount

prevail upon affect, bait *(lure)*, browbeat, coax, constrain *(compel)*, convince, exhort, incite, induce, influence, inspire, motivate, persuade, reason *(persuade)*, urge

prevail with arbitrate *(conciliate)*

prevailing accustomed *(customary)*, cardinal *(outstanding)*, coercion, common *(customary)*, convincing, current, customary, dominant, familiar *(customary)*, force *(compulsion)*, general, influential, leading *(ranking first)*, master, ordinary, orthodox, popular, potent, powerful, predominant, prevalent, prime *(most valuable)*, principal, regular *(conventional)*, rife, successful, typical, usual

prevailing attitudes climate

prevailing conditions climate

prevailing form protocol *(etiquette)*

prevailing idea motif

prevailing standards climate

prevailing style mode

prevailing taste custom, mode

prevalence boom *(prosperity)*, custom, frequency, mode, preponderance, usage

prevalent common *(customary)*, conventional, current, customary, dominant, extensive, familiar *(customary)*, frequent, general, habitual, household *(familiar)*, influential, master, material *(important)*, ordinary, popular, predominant, present *(current)*, prevailing *(current)*, proverbial, rampant, regular *(conventional)*, rife, routine, typical, usual

prevaricate bear false witness, cheat, circumvent, deceive, equivocate, evade *(deceive)*, fabricate *(make up)*, feign, invent *(falsify)*, lie *(falsify)*, mislead, misrepresent, misstate, palter, pettifog, pretend

prevaricating deceptive, disingenuous, disreputable, equivocal, mendacious, oblique *(evasive)*, untrue

prevarication ambivalence, deceit, deception, dishonesty, evasion, false pretense, falsehood, falsification, fiction, fraud, indirection *(deceitfulness)*, lie, perjury, story *(falsehood)*, subreption, subterfuge

prévenance comity

prevene antecede

prevenience expectation

prevenient aforesaid, antecedent, before mentioned, precursory, preliminary, previous, prior, said

prevent arrest *(stop)*, avert, balk, ban, bar *(exclude)*, bar *(hinder)*, block, censor, clog, condemn *(ban)*, constrain *(restrain)*, counter, counteract, countervail, debar, delay, detain *(restrain)*, disqualify, disrupt, eliminate *(exclude)*, enjoin, estop, exclude, fight *(counteract)*, foil, forbid, forestall, frustrate, halt, hamper, impede, inhibit, interdict, interfere, interpose, keep *(restrain)*, obstruct, obturate, occlude, oppose, parry, preclude, prohibit, proscribe *(prohibit)*, repel *(drive back)*, resist *(oppose)*, restrain, restrict, stave, stay *(halt)*, stem *(check)*, stifle, stop, suppress, thwart, withstand

prevent crime police

prevent from being discovered enshroud

prevent from being seen enshroud

prevent offenses against the state police

prevent passage clog, shut

prevent publication censor

prevent temporarily hinder

preventative offset, preventive, prophylactic, restrictive

prevented arrested *(checked)*

preventing prohibitive *(restrictive)*

prevention bar *(obstruction)*, barrier, constraint *(restriction)*, control *(restriction)*, damper *(stopper)*, deterrence, deterrent, disadvantage, fetter, frustration, halt, impediment, obstruction, obviation, prohibition, restraint, stay, veto

prevention of accomplishment frustration

prevention of congressional action filibuster

prevention of waste economy *(frugality)*

preventive barrier, prohibitive *(restrictive)*, prophylactic, protective, restrictive, salutary

preventive custody constraint *(imprisonment)*, detention

preventive detention constraint *(imprisonment)*

preventive measure panoply, safeguard

preventive measures precaution

preview precursor

previous aforesaid, antecedent, before mentioned, former, last *(preceding)*, late *(defunct)*, precursory, preexisting, preliminary, prior, said

previous consideration forethought

previous deliberation premeditation

previous design forethought

previous reflection forethought, premeditation

previous to heretofore, theretofore

previously heretofore

previously called alias

previously in mind aforethought

previously mentioned previous, said

previously named said

previously referred to said

previously specified aforesaid

prevision premonition

prewarn admonish *(warn)*, caution, forewarn, presage

prewarning caveat, premonition

prey pillage, prize, victim

prey on plague, plunder

prey on the mind obsess

prey upon bait *(harass)*, endanger, harass, loot

preyed upon aggrieved *(harmed)*

preying rapacious

price bid, charge *(cost)*, collection *(payment)*, evaluate, expenditure, expense *(cost)*, fare, fee *(charge)*, gratuity *(bribe)*, par *(face amount)*, rate, rate, recompense, value, worth

price charged face value *(price)*

price increase inflation *(decrease in value of currency)*

price list tariff *(bill)*

price of a ticket fare

price of corruption gratuity *(bribe)*

price of passage fare

price of redemption ransom

price of retaking ransom

price of retrieval ransom

priceless inestimable, invaluable, prime *(most valuable)*, rare

pricing charge *(assess)*

prick enter *(penetrate)*, lancinate, penetrate, pierce *(lance)*, provocation

pricking bitter *(penetrating)*

prideful inflated *(vain)*, orgulous, pretentious *(pompous)*, proud *(conceited)*, supercilious

prig steal

prim formal, pretentious *(pompous)*

prima facie content *(meaning)*

primacy advantage, dominance, dominion *(supreme authority)*, emphasis, force *(strength)*, importance, magnitude, power, precedence, prestige, priority, regime, significance, stress *(accent)*, supremacy

primal cardinal *(basic)*, central *(essential)*, incipient, initial, original *(initial)*, prime *(original)*, primordial, principal, rudimentary, underlying

primarily a fortiori, ab initio, particularly

primarius leading *(ranking first)*

primary cardinal *(basic)*, causative, central *(essential)*, critical *(crucial)*, dominant, elementary, essential *(inherent)*, essential *(required)*, fundamental, important *(significant)*, inchoate, incipient, indispensable, initial, integral, leading *(ranking first)*, master, material *(important)*, organic, original *(initial)*, paramount, preliminary, prime *(original)*, primordial, principal, rudimentary, salient, simple, stellar, sub-

stantive, ultimate, underlying, vital
primary constituent necessity
primary element center *(essence)*, consequence *(significance)*, content *(meaning)*
primary meaning connotation, content *(meaning)*, gist *(substance)*
primate chief
prime bonus
prime cardinal *(basic)*, cardinal *(outstanding)*, dominant, edify, educate, important *(significant)*, initiate, instruct *(teach)*, leading *(ranking first)*, major, master, meritorious, necessary *(required)*, notable, original *(initial)*, paramount, premium, primary, primordial, principal, professional *(stellar)*, ripe, salient, select, sterling, superlative
prime constituent center *(essence)*, main point, sine qua non
prime ingredient center *(essence)*, main point, sine qua non
prime ingredients character *(personal quality)*
prime motive derivation
prime mover aggressor, architect, author *(originator)*, determinant, promoter, protagonist, reason *(basis)*
primed acquainted, fit, informed *(having information)*, ready *(prepared)*, ripe
primer hornbook
primeval incipient, original *(initial)*, prime *(original)*, primordial
primigenial original *(initial)*, primordial
primitive brutal, elementary, incipient, obsolete, organic, original *(initial)*, outdated, outmoded, prime *(original)*, primordial, rudimentary
primogenitor ancestor, derivation, progenitor
primogenitors parentage
primogeniture birthright
primordial original *(initial)*, prime *(original)*, rudimentary
primus cardinal *(basic)*, cardinal *(outstanding)*, elementary, fundamental, initial, primary, prime *(original)*, principal
princeliness philanthropy
princely charitable *(benevolent)*, liberal *(generous)*, magnanimous, meritorious, outstanding *(prominent)*, philanthropic
princeps chief, leading *(ranking first)*, principal
principal accomplice, assets, cardinal *(basic)*, cash, central *(essential)*, chairman, chief, corpus, critical *(crucial)*, director, dominant, fundamental, important *(significant)*, leading *(ranking first)*, major, material *(important)*, necessary *(required)*, noteworthy, outstanding *(prominent)*, paramount, predominant, primary, prime *(most valuable)*, professional *(stellar)*, prominent, protagonist, salient, stellar, substantive, superlative, vital
principal backer mainstay
principal character protagonist
principal item feature *(special attraction)*
principal maintainer mainstay
principal part body *(main part)*,

bulk, center *(essence)*, cornerstone, generality *(bulk)*, gist *(ground for a suit)*, gravamen, majority *(greater part)*, principal *(capital sum)*
principal person chief
principal point gist *(ground for a suit)*, main point
principal support mainstay
principal supporter mainstay
principal sustainer mainstay
principal thoroughfare avenue *(route)*
principalis fundamental, primary, principal
principally ab initio, as a rule, generally, particularly
principatus predominance, supremacy
principia premises *(hypotheses)*
principium maxim
principium origin *(source)*
principle article *(precept)*, basis, belief *(something believed)*, color *(complexion)*, conscience, consequence *(significance)*, conviction *(persuasion)*, cornerstone, corpus, criterion, doctrine, dogma, generality *(vague statement)*, ground, honor *(good reputation)*, integrity, law, maxim, precept, prescription *(directive)*, probity, reason *(basis)*, rectitude, right *(righteousness)*, rule *(legal dictate)*, substance *(essential nature)*, thesis, veracity
principle of law stare decisis
principle part component
principled bona fide, conscientious, equitable, ethical, high-minded, honest, juridical, just, law-abiding, meritorious, moral, reputable, scrupulous, strict
principles code, ethics, honesty, pandect *(code of laws)*, platform, policy *(plan of action)*, polity
principles of government constitution
principles of morality ethics
print brand *(mark)*, circulate, copy, copy, impression, issue *(publish)*, post, publish, stamp
printed holographic
printing publication *(printed matter)*, script
prints fingerprints
prior aforesaid, antecedent, back *(in arrears)*, before mentioned, former, precursory, preexisting, preferred *(given priority)*, preliminary, preparatory, previous, said
prior last *(preceding)*
prior condition prerequisite
prior determination premeditation
prior instance authority *(documentation)*, precedent
prior measure precaution, preparation
prior planning forethought
prior right prerogative, priority
prior thought forethought
prior to heretofore, theretofore
priority importance, magnitude, materiality *(consequence)*, precedence, preferential, prerogative, privilege, significance
prison bondage, captivity, cell, constraint *(imprisonment)*, detention, jail, penitentiary, reformatory
prison house cell, prison
prisonbreaker fugitive

prisoner captive, convict, hostage, inmate
prisoner at the bar convict
prisoner behind bars convict
prisoner of state convict
prisonhouse jail, penitentiary
pristine initial, original *(initial)*, primordial
pristinus former
privacy concealment, confidence *(relation of trust)*, obscuration
private blind *(concealed)*, confidence *(relation of trust)*, confidential, covert, esoteric, furtive, interior, internal, intimate, obscure *(remote)*, personal *(individual)*, privy, remote *(secluded)*, residential, secret, several *(separate)*, solitary, surreptitious
private affair confidence *(relation of trust)*, secret
private communication secret
private enterprise business *(commercial enterprise)*, commerce
private language jargon *(technical language)*
private matter secret
private property possessions
private understanding contract
private war feud
private wrong tort
privateering larcenous
privately alone *(solitary)*, in person
privateness privacy
privation abridgment *(disentitlement)*, bankruptcy, cost *(penalty)*, curtailment, dearth, deficiency, denial, detriment, expense *(sacrifice)*, foreclosure, indigence, injury, loss, need *(deprivation)*, paucity, poverty
privation of seisin disseisin
privatus personal *(private)*, private *(not public)*
privilege advantage, allow *(authorize)*, authorize, birthright, capacity *(authority)*, charter *(sanction)*, claim *(right)*, concession *(authorization)*, dispensation *(exception)*, droit, easement, empower, enable, exclusion, exemption, franchise *(license)*, franchise *(right to vote)*, free, freedom, grant *(concede)*, immunity, impunity, invest *(vest)*, let *(permit)*, liberty, license, option *(contractual provision)*, palliate *(excuse)*, patent, permit, prerogative, prize, right *(entitlement)*, sanction
privilege to publish copyright
privilege to reproduce copyright
privileged entitled, exempt, free *(not restricted)*, immune, preferential, rightful, unalienable
privileged class elite, society
privileged communication confidence *(relation of trust)*, secret
privileged information secret
privity chain *(nexus)*, nexus
privy mysterious, personal *(private)*, private *(confidential)*, secret, stealthy
privy council bench
privy to familiar *(informed)*
prizable valuable
prize bounty, consideration *(recompense)*, honor, hush money, paragon, prefer, preferential, premium *(excess value)*, prime *(most valuable)*, profit, raise *(advance)*, recognition, recommend, regard *(hold in esteem)*, reward,

select, spoils, stake *(award)*
pro rata per capita
pro re valere equivalent
pro tem pro tempore
probabilis plausible
probabilitas likelihood
probability chance *(possibility),* expectation, likelihood, possibility, presumption, prospect *(outlook),* supposition
probable apparent *(presumptive),* believable, circumstantial, constructive *(inferential),* deductible *(provable),* foreseeable, future, possible, presumptive, reasonable *(rational)*
probare approve, establish *(show),* evince, prove, recommend, verify *(confirm),* vindicate
probatio probation
probation examination *(test),* preparation
probationary tentative
probationer apprentice, novice
probative tentative
probative matter evidence
probatory probative
probe analysis, analyze, audit, canvass, check *(inspect),* consider, cross-examination, cross-examine, cross-questioning, delve, examine *(interrogate),* examine *(study),* frisk, hearing, hunt, indagation, inquire, inquiry *(request for information),* inquiry *(systematic investigation),* interrogation, investigate, investigation, penetrate, peruse, pursuit *(chase),* pursuit *(effort to secure),* question *(inquiry),* research, scrutinize, scrutiny, search, study, trace *(follow),* traverse, trial *(experiment)*
probe into research
probe to the bottom delve
prober detective
probing interrogative, judgment *(discernment)*
probitas honesty, integrity, probity, rectitude
probity candor *(impartiality),* conscience, credibility, ethics, fairness, good faith, honesty, honor *(good reputation),* integrity, justice, principle *(virtue),* rectitude, right *(righteousness),* trustworthiness, truth, veracity
problem disadvantage, enigma, foible, grievance, hindrance, impasse, issue *(matter in dispute),* matter *(subject),* misfortune, nuisance, pitfall, plight, quagmire, question *(issue),* thesis, trouble
problematic debatable, difficult, disputable, doubtful, inauspicious, uncertain *(questionable)*
problematical controversial, debatable, inauspicious, moot, problematic, uncertain *(questionable),* undecided, vague
probrosus disgraceful, scandalous, scurrilous
probrum discredit, infamy, reproach
probus honest, moral, upright
procacious bumptious, impertinent *(insolent),* insolent
procacity temerity
procedural law adjective law
procedure agenda, avenue *(means of attainment),* campaign, conduct, con-

stant, course, direction *(course),* expedient, form *(arrangement),* maneuver *(tactic),* manner *(behavior),* matter of course, method, mode, modus operandi, operation, policy *(plan of action),* polity, practice *(custom),* proceeding, process *(course),* rule *(guide),* scheme, step, strategy, system
proceed accrue *(arise),* arise *(occur),* continue *(resume),* develop, emanate, ensue, occur *(happen),* pass *(advance),* progress, pursue *(carry on),* redound, remain *(continue),* reopen, result, resume, stem *(originate)*
proceed against civilly prosecute *(charge)*
proceed against criminally prosecute *(charge)*
proceed by stratagem circumvent, devise *(invent),* maneuver
proceed from arise *(originate),* result
proceed to assume *(undertake)*
proceed with conduct, discharge *(perform),* maintain *(carry on),* prosecute *(carry forward),* transact
proceeding business *(affair),* continuation *(resumption),* day in court, event, expedient, experience *(encounter),* happening, incident, lawsuit, manner *(behavior),* occurrence, operation, procedure, progressive *(going forward),* step, suit, transaction, trial *(legal proceeding)*
proceeding from antecedent to consequent a priori
proceeding without cessation continual *(connected)*
proceeding without interruption continual *(connected)*
proceedings affairs, case *(lawsuit),* cause *(lawsuit),* dealings, matter *(case),* record, register, strategy
proceeds commission *(fee),* earnings, income, output, product, profit, rent, revenue
process avenue *(means of attainment),* conduit *(channel),* course, expedient, instrumentality, manufacture, method, mode, modus operandi, operation, practice *(procedure),* procedure, proceeding, search warrant, step, subpoena, system, transaction, treatment, warrant *(judicial writ)*
process in law controversy *(lawsuit)*
process of extinguishment of rights foreclosure
process of governing bureaucracy
process of proving proof
processing treatment
procession chain *(series),* order *(arrangement),* sequence, serial, succession
proclaim affirm *(claim),* annunciate, appoint, argue, avouch *(avow),* avow, bear *(adduce),* certify *(attest),* circulate, command, communicate, convey *(communicate),* declaim, declare, decree, disclose, divulge, enunciate, express, herald, inform *(notify),* issue *(publish),* manifest, notify, observe *(remark),* plead *(allege in a legal action),* posit, post, prescribe, profess *(avow),* promulgate, pronounce *(speak),* propagate *(spread),* publish, report *(disclose),* signify *(inform),* speak, utter
proclaimed alleged, public *(known)*
proclaimer harbinger, informant, in-

former *(a person who provides information)*
proclaimor declarant
proclamation adjudication, avouchment, canon, charge *(command),* charter *(declaration of rights),* communication *(statement),* declaration, decree, dictate, directive, disclosure *(act of disclosing),* disclosure *(something disclosed),* divulgation, issuance, notice *(announcement),* notification, order *(judicial directive),* ordinance, publication *(disclosure),* publicity, report *(detailed account)*
proclamatory declaratory
proclivis inclined, prone
proclivitas predisposition, proclivity, propensity, tendency
proclivity affinity *(regard),* bias, character *(personal quality),* characteristic, conatus, conviction *(persuasion),* desire, dispositition *(inclination),* favor *(partiality),* favoritism, frame *(mood),* habit, inclination, instinct, liability, partiality, penchant, position *(point of view),* predisposition, preference *(choice),* propensity, standpoint, tendency
procrastinare procrastinate
procrastinate defer *(put off),* hesitate, hold up *(delay),* neglect, protract *(prolong),* stall
procrastinating dilatory
procrastination cessation *(interlude),* deferment, delay, laches, neglect, pause
procrastinative dilatory, indolent, remiss
procrastinatory dilatory
procreant fertile
procreare propagate *(increase)*
procreate bear *(yield),* create, produce *(manufacture),* propagate *(increase),* pullulate, reproduce
procreation creation
procreative causative, fertile, prolific
procreator ancestor, ascendant, parents, predecessor, primogenitor, progenitor
procreators ancestry
proctor advocate *(counselor),* deputy, director, factor *(commission merchant),* plenipotentiary, procurator, superintendent
proctorage supervision
proctorship control *(supervision)*
procurable disposable, open *(accessible)*
procuracy agency *(legal relationship),* delegation *(envoy)*
procurare administer *(conduct),* administer *(tender),* oversee, superintend
procuratio administration, government *(administration),* supervision
procuration acquisition, agency *(legal relationship),* delegation *(assignment),* deputation *(selection of delegates),* recovery *(repossession)*
procurator agent, attorney, barrister, deputy, director, jurist, proctor
procurator factor *(commission merchant),* proxy
procuratory vicarious *(delegated)*
procure acquire *(secure),* attain, buy, coax, contrive, derive *(receive),* educe, engage *(hire),* evoke, gain, glean, hire, lobby, obtain, occupy *(take possession),*

pander, purchase, raise *(collect)*, realize *(obtain as a profit)*, reap, receive *(acquire)*, recover

procure another to commit perjury suborn

procure by effort earn

procure indirectly suborn

procure title to buy, purchase

procurement acquisition, adverse possession, provision *(act of supplying)*, recovery *(repossession)*, takeover

procurer consumer, go-between

prod coax, coerce, constrain *(compel)*, impel, jostle *(bump into)*, press *(goad)*, pressure, prompt, remind, reminder, spirit, stimulate, stimulus, urge

prodding provocation

prodere betray *(disclose)*, deliver, give *(grant)*

prodesse avail *(be of use)*, contribute *(assist)*

prodigal dissolute, improvident, inordinate, liberal *(generous)*, needless, portentous *(eliciting amazement)*, profligate *(extravagant)*, profuse, superfluous, unrestrained *(not repressed)*

prodigality delinquency *(misconduct)*, inconsideration, largess *(generosity)*, misapplication, neglect, waste

prodigalize dissipate *(expend foolishly)*

prodigious far reaching, noteworthy, portentous *(eliciting amazement)*, special, unusual

prodigium phenomenon *(unusual occurrence)*

prodigy mastermind

prodition bad repute, bribery

prodromal before mentioned

prodrome precursor

produce adduce, avail *(bring about)*, bear *(adduce)*, bear *(yield)*, build *(construct)*, cargo, cause, commodities, compose, conjure, constitute *(compose)*, create, develop, discharge *(perform)*, effectuate, engender, evoke, exhibit, fabricate *(construct)*, form, formulate, frame *(construct)*, frame *(formulate)*, furnish, generate, germinate, goods, induce, inspire, invent *(produce for the first time)*, make, manufacture, merchandise, occasion, offer *(tender)*, originate, output, perpetrate, proceeds, product, profit, propagate *(increase)*, provide *(supply)*, pullulate, realize *(make real)*, realize *(obtain as a profit)*

produce a change affect

produce a good effect profit

produce a good result profit

produce an effect affect

produce an example illustrate

produce an instance exemplify, quote

produce conviction convince

produce counterfeit money forge *(counterfeit)*

produce equilibrium compensate *(counterbalance)*

produce evidence verify *(confirm)*

produce injury inflict

produce rapidly proliferate

produce the evidence bear *(adduce)*

produced alleged

produced materials commodities

producer author *(originator)*, derivation, determinant, maker

producere adduce, promote *(advance)*

producing creation

producing a powerful effect forcible

producing abundantly copious

producing boredom lifeless *(dull)*

producing ennui lifeless *(dull)*

product amount *(result)*, conclusion *(outcome)*, consequence *(conclusion)*, development *(outgrowth)*, effect, invention, item, outcome, output, proceeds, result

product of imagination fiction, idea

product of the imagination figment

production boom *(increase)*, boom *(prosperity)*, building *(business of assembling)*, business *(commerce)*, composition *(makeup)*, creation, discharge *(performance)*, disclosure *(act of disclosing)*, formation, fruition, industry *(business)*, manifestation, manufacture, operation, origination, outcome, output, performance *(execution)*, performance *(workmanship)*, realization

production and distribution commerce

productive beneficial, causal, causative, constructive *(creative)*, copious, effective *(efficient)*, efficient, fertile, gainful, lucrative, operative, original *(creative)*, potent, profitable, prolific, purposeful

productiveness creation, efficiency, utility *(usefulness)*

productivity boom *(prosperity)*, creation, utility *(usefulness)*

products commodities, goods, stock in trade

proelium committere fight *(battle)*

proem overture, preamble, preface, prelude

proemial elementary, incipient, original *(initial)*, preliminary, preparatory, prior

profanation blasphemy, profanity

profane abuse *(violate)*, contaminate, debase, diabolic, mundane, obscene, pollute

profane interjection expletive

profane language profanity

profane oath blasphemy

profaneness blasphemy, profanity

profanity imprecation

profanus profane

profectio start

proferre adduce, postpone, publish, quote

profess affirm *(claim)*, allege, annunciate, assert, assume *(simulate)*, assure *(insure)*, avouch *(avow)*, avow, bear *(adduce)*, claim *(maintain)*, concede, contend *(maintain)*, declare, depose *(testify)*, enunciate, palter, posit, pretend, purport, testify

professed alleged, ostensible, purported, putative, specious

professed belief doctrine, dogma, principle *(axiom)*

professed purpose pretense *(pretext)*, pretext

professio profession *(declaration)*

profession admission *(disclosure)*, affirmation, appointment *(position)*, assertion, asseveration, averment, avowal, business *(occupation)*, calling, career, conviction *(persuasion)*, cover *(pretext)*, declaration, disclosure *(act of*

disclosing)*, disclosure *(something disclosed)*, employment, expression *(comment)*, industry *(business)*, job, labor *(work)*, livelihood, mission, occupation *(vocation)*, office, position *(business status)*, post, pretext, pronouncement, pursuit *(occupation)*, testimony, trade *(occupation)*, work *(employment)*

profession of faith principle *(axiom)*

professional ethical, expert, expert, learned, practitioner, specialist, technical

professional advice holding *(ruling of a court)*

professional decision holding *(ruling of a court)*

professional error of judgment malpractice

professional ethics conscience

professional fee retainer

professional force staff

professional language jargon *(technical language)*

professional laxness malpractice

professional misconduct malpractice

professional neglect malpractice

professional negligence malpractice

professional staff staff

professional standards ethics

professional vocabulary jargon *(technical language)*

professionalism specialty *(special aptitude)*

professor pedagogue, specialist

professorate faculty *(teaching staff)*

professorial learned

professors faculty *(teaching staff)*

proffer adduce, bestow, bid, contribute *(supply)*, extend *(offer)*, give *(grant)*, hold out *(deliberate on an offer)*, introduce, invitation, offer *(propose)*, offer *(tender)*, overture, pose *(propound)*, present *(make a gift)*, proposal *(suggestion)*, propose, propound, remit *(submit for consideration)*, tender

proffer payment offer *(tender)*

proffered unsolicited

proficere profit, progress

proficiency ability, caliber *(mental capacity)*, capacity *(aptitude)*, competence *(ability)*, efficiency, experience *(background)*, facility *(easiness)*, faculty *(ability)*, force *(strength)*, gift *(flair)*, knowledge *(learning)*, performance *(workmanship)*, potential, prowess *(ability)*, science *(technique)*, skill, specialty *(special aptitude)*

proficient artful, capable, cognizant, competent, deft, effective *(efficient)*, efficient, expert, familiar *(informed)*, informed *(educated)*, learned, literate, practiced, professional *(trained)*, qualified *(competent)*, resourceful, sciential, specialist, veteran

proficient person expert, specialist

proficient practitioner professional

proficisci leave *(depart)*

proficuous beneficial

profile brief, characterize, configuration *(form)*, contour *(outline)*, contour *(shape)*, cross section, delineate, delineation, description, outline *(boundary)*

profit advantage, avail *(bring about)*, bear *(yield)*, behalf, benefit *(betterment)*, boom *(prosperity)*, capitalize *(seize the chance)*, collect *(recover* *money),* commission *(fee),* dividend, earn, earnings, edification, gain, inure *(benefit),* output, pay, perquisite, proceeds, prosperity, realization, realize *(obtain as a profit),* reap, revenue, succeed *(attain),* utility *(usefulness),* worth

profit and loss account budget

profit and loss statement ledger

profit by employ *(make use of),* exploit *(make use of)*

profit by cheating prey

profit by swindling prey

profit from conversion of assets income

profit from money loaned interest *(profit)*

profit from sale income

profit making boom *(prosperity)*

profitability utility *(usefulness)*

profitable beneficial, constructive *(creative),* copious, effective *(efficient),* favorable *(advantageous),* fertile, functional, gainful, lucrative, practical, productive, salutary, successful, valuable

profitableness expedience, feasibility, worth

profiteering exploitation, graft, mercenary

profiteri avow, declare, offer *(propose)*

profiting prosperous

profitless barren, disadvantageous, futile, ineffective, ineffectual, unavailing, unproductive

profits earnings, income

profits from employment earnings

profits of commerce income

profligacy bad repute, debauchery, delinquency *(misconduct),* vice

profligate delinquent *(guilty of a misdeed),* depraved, disreputable, dissolute, immoral, improvident, iniquitous, lawless, lecherous, lewd, licentious, nefarious, obscene, prodigal, profuse, promiscuous, reprobate, salacious, scandalous, tainted *(corrupted),* unscrupulous, vicious, wrongdoer

profligatus profligate *(extravagant),* reprobate

profluence boom *(prosperity)*

profluency boom *(prosperity)*

profluent progressive *(going forward)*

profound convincing, esoteric, intense, learned, obscure *(abstruse),* recondite, sapient

profound application diligence *(care)*

profound attention diligence *(care)*

profound study diligence *(care)*

profound thought diligence *(care),* preoccupation

profugus fugitive

profundity sagacity

profuse copious, excess, excessive, inordinate, liberal *(generous),* loquacious, manifold, multiple, prolific, replete, rife, superfluous, undue *(excessive),* voluble

profuseness boom *(prosperity),* plethora, sufficiency, surfeit, tautology

profusion boom *(prosperity),* overage, plethora, quantity, spate, store *(depository),* sufficiency, surfeit, waste

profusive copious

profusus profuse

progenerate propagate *(increase),* reproduce

progenerative fertile

progenies issue *(progeny),* offspring, progeny

progenitive prolific

progenitor ancestor, ascendant, derivation, forerunner, parents, predecessor

progenitors lineage, parentage

progenitorship paternity

progeniture bloodline

progeny child, children, descendant, family *(household),* offspring, posterity, succession

prognose predict

prognosis caution *(warning)*

prognostic caution *(warning),* harbinger, indicant, indication, indicator, menace, oracular, precursor, prophetic, provident *(showing foresight),* symptom, warning

prognosticate expect *(consider probable),* forewarn, herald, portend, predict, presage, promise *(raise expectations)*

prognostication prognosis

prognosticative precursory, prophetic

program arrange *(methodize),* arrange *(plan),* calendar *(record of yearly periods),* campaign, course, direction *(course),* docket, enterprise *(undertaking),* method, plan, platform, policy *(plan of action),* polity, practice *(procedure),* procedure, prospectus, register, schedule, set down, strategy, system, undertaking *(enterprise)*

program of action arrangement *(plan),* device *(contrivance),* method, proposition, scheme

program of business agenda

program of operation agenda

progredi progress

progress accession *(enlargement),* accrue *(arise),* advance *(progression),* advancement *(improvement),* augmentation, boom *(increase),* boom *(prosperity),* civilization, continue *(persevere),* develop, development *(progression),* edification, endure *(last),* enlarge, evolve, expand, germinate, growth *(evolution),* headway, increase, inflow, keep *(continue),* move *(alter position),* pass *(advance),* persist, proceed *(go forward),* promotion *(advancement),* pursue *(strive to gain),* reform, remain *(continue),* renew *(begin again),* resume, succeed *(attain),* transition

progress to maturity development *(progression)*

progressing live *(existing)*

progression accession *(enlargement),* advance *(progression),* advancement *(improvement),* array *(order),* boom *(increase),* boom *(prosperity),* chain *(series),* civilization, continuity, cycle, gamut, headway, hierarchy *(arrangement in a series),* order *(arrangement),* progress, promotion *(advancement),* reform, sequence, serial, step, succession, way *(manner)*

progressive continuous, corrigible, direct *(uninterrupted),* liberal *(broad minded),* radical *(favoring drastic change),* sophisticated

progressive course process *(course)*

progressive growth development *(progression)*

progressiveness boom *(prosperity)*

progressivism reform

progressus advance *(progression),* development *(progression),* progress

prohibere avert, debar, exclude, hinder, preclude, prevent, stop

prohibit abolish, abrogate *(annul),* abrogate *(rescind),* ban, bar *(exclude),* bar *(hinder),* block, censor, clog, condemn *(ban),* constrain *(restrain),* contain *(restrain),* control *(restrain),* counter, curb, debar, deny *(refuse to grant),* disfranchise, disqualify, dissent *(withhold assent),* eliminate *(exclude),* enjoin, estop, exclude, fetter, forbid, forestall, halt, inhibit, interdict, interfere, keep *(restrain),* lock, negate, obstruct, occlude, oppose, preclude, prevent, refuse, reject, repel *(drive back),* repress, restrain, restrict, revoke, stay *(halt),* stop, suppress, withhold

prohibit by legal injunction enjoin

prohibited barred, illegal, illegitimate *(illegal),* illicit, impermissible, improper, inadmissible, irregular *(improper),* unauthorized, unlawful

prohibited articles contraband

prohibited by law illegal, illegitimate *(illegal)*

prohibited import contraband

prohibiting penal

prohibition bar *(obstruction),* barrier, censorship, check *(bar),* coercion, constraint *(imprisonment),* constraint *(restriction),* control *(restriction),* countermand, denial, deterrence, embargo, estoppel, exclusion, fetter, halt, injunction, limitation, obstacle, obstruction, ostracism, proscription, refusal, rejection, restraint, restriction, temperance, veto

prohibitionary restrictive

prohibitive exclusive *(limited),* inordinate, preventive, restrictive

prohibitory prohibitive *(restrictive),* restrictive

project arrange *(plan),* campaign, cast *(throw),* contrive, device *(contrivance),* emanate, endeavor, enterprise *(undertaking),* impel, overlap, plan, prearrange, precipitate *(throw down violently),* predetermine, program, program, proposition, propound, pursuit *(occupation),* scheme, scheme, send, undertaking *(business),* undertaking *(enterprise),* venture

projected forthcoming, prospective, speculative

projected campaign project

projected goal design *(intent)*

projected law bill *(proposed act)*

projected scheme project

projecting prominent

projection design *(construction plan),* plan

projector architect

prolatio extension *(expansion)*

prolegomenon preamble, preface

proles offspring

proletarian ignoble

proletariat populace

proliferate bear *(yield),* increase, propagate *(increase),* pullulate, reproduce

proliferation augmentation, boom *(increase),* boom *(prosperity)*

proliferative productive, prolific

proliferous productive, prolific

prolific beneficial, copious, fertile, productive, profuse, rampant

prolix flatulent, loquacious, profuse, prosaic, protracted, turgid

prolocutor procurator, spokesman

prologue preamble, prelude, threshold (*commencement*)

prolong compound, conserve, defer (*put off*), delay, dwell (*linger over*), expand, hold up (*delay*), increase, keep (*continue*), last, maintain (*carry on*), perpetuate, persevere, preserve, procrastinate, remain (*continue*), stay (*continue*)

prolongate dwell (*linger over*)

prolongation adjournment, advance (*increase*), boom (*increase*), continuance, deferment, delay, extension (*postponement*), longevity, survival

prolonged chronic, continuous, prolix, protracted

prolonged outburst of denunciation diatribe

prolusion preface

promenade perambulate

prominence character (*reputation*), clout, consequence (*significance*), distinction (*reputation*), eminence, emphasis, honor (*outward respect*), importance, materiality (*consequence*), notoriety, prestige, reputation, significance, status, stress (*accent*), weight (*importance*)

prominens prominent

prominent appreciable, blatant (*conspicuous*), clear (*apparent*), conspicuous, critical (*crucial*), famous, flagrant, illustrious, important (*significant*), influential, leading (*ranking first*), manifest, momentous, naked (*perceptible*), notable, noteworthy, notorious, obtrusive, obvious, open (*in sight*), palpable, paramount, particular (*specific*), patent, perceivable, perceptible, primary, prime (*most valuable*), principal, remarkable, renowned, reputable, salient, stellar, unusual

prominent aspect main point

prominent detail highlight

prominent object landmark (*conspicuous object*)

prominent part highlight

prominent point main point

prominently fairly (*clearly*), particularly

promiscuous haphazard, immoral, indiscriminate, lascivious, licentious, random

promiscuus indiscriminate, miscellaneous, promiscuous

promise agree (*contract*), allegiance, assurance, assure (*insure*), bestow, bind (*obligate*), bond, bond (*secure a debt*), commitment (*responsibility*), compact, condition (*contingent provision*), contract, contract, cosign, covenant, coverage (*insurance*), depose (*testify*), duty (*obligation*), ensure, expectation, guarantee, insurance, oath, obligation (*duty*), pact, pledge (*binding promise*), possibility, potential, predict, presage, probability, proffer, prognosis, prognosticate, prospect (*outlook*), recognizance, responsibility (*accountability*), security (*pledge*), stipulate, stipulation, swear, testament, undertake, undertaking

(*pledge*), underwrite, vouch, vow, warrant (*guaranty*), warranty

promise ill impend

promise solemnly pledge (*promise the performance of*)

promise to contribute subscribe (*promise*)

promise to pay coverage (*insurance*)

promise to pay another's debt guaranty

promise to set aside reservation (*engagement*)

promise under seal specialty (*contract*)

promised contractual, forseen, forthcoming, indentured, prospective

promising auspicious, favorable (*advantageous*), possible, probable, promissory, propitious, viable

promising to underwrite promissory

promisor surety (*guarantor*)

promissory note bond, draft, security (*pledge*)

promissory oath pledge (*binding promise*)

promissory obligation bill (*formal declaration*)

promissum pledge (*binding promise*), promise, vow

promittere hold out (*deliberate on an offer*), proffer

promote advocate, aid, ameliorate, assist, avail (*be of use*), bear (*support*), capitalize (*provide capital*), conduce, continue (*persevere*), cultivate, develop, elevate, enhance, expedite, facilitate, favor, foment, foster, further, hasten, heighten (*augment*), help, honor, inure (*benefit*), lobby, motivate, notify, nurture, originate, prefer, preserve, prompt, propagate (*spread*), provoke, raise (*advance*), recommend, sanction, serve (*assist*), side, sponsor, subsidize, support (*assist*), sustain (*prolong*), urge

promote a cause defend

promote public health and safety police

promote racial harmony desegregate

promote racial mixing desegregate

promoter abettor, advocate (*espouser*), backer, benefactor, coactor, conspirer, developer, disciple, partisan, patron (*influential supporter*), sponsor

promoting beneficial

promoting health salutary

promotion advance (*progression*), advancement (*improvement*), advocacy, aid (*help*), behalf, benefit (*betterment*), development (*progression*), elevation, headway, progress, propaganda, publicity, relief (*aid*), support (*assistance*)

promotor coactor

promovere promote (*advance*)

prompt abet, acute, advocate, agitate (*activate*), cause, coax, convince, counsel, enjoin, evoke, exhort, expeditious, hint, immediate (*at once*), impel, incite, indication, induce, influence, initiate, inspire, instantaneous, instruct (*direct*), motivate, originate, persuade, prevail (*persuade*), provoke, punctual, ready (*prepared*), recommend, remind, reminder, spirit, stimulate, summary, urge

prompte readily

prompted inclined

prompter abettor, advocate (*counselor*), catalyst, special interest

prompting advice, cause (*reason*), guidance, impulsive (*impelling*), incentive, inducement, instigation, invitation, moving (*evoking emotion*), persuasion, provocation, suggestion

promptitude dispatch (*promptness*)

promptly as soon as feasible, forthwith, instantly, readily

promptuary bank, cache (*storage place*), repository

prompture suggestion

promptus expeditious, prompt, ready (*prepared*)

promulgare promulgate

promulgate annunciate, bear (*adduce*), circulate, convey (*communicate*), decree, diffuse, disclose, disseminate, divulge, enunciate, herald, inform (*notify*), issue (*publish*), notify, posit, proclaim, propagate (*spread*), report (*disclose*), reveal, signify (*inform*), spread

promulgate a decree instruct (*direct*)

promulgate an order command, instruct (*direct*)

promulgated alleged, public (*known*)

promulgatio notice (*announcement*), notice (*give formal warning*), notification

promulgation charter (*declaration of rights*), declaration, divulgation, issuance, notification, proclamation, pronouncement, publication (*disclosure*), publicity

promulgatory declaratory

prone inclined, partial (*biased*), ready (*willing*), subject (*exposed*)

prone to addicted

prone to believe credulous

prone to display of feeling demonstrative (*expressive of emotion*)

prone to emotional display demonstrative (*expressive of emotion*)

prone to error fallible

prone to inaccuracy fallible

proneness affection, bias, character (*personal quality*), characteristic, conatus, disposition (*inclination*), favor (*partiality*), favoritism, frame (*mood*), inclination, instinct, liability, penchant, position (*point of view*), predilection, predisposition, preference (*choice*), proclivity, propensity, tendency

proneness to error frailty

pronounce adjudicate, affirm (*claim*), affirm (*declare solemnly*), allege, annunciate, argue, assert, avouch (*avow*), avow, award, certify (*attest*), communicate, convey (*communicate*), decide, declare, decree, determine, enunciate, express, issue (*publish*), judge, pass (*determine*), phrase, posit, profess (*avow*), recite, rule (*decide*), speak, try (*conduct a trial*), utter

pronounce a judgment conclude (*decide*), determine

pronounce as an official act find (*determine*)

pronounce distinctly enunciate

pronounce formally adjudge, arbitrate (*adjudge*)

pronounce free from guilt exonerate

pronounce guilty determine, sen-

tence
pronounce in a distinct manner enunciate
pronounce innocent of wrong excuse
pronounce judgment arbitrate (adjudge), award, condemn (punish), convict, deem, opine, pass (determine), rule (decide), sentence
pronounce legal authorize, certify (approve), legalize, notarize
pronounce not guilty acquit, clear, vindicate
pronounce on award
pronounce sentence condemn (punish), convict
pronounced alleged, clear (apparent), conspicuous, distinct (clear), evident, flagrant, lucid, manifest, nuncupative, obvious, open (in sight), palpable, prominent, salient, unmistakable, verbal
pronouncement adjudication, affirmance (authentication), affirmance (legal affirmation), affirmation, allegation, assertion, asseveration, averment, avouchment, avowal, award, charter (declaration of rights), choice (decision), conclusion (determination), confession, declaration, decree, determination, dictum, disposition (determination), edict, fiat, finding, holding (ruling of a court), issuance, judgment (formal court decree), law, notice (announcement), notification, observation, opinion (judicial decision), order (judicial directive), proclamation, profession (declaration), publication (disclosure), remark, resolution (formal statement), ruling, sentence, speech, statement, surety (certainty)
pronouncement by a court award, holding (ruling of a court)
pronouncement of a jury verdict
pronunciamiento canon, issuance, pronouncement
pronunciamiento decree
pronunciation speech, stress (accent)
pronuntiare enunciate, issue (publish), proclaim, pronounce (pass judgment)
pronuntiatio declamation, publication (disclosure)
pronus prone, propensity
prooemium preface, prelude
proof certification (attested copy), certification (certainness), confirmation, corroboration, counterargument, data, design (construction plan), document, documentation, evidence, ground, safe, strength, testimony, token
proof by a witness deposition, testimony
proof legally presented at trial evidence
proof of absence alibi
proof of authority credentials
proof of delivery receipt (proof of receiving)
proof of facts evidence
proof of guilt conviction (finding of guilt)
proof of identity identification
proof of payment receipt (proof of receiving)
proof of the validity of a will probate

proof of the will probate
prop bear (support), bolster, elevate, help, mainstay, reinforcement, rest (be supported by), uphold
propaedeutic didactic, informative
propaedeutical informative
propaedeutics education
propaganda persuasion
propagandist advocate (espouser)
propagandistic persuasive
propagandize convert (persuade), convince, inculcate, instill, misinform, persuade, prevail (persuade), promote (organize)
propagare extend (enlarge)
propagate bear (yield), circulate, diffuse, disperse (disseminate), disseminate, notify, originate, proclaim, produce (manufacture), proliferate, promulgate, reproduce, spread
propagated public (known)
propagatio extension (expansion)
propagation maternity, publication (disclosure), publicity, report (detailed account), transmittal
propagator advocate (espouser)
propel cast (throw), constrain (compel), dispatch (send off), impel, launch (project), move (alter position), precipitate (throw down violently), project (impel forward), provoke, send, spirit, stimulate, urge
propel oneself proceed (go forward)
propellant impetus
propellants ammunition
propense prone, ready (willing)
propenseness predisposition, propensity
propensio penchant
propensio animi bias
propension character (personal quality), penchant, predisposition, propensity
propensity affinity (regard), animus, aptitude, bias, character (personal quality), characteristic, conatus, conviction (persuasion), desire, disposition (inclination), favor (partiality), frame (mood), habit, inclination, instinct, partiality, penchant, position (point of view), predilection, predisposition, preference (choice), proclivity, standpoint, tendency
propensus inclined, propensity
proper accurate, admissible, allowable, applicable, appropriate, due (regular), eligible, equitable, evenhanded, fit, fitting, formal, honest, juridical, just, justifiable, lawful, legal, licit, meritorious, moral, official, orthodox, permissible, precise, reasonable (fair), reasonable (rational), relevant, right (suitable), rightful, seasonable, several (separate), suitable, tenable, unprejudiced
proper behavior protocol (etiquette)
proper for judicial examination justiciable
proper for judicial review justiciable
proper formality propriety (correctness)
proper name call (title)
proper occasion opportunity
proper thing to do decorum
proper time opportunity, timeliness

proper title heading
proper to be examined in courts of justice justiciable
proper to public debate forensic
properantia haste
properare hasten
properatio dispatch (promptness), haste
properly as a matter of right, fairly (impartially)
properly qualified competent
properly timed punctual, seasonable
properness decorum, propriety (appropriateness), propriety (correctness)
propertied opulent
properties commodities
property assets, capital, characteristic, chattel, demesne, differential, domain (land owned), dominion (absolute ownership), effects, fee (estate), freehold, goods, holding (property owned), interest (ownership), land, merchandise, money, paraphernalia (personal belongings), parcel, personalty, plot (land), possessions, premises (buildings), principal (capital sum), quality (attribute), quality (grade), real estate, realty, remainder (estate in property), resource, securities, share (stock), specialty (distinctive mark), stock (shares), substance (material possessions), territory, trait
property holder landholder, landowner, lessee
property illegally acquired graft
property leased leasehold
property obtained by descent inheritance
property obtained by devise inheritance
property owner landholder, landowner, lessor, shareholder
property permanently affixed to the realty immovable
property right lien
property saved salvage
property which may descend to an heir hereditament
prophesied foreseeable, forseen
prophesy anticipate (prognosticate), expect (consider probable), forewarn, portend, predict, presage, prognosis, prognosticate, promise (raise expectations)
prophetic oracular, portentous (ominous)
prophetical portentous (ominous), prophetic
prophylactic preventive, protective, remedial, salutary
prophylaxis deterrence
propiatory penitent
propietory owner landlord
propinquitas affinity (family ties), relationship (family tie)
propinquity blood, connection (relation), corollary, kinship, relation (connection), vicinity
propinquus approximate, close (near), related, relation (kinship), relative
propitiable nonmilitant
propitiare propitiate
propitiate arbitrate (conciliate), disarm (set at ease), mollify, pacify, placate, reconcile, redeem (satisfy debts), redress, soothe

propitiated agreed *(harmonized)*
propitiating compensatory
propitiation collection *(payment)*, conciliation, expiation, mollification, reconciliation
propitiator go-between, intermediary, referee
propitiatory nonmilitant
propitious auspicious, beneficial, favorable *(advantageous)*, fitting, opportune, seasonable, viable
propitiousness expedience, opportunity
propitius propitious
propone hold out *(deliberate on an offer)*
proponent advocate *(espouser)*, apologist
proponere exhibit, issue *(publish)*
proporting distribution *(apportionment)*
proportion allotment, caliber *(measurement)*, coordinate, differential, quota, ration, regularity, share *(interest)*
proportionable cognate, proportionate
proportional commensurable, commensurate, congruous, harmonious, proportionate, relative *(comparative)*
proportionate adequate, commensurable, commensurate, congruous, correlative, dispense, harmonious, pro rata, relative *(comparative)*, suitable
proportionately per capita, pro rata
proportioned coextensive, elegant
proportionment apportionment
proportions area *(surface)*, degree *(magnitude)*, dimension, magnitude
proposal advice, agenda, application, bid, bill *(proposed act)*, campaign, conspiracy, invitation, measure, motion, motive, nomination, overture, plan, platform, policy *(plan of action)*, prescription *(directive)*, program, project, proposition, recommendation, request, resolution *(formal statement)*, strategy, suggestion
propose advise, advocate, argue, counsel, extend *(offer)*, hold out *(deliberate on an offer)*, initiate, intend, move *(judicially request)*, nominate, plan, pose *(propound)*, posit, present *(introduce)*, proffer, propound, raise *(advance)*, recommend, remit *(submit for consideration)*, resolve *(decide)*, submit *(give)*, tender
propose a motion move *(judicially request)*
propose a question inquire
propose an action formally move *(judicially request)*
propose as a candidate nominate
propose legal instructions charge *(instruct on the law)*
proposed apparent *(presumptive)*, tentative
proposed act measure
proposed action agenda, design *(intent)*, plan, platform, policy *(plan of action)*, strategy
proposed enactment bill *(proposed act)*
proposed law bill *(proposed act)*
proposed measure motion
proposed regulation bill *(proposed act)*

act)
proposed rule bill *(proposed act)*
proposed sequence of action design *(intent)*
proposed statute bill *(proposed act)*
proposer of a law lawmaker
proposer of legislation lawmaker
propositio proposition
proposition advice, affirmance *(legal affirmation)*, agenda, application, basis, bid, business *(affair)*, campaign, claim *(assertion)*, clause, contention *(argument)*, invitation, issue *(matter in dispute)*, matter *(subject)*, measure, motion, overture, plan, platform, policy *(plan of action)*, principle *(axiom)*, project, proposal *(suggestion)*, question *(issue)*, rationale, recommendation, resolution *(formal statement)*, strategy, suggestion, theory, thesis, ultimatum
propositional apparent *(presumptive)*
propositum intention, matter *(subject)*, object, project, purpose, strategy
propound adduce, admonish *(advise)*, advocate, allege, annunciate, argue, assert, avouch *(avow)*, avow, bear *(adduce)*, claim *(maintain)*, defend, hold *(decide)*, issue *(publish)*, offer *(propose)*, posit, postulate, proffer, propose, submit *(give)*, utter
propounded alleged
proprietary ownership, proprietor
proprietary rights occupation *(possession)*
proprietas character *(personal quality)*, characteristic, feature *(characteristic)*, property *(distinctive attribute)*, trait
proprieties protocol *(etiquette)*
proprietor employer, landholder, landlord, landowner, principal *(director)*, tenant
proprietorship adverse possession, dominion *(absolute ownership)*, enjoyment *(use)*, interest *(ownership)*, occupancy, occupation *(possession)*, ownership, possession *(ownership)*, tenancy, title *(right)*
propriety admissibility, aptitude, behalf, behavior, conduct, decorum, deportment, expedience, formality, integrity, justice, qualification *(fitness)*, rectitude, right *(righteousness)*
proprius distinctive, essential *(required)*, individual, inherent, innate, particular *(specific)*, specific, typical
propugnaculum bulwark, safeguard
propulsare parry, repulse, stave
propulsion impetus
propulsive compelling, impulsive *(impelling)*
propulsive force impetus
prorate allocate, allot, apportion, charge *(assess)*, disburse *(distribute)*, distribute, divide *(distribute)*, parcel, partition
prorogare prolong
prorogate postpone
prorogation adjournment, cloture, deferment, delay, dissolution *(termination)*
prorogue adjourn, continue *(adjourn)*, defer *(put off)*, postpone, procrastinate, recess
prorsus in toto
proruption outbreak, outburst
prosaic average *(standard)*, jejune

(dull), languid, lifeless *(dull)*, mediocre, mundane, nondescript, ordinary, pedestrian, ponderous, stale, trite, typical, usual
prosaical mediocre, ordinary, prosaic
proscribe ban, bar *(hinder)*, block, border *(bound)*, censor, condemn *(ban)*, constrain *(restrain)*, debar, eliminate *(exclude)*, enjoin, exclude, forbid, forswear, inhibit, interdict, limit, order, outlaw, prohibit, reject, relegate, renounce, repudiate, restrain, restrict, sentence
proscribed barred, illegal, illegitimate *(illegal)*, illicit, impermissible, unauthorized
proscribed form procedure
proscribed person pariah
proscribere outlaw, proscribe *(prohibit)*
proscriptio proscription
proscription bar *(obstruction)*, boycott, check *(bar)*, constraint *(restriction)*, deterrence, deterrent, direction *(order)*, injunction, limitation, mandate, obstacle, obstruction, ostracism, prohibition, refusal, rejection, renunciation, restraint, veto
proscriptive prohibitive *(restrictive)*, restrictive
proscriptus outlaw
proscrit discard
prosecute accuse, arraign, complain *(charge)*, incriminate, lodge *(bring a complaint)*, pursue *(carry on)*
prosecute an inquiry delve
prosecute one's case plead *(argue a case)*
prosecute to a conclusion close *(terminate)*, conclude *(complete)*, consummate, follow-up
prosecuting attorney district attorney, prosecutor
prosecution action *(proceeding)*, arraignment, complainant, complaint, cross-examination, proceeding, prosecutor, pursuit *(chase)*
prosecutor accuser, complainant, district attorney, jurist
prosecutorial complaint information *(charge)*
proselyte partisan, persuade
proselytism persuasion
proselytize convert *(persuade)*, persuade
prosequi pursue *(chase)*
prospect chance *(possibility)*, contemplation, customer, expectation, likelihood, motive, opportunity, possibility, potential, probability
prospection expectation
prospective apparent *(presumptive)*, forthcoming, future, immediate *(imminent)*, imminent, pending *(imminent)*, proximate
prospective buyer patron *(regular customer)*
prospective client prospect *(prospective patron)*
prospective customer prospect *(prospective patron)*
prospector speculator
prospectus issuance, plan, program, proposition
prosper earn, gain, prevail *(triumph)*, progress, succeed *(attain)*

prosper auspicious
prospering successful
prosperitas prosperity
prosperity welfare
prosperous beneficial, opulent, successful
prosperous issue boom *(prosperity)*
prosperous outcome boom *(prosperity)*
prosperousness boom *(prosperity)*, prosperity, welfare
prosperus favorable *(advantageous)*, prosperous
prospicience expectation
prostitute betray *(lead astray)*, corrupt, deteriorate, misemploy, mistreat, pervert, pollute
prostitution misusage, perversion
prostrate disable, helpless *(powerless)*, overcome *(overwhelm)*, overthrow, servile, subservient
prostration impuissance
prosy jejune *(dull)*, mundane, pedestrian, prolix, prosaic, stale, usual
protagonist abettor, backer
protean aleatory *(uncertain)*, mutable, pliable, variable
protect care *(be cautious)*, care *(regard)*, conceal, conserve, cover *(guard)*, defend, ensconce, enshroud, ensure, envelop, foster, harbor, hedge, keep *(shelter)*, maintain *(sustain)*, patrol, police, preserve, save *(rescue)*, screen *(guard)*, shroud, side, sponsor, support *(assist)*, sustain *(prolong)*, uphold
protect against loss insure
protect from injury preserve
protected exempt, guarded, immune, impervious, inexpugnable, insusceptible *(resistant)*, safe, secure *(free from danger)*
protecting conservation, preventive
protection adoption *(affiliation)*, advantage, auspices, behalf, blackmail, bulwark, charge *(custody)*, conservation, coverage *(insurance)*, custody *(supervision)*, defense, direction *(guidance)*, ecology, gratuity *(bribe)*, haven, immunity, impunity, inviolability, lodging, panoply, patronage *(support)*, precaution, preservation, refuge, reinforcement, safeguard, safekeeping, security *(safety)*, shield, support *(assistance)*, surveillance, trust *(custody)*, veil, ward
protection against loss indemnity, insurance
protection money bribe
protective paternal, preventive, prophylactic, salutary
protective covering panoply
protective custody constraint *(imprisonment)*, detention, preservation, safekeeping
protective device barrier
protective fire barrage
protective outfit panoply
protector advocate *(counselor)*, apologist, backer, benefactor, guardian, peace officer, proponent, samaritan, shield, sponsor, warden
protectorship adoption *(affiliation)*, auspices, control *(supervision)*, management *(supervision)*, patronage *(support)*
protectory cache *(hiding place)*
protegé disciple
proteiform pliable, protean

protervitas audacity
protest admonition, avow, challenge, complain *(criticize)*, complaint, conflict, confront *(oppose)*, counter, counteract, cross *(disagree with)*, demur, denial, deprecate, differ *(disagree)*, disaccord, disaccord, disaffirm, disagree, disallow, disapprobation, disapprove *(reject)*, disavow, disown *(deny the validity)*, disparagement, dissension, dissent *(withhold assent)*, drawback, except *(object)*, exception *(objection)*, expostulate, fight *(counteract)*, gainsay, impugnation, negate, negation, nonconformity, object, objection, oppose, opposition, oppugn, outcry, picket, prohibit, reaction *(opposition)*, refuse, reject, remonstrance, remonstrate, renounce, reprehend, repudiate, resist *(oppose)*, resistance
protest against counter, counteract, decry, denounce *(condemn)*, inveigh, reproach
protest against a ruling exception *(objection)*
protest frivolously cavil
protestant dissident, heretic, recusant, reluctant
protestation avowal, complaint, contention *(opposition)*, criticism, denial, disapprobation, disapproval, dissension, drawback, exception *(objection)*, impugnation, negation, nonconformity, opposition, outcry, remonstrance
protested bill bad debt
protester malcontent
protesting dissenting, dissident, nonconsenting, remonstrative
prothonotary clerk
protocol bill *(proposed act)*, decorum, mode, practice *(procedure)*, rule *(guide)*, treaty
protogenic primordial
protomorphic rudimentary
protoplast prototype
prototypal primordial
prototype constant, exemplar, model, paradigm, pattern, rule *(guide)*, sample, standard
protract compound, continue *(prolong)*, delay, enlarge, extend *(enlarge)*, hold up *(delay)*, increase, last, procrastinate, prolong, sustain *(prolong)*
protracted chronic, profuse, prolix
protraction adjournment, advance *(increase)*, boom *(increase)*, continuance, continuation *(prolongation)*, continuity, filibuster, longevity
protrude overlap, project *(extend beyond)*
protrudent salient
protruding obtrusive, prominent, salient
protrusive obtrusive, prominent, salient
protuberant obtrusive, prominent, salient
protuberate project *(extend beyond)*
proud disdainful, inflated *(vain)*, supercilious
proud contempt disdain
provable convincing
prove ascertain, bear *(adduce)*, cite *(state)*, confirm, convince, corroborate, demonstrate *(establish)*, disabuse, document, establish *(show)*, evince, mani-

fest, reason *(persuade)*, substantiate, support *(corroborate)*, sustain *(confirm)*, testify, validate, verify *(confirm)*
prove acceptable satisfy *(fulfill)*
prove blameless exonerate
prove false disprove, rebut, refute
prove guiltless exculpate
prove inadequate fail *(lose)*
prove innocent absolve, acquit, clear
prove not guilty absolve, exculpate, exonerate
prove one's point convince
prove the contrary contradict, disprove, negate
prove the truth of justify
prove the validity of a will probate
prove to be a participant in involve *(implicate)*
prove to be wrong disprove
prove to the contrary disprove
prove treacherous defect
prove unreliable fail *(neglect)*
prove unsatisfactory fail *(lose)*
prove useless fail *(lose)*
prove warranted justify
proved dependable, reliable, unrefutable, valid
proved innocent acquitted
proved strength proof
provehere promote *(advance)*, raise *(advance)*
proven dependable, irrefutable, official, sound, undeniable, unrefutable
proven name goodwill
provenance birth *(lineage)*, derivation, genesis, origination, source
provender replenish
provenience derivation, origination, source
proverb maxim, phrase
proverbial trite
proverbial saying maxim
provide accommodate, avail *(bring about)*, bear *(yield)*, bequeath, bestow, clothe, dispense, enable, endow, endue, fund, furnish, give *(grant)*, hoard, impart, lend, make, pander, present *(make a gift)*, procure, produce *(manufacture)*, recruit, render *(administer)*, replenish, sell, stipulate, supply, transmit, yield *(produce a return)*
provide against forestall
provide an answer respond
provide an opportunity extend *(offer)*
provide capital finance, invest *(fund)*
provide capital again refinance
provide capital for capitalize *(provide capital)*, subsidize
provide financing subsidize
provide for bear *(support)*, capitalize *(provide capital)*, expect *(anticipate)*, fund, maintain *(sustain)*, nurture, plan, preserve, sponsor, subsidize, support *(assist)*
provide funds finance
provide funds for capitalize *(provide capital)*, subsidize
provide funds for again refinance
provide justification palliate *(excuse)*, support *(justify)*
provide means enable
provide money finance, fund, invest *(fund)*
provide money for capitalize *(provide capital)*, subsidize

provide refuge harbor

provide safety harbor

provide sanctuary harbor, preserve

provide subvention finance

provide the answer countercharge, resolve *(solve)*

provide the means implement

provide the wherewithal fund

provide with administer *(tender)*, lend, render *(administer)*

provide with a motive motivate

provide with an alibi excuse

provide with documents document

provide with information instruct *(teach)*

provide with nomenclature call *(title)*, identify, label

provide with proof document

provided with arms armed

provided without charge free *(at no charge)*, gratuitous *(given without recompense)*

providence discretion *(quality of being discreet)*, economy *(frugality)*, precaution, preparation, provision *(act of supplying)*, prudence

provident acute, careful, economical, frugal, judicious, juridical, politic, preparatory, preventive, prudent, vigilant

providentia forethought

providential auspicious, favorable *(advantageous)*, fitting, fortuitous, opportune, propitious, prosperous

provider materialman, supplier

providere provide *(arrange for)*

providing donative

providing evidence probative

providing proof probative

providing sanctuary conservation

providus circumspect, vigilant

province ambit, bailiwick, capacity *(sphere)*, circuit, coverage *(scope)*, department, district, division *(administrative unit)*, domain *(sphere of influence)*, jurisdiction, locality, part *(role)*, pursuit *(occupation)*, purview, realm, region, role, section *(vicinity)*, sphere, territory

provincia department, province, sphere

provincial local, naive, narrow, parochial, regional

provincialism prejudice *(preconception)*

proving cogent, convincing

provise stipulation

provision accommodation *(adjustment)*, aid, alimony, article *(distinct section of a writing)*, attornment, bear *(yield)*, bestow, budget, clause, condition *(contingent provision)*, contribution *(donation)*, dispensation *(act of dispensing)*, donation, endowment, forethought, fund, furnish, inheritance, limitation, precaution, preparation, principle *(axiom)*, qualification *(condition)*, ration, replenish, reservation *(condition)*, reserve, resource, safeguard, stock *(store)*, supply, title *(division)*, ultimatum

provision for damages ad damnum clause

provision of the law statute

provisional conditional, contingent, dubious, empirical, interim, interlocutory, qualified *(conditioned)*, restrictive, speculative, subject *(conditional)*, surro-

gate, temporary, tentative, transient, transitory, uncertain *(questionable)*, vicarious *(substitutional)*

provisional hypothesis proposition

provisional measure stopgap

provisional settlement modus vivendi

provisionally pro tempore, provided

provisionary conditional, qualified *(conditioned)*

provisioner supplier

provisioning equipment

provisions ammunition, cargo, maintenance *(support of spouse)*, merchandise, stock in trade, store *(depository)*, sustenance

provisions of a law legislation *(enactments)*

proviso arrangement *(understanding)*, article *(distinct section of a writing)*, attornment, clause, condition *(contingent provision)*, need *(requirement)*, option *(contractual provision)*, prerequisite, provision *(clause)*, qualification *(condition)*, requirement, reservation *(condition)*, salvo, specification, term *(provision)*, ultimatum

provisory conditional, dependent, interim, interlocutory, provisional, qualified *(conditioned)*, restrictive, tentative, transient

provocare defy

provocateur catalyst

provocatio appeal, defiance

provocation aggravation *(annoyance)*, catalyst, incentive, inducement, influence, instigation, motive, reason *(basis)*, stimulus

provocative catalyst, impertinent *(insolent)*, incentive, inducement, invitation, moving *(evoking emotion)*, offensive *(taking the initiative)*, persuasive, presumptuous, provocation, salacious, sapid, suggestive *(evocative)*, suggestive *(risqué)*, vexatious

provocator aggressor, demagogue

provoke aggravate *(annoy)*, agitate *(activate)*, annoy, antagonize, badger, bait *(harass)*, bait *(lure)*, cause, coax, contrive, discommode, discompose, evoke, exacerbate, foment, generate, harass, harrow, harry *(harass)*, hector, incense, incite, inspire, irritate, lobby, mistreat, molest *(annoy)*, occasion, offend *(insult)*, originate, persecute, perturb, pique, plague, press *(goad)*, prompt, spirit, stimulate, urge

provoke desire lure, motivate

provoke hatred alienate *(estrange)*, incense

provoke hatred against disaffect

provoke ire incense

provoked aggrieved *(harmed)*, bitter *(reproachful)*

provoker demagogue

provoking moving *(evoking emotion)*, offensive *(taking the initiative)*, persuasive, provocative, sapid, vexatious

provost plenipotentiary

prowess ability, efficiency, skill

prowl lurk, perambulate, pursue *(chase)*

prowl after hunt

prowler burglar

prowling burglary, stealthy

proxies deputation *(delegation)*

proximal adjacent, approximate, close *(near)*, contiguous, proximate

proximate approximate, border *(approach)*, close *(near)*, contiguous, immediate *(not distant)*, present *(attendant)*

proximate to situated

proximity presence *(attendance)*, propinquity *(similarity)*, vicinity

proximity of blood degree *(kinship)*

proximus proximate, related

proxy agency *(legal relationship)*, agent, attorney in fact, conduit *(intermediary)*, deputy, plenipotentiary, proctor, procurator, replacement, substitute, surrogate

proxyship delegation *(assignment)*

prudence caution *(vigilance)*, common sense, continence, deliberation, diligence *(care)*, discretion *(quality of being discreet)*, discrimination *(good judgment)*, economy *(frugality)*, expedience, precaution, preparation, sagacity, sense *(intelligence)*, temperance

prudens circumspect, deliberate, discreet, judicious, knowing, politic, prudent, reasonable *(rational)*, sensible, tactical

prudent acute, careful, circumspect, deliberate, diplomatic, discreet, economical, frugal, guarded, judicial, judicious, juridical, noncommittal, politic, provident *(frugal)*, provident *(showing foresight)*, responsive, safe, sensible, solid *(sound)*, vigilant

prudent conduct management *(judicious use)*

prudentia caution *(vigilance)*, discretion *(quality of being discreet)*, discrimination *(good judgment)*, prudence, sagacity, sense *(intelligence)*

prudential judicial, judicious, juridical, politic, provident *(showing foresight)*, prudent, solid *(sound)*

prudently contrived politic

prune decrease, diminish, minimize, retrench

prurience pornography

prurient dissolute, immoral, lascivious, lecherous, lewd, salacious

pry delve, force *(break)*, hunt, research, spy

pry into examine *(study)*, frisk, inquire, peruse, probe, scrutinize, search

prying encroachment, interest *(concern)*, interrogative, obtrusive

pseudo false *(not genuine)*, imitation, quasi, spurious, surrogate, synthetic

pseudonym sobriquet

pseudonymous quasi

psyche spirit

psychiatric hospital asylum *(hospital)*

psychiatric ward asylum *(hospital)*

psychological habits character *(personal quality)*

psychologically abnormal non compos mentis

psychopathic non compos mentis

psychotic non compos mentis

puberty adolescence

pubes adult

pubescence adolescence

pubescent juvenile, minor

public blatant *(conspicuous)*, civic, common *(shared)*, competitive *(open)*, conspicuous, famous, manifest, national, open *(accessible)*, overt, patent, political, populace, population

public address peroration

public announcement canon, charter *(declaration of rights)*, declaration, issuance, proclamation, publication *(disclosure)*

public attorney district attorney, jurist

public avowal proclamation

public building edifice

public business utility *(public service)*

public company utility *(public service)*

public corporation utility *(public service)*

public declaration avouchment

public disclosure common knowledge

public disgrace dishonor *(shame)*

public distribution publicity

public disturbance commotion

public economy finance

public enemy convict, criminal, foe, outlaw

public esteem character *(reputation)*, distinction *(reputation)*

public favor goodwill, prestige

public industry utility *(public service)*

public inquest hearing

public knowledge common knowledge

public manners conduct

public notice common knowledge, declaration, notoriety, proclamation, publicity

public office holder official

public opinion poll *(canvass)*

public opponent foe

public pleader district attorney

public proceeding hearing

public prosecutor complainant, district attorney, prosecutor

public recognition mention *(tribute)*

public relations publicity

public reproach bad repute, infamy

public revenue finance

public sale auction

public sale of property auction

public servant caretaker *(one fulfilling the function of office)*, legislator, politician

public servants government *(political administration)*

public service nonprofit, politics

public speaking declamation, rhetoric *(skilled speech)*

public spirit philanthropy

public statement charter *(declaration of rights)*

public support goodwill

public treasury bank

public uprising revolution

public wrong crime

public-spirited philanthropic

publicare condemn *(seize)*, confiscate

publication charter *(declaration of rights)*, declaration, disclosure *(act of disclosing)*, disclosure *(something disclosed)*, issuance, pandect *(treatise)*, proclamation, pronouncement, publicity

publicist attorney, barrister, promoter

publicists press

publicity issuance, notice *(announce-*

ment), notification, notoriety, promotion *(encouragement)*, story *(narrative)*

publicize annunciate, bare, communicate, correspond *(communicate)*, denude, disseminate, divulge, herald, issue *(publish)*, notify, proclaim, promulgate, propagate *(spread)*, publish, spread, utter

publicized notorious

publicizer harbinger

publicly accuse condemn *(blame)*, denounce *(condemn)*, denounce *(inform against)*

publicly indecent lewd

publicly known common *(customary)*

publicly owned national

publicly recognized standing character *(reputation)*

publicness common knowledge

publicus common *(shared)*, official, political, public *(known)*

publish annunciate, apprise, bear *(adduce)*, circulate, convey *(communicate)*, disclose, disseminate, divulge, enunciate, expose, herald, inform *(notify)*, manifest, notice *(give formal warning)*, notify, post, proclaim, promulgate, propagate *(spread)*, report *(disclose)*, reveal, signify *(inform)*, speak, spread, utter

publish a falsehood libel

publish abroad disseminate

published patent, public *(known)*

publishers press

puckishness mischief

pudency embarrassment

pueri child, children

puerile inept *(incompetent)*, jejune *(lacking maturity)*

puerile person juvenile

puerilis juvenile, juvenile, puerile

puerility adolescence, minority *(infancy)*

puff up inflate

puffed inflated *(enlarged)*

puffed up inflated *(enlarged)*, proud *(conceited)*, supercilious, turgid

puffery overstatement, rodomontade

puffy inflated *(enlarged)*

pugilatio fight *(battle)*

pugilist contender

pugna affray, fight *(argument)*, fray

pugnacious argumentative, contentious, hostile, litigious, perverse, petulant, polemic, querulous, spartan

pugnaciousness belligerency

pugnacity belligerency

pugnare contend *(dispute)*

pugnax contentious

puisne inferior *(lower in position)*

puissance clout, dint, influence, main force, potential, power, predominance, quality *(excellence)*, strength, validity

puissant cogent, compelling, considerable, efficient, in full force, indomitable, inexpugnable, influential, irresistible, omnipotent, potent, powerful, predominant, strong

puissant prevailing *(having superior force)*

puling querulous

pull draw *(attraction)*, draw *(extract)*, educe, evulsion, extract, predominance, pressure, stress *(strain)*

pull aside divert

pull back retreat, withdraw

pull different ways bicker

pull down derogate, subvert

pull in discipline *(control)*, inhibit

pull into shape frame *(formulate)*

pull out abandon *(withdraw)*, disinter, educe, eviscerate, extirpate, extract, leave *(depart)*, quit *(evacuate)*, relinquish, renege, secede

pull strings influence, lobby, manipulate *(control unfairly)*

pull strings for prefer

pull the strings predominate *(command)*

pull together cooperate, unite

pull up disinter

pull up by the roots extirpate, obliterate

pull wires manipulate *(control unfairly)*

pullalare pullulate

pulling out evulsion

pullulate germinate, increase, propagate *(increase)*

pulsare beat *(strike)*

pulse beat *(pulsate)*

pulseless lifeless *(dead)*

pulverize break *(fracture)*, destroy *(efface)*

pulverized broken *(fractured)*

pummel beat *(strike)*, fight *(battle)*, lash *(strike)*

pump up inflate

punch beat *(strike)*

punctilio decorum, formality, particular, protocol *(etiquette)*

punctilious accurate, close *(rigorous)*, conscientious, detailed, diligent, draconian, exact, meticulous, painstaking, particular *(exacting)*, precise, rigid, strict

punctiliously faithfully

punctiliousness decorum, particularity

punctual exact, expeditious, instant, precise, prompt

punctuality dispatch *(promptness)*, regularity

punctualness dispatch *(promptness)*

punctuate discontinue *(break continuity)*, interrupt, reaffirm

punctuated disjunctive *(tending to disjoin)*

punctum vote

punctum temporis instant

puncture break *(fracture)*, debunk, enter *(penetrate)*, lancinate, penetrate, pierce *(lance)*

pundit mastermind

pungent bitter *(acrid tasting)*, caustic, incisive, mordacious, trenchant

punic faith bad faith

punire condemn *(punish)*

punish beat *(strike)*, convict, fine, inflict, mulct *(fine)*, penalize, repay, reprehend

punish by pecuniary penalty fine

punish with death execute *(sentence to death)*

punishable culpable, delinquent *(guilty of a misdeed)*, illegal, impermissible

punishable act tortious act

punishable by law illicit

punishable offense misdemeanor

punishing cruel, disciplinary *(punitory)*, harsh, penal, punitive

punishing experience condemnation (*punishment*)

punishment condemnation (*punishment*), conviction (*finding of guilt*), cost (*penalty*), expiation, forfeiture (*act of forfeiting*), forfeiture (*thing forfeited*), infliction, penalty, reprisal, retribution, revenge, sentence, vengeance

punishment fixed by law penalty

punishment prescribed by law penalty

punishment without trial lynch law

punition condemnation (*punishment*), conviction (*finding of guilt*), correction (*punishment*), punishment, reprisal

punitive disciplinary (*punitory*), penal, severe, vindictive

punitive action reprisal, retribution, revenge

punitory penal, punitive, vindictive

punt bet

punter bettor

puny negligible, null (*insignificant*), paltry, petty

pupil disciple, neophyte, novice, protégé

purblind opaque

purchasable mercenary, venal

purchase acquire (*secure*), buy, deal, leverage, procure, takeover, trade (*commerce*), trade, transaction

purchase from patronize (*trade with*)

purchase money price

purchase on time credit (*delayed payment*)

purchase on trust credit (*delayed payment*)

purchase price cost (*price*)

purchase without a guaranty caveat emptor

purchase without a warranty caveat emptor

purchased at one's risk caveat emptor

purchaser client, consumer, customer, patron (*regular customer*)

purchaser of goods consumer

purchaser of goods from another customer

purchaser of stolen goods fence

purchaser of stolen property fence

pure absolute (*ideal*), authentic, blameless, clean, clear (*apparent*), genuine, honest, inculpable, inviolate, moral, natural, original (*initial*), pellucid, simple, stark, sterling, theoretical, true (*authentic*), unadulterated, unblemished, upright

pure in heart clean

pure-hearted clean

purebred genuine

purely only, solely (*purely*)

purgare absolve, acquit, justify, vindicate

purgatio justification

purgation absolution, acquittal, catharsis, clemency, confession

purgatorial penitent

purge absolve, catharsis, clear, decontaminate, deplete, deportation, discharge (*liberate*), dismiss (*discharge*), displace (*remove*), eliminate (*eradicate*), eradicate, exclusion, exonerate, expel, expulsion, expurgate, extirpate, free, oust, pardon, removal, remove (*eliminate*)

purge oneself confess

purged clear (*free from criminal charges*)

purified sacrosanct

purify decontaminate, expurgate, fix (*repair*), meliorate

purify by removing the foreign and nonessential distill

purifying medicinal, remedial

puritanic severe, uncompromising

puritanical draconian, rigid, severe, strict, stringent, tartuffish, uncompromising

purity honor (*good reputation*), integrity, rectitude

purlieu bailiwick, periphery, vicinity

purlieus border, locality, location, part (*place*), region, section (*vicinity*)

purloin abduct, bilk, carry away, cheat, defalcate, deprive, despoil, embezzle, hold up (*rob*), impropriate, jostle (*pickpocket*), loot, peculate, pilfer, pirate (*reproduce without authorization*), plunder, poach, rob, steal

purloiner embezzler, hoodlum, thief

purloining embezzlement, theft

purloinment burglary, theft

purport amount (*result*), bespeak, connotation, consequence (*significance*), content (*meaning*), context, cornerstone, design (*intent*), gist (*substance*), import, intent, main point, materiality (*consequence*), meaning, point (*purpose*), pretend, signification, signify (*denote*), spirit, substance (*essential nature*), tenor, value

purported ostensible, putative, specious

purpose animus, basis, cause (*reason*), contemplation, content (*meaning*), cornerstone, design (*intent*), destination, end (*intent*), forethought, function, goal, ground, idea, impetus, intend, intent, intention, mission, motive, object, objective, plan, predetermination, project, pursuit (*goal*), purview, reason (*basis*), resolution (*decision*), resolve (*decide*), signification, undertaking (*attempt*), use, volition, will (*desire*)

purpose in view design (*intent*)

purposed aforethought, deliberate, intentional, tactical, willful

purposeful decisive, deliberate, earnest, express, industrious, intense, intentional, knowing, persistent, pertinacious, resolute, serious (*devoted*), tactical, voluntary, willful

purposefully knowingly, purposely

purposefulness diligence (*perseverance*)

purposeless arbitrary and capricious, casual, expendable, nugatory, random, unavailing, unintentional, unwitting, vacuous

purposive aforethought, express, purposeful

purse reward, stake (*award*), treasury

purser comptroller

pursuance course, endeavor, industry (*activity*)

pursue adhere (*persist*), approach, assume (*undertake*), attempt, bait (*harass*), chase, continue (*persevere*), delve, desire, endeavor, exercise (*discharge a function*), follow-up, hunt, inquire, keep (*continue*), maintain (*carry on*), perse-

vere, ply, practice (*engage in*), prosecute (*carry forward*), race, remain (*continue*), research, resume, search, specialize, strive, study, trace (*follow*), undertake

pursue a claim sue

pursue a course perform (*execute*)

pursue an inquiry audit, canvass, investigate, probe, research

pursue in court litigate

pursue relentlessly persist

pursuer addict

pursuit activity, assignment (*task*), business (*occupation*), calling, career, course, design (*intent*), employment, endeavor, enterprise (*undertaking*), function, industry (*activity*), industry (*business*), inquiry (*systematic investigation*), labor (*work*), livelihood, market (*demand*), mission, objective, occupation (*vocation*), operation, position (*business status*), post, practice (*professional business*), probe, profession (*vocation*), project, quest, research, specialty (*special aptitude*), struggle, trade (*occupation*), undertaking (*business*), undertaking (*enterprise*), work (*employment*)

pursuit by a law enforcement agency prosecution (*criminal trial*)

pursuits affairs

purulent toxic

purus clean, pure, unblemished, unconditional

purvey bear (*yield*), fund, furnish, pander, provide (*supply*), replenish, supply

purveyance provision (*act of supplying*)

purveyor supplier

purview area (*province*), coverage (*scope*), jurisdiction, scope

push cajole, coerce, constrain (*compel*), dispatch (*send off*), exhort, foray, force (*coerce*), impact, impel, impetus, importune, impulse, incite, jostle (*bump into*), launch (*project*), main force, pressure, pressure, project (*impel forward*), promote (*organize*), prompt, provoke, spirit, stimulus, struggle, urge

push ahead expedite, proceed (*go forward*)

push aside divert, doubt (*hesitate*), hold up (*delay*), ignore, misprize, postpone, procrastinate, relegate

push away dispel, eject (*expel*), parry, stave

push back repel (*drive back*), repulse

push forward expedite, facilitate

push into browbeat

push on hasten, move (*alter position*), proceed (*go forward*), progress

push out dislodge, eject (*expel*)

push through dispatch (*send off*), expedite

push together impact

push too far incense, tax (*overwork*)

push toward pursue (*strive to gain*)

push up promote (*advance*)

pushing impulsive (*impelling*)

pushy eager, obtrusive

pusillanimity fear

pusillanimous caitiff, recreant

pusillus paltry

put deposit (*place*), dispose (*incline*), impute, introduce, locate, lodge (*house*), phrase, plant (*place firmly*), raise (*ad-

vance), repose *(place)*, situated, submit *(give)*

put a barrier around enclose, include

put a damper on discourage

put a false appearance on misrepresent

put a false appearance upon disguise

put a false construction on distort, misconceive, misread, misrepresent, misunderstand

put a false construction upon perjure, profess *(pretend)*

put a false sense on distort, misconstrue, mistake

put a mark on brand *(mark)*

put a mark upon label

put a meaning on comment, construe *(translate)*

put a restraint upon check *(restrain)*

put a stop to cease, check *(restrain)*, clog, close *(terminate)*, condemn *(ban)*, constrain *(restrain)*, desist, deter, eliminate *(eradicate)*, enjoin, estop, finish, hold up *(delay)*, interrupt, quit *(discontinue)*, strangle, toll *(stop)*

put a wrong construction on misread, misunderstand

put aboard load

put about circulate

put across explain

put ahead conduce

put along side border *(approach)*

put alongside compare, juxtapose

put an approximate price on estimate

put an embargo on bar *(hinder)*, condemn *(ban)*

put an end to abate *(extinguish)*, annul, cancel, cease, check *(restrain)*, condemn *(ban)*, destroy *(void)*, discontinue *(abandon)*, dispatch *(put to death)*, eliminate *(eradicate)*, enjoin, estop, expunge, extinguish, extirpate, finish, halt, interrupt, quash, quit *(discontinue)*, stay *(halt)*, stop, subvert, terminate

put an erroneous construction on distort, misunderstand

put an indication on brand *(mark)*

put an interpretation construe *(translate)*

put an obligation upon commit *(entrust)*

put aside abandon *(relinquish)*, defer *(put off)*, eliminate *(exclude)*, except *(exclude)*, exclude, forfeit, hoard, hold up *(delay)*, isolate, keep *(shelter)*, postpone, pretermit, reserve, select, set aside *(reserve)*, waive

put asunder disconnected, divorce

put at a disadvantage embarrass, penalize

put at ease assure *(give confidence to)*

put at hazard compromise *(endanger)*, pawn

put at interest deposit *(submit to a bank)*

put at stake pawn

put away keep *(shelter)*, preserve, retain *(keep in possession)*, set aside *(reserve)*

put back reconstitute, reinstate, renew *(begin again)*, replace, restore *(return)*

put back into service reinstate

put before instruct *(teach)*

put behind bars imprison, jail, lock

put beside juxtapose

put between interject, intersperse

put beyond the protection of the law outlaw

put by store

put close together juxtapose

put confidence in rely, trust

put down cast *(register)*, defeat, demean *(make lower)*, derogate, dispatch *(put to death)*, enter *(record)*, humiliate, kill *(defeat)*, quash, repress, stifle, subdue, subjugate

put faith in confide *(trust)*, rely

put first preface

put forth argue, communicate, emit, exert, extend *(offer)*, issue *(publish)*, move *(judicially request)*, offer *(propose)*, pass *(determine)*, plead *(allege in a legal action)*, posit, postulate, present *(introduce)*, profess *(avow)*, propound, publish, pullulate, submit *(give)*

put forth an effort attempt, strive

put forth effort try *(attempt)*

put forth for acceptance offer *(propose)*

put forth for consideration offer *(propose)*

put forward alleged, circulate, claim *(maintain)*, conduce, declare, extend *(offer)*, flaunt, hold out *(deliberate on an offer)*, introduce, issue *(publish)*, move *(judicially request)*, offer *(propose)*, plead *(allege in a legal action)*, pose *(propound)*, posit, postulate, prefer, profess *(avow)*, proffer, propose, propound, submit *(give)*, tender

put forward for consideration extend *(offer)*, introduce, offer *(propose)*

put forward in opposition object

put goods in load

put in enter *(insert)*, interpose, introduce

put in a bad light defame, denounce *(condemn)*, pillory

put in a cell constrain *(imprison)*, imprison

put in a claim for call *(demand)*, desire

put in a conspicuous place expose

put in accord arbitrate *(conciliate)*

put in action apply *(put in practice)*, employ *(make use of)*, enforce, execute *(accomplish)*, exercise *(use)*, exert, manipulate *(utilize skillfully)*

put in an affidavit avouch *(avow)*, plead *(allege in a legal action)*

put in an appearance appear *(attend court proceedings)*, emerge, issue *(send forth)*, report *(present oneself)*

put in array classify, file *(arrange)*, organize *(arrange)*

put in bodily fear menace

put in care of charge *(empower)*, confide *(trust)*

put in charge entrust

put in check balk, counter

put in commission assign *(designate)*, delegate, invest *(vest)*

put in concealment blind *(obscure)*, camouflage, plant *(covertly place)*

put in condition fix *(repair)*

put in custody commit *(institutionalize)*

put in danger expose

put in durance arrest *(apprehend)*

put in duress arrest *(apprehend)*, seize *(apprehend)*

put in execution commence

put in fear browbeat, intimidate, menace

put in for request

put in force administer *(conduct)*, authorize, constitute *(establish)*, effectuate, enact, enforce, execute *(accomplish)*, implement, impose *(enforce)*, legislate, pass *(approve)*, perform *(adhere to)*, perform *(execute)*

put in good condition fix *(repair)*

put in hazard endanger

put in in a bad light denigrate

put in irons fetter, handcuff, imprison, trammel

put in jeopardy compromise *(endanger)*, endanger

put in motion agitate *(shake up)*, dispatch *(send off)*, establish *(launch)*, exercise *(discharge a function)*, impel, launch *(initiate)*, move *(alter position)*

put in one's hands delegate

put in operation apply *(put in practice)*, capitalize *(seize the chance)*, employ *(make use of)*, enforce

put in opposition confront *(oppose)*, oppose, polarize

put in order classify, emend, file *(arrange)*, fix *(arrange)*, fix *(repair)*, marshal, orchestrate, organize *(arrange)*, pigeonhole, regulate *(adjust)*, repair, restore *(renew)*, settle, sort

put in other words construe *(translate)*, elucidate, explain

put in pawn pledge *(deposit)*

put in peril expose

put in place locate

put in pledge pawn

put in possession bequeath, devolve, grant *(transfer formally)*, instate, seize *(confiscate)*, vest

put in practice exercise *(use)*, exploit *(make use of)*, implement, perform *(adhere to)*, ply

put in production manufacture

put in proper order fix *(arrange)*

put in readiness arrange *(methodize)*

put in repair fix *(repair)*, restore *(renew)*

put in restraint apprehend *(arrest)*

put in safekeeping delegate

put in shape fix *(repair)*

put in slyly foist

put in stealthily foist

put in the hands of commit *(entrust)*, endow

put in the place of change, displace *(replace)*, supersede

put in uniform clothe

put in view expose

put in words communicate, enunciate, express

put in writing enter *(record)*, inscribe, note *(record)*, record

put into inject

put into a cage imprison

put into a receptacle enclose

put into a systematic form orchestrate

put into a temper incense

put into action exercise *(discharge a function)*, expedite, exploit *(make use*

of), perpetrate
put into bodily form embody
put into circulation circulate, diffuse, dispel, issue *(publish)*, publish
put into condition remedy
put into disorder confound
put into effect enact, enforce, exercise *(discharge a function)*, implement, operate, pass *(approve)*, perpetrate, ply, render *(administer)*
put into execution enforce
put into force inflict
put into isolation confine
put into language phrase
put into motion cast *(throw)*
put into operation exploit *(make use of)*, manipulate *(utilize skillfully)*
put into practice exercise *(discharge a function)*, operate, transact
put into shape formulate, frame *(formulate)*, organize *(arrange)*, remedy, renew *(refurbish)*, repair
put into the hands of deliver
put into words observe *(remark)*, phrase, relate *(tell)*, speak
put money down bet
put off adjourn, delay, deter, hold up *(delay)*, pause, postpone, pretermit, procrastinate, stall, stave, suspend
put off a decision doubt *(hesitate)*
put off the scent misdirect
put off the track divert, obfuscate
put off to a future time hold up *(delay)*
put on betray *(lead astray)*, levy, pretend, prevaricate, specious
put on a false front pretend
put on a firm basis establish *(entrench)*
put on a pedestal elevate, honor
put on an act fake
put on board load
put on deceitfully assume *(simulate)*
put on display produce *(offer to view)*
put on guard caution, forewarn, portend
put on one's guard alert, notice *(give formal warning)*
put on paper note *(record)*, record
put on payroll hire
put on record cast *(register)*, enter *(record)*, file *(place among official records)*, note *(record)*, record, set down
put on sale sell
put on speed hasten
put on the retired list discharge *(dismiss)*
put on the scale weigh
put on the stage produce *(offer to view)*
put on trial hear *(give a legal hearing)*, impeach, sue
put one's case plead *(argue a case)*
put one's mind to concentrate *(pay attention)*
put one's trust in swear
put one's veto to condemn *(ban)*
put one's veto upon bar *(hinder)*
put oneself out endeavor
put out depose *(remove)*, disadvantage, disappointed, discompose, dislodge, disoblige, displace *(remove)*, eject *(evict)*, exclude, expel, extinguish, issue *(publish)*, oust, perturb, provoke, publish, remove *(dismiss from office)*
put out at interest invest *(fund)*

put out of action disable
put out of combat disarm *(divest of arms)*
put out of commission impair
put out of countenance bait *(harass)*, humiliate, pique
put out of house by legal process evict
put out of humor irritate, provoke
put out of joint luxate
put out of matrimony divorce
put out of mind dismiss *(put out of consideration)*
put out of order disorganize, upset
put out of place luxate
put out of possession depose *(remove)*, eject *(evict)*
put out of sight blind *(obscure)*, cloak, cover *(conceal)*, hide, plant *(covertly place)*
put out of the way dispatch *(put to death)*
put out of wedlock divorce
put over continue *(adjourn)*
put over to a future date continue *(adjourn)*
put pressure on bait *(harass)*, browbeat, coerce, constrain *(compel)*, enforce, insist, lobby, press *(constrain)*, press *(goad)*
put questions to examine *(interrogate)*
put right disabuse, edit, emend, help, redress, repair, restore *(renew)*
put side by side juxtapose
put something across bilk
put something over bilk, dupe, illude
put something over on betray *(lead astray)*
put straight disabuse
put the blame on charge *(accuse)*, convict, impeach
put through attain, pass *(approve)*, prosecute *(carry forward)*
put through a deal dicker
put through paces discipline *(train)*
put to call *(appeal to)*, pose *(propound)*
put to a wrong use convert *(misappropriate)*
put to advantage capitalize *(seize the chance)*
put to death destroy *(efface)*, dispatch *(put to death)*, execute *(sentence to death)*, extinguish, kill *(murder)*, slay
put to death according to law execute *(sentence to death)*
put to flight repel *(drive back)*, repulse
put to inconvenience discommode
put to press publish
put to rest lull
put to rights rectify
put to rout beat *(defeat)*
put to service capitalize *(seize the chance)*, employ *(make use of)*, exploit *(make use of)*
put to shame brand *(stigmatize)*, denigrate, humiliate, pillory, reproach, sully
put to sleep drug, lull
put to the proof prove
put to the test probe, prove
put to the vote choose
put to use apply *(put in practice)*, em-

ploy *(make use of)*, exercise *(use)*, exploit *(make use of)*, profit, resort
put to work employ *(engage services)*, engage *(hire)*, exercise *(use)*, exploit *(make use of)*, hire, retain *(employ)*
put to wrong use exploit *(take advantage of)*
put together affix, annex *(add)*, attach *(join)*, cement, collect *(gather)*, commingle, connect *(join together)*, consolidate *(strengthen)*, consolidate *(unite)*, constitute *(compose)*, create, devise *(invent)*, fabricate *(construct)*, forge *(produce)*, form, formulate, frame *(construct)*, incorporate *(include)*, join *(bring together)*, make, manufacture
put under an injunction condemn *(ban)*, enjoin, forbid
put under an interdiction condemn *(ban)*, enjoin
put under arrest apprehend *(arrest)*, confine, constrain *(imprison)*, detain *(hold in custody)*, immure
put under contract engage *(hire)*
put under duress kidnap
put under embargo enjoin
put under lock and key imprison
put under obligation compel, constrain *(compel)*, force *(coerce)*, press *(constrain)*
put under prohibition condemn *(ban)*
put under restraint arrest *(apprehend)*, check *(restrain)*, coerce, confine, constrain *(imprison)*, constrain *(restrain)*, control *(restrain)*, detain *(hold in custody)*, fetter, hold up *(delay)*, imprison, jail, restrict
put under suspicion compromise *(endanger)*
put under the ban enjoin
put under water immerse *(plunge into)*
put up build *(construct)*, invest *(fund)*, nominate, pledge *(deposit)*, proffer
put up a front fake
put up a petition move *(judicially request)*
put up a request call *(appeal to)*, plead *(implore)*
put up a sign post
put up a struggle parry
put up for sale handle *(trade)*, sell, vend
put up petitions pray
put up the money finance, lend, sponsor
put up with authorize, bear *(tolerate)*, endure *(suffer)*, forbear, submit *(yield)*, suffer *(permit)*, tolerate
put upon record inscribe
putare impression
putative plausible, presumptive
putrefaction deterioration, spoilage
putrefied tainted *(contaminated)*
putrefy decay, degenerate, infect, spoil *(impair)*, taint *(contaminate)*
putrescence spoilage
putrid loathsome, offensive *(offending)*, tainted *(contaminated)*
putridity deterioration
putting in custody commitment *(confinement)*
putting in order disposition *(determination)*

putting off deferment, delay
putting out expulsion
putting together accession *(annexation)*
puzzle complication, confound, confuse *(bewilder)*, confusion *(ambiguity)*, dilemma, disconcert, disturb, enigma, hoodwink, involution, muddle, mystery, obfuscate, paradox, perplex, pose *(propound)*, problem, question *(issue)*, secret
puzzle out solve
puzzle over doubt *(hesitate)*, ponder, reflect *(ponder)*, speculate *(conjecture)*
puzzled lost *(disoriented)*
puzzlement ambiguity, cloud *(suspicion)*, confusion *(ambiguity)*, dilemma, quandary
puzzling debatable, difficult, elusive, enigmatic, equivocal, esoteric, hidden, inapprehensible, incomprehensible, indefinable, inexplicable, inexpressive, inscrutable, labyrinthine, mysterious, opaque, peculiar *(curious)*, problematic, recondite, uncertain *(ambiguous)*
puzzling alternative dilemma
puzzling problem enigma
pylon portal
pyramid build *(augment)*, parlay *(exploit successfully)*
pyromania arson
pyrotic caustic
pythonic ominous, portentous *(ominous)*, prophetic

Q

quack fake
quackery abortion *(fiasco)*, fraud, hypocrisy
quadrate comport *(agree with)*
quadrate with cohere *(adhere)*
quaerere investigate, speculate *(conjecture)*
quaesitor judge
quaestio inquest, inquiry *(systematic investigation)*, interrogation, question *(inquiry)*, subject *(topic)*, trial *(legal proceeding)*
quaestuosus gainful, lucrative
quaestus earnings, income, profit
quaff carouse
quagmire impasse, pitfall, plight, quandary
quaint eccentric, nonconforming, novel, outdated, outmoded
quake beat *(pulsate)*, cataclysm
quaking trepidation
qualification caliber *(mental capacity)*, capacity *(aptitude)*, capacity *(authority)*, clause, condition *(contingent provision)*, control *(restriction)*, correction *(change)*, degree *(academic title)*, discipline *(training)*, discretion *(quality of being discreet)*, doubt *(indecision)*, drawback, education, experience *(background)*, extenuating circumstances, faculty *(ability)*, gift *(flair)*, limitation, modification, necessary, necessity, performance *(workmanship)*, potential, preparation, propensity, provision *(clause)*, reservation *(condition)*, restriction, salvo, sine qua non, specialty *(special aptitude)*, term *(provision)*
qualifications competence *(ability)*
qualified admissible, capable, compe-

tent, conditional, deft, dependent, desirable *(qualified)*, eligible, entitled, expert, familiar *(informed)*, fit, literate, practiced, professional *(trained)*, proficient, sciential, suitable, veteran
qualified endorsement without recourse
qualified person expert, mastermind, specialist
qualified practitioner professional
qualify allay, allow *(authorize)*, alter, delegate, discipline *(train)*, empower, enable, enfranchise, extenuate, instill, instruct *(teach)*, lessen, moderate *(temper)*, modify *(alter)*, modify *(moderate)*, palliate *(abate)*, pass *(satisfy requirements)*, restrict, satisfy *(fulfill)*, specialize, validate
qualifying mitigating, palliative *(excusing)*, preparatory, restrictive
qualifying factors circumstances
qualifying reasons extenuating circumstances
qualities character *(personal quality)*, temperament
quality characteristic, color *(complexion)*, complexion, condition *(state)*, differential, feature *(characteristic)*, gift *(flair)*, intonation, merit, meritorious, premium, property *(distinctive attribute)*, select, speciality, specialty *(distinctive mark)*, status, sterling, trait, value, weight *(importance)*, worth
quality of being certain certainty
quality of being equal and fair equity *(justice)*
quality of being singular identity *(individuality)*
quality of execution performance *(workmanship)*
quality of work performance *(workmanship)*
quality-minded particular *(exacting)*
qualm apprehension *(fear)*, doubt *(indecision)*, doubt *(suspicion)*, fear, hesitation, misgiving, scruple, suspicion *(mistrust)*
qualmish diffident, disinclined, hesitant
qualmishness doubt *(indecision)*, doubt *(suspicion)*
qualms reluctance
quandary complication, confusion *(ambiguity)*, deadlock, dilemma, disturbance, doubt *(indecision)*, imbroglio, impasse, incertitude, indecision, plight, predicament, problem, quagmire
quantification appraisal, measurement, rating
quantified definite
quantify calculate, measure, pinpoint, rate
quantitas quantity
quantity bulk, conglomeration, corpus, extent, measurement, part *(portion)*, quota, ration, selection *(collection)*, unit *(item)*
quantity produced output
quantum bulk, proportion, quantity, quota
quarantine captivity, confine, constraint *(imprisonment)*, contain *(enclose)*, detain *(hold in custody)*, detention, durance, exclude, immure, insulate, isolate, ostracism, seclude, sequester *(seclude)*

quarantine station captivity
quarrel altercation, argument *(contention)*, bicker, brawl, challenge, collide *(clash)*, commotion, conflict, conflict, confrontation *(altercation)*, contend *(dispute)*, contention *(opposition)*, contest *(dispute)*, contradict, contravention, controversy *(argument)*, disaccord, disaccord, disagree, disagreement, dissension, dissent *(differ in opinion)*, dissidence, embroilment, feud, fight *(argument)*, fracas, fray, incompatibility *(difference)*, object, outbreak, split, strife, struggle, variance *(disagreement)*
quarrel noisily brawl
quarrel over contest, dispute *(contest)*
quarreling abusive, argument *(contention)*, conflict, contention *(opposition)*, discord, dissenting, dissident
quarrelsome argumentative, contentious, disorderly, dissenting, fractious, litigious, negative, petulant, polemic, pugnacious, querulous
quarrelsomeness contention *(opposition)*
quarry extract, victim
quarter circuit, deposit *(place)*, disjoint, district, dwell *(reside)*, harbor, indulgence, lenience, locality, locate, location, lodge *(house)*, lodge *(reside)*, part *(place)*, pity, region, territory
quartered situated
quarters building *(structure)*, domicile, dwelling, habitation *(dwelling place)*, home *(domicile)*, house, inhabitation *(place of dwelling)*, lodging, premises *(buildings)*, residence
quash abate *(extinguish)*, abolish, abrogate *(annul)*, cancel, censor, condemn *(ban)*, contain *(restrain)*, discharge *(release from obligation)*, disinherit, dissolve *(terminate)*, eliminate *(eradicate)*, enjoin, expunge, extinguish, extirpate, invalidate, kill *(defeat)*, negate, nullify, obliterate, overcome *(surmount)*, overthrow, overwhelm, prohibit, refute, repeal, rescind, revoke, subjugate, suppress, upset, vacate *(void)*, vitiate, withdraw
quash the conviction clear
quashed invalid, lifeless *(dead)*, null *(invalid)*, null and void
quashing avoidance *(cancellation)*, deterrence, dismissal *(termination of a proceeding)*, rescission
quasi imitation, spurious, synthetic
quasi pendent
quaver beat *(pulsate)*
queer eccentric, irregular *(not usual)*, ludicrous, noteworthy, peculiar *(curious)*, prodigious *(amazing)*, singular, unaccustomed
queerness quirk *(idiosyncrasy)*
quell abate *(extinguish)*, allay, alleviate, arrest *(stop)*, assuage, beat *(defeat)*, cancel, cease, condemn *(ban)*, contain *(restrain)*, decrease, defeat, destroy *(efface)*, deter, diminish, eliminate *(eradicate)*, enjoin, expunge, extinguish, extirpate, halt, impede, kill *(defeat)*, lull, moderate *(temper)*, mollify, obliterate, obtund, overcome *(surmount)*, override, overthrow, overturn, overwhelm, pacify, palliate *(abate)*, prevail *(triumph)*, prohibit, quash, remit *(relax)*, repress,

restrain, soothe, stay *(halt)*, stem *(check)*, stifle, stop, strangle, subdue, subject, subjugate, suppress

quell suspicion   disarm *(set at ease)*

quelling   palliative *(abating)*

quench   allay, assuage, cancel, deter, discourage, extinguish, inhibit, quash, repress, satisfy *(fulfill)*, soothe, stifle, suppress

quenchless   hot-blooded, indomitable, insatiable

querela   grievance, plaint

queribundus   querulous

querimonia   complaint, grievance, plaint

querimonious   querulous

querulous   fractious, froward, litigious, particular *(exacting)*, petulant, reluctant, resentful

querulousness   dissatisfaction

querulus   querulous

query   challenge, check *(inspect)*, cross-examination, cross-examine, cross-questioning, dispute *(contest)*, doubt *(distrust)*, examine *(interrogate)*, impugn, inquire, inquiry *(request for information)*, interrogation, pose *(propound)*, question *(inquiry)*

quest   agency *(legal relationship)*, attempt, campaign, cross-examination, delve, discovery, endeavor, hunt, indagation, inquest, probe, pursue *(chase)*, pursuit *(chase)*, pursuit *(effort to secure)*, research, research, undertaking *(attempt)*, undertaking *(enterprise)*, venture

question   analyze, canvass, challenge, check *(inspect)*, consult *(ask advice of)*, contest, cross-examine, disbelieve, discount *(disbelieve)*, doubt *(indecision)*, doubt *(distrust)*, enigma, examine *(interrogate)*, hesitate, impugn, incertitude, incredulity, inquire, inquiry *(request for information)*, inquiry *(systematic investigation)*, investigate, issue *(matter in dispute)*, matter *(subject)*, misdoubt, mistrust, pose *(propound)*, probe, problem, qualm, scruple, scrutinize, suspect *(distrust)*, suspicion *(uncertainty)*, thesis

question and answer   interview

question at issue   conflict, controversy *(argument)*, issue *(matter in dispute)*

question in one's mind   doubt *(suspicion)*

question the truth of   dispute *(contest)*

question under oath   examine *(interrogate)*

questionability   cloud *(suspicion)*, ill repute, improbability

questionable   blameworthy, contestable, controversial, debatable, disputable, doubtful, dubious, dubitative, equivocal, implausible, indefinite, lewd, ludicrous, moot, outrageous, problematic, speculative, tentative, unbelievable, undecided, unethical, unscrupulous, unsound *(fallacious)*, unsustainable, untenable, untrustworthy, vague

questionableness   ill repute

questionary   form *(document)*, poll *(canvass)*

questioned   moot

questioning   conversation, cross-

examination, cross-questioning, cynical, dissenting, doubtful, inconvincible, incredulous, indagation, inquest, inquisitive, interest *(concern)*, interrogation, interrogative, interrogatories, investigation, leery, research, skeptical, test

questioning integrity   impeachment

questioning under oath   examination *(test)*

questioning witness's veracity   impeachment

questionless   axiomatic, certain *(positive)*, clear *(certain)*, decisive, definite, incontrovertible, irrefutable, undisputed, unimpeachable

questionlessness   certainty

questionnaire   blank *(form)*, form *(document)*, poll *(canvass)*

questions   interrogatories

queue   assemblage, lineup

qui conventui praeest   chairman

qui facit   actor

qui oppugnat   assailant

qui sibi placet   complacent

qui vulnerari potest   vulnerable

quibble   equivocate, haggle, prevaricate, tergiversate

quibbling excuse   salvo

quick   alert *(agile)*, artful, born *(alive)*, brief, cursory, deft, expeditious, facile, immediate *(at once)*, impulsive *(rash)*, instantaneous, live *(conscious)*, perfunctory, perspicacious, precipitate, proficient, prompt, rapid, ready *(prepared)*, summary, volatile

quick discharge   dispatch *(promptness)*

quick judgment   discretion *(quality of being discreet)*

quick of apprehension   perceptive, sapient, sensitive *(discerning)*

quick riddance   dispatch *(promptness)*

quick sense   perception

quick-tempered   hot-blooded, sensitive *(easily affected)*

quick-witted   acute, perspicacious, sapient

quicken   expedite, facilitate, precipitate *(hasten)*, promise *(raise expectations)*

quickening   acceleration, cumulative *(intensifying)*, revival

quickly   forthwith, instantly, readily

quickly executed   summary

quickly performed   summary

quickness   dispatch *(promptness)*, efficiency, facility *(easiness)*, haste, judgment *(discernment)*, sagacity, skill

quickness of perception   intelligence *(intellect)*

quid   center *(essence)*

quid pro quo   collection *(payment)*

quidam   certain *(specific)*

quiddity   center *(essence)*, character *(personal quality)*, content *(meaning)*, essence, gist *(substance)*, main point

quies   ease, inaction

quiescence   cessation *(interlude)*, composure, inaction, inertia, languor, lull, peace, silence

quiescency   abeyance, lull, silence

quiescent   dormant, lifeless *(dull)*, mute, passive, patient, peaceable, placid, stagnant, static

quiet   allay, alleviate, diffident, dimin-

ish, dormant, ease, inconspicuous, laconic, lifeless *(dull)*, lull, lull, moderate *(temper)*, moderation, mollify, mute, obtund, pacify, palliate *(abate)*, patient, peace, peaceable, placate, placid, private *(secluded)*, remit *(relax)*, repress, silence, solemn, soothe, speechless, static, strangle, subdue, subside, taciturn, unobtrusive, unpretentious

quiet down   lull

quieten   lull

quieting   palliative *(abating)*

quietly persevering   patient

quietness   peace, silence

quietude   composure, privacy, silence

quietus   extremity *(death)*, release, remission

quietus   denouement, inactive, placid

quintessence   center *(essence)*, character *(personal quality)*, characteristic, consequence *(significance)*, content *(meaning)*, cornerstone, corpus, essence, gist *(substance)*, main point, spirit

quintessential   best

quirk   compulsion *(obsession)*, speciality, specialty *(distinctive mark)*

quit   abandon *(physically leave)*, abandon *(relinquish)*, abandon *(withdraw)*, cease, comport *(behave)*, defect, demean *(deport oneself)*, demit, discontinue *(abandon)*, evacuate, forfeit, forgo, forswear, halt, leave *(depart)*, part *(leave)*, pay, recoup *(reimburse)*, relinquish, remise, renege, renounce, resign, retire *(conclude a career)*, retreat, secede, shirk, stop, vacate *(leave)*, withdraw, yield *(submit)*

quit of   free *(relieved from a burden)*

quit work   strike *(refuse to work)*

quitclaim   cede, remise

quite the contrary   contra

quittance   acquittal, amnesty, collection *(payment)*, compensation, contribution *(indemnification)*, expiation, honorarium, payment *(act of paying)*, payment *(remittance)*, quitclaim, receipt *(proof of receiving)*, recompense, remission, remittance, remuneration, reparation *(indemnification)*, reprieve, requital, restitution, revenge, reward, satisfaction *(discharge of debt)*, trover, wage

quitting   abdication, desertion, resignation *(relinquishment)*

quiver   beat *(pulsate)*

quivering   trepidation

quixotical   quixotic

quiz   check *(inspect)*, cross-examine, examination *(test)*, examine *(interrogate)*, inquire, test

quizzical   inquisitive, interrogative, ironic, skeptical, suspicious *(distrustful)*

quo nihil efficitur   inconclusive

quod abalienari non potest   inalienable

quod comprehendi   incomprehensible

quod contra dicitur   objection

quod contra leges fit   illegal, illicit

quod defendi non potest   indefensible

quod eodem tempore est   contemporaneous

quod est admirabile contraque opinionem omnium   paradox

quod everti non potest   indestructible

quod ex lege   legal, licit

quod fiere non potest   impracticable

quod fieri non potest   impossible

quod indecorum est impropriety
quod nihil ad rem est impertinent *(irrelevant)*
quod nihil excusationis habet inexcusable
quod refutari non potest inappealable, incontrovertible
quod restat remainder *(remaining part)*
quod satis est sufficiency
quod tangi non potest impalpable
quondam former, prior
quorum minimum
quota quorum, ration
quotation attribution, bid, charge *(cost)*, citation *(attribution)*, cost *(price)*, estimate *(approximate cost)*, excerpt, price, rate, reference *(citation)*, value, worth
quote cite *(state)*, excerpt, extract, recite, refer *(direct attention)*, repeat *(state again)*
quoted passage excerpt, reference *(citation)*
quoted price bid, cost *(price)*, face value *(price)*, tariff *(bill)*
quotidian daily
quotidianus customary, ordinary
quotidie daily
quoting reference *(citation)*
quotum proportion, share *(interest)*

R

rabble-rouser demagogue, malcontent
rabid deranged, extreme *(exaggerated)*, fanatical, outrageous, vehement, zealous
rabidity furor, passion
race competition, contest *(competition)*, descent *(lineage)*, hasten, origin *(ancestry)*, strife
race hatred discrimination *(bigotry)*
race prejudice discrimination *(bigotry)*
racial balance integration *(assimilation)*
racial harmonization integration *(assimilation)*
racial harmony integration *(assimilation)*
racial prejudice segregation *(isolation by races)*
racialism discrimination *(bigotry)*, segregation *(isolation by races)*
racism discrimination *(bigotry)*, intolerance, segregation *(isolation by races)*
rack plague
rack the brains ponder
racket bluster *(commotion)*, brawl, bunko, commotion, disorder *(lack of order)*, noise, outcry, pandemonium
racketeer malefactor, outlaw
rackety disorderly
racking insufferable
racy lurid, suggestive *(risqué)*
radiant ecstatic, illustrious
radiare radiate
radiate cast *(throw)*, circulate, deploy, diffuse, dispel, disseminate, dissipate *(spread out)*, dissolve *(disperse)*, emanate, emit, pervade, spread, transmit
radiating divergent
radical demagogue, drastic, extreme *(exaggerated)*, fanatical, insurgent, mal-

content, outrageous, total, unusual, vital
radically new measure innovation
radicated permanent
radius boundary
raffish blatant *(obtrusive)*, caitiff, ignoble
raffle bet, lottery
rag mock *(deride)*
rage furor, mode, outbreak, outburst, passion, style, violence
rage against inveigh
raging disorderly, lunatic, outrageous, severe
raid attack, bait *(harass)*, depredation, despoil, devastate, encroach, encroachment, foray, harry *(plunder)*, impinge, incursion, invade, invasion, loot, onset *(assault)*, outbreak, pillage, pillage, plunder, plunder, prey, spoil *(pillage)*, spoliation
raider burglar, vandal
raiding burglary, housebreaking, predatory
rail demonstrate *(protest)*, inveigh
rail at flout, reprimand, reproach
railing aspersion, diatribe
raillery ridicule
raise accrue *(increase)*, adopt, ameliorate, boom *(increase)*, build *(augment)*, build *(construct)*, collect *(recover money)*, compound, develop, discipline *(train)*, elevate, enhance, enlarge, excise *(levy a tax)*, expand, foster, frame *(construct)*, heighten *(augment)*, heighten *(elevate)*, honor, increase, increment, levy, magnify, meliorate, originate, parlay *(exploit successfully)*, prefer, produce *(manufacture)*, promote *(advance)*, promotion *(advancement)*, recruit, uphold
raise a demand necessitate
raise a hue and cry against censure, decry, impugn
raise a question challenge, doubt *(distrust)*
raise a question as to impugn
raise a suspicion doubt *(distrust)*
raise above the proper value inflate
raise aloft elevate, heighten *(elevate)*
raise anger incense
raise apprehension dissuade, frighten
raise apprehensions browbeat, menace
raise contributions collect *(recover money)*
raise expectations assure *(give confidence to)*
raise frivolous objection to cavil
raise funds collect *(recover money)*
raise hopes promise *(raise expectations)*
raise objections challenge, counter, demur, differ *(disagree)*, disaffirm, disagree, dissent *(withhold assent)*, protest, remonstrate
raise objections frivolously cavil
raise one's voice against challenge, decry, dissent *(withhold assent)*, impugn, inveigh
raise questions impugn
raise specious objection to cavil
raise spirits invoke
raise taxes toll *(exact payment)*
raise to a higher position elevate

raise to distinction honor
raise troops recruit
raise up one's voice pray
raised prominent
raised path causeway
raised road causeway
raised voice outcry
raison d'être basis
rake off decrease
rake through frisk
rakeoff gratuity *(bribe)*
rakish dissolute, lecherous, licentious
rally assemblage, call *(summon)*, caucus, coax, collection *(assembly)*, combine *(act in concert)*, congregate, convene, help, incite, join *(bring together)*, meet, provoke, reassure, stimulate
rally around side
rally round cooperate
rally to bear *(support)*, maintain *(sustain)*
ram constrict *(compress)*, impact
ram in inject
ramble detour, digress, perambulate, prowl
rambler itinerant
rambling circuitous, desultory, discursive *(digressive)*, indirect, labyrinthine, loquacious, profuse, prolix, sinuous, voluble
rambling talk jargon *(unintelligible language)*
ramification organ
ramified divergent
ramify bifurcate, radiate, spread
rammed compact *(dense)*
rampage bluster *(commotion)*, brawl, brawl, commotion, confusion *(turmoil)*, outburst, pandemonium, passion, violence
rampageous uncontrollable
rampancy passion
rampant disorderly, hot-blooded, predominant, prevailing *(current)*, prevalent, rife, uncontrollable, unrestrained *(not repressed)*, unruly, vehement
rampart barrier, buffer zone, bulwark, mainstay, security *(safety)*, shield
ramshackle dilapidated
rancid loathsome, stale, tainted *(contaminated)*
rancor alienation *(estrangement)*, cruelty, feud, ill will, malice, odium, spite, umbrage, vengeance
rancorous bitter *(reproachful)*, caustic, harsh, hostile, invidious, malevolent, malignant, mordacious, negative, relentless, ruthless, scathing, spiteful, vindictive, virulent
random astray, desultory, discursive *(digressive)*, disordered, disorderly, fortuitous, haphazard, indiscriminate, unpredictable
random luck act of god, happenstance
random sample cross section
randomness incoherence
range area *(province)*, capacity *(aptitude)*, chain *(series)*, circuit, classify, coverage *(scope)*, degree *(magnitude)*, direction *(course)*, extent, file *(arrange)*, fix *(arrange)*, gamut, hierarchy *(arrangement in a series)*, jurisdiction, latitude, magnitude, perambulate, prowl,

purview, region, scene, scope, sort, space, sphere

range of choice latitude

range of meaning connotation, context

range of view coverage *(scope)*, perspective

range of vision perspective

range together juxtapose

ranger migrant

ranging discursive *(digressive)*

rank calculate, class, classify, codify, condition *(state)*, credit *(recognition)*, criticize *(evaluate)*, degree *(station)*, depraved, estimate, evaluate, excessive, fertile, file *(arrange)*, fix *(arrange)*, gauge, loathsome, marshal, materiality *(consequence)*, measure, obnoxious, odious, organize *(arrange)*, pigeonhole, precedence, prestige, productive, quality *(excellence)*, rate, rating, repulsive, reputation, sort, status, tabulate, title *(position)*, unmitigated

rank first surpass

ranking classification, degree *(station)*, master, outstanding *(prominent)*, rating

rankle affront, aggravate *(annoy)*, annoy, bait *(harass)*, harass, irritate

rankling malice, resentment

ransack despoil, devastate, foray, harry *(plunder)*, loot, pillage, pillage, pirate *(take by violence)*, plunder, prey, spoil *(pillage)*, spoliation

ransom blackmail, extricate, free, pay, redeem *(repurchase)*, rescue

ransomed free *(relieved from a burden)*

rant bombast, declaim, fustian, outpour, reprimand, rodomontade

rant at reproach

ranter bigot, demagogue

ranting bluster *(speech)*, fustian, incoherence, lunatic

rap beat *(strike)*

rapacious confiscatory, insatiable, larcenous, mercenary, predatory

rapaciousness desire, extortion

rapacity bad repute, extortion, larceny, pillage

rapax rapacious

rape molest *(subject to indecent advances)*

rapere rape, seize *(apprehend)*

rapid cursory, expeditious, impulsive *(rash)*, instantaneous, precipitate, summary

rapidity dispatch *(promptness)*, haste

rapidly instantly

rapidus rapid

rapina pillage, plunder, robbery

rapine depredation, larceny, pillage, plunder, rape, spoliation

rapport accordance *(understanding)*, compatibility, concert, concordance, connection *(relation)*, contact *(association)*, peace, rapprochement, relationship *(connection)*, understanding *(agreement)*

rapprochement arbitration, comparison

rapprochement reconciliation

rapscallion degenerate, malefactor

rapt ecstatic, pensive

rapt attention diligence *(care)*, obsession, preoccupation

raptorial predatory

rapture passion

rapturous ecstatic

raptus abduction

rare extraordinary, individual, inestimable, infrequent, meritorious, nonconforming, notable, noteworthy, novel, obscure *(remote)*, original *(creative)*, peculiar *(curious)*, portentous *(eliciting amazement)*, priceless, remarkable, scarce, select, singular, special, sporadic, unaccustomed, uncanny, uncommon, unique, unprecedented, unusual, valuable

rare occurrence improbability, phenomenon *(unusual occurrence)*

rarefy cultivate, decontaminate

rareness dearth, paucity

rari aditus inaccessible, unapproachable

rarity exception *(exclusion)*, improbability, irregularity, phenomenon *(unusual occurrence)*, specialty *(distinctive mark)*

rarus infrequent, rare, scarce, sporadic, uncommon

rascal malefactor

rascality artifice, deception, ill repute, improbity, knavery, mischief, misdoing

rascally artful, lawless, machiavellian, profligate *(corrupt)*, reprobate, sinister, unconscionable

rash blind *(not discerning)*, careless, heedless, hot-blooded, ill-advised, ill-judged, impolitic, improvident, imprudent, irresponsible, negligent, precipitate, premature, presumptuous, spontaneous, thoughtless, unpolitic, unpremeditated

rashness audacity, haste, inconsideration, indiscretion, inexpedience, neglect, temerity

rasp erode, irritate

rasure annulment, cancellation

ratable ad valorem

rate amount *(sum)*, assess *(appraise)*, assessment *(levy)*, calculate, caliber *(quality)*, charge *(cost)*, charge *(assess)*, classify, criticize *(evaluate)*, differential, duty *(tax)*, earnings, estimate *(approximate cost)*, estimate, evaluate, expense *(cost)*, frequency, gauge, inveigh, measure, organize *(arrange)*, par *(face amount)*, pigeonhole, price, rebuke, reprehend, worth

rate below the true value underestimate

rate incorrectly misjudge

rate of pay wage

rate too low underestimate

rather than in lieu of

rather well fairly *(moderately)*

ratification acceptance, acknowledgment *(acceptance)*, adoption *(acceptance)*, affirmance *(authentication)*, affirmation, approval, assent, certification *(attested copy)*, charter *(sanction)*, confirmation, consent, corroboration, indorsement, jurat, legalization, proof, sanction *(permission)*, stamp, subscription, support *(corroboration)*

ratified allowed, choate lien, nunc pro tunc

ratified agreement contract

ratifier surety *(guarantor)*, under-

signed

ratify accept *(assent)*, accredit, acknowledge *(respond)*, affirm *(uphold)*, agree *(comply)*, approve, assent, attest, bear *(adduce)*, bestow, certify *(approve)*, certify *(attest)*, concur *(agree)*, confirm, consent, corroborate, cosign, countenance, countersign, embrace *(accept)*, endorse, fix *(make firm)*, indorse, pass *(approve)*, recommend, sanction, seal *(solemnize)*, sign, subscribe *(sign)*, substantiate, support *(corroborate)*, sustain *(confirm)*, validate

rating assessment *(estimation)*, class, disapprobation, estimate *(approximate cost)*, estimation *(calculation)*, measurement, reprimand, reproach, status

ratio differential, proportion, quota, share *(interest)*

ratio account *(evaluation)*, expedient, ground, method, mode, motive, phase *(aspect)*, process *(course)*, reason *(basis)*, reference *(allusion)*, reflection *(thought)*, scheme (noun), scheme (verb), style, theoretical, theory

ratio decidendi authority *(documentation)*

ratio iudiciorum judicatory

ratiocinari reason *(conclude)*

ratiocinate debate, deduce, deliberate, ponder, reason *(conclude)*

ratiocinatio ratiocination

ratiocination contemplation, deduction *(conclusion)*, deliberation, dialectic, judgment *(discernment)*

ratiocinative deductible *(provable)*, discursive *(analytical)*, logical, pensive, rational, reasonable *(rational)*, sensible

ratiocinatory discursive *(analytical)*, logical, pensive

ration allocate, allot, allotment, budget, disburse *(distribute)*, dispense, distribute, divide *(distribute)*, dole, mete, moiety, parcel, provision *(something provided)*, quota, reapportion, share *(interest)*

rational colorable *(plausible)*, conscious *(aware)*, convincing, deductive, discriminating *(judicious)*, discursive *(analytical)*, judicial, judicious, juridical, justifiable, logical, lucid, normal *(sane)*, plausible, possible, pragmatic, reasonable *(rational)*, sane, sapient, sensible, solid *(sound)*, tenable

rational faculty common sense, intellect, intelligence *(intellect)*, judgment *(discernment)*, sense *(intelligence)*

rationale argument *(pleading)*, basis, cause *(reason)*, construction, explanation, ground, motive, reason *(basis)*

rationalism dialectic

rationalistic discursive *(analytical)*

rationality coherence, common sense, competence *(sanity)*, comprehension, discrimination *(good judgment)*, intellect, intelligence *(intellect)*, judgment *(discernment)*, pragmatism, ratiocination, reason *(sound judgment)*, sagacity, sanity, sense *(intelligence)*

rationalization deduction *(conclusion)*, dialectic, excuse, justification, ratiocination

rationalize comment, deduce, deduct *(conclude by reasoning)*, ponder, reason *(conclude)*

rationalizing dialectic

rationcinate construe *(comprehend)*, deduct *(conclude by reasoning)*

ratione praeditus rational

rationem inire embark

rationem rei responsibility *(accountability)*

rationes dispungere audit

rationi consentaneus reasonable *(fair)*

rationing control *(restriction)*, distribution *(apportionment)*, division *(act of dividing)*

rationis expers irrational

rationis particeps reasonable *(rational)*

rattle confuse *(bewilder)*, discompose, perplex

rattle the saber brandish

ratum facere sanction

ravage beat *(defeat)*, catastrophe, consumption, damage, debacle, despoil, destroy *(efface)*, devastate, disaster, extirpate, harm, harry *(plunder)*, havoc, loot, obliterate, overthrow, pillage, plunder, prejudice *(injure)*, prey, prostration, rape, spoil *(pillage)*, wear and tear

ravagement defilement

ravager aggressor, assailant, vandal

ravaging depredation, disastrous, larcenous, predatory

rave against lash *(attack verbally)*

ravel ascertain, disorganize, elucidate, snarl

raveled disordered, inextricable, labyrinthine, problematic

raven despoil, prey

ravening predatory, rapacious

ravenous eager, gluttonous, predatory, rapacious

ravenousness greed

ravin plunder, spoils

raving bluster *(speech)*, bombast, frenetic, incoherence, insanity, lunatic, non compos mentis, zealous

ravish abduct, carry away, mishandle *(maltreat)*, molest *(subject to indecent advances)*, prey

ravishing attractive, provocative

ravishment abduction, rape

raw imperfect, incompetent, inept *(incompetent)*, inexperienced, mordacious, premature, puerile, unaccustomed, unversed

raw materials commodities

rawness ignorance, nescience

raze abolish, destroy *(efface)*, devastate, eliminate *(eradicate)*, expunge, extinguish, extirpate, obliterate, plunder

razzia foray, pillage, plunder

re carere dispense

re liber free *(relieved from a burden)*

re multari forfeit

re uti avail *(bring about)*

re vacuus devoid

re-charged double jeopardy

re-litigated double jeopardy

re-prosecuted double jeopardy

re-tried double jeopardy

reach abut, accede *(succeed)*, attain, capacity *(aptitude)*, capacity *(maximum)*, capacity *(sphere)*, contact *(communicate)*, contact *(touch)*, coverage *(scope)*, degree *(magnitude)*, extent, gamut, impress *(affect deeply)*, jurisdiction, magnitude, obtain, pass *(satisfy requirements)*, purview, range, scope,

succeed *(attain)*

reach a compromise settle

reach a conclusion infer

reach a decision decide

reach a new high surpass

reach a peak culminate

reach a verdict decide

reach an official decision rule *(decide)*

reach beyond overreach

reach manhood develop

reach of mind caliber *(mental capacity)*, comprehension, intellect, intelligence *(intellect)*

reach one's goal attain

reach over overlap, overreach

reach the end of exhaust *(deplete)*

reach the goal consummate

reach the highest point culminate

reach the zenith culminate

reach to adjoin

reach too far overreach

reachable available, disposable, open *(accessible)*, passable, public *(open)*, vulnerable

reacknowledge reconfirm

reacquire collect *(recover money)*, reclaim, recoup *(regain)*, recover, repossess

react perceive, reply, respond, return *(respond)*

reacting responsive

reaction answer *(reply)*, consequence *(conclusion)*, effect, emotion, estimate *(idea)*, impression, opinion *(belief)*, repercussion, reply, reprisal, response

reactionary hostile, illiberal, malcontent, renitent

reactionist malcontent

reactivate reconstitute

reactivation recrudescence

reactive responsive, sensitive *(easily affected)*, susceptible *(responsive)*

read peruse, predict, study

read as one pari materia

read back repeat *(state again)*

read in tandem pari materia

read incorrectly misread

read the future predict

read together pari materia

read up on research

read with respect of another pari materia

readable cognizable

readapt attune

readdress redirect

readily impressed susceptible *(responsive)*

readily influenced pliant

readily mastered facile

readily perceived palpable

readily seen palpable

readily wrought tractable

readiness amenability, diligence *(care)*, dispatch *(promptness)*, facility *(easiness)*, faculty *(ability)*, gift *(flair)*, inclination, maturity, opportunity, plan, predisposition, preparation, proclivity, propensity, qualification *(fitness)*

readiness to believe credulity

readiness to give largess *(generosity)*

reading declamation, rendition *(explication)*

reading matter publication *(printed matter)*

readjust adapt, attune, modify *(alter)*, redress, rehabilitate, remedy, renovate, repair

readjust downward depreciate

readjustment accommodation *(adjustment)*, correction *(change)*, reconversion, rehabilitation, renewal, reorganization, reparation *(keeping in repair)*

readminister redistribute

readmit renew *(begin again)*

ready artful, available, competent, discipline *(train)*, eager, expeditious, facile, fit, inclined, instant, present *(current)*, proficient, prompt, prone, provide *(arrange for)*, provident *(showing foresight)*, punctual, ripe, willing *(desirous)*, zealous

ready ability facility *(easiness)*

ready cash capital

ready for use disposable, effective *(operative)*

ready money cash, currency

ready-tongued voluble

readying discipline *(training)*, preparation

reaffirm avouch *(avow)*, certify *(attest)*, plead *(allege in a legal action)*, reconfirm, reiterate, repeat *(state again)*

reaffirmation recital, restatement

reaffirmed nunc pro tunc

real absolute *(conclusive)*, actual, apparent *(perceptible)*, authentic, bona fide, certain *(positive)*, concrete, convincing, corporeal, de facto, definite, documentary, factual, faithful *(true to fact)*, genuine, legitimate *(rightful)*, material *(physical)*, natural, objective, peremptory *(absolute)*, physical, ponderable, pure, realistic, reliable, rightful, sterling, substantial, substantive, tangible, true *(authentic)*, veridical

real content gist *(substance)*

real episode fact

real estate demesne, domain *(land owned)*, estate *(property)*, fee *(estate)*, holding *(property owned)*, immovable, land, parcel, premises *(buildings)*, property *(land)*, realty

real estate trespass encroachment

real experience fact

real interpretation connotation

real meaning connotation

real property demesne, domain *(land owned)*, fee *(estate)*, freehold, holding *(property owned)*, immovable, property *(land)*, real estate, realty

real property capable of being inherited hereditament

real property holder landholder, landowner

real property owner landholder, landowner

real property subject to a lease leasehold

real security bond, charge *(lien)*, cloud *(incumbrance)*, hostage, lien, mortgage, pledge *(security)*

real sense connotation

real size area *(surface)*

realignment transition

realism pragmatism, truth

realistic accurate, actual, candid, descriptive, factual, faithful *(true to fact)*, natural, pragmatic, reasonable *(rational)*, sane, true *(authentic)*

realistic attitude pragmatism

realisticness pragmatism

reality fact, fait accompli, gist *(substance)*, honesty, materiality *(physical existence)*, substance *(essential nature)*, truth, validity

realizable cognizable, coherent *(clear)*, comprehensible, disposable, passable, possible, potential, practicable

realization acquisition, appreciation *(increased value)*, cessation *(termination)*, cognition, commission *(act)*, comprehension, conclusion *(determination)*, creation, denouement, development *(outgrowth)*, discharge *(performance)*, embodiment, end *(termination)*, fait accompli, fruition, insight, knowledge *(awareness)*, occurrence, outcome, perception, performance *(execution)*, phenomenon *(manifestation)*, profit, recognition, satisfaction *(fulfilment)*, sense *(feeling)*, understanding *(comprehension)*

realization in advance advancement *(loan)*

realize accomplish, acquire *(secure)*, appreciate *(comprehend)*, apprehend *(perceive)*, attain, avail *(bring about)*, collect *(recover money)*, commit *(perpetrate)*, complete, comprehend *(understand)*, conceive *(comprehend)*, conjure, construe *(comprehend)*, consummate, detect, discern *(detect with the senses)*, discharge *(perform)*, discover, dispatch *(dispose of)*, earn, effectuate, execute *(accomplish)*, find *(discover)*, fulfill, gain, implement, invent *(produce for the first time)*, note *(notice)*, notice *(observe)*, obtain, pass *(satisfy requirements)*, perceive, pierce *(discern)*, procure, produce *(manufacture)*, profit, reap, receive *(acquire)*, recognize *(acknowledge)*, recover, solve, substantiate, succeed *(attain)*

realize in cash liquidate *(convert into cash)*

realize the worth of appreciate *(value)*

realized cognizable, complete *(ended)*, fully executed *(consummated)*

realized from accompanying words noscitur a sociis

reallocate reapportion, reassign

reallocation reclassification, removal

reallot reapportion, reassign, redistribute

reallotment reclassification

really purely *(positively)*

realm ambit, area *(province)*, bailiwick, capacity *(sphere)*, circuit, coverage *(scope)*, demesne, department, district, domain *(sphere of influence)*, jurisdiction, part *(role)*, province, region, scope, sphere, territory

realness honesty, legitimacy, reality, validity

realtor broker

realty demesne, domain *(land owned)*, estate *(property)*, fee *(estate)*, freehold, holding *(property owned)*, property *(land)*, real estate

reanalysis reclassification

reanalyze reexamine

reanimate recall *(call back)*, recreate, renew *(refurbish)*, renovate, restore *(renew)*, resurrect

reanimated renascent

reanimation recrudescence, renewal, repair, resurgence, revival

reap acquire *(receive)*, attain, earn, gain, procure, profit, realize *(obtain as a profit)*, receive *(acquire)*, succeed *(attain)*

reap profits gain

reap rewards gain

reap the benefit of capitalize *(seize the chance)*, gain

reap the fruits profit

reappear recur, return *(go back)*

reappearance recrudescence, resurgence, revival

reappearing periodic, renascent

reappoint reapportion, reassign, reinstate

reapportion redistribute

reapportionment reclassification

reappraise reassess

reappreciate reassess

reapprise reassess

reappropriate reassign

reapprove reconfirm

rear discipline *(train)*, educate, foster, last *(final)*, nurture

rearmost back *(in reverse)*, final

rearrange alter, convert *(change use)*, disturb, edit, modify *(alter)*, reapportion, reconstruct, redistribute, reform, restore *(renew)*

rearrangement exchange, interchange, reclassification, renewal, reorganization

rearward back *(in reverse)*

reason analyze, answer *(solution)*, basis, common sense, competence *(sanity)*, comprehension, construe *(comprehend)*, contention *(argument)*, debate, deduce, deduct *(conclude by reasoning)*, deliberate, derive *(deduce)*, discrimination *(good judgment)*, end *(intent)*, excuse, gist *(ground for a suit)*, ground, impetus, incentive, infer, intellect, intelligence *(intellect)*, justice, justification, motive, point *(item)*, point *(purpose)*, ponder, postulate, rationale, rationalize, read, reflect *(ponder)*, sagacity, sanity, sense *(intelligence)*, solution *(answer)*, stimulus, treat *(process)*, understanding *(comprehension)*

reason about discuss, treat *(process)*

reason against oppugn

reason earnestly against expostulate

reason for action motive

reason for disapproval objection

reason for legal pursuit cause of action

reason for relief cause of action

reason for which suit is commenced gist *(ground for a suit)*

reason out deliberate, solve

reason the point deliberate

reason to believe clue

reason to complain grievance

reason upon argue

reason with counsel, discuss

reasonability admissibility, competence *(sanity)*

reasonable adequate, amenable, colorable *(plausible)*, considerable, convincing, discriminating *(judicious)*, equitable, fair *(satisfactory)*, impartial, judicial, judicious, just, justifiable, logical, normal *(sane)*, objective, open-minded, ostensible, peaceable, placable,

plausible, possible, practicable, pragmatic, probable, rational, receptive, right *(correct)*, right *(suitable)*, rightful, sane, sensible, solid *(sound)*, suitable, tenable, unprejudiced, upright, viable

reasonable chance likelihood, opportunity, probability, prospect *(outlook)*

reasonable claim cause of action

reasonable excuse justification

reasonable ground likelihood

reasonable presumption likelihood

reasonable prospect likelihood

reasonable supposition presumption

reasonableness common sense, equity *(justice)*, expedience, fairness, feasibility, justice, moderation, pragmatism, probability, propriety *(appropriateness)*, sanity

reasonably anticipated foreseeable

reasonably good fair *(satisfactory)*

reasonably sufficient adequate

reasoned deductive, deliberate, intentional, judicial, logical, premeditated

reasoned judgment adjudication, conclusion *(determination)*, deduction *(conclusion)*, determination

reasoning contemplation, dialectic, discursive *(analytical)*, judgment *(discernment)*, justification, pensive, ratiocination, rational, rationale, reflection *(thought)*, speculation *(conjecture)*

reasoning faculties judgment *(discernment)*

reasoning faculty intellect, intelligence *(intellect)*

reasoning power intellect, intelligence *(intellect)*, judgment *(discernment)*, sagacity

reasonless deranged, irrational, lunatic, misadvised

reassemble recall *(call back)*

reassembling repair

reassembly collection *(assembly)*

reassert avouch *(avow)*, plead *(allege in a legal action)*, reaffirm, reiterate, repeat *(state again)*

reassertation recital

reassertion restatement

reassessment rehearing

reassign reapportion, recover, redistribute, relocate, remand

reassignment reclassification

reassort reapportion, redistribute

reassorting reclassification

reassortment reclassification

reassume recoup *(regain)*

reassurance assurance, certainty, certification *(attested copy)*, coverage *(insurance)*, solace, surety *(certainty)*, trust *(confidence)*

reassure assure *(give confidence to)*, certify *(attest)*, corroborate, insure

reassure oneself ascertain

reassured positive *(confident)*, sanguine, secure *(confident)*

reassurement certification *(attested copy)*

reassuring favorable *(expressing approval)*, propitious

reauthenticate reconfirm

reave hold up *(rob)*, pillage, plunder

reawaken renew *(refurbish)*

reawakening revival

rebate discount *(reduce)*, refund, refund, reimburse, reimbursement, repay, restitution

rebegin continue (resume)

rebel defect, defy, demagogue, disobey, fight (battle), insurgent, malcontent, pariah, resist (oppose), secede, strike (refuse to work)

rebellio insurrection

rebellion anarchy, commotion, defiance, disloyalty, disturbance, infidelity, insurrection, mutiny, outbreak, outburst, resistance, revolt, revolution, riot, sedition, subversion, treason

rebellion against the government treason

rebellious contumacious, disobedient, disorderly, dissident, fractious, froward, impertinent (insolent), insubordinate, intractable, irresponsible, lawless, pugnacious, radical (favoring drastic change), recalcitrant, recusant, restive, unruly

rebelliousness defiance

rebellis insurgent

rebirth reconversion, renewal, resurgence, revival

reborn renascent

rebound reaction (opposition), reflect (mirror), repercussion, return (go back)

rebounding resounding

rebuff abrogate (annul), censure, check (bar), confront (oppose), contemn, contempt (disdain), controvert, counter, counteract, decline (reject), disallow, disapprove (condemn), disapprove (reject), disdain, disdain, disfavor, disoblige, disown (refuse to acknowledge), disrespect, dissent (withhold assent), eliminate (exclude), exclude, fight (counteract), impeach, parry, reaction (opposition), rebut, refusal, refuse, reject, rejection, renounce, renunciation, repel (drive back), repulse, resist (oppose), resistance, reversal, shun, spurn

rebuffing negative

rebuild copy, fix (repair), reclaim, reconstitute, reconstruct, recreate, rehabilitate, renew (refurbish), renovate, repair, reproduce, restore (renew), resurrect

rebuilding rehabilitation, reorganization, reparation (keeping in repair)

rebukable reprehensible

rebuke admonish (warn), admonition, aspersion, bad repute, blame (culpability), blame, castigate, censure, complain (criticize), condemn (blame), condemnation (blame), criticize (find fault with), denounce (condemn), denunciation, diatribe, disapprobation, disapprove (condemn), disparagement, exception (objection), impeachment, lash (attack verbally), objection, objurgation, odium, outcry, penalize, rebuff, rebuff, remonstrance, remonstrate, reprehend, reprimand, reprimand, reproach, reproach, reversal, stricture

rebuking critical (faultfinding), remonstrative

rebut answer (reply), answer (respond legally), contradict, contravene, controvert, countercharge, countervail, disaccord, disaffirm, disallow, disown (deny the validity), disprove, dispute (debate), gainsay, impugn, negate, oppose, refute, reply, respond, retaliate, retort, return (respond)

rebut the charge countercharge

rebuttal answer (judicial response), answer (reply), argument (pleading), confutation, contradiction, contravention, counterargument, defense, denial, disagreement, plea, pleading, reply, response

rebutter confutation, counterargument

rebutting contradictory, contrary, negative

rebutting evidence answer (judicial response), contradiction

recalcitrance contempt (disobedience to the court), contest (dispute), defiance, resistance, revolt, tenacity

recalcitrancy defiance

recalcitrant adverse (hostile), contentious, contumacious, deviant, disinclined, disobedient, disorderly, dissident, fractious, incorrigible, indomitable, insubordinate, insusceptible (uncaring), intractable, lawless, nonconsenting, obdurate, recusant, reluctant, renitent, restive, uncontrollable, unreasonable, unruly, unyielding, vicious

recalcitrantly unwillingly

recalcitrate confront (oppose), disobey, oppose, oppugn, rebel, resist (oppose)

recalcitration defiance, opposition, reaction (opposition)

recalculate reassess

recall abjuration, abrogate (rescind), ademption, annul, cancel, cancellation, countermand, defeasance, depose (remove), disavow, discharge (annulment), discharge (release from obligation), disinherit, hindsight, nullify, recant, reclaim, recognition, recognize (perceive), recollect, recollection, redeem (repurchase), remember, remembrance (recollection), renege, repeal, repossess, rescind, rescission, retain (keep in possession), retraction, retrospect, revocation, revoke, withdraw

recall to life cure, resurrect

recalling cancellation, memory (retention)

recalling to mind honorary

recant abrogate (rescind), cancel, disaffirm, disavow, disclaim, disinherit, disown (deny the validity), negate, nullify, renounce, repent, repudiate, rescind, revoke, tergiversate, vacate (void), withdraw

recantare recant

recantation abjuration, abolition, bad faith, cancellation, countermand, denial, disclaimer, negation, rejection, renunciation, repudiation, rescission, retraction, reversal, revocation

recap scenario, summary

recapitulate compile, copy, digest (summarize), itemize, quote, recite, recount, reiterate, repeat (state again), review

recapitulated compact (pithy)

recapitulation account (report), capsule, compendium, digest, hornbook, narration, outline (synopsis), paraphrase, recital, report (detailed account), restatement, retrospect, review (official reexamination), scenario, statement, story (narrative), summary, synopsis

recapitulatory repetitious

recapture rearrest, recoup (regain), recover, recovery (repossession), redeem (repurchase), repossess, rescue, salvage

recast alter, change, convert (change use), modify (alter), reconstruct, recreate, reform, reform, revise, tempered, transform

recasting reorganization

recede decrease, depart, diminish, ebb, erode, escheat, regress, retire (retreat), retreat, revert, subside, withdraw

recede from view disappear

recedence capitulation

recedere ebb, retire (retreat)

receding regressive

receipt acceptance, binder, quitclaim, realization

receipt for payment binder

receipt in full payment (act of paying)

receipted payment collection (payment), satisfaction (discharge of debt)

receipts capital, earnings, income, proceeds, profit, revenue

receivable delinquent (overdue), passable

receival acquisition

receive accept (take), congregate, draw (extract), embrace (encircle), endure (suffer), gain, hold (possess), inherit, instate, obtain, partake, possess, procure, realize (obtain as a profit), reap, tolerate

receive a false idea misconstrue

receive a false impression err, misapprehend, miscalculate, misconceive, misconstrue, misinterpret, misread, mistake

receive a legacy inherit

receive a wrong idea misinterpret

receive a wrong impression misconceive, misread, mistake, misunderstand

receive an endowment inherit

receive an incorrect impression misinterpret, misread

receive an instrument officially file (place among official records)

receive as right inherit

receive by bequest inherit

receive by devise inherit

receive by law of descent inherit

receive by succession inherit

receive compensation earn

receive information overhear

receive information aurally hear (perceive by ear)

receive knowledge of overhear

receive money collect (recover money)

receive notice beware

receive payment collect (recover money)

receive property as an heir inherit

receive with approval accept (take)

received common (customary), popular

received maxim principle (axiom)

receiver assignee, bearer, beneficiary, catchall, disciple, fence, feoffee, heir, holder, recipient

receiver of stolen goods fence

receiver of stolen property fence

receiving acquisition, assumption (adoption), receptive

recent current, novel, present (cur-

rent)

receptacle catchall, coffer, depository, enclosure, receiver, repository, treasury

receptaculum depository, refuge, repository, shelter *(protection)*

reception acquisition, adoption *(acceptance),* assumption *(adoption),* ceremony, entrance, receipt *(act of receiving)*

reception room chamber *(compartment)*

receptive available, inclined, liberal *(broad minded),* open *(persuasible),* open-minded, passive, penetrable, perceptive, pliable, pliant, responsive, suasible, susceptible *(responsive),* willing *(not averse)*

receptiveness acceptance, amenability

receptor receiver

recertify reconfirm

recess abeyance, adjourn, adjournment, cloture, continue *(adjourn),* defer *(put off),* discontinuance *(act of discontinuing),* discontinue *(break continuity),* extension *(postponement),* furlough, halt, hiatus, holiday, interruption, interval, lapse *(break),* leave *(absence),* lull, moratorium, pause, pendency, remission, respite *(interval of rest),* rest *(cease from action)*

recession capitulation, decline, erosion, outflow

recessive regressive

rechannel recover

recharge reassess, replenish

recharging renewal

recheck reconfirm, reexamine, review

recidere relapse, relapse

recidivate relapse, return *(go back)*

recidivation recrudescence, relapse

recidivism relapse, reversion *(act of returning)*

recidivist convict, criminal, delinquent, felon, malefactor, outlaw

recidivistic regressive

recidivous incorrigible, regressive, reprobate

recipe system

recipere admit *(give access),* enfranchise

recipience acquisition, assumption *(adoption),* receipt *(act of receiving)*

recipient assignee, bearer, beneficiary, devisee, donee, grantee, heir, holder, legatee, payee, receiver, receptive, subject *(object),* transferee, trustee

recipient of a fee feoffee

recipient of stolen goods fence

recipient of stolen property fence

reciprocal coequal, cognate, common *(shared),* complement, correlate, correlative, counterpart *(complement),* equivalent, related, same

reciprocal action reaction *(response),* repercussion

reciprocal agreement mutual understanding

reciprocal commitment mutual understanding

reciprocal concession composition *(agreement in bankruptcy)*

reciprocal exchange interchange

reciprocal feeling consortium *(marriage companionship)*

reciprocal trade commerce

reciprocality mutuality, quid pro quo, reciprocity

reciprocalize correspond *(be equivalent)*

reciprocally attached conjoint

reciprocalness mutuality, reciprocity

reciprocate beat *(pulsate),* repay, retaliate, return *(respond)*

reciprocating mutual *(reciprocal)*

reciprocation exchange, interchange, mutuality, quid pro quo, reciprocity, reply, reprisal, retribution, revenge

reciprocative convertible, mutual *(reciprocal),* reciprocal, responsive

reciprocator correlate

reciprocity comity, exchange, mutuality, quid pro quo, rapprochement, relationship *(connection)*

reciprocity of obligation agreement *(concurrence)*

recision abolition, retraction

recission revocation

recital account *(report),* declamation, delineation, disclosure *(act of disclosing),* disclosure *(something disclosed),* discourse, instruction *(teaching),* mention *(reference),* narration, report *(detailed account),* restatement, specification, speech, statement, story *(narrative)*

recitation declamation, declaration, delineation, disclosure *(act of disclosing),* discourse, instruction *(teaching),* mention *(reference),* narration, parlance, peroration, proclamation, recital, reference *(citation),* remark, report *(detailed account),* rhetoric *(skilled speech),* speech, statement, story *(narrative)*

recite allege, assert, cite *(state),* converse, convey *(communicate),* declaim, delineate, depict, detail *(particularize),* discourse, discuss, inform *(notify),* mention, phrase, pronounce *(speak),* quote, recapitulate, recount, relate *(tell),* remark, repeat *(state again),* report *(disclose),* speak, utter

recite a spell invoke

recite an incantation invoke

recited aforesaid, repeated, verbal

reckless careless, heedless, hotblooded, ill-advised, ill-judged, impolitic, improvident, imprudent, impulsive *(rash),* injudicious, misadvised, negligent, precipitate, prodigal, profligate *(extravagant),* profuse, remiss, thoughtless, unpolitic, wanton

reckless expenditure misapplication

reckless homocide manslaughter

recklessness audacity, inconsideration, indiscretion, neglect, negligence, temerity

reckon assess *(appraise),* calculate, consider, criticize *(evaluate),* determine, estimate, evaluate, guess, infer, judge, measure, opine, presuppose, rate, speculate *(conjecture),* suspect *(think)*

reckon among contain *(comprise)*

reckon from some point in time date

reckon on expect *(anticipate)*

reckon up sum

reckon with pay

reckoner accountant, comptroller

reckoning accounting, amount *(sum),* appraisal, assessment *(estimation),* bill

(invoice), census, computation, consideration *(contemplation),* consideration *(recompense),* contribution *(indemnification),* cost *(price),* determination, dun, estimate *(approximate cost),* estimate *(idea),* estimation *(calculation),* expiation, invoice *(bill),* measurement, pay, payment *(act of paying),* recovery *(award)*

reclaim claim *(demand),* collect *(recover money),* cure, fix *(repair),* meliorate, purge *(wipe out by atonement),* reconstruct, recoup *(regain),* recover, redeem *(repurchase),* reform, rehabilitate, renew *(refurbish),* repossess, rescue

reclaimable corrigible

reclaimed renascent, repentant

reclaimed materials salvage

reclamare remonstrate

reclamatio remonstrance

reclamation compensation, progress, recovery *(award),* recovery *(repossession),* redemption, reform, rehabilitation, renewal, replacement, replevin, restitution, revival, salvage

reclass reassess, redistribute

reclassify reapportion, redistribute

recline repose *(rest),* rest *(be supported by)*

reclusive solitary

recognition acknowledgment *(acceptance),* adoption *(acceptance),* appreciation *(perception),* apprehension *(perception),* approval, assent, certification *(certification of proficiency),* character *(reputation),* charter *(sanction),* cognition, comprehension, concession *(compromise),* franchise *(license),* identification, knowledge *(awareness),* notice *(heed),* notoriety, perception, realization, reason *(sound judgment),* recollection, remembrance *(recollection),* respect, reward, scienter, sense *(intelligence),* understanding *(comprehension)*

recognizable apparent *(perceptible),* appreciable, arrant *(definite),* ascertainable, cognizable, coherent *(clear),* comprehensible, conspicuous, discernible, distinct *(clear),* explicit, manifest, naked *(perceptible),* obvious, open *(in sight),* palpable, pellucid, perceivable, perceptible, ponderable, prominent, solvable, unambiguous, unmistakable, visible *(noticeable)*

recognizably fairly *(clearly)*

recognizance binder, concession *(compromise),* guaranty, identification, remembrance *(recollection),* specialty *(contract)*

recognize acknowledge *(verify),* admit *(concede),* appreciate *(comprehend),* apprehend *(perceive),* assent, authorize, bear *(tolerate),* bestow, comprehend *(understand),* concede, confirm, countenance, detect, diagnose, discern *(detect with the senses),* find *(discover),* grant *(concede),* hear *(perceive by ear),* heed, identify, notice *(observe),* perceive, pierce *(discern),* realize *(understand),* recall *(remember),* recollect, remember, spy, witness *(have direct knowledge of)*

recognize as different distinguish

recognize as distinct discern *(discriminate)*

recognize as separate differentiate,

discriminate *(distinguish)*

recognize authority of acknowledge *(verify)*

recognize the worth of appreciate *(value)*

recognized allowed, common *(customary)*, customary, familiar *(customary)*, famous, household *(familiar)*, influential, master, ordinary, orthodox, outstanding *(prominent)*, predominant, prescriptive, proverbial, public *(known)*, putative, renowned, right *(suitable)*, salient

recognized because of continued possession prescriptive

recognized by law jural, legitimate *(rightful)*

recognized by the law legal

recognized condition necessity

recognized from accompanying words noscitur a sociis

recognized maxim principle *(axiom)*

recognized principles polity

recognized through use prescriptive

recoil rebuff, refuse, repercussion, retreat, revert

recoil from eschew, shun

recoil from with pride disdain

recoiling reluctance, resilient

recolere resume

recollect identify, recall *(remember)*, recognize *(perceive)*, remember, retain *(keep in possession)*

recollection hindsight, identification, memory *(retention)*, recognition, retrospect

recollective suggestive *(evocative)*

recommence continue *(resume)*, proceed *(continue)*, renew *(begin again)*, reopen, resume

recommencement continuation *(resumption)*, renewal

recommend admonish *(advise)*, advise, advocate, authorize, bestow, coax, counsel, countenance, exhort, incite, indorse, instruct *(direct)*, offer *(propose)*, prefer, prompt, propose, propound, refer *(send for action)*, urge

recommend against expostulate

recommend points of law charge *(instruct on the law)*

recommend to pardon condone

recommendable desirable *(qualified)*

recommendation advice, advocacy, auspices, determination, dictum, direction *(guidance)*, guidance, holding *(ruling of a court)*, judgment *(formal court decree)*, patronage *(support)*, proposal *(suggestion)*, proposition, suggestion, tip *(clue)*

recommendations credentials

recommendatory advisory, favorable *(expressing approval)*

recommended preferential

recommender arbiter

recommission reassign

recommit confine, rearrest, remand

recommit to custody commit *(institutionalize)*

recommitment rendition *(restoration)*

recompensation in value compensation

recompense alimony, bear the expense, brokerage, collect *(recover money)*, collection *(payment)*, commission *(fee)*, compensate *(remunerate)*,

compensation, contribute *(indemnify)*, contribution *(indemnification)*, cover *(provide for)*, damages, disburse *(pay out)*, disbursement *(funds paid out)*, discharge *(payment)*, discharge *(pay a debt)*, earnings, expiation, fee *(charge)*, honorarium, indemnification, indemnify, indemnity, pay, pay, payment *(act of paying)*, payment *(remittance)*, payroll, perquisite, price, prize, quit *(repay)*, reciprocate, recoup *(reimburse)*, recovery *(award)*, refund, refund, reimburse, reimbursement, relief *(legal redress)*, remedy *(legal means of redress)*, remit *(send payment)*, remittance, remunerate, remuneration, reparation *(indemnification)*, repay, requital, restitution, restore *(return)*, retainer, revenue, reward, satisfaction *(discharge of debt)*, satisfy *(discharge)*, trover, wage

recompense for past loss indemnify

recompenser insurer

recompensive compensatory

recompose reconstruct

reconcilable apposite, concordant, congruous, consonant, correlative, placable, suitable

reconcile adapt, agree *(comply)*, arbitrate *(conciliate)*, comport *(agree with)*, compromise *(settle by mutual agreement)*, conform, correspond *(be equivalent)*, disarm *(set at ease)*, mediate, mollify, pacify, placate, propitiate, rationalize, settle, unite

reconcile oneself to submit *(yield)*

reconciled agreed *(harmonized)*, consensual, patient, resigned

reconcilement accordance *(compact)*, accordance *(understanding)*, adjustment, conciliation, condonation, consensus, intercession, rapprochement, reconciliation

reconciler adjuster, arbiter, arbitrator, go-between, intermediary, referee, umpire

reconciliatio accommodation *(adjustment)*

reconciliation accordance *(compact)*, accordance *(understanding)*, adjustment, arrangement *(understanding)*, compatibility, concession *(compromise)*, conciliation, expiation, intercession, mediation, mollification, pact, peace, rapprochement, settlement

reconcinnare renew *(refurbish)*

recondite complex, difficult, equivocal, esoteric, hidden, inapprehensible, incomprehensible, inexplicable, learned, mysterious, nebulous, oblique *(evasive)*, obscure *(abstruse)*, opaque, private *(confidential)*, privy, profound *(esoteric)*, secret

recondite knowledge secret

reconditeness ambiguity

recondition change, fix *(repair)*, reconstitute, reconstruct, rehabilitate, renew *(refurbish)*, renovate, repair, restore *(renew)*, resurrect, transform

reconditioned renascent

reconditioning repair, reparation *(keeping in repair)*

reconditus recondite

reconfine rearrest

reconfirmed nunc pro tunc

reconnaissance examination *(study)*, inspection, observation, research

reconnoiter check *(inspect)*, examine *(study)*, investigate, observe *(watch)*, oversee, patrol, perambulate, spy, study, survey *(examine)*

reconnoiterer spy

reconnoitering discovery

reconsider appeal, reexamine, review, revise

reconsideration appeal, hindsight, retrospect, review *(official reexamination)*

reconstitute convert *(change use)*, reconstruct, reform, rehabilitate, reinforce, reinstate, renew *(refurbish)*, renovate, reproduce, restore *(renew)*

reconstituted renascent

reconstitution reclassification, reform, rehabilitation, renewal, reorganization, replacement

reconstruct alter, change, convert *(change use)*, copy, emend, fix *(repair)*, modify *(alter)*, reconstitute, recreate, reform, rehabilitate, renew *(refurbish)*, renovate, repair, repeat *(do again)*, reproduce, restore *(renew)*, revise, transform

reconstructed renascent, tempered

reconstruction conversion *(change)*, correction *(change)*, reform, rehabilitation, remembrance *(recollection)*, renewal, reorganization, repair, reparation *(keeping in repair)*, replacement

reconvene recall *(call back)*

reconvert reconstitute, rehabilitate, renew *(refurbish)*, renovate, transform

record account *(report)*, bill *(invoice)*, book, calendar *(list of cases)*, calendar *(record of yearly periods)*, cast *(register)*, ceiling, date, deed, docket, document, documentation, dossier, enroll, evidence, file, form *(document)*, impanel, index *(relate)*, inscribe, inscription, instrument *(document)*, inventory, journal, ledger, marginalia, memorandum, notation, note *(brief comment)*, register, register, render *(depict)*, report *(detailed account)*, roll, set down, story *(narrative)*, transcript

record book ledger

record keeper clerk

record keeping registration

record of credits and debits ledger

record of money transactions ledger

record of proceedings docket

record of the court file

record of yearly periods calendar *(record of yearly periods)*

record the vote poll

record-breaking best

recordari recall *(remember)*, recollect, remember

recordatio recollection

recorded documentary, in writing

recorded expression of a formal judgment award, holding *(ruling of a court)*

recorded information dossier, file

recorded item entry *(record)*

recorded material document, documentation, dossier

recorder accountant, amanuensis, clerk, notary public

recording record, registration, transcript

recording secretary amanuensis

records credentials, proof
recount census, converse, convey *(communicate)*, delineate, depict, detail *(particularize)*, disabuse, inform *(notify)*, itemize, mention, notify, quote, recapitulate, recite, relate *(tell)*, repeat *(state again)*, report *(disclose)*
recountal narration, recital, restatement, story *(narrative)*
recounted narrative
recounting narration, recital, report *(detailed account)*, restatement
recoup collect *(recover money)*, outbalance, recover, redeem *(repurchase)*, repossess, restore *(return)*
recoupable deductible *(capable of being deducted from taxes)*
recouping recovery *(repossession)*
recoupment compensation, expiation, indemnity, recompense, recovery *(award)*, refund, reimbursement, replevin, restitution, salvage, satisfaction *(discharge of debt)*, setoff, trover
recourse alternative *(option)*, tool
recourse to some higher power appeal
recourse to the principles of natural justice equity *(justice)*
recover collect *(recover money)*, cure, hold *(possess)*, obtain, occupy *(take possession)*, reap, reclaim, recoup *(regain)*, redeem *(repurchase)*, renew *(refurbish)*, repossess, rescue
recover knowledge recognize *(perceive)*
recover knowledge of recall *(remember)*, remember
recover property evict
recoverable corrigible
recovery adverse possession, boom *(prosperity)*, compensation, cure, damages, expiation, improvement, out of pocket, progress, recompense, redemption, reform, repair, replacement, replevin, restitution, resurgence, revival, salvage, trover
recovery of property replevin
recovery of property from another's possession eviction
recreance sedition
recreancy bad faith, desertion, disloyalty, infidelity, lapse *(expiration)*, recidivism, sedition
recreant caitiff, convict, criminal, degenerate, delinquent, disgraceful, disreputable, faithless, false *(disloyal)*, felon, iniquitous, lawless, peccable, reprehensible, reprobate, untrue
recreare reassure
recreate copy, portray, reconstruct, renew *(refurbish)*, renovate, repeat *(do again)*, reproduce, restore *(renew)*
recreated renascent
recreation enjoyment *(pleasure)*, reform, rehabilitation, revival
recreation time leave *(absence)*
recremental excess
recrementitial excess
recrementitious excess
recriminate answer *(respond legally)*, blame, censure, charge *(accuse)*, countercharge, denounce *(condemn)*, dispute *(contest)*, impeach, reprehend, reprimand, return *(respond)*
recrimination answer *(judicial response)*, charge *(accusation)*, condemna-

tion *(blame)*, contention *(opposition)*, denunciation, incrimination
recriminative critical *(faultfinding)*
recrudesce recur, relapse
recrudescence relapse, renewal
recrudescency recrudescence, relapse, renewal
recruit disciple, employ *(engage services)*, enroll, hire, induct, novice, prospect *(prospective patron)*, retain *(employ)*, supply, volunteer
rectifiable corrigible
rectification accommodation *(adjustment)*, adjustment, collection *(payment)*, compensation, correction *(change)*, reform, relief *(legal redress)*, remedial statute, remedy *(legal means of redress)*, reorganization, repair, reparation *(keeping in repair)*, revision *(process of correcting)*
rectify adjust *(resolve)*, ameliorate, amend, attune, cure, disabuse, edit, emend, fix *(repair)*, meliorate, modify *(alter)*, purge *(purify)*, redress, reform, regulate *(adjust)*, rehabilitate, remedy, renew *(refurbish)*, repair, restore *(renew)*, revise, settle
rectilineal direct *(straight)*
rectitude conscience, credibility, ethics, fairness, good faith, honor *(good reputation)*, integrity, justice, merit, principle *(virtue)*, probity, propriety *(correctness)*, right *(righteousness)*, trustworthiness, veracity
rectus direct *(forthright)*, proper, right *(righteousness)*
recumbency abeyance, prostration
recumbent inactive, passive
recuperare recover
recuperate cure, progress
recuperation cure, rehabilitation, resurgence, revival
recuperative medicinal, remedial, salubrious
recuperatory medicinal
recur occur *(happen)*, repeat *(do again)*
recurrence continuation *(resumption)*, cycle, frequency, habit, recrudescence, redundancy, regularity, relapse, renewal, resurgence, revival
recurrent chronic, consecutive, habitual, incessant, insistent, intermittent, iterative, periodic, repeated, repetitious, routine, sporadic, typical, usual
recurring chronic, habitual, intermittent, iterative, periodic, regular *(orderly)*, repeated, repetitious, routine, sporadic
recurring period cycle
recurring theme motif
recusancy contempt *(disobedience to the court)*, contest *(dispute)*, defiance, disagreement, dissidence, nonconformity, resistance, schism, sedition, violation
recusant contumacious, disobedient, dissenting, dissident, insubordinate, lawless, malcontent, nonconsenting, radical *(favoring drastic change)*, recalcitrant, restive
recusare decline *(reject)*, protest
recusatio protest, refusal
red neck bigot
red tape bureaucracy
redact edit, formulate, revise

redaction correction *(change)*
redargue disaccord
redarguere disprove, rebut, refute
redargution confutation
reddere refund, reimburse, render *(deliver)*, repay, restore *(return)*, return *(refund)*
reddition restitution
rede advice
redeem buy, collect *(recover money)*, cure, defray, discharge *(pay a debt)*, disenthrall, extricate, free, fulfill, indemnify, liberate, liquidate *(convert into cash)*, outbalance, pardon, purchase, purge *(wipe out by atonement)*, reclaim, recoup *(regain)*, recover, reform, refund, rehabilitate, renovate, repossess, rescue, restore *(return)*, save *(conserve)*
redeemable corrigible, payable, receivable
redeemable part coupon
redeemer benefactor, customer, good samaritan
redeliberate reconsider
redelivery replevin
redemption discharge *(payment)*, freedom, indemnification, indemnity, liberation, progress, ransom, recovery *(repossession)*, rehabilitation, replevin, restitution, salvage
redemption slip coupon
redemptive compensatory
redesign renew *(refurbish)*
redetain rearrest
redimire intertwine
redintegrare renew *(begin again)*
redintegrate fix *(repair)*, rehabilitate, renew *(refurbish)*, renovate, restore *(renew)*
redintegrated renascent
redintegration reconversion, rehabilitation, repair, revival
redire return *(go back)*
redirect divert
redisperse reapportion
redistribute reapportion, reassign, subdivide
redistributing reclassification
redistribution reclassification
redistrict reapportion
reditus proceeds, rent, revenue
redivide reapportion, reassign, redistribute, subdivide
redivivus renascent
redo emend, reconstitute, reconstruct, recreate, reform, renew *(refurbish)*, repeat *(do again)*, reproduce, restore *(renew)*, transform
redolent suggestive *(evocative)*
redone repeated
redouble accrue *(increase)*, accumulate *(enlarge)*, expand, intensify, reinforce, reiterate
redoubled repeated
redoubling augmentation, renewal
redoubtable formidable, indomitable, inexpugnable
redound result
redraft edit, redact
redress adjust *(resolve)*, collection *(payment)*, compensate *(remunerate)*, contribution *(indemnification)*, cure, cure, disbursement *(funds paid out)*, equity *(justice)*, fix *(repair)*, habeas corpus, help, recompense, recourse, recov-

ery *(award)*, rectify, reform, reimburse, reimbursement, remedy, renew *(refurbish)*, repair, reparation *(indemnification)*, repent, requital, restitution, restore *(return)*, satisfaction *(discharge of debt)*, trover

redressible wrong cause of action

reduce abate *(lessen)*, abridge *(shorten)*, abstract *(summarize)*, allay, alleviate, assuage, attenuate, beat *(defeat)*, commute, condense, constrict *(compress)*, curtail, debilitate, decrease, demean *(make lower)*, demote, deplete, depose *(remove)*, depress, derogate, digest *(summarize)*, diminish, discount *(minimize)*, divest, erode, expend *(consume)*, extenuate, impair, lessen, minimize, mitigate, moderate *(temper)*, modify *(moderate)*, mollify, palliate *(abate)*, rebate, relax, remit *(relax)*, restrict, retrench, subdue, subjugate

reduce a punishment commute

reduce expenses retrench

reduce forces disarm *(divest of arms)*

reduce in asperity commute

reduce in intensity attenuate

reduce in quality debase

reduce in severity allay

reduce in strength attenuate, disarm *(divest of arms)*, extenuate

reduce tension ease

reduce the armament disarm *(divest of arms)*

reduce the edge obtund

reduce the mark-up discount *(reduce)*

reduce the purchasing value of depreciate

reduce the strength of depreciate, dilute

reduce the violence obtund

reduce to a code codify

reduce to a digest codify

reduce to a formula formulate

reduce to ashes deflagrate

reduce to chaos mismanage

reduce to extreme purity and strength distill

reduce to inferior rank demote

reduce to method regulate *(adjust)*

reduce to nothing annul, destroy *(efface)*, extinguish

reduce to nought annul

reduce to order arrange *(methodize)*, classify, codify, file *(arrange)*, orchestrate, organize *(arrange)*, pigeonhole, sort

reduce to subjection repress

reduce to the ranks demote, humiliate

reduce volume constrict *(compress)*

reduced brief, inferior *(lower in position)*, insolvent, minimal, nominal, poor *(underprivileged)*

reduced circumstances poverty, privation

reduced in means destitute

reduced to a writing in writing

reduced to beggary poor *(underprivileged)*

reducing mitigating

reducing to order classification

reductio ad absurdum counterargument

reduction abatement *(reduction)*, abridgment *(condensation)*, abstract,

capsule, curtailment, decrease, deduction *(diminution)*, deterioration, diminution, discount, erosion, mitigation, moderation, mollification, rebate, refund, relief *(release)*, remission

reduction in rank degradation

reduction to order method

redundance overage, redundancy, sufficiency, surfeit, surplus

redundancy overage, prolixity, surplus, tautology

redundant excess, excessive, expendable, extraneous, inordinate, iterative, needless, nonessential, profuse, prolix, repetitious, superfluous, turgid, unnecessary

redundantia redundancy

redundare redound

redundent repeated

reduplicate copy, plagiarize, repeat *(do again)*, reproduce

reduplicated repeated

reduplicative repeated, repetitious

reecho copy

reechoed repetitious

reeducation rehabilitation

reeking offensive *(offending)*

reel off recite

reembark renew *(begin again)*, reopen

reenact repeat *(do again)*

reenactment duplicate

reendorse reconfirm

reendorsed nunc pro tunc

reenforce reconfirm, relieve *(give aid)*

reengage reassign

reenter renew *(begin again)*, return *(go back)*

reestablish continue *(resume)*, copy, reclaim, reconfirm, reconstitute, reconstruct, recreate, reform, rehabilitate, reinforce, reinstate, relocate, renovate, reopen, restore *(return)*, return *(go back)*

reestablished nunc pro tunc, renascent

reestablishment continuation *(resumption)*, reclassification, reconversion, rehabilitation, renewal, reorganization, resurgence, revival

reestimate reassess

reevaluate reassess, reconsider

reexamination appeal, cross-examination, cross-questioning, hindsight, rehearing, retrospect

reexamine appeal, audit, check *(inspect)*, cross-examine, reconsider, review, revise

reface meliorate

refashion amend, convert *(change use)*, copy, fix *(repair)*, reconstruct, recreate, reform, rehabilitate, renew *(refurbish)*, renovate, reproduce, restore *(renew)*

refashioned renascent

refellere controvert, disprove, refute

refer appertain, apply *(pertain)*, assign *(transfer ownership)*, confer *(consult)*, delegate, hint, pertain, quote, relegate, remit *(submit for consideration)*, submit *(give)*

refer back recommit

refer to allude, appeal, ascribe, bear *(adduce)*, cite *(state)*, concern *(involve)*, connote, consult *(seek information*

from), denote, mention, specify

refer to for information consult *(seek information from)*

refer to legal authorities cite *(state)*

referable to comparative

referee adjudicate, arbiter, arbitrate *(conciliate)*, arbitrator, decide, determine, go-between, hear *(give a legal hearing)*, intercede, intermediary, judge, judge, mediate, negotiate, umpire

reference attribution, citation *(attribution)*, connection *(relation)*, connotation, derivation, documentation, excerpt, guidance, indication, innuendo, insinuation, intimation, recommendation, referral, relation *(connection)*, relevance, reminder

reference book directory

reference form form *(document)*

reference work directory

references credentials

referendary arbitrator

referendum election *(selection by vote)*, plebiscite, poll *(casting of votes)*

referent mention *(reference)*

referential comparative, leading *(guiding)*, suggestive *(evocative)*

referment reference *(allusion)*, reference *(citation)*, referral

referral reference *(citation)*

referre enter *(record)*, move *(judicially request)*, recapitulate, recount, refer *(send for action)*, render *(deliver)*, report *(disclose)*, restore *(return)*, submit *(give)*

referrence delegation *(assignment)*

referrential pertinent

referring comparative, delegation *(assignment)*, germane, pertinent, relative *(relevant)*

referring to relevant

reficere fix *(repair)*, reconstruct, renew *(refurbish)*, renovate, repair

refill replenish, supply

refilled replete

refine amend, clarify, compound, cultivate, decontaminate, develop, edit, elaborate, emend, enhance, expurgate, meliorate, modify *(alter)*, perfect, purge *(purify)*, reform

refined aesthetic, choate lien, civil *(polite)*, discreet, elegant, meritorious, punctilious

refined discrimination discretion *(quality of being discreet)*

refined manners decorum

refined taste decorum

refinement amendment *(correction)*, amenity, civilization, clarification, courtesy, decorum, development *(progression)*, discretion *(quality of being discreet)*, presence *(poise)*, propriety *(correctness)*, reform

refining revision *(process of correcting)*

refinish renew *(refurbish)*

refit fix *(repair)*, rehabilitate, renew *(refurbish)*, renovate, repair, restore *(renew)*

refitting renewal, repair

reflect brood, characterize, deliberate, muse, pause, radiate, rationalize, reason *(conclude)*

reflect again reconsider

reflect discredit upon discommend,

disgrace, dishonor *(deprive of honor)*
reflect dishonor upon discredit, disgrace
reflect honor on dedicate
reflect honor upon bestow
reflect over deliberate
reflect poorly upon denigrate, disparage
reflect shame upon disgrace
reflect upon brand *(stigmatize)*, consider, deliberate, denounce *(condemn)*, ponder, study, weigh
reflecting circumspect, discreet, judicious, juridical
reflection apprehension *(perception)*, bad repute, comment, concept, consideration *(contemplation)*, contemplation, criticism, deliberation, dialectic, discredit, hindsight, idea, impression, innuendo, introspection, memory *(retention)*, observation, opinion *(belief)*, penumbra, remark, repercussion, resemblance
reflective aforethought, circumspect, cogitative, deliberate, pensive, profound *(esoteric)*, rational, solemn
reflex controlled *(restrained)*, repercussion
reflex action instinct
refluence outflow
refluent regressive
reflux decrease, outflow
refocillate recreate
reform ameliorate, amend, change, convert *(change use)*, convert *(persuade)*, correction *(change)*, development *(progression)*, emend, fix *(repair)*, meliorate, modify *(alter)*, progress, reconstitute, reconstruct, recreate, rectify, redeem *(satisfy debts)*, repair, repair, repent, reproduce, restore *(renew)*, revision *(process of correcting)*, transform
reform school reformatory
reformable corrigible
reformation amendment *(correction)*, correction *(change)*, development *(progression)*, reform, rehabilitation, renewal, reorganization, repair
reformational corrigible, disciplinary *(punitory)*, progressive *(advocating change)*
reformative disciplinary *(punitory)*, medicinal, progressive *(advocating change)*, remedial, repentant
reformatory corrigible, disciplinary *(punitory)*, jail, penitentiary, prison, progressive *(advocating change)*, repentant
reformed penitent, renascent, repentant
reformed character penitent
reformer insurgent, malcontent
reformers lobby
refractoriness contempt *(disobedience to the court)*
refractory contumacious, difficult, disobedient, disorderly, fractious, froward, hostile, incorrigible, indomitable, inflexible, insubordinate, intractable, lawless, obdurate, perverse, recalcitrant, restive, uncontrollable, unruly, unyielding, vicious
refrain cease, desist, eschew, forbear, shun, stop, withhold
refrain from avoid *(evade)*, forgo, forswear, waive

refrain from action forbear
refrain from noticing ignore
refrain from punishing condone
refrain from using conserve
refrain from working strike *(refuse to work)*
refraining avoidance *(evasion)*
refraining from involvement laissez faire
refraining from utterance mute
refrainment abstention
refresh meliorate, reassure, reconstruct, recreate, renew *(refurbish)*, renovate, repair, replenish, restore *(renew)*
refresh one's memory recall *(remember)*
refresh the memory remind
refreshed renascent
refreshing palatable, sapid, unusual
refreshment enjoyment *(pleasure)*, renewal, revival, solace, treat
refuel replenish
refuge asylum *(hiding place)*, asylum *(protection)*, bulwark, cache *(hiding place)*, haven, home *(domicile)*, inhabitation *(place of dwelling)*, lodging, protection, shelter *(protection)*, shelter *(tax benefit)*, shield
refugee alien
refugee prisoner fugitive
refugium refuge
refulgent lucid
refund bear the expense, compensate *(remunerate)*, consideration *(recompense)*, defray, discharge *(payment)*, discharge *(pay a debt)*, indemnify, indemnity, quit *(repay)*, rebate, rebate, reciprocate, recoup *(reimburse)*, reimburse, reimbursement, repay, replace, replacement, restitution, restore *(return)*
refunding compensatory
refundment refund
refurbish fix *(repair)*, meliorate, reconstruct, rehabilitate, reinforce, renew *(refurbish)*, renovate, repair
refurbishment reparation *(keeping in repair)*
refusal bar *(obstruction)*, declination, disapproval, disclaimer, exclusion, negation, noncompliance *(nonobservance)*, ostracism, prohibition, rebuff, rejection, renunciation, repudiation, resistance
refusal of agreement dissension
refusal of approval veto
refusal of bail bondage
refusal of consent declination
refusal to accept dishonor *(nonpayment)*
refusal to answer demurrer
refusal to be provoked longanimity
refusal to become involved laissez faire
refusal to believe cloud *(suspicion)*, doubt *(suspicion)*
refusal to comply mutiny
refusal to do business boycott
refusal to furnish work lockout
refusal to obey disregard *(omission)*, infraction
refusal to obey orders contempt *(disobedience to the court)*
refusal to pay default, dishonor *(nonpayment)*, nonpayment
refusal to sanction veto
refuse abrogate *(annul)*, ban, bar *(ex-*

clude), censor, condemn *(ban)*, constrain *(restrain)*, debar, decline *(reject)*, disaffirm, disallow, disapprove *(reject)*, disavow, dismiss *(put out of consideration)*, disobey, disoblige, dissent *(withhold assent)*, forbid, forgo, forswear, hold out *(resist)*, prohibit, proscribe *(prohibit)*, protest, rebuff, refrain, reject, renounce, shirk, spurn, waive, withhold
refuse approval forbid
refuse assent disaccord, disagree, dissent *(withhold assent)*
refuse assent to disapprove *(reject)*
refuse bail imprison
refuse consent disapprove *(reject)*, forbid, hold out *(resist)*
refuse credence disavow, disbelieve, disown *(deny the validity)*, impugn
refuse payment dishonor *(refuse to pay)*
refuse permission ban, censor, interdict, prohibit, proscribe *(prohibit)*
refuse to accept contest, contradict, decline *(reject)*, disaccord, disavow, disown *(deny the validity)*, except *(object)*, reject, repudiate, spurn
refuse to acknowledge deny *(contradict)*, disaccord, disallow, disavow, ignore, repudiate
refuse to admit contest, deny *(contradict)*, disaccord, disavow, disbelieve, disown *(deny the validity)*, dissent *(withhold assent)*, exclude, gainsay, ignore
refuse to agree disagree
refuse to allow deny *(contradict)*, deny *(refuse to grant)*, disallow, forbid, inhibit
refuse to associate with isolate
refuse to authorize forbid
refuse to believe disbelieve, doubt *(distrust)*
refuse to bestow deny *(refuse to grant)*
refuse to confirm disapprove *(reject)*
refuse to conform cross *(disagree with)*, rebel
refuse to consent disaccord
refuse to consider exclude, reject
refuse to corroborate disallow, disavow, disown *(deny the validity)*
refuse to credit disbelieve
refuse to disclose withhold
refuse to give deny *(refuse to grant)*
refuse to give permission forbid
refuse to give up endure *(last)*, persevere, persist
refuse to grant constrain *(restrain)*, disallow
refuse to hear disregard, ignore
refuse to honor dishonor *(refuse to pay)*
refuse to honor a commitment renege
refuse to honor a promise renege
refuse to include exclude
refuse to know disregard
refuse to notice ignore
refuse to obey disobey
refuse to oblige disoblige
refuse to permit deny *(refuse to grant)*, forbid
refuse to ratify disapprove *(reject)*
refuse to receive disapprove *(reject)*
refuse to recognize disown *(refuse to*

acknowledge), neglect
refuse to regard disregard
refuse to sanction disapprove *(reject)*
refuse to see exclude
refuse to submit resist *(withstand),* withstand
refuse to supply deny *(refuse to grant)*
refuse to support rebel, secede
refuse to sustain overrule
refuse to tolerate persecute
refuse to trust doubt *(distrust)*
refuse to waste conserve
refuse to yield endure *(last),* persevere, resist *(oppose)*
refused inadmissible
refusing disinclined, dissident, nonconsenting, reluctant
refusing to admit dissenting
refusing to agree dissenting, irreconcilable
refusing to harmonize irreconcilable
refusing to obey contumacious
refusing to relent persistent
refutability cloud *(suspicion)*
refutable contestable, controversial, debatable, defeasible, disputable, dubious, dubitative, litigable, untenable
refutal answer *(reply),* contradiction
refutare controvert
refutation answer *(judicial response),* argument *(pleading),* confutation, contradiction, counterargument, defeat, demurrer, denial, negation, opposition, plea, repudiation
refutative contradictory, contrary
refutatory contradictory, contrary
refute answer *(reply),* avoid *(cancel),* conflict, contradict, contravene, controvert, countercharge, countervail, cross *(disagree with),* debate, defeat, disaccord, disaffirm, disagree, disallow, disown *(deny the validity),* disprove, dispute *(contest),* dispute *(debate),* gainsay, impugn, invalidate, negate, oppose, oppugn, overthrow, parry, rebut, reply
refute by argument countercharge
refuting contradictory, contrary, dissenting, negative
regain collect *(recover money),* reclaim, recover, redeem *(repurchase),* repossess
regaining recovery *(repossession)*
regainment recovery *(repossession)*
regard affection, appertain, apply *(pertain),* aspect, caution *(vigilance),* character *(reputation),* complexion, concern *(interest),* concern *(care),* concern *(involve),* consider, consideration *(sympathetic regard),* credit *(recognition),* deem, defer *(yield in judgment),* deference, diligence *(care),* discern *(detect with the senses),* estimation *(esteem),* hear *(give attention to),* heed, homage, honor *(good reputation),* honor *(outward respect),* honor, interest *(concern),* keep *(fulfill),* mention *(tribute),* note *(notice),* notice *(heed),* notice *(observe),* observation, observe *(watch),* opine, outlook, perceive, perception, prestige, presuppose, prudence, recognition, reputation, respect, surmise, worth
regard as apprehend *(perceive)*
regard as axiomatic postulate, presume

regard as wrong disapprove *(condemn)*
regard carefully check *(inspect),* concentrate *(pay attention),* examine *(study),* focus, scrutinize
regard indulgently excuse
regard likely expect *(consider probable)*
regard studiously peruse
regard unfavorably disfavor
regard upon deliberate
regard with blame disapprove *(condemn)*
regard with favor favor
regard with kindness favor
regard with proud contempt disdain
regard with sorrow deplore
regard with suspicion doubt *(distrust),* mistrust
regardful careful, circumspect, cognizant, conscientious, conscious *(aware),* discreet, judicious, meticulous, obedient, painstaking, particular *(exacting),* politic, preventive, prudent, vigilant
regardfully respectfully
regardfulness discretion *(quality of being discreet),* interest *(concern),* notice *(heed)*
regarding pertinent, wherein
regardless careless, cursory, derelict *(negligent),* inadvertent, insusceptible *(uncaring),* lax, negligent, perfunctory, thoughtless
regardless of irrespective
regardlessness disregard *(lack of respect),* disregard *(omission),* disregard *(unconcern),* inconsideration, negligence
regauge reassess
regency dominion *(supreme authority),* hegemony, hierarchy *(persons in authority),* predominance, regime
regeneracy revival
regenerate change, convert *(change use),* cure, fix *(repair),* meliorate, penitent, reclaim, reconstitute, reconstruct, recreate, reform, renew *(begin again),* renew *(refurbish),* renovate, repeat *(do again),* restore *(renew),* resurrect, transform
regenerated renascent
regenerateness reconversion
regeneration development *(progression),* reconversion, reform, rehabilitation, renewal, resurgence, revival
regenesis reconversion, resurgence, revival
regent plenipotentiary, sovereign *(absolute),* substitute
regere direct *(supervise),* govern, manage
regignere reproduce
regime hierarchy *(persons in authority),* management *(directorate),* system, tenure
regimen control *(supervision)*
regimen regime, regulation *(rule),* system
regiment control *(regulate),* manage, marshal, orchestrate, organize *(arrange),* oversee
regimentation distribution *(arrangement),* form *(arrangement),* regulation *(management)*
regio direction *(course),* district, region, section *(vicinity),* territory

region area *(province),* bailiwick, capacity *(sphere),* circuit, coverage *(scope),* district, division *(administrative unit),* domain *(sphere of influence),* locality, location, parcel, province, realm, scope, seat, section *(vicinity),* sphere, territory, vicinity, zone
regional local, native *(domestic),* parochial, provincial
register account *(evaluation),* book, calendar *(list of cases),* calendar *(record of yearly periods),* date, digest *(comprehend),* docket, document, empanel, enroll, enter *(record),* file, file *(place among official records),* form *(document),* impanel, inscribe, inventory, itemize, join *(associate oneself with),* journal, ledger, marginalia, notary public, notation, poll *(canvass),* poll, program, record, record, roll, set down, subscribe *(promise),* survey *(poll),* tabulate
register of cases calendar *(list of cases)*
register one's vote cast *(register)*
registered person member *(individual in a group)*
registerer notary public
registering census
registrar accountant, clerk, comptroller, notary public
registration census, entry *(record),* poll *(canvass),* reservation *(engagement),* subscription
registration book register
registry docket, file, form *(document),* ledger, registration, roll
règlement act *(enactment)*
reglement bylaw
regnancy government *(administration)*
regnant dominant, master, paramount, powerful, predominant, rife, sovereign *(absolute)*
régnant prevailing *(having superior force)*
regnare rule *(govern)*
regradation reclassification
regrade retreat
regrater broker
regress decline, deteriorate, escheat, recidivate, relapse, relapse, reversion *(act of returning),* revert
regression decline, lapse *(expiration),* recidivism, recrudescence, relapse, reversion *(act of returning)*
regressive decadent
regret deplore, dissatisfaction, refuse, remorse, repent
regret profoundly deplore
regretful contrite, penitent, remorseful, repentant
regretfulness remorse
regrets refusal
regrettable deplorable, lamentable
regretted regrettable
regretting contrite, repentant
regroup redistribute
regrouping reclassification
regula canon, law, maxim, principle *(axiom),* rule *(guide),* standard
regular accustomed *(customary),* chronic, consistent, constant, continual *(connected),* conventional, customary, daily, familiar *(customary),* general, habitual, household *(familiar),* mun-

dane, natural, ordinary, periodic, prevailing *(current)*, prevalent, punctual, repeated, routine, systematic, traditional, typical, uniform, usual
regular arrangement method
regular employment pursuit *(occupation)*
regular performance norm
regular procedure matter of course
regular proceeding process *(course)*
regular recurrence regularity
regular return cycle, regularity
regularity arrangement *(ordering)*, array *(order)*, constant, form *(arrangement)*, frequency, method, organization *(structure)*, system, uniformity
regularity of action method
regularity of recurrence cycle, frequency
regularize adapt, codify, coordinate, modify *(alter)*, naturalize *(acclimate)*, regulate *(adjust)*
regularly as a rule, generally, invariably
regularness regularity
regulate administer *(conduct)*, arbitrate *(conciliate)*, arrange *(methodize)*, attune, check *(inspect)*, conduct, coordinate, determine, direct *(supervise)*, discipline *(control)*, file *(arrange)*, fix *(arrange)*, govern, handle *(manage)*, manage, manipulate *(utilize skillfully)*, marshal, mitigate, moderate *(preside over)*, modify *(moderate)*, officiate, operate, orchestrate, organize *(arrange)*, oversee, palliate *(abate)*, police, preclude, prescribe, preside, prohibit, qualify *(condition)*, rule *(govern)*, superintend
regulated periodic, regular *(orderly)*, safe, systematic
regulated by conditional, dependent
regulating adjustment, leading *(guiding)*
regulation act *(enactment)*, administration, boiler plate, bureaucracy, bylaw, canon, check *(bar)*, codification, condition *(contingent provision)*, constitution, control *(supervision)*, criterion, custody *(supervision)*, dictate, direction *(guidance)*, direction *(order)*, discipline *(training)*, disposition *(final arrangement)*, edict, enactment, familiar *(customary)*, fiat, government *(administration)*, instruction *(direction)*, law, management *(supervision)*, mandate, measure, moderation, ordinance, ordinary, precept, prescription *(directive)*, principle *(axiom)*, quota, requirement, restriction, rubric *(authoritative rule)*, rule *(legal dictate)*, statute, supervision, supremacy, writ
regulation by a system classification
regulation by law code, edict
regulation by statute code, edict, legalization
regulation of finances economy *(economic system)*
regulations code, legislation *(enactments)*, mode, protocol *(etiquette)*
regulative administrative
regulatory civic, disciplinary *(punitory)*
rehabilitate cure, fix *(repair)*, meliorate, reconstruct, recreate, rectify, reform, reinstate, renew *(refurbish)*,

renovate, repair, restore *(renew)*
rehabilitated renascent
rehabilitation correction *(change)*, improvement, progress, reconversion, remedy *(legal means of redress)*, rendition *(restoration)*, renewal, reorganization, repair, reparation *(keeping in repair)*
rehash copy, repeat *(state again)*, restatement
rehear appeal, reconsider
rehearing appeal
rehearsal discipline *(training)*, preparation
rehearse practice *(train by repetition)*, recite, review
rehearsed repeated
rehire reinstate
rei adiacere abut
rei adversari militate
rei deditus addicted
rei obstare militate
reicere rebuff, reject, repudiate
reidentification remembrance *(recollection)*
reidentify recognize *(perceive)*, remember
reiectio rejection, renunciation
reify substantiate
reign dominion *(supreme authority)*, govern, government *(administration)*, hegemony, influence, jurisdiction, power, predominance, predominate *(command)*, preside, prevail *(triumph)*, regime, rule *(govern)*, term *(duration)*
reign of terror lynch law, oppression
reign over dominate, handle *(manage)*
reigning influential, master, paramount, powerful, predominant, rife, sovereign *(absolute)*
reimburse bear the expense, compensate *(remunerate)*, contribute *(indemnify)*, defray, disburse *(pay out)*, indemnify, pay, quit *(repay)*, rebate, reciprocate, refund, remunerate, repay, replace, restore *(return)*, return *(refund)*, satisfy *(discharge)*
reimbursement collection *(payment)*, commission *(fee)*, compensation, consideration *(recompense)*, contribution *(indemnification)*, damages, disbursement *(funds paid out)*, discharge *(payment)*, honorarium, indemnification, indemnity, pay, payment *(act of paying)*, payment *(remittance)*, rebate, receipt *(voucher)*, recompense, refund, remittance, remuneration, reparation *(indemnification)*, restitution, satisfaction *(discharge of debt)*
reimbursing compensatory
reimprison rearrest
rein constraint *(restriction)*, damper *(stopper)*, disadvantage, fetter, hamper, oversee, subdue
rein in constrict *(inhibit)*, detain *(restrain)*, discipline *(control)*, inhibit, repress, stem *(check)*, withhold
reinaugurate reinstate
reincarcerate remand
reincarnate resurrect
reincarnation revival
reindoctrination rehabilitation
reinfection recrudescence
reinforce accumulate *(enlarge)*, aid, assist, bear *(support)*, bear *(yield)*, com-

pound, corroborate, develop, enhance, heighten *(augment)*, help, preserve, side, supplement, support *(assist)*, support *(corroborate)*, sustain *(confirm)*, sustain *(prolong)*
reinforced strong
reinforcement aid *(help)*, assistance, augmentation, boom *(increase)*, help, mainstay, relief *(aid)*
reinless lawless, uncurbed
reinquire reexamine
reinquiry rehearing, review *(official reexamination)*
reins bondage
reins of government bureaucracy
reinstall reassign, reinstate, renew *(begin again)*, replace, restore *(return)*
reinstate continue *(resume)*, proceed *(continue)*, reclaim, remit *(release from penalty)*, renew *(begin again)*, replace, restore *(return)*, surrender *(give back)*
reinstatement continuation *(resumption)*, rehabilitation, renewal, replacement, restitution
reinstitute continue *(resume)*, renew *(begin again)*, reopen, repeat *(do again)*
reinstitution continuation *(resumption)*
reinstitutionalize remand
reinsurance coverage *(insurance)*
reinsure certify *(attest)*
reintegrate reconstitute, rehabilitate, renew *(refurbish)*
reintroduce renew *(begin again)*
reinvest refinance, reinstate
reinvest with restore *(return)*
reinvestigate reexamine
reinvigorate fix *(repair)*, meliorate, recruit, rehabilitate, reinforce, remedy, renew *(refurbish)*, renovate, restore *(renew)*
reinvigoration rehabilitation, renewal
reipublicae forma organization *(association)*, polity
reissue circulate, copy, redistribute, renewal
reiterant iterative, repetitious
reiterate copy, dwell *(linger over)*, quote, reaffirm, recapitulate, recite, recount, repeat *(state again)*, review
reiterated repeated
reiteration narration, platitude, recital, redundancy, restatement
reiterative frequent, incessant, insistent, repetitious
reive hold up *(rob)*
rejail rearrest
reject abrogate *(annul)*, bar *(exclude)*, censor, challenge, condemn *(ban)*, contemn, decry, defect, demonstrate *(protest)*, demur, deny *(refuse to grant)*, deprecate, differ *(disagree)*, disaccord, disaffirm, disallow, disavow, disbelieve, discard, disclaim, discriminate *(treat differently)*, disdain, disfavor, dismiss *(put out of consideration)*, disobey, disoblige, disown *(deny the validity)*, disqualify, dissent *(withhold assent)*, eliminate *(exclude)*, eschew, exclude, expel, fight *(counteract)*, forgo, forswear, gainsay, ignore, oppose, outlaw, overrule, prohibit, proscribe *(denounce)*, rebuff, refuse, relegate, relinquish, remove *(eliminate)*, renounce, repudiate, repulse, resign, select, set aside

(annul), spurn, waive

reject as erroneous deny *(contradict)*

reject as inadmissable disapprove *(reject)*

reject as untrue disbelieve

reject by subsequent action overrule

reject by subsequent decision overrule

rejected derelict *(abandoned)*, disreputable, inadmissible, ineligible, obsolete, outdated, outmoded, poor *(inferior in quality)*, undesirable, unsatisfactory

rejecting disqualification *(rejection)*, negative

rejection abandonment *(repudiation)*, abjuration, bar *(obstruction)*, boycott, breach, check *(bar)*, criticism, declination, denial, disapprobation, disapproval, disclaimer, disdain, dishonor *(nonpayment)*, dismissal *(termination of a proceeding)*, disparagement, disqualification *(rejection)*, exception *(objection)*, exclusion, expulsion, impugnation, intolerance, layoff, negation, nonconformity, objection, ostracism, prohibition, proscription, rebuff, refusal, removal, renunciation, repudiation, reversal, veto

rejective reluctant

rejoice in relish

rejoicing enjoyment *(pleasure)*

rejoin acknowledge *(respond)*, answer *(reply)*, answer *(respond legally)*, countercharge, meet, rebut, reply, respond, retort, return *(respond)*

rejoinder answer *(judicial response)*, answer *(reply)*, confutation, contradiction, counterargument, counterclaim, reaction *(response)*, reply, response

rejoining responsive

rejudge reassess, reconsider

rejuvenate cure, fix *(repair)*, recreate, renew *(refurbish)*, renovate, repair, restore *(renew)*, resurrect

rejuvenated renascent

rejuvenation renewal, reparation *(keeping in repair)*, resurgence, revival

rejuvenescence revival

rekindle renew *(refurbish)*, resurrect

relabi relapse

relapse crossroad *(turning point)*, decline, escheat, lapse *(expiration)*, recidivate, recidivism, recrudescence, regress, renewal, repeat *(do again)*, return *(go back)*, reversion *(act of returning)*

relapsing regressive

relate admit *(concede)*, allege, allude, appertain, apply *(pertain)*, assert, communicate, compare, connect *(relate)*, contact *(communicate)*, converse, convey *(communicate)*, correspond *(be equivalent)*, correspond *(communicate)*, delineate, depict, depose *(testify)*, detail *(particularize)*, disabuse, divulge, impart, inform *(notify)*, involve *(implicate)*, involve *(participate)*, notify, pertain, phrase, recapitulate, recite, recount, refer *(direct attention)*, remark, repeat *(state again)*

relate ideas converse

relate to affiliate, concern *(involve)*

related affiliated, akin *(germane)*, allied, analogous, associated, coadunate, cognate, collateral *(accompanying)*,

comparable *(capable of comparison)*, consanguineous, consonant, correlative, germane, interrelated, pertinent, relative *(relevant)*, relevant, similar, tangential

related by affinity next of kin

related to incident

relatedness association *(connection)*, chain *(nexus)*, connection *(relation)*, degree *(kinship)*

relater informer *(a person who provides information)*

relating akin *(germane)*, germane, pertinent, reference *(citation)*, relative *(relevant)*

relating to apposite, cognate, comparative, correlative, incident

relating to a penalty penal

relating to a will testate

relating to accounts fiscal

relating to method procedural

relating to money matters fiscal

relating to moral action ethical

relating to one side only ex parte

relating to the family domestic *(household)*

relating to the home domestic *(household)*

relating to the management of revenue fiscal

relating to the mechanics of a lawsuit procedural

relating to traffic industrial

relatio report *(detailed account)*

relation affiliation *(bloodline)*, affiliation *(connectedness)*, affinity *(family ties)*, analogy, association *(connection)*, attribution, chain *(nexus)*, collation, contact *(association)*, correlate, delineation, disclosure *(act of disclosing)*, kinship, mention *(reference)*, narration, nexus, privity, proportion, recital, relationship *(connection)*, relationship *(family tie)*, relative, relevance, report *(detailed account)*, representation *(statement)*, story *(narrative)*

relation by birth kindred

relation by blood affinity *(family ties)*, kindred, next of kin

relation by consanguinity kindred

relational comparative, pertinent, relative *(relevant)*

relations blood, dealings, kindred, next of kin

relationship affiliation *(bloodline)*, affiliation *(connectedness)*, affinity *(family ties)*, association *(connection)*, chain *(nexus)*, connection *(relation)*, contact *(association)*, filiation, kinship, nexus, privity, propinquity *(kinship)*, proportion, rapport, relation *(connection)*, relation *(kinship)*, relevance

relationship between persons degree *(kinship)*

relative apposite, cognate, commensurable, commensurate, comparative, consanguineous, correlative, germane, proportionate, related, relation *(kinship)*, relevant

relative estimate comparison, proportion

relative estimation comparison

relative position aspect, degree *(station)*, relation *(connection)*

relative quantity differential

relative to incident

relative to the manner of proceeding procedural

relativeness analogy

relatives kindred, next of kin

relativity analogy, chain *(nexus)*, proportion

relator complainant, informant

relax ease, impair, lull, mollify, recess, relent, relieve *(free from burden)*, repose *(rest)*, rest *(cease from action)*, soothe, subside

relax severity commute

relaxation enjoyment *(pleasure)*, informality, leave *(absence)*, mitigation, mollification, pause, remission, respite *(interval of rest)*

relaxation of control freedom

relaxation of law dispensation *(exception)*

relaxed informal

relay deliver, disseminate, pass *(advance)*, send

relay ideas converse

release absolution, acquit, acquittal, amnesty, assign *(transfer ownership)*, authorize, bestow, catharsis, cede, cession, clear, clemency, composition *(agreement in bankruptcy)*, condone, deed, disband, discharge *(liberation)*, discharge *(dismiss)*, discharge *(liberate)*, disencumber, disengage, disentangle, disenthrall, dismiss *(discharge)*, dispel, disposition *(transfer of property)*, dissociate, emancipation, enable, enfranchise, excuse, exemption, exoneration, extricate, exude, free, freedom, immunity, issuance, issue *(publish)*, layoff, let *(permit)*, liberate, liberation, notice *(announcement)*, notification, palliate *(excuse)*, pardon, pardon, parole, parole, privilege, probation, proclaim, publication *(disclosure)*, publicity, quit *(free of)*, receipt *(proof of receiving)*, redeem *(repurchase)*, redemption, relieve *(free from burden)*, relinquish, remise, remission, remit *(release from penalty)*, report *(detailed account)*, rescue, respite *(reprieve)*, settlement, terminate, vindicate, waiver

release conditionally parole

release from an obligation exonerate

release from attachment disengage

release from bondage disenthrall

release from charge immunity

release from custody discharge *(liberation)*, emancipation, liberate

release from debt satisfaction *(discharge of debt)*

release from duty immunity

release from employment dismissal *(discharge)*

release from imprisonment parole

release from imputation absolve

release from liability exemption, exonerate

release from matrimonial status divorce

release from matrimony divorce

release from obligation dispensation *(exception)*, excuse, exemption, palliate *(excuse)*

release from penalty pardon

release from pressure ease

release from prison parole

release from punishment absolution,

pardon, pardon

release from restraint disenthrall, extricate, free

release from wedlock divorce

released clear *(free from criminal charges)*, exempt, free *(relieved from a burden)*, immune, public *(known)*, unbound

released convict probationer *(released offender)*

released criminal probationer *(released offender)*

released felon probationer *(released offender)*

released lawbreaker probationer *(released offender)*

released malefactor probationer *(released offender)*

released prisoner probationer *(released offender)*

released transgressor probationer *(released offender)*

released wrongdoer probationer *(released offender)*

releasing from custody liberation

releasor licensor

relegate assign *(transfer ownership)*, bar *(exclude)*, delegate, detail *(assign)*, dislodge, remand, remit *(submit for consideration)*, seclude, set aside *(annul)*

relegate to commit *(entrust)*

relegatio banishment

relegation assignment *(transfer of ownership)*, proscription, rejection, removal

relent comply, condone, relax, submit *(yield)*, succumb, surrender *(yield)*, yield *(submit)*

relentless callous, close *(rigorous)*, cold-blooded, cruel, dictatorial, diligent, draconian, faithful *(diligent)*, immutable, implacable, inexorable, inflexible, ironclad, malicious, obdurate, patient, persistent, pertinacious, recalcitrant, remorseless, resolute, rigid, ruthless, sedulous, serious *(devoted)*, severe, stable, steadfast, unalterable, unbending, uncompromising, unrelenting, unyielding

relentlessness cruelty, diligence *(perseverance)*, rigor, severity

relet sublet

relevance connection *(relation)*, consequence *(significance)*, importance, interest *(concern)*, materiality *(consequence)*, propriety *(appropriateness)*, qualification *(fitness)*, relation *(connection)*, relationship *(connection)*, significance

relevancy relationship *(connection)*

relevant akin *(germane)*, applicable, apposite, appropriate, congruous, correlative, felicitous, fit, fitting, germane, important *(significant)*, interrelated, material *(important)*, pertinent, proper, related, suitable, valuable

relevant fact evidence

relevant instance illustration

relevant material evidence

relevant to all general

relevy reassess

reliability adhesion *(loyalty)*, candor *(straightforwardness)*, certainty, certification *(certainness)*, constant, credibility, honor *(good reputation)*, loyalty,

trustworthiness

reliable accurate, authentic, believable, bona fide, candid, certain *(fixed)*, certain *(positive)*, cogent, conscientious, constant, convincing, credible, definite, dependable, diligent, factual, faithful *(loyal)*, fiduciary, honest, incorruptible, indestructible, infallible, loyal, meritorious, official, positive *(incontestable)*, reputable, safe, scrupulous, secure *(sound)*, solid *(sound)*, stable, staunch, steadfast, strong, tenable, true *(authentic)*, true *(loyal)*

reliableness certification *(certainness)*

reliably faithfully

reliance confidence *(faith)*, credence, credit *(delayed payment)*, faith, mainstay, prospect *(outlook)*, security *(safety)*, trust *(confidence)*, weight *(credibility)*

reliance on principle *(axiom)*, surety *(certainty)*

reliant dependent

relic holdover, reminder, token

relief abatement *(reduction)*, aid *(help)*, aid *(subsistence)*, benefit *(betterment)*, benevolence *(act of kindness)*, charity, contour *(outline)*, contour *(shape)*, cure, help, immunity, mitigation, mollification, panacea, reinforcement, remedial statute, remedy *(legal means of redress)*, remedy *(that which corrects)*, remission, reparation *(indemnification)*, replacement, service *(assistance)*, solace, substitute, support *(assistance)*

relief from exoneration

relieve abate *(lessen)*, aid, allay, alleviate, assist, assuage, commute, cure, demote, diminish, discharge *(dismiss)*, discharge *(liberate)*, discharge *(release from obligation)*, disencumber, disentangle, divest, ease, excuse, exonerate, extricate, free, help, meliorate, mitigate, mollify, pacify, palliate *(abate)*, redress, release, remedy, remove *(dismiss from office)*, soothe, succeed *(follow)*

relieve from accusation exonerate

relieve of dispossess

relieve of blame exonerate

relieve of burden vindicate

relieve of complication disentangle

relieve of liability exonerate

relieve of obligation disengage

relieve of responsibility discharge *(release from obligation)*

relieve of something detrimental cure

relieve pressure soothe

relieved free *(relieved from a burden)*, prominent

relieved from liability exempt

reliever backer

relieving curative, mitigating, palliative *(abating)*

religiosus conscientious, scrupulous

religious sacrosanct, solemn

religious order denomination, society

religiously faithfully

relinguish bestow

relinquere leave *(give)*, relinquish

relinquish annul, attorn, cease, cede, confer *(give)*, contribute *(supply)*, convey *(transfer)*, demit, disavow, discontinue *(abandon)*, disown *(refuse to ac-*

knowledge), forfeit, forgo, forswear, lapse *(cease)*, leave *(allow to remain)*, quit *(discontinue)*, release, remise, remit *(relax)*, renounce, resign, retire *(conclude a career)*, secede, set aside *(annul)*, surrender *(give back)*, vacate *(leave)*, vacate *(void)*, waive, withdraw, yield *(submit)*

relinquish life die, perish

relinquished derelict *(abandoned)*

relinquishing claim to cession

relinquishment abandonment *(desertion)*, abandonment *(discontinuance)*, abdication, cancellation, capitulation, cession, concession *(compromise)*, denial, dereliction, desuetude, disclaimer, disposition *(transfer of property)*, expense *(sacrifice)*, pardon, release, remission, renunciation, waiver

relinquishment by gift disposition *(transfer of property)*

reliquum remainder *(remaining part)*

reliquus balance *(amount in excess)*

relish enjoyment *(pleasure)*, penchant, propensity

relishable palatable, preferable, sapid

relive recall *(remember)*, recollect, remember

reload replenish

relocate remove *(transfer)*

reluct contend *(dispute)*, demonstrate *(protest)*, fight *(battle)*, oppugn, parry

reluctance disincentive, doubt *(indecision)*, hesitation, misgiving, resistance, scruple

reluctance to believe cloud *(suspicion)*, doubt *(suspicion)*, incredulity

reluctant averse, disinclined, disobedient, hesitant, renitent, restive

reluctant to punish placable

reluctantly unwillingly

reluctate oppugn, parry, resist *(oppose)*

relume burn

rely on confide *(trust)*, rely, trust

rely on fortune bet

rely upon confide *(trust)*

relying on based on

relying upon subject *(conditional)*

rem administrare administer *(conduct)*

rem amittere forfeit

rem attingere abut

rem bene succeed *(attain)*

rem concedere waive

rem dissimulare connive, disguise

rem faciliorem reddere facilitate

rem hereditate accipere inherit

rem hominem flagitare importune

rem homini adsignare assign *(allot)*

rem integram relinquere abeyance

rem invenire detect

rem longius prosequi dwell *(linger over)*

rem praestare vouch

rem pro re pacisci barter

rem re mutare barter

rem relinquere abandon *(withdraw)*

rem sibi adrogare assume *(seize)*

rem simulare appearance *(look)*

rem tempore tribuere date

rem tempori adsignare date

rem testari attest

remade renascent

remail redirect

remain cease, dwell *(reside)*, endure *(last)*, exist, halt, inhabit, keep *(con-*

tinue), last, lodge *(reside),* persevere, persist, reside, resist *(withstand),* stay *(continue),* stay *(rest),* subsist

remain alive endure *(last),* exist, subsist

remain firm determine, hold out *(resist)*

remain hidden elude

remain unchanged persist

remain unconverted disbelieve

remain undiscovered elude

remain valid endure *(last)*

remainder balance *(amount in excess),* complement, discard, dower, holdover, overage, residual, surplus

remainder over reversion *(remainder of an estate)*

remaining durable, habitation *(act of inhabiting),* lasting, live *(existing),* net, permanent, persistent, residuary, superfluous

remaining course alternative *(option)*

remaining courses choice *(alternatives offered)*

remaining options choice *(alternatives offered)*

remaining period unexpired term

remaining portion balance *(amount in excess),* holdover, remainder *(remaining part)*

remaining time unexpired term

remains balance *(amount in excess),* corpse, remainder *(remaining part),* residual, salvage

remake change, convert *(change use),* copy, fix *(repair),* reconstitute, reconstruct, recreate, reform, rehabilitate, renew *(refurbish),* renovate, repeat *(do again),* reproduce, restore *(renew),* transform

remaking reform, rehabilitation, reorganization

remand bondage, confine, constraint *(imprisonment),* detain *(hold in custody),* recommit, relegate, remit *(submit for consideration)*

remand to custody commit *(institutionalize)*

remanded arrested *(apprehended)*

remanded into custody arrested *(apprehended)*

remanding to custody commitment *(confinement)*

remanent superfluous

remanere remain *(stay)*

remark acknowledge *(respond),* comment, comment, convey *(communicate),* dictum, disclosure *(something disclosed),* express, expression *(comment),* mention *(reference),* muse, observation, phrase, pronouncement, speak, statement

remark on mention

remark upon comment

remarkable considerable, conspicuous, egregious, extraordinary, famous, illustrious, important *(significant),* major, material *(important),* meritorious, momentous, nonconforming, notable, noteworthy, outstanding *(prominent),* paramount, peculiar *(curious),* perceivable, portentous *(eliciting amazement),* prime *(most valuable),* prodigious *(amazing),* prominent, renowned, salient, singular, special, un-

accustomed, uncanny, uncommon, unusual

remarkably particularly

remarriage digamy

remeasure reapportion, reassess

remediable corrigible

remediable by an action at law actionable

remedial curative, medicinal, progressive *(advocating change),* salubrious, salutary

remedial justice equity *(justice)*

remedial measure remedial statute, remedy *(legal means of redress),* remedy *(that which corrects)*

remediless inoperable *(incurable),* irredeemable, irremediable, irreparable, irreversible, irrevocable

remedium relief *(release),* remedy *(that which corrects),* remedy

remedy adjust *(resolve),* alleviate, amend, amendment *(correction),* assuage, correction *(change),* cure, cure, disabuse, drug, emend, fix *(repair),* habeas corpus, help, help, panacea, recourse, rectify, redress, reform, regulate *(adjust),* relief *(legal redress),* relieve *(give aid),* remedial statute, repair, repair, reparation *(indemnification),* reparation *(keeping in repair),* restore *(renew)*

remember occur *(come to mind),* recognize *(perceive),* recollect, retain *(keep in possession),* review

remember with sorrow repent

rememberable notable

remembrance contribution *(donation),* hindsight, impression, memory *(commemoration),* monument, recognition, recollection, reminder, retrospect, reward, token

rememoration retrospect

remind advise, notify, prompt

remind oneself remember

reminder admonition, monument, note *(brief comment),* notice *(announcement),* suggestion

remindful suggestive *(evocative)*

reminisce recall *(remember),* recollect, remember

reminiscence recollection, remembrance *(recollection),* retrospect

reminiscent suggestive *(evocative)*

reminiscential suggestive *(evocative)*

reminisci recollect, remember

remise alienate *(transfer title),* cede, pass *(advance)*

remiss careless, delinquent *(guilty of a misdeed),* delinquent *(overdue),* derelict *(negligent),* dilatory, disobedient, improvident, lax, negligent, oblivious, overdue, perfunctory, slipshod, thoughtless, truant

remissio abatement *(extinguishment),* abatement *(reduction),* remission

remission absolution, acquittal, cessation *(interlude),* collection *(payment),* diminution, discontinuance *(act of discontinuing),* exoneration, halt, lull, pause, relief *(release)*

remission of guilt pardon

remissness culpability, dereliction, disregard *(omission),* laches, laxity, neglect, negligence, omission, oversight *(carelessness)*

remissus languid, lax, negligent

remit absolve, acquit, alleviate, bear *(yield),* bear the expense, bequeath, bestow, compensate *(remunerate),* condone, contribute *(indemnify),* contribute *(supply),* defray, delay, deliver, diminish, discontinue *(break continuity),* dispatch *(send off),* excuse, free, give *(grant),* lessen, lull, offer *(tender),* present *(make a gift),* recommit, reimburse, reinstate, relax, release, relent, remand, remise, remunerate, restore *(return),* satisfy *(discharge),* subside, suspend, transmit

remit a penalty exonerate

remit the penalty palliate *(excuse)*

remit to custody commit *(institutionalize)*

remittal recovery *(award)*

remittance amortization, benefit *(conferment),* collection *(payment),* consideration *(recompense),* delivery, disbursement *(funds paid out),* discharge *(payment),* expenditure, expense *(cost),* installment, pay, payment *(act of paying),* payment *(remittance),* pension, transmittal

remittance for delay demurrage

remitted clear *(free from criminal charges)*

remittent intermittent, periodic, sporadic

remitter restitution

remittere abate *(lessen),* remand, remit *(relax)*

remitting compensatory

remitting to custody commitment *(confinement)*

remnant balance *(amount in excess),* discard, end *(termination),* overage

remodel convert *(change use),* emend, modify *(alter),* reconstitute, reconstruct, recreate, reform, renew *(refurbish),* renovate, restore *(renew),* transform

remodeling development *(progression),* rehabilitation, reorganization, repair

remold convert *(change use),* modify *(alter),* reconstitute, reconstruct, revise, transform

remolded tempered

remonstrance admonition, blame *(culpability),* complaint, criticism, diatribe, disapprobation, disapproval, discredit, dispute, dissension, exception *(objection),* objection, opposition, protest, reply, reprimand

remonstrant remonstrative

remonstrate admonish *(warn),* argue, blame, castigate, caution, censure, challenge, complain *(criticize),* demonstrate *(protest),* denounce *(condemn),* deter, disaccord, disagree, disapprove *(condemn),* discourage, dissuade, expostulate, fault, oppose, oppugn, protest, reason *(persuade),* reprimand

remonstrate against decry

remonstrate with rebuke

remonstration disapprobation, disapproval, dispute, opposition, protest

remonstrative hortative

remora handicap, obstacle, obstruction

remorseful contrite, penitent, repentant

remorseful person penitent

remorsefulness remorse

remorseless brutal, callous, cold-blooded, cruel, incorrigible, obdurate, relentless, ruthless, sinister, unaffected *(uninfluenced)*, unrelenting
remorselessness cruelty
remote foreign, immaterial, impertinent *(irrelevant)*, inaccessible, inapposite, inappropriate, inconsequential, irrelevant, private *(secluded)*, remote *(secluded)*, solitary, unapproachable
remote district frontier
remotion removal
remotus remote *(not proximate)*
removable deductible *(capable of being deducted from taxes)*, defeasible, moving *(in motion)*
removal absence *(nonattendance)*, avoidance *(cancellation)*, banishment, deduction *(diminution)*, defeasance, deportation, discharge *(dismissal)*, distress *(seizure)*, eviction, evulsion, exception *(exclusion)*, exclusion, expropriation *(divestiture)*, expulsion, flight, foreclosure, homicide, layoff, leave *(absence)*, loss, obviation, ouster, rejection, replacement
removal from a job dismissal *(discharge)*
removal from a position dismissal *(discharge)*
removal from employment discharge *(dismissal)*
removal from office dismissal *(discharge)*
removal of a cause out of court dismissal *(termination of a proceeding)*
removal of discrimination integration *(assimilation)*
removal of errors correction *(change)*, revision *(process of correcting)*
remove abscond, abstract *(separate)*, adeem, bowdlerize, cancel, carry away, debar, deduct *(reduce)*, delete, deport *(banish)*, detach, discharge *(dismiss)*, discharge *(release from obligation)*, disencumber, disinter, dislocate, dislodge, dismiss *(discharge)*, dispel, dispossess, dissociate, divest, eject *(evict)*, eject *(expel)*, eliminate *(eradicate)*, eliminate *(exclude)*, eradicate, evacuate, evict, except *(exclude)*, excise *(cut away)*, exclude, expel, expunge, extirpate, extract, hold up *(rob)*, impound, move *(alter position)*, obliterate, oust, overthrow, part *(leave)*, reject, relegate, rescind, retire *(retreat)*, retrench, revoke, seclude, sequester *(seclude)*, succeed *(follow)*, superannuate, supersede, supplant, suspend, transfer, transport, vacate *(leave)*, withdraw
remove a disability enable
remove a hindrance disencumber
remove a restraint disencumber
remove all sign of expunge
remove all trace of expunge
remove an essential part eviscerate
remove an impediment disencumber
remove bodily carry away
remove doubt ascertain, reassure
remove errors edit, emend
remove falsehood disabuse
remove faults amend
remove fear reassure
remove from abandon *(physically leave)*
remove from legal office disbar

remove from life dispatch *(put to death)*
remove from office demote, discharge *(dismiss)*, dismiss *(discharge)*, oust
remove from premises eject *(evict)*
remove from private ownership nationalize
remove from the practice of law disbar
remove from the roll of attorneys disbar
remove misunderstanding resolve *(solve)*
remove one's anxieties lull
remove one's fears lull
remove oneself flee, quit *(evacuate)*, retreat, secede
remove pollutants decontaminate
remove suspicion disarm *(set at ease)*
remove the errors fix *(repair)*
remove the obstacles permit
remove the traces obliterate
remove unhealthy agents decontaminate
remove utterly eradicate
removed alone *(solitary)*, apart, discrete, distinct *(distinguished from others)*, inaccessible, insular, insusceptible *(uncaring)*, irrelative, obscure *(remote)*, private *(secluded)*, remote *(not proximate)*, remote *(secluded)*, separate, solitary, unapproachable
removed from bondage free *(enjoying civil liberty)*, sovereign *(independent)*
removere remove *(transfer)*, seclude
rempublicam gubernare administer *(conduct)*
remunerari compensate *(remunerate)*, remunerate
remunerate bear the expense, contribute *(indemnify)*, defray, disburse *(pay out)*, indemnify, pay, quit *(repay)*, recoup *(reimburse)*, reimburse, remit *(send payment)*, repay, satisfy *(discharge)*
remunerate for injury compensate *(remunerate)*
remuneratio recompense, remuneration
remuneration advance *(allowance)*, alimony, annuity, boom *(prosperity)*, brokerage, collection *(payment)*, commission *(fee)*, compensation, consideration *(recompense)*, contribution *(indemnification)*, disbursement *(funds paid out)*, earnings, fee *(charge)*, honorarium, income, indemnification, indemnity, out of pocket, pay, payment *(remittance)*, payroll, pension, perquisite, profit, recompense, recovery *(award)*, reimbursement, remittance, rent, requital, restitution, retainer, revenue, reward, satisfaction *(discharge of debt)*, wage
remuneration for injury compensation
remuneration for injury suffered damages
remunerative beneficial, compensatory, gainful, lucrative, productive, profitable, valuable
remunerator insurer
renaissance reconversion, renewal,

resurgence, revival
renascence renewal, resurgence, revival
rencounter conflict, confrontation *(act of setting face to face)*, confrontation *(altercation)*, fight *(battle)*, struggle
rend break *(fracture)*, destroy *(efface)*, dichotomize, disjoint, disperse *(scatter)*, force *(break)*, lancinate, luxate, separate, sever, split
rend asunder disrupt, sever
render administer *(tender)*, allocate, avail *(bring about)*, bear *(yield)*, bear the expense, bequeath, bestow, cede, construe *(translate)*, contribute *(supply)*, define, discharge *(perform)*, dispense, offer *(tender)*, pay, present *(make a gift)*, proffer, rebate, recite, recount, remit *(send payment)*, satisfy *(discharge)*, supply, tender, transact, yield *(produce a return)*
render a decision pass *(determine)*
render a document imperfect mutilate
render a judgment pass *(determine)*
render a service accommodate, function
render a service to promote *(organize)*
render a task easier facilitate
render accordant adapt, attune, comport *(agree with)*, conform, regulate *(adjust)*
render an account convey *(communicate)*, depict
render an account of speak
render an attorney's license null and void disbar
render assistance enable, facilitate, help, relieve *(give aid)*, subsidize
render averse deter, disaffect, discourage, dissuade
render better emend, meliorate, nurture, repair
render broad expand
render central focus
render certain ascertain, assure *(give confidence to)*, assure *(insure)*
render chaotic degenerate
render clear explicate
render compatible arbitrate *(conciliate)*
render competent empower, enable
render complete conclude *(complete)*, consummate
render concordant arbitrate *(conciliate)*, reconcile
render deathless perpetuate
render defective vitiate
render definite ascertain
render different convert *(change use)*, transform
render difficult encumber *(hinder)*, hinder
render dim blind *(obscure)*
render evil brutalize, pervert
render eyeless blind *(deprive of sight)*
render feeble impair
render few deduct *(reduce)*, diminish
render filthy pollute
render flustered embarrass
render free clear, discharge *(liberate)*, disenthrall, quit *(free of)*
render harmless decontaminate, disarm *(divest of arms)*

render help aid, contribute *(assist)*, serve *(assist)*

render helpless disable

render honor to dedicate

render humble humiliate

render ill at ease embarrass

render illegible deface, expunge, obliterate

render impassable stop

render imperceptible obliterate

render imperfect mutilate

render impossible forbid

render impotent disable, disqualify

render impure taint *(contaminate)*

render in a better form modify *(alter)*

render incompetent disable

render ineffective destroy *(void)*

render inefficacious vitiate

render inert dissolve *(terminate)*, neutralize

render inimical antagonize

render innocuous disarm *(divest of arms)*

render inoperative neutralize, vacate *(void)*

render insufficient deplete

render intelligible clarify, comment, construe *(translate)*, solve

render invalid cancel, frustrate, nullify, repeal, rescind

render invisible blind *(obscure)*, cloak, conceal, enshroud, hide, plant *(covertly place)*, shroud

render judgment adjudicate

render larger expand

render less decrease, discount *(minimize)*, minimize

render less difficult commute, ease, facilitate

render less excusable aggravate *(exacerbate)*

render less painful soothe

render less tolerable aggravate *(exacerbate)*

render lip service palter

render manifest exemplify

render more compact condense

render necessary call *(demand)*, necessitate

render neutral neutralize

render no longer opposed arbitrate *(conciliate)*

render null extirpate, perish

render null and void abolish, adeem, annul, disown *(deny the validity)*, frustrate, negate

render payment disburse *(pay out)*, expend *(disburse)*

render powerless disable, disarm *(divest of arms)*, handcuff, stall

render precise characterize, define

render putrid decay

render safe assure *(insure)*, hedge, police

render sanitary decontaminate

render service pander

render sightless blind *(deprive of sight)*

render smaller diminish

render solid consolidate *(strengthen)*, fix *(make firm)*

render spurious adulterate, fake

render sterile decontaminate

render strong nurture

render suspect impugn

render threadlike attenuate

render uncertain blind *(obscure)*, confuse *(bewilder)*, disorganize, disorient, perplex

render unclean infect, smear

render unfit disable, disqualify

render up abandon *(relinquish)*, restore *(return)*, surrender *(give back)*

render useful capitalize *(seize the chance)*, inure *(benefit)*

render useless cancel, eliminate *(eradicate)*

render vain foil

render visionless blind *(deprive of sight)*

render void adeem, annul, cancel, discharge *(release from obligation)*

render weak debilitate, dilute, disarm *(divest of arms)*

render worse aggravate *(exacerbate)*, exacerbate

renderable accountable *(explainable)*

rendered stable fixed *(securely placed)*

rendering delivery, design *(construction plan)*, explanation, paraphrase, rendition *(explication)*

rendering explicit clarification

rendering incisive clarification

rendering legal advice representation *(acting for others)*

rendering legal assistance representation *(acting for others)*

rendering unequivocal clarification

rendering unmistakable clarification

rendering void avoidance *(cancellation)*

rendezvous appointment *(meeting)*, meeting *(encounter)*, session

rending separation

rendition delineation, explanation, narration, paraphrase, performance *(execution)*, recital

renegade fugitive, insurgent, malcontent, pariah, recreant

renege abandon *(withdraw)*, annul, cancel, default, defect, deny *(refuse to grant)*, nullify, refuse, renounce, rescind, revoke, tergiversate, withdraw

renew amend, continue *(resume)*, cure, fix *(repair)*, meliorate, proceed *(continue)*, recollect, reconstitute, reconstruct, recreate, recur, reform, rehabilitate, relapse, remedy, renovate, reopen, repair, repeat *(do again)*, replenish, reproduce, resume, resurrect

renew memories remind

renewable corrigible

renewal continuation *(resumption)*, recrudescence, reform, rehabilitation, repair, reparation *(keeping in repair)*, replacement, resurgence, revival

renewed renascent, repeated

renitant contumacious

renitence reaction *(opposition)*, reluctance, resistance

renitency conflict, reaction *(opposition)*, reluctance

renitent adverse *(hostile)*, disinclined, disobedient, hostile, insusceptible *(uncaring)*, recalcitrant, reluctant, restive, rigid, unbending, unyielding

renounce abandon *(relinquish)*, abrogate *(annul)*, cede, decline *(reject)*, defect, demit, deny *(refuse to grant)*, disaffirm, disapprove *(reject)*, disavow,

disclaim, discontinue *(abandon)*, disdain, disinherit, disown *(refuse to acknowledge)*, eliminate *(exclude)*, exclude, forbear, forfeit, forgo, forswear, leave *(allow to remain)*, negate, overrule, quit *(discontinue)*, rebel, rebuff, recant, refrain, refuse, reject, relinquish, repel *(drive back)*, repudiate, rescind, resign, revoke, set aside *(annul)*, spurn, surrender *(give back)*, tergiversate, waive, yield *(submit)*

renounce citizenship expatriate

renounce claim to cede, forgo

renounce rights of citizenship expatriate

renouncement abandonment *(repudiation)*, abjuration, ademption, denial, desertion, disclaimer, rebuff, refusal, renunciation, repudiation, resignation *(relinquishment)*, reversal, revocation

renovare continue *(resume)*, recreate, renew *(refurbish)*

renovate convert *(change use)*, fix *(repair)*, meliorate, reconstitute, reconstruct, recreate, rectify, reform, rehabilitate, renew *(refurbish)*, restore *(renew)*, transform

renovated renascent

renovatio renewal

renovation correction *(change)*, development *(progression)*, reform, rehabilitation, renewal, repair, reparation *(keeping in repair)*, replacement

renovize renovate

renown character *(reputation)*, distinction *(reputation)*, eminence, notoriety, prestige, reputation

renowned conspicuous, famous, household *(familiar)*, illustrious, influential, notable, noteworthy, notorious, outstanding *(prominent)*, prodigious *(amazing)*, prominent, public *(known)*, reputable

rent charge *(cost)*, lease, let *(lease)*, rift *(gap)*, schism, split, sublease, sublet

rent out lease, let *(lease)*, sublease, sublet

rent payer lessee, lodger, tenant

rental rent

rentee lessee

renter lessee, lodger, occupant, tenant

renting tenancy

renueve decline *(reject)*

renumeration proceeds

renunciate disallow

renunciation abandonment *(repudiation)*, abdication, abjuration, ademption, cancellation, confutation, continence, declination, denial, desertion, disclaimer, disdain, expense *(sacrifice)*, rebuff, refusal, rejection, repudiation, rescision, resignation *(relinquishment)*, retraction, reversal, waiver

renunciatory ambulatory

renuntiare report *(disclose)*, revoke

renuntiatio report *(detailed account)*

reobtain recoup *(regain)*, recover

reoccupation salvage

reoccupy reclaim

reoccur recur

reoccurrence relapse

reopen appeal, continue *(resume)*, renew *(begin again)*

reopening appeal, continuation *(resumption)*, renewal

reordering reclassification

reorganization development *(progression)*, progress, reclassification, reconversion, rehabilitation, repair, replacement

reorganize alter, change, convert *(change use)*, emend, meliorate, reconstitute, reconstruct, recreate, reform, reinforce, renew *(begin again)*, renovate, restore *(renew)*, resurrect, transform, vary

repair correction *(change)*, cure, emend, maintenance *(upkeep)*, meliorate, rectify, redress, reform, reform, rehabilitate, rehabilitation, remedy, renew *(refurbish)*, renewal, renovate, reparation *(keeping in repair)*, restore *(renew)*

repairable corrigible

repaired renascent

repairing correction *(change)*

reparable corrigible

reparare fix *(repair)*, recover, repair

reparation collection *(payment)*, compensation, consideration *(recompense)*, contribution *(indemnification)*, damages, discharge *(payment)*, indemnification, justice, payment *(remittance)*, recompense, recovery *(award)*, redemption, rehabilitation, reimbursement, relief *(legal redress)*, remedy *(legal means of redress)*, remittance, rendition *(restoration)*, repair, replacement, requital, restitution, retribution, satisfaction *(discharge of debt)*, satisfaction *(fulfilment)*, trover

reparation for loss out of pocket

reparative compensatory, curative, remedial, salubrious, salutary

reparative measure remedy *(legal means of redress)*

reparatory remedial, salutary

repartee answer *(reply)*

repartition dispensation *(act of dispensing)*, distribution *(apportionment)*, reapportion, redistribute

repast treat

repay bear the expense, compensate *(remunerate)*, defray, disburse *(pay out)*, discharge *(pay a debt)*, indemnify, rebate, reciprocate, recoup *(reimburse)*, refund, reimburse, remit *(send payment)*, remunerate, replace, restore *(return)*, retaliate, return *(refund)*, satisfy *(discharge)*

repay for a loss compensate *(remunerate)*

repay in kind retaliate

repaying compensatory

repayment collection *(payment)*, commission *(fee)*, compensation, consideration *(recompense)*, contribution *(indemnification)*, disbursement *(funds paid out)*, discharge *(payment)*, expiation, indemnification, indemnity, out of pocket, pay, rebate, recompense, recovery *(award)*, refund, reimbursement, reparation *(indemnification)*, reprisal, requital, restitution, retribution, revenge, satisfaction *(discharge of debt)*, vengeance

repayment for injury sustained damages

repayment for loss damages

repeal abate *(extinguish)*, abatement *(extinguishment)*, abolish, abolition, abrogate *(rescind)*, adeem, ademption,

annul, cancel, cancellation, countermand, defeasance, discharge *(annulment)*, discharge *(release from obligation)*, discharge *(release from obligation)*, discontinue *(abandon)*, dissolution *(termination)*, invalidate, negate, negation, nullify, overrule, quash, renege, repudiate, repudiation, rescind, rescision, retraction, reversal, revocation, revoke, supersede, vacate *(void)*, withdraw

repealed lifeless *(dead)*, null *(invalid)*, null and void

repeat circulate, copy, insist, mock *(imitate)*, propagate *(spread)*, quote, reaffirm, recapitulate, recite, recount, recur, reflect *(mirror)*, reiterate, relate *(tell)*, renew *(begin again)*, reopen, reproduce, speak

repeat by rote recite

repeat from memory recite

repeat offender recidivist

repeated consecutive, continuous, frequent, habitual, incessant, insistent, iterative, ordinary, periodic, persistent, repetitious, routine, usual

repeated relapse into crime recidivism

repeatedly invariably

repeatedly recognized common *(customary)*

repeater gun

repeating chronic, repetitious

repel alienate *(estrange)*, antagonize, arrest *(stop)*, confront *(oppose)*, counter, decline *(reject)*, deter, disapprove *(reject)*, disavow, discourage, disfavor, disoblige, exclude, forswear, hold out *(resist)*, oppose, outlaw, parry, rebuff, refuse, refute, reject, renounce, repulse, resist *(oppose)*, spurn, stave, stem *(check)*, withstand

repelled averse

repellence repudiation

repellent antipathetic *(distasteful)*, contemptible, contemptuous, insusceptible *(resistant)*, loathsome, obnoxious, odious, offensive *(offending)*, repugnant *(exciting aversion)*, repulsive, sordid, undesirable

repellere parry, rebuff, rebut, repel *(drive back)*, repulse, stave

repelling loathsome, offensive *(offending)*, repugnant *(exciting aversion)*, repulsive, unsavory

repent reform, regret

repentance remorse

repentant contrite, penitent, remorseful

repentant person penitent

repenting remorseful

repercuss repel *(drive back)*, repulse

repercussion conclusion *(outcome)*, effect, outgrowth, reaction *(response)*

repercussive resounding

reperire detect, invent *(produce for the first time)*

reperta invention

repertory cache *(storage place)*, depository, treasury

repetere renew *(begin again)*, resume

repetition copy, duplicate, frequency, habit, narration, redundancy, relapse, renewal, restatement, tautology

repetitional insistent, repeated, repetitious

repetitionary insistent, repeated, repetitious

repetitious chronic, incessant, iterative, repeated

repetitive chronic, consecutive, frequent, iterative, prolix, redundant, repeated, repetitious

repetitiveness cycle, frequency

rephrase construe *(translate)*, elucidate, explain, quote, recapitulate, reiterate, repeat *(state again)*

rephrasing restatement

repine complain *(criticize)*, deplore, languish, regret

repiner malcontent

repititious redundant

replace accede *(succeed)*, change, convert *(change use)*, cover *(provide for)*, discharge *(dismiss)*, disinherit, rebate, reconstitute, recoup *(regain)*, recoup *(reimburse)*, redistribute, refund, reimburse, reinstate, relocate, remand, remove *(dismiss from office)*, renew *(refurbish)*, renovate, repay, replenish, represent *(substitute)*, restore *(return)*, succeed *(follow)*, superannuate, supersede, supplant

replace with displace *(replace)*

replaceable corrigible, expendable

replacement alternative *(substitute)*, correction *(change)*, cover *(substitute)*, defeasance, discharge *(dismissal)*, exchange, novation, preemption, refund, reimbursement, reparation *(keeping in repair)*, restitution, stopgap, subrogation, substitute, succedaneum, successor

replacing acting, subrogation

replay restatement

replenish bear *(yield)*, bestow, provide *(supply)*, recruit, reinforce, renew *(refurbish)*, supply

replenished replete

replenishment reinforcement, renewal

replere replenish

replete copious, detailed, full, intact, profuse, rife

repleteness plethora

repletion overage, plethora, sufficiency, surfeit

repletus full

replevied attached *(seized)*

replevin reclaim, recoup *(regain)*, recovery *(repossession)*, redeem *(repurchase)*, redemption

replevy attach *(seize)*, distrain, reclaim, recoup *(regain)*, recover, recovery *(repossession)*, redeem *(repurchase)*, repossess, sequester *(seize property)*

replica copy, counterpart *(parallel)*, duplicate, facsimile, fake, model, resemblance, semblance

replicate copy, repeat *(do again)*, reproduce, retort

replication acknowledgment *(acceptance)*, answer *(judicial response)*, answer *(reply)*, counterargument, reply, response

replier respondent

reply acknowledge *(respond)*, acknowledgment *(acceptance)*, answer *(respond legally)*, confutation, correspond *(communicate)*, counterargument, countercharge, plea, pleading, reaction *(response)*, rebut, rejoinder, respond, re-

sponse, retort, return *(respond)*
reply to a charge answer *(judicial response)*
replying responsive
reponder reconsider
reponere repay, replace, reserve
report annunciate, apprise, betray *(disclose)*, bill *(invoice)*, book, canvass, comment, communication *(statement)*, conclusion *(determination)*, convey *(communicate)*, delineate, delineation, depict, detail *(particularize)*, disabuse, disclose, disclosure *(something disclosed)*, dispatch *(message)*, disseminate, divulge, document, enlighten, enter *(record)*, entry *(record)*, file, finding, form *(document)*, hearsay, herald, holding *(ruling of a court)*, inform *(notify)*, intelligence *(news)*, issuance, judgment *(formal court decree)*, memorandum, mention *(reference)*, mention, narration, notice *(announcement)*, notification, notify, observation, opinion *(judicial decision)*, outline *(synopsis)*, portray, post, proclaim, promulgate, pronouncement, propagate *(spread)*, publication *(disclosure)*, publicity, publish, quote, recital, recite, record, recount, relate *(tell)*, rendition *(explication)*, repeat *(state again)*, repercussion, report *(disclose)*, representation *(statement)*, reputation, review *(critical evaluation)*, scenario, signify *(inform)*, speak, statement, story *(narrative)*, summary, tip *(clue)*
report against accuse, denounce *(inform against)*, inform *(betray)*
report inaccurately misinform
report intended to delude canard
reported alleged, documentary, narrative, public *(known)*, putative, stated
reportedly reputedly
reporter bystander, deponent, informant, informer *(a person who provides information)*, spy, witness
reporters press
reporting informatory
repose abeyance, composure, desist, leave *(absence)*, lull, pause, peace, prostration, recess, remain *(stay)*, rest *(cease from action)*, stay *(rest)*
reposeful complacent, placid
reposing inactive
reposit deposit *(place)*, hoard, repose *(place)*, store
reposition relocate
repository arsenal, bank, cache *(storage place)*, catchall, depository, hoard, recipient, treasury
repossess reclaim, recoup *(regain)*, recover, redeem *(repurchase)*
repossession redemption, replevin, salvage
reprehend admonish *(warn)*, blame, castigate, cavil, censure, charge *(accuse)*, complain *(charge)*, complain *(criticize)*, condemn *(blame)*, criticize *(find fault with)*, decry, defame, denounce *(condemn)*, disapprove *(condemn)*, discredit, fault, lash *(attack verbally)*, protest, rebuke, remonstrate, reprimand, reproach
reprehendendus reprehensible
reprehendere blame, censure, criticize *(find fault with)*, rebuke, reprehend, reprimand

reprehensibility culpability, guilt
reprehensible bad *(offensive)*, blameful, blameworthy, contemptible, delinquent *(guilty of a misdeed)*, disreputable, gross *(flagrant)*, guilty, heinous, inexcusable, inexpiable, iniquitous, loathsome, nefarious, obnoxious, odious, offensive *(offending)*, outrageous, peccable, peccant *(culpable)*, scandalous, sinister, unjustifiable, unseemly, vicious
reprehensio blame *(culpability)*, reprimand, stricture
reprehension bad repute, blame *(culpability)*, condemnation *(blame)*, conviction *(finding of guilt)*, criticism, denunciation, diatribe, disapprobation, disapproval, discredit, disparagement, impugnation, objurgation, onus *(blame)*, reprimand, reproach, revilement, stricture
reprehensive critical *(faultfinding)*
represent advise, bare, bear *(adduce)*, characterize, comport *(behave)*, connote, construe *(comprehend)*, convey *(communicate)*, copy, delineate, denote, depict, draw *(depict)*, exemplify, illustrate, impersonate, lobby, manifest, portray, purport, render *(depict)*, replace, signify *(denote)*, simulate, specify
represent as assume *(simulate)*
represent as resembling compare
represent by diagram delineate
represent by outlines delineate
represent by words describe
represent falsely cheat, falsify, lie *(falsify)*, misrepresent, palter
represent fictitiously feign, profess *(pretend)*
represent fraudulently misrepresent
represent in words portray, relate *(tell)*
represent incorrectly mislabel, misrepresent
represent oneself demean *(deport oneself)*
represent oneself to be impersonate
represent pictorially delineate
represent to oneself conjure
representation agency *(legal relationship)*, assertion, brief, color *(deceptive appearance)*, concept, copy, cross section, definition, delineation, deputation *(delegation)*, design *(construction plan)*, designation *(symbol)*, disclosure *(act of disclosing)*, disguise, duplicate, election *(selection by vote)*, embodiment, example, illustration, indicant, manifestation, model, narration, paraphrase, part *(role)*, performance *(workmanship)*, profession *(declaration)*, proxy, recital, rendition *(explication)*, resemblance, role, sample, semblance, substitute, suggestion, symbol
representation by words delineation
representation in language expression *(comment)*
representational descriptive, detailed, realistic, representative, vicarious *(substitutional)*
representative acting, advocate *(counselor)*, agent, broad, broker, case *(example)*, conduit *(intermediary)*, congruous, demonstrative *(illustrative)*, deputy, descriptive, employee, epitome, example, exemplary, factor *(commission merchant)*, functionary, general,

indicant, instance, intermediary, lawmaker, legislator, liaison, nominee *(delegate)*, normal *(regular)*, ordinary, plenipotentiary, politician, proctor, procurator, proxy, realistic, replacement, sample, several *(separate)*, specimen, spokesman, substitute, surrogate, typical, usual
representative in Congress lawmaker
representative of the decedent executor
representative sampling cross section
representative section cross section
representative selection case *(example)*, cross section, example, excerpt, instance, sample, specimen
representatives chamber *(body)*, commission *(agency)*, committee, delegation *(envoy)*, deputation *(delegation)*, government *(political administration)*
representing acting, congruous, in lieu of
repress allay, ban, bar *(hinder)*, bind *(restrain)*, capture, clog, condemn *(ban)*, confine, constrain *(restrain)*, constrict *(inhibit)*, contain *(restrain)*, counteract, curb, deter, disadvantage, dominate, enjoin, extinguish, hamper, hold up *(delay)*, inhibit, interdict, kill *(defeat)*, limit, moderate *(temper)*, overturn, prevent, prohibit, quash, restrain, restrict, stifle, stop, strangle, subdue, subject, suppress, trammel, withhold
repressed arrested *(checked)*
repressing limiting
repressing emotion stoical
repression censorship, coercion, constraint *(restriction)*, control *(restriction)*, deterrence, deterrent, disadvantage, discipline *(obedience)*, duress, fetter, force *(compulsion)*, oppression, prohibition, restraint
repressive dictatorial, prohibitive *(restrictive)*, restrictive
repressive governor dictator
reprieve abeyance, absolution, absolve, acquit, acquittal, amnesty, clear, clemency, compurgation, condonation, condone, discharge *(liberation)*, discharge *(release from obligation)*, emancipation, excuse, exoneration, forgive, grace, grace period, immunity, impunity, palliate *(excuse)*, pardon, pardon, parole, postpone, release, relief *(release)*, remission, remit *(release from penalty)*, stay, stay *(halt)*, vindicate
reprieved blameless, clear *(free from criminal charges)*, free *(relieved from a burden)*
reprimand admonish *(warn)*, admonition, bad repute, blame, castigate, censure, complain *(criticize)*, condemn *(punish)*, condemnation *(blame)*, criticism, criticize *(find fault with)*, denounce *(condemn)*, denunciation, diatribe, disapprobation, disapprove *(condemn)*, discipline *(punishment)*, disparagement, fault, impeach, impeachment, lash *(attack verbally)*, objurgation, outcry, penalize, punish, punishment, rebuff, rebuke, remonstrance, reprehend, reproach, reproach
reprimanded blameful, blameworthy
reprimanding remonstrative

reprimere restrain, stifle, suppress

reprint copy, copy, transcript

reprisal conviction *(finding of guilt)*, counterattack, exchange, penalty, reaction *(opposition)*, requital, retribution, revenge, vengeance

reproach admonition, aspersion, attaint, bad repute, blame *(culpability)*, blame, castigate, censure, charge *(accusation)*, complain *(charge)*, complain *(criticize)*, condemn *(blame)*, condemnation *(blame)*, contemn, contempt *(disdain)*, contempt *(disobedience to the court)*, contumely, criticism, criticize *(find fault with)*, denigrate, denounce *(condemn)*, denunciation, diatribe, disapprobation, disapproval, disapprove *(condemn)*, discredit, disgrace, dishonor *(shame)*, dishonor *(deprive of honor)*, disparagement, guilt, ignominy, impeach, impeachment, incrimination, indictment, infamy, lash *(attack verbally)*, notoriety, objurgation, obloquy, odium, onus *(stigma)*, opprobrium, outcry, rebuff, rebuke, remonstrance, remonstrate, reprehend, reprimand, reprimand, revilement, scandal, shame, slander, stigma, stricture

reproach oneself regret

reproachability bad character

reproachable blameful, blameworthy, delinquent *(guilty of a misdeed)*, guilty, reprehensible

reproachableness culpability

reproached accused *(attacked)*, disreputable

reproachful blameful, contemptible, contemptuous, critical *(faultfinding)*, ignoble, remonstrative

reproachful accusation incrimination

reproaching contemptuous

reprobacy bad faith, delinquency *(misconduct)*

reprobate bad *(offensive)*, blame, blameful, blameworthy, censure, complain *(charge)*, condemn *(ban)*, convict, criminal, criticize *(find fault with)*, delinquent *(guilty of a misdeed)*, delinquent, denounce *(condemn)*, disapprove *(condemn)*, disgraceful, dissolute, felon, immoral, incorrigible, inexcusable, iniquitous, judge, lecherous, lewd, malefactor, nefarious, peccable, peccant *(culpable)*, perverse, rebuff, recidivist, recreant, reject, reprehend, reprehensible, reprimand, reproach, sentence, spurn, tainted *(corrupted)*, vandal, vicious, wrongdoer

reprobation abandonment *(repudiation)*, admonition, bad repute, blame *(culpability)*, condemnation *(blame)*, contempt *(disdain)*, conviction *(finding of guilt)*, correction *(punishment)*, denunciation, discredit, disdain, disparagement, impugnation, ostracism, outcry, phillipic, rejection, remonstrance, renunciation, reprimand, reproach, revilement, stricture

reprobative blameful, blameworthy, contemptible, critical *(faultfinding)*, remonstrative

reprobatory remonstrative

reprobe reexamine

reproduce bear *(yield)*, copy, mock *(imitate)*, portray, proliferate, propagate *(increase)*, pullulate, quote, recreate, reflect *(mirror)*, rehabilitate, reiterate, render *(depict)*, renew *(refurbish)*, repeat *(do again)*, trace *(delineate)*

reproduce fraudulently forge *(counterfeit)*

reproduce in kind proliferate

reproduce rapidly proliferate

reproduced renascent, repeated

reproducing plagiarism

reproduction boom *(increase)*, copy, counterpart *(parallel)*, duplicate, facsimile, fake, maternity, plagiarism, renewal, replacement, resemblance, revival, sham, transcript

reproof admonition, aspersion, bad repute, blame *(culpability)*, charge *(accusation)*, condemnation *(blame)*, contempt *(disdain)*, conviction *(finding of guilt)*, criticism, denunciation, diatribe, disapprobation, discipline *(punishment)*, disparagement, impeachment, objurgation, ostracism, rebuff, remonstrance, reprimand, reproach, revilement, stricture

reprovable blameful, blameworthy, guilty, reprehensible

reproval contempt *(disdain)*, correction *(punishment)*, disapprobation, objurgation, remonstrance, reprimand

reprove admonish *(warn)*, advise, blame, browbeat, castigate, censure, comment, complain *(criticize)*, condemn *(blame)*, condemn *(punish)*, criticize *(find fault with)*, denigrate, deter, disapprove *(condemn)*, discipline *(punish)*, discourage, fault, impeach, lash *(attack verbally)*, penalize, rebuff, rebuke, remonstrate, reprehend, reprimand, reproach

reproved accused *(attacked)*

reproving critical *(faultfinding)*, remonstrative

reptilian heinous

republic polity

republish copy

repudiare disclaim, disown *(deny the validity)*, disown *(refuse to acknowledge)*, reject, repudiate

repudiate abandon *(relinquish)*, abolish, abrogate *(annul)*, abrogate *(rescind)*, adeem, annul, answer *(reply)*, cancel, challenge, condemn *(blame)*, contemn, contradict, controvert, cross *(disagree with)*, decline *(reject)*, default, defect, demur, deny *(contradict)*, deprecate, differ *(disagree)*, disaccord, disaffirm, disagree, disallow, disapprove *(condemn)*, disapprove *(reject)*, disavow, disclaim, disdain, dishonor *(refuse to pay)*, disinherit, disobey, disoblige, disown *(deny the validity)*, disown *(refuse to acknowledge)*, dissent *(withhold assent)*, except *(object)*, exclude, forfeit, forswear, gainsay, ignore, invalidate, leave *(allow to remain)*, negate, nullify, oust, overrule, picket, prohibit, proscribe *(prohibit)*, protest, rebuff, rebut, recall *(call back)*, recant, refuse, refute, reject, renounce, repel *(drive back)*, repulse, rescind, resign, revoke, secede, set aside *(annul)*, spurn, waive

repudiated broken *(unfulfilled)*, derelict *(abandoned)*

repudiating dissenting, negative

repudiatio denial, rejection, renunciation, repudiation

repudiation abandonment *(desertion)*, abjuration, abolition, ademption, breach, cancellation, condemnation *(blame)*, confutation, contempt *(disobedience to the court)*, countermand, declination, default, denial, desertion, disapprobation, disapproval, discharge *(annulment)*, disclaimer, discredit, disdain, disqualification *(rejection)*, dissent *(nonconcurrence)*, exclusion, impugnation, infringement, negation, nonpayment, ouster, prohibition, protest, rebuff, refusal, rejection, renunciation, rescision, retraction, reversal, revocation

repudiation of a marriage divorce

repudiation of employment lockout

repudiation of one's duty delinquency *(failure of duty)*

repudiation of payment dishonor *(nonpayment)*

repudiation of the allegations demurrer

repudiative ambulatory

repudiatory ambulatory

repudium divorce

repugn disaccord, disagree, expostulate, oppose

repugnance antipode, contempt *(disdain)*, disapprobation, incompatibility *(difference)*, malice, odium, phobia, reluctance, resistance

repugnancy disapprobation

repugnans contradictory, repugnant *(exciting aversion)*

repugnant adverse *(hostile)*, antipathetic *(distasteful)*, averse, bad *(offensive)*, contemptible, contemptuous, contradictory, heinous, inimical, loathsome, malevolent, negative, objectionable, obnoxious, odious, offensive *(offending)*, repulsive, unacceptable, unfavorable, unsavory

repugnantia contradiction, incongruity

repugnare conflict, object

repugning dissenting

repulsa defeat, rebuff

repulse beat *(defeat)*, block, contemn, disallow, disavow, disdain, disdain, disfavor, disown *(refuse to acknowledge)*, dissent *(withhold assent)*, eliminate *(exclude)*, exclude, fight *(counteract)*, kill *(defeat)*, oppose, parry, rebuff, rebuff, refusal, reject, rejection, renounce, repel *(disgust)*, repel *(drive back)*, resist *(oppose)*, spurn, stem *(check)*, withstand

repulsion contempt *(disobedience to the court)*, disdain, malice, renunciation, resistance

repulsive antipathetic *(distasteful)*, bad *(offensive)*, contemptible, contemptuous, contumacious, loathsome, lurid, objectionable, obnoxious, odious, offensive *(offending)*, repugnant *(exciting aversion)*, undesirable

repulsiveness odium

repurchase redemption

reputability distinction *(reputation)*, honesty, honor *(good reputation)*, integrity, probity, rectitude, regard *(esteem)*

reputable conscientious, credible, dependable, high-minded, honest, incorruptible, influential, law-abiding, meritorious, moral, outstanding *(promi-*

nent), reliable, renowned, scrupulous, unimpeachable, upright

reputableness character *(reputation)*, credit *(recognition)*

reputare reconsider, weigh

reputation credit *(recognition)*, notoriety, prestige, regard *(esteem)*

repute character *(reputation)*, credit *(recognition)*, distinction *(reputation)*, eminence, honesty, honor *(good reputation)*, importance, notoriety, prestige, regard *(esteem)*, reputation, respect

reputed putative

request application, call *(appeal)*, call *(appeal to)*, canvass, charge *(command)*, claim *(demand)*, demand, desire, dun, dun, entreaty, importune, invitation, lobby, mandate, market *(demand)*, motion, move *(judicially request)*, petition, petition, plead *(implore)*, prayer, press *(beseech)*, pressure, require *(need)*, requirement, requisition, solicit, subpoena, urge

request another decision appeal

request for another decision appeal

request for payment bill *(invoice)*

request for relief petition, prayer

request for retrial appeal

request for review appeal

request for the aid of the court prayer

request reexamination appeal

request reopening of a case appeal

request the presence of call *(summon)*

request to appear summons

request to perform demand

requested important *(urgent)*, popular

requesting insistent

requestion reexamine

require appoint, bind *(obligate)*, call *(demand)*, claim *(demand)*, coerce, command, compel, constrain *(compel)*, decree, demand, dictate, dun, enforce, enjoin, entail, exact, force *(coerce)*, impose *(enforce)*, impose *(subject)*, insist, instruct *(direct)*, lack, levy, necessitate, need, order, prescribe, press *(constrain)*, request, tax *(levy)*, tax *(overwork)*

require a tax excise *(levy a tax)*

require authoritatively dictate, exact

require compliance impose *(enforce)*, subpoena, summon

require of others call *(demand)*

require to attend subpoena, summon

required binding, bound, compulsory, exigent, forcible, fundamental, imperative, important *(urgent)*, indispensable, integral, mandatory, obligatory, positive *(prescribed)*, requisite, urgent, vital

required assumption presumption

required by custom prescriptive

required by law legal

required item necessity, need *(requirement)*

required legal assumption presumption

required manner practice *(procedure)*

required to attend venire

requirement appointment *(act of designating)*, article *(precept)*, burden, call *(appeal)*, call *(option)*, canon, charge

(command), claim *(legal demand)*, compulsion *(coercion)*, condition *(contingent provision)*, demand, desideratum, dictate, directive, duress, enforcement, exigency, instruction *(direction)*, mandate, market *(demand)*, necessary, necessity, ordinance, precept, prerequisite, provision *(clause)*, qualification *(condition)*, request, requisition, sine qua non, ultimatum, writ

requirement of polite society decorum

requirement to appear process *(summons)*

requirement to attend subpoena

requirere require *(need)*

requiring perfunctory

requiring immediate attention exigent, imperative

requiring immediate care exigent

requiring no effort convenient

requiring prompt action exigent

requisite attornment, binding, burden, central *(essential)*, compulsory, condition *(contingent provision)*, demand, desideratum, essential *(required)*, fundamental, imperative, important *(urgent)*, indispensable, integral, mandatory, necessary *(required)*, necessary, necessity, need *(requirement)*, obligatory, positive *(prescribed)*, prerequisite, primary, qualification *(condition)*, requirement, requisition, reservation *(condition)*, substantive, ultimatum, vital

requisiteness need *(requirement)*, priority

requisition application, arrogation, call *(appeal)*, call *(option)*, call *(demand)*, canon, charge *(command)*, claim *(demand)*, desideratum, dun, exact, excise *(levy a tax)*, importune, mandate, market *(demand)*, monition *(legal summons)*, move *(judicially request)*, petition, petition, pray, prayer, request, request, require *(compel)*, requirement

requisition to the court application

requisitioned necessary *(required)*

requisitory confiscatory, requisite

requital collection *(payment)*, compensation, consideration *(recompense)*, contribution *(indemnification)*, exchange, expiation, honorarium, indemnification, interchange, recompense, remuneration, reprisal, restitution, retribution, revenge, reward, satisfaction *(discharge of debt)*, trover

requite defray, disburse *(pay out)*, indemnify, reciprocate, recoup *(reimburse)*, recriminate, refund, reimburse, remit *(send payment)*, remunerate, repay, retaliate, retort, satisfy *(discharge)*

requited reciprocal

requitement contribution *(indemnification)*, indemnification, indemnity, recompense, requital, restitution, retribution, reward, satisfaction *(discharge of debt)*, trover

rerank reassess

reresentative amicus curiae

rereside relocate

res corpus

res article *(commodity)*, article *(distinct section of a writing)*, commodities,

effects, fact, issue *(matter in dispute)*, item, matter *(subject)*, occurrence, point *(item)*, possession *(property)*, possessions, substance *(essential nature)*

res adversae adversity

res arcana secret

res atrox atrocity

res commodata loan

res cuius actio est actionable

res ficta fiction

res judicata adjudication

res mira phenomenon *(unusual occurrence)*

res occulta mystery, secret

res repetundae extortion

res secundae prosperity

res simillima counterpart *(parallel)*

res summa main point

res venales merchandise

resanction reconfirm

rescind abate *(extinguish)*, abolish, adeem, annul, cancel, disavow, discharge *(release from obligation)*, disclaim, disinherit, disown *(deny the validity)*, invalidate, negate, nullify, overrule, quash, recall *(call back)*, recant, renege, repeal, revoke, vacate *(void)*, vitiate, withdraw

rescind an attorney's license to practice disbar

rescinded null *(invalid)*, null and void

rescindere abrogate *(rescind)*, invalidate, quash, repeal, rescind, revoke

rescinding cancellation

rescindment abatement *(extinguishment)*, abolition, ademption, annulment, cancellation, countermand, defeasance, rescision, retraction, revocation

rescission abandonment *(repudiation)*, abolition, ademption, avoidance *(cancellation)*, cancellation, countermand, defeasance, discharge *(annulment)*, discharge *(release from obligation)*, dissolution *(termination)*, negation, repudiation, reversal

rescribere answer *(reply)*

rescript canon, citation *(charge)*, correction *(change)*, dictate, direction *(order)*, directive, fiat, issuance, law, monition *(legal summons)*, order *(judicial directive)*, proclamation, requirement, revision *(corrected version)*, transcript

rescrutinize reexamine

rescuable corrigible

rescue aid *(help)*, aid, clear, disencumber, disenthrall, extricate, free, help, liberate, liberation, palliate *(excuse)*, preserve, quit *(free of)*, ransom, recovery *(repossession)*, redeem *(repurchase)*, redemption, relief *(aid)*, salvage

rescue from imprisonment disenthrall

rescue from oppression disenthrall

rescue from slavery disenthrall

rescued free *(relieved from a burden)*

rescuer benefactor, good samaritan

research analysis, analyze, audit, canvass, delve, examination *(study)*, examine *(study)*, experiment, indagation, inquire, inquiry *(systematic investigation)*, investigation, peruse, probe, quest, scrutinize, scrutiny, study, test

reseat reinstate

resell recover
resemblance analogy, comparison, correspondence *(similarity)*, identity *(similarity)*, parity, propinquity *(similarity)*, relation *(connection)*, same, semblance
resemble appear *(seem to be)*, approximate, correspond *(be equivalent)*, demean *(deport oneself)*
resembling akin *(germane)*, analogous, comparable *(capable of comparison)*, congruous, correlative, identical, similar
resembling truth specious
resent contemn
resentful bitter *(reproachful)*, malevolent, malicious, malignant, restive, spiteful, vindictive
resentfulness resentment
resentive resentful
resentment dissension, ground, ill will, malice, odium, rancor, spite, umbrage
reservation adjournment, condition *(contingent provision)*, doubt *(indecision)*, limitation, misgiving, modification, objection, provision *(clause)*, qualification *(condition)*, registration, restriction, retention, salvo, selection *(choice)*
reservations reluctance
reservatory repository, treasury
reserve adjourn, bank, cash, composure, cumulation, doubt *(indecision)*, engage *(hire)*, fund, fund, garner, hoard, hold up *(delay)*, keep *(shelter)*, margin *(spare amount)*, misgiving, predetermine, provision *(something provided)*, register, resource, restraint, retain *(employ)*, retain *(keep in possession)*, save *(hold back)*, stock *(store)*, stopgap, store *(depository)*, store, strangle, treasury, withhold
reserve fund resource, treasury
reserved diffident, discreet, formal, guarded, inarticulate, laconic, mute, noncommittal, private *(not public)*, privy, taciturn, unapproachable, unobtrusive, unresponsive
reserved amount margin *(spare amount)*
reserves assets, capital, hoard
reservoir arsenal, cache *(storage place)*, depository, fund, repository, stock *(store)*, store *(depository)*, sufficiency
reset adjust *(regulate)*
resettle relocate
reshape camouflage, convert *(change use)*, distort, modify *(alter)*, reform, repair
reshaped tempered
reship redirect
reside dwell *(reside)*, lodge *(reside)*, remain *(occupy)*
reside in inhabit, occupy *(take possession)*
reside together cohabit
residence abode, address, apartment, building *(structure)*, domicile, dwelling, habitation *(act of inhabiting)*, habitation *(dwelling place)*, headquarters, home *(domicile)*, homestead, house, household, inhabitation *(place of dwelling)*, lodging, occupancy, occupation *(possession)*, seat

residencer citizen
residences premises *(buildings)*
residency abode, domicile, inhabitation *(place of dwelling)*, residence, tenancy
resident citizen, constituent *(member)*, denizen, domiciliary, habitant, inhabitant, inmate, lessee, lodger, occupant, tenant
residential habitable, household *(domestic)*
residential building development *(building)*
residentiary denizen, habitant, household *(domestic)*, inhabitant, lodger, occupant, resident
residents populace, population
resider citizen, habitant, lodger, occupant, resident
residere subside
residing habitation *(act of inhabiting)*
residing together cohabitation *(living together)*
residual balance *(amount in excess)*, net, residuary, superfluous
residual estate remainder *(estate in property)*
residual portion balance *(amount in excess)*
residual time unexpired term
residuals remainder *(remaining part)*
residuary alluvion, net, residual, superfluous
residue balance *(amount in excess)*, overage, remainder *(remaining part)*, residual, reversion *(remainder of an estate)*, surplus
residuum balance *(amount in excess)*, residual
residuum remainder *(remaining part)*, surplus
resign abandon *(relinquish)*, cede, defect, demit, depart, discontinue *(abandon)*, forgo, leave *(depart)*, quit *(discontinue)*, reconcile, relent, relinquish, remise, renounce, retire *(conclude a career)*, secede, submit *(yield)*, succumb, surrender *(give back)*, withdraw, yield *(submit)*
resign oneself bear *(tolerate)*
resign oneself to comply, endure *(suffer)*
resignation abdication, acceptance, capitulation, cession, desertion, longanimity, renunciation, sufferance, tolerance
resigned complacent, passive, patient, stoical
resignedness acquiescence, capitulation
resilient corrigible
resist challenge, collide *(clash)*, conflict, confront *(oppose)*, contest, counter, counteract, countervail, cross *(disagree with)*, decline *(reject)*, defy, demonstrate *(protest)*, disaccord, disaffirm, disallow, disapprove *(reject)*, disobey, dissent *(withhold assent)*, fight *(battle)*, fight *(counteract)*, hamper, hold up *(delay)*, object, oppose, oppugn, parry, rebel, rebuff, refuse, repel *(drive back)*, repulse, stem *(check)*, withstand
resist change persevere
resist lawful authority rebel
resist openly defy
resistance conflict, contempt *(disobe-*

dience to the court)*, contention *(opposition)*, contest *(dispute)*, contravention, defiance, deterrence, disadvantage, disapproval, fight *(battle)*, impediment, impugnation, mutiny, negation, opposition, protest, reaction *(opposition)*, rebellion, rebuff, refusal, reluctance, revolt, struggle
resistance against attack defense
resistance movement rebellion
resistance to authority contempt *(disobedience to the court)*, sedition
resistance to change inertia
resistance to government insurrection, revolution
resistant antipathetic *(oppositional)*, contumacious, disobedient, dissident, durable, inexorable, infrangible, nonconsenting, recalcitrant, recusant, renitent, rigid, unbending
resistence collision *(dispute)*
resister adversary, disputant, malcontent
resistere counteract, hold out *(resist)*, withstand
resisting chronic, cohesive *(sticking)*, disorderly, dissenting, indomitable, opposite, renitent, spartan, unyielding
resisting authority contumacious
resisting control contumacious, restive
resistive adverse *(hostile)*, disobedient, insubordinate, intractable, negative, opposite, perverse, preventive, recalcitrant, unruly
resistless forcible, indomitable, inexpugnable, invincible, irresistible, passive, resigned, susceptible *(unresistent)*, unavoidable *(inevitable)*
resite relocate
resolute decisive, definite, diligent, earnest, faithful *(loyal)*, fanatical, heroic, indomitable, inexorable, inflexible, loyal, obdurate, patient, peremptory *(absolute)*, persistent, pertinacious, purposeful, relentless, sedulous, serious *(devoted)*, spartan, staunch, steadfast, strong, true *(loyal)*, unalterable, unbending, uncompromising, undaunted, unyielding
resolutely faithfully
resoluteness prowess *(bravery)*, resolution *(decision)*, spirit, tenacity, will *(desire)*
resolution act *(enactment)*, adhesion *(loyalty)*, adjudication, animus, answer *(solution)*, arbitration, award, bill *(proposed act)*, choice *(decision)*, conclusion *(determination)*, consequence *(conclusion)*, decision *(judgment)*, declaration, decree, denouement, determination, diligence *(perseverance)*, disposition *(determination)*, finding, forethought, goal, holding *(ruling of a court)*, intent, intention, judgment *(formal court decree)*, key *(solution)*, opinion *(judicial decision)*, outcome, project, proposition, purpose, result, ruling, solution *(answer)*, spirit, suggestion, tenacity, volition, will *(desire)*
resolution by a jury verdict
resolution of the court finding
resolvable determinable *(ascertainable)*, solvable
resolve animus, arbitrate *(adjudge)*, arrange *(methodize)*, ascertain, choice

(decision), choose, conclude *(decide)*, conclusion *(determination)*, contemplation, decide, design *(intent)*, determination, determine, discharge *(perform)*, endeavor, find *(determine)*, fix *(settle)*, forethought, goal, hold *(decide)*, intend, intent, intention, judge, plan, plan, predetermination, purpose, reason *(conclude)*, resolution *(decision)*, rule *(decide)*, settle, solve

resolve a discord attune

resolve beforehand prearrange, predetermine, prejudge, preordain

resolve into change

resolved decisive, deliberate, indomitable, inexorable, inflexible, intense, intentional, patient, peremptory *(absolute)*, persistent, pertinacious, purposeful, res judicata, resolute, sedulous, serious *(devoted)*, spartan, steadfast, uncompromising, unrelenting, unyielding

resonance intonation

resonant full, orotund

resort device *(contrivance)*, expedient, refuge, resource, stopgap

resort to employ *(make use of)*, exploit *(make use of)*

resort to arms belligerency, fight *(battle)*

resort to superior authority appeal

resounding powerful

resource chattel, expedient, help, holding *(property owned)*, instrumentality, means *(funds)*, possession *(property)*, recourse, reserve, tool

resourceful artful, competent, deft, original *(creative)*, practiced, productive

resourcefulness common sense, discretion *(quality of being discreet)*, efficiency

resourceless helpless *(defenseless)*

resources advantage, assets, capital, cash, effects, estate *(property)*, finance, fund, goods, livelihood, means *(funds)*, money, paraphernalia *(personal belongings)*, personalty, possessions, principal *(capital sum)*, property *(possessions)*, provision *(something provided)*, reserve, stock in trade, substance *(material possessions)*

respect abide, character *(reputation)*, comity, complexion, comply, concede, concern *(care)*, concern *(involve)*, consideration *(sympathetic regard)*, courtesy, credit *(recognition)*, decorum, defer *(yield in judgment)*, deference, estimation *(esteem)*, fealty, heed, homage, honor, keep *(fulfill)*, mention *(tribute)*, obey, observe *(obey)*, particular, perform *(adhere to)*, prestige, regard *(esteem)*, regard *(hold in esteem)*, reputation, worth

respectability character *(reputation)*, decorum, distinction *(reputation)*, honesty, honor *(good reputation)*, propriety *(correctness)*, reputation

respectable considerable, ethical, fair *(satisfactory)*, high-minded, honest, incorruptible, influential, law-abiding, moral, proper, reliable, reputable, upright

respected influential, outstanding *(prominent)*, popular, prominent, reputable

respectful civil *(polite)*, obedient, obeisant, servile

respectful deportment decorum

respectfulness comity, deference

respecting relative *(relevant)*, wherein

respective certain *(specific)*, particular *(individual)*, specific

respectively per capita, pro rata

respectlessness ingratitude

respectus regard *(esteem)*, retrospect

respicere consider, regard *(hold in esteem)*

respite abeyance, adjournment, cessation *(interlude)*, clemency, continue *(adjourn)*, defer *(put off)*, deferment, extension *(postponement)*, furlough, halt, hiatus, immunity, interruption, interval, leave *(absence)*, lull, moratorium, pause, pendency, recess, relief *(aid)*, relief *(release)*, remission, remit *(release from penalty)*, reprieve, stay, stay *(halt)*

respite from impending punishment reprieve

resplendent illustrious

respond answer *(reply)*, correspond *(communicate)*, countercharge, obey, rebut, reciprocate, remark, reply, retort

respond conclusively countercharge

responded to reciprocal

respondence answer *(reply)*, response

respondent contender, defendant, litigant, open *(persuasible)*, party *(litigant)*, responsive

responder respondent

respondere answer *(reply)*, reply, retort, return *(respond)*

responsal response

response acknowledgment *(acceptance)*, answer *(reply)*, consequence *(conclusion)*, counterargument, effect, emotion, impression, plea, rejoinder, repercussion, reply, sensibility

response to an action appearance *(coming into court)*

responsibility agency *(legal relationship)*, allegiance, assignment *(task)*, burden, business *(affair)*, competence *(ability)*, duty *(obligation)*, function, integrity, job, labor *(work)*, liability, obligation *(duty)*, onus *(blame)*, onus *(burden)*, part *(role)*, position *(business status)*, rectitude, requirement, trust *(custody)*, weight *(burden)*

responsible actionable, amenable, blameful, blameworthy, bound, causative, competent, culpable, dependable, diligent, liable, lucid, moral, normal *(sane)*, reliable, sane, solid *(sound)*, true *(loyal)*

responsible for at fault

responsibleness charge *(responsibility)*

responsibly faithfully

responsio reply

responsive favorable *(expressing approval)*, flexible, open *(persuasible)*, open-minded, perceptive, pliable, pliant, receptive, resilient, sensitive *(discerning)*, suasible, willing *(not averse)*

responsive allegations pleading

responsive offer counteroffer

responsive to change flexible, resilient

responsiveness amenability, sensibility

responsum reply

respublica community, realm

rest abeyance, cessation *(interlude)*, complement, composure, deposit *(place)*, desist, extension *(postponement)*, furlough, halt, halt, hiatus, holiday, inaction, inertia, interval, leave *(absence)*, lodge *(reside)*, lull, moratorium, pause, pause, recess, recess, relief *(release)*, remain *(stay)*, remainder *(remaining part)*, remission, repose *(rest)*, respite *(interval of rest)*, stop

rest assured opine

rest in peace die

rest period pause

restate construe *(translate)*, copy, elucidate, explain, quote, reaffirm, recapitulate, reiterate, repeat *(state again)*

restate briefly review

restated repeated

restatement narration, paraphrase, recital, redundancy, summary

restation relocate

rested on based on

restful placid

restiff restive

resting dormant, inactive, static

resting place destination, haven, home *(domicile)*

restinguere extinguish

restituere fix *(repair)*, reconstruct, redress, rehabilitate, reinstate

restitute bear the expense, recoup *(reimburse)*, replace, restore *(renew)*

restitution collection *(payment)*, consideration *(recompense)*, contribution *(indemnification)*, damages, disbursement *(funds paid out)*, discharge *(payment)*, expiation, indemnification, indemnity, out of pocket, payment *(act of paying)*, payment *(remittance)*, recompense, recovery *(award)*, refund, rehabilitation, reimbursement, relief *(legal redress)*, remedy *(legal means of redress)*, remuneration, rendition *(restoration)*, reparation *(indemnification)*, replacement, requital, satisfaction *(discharge of debt)*, trover

restitutive compensatory, medicinal, remedial

restitutory compensatory

restive adverse *(hostile)*, contumacious, disinclined, disobedient, disorderly, fractious, froward, insubordinate, intractable, lawless, recalcitrant, recusant, uncontrollable, unruly, willful

restiveness contempt *(disobedience to the court)*, disturbance

restless frenetic, moving *(in motion)*, restive, unsettled

restlessness commotion, diligence *(perseverance)*, disturbance, outburst, trepidation

restock replenish

restorable corrigible

restoral reparation *(keeping in repair)*

restoration acquittal, collection *(payment)*, compensation, continuation *(resumption)*, contribution *(indemnification)*, correction *(change)*, damages, indemnification, indemnity, out of pocket, progress, reconversion, recovery *(repossession)*, redemption, rehabilitation, reimbursement, relief *(legal redress)*, renewal, reorganization, repair, reparation *(indemnification)*, reparation *(keeping in repair)*, replacement, restitution, resurgence, revival

restoration of harmony arrangement (*understanding*), reconciliation

restoration to health cure

restorative curative, cure, medicinal, palliative (*abating*), panacea, remedial, remedy (*that which corrects*), salubrious, salutary

restorative agent panacea

restore bear (*yield*), bestow, continue (*resume*), contribute (*indemnify*), cure, emend, fix (*repair*), indemnify, meliorate, quit (*repay*), rebate, reconstitute, reconstruct, recoup (*reimburse*), recreate, rectify, redress, reform, refund, rehabilitate, reimburse, reinstate, remand, remedy, renew (*refurbish*), renovate, repair, repay, resurrect, return (*refund*), surrender (*give back*)

restore courage to reassure

restore equilibrium adjust (*regulate*), regulate (*adjust*)

restore harmony arbitrate (*conciliate*), attune, disarm (*set at ease*), mediate, pacify, placate, reconcile, settle

restore one's faith assure (*give confidence to*)

restore permission authorize

restore to a state of peace pacify

restore to a state of tranquillity pacify

restore to assurance reassure

restore to confidence reassure

restore to equilibrium compensate (*counterbalance*)

restore to friendship reconcile

restore to liberty enfranchise

restore to office reinstate

restore to power reinstate

restored renascent

restrain allay, apprehend (*arrest*), arrest (*apprehend*), arrest (*stop*), balk, ban, bar (*hinder*), block, border (*bound*), cancel, capture, censor, check (*restrain*), clog, commit (*institutionalize*), condemn (*ban*), confine, constrain (*imprison*), constrain (*restrain*), constrict (*inhibit*), continue (*adjourn*), curb, debar, deter, diminish, discipline (*control*), discourage, disqualify, enclose, enjoin, estop, fetter, foil, forbear, forbid, govern, halt, hamper, hinder, hold up (*delay*), immure, impede, imprison, inhibit, interdict, jail, limit, lock, mitigate, moderate (*temper*), mollify, obstruct, occlude, police, preclude, prevent, prohibit, proscribe (*prohibit*), repress, restrict, rule (*govern*), stay (*halt*), stem (*check*), stifle, stop, strangle, subdue, subjugate, suppress, thwart, toll (*stop*), trammel, withhold

restrain by injunction enjoin

restrain motion fetter

restrain movement fetter

restrained arrested (*apprehended*), arrested (*checked*), bound, controlled (*restrained*), frugal, limited, passive, patient, peaceable, reasonable (*fair*), taciturn, unobtrusive

restraining compulsory, limiting, preventive, prohibitive (*restrictive*), restrictive

restraining device barrier

restraining order injunction

restraint apprehension (*act of arresting*), arrest, bar (*obstruction*), barrier,

bondage, captivity, censorship, check (*bar*), cloud (*incumbrance*), coercion, commitment (*confinement*), composure, compulsion (*coercion*), constraint (*restriction*), continence, control (*restriction*), custody (*incarceration*), damper (*stopper*), detention, deterrence, deterrent, disadvantage, discipline (*obedience*), disincentive, durance, embargo, estoppel, fetter, force (*compulsion*), handicap, hindrance, impediment, incarceration, incumbrance (*lien*), injunction, limitation, moderation, obstacle, obstruction, prohibition, propriety (*correctness*), quota, restriction, retention, servitude, stay, temperance, veto

restraint of movement quarantine

restraints confines

restrengthen compound

restrict abridge (*divest*), bar (*exclude*), block, border (*bound*), capture, censor, check (*restrain*), clog, compel, condemn (*ban*), confine, constrain (*imprison*), constrain (*restrain*), constrict (*inhibit*), contain (*restrain*), control (*restrain*), debar, detain (*restrain*), deter, disadvantage, discipline (*control*), disfranchise, disqualify, enclose, enjoin, estop, exclude, fetter, forbid, halt, hamper, hinder, impede, inhibit, interdict, jail, keep (*restrain*), limit, lock, modify (*moderate*), occlude, preclude, prevent, prohibit, proscribe (*prohibit*), qualify (*condition*), repress, restrain, specialize, toll (*stop*), trammel, withhold

restrict access condemn (*ban*), confine, constrain (*restrain*), picket, police

restrict in area constrict (*compress*)

restricted arrested (*checked*), certain (*specific*), conditional, confidential, dependent, exclusive (*limited*), limited, local, narrow, partial (*biased*), personal (*private*), private (*not public*), privy, qualified (*conditioned*), regional, specific, without recourse

restricted goods contraband

restricted to a small area parochial

restricted to a small scope parochial

restricting limiting

restriction abridgment (*disentitlement*), arrest, barrier, blockade (*limitation*), bondage, censorship, check (*bar*), commitment (*confinement*), compulsion (*coercion*), condition (*contingent provision*), constraint (*imprisonment*), custody (*incarceration*), damper (*stopper*), decrease, detention, deterrence, deterrent, disadvantage, duress, economy (*frugality*), embargo, enclosure, encumbrance, estoppel, fetter, force (*compulsion*), guideline, hindrance, impediment, incarceration, injunction, limitation, moderation, modification, obstacle, obstruction, prohibition, provision (*clause*), qualification (*condition*), quota, reservation (*condition*), restraint, salvo, veto

restriction on movement bondage, detention, durance

restriction on personal liberty incarceration

restrictive arbitrary and capricious, binding, compulsory, exclusive (*limited*), limiting, preventive, proprietary

restrictive practice constraint (*restriction*), control (*restriction*)

restrictus parsimonious

restringe restrict

restructuring reorganization

restudy reexamine

restyle change, convert (*change use*), transform

restyling revision (*process of correcting*)

resubstantiate reconfirm

result adjudication, answer (*solution*), award, conclusion (*determination*), conclusion (*outcome*), consequence (*conclusion*), denouement, destination, determination, development (*outgrowth*), effect, emanate, end (*termination*), ensue, evolve, finding, follow-up, holding (*ruling of a court*), issuance, judgment (*formal court decree*), occur (*happen*), outcome, outgrowth, output, proceeds, product, redound, stem (*originate*), supervene, toll (*effect*)

result ascertained conclusion (*determination*), determination

result from accrue (*arise*)

result in produce (*manufacture*)

result of judicial inquest conclusion (*determination*)

resultance conclusion (*outcome*), outgrowth

resultant amount (*result*), ancillary (*subsidiary*), consequential (*deducible*), constructive (*creative*), deductive, derivative, development (*outgrowth*), effect, end (*termination*), ensuing, outcome, outgrowth, residuary, result

resultant action conclusion (*outcome*), consequence (*conclusion*), effect

resulting ancillary (*subsidiary*), derivative, ensuing

resulting from contingent, dependent

resultless futile, otiose

resume brief

resumé capsule, dossier

resume proceed (*continue*), recur, renew (*begin again*), reopen, repeat (*do again*), return (*go back*)

resumption recrudescence, renewal, resurgence, revival

resupply replenish

resurge renew (*refurbish*)

resurgence recrudescence, resurgence, revival

resurgent corrigible, renascent

resurrect disinter, renew (*refurbish*), renovate, repair

resurrected renascent

resurrection rehabilitation, renewal, repair, resurgence, revival

resuscitate cure, recall (*call back*), remedy, renew (*refurbish*), restore (*renew*), resurrect

resuscitated renascent

resuscitation rehabilitation, renewal, resurgence, revival

retabulating reclassification

retail recount, vend

retail store market (*business*)

retailer dealer, merchant, vendor

retain continue (*prolong*), detain (*hold in custody*), employ (*engage services*), enclose, engage (*hire*), fund, hire, hoard, hold (*possess*), keep (*shelter*), occupy (*take possession*), own, perpetuate, possess, prolong, recall (*remember*), remain (*occupy*), remember, reserve, save (*hold back*), store, understand

retain exclusive control monopolize

retain exclusive possession monopolize

retain in custody impound

retain the impression of recognize *(perceive)*

retain the services of employ *(engage services)*

retainer compensation, consociate, deposit, downpayment, honorarium

retainer of counsel client

retaining reservation *(engagement)*

retaining fee compensation, retainer

retainment employment, reservation *(engagement)*, retention

retake attach *(seize)*, reclaim, recoup *(regain)*, recover, rescue

retaking replevin

retaliate answer *(reply)*, penalize, punish, rebut, reciprocate, recriminate, repay, resist *(oppose)*, return *(respond)*

retaliation counterattack, exchange, interchange, reaction *(opposition)*, reprisal, requital, retribution, revenge, vengeance

retaliative malevolent, reciprocal, ruthless, vindictive

retaliatory disciplinary *(punitory)*, malevolent, penal, punitive, reciprocal, vindictive

retaliatory punishment revenge

retard bar *(hinder)*, block, check *(restrain)*, clog, condemn *(ban)*, constrict *(inhibit)*, control *(restrain)*, curb, debar, defer *(put off)*, delay, diminish, disadvantage, discontinue *(break continuity)*, encumber *(hinder)*, enjoin, foil, hamper, hinder, hold up *(delay)*, impede, inhibit, interfere, interrupt, keep *(restrain)*, obstruct, occlude, preclude, prevent, procrastinate, protract *(prolong)*, stall, stem *(check)*, thwart, trammel, withstand

retard decay keep *(shelter)*

retard flow shut

retardant preventive

retardare hinder, impede

retardation check *(bar)*, damper *(stopper)*, delay, deterrent, disadvantage, encumbrance, filibuster, hindrance, impediment, restraint

retarded arrested *(checked)*, disadvantaged, late *(tardy)*

retardment check *(bar)*, disadvantage, filibuster, hindrance, impediment

retax reassess

retell copy, quote, reaffirm, recapitulate, recite, recount, reiterate, relate *(tell)*, repeat *(state again)*, review

retelling narration, recital, redundancy, restatement

retentio detention, retention

retention apprehension *(act of arresting)*, arrest, enjoyment *(use)*, occupancy, occupation *(possession)*, remembrance *(recollection)*, reservation *(engagement)*

retentive memory retrospect

rethink reconsider

reticent discreet, guarded, inarticulate, laconic, mute, noncommittal, taciturn, unobtrusive, unresponsive

reticular sinuous

reticulate intertwine

retinere detain *(restrain)*, hold up

(delay), keep *(fulfill)*, keep *(restrain)*, restrain, withhold

retire abandon *(withdraw)*, demit, depart, discharge *(dismiss)*, discontinue *(abandon)*, dislodge, ebb, flee, leave *(depart)*, part *(leave)*, quit *(discontinue)*, quit *(evacuate)*, recess, rest *(cease from action)*, retreat, secede, seclude, sequester *(seclude)*, superannuate, supplant, withdraw

retire from office demit

retire from sight seclude

retired former, obsolete, outmoded

retirement abandonment *(desertion)*, cessation *(termination)*, end *(termination)*, expiration, layoff, leave *(absence)*, obscuration, privacy, removal, resignation *(relinquishment)*

retirement benefits pension

retirement income annuity, pension

retirement of a debt discharge *(payment)*

retiring diffident, inconspicuous, unobtrusive, unpretentious

retold repeated

retort answer *(reply)*, answer *(reply)*, confutation, counterargument, counterattack, countercharge, plea, rebut, recriminate, refute, rejoinder, reply, reply, respond, response, return *(respond)*

retort a charge recriminate

retortion counterattack

retouch emend, enhance, fix *(repair)*, renew *(refurbish)*, repair, restore *(renew)*

retouching repair

retrace copy, recall *(remember)*, reexamine, repeat *(do again)*, review

retrace one's steps return *(go back)*

retract abandon *(withdraw)*, abolish, abrogate *(annul)*, abrogate *(rescind)*, adeem, annul, cancel, disaffirm, disavow, discharge *(release from obligation)*, disclaim, disinherit, disown *(deny the validity)*, invalidate, negate, nullify, overrule, recant, renege, repeal, repudiate, rescind, revoke, secede, vacate *(void)*, withdraw

retractare recant, revise

retractation defeasance, discharge *(annulment)*, negation, repudiation, retraction, revocation

retracting cancellation

retraction abjuration, abolition, ademption, annulment, breach, cancellation, correction *(change)*, countermand, defeasance, denial, negation, renunciation, repudiation, rescision, reversal, revocation

retractory willful

retranslate construe *(translate)*

retransmit recover

retread repair

retreat abandon *(physically leave)*, abandon *(withdraw)*, asylum *(hiding place)*, avoid *(evade)*, avoidance *(evasion)*, chamber *(compartment)*, decline, disappear, ebb, evacuate, flee, flight, give *(yield)*, haven, leave *(absence)*, leave *(depart)*, part *(leave)*, privacy, quit *(evacuate)*, refuge, removal, renege, resign, return *(go back)*, revert, seclude, shelter *(protection)*, vacate *(leave)*, withdraw

retrench curtail, decrease, diminish

retrenchment curtailment, decrease

retrial appeal, rehearing

retribution condemnation *(punishment)*, conviction *(finding of guilt)*, correction *(punishment)*, discipline *(punishment)*, justice, punishment, relief *(legal redress)*, reprisal, revenge, vengeance

retributive compensatory, disciplinary *(punitory)*, penal, punitive, reciprocal, vindictive

retributive action sanction *(punishment)*

retributive justice condemnation *(punishment)*, conviction *(finding of guilt)*, correction *(punishment)*, discipline *(punishment)*, penalty, punishment, reprisal, retribution

retributive punishment revenge, vengeance

retrievable corrigible

retrieval compensation, out of pocket, recovery *(repossession)*, redemption, replevin, restitution, salvage, trover

retrieve collect *(recover money)*, reap, reclaim, recoup *(regain)*, recover, redeem *(repurchase)*, remedy, repossess, rescue

retrievement trover

retroaction decline, reaction *(opposition)*, repercussion, reversion *(act of returning)*

retroactive ex post facto

retroactive effect nunc pro tunc

retrocede escheat, regress, relapse, retire *(retreat)*, retreat

retrocedent regressive

retrocession decline, relapse, reversion *(act of returning)*

retrogradation decline, degradation, deterioration, lapse *(expiration)*, recidivism, relapse, reversion *(act of returning)*

retrograde decadent, decay, depreciate, deteriorate, recidivate, regress, regressive, relapse, return *(go back)*, revert

retrogress decay, degenerate, deteriorate, regress, relapse, revert

retrogression decline, degradation, deterioration, lapse *(expiration)*, recidivism, reconversion, relapse, reversion *(act of returning)*

retrogressive back *(in reverse)*, bad *(offensive)*, decadent, regressive

retrospect hindsight, recall *(remember)*, recapitulate, recollect, remembrance *(recollection)*

retrospection hindsight, recollection, remembrance *(recollection)*

retrospective back *(in reverse)*

retrospective effect nunc pro tunc

retrospectively heretofore

retroversion reconversion, relapse, reversion *(act of returning)*

retrovert escheat, relapse, revert

retrude repel *(drive back)*, repulse

retry appeal, reconsider

return annuity, answer *(reply)*, answer *(reply)*, bear *(yield)*, benefit *(betterment)*, commission *(fee)*, compensate *(remunerate)*, compensation, consideration *(recompense)*, continuation *(resumption)*, contribute *(indemnify)*, contribution *(indemnification)*, discharge *(payment)*, dividend, escheat, indemnification, indemnity, output, pay, payment *(act of paying)*, perquisite, poll *(canvass)*, proceed *(continue)*, profit, quit *(repay)*, reaction *(response)*, rebate, reciprocate, reciprocity, recommit, recompense, reconversion, recoup *(reimburse)*, recovery *(repossession)*, recrudescence, recur, redemption, refund, refund, regress, rehabilitation, reinstate, relapse, relapse, remand, remuneration, rendition *(restoration)*, renewal, rent, reparation *(indemnification)*, repay, repeat *(do again)*, reply, reply, reprisal, requital, response, restitution, retaliate, retort, retribution, revenue, reversion *(act of returning)*, revert, revival, reward, salvage, satisfaction *(discharge of debt)*, surrender *(give back)*, trover, yield *(produce a return)*

return an accusation recriminate
return an answer respond
return in money income
return money paid out indemnify
return on capital income
return the charge recriminate
return to continue *(resume)*, renew *(begin again)*, reopen, resume
return to prison remand
return to the original state fix *(repair)*
returned reciprocal
returned check bad check
returning chronic, incessant, periodic
returning at intervals chronic, periodic
returns earnings, proceeds
retusus obtuse
réunion assemblage
reunion collection *(assembly)*, conciliation, congregation, meeting *(conference)*, rapprochement, reconciliation
reunite call *(summon)*, collect *(gather)*, conjoin, convene, meet, pacify, reconcile
reus criminal
reutter recapitulate, reiterate
reuttered repeated
revalidate reconfirm
revalidated nunc pro tunc
revalue reassess
revamp amend, convert *(change use)*, edit, emend, fix *(repair)*, modify *(alter)*, reconstruct, recreate, redact, rehabilitate, renew *(refurbish)*, renovate, repair, revise, transform
revamping renewal, reparation *(keeping in repair)*
revampment amendment *(correction)*, correction *(change)*
reveal adduce, admit *(concede)*, apprise, bare, betray *(disclose)*, circulate, communicate, confess, construe *(translate)*, convey *(communicate)*, declare, denude, depict, detect, disabuse, disclose, disinter, display, divulge, enlighten, evidence, exhibit, explain, explicate, expose, expound, find *(discover)*, impart, inform *(betray)*, inform *(notify)*, interpret, issue *(publish)*, locate, manifest, mention, notice *(give formal warning)*, notify, produce *(offer to view)*, profess *(avow)*, promulgate, publish, relate *(tell)*, report *(disclose)*, resolve *(solve)*, signify *(denote)*, signify *(inform)*, speak, unveil, utter
reveal itself arise *(appear)*, occur

(come to mind)
reveal oneself report *(present oneself)*
reveal something private confide *(divulge)*
reveal the answer resolve *(solve)*
reveal to public notice exhibit
revealed comprehensible, evident, manifest, naked *(perceptible)*, obvious, open *(in sight)*, overt, palpable, patent, pellucid, perceivable, perceptible, public *(known)*
revealing demonstrative *(illustrative)*, descriptive, disclosure *(act of disclosing)*, informative, informatory
revealment admission *(disclosure)*, confession, disclosure *(act of disclosing)*, disclosure *(something disclosed)*, discovery, expression *(manifestation)*, publication *(disclosure)*, publicity
revel carouse
revel in relish
revelation admission *(disclosure)*, answer *(solution)*, communication *(statement)*, declaration, disclosure *(something disclosed)*, discovery, exhibit, expression *(manifestation)*, information *(knowledge)*, manifestation, notice *(announcement)*, notification, publication *(disclosure)*, publicity, report *(detailed account)*, testimony, vision *(dream)*
revelatory informatory
revelry treat
revenant phantom, specter
revenge counterattack, penalize, rancor, repay, reprisal, retaliate, retribution, vengeance
revengeful malevolent, malignant, resentful, ruthless, spiteful, vindictive
revengefulness belligerency, rancor, reprisal, revenge, spite, vengeance
revenue boom *(prosperity)*, capital, duty *(tax)*, earnings, finance, income, money, pay, perquisite, proceeds, profit, rent, resource, substance *(material possessions)*, wage
reverberant resounding
reverberating resounding
reverberation reaction *(response)*, repercussion
reverberatory resounding
revere honor, regard *(hold in esteem)*
revered outstanding *(prominent)*, reputable, sacrosanct
reverence courtesy, estimation *(esteem)*, fealty, homage, honor *(outward respect)*, honor, interest *(concern)*, regard *(esteem)*, regard *(hold in esteem)*, respect
reverenced reputable
reverend sacrosanct
reverent obeisant
reverenter respectfully
reverential obedient, obeisant, sequacious, solemn
reverently respectfully
reverie contemplation, figment, introspection, preoccupation, reflection *(thought)*
reversal annulment, cancellation, countermand, defeasance, discharge *(annulment)*, negation, nollo prosequi, reconversion, recrudescence, relapse, repudiation, rescision, retraction, reversion *(act of returning)*, revocation
reverse abrogate *(annul)*, abrogate *(rescind)*, adverse *(opposite)*, annul, an-

tipathetic *(oppositional)*, antipode, antithesis, cancel, contra, contradict, contradictory, contraposition, contrary, counteract, counterpart *(complement)*, debacle, disaffirm, discharge *(release from obligation)*, disown *(deny the validity)*, escheat, hostile, invalidate, inverse, misfortune, negate, negative, nullify, opposite, override, overrule, overthrow, overturn, plight, quash, recant, recrudescence, regress, regressive, relapse, relapse, renege, repeal, repudiate, rescind, retreat, reversion *(act of returning)*, revert, revoke, tragedy, trouble, upset, vacate *(void)*, vitiate, withdraw
reverse direction return *(go back)*
reversed back *(in reverse)*, inverse, null *(invalid)*, null and void, opposite, regressive
reverseless indefeasible, indelible, irreversible, irrevocable, permanent
reversible ambulatory, capricious, convertible
reversing cancellation
reversion continuation *(resumption)*, decline, defeasance, devolution, heritage, lapse *(expiration)*, nollo prosequi, recidivism, reconversion, recovery *(repossession)*, recrudescence, relapse, remainder *(remaining part)*, restitution, resurgence, reversal
reversion to the government escheatment
reversion to the state escheatment
reversional ambulatory, regressive
reversionary regressive
reversionary estate remainder *(estate in property)*
revert disorganize, escheat, recur, regress, relapse, repeat *(do again)*, return *(go back)*, revoke
revert to the state escheat
reverti lapse *(cease)*, return *(go back)*
reverting reversion *(act of returning)*
revest reinstate, restore *(return)*
review account *(report)*, analysis, analyze, appeal, appeal, audit, canvass, capsule, censor, check *(inspect)*, comment, compendium, consideration *(contemplation)*, contemplation, criticism, criticize *(evaluate)*, cross-questioning, deliberate, digest, diligence *(care)*, discretion *(power of choice)*, discuss, evaluate, examination *(study)*, examine *(study)*, frisk, habeas corpus, hindsight, hornbook, indagation, inquest, inspection, investigate, judge, judgment *(discernment)*, monitor, muse, narration, notice *(observe)*, observe *(watch)*, overlook *(superintend)*, peruse, ponder, probe, probe, recall *(remember)*, recapitulate, recital, recollect, reconsider, reexamine, reiterate, remember, repeat *(state again)*, report *(detailed account)*, restatement, retrospect, revise, revision *(process of correcting)*, scenario, scrutinize, scrutiny, study, summary, survey *(examine)*, survey *(poll)*, synopsis, test, trial *(experiment)*
review of things past hindsight
reviewer juror
reviewers of fact jury
revile attack, blame, condemn *(blame)*, contemn, decry, defame, denigrate, denounce *(condemn)*, derogate,

disapprove *(condemn)*, discommend, flout, inveigh, lash *(attack verbally)*, libel, malign, rebuke, reprimand, reproach

revilement bad repute, contempt *(disdain)*, contumely, criticism, denunciation, diatribe, disapprobation, discredit, disdain, disparagement, libel, malediction, obloquy, outcry, phillipic, rejection, reprimand, reproach, slander, vilification

revilement of religion blasphemy

reviling abusive, aspersion, contemptuous, diatribe

revindication recovery *(repossession)*

revisable corrigible

revisal amendment *(correction)*, correction *(change)*, revision *(process of correcting)*

revise adapt, amend, change, convert *(change use)*, edit, emend, modify *(alter)*, qualify *(condition)*, rectify, reform, remedy, renew *(refurbish)*, review, transform, treat *(process)*

revise one's thoughts reconsider

revised current, tempered

revised edition correction *(change)*, revision *(corrected version)*

revising reorganization

revision amendment *(correction)*, correction *(change)*, development *(progression)*, innovation, reform, renewal, reorganization

revisional ambulatory, corrigible

revisionist malcontent

revisit return *(go back)*

revisory ambulatory

revitalize renew *(refurbish)*, resurrect

revival recrudescence, rehabilitation, renewal, repair, resurgence

revival in the mind remembrance *(recollection)*

revive change, copy, cure, develop, fix *(repair)*, meliorate, recall *(call back)*, recall *(remember)*, recollect, recreate, rehabilitate, reinstate, remedy, renew *(begin again)*, renew *(refurbish)*, renovate, reopen, repair, restore *(renew)*, resurrect

revived de novo, renascent

revivement rehabilitation

revivification recrudescence, rehabilitation, renewal, resurgence, revival

revivified renascent

revivify cure, fix *(repair)*, recall *(call back)*, rehabilitate, remedy, renovate, restore *(renew)*, resurrect

revivifying remedial

reviviscence recrudescence, revival

reviviscency recrudescence

reviviscent salubrious

revocable ambulatory, defeasible, voidable

revocare recall *(call back)*

revocatio revocation

revocation abatement *(extinguishment)*, abjuration, abolition, annulment, cancellation, countermand, defeasance, denial, discharge *(annulment)*, discharge *(release from obligation)*, disclaimer, dissolution *(termination)*, mistrial, negation, repudiation, rescision, retraction, reversal

revocation of orders countermand

revocatory ambulatory

revoke abate *(extinguish)*, abolish,

abrogate *(rescind)*, adeem, annul, bear false witness, cancel, debar, disavow, discharge *(release from obligation)*, discontinue *(abandon)*, disinherit, disown *(deny the validity)*, dissolve *(terminate)*, invalidate, kill *(defeat)*, negate, nullify, override, overrule, prohibit, proscribe *(prohibit)*, recall *(call back)*, recant, refuse, renege, repeal, repudiate, rescind, vacate *(void)*, withdraw

revoke one's license to practice law disbar

revoked null *(invalid)*, null and void

revokement abjuration, abolition, ademption, annulment, cancellation, countermand, defeasance, dissolution *(termination)*, negation, rescision, reversal, revocation

revoking cancellation, revocation

revolt conflict, contest *(dispute)*, defect, defiance, disagree, disloyalty, disobey, disturbance, fight *(battle)*, infidelity, insurrection, mutiny, outbreak, outburst, overthrow, protest, rebel, rebellion, reject, rejection, repel *(disgust)*, resistance, revolution, riot, secede, sedition, strike *(refuse to work)*, subversion, treason

revolted averse

revolter insurgent, malcontent

revolting bad *(offensive)*, heinous, loathsome, lurid, objectionable, obnoxious, odious, offensive *(offending)*, repugnant *(exciting aversion)*, repulsive, unsavory

revolution anarchy, cycle, defiance, disturbance, innovation, insurrection, mutiny, outbreak, outburst, rebellion, resistance, revolt, sedition, subversion, treason

revolutionary demagogue, disorderly, incendiary, insubordinate, insurgent, lawless, malcontent, radical *(favoring drastic change)*, restive

revolutionist insurgent, malcontent

revolutionize change, disobey, overthrow, rebel, reform, transform

revolve muse

revolve in the mind ponder, reflect *(ponder)*, study

revolver gun

revulsion contempt *(disdain)*, disapprobation, hatred, odium

reward benefit *(conferment)*, bonus, bounty, commission *(fee)*, compensate *(remunerate)*, compensation, consideration *(recompense)*, disburse *(pay out)*, earnings, fee *(charge)*, grant, gratuity *(present)*, pay, pay, perquisite, prize, profit, recognition, recompense, remunerate, remuneration, repay, requital, retribution, revenue, tip *(gratuity)*

reward for a loss compensate *(remunerate)*

reward for an injury compensate *(remunerate)*

reward for injury compensation

reward for loss compensation

reward for service bounty, compensation, honorarium, perquisite, wage

reward of labor earnings

reward of office earnings

rewarder donor, grantor

rewardful compensatory, lucrative

rewarding compensatory, gainful, lucrative, profitable, valuable

reweigh reconsider

reword construe *(translate)*, quote, recapitulate, recount, reiterate, repeat *(state again)*, review

reworded repeated

rewording paraphrase, rendition *(explication)*, restatement

rework amend, edit, emend, modify *(alter)*, reconsider, reconstruct, redact, reform, renew *(refurbish)*, revise

rewrite amend, copy, correction *(change)*, edit, emend, modify *(alter)*, redact, revise, revision *(corrected version)*

rewriting revision *(process of correcting)*

rezone reapportion, reassign

rhapsodical ecstatic

rhetoric bombast, declamation, fustian, language, parlance, phraseology, speech

rhetorica rhetoric *(skilled speech)*

rhetorical flatulent, inflated *(bombastic)*, orotund, turgid, voluble

rhetorical discourse peroration

rhetorical phrase expletive

rhetorical presentation discourse

rhetorical word expletive

rhetoricalness bombast

rhetorize declaim

rhythm regularity

rhythmic intermittent, periodic, regular *(orderly)*

rhythmical periodic

rialto market *(business)*

ribald blameworthy, blatant *(obtrusive)*, disreputable, inelegant, lascivious, lewd, obscene, offensive *(offending)*, prurient, salacious, scurrilous, suggestive *(risqué)*

ribaldry obscenity

rich copious, elaborate, eloquent, fertile, full, nectareous, opulent, productive, profuse, prolific, prosperous, resounding, savory, strong, successful

riches assets, cash, hoard, money, prosperity, substance *(material possessions)*

richly endowed opulent

richness boom *(prosperity)*, plethora, prosperity

rickety imperfect

ricochet repercussion

rid dislodge, eject *(evict)*, extirpate, free *(relieved from a burden)*, relieve *(free from burden)*, relinquish

rid of deception disabuse

rid of defects emend

rid oneself of forgo, jettison, renounce

riddance catharsis, deportation, estrangement, exclusion, layoff, privation, rejection, removal

riddle enigma, mystery, penetrate, problem

riddled penetrable

rider addendum, allonge, amendment *(legislation)*, appendix *(supplement)*

ridicile discommend

ridicula imitatio parody

ridicule contemn, contempt *(disdain)*, decry, derogate, disdain, disgrace, dishonor *(shame)*, disparage, disparagement, disrespect, flout, humiliate, illude, impeach, jape, jeer, libel, malign, minimize, misprize, mock *(deride)*, offend *(insult)*, parody, pillory, smear, travesty

ridicule irresponsibly cavil

ridiculing cynical, disdainful

ridiculous fatuous, incredible, inept *(inappropriate)*, irrational, ludicrous, unreasonable, untenable

ridiculousness incongruity

ridiculum ridicule

ridiculus jocular

rife general, ordinary, populous, predominant, prevailing *(current)*, prevalent, profuse, rampant, replete, usual

rifle despoil, gun, loot, pirate *(take by violence)*, plunder, poach, steal

rifler burglar

rift alienation *(estrangement)*, disaccord, disassociation, dissension, estrangement, flaw, hiatus, schism, split, split, strife

rig furnish, manipulate *(control unfairly)*

right accurate, actual, allowable, applicable, appropriate, birthright, capacity *(authority)*, cause of action, certain *(positive)*, condign, cure, dominion *(absolute ownership)*, droit, due, eligible, emend, equitable, equity *(share of ownership)*, ethical, exact, factual, fairness, fit, fix *(repair)*, franchise *(license)*, honest, intangible, interest *(ownership)*, juridical, just, justice, liberty, license, licit, option *(contractual provision)*, patent, possession *(ownership)*, prerogative, prescription *(claim of title)*, privilege, proper, propriety *(appropriateness)*, qualification *(fitness)*, real, reasonable *(rational)*, rectify, rectitude, redress, remedy, repair, rightful, share *(interest)*, sound, stake *(interest)*, suitable, title *(right)*, true *(authentic)*, truth, undistorted

right answer solution *(answer)*

right arm mainstay

right away instantly

right dealing equity *(justice)*

right hand mainstay

right note decorum

right now instantly

right of action cause of action

right of choice discretion *(power of choice)*, franchise *(right to vote)*, latitude, liberty, option *(choice)*, patronage *(power to appoint jobs)*

right of entry access *(right of way)*, ingress

right of future enjoyment reversion *(remainder of an estate)*

right of future possession reversion *(remainder of an estate)*

right of literary property copyright

right of ownership interest *(ownership)*

right of passage easement

right of possession dominion *(absolute ownership)*, fee *(estate)*, ownership

right of put and call call *(option)*

right of recovery cause of action

right of representation franchise *(right to vote)*

right of retention possession *(ownership)*

right of succession reversion *(remainder of an estate)*

right of use easement

right of way easement

right thing to do decorum

right time opportunity

right to adjudicate authority *(right)*

right to buy or sell option *(contractual provision)*

right to command authority *(right)*

right to decide freedom

right to determine authority *(right)*

right to dispose of property charge *(lien)*

right to enforce charge on property mechanics lien

right to enforce charge upon property lien

right to enter ingress

right to personal things intangible

right to precedence priority

right to preference priority

right to profits accruing patent

right to property dominion *(absolute ownership)*

right to recovery intangible

right to relief cause of action

right to retain occupation *(possession)*

right to settle issues authority *(right)*

right to vote suffrage

right, title and interest in land estate *(property)*

right-hand man assistant

right-minded clean, high-minded, law-abiding, meritorious, moral

right-of-way priority

righteous clean, conscientious, equitable, ethical, high-minded, just, law-abiding, meritorious, moral, proper, pure, reputable, right *(correct)*, upright

righteously fairly *(impartially)*

righteousness equity *(justice)*, ethics, honor *(good reputation)*, integrity, justice, merit, principle *(virtue)*, probity, rectitude

rightful actual, allowed, appropriate, blameless, bona fide, due *(regular)*, felicitous, genuine, juridical, just, legal, legitimate *(rightful)*, licit, right *(correct)*, sound, suitable, true *(authentic)*, unalienable

rightful possession dominion *(absolute ownership)*, interest *(ownership)*

rightful power authority *(right)*, prerogative

rightful strength force *(legal efficacy)*

rightfully as a matter of right, duly, fairly *(impartially)*

rightfulness equity *(justice)*, fairness, justice, legality, legitimacy, principle *(virtue)*

righting correction *(change)*

rightly fairly *(impartially)*

rightness expedience, fairness, honesty, propriety *(appropriateness)*, qualification *(fitness)*

rights and privileges birthright

rigid close *(rigorous)*, draconian, exact, factual, firm, fixed *(securely placed)*, formal, inflexible, ironclad, irreconcilable, literal, meticulous, narrow, orthodox, particular *(exacting)*, pertinacious, precise, provincial, punctilious, relentless, renitent, severe, solid *(compact)*, static, strict, stringent, unalterable, unbending, uncompromising, unmitigated, unrelenting, unyielding

rigid control censorship

rigid routine bureaucracy

rigidity formality, rigor

rigidly faithfully, invariably

rigidness formality, particularity, rigor

rigidus inflexible, rigid, stark, strict, unbending

rigor severity

rigorist bigot

rigorous accurate, callous, draconian, harsh, inflexible, intense, ironclad, meticulous, onerous, oppressive, particular *(exacting)*, precise, punctilious, rigid, severe, strict, stringent, unrelenting

rigorous proof certification *(certainness)*

rigorous search indagation, probe

rigorousness rigor, severity

rile badger, bait *(harass)*, disaffect, discompose, harry *(harass)*, incense, irritate, offend *(insult)*, pique

rim border, boundary, edge *(border)*, frontier, limit, margin *(outside limit)*, mete, outline *(boundary)*, periphery

rima rift *(gap)*, split

rimari ferret, probe, probe

ring cabal, enclose, encompass *(surround)*, hedge, league, syndicate

ringing resounding

ringleader demagogue, pioneer

riot anarchy, belligerency, bluster *(commotion)*, brawl, brawl, disorder *(lack of order)*, embroilment, fracas, imbroglio, insurrection, outbreak, pandemonium, rebel, rebellion, sedition

rioter insurgent, malcontent

riotous disobedient, disorderly, drunk, lawless, licentious, uncontrollable, unruly

rip lancinate, rend, split, split

rip out eviscerate

riparian fluvial, littoral

ripe ready *(prepared)*

ripe to submit for judicial review justiciable

ripen develop, mature, progress

ripeness opportunity

ripening growth *(evolution)*

riposte answer *(reply)*, answer *(reply)*, counterattack, countercharge, reply, response, retort, return *(respond)*

ripping out avulsion, evulsion

rise advancement *(improvement)*, appearance *(emergence)*, appreciate *(increase)*, appreciation *(increased value)*, augmentation, boom *(increase)*, build *(augment)*, commence, disobey, elevation, emerge, genesis, growth *(increase)*, inception, increase, increment, inflate, inflation *(increase)*, nascency, onset *(commencement)*, origination, outset, progress, progress, promotion *(advancement)*, pullulate, rebel, result, start, stem *(originate)*

rise above outbalance, outweigh, overcome *(surmount)*, predominate *(outnumber)*, surmount, surpass, transcend

rise against confront *(oppose)*

rise and fall fluctuate

rise from accrue *(arise)*

rise in arms rebel

rise in hostility before accost

rise in value appreciate *(increase)*, appreciation *(increased value)*

risible ludicrous

rising insurrection, outbreak, outburst, progressive *(going forward)*, prominent, prosperous, rebellion, revolt, sedition

rising generation children

rising insubordination commotion

rising prices boom *(prosperity)*

risk bet, compromise *(endanger)*, danger, endanger, endeavor, expose, gamble, hazard, invest *(fund)*, jeopardize, jeopardy, parlay *(bet)*, pawn, peril, pitfall, speculate *(chance)*, threat, venture

risk exposure to harm endanger

risk one's money invest *(fund)*

risk taker speculator

risk-taker bettor

risk-taking hot-blooded, impulsive *(rash)*

riskful aleatory *(perilous)*, precarious

risks pitfall

risky aleatory *(perilous)*, dangerous, impulsive *(rash)*, insalubrious, insecure, noxious, precarious, speculative, toxic, vulnerable

risky undertaking venture

risqué brazen

risque improper, lewd, lurid, obscene, salacious, scurrilous

rite ceremony, custom, form *(arrangement)*, formality

ritual behavior, ceremony, custom, form *(arrangement)*, formal, formality, process *(course)*, propriety *(correctness)*, remembrance *(commemoration)*, routine, solemn, way *(manner)*

ritualism behavior

ritualistic formal

ritualistically pro forma

ritualize formalize

ritually pro forma

ritus ceremony, formality

rival adversary, antagonize, compete, competitive *(antagonistic)*, conflict, confront *(oppose)*, contend *(dispute)*, contender, contestant, counteract, disputant, foe, jealous, outbalance, peer, resist *(oppose)*, surpass, transcend

rivaling comparative, competitive *(antagonistic)*

rivalry belligerency, competition, conflict, contention *(opposition)*, contest *(competition)*, impugnation, strife

rivalship contest *(competition)*

rive break *(separate)*, dichotomize, disjoint, disperse *(scatter)*, force *(break)*, lancinate, luxate, rend, separate, sever, split

riven broken *(fractured)*

riverine fluvial

rivery fluvial

rivet the attention occupy *(engage)*

rivet the mind occupy *(engage)*

rivet the thoughts occupy *(engage)*

riveted immutable, stable, steadfast

rixa affray, altercation, brawl

rixari brawl, dispute *(contest)*

road access *(right of way)*, admission *(entry)*, admittance *(means of approach)*, avenue *(route)*, causeway, course, way *(channel)*

roadway admission *(entry)*, avenue *(route)*, causeway, way *(channel)*

roam perambulate, prowl

roamer itinerant, pedestrian

roaming discursive *(digressive)*, mov-

ing *(in motion)*, shifting, transient, vagrancy

roar barrage, pandemonium

rob defalcate, deprive, despoil, harry *(plunder)*, hold up *(rob)*, impropriate, loot, peculate, pilfer, pillage, pirate *(take by violence)*, plunder, prey, purloin, spoil *(pillage)*, steal

rob of freedom subjugate

robber burglar, criminal, outlaw, thief, vandal

robbery burglary, housebreaking, plunder, spoliation, theft

robbing burglary

robe clothe

roborant medicinal, remedial, salubrious, salutary

robur strength

robust durable, strong

robustness health, puissance, sinew, strength

robustus strong

rock lull, oscillate, vacillate

rocklike durable

rodomontade bombast, exaggeration, fustian, jactation

rogare petition, pray, request, sue

rogatio bill *(proposed act)*, motion, proposition, question *(inquiry)*, request

rogue convict, delinquent, hoodlum, malefactor

roguery deception, improbity, knavery, mischief, misdoing

roguish false *(disloyal)*, immoral, jocular, machiavellian, reprobate, unscrupulous

roguishness knavery, mischief

roil agitate *(activate)*, annoy, badger, discompose, disturb, hector, pique, plague, provoke

roisterer hoodlum

role agency *(legal relationship)*, assignment *(task)*, capacity *(job)*, conduct, duty *(obligation)*, function, job, office, position *(business status)*, profession *(vocation)*

roll docket, file, record, register, schedule

roll back decrease, diminish

roll into one collect *(gather)*, consolidate *(unite)*

roll on proceed *(go forward)*

roll out spread

rollicking jocular

rolling fluvial

rolling in riches opulent

romance figment

romantic quixotic

rompish jocular

roof ceiling, shelter *(protection)*

rookie novice

room capacity *(maximum)*, chamber *(compartment)*, coverage *(scope)*, dwell *(reside)*, freedom, inhabit, latitude, margin *(spare amount)*, part *(place)*, scope, space

room for improvement foible

room in which a court of law is held courtroom

room in which a lawcourt is held courtroom

room to spare margin *(spare amount)*

room together cohabit

room used for the application of the laws courtroom

room used for the public administration of justice courtroom

room where justice is administered courtroom

roomer inmate, lessee, lodger, occupant

rooming together cohabitation *(living together)*

rooms lodging

roomy capacious

roorback canard

root basis, bloodline, cause *(reason)*, derivation, determinant, embed, establish *(entrench)*, fix *(make firm)*, foundation *(basis)*, genesis, gist *(substance)*, gravamen, ground, hunt, origin *(source)*, origination, plant *(place firmly)*, reason *(basis)*, source

root of dissension contention *(argument)*

root out destroy *(efface)*, disinter, extirpate, ferret, solve

root up disinter

rooted firm, fixed *(settled)*, habitual, immutable, indelible, ingrained, inveterate, organic, permanent, prescriptive, situated, stable, steadfast, traditional

rooted belief conviction *(persuasion)*

rootless baseless, solitary

rope handcuff

rope off demarcate, isolate, seclude

roseate auspicious, propitious

roster record, register, roll

rot decay, degenerate, spoil *(impair)*, spoilage, taint *(contaminate)*

rotate oscillate, vary

rotation cycle, order *(arrangement)*, sequence

rotten heinous, marred, odious, profligate *(corrupt)*, repulsive, stale, tainted *(contaminated)*, tainted *(corrupted)*

rotting decadent, dissolution *(disintegration)*

rough astringent, blatant *(obtrusive)*, brutal, disorderly, harsh, hoodlum, imperfect, impertinent *(insolent)*, inelegant, inexact, mishandle *(maltreat)*, mordacious, provincial, severe, stringent, uncouth

rough calculation estimate *(approximate cost)*, estimation *(calculation)*

rough cast design *(construction plan)*

rough copy design *(construction plan)*

rough draft delineation

rough guess estimate *(approximate cost)*, estimation *(calculation)*

rough outline configuration *(form)*

rough representation design *(construction plan)*

rough sketch contour *(outline)*

roughness irregularity

round chain *(series)*, cycle, stabilize

round body sphere

round table panel *(discussion group)*, session

round up convene, cull

round-about astray

roundabout circuitous, devious, discursive *(digressive)*, indirect, labyrinthine, oblique *(evasive)*, sinuous, tortuous *(bending)*

roundabout action indirection *(indirect action)*

roundabout course detour

roundabout way digression

roundaboutness indirection *(indirect action)*

roundly wholly

rouse agitate *(activate)*, bait *(harass)*, coax, disturb, evoke, exhort, foment, hasten, impel, impress *(affect deeply)*, incite, interest, motivate, persuade, perturb, pique, prompt, provoke, spirit, stimulate, urge

rouser demagogue

rousing moving *(evoking emotion)*, persuasive

rout beat *(defeat)*, debacle, defeat, dispel, miscarriage, overcome *(surmount)*, prostration, repel *(drive back)*, repulse, subjugate, surmount

rout out expel, purge *(purify)*

route access *(right of way)*, admission *(entry)*, admittance *(means of approach)*, conduit *(channel)*, course, direction *(course)*, send, way *(channel)*

routes approaches

routine accustomed *(customary)*, behavior, conventional, custom, customary, daily, familiar *(customary)*, habit, habitual, manner *(behavior)*, matter of course, method, mode, modus operandi, mundane, normal *(regular)*, operation, perfunctory, practice *(custom)*, practice *(procedure)*, procedure, process *(course)*, regular *(conventional)*, rule *(guide)*, system, systematic, trite, usage, usual

routine event matter of course

routine happening matter of course

routine procedure custom

routinely invariably

rove digress, perambulate, prowl

rover itinerant, migrant, pedestrian

roving circuitous, discursive *(digressive)*, moving *(in motion)*, shifting, transient, vagrancy

row affray, altercation, bluster *(commotion)*, brawl, brawl, chain *(series)*, commotion, confrontation *(altercation)*, disaccord, embroilment, fight *(argument)*, fracas, fray, imbroglio, pandemonium, riot, strife, trouble, turmoil

rowdiness brawl, fracas

rowdy blatant *(obtrusive)*, disorderly, pugnacious, uncontrollable, unruly

royal outstanding *(prominent)*, sovereign *(absolute)*

rub contact *(touch)*

rub away diminish, erode

rub off deface, obliterate

rub out censor, deface, delete, destroy *(efface)*, expunge, extirpate, obliterate

rub the wrong way irritate

rubber check bad check

rubbery resilient

rubbing away erosion

rubric article *(precept)*, bylaw, caption, code, constitution, dictate, direction *(order)*, law, measure, precept, prescription *(directive)*, principle *(axiom)*, statute, title *(designation)*

rubricate embellish

ruckus noise

ruction brawl, commotion, fracas, fray, noise, pandemonium

rude blatant *(obtrusive)*, brazen, caitiff, caustic, contemptuous, disdainful, disorderly, impertinent *(insolent)*, inelegant, insolent, obtrusive, offensive *(offending)*, perverse, presumptuous, provincial, uncouth, unseemly

rude behavior disrespect

rude reproach disparagement

rudeness contempt *(disobedience to the court)*, contumely, disparagement, disregard *(lack of respect)*, disrespect, ingratitude, rebuff, temerity

rudiment cornerstone, element, embryo, foundation *(basis)*, necessity

rudimental elementary, inchoate, incipient, original *(initial)*, rudimentary, ultimate

rudimentary cardinal *(basic)*, elementary, fundamental, inchoate, incipient, initial, minimal, organic, original *(initial)*, prime *(original)*, primordial, simple, ultimate, underlying

rudimentary state embryo

rudis inexperienced, novice, uncouth, unversed

rue deplore, regret, remorse, repent

rueful contrite, despondent, lamentable, penitent, remorseful, repentant

ruffian aggressor, delinquent, hoodlum, malefactor

ruffianism brutality, misdoing

ruffianly disorderly

ruffle aggravate *(annoy)*, agitate *(shake up)*, annoy, badger, discompose, disconcert, disorient, disrupt, disturb, harry *(harass)*, incense, irritate, molest *(annoy)*, perturb, pique, plague

rugged brutal, powerful, severe, solid *(sound)*, strong

ruggedness health

ruin bankruptcy, betray *(lead astray)*, catastrophe, consumption, damage, damage, debacle, debauch, decay, decline, defeat, despoil, destroy *(efface)*, destruction, deterioration, detriment, devastate, disable, disaster, dissolution *(termination)*, extinguish, failure *(lack of success)*, fatality, foil, harm, harm, havoc, impair, loss, miscarriage, mischief, misemploy, misfortune, obliterate, overturn, pervert, pillage, plunder, prejudice *(injure)*, prostration, spoil *(impair)*, stain, subversion, subvert, thwart, upset

ruin one's eyesight blind *(deprive of sight)*

ruin one's prospects disappoint

ruinable destructible

ruinate despoil, destroy *(efface)*, pillage, spoil *(impair)*

ruination adversity, bankruptcy, catastrophe, consumption, damage, debacle, defeat, defilement, destruction, deterioration, detriment, disaster, disrepair, dissolution *(termination)*, havoc, prostration, subversion, waste, wear and tear

ruined bad *(inferior)*, bad *(offensive)*, bankrupt, depraved, dilapidated, imperfect, insolvent, irredeemable, irremediable, irreparable, marred, poor *(underprivileged)*

ruiner vandal

ruining disastrous, fatal

ruinous adverse *(negative)*, bad *(offensive)*, deadly, deleterious, diabolic, dire, disastrous, fatal, harmful, insalubrious, malevolent, malignant, noxious, pernicious, regrettable

ruinous price toll *(effect)*

ruinousness adversity, disaster

rule act *(enactment)*, adjudge, adjudi-

cate, arbitrate *(adjudge)*, array *(order)*, award, belief *(something believed)*, brevet, bureaucracy, bylaw, canon, codification, coerce, command, conclude *(decide)*, condition *(contingent provision)*, constant, control *(regulate)*, criterion, decide, decree, determine, dictate, dictate, direct *(order)*, direct *(supervise)*, direction *(order)*, doctrine, dogma, dominate, dominion *(supreme authority)*, edict, enactment, enjoin, fiat, find *(determine)*, govern, government *(administration)*, habit, handle *(manage)*, hegemony, hold *(decide)*, influence, instruction *(direction)*, law, legislate, manage, mandamus, mandate, manipulate *(control unfairly)*, matter of course, maxim, measure, measure, method, mode, norm, occupation *(possession)*, operate, opinion *(judicial decision)*, order *(judicial directive)*, order, ordinance, oversee, pass *(determine)*, pattern, police, power, practice *(procedure)*, precedent, precept, predominance, predominate *(command)*, prescription *(directive)*, preside, prevail *(triumph)*, primacy, principle *(axiom)*, procedure, pronounce *(pass judgment)*, regime, regulate *(manage)*, rubric *(authoritative rule)*, ruling, stare decisis, statute, subject, superintend, supremacy, technicality, try *(conduct a trial)*, wield

rule against overrule

rule dishonestly misgovern

rule for future determinations precedent

rule for future guidance precedent

rule of action platform, policy *(plan of action)*, principle *(axiom)*

rule of conduct canon, law

rule of might oppression

rule of proceeding formality

rule on judge

rule out delete, deter, dismiss *(put out of consideration)*, disqualify, eliminate *(exclude)*, exclude, negate, obliterate, overrule, prevent

rule over dominate, predominate *(command)*, subjugate

rule upon adjudicate

rule-abiding obedient

ruled positive *(prescribed)*

ruler arbitrator

rulers authorities, hierarchy *(persons in authority)*

rulership government *(administration)*

rules code, mode, protocol *(etiquette)*

rules and regulations codification, criterion

rules of business practice *(procedure)*

rules of conduct decorum

rules of war strategy

ruling act *(enactment)*, adjudication, authority *(documentation)*, award, canon, central *(essential)*, code, conclusion *(determination)*, condition *(contingent provision)*, conviction *(finding of guilt)*, decree, determination, dictate, dominant, edict, enactment, finding, influential, judgment *(formal court decree)*, mandate, master, measure, omnipotent, opinion *(judicial decision)*, order *(judicial directive)*, potent, powerful, predominant, prescription *(direc-*

tive), prevailing *(having superior force)*, primary, principal, pronouncement, requirement, rubric *(authoritative rule)*, sentence, sovereign *(absolute)*, verdict

ruling of the court award, decree

ruling passion obsession

ruling power government *(political administration)*

ruling whim obsession

rulings codification, legislation *(enactments)*

ruminant cogitative, pensive

ruminate brood, concentrate *(pay attention)*, consider, deliberate, muse, ponder, reflect *(ponder)*, speculate *(conjecture)*, study, weigh

rumination consideration *(contemplation)*, contemplation, deliberation, dialectic, hindsight, reflection *(thought)*, speculation *(conjecture)*

ruminative cogitative, pensive

rummage delve

rumor canard, circulate, spread

rumor hearsay

rumor about circulate

rumored reputedly

rumpere infringe, violate

rumpus bluster *(commotion)*, fray, furor, imbroglio, pandemonium, riot, turmoil

run abscond, chain *(series)*, conduct, exude, flee, function, hierarchy *(arrangement in a series)*, manage, manipulate *(utilize skillfully)*, market *(demand)*, moderate *(preside over)*, officiate, operate, race, rule *(govern)*

run a race race

run across find *(discover)*

run afoul of collide *(clash)*

run after chase, hunt, pursue *(chase)*

run against collide *(clash)*, conflict, counteract, fight *(counteract)*, jostle *(bump into)*, oppugn

run at attack

run at cross purposes conflict

run at cross-purposes collide *(clash)*

run away abandon *(physically leave)*, abscond, defect, escape, evacuate, flee, leave *(depart)*, quit *(evacuate)*, retreat

run away with jostle *(pickpocket)*, kidnap

run checks on check *(inspect)*, poll, probe

run counter check *(restrain)*, confront *(oppose)*, counteract

run counter to antagonize, collide *(clash)*, conflict, confront *(oppose)*, contradict, contravene, counteract, countervail, cross *(disagree with)*, disaccord, disaffirm, except *(object)*, fight *(counteract)*, oppugn

run down brutalize, decrease, defame, degenerate, denigrate, deplete, depreciate, derogate, diminish, disapprove *(condemn)*, disparage, lessen, minimize, misprize, mistreat, old, pillory, pursue *(chase)*, reprehend, reprimand, sully, underestimate

run foul of collide *(clash)*

run from shirk

run in opposition to conflict, counter, counteract

run in pursuit chase

run into impinge, pervade

run into debt overdraw

run into each other collide *(crash*

against)

run its course cease

run low diminish

run of luck prosperity

run of the mill mediocre, prevalent, regular *(conventional)*, trite

run off flee, publish

run off with carry away, hold up *(rob)*, jostle *(pickpocket)*, kidnap, poach

run on keep *(continue)*, persevere

run out close *(terminate)*, expire, lapse *(cease)*, terminate

run over inundate, invade, overlap, overstep, recapitulate, repeat *(state again)*, review

run parallel to correspond *(be equivalent)*

run riot brawl

run swiftly race

run tests on check *(inspect)*

run the chance incur

run the risk bet

run through exhaust *(deplete)*, penetrate, permeate, pervade, pierce *(lance)*, spend

run together collide *(crash against)*, commingle

runabout itinerant

runagate fugitive

runaway elusive, fugitive

rundle step

rung degree *(station)*, step

runic mysterious

runner bootlegger, candidate

running consecutive, continuous, fluvial, management *(judicious use)*

running account ledger

running away flight

running counter to dissenting, opposition

running expense cost *(expenses)*

running expenses maintenance *(upkeep)*

running out expiration

runoff outflow

runthrough hornbook

rupture alienation *(estrangement)*, break *(fracture)*, controversy *(argument)*, disassociation, disrupt, embroilment, estrangement, feud, force *(break)*, rend, rift *(gap)*, schism, separate, separation, sever, split, variance *(disagreement)*

ruptured broken *(fractured)*

ruse artifice, bunko, canard, deception, device *(contrivance)*, evasion, expedient, fake, false pretense, fraud, hoax, imposture, machination, maneuver *(trick)*, plot *(secret plan)*, ploy, pretense *(pretext)*, pretext, stratagem, subterfuge

rush dispatch *(promptness)*, dispatch *(send off)*, expedite, haste, hasten, outbreak, outburst, precipitate *(hasten)*, race, spate

rush off dispatch *(send off)*

rush through hasten

rush to a conclusion presuppose

rush to conclusion prejudge

rush upon assail, attack, inundate

rushed perfunctory, precipitate

rushing rapid

rushing in incursion

rustic inelegant, ingenuous, simple, uncouth

rusticate retreat

rusty old

ruth lenience, pity

ruthful placable

ruthless brutal, cold-blooded, cruel, diabolic, draconian, harsh, malevolent, malicious, malignant, relentless, remorseless, severe, uncompromising, unrelenting, unscrupulous

ruthlessness atrocity, brutality, cruelty, oppression, rancor, severity, violence

ruttish lecherous, lewd, licentious, salacious

rutty lewd

S

sabotage damage, disable, disloyalty, pillage, spoil *(impair)*, subversion

saboteur conspirer

saccharine nectarious

sack depredation, despoil, devastate, foray, harry *(plunder)*, havoc, hold up *(rob)*, loot, pillage, pillage, pirate *(take by violence)*, plunder, plunder, spoliation

sacrament of marriage matrimony

sacramental sacrosanct, solemn

sacred ineffable, infrangible, inviolate, sacrosanct, solemn

sacrifice abandon *(relinquish)*, cost *(penalty)*, extirpate, forbear, forfeit, forswear, lose *(be deprived of)*, loss, relinquish, renunciation, suffer *(sustain loss)*, waive, yield *(submit)*

sacrifice pride condescend *(deign)*

sacrificed lost *(taken away)*

sacrilege blasphemy

sacrilegious profane

sacrilegiousness blasphemy

sacrosanct infrangible

sad deplorable, despondent, disconsolate, grave *(solemn)*, lamentable, lugubrious, pessimistic, regrettable, remorseful

sadden depress, discourage, distress

saddening lamentable

saddle disadvantage, encumber *(hinder)*, load, overcome *(overwhelm)*, overload

saddle with tax *(overwork)*

sadistic brutal, cruel, diabolic, ruthless

sadness damper *(depressant)*, distress *(anguish)*

saepire enclose

safe bank, cache *(storage place)*, coffer, depository, guarded, immune, impervious, indubious, inexpugnable, innocuous, intact, nontoxic, reliable, repository, salutary, secure *(free from danger)*, solid *(sound)*, treasury

safe conduct protection, security *(safety)*

safe deposit box coffer

safe place cache *(hiding place)*, cache *(storage place)*, refuge

safe retreat cache *(hiding place)*

safe-deposit box depository

safe-deposit vault bank

safebreaker burglar

safecracker burglar

safeguard asylum *(protection)*, auspices, barrier, bear *(support)*, bulwark, concern *(care)*, conserve, cover *(protection)*, cover *(guard)*, coverage *(insur-*

ance), custody *(supervision)*, defend, discretion *(quality of being discreet)*, ensconce, ensure, foster, guarantee, guaranty, guardian, harbor, hedge, keep *(shelter)*, maintain *(sustain)*, panoply, patrol, police, precaution, preparation, preserve, protect, protection, rescue, save *(rescue)*, screen *(guard)*, security *(safety)*, shield, ward

safeguarded guarded, safe

safeguarding conservation, preservation, preventive, prophylactic, protective

safehold asylum *(hiding place)*

safekeeper guardian

safekeeping charge *(custody)*, conservation, custody *(incarceration)*, custody *(supervision)*, preservation, protection, ward

safeness security *(safety)*

safety asylum *(protection)*, inviolability, preservation, protection, refuge, shelter *(protection)*, trust *(custody)*

safety from prosecution immunity

sag give *(yield)*, languish

saga account *(report)*, report *(detailed account)*, story *(narrative)*

sagacious cognizant, discriminating *(judicious)*, judicial, judicious, juridical, learned, lucid, omniscient, perspicacious, politic, profound *(esoteric)*, prudent, rational, reasonable *(rational)*, resourceful, sapient, sensible, solid *(sound)*, subtle *(refined)*

sagaciousness insight, perception, sagacity, sense *(intelligence)*

sagacitas perception, sagacity

sagacity caliber *(mental capacity)*, common sense, comprehension, discretion *(quality of being discreet)*, discrimination *(good judgment)*, insight, intelligence *(intellect)*, judgment *(discernment)*, perception, reason *(sound judgment)*, sense *(intelligence)*

sagax acute, judicious, perceptive, perspicacious

sage cognizant, expert, judicial, judicious, juridical, learned, lucid, mastermind, oracular, pedagogue, perspicacious, profound *(esoteric)*, prudent, rational, sapient, sensible, solid *(sound)*

sage maxim principle *(axiom)*

sage reflection maxim

sageness comprehension

sagesse discretion *(quality of being discreet)*

said aforesaid, before mentioned, oral, stated

said again repeated

said aloud oral

said in a preceding part aforesaid

sainted sacrosanct

saintly laudable

sake advantage, reason *(basis)*

salable disposable, marketable, negotiable, valuable

salable commodities merchandise

salable commodity item, product

salacious depraved, dissolute, immoral, lascivious, lecherous, lewd, lurid, obscene, prurient, scurrilous, suggestive *(risqué)*

salaciousness obscenity, pornography

salacity debauchery, obscenity, pornography

salaried worker employee

salary commission *(fee)*, compensate *(remunerate)*, compensation, earnings, honorarium, income, pay, payment *(remittance)*, payroll, recompense, revenue, wage

sale conveyance, disposition *(transfer of property)*, trade *(commerce)*, transaction

sale by bid auction

sale by outcry auction

sale proceeds income

sale to the highest bidder auction

sales trade *(commerce)*

salesman dealer, vendor

salesmanship persuasion

salesperson dealer, merchant

saleswoman dealer

salience emphasis, importance, interest *(concern)*, materiality *(consequence)*, significance

saliency emphasis

salient arrant *(definite)*, clear *(apparent)*, distinctive, evident, important *(significant)*, manifest, material *(important)*, notable, noteworthy, open *(in sight)*, outstanding *(prominent)*, palpable, paramount, perceivable, perceptible, prominent, remarkable

salient characteristic aspect

salient feature main point

salient point content *(meaning)*, cornerstone, feature *(characteristic)*, gist *(ground for a suit)*, gravamen, highlight, landmark *(significant change)*, main point, significance

salient quality feature *(characteristic)*

salire frisk

salle chamber *(compartment)*

sally outburst

salubrious beneficial, medicinal, remedial, safe, salutary

salubriousness health

salubrity health

salus health, maintenance *(upkeep)*, security *(safety)*

salutaris beneficial, remedial, salutary

salutary beneficial, contributory, favorable *(advantageous)*, medicinal, profitable, prophylactic, remedial, salubrious

salutation remembrance *(commemoration)*

salute honor, recognize *(acknowledge)*, salvo

salutiferous beneficial, medicinal, remedial, salubrious, salutary

salvage recover, recovery *(repossession)*, rehabilitate, renew *(refurbish)*, renewal, renovate, repair, reparation *(keeping in repair)*, replevin, rescue, save *(conserve)*

salvageable corrigible

salvaged renascent

salvation discharge *(liberation)*, emancipation, mainstay, preservation, protection, redemption, rehabilitation, release, relief *(aid)*, safekeeping, salvage, security *(safety)*

salve assuage, cure, cure, pacify, placate, relieve *(give aid)*, soothe

salvo barrage, discharge *(shot)*, reservation *(condition)*

salvus intact

Samaritanism benevolence *(disposition to do good)*

same analogous, cognate, equal, equivalent, similar, uniform

same conditions status quo

same line of descent family *(common ancestry)*

same strain family *(common ancestry)*

sameness constant, correspondence *(similarity)*, facsimile, identity *(similarity)*, par *(equality)*, parity, regularity, resemblance, semblance

sample case *(example)*, check *(inspect)*, cross section, example, exemplary, illustration, instance, model, paradigm, partake, pattern, poll, prototype, representative, representative *(example)*, specimen

samples selection *(collection)*

sanare cure

sanatio cure

sanative medicinal, remedial, salutary

sanatory medicinal, remedial, salubrious, salutary

sancire confirm, sanction

sanctification elevation

sanctified inviolate, sacrosanct, solemn

sanctify authorize, elevate, purge *(purify)*

sanctify by custom inure *(accustom)*

sanctimonious tartuffish

sanctimoniousness blasphemy, hypocrisy

sanctimony hypocrisy

sanctio enactment, ratification

sanction abide, accept *(assent)*, acceptance, accredit, acquiescence, adoption *(acceptance)*, advantage, advocacy, advocate, allow *(authorize)*, appoint, approval, approve, assent, assent, authority *(documentation)*, authorize, bear *(support)*, bear *(tolerate)*, bestow, bind *(obligate)*, brevet, capacity *(authority)*, certify *(approve)*, concede, concession *(authorization)*, concur *(agree)*, confirm, confirmation, consent, consent, constitute *(establish)*, copyright, corroborate, countenance, countersign, decree, delegate, discretion *(power of choice)*, dispensation *(exception)*, droit, embrace *(accept)*, empower, enable, endorse, enfranchise, favor, fiat, force *(compulsion)*, franchise *(license)*, grant *(concede)*, indorse, indorsement, indulgence, invest *(vest)*, leave *(permission)*, legality, legalization, legalize, legislate, legitimate, let *(permit)*, liberty, license, option *(contractual provision)*, pass *(approve)*, permission, permit, permit, prefer, prerogative, privilege, promote *(organize)*, qualify *(meet standards)*, ratification, reassure, recommend, recommendation, right *(entitlement)*, seal *(solemnize)*, sign, subscription, sufferance, sustain *(confirm)*, title *(right)*, tolerate, uphold, validate, vest, warrant *(authorization)*

sanction a claim authorize

sanction by law legalize

sanctionability admissibility

sanctionable admissible, allowable, licit

sanctionableness admissibility, legality

sanctioned admissible, allowable, allowed, due *(regular)*, entitled, juridical, justifiable, lawful, legal, legitimate *(rightful)*, licit, official, permissible, privileged, rightful, statutory, traditional, valid

sanctioned by custom legitimate *(rightful)*

sanctioned by law de jure, jural, lawful, legitimate *(rightful)*, permissible

sanctioned by legal authority legitimate *(rightful)*

sanctioned by the law allowed

sanctioned effectiveness force *(legal efficacy)*

sanctioned potency force *(legal efficacy)*

sanctions codification

sanctitas inviolability

sanctity good faith, honesty

sanctuary asylum *(hiding place)*, asylum *(protection)*, bulwark, haven, preservation, protection, refuge, security *(safety)*, shelter *(protection)*, shield

sanctum sanctorum asylum *(hiding place)*

sanctus conscientious, incorruptible, inculpable, irreprehensible, moral, unimpeachable

sane lucid, rational, sensible

sanemindedness competence *(sanity)*

saneness competence *(sanity)*, sanity

sang-froid dispassionate

sanguinary deadly, ruthless

sanguine expectation faith

sanguineness belief *(state of mind)*, confidence *(faith)*, faith

sanguineous sanguine

sanguis blood

sanitary remedial, salutary

sanitary cordon quarantine

sanitas health

sanitize decontaminate

sanitorium asylum *(hospital)*

sanity reason *(sound judgment)*

sans pareil best

sansculottic insubordinate

sanus sane

sap eviscerate, exhaust *(deplete)*, impair

sap the strength of debilitate

sapid palatable, savory

sapience caliber *(mental capacity)*, common sense, judgment *(discernment)*, sagacity, sense *(intelligence)*

sapiency sagacity

sapiens judicious, sapient

sapient acute, discriminating *(judicious)*, judicial, judicious, juridical, learned, literate, omniscient, oracular, perspicacious, prudent, reasonable *(rational)*, sensible, solid *(sound)*

sapiential sensible

sapless languid, powerless

saporous sapid

sarcasm diatribe, irony, ridicule

sarcastic bitter *(reproachful)*, cynical, incisive, insolent, ironic, offensive *(offending)*, trenchant

sarcastical cynical, incisive, ironic

sardonic bitter *(reproachful)*, cynical, disdainful, ironic

satanic cruel, heinous, malevolent, malignant, sinister

Satanic diabolic

sate assuage, satisfy *(fulfill)*

sated full

satellite offshoot, partisan

satiate assuage, pacify, satisfy *(fulfill)*

satiate to excess overindulge

satiated full, replete

satiation plethora, surfeit

satietas surfeit

satiety plethora, sufficiency, surfeit

satire caricature, distortion, irony, parody, ridicule

satiric incisive, ironic

satirical incisive, ironic

satirize jape, mock *(deride)*, mock *(imitate)*

satisdatio warranty

satisfactio reparation *(indemnification)*

satisfaction amortization, benefit *(betterment)*, compensation, conciliation, consideration *(recompense)*, contribution *(indemnification)*, discharge *(payment)*, enjoyment *(pleasure)*, expiation, fruition, indemnification, offset, out of pocket, payment *(act of paying)*, pride, proof, recompense, recovery *(award)*, refund, relief *(legal redress)*, remuneration, reparation *(indemnification)*, requital, restitution, retribution, revenge, settlement, surfeit, trover

satisfaction for damage compensation

satisfaction for injury compensation

satisfaction in full payoff *(payment in full)*

satisfactorily fairly *(moderately)*

satisfactoriness mediocrity, sufficiency

satisfactory adequate, ample, competent, eligible, mediocre, palatable, prima facie *(legally sufficient)*, right *(suitable)*, suitable, unobjectionable

satisfactory evidence proof

satisfactory notice adequate notice

satisfiable placable

satisfied certain *(positive)*, complacent, definite, full, indubious, peaceable, positive *(confident)*, proud *(self-respecting)*, replete, successful

satisfy assuage, assure *(give confidence to)*, compensate *(remunerate)*, comply, contribute *(indemnify)*, convince, disarm *(set at ease)*, discharge *(pay a debt)*, fulfill, keep *(fulfill)*, liquidate *(determine liability)*, obey, observe *(obey)*, pacify, pander, pay, perform *(adhere to)*, placate, propitiate, reassure, recoup *(reimburse)*, redeem *(satisfy debts)*, redress, refund, reimburse, remedy, remit *(send payment)*, remunerate, repay, restore *(return)*, return *(refund)*, supply, vouchsafe

satisfy a claim defray

satisfy by evidence convince, persuade

satisfy by proof convince, persuade

satisfy desires pander

satisfy in advance prepay

satisfy in full discharge *(pay a debt)*

satisfy oneself ascertain

satisfy requirements pass *(satisfy requirements)*

satisfy to excess overindulge

satisfying adequate, compensatory, sapid

saturate imbue, inject, inundate, overload, penetrate, permeate, pervade, replenish

saturated drunk, full, replete

saturation maximum *(amplitude)*, osmosis, plethora, sufficiency, surfeit

saturnine disconsolate, grave *(solemn)*, lugubrious

satyric dissolute, lascivious, prurient, salacious

satyrical lascivious, salacious

sauciness disrespect

saucy brazen, impertinent *(insolent)*, insolent, obtrusive, offensive *(offending)*, presumptuous

saunter perambulate

savage assail, brutal, cold-blooded, cruel, disorderly, harsh, hot-blooded, malevolent, malicious, malignant, mistreat, ruthless, severe, vicious

savageness brutality, cruelty

savagery atrocity, bestiality, brutality, cruelty, severity, violence

savant expert, mastermind, specialist

save conserve, deposit *(submit to a bank)*, extricate, free, fund, garner, glean, hold *(possess)*, keep *(shelter)*, maintain *(sustain)*, perpetuate, preserve, protect, release, remedy, renew *(refurbish)*, rescue, reserve, retain *(keep in possession)*, store, sustain *(prolong)*, unless

save from disencumber

save from loss conserve

save harmless indemnify

save up fund, hoard, set aside *(reserve)*

saved free *(relieved from a burden)*

saved from bondage free *(enjoying civil liberty)*

saving conservation, economical, economy *(frugality)*, hoard, penurious, preservation, provident *(frugal)*, prudent, reservation *(engagement)*

saving clause loophole, reservation *(condition)*, salvo

savings capital, fund, reserve, store *(depository)*

savior samaritan

savoir faire common sense, discretion *(quality of being discreet)*

savor partake, relish

savorless insipid, stale

savory palatable, sapid

saw maxim, phrase

say allege, claim *(maintain)*, comment, communicate, contend *(maintain)*, converse, declare, enunciate, express, observe *(remark)*, phrase, posit, pronounce *(speak)*, purport, referendum, relate *(tell)*, remark, speak, speech, suffrage

say again recapitulate, reiterate, repeat *(state again)*

say by heart recite

say in advance preface

say in defense support *(justify)*

say in reply answer *(reply)*, countercharge, retort, return *(respond)*

say less than the truth perjure

say no challenge

say no to ban

say over repeat *(state again)*

say repeatedly reiterate

say under oath depose *(testify)*, witness *(attest to)*

say yes concur *(agree)*

saying catchword, expression *(comment)*, maxim, phrase, remark
scab pariah
scabrous lurid, obscene, salacious, scurrilous
scaena scene
scaenicus histrionic, histrionics
scald burn
scalding caustic
scale caliber *(measurement)*, chain *(series)*, differential, index *(gauge)*, magnitude, surmount
scale down decrease, diminish, discount *(minimize)*, minimize
scale of prices tariff *(bill)*
scaled proportionate
scamp degenerate, derelict, malefactor
scamper race
scampish disorderly, profligate *(corrupt)*
scampishness knavery
scan analyze, canvass, check *(inspect)*, frisk, investigate, monitor, observe *(watch)*, patrol, peruse, probe, read, regard *(pay attention)*, research, scrutinize, search, study, survey *(examine)*
scandal defamation, discredit, disgrace, dishonor *(shame)*, ignominy, infamy, notoriety, odium, opprobrium, shame, slander
scandalize contemn, defame, discredit, disgrace, libel, pillory, repel *(disgust)*
scandalizing flagrant
scandalous arrant *(onerous)*, bad *(offensive)*, blameworthy, calumnious, contemptuous, delinquent *(guilty of a misdeed)*, disgraceful, disorderly, flagrant, ignoble, inexpiable, iniquitous, lewd, libelous, licentious, nefarious, notorious, outrageous, peccant *(culpable)*, regrettable, vicious
scandalum magnatum stigma
scant deficient, inadequate, inappreciable, insubstantial, insufficient, marginal, minimal, minor, negligible, nonsubstantial *(not sufficient)*, paltry, petty, poor *(inferior in quality)*, remote *(small)*, scarce, slight, tenuous
scant of devoid
scant respect disparagement
scantiness austerity, dearth, deficit, delinquency *(shortage)*, insignificance, insufficiency, need *(deprivation)*, paucity, poverty
scantity poverty
scantling minimum
scantness dearth, insufficiency, paucity, poverty
scanty de minimus, deficient, imperfect, inappreciable, insufficient, marginal, minimal, negligible, nominal, nonsubstantial *(not sufficient)*, paltry, partial *(relating to a part)*, petty, trivial
scapegrace degenerate
scar deface, defacement, onus *(stigma)*, stigma
scarce barren, deficient, infrequent, insufficient, minimal, nonsubstantial *(not sufficient)*, paltry, rare, uncommon, unusual
scarcely almost
scarceness dearth, insignificance, paucity, poverty

scarcity dearth, deficiency, deficit, delinquency *(shortage)*, indigence, insufficiency, need *(deprivation)*, paucity, poverty
scare browbeat, discourage, fear, fright, frighten, intimidate, menace, start, trepidation
scared caitiff
scarify lash *(attack verbally)*
scarifying critical *(faultfinding)*
scarlet lewd, licentious, salacious
scarred marred
scathe damage, disable, harm, harm, lash *(attack verbally)*, persecute
scathed marred
scatheful adverse *(negative)*, malevolent, malignant, noxious, scathing, sinister
scatheless inviolate, safe
scathing bitter *(penetrating)*, critical *(faultfinding)*, harsh, incisive, mordacious, trenchant
scatter break *(fracture)*, deploy, diffuse, disband, disburse *(distribute)*, dislocate, disorganize, dispel, dispense, dissipate *(spread out)*, dissociate, dissolve *(disperse)*, distribute, intersperse, radiate, repel *(drive back)*, spread
scatter abroad disperse *(disseminate)*, disperse *(scatter)*
scatter thinly dissipate *(spread out)*
scatter to the winds dissipate *(spread out)*
scatter widely dissipate *(spread out)*
scatterbrained fatuous, thoughtless
scattered disconnected, sporadic
scattering circulation, decentralization, havoc
scavenge prowl
sceleratus criminal, felon, guilty
scelestus felon
scene locality, location, region, territory, vicinity
scene of destruction shambles
scene of disorder shambles
scent clue, trace *(follow)*
scepter supremacy
schedule agenda, arrange *(plan)*, book, calendar *(list of cases)*, calendar *(record of yearly periods)*, docket, empanel, impanel, invoice *(itemized list)*, plan, plan, policy *(contract)*, program, program, register, register, roll, scheme, set down
schedule of affairs agenda
schedule of articles inventory
schedule of duties tariff *(duties)*
schedule of events calendar *(record of yearly periods)*
schedule of items and their respective prices invoice *(itemized list)*
scheduled forthcoming, future, prospective
scheduling codification, economy *(frugality)*
schema arrangement *(plan)*
schematic arrangement array *(order)*
schematism arrangement *(ordering)*
schematize arrange *(methodize)*, coordinate, devise *(invent)*
scheme agenda, arrangement *(plan)*, artifice, avenue *(means of attainment)*, blueprint, cabal, campaign, circumvent, codification, connivance, connive, conspiracy, conspire, contrivance, contrive,

course, design *(intent)*, device *(contrivance)*, devise *(invent)*, direction *(course)*, endeavor, enterprise *(undertaking)*, expedient, forethought, form *(arrangement)*, frame *(formulate)*, goal, hoax, intend, intent, machination, maneuver *(tactic)*, maneuver *(trick)*, maneuver, mode, organization *(structure)*, plan, plan, platform, plot *(secret plan)*, plot, ploy, policy *(plan of action)*, practice *(procedure)*, procedure, process *(course)*, program, project, proposal *(suggestion)*, proposition, prospectus, racket, ruse, stratagem, strategy, suggestion, system
scheme of arrangement configuration *(form)*, method
schemeful collusive
schemer architect, coactor, conspirator, conspirer
schemery collusion, confederacy *(conspiracy)*, strategy
scheming artful, collusion, collusive, deceptive, devious, diplomatic, dishonest, disingenuous, evasive, fraudulent, insidious, machiavellian, perfidious, recreant, sinister, sly, unconscionable, untrue
schism alienation *(estrangement)*, contention *(opposition)*, difference, disaccord, disassociation, discord, dissension, dissent *(difference of opinion)*, dissidence, division *(act of dividing)*, estrangement, fight *(argument)*
schisma schism
schismatic contentious, divisive, heretic, hostile, polemic, recusant
schismatize conflict
scholar disciple, expert, pedagogue, specialist
scholarly didactic, diligent, disciplinary *(educational)*, learned, literate, profound *(esoteric)*
scholarship education, knowledge *(learning)*
scholastic didactic, disciplinary *(educational)*, informative, literate
scholium clarification, comment, note *(brief comment)*
school discipline *(train)*, edify, educate, instill, institute, instruct *(teach)*, organization *(association)*, practice *(train by repetition)*, style
school oneself study
schooled familiar *(informed)*, informed *(educated)*, knowing, learned, literate, sciential
schooling discipline *(training)*, edification, education, experience *(background)*, guidance, instruction *(teaching)*
schoolman pedagogue
schoolmaster pedagogue
schoolteacher pedagogue
science of law jurisprudence
science of legal relations jurisprudence
science of monetary relations finance
science of oratory rhetoric *(skilled speech)*
science of teaching education
science of wealth finance
sciens expert, familiar *(informed)*, knowing, proficient
scientia knowledge *(learning)*, science

(study), skill

scientific objective, precise, real, sound, technical, valid

scientific determination diagnosis

scindere split

scintilla iota, minimum

sciolist pedant

sciolistic superficial

scion child, descendant, heir, offshoot, offspring, posterity, successor

scions progeny

scissile destructible, divisible, severable

scission decentralization, division *(act of dividing)*, severance, split

scissura split

scissure rift *(gap)*, split

scitum resolution *(decision)*

scoff derogate, disdain, disdain, disparage, flout, humiliate, jape, jeer, mock *(deride)*

scoff at contemn, discommend, reject

scoffing cynical, disregard *(lack of respect)*, disrespect, impertinent *(insolent)*, skeptical

scofflaw delinquent

scold castigate, denounce *(condemn)*, disapprove *(condemn)*, fault, inveigh, rebuke, remonstrate, reprehend, reprimand, reproach

scolding critical *(faultfinding)*, criticism, diatribe, disparagement, objurgation, obloquy, outcry, rebuff, reprimand, reproach

sconce fine, penalty

scope area *(province)*, capacity *(aptitude)*, capacity *(maximum)*, capacity *(sphere)*, connotation, content *(meaning)*, contents, context, degree *(magnitude)*, extent, gamut, intent, latitude, magnitude, opportunity, province, purview, range, region, scene, space, sphere

scope of vision perspective

scorch burn, deflagrate

scorching bitter *(penetrating)*

score bill *(invoice)*, calculate, carry *(succeed)*, census, computation, inveigh, poll, sum *(tally)*

score a success attain, succeed *(attain)*

scorify burn

scorn affront, contemn, contempt *(disdain)*, decry, disapprove *(reject)*, disavow, disdain, disdain, dishonor *(shame)*, disoblige, disown *(refuse to acknowledge)*, disparage, disparagement, disregard *(lack of respect)*, disrespect, exclude, flout, forswear, humiliate, ignore, illude, infamy, minimize, misprize, mock *(deride)*, odium, pillory, rebuff, rejection, renounce, repulse, ridicule, shame, spurn, vilification

scorn of the consequences audacity

scorned derelict *(abandoned)*, undesirable

scornful bitter *(reproachful)*, contemptuous, cynical, disdainful, inflated *(vain)*, orgulous, pejorative, supercilious

scornful imitation ridicule

scornful insolence contumely

scornful treatment contumely

scornfulness contumely, disdain

scorning disdain

scorse trade

scot tax

scotch stem *(check)*

scoundrel convict, hoodlum, malefactor, wrongdoer

scoundrelism corruption, knavery

scoundrelly sinister

scour decontaminate, frisk, perambulate, purge *(purify)*, search

scourge catastrophe, disaster, discipline *(punishment)*, discipline *(punish)*, disease, harm, harm, lash *(strike)*, nuisance, persecute, plague, punish

scourging correction *(punishment)*

scout forerunner, observe *(watch)*, patrol, pioneer, precede, precursor, reject, search, spurn, spy

scramble bluster *(commotion)*, brawl, commingle, competition, confound, disorganize, disorient, dispatch *(promptness)*, fracas, fray, muddle, race

scrambled composite, miscellaneous, promiscuous

scrap bicker, brawl, reject, salvage

scrape entanglement *(involvement)*, erode, imbroglio, misdeed, misdoing, plight, predicament, quagmire

scrape together glean

scraping obsequious

scrapped derelict *(abandoned)*

scrappy sporadic

scratch deface, defacement

scratch out censor, deface, delete, destroy *(efface)*, expunge, obliterate

scratched marred

scrawl script

scream outcry

screaming blatant *(obtrusive)*, flagrant

screed declamation, phillipic

screen blind *(obscure)*, buffer zone, camouflage, cloak, conceal, cover *(pretext)*, cover *(conceal)*, disguise, disguise, ensconce, enshroud, envelop, harbor, hedge, hide, lodge *(house)*, maintain *(sustain)*, obfuscate, obliterate, obnubilate, obscure, panoply, plant *(covertly place)*, preserve, protect, safeguard, shelter *(protection)*, shield, shroud, sort, suppress, veil

screen from observation blind *(obscure)*, camouflage

screen from sight blind *(obscure)*, camouflage

screen off insulate

screen out reject, seclude

screened allusive, blind *(concealed)*, clandestine, covert, hidden, immune, impalpable, indiscernible, latent, mysterious, safe

screened from danger safe

screening protective

scriba clerk, notary public

scribbled holographic

scribe amanuensis, clerk, inscribe, notary public, note *(record)*

scribere legislate

scrimmage affray, brawl, brawl, fight *(battle)*, fray, struggle

scrimping austerity, parsimonious

scrinium portfolio

script handwriting, scenario

scription handwriting, script

scriptor author *(writer)*

scriptorial holographic

scriptory in writing

scriptural holographic

scrivener amanuensis, clerk, notary

public

scrofulous lurid, salacious

scrounger parasite

scrub decontaminate, poor *(inferior in quality)*

scrubby ignoble, poor *(inferior in quality)*

scrumptious palatable, sapid

scruple demur, doubt *(hesitate)*, hesitate, hesitation, misdoubt, qualm, refuse

scruples conscience, integrity, reluctance, responsibility *(conscience)*

scrupulosity honesty, particularity

scrupulous accurate, bona fide, candid, careful, clean, close *(rigorous)*, conscientious, credible, equitable, even-handed, exact, factual, fair *(just)*, high-minded, honest, impartial, incorruptible, just, law-abiding, literal, meticulous, moral, orthodox, painstaking, particular *(exacting)*, precise, punctilious, punctual, reliable, reputable, right *(correct)*, straightforward, strict, undistorted, upright, vigilant

scrupulously fairly *(impartially)*, faithfully

scrupulousness adhesion *(loyalty)*, fairness, honesty, honor *(good reputation)*, integrity, particularity, principle *(virtue)*, probity, rectitude, responsibility *(conscience)*, rigor

scrupulus embarrassment

scrutable cognizable, coherent *(clear)*, solvable

scrutari probe, probe

scrutation indagation, scrutiny

scrutinization analysis, investigation

scrutinize analyze, audit, canvass, check *(inspect)*, concentrate *(pay attention)*, consider, criticize *(evaluate)*, discern *(detect with the senses)*, examine *(study)*, frisk, inquire, investigate, monitor, notice *(observe)*, observe *(watch)*, overlook *(superintend)*, oversee, peruse, probe, regard *(pay attention)*, research, review, search, spy, study, survey *(examine)*

scrutinizing circumspect, inquisitive, interrogative

scrutiny analysis, contemplation, cross-examination, cross-questioning, diligence *(care)*, discovery, examination *(study)*, indagation, inquiry *(request for information)*, inquiry *(systematic investigation)*, inspection, interrogation, investigation, notice *(heed)*, observation, perception, probe, question *(inquiry)*, regard *(attention)*, research, review *(official reexamination)*, surveillance, test, trial *(experiment)*

scud race

scuffle affray, altercation, belligerency, brawl, brawl, commotion, confrontation *(altercation)*, fight *(battle)*, fight *(battle)*, fracas, fray, struggle

sculpture contour *(shape)*

scurrile calumnious, libelous, salacious, scurrilous

scurrilis scurrilous

scurrility aspersion, bad repute, contempt *(disdain)*, contumely, diatribe, disapprobation, expletive, slander

scurrillity obscenity

scurrilous blatant *(obtrusive)*, calumnious, ignoble, lewd, libelous,

malignant, salacious, scandalous
scurry dispatch *(promptness)*
scurvy iniquitous, objectionable, odious, poor *(inferior in quality)*
scuttlebutt report *(rumor)*
scutum shield
se abstinere refrain
se applicare recourse
se conferre recourse
se coniungere join *(associate oneself with)*
se continere refrain
se defendere answer *(reply)*
se interponere intrude, mediate
se opponere confront *(oppose)*
se recipere retreat
se rei dedere address *(talk to)*
se submittere condescend *(deign)*
seaboard littoral
seacoast littoral
seal bar *(hinder)*, brand, brand *(mark)*, complete, conclude *(complete)*, conclude *(decide)*, confirm, confirmation, determine, fix *(settle)*, lock, notarize, occlude, sanction *(permission)*, shut, sign, stamp, subscribe *(sign)*, symbol, validate
seal of secrecy censorship
seal the doom of determine
seal up contain *(enclose)*, immure, repress
sealed blind *(impassable)*, impervious, necessary *(inescapable)*, undisclosed
sealing off blockade *(enclosure)*
sear burn, deflagrate
search audit, canvass, chase, cross-examination, delve, endeavor, examination *(study)*, experiment, ferret, indagation, inquest, inquire, inquiry *(request for information)*, inquiry *(systematic investigation)*, interrogation, investigation, market *(demand)*, peruse, probe, pursue *(chase)*, pursuit *(chase)*, pursuit *(effort to secure)*, quest, question *(inquiry)*, research, research, scrutinize, scrutiny, survey *(examine)*, test, trace *(follow)*, undertaking *(attempt)*, undertaking *(enterprise)*
search for delve, hunt
search for an answer consult *(seek information from)*
search for information inquiry *(request for information)*
search into check *(inspect)*, inquire, investigate, probe, scrutinize, study
search into facts cross-examination, inquest
search laboriously delve
search made for useful military information espionage
search one's pockets frisk
search out hunt, locate, spy
search through delve, frisk
searching inquisitive, interrogative, quest, vigilant
searching examination probe
searching inquiry analysis, cross-examination, hearing, investigation
searching investigation indagation
seared callous, impervious
searing insufferable, scathing
seashore littoral
seaside littoral
season duration, inure *(accustom)*, lifetime, mature, moderate *(temper)*, period, phase *(period)*, term *(duration)*

seasonable apposite, favorable *(advantageous)*, fit, fitting, opportune, prompt, proper, propitious, punctual, relevant, suitable
seasonableness timeliness
seasonal intermittent, periodic, regular *(orderly)*
seasoned elderly, expert, practiced, ripe, sapid, veteran
seasoning experience *(background)*
seat address, embed, headquarters, instate, locality, standpoint, venue
seat of judgment bench
seat of justice bar *(court)*, bench
seated situated
secede defect, leave *(depart)*, quit *(discontinue)*, renege, withdraw
secede from abandon *(physically leave)*, relinquish
secernere distinguish, isolate
secession desertion, lapse *(expiration)*, resignation *(relinquishment)*, revolt, schism
seclude blind *(obscure)*, camouflage, cloak, conceal, condemn *(ban)*, confine, cover *(conceal)*, ensconce, enshroud, harbor, hide, immure, insulate, isolate, protect, shroud
seclude oneself lurk, retire *(retreat)*, retreat
secluded clandestine, covert, evasive, hidden, obscure *(remote)*, secret, separate, solitary, unapproachable
secludere seclude
seclusion concealment, exclusion, obscuration, privacy, quarantine
seclusive private *(secluded)*, remote *(secluded)*
second abet, abettor, advocate, aid, approve, assist, assistant, backer, bear *(support)*, concur *(agree)*, confirm, countersign, deputy, endorse, help, indorse, justify, point *(period of time)*, proctor, promote *(organize)*, recommend, replacement, side, support *(assist)*, uphold
second best poor *(inferior in quality)*
second examination review *(official reexamination)*
second legal marriage digamy
second marriage digamy
second nature habit
second rank circumstantial
second self alter ego
second thoughts hesitation, hindsight
second time de novo
second to none best, cardinal *(outstanding)*, paramount, premium, primary, superior *(excellent)*, superlative
second view hindsight
second-rate inferior *(lower in quality)*, mediocre, poor *(inferior in quality)*
second-story thief burglar
secondary ancillary *(subsidiary)*, circumstantial, collateral *(immaterial)*, contributory, deputy, derivative, extrinsic, incidental, inferior *(lower in position)*, minor, null *(insignificant)*, pendent, peripheral, plenipotentiary, replacement, slight, subaltern, subordinate, subservient, subsidiary, succedaneum, supplementary, unessential
secondary evidence hearsay
secondary group minority *(outnum-*

bered group)
secondary implied meaning connotation
seconder advocate *(counselor)*, advocate *(espouser)*, assistant, backer, benefactor, colleague, partisan, proponent
secondhand evidence hearsay
seconding accommodation *(backing)*, advocacy, help
secrecy concealment, confidence *(relation of trust)*, evasion, mystery, obscuration, privacy
secret anonymous, clandestine, confidence *(relation of trust)*, confidential, covert, enigma, enigmatic, esoteric, furtive, hidden, inscrutable, interior, intimate, mysterious, mystery, personal *(private)*, private *(confidential)*, privy, recondite, seal *(close)*, sequester *(seclude)*, sly, stealthy, surreptitious, ulterior, uncanny, undisclosed
secret agent spy
secret approval connivance
secret association collusion
secret communication confidence *(relation of trust)*
secret fraudulent understanding collusion
secret group cabal
secret observation espionage
secret place cache *(hiding place)*
secret plot cabal
secret storehouse cache *(storage place)*
secret understanding collusion
secret understanding for fraud collusion
secret watching espionage
secretary amanuensis, clerk
secrete blind *(obscure)*, camouflage, cloak, conceal, cover *(conceal)*, emit, ensconce, enshroud, exude, harbor, hide, plant *(covertly place)*
secrete oneself lurk
secreted blind *(concealed)*, hidden
secretion concealment
secretive clandestine, evasive, furtive, laconic, mysterious, noncommittal, oblique *(evasive)*, sly, stealthy, surreptitious, taciturn, unresponsive
secretiveness concealment, evasion, mystery, privacy
secretness evasion
secretus mysterious, secret, separate
sect class, denomination, side, society, split
sectarian heretic, one-sided, parochial, partisan, partisan, specific
sectarianism intolerance, schism
sectarism schism
sectarist pariah
sectary advocate *(espouser)*, backer, pariah, partisan
section article *(distinct section of a writing)*, chamber *(compartment)*, chapter *(branch)*, chapter *(division)*, circuit, clause, component, constituent *(part)*, cross *(intersect)*, decentralization, denomination, department, detail, dichotomize, disjoint, district, divide *(separate)*, division *(act of dividing)*, element, heading, ingredient, installment, locality, location, member *(constituent part)*, moiety, organ, parcel, part *(place)*, part *(portion)*, part *(separate)*, partition, phase *(aspect)*, pigeonhole,

province, region, segment, separate, share *(interest)*, split, subdivision, subheading, territory, title *(division)*
section head caption
section head caption
sectional broken *(fractured)*, local, partial *(part)*, partial *(relating to a part)*, provincial, regional
sectionalism intolerance
sectionalize dichotomize, divide *(separate)*, parcel, partition, separate
sector chapter *(division)*, component, constituent *(part)*, department, ingredient, locality, parcel, region, segment, subdivision
secular civil *(public)*, material *(physical)*, mundane, profane
secundarius secondary
secundum leges fit legal
secundus fair *(satisfactory)*, prosperous
securable available, disposable, open *(accessible)*
secure accept *(take)*, adhere *(fasten)*, affix, arrest *(apprehend)*, attach *(join)*, attach *(seize)*, attain, bar *(hinder)*, bind *(restrain)*, bond *(hold together)*, bond *(secure a debt)*, buy, cement, certain *(positive)*, collect *(recover money)*, combine *(join together)*, conserve, convincing, cosign, cover *(guard)*, definite, derive *(receive)*, detain *(hold in custody)*, earn, educe, employ *(engage services)*, engage *(hire)*, ensconce, ensure, evoke, fetter, firm, fix *(make firm)*, fixed *(securely placed)*, gain, guarantee, handcuff, harbor, hijack, hold *(possess)*, inexpugnable, infallible, infrangible, inviolate, keep *(shelter)*, lock, maintain *(sustain)*, obtain, permanent, police, positive *(confident)*, possess, preserve, procure, protect, purchase, reap, receive *(acquire)*, recover, reliable, repossess, restrict, retain *(employ)*, retain *(keep in possession)*, safe, seal *(close)*, shut, solid *(sound)*, sponsor, stabilize, stable, steadfast, strong, succeed *(attain)*, underwrite, vouch
secure against damage indemnify
secure against loss assure *(insure)*, indemnify, insure
secure by force constrain *(compel)*
secure exclusive control monopolize
secure exclusive possession monopolize
secure for a consideration buy, purchase
secure from capture inexpugnable, invincible
secure payment collect *(recover money)*
secure retreat asylum *(hiding place)*
secure the services of hire
secure with chains fetter
secured firm, guarded
secured by law inalienable
secured debenture security *(stock)*
securely fixed firm
securement distraint
secureness certainty, security *(safety)*
securing accession *(annexation)*
securities portfolio
securities law blue sky law
securities oversight blue sky law
securities rules blue sky law
securities statutes blue sky law
security accommodation *(backing)*, assurance, asylum *(protection)*, bail,

binder, bond, bulwark, certainty, charge *(lien)*, check *(instrument)*, cloud *(incumbrance)*, confidence *(faith)*, deposit, guaranty, handsel, hostage, hypothecation, indemnity, inviolability, letter of credit, lien, mainstay, mortgage, pledge *(security)*, precaution, preservation, protection, recognizance, refuge, reliance, safeguard, safekeeping, share *(stock)*, shelter *(protection)*, shelter *(tax benefit)*, shield, specialty *(contract)*, stock *(shares)*, undertaking *(bond)*, undertaking *(pledge)*, ward, warrant *(guaranty)*
security against damage indemnity
security against loss coverage *(insurance)*, indemnity, insurance
security against violence inviolability
security for a debt mortgage
security officer peace officer
security on property charge *(lien)*, cloud *(incumbrance)*, lien, mechanics lien
securus safe
secus procedere miscarriage
sedare allay, assuage, lull
sedate peaceable, phlegmatic, solemn
sedateness composure, decorum, moderation
sedative drug, narcotic, narcotic, palliative *(abating)*
sedentary inactive, torpid
sedes dwelling, foundation *(basis)*, inhabitation *(place of dwelling)*, residence, seat
sediment alluvion
seditio insurrection, mutiny, rebellion, revolt, sedition
sedition anarchy, bad faith, bad repute, defiance, disloyalty, infidelity, insurrection, mutiny, rebellion, resistance, revolt, subversion, treason
seditionary insurgent, malcontent
seditionem rebel
seditionist malcontent
seditiosus insubordinate
seditious lawless, nonconsenting, restive
seditiousness bad faith, disloyalty, infidelity, sedition
seduce bait *(lure)*, betray *(lead astray)*, brutalize, corrupt, entice, inveigle, lure, mislead, persuade, prevail *(persuade)*, suborn
seducement bribery, seduction
seduction debauchery, debauchment, rape
seductive attractive, provocative, suggestive *(risqué)*
sedulity diligence *(perseverance)*, industry *(activity)*
sedulous active, diligent, faithful *(diligent)*, industrious, painstaking, patient, persistent, pertinacious, purposeful, relentless, resolute, stable, steadfast, unrelenting, unremitting, unyielding, zealous
sedulousness diligence *(perseverance)*, industry *(activity)*
sedulus industrious, painstaking, sedulous
see apprehend *(perceive)*, comprehend *(understand)*, conceive *(comprehend)*, detect, discern *(detect with the senses)*, discover, note *(notice)*, notice *(observe)*,

observe *(watch)*, perceive, pierce *(discern)*, realize *(understand)*, recognize *(perceive)*, regard *(pay attention)*, spy, witness *(have direct knowledge of)*
see about check *(inspect)*
see as distinct discern *(discriminate)*
see at a glance discern *(detect with the senses)*
see in retrospect recall *(remember)*
see the difference diagnose, discern *(discriminate)*, discriminate *(distinguish)*
see through construe *(comprehend)*, dispatch *(dispose of)*, execute *(accomplish)*, follow-up, implement
see to attend *(take care of)*, handle *(manage)*, maintain *(sustain)*, manage, superintend
seeable appreciable, discernible, manifest, open *(in sight)*, ostensible, palpable, perceivable, perceptible, scrutable, visible *(in full view)*
seed children, embryo, inseminate, posterity, progeny
seedy poor *(inferior in quality)*
seek apply *(request)*, chase, delve, endeavor, ferret, frisk, hunt, petition, probe, pursue *(chase)*, pursue *(strive to gain)*, request, research, search, strive, trace *(follow)*, try *(attempt)*
seek a clue delve
seek accord close *(agree)*
seek advice confer *(consult)*, counsel, refer *(send for action)*
seek as due claim *(demand)*
seek by request sue
seek counsel consult *(ask advice of)*
seek facts from consult *(seek information from)*
seek guidance consult *(ask advice of)*
seek information inquire
seek information regarding investigate, probe
seek legal redress litigate
seek redress address *(petition)*
seek reexamination appeal
seek reference of a case from one court to another appeal
seek review of a case appeal
seek the opinion of consult *(ask advice of)*
seek to attempt
seek to attain pursue *(strive to gain)*
seek to persuade counsel
seeker candidate, special interest, suitor
seeking inquisitive, quest
seeking to avoid evasive
seeking to elude evasive
seeking to evade evasive
seem comport *(behave)*, demean *(deport oneself)*, pretend
seem like appear *(seem to be)*
seem to be demean *(deport oneself)*
seeming apparent *(presumptive)*, colorable *(plausible)*, constructive *(inferential)*, deceptive, ostensible, plausible, presumptive, probable, specious
seeming contradiction paradox
seemingly prima facie *(self-evident)*, reputedly
seemingly but not actually quasi
seemingly fair colorable *(plausible)*
seemingly sound colorable *(plausible)*
seemingly valid colorable *(plausible)*

seemingly worthy of acceptance plausible

seemliness conduct, decorum, expedience, propriety *(appropriateness)*

seemly appropriate, felicitous, fit, fitting, proper, right *(suitable)*, rightful, seasonable, suitable

seep exude, outflow, permeate

seep in penetrate, pervade

seepage osmosis

seer bystander, eyewitness

seesaw beat *(pulsate)*, oscillate, vacillate

seethe burn

segment chapter *(division)*, component, constituent *(part)*, cross *(intersect)*, dichotomize, disjoint, divide *(separate)*, element, factor *(ingredient)*, installment, member *(constituent part)*, moiety, parcel, parcel, part *(portion)*, partition, section *(division)*, separate, sever, share *(interest)*, split, subdivision, subheading

segmental partial *(relating to a part)*

segmentation disassociation, division *(act of dividing)*, split

segmentum segment

segnitia sloth

segregare seclude

segregate classify, demarcate, differentiate, dissociate, divide *(separate)*, estrange, exclude, insulate, isolate, relegate, remove *(eliminate)*, screen *(select)*, seclude, select, separate, sequester *(seclude)*, sever, sort, split

segregated remote *(secluded)*, separate

segregation discrimination *(differentiation)*, division *(act of dividing)*, estrangement, exception *(exclusion)*, exclusion, expulsion, intolerance, ostracism, quarantine, removal, selection *(choice)*, severance, split

seigniory domain *(land owned)*

seignorage dominion *(absolute ownership)*

seisin dominion *(absolute ownership)*, enjoyment *(use)*, holding *(property owned)*, inheritance, interest *(ownership)*, land, ownership, paraphernalia *(personal belongings)*, possession *(ownership)*

seiunctio segregation *(separation)*

seiungere detach, isolate

seize abridge *(divest)*, adopt, annex *(arrogate)*, apprehend *(arrest)*, arrest *(apprehend)*, capture, carry away, confiscate, construe *(comprehend)*, deprive, despoil, distrain, divest, embrace *(accept)*, garnish, grapple, harry *(plunder)*, hijack, impound, impress *(procure by force)*, impropriate, kidnap, levy, loot, obsess, obtain, occupy *(take possession)*, pilfer, pirate *(take by violence)*, plunder, possess, preempt, prey, procure, purloin, receive *(acquire)*, repossess, rob, takeover, usurp

seize again rearrest

seize and appropriate confiscate, garnish

seize as forfeited to the public treasury confiscate

seize by authority confiscate

seize by legal warrant arrest *(apprehend)*

seize for public use nationalize

seize for the government nationalize

seize from private control federalize *(place under federal control)*

seize from state control federalize *(place under federal control)*

seize legally book

seize power federalize *(place under federal control)*, usurp

seize summarily attach *(seize)*

seize the advantage beat *(defeat)*

seize wrongfully infringe

seized arrested *(apprehended)*

seized articles contraband

seized goods contraband

seizing attachment *(seizure)*, confiscatory, distress *(seizure)*

seizure adverse possession, apprehension *(act of arresting)*, appropriation *(taking)*, arrest, arrogation, disseisin, forfeiture *(act of forfeiting)*, garnishment, infringement, levy, occupation *(possession)*, onset *(assault)*, plunder, sequestration, taking

seizure and appropriation distraint

seizure and transference extradition

seizure of a privilege forfeiture *(act of forfeiting)*

seizure of private property for public use expropriation *(right of eminent domain)*

seizure of property by the government expropriation *(right of eminent domain)*

seizure of property in the public interest expropriation *(right of eminent domain)*

seizure to procure satisfaction of a debt distraint

sejunction division *(act of dividing)*

seldom happening infrequent

seldom met with scarce, uncommon

seldom occurring infrequent

seldom seen infrequent, rare

select adopt, appoint, best, cast *(register)*, certain *(specific)*, choose, compile, cull, decide, delegate, designate, digest *(summarize)*, edit, elect *(choose)*, exclusive *(limited)*, extract, inestimable, meritorious, nominate, particular *(specific)*, personal *(individual)*, prefer, preferential, premium, prime *(most valuable)*, private *(not public)*, rare, recruit, restrictive, specialize, specific, specify, valuable

select and arrange compile

select as one's own adopt

select body elite

select boundaries locate

select few elite

select for office elect *(select by a vote)*

select jurors empanel

select passage excerpt

selected particular *(specific)*, preferable, preferential, preferred *(favored)*, select

selectee licensee, nominee *(delegate)*

selection adoption *(acceptance)*, alternative *(option)*, appointment *(act of designating)*, assignment *(designation)*, assumption *(adoption)*, choice *(alternatives offered)*, choice *(decision)*, compilation, decision *(election)*, designation *(naming)*, discretion *(power of choice)*, election *(choice)*, excerpt, manner *(kind)*, nomination, nominee *(candi-*

date), option *(choice)*, patronage *(power to appoint jobs)*, poll *(casting of votes)*, preference *(choice)*, primary, referendum, volition, vote

selection for office by vote election *(selection by vote)*

selection of words phraseology

selective adoptive, discretionary, discriminating *(distinguishing)*, discriminating *(judicious)*, disjunctive *(alternative)*, exclusive *(limited)*, particular *(exacting)*, preferential, restrictive

selectiveness particularity

selector licensor

self identity *(individuality)*

self consistent consonant

self-abasing obeisant, repentant

self-abnegation capitulation

self-absorption introspection

self-accusation confession, remorse

self-accusatory remorseful, repentant

self-accusing contrite, penitent

self-acting spontaneous

self-admiration pride

self-admiring pretentious *(pompous)*

self-applauding inflated *(vain)*, orgulous, pretentious *(pompous)*, proud *(conceited)*

self-applause pride

self-approval pride

self-assertive obtrusive

self-assurance composure, surety *(certainty)*

self-assured assertive, positive *(confident)*

self-centered inflated *(vain)*

self-centred orgulous

self-command composure, continence, discipline *(obedience)*

self-communing pensive, reflection *(thought)*

self-communion introspection

self-condemnation confession, remorse

self-condemnatory contrite, remorseful, repentant

self-condemned penitent

self-confident positive *(confident)*

self-conquest discipline *(obedience)*

self-conscious diffident, histrionic

self-consciousness embarrassment

self-consequence consequence *(significance)*

self-consistent consistent

self-contained autonomous *(independent)*

self-containment home rule

self-content complacent

self-contradiction paradox

self-contradictory illogical, impossible

self-control continence, longanimity, moderation, restraint, sufferance, temperance, will *(desire)*

self-controlled controlled *(restrained)*, dispassionate, nonchalant, patient, stoical

self-convicted contrite, penitent, repentant

self-conviction remorse, surety *(certainty)*

self-counsel introspection, reflection *(thought)*

self-criticism remorse

self-denial austerity, continence, discipline *(obedience)*, restraint, temper-

ance
self-denouncing repentant
self-denunciatory contrite
self-derived power home rule
self-determination discretion *(power of choice)*, freedom, home rule, liberty, suffrage
self-determined autonomous *(self governing)*, nonpartisan, sovereign *(independent)*, spontaneous
self-determined being character *(an individual)*
self-directing autonomous *(self governing)*, free *(enjoying civil liberty)*, nonpartisan, sovereign *(independent)*
self-direction discipline *(obedience)*, home rule, liberty
self-discipline continence, will *(desire)*
self-disciplined stoical
self-doubt doubt *(indecision)*
self-effacing diffident, unobtrusive
self-esteem pride
self-esteeming pretentious *(pompous)*
self-evident apparent *(perceptible)*, axiomatic, certain *(positive)*, clear *(apparent)*, coherent *(clear)*, comprehensible, conspicuous, convincing, discernible, distinct *(clear)*, ostensible, palpable
self-evident proposition principle *(axiom)*
self-evident truth principle *(axiom)*
self-exaltation pride
self-examination introspection
self-existent peremptory *(absolute)*
self-explanatory comprehensible
self-flattering orgulous
self-glorification jactation, pride
self-glorifying inflated *(vain)*, orgulous, pretentious *(pompous)*
self-governed sovereign *(independent)*
self-governing free *(enjoying civil liberty)*, independent, nonpartisan
self-government freedom, home rule, liberty, suffrage
self-importance consequence *(significance)*, pride
self-important consequential *(substantial)*, inflated *(vain)*, orgulous, pretentious *(pompous)*, proud *(conceited)*
self-imposed task campaign
self-inspection introspection
self-knowledge introspection
self-lauding inflated *(vain)*, orgulous
self-legislation home rule
self-magnifying orgulous
self-mastery discipline *(obedience)*
self-possession composure, sufferance
self-praising orgulous
self-regulation discipline *(obedience)*
self-reliance home rule
self-reliant autonomous *(independent)*, independent, spartan
self-reproach remorse
self-reproachful contrite, penitent, repentant
self-reproaching remorseful
self-reproof remorse
self-reproving repentant
self-respect integrity
self-restraint austerity, composure, continence, discipline *(obedience)*, sufferance, temperance
self-rule freedom
self-ruling autonomous *(self govern-*

ing), free *(enjoying civil liberty)*, sovereign *(independent)*
self-sacrifice philanthropy
self-satisfaction pride
self-satisfied complacent, inflated *(vain)*, orgulous, pretentious *(pompous)*, proud *(conceited)*
self-scrutiny introspection
self-seeking venal
self-study introspection
self-subsistence home rule
self-subsistent independent
self-sufficiency home rule
self-sufficient autonomous *(independent)*, insular
self-support home rule
self-supporting autonomous *(independent)*, independent
self-willed pertinacious, perverse, voluntary
selfhood identity *(individuality)*, personality
selfish illiberal, insatiable, mercenary, parsimonious, penurious, thoughtless
selfishness greed
selfless dispassionate, liberal *(generous)*, philanthropic
selflessness largess *(generosity)*, philanthropy
selfness identity *(individuality)*, personality
selfsameness resemblance
sell deal, handle *(trade)*, liquidate *(convert into cash)*, persuade, trade, vend
sell assets liquidate *(convert into cash)*
sell at the market handle *(trade)*
sell below par discount *(reduce)*
sell into slavery subjugate
sell out betray *(disclose)*, betray *(lead astray)*
seller creditor, dealer, merchant, supplier, vendor
selling alienation *(transfer of title)*
selling price price
selvedge border
semantics meaning
semaphore indicator
semasiology meaning
semblance analogy, complexion, correspondence *(similarity)*, disguise, face value *(first blush)*, facsimile, identity *(similarity)*, parity, presence *(poise)*, pretense *(pretext)*, pretext, propinquity *(similarity)*, reflection *(image)*, resemblance
seminal original *(initial)*
seminar conference, meeting *(conference)*, panel *(discussion group)*, parley
semiprocessed inchoate
sempiternal constant, continual *(perpetual)*, durable, infinite, permanent, perpetual
sempiternus indelible, perpetual
senate legislature
senator lawmaker, legislator
senatus consultum decree
send consign, delegate, deliver, dispatch *(send off)*, dispel, displace *(remove)*, project *(impel forward)*, radiate, refer *(send for action)*, remand, remit *(submit for consideration)*, remove *(transfer)*, transfer, transmit, transport
send a final demand charge *(assess)*

send a message correspond *(communicate)*, transmit
send abroad diffuse
send an order instruct *(direct)*
send an order for call *(demand)*
send as deputy delegate
send away deport *(banish)*, dislodge, dismiss *(discharge)*, dispatch *(send off)*, displace *(remove)*, evacuate, expatriate, rebuff, relegate, repulse
send back disavow, recommit, reflect *(mirror)*, remand, restore *(return)*
send flying dispel, launch *(project)*, precipitate *(throw down violently)*
send for call *(summon)*, request, subpoena, summon
send forth cast *(throw)*, circulate, diffuse, discharge *(shoot)*, dispatch *(send off)*, emit, launch *(project)*, outpour, precipitate *(throw down violently)*, radiate, remove *(transfer)*, send
send forward redirect
send headlong impel, launch *(project)*, precipitate *(throw down violently)*
send home dispel
send money remit *(send payment)*
send off cast *(throw)*, dismiss *(discharge)*, launch *(project)*, project *(impel forward)*
send on redirect, transmit
send on a commission delegate
send on a mission delegate
send on an errand delegate
send out delegate, emit, issue *(publish)*, outpour, send
send payment remit *(send payment)*
send regrets refuse
send through the mail dispatch *(send off)*
send to an asylum commit *(institutionalize)*
send to jail arrest *(apprehend)*, commit *(institutionalize)*, confine, imprison
send to prison apprehend *(arrest)*, commit *(institutionalize)*, constrain *(imprison)*, immure, imprison, jail
send to the bottom immerse *(plunge into)*
send word communicate, inform *(notify)*
sending consignment, delivery, transmittal
sending away deportation
sending to another state for trial extradition
sending to jail commitment *(confinement)*
senescence deterioration
senescent elderly
senility caducity
senior adult, chief, principal *(director)*, superior *(higher)*
senior court appellate court
senior statesman veteran
seniority age, authority *(power)*, longevity, precedence, predominance, preference *(priority)*, primacy, priority
sensation emotion, impression, reaction *(response)*, sense *(feeling)*, sensibility
sensational blatant *(conspicuous)*, lurid, moving *(evoking emotion)*
sensationalism exaggeration
sense apprehend *(perceive)*, apprehension *(perception)*, competence *(sanity)*, comprehension, connotation, construc-

tion, content (meaning), contents, context, detect, expedience, gist (substance), import, impression, intellect, intelligence (intellect), main point, meaning, perceive, perception, prudence, reaction (response), reason (sound judgment), sagacity, sanity, signification, spirit, substance (essential nature), tenor, understanding (comprehension)

sense of danger apprehension (fear)

sense of disgrace ignominy

sense of duty adhesion (loyalty), allegiance, charge (responsibility), commitment (responsibility), conscience, responsibility (conscience)

sense of language parlance

sense of moral right conscience

sense of obligation responsibility (conscience)

sense of proportion perspective

sense of responsibility adhesion (loyalty), honor (good reputation)

sense of right and wrong conscience, ethics, responsibility (conscience)

sense of shame disgrace, ignominy

sense perception impression

senseless fatuous, frivolous, ill-advised, impolitic, inexpressive, insensible, irrational, ludicrous, lunatic, misadvised, non compos mentis, obtuse, opaque, puerile, unpolitic, unreasonable, unsound (fallacious), vacuous

senseless prate platitude

senseless talk jargon (unintelligible language)

senselessness inexpedience, insentience

senses competence (sanity)

sensibility cognition, perception, pragmatism, realization, reason (sound judgment)

sensible colorable (plausible), conscious (aware), discreet, familiar (informed), functional, judicial, judicious, justifiable, lucid, normal (sane), perceptive, perspicacious, physical, plausible, politic, pragmatic, prudent, rational, reasonable (rational), responsive, sane, sapient, solid (sound), viable

sensible to cognizant

sensibleness common sense, expedience, pragmatism, reason (sound judgment), sanity

sensilis sensitive (discerning)

sensitive charitable (lenient), circumspect, discreet, hot-blooded, moving (evoking emotion), open (persuasible), perceptive, receptive, responsive, susceptible (responsive), susceptible (unresistant)

sensitiveness discretion (quality of being discreet), emotion, sensibility

sensitivity discretion (quality of being discreet), insight, sensibility, understanding (tolerance)

sensory experience perception

sensory perception impression

sensu carere insensible, insusceptible (uncaring)

sensual dissolute, mundane, obscene, physical, salacious

sensuous lascivious, physical

sensus content (meaning), sense (feeling)

sent to prison arrested (apprehended)

sentence adjudge, adjudication, clause, condemn (punish), condemnation (punishment), convict, conviction (finding of guilt), decide, decree, determination, discipline (punish), finding, holding (ruling of a court), judge, judgment (formal court decree), opinion (judicial decision), penalize, penalty, punish, ruling, verdict

sentenced blameworthy

sentencing commitment (confinement), conviction (finding of guilt)

sententia content (meaning), conviction (persuasion), expression (comment), holding (ruling of a court), meaning, motion, opinion (judicial decision), resolution (decision), standpoint, tenor, verdict, vote

sententiam dicere comment

sententiosus sententious

sententious axiomatic, brief, compact (pithy), incisive, laconic, pithy, proverbial, succinct

sententious saying maxim

sententious utterance maxim

sentient conscious (aware), perceptive, responsive, sensitive (discerning)

sentiment affection, conviction (persuasion), emotion, idea, notion, opinion (belief), position (point of view), posture (attitude), reaction (response), spirit

sentimental sensitive (easily affected)

sentimental attachment affection

sentimentality affection

sentinel guardian, protect

sentire perceive

sentry caretaker (one caring for property), guardian, warden

separabilis severable

separable divisible, divisive, moving (in motion), severable

separable part of a certificate coupon

separare apart, detach, divide (separate), part (separate), separate, sever

separate alienate (estrange), alone (solitary), apart, bifurcate, bipartite, classify, cross (intersect), cull, demarcate, detach, dichotomize, different, disaffect, disband, disconnected, discontinue (abandon), discontinue (break continuity), discrete, discriminate (distinguish), disengage, disentangle, disjoint, disjunctive (tending to disjoin), disorganize, disparate, disperse (scatter), dissociate, distill, distinct (distinguished from others), distinguish, divide (separate), estrange, except (exclude), excise (cut away), exclusive (singular), extract, extrinsic, foreign, impertinent (irrelevant), individual, insular, insulate, interrupt, irrelative, isolate, liberate, luxate, particular (individual), particular (specific), private (secluded), purge (purify), relegate, remove (eliminate), screen (select), secede, seclude, sequester (seclude), sequester (seize property), sever, singular, sole, solitary, sort, split, sporadic, subdivide, substantive, unrelated, withdraw

separate as different differentiate

separate existence entity

separate from quit (evacuate)

separate in two dichotomize

separate into categories organize

(arrange)

separate maintenance alimony, estrangement

separate oneself retire (retreat)

separate oneself from part (leave)

separate paragraph item

separate part chamber (compartment), chapter (division), section (division)

separate ticket coupon

separated apart, bicameral, bipartite, broken (fractured), disconnected, discrete, inaccessible, individual, irrelative, peculiar (distinctive), remote (secluded), separate, solitary, unapproachable

separately respectively

separateness difference, nonconformity, privacy

separating divergent

separatio separation

separation alienation (estrangement), decentralization, dichotomy, disassociation, discrimination (differentiation), dissolution (disintegration), diversification, division (act of dividing), estrangement, evulsion, exception (exclusion), exclusion, expulsion, hiatus, liberation, ostracism, privacy, quarantine, removal, rift (gap), schism, section (division), selection (choice), severance, split, subdivision

separation by races segregation (isolation by races)

separation money alimony

separatism nonconformity

separatist heretic

separative discriminating (distinguishing), distinctive

separatus distinct (distinguished from others), particular (specific), separate

seperate select

sept family (common ancestry)

septic deleterious, peccant (unhealthy)

sequacious passive, pliable, pliant, resilient

sequel codicil, development (outgrowth), effect, follow-up, outgrowth

sequela codicil

sequence array (order), chain (series), continuity, cycle, method, order (arrangement), outcome, succession

sequence of events calendar (record of yearly periods)

sequent consecutive, corollary, derivative, future, outcome, proximate, subsequent, successive

sequential ancillary (subsidiary), consecutive, consequential (deducible), continuous, ensuing, narrative, subsequent, successive

sequester attach (seize), collect (recover money), confiscate, deprive, distrain, exclude, garnish, impound, impress (procure by force), insulate, isolate, remove (eliminate), seclude, seize (confiscate), withdraw

sequestered attached (seized), privy, remote (secluded)

sequestrate attach (seize), condemn (seize), confiscate, deprive, distrain, garnish, impound, impress (procure by force), remove (eliminate), seize (confiscate), sequester (seize property), withdraw

sequestrating confiscatory

sequestration attachment *(seizure)*, disseisin, distraint, distress *(seizure)*, expropriation *(divestiture)*, privation, removal, taking
sequi pursue *(chase)*, pursue *(strive to gain)*
serendipitous beneficial
serendipity happenstance
serene complacent, patient, peaceable, phlegmatic, placid
serenity composure, peace
serere propagate *(spread)*
serial cognate, consecutive, intermittent, journal, periodic, progressive *(going forward)*
serialization distribution *(arrangement)*, sequence
serialized consecutive
seriate classify, consecutive
seriatim consecutive
seriation hierarchy *(arrangement in a series)*
series assemblage, hierarchy *(arrangement in a series)*, serial, succession
series chain *(series)*, sequence
series of events proceeding, program
series of measures process *(course)*
serious chronic, critical *(crucial)*, dangerous, dire, earnest, exigent, grave *(important)*, grave *(solemn)*, important *(significant)*, insistent, major, momentous, pensive, pernicious, persistent, pertinacious, purposeful, resolute, solemn, steadfast, urgent
serious accident casualty
serious calamity catastrophe
serious infraction of the law crime
serious thought consideration *(contemplation)*
seriously purely *(positively)*
seriously dangerous deadly
seriousness consequence *(significance)*, contemplation, degree *(magnitude)*, diligence *(care)*, import, importance, magnitude, severity, significance, solemnity, weight *(importance)*
serius grave *(important)*, serious *(grave)*
sermo discourse, language
sermon declamation, diatribe, instruction *(teaching)*, objurgation, peroration, reprimand, speech
sermonize address *(talk to)*, declaim, discourse, inculcate, speak
serpentiform circuitous
serpentile circuitous
serpentine artful, circuitous, devious, indirect, insidious, labyrinthine, sinuous, subtle *(insidious)*, tortuous *(bending)*
serpentoid circuitous
serried compact *(dense)*, solid *(compact)*
servant employee
servantry personnel
servants personnel, staff
servare conserve, preserve
serve abet, accommodate, aid, assist, attend *(take care of)*, avail *(be of use)*, bestow, care *(regard)*, contribute *(assist)*, dispense, divide *(distribute)*, fulfill, function, help, inure *(benefit)*, obey, officiate, order, pander, perform *(execute)*, promote *(organize)*, provide *(arrange for)*, supply

serve as exercise *(discharge a function)*
serve as a substitute succeed *(follow)*
serve in the capacity of perform *(execute)*
serve notice caution, communicate, contact *(communicate)*, notify
serve the people rule *(govern)*
serve the purpose satisfy *(fulfill)*
serve with a writ call *(summon)*
service adhesion *(loyalty)*, agency *(legal relationship)*, aid *(help)*, aid, avail *(be of use)*, benevolence *(act of kindness)*, bureaucracy, employment, fix *(repair)*, help, homage, maintain *(sustain)*, maintenance *(upkeep)*, office, post, profit, promotion *(encouragement)*, purpose, repair, reparation *(keeping in repair)*, servitude, usage, use, utility *(usefulness)*, worth
service road causeway
serviceability means *(opportunity)*, use, utility *(usefulness)*, utilization
serviceable constructive *(creative)*, convenient, disposable, effective *(efficient)*, functional, instrumental, ministerial, operative, passable, practical, pragmatic, profitable, subservient, valuable
serviceableness worth
services agency *(legal relationship)*
serviceway easement
servicing provision *(act of supplying)*
servile dependent, ignoble, obedient, obsequious, passive, pliable, pliant, sequacious, subaltern, subservient
servilis servile
servility amenability, discipline *(obedience)*, fealty, homage
serving adequate, part *(portion)*, provision *(act of supplying)*, ration
serving as a deterrent exemplary
serving as a model exemplary
serving as a pattern exemplary
serving as a sample exemplary
serving as a warning exemplary
serving as an adjunct ancillary *(auxiliary)*
serving as an aid ancillary *(auxiliary)*
serving as an instance exemplary
serving to commemorate honorary
serving to declare declaratory
serving to distinguish distinctive
servire serve *(assist)*
servitium servitude
servitude adhesion *(loyalty)*, bondage, homage, restraint, subjection, thrall
servitus servitude, subjection, thrall
sescenti myriad
sesquipedalian turgid
sesquipedalian words bombast
sesquipedalianism fustian
sesquipedalism bombast
sesquipedality bombast
session caucus, chamber *(body)*, congregation, meeting *(conference)*, phase *(period)*, term *(duration)*
session of the court forum *(court)*
sessions bar *(court)*
set adjust *(resolve)*, assemblage, assess *(appraise)*, assign *(designate)*, cement, chain *(series)*, chronic, class, confederacy *(compact)*, crystallize, customary, deposit *(place)*, designate, embed, firm, fix *(make firm)*, fix *(settle)*, fixed *(se-*

curely placed)*, formal, habitual, inexorable, ingrained, instate, inveterate, levy, locate, permanent, pertinacious, plant *(place firmly)*, positive *(prescribed)*, prescribe, prescriptive, prevalent, ready *(prepared)*, repose *(place)*, resolute, rigid, routine, situated, society, stabilize, unyielding, usual
set a figure evaluate
set a name to subscribe *(sign)*
set a price on estimate, evaluate
set a question at rest find *(determine)*
set a snare for entrap
set a task bind *(obligate)*, direct *(order)*
set a trap for ambush, dupe, ensnare, entrap, hunt
set a value on calculate, estimate, evaluate, gauge, measure, rate
set about assume *(undertake)*, endeavor, occupy *(engage)*, undertake
set above others prefer
set abroach dispel
set adrift derelict *(abandoned)*
set afloat originate
set afoot initiate
set against alienate *(estrange)*, antagonize, counter, counteract, disaffect, discourage, estrange, oppose
set an earlier date antedate
set apart allocate, characterize, choose, dedicate, demarcate, designate, devote, different, disconnected, discriminate *(distinguish)*, distinct *(distinguished from others)*, distinguish, estrange, except *(exclude)*, exclude, exempt, hoard, hold *(possess)*, insulate, isolate, label, preferred *(favored)*, relegate, remove *(eliminate)*, reserve, sacrosanct, seclude, select, separate, separate, sequester *(seize property)*, set aside *(reserve)*, sever
set apart as different differentiate
set apart for special use dedicate
set aright fix *(repair)*
set as a goal intend, pursue *(strive to gain)*
set aside abandon *(relinquish)*, abolish, abrogate *(rescind)*, allocate, annul, cancel, dedicate, defer *(put off)*, designate, devote, disapprove *(reject)*, disavow, discharge *(release from obligation)*, disclaim, dismiss *(put out of consideration)*, disown *(deny the validity)*, dispel, eliminate *(exclude)*, exclude, hoard, hold *(possess)*, hold up *(delay)*, isolate, leave *(allow to remain)*, negate, null *(invalid)*, null and void, override, overrule, postpone, rebuff, reject, repeal, repudiate, rescind, reserve, seclude, sequester *(seize property)*, succeed *(follow)*, supersede, vacate *(void)*, waive
set astir foment, inspire, promise *(raise expectations)*
set asunder disconnected, dispel, dissolve *(separate)*
set at ease assure *(give confidence to)*, satisfy *(fulfill)*
set at large clear, disencumber, disenthrall, extricate, free, liberate, release
set at liberty acquit, clear, discharge *(liberate)*, disengage, disenthrall, enfranchise, extricate, free, liberate, par-

don, parole, quit *(free of)*, release
set at naught counteract, disavow, lessen, minimize, misprize, underestimate
set at nought decry, disown *(deny the validity)*, spurn
set at odds alienate *(estrange)*, antagonize, disaffect
set at rest complete *(ended)*, conclude *(complete)*, dispatch *(dispose of)*, settle, through
set at variance alienate *(estrange)*, estrange
set back check *(restrain)*, constrict *(inhibit)*, delay, hinder
set before pose *(propound)*
set bounds limit
set bounds to demarcate
set by hoard
set conflagration arson
set down alight, avow, browbeat, enter *(record)*, express, formulate, itemize, note *(record)*, record, render *(deliver)*
set down to attribute
set eyes on discern *(detect with the senses)*
set firmly embed, plant *(place firmly)*
set foot in enter *(go in)*
set for a later time continue *(adjourn)*
set form formality, matter of course, procedure
set format procedure
set forth allege, alleged, argue, assert, cite *(state)*, commence, communicate, contend *(maintain)*, declare, delineate, demonstrate *(establish)*, depict, detail *(particularize)*, exhibit, exposit, expound, express, interject, issue *(publish)*, manifest, pass *(determine)*, plead *(allege in a legal action)*, portray, posit, present *(introduce)*, proclaim, profess *(avow)*, proffer, promulgate, propose, propound, quit *(evacuate)*, reason *(persuade)*, recite, recount, relate *(tell)*, render *(depict)*, report *(disclose)*, signify *(inform)*, stated, trace *(delineate)*
set forth evidence bare
set forth in a will testamentary
set forth in words express
set forth the character of characterize
set forth the meaning interpret
set free absolve, acquit, clear, condone, discharge *(liberate)*, disencumber, disengage, disentangle, disenthrall, dismiss *(discharge)*, dissociate, enfranchise, exculpate, exonerate, extricate, free *(relieved from a burden)*, free, liberate, palliate *(excuse)*, pardon, parole, quit *(free of)*, release, relieve *(free from burden)*, rescue, unbound, vindicate
set going create, dispatch *(send off)*, establish *(launch)*, impel, initiate, launch *(initiate)*, originate
set going again renew *(begin again)*
set guidelines organize *(arrange)*
set in remain *(stay)*
set in array organize *(arrange)*
set in motion expedite, exploit *(make use of)*, generate, impel, implement, incite, launch *(initiate)*, launch *(project)*, maintain *(commence)*, manipulate *(utilize skillfully)*, motivate, originate, preface, undertake

set in operation commence, establish *(launch)*, maintain *(commence)*
set in opposition contrast
set in order apportion, arrange *(methodize)*, classify, coordinate, distribute, file *(arrange)*, fix *(arrange)*, marshal, orchestrate, organize *(arrange)*
set in place locate, settle
set limitations constrict *(inhibit)*
set limits constrict *(inhibit)*
set little store by underestimate
set loose release, rescue
set moving impel
set no store by disbelieve, flout
set no value on decry
set of facts case *(set of circumstances)*
set of maneuvers strategy
set of questions examination *(test)*
set of rules codification, law, protocol *(etiquette)*
set of standards protocol *(etiquette)*
set of tactics program
set of terms article *(precept)*, counteroffer, settlement
set off abandon *(physically leave)*, compensate *(counterbalance)*, countervail, demarcate, differentiate, discriminate *(distinguish)*, offset, outbalance, part *(leave)*
set off against contrast
set off by opposition contrast
set one back deter, hold up *(delay)*, impede
set one's hand and seal notarize
set one's hand and seal to certify *(attest)*
set one's name to sign
set oneself against conflict, confront *(oppose)*, disapprove *(condemn)*
set out allocate, depart, embark, leave *(depart)*, manifest, part *(leave)*, produce *(offer to view)*, quit *(evacuate)*
set out to attempt
set phrase expression *(comment)*
set purpose animus, design *(intent)*, goal, intention, objective, project
set right attune, debunk, disabuse, emend, fix *(repair)*, inform *(notify)*, rectify, redress, regulate *(adjust)*, reveal
set side by side compare, juxtapose
set straight disabuse, emend, inform *(notify)*, informed *(having information)*, redeem *(satisfy debts)*, reform, remedy
set terms contract
set the date date
set to brawl, fight *(battle)*
set to music orchestrate
set to rights file *(arrange)*, rectify
set to work employ *(engage services)*, engage *(hire)*, exert, exploit *(make use of)*, hire, manipulate *(utilize skillfully)*, occupy *(engage)*
set too high an estimate overestimate
set up build *(construct)*, capitalize *(provide capital)*, constitute *(establish)*, create, devise *(invent)*, establish *(launch)*, fabricate *(construct)*, frame *(construct)*, frame *(formulate)*, initiate, make, marshal, organize *(unionize)*, originate, plan, plant *(place firmly)*, structure *(composition)*
set up an inquiry analyze, canvass, delve

set up housekeeping lodge *(reside)*
set up in business capitalize *(provide capital)*, finance
set upon accost, assail, assault, earnest, oppugn, persistent
set upon with force assault, attack
set upon with violence assail, assault
set-off counterclaim, drawback
set-to affray, controversy *(argument)*, fracas
setback adversity, casualty, damper *(depressant)*, debacle, decline, defeat, delay, disadvantage, disaster, hindrance, impediment, misfortune, plight, relapse, toll *(effect)*, trouble
setdown disgrace
setoff indemnity
setting atmosphere, case *(set of circumstances)*, posture *(situation)*, scene, site, vicinity
setting a price appraisal
setting apart appropriation *(allotment)*, dedication, discrimination *(differentiation)*, segregation *(separation)*
setting aside avoidance *(cancellation)*, repudiation
setting aside for a particular purpose dedication
setting aside of specific property levy
setting forth narration, representation *(statement)*
setting forth in words expression *(comment)*
setting free discharge *(liberation)*, emancipation, parole, release
setting the value appraisal
settle accommodate, adjudge, adjudicate, adjust *(resolve)*, administer *(conduct)*, agree *(comply)*, agree *(contract)*, arbitrate *(adjudge)*, arbitrate *(conciliate)*, arrange *(methodize)*, award, choose, close *(agree)*, compromise *(settle by mutual agreement)*, concede, conclude *(complete)*, conclude *(decide)*, decide, deposit *(place)*, determine, discharge *(pay a debt)*, dwell *(reside)*, embed, hold *(decide)*, intercede, judge, liquidate *(determine liability)*, locate, lodge *(reside)*, lull, mediate, negotiate, pacify, pay, plant *(place firmly)*, reconcile, recoup *(reimburse)*, refund, reimburse, remit *(send payment)*, remunerate, repose *(place)*, repose *(rest)*, reside, rest *(cease from action)*, return *(refund)*, rule *(decide)*, satisfy *(discharge)*, settle, stabilize, stipulate, subside, sustain *(confirm)*
settle a debt quit *(repay)*
settle a dispute mediate
settle accounts discharge *(pay a debt)*, satisfy *(discharge)*
settle accounts with collect *(recover money)*, compensate *(remunerate)*
settle accounts with the debtors and creditors liquidate *(determine liability)*
settle amicably accommodate
settle an account quit *(repay)*
settle by authoritative decision arbitrate *(adjudge)*
settle by conciliation mediate
settle by covenant agree *(contract)*
settle by decree rule *(decide)*
settle differences arbitrate *(concili-*

ate), compromise *(settle by mutual agreement),* mediate, pacify

settle disputes negotiate

settle firmly consolidate *(strengthen)*

settle in occupy *(take possession)*

settle in advance prepay

settle in one's mind conclude *(decide),* determine

settle on elect *(choose)*

settle on by deliberate will resolve *(decide)*

settle order on notice settle

settle terms stipulate

settle upon conclude *(decide),* descend, determine, fund, leave *(give),* resolve *(decide)*

settled absolute *(conclusive),* agreed *(harmonized),* categorical, certain *(fixed),* certain *(positive),* certain *(specific),* chronic, complete *(ended),* contractual, definite, durable, firm, immutable, incontrovertible, indefeasible, ingrained, irrevocable, necessary *(inescapable),* prescriptive, resolute, serious *(devoted),* situated, stable, standing, stated, steadfast, through, unalterable, unavoidable *(not voidable),* unyielding

settled belief conviction *(persuasion)*

settled decision adjudication, holding *(ruling of a court)*

settled determination intention

settled disposition practice *(custom)*

settled judgment conviction *(persuasion)*

settled law code

settled method formality

settled principle law, principle *(axiom)*

settled procedure method, system

settled purpose animus, design *(intent),* objective

settled upon preferred *(favored)*

settled without appeal clear *(certain)*

settlement accommodation *(adjustment),* accord, accordance *(compact),* adjustment, agreement *(concurrence),* agreement *(contract),* alimony, alluvion, arbitration, arrangement *(understanding),* bargain, choice *(decision),* compensation, composition *(agreement in bankruptcy),* compromise, concession *(compromise),* conciliation, consequence *(conclusion),* consideration *(recompense),* contract, denouement, descent *(declination),* determination, discharge *(payment),* disposition *(determination),* disposition *(final arrangement),* dower, expiation, habitation *(act of inhabiting),* habitation *(dwelling place),* honorarium, nollo contendere, outcome, pact, pay, payment *(act of paying),* payoff *(payment in full),* recompense, reconciliation, refund, remuneration, reparation *(indemnification),* restitution, satisfaction *(discharge of debt),* treaty

settlement by authoritative decision holding *(ruling of a court),* opinion *(judicial decision)*

settlement by mutual agreement composition *(agreement in bankruptcy)*

settlement of an estate administration

settlement of differences conciliation

settlement of difficulties mediation

settlement of dispute mediation

settlement on account composition *(agreement in bankruptcy),* discharge *(payment)*

settler domiciliary, habitant, inhabitant, migrant, pioneer, referee, resident

settling conclusion *(determination)*

settlings alluvion

setup content *(structure),* device *(contrivance),* method, order *(arrangement)*

sever break *(separate),* detach, dichotomize, disband, discontinue *(abandon),* discontinue *(break continuity),* disengage, disjoint, dissociate, dissolve *(separate),* divide *(separate),* divorce, estrange, excise *(cut away),* interrupt, isolate, luxate, part *(separate),* partition, rend, separate, split, subdivide

sever one's connections secede

sever the unity of possession partition

severable divisible, divisive, separable

several diverse, manifold, multiple

severally respectively

severance decentralization, dichotomy, dismissal *(discharge),* division *(act of dividing),* estrangement, exception *(exclusion),* interruption, schism, separation, split

severance of relations estrangement

severe astringent, bitter *(penetrating),* brutal, callous, caustic, close *(rigorous),* critical *(faultfinding),* crucial, cruel, dictatorial, draconian, drastic, harsh, incisive, inexorable, insufferable, intense, mordacious, onerous, oppressive, pejorative, precise, relentless, rigid, scathing, serious *(grave),* spartan, strict, trenchant, tyrannous, uncompromising, unmitigated, unrelenting

severe censure denunciation

severe discipline austerity

severed bipartite, broken *(fractured),* disconnected, disjunctive *(tending to disjoin),* separate

severence disassociation

severitas austerity, rigor, severity, solemnity

severity austerity, cruelty, oppression, violence

severus rigid, serious *(grave),* severe, solemn, strict

sex-ridden lascivious

sexton caretaker *(one caring for property)*

sexual assault rape

sexual deviation sodomy

sexual unfaithfulness of a married person adultery

sexually abuse molest *(subject to indecent advances)*

sexually assault molest *(subject to indecent advances)*

sexually impure lewd

sexually indecent lewd

sexually indulgent lecherous

sexy obscene, salacious, suggestive *(risqué)*

shabby decadent, dilapidated, inferior *(lower in quality),* penurious, poor *(inferior in quality),* slipshod

shabby work noncompliance *(improper completion)*

shackle arrest *(apprehend),* constrain *(imprison),* contain *(restrain),* detain

(restrain), disadvantage, encumber *(hinder),* estop, fetter, fetter, hamper, handcuff, handcuff, hinder, hindrance, impede, impediment, lock, obstruction, repress, restrain, restraint, restrict, trammel

shade blind *(obscure),* camouflage, cloak, conceal, ensconce, enshroud, hide, minimum, nuance, obfuscate, obnubilate, obscuration, obscure, penumbra, phantom, plant *(covertly place),* protect, screen *(guard),* veil

shade into consolidate *(unite)*

shade of difference differential, nuance

shade of meaning nuance

shaded impalpable

shadiness ill repute, improbity, knavery

shading obscuration

shadow alter ego, blind *(obscure),* cloak, conceal, damper *(depressant),* ensconce, hide, indistinctness, nuance, obnubilate, penumbra, specter, spy, trace *(follow)*

shadowed nebulous

shadowiness indistinctness

shadowing obscuration

shadowy blind *(concealed),* dubious, elusive, equivocal, impalpable, inconspicuous, intangible, mysterious, nebulous, obscure *(faint),* opaque, unclear, vague

shady furtive, machiavellian, unethical

shady reputation disrepute, opprobrium, turpitude

shake beat *(pulsate),* brandish, discompose, disturb, intersperse, jostle *(bump into),* perturb

shake off dispel

shake one's faith deter

shake up agitate *(perturb),* churn, discompose, disturb, perturb

shakedown blackmail

shaking trepidation

shaky diffident, insecure, precarious

shallow barren, cursory, fatuous, frivolous, puerile, superficial, trivial, volatile

shallowness immateriality, insignificance

sham artifice, bogus, cloak, colorable *(specious),* cover *(pretext),* deceit, deception, deceptive, delusive, disguise, duplicity, evasion, fabricate *(make up),* fake, false *(not genuine),* false pretense, feign, fictitious, forgery, fraud, fraudulent, hoax, imitation, imposture, invent *(falsify),* mendacious, meretricious, misrepresent, pretend, pretense *(ostentation),* pretense *(pretext),* pretext, prevaricate, profess *(pretend),* recreant, role, ruse, spurious, subterfuge

shambles havoc

shame attaint, bad repute, defame, degradation, demean *(make lower),* denigrate, derogate, discredit, disgrace, disgrace, disparage, disrepute, embarrass, embarrassment, expose, humiliate, ignominy, ill repute, infamy, notoriety, obloquy, odium, onus *(stigma),* opprobrium, ostracism, reproach, scandal, stigma, sully, tarnish

shame into browbeat

shamefacedness disgrace

shameful arrant *(onerous)*, contemptible, depraved, diffident, disgraceful, disreputable, gross *(flagrant)*, heinous, ignoble, inexcusable, inexpiable, iniquitous, nefarious, notorious, obscene, paltry, peccant *(culpable)*, profligate *(corrupt)*, reprehensible, salacious, scandalous, unseemly
shameful notoriety disgrace
shamefulness bad repute, defilement, dishonor *(shame)*, disrepute
shameless arrant *(onerous)*, brazen, contemptible, depraved, dishonest, disreputable, dissolute, flagrant, immoral, impertinent *(insolent)*, insolent, lascivious, lewd, machiavellian, notorious, obscene, outrageous, presumptuous, profane, profligate *(corrupt)*, prurient, remorseless, reprobate, salacious, scurrilous, suggestive *(risqué)*, tainted *(corrupted)*, unabashed, vicious
shamelessness temerity
shanghai abduct, carry away, kidnap
shanghaiing abduction
shape body *(main part)*, build *(construct)*, color *(complexion)*, complexion, compose, condition *(state)*, configuration *(form)*, create, criterion, delineate, delineation, devise *(invent)*, dimension, fabricate *(construct)*, feature *(appearance)*, forge *(produce)*, form *(arrangement)*, form, formalize, formulate, frame *(construct)*, frame *(formulate)*, influence, make, militate, mode, motif, organization *(structure)*, pattern, phenomenon *(manifestation)*, posture *(situation)*, specter, state *(condition)*, structure *(composition)*, style, vision *(dream)*
shape a course arrange *(plan)*, plan
shape out a course contrive
shape up crystallize, develop
shapeless disordered, indefinite, indeterminate
shapelessness confusion *(turmoil)*
shaping building *(business of assembling)*, creation, determinative
share allocate, allot, apportion, assign *(allot)*, claim *(right)*, contribute *(supply)*, convey *(communicate)*, disburse *(distribute)*, dispensation *(act of dispensing)*, dispense, distribute, divide *(distribute)*, dividend, dole, engage *(involve)*, holding *(property owned)*, interest *(ownership)*, involve *(participate)*, member *(constituent part)*, moiety, part *(portion)*, partake, participate, partition, pool, proportion, quota, ration, reciprocate, segment, split, stake *(interest)*, subdivide
share an address cohabit
share and share alike per capita
share bed and board cohabit
share buyer customer
share grief sympathize
share in cooperate, partake, participate
share of profits commission *(fee)*
share out mete
share secrets confide *(divulge)*
share sorrow sympathize
share-out coupon
shared concurrent *(united)*, joint, mutual *(collective)*
shared among several common *(shared)*
shared by two or more common

(shared)
shareholder contributor *(contributor)*, member *(individual in a group)*, participant
shareholding contribution *(participation)*
sharer contributor *(contributor)*, copartner *(business associate)*, member *(individual in a group)*, participant, partner, party *(participant)*
shares securities
sharing cognate, contribution *(participation)*, distribution *(apportionment)*, division *(act of dividing)*
sharp acute, artful, bitter *(acrid tasting)*, caustic, cheat, close *(rigorous)*, cognizant, deft, distinct *(clear)*, harsh, incisive, intensive, machiavellian, mordacious, mulct *(defraud)*, perceptive, perspicacious, politic, profound *(intense)*, resourceful, responsive, sapient, scathing, severe, sly, subtle *(refined)*, trenchant, vigilant
sharp censure reprimand
sharp criticism reproach
sharp practice artifice, knavery, maneuver *(trick)*, misdoing, pettifoggery, ruse
sharp sight perception
sharp words reprimand
sharp-edged acute
sharp-sighted perspicacious
sharp-tempered fractious
sharp-witted acute, artful, perspicacious
sharpen enhance, intensify
sharpening cumulative *(intensifying)*
sharper bettor
sharply defined precise
sharpness discretion *(quality of being discreet)*, insight, perception, propensity, rigor, sagacity, sensibility, severity
sharpness of mind judgment *(discernment)*
shatter break *(fracture)*, discompose, disintegrate, extinguish, extirpate, force *(break)*, overcome *(overwhelm)*, overthrow, rend
shattered broken *(fractured)*, disabled *(made incapable)*
shave decrease, minimize
shave off diminish
she who has expired decedent
sheaf assemblage
sheath cover *(protection)*
sheathe cover *(guard)*, ensconce, enshroud, envelop, protect, shroud
shed cast *(throw)*, denude, eliminate *(exclude)*, emit, outpour, radiate
shed light on clarify
shed light upon comment, elucidate, enlighten, explain, explicate, exposit, resolve *(solve)*, solve
shed tears over deplore
sheepish diffident
sheer absolute *(complete)*, mere, naked *(lacking embellishment)*, outright, pure, stark, thorough, unmitigated
sheer force main force
sheer power main force
sheer terror panic
sheet of flame conflagration
shell bomb, frame *(structure)*
shelling barrage

shelter asylum *(hiding place)*, asylum *(protection)*, building *(structure)*, bulwark, cache *(hiding place)*, cloak, cover *(protection)*, cover *(guard)*, dwelling, ensconce, enshroud, harbor, haven, hedge, hide, house, immure, keep *(shelter)*, lodging, maintain *(sustain)*, panoply, preserve, protect, protection, receive *(permit to enter)*, refuge, safekeeping, screen *(guard)*, security *(safety)*, shield, shroud, veil
shelter for the afflicted asylum *(hospital)*
sheltered blind *(concealed)*, covert, guarded, immune, safe, secure *(free from danger)*
sheltering conservation, protective
shelterless helpless *(defenseless)*
shelve continue *(adjourn)*, defer *(put off)*, delay, hold up *(delay)*, postpone, pretermit, procrastinate, protract *(stall)*, reserve, retire *(retreat)*, set aside *(reserve)*, superannuate, suspend
shepherd protect
sheriff peace officer
shibboleth catchword
shield blind *(obscure)*, bulwark, conceal, conserve, cover *(protection)*, cover *(guard)*, defend, disguise, disguise, ensconce, enshroud, envelop, harbor, hedge, lodge *(house)*, maintain *(sustain)*, obfuscate, panoply, preserve, protect, protection, safeguard, save *(rescue)*, screen *(guard)*, shelter *(protection)*, veil
shield from danger preserve
shield from injury preserve
shielded exempt, guarded, immune, impervious, safe
shielding conservation, preservation, preventive, protective
shift conversion *(change)*, convert *(change use)*, convey *(transfer)*, conveyance, digress, diversification, divert, equivocate, exchange, expedient, fluctuate, hoax, innovation, maneuver, oscillate, palter, period, phase *(period)*, pretext, prevaricate, reconversion, removal, remove *(transfer)*, replacement, ruse, stratagem, subterfuge, tergiversate, transfer, transform, transition, vacillate, vary
shift from its place displace *(remove)*
shift in topic digression
shift the blame recriminate
shifting discursive *(digressive)*, faithless, moving *(in motion)*, sporadic, temporary, variable
shiftless idle, improvident, indolent, irresponsible, remiss, truant
shiftlessness sloth, vagrancy
shifty dishonest, disingenuous, evasive, fraudulent, furtive, machiavellian, perfidious, sly, subtle *(insidious)*, undependable, unreliable, unscrupulous, untrue, untrustworthy
shillelagh cudgel
shindy riot
shining illustrious
shining example exemplar
ship consign, deliver, dispatch *(send off)*, send, transmit, transport
shipload cargo
shipment cargo, carriage, consignment, delivery, freight
shipments outflow

shipper carrier, dealer

shipping cargo, carriage, consignment

shirk default, disobey, fail *(neglect),* neglect, refuse, shun

shirk one's duty default

shirking disinclined, truant

shiver beat *(pulsate),* break *(fracture),* rend, split

shivered broken *(fractured)*

shoal plurality, superficial

shock bombshell, collision *(accident),* frighten, intimidate, overwhelm, perturb, repel *(disgust),* repercussion, stimulus, surprise, upset

shock with sudden fear frighten

shock-proof callous

shocking arrant *(onerous),* deplorable, disgraceful, flagrant, gross *(flagrant),* heinous, immoral, loathsome, lurid, notorious, odious, offensive *(offending),* outrageous, portentous *(eliciting amazement),* reprehensible, repulsive, scandalous, unexpected

shoddiness disrepute

shoddy inferior *(lower in quality),* poor *(inferior in quality),* tawdry

shoot emit, inject, launch *(project),* precipitate *(throw down violently),* send

shoot at attack

shoot forth pullulate

shoot forward project *(impel forward)*

shoot upward expand

shop business *(commercial enterprise),* market *(business),* store *(business),* trade

shop at patronize *(trade with)*

shop goods merchandise

shop with patronize *(trade with)*

shopkeeper dealer, merchant

shoplift steal

shopman dealer, merchant

shopper consumer, customer, patron *(regular customer)*

shopperson dealer

shopping center market *(business),* market place

shopwoman dealer

shopworn stale, trite

shore margin *(outside limit)*

shore up bolster, maintain *(carry on)*

short brief, caustic, compact *(pithy),* concise, cursory, deficient, delinquent *(overdue),* devoid, ephemeral, impecunious, imperfect, inadequate, incommensurate, insufficient, laconic, minimal, perfunctory, petulant, poor *(underprivileged),* scarce, succinct, transient

short fall insufficiency

short letter note *(brief comment)*

short lived transitory

short measure delinquency *(shortage),* insufficiency

short of devoid, save

short of cash impecunious

short of funds impecunious, indebted

short of money destitute, impecunious, poor *(underprivileged)*

short supply dearth, deficiency, delinquency *(shortage),* insufficiency

short version summary

short-lived ephemeral, temporary, transient, volatile

short-tempered fractious, hot-blooded, petulant

short-term acting, brief

shortage absence *(omission),* dearth, deficiency, deficit, delinquency *(shortage),* insufficiency, need *(deprivation),* paucity, poverty

shortcoming breach, decrement, defect, deficiency, deficit, disadvantage, disqualification *(factor that disqualifies),* failure *(falling short),* fault *(weakness),* flaw, foible, frailty, handicap, inability, insufficiency, lapse *(expiration),* onus *(blame),* vice

shorten abstract *(summarize),* commute, condense, constrict *(compress),* curtail, decrease, digest *(summarize),* diminish, discount *(minimize),* lessen, minimize, reduce, retrench

shortened compact *(pithy),* concise, minimal

shortening curtailment, decrease, decrement, deduction *(diminution)*

shortening of time acceleration

shortly in due course, instantly

shortness deficit, delinquency *(shortage),* disrespect

shortness of supply need *(deprivation)*

shortsighted ill-advised, ill-judged, imprudent, misadvised

shotgun gun

shoulder assume *(undertake),* bear *(support),* bolster, maintain *(sustain),* underwrite

shout outcry

shove impact, impel, impetus, jostle *(bump into)*

shove aside avert

show adduce, appearance *(look),* argue, bare, bear *(adduce),* betray *(disclose),* brandish, cite *(state),* clarify, color *(deceptive appearance),* demean *(deport oneself),* demonstrate *(establish),* denote, denude, depict, designate, detail *(particularize),* discipline *(train),* disinter, display, document, edify, educate, emerge, evince, exhibit, explain, expose, express, expression *(manifestation),* flaunt, histrionics, hypocrisy, illustrate, indicate, instruct *(teach),* manifest, manifestation, performance *(workmanship),* phenomenon *(manifestation),* portray, present *(introduce),* pretense *(ostentation),* pretense *(pretext),* pretext, produce *(offer to view),* prove, purport, render *(depict),* represent *(portray),* semblance, signify *(denote),* specify, testify, unveil

show a difference differentiate

show a relationship connect *(relate)*

show affinity connect *(relate)*

show an aversion discriminate *(treat differently)*

show an image reflect *(mirror)*

show as cognate connect *(relate)*

show as kindred connect *(relate)*

show bias discriminate *(treat differently)*

show by example demonstrate *(establish),* exemplify, illustrate

show clearly prove

show clemency relax, remit *(release from penalty)*

show concern for deplore

show consideration for favor

show contempt for flout

show contrast differ *(vary)*

show correspondence compare

show courtesy defer *(yield in judgment)*

show determination adhere *(persist)*

show devotion adhere *(maintain loyalty)*

show disagreement demonstrate *(protest)*

show disapproval blame, demonstrate *(protest)*

show disrespect humiliate

show evidence cite *(state)*

show favor bestow, vouchsafe

show favor to favor

show forbearance bear *(tolerate)*

show grounds for show cause

show hostility collide *(clash),* menace

show ill will antagonize, ill use, mistreat

show improvement develop

show in receive *(permit to enter)*

show indecision alternate *(fluctuate),* vacillate

show indignation resent

show indirectly imply

show itself arise *(appear),* occur *(come to mind)*

show manner comport *(behave)*

show mercy condone, palliate *(excuse),* relent, remit *(release from penalty),* sympathize

show mien comport *(behave)*

show no mercy persecute

show no pity persecute

show no respect minimize

show off expose, flaunt

show oneself report *(present oneself)*

show opinion publicly demonstrate *(protest)*

show opposition demonstrate *(protest)*

show phases change

show pity relax

show preference discriminate *(treat differently),* prefer

show prejudice discriminate *(treat differently)*

show promise portend

show proof cite *(state)*

show regard for observe *(obey)*

show regret for repent

show relation connect *(relate)*

show reluctance challenge

show resemblance connect *(relate)*

show respect defer *(yield in judgment),* honor

show signs evince

show signs of promise *(raise expectations)*

show similarity connect *(relate)*

show tenderness sympathize

show the fallacy of disprove

show the meaning of construe *(comprehend)*

show to be an abettor involve *(implicate)*

show to be analogous compare

show to be false disprove

show to be just justify

show to be similar compare

show unfair bias favor

show up emerge

show variety deviate, differ *(vary),* fluctuate, vary

showable manifest

shower barrage, sufficiency

shower upon bestow, load

showiness pretense *(ostentation)*

showing apparent *(perceptible)*, clear *(apparent)*, demonstrative *(illustrative)*, disclosure *(act of disclosing)*, evident, exhibit, explanation, expression *(manifestation)*, illustration, lineup, manifestation, perceivable, perceptible, proof, salient, visible *(in full view)*

showing homage obeisant

showing lack of judgment injudicious

showing of criminal defendants lineup

showing of criminals for inspection and identification lineup

showing of possible suspects lineup

showing of suspected criminals lineup

showing poor judgment ill-judged, injudicious

showmanship histrionics

shown clear *(apparent)*, ostensible, perceptible

showpiece sample

showy elaborate, flagrant, grandiose, histrionic, inflated *(vain)*, meretricious, orotund, pretentious *(ostentatious)*, prominent, tawdry

shred iota

shrewd artful, judicious, machiavellian, perceptive, perspicacious, politic, practiced, prudent, resourceful, sapient, sensible, sly, subtle *(insidious)*

shrewd diagnosis discretion *(quality of being discreet)*

shrewdness discretion *(quality of being discreet)*, discrimination *(good judgment)*, forethought, insight, perception, prudence, sagacity, sense *(intelligence)*

shrewish fractious, petulant, querulous

shrine monument, reminder

shrink abridge *(shorten)*, commute, condense, constrict *(compress)*, decrease, deduct *(reduce)*, depreciate, depress, diminish, disoblige, ebb, erode, lessen, minimize, reduce, retreat, shirk, subside

shrink from eschew, mistrust, shun

shrinkage curtailment, decline, decrease, decrement, deduction *(diminution)*, diminution, erosion

shrinking decrease, diffident, disinclined, hesitant, reluctant, unobtrusive

shrive clear, excuse, forgive, palliate *(excuse)*, purge *(wipe out by atonement)*, redeem *(satisfy debts)*

shrivel decay, degenerate

shriver penitent

shroud blind *(obscure)*, camouflage, cloak, conceal, cover *(conceal)*, disguise, ensconce, enshroud, envelop, harbor, hide, obfuscate, obliterate, obnubilate, obscure, plant *(covertly place)*, protect, screen *(guard)*, suppress, veil

shrouded blind *(concealed)*, clandestine, covert, esoteric, furtive, hidden, impalpable, inconspicuous, secret, stealthy

shrouded in mystery esoteric, inexplicable, problematic

shrug off ignore

shrunk compact *(pithy)*

shuck denude

shuffle beat *(pulsate)*, bilk, equivo-

cate, evade *(deceive)*, exchange, palter, prevaricate

shun avoid *(evade)*, default, disapprove *(reject)*, disavow, discriminate *(treat differently)*, disdain, elude, eschew, forgo, forswear, leave *(allow to remain)*, neglect, refrain, refuse, reject, repulse, shirk, spurn, stave

shunned derelict *(abandoned)*, undesirable

shunning avoidance *(evasion)*, boycott, disapprobation, disapproval, elusive, reluctant

shunt avert, divert, set aside *(annul)*

shut blind *(impassable)*, impervious, obturate, occlude

shut away remote *(secluded)*

shut down close *(terminate)*, conclude *(complete)*, discontinue *(abandon)*, shut

shut in bind *(restrain)*, border *(bound)*, circumscribe *(surround by boundary)*, confine, contain *(enclose)*, detain *(hold in custody)*, enclose, encompass *(surround)*, fetter, jail, keep *(restrain)*, occlude

shut off ban, bar *(hinder)*, block, clog, occlude

shut out ban, bar *(exclude)*, barred, condemn *(ban)*, debar, discharge *(dismiss)*, eliminate *(exclude)*, exclude, lock, prohibit, relegate, restrict, seclude, select

shut up block, immure, jail, keep *(restrain)*, lock

shut-in patient

shut-off blind *(impassable)*

shutdown blockade *(limitation)*, close *(conclusion)*, halt, strike

shutter protect

shutting out renunciation

shy deficient, diffident, guarded, hesitant, insufficient, precipitate *(throw down violently)*

shy at refuse

shy away from avoid *(evade)*, shun

shy from mistrust

shy of leery

shyness reluctance

sib interrelated, relative

sibi adsumere usurp

sibylic prophetic

sibylline oracular, portentous *(ominous)*, prophetic

sick individual patient

sick person patient

sicken degenerate, disable, languish, repel *(disgust)*

sickening heinous, loathsome, objectionable, odious, offensive *(offending)*, repulsive, unsavory

sickling patient

sickly languid, powerless, unsound *(not strong)*

sickness disability *(physical inability)*, disease, disorder *(abnormal condition)*, pain, prostration

side border, choose, edge *(border)*, faction, phase *(aspect)*

side against counter, counteract, disapprove *(reject)*, fight *(counteract)*, oppugn

side by side along, contiguous

side issue development *(outgrowth)*

side road causeway

side with concur *(agree)*, conform, cooperate, espouse, involve *(participate)*,

join *(associate oneself with)*, maintain *(sustain)*, unite

side-partner consociate

sidelong indirect

sidereal stellar

sideslip digression

sidestep avoidance *(evasion)*, detour, digress, digression, parry

sidetrack digress, divert

siege assault, barrage, belligerency, invasion, onset *(assault)*, outbreak

sieve screen *(select)*, sort

sift analyze, censor, cull, discriminate *(distinguish)*, screen *(select)*, scrutinize, select, sort, study

sifting analysis

sigh plaint

sigh for deplore

sight appearance *(look)*, detect, discern *(detect with the senses)*, notice *(observe)*, perception, phenomenon *(manifestation)*, phenomenon *(unusual occurrence)*, recognize *(perceive)*, scene, spy, witness *(have direct knowledge of)*

sight draft check *(instrument)*

sighted perceivable, perceptible

sighting detection, discovery

sightly attractive

sigil brand, stamp

sigmoid circuitous

sign authorize, brand, brand *(mark)*, call *(title)*, clue, designation *(symbol)*, device *(distinguishing mark)*, earmark, expression *(manifestation)*, forerunner, harbinger, index *(catalog)*, indicant, indication, indicator, indorse, label, manifestation, notarize, phenomenon *(manifestation)*, precursor, premonition, seal *(solemnize)*, symbol, symptom, threat, title *(designation)*, token, witness *(attest to)*

sign a name to subscribe *(sign)*

sign and seal notarize

sign away alienate *(transfer title)*, cede, devolve, forgo, relinquish

sign in empanel, register

sign legally notarize

sign on join *(associate oneself with)*

sign one's name on indorse

sign over alienate *(transfer title)*, assign *(transfer ownership)*, grant *(transfer formally)*, lend

sign up employ *(engage services)*, enroll, recruit, register

signal admonition, clue, contact *(communicate)*, denote, direct *(order)*, forewarn, illustrious, important *(significant)*, indicant, indicate, indication, manifestation, material *(important)*, momentous, notable, noteworthy, notify, particular *(specific)*, peculiar *(curious)*, remarkable, symbol, symptom

signal by which one is summoned process *(summons)*

signalize indicate

signally particularly

signatory surety *(guarantor)*, undersigned

signature call *(title)*, indicant, subscription

signboard indicant

signed contractual

signed and delivered instrument deed

signed and sealed contractual

signed notice receipt *(proof of receiv-*

ing)

signer affiant, surety *(guarantor)*, undersigned

signet brand, trademark

significance clout, connotation, construction, content *(meaning)*, degree *(magnitude)*, distinction *(reputation)*, import, importance, interest *(concern)*, magnitude, main point, materiality *(consequence)*, meaning, notoriety, point *(purpose)*, prestige, purpose, relevance, signification, spirit, stress *(accent)*, substance *(essential nature)*, tenor, validity, value, weight *(importance)*

significant central *(essential)*, consequential *(substantial)*, considerable, constructive *(creative)*, critical *(crucial)*, crucial, decisive, determinative, indispensable, key, major, material *(important)*, momentous, necessary *(required)*, notable, noteworthy, outstanding *(prominent)*, paramount, prominent, remarkable, salient, special, strategic, substantial, unusual, valuable

significant detail necessity

significant event landmark *(significant change)*

significant feature highlight

significant occurrence landmark *(significant change)*

significant part content *(meaning)*

significare allude, denote, express, hint, imply, indicate, portend, purport

significatio content *(meaning)*, hint, import, indication, innuendo, insinuation, intimation, meaning, significance, signification

signification assignment *(designation)*, connotation, consequence *(significance)*, content *(meaning)*, corpus, designation *(naming)*, implication *(inference)*, import, manifestation, meaning, significance, substance *(essential nature)*, symbol, tenor, title *(designation)*

signified implied

signify allude, bear *(adduce)*, bespeak, communicate, connote, construe *(translate)*, convey *(communicate)*, denominate, denote, depict, designate, evidence, exemplify, hint, indicate, inform *(notify)*, manifest, notify, portend, predict, presage, prognosticate, promise *(raise expectations)*, purport, refer *(direct attention)*, represent *(portray)*

signify assent acknowledge *(respond)*, concur *(agree)*

signing up registration

signit stamp

signory domain *(sphere of influence)*

signpost indication, landmark *(conspicuous object)*

signs indicia

signum stamp, symbol

silence allay, concealment, lull, lull, peace, placate, repress, stifle, stop, strangle, subdue, suppress

silent inarticulate, mute, noncommittal, speechless, stealthy, tacit, taciturn

silentium silence

silhouette configuration *(form)*, contour *(outline)*, contour *(shape)*, delineate, delineation

sill threshold *(entrance)*

silly fatuous, frivolous, inept *(inappropriate)*, ludicrous, puerile, superficial,

vacuous

silly talk jargon *(unintelligible language)*

similar akin *(germane)*, analogous, approximate, cognate, commensurable, commensurate, comparable *(capable of comparison)*, congruous, consonant, correlative, equal, equivalent, identical, pendent, same, tantamount, uniform

similar appearance analogy

similar form analogy

similar item cover *(substitute)*

similar relation analogy

similar to comparative

similarity analogy, conformity *(agreement)*, identity *(similarity)*, par *(equality)*, parity, relation *(connection)*, resemblance, same, semblance

similarly also

similative congruous

simile example

similis analogous, similar

similitude analogy, correlate, correspondence *(similarity)*, identity *(similarity)*, propinquity *(similarity)*, relation *(connection)*, resemblance, semblance

similitudinous comparative

similitudo analogy, resemblance

similtude parity

simoniacal mercenary

simple coherent *(clear)*, comprehensible, credulous, elementary, facile, fatuous, genuine, household *(familiar)*, ingenuous, innocuous, lucid, mere, mundane, naive, naked *(lacking embellishment)*, narrow, nominal, obtuse, only *(no more than)*, opaque, ordinary, pellucid, puerile, pure, rudimentary, stark, unadulterated, unaffected *(sincere)*, unobtrusive, unpretentious, unsuspecting

simple job sinecure

simple meaning connotation

simple-minded non compos mentis, obtuse, opaque, simple

simpleness credulity, ignorance

simplex candid, categorical, honest, ingenuous, naive, open *(persuasible)*, simple, straightforward, unaffected *(sincere)*, unconditional, unpretentious

simplicity credulity, honesty, ignorance, informality, opacity

simplification clarification, definition, explanation, illustration, paraphrase

simplified elementary, simple

simplify clarify, elucidate, enlighten, explain, explicate, exposit, expound, facilitate, interpret

simplistic statement generality *(vague statement)*

simply only, solely *(purely)*

simul simultaneous

simulacrum deception, distortion, imitation, semblance, sham

simulacrum color *(deceptive appearance)*, disguise, embodiment

simulare feign, pretend

simulate copy, disguise, fake, feign, forge *(counterfeit)*, misrepresent, mock *(imitate)*, pose *(impersonate)*, pretend, profess *(pretend)*, reflect *(mirror)*

simulated artificial, false *(not genuine)*, imitation, specious, spurious, surrogate

simulatio disguise, pretext

simulation color *(deceptive appearance)*, copy, counterfeit, decoy, disguise, fake, false pretense, plagiarism, pretense *(pretext)*, pretext, sham

simulatione pretense *(pretext)*

simulative artificial

simulatus false pretense, ostensible

simultaneity synchronism

simultaneous coincidental, collateral *(accompanying)*, concerted, concomitant, contemporaneous, instant, instantaneous

simultaneous discharge of shots salvo

simultaneousness synchronism

simultas feud

sin guilt, misdeed, transgression, trespass, vice, wrong

sin-laden diabolic

since thereafter

sincere candid, direct *(forthright)*, earnest, faithful *(loyal)*, fervent, genuine, honest, ingenuous, pure, reliable, scrupulous, serious *(devoted)*, simple, straightforward, true *(loyal)*, veridical

sincerely faithfully

sinceritas honesty

sincerity candor *(straightforwardness)*, honesty, integrity, probity, truth, veracity

sincerus genuine, honest, real, simple, unadulterated

sine certamine uncontested

sine corpore immaterial

sine nomine anonymous

sine qua non center *(essence)*, cornerstone

sinere let *(permit)*, suffer *(permit)*

sinew prowess *(bravery)*

sinewless languid, powerless

sinewy powerful

sinful arrant *(onerous)*, bad *(offensive)*, delinquent *(guilty of a misdeed)*, depraved, diabolic, disgraceful, immoral, iniquitous, malignant, nefarious, outrageous, peccant *(culpable)*, profane, profligate *(corrupt)*, reprehensible, reprobate, salacious, sinister

sinfulness guilt, vice

sing out proclaim

sing the praises of belaud

singe burn, deflagrate

single exclusive *(singular)*, express, individual, particular *(individual)*, particular *(specific)*, simple, singular, sole, solitary, sporadic, unilateral, unique, whole *(unified)*

single case particular

single item entity

single out cull, differentiate, except *(exclude)*, extract, label, prefer, screen *(select)*, select

single piece entity

single-minded intense, pertinacious, purposeful, steadfast

single-mindedness adhesion *(loyalty)*, diligence *(care)*, loyalty, obsession

singled out preferred *(favored)*

singlehearted faithful *(loyal)*

singleness identity *(individuality)*, particularity, purpose, uniformity

singleness of heart loyalty

singleness of purpose diligence *(perseverance)*

singleton item

singly only, respectively, retail
singula detail
singular certain *(particular)*, certain *(specific)*, different, distinct *(distinguished from others)*, distinctive, eccentric, extraordinary, individual, infrequent, irregular *(not usual)*, nonconforming, notable, noteworthy, novel, only *(sole)*, original *(creative)*, particular *(individual)*, particular *(specific)*, peculiar *(curious)*, peculiar *(distinctive)*, personal *(private)*, portentous *(eliciting amazement)*, prodigious *(amazing)*, rare, remarkable, renowned, several *(separate)*, sole, special, unaccustomed, uncommon, unilateral, unique, unprecedented, unusual
singularis individual, rare, remarkable, singular, unique
singularity differential, feature *(characteristic)*, identity *(individuality)*, irregularity, nonconformity, particularity, personality, property *(distinctive attribute)*, quality *(attribute)*, quirk *(idiosyncrasy)*, speciality, specialty *(distinctive mark)*, technicality, trait
singularly particularly
sinister arrant *(onerous)*, bad *(offensive)*, blameworthy, diabolic, dire, heinous, malevolent, malignant, nefarious, odious, ominous, pernicious, portentous *(ominous)*, unfavorable, unpropitious
sinistrous disastrous
sink decay, decrease, degenerate, depreciate, depress, ebb, immerse *(plunge into)*, invest *(fund)*, languish, subside
sink away perish
sink back relapse
sink in penetrate
sink into enter *(penetrate)*
sink to a lower condition degenerate
sinkage decline
sinking decadent, decline, decrease, depression, descent *(declination)*, relapse
sinless blameless, incorruptible, inculpable, innocent, irreprehensible, not guilty, pure, unblemished, unimpeachable
sinlessness innocence
sinner convict, offender, wrongdoer
sinning diabolic, iniquitous
sinuate circuitous, sinuous, tortuous *(bending)*
sinuated tortuous *(bending)*
sinuation involution
sinuosity complication, involution
sinuosus sinuous
sinuous circuitous, complex, devious, indirect, labyrinthine, oblique *(evasive)*, tortuous *(bending)*
sire ascendant, author *(originator)*, generate, originate, progenitor, propagate *(increase)*, reproduce
sired in wedlock legitimate *(lawfully conceived)*
Sisyphean operose
sit in conclave deliberate
sit in council deliberate
sit in judgment adjudge, adjudicate, arbitrate *(adjudge)*, decide, determine, find *(determine)*, hear *(give a legal hearing)*, judge, try *(conduct a trial)*
site building *(structure)*, circuit, habitation *(dwelling place)*, locality, loca-

tion, part *(place)*, pinpoint, scene, seat, situs, venue
sitting session
sitting room chamber *(compartment)*
situate allocate, deposit *(place)*, establish *(entrench)*, locate, lodge *(house)*, pinpoint, plant *(place firmly)*, site
situated at the farthest limit extreme *(last)*
situation aspect, capacity *(job)*, career, case *(set of circumstances)*, condition *(state)*, degree *(station)*, employment, environment, experience *(encounter)*, livelihood, locality, occasion, occupation *(vocation)*, occurrence, office, perspective, plight, position *(business status)*, post, predicament, pursuit *(occupation)*, region, site, situs, standpoint, state *(condition)*, status, title *(position)*, trade *(occupation)*
situations circumstances
situs circuit, site
situs locality, situated, situation
sizable appreciable, considerable, major, prodigious *(enormous)*, substantial
sizableness mass *(weight)*
size arrange *(methodize)*, bulk, calculate, caliber *(measurement)*, classify, dimension, extent, magnitude, mass *(weight)*, maximum *(amplitude)*, measure, measurement, sort, space
size up gauge
sizzle burn
skeleton capsule, configuration *(form)*, contour *(outline)*, design *(construction plan)*, foundation *(basis)*, frame *(structure)*, outline *(synopsis)*, summary
skeleton plan delineation
skeptic heretic
skeptical cynical, dubious, inconvincible, incredulous, leery, suspicious *(distrustful)*
skepticalness doubt *(suspicion)*, incredulity, misgiving
skepticism cloud *(suspicion)*, doubt *(suspicion)*, incredulity, misgiving, qualm, reluctance, suspicion *(mistrust)*
sketch abridge *(shorten)*, abridgment *(condensation)*, blueprint, brief, capsule, contour *(outline)*, contrive, delineate, delineation, depict, description, design *(construction plan)*, draw *(depict)*, frame *(construct)*, frame *(formulate)*, indicate, narration, outline *(synopsis)*, portray, program, prospectus, render *(depict)*, scenario, story *(narrative)*, trace *(delineate)*
sketch in outline delineate
sketch out arrange *(plan)*, delineate, devise *(invent)*
sketchy deficient, inchoate, partial *(relating to a part)*, perfunctory, unclear
skewer penetrate, pierce *(lance)*
skill ability, capacity *(aptitude)*, competence *(ability)*, discretion *(quality of being discreet)*, efficiency, experience *(background)*, facility *(easiness)*, faculty *(ability)*, gift *(flair)*, knowledge *(learning)*, performance *(workmanship)*, potential, propensity, prowess *(ability)*, qualification *(fitness)*, science *(technique)*, specialty *(special aptitude)*
skilled competent, deft, efficient, ex-

pert, facile, familiar *(informed)*, learned, literate, practiced, professional *(trained)*, proficient, qualified *(competent)*, veteran
skilled hand expert, specialist
skilled in commerce commercial
skilled laborer artisan
skilled occupation career
skilled person specialist
skilled practitioner expert, professional, specialist
skilled technician professional
skilled worker artisan, specialist
skillful artful, capable, competent, deft, effective *(efficient)*, efficient, expert, facile, familiar *(informed)*, practiced, professional *(trained)*, proficient, qualified *(competent)*, resourceful, sciential, subtle *(refined)*, tactical
skillful in handling others diplomatic
skillful management strategy
skillful treatment management *(judicious use)*
skillfulness competence *(ability)*, efficiency, experience *(background)*, faculty *(ability)*, gift *(flair)*, performance *(workmanship)*, prowess *(ability)*, science *(technique)*, specialty *(special aptitude)*
skim border *(approach)*, read, review
skimpy deficient, marginal, petty, scarce
skin denude
skin-deep superficial
skip ignore, neglect, omit, pretermit
skirmish affray, collision *(dispute)*, commotion, confront *(oppose)*, confrontation *(altercation)*, contend *(dispute)*, contest *(dispute)*, disaccord, fight *(battle)*, fight *(battle)*, fray
skirt border, border *(approach)*, detour, digress, embrace *(encircle)*, margin *(outside limit)*, outline *(boundary)*
skirting circuitous
skirts confines, edge *(border)*, periphery
skittish restive
skulduggery bunko, knavery
skulk lurk, prowl
skulking recreant, sly, stealthy
skyrocket increase
skyscraper edifice
slab part *(portion)*
slack careless, derelict *(negligent)*, indolent, languid, lax, negligent, otiose, remiss, truant
slack off subside
slacken alleviate, commute, decrease, delay, ease, hold up *(delay)*, impede, lessen, moderate *(temper)*, pause, relax, subdue, subside
slackening mollification
slackness informality, laxity, neglect, negligence, sloth
slake allay, assuage, satisfy *(fulfill)*, soothe
slam beat *(strike)*
slam into collide *(crash against)*
slander aspersion, defamation, defame, denigrate, disparage, libel, malign, smear, tarnish, vilification
slanderous calumnious, derogatory
slant aspect, character *(personal quality)*, complexion, favoritism, inclination, intolerance, misrepresent, outlook, per-

spective, position (point of view), prejudice (preconception), prejudice (influence), side, stand (position), tendency

slanted inclined, one-sided, prejudicial

slanting oblique (slanted)

slap beat (strike), lash (strike), strike (assault)

slapdash cursory, superficial

slash commute, decrease, deduct (reduce), lancinate, minimize, rebate, rend, split

slash prices discount (reduce)

slashing incisive, mordacious

slate docket, lash (attack verbally), program, punish, rebuke, reprehend, reproach, set down

slatternly sordid

slaughter aberemurder, dispatch (put to death), eliminate (eradicate), extinguish, homicide, kill (murder), killing, slay

slaughtering killing, lethal

slaughterous deadly, fatal

slave captive

slavery bondage, captivity, restraint, servitude, subjection, thrall

slavish loyal, obsequious, pliable, pliant, sequacious, servile, subservient

slavishness bondage

slay destroy (efface), dispatch (put to death), execute (sentence to death), extinguish, kill (murder)

slaying aberemurder, assassination, homicide, killing

sleave involution

sleazy poor (inferior in quality), tawdry

sleep repose (rest)

sleep at lodge (reside)

sleeping dormant

sleepless industrious

sleepy torpid

sleight false pretense, imposture, maneuver (trick)

sleight of hand prestidigitation

sleightful delusive, evasive

slender insubstantial, insufficient, minimal, slight, subtle (refined), tenuous

slender means poverty

sleuth research, spy

slice part (portion), ration, rend, segment, share (interest), split

slick deft, machiavellian

slide ebb

slide back relapse

slight affront, aspersion, bad repute, brief, contemn, de minimus, deficient, delinquency (failure of duty), depreciate, discommend, discount (disbelieve), disdain, disoblige, disparage, disregard (lack of respect), disrespect, flout, frivolous, humiliate, ignore, impalpable, inappreciable, inconsequential, inconsiderable, insubstantial, insufficient, lessen, minimal, minimize, minor, misprize, neglect, neglect, negligible, nominal, nonsubstantial (not sturdy), nugatory, offend (insult), omit, paltry, pardonable, petty, pretermit, rebuff, rebuff, reject, rejection, remote (small), spurn, superficial, tenuous, trivial, underestimate

slight change modification

slight indication hint

slight mention hint

slight trace suggestion

slighting calumnious, contemptuous, derogatory, pejorative

slighting language disparagement

slim insubstantial, insufficient, minimal, remote (small), slight, trivial

sling project (impel forward)

slink lurk, prowl

slink away shirk

slip coupon, delinquency (failure of duty), deviate, ebb, err, error, failure (falling short), fault (mistake), indiscretion, label, lapse (expiration), lapse (fall into error), miscalculate, miscue, misdeed, misdoing, misstatement, omission, oversight (carelessness), receipt (proof of receiving), transgression

slip away elude, escape, leave (depart), move (alter position), retreat

slip away from abandon (physically leave)

slip back ebb, escheat, recidivate, relapse

slip from virtue lapse (fall into error)

slip into penetrate

slip off move (alter position)

slip out elude, evade (elude)

slip up miscalculate, mistake

slippery deceptive, elusive, evasive, insecure, machiavellian, perfidious, precarious, sly, undependable, untrustworthy

slipshod careless, cursory, inaccurate, lax, negligent

slipshodness disorder (lack of order)

slit lancinate, sever, split, split

sliver minimum

slivered broken (fractured)

slogan catchword, phrase

sloping oblique (slanted)

sloppiness laxity

sloppy careless, repulsive, slipshod

slot split

sloth inaction, inertia, languor, laxity, neglect

slothful idle, inactive, indolent, lax, lifeless (dull), negligent, otiose, remiss, truant

slough denude, jettison

slovenliness laxity, neglect

slovenly disorderly, lax, negligent, slipshod, sordid

slow check (restrain), constrict (inhibit), delay, deliberate, hesitant, languid, late (tardy), obtuse, otiose, phlegmatic, torpid

slow down alleviate, check (restrain), delay, diminish, encumber (hinder), hinder, impede, moderate (temper), obstruct, prolong

slow in understanding opaque

slow motion languor

slow pace languor

slow to believe inconvincible, incredulous

slow to take offense peaceable

slow up delay, hold up (delay)

slow-moving deliberate, ponderous

slow-paced deliberate

slow-wittedness opacity

slowed down arrested (checked)

slowing down decrease

slowness delay, hesitation, languor, opacity

slug beat (strike)

sluggish despondent, inactive, indolent, languid, lax, lifeless (dull), otiose, phlegmatic, ponderous, stagnant, torpid

sluggishness inaction, inertia, languor, sloth

slumber repose (rest)

slumbering dormant

slumberous narcotic

slump decline, decrease, decrease, depress, depression, languish

slur aspersion, brand (stigmatize), contemn, defamation, defame, denounce (condemn), denunciation, depreciate, discommend, discredit, disgrace, disgrace, dishonor (shame), dishonor (deprive of honor), disparage, ignominy, libel, libel, malign, notoriety, obloquy, onus (stigma), opprobrium, reproach, scandal, slander, smear, spurn, stigma, sully, tarnish

slur over ignore, minimize

slush fund hush money

sly artful, covert, deceptive, devious, disingenuous, furtive, insidious, machiavellian, mendacious, secret, stealthy, subtle (insidious), unscrupulous

slyness artifice, evasion, indirection (deceitfulness), knavery

smack beat (strike)

small brief, deficient, impalpable, inappreciable, inconsiderable, minimal, minor, negligible, nominal, null (insignificant), paltry, petty, remote (small), slight, tenuous, trivial

small amount iota, minimum, modicum, scintilla

small cavity cell

small chance improbability

small group minority (outnumbered group)

small hope improbability

small number minority (outnumbered group), paucity

small parcel of land lot

small part member (constituent part), segment

small percentage minority (outnumbered group)

small proportion minority (outnumbered group)

small quantity iota, minimum, minority (outnumbered group), modicum, paucity, scintilla

small room cell

small-minded parochial, parsimonious, provincial

smaller minor

smaller group minority (outnumbered group)

smaller part minority (outnumbered group)

smallest minimal

smallness inconsequence, insignificance

smallness of number dearth

smart omniscient, rapid, resourceful

smarten embellish

smarting bitter (penetrating), painful

smartness perception, sagacity, sense (intelligence)

smash break (fracture), debacle, defeat, extirpate, force (break), obliterate, spoil (impair), strike (assault), strike (collide), subdue

smash into collide (crash against)

smash up collide (clash)

smear attaint, brand *(stigmatize),* contemn, deface, defacement, defamation, defame, denigrate, denounce *(condemn),* denunciation, disgrace, dishonor *(shame),* dishonor *(deprive of honor),* disparage, libel, libel, malign, pillory, slander, spread, stain, stigma, sully, tarnish, vilification
smearing calumnious, defilement, pejorative
smelt burn
smirch attaint, brand, brand *(stigmatize),* defamation, defame, denigrate, derogate, disgrace, disgrace, dishonor *(deprive of honor),* ignominy, infect, malign, onus *(stigma),* opprobrium, pillory, pollute, shame, smear, stain, stigma, sully, tarnish
smirched tainted *(contaminated)*
smite beat *(strike),* harm, impress *(affect deeply),* kill *(murder),* lash *(strike),* plague, punish, strike *(assault)*
smoke out expose
smoke screen disguise, subterfuge
smokiness indistinctness
smoky indistinct
smolder burn
smoldering dormant
smooth allay, alleviate, deft, facile, facilitate, help, machiavellian, moderate *(temper),* mollify, pacify, placate, placid, practiced, soothe
smooth over disarm *(set at ease)*
smoothe expedite
smoothly diplomatic, readily
smoothness facility *(easiness),* uniformity
smother assuage, extinguish, hamper, inhibit, prohibit, repress, stifle, strangle, subdue, suppress, withhold
smudge brand *(stigmatize),* deface, defacement, onus *(stigma),* stain, sully, tarnish
smug complacent, pretentious *(pompous)*
smuggle hide
smuggled commerce contraband
smuggled goods contraband
smuggled trade contraband
smuggled traffic contraband
smuggler bootlegger, criminal
smugness pride
smut obscenity, pornography
smutch onus *(stigma)*
smuttiness obscenity
smutty profane, prurient, salacious, suggestive *(risqué)*
snag block, complex *(entanglement),* damper *(stopper),* entanglement *(confusion),* impediment, obstacle, obstruct, obstruction, snarl, trouble
snakelike circuitous, tortuous *(bending)*
snaky circuitous, malevolent, sinuous
snap impulsive *(rash),* rend, split, spontaneous, unpremeditated
snap back retort
snappish fractious, perverse, petulant
snappy expeditious, petulant
snare ambush, artifice, bait *(lure),* deceive, deception, ensnare, entrap, hunt, inveigle, mislead, pitfall, ruse, trap, trap
snaring bribery
snarl altercation, complex *(entanglement),* confuse *(create disorder),* entan-

glement *(confusion),* involution, perplex, perturb
snarled complex, inextricable, labyrinthine, problematic
snarling perverse, petulant
snatch hijack, kidnap, poach, purloin, steal, trap
snatching appropriation *(taking),* distress *(seizure)*
sneak cloak, deceive, lurk, prowl
sneak off escape
sneak thief burglar, criminal
sneakiness deceit, fraud
sneaking clandestine, devious, furtive, machiavellian, perfidious, recreant, sly, stealthy
sneaky covert, deceptive, evasive, fraudulent, furtive, lying, machiavellian, perfidious, sly, stealthy, surreptitious
sneer disdain, disparage, disrespect, flout, humiliate, jeer, mock *(deride),* ridicule, spurn
sneer at denigrate, derogate, discommend, disdain, minimize, misprize
sneering cynical, disdainful
snicker mock *(deride)*
snigger mock *(deride)*
sniggering ridicule
snobbery pride
snobbish disdainful, exclusive *(limited),* pretentious *(pompous)*
snobby disdainful, exclusive *(limited)*
snoop spy, spy
snooper spy
snooty disdainful
snowy clean
snub affront, curb, disdain, disregard *(lack of respect),* disregard, disrespect, humiliate, ignore, offend *(insult),* ostracism, rebuff, rebuff, reject, rejection, repulse, shun, spurn
snuff out obliterate, stifle, strangle
so-called ostensible, purported, specious
so-so mediocre
soak imbue, immerse *(plunge into),* overload, permeate, pervade
soak through penetrate
soaked full
sober deliberate, disconsolate, discriminating *(judicious),* earnest, grave *(solemn),* lucid, major, moderate *(temper),* objective, peaceable, pensive, phlegmatic, prudent, rational, sane, sensible, serious *(grave),* solemn
sober-minded sane
sober-mindedness common sense
sobered penitent
soberness solemnity, temperance
sobriety common sense, continence, deliberation, moderation, reason *(sound judgment),* sagacity, solemnity, temperance
sobriquet call *(title),* cognomen
sociable amicable, harmonious
social civil *(public),* public *(affecting people)*
social adjustment civilization
social behavior conduct
social climber philistine
social code decorum
social conduct decorum
social elevation civilization
social graces conduct, decorum

social group public, sodality
social procedures decorum
social rank class
social responsibility obligation *(duty)*
social status class
social usage custom, decorum
socialize nationalize
societal civil *(public),* national, public *(affecting people)*
societas association *(connection),* combination, company *(assemblage),* confederacy *(compact),* league, partnership, syndicate
societas clandestina cabal
society chamber *(body),* civilization, coalition, community, confederacy *(compact),* institute, league, nationality, populace, population, public, sodality
socius associate, consort, partner
socius criminis accessory, accomplice, cohort, colleague, copartner *(coconspirator)*
sodalis associate
sodalitas facility *(institution),* foundation *(organization),* institute
sodality body *(collection),* cartel, coalition, corporation, league, organization *(association),* partnership, society, union *(labor organization)*
soft charitable *(lenient),* flexible, lenient, malleable, pliant, yielding
soft job sinecure
soften allay, alleviate, assuage, commute, ease, extenuate, give *(yield),* mitigate, moderate *(temper),* modify *(moderate),* mollify, obtund, palliate *(abate),* propitiate, relax, relent, remit *(relax),* soothe, subdue
softened malleable
softening mitigating, mitigation, mollification, palliative *(abating)*
softening circumstances extenuating circumstances
softhearted benevolent, charitable *(lenient),* lenient, placable, sensitive *(easily affected)*
softheartedness benevolence *(disposition to do good),* lenience
softness lenience, mollification
soil brand *(stigmatize),* debase, deface, denigrate, depreciate, disgrace, infect, onus *(stigma),* pervert, pillory, pollute, smear, stain, sully, taint *(contaminate),* tarnish
soiled blemished, tainted *(contaminated)*
soiling defacement
sojourn dwell *(reside),* habitation *(act of inhabiting),* inhabit, inhabitation *(act of dwelling in),* lodge *(reside),* reside, stop
sojourner denizen, habitant, inhabitant, lodger, occupant, resident
sojournment habitation *(act of inhabiting),* presence *(attendance)*
solace alleviate, assuage, assure *(give confidence to),* benefit *(betterment),* reassure, sympathize
solatium compensation, consideration *(recompense),* expiation, pay, payment *(remittance),* recompense, reward, satisfaction *(discharge of debt),* trover
solatium solace
solder cement, connect *(join together)*

soldier-like spartan

soldierly heroic, spartan

soldiership strategy

sole exclusive *(singular)*, individual, singular, solitary, unique

sole control of a commodity monopoly

solecism catachresis, irregularity, misuse

solecistic anomalous, faulty, incorrect

solecistical faulty, incorrect

solely only

solemn critical *(crucial)*, earnest, important *(significant)*, major, sacrosanct, serious *(grave)*

solemn affirmation affidavit, affirmation, averment, oath

solemn agreement testament

solemn appropriation dedication

solemn assertion assurance, vow

solemn averment affirmance *(legal affirmation)*, affirmation, asseveration, attestation, avouchment, confirmation, declaration, surety *(certainty)*

solemn avowal adjuration, affirmance *(legal affirmation)*, affirmation, asseveration, attestation, avouchment, confirmation, declaration, oath, surety *(certainty)*

solemn declaration affirmation, asseveration, attestation, avouchment, certification *(attested copy)*, commitment *(responsibility)*, confirmation, deposition, jurat, oath, pledge *(binding promise)*, surety *(certainty)*, vow

solemn entreaty call *(appeal)*, prayer

solemn feeling solemnity

solemn invocation oath

solemn mockery blasphemy

solemn observance ceremony

solemn promise assurance, testament, vow

solemn request petition

solemn word pledge *(binding promise)*

solemn writing instrument *(document)*

solemnity ceremony, formality, importance

solemnization ceremony, remembrance *(commemoration)*

solemnize formalize, keep *(fulfill)*

solemnly affirm avouch *(avow)*, certify *(attest)*

solemnly promise assure *(insure)*

solemnly request petition

solicit apply *(request)*, bait *(lure)*, call *(appeal to)*, desire, importune, inquire, lobby, petition, plead *(implore)*, pray, pressure, pursue *(strive to gain)*, request, urge

solicit earnestly importune

solicit insistently bait *(harass)*, importune

solicit votes lobby

solicitant applicant *(petitioner)*, claimant, petitioner

solicitation call *(appeal)*, dun, entreaty, instigation, invitation, persuasion, request, seduction

solicitor advocate *(counselor)*, agent, attorney, barrister, claimant, counsel, counselor, esquire, jurist, lawyer, petitioner, practitioner, procurator, representative *(proxy)*, special interest, suitor

solicitorial forensic, juridical

solicitors bar *(body of lawyers)*

solicitous benevolent, interested, protective, zealous

solicitousness benevolence *(disposition to do good)*, consideration *(sympathetic regard)*

solicitude benevolence *(disposition to do good)*, concern *(interest)*, consideration *(sympathetic regard)*, interest *(concern)*, precaution

solid authentic, axiomatic, bodily, cogent, cohesive *(compact)*, compact *(dense)*, compound, concrete, corporeal, dependable, firm, fixed *(securely placed)*, indomitable, inflexible, infrangible, intact, material *(physical)*, meritorious, ossified, secure *(sound)*, sound, stable, staunch, strong, substantive, tangible, unyielding, valid, well-grounded, whole *(undamaged)*

solid substance corpus

solid vote consensus

solidarity coaction, conciliation, confederacy *(compact)*, corpus, integration *(assimilation)*, merger

solidification adhesion *(affixing)*, agglomeration, coalescence, congealment, consolidation

solidified compact *(dense)*, concrete, ossified, solid *(compact)*

solidify amalgamate, cement, cohere *(adhere)*, consolidate *(strengthen)*, consolidate *(unite)*, crystallize, establish *(entrench)*, fix *(make firm)*, unite

solidity certainty, common sense, congealment, density, materiality *(physical existence)*, strength

solidness congealment

solidus concrete, durable, firm, solid *(sound)*

soliloquize recite

soliloquy peroration

solitariness privacy

solitary derelict *(abandoned)*, exclusive *(singular)*, individual, insular, nonconforming, only *(sole)*, private *(secluded)*, remote *(secluded)*, separate, sole

solitary abode cell

solitude privacy

solitudo privacy

solitus accustomed *(customary)*, typical

sollemnis periodic

sollers resourceful

sollertia skill

sollicitare harass, molest *(annoy)*, perplex, pique

sollicitudo concern *(interest)*, misgiving, trouble

sollicitus solicitous

solo alone *(solitary)*, apart, solitary

soluble solvable

solus apart, sole, solitary

solutio solution *(answer)*

solution conclusion *(determination)*, denouement, determination, disposition *(determination)*, explanation, finding, opinion *(judicial decision)*, outcome, panacea, remedy *(legal means of redress)*

solution to difficulties panacea

solutus exempt, free *(not restricted)*, independent

solvable determinable *(ascertainable)*

solve adjust *(resolve)*, ascertain, construe *(comprehend)*, elucidate, explain, expound, find *(discover)*, interpret, remedy, settle

solvent solid *(sound)*, solution *(substance)*

solvere annul, defray, disburse *(pay out)*, disengage, free

somatic bodily, corporal, physical, tangible

somatical bodily

somber bleak *(not favorable)*, bleak *(severely simple)*, despondent, disconsolate, grave *(solemn)*, lifeless *(dull)*, lugubrious, ominous, portentous *(ominous)*, solemn

sombrous bleak *(not favorable)*, bleak *(severely simple)*

some several *(plural)*

somebody character *(an individual)*, person

someone character *(an individual)*, person

something added appurtenance, augmentation

something constructively affixed to real property fixture

something equivalent quid pro quo

something for something quid pro quo

something immovable from realty fixture

something like cognate, pendent

something of value consideration *(recompense)*

something over and above bonus

something owed due

something owing mortgage

something physically annexed to realty fixture

something produced by capital income

something to be imitated example

somewhat fairly *(moderately)*, in part

somewhere about on or about

somnifacient narcotic

somniferous narcotic

somnific narcotic

somnolence languor

somnolency languor

somnolent torpid

sonitus noise

sonorous orotund, resounding, sesquipedalian

sons progeny

soon in due course, instantly

soon to be prospective

soon to happen prospective

sooner than due premature

sooner than intended premature

soothe allay, alleviate, assuage, cure, lessen, lull, moderate *(temper)*, mollify, pacify, placate, propitiate, relieve *(give aid)*, remedy, remit *(relax)*, sympathize

soother narcotic

soothing medicinal, mitigation, mollification, narcotic, palliative *(abating)*, placid, remedial

soothsay predict, presage, prognosticate

sop bribe, gratuity *(bribe)*

sophism fallacy, non sequitur

sophistic deceptive, ill-founded, illogical, illusory, incorrect, specious

sophistical deceptive, fallacious, ill-founded, illogical, illusory, incorrect,

sophistic, specious, subtle *(insidious)*, unsound *(fallacious)*
sophistical excuse evasion
sophisticate denature, evade *(deceive)*, expert, mislead, pervert, prevaricate, veteran
sophisticated elegant, practiced, subtle *(refined)*, veteran
sophistication civilization, experience *(background)*, perversion
sophistry casuistry, fallacy, non sequitur, subterfuge
sophomoric inexperienced
soporiferous narcotic
soporific drug, narcotic, narcotic, pedestrian
sorcery prestidigitation
sordid penurious, poor *(inferior in quality)*
sordidus illiberal, sordid
sore bitter *(penetrating)*, pain, painful, resentful
soreness pain, resentment, umbrage
sorosis sodality
sorriness remorse
sorrow distress *(anguish)*, pain, plaint, remorse, tragedy
sorrow for regret
sorrow over deplore
sorrowful bitter *(reproachful)*, contrite, deplorable, despondent, disconsolate, grave *(solemn)*, lamentable, lugubrious, penitent, pessimistic, remorseful, repentant
sorrowfulness pessimism
sorry contrite, deplorable, ignoble, lamentable, nonsubstantial *(not sturdy)*, paltry, penitent, poor *(inferior in quality)*, remorseful, repentant
sorry plight predicament
sors capital, lottery, principal *(capital sum)*
sort class, classify, codify, distribute, file *(arrange)*, fix *(arrange)*, form *(arrangement)*, kind, manner *(kind)*, organize *(arrange)*, pigeonhole, screen *(select)*, tabulate
sort out cull, diagnose, differentiate, discriminate *(distinguish)*, fix *(arrange)*, part *(separate)*, select
sort systematically fix *(arrange)*
sortable applicable, fit
sortie affray, incursion
sortitio lottery
sottish drunk
sought after popular
soul center *(essence)*, consequence *(significance)*, essence, person, personality, spirit, substance *(essential nature)*
soul-searching contrite
soul-stirring profound *(intense)*
soulless cold-blooded
sound authentic, cogent, communicate, credible, defensible, discriminating *(judicious)*, durable, fiduciary, firm, fixed *(securely placed)*, honest, indomitable, intact, intonation, inviolate, judicious, juridical, justifiable, legitimate *(rightful)*, licit, logical, lucid, meritorious, noise, normal *(sane)*, persuasive, phrase, plausible, positive *(incontestable)*, pragmatic, pronounce *(speak)*, rational, reasonable *(rational)*, reliable, safe, sane, scrupulous, secure *(sound)*, sensible, stable, staunch, strong, thor-

ough, true *(authentic)*, unblemished, undeniable, utter, valid, viable, well-grounded
sound forth proclaim
sound judgment discretion *(quality of being discreet)*, expedience
sound mind competence *(sanity)*
sound moral principle integrity
sound out inquire
sound perception common sense
sound reasoning discretion *(quality of being discreet)*, discrimination *(good judgment)*
sound sense common sense
sound stewardship economy *(frugality)*
sound the alarm alert, caution
sound thinking pragmatism
sound understanding common sense, sanity
sounded oral
sounding resounding
soundless mute, speechless
soundlessness lull, silence
soundmindedness competence *(sanity)*, sanity
soundness certainty, competence *(sanity)*, health, honesty, legitimacy, quality *(excellence)*, sanity, strength, validity, welfare
soundness of body health
soundness of mind competence *(sanity)*
sour aggravate *(annoy)*, bitter *(acrid tasting)*, dyseptic, petulant, severe, spoil *(impair)*, stale
sour-tempered bitter *(reproachful)*, dyseptic, petulant
source authority *(power)*, basis, cause *(reason)*, citation *(attribution)*, connotation
source derivation
source determinant, documentation, embryo, genesis, inception, informant, informer *(a person who provides information)*, onset *(commencement)*, origination, parentage, progenitor, prototype, reason *(basis)*, reference *(citation)*, resource, spy, start
source material derivation, reference *(citation)*
source of danger peril
source of income livelihood
source of perplexity problem
source of risk hazard, peril
soured bitter *(acrid tasting)*, stale
sourish bitter *(acrid tasting)*
souse immerse *(plunge into)*, permeate
souvenir remembrance *(commemoration)*, reminder, token
sovereign autonomous *(self governing)*, dominant, free *(enjoying civil liberty)*, government *(political administration)*, independent, master, national, nonpartisan, omnipotent, paramount, powerful, predominant, superlative
sovereign state nationality
sovereign unit state *(political unit)*
sovereignty bureaucracy, capacity *(authority)*, dominance, dominion *(supreme authority)*, hierarchy *(persons in authority)*, home rule, influence, jurisdiction, polity, predominance, primacy, regime, supremacy
sow diffuse, dissipate *(spread out)*,

distribute, inseminate, plant *(place firmly)*, spread
sow dissension alienate *(estrange)*, disaffect
sow the seeds of cause
space arrange *(methodize)*, atmosphere, coverage *(scope)*, distribute, extent, latitude, margin *(spare amount)*, pause, range, region, scope
space of time duration, phase *(period)*
space saving compact *(dense)*
spacious broad, capacious, open *(unclosed)*
spaciousness capacity *(maximum)*, extent, space
span comprehend *(include)*, connect *(relate)*, duration, encompass *(include)*, extent, gamut, include, life *(period of existence)*, lifetime, magnitude, measure, measurement, period, phase *(period)*, purview, range, scope, space, term *(duration)*
span of years lifetime
spangle embellish
spar bicker, compete, contend *(dispute)*, fight *(battle)*
spare ancillary *(auxiliary)*, balance *(amount in excess)*, bear *(tolerate)*, bestow, condone, conserve, dole, excess, excessive, expendable, fund, insufficient, keep *(shelter)*, needless, nonessential, overage, palliate *(excuse)*, preserve, release, relent, relinquish, remit *(release from penalty)*, residuary, superfluous, supplementary, surplus, sustain *(prolong)*, unnecessary
spare no effort endeavor, persevere
spare no pains endeavor
spared clear *(free from criminal charges)*, free *(relieved from a burden)*, immune
spargere disseminate, spread
sparing conservation, deficient, devoid, economical, economy *(frugality)*, frugal, illiberal, lenient, parsimonious, penurious, placable, provident *(frugal)*, prudent, release, scarce
sparing no pains painstaking
sparing of words brief, inarticulate, laconic, sententious, taciturn
sparing use temperance
spark iota, scintilla
sparkle spirit
sparring belligerency
sparse barren, deficient, infrequent, insufficient, petty, scarce, sporadic
sparseness delinquency *(shortage)*, insignificance, insufficiency, paucity, poverty
sparsity dearth, deficiency, delinquency *(shortage)*, paucity
Spartan draconian
spartan frugal, stoical
spasm outbreak, outburst
spasmodic broken *(interrupted)*, desultory, disjointed, disjunctive *(tending to disjoin)*, intermittent, periodic, sporadic, unpredictable, variable
spat bicker, brawl, contend *(dispute)*
spate plethora
spatium magnitude, space
spatium interiectum interval
spatium temporis term *(duration)*
spatter defame, diffuse, pillory, pollute, stain, sully

spawn create, engender, offspring, proliferate, propagate *(increase)*, reproduce

spe depellere disappoint

speak avow, communicate, convey *(communicate)*, declaim, discourse, enunciate, express, phrase, recite, relate *(tell)*, remark, utter

speak about report *(disclose)*

speak against cross *(disagree with)*, disapprove *(reject)*, gainsay, protest

speak clearly enunciate

speak derisively jeer

speak disparagingly of decry

speak evil defame

speak evil of derogate, malign, smear

speak falsely bear false witness, feign, misrepresent, perjure, prevaricate

speak for plead *(argue a case)*, promote *(organize)*, represent *(substitute)*, uphold

speak formally pronounce *(speak)*

speak highly of recommend

speak ill defame

speak ill of censure, complain *(criticize)*, decry, defame, denigrate, denounce *(condemn)*, derogate, discommend, dishonor *(deprive of honor)*, disparage, malign, pillory, reproach, sully

speak in favor of advocate, justify

speak logically reason *(persuade)*

speak of bespeak, circulate, connote, discuss, mention

speak of slightingly defame

speak on discuss

speak on oath attest

speak one's mind communicate

speak out disclose, manifest

speak publicly declaim

speak rhetorically declaim

speak slightingly jeer, lessen

speak slightingly of decry, derogate, discommend, misprize

speak the truth disclose

speak to address *(talk to)*

speak up for plead *(argue a case)*

speak well of recommend

speak with converse

speaker amicus curiae, chairman, plenipotentiary, spokesman

speaking conversation

speaking by delegated authority acting

speaking for another representation *(acting for others)*

spear penetrate, pierce *(lance)*

special ad hoc, certain *(particular)*, certain *(specific)*, considerable, distinct *(distinguished from others)*, distinctive, exclusive *(singular)*, extraordinary, individual, momentous, nonconforming, notable, noteworthy, outstanding *(prominent)*, particular *(individual)*, particular *(specific)*, peculiar *(distinctive)*, preferential, preferred *(favored)*, rare, remarkable, singular, specific, technical, uncommon, unique, unusual

special ability gift *(flair)*

special attention emphasis

special attraction feature *(special attraction)*

special case exception *(exclusion)*

special characteristic specialty *(distinctive mark)*

special concern emphasis

special dispensation variance *(exemption)*

special endowment gift *(flair)*

special favor distinction *(reputation)*

special interest group lobby

special interests lobby

special intonation emphasis

special item specialty *(distinctive mark)*

special line of work specialty *(special aptitude)*

special marking distinction *(difference)*

special matter specialty *(distinctive mark)*

special occurrence phenomenon *(unusual occurrence)*

special point detail, particular, particularity, specialty *(distinctive mark)*, specification, technicality

special points circumstances

special price discount

special privilege dispensation *(exception)*, exemption, immunity, license

special privileges patronage *(support)*

special project specialty *(special aptitude)*

special right prerogative

special significance emphasis

special skill specialty *(special aptitude)*

special study specialty *(special aptitude)*

specialist expert, mastermind, practitioner, professional

speciality characteristic, identity *(individuality)*, technicality

specialization calling, pursuit *(occupation)*, specialty *(special aptitude)*

specialize practice *(engage in)*, restrict, select, study

specialize in occupy *(engage)*, practice *(engage in)*

specialized professional *(trained)*, technical

specialized administrative unit bureau

specialized language jargon *(technical language)*

specialized terminology jargon *(technical language)*

specialized unit bureau

specialized vocabulary jargon *(technical language)*

specializer expert, specialist

specially particularly

specially prepared express

specially provided for privileged

specially selected premium, prime *(most valuable)*

specially trained person expert

specialness speciality

specialties commodities

specialty bailiwick, business *(occupation)*, caliber *(mental capacity)*, calling, capacity *(sphere)*, career, characteristic, department, employment, feature *(special attraction)*, identity *(individuality)*, merchandise, occupation *(vocation)*, penchant, position *(business status)*, practice *(professional business)*, profession *(vocation)*, province, pursuit *(occupation)*, trade *(occupation)*, trait, work *(employment)*

specie cash, currency, money

species denomination, kind, manner *(kind)*

species apparent *(perceptible)*, appearance *(look)*, color *(complexion)*, pretext, semblance

species of proof evidence

specific actual, certain *(particular)*, concrete, descriptive, detailed, exact, explicit, express, particular *(individual)*, particular, personal *(individual)*, point *(item)*, precise, regional, said, special, technical, technicality

specific aptness penchant

specific confinement limitation

specific curtailment limitation

specific moment point *(period of time)*

specific quality characteristic, identity *(individuality)*, particularity, penchant, property *(distinctive attribute)*, specialty *(distinctive mark)*

specifically particularly

specification assignment *(designation)*, caption, clarification, classification, clause, condition *(contingent provision)*, delineation, description, designation *(naming)*, detail, diagnosis, item, limitation, particular, prerequisite, provision *(clause)*, qualification *(condition)*, report *(detailed account)*, requirement, reservation *(condition)*, selection *(choice)*, stipulation, technicality, term *(provision)*, ultimatum

specification of details bill *(formal declaration)*

specifications pattern

specificity identity *(individuality)*

specificness specialty *(distinctive mark)*

specifics data, information *(facts)*

specified aforesaid, certain *(particular)*, certain *(specific)*, conditional, express, stated

specified income payable for life annuity, pension

specified period of time date

specify allocate, allot, amplify, annunciate, assign *(designate)*, call *(title)*, characterize, cite *(state)*, classify, communicate, convey *(communicate)*, define, delineate, denominate, depict, describe, designate, detail *(particularize)*, diagnose, disabuse, distinguish, enumerate, explain, identify, index *(relate)*, interject, itemize, label, mention, nominate, pinpoint, portray, postulate, qualify *(condition)*, quote, report *(disclose)*, select, signify *(inform)*, stipulate

specify in greater detail amplify

specify limits border *(bound)*

specify the particulars of delineate

specify the peculiarities of characterize

specimen case *(example)*, entity, example, illustration, instance, model, representative *(example)*

specimen paragon, pattern, sample

speciosus specious

specious deceptive, delusive, ostensible, purported, sophistic, untenable

specious argument non sequitur

specious reasoning non sequitur, sophistry

speciously attractive meretricious

speckled marred

spectacle phenomenon *(manifestation)*, phenomenon *(unusual occurrence)*, scene, vision *(dream)*
spectacular conspicuous
spectare aspect, observe *(watch)*, survey *(examine)*, witness *(have direct knowledge of)*
spectator bystander, eyewitness
spectator et testis eyewitness
specter phantom, reflection *(image)*, spirit, vision *(dream)*
spectral immaterial, insubstantial
speculari spy
speculate bet, gamble, guess, invest *(fund)*, muse, opine, parlay *(bet)*, ponder, postulate, presume, presuppose, prognosticate, reflect *(ponder)*, surmise, suspect *(think)*
speculate with endanger
speculation conjecture, consideration *(contemplation)*, contemplation, estimate *(idea)*, estimation *(calculation)*, hypothesis, inference, investment, opinion *(belief)*, postulate, presumption, prospect *(outlook)*, rationale, reflection *(thought)*, risk, sense *(feeling)*, supposition, suspicion *(uncertainty)*, theory, thesis, venture
speculatist bettor
speculative cogitative, controversial, debatable, deliberate, disputable, doubtful, dubious, hypothetical, indeterminate, inquisitive, insecure, moot, pensive, presumptive, putative, tentative, theoretical, undecided, unpredictable, unsettled, unsound *(fallacious)*
speculator bettor
speculator spy
speculatory presumptive, speculative, theoretical
speech declamation, discourse, language, parlance, peroration, phraseology, remark
speech-making rhetoric *(skilled speech)*
speechification declamation
speechless mute, taciturn
speechlessness silence
speechmaker spokesman
speed dispatch *(promptness)*, dispatch *(send off)*, expedite, haste, help, precipitate *(hasten)*, promote *(organize)*, race
speed along dispatch *(send off)*, hasten
speed on its way dispatch *(send off)*
speed track causeway
speed up expedite, facilitate, precipitate *(hasten)*
speeded adjudication accelerated judgment
speedily instantly
speediness dispatch *(promptness)*
speedup acceleration
speedway causeway
speedy brief, cursory, expeditious, immediate *(at once)*, instant, instantaneous, perfunctory, precipitate, prompt, rapid, ready *(prepared)*, summary
speedy completion dispatch *(promptness)*
speedy disposition dispatch *(promptness)*
speedy transaction dispatch *(promptness)*
spell duration, hiatus, interval, period, phase *(period)*, prognosticate, re-

cess, respite *(interval of rest)*, term *(duration)*
spell danger caution
spell out clarify, comment, define, describe, elucidate, enlighten, explain, explicate, exposit, expound
spellbind coax
spellbinding eloquent
spend bestow, consume, defray, deplete, disburse *(pay out)*, dissipate *(expend foolishly)*, exert, exhaust *(deplete)*, expend *(consume)*, expend *(disburse)*, pay
spend lavishly dissipate *(expend foolishly)*
spend more than one has overdraw
spend one's time in occupy *(engage)*
spend wastefully dissipate *(expend foolishly)*
spendable disposable
spending outlay, payment *(act of paying)*
spendings disbursement *(funds paid out)*, expenditure, overhead
spendthrift improvident, prodigal, profligate *(extravagant)*, profuse
spent irredeemable, irretrievable, powerless
sperare expect *(anticipate)*
spernere disdain
spes chance *(possibility)*, expectation
sphaera sphere
sphere ambit, area *(province)*, bailiwick, circuit, coverage *(scope)*, department, district, jurisdiction, position *(business status)*, province, pursuit *(occupation)*, purview, range, realm, region, scene, scope, zone
sphere of activity calling
sphere of occupation appointment *(position)*
spheroid sphere
sphinx-like mysterious
sphinxian mysterious
spice spirit
spicy obscene, salacious, suggestive *(risqué)*
spike penetrate, pierce *(lance)*
spill outflow, outpour
spill over inundate
spin out prolong
spineless irresolute, obsequious, powerless
spiral sinuous
spiral inflation boom *(prosperity)*
spiriferous circuitous
spirit ardor, complexion, connotation, content *(meaning)*, disposition *(inclination)*, emotion, frame *(mood)*, gist *(substance)*, gravamen, life *(vitality)*, motivate, phantom, prowess *(bravery)*, specter, tenor
spirit away abduct, carry away, hold up *(rob)*, kidnap, purloin
spirit of the law equity *(justice)*
spirited alert *(agile)*, eager, expeditious, fervent, trenchant, unrestrained *(not repressed)*, volatile
spiritedness life *(vitality)*
spiriting away abduction
spiritless caitiff, disconsolate, grave *(solemn)*, inactive, inexpressive, insensible, insipid, lifeless *(dull)*, nonchalant, otiose, pedestrian, phlegmatic, prosaic, recreant, torpid
spiritlessness disinterest *(lack of in-*

terest)
spirits alcohol
spiritual incorporeal, intangible, sacrosanct, solemn
spiritual upbuilding edification
spirituality immateriality
spiritualness immateriality
spit pierce *(lance)*
spite antagonize, cruelty, disoblige, harass, harrow, ill will, malice, mistreat, plague, rancor, resentment
spiteful bilious, bitter *(reproachful)*, contemptuous, cruel, dyseptic, harmful, hostile, invidious, malevolent, malicious, malignant, mordacious, outrageous, pejorative, perverse, petulant, resentful, scathing, sinister, vicious, vindictive, virulent
spitefulness ill will, malice, rancor, spite
splash pretense *(ostentation)*, sully
splay deploy, radiate, spread
spleen resentment, umbrage
spleenful bilious, fractious, malevolent, malignant, perverse, petulant
spleeny fractious, perverse
splendid elegant, illustrious, meritorious, premium, prime *(most valuable)*, proud *(self-respecting)*, sterling
splendidus illustrious
splendor prestige
splendorous illustrious
splenetic bitter *(reproachful)*, fractious, froward, perverse, petulant, querulous, resentful, restive
splenetical petulant
splice combine *(join together)*, connection *(fastening)*, intertwine, join *(bring together)*
spliced conjoint
splinter break *(fracture)*, rend, separate, sever, split
splinter party faction
splintered broken *(fractured)*
split alienation *(estrangement)*, apportion, bifurcate, break *(separate)*, controversy *(argument)*, cross *(intersect)*, detach, dichotomize, dichotomy, disaccord, disaccord, disagree, disassociation, discord, discrepancy, disjoint, divide *(separate)*, division *(act of dividing)*, divisive, estrangement, feud, force *(break)*, isolate, mete, part *(separate)*, partial *(part)*, rend, rift *(disagreement)*, rift *(gap)*, schism, separate, separate, separation, sever, sort, subdivide, variance *(disagreement)*
split again reapportion
split hairs bicker, pettifog
split off break *(separate)*
split up disintegrate, disperse *(scatter)*, disrupt, dissolve *(separate)*, dissolve *(terminate)*, divorce, parcel, partition, prorate, separate
splitting division *(act of dividing)*
splotch defacement, stain
splurge pretense *(ostentation)*, spend
spoil adulterate, corrupt, damage, decay, deface, depreciate, deteriorate, disable, eviscerate, foil, frustrate, harm, hold up *(rob)*, infect, loot, misemploy, mismanage, pervert, pillage, pirate *(take by violence)*, pollute, prejudice *(injure)*, prey, prize, stain, sully, taint *(contaminate)*, thwart, vitiate

spoil excessively overindulge

spoil the look of deface

spoilage decrement, dissolution (disintegration)

spoilate pirate (take by violence)

spoiled decadent, marred, stale, tainted (contaminated)

spoiler burglar, vandal

spoiling burglary, damage, decadent

spoils plunder, stake (award)

spoken nuncupative, oral, verbal

spoken expression language

spoken in confidence confidential

spoken language speech

spoken out loud oral

spoken word language, parlance, speech

spokesman advocate (counselor), advocate (espouser), go-between, informer (a person who provides information), interagent, liaison, plenipotentiary, procurator, proponent, representative (proxy)

spokesperson liaison, medium, plenipotentiary

spokeswoman advocate (counselor), advocate (espouser)

spolia spoils

spoliare spoil (pillage)

spoliate despoil, harry (plunder), loot, pillage, plunder, prey, spoil (pillage)

spoliatio robbery

spoliation depredation, deterioration, dissolution (disintegration), havoc, pillage, plunder, rape

spoliatory predatory

sponge parasite

spongy resilient

sponsio guarantee, recognizance

sponsor avouch (guarantee), backer, bestow, capitalize (provide capital), creditor, espouse, finance, guarantee, guardian, invest (fund), nurture, partisan, patron (influential supporter), promote (organize), promoter, proponent, protect, surety (guarantor), underwrite

sponsor again refinance

sponsorship accommodation (backing), advocacy, aid (help), appropriation (donation), auspices, behalf, favor (sanction), goodwill, guidance, indorsement, patronage (support), promotion (encouragement)

spontaneity impulse

spontaneous elective (voluntary), fortuitous, impulsive (rash), informal, ingenuous, prompt, unaffected (sincere), unintentional, unpremeditated

spontaneous inclination impulse

spontaneus spontaneous

sporadic broken (interrupted), infrequent, intermittent, periodic

sporadical sporadic

sport bet, contest (competition), flaunt, ridicule

sport with dupe

sporting fair (just)

sporting event contest (competition)

sportive jocular

sportsmanlike fair (just)

spot deface, defacement, detect, discern (detect with the senses), locality, location, notice (observe), onus (stigma), part (place), position (situation), quagmire, region, seat, stain, standpoint, stigma, sully, tarnish, witness (have direct knowledge of)

spotless absolute (ideal), clean, inviolate, irreprehensible, moral, pure, unblemished, unimpeachable

spotlight publicity

spotted blemished, marred

spotting detection

spotty sporadic

spousal marriage (wedlock), matrimony

spouse consort

spout exude, outflow, outlet, outpour, recite

sprawl expand, spread

spray barrage, discharge (shot)

spread accumulate (enlarge), augmentation, boom (increase), cast (throw), circulate, circulation, coverage (scope), deploy, diffuse, disburse (distribute), dispel, disperse (disseminate), dissipate (spread out), dissolve (disperse), distribute, division (act of dividing), enlarge, expand, growth (increase), herald, increase, inflate, inflated (enlarged), inflation (increase), issue (publish), magnify, pervade, post, proliferate, promulgate, publish, radiate, scope, utter

spread a report circulate, disseminate

spread about diffuse

spread abroad circulate, diffuse, disperse (disseminate), divulge, post, proclaim, promulgate, propagate (spread), public (known)

spread an evil report malign

spread around diffuse

spread far and wide diffuse, disseminate

spread out compound, disperse (disseminate), expand, far reaching, open (unclosed), prolix

spread out in area extend (enlarge)

spread out in battle formation deploy

spread over dissipate (spread out), expand, overlap

spread through permeate, pervade

spread too far overextend

spread too thin overextend

spread widely diffuse, disperse (scatter)

spread-out extensive

spreading boom (increase), broad, circulation, contagious, extension (expansion), extensive, rampant

spreading abroad divulgation

spree carouse

sprightliness life (vitality)

sprightly alert (agile), jocular, resilient, volatile

spring accrue (arise), derivation, ensue, fund, origination, proceed (go forward), reason (basis), redound, result, source, stem (originate)

spring forth arise (originate)

spring from emanate, evolve

spring up arise (originate), issue (send forth), pullulate, supervene

spring upon attack

springhead derivation, source

springy resilient

sprinkle dissipate (spread out), distribute, intersperse, spread

sprinkling minimum

sprint race

sprite phantom, specter

sprout germinate, outgrowth, proliferate, pullulate, stem (originate)

sprout from redound

sprouting boom (increase), growth (evolution)

spruce up embellish

spry alert (agile)

spun out prolix

spunk resolution (decision)

spunkless languid, phlegmatic

spur abet, agitate (activate), bait (harass), catalyst, cause (reason), exhort, hasten, impel, impetus, incentive, motivate, precipitate (hasten), prevail upon, provocation, provoke, spirit, stimulate, stimulus, urge

spur of necessity compulsion (coercion), force (compulsion)

spur on incite, prompt

spurious artificial, assumed (feigned), bogus, deceptive, delusive, dishonest, disingenuous, disreputable, erroneous, false (not genuine), fictitious, fraudulent, imitation, lying, mendacious, meretricious, specious, synthetic, unfounded, untrue

spurious issue bastard

spuriousness bad faith, false pretense

spurn bar (exclude), condescend (patronize), contemn, decline (reject), decry, demonstrate (protest), disallow, disapprove (reject), disavow, disclaim, discommend, discount (disbelieve), disdain, disoblige, disown (refuse to acknowledge), disregard, disrespect, dissent (withhold assent), eliminate (exclude), exclude, fight (counteract), flout, forswear, humiliate, mock (deride), rebuff, rebuff, refuse, reject, renounce, repel (drive back), repudiate, repulse, set aside (annul), shun

spurning denial, disdain, negative, rejection, renunciation

spurt acceleration, dispatch (promptness), emit, outburst, outflow, outpour, race

spy conspirator, discern (detect with the senses), informant, observe (watch), recognize (perceive)

spy against subvert

spy upon spy

spying espionage

squabble affray, altercation, bicker, brawl, brawl, confrontation (altercation), contend (dispute), contest (dispute), controversy (argument), disaccord, disaccord, embroilment, fight (argument), fight (battle), fracas, strife

squad assemblage, band

squalid destitute, repulsive, sordid

squall fracas

squander consume, lose (be deprived of), misemploy, mishandle (mismanage), overdraw

squandered irredeemable, lost (taken away)

squandering consumption, improvident, misapplication, prodigal, profligate (extravagant), profuse, waste

square close (enclosed area), compensate (counterbalance), fair (just), market place, parcel, pay, refund, regulate (adjust), rightful, upright

square accounts discharge (pay a

debt), pay, repay
square measure dimension
square with comport *(agree with)*
squash depress, extinguish, kill *(defeat)*, obliterate, repress, stifle
squat inhabit, lodge *(reside)*, reside, rest *(be supported by)*, usurp
squatter habitant
squeal divulge
squealer informer *(one providing criminal information)*
squeamish disinclined, reluctant
squeamishness reluctance
squeeze constrain *(compel)*, constrict *(compress)*, exact, impact
squeeze out distill
squeeze together consolidate *(strengthen)*
squeezed together compact *(dense)*
squelch abolish, counteract, defeat, extinguish, quash, refute, stifle, strangle
squib parody, ridicule
squirt emit
stab enter *(penetrate)*, lancinate, penetrate, pierce *(lance)*
stabbing bitter *(penetrating)*
stabile stable
stabilire establish *(entrench)*, instate
stabilis constant, constant, durable, firm, immovable, immutable, permanent, solid *(sound)*, stable, steadfast
stabilitate establish *(entrench)*
stability certainty, composure, constant, equipoise, indestructibility, prowess *(bravery)*, responsibility *(conscience)*, security *(safety)*, uniformity
stabilization balance *(equality)*
stabilize adjust *(regulate)*, compensate *(counterbalance)*, establish *(entrench)*, fix *(make firm)*, settle
stable certain *(fixed)*, constant, demonstrable, dependable, durable, firm, fixed *(securely placed)*, indelible, indomitable, infallible, irrevocable, permanent, perpetual, rational, regular *(orderly)*, reliable, secure *(free from danger)*, secure *(sound)*, solid *(sound)*, static, staunch, steadfast, strong, unalterable, unyielding
stable equilibrium balance *(equality)*
stable state status quo
stabulare stall
stack assemblage, bulk, hoard, load, store *(depository)*
staff committee, cudgel, employ *(engage services)*, hire, mainstay, personnel, unit *(department)*
staff members staff
staff person employee
staff with engage *(hire)*
stage degree *(station)*, direct *(supervise)*, duration, period, phase *(period)*, point *(period of time)*, portray, scene, term *(duration)*
stage of advancement degree *(station)*
stage of life age
stage setting scene
stagecraft histrionics
stagger overcome *(overwhelm)*, vacillate
staggering incredible, ineffable, portentous *(eliciting amazement)*, unbelievable
staggering belief ludicrous

stagnans stagnant
stagnant inactive, indolent, languid, lifeless *(dull)*, static, torpid
stagnate languish
stagnating barren, otiose, stagnant
stagnation desuetude, inaction, inertia, languor
stagy histrionic
staid earnest, phlegmatic, solemn
stain attaint, brand, brand *(stigmatize)*, damage, debase, deface, defacement, demean *(make lower)*, denigrate, depreciate, derogate, discredit, discredit, disgrace, disgrace, dishonor *(shame)*, dishonor *(deprive of honor)*, disparage, disrepute, flaw, humiliate, ignominy, infamy, infect, onus *(stigma)*, opprobrium, pervert, pillory, pollute, scandal, shame, smear, stigma, sully, tarnish
stain one's reputation malign
stain the character of defame
stained blemished, marred, tainted *(contaminated)*
stainless absolute *(ideal)*, blameless, clean, honest, infallible, inviolate, irreprehensible, meritorious, pure, unblemished, unimpeachable
stainlessness honesty
stake bet, binder, bond *(secure a debt)*, claim *(right)*, compromise *(endanger)*, deposit, dominion *(absolute ownership)*, downpayment, endanger, equity *(share of ownership)*, gamble, guarantee, guaranty, holding *(property owned)*, interest *(ownership)*, jeopardize, lien, loan, parlay *(bet)*, pawn, pledge *(security)*, pledge *(deposit)*, right *(entitlement)*, risk, speculate *(chance)*, title *(right)*
stake money handsel, pledge *(security)*
stake one's credit promise *(vow)*
stake out border *(bound)*, demarcate
stale dilapidated, languid, lifeless *(dull)*, mundane, obsolete, old, ordinary, outdated, outmoded, pedestrian, prosaic, repetitious, trite, usual
stale comment platitude
stalemate abeyance, check *(restrain)*, deadlock, draw *(tie)*, halt, impasse, impede, stall
staleness disuse
stalk approach, hunt, perambulate, pursuit *(chase)*
stall arrest *(stop)*, balk, block, chamber *(compartment)*, clog, constrict *(inhibit)*, continue *(adjourn)*, debar, defer *(put off)*, delay, delay, detain *(restrain)*, disadvantage, extension *(postponement)*, hold up *(delay)*, impasse, inconvenience, obstruct, pause, postpone, procrastinate, remit *(relax)*, stand *(witness' place in court)*, stem *(check)*, stop, store *(business)*, suspend
stall for time delay
stalling filibuster
stalwart cohort, colleague, heroic, indomitable, pertinacious, powerful, purposeful, sedulous, spartan, stable, staunch, strong, undaunted
stalwartness strength
stamina force *(strength)*, health, longanimity, prowess *(bravery)*, puissance, sinew, strength, tenacity, tolerance

stamp brand, brand *(mark)*, embed, indicant, indicator, label, label, seal *(solemnize)*, speciality, specialty *(distinctive mark)*, tenor, validate
stamp incorrectly mislabel
stamp of approval confirmation, indorsement, ratification, sanction *(permission)*
stamp out eliminate *(eradicate)*, eradicate, extirpate, obliterate
stamped monetary
stamped with approval permissible, popular
stampede panic
stance manner *(behavior)*, opinion *(belief)*
stanch cease, firm, incorruptible, indomitable, infallible, occlude, pertinacious, reliable, resolute, solid *(sound)*, stable, stem *(check)*, stop, true *(loyal)*, unyielding
stanchly faithfully
stanchness adhesion *(loyalty)*, fidelity, loyalty
stand bear *(tolerate)*, desist, endure *(last)*, endure *(suffer)*, halt, lie *(be sustainable)*, opine, opinion *(belief)*, outlook, remain *(stay)*, resist *(withstand)*, resistance, stay *(rest)*, thesis, tolerate
stand against counter, counteract, disapprove *(reject)*, fight *(counteract)*, oppugn
stand aghast fear
stand aloof eschew
stand apart deviate
stand around loiter
stand aside abandon *(withdraw)*, demit, quit *(discontinue)*, resign, retire *(conclude a career)*
stand behind espouse, preserve, sanction, side, sponsor, subsidize
stand between intercede, part *(separate)*
stand by adhere *(maintain loyalty)*, adjoin, assist, contribute *(assist)*, countenance, help, indorse, keep *(fulfill)*, maintain *(sustain)*, recommend, side, subsidize, uphold
stand clear eschew
stand down demit
stand facing confront *(encounter)*
stand fast endure *(last)*, hold out *(resist)*, persevere, remain *(continue)*, remain *(stay)*, resist *(withstand)*, subsist, withstand
stand firm adhere *(persist)*, bear *(adduce)*, claim *(maintain)*, confront *(oppose)*, hold out *(resist)*, insist, last, maintain *(sustain)*, persevere, remain *(continue)*, resist *(withstand)*, withstand
stand firm against oppose
stand for connote, denote, exemplify, indicate, replace, represent *(portray)*, signify *(denote)*
stand guard patrol, police
stand in replacement
stand in awe fear
stand in for displace *(replace)*
stand in need of require *(need)*
stand in relation concern *(involve)*
stand in relation to pertain
stand in stead of supersede
stand in the place of represent *(substitute)*
stand in the way balk, bar *(hinder)*, block, check *(restrain)*, delay, estop,

hinder, hold up (delay), impede, inconvenience, interpose, obstruct
stand in the way of clog
stand off deadlock
stand one's ground maintain (sustain)
stand opposite confront (encounter)
stand out project (extend beyond)
stand out in opposition contrast
stand over discipline (control), moderate (preside over)
stand sentinel patrol, police
stand still halt, pause, rest (cease from action)
stand the cost bear the expense, defray
stand the cost of disburse (pay out)
stand the hazard bet
stand the strain bear (tolerate)
stand the test pass (satisfy requirements)
stand together conform, cooperate
stand up against challenge, defy
stand up for defend, espouse, justify, plead (argue a case), support (justify), uphold
stand up to disown (deny the validity), fight (battle), fight (counteract), oppugn, resist (withstand), withstand
stand-by colleague
stand-in alter ego, cover (substitute), substitute, surrogate
standard broad, bylaw, canon, code, constant, conventional, cornerstone, criterion, customary, decorum, designation (symbol), epitome, example, exemplar, familiar (customary), general, habitual, household (familiar), law, mediocre, model, mundane, norm, normal (regular), ordinary, paradigm, paragon, pattern, popular, precedent, prevalent, principle (axiom), pro forma, prototype, rate, regular (conventional), repeated, representative, routine, rule (guide), stare decisis, typical, uniform, usual
standard for comparison exemplar, paragon
standard for imitation exemplar
standard letter form (document)
standard of comparison criterion, example, sample
standard of criticism criterion, pattern
standard of judgment criterion, pattern
standard of perfection exemplar
standard of value money
standard practice constant
standard procedure avenue (means of attainment), constant, modus operandi
standardization uniformity
standardization of laws codification
standardize adapt, adjust (regulate), conform, orchestrate, organize (arrange), regulate (adjust)
standardized boiler plate, industrial, normal (regular), systematic, typical
standardness mediocrity
standards conscience, ethics
standards of conduct ethics
standards of professional behavior ethics
standing caliber (quality), case (set of circumstances), character (reputation), class, credit (recognition), degree (sta-

tion), eminence, extant, honor (good reputation), lasting, posture (situation), prestige, quality (excellence), quality (grade), reputation, situation, stagnant, state (condition), static, status
standing apart distinct (distinguished from others)
standing by ready (prepared)
standing committee commission (agency)
standing in the place of acting
standing order decree, law, rule (guide), rule (legal dictate)
standing out conspicuous, evident, manifest, noteworthy, obvious, patent, salient
standing out clearly evident
standoff draw (tie)
standoffish unapproachable
standpoint conviction (persuasion), outlook, perspective, position (point of view), posture (attitude), side, stand (position)
standstill cessation (interlude), check (bar), cloture, deadlock, desuetude, halt, hiatus, impasse, interruption, lull, moratorium, pause, remission
staple item, stock in trade
staples commodities, goods, merchandise, provision (something provided)
star feature (special attraction), master
starched formal, punctilious, rigid
starchy rigid
stare abide, continue (prolong)
stare scrutinize
staring stark
stark naked (lacking embellishment), palpable, severe, unmitigated
starlike stellar
starring outstanding (prominent)
starry stellar
start arise (originate), cause, commence, conceive (invent), create, embark, embryo, establish (launch), generate, genesis, impel, impetus, inception, incite, initiate, launch (initiate), maintain (commence), nascency, onset (commencement), originate, origination, outset, overt act, postulate, preface, prelude, stem (originate), threshold (commencement), undertake, unveil
start a corporation incorporate (form a corporation)
start a fight attack
start a lawsuit litigate
start a war attack
start afresh resume
start again relapse, renew (begin again), resume
start an action complain (charge), litigate
start forward again resume
start fresh relapse
start out arise (originate), depart, embark
start over reopen
start up induct
starting elementary, incipient, initial, nascency, original (initial), preliminary, preparatory, prime (original), rudimentary
starting before retroactive
starting point base (foundation), derivation, embryo, inception, onset (commencement), origin (source), origina-

tion, outset, postulate
startle disconcert, disturb, frighten, menace, upset
startler bombshell
startling lurid, peculiar (curious), portentous (eliciting amazement), prodigious (amazing), unanticipated, uncommon, unexpected, unforeseeable, unusual
starvation poverty, privation
starved deficient, poor (underprivileged)
stash deposit (place)
state acknowledge (declare), adduce, affirm (claim), allege, annunciate, aspect, assert, avouch (avow), avow, caliber (quality), case (set of circumstances), claim (maintain), comment, contend (maintain), converse, convey (communicate), declare, disabuse, enunciate, exposit, express, inform (notify), interject, issue (publish), mention, notify, observe (remark), phase (period), phrase, plead (allege in a legal action), plight, polity, pose (propound), posit, position (situation), posture (situation), predicament, proclaim, profess (avow), pronounce (speak), public (affecting people), publish, purport, quagmire, recite, recount, relate (tell), remark, remind, report (disclose), signify (inform), situation, speak, status, stipulate, swear, testify, utter, verify (swear)
state a fact testify
state a grievance complain (charge)
state a truth testify
state affairs politics
state again reiterate
state an untruth misrepresent
state as fact bear (adduce)
state as true allege, assert, avouch (avow), avow
state authoritatively command
state by items itemize
state by way of objection object
state directly express
state emphatically certify (attest), contend (maintain), plead (allege in a legal action), speak
state falsely misrepresent
state fully expound
state highway causeway
state hospital asylum (hospital)
state in detail expound, specify
state in nonexplicit terms imply
state incorrectly misstate
state institution asylum (hospital)
state management bureaucracy, government (administration)
state managers government (political administration)
state misleadingly misstate
state occasion ceremony
state of a married woman coverture
state of affairs case (set of circumstances), circumstances, plight, posture (situation)
state of anxiety fear
state of being condition (state)
state of being different difference
state of being equal parity
state of being public common knowledge
state of being unused desuetude
state of disorder disturbance
state of doubt quandary

state of equilibrium balance *(equality)*
state of excitability ardor
state of excitement affection
state of feeling frame *(mood)*
state of health health
state of inaction deadlock, impasse
state of indebtedness arrears, cloud *(incumbrance)*, mortgage
state of indecision deadlock
state of inertia deadlock
state of matrimony cohabitation *(married state)*, coverture
state of mind frame *(mood)*
state of neutralization deadlock
state of no progress impasse
state of not being satisfied dissatisfaction
state of order array *(order)*, system
state of refinement civilization
state of siege belligerency
state of suspense doubt *(indecision)*
state of terror panic
state of violence shambles
state of war belligerency
state on oath bear *(adduce)*
state one's case plead *(argue a case)*, speak
state one's terms dicker
state opposition demonstrate *(protest)*, object
state positively affirm *(claim)*
state precisely specify
state servant caretaker *(one fulfilling the function of office)*
state something in detail elaborate
state systematically formulate
state the meaning of define
state the meaning precisely define
state under oath swear
state with conviction affirm *(claim)*, argue, avouch *(avow)*, avow, certify *(attest)*, express, speak
state's attorney district attorney, prosecution *(government agency)*, prosecutor
statecraft government *(administration)*
stated alleged, assumed *(inferred)*, certain *(positive)*, certain *(specific)*, convincing, definite, nuncupative, verbal
stated as a premise theoretical
stated authoritatively positive *(prescribed)*
stated in a writing in writing
stated in writing in writing
stated maintenance pension
stated term condition *(contingent provision)*
stated terms contract
statehood nationality
stateliness solemnity
stately elegant, proud *(self-respecting)*, solemn
statement account *(evaluation)*, acknowledgment *(avowal)*, admission *(disclosure)*, affidavit, affirmation, allegation, amount *(sum)*, assertion, attestation, avowal, bill *(invoice)*, budget, caption, census, certification *(attested copy)*, claim *(assertion)*, comment, confession, declaration, dictum, disclosure *(something disclosed)*, dispatch *(message)*, dun, expression *(comment)*, invoice *(bill)*, issuance, ledger, mention *(reference)*, note *(brief comment)*, notice

(announcement), notification, observation, postulate, proclamation, profession *(declaration)*, pronouncement, prospectus, publication *(disclosure)*, recital, remark, rendition *(explication)*, report *(detailed account)*, resolution *(formal statement)*, speech, suggestion, testimony, title *(division)*
statement alleged in defense plea
statement alleged in justification plea
statement by way of illustration dictum
statement of a cause of action count
statement of account budget, invoice *(bill)*
statement of belief principle *(axiom)*
statement of claim demand
statement of debits and credits account *(evaluation)*
statement of defense argument *(pleading)*, justification, plea, pleading
statement of facts averment, avouchment, bill *(formal declaration)*, declaration, testimony
statement of general truth maxim
statement of indebtedness bill *(invoice)*
statement of meaning definition
statement of obligations invoice *(bill)*
statement of particulars specification
statement of pecuniary transactions account *(evaluation)*
statement of position principle *(axiom)*
statement of the case brief
statement of the costs estimate *(approximate cost)*
statement of the plaintiff's cause complaint
statement offered in proof argument *(pleading)*
statement on oath affirmance *(legal affirmation)*, affirmation, averment, avowal, deposition, pledge *(binding promise)*
statement particularizing debts due invoice *(bill)*
statement recorded in a book entry *(record)*
statement tending to prove a point argument *(pleading)*
statement under oath affidavit, deposition
statement which answers the charges plea
statement which confirms information on an affidavit jurat
statements on behalf of the defense plea
statements that describe delineation
statemongers government *(political administration)*
stateroom chamber *(compartment)*
statesman politician
statesmanship discretion *(quality of being discreet)*, government *(administration)*, politics
statesmen government *(political administration)*
static certain *(fixed)*, dormant, immutable, inactive, permanent, rigid, stagnant, torpid

static condition status quo
statical static
statim instantly
station appointment *(position)*, base *(place)*, building *(structure)*, caliber *(quality)*, character *(reputation)*, class, condition *(state)*, department, locality, locate, location, lodge *(house)*, lodge *(reside)*, office, plant *(place firmly)*, plight, position *(business status)*, position *(situation)*, post, posture *(situation)*, prestige, reputation, seat, situation, stand *(witness' place in court)*, standpoint, state *(condition)*, status, title *(position)*, venue
stationary firm, permanent, stable, stagnant, standing, static, steadfast
stationed situated
statistic computation, poll *(canvass)*
statistical inquiry census, investigation
statistician accountant, actuary
statistics census, information *(facts)*
statuere constitute *(establish)*, determine, establish *(launch)*, fix *(settle)*, instate, resolve *(decide)*
stature capacity *(authority)*, elevation, magnitude
status caliber *(quality)*, case *(set of circumstances)*, character *(reputation)*, class, credit *(recognition)*, degree *(station)*, honor *(good reputation)*, precedence, prestige, quality *(excellence)*, rating, reputation, situation, title *(position)*
status condition *(state)*, phase *(aspect)*, position *(situation)*, posture *(situation)*, state *(condition)*
statutable law-abiding, lawful, legitimate *(rightful)*, licit
statute act *(enactment)*, authority *(documentation)*, canon, code, codification, constitution, edict, enactment, law, measure, ordinance, precept, prescription *(directive)*, regulation *(rule)*, rubric *(authoritative rule)*, rule *(legal dictate)*
statute book code, codification, pandect *(code of laws)*
statute law code, codification
statutes legislation *(enactments)*
statutory due *(regular)*, forensic, law-abiding, lawful, legal, legislative, legitimate *(rightful)*, licit, rightful, valid
statutory cogency force *(legal efficacy)*
statutory law enactment
staunch constrict *(inhibit)*, dependable, faithful *(loyal)*, loyal, purposeful, steadfast, strong
staunch belief conviction *(persuasion)*, faith
staunch loyalty faith
staunchness constant
stave in break *(fracture)*
stave off avert, contain *(restrain)*, defer *(put off)*, deter, dissuade, forestall, hold up *(delay)*, parry, postpone, prevent, procrastinate, repel *(drive back)*, thwart, withstand
stay abeyance, adjournment, arrest *(stop)*, balk, ban, bar *(hinder)*, barrier, block, cease, cessation *(interlude)*, clog, cloture, cohere *(adhere)*, constrict *(inhibit)*, continuance, continue *(adjourn)*,

curb, defer *(put off)*, delay, delay, desist, detain *(restrain)*, dwell *(reside)*, encumbrance, endure *(last)*, estop, exist, extension *(postponement)*, forestall, halt, halt, impede, inhabit, inhabitation *(act of dwelling in)*, keep *(continue)*, keep *(restrain)*, last, lodge *(reside)*, lull, mainstay, obstruct, occupy *(take possession)*, pause, pause, persevere, persist, postpone, preclude, prevent, prohibit, prohibition, remain *(continue)*, remission, repress, reprieve, reside, resist *(withstand)*, respite *(interval of rest)*, rest *(cease from action)*, restraint, stem *(check)*, stop, subsist, suspend, toll *(stop)*, uphold, withstand

stay alive exist, subsist

stay away shirk

stay away from shun

stay incognito prowl

stay of execution reprieve, respite *(reprieve)*

stay on continue *(persevere)*, last

stay order injunction

stay together cohabit, consolidate *(unite)*

stayed arrested *(checked)*

staying durable, infallible, lasting, live *(existing)*, permanent, persistent

staying power diligence *(perseverance)*, resolution *(decision)*, sinew

stead behalf, help, help, site

steadfast chronic, constant, continual *(connected)*, dependable, diligent, durable, faithful *(loyal)*, firm, fixed *(securely placed)*, immutable, indelible, industrious, inexorable, inflexible, loyal, patient, permanent, persistent, pertinacious, purposeful, relentless, reliable, resolute, sedulous, serious *(devoted)*, solid *(sound)*, stable, staunch, strong, true *(loyal)*, uncompromising, unrelenting, unyielding

steadfast belief faith

steadfastly faithfully

steadfastness adherence *(devotion)*, adhesion *(loyalty)*, allegiance, constant, diligence *(perseverance)*, faith, fealty, fidelity, industry *(activity)*, loyalty, resolution *(decision)*, tenacity

steadily faithfully, in good faith, invariably

steadiness constant, diligence *(perseverance)*, indestructibility, longanimity, moderation, regularity, resolution *(decision)*

steady bear *(support)*, consecutive, constant, continual *(connected)*, continuous, controlled *(restrained)*, dependable, direct *(uninterrupted)*, dispassionate, establish *(entrench)*, firm, fixed *(securely placed)*, immutable, incessant, industrious, inexorable, infallible, loyal, patient, permanent, persistent, pertinacious, punctual, purposeful, regular *(orderly)*, reliable, resolute, serious *(devoted)*, solid *(sound)*, stabilize, stable, staunch, steadfast, strong, true *(loyal)*, undaunted, uniform, unyielding, well-grounded

steady advance progress

steady application diligence *(perseverance)*

steady demand market *(demand)*

steal acquire *(secure)*, carry away, convert *(misappropriate)*, defalcate, de-

prive, despoil, impropriate, jostle *(pickpocket)*, loot, lurk, mulct *(defraud)*, peculate, pilfer, pillage, pirate *(reproduce without authorization)*, pirate *(take by violence)*, plagiarize, plunder, poach, prowl, purloin, rob, spoil *(pillage)*, usurp

steal away abscond, elude, escape, kidnap

stealer burglar, hoodlum, thief

stealing acquisition, burglary, embezzlement, housebreaking, misappropriation, plagiarism, robbery, theft

stealth evasion

stealthful stealthy

stealthiness concealment, evasion

stealthy artful, clandestine, covert, evasive, furtive, insidious, machiavellian, mysterious, privy, sly, subtle *(insidious)*, surreptitious

steamship company carrier

steeled impervious

steeled against callous

steely rigid, unaffected *(uninfluenced)*

steep immerse *(plunge into)*, oblique *(slanted)*, permeate, pervade

steeped in poison deadly

steeped in vice vicious

steepness elevation

steer administer *(conduct)*, direct *(show)*, direct *(supervise)*, govern, manage, manipulate *(utilize skillfully)*, militate, moderate *(preside over)*, officiate, operate, overlook *(superintend)*, oversee, prescribe, preside, regulate *(manage)*, superintend

steer clear shirk

steer clear of shun

steer for pursue *(strive to gain)*

steerage direction *(guidance)*, management *(judicious use)*, regulation *(management)*, supervision

steered direct *(straight)*

steering guidance, leading *(guiding)*, management *(supervision)*

steering committee management *(directorate)*

steeve load

stellar leading *(ranking first)*, master, principal

stem block, bloodline, cease, check *(restrain)*, confront *(oppose)*, constrict *(inhibit)*, derivation, enjoin, halt, obstruct, parentage, race, repulse, resist *(oppose)*, source, stay *(halt)*, stop, withstand

stenographic copy transcript

stentorian powerful

step act *(undertaking)*, degree *(station)*, expedient, operation, perambulate, phase *(period)*, procedure, proceeding, venture

step aside deviate

step down alight, diminish, quit *(discontinue)*, resign

step in enter *(go in)*, intercede, intervene

step up expand, increase, intensify

step up to approach

stepping up a pace acceleration

steps campaign

steps in the prosecution of an action proceeding

stereotyped boiler plate, familiar *(customary)*, mundane, ordinary, routine, trite, typical, usual

stereotyped saying platitude

sterile barren, ineffective, ineffectual, otiose, unproductive

sterilis unproductive

sterilize decontaminate

sterilized pure

sterling genuine, high-minded, honest, laudable, meritorious, priceless, professional *(stellar)*

stern astringent, bitter *(penetrating)*, harsh, particular *(exacting)*, relentless, rigid, serious *(grave)*, severe, solemn, strict, stringent, unapproachable, unbending, unrelenting, unyielding

sternly just inexorable

sternness cruelty, rigor, severity

stew imbroglio

steward caretaker *(one caring for property)*, proctor, procurator, substitute, superintendent, supplier

stewards management *(directorate)*

stewardship control *(supervision)*, custody *(supervision)*, generalship, government *(administration)*, management *(supervision)*, supervision, surveillance

stick bond *(hold together)*, cement, cohere *(adhere)*, cudgel, lancinate, pierce *(lance)*

stick at refuse

stick close cohere *(adhere)*

stick in enter *(insert)*, plant *(place firmly)*

stick on to cohere *(adhere)*

stick out project *(extend beyond)*

stick to adhere *(fasten)*, adhere *(persist)*, keep *(continue)*, maintain *(carry on)*, maintain *(sustain)*, persevere, persist, pursue *(carry on)*

stick together adhere *(fasten)*, cohere *(adhere)*, combine *(join together)*, consolidate *(unite)*

stick up hold up *(rob)*

stick up for side

sticker brand, label

stickiness adhesion *(affixing)*

sticking coherent *(joined)*, cohesive *(sticking)*

sticking out manifest

sticking together adherence *(adhesion)*, coherence, coherent *(joined)*

stickle haggle, refuse, remonstrate

stickler bigot

stickling restive

stickup man burglar

stiff close *(rigorous)*, draconian, formal, immutable, indomitable, inflexible, ossified, ponderous, potent, precise, punctilious, renitent, restrictive, rigid, severe, solid *(compact)*, strict, stringent, strong, unbending, unyielding

stiffen fix *(make firm)*

stiffened ossified

stiffness formality

stifle arrest *(stop)*, cloak, clog, constrict *(inhibit)*, debar, diminish, extinguish, forestall, impair, inhibit, keep *(restrain)*, repress, restrain, restrict, stop, suppress, thwart, withhold

stifle competition monopolize

stifled clandestine

stifling censorship, deadly, disadvantage, oppressive

stigma attaint, bad repute, brand, discredit, disgrace, dishonor *(shame)*, disparagement, ignominy, infamy, notoriety, obloquy, opprobrium, reproach,

scandal, shame
stigmatism brand
stigmatization denunciation, notoriety
stigmatize charge (accuse), defame, denigrate, denounce (condemn), discredit, disgrace, dishonor (deprive of honor), disparage, humiliate, incriminate, involve (implicate), lessen, pillory, smear, stain, sully, tarnish
stigmatizing calumnious
still allay, alleviate, assuage, dead, dormant, idle, lull, moderate (temper), mollify, mute, notwithstanding, pacify, palliate (abate), peaceable, placate, placid, regardless, repress, soothe, stagnant, stall, standing, static, stifle, strangle, suppress
still existing extant
still in debate pending (unresolved)
still to be found extant
stillare distill
stilling palliative (abating)
stillness abeyance, inaction, insentience, lull, pause, peace, silence
stilted formal, histrionic, inflated (bombastic), orotund, pretentious (pompous), turgid
stiltedness formality
stimulant catalyst, cause (reason), drug, impulse, incentive, inducement, motive, provocation, stimulus
stimulare spirit
stimulate abet, agitate (activate), bait (lure), cause, coax, develop, elicit, evoke, exhort, expedite, foment, foster, impel, incite, induce, influence, inspire, motivate, originate, promise (raise expectations), prompt, provoke, renew (begin again), spirit, urge
stimulated inclined
stimulater inducement
stimulating causative, constructive (creative), impulsive (impelling), moving (evoking emotion), provocative, remedial, salubrious
stimulation aggravation (exacerbation), cause (reason), development (progression), inducement, instigation, motive, origination, provocation, reason (basis), stimulus
stimulative inducement, moving (evoking emotion), provocative, stimulus
stimulator catalyst, stimulus
stimulus cause (reason), impetus, incentive, inducement, motive, origination, provocation
stimulus instigation
sting affront, aggravate (annoy), irritate, pique, provoke, stimulus
stinginess austerity
stinging bitter (penetrating), caustic, harsh, incisive, mordacious, offensive (offending), scathing, severe, trenchant
stinging words diatribe
stingy illiberal, nonsubstantial (not sufficient), parsimonious, penurious, provident (frugal)
stint assignment (task), austerity, insufficiency, period
stinted devoid, limited, slight
stinting frugal, illiberal, limiting, parsimonious
stintless liberal (generous)
stipend alimony, annuity, commission

(fee), consideration (recompense), endowment, honorarium, loan, pay, payment (remittance), payroll, pension, perquisite, subsidy, wage
stipendium campaign, pay
stipulari stipulate
stipulate agree (contract), bear (adduce), designate, determine, mention, posit, promise (vow), select, signify (inform), specify
stipulated agreed (promised), contractual, stated
stipulatio stipulation
stipulation adjustment, agreement (contract), assignment (designation), attornment, bargain, clause, compact, condition (contingent provision), consent, contract, covenant, designation (naming), indenture, option (contractual provision), pact, prerequisite, promise, protocol (agreement), provision (clause), qualification (condition), reservation (condition), security (pledge), selection (choice), specialty (contract), specification, term (provision), ultimatum, undertaking (pledge)
stipulation to compensate for loss insurance
stipulative conditional
stipulatory qualified (conditioned)
stir agitate (shake up), commingle, commotion, discompose, emotion, foment, furor, impress (affect deeply), incite, industry (activity), interest, noise, outburst, pandemonium, perturb, prompt, provoke, turmoil
stir to anger irritate
stir up agitate (activate), churn, disrupt, disturb, engender, foment, incite, motivate, perturb, pique, press (goad), promote (organize), provoke, spirit, stimulate
stirps ancestry, family (common ancestry), race
stirps issue (progeny), lineage, offspring, parentage
stirring momentous, moving (evoking emotion), noteworthy, portentous (eliciting amazement), provocative, sapid, solemn
stock average (standard), blood, bloodline, boiler plate, cargo, commodities, cumulation, derivation, descent (lineage), familiar (customary), family (common ancestry), fund, fund, furnish, garner, goods, hoard, household (familiar), kindred, merchandise, nationality, nondescript, ordinary, origin (ancestry), parentage, possessions, posterity, prevailing (current), prevalent, progeny, prosaic, provide (supply), provision (something provided), race, regular (conventional), repeated, replenish, reserve, resource, routine, stock in trade, store (depository), store, supply, trite, typical, usual
stock agreement call (option)
stock book inventory
stock company corporation
stock in trade commodities, goods, merchandise, possessions, product, resource
stock list inventory
stock market exchange
stock pile reserve
stock saying catchword

stock sheet inventory
stock up hoard
stockade bulwark, jail
stocked replete
stockholder member (individual in a group), shareholder
stockholder of record shareholder
stockholding share (stock)
stockowner shareholder
stockpile accumulate (amass), collection (accumulation), cumulation, fund, garner, hoard, hoard, provision (something provided), store (depository), store
stockroom cache (storage place)
stocks portfolio, securities
stocks and bonds portfolio
stodgy lifeless (dull), pedestrian
stoic patient, resigned, spartan, unaffected (uninfluenced)
stoical controlled (restrained), dispassionate, patient, phlegmatic, resigned, spartan, unaffected (uninfluenced)
stoicism continence, discipline (obedience), longanimity, resignation (passive acceptance), sufferance, tolerance
stolen article contraband
stolen articles plunder
stolen goods contraband, plunder, spoils
stolid dispassionate, jejune (dull), opaque, phlegmatic, ponderous
stolidity opacity
stolidness opacity
stomach endure (suffer), tolerate
stomachus resentment
stony insensible, obdurate, ossified, phlegmatic, rigid, severe, unaffected (uninfluenced)
stony-hearted relentless, ruthless, severe
stonyhearted brutal, malignant
stool pigeon informant
stoop comply, condescend (deign), decline (fall), deign, succumb, vouchsafe
stop adjourn, balk, ban, bar (hinder), barrier, block, blockade (barrier), cease, cessation (interlude), check (bar), check (restrain), clog, close (terminate), cloture, conclude (complete), condemn (ban), constrict (inhibit), contain (restrain), debar, delay, desist, destination, desuetude, detain (restrain), deter, deterrence, discontinuance (act of discontinuing), discontinue (abandon), disqualify, disrupt, dissolve (terminate), dwell (reside), embargo, encumbrance, end (termination), enjoin, estop, expiration, expire, finality, finish, forbear, forbid, forestall, forgo, halt, halt, hesitate, hiatus, hold up (delay), impasse, impede, impediment, inhibit, interdict, interfere, interrupt, interruption, keep (restrain), kill (defeat), lapse (cease), leave (allow to remain), lock, lodge (reside), lull, moratorium, obstacle, obstruct, obstruction, occlude, palliate (abate), parry, preclude, prevent, prohibit, prohibition, quash, quit (discontinue), recess, recess, refrain, remission, remit (relax), reprieve, resist (oppose), respite (interval of rest), rest (cease from action), restrain, restraint, restrict, shut, stall, stay, stay (halt), stay (rest), stem (check), stifle, strangle, suppress, suspend, terminate, thwart, withstand

stop an advance halt

stop and consider pause

stop at nothing persevere

stop in progress by hindrances impede

stop look and listen beware

stop payment default, dishonor (refuse to pay)

stop short balk, clog, halt

stop the progress of estop

stop the way estop

stop to consider doubt (hesitate)

stop up block, clog, obstruct, obturate, occlude, shut

stop work cease, rest (cease from action), strike (refuse to work)

stopgap expedient, substitute, temporary

stopover halt

stoppage abeyance, bar (obstruction), blockade (limitation), cessation (termination), check (bar), close (conclusion), cloture, damper (stopper), deadlock, defeasance, deferment, desuetude, discontinuance (act of discontinuing), embargo, encumbrance, end (termination), expiration, extremity (death), filibuster, finality, halt, hiatus, impediment, interruption, layoff, lull, miscarriage, moratorium, obstacle, obviation, pause, prohibition, recess, remission, restraint, stay, strike

stoppage of use desuetude

stoppage of work lockout

stopped arrested (checked), broken (interrupted)

stopped-up blind (impassable)

stopper bar (obstruction), check (bar), damper (stopper), obstacle, obstruction, obturate, shut, stop

stopping-place destination

stopple damper (stopper), stop

storage arsenal, cache (storage place), coffer, conservation, cumulation, depository, preservation

store business (commercial enterprise), collection (accumulation), conceal, cumulation, deposit (place), depository, fund, fund, garner, hoard, hoard, keep (shelter), load, market (business), merchandise, provision (something provided), quantity, replenish, repose (place), reserve, reserve, resource, stock in trade, sufficiency, treasury

store away reserve

store in the archives file (place among official records)

store of knowledge education

store of provisions cache (storage place)

store secretly hoard

store up accumulate (amass), conserve, hoard, reserve, set aside (reserve)

storehouse bank, cache (storage place), depository, repository, reserve, store (depository), treasury

storehouse for safekeeping cache (storage place)

storekeeper dealer, merchant

storeroom cache (storage place), repository

storm assail, attack, barrage, bluster (commotion), cataclysm, demonstrate (protest), furor, incursion, onset (assault), pandemonium, passion, strike (assault), turmoil

storm against inveigh

stormer aggressor

storming barrage

stormless placid

stormy disorderly, severe, unruly

story falsehood, figment, item, myth, recital, scenario, statement

storylike narrative

storytelling narration

stout firm, heroic, indomitable, ponderous, powerful, spartan, strong

stout heart prowess (bravery)

stout-hearted spartan

stouthearted heroic, undaunted

stoutness puissance, strength

stow deposit (place), garner, hoard, load

stow away harbor, hide, hoard, store

straddle pause, tergiversate

strages havoc

straggle spread

straight clean, direct (uninterrupted), ethical, naked (lacking embellishment), right (direct), straightforward, unadulterated, unbending, undistorted

straight course rectitude, right (righteousness)

straight out outright

straight-thinking pragmatic

straightaway direct (straight), forthwith, right (direct)

straighten fix (repair), organize (arrange), rectify

straighten out arrange (methodize), disabuse, disentangle, fix (arrange), fix (settle), negotiate, regulate (adjust), settle

straightforward absolute (conclusive), bona fide, candid, clear (apparent), cognizable, coherent (clear), compact (pithy), credible, direct (forthright), explicit, honest, ingenuous, irreprehensible, law-abiding, lucid, outright, pellucid, right (direct), simple, unaffected (sincere), unequivocal, upright

straightforwardness probity, rectitude

straightness rectitude

straightway instantly

strain aggravation (annoyance), ancestry, blood, bloodline, burden, descent (lineage), distill, distort, effort, encumber (hinder), endeavor, endeavor, exert, exhaust (deplete), family (common ancestry), feud, force (break), harass, ill will, labor (exertion), labor, mistreat, overextend, overload, overstep, pressure, purge (purify), race, screen (select), strive, struggle, tax (overwork), try (attempt), work (effort)

strain of invective diatribe

strain out distill

strain the meaning distort

strain the sense distort

strain the truth distort, perjure

strained relations contest (dispute), disaccord, discord

strained sense catachresis, distortion

straining operose

strait emergency, entanglement (involvement), plight, quagmire

strait-laced provincial, severe, stringent

straitened poor (underprivileged)

straitened circumstances poverty

straitened means privation

straitlaced restrictive, rigid, strict, unbending

straits poverty, predicament

strange eccentric, extraneous, extrinsic, foreign, incongruous, ineffable, inexplicable, irregular (not usual), irrelative, ludicrous, mysterious, noteworthy, novel, obscure (remote), peculiar (curious), prodigious (amazing), rare, remarkable, suspicious (questionable), unaccustomed, unacquainted, uncanny, uncommon, uncouth, unrelated, unusual

strange behavior quirk (idiosyncrasy)

strange occurrence quirk (idiosyncrasy)

strange person stranger

strangeness irregularity, nonconformity, quirk (idiosyncrasy)

stranger alien

strangle extinguish, inhibit, repress, stifle, suppress

strangulare strangle

strangulate constrict (inhibit), stifle

strangulation blockade (limitation), constraint (restriction)

strap fetter, handcuff

strapped impecunious, poor (underprivileged)

strapping powerful, strong

stratagem act (undertaking), artifice, campaign, contrivance, deception, design (intent), device (contrivance), expedient, false pretense, hoax, instrumentality, machination, maneuver (tactic), maneuver (trick), operation, plot (secret plan), ploy, policy (plan of action), practice (procedure), pretext, ruse, scheme, trap

strategem plan, subterfuge

strategic cardinal (basic), critical (crucial), diplomatic, necessary (required), subtle (refined), tactical

strategic item necessity, need (requirement)

strategical necessary (required), strategic, tactical

strategics contrivance

strategist catalyst, coactor, conspirator, conspirer, expert, mastermind

strategists management (directorate)

strategy campaign, design (intent), direction (course), discretion (quality of being discreet), expedient, forethought, machination, maneuver (tactic), plan, practice (procedure), procedure, process (course), program, proposition, ruse, scheme, stratagem, system

stratification order (arrangement)

stratum class

stray detour, deviant, deviate, digress, lapse (fall into error), miscalculate, prowl, random, sporadic

strayed lost (disoriented)

straying astray, deviation, discursive (digressive), divergent, indirection (indirect action), shifting, truant

streak frame (mood)

stream issue (send forth), outflow, outpour

stream of abuse diatribe

stream of correspondence dispatch (message)

stream out emanate

streaming copious, fluvial
streamline simplify *(make easier)*
streamy fluvial
street avenue *(route)*, causeway
street number address
street vendor dealer
strenghten sustain *(confirm)*
strength amount *(quantity)*, degree *(magnitude)*, dint, emphasis, faculty *(ability)*, health, main force, mainstay, potential, predominance, protection, prowess *(bravery)*, puissance, sinew, tenacity, tolerance, validity
strength of character discipline *(obedience)*
strength of will diligence *(perseverance)*, discipline *(obedience)*
strengthen aid, bear *(support)*, compound, concentrate *(consolidate)*, corroborate, develop, document, edify, empower, enable, endue, enforce, enhance, establish *(entrench)*, heighten *(augment)*, help, intensify, justify, magnify, nurture, reassure, recruit, reinforce, side, supplement, support *(corroborate)*, sustain *(prolong)*
strengthened insusceptible *(resistant)*, protective
strengthener reinforcement
strengthening boom *(increase)*, consolidation, corroboration, cumulative *(increasing)*, cumulative *(intensifying)*, development *(progression)*, enforcement, help, remedial, support *(corroboration)*
strengthful strong
strengthless helpless *(powerless)*, languid, nonsubstantial *(not sturdy)*, null *(invalid)*, null and void, powerless
strengthlessness impotence, impuissance
strenuous difficult, intense, intensive, onerous, operose, oppressive, painstaking
strenuous effort endeavor, pursuit *(effort to secure)*
strenuousness effort, industry *(activity)*
strenuus spartan
strepitus noise
stress aggravation *(annoyance)*, argue, assert, certify *(attest)*, compulsion *(coercion)*, contend *(maintain)*, duress, dwell *(linger over)*, emphasis, enunciate, force *(compulsion)*, inflection, insist, plead *(allege in a legal action)*, pressure, pressure, pronounce *(speak)*, reaffirm, remind, work *(effort)*
stressed alleged
stretch capacity *(maximum)*, capacity *(sphere)*, develop, distort, distortion, duration, embellish, enlarge, exaggeration, expand, extend *(enlarge)*, extent, falsify, gamut, increase, inflate, magnify, magnitude, overextend, overstep, period, phase *(period)*, prolong, purview, range, scope, slant, space, spread, stress *(strain)*, sustain *(prolong)*
stretch a point magnify
stretch out deploy, expand, extend *(enlarge)*, spread
stretch the meaning distort
stretch the truth fabricate *(make up)*, perjure, prevaricate
stretch too far overextend
stretchable flexible, malleable, plia-

ble
stretched inflated *(enlarged)*
stretching continuation *(prolongation)*, extension *(expansion)*
strew diffuse, dispel, disperse *(disseminate)*, disseminate, dissipate *(spread out)*, spread
stricken disconsolate
strict astringent, close *(rigorous)*, conscientious, draconian, drastic, exact, explicit, factual, faithful *(true to fact)*, inflexible, intense, ironclad, literal, meticulous, narrow, orthodox, painstaking, particular *(exacting)*, precise, punctilious, punctual, rigid, severe, stringent, tyrannous, unbending, uncompromising
strict control force *(compulsion)*
strict disciplinarian dictator
strict examination indagation, probe
strict honesty integrity
strict inquiry analysis, examination *(study)*, hearing, indagation, investigation
strict interpretation explanation
strict isolation quarantine
strict order array *(order)*
strict procedure bureaucracy
strict search indagation
striction deterrence, hindrance
strictly faithfully
strictly defined definite
strictly honest clean
strictly to the letter verbatim
strictness austerity, particularity, rigor, severity
stricture admonition, aspersion, bad repute, condemnation *(blame)*, correction *(punishment)*, denunciation, discredit, obloquy, obstruction, ostracism, outcry, reprimand, revilement, slander
stride perambulate, step
strident discordant, harsh
stridulous harsh
strife altercation, argument *(contention)*, belligerency, competition, contention *(opposition)*, contest *(dispute)*, controversy *(argument)*, discord, disagreement, discord, dispute, dissension, dissidence, embroilment, feud, fight *(argument)*, fray, labor *(exertion)*, outbreak, outburst, resistance, revolt, variance *(disagreement)*, work *(effort)*
strike assault, assault, attack, beat *(pulsate)*, boycott, collide *(crash against)*, contact *(touch)*, defiance, fight *(battle)*, find *(discover)*, impact, impinge, impress *(affect deeply)*, inflict, mistreat, onset *(assault)*, reach, rebel, rebellion, resist *(oppose)*, resistance, revolt
strike a balance adjust *(regulate)*, compensate *(counterbalance)*, compromise *(settle by mutual agreement)*, discharge *(pay a debt)*
strike a bargain barter, close *(agree)*, dicker, settle
strike a light burn
strike against collide *(crash against)*, jostle *(bump into)*
strike at accost, collide *(crash against)*, contend *(dispute)*, oppugn
strike back conflict, confront *(oppose)*, counter, recriminate, resist *(oppose)*, retaliate
strike forcibly against each other collide *(crash against)*

strike hard impress *(affect deeply)*
strike home impress *(affect deeply)*
strike in with involve *(participate)*
strike off decrease, deduct *(reduce)*, delete, discount *(reduce)*, rebate
strike off the roll discharge *(dismiss)*
strike off the roll of lawyers disbar
strike one as being appear *(seem to be)*
strike out annul, deface, delete, edit, eliminate *(eradicate)*, eradicate, expunge, expurgate, obliterate, redact
strike sightless blind *(deprive of sight)*
strike the first blow attack
strike together jostle *(bump into)*
strike visionless blind *(deprive of sight)*
strike with overwhelming fear frighten, menace
striking arrant *(definite)*, clear *(apparent)*, conspicuous, distinct *(clear)*, eloquent, flagrant, insistent, manifest, notable, obvious, open *(in sight)*, palpable, particular *(specific)*, portentous *(eliciting amazement)*, powerful, prodigious *(amazing)*, prominent, remarkable, salient, special, unusual
striking part highlight
striking qualities character *(personal quality)*
striking together collision *(accident)*
strikingly particularly
string assemblage, handcuff, sequence
string out dispel, protract *(stall)*
stringency austerity, rigor, severity
stringent astringent, close *(rigorous)*, compulsory, draconian, harsh, inflexible, ironclad, particular *(exacting)*, relentless, rigid, severe, strict, uncompromising
strip abridge *(divest)*, deduct *(reduce)*, demote, denude, deprive, despoil, disarm *(divest of arms)*, divest, erode, expose, harry *(plunder)*, loot, minimize, pillage, plunder, prey, remove *(eliminate)*, unveil
strip of disguise expose
strip of right disqualify
stripling juvenile
strive attempt, compete, contend *(dispute)*, endeavor, exert, labor, oppose, try *(attempt)*, undertake
strive against conflict, dispute *(contest)*, oppose, oppugn, repel *(drive back)*, resist *(oppose)*
strive for pursue *(strive to gain)*
striver contender
striving competitive *(antagonistic)*, struggle
striving for effect flagrant, histrionic
striving for superiority competition
stroke calamity, expedient, maneuver *(tactic)*, operation
stroll perambulate, prowl
strong assertive, categorical, cogent, cohesive *(compact)*, compelling, convincing, disorderly, drastic, durable, firm, forcible, in full force, indomitable, inexpugnable, influential, infrangible, insusceptible *(resistant)*, intense, intensive, irresistible, omnipotent, orotund, persuasive, potent, powerful, predominant, prevailing *(having superior force)*, profound *(intense)*, reliable, resilient, resounding, secure *(sound)*, solid

(sound), sound, spartan, stable, staunch, steadfast, substantial, tenable, unyielding, valid, vehement, well-grounded
strong arm tactics coercion
strong aversion odium
strong connection adhesion *(loyalty)*
strong contrast antithesis
strong demand market *(demand)*
strong discomfort pain
strong dissension dissension
strong feeling passion
strong language expletive
strong point specialty *(special aptitude)*
strong probability presumption
strong request dun
strong-minded inexorable, obdurate, purposeful, unbending
strong-willed earnest, hot-blooded, inexorable, inflexible, obdurate, persistent, pertinacious, purposeful, resolute, steadfast
strongbox coffer, treasury
stronghold bulwark, mainstay, protection, refuge, shelter *(protection)*
strongly attached close *(intimate),* intimate
strongroom bank
structural fundamental, organic
structural composition configuration *(form)*
structural design configuration *(form)*
structure body *(main part),* complex *(development),* composition *(makeup),* configuration *(form),* construction, contour *(outline),* contour *(shape),* corpus, delineation, edifice, fabricate *(construct),* form, formation, motif, order *(arrangement),* temperament
structures premises *(buildings)*
structuring building *(business of assembling)*
struggle affray, campaign, commotion, compete, conflict, confront *(oppose),* confrontation *(altercation),* contend *(dispute),* contention *(opposition),* contest *(competition),* contest, effort, embroilment, endeavor, endeavor, engage *(involve),* fight *(battle),* grapple, labor, onus *(burden),* opposition, persevere, pursuit *(effort to secure),* resistance, strife, strive, work *(effort)*
struggle against dispute *(contest),* fight *(battle)*
struggle for pursue *(strive to gain)*
struggle for superiority competition
struggler candidate
strut flaunt, perambulate
strutting inflated *(vain)*
stub coupon, receipt *(proof of receiving)*
stubborn callous, chronic, contentious, difficult, disobedient, fractious, froward, impervious, incorrigible, indomitable, inexorable, inflexible, insusceptible *(uncaring),* intractable, obdurate, persistent, pertinacious, perverse, pugnacious, purposeful, recalcitrant, relentless, resolute, restive, rigid, severe, unbending, uncontrollable, unrelenting, unruly, unyielding
stubborn person bigot
stubbornly disobedient contumacious

stubbornly rebellious contumacious
stubbornness defiance, diligence *(perseverance),* tenacity
stuck inextricable
student disciple, neophyte, novice, protégé
studere adhere *(maintain loyalty),* favor, study
studied aforethought, deliberate, elaborate, intentional, literate, nonchalant, premeditated, purposeful, tactical, willful
studies education
studiosus partial *(biased),* zealous
studious diligent, industrious, learned, literate, pensive
studiously purposely
studiousness diligence *(care),* interest *(concern)*
studium ardor, inclination, interest *(concern),* predilection, predisposition, pursuit *(chase),* regard *(esteem)*
study analysis, analyze, audit, brood, canvass, check *(inspect),* consider, consideration *(contemplation),* contemplation, deliberate, deliberation, diligence *(care),* hornbook, indagation, inquire, inquiry *(systematic investigation),* inspection, knowledge *(learning),* monitor, observation, overlook *(superintend),* pandect *(treatise),* peruse, ponder, preoccupation, probe, read, reason *(conclude),* reflect *(ponder),* reflection *(thought),* research, research, review *(official reexamination),* review, scrutinize, scrutiny, subject *(topic),* survey *(examine),* test, treatment, trial *(experiment),* weigh
study book hornbook
study deeply concentrate *(pay attention)*
study in detail investigate, probe
study in silence muse
study of ecosystems ecology
study of environs ecology
study of surroundings ecology
study quietly muse
study systematically examine *(study)*
stuff load
stuffed compact *(dense),* full, replete
stuffy orotund, pedestrian
stultification constraint *(restriction)*
stultify balk, check *(restrain),* clog, deter, disable, foil, frustrate, thwart
stultus irrational
stumble miscalculate, miscue, mistake
stumble on find *(discover),* locate
stumbling incompetent
stumbling block bar *(obstruction),* barrier, blockade *(barrier),* complication, deadlock, deterrence, disadvantage, handicap, obstacle
stump confuse *(bewilder)*
stumper enigma, problem
stun drug, impress *(affect deeply),* overcome *(overwhelm),* overwhelm
stunned speechless
stunt lessen
stupefacient drug, narcotic
stupefaction bombshell
stupefactive narcotic
stupefied insensible, lifeless *(dull),* phlegmatic, speechless, torpid
stupefy confuse *(bewilder),* drug, lull,

muddle, obfuscate
stupendous grandiose, portentous *(eliciting amazement),* prodigious *(enormous),* remarkable, special
stuperous torpid
stupid fatuous, impolitic, incompetent, inexpressive, irrational, obtuse, opaque, thoughtless, torpid, unpolitic, vacuous
stupidity opacity
stupidness opacity
stupor inertia, insentience, prostration, sloth
stuprare dishonor *(deprive of honor)*
stuprate debauch
stupration rape
stuprum debauchery, seduction
sturdiness health, prowess *(bravery),* strength
sturdy durable, firm, indestructible, inexpugnable, solid *(sound),* stable, strong
style call *(title),* character *(personal quality),* cognomen, color *(complexion),* complexion, conduct, custom, denominate, form *(arrangement),* habit, identify, manner *(behavior),* manner *(kind),* means *(opportunity),* mode, modus operandi, motif, nominate, parlance, personality, phrase, phraseology, practice *(custom),* presence *(poise),* property *(distinctive attribute),* structure *(composition),* temperament, usage
style of arrangement content *(structure),* organization *(structure)*
style of penmanship handwriting
styleless outdated, outmoded
stylish current, elegant, popular
stymie balk, clog, constrict *(inhibit),* debar, delay, disadvantage, estop, forestall, frustrate, hamper, imbroglio, inconvenience, keep *(restrain),* obstruct, parry, stay *(halt),* stifle, stop, thwart
sua sponte free *(enjoying civil liberty)*
sua voluntate free *(enjoying civil liberty)*
suable actionable
suadere advocate
suasible amenable, open *(persuasible),* pliable
suasion instigation, persuasion
suasive cogent, convincing, hortative, persuasive
suasor advocate *(counselor),* spokesman
suavis palatable
suavity courtesy
sub hasta vendere auction
subaltern ancillary *(subsidiary),* assistant, ignoble, inferior *(lower in position),* minor, secondary, slight, subordinate, subservient
subalternate subaltern
subauscultare overhear
subcategory subdivision
subcenturio subaltern
subclass subdivision
subcommittee caucus
subconscious perception impression
subdere foist
subditus false *(not genuine)*
subdivide apportion, break *(separate),* codify, dichotomize, disjoint, file *(arrange),* parcel, part *(separate),* partition, pigeonhole, sever, sort, split
subdivided bipartite

subdivisible divisible
subdivision affiliate, chapter *(branch)*, chapter *(division)*, class, component, constituent *(part)*, decentralization, denomination, department, detail, dichotomy, lot, member *(constituent part)*, offshoot, organ, part *(portion)*, province, section *(division)*, segment, split, subheading
subdivisional local, regional
subdivisive divisive
subdolous deceptive, machiavellian, surreptitious
subdolus sly
subdual control *(restriction)*, subjection
subduce withdraw
subducere steal
subduct decrease, deduct *(reduce)*, discount *(reduce)*, except *(exclude)*, excise *(cut away)*, retrench, withdraw
subduction curtailment, decrease, deduction *(diminution)*
subdue allay, alleviate, arrest *(stop)*, beat *(defeat)*, browbeat, capture, confine, constrain *(restrain)*, contain *(restrain)*, control *(restrain)*, defeat, diminish, disarm *(set at ease)*, dominate, extinguish, foil, halt, impose *(subject)*, lessen, lull, moderate *(temper)*, modify *(moderate)*, mollify, overcome *(surmount)*, override, overthrow, overturn, overwhelm, pacify, palliate *(abate)*, prevail *(triumph)*, quash, repress, restrain, stifle, strangle, subject, subjugate, suppress, surmount
subdued dispassionate, passive, placid, solemn, unobtrusive
subduing bondage, mitigating, palliative *(abating)*
subgrade poor *(inferior in quality)*
subgroup chapter *(division)*, class, classification, part *(portion)*, section *(division)*, subdivision, subheading
subhead caption
subheading caption, subdivision
subicere forge *(counterfeit)*, hint, subject
subiectio forgery
subiectus subject *(conditional)*
subigere compel
subit occur *(come to mind)*
subitaneous unexpected, unforeseeable
subitus instantaneous
subiungere subdue
subject article *(commodity)*, article *(distinct section of a writing)*, captive, compel, constrain *(compel)*, content *(meaning)*, contents, dependent, dominate, inferior *(lower in position)*, object, passive, question *(issue)*, require *(compel)*, servile, subdue, subjugate, subordinate, subservient, thesis
subject for inquiry issue *(matter in dispute)*, matter *(subject)*
subject matter content *(meaning)*, contents, context, matter *(subject)*, tenor
subject of controversy discrepancy
subject of dispute cause *(lawsuit)*, conflict, controversy *(argument)*, discrepancy, problem
subject of inquiry question *(inquiry)*
subject of thought contents
subject to conditional, contingent, de-

pendent, incident, liable, provided
subject to a charge encumber *(financially obligate)*
subject to a handicap penalize
subject to a liability encumber *(financially obligate)*
subject to a pecuniary penalty fine
subject to action of court of justice justiciable
subject to analysis examine *(study)*
subject to another jurisdiction foreign
subject to argument debatable, disputable
subject to authority impose *(subject)*
subject to be concluded determinable *(liable to be terminated)*
subject to being abrogated defeasible
subject to being annulled defeasible
subject to being cancelled defeasible
subject to being divested defeasible
subject to being invalidated defeasible
subject to being repealed defeasible
subject to being retracted defeasible
subject to being revoked defeasible, voidable
subject to being taken away defeasible
subject to being withdrawn defeasible
subject to cancellation determinable *(liable to be terminated)*, voidable
subject to chance conditional, insecure
subject to change ambulatory, conditional, indefinite, insecure, mutable, provisional
subject to contention debatable, forensic
subject to contravention debatable
subject to control impose *(subject)*
subject to controversy debatable, disputable, forensic, moot, polemic
subject to dependence impose *(subject)*
subject to discontinuance determinable *(liable to be terminated)*
subject to examination analyze, audit, canvass, cross-examine, monitor
subject to influence impose *(subject)*
subject to loss endanger
subject to measurement determinable *(ascertainable)*
subject to penalty condemn *(punish)*, penalize, punish
subject to preference disjunctive *(alternative)*
subject to pressure enforce
subject to punishment discipline *(punish)*, penalize
subject to questioning examine *(interrogate)*
subject to revisal corrigible
subject to scrutiny check *(inspect)*, examine *(study)*, frisk, inquire, monitor, peruse, probe
subject to strain distress
subject to termination determinable *(liable to be terminated)*
subject to terms conditional, contingent, provisional, qualified *(conditioned)*, without recourse
subject to verification inconclusive

subjected subordinate
subjection acquiescence, allegiance, bondage, captivity, duress, force *(compulsion)*, homage, oppression, prostration, servitude, thrall
subjection to responsibility *(accountability)*
subjection to death mortality
subjection to fate fatality
subjection to force compulsion *(coercion)*
subjective partial *(biased)*, personal *(private)*
subjective belief credence
subjectivity intolerance, prejudice *(preconception)*
subjoin affix, annex *(add)*, append, attach *(join)*, compound, connect *(join together)*, join *(bring together)*
subjoined attached *(annexed)*
subjoiner adjoiner
subjoining accession *(annexation)*
subjugate abduct, beat *(defeat)*, coerce, confine, constrain *(restrain)*, defeat, discipline *(control)*, dominate, impose *(subject)*, jail, manage, overcome *(surmount)*, overthrow, overwhelm, repress, restrain, subdue, subject, surmount
subjugated to inferior *(lower in position)*
subjugation abduction, bondage, captivity, duress, force *(compulsion)*, oppression, servitude, subjection, thrall
subjunction accession *(annexation)*, addition, attachment *(act of affixing)*, rider
sublation removal
sublease rent, sublet
sublet lease, rent, sublease
sublevatio relief *(release)*
sublimate elevate, purge *(purify)*
sublime illustrious, meritorious, outstanding *(prominent)*
sublunar mundane
sublunary mundane
submerge censor, immerse *(engross)*, immerse *(plunge into)*, overcome *(overwhelm)*, overwhelm
submerged latent
submerse immerse *(plunge into)*
submission acquiescence, adhesion *(loyalty)*, allegiance, amenability, application, argument *(pleading)*, assent, bid, capitulation, compliance, concession *(compromise)*, conciliation, conformity *(obedience)*, deference, discipline *(obedience)*, homage, longanimity, proposal *(suggestion)*, proposition, prostration, rendition *(restoration)*, resignation *(passive acceptance)*, servitude, subjection, sufferance, thrall, tolerance
submission to a court's jurisdiction appearance *(coming into court)*
submissive malleable, obedient, obeisant, obsequious, passive, patient, pliable, pliant, powerless, resigned, sequacious, servile, subordinate, subservient, tractable, yielding
submissive to correction corrigible
submissively faithfully, respectfully
submissiveness acquiescence, adhesion *(loyalty)*, amenability, capitulation, conformity *(obedience)*, deference, discipline *(obedience)*, homage, loyalty, resignation *(passive acceptance)*

submit abide, accede *(concede)*, admonish *(advise)*, advise, argue, bear *(adduce)*, bestow, cede, concede, conform, counsel, defer *(yield in judgment)*, extend *(offer)*, forbear, give *(grant)*, hear *(give attention to)*, hold out *(deliberate on an offer)*, index *(docket)*, introduce, move *(judicially request)*, obey, offer *(propose)*, offer *(tender)*, pose *(propound)*, posit, proffer, propose, propound, refer *(send for action)*, render *(deliver)*, serve *(assist)*, succumb, surrender *(yield)*, tender

submit a formal request move *(judicially request)*

submit for determination defer *(yield in judgment)*

submit in evidence exhibit

submit in judgment to defer *(yield in judgment)*

submit oneself to appear *(attend court proceedings)*

submit the case rest *(end a legal case)*

submit to allow *(endure)*, bear *(tolerate)*, comply, concede, endure *(suffer)*, tolerate

submit without complaint forbear

submittal acquiescence, capitulation, cession, deference

suborder class

subordinate ancillary *(subsidiary)*, assistant, coadjutant, dependent, derivative, employee, extrinsic, impose *(subject)*, incidental, inferior *(lower in position)*, minor, obsequious, passive, pliant, secondary, sequacious, servile, slight, subaltern, subject *(conditional)*, subject, subservient, subsidiary, supplementary, tangential

subordinate group minority *(outnumbered group)*

subordinate part adjunct, member *(constituent part)*

subordinate position subordinate

subordination allegiance, array *(order)*, bondage, conformity *(obedience)*, servitude, subjection

subordination to rules discipline *(obedience)*

suborn bait *(lure)*, coax, convince, corrupt, inveigle, persuade, taint *(corrupt)*

subornare suborn

subornation gratuity *(bribe)*

subornative persuasive

subpoena call *(summon)*, charge *(command)*, citation *(charge)*, direction *(order)*, monition *(legal summons)*, process *(summons)*, serve *(deliver a legal instrument)*, summon, venire, warrant *(judicial writ)*

subrent lease, rent, sublease, sublet

subreption deceit, fraud, misstatement

subreptitious collusive

subrogate change, replace, succeed *(follow)*, supersede, supplant

subrogation replacement

subscribe attest, bear *(adduce)*, close *(agree)*, corroborate, enroll, hear *(give attention to)*, join *(associate oneself with)*, notarize, register, sign, subsidize

subscribe to abide, accede *(concede)*, advocate, agree *(comply)*, assent, assure *(insure)*, authorize, coincide *(concur)*,

concur *(agree)*, contribute *(assist)*, countenance, defer *(yield in judgment)*, embrace *(accept)*, espouse, indorse, maintain *(sustain)*, profess *(avow)*, promote *(organize)*, sanction, sponsor

subscriber affiant, contributor *(giver)*, donor, notary public, proponent, surety *(guarantor)*, undersigned

subscribere sign

subscript addendum, codicil, rider

subscription advance *(allowance)*, advocacy, affirmance *(judicial sanction)*, aid *(help)*, confirmation, consent, favor *(sanction)*, grant, sanction *(permission)*, vow

subsection department, subheading

subsequent consecutive, derivative, ensuing, future, prospective, proximate, secondary, successive

subsequent meditation hindsight

subsequent reflection hindsight

subsequently thereafter

subsequently set down a savoir

subserve aid, assist, avail *(be of use)*, foster, inure *(benefit)*, pander, promote *(organize)*, subsidize

subservience adhesion *(loyalty)*, bondage, homage, servitude

subserviency subjection

subservient dependent, inferior *(lower in position)*, obedient, obeisant, obsequious, passive, pliant, subordinate, subsidiary

subside decrease, diminish, ebb, lessen

subsidence decline, decrease, descent *(declination)*, lull, remission

subsidiarius subsidiary

subsidiary affiliate, appurtenance, appurtenant, chapter *(branch)*, circumstantial, contingent, derivative, extraneous, extrinsic, incident, incidental, inferior *(lower in position)*, minor, offshoot, organ, pendent, secondary, slight, subaltern, subordinate, subservient, supplementary

subsidiary group minority *(outnumbered group)*

subsidiary law code

subsidium help, relief *(aid)*, support *(assistance)*

subsidization alimony, pension

subsidize assist, capitalize *(provide capital)*, contribute *(supply)*, endow, finance, fund, maintain *(sustain)*, pay, supplement, support *(assist)*

subsidize again refinance

subsidizer backer

subsidy aid *(help)*, aid *(subsistence)*, alimony, annuity, assistance, benefit *(conferment)*, commission *(fee)*, consideration *(recompense)*, contribution *(donation)*, donation, endowment, grant, loan, maintenance *(support of spouse)*, payment *(act of paying)*, pension, perquisite

subsist continue *(persevere)*, endure *(last)*, exist, last, remain *(continue)*, stay *(continue)*

subsist of contain *(comprise)*

subsistence aid *(help)*, livelihood, maintenance *(support of spouse)*, subsidy, support *(assistance)*, sustenance

subsistence level austerity, poverty

subsistent extant, inherent

subsistere halt

subspecies class

substance amount *(quantity)*, article *(commodity)*, body *(main part)*, bulk, capsule, center *(essence)*, connotation, consequence *(significance)*, construction, content *(meaning)*, contents, contour *(shape)*, cornerstone, corpus, element, essence, gist *(ground for a suit)*, gravamen, import, importance, main point, materiality *(physical existence)*, meaning, money, object, point *(purpose)*, property *(possessions)*, reality, significance, signification, spirit, structure *(composition)*, sum *(tally)*, value

substance of a charge complaint

substandard deficient, perfunctory, poor *(inferior in quality)*

substantiable deductible *(provable)*

substantial actual, appreciable, capacious, cardinal *(basic)*, cogent, cohesive *(compact)*, concrete, considerable, convincing, corporal, corporeal, critical *(crucial)*, durable, far reaching, firm, grave *(important)*, important *(significant)*, major, material *(important)*, material *(physical)*, meritorious, momentous, opulent, organic, outstanding *(prominent)*, physical, pithy, prodigious *(enormous)*, secure *(sound)*, solid *(sound)*, sound, stable, staunch, substantive, tangible, valid

substantial cause gravamen

substantial form contour *(shape)*

substantial meaning connotation, content *(meaning)*, gist *(substance)*

substantial number bulk

substantial part bulk

substantial part of a complaint gist *(ground for a suit)*

substantial quantity bulk

substantial rise of prices inflation *(decrease in value of currency)*

substantiality certainty, character *(personal quality)*, cornerstone, corpus, embodiment, importance, materiality *(consequence)*, materiality *(physical existence)*, reality, significance, strength

substantialize embody, substantiate

substantially as a rule

substantially true candid

substantialness materiality *(physical existence)*, reality, strength

substantiate affirm *(uphold)*, attest, bear *(adduce)*, cite *(state)*, corroborate, demonstrate *(establish)*, document, establish *(show)*, maintain *(sustain)*, probate, prove, quote, realize *(make real)*, seal *(solemnize)*, support *(corroborate)*, sustain *(confirm)*, uphold, validate, verify *(confirm)*, witness *(attest to)*

substantiated incident fact

substantiation affirmance *(authentication)*, affirmation, attestation, certification *(attested copy)*, confirmation, corroboration, documentation, evidence, jurat, proof, ratification, realization, reference *(citation)*, reference *(recommendation)*, support *(corroboration)*

substantiative demonstrative *(illustrative)*

substantive actual, appreciable, cardinal *(basic)*, concrete, corporeal, de facto, necessary *(required)*, organic, physical, ponderable, solid *(sound)*, substantial, tangible, virtual

substituere replace

substitutable equivalent, expendable

substitute agent, alienate *(transfer title)*, alternate *(take turns)*, change, commute, conduit *(intermediary)*, convert *(change use)*, cover *(provide for)*, delegate, deputy, devolve, disjunctive *(alternative)*, displace *(replace)*, exchange, false *(not genuine)*, imitation, liaison, offset, plenipotentiary, procurator, provisional, proxy, quid pro quo, replace, replacement, representative *(proxy)*, secondary, stopgap, succedaneum, supersede, supplant, surrogate, transform

substitute for succeed *(follow)*

substitutes choice *(alternatives offered)*

substituting for acting

substitution contribution *(indemnification)*, cover *(substitute)*, devolution, exchange, novation, preemption, proxy, recompense, replacement, representation *(acting for others)*, representative *(proxy)*, stopgap, subrogation, substitute, succedaneum

substitutional disjunctive *(alternative)*, surrogate

substitutive convertible, disjunctive *(alternative)*

substructure foundation *(basis)*

subsume classify, comprise, encompass *(include)*, include, pigeonhole

subterfuge artifice, bad faith, color *(deceptive appearance)*, concealment, contrivance, cover *(pretext)*, deception, evasion, excuse, expedient, false pretense, hoax, imposture, machination, maneuver *(trick)*, pretense *(pretext)*, pretext, ruse, scheme, stratagem

subterranean clandestine

subtile imponderable, subtle *(refined)*

subtilis acute, exact

subtilize clarify, differentiate

subtitle caption

subtle artful, discreet, furtive, impalpable, inconspicuous, insidious, obscure *(faint)*, politic, recondite, sly, surreptitious

subtle communication reference *(allusion)*

subtle difference differential, nuance

subtle maneuver device *(contrivance)*

subtlety discretion *(quality of being discreet)*, evasion, nuance, subterfuge, technicality

subtract abridge *(shorten)*, curtail, decrease, deduct *(reduce)*, dilute, diminish, discount *(reduce)*, eradicate, except *(exclude)*, excise *(cut away)*, lessen, minimize, rebate, remove *(eliminate)*, retrench, withdraw

subtract from derogate

subtraction curtailment, decrease, decrement, deduction *(diminution)*, discount, exception *(exclusion)*, removal

suburbs vicinity

subvenire assist, help

subvention alimony, annuity, benefit *(conferment)*, contribution *(donation)*, dispensation *(act of dispensing)*, donation, grant, help, pension, subsidy

subventionize subsidize

subversion bad faith, counterargument, disloyalty, mutiny, rebellion, revolt, sedition, treason

subversionary harmful

subversive conspirer, harmful, lawless

subversive activities subversion

subversive activity bad faith, disloyalty, espionage

subvert corrupt, destroy *(efface)*, disturb, harm, overthrow, overturn, pervert, supplant, upset

subverter insurgent

subvertere abolish, overturn, subvert, upset

succedaneum alternative *(substitute)*, stopgap

succedere succeed *(follow)*, supersede

succeed accomplish, attain, avail *(bring about)*, carry *(succeed)*, complete, discharge *(perform)*, dispatch *(dispose of)*, displace *(replace)*, effectuate, ensue, execute *(accomplish)*, gain, implement, pass *(satisfy requirements)*, prevail *(triumph)*, reach, replace, supersede, supervene, supplant

succeed in reaching attain, earn

succeed to inherit

succeeding consecutive, ensuing, future, proximate, subsequent, successive

succeeding generation descendant

succeeding generations posterity, progeny

success advantage, benefit *(betterment)*, fruition, progress, prosperity, satisfaction *(fulfilment)*, welfare

successful auspicious, effective *(efficient)*, felicitous, lucrative, operative, prevailing *(having superior force)*, profitable, prosperous

successful remedial treatment cure

successfulness prosperity

succession birth *(lineage)*, bloodline, chain *(series)*, continuity, cycle, devolution, frequency, hierarchy *(arrangement in a series)*, sequence, subrogation

succession of acts course

succession of property inheritance

succession of property rights devolution

successions vicissitudes

successive consecutive, direct *(uninterrupted)*, disjunctive *(tending to disjoin)*, ensuing, periodic, progressive *(going forward)*, regular *(orderly)*, repeated

successive phases vicissitudes

successive portion installment, serial

successive relationship privity

successively gaining in force cumulative *(increasing)*

successively waxing in force cumulative *(increasing)*

successiveness continuity

successless disappointed, unavailing

successlessness miscarriage

successor descendant, devisee, heir, offspring, replacement, transferee

successors posterity

successorship succession

succinct brief, compact *(pithy)*, concise, laconic, pithy, proverbial, sententious

succor abet, accommodation *(backing)*, aid *(help)*, aid, alleviate, assist, assistance, avail *(be of use)*, bear *(support)*, benefit *(betterment)*, benevolence *(act of kindness)*, bolster, contribute *(assist)*, contribution *(donation)*, favor,

foster, help, help, nurture, relief *(aid)*, relieve *(give aid)*, remedy, serve *(assist)*, service *(assistance)*, soothe, support *(assistance)*

succorer benefactor, good samaritan, samaritan, sponsor

succulent palatable, sapid

succumb accede *(concede)*, cede, comply, concede, decease, expire, fail *(lose)*, hear *(give attention to)*, languish, lose *(undergo defeat)*, obey, perish, quit *(discontinue)*, relent, submit *(yield)*, surrender *(yield)*, yield *(submit)*

succumb to death die

succumbere succumb

succurrere help

suceed in winning beat *(defeat)*

such being the case consequently

sudden brief, immediate *(at once)*, impulsive *(rash)*, precipitate, spontaneous, summary, unanticipated, unexpected, unforeseeable, unforeseen

sudden attack assault, bombshell, foray

sudden burst bombshell

sudden contact collision *(accident)*

sudden death fatality

sudden desire impulse

sudden excursion outburst

sudden fear consternation, panic

sudden force impulse

sudden happening accident *(chance occurrence)*

sudden misfortune disaster

sudden peril emergency

sudden terror fright

suddenness dispatch *(promptness)*

sue appeal, call *(appeal to)*, claim *(demand)*, complain *(charge)*, importune, litigate, prosecute *(charge)*

sue a third party implead

sue for request

suffer abide, allow *(endure)*, bear *(tolerate)*, consent, forbear, languish, let *(permit)*, permit, recognize *(acknowledge)*, sanction, tolerate, vouchsafe

suffer a deprivation lose *(be deprived of)*

suffer a relapse relapse

suffer by comparison lose *(undergo defeat)*

suffer death die

suffer defeat lose *(undergo defeat)*, quit *(discontinue)*, yield *(submit)*

suffer loss decrease, lose *(be deprived of)*

suffer pain endure *(suffer)*

suffer privation lack

suffer to occur allow *(endure)*, authorize

sufferable allowable, permissible

sufferance acquiescence, charter *(sanction)*, consent, dispensation *(exception)*, franchise *(license)*, indulgence, leave *(permission)*, longanimity, resignation *(passive acceptance)*, sanction *(permission)*, tolerance, understanding *(tolerance)*

suffered allowable

sufferer victim

suffering adversity, discipline *(punishment)*, distress *(anguish)*, hardship, misfortune, pain, prostration, sanction *(punishment)*, sufferance, toll *(effect)*, trouble

suffering privation poor *(underprivi-*

leged)

suffice avail *(bring about)*, bear *(tolerate)*, fulfill, satisfy *(fulfill)*
suffice to defray cover *(provide for)*
sufficience quorum
sufficiency admissibility, competence *(ability)*, minimum, quorum, satisfaction *(fulfilment)*, store *(depository)*
sufficient adequate, ample, commensurate, competent, fair *(satisfactory)*, operative, suitable
sufficient amount minimum
sufficient evidence proof
sufficient for the purpose adequate
sufficient in law legal
sufficient notice adequate notice
sufficient number quorum
sufficient on its face prima facie *(legally sufficient)*
sufficient on the pleadings prima facie *(legally sufficient)*
sufficient quantity quorum
sufficient to make out a case prima facie *(legally sufficient)*
sufficiently strong prima facie *(legally sufficient)*
sufficientness sufficiency
sufficing adequate, commensurate
suffisant complacent
suffix codicil
sufflate inflate
sufflation inflation *(increase)*
suffocate extinguish, impede, repress, stifle
suffocating deadly, oppressive
suffragari favor, support *(assist)*
suffrage discretion *(power of choice)*, franchise *(right to vote)*
suffragia election *(choice)*
suffragium suffrage, vote
suffragium ferre vote
suffuscus dun
suffuse penetrate, permeate, pervade, spread
sugary nectarious
suggest admonish *(advise)*, advise, advocate, allude, bespeak, charge *(instruct on the law)*, coax, connote, convey *(communicate)*, counsel, denote, evidence, hint, hold out *(deliberate on an offer)*, implicate, imply, indicate, instruct *(direct)*, mention, nominate, offer *(propose)*, pose *(propound)*, postulate, present *(introduce)*, proffer, promise *(raise expectations)*, prompt, propose, propound, purport, raise *(advance)*, recommend, refer *(direct attention)*, remark, remind, signify *(denote)*, submit *(give)*
suggest a proposed claim counsel
suggest a proposed contention counsel
suggest conclusions of law charge *(instruct on the law)*
suggest itself occur *(come to mind)*
suggested constructive *(inferential)*, implicit, implied, tacit
suggested meaning implication *(inference)*
suggested plan suggestion
suggester catalyst, special interest
suggestibility credulity
suggestible open *(persuasible)*, pliant
suggesting advisory, demonstrative *(illustrative)*, precatory
suggestio falsi color *(deceptive appear-

ance)
suggestion advice, advocacy, connotation, expedient, guidance, hint, hypothesis, implication *(inference)*, indicant, indication, innuendo, insinuation, intimation, mention *(reference)*, notion, nuance, plan, possibility, postulate, proposal *(suggestion)*, proposition, recommendation, reference *(allusion)*, reminder, request, suspicion *(uncertainty)*, tip *(clue)*
suggestive allusive, apparent *(presumptive)*, circumstantial, demonstrative *(illustrative)*, implicit, leading *(guiding)*, lewd, portentous *(ominous)*, precatory, provocative, prurient, salacious
sui iuris sovereign *(independent)*
suit accommodate, action *(proceeding)*, agree *(comply)*, calculate, call *(appeal)*, case *(lawsuit)*, cause *(lawsuit)*, chain *(series)*, claim *(legal demand)*, clothe, comport *(agree with)*, concur *(agree)*, conform, entreaty, matter *(case)*, proceeding, prosecution *(criminal trial)*, satisfy *(fulfill)*, trial *(legal proceeding)*
suit at law action *(proceeding)*, case *(lawsuit)*, cause *(lawsuit)*, lawsuit, matter *(case)*, proceeding, trial *(legal proceeding)*
suit in equity lawsuit
suit in law action *(proceeding)*, controversy *(lawsuit)*, suit
suit one's purpose avail *(be of use)*
suit to extinguish the equity of redemption foreclosure
suitability admissibility, aptitude, competence *(ability)*, decorum, expedience, propriety *(appropriateness)*, qualification *(fitness)*, relevance, timeliness, use, utility *(usefulness)*
suitable adequate, admissible, allowable, allowed, applicable, apposite, appropriate, available, commensurate, competent, condign, consonant, constructive *(creative)*, convenient, correlative, desirable *(qualified)*, disposable, eligible, entitled, fair *(just)*, fair *(satisfactory)*, favorable *(advantageous)*, felicitous, fit, fitting, habitable, harmonious, just, justifiable, opportune, pertinent, practical, prima facie *(legally sufficient)*, proper, qualified *(competent)*, reasonable *(fair)*, relative *(relevant)*, relevant, right *(suitable)*, rightful, scientific, seasonable, valuable, viable
suitable circumstance chance *(fortuity)*, opportunity
suitable for living in habitable
suitable for use functional
suitable notice adequate notice
suitable occasion opportunity
suitable time occasion, opportunity, timeliness
suitableness decorum, expedience, propriety *(appropriateness)*, qualification *(fitness)*, relevance
suite chain *(series)*
suited agreed *(harmonized)*, apposite, appropriate, capable, convenient, correlative, fit, fitting, opportune, proper, scientific, suitable
suited to youth juvenile
suitedness qualification *(fitness)*
suiting congruous, felicitous, harmonious

suitor appellant, claimant, complainant, contender, contestant, litigant, party *(litigant)*, plaintiff, special interest
sulk brood
sulky resentful, restive
sullen despondent, resentful, restive
sullied blemished, marred, tainted *(contaminated)*
sully brand *(stigmatize)*, contaminate, debauch, deface, defame, denigrate, depreciate, derogate, disapprove *(condemn)*, disgrace, disparage, humiliate, infect, pillory, pollute, smear, stain, taint *(contaminate)*, tarnish, vitiate
sullying defilement
sum aggregate, amount *(quantity)*, amount *(result)*, computation, consideration *(recompense)*, content *(meaning)*, corpus, entirety, expenditure, expense *(cost)*, face amount, face value *(price)*, import, principal *(capital sum)*, quantity, substance *(essential nature)*, totality
sum and substance capsule, center *(essence)*, content *(meaning)*, context, corpus, gist *(ground for a suit)*, gist *(substance)*, gravamen, materiality *(consequence)*, scenario
sum asked for cost *(price)*
sum charged expense *(cost)*
sum derived from a sale proceeds
sum entrusted loan
sum of money fund
sum of money borrowed loan
sum of money lent loan
sum owed debt
sum owing debit
sum paid for carrying a passenger fare
sum shown face amount
sum stated face amount
sum total aggregate, amount *(result)*, corpus, in solido, principal *(capital sum)*, quantity, sum *(total)*, whole
sum up condense, criticize *(evaluate)*, digest *(summarize)*, recapitulate, repeat *(state again)*, review
sumere presume
sumless innumerable, myriad
summa amount *(quantity)*
summarily dispossess eject *(evict)*
summariness dispatch *(promptness)*
summarium epitome, summary, synopsis
summarization narration
summarize abridge *(shorten)*, condense, extract, lessen, recapitulate, recount, repeat *(state again)*, review
summarized brief, compact *(pithy)*, concise, laconic, sententious
summary abridgment *(condensation)*, abstract, account *(report)*, brief, brief, capsule, compact *(pithy)*, compendium, concise, cursory, decisive, digest, direct *(forthright)*, narration, pandect *(treatise)*, paraphrase, pithy, prompt, proposal *(report)*, prospectus, recital, report *(detailed account)*, restatement, scenario, statement, succinct, sum *(tally)*, synopsis
summary of facts story *(narrative)*
summary on the law brief
summary punishment by mob lynch law
summate sum

summation account (report), amount (sum), computation, corpus, denouement, outline (synopsis), synopsis
summed up compact (pithy)
summing up recital
summisse respectfully
summit caucus, ceiling, culmination, meeting (conference), panel (discussion group), paragon, parley, pinnacle
summit conference parley
summit talk parley
summital cardinal (basic)
summitry negotiation
summon convene, evoke, invoke, prosecute (charge), request, require (compel), serve (deliver a legal instrument), subpoena
summon back recall (call back)
summon by incantation invoke
summon forth call (summon), educe, elicit, evoke
summon to court subpoena
summon up evoke, recall (remember), recollect, remember
summons charge (accusation), charge (command), direction (order), invitation, monition (legal summons), subpoena, venire, warrant (judicial writ)
summons to appear and answer monition (legal summons)
summus ascendant, extreme (last), paramount, unqualified (unlimited)
sumptio assumption (supposition), postulate
sumptious profuse
sumptuary financial, pecuniary
sumptuous elaborate
sumptus outlay, waste
sumptus minuere retrench
sunder bifurcate, break (separate), disband, discontinue (abandon), discontinue (break continuity), disengage, disjoint, disrupt, dissociate, dissolve (separate), divide (separate), divorce, estrange, interrupt, isolate, lancinate, luxate, part (separate), rend, separate, sever, split, subdivide
sunderance disassociation, division (act of dividing), interruption, severance, split
sundered disconnected, discrete, separate
sundering estrangement, separation
sundry composite, diverse, manifold, miscellaneous, multiple, several (plural)
sung famous
suo arbitrio discretion (power of choice)
super superlative
superable possible
superabundance boom (prosperity), plethora, redundancy, sufficiency, surfeit, surplus
superabundant copious, excess, excessive, expendable, inordinate, multiple, needless, redundant, superfluous, unwarranted
superadd compound, supplement
superadded additional
superannuated antique, old, outdated, outmoded, powerless
superare beat (defeat), defeat, outweigh, predominate (command), prevail (triumph)
superb meritorious, portentous (elicit-

ing amazement), preferential, premium, prime (most valuable), professional (stellar), sterling
superbia intolerance
superbire rampant
superbus supercilious
supercharge overload
supercherie bunko
supercilious cynical, disdainful, insolent, orgulous, presumptuous, proud (conceited)
superciliousness disdain, disrespect, pride
superego conscience
supereminence eminence, primacy
supereminent cardinal (outstanding), master, outstanding (prominent), paramount, primary, prime (most valuable), principal
supererogate surpass
supererogative excess, superfluous, unnecessary
supererogatory excess, excessive, expendable, inordinate, needless, nonessential, superfluous, unnecessary
superexcellent superior (excellent), superlative
superficial artificial, careless, casual, cursory, frivolous, inconsequential, insubstantial, minor, nominal, nugatory, null (insignificant), perfunctory, pretentious (ostentatious), remote (small), trivial
superficially pro forma
superficies area (surface)
superfine best, premium, subtle (refined), superlative
superfluity balance (amount in excess), boom (prosperity), exaggeration, plethora, redundancy, remainder (remaining part), surfeit, surplus
superfluous disproportionate, excess, excessive, expendable, extraneous, gratuitous (unwarranted), inordinate, needless, nonessential, profuse, redundant, undue (excessive), unessential, unnecessary, unwarranted
superfluousness balance (amount in excess), exaggeration, plethora, tautology
superhighway causeway
superimpose overlap
superinduce affect, cause
superintend administer (conduct), check (inspect), conduct, control (regulate), direct (supervise), discipline (control), govern, handle (manage), manage, officiate, operate, oversee, patrol, police, prescribe, preside, regulate (manage), rule (govern)
superintendence administration, agency (legal relationship), auspices, charge (custody), control (supervision), custody (supervision), direction (guidance), government (administration), jurisdiction, management (supervision), occupation (possession), oversight (control), regulation (management), safekeeping, supervision, supremacy, surveillance
superintendency generalship
superintendent caretaker (one caring for property), caretaker (one fulfilling the function of office), director, employer, guardian, official, principal (director), procurator, warden

superintendents management (directorate)
superintending administrative
superior absolute (ideal), best, chief, disdainful, dominant, employer, important (significant), inflated (vain), irresistible, meritorious, notable, outstanding (prominent), paramount, predominant, preferable, preferential, premium, prime (most valuable), principal (director), professional (stellar), select, special, sterling, superlative, unapproachable, valuable
superior ascendant, prior
superior group elite
superior individual paragon
superior situation advantage
superiority advantage, dint, distinction (reputation), edge (advantage), eminence, hegemony, importance, influence, merit, precedence, predominance, preponderance, prestige, pride, primacy, priority, quality (excellence), status, strength, stress (accent), supremacy, value
superiority in number plurality
superlatio exaggeration
superlative absolute (ideal), best, bombast, cardinal (outstanding), exaggeration, meritorious, outstanding (prominent), paramount, portentous (eliciting amazement), premium, prime (most valuable), rare, sterling, superior (excellent), unapproachable, utmost
supernatural mysterious, peculiar (curious), uncanny
supernatural being spirit
supernormal best, extraordinary, mysterious, prodigious (amazing), unusual
supernumerary ancillary (auxiliary), copious, excess, excessive, expendable, needless, redundant, superfluous, unwarranted
superplus balance (amount in excess), surplus
supersaturate overload
supersaturated inordinate
supersaturation overage, plethora, surfeit, surplus
superscription caption, heading, inscription, label, rubric (title), title (designation)
supersede abolish, abrogate (rescind), accede (succeed), annul, disinherit, dislodge, displace (replace), leave (allow to remain), override, overrule, replace, succeed (follow), supplant, upset
superseded null (invalid), null and void, outdated, outmoded
supersedence preemption
superseder alternative (substitute)
supersedere forbear
supersedure replacement, subrogation
supersession cancellation, defeasance, preemption, replacement, subrogation
superstruct build (construct)
superstructure building (structure)
supervacaneous superfluous
supervacaneus redundant, superfluous, unnecessary
supervacuus superfluous, unnecessary
supervene ensue, succeed (follow)
supervenient additional, extraneous,

incidental, needless, nonessential, supplementary

supervenire intervene, supervene

supervention preemption

supervise administer *(conduct)*, care *(regard)*, check *(inspect)*, conduct, control *(regulate)*, discipline *(control)*, govern, handle *(manage)*, manage, moderate *(preside over)*, officiate, operate, overlook *(superintend)*, oversee, police, predominate *(command)*, preside, regulate *(manage)*, rule *(govern)*, superintend

supervise communications censor

supervising administrative, leading *(guiding)*

supervising director chief

supervision administration, agency *(legal relationship)*, auspices, charge *(custody)*, direction *(guidance)*, generalship, guidance, jurisdiction, observation, oversight *(carelessness)*, oversight *(control)*, protection, regime, regulation *(management)*, safekeeping, supremacy, surveillance

supervisor administrator, caretaker *(one caring for property)*, chairman, director, employer, guardian, official, principal *(director)*, procurator, superintendent, warden

supervisor of accounts comptroller

supervisor of an estate administrator

supervisors management *(directorate)*

supervisorship generalship

supervisory administrative, leading *(guiding)*, predominant

supervisory official warden

supine inactive, indolent, insensible, languid, lifeless *(dull)*, otiose, passive, phlegmatic, ponderous, stagnant, torpid

supineness disinterest *(lack of interest)*, inertia, languor, sloth

suppeditare defray, furnish, provide *(supply)*, supply

suppeditate supply

supplant abolish, accede *(succeed)*, dislodge, displace *(replace)*, replace, succeed *(follow)*, supersede

supplantation replacement, subrogation

supplanter alternative *(substitute)*, replacement, substitute

supplanting exchange, preemption, subrogation

supple flexible, malleable, obedient, passive, pliable, pliant, servile, yielding

supplement accrue *(increase)*, addendum, addition, additive, adjunct, affix, aid, allonge, amendment *(correction)*, amendment *(legislation)*, annex *(add)*, append, appurtenance, attach *(join)*, attachment *(thing affixed)*, augmentation, boom *(increase)*, codicil, complement, compound, corollary, correlate, enlarge, expand, extend *(enlarge)*, increase, increment, insertion, offshoot, reinforce, reinforcement, replenish, rider

supplement to a will codicil

supplemental additional, ancillary *(auxiliary)*, collateral *(accompanying)*, expendable, extrinsic, incidental, nonessential, pendent, subsidiary, superfluous, supplementary, unnecessary

supplementary additional, ancillary *(auxiliary)*, collateral *(accompanying)*, expendable, extraneous, incidental, nonessential, subsidiary, unnecessary

supplementary device attachment *(thing affixed)*

supplementation accession *(annexation)*, accession *(enlargement)*, addendum, continuation *(resumption)*, development *(progression)*, extension *(expansion)*, insertion

supplementum reinforcement

supplere replenish

suppletive supplementary

suppletory supplementary

supplex petitioner

suppliant special interest, suitor

supplicant petitioner, suitor

supplicate call *(appeal to)*, desire, importune, plead *(implore)*, pray, press *(beseech)*, request, solicit, sue

supplication call *(appeal)*, entreaty, intercession, prayer, request

supplicatory solicitous

supplicium execute *(sentence to death)*

supplied with arms armed

supplier contributor *(giver)*, materialman

supplies equipment, goods, merchandise, paraphernalia *(apparatus)*, store *(depository)*, sustenance

supply bear *(yield)*, bestow, clothe, contribute *(supply)*, cumulation, dole, endow, endue, fund, fund, furnish, give *(grant)*, hoard, lend, maintain *(sustain)*, pander, present *(make a gift)*, provision *(something provided)*, quantity, recruit, replenish, reserve, resource, stock *(store)*, stock in trade, store *(depository)*, sufficiency, yield *(produce a return)*

supply accommodations for lodge *(house)*

supply aid abet, assist, bear *(support)*, capitalize *(provide capital)*, inure *(benefit)*, lend, nurture, serve *(assist)*, subsidize

supply an equivalent replace

supply base headquarters

supply deficiencies replenish

supply funds loan

supply money finance

supply on hand stock in trade

supply or furnish with reference index *(relate)*

supply support bear *(support)*, capitalize *(provide capital)*, subsidize

supply the necessities of support *(assist)*

supply the wants of accommodate

supply with a subsidy capitalize *(provide capital)*

supply with an epithet call *(title)*

supply with means enable, endow

supplying commercial, donative

supplying another's place representation *(acting for others)*

supponere foist, forge *(counterfeit)*

support abet, abettor, accommodate, accommodation *(backing)*, adhere *(maintain loyalty)*, adhesion *(loyalty)*, advantage, advocacy, advocate *(espouser)*, advocate, affirm *(uphold)*, aid *(help)*, aid *(subsistence)*, aid, alimony, allegiance, allow *(authorize)*, approval, approve, assist, assistance, attest, auspices, base *(foundation)*, basis, bear *(tolerate)*, behalf, benevolence *(act of*

kindness)*, bolster, bulwark, capitalize *(provide capital)*, care *(regard)*, certification *(attested copy)*, charity, charter *(sanction)*, choose, concur *(agree)*, confederate, confirm, confirmation, conform, consent, consent, conservation, contribute *(assist)*, cornerstone, corroborate, corroboration, cosign, countenance, countersign, coverage *(insurance)*, defend, defense, demonstrate *(establish)*, document, documentation, ecology, embrace *(accept)*, enable, encourage, endorse, enforcement, espouse, expedite, favor *(sanction)*, favor, fealty, finance, foster, foundation *(basis)*, frame *(structure)*, goodwill, grant *(concede)*, ground, guarantee, guaranty, help, help, indorse, indorsement, invest *(fund)*, involve *(participate)*, justify, keep *(continue)*, keep *(shelter)*, let *(permit)*, livelihood, loyalty, mainstay, maintain *(sustain)*, nurture, palliate *(excuse)*, partisan, pass *(approve)*, patronage *(support)*, patronize *(trade with)*, pay, pay, pension, preservation, preserve, promote *(organize)*, protect, protection, prove, quote, reassure, recommend, recommendation, reinforce, reinforcement, reliance, relief *(aid)*, resource, safekeeping, sanction *(permission)*, sanction, seal *(solemnize)*, security *(safety)*, service *(assistance)*, shelter *(protection)*, side, sponsor, subscribe *(promise)*, subsidize, substantiate, sustain *(confirm)*, sustenance, underwrite, uphold, verify *(confirm)*, vouch

support again refinance

support an analogy correspond *(be equivalent)*

support by authority authorize

support the expense of disburse *(pay out)*, expend *(disburse)*

supportability corroboration

supportable convincing, deductible *(provable)*, defensible, provable, tenable

supportable by law valid

supported by authority allowed

supporter abettor, accomplice, advocate *(espouser)*, apologist, assistant, backer, benefactor, coactor, coadjutant, coconspirator, cohort, confederate, contributor *(giver)*, copartner *(coconspirator)*, disciple, partisan, patron *(influential supporter)*, patron *(regular customer)*, promoter, proponent, surety *(guarantor)*, undersigned

supporting ancillary *(auxiliary)*, instigation, propitious, underlying

supporting evidence corroboration, documentation

supporting structure foundation *(basis)*

supportive benevolent, demonstrative *(illustrative)*

supposable apparent *(presumptive)*, colorable *(plausible)*, constructive *(inferential)*, ostensible, possible, theoretical

supposal assumption *(supposition)*, condition *(contingent provision)*, conjecture, deduction *(conclusion)*, estimate *(idea)*, estimation *(calculation)*, generalization, hypothesis, inference, postulate, supposition

suppose anticipate *(expect)*, deduce, deduct *(conclude by reasoning)*, deem, estimate, expect *(consider probable)*, gauge, generalize, guess, infer, opine, presume, presuppose, reason *(conclude)*, speculate *(conjecture)*, surmise, suspect *(think)*

supposed apparent *(presumptive)*, assumed *(inferred)*, hypothetical, ostensible, plausible, presumptive, probable, putative

supposedly reputedly

supposition concept, condition *(contingent provision)*, conjecture, conviction *(persuasion)*, deduction *(conclusion)*, estimate *(idea)*, estimation *(calculation)*, generalization, ground, hypothesis, idea, inference, notion, opinion *(belief)*, perception, postulate, presumption, prognosis, proposition, speculation *(conjecture)*, suspicion *(uncertainty)*, theory, thesis

suppositional apparent *(presumptive)*, assumed *(inferred)*, disputable, doubtful, dubious, hypothetical, ill-founded, illusory, indefinite, moot, plausible, presumptive, speculative, theoretical, unfounded, unsupported

suppositionary apparent *(presumptive)*

suppositious debatable

suppositious check bad check

supposititious presumptive, unfounded, unsupported

suppositive apparent *(presumptive)*, hypothetical, presumptive, theoretical

suppress abate *(lessen)*, abolish, allay, arrest *(stop)*, ban, beat *(defeat)*, camouflage, censor, check *(restrain)*, cloak, clog, coerce, conceal, condemn *(ban)*, confine, constrain *(restrain)*, constrict *(inhibit)*, contain *(restrain)*, control *(restrain)*, counter, countervail, curb, debar, defeat, detain *(restrain)*, disadvantage, eliminate *(eradicate)*, enjoin, ensconce, expurgate, extinguish, fetter, forestall, hamper, hide, hold up *(delay)*, inhibit, keep *(restrain)*, limit, moderate *(temper)*, negate, obliterate, obscure, obstruct, overthrow, overturn, overwhelm, palliate *(abate)*, prevail *(triumph)*, prohibit, quash, repress, restrain, restrict, revoke, shroud, stay *(halt)*, stem *(check)*, stifle, stop, strangle, subdue, subject, subjugate, trammel, withhold

suppress competition monopolize

suppressed arrested *(checked)*, clandestine, hidden, inadmissible, inconspicuous, undisclosed

suppressing limiting

suppressio veri color *(deceptive appearance)*

suppression abatement *(reduction)*, bar *(obstruction)*, censorship, concealment, constraint *(restriction)*, control *(restriction)*, countermand, defeasance, deterrence, deterrent, disadvantage, dissolution *(termination)*, fetter, obstacle, oppression, prohibition, quota, removal, restraint, servitude

suppression of sound silence

suppression of the truth concealment

suppression of truth bad faith, false pretense, misstatement, story *(falsehood)*

suppressive dictatorial, prohibitive

(restrictive), restrictive

supprimere suppress, withhold

supputation census

supremacy advantage, authority *(power)*, capacity *(authority)*, dominance, dominion *(supreme authority)*, eminence, force *(strength)*, hegemony, importance, influence, possession *(ownership)*, power, precedence, predominance, primacy, priority, regime, significance

supreme absolute *(ideal)*, best, cardinal *(outstanding)*, central *(essential)*, crucial, definitive, dictatorial, dominant, final, important *(significant)*, influential, leading *(ranking first)*, major, master, meritorious, omnipotent, outstanding *(prominent)*, paramount, predominant, prevailing *(having superior force)*, primary, prime *(most valuable)*, principal, sovereign *(absolute)*, superior *(excellent)*, superlative, ultimate, unapproachable, utmost

supreme authority predominance, supremacy

supreme contempt disdain

supreme law constitution

supremely particularly

supremeness power, primacy, supremacy

surcease cease, cessation *(termination)*, close *(terminate)*, conclude *(complete)*, desist, expire, quit *(discontinue)*

surcharge overload

sure affirmative, axiomatic, believable, certain *(fixed)*, certain *(positive)*, clear *(certain)*, constant, dependable, dogmatic, explicit, incontrovertible, indubious, inevitable, infallible, irrefutable, necessary *(inescapable)*, pertinacious, positive *(confident)*, positive *(incontestable)*, real, reliable, safe, secure *(confident)*, stable, staunch, true *(loyal)*, unambiguous, unavoidable *(inevitable)*, unequivocal, unmistakable, unrefutable

sure assumption certitude

sure presumption certainty, certitude

sure to happen inevitable

surely admittedly, fairly *(clearly)*

sureness certainty, certification *(certainness)*, certitude, confidence *(faith)*, conviction *(persuasion)*, credence, faith, reliance, surety *(certainty)*, trust *(confidence)*

surety accommodation *(backing)*, assurance, bail, bond, certainty, certitude, confidence *(faith)*, coverage *(insurance)*, credence, deposit, downpayment, faith, guaranty, insurer, recognizance, safeguard, security *(pledge)*, sponsor, warrant *(guaranty)*

surface bare, cursory, dimension, emerge, issue *(send forth)*, ostensible, side, superficial

surfeit balance *(amount in excess)*, overage, overload, plethora, satisfy *(fulfill)*, sufficiency, surplus, tautology

surfeited full, replete

surge growth *(increase)*, increase, increment, inflate, inflation *(increase)*, inundate, issue *(send forth)*

surging fluvial

surly fractious, froward, harsh, impertinent *(insolent)*, perverse, petulant, re-

sentful

surmisable colorable *(plausible)*, ostensible, presumptive, probable

surmisal estimate *(idea)*, estimation *(calculation)*

surmise anticipate *(expect)*, apprehend *(perceive)*, assumption *(supposition)*, concept, conclusion *(determination)*, conjecture, deduce, deduct *(conclude by reasoning)*, deduction *(conclusion)*, deem, estimate *(idea)*, estimation *(calculation)*, expect *(consider probable)*, gauge, generalize, guess, hypothesis, idea, infer, inference, opine, opinion *(belief)*, perception, postulate, postulate, preconceive, presume, presumption, presuppose, prognosticate, rationale, speculate *(conjecture)*, speculation *(conjecture)*, supposition, suspect *(think)*, suspicion *(uncertainty)*, theory

surmised approximate, inexact

surmount beat *(defeat)*, defeat, kill *(defeat)*, negotiate, overthrow, overwhelm, prevail *(triumph)*, transcend

surmount obstacles succeed *(attain)*

surmountable possible

surname call *(title)*

surpass beat *(defeat)*, outbalance, outweigh, override, predominate *(outnumber)*, prevail *(triumph)*, surmount, transcend

surpassing best, infringement, preferable, superlative

surplus balance *(amount in excess)*, bonus, boom *(prosperity)*, excess, excessive, expendable, needless, net, overage, plethora, profuse, redundancy, redundant, remainder *(estate in property)*, remainder *(remaining part)*, residual, residuary, superfluous, surfeit, unnecessary

surplus time unexpired term

surplusage balance *(amount in excess)*, bonus, overage, plethora, surfeit, surplus

surprisal bombshell

surprise bombshell, fortuitous, overwhelm, unforeseeable, unforeseen

surprise package bombshell

surprised unaware

surprising coincidental, fortuitous, noteworthy, peculiar *(curious)*, portentous *(eliciting amazement)*, prodigious *(amazing)*, remarkable, unaccustomed, unanticipated, uncommon, unexpected, unusual

surrebut rebut, reply, retort, return *(respond)*

surrebuttal answer *(judicial response)*, counterargument, reply

surrebutter answer *(judicial response)*, counterargument, response

surrejoin answer *(respond legally)*, rebut, reply, retort, return *(respond)*

surrejoinder answer *(judicial response)*, confutation, counterargument, response

surrender abandon *(relinquish)*, abandonment *(discontinuance)*, abdication, accede *(concede)*, alienate *(transfer title)*, alienation *(transfer of title)*, bear *(yield)*, cancellation, capitulation, cede, cession, concession *(compromise)*, deliver, delivery, desuetude, discontinue *(abandon)*, disposition *(transfer of property)*, expense *(sacrifice)*, forfeit, forgo,

give *(grant)*, give *(yield)*, introduce, leave *(allow to remain)*, obey, perish, prostration, quit *(discontinue)*, relinquish, remise, render *(deliver)*, rendition *(restoration)*, renounce, resign, resignation *(passive acceptance)*, resignation *(relinquishment)*, submit *(yield)*, succumb, vacate *(leave)*, waive, waiver, withdraw, yield *(submit)*
surrender of an individual extradition
surrender of control abdication
surrender to another assign *(transfer ownership)*
surrendered resigned
surrendered to addicted
surrendering obeisant
surreptitious clandestine, collusive, covert, dishonest, disingenuous, evasive, fraudulent, furtive, hidden, insidious, mysterious, privy, secret, sly, stealthy, unobtrusive
surreptitiousness bad faith, deceit, dishonesty, false pretense, fraud, improbity
surripere pilfer, purloin, steal
surrogate attorney in fact, conduit *(intermediary)*, deputy, judge, plenipotentiary, proctor, proxy, replace, replacement, substitute
surrogation replacement, subrogation
surround border *(bound)*, circumscribe *(surround by boundary)*, contain *(enclose)*, delimit, detain *(hold in custody)*, embrace *(encircle)*, enclose, enshroud, envelop, hedge, include
surrounded by difficulties difficult
surrounding blockade *(enclosure)*, local
surrounding area periphery
surrounding facts circumstances
surrounding influence climate
surrounding space periphery
surroundings atmosphere, circumstances, climate, context, environment, locality, scene, section *(vicinity)*, vicinity
surveillance bondage, contemplation, direction *(guidance)*, espionage, inspection, management *(supervision)*, notice *(heed)*, observation, precaution, scrutiny, supervision
survey analysis, analyze, appraisal, assessment *(estimation)*, canvass, check *(inspect)*, compendium, delineate, digest *(summarize)*, estimate, examination *(study)*, examine *(study)*, gauge, inquire, inquiry *(request for information)*, inquiry *(systematic investigation)*, inspection, investigate, measure, measurement, monitor, observation, observe *(watch)*, overlook *(superintend)*, pandect *(treatise)*, peruse, poll *(canvass)*, poll, question *(inquiry)*, regard *(pay attention)*, research, retrospect, review *(official reexamination)*, review, scrutinize, scrutiny, study, test
survey carefully traverse
survey of time past hindsight
surveyable appreciable, determinable *(ascertainable)*
surveying discovery
surviorship longevity
survival life *(period of existence)*, longevity
survival studies ecology

survivance longevity
survive endure *(last)*, exist, keep *(continue)*, last, persevere, persist, remain *(continue)*, subsist
surviving durable, extant, lasting, live *(existing)*, net, outstanding *(unpaid)*, permanent, perpetual
survivor heir
susceptibility bias, character *(personal quality)*, credulity, danger, peril, predisposition, probability, sensibility, tendency
susceptible liable, open *(accessible)*, open *(persuasible)*, penetrable, pliant, receptive, responsive, sensitive *(easily affected)*, subject *(exposed)*, vulnerable, willing *(not averse)*
susceptible of apportionment divisible
susceptible of division divisible
susceptible of proof provable
susceptibleness peril
susceptive pliant, sensitive *(easily affected)*, susceptible *(responsive)*
susceptivity credulity, peril
suscipere assume *(undertake)*, incur, undertake
suspect assume *(suppose)*, controversial, debatable, deem, disbelieve, discount *(disbelieve)*, disputable, doubt *(distrust)*, dubitative, expect *(consider probable)*, guess, incredible, infer, leery, ludicrous, misdoubt, mistrust, opine, presume, presumptive, presuppose, surmise, suspicious *(questionable)*, unbelievable, uncertain *(questionable)*
suspected criminal suspect
suspecting cynical, inconvincible, incredulous, leery, skeptical, suspicious *(distrustful)*
suspectum reddere incriminate
suspend adjourn, arrest *(stop)*, balk, bar *(exclude)*, cancel, cease, close *(terminate)*, continue *(adjourn)*, debar, defer *(put off)*, desist, discharge *(dismiss)*, discontinue *(abandon)*, discontinue *(break continuity)*, dismiss *(discharge)*, disrupt, forestall, halt, hold up *(delay)*, impede, inhibit, interrupt, leave *(allow to remain)*, negate, nullify, obstruct, palliate *(abate)*, pause, postpone, pretermit, procrastinate, prohibit, quit *(discontinue)*, recess, remit *(relax)*, remove *(dismiss from office)*, revoke, stop, toll *(stop)*
suspend charges pardon
suspend from the practice of law disbar
suspend from the profession of law disbar
suspend operation close *(terminate)*
suspend work strike *(refuse to work)*
suspended arrested *(checked)*, broken *(interrupted)*, disjunctive *(tending to disjoin)*, dormant, inactive, null *(invalid)*, null and void, static
suspended animation inaction
suspended judgment doubt *(indecision)*
suspense doubt *(indecision)*, expectation, pendency, remission
suspenseful conditional, pending *(unresolved)*
suspension abandonment *(discontinuance)*, abeyance, adjournment, cancellation, cessation *(interlude)*, check *(bar)*,

cloture, deferment, delay, desuetude, discontinuance *(act of discontinuing)*, disuse, expulsion, extension *(postponement)*, halt, hiatus, inaction, interruption, lull, moratorium, nonuse, ostracism, pause, pendency, remission, rescision, respite *(interval of rest)*, solution *(substance)*, stay
suspension of activity extension *(postponement)*
suspension of business failure *(bankruptcy)*
suspension of consciousness insentience
suspension of disbelief credence
suspension of employment layoff
suspension of execution reprieve
suspension of hostilities peace
suspension of punishment reprieve
suspension of work furlough, leave *(absence)*, strike
suspicari surmise, suspect *(think)*
suspicio doubt *(suspicion)*, notion, suspicion *(mistrust)*
suspicion apprehension *(fear)*, conjecture, idea, incredulity, inference, opinion *(belief)*, qualm, speculation *(conjecture)*, suggestion, supposition
suspicionem habere suspect *(think)*
suspiciosus suspicious *(distrustful)*
suspicious cynical, debatable, disputable, disreputable, guarded, implausible, inconvincible, incredible, incredulous, jealous, leery, resentful, skeptical, unbelievable, uncertain *(questionable)*, vigilant
suspiciousness bad faith, bad repute, doubt *(suspicion)*, incredulity, suspicion *(mistrust)*
sustain adhere *(persist)*, affirm *(uphold)*, aid, allow *(authorize)*, allow *(endure)*, approve, authorize, bear *(adduce)*, bear *(support)*, bear *(tolerate)*, bolster, care *(regard)*, certify *(attest)*, concur *(agree)*, confirm, conserve, continue *(persevere)*, continue *(prolong)*, corroborate, countenance, defend, demonstrate *(establish)*, document, endure *(last)*, endure *(suffer)*, finance, foster, fund, harbor, help, indorse, justify, keep *(continue)*, keep *(shelter)*, last, nurture, pass *(approve)*, perpetuate, persevere, persist, preserve, prolong, promote *(organize)*, protect, provide *(supply)*, reaffirm, reassure, remain *(continue)*, retain *(keep in possession)*, side, sponsor, subsidize, supply, support *(assist)*, support *(corroborate)*, uphold, vouch, witness *(attest to)*
sustain by authority authorize
sustain damage suffer *(sustain loss)*
sustainable convincing, deductible *(provable)*, provable
sustainable in law valid
sustained chronic, constant, continual *(connected)*, continuous, durable, habitual, incessant, lasting, live *(existing)*, permanent, persistent, safe
sustained action continuance
sustained by dependent
sustained trial endeavor, pursuit *(effort to secure)*
sustainer abettor, backer, benefactor, mainstay, partisan
sustaining conservation, continuation *(prolongation)*, corroboration, salutary

sustainment aid *(help)*, aid *(subsistence)*, ecology, livelihood, tolerance
sustenance aid *(help)*, aid *(subsistence)*, alimony, behalf, continuation *(prolongation)*, contribution *(donation)*, ecology, help, livelihood, mainstay, maintenance *(support of spouse)*, relief *(aid)*, support *(assistance)*
sustentare sustain *(prolong)*, uphold
sustentation alimony, conservation, sustenance
sustentative salubrious, salutary
sustinere bear *(tolerate)*, endure *(suffer)*, preserve, sustain *(prolong)*, uphold
swaddle envelop
swag contraband, spoils
swagger flaunt, jactation, pride, rodomontade
swaggering bluster *(speech)*, inflated *(vain)*, insolent
swallow consume, endure *(suffer)*, tolerate
swallow up obliterate, overcome *(overwhelm)*
swamp immerse *(plunge into)*, inundate, overcome *(overwhelm)*
swank jactation
swap barter, exchange, interchange, replace, replacement, trade *(commerce)*
swarm assemblage, mass *(body of persons)*, meet
swarming populous, profuse, rife
swashbuckling rodomontade
swatch sample
swathe enshroud, envelop
sway advantage, authority *(power)*, bailiwick, beat *(pulsate)*, coax, convert *(persuade)*, convince, dint, dispose *(incline)*, dominance, dominate, dominion *(supreme authority)*, force *(strength)*, government *(administration)*, hegemony, induce, influence, influence, inspire, inveigle, lobby, manage, motivate, oscillate, patronage *(power to appoint jobs)*, persuade, power, predominance, predominate *(command)*, prejudice *(influence)*, preside, pressure, prestige, prevail *(persuade)*, prevail upon, primacy, supremacy, vacillate, wield
swayable open *(persuasible)*, pliable, pliant, suasible, susceptible *(responsive)*
swayed one-sided, partial *(biased)*, partisan
swaying convincing, persuasive
swear acknowledge *(declare)*, assure *(insure)*, attest, avouch *(avow)*, avow, bear *(adduce)*, certify *(attest)*, depose *(testify)*, evidence, plead *(allege in a legal action)*, promise *(vow)*, testify, witness *(attest to)*
swear an affidavit certify *(attest)*
swear an oath avouch *(avow)*, promise *(vow)*
swear by trust
swear falsely bear false witness, cloak, frame *(charge falsely)*, lie *(falsify)*, perjure
swear in delegate
swear off forgo, refrain, renounce
swear the truth avouch *(avow)*
swear to vouch
swear under oath depose *(testify)*
swearer affiant, bystander, deponent, juror, witness
swearing adjuration, affirmation, attestation, averment, avouchment, blas-

phemy, certification *(attested copy)*, confirmation, expletive, imprecation, oath, profanity
swearing off denial, renunciation
sweep coverage *(scope)*, extent, gamut, range, scope, space
sweep aside rescind
sweep away eliminate *(eradicate)*, eradicate, obliterate
sweep out purge *(purify)*
sweep through patrol, perambulate
sweeping broad, complete *(all-embracing)*, comprehensive, extensive, far reaching, general, generic, inclusive, omnibus, outright, prevailing *(current)*, prevalent, radical *(extreme)*, thorough, unqualified *(unlimited)*
sweeping change revolution
sweepstake lottery
sweet attractive, nectarious, sapid, savory
sweet-tempered benevolent
swell accrue *(increase)*, accumulate *(enlarge)*, boom *(increase)*, build *(augment)*, develop, enlarge, expand, extend *(enlarge)*, growth *(increase)*, increase, inflate, inflation *(increase)*, magnify, proliferate, spread
swell the ranks recruit
swelled inflated *(enlarged)*, turgid
swelling accession *(enlargement)*, boom *(increase)*, cumulative *(increasing)*, growth *(increase)*, inflation *(increase)*, orotund, plethora
swelling utterance bombast
swerve depart, detour, deviate, deviation, digress, digression, divert, indirection *(indirect action)*, oscillate
swerving deviation
swift brief, expeditious, impulsive *(rash)*, instantaneous, precipitate, prompt, rapid, ready *(prepared)*, summary
swift execution dispatch *(promptness)*
swift rate dispatch *(promptness)*
swiftly instantly
swiftness haste
swindle bait *(lure)*, betray *(lead astray)*, bilk, bunko, cheat, circumvent, deceive, deception, defalcate, defraud, delude, dupe, embezzle, embezzlement, fake, false pretense, hoax, hoodwink, illude, imposture, larceny, misappropriation, mislead, mulct *(defraud)*, peculate, purloin
swindled aggrieved *(harmed)*
swindler criminal, delinquent, embezzler, outlaw, thief
swindling fraud, imposture, larceny, theft
swing beat *(pulsate)*, beat *(strike)*, brandish, fluctuate, oscillate, vacillate, wield
switch alternate *(take turns)*, barter, change, conversion *(change)*, convert *(change use)*, displace *(replace)*, lash *(strike)*, reciprocate, remove *(transfer)*, replace, replacement, subrogation, transform
switch around change
switched off disconnected
swollen full, fustian, inflated *(enlarged)*, orotund, pretentious *(pompous)*, proud *(conceited)*, supercilious, turgid

swollen diction bombast
swollen language fustian
swoon prostration
sworn agreed *(promised)*
sworn enemy foe
sworn evidence affidavit, affirmance *(legal affirmation)*, affirmation, attestation, certification *(attested copy)*, deposition
sworn pledge oath
sworn promise oath
sworn statement adjuration, affidavit, affirmation, asseveration, oath
sycophant parasite
sycophantic obsequious, sequacious, servile, subservient
syllabus capsule, compendium, outline *(synopsis)*, pandect *(treatise)*, plan, program, prospectus, summary
syllogism corollary
symbiosis coalescence
symbol device *(distinguishing mark)*, earmark, indicant, indication, indicator, manifestation, representative *(example)*, substitute, suggestion, token, trademark
symbolic nominal, representative, suggestive *(evocative)*
symbolical representative
symbolization connotation
symbolize connote, denote, depict, exemplify, personify, replace, represent *(portray)*, signify *(denote)*
symbolized tacit
symbols indicia
symbolum symbol
symmetric equal
symmetrical coequal, coextensive, equal, regular *(orderly)*
symmetrical scales balance *(equality)*
symmetry analogy, arrangement *(ordering)*, balance *(equality)*, constant, correspondence *(similarity)*, equipoise, parity, proportion, regularity, uniformity
sympathetic charitable *(lenient)*, concerted, concordant, consensual, lenient, open *(persuasible)*, patient, propitious, receptive, sensitive *(easily affected)*, susceptible *(responsive)*, vicarious *(delegated)*
sympathetic perception discretion *(quality of being discreet)*
sympathize relent, sponsor
sympathize with concur *(agree)*
sympathizer advocate *(espouser)*, backer, disciple, partisan, proponent, samaritan, sponsor
sympathizing benevolent, charitable *(lenient)*, vicarious *(delegated)*
sympathy affinity *(regard)*, concordance, condonation, goodwill, humanity *(humaneness)*, lenience, pity, sensibility, solace, tolerance, understanding *(tolerance)*
symphonize orchestrate
symphysis concrescence
symposiac parley
symposiarch chairman
symposium assemblage, conference, meeting *(conference)*, panel *(discussion group)*, parley
symptom indicant, indication, indicator, manifestation, symbol, warning
symptomatology diagnosis

synchronal commensurate, concurrent *(at the same time)*, consonant, contemporaneous, simultaneous
synchronic simultaneous
synchronical simultaneous
synchronistic concurrent *(at the same time)*, contemporaneous, simultaneous
synchronistical concurrent *(at the same time)*, simultaneous
synchronization consensus
synchronize coincide *(concur)*, conform, coordinate
synchronized congruous, consonant
synchronous concurrent *(at the same time)*, congruous, contemporaneous, simultaneous
syncophantic vexatious
syncretize combine *(act in concert)*, embody, federalize *(associate)*, unite
syndic functionary, procurator
syndicate amalgamate, association *(alliance)*, business *(commercial enterprise)*, cartel, coalition, combine *(act in concert)*, committee, confederacy *(compact)*, consortium *(business cartel)*, corporation, enterprise *(economic organization)*, federation, institute, merger, organization *(association)*, partnership, pool, trust *(combination of businesses)*
synergetic associated, joint
synergic concerted, concomitant, concurrent *(united)*, consensual
synergism collusion, synergy
synergy collusion, concert
syngrapha bill *(invoice)*, bond, instrument *(document)*
synod council *(assembly)*, meeting *(conference)*, session
synonym call *(title)*, definition, same
synonymity identity *(similarity)*, propinquity *(similarity)*
synonymous coequal, coextensive, cognate, congruous, equivalent, identical, same, similar, tantamount
synopsis abridgment *(condensation)*, abstract, brief, capsule, compendium, digest, pandect *(treatise)*, paraphrase, prospectus, restatement, scenario, summary
synopsize abridge *(shorten)*, abstract *(summarize)*, condense
synoptic broad, compact *(pithy)*, comprehensive, concise, succinct
syntaxis classification
synthesis building *(business of assembling)*, centralization, coalescence, composition *(makeup)*, embodiment, formation, manufacture
synthesize consist, consolidate *(unite)*, embody, make
synthetic assumed *(feigned)*, false *(not genuine)*, imitation, spurious
system arrangement *(plan)*, array *(order)*, avenue *(means of attainment)*, bureaucracy, codification, complex *(development)*, course, device *(contrivance)*, doctrine, form *(arrangement)*, hierarchy *(arrangement in a series)*, institute, means *(opportunity)*, method, mode, modus operandi, order *(arrangement)*, practice *(procedure)*, procedure, process *(course)*, program, rule *(guide)*, scheme, strategy, usage
system of belief doctrine
system of distributing wealth economy *(economic system)*

system of drill discipline *(training)*
system of exchanges commerce
system of government polity
system of knowledge education, science *(study)*
system of law code
system of laws codification, jurisprudence
system of morals ethics
system of reckoning time calendar *(record of yearly periods)*
system of regulations codification
system of rules code, protocol *(etiquette)*
systematic formal, periodic, procedural, punctilious, punctual, regular *(orderly)*, thorough, uniform
systematic arrangement of cases calendar *(list of cases)*
systematic arrangement of laws codification
systematic search indagation, investigation
systematic secret observation of the words and conduct of others espionage
systematic training discipline *(training)*, education
systematical systematic
systematically invariably
systematization arrangement *(ordering)*, array *(order)*, centralization, classification, distribution *(arrangement)*, form *(arrangement)*, formation, order *(arrangement)*, organization *(structure)*, regulation *(management)*
systematization of laws codification
systematize adjust *(regulate)*, arrange *(methodize)*, classify, codify, conform, contrive, coordinate, distribute, file *(arrange)*, fix *(arrange)*, frame *(construct)*, marshal, orchestrate, organize *(arrange)*, pigeonhole, police, regulate *(adjust)*, sort, tabulate
systematized tactical
systemic physical
systemize codify
systemless haphazard, indiscriminate

T

T.N.T. bomb
tab invoice *(bill)*
tabernacle domicile, dwelling, habitation *(dwelling place)*
tabescere languish
tabid dilapidated
table calendar *(record of yearly periods)*, continue *(adjourn)*, defer *(put off)*, delay, doubt *(hesitate)*, hold up *(delay)*, postpone, procrastinate, suspend
table of cases calendar *(list of cases)*
table of charges tariff *(bill)*
tables census
tabling deferment
taboo ban, exclude, forbid, illicit, inhibit, prohibition, proscribe *(prohibit)*, restraint, restrict, veto
tabula document, instrument *(document)*, inventory, roll, schedule
tabula rasa blank *(emptiness)*
tabulae register
tabular register of the year calendar *(record of yearly periods)*
tabulas referre register
tabulate book, cast *(register)*, codify,

enter *(record)*, enumerate, fix *(arrange)*, itemize, pigeonhole, poll, record, register, sort, survey *(poll)*
tabulation census, codification, poll *(canvass)*, registration
tacere speechless
tacit allusive, constructive *(inferential)*, covert, implicit, implied, indirect, undisclosed
tacit assent acquiescence
tacit inference implication *(inference)*
tacitly assumed constructive *(inferential)*
taciturn inarticulate, laconic, mute, noncommittal, unresponsive
taciturnitas silence
taciturnus taciturn
tacitus implicit, tacit
tack avenue *(means of attainment)*
tack together combine *(join together)*
tackle attack, endeavor, grapple, occupy *(engage)*, ply, strive, try *(attempt)*, undertake
tact consideration *(sympathetic regard)*, courtesy, decorum, discretion *(quality of being discreet)*, prudence
tactful diplomatic, judicious, politic, subtle *(refined)*
tactfulness discretion *(quality of being discreet)*
tactic expedient, machination, method, plan, plot *(secret plan)*, stratagem
tactical strategic
tactician mastermind
tactics artifice, campaign, contrivance, direction *(course)*, manner *(behavior)*, modus operandi, practice *(procedure)*, procedure, process *(course)*, scheme, strategy
tactile bodily, material *(physical)*, palpable, tangible
taction contact *(touching)*
tactless thoughtless, unpolitic
tactlessness disrespect, impropriety, indiscretion
tactual tangible
taeter loathsome
tag brand, brand *(mark)*, call *(title)*, catchword, classify, label, label, nominate, pigeonhole, rate, title *(designation)*
tag incorrectly mislabel
tail end *(termination)*
tail end extremity *(furthest point)*
tailor conform, transform
tailor-made fit
taint adulterate, attaint, bad repute, brand, brand *(stigmatize)*, contaminate, contaminate, contemn, corrupt, damage, debase, defame, degenerate, depreciate, derogate, deteriorate, disadvantage, discredit, discredit, disease, disgrace, disgrace, dishonor *(shame)*, dishonor *(deprive of honor)*, disparage, disrepute, humiliate, ignominy, impair, infamy, infect, misemploy, notoriety, onus *(stigma)*, opprobrium, pervert, pillory, pollute, prejudice *(injure)*, reproach, scandal, shame, smear, stain, stigma, sully, tarnish
tainted blameworthy, blemished, imperfect, marred, odious, peccable, peccant *(unhealthy)*, sinister, unsound *(not strong)*
taintless absolute *(ideal)*, blameless,

clean, pure, unblemished

take acquire *(secure)*, adopt, apprehend *(arrest)*, appropriate, attach *(seize)*, carry *(transport)*, derive *(receive)*, despoil, endure *(suffer)*, excise *(levy a tax)*, gain, hijack, impound, impress *(procure by force)*, inherit, loot, obtain, partake, pilfer, plunder, preempt, procure, profit, purloin, reap, receive *(acquire)*, seize *(apprehend)*, seize *(confiscate)*, sequester *(seize property)*, spoils, transport, trust, usurp

take a beating lose *(undergo defeat)*

take a break rest *(cease from action)*

take a breather pause

take a census poll

take a chance bet, gamble, parlay *(bet)*, speculate *(chance)*, try *(attempt)*

take a circuitous route detour

take a constitutional perambulate

take a crack at endeavor

take a decisive step choose, conclude *(decide)*, determine

take a different course deviate

take a dim view of disapprove *(condemn)*

take a fancy to prefer

take a lease rent

take a life slay

take a part in participate

take a part of participate

take a recess recess

take a rest recess

take a roll call poll

take a roundabout course detour

take a share of partake

take a stand posit, resolve *(decide)*

take a stand against counter, disagree, oppose, rebut

take a temporary route detour

take a turn reciprocate

take a vow promise *(vow)*

take a walk perambulate

take account of note *(notice)*, ponder

take action complain *(charge)*, endeavor, execute *(accomplish)*, implement, militate, perform *(execute)*, strive

take advantage deceive

take advantage of bait *(lure)*, bilk, capitalize *(seize the chance)*, defraud, delude, dupe, employ *(make use of)*, ensnare, exploit *(make use of)*, illude, manipulate *(control unfairly)*, mislead

take after copy, mock *(imitate)*

take alarm fear

take amiss misapprehend, resent

take an account of calculate

take an active part in contribute *(assist)*, partake, participate

take an advance borrow

take an airing perambulate

take an alternate highway detour

take an alternate route detour

take an indirect way detour

take an interest in participate

take an oath promise *(vow)*

take another's place displace *(replace)*

take apart break *(separate)*, disjoint, dissolve *(separate)*

take as an axiom postulate

take as an heir inherit

take as one's own assume *(seize)*, impropriate

take authority hold *(possess)*

take away abduct, abridge *(divest)*,

abridge *(shorten)*, adeem, carry away, decrease, deduct *(reduce)*, depreciate, deprive, dilute, diminish, dislodge, displace *(remove)*, distrain, divest, excise *(cut away)*, hijack, hold up *(rob)*, jostle *(pickpocket)*, kidnap, lessen, plunder, remove *(eliminate)*, withdraw

take away an essential part eviscerate

take away from confiscate, disinherit

take back adeem, bear false witness, disavow, disclaim, recall *(call back)*, recant, recoup *(regain)*, repossess, rescind, withdraw

take back again collect *(recover money)*

take birth arise *(originate)*

take by assault capture, carry away, hijack

take by authority apprehend *(arrest)*, arrest *(apprehend)*

take by craft ensnare

take by descent inherit

take by force abduct, capture, despoil, hijack, kidnap, levy, pirate *(take by violence)*, rob

take by fraud defalcate, defraud, dupe, embezzle, purloin

take by illegal methods poach

take by inheritance inherit

take by stealth carry away

take by strategem ensnare

take by succession inherit

take by theft hold up *(rob)*

take by unfair methods poach

take captive apprehend *(arrest)*, arrest *(apprehend)*, capture, carry away, constrain *(imprison)*, detain *(hold in custody)*, hijack, immure

take care beware, heed

take care of assume *(undertake)*, concern *(care)*, conduct, control *(regulate)*, cover *(guard)*, foster, keep *(shelter)*, maintain *(sustain)*, operate, preserve, preside, protect, serve *(assist)*, support *(assist)*

take charge assume *(undertake)*, command, govern, preside, takeover, usurp

take charge of arrest *(apprehend)*, conduct, maintain *(sustain)*, manage, moderate *(preside over)*, operate

take cognizance notice *(observe)*

take cognizance of hear *(perceive by ear)*, heed, note *(notice)*, observe *(watch)*, regard *(pay attention)*, witness *(have direct knowledge of)*

take command direct *(supervise)*, federalize *(place under federal control)*, govern, hold *(possess)*, takeover

take control federalize *(place under federal control)*

take control of accept *(take)*

take counsel confer *(consult)*, consult *(ask advice of)*

take counsel with oneself deliberate

take disciplinary action condemn *(punish)*

take dishonestly hold up *(rob)*, purloin

take down demean *(make lower)*, demote, enter *(record)*, note *(record)*, record

take effect occur *(happen)*

take employment occupy *(engage)*

take evasive action counter, elude,

parry

take evidence investigate

take exception complain *(criticize)*, conflict, cross *(disagree with)*, demur, differ *(disagree)*, differ *(vary)*, disaccord, disagree, disapprove *(reject)*, dispute *(contest)*, dissent *(differ in opinion)*, except *(object)*, expostulate, object, oppugn, protest, remonstrate, reprehend

take exception to challenge, complain *(criticize)*, confront *(oppose)*, contest, denounce *(condemn)*, disapprove *(condemn)*, disapprove *(reject)*, disclaim, gainsay, oppose, reject, renounce, resent

take exception to the allegations demurrer

take feloniously embezzle, hold up *(rob)*, purloin

take flight abscond, disappear, escape, evacuate, flee, move *(alter position)*, quit *(evacuate)*, retreat

take for deem

take for granted assume *(suppose)*, guess, postulate, presume, presuppose, suspect *(think)*, trust

take for oneself impropriate

take for public use condemn *(seize)*

take forcibly carry away

take form crystallize, develop, evolve

take fright fear

take from adeem, diminish, discount *(reduce)*, occupy *(take possession)*

take heed beware

take hold of accept *(take)*, grapple, sequester *(seize property)*

take illegally convert *(misappropriate)*, pirate *(reproduce without authorization)*, poach

take in acquire *(receive)*, betray *(lead astray)*, bilk, comprehend *(include)*, comprehend *(understand)*, defraud, delude, dupe, embrace *(encircle)*, encompass *(include)*, entrap, illude, include, incorporate *(include)*, instate, mislead, realize *(understand)*, reap, receive *(acquire)*, receive *(permit to enter)*, recruit, seize *(apprehend)*

take in exchange displace *(replace)*

take in hand undertake

take into account calculate, consider, discuss, heed, notice *(observe)*, provide *(arrange for)*

take into consideration appreciate *(comprehend)*, concern *(care)*, deliberate, muse, notice *(observe)*

take into custody apprehend *(arrest)*, arrest *(apprehend)*, book, capture, confine, constrain *(imprison)*, detain *(hold in custody)*, distrain, enclose, immure, impound, jail, restrain, seize *(apprehend)*

take into employ employ *(engage services)*

take into legal custody impound

take into one's employ engage *(hire)*

take into preventive custody arrest *(apprehend)*

take into protective custody arrest *(apprehend)*

take into service employ *(engage services)*, engage *(hire)*, hire

take issue collide *(clash)*, differ *(disagree)*, differ *(vary)*, disagree

take issue with antagonize, contra-

dict, counter, counteract, demurrer, disown *(deny the validity)*, dispute *(contest)*, dissent *(differ in opinion)*, gainsay, impugn, oppose
take it to be deem
take its course occur *(happen)*
take leave abandon *(physically leave)*, dissociate, leave *(depart)*, part *(leave)*, quit *(evacuate)*, retire *(conclude a career)*, retire *(retreat)*
take leave of quit *(evacuate)*
take liberties infringe
take life dispatch *(put to death)*
take lodgings lodge *(reside)*
take measures frame *(formulate)*, perpetrate, plan, plot, provide *(arrange for)*
take minutes record
take no account of disregard, flout, override
take no denial compel, constrain *(compel)*, insist, persevere, persist, press *(constrain)*
take no interest disregard
take no note ignore, neglect
take no note of disregard
take no notice dismiss *(put out of consideration)*, ignore, neglect, overlook *(disregard)*
take no notice of disregard
take no part in refrain
take no stock in disbelieve
take note heed, observe *(watch)*, spy
take note of concern *(care)*, peruse
take notice appreciate *(comprehend)*, heed, note *(notice)*, observe *(watch)*, perceive, regard *(pay attention)*
take notice of attend *(heed)*
take off decrease, deduct *(reduce)*, diminish, discount *(reduce)*, rebate
take off on mock *(imitate)*
take offense resent
take offensive action attack
take on adopt, attempt, contend *(dispute)*, embark, endeavor, engage *(involve)*, fight *(battle)*, grapple, hire, occupy *(engage)*
take on cargo load
take on character crystallize
take on credit borrow
take on loan borrow
take on oneself assume *(undertake)*
take on the aspect appear *(seem to be)*
take on the manner appear *(seem to be)*, demean *(deport oneself)*
take one to court prosecute *(charge)*
take one's choice choose
take one's departure abandon *(physically leave)*, part *(leave)*
take one's leave abandon *(physically leave)*
take one's life away dispatch *(put to death)*
take one's meaning construe *(comprehend)*
take one's oath affirm *(declare solemnly)*, attest, avow, bear *(adduce)*, certify *(attest)*, testify, witness *(attest to)*
take one's stand against antagonize, counteract
take oneself away quit *(evacuate)*
take order crystallize
take orders obey
take origin arise *(originate)*

take out delete, distill, except *(exclude)*, excise *(cut away)*, exclude, expunge, extract, remove *(eliminate)*, select
take out of context abstract *(separate)*
take out of the place of interment disinter
take over accroach, annex *(arrogate)*, appropriate, attach *(seize)*, condemn *(seize)*, confiscate, distrain, hold *(possess)*, impound, impropriate, manage, obtain, occupy *(take possession)*, preempt, preside, prevail *(triumph)*, succeed *(follow)*, supplant
take over another's duties displace *(replace)*
take pains endeavor, strive
take part combine *(act in concert)*, compete, engage *(involve)*, involve *(participate)*, join *(associate oneself with)*, occupy *(engage)*, participate
take part in conspire, cooperate, espouse, partake
take part in a demonstration picket
take part with assist, conspire, cooperate
take patiently allow *(endure)*, bear *(tolerate)*, endure *(suffer)*, tolerate
take place arise *(occur)*, occur *(happen)*, supervene
take pleasure in relish
take poorly resent
take possession acquire *(secure)*, annex *(arrogate)*, collect *(recover money)*, condemn *(seize)*, evict, obtain, possess, receive *(acquire)*, takeover, usurp
take possession for public use eminent domain
take possession of accept *(take)*, adopt, attach *(seize)*, capture, confiscate, distrain, hold up *(rob)*, impound, impress *(procure by force)*, impropriate, preempt, procure, repossess, seize *(confiscate)*
take precautions beware, care *(be cautious)*, caution, forestall
take precedence beat *(defeat)*, override, surpass, transcend
take precedence over outweigh
take prisoner apprehend *(arrest)*, arrest *(apprehend)*, capture, carry away, confine, detain *(hold in custody)*, hijack, restrain, seize *(apprehend)*
take prisoner again rearrest
take responsibility underwrite
take responsibility for sponsor
take retribution retaliate
take revenge retaliate
take rooms lodge *(reside)*
take shape crystallize, develop, evolve
take sides bicker, involve *(participate)*
take something from derogate
take steps devise *(invent)*, frame *(formulate)*, maneuver, perform *(execute)*, plot, proceed *(go forward)*, provide *(arrange for)*, strive
take stock calculate, check *(inspect)*, observe *(watch)*, survey *(poll)*
take stock of criticize *(evaluate)*, examine *(study)*, muse, notice *(observe)*, peruse
take summarily annex *(arrogate)*, at-

tach *(seize)*, confiscate
take surreptitiously abduct
take the chair officiate
take the chances of bet
take the dimensions calculate
take the edge off obtund
take the first step embark, launch *(initiate)*, originate
take the initiative attack, commence, initiate, originate
take the lead command, initiate, launch *(initiate)*, originate, precede, predominate *(command)*
take the offensive attack, fight *(battle)*, oppugn
take the opportunity capitalize *(seize the chance)*
take the part of assume *(simulate)*, impersonate, pose *(impersonate)*, represent *(substitute)*, side, support *(assist)*
take the place of accede *(succeed)*, displace *(replace)*, succeed *(follow)*, supersede, supplant
take the semblance of assume *(simulate)*
take the stand testify
take the yield reap
take time stall
take time out pause, recess, rest *(cease from action)*
take to prefer
take to account impeach
take to court litigate, sue
take to mean understand
take to one's heels flee
take to oneself embrace *(accept)*, impropriate
take to pieces break *(separate)*, disable
take to safety rescue
take to task castigate, condemn *(blame)*, denounce *(condemn)*, disapprove *(condemn)*, discipline *(punish)*, fault, lash *(attack verbally)*, punish, rebuke, reprehend, reproach
take training practice *(train by repetition)*
take trouble strive
take umbrage alienate *(estrange)*, resent
take under consideration deliberate, ponder
take unlawful possession rob
take unlawfully steal
take up adopt, assume *(undertake)*, discharge *(pay a debt)*, embark, embrace *(accept)*, endeavor, espouse, immerse *(engross)*, levy, occupy *(engage)*, ply, specialize, undertake
take up abode locate, reside
take up again continue *(resume)*, proceed *(continue)*, resume
take up an inquiry canvass, probe
take up an option choose
take up arms fight *(battle)*, rebel
take up in conference discuss
take up membership join *(associate oneself with)*
take up one's abode dwell *(reside)*
take up quarters lodge *(reside)*
take up residence dwell *(reside)*, inhabit, reside
take up residence in lodge *(reside)*, occupy *(take possession)*
take upon oneself endeavor, pledge *(promise the performance of)*, promise

(vow), undertake

take vengeance retaliate

take vengeance on punish

take warning beware

take wing disappear

take without proof assume *(suppose)*, presume

take wrongfully hold up *(rob)*, purloin

take wrongly misapprehend

take-off travesty

take-over disseisin, sequestration

take-over of property eviction

taken lost *(taken away)*, preferred *(favored)*

taken advantage of aggrieved *(victimized)*

taken by force by the authorities arrested *(apprehended)*

taken for granted apparent *(presumptive)*, assumed *(inferred)*, ordinary, tacit

taken into custody arrested *(apprehended)*

taken prisoner arrested *(apprehended)*

takeover condemnation *(seizure)*

taker bearer, customer, extortionist, grantee, payee, volunteer

taking acquisition, apprehension *(act of arresting)*, arrogation, confiscatory, disseisin, distress *(seizure)*, plagiarism

taking away abduction, removal

taking back retraction

taking by undue exercise of power blackmail, extortion

taking counsel deliberation

taking different courses divergent

taking effect before retroactive

taking exception dissenting

taking for public use expropriation *(right of eminent domain)*

taking hold apprehension *(act of arresting)*

taking information interrogation

taking issue with dissenting

taking of human life murder

taking of life aberemurder

taking of private land by the government expropriation *(right of eminent domain)*

taking of property for public use condemnation *(seizure)*

taking on assumption *(adoption)*

taking possession appropriation *(taking)*, condemnation *(seizure)*, disseisin

taking the law in one's own hands lynch law

taking the place of another vicarious *(delegated)*

taking without compensation disseisin

takings earnings, spoils

tale falsehood, myth, narration, story *(narrative)*

tale telling narration

talebearer informant

talent aptitude, caliber *(mental capacity)*, capacity *(aptitude)*, competence *(ability)*, faculty *(ability)*, gift *(flair)*, penchant, performance *(workmanship)*, potential, proclivity, propensity, sense *(intelligence)*, skill, specialty *(special aptitude)*

talented artful, deft, practiced, proficient, resourceful, veteran

talesmen jury

talion punishment, reprisal

talionic disciplinary *(punitory)*, punitive

talk communicate, conversation, converse, declaim, declamation, discourse, discourse, interview, language, parlance, parley, peroration, phrase, recite, recount, report *(detailed account)*, report *(rumor)*, scandal, speak, speech, utter

talk about discuss, mention, remark

talk down to condescend *(patronize)*, patronize *(condescend toward)*

talk insincerely palter

talk into convert *(persuade)*, exhort, induce, influence, motivate, prevail upon

talk it over discuss

talk nonsense prattle

talk of circulate, discuss

talk out discuss

talk out of dissuade, expostulate

talk over confer *(consult)*, consult *(ask advice of)*, discourse, discuss, reason *(persuade)*

talk together discourse, discuss

talkative demonstrative *(expressive of emotion)*, flatulent, loquacious, voluble

talked about renowned

talked of famous, illustrious, notable

talked-about household *(familiar)*

talked-of household *(familiar)*

talking loquacious

talking big bluster *(speech)*

talks conference

tall story myth

tall talk rodomontade

tallage assessment *(levy)*, duty *(tax)*

tallness elevation

tally account *(evaluation)*, amount *(sum)*, bill *(invoice)*, calculate, census, comport *(agree with)*, computation, poll *(canvass)*, poll, record

tally sheet inventory

tame alleviate, dominate, harmless, insipid, jejune *(dull)*, lifeless *(dull)*, malleable, moderate *(temper)*, obedient, passive, peaceable, pedestrian, phlegmatic, placid, prosaic, resigned, soothe, subdue, subject, subjugate

tameable corrigible

tamper disturb

tamper with adulterate, contaminate, damage, denature, falsify, pervert, suborn, vitiate

tangency connection *(abutment)*, contact *(touching)*

tangent close *(near)*, proximate, tangential

tangential proximate

tangere adjoin, affect

tangibility embodiment, materiality *(physical existence)*

tangible actual, apparent *(perceptible)*, appreciable, bodily, certain *(positive)*, concrete, corporal, corporeal, de facto, manifest, material *(physical)*, palpable, perceivable, perceptible, physical, substantive

tangible assets estate *(property)*, merchandise, principal *(capital sum)*, property *(possessions)*

tangible form embodiment

tangible object entity

tangible proof fact

tangibles estate *(property)*, property *(possessions)*

tangibly fairly *(clearly)*

tangle complex *(entanglement)*, disorganize, engage *(involve)*, implicate, intertwine, involution, perplex, snarl

tangled complex, compound, disordered, disorderly, inextricable, intricate, labyrinthine, problematic, recondite, sinuous

tangly inextricable

tangy palatable

tankage capacity *(maximum)*

tantalization bribery, incentive, seduction

tantalize bait *(lure)*, interest, lure

tantalized eager

tantalizing provocative, sapid

tantamount coequal, comparable *(equivalent)*, equal, equivalent, identical

tantamount to constructive *(inferential)*, virtual

tap impinge

tap the lines eavesdrop

taper attenuate, converge, decrease, diminish, lessen

taper off subside

tapering narrow

tar brand *(stigmatize)*

tardare delay, hold up *(delay)*

tardiness delay

tardus phlegmatic

tardy back *(in arrears)*, dilatory, overdue, remiss

targe panoply

target design *(intent)*, destination, end *(intent)*, goal, intention, object, objective, purpose, pursuit *(goal)*, victim

tariff duty *(tax)*, excise, fare, imposition *(tax)*, levy, tax

tarnish attaint, brand *(stigmatize)*, contaminate, debase, deface, defacement, defame, demean *(make lower)*, denigrate, depreciate, derogate, discredit, discredit, disgrace, disgrace, dishonor *(shame)*, dishonor *(deprive of honor)*, disparage, humiliate, ignominy, infamy, infect, onus *(stigma)*, opprobrium, pillory, pollute, reproach, scandal, shame, smear, stain, stigma, sully, taint *(corrupt)*

tarnished blemished, disgraceful, marred

tarnished honor attaint, disgrace, dishonor *(shame)*, ignominy, scandal, shame

tarriance delay

tarry delay, dwell *(reside)*, lodge *(reside)*, loiter, pause, procrastinate, prolong, reside, stop

tarrying deferment

tart astringent, bitter *(acrid tasting)*, caustic

task act *(undertaking)*, agency *(legal relationship)*, burden, business *(affair)*, calling, campaign, capacity *(job)*, charge *(responsibility)*, duty *(obligation)*, duty *(tax)*, employment, endeavor, enterprise *(undertaking)*, exact, function, job, labor *(work)*, mission, operation, part *(role)*, post, project, pursuit *(occupation)*, role, specialty *(special aptitude)*, tax *(overwork)*, trade *(occupation)*, undertaking *(business)*, undertaking *(enterprise)*, venture, work *(em-*

ployment)

task undertaken undertaking *(attempt)*

taskmaster employer, principal *(director)*, superintendent

taste discretion *(quality of being discreet)*, mode, partake, partiality, predilection, predisposition, propensity, propriety *(correctness)*, sensibility, style

tasteful aesthetic, attractive, elegant, felicitous, fit, palatable, proper

tastefulness decorum

tasteless disreputable, inelegant, insipid, jejune *(dull)*, pedestrian, stale, tawdry

tastelessness indecency

tasty nectarious, palatable, sapid, savory

tattle betray *(disclose)*, divulge, inform *(notify)*, report *(rumor)*

taught informed *(educated)*, knowing

taunt badger, bait *(harass)*, denigrate, discompose, disparage, jape, jeer, mock *(deride)*, offend *(insult)*, pique, plague, press *(goad)*, provocation, provoke, ridicule

taunting critical *(faultfinding)*, instigation

taut firm, rigid

tautness stress *(strain)*

tautologic redundant

tautological iterative, redundant

tautology redundancy

tawdry blatant *(obtrusive)*, meretricious, poor *(inferior in quality)*, pretentious *(ostentatious)*

tax assessment *(levy)*, charge *(cost)*, charge *(assess)*, encumber *(hinder)*, exact, excise, excise *(levy a tax)*, exhaust *(deplete)*, fine, force *(coerce)*, impose *(enforce)*, levy, levy, rebuke, reproach, require *(compel)*, tariff *(duties)*, toll *(exact payment)*

tax collector assessor

tax gatherer assessor

tax haven shelter *(tax benefit)*

tax man assessor

tax on demand duty *(tax)*

tax one's energies strive

tax receiver assessor

tax sanctuary shelter *(tax benefit)*

tax taker assessor

taxation ad valorem, duty *(tax)*, excise, levy, tax

taxer assessor

taxing onerous, oppressive

taxis classification

teach communicate, convey *(communicate)*, disabuse, edify, educate, elucidate, enlighten, explain, impart, inculcate, inform *(notify)*, initiate, instill, nurture

teach a lesson to punish

teach by example demonstrate *(establish)*

teach by examples illustrate

teach wickedness brutalize, pervert

teachable corrigible, malleable, pliable, sequacious, tractable

teacher pedagogue

teachers faculty *(teaching staff)*

teaching didactic, direction *(guidance)*, discipline *(field of study)*, doctrine, edification, education, experience *(background)*, guidance, informatory, maxim, precept, preparation, propa-

ganda

teaching body faculty *(teaching staff)*

teaching personnel faculty *(teaching staff)*

teachings doctrine

team band

team of employees personnel

team up federalize *(associate)*, involve *(participate)*

team up with combine *(act in concert)*, join *(associate oneself with)*

teammate coadjutant, contributor *(contributor)*, member *(individual in a group)*, partner

teamwork coaction, concert, contribution *(participation)*, cooperative

teamworker contributor *(contributor)*, partner

tear divide *(separate)*, lancinate, mutilate, race, rend, separate, sever, split

tear apart disjoint, mutilate

tear assunder part *(separate)*

tear asunder force *(break)*, rend

tear away deprive

tear down obliterate, refute

tear into attack

tear loose extricate

tear off denude

tear oneself away part *(leave)*

tear out eliminate *(eradicate)*, eviscerate, excise *(cut away)*, extirpate

tear to pieces extirpate

tear up disorganize

tearable divisible

tearful disconsolate, lugubrious, querulous

tearing division *(act of dividing)*, separation

tearing away avulsion

tearing down destruction

tearing off avulsion

tearless callous

tease badger, bait *(harass)*, bait *(lure)*, cajole, discompose, harrow, harry *(harass)*, hector, irritate, jape, mock *(deride)*, molest *(annoy)*, offend *(insult)*, perplex, pique, plague, press *(goad)*, provoke

teaser enigma

technic instrumentality

technical industrial

technical term technicality

technicality detail

technician artisan, expert, specialist

technique avenue *(means of attainment)*, discretion *(quality of being discreet)*, expedient, facility *(instrumentality)*, instrumentality, method, mode, modus operandi, performance *(workmanship)*, specialty *(special aptitude)*, strategy, style, system, treatment

technological industrial

tectum ceiling, habitation *(dwelling place)*, inhabitation *(place of dwelling)*

tectus inscrutable

tedious jejune *(dull)*, lifeless *(dull)*, mundane, onerous, pedestrian, ponderous, prolix, prosaic, repetitious, trite, usual

teem propagate *(increase)*, pullulate

teeming copious, full, manifold, populous, productive, profuse, prolific, replete, rife

teemless barren

teen juvenile

teenager adolescent, juvenile, minor

teeter beat *(pulsate)*

teetotalism temperance

tegere cloak, shroud

telegram dispatch *(message)*

telegraphic laconic, sententious

telescope abridge *(shorten)*, abstract *(summarize)*, constrict *(compress)*

telescoped compact *(pithy)*

telic purposeful

tell annunciate, apprise, betray *(disclose)*, communicate, constrain *(compel)*, convey *(communicate)*, declare, depict, detail *(particularize)*, direct *(order)*, disclose, divulge, enunciate, express, herald, impart, inform *(notify)*, instruct *(direct)*, mention, notify, observe *(remark)*, order, phrase, posit, proclaim, profess *(avow)*, pronounce *(speak)*, propagate *(spread)*, publish, recite, recount, remark, remind, report *(disclose)*, reveal, signify *(inform)*, speak, utter

tell a falsehood fabricate *(make up)*, falsify, lie *(falsify)*, misguide, mislead, misrepresent, misstate, perjure, prevaricate

tell a lie bear false witness, fabricate *(make up)*, misguide, misstate, perjure, prevaricate

tell a secret confide *(divulge)*

tell again recapitulate, repeat *(state again)*

tell all confess

tell an untruth lie *(falsify)*, misguide, mislead, misstate, prevaricate

tell apart differentiate, discriminate *(distinguish)*

tell details detail *(particularize)*

tell falsehoods about frame *(charge falsely)*

tell fortunes predict, prognosticate

tell from differentiate

tell fully detail *(particularize)*

tell how explain

tell in detail recount

tell lies misrepresent

tell lies about frame *(charge falsely)*

tell of bespeak, connote, evidence, signify *(denote)*

tell on betray *(disclose)*

tell over repeat *(state again)*

tell particulars detail *(particularize)*

tell secrets inform *(betray)*

tell the future predict

tell the meaning define

tell the meaning of denote

tell the truth bare, disabuse

tell vividly delineate, depict, portray

tell with assurance of secrecy confide *(divulge)*

teller bystander, deponent, harbinger, informer *(a person who provides information)*

telling caveat, cogent, conversation, demonstrative *(illustrative)*, determinative, disclosure *(act of disclosing)*, eloquent, incisive, informatory, noteworthy, persuasive, potent, powerful, recital, strategic, trenchant

tellurian mundane

telluric mundane

temblor cataclysm

temerarious careless, hot-blooded, impolitic, improvident, imprudent, impulsive *(rash)*, injudicious, lax, negligent, remiss, unpolitic

temerarius heedless, ill-advised, imprudent, injudicious, precipitate
temeritas temerity
temerity audacity
temerous negligent, reckless
temper abate *(lessen)*, adapt, adjust *(regulate)*, allay, alleviate, alter, animus, assuage, character *(personal quality)*, commute, complexion, curb, disposition *(inclination)*, extenuate, frame *(mood)*, lessen, mitigate, modify *(moderate)*, mollify, palliate *(abate)*, passion, posture *(attitude)*, qualify *(condition)*, regulate *(adjust)*, relax, soothe, spirit, subdue
temperament character *(personal quality)*, color *(complexion)*, conatus, condition *(state)*, disposition *(inclination)*, frame *(mood)*, personality, posture *(attitude)*, predisposition, property *(distinctive attribute)*, spirit, tendency, trait
temperamental fractious, sensitive *(easily affected)*
temperance austerity, clemency, constraint *(restriction)*, continence, longanimity, moderation, prudence, restraint
temperantia continence, control *(supervision)*, moderation, temperance
temperare control *(restrain)*, forbear, modify *(moderate)*
temperate charitable *(lenient)*, controlled *(restrained)*, dispassionate, judicious, normal *(sane)*, peaceable, reasonable *(fair)*
temperateness continence, moderation, temperance
temperatio organization *(structure)*
tempered reasonable *(fair)*
tempering abatement *(reduction)*, mitigating, palliative *(abating)*
tempermental demonstrative *(expressive of emotion)*
tempest bluster *(commotion)*, commotion, furor, outburst, turmoil
tempestivus ripe, seasonable
tempestuous disorderly, outrageous, severe, vehement
template pattern
tempo rate
temporal civil *(public)*, corporeal, ephemeral, material *(physical)*, mundane, physical, profane, temporary, transient, transitory
temporarily pro tempore
temporarily established provisional
temporary acting, brief, ephemeral, interim, interlocutory, provisional, tentative, transient, transitory, vicarious *(substitutional)*
temporary accommodation loan
temporary agreement modus vivendi
temporary arrangement modus vivendi, stopgap
temporary closing lockout
temporary deprivation layoff
temporary discharge layoff
temporary escape reprieve
temporary existence mortality
temporary expedient replacement, stopgap, substitute
temporary halt moratorium
temporary inaction cessation *(interlude)*
temporary possession occupancy,

tenancy
temporary quiet lull
temporary refuge asylum *(hiding place)*
temporary relief moratorium, reprieve
temporary route detour
temporary settlement modus vivendi
temporary stillness lull
temporary stop extension *(postponement)*, hiatus, pendency
temporary stoppage respite *(interval of rest)*
temporary substitute stopgap
temporary suspension extension *(postponement)*, layoff
temporary suspension of the execution of a sentence reprieve
temporis intervallum interim
temporis spatium duration
temporize delay, stall, suspend
tempt bait *(lure)*, cajole, coax, entice, entrap, interest, inveigle, lure, motivate, prompt
temptare attempt, try *(attempt)*
temptation bribery, cause *(reason)*, hush money, incentive, provocation, seduction
tempted eager
temptestuousness bluster *(commotion)*
tempting attractive, bribery, palatable, persuasive, provocative, sapid, savory
tempus date, emergency, occasion
temulentus drunk
tenability credibility
tenable believable, colorable *(plausible)*, convincing, defensible, inexpugnable, persuasive, reasonable *(rational)*
tenableness credibility
tenacious chronic, cohesive *(sticking)*, diligent, dogmatic, durable, indestructible, indivisible, industrious, inexorable, infallible, inflexible, inseparable, insistent, intractable, obdurate, patient, permanent, persistent, purposeful, relentless, resolute, sedulous, serious *(devoted)*, stable, steadfast, strong, unrelenting, unremitting, unyielding, willful
tenaciousness adherence *(adhesion)*, adherence *(devotion)*, adhesion *(loyalty)*, diligence *(perseverance)*, strength, tenacity
tenacitas tenacity
tenacity adherence *(adhesion)*, adherence *(devotion)*, adhesion *(loyalty)*, diligence *(perseverance)*, industry *(activity)*, longanimity, purpose, resolution *(decision)*, retention, rigor, strength
tenancy duration, enjoyment *(use)*, habitation *(act of inhabiting)*, inhabitation *(act of dwelling in)*, ownership, possession *(ownership)*, seisin, term *(duration)*, time
tenant denizen, dwell *(reside)*, habitant, inhabit, inhabitant, lessee, lodge *(reside)*, lodger, occupant, reside, resident
tenant-landlord agreement lease
tenantable habitable
tenanted populous
tenantless devoid
tenantry inhabitation *(act of dwelling*

in)
tenative interim
tenax close *(rigorous)*, parsimonious, penurious
tend care *(regard)*, concern *(care)*, contribute *(assist)*, dispose *(incline)*, foster, gravitate, keep *(shelter)*, pander, prefer, preserve, serve *(assist)*
tend to conduce
tend to show evidence
tend toward discriminate *(treat differently)*, gravitate
tendency animus, aptitude, bias, character *(personal quality)*, characteristic, color *(complexion)*, conatus, direction *(course)*, disposition *(inclination)*, habit, inclination, instinct, mode, penchant, position *(point of view)*, predilection, predisposition, probability, proclivity, propensity, quality *(grade)*, standpoint, temperament, tenor
tendency to change the mind indecision
tendency to waver indecision
tender benevolent, bestow, bid, cede, confer *(give)*, contribute *(indemnify)*, contribute *(supply)*, dispense, extend *(offer)*, introduce, invitation, overture, pay, pose *(propound)*, present *(make a gift)*, proffer, proposal *(suggestion)*, propose, proposition, propound, remit *(send payment)*, remit *(submit for consideration)*, satisfy *(discharge)*, submit *(give)*
tender age nonage
tender feeling affection
tender in advance prepay
tender one's resignation abandon *(withdraw)*, demit, resign, retire *(conclude a career)*
tender passion affection
tender payment disburse *(pay out)*
tender performance offer *(tender)*
tenderfoot neophyte
tenderhearted sensitive *(easily affected)*
tenderness affection, affinity *(regard)*, benevolence *(disposition to do good)*, consideration *(sympathetic regard)*
tending inclined, prone
tending to attract attention conspicuous
tending to cause death deadly, malignant, pernicious, pestilent
tending to elude elusive
tending to escape elusive
tending to evade evasive
tending to excite lustful desires obscene
tending to impair prejudicial
tending to obstruct prejudicial
tending to slip away elusive
tenement estate *(property)*
tenere detain *(restrain)*, hold *(possess)*, interest, occupy *(engage)*, own, possess, restrain, retain *(keep in possession)*
tenet article *(precept)*, belief *(something believed)*, concept, conviction *(persuasion)*, doctrine, dogma, idea, law, precept, principle *(axiom)*, rule *(legal dictate)*, thesis
tenets platform
tenor complexion, condition *(state)*, connotation, content *(meaning)*, context, degree *(magnitude)*, gist *(substance)*, import, main point, meaning,

mode, signification, spirit, substance
(essential nature), temperament
tense rigid
tenseness stress (strain)
tension conflict, disaccord, feud, ill
will, pressure, stress (strain)
tensity stress (strain)
tentative conditional, hesitant, interlocutory, problematic, provisional, speculative, uncertain (questionable), undecided, unsettled, vicarious (substitutional)
tentative approach proposition
tentative explanation hypothesis
tentative law hypothesis
tentative statement proposition, suggestion
tentativeness hesitation
tenuis inconsiderable, negligible,
petty, poor (inferior in quality), slight
tenuitas poverty
tenuous illusory, insubstantial, marginal, nonsubstantial (not sturdy), null
(insignificant), slight
tenure domain (land owned), duration, enjoyment (use), occupancy, occupation (possession), ownership, period,
phase (period), seisin, tenancy, term
(duration), time, title (right)
tenure by lease leasehold
tepidity disinterest (lack of interest)
tergiversari equivocate, prevaricate
tergiversate abandon (relinquish), defect, equivocate, leave (depart), palter,
prevaricate, quit (discontinue), rebel,
recant, secede
tergiversating false (disloyal), regressive, undependable, unreliable, untrustworthy
tergiversatio evasion
tergiversation breach, evasion, reversal, revolt, sedition
tergiversator pariah
term call (title), call (title), clause,
condition (contingent provision), define,
denominate, denomination, duration,
expiration, finality, identify, label, life
(period of existence), lifetime, option
(contractual provision), period, phase
(period), phrase, provision (clause), purview, qualification (condition), session,
technicality, tenure, time, title (division)
term of activity life (period of existence)
term of effectiveness life (period of
existence)
term of imprisonment captivity
term of life age
term of reference article (distinct
section of a writing)
terminable defeasible, determinable
(liable to be terminated)
terminal border, conclusive (settled),
destination, end (termination), extreme
(last), final, finality, last (final), mete,
ultimate
terminal point destination, end (termination), extremity (furthest point),
objective
terminally ill in extremis
terminare finish, limit
terminate abate (extinguish), abolish,
abrogate (rescind), adjourn, annul, cancel, cap, cease, complete, conclude
(complete), consummate, culminate, de-

cide, desist, destroy (void), discontinue
(abandon), eliminate (eradicate), expire, extinguish, finish, halt, lapse
(cease), liquidate (convert into cash),
obstruct, overthrow, palliate (abate),
quash, quit (discontinue), rest (cease
from action), result, shut, slay, stop
terminate a trial rest (end a legal
case)
terminate business affairs liquidate
(convert into cash)
terminate work strike (refuse to
work)
terminated complete (ended), dead,
defunct, through
terminated trial mistrial
terminating final, last (final)
termination abatement (extinguishment), adjournment, barrier, border,
cancellation, close (conclusion), conclusion (outcome), denouement, destination, desuetude, discharge (performance), discontinuance (act of discontinuing), discontinuance (interruption of
a legal action), effect, end (termination), expiration, extremity (death), extremity (furthest point), finality, frontier, halt, lapse (expiration), layoff,
moratorium, rescision, resignation (relinquishment), result
termination of a pregnancy abortion (feticide)
termination of an action dismissal
(termination of a proceeding), nonsuit
termination of cohabitation estrangement
termination of employment layoff
termination of life death, homicide
termination of marital cohabitation
separation
termination of membership expulsion
terminational complete (ended), definitive, final, last (final)
terminative complete (ended), conclusive (settled), definitive, extreme (last),
final, last (final), ultimate
terminology denomination, language,
parlance, phraseology
terminus cessation (termination), destination, end (termination), extremity
(furthest point), finality, mete, periphery
terminus boundary, close (conclusion),
denouement, limit
termless indeterminate, infinite,
open-ended, unlimited
termly intermittent
termor lodger
terms adjustment, arrangement (understanding), case (set of circumstances), compromise, posture (situation), premises (hypotheses), settlement
terms for agreement contract
terms imposed circumstances
terms proposed counteroffer, proposition
terra district
terra firma cornerstone
terrae filius nonentity
terrain land, locality, parcel, region,
territory, zone
terrene mundane
terrestrial mundane
terrible deplorable, dire, formidable,
gross (flagrant), heinous, lamentable,

loathsome, nefarious, pestilent, regrettable, sinister
terrible accident disaster
terrifc meritorious
terrific prodigious (enormous)
terrify endanger, frighten, intimidate,
menace
terrifying formidable
territorial local, regional
territorial division district
territorial range of authority jurisdiction
territorial shape dimension
territory area (province), bailiwick,
capacity (sphere), circuit, district, domain (sphere of influence), dominion
(absolute ownership), estate (property),
freehold, jurisdiction, locality, location,
parcel, possessions, property (land),
province, purview, realm, region, scope,
section (vicinity), site, space, venue, vicinity, zone
territory for defense buffer zone
terror fear, panic, phobia, trepidation
terror fright
terrorism anarchy, lynch law
terrorist assailant, criminal
terrorize bait (harass), coerce, endanger, frighten, harass, intimidate,
threaten
terse cohesive (compact), compact
(pithy), laconic, pithy, sententious, succinct
test attempt, canon, check (inspect),
criterion, endeavor, experiment,
indagation, question (inquiry), research, survey (poll), trial (experiment),
try (attempt), venture
test case criterion
test of endurance contest (competition)
testable deductible (provable), incontrovertible, irrefutable
testament certificate, codicil, will
(testamentary instrument)
testamentary heritable
testamentary declaration testament
testamentary decree testament
testamentary disposition bequest,
conveyance, demise (conveyance)
testamentary gift bequest, legacy
testamentum testament, will (testamentary instrument)
testari depose (testify), testify, witness
(attest to)
testator contributor (giver), decedent,
grantor
tested conclusive (determinative), definite, dependable, genuine, indubious,
meritorious, safe
testee subject (object)
testem facere attest
testificari attest, depose (testify), testify, witness (attest to)
testificatio attestation
testification affirmation, attestation,
averment, avouchment, certification
(attested copy), corroboration, deposition, reference (recommendation)
testification under oath affidavit
testified to alleged
testifier affiant, affirmant, bystander,
deponent, eyewitness, witness
testify acknowledge (verify), affirm
(declare solemnly), avouch (avow),
avow, bear (adduce), bespeak, certify

(attest), inform *(notify)*, manifest, posit, promise *(vow)*, verify *(swear)*, vouch

testify against inform *(betray)*

testify to attest, corroborate, establish *(show)*, report *(disclose)*, witness *(attest to)*

testimonial affirmation, deposition, monument, recommendation, remembrance *(commemoration)*, reminder, respect

testimonial averment admission *(disclosure)*

testimonials credentials

testimonium affirmation

testimonium attestation, deposition, evidence, evidence, proof, testimony

testimonium dicere witness *(attest to)*

testimonium per tabulas datum affidavit

testimony adjuration, admission *(disclosure)*, affirmance *(legal affirmation)*, affirmation, attestation, avowal, certification *(attested copy)*, corroboration, deposition, disclosure *(something disclosed)*, proof, reference *(recommendation)*, statement

testing trial *(experiment)*

testing program experiment, research

testis witness

testy fractious, perverse, petulant, querulous, spiteful

tether fix *(make firm)*, handcuff, restrict, trammel

tethered fixed *(securely placed)*

text content *(meaning)*, contents, context, hornbook, meaning, phraseology, scenario, script, subject *(topic)*

textbook hornbook

textual literal

thalamus chamber *(compartment)*

thankful indebted

thankless undesirable, unrequited

thanklessness ingratitude

thanks recognition

that being so consequently

that being the case consequently

that is a savoir

that is to say a savoir

that may be determined determinable *(ascertainable)*

that which a person owes to another obligation *(duty)*

that which attaches attachment *(act of affixing)*

that which furnishes proof evidence

that which is comprehended coverage *(scope)*

that which is decided holding *(ruling of a court)*

that which is due from a person obligation *(duty)*

that which is owed debit

that which is owing due, obligation *(liability)*, responsibility *(accountability)*

that which is proper decorum

that which tends to prove evidence

thaumaturgy mystery

the accused defendant

the act of tracing delineation

the bench forum *(court)*

the case basic facts

the court judge

the deceased dead

the defense litigant

the defunct dead

the departed dead

the entirety in solido

the facts in the matter basic facts

the facts of the case basic facts

the following a savoir

the government prosecution *(government agency)*

the late dead

the late lamented dead

the legal fraternity bar *(body of lawyers)*

the most possible utmost

the other side contra

the outvoted minority *(outnumbered group)*

the people district attorney, prosecution *(government agency)*

the prosecuting attorney prosecution *(government agency)*

the prosecution contender, district attorney

the state district attorney, prosecution *(government agency)*

the succeeding a savoir

the unforeseen bombshell

the whole sum *(total)*

the whole story basic facts

theater scene

theatralis pretentious *(pompous)*

theatrecraft histrionics

theatric histrionic

theatrical grandiose, histrionic, meretricious, orotund

theatricalism histrionics

theatricality histrionics, pretense *(ostentation)*

theatricalness histrionics

theft burglary, conversion *(misappropriation)*, embezzlement, housebreaking, larceny, misappropriation, plunder, robbery, spoliation

theft of money entrusted to one's care embezzlement

theft of money entrusted to one's management embezzlement

theistic sacrosanct

theme content *(meaning)*, motif, question *(issue)*, subject *(topic)*, thesis

theme of inquiry question *(inquiry)*

themes contents

then late *(defunct)*

then again also

theologic sacrosanct

theological sacrosanct

theorem inference, postulate, prescription *(directive)*, principle *(axiom)*, supposition

theorems premises *(hypotheses)*

theoretical debatable, disputable, indefinite, intangible, moot, nonexistent, presumptive, speculative

theorization generalization, speculation *(conjecture)*

theorize assume *(suppose)*, derive *(deduce)*, generalize, guess, opine, ponder, postulate, presume, presuppose, prognosticate, rationalize, reason *(conclude)*, reflect *(ponder)*, speculate *(conjecture)*, surmise, suspect *(think)*

theory assumption *(supposition)*, concept, conjecture, conviction *(persuasion)*, deduction *(conclusion)*, generalization, hypothesis, idea, inference, opinion *(belief)*, perception, proposition, rationale, speculation *(conjecture)*, supposition, thesis

theory of business finance

theory of fiscal relations finance

therapeutic curative, cure, medicinal, palliative *(abating)*, remedial, salubrious, salutary

therapeutical medicinal, salubrious

therapy treatment

thereafter ex post facto

therefore consequently

therein herein, wherein

thersitical scandalous

thesaurus treasury

theses premises *(hypotheses)*

thesis conjecture, contents, deduction *(conclusion)*, hypothesis, inference, opinion *(belief)*, postulate, proposition, subject *(topic)*, supposition, theory

thews sinew

thick cohesive *(compact)*, compact *(dense)*, impervious, obtuse, opaque, ossified, populous, rife, solid *(compact)*

thick-headed opaque

thick-skinned callous, impervious

thick-witted opaque

thick-wittedness opacity

thicken crystallize

thickened ossified

thickening congealment

thicket assemblage

thickheaded obtuse

thickheadedness opacity

thickly settled populous

thickness caliber *(measurement)*, congealment, density, opacity

thief burglar, convict, criminal, embezzler, hoodlum, lawbreaker, outlaw

thieve carry away, defalcate, despoil, embezzle, hold up *(rob)*, impropriate, loot, pilfer, pillage, pirate *(take by violence)*, plunder, purloin, steal

thievery burglary, conversion *(misappropriation)*, embezzlement, housebreaking, larceny, misappropriation, plagiarism, racket, robbery, spoliation, theft

thieving larcenous

thievish furtive, larcenous, stealthy

thievishness dishonesty

thin deficient, dilute, diminish, excise *(cut away)*, extenuate, insubstantial, insufficient, jejune *(dull)*, lessen, minimal, minimize, narrow, nonsubstantial *(not sufficient)*, reduce, slight, tenuous

thin out deploy, dilute, diminish, lessen

thin with liquid dilute

thing article *(commodity)*

things effects

things as they are status quo

things for sale goods

think deduce, deduct *(conclude by reasoning)*, deem, expect *(consider probable)*, guess, muse, opine, presume, presuppose, rationalize, reason *(conclude)*, reflect *(ponder)*, speculate *(conjecture)*, surmise

think about consider, devote, digest *(comprehend)*, muse, regard *(pay attention)*, study

think ahead plan, scheme

think anxiously brood

think back remember

think back to recall *(remember)*

think better prefer

think better of reconsider, repent

think carefully deliberate

think credible assume *(suppose)*

think deeply ponder

think differently differ *(disagree)*, differ *(vary)*, disagree

think highly of recommend, regard *(hold in esteem)*

think ill of disapprove *(condemn)*

think intensely concentrate *(pay attention)*

think it over doubt *(hesitate)*

think likely assume *(suppose)*, deduce, deduct *(conclude by reasoning)*, expect *(consider probable)*, guess, presume

think little of disparage, disregard, minimize

think logically rationalize

think no more of dismiss *(put out of consideration)*

think nothing of disdain, disregard, minimize

think of conjure, initiate, invent *(produce for the first time)*, recollect

think on ponder

think one deserves claim *(demand)*

think out calculate, scheme, solve

think over brood, deliberate, muse, pause, reconsider

think probable assume *(suppose)*

think reprehensible disapprove *(condemn)*

think through reason *(conclude)*

think too little of underestimate

think twice beware, hesitate, pause

think unworthy of notice disdain

think up conjure, create, frame *(formulate)*, invent *(produce for the first time)*, make, originate

think well of regard *(hold in esteem)*

think wrong disapprove *(condemn)*

thinkable colorable *(plausible)*, plausible, possible, potential, viable

thinker mastermind

thinking assumption *(supposition)*, circumspect, cogitative, conviction *(persuasion)*, dialectic, opinion *(belief)*, ratiocination, rational, reason *(sound judgment)*, reflection *(thought)*, sapient, sensible

thinking out deliberation

thinly scattered scarce

thinness immateriality, paucity

thinning out erosion

thoroughfare causeway

thirst desire, need *(deprivation)*

thirst for need

thorny impracticable, precarious

thorough accurate, circumspect, complete *(all-embracing)*, comprehensive, conscientious, definitive, detailed, diligent, faithful *(diligent)*, industrious, ingrained, intensive, judicious, meticulous, outright, painstaking, particular *(exacting)*, plenary, precise, punctilious, radical *(extreme)*, scrupulous, systematic, total, unmitigated

thoroughfare causeway

thoroughgoing circumspect, complete *(all-embracing)*, comprehensive, diligent, intensive, meticulous, particular *(exacting)*, radical *(extreme)*, systematic, thorough, total, trenchant

thoroughgoingness diligence *(care)*

thoroughly in toto, purely *(positively)*

thoroughness caution *(vigilance)*, diligence *(care)*

those holding power authorities

those in command authorities

those in control authorities

those of influence authorities

those who rule authorities

though regardless

thought apprehension *(perception)*, concept, consideration *(sympathetic regard)*, contemplation, deliberation, idea, notice *(heed)*, notion, opinion *(belief)*, perspective, point *(item)*, proposal *(suggestion)*, ratiocination, reason *(sound judgment)*, remark, suggestion, theory

thought beforehand forethought

thought out intentional, premeditated

thought-out deliberate

thought-provoking sapid, suggestive *(evocative)*

thoughtful benevolent, careful, circumspect, cogitative, deliberate, discreet, discriminating *(judicious)*, earnest, intentional, judicial, judicious, pensive, politic, profound *(esoteric)*, provident *(showing foresight)*, prudent, rational, sensible

thoughtful regard consideration *(sympathetic regard)*

thoughtfulness benevolence *(disposition to do good)*, consideration *(sympathetic regard)*, contemplation, courtesy, deliberation, discretion *(quality of being discreet)*, discrimination *(good judgment)*, forethought, interest *(concern)*, introspection, largess *(generosity)*

thoughtless blind *(not discerning)*, careless, casual, cursory, derelict *(negligent)*, fatuous, heedless, hot-blooded, ill-judged, impolitic, improvident, imprudent, impulsive *(rash)*, inadvertent, injudicious, irrational, irresponsible, lax, misadvised, negligent, oblivious, perfunctory, perverse, precipitate, reckless, remiss, slipshod, unpremeditated, unwitting, vacuous

thoughtlessness disinterest *(lack of interest)*, disregard *(lack of respect)*, inconsideration, indiscretion, ingratitude, laxity, neglect, oversight *(carelessness)*, temerity

thoughts of the past hindsight, retrospect

thrall captive, durance, servitude, subjection

thralldom bondage, custody *(incarceration)*, durance, servitude, thrall

thrash beat *(strike)*, lash *(strike)*

thrashing battery

thrasonical orgulous

thread nexus

threadbare trite

threadbare phrase platitude

threat apprehension *(fear)*, coercion, danger, dun, duress, hazard, jeopardy, menace, peril, pitfall, ultimatum, warning

threaten bait *(harass)*, brandish, challenge, coerce, compel, endanger, exact, forewarn, frighten, hector, impend, intimidate, jeopardize, menace, portend, presage, promise *(raise expectations)*

threatening abusive, chilling effect, dangerous, formidable, imminent, insalubrious, noxious, ominous, pending *(imminent)*, pestilent, portentous *(ominous)*, precarious, pugnacious, sinister, unpropitious

threatening harm imminent

threatful ominous

thresh beat *(strike)*

threshold cornerstone, entrance, margin *(outside limit)*, onset *(commencement)*, outline *(boundary)*, outset, start

thrift austerity, economy *(frugality)*, moderation, prudence

thriftiness austerity, economy *(frugality)*, moderation

thriftless improvident, prodigal, profligate *(extravagant)*, profuse

thrifty economic, economical, frugal, parsimonious, provident *(frugal)*, prudent

thrifty use management *(judicious use)*

thrill enjoyment *(pleasure)*, passion

thrilled ecstatic, proud *(self-respecting)*

thrilling moving *(evoking emotion)*, provocative

thrive gain, germinate, increase, prevail *(triumph)*, proliferate, succeed *(attain)*

thriving cumulative *(increasing)*, prosperous, successful

thriving condition prosperity

thriving conditions boom *(prosperity)*

thriving economy boom *(prosperity)*

throb beat *(pulsate)*

throbbing painful

throe outbreak, outburst

throng assemblage, collection *(assembly)*, congregate, mass *(body of persons)*, meet

thronged populous

throttle occlude, shut, stifle

throttle down curb

through arrant *(definite)*, complete *(ended)*, hereby, thereby

through and through outright

through road causeway

through the medium of hereby, thereby

throughout ad interim, wholly

throughway way *(channel)*

throw emit, impel, launch *(project)*, project *(impel forward)*, send

throw a veil over camouflage, conceal

throw aside forgo, reject

throw away abandon *(relinquish)*, dislodge, dispel, jettison, relinquish

throw back reflect *(mirror)*, repulse

throw dishonor upon brand *(stigmatize)*, disgrace

throw doubt upon impugn

throw down overthrow, precipitate *(throw down violently)*, subvert

throw headlong precipitate *(throw down violently)*

throw into confusion agitate *(perturb)*, confound, confuse *(bewilder)*, confuse *(create disorder)*, discompose, disconcert, dislocate, disorganize, disorient, misdirect, muddle, obfuscate, perturb

throw into disorder confuse *(create disorder)*, disorganize, disorient

throw into prison arrest *(apprehend)*, immure

throw light upon define, elucidate, explain, explicate, exposit, interpret, resolve (*solve*), solve

throw off abandon (*relinquish*), dispel, emit, repel (*drive back*)

throw off heat radiate

throw off the scent obfuscate

throw oneself upon attack

throw open admit (*give access*), manifest

throw open to inquiry canvass

throw out discharge (*dismiss*), dislodge, displace (*remove*), eject (*evict*), eject (*expel*), eliminate (*exclude*), emit, exclude, expel, oust, pose (*propound*), propound, radiate, reject, relegate

throw out of gear luxate

throw out of joint dislocate

throw out of order agitate (*shake up*), dislocate, disorganize, disorient, muddle

throw over overthrow

throw overboard jettison

throwback reversion (*act of returning*)

throwing out disqualification (*rejection*), expulsion

thrown away lost (*taken away*)

thrown overboard derelict (*abandoned*)

thrust emphasis, foray, gravamen, impetus, impinge, impulse, launch (*project*), onset (*assault*), operation, project (*impel forward*)

thrust at accost, assail, assault, oppugn

thrust back repel (*drive back*)

thrust in impact, inject, interject, interpose, intrude, plant (*place firmly*)

thrust oneself intrude

thrust oneself in impose (*intrude*)

thrust out deport (*banish*), dislodge, eject (*evict*), eject (*expel*), eliminate (*exclude*), evict, exclude, expel, oust

thrust under immerse (*plunge into*)

thrust upon surreptitiously foist

thrustful compelling, decisive

thrusting out deportation

thruway causeway

thug assailant

thumb peruse

thumb through read

thumbnail sketch brief

thump beat (*pulsate*)

thumping prodigious (*enormous*)

thunder barrage, outbreak, outburst

thunder against inveigh, reprimand

thunder forth proclaim

thunderbolt bombshell

thunderclap bombshell

thunderous resounding

thunderstruck speechless

thus a fortiori, consequently

thusly a priori, consequently

thwart annoy, arrest (*stop*), avert, balk, bar (*hinder*), beat (*defeat*), block, check (*restrain*), circumvent, condemn (*ban*), constrict (*inhibit*), contain (*restrain*), contravene, counter, countervail, defeat, deter, disadvantage, discontinue (*break continuity*), discourage, disrupt, encumber (*hinder*), enjoin, estop, fight (*counteract*), foil, forestall, frustrate, halt, hamper, hold up (*delay*), impede, inconvenience, interdict, interfere, interrupt, keep (*restrain*), kill (*defeat*), obstruct, occlude, oppugn, overreach, override, parry, preclude, pre-

vent, prohibit, repulse, resist (*oppose*), stay (*halt*), stem (*check*), stop, toll (*stop*), trammel, withstand

thwarted disappointed

thwarted expectation frustration

thwarter deterrence, deterrent

thwarting defeat, disadvantageous, frustration, preventive

ticket brand, coupon, fare, key (*passport*), label, label, pigeonhole, trademark

ticket incorrectly mislabel

ticket of leave permit

ticklish insecure, precarious

tidal wave cataclysm

tide outflow

tide over continue (*adjourn*)

tidewater littoral

tidings intelligence (*news*), report (*detailed account*), story (*narrative*)

tidy compact (*pithy*), meticulous

tie adherence (*adhesion*), adherence (*devotion*), adhesion (*loyalty*), attachment (*act of affixing*), chain (*nexus*), charge (*lien*), combine (*join together*), connect (*join together*), connection (*fastening*), connection (*relation*), contact (*association*), deadlock, fetter, fetter, handcuff, kinship, liaison, marriage (*intimate relationship*), nexus, prevent, privity, propinquity (*kinship*), relate (*establish a connection*), relation (*connection*), relationship (*connection*), restrain, trammel

tie down fetter

tie in with correspond (*be equivalent*), involve (*implicate*), pertain

tie one's hands handcuff

tie the hands of handcuff

tie together intertwine

tie up constrict (*inhibit*), encumber (*hinder*), handcuff, restrict, trammel

tie-in relation (*connection*), relevance

tied bound, cohesive (*sticking*), compound, equal, inextricable, interrelated, related

tied down indentured

tied in with relevant

tied together conjoint

tier degree (*station*)

ties of blood affiliation (*bloodline*), degree (*kinship*), filiation

ties of family blood

ties of race affiliation (*bloodline*)

tiff bicker, brawl

tight cohesive (*compact*), compact (*dense*), fixed (*securely placed*), illiberal, impervious, parsimonious, solid (*compact*)

tight situation predicament, problem, quagmire

tight spot imbroglio, predicament

tight-lipped mute

tighten adhere (*fasten*), constrict (*compress*)

tightfisted illiberal

tightly knit compact (*dense*)

tightness stress (*strain*)

til until

till ad interim, bank, coffer, cultivate, treasury

tilt bicker, compete

tilted oblique (*slanted*)

timbre intonation

time annum, chance (*fortuity*), date, date, duration, life (*period of existence*),

lifetime, occasion, opportunity, period, phase (*period*), point (*period of time*), term (*duration*), timeliness

time ahead prospect (*outlook*)

time during which anything occurs date

time from birth to death life (*period of existence*)

time interval period

time of life age

time of war belligerency

time off furlough, holiday

time out halt, pause, recess

time payment loan

time saving economic

time stretch period

time without end perpetuity

time worn antique

time-honored conventional, familiar (*customary*), illustrious, inveterate, prescriptive, traditional

time-saving economical

timed punctual

timeful seasonable

timeless durable, incessant, infinite

timelessness perpetuity

timeliness dispatch (*promptness*), expedience

timely apposite, appropriate, favorable (*advantageous*), felicitous, fitting, opportune, prompt, propitious, punctual, seasonable, suitable

timely care precaution

timere fear

timeserving undependable

timetable calendar (*list of cases*), calendar (*record of yearly periods*), schedule

timeworn dilapidated, obsolete, old, stale

timid diffident, hesitant, irresolute, recreant

timidity fear

timor fear

timorous diffident, recreant

timorousness fear

tincture minimum, penetrate

tinge minimum, stain

tingere imbue

tingling ecstatic

tinker repair

tinsel meretricious, tawdry

tint stain

tiny impalpable, minimal, remote (*small*), tenuous

tip bonus, bounty, edge (*border*), end (*termination*), extremity (*furthest point*), gratuity (*present*), herald, inform (*notify*), intelligence (*news*), perquisite, pinnacle, recommendation, reward, suggestion

tip off notify

tip over upset

tipped informed (*having information*), oblique (*slanted*)

tipper informant, informer (*a person who provides information*)

tipping oblique (*slanted*)

tipple carouse

tipster bystander, informant, informer (*one providing criminal information*), informer (*a person who provides information*)

tiptop superlative

tirade bombast, declamation, denunciation, diatribe, disparagement, harangue, obloquy, phillipic, revilement, stricture

tire exhaust *(deplete)*, succumb

tire out tax *(overwork)*

tired languid, lifeless *(dull)*

tiredness languor, prostration

tireless diligent, faithful *(diligent)*, industrious, persistent, undaunted

tirelessness diligence *(perseverance)*

tiresome irksome, jejune *(dull)*, lifeless *(dull)*, operose, painful, pedestrian, prolix, prosaic, vexatious

tiring irksome, operose, oppressive

tiro probationer *(one being tested)*

titallative sapid

titanic prodigious *(enormous)*, strong

tithe tax, toll *(tax)*

titillate bait *(lure)*, interest

titillating attractive, provocative, salacious, sapid, suggestive *(risqué)*

title caption, claim *(right)*, degree *(academic title)*, denominate, denomination, designation *(symbol)*, dominion *(absolute ownership)*, fee *(estate)*, heading, interest *(ownership)*, label, nominate, ownership, possession *(ownership)*, prerogative, privilege, prize, right *(entitlement)*, seisin, stake *(interest)*, subheading, term *(expression)*

title deed debenture

title impairment incumbrance *(lien)*

title incorrectly mislabel

title of honor degree *(academic title)*

titleholder landholder, landowner

tittle iota, minimum, scintilla

titular nominal

titulary nominal

titulus inscription

to until

to a certain extent in part, quasi

to a degree fairly *(moderately)*, in part

to a limited extent fairly *(moderately)*, in part

to all appearances prima facie *(self-evident)*

to all intents and purposes as a rule

to be future, prospective

to be believed convincing

to be decided disputable

to be depended on credible, official

to be expected foreseeable, probable

to be had available, disposable

to be paid delinquent *(overdue)*, due *(owed)*

to be relied upon credible

to be similiar correspond *(be equivalent)*

to be supposed apparent *(presumptive)*

to be trusted official

to blame delinquent *(guilty of a misdeed)*, guilty

to bring to completion consummate

to bring together desegregate

to come forthcoming, future, immediate *(imminent)*, inevitable, prospective

to each according to his share per capita, pro rata

to infinity ad infinitum

to no end unavailing

to no purpose unavailing

to one's advantage beneficial

to one's liking attractive

to some extent fairly *(moderately)*

to that end a priori, consequently

to the contrary contra

to the end throughout *(all over)*

to the letter faithfully, literal, verbatim

to the point applicable, apposite, brief, cogent, cohesive *(compact)*, compact *(pithy)*, concise, explicit, felicitous, germane, laconic, pertinent, relevant, sententious, succinct

to the purpose apposite, effective *(efficient)*, felicitous, fit, pertinent, practical, relevant

to the same degree equal

to the time when until

to this day through *(until now)*

to wit a savoir

toady pander, truckle

toadying obsequious, sequacious, subservient

toast honor

toddler infant

together along, conjoint, en masse, intact

together with also

togetherness integration *(assimilation)*

toil effort, endeavor, endeavor, industry *(activity)*, labor *(work)*, labor, persevere, strive, work *(effort)*

toil unceasingly persist

toiler employee

toilsome onerous, operose, oppressive

token binder, bounty, brand, clue, coupon, denote, designation *(symbol)*, device *(distinguishing mark)*, expression *(manifestation)*, guaranty, indicant, indication, indicator, money, nominal, null *(insignificant)*, perquisite, precursor, prize, remembrance *(commemoration)*, security *(pledge)*, specialty *(distinctive mark)*, symbol, symptom

token payment binder, installment, pledge *(security)*

tokens indicia

told acquainted, informed *(having information)*, narrative, oral, parol, stated

told in confidence confidential

tolerability admissibility, mediocrity

tolerable admissible, allowable, allowed, considerable, fair *(satisfactory)*, imperfect, marginal, mediocre, passable, permissible, reasonable *(fair)*, unobjectionable

tolerableness mediocrity

tolerably fairly *(moderately)*

tolerance acceptance, benevolence *(disposition to do good)*, charter *(sanction)*, clemency, composure, consent, disinterest *(lack of prejudice)*, dispensation *(exception)*, franchise *(license)*, goodwill, indulgence, leave *(permission)*, lenience, longanimity, permission, privilege, resignation *(passive acceptance)*, sanction *(permission)*, sufferance, temperance

tolerans patient

tolerant benevolent, charitable *(lenient)*, dispassionate, lenient, liberal *(broad minded)*, nonmilitant, open-minded, patient, peaceable, permissive, receptive, resigned, stoical, unbiased, unprejudiced

tolerantia tolerance

tolerantly fairly *(impartially)*

tolerare bear *(tolerate)*, endure *(suffer)*, tolerate

tolerate abide, accept *(assent)*, allow *(endure)*, authorize, concede, condescend *(deign)*, condone, consent, endure *(suffer)*, forbear, let *(permit)*, palliate *(excuse)*, permit, receive *(permit to enter)*, recognize *(acknowledge)*, resist *(withstand)*, sanction, submit *(yield)*, suffer *(permit)*, vouchsafe

tolerated allowable, allowed

tolerating permissive

toleratio sufferance

toleration acceptance, approval, charter *(sanction)*, clemency, consent, disinterest *(lack of prejudice)*, dispensation *(exception)*, indulgence, lenience, longanimity, resignation *(passive acceptance)*, sanction *(permission)*, sufferance, temperance, tolerance, understanding *(tolerance)*

toll assessment *(levy)*, charge *(cost)*, duty *(tax)*, exact, excise, fare, fee *(charge)*, imposition *(tax)*, levy, price, tax

tollere abolish, cancel

tome publication *(printed matter)*

tonality intonation

tone character *(personal quality)*, color *(complexion)*, complexion, inflection, intonation, manner *(behavior)*, means *(opportunity)*, parlance, phraseology, property *(distinctive attribute)*, stress *(accent)*, style, tenor

tone down allay, commute, diminish, moderate *(temper)*, modify *(moderate)*, mollify, subdue

tone of voice intonation

tongue language, speech

tongue lash reproach

tongue-lashing denunciation, diatribe, malediction, obloquy, phillipic

tongue-tied inarticulate, mute, speechless

tonguey loquacious

tonic cure, medicinal, panacea, remedial, salubrious, salutary

tonnage cargo

too also

too difficult insurmountable

too early premature

too familiar trite

too few insufficiency

too hard difficult, impracticable, insurmountable

too little deficient, insufficient, nonsubstantial *(not sufficient)*

too many overage

too much disproportionate, overage

too small nonsubstantial *(not sufficient)*

too soon premature

too zealous perfervid

tool appliance, device *(mechanism)*, embellish, expedient, facility *(instrumentality)*, instrumentality, medium, resource

tools paraphernalia *(apparatus)*

toothsome palatable

top cardinal *(outstanding)*, ceiling, culminate, culmination, leading *(ranking first)*, major, outbalance, outweigh, paramount, pinnacle, prime *(most valuable)*, surmount, surpass, transcend

top people elite

top person key man
top-flight master, renowned
top-level best, major
top-level meeting caucus
top-notch best, premium, select
top-rank notable
top-secret confidential
topic caption, context, heading, matter (subject), question (issue), thesis
topic for discussion matter (subject)
topic under consideration issue (matter in dispute)
topical current, present (current)
topical outline hornbook
topics affairs, contents
toploftiness pride
toplofty insolent, supercilious
topmost best, leading (ranking first), primary
topmost point culmination
topping superior (excellent)
topple obliterate, overthrow, overturn, subvert, upset
torment annoy, badger, bait (harass), discompose, distress (anguish), distress, endanger, harass, harrow, harry (harass), hector, ill use, inflict, infliction, irritate, mistreat, molest (annoy), obsess, oppression, pain, persecute, pique, plague, press (goad), prey, provoke, trouble
tormenting caustic, painful
tormentum gun
torpedo bomb
torpescence sloth
torpescent lifeless (dull), otiose, torpid
torpid dormant, inactive, indolent, insipid, jejune (dull), languid, lifeless (dull), otiose, phlegmatic, powerless, stagnant, static
torpidity inaction, languor, sloth
torpidness languor
torpor inaction, inertia, languor, sloth
torporifc narcotic
torporific insensible, obtuse, stagnant, torpid
torquere harrow, harry (harass)
torrefy deflagrate
torrent outbreak, outburst, spate
torrid hot-blooded
torsion involution
torsional tortuous (bending)
tort delict, delinquency (misconduct), misconduct
tortile circuitous, sinuous, tortuous (bending)
tortility involution
tortious illicit
tortiously illegally
tortuose indirect
tortuosity involution
tortuous caustic, circuitous, complex, cruel, devious, labyrinthine, machiavellian, sinuous
tortuousness involution
torture badger, cruelty, endanger, ill use, inflict, infliction, irritate, mistreat, pique, plague, prey, punish
torturous insufferable, painful
toss beat (pulsate), cast (throw), launch (project), precipitate (throw down violently), send
toss aside forswear
toss out jettison

toss overboard jettison
toss up bet
tot infant
total absolute (complete), aggregate, aggregate, amount (quantity), categorical, collective, complete (all-embracing), comprehensive, comprise, computation, corpus, detailed, entirety, face amount, face value (price), full, in solido, inclusive, maximum (amplitude), outright, peremptory (absolute), plenary, poll, pure, radical (extreme), stark, sum, survey (poll), thorough, unqualified (unlimited), whole (undamaged), whole (unified)
total loss miscarriage
totalitarian dictator, dictatorial
totalitarianism oppression
totality aggregate, complex (development), corpus, entirety, finality, in solido, principal (capital sum), quantity, sum (total), whole
totalize calculate
totally in toto, purely (positively), wholly
totalness entirety, totality
tote carry (transport), transport
totem designation (symbol)
totter vacillate
tottering insecure, precarious
totus entirety, total
touch abut, adjoin, appertain, apply (pertain), connect (join together), correspond (be equivalent), disarm (set at ease), impinge, impress (affect deeply), interest, minimum, nuance, overlap, reach, suggestion
touch off launch (initiate)
touch on connote, indicate, refer (direct attention)
touch up embellish, emend, enhance, fix (repair), meliorate, modify (alter), repair, revise
touch upon allude, comment, mention, pertain
touchable palpable, tangible
touched lunatic
touching adjacent, close (near), contiguous, moving (evoking emotion), persuasive, profound (intense), proximate, tangential, wherein
touchstone standard
touchy fractious, perverse, petulant, querulous, resentful, sensitive (easily affected)
tough durable, indestructible, indomitable, insusceptible (resistant), insusceptible (uncaring), ossified, pertinacious, rigid, severe, strong, unyielding
toughen inure (accustom)
toughened callous, incorrigible, insusceptible (uncaring), ossified
toughness main force, strength, tenacity
tour perambulate, period, phase (period)
touring moving (in motion)
tournament contest (competition)
tourner la loi circumvent
tourney contest (competition), fight (battle), oppose
tournure contour (outline)
tousle agitate (shake up), discompose
tout bystander, inform (notify)
tout au contraire contradictory
tout le contraire contrary

towardly seasonable
tower edifice
tower above overcome (surmount), transcend
tower of strength mainstay
tower over surpass
towering prodigious (enormous), salient
town civic, community
townsman denizen, habitant, resident
toxic deadly, deleterious, detrimental, fatal, harmful, insalubrious, lethal, malignant, noxious, peccant (unhealthy), pernicious, pestilent, virulent
toxicant deadly, pernicious, pestilent
toxiferous lethal, malignant, pernicious, pestilent
trace copy, deduce, deduct (conclude by reasoning), delineate, derive (deduce), detect, ferret, find (discover), follow-up, hint, hunt, impression, indication, iota, locate, minimum, pursue (chase), research, scintilla, search, solve, suggestion, suspicion (uncertainty)
trace out delineate
trace the outline of delineate
trace to ascribe
traceable deductible (provable)
tracing copy, delineation, outline (boundary), pattern
tracing back derivation
track chase, delve, detect, follow-up, investigate, pursue (chase), research, search, trace (follow)
track down ferret, hunt, locate, search, trace (follow)
track mentally investigate
tract district, land, lot, pandect (treatise), parcel, plot (land), property (land), province, section (vicinity), territory, thesis
tract of land premises (buildings)
tractabilis palpable, tangible, tractable
tractability amenability, compliance, credulity
tractable amenable, corrigible, facile, flexible, malleable, obedient, open (persuasible), passive, patient, pliable, pliant, receptive, resigned, resilient, sequacious, servile, suasible, subservient, willing (not averse), yielding
tractableness compliance
tractare manage, manipulate (utilize skillfully), wield
tractate pandect (treatise)
tractatio management (supervision)
tractile pliable, pliant, tractable
traction stress (strain)
tractus region
tradable marketable
trade barter, business (commerce), business (occupation), buy, calling, career, commerce, commercial, deal, deal, dealings, devolve, dicker, employment, exchange, handle (trade), industry (business), interchange, job, labor (work), livelihood, mercantile, occupation (vocation), office, position (business status), practice (professional business), profession (vocation), pursuit (occupation), reciprocate, sale, vend, work (employment)
trade association union (labor organization)

trade by exchange barter
trade fair market *(business)*
trade in handle *(trade)*, sell
trade name brand
trade off barter
trade sign trademark
trade with deal
trademark brand, denomination, designation *(symbol)*, device *(distinguishing mark)*, indicant, symbol
trader broker, dealer, merchant, speculator, supplier, vendor
tradere deliver, surrender *(yield)*
tradesman artisan, dealer, vendor
tradesperson dealer, merchant
tradeswoman dealer
trading business *(commerce)*, commerce, commercial
trading house market *(business)*
trading place market place
trading post market *(business)*
tradition custom, habit, myth, prescription *(custom)*, propriety *(correctness)*, solemnity, usage
tradition-bound conventional
traditional accustomed *(customary)*, common *(customary)*, conventional, customary, familiar *(customary)*, formal, habitual, hereditary, ordinary, orthodox, prescriptive, proverbial, regular *(conventional)*, standing, typical, usual
traditionalism custom
traditionalist philistine
traditionality custom
traditionally invariably
traditionary traditional
traditive prescriptive, traditional
traduce defame, denigrate, denounce *(condemn)*, deprecate, depreciate, derogate, discommend, disoblige, disparage, lessen, libel, malign, pillory, reproach, smear, sully
traducement aspersion, bad repute, defamation, denunciation, dishonor *(shame)*, obloquy, revilement, slander, vilification
traducere transfer
traducing libelous
traffic business *(commerce)*, commerce, deal, dealings, exchange, trade *(commerce)*, trade
traffic by exchange barter
traffic in deal, handle *(trade)*, sell
traffic of commodities commerce
traffic with communicate, patronize *(trade with)*
trafficker dealer
tragedy adversity, calamity, casualty, catastrophe, debacle, disaster, fatality, misfortune
tragic deplorable, dire, disastrous, fatal, lamentable
tragical deplorable, dire, disastrous
tragoedia tragedy
trahere derive *(receive)*, prolong
traiectio exaggeration
trail chase, delve, follow-up, hunt, pursue *(chase)*, search, spy, stem *(originate)*, trace *(follow)*
trail blazer pioneer
trailing subsequent
train chain *(series)*, cultivate, edify, educate, empower, foster, inculcate, initiate, instill, instruct *(teach)*, nurture, specialize, succession
train by instruction discipline *(train)*

train in study
train of thought idea
trained competent, expert, familiar *(informed)*, informed *(educated)*, literate, practiced, professional *(trained)*, proficient, qualified *(competent)*, resourceful, sciential, technical, veteran
trained person expert, practitioner, professional, specialist
trained personnel expert
trainee neophyte, novice, protégé
trainer pedagogue
training competence *(ability)*, direction *(guidance)*, disciplinary *(educational)*, edification, education, experience *(background)*, guidance, instruction *(teaching)*, preparation
trainload cargo
trait character *(personal quality)*, characteristic, differential, feature *(characteristic)*, habit, particularity, property *(distinctive attribute)*, quality *(attribute)*, specialty *(distinctive mark)*, symptom
traitor conspirer, insurgent, malcontent
traitoriousness disloyalty
traitorous disobedient, faithless, false *(disloyal)*, perfidious, recreant, untrue
traitorousness bad faith, infidelity
traits personality
traject deliver, project *(impel forward)*
trammel bar *(hinder)*, block, check *(bar)*, confine, constrain *(imprison)*, constraint *(restriction)*, contain *(restrain)*, control *(restrain)*, curb, debar, detain *(hold in custody)*, detain *(restrain)*, disadvantage, enclose, enclosure, encumber *(hinder)*, fetter, fetter, hamper, handcuff, handcuff, hinder, impede, impediment, obstacle, obstruct, obstruction, occlude, repress, restrain, restrict
tramontane stranger
tramp perambulate, prowl, step, traverse
tramper derelict
trample spurn, subjugate
trample on damage, mistreat, violate
trample upon beat *(defeat)*, break *(violate)*
trance insentience, preoccupation
trangression infringement
tranmission conveyance
tranquil complacent, dispassionate, patient, peaceable, placid
tranquil mind composure
tranquility longanimity, peace, solace
tranquilization mollification, remission
tranquilize allay, alleviate, assuage, disarm *(set at ease)*, lull, moderate *(temper)*, mollify, pacify, placate, propitiate, remit *(relax)*, soothe, subdue
tranquilizer narcotic
tranquilizing narcotic, palliative *(abating)*
tranquillitas composure, ease
tranquillity composure, lull
tranquillus dispassionate, placid
transact commit *(perpetrate)*, conduct, dicker, discharge *(perform)*, execute *(accomplish)*, manage, negotiate, perform *(adhere to)*, perpetrate, trade
transact business handle *(trade)*

transact business with patronize *(trade with)*
transact with patronize *(trade with)*
transaction act *(undertaking)*, agreement *(contract)*, business *(commerce)*, commission *(act)*, deal, event, exchange, interchange, occurrence, operation, proceeding, process *(course)*, sale, trade *(commerce)*, treatment, undertaking *(business)*
transactions affairs, dealings
transcedent sacrosanct
transcend beat *(defeat)*, outbalance, outweigh, overcome *(surmount)*, overstep, prevail *(triumph)*, surmount, surpass
transcendant prime *(most valuable)*
transcendence infringement, supremacy
transcendency supremacy
transcendent best, notable, outstanding *(prominent)*, paramount, primary, superior *(excellent)*, superlative
transcendental mysterious, obscure *(abstruse)*, paramount, recondite
transcendere surmount
transcending infringement
transcribe copy, enter *(record)*
transcript copy, record
transcript of minutes of commitment mittimus
transcript of testimony deposition
transcription record, transcript
transcursion transgression
transect dichotomize
transfer abalienate, assignment *(transfer of ownership)*, attorn, bear *(yield)*, cargo, carriage, cede, cession, confer *(give)*, consign, consignment, convert *(change use)*, conveyance, copy, deed, defect, delegate, delivery, demise *(conveyance)*, deport *(banish)*, devise *(give)*, devolution, devolve, dispatch *(send off)*, dispensation *(act of dispensing)*, displace *(remove)*, displace *(replace)*, disposition *(transfer of property)*, exchange, give *(grant)*, grant *(transfer formally)*, impart, move *(alter position)*, reassign, refer *(send for action)*, relegate, remand, removal, replacement, sale, send, subrogation, supplant, transmit, transmittal, transport
transfer again recover
transfer among the living inter vivos
transfer back recover
transfer by deed abalienate, deliver
transfer by will abalienate, demise
transfer by writing grant *(transfer formally)*
transfer control to the government nationalize
transfer for a consideration sell
transfer for sale consign
transfer of property conveyance, devolution, feoffment
transfer of property as security for a debt mortgage
transfer of security mortgage
transfer of title conveyance
transfer ownership alienate *(transfer title)*, bequeath, demise, devolve, grant *(transfer formally)*, pass *(advance)*
transfer ownership to the government nationalize
transfer property deliver

transfer right deliver
transfer title convey *(transfer)*, pass *(advance)*
transfer to devolve
transfer to an earlier date antedate
transfer to another assign *(transfer ownership)*
transfer to another authority extradition
transferable assignable, contagious, heritable, negotiable
transferee assignee, bearer, consumer, devisee, feoffee, heir, legatee, licensee, payee, recipient
transference alienation *(transfer of title)*, assignment *(transfer of ownership)*, carriage, consignment, conveyance, deed, delivery, demise *(conveyance)*, devolution, disposition *(transfer of property)*, extradition, removal, subrogation, takeover, transition, transmittal
transferor carrier, feoffor, licensor
transferral delivery
transferre transfer
transferred bailment
transferred by a legacy testamentary
transferred by bequest testamentary
transferred by devise testamentary
transferring consignment
transfigere pierce *(lance)*
transfiguration development *(progression)*
transfigure affect, change, convert *(change use)*, denature, distort, meliorate, modify *(alter)*, transform, vary
transfix pierce *(lance)*
transform adapt, alter, change, convert *(change use)*, denature, distort, meliorate, modify *(alter)*, renew *(begin again)*, vary
transformable convertible, protean
transformation conversion *(change)*, development *(progression)*, reconversion, reorganization, transition
transformations vicissitudes
transformed tempered
transfuse deliver, inject, permeate, pervade
transfuse the sense construe *(translate)*
transgredi pass *(advance)*
transgress accroach, break *(violate)*, contravene, disobey, encroach, impose *(intrude)*, infringe, lapse *(fall into error)*, offend *(violate the law)*, overstep, trespass, violate
transgress established bounds impinge
transgressed broken *(unfulfilled)*
transgressing blameworthy, culpable, delinquent *(guilty of a misdeed)*, diabolic, felonious, guilty, peccant *(culpable)*
transgression bad repute, breach, contravention, criminality, culpability, delinquency *(misconduct)*, disregard *(omission)*, encroachment, fault *(responsibility)*, felony, guilt, illegality, infraction, injustice, invasion, malfeasance, mischief, misconduct, misdeed, misdemeanor, misdoing, misfeasance, misprision, offense, onus *(blame)*, tort,

vice, violation, wrong
transgressive disobedient, lawless, unlawful
transgressor convict, criminal, degenerate, delinquent, felon, lawbreaker, malefactor, offender, outlaw, recidivist, vandal, wrongdoer
transhipment removal
transient acting, brief, ephemeral, interim, interlocutory, lodger, moving *(in motion)*, mutable, profane, provisional, shifting, temporary, transitory, unsettled, volatile
transient arrangement modus vivendi
transientness insignificance, mortality
transigere transact
transire omit, pass *(advance)*
transit circulation, reconversion, transition
transitio transition
transition circulation, conversion *(change)*, reconversion
transitional intermediate, mesne, moving *(in motion)*, progressive *(going forward)*, provisional, temporary
transitive temporary
transitorily pro tempore
transitoriness mortality
transitory brief, ephemeral, interlocutory, profane, provisional, shifting, temporary, transient, volatile
translatable accountable *(explainable)*, determinable *(ascertainable)*
translate define, deliver, elucidate, explain, explicate, interpret, render *(depict)*, transform
translate incorrectly misread
translate into action exercise *(discharge a function)*
translate orally interpret
translaticius conventional, ordinary
translation construction, definition, explanation, paraphrase, rendition *(explication)*, restatement
translocate deliver, move *(alter position)*
translocation carriage, extradition, removal, transmittal
transmigration circulation, immigration, transition
transmigratory moving *(in motion)*
transmissible assignable, contagious, hereditary, heritable, negotiable
transmission alienation *(transfer of title)*, assignment *(transfer of ownership)*, circulation, consignment, contact *(association)*, conveyance, delivery, demise *(conveyance)*, devolution, osmosis, publication *(disclosure)*, transmittal
transmission of knowledge declaration, notification
transmission of title feoffment
transmissive contagious
transmit annunciate, assign *(transfer ownership)*, bestow, cede, circulate, communicate, confer *(give)*, consign, contribute *(supply)*, convey *(communicate)*, convey *(transfer)*, correspond *(communicate)*, delegate, deliver, demise, descend, devise *(give)*, devolve, dispatch *(send off)*, disseminate, give *(grant)*, grant *(transfer formally)*, impart, issue *(send forth)*, leave *(give)*, notify, pass *(advance)*, propagate *(spread)*,

radiate, redirect, remit *(submit for consideration)*, remove *(transfer)*, send, transfer, transport
transmit by will devise *(give)*
transmit disease infect
transmit payment remit *(send payment)*
transmittable assignable
transmittal assignment *(transfer of ownership)*, conveyance, delivery, demise *(conveyance)*, remittance
transmittance delivery, transmittal
transmittere transfer, transmit, transport
transmittible negotiable
transmogrify alter, change, convert *(change use)*, transform
transmutable convertible
transmutation conversion *(change)*, transition
transmute alter, change, convert *(change use)*, denature, modify *(alter)*, transform, vary
transparent clear *(apparent)*, direct *(forthright)*, evident, explicit, ingenuous, lucid, manifest, obvious, open *(in sight)*, pellucid, perceivable, unambiguous
transpierce enter *(penetrate)*, lancinate, penetrate, pierce *(lance)*
transpiration experience *(encounter)*, happening
transpire arise *(occur)*, ensue, occur *(happen)*, pass *(advance)*
transplacement removal
transplant consign, deliver, transport
transplantation insertion, removal, transmittal
transplendent illustrious
transport carry *(transport)*, consign, convey *(transfer)*, deliver, deport *(banish)*, expatriate, move *(alter position)*, passion, relegate, transfer, transmit
transport back recover
transport company carrier
transportable property movable
transportables movable
transportare transport
transportation carriage, removal, transmittal
transportation charge fare
transportation fee fare
transportation of commodities commerce
transportation of goods commerce
transported ecstatic
transposable convertible
transposal delivery, exchange
transpose convert *(change use)*, convey *(transfer)*, displace *(replace)*, move *(alter position)*
transposed inverse
transposition delivery, exchange, replacement
transshape convert *(change use)*, transform
transshipment carriage
transubstantiate change, convert *(change use)*, modify *(alter)*, transform
transudation outflow
trap ambush, artifice, bait *(lure)*, deceive, deception, decoy, dupe, ensnare, entrap, frame up, hunt, imposture, inveigle, lock, maneuver *(trick)*, mislead, obstruct, occlude, pitfall, stratagem
trapping chattel

trappings paraphernalia *(personal belongings)*

trashy inferior *(lower in quality)*, poor *(inferior in quality)*, trivial

traumatize damage

travail disaster, effort, endeavor, hardship, labor, strive

travel perambulate

travel over traverse

travelable passable

traveled passable

traveler afoot pedestrian

traveling moving *(in motion)*, progressive *(going forward)*

traveller itinerant

travelling itinerant

traversable passable

traversal contravention, counterargument, demurrer, disapproval, impugnation, intersection, negation, opposition, prohibition

traverse answer *(reply)*, balk, circumvent, collide *(clash)*, contest, contradict, contravene, counteract, countervail, cross *(disagree with)*, cross *(intersect)*, demonstrate *(protest)*, demur, deny *(contradict)*, disaccord, disaffirm, disagree, disavow, disobey, disown *(deny the validity)*, disprove, dispute *(contest)*, fight *(counteract)*, gainsay, hinder, negate, oppugn, patrol, perambulate, prohibit, protest, refuse, refute, reject, repel *(drive back)*, thwart

traverse the outline of delineate

traversing negative

travesty caricature, distortion, jape, mock *(imitate)*, parody, ridicule

treacherous aleatory *(perilous)*, bad *(offensive)*, collusive, cruel, dangerous, detrimental, dishonest, faithless, false *(disloyal)*, fraudulent, harmful, insecure, insidious, insubordinate, irresponsible, lying, machiavellian, malevolent, malicious, malignant, nefarious, perfidious, pernicious, precarious, recreant, ruthless, sinister, sly, tortuous *(corrupt)*, undependable, unreliable, unscrupulous, untrue, untrustworthy, vicious, virulent

treacherous killing assassination

treacherousness bad faith, dishonesty, false pretense, improbity

treachery bad faith, collusion, deceit, disloyalty, false pretense, fraud, infidelity, knavery, machination, pettifoggery, sedition, treason

tread perambulate, step

tread on mistreat, spurn

treading warily diffident

treason disloyalty, infidelity, mutiny, rebellion, sedition

treasonable faithless, false *(disloyal)*, perfidious, recreant, untrue

treasonable activities disloyalty

treasonable alliance confederacy *(conspiracy)*, conspiracy

treasonous disobedient, faithless, false *(disloyal)*, insubordinate, perfidious

treasure cash, conserve, foster, fund, garner, hoard, keep *(shelter)*, money, possession *(property)*, possessions, preserve, protect, regard *(hold in esteem)*, store *(depository)*, store, substance *(material possessions)*, sufficiency

treasure house treasury

treasure up hoard

treasured valuable

treasurehouse repository

treasurer comptroller

treasury arsenal, coffer, repository, selection *(collection)*, store *(depository)*

treasury note check *(instrument)*

treat adjust *(resolve)*, comment, cure, drug, enjoyment *(pleasure)*, manage, relieve *(give aid)*, remedy

treat abusively mishandle *(maltreat)*

treat as a special case except *(exclude)*, exclude

treat as human personify

treat badly mistreat

treat cruelly ill use

treat differently favor

treat ill mishandle *(maltreat)*

treat improperly mishandle *(maltreat)*, violate

treat in a condescending way patronize *(condescend toward)*

treat poorly persecute

treat rudely ignore

treat thoroughly exhaust *(try all possibilities)*

treat unfairly ill use

treat unkindly ill use

treat with contempt disdain, flout, mock *(deride)*

treat with derision mock *(deride)*

treat with discourtesy offend *(insult)*

treat with disdain flout, spurn

treat with disfavor disgrace

treat with disrespect humiliate, mock *(deride)*

treat with indignity disoblige, humiliate, offend *(insult)*

treat with indulgence bear *(tolerate)*, forbear

treat with insolence hector, jeer

treat with partiality favor, prefer

treat with reserve mistrust

treat with scorn mock *(deride)*

treat without due respect disregard

treat without reverence violate

treated tempered

treatise hornbook

treatise on the law hornbook

treatment analysis, design *(construction plan)*, expedient, management *(judicious use)*, pandect *(treatise)*, practice *(procedure)*, process *(course)*, relief *(aid)*, usage

treaty bargain, compact, league, mutual understanding, pact, peace, promise, protocol *(agreement)*, stipulation

treaty-making negotiation

trek perambulate, traverse

trekker migrant

tremble beat *(pulsate)*

trembling trepidation

tremendous far reaching, major, portentous *(eliciting amazement)*, prodigious *(enormous)*

tremor cataclysm, trepidation

tremulous diffident

tremulousness trepidation

trench on intrude, overstep

trench upon impinge

trenchant active, acute, bitter *(penetrating)*, brief, caustic, cogent, compelling, concise, eloquent, incisive, mordacious, pithy, potent, powerful, scathing, succinct

trend bias, conatus, direction *(course)*, gravitate, mode, style, tendency, tenor

trend downward decline *(fall)*

trending inclined

trepan bait *(lure)*, deception, ensnare

trepidatio trepidation

trepidation apprehension *(fear)*, cloud *(suspicion)*, consternation, disturbance, fear, fright, misgiving, panic, phobia, stress *(strain)*, suspicion *(mistrust)*

trepidity trepidation

trespass accroach, breach, break *(violate)*, delinquency *(misconduct)*, disobey, disregard *(omission)*, encroach, encroachment, impinge, impose *(intrude)*, infraction, infringe, infringement, intrude, intrusion, invade, invasion, lapse *(fall into error)*, misdeed, misdoing, obtrude, offend *(violate the law)*, overstep, transgression, violate, violation, wrong

trespasser malefactor

trespassing disobedient, housebreaking, infringement, intrusive, peccant *(culpable)*

triable illicit, justiciable

triable act tortious act

trial action *(proceeding)*, cause *(lawsuit)*, conatus, contest *(competition)*, cross-examination, day in court, discipline *(punishment)*, distress *(anguish)*, effort, endeavor, experiment, grievance, hearing, indagation, infliction, inquiry *(systematic investigation)*, inspection, lawsuit, matter *(case)*, misfortune, nuisance, plight, predicament, preliminary, proceeding, prosecution *(criminal trial)*, quagmire, stress *(strain)*, suit, tentative, test, trouble, undertaking *(attempt)*, undertaking *(enterprise)*, venture

trial at the bar hearing

trial by jury hearing

trial in court hearing

trial list calendar *(list of cases)*

trial of a case action *(proceeding)*

trial of superiority competition

trial of the issues action *(proceeding)*

tribe affinity *(family ties)*, assemblage, band, blood, family *(common ancestry)*, house, origin *(ancestry)*, parentage, progeny, society

tribuere attribute, render *(deliver)*

tribulation burden, distress *(anguish)*, misfortune, quagmire, trouble

tribunal bar *(court)*, bench, board, chamber *(body)*, council *(assembly)*, court, forum *(court)*, judicatory, judicature, judiciary, jury

tributary contributory, inferior *(lower in position)*

tribute bounty, contribution *(donation)*, duty *(tax)*, gift *(present)*, honor *(outward respect)*, payment *(remittance)*, recognition, recommendation, remembrance *(commemoration)*, respect, reward, tax

trick artifice, bait *(lure)*, betray *(lead astray)*, bilk, bunko, canard, circumvent, deceive, deception, decoy, defraud, delude, device *(contrivance)*, dupe, ensnare, evade *(deceive)*, evasion, expedient, fake, false pretense, foist, hoax, hoodwink, illude, imposture, inveigle, knavery, machination, maneuver, mislead, misrepresent, mulct *(defraud)*, overreach, pettifog, plot *(secret plan)*, ploy, pretense *(pretext)*, pretext, racket, ruse, sham, stratagem, subterfuge

trickery artifice, collusion, deceit, deception, duplicity, falsification, frame up, fraud, hoax, hypocrisy, imposture, knavery, pettifoggery, prestidigitation, pretense *(pretext)*, pretext, ruse, sham

trickiness deception, dishonesty, fraud, improbity, knavery, pettifoggery

trickish fraudulent, machiavellian

trickle distill, exude, paucity

tricksy jocular

tricky deceptive, delusive, devious, disingenuous, evasive, fraudulent, illusory, insidious, intricate, lying, machiavellian, perfidious, sly, sophistic, strategic, subtle *(insidious)*, surreptitious, unconscionable

tried conclusive *(determinative)*, convincing, dependable, expert, indubious, loyal, reliable, staunch, steadfast, true *(loyal)*, veteran

tried for the same crime double jeopardy

trier array *(jury)*

trier of fact juror

trier of the facts array *(jury)*

triers of fact jury, panel *(jurors)*

trifle palter, paucity, pettifog, scintilla, technicality

trifle amount modicum

trifle with mock *(deride)*

trifling collateral *(immaterial)*, de minimus, expendable, frivolous, inappreciable, inconsequential, inconsiderable, insubstantial, marginal, minor, negligible, nominal, nonessential, nugatory, null *(insignificant)*, paltry, petty, slight, superficial, tenuous, trivial, unessential

trigger launch *(initiate)*, originate

trim abridge *(shorten)*, color *(complexion)*, commute, compact *(pithy)*, curtail, decrease, deduct *(reduce)*, edit, embellish, lessen

trimming curtailment, reprimand

trip misguide, overreach

trip up entrap

triste disconsolate

tristis grave *(important)*, solemn

tristitia depression, solemnity

trite inexpressive, lifeless *(dull)*, mediocre, mundane, nondescript, ordinary, pedestrian, prosaic, stale

trite expression phrase, platitude

trite phrase platitude

trite remark platitude

trite saying platitude

tritus customary, trite

triumph carry *(succeed)*, kill *(defeat)*, pass *(satisfy requirements)*, reach, succeed *(attain)*, supremacy

triumph over beat *(defeat)*, defeat, overcome *(surmount)*, overwhelm, subdue, subject, subjugate, surmount, surpass

triumphal prevailing *(having superior force)*

triumphant prevailing *(having superior force)*, successful

trivia detail

trivial collateral *(immaterial)*, de minimus, frivolous, immaterial, inapposite, inconsequential, inconsiderable, insubstantial, mediocre, minor, negligible, nominal, nonessential, nugatory, null

(insignificant), paltry, peripheral, petty, remote *(small)*, slight, superficial, tenuous, unessential, usual

triviality immateriality, inconsequence, insignificance, mediocrity, platitude, technicality

troop assemblage, band

trope call *(title)*

trophy prize

troth adherence *(devotion)*, adhesion *(loyalty)*, faith, loyalty, profession *(declaration)*, reliance, undertaking *(pledge)*

trothless faithless, false *(disloyal)*, perfidious

trouble aggravate *(annoy)*, agitate *(perturb)*, annoy, badger, bait *(harass)*, burden, disaster, discommode, discompose, disorient, distress *(anguish)*, distress, disturb, embarrass, emergency, encumber *(hinder)*, fracas, grievance, harass, hector, inconvenience, mischief, misfortune, molest *(annoy)*, nuisance, obsess, pandemonium, perplex, persecute, perturb, pique, plague, plight, predicament, press *(goad)*, problem, quagmire, strife, turmoil

trouble maker delinquent

trouble oneself endeavor, strive

trouble-maker demagogue

troubled disconsolate, pessimistic, unsettled

troublemaker malcontent

troublesome difficult, froward, invidious, irksome, operose, oppressive, painful, perverse, problematic, uncontrollable, undesirable, unruly, vexatious

troubling painful

troublous bad *(offensive)*, harmful

trounce beat *(strike)*, browbeat, defeat, lash *(strike)*, punish, reprehend, reprimand

troupe assemblage, band, body *(collection)*, organization *(association)*

trover recovery *(repossession)*

trow presuppose, surmise

truancy absence *(nonattendance)*, dereliction, nonappearance, nonperformance

truant disobedient

truce cessation *(interlude)*, conciliation, halt, interruption, interval, lull, pause, peace, treaty

trucidare kill *(defeat)*

truck trade *(commerce)*

truckage carriage

truckle to pander

truckling servile, subservient

truckload cargo

truculence atrocity, brutality

truculency brutality

truculent brutal, cold-blooded, harsh, hostile, malevolent, malicious, malignant, offensive *(offending)*, perverse, relentless, ruthless, sinister

trudge perambulate

true absolute *(conclusive)*, accurate, actual, authentic, candid, convincing, credible, de facto, definite, dependable, direct *(straight)*, documentary, factual, faithful *(loyal)*, faithful *(true to fact)*, genuine, honest, incontrovertible, literal, loyal, positive *(incontestable)*, proper, pure, real, reliable, rightful, serious *(devoted)*, solid *(sound)*, sound, staunch, steadfast, sterling, unadulter-

ated, undistorted, unrefutable, unyielding, valid, veridical

true believer disciple

true bill accusation

true charge accusation

true dimensions area *(surface)*

true incident fact

true meaning connotation, gist *(substance)*

true to fact exact, literal

true to form normal *(regular)*

true to life descriptive, natural

true to nature undistorted

true to scale candid

true to the facts actual, candid, certain *(positive)*, honest

true to the letter actual, verbatim

true to type typical

truehearted honest, loyal, moral, true *(loyal)*

trueness adhesion *(loyalty)*, allegiance, fidelity, loyalty, validity

truism platitude, postulate, principle *(axiom)*

truly admittedly, de facto, faithfully, in good faith, ipso facto

trump outbalance

trump up fabricate *(make up)*, frame *(prearrange)*, invent *(falsify)*, misrepresent, palter, perjure

trump up a charge frame *(charge falsely)*

trumped up colorable *(specious)*, ill-founded, lying, unfounded, untrue

trumped up story myth

trumped-up fictitious

trumped-up charge frame up

trumped-up story frame up

trumpery deception, falsification

trumpet circulate, herald, inform *(notify)*, proclaim, propagate *(spread)*, publish

truncare mutilate

truncate commute, condense, deduct *(reduce)*, excise *(cut away)*, mutilate, remove *(eliminate)*

truncheon beat *(strike)*, cudgel, lash *(strike)*

trunk road causeway

truss bear *(support)*

trust agency *(legal relationship)*, cartel, charge *(custody)*, commit *(entrust)*, commitment *(responsibility)*, confederacy *(compact)*, confidence *(faith)*, consortium *(business cartel)*, credence, credulity, entrust, expectation, faith, league, loan, mission, office, pool, prospect *(outlook)*, protégé, reliance, rely, security *(safety)*

trust to chance bet, parlay *(bet)*

trust to keep secret confide *(divulge)*

trust with delegate

trustable dependable, incorruptible

trusted authentic, convincing, credible, dependable, fiduciary, intimate, undisputed

trustee administrator, comptroller, executor, fiduciary, guardian, nominee *(delegate)*, receiver, representative *(proxy)*, substitute, transferee

trustees commission *(agency)*, committee

trusteeship charge *(custody)*, custody *(supervision)*, ward

truster disciple

trustful sanguine, unsuspecting

trustfulness credulity

trustiness adhesion *(loyalty)*, fidelity, honor *(good reputation)*, probity

trusting convincing, credulous, naive, positive *(confident)*, sanguine, unsuspecting

trustingly faithfully

trustless irresponsible

trustworthily faithfully

trustworthiness adhesion *(loyalty)*, certification *(certainness)*, credibility, fidelity, honesty, honor *(good reputation)*, integrity, loyalty, principle *(virtue)*, probity, rectitude, responsibility *(conscience)*, trust *(confidence)*, veracity, weight *(credibility)*

trustworthy accurate, authentic, believable, bona fide, candid, cogent, conscientious, convincing, credible, demonstrable, dependable, diligent, factual, faithful *(loyal)*, fiduciary, harmless, high-minded, honest, incorruptible, infallible, ingenuous, law-abiding, loyal, moral, official, positive *(incontestable)*, real, reliable, reputable, safe, scrupulous, secure *(sound)*, solid *(sound)*, staunch, steadfast, tenable, thorough, true *(authentic)*, true *(loyal)*, upright

trusty believable, conscientious, dependable, incorruptible, infallible, law-abiding, loyal, reliable, secure *(sound)*, solid *(sound)*, staunch, true *(loyal)*

truth fact, honesty, maxim, principle *(virtue)*, probity, reality, right *(righteousness)*, validity, veracity

truth telling credible

truth-speaking straightforward

truth-telling veridical

truthful accurate, actual, candid, credible, direct *(forthright)*, honest, ingenuous, literal, precise, real, realistic, reliable, right *(correct)*, scrupulous, sound, straightforward, true *(authentic)*, unaffected *(sincere)*, undistorted, upright, valid, veridical

truthfully faithfully

truthfulness credibility, honesty, integrity, probity, veracity

truthless dishonest, disingenuous, evasive, fallacious, false *(inaccurate)*, fraudulent, lying, mendacious, untrue

truthlessness bad faith, dishonesty, improbity

try adjudicate, adopt, attempt, check *(inspect)*, endeavor, endeavor, exert, harrow, harry *(harass)*, hear *(give a legal hearing)*, judge, pursuit *(effort to secure)*, resort, strive, test, undertake

try a case hear *(give a legal hearing)*, judge

try conclusions reason *(conclude)*

try for pursue *(strive to gain)*, strive

try hard attempt

try one's best attempt, pursue *(strive to gain)*, strive

try one's fortune bet

try one's luck bet, gamble, speculate *(chance)*

try one's patience badger, bait *(harass)*, provoke

try the cause adjudicate, hear *(give a legal hearing)*

try the patience discompose, pique, plague

try to find hunt

try to obtain pursue *(strive to gain)*

try to overtake chase

trying onerous, operose, oppressive, painful, severe, vexatious

trying situation predicament

tryout experiment, test

tryst appointment *(meeting)*, rendezvous

tueri preserve

tuitio preservation

tuition direction *(guidance)*, edification, education, experience *(background)*, guidance

tuitionary disciplinary *(educational)*

tumble agitate *(shake up)*, disorganize, subvert, upset

tumid flatulent, fustian, grandiose, inflated *(bombastic)*, inflated *(enlarged)*, orotund, pretentious *(pompous)*, turgid

tumidity bombast

tumidness bombast

tumidus inflated *(bombastic)*, inflated *(enlarged)*, pretentious *(pompous)*

tumult affray, anarchy, belligerency, bluster *(commotion)*, brawl, commotion, confusion *(turmoil)*, disorder *(lack of order)*, disturbance, embroilment, entanglement *(confusion)*, fracas, fray, furor, imbroglio, noise, outcry, pandemonium, revolution, riot, turmoil

tumultous disorderly

tumultuary disordered, disorderly

tumultuous disordered

tumultuous assault affray

tumultuousness bluster *(commotion)*, disorder *(lack of order)*

tumultus affray, commotion, disturbance, revolt, riot

tune adjust *(regulate)*

tune down diminish

tunnel penetrate

turba band, commotion, riot, turmoil

turbare muddle

turbatio disturbance

turbid inextricable, opaque, unclear

turbulence bluster *(commotion)*, commotion, confusion *(turmoil)*, disorder *(lack of order)*, disturbance, embroilment, furor, irregularity, pandemonium, revolution, severity, turmoil

turbulency turmoil

turbulent disordered, disorderly, hot-blooded, unruly, vehement

turbulentus insubordinate

turgent turgid

turgescence bombast, inflation *(increase)*, plethora, rodomontade

turgescent orotund, pretentious *(pompous)*, proud *(conceited)*

turgid flatulent, fustian, grandiose, inflated *(bombastic)*, inflated *(enlarged)*, orotund, pretentious *(pompous)*, proud *(conceited)*

turgid language fustian

turgidity bombast, inflation *(increase)*

turgidness inflation *(increase)*

turgidus inflated *(enlarged)*

turmoil affray, anarchy, bluster *(commotion)*, brawl, commotion, conflict, disorder *(lack of order)*, disturbance, embroilment, emotion, fracas, fray, furor, havoc, imbroglio, misrule, outcry, pandemonium, panic, riot, shambles

turn alter, avert, contort, contour *(shape)*, convert *(change use)*, crossroad *(turning point)*, deviate, digress, gift

(flair), occurrence, opportunity, oscillate, posture *(situation)*, predisposition, prejudice *(influence)*, proclivity, quirk *(accident)*, slant, spoil *(impair)*, tendency, transform, transition

turn a deaf ear to ignore

turn adrift dispel, evict

turn against antagonize, confront *(oppose)*, rebel

turn aside avert, deter, detour, deviate, discourage, divert, eschew, estop, expostulate, impede, parry, prevent, shun, stave, thwart

turn attention devote

turn attention to note *(notice)*

turn away abandon *(relinquish)*, alienate *(estrange)*, avert, decline *(reject)*, depose *(remove)*, disaffect, disapprove *(reject)*, disclaim, disfavor, dismiss *(discharge)*, exclude, parry, prevent, rebuff, repulse

turn away from disavow, eschew, shun

turn awry distort

turn back disavow, escheat, parry, regress, revert

turn down decline *(reject)*, disapprove *(reject)*, disoblige, refuse, spurn

turn from change, disapprove *(reject)*, disavow, discourage, disfavor, refuse, renounce

turn from a purpose dissuade

turn from sin redeem *(satisfy debts)*

turn in retire *(retreat)*

turn informer betray *(disclose)*, denounce *(inform against)*

turn into change, evolve, vary

turn into cash realize *(obtain as a profit)*

turn into money liquidate *(convert into cash)*, realize *(obtain as a profit)*

turn loose discharge *(dismiss)*, discharge *(liberate)*, disenthrall, free, liberate, parole

turn of expression phrase, phraseology

turn of mind disposition *(inclination)*, position *(point of view)*, spirit

turn of the tide crossroad *(turning point)*

turn off alienate *(estrange)*, shut

turn on recriminate

turn one's back on abandon *(physically leave)*, ignore, quit *(evacuate)*, relinquish

turn one's back upon disdain

turn one's gaze upon peruse

turn out deport *(banish)*, depose *(remove)*, discharge *(dismiss)*, disinherit, dislodge, dismiss *(discharge)*, displace *(remove)*, dispossess, eject *(evict)*, eliminate *(exclude)*, evict, exclude, expel, expose, fabricate *(construct)*, formulate, make, manufacture, oust, produce *(manufacture)*, remove *(dismiss from office)*, result, supplant

turn out by industrial process manufacture

turn out of doors evict

turn out of house and home evict

turn out of one's way deviate

turn out of possession eject *(evict)*

turn over alienate *(transfer title)*, attorn, cede, consign, deal, deliver, devolve, give *(grant)*, lend, muse, reflect *(ponder)*, serve *(deliver a legal instru-*

turn over for safekeeping entrust
turn over in one's mind consider
turn over in the mind ponder, reason *(conclude)*, speculate *(conjecture)*
turn over to commit *(entrust)*, delegate, relegate
turn renegade tergiversate
turn selfishly to one's own account exploit *(take advantage of)*
turn state's evidence confess
turn tail retreat
turn the attention to observe *(watch)*, occupy *(engage)*
turn the eyes on observe *(watch)*
turn the leaves of peruse
turn the mind to occupy *(engage)*
turn the tables on recriminate
turn to call *(appeal to)*, consult *(ask advice of)*
turn to account employ *(make use of)*, exercise *(use)*, expend *(consume)*, exploit *(make use of)*, gain, inure *(benefit)*, profit
turn to for help resort
turn to for support resort
turn to good account capitalize *(seize the chance)*
turn to one's advantage capitalize *(seize the chance)*
turn to scorn disdain
turn to the side avert
turn to use employ *(make use of)*
turn up discover, disinter, emerge
turn upside down overthrow, upset
turnabout reversal, reversion *(act of returning)*
turnaround reversion *(act of returning)*
turned about inverse
turned around back *(in reverse)*
turned to bone ossified
turning circuitous, critical *(crucial)*, indirect, sinuous, strategic, tortuous *(bending)*
turning aside obviation
turning over to a foreign state extradition
turning to account exploitation
turnkey warden
turnout result
turnpike causeway
turpis disgraceful, obscene, scandalous, vicious
turpitude bad faith, bad repute, corruption, defilement, delinquency *(misconduct)*, discredit, dishonor *(shame)*, disrepute, guilt, knavery, misconduct, misdoing, perversion, shame, vice, wrong
turpitudinous bad *(offensive)*
turpitudo disgrace, dishonor *(shame)*, ignominy, obscenity
tussle affray, belligerency, commotion, fight *(battle)*, fight *(battle)*, fracas, grapple, struggle
tutari protect
tutela charge *(custody)*, protection
tutelage aid *(help)*, auspices, charge *(custody)*, direction *(guidance)*, edification, education, guidance, instruction *(teaching)*, patronage *(support)*, protection, safekeeping, ward
tutelar guardian
tutelary protective
tutor edify, educate, enlighten, instill,

instruct *(teach)*, nurture, pedagogue
tutored familiar *(informed)*
tutorial didactic, disciplinary *(educational)*
tutoring direction *(guidance)*, education, guidance, instruction *(teaching)*
tutors faculty *(teaching staff)*
tutus safe
twaddle prattle
twelve months annum
twice-bereaved child orphan
twice-told repeated
twin alter ego, correlate, counterpart *(parallel)*, duplicate, identical, same, similar
twine contort
twine together intertwine
twinge of conscience qualm
twining circuitous
twist camouflage, complex *(entanglement)*, contort, disorganize, distort, distortion, falsify, intertwine, involution, mutilate, palter, prejudice *(influence)*, quirk *(accident)*, quirk *(idiosyncrasy)*, slant, snarl, tendency
twist and turn contort
twist the meaning distort, misinterpret, misstate, misunderstand
twist the meaning of camouflage, misread, misrepresent
twist the sense distort
twist the truth pretend, prevaricate
twist the words distort, misconstrue
twistable malleable
twisted disordered, inextricable, labyrinthine, peccable, sinuous, tortuous *(bending)*, unreasonable
twisting circuitous, indirect, labyrinthine, sinuous, tortuous *(bending)*
twit jape, jeer, mock *(deride)*
two-faced faithless, false *(disloyal)*, machiavellian, recreant, tartuffish, undependable, unreliable, unscrupulous, untrue, untrustworthy
two-facedness duplicity
two-sided bilateral, mutual *(reciprocal)*, reciprocal
two-way mutual *(reciprocal)*
type case *(example)*, characteristic, class, classification, classify, color *(complexion)*, criterion, denomination, designation *(symbol)*, form *(arrangement)*, instance, kind, manner *(kind)*, personality, pigeonhole, resemblance, style
typical average *(standard)*, boiler plate, broad, common *(customary)*, conventional, customary, demonstrative *(illustrative)*, familiar *(customary)*, general, habitual, mediocre, mundane, natural, nondescript, normal *(regular)*, ordinary, orthodox, prevailing *(current)*, prevalent, regular *(conventional)*, representative, usual
typical component epitome
typical example representative *(example)*, sample
typical instance example, representative *(example)*
typical part epitome
typical performance norm
typicus typical
typification epitome
typify depict, exemplify, personify, represent *(portray)*, signify *(denote)*
typifying exemplary, representative
tyrannical brutal, cruel, dictatorial,

oppressive, relentless, severe, strict, stringent, tyrannous
tyrannical leader dictator
tyrannize bait *(harass)*, harass, mishandle *(maltreat)*, mistreat, tax *(overwork)*
tyrannized aggrieved *(harmed)*
tyrannous brutal, dictatorial
tyranny cruelty, injustice, oppression, severity, thrall
tyrant dictator
tyro neophyte, novice
tyrranize brutalize, dominate

U

uber productive
ubiquitary present *(current)*, ubiquitous
ubiquitous broad, present *(current)*
ugly loathsome, odious, repulsive, scandalous
ukase citation *(charge)*, declaration, decree, directive, fiat, order *(judicial directive)*, requirement
ulciscendi cupidus vindictive
ulcisci punish, retaliate
ullage deficiency
ulterior additional, undisclosed
ultimate categorical, ceiling, conclusive *(determinative)*, conclusive *(settled)*, definitive, extreme *(last)*, final, forthcoming, future, last *(final)*, prospective
ultimate cause derivation, determinant, gist *(ground for a suit)*
ultimate end design *(intent)*
ultimate motive determinant
ultimate point extremity *(furthest point)*
ultimate purpose intention, object
ultimate result issuance
ultimately hereafter *(eventually)*, in due course
ultimatum canon, charge *(command)*, claim *(legal demand)*, condition *(contingent provision)*, demand, dictate, dun, mandate, notice *(warning)*, requirement, warning
ultimus extreme *(last)*, final, ultimate
ultio revenge, vengeance
ultracritical critical *(faultfinding)*
ultraist radical *(favoring drastic change)*
ultramodern sophisticated
ultrareligious fanatical
ululant blatant *(obtrusive)*
umbrage alienation *(estrangement)*, dissatisfaction, malice, offense, resentment
umbrageous mysterious, resentful
umpirage collective bargaining
umpire decide, go-between, intercede, judge, judge, mediate, negotiate, referee, rule *(decide)*
unabashed brazen, impertinent *(insolent)*, insolent, presumptuous
unabated undiminished, unremitting
unabetted alone *(unsupported)*, solitary, unsupported
unable disabled *(deprived of legal right)*, helpless *(powerless)*, inadept, inadequate, incapable, incompetent, inept *(incompetent)*, otiose, powerless, unfit, unqualified *(not competent)*
unable to be annulled irrevocable,

unavoidable *(not voidable)*
unable to be bought inalienable, incorruptible
unable to be corrected irremediable
unable to be discredited unimpeachable
unable to be disposed of inalienable
unable to be evaded compulsory
unable to be expressed ineffable
unable to be fixed irremediable
unable to be investigated inscrutable
unable to be overcome invincible
unable to be pacified irreconcilable
unable to be quelled invincible
unable to be remedied irremediable
unable to be spoken ineffable
unable to be subjugated invincible
unable to exist without dependent
unable to find the way lost *(disoriented)*
unable to make both ends meet bankrupt
unable to make ends meet impecunious, poor *(underprivileged)*
unable to pay indebted, insolvent
unable to pay matured debts bankrupt
unable to resist eager
unable to satisfy creditors bankrupt
unable to speak mute, speechless
unable to utter articulate sound mute
unable to yield barren
unabridged full, gross *(total)*, intact, thorough
unabridgedly in toto
unacceptable blameful, ineligible, inferior *(lower in quality)*, invidious, nonsubstantial *(not sufficient)*, objectionable, repugnant *(exciting aversion)*, undesirable, unendurable, unsatisfactory, unsuitable
unacceptableness bad repute
unacceptance disapproval
unaccepted outdated, outmoded, unorthodox
unaccessible inaccessible
unaccidental voluntary
unaccommodating disinclined, froward, invidious, perverse, restive, thoughtless
unaccompanied alone *(unsupported)*, separate, singular, sole, solitary
unaccomplished amateur, executory, inadept
unaccountable arbitrary, clear *(unencumbered)*, immune, inapprehensible, incomprehensible, indefinable, inexplicable, inscrutable, lawless, mysterious, nonconforming, peculiar *(curious)*, prodigious *(amazing)*, uncanny, uncurbed, unforeseeable, unpredictable
unaccredited unauthorized
unaccustomed extraordinary, inexperienced, nonconforming, peculiar *(curious)*, prodigious *(amazing)*, special, unacquainted, uncommon, unusual
unachievability impossibility
unachievable difficult, impossible, impracticable, inaccessible, infeasible, insuperable, insurmountable, unattainable
unacknowledged anonymous, unrequited, unspecified
unacquaintance ignorance

unacquainted blind *(not discerning)*, incognizant, inexperienced, insensible, unaccustomed, unaware, unversed
unacquirability unavailability
unacquirable inaccessible, unattainable
unacquired devoid
unactivated lifeless *(dull)*
unactivity neglect
unactual delusive, illusory, nominal
unadaptable nonconforming, otiose, rigid
unadapted improper, incompetent, ineligible, inexperienced, unfit, unqualified *(not competent)*
unadjustable irreconcilable, nonconforming
unadjusted outstanding *(unresolved)*, unsettled
unadministered executory
unadorned clear *(apparent)*, naked *(lacking embellishment)*, nondescript, simple
unadroit amateur, inadept, inept *(incompetent)*
unadult juvenile
unadulterate decontaminate
unadulterated authentic, genuine, honest, naked *(lacking embellishment)*, natural, pure, simple, sterling, true *(authentic)*
unadulteration honesty
unadvantageous deleterious
unadventurous careful, safe
unadvertised ulterior
unadvisable adverse *(negative)*, disadvantageous, inappropriate, injudicious
unadvised hot-blooded, imprudent, impulsive *(rash)*, incognizant, unaware
unaffected bona fide, direct *(forthright)*, dispassionate, exempt, genuine, honest, impartial, impervious, inexpressive, ingenuous, insensible, insusceptible *(uncaring)*, irreconcilable, naive, neutral, nonchalant, simple, straightforward, true *(authentic)*, unpretentious
unaffected by immune
unaffected by injury intact, inviolate
unaffectedness candor *(straightforwardness)*, honesty, informality
unaffiliated alien *(unrelated)*, apart, disconnected, extraneous, foreign, independent, irrelative, separate, unrelated
unaffirmative negative
unaffirmed debatable, disputable, unauthorized
unafraid secure *(confident)*, spartan, unabashed, undaunted
unaggressive harmless, nonmilitant
unaging immutable
unagitated peaceable, phlegmatic, placid
unagreeing discordant
unaggressive languid
unaided alone *(unsupported)*, helpless *(defenseless)*, solitary, unilateral, unsupported
unaimed haphazard, indiscriminate, random
unaired undisclosed
unalarmed undaunted
unalert negligent
unalertness neglect, negligence
unalike atypical, dissimilar, heteroge-

neous
unallayed persistent, undiminished
unalleviated chronic
unallied alien *(unrelated)*, apart, disconnected, extraneous, foreign, impertinent *(irrelevant)*, inapposite, independent, individual, irrelative, irrelevant, separate, unrelated
unallocated unclaimed
unallowable impermissible, improper, inexcusable, inexpiable, unjustifiable
unallowed felonious, illegitimate *(illegal)*, illicit, ultra vires, unlawful
unalloyed genuine, simple, sterling, unadulterated
unalluring undesirable, unsavory
unalterability indestructibility
unalterable firm, immutable, indefeasible, indelible, inevitable, inexorable, inflexible, ironclad, irreconcilable, irreversible, irrevocable, necessary *(inescapable)*, obdurate, peremptory *(absolute)*, permanent, resolute, rigid, stable, steadfast, unalienable
unalterableness resistance
unalterably invariably
unaltered certain *(positive)*, durable, intact, inviolate, unaffected *(uninfluenced)*, uniform
unambiguity certification *(certainness)*, certitude
unambiguous accurate, axiomatic, categorical, certain *(fixed)*, certain *(positive)*, clear *(apparent)*, coherent *(clear)*, comprehensible, conclusive *(determinative)*, demonstrable, direct *(forthright)*, distinct *(clear)*, explicit, express, incontestable, incontrovertible, lucid, pellucid, precise, unequivocal, unmistakable
unambiguously fairly *(clearly)*
unambitious diffident, lax
unamenable impervious, inflexible
unamiable bitter *(reproachful)*
unamicable malevolent
unample deficient
unamusing pedestrian
unanimated inexpressive, insipid, languid, lifeless *(dead)*
unanimity accordance *(understanding)*, agreement *(concurrence)*, compatibility, concert, conciliation, consensus, peace, rapprochement, understanding *(agreement)*
unanimous concordant, consensual, harmonious
unanimously in toto
unannexed disconnected, discrete, disjunctive *(tending to disjoin)*, individual
unannounced undisclosed, unexpected
unanswerable certain *(fixed)*, cogent, immune, incontrovertible, irrefutable, positive *(incontestable)*, sound, uncurbed, undeniable, undisputed, unequivocal, unrefutable
unanswered unrequited
unanswering unresponsive
unanticipated impulsive *(rash)*, premature, unexpected, unforeseeable, unforeseen
unanticipated event accident *(chance occurrence)*
unanxious peaceable, phlegmatic, secure *(confident)*

unapologizing incorrigible
unapparent blind *(concealed)*, hidden, impalpable, inconspicuous, indiscernible, intangible, latent, obscure *(abstruse)*, obscure *(faint)*, potential, undisclosed
unappealable certain *(fixed)*, final
unappealing objectionable, unacceptable, undesirable
unappeasability contention *(opposition)*
unappeasable implacable, insatiable, irreconcilable, relentless, remorseless, uncontrollable, unrelenting
unappetizing bitter *(acrid tasting)*, repugnant *(exciting aversion)*, unsavory
unapplied theoretical, unclaimed
unappreciable paltry
unappreciativeness ingratitude
unapprehensive careless, lax, phlegmatic, spartan, unabashed, undaunted
unapprised blind *(not discerning)*, unaware
unapprized incognizant, unacquainted, unwitting
unapproachability unavailability
unapproachable difficult, disdainful, inaccessible, remote *(secluded)*, unattainable
unapproached best, paramount
unappropriated unclaimed
unapprovable undesirable
unapproved unauthorized, unorthodox
unapproving hostile, nonconsenting
unapt disproportionate, impertinent *(irrelevant)*, inadept, inadequate, inapplicable, inapposite, inappropriate, inapt, incompetent, inept *(inappropriate)*, inept *(incompetent)*, irrelevant, powerless, unbecoming, unsatisfactory, unseemly, unsuitable
unaptness disqualification *(factor that disqualifies)*, impropriety
unarm disarm *(divest of arms)*
unarmed helpless *(defenseless)*, powerless
unarmored helpless *(defenseless)*
unaroused dormant, insensible, insusceptible *(uncaring)*, lifeless *(dull)*, nonchalant
unarranged casual, complex, disordered, haphazard, random
unartificial natural
unascertained debatable, disputable, dubious, inconclusive, indefinite, outstanding *(unresolved)*, pending *(unresolved)*, provisional, unconfirmed, undecided
unashamed brazen, dissolute, unabashed
unasked unsolicited
unasked for unclaimed
unaspiring lax
unassailability incontestability, inviolability, security *(safety)*
unassailable categorical, certain *(positive)*, clear *(certain)*, defensible, definitive, immune, inappealable, incontestable, inexpugnable, infallible, insuperable, insurmountable, invincible, irreprehensible, safe, secure *(free from danger)*, tenable, unimpeachable
unassembled disordered
unassenting dissident, involuntary
unassertive obsequious, passive, pli-

ant, resigned, sequacious, servile, subservient
unassimilated discrete, individual
unassisted alone *(unsupported)*, solitary, unsupported
unassociated alien *(unrelated)*, apart, disconnected, discrete, disjunctive *(tending to disjoin)*, extraneous, foreign, independent, individual, irrelative, remote *(secluded)*, separate, unrelated
unassumed honest
unassuming diffident, direct *(forthright)*, honest, inconspicuous, ordinary, unaffected *(sincere)*, unobtrusive, unpretentious
unassumingly respectfully
unassumingness informality
unassured conditional, dubious, hesitant, insecure, noncommittal, precarious, provisional
unassured purchase caveat emptor
unatonable inexcusable, inexpiable
unattach disengage, remove *(eliminate)*
unattached apart, disconnected, discrete, free *(not restricted)*, independent, individual, irrelative, moving *(in motion)*, separate, sovereign *(independent)*, unrelated, unsettled
unattackability security *(safety)*
unattackable defensible, immune, inexpugnable, insuperable, insurmountable, safe, secure *(free from danger)*, tenable
unattainability impossibility, unavailability
unattainable impossibility, impossible, inaccessible, infeasible, insuperable, insurmountable, unapproachable
unattended alone *(unsupported)*, separate, sole, solitary
unattended to perfunctory
unattested unconfirmed, uncorroborated, unfounded, unsupported
unattractive unacceptable, undesirable, unsavory
unauthentic artificial, assumed *(feigned)*, bogus, dishonest, dubious, fraudulent, illusory, imitation, invalid, spurious, unsound *(fallacious)*, unsustainable
unauthenticated dubious, unconfirmed, uncorroborated, unfounded, unsupported, untrustworthy
unauthenticity bad faith
unauthorative uncorroborated
unauthoritative dubious, ineffective, ineffectual, unofficial
unauthorization illegality
unauthorized disorderly, felonious, illegal, illegitimate *(illegal)*, illicit, impermissible, improper, irregular *(improper)*, null *(invalid)*, null and void, ultra vires, unlawful, unofficial, unwarranted, wrongful
unauthorized assumption of property conversion *(misappropriation)*
unauthorized borrowing plagiarism
unauthorized copy counterfeit
unauthorized reproduction fake
unavailability absence *(omission)*, impossibility
unavailable difficult, inaccessible, scarce, unattainable
unavailing disadvantageous, expend-

able, futile, ineffective, ineffectual, needless, nugatory, null *(insignificant)*, otiose, powerless, unproductive
unavoidable certain *(fixed)*, certain *(positive)*, compelling, compulsory, exigent, forthcoming, imperative, important *(urgent)*, indispensable, inevitable, irrevocable, mandatory, necessary *(inescapable)*, obligatory, peremptory *(imperative)*, undeniable
unavowed ulterior
unawaited unexpected
unawaited event bombshell
unawakened dormant
unaware heedless, incognizant, insensible, lax, oblivious, reckless, unacquainted, unsuspecting, unwitting
unawareness ignorance, insentience, nescience
unawares unknowingly
unawed unabashed
unbacked unsound *(not strong)*, unsupported
unbalance discompose, disorganize, disorient, disturb, inequality, obsess
unbalanced deranged, disproportionate, inequitable, insecure, non compos mentis, partial *(biased)*, unequal *(unequivalent)*, unsettled
unbalanced mind insanity
unbar disencumber, disengage, disenthrall
unbarred open *(accessible)*, public *(open)*
unbased baseless, ill-founded, insubstantial
unbearable deplorable, insufferable, intolerable, loathsome, objectionable, obnoxious, odious, offensive *(offending)*, onerous, oppressive, painful, repulsive, unendurable
unbeatable indomitable, inexpugnable, infallible, insuperable, insurmountable, invincible, irresistible, premium
unbeaten prosperous, successful
unbecoming improper, inapposite, inappropriate, inapt, incongruous, inept *(inappropriate)*, objectionable, undesirable, undue *(excessive)*, unfit, unseemly, unsuitable
unbefitting disproportionate, improper, inapposite, inappropriate, inapt, inept *(inappropriate)*, unbecoming, undesirable, undue *(excessive)*, unfit, unprofessional, unsatisfactory, unseemly
unbefriended helpless *(defenseless)*
unbeguile disabuse
unbeholdable indiscernible, intangible
unbelief cloud *(suspicion)*, doubt *(suspicion)*, suspicion *(mistrust)*
unbelievable debatable, disputable, doubtful, implausible, impossible, incredible, ludicrous, remarkable, suspicious *(questionable)*, uncanny
unbeliever heretic
unbelieving cynical, inconvincible, incredulous, leery, skeptical
unbellicose nonmilitant, peaceable
unbelligerent nonmilitant, peaceable
unbend condescend *(deign)*, relent
unbending callous, draconian, firm, formal, immutable, implacable, inexorable, inflexible, insusceptible *(uncaring)*, intractable, ironclad, irreconcila-

ble, obdurate, orthodox, parochial, pertinacious, precise, relentless, resolute, rigid, severe, strict, unalterable, uncompromising, unrelenting, unyielding
unbenevolent cruel, scathing, sinister
unbent direct *(straight)*
unbeseeming unbecoming, unsuitable
unbetraying loyal, true *(loyal)*
unbias candor *(impartiality)*
unbiased broad, discriminating *(judicious)*, dispassionate, equal, equitable, evenhanded, factual, fair *(just)*, honest, impartial, judicial, juridical, just, liberal *(broad minded)*, neutral, nonpartisan, objective, open-minded, receptive, undistorted, unprejudiced
unbiased impulse common sense
unbiasedly fairly *(impartially)*
unbiasedness disinterest *(lack of prejudice)*, fairness
unbidden lawless, spontaneous, unsolicited, voluntary, willing *(uncompelled)*
unbigoted equitable, impartial, judicial, just, liberal *(broad minded)*, neutral, nonpartisan, objective, open-minded, unbiased, unprejudiced
unbind break *(separate)*, disband, disencumber, disengage, disenthrall, dissociate, divide *(separate)*, extricate, free, liberate, remove *(eliminate)*, rescue, separate, sever, split
unbinding liberation
unblamable blameless, clean, inculpable, innocent, irreprehensible, pardonable, unimpeachable
unblameworthy blameless, inculpable, irreprehensible, unimpeachable, unobjectionable
unblemished absolute *(ideal)*, blameless, clean, incorruptible, intact, inviolate, irreprehensible, not guilty, pure, unimpeachable
unblenched undaunted
unblenching heroic, spartan
unblended simple
unblest profane
unblindfold disabuse
unblocked open *(accessible)*
unblurred clear *(apparent)*, cognizable, coherent *(clear)*, conspicuous
unblushing brazen, callous, lascivious, nonchalant, salacious, unabashed
unboastful diffident
unbodied incorporeal
unbolt disengage, parole
unborn nonexistent
unborrowed native *(domestic)*, original *(creative)*
unbosom divulge
unbought free *(at no charge)*, gratis, gratuitous *(given without recompense)*, impartial, just, loyal
unbound clear *(unencumbered)*, exempt, free *(not restricted)*, independent, sovereign *(independent)*, uncurbed, unqualified *(unlimited)*, unrestricted
unbounded absolute *(complete)*, competitive *(open)*, excessive, indefinite, indeterminate, infinite, open-ended, unconditional, unlimited, unmitigated, unrestrained *(not in custody)*, unrestricted
unbowdlerized salacious
unbreakable indivisible,

inexpugnable, infrangible, ironclad
unbreathed undisclosed
unbribable honest, incorruptible, just, law-abiding
unbribed clean, evenhanded, impartial, just, loyal
unbridgeable insuperable
unbridled clear *(unencumbered)*, disorderly, dissolute, free *(not restricted)*, hot-blooded, incendiary, independent, inordinate, intemperate, lecherous, open-ended, prodigal, profuse, uncurbed, unrestrained *(not in custody)*, unrestrained *(not repressed)*, unrestricted, unruly
unbroadened provincial
unbroken consecutive, continual *(connected)*, continuous, direct *(straight)*, direct *(uninterrupted)*, gross *(total)*, incessant, intact, inviolate, safe, unremitting
unbroken line chain *(series)*
unbroken order array *(order)*
unbruised intact
unbuckle disengage
unburden alleviate, disencumber, ease, free, mitigate, release, relieve *(free from burden)*
unburdened clear *(free from criminal charges)*, clear *(unencumbered)*, free *(relieved from a burden)*
unbury disinter
unbusied inactive
unbusinesslike inexperienced, unprofessional
uncage parole
uncalculated fortuitous, imprudent, unintentional, unpremeditated
uncalculating careless, impulsive *(rash)*, injudicious, negligent, precipitate
uncalled for disproportionate, excessive, extraneous, gratuitous *(unwarranted)*, inapplicable, inappropriate, nonessential
uncalled-for exorbitant, expendable, inordinate, needless, otiose, redundant, superfluous, unclaimed, undue *(excessive)*, unessential, unnecessary, unsolicited, unwarranted
uncamouflaged obvious, patent
uncandid devious, disingenuous, lying, mendacious, sly, untrue
uncanny mysterious
uncanonical unorthodox
uncaptivating insipid, lifeless *(dull)*, pedestrian
uncared for derelict *(abandoned)*
uncareful slipshod
uncaring callous, cold-blooded, heedless, lax, nonchalant, obdurate, oblivious, obtuse, perfunctory, phlegmatic, slipshod, unaffected *(uninfluenced)*
uncase denude, unveil
uncatholic parochial
uncaught free *(not restricted)*, unbound
uncaused baseless
unceasing chronic, continual *(connected)*, continual *(perpetual)*, continuous, durable, incessant, industrious, infinite, live *(existing)*, open-ended, patient, permanent, perpetual, persistent, standing, undiminished, unremitting
uncensored intact, lurid
uncensurable blameless, clear *(free*

from criminal charges), irreprehensible, laudable, meritorious, unimpeachable, unobjectionable
unceremonial informal
unceremonious informal, presumptuous
unceremoniousness informality
uncertain ambiguous, approximate, capricious, casual, conditional, controversial, debatable, difficult, disputable, dubious, elusive, equivocal, fallible, hesitant, inconclusive, inconvincible, indefinite, indeterminate, insecure, intangible, irresolute, leery, moot, mutable, nebulous, noncommittal, pending *(unresolved)*, precarious, problematic, reluctant, shifting, skeptical, speculative, sporadic, subject *(conditional)*, suspicious *(questionable)*, unclear, unconfirmed, undecided, undependable, unforeseeable, unpredictable, unsettled, untrustworthy, vague
uncertain event condition *(contingent provision)*, contingency
uncertain state doubt *(indecision)*
uncertainness doubt *(indecision)*, hesitation, incertitude, quandary
uncertainty ambivalence, chance *(possibility)*, confusion *(ambiguity)*, contingency, dilemma, doubt *(indecision)*, hazard, hesitation, improbability, incertitude, incredulity, indecision, jeopardy, misgiving, peril, possibility, qualm, quandary, reluctance, risk, scruple, speculation *(risk)*, venture
uncertainty of meaning ambiguity
uncertified controversial, dubious, unauthorized, unconfirmed, unsupported
unchain break *(separate)*, disencumber, disengage, disenthrall, dissociate, free, liberate, parole, rescue
unchained free *(not restricted)*, unbound, uncurbed
unchaining liberation, release
unchallengeable axiomatic, clear *(certain)*, conclusive *(determinative)*, equitable, evenhanded, incontrovertible, indefeasible, inexpugnable, irrebuttable, irrefutable, irreprehensible, just, positive *(incontestable)*, sound, tenable, unalienable, uncontested, undisputed, unimpeachable
unchallenged accurate, consensual, permissible, uncontested, uncontroverted, undisputed, unequivocal
unchangeability indestructibility
unchangeable categorical, certain *(positive)*, conclusive *(determinative)*, consonant, durable, fixed *(settled)*, immutable, inappealable, indefeasible, indelible, inevitable, inflexible, infrangible, ironclad, irreconcilable, irredeemable, irreversible, irrevocable, loyal, noncancellable, obdurate, orthodox, patient, permanent, stable, unalterable, unavoidable *(not voidable)*, unbending, uncompromising, unyielding
unchangeableness constant
unchangeably invariably
unchanged consonant, infallible, literal, regular *(conventional)*, unaffected *(uninfluenced)*
unchanging certain *(fixed)*, consis-

tent, consonant, constant, continual *(connected)*, definite, dependable, equal, fixed *(settled)*, immutable, inexorable, infallible, ironclad, loyal, permanent, persistent, resolute, stable, standing, steadfast, uniform, unremitting
uncharacteristic improper, novel
uncharged free *(at no charge)*
uncharitable exclusive *(limited)*, illiberal, mordacious, parsimonious, scathing
uncharitableness rancor
uncharming pedestrian
unchartered illegal, impermissible, ultra vires, unauthorized, unsettled
unchary impulsive *(rash)*
unchaste dissolute, immoral, lascivious, lecherous, lewd, licentious, obscene, peccable, promiscuous, prurient, salacious
unchastised clear *(free from criminal charges)*
unchastity obscenity, vice
unchecked exempt, free *(not restricted)*, independent, intemperate, live *(existing)*, permanent, persistent, rampant, unbound, unconditional, unconfirmed, uncurbed, unlimited, unqualified *(unlimited)*, unrestrained *(not in custody)*, unrestrained *(not repressed)*, unrestricted
uncheerful grave *(solemn)*, pessimistic
uncheerfulness pessimism
uncheery grave *(solemn)*, pessimistic
unchivalrous ignoble, illiberal
unchosen ineligible
uncircumscribed far reaching, omnipotent
uncircumspect careless, derelict *(negligent)*, hot-blooded, imprudent, impulsive *(rash)*, lax, negligent, reckless, remiss
uncircumspection indiscretion
uncivil blatant *(obtrusive)*, contemptuous, disdainful, disorderly, impertinent *(insolent)*, offensive *(offending)*, perverse, uncouth
uncivilized brutal, caitiff, disorderly, vicious
unclaimed anonymous, derelict *(abandoned)*
unclarified equivocal, opaque
unclarity opacity
unclasp disengage
unclassifiable individual, nonconforming, nondescript, unusual
unclassified complex, disjointed, disordered, miscellaneous, peculiar *(curious)*
unclean insalubrious, lewd, prurient, repulsive, salacious, tainted *(contaminated)*
uncleanliness defilement
uncleanness defilement
unclear difficult, elusive, equivocal, impalpable, inarticulate, incomprehensible, inconspicuous, indefinable, indefinite, indeterminate, indistinct, inexact, inscrutable, nebulous, oblique *(evasive)*, obscure *(faint)*, opaque, pending *(unresolved)*, uncertain *(ambiguous)*, unspecified, vague
unclearness confusion *(ambiguity)*, incoherence, indistinctness, obscuration, opacity

unclever inadept, inept *(incompetent)*, unversed
unclinch break *(separate)*
uncloak bare, denude, expose, find *(discover)*, reveal, unveil
unclog disencumber
unclogged open *(unclosed)*
unclosed competitive *(open)*, penetrable
unclothe bare, denude
unclouded clear *(apparent)*, comprehensible, conspicuous, distinct *(clear)*, manifest, open *(in sight)*, perceivable, pure
uncoerced autonomous *(independent)*, free *(not restricted)*, voluntary
uncohesive desultory, disconnected, disjointed
uncoil spread
uncollaborated unsupported
uncollected outstanding *(unpaid)*, payable, unpaid, unsettled
uncollectible debt bad debt
uncolored accurate, factual, fair *(just)*, genuine, honest, impartial, just, objective, open-minded, true *(authentic)*, unbiased, unprejudiced
uncombined simple, unadulterated
uncomely unbecoming
uncomfortable egregious, lamentable, oppressive, painful
uncomfortableness dissatisfaction
uncomforting callous, harsh
uncommanded unauthorized
uncommendable blameful, blameworthy, disorderly, inappropriate, objectionable, peccable, reprehensible, scandalous, sinister, unethical
uncommissioned unauthorized
uncommitted impartial, independent, neutral, noncommittal, nonpartisan
uncommon anomalous, distinct *(distinguished from others)*, distinctive, eccentric, extraordinary, individual, infrequent, momentous, nonconforming, noteworthy, novel, original *(creative)*, particular *(specific)*, peculiar *(distinctive)*, prodigious *(amazing)*, rare, remarkable, scarce, singular, special, specific, unaccustomed, uncanny, unique, unorthodox, unusual
uncommonly particularly
uncommonness paucity
uncommunicated undisclosed
uncommunicative laconic, mute, noncommittal, phlegmatic, surreptitious, taciturn, unresponsive
uncommunicativeness loophole
uncompassionate callous, cruel, draconian, inexorable, obdurate, relentless, remorseless, ruthless, unaffected *(uninfluenced)*, unrelenting, unresponsive
uncompassionateness cruelty
uncompelled autonomous *(independent)*, impartial, nonpartisan, spontaneous, voluntary
uncompensated due *(owed)*, unpaid, unrequited
uncomplaining patient, resigned
uncomplaisant perverse, reluctant, restive
uncompleted deficient, executory, imperfect, inchoate, incipient, insufficient, partial *(part)*, partial *(relating to a part)*, rudimentary
uncomplex elementary

uncompliant broken *(unfulfilled)*, disobedient, lawless, perverse, recalcitrant, recusant, restive, unruly
uncomplicate simplify *(make easier)*
uncomplicated elementary, naked *(lacking embellishment)*, simple
uncomplimentary critical *(faultfinding)*, derogatory, pejorative
uncomplimentary remark disparagement
uncomplying contumacious, disobedient, insubordinate, lawless, nonconsenting, recalcitrant, reluctant, restive, unruly
uncompounded simple, unadulterated
uncomprehended hidden
uncomprehending blind *(not discerning)*, obtuse, opaque
uncomprehension nescience
uncompromising close *(rigorous)*, dictatorial, draconian, formal, immutable, implacable, inexorable, inflexible, ironclad, irreconcilable, obdurate, orthodox, particular *(exacting)*, patient, pertinacious, precise, punctilious, purposeful, radical *(favoring drastic change)*, relentless, resolute, rigid, scathing, sedulous, serious *(devoted)*, severe, stable, steadfast, strict, stringent, thorough, tyrannous, unbending, unrelenting, unyielding, willful
uncompromisingness rigor
unconceal bare, expose, find *(discover)*, manifest, unveil
unconcealed comprehensible, evident, manifest, naked *(perceptible)*, obvious, open *(in sight)*, overt, palpable, patent, pellucid, perceivable, perceptible, salient, scrutable, unmistakable
unconcern dereliction, disinterest *(lack of interest)*, indifference, laxity, neglect, negligence, sloth
unconcerned careless, casual, cold-blooded, controlled *(restrained)*, derelict *(negligent)*, heedless, insusceptible *(uncaring)*, lax, negligent, neutral, nonchalant, obdurate, perfunctory, phlegmatic, reckless, remiss, secure *(confident)*, thoughtless, torpid, truant, unabashed, unaffected *(uninfluenced)*, undaunted, unresponsive
unconcise prolix
unconcluded outstanding *(unresolved)*, pending *(unresolved)*
unconcrete intangible
unconcreteness impalpability
uncondemned blameless, clear *(free from criminal charges)*
unconditional absolute *(complete)*, categorical, complete *(all-embracing)*, comprehensive, outright, peremptory *(absolute)*, strict, unlimited, unmitigated, unqualified *(unlimited)*, unrestricted
unconditional inheritance fee *(estate)*
unconditionally purely *(positively)*
unconditioned absolute *(conclusive)*, categorical, peremptory *(absolute)*
uncondoling callous
unconfident dubious, hesitant, insecure
unconfined broad, competitive *(open)*, exempt, free *(not restricted)*, open-ended, plenary, unbound, uncondi-

tional, uncurbed, unlimited, unrestrained *(not in custody)*, unrestricted

unconfirmable unsustainable

unconfirmed debatable, disputable, dubious, ill-founded, inconclusive, provisional, speculative, uncertain *(questionable)*, uncorroborated, unsupported

unconfirmed account hearsay

unconfirmed report hearsay, report *(rumor)*

unconformable disparate, disproportionate, dissident, dissimilar, inapplicable, inapposite, inappropriate, incommensurate, irreconcilable, irregular *(not usual)*, lawless, nonconforming, original *(creative)*, peculiar *(curious)*, peculiar *(distinctive)*, recusant, repugnant *(incompatible)*, rigid, unique, unorthodox, unrelated

unconforming eccentric, peculiar *(distinctive)*, recusant

unconformity breach, controversy *(argument)*, deviation, difference, disaccord, disagreement, discrepancy, disparity, dissent *(difference of opinion)*, dissidence, distinction *(difference)*, diversity, exception *(exclusion)*, incompatibility *(inconsistency)*, incongruity, inconsistency, inequality, irregularity, nonconformity, quirk *(idiosyncrasy)*, variance *(disagreement)*

unconfused coherent *(clear)*, comprehensible, distinct *(distinguished from others)*, unambiguous

unconfusedly fairly *(clearly)*

unconfusing explicit, unmistakable

unconfutability certainty

unconfutable clear *(certain)*, convincing, incontrovertible, irrefutable, positive *(incontestable)*, solid *(sound)*, sound, unimpeachable, unrefutable

unconfuted certain *(positive)*, cogent, definite

uncongenial inapposite, inapt, incongruous, inept *(inappropriate)*, offensive *(offending)*, unsuitable

unconnected alien *(unrelated)*, apart, collateral *(immaterial)*, desultory, disconnected, discrete, disjunctive *(tending to disjoin)*, foreign, gratuitous *(unwarranted)*, impertinent *(irrelevant)*, inapposite, inconsequential, independent, individual, irrelative, irrelevant, obscure *(remote)*, remote *(secluded)*, separate, solitary, unrelated

unconquerable formidable, indomitable, inexpugnable, infallible, insuperable, insurmountable, invincible, irresistible, powerful, spartan

unconquered independent, sovereign *(independent)*

unconscienced recreant, unconscionable

unconscientious inaccurate

unconscientiousness bad faith, neglect

unconscionable excessive, exorbitant, immoral, inordinate, outrageous, perfidious, prohibitive *(costly)*, reprobate, unethical, unwarranted, usurious

unconscionable delay laches

unconscionable rate of interest usury

unconscious blind *(not discerning)*, incognizant, insensible, involuntary, oblivious, torpid, unaware, uninten-

tional, unsuspecting, unwitting

unconsciously unknowingly

unconsciousness disregard *(unconcern)*, ignorance, insentience

unconsecrated profane

unconsenting disinclined, disobedient, dissenting, dissident, nonconsenting, recusant, reluctant, restive

unconsentingly unwillingly

unconsidered haphazard, ill-advised, ill-judged, impulsive *(rash)*, injudicious, irrational, misadvised, unpremeditated

unconsolable disconsolate

unconsoling callous, harsh

unconsonant hostile, inapplicable, inapposite, inappropriate, inapt, inept *(inappropriate)*

unconspicuous unobtrusive

unconstitutional illegal, illicit, impermissible, unauthorized, unlawful

unconstitutionality prohibition

unconstrained absolute *(complete)*, autonomous *(independent)*, candid, clear *(unencumbered)*, direct *(forthright)*, ingenuous, lawless, open-ended, simple, spontaneous, unbound, uncurbed, unqualified *(unlimited)*, unrestrained *(not in custody)*, unrestrained *(not repressed)*, unrestricted, voluntary, willful

unconstraint freedom, honesty, informality, latitude, liberty

uncontained unrestricted

uncontaminated pure, unadulterated

uncontemplated unanticipated, unexpected

uncontemporary outdated

uncontentious nonmilitant, peaceable

uncontestable arrant *(definite)*, irrefutable, manifest, palpable, unmistakable

uncontested axiomatic, categorical, clear *(certain)*, conclusive *(determinative)*, consensual, definite, definitive, indubious, uncontroverted

uncontradictable incontestable, incontrovertible

uncontradicted consensual, uncontested, uncontroverted

uncontrite incorrigible

uncontrived spontaneous, straightforward

uncontrollable hot-blooded, incorrigible, inexorable, intractable, necessary *(inescapable)*, obdurate, recalcitrant, restive, unavoidable *(inevitable)*, unruly, unyielding

uncontrolled autonomous *(independent)*, capricious, disorderly, drunk, exempt, impulsive *(rash)*, independent, intemperate, irresponsible, lawless, licentious, open-ended, rampant, sensitive *(easily affected)*, sovereign *(independent)*, spontaneous, unbound, uncurbed, unlimited, unqualified *(unlimited)*, unrestrained *(not repressed)*, unrestricted

uncontroversial clear *(certain)*, consensual, inappealable, irrefutable, uncontested, undisputed, unrefutable

uncontroverted consensual, uncontested

unconventional anomalous, deviant, divergent, eccentric, individual, informal, irregular *(not usual)*, licentious, nonconforming, novel, original *(crea-*

tive)*, peculiar *(curious)*, prodigious *(amazing)*, unaccustomed, uncommon, unorthodox, unusual

unconventionality exception *(exclusion)*, informality, nonconformity, quirk *(idiosyncrasy)*

unconversable unresponsive

unconversant blind *(not discerning)*, inexperienced, unaccustomed, unacquainted, unversed

unconverted negative

unconveyed undisclosed

unconvinced incredulous, leery, negative, undecided

unconvincing doubtful, implausible, incredible, ludicrous, problematic, suspicious *(questionable)*, unbelievable

uncooperated reluctant

uncooperative adverse *(hostile)*, contentious, disinclined, disobedient, froward, hostile, perverse, recalcitrant, unresponsive

uncoordinated disordered, incongruous, random, slipshod

uncopied honest, original *(creative)*

uncorked open *(unclosed)*

uncorrectable chronic

uncorrectness misestimation

uncorroborated baseless, inconclusive, unconfirmed, unsupported

uncorrupt blameless, conscientious, credible, decontaminate, ethical, evenhanded, high-minded, impartial, incorruptible, inculpable, just, moral, pure, reputable, straightforward, upright

uncorrupted blameless, clean, dispassionate, ethical, evenhanded, fair *(just)*, high-minded, impartial, inviolate, just, law-abiding, literal, moral, pure, unadulterated

uncorruptibility rectitude

uncorruptible credible

uncountable innumerable, myriad

uncounted innumerable, multiple, myriad

uncounterfeited authentic, bona fide, genuine, honest, unaffected *(sincere)*, veridical

uncouple break *(separate)*, detach, disband, disjoint, dissociate, dissolve *(separate)*, divide *(separate)*, divorce, separate, sever

uncoupled disconnected

uncoupling division *(act of dividing)*, separation

uncourageous caitiff, recreant

uncourteous uncouth

uncourtliness disrespect

uncourtly disorderly, inelegant, presumptuous, provincial, uncouth

uncouth blatant *(obtrusive)*, ignoble, impertinent *(insolent)*, inelegant, provincial

uncovenanted purchase caveat emptor

uncover bare, betray *(disclose)*, convey *(communicate)*, denude, detect, disabuse, disclose, discover, disinter, divest, divulge, evidence, exhibit, expose, find *(discover)*, inform *(betray)*, locate, manifest, present *(introduce)*, produce *(offer to view)*, reveal, unveil

uncovered apparent *(perceptible)*, clear *(apparent)*, conspicuous, distinct *(clear)*, helpless *(defenseless)*, open *(in sight)*, open *(unclosed)*, overt, palpable

uncovering disclosure *(act of disclosing)*, discovery, expression *(manifestation)*, manifestation
uncovery disclosure *(act of disclosing)*
uncreated nonexistent
uncreative trite
uncredulousness cloud *(suspicion)*, doubt *(suspicion)*
uncringing unabashed
uncritical casual, favorable *(expressing approval)*, indiscriminate, promiscuous, unnecessary
uncritical acceptance credulity
uncrown overthrow
uncrowning abdication
unctious subservient
unculpable blameless, clean, pardonable
uncultivated idle, ignoble, inelegant, natural, uncouth
uncultured blatant *(obtrusive)*, imperfect, inelegant, uncouth
uncurbed clear *(unencumbered)*, disorderly, dissolute, free *(not restricted)*, independent, inordinate, intemperate, intractable, irresponsible, lawless, licentious, prodigal, profuse, unrestrained *(not in custody)*, unrestrained *(not repressed)*, unruly
uncurrent outdated, outmoded
uncurtain bare, denude, manifest, reveal, unveil
uncurtained palpable
uncustomarily particularly
uncustomary anomalous, extraordinary, informal, infrequent, nonconforming, noteworthy, novel, original *(creative)*, peculiar *(curious)*, portentous *(eliciting amazement)*, prodigious *(amazing)*, rare, singular, special, unaccustomed, uncommon, unprecedented, unusual
uncut gross *(total)*, intact, undiminished
undamaged intact, safe, undiminished
undaring judicious, noncommittal, safe
undaunted diligent, heroic, indomitable, patient, persistent, pertinacious, relentless, resolute, spartan, steadfast, unabashed
undauntedness audacity, diligence *(perseverance)*
undebased unadulterated
undebatable undisputed
undecayed intact
undeceitful direct *(forthright)*
undeceitfulness honesty
undeceive debunk, disabuse, inform *(notify)*, reveal
undeceived conscious *(aware)*, informed *(having information)*
undeceiving direct *(forthright)*
undeceptive direct *(forthright)*, unaffected *(sincere)*
undeceptiveness honesty, probity
undecided aleatory *(uncertain)*, conditional, controversial, debatable, disputable, equivocal, hesitant, impartial, indefinite, indeterminate, irresolute, moot, mutable, noncommittal, outstanding *(unresolved)*, pending *(unresolved)*, pliant, problematic, provisional, tentative, uncertain *(questiona-*

ble), unsettled
undecidedness ambivalence, doubt *(indecision)*, qualm
undecipherability incoherence
undecipherable complex, inapprehensible, indistinct, inexplicable, inexpressive
undeciphered hidden, mysterious
undeclared implied, tacit, undisclosed
undecorated naked *(lacking embellishment)*, simple
undeducted from gross *(total)*
undefaced intact
undefeatable indefeasible, insuperable, insurmountable
undefeated prosperous, successful
undefended helpless *(defenseless)*, open *(accessible)*, susceptible *(unresistent)*, untenable
undefiled blameless, inviolate, pure, unadulterated, unblemished
undefinable inapprehensible, ineffable
undefined equivocal, inconspicuous, indefinite, indeterminate, indistinct, nebulous, open-ended, unclear, unspecified, vague
undeflected direct *(straight)*
undefrayed delinquent *(overdue)*
undeft inadept, inept *(incompetent)*
undeftness disqualification *(factor that disqualifies)*, inability, incompetence
undelectable unsavory
undeleted gross *(total)*
undeliberate unintentional
undemanded unclaimed
undemanding facile, lax, lenient
undemanding chore sinecure
undemanding job sinecure
undemanding task sinecure
undemocratic dictatorial
undemolished intact
undemonstrable debatable, disputable, problematic, unsustainable, untenable
undemonstrated debatable, disputable, dubious, inconclusive, speculative, unconfirmed, uncorroborated, unsupported
undemonstrative controlled *(restrained)*, dispassionate, passive, phlegmatic, placid, stoical
undeniability certainty, certitude, incontestability
undeniable axiomatic, believable, categorical, certain *(fixed)*, certain *(positive)*, clear *(certain)*, cogent, conclusive *(determinative)*, convincing, credible, definite, definitive, evident, factual, incontestable, incontrovertible, indefeasible, indubious, irrefutable, lucid, necessary *(inescapable)*, noncontestable, obvious, official, positive *(incontestable)*, real, reliable, uncontested, undisputed, unequivocal, unimpeachable, unmistakable, unrefutable
undeniable fact fait accompli
undeniably admittedly, fairly *(clearly)*
undenied accurate
undenominational nonsectarian
undependability dishonesty, improbity

undependable dishonest, disobedient, faithless, fallible, false *(disloyal)*, insecure, irresponsible, machiavellian, perfidious, precarious, recreant, unpredictable, unreliable, untrustworthy
under inferior *(lower in position)*, subaltern
under a sense of impending death in extremis
under a vow bound
under advisement at issue
under arms armed
under arrest arrested *(apprehended)*, in custody
under average poor *(inferior in quality)*
under ban illicit, impermissible
under compulsion bound
under consideration at issue, pending *(unresolved)*
under control bailment, systematic
under cover safe
under discussion debatable, disputable, moot
under examination at issue, debatable
under fiduciary control in trust
under inquiry controversial
under legal obligation actionable, liable
under lock and key in custody
under necessity bound
under oath promissory
under obligation accountable *(responsible)*, actionable, bound, indebted, indentured, liable
under one's hand holographic
under par minimal
under shelter immune
under surveillance guarded
under the circumstances consequently
under the control of conditional
under the influence of addicted
under the influence of liquor drunk
under the mark minimal
under the surface internal, latent
underage juvenile
underage person minor
underbid haggle
underbred ignoble
undercover cache *(hiding place)*, clandestine, collusive, confidential, covert, furtive, hidden, mysterious, private *(confidential)*, sly, stealthy, surreptitious, unobtrusive
undercover agent spy
undercover man bystander, spy
undercover work espionage
underestimate depreciate, derogate, discount *(minimize)*, lessen, minimize, misprize
underestimating pejorative
underestimation disregard *(lack of respect)*, understatement
undergo allow *(endure)*, bear *(tolerate)*, endure *(suffer)*, tolerate
undergo eclipse disappear
undergo evolution evolve
undergo the cost of disburse *(pay out)*
undergo the expense of disburse *(pay out)*
undergrade poor *(inferior in quality)*
underground clandestine, covert, furtive, hidden, surreptitious, unobtrusive

underground activity sedition
underhand clandestine, covert, furtive, machiavellian, mysterious, oblique *(evasive)*, sly, stealthy, subtle *(insidious)*, surreptitious, unscrupulous
underhand dealing bad faith, collusion, dishonesty, evasion, knavery, pettifoggery
underhand participation connivance
underhand practice pettifoggery
underhanded clandestine, collusive, deceptive, dishonest, disingenuous, false *(disloyal)*, fraudulent, hidden, insidious, machiavellian, oblique *(evasive)*, sly, unethical
underhanded act maneuver *(trick)*
underhanded complicity connivance
underhanded practice deceit
underhandedness deceit, dishonesty, false pretense, fraud, illegality, improbity, indirection *(deceitfulness)*
underived original *(creative)*, primordial
underlease rent
underlet rent, sublease, sublet
underlie inspire
underline insist, reaffirm
underling assistant, coadjutant
underlining emphasis
underlying cardinal *(basic)*, central *(essential)*, fundamental, latent, organic, original *(initial)*, primary, rudimentary, substantive, virtual
underlying principle basis, cause *(reason)*, foundation *(basis)*
undermine check *(restrain)*, corrupt, countervail, debilitate, disable, disarm *(divest of arms)*, discommode, disqualify, foil, frustrate, hamper, hold up *(delay)*, impair, invalidate, overreach, plot, pollute, rebel, smear, subvert, supplant, thwart
undermine one's belief deter, impugn
undermining detrimental
undermost cardinal *(basic)*, underlying
underpin bolster
underpinning foundation *(basis)*
underplot collusion, connivance, conspiracy, machination
underpraise depreciate, minimize
underprice discount *(reduce)*, minimize, underestimate
underprize depreciate, misprize, underestimate
underrate depreciate, derogate, discommend, disparage, lessen, minimize, misprize, underestimate
underreckon depreciate, derogate, minimize, misprize, underestimate
underripe premature
underscoring emphasis
undersell discount *(reduce)*
undersign corroborate, cosign, indorse, notarize, seal *(solemnize)*, sign, subscribe *(sign)*, witness *(attest to)*
undersized minimal
understand agree *(comply)*, appreciate *(comprehend)*, apprehend *(perceive)*, conceive *(comprehend)*, construe *(comprehend)*, deduce, deduct *(conclude by reasoning)*, digest *(comprehend)*, discover, find *(discover)*, infer, interpret, perceive, pierce *(discern)*, presume, presuppose, read, recognize *(perceive)*, re-

solve *(solve)*, solve, surmise, suspect *(think)*, sympathize
understand by construe *(comprehend)*
understand fully comprehend *(understand)*
understand improperly misconstrue
understand incorrectly miscalculate, misinterpret, misread
understand the meaning of construe *(comprehend)*
understand wrongly misunderstand
understandability coherence
understandable ascertainable, cognizable, coherent *(clear)*, comprehensible, elementary, explicit, lucid, obvious, pardonable, pellucid, perceptible, ponderable, reasonable *(rational)*, scrutable, simple, unambiguous
understandable language plain language
understandably fairly *(clearly)*
understanding accord, accordance *(understanding)*, adjustment, affection, agreement *(concurrence)*, agreement *(contract)*, apprehension *(perception)*, attornment, bargain, belief *(state of mind)*, benevolence *(disposition to do good)*, benevolent, caliber *(mental capacity)*, charitable *(lenient)*, cognition, cognizant, common sense, compact, comprehension, concept, conciliation, concordance, conscious *(aware)*, consideration *(sympathetic regard)*, consortium *(marriage companionship)*, construction, contract, conviction *(persuasion)*, covenant, deal, discrimination *(good judgment)*, estimate *(idea)*, experience *(background)*, humanity *(humaneness)*, inference, information *(knowledge)*, insight, intellect, intelligence *(intellect)*, judgment *(discernment)*, juridical, knowing, knowledge *(awareness)*, league, lenience, longanimity, notion, omniscient, option *(contractual provision)*, pact, patient, perception, perceptive, perspicacious, placable, policy *(contract)*, promise, protocol *(agreement)*, quid pro quo, rapport, rapprochement, rational, realization, reason *(sound judgment)*, receptive, reconciliation, sagacity, sane, sanity, scienter, sense *(feeling)*, sense *(intelligence)*, sensible, sensitive *(discerning)*, settlement, specialty *(contract)*, stipulation, term *(provision)*, tolerance, treaty, vicarious *(delegated)*
understanding before marriage antenuptial agreement
understandings dealings
understate discount *(minimize)*, distort, minimize, misrepresent
understood assumed *(inferred)*, clear *(apparent)*, cognizable, coherent *(clear)*, consensual, constructive *(inferential)*, contractual, familiar *(customary)*, implicit, implied, indirect, lucid, prescriptive, tacit
understood by a select few esoteric
understood by the initiated esoteric
understood from accompanying words noscitur a sociis
understudy replace, replacement, substitute
understudy for displace *(replace)*
undertake agree *(contract)*, attempt,

close *(agree)*, commence, contract, embark, endeavor, engage *(involve)*, generate, incur, initiate, launch *(initiate)*, maintain *(commence)*, occupy *(engage)*, originate, participate, pledge *(promise the performance of)*, ply, practice *(engage in)*, promise *(vow)*, strive, try *(attempt)*, underwrite
undertake by contract contract
undertake responsibility answer *(be responsible)*
undertaking activity, agreement *(contract)*, appointment *(position)*, assumption *(adoption)*, bail, burden, business *(affair)*, business *(occupation)*, calling, campaign, charge *(responsibility)*, commitment *(responsibility)*, contract, covenant, coverage *(insurance)*, endeavor, enterprise *(undertaking)*, expedient, indenture, industry *(business)*, job, labor *(work)*, livelihood, maneuver *(tactic)*, mission, occupation *(vocation)*, operation, part *(role)*, plan, pledge *(binding promise)*, post, practice *(professional business)*, proceeding, profession *(vocation)*, project, prosecution *(criminal trial)*, pursuit *(effort to secure)*, pursuit *(occupation)*, role, specialty *(contract)*, transaction, vow, work *(effort)*
undertakings dealings
undervaluation disregard *(lack of respect)*, understatement
undervalue depreciate, derogate, discommend, discount *(minimize)*, discount *(reduce)*, disparage, humiliate, lessen, minimize, misprize, underestimate
underworker assistant
underworld activity racket
underworld character criminal, outlaw, racketeer
underworld gangster racketeer
underwrite assure *(insure)*, authorize, avouch *(guarantee)*, bond *(secure a debt)*, close *(agree)*, cosign, ensure, guarantee, indorse, promise *(vow)*, sign, sponsor, subscribe *(sign)*, subsidize, vouch
underwrite again refinance
underwrite against loss insure
underwriter insurer, surety *(guarantor)*
underwriting coverage *(insurance)*
undeserved disproportionate, undue *(excessive)*, unjust
undeserving disproportionate, unworthy
undeserving of censure irreprehensible
undesignated anonymous, unspecified
undesigned fortuitous, inadvertent, random, unexpected, unforeseen, unintentional, unpremeditated, unwitting
undesigned occurrence accident *(chance occurrence)*, quirk *(accident)*
undesigning direct *(forthright)*, ingenuous, simple, straightforward, unaffected *(sincere)*
undesirability bad character, detriment, disqualification *(factor that disqualifies)*, inexpedience
undesirable antipathetic *(distasteful)*, bad *(inferior)*, bad *(offensive)*, delinquent, deplorable, gratuitous *(unwar-*

ranted), ill-advised, improper, imprudent, inadvisable, inappropriate, inapt, ineligible, inept *(inappropriate),* inferior *(lower in quality),* injudicious, inopportune, loathsome, needless, objectionable, repugnant *(exciting aversion),* sordid, unacceptable, unendurable, unfit, unsatisfactory, unsavory, unsuitable

undesirableness inexpedience

undesired unacceptable, unsolicited

undesirous averse

undespairing sanguine

undestroyable indelible, indestructible, infallible, noncancellable, permanent, perpetual

undestroyed chronic, extant, intact, inviolate, lasting, live *(existing)*

undestructive nontoxic

undetached interested, one-sided, partisan

undetachment bias, inequity, nepotism, predetermination

undetected blind *(concealed),* hidden, latent, potential, undisclosed

undetermination ambivalence

undetermined casual, conditional, debatable, disputable, dubious, equivocal, indefinite, irresolute, moot, outstanding *(unresolved),* pending *(unresolved),* problematic, provisional, speculative, uncertain *(questionable),* undecided, unsettled, vague

undeterminedness doubt *(indecision)*

undeveloped deficient, dormant, imperfect, inadequate, inexperienced, juvenile, latent, partial *(relating to a part),* premature, rudimentary

undeveloped stage embryo

undeviating accurate, boiler plate, certain *(positive),* comparable *(equivalent),* consistent, consonant, constant, direct *(straight),* equal, exact, factual, immutable, industrious, intense, literal, loyal, patient, persistent, pertinacious, purposeful, regular *(conventional),* relentless, resolute, right *(direct),* rigid, sedulous, sequacious, stable, steadfast, straightforward, unalterable, undistorted, uniform, unrelenting, unyielding

undeviatingly faithfully, invariably

undevout profane

undexterous inadept

undextrous amateur

undifferentiating indiscriminate

undignified blatant *(obtrusive),* disreputable, inappropriate, inelegant, unbecoming, unprofessional, unseemly

undiligent negligent

undiluted honest, unadulterated

undiminished complete *(all-embracing),* gross *(total),* intact, outright, plenary, whole *(undamaged)*

undiminished quantity entirety

undiplomatic impolitic, unpolitic

undirected astray, casual, discursive *(digressive),* fortuitous, haphazard, indiscriminate, random

undiscernable impalpable

undiscernible inconspicuous, indefinite, intangible, nebulous

undiscerning blind *(not discerning),* cursory, heedless, ill-judged, inadvertent, injudicious, insensible, oblivious, obtuse, perfunctory, promiscuous, una-

ware

undischarged unpaid

undisciplined capricious, disobedient, disordered, disorderly, inexperienced, intractable, irresponsible, lawless, licentious, uncurbed, unrestrained *(not repressed),* unversed

undisclosable private *(confidential)*

undisclosed clandestine, covert, esoteric, furtive, hidden, mysterious, personal *(private),* potential, privy, secret, stealthy, surreptitious, ulterior

undiscordant consonant

undiscouraged patient, persistent, undaunted

undiscoverability mystery

undiscoverable inapprehensible, indiscernible, inexplicable, inscrutable

undiscovered latent, potential

undiscriminating promiscuous

undisguise bare

undisguised accurate, apparent *(perceptible),* authentic, bona fide, candid, clear *(apparent),* coherent *(clear),* conspicuous, distinct *(clear),* evident, explicit, factual, genuine, honest, ingenuous, lucid, manifest, naked *(lacking embellishment),* obvious, open *(in sight),* overt, palpable, patent, pellucid, realistic, true *(authentic),* undistorted, unmistakable

undisguising direct *(forthright),* honest

undismayed unabashed, undaunted

undispassionate one-sided, partisan

undispassionateness bias, inequity

undisputable indefeasible, sound

undisputed accurate, axiomatic, categorical, certain *(fixed),* certain *(positive),* clear *(certain),* consensual, convincing, definite, definitive, factual, general, resounding, true *(authentic),* uncontested, uncontroverted, unequivocal, unimpeachable

undissembling bona fide, candid, honest, straightforward

undissimulating honest

undissolvable inseparable

undissolved solid *(compact)*

undistinctive usual

undistinguished marginal, mediocre, mundane, nondescript, obscure *(faint),* ordinary, unpretentious, usual

undistorted accurate, authentic, bona fide, candid, direct *(straight),* distinct *(clear),* factual, genuine, honest, literal, realistic, sound, straightforward, true *(authentic),* unadulterated

undistracted pertinacious, steadfast

undisturbed dispassionate, inviolate, patient, peaceable, phlegmatic, placid, sane, secure *(confident),* stoical

undiversified uniform

undividable indivisible, inseparable

undivided complete *(all-embracing),* concurrent *(united),* gross *(total),* intact, outright, total, undiminished

undivided attention diligence *(care),* diligence *(perseverance),* interest *(concern),* obsession

undividedly in toto

undividedness entirety, integration *(assimilation),* whole

undivisible whole *(unified)*

undivulgable private *(confidential)*

undivulged esoteric, hidden, secret,

ulterior, undisclosed

undo abolish, abrogate *(annul),* beat *(defeat),* betray *(lead astray),* counteract, denude, disengage, disorganize, disown *(deny the validity),* dissociate, dissolve *(separate),* dissolve *(terminate),* frustrate, invalidate, liberate, overreach, overrule, part *(separate),* subvert, upset, vitiate

undoable impracticable, inoperable *(impracticable)*

undogmatic open-minded

undoing annulment, defeasance, defeat, destruction, detriment, disaster, dissolution *(disintegration),* prostration, reversal

undone irredeemable, irreparable

undoubtable cogent, irrefutable, noncontestable, palpable, real

undoubted absolute *(conclusive),* axiomatic, certain *(positive),* clear *(certain),* cogent, conclusive *(determinative),* decisive, definitive, uncontested, uncontroverted, undisputed, unimpeachable, unmistakable

undoubtedly admittedly, fairly *(clearly)*

undoubtful certain *(positive),* indubious

undoubting affirmative, certain *(positive),* credulous, definite, pertinacious, positive *(confident),* sanguine, unsuspecting

undramatic insipid, jejune *(dull)*

undrape bare, denude, expose, manifest, unveil

undress denude, expose, unveil

undrilled inexperienced, unversed

undue disproportionate, drastic, excess, excessive, exorbitant, extreme *(exaggerated),* gratuitous *(unwarranted),* improper, inadmissible, inapposite, inappropriate, inapt, inept *(inappropriate),* inordinate, outrageous, prohibitive *(costly),* redundant, unauthorized, unfit, unreasonable, unseemly, unwarranted, usurious, wrongful

undue amount overage, plethora

undue delay laches

undue expansion of currency inflation *(decrease in value of currency)*

undue influence coercion, pressure

undueness breach, exaggeration, inequity

undulate beat *(pulsate),* circuitous, oscillate, vacillate

undulated circuitous

undulating circuitous

undulative circuitous

undulatory circuitous, tortuous *(bending)*

unduly arbitrary and capricious

unduteousness breach, nonperformance

undutiful broken *(unfulfilled),* disobedient, irresponsible, untrue

undutifulness breach, contempt *(disobedience to the court),* infidelity, nonperformance

undying chronic, constant, durable, immutable, incessant, indestructible, infallible, infinite, permanent, persistent

unearned increment gratuity *(present)*

unearth ascertain, betray *(disclose),*

delve, detect, disclose, discover, disinter, educe, expose, ferret, find *(discover)*, locate, manifest, probe, research, reveal, solve, trace *(follow)*
unearthing detection, discovery
unearthly intangible, nonsubstantial *(not sturdy)*, uncanny
unease pain, scruple
uneasiness apprehension *(fear)*, concern *(interest)*, distress *(anguish)*, embarrassment, fear, misgiving, qualm, scruple, trepidation
uneasiness of mind dissatisfaction
uneasy restive, unsettled
uneconomical improvident, prodigal, prolix
unedited intact
uneducated unversed
uneffective unqualified *(not competent)*
unelaborate unpretentious
unelapsed period unexpired term
unelevated insipid
unembarrassed brazen, unabashed
unembellished naked *(lacking embellishment)*, simple
unembodied incorporeal
unembroidered honest, literal, undistorted
unemotional clinical, cold-blooded, controlled *(restrained)*, dispassionate, inexpressive, insusceptible *(uncaring)*, phlegmatic, unresponsive
unemotional consideration common sense
unemphatic insipid
unemployable impracticable
unemployed idle, inactive, otiose, truant, vacant
unemployment disuse, inaction
unempowered inadequate, incapable, ineffectual, powerless, unauthorized
unenclosed open *(accessible)*
unencumbered exempt, free *(relieved from a burden)*, immune, independent, unbound, unrestrained *(not in custody)*
unendangered safe
unended live *(existing)*
unending chronic, continual *(perpetual)*, continuous, direct *(uninterrupted)*, durable, far reaching, immutable, incessant, infinite, myriad, open-ended, permanent, perpetual, protracted, rife, unlimited
unendorsed unauthorized, unofficial
unendorsed purchase caveat emptor
unendowed disabled *(deprived of legal right)*, disabled *(made incapable)*, inadept, powerless
unendowment incompetence
unendurable insufferable, intolerable, loathsome, objectionable, obnoxious, odious, offensive *(offending)*, oppressive, painful
unenduring ephemeral, temporary, transient, transitory
unenforceable void *(invalid)*
unengaged unemployed
unenlightened blind *(not discerning)*, ill-judged, incognizant, insensible, opaque, unacquainted, unaware
unenlightenment ignorance, nescience
unenlivened jejune *(dull)*, lifeless *(dull)*, nondescript, pedestrian
unenslaved free *(enjoying civil lib-*

erty)*, independent, sovereign *(independent)*
unentangled free *(not restricted)*
unenterprising careful, indolent, lax, lifeless *(dull)*
unentertaining insipid, jejune *(dull)*, lifeless *(dull)*, pedestrian, prosaic
unenthralled free *(enjoying civil liberty)*, independent
unenthusiastic disinclined, lifeless *(dull)*, nonchalant, perfunctory
unentitled impermissible, ineligible, unauthorized, unwarranted
unequal broken *(interrupted)*, disparate, disproportionate, heterogeneous, incommensurate, incompetent, insufficient, partial *(biased)*, peculiar *(distinctive)*, unconscionable, unfair, unjust
unequal to deficient, inadept, inadequate
unequaled absolute *(ideal)*, best, cardinal *(outstanding)*, leading *(ranking first)*, noteworthy, paramount, premium, priceless, prime *(most valuable)*, professional *(stellar)*, rare, select, singular, superior *(excellent)*, superlative, unapproachable, unique, unprecedented, unusual
unequalled extraordinary, inestimable, invaluable
unequalness difference
unequipped incapable, incompetent, ineligible, powerless, unfit, unqualified *(not competent)*
unequivocal absolute *(conclusive)*, axiomatic, categorical, certain *(positive)*, clear *(apparent)*, clear *(certain)*, cogent, cognizable, coherent *(clear)*, conclusive *(determinative)*, constant, credible, decisive, definite, demonstrable, distinct *(clear)*, dogmatic, evident, explicit, express, incontestable, incontrovertible, indubious, irrefutable, lucid, official, outright, palpable, peremptory *(absolute)*, positive *(incontestable)*, precise, reliable, unambiguous, unmistakable, unrefutable, vehement
unequivocally fairly *(clearly)*, purely *(positively)*
unequivocalness belief *(state of mind)*, certainty, certitude, incontestability, surety *(certainty)*
uneradicated lasting
unerasable chronic, indelible, permanent, perpetual
unerased lasting
unerring absolute *(conclusive)*, accurate, actual, certain *(fixed)*, certain *(positive)*, clean, clear *(certain)*, definite, effective *(efficient)*, exact, factual, incorruptible, inculpable, infallible, irreprehensible, literal, moral, positive *(incontestable)*, precise, reliable, secure *(sound)*, solid *(sound)*, strict, unblemished
unerringly faithfully
unerroneous actual, factual, real
unescorted solitary
unessayed unsettled
unessential collateral *(immaterial)*, expendable, extraneous, extrinsic, gratuitous *(unwarranted)*, immaterial, inapposite, inconsequential, inconsiderable, irrelevant, minor, needless, negligible, nonessential, null *(insignificant)*, petty, remote *(small)*, secondary, slight,

superfluous, supplementary, unnecessary
unestablished inconclusive, unconfirmed, unfounded
unethical dishonest, disingenuous, disreputable, fraudulent, immoral, machiavellian, profligate *(corrupt)*, unconscionable, unprofessional, unscrupulous
unethical use exploitation
unevasible necessary *(inescapable)*
unevasive clear *(apparent)*, cognizable
uneven broken *(interrupted)*, disordered, disorderly, disparate, disproportionate, inequitable, one-sided, partial *(biased)*, sporadic, unequal *(unequivalent)*, unfair, unpredictable, variable
unevenness diversity, flaw, incoherence, inequality, irregularity
uneventful mundane, unavailing
unevident impalpable, inconspicuous, ulterior, unclear
unexact indefinite
unexacted unclaimed
unexacting casual, flexible
unexaggerated authentic, bona fide, exact, factual, honest, literal, naked *(lacking embellishment)*, sound, true *(authentic)*, undistorted
unexalted mundane
unexamined perfunctory
unexampled extraordinary, original *(creative)*, peculiar *(curious)*, portentous *(eliciting amazement)*, prodigious *(amazing)*, rare, renowned, singular, special, uncommon, unique, unprecedented
unexcelled absolute *(ideal)*, cardinal *(outstanding)*, leading *(ranking first)*, paramount, professional *(stellar)*, select, superior *(excellent)*, superlative, unapproachable
unexceptionability admissibility
unexceptionable admissible, clean, irreprehensible, mediocre, unimpeachable, unobjectionable
unexceptional average *(standard)*, fair *(satisfactory)*, familiar *(customary)*, nondescript, normal *(regular)*, ordinary, regular *(conventional)*, typical, usual
unexceptionality mediocrity
unexcercised unversed
unexcessiveness temperance
unexcitable controlled *(restrained)*, peaceable, phlegmatic
unexcited dispassionate, nonchalant, peaceable, phlegmatic, placid, unaffected *(uninfluenced)*
unexciting insipid, jejune *(dull)*, mediocre, nondescript, ordinary, trite
unexclusive comprehensive
unexcused delay laches
unexecuted executory, inchoate
unexempt from actionable, subject *(exposed)*
unexercised inactive
unexisting devoid, nonexistent
unexpectant unsuspecting
unexpected coincidental, fortuitous, impulsive *(rash)*, nonconforming, original *(creative)*, peculiar *(curious)*, precipitate, unanticipated, unforeseeable, unforeseen, unintentional, unprecedented, unpredictable, unusual, unwitting

unexpected event bombshell, surprise
unexpected happening emergency
unexpected misfortune accident *(chance occurrence)*
unexpected occurrence accident *(chance occurrence)*, happenstance, surprise
unexpectedness chance *(possibility)*
unexpended net
unexplainable inapprehensible, inexplicable, mysterious, undefinable
unexplained dubious, equivocal, hidden, mysterious, undisclosed
unexplained delay laches
unexplicit impalpable, unclear
unexplored unsettled
unexplored ground mystery
unexposed blind *(concealed)*, hidden, immune, latent, potential, safe, undisclosed
unexpressed implicit, indirect, potential, tacit, ulterior, undisclosed
unexpressive mute
unexpurgated gross *(total)*, intact, lurid, salacious
unextravagant reasonable *(fair)*
unextreme reasonable *(fair)*
unfabricated authentic, factual, genuine, honest, true *(authentic)*
unfacile inadept, inept *(incompetent)*
unfactual inaccurate, incorrect, lying
unfactualness error
unfaded intact, undiminished
unfading chronic, durable, indelible, indestructible, infallible, live *(existing)*, permanent, perpetual
unfailing certain *(fixed)*, certain *(positive)*, credible, definite, dependable, durable, faithful *(loyal)*, inevitable, infallible, lasting, live *(existing)*, loyal, permanent, perpetual, persistent, reliable, secure *(sound)*, solid *(sound)*, stable, staunch, steadfast, true *(loyal)*, unremitting
unfair inequitable, iniquitous, one-sided, partial *(biased)*, sinister, unconscionable, unequal *(unjust)*, unethical, unjust, unreasonable, unscrupulous, unwarranted, wrongful
unfair action injustice
unfair choice dilemma
unfair judgment misjudgment
unfairly call to account frame *(charge falsely)*
unfairness bad faith, discrimination *(bigotry)*, grievance, inequality, inequity, injustice, misjudgment, nepotism, prejudice *(injury)*, wrong
unfaith bad faith
unfaithful broken *(unfulfilled)*, derelict *(negligent)*, dishonest, disobedient, faithless, false *(disloyal)*, fraudulent, perfidious, recreant, untrue, untrustworthy
unfaithfulness adultery, bad faith, breach, dereliction, disloyalty, infidelity
unfaithworthiness bad faith
unfaithworthy irresponsible, precarious
unfaked authentic, bona fide, genuine, honest, undistorted, veridical
unfallacious actual, real, true *(authentic)*
unfallen blameless, irreprehensible
unfalse actual, credible, true *(loyal)*

unfaltering continuous, definite, diligent, direct *(uninterrupted)*, industrious, inexorable, infallible, patient, persistent, pertinacious, purposeful, relentless, resolute, sedulous, serious *(devoted)*, stable, staunch, steadfast, undaunted
unfamiliar extraordinary, foreign, incognizant, inexperienced, inexplicable, noteworthy, novel, peculiar *(curious)*, prodigious *(amazing)*, rare, recondite, special, unaccustomed, unacquainted, uncanny, uncommon, unprecedented, unusual, unversed
unfamiliar with unaware
unfamiliarity ignorance, insentience
unfamiliarly particularly
unfashionable deviant, eccentric, nonconforming, obsolete, original *(creative)*, outdated, outmoded, unorthodox
unfasten detach, disencumber, disengage, disentangle, disjoint, free, liberate, remove *(eliminate)*, sever
unfastened discrete, free *(not restricted)*, insecure, moving *(in motion)*, open *(unclosed)*, unbound
unfathomability mystery
unfathomable complex, inapprehensible, inarticulate, incomprehensible, indefinable, indeterminate, inexpressive, innumerable, inscrutable, myriad, mysterious, opaque, profound *(intense)*, unlimited
unfathomableness mystery, opacity
unfavorable adverse *(negative)*, averse, bleak *(not favorable)*, deleterious, derogatory, disadvantageous, disastrous, harmful, inadvisable, inapposite, inauspicious, inimical, inopportune, lamentable, noxious, prejudicial, regrettable, sinister, unpropitious, unsatisfactory, unsuitable, untimely
unfavorable circumstance disadvantage
unfavorable remark stricture
unfavorable to health insalubrious, peccant *(unhealthy)*
unfavorable verdict conviction *(finding of guilt)*
unfavorableness disadvantage
unfavorably known notorious
unfearing unabashed, undaunted
unfeasable insuperable
unfeasibility impossibility
unfeasible impossible, impracticable, inoperable *(impracticable)*, insurmountable, unattainable
unfeeling brutal, callous, cold-blooded, cruel, dispassionate, harsh, insensible, insusceptible *(uncaring)*, lifeless *(dead)*, lifeless *(dull)*, malevolent, malicious, nonchalant, obdurate, obtuse, perfunctory, phlegmatic, relentless, ruthless, severe, torpid, unaffected *(uninfluenced)*, unresponsive
unfeelingness brutality, ingratitude, insentience
unfeigned authentic, bona fide, genuine, honest, naive, real, straightforward, true *(authentic)*
unfeigning direct *(forthright)*, genuine, honest, unaffected *(sincere)*
unfenced open *(accessible)*
unfertile barren, lifeless *(dull)*, otiose
unfetter break *(separate)*, disencumber, disengage, disentangle, disenthrall,

extricate, free, liberate, parole, release, rescue
unfettered clear *(unencumbered)*, free *(not restricted)*, independent, lawless, unbound, unrestrained *(not in custody)*, unrestrained *(not repressed)*, unrestricted
unfettering freedom, liberation, release
unficticious veridical
unfictitious authentic, genuine, honest, true *(authentic)*, undistorted
unfigurative literal
unfilled available, insatiable, vacant, vacuous, void *(empty)*
unfilled place access *(opening)*
unfinalized inchoate, partial *(relating to a part)*
unfinished defective, deficient, executory, imperfect, inchoate, insufficient, interim, outstanding *(unresolved)*, partial *(part)*, partial *(relating to a part)*, rudimentary, semi
unfirm insubstantial
unfit amateur, bad *(inferior)*, bad *(offensive)*, detrimental, disabled *(deprived of legal right)*, disabled *(made incapable)*, disqualify, faulty, ill-advised, improper, inadept, inadequate, inadmissible, inapplicable, inapposite, inappropriate, inapt, incapable, incompetent, incongruous, ineligible, inept *(inappropriate)*, injudicious, inopportune, insufficient, powerless, unable, unbecoming, undesirable, undue *(excessive)*, unqualified *(not competent)*, unsatisfactory, unseemly, unsuitable, unworthy
unfitness disability *(legal disqualification)*, disability *(physical inability)*, disqualification *(factor that disqualifies)*, illegality, impotence, impropriety, inability, incapacity, incompetence, incongruity, inexpedience
unfitted disabled *(made incapable)*, inadept, inadequate, inadmissible, inapplicable, inappropriate, incompetent, ineligible, insufficient, unbecoming
unfittedness disqualification *(factor that disqualifies)*
unfitting disproportionate, improper, inadvisable, inapplicable, inapposite, inappropriate, inapt, incongruous, ineligible, inept *(inappropriate)*, unfit, unprofessional, unseemly, unsuitable
unfittingness impropriety, incongruity, inexpedience
unfix disengage, free
unfixable irremediable
unfixed casual, debatable, disputable, free *(not restricted)*, indeterminate, irresolute, pending *(unresolved)*, unbound, undecided, unsettled, unspecified
unflagging faithful *(diligent)*, industrious, infallible, patient, permanent, persistent, pertinacious, purposeful, sedulous, stable, steadfast
unflappable nonchalant
unflattering calumnious, derogatory, harsh, pejorative
unfledged inexperienced, jejune *(lacking maturity)*, juvenile
unfleshly incorporeal, intangible
unflimsy strong
unflinching heroic, indomitable, pa-

tient, pertinacious, purposeful, relentless, resolute, spartan, stable, steadfast, unabashed, undaunted

unflowing stagnant

unfluctuating equal

unflustered phlegmatic

unfold bare, betray *(disclose)*, clarify, construe *(translate)*, crystallize, denude, deploy, develop, disabuse, disclose, educe, elucidate, evolve, expand, explain, explicate, expose, exposit, expound, find *(discover)*, interpret, manifest, produce *(offer to view)*, recount, reveal, simplify *(clarify)*, solve, spread, unveil

unfold the meaning of explicate

unfold the sense of explicate

unfolding denouement, detection, development *(progression)*, disclosure *(act of disclosing)*, explanation, growth *(evolution)*, happening, manifestation

unfoldment disclosure *(act of disclosing)*

unfool disabuse

unforbidden admissible, allowable, allowed, permissible, unrestricted

unforced ingenuous, nonpartisan, spontaneous, voluntary, willing *(uncompelled)*

unforeseeable unpredictable

unforeseen fortuitous, haphazard, unanticipated, unexpected, unintentional

unforeseen accident casualty

unforeseen adversity misfortune

unforeseen circumstance complication

unforeseen condition emergency

unforeseen contingency surprise

unforeseen event quirk *(accident)*, surprise

unforeseen occurrence accident *(chance occurrence)*, contingency, emergency, happenstance, quirk *(accident)*, surprise

unforewarned unaware

unforfeitable inalienable

unforgettable indelible, notable, noteworthy, outstanding *(prominent)*, remarkable, special

unforgivable inexcusable, inexpiable, peccant *(culpable)*, unjustifiable

unforgiving callous, implacable, irreconcilable, obdurate, relentless, remorseless, resentful, ruthless, unrelenting, vindictive

unforgoable obligatory

unforgotten indelible

unformed premature

unforthcoming noncommittal

unfortified disabled *(made incapable)*, helpless *(defenseless)*, indefensible, open *(accessible)*, powerless, untenable

unfortunate adverse *(negative)*, deplorable, derelict *(abandoned)*, dire, harmful, inopportune, lamentable, ominous, regrettable, unfavorable, unpropitious, unsuitable

unfortunate accident casualty

unfortunate consequence cost *(penalty)*

unfortunate event accident *(misfortune)*, disaster

unfortunate occurrence casualty, misfortune

unfortunate person victim

unfounded baseless, delusive, errone-

ous, fallacious, false *(inaccurate)*, fictitious, gratuitous *(unwarranted)*, ill-founded, illogical, inaccurate, insubstantial, sophistic, specious, unsupported, untrue, unwarranted

unfounded conclusion non sequitur

unfounded story canard

unfrequent infrequent

unfrequented private *(secluded)*, remote *(secluded)*

unfriended derelict *(abandoned)*

unfriendliness alienation *(estrangement)*, estrangement, ill will, incompatibility *(difference)*, ostracism, rancor

unfriendly adverse *(hostile)*, antipathetic *(oppositional)*, contentious, inimical, malevolent, perverse, pugnacious, recusant, unfavorable, vicious, virulent

unfriendly feeling ill will

unfrightened secure *(confident)*, undaunted

unfrock denude

unfrugal improvident, prodigal

unfruitful barren, disadvantageous, futile, ineffective, ineffectual, nugatory, otiose, unproductive

unfruitfulness inefficacy

unfulfilled deficient, executory

unfulfillment nonperformance

unfulfillment of an assignment delinquency *(failure of duty)*

unfulfillment of duty delinquency *(failure of duty)*

unfunctional impracticable

unfurl bare, deploy, spread

unfurled open *(unclosed)*

unfurnished deficient, void *(empty)*

unfussy inaccurate

ungainly incompetent, inelegant, inept *(incompetent)*, uncouth

ungallant perverse

ungallantness disrespect

ungarbled honest, literal

ungarrulous laconic, taciturn

ungathered outstanding *(unpaid)*

ungenerous illiberal, parsimonious, penurious

ungenteel blatant *(obtrusive)*, disorderly, ignoble, inelegant, presumptuous, unbecoming, unseemly

ungentle brutal, caustic, disorderly, harsh, hot-blooded, scathing, severe

ungentlemanlike disorderly

ungentlemanliness disrespect

ungentlemanly blatant *(obtrusive)*, disorderly, illiberal, uncouth

ungenuine artificial, assumed *(feigned)*, bogus, dishonest, disingenuous, fraudulent, imitation, mendacious, spurious

ungenuineness bad faith

ungermane alien *(unrelated)*, inapplicable, inapposite, inappropriate, inconsequential, nonessential, peripheral, unrelated

ungerminating barren

ungettable unattainable

ungifted amateur, inadept

ungiving insusceptible *(uncaring)*

unglue disengage

ungodly mundane, profane

ungovernable contumacious, disobedient, froward, hot-blooded, incorrigible, indomitable, insubordinate, intractable, lawless, obdurate, perverse, recalcitrant, restive, uncontrollable, un-

ruly, unyielding

ungoverned disorderly, lawless, licentious, uncurbed, unrestrained *(not repressed)*

ungraceful inelegant, provincial

ungracious abusive, blatant *(obtrusive)*, harsh, impertinent *(insolent)*, invidious, offensive *(offending)*, perverse, severe

ungraciousness disrespect

ungratefulness ingratitude

ungratifying nonsubstantial *(not sufficient)*, unsatisfactory

ungrounded baseless, erroneous, fallacious, false *(inaccurate)*, ill-founded, illogical, incorrect, insubstantial, nonsubstantial *(not sturdy)*, sophistic, unfounded, unsound *(fallacious)*

ungrudging benevolent, dispassionate, liberal *(generous)*, magnanimous, philanthropic

ungrudgingness philanthropy

unguaranteed purchase caveat emptor

unguarded careless, helpless *(defenseless)*, improvident, imprudent, indefensible, lax, open *(accessible)*, perfunctory, unaware, unsuspecting, untenable, vulnerable

unguardedness danger

unguided astray, haphazard, ill-judged, random

unguilty blameless, clean

unhabitual unusual

unhabituated inexperienced, unaccustomed

unhallow pollute

unhallowed mundane, profane

unhamper disencumber, disengage, disentangle, extricate

unhampered clear *(unencumbered)*, free *(not restricted)*, unrestrained *(not in custody)*, unrestrained *(not repressed)*

unhandsome unbecoming, unseemly

unhandy impracticable, incompetent, inept *(incompetent)*

unhappiness damper *(depressant)*, dissatisfaction, distress *(anguish)*, pessimism

unhappiness with one's lot dissatisfaction

unhappy bitter *(reproachful)*, deplorable, despondent, disconsolate, lamentable, lugubrious, pessimistic, regrettable

unharmable secure *(free from danger)*

unharmed intact, inviolate, safe

unharmonious hostile, inapplicable, inapposite, inappropriate

unharmoniousness conflict, discord

unharness disencumber, extricate, parole

unharnessing release

unhasty deliberate

unhazarded safe

unhazardous harmless, nontoxic, reliable

unhealable chronic

unhealthful deleterious, insalubrious, pernicious, pestilent

unhealthiness disease

unhealthy deadly, deleterious, detrimental, disadvantageous, harmful, inadvisable, insalubrious, lethal, noxious, pernicious, pestilent, unsound *(not*

strong)
unhealthy air air pollution
unhealthy situation peril
unheard diffident, ineffable
unheard of extraordinary, implausible, ludicrous, noteworthy, novel, original *(creative),* peculiar *(curious),* portentous *(eliciting amazement),* prodigious *(amazing),* uncanny, uncommon, unprecedented, unusual
unhearing heedless, insensible
unheeded perfunctory
unheedful derelict *(negligent),* heedless, inadvertent, negligent, perfunctory
unheedfulness disregard *(lack of respect),* disregard *(unconcern),* neglect
unheeding derelict *(negligent),* heedless, inadvertent, lax, negligent, oblivious, perfunctory, reckless, remiss, unaware
unhelpful detrimental, disadvantageous, inadvisable, perverse
unheralded undisclosed, unexpected, unforeseen
unheroic peccable
unhesitating categorical, certain *(positive),* clear *(certain),* decisive, definite, immediate *(at once),* positive *(confident),* prompt, purposeful, secure *(confident),* stable, steadfast
unheterodox orthodox
unhidden comprehensible, conspicuous, distinct *(clear),* evident, manifest, obvious, open *(in sight),* overt, palpable, patent, pellucid, perceivable, perceptible, scrutable
unhindered clear *(unencumbered),* free *(not restricted),* independent, unbound, uncurbed, unrestrained *(not in custody),* unrestrained *(not repressed)*
unhinge confuse *(bewilder),* discompose, disjoint, impair, luxate, obsess
unhinged lunatic
unhistorical fictitious
unhitch disengage
unholiness blasphemy
unholy mundane, profane
unhook disengage
unhopeful despondent
unhostile amicable, nonmilitant, propitious
unhouse displace *(remove)*
unhurried deliberate
unhurriedness deliberation
unhurt intact, inviolate, safe, whole *(undamaged)*
unhygienic insalubrious, peccant *(unhealthy)*
unicus singular, sole, unique
unidealism pragmatism
unidealistic mercenary, pragmatic, realistic
unidentical different, dissimilar, diverse
unidentifiable nondescript
unidentified anonymous
unification accession *(annexation),* affiliation *(amalgamation),* centralization, coalescence, coalition, combination, confederacy *(compact),* consolidation, federation, incorporation *(blend),* incorporation *(formation of a business entity),* integration *(amalgamation),* joinder, league, meeting *(encounter),* merger, pool, relationship *(connection),* sodality,

union *(unity)*
unified coadunate, collective, concurrent *(united),* conjoint, consonant, intact, joint, mutual *(collective)*
unifier connection *(fastening)*
uniform boiler plate, clothe, coequal, comparable *(equivalent),* concordant, consistent, consonant, equal, identical, proportionate, regular *(orderly),* repeated, routine, same, similar, systematic
uniformity adjustment, agreement *(concurrence),* arrangement *(ordering),* array *(order),* conciliation, conformity *(agreement),* consensus, constant, correspondence *(similarity),* identity *(similarity),* method, parity, regularity, resemblance, semblance, union *(unity)*
uniformly invariably
unify amalgamate, cohere *(adhere),* collect *(gather),* combine *(join together),* conjoin, consolidate *(strengthen),* conspire, crystallize, desegregate, federalize *(associate),* federate, include, join *(bring together),* merge, organize *(unionize),* pool, unite
unilateral ex parte, ex parte
unimaginable implausible, impossible, incomprehensible, incredible, ineffable, infeasible, peculiar *(curious),* prodigious *(amazing),* unbelievable
unimaginative lifeless *(dull),* mundane, obtuse, ordinary, parochial, pedestrian, prosaic, sequacious, stale, trite
unimagined actual, factual, real, sound, true *(authentic)*
unimaginitive usual
unimitated distinct *(distinguished from others),* distinctive, genuine, individual, noteworthy, original *(creative),* peculiar *(distinctive),* uncommon, unique
unimitative eccentric, special
unimpaired complete *(all-embracing),* intact, inviolate, safe, undiminished, whole *(undamaged)*
unimparted undisclosed
unimpassioned dispassionate, insipid, insusceptible *(uncaring),* jejune *(dull),* languid, lifeless *(dull),* nonchalant, open-minded, phlegmatic, placid, prosaic, stoical
unimpeachability certainty, certification *(certainness),* certitude, incontestability
unimpeachable absolute *(conclusive),* accurate, actual, axiomatic, believable, blameless, certain *(positive),* clean, clear *(certain),* conclusive *(determinative),* definite, definitive, demonstrable, ethical, factual, genuine, inappealable, incontestable, incontrovertible, incorruptible, infallible, irrebuttable, irrefutable, irreprehensible, just, laudable, law-abiding, loyal, meritorious, not guilty, official, positive *(incontestable),* provable, real, reputable, secure *(sound),* solid *(sound),* sound, true *(authentic),* unalienable, undeniable, unobjectionable, unrefutable, upright
unimpeached inculpable
unimpeded exempt, free *(not restricted),* free *(relieved from a burden),* passable, uncurbed, unrestrained *(not in custody)*

unimperiled secure *(free from danger)*
unimportance immateriality, inconsequence, insignificance, mediocrity
unimportant collateral *(immaterial),* expendable, frivolous, futile, immaterial, inapposite, inappreciable, inconsequential, inconsiderable, inferior *(lower in position),* insubstantial, irrelevant, mediocre, minimal, minor, negligible, nominal, nonessential, nugatory, null *(insignificant),* paltry, peripheral, petty, remote *(small),* secondary, slight, tenuous, trivial, unessential, unnecessary
unimposing diffident, unobtrusive
unimpressed callous, nonchalant, unaffected *(uninfluenced)*
unimpressible callous, cold-blooded, dispassionate, inexorable, insusceptible *(uncaring),* stoical, unresponsive, unyielding
unimpressionable callous, clinical, dispassionate, unresponsive
unimpressive poor *(inferior in quality),* usual
unimprison free
unimprovable irremediable
uninclined disinclined, reluctant
unincreased undiminished
unindebted compensatory, solvent
unindoctrinated unversed
uninduced nonpartisan
uninfluenceable impervious, unresponsive, unyielding
uninfluenced dispassionate, fair *(just),* impartial, impervious, independent, judicial, just, liberal *(broad minded),* loyal, neutral, nonpartisan, objective, open-minded, unbiased, unprejudiced
uninfluential ineffective, ineffectual, minor, null *(insignificant),* powerless
uninfluential group minority *(outnumbered group)*
uninformed blind *(not discerning),* incognizant, inexperienced, unacquainted, unaware, unversed, unwitting
uninformedness nescience
uninhabited devoid, solitary, unsettled, vacant, void *(empty)*
uninhibited candid, intemperate, uncurbed
uninhibitedness freedom, latitude, liberty
uniniquitous blameless
uninitiated incompetent, inexperienced, unaccustomed, unversed
uninjured intact, inviolate, safe, unblemished
uninjurious harmless, innocuous, nontoxic, salutary
uninspired insipid, jejune *(dull),* languid, lifeless *(dull),* mundane, perfunctory, unaffected *(uninfluenced)*
uninspiring insipid, jejune *(dull),* lifeless *(dull),* mediocre, pedestrian, prosaic
uninstructed incognizant
unintellectualism illiteracy
unintellectuality ignorance
unintelligence ignorance, nescience
unintelligent fatuous, irrational, obtuse, opaque, vacuous
unintelligibility ambiguity, incoherence, opacity

unintelligible ambiguous, disconnected, equivocal, inapprehensible, inarticulate, incomprehensible, indefinite, indistinct, inexplicable, inexpressive, inscrutable, mysterious, nebulous, obscure *(abstruse),* opaque, recondite, uncertain *(ambiguous),* unclear
unintelligible talk jargon *(unintelligible language)*
unintelligibleness obscuration
unintended fortuitous, haphazard, inadvertent, involuntary, unexpected, unforeseeable, unforeseen, unintentional, unpremeditated, unwitting
unintentional fortuitous, haphazard, inadvertent, involuntary, spontaneous, unexpected, unpremeditated, unwitting
unintentional happening contingency
unintentional homocide manslaughter
unintentional mistake oversight *(carelessness)*
unintentional murder manslaughter
unintentional omission oversight *(carelessness)*
unintentionality quirk *(accident)*
unintentionally unknowingly
uninterested cold-blooded, derelict *(negligent),* insusceptible *(uncaring),* languid, lax, nonchalant, perfunctory, unresponsive
uninteresting insipid, lifeless *(dull),* mediocre, mundane, nondescript, pedestrian, prosaic, stale, usual
unintermitted continual *(connected)*
unintermitted continuance perpetuity
unintermittedness continuity
unintermittent continuous, incessant, unremitting
unintermitting chronic, continuous, durable, incessant, relentless
uninterrupted chronic, consecutive, constant, continual *(connected),* continuous, durable, incessant, permanent, perpetual, progressive *(going forward),* unremitting
uninterrupted connection continuity
uninterrupted existence perpetuity
uninterrupted in course consecutive
uninterruptedness continuity, perpetuity
uninterruption continuity
uninured unaccustomed
uninvented genuine, honest
uninventive lifeless *(dull),* pedestrian
uninvited unsolicited
uninvited attendance intrusion
uninvited entry intrusion
uninviting antipathetic *(distasteful),* bleak *(severely simple),* objectionable, repulsive, unacceptable, undesirable, unsavory
uninvolved clean, cognizable, dispassionate, irreprehensible, neutral, noncommittal, not guilty, perfunctory, simple
union accession *(annexation),* adhesion *(affixing),* adhesion *(loyalty),* affiliation *(amalgamation),* assemblage, association *(alliance),* cabal, cartel, centralization, chain *(nexus),* chamber *(body),* coaction, coalescence, coalition, cohabitation *(married state),* coherence, collusion, combination, compatibility,

composition *(makeup),* conciliation, confederacy *(compact),* conformity *(agreement),* conjunction, connection *(abutment),* connection *(fastening),* consensus, consolidation, consortium *(business cartel),* contact *(association),* contact *(touching),* contribution *(participation),* cooperative, corporation, coverture, federation, incorporation *(blend),* incorporation *(formation of a business entity),* institute, integration *(amalgamation),* intersection, joinder, league, marriage *(intimate relationship),* matrimony, meeting *(encounter),* melange, merger, nexus, pact, pool, reconciliation, relationship *(connection),* session, society, sodality, syndicate
union of action coaction
union of factions coalition
unionize consolidate *(unite),* federalize *(associate),* federate
unions ties
unique certain *(particular),* different, distinct *(distinguished from others),* distinctive, eccentric, exclusive *(singular),* extraordinary, individual, inestimable, irregular *(not usual),* nonconforming, noteworthy, novel, only *(sole),* original *(creative),* particular *(individual),* particular *(specific),* peculiar *(distinctive),* portentous *(eliciting amazement),* prodigious *(amazing),* rare, remarkable, renowned, scarce, several *(separate),* singular, sole, special, specific, unaccustomed, unapproachable, uncommon, unprecedented, unusual
unique feature distinction *(difference)*
uniquely particularly
uniqueness characteristic, difference, distinction *(difference),* identity *(individuality),* irregularity, nonconformity, particularity, personality, specialty *(distinctive mark)*
unirritable dispassionate
unison accordance *(compact),* agreement *(concurrence),* concert, consensus, consent, rapprochement, synchronism, union *(unity)*
unisonant consonant
unisonous consonant
unit band, component, entity, factor *(ingredient),* ingredient, item, member *(constituent part),* organ
unit of being entity
unit of composition component, ingredient
unite accumulate *(amass),* adhere *(fasten),* affiliate, affix, aggregate, agree *(comply),* amalgamate, annex *(add),* attach *(join),* bond *(hold together),* border *(approach),* call *(summon),* cement, cohere *(adhere),* coincide *(concur),* collect *(gather),* combine *(act in concert),* combine *(join together),* commingle, compile, concentrate *(consolidate),* congregate, conjoin, connect *(join together),* conspire, contact *(touch),* convene, converge, correspond *(be equivalent),* desegregate, federalize *(associate),* federate, include, incorporate *(include),* involve *(participate),* join *(associate oneself with),* join *(bring together),* lock, meet, merge, organize *(unionize),* pool, reconcile, relate *(establish a connection)*

unite by compact federate
unite efforts concur *(agree)*
unite efforts with participate
unite for a common purpose organize *(unionize)*
unite in a federation federate
unite in a league federalize *(associate),* federate
unite ones efforts cooperate
unite with concur *(agree),* cooperate, participate, side
united affiliated, associated, attached *(annexed),* coadunate, coherent *(joined),* cohesive *(sticking),* collective, composite, compound, concerted, concordant, concurrent *(united),* conglomerate, conjoint, conjugal, consensual, federal, harmonious, indivisible, infrangible, inseparable, interrelated, joint, mutual *(collective),* nuptial, solid *(compact)*
united action coaction, conjunction, synergy
united body faction
united front merger
uniting accession *(annexation),* concerted, concordant, concrescence
unity accordance *(compact),* adhesion *(affixing),* affiliation *(amalgamation),* agreement *(concurrence),* cartel, centralization, coalition, coherence, compatibility, complex *(development),* concert, conciliation, concordance, consent, identity *(similarity),* peace, propinquity *(similarity),* rapprochement, relationship *(connection),* totality, uniformity
unius diei ephemeral
universal boiler plate, collective, common *(shared),* competitive *(open),* comprehensive, familiar *(customary),* general, generic, nonsectarian, prevailing *(current),* prevalent, proverbial, rife, total, ubiquitous, uniform, unlimited, usual, whole *(unified)*
universal cure panacea
universal forgiveness of past offenses amnesty
universal principle doctrine
universal remedy panacea
universality generality *(bulk),* whole
universalize generalize
universally always *(without exception)*
universally known common *(customary)*
universally recognized familiar *(customary),* famous, household *(familiar)*
universe generalize
university institute
universus total
univocal definite, unambiguous
unjaundiced impartial, neutral, objective, open-minded, reasonable *(rational),* receptive, unbiased, undistorted, unprejudiced
unjealous dispassionate
unjoined apart, disconnected, discrete, disjunctive *(tending to disjoin),* individual
unjoint disjoint, displace *(remove),* luxate
unjoyful pessimistic
unjust delinquent *(guilty of a misdeed),* inequitable, iniquitous, onesided, partial *(biased),* peccant *(culpable),* prejudicial, severe, unconsciona-

ble, unfair, unjustifiable, unreasonable, unscrupulous, unwarranted, wrongful
unjust acquisition graft
unjust action injustice
unjust burden imposition *(excessive burden)*
unjust decision inequity
unjust deed ground
unjust opinion misjudgment
unjust performance malfeasance
unjust requirement imposition *(excessive burden)*
unjustifiable baseless, blameful, blameworthy, disproportionate, immoral, indefensible, inexcusable, inexpiable, iniquitous, peccant *(culpable)*, reprehensible, sinister, unequal *(unjust)*, unjust, unreasonable, untenable, unwarranted, wanton
unjustified arbitrary, gratuitous *(unwarranted)*, illegal, partial *(biased)*, unauthorized, undue *(excessive)*, unjustifiable, unwarranted
unjustly call to account frame *(charge falsely)*
unjustly involve frame *(charge falsely)*
unjustly severe tyrannous
unjustness ground, inequity, nepotism
unkempt disordered, inelegant
unkind caustic, cold-blooded, cruel, harsh, invidious, malevolent, mordacious, pernicious, ruthless, scathing, severe
unkindly harsh
unkindness cruelty, disservice, ill will, inconsideration, severity
unknot break *(separate)*, disengage, disentangle, extricate
unknowable inapprehensible, incomprehensible, inexplicable, inscrutable
unknowing blind *(not discerning)*, incognizant, insensible, unacquainted, unaware, unintentional, unversed, unwitting
unknowingness ignorance, nescience
unknowledgeable unversed
unknown anonymous, blind *(concealed)*, clandestine, covert, defunct, disputable, hidden, inexplicable, mysterious, obscure *(remote)*, secret, surreptitious, ulterior, undisclosed, unprecedented
unknown information secret
unknown person stranger
unlace disengage
unladylike blatant *(obtrusive)*, disorderly, unbecoming
unlatch disengage
unlatched open *(unclosed)*
unlavish economical, provident *(frugal)*
unlawful broken *(unfulfilled)*, delinquent *(guilty of a misdeed)*, felonious, illegal, illegitimate *(illegal)*, illicit, immoral, impermissible, unauthorized, unscrupulous, unwarranted, wrongful
unlawful acquisition larceny
unlawful act burglary, miscarriage, offense, tortious act
unlawful action malfeasance
unlawful appropriation conversion *(misappropriation)*
unlawful bait bribe
unlawful begetting bar sinister

unlawful breaking and entering burglary
unlawful carnal connection adultery
unlawful carnal knowledge adultery
unlawful carnality adultery
unlawful combination conspiracy
unlawful compensation bribe
unlawful compulsion coercion
unlawful contrivance conspiracy
unlawful conversion larceny
unlawful departure desertion
unlawful detention detainer
unlawful encouragement bribery
unlawful entry intrusion
unlawful force violence
unlawful gain graft
unlawful gift bribe
unlawful gratuity bribe
unlawful hitting battery
unlawful homicide aberemurder, assassination
unlawful invasion encroachment
unlawful killing murder
unlawful obstruction nuisance
unlawful obtainer extortionist
unlawful plan conspiracy
unlawful practice guilt
unlawful restriction detainer
unlawful retention detainer
unlawful scheme conspiracy
unlawful sexual intercourse sodomy
unlawful striking battery
unlawful taking extortion, larceny
unlawful touching battery
unlawful use of another's property conversion *(misappropriation)*
unlawful use of power misfeasance
unlawfully illegally
unlawfully begotten illegitimate *(born out of wedlock)*
unlawfully deprive purloin
unlawfully seize kidnap
unlawfulness burglary, criminality, illegality, injustice, prohibition
unlearned jejune *(lacking maturity)*, unversed
unlearnedness ignorance, illiteracy, nescience
unleash free
unlegalized illicit
unlegislated illicit
unlessened undiminished
unlettered unversed
unliable immune
unliberal parochial
unlicensed felonious, illegitimate *(illegal)*, impermissible, inexperienced, ultra vires, unauthorized, unlawful
unlikable objectionable, undesirable
unlike different, disparate, dissimilar, distinct *(distinguished from others)*, distinctive, diverse, heterogeneous, peculiar *(distinctive)*, unequal *(unequivalent)*, unrelated
unlike others distinct *(distinguished from others)*
unlikelihood improbability
unlikeliness improbability
unlikely disputable, doubtful, dubious, implausible, impossible, incredible, infeasible, unbelievable, unfit
unlikely to cause harm innocuous
unlikely to cause injury innocuous
unlikeness contraposition, deviation,

difference, discrepancy, disparity, distinction *(difference)*, distortion, diversity, identity *(individuality)*, incompatibility *(inconsistency)*, incongruity, inconsistency, inequality, nonconformity, specialty *(distinctive mark)*
unlimited absolute *(complete)*, copious, dictatorial, far reaching, indefinite, indeterminate, infinite, innumerable, inordinate, intemperate, myriad, omnibus, open-ended, peremptory *(absolute)*, perpetual, plenary, unbound, unrestrained *(not in custody)*, unrestrained *(not repressed)*, unrestricted
unlimited in power omnipotent
unlimited inheritance fee *(estate)*
unlimited sovereignty home rule
unlink detach
unlinked disconnected
unliquidated delinquent *(overdue)*, outstanding *(unpaid)*
unliquidated claim liability, obligation *(liability)*
unlively grave *(solemn)*, jejune *(dull)*, lifeless *(dull)*, pedestrian, ponderous
unload alleviate, deplete, diminish, disencumber, dislodge, ease, relieve *(free from burden)*, remove *(eliminate)*, vend
unlock disencumber, disengage, disenthrall, dissociate, find *(discover)*, solve
unlocked open *(accessible)*, open *(unclosed)*
unlooked for fortuitous, unanticipated, unexpected, unforeseeable
unloose break *(separate)*, diffuse, disencumber, disengage, disentangle, dissociate, extricate, liberate, part *(separate)*, rescue, separate
unloosen disjoint, extricate
unloquacious laconic, mute, taciturn
unlovable odious
unloyal broken *(unfulfilled)*, faithless
unloyalty bad faith
unlucid blind *(not discerning)*
unlucky dire, harmful, inauspicious, ominous, regrettable, unfavorable
unlucky accident misfortune
unlucky happening misfortune
unlucky person victim
unmaintainable unsustainable, untenable
unmake annul, destroy *(void)*, disorganize, extirpate, obliterate
unmaking cancellation, destruction
unmalleable immutable, inflexible, intractable, ironclad, obdurate, rigid, uncontrollable
unmanacle disenthrall, free
unmanageable contumacious, disobedient, disordered, disorderly, fractious, froward, impossible, impracticable, incorrigible, indomitable, inexorable, inflexible, intractable, obdurate, perverse, ponderous, recalcitrant, restive, uncontrollable, unruly, unyielding, wanton
unmanifested latent, potential
unmanly ignoble, recreant, unseemly
unmanned devoid
unmannered disorderly, offensive *(offending)*
unmannerliness disrespect
unmannerly brazen, disdainful, disorderly, impertinent *(insolent)*, inelegant, insolent, obtrusive, offensive *(offend-

ing), perverse, uncouth

unmannerly conduct disrespect

unmarked intact, usual

unmarketable check bad check

unmarred intact, pure, unblemished, unimpeachable

unmarry divorce, separate

unmask admit *(concede),* bare, betray *(disclose),* clarify, detect, disabuse, disclose, divulge, expose, find *(discover),* inform *(betray),* manifest, produce *(offer to view),* report *(disclose),* reveal, unveil

unmasked naked *(lacking embellishment),* obvious, palpable, patent, scrutable

unmasking admission *(disclosure),* disclosure *(act of disclosing),* manifestation

unmasterable insuperable, insurmountable

unmatched different, disparate, dissimilar, diverse, heterogeneous, inestimable, leading *(ranking first),* only *(unrepeated),* original *(creative),* paramount, premium, prime *(most valuable),* solitary, superlative, unequal *(unequivalent),* unique, unprecedented, unrelated, unusual

unmatured premature

unmeaningful null *(insignificant)*

unmeant fortuitous, inadvertent, unintentional, unpremeditated, unwitting

unmeasured copious, indeterminate, infinite, innumerable, intemperate, open-ended

unmeditated involuntary

unmeet improper, inappropriate, inapt, inept *(inappropriate),* unbecoming, undesirable, unseemly

unmelting callous

unmemorable usual

unmentionable confidential, ineffable

unmentioned tacit, ulterior, undisclosed

unmerciful brutal, callous, cold-blooded, cruel, harsh, inexorable, malignant, obdurate, relentless, remorseless, ruthless, severe, unrelenting

unmeretricious elegant

unmerited undue *(excessive),* unjust

unmetaphorical literal

unmethodical capricious, casual, desultory, disordered, disorderly, haphazard, indiscriminate, informal, unpredictable

unmeticulous casual, inexact, slipshod

unmilitant harmless, nonmilitant, peaceable

unmindful blind *(not discerning),* careless, casual, cold-blooded, cursory, derelict *(negligent),* disobedient, dispassionate, heedless, impulsive *(rash),* inadvertent, incognizant, insensible, lax, negligent, nonchalant, oblivious, perfunctory, reckless, remiss, thoughtless, unaware, unwitting

unmindfully unknowingly

unmindfulness disinterest *(lack of interest),* disregard *(lack of respect),* disregard *(unconcern),* neglect, negligence

unmingled pure, simple, sterling, unadulterated

unmistakability certainty

unmistakable absolute *(conclusive),*

arrant *(definite),* axiomatic, certain *(fixed),* certain *(positive),* clear *(apparent),* clear *(certain),* cognizable, coherent *(clear),* comprehensible, conclusive *(determinative),* conspicuous, definite, demonstrable, evident, explicit, factual, incontrovertible, irrefutable, lucid, manifest, naked *(perceptible),* obvious, open *(in sight),* palpable, particular *(specific),* perceivable, perceptible, positive *(incontestable),* salient, unambiguous, unequivocal

unmistakableness surety *(certainty)*

unmistakably fairly *(clearly)*

unmistakably bad arrant *(onerous)*

unmistaken accurate, actual, proper, real, true *(authentic)*

unmitigable hot-blooded, relentless

unmitigated absolute *(conclusive),* categorical, chronic, comprehensive, disorderly, drastic, gross *(flagrant),* harsh, intensive, outright, pure, rigid, severe, stark, thorough, unqualified *(unlimited)*

unmitigating chronic

unmixed absolute *(conclusive),* pure, simple, strong, unadulterated

unmodern obsolete

unmodest brazen

unmodifiable irrevocable, permanent, unalterable

unmodified unqualified *(unlimited)*

unmolested safe

unmoneyed bankrupt, destitute, impecunious, poor *(underprivileged)*

unmoral immoral

unmotivated fortuitous

unmovable firm, impervious, inexorable, inflexible, permanent, pertinacious

unmoved callous, cold-blooded, impervious, inexpressive, insensible, insusceptible *(uncaring),* irreconcilable, nonchalant, peaceable, placid, steadfast, stoical, unaffected *(uninfluenced),* unresponsive

unmoved by entreaties inexorable

unmoved by pity relentless

unmoving firm, inactive, rigid, stagnant, static

unmuddied clean

unmurmuring patient

unmuzzled uncurbed

unnamable ineffable

unnamed anonymous, unspecified

unnatural anomalous, artificial, cruel, diabolic, histrionic, illegitimate *(born out of wedlock),* irregular *(not usual),* peculiar *(curious),* synthetic, unaccustomed, uncanny, unusual

unnatural carnal intercourse sodomy

unnatural habit perversion

unnatural sexual intercourse sodomy

unnaturalized alien *(foreign)*

unnaturalness bestiality, false pretense, irregularity, pretense *(ostentation)*

unnavigable impervious

unneat slipshod

unnecessary circumstantial, excess, excessive, expendable, extraneous, gratuitous *(unwarranted),* inconsequential, inordinate, minor, needless, nonessential, null *(insignificant),* otiose, redundant, superfluous, undue *(excessive),*

unessential, unwarranted

unnecessary addition expletive

unnecessary inclusion expletive

unnecessary loss waste

unnecessary prolongation laches

unneeded excess, excessive, expendable, extraneous, gratuitous *(unwarranted),* needless, nonessential, otiose, undue *(excessive),* unessential, unnecessary

unnerve disable, discommode, discourage, disturb, frighten, intimidate, menace, perturb, upset

unnerved disconsolate, powerless, unsettled

unnerving formidable

unnervous dispassionate

unnotable petty

unnoteworthiness immateriality, inconsequence, insignificance, mediocrity

unnoteworthy average *(standard),* inapposite, mediocre, minor, negligible, nonessential

unnoticeable impalpable, inconspicuous, indiscernible, minor

unnoticed inconspicuous, latent

unnoticing heedless, inadvertent, oblivious

unnourishing deficient

unnumberable myriad

unnumbered infinite, innumerable, multiple, myriad, profuse

unobjectionability admissibility

unobjectionable admissible, allowable, blameless, clean, fair *(satisfactory),* innocuous, irreprehensible, mediocre, nontoxic, palatable, pardonable, unimpeachable

unobliging thoughtless

unobnoxious innocuous

unobscure comprehensible, palpable

unobscured palpable

unobservable impalpable

unobservance breach, contempt *(disobedience to the court),* neglect, negligence

unobservant blind *(not discerning),* broken *(unfulfilled),* careless, derelict *(negligent),* heedless, inadvertent, lax, oblivious, perfunctory, reckless, thoughtless, unaware, unorthodox

unobserved blind *(concealed),* defunct, hidden, inconspicuous

unobserving blind *(not discerning),* lax

unobstructed clear *(unencumbered),* free *(not restricted),* open *(accessible),* open *(in sight),* passable, patent, unbound, uncurbed, unrestrained *(not in custody),* unrestricted

unobtrusive diffident

unobtainability impossibility, unavailability

unobtainable impossible, inaccessible, infeasible, insuperable, scarce, unapproachable, unattainable

unobtainableness impossibility

unobtrusive covert, furtive, inconspicuous, unpretentious

unobvious impalpable, inconspicuous, ulterior, unclear

unoccupied devoid, idle, open *(accessible),* otiose, solitary, unemployed, unsettled, vacant, vacuous, void *(empty)*

unoffended dispassionate

unoffending blameless, clean, innocent, innocuous, irreprehensible

unofficered devoid

unofficial informal, interim, private *(not public)*, uncorroborated

unopened impervious

unoperative ineffective, ineffectual

unopinionated impartial, liberal *(broad minded)*

unopinioned impartial

unopposed consensual

unopposing passive

unordered casual, indeterminate

unordinary extraordinary, momentous, nonconforming, novel, original *(creative)*, unaccustomed

unorganized casual, complex, disordered, haphazard, indiscriminate, random, slipshod

unoriginal familiar *(customary)*, lifeless *(dull)*, ordinary, pedestrian, prosaic, trite, usual

unornamented naked *(lacking embellishment)*

unorthodox deviant, eccentric, informal, nonconforming, novel, original *(creative)*, peculiar *(curious)*, skeptical, uncommon, unusual

unorthodoxness nonconformity

unorthodoxy blasphemy, deviation, informality, irregularity, nonconformity, quirk *(idiosyncrasy)*

unostentatious diffident, inconspicuous, unobtrusive, unpretentious

unovercomable insuperable

unowed undue *(not owing)*

unowned derelict *(abandoned)*

unpacifiable implacable

unpacific contentious, offensive *(taking the initiative)*, pugnacious

unpaid delinquent *(overdue)*, due *(owed)*, free *(at no charge)*, gratuitous *(given without recompense)*, overdue, payable, receivable, unsettled

unpaid amount delinquency *(shortage)*

unpaid bill arrears

unpaid debt arrears, obligation *(liability)*

unpaid dues nonpayment

unpaid for gratis, gratuitous *(given without recompense)*

unpaid worker volunteer

unpainstaking inaccurate

unpaired dissimilar, solitary

unpalatable bitter *(acrid tasting)*, loathsome, objectionable, odious, offensive *(offending)*, repugnant *(exciting aversion)*, repulsive, undesirable, unendurable, unsavory

unparalled renowned

unparalleled best, cardinal *(outstanding)*, extraordinary, inestimable, invaluable, leading *(ranking first)*, major, nonconforming, noteworthy, only *(unrepeated)*, original *(creative)*, outstanding *(prominent)*, paramount, portentous *(eliciting amazement)*, premium, prime *(most valuable)*, rare, remarkable, singular, special, superior *(excellent)*, superlative, unapproachable, uncommon, unique, unprecedented, unusual

unpardonable blameful, felonious, inexcusable, inexpiable, peccant *(culpable)*, reprehensible, unjustifiable

unpardoning callous

unparticular casual, indiscriminate

unpassable impervious

unpassionate dispassionate

unpatent impalpable

unpatriotic faithless

unpatterned disordered

unpayable irredeemable

unpeaceful contentious, litigious, offensive *(taking the initiative)*, pugnacious

unpeacefulness belligerency

unpent free *(not restricted)*

unpeopled devoid

unperceivability nonappearance

unperceivable impalpable, inconspicuous, indiscernible, intangible

unperceived blind *(concealed)*, hidden, ulterior

unperceiving blind *(not discerning)*, heedless

unperceptive inadvertent, insensible

unperfected partial *(relating to a part)*

unperfidious bona fide, candid, loyal, true *(loyal)*

unperfidiousness responsibility *(conscience)*

unperforated impervious

unperformability impossibility

unperformable impracticable, insurmountable, unattainable

unperformed executory, partial *(part)*

unperilous reliable

unperjured accurate, bona fide, candid, honest, straightforward, true *(authentic)*, veridical

unpermitted unauthorized

unpersevering otiose, truant

unpersuadable inexorable

unpersuaded disinclined

unperturbed cold-blooded, dispassionate, patient, phlegmatic

unperverted undistorted

unphysical intangible

unpierceable impervious

unpin disengage

unpitying callous, cruel, harsh, obdurate, relentless, remorseless, ruthless, unrelenting

unplagiarized authentic

unplain equivocal, impalpable, inarticulate, indefinable, indistinct, obscure *(faint)*, opaque, unclear

unplainness indistinctness, opacity

unplanned coincidental, fortuitous, haphazard, spontaneous, unforeseeable, unpremeditated

unplanned happening quirk *(accident)*

unplausible suspicious *(questionable)*

unpleasant bitter *(acrid tasting)*, deplorable, invidious, loathsome, objectionable, obnoxious, odious, offensive *(offending)*, outrageous, painful, repugnant *(exciting aversion)*, repulsive, unacceptable, undesirable, unendurable, unsatisfactory, unsavory

unpleasant sound noise

unpleasing deplorable, objectionable, obnoxious, offensive *(offending)*, unacceptable, undesirable, unsavory

unplentiful scarce

unpliable immutable, inflexible, unyielding

unpliant inflexible, ironclad, rigid,

strong, unalterable, unbending

unplug detach

unpoetic prosaic

unpoetical mundane, pedestrian, prosaic

unpointed jejune *(dull)*

unpolished blatant *(obtrusive)*, caitiff, imperfect, impertinent *(insolent)*, inelegant, provincial, uncouth

unpolite perverse

unpoliteness disrespect

unpollute decontaminate

unpolluted inviolate, pure

unpopular odious, repugnant *(exciting aversion)*, unacceptable, undesirable

unpopularity ill repute, ill will, odium

unpopulated bleak *(exposed and barren)*

unpositive conditional

unpossessed derelict *(abandoned)*, unclaimed, vacant

unpossessed of devoid

unpowerful incapable

unpracticability impossibility

unpracticed inexperienced, outdated, outmoded, unaccustomed, unversed

unpraiseworthy blameful, blameworthy, unbecoming, unseemly

unprecedented extraordinary, nonconforming, noteworthy, novel, portentous *(eliciting amazement)*, prodigious *(amazing)*, renowned, singular, special, uncommon, unforeseeable, unique, unusual

unprecise approximate, casual, faulty, liberal *(not literal)*

unpreciseness misestimation, misjudgment

unpredictability chance *(possibility)*, happenstance

unpredictable conditional, debatable, fallible, haphazard, undependable, unforeseeable, unreliable

unpredicted fortuitous, unexpected, unforeseeable, unforeseen

unprejudice disinterest *(lack of prejudice)*

unprejudiced dispassionate, equal, equitable, evenhanded, factual, fair *(just)*, impartial, judicial, juridical, just, liberal *(broad minded)*, neutral, nonpartisan, objective, reasonable *(rational)*, receptive, unbiased, undistorted

unprejudicedness candor *(impartiality)*

unpremeditated fortuitous, haphazard, impulsive *(rash)*, inadvertent, involuntary, random, spontaneous, unexpected, unintentional, unwitting

unpremeditated murder manslaughter

unpremeditation inconsideration, quirk *(accident)*

unprepared impulsive *(rash)*, lax, premature, spontaneous, unaware, unfit, unpremeditated, unqualified *(not competent)*, unversed, vulnerable

unprepared for precipitate, unexpected, unforeseeable

unpreparedness disqualification *(factor that disqualifies)*, laxity

unpreparing improvident

unprepossessed dispassionate, impartial, neutral, open-minded, unpreju-

diced
unprepossessing repulsive
unpresentable blatant *(obtrusive)*, unseemly
unpretended bona fide, genuine, honest, true *(authentic)*
unpretending direct *(forthright)*, genuine, honest, unaffected *(sincere)*, veridical
unpretentious bona fide, diffident, direct *(forthright)*, genuine, honest, inconspicuous, simple, unaffected *(sincere)*
unpretentiousness candor *(straightforwardness)*
unprevalent unusual
unpreventable certain *(fixed)*, compulsory, inevitable, necessary *(inescapable)*, unavoidable *(inevitable)*
unprevented free *(not restricted)*, unbound, uncurbed, unrestrained *(not in custody)*
unprincipaled dissolute
unprincipled baseless, delinquent *(guilty of a misdeed)*, depraved, diabolic, dishonest, disingenuous, disreputable, false *(disloyal)*, heinous, illicit, immoral, inexcusable, iniquitous, lawless, machiavellian, peccable, peccant *(culpable)*, perfidious, profligate *(corrupt)*, reprehensible, reprobate, sinister, unconscionable, unethical, unfair, unjust, unscrupulous, vicious
unprincipled politician demagogue
unprintable profane, salacious
unprocessed inchoate
unproclaimed undisclosed
unprocreant barren
unprocurable inaccessible, unattainable
unproductive barren, futile, ineffective, ineffectual, inept *(incompetent)*, nugatory, otiose, unavailing
unproductive trial mistrial
unproductivity miscarriage
unprofaned inviolate
unprofessional unethical
unprofessional conduct incompetence, malpractice, misconduct
unprofessional treatment malpractice
unproficiency disqualification *(factor that disqualifies)*, inability, incapacity, incompetence, maladministration
unproficient inadept, inept *(incompetent)*, unversed
unprofitability detriment, inexpedience
unprofitable barren, detrimental, disadvantageous, expendable, futile, idle, inadvisable, ineffective, ineffectual, injudicious, needless, nugatory, otiose, unavailing, unproductive
unprogressive decadent, static
unprogressiveness inaction
unprohibited admissible, allowable, allowed, lawful, licit, permissible, public *(open)*
unprolific barren, otiose, unproductive
unprolonged brief
unpromising inauspicious, ominous, pessimistic, sinister, unfavorable, unfit, unpropitious, untimely
unprompted impulsive *(rash)*, spontaneous, voluntary

unprompted will conatus
unpronounceable ineffable
unpronounced impalpable, implicit, inconspicuous, tacit, undisclosed
unpropitiating implacable
unpropitious adverse *(hostile)*, antipathetic *(oppositional)*, detrimental, dire, disadvantageous, harmful, inauspicious, inimical, inopportune, ominous, pernicious, portentous *(ominous)*, regrettable, sinister, unfavorable, untimely
unprosperous impecunious, poor *(underprivileged)*
unprosperousness poverty
unprotected dangerous, helpless *(defenseless)*, indefensible, insecure, open *(in sight)*, precarious, susceptible *(unresistent)*, untenable, vulnerable
unprovable unsustainable
unproved inconclusive, theoretical, unconfirmed, unsupported
unproved theory hypothesis
unproven debatable, disputable, inconclusive, speculative, theoretical, unconfirmed, uncorroborated, unfounded, unsupported
unprovided deficient, devoid
unprovided for poor *(underprivileged)*
unproviding improvident
unprovocativeness disincentive
unprovoked gratuitous *(unwarranted)*, wanton
unpublicized undisclosed
unpublished secret, undisclosed
unpugnacious nonmilitant, peaceable
unpunctilious casual
unpunctual back *(in arrears)*, dilatory, late *(tardy)*, untimely
unpunctuality irregularity
unpunishable immune
unpunished clear *(free from criminal charges)*
unpurposed unwitting
unpurposeful unintentional, unpremeditated
unpushing diffident
unqualification certainty, disability *(legal disqualification)*
unqualified absolute *(complete)*, affirmative, categorical, certain *(positive)*, clear *(certain)*, complete *(all-embracing)*, comprehensive, decisive, definite, demonstrable, disabled *(deprived of legal right)*, disabled *(made incapable)*, free *(not restricted)*, inadept, inadmissible, inapplicable, inapt, incapable, incompetent, ineligible, inept *(inappropriate)*, inept *(incompetent)*, inexperienced, insufficient, omnibus, outright, peremptory *(absolute)*, plenary, positive *(incontestable)*, powerless, stark, thorough, total, unable, unconditional, unequivocal, unfit, unmitigated, unrestricted, unversed, unworthy
unqualifiedness disability *(legal disqualification)*, disqualification *(factor that disqualifies)*, incompetence
unquashable noncancellable
unquelled disorderly, hot-blooded
unquenchable indomitable, insatiable, powerful
unquenched hot-blooded
unquestionability certainty, certification *(certainness)*, incontestability

unquestionable absolute *(conclusive)*, accurate, authentic, axiomatic, believable, categorical, certain *(fixed)*, certain *(positive)*, clear *(certain)*, cogent, conclusive *(determinative)*, de facto, decisive, definitive, demonstrable, evident, factual, genuine, incontestable, incontrovertible, indefeasible, inevitable, infallible, irrebuttable, irrefutable, lucid, manifest, noncontestable, obvious, palpable, pellucid, peremptory *(absolute)*, positive *(incontestable)*, probable, real, reliable, solid *(sound)*, tenable, true *(authentic)*, uncontested, undeniable, unequivocal, unimpeachable, unmistakable, unrefutable
unquestionableness certainty, certification *(certainness)*, certitude, surety *(certainty)*
unquestionably admittedly, fairly *(clearly)*
unquestioned axiomatic, certain *(fixed)*, certain *(positive)*, clear *(certain)*, consensual, decisive, definite, infallible, proverbial, uncontested, uncontroverted, undisputed
unquestioning categorical, credulous, positive *(confident)*, unsuspecting
unquestioning acceptance faith
unquestioning belief credulity
unquiet restive
unratified unauthorized, unconfirmed, uncorroborated
unravel ascertain, clarify, construe *(translate)*, detect, discover, disengage, disentangle, elucidate, explain, extricate, find *(discover)*, interpret, resolve *(solve)*, separate, simplify *(make easier)*, solve, spread
unraveled elementary
unraveling denouement
unraveling of plot denouement
unravelment development *(progression)*, evulsion
unreachable impervious, inaccessible, unapproachable, unattainable
unreacting unresponsive
unread unversed
unreadable inapprehensible, pedestrian, unclear
unready back *(in arrears)*, late *(tardy)*, premature, unqualified *(not competent)*
unreal artificial, assumed *(feigned)*, bogus, delusive, dishonest, erroneous, false *(not genuine)*, fictitious, fraudulent, hypothetical, illusory, impalpable, inaccurate, insubstantial, nonexistent, spurious, unsound *(fallacious)*, untrue
unrealistic infeasible, quixotic, subjective
unreality figment, myth, phantom
unrealizable impracticable, inaccessible, insurmountable
unrealized possible, potential
unrealizing incognizant, insensible, unaware
unreasonable arbitrary, baseless, contumacious, disproportionate, drastic, excessive, exorbitant, extreme *(exaggerated)*, fanatical, ill-advised, ill-judged, impolitic, impossible, impracticable, improper, inexcusable, inexpiable, infeasible, inordinate, irrational, ludicrous, misadvised, oppressive, outrageous, partial *(biased)*, perverse, prohibitive

(costly), sophistic, unconscionable, undue *(excessive)*, unfair, unjust, unjustifiable, unsound *(fallacious)*, untenable, unwarranted, usurious

unreasonable amplification exaggeration

unreasonable bias prejudice *(preconception)*

unreasonable delay laches

unreasonable fear paranoia

unreasonable fright paranoia

unreasonably resolute fanatical

unreasoned arbitrary, injudicious, irrational, unsound *(fallacious)*

unreasoned alarm phobia

unreasoned fear phobia

unreasoning fatuous, ill-judged, irrational, opaque, thoughtless, vacuous

unreasoning fear panic

unreceivable inadmissible

unreceptive impervious

unrecognizable impalpable, inapprehensible, incomprehensible, indiscernible, indistinct, inexplicable, unclear

unrecognizing oblivious

unrecompensed gratis, gratuitous *(given without recompense)*, outstanding *(unpaid)*, unpaid, unrequited

unreconciled adverse *(hostile)*, contradictory, disinclined, irreconcilable, polemic

unrecoverable irretrievable

unredeemable profligate *(corrupt)*

unredeemed diabolic

unreduced complete *(all-embracing)*, gross *(total)*, intact, undiminished, whole *(undamaged)*

unrefined blatant *(obtrusive)*, disreputable, impertinent *(insolent)*, improper, inelegant, provincial, uncouth, unseemly

unreflecting blind *(not discerning)*, irrational, misadvised, thoughtless

unreflective thoughtless

unreformable incorrigible

unrefreshed languid

unrefutability incontestability

unrefutable clear *(certain)*, convincing, inappealable, positive *(incontestable)*, solid *(sound)*, unimpeachable

unrefuted accurate, actual, certain *(positive)*, definite, factual

unregarded indiscernible, perfunctory

unregenerate lascivious, lecherous, profligate *(corrupt)*, remorseless, reprobate

unregretful incorrigible

unregretting incorrigible

unregular intermittent

unregulated disorderly

unrehearsed fortuitous, spontaneous, unpremeditated

unreined free *(not restricted)*, independent, intemperate, lawless, licentious, uncurbed, unrestrained *(not repressed)*

unrelated alien *(unrelated)*, different, disconnected, dissimilar, extraneous, foreign, gratuitous *(unwarranted)*, heterogeneous, immaterial, impertinent *(irrelevant)*, inapposite, inconsequential, individual, irrelative, irrelevant

unrelatedness difference, inconsequence

unrelaxed rigid

unrelaxing industrious, patient, persistent, pertinacious

unrelenting brutal, callous, cold-blooded, constant, cruel, dictatorial, diligent, faithful *(diligent)*, immutable, implacable, inexorable, inflexible, ironclad, obdurate, patient, pertinacious, recalcitrant, relentless, remorseless, resolute, rigid, ruthless, sedulous, severe, unbending, uncompromising, undaunted, vindictive

unreliability dishonesty, improbity, knavery

unreliable capricious, dangerous, debatable, dishonest, disobedient, disputable, dubious, faithless, fallible, false *(disloyal)*, false *(inaccurate)*, fraudulent, insecure, irresponsible, mutable, perfidious, precarious, recreant, uncertain *(questionable)*, undependable, unpredictable, unsound *(not strong)*, untrustworthy, variable

unrelievable chronic

unreligious profane

unreluctant willing *(not averse)*

unremarkable mediocre, nondescript, usual

unremarkableness mediocrity

unremedied chronic

unremittent chronic

unremitting chronic, close *(rigorous)*, consecutive, continual *(connected)*, continuous, diligent, faithful *(diligent)*, incessant, industrious, patient, persistent, pertinacious, relentless, sedulous, stable, strong, uncompromising

unremorseful remorseless

unremorsefulness cruelty

unremoved lasting, present *(attendant)*, present *(current)*

unremunerated unpaid, unrequited

unremunerative unproductive

unrenowned obscure *(remote)*

unrepaid unrequited

unrepair deterioration

unrepealable irrevocable, permanent, perpetual

unrepealed lasting

unrepeated desultory, unique

unrepentant incorrigible, profligate *(corrupt)*, recusant, remorseless

unrepining resigned

unreplenished devoid, inadequate

unreplying unresponsive

unrepresentative anomalous, atypical

unrepressed disorderly, hot-blooded, uncurbed, unrestrained *(not repressed)*

unreproachable blameless

unreproached blameless, inculpable

unreproved blameless, inculpable

unrequested unsolicited

unrequired expendable, needless, nonessential, redundant, unnecessary

unrequisitioned unclaimed

unrequited outstanding *(unpaid)*, unpaid

unresembling dissimilar

unresentful placable

unreserve honesty

unreserved absolute *(complete)*, bona fide, brazen, candid, complete *(all-embracing)*, comprehensive, direct *(forthright)*, ingenuous, public *(open)*, unaffected *(sincere)*, unqualified *(un-*

limited), unrestrained *(not repressed)*

unreservedly in toto

unresigned recusant

unresistant passive, yielding

unresisting obedient, obeisant, passive, patient, peaceable, resigned, servile, stoical, yielding

unresistingness capitulation

unresolved debatable, disputable, doubtful, dubious, equivocal, hesitant, indefinite, indeterminate, irresolute, noncommittal, undecided, unsettled

unrespectability bad character, bad repute, ignominy, notoriety

unrespectable disreputable, ignoble, notorious

unrespected blameworthy

unresponding unresponsive

unresponsive cold-blooded, dispassionate, impervious, insensible, insusceptible *(uncaring)*, lifeless *(dull)*, noncommittal, obdurate, perfunctory, phlegmatic, unaffected *(uninfluenced)*

unrest confusion *(turmoil)*, disorder *(lack of order)*, disturbance, embroilment, strife, trepidation, turmoil

unrestful restive

unrestorable irreversible, irrevocable

unrestored languid

unrestrainable uncontrollable

unrestrained absolute *(complete)*, capricious, clear *(unencumbered)*, competitive *(open)*, demonstrative *(expressive of emotion)*, direct *(forthright)*, dissolute, exempt, free *(not restricted)*, gluttonous, immune, informal, ingenuous, inordinate, intemperate, irresponsible, lecherous, licentious, privileged, prodigal, profligate *(extravagant)*, rampant, unbound, uncurbed, unlimited, unqualified *(unlimited)*, unrestricted, unruly, unscrupulous, voluntary

unrestraint debauchery, freedom, honesty, latitude

unrestricted absolute *(complete)*, autonomous *(independent)*, competitive *(open)*, complete *(all-embracing)*, comprehensive, copious, dictatorial, exempt, general, immune, omnibus, open *(accessible)*, open-ended, peremptory *(absolute)*, plenary, public *(open)*, sovereign *(independent)*, unbound, unconditional, unlimited, unqualified *(unlimited)*

unrestricted inheritance fee *(estate)*

unretarded undiminished

unreturnable irreversible

unreturned unrequited

unrevealable private *(confidential)*

unrevealed blind *(concealed)*, clandestine, confidential, furtive, hidden, impalpable, inscrutable, latent, mysterious, personal *(private)*, privy, secret, stealthy, ulterior, undisclosed

unrevengeful placable

unreversed live *(existing)*

unrevised inexact

unrevived lifeless *(dead)*

unrevoked live *(existing)*

unrewarded barren, due *(owed)*, unpaid, unrequited

unrewarding barren, needless, unproductive

unriddle ascertain, elucidate, explicate, expound, solve

unrighteous blameworthy, culpable,

diabolic, immoral, iniquitous, lawless, nefarious, peccable, peccant *(culpable)*, reprehensible, reprobate, sinister, vicious

unrighteousness guilt, injustice, misdoing, offense, wrong

unrigorous liberal *(not literal)*

unrigorousness informality, laxity

unripe inexperienced, premature

unripeness minority *(infancy)*

unrivaled absolute *(ideal)*, best, paramount, premium, prime *(most valuable)*, professional *(stellar)*, superlative, unique, unprecedented, unusual

unrivaled effort main force

unrivalled leading *(ranking first)*, superior *(excellent)*

unrobe denude, unveil

unroll spread

unromantic pragmatic, realistic

unroot disinter, eradicate

unrooted unsettled

unrooting evulsion

unroutine unusual

unruffled callous, controlled *(restrained)*, dispassionate, nonchalant, patient, peaceable, phlegmatic, placid, stoical

unruliness anarchy, commotion, contempt *(disobedience to the court)*, defiance, disturbance, irregularity, lynch law, misrule, outbreak, outburst, pandemonium, riot

unruly disobedient, disordered, disorderly, fractious, froward, indomitable, insubordinate, intemperate, intractable, licentious, perverse, restive, uncontrollable, uncurbed, vicious

unsacred mundane, profane

unsacredness blasphemy

unsafe aleatory *(perilous)*, dangerous, deadly, destructible, harmful, insalubrious, insecure, noxious, precarious, speculative, susceptible *(unresistent)*, toxic, unsound *(not strong)*, untrustworthy, vulnerable

unsafe object hazard

unsafety jeopardy, peril

unsagacious unpolitic

unsaid implicit, tacit, undisclosed

unsaintly profane

unsalable barren, unmarketable

unsalaried unpaid

unsame dissimilar

unsanctified mundane, profane

unsanctioned illegal, illegitimate *(illegal)*, illicit, impermissible, null *(invalid)*, null and void, ultra vires, unauthorized, unlawful, unwarranted

unsanitary insalubrious

unsated insatiable

unsatisfaction dissatisfaction

unsatisfactoriness mediocrity

unsatisfactory antipathetic *(distasteful)*, deficient, deleterious, deplorable, detrimental, faulty, imperfect, inadequate, inadvisable, inferior *(lower in quality)*, nonsubstantial *(not sufficient)*, objectionable, paltry, poor *(inferior in quality)*, unacceptable, undesirable, unfavorable, unsuitable

unsatisfied delinquent *(overdue)*, disappointed, insatiable, outstanding *(unpaid)*, payable

unsatisfied hopes frustration

unsatisfying nonsubstantial *(not suf-*

ficient), unsatisfactory, unsuitable

unsavory bitter *(acrid tasting)*, disreputable, insipid, loathsome, objectionable, offensive *(offending)*, repugnant *(exciting aversion)*, repulsive, unendurable

unsay disclaim, recall *(call back)*, recant

unsaying retraction

unscarred intact

unscathed intact, inviolate, safe

unscholarliness ignorance, illiteracy

unscholarly unprofessional

unschooled inexperienced, naive, unversed

unscientific illogical, inexact

unscintillating insipid, pedestrian

unscramble ascertain, clarify, elucidate, explain, find *(discover)*, interpret, resolve *(solve)*, solve

unscratched intact

unscreen bare, denude, disclose, find *(discover)*, manifest, produce *(offer to view)*

unscreened obvious, palpable

unscrew disengage

unscrupulous arrant *(onerous)*, delinquent *(guilty of a misdeed)*, depraved, diabolic, dishonest, disingenuous, disreputable, faithless, false *(disloyal)*, fraudulent, immoral, insidious, lawless, machiavellian, peccant *(culpable)*, perfidious, recreant, sly, tortuous *(corrupt)*, unconscionable, unethical

unscrupulous agitator demagogue

unscrupulous haranguer demagogue

unscrupulousness bad faith, bad repute, corruption, dishonesty, fraud, improbity

unseal bare, disclose, reveal, unveil

unsealed open *(accessible)*, open *(unclosed)*

unsearchable inscrutable

unsearchableness opacity

unseasonable improper, inapposite, inappropriate, inapt, inept *(inappropriate)*, inopportune, premature, undue *(not owing)*, unsuitable, untimely

unseasoned inexperienced, juvenile, unaccustomed

unseat demote, depose *(remove)*, discharge *(dismiss)*, dislocate, dislodge, dismiss *(discharge)*, displace *(remove)*, disturb, divest, oust, overthrow, supplant

unseating discharge *(dismissal)*, removal

unsecluded open *(in sight)*

unseconded alone *(unsupported)*, solitary, unsupported

unsecurable inaccessible, unattainable

unseeable inconspicuous, indiscernible, intangible

unseeableness nonappearance

unseeing blind *(not discerning)*, blind *(sightless)*, heedless, inadvertent, incognizant, insensible

unseemingliness indecency

unseemliness impropriety

unseemly blatant *(obtrusive)*, brazen, delinquent *(guilty of a misdeed)*, disgraceful, disorderly, disproportionate, ill-advised, illicit, improper, inappropriate, inapt, inelegant, inept *(inappropriate)*, notorious, objectionable, slipshod,

unbecoming, uncouth, undesirable, undue *(excessive)*, unfit, unprofessional, unsatisfactory, unsuitable, wrongful

unseen blind *(concealed)*, clandestine, covert, furtive, hidden, inconspicuous, latent, potential, secret, stealthy, surreptitious, ulterior, underlying, undisclosed, unobtrusive

unselected miscellaneous

unselective promiscuous

unselfconscious ingenuous

unselfish benevolent, charitable *(benevolent)*, humane, liberal *(generous)*, magnanimous, meritorious, philanthropic

unselfish person good samaritan

unselfishness benevolence *(disposition to do good)*, charity, consideration *(sympathetic regard)*, disinterest *(lack of prejudice)*, humanity *(humaneness)*, largess *(generosity)*, philanthropy

unsensible ill-judged, impolitic, inadvisable, irrational, misadvised, unreasonable

unsensibleness inexpedience

unsentimental dispassionate, pragmatic

unsentimentality pragmatism

unseparated composite

unsepulcher disinter

unserious frivolous

unserviceable impracticable, ineffective, ineffectual, nugatory, otiose, unavailing

unserviceable check bad check

unsettle agitate *(perturb)*, confuse *(bewilder)*, confuse *(create disorder)*, discompose, dislocate, disorganize, disorient, disrupt, disturb, inconvenience, muddle, obfuscate, perplex, perturb, upset

unsettled aleatory *(uncertain)*, conditional, debatable, delinquent *(overdue)*, deranged, disorderly, disputable, due *(owed)*, frenetic, hesitant, inconclusive, indefinite, indeterminate, insecure, irresolute, lunatic, moot, moving *(in motion)*, mutable, non compos mentis, noncommittal, outstanding *(unpaid)*, outstanding *(unresolved)*, payable, pending *(unresolved)*, precarious, problematic, protean, provisional, restive, speculative, tentative, uncertain *(questionable)*, unconfirmed, undecided, unpaid, unsound *(not strong)*, unspecified, vague, variable

unsettled in one's mind non compos mentis

unsettled in opinion doubtful

unsettled opinion doubt *(indecision)*, indecision

unsettlement confusion *(turmoil)*, disturbance, doubt *(indecision)*

unsevered complete *(all-embracing)*, intact, undiminished

unshacking liberation

unshackle disencumber, disengage, disenthrall, extricate, free, liberate, parole, rescue

unshackled free *(not restricted)*, independent, uncurbed, unrestrained *(not in custody)*, unrestricted

unshackling emancipation

unshaded candid, patent

unshakable certain *(positive)*, dogmatic, incontrovertible, indubious, pertinacious, safe

unshakable opinion conviction *(persuasion)*

unshakable trust faith

unshakeable infrangible, ironclad, stable, staunch

unshaken constant, definite, dispassionate, inexorable, patient, pertinacious, positive *(confident)*, resolute, secure *(confident)*, stable, steadfast, unabashed, undaunted

unshaken belief credence

unshape deface, mutilate

unshared personal *(private)*, solitary

unshatterable infrangible

unshattered intact

unsheathe bare, denude, evidence, expose, withdraw

unsheltered bleak *(exposed and barren)*, dangerous, helpless *(defenseless)*, insecure, open *(in sight)*, precarious

unshield bare

unshielded helpless *(defenseless)*, insecure, open *(accessible)*, open *(in sight)*, precarious, vulnerable

unshifting chronic, fixed *(settled)*, permanent, unremitting

unshocked nonchalant

unshorn gross *(total)*

unshortened gross *(total)*

unshown unconfirmed

unshrewd unpolitic

unshrinking heroic, indomitable, pertinacious, purposeful, relentless, spartan, unabashed, undaunted

unshroud bare, denude, disclose, find *(discover)*, manifest, reveal

unshrouded palpable

unshut open *(unclosed)*

unsightliness defacement

unsightly poor *(inferior in quality)*, repulsive, unseemly

unsigned anonymous

unsimilar dissimilar

unsimulated authentic, bona fide, genuine, honest, real, unaffected *(sincere)*

unskilled amateur, incompetent, inexperienced, unaccustomed, unversed

unskilled person novice

unskilled practitioner layman

unskillful inadept, incapable, incompetent, inept *(incompetent)*

unskillfulness abortion *(fiasco)*, disqualification *(factor that disqualifies)*, inability, incapacity, inefficacy

unslackening chronic

unslanted objective, unbiased, unprejudiced

unslantedness disinterest *(lack of prejudice)*

unsleeping industrious, vigilant

unslumbering vigilant

unsmoothness irregularity

unsnap disengage

unsober drunk

unsociable disdainful, taciturn, unapproachable, unresponsive

unsociableness ostracism

unsoftened unmitigated

unsoftening unrelenting

unsoiled blameless, clean, unblemished

unsolicitous cold-blooded, heedless, remiss

unsolicitousness disinterest *(lack of*

interest)

unsolid insubstantial, intangible, nonsubstantial *(not sturdy)*

unsolidity impalpability

unsolvable insurmountable

unsolved doubtful, equivocal, pending *(unresolved)*

unsophisticated credulous, elementary, honest, inexperienced, ingenuous, naive, provincial, simple, unadulterated, unaffected *(sincere)*, usual

unsophistication credulity

unsorted disjointed, haphazard, miscellaneous

unsought unclaimed, undesirable, unsolicited

unsound bad *(inferior)*, baseless, defective, deficient, dubious, erroneous, fallacious, false *(inaccurate)*, faulty, ill-judged, illogical, imperfect, impolitic, improper, inaccurate, inadvisable, inconsequential, incorrect, injudicious, insecure, insubstantial, insufficient, irrational, misadvised, non compos mentis, nonsubstantial *(not sturdy)*, peccable, precarious, sophistic, unreasonable, unreliable, untenable, untrustworthy

unsound argument fallacy

unsound check bad check

unsound mind insanity

unsoundness disability *(physical inability)*, disease, frailty, inexpedience, invalidity

unsoundness of mind insanity, lunacy

unsparing benevolent, charitable *(benevolent)*, close *(rigorous)*, copious, liberal *(generous)*, philanthropic, profuse, relentless, ruthless, severe, trenchant, unqualified *(unlimited)*, unrelenting

unsparingness philanthropy

unsparkling insipid, lifeless *(dull)*, pedestrian

unspeakable ineffable, offensive *(offending)*, profane, remarkable

unspecific indiscriminate

unspecified anonymous, broad, collective, generic, indefinite, indeterminate, inexact, nonsectarian, vague

unspecious authentic, bona fide, honest

unspeciousness honesty

unspent net, residuary

unspiced insipid

unspied latent, surreptitious

unspirited inactive, insipid, jejune *(dull)*, languid, lifeless *(dull)*, nonchalant

unspiritual civil *(public)*, corporeal, lecherous, material *(physical)*, mundane, physical

unspoiled intact

unspoken implicit, implied, tacit

unsporting unfair

unspotted blameless, clean, infallible, inviolate, pure, unblemished

unspurious authentic, bona fide, factual, genuine, honest, real, true *(authentic)*

unspuriousness honesty

unstable aleatory *(uncertain)*, capricious, dangerous, ephemeral, faithless, fallible, inconsistent, indefinite, insecure, irresponsible, mutable, non compos mentis, nonsubstantial *(not sturdy)*, peccable, precarious, temporary, tran-

sient, transitory, undependable, unpredictable, unreliable, unsettled, unsound *(not strong)*, untrustworthy, variable, volatile

unstaffed devoid

unstaid moving *(in motion)*, unsettled

unstained clean, inviolate, pure

unstated tacit

unstationary moving *(in motion)*

unsteadfast faithless, false *(disloyal)*, insecure, irresolute, mutable, noncommittal, precarious, undependable, unpredictable, untrustworthy, variable

unsteadfastness bad faith, disloyalty

unsteadiness doubt *(indecision)*, inconsistency, indecision, irregularity

unsteady broken *(interrupted)*, dangerous, disorderly, inconsistent, infrequent, insecure, irresolute, irresponsible, mutable, noncommittal, powerless, precarious, sporadic, undependable, unpredictable, unreliable, unsettled, unsound *(not strong)*, variable, volatile

unstereotyped informal

unstick detach, disengage

unstinted absolute *(complete)*, full, profuse, unqualified *(unlimited)*

unstinting benevolent, charitable *(benevolent)*, copious, liberal *(generous)*, philanthropic, profuse

unstirred callous, dispassionate, inactive, insusceptible *(uncaring)*, nonchalant, obdurate, unaffected *(uninfluenced)*

unstirring placid, stagnant

unstoppable infallible

unstopped chronic, continual *(connected)*, continual *(perpetual)*, continuous, direct *(uninterrupted)*, free *(not restricted)*, live *(existing)*, rampant

unstoppered open *(unclosed)*

unstopping chronic, persistent

unstraightforward devious, disingenuous, oblique *(evasive)*

unstraightforward action indirection *(indirect action)*

unstraightforwardness dishonesty, improbity, indirection *(deceitfulness)*

unstrain ease

unstrained harmonious

unstrained meaning connotation

unstrap disengage

unstrengthened dangerous, helpless *(defenseless)*, insipid, languid, powerless

unstrict flexible, inaccurate, informal, lax, lenient, liberal *(not literal)*

unstrictness latitude

unstruck unaffected *(uninfluenced)*

unstrung powerless

unstudied casual, ingenuous, perfunctory, simple, spontaneous, unpremeditated, unversed

unsturdy nonsubstantial *(not sturdy)*

unstylish outdated, outmoded

unsubduable indomitable, inexpugnable, insurmountable, invincible

unsubdued undaunted

unsubject immune

unsubjected free *(enjoying civil liberty)*, independent, sovereign *(independent)*

unsubmissive contumacious, disobedient, disorderly, incorrigible, indomitable, intractable, lawless, nonconforming, nonconsenting, recalcitrant, recusant, renitent, restive, uncontrollable, unruly

unsubmissiveness contempt *(disobedience to the court)*

unsubsiding chronic

unsubstantial baseless, delusive, erroneous, futile, ill-founded, illusory, immaterial, impalpable, imponderable, incorporeal, insubstantial, intangible, negligible, nominal, nonsubstantial *(not sturdy)*, null *(insignificant)*, otiose, precarious, slight, tenuous, unfounded, unsound *(fallacious)*, unsound *(not strong)*, untrue

unsubstantiality blank *(emptiness)*, immateriality, nonentity

unsubstantialness impalpability, nonentity

unsubstantiated baseless, implausible, inconclusive, theoretical, unconfirmed, uncorroborated, unsupported

unsuccessful disappointed, futile, inadept, ineffective, ineffectual, otiose, regrettable, unavailing, unproductive

unsuccessful attempt failure *(lack of success)*

unsuccessful trial mistrial

unsuccessfulness frustration

unsuccessive broken *(interrupted)*, desultory, disjointed, disjunctive *(tending to disjoin)*, intermittent, sporadic

unsufferable painful

unsufficing deficient, inadequate, insufficient, nonsubstantial *(not sufficient)*

unsuitability disability *(legal disqualification)*, disqualification *(factor that disqualifies)*, impropriety, incongruity, inexpedience, misdoing

unsuitable bad *(inferior)*, bad *(offensive)*, detrimental, disproportionate, gratuitous *(unwarranted)*, ill-advised, imperfect, improper, inadmissible, inadvisable, inapplicable, inapposite, inappropriate, inapt, incapable, incompetent, incongruous, inconsistent, ineligible, inept *(inappropriate)*, injudicious, inopportune, irrelevant, objectionable, unacceptable, unauthorized, unbecoming, undesirable, undue *(excessive)*, unfit, unprofessional, unsatisfactory, unseemly, wrongful

unsuitable action impropriety

unsuitable for practical use impracticable

unsuitableness disability *(legal disqualification)*, impropriety, incompatibility *(inconsistency)*, inconsistency

unsuitably timed untimely

unsuited gratuitous *(unwarranted)*, improper, inapplicable, inapposite, inappropriate, incapable, ineligible, inept *(inappropriate)*, inopportune, insufficient, unbecoming, unfavorable, unfit, unqualified *(not competent)*, unsuitable

unsuitedness disability *(legal disqualification)*

unsullied blameless, clean, irreprehensible, pure, unblemished

unsunderable indivisible, inseparable

unsupplied deficient, devoid, void *(empty)*

unsupportable baseless, ill-founded, illusory, insubstantial, unfounded

unsupported baseless, helpless *(de-*

fenseless)*, ill-founded, inconclusive, powerless, solitary, unauthorized, unconfirmed, uncorroborated, unfounded

unsupported by evidence inconclusive

unsupposed actual

unsuppressed chronic, intemperate, lawless, uncurbed, unmitigated, unrestrained *(not in custody)*, unrestrained *(not repressed)*

unsure aleatory *(uncertain)*, conditional, controversial, debatable, disputable, doubtful, dubious, equivocal, fallible, hesitant, inconclusive, indefinite, insecure, leery, noncommittal, precarious, skeptical, uncertain *(questionable)*, undecided, undependable, unpredictable, vague

unsure of oneself diffident

unsureness doubt *(indecision)*, hazard, hesitation, incertitude, indecision, peril, suspicion *(uncertainty)*

unsurmountable insurmountable

unsurpassable inestimable, prime *(most valuable)*

unsurpassed absolute *(ideal)*, cardinal *(outstanding)*, dominant, infallible, leading *(ranking first)*, paramount, premium, primary, prime *(most valuable)*, professional *(stellar)*, superior *(excellent)*, superlative, unapproachable

unsurprising usual

unsusceptibility resistance

unsusceptible callous, cold-blooded, dispassionate, immune, obdurate, phlegmatic

unsusceptible of change certain *(positive)*

unsuspected blind *(concealed)*, covert, latent, surreptitious

unsuspected event surprise

unsuspecting credulous, definite, incognizant, insensible, naive, secure *(confident)*, unaware, unsuspecting, unwitting

unsuspectingly unknowingly

unsuspectingness credulity

unsuspicious credulous, definite, ingenuous, naive, unsuspecting

unsuspiciousness credulity

unsustainable baseless, debatable, disputable, doubtful, dubitative, erroneous, ill-founded, illogical, insubstantial, untenable

unsustained baseless, debatable, disputable, unsupported

unswayable impervious, inflexible

unswayed dispassionate, fair *(just)*, impartial, judicial, just, liberal *(broad minded)*, loyal, neutral, nonpartisan, objective, open-minded, receptive, unaffected *(uninfluenced)*, unbiased, unprejudiced

unsweet bitter *(acrid tasting)*

unswerring purposeful

unswerving constant, direct *(straight)*, industrious, loyal, patient, persistent, pertinacious, relentless, resolute, right *(correct)*, right *(direct)*, sedulous, serious *(devoted)*, stable, steadfast, straightforward, true *(loyal)*, undistorted, uniform, unremitting

unswerving fidelity adhesion *(loyalty)*

unswervingly faithfully

unsymmetric irregular *(not usual)*

unsymmetrical disproportionate, irregular *(not usual)*

unsympathetic callous, cold-blooded, cruel, harsh, insusceptible *(uncaring)*, obdurate, relentless, ruthless, unaffected *(uninfluenced)*, unrelenting, unresponsive

unsympathizing callous, cruel

unsynthetic authentic, genuine, honest, natural, real, sterling, unaffected *(sincere)*, veridical

unsystematic capricious, casual, desultory, discursive *(digressive)*, disjointed, disordered, disorderly, haphazard, indiscriminate, sporadic, unpredictable

untactful impolitic, unpolitic

untaint decontaminate

untainted absolute *(ideal)*, blameless, infallible, pure, unblemished, unimpeachable

untaken available, unclaimed

untalented amateur, inadept

untalkative laconic, mute, taciturn

untalked of undisclosed

untamed brutal, lawless, unmitigated, vicious

untangle ascertain, elucidate, explain, explicate, rectify, resolve *(solve)*, solve

untarnishable incorruptible

untarnished absolute *(ideal)*, clean, pure, unblemished

untasteful inelegant, unbecoming, unseemly

untastefulness indecency

untaught spontaneous, unversed

untaught state ignorance

untaxed free *(at no charge)*

untempered intemperate, unmitigated

untenable baseless, disabled *(deprived of legal right)*, doubtful, helpless *(defenseless)*, ill-founded, illogical, implausible, inadequate, indefensible, insubstantial, invalid, ludicrous, nonsubstantial *(not sturdy)*, sophistic, unbelievable, unfounded, unreasonable, unsound *(fallacious)*, unsupported, unsustainable, vulnerable

untenableness invalidity

untenanted devoid, vacant, void *(empty)*

untender harsh

unterrified undaunted

untested inconclusive, novel

untested opinion theory

unthankfulness ingratitude

unthinkability impossibility

unthinkable implausible, impossible, incomprehensible, incredible, infeasible, ludicrous, prodigious *(amazing)*, unbelievable

unthinking careless, fatuous, heedless, ill-judged, impolitic, impulsive *(rash)*, inadvertent, involuntary, irrational, lax, misadvised, negligent, opaque, perfunctory, reckless, remiss, spontaneous, superficial, thoughtless, unintentional, unpremeditated, unwitting, vacuous

unthinkingness disregard *(unconcern)*

unthorough cursory, lax, negligent, partial *(relating to a part)*, perfunctory

unthought of perfunctory, unanticipated, unexpected, unforeseeable, unforeseen

unthoughtful ill-judged, irrational, lax, misadvised, thoughtless

unthoughtfulness inexpedience, temerity

unthreatened immune, safe, secure *(free from danger)*

unthreatening harmless

unthriftiness waste

unthrifty improvident, prodigal, profligate *(extravagant)*, profuse

untidiness laxity

untidy disordered, disorderly, lax, slipshod

untie break *(separate)*, disencumber, disengage, disentangle, disenthrall, extricate, free, liberate, remove *(eliminate)*, separate, sever, split

untied free *(not restricted)*, unbound

until ad interim

until the conclusion of throughout *(during)*

untimeliness impropriety, inexpedience

untimely improper, inapposite, inappropriate, inapt, inauspicious, inept *(inappropriate)*, inopportune, overdue, premature, regrettable, undue *(not owing)*, unexpected, unfavorable, unsuitable

untimid undaunted

untiring diligent, faithful *(diligent)*, incessant, industrious, painstaking, patient, persistent, pertinacious, resolute, sedulous, stable, steadfast, unremitting

untitled ignoble

untold esoteric, hidden, indefinite, innumerable, multiple, myriad, mysterious, personal *(private)*, secret, tacit, undisclosed, unlimited

untolerating parochial

untomb disinter

untorn intact

untouchable dispassionate, immune, impalpable, inalienable, intangible

untouched cold-blooded, immune, impartial, insensible, insusceptible *(uncaring)*, intact, inviolate, natural, nonchalant, obdurate, pure, unadulterated, unaffected *(uninfluenced)*

untoward adverse *(hostile)*, deplorable, detrimental, disproportionate, inadvisable, inapposite, inappropriate, inapt, inauspicious, inept *(inappropriate)*, lawless, perverse, regrettable, uncontrollable, unfavorable, unpropitious, unruly, unsatisfactory, unsuitable

untraceable irretrievable

untractable fractious, immutable

untraditional divergent, unprecedented, unusual

untrained disorderly, incompetent, inexperienced, unaccustomed

untrained individual novice

untrained person layman

untrammel disencumber, rescue

untrammeled clear *(unencumbered)*, free *(not restricted)*, unbound, unrestrained *(not in custody)*, unrestricted

untransferable unalienable

untranslatable indefinable, ineffable, undefinable

untransparent equivocal, opaque

untraveled provincial

untreacherous candid, incorruptible,

loyal, true *(loyal)*

untreacherousness responsibility *(conscience)*

untried inconclusive, inexperienced, moot, novel, unaccustomed, unconfirmed, unsettled

untrodden unsettled

untroubled cold-blooded, harmonious, peaceable, phlegmatic, placid, positive *(confident)*

untrue bogus, broken *(unfulfilled)*, colorable *(specious)*, deceptive, delusive, dishonest, erroneous, faithless, fallacious, false *(disloyal)*, false *(inaccurate)*, fictitious, fraudulent, inaccurate, incorrect, invalid, lying, mendacious, perfidious, recreant, spurious, unfounded, unreliable, unsound *(fallacious)*, unsustainable, untrustworthy

untrue declaration falsehood

untrue statement misrepresentation, story *(falsehood)*

untrue story myth

untrueness bad faith

untrustful cynical, suspicious *(distrustful)*

untrustiness bad faith

untrusting incredulous, skeptical, suspicious *(distrustful)*

untrustworthiness bad faith, dishonesty, improbity, indirection *(deceitfulness)*, knavery

untrustworthy dangerous, dishonest, disingenuous, disreputable, faithless, fallible, false *(disloyal)*, fraudulent, inaccurate, insecure, irresponsible, machiavellian, perfidious, precarious, recreant, sinister, suspicious *(distrustful)*, uncertain *(questionable)*, undependable, unreliable, unsound *(not strong)*, unsustainable, untrue

untrusty irresponsible

untruth canard, deceit, deception, defamation, dishonesty, false pretense, falsehood, fiction, figment, lie, misrepresentation, misstatement, myth, perjury, pretense *(pretext)*, pretext, story *(falsehood)*, subreption, subterfuge

untruthful dishonest, disingenuous, disreputable, evasive, fraudulent, lying, machiavellian, mendacious, perfidious, untrue

untruthful report canard, fiction

untruthfulness bad faith, deceit, deception, dishonesty, false pretense, falsification, fraud, improbity, indirection *(deceitfulness)*, misrepresentation, misstatement

unturned direct *(straight)*, straightforward

untutored inexperienced

untutored intelligence instinct

untwist disentangle, simplify *(clarify)*

untying division *(act of dividing)*, liberation, release

untypical anomalous, dissimilar, infrequent, unusual

ununiformity inequality, irregularity

unus sole

unusable expendable, impracticable, inapplicable, otiose, unfit

unused defunct, expendable, idle, inexperienced, novel, unemployed, vacant

unusual anomalous, different, distinct *(distinguished from others)*, eccentric, extraordinary, foreign, individual, in-

frequent, irregular *(not usual)*, lurid, momentous, nonconforming, noteworthy, novel, original *(creative)*, particular *(individual)*, particular *(specific)*, patent, peculiar *(distinctive)*, portentous *(eliciting amazement)*, rare, remarkable, scarce, singular, special, specific, unaccustomed, uncommon, unexpected, unforeseeable, unique, unorthodox, unprecedented

unusual circumstance phenomenon *(unusual occurrence)*

unusual happening phenomenon *(unusual occurrence)*

unusual incident phenomenon *(unusual occurrence)*

unusual occurrence surprise

unusual task onus *(burden)*

unusually particularly

unusualness irregularity, quirk *(idiosyncrasy)*

unutilized vacant

unutterable ineffable

unutterable contempt disdain

unvalidated unconfirmed, uncorroborated, unsupported

unvanquishable insurmountable, invincible

unvanquished independent, prevailing *(having superior force)*, sovereign *(independent)*, successful

unvaried boiler plate, equal, literal, ordinary, pedestrian, prosaic, stale, uniform, usual

unvarnished accurate, genuine, honest, literal, naked *(lacking embellishment)*, simple, true *(authentic)*, unadulterated

unvarnished truth honesty

unvarying certain *(positive)*, chronic, comparable *(equivalent)*, constant, continual *(perpetual)*, equal, fixed *(settled)*, invariably, normal *(regular)*, permanent, persistent, regular *(orderly)*, steadfast, uniform, unremitting

unveil admit *(concede)*, bare, clarify, denude, detect, disabuse, disclose, disinter, divulge, educe, exhibit, expose, find *(discover)*, manifest, present *(introduce)*, produce *(offer to view)*, reveal

unveiled comprehensible, naked *(lacking embellishment)*, palpable, scrutable

unveiling admission *(disclosure)*, denouement, disclosure *(act of disclosing)*, manifestation

unvenal incorruptible

unvendible unmarketable

unventilated impervious

unventured unsettled

unveracious dishonest, evasive, false *(inaccurate)*, fraudulent, incorrect, lying, mendacious, untrue

unveraciousness bad faith

unveracity bad faith, deception, false pretense, misrepresentation

unveridical mendacious

unverifiable controversial, debatable, disputable, dubious, hypothetical, unsustainable

unverified inconclusive, unconfirmed, uncorroborated, unsupported

unverified comments hearsay

unverified news hearsay, report *(rumor)*

unverified supposition conjecture

unverity bad faith

unversed blind *(not discerning)*, inexperienced, unaccustomed, unacquainted, unaware

unvexed complacent, patient

unviable impracticable, insurmountable

unvindictive placable

unviolated clean, inviolate

unvirtuous bad *(offensive)*, blameworthy, delinquent *(guilty of a misdeed)*, diabolic, dishonest, dissolute, fraudulent, immoral, lewd, peccable, peccant *(culpable)*, profane, promiscuous, prurient, salacious

unvirtuousness delinquency *(misconduct)*

unvisited solitary

unvivid insipid, lifeless *(dull)*, pedestrian

unvocal inarticulate, mute, speechless, taciturn

unvocalizing mute

unvoiced implicit, tacit, undisclosed

unvoidable noncancellable

unwakened dormant

unwanted derelict *(abandoned)*, ineligible, needless, otiose, unacceptable, undesirable, unsolicited

unwariness disregard *(unconcern)*, inconsideration, indiscretion, neglect, negligence

unwarlike nonmilitant

unwarned unaware, unsuspecting

unwarped direct *(straight)*, nonpartisan, objective, open-minded, unbiased, undistorted, unprejudiced

unwarrantable disproportionate, felonious, illegal, illicit, improper, indefensible, inexcusable, lawless, untenable, unwarranted

unwarrantable intrusion nuisance

unwarranted baseless, disproportionate, exorbitant, extreme *(exaggerated)*, ill-founded, illegal, illicit, inconsequential, inexcusable, irregular *(improper)*, irrelevant, lawless, nonessential, outrageous, profuse, prohibitive *(costly)*, sophistic, ultra vires, unauthorized, unconscionable, undue *(excessive)*, unfounded, unjust, unlawful, unreasonable, unsound *(fallacious)*

unwarranted conclusion anacoluthon, non sequitur

unwarranted purchase caveat emptor

unwary careless, heedless, hot-blooded, impolitic, improvident, imprudent, injudicious, lax, misadvised, negligent, reckless, unaware, unpolitic

unwasteful economical, frugal

unwastefulness austerity

unwatchful derelict *(negligent)*, heedless, lax, negligent, perfunctory, reckless, remiss, thoughtless

unwatchfulness disregard *(unconcern)*, laxity, neglect, negligence

unwavering certain *(positive)*, constant, definite, diligent, faithful *(diligent)*, faithful *(loyal)*, fixed *(settled)*, indomitable, industrious, inexorable, infallible, intense, loyal, patient, permanent, persistent, pertinacious, positive *(confident)*, purposeful, resolute, stable, staunch, steadfast, straightforward, true *(loyal)*, unalterable, unrelenting,

unyielding

unweakened powerful, undiminished

unwearied patient, unremitting

unwearying diligent, incessant, patient, persistent, pertinacious, sedulous

unweighable imponderable

unweighed casual, perfunctory

unwelcome invidious, unacceptable, undesirable, unsatisfactory, unsolicited

unwelcome suggestion intrusion

unwell unsound *(not strong)*

unwholesome detrimental, harmful, immoral, insalubrious, noxious, obnoxious, obscene, peccant *(unhealthy)*, pernicious, sinister

unwholesome condition disease

unwieldy impracticable, onerous, ponderous

unwilled involuntary

unwilling adverse *(hostile)*, averse, disinclined, disobedient, dissident, evasive, intractable, involuntary, nonconsenting, recalcitrant, recusant, reluctant, remiss, renitent, restive

unwilling to accept inconvincible, incredulous

unwilling to care insusceptible *(uncaring)*

unwilling to give parsimonious

unwilling to pay penurious

unwillingness contempt *(disobedience to the court)*, declination, disincentive, hesitation, refusal, reluctance, resistance, scruple

unwillingness to believe incredulity

unwind spread

unwise detrimental, disadvantageous, fatuous, ill-advised, ill-judged, impolitic, imprudent, inadvisable, inapt, inept *(inappropriate)*, injudicious, irrational, misadvised, puerile, reckless, unfit, unpolitic, unreasonable

unwiseness indiscretion, inexpedience

unwished undesirable, unsolicited

unwitnessed unconfirmed

unwitting incognizant, insensible, unintentional

unwittingly unknowingly

unwitty pedestrian

unwonted different, nonconforming, original *(creative)*, unforeseeable, unusual

unworkability impossibility

unworkable impossible, impracticable, infeasible, inoperable *(impracticable)*, insurmountable, otiose

unworldliness ignorance

unworldly incorporeal, inexperienced, naive

unworn intact, undiminished

unworried nonchalant, phlegmatic

unworthiness frailty

unworthy blameful, blameworthy, contemptible, delinquent *(guilty of a misdeed)*, disgraceful, disreputable, ignoble, odious, peccant *(culpable)*, poor *(inferior in quality)*, reprehensible, scandalous, undesirable, unethical, unfit, unsatisfactory

unworthy of belief suspicious *(questionable)*

unworthy of confidence untrustworthy

unworthy of consideration inappreciable, inconsiderable

unworthy of notice inappreciable,

inconsiderable

unworthy of regard negligible, petty

unworthy of respect notorious

unworthy of serious consideration de minimus, paltry, puerile

unworthy of serious notice frivolous

unworthy of trust untrustworthy

unwrap bare, denude, expose, unveil

unwritten nuncupative, oral, parol, prescriptive, verbal

unwritten law custom, equity *(justice)*

unyielding barren, callous, chronic, disobedient, dogmatic, durable, fanatical, firm, formidable, froward, immutable, impervious, implacable, impossible, indelible, indestructible, indomitable, industrious, inexorable, inexpugnable, infallible, inflexible, insusceptible *(resistant)*, insusceptible *(uncaring)*, intractable, invincible, ironclad, irreconcilable, obdurate, oppressive, parsimonious, particular *(exacting)*, patient, permanent, persistent, pertinacious, perverse, recalcitrant, relentless, resolute, restive, rigid, sedulous, serious *(devoted)*, severe, solid *(compact)*, stable, staunch, steadfast, strict, stringent, strong, unaffected *(uninfluenced)*, unalterable, unbending, uncompromising, unmitigated, unproductive, unrelenting, unruly, willful

unyieldingness resistance, rigor, tenacity

unyoke disencumber, dissociate, divorce, separate

unzealous disinclined

up for discussion arguable, debatable

up in arms inimical, resentful

up in the air debatable

up to effective *(efficient)*, proficient, sciential, until

up to date contemporary, current, progressive *(advocating change)*, sophisticated

up to par palatable

up to standard fairly *(moderately)*

up to the mark coequal

up to the minute contemporary, current, sophisticated

up to the time of until

up to this time heretofore

up-to-date novel, present *(current)*, prevailing *(current)*, recent

up-to-the-minute novel, present *(current)*

upbear bear *(support)*

upbraid blame, castigate, cavil, censure, complain *(criticize)*, condemn *(blame)*, criticize *(find fault with)*, denounce *(condemn)*, disapprove *(condemn)*, fault, harass, impeach, lash *(attack verbally)*, rebuke, remonstrate, reprehend, reprimand, reproach

upbraiding critical *(faultfinding)*, criticism, denunciation, diatribe, objurgation, outcry, reprimand, reproach, revilement

upbringing education, instruction *(teaching)*

upbuild build *(construct)*, edify

upcoming forthcoming, future, immediate *(imminent)*, imminent, instant, pending *(imminent)*, prospective, proximate

updated version revision *(corrected version)*
upend overthrow, overturn, upset
upgrade ameliorate, amend, elevate, enhance, inure *(benefit)*, meliorate, promote *(advance)*
upgrading boom *(prosperity)*
upgrowth boom *(increase)*, boom *(prosperity)*, development *(progression)*
upheaval bluster *(commotion)*, cataclysm, commotion, confusion *(turmoil)*, disaster, furor, havoc, mutiny, outburst, rebellion, revolution, shambles, strife, subversion, turmoil
uphill operose
uphold adhere *(maintain loyalty)*, advocate, aid, approve, bear *(support)*, bolster, certify *(approve)*, concur *(agree)*, confirm, continue *(prolong)*, corroborate, defend, demonstrate *(establish)*, document, espouse, establish *(show)*, indorse, justify, maintain *(sustain)*, pass *(approve)*, preserve, promote *(organize)*, prove, reassure, recommend, sanction, side, sponsor, subsidize, substantiate, support *(assist)*, sustain *(confirm)*, sustain *(prolong)*, underwrite, vouch, witness *(attest to)*
uphold in evidence corroborate, establish *(show)*, support *(corroborate)*, sustain *(confirm)*
upholder abettor, advocate *(counselor)*, advocate *(espouser)*, apologist, backer, benefactor, mainstay, partisan, patron *(influential supporter)*, proponent
upholding conservation, corroboration
upkeep alimony, conservation, maintenance *(support of spouse)*, overhead, preservation, promotion *(encouragement)*, safekeeping, support *(assistance)*, sustenance
uplift edify, elevate, elevation, enhance, heighten *(elevate)*, meliorate, promotion *(advancement)*, raise *(advance)*, reassure, reform
uplifting edification
upmost prominent
upper circles elite
upper class society
upper classes elite
upper extremity maximum *(pinnacle)*, pinnacle
upper hand advantage, edge *(advantage)*, predominance
upper limit capacity *(maximum)*
upperhand supremacy
uppermost best, cardinal *(basic)*, cardinal *(outstanding)*, primary
uppish proud *(conceited)*, supercilious
uppity proud *(conceited)*, supercilious
upraise elevate, enhance, heighten *(elevate)*, raise *(advance)*, uphold
upright blameless, clean, conscientious, credible, dependable, equitable, ethical, evenhanded, fair *(just)*, high-minded, incorruptible, innocent, irreprehensible, just, law-abiding, licit, meritorious, moral, pure, reliable, reputable, right *(correct)*, scrupulous, sterling, straightforward, unaffected *(sincere)*, unimpeachable
upright distance elevation
upright moral character integrity
uprighteousness justice
uprightly faithfully

uprightness candor *(straightforwardness)*, conscience, credibility, equity *(justice)*, ethics, fairness, good faith, honesty, honor *(good reputation)*, integrity, merit, principle *(virtue)*, probity, rectitude, responsibility *(conscience)*, right *(righteousness)*, trustworthiness
uprightness of character integrity
uprisen disorderly
uprising anarchy, commotion, defiance, disturbance, insurrection, mutiny, outbreak, rebellion, resistance, revolt, revolution, riot, sedition, subversion
uproar bluster *(commotion)*, brawl, commotion, confusion *(turmoil)*, disorder *(lack of order)*, disturbance, embroilment, fracas, fray, furor, imbroglio, noise, outbreak, outburst, outcry, pandemonium, riot, shambles, turmoil
uproarious disorderly
uproariousness noise, pandemonium
uproot destroy *(efface)*, dislodge, eliminate *(eradicate)*, eradicate, evict, exclude, extirpate, overthrow, overturn, reject, remove *(eliminate)*, supplant
uprooting evulsion, rejection
ups and downs vicissitudes
upset agitate *(perturb)*, annoy, beat *(defeat)*, counterargument, debacle, defeat, disaster, discommode, discompose, disconcert, discourage, dislocate, disorganize, disorient, disrupt, distress, disturb, embarrass, foil, harrow, hold up *(delay)*, kill *(defeat)*, muddle, obfuscate, override, overrule, overthrow, overturn, perplex, perturb, pique, prostration, rebellion, subversion, subvert, supplant, surmount, unsettled
upsetting oppressive, unsatisfactory
upshot amount *(result)*, conclusion *(outcome)*, consequence *(conclusion)*, denouement, development *(outgrowth)*, effect, end *(termination)*, holding *(ruling of a court)*, issuance, outcome, result
upstanding high-minded, law-abiding, moral, right *(correct)*, upright
upstandingness honesty, integrity, rectitude
upsurge advance *(progression)*, boom *(increase)*, boom *(prosperity)*, inflate, inflation *(increase)*
upswing headway
uptrend development *(progression)*
upturn in prices inflation *(decrease in value of currency)*
upward curve boom *(prosperity)*
upward trend boom *(prosperity)*
uranic stellar
urban civic, civil *(public)*
urban district city
urban place city
urbana record
urbane civil *(polite)*, sophisticated
urbanitas courtesy
urbanity courtesy
urbanization city, development *(building)*
urbs city
urge abet, admonish *(advise)*, advocate, argue, assert, bait *(harass)*, bait *(lure)*, cajole, call *(appeal to)*, caution, charge *(instruct on the law)*, coax, compel, constrain *(compel)*, counsel, demand, desire, desire, exact, exhort, foment, force *(coerce)*, hold out *(deliberate on an offer)*, impel, impetus, importune,

incite, inculcate, influence, insist, inspire, inveigle, lobby, motivate, persuade, petition, plead *(implore)*, pray, press *(beseech)*, pressure, prevail *(persuade)*, prevail upon, promote *(organize)*, prompt, provocation, reason *(persuade)*, recommend, request, solicit, stimulus
urge against expostulate, forewarn, remonstrate
urge as a reason allege
urge forward compel, constrain *(compel)*, expedite, impel, precipitate *(hasten)*, press *(constrain)*
urge in court litigate
urge not to dissuade
urge on agitate *(activate)*, expedite, hasten, spirit
urge persistently pray
urge reasons for assert, defend, justify, plead *(argue a case)*
urge repeatedly pray
urge to take heed forewarn
urge upon offer *(propose)*, tender
urgency compulsion *(coercion)*, dispatch *(promptness)*, emergency, exigency, force *(compulsion)*, haste, importance, necessity, need *(requirement)*, pressure, priority, requirement, stress *(accent)*, stress *(strain)*
urgent compulsory, critical *(crucial)*, crucial, essential *(required)*, exigent, grave *(important)*, imperative, indispensable, insistent, mandatory, necessary *(required)*, obligatory, peremptory *(imperative)*, provocative, requisite, vehement, vital
urgent need exigency
urgent request prayer
urgent requirement necessity, need *(requirement)*
urger demagogue
urgere impel, press *(beseech)*, urge
urging impulsive *(impelling)*, inducement, influence, instigation, invitation
urging by force compulsion *(coercion)*
urging by moral constraint compulsion *(coercion)*
urging by physical constraint compulsion *(coercion)*
usability utility *(usefulness)*, utilization
usable applicable, available, beneficial, constructive *(creative)*, disposable, effective *(operative)*, eligible, functional, malleable, passable, ripe, viable
usage consumption, custom, function, management *(judicious use)*, manner *(behavior)*, means *(opportunity)*, mode, phraseology, practice *(custom)*, prescription *(custom)*, procedure, use
use apply *(put in practice)*, consumption, employ *(make use of)*, exert, exhaust *(deplete)*, expend *(consume)*, exploit *(make use of)*, exploitation, function, handle *(manage)*, help, impropriate, manipulate *(control unfairly)*, manipulate *(utilize skillfully)*, means *(opportunity)*, ownership, parlay *(exploit successfully)*, patronize *(trade with)*, ply, practice *(custom)*, prescription *(custom)*, profit, purpose, resort, spend, treat *(process)*, usage, utility *(usefulness)*, value, wield, worth
use and title patent

use another's services employ *(engage services)*
use arguments plead *(argue a case)*
use as an agent employ *(engage services)*
use badly exploit *(take advantage of)*, ill use
use carefully conserve
use dispiteously mishandle *(maltreat)*, mistreat, persecute
use evasions tergiversate
use false evidence frame *(prearrange)*
use for one's own needs bilk
use force upon coerce
use frugally conserve
use hard mistreat, tax *(overwork)*
use improperly abuse *(misuse)*, exploit *(take advantage of)*
use in support of propositions of law cite *(state)*
use of words parlance, phraseology
use one's authority police
use one's best endeavors attempt
use one's discretion choose
use one's imagination compose
use one's influence lobby
use one's option choose
use premises rent
use selfishly exploit *(take advantage of)*
use sparingly conserve
use subterfuge tergiversate
use threats threaten
use thriftily conserve
use trickery palter
use up consume, deplete, diminish, dissipate *(expend foolishly)*, exhaust *(deplete)*, expend *(consume)*, spend
use up available remedies exhaust *(try all possibilities)*
use violence force *(coerce)*
use wrongfully infringe
use wrongly abuse *(misuse)*, exploit *(take advantage of)*, ill use, misemploy, mishandle *(maltreat)*, mishandle *(mismanage)*, mistreat
useable operative, purposeful
used dilapidated, old, trite
used as a deterrent exemplary
used as a model exemplary
used as a specimen exemplary
used by all common *(shared)*
used to familiar *(informed)*
used up irredeemable
used with another thing appurtenant
useful applicable, beneficial, constructive *(creative)*, contributory, convenient, disposable, effective *(efficient)*, favorable *(advantageous)*, functional, gainful, instrumental, lucrative, ministerial, operative, potent, practical, pragmatic, productive, profitable, purposeful, salutary, subservient, valuable, viable
useful office service *(assistance)*
usefulness consequence *(significance)*, expedience, feasibility, importance, service *(assistance)*, use, utilization, value
useless disabled *(made incapable)*, expendable, futile, impracticable, inadequate, incapable, incompetent, ineffective, ineffectual, inept *(incompetent)*, invalid, needless, nugatory, null *(insignificant)*, null *(invalid)*, null and void, otiose, paltry, powerless, redundant, su-

perfluous, trivial, unable, unavailing, unfit, unproductive, unsatisfactory, void *(invalid)*
useless check bad check
useless consumption waste
useless expenditure misapplication
useless trial mistrial
user customer
usher conduct, harbinger, precursor
usher in herald, induct, initiate, introduce, originate, precede, preface, receive *(permit to enter)*
using through *(by means of)*
using evasion evasive
using the help of through *(by means of)*
using up consumption
usitatus current, customary, habitual
usuage enjoyment *(use)*
usual accustomed *(customary)*, average *(standard)*, common *(customary)*, conventional, customary, daily, familiar *(customary)*, frequent, general, habitual, household *(familiar)*, jejune *(dull)*, lifeless *(dull)*, mediocre, mundane, nondescript, normal *(regular)*, ordinary, orthodox, pedestrian, prescriptive, prevailing *(current)*, pro forma, prosaic, regular *(conventional)*, rife, routine, typical
usual custom matter of course, practice *(custom)*
usual manner custom
usual method practice *(custom)*
usual occurrence matter of course
usual practice matter of course
usual procedure habit, matter of course
usual thing matter of course
usual way practice *(procedure)*
usually as a rule, generally, invariably
usually understood common *(customary)*
usualness frequency
usufruct benefit *(betterment)*
usufructuary beneficiary
usura interest *(profit)*
usurious mercenary
usurp abridge *(divest)*, accroach, adopt, annex *(arrogate)*, assume *(seize)*, attach *(seize)*, condemn *(seize)*, depose *(remove)*, deprive, dislodge, impropriate, infringe, invade, levy, overstep, preempt, seize *(confiscate)*, steal, supplant, takeover, trespass
usurp for public use eminent domain
usurpation arrogation, assumption *(seizure)*, distress *(seizure)*, infringement
usurpatory confiscatory
usurped attached *(seized)*
usury exploitation
usus misuse, practice *(procedure)*, routine, use
usus perversus abuse *(corrupt practice)*, misapplication
utensil appliance, device *(mechanism)*, expedient, instrument *(tool)*, tool
utensils paraphernalia *(apparatus)*
utile functional
utilis beneficial, profitable, salutary
utilitarian beneficial, disposable, effective *(efficient)*, functional, practical, pragmatic, purposeful, subservient, val-

uable
utilitarianism casuistry
utilitas expedience, use
utility advantage, appliance, behalf, benefit *(betterment)*, expedience, feasibility, function, help, instrument *(tool)*, profit, propriety *(appropriateness)*, use, value, worth
utilizable applicable, disposable, functional, practical
utilization benefit *(betterment)*, consumption, enjoyment *(use)*, exploitation, management *(judicious use)*, usage, use
utilization for profit exploitation
utilize adopt, apply *(put in practice)*, capitalize *(seize the chance)*, consume, employ *(make use of)*, exercise *(use)*, exert, exploit *(make use of)*, manipulate *(utilize skillfully)*, ply, profit, resort, wield
utilize for profit bilk, capitalize *(seize the chance)*
utmost cardinal *(basic)*, cardinal *(outstanding)*, ceiling, extreme *(last)*, maximum *(amplitude)*, primary, prime *(most valuable)*, superlative
utmost care diligence *(care)*
utmost extent ceiling, pinnacle
utmost height ceiling, culmination, pinnacle
utmost point extremity *(furthest point)*
utopian quixotic
utter absolute *(complete)*, arrant *(definite)*, comment, communicate, complete *(all-embracing)*, confess, converse, declare, disclose, disseminate, enunciate, express, gross *(flagrant)*, mention, observe *(remark)*, outright, phrase, proclaim, profess *(avow)*, pronounce *(speak)*, publish, pure, recite, relate *(tell)*, remark, reveal, speak, stark, thorough, total, unconditional, unequivocal, unmitigated, unqualified *(unlimited)*
utter a falsehood bear false witness, misrepresent, palter, perjure
utter again repeat *(state again)*
utter an oath swear
utter contempt disdain
utter disapproval denunciation
utter force main force
utter formally pronounce *(pass judgment)*, pronounce *(speak)*
utter forth pronounce *(speak)*, speak
utter invective inveigh
utter judicial sentence pronounce *(pass judgment)*
utter judicial sentence against convict, determine
utter reliability certification *(certainness)*
utter with conviction certify *(attest)*, claim *(maintain)*, contend *(maintain)*, issue *(publish)*, posit, speak
utter words speak
utterance comment, communication *(statement)*, confession, disclosure *(something disclosed)*, observation, parlance, phrase, pronouncement, publicity, remark, speech, statement
uttered nuncupative, oral, parol, stated, verbal
uttered with conviction alleged
uttering disclosure *(act of disclosing)*

utterly in toto, purely *(positively)*, wholly
utterly disperse dispel
utterly illogical irrational
utterly overlook ignore
utterly senseless non compos mentis
uttermost ceiling, extreme *(last)*

V

vacancy access *(opening)*, blank *(emptiness)*
vacant available, barren, devoid, idle, inexpressive, thoughtless, vacuous, void *(empty)*
vacate abolish, abrogate *(rescind)*, adeem, avoid *(cancel)*, cancel, cease, depart, disappear, discontinue *(abandon)*, dismiss *(discharge)*, disown *(deny the validity)*, evacuate, leave *(depart)*, move *(alter position)*, negate, nullify, quash, quit *(evacuate)*, recant, relinquish, renege, repeal, rescind, resign, retire *(conclude a career)*, retire *(retreat)*, retreat, revoke, secede, withdraw
vacate office abandon *(withdraw)*, demit
vacate one's seat demit
vacated null *(invalid)*, null and void, open *(accessible)*
vacating abandonment *(desertion)*, abdication, avoidance *(cancellation)*
vacatio exemption, immunity
vacation abdication, abolition, ademption, avoidance *(cancellation)*, cancellation, countermand, defeasance, furlough, holiday, leave *(absence)*, pause, recess, recess, resignation *(relinquishment)*
vacatur ademption, cancellation, revocation
vaccinate inject
vacillant irresolute
vacillare vacillate
vacillate alternate *(fluctuate)*, beat *(pulsate)*, doubt *(hesitate)*, hesitate, oscillate, pause, tergiversate, vary
vacillating capricious, dubious, faithless, hesitant, inconsistent, irresolute, irresponsible, moving *(in motion)*, mutable, noncommittal, shifting, undecided, undependable, unreliable, unsettled, volatile
vacillation ambivalence, doubt *(indecision)*, hesitation, incertitude, inconsistency, indecision
vacillatory irresolute, undecided
vacuefacere vacate *(leave)*
vacuitas exemption
vacuity nullity, opacity
vacuous barren, devoid, fatuous, inexpressive, jejune *(dull)*, opaque, thoughtless, vacant, void *(empty)*
vacuousness blank *(emptiness)*
vacuum blank *(emptiness)*, need *(deprivation)*
vacuus blank *(emptiness)*, free *(relieved from a burden)*, idle, unemployed, vacant, void *(empty)*
vadimonium guarantee
vadimonium deserere default
vadium promise, security *(pledge)*
vadium mortuum charge *(lien)*, cloud *(incumbrance)*
vadium vivum charge *(lien)*
vafer sly

vagabond moving *(in motion)*
vagabondage vagrancy
vagabondism vagrancy
vagari err, prowl
vagarious capricious
vagary notion, quirk *(idiosyncrasy)*
vagrant derelict, indirect, moving *(in motion)*, variable
vague allusive, ambiguous, broad, debatable, disputable, dubious, equivocal, evasive, impalpable, imponderable, inapprehensible, inarticulate, incomprehensible, inconspicuous, indefinite, indeterminate, indistinct, inexact, inexpressive, inscrutable, insubstantial, intangible, nebulous, noncommittal, oblique *(evasive)*, obscure *(faint)*, opaque, open-ended, problematic, uncertain *(ambiguous)*, unclear, undecided, undefinable, unspecified
vague impression hint
vague suggestion hint
vagueness ambiguity, confusion *(ambiguity)*, doubt *(indecision)*, ignorance, incertitude, indistinctness, obscuration, opacity
vagus discursive *(digressive)*
vail largess *(gift)*
vain baseless, futile, ineffective, ineffectual, invalid, nugatory, orgulous, otiose, presumptuous, pretentious *(pompous)*, proud *(conceited)*, unavailing
vain attempt abortion *(fiasco)*, failure *(lack of success)*, miscarriage
vain effort abortion *(fiasco)*, miscarriage
vain pretensions pride
vainglorious grandiose, inflated *(bombastic)*, orgulous, orotund, pretentious *(pompous)*, proud *(conceited)*, supercilious
vainglorious boasting rodomontade
vainglory bombast, jactation, pride, rodomontade
valens strong
valere avail *(be of use)*
valetudo health
valiancy prowess *(bravery)*
valiant heroic, indomitable, spartan, undaunted
valid accurate, actual, adequate, allowed, authentic, certain *(positive)*, cogent, convincing, de facto, deductible *(provable)*, demonstrable, documentary, effective *(efficient)*, effective *(operative)*, factual, genuine, honest, lawful, legal, legitimate *(rightful)*, licit, official, operative, persuasive, potent, real, reasonable *(rational)*, right *(correct)*, right *(suitable)*, rightful, solid *(sound)*, substantial, suitable, true *(authentic)*, unrefutable, viable
valid notice adequate notice
valid potentiality force *(legal efficacy)*
validate accredit, affirm *(uphold)*, approve, attest, authorize, bear *(adduce)*, certify *(approve)*, certify *(attest)*, confirm, constitute *(establish)*, corroborate, cosign, demonstrate *(establish)*, document, endorse, establish *(show)*, formalize, indorse, legalize, legitimate, notarize, pass *(approve)*, prove, quote, sanction, seal *(solemnize)*, sign, substantiate, support *(corroborate)*, sustain *(confirm)*, verify *(confirm)*, witness *(at-*

test to)
validate a will probate
validated allowed, choate lien
validation acknowledgment *(avowal)*, affirmance *(authentication)*, affirmation, approval, avowal, certification *(attested copy)*, confirmation, consent, corroboration, documentation, evidence, legalization, ratification, sanction *(permission)*, stamp, subscription, support *(corroboration)*
validation of a testament probate
validification attestation, corroboration, reference *(recommendation)*
validity honesty, legality, legitimacy, quality *(excellence)*, strength, weight *(credibility)*
validity proceedings probate
validly admittedly
validus compelling
valor prowess *(bravery)*
valorization ad valorem, rating
valorize calculate, gauge
valorous heroic, spartan, undaunted
valorousness prowess *(bravery)*
valuable beneficial, chattel, considerable, constructive *(creative)*, crucial, functional, gainful, important *(significant)*, inestimable, instrumental, invaluable, lucrative, material *(important)*, meritorious, possession *(property)*, practical, priceless, productive, profitable, purposeful, sterling, subservient
valuables assets, estate *(property)*, property *(possessions)*
valuate assess *(appraise)*, calculate, gauge
valuation account *(evaluation)*, appraisal, appreciation *(perception)*, assessment *(estimation)*, census, charge *(cost)*, computation, conclusion *(determination)*, cost *(price)*, estimate *(approximate cost)*, estimation *(calculation)*, expense *(cost)*, idea, measurement, par *(face amount)*, price, rate, rating, regard *(esteem)*, value, worth
value amount *(sum)*, assess *(appraise)*, calculate, caliber *(quality)*, charge *(cost)*, charge *(assess)*, cost *(price)*, criticize *(evaluate)*, degree *(magnitude)*, emphasis, estimate *(approximate cost)*, estimate, evaluate, expense *(cost)*, gauge, honor, importance, judge, magnitude, materiality *(consequence)*, measure, merit, par *(face amount)*, prefer, price, quality *(excellence)*, rate, rate, recommend, regard *(esteem)*, regard *(hold in esteem)*, significance, signification, utility *(usefulness)*, weight *(importance)*, worth
value added tax ad valorem
value in exchange par *(face amount)*
value incorrectly misconceive
value received income, proceeds, profit
valued at ad valorem
valueless barren, expendable, futile, needless, negligible, nugatory, null *(insignificant)*, null *(invalid)*, null and void, otiose, paltry, poor *(inferior in quality)*, unavailing, unfit
valueless check bad check
values ethics
vamp modify *(alter)*, repair
vandalism defacement, pillage
vandalize damage

vandimonium deserere default
vanguard forerunner, pioneer, precursor
vanish depart, disappear, dissipate *(spread out)*, evacuate, expire, leave *(depart)*, perish, quit *(evacuate)*
vanished defunct, irretrievable, lost *(taken away)*
vanishing elusive, ephemeral, transient
vanishment nonappearance
vanitas nullity
vanity jactation, pride
vanload cargo
vanquish beat *(defeat)*, defeat, demean *(make lower)*, foil, humiliate, kill *(defeat)*, overcome *(surmount)*, overturn, overwhelm, repress, restrain, subdue, subject, subjugate, succeed *(attain)*, suppress, surmount, upset
vanquishment defeat, prostration
vantage edge *(advantage)*, leverage
vantage point perspective, stand *(position)*, standpoint
vanus delusive, fallacious, futile, illusory, unavailing, unfounded, void *(invalid)*
vapid insipid, jejune *(dull)*, languid, lifeless *(dull)*, prosaic, stale
vapid expression platitude
vapidity opacity
vapor phantom
vaporable volatile
vaporing inflated *(vain)*, rodomontade
vaporizable volatile
vaporize disappear
vaporize and condense distill
vaporous immaterial, volatile
variability deviation, diversity, irregularity
variable aleatory *(uncertain)*, ambulatory, atypical, broken *(interrupted)*, capricious, faithless, inconsistent, mutable, open-ended, periodic, pliable, protean, sporadic, undependable, unpredictable, untrustworthy
variableness irregularity
variance alienation *(estrangement)*, argument *(contention)*, conflict, contest *(dispute)*, contradiction, contravention, controversy *(argument)*, deviation, difference, digression, disaccord, disagreement, discord, discrepancy, disparity, dispute, dissent *(difference of opinion)*, dissent *(nonconcurrence)*, dissidence, distinction *(difference)*, estrangement, feud, fight *(argument)*, incompatibility *(difference)*, incompatibility *(inconsistency)*, incongruity, inconsistency, inequality, nonconformity, nuance, rift *(disagreement)*, split, strife
variant deviant, different, differential, discordant, distinction *(difference)*, divergent, diverse, heterogeneous, peculiar *(distinctive)*, variable
variare vary
variation deviation, difference, digression, discrepancy, disparity, distinction *(difference)*, diversification, diversity, inequality, innovation, irregularity, modification, nonconformity
variations vicissitudes
varied complex, composite, compound, conglomerate, different, disparate, dissimilar, diverse, heterogeneous, miscellaneous, multifarious, multifold, multi-

ple
variegate alter, change, vary
variegated composite, compound, dissimilar, diverse, heterogeneous, manifold, miscellaneous, multifarious, multifold, promiscuous
variegation difference, diversity
varietal different
varietas difference
variety class, color *(complexion)*, denomination, difference, diversity, kind, manner *(kind)*, nonconformity, selection *(collection)*
variety store market *(business)*
variform dissimilar, heterogeneous, miscellaneous, multifold
various different, dissimilar, diverse, heterogeneous, manifold, miscellaneous, multifarious, multiple
variously called alias
variously known as alias
variousness diversity
varius discursive *(digressive)*, manifold, miscellaneous, multifarious, unsettled
varnish embellish, invent *(falsify)*, mislead, slant
varnished mendacious
vary alter, alternate *(fluctuate)*, change, collide *(clash)*, conflict, convert *(change use)*, detour, deviate, differ *(vary)*, disaccord, disagree, fluctuate, modify *(alter)*, oscillate, replace, transform
vary from depart
varying desultory, different, dissenting, divergent, diverse, heterogeneous, protean, shifting
vassal dependent
vassalage thrall
vast capacious, extensive, far reaching, general, inclusive, prodigious *(enormous)*, unlimited
vastatio havoc
vastness degree *(magnitude)*, gamut, magnitude, measurement, space
vasty capacious
vatic ominous, oracular, prophetic
vaticinal foreseeable, ominous, oracular, prophetic
vaticinari predict
vaticinate anticipate *(prognosticate)*, forewarn, portend, predict, presage, prognosticate
vaticination prognosis
vault bank, coffer, depository, surmount, treasury
vaunt jactation
vauntful inflated *(vain)*
vaunting orgulous
vecordia insanity
vectigal duty *(tax)*, income, revenue, tax, toll *(tax)*
vectura fare
veer detour, deviate, digress, divert, slant, vary
vegatating lifeless *(dull)*
vegetate germinate, languish, pullulate
vegetating insensible
vegetation inaction, inertia, languor
vegetative inactive, lifeless *(dull)*
vehemence force *(compulsion)*, outburst, passion, violence
vehemens compelling
vehement categorical, demonstrative

(expressive of emotion), eager, fervent, forcible, hot-blooded, incisive, insistent, intense, intensive, powerful
vehement condemnation denunciation
vehement desire passion
vehement speech harangue
vehicle expedient, forum *(medium)*, go-between, instrument *(tool)*, instrumentality, interagent, intermediary, medium, tool
vehicle for escape loophole
vehiculum carriage
veil blind *(obscure)*, camouflage, cloak, conceal, cover *(conceal)*, disguise, ensconce, enshroud, envelop, hide, obfuscate, obnubilate, obscure, plant *(covertly place)*, protect, screen *(guard)*, shroud, suppress
veil the brightness blind *(obscure)*
veiled allusive, clandestine, covert, enigmatic, equivocal, esoteric, furtive, hidden, impalpable, inconspicuous, indiscernible, latent, mysterious, oblique *(evasive)*, obscure *(faint)*, personal *(private)*, secret, stealthy, surreptitious
veiled information secret
veiled observation insinuation
veiled remark insinuation
vein phraseology, tenor
velare cover *(pretext)*, cover *(conceal)*, shroud
velitation confrontation *(altercation)*, contention *(opposition)*
velleity will *(desire)*
vellicare cavil
velocity haste, rate
velox rapid
venal bad *(offensive)*, blameful, blameworthy, lawless, machiavellian, mercenary, penurious, unjust
venalis marketable, mercenary, venal
venality bad faith, bad repute, bribery, corruption, disloyalty
venari hunt
vend barter, handle *(trade)*, sell
vendee consumer, customer, patron *(regular customer)*
vendere sell
vendetta feud, rancor, reprisal, revenge, vengeance
vendible item, marketable, negotiable
vendibles commodities, goods, merchandise, stock in trade
venditation jactation
vendition sale
vendor dealer, merchant
vendor of stolen goods fence
vendor of stolen property fence
vendue auction
veneer cover *(protection)*, disguise
venemous malicious, scathing, spiteful
venerable antique, outstanding *(prominent)*, popular, sacrosanct, solemn
venerate defer *(yield in judgment)*, honor, regard *(hold in esteem)*
venerated reputable, sacrosanct
venerating obedient
veneration estimation *(esteem)*, fealty, homage, honor *(outward respect)*, interest *(concern)*, regard *(esteem)*, respect
vengeance punishment, rancor, reprisal, retribution, revenge, spite

vengeful resentful, ruthless, vindictive

vengefulness rancor, reprisal, resentment, retribution, revenge, vengeance

venia amnesty, indulgence, pardon, remission

venial allowable

venom malice, odium, rancor, resentment, severity, spite

venomous bitter *(penetrating)*, bitter *(reproachful)*, caustic, dangerous, deadly, deleterious, fatal, harmful, insalubrious, lethal, malevolent, malignant, peccant *(unhealthy)*, pejorative, pernicious, perverse, pestilent, resentful, ruthless, sinister, toxic, vicious, virulent

venomousness rancor

vent bare, convey *(communicate)*, denude, disabuse, disclose, expose, express, exude, outlet, outpour, promulgate, propagate *(spread)*, relate *(tell)*, reveal, signify *(inform)*, spread, utter

ventilate bare, circulate, consult *(ask advice of)*, proclaim, propagate *(spread)*, publish, relate *(tell)*

ventilate a question reason *(persuade)*

ventilated public *(known)*

ventilation catharsis, publicity, report *(detailed account)*

venture activity, attempt, bet, business *(commercial enterprise)*, compromise *(endanger)*, embark, endeavor, endeavor, enterprise *(undertaking)*, experience *(encounter)*, experiment, invest *(fund)*, investment, livelihood, mission, occupation *(vocation)*, occurrence, offer *(propose)*, operation, parlay *(bet)*, presume, project, pursuit *(effort to secure)*, pursuit *(occupation)*, risk, speculate *(chance)*, speculate *(conjecture)*, speculation *(risk)*, strive, try *(attempt)*, undertake, undertaking *(business)*, undertaking *(enterprise)*

venture a conjecture postulate

venture a supposition postulate

venture capital capitalize *(provide capital)*

venture on commence

venture upon assume *(undertake)*

venturer bettor, speculator

ventures business *(commerce)*

venturesome aleatory *(perilous)*, hotblooded, imprudent, impulsive *(rash)*, insecure, resourceful

venturesomeness temerity

venturous aleatory *(perilous)*, imprudent, impulsive *(rash)*, insecure

venue locality

venustus felicitous

veracious accurate, actual, bona fide, candid, certain *(positive)*, clean, credible, demonstrable, dependable, direct *(forthright)*, documentary, factual, honest, incontrovertible, ingenuous, literal, real, realistic, reliable, right *(correct)*, sound, straightforward, strict, true *(authentic)*, undistorted, unrefutable, upright, veridical

veraciously faithfully

veraciousness honesty, probity, veracity

veracity credibility, honesty, probity, reality, rectitude, truth, validity

verbal loquacious, nuncupative, oral, parol

verbal abuse malediction, obloquy, phillipic, revilement

verbal assault barrage, malediction

verbal attack malediction, vilification

verbal communication discourse

verbal conflict argument *(contention)*

verbal contention contest *(dispute)*, dispute

verbal contest fight *(argument)*

verbal controversy dispute

verbal engagement contest *(dispute)*, dispute

verbal evidence affirmance *(legal affirmation)*

verbal exposition discourse

verbal expression speech

verbal intercourse conversation, discourse, interview, language, parlance, parley, speech

verbal onslaught diatribe

verbal portraiture delineation

verbalism expression *(comment)*, term *(expression)*

verbalize communicate, enunciate, express, phrase, pronounce *(speak)*, relate *(tell)*, remark

verbatim accurate, exact, faithfully, literal

verberare beat *(strike)*, lash *(strike)*

verbiage bombast, fustian, language, prattle, prolixity, tautology

verbose flatulent, inflated *(bombastic)*, loquacious, profuse, prolific, prolix, redundant, voluble

verbosity fustian, prolixity, tautology

verbosus loquacious, prolix

verbum expression *(comment)*, term *(expression)*, verbal

verdant inexperienced

verdict adjudication, answer *(solution)*, award, conclusion *(determination)*, consequence *(conclusion)*, conviction *(finding of guilt)*, decision *(judgment)*, decree, determination, finding, holding *(ruling of a court)*, result, ruling, sentence

verdict after judicial inquiry finding

verdict of not guilty acquittal, compurgation

verecunde respectfully

verecundia homage

verecundus diffident

vereri fear

verge border, border *(approach)*, boundary, dispose *(incline)*, edge *(border)*, extremity *(furthest point)*, limit, margin *(outside limit)*, outline *(boundary)*, periphery, side

verge on abut, approach, connect *(join together)*

verge upon border *(approach)*, contact *(touch)*

verging contiguous, immediate *(not distant)*, proximate

verging on adjacent

veri similis probable

veri similitudo likelihood, probability

veridical bona fide, candid, cogent, direct *(forthright)*, factual, genuine, honest, reliable, straightforward, true *(authentic)*

veridicality honesty, integrity, veracity

verifiability corroboration

verifiable accurate, ascertainable, authentic, certain *(positive)*, deductible *(provable)*, determinable *(ascertainable)*, indubious, provable, tangible, true *(authentic)*, veridical

verifiable excuse alibi

verifiable happening fact

verification acknowledgment *(acceptance)*, affirmance *(authentication)*, affirmation, approval, attestation, avowal, certainty, certification *(attested copy)*, confirmation, consent, corroboration, document, documentation, evidence, experiment, jurat, proof, reference *(recommendation)*, support *(corroboration)*

verificative demonstrative *(illustrative)*, probative

verificative excuse alibi

verificatory provable

verified official

verify affirm *(uphold)*, ascertain, assure *(insure)*, attest, avouch *(guarantee)*, bear *(adduce)*, certify *(attest)*, check *(inspect)*, confirm, corroborate, demonstrate *(establish)*, depose *(testify)*, document, ensure, establish *(show)*, evidence, find *(discover)*, identify, prove, quote, recognize *(perceive)*, reveal, seal *(solemnize)*, substantiate, support *(corroborate)*, sustain *(confirm)*, testify, validate, witness *(attest to)*

verify a testament probate

verify again reconfirm

verifying convincing, demonstrative *(illustrative)*

verifying statement jurat

verisimilar believable, circumstantial, credible, probable

verisimilis colorable *(plausible)*, plausible

verisimilitude credibility, probability

verisimilous probable

veritable absolute *(conclusive)*, actual, authentic, candid, de facto, definite, documentary, genuine, honest, real, sound, true *(authentic)*, unrefutable, valid

veritably admittedly

veritas reality, truth, veracity

verity honesty, reality, truth, validity, veracity

vermicular tortuous *(bending)*

vermiculate tortuous *(bending)*

vermiculated tortuous *(bending)*

vernacular language, native *(domestic)*, ordinary, prevailing *(current)*, prevalent, regional, usual

vernal juvenile

vernile servile

versant learned

versari employ *(engage services)*

versari in re concern *(involve)*

versatile artful, mutable, pliable, protean, resourceful

versatility ability, amenability

verse maker author *(writer)*

versed cognizant, competent, expert, familiar *(informed)*, informed *(educated)*, learned, qualified *(competent)*

version construction, paraphrase

versus contra

versus contra

versutus artful

vertex ceiling, crossroad *(intersection)*

verus actual, authentic, candid, essential *(required)*, real, right *(righteousness)*, sterling, true *(authentic)*

verve ardor, emotion, life *(vitality)*, passion, spirit

very stark

very fine impalpable, premium

very thorough complete *(all-embracing)*

vesanus frenetic

vesicate burn

vest admit *(give access)*, bestow, dedicate, empower

vest in bequeath, commit *(entrust)*, delegate, repose *(place)*

vest with a title authorize

vested immutable, prescriptive

vested interest birthright, claim *(right)*, equity *(share of ownership)*, prescription *(claim of title)*, right *(entitlement)*, title *(right)*

vested interest in land fee *(estate)*, freehold

vested right birthright, charter *(sanction)*, droit, due, prerogative, prescription *(claim of title)*

vestibule entrance

vestigium indication

vestire clothe

vestis mutata disguise

vetare condemn *(ban)*, disallow, forbid

veteran expert, expert, practiced, specialist

vetitus felonious, illegal, illicit, unlawful

veto ban, countermand, debar, decline *(reject)*, disapproval, disapprove *(reject)*, disavow, exclude, forbid, forestall, inhibit, interdict, negate, nonconformity, prevent, prohibit, prohibition, protest, refusal, refuse, reject, rejection, renunciation, repudiation, restraint, restrict, stem *(check)*

vetoed impermissible

vetus old, stale

vetustus old

vex affront, aggravate *(annoy)*, annoy, badger, bait *(harass)*, discommode, discompose, distress, disturb, embarrass, harass, harrow, harry *(harass)*, hector, incense, inconvenience, irritate, mistreat, molest *(annoy)*, obsess, offend *(insult)*, perplex, perturb, pique, plague, press *(goad)*, provoke, repel *(disgust)*

vexare harass, harrow, harry *(harass)*, molest *(annoy)*, persecute, pique, plague

vexatio molestation, oppression

vexation burden, damage, dissatisfaction, distress *(anguish)*, grievance, molestation, nuisance, provocation

vexatious invidious, operose, oppressive, perverse, provocative

vexed aggrieved *(harmed)*, bitter *(reproachful)*

vexed question dilemma, problem

vexing provocative, unsatisfactory

via direction *(course)*, facility *(instrumentality)*, method, mode

via through *(from beginning to end)*

viability feasibility, possibility

viable live *(conscious)*, permissible, possible, virtual

viableness possibility

vibrant strong

vibrare brandish

vibrate beat *(pulsate)*, vacillate

vicar deputy, proctor, spokesman

vicarial surrogate

vicarious derivative, secondary, surrogate

vicarius deputy, proxy, representative *(proxy)*, surrogate

vice bad repute, flaw, foible, guilt, mens rea, mischief, misdoing, sodomy, wrong

vice versa contra, contrary

vice-ridden profane, profligate *(corrupt)*

vicegerent deputy

viceregent procurator

viceroy plenipotentiary

vicinage area *(province)*, locality, location, propinquity *(proximity)*, region, section *(vicinity)*

vicinal adjacent, close *(near)*, present *(attendant)*, proximate

vicinitas section *(vicinity)*

vicinity area *(province)*, locality, location, region, site

vicinus adjacent

vicious bad *(offensive)*, brutal, cruel, dangerous, delinquent *(guilty of a misdeed)*, diabolic, harmful, heinous, hostile, inexcusable, inexpiable, iniquitous, malevolent, malicious, malignant, noxious, peccant *(culpable)*, pernicious, profligate *(corrupt)*, reprehensible, reprobate, ruthless, severe, spiteful, tainted *(corrupted)*, unjustifiable, unscrupulous

viciousness bestiality, cruelty, delinquency *(misconduct)*, guilt, malice, spite

vicissitudes circumstances

vicissitudinous unpredictable

vicissitudo reciprocity

vicitimize ill use

victim cadaver, captive, corpse, patient, subject *(object)*

victima victim

victimization abuse *(physical misuse)*, atrocity, bunko, cruelty, oppression

victimize bait *(harass)*, betray *(lead astray)*, bilk, deceive, defeat, dupe, endanger, ensnare, exploit *(take advantage of)*, extort, harass, illude, inveigle, mishandle *(maltreat)*, mistreat, palter, persecute, prey, slay

victorious prevailing *(having superior force)*, successful

victory supremacy

victual nurture, supply

victualer supplier

victuals sustenance

victus livelihood, maintenance *(support of spouse)*, sustenance

videlicet a savoir

videor apparent *(perceptible)*

videre witness *(have direct knowledge of)*

videri appear *(seem to be)*

vie strive

vie for endeavor

vie with compete, contend *(dispute)*, contest, fight *(battle)*, grapple

view advice, apprehend *(perceive)*, apprehension *(perception)*, aspect, assumption *(supposition)*, complexion, concept, conclusion *(determination)*, conviction *(persuasion)*, coverage *(scope)*, credence, design *(intent)*, de-

tect, discern *(detect with the senses)*, estimate *(idea)*, idea, intent, notice *(observe)*, notion, observation, observe *(watch)*, opine, opinion *(belief)*, perception, perspective, pierce *(discern)*, platform, position *(point of view)*, posture *(attitude)*, purview, reaction *(response)*, recognize *(perceive)*, regard *(pay attention)*, scene, scrutinize, side, spy, stand *(position)*, standpoint, study, surmise, survey *(examine)*, suspect *(think)*, theory, witness *(have direct knowledge of)*

view as deem

view from all sides ponder

view retrospectively review

view with a scornful eye disdain, flout

view with deliberation ponder

view with disfavor censure, deprecate, disapprove *(condemn)*, discommend, disfavor, expostulate

view with dissatisfaction resent

view with favor countenance

view with regret deplore

viewable apparent *(perceptible)*, discernible, perceivable, perceptible, visible *(in full view)*

viewer bystander, eyewitness

viewership bystander

viewless inconspicuous

viewpoint aspect, conviction *(persuasion)*, idea, opinion *(belief)*, outlook, perception, perspective, position *(point of view)*, posture *(attitude)*, side, stand *(position)*, standpoint

vigil notice *(heed)*, precaution, surveillance

vigilance diligence *(care)*, notice *(heed)*, precaution, prudence, regard *(attention)*, surveillance, ward

vigilans vigilant

vigilant careful, circumspect, conscious *(aware)*, discreet, guarded, leery, meticulous, protective, provident *(showing foresight)*

vigilence diligence *(perseverance)*

vignette brief

vigor ardor, diligence *(perseverance)*, dint, effort, force *(strength)*, health, industry *(activity)*, life *(vitality)*, main force, prowess *(bravery)*, puissance, sinew, spirit, strength

vigorless powerless

vigorous active, compelling, forcible, indomitable, intense, intensive, irresistible, potent, powerful, resolute, resounding, strong, trenchant

vigorous enunciation emphasis

vigorously effective drastic

vigorousness ardor, effort, force *(strength)*, sinew

vile arrant *(onerous)*, bad *(offensive)*, blameful, caitiff, contemptible, contemptuous, deplorable, depraved, disgraceful, heinous, ignoble, iniquitous, loathsome, machiavellian, malignant, nefarious, objectionable, obnoxious, obscene, odious, offensive *(offending)*, paltry, peccant *(culpable)*, profligate *(corrupt)*, reprobate, repulsive, scurrilous, vicious

vileness delinquency *(misconduct)*, dishonor *(shame)*, disrepute, obscenity, shame, turpitude, vice

vilification aspersion, bad repute, condemnation *(blame)*, contumely, denunciation, diatribe, dishonor *(shame)*, disparagement, disrespect, impeachment, imprecation, libel, malediction, obloquy, opprobrium, outcry, phillipic, profanity, reproach, revilement, scandal, slander

vilify brand *(stigmatize)*, condemn *(blame)*, contemn, decry, defame, denigrate, denounce *(condemn)*, derogate, discommend, dishonor *(deprive of honor)*, disparage, humiliate, inveigh, lash *(attack verbally)*, lessen, libel, malign, pillory, reprimand, reproach, smear, sully, tarnish

vilifying calumnious, libelous, pejorative

vilipend blame, brand *(stigmatize)*, censure, contemn, decry, defame, denigrate, denounce *(condemn)*, deprecate, derogate, disapprove *(condemn)*, discommend, disoblige, disparage, lash *(attack verbally)*, lessen, malign, reprimand, reproach, smear, sully

vilipendency bad repute, disapprobation, disparagement, disrespect

vilis paltry

villa estate *(property)*

villager habitant, resident

villain convict, criminal, hoodlum, malefactor, wrongdoer

villainous bad *(offensive)*, contemptible, delinquent *(guilty of a misdeed)*, felonious, heinous, inexpiable, iniquitous, malevolent, malignant, nefarious, notorious, obnoxious, outrageous, peccant *(culpable)*, recreant, reprehensible, sinister, unscrupulous, vicious

villainousness corruption, delinquency *(misconduct)*, knavery

villainy atrocity, corruption, delinquency *(misconduct)*, knavery, mischief, misdeed, misdoing, wrong

vim industry *(activity)*, life *(vitality)*, spirit

vincere beat *(defeat)*, defeat, establish *(show)*, outweigh, overrule, predominate *(command)*, prevail *(triumph)*

vincibility danger

vincible disabled *(made incapable)*, helpless *(defenseless)*, inadequate, indefensible, penetrable, powerless, untenable, vulnerable

vincibleness danger

vincula fetter, incarceration

vincula ties

vinculo matrimonii cohabitation *(married state)*

vinculum chain *(series)*, fetter

vinculum nexus

vindicable defensible, justifiable, pardonable, tenable, unobjectionable

vindicate absolve, acquit, bear *(adduce)*, bear *(support)*, clear, condone, exculpate, excuse, exonerate, extenuate, forgive, free, justify, liberate, maintain *(sustain)*, palliate *(excuse)*, pardon, rationalize, remit *(release from penalty)*, substantiate, support *(corroborate)*, support *(justify)*, sustain *(confirm)*, uphold

vindicate a right claim *(demand)*

vindicate a title claim *(demand)*

vindicate from unjust reproach exculpate

vindicated acquitted, blameless, clear *(free from criminal charges)*

vindicating palliative *(excusing)*

vindicatio assertion

vindication absolution, acquittal, advocacy, compurgation, condonation, corroboration, exoneration, indemnity, justification, liberation, pardon, reason *(basis)*, support *(corroboration)*

vindicative palliative *(excusing)*

vindicator proponent

vindicatory defensible, palliative *(excusing)*, vindictive

vindicta revenge, vengeance

vindictive implacable, malevolent, malicious, malignant, punitive, relentless, resentful, ruthless, severe, spiteful

vindictive oath imprecation

vindictiveness rancor, reprisal, resentment, retribution, revenge, spite, vengeance

vinegarish bitter *(acrid tasting)*

vintage age, old

violare infringe, offend *(violate the law)*, violate

violate betray *(lead astray)*, contravene, damage, debauch, disobey, encroach, endanger, impinge, impose *(intrude)*, infringe, invade, misemploy, mishandle *(maltreat)*, mistreat, molest *(subject to indecent advances)*, overstep, pollute, taint *(corrupt)*, trespass

violate a confidence betray *(disclose)*, inform *(betray)*

violate a contract infringe

violate a law infringe

violate a privilege infringe

violate a regulation infringe

violate one's oath defect

violate rules mismanage

violate the confidence of inform *(betray)*

violate the truth falsify

violated broken *(unfulfilled)*

violating disobedient

violatio infraction, infringement

violation abuse *(corrupt practice)*, abuse *(physical misuse)*, breach, contravention, debauchment, defilement, delict, delinquency *(misconduct)*, disregard *(omission)*, encroachment, guilt, incursion, infraction, infringement, invasion, irregularity, misdeed, misdoing, misprision, misusage, misuse, offense, perversion, rape, rebellion, sedition, transgression, wrong

violation of a contract infringement

violation of a duty delict

violation of a law infringement

violation of a legal duty tort

violation of a privilege infringement

violation of a regulation infringement

violation of allegiance bad faith, disloyalty, treason

violation of an oath perjury

violation of another's rights assault

violation of duty bad faith, default

violation of law breach, crime, felony, guilt, infraction, misdemeanor, misfeasance, offense

violation of oath infidelity

violation of orders contempt *(disobedience to the court)*, infraction, offense

violation of professional code malpractice

violation of professional duty malpractice

violation of right injustice, wrong

violation of the law illegality

violation of the marriage vows adultery

violation of trust dishonesty, disloyalty

violative broken *(unfulfilled)*, disobedient, lawless

violator aggressor, assailant, offender

violator of laws malefactor

violator of the law outlaw

violence affray, belligerency, brutality, commotion, cruelty, embroilment, havoc, infliction, infringement, injury, outburst, passion, severity, strife

violent brutal, demonstrative *(expressive of emotion)*, disorderly, drastic, extreme *(exaggerated)*, forcible, hot-blooded, malignant, pernicious, pestilent, precipitate, severe, strong, uncontrollable, vehement, virulent

violent anger passion

violent animosity malice

violent behavior outbreak

violent change revolution

violent contact collision *(accident)*

violent death fatality, homicide, killing, murder

violent disagreement dissension

violent separation avulsion

violent upheaval cataclysm

violentia violence

viperine dangerous

viperous dangerous, malevolent, spiteful

vires ability, strength

virgin unadulterated

virile potent, spartan, strong

virility strength

virtual constructive *(inferential)*

virtue caliber *(quality)*, ethics, honesty, honor *(good reputation)*, integrity, merit, probity, rectitude, right *(righteousness)*, veracity

virtueless bad *(offensive)*, base *(bad)*, delinquent *(guilty of a misdeed)*, diabolic, inexpiable, peccable, profane, salacious

virtuosity performance *(workmanship)*, prowess *(ability)*, specialty *(special aptitude)*

virtuoso expert, specialist

virtuous blameless, clean, conscientious, ethical, evenhanded, high-minded, incorruptible, inculpable, innocent, innocuous, irreprehensible, just, laudable, law-abiding, meritorious, moral, proper, pure, reputable, right *(correct)*, right *(suitable)*, sterling, upright

virtuous conduct ethics

virtuously faithfully

virtuousness ethics, integrity, principle *(virtue)*

virtus merit, prowess *(bravery)*, worth

virulence fatality, force *(strength)*, harm, rancor, severity, spite

virulency fatality, spite

virulent antipathetic *(distasteful)*, bitter *(penetrating)*, caustic, chronic, dangerous, deleterious, fatal, harsh, insalubrious, lethal, malevolent, malicious, malignant, mordacious, noxious, peccant *(unhealthy)*, pernicious, pestilent, ruthless, scathing, sinister, spiteful, toxic, vicious

virulently inimical malignant

virus disease

vis compulsion *(coercion)*, efficiency, essence, faculty *(ability)*, force *(strength)*, impetus, import, importance, influence, life *(vitality)*, meaning, power, pressure, significance, signification, stock *(store)*

vis-à-vis antipode, contra, contrary, hostile

visa permission, permit

visage aspect, complexion, feature *(appearance)*, presence *(poise)*, semblance

viscidity adhesion *(affixing)*

viscosity adhesion *(affixing)*

viscous coherent *(joined)*

visé confirmation

visible apparent *(perceptible)*, appreciable, bodily, clear *(apparent)*, coherent *(clear)*, conspicuous, discernible, distinct *(clear)*, evident, extant, flagrant, manifest, naked *(perceptible)*, obvious, open *(in sight)*, ostensible, overt, palpable, patent, perceivable, perceptible, prominent, remarkable, salient, tangible, unmistakable

visible effect impression

visible form embodiment

visible sign symbol

visible token indicant

visibly fairly *(clearly)*

vision phantom, phenomenon *(manifestation)*, sagacity, standpoint

visionary delusive, illusory, impossible, infeasible, insubstantial, nonexistent, quixotic, theoretical

visioned original *(creative)*

visionless blind *(sightless)*

visit appointment *(meeting)*, attend *(be present at)*, inhabit

visit punishment discipline *(punish)*, penalize

visitation adversity, misfortune, presence *(attendance)*

visor enshroud, veil

vista aspect, scene, vision *(sight)*

visual discernible, perceivable, perceptible

visual examination inspection

visual impact face value *(first blush)*

visualization concept, perception

visualize compose, conceive *(comprehend)*, conjure, discern *(detect with the senses)*, invent *(produce for the first time)*

visualized distinct *(clear)*

visualizing original *(creative)*

vita life *(period of existence)*

vita decedere die

vital born *(alive)*, cardinal *(basic)*, central *(essential)*, compulsory, critical *(crucial)*, crucial, exigent, fundamental, important *(urgent)*, indispensable, integral, live *(conscious)*, major, mandatory, material *(important)*, necessary *(required)*, obligatory, primary, requisite, strategic, substantive, urgent, viable

vital center seat

vital concern main point, sine qua non

vital element center *(essence)*

vital essence spirit

vital part center *(essence)*, consequence *(significance)*, ingredient, neces-

sity, need *(requirement)*, prerequisite, requirement, substance *(essential nature)*

vital principle gist *(substance)*

vital statistics census

vitalic vital

vitalis vital

vitality ardor, force *(strength)*, health, prowess *(bravery)*, puissance, spirit, strength

vitalization birth *(beginning)*

vitalize generate, stimulate

vitalized born *(alive)*

vitalness need *(requirement)*, priority

vitals necessary, necessity

vitare avoid *(evade)*, eschew, shun

vitiare adulterate, corrupt, debase, debauch, falsification, falsify, vitiate

vitiate abolish, adulterate, annul, contaminate, corrupt, damage, debase, debauch, degenerate, denature, deteriorate, disable, dissolve *(terminate)*, infect, invalidate, neutralize, nullify, pervert, pollute, revoke, spoil *(impair)*, subvert, sully, taint *(corrupt)*

vitiated depraved, profligate *(corrupt)*, reprobate, stale, tainted *(corrupted)*

vitiation annulment, contaminate, damage, debauchment, fault *(weakness)*, invalidity, perversion, rescision

vitiis inficere infect

vitiosus faulty, vicious

vitium fallacy, flaw, foible, guilt

vitriol disapprobation

vitriolic bitter *(reproachful)*, malevolent, malignant, mordacious, scathing

vituperare blame, censure, condemn *(blame)*, decry, rebuke, reprimand

vituperate castigate, condemn *(blame)*, contemn, defame, denigrate, denounce *(condemn)*, impeach, inveigh, lash *(attack verbally)*, malign, pillory, rebuke, reprimand, reproach

vituperatio blame *(culpability)*, obloquy, reprimand

vituperation aspersion, condemnation *(blame)*, contumely, denunciation, diatribe, disparagement, imprecation, malediction, obloquy, outcry, phillipic, profanity, revilement, stricture, vilification

vituperative calumnious, contemptuous, harsh, libelous, pejorative

vivacity ardor, life *(vitality)*, spirit

vivid acute, clear *(apparent)*, coherent *(clear)*, descriptive, detailed, distinct *(clear)*, eloquent, intense, profound *(intense)*, strong, suggestive *(evocative)*

vividly fairly *(clearly)*

vividness strength

vivification birth *(emergence of young)*, revival

vivified conscious *(awake)*

vivify generate, heighten *(augment)*, stimulate

vixenish petulant, querulous

vizard veil

vocable term *(expression)*

vocabulary language, parlance, phraseology

vocabulum term *(expression)*

vocal nuncupative, oral, parol

vocal embodiment of thought expression *(comment)*

vocalism intonation

vocalization parlance, speech

vocalize communicate, enunciate, ob-

serve *(remark)*, phrase, pronounce *(speak)*, remark

vocalized oral

vocare call *(title)*

vocation appointment *(position)*, business *(occupation)*, calling, career, employment, job, labor *(work)*, livelihood, mission, position *(business status)*, post, practice *(professional business)*, profession *(vocation)*, pursuit *(occupation)*, specialty *(special aptitude)*, trade *(occupation)*, work *(employment)*

vocational technical

voces outcry

vociferance noise

vociferate interject

vociferatio outcry

vociferation noise, outcry, pandemonium

vociferous blatant *(obtrusive)*, loquacious

vogue custom, market *(demand)*, mode, style, usage

vogue word catchword

voice circulate, communicate, disclose, divulge, enunciate, express, intonation, mention, observe *(remark)*, phrase, poll *(casting of votes)*, pronounce *(speak)*, propose, propound, recite, referendum, remark, report *(disclose)*, reveal, signify *(inform)*, spokesman, suffrage, utter

voice change inflection

voice disapproval reprehend

voiced nuncupative, oral, parol, stated, verbal

voiceless mute, speechless

voicing expression *(comment)*

void abate *(extinguish)*, abolish, abrogate *(annul)*, abrogate *(rescind)*, absence *(omission)*, adeem, annul, avoid *(cancel)*, barren, blank *(emptiness)*, cancel, defunct, deplete, discontinue *(abandon)*, disown *(deny the validity)*, eliminate *(eradicate)*, eradicate, inactive, ineffective, ineffectual, inexpressive, invalid, lifeless *(dead)*, nugatory, null *(invalid)*, null and void, nullify, nullity, overrule, recall *(call back)*, recant, repeal, rescind, revoke, supersede, vacant, vacuous

void check bad check

void of deficient, devoid

void of contents barren

void of feeling insensible

void of reason irrational

void of suspicion certain *(positive)*, credible, naive

void of taste insipid

void of truth dishonest, fraudulent, mendacious

void the license of an attorney disbar

void trial mistrial

voidable defeasible

voidance abatement *(extinguishment)*, abolition, ademption, annulment, avoidance *(cancellation)*, cancellation, countermand, defeasance, discharge *(annulment)*, discharge *(release from obligation)*, dissolution *(termination)*, exclusion, repudiation, rescision, retraction, reversal

voiding cancellation, reversal

voidness invalidity

volaticus volatile

volatile brief, ephemeral, inconsistent, irresolute, mutable, temporary, transient, transitory, variable
volatility inconsistency
volcanic vehement
volcano outburst
volens voluntary
volitient deliberate, spontaneous, voluntary
volition animus, conatus, discretion *(power of choice)*, election *(choice)*, forethought, intent, purpose, will *(desire)*
volitional deliberate, discretionary, spontaneous, voluntary, willful, willing *(desirous)*
volitionally purposely
volitionary voluntary
volitive deliberate, discretionary, permissive, spontaneous, willful
volley barrage, discharge *(shot)*, salvo
voluble loquacious
volume bulk, capacity *(maximum)*, coverage *(scope)*, degree *(magnitude)*, magnitude, publication *(printed matter)*, quantity
voluminous capacious, copious
voluntarily purposely, readily
voluntariness conatus, purpose
voluntarius spontaneous, voluntary
voluntary consenting, deliberate, gratis, gratuitous *(given without recompense)*, spontaneous, unsolicited, willful, willing *(not averse)*
voluntary acknowledgment admission *(disclosure)*
voluntary activity conatus
voluntary association affiliation *(amalgamation)*, merger
voluntary attestment under oath affidavit
voluntary conveyance largess *(gift)*
voluntary decision alternative *(option)*
voluntary exile privacy
voluntary oversight connivance
voluntary relinquishment waiver
voluntary work campaign
voluntary worker volunteer
voluntas inclination, volition, will *(desire)*
volunteer hold out *(deliberate on an offer)*, pose *(propound)*, proffer, tender, unpaid
volunteered unsolicited
volute sinuous
voracious eager, gluttonous, predatory, rapacious
voraciousness greed
voracity greed
votary addict, advocate *(counselor)*, advocate *(espouser)*, colleague, disciple, partisan, proponent
vote cast *(register)*, decide, franchise *(right to vote)*, plebiscite, poll *(casting of votes)*, primary, referendum, suffrage
vote against disapprove *(reject)*, protest, reject
vote down disapprove *(reject)*, fight *(counteract)*
vote favorably pass *(approve)*
vote for confirm, side
vote in legislate, pass *(approve)*
vote into office elect *(select by a vote)*, nominate
vote of confidence adhesion *(loyalty)*
vote to accept adopt

vote-casting election *(selection by vote)*
voted consensual
voter constituent *(member)*
voters constituency
voting age majority *(adulthood)*
voting district constituency
voting list constituency
voting power franchise *(right to vote)*
votum prayer
vouch affirm *(declare solemnly)*, avouch *(avow)*, avouchment, avow, certify *(attest)*, contend *(maintain)*, depose *(testify)*, posit, promise *(vow)*, seal *(solemnize)*, swear, vow
vouch for accredit, affirm *(uphold)*, assure *(insure)*, attest, authorize, avouch *(guarantee)*, bear *(adduce)*, certify *(attest)*, confirm, corroborate, cosign, depose *(testify)*, guarantee, indorse, recommend, side, sponsor, support *(corroborate)*, underwrite, verify *(swear)*, witness *(attest to)*
vouch for as genuine certify *(attest)*
vouched alleged
vouched for promissory
voucher affiant, affirmant, assurance, bond, certificate, corroboration, coupon, deponent, draft, guaranty, note *(written promise to pay)*, permit, receipt *(proof of receiving)*, reference *(recommendation)*, security *(pledge)*, surety *(guarantor)*, warrant *(authorization)*, warranty
vouchers credentials
vouching adjuration, advocacy, averment, deposition, reference *(recommendation)*
vouchsafe accede *(concede)*, allow *(authorize)*, authorize, bestow, cede, condescend *(deign)*, deign, give *(grant)*, grant *(concede)*, let *(permit)*, patronize *(condescend toward)*, present *(make a gift)*, sanction
vouchsafed allowed
vouchsafement concession *(authorization)*, consent, disposition *(transfer of property)*, indulgence, leave *(permission)*, license, privilege, sanction *(permission)*
vouchsafer contributor *(giver)*, donor
vow adjuration, asseveration, assurance, assure *(insure)*, avouch *(avow)*, avouchment, avow, bear *(adduce)*, claim *(maintain)*, commitment *(responsibility)*, oath, pledge *(binding promise)*, pledge *(promise the performance of)*, profession *(declaration)*, promise, promise *(vow)*, surety *(certainty)*, swear, undertake, undertaking *(pledge)*, verify *(swear)*
vox call *(appeal)*, expression *(comment)*, verbal
voyager itinerant
voyaging moving *(in motion)*
vulgar blatant *(obtrusive)*, caitiff, depraved, ignoble, impertinent *(insolent)*, inelegant, lewd, licentious, lurid, meretricious, obnoxious, obscene, odious, poor *(inferior in quality)*, profane, scurrilous, tawdry, unbecoming, uncouth, unseemly
vulgare propagate *(spread)*
vulgarian blatant *(obtrusive)*
vulgarity indecency, obscenity, pornography, profanity
vulgarize corrupt, debase

vulgus mass *(body of persons)*
vulnerability danger, frailty, jeopardy, liability, peril, risk
vulnerable destructible, helpless *(defenseless)*, inadequate, indefensible, insecure, liable, open *(accessible)*, penetrable, precarious, subject *(exposed)*, susceptible *(unresistent)*, untenable
vulnerable point fault *(weakness)*, peril
vulnerableness frailty
vulnerary medicinal
vulpine artful, insidious, machiavellian, sly, subtle *(insidious)*, surreptitious
vulturine predatory, rapacious
vulturish predatory
vulturous predatory, rapacious
vying competitive *(antagonistic)*
vying for ascendance competition
vying with comparative, contravention

W

wag brandish
wage commission *(fee)*, exercise *(discharge a function)*, fee *(charge)*, income, payment *(remittance)*, perquisite, ply, recompense
wage earner employee
wage war engage *(involve)*, fight *(battle)*
wager bet, gamble, lottery, parlay *(bet)*, pawn, risk, speculate *(chance)*, speculation *(risk)*, stake *(award)*, venture
wagerer bettor, speculator
wages compensation, earnings, income, pay, payroll, revenue
waggery mischief
waggish jocular
waggishness mischief
waggle brandish
waif orphan
wail outcry, plaint
wailful querulous
wait cessation *(interlude)*, defer *(put off)*, deferment, delay, discontinue *(break continuity)*, forbear, halt, halt, hesitate, last, moratorium, pause, procrastinate, remain *(stay)*, respite *(interval of rest)*, stay, stay *(rest)*
wait for anticipate *(expect)*, expect *(anticipate)*, forestall
wait on pander, serve *(assist)*
wait upon attend *(take care of)*
waiting expectation, ready *(prepared)*
waiting period moratorium
waive abrogate *(rescind)*, discontinue *(abandon)*, discontinue *(break continuity)*, forbear, forfeit, forgo, forswear, leave *(allow to remain)*, refrain, reject, relinquish, remit *(release from penalty)*, renounce, surrender *(give back)*, yield *(submit)*
waive privilege condescend *(deign)*
waive punishment condone
waived exempt
waiver cancellation, cession, quitclaim, rejection, release, renunciation
wake incite, inspire
wake up foment
wakeful vigilant
wakefulness diligence *(care)*

waken foment
walk patrol, perambulate
walk a beat patrol
walk away move *(alter position)*, quit *(evacuate)*
walk in enter *(go in)*
walk of life business *(occupation)*, calling, position *(business status)*, profession *(vocation)*
walk off move *(alter position)*
walk off with hold up *(rob)*, jostle *(pickpocket)*, poach
walk out quit *(evacuate)*, secede, strike *(refuse to work)*
walk through perambulate
walker pedestrian
walkout strike
wall barrier
wall in enclose, encompass *(surround)*, envelop, restrain, restrict
wall of flame conflagration
wall up block, immure
walled in area enclosure
wallow carouse
wan disconsolate, languid
wander digress, perambulate
wander about prowl
wander aimlessly loiter
wander from the subject deviate
wanderer derelict, itinerant, migrant
wandering circuitous, discursive *(digressive)*, incoherence, indirect, itinerant, labyrinthine, lost *(disoriented)*, lunatic, moving *(in motion)*, prolix, shifting, truant, unsettled, vagrancy
wane decline, decline *(fall)*, decrease, decrease, degenerate, deteriorate, diminish, ebb, end *(termination)*, lessen, outflow, relapse, subside
waning attrition, decrease, old
want absence *(omission)*, conatus, dearth, deficiency, desideratum, desire, desire, exigency, failure *(falling short)*, foible, indigence, insufficiency, lack, market *(demand)*, need *(deprivation)*, need, paucity, poverty, privation, request, require *(need)*, requirement, requisition, will *(desire)*
want of ability disqualification *(factor that disqualifies)*, inability
want of activity inertia
want of adaptation incompatibility *(difference)*
want of agreement incompatibility *(difference)*, incompatibility *(inconsistency)*
want of attention disinterest *(lack of interest)*
want of authority want of jurisdiction
want of capacity inability
want of caution audacity, impropriety, temerity
want of certainty cloud *(suspicion)*
want of circumspection impropriety
want of comprehension insanity
want of confidence cloud *(suspicion)*, doubt *(indecision)*, doubt *(suspicion)*, fear, qualm
want of consideration ingratitude
want of duty laches, maladministration
want of esteem disrepute, disrespect
want of faith cloud *(suspicion)*, doubt *(indecision)*, doubt *(suspicion)*, incredulity

want of fidelity story *(falsehood)*
want of forbearance discrimination *(bigotry)*, intolerance
want of formality informality
want of harmony conflict, impugnation, inconsistency, opposition
want of integrity dishonesty
want of interest disinterest *(lack of interest)*
want of knowledge ignorance
want of legal capacity disability *(legal disqualification)*
want of legal qualification disability *(legal disqualification)*
want of loyalty disloyalty
want of method irregularity, pandemonium
want of moral strength frailty
want of notice disregard *(unconcern)*
want of originality platitude
want of power inability
want of principle abuse *(corrupt practice)*, bad repute, corruption, perversion
want of reason insanity
want of respect disparagement
want of sensibility insentience
want of skill disqualification *(factor that disqualifies)*, inability
want of success abortion *(fiasco)*
want of thought disregard *(lack of respect)*, disregard *(unconcern)*, negligence
want of toleration intolerance
want of transparency opacity
want of trust doubt *(suspicion)*
wantage dearth, need *(deprivation)*
wanted important *(urgent)*, indispensable, popular, requisite
wanting defective, deficient, delinquent *(overdue)*, destitute, devoid, faulty, imperfect, inadept, inadequate, insufficient, marginal, nonsubstantial *(not sufficient)*, paltry, partial *(part)*, partial *(relating to a part)*, perfunctory, poor *(inferior in quality)*, scarce, solicitous, unsatisfactory, vacuous, void *(empty)*
wanting discretion imprudent
wanting in candor disingenuous
wanting in probity dishonest, fraudulent
wanting in proportion disproportionate
wanton flagrant, hot-blooded, imprudent, lascivious, lecherous, lewd, licentious, malicious, needless, obscene, outrageous, prodigal, profuse, promiscuous, prurient, reckless, salacious, suggestive *(risqué)*, unrestrained *(not repressed)*, unruly, unscrupulous
wanton destruction waste
wanton disregard malice
wantonly wicked conduct atrocity
wantonness delinquency *(misconduct)*, vice
war contend *(dispute)*, contest *(dispute)*, fight *(battle)*, strife
war hammer cudgel
war of words argument *(contention)*, contest *(dispute)*, fight *(argument)*
war with engage *(involve)*
ward bailiwick, charge *(custody)*, control *(supervision)*, dependent, district, division *(administrative unit)*, juvenile, minor, orphan, preservation, protect,

protégé, region
ward off avert, contain *(restrain)*, counter, debar, deter, estop, forestall, parry, prevent, repel *(drive back)*, repulse, shun, stall, stave, stop, thwart
warden caretaker *(one caring for property)*, guardian, superintendent
wardenship auspices, control *(supervision)*
warder guardian, warden
warding off defense, preventive
wardship adoption *(affiliation)*, auspices, charge *(custody)*, control *(supervision)*, custody *(supervision)*, management *(supervision)*, preservation, protection, safekeeping
ware cargo, item
warehouse cache *(storage place)*, depository, repository, store
wares cargo, commodities, merchandise, stock in trade
warfare belligerency, campaign, fight *(battle)*, outbreak, strife
wariness caution *(vigilance)*, deliberation, diligence *(care)*, discretion *(quality of being discreet)*, doubt *(suspicion)*, notice *(heed)*, precaution
warlike disorderly, inimical, litigious, malevolent, offensive *(taking the initiative)*, pugnacious, spartan
warlikeness belligerency
warm benevolent, charitable *(lenient)*, moving *(evoking emotion)*
warmhearted benevolent, humane
warmheartedness benevolence *(disposition to do good)*
warmth affection
warmth of feeling ardor
warn advise, alert, apprise, caution, counsel, deter, discourage, exhort, forewarn, herald, inform *(notify)*, notice *(give formal warning)*, notify, portend, predict, presage, remind, remonstrate, reprimand
warn against admonish *(warn)*
warn beforehand forewarn
warn in advance forewarn
warned informed *(having information)*
warner informer *(a person who provides information)*
warning admonition, advice, caveat, deterrent, forerunner, harbinger, hortative, indication, indicator, intelligence *(news)*, notification, precaution, precursor, premonition, remonstrance, remonstrative, reprimand, symptom, threat, tip *(clue)*, ultimatum
warning notice dun
warning sign caveat, symptom
warp corrupt, deface, distort, mutilate, pervert, predisposition, prejudice *(influence)*, propensity, slant, tendency
warped defective, depraved, dissolute, faulty, imperfect, one-sided, peccable, tainted *(corrupted)*, unjust, unsound *(not strong)*
warped idea misestimation
warped impression misestimation
warped judgment distortion, misestimation
warrant affirm *(uphold)*, allow *(authorize)*, assure *(insure)*, authorize, avouch *(guarantee)*, award, basis, bear *(adduce)*, bind *(obligate)*, bond, bond *(secure a debt)*, brevet, canon, capacity

(authority), certificate, certify *(attest)*, charge *(empower)*, citation *(charge)*, claim *(maintain)*, commitment *(responsibility)*, concession *(authorization)*, confirmation, consent, consent, contend *(maintain)*, corroborate, coverage *(insurance)*, delegate, delegation *(assignment)*, direction *(order)*, dispensation *(exception)*, draft, droit, empower, ensure, fiat, grant *(concede)*, guarantee, guaranty, indorsement, injunction, justify, leave *(permission)*, let *(permit)*, license, monition *(legal summons)*, order, permit, permit, pledge *(promise the performance of)*, power, precept, prerogative, privilege, promise *(vow)*, proof, reassure, requirement, right *(entitlement)*, sponsor, subscribe *(promise)*, surety *(certainty)*, undertaking *(pledge)*, uphold, validate, verify *(swear)*, vouch, vow, witness *(attest to)*

warrant of commitment mittimus
warrantability admissibility
warrantable admissible, allowable, colorable *(plausible)*, defensible, justifiable, licit, permissible, reasonable *(rational)*, tenable
warrantableness admissibility, legality
warranted admissible, agreed *(promised)*, allowed, condign, entitled, fully secured, juridical, justifiable, legal, licit, rightful, valid
warranted by law lawful
warranting advocacy
warrantor backer, surety *(guarantor)*
warranty assurance, bond, certainty, consent, contract, covenant, coverage *(insurance)*, guaranty, pact, pledge *(binding promise)*, promise, recognizance, security *(pledge)*, specialty *(contract)*, warrant *(guaranty)*
warranty against loss insurance
wartime belligerency
wary alert *(vigilant)*, circumspect, deliberate, diffident, guarded, inconvincible, leery, noncommittal, provident *(showing foresight)*, prudent, skeptical, suspicious *(distrustful)*, vigilant
wash permeate
wash away purge *(purify)*
waspish fractious, perverse, petulant, querulous, resentful
wastage consumption, decrement, spoilage, waste, wear and tear
waste barren, bleak *(exposed and barren)*, consume, consumption, decrement, degenerate, deplete, destroy *(efface)*, deteriorate, diminish, discard, dissipate *(expend foolishly)*, erode, erosion, exhaust *(deplete)*, expend *(consume)*, havoc, impair, lose *(be deprived of)*, loss, misapplication, misemploy, mishandle *(mismanage)*, mistreat, pillage, prey, prostration, spoil *(pillage)*, spoilage
waste away decay, diminish, ebb, languish, lessen
waste time procrastinate
wasted futile, irredeemable, lost *(taken away)*, otiose, stale, unavailing, unsound *(not strong)*
wasteful barren, careless, improvident, inordinate, intemperate, needless, prodigal, profligate *(extravagant)*, pro-

fuse, superfluous, unavailing, unproductive
wasteful expenditure misapplication
wastefulness consumption, misapplication, waste
wasting decadent, deleterious, fatal, waste
wasting away decadent
wastrel degenerate, derelict
watch charge *(custody)*, check *(inspect)*, concern *(care)*, custody *(supervision)*, harbor, heed, monitor, note *(notice)*, notice *(heed)*, notice *(observe)*, observation, oversee, patrol, peruse, police, precaution, preserve, regard *(attention)*, regard *(pay attention)*, safekeeping, scrutinize, spy, superintend, surveillance, survey *(examine)*, ward, witness *(have direct knowledge of)*
watch closely examine *(study)*
watch diligently police
watch for expect *(anticipate)*
watch out beware
watch out for care *(be cautious)*
watch over attend *(take care of)*, care *(be cautious)*, care *(regard)*, cover *(guard)*, ensconce, foster, keep *(shelter)*, maintain *(sustain)*, overlook *(superintend)*, oversee, preserve, protect
watch secretly spy
watched over guarded
watcher bystander, eyewitness, spy
watchful alert *(vigilant)*, careful, circumspect, conscious *(aware)*, diligent, discreet, guarded, leery, meticulous, noncommittal, precise, preventive, protective, provident *(showing foresight)*, suspicious *(distrustful)*, vigilant
watchful care oversight *(control)*
watchfulness caution *(vigilance)*, deliberation, diligence *(care)*, discretion *(quality of being discreet)*, notice *(heed)*, observation, oversight *(control)*, precaution, prudence, regard *(attention)*, surveillance, ward
watchman caretaker *(one caring for property)*, guardian, warden
watchword catchword, indicant, phrase
water dilute
water down denature, lessen
waterfront littoral
waterlog permeate
watermark brand
waterproof impervious
watershed crossroad *(turning point)*
waterside littoral
watertight impervious
wave beat *(pulsate)*, brandish, display, flaunt, fluctuate
wave brazenly flaunt
wave conspicuously flaunt
wave ostentatiously flaunt
waver alternate *(fluctuate)*, beat *(pulsate)*, doubt *(hesitate)*, fluctuate, hesitate, misdoubt, oscillate, pause, vacillate, vary
wavering capricious, doubt *(indecision)*, dubious, faithless, hesitant, hesitation, intermittent, irresolute, irresponsible, moving *(in motion)*, mutable, noncommittal, shifting, sporadic, undecided, undependable, unpredictable, unreliable, unsettled, untrustworthy, variable, volatile
wax expand, inflate, proliferate,

pullulate
waxen flexible
waxing inflation *(increase)*
way access *(right of way)*, admission *(entry)*, admittance *(means of approach)*, avenue *(means of attainment)*, avenue *(route)*, conduct, conduit *(channel)*, demeanor, deportment, direction *(course)*, expedient, facility *(instrumentality)*, form *(arrangement)*, habit, instrumentality, key *(solution)*, manner *(behavior)*, method, mode, modus operandi, ploy, practice *(custom)*, practice *(procedure)*, presence *(poise)*, procedure, process *(course)*, state *(condition)*, style, system, temperament, treatment
way in access *(right of way)*, entrance, ingress
way of acting behavior, conduct
way of approach access *(right of way)*
way of doing things design *(intent)*, practice *(procedure)*
way of escape loophole
way of life behavior, modus vivendi
way of living modus vivendi
way of operation procedure
way of thinking conviction *(persuasion)*, outlook, perspective, position *(point of view)*, posture *(attitude)*, principle *(axiom)*
way out egress, loophole, outlet
way over land easement
way through access *(right of way)*
way to ingress
wayfaring itinerant, moving *(in motion)*, vagrancy
waylay accost, ambush, assail, attack, carry away, ensnare, jostle *(pickpocket)*, kidnap
waymark landmark *(conspicuous object)*
ways approaches, conduct, deportment, means *(opportunity)*, policy *(plan of action)*, presence *(poise)*
ways and means avenue *(means of attainment)*, modus operandi, process *(course)*
wayward disobedient, disorderly, dissolute, eccentric, froward, insubordinate, intractable, lawless, opposite, peccable, perverse, restive, unruly, unyielding, variable
waywardness delinquency *(misconduct)*
weak defective, deficient, dependent, fallible, harmless, helpless *(powerless)*, imperfect, inactive, inadequate, incapable, inconclusive, indistinct, ineffective, ineffectual, insipid, insubstantial, insufficient, invalid, jejune *(dull)*, languid, lifeless *(dull)*, marginal, nonsubstantial *(not sturdy)*, obscure *(faint)*, poor *(inferior in quality)*, powerless, unsatisfactory, unsound *(not strong)*, untenable, vulnerable
weak group minority *(outnumbered group)*
weak point disadvantage, fault *(weakness)*, flaw, foible, frailty, vice
weak side foible, frailty
weak spot flaw
weak-eyed blind *(sightless)*
weak-minded caitiff
weaken adulterate, alleviate, attenuate, countervail, damage, debase, debil-

itate, denature, deplete, depreciate, depress, derogate, deteriorate, dilute, diminish, disable, disadvantage, disarm *(divest of arms),* encumber *(hinder),* erode, eviscerate, exhaust *(deplete),* extenuate, impair, languish, lapse *(fall into error),* lessen, moderate *(temper),* mollify, obtund, prejudice *(injure),* relapse, relax, remit *(relax),* tax *(overwork),* vitiate

weaken in force attenuate

weaken the resolution of discourage

weakened decadent, disadvantaged, old

weakening damage, decrease, disabling, mitigation, operose, relapse

weakly nonsubstantial *(not sturdy)*

weakness caducity, defect, deficiency, detriment, disability *(physical inability),* disadvantage, disease, flaw, foible, frailty, impotence, impuissance, incapacity, inefficacy, languor, penchant, predisposition, propensity, prostration, vice

weakness of character foible

weal boom *(prosperity),* prosperity, welfare

wealth assets, boom *(prosperity),* economy *(economic system),* effects, finance, income, means *(funds),* money, personalty, possessions, principal *(capital sum),* prosperity, resource, store *(depository),* substance *(material possessions),* sufficiency

wealthy prosperous, successful

wean alienate *(estrange),* withdraw

wean away disaffect

weapon bomb, cudgel, gun

weaponless powerless

weapons ammunition

wear consumption, degenerate, depreciate, endure *(last),* erode, erosion, flaunt, keep *(continue),* usage

wear and tear decrement, defacement

wear away consume, decay, degenerate, diminish, erode, expire, languish, lessen, spend

wear down diminish, erode, harass, prevail *(persuade),* tax *(overwork)*

wear down by friction erode

wear out consume, deplete, diminish, exhaust *(deplete),* impair, misemploy, mistreat, spend, tax *(overwork)*

wear the aspect appear *(seem to be)*

weariful irksome

weariness inertia, languor, prostration

wearing chronic, irksome, operose, oppressive

wearing away attrition, erosion

wearing down by friction erosion

wearisome irksome, jejune, *(dull),* lifeless *(dull),* mundane, onerous, operose, oppressive, ordinary, painful, pedestrian, ponderous, prolix, prosaic, trite, vexatious

weary exhaust *(deplete),* lugubrious, otiose, tax *(overwork)*

weary load onus *(burden)*

wearying irksome, lifeless *(dull),* operose, ponderous

weather atmosphere, bear *(tolerate),* endure *(last),* endure *(suffer),* erode, maintain *(sustain),* resist *(withstand),* withstand

weatherbeaten dilapidated

weathered old

weave incorporate *(include)*

weave a plot scheme

web intertwine, involution

wed connect *(join together),* join *(bring together),* unite

wedded composite, concurrent *(united),* conjoint, conjugal, nuptial

wedded state cohabitation *(married state),* coverture, marriage *(wedlock),* matrimony

wedded status cohabitation *(married state)*

wedded to addicted

wedding marriage *(wedlock)*

wedding a second time digamy

wedge impact

wedged inextricable

wedlock cohabitation *(married state),* matrimony

weed cannabis, delete, edit, eliminate *(exclude),* excise *(cut away),* exclude, expurgate, screen *(select)*

weed out diminish, eliminate *(eradicate),* eradicate, expel, extirpate, lessen, reject, select

ween opine, surmise

weep exude

weep over deplore, regret, repent

weeping disconsolate, outcry, repentant

weigh assess *(appraise),* brood, compare, consider, criticize *(evaluate),* debate, deliberate, determine, diagnose, digest *(comprehend),* estimate, gauge, judge, measure, muse, pause, ponder, rate, reason *(conclude),* reflect *(ponder),* review, speculate *(conjecture),* study, survey *(examine)*

weigh against countervail

weigh down disadvantage, encumber *(hinder),* load, overcome *(overwhelm),* overload, overwhelm, tax *(overwork)*

weigh in the mind deliberate

weigh more than outweigh

weigh on harass

weigh on the mind obsess

weigh out mete

weighable appreciable, ponderable

weighed deliberate, tactical

weighing contemplation, deliberation, discrimination *(differentiation),* estimation *(calculation),* judgment *(discernment),* reflection *(thought)*

weight burden, clout, corpus, degree *(magnitude),* dint, dominance, eminence, emphasis, import, importance, incumbrance *(burden),* influence, interest *(concern),* load, magnitude, materiality *(consequence),* onus *(burden),* power, predominance, pressure, prestige, primacy, significance, stress *(accent)*

weight of numbers majority *(greater part),* plurality

weighted inequitable, unfair

weightiness import, importance, interest *(concern),* magnitude, materiality *(consequence),* significance

weightless intangible

weighty cogent, compelling, consequential *(substantial),* critical *(crucial),* determinative, dominant, grave *(important),* important *(significant),* key, major, material *(important),* momen-

tous, onerous, oppressive, persuasive, ponderous, potent, powerful, predominant, prevailing *(having superior force),* prominent, serious *(grave),* solid *(sound),* sound, urgent

weird mysterious, peculiar *(curious),* prodigious *(amazing),* uncanny

welcome desirable *(pleasing),* embrace *(accept),* palatable, sapid

welcoming receptive

weld cement, join *(bring together),* lock, merge

welded conjoint, inseparable

welfare advantage, behalf, benefit *(betterment),* boom *(prosperity)*

well fund, source

well based well-grounded

well being prosperity

well defined visible *(in full view)*

well done professional *(stellar)*

well enough fairly *(moderately)*

well established fixed *(settled)*

well founded well-grounded

well off prosperous

well provided for opulent

well thought of popular, reputable

well thought out strategic

well to do prosperous

well-acquainted familiar *(informed)*

well-adapted apposite, politic

well-advised cognizant, discreet, discriminating *(judicious),* juridical, politic, prudent, reasonable *(rational),* sensible

well-armed armed

well-balanced proportionate

well-based authentic, true *(authentic)*

well-behaved civil *(polite),* malleable, obedient

well-being benefit *(betterment),* boom *(prosperity),* health, welfare

well-bred civil *(polite),* proper

well-brought up civil *(polite)*

well-built solid *(sound),* stable, strong

well-chosen felicitous

well-chosen moment crossroad *(turning point)*

well-conducted moral

well-considered aforethought, circumspect, deliberate, judicious, premeditated

well-constructed solid *(sound)*

well-defined absolute *(conclusive),* accurate, certain *(specific),* clear *(apparent),* coherent *(clear),* conspicuous, definite, distinct *(clear),* manifest, obvious, perceivable, perceptible, precise, tangible, unambiguous, unmistakable

well-deserved condign

well-developed explicit, ripe

well-devised politic, premeditated

well-disciplined spartan

well-disposed inclined, peaceable, prone, propitious

well-doer benefactor

well-done meritorious, right *(suitable)*

well-drawn descriptive, distinct *(clear)*

well-earned condign

well-educated cognizant, familiar *(informed),* informed *(educated),* learned, literate

well-established ingrained, solid *(sound)*

well-expressed felicitous

well-fitted competent, fit
well-fixed opulent
well-founded actual, authentic, axiomatic, believable, cogent, convincing, de facto, legitimate *(rightful)*, presumptive, provable, reasonable *(rational)*, solid *(sound)*, sound, tenable, true *(authentic)*
well-founded opinion conviction *(persuasion)*
well-grounded actual, authentic, believable, cogent, cognizant, convincing, credible, de facto, informed *(educated)*, justifiable, legitimate *(rightful)*, presumptive, provable, rational, solid *(sound)*, sound, stable, tenable, true *(authentic)*, valid
well-grounded hope likelihood, prospect *(outlook)*
well-grounded possibility likelihood
well-informed cognizant, knowing, learned, literate, omniscient, politic
well-intentioned benevolent, meritorious, propitious
well-judged politic
well-knit cohesive *(compact)*
well-known blatant *(conspicuous)*, common *(customary)*, customary, familiar *(customary)*, famous, household *(familiar)*, illustrious, important *(significant)*, influential, master, mundane, prevailing *(current)*, prevalent, prominent, proverbial, public *(known)*, renowned, reputable, salient, trite, usual
well-liked popular
well-made solid *(sound)*, strong
well-mannered civil *(polite)*
well-marked clear *(apparent)*, coherent *(clear)*, conspicuous, definite, distinct *(clear)*, manifest, perceivable, perceptible, prominent
well-matched concurrent *(united)*, uniform
well-meaning benevolent, propitious
well-meant benevolent
well-off opulent, successful
well-ordered systematic
well-organized systematic
well-paying gainful, lucrative, profitable
well-performed right *(suitable)*
well-planned artful, tactical
well-pleased proud *(self-respecting)*
well-populated populous
well-posted knowing
well-principled honest, law-abiding
well-provided copious, full, replete
well-qualified expert, fit, practiced, professional *(trained)*, proficient
well-read cognizant, informed *(educated)*, learned, literate
well-received popular
well-recognized household *(familiar)*, influential
well-regarded influential
well-regulated regular *(orderly)*, right *(suitable)*, systematic
well-rounded informed *(educated)*, learned
well-satisfied proud *(self-respecting)*
well-seen clear *(apparent)*, conspicuous, manifest, prominent
well-situated opulent, prosperous, successful
well-spoken civil *(polite)*
well-stocked copious, full, replete

well-suited appropriate, fit, qualified *(competent)*, sciential
well-supplied full, rife
well-taught learned, literate
well-thought-out tactical
well-timed felicitous, fit, opportune, punctual, seasonable
well-timed initiative crossroad *(turning point)*
well-to-do opulent, successful
well-trained learned
well-trodden familiar *(customary)*, mundane, ordinary, routine, usual
well-versed cognizant, familiar *(informed)*, informed *(educated)*, knowing, proficient
well-wisher proponent, samaritan
well-worn ordinary
well-written cognizable
wellhead source
wellspring origin *(source)*, origination, source
welter commotion, imbroglio, shambles, turmoil
wergild reparation *(indemnification)*
whack lash *(strike)*
whatsoever whatever
wheedle inveigle
whelm overcome *(overwhelm)*
when ad interim, whenever
whereabouts locality, scene
whereby hereby, thereby
wherefore consequently, reason *(basis)*
wherein herein
whereon wherein
whereupon wherein
wherewithal assets, expedient, instrumentality, means *(funds)*, means *(opportunity)*, money, resource, substance *(material possessions)*, sufficiency
whet stimulate, stimulus
whet one's interest interest
whichever whatever
while ad interim, duration, period
whilom former
whim notion
whimpering querulous
whimsical arbitrary and capricious, capricious, original *(creative)*
whine plaint
whiner malcontent
whining querulous
whiny petulant, querulous
whip beat *(strike)*, churn, punish
whirl commotion
whisper imply, report *(rumor)*, suggestion, tip *(clue)*
whit iota, minimum, scintilla
white clean
whittle abridge *(shorten)*, diminish
whiz race
whole absolute *(complete)*, aggregate, amount *(quantity)*, collective, corpus, detailed, entirety, full, gross *(total)*, intact, inviolate, plenary, principal *(capital sum)*, pure, radical *(extreme)*, safe, total, totality, undiminished
whole attention diligence *(care)*, obsession
whole mind diligence *(care)*
whole range gamut
wholeness body *(collection)*, corpus, entirety, finality, sum *(total)*, whole
wholesale destruction conflagration

wholesale trader dealer
wholesaler dealer
wholesome clean, remedial, salubrious, salutary, unaffected *(sincere)*
wholesomeness health
wholly in toto, solely *(singly)*
whomever whoever
whomsoever whoever
whopping prodigious *(enormous)*
whorled circuitous
whosoever whoever
wicked arrant *(onerous)*, bad *(offensive)*, base *(bad)*, contemptible, delinquent *(guilty of a misdeed)*, depraved, diabolic, felonious, harmful, heinous, ignoble, illicit, immoral, impermissible, incorrigible, inexpiable, iniquitous, irregular *(improper)*, malevolent, malicious, malignant, nefarious, outrageous, peccant *(culpable)*, pernicious, perverse, profane, profligate *(corrupt)*, reprehensible, reprobate, scandalous, sinister, tainted *(corrupted)*, unjust, unjustifiable, unscrupulous, vicious
wicked action misdeed
wicked deed misdeed, misdemeanor, misdoing
wickedness atrocity, corruption, delinquency *(misconduct)*, dishonor *(shame)*, disrepute, mischief, misdoing, perversion, turpitude, vice, wrong
wide broad, capacious, comprehensive, copious, extensive, far reaching, generic, inclusive, liberal *(not literal)*, open *(unclosed)*
wide awake vigilant
wide currency coverage *(scope)*
wide of the mark improper
wide open penetrable
wide-awake careful
wide-embracing complete *(all-embracing)*
wide-open open-ended, patent
wide-reaching comprehensive, extensive, omnibus
widely accepted prevailing *(current)*, prevalent
widely extended extensive
widely known common *(customary)*, household *(familiar)*, illustrious, prevalent, proverbial, public *(known)*, trite
widely read informed *(educated)*, learned, literate
widely recognized predominant
widely used conventional
widen accrue *(increase)*, compound, deploy, develop, enlarge, expand, extend *(enlarge)*, increase, magnify, project *(extend beyond)*, spread, supplement
widening augmentation, cumulative *(increasing)*, extension *(expansion)*
widespread broad, collective, common *(customary)*, comprehensive, current, extensive, familiar *(customary)*, far reaching, general, household *(familiar)*, omnibus, ordinary, predominant, prevailing *(current)*, prevalent, rampant, rife
widow's estate dower
widow's portion dower
width caliber *(measurement)*, extent, gamut
wield brandish, employ *(make use of)*, exercise *(use)*, exert, exploit *(make use of)*, handle *(manage)*, manipulate *(utilize skillfully)*, militate, ply

wield authority govern, handle *(manage)*, manage, preside
wield influence prevail upon
wield restraint over hold *(possess)*
wielding power forcible
wieldy flexible
wife consort, spouse
wifedom coverture
wild disobedient, disorderly, ill-judged, licentious, ludicrous, lunatic, outrageous, precipitate, promiscuous, rampant, reckless, uncontrollable, unrestrained *(not repressed)*, unruly, vehement
wild being animal
wild confusion riot
wild uproar pandemonium
wild-fire conflagration
wildness furor, irregularity, pandemonium, violence
wile artifice, bunko, contrivance, deception, device *(contrivance)*, false pretense, hoax, imposture, machination, maneuver *(trick)*, ploy, pretext, ruse, stratagem
wiles knavery
wiliness artifice, dishonesty, fraud
will animus, choose, conatus, contribute *(supply)*, decision *(election)*, demise, descend, design *(intent)*, desire, determine, discretion *(power of choice)*, elect *(choose)*, forethought, give *(grant)*, latitude, leave *(give)*, predetermination, purpose, resolution *(decision)*, resolve *(decide)*, tenacity, testament, volition
will addendum codicil
will and bequeath descend, devise *(give)*
will power discipline *(obedience)*, resolution *(decision)*
will supplement codicil
will to bequeath, devise *(give)*
will validation proceeding probate
will verification proceeding probate
willed deliberate
willful arbitrary and capricious, deliberate, disobedient, express, froward, hot-blooded, inexorable, inflexible, intentional, intractable, obdurate, pertinacious, premeditated, purposeful, recalcitrant, restive, spontaneous, unbending, uncontrollable, unruly, unyielding, voluntary
willful abandonment desertion
willful burning of property arson
willful disregard contempt *(disobedience to the court)*
willful distortion of the truth perjury
willful falsehood perjury
willful telling of a falsehood perjury
willful telling of a lie perjury
willfully purposely
willfully contrary froward
willfully disregard ignore
willfully disrespectful contumacious
willfulness forethought
willing available, consenting, eager, favorable *(expressing approval)*, inclined, malleable, obedient, obeisant, pliable, pliant, prone, receptive, resigned, solicitous, tractable, zealous
willing consent assent
willing help aid *(help)*, charity
willing to forgive lenient, placable
willing to yield to influence of oth-

ers flexible
willingly purposely, readily
willingness acquiescence, adhesion *(loyalty)*, amenability, assent, conformity *(obedience)*, consent, deference, goodwill, predisposition, sanction *(permission)*, volition
willingness to comply compliance
willingness to forgive clemency, condonation
willingness to please consideration *(sympathetic regard)*
willingness to purchase market *(demand)*
willowy flexible
willpower strength
wilt languish, perish
wilted dilapidated, stale
wily artful, collusive, deceptive, delusive, devious, disingenuous, fraudulent, insidious, machiavellian, politic, sly, subtle *(insidious)*, surreptitious
wily device contrivance, machination
win acquire *(receive)*, carry *(succeed)*, earn, gain, inveigle, obtain, prevail *(triumph)*, reap, receive *(acquire)*, succeed *(attain)*
win an argument convert *(persuade)*
win back recoup *(regain)*, recover
win over convert *(persuade)*, convince, disarm *(set at ease)*, persuade, placate, prejudice *(influence)*, prevail *(persuade)*, prevail upon, propitiate, reason *(persuade)*, reconcile
win the battle beat *(defeat)*
wind contort
wind up close *(terminate)*, complete, expire, finish, terminate
windfall profit
winding circuitous, indirect, labyrinthine, sinuous, tortuous *(bending)*
window-dressing pretense *(ostentation)*
windup close *(conclusion)*, defeasance, denouement
windy loquacious, orotund
wing affiliate, organ, protection
winged rapid
winning popular, prevailing *(having superior force)*, prize, sapid, successful
winning over persuasion
winnings earnings, profit, spoils, stake *(award)*
winnow cull, distinguish, screen *(select)*, select, separate
winsome sapid
wipe away deface, expunge
wipe off expunge
wipe out delete, destroy *(efface)*, dissolve *(terminate)*, eliminate *(eradicate)*, expunge, extinguish, extirpate, obliterate, rescind, revoke, stop
wipe out illiteracy educate
wiretap eavesdrop
wiry resilient, strong
wisdom caliber *(mental capacity)*, cognition, common sense, comprehension, discretion *(quality of being discreet)*, experience *(background)*, information *(knowledge)*, insight, intelligence *(intellect)*, knowledge *(learning)*, reason *(sound judgment)*, sagacity, sense *(intelligence)*, understanding *(comprehension)*
wise cognizant, conduct, discreet, discriminating *(judicious)*, expert, favora-

ble *(advantageous)*, fit, judicial, judicious, learned, manner *(behavior)*, omniscient, oracular, perceptive, perspicacious, politic, profound *(esoteric)*, prudent, rational, reasonable *(rational)*, sapient, sensible, solid *(sound)*
wise man mastermind
wise saying maxim
wiseness sense *(intelligence)*
wish conatus, desire, end *(intent)*, market *(demand)*, predisposition, purpose, request, volition, will *(desire)*
wish for desire, lack
wishful eager
wistful pensive
with along
with a high degree of certainty high probability
with a valid will testate
with alacrity expeditious
with all reasonable speed forthwith
with all respect respectfully
with allegiance faithfully
with an executed will testate
with an iron hand dictatorial
with assurance fairly *(clearly)*
with authority as a matter of right
with cause for cause
with certainty fairly *(clearly)*
with compliance respectfully
with confidence fairly *(clearly)*
with constancy faithfully
with deference respectfully
with dispatch expeditious
with due deference respectfully
with due respect respectfully
with fealty faithfully
with fidelity faithfully
with force of law obligatory
with forethought aforethought, deliberate, express, premeditated, purposely
with free will purposely
with full effect in full force
with full force in full force
with funds solvent
with good credit solvent
with good faith faithfully
with intent purposely
with justice fairly *(impartially)*
with justification for cause
with knowledge knowingly
with license liberal *(not literal)*
with meager funds poor *(underprivileged)*
with means opulent
with no exception complete *(all-embracing)*, total
with no mistake exact
with nothing missing intact
with premeditation purposely
with reasonable dispatch forthwith, immediate *(at once)*
with reference to apposite, comparative, pertinent
with regard to comparative
with relation to comparative
with scanty funds poor *(underprivileged)*
with secret design clandestine
with simplicity ingenuous
with speed expeditious, instantly
with the aid of thereby
with the end in sight determinable *(liable to be terminated)*
with the greater force a fortiori
with the highest respect respectfully

with the stipulation provided
with the understanding provided
with this proviso provided
with validity de facto
withdraw abolish, abscond, adeem, annul, cancel, cease, debar, deduct *(reduce)*, demit, depart, diminish, disavow, discontinue *(abandon)*, disengage, disinherit, disinter, dissociate, ebb, evacuate, excise *(cut away)*, extract, flee, forfeit, hold up *(rob)*, invalidate, leave *(depart)*, part *(leave)*, quash, quit *(discontinue)*, quit *(evacuate)*, recall *(call back)*, recant, recess, refrain, refuse, relinquish, remove *(eliminate)*, renege, repeal, repudiate, rescind, resign, retire *(retreat)*, retreat, revoke, secede, seclude, excise *(seclude)*, superannuate, vacate *(leave)*
withdraw clandestinely abscond
withdraw from eschew, forgo, forswear, stop
withdraw from association disband
withdraw from observation conceal
withdraw from one's native land expatriate
withdraw one's objections concede
withdraw one's support defect
withdraw the affections of alienate *(estrange)*, disaffect
withdrawal abandonment *(desertion)*, abandonment *(discontinuance)*, abdication, absence *(nonattendance)*, ademption, alienation *(estrangement)*, cancellation, cloture, countermand, deduction *(diminution)*, defeasance, discontinuance *(act of discontinuing)*, discontinuance *(interruption of a legal action)*, egress, estrangement, evulsion, exception *(exclusion)*, outflow, privacy, recess, removal, renunciation, repudiation, rescision, resignation *(relinquishment)*, retraction, revocation, schism, severance
withdrawal of a sentence reprieve
withdrawal of the charge compurgation, exoneration
withdrawing cancellation
withdrawment ademption
withdrawn inarticulate, null *(invalid)*, null and void, taciturn, unapproachable
wither decay, decline *(fall)*, degenerate, diminish, languish, perish
withered ineffective, ineffectual, stale
withering bitter *(penetrating)*, consumption, decadent, dilapidated, harsh, regressive, scathing, supercilious
withheld arrested *(checked)*
withhold arrest *(stop)*, condemn *(ban)*, constrain *(restrain)*, constrict *(inhibit)*, debar, defer *(put off)*, deny *(refuse to grant)*, disinherit, forbear, hamper, hide, hoard, hold up *(delay)*, inhibit, keep *(restrain)*, refrain, repress, reserve, restrain, retain *(keep in possession)*, stifle, strangle
withhold action forbear
withhold approval disaccord, disallow
withhold approval from disapprove *(reject)*
withhold assent demur, differ *(disagree)*, differ *(vary)*, disaccord, disbelieve, expostulate, hold out *(resist)*
withhold consent disoblige, forbid,

hold out *(resist)*, refuse
withhold judgment doubt *(hesitate)*, misdoubt
withhold one's assent disapprove *(reject)*
withhold payment default, dishonor *(refuse to pay)*
withhold permission ban, censor, disapprove *(reject)*, forbid
withhold reliance doubt *(distrust)*
withholding reservation *(engagement)*
withholding approval dissenting
withholding assent dissenting
withholding of patronage boycott
within herein, wherein
within appropriate time provided timeliness
within boundary lines internal
within bounds fairly *(moderately)*
within reach available, disposable, facile, open *(accessible)*, passable, possible, practicable, present *(attendant)*
within reason fairly *(moderately)*
within sight of almost
within the bounds of possiblity practicable
within the law allowed, de jure, jural, juridical, law-abiding, lawful, legal, legitimate *(rightful)*, licit, permissible, rightful, statutory
within the range of possibility possible
within the realm of possibility plausible, possible
withold conceal
withold information conceal
without devoid, peripheral, save, unless
without a bend direct *(straight)*
without a name anonymous
without a penny poor *(underprivileged)*
without a preference impartial
without a shade of doubt categorical
without a sign of life dead
without a stain clean
without a wait instantly
without adequate ability incompetent
without adequate determining principle arbitrary
without aid helpless *(defenseless)*
without airs unpretentious
without animation languid
without any lapse of time instantly
without appeal categorical, final, irrevocable, mandatory, obligatory
without assent unwillingly
without authority illegal, illicit, null *(invalid)*, null and void, powerless, unofficial
without base baseless
without basis baseless, gratuitous *(unwarranted)*, ill-founded, illogical, insubstantial, unfounded, unsupported
without bearings lost *(disoriented)*
without belief incredulous, leery
without bias fairly *(impartially)*
without blame blameless
without blemish infallible
without body incorporeal
without bound indeterminate, profuse
without cause baseless
without caution reckless

without ceasing incessant
without ceremony informal, unofficial
without cessation continuous
without charge gratis, gratuitous *(given without recompense)*
without choice compulsory, mandatory, obligatory
without circumlocution direct *(straight)*
without companions solitary
without company solitary
without comparison best, prime *(most valuable)*
without compensation gratuitous *(given without recompense)*
without compulsion voluntary
without concern perfunctory
without conditions unconditional
without confusion simple
without connection foreign, impertinent *(irrelevant)*, irrelative
without consent involuntary, unwillingly
without consequence null *(insignificant)*
without consideration arbitrary, gratis, gratuitous *(given without recompense)*, heedless, oblivious, thoughtless
without constraint voluntary
without content devoid
without contents void *(empty)*
without context alien *(unrelated)*
without current stagnant
without date sine die
without deductions gross *(total)*
without defect unblemished
without defense blameful, blameworthy, inexcusable, inexpiable
without delay as soon as feasible, immediate *(at once)*, instant, instantaneous, instantly, prompt
without depth immaterial
without dexterity inadept
without difference equivalent, same
without distinction comparable *(equivalent)*, fairly *(impartially)*, identical
without divergence direct *(straight)*
without doubt decisive, definitive, demonstrable, indubious, undisputed
without effect ineffective, ineffectual
without employment unemployed
without end ad infinitum, durable, indeterminate, infinite, permanent, perpetual, profuse
without enthusiasm perfunctory
without equal inestimable
without error exact
without exaggeration literal
without exception invariably
without excuse blameful, inexcusable, inexpiable, peccant *(culpable)*, unjustifiable
without exit blind *(impassable)*
without experience inexperienced
without faith inconvincible, incredulous, leery
without fault blameless
without favor fairly *(impartially)*
without favoritism impartial
without force helpless *(powerless)*, insipid, languid, nonsubstantial *(not sturdy)*, powerless
without foresight improvident

without form intangible
without formality informal
without foundation gratuitous *(un-warranted)*, ill-founded, illogical, insubstantial, nonsubstantial *(not sturdy)*, unfounded, unsupported
without funds impecunious
without guile ingenuous
without harm innocent
without heart cold-blooded
without hesitation instantly
without honor perfidious, recreant
without hope irredeemable
without insight blind *(not discerning)*
without integrity immoral, unscrupulous
without interruption continuous, incessant
without issue barren
without judgment irrational
without judicial authority want of jurisdiction
without knowledge inexperienced
without law lawless
without legal authority illegally
without legal effect null *(invalid)*, null and void
without legal efficacy invalid
without legal force null *(invalid)*, null and void, void *(invalid)*
without legal sanction illegally
without life dead, defunct, lifeless *(dead)*
without limit indeterminate, infinite, profuse
without limitation peremptory *(absolute)*
without limits open-ended
without loss intact, undiminished, whole *(undamaged)*
without meaning null *(insignificant)*
without measure indeterminate, infinite
without method disordered
without modesty proud *(conceited)*
without monetary inducement gratis
without monetary reward gratis
without money impecunious
without motion stagnant
without nerves dispassionate
without notice instantly, unaware
without novelty stale
without number infinite, myriad, unlimited
without offense innocent
without omission in toto, total
without omissions complete *(all-embracing)*
without order haphazard
without originality sequacious
without parallel paramount, superlative
without particularizing generally
without pecuniary gain gratis
without perceptible time lapse instantaneous
without physical substance intangible
without pity ruthless
without plausibility insubstantial
without potency null *(invalid)*, null and void
without power of appeal inappealable
without power of choice involuntary

without power to harm innocuous
without precision inexact
without prejudice fairly *(impartially)*
without price inestimable, invaluable, priceless
without probity dishonest, fraudulent
without prudence impulsive *(rash)*, reckless
without qualification absolute *(complete)*
without question decisive, definitive, indubious, undisputed
without rational basis capricious
without reality baseless, insubstantial, unfounded
without reason arbitrary, baseless, irrational, ludicrous
without recompense gratis
without reference irrespective
without reference to irrelevant
without regard insusceptible *(uncaring)*
without regard to regardless
without regrets relentless
without relation alien *(unrelated)*, heterogeneous, irrelative
without reliance in suspect *(distrust)*
without reproach blameless, clean
without repute notorious
without reservations unconditional
without reserve categorical, demonstrative *(expressive of emotion)*
without resources destitute, devoid
without respect or regard to irrespective
without respect to regardless
without restraint inordinate
without results unproductive
without reward gratis
without rhyme or reason irrational
without risk harmless, immune, nontoxic, safe
without scruples unscrupulous
without shame unabashed
without significance null *(insignificant)*
without sound basis ill-founded
without specified limits open-ended
without spirit languid
without stain unblemished
without stint profuse
without stopping incessant
without strings unrestricted
without substance ill-founded, immaterial, incorporeal, null *(insignificant)*, unfounded
without substantial cause arbitrary
without succor helpless *(defenseless)*
without suspicion unsuspecting
without taste inelegant, insipid
without tendency to harm innocuous
without the appearance of life dead
without the name of the author anonymous
without thought impulsive *(rash)*
without truth dishonest, disingenuous, fraudulent
without value null *(invalid)*, null and void
without vanity diffident
without vitality powerless
without warmth cold-blooded, dispassionate

without warranty as is
without weight immaterial, ineffective, ineffectual
without will involuntary
withstand allow *(endure)*, collide *(clash)*, counteract, defy, endure *(last)*, endure *(suffer)*, hold out *(resist)*, last, parry, repel *(drive back)*, repulse
withstanding resistance
witless fatuous, irrational, obtuse, opaque
witlessly unknowingly
witness attest, avow, bystander, bystander, corroboration, declarant, deponent, depose *(testify)*, discern *(detect with the senses)*, indicator, informant, notarize, note *(notice)*, notice *(observe)*, perceive, pierce *(discern)*, regard *(pay attention)*, subscribe *(sign)*, verify *(swear)*, vouch
witness against informer *(one providing criminal information)*
witness as to character bystander
witness box stand *(witness' place in court)*
witness stand stand *(witness' place in court)*
witness to bear *(adduce)*
witness to a crime bystander
witness who gives testimony deponent
witnessing attestation, observation, reference *(recommendation)*
wittingly knowingly, purposely
witty jocular
wizardry prowess *(ability)*
wobbly insubstantial, nonsubstantial *(not sturdy)*
woe disaster, distress *(anguish)*, pain, plaint, tragedy
woebegone disconsolate, lugubrious
woeful blameworthy, dire, disconsolate, lamentable, lugubrious, regrettable
wolfish predatory, rapacious
womanhood majority *(adulthood)*
wonder phenomenon *(unusual occurrence)*, reflect *(ponder)*, surprise
wonder about ponder, speculate *(conjecture)*
wonderful meritorious, noteworthy, portentous *(eliciting amazement)*, prodigious *(amazing)*, remarkable, special
wondering incredulous
wonderment phenomenon *(unusual occurrence)*, surprise
wonderwork phenomenon *(unusual occurrence)*
wondrous noteworthy, portentous *(eliciting amazement)*, prodigious *(amazing)*, remarkable
wont custom, manner *(behavior)*, usage
wonted boiler plate, conventional, customary, familiar *(customary)*, habitual, inveterate, ordinary, orthodox, prescriptive, prevailing *(current)*, regular *(conventional)*, usual
wontedness custom
woo persuade, prevail *(persuade)*
wooden rigid
word canon, disclosure *(something disclosed)*, intelligence *(news)*, phrase, pledge *(binding promise)*, profession *(declaration)*, promise, remark, term *(expression)*, undertaking *(pledge)*, vow

word for word faithfully, literal, verbatim, verbatim

word group phrase

word of command instruction *(direction)*

word of explanation comment, note *(brief comment)*

word of honor pledge *(binding promise)*, profession *(declaration)*, vow

word picture delineation

wordage language, parlance

wordiness fustian, prolixity

wording language, phraseology, rhetoric *(skilled speech)*

wordless mute, speechless, tacit

wordlessness silence

words speech

wordy flatulent, loquacious, profuse, prolific, prolix, redundant, turgid, voluble

work activity, appointment *(position)*, assignment *(task)*, burden, business *(occupation)*, calling, career, cultivate, duty *(obligation)*, effectuate, employ *(make use of)*, employment, endeavor, exert, exploit *(make use of)*, function, function, industry *(activity)*, industry *(business)*, job, labor, livelihood, manage, manipulate *(utilize skillfully)*, militate, mission, occupation *(vocation)*, office, operate, perform *(execute)*, performance *(execution)*, performance *(workmanship)*, perpetrate, ply, position *(business status)*, post, profession *(vocation)*, publication *(printed matter)*, pursuit *(occupation)*, role, strive, struggle, wield

work a change adapt, affect

work a cure remedy

work against antagonize, collide *(clash)*, counter, counteract, countervail, fight *(counteract)*, hinder, interfere

work as a team cooperate, federalize *(associate)*

work at endeavor, occupy *(engage)*, practice *(engage in)*, practice *(train by repetition)*

work at cross purposes counter

work done fait accompli

work evil mistreat

work for foster, help, pursue *(strive to gain)*, serve *(assist)*

work for a judge clerk

work force personnel

work hard labor, strive

work in interject, intersperse

work in the service of pander

work in unison combine *(act in concert)*

work into a passion incense, provoke

work jointly concur *(agree)*

work on lobby, treat *(process)*

work out calculate, compose, devise *(invent)*, dispatch *(dispose of)*, fix *(settle)*, implement, maneuver, negotiate, perpetrate, plan, plot, program, scheme, settle, solve

work out differences mediate

work out in detail develop

work over emend, modify *(alter)*, redact, revise

work party personnel

work place office

work side by side with cooperate

work stoppage lockout, strike

work to excess overload

work together combine *(act in concert)*, consolidate *(unite)*, cooperate, federalize *(associate)*, involve *(participate)*, participate

work toward conduce

work unceasingly adhere *(persist)*, persevere, persist

work unflaggingly persevere, persist

work up churn, compose, foment, frame *(formulate)*, perturb, pique, provoke, scheme, stimulate

work upon affect, constrain *(compel)*, influence, motivate

workability feasibility, potential

workable demonstrable, determinable *(ascertainable)*, fit, functional, operative, possible, potential, practicable, practical, solvable, viable

workableness feasibility

workaday household *(familiar)*, ordinary, prevailing *(current)*, regular *(conventional)*, usual

workday mundane

worked up frenetic

worker apprentice, artisan, employee

worker of iniquity criminal, delinquent

workers personnel, staff

workfellow contributor *(contributor)*, partner

working active, effective *(operative)*, functional, operative

working ability performance *(workmanship)*

working arrangement modus vivendi

working assets capital, cash

working capital finance, money, principal *(capital sum)*

working in concert association *(connection)*

working people personnel

working plan device *(contrivance)*, method

working proposition device *(contrivance)*

working together coaction, connivance

workingman artisan

workingwoman artisan

workless idle, unemployed

workman artisan, employee

workwoman artisan

world-wide nonsectarian, ubiquitous

world-wise veteran

worldliness experience *(background)*

worldly civil *(public)*, material *(physical)*, mundane, physical, profane

worldly belongings possessions

worldly substance effects

worldly wisdom common sense

worldly-minded mundane

worldwide prevailing *(current)*, prevalent, rife

worn dilapidated, old, trite, unsound *(not strong)*

worn out decadent, dilapidated, old, stale, trite

worrisome problematic

worry agitate *(perturb)*, apprehension *(fear)*, badger, bait *(harass)*, concern *(interest)*, discommode, discompose, distress *(anguish)*, distress, disturb, embarrass, fear, harry *(harass)*, hector, interest *(concern)*, mistreat, molest *(annoy)*, nuisance, pain, perplex, perturb, pique, plague, press *(goad)*, qualm

worsen aggravate *(exacerbate)*, decay, degenerate, depreciate, deteriorate, exacerbate, harm, impair

worsening aggravation *(exacerbation)*

worship honor *(outward respect)*, regard *(hold in esteem)*, respect

worshiped sacrosanct

worshipful solemn

worst dire, subdue, subject, upset

worth advantage, amount *(sum)*, benefit *(betterment)*, caliber *(quality)*, charge *(cost)*, connotation, credit *(recognition)*, emphasis, estimate *(approximate cost)*, expense *(cost)*, face value *(price)*, magnitude, materiality *(consequence)*, merit, par *(face amount)*, prestige, price, quality *(excellence)*, quality *(grade)*, rate, respect, significance, signification, value

worth a great deal opulent

worth considering material *(important)*

worth imitating meritorious

worthiness expedience, honesty, integrity, merit, qualification *(fitness)*, rectitude, right *(righteousness)*, value, worth

worthless barren, contemptible, delinquent *(guilty of a misdeed)*, expendable, frivolous, futile, ignoble, immaterial, inconsequential, inconsiderable, ineffective, ineffectual, insubstantial, needless, nugatory, null *(insignificant)*, null *(invalid)*, null and void, otiose, paltry, petty, poor *(inferior in quality)*, reprobate, trivial, unable, unavailing, unproductive, unsound *(fallacious)*, unworthy

worthless argument fallacy

worthless check bad check

worthless person degenerate

worthless trial mistrial

worthlessness immateriality

worthwhile beneficial, gainful, laudable, lucrative, meritorious, productive, profitable, purposeful

worthy capable, condign, constructive *(creative)*, desirable *(qualified)*, entitled, exemplary, fit, high-minded, justifiable, laudable, meritorious, moral, premium, qualified *(competent)*, reputable, scrupulous, sterling, suitable, unimpeachable, upright, valuable

worthy of attention extraordinary

worthy of belief authentic, credible, fiduciary

worthy of blame culpable, sinister

worthy of choice preferable, qualified *(competent)*

worthy of confidence credible, loyal, official

worthy of consideration considerable, major

worthy of contempt disgraceful

worthy of credence convincing, credible, fiduciary, plausible

worthy of estimation laudable

worthy of fame meritorious

worthy of imitation exemplary

worthy of note remarkable

worthy of notice influential, notable, noteworthy, paramount, salient

worthy of praise meritorious
worthy of regard extraordinary
worthy of remark major, notable, noteworthy, paramount, salient
worthy of trust reliable
would-be specious
wound damage, disable, harm, inflict, infliction, maim, mistreat, mutilate, offend *(insult)*, prejudice *(injure)*, provoke
wound the feelings affront
woundable vulnerable
wounded aggrieved *(harmed)*, marred
wounded pride resentment
wounding harmful, offensive *(offending)*
woven compound
wrack prostration
wraith phantom
wrangle altercation, argument *(contention)*, belligerency, bicker, brawl, brawl, challenge, collide *(clash)*, conflict, conflict, confront *(oppose)*, confrontation *(altercation)*, contend *(dispute)*, contest *(dispute)*, contravention, controversy *(argument)*, debate, dicker, disaccord, disagree, dispute, dispute *(debate)*, dissidence, fight *(argument)*, fracas, haggle, oppugn, strife
wrangler disputant, malcontent
wrangling altercation, argument *(contention)*, contention *(opposition)*, contentious, discord, dissension, dissenting, hostile
wrap clothe, cover *(guard)*, encompass *(surround)*, ensconce, enshroud, envelop, hide, obnubilate, obscure, plant *(covertly place)*, shroud
wrap around envelop
wrapper enclosure
wrath ill will, malice, passion, resentment, umbrage
wreak inflict
wreathe intertwine
wreathed tortuous *(bending)*
wreck damage, damage, debacle, despoil, destroy *(efface)*, devastate, disable, mutilate, obliterate, pillage, prejudice *(injure)*, prostration, spoil *(impair)*
wrecker vandal
wrecking activities defacement
wrench contort, deprive, distort, exact, force *(break)*, luxate, sever
wrench away from confiscate
wrench the meaning distort
wrench the sense distort
wrenching extortion
wrest contort, deprive, exact, extort, levy, seize *(confiscate)*, sequester *(seize property)*, slant, succeed *(attain)*, usurp
wrest away from confiscate
wrest from abridge *(divest)*, acquire *(secure)*, coerce
wrest property from evict
wrester extortionist
wresting avulsion, extortion
wresting money by force extortion
wrestle compete, grapple
wrestle with confront *(oppose)*, fight *(battle)*
wretched deplorable, derelict *(abandoned)*, disconsolate, heinous, lamentable, lugubrious, obnoxious, paltry, peccant *(culpable)*, pessimistic, poor *(inferior in quality)*
wretchedness disrepute, distress *(anguish)*, pessimism, prostration

wring distill, exact, extort, press *(constrain)*
wring away from confiscate
wringing extortion
wrinkle artifice, contort
writ brevet, canon, certificate, charge *(command)*, citation *(charge)*, direction *(order)*, directive, document, habeas corpus, monition *(legal summons)*, precept, process *(summons)*, search warrant, subpoena, summons
writ for deliverance from illegal confinement habeas corpus
writ of summons citation *(charge)*
writ to gain freedom habeas corpus
write communicate, compile, compose, correspond *(communicate)*, frame *(construct)*, inscribe, note *(record)*, record, subscribe *(sign)*
write a prescription prescribe
write about treat *(process)*
write down book, enter *(record)*, note *(record)*, record
write in enter *(record)*
write notes for edit
write off obliterate
write up report *(disclose)*
write-off bad debt
write-up publicity
writer amanuensis
writhe beat *(pulsate)*, contort
writing charter *(declaration of rights)*, communication *(statement)*, entry *(record)*, handwriting, instrument *(document)*, memory *(commemoration)*, proposal *(report)*, publication *(printed matter)*, script, testament
writing delivered as the evidence of an agreement instrument *(document)*
writing that discredits libel
writing which gives formal expression to a legal act instrument *(document)*
writings correspondence *(communication by letters)*
written documentary, holographic
written accusation indictment, information *(charge)*, libel
written agreement covenant, lease
written announcement resolution *(formal announcement)*
written application for relief petition
written assurance vow
written authorization proxy
written certificate bill *(formal declaration)*
written characters script
written complaint bill *(formal declaration)*
written constitution code
written contract certificate
written copy transcript
written declaration under oath deposition
written declaration upon oath affidavit
written discourse publication *(printed matter)*
written document form *(document)*
written evidence affirmance *(legal affirmation)*, certificate, certification *(attested copy)*
written expression language
written formal expression instrument *(document)*

written instrument coupon
written instrument of contingency escrow
written law act *(enactment)*, code, codification, constitution, statute
written material document, record
written matter inscription, script
written notification to appear in court summons
written off derelict *(abandoned)*
written order holding *(ruling of a court)*, instruction *(direction)*, mandate
written permission charter *(license)*, license
written pledge covenant
written precept of imprisonment mittimus
written record entry *(record)*, register
written requests for information interrogatories
written requirement specification
written statement averment
written statement of defense pleading
written statement under oath affidavit
written statements of accusation pleading
written terms contract
written word language
wrong abuse *(violate)*, affront, arrant *(onerous)*, at fault, blame *(culpability)*, blameworthy, crime, culpable, damage, damage, delict, delinquency *(misconduct)*, disserve, errant, erroneous, fallacious, false *(inaccurate)*, faulty, felonious, grievance, ground, guilt, harm, harrow, heinous, illicit, immoral, impermissible, improper, inaccurate, inadmissible, inadvisable, inapplicable, inapposite, incorrect, infraction, infringement, iniquitous, injury, injustice, inopportune, irregular *(improper)*, mendacious, mens rea, mischief, misconduct, misdeed, misdemeanor, misdoing, misfeasance, mishandle *(maltreat)*, mistreat, nefarious, objectionable, offense, peccant *(culpable)*, persecute, perverse, prejudice *(injury)*, prejudice *(injure)*, reprehensible, sinister, sophistic, tort, transgression, unethical, unfit, unjust, unjustifiable, unseemly, unsound *(fallacious)*, unsustainable, untenable, untrue, vice, vicious, violation, wrongful
wrong application misapplication
wrong arising from affirmative action misfeasance
wrong course detour, error
wrong designation misnomer
wrong doing infringement
wrong estimation misjudgment
wrong implementation noncompliance *(improper completion)*
wrong impression error, misestimation
wrong interpretation catachresis, distortion, misapplication
wrong name misnomer
wrong reasoning non sequitur
wrong statement misstatement
wrong usage catachresis, misapplication
wrong use abuse *(corrupt practice)*, misapplication, misusage, misuse

wrong verdict injustice
wrong-doer delinquent
wrongdoer convict, criminal, felon, hoodlum, lawbreaker, malefactor, offender, recidivist
wrongdoer released from prison probationer *(released offender)*
wrongdoing criminality, culpability, delinquency *(misconduct)*, felony, guilt, injustice, knavery, mens rea, mischief, misconduct, misdeed, misfeasance, offense, tort, transgression, turpitude, vice
wronged aggrieved *(victimized)*
wrongful arrant *(onerous)*, blameful, blameworthy, felonious, illegal, illegitimate *(illegal)*, illicit, impermissible, improper, irregular *(improper)*, lawless, outrageous, peccant *(culpable)*, unauthorized, unjust, unlawful, unscrupulous, unwarranted
wrongful act tort, tortious act
wrongful action malfeasance
wrongful action of a public official misprision
wrongful appropriation embezzlement
wrongful assumption conversion *(misappropriation)*
wrongful conduct malfeasance
wrongful conversion of property misappropriation
wrongful displacement asportation
wrongful dispossession disseisin
wrongful entry encroachment
wrongful exaction extortion
wrongful exercise of dominion conversion *(misappropriation)*
wrongful impoundment detainer
wrongful ingress encroachment
wrongful keeping detainer
wrongful performance of a normally legal act misfeasance
wrongful removal asportation
wrongful taking larceny, theft
wrongful transfer asportation
wrongful use misapplication, misappropriation
wrongfully illegally
wrongfulness infringement, misdoing, misfeasance, offense
wrongheaded perverse
wrongly advised misadvised
wrongly timed inappropriate
wrongness error
wrongous unlawful
wrought up frenetic
wrought with labor elaborate

Y

yard close *(enclosed area)*, curtilage
yardage space
yardstick criterion

yarn myth
yawning open *(unclosed)*, penetrable
year annum
yearly per annum
yearly payment annuity, premium *(insurance payment)*
yearn for lack, need
yearning desire, eager, predisposition, solicitous, will *(desire)*
years age, longevity
years of existence lifetime
yell outcry
yellow recreant
yen desire
yet notwithstanding
yet to be forthcoming
yield abandon *(relinquish)*, abide, accede *(concede)*, accommodate, accrue *(arise)*, acknowledge *(verify)*, allow *(endure)*, bestow, cede, concede, concur *(agree)*, condescend *(deign)*, condone, confer *(give)*, confess, conform, consent, defer *(yield in judgment)*, engender, forfeit, forgo, forswear, fund, furnish, germinate, grant *(concede)*, hear *(give attention to)*, let *(permit)*, lose *(undergo defeat)*, obey, outcome, outgrowth, output, proceeds, produce *(manufacture)*, product, profit, quit *(discontinue)*, redound, relax, release, relent, relinquish, resign, result, revenue, succumb, supply, vouchsafe, waive
yield assent accede *(concede)*, agree *(comply)*, certify *(approve)*, coincide *(concur)*, conform, grant *(concede)*, permit
yield gain inure *(benefit)*
yield in opinion to defer *(yield in judgment)*
yield passage to admit *(give access)*
yield profit inure *(benefit)*
yield results make
yield returns gain, profit
yield to comply, observe *(obey)*, recognize *(acknowledge)* •
yield to the wishes of others truckle
yielding amenable, capitulation, cession, charitable *(lenient)*, compliance, concession *(compromise)*, conformity *(obedience)*, consenting, constructive *(creative)*, disposition *(transfer of property)*, facile, fertile, flexible, lenient, malleable, obedient, obeisant, obsequious, operative, passive, patient, permissive, pliable, pliant, powerless, productive, prolific, release, renunciation, resignation *(passive acceptance)*, resignation *(relinquishment)*, resigned, resilient, sequacious, subjection, susceptible *(unresistent)*, tractable, willing *(not averse)*
yielding abundantly copious
yieldingness amenability, compliance

yoke bondage, curb, fetter, incorporate *(include)*, join *(bring together)*, lock, subjection, thrall
young child, inexperienced, juvenile, progeny
young boy child
young descendant child
young girl child
young people children
young person adolescent, infant, juvenile, minor
younger generation children, offspring
youngling adolescent, child, juvenile, minor
youngster adolescent, child, infant, juvenile, minor
youngsters children
your honor judge
youth adolescence, adolescent, child, children, infant, juvenile, minor, minority *(infancy)*, nonage
youthful inexperienced, juvenile
youthfulness minority *(infancy)*

Z

zeal adhesion *(loyalty)*, ardor, compulsion *(obsession)*, diligence *(perseverance)*, emotion, industry *(activity)*, life *(vitality)*, loyalty, passion, predisposition, purpose, spirit
zealot addict, bigot, partisan
zealotist partisan
zealotry resolution *(decision)*
zealous eager, earnest, faithful *(loyal)*, fanatical, fervent, hot-blooded, industrious, intense, intensive, painstaking, pertinacious, purposeful, ready *(willing)*, resolute, sedulous, serious *(devoted)*, steadfast, thorough, true *(loyal)*, unyielding, vehement, willing *(desirous)*
zealous advocates lobby
zealous attachment affection
zealousness diligence *(perseverance)*, industry *(activity)*
zenith ceiling, culmination, pinnacle
zero blank *(emptiness)*
zest enjoyment *(pleasure)*, life *(vitality)*
zestful eager, fervent, ready *(willing)*
zestfulness life *(vitality)*
zigzag circuitous, indirect, indirection *(indirect action)*, sinuous, tortuous *(bending)*
zonal regional
zone area *(province)*, circuit, coverage *(scope)*, demarcate, department, district, division *(administrative unit)*, enclosure, insulate, locality, location, purview, region, scope, territory, vicinity